單文華

国际法与比较法论集（上）

Wenhua Shan's Essays on International and Comparative Law

单文华 著
杜 娟 编

法律出版社
LAW PRESS·CHINA

编者说明

《单文华国际法与比较法论集》是单文华教授在多年从事国际法与比较法的研究中形成的主要学术成果的凝练和总结。本书自 2015 年 7 月开始筹备工作，历经年余，终于 2016 年 11 月得以问世。其间通过与单文华老师的反复沟通，在法律出版社人员的帮助下，最终确定了本《论集》收录的学术成果范围、编章目次，以及本书(上卷)、(中卷)、(下卷)三卷本的编排体例。

在成果类别方面，本书主要涵盖了单文华教授自 1994 年至 2016 年间发表在中外重要学术刊物上的中英文论文，以及撰写的书籍章节、案件报告、专家意见、仲裁裁决等，同时还包括了一些报刊评论文章和个人专访等内容。在商定本书论文范围时，单文华教授剔除了不少文章，仅保留了比较有代表性的论文。显然，本书并不包括单文华教授截至 2016 年已经出版的十二部中、英文专著及译著的全部内容。

在编章目次和编排体例的安排方面，本书主要根据单文华教授研究成果涉及的不同学术领域，划分为三卷八编，依次分别为上卷(国际法与比较法通论、欧洲联盟与中欧关系法)、中卷(国际投资法)、下卷(国际贸易法、一带一路建设与国际能源法、法学教育、仲裁实践、人物专访)。其中上卷的第一、二编主要从总体角度出发，立足中国国情，从中国视角探讨论证了当代国际经济法领域的基本理论问题，以及目前热议的欧盟投资体系与中欧投资关系的热点问题；中卷的第三编主要涉及近年来国际投资法领域中的热点难点等理论与实践问题，因其内容丰富、研究翔实、成果多样，故安排其独立成卷；下卷的第四至八编则主要是关于国际贸易法方面的一些早期成果，丝绸之路建设、国际能源投资等国家大政方针政策的成果总结，以及单文华教授在国内外从事法学教育的过程中积累的对中国法学教育问题的一些认识、意见和建议，同时，也收录其作为各仲裁机构仲裁员与仲裁参与人的角色中形成的一些仲裁裁决和专家报告等内容，以及近年来其针对法学院建设等方面接受媒体专访的内容摘选。

值此西安交通大学丝绸之路国际法与比较法研究所十周年所庆之际，作为对研究所十年庆典的献礼，同时也是对单文华教授二十多年学术历程的一次回顾与总结，我们很期待并欣喜能让《单文华国际法与比较法论集》在这个意义非凡的时刻首发问世，这应该是西安交大国际法人共同的纪念，更是我们学术征程上的另一个新的开始！

本论集在正式出版前，已征得中外各期刊、出版社关于单文华教授已发表的学术成果再版出书的版权同意。

编者　杜　娟

2016 年 10 月 22 日

目 录

Contents

上 卷

第一编

国际法与比较法通论

第二编

欧洲联盟与中欧关系法

中　卷

第三编
国际投资法

下　卷

第四编

国际贸易法

第五编

"一带一路" 建设与国际能源法

第六编

法学教育

第七编

仲裁实践

上　　卷

第一编
国际法与比较法通论

Part Ⅰ

003 -058

Redefining the Chinese Concept of Sovereignty*

The concept of sovereignty and the debates about it have always been at the center of the system of public international law. Views about the nature and purposes of sovereignty and its rightful place in international law have varied from time to time and from place to place.[1] In this regard, the Chinese concept of sovereignty is particularly interesting, not only because it differs significantly from that of other major states, but also because it has significant bearings on the future international behavior of China, which is poised to play a major leading role on the world stage.

In this chapter, I will first briefly introduce the much debated concept of sovereignty and the traditional Chinese version thereof. Then I will proceed to explore whether and to what extent such traditional Chinese concept of sovereignty has been changed and challenged since China decided to open up to the outside world. I will do so mainly by referring to China's practices in international economic treaties and organizations, notably the bilateral investment treaties and the World Trade Organization. I will then analyze some recent statements by Chinese government officials, with a view to ascertaining whether and to what extent the official Chinese views toward the concept of sovereignty have been changed. My finding is that, despite significant concessions of important sovereign powers through those treaties and organizations, China's official perception of "sovereignty" has hardly changed.

In an effort to explain such disparity between the official opinions and state practices, I will finally revisit the concept of sovereignty, and argue for a doublelayer definition of sovereignty: abstract sovereignty and concrete sovereignty. I will conclude that, whereas the "concrete sovereignty"(as specific powers that implement sovereign authority) keeps changing to suit the need of times, the "abstract sovereignty"(as the ultimate and final source of authority) of a state remains unchanged as long as it remains a sovereign state.

---

* In Wang Gungwu and Zheng Yongnian (eds.), China and the New International Order, Part I, Routledge, 2008.

[1] Oppenheim stated in his celebrated treatise on international law that "[T] here exists perhaps no conception, the meaning of which is more controversial than that of sovereignty. It is an indisputable fact that this conception, from the moment when it was introduced into political science until the present day, has never had a meaning which was universally agreed upon. " See Lassa Oppenheim, *International Law*, ed. Sir Arnold D. McNair, 4th edn , Longmans, 1928, p. 137. Louis Henkin also pointed out that sovereignty "means many things, some essential, some insignificant; some agreed, some controversial; some that are not warranted and should not be accepted"; Louis Henkin, *International Law: Politics and Values*, Martinus Nijhoff, 1995, p. 8. In his insightful paper, Sir Robert Jennings described vividly how different times have nourished different perceptions of sovereignty; see Robert Jennings, "Sovereignty and International Law, " in Gerard Kreijen, Marcel Brus, Jorris Duursma, Elizabeth De Vos, and John Dugard, ed., *State, Sovereignty, and International Governance*, Oxford University Press, 2002.

Sovereignty and the Chinese Concept Thereof

Sovereignty: the concept thereof and the challenges thereto

The concept of sovereignty is like the concept of God. Every so often people refer to it, yet nobody seems to be very clear what it exactly means.[2] It is generally accepted that the concept was first formulated by a political scientist, Jean Bodin in 1576 in his work *De Republica*.[3] Bodin's theory on sovereignty(*summa potestas*) was based on the situation of states in Europe in his time and on the need to have a means for the restoration of some sort of internal order within Europe.[4] As observed by Brierly,

> Bodin was convinced that a confusion of uncoordinated independent authorities must be fatal to a State, and that there must be one final source and no more than one from which its laws proceed. The essential manifestation of sovereignty, he thought, is the power to make the laws, and since the sover-eign makes the law, he clearly cannot be bound by the laws that he makes.[5]

Thus the essence of sovereignty, according to Bodin, is the possession of the "one and only final source of authority" and the essential manifestation of such authority is the making of laws, by which the authority is not bound.[6] Such a conception of sovereignty has become the starting point of almost any discussion of the definition of state sovereignty in international relations and international law, and is still very much valid today.

The concept of sovereignty in international law is believed to begin with the 1648 Treaty of Westphalia.[7] As a "Peace Treaty between the Holy Roman Emperor and the King of France and Their Respective Allies," the agreement represented the transfer of some powers from the Emperor to certain kings and lords; over time, this was developed into the notion of the absolute right of the sovereign, or what is called "Westphalian Sovereignty."[8] By the nineteenth century, such a notion of absolute sovereignty gained currency in international law. Henry Wheaton, for example, a leading international lawyer of his time, claimed that each state "possesses and exercises exclusive sovereignty and jurisdiction throughout the full extent of its territory... No state can, by its laws, directly affect, bind, or regulate property beyond its own territory, or control persons that do not reside within it, whether they be native-born subjects or not."[9] Such a concept of sover-

---

[2] Sarooshi has observed, for instance, that the meaning of the concept of sovereignty is largely contingent on the text in which it figures and there is no objective concept as such that is universally applicable. Schermers noted that "Sovereignty has many different aspects and none of these aspects is stable. The content of the notion of 'sovereignty' is continuously changing, especially in recent years." Dan Sarooshi, *International Organisations and their Exercise of Sovereign Powers*, Oxford University Press, 2005, p. 3; Henry Schermers, "Different Aspects of Sovereignty," in Kreijen *et al.*, *State, Sovereignty, and International Governance*, pp. 185, 192.

[3] Jennings, "Sovereignty and International Law," p. 27.

[4] Ibid.

[5] J. L. Brierly, *The Law of Nations*, Oxford University Press, 1955, p. 7.

[6] Bodin nevertheless acknowledged that even the sovereign would be bound by certain laws, such as "the divine law, the law of nature or reason, the law that is common to all nations, and also certain laws which he calls *leges imperii*, the law of government." Brierly, *The Law of Nations*, p. 9.

[7] John H. Jackson, "Sovereignty-Modern: A New Approach to an Outdated Concept," *The American Journal of International Law*, 97: 782-(2003), p. 786.

[8] John H. Jackson, "Sovereignty-Modern: A New Approach to an Outdated Concept," *The American Journal of International Law*, 97: 782-(2003), p. 786.

[9] Henry Wheaton, *Elements of International Law*, 8th edn., Dana, 1866, Sec. 78.

eignty is sometimes further summarized as having four main components: internal authority, border control, policy autonomy, and non-intervention:

> Historically, sovereignty has been associated with four main characteristics: First, a sovereign state is one that enjoys supreme political authority and monopoly over the legitimate use of force within its territory. Second, it is capable of regulating movements across its borders. Third, it can make its foreign policy choices freely. Finally, it is recognized by other governments as an independent entity entitled to freedom from external intervention. These components of sovereignty were never absolute, but together they offered a predictable foundation for world order.[10]

Among the four components identified above, only the first refers to what Sir Elihu Lauterpacht called "internal sovereignty"(as sovereignty within the national sphere), whereas the other three refer to what he called "external sovereignty"(as sovereignty on the international plane).[11]

Although the absolute concept of sovereignty has always been a subject of debate and controversy, it is now "being challenged in unprecedented ways".[12] Since World War II, particularly in recent years, there has been a proliferation of international treaties and international organizations, each of which allegedly constitutes a limit or challenge to state sovereignty. State sovereignty is, in particular, severely challenged by the human rights movement, regional integration, humanitarian intervention activities, and influential trade and investment treaties and institutions as a result of economic globalization. Consequently, there has been a wealth of literature dealing with the issue of "sovereignty, "[13] most of which seems to be very critical of the traditional idea of "abso-

---

[10] Richard N. Haass, "Sovereignty: Existing Rights, Evolving Responsibilities, " remarks at the School of Foreign Service and the Mortara Center for International Studies, Georgetown University, 14 January 2003, p. 2, as cited in Jackson, "Sovereignty-Modern, " p. 786.

[11] Sir Elihu Lauterpacht, "Sovereignty: Myth or Reality, " *International Affairs* 73(1), pp. (1997), p. 138.

[12] Haas, as cited in Jackson, "Sovereignty-Modern, " p. 786.

[13] See for example Daniel Philpott, *Revolutions in Sovereignty*, Princeton University Press, 2001; the special issues of *Chicago Journal of International Law* (2000, 2001); Claude Barfield, *Free Trade, Sovereignty, Democracy: The Future of the World Trade Organisation*, AEI Press, 2001; Marcus Krajewski, "Democratic Legitimacy and Constitutional Perspectives of WTO Law, " *Journal of World Trade*, 35(2001); Jeff Atik, "Democratising the WTO, " *George Washington International Law Review*, 33(3 - 4)(2001); Thomas Franck, ed., *Delegating State Powers: The Effect of Treaty Regimes on Democracy and Sovereignty*, Transnational, 2000; Neil MacCormick, Questioning Sovereignty(Oxford: Oxford University Press, 1999); Marco C. E. J. Bronckers, "Better Rules for a New Millennium: A Warning Against Undemocratic Developments in the WTO?, " *Journal of International Economic Law*, 2, 547(1999); Paul Stephan, "Legitimacy, Accountability, Authority, and Freedom in the New Global Order, " *University of Colorado Law Review*, 70(1999); Benedict Kingsbury, "Sovereignty and Inequality, " *European Journal of International Law*, 9(1998); Jeremy Rabkin, *Why Sovereignty Matters*, AEI Press, 1998; Saskia Sassen, *Losing Control? Sovereignty in an Age of Globalisation*, Columbia University Press, 1996; Robert O. Keohane, "Sovereignty, Interdependence and International Institutions, " in Linda B. Miller and Michael Smith, ed., *Ideas and Ideals: Essays on Politics in Honor of Stanley Hoffmann*, Westview, 1993; Christopher Schreur, "The Waning of the Sovereign State, " *European Journal of International Law*, 4(4): pp(1993); Giandomenico Majone, "Europe's ' Democratic Deficit': The Question of Standards, " *European Law Journal*, 4(5) 18 - 22 (1998); Michael Ross Fowler and Julie Marie Bunck, *Law, Power, and the Sovereign State*, Penn State Press, 1995; Thomas L. Friedman, *The Lexus and the Olive Tree: Understanding Globalization*, Farrar Strauss Giroux, 1999; Karen T. Liftin, ed., *The Greening of Sovereignty in World Politics*, MIT Press, 1998; Stephen D. Krasner, *Sovereignty: Organized Hypocrisy*, Princeton University Press, 1999; Kreijen *et al.*, *State, Sovereignty, and International Governance*; Thomas J. Biersteker and Cynthia Weber, ed., *State Sovereignty as Social Construct*, Cambridge University Press, 1996; Ute Collier, Jonathan Golub, and Alexander Kreher, ed., *Subsidiarity and Shared Responsibility: New Challenges for EU Environmental Policy*, Nomos, 1997; Centre for Economic Policy Research [CEPR], "Making Sense of Subsidiarity, " in *Annual Report: Monitoring European Integration*, 4(1993); see also Abram Chayes and Antonia Handler Chayes, *The New Sovereignty*, Harvard University Press, 1995.

lute sovereignty."[14] Among them, the most serious attack came from Louis Henkin, who declared that "[s] overeignty is a bad word, not only because it has served terrible national mytholo-gies in international relations, and even in international law, but also because it is often a catchword, or a substitute for thinking and precision."[15] He reasoned that "Sovereignty is essentially an internal concept, the locus of ultimate authority in a society... [s] urely, as applied to the modern secular state in relation to other secular states, it is not meaningful to speak of the state as sovereign. Sovereignty, I conclude is not per se a normative conception in international law."[16] Further, he advocated that "[f] or legal purposes at least, we might do well to relegate the term sovereignty to the shelf of history as a relic from an earlier era."[17] Sir Elihu also considers that sovereignty "on the international plane" "must be seen largely as myth-except when it is used to describe a state's title to territory."[18] Sarooshi argued that sovereignty is an "essentially contested concept," the elements of which "have always been contested within politics."[19] Another eminent scholar has gone as far as to describe the sovereignty concept as "organized hypocrisy."[20] Some other authors have referred to it as being "of more value for purposes of oratory and persuasion than of science and law."[21] John Jackson, who may be regarded as a mild critic of the traditional concept of sovereignty, argues that the Westphalian sovereignty concept has been outmoded and needs replacing by what he terms "sovereignty-modern," which is not something that has been clearly defined but encourages disaggregating and analysis by employing "power allocation analy-sis" as the core analytical tool.[22]

Some world leaders have also joined in the critique of the sovereignty idea, while still recognizing the importance of some attributes of the concept. Boutros Boutros-Ghali, then Secretary-General of the United Nations, said in 1992 in his report to the Security Council that "[R] espect for [the state's] fundamental sovereignty and integrity [is] crucial to any common international progress. The time of absolute and exclusive sovereignty, however, has passed; its theory was never matched by reality."[23]

Unsurprisingly there are also voices against such denial of the traditional concept of sovereignty. Sir Robert Jennings, for example, after having carefully examining, *inter alia*, the chaotic situation in many parts of Africa and some parts of Asia, the impact of technological advancements, and the proliferation of international governmental and non-governmental organizations on state sovereignty, concluded that:

> [t] he current fashionable suggestions that State sovereignty is a thing of the past

---

[14] Jackson, "Sovereignty-Modern," p. 786.

[15] Henkin, *International Law*, p. 8.

[16] Ibid., p. 10.

[17] Ibid., p. 6.

[18] Lauterpecht, "Sovereignty," p. 149.

[19] Sarooshi, *International Organisations*, p. 4.

[20] Krasner, *Sovereignty*, p. 9.

[21] Fowler and Bunck, *Law, Power, and the Sovereign State*, p. 21.

[22] Jackson, "Sovereignty-Modern," particularly Parts I-III.

[23] *An Agenda for Peace-Preventive Diplomacy, Peacemaking, and Peace-Keeping*, Report of The Secretary-General, UN Doc. A/47/277 – S/24111, para. 17(1992).

are to be understood with some caution and perhaps some qualification.[24]

[...]

It is indeed odd that State sovereignty should at the present be supposed by some to be in serious decline... Looking even briefly at such international constitutional law as we have, one can only conclude that the suggested demise of national State sovereignty has been much exaggerated.[25]

Moreover, he pointed out that the fashionable "sovereignty outdated" suggestion "is partly no doubt a result of the present prevalent habit in the north and the west-and international lawyers are by no means free from this tendency-of regarding what happens in the north and the west as the normal situation, and therefore as the provider of the practice to be taken into account in the interpretation and development of our supposedly ' universal' system of international law."[26] He continued that:

No doubt we who are fortunate enough to be part of this highly developed and relatively very rich area, think the world would be a better place if our ideas were indeed universally shared even where there they are not actually at present realised. But the fact is that a large part of the world, including the most populated parts, would not necessarily agree with that.[27]

As a matter of fact, some scholars from the third world did voice strongly again the theory that completely denies state sovereignty. Chen An, an eminent international lawyer from China, for example, considered Henkin's argument to "do away with the ' S' word"[28] a hegemonist "spear" to attack and penetrate the sovereignty of other states, particularly the small and weak states in the Third World. He wrote,

For the third world, it seems necessary to advocate: Never away with the "S" word in current time! They must firmly cling to the "S" word, so as to use their sovereignty, separately and/or jointly, to fight against the political and economic hegemony, when the political and economic hegemony have still existed in contemporary world.[29]

The heat of the debate on the relegation of or insistence on the concept of sovereignty can

---

[24] This is because, he said, "[T] hey fail to provide for, or even take adequate account of, one of the most pressing and distressing problems of our times." These problems lie in the fact that, "at the beginning of the new millennium, in far too many parts of Africa and in some parts of Asia, there is a situation that is disturbingly reminiscent of the chaotic situation in Europe in the sixteenth century which informed Bodin's seminal study of the State and of sovereignty in the State." He then pointed out that "[T] he basic problem in the big trouble spots of this present time-Somalia. Rwanda, Bosnia, Sierra Leone, East Timor, and the like-has been above all lack of a government with real sovereign power." And in this regard, "[T] he at present much approved notion of globalisation is not very helpful and indeed hardly relevant at all." He asserted that "[I] t can hardly be argued that a highly dangerous situation, for which a restoration of some sovereign governmental power is manifestly the remedy, can be said to demonstrate a decline of the importance of the idea of State sovereignty, but rather the contrary."

[25] Jennings, "Sovereignty and International Law," pp. 30 – 5.

[26] Jennings, "Sovereignty and International Law," p. 31.

[27] He also disagreed with Sir Elihu Lauterpacht's views that sovereignty can be divided into "internal sovereignty" and "external sovereignty" and that external sovereignty is largely a "myth." Jennings, ibid., pp. 31 – 3.

[28] Louis Henkin, "The Mythology of Sovereignty," *American Society of International Law Newsletter*, vol: 1 – 2(1993), available at www.asil.org/.

[29] Chen An, "The Three Big Rounds of U. S. Unilateralism versus WTO Multilateralism During the Last Decade: A Combined Analysis of the Great 1994 Sovereignty Debate, Section 301 Disputes(1998 – 2000), and Section 201 Disputes(2002 – 2003) (Third Draft)," paper presented at the ASIL/IELG Meeting 2005 "Trade as the Guarantor of Peace, Liberty and Security?," Part IV. 3.

thus be clearly seen.[30] Although it is unclear which view will win eventually, it is clear that the traditional absolute concept of sovereignty is no longer the generally accepted concept, but one subject to severe and increasing challenges.

The Chinese concept of sovereignty: from "tributary system" to "inviolable sovereignty"

To the Chinese, the modern concept of "sovereignty," together with many other concepts of modern international law, was an "imported" Western plant. And the importing process was not a pleasant one. Until the expansionist Western powers arrived at China in the middle of the nineteenth century, China's foreign relations had been managed under an indigenous system known as the "tributary system," whereby China, occupying the patriarchal position, assumed the leadership and, in return, tributary states came into contact with China as part of the Chinese family of nations but in a subordinate position.[31] Under such a Sino-centric system, only China, the "Middle Kingdom," enjoyed full "sovereignty" and there was no such thing as "equality of sovereignty" between China and the tributary states. After the First Opium War (1839 - 42), however, such Sino-centric world order was broken down by Western imperialist powers and was replaced with an "unequal treaty regime."[32] Thus the "Middle Kingdom" at the center of the universe was downgraded into a "semicolonial society" at the hands of foreign imperialism. It was against this background and in an effort to seek a way of survival in what was described as "a great change in more than three thousand years of history" that the concept of state sovereignty and other norms of modern international law were first formally introduced into China.[33]

As a result, it is hardly surprising that the Chinese perspective on international law presents three main "Chinese characteristics." First of all, the Chinese concept of sovereignty features a "sovereignty-bound thinking" on international law, which places the principle of sovereignty at the very center of international law.[34] Indeed, since the fall of the Qing dynasty in 1911, the ability to maintain China's sovereignty internally and externally has become the *raison d'être* of any Chinese government regardless of its ideological standing. Thus even during the heyday of the Sino-Soviet alliance in the 1950s, Chinese leaders asserted that such an alliance had to be formed on the basis of sovereign

---

[30] Some commentators have gone further to argue that, rather than undermining sovereignty as commonly held, institutions such as the World Trade Organization actually strengthen sovereignty. See for example Kal Raustiala, "Rethinking the Sovereignty Debate in International Economic Law," *Journal of International Economic Law*, 6: 841 (2003).

[31] Li Zhaojie, "Legacy of Modern Chinese History: Its Relevance to the Chinese Perspective of the Contemporary International Legal Order," *Singapore Journal of International and Comparative Law*, 5: 314, p. 316.

[32] Ibid.

[33] However, the Western powers did not intend to apply international law to their relations with China in the same way that they did among themselves, even if their demands were often couched in terms of the Western system of international law. Although they introduced this Western legal concept to China, they did so largely as part of their efforts to dismantle the traditional Chinese world order and put China under the rule of the Euro-centric system of international relations, making the Chinese follow the rules that a semicolonial state was supposed to follow. Li, "Legacy of Modern Chinese History," p. 317.

[34] Li, "Legacy of Modern Chinese History," p. 318.

equality and independence.[35] Again, in negotiating China's restoration of its sovereignty over Hong Kong, Deng Xiaoping made it clear that the present Chinese government was resolved to resume exercise of its sovereignty over Hong Kong; otherwise it would become another Qing government and Chinese leaders would become Li Hongzhang's followers-the Chinese people would have every reason to overthrow them.[36] As a result, in its diplomatic announcements, China has constantly appraised sovereignty as the basis of the contemporary international relations and the cornerstone of the entire edifice of international law, and professes to be "the most enthusiastic champion of that principle."[37] Indeed, as Kim observed,

> If China's foreign policy pronouncements and protestations are taken at face value, sovereignty remains the lingua franca of its international comportment and the chrysalis of international order. Despite the twists and turns in international conduct over the years, the Chinese Government has remained compulsively sovereignty-bound on most basic global issues and problems. In the normative domain of global politics, China is perhaps beyond compare. Some wayward stranger from another planet, doing a content analysis of the annual UN debate on the state of the world, could easily take sovereignty as a quintessentially Chinese idea.[38]

Faithful adherence to the principle of inviolability of state sovereignty has therefore become a second distinctive feature of the Chinese concept of sovereignty and international law. In scholarly writings of earlier days of the People's Republic, Chinese publicists likewise uphold the inviolability of state sovereignty. In an article published in 1960, Ying T'ao wrote:

> In the course of cooperation and struggle in international relations, sovereignty is a question of paramount importance. Therefore, peoples of the various countries handling high the banner of "inviolability of sovereignty" and the oppressed nations of the world in the past and at present, have launched stubborn struggles against imperialism in defence of their country's sovereignty... But bourgeois international law, dictated by the needs of bourgeois interests, vacillates and contradicts itself, and nowadays even openly attempts to bury the principles of inviolability of sovereignty in order to meet the practices of

---

[35] Premier Zhou Enlai repeatedly stated, for example, that "the Chinese people must use their own brain for thinking and their own legs for walking." "We adhere to a basic position in the conduct of China's foreign affairs," said Zhou, "that is to maintain China's national independence. No country is permitted to intervene in China's internal affairs." Xue Mouhong, ed., *Dangdai Zhongguo Waijiao* (*Diplomacy in Contemporary China*), China Social Sciences Academy Press, 1986, p. 30.

[36] *Renmin Ribao* (*People's Daily*), overseas edition, 23 March 1994. Viceroy Li Hongzhang was the person in the Qing government taking charge of China's negotiations with foreign powers. He was therefore often blamed as a national traitor for "selling the country" by the many unequal treaties resulting from such negotiations.

[37] Wang Tieya, "International Law in China," 221 *Receuil des cours* (*Collected Courses of The Hague Academy of International Law*), No. 2(1991), p. 288.

[38] Samuel S. Kim, "Sovereignty in the Chinese Image of World Order," in R. St. J. Macdonald, ed., *Essays in Honour of Wang Tieya*, Martinus Nijhoff, 1994, p. 428.

imperialist aggression.[39]

A third and final feature of the Chinese concept of sovereignty is that it has in it an element of and indeed, an emphasis on "reciprocity" or "mutuality." This is most clearly elaborated in the principle of "mutual respect of sovereignty and territorial integrity," as one of the Five Principles of Peaceful Co-existence(FPPC), which were jointly initiated by China and India more than 50 years ago.[40] In other words, the "inviolability of sovereignty" doctrine is not equal to the Westphalian concept of "absolute sovereignty" and has not prevented the Chinese from acknowledging and respecting the sovereignty of other states and rules of international law.[41] As two Chinese scholars commented in 1964,

> Quite obviously, the theories of absolute sovereignty, restrictive sovereignty and the denial of sovereignty advocated by imperialist jurists are completely different from the principle of mutual respect for sovereignty which we advocate. Mutual respect for sovereignty absolutely does not mean that a state(regardless of how strong and large it is) may do whatever it wishes to other states on the pretext of exercising its sovereignty. Respect for sovereignty must be mutual: the principle that other states respect our sovereignty and we respect the sovereignty of other states. The exercise of sovereignty should be based upon the premise of not impairing the sovereignty of other states.[42]

It can therefore be concluded that the earlier Chinese concept of sovereignty and, in particular, the doctrine of "inviolability of sovereignty," are developed as a "defensive weapon" to protect against interference in domestic affairs[43] and do not necessarily exclude respect for the sovereignty of other states and norms of international law. But two important questions remain: What is the scope of "interference in domestic affairs" that is regarded as violating state sovereignty? And more generally, what are the norms of in-

---

〔39〕 Ying T'ao, "A Criticism of Bourgeois International Law Concerning the Question of State Sovereignty," *Guoji Wenti Yanjiu* (*International Studies*), 3(1960): 47 – 49, 50 – 52, as translated and reprinted in Jeremy Alan Cohen and Hungdah Chiu, *People's China and International Law: A Documentary Study* (Princeton, NJ: Princeton University Press, 1974), 2 volumes, Vol. 1, p. 106.

〔40〕 As noted by Kim("Sovereignty in the Chinese Image of World Order," p. 431), the FPPC have become the defining criterion of Chinese characteristics in the recent world order debate. For further details on the FPPC, see Cohen and Chiu, *People's China and International Law*, pp. 119 – 155. For more recent materials and discussion on the FPPC, see the special column for "The Five Principles of Peaceful Coexistence: A 50th Anniversary Celebration," *Chinese Journal of International Law*, 3(2): pp(2004).

〔41〕 After examining a range of Chinese literature, Cohen and Chiu observed that, although some, such as Soviet writers, suggested that a state's sovereignty is not subject to the supremacy of international law, a number of them did recognize the untenability of such a position. Cohen and Chiu, *People's China and International Law*, p. 118.

〔42〕 Yang Hsin and Chien Chien, "Expose and Criticize the Imperialist Fallacy Concerning the Question of State Sovereignty," *Zhengfa Yanjiu* (now *CASS Journal of Law*) 4: 6 – 11(1964), translated and reprinted in Cohen and Chiu, *People's China and International Law*, Vol. 1, p. 112.

〔43〕 Cohen and Chiu, *People's China and International Law*, pp. 117 – 118.

ternational law to which the Chinese state sovereignty is properly subject?[44] These questions have been more and more important for the international community and for China herself, as she emerges onto the world stage as already an existing economic power and a potential superpower, in this rapidly globalizing world. Although the second question is too big a question to be effective to answer in this chapter, the following sections of the chapter will attempt to address the first question by exploring and analyzing recent practice and opinions relating to concept of state sovereignty.

Chinese Practice in International Economic Law in Relation to State Sovereignty: Giving Up State Sovereignty?

Given that sovereignty constitutes the very foundation of international law and international relations, China's every conduct in foreign affairs is related to state sovereignty. It is therefore only possible for the following to highlight the most important and highly relevant aspects of China's practice, with a view to ascertaining its current position toward the principle of state sovereignty. This chapter will therefore focus on two major aspects of international economic law, namely international treaty-making and participation in international organization.

International treaty-making: investment treaties as an example

Each international treaty, as a matter of fact, has the effect of "ceding" or "eroding" certain powers of the state party concerned. Growingly, however, people have also come to notice that this is not a zero-sum game. As a return of such "cession" or "erosion," state parties may also gain some benefits.[45] The problem is, although the "cost" (such as erosion or cession of powers) is often manifest and realizable, the "benefit" might not always be as clear-cut or able to be effectively materialized.[46] A case in point is bilateral investment treaties(BITs).

Such treaties are typically entered into between a capital exporting state and capital importing state.[47] The capital exporting state wants the BIT to offer protection of its investment in the capital importing state. And the capital importing state hopes that such protection offered will attract the much needed foreign investment to come. What is written in such a treaty is, however, normally only concrete commitments of investment protection offered by the host state. No promise of certain inflow from the capital exporting country concerned is stipulated therein, apart from the hortatory statement in the pream-

---

[44] Cohen and Chiu, for instance, have commented that the recognition that state sovereignty is subject to generally accepted norms of international law is encouraging but of no great significance, as it is unclear what is the content of the international law that China is willing to be subject to. Cohen and Chiu, *People's China and International Law*, p. 118.

[45] One might argue that, for example, a state's sovereignty has also been expanded by successfully limiting acts of(an) other state(s).

[46] For instance, a small country that could not afford an office at Geneva might not be able to effectively assert her rights resulting from her membership of the World Trade Organization.

[47] See generally on BITs, Rudolf Dolzer and Margaret Stevens, *Bilateral Investment Treaties*, Kluwer Law International, 1995. For Chinese BITs, see Wenhua Shan, *The Legal Framework of EU-China Investment Relations: A Critical Appraisal*, Hart Publishing, 2005.

ble requiring state parties to "encourage" investment flows between the two parties.[48] And, as a matter of fact, studies show that BITs indeed do not help much in attracting foreign investment. In 2001, I personally did a survey among EU investors in China, about their awareness of BITs, among other things.[49] Fewer than half of EU investors knew of the existence of BITs when making the decision to invest in China.[50]

Now let us move to the specific sovereign powers that are affected in these BITs. State sovereign powers are sometimes divided into legislative power, executive power, and judicial power(sometimes also referred to as "legislative sovereignty," "executive sovereignty," and "judicial sovereignty').[51] Now let us pay a close look at the Chinese BITs and see whether and to what extent the sovereign powers of China have been altered as a result of such BITs.

To give an overview, by now China has entered into 125 BITs(including nine renegotiated BITs and protocols), which effectively cover at least most if not all states with which China has a meaningful investment relationship, and which make it the number two in the league table for BIT numbers, second only to Germany.[52] The first BIT was signed in 1982 with Sweden, but the bulk of them(over 80 percent) were signed since 1990, from which one can see the influence of economic globalization. Among them, 44 are entered into with European states, 38 with Asian states, 29 with African states, 11 with American states, and three with states in Oceania.[53]

Such BITs typically address two categories of issues, substantive and procedural ones. The substantive provisions tend to have the effect to limit legislative and executive powers, whereas the procedural provisions may affect the judicial powers. In terms of substantive provisions, for example, a BIT will normally provide certain general standards of treatment of foreign investors and their investment, such as national treatment standard and most-favored-nation(MFN) standard.

National treatment

The national treatment requirement, for example, poses a significant challenge and pressure for the Chinese government, as China has had a planned economy under which even the national investors were treated in different ways. For instance, for a considerable time, the tax burdens were different for state-owned enterprise(SOEs), collectively owned enterprises(COEs), and private enterprises. So are access to and charges for public utility supplies such as water, gas, and electricity. Under such circumstances, China has practical difficulty in choosing an appropriate "national investor" as the basis for the implementation of the "national treatment" to foreign investors. For example, if SOEs,

---

[48] And this is legitimate, because a state cannot force its private companies to invest in a particular country.

[49] For details of the survey see Wenhua Shan, *The Legal Framework of EU-China Investment Relations*, pp. 25 - 6.

[50] See Shan, *Legal Framework*, pp. 250 - 1.

[51] See for example Oscar Schachter, "International Law in Theory and Practice," *Developments in International Law*, 13: pp(1991).

[52] Data on the Chinese BITs available from my personal files. UNCTAD has made most signed Chinese BITs available online, as posted at www. unctad. org/(accessed on 23 December 2006).

[53] Ibid.

the then most important form of domestic enterprises, were chosen as the comparable "national investors," there would still be further problems such as whether foreign investors would like also to take care of the special public obligations undertaken by such SOEs, including education, health care, and housing. Indeed, it would be a "mission impossible" to implement a national treatment under such circumstances. Yet often some capital exporting states pressed on. For instance, the US insisted on the inclusion of such a standard in its negotiations in the 1980s, which led to a complete halt of the negotiations.[54] The UK government was more diplomatic, as it is, and managed to include this standard in the 1986 Sino-UK BIT, but with substantial qualifications, such as "to the extent possible" and "in accordance with the stipulations of its laws and regulations."[55] Indeed, as I argued elsewhere, the qualifications are so substantial that such national treatment clause does not impose any material restrictions on the way in which China may treat UK investment.[56] Such qualifications, however, have been materially reduced in the new Sino-German BIT signed in 2003, which, according to the UNCTAD, entered into force in November 2005. This BIT adopted the national treatment (NT) standard without the above mentioned qualifying phrases, but a "grandfather clause".[57] In other words, it permits all existing discriminatory measures against foreign investment maintained in China, but prohibits the introduction of any new derogatory measures.[58] Moreover, it requires China to gradually phase out such incompatible measures.[59] It is beyond doubt that such "stand-still" and "roll-back" provisions will, once effected, place substantial limits on the discretion that Chinese government would otherwise have in treating foreign investment in general and German investment in particular.[60] In this context, it is relevant to recall that China has massively revised its foreign investment laws, at least partly because of the obligations and pressures based on such BITs and ongoing BIT negotiations.[61]

Most-favored-nation treatment

The reason that the new Sino-German BIT would affect China's discretion to regulate foreign investment in general is mainly because in every Chinese BIT there is an MFN clause, which is another key clause of BITs. This clause requires that all the benefits and privileges that China grants to investors and investment from any other states must be also given to the investors and investment from the counter-state party with which China has a BIT arrangement. In other words, the aforementioned expanded bene-

---

[54] See Timothy A. Steinert, "If the BIT Fits: The Proposed Bilateral Investment Treaty between the United States and the People's Republic of China," *Journal of Chinese Law*, 2: 434(1988).

[55] See Article 3(3) of the 1986 Sino-British BIT.

[56] Shan, *Legal Framework*, p. 153.

[57] Article 2(2), Sino-German BIT 2003.

[58] Point 3(Re: Arts. 2 and 3), Protocol to the new Sino-German BIT.

[59] Ibid.

[60] Nevertheless, regulation of investment admission or establishment is not subject to NT obligations, and NT obligations do not require the extension of a tax privilege, exemption or reduction to domestic investors to foreign investors. Point 4(Re: Art. 3), Protocol to the new Sino-Germany BIT.

[61] For further details on these changes, see Wenhua Shan, *Legal Framework*, pp. 46 –51, 165 –6.

fit of national treatment, although only stipulated in the new Sino-German BITs, once it came into effect, should be extended to all other states with which China has a BIT arrangement. Therefore, UK investors who enjoyed little if any national treatment from China could expect the treatment to be upgraded to the level provided for in the new Sino-German BIT. French investors who previously did not enjoy national treatment at all could also expect the same level of national treatment from China. Although this is only about substantive benefits, the MFN clause may also have the power to multiply the benefits contained in procedural provisions. I will come back to this issue later, but suffice it to say that the MFN clause has the magical effect of multiplying and therefore further strengthening the limitations and restrictions that other treaty provisions might place on a state party, such as China.

Expropriation and compensation

Another essential provision in BITs is about expropriation and its compensation, which deals with whether and under what conditions a host state may nationalize foreign property. In this regard, Chinese BITs typically adopt an open definition of what constitutes "expropriation," which includes "expropriation, nationalization and measures of similar effect."[62] Such open-ended definition may, in fact, be interpreted very broadly to embrace, as in the judgment in the well-publicized *Metaclad* case (decided under NAFTA Chapter 11),

> not only open, deliberate and acknowledged takings of property, such as outright seizure or formal or obligatory transfer of title in favour of the host State, but also *covert or incidental interference with the use of property which has the effect of depriving the owner, in whole or in significant part, of the use or reasonably-to-be-expected economic benefit of property* even if not necessarily to the obvious benefit of the host State.[63]

It is beyond doubt that such broad reach of the definition of "expropriation" has the effect of significantly limiting the ability of host governments to regulate foreign investment. It also encourages foreign investors to file "frivolous claims' against local government. Partly on account of such an investor-friendly approach taken by international investment arbitration tribunals, recent years have seen a dramatic increase of investment treaty-based arbitration cases.[64]

Once expropriation is established, there comes the question of compensation. On this issue, Chinese BITs, like most BITs, guarantee that foreign investors will obtain compensation

---

[62] For example, all BITs between China and the EU member states have adopted such a broad definition of "expropriation." For details see Wenhua Shan, *Legal Framework*, pp. 194, 315.

[63] *Metalclad Corporation* v. *The United Mexican States*, ICSID CASE No. ARB(AF)/97/1, para. 103, emphasis added.

[64] According to UNCTAD, by November 2005 there had been 219 investment treatybased arbitration cases, among which more than two thirds were initiated since 2002. In other words, on average more than 30 cases had been launched each year in the last four years. Almost all these cases were brought by investors against states, and developing states are the worst victims. Among them, Argentina topped the league table with 42 cases, which accounted for nearly 20 percent of the total caseload. In the year 2003 alone, there were 20 cases against Argentina, accounting for nearly half of the total investment arbitration caseload worldwide, creating a miracle in world arbitration history!

that is "equivalent to the value of the expropriated investment," and is paid without undue delay, and is realizable and freely transferable.[65] Such a high standard of compensation appears reasonable, but in times may put the host government in a "Catch-22" situation. What happened in Argentina provides an example in point. In response to a major economic crisis, the Argentine government issued the Emergency Law 25561 in January 2002, which had the effect of freezing local tariff and abolishing the one-to-one US dollar-peso convertibility. Such measures had significant negative impact on foreign investors,[66] who then sued the host government for breach of BITs, particularly the expropriation clauses. As of today, Argentina has more than 40 pending cases before the ICSID. Such a huge caseload for one single country constitutes a significant burden, politically as well as financially. It is estimated that on average lawyers' charges alone for an investment treaty-based arbitration would amount to US $ 1 or 2 million; then there would be costs for the tribunals, which would need about US $ 400,000.[67] This means Argentina would have to pay tens of millions of dollars annually in order to cope with the cases. If it lost the cases, the compensation would amount to US $ 17 billion,[68] which, as alleged by Argentina, exceeds its annual financial budget.[69] In other words, the Argentine government might effectively go bankrupt because of such compensation for expropriation!

Although there has been no investment arbitration case against China so far, no one can guarantee that it will not happen in the future. Given the huge number of BITs and the recently adopted very liberal approach in terms of substantive protection and procedural access, it is indeed very likely that China will have to face such cases in the near future. Even if this never happened, the limits and restraints such provisions place on Chinese sovereign power are undoubtedly significant.

Access to international arbitration

I shall now finally turn to procedural provisions. The key question here is whether and to what extent foreign investors can resort to international arbitration tribunals, rather than local courts. In other words, this is about the degree of concession on the "judicial sovereignty" of the host state. China has been very cautious on this and has placed significant limits on access to international tribunals. For example, in the Sino-UK BIT signed in 1986, China only agreed to submit issues about the "amount of compensation" in case of expropriation to international arbitration tribunals.[70] Later on, since the early

[65] See Wenhua Shan, *Legal Framework*, pp. 201, 318.

[66] One commentator observed that the net consequence of these measures for the utility companies was "a roughly two-thirds reduction in income."

[67] The lawyers' charge for the plaintiffs are about the same amount. See UNCTAD, *Issues Related to Investment Arrangements: Investor-State Disputes and Policy Implication*, TD/B/COM. 2/62(14 January 2005), p. 7.

[68] Indeed, the CMS award, the first of the many Argentine cases, has required Argentina to pay the company US $ 1330 million. See UNCTAD, *Latest Developments in Investor-State Disputes Settlement*, IIA Monitor No. 4(2005) (UNCTAD/WEB/ITE/ IIT/2005/2), p. 6. See also Luke Peterson, "Argentina moves to annul award in dispute with CMS Company over financial crisis," *Investment Treaty News(ITN)*, 26 October 2005, posted at www.iisd.org/pdf/2005/(accessed on 11 February 2006), pp. 4 – 6.

[69] Luke Peterson, ibid.

[70] Article 7, Sino-UK BIT.

1990s, after China ratified the Convention for the Settlement of Disputes between States and Nationals of Other States(the ICSID Convention), China has broadened the scope of disputes that may be submitted to international arbitration to "any investment disputes" although still requiring China's consent on the submission of disputes that do not concern amount of compensation.[71]

A final breakthrough took place in 1998, when China, for the first time, agreed in the Sino-Barbadian BIT that foreign investors may submit all investment disputes to the ICSID or other international tribunals without a specific consent from the Chinese government. Such open access to international arbitration thus opened a wide door for foreign investors to avoid the domestic judicial system and resort directly to international courts and tribunals. Since the Sino-Barbadian BIT, China has signed another 27 BITs that accept such open access to international arbitration.[72] Among the total 28 BITs, eight have already entered into force.[73]

If the Maffezini doctrine[74] is to be applied, which at the moment is still uncertain,[75] such open access would be extended to all the 116 states with which China has a BIT arrangement. This may entail serious consequences. As a matter of fact, the reason that China has not been sued in any international investment arbitration tribunal is at least partly because China had adopted a "limited access" policy and such policy is still applicable with regard to major foreign investors in China. By now most of such major foreign investors in China have renegotiated their BITs with China, and once such new BITs with higher substantive standards and open access to international arbitration has entered into force, or once the Maffezini doctrine is clearly and conclusively established, it is almost inevitable that China will have to face waves of investment treaty-based arbitration cases. In times this might become a severe challenge to the Chinese government,

---

〔71〕 For details see Wenhua Shan, *Legal Framework*, pp. 212, 321.

〔72〕 The 27 BITs are with Benin, Bosnia and Herzegovina, Botswana, Congo, Côte d'Ivoire, Cyprus, the Czech Republic(2005), Djibouti, Finland(2004), Germany(2003), Guyana, Jordan(2001), Kenya, Latvia, Mozambique, Myanmar, the Netherlands(2001), Portugal(2005), Russia, Seychelles, Sierra Leone, Spain(2005), Sweden(2004), Trinidad and Tobago, Tunisia, Uganda, and Vanuatu. Seven Chinese BITs offer access to ad hoc international arbitration for all investment disputes without referring to the ICSID arbitration. They are BITs with Brunei Darussalam, North Korea, India, Iran, Namibia, Nigeria(2001), and South Africa. The Sino-Indian BIT also indicates that, in case both parties become member states of the ICSID Convention, state-investor disputes can be submitted to the ICSID for arbitration. (India has not yet joined the ICSID Convention.)

〔73〕 The eight BITs are with Barbados, Cyprus, Germany(2003), Guyana, Myanmar, the Netherlands(2001), Trinidad and Tobago, and Tunisia.

〔74〕 In the case of *Emilio Agustin Maffezini* v. *Spain*, the ICSID tribunal decided that the MFN in a BIT may have the effect of extending benefits contained in procedural provisions. See *Emilio Agustin Maffezini* v. *Spain* Case, ICSID Case No. ARB/97/7, paras. 38 – 64.

〔75〕 Some cases are affirmative of the doctrine, such as *Siemens A. G.* v. *Argentine Republic* (Case No. ARB/02/8), Decision on Jurisdiction of 3 August 2004(*Siemens* v. *Argentina*), para. 103; *Camuzzi International S. A.* v. *Argentine Republic* (Case No. ARB/03/7), Decision on Jurisdiction of 11 May 2005, paras. 120 – 1. Other cases actually answered in the negative, such as *Salini Construttori S. p. A. and Italstrade S. p. A.* v. the *Hashemite Kingdom of Jordan* (Case No. ARB/02/13), Decision of the Tribunal on Jurisdiction of 29 November 2004(*Salini* v. *Jordan*), paras. 117 – 18; *Plama Consortium Limited* v. *Republic of Bulgaria* (Case No. ARB/03/24), Decision on Jurisdiction of 8 February 2005(*Plama* v. *Bulgaria*), paras. 183 – 227.

as it is now to Argentina. One may argue that by then China should be ready for such challenge. I hope so but I sincerely doubt it, because I recall that states as powerful as the USA have from time to time to revise their model BITs to protect the state's sovereign rights to regulate foreign investment. I see no much reason why a developing state such as China should not take these potential challenges seriously and take prompt and decisive counter-measures.

Summary and assessment

To summarize, international treaties such as investment treaties do have significant impact on China's state sovereignty, notably by limiting the government's power to regulate foreign investment, through the operation of substantive provisions such as national treatment and MFN treatment standards, and more concrete clauses such as that of expropriation and compensation. Chinese investment treaties also significantly limited China's adjudicative sovereignty by effectively diverting all foreign investment cases to international arbitration forums such as the ICSID.

Such limitations and restrictions on sovereignty by treaties, serious as they are, are nevertheless, manageable, particularly given that they are bilateral treaties, which are bilaterally negotiated and can be renegotiated and modified as parties see necessary. In other words, no matter how far such treaties might have altered the courses of exercise of state sovereignty, they are still under the ultimate control of the state concerned. The state remains the "marker and changer" of such treaties. It can therefore be argued that such treaties can only change the way sovereignty powers are exercised, but not sovereignty per se, as the "final source of authority."

International organizations: WTO as an example

Compared with treaties, international organizations pose even stronger challenges to state sovereignty. Although international organizations are often established on the basis of treaties, they prove to be much more difficult to handle than treaties themselves. Indeed, a treaty is like a marriage certificate, yet an international organization is like a baby born of such a marriage—although they are both the outcomes of the same marriage, they are outcomes of greatly different type, and as a result, it is far easier to deal with a certificate than handling a lively baby.

Since World War II, many international organizations have come into being. Many of them are economic organizations, including the now much talked about "Bretton Woods system" organizations, namely the World Bank (IBRD), the International Monetary Fund (IMF), and the General Agreement on Tariffs and Trade (GATT), which was the subtitle of the International Trade Organization conceived at Bretton Woods and which has now been replaced by the World Trade Organization (WTO). China has acceded by now to all these major international economic organizations. I shall now take the WTO as an example to illustrate the impact that a powerful international organization may have on state sovereignty in general and Chinese state sovereignty in particular.

The WTO is often blamed for threatening state sovereignty by its invasion into all the three major aspects of sovereign powers: legislative, executive, and adjudicative ones. More specifically, the three aspects refer to the WTO agreements, its decision-making procedures, and its dispute-settlement mechanism. Such threats were amply discussed and hotly debated in the 1994 Sovereignty Debate within the Congress of the United States, when it was to decide whether or not the US should accept the WTO agreements, as the final result of the Uruguay Round of GATT negotiations.[76] I shall now assess the impact of the WTO on Chinese sovereignty by referring to these three aspects of the WTO system.

The WTO agreements

First of all, the WTO agreements, like the investment treaties we just discussed, represent a significant intrusion into the legislative power of member states. Article 16 of the Agreement Establishing the World Trade Organization (the WTO Agreement, sometimes referred to as the "WTO Charter") expressly requires that "[E]ach Member shall ensure the conformity of its laws, regulations and administrative procedures with its obligations as provided in the annexed Agreements."[77] It further stipulates that "[N]o reservations may be made in respect of any provision of this Agreement."[78] Thus, the WTO Charter abandoned the "grandfather provision" in the GATT, which permitted all existing incompatible measures of domestic laws to continue to exist and function. As a matter of fact, China promulgated a wide range of new laws and regulations and revised a number of existing laws, in order to comply with the obligation undertaken under the WTO Agreement, as detailed in its Accession Protocol.[79] For example, China revised its Foreign Trade Law and all the major laws of foreign investment.[80] China also passed a number of new laws to implement her commitments with regard to a range of service areas, such as banking, insurance, cargo transportation, telecommunication, printing, cinema, distribution, venture capital, and leasing.[81] It would not an exaggeration to say that such vast legislative changes were unprecedented in modern Chinese history. Yet China did it, without much heard complaint about the loss of her sovereignty.

The WTO decision-making mechanism

The second important challenge of the WTO to state sovereignty is an institutional challenge, which may be regarded as a challenge more to the executive power of member states. Unlike its predecessor, the GATT, which did not form an organization in a legal sense, the WTO is a powerful formal international organization with a proper internation-

---

〔76〕 John H Jackson, "The Great 1994 Sovereignty Debate: United States Acceptance and Implementation of the Uruguay Round Results," *Columbia Journal of Transnational Law*, 36(157): 170 – 88.

〔77〕 Article 16(4), Agreement Establishing the World Trade Organization, available at www.wto.org/English/docs_e/legal_e/04-wto.pdf (accessed on 25 December 2006).

〔78〕 Ibid, Article 16(5).

〔79〕 The Protocol of Accession of the People's Republic of China, together with the Working Party Report and schedules of commitments, is available at the WTO website: www.wto.org/English/thewto_e/acc_e/completeacc_e.htm (accessed on 25 December 2006).

〔80〕 The Foreign Trade Law was revised in April 2004 and is available at www.law-lib.com/law/ (visited on 25 December 2006). For details of the changes to Chinese FDI laws see Wenhua Shan, *Legal Framework*, pp. 46 – 51.

〔81〕 For details of such new legislation, see *The New Compilation of Laws, Regulations and Ministerial Rules on Foreign Trade and Economic Co-operation of the People's Republic of China* (hereinafter "the New Compilation"), edited by the Ministry of Foreign Trade and Economic Co-operation (now the Ministry of Commerce, the MOFCOM), in Chinese Law Press, 2002.

al legal personality.[82] What is most important in the context of this discussion is that it has its own decision-making bodies and procedures and, according to the WTO Charter, such decisions may constitute part of the overall obligations binding on all member states.[83] The ultimate decision-making body within the WTO is the Ministerial Conference, and the WTO Charter stipulates that the Ministerial Conference "shall carry out the functions of the WTO and take actions necessary to this effect" and "shall have the authority to take decisions on all matters under any of the Multilateral Trade Agreements."[84] Moreover, the Ministerial Conference and the General Council(a permanent decisionmaking body established under the Ministerial Conference, which is composed of representatives of WTO members) have the "exclusive authority to adopt formal interpretations of the WTO Agreement the annexed Multilateral Agreement."[85] Although the WTO tends to work on a consensus basis, the existence of formal voting procedures suggests that the decisions made by the WTO may not always be consistent with a particular member's wishes.[86] Yet all the members shall carry out such decisions, regardless whether they voted for or against it. In this sense, it can be regarded as another major threat to national sovereignty, particularly the "executive sovereignty."

The WTO dispute settlement mechanism

The WTO's final and probably most significant threat to state sovereignty, however, is its powerful dispute settlement mechanism(DSM). Widely heralded as the most important and unique contribution of the WTO to global economy,[87] the WTO DSM features four automaticities: automatic jurisdiction, automatic acceptance of panel report, automatic acceptance of Appellate Body reports, and automatic authorization of retaliation. Among them, automatic jurisdiction refers to the fact that almost every request for the setting up of a dispute settlement panel will be accepted. In other words, each WTO member, once it has a complaint against any other member, can bring a litigation against the other member, with the need to seek "consent" from its counter-party, as is normally required by statutes of other international courts and tribunals. This is because the WTO adopts a "reverse consensus" rule in this process. Thus when a member has a dispute, it shall first seek consultation with its counter-party.[88] Failing to achieve an agreement

[82] The WTO Agreement expressly confirms that "The WTO shall have legal personality, and shall be accorded by each of its Members such legal capacity as may be necessary for the exercise of its functions." See Article 8 (1), the WTO Agreement.

[83] The WTO Ministerial Conference and the General Council, for example, have the exclusive authority to adopt interpretations of the WTO Agreement and of the Multilateral Trade Agreements. Further, in exceptional circumstances, the Ministerial Conference may decide to waive an obligation imposed on a Member by this Agreement or any of the Multilateral Trade Agreements. See Article 9(2 – 3), the WTO Agreement.

[84] Article 6(1), the WTO Agreement.

[85] See Article 9(2), the WTO Agreement.

[86] For details of the WTO voting system see Article 9(1 – 5), the WTO Agreement.

[87] The WTO itself considers that "Dispute settlement is the central pillar of the multilateral trading system, and the WTO's unique contribution to the stability of the global economy." The WTO: Understanding the WTO: Settling Disputes, posted at www.wto.org/english/thewto_e/whatis_e/tif_e/disp1_e.htm(accessed on 25 December 2006).

[88] Article 4, Understanding on Rules and Procedures Governing the Settlement of Disputes(the DSU), available at www.wto.org/english/docs_e/legal_e/28 – dsu.doc(accessed on 25 December 2006).

through such consultation, the claimant can formally launch the "judicial process" by requesting the WTO Dispute Settlement Body, which is the General Council wearing another hat, to set up a panel to hear the case.[89] The request will be accepted, unless there is a consensus to the opposite result.[90] As at least the claimant member will for sure uphold such a request, it can be practically certain that such a request will be accepted. Same "reverse consensus" rule applies to the approval of the "decisions"("recommendations" in the formal words) of the panel, and in case of an appeal, of the Appellate Body.[91] Likewise, in case a member loses the case and fail to comply with the DSB rulings, the winning party may request an authorization of trade "retaliation"(mainly in the form of withdrawal of commitments made to the counter party).[92] Again, such request will "automatically" be approved, as the same "reverse consensus" rule applies thereto.[93] The four "automaticities" have the merit of maintaining "judicial independence," but meanwhile, have the effect of depriving states of the opportunity to give "consent" to a particular case involved. Therefore, they represent a remarkable restraint on members' sovereignty, particularly "adjudicative sovereignty." There are also other sovereignty concerns such as judicial activism, by which panels might stretch interpretations to achieve certain policy results they favor, standard of review, by which the WTO panels examine national government actions such as anti-dumping actions, the obligation to comply with panel rulings, and the legal precedent effect of panel reports and appellate body(AB) recommendations.

Indeed, the concerns on the interference of the WTO DSM over national sovereignty have been so grave in the 1994 US Congress Sovereignty Debate that a bill was proposed to set up a Commission to review every panel report adverse to US interests, judging against four criteria.[94] The draft bill stated that:

> [t]he continued support of the Congress for the WTO is dependent upon a WTO dispute settlement system that:
>
> A) operates in a fair and impartial manner;
>
> B) does not add to the obligations of or diminish the rights of the United States under the Uruguay Round agreements; and
>
> C) does not exceed its authority, scope, or established standard of review.[95]

The bill thus effective places WTO DSB decisions, as a part of compact of the WTO Agreement, under the scrutiny of a national organ against national law. Al-

---

[89] Ibid., Article 6.

[90] Ibid.

[91] Ibid., Articles 16 and 19.

[92] Ibid., Article 22.

[93] Ibid., Article 22(6).

[94] The four specific criteria check whether the panel had: (1) exceeded its authority or terms of reference; (2) added to the obligations, or diminished the rights, of the United States; (3) acted arbitrarily or capriciously or engaged in misconduct, etc.; or(4) deviated from the applicable standard of review including that in Article 17(6) of the antidumping text. Jackson, "Sovereignty Debate," pp. 186 –7.

[95] Ibid., p. 186.

though it does not seem to have been materialized, such an attempt demonstrates very clearly that states have been deeply concerned about this new and powerful invention of the WTO.

China has not passed or considered such a bill. Nor has there been such a great debate about sovereignty and the WTO accession, which may or may not be a good thing. China has, nevertheless, passed an Order, by the Supreme People's Court, to the effect of ruling out the "direct effect" of the WTO agreements.[96] Although this is consistent with practices of other major trading powers such as the US and the EU, it nevertheless signals an attitude of caution towards the rules of the WTO.

To sum up, it is not an exaggeration to say that the WTO, together with the treaties establishing it, has an unprecedented impact on China's sovereign powers to regulate international trade relations, ranging from legislative power to executive and adjudicative powers. WTO accession has already resulted in massive legislative activities in China; decisions made by the WTO are binding on China; and the DSM of the WTO challenges China's long held concept of "state consent" in establishing jurisdiction of international courts and tribunals over states. Although there has been no great sovereignty debate as in the US in 1994 over acceptance of WTO obligations, the Chinese have been cautious of the potential negative impacts of the WTO membership, as witnessed by the recently promulgated Order by the Supreme People's Court.

Observations

It can be concluded that, despite hesitations and reservations in the earlier years of opening up to the outside world, China now has little if any difficulty in accepting limitations and restrictions on its sovereign powers, legislative, executive, or adjudicative, in international economic relations, particularly in international investment and trade relations.[97] In other words, China seems to have become ready to give up certain "economic sovereignty" in return for perceived opportunities of economic development. This pro-

---

[96] Article 7 of the Order prescribes that:

"[w]hen a people's court hears international trade administration cases, it shall apply the laws and administrative regulations of the People's Republic of China, and local regulations relating to or having an effect on international trade, as laid down by local legislatures within their legislative competence. Such local legislation applies only to its own local administrative regions."

Thus it does not uphold the direct applicability of international trade treaties such as the WTO Agreement. The Order, nevertheless, provides that:

"[I]n case there are two or more interpretations of the concrete provisions in applicable laws and regulations, and one of such interpretations is in conformity with relevant provisions of an international treaty that China has concluded or participated in, the people's court shall choose the interpretation that conforms to the international treaty provisions, except the case that China has lodged a reservation to such provisions."

See Articles 7 and 9, the Supreme People's Court Order on Certain Issues Concerning the Hearing of International Trade Administration Cases, The Supreme People's Court Fashi No. [2002] 27(27 August 2002).

[97] In other international economic areas, we can also see China being a very active participant. For example, in the banking and financial law area, China is an active member of the IMF and the IBRD, as well as of the ICSID and the Multilateral Investment Guarantee Agency(MIGA). In regional economic integration, which China opposed initially, China has take impressive steps, particularly in engaging in free trade agreement negotiations with countries in the Asia-Pacific regions, such as ASEAN, Australia, New Zealand, and with Middle Asian states under the "Shanghai Five" mechanism.

vides a sharp contrast with China's standing on sovereignty in general, which still sticks to the traditional concept of "inviolable sovereignty", particularly when issues such as territorial sovereignty and integrity, humanitarian intervention, and universal human rights are concerned. China's recent general opinions on sovereignty are discussed below.

Recent Official Statements on State Sovereignty: Insisting on Inviolable Sovereignty

Despite significant concessions in "economic sovereignty", China's general opinion on state sovereignty seems to have hardly changed. Still, the FPPC is dearly upheld with state sovereignty lying at its heart. Still, China opposes any interference in domestic affairs, including those with the excuse of humanitarian intervention.[98] In the 46th Session of the United Nations General Assembly, when Boutros Boutros-Ghali rejected the Westphalian concept of "absolute sovereignty" whilst upholding the important of state sovereignty in general, the Chinese Foreign Minister, Qian Qichen, stated:

> The turbulent and complex international situation has further awakened all countries and people of the world to the demand for the establishment of a new international order, making it more urgent and stronger... *A new international order should be established on the basis of mutual respect for sovereignty and territorial integrity, mutual non-aggression, non-interference in each other's internal affairs, equality and mutual benefit, and peaceful coexistence*.... Only when all states promise to implement these principles will it be likely to establish genuine democracy in international relations.[99]

In 2004, a major celebration of the fiftieth anniversary of the FPPC was held in Beijing, where Chinese Premier Wen Jiabao stated:

> *Sovereignty is the birthmark of any independent state*, the crystallization of its national interests and the best safeguard of all it holds dear. *The increasing interaction and interdependence among countries,* thanks to surging economic globalization and technological revolution, *does not mean that the status and role of sovereignty can in any way be neglected or weakened ... No country has the right to impose its will on others, nor can it undermine or deny other countries' sovereignty under whatever excuse.* Facts have proven that such practices as disregarding other's sovereignty, bullying the small and the weak by dint of one's size and power, and pursuing hegemony and power politics would

[98] It is notable that China's general opposition to humanitarian intervention activities does not prevent her from increasingly participating in UN peacekeeping activities. Since 1990, China has sent 465 Military Observers to UN-led authorities such as UNSTO, UNIKOM, UNTAC, MINURSO, ONUMOZ, UNOMIL and UNOMSIL. In 1992, she sent an army of 800 engineers to the UNTAC. In 1997, China decided that she should, in principle, participate in UN peacekeeping arrangements, and provide, when appropriate, military observers, civil police force, engineering, medical, transportation, and other logistic personnel. So far four Chinese peacekeeping personnel have died when performing their duties. See *PLA Daily*, "China Participates in Peacekeeping Activities in a Positive and Practical Manner," posted at www. pladaily. com. cn/item/peace/(accessed on 23 December 2006).

[99] *Renmin Ribao* (*People's Daily*), 26 September 1991, emphasis added.

not get anywhere... *China will firmly safeguard its sovereignty and territorial integrity, tolerating no one to interfere in its internal affairs.* At the same time, it will respect the sovereignty and territorial integrity of others.[100]

The FPPC was also reiterated in the White Paper on "China's Approach of Peaceful Development(CAPD)" as the basis upon which China shall develop its relationship with other states.[101] The CAPD also reiterates that China shall "insist on the peaceful settlement of international disputes or conflicts through equal negotiations and consultations; oppose the practices of invading other sovereign states; oppose intervening into domestic affairs of other states; and oppose the arbitrary use of force or threat by force." A most recent development thereon is the CPC Foreign Affairs Meeting, during which President Hu Jintao emphasized that, in the conducting of foreign affairs, China should "protect state sovereignty, security and development interests."[102] A more sophisticated assessment of sovereignty and international law in the post-Cold War world is found in an article by Liu Zhenmin, the then Legal Advisor to the Chinese Ministry of Foreign Affairs (now Deputy Ambassador of China to the United Nations). He wrote,

> "Since the Cold War ended, the UN Charter and international law have been challenged. Western countries raised the theories of "humanitarian intervention" and "primacy of human rights over sovereignty" and put them in continuous practice. In 1999, NATO headed by the United States waged the Kosovo war on the excuse of "humanitarian intervention," and caused objections from the majority of the states of the world. In 2003, the US breached the UN Charter, disregarded the Security Council, and launched the Iraqi War on the excuse of "eliminating weapons of mass destruction," and resulted in an anti-war campaign unprecedented in human history. On the surface, the aforementioned wars have seriously challenged international law—international law no longer seems to be working. But in fact, such wars were only acts in violation of international law, and they did not change the contents of the principle of international relations, nor did they shake the foundation of international law. Although sovereign acts of states are increasingly subject to the influence of the institutionalization of the international community, economic globalization and regional integration, principles such as sovereign equality, non-intervention into domestic affairs, non-use of force, and peaceful settlement of disputes are still irreplaceable norms guiding cotemporary international relations.[103]

---

[100] Wen Jiabao, "Carrying Forward the Five Principles of Peaceful Coexistence in the Promotion of Peace and Development, Speech at a Rally Commemorating the 50th Anniversary of the Five Principles of Peaceful Coexistence," reprinted in the *Chinese Journal of International Law* 3(363):365(2004), emphasis added.

[101] State Council Press Office, *China's Approach of Peaceful Development* (December 2005), parts II and V.

[102] China News Agency, "Hu Made Important Speech at the CPC Foreign Affairs Meeting," 23 August 2006, posted at www.chinanews.com.cn/(accessed on 16 September 2006).

[103] Liu Zhenmin, "Guoji Zhixu yu Zhongguo de Heping Fazhan"(International Order and China's Peaceful Development), *Qiushi* (*Seeking Truth*), 10(2005), part II. Also available at http://theory.people.com.cn/GB/(accessed on 15 September 2007).

Ambassador Liu's remarks not only provide us a vivid Chinese evaluation of the current international order and the role of international law, but also, once again, demonstrate China's unambiguous opposition to certain Western doctrines such as "humanitarian intervention" and "primacy of human rights over sovereignty." Whereas China's opposition to intervention into domestic affairs is already wellknown and has been documented by the previously cited official statements,[104] China's rejection of the idea of the "primacy of human rights over sovereignty" is equally, if not even more, notorious in the world. Although China has now acceded to all major UN-sponsored multilateral human rights conventions[105] and included human rights protection in the recently modified Constitution, China still finds it uneasy to entertain the primacy of human rights over state sovereignty. For the Chinese, the opposite is right: no state sovereignty, no human rights. This is at least partly due to Chinese history and culture, which are vastly different from the West, where the concept of human rights was originally conceived and flourished.[106]

Another area that also clearly manifests China's insistence on the "inviolability of sovereignty" doctrine is territorial integrity and sovereignty. This is amply demonstrated by the saying by Deng Xiaoping during talks with British leaders on the handover of Hong Kong, which has been frequently repeated now by Chinese officials when asked about talks with Taiwan on the terms of reunification: "Sovereignty is not an issue open for negotiation!"

It may be safe to conclude that China still adheres to a sovereignty-bound thinking and generally the "inviolability of sovereignty" doctrine. However, when it comes to more specific areas of the exercise of state sovereignty, China displays a certain inconsistency in her approach: although she is ready to give up "economic sovereignty" by signing up to numerous international economic treaties and organizations, she seems to be rather stubborn about compromising sovereignty in politically sensitive areas, or "political sov-

---

[104] It is drawn on the basis of the bitter semicolonial history, and constitutes the very core of the "inviolability of sovereignty" doctrine.

[105] Most of these conventions are on collective or group human rights treaties with regard to women, racial discrimination, refugees, apartheid, torture, and children. In this respect, the most remarkable development is reflected in China's signing in 1998 of the two basic human rights covenants, of which one, the International Covenant on Economic, Social and Cultural Rights, has been ratified by the Chinese government recently. Steps are also being seriously taken for ratifying the other, namely the International Covenant on Civil and Political Rights.

[106] Li commented,

"A century of humiliation, domination, and oppression at the hands of foreign imperialism, has convinced the Chinese that, without national independence, there would be no guarantee for their basic human rights... Culturally, the traditional Chinese notion perceived the meaning of human beings from their social being in an intricate web of social relationship rather than from their atomized autonomy. Thus, values such as liberty and autonomy were not prized as the ends in themselves in the way as they have been in the Western nations. This does not suggest that there is no respect for human dignity in the Chinese cultural context, but rather its basis is different. Respect for human dignity as viewed by the Chinese, lies in the integrity of harmonic and orderly social bonds and is meant to be exercised for the purpose of fostering collective welfare through both moral exhortation internalized in the individual and by means of the legal restriction of government power vis-à-vis individual."

See Zhaojie Li, "Legacy of Modern Chinese History: Its Relevance to the Chinese Perspective of the Contemporary International Legal Order," *Singapore Journal of International and Comparative Law* 5(314): 325.

ereignty," including humanitarian intervention, human rights, and territorial integrity. Such inconsistency takes me into the concluding part, revisiting the concept of sovereignty, in an effort to understand or explain the seemingly contradictory Chinese position state sovereignty.

Concluding Remarks: the Concept of Sovereignty Revisited

My explanation of the seemly contradicting approaches of China towards sovereignty is actually neither completely novel[107] nor very complicated, although I consider it of considerable importance in the current general debate on the concept of sovereignty. Much of the confusions surrounding the concept of sovereignty in the current sovereignty debate have resulted from a confusion of two concepts of sovereignty at two different levels.

On the one hand, at the conceptual level, there is the concept of sovereignty in the abstract, which may be called "abstract sovereignty." It inherits the concept first conceived by Jean Bodin as the "final (or 'ultimate') source of authority." That who possess such authority is the "Sovereign," be it the king/queen, a state, a people, or a multinational. If the world remains a land of order, or order of certain degree, there must be "sovereignty" or "sovereignties" of some kind. In this sense, the concept of "sovereignty" has hardly changed, and will not change in a foreseeable future. Strictly speaking, only such "abstract sovereignty" is real "sovereignty," as only it possesses the essential character of "sovereignty," which is "the final source of authority." In the current world, although other players such as people, multinationals, and international organizations, are playing more and more important roles, it cannot be denied that states remain the center of the framework of the entire world order. Much has been changed in the world, but the core still remains the same. In this sense, Sir Robert Jennings is right to point out that,

> If one looks at the Charter of the United Nations, the very title assumes that it is an organisation of sovereignty and equal States. The delegation which composes the General Assembly and the Security Council are the representatives of sovereign States. And this is broadly true of all the organizations that form part of the United Nations system. The International Court of Justice, the principal judicial organ of the United Nations, by Article 34 of its Statute is still, in its contentious jurisdiction, confined to disputes between States. Looking even briefly at such international constitutional law as we have, one can only conclude that the suggested demise of national State sovereignty has been much exaggerated.[108]

---

[107] My double-layer approach is largely inspired by Rousseau's *Social Contract* and the *Discourses*, in which, in upholding his view that sovereignty is indivisible, he criticized political theorists for dividing sovereignty according to its object, and for taking the application of sovereignty as components of sovereignty itself. Jean-Jacques Rousseau, *The Social Contract and the Discourses*, translated by G. G. H. Cole, revised edition (place: David Campbell Publishers, 1993), pp. 200 - 1.

[108] Jennings, "Sovereignty and International Law," pp. 34 - 5.

Yet there is also the concept(or, perhaps more accurately, the conception) of sovereignty in the concrete(or "concrete sovereignty"), at the operational level, which refers to the actual powers that derive from and implement the "final source of authority"("abstract sovereignty"), and which may be "decomposed" and divided into legislative, executive, and adjudicative powers(or "sovereignty" as often used or rather "misused"), or economic, political, social, and cultural powers. It might also be decomposed "vertically" into supranational, national, federal, or provincial powers. In a strict sense, "concrete sovereignty" is not "sovereignty" per se, but subordinate powers or rights, which always imply sovereignty of which they only sanction the execution.[109] To avoid confusion, it would be better use the term "power," rather than "sovereignty," to describe such decomposed authorities. Sovereign powers so decomposed or "sliced" may then be allocated, delegated or transferred, in the process of which the "power allocation analysis" that John Jackson advocated may be applied.

Looking through the double-layer concept of sovereignty, one may find it easier to understand and explain the current Chinese concepts of sovereignty. China's generally sovereignty-centered thinking and obsession with the "inviolability of sovereignty" doctrine actually refer to the "abstract sovereignty" concept, which essentially means that China, as a sovereign state, should retain the ultimate control over the domestic affairs within the country and enjoy an equal standing in the international community. In other words, what such thinking and doctrine demand is nothing more than a rightful place and equal status of the state of China on the international stage. And in this sense, it cannot be violated, divided, or transferred. Because once abstract sovereignty was violated or divided or transferred, the very foundation of the sovereign state would have been shaken, and as a result, the state would no longer able to hold itself as a sovereign entirety, but face the fate of falling into pieces.

On the other hand, the economic "sovereignty," and the political, refer to the "concrete sovereignty" or, more precisely, specific sovereign powers. They can be divided, allocated, delegated, or transferred, perhaps after weighing up the costs and benefits of such allocation, delegation, or transfer. For example, after conducting such a cost-benefit analysis, China might have been convinced that giving up certain economic powers in return of potential increase in investment and trade was worthwhile, and therefore it decided to go down the route of trade and investment liberalization. With regard to specific treaty provisions, this "cost-benefit analysis" may also have been used. Thus China rejected the provisions in her BITs to grant national treatment as a principle and access to international dispute settlement forums in the 1980s, as such provisions were things that China could not realistically afford then. However, since the 1990s, when the general conditions in China had been greatly improved, China decided to accept both provisions in its BIT practice.

---

[109] Rousseau wrote in *Social Contract and Discourses* (p. 21) that, "If we examined the other divisions in the same manner, we should find that, whenever Sovereignty seems to be divided, there is an illusion: the rights which are taken as being part of Sovereignty are really all subordinate, and always imply supreme will of which they only sanction the execution."

The bottom line of such power allocation, delegation or transfer, however, is that China shall retain the ultimate control over powers so allocated, delegated or transferred, to ensure that the "abstract sovereignty" or the foundation of all sovereign powers is not replaced. Thus China needs to, for example, retain the right to withdraw from these international treaties and organization. She may also want to maintain control to a certain degree of the operation of such treaty regimes or the decision-making of such organizations. On the other hand, so long as China remains abstract sovereignty, she shall have every confidence to continue her "power allocation" activities.

The same double-layer analysis can be made of the aforementioned aspects of the application of "political sovereignty," including human rights, humanitarian interventions, and territorial disputes. In the general rhetoric of the "primary of sovereignty over human rights," China actually refers to the "abstract sovereignty," which means that, however important human rights may be, their actual implementation has to be done within the current political reality of the world, that is to say, under the sovereignty of states. It does not exclude China from joining in concrete actions to implement specific norms of human rights, such as joining international conventions or engaging in rights dialogues.

Partly because of China's insistence on the "primacy of sovereignty over human rights," China unreservedly rejects the idea of "humanitarian intervention." Another reason is that such interventions often take the form of armed invasion into territories of other sovereign states, and therefore violates another much cherished principle: "territorial integrity."

"Territorial integrity", or "territorial sovereignty", as part of the "abstract sovereignty," is certainly inviolable and as such closed for "negotiation." This, however, does not prevent China to give up certain important powers relating to the specific execution of such sovereignty. This is most amply witnessed by the high autonomy China's two Special Administrative Regions now enjoy, under the much celebrated "one country, two systems" arrangement.

Such is my "double-layer" approach to the understanding and explanation of the Chinese concept of sovereignty, which I hope will also be helpful in the current debate on the general concept of state sovereignty.

Introduction to "The Pacific Rim and International Economic Law: Opportunities and Risks of the Pacific Century"*

Recent State practice strongly suggests that the international economic law architecture for the 21st century largely will be shaped in the Pacific Rim region. Negotiations of two "mega-regional" free trade agreements—the Trans-Pacific Partnership(TPP) and the Regional Comprehensive Economic Partnership(RCEP) —continue to advance. Japan, Korea, and China recently concluded a trilateral investment agreement. The world's two largest economies—China and the United States—held their 17th round of bilateral investment treaty negotiations in December. Japan has announced a "Revitalization Strategy, " identifying a number of economic priorities, including the negotiation of new investment agreements. Asia-Pacific Economic Cooperation(APEC) members recently agreed to launch a feasibility study, proposed by China, to consider a potential Free Trade Area of the Asia-Pacific agreement(FTAAP) .

At the same time, however, international economic law challenges in the Pacific Rim region remain significant. Overlapping treaties can create a "noodle bowl" of complex, unpredictable rules. Japan and Australia recently opted not to include an investor-state dispute settlement mechanism in their free trade agreement, and Indonesia has announced that it will not renew its existing bilateral investment treaties. The impact of certain rapidly developing areas of law in the Pacific Rim region, such as anti-corruption and intellectual property law, is only beginning to emerge. Treaty practice aimed at achieving a level playing field between state-owned and privately-owned enterprises remains, to date, limited.

This TDM Special Issue collects views of more than thirty contributors, based in more than ten countries, on these and other key international economic law issues facing the Pacific Rim region.

The Pacific Rim special begins with introductory remarks by J. Christopher Thomas, Q. C. , who observes that "*plurilateral* treaty negotiations such as the TPP, if successful, will usher in a new era" of treaty practice, which holds great potential for achieving "a much greater degree of investment treaty policy convergence between North America, the European Union and Asia than has previously been the case. " Current treaty practice—particularly in the Pacific Rim region, where investment treaty—making "continues unabated"—also is raising important "new issues, " such as how investment obligations should be applied in cases involving state-owned enterprises or corrupt actors. The papers collected in the Pacific Rim special contribute to "our collective understanding" of this "new world of investment treaty-making and investment treaty arbitration. "

---

* Transnational Dispute Management 1, 2015. The authors are Feldman, Mark and Shan Wenhua.

Regarding negotiations of "mega-regional" trade agreements in the Pacific Rim region, the Special Issue includes three articles addressing the TPP and one article addressing the RCEP. In "*The Case Against China's Joining the Trans-Pacific Partnership*," Ming Du maintains that the TPP poses "a serious policy challenge to China as a new rising power" and recommends, in light of several factors including the potential for significant concessions and regulatory reform, that China not join the TPP negotiations. Christopher Hunt and Colin Trehearne explore Japan's interest in the TPP in "*Japan in the Pacific Century: Opportunities and Challenges arising from the TPP.*" In that article, Hunt and Trehearne examine several economic and political factors driving Japan's participation in the TPP negotiations. Alastair Henderson and GittaSatryani, in "*Regulating State Owned Enterprises in the TPP: The View from South East Asia*," analyze the TPP as an instrument that likely will, for the first time, establish a set of binding rules applicable to SOEs that are agreed to by a large number of States. TeerawatWongkaew, in "*Disentangling the RCEP Noodle Bowl: Legal and Policy Challenges*," recommends that RCEP negotiators include consideration of the "noodle bowl effect"—the complexity and lack of predictability that can result from a multi-layered investment agreement regime. Wongkaew analyzes whether a consolidation approach would be the most effective response by RCEP negotiators to the existence of overlapping treaties.

Two contributors address the ongoing US-China BIT negotiations. Kristina Andjelic, in "*A U. S. -China BIT-Resolution of Investment Disputes in Context of Transparency Issues*," analyzes the role that a U. S. -China BIT could play in contributing to the social legitimacy of investor-State arbitration. In "*Political Economy of China-U. S. BIT Negotiation: Whose Decisive Pursuit of Leadership inInstitutional Transformation?*" Wang Peng addresses how an evolving power dynamic between the United States and China might impact U. S. -China BIT negotiations.

A set of articles analyzes key international economic law developments in individual Pacific Rim countries(Australia, Indonesia, Canada, China, and Japan) and groups of countries(China/Korea/Japan; The Pacific Islands). Three of those articles focus on Australia: "*Investor-State Dispute Resolution in Australia: A Changing Landscape for Investors*, " by Leon Chung, Donald Robertson, Kate Lindeman, and Anne Hoffmann, "*Do Many of Australia's Bilateral Investment Treaties Really Not Provide Full Advance Consent to Investor-State Arbitration? Analysis of* Planet Mining v. Indonesia *and Regional Implications*, " by Luke Nottage, and "*Locating Australia on the Pacific Rim*, "by Leon Trakman and Kunal Sharma. Chung, Robertson, Lindeman, and Hoffmann analyze Australia's new "case-by-case" approach to ISDS, including options for the use of provisions intended to safeguard against ISDS-related risks. Nottage discusses implications for Australian investment treaties arising from the recent *Planet Mining v. Indonesia* Decision on Jurisdiction, where the Tribunal found the Australia-Indonesia BIT did not include a full, advance consent to arbitrate by Indonesia. Trakman and Sharma consider Australia's ISDS policy in light of Australia's political and economic interests, particularly in connection with key trading partners in the Pacific region.

Michael Ewing-Chow and Junianto James Losari consider recent international investment law developments in Indonesia in "*Reflective or Reactionary? Indonesia's Approaches to International Investment Agreements and Recommendations for the Future.*" Following consideration of Indonesia's investment policies and experience as a respondent in investor-state arbitration, Ewing-Chow and Losari offer recommendations for a new Indonesian model BIT.

Matthew Levine examines Canada's treaty practice in the Pacific Rim region in "*Canada-China FIPPA & Canada-Korea FTA: Recent Canadian Pieces in the Pacific Rim Investment Treaty Jigsaw.*" Levine observes that Canada's recent treaty practice reflects a "fluid negotiating dynamic" by taking a "case-by-case approach to key" investment treaty provisions.

Two articles consider the future of investment law in China. In "*Investor Protection in the Chi-*

na(Shanghai) Pilot Free Trade Zone," Shu Shang recommends that greater investor protections, including an integrated foreign investment insurance system, should be available within the Shanghai Free Trade Zone. In "*Pending Issues in China's BITs: National Treatment, Environmental Protection and Enforcement of Award*," Li Li analyzes how China's investment treaty program will need to adapt to a rapidly increasing level of Chinese outbound foreign direct investment.

Two articles examine Japan's international investment regime. In "*Japan's Ambitious International Investment Agreement Policy-Laying the Groundwork for Future Disputes?*" Jonathan Stoel, Tomoko Ishikawa, and Michael Jacobson predict that Japan will secure treaty coverage for its investors "in the major sites of Japanese foreign investment around the world" and that Japanese investors will capitalize on such expanded coverage by bringing investment treaty claims. In "*What (Japanese) Investors Should Consider Before Commencing an Investment Arbitration*," Lars Markert analyzes key factors for Japanese investors to consider when preparing an investment arbitration claim, including available treaty coverage, early consultations with damages experts, forms of home State assistance, and third-party financing.

In "*Coordinating Exceptions in Domestic Instruments and International Investment Law: Insight into the Japan-China-Korea Trilateral Investment Treaty*," QiangRen analyzes, with respect to foreign investment protections, exceptions available under Chinese domestic law and the Japan-China-Korea trilateral investment treaty. Ren argues that China's increasing reliance on exceptions in its international investment treaty practice will serve as a counterbalance to China's decreasing reliance on exceptions in its domestic law, such as applicable law in the Shanghai FTZ.

With respect to securing protections for international trade in services, Bregt Natens and Radika Kumar address strategic considerations for States located in the Pacific Islands region. In "*The Pacific Islands and Trade in Services: One Step Back to Take Two Steps Forward*," Natens and Kumar recommend that fourteen States in the Pacific Islands region join either the TPP or RCEP negotiations in order to ensure "easy integration of the Pacific services trading system" into a larger market.

A set of articles examines particular disciplines and protections that are of central importance for ongoing treaty negotiations in the Pacific Rim region(state-controlled entities, fair and equitable treatment, anti-corruption, and intellectual property). Two articles examine disciplines and protections applicable to state-controlled entities: "*Competitive Neutrality in the Trans-Pacific Partnership(TPP) Negotiations on International Investment*" by Bao Jin, and "*State-Controlled Entities as Qualified 'Investors': Implications for the Pacific Region Investment Treaty Making*" by Lu Wang. Jin analyzes the regulatory efficacy of an emerging set of disciplines applicable to State-owned entities and prospects for including such disciplines in a TPP agreement. Wang recommends—given the sharp growth in outbound investment by state-controlled entities and existing uncertainty with respect to the availability of investment treaty protections for such investment-that States in the Pacific Rim region clarify the applicability of treaty protections to investments by state-controlled entities.

Two articles address the content of the fair and equitable treatment obligation: Patrick Dumberry, in "*Drafting the Fair and Equitable Treatment Clause in the TPP and RCEP: Lessons Learned from the NAFTA Article* 1105 *Experience*," and Wenjuan Zhang, in "*Will Greater Specificity with Respect to the Fair and Equitable Treatment Obligation Lead to Greater Predictability in Investment Treaty Cases?*" Dumberry recommends that drafters of the TPP and RCEP agreements build on the experience of NAFTA jurisprudence and current EU-Canada Comprehensive Economic and Trade Agreement(CETA) negotiations by expressly listing particular elements included within the obligation. Zhang also addresses the CETA approach of specifying particular elements of the fair and equitable treatment obligation, concluding that such an approach might contribute to, but cannot guarantee, greater predictability and consistence in arbitral practice.

Two articles address the rapidly developing area of anti-corruption measures: "*Anti-Corruption Legislation in the Asia-Pacific: Disparate Extraterritorial Measures*" by Cecilia Nassare, and "*Canada's Anti-Corruption Framework and the Relevance to the Pacific Rim and TPP Negotiations*" by Noemi Gal-Or. Gal-Or discusses Canada's active anti-corruption efforts, which are reflected not only in domestic legislation but also international trade policy, including, potentially, disciplines in a TPP agreement. Nassare explores the relationship between the extraterritoriality of domestic anti-corruption measures in certain States in the Asia-Pacific region and corruption rates in those States.

Regarding the emerging international intellectual property regime in the Pacific Rim region, AnleiZuo considers the potential impact of the "institutional fragmentation" of the regime on its authority and legitimacy.

Taken together, these contributions—by more than thirty authors based in more than ten countries—address key issues facing the Pacific Rim region at a particularly opportune time: a moment when the Pacific Rim region is shaping, to a very significant extent, the international economic law architecture for the 21st century.

中国国际经济法学的创立与发展*

在世界范围,国际经济法作为独立的法律部门,形成于19世纪末;国际经济法学作为独立的法学学科,直至第二次世界大战后才逐渐形成和发展起来。1978年党的十一届三中全会确定实行改革开放政策以来,国际经济法学在中国应运而生,蓬勃发展,取得了令人瞩目的丰硕成果。

一、中国国际经济法学的初步创立

20世纪70年代末80年代初,中国法学界的一些学者深切感受到改革开放新形势下的迫切需求,开始进行国际经济法学的研究和传播。这一时期的代表作有武汉大学姚梅镇教授发表在《武汉大学学报》和《中国国际法年刊》的一系列研究国际经济法的论文、译文和厦门大学陈安教授1982年编译出版的《国际经济立法的历史和现状》等。

在《中国国际法年刊》(1983)发表的一组"国际经济法讨论"文章中,反映了中国法学界关于国际经济法的概念和体系的不同主张。其中,汪暄、史久镛教授主张国际经济法是国际公法的一个分支,是"经济的国际法"姚梅镇、王名扬教授则主张国际经济法是调整国际经济关系的国际法和国内法规范的总称,是独立的新兴的法学部门。上述和其后的继续讨论,在一定程度上促进了全国性国际经济法学习和研究热潮的形成。

1984年5月8日至6月5日,经武汉大学、上海社会科学院、厦门大学、南开大学、安徽大学、中山大学和江西大学发起组织,在庐山举办了国际经济法讲习班,来自全国53个单位的90多名代表参加。这是全国国际经济法学者的第一次盛会。在讲习班上,代表们倡议成立全国性的国际经济法学术团体。经讨论,决

---

* 本文发表在《中国法学》1998年第5期。作者曾华群、单文华。

定成立中国国际经济法研究会,并通过研究会章程和组成第一届理事会,推选姚梅镇教授为会长。

庐山国际经济法讲习班的举办和中国国际经济法研究会的成立标志着中国国际经济法学的初步创立。

二、中国国际经济法学的全面发展

中国国际经济法学初步创立之后,在学科体系的确立、学科建设和人才培养、专题研究以及学术团体活动等方面取得了全面的发展,呈现出良好的发展势头。

(一)中国国际经济法学科体系的初步确立

20 世纪 80 年代中期以来,在借鉴和吸收外国有关研究成果的基础上,中国国际经济法学界陆续出版了国际经济法概论性著作、国际经济法各分支的专著或教材和国际经济法系列专著或教材。

1984 年刘丁教授编著的《国际经济法》是我国第一部国际经济法的概论性著作。沈达明、冯大同教授编著的《国际贸易法》(1983 年)和姚梅镇教授著《国际投资法》(1985)是最早系统论述国际经济法分支的教材或专著。

1987 年陈安教授主编的国际经济法系列专著,包括《国际贸易法》《国际投资法》《国际货币金融法》《国际税法》《国际海事法》等 5 部,是中国第一套国际经济法系列专著。1988 ~ 1991 年为适应国际经济法专业本科教学的需要,司法部法学教材编辑部组织编写了一套高等学校法学试用教材,包括《国际经济法总论》《国际贸易法新论》《国际金融法》《国际税法》《国际技术转让》《海商法学》《冲突法》《涉外法律文书》等 8 部著作。

1996 ~ 1998 年,该编辑部又编审出版了"'九五'规划高等学校法学教材——国际经济法系列",包括《国际经济法导论》《国际贸易法》《国际金融法》《国际投资法》《国际技术转让法》《国际税法》《世界贸易组织》《国际商事争议解决程序》《国际环境法》等 9 部著作。

贯穿于上述论著中的共同观点是,国际经济法学是由调整国际经济关系的国际法和国内法规范构成的学科体系;该体系由国际经济法基本理论和国际贸易法、国际投资法、国际货币金融法、国际税法、国际海事法、国际经济组织法和国际经济争端解决法等主要分支组成;中国国际经济法学应紧密联系中国实际,以中国已经参加或准备参加的国际经济条约、中国涉外经济立法、国际商务惯例和涉外经贸合同实务为研究重点,同时,应站在发展中国家立场,坚持建立国际经济新秩序的目标。

上述论著,大体上确立了具有中国特色的国际经济法学科体系,同时,在相当程度上满足了国际经济法的教学需要和实务参考需要。

(二)具有中国特色的学科建设和人才培养

与发达国家比较,中国国际经济法学的学科建设和人才培养具有明显的特色。主要表现在,由于国家教育行政主管部门重视,学科建设后来居上,发展迅速。国际经济法专门人才培养规范化、系统化。

近十多年来,许多法律院校经国家教委批准,相继设立国际经济法专业本科和国际经济法专业硕士学位授予点。北京大学(1982 年)、对外经济贸易大学(1984 年)、武汉大学(1984 年)和厦门大学(1986 年)先后获准设立国际经济法博士学位授予点。目前,中国各大学的法律院系、各政法院校(以下统称高校)一般都将国际经济法作为一门主要的专业课程。一些高校的国际金融、世界经济、国际经济合作等专业也将国际经济法作为一门主要的专业必修课程。国际经济法各层次专业课程的设置和教材建设渐趋成熟和规范化。

国际经济法专业各层次专门人才因其"懂法律、懂经济、懂外语"的优势而受到涉外经贸管理部门、涉外经贸企业和法律实务界的普遍欢迎和重视。一些较早毕业的国际经济法专业的硕士、博士从事教学和研究工作,逐渐成长为新一代的学术带头人。实践表明,在中国实行对外开放政策、建设社会主义市场经济体制和建设社会主义法治国家的大背景下,国际经济法的专门人才切合市场急需,大有用武之地。

(三)理论联系实际的专题研究

在"七五"、"八五"和"九五"期间,中国国际经济法学界承担了许多国家和省部级重点科研项目,紧密联系改革开放的实际,在国际经济法基本理论和国际经济法各分支领域进行了开拓性的专题研究。

在此期间出版的国际经济法专题研究著作甚多,仅以国际投资法和国际贸易法领域为例:国际投资法领域,陈安教授著《美国对海外私人投资的法律保护及典型案例分析》(1985 年)以案例研究的方法,对美国海外私人投资保证制度作了深入的研究。姚梅镇教授主编的《比较外资法》(1993 年)采用比较研究的方法,把中国外资法的研究提高到一个新水平。余劲松博士著《跨国公司法律问题研究》(1989 年)和曾华群博士著《中外合资企业法律的理论与实务》(1991 年)均采取综合研究的方法,从国际法和国内法角度,分别对跨国公司和中外合资企业的法律问题作了系统探讨。陈安教授主编的《"解决投资争端国际中心"述评》(1989 年)和《MIGA 与中国:多边投资担保机构述评》(1995 年)对现有两个多边投资法律体制进行了较深入的剖析,对我国是否接受和如何利用该体制提出了建设性意见。

在国际贸易法领域,冯大同教授主编的《国际货物买卖法》(1992 年)和张玉卿教授编著的《联合国国际货物销售合同公约释义》(1988年)是研究国际货物销售合同公约的重要著作。研究关税及贸易总协定和世界贸易组织的主要著作有赵维田教授的《最惠国与多边贸易体制》(1996年)、曹建明教授主编的《关税及贸易总协定》(1994年)、张克文博士的《关税及贸易总协定及其最惠国待遇制度》(1992年)、冯予蜀博士的《GATT与中国》(1992年)、曾令良教授的《世界贸易组织法》(1996年)和汪尧田、周汉民教授主编的《世界贸易组织总论》(1995年)等。

与此同时,我国国际经济法学者还在国内外重要学术刊物上发表了一系列高水平的学术论文,涉及国际经济法的基本理论和国际经济法各分支的重要专题。

1998年,中国国际经济法学界的学术著述汇辑《国际经济法论丛》第一卷出版,预期每年推出两卷(每卷约42万~45万字),此举将进一步推动国际经济法的专题研究。

此外,中国国际经济法学界还积极承担国家有关机构委托研究的项目或咨询项目。例如,厦门大学法学院、中国社会科学院法学研究所和对外经贸大学等有关专家分别受国家外经贸部委托,先后就"中国加入1965年《华盛顿公约》的利弊得失""'九七'后中国参加的国际经济条约在香港的适用问题""外资国民待遇问题""'解决投资争端国际中心'案例研究""外贸代理制""知识产权保护""公司法适用于'三资'企业"等专题提出咨询研究报告,供有关机构决策参考。

(四)生机勃勃的学术团体活动

自1984年庐山国际经济法讲习班以来,中国国际经济法学术团体主持开展了一系列卓有成效的学术交流活动,促进了中国国际经济法研究和教学的发展。

1987年,全国国际经济法教学研讨会在武汉大学召开,来自全国30多所大学和科研机构的40多名专家学者参加。会议决定加强中国国际经济法研究会(以下简称研究会)的机构建设。1993年,研究会在珠海召开中国国际经济法学术研讨会暨会员代表大会,通过决议将研究会更名为中国国际经济法学会(以下简称学会)。陈安教授当选为会长。学会秘书处设于厦门大学。

中国国际经济法学术团体的建立和健全,对促进全国国际经济法的教学和研究起了重要的作用。目前,在一年一度的中国国际经济法学术研讨会上,来自全国高校和科研机构的国际经济法教学和研究人员以及来自涉外经贸管理部门的实务工作者聚集一堂,相互交流国际经济法学术研究成果和讨论我国对外经济交往中面临的重要法律问题。理论紧密联系实际,成为学会学术活动的重要特色。

三、促进中国国际经济法学进一步发展

中国国际经济法学虽然走过了20年历程,但从历史的观点看,尚处于艰苦创

业的阶段。无论是从学科建设本身,还是从改革开放的现实需要看,中国国际经济法学者任重道远,为争取中国国际经济法学的更大发展,尤其需要从以下三个方面努力:

(一)加强中国国际经济法学基本理论的研究

由于亟待解决的国际经济法实际问题很多,中国国际经济法学者在一定程度上忽略了对国际经济法学基本理论的继续研究。在1996年中国国际法学会年会上,重新提出了国际经济法学的基本理论问题,特别是国际经济法的学科体系问题,引起了热烈的讨论。这从一个侧面反映了深入进行国际经济法学理论研究的重要性。基本理论的研究是学科发展的前提和基础。作为新兴的学科,对中国国际经济法学的基本理论应予以持续的关注和研究,经过长期的努力和积累,才能不断发展和日臻成熟。与此同时,鉴于强调建立国际经济新秩序是有中国特色的国际经济法学的重要标志,在中国国际经济法学基本理论研究中,国际经济法的基本原则和国际经济新秩序理论研究也是重要的课题。

(二)深入进行国际经济法专题研究

在当前国际经济关系迅速发展的情况下,调整国际经济关系的国际法规范和国内法规范不断发展和加强,国家之间、不同国籍私人之间和一国与他国私人之间等不同层面的国际经济合作新形式不断涌现。从理论的角度考虑,只有深入进行国际经济法专题研究,才能丰富国际经济法学各分支的内容,从而进一步确立中国国际经济法的学科体系。从务实的角度考虑,高质量的国际经济法专题研究成果将为我国国际经济条约实践和涉外经济立法提供理论依据和决策参考意见。

在今后一段时期内,中国国际经济法学者需要特别关注和加强研究的国际经济法专题可大致归纳为以下五个方面:

1. 世界性国际经济组织的法律体制。一些世界性国际经济组织,如国际货币基金组织(IMF)、国际复兴开发银行(IBRD)、解决投资争端国际中心(ICSID)、多边投资担保机构(MIGA)和世界贸易组织(WTO)的法律体制在调整国际经济关系中起了重要的作用,中国作为这些组织的成员或潜在参与者,对这些组织的法律体制及其发展应有全面、深入、持续的跟踪研究。

2. 区域性国际经济组织的法律体制。区域性国际经济组织近年来有了重大的发展,《北美自由贸易区协定》(NAFTA)开了南北国家组成区域性国际经济组织的先河,欧洲联盟(EU)的发展超越了区域性经济一体化组织的范畴,亚太经合组织(APEC)则创设了区域性经济合作的新模式。中国作为这些组织的经济合作伙伴或成员,有必要深入研究这些组织的法律体制及其对外关系。目前经合组织(OECD)成员国正在谈判中的《多边投资协定》(MAI)(草案)是国际投资法的新发展，也需要认真研究和密切注视其发展动向。

3. 中外双边经济条约。中国近十多年来，与外国签订了大量的双边经济条约，主要是双边投资条约和双边税收条约。为了今后能更有效地通过中外双边经济条约维护经济主权和促进中外经济合作，这些条约的内容、依据和利弊得失值得探讨和总结。

4. 涉外经济立法。中国正处于向社会主义市场经济过渡的历史时期，应从建设社会主义法治国家的目标出发，借鉴外国的立法经验，就健全和完善我国的涉外经济立法、特别是有关投资、贸易、融资、税收等的监管法律制度进行深入的研究，提出建设性的立法建议。

5. 国际经贸惯例或法律实务。不同国籍私人之间的经济交往是国际经济关系最重要的表现形式，也衍生了一系列法律问题。对国际经贸惯例或法律实务、特别是新的国际经济合作形式，如"建造—经营—转让"（BOT）、"外资并购"（M&A）、"电子数据交换"（EDI）合同等的法律实务，需要进行深入的专题研究。

（三）坚持和发展中国国际经济法学的研究方法

中国属于发展中的社会主义国家，中国国际经济法的研究服务于建立国际经济新秩序和建立社会主义市场经济体制的目标，这决定了中国国际经济法学界在吸收西方国家有关研究成果的同时，应有符合本国国情和目标的研究方法。从中国国际经济法学发展的经验看，今后应继续坚持和发展的研究方法主要是：

1. 立足本国实际的方法。从各国国际经济法的研究现状看，各国学者都是从本国实际出发，研究本国政府和私人在对外经济交往活动中所涉及的国际法和国内法问题。如前所述，中国国际经济法学应改革开放之运而生，也只有紧密联系改革开放的实际才能获得更大的发展。因此，中国国际经济法的研究，应以中国已经参加或准备参加的国际经济条约、中国涉外经济立法与涉外经贸合同实务为重点，为中国的国际经济条约实践、涉外经济立法和涉外经贸合同实务提供科学的理论依据，以维护国家的利益和中外当事人的合法权益，促进中国的改革开放事业进一步发展。

2. 历史和现实结合的方法。国际经济法是历史发展到一定阶段的产物，并随历史的发展而发展。在研究国际经济法的理论问题时，特别应该注重以历史的观点分析现实问题，不能割断历史，不能孤立地就事论事，无原则地迎合所谓"国际惯例"或"时代潮流"。

只有这样，才能较准确地理解和把握南北矛盾、新旧国际经济秩序斗争的实质和发展方向，才能较好地站在发展中国家的立场，坚持原则，为争取建立国际经济新秩序的伟大事业作出贡献。

3. 综合研究的方法。国际经济法是包含国际法规范和国内法规范的综合性、边缘性的法学学科。在研究特定国际经济法问题时,应采取综合研究的方法。具体说来,在研究国际经济条约问题时,应同时研究有关国家的国内法规范,以后者作为前者的基础;在研究涉外经济法律或合同实务问题时,也不能忽略有关的国际法规范,以后者作为前者的背景。这样,以问题为中心,不受传统法律部门划分的束缚,才能对研究对象有一个全面、整体的了解和认识,避免顾此失彼、失之偏颇。

4. 比较研究的方法。取决于国际经济关系的复杂性和相互联系的性质,比较研究的方法对国际经济法的研究十分重要。例如,在双边经济条约实践的研究中,比较分析同类双边经济条约的有关规定,可了解该领域普遍的或不同的国家实践及其发展趋向,由此判断是否形成习惯国际经济法,以便根据本国的实际情况采取符合本国利益的立场和原则。在涉外经济法律的研究中,比较分析不同国家的有关法制,有助于借鉴国外先进的立法经验,进一步健全和完善本国的涉外经济法制。此外,对本国和外国涉外经济法的比较研究,可为当事人进行国际经济交往活动的合同实务、特别是在法律选择方面提供必要的指导。

5. 法律与经济相结合的方法。国际经济法是以国际经济关系为调整对象的,因此,国际经济法的研究应注意密切结合国际经济现象、国际经济关系的研究。如果就法论法,忽视决定国际经济法的发展变化的国际经济关系,就不可能深刻了解和掌握国际经济法的发展变化规律,其研究也无法深入和取得成效。

在强调"中国特色"的国际经济法学的同时,还应当明确,国际经济法学是世界性的,中国国际经济法学是世界性国际经济法学的一个重要组成部分。中国国际经济法学的发展和繁荣在一定程度上有赖于世界性国际经济法学的发展和繁荣,世界性国际经济法学的发展和繁荣也不能缺少中国国际经济法学的参与和奉献。因此,中国国际经济法学者理应继续借鉴和吸收外国的相关研究成果,积极主动地开展国际学术交流和合作,在国际学术论坛上,对国际经济法学的重要理论和实践问题提出中国学者的见解,表明中国的立场,为世界性国际经济法学的发展和繁荣做出应有的贡献。

中国有关国际惯例的立法评析*

——兼论国际惯例的适用

迄今为止,我国关于国际惯例的国内立法主要有五部法律。1985 年,我国的《涉外经济合同法》第 5 条率先规定:“合同当事人可以选择处理合同争议所适用的法律。当事人没有选择的,适用与合同有最密切联系的国家的法律。在中华人民共和国境内履行的中外合资经营企业合同、中外合作经营企业合同、中外合作勘探开采自然资源合同,适用中华人民共和国法律。中华人民共和国法律未作规定的,可以适用国际惯例。”次年,《民法通则》第 8 章第 142 条规定:“涉外民事关系的法律适用,依照本章的规定确定。中华人民共和国缔结或参加的国际条约同中华人民共和国的民事法律有不同规定的,适用国际条约的规定,但中华人民共和国声明保留的条款除外。中华人民共和国法律和中华人民共和国缔结或参加的国际条约没有规定的,可以适用国际惯例。”第 150 条进而规定,“依照本章规定不得违背中华人民共和国的社会公共利益”。1992 年的《海商法》第 268、276 条和 1995 年的《民用航空法》第 184、190 条的规定与《民法通则》的上述两条规定几乎完全一样,只是少了《民法通则》第 142 条第 1 款的规定。1995 年颁布的《票据法》第 96 条也有关于国际条约优先及国际惯例补缺的涉外法律适用规定,所不同的是:一方面,它所规定的“适用国际惯例”的条件,是“本法”和中华人民共和国缔结或者参加的国际条约没有规定,而未采用通用的“中华人民共和国法律”这一措辞;另一方面,它也没有规定关于适用国际惯例时的公共秩序保留问题。

我国上述涉外法律中关于可以适用国际惯例的规定受到了海内外“现代商人法”的倡导者们的热烈欢迎与充分肯定。台湾地区学者柯泽东称赞该规定做到了

---

* 本文发表在《中国法学》1997 年第 3 期。

“国际化”“相当进步”;[1]德国的霍恩(N. Horn)则认为,这种规定不仅表明了中国立法者对于国际公认的法律意识的友好态度,而且也是中国在对于现代商人法这一概念的解释方面所作出的一项重要贡献。[2] 但国内学者对这些规定深感困惑。主要的问题有四:第一,这里的“国际惯例”的含义是什么,是冲突规则中的国际惯例,还是实体规则中的国际惯例?第二,这里的“国际惯例”的性质是什么,是国际法?国内法?还是别的什么规范?第三,这种国际惯例在我国适用时,应具备什么条件?以公共秩序排除国际惯例适用的立法究竟是否合理?第四,我国有关国际惯例立法与《联合国国际货物销售合同公约》(以下简称《公约》)有关规定[3]之间是什么样的关系?本文结合中外有关法律与实践对这些问题逐一进行探讨。

一、“国际惯例”的含义

我国上述立法中的“国际惯例”的含义问题是我国民法学与国际私法、国际经济法学者争论最多的相关问题之一。有学者提出,这里的“国际惯例”只能是冲突法上的国际惯例;[4]有学者则反之,认为它只能是实体法上的国际惯例;[5]还有学者则认为二者兼有,即既包括冲突法上的国际惯例,也包括实体法上的国际惯例。[6] 我们赞成第二种观点,认为这里的“国际惯例”指的是实体“法”意义上的国际惯例。其理由有三:

第一,我国有关立法背景及司法解释表明,这里的“国际惯例”只能是实体法意义上的国际惯例。首先,我国最早的有关国际惯例的立法——《涉外经济合同法》的立法过程表明,提出用“国际惯例”来补充法律主要是考虑到我国涉外经济法律尚不完备,在我国法被确定为合同准据法时可能出现“无法可依”的情况。[7]再者,最高人民法院《关于适用〈涉外经济合同法〉若干问题的解答》(以下简称

---

〔1〕 参见柯泽东:《从国际私法方法论探讨契约准据法发展新趋势——并略评两岸现行法》,载《台大法学论丛》1996年第23卷第1期。

〔2〕 转自徐国建:《现代商人法论》,载《中国社会科学》1993年第3期。

〔3〕 由于我国已批准了《联合国国际货物销售合同公约》(以下简称《公约》)而成为其缔约国之一,《公约》已成为中国法律的有机组成部分。因此《公约》有关“惯例”的规定也可算作中国有关立法的一种表现形式。

〔4〕 参见李双元:《国际私法(冲突法篇)》,武汉大学出版社1987年版,第42页。作者指出,我国《民法通则》中关于“国际惯例”的规定是在“涉外民事关系的法律适用”一章中作出的,“似应理解为是有关冲突法的国际惯例”。

〔5〕 参见佟柔主编:《中华人民共和国民法通则简论》,中国政法大学出版社1987年版,第287页;浦伟良:《论〈民法通则〉中关于冲突法总则性规定》,载《法学评论》1990年第5期。

〔6〕 参见王常营主编:《中国国际私法的理论与实践》,人民法院出版社1993年第1版,第35页。

〔7〕 参见《全国人大法律委员会对〈中华人民共和国涉外经济合同法(草案)〉审议结果的报告》(1985年3月13日)之第一部分。

《解答》)第二部分第(九)项也确认,国际惯例的适用以我国法为准据法,而以我国法没有规定为前提。与此同时,依该《解答》第二部分第(九)项规定,依选择或最密切联系原则所确定的合同争议准据法,“是指现行的实体法,而不包括冲突规范和程序法”。可见,这里作为准据法的补充而适用的国际惯例也只能是实体性规范,不包括程序法与冲突规范。换言之,《涉外经济合同法》中的“国际惯例”只可能是实体法意义上的国际惯例。

第二,根据法律体系的内在统一性原理,〔8〕既然最初的《涉外经济合同法》中的“国际惯例”是指实体法意义上的国际惯例,则其他法律中的“国际惯例”也应为实体法意义上的国际惯例。上述的几部法律都属于我国涉外民商事(经济)立法的范畴,都是整个国内法律体系的构成部分,它们之间在概念、术语上应是协调统一的,这是作为一个统一的法律体系的基本要求。事实上,上述几部法律中的类似或相同的规定是相互参照制订的。例如《关于〈中华人民共和国票据法(草案)〉的说明》就指出,其关于涉外票据的法律适用一章是“根据民法通则的有关规定”制定的。〔9〕 在这种情况下,这几部法律中的“国际惯例”在内涵上的一致性应无疑义。即它们都应该指的是实体法意义上的“国际惯例”。那种主张《涉外经济合同法》中的“国际惯例”是指实体法,而《民法通则》中的“国际惯例”是指冲突法的观点比较令人费解。

第三,从实践上考察,各国普遍认为,目前世界上只有冲突规范的国际条约,而不存在冲突规范的国际惯例。〔10〕 尽管随着国际民事经济生活的发展,各国国内法和若干国际条约常有一些共同采用的冲突规则,但多数学者都不承认在法律适用上存在某种私法关系必须适用某种国家法律的国际惯例,充其量只能说有了一些国际上比较普遍的实践或习惯做法。〔11〕 相反,实体法领域中的国际惯例却大量存在。可见,我国有关立法中的“国际惯例”只能是指实体法意义上的国际惯例。而这种国际惯例的主体部分,正是国际贸易惯例。值得一提的是,这里,通行的“实体法国际惯例”的提法并不妥当。因为,国际经济贸易领域中的这种“国际惯例”多为本身不具备法律拘束力的习惯做法,本质上尚不是“法律”,〔12〕所以也就不能称之为“实体法”或“实体法国际惯例”。为区别计,不妨称“实体性国际惯例”。

---

〔8〕 参见孙国华主编:《法理学》,法律出版社 1995 年版,第 288 ~ 290 页。

〔9〕 参见国务院法制局财政金融法规司编:《〈中华人民共和国票据法〉讲解》,法律出版社 1995 年版,第 284 页。

〔10〕 参见浦伟良:《论〈民法通则〉中关于冲突法总则性规定》,载《法学评论》1990 年第 5 期。

〔11〕 参见李双元主编:《中国与国际私法统一化进程》,武汉大学出版社 1993 年版 第 57 页。

〔12〕 单文华:《国际贸易惯例基本理论问题研究》,1996 年厦门大学博士学位论文。

那么,这种实体性国际惯例究竟包括哪些?显然,这里不可能也没必要一一加以罗列。但学者多同意,对这里的“国际惯例”应作广义理解,即不单单包括那些严格意义上的,具有任意性、自发性与明确性的国际惯例,如《国际贸易术语解释通则》(INCOTERMS)、《跟单信用证统一惯例》(UCP)等国际贸易惯例。对于那些中国没有缔结或尚未参加的国际公约,甚至于国外先进的立法通例,或体现在各国法律与国际立法中的具有进步意义的一般法律原则,等等,只要经过深入的研究和认真的鉴别,确认它们不致违反我国强制性立法与我国的社会公共利益,而又确实为我国司法实践所需要,也可以视为“国际惯例”而“拿来”适用,以补我国有关立法的漏洞与不足。〔13〕 从这一意义上看,霍恩对我国立法中的“国际惯例”内容的理解〔14〕是有一定道理的。然而,从现代商人法的发展现状与我国的实际认识程度来看,将我国上述立法中的“国际惯例”等同于西方学者所主张的“现代商人法”至少在目前是我们难以接受的。

二、“国际惯例”的性质

关于我国立法中的“国际惯例”的性质,主要有两种观点:一种认为这里的“国际惯例”“显然就是我国公法学家们所称的‘国际惯例’”,〔15〕质言之,这里的“国际惯例”属于国际公法的范畴;另一种观点认为,上述国际惯例可以补充我国法律的规定意味着我国对国际惯例效力的立法承认,因此,这里的“国际惯例”是我国法律的渊源之一。〔16〕 我们认为,这两种观点都是值得商榷的。

首先,这里的“国际惯例”不可能是作为国际法渊源之一的国际惯例(InternationalCustom)。道理很简单,如果这里的国际惯例已上升为国际法,则按国际法优先的原则,国际惯例应先于国内法而得到适用,而且是必须得到适用,决不至于等到在国内法中找不到规定以后,才“可以适用”。同时,从事实上说,正如我国国际私法与国际经济法学者们所公认的,在国际经济贸易领域,像“国家主权豁免”这样的强制性国际惯例很少,而大量存在的是任意性的国际惯例。〔17〕

---

〔13〕 例如,陈安教授就认为,对我国有关立法中的国际惯例,“似宜作广义理解”,“举凡中国并未缔结或参加的国际条约、一切外国的法律、一切国际民间团体编纂的规则,其中所包含的国际经贸行为规范或行为准则”,都可以视为“国际惯例”,“只要它确实有利于促进我国社会主义市场经济体制的建立,就应当奉行‘拿来主义’,尽可能地博采众长,大胆采用”。参见陈安:《论适用国际惯例与有法必依的统一》,载《中国社会科学》1994 年第 4 期。

〔14〕 霍恩曾提出,我国《涉外经济合同法》中的“国际惯例”实质上就是指以调整国际贸易和经济关系的统一的法律基本原则为指导思想和全部内容的“现代商人法”,它既包括法律规范(以国际条约为基础的统一立法或习惯法),也包括对合同和法律规范的解释起帮助作用的实际行动的规范和习惯。转引自徐国建:《现代商人法论》,载《中国社会科学》1993 年第 3 期。

〔15〕 参见李双元主编:《中国与国际私法统一化进程》,武汉大学出版社 1993 年版,第 108 页。

〔16〕 参见张坦:《论习惯在民法典中的地位》,载《河北法学》1996 年第 1 期。

〔17〕 参见韩德培主编:《国际私法》,武汉大学出版社 1989 年修订本,第 28 页。

与此同时，在我们看来，这里的规定似乎也不宜理解为我国对国际惯例的立法承认，从而也不能据此认定"国际惯例"为我国法律的正式渊源之一。因为，首先，国际惯例是一个内容十分庞杂，发展程度各异的习惯性规范群体，这里面有世界性惯例、地区性惯例，还有行业性的惯例，甚至还包括某特定双方当事人之间的"交易做法"与"履约做法"，而且每项惯例的确切内容、适用范围、被接受程度等等也相去甚远。由一项立法统一予以承认既不现实，也不可取。其次，从国际惯例的发展历史来看，国际经济贸易领域的惯例主要是西方国家贸易实践经验的总结与提炼，其内容不仅为发展中国家所不熟悉，而且不免带有维护其贸易优势地位的倾向。这一点西方学者也不否认，例如，伯奈尔（Bonell）就曾指出："事实上，由于现存于国际贸易中的大多数惯例是在主要发达国家的商品市场与交易中发展起来的，它们不仅在内容上是片面的，而且对于来自其他国家的商人来说，几乎是一无所知"。[18] 诚然，经过发展中国家的不断学习与不懈斗争，这种片面性与一无所知的状况已有所改变，但根本改观在短期中无疑是不可能完成的。所以迄今为止，发展中国家（包括中国）对这些惯例的掌握仍不能说是很全面与熟练，而这种利益上的片面性也未能完全纠正过来。在这种背景之下，如果我们不问良莠，一律予以承认，奉之为"法律"，无异于自投罗网，作茧自缚，不仅难以达到促进"对外开放"的初衷，反而会束缚我国外经贸当事人的手脚，对我国的改革开放事业造成不可忽视的负面影响。最后，从各国的实践来看，目前似乎也没有任何一个国家曾经"一揽子"式地承认所有的国际惯例，伊拉克与西班牙对 INCOTERMS 的承认[19]都是鲜见的例子，而且是对个别惯例的具体承认。而许多国家民法典中对"惯例"或"习惯"补充法律的功能的确认，一般也被认为是国家对"惯例"或"习惯"作为法律漏洞的补充工具的功能的承认，而不是对其"法律"地位的一般认可。事实上，许多发达国家至今仍在为贸易惯例是不是法律、构不构成法律的真正渊源的问题争论不休。国际商会作为最具权威性的国际贸易惯例编纂机构，也曾特别警告说，它所制定的这些惯例仅仅是私人机构所制定的，只有在当事人直接或间接采用时，才对他们有拘束力。不可轻率地肯定其具有法源地位或法律拘束力。[20] 在这种情况下，如认为我国已经笼统地承认所有由这些发达国家所发展起来的，片面而为我们所不熟悉的"国际惯例"，是不合理的。

---

〔18〕 Bianca Bonell, Commentary on the International Sales Law, the 1980 Vienna Sales Convention, 1987, p. 105.

〔19〕 伊拉克与西班牙都曾立法确认 INCOTERM S 的法律效力。See C. M. Schmitthoff, Schmitthoff's Export Trade: The law and Practice of International Trade, 9th ed. (1990), pp. 66－67.

〔20〕 参见张锦源：《贸易契约理论与实务》，三民书局 1988 年版，第 55～56 页。

基于上述理由,我们认为,我国有关立法中的"国际惯例"的规定不应理解为对国际惯例的效力及其法源地位的普遍立法承认。那么,究竟该怎么理解呢?我们认为,实质上,我国的有关国内立法赋予"国际惯例"的只是作为我国法律漏洞补充工具的性质与地位。

任何法律皆有漏洞,这是当今判例学说所公认的事实。[21] 所谓法律漏洞,是指现行法律体系上存在影响法律功能,且违反立法意旨的不完全性。[22] 这种漏洞的产生,或者因为立法者考虑不周,根本未考虑到,或虽考虑到但不周详;或者由于情事发生变化;或者由于立法者自觉其对所要规范的情形了解不够,而不加规范。[23] 但无论其因何而生,有漏洞就应予补充,这样才能实现法律维护公平正义及法律秩序的目的,同时确保法律体系的完整与协调。[24]

关于法律漏洞补充的性质,有两种观点:一种观点认为,法律漏洞的补充是法律解释活动的继续。法院审理具体案件的第一步,就是找寻所应适用的法律规范,即进行"三段论"推理中的大前提,称"找法活动",找法活动又可区分为法律解释与漏洞补充两个阶段。二者的区分点在于法条可能的文义。在可能的文义内找法,为法律解释;在可能文义之外找法,即为漏洞补充。但通说又认为二者不能截然分开,而有交叉地带,即所谓的法内漏洞的补充。因为法内漏洞的补充,即可算是在法条可能文义范围之内,也可说是在可能文义范围之外。[25] 但一般来说,法律漏洞补充是在法律解释活动不足以解决的可能文义范围之外的问题时,才发挥其功能,即法律漏洞补充是法律解释活动的继续。[26] 另一种观点则认为法律漏洞补充是造法的尝试,而不是立法活动。因为,第一,法律漏洞补充是针对一件待决案件,取向于法律体系与价值而采取一个法律见解,将其作为裁判依据,并在裁判中表现出来。因此,它只是作为一个裁判,属于行使司法权的活动,而不是针对某一类案件补充地制定一般性规范的活动。其次,虽然作为判决先例在事实上有类似法律的效力,但事实上的效力毕竟不同于法律的规范效力。因此,判决先例并不构成法源,违反判例也不构成违法。最后,法院对既存判决先例无遵守的义务,仅有斟酌的义务。由此产生法院对于采纳或不采纳判决先例中的法律见解负有说理义务。可见法院的法律漏洞补充活动,在性质上充其量只能说是一

---

〔21〕 参见王泽鉴:《民法学说与判例研究》(第1册),载《台大法学丛书》(十六),第303页。

〔22〕 参见梁慧星:《法律漏洞及其补充方法》,载梁慧星主编:《民商法论丛》(第1卷),法律出版社1994年版,第7页。

〔23〕 参见黄茂荣:《法学方法与现代民法》,载《台大法学丛书》(三十二),第353页。

〔24〕 参见梁慧星:《法律漏洞及其补充方法》,载《民商法论丛》(第1卷),法律出版社1994年版,第19页。

〔25〕 参见黄茂荣:《法学方法与现代民法》,载《台大法学丛书》(三十二),第370~371页。

〔26〕 参见黄建辉:《法律漏洞·类推适用》,蔚理法律出版社1988年版,第69~70页。

种"造法的尝试",而非终局的法律制定。由这种造法活动所表现于判决先例中的法律见解,将来有可能转化为习惯法,也可能迟早被抛弃。[27]

总而言之,无论是作为法律解释的继续,还是作为造法的尝试,法律漏洞补充都不是国家的立法活动,而是司法机关具体适用法律的活动。相应地,补充法律漏洞的依据或工具,也就不能视为法律,不属于法律渊源的范畴。

法律漏洞的补充方法大致有三种,一种就是依习惯补充,另外两种为依法理补充与依判例补充。[28]

依习惯补充法律漏洞,其根据通常在于各国民法均以明文规定,在一定条件下习惯有与法律同一的效力。例如,《瑞士民法典》第1条规定,"如本法无相应规定时,法官应依据惯例;无惯例时,依据自己作为立法者所提出的规则裁判"。此外,土耳其、泰国、阿根廷、奥地利等国的民法也都有类似的规定。我国清末的民法草案也曾采用这一外国立法例。这种立法迄今在我国台湾地区的"民法"中仍得以维持。现行我国台湾地区"民法"第1条规定:"民事,法律所未规定者,依习惯;无习惯者,依法理。"依我国台湾地区权威学者的解释,这里的"习惯"乃指"事实上的惯行",而不是已经上升为法律的"习惯法"。[29]

我国《民法通则》虽然没有一般性地赋予"习惯"或"惯例"以补充法律漏洞的功能,但《民法通则》第142条第3款及《涉外经济合同法》等涉外立法的有关规定,却显然是承认了"国际惯例"对我国涉外民商事法律漏洞的补充意义。换言之,我国法律只是不承认"国内惯例"对法律漏洞具有补充功能,而对于"国际惯例"的补充功能则是承认的。这一点如果说仅仅从法条本身还难以明确的话,从有关的立法背景与司法解释中则可以找到明确的肯定的证据。回顾我国最早的关于"国际惯例"的立法——《涉外经济合同法》的立法过程,就可以知道,"中华人民共和国法律没有规定的,可以适用国际惯例"这一款的提出,乃是有关部门考虑到"目前我国涉外经济法律还不够完备,处理合同争议适用我国法律时,有的可能找不到依据"而建议增写的。[30] 随后,前面提到的最高人民法院《关于适用〈涉外经济合同法〉若干问题的解答》第二部分第(9)项再次明确,上款的意思在于"在应当适用我国法律的情况下,如果我国法律对于合同争议的问题未作规定的,可以适用国际惯例"。可见,无论是"立法者"还是司法机构都把"国际惯例"当作

〔27〕 参见黄茂荣:《法学方法与现代民法》,载《台大法学丛书》(三十二),第373~375、378页。

〔28〕 参见梁慧星:《法律漏洞及其补充方法》,载梁慧星主编:《民商法论丛》(第1卷),法律出版社1994年版,第23页。

〔29〕 参见黄茂荣:《民法总则》,三民书局1984年版,第7页。

〔30〕 参见《全国人大法律委员会对〈中华人民共和国涉外经济合同法〉草案审议结果的报告》,载宋汝棼:《参加立法工作琐记》,中国法制出版社1994年版,第60页。

补充我国涉外法律漏洞（“法律不够完备”即谓存在着法律漏洞）的具体“依据”，而并无意使之统统成为有当然法律约束力的“法律”和正式的法源。霍恩（N. Horn）显然也意识到了这一点，他提出，中国法律实际上是承认了国际惯例（他所理解的“现代商人法”）是本国涉外经济合同法的一个“替补渊源”[31]——“替补渊源”显然不是法律的正式渊源，而只是正式法律渊源的补充，确言之，是正式法律渊源中的法律漏洞的补充工具。

作为法律漏洞补充工具的国际惯例与作为法律的国际惯例是有明显区别的：前者可能只有个别意义，即可能只在个案中偶尔得到采用，不能必然地适用于所有同类案件；后者则具有普遍意义，对于同类情况均有规范效力。前者是有条件的、附从的，即只有在法律没有规定，“无法可依”的条件下，方可适用，它服从于法律或者整个法律秩序的目的，而不具备独立的法律性格；后者则一般是无条件的、主动的和独立的，基于自身的法律价值而存在，而不必然地服从于某一或某类法律的目的与价值。质言之，后者是法，所以具有法律的全部普遍性、规范性、抽象性；前者不是法，而只是一种“事实上惯行”，本质上仍是“事实”，故不具有法的一般抽象性与普遍规范力。

值得一提的是，“国际惯例”或“习惯”作为法律漏洞的补充工具之一，与学理、判例等其他补充工具又是有区别的。如前所述，“习惯”特别是“国际（贸易）惯例”是特殊的社会机制所形成的一种具有事实上的约束力的社会行为规范，其中不少已为国际（商业）社会所“广泛知悉”并“经常遵守”，其规范效力与学理、判例等是不可同日而语的。正因为如此，在上述各国的民法典中，习惯居于优先补充的地位。也正是因为这一点，才使人们误认为我国立法中的上述有关规定实质上就是对其法律效力与法源地位的承认。然而，从本质上说，“国际惯例”对我国法律的补充意义与“习惯”“学理”“判例”等对上述其他国家法律的补充意义是没有区别的。

确立“国际惯例”的法律漏洞补充工具性质与地位在理论上与实践上都颇有意义。在理论上，它可以比较圆满地解释我国既然普遍不承认国际惯例是法律又何以规定“可以适用国际惯例”这一看似矛盾的现象，有利于澄清种种观念上、思想上的模糊与混乱；在实践上，则不仅有利于我国外经贸事业的开展，也有利于司法活动中对“国际惯例”的科学、准确适用，避免将“适用国际惯例”凌驾于“有法必依”之上的错误做法。实际上，目前我国采用“按照国际通行规则”取代以往“与国际惯例接轨”的提法这一事实就表明我国已经意识到“国际惯例”的任意性

---

〔31〕 转引自徐国建：《现代商人法论》，载《中国社会科学》1993 年第 3 期。

质与补充地位，在认识上已向前迈进了一大步。

三、“国际惯例”适用的条件

从上面的分析可以看出，在我国，国际惯例要得到适用必须同时具备六个条件：第一，该争议问题的准据法是中国法；第二，中国法律和中国缔结或参加的国际条约对该争议问题没有规定；第三，对于该争议问题存在着国际惯例；第四，该惯例未为当事人所明示排除；第五，该国际惯例的适用不会违反中国的社会公共利益；第六，中国的司法机关决定适用该国际惯例来补充法律。

第一，国际惯例在我国的适用须以我国法为争议问题的准据法为前提。如果该争议的准据法为外国法，或者港澳地区的法律，则“国际惯例”之能适用与否须视该准据法的规定。如果该准据法允许适用国际惯例，国际惯例方有可能得到适用，反之，则不能适用。与此同时，依我国《涉外经济合同法》《民法通则》及其司法解释，涉外经济合同与涉外合同当事人均可以选择处理合同争议所适用的法律，这种法律“可以是中国法，也可以是港澳地区的法律或外国法”，[32] 而未提及“国际惯例”。但是从我国对“国际惯例”性质的一般认定及我国立法对其法律漏洞补充地位的确定来看，我国似乎是不太可能同意当事人选择适用“国际惯例”的。至于依据“最密切联系原则”所确立的准据法，则更不可能是“国际惯例”，[33] 因为《民法通则》与《涉外经济合同法》都明确规定，合同当事人没有选择时，适用的是与合同有最密切联系的“国家的法律”，换言之，这里明确肯定所适用的只能是内国法，而不包括不属于任何国家的“国际惯例”。

第二，国际惯例在我国的适用须以我国法律与我国缔结或参加的国际条约对争议问题没有规定为条件。这显然是由“国际惯例”在我国法律中的补充适用地位所决定的。由于香港、澳门是独立的两个法域，这里的“中国法律”应不包括香港地区法与澳门地区法。[34] 而这里的“没有规定”应指无论是中国法中的强制性规范还是任意性规范都没有相应的规定。[35]

第三，适用国际惯例固须以相关领域国际惯例的存在为前提。显然，这时就

---

〔32〕 参见最高人民法院《关于适用〈涉外经济合同法〉若干问题的解答》第二部分第（二）点。

〔33〕 参见韩健：《现代国际商事仲裁法的理论与实践》，法律出版社1993年版，第254页。

〔34〕 准确地说，应为中国大陆的法律。这里从我国立法上的习惯表达。以下有关内容，如未特别声明，均作此解。

〔35〕 日本学者石田穰先生将习惯区分为三种情形而论其效力：其一，既不违反法律强行规定，也不违反任意规定的习惯，有与法律同一之效力；其二，不违反法律强行规定，而违反任意规定的习惯，以当事人认可为条件，有与法律同一之效力；其三，违反法律强行规定的习惯，无与法律同一之效力。因此，他总结道，依习惯补充法律漏洞，须以该习惯不违反法律强行性规定及任意性规定为条件。参见[日]石田穰：《法解释学的方法》，第34页，转引自梁慧星：《法律漏洞及其补充方法》，载梁慧星主编：《民商法论丛》（第1卷），法律出版社1994年版，第24页。

存在“国际惯例”的查明问题，其具体方法大致可参考国际贸易惯例的证明方法。[36] 不过，对于我国未缔结或参加的国际公约、国际统一示范法等国际立法规范，如若也视同国际惯例而予以适用，一般来说就不存在上述查明或证明问题了。至于在查明不存在适用的国际惯例的情况下，该依据什么判决的问题似乎已超出本文的范围，兹不赘述。[37]

第四，国际惯例的适用还应以该惯例未被当事人所明示排除为前提。这主要是由这里的“国际惯例”的任意性质使然。各国普遍认为，国际（贸易）惯例属于当事人意思自治的范畴，如当事人在合同中已明示排除某惯例的适用，则无论该惯例如何广为人知且被普遍遵守，均不可拘束此合同的当事人。[38] 我国法律既承认合同自由，对此当无异议。故在考虑补充适用国际惯例时，如可适用的惯例已为当事人所明示排除，则该惯例不应得到适用。

第五，按我国《民法通则》等立法规定，适用的国际惯例还不得与我国的社会公共利益相违背，否则应予排除。这一公共秩序保留条款在国内似乎备受攻击，认为系世所罕见。[39] 因为各国一般认为适用国际惯例不会损害公共秩序；而一旦当事人选择了某一国际惯例，就取得了高于国内法的效力，即使其适用有可能导致损害公共秩序的后果，也不能供国内立法限制其适用。[40] 我们认为这种看法颇值商榷。诚然，国际（贸易）惯例由于一般是在与国家没有原则性利害关系的领域内自发形成的，一般不会危及公共秩序。然而，并不能因此绝对排除其有危害公共秩序的可能。由于各国历史、文化及经济、社会的巨大差别，在一时一地为合理合法，成为“惯例”的东西，到另一地另一时很可能是完全无法接受的。特别是许多由发达国家提出的所谓的“国际惯例”，往往带有霸权主义色彩，为发展中国家所无法接受。对于这样的“国际惯例”，我们显然不能不分青红皂白地照单全收，而应充分意识到其危害性，运用公共秩序保留予以坚决的抵制。实际上，在西方国家，也并未放弃公共秩序保留的权利。例如，施米托夫与哥尔德斯坦均认为，现代商人法可能因主权国家的公共秩序而失效，也可能因公共秩序而受到

---

〔36〕 关于国际贸易惯例的证明，可参见单文华：《国际贸易惯例基本理论问题研究》第三章，厦门大学1996年博士学位论文。

〔37〕 有人曾提出可以依“政策”来补充国际惯例。参见溥伟良：《论〈民法通则〉中关于冲突法总则性规定》，载《法学评论》1990年第5期。我们认为，也不妨以法理及判例来补充。关于依法理及判例的补充，可参见梁慧星：《法律漏洞及其补充方法》，载梁慧星主编：《民商法论丛》（第1卷），法律出版社1994年版；另见徐国栋：《民法基本原则解释——成文法局限性之克服》，中国政法大学出版社1992年版。

〔38〕 Cf. C. M. Schmitthoff, International Trade Usage, 1987, p. 15.

〔39〕 参见胡振杰：《国际惯例立法修订的法律思考》，载《法学》1993年第2期；另见李双元主编：《中国与国际私法统一化进程》，武汉大学出版社1993年版，第123页。

〔40〕 胡振杰：《国际惯例立法修订的法律思考》，载《法学》1993年第2期。

限制。[41] 就连自治商人法理论的积极鼓吹者戈德曼（B. Goldman）也认为商人法的适用应受公共秩序的限制，尽管他使用的是所谓的"跨国公共秩序"的概念。[42] 至于国际惯例一经选择即取得优于国内法的效力的提法，我们更不敢苟同。国际惯例多为任意性的规范，即使经当事人采用，也只取得优于任意法的效力，而无论如何应受强行法的约束。换言之，如果此说只是对任意法而言，则可以成立；如果系针对所有国内法而言，则显然是不能成立的。我们认为，既然对国际惯例的公共秩序保留为世所公认，则我国有关立法的合理性应无疑问，即便是这种规定真的是"世所罕见"。

第六，国际惯例的适用还取决于司法机关对补充适用国际惯例的选择。这一点常为人们所忽视。实际上，我国所有有关立法，无不是规定"可以适用"国际惯例，换言之，也可以不予适用——事实上，基于公共秩序原因而不适用即其表现之一。"用与不用，悉听司法、执法者的自由裁断。"[43] 在我们看来，可以用"三个有利于"标准来衡量取舍，凡是有利于发展社会生产力，有利于改革开放，有利于建设社会主义市场经济的国际惯例，我们就应大胆拿来，取长补短；反之，凡是不利于发展社会生产力，不利于改革开放，不利于建设社会主义市场经济，违反我国社会公共利益的国际惯例，我们则应弃之如敝屣，毫不足惜。有"惯例"而不予适用固然可能导致司法过程复杂化，但不加区别地盲目适用那些不合时宜、甚至严重损害国家主权与社会公益的所谓的"国际惯例"无疑会危害更大。

四、《联合国国际货物销售合同公约》关于"惯例"的规定与我国关于"国际惯例"的国内立法

《联合国国际货物销售合同公约》（以下简称《公约》）主要有三个条款与国际惯例直接相关。《公约》第 4 条规定，本公约除非另有明文规定外，与任何合同、任何条款或任何惯例的有效性问题无关。换言之，合同、合同条款或惯例是否合法、有效，《公约》并无意作统一规定，而留待各国国内法具体解决。这一条实质上使得惯例必须受国内强行法以及公共秩序的制约。例如，按照我国《涉外经济合同法》第 9 条的规定，违反中华人民共和国法律或者社会公共利益的合同无效。显然，这里的"法律"指的是强制性法律，而不包括任意性法律。

《公约》第 8 条、第 9 条是关于合同的解释与补充规则的规定。其中，第 8 条

〔41〕 Cf. C. M. Schmitthoff, "The Unification of the Law of International Trade", in Chia-Jui Cheng ed., Clive M. Schmitthoff's Select Essags on International Trade Law, 1988, p. 209.

〔42〕 Cf. Filip De Ly, Interantional Business Law and Lex Mercatoria, 1992, p. 215.

〔43〕 参见陈安：《论适用国际惯例与有法必依的统一》，载《中国社会科学》1994 年第 4 期。

第3款规定在解释合同时,“应适当地考虑到与事实有关的一切情况”,其中应包括当事人之间确立的任何习惯做法或惯例。也就是说,该款规定“惯例”是解释合同的重要因素之一。《公约》第9条实质上是关于惯例对合同的补充功能的规定。由于合同补充也可以说是解释的延长,故总体上仍属于合同解释的范畴。该条第1款规定,当事人之间业已同意的任何惯例和他们之间确立的任何习惯做法,对双方当事人均有约束力。第2款则规定除非另有协议,双方当事人应视为已默示地同意对他们的合同或其成立适用双方当事人已经知道或理应知道的惯例,条件是这种惯例必须是在国际贸易上已为有关特定贸易所涉同类合同的当事人所广泛知道并为他们经常遵守。质言之,双方当事人明示或默示同意纳入其合同的惯例均构成合同的一部分,从而对合同具有补充的功能。而这种“默示同意”的判断标准便是这种惯例必须是在国际贸易中被广泛使用,并被认为是约定俗成的习惯做法。[44] INCOTERMS 以及 UCP 就是这样的惯例。这里的“经常遵守”条件是继承了《国际货物买卖统一法》第9条第2款的规定,而“广泛知道”条件则是《公约》的创新。其意旨在于避免原限于国内使用的惯例被任意推广适用于与外国贸易商的交易之中。这样一来,英国的设备出口商在与印度商人交易时,就不能援用英国国内设备买卖中的惯例,即使该惯例在英国是尽人皆知以至于外方当事人“已经知道”或者至少“理应知道”这些惯例。[45]

不过,也有学者提出,《公约》这一条款也并不排除在某些情况下,地方或国内惯例适用于与外国交易的可能。例如,某些商品交易所、贸易洽谈会中的惯例,如果在与外国人的交易中也得到经常遵守,也可以在同类国际贸易当事人之间产生约束力。又如,某外商曾与一国当事人签订过大量同类合同,则有关该类合同的既定惯例对于该外商也是有约束力的。但无论如何,《公约》“只给了地方性惯例以非常有限的承认”。[46]

值得注意的是,“广泛知道”与“经常遵守”不仅仅是推定当事人“理应知道”的客观标准,在当事人“已经知道”某惯例的情况下,它也必须同时具备这两个条件。这一点从上文关于英国设备买卖国内惯例一般不能约束国外的当事人(即使他们已经知道该惯例)的例子足以证明。显然,《公约》的这一规定对来自发展中国家的贸易新手来说是十分有利也十分必要的。也正因如此,它才成了包括中国

〔44〕 参见王贵国:《〈联合国国际货物销售合同公约〉的适用原则及解释原则》,载《中国国际法年刊》1989年卷。

〔45〕 Bianca, Bonell, Commentary on the Inernational Sales Law, the 1980 Vienna Sales Convention, 1987, p. 109.

〔46〕 Ibid.

在内的许多发展中国家积极参加的一个公约。

《公约》关于惯例的这些规定与我国国内法上的有关国际惯例的规定既互相区别，又相互联系、相互补充。《公约》的规定是对特定惯例对合同的解释与补充功能的确认，本质上属于合同解释的范畴；我国国内法的有关国际惯例的规定是关于国际惯例对我国法律的补充的功能，本质上属于法律解释的范畴；二者属于不同的法律层面。但同时这两种规定又是互相联系、互相补充的。《公约》关于特定惯例的补充功能的规定使国际惯例中的一部分可作为合同的默示条款而直接补充合同的内容，从而取得优于《公约》及国内任法律规范的法律效力。而我国国内法的规定则使所有未依《公约》而明示或默示地纳入合同，且不违反我国社会公共利益的国际惯例可以用来补充国内法的不足。对于某一具体惯例而言，一旦它符合《公约》规定的条件而构成某合同的一部分，则通常不会再被用作该合同争议的法律补充工具，因为它已经在合同解释与补充中得到了先期适用，从而实现了其规范功能，自不必待到无法可依后再行适用；但如果它不符合《公约》规定的条件，不能直接补充该合同，不构成该合同的一部分，则它只能在"无法可依"的情况下，才可能得到适用。对于某一类合同中所有惯例而言，只有那些符合《公约》规定条件的国际惯例构成该类合同的一部分，可对合同内容进行直接补充；而不符合《公约》规定条件，不构成该类合同的一部分的国际惯例在我国法律不敷适用时，则可以用来补充法律的不足而适用于该类合同争议。换言之，《公约》与我国国内法的结合，实质上使"国际惯例"分割成两大部分，符合《公约》条件的部分可直接补充合同，构成合同的组成部分而先期得到适用；不符合《公约》规定条件的国际惯例则只能作为漏洞补充的工具而得到补充适用。这也就意味着，事实上，对法律起补充作用的"国际惯例"不仅仅应没有被吸收进入我国的国内法或上升而为我国缔结或参加的国际条约，而且应没有根据《公约》的规定而被纳入合同，成为合同明示或默示条款。这无疑是对补充适用的国际惯例的一种事实上的限制。

基于上述分析，我们认为，国际惯例与《公约》及我国国内法三者之间的效力等级与适用顺次大致可归纳如下，即先后依次是：我国法的强制性规定——依《公约》规定而成为合同明示或默示条款的惯例——《公约》的规定[47]——我国法中的任意性规定——依《公约》规定不构成合同明示或默示条款的国际惯例。

由此可见，《公约》有关惯例的规定与我国有关国际惯例的国内立法相结合实际上使得国际惯例在我国涉外民商事（特别是合同）法律适用过程中占有十分重要的地位。

---

〔47〕 这里需注意的是，《公约》中我国已作出保留的部分将不对我国产生约束力。

综上所述，我们认为：我国有关国内立法中的“国际惯例”当仅指实体意义上的国际惯例；它既不属国际法，也不属国内法，而只是国际法与国内法的补充，是法律漏洞补充的工具；国际惯例在我国的适用以我国法为准据法而我国有关国内法与国际条约未作规定，且当事人对其适用未予明示排除作为前提，同时，国际惯例的适用尚不能违反我国的社会公共利益；此外，我国所参加的《联合国国际货物销售合同公约》的有关规定则赋予了“惯例”以解释与补充合同的法律意义，这使得国际惯例在我国对外经济交往中具备了更重要的法律意义。

进而言之，我国现行有关“国际惯例”的立法是否真如某些学者所主张的，需要作根本性的修改呢？在我们看来，我国现行有关立法既体现了尊重国际惯例的时代精神，也适应与国际通行规则接轨，弥补国内法律不足的现实需要，是必要的，也是合理的，无须作大的修改。不过，考虑到理论与实践中存在的种种歧异，我们似有必要对其作出科学、权威的法律解释，以明确其含义、性质、适用条件诸项，从而统一认识，使相关法学理论研究与立法司法实践得以明确化、深层化与科学化。

法治中国的国际维度*

依法治国是“法治中国”建设史的一座丰碑，是中国迈进“法治时代”的标志性事件。外交是内政的延伸。十八届四中全会决定所描绘的法治中国蓝图不仅为“国内法治”提供了路线图，也为“国际法治”建设和发展指明了方向。

作为世界和平的积极维护者和全球发展的主要动力，世界各国人民对中国寄予厚望。在改革不合理的国际政治经济旧秩序和建立国际政治经济新秩序过程中，中国的作用不可替代，中国的方法举世瞩目。毫无疑义，在中国处理国际关系和对外事务的过程中，首善的方法应该也是法治。

首先，推动国际法治必须要在宪法赋予的权限内进行。国际交往关涉国家的重大利益，是党和国家治国理政的重要内容之一。我国《宪法》在多个条款中对开展国际交往做出了规定，这些规定构成了外事、外贸活动的宪法性规范，必须予以遵守。

其次，推动国际法治必须要坚持推动高质量的国际“立法”工作，即国际法律规范体系的制定、改进和完善工作。就此，四中全会决定明确提出要“适应对外开放不断深化，完善涉外法律法规体系，促进构建开放型经济新体制。积极参与国际规则制定，推动依法处理涉外经济、社会事务，增强我国在国际法律事务中的话语权和影响力”。

再次，推动国际法治必须推动国际法的有效实现，即国际法的“运用”“实施”或“执法”。对此，全会决定做了明确部署，提出不仅要“运用法律手段维护我国主权、安全、发展利益”，要“强化涉外法律服务，维护我国公民、法人在海外及外国公民、法人在我国的正当权益，依法维护海外侨胞权益”，还要“积极参与执法

* 本文发表在《光明日报》2014 年 11 月 5 日第 2 版。

安全国际合作,共同打击暴力恐怖势力、民族分裂势力、宗教极端势力和贩毒走私、跨国有组织犯罪”。

此外,推动国际法治还要求我们积极参与国际“司法”,努力维护国际公平正义。当代司法化或类司法的国际机制获得长足发展,已成为国际法保障机制的重要特征。在今后的国际司法治理中,中国有必要正确研判有关规则,更加积极地推进对国际司法机制的深度参与。与此同时,还要根据全会决定部署,“深化司法领域国际合作,完善我国司法协助体制,扩大国际司法协助覆盖面”。

最后,推动国际法治还必须推动国际“守法”。“有法必依”既是国内法上的普遍原则,也是国际法上的一般义务。中国作为国际社会的重要一分子,坚持信守国际承诺,切实履行国际法律义务和责任。中国对国际法的“守法”有助于推动国际法治的转型升级,有助于营造有利于我国和平发展的良好外部环境。

十八届四中全会决定中直接论述涉外和国际法治的篇幅虽然不大,但在推动“法治中国”的同时,推动“法治世界”,这是全面推进依法治国的题中应有之义,也是世界政府和人民的殷切期待。

更加积极地参与全球经济治理*

随着全球经济格局调整和自身经济实力提升，中国更加主动地发出自己的声音，既是深化对外开放的内在要求，也是促进世界经济和谐发展的客观需要，有助于打破少数国家对全球经济法律规则的“垄断”，使规则向更为合理均衡的方向发展

近期，北京 APEC 会议、G20 集团领导人峰会、第九届东亚峰会、中国—东盟领导人会议等一系列国际会议密集召开。中国领导人亲自与会并发表重要讲话，就促进世界经济增长、推动区域合作、完善全球经济治理等阐述主张，引发国际舆论高度关注。与以往不同的是，中国在这些会议上不仅广泛宣示自身内外政策，还积极发出中国倡议、提出中国方案，体现出自身作为一个负责任的大国，更加主动自信地参与全球经济治理的良好形象。

改革开放以来，中国在国际经济事务中更多以接受既有规则为主。随着全球经济格局调整和自身经济实力提升，中国更加主动地发出自己的声音，既是深化对外开放的内在要求，也是促进世界经济和谐发展的客观需要，有助于打破少数国家对全球经济法律规则的“垄断”，使规则向更为合理均衡的方向发展。

自 2001 年加入 WTO 以来，中国主动履行世贸组织成员国义务，在减免关税、开放市场、完善法律方面做出了巨大努力。多哈回合谈判陷入僵局后，中国积极寻求区域合作法制的完善。中国牵头推动世界上最大的贸易协定之一的“区域全面经济伙伴关系”谈判，顺利结束了第四轮谈判，有望在 2015 年前达成在亚太地区降低贸易壁垒的协定。

刚结束不久的亚太经合组织（APEC）第二十二次领导人非正式会议，在中国

* 本文发表在《经济日报》2014 年 12 月 1 日第 6 版。

的努力推动下,决定启动亚太自由贸易区进程。会议批准亚太经合组织推动实现亚太自由贸易区路线图,标志着亚太自贸区进程正式启动,朝着实现亚太自贸区方向迈出了历史性一步。

中国政府提出的“一带一路”重要倡议,对促进全球经济增长具有重要意义。习近平主席立足我国对外开放和区域发展新形势,放眼全球经济增长和发展,提出建设“一带一路”的重要倡议,得到国际社会的广泛响应和支持。后续的落实和建设,应以区域经济一体化为手段,以经贸合作为主要形式,以共同规则为主要保障。具体路径为贸易合作、能源合作、基础建设、文化交流和政治互信与合作,并通过各种完善的法律协定来实现。随着亚投行、丝路基金等措施的筹划和设置,未来充满期待。

如果说中国对全球贸易领域的影响,主要通过区域性协定实现,那么国际投资法领域则有望在中国的推动下,实现一个全球性的多边投资协定。中国是世界上拥有双边投资条约数量第二多的国家。中国正与美国和欧盟分别展开双边投资协定的谈判,这两个谈判必然会对国际投资法的发展方向产生重要影响。

中国是世界上最大的发展中国家,美国是世界上最大的发达国家,欧盟是世界上最大的经济体,相互之间的投资条约谈判,体现的不仅是发展中国家与发达国家相关经济利益的考虑,更是共同应对当前国际投资法所面临问题的正面回应。通过这两个协定的示范作用,将推动全球投资领域成功订立多边协定。

党的十八届四中全会决定明确指出,要“积极参与国际规则制定,推动依法处理涉外经济社会事务,增强我国在国际法律事务中的话语权和影响力,运用法律手段维护我国的主权、安全和发展利益”。中国更加积极主动参与全球经济治理的完善,促进更为公平合理的国际经济政治秩序,既是实现中华民族伟大复兴“中国梦”的必然要求,也为推动全球经济发展、维护世界和平提供了重要保障,必然会赢得更多的国际理解和支持。

第二编 欧洲联盟与中欧关系法 Part II

059－283

The Treaty of Lisbon: Halfway toward a Common Investment Policy*

The Treaty of Lisbon finally entered into force on 1 December 2009, marking a fortunate turn for European integration from an institutional crisis and effectuating a number of significant changes in the constitutional structure of the EU. Among them the inclusion of foreign direct investment (FDI) in the Common Commercial Policy (CCP) is perhaps 'the largest but still the least discussed'[1] change. In a 300-page impact assessment on the treaty provided by the House of Lords, for instance, this change received only a passing comment.[2] Indeed, when preparing the European Constitution, the predecessor of the Lisbon Treaty, no discussion had been held on the extension of the CCP to investment.[3]

As a follow-up study[4] on the external investment policy of the EU, this article attempts to analyse the relevant provisions in the Lisbon Treaty and assesses their legal implication on the international investment treaty practice of the Union and its Member States. It first briefly reviews the EU's foreign investment competence before the Treaty of the Lisbon. Then it assesses the different views concerning the interpretation of the Lisbon Treaty provisions with regard to the inclusion of FDI in the CCP. The practical legal implications of the change are discussed in the third part, including intra-and extra-EU investment treaty practice. It is concluded that whilst the change is significant

---

* Shan Wenhua and Zhang Sheng, *European Journal of International Law*, Volume 21 Issue 4, 2010.

Zhang Sheng, Research Assistant and PhD Candidate, Silk Road Institute for International and Comparative Law, Xi'an Jiaotong University; and Visiting Student of the Max Planck Institute for Comparative and International Private Law, Germany. Email: zhang. sheng@ stu. xjtu. edu. cn.

[1] Bungenberg, Going Global? The EU Common Commercial Policy After Lisbon, in C. Herrmann and J. P. Terhechte(eds), *European Yearbook of International Economic Law* 2010 (2010) 123, p. 151.

[2] The Treaty of Lisbon: an Impact Assessment, available at: www. publications. parliament. uk/pa/ld200708/ldselect/ldeucom/62/62. pdf(accessed on 26 May 2010).

[3] Though the Treaty of Lisbon made some modifications compared with the European Constitution, the stipulation concerning the CCP remained intact. It was pointed out that in the first stage of the Constitution deliberations this issue was not raised, nor did the Working Group on External Action suggest such an expansion: see Krajewiki, External Trade Law and the Constitution Treaty: Towards a Federal and More Democratic Common Commercial Policy?, 42 *CML Rev* (2005) 91, at 100 – 102.

[4] See Shan, Towards a Common European Community Policy on Investment Issues, 2 *J World Investment* (2001) 603.

and will greatly enhance the treaty-making competence of the EU in the external investment area, it is only half way toward a full common investment policy(CIP). Potential paths to achieve this goal are explored in the end.

1 The EC's International Investment Competence Before Lisbon: Recent Practices

As has been written before, the EC did not have exclusive, but shared, competence in international investment matters.[5] This is because the Community had not established either express or implied exclusive competence in this area, as none of the express treaty provisions or the measures adopted under such provisions covered the entire field of international investment.[6] In *Opinion* 2/92, for instance, the Court held that the national treatment rule, which was basically a rule on FDI activities, related only partially to international trade with non-member countries, and therefore Article 113 TEC(on CCP) could not be used as the legal basis for the exclusive Community competence thereon.[7] It also observed that "although the Community has adopted measures capable of serving as basis for an exclusive external competence in accordance with the aforesaid case-law and falling in particular within the scope of Articles 57(2), 75, 84 and 100a of the EC Treaty, it is undisputed that those measures do not cover all the fields of activity to which the Third Decision relates".[8]

This shared competence has witnessed some notable practices in recent years,[9] including the 2006 Minimum Platform on Investment for EU Free Trade Agreements (MPoI), and a few cases before the European Courts[regarding BITs between EU Member States and third states(extra-EU BITs)] and investment arbitration tribunals[relating to BITs between different EU Member States(intra-EU BITs)].

A The MPoI and Recent Treaty Practice

The Minimum Platform on Investment for EU FTAs[10] was adopted by the Council of the EU on 27 November 2006. As a standardized negotiation proposal for current and future free trade agreement negotiations with third countries, it intends to satisfy the need of the EC to agree on an investment chapter when a potential FTA is under negotiation.[11] The Platform's scope of application is confined to "measures by the Parties affecting establishment". It is therefore targeted at foreign direct investment, and does not

---

〔5〕 See Shan, Towards a Common European Community Policy on Investment Issues, 2 *J World Investment* (2001)603.

〔6〕 Exclusive competence might also be established on the basis of the nature of the measure to be adopted, as established in *Opinion* 1/76 [1977] ECR 741. However, as confirmed by the ECJ in its *Opinions* 1/94 and 2/92, this principle does not apply to international investment treaty-making: see *Opinion* 1/94, *WTO* [1994] ECR I-5267, at paras 84-86; *Opinion* 2/92, *OECD-National Treatment Investment* [1995] ECR I-521, at para. 32.

〔7〕 Opinion 2/92, *supra* note 6, at paras 18-28.

〔8〕 Ibid., at para. 34.

〔9〕 For an analysis of the law and practice up to 2000 see Shan, *supra* note 4.

〔10〕 Council of the European Union, 15375/06, 27 Nov. 2006.

〔11〕 Maydell, The European Community's Minimum Platform on Investment or the Trojan Horse of Investment Competence, in A. Reinisch and C. Knahr(eds), *International Investment Law in Con-text* (2007) 73, at 75.

include measures relating to expropriation and settlement of investor-state disputes.

The MPoI was intended to be the basis on which 'an ambitious investment policy' was to be built.[12] It represented the first formalized and systematic EC approach towards international investment treaty making, and was the most significant proof of the EC's recent willingness to intervene in an external economic policy field so far predominantly left to the Member States.[13] The Platform, however, is unlikely to have a direct impact on the competence division between the Community and the Member States, as some have suggested.[14] Legally it is only a negotiation template which has not been formally published, not a formal EU regulation. It therefore does not have the effect of increasing or decreasing the competence of the Union *vis-à-vis* its Member States. Its symbolic implications may be much more significant than its actual legal impact. Indeed, as the Commission has stressed, any EU-negotiated FTA including BIT like investor protection would require approval by all Member States.[15] Clearly foreign investment remains an area of shared competence between the Union and its Member States.

In this connection, it is noted that the EU has already started to negotiate relatively ambitious investment agreements (or chapters within comprehensive agreements) in recent years. The EC-Chile Association Agreement, for example, grants full national treatment at the pre-and post-entry stage for both natural and legal persons from the other contracting party, together with consent to state-to-state dispute settlement by arbitration.[16] The EU-CARIFORUM EPA signed in 2008 includes a chapter on liberalization of investment based on a positive listing of coverage, protection for current payments and capital movements related to FDI, and some provisions on investor behaviour.[17] In February 2009, the EU and Canada published a joint report concerning the economic and trade relationship, in which investment rules might "cover pre-and post-establishment in all sectors in order to improve market access and provide for the non-discriminatory treatment of investors and investments, and to improve transparency."[18] The EU-MERCOSUR Bi-regional Agreement is also intended to include obligations on invest-

---

[12] *See* "Remarks" in the draft "Minimum Platform on Investment for EU Free Trade Agreements", by the Commission for the discussion of the 133 Committee, 28 July 2006, available at: www. iisd. org/pdf/2006/itn_ ecom. pdf(accessed on 26 May 2010).

[13] Maydell, *supra* note 11, at 73.

[14] Niklas Maydell, e. g., considers that the MPoI would have serious consequences for the Member States' competence to enter into international investment agreements, particularly in the area of admission for investment. *See* ibid., at 91.

[15] Vis-Dunbar, European Governments Remain Split Over Extent of Investor Provisions in EU FTAs, *Investment Treaty News*, 16 Mar. 2007, available at: www. iisd. org/pdf/2007/itn_mar16 _2007. pdf(accessed on 26 May 2010).

[16] Agreement establishing an association between the European Community and its Member States, of the one part, and the Republic of Chile, of the other part, available at: http://eur-lex. eu ropa. eu/LexUriServ/LexUriServ. do? uri = OJ: L: 20 02: 352: 0003: 1439: EN: PDF(accessed on 26 May 2010).

[17] Woolcock, The Treaty of Lisbon and the European Union as an Actor in International Trade, ECIPE Working Paper no. 1/2010, at 10, available at: www. ecipe. org/the-treaty-of-lisbon-and-the-european-union-as-an-actor-in-international-trade(accessed on 26 May 2010).

[18] Joint Report on the EU-Canada Scoping Exercise, 5 Mar. 2009, at 5 - 6, available at: http:// trade. ec. europa. eu/doclib/docs/2009/ march/ tradoc_142470. pdf(accessed on 26 May 2010).

ment.[19] The same is to be seen in the EC's new neighborhood policy aiming to create a Pan-Euro-Mediterranean market[20] and the current EU-India FTA negotiations, which plan to include an entire chapter on investment.[21] All this treaty practice further confirms the EU's competence in foreign investment matters, though such competence is not complete or comprehensive enough for it to sign BIT-style investment treaties on its own.

B Extra-EU BITs and the ECJ Cases

Another important recent development in the Commission's effort to assert investment competence is the cases it brought against Sweden, Austria, and Finland before the European Court of Justice (ECJ). In 2004, the Commission notified Austria, Finland, Sweden, and Denmark that some of their preaccession BITs with non-EU countries (extra-EU BITs) might be in conflict with certain powers reserved to the EU.[22] The EC Treaty permits wide-ranging freedom for movement of capital and payments but allows the Council of Ministers, in exceptional circumstances, to take certain restrictive measures in relation to movements of capital to or from non-EU countries. The EC considered that the BITs in question, particularly the free transfer provisions, might hinder the application of these restrictive measures. According to Article 307 of the EC Treaty, Community law does not automatically prevail over international agreements concluded by Member States prior to their accession.[23] Member States are, however, obliged to take all appropriate steps to eliminate possible incompatibilities contained in such prior international agreements.[24]

The EC's request for BIT modification was rejected by the Member States concerned. The Commission therefore took Sweden and Austria to the ECJ in 2006 and began a similar case against Finland later.[25] The case against Denmark was dropped fol-

---

[19] The agenda of investment is discussed in the 12th and the 13th negotiations. The EU-Mercosur FTA negotiations were launched in 1999 but were suspended in October 2004 due to important divergences relating to the trade pillar of the agreement. The negotiations re-launched when the EU-LAC Summit took place on 18 May 2010 in Madrid. More details are available at: http://ec.europa.eu/trade/creating-opportunities/bilateral-relations/regions/mercosur/ (accessed on 26 May 2010).

[20] Gavin, Trade and Investment in the Wider Europe: EU Neighborhood Policy for Enhanced Regional Integration, 4 *J World Investment* (2003) 893, 902.

[21] Bungenberg, *supra* note 1, at 140. More information on this FTA can be found at: http://ec.europa.eu/trade/creating-opportunities/bilateral-relations/countries/india/ and http://trade.ec.europa.eu/doclib/docs/2007/june/tradoc_135101.pdf (accessed on 26 May 2010).

[22] Vis-Dunbar, European Governments Defend BITs in Lawsuit Brought by EU Executive Branch, *Investment Treaty News*, 16 Mar. 2007, available at: www.iisd.org/pdf/2007/itn_mar16_2007.pdf (accessed on 26 May 2010).

[23] Art. 307 TEC, OJ (2006) C 321E/1, available at: http://eur-lex.europa.eu/LexUriServ/LexUriServ.do?uri=OJ:C:2006:321E:0001:0331:EN:PDF (accessed on 26 May 2010).

[24] Ibid.

[25] Vis-Dunbar, European Court of Justice Rules that Certain Swedish and Austrian BITs are Incompatible with the EC Treaty, *Investment Treaty News*, 4 Mar. 2009, available at: www.investmenttreatynews.org/cms/news/archive/2009/03/04/european-court-of-justice-rulesthat-certain-swedish-and-austrian-bits-areincompatible-with-the-ec-treaty.aspx (accessed on 26 May 2010).

lowing Denmark's notification that it would terminate the BIT in question.[26]

For their part, Sweden and Austria argued that until measures to restrict capital flows were enacted, there was no incompatibility between their bilateral investment treaties and the EC Treaty.[27] The ECJ sided with the Commission in its 3 March 2009 ruling, in which it argued that, should the European Community decide to restrict capital flows, it would be impractical for Sweden and Austria quickly to resolve the conflict that would arise with respect to the commitments made to foreign investors under their bilateral investment treaties.[28] Accordingly, the ECJ ruled that Austria and Sweden had not fulfilled their obligations under Article 307 TEC.[29] Importantly, the ECJ explicitly held that its findings were "not limited to the Member State which is the defendant in the present case".[30] This appears to be a suggestion by the ECJ that the more than 1,300 EU Member State BITs may also be deemed to be in violation of the EC Treaty to the extent that they contain similar free transfer provisions.

On 19 November 2009, a similar ruling was delivered in *Commission* v. *Finland*.[31] The ECJ again rejected Finland's assertion that the BIT provisions were not incompatible with Article 307 TEC because they were stated to be subject to the limits authorized by the laws of the contracting parties, of which Community law was a part.[32] The Court considered that the scope, interpretation, and effects of those provisions were too uncertain, and therefore they were not sufficient to ensure compatibility with Article 307 TEC.[33] Accordingly, Finland should have renegotiated the treaties to bring them into line with the EC Treaty.[34]

The success of the Union in these extra-EU BIT cases has confirmed a basic principle of EC law, namely the supremacy of EC law over national law (BITs of Member States can be considered as part of the national legal order). It also demonstrates that the Union does possess competence in foreign investment matters, which may not be violated even where such competence has not been exercised by the Union.

To avoid conflicts, some non-EU states took more deliberate steps before the prob-

---

[26] Antell, Carlson, and McCandless, The European Commission and Investment Treaties, *The European & Middle Eastern Arbitration Review* 2010, available at: www. globalarbitration review. com/reviews/22/sections/81/chapters/829/the-european-commission-investmenttreaties/(accessed on 26 May 2010).

[27] Vis-Dunbar, *supra* note 25.

[28] Ibid.

[29] Ibid.

[30] Case C - 249/06, *EC Commission v. Sweden*, judgment of 3 Mar. 2009, at para. 43, available at: http://curia. europa. eu/jurisp/cgi-bin/form. pl? l ang = EN&Submit = Rechercher $ docrequire = a lldocs&numaff = C-249/06&datefs = &datefe = &nomusuel = &domaine = &mots = &resmax = 100(accessed on 26 May 2010); Case C - 205/06, *EC Commission v. Austria*, judgment of 3 Mar. 2009, at para. 43, available at: http://curia. europa. eu/jurisp/cgi-bin/form. pl? lang = EN&Submit = Rechercher $ docrequire = alldocs&numaff = C-205/06-&datefs = &datefe = &nomusuel = &domaine = &m ots = &resmax = 100(accessed on 26 May 2010).

[31] Case C - 118/07, *C Commission v. Finland*. See PLC Arbitration, ECJ finds Finland's BITs breach article 307 of the EC Treaty, available at: http:// arbitration. practicallaw. com/1-500-8076(accessed on 26 May 2010).

[32] Ibid.

[33] Ibid.

[34] Ibid.

lem arose. The US, for example, engaged in extensive negotiations with the Commission, aimed at amending its BITs with the acceding states and adjusting them to the requirement of the EU before the 2004 enlargement. The negotiations ended with a Memorandum of Understanding(MOU) signed by the US, the Commission, and the acceding states regarding the revision of the BITs. Subsequently, the US entered into protocols with some of the acceding states and modified relevant BITs. Canada followed suit and reached an agreement with the EU soon after the 2004 enlargement to develop amendments to its investment treaties with new Member States.[35] In 2007, Hungary terminated its BIT with Israel.[36] In 2008, the Czech Republic concluded five protocols on the amendments to original BITs signed with other third countries.[37]

C Intra-EU BITs and Recent Arbitration Cases

While the above-mentioned ECJ rulings concern BITs between EU Member States and non-EU states, the Commission has also raised concerns over BITs between EU Member States(intra-EU BITs) on the grounds that they overlap with EC law. It is estimated that there are nearly 200 such BITs between pairs of EU Member States, many of which pre-date at least one state's EU accession.[38] As noted below, some of these BITs have been invoked by investors in recent years in investment treaty arbitration cases.

In 2006, the Commission submitted an informal note to the Economic and Financial Committee of the Council(EFC) of the EU regarding the continued existence of intra-EU BITs. The Commission suggested in that note that "[t] here appears to be no need for agreements of this kind in the single market and their legal character after accession is not entirely clear. It would appear that most of their content is superseded by Community law upon accession of the respective Member State."[39] Commission officials also warned that "investors could try to practice forum shopping by submitting claims to BIT arbitration instead of—or in addition to—national courts. This could lead to BIT arbitration taking place without relevant questions of EC law being submitted to the ECJ, with unequal treatment of investors among Member States a possible outcome."[40] However, this note seems to have had little effect in persuading the EU Member States. After receiving comments from Member States regarding the Commission's proposal, the EFC wrote a letter in February 2009 to the President of the Council of the European Union and noted that "[m] ost member states did not share the Commission's concern regarding

---

〔35〕 *See* Canada - Europe Union Reach Deal to Amend Six Investment Treaties, *INVESTSD: Investment Law and Policy Weekly News Bull*, 13 Oct. 2004, available at: www. iisd. org/pdf/2004/investment_investsd_oct13_2004. pdf(accessed on 26 May 2010).

〔36〕 *See* Recent Developments in International Investment Agreements (2008 - June 2009), *IIA Monitor* No. 3(2009), at 5, available at: www. unctad. org/en/docs/webdiaeia20098_en. pdf(accessed on 26 May 2010).

〔37〕 Ibid.

〔38〕 Antell, Carlson, and McCandless, *supra* note 26.

〔39〕 Vis-Dunbar, EU Members Review Intra-European BITs in Light of Potential Overlap with EU Law, *In-vestment Treaty News*, 30 June 2007, available at: www. iisd. org/pdf/2007/itn_june30_2007. pdf(accessed on 26 May 2010).

〔40〕 Vis-Dunbar, EU Member States Reject the Call to Terminate Intra-EU Bilateral Investment Treaties, *Investment Treaty News*, 10 Feb. 2009, available at: www. investmenttreatynews. org/cms/news/ archive/2009/02/10/ eu-member-statesreject-the-call-to-terminate-intra-eu-bilateralinvestment-treaties. aspx(accessed on 26 May 2010).

arbitration risks and discriminatory treatment of investors and a clear majority of member states preferred to maintain the existing agreements".[41]

In the few investment arbitration cases involving this issue, arbitral tribunals have determined that intra-EU BITs were not implicitly terminated when those countries acceded to the EU. The *Eastern Sugar* v. *Czech Republic* tribunal, for instance, recently rejected the Czech Republic's argument that all of its BITs with other EU Member States were implicitly terminated when it acceded to the EU.[42] A similar conclusion has reportedly been reached by another tribunal.[43] The Czech Republic has appealed at least one of these decisions to local courts.[44] Such arbitration decisions confirmed what the EC had worried and warned in the informal note-BIT arbitration did take place ' without relevant questions of EC law being submitted to the ECJ' .

Several EU Member States have announced their plans to terminate their intra-EU BITs. The Czech Republic is understandably leading this effort, and announced in 2005 its intention to terminate all of its BITs with other EU Member States.[45] The Italy-Czech Republic BIT has already been terminated, while the termination of Denmark-Czech Republic BIT is on the way.[46] Recently Slovenia and Malta announced that they intended to terminate their own BITs.[47] Italy has also evinced the same intention.[48] However, some EU Member States do not agree with the Czech Republic's approach. They reportedly include Belgium, Germany, the Netherlands, and the United Kingdom.[49] It is noted that many of the recent disputes brought against the Czech Republic arose under BITs with some of those countries.

Recently, the Commission successfully applied to intervene in two investment treaty arbitration cases, both relating to power generation in Hungary.[50] The claims were tar-

---

〔41〕 Vis-Dunbar, EU Member States Reject the Call to Terminate Intra-EU Bilateral Investment Treaties, *Investment Treaty News*, 10 Feb. 2009, available at: www. investmenttreatynews. org/cms/news/ archive/2009/02/10/eu-member-statesreject-the-call-to-terminate-intra-eu-bilateralinvestment-treaties. aspx(accessed on 26 May 2010).

〔42〕 *Eastern Sugar BV(Netherlands) v. The Czech Re-public*, SCC No. 088/2004, available at: http://ita. law. uvic. ca/documents/EasternSugar. pdf(accessed on 26 May 2010).

〔43〕 Vis-Dunbar, Czech Republic Quietly Pursues Challenge to Jurisdictional Ruling in Prague Court, *Investment Treaty News*, 17 Jan. 2008, available at: www. iisd. org/pdf/2008/itn_jan17_2008. pdf(accessed on 26 May 2010).

〔44〕 Ibid.

〔45〕 Vis-Dunbar, Czech Republic Pursues Shake-up of Its Bilateral Investment Treaties, *Investment Treaty News*, 21Nov. 2005, availableat: www. iisd. org/pdf/2005/investment_investsd_nov21_2005. pdf(accessed on 26 May 2010).

〔46〕 *See* Italy, Slovenia and Malta concur with Czech Republic on lack of necessity for intra-EU BITs; Italy-Czech treaty has been terminated *and* Denmark and Czech Republic working to terminate investment treaty; not all EU member-states agree with the Czech view that intra-EU treaties are unnecessary, *Investment Arbitration Reporter*, 6 Aug. 2009 and 17 July 2009.

〔47〕 Italy, Slovenia and Malta concur with Czech Republic on lack of necessity for intra-EU BITs; Italy-Czech treaty has been terminated, *Investment Arbitration Reporter*, 6 Aug. 2009.

〔48〕 Ibid.

〔49〕 See the articles, *supra* note 46.

〔50〕 *AES Summit Generation Limited and AES-Tisza Erömü Kft v. Republic of Hungary* (ICSID Case No. ARB/07/22), award of 23 Sept. 2010, available at: http://icsid. worldbank. org/ICSID/FrontServlet? requestType = CasesRH&actionVal = showDoc&d ocId = DC1730_En&caseId = C114 (accessed on 10 Oct. 2010); and *Electrabel SA v. Republic of Hungary* (ICSID Case No. ARB/07/19) (pending).

geted at Hungarian government requirements that the Hungarian purchasers of electricity make changes to long-term contracts('power purchase agreements') entered into before Hungarian accession to the EU. Part of the Hungarian defence was that it had to make the changes required under EU law, since the Commission had determined that such agreements were illegal under EU law.[51] In both cases, the Commission was granted permission to file non-party submissions.[52] While the submissions have not yet been made public, it is generally understood that the Commission intervened to defend Hungary's actions as being required by EU law.[53] The Commission also reportedly sought to challenge the jurisdiction of the tribunal on the ground that some aspects of the dispute and the underlying contract from which the dispute arose were subject to EU law, and therefore within the jurisdiction of the Commission.[54]

D Summary and Comments

The preceding paragraphs reveal that there have been notable practices relating to the international investment competence of the EU in recent years. While it is not surprising to see that the Commission has been making continuous efforts to assert and expand its foreign investment competence, it appears to be dramatic to find out that the European Courts and the international arbitration tribunals seem to have adopted opposite views with regard to the relationship between EC law and international law. In the ECJ cases the decisions were based on EC law, upholding the Commission's power to intervene into at least some provisions of the BITs which the Member States have entered into. In contrast, the arbitration tribunals ruled that the BITs should be interpreted in accordance with principles of international law, and thus accession to the EU of one Member State did not implicitly terminate the BITs which that Member State had entered into with other Member States.

While the two sets of cases certainly have exposed the tension between the two different legal orders, EU law and international law, a closer look at them demonstrates that they are not as contradictory as they appear. In the ECJ cases the Court was dealing with essentially a question of EC law, i. e., whether the EU Member States had violated the EC Treaty by refusing to take measures to bring certain BITs provisions into conformity with EC law. It was not directly dealing with any question of international law, e. g, whether EC law was superior to international law(BITs). It is therefore only natural that it applied EC law principles and arrived at a decision which happened to be favourable to the Commission. In contrast, the investment arbitration tribunals were dealing with an essentially international law question whether the effective application

---

[51] This is because they 'constitute[d] unlawful and incompatible state aid to the power generators', and because they unduly restricted competition by preventing new entrants: *see* European Commission seeks to intervene as amicus curiae in ICSID arbitrations to argue that long-term power purchase agreements between Hungary and foreign investors are contrary to European Community Law, *Investment Treaty News*, 17 Sept. 2008.

[52] *See* ICSID tribunal will permit European Com-mission to file legal brief in Energy Charter Treaty arbitration, *Investment Treaty News*, 11 Dec. 2008; European Commission moves to intervene in another ICSID arbitration, *Investment Arbitration Reporter*, 11 May 2009.

[53] Ibid.

[54] Ibid.

of the EC Treaty to an EU Member State effectuated the implicit termination of the BITs entered into by the Member State with other Member States. Such a question can be answered only by applying international law principles, rather than EC law principles. Even though EC law, particularly the EC Treaty, is relevant, it is relevant as a matter of legal fact, not as the primary governing law. The same applies to the BIT provisions in the ECJ cases-they were relevant only as matter of fact, not as directly applicable law to the dispute, since the dispute was not a BIT dispute but an EC law dispute.

The two sets of cases can not only be reconciled with each other, but can jointly serve to strengthen the call for a common investment policy (CIP).[55] The ECJ cases serve as a positive confirmation of the power the EU already had in foreign investment matters; the arbitration decisions demonstrate from a negative perspective what kind of troubles and complications the EU and its Member State had to confront without a common investment policy at the Union level. It is therefore a great achievement for the Union to include 'foreign direct investment' in its common commercial policy, even though it may not be a ideal solution, as discussed below.

2 The EC's International Investment Competence under the Lisbon Treaty: Different Interpretations

A The Relevant Articles

The Lisbon Treaty has managed to include 'foreign direct investment' in the 'common commercial policy' of the EC Treaty, which is now named the Treaty on the Functioning of the European Union (TFEU). The most directly related provisions are contained in Articles 206 and 207 TFEU. They are as follows:

Article 206

By establishing a customs union in accordance with Articles 28 to 32, the Union shall contribute, in the common interest, to the harmonious development of world trade, the progressive abolition of restrictions on international trade *and on foreign direct investment*, and the lowering of customs and other barriers.

Article 207

1. The common commercial policy shall be based on uniform principles, particularly with regard to changes in tariff rates, the conclusion of tariff and trade agreements relating to trade in goods and services, and the commercial aspects of intellectual property, *foreign direct investment*, the achievement of uniformity in measures of liberalisation, export policy and measures to protect trade such as those to be taken in the event of dumping or subsidies. The common commercial policy shall be conducted in the context of the principles and objectives of the Union's external action.

...

6. The exercise of the competences conferred by this Article in the field of the com-

[55] For an earlier call for a common investment policy of the EU see Shan, *supra* note 4, at 623 – 625.

mon commercial policy *shall not affect the delimitation of competences between the Union and the Member States*, and shall not lead to harmonisation of legislative or regulatory provisions of the Member States in so far as the Treaties exclude such harmonisation [emphasis added].

Clearly Article 206 TFEU sets out the objectives of the common commercial policy. It follows the former Article 131 TEC but adds "foreign direct investment" in parallel to "international trade" as the areas in which the Union intends progressively to prohibit restrictions. As discussed below, this parallel phrasing has implications in the interpretation of Article 207 TFEU, particularly with regard to the question whether the FDI mentioned in Article 207(1) TFEU should be interpreted to cover the entire area of FDI or only "trade-related aspects" of FDI.

Article 207 TFEU is the body Article of the common commercial policy and deserves close examination. It generally follows the former Article 133 TEC (with some modifications, e. g., in the last paragraph), but again adds "foreign direct investment" to the coverage of the CCP. Paragraph 1 is the most important as it sets out the scope of the policy. While it is clear that FDI is included in the CCP, there is no definition of the term "foreign direct investment", nor is there any clarification of the exact scope of FDI under the CCP. It is therefore desirable to discuss how the term 'FDI' should be defined and how the entire provision should be interpreted.

B The Meaning of "Foreign Direct Investment"

The Treaty of Lisbon, however, included FDI under the CCP, but did not define it.[56] In contrast, most BITs, including those signed by EU Member States, contain a definition clause on "investment", which usually refers to every kind of asset having an economic value, regardless of whether the investor has taken managerial control of an undertaking. The concept of FDI under the Lisbon Treaty must therefore be interpreted in accordance with international law and community law.

At international level, both the International Monetary Fund (IMF)[57] and the Organization for Economic Co-operation and Development (OECD)[58] have attempted to define FDI, and have characterized FDI as a lasting interest with a long-term relationship and influence. Such definition has been reflected in the ECJ's interpretation of the

[56] When discussing amendment to the CCP, some commissioner pointed out that the term Foreign Direct Investment requires more precise formulation, see http://european-convention.eu.int/Docs/Treaty/pdf/866/Art24Hain.pdf (accessed on 26 May 2010).

[57] The International Monetary Fund (IMF) defines 'direct investment' as reflecting the objective of obtaining a lasting interest by an entity resident in one country in an enterprise resident in another economy. The lasting interest implies the existence of a long-term relationship between the direct investor and the enterprise and a significant degree of influence by the investor on the management of the enterprise: IMF, *Balance of Payment Manual* (5th edn, 1993), available at: www.imf.org/external/pubs/ft/bopman/bopman.pdf (accessed on 10 Oct. 2010).

[58] According to the definition of the OECD, foreign direct investment reflects the objective of establishing a lasting interest by a resident enterprise in one economy (direct investor) in an enterprise (direct investment enterprise) which is resident in an economy other than that of the direct investor. The lasting interest implies the existence of a long-term relationship between the direct investor and the direct investment enterprise and a significant degree of influence on the management of the enterprise. *See* OECD, Benchmark Definition of Foreign Direct Investment (4th edn, 2008), at 48.

term ' direct investment' (used in former Article 57(2) TEC, now Article 64(2) TFEU) in accordance with Directive 88/361/EEC.[59] The definition goes as follows:

investments of all kinds by natural persons or commercial, industrial or financial undertakings, and which serve to establish or to maintain lasting and direct links between the person providing the capital and the entrepreneur to whom or the undertaking to which the capital is made available in order to carry on an economic activity. This concept must therefore be understood in its widest sense.

This provides for a Community law definition which may be used when defining the same term included in the CCP. Like the IMF and OECD definitions, it stresses a ' lasting and direct link' between the investor and the investment. Although there has been no further clarification on the definition, it is understood that indirect or portfolio investment, such as short-term loans, contractual claims, and intellectual property rights, is not covered as FDI under the CCP.[60] Accordingly, while this new competence covers current EU investment activities such as the WTO Doha Round mandate, the EU bilateral agreements, and potentially an EU investment insurance scheme, it only partially covers conventional BITs and other comprehensive bilateral or multilateral investment instruments protecting and promoting both direct and indirect foreign investments.

However, this does not mean that the EU is prohibited from concluding comprehensive investment treaties such as BITs. It just has to do so with the participation of its Member States, since regulation of indirect or portfolio investment is still a competence shared with the Member States. The EU's competence on portfolio investment is founded on Article 64 TFEU(ex Article 57 TEC). Indeed, this provision has been used, as confirmed by the ECJ, as the legal basis for the EC to participate in the negotiation of comprehensive investment instruments such as OECD National Treatment and the MAI of the OECD, which cover almost every category of foreign investment.

C The Scope of the New FDI Competence: Varied Interpretations

The inclusion of FDI in the CCP has attracted great interest among European and international scholars. As a result, five main interpretations have been given to the scope of the new FDI competence, some narrower, some broader. They are discussed below.

1 The ' Trade-related Aspects' of Interpretation

This is perhaps the narrowest interpretation on the CCP coverage of investment matter under the Lisbon Treaty. Krajewiki, for example, considers that only those aspects of FDI which are directly linked to international trade agreements would fall within the EU's exclusive competence, on the basis of the context, object, and purpose as well as negotiating history of the Treaty.[61] He noted that no discussion was held on the extension of CCP to FDI during the deliberations which prepared for the European Constitu-

---

[59] Council Dir. 88/361/EEC of 24 June 1988 for the implementation of Art. 67 of the Treaty, OJ(1988) L178/11, available at: http://eur-lex.eu ropa.eu/LexUriServ/LexUriServ.do?uri=CELEX:31988L0361:EN:HTML(accessed on 26 May 2010).

[60] Ceyssens, Towards a Common Foreign Investment Policy? Foreign Investment in the European Commission, 32 *Legal Issues of Economic Integration* (2005) 259, at 274.

[61] Krajewiki, *supra* note 3, at 112 – 114.

tion, which suggested that it was not meant to go beyond trade-related aspects of FDI.[62] This interpretation, however, is probably too restrictive. First, although in the immediate context the CCP is termed "commercial", which traditionally means "trade" (or indeed "trade in goods"), its coverage has been significantly expanded to embrace all kinds of economic activities, including the so-called "trade in services" aspects of intellectual property rights, and foreign investment. A clear demonstration is the attempt by the WTO (a "trade" organization) to negotiate a multilateral agreement on investment.[63] Although the initiative was dropped in the Doha round negotiations, it is not disputed that a proper investment agreement could be included under the umbrella of a "trade"[64] organization, the WTO. Indeed should the Member States wish to confine it to trade related aspects of FDI, the Lisbon Treaty should have stated this explicitly by using the "trade related aspects" qualification, as it did with regard to intellectual property rights. Secondly, the object and purpose of the CCP under the Lisbon Treaty, as noted above, listed the prohibition of restriction on both "international trade" and "foreign direct investment" in parallel, suggesting that the latter must go beyond the traditional boundary of the former and should not be confined to just "trade-related aspects" of FDI issues. Finally, although the inclusion of FDI may not have been specifically debated in the course of preparation of the Constitution which formed the basis of the Lisbon Treaty, it was extensively discussed and debated during the inter-governmental conferences leading to the Treaties of Amsterdam and Nice.[65] In the Laeken Declaration of December 2001 the European Council argued that the EU was "confronted with a fast-changing, globalised world".[66] A better division and definition of competence was therefore needed to achieve a more democratic, transparent, and efficient European Union.[67] In the 2006 Commission Communication entitled "Global Europe, Competing in the World", the European Commission proposed a suggestion that it develop a new, ambitious model EU investment agreement.[68] It may be that by the time the Constitution was under deliberation a general consensus had been reached on this, and hence no need was felt for further discussion. The narrow interpretation of the inclusion of FDI

---

〔62〕 Krajewiki, *supra* note 3, at 114.

〔63〕 Wouters, Coppens, and De Meester, The European Union's External Relations after the Lisbon Treaty, in S. Griller and J. Ziller(eds), *The Lisbon Treaty: EU Constitutionalism with-out a Constitutional Treaty*? (2008) 143, at 172. n. 130. The multilateral framework of investment was first proposed in the Singapore Ministerial Declaration in 1996: Singapore Ministerial Declaration, WT/MIN(96)/DEC/W, 13 Dec. 1996, at para. 20. The Doha WTO Ministerial Declaration argued that the multilateral negotiations of investment would take place after the Fifth Session: Doha WTO Ministerial 2001: Ministerial Declaration, WT/MIN(01)/DEC/1, 20 Nov. 2001. This proposal, nevertheless, was suspended in the General Council Decision of 31 July 2004: General Council Decision, WT/ GC/W/535, at para. 3.

〔64〕 Wouters, Coppens and De Meester, s*upra* note 63.

〔65〕 *See* European Commission, Report on the operation of the Treaty on European Union, SEC(95) 731, at 57 – 60, and European Commission, Commission Opinion in accordance with Article 48 EU, COM(2000)34, at 27.

〔66〕 Laken Declaration on The Future of The Europe Union, at 2, available at: http://europeanconvention. eu. int/pdf/LKNEN. pdf(accessed on 26 May 2010).

〔67〕 Ibid.

〔68〕 European Commission Staff Working Document, SEC(2006) 1230, at 18, available at: http://trade. ec. europa. eu/doclib/html/130370. htm(accessed on 26 May 2010).

confining it to only "trade-related aspects of FDI" must therefore be rejected.

2 The "Investment Liberalization" Interpretation

A second interpretation is that the inclusion of FDI brings under the CCP only measures and instruments of "investment liberalization" or "market access", and does not cover those of "investment protection". Leczykiewicz seems to be of this view. Relying on the object of the CCP under Article 206 TFEU, she argued that "foreign investment is only part of the common commercial policy as far as restrictions on foreign direct investment are concerned, but not where investment protection against expropriation is concerned".[69] This interpretation, again, is too narrow to be accepted. There are three main reasons supporting the rejection. First, as UNCTAD research has revealed, the lack of predictability of the host state regulatory environment is among the major factors restricting international investment flows.[70] Non-liberalization measures(such as expropriation and compensation rules), just like liberalization rules, are therefore part and parcel of the entire investment regime which helps to reduce restrictions on FDI. Secondly, it is difficult to draw a fine line between foreign investment policies which deal with mark access and those dealing with post-access conditions.[71] A significant increase in company income tax, for example, may be considered a post-admission investment measure, yet it certainly has important implications on potential investors in the process of deciding whether or not to invest in the state taking that measure. Finally, as demonstrated in its *Opinion* 1/78, the ECJ has held that the objective of the CCP was not confined to trade liberalization, but also covered trade regulation.[72] By analogy, now that FDI is included under the CCP, it should be interpreted as covering not only investment liberalization measures, i. e., market access measures, but also investment protection and regulation measures.[73]

3 The "Substantially Limited Comprehensive Competence" Interpretation

The third interpretation is provided by Ceyssens who supports a broad reading of the new FDI competence to cover both investment liberalization and regulation, but excludes two important areas: investment protection against expropriation and a general standard of fair and equitable treatment.[74] Ceyssens's interpretation largely relies on

---

[69] *See* Krajewiki, *supra* note 3, at 114. See also Leczykiewicz, "Common Commercial Policy: The Expanding Competence of the European Union in the Area of International Trade", 6 *German LJ* (2005) 1673, at 1678.

[70] Ceyssens, *supra* note 60, at 277. See also United Nations, *World Investment Report* 2003. *FDI Policies for Development: National and International Perspective* (2003), at 85.

[71] Ceyssens, *supra* note 60, at 277.

[72] Ibid. *See* also *Opinion 1/78, Nature Rubber Agreement* [1979] ECR 2871, at paras 39 – 49. In this opinion, the ECJ stated: "A ' commercial policy' understood in that sense would be des-tined to become nugatory in the course of time. Although it may be thought that at the time when the EC treaty was drafted liberalization of trade was the dominant idea, it nevertheless does not form a barrier to the possibility of the Community's developing a commercial policy aiming at a regulation of the world market for certain products rather than at a mere liberalization of trade."

[73] Indeed, since FDI is more closely linked to public interest regulations for labour, environmental, and human rights consideration than trade, it makes more sense to treat both investment liberalization and regulation together. *See* Ceyssens, *supra* note 60, at 282.

[74] Ibid., at 279 – 281.

Article 207(6) TFEU.[75] Based on the principle of "parallelism" alluded to by the ECJ in *Opinion* 1/94, he argues that "where the EU does not even have internal competences, there is no need to protect the uniformity of EU rules by conducting a common commercial policy".[76] And because the above-mentioned two policies "do not exist within the internal market",[77] these two areas should be excluded from the new competence on FDI.

This restrictive interpretation, however, also has to be rejected. In the first place, as Wouters, Coppens, and De Meester have pointed out, the principle of parallelism could not be supported by Article 207(6) TFEU because the principle involves the determination of implicit external competence, not express external competence.[78] Article 207 (1) TFEU grants "an explicit exclusive external competence, even in the absent of existing internal measures".[79] Therefore, the scope of the Union's competence on FDI should not be limited to those areas where the Union has already exercised its internal competence.[80] This interpretation finds support in the fact that the requirement of unanimity for the adoption of commercial policy measures in cases where no internal measures have been adopted has not been incorporated in Article 207(4) TFEU, which proves that the lack of internal rules is no impediment to the adoption of external action, even at a procedural level. Indeed, Article 207(6) TFEU is better read as a principle of "reverse parallelism", since "parallelism" usually refers to an implicit conferment of external power in areas where internal power has been exercised. Here it is the other way round. The purpose of this provision seems to be to prevent a situation where the exercise of the Union's CCP including FDI competence affects the fine balance of competence division between the Union and the Member States within the Union's internal order.

Secondly, as noted by Dimopoulos, Article 345 TFEU (ex Article 295 TEC) has been interpreted narrowly to reserve for the Member States only the power to decide whether and when expropriation occurs, not the conditions under which such expropriation takes place.[81] It can therefore be argued that the EU has the right to determine the conditions of indirect expropriation of foreign investment resulting from Union measures, and to harmonize Member States' laws on conditions of expropriation resulting from national measures.[82] Finally, fair and equitable treatment (FET) has already become a rule of international law and is not determined by the laws of the host state. Tri-

---

[75] Art. 207(6) states: "The exercise of the competences conferred by this Article in the field of the common commercial policy shall not affect the delimitation of competences between the Union and the Member States, and shall not lead to harmonisation of legislative or regulatory provisions of the Member States in so far as the Treaties exclude such harmonisation."

[76] Ceyssens, *supra* note 60, at 281.

[77] Ibid.

[78] See Wouters, Coppens, and De Meester, *supra* note 63, at 173.

[79] Ibid.

[80] Ibid.

[81] Dimopoulos, "The Common Commercial Policy After the Lisbon Treaty: Establishing Parallelism Between Internal and External Economic Rela-tions?", 4 *Croatian Yrbk European L and Policy* (2008) 101. See also Bungenberg, *supra* note 1, at 144.

[82] Dimopoulos, *supra* note 81.

bunals have repeatedly emphasized that this treatment standard is independent of the national treatment standard.[83] Notes and comments on the OECD Draft Convention on the Protection of Foreign Property of 1967[84] indicate that the FET treatment standard is set by customary international law. The Free Trade Commission(FTC) of NAFTA also points out that the FET standard in Article 1105(1) reflects the customary international law minimum standard and does not require treatment in addition to or beyond that which is required by customary international law.[85] As part of customary international law, the FET treatment shall be upheld within and beyond the EU regardless of the division of competence between it and its Member States. The exclusion of the FET standard therefore does not make sense in practical terms. For the above considerations, the exception of expropriation and FET from the coverage of the EU's FDI competence should be rejected.

4 The "Negotiation Competence" Interpretation

A fourth view argued that the inclusion of FDI enables the EU competence only to negotiate and conclude agreements in this area, not to enter into substantive rights and obligations. In other words, the EU has only "negotiation competence", but no "substantive competence". According to Mola, for instance, Article 207 TFEU means that the Member States retain competence in FDI and act by unanimity, and the Commission has the right only to speak on behalf of the Member States.[86] If agreement cannot be found among Member States, the Commission should negotiate a commitment which allows for national differentiation.[87] However, this approach cannot be supported. Clearly, Article 207(particularly Article 207(3) –(4)) TFEU covers both internal acts such as legislation and external acts including the negotiation and conclusion of treaties. Accordingly, the Article confers on the Union not only procedural rights such as treaty negotiation, but also substantive rights such as investment regulation. When negotiating an investment treaty, the Union can not only represent the Union and its Member States as a "speaker" on their behalf, but can also decide on the substantive terms of the treaties as far they fall within the Union's competence. Otherwise the inclusion of FDI would do little, if anything, to enhance the efficiency of the EU, which is one of the major purposes of the Lisbon Treaty.

5 The "Comprehensive FDI Competence" Interpretation

Some commentators have argued for a comprehensive EU competence in FDI, enabling the Union to enter into international obligation similar to those included in the US free-trade agreements.[88] Dimopoulos, for example, is of the view that the new EU FDI competence should cover admission, capital movement(transfer), post-admission treat-

---

[83] R. Dolzer and C. Schreuer, *Principles of International Investment Law* (2008), at 123.

[84] OECD, Fair and Equitable Treatment Standard in International Investment Law, Sept. 2004, available at: www. oecd. org/dataoecd/22/53/ 33776498. pdf(accessed on 10 Oct. 2010).

[85] Dolzer and Schreuer, *supra* note 83, at 124 – 125.

[86] Mola, Which Role for the EU in the Development of International Investment Law?, Society of International Economic Law Inaugural Conference, Geneva, 15 – 17 July 2008, availableat: http://papers. ssrn. com/sol3/papers. cfm? abstract_id = 1154583(accessed on 10 Oct. 2010).

[87] Ibid.

[88] Bungenberg, *supra* note 1, at 143.

ment including FET treatment, performance requirements and free movement of key personnel, expropriation, and investor – state dispute settlement.[89] This effectively covers all major aspects covered by a typical BIT.

Given that the term "foreign direct investment" was not unqualified under the CCP, and taking into account the need for the Union to be able to act effectively in the entire area of international investment law-making, this broad interpretation should be preferred. This, however, does not mean that the Union could, on its own, enter into investment treaties in exactly the same way as ordinary BITs.

One must note that the Union's exclusive competence on investment has been confined to "foreign direct investment", while BITs typically cover both direct and indirect investment. The latter, which is also termed "portfolio investment", lies beyond the exclusive competence of the Union. Indirect(as well as direct) investment may, arguably, be covered by Article 64 TFEU(ex Article 57 TEC) concerning free movement of capital. However, as noted by the ECJ, it does not confer express exclusive competence on the EU, nor does it provide sufficient legal basis for an implicit exclusive competence of the EU in this area.[90] It therefore follows that to sign a BIT in its conventional sense the Union would have to act jointly with the Member States. It might nevertheless be possible for the Union to choose to sign a BIT to cover only FDI, leaving portfolio investment aside. This however does not seems to be a very appealing choice, given the increasing importance of portfolio investment, particularly in an economy as developed as that of the EU. It is therefore more likely that the Union will have to team up with its Member States to enter into comprehensive investment treaties anyway. The Union has gone a long way toward achieving this competence on FDI, yet it is still only half way toward a full "common investment competence".

D Summary: Half Way toward a Common Investment Policy of the EU

The inclusion of FDI in the CCP has conferred on the EU exclusive competence on FDI. This competence should be interpreted as a comprehensive competence on all FDI matters, rather than being restrictively interpreted to cover only trade-related aspects of FDI, or matters relating to investment liberalization, or the negotiation of FDI agreements, or an FDI competence excluding essential components such as expropriation and fair and equitable treatment. Such a comprehensive competence, however, does not cover foreign indirect or portfolio investments, which remain a shared competence between the Union and its Member States. The new competence is therefore only half way toward a complete "common investment policy". The legal implications of the new competence on the BIT practices within the EU are further explored below.

3 The EC's International Investment Competence after Lisbon: The Legal Implications for Intra and Extra-EU BITs

As noted above, there were notable practices relating to both BITs between EU

[89] Dimopoulos, *supra* note 81, at 23 – 25.

[90] *Opinion* 2/92, *supra* note 6, at para. 34.

Member States (intra-EU BITs) and BITs between EU Member States and third states (extra-EU BITs) in the years preceding the entry into force of the Lisbon Treaty. Whether and to what extent the new FDI competence under the CCP may change the legal landscapes in the two areas merits further discussion.

A Intra-EU BITs after Lisbon

Bilateral investment treaties between Member States of the EU have long been all but non-existent.[91] Before the 2004 enlargement, there were only two intraEU BITs.[92] However, the number dramatically increased to about 150 after the accession of 10 new Member States in 2004.[93] Most of these BITs were signed in the 1990s when the Eastern European countries began to transform into market economies. In 2007, the total number reached 191 following the accessions of Bulgaria and Romania. Apart from Ireland and Portugal, all the old EU Member States had entered into BITs with all these new EU Member States, and most of these BITs have already entered into force.[94]

The dramatic increase of the intra-EU BITs has elevated the conflict between intra-EU BITs and EU law from fiction to reality. As noted above, the Commission was of the view that the intra-EU BITs were no longer needed and hence implicitly terminated after the accession of the Eastern European States to the EU, a suggestion which was rejected by the Member States. In *Eastern Sugar BV (Netherlands) v. The Czech Republic*, the tribunal refused the Czech Republic's argument that its BITs with other EU Members had become inapplicable following its accession.[95] Other cases such as *R. J. Binder v. The Czech Republic*,[96] *Saluka v. The Czech Republic*,[97] and *Micula v. Romania*[98] have also touched upon similar issues.

Whether the EU's new FDI competence under the CCP could change the answer given by the tribunal in the *Eastern Sugar* case, in other words, whether the intra-EU BITs would become automatically and implicitly terminated or suspended after Lisbon, is a new question which needs to be answered here. As pointed out by the *Eastern Sugar* tribunal, this question must be assessed in accordance with general principles of interna-

---

[91] Wehland, Intra-EU Investment Agreements and Arbitration: Is European Community Law an Obstacle?, 58 *ICLQ* (2009) 297.

[92] These two BITs were signed separately by Germany with Greece and Portugal. Actually, both of them were concluded before Greece and Portugal became Member States of the EC in 1981 and 1986 respectively.

[93] The 10 countries, which are mainly from Eastern Europe, are Cyprus, the Czech Republic, Estonia, Hungary, Latvia, Lithuania, Malta, Poland, Slovakia, and Slovenia.

[94] Ireland has only one BIT with the Czech Republic and Portugal does not have one with Estonia. As of July 2009, all these intra-EU BITs had entered into force except the Cyprus – Italy BIT, which was signed on 27 April 2004: *see* Wehland, *supra* note 90, at 298.

[95] *Supra* note 42, at paras 95 – 181.

[96] *See* Vis-Dunbar, *supra* note 43. There appears to be no public information available with regard to the progress of the court proceedings in Prague, so it can only be inferred from the relative report.

[97] *See* Permanent Court of Arbitration, *Saluka Investments BV v. Czech Republic*, available at: www. pca-cpa. org/showpage. asp? pag_id = 1149 (accessed on 26 May 2010). The case was finally settled and resolved following issue of the Partial Award.

[98] *Ioan Micula, Viorel Micula and others v. Romania* (ICSID Case No. ARB/05/20). This case is pending. The Tribunal issued a procedural order concerning confidentiality on 3 Mar. 2010, available at: http://icsid. worldbank. org/ICSID/FrontServlet? requestType = GenCaseDtlsRH&actionVal = L istPending (accessed on 26 May 2010).

tional law as expressed in the Vienna Convention on the Law of Treaties(VCLT), particularly Article 59.[99] The Article reads:

Article 59

Termination or suspension of the operation of a treaty implied by conclusion of a later treaty

1. A treaty shall be considered as terminated if all the parties to it conclude a later treaty relating to the s*ame subject-matter* and:

a. It appears from the later treaty or is otherwise established that the parties *intended* that the matter should be governed by that treaty; or

b. The provisions of the later treaty are so far *incompatible* with those of the earlier one that the two treaties are not capable of being applied at the same time.

2. The earlier treaty shall be considered as only suspended in operation if it appears from the later treaty or is otherwise established that such was the intention of the parties [emphasis added].

It appears that the VCLT applies three tests for this issue. First, as a precondition, the two treaties must cover the "same subject matter"; secondly, a common "intention" of termination can be established; or, thirdly, the two treaties are clearly "incompatible". The *Eastern Sugar* tribunal looked at and answered in the negative all the three tests. Below is a discussion of any changes which may have resulted from the inclusion of FDI in the CCP by the Lisbon Treaty by using the three tests.

First, a precondition for the implicit termination of a treaty(e. g. , an intra-EU BIT) by the conclusion of a later treaty(the EC Treaty) is that both the earlier and later treaties cover the "same subject matter". The *Eastern Sugar* tribunal examined this issue and concluded in the negative on the basis that the applicable BIT and EC law(Article 57 TEC(Article 64 TFEU)) did not cover the "same precise subject-matter" even though both dealt with intra-EC investment.[100] Most importantly, the tribunal noted that EC law did not provide the investor – state dispute resolution mechanism found in BITs, which it considered "the best guarantee that the investment will be protected against potential undue infringements by the host state".[101] As argued above, the new EU competence on FDI is comprehensively capable of offering guarantees provided by BITs including the investor – state dispute resolution mechanism. It is therefore tempting to argue that after Lisbon the EU Treaty now covers or is able to cover the same subject matter as that under traditional intra-EU BITs. However, since the EU's exclusive FDI competence does not cover indirect investment, BIT protection over indirect investments remains out of the exclusive competence of the EU. It is therefore difficult to argue that EU law and BITs are now covering the "same precise subjectmatter". Accordingly it remains difficult to argue that intra-EU BITs should be superseded by the new EU competence on FDI.

Secondly, the EU Member States remain divided in their approach to this question.

---

〔99〕 Vienna Convention on the Law of Treaties 1969, available at: http://untreaty. un. org/ilc/texts/ instruments/english/conventions/1_1_1969. pdf(accessed on 10 Oct. 2010).

〔100〕 *Eastern Sugar BV(Netherlands) v. The Czech Re-public*, *supra* note 42, at paras 95 – 181.

〔101〕 *Ibid.* , at para. 165.

In the *Eastern Sugar* case, the tribunal held that a common intention of the Czech Republic and the Netherlands to terminate the BIT or to supersede it by EC law could not be established.[102] This is still the case today, as noted above.[103] Although FDI has been included in the CCP, EU Member States are yet to reach a consensus (or a common *intention*) to terminate existing intra-EU BITs and to replace them with Community law. This certainly does not help in establishing a case for the explicit termination of existing intra-EU BITs.

Thirdly, it is important to examine whether the two treaties are "incompatible". In *Eastern Sugar*, the tribunal found that the BIT and the EC Treaty are not *incompatible*, because free movement of capital and protection of investment are "different but complementary things".[104] Now that FDI is included in the CCP, the bases of comparison have been changed. Again, as argued above, the new extension of EU exclusive competence on FDI is a comprehensive competence capable of covering all BITs' aspects including admission, treatment, expropriation, and dispute settlement. Since it is an exclusive competence of the Union, it excludes its Member States from interfering in FDI activities, including the conclusion of BITs protecting FDI. In other words, this means that the EU Member States are no longer able to conclude BITs protecting FDI with either EU or non-EU states. The power to enter into BITs protecting FDI has been transferred to the Union from the Member States. This does not mean, nevertheless, that the EU Member States will have no role to play in future BIT negotiations. As noted above, foreign indirect investment remains a shared competence between the Union and its Member States. If the Union is to conclude conventional BITs covering both direct and indirect investments Member States' participation will be essential.

However, the transfer of power to conclude BITs on FDI from the Member States to the EU does not necessarily mean that existing intra-EU BITs are incompatible with the new EU Treaty. The Lisbon Treaty confers on the EU only a general (albeit exclusive) competence on FDI but does not offer any further details as to how the EU should treat and regulate FDI. Since the EU has not yet taken action to enter into BITs covering the same content as traditional BITs by Member States, one cannot claim that existing intra-EU BITs are incompatible with the new EU Treaty. FDI competence and FDI regulation are two different things. Until the competence is exercised, and in a way which conflicts in an irreconcilable manner with the existing intra-EU BITs, such incompatibility may not be established.

For the above reasons, it can be concluded that the new FDI competence of the EU does not require the automatic or implicit termination of existing intra-EU BITs, even though it does deprive the EU Member States of their power to enter into new intra-EU BITs covering FDI.

B Extra-EU BITs after Lisbon

Old EU Member States are among the pioneer states in BIT practice. The very first

[102] *Ibid.*, at para. 167.

[103] See sect. 1C above.

[104] *Eastern Sugar, supra* note 42, at paras 168 – 169.

BIT was signed by Germany with Pakistan in 1959. According to UNCTAD, seven of the top ten signatories of BITs are from the EU including Germany, the UK, Italy, France, the Netherlands, Belgium, and Luxembourg, with Germany leading the world league table.[105] The total number of BITs between EU Member States and a non-EU state (extra-EU BITs) is believed to have exceeded 1300, nearly half of the total number of BITs in the world. This background highlights the role EU Member States have played in international investment treaty-making practice in the past. But the question here is: is this going to be changed by the new FDI competence of the EU? The question can be assessed from two angles: existing and future extra-EU BITs.

1 Existing Extra-EU BITs

A short answer to the question of the impact of the EU's FDI competence on existing extra-EU BITs is that they will not be required to be terminated or superseded under either international or EU law. However, they may have to be modified in accordance with the requirements of EU law, as confirmed by the recent ECJ cases mentioned above.

The legal basis for the continued validity of extra-EU BITs can be found in general international law as expressed in Article 30(4) of the VCLT,[106] which essentially establishes that "a treaty between two parties will not be superseded by a subsequent treaty that one of the parties enters into with a third party".[107] It is also supported by Article 351 TFEU (ex Article 307 TEC), which expressly states that the rights and obligations arising from agreements between a Member State and a third state concluded before the entry into force of the present treaty "shall not be affected by the provisions of the Treaties".[108] However, the Member States may be required by the European Commission to "take appropriate steps to eliminate the incompatibilities established" between EC law and the BITs with non-EU states.[109] In this regard, it is noted that the EU has taken Sweden, Denmark, and Finland to the ECJ for the inconsistency of their BITs with EC law requirements particularly relating to possible restrictions on monetary transfers.[110]

If such extra-EU BITs are amended to "eliminate the incompatibilities estab-

---

[105] *Supra* note 36, at 3.

[106] Art. 30(4) VCLT states: "4. When the parties to the later treaty do not include all the parties to the earlier one: (a) as between States Parties to both treaties the same rule applies as in paragraph 3; (b) as between a State party to both treaties and a State party to only one of the treaties, the treaty to which both States are parties governs their mutual rights and obligations."

[107] Alexandrov, Carlson, and Robbins, "The Future of Investment Treaty Protection in Eastern Europe", available at: www.globalarbitrationreview.com/reviews/14/sections/53/chapters/511/ www.sidley.com (accessed on 26 May 2010). *See also* Eilmansberger, "Bilateral Investment Treaties and EU Law", 46 *CMLRev* (2009) 383, at 398.

[108] The Art. states: "The rights and obligations arising from agreements concluded before 1 January 1958 or, for acceding States, before the date of their accession, between one or more Member States on the one hand, and one or more third countries on the other, shall not be affected by the provisions of the Treaties. To the extent that such agreements are not compatible with the Treaties, the Member State or States concerned shall take all appropriate steps to eliminate the incompatibilities established. Member States shall, where necessary, assist each other to this end and shall, where appropriate, adopt a common attitude."

[109] Ibid.

[110] *See* sect 1B above.

lished", one has to note that most of the BITs stipulate that the treaty will remain in effect for a period, even though it has been terminated.[111] For instance, foreign investment established in the territory of EU Member States may be affected by the provisions in the amended BITs, especially when new exceptions are added to the investment treatment, such as most favoured nation treatment and national treatment. In this case, the US MOU with the European Commission and eight EU Member States may serve as a reference. It stipulates that any exception set by the Member State to MFN and NT in accordance with the new laws and regulations shall not apply to investments of nationals or companies in the relevant sector for a period of ten years from the effective date of the relevant law or regulation, or twenty years from the date of entry into force of the BIT, whichever date is later.[112] In no case may an exception apply to an existing investment to the extent that it would require divestment, in whole or part, of such an existing investment.[113]

2 Future Extra-EU BITs

As mentioned above, since the EU has acquired exclusive competence on FDI since the entry into force of the Treaty of Lisbon, EU Member States no longer possess the power to enter into new BITs covering FDI with either fellow EU Member States or third states. EU Member States nevertheless have shared competence on foreign indirect investment matters, which means that they still have an essential role to play when the EU is to enter into a conventional BIT covering both foreign direct and indirect investment.

However, while it is clear that the EU now has exclusive competence on FDI treaty-making, it is unclear how this new competence may be exercised, particularly when it comes to the question of investment dispute resolution. Most important questions include: whether the EU as a regional community could negotiate investor-state dispute resolution provisions? In the event of a dispute which one, the Union or any Member State, will be the respondent?

With regard to the first question, some have argued that the EU could not negotiate an investor-state dispute settlement mechanism clause because it is not a "state", whereas only a state can participate in the ICSID Convention.[114] However, this does not appear to be a real problem. The EU may, for instance, agree with the other contracting party that the foreign investor can submit a dispute to *ad hoc* arbitration under the UNCITRAL rules. Alternatively, the EU can also seek revision of the ICSID Convention to allow it to become a party.

The question about the respondent party in a dispute brought by an investor under

---

[111] *See*, e. g., Art. 15(3) of the China – Finland BIT which states "[i]n respect of investment made prior to the date of termination of this Agreement the provisions of Articles 1 through 14 shall remain in force for a further period of twenty(20) years from the date of termination of this Agreement". The treaty is available at: http://tfs.mofcom.gov.cn/aarticle/h/au/201001/20100106725240.html(accessed on 26 May 2010).

[112] *See* Radu, "Foreign Investors in the EU-Which 'Best Treatment'? Interactions Between Bilateral Investment Treaties and EU Law", 14 *European LJ* (2008) 237, at 258.

[113] *See* Radu, "Foreign Investors in the EU-Which 'Best Treatment'? Interactions Between Bilateral Investment Treaties and EU Law", 14 *European LJ* (2008) 237, at 258.

[114] *See*, e. g., Bungenberg, *supra* note 1, at 149.

an EU BIT appears more complex. In this regard, the practice of the EU with the Energy Charter Treaty(ECT) may be helpful. Both the European Communities and the Member States are members of the ECT. In order to solve the respondent problem, the Communities submitted a Statement to the Secretariat of the Energy Charter in 1998 which included the following:

The Communities and the Member States will, if necessary, determine among them who is the respondent party to arbitration proceedings initiated by an Investor of another Contracting Party. In such case, upon the request of the Investor, the Communities and the Member States concerned will make such determination within a period of 30 days.[115]

In the current negotiation of the FTA between the EU and Canada, the text concerning the investment proposed by Canada has proved to consist essentially of its Model BIT language for investor and investment protection, including investor-to-state arbitration.[116] It is therefore interesting to see how such provisions will finally turn out. What can be ascertained now is that the EU could sign BITs protecting FDI, even though it needs cooperation from its Member States if it wants to enter into conventional BITs covering both direct and indirect foreign investments.

C Summary

The new FDI competence of the EU does not legally require the automatic and implicit termination of existing intra-EU BITs, because the new competence does not cover exactly the same subject matter as existing intra-EU BITs; because a consensus is yet to be established among EU Member States on this; and because the incompatibility of the existing intra-EU BITs with the new competence is yet to be established.

In a similar vein, the new FDI competence of the EU does not require the termination of existing extra-EU BITs either, in accordance with both national and Community law. However, after Lisbon, EU Member States have lost their power to conclude(both intra-and extra-EU) BITs protecting FDI, given that that now falls within the exclusive competence of the EU. Member States nevertheless still have an essential role to play when the EU intends to conclude conventional BITs covering both direct and indirect foreign investments. It is possible for the EU to enter into BITs including investor – state dispute resolution provisions. The EU's experience with the ECT offers a good example of how the respondent issue may be solved.

4 Conclusion: Towards a Complete Common Investment Policy of the EU

The Lisbon Treaty has achieved only half a success for a common investment poli-

---

〔115〕 Statement submitted by the European Communities to the Secretariat of the Energy Charter pursuant to Art. 26(3)(b)(ii) of the Energy Charter Treaty, OJ(1994) L 380/115. In this statement, a footnote goes on to state "this is without prejudice to the right of the investor to indicate proceedings against both the Communities and their Member States".

〔116〕 Dispute Settlement, draft text of the Canada – EU FTA(12 Jan. 2010), published on 20 Apr. 2010 by Transnational Dispute Management.

cy(CIP) . Foreign direct investment(FDI) is now covered by the CCP, enabling the EU to take a uniform policy on FDI in the international arena. However, foreign indirect investment is still outside the reach of the EU's exclusive competence. The EU therefore has to seek cooperation from its Member States when entering into conventional BITs covering both direct and indirect investment.

This is a significant step forward, but is not an ideal solution. As mentioned above, the EU is more likely to enter into comprehensive investment treaties(bilateral or multilateral) covering both direct and indirect investments, which means that the EU has to seek cooperation from its Member States when concluding most investment treaties. This situation needs to change. As argued elsewhere, a common investment policy is essential for the EU to deal with an increasingly competitive world. First, a complete CIP would improve the policy coherence, thus reducing asymmetries and uncertainties with the different policies existing in the EU becoming integrated and transparent. A transparent investment environment is crucial to attracting foreign investors from third countries, and *vice versa*. And this will eventually strengthen EU trade policy as trade and investment are strong linked. Secondly, it would increase the attractiveness of the EU as an investment destination, because a harmonized investment scheme on an EU level would create a fair level playing field for foreign investors. Thirdly, it would enhance the bargaining power of the EU, as the negotiating power of the EU together would be much stronger than those of individual EU Member States.[117]

A CIP of the EU will benefit not only the EU, but also the rest of the world. On the one hand, with a CIP the EU is better positioned to push forward a global investment treaty. A multilateral investment treaty is not a new topic. This proposal has been tried and failed in both the OECD and the WTO, of both of which the EU and its Member States are the main supporters. It should be pointed out that a multilateral investment treaty is still needed despite these failures and the "new regionalism". The fragmentation and "legitimacy crisis" of bilateral and regional investment treaties have put the "spaghetti bowl" of investment treaties under severe criticism. In the current economic downturn, investment protectionism has gained the upper hand in some quarters of the world. As a response, there are renewed calls for a global investment regime. The OECD, for example, recently announced that it was considering the feasability of a non-binding "Model Investment Treaty" to avoid an escalation of investment restrictions.[118] A complete CIP of the EU would certainly help in facilitating the negotiation process avoiding the MAI debacle happening again. In this respect, the great success of the OECD Model Tax Convention, which serves as the basis for the more than 3, 000 bilateral tax treaties in

[117] Shan, *supra* note 4. See also Hjalmroth and Westerberg, "A Common Investment Policy for the EU", in *The Contribution of Trade to a New EU Growth Strategy, Ideas for a More Open European Economy*, Part 1, at 22, available at: www. kommers. se/upload/Analysarkiv/In% 20English/Analyses/LS% 20Investments. pdf(accessed on 26 May 2010), and Karl, "The Competence for Foreign Direct Investment, New Powers for the European Union?", 5 *J World Investment and Trade* (2004) 413, at 424 – 429.

[118] Gurría, "The Global Economy and the Global Investment Agenda – an OECD Perspective", available at: www. oecd. org/document/0/0, 3343, en_2649_34529562_44775040_1_1_1_1, 00. html(accessed on 26 May 2010).

force today in the world, may provide positive experience.[119]

A complete CIP of the EU might help in the development of a more balanced investment treaty regime.[120] Article 21 TFEU states that the Union's action shall be guided by the principles of "democracy, the rule of law, the universality and indivisibility of human rights and fundamental freedoms, respect of human dignity, the principles of equality and solidarity, and respect for the principles of the United Nations Charter and international law". Article 205 TFEU, under the title of "Common Commercial Policy", clearly refers to Article 21 TEU, pointing out that the Union's action "shall be guided by the principles, pursue the objectives and be conducted in accordance with the general provisions laid down" in Article 21 TEU. This makes it clear that the Union does have not only a liberalization agenda, but also the other objectives-human rights, good governance, environmental protection, sustainable development-in the negotiation of investment agreements. It is reported that, for example, the EU in 2007 proposed a clause on human rights in the trade negotiations between the EU and India.[121] In April 2008—before the second Irish plebiscite—the Parliament declared in a resolution that it would give its consent to the conclusion of a Free Trade Agreement between the EC and the Gulf Cooperation Council only if those objectives laid down in Article 21 TEU were sufficiently taken into account.[122] It is hoped that the EU's emphasis on social responsibilities will eventually help to build a more balanced global investment regime.

To achieve a complete CIP, two approaches could be used. On the one hand, it might be achieved by implication through the operation of "parallelism" principle. In other words, the EU could adopt measures and acts to harmonize foreign investment policies within the EU aiming at establishing a uniform Union foreign investment policy. Then through the operation of the parallelism principle, the EU would acquire exclusive competence in the area. This possibility has been confirmed by the ECJ in, for example, *Opinion 2/92*.[123] However, it might take a series of measures and a long time to achieve the desired effect. The preferred route obviously is to confer the EU express exclusive competence in the entire area of foreign investment including both direct and indirect investments by, for example, revising the CCP provision under the TFEU replacing the current FDI with "foreign investment". Until this is done, the EU international investment treaty operations will remain seriously constrained.

---

〔119〕 Gurría, "The Global Economy and the Global Investment Agenda - an OECD Perspective", available at: www.oecd.org/document/0/0,3343,en_2649_34529562_44775040_1_1_1_1,00.html(accessed on 26 May 2010).

〔120〕 *See*, e.g., Shan, "From 'South - North Contradiction' to 'Public - Private Conflict': Revival of the Calvo Doctrine and New View of International Investment Law", 27 *Northwest J Int'l L and Business* (2007) 631.

〔121〕 Cabrera Diaz, "EU Trade negotiations with India stumble over human rights, proliferation issues", *Investment Treaty News*, 6 Mar. 2007.

〔122〕 Bungenberg, *supra* note 1, at130.

〔123〕 *Opinion* 2/92, *supra* note 6, at para. 34.

Towards a Common European Community Policy on Investment Issues*

On the world stage, trade and foreign direct investment(FDI) are inextricably intertwined as the lifeblood of the emerging integrated international production systems.[1] Accordingly, the development of the trading system must co-ordinate with that of the investment regime. In this regard, an outstanding example is the extension of the jurisdiction of the World Trade Organization from an instrument dealing purely with trade in goods[the General Agreement on Tariffs and Trade(GATT)], to a system also embracing an Agreement on Trade-Related Investment Measures(TRIMs) and many investment-related agreements.[2]

However, this has not happened within the framework of the European Community (the EC or the Community), one of world's most important trading and investment blocks. While the Community's exclusive competence on trade has long been well established, its competence on FDI remains fairly vague and often ignored, despite the persistent efforts of the European Commission(the Commission).[3] For instance, in the proceedings of the WTO case before the Court of Justice for the European Communities (CJEC or the Court), the EC's external investment competence[4] was totally neglected, while its competence on the other two "new issues" of the WTO were hotly debated and carefully addressed.[5] Likewise, attention has hardly been paid to the influence of Court *Opinion 2/92*, which dealt with the Community's competence in participating in a binding instrument on FDI activities.[6]

---

* 2 *Journal of World Investment*(Geneva) 3, September 2001.

[1] See *World Investment Report* 1996—*Investment, Trade and Investment Policy Arrangements: Overview*, UNCTAD/DTCI/32(Overview), p. 16.

[2] For more about trade and investment relations within the WTO Agreements, see Section III. C. 1 of this article.

[3] For the EC's practice in investment matters, see Section 111 of this article.

[4] This may include the EC's power to enter into international agreements, to foster international co-operation or to co-operate with international organizations on investment issues. However, here the focus is to look at its competence to conclude international investment agreements.

[5] Opinion 1/94 *(Re* WTO), [1994] ECR 1 -5267. The other two "new issues" are "trade in services" and "trade in intellectual property rights"; see, further, Section Ⅲ. C. 1 of this article.

[6] See Section III. C. 3 of this article for details.

As the call for a multilateral agreement on investment(MAl) is compelling and the EC is a very positive player in this regard,[7] it is necessary and indeed very important to clarify its competence on investment matters.

Such is the purpose of this article.[8] Following Professor Alan Dashwood's formula,[9] it first discusses the question of the existence of such competence, then analyses its exclusivity. In the third part, the EC's practice in this regard is explored and summarized, and some conclusions are drawn in the last part, which proposes the establishment of a common investment policy and an exclusive investment competence of the Community.

I. The Existence Of The EC's External Investment Competence

A. A Brief Look at the Sources

Where does the EC's competence come from? A simple answer would be the Treaty Establishing the European Community(the EC Treaty or the Treaty), as well as the objectives set forth therein. This constitutes the principle of the attribution of powers. This principle applies to both actions by the Community in the sphere of international law and actions taken within the internal legal order.[10] However, according to the CJEC, the requisite authorization for the acceptance of international commitments by the Community need not be expressly given by the specific provision relied on as the legal basis (express external power); it may be implied from these provisions(implied external power).[11]

Such an implication would be drawn, where the Community institutions had been given powers within the internal order to pursue a specific objective, as to the possibility of entering into the international commitments necessary for the attainment of that spe-

〔7〕 The EC is a very active advocate of a multilateral investment framework; see *Trade and Investment: The International Dimension*, at http: / /europa. eu. int/ comm/trade/miti/invest/overview. htm, 22 May 2000.

〔8〕 Few articles have examined the Community's competence in investment matters. See, for example, Jurgen Voss, *The Protection and Promotion of European Private Investment in Developing Countries-An Approach Towards a Concept for a European Policy on Foreign Investment: A German Contribution*, Common Market Law Review, Vol. 18, 1981, pp. 363 – 395; Thomas Brewer and Stephen Young, *European Union Policies and the Problems of Multilateral Enterprises*, 29 J. W. T. 1, 1995, pp. 33 – 52; and Alasdair R. Young, *The Adaptation of European Foreign Economic Policy: From Rome to Seattle*, 39 Journal of Common Market Studies, No. 1, 2000, pp. 93 – 116. A recent article by the author also touched on this matter; see Wenhua Shan, *Towards a New Legal Framework for EU-China Investment Relations*, 34 J. W. T. 5, 2000, pp. 137 – 179.

〔9〕 The distinction between the "existence question" and the "exclusivity question" was first drawn by Professor Alan Dashwood, *Implied External Competence of the EC*, in Martii Koskenniemi(ed.), *International Law Aspects of the European Union*, Kluwer, 1998, p. 113.

〔10〕 Alan Dashwood, *The Attribution of External Relations Competence*, in A. Dashwood and C. Hillion(eds.), *The General Law of EC External Relations*, Sweet & Maxwell, 2000. See also *Opinion 2/94 (Re* ECHR), [1996] ECR 1 – 1759, at para. 24. Other important Court decisions and opinions related to external competence include Case 22/70, *Commission v. Council(AETR)*, [1971] ECR 263; Joined cases 3, 4 and 6/76, *Cornelis Kramer*, [1976] ECR 1279; Opinion 2/91 *(Re Iw Convention)*, [1993] ECR 1 – 1061; *Opinion2/92 (Re OECD National Treatment Instrument)*, [1995] ECR 1 – 521; Opinion 1/94, *supra*, footnote 5; and *Opinion 1/76 (Re Inland Waterway Vessels)*, [1997] ECR 741.

〔11〕 *Opinion 2/94*, ibid., para. 26.

cific objective.[12] In other words, if the Community has been conferred internal power to pursue certain specific objectives and it is necessary to extend that power to international order for the same objectives, it may enjoy the external power by implication, i. e. without the express conferment of that power by the Treaty.

Needless to say, here the definition of "necessary" is crucial. There are basically two tests for it: either the test of indispensability or the test of facilitation.[13] By "indispensability test" is meant that international action and internal action are inextricably linked so that authorization of the former must be taken to extend to the latter, since otherwise it would have been futile. On the other hand, the "facilitation test" means that external power is needed by the Community to ensure the optimal use, over time, of its expressly conferred internal competence.[14]

Both tests seem to have been supported by the CJEC in certain cases. For example, in *Opinion 1/76*, the Court stated:

"It is *impossible* fully to attain the objective pursued by means of the establishment of common rules pursuant to Article 75 of the Treaty, because of the traditional participation of vessels from a third country, Switzerland, in navigation by the principal waterways in question, which are subject to the system of freedom of navigation established by international agreements of long standing. It has thus been *necessary* to bring Switzerland into the scheme in question by means of an international agreement with this third country. "(emphasis added)[15]

That is to say, it employed the "indispensability test". In *Opinion 2/91*, however, the Court held that:

"The Community thus enjoys an internal legislative competence in the area of social policy. *Consequently*, Convention No. 170, whose subject-matter *coincides, moreover*, with that of several Directives adopted under Article 118a, falls within the Conununity's area of competence. "(emphasis added).[16]

Obviously, in this case, the Court merely used the test of "facilitation" rather than that of indispensability.

Nevertheless, it might be argued that, in the CJEC cases, only the "facilitation test" has been used as the test to justify the necessity of the existence of the EC's external competence. In fact, when the test of indispensability was used, it was actually used to justify the exclusivity, rather than the existence, of its external competence. The reason that people are somewhat confused is that the Court, as in the *Kramer* case and in Opinion 1/76, sometimes did not split the existence question and the exclusivity question and treat them separately.[17]

---

[12] Dashwood, *supra*, footnote 10, p. 5.

[13] Ibid., pp. 32 – 33.

[14] Ibid.

[15] *Opinion 1/76*, *supra*, footnote 10, para. 2.

[16] *Opinion 2/91*, *supra*, footnote 10, para. 17.

[17] The Court shall be regarded as having done this with good excuse: once the exclusivity has been established, it is no longer necessary to question its existence.

It is true that, by employing the "facilitation test", the scope of the Community's external competence is almost the same, or might eventually be the same, as that of its internal competence, since it adds no substantial qualification on the extension of the latter to the former. It is in this sense that "parallelism"[18] might make sense. Here again, the paragraph of Court *Opinion 2/91* cited above can serve as an example.

In short, to answer the question of the existence of the EC's external competence in a certain field, it is necessary first to look at the Treaty for provisions conferring express external powers. Failing this, one should try to identify whether that power exists by implication, i. e. if the EC has been conferred power for the same objectives in the internal legal order and if it is necessary(by the "facilitation test") to extend it to entering into international commitments.

B. Express Or Implied?

1. *Express External Investment Competence*

Has the EC's competence on investment issues explicitly been conferred by the EC Treaty? The answer relates to the definition of the scope of the EC's express external competence. As observed, so far the EC Treaty has vested the Community external competence in fields such as common commercial policy(with the potential to cover services and intellectual property rights issues), research and technological development co-operation, environmental matters, development co-operation, association agreements and the monetary and foreign exchange regime.[19]

Admittedly, almost all of these, especially common commercial policy(CCP), the monetary and foreign exchange regime and association agreements, are closely related to investment issues and are therefore analysed herein.

First of all, the CCP has significant implications on FDI activities. Most foreign-invested companies will have to import materials or technologies and export their products or services. Furthermore, investment is particularly relevant to trade in services which, according to the definition of the General Agreement on Trade in Services(GATS) embraces all sorts of "commercial presence",[20] i. e. foreign-funded companies or their subsidiaries or branches. At most, based on a broad definition of the CCP, it may, as the Commission[21] and the European Parliament[22] have proposed, include the entirety of

---

[18] By "parallelism", every substantive attribution of powers of action on the internal level implicitly entails the attribution of powers, in the same field of policy, on the international level; see Dashwood, *supra*, footnote 10, p. 24.

[19] Dashwood, *supra*, footnote 10, pp. 8 – 17. See also I. Macleod, I D. Hendry and Stephen Hyett, *The External Relations of the European Community*, Clarendon Press, Oxford, 1996, pp. 45 – 47.

[20] According to Article XXVIII of GATS, "commercial presence" means any type of business or professional establishment, including through(i) the constitution, acquisition or maintainance of a juridical person, or(ii) the creation or maintenance of a branch or a representative office, within the territory of a Member for the purpose of supplying a service.

[21] In Part 11(2) of the Commission Opinion on the 1996 Intergovernmental Conference, the Commission said that the common commercial policy should be clarified so as to "take account of the radical changes in the structure of the world economy, in which services, intellectual property and direct foreign investment play an increasingly important role."

[22] See Elmar Brok and Dimitrios Tsatsos, Representatives of the European Parliament at the Intergovernmental Conference, *IGC 2000—Commercial Policy and International Agreements*, CONFER 4759/00, Brussels, 11 July 2000. It proposed to extend the CCP to include investment as well as services and intellectual property.

all investment issues.

However, this broad interpretation has been rejected by the Court, first in Opinion 1/94 and then in *Opinion 2/92*. In *Opinion 1/94*, the Court ruled, in particular, that services offered through "commercial presence" were not covered in the CCP.[23] More recently, in its *Opinion 2/92*, the Court held that the national treatment rule, which was basically a rule on FDI activities, related only partially to international trade with non-Member countries and, therefore, Article 113(now Article 133) could not be used as the legal basis for the exclusive Community competence thereon.[24] It is clear, therefore, that, unless the Treaty has been amended, the EC probably has to resort to other legal bases to establish its competence on investment matters.

Second, as the monetary and foreign exchange regime plays an important role in investment activities, the EC's competence in this field can, to a certain extent, justify its competence on investment issues. Nevertheless, foreign investment does not just mean monetary and foreign exchange but also relates to many other aspects, such as the right of establishment, employment, purchase and sale, taxation, etc. Hence, the EC probably cannot establish its competence on this single legal basis either.

Last but not least, association agreements may cover investment issues. An example of this is the EC's co-operation with the African, Caribbean and Pacific(ACP) countries based on the Lome Conventions which, from the second Convention, have included extensive investment clauses.[25] However, again the Community probably cannot claim a general investment competence simply based on its practice of an association agreement which, as the Court said, creates "special, privileged links with a non-Member country, which must, at least to certain extent, take part in the Community system".[26]

To summarize, it can be argued that, within the state of play of EC law as interpreted by the Court, the EC probably cannot establish its power on external investment relations simply on the ground of express Treaty provisions. Although these provisions may be closely related to investment, none of them has been sufficiently developed, or clearly identified by the Court, to cover investment issues in general. Therefore, none of them alone may be relied upon as a single legal basis of the Community's competence on investment matters, nor do all those provisions combined seem to have that effect. Therefore, it is probably necessary to take into account the principle of implied power to justify the EC's general competence on investment matters.

2. *Implied External Investment Competence*

(a) *Articles* 56 *and* 57 *of the EC Treaty*

To identify the EC's implied external competence on investment matters, Chapter 4 of the EC Treaty, regarding capital and payment, particularly Articles 56(ex Article 73b) and 57(ex Article 73c), may be of primary importance. Article 56 rules that:

"1. Within the framework of the provisions set out in the Chapter, all restrictions on

[23] Opinion 1/94, *supra*, footnote 5, paras. 36 – 53.

[24] Opinion 2/92, *supra*, footnote 10, paras. 18 – 28.

[25] For details see Section III. B. 2 of this article.

[26] See Case 12/86, *Demirel v. Stadt Schwabisch Gmund*, [1987] ECR 3719, at para. 9.

the movement of capital between Member States and between Member States and third countries shall be prohibited.

2. Within the framework of the provisions set out in the Chapter, all restrictions on payments between Member States and between Member States and third countries shall be prohibited."

Actually, the Treaty does not treat the movement of capital and payments between Member States and third countries exactly the same as those between Member States, as the former are subject to certain extra restrictions set forth in the Chapter. Nevertheless, the absolute terms used distinguish them from those used in preceding Chapters on the right of establishment and services.

As observed by the Court in *Opinion 1/94*, the sole objective of the Treaty Chapters on the right of establishment and on freedom of providing services is to secure the right of establishment and the freedom to provide services "for nationals of Member States" [27] They do not contain any express provisions extending the competence of the Community to "relationships arising from international law". [28] Nor does Chapter 2 have provisions on the right of first establishment of non-Member country nationals or on their access to self-employed activities. [29]

In comparison, Article 56 not only expressly extends the freedom of capital movement and payments from those between Member States to those between Member States and third countries but also, in absolute terms, puts them in parallel. These terms may have implications that the Community shall have powers on internal capital movement and payments, as well as on external ones. This has, in fact, been confirmed in the next provision, Article 57(2) (ex Article 73c), which reads:

"Whilst endeavouring to achieve the objective of free movement of capital between Member States and third countries to the extent possible and without prejudice to the other Chapters of this Treaty, the Council may, acting by a qualified majority on a proposal from the Commission, adopt measures on the movement of capital to or from third countries involving direct investment—including investment in real estate—establishment, the provision of financial services or the admission of securities to capital markets. Unanimity shall be required for measures under this paragraph which constitute a step back in Community law as regards the liberalization of the movement to or from third countries."

Most importantly for the present purposes, this provision directly empowers the Community to adopt "measures" to facilitate the flow of direct investment. Here, the "measures" are not defined but, from the wording of Articles 56 and 57, they probably include internal measures on the functioning of the internal market, as well as external measures "arising from international law".

This understanding has been supported by the fact that Article 57 was used by the EC among the legal bases for the conclusion of WTO Agreements, including the GATS

[27] *Opinion 1/94*, *supra*, footnote 5, para. 81.

[28] Ibid.

[29] Ibid.

and TRIMs Agreements, as well as the Energy Charter Treaty(ECT) and other co-operation and partnership agreements with third countries.[30]

Such power as conferred by Article 57(2) is, however, subject to certain exceptions stipulated in Article 57(1) and Article 58(ex Article 73d). Article 57(1) grandfathers all the restrictions on the external movement of capital involving direct investment existing as at the end of 1993. It is therefore observed that the Community is given power to act only in those areas where the Treaty itself does not automatically require existing restrictions to be eliminated by the Member States.[31]

Exceptions under Article 58 include, among others,[32] national taxation law and restrictions on the right of establishment, which are both of great importance to FDI. Thus, a closer look at relevant Treaty provisions is worthwhile.

(b) *National taxation law and the right of establishment*

Chapter 2 of Title VI(ex Title v) deals specifically with national taxation law. Article 93(ex Article 99), in particular, states that the Council shall adopt provisions for "the harmonization of legislation concerning turnover taxes, excise duties and other forms of indirect taxation to the extent that such harmonization is necessary to ensure the establishment and the functioning of the internal market." Therefore, according to the Court, the Community might have competence on indirect taxation once such harmonization has been achieved. Nevertheless, it only covers forms of indirect taxation, rather than direct taxation such as income tax, which is also very important for FDI operations. In other words, the Community has limited competence on national taxation laws.

As for the right of establishment, as the Court has made clear in its *Opinion 1/94*, the Treaty contains neither provision on the first establishment of nationals of non-Member countries nor the rules on their access to self-employed activities. It therefore follows that the Community does not have express competence on the right of establishment of non-Member-country nationals.

(c) *Articles* 94, 95 *and* 308 *of the EC Treaty*

These deficiencies of competence, however, may be complemented by Articles 94 (ex Article 100), 95(ex Article 100a) and, finally, 308(ex Article 235).

As a general entitlement, Articles 95 and 96 confer on the Council the right to adopt measures for the approximation of the provisions laid down by law, regulation or administrative action in Member States "which have as their object the establishment and functioning of the internal market". Thus, the Community may take actions on FDI-related issues like direct taxation, and such actions will have the effect to deprive Member

---

[30] Section III of this article will discuss the EC's external practices related to investment issues in detail. See also letter from Mr Carlo Pettinato to the author of 14 August 2000.

[31] J. A. Usher, *The Law of Money and Financial Services in the EC*, second edition, Oxford University Press, Oxford, 2000, p. 232.

[32] Including "all requisite measures to prevent infringements of national law and regulations, in particular in the field of taxation and the prudential supervision of financial institutions, or to lay down procedures for the declaration of capital movements for purposes of administrative or statistic information, or to take measures which are justified on grounds of public policy or public security." See Article 58(1)(b).

States of their powers thereon.[33]

Also, more generally, Article 308 grants the Community power to take appropriate measures "if action by the Community should prove necessary to attain, in the course of the operation of the Common Market, one of the objectives of the Community and this Treaty has not provided the necessary powers." For instance, in Opinion 1/94, the Court stated that:

"Although the only objective expressly mentioned in the Chapters on the rights of establishment and the freedom to provide services is the attainment of those freedoms for nationals of the Member States, it does not follow that the Community institutions are prohibited from using the powers conferred on them in that field[34] in order to specify the treatment which is to be accorded to nationals of non-Member countries."[35]

Instead, according to the Court Opinion, the Community might adopt such measures and, once they were adopted, it would acquire (exclusive) external competence in the sphere they covered.[36]

In conclusion, based on Article 57(2), supplemented by all the other related provisions mentioned, it would be tempting to argue that the EC shall have in general external competence on investment matters. The participation of the EC in investmentrelated treaties such as the WTO Agreements and the ECT could serve as practical examples.

Ⅱ. The Exclusivity of the EC's External Investment Competence

A. The General Criteria

However, is the EC's external investment competence exclusive, i. e. do Member States still possess external power on investment issues, given that the Community has established its external competence in this field? To answer this question, first of all, it is necessary to have a look at the general criteria of the exclusivity of the Community's external competence.

So far, the EC Treaty has said nothing explicitly on the nature of the EC's external competence. The criteria of the exclusivity of external competence are therefore developed by the Court in its opinions and judgments. Despite some inconsistencies among these opinions and judgments, it seems that the general idea is, as stated by Jacobs, Advocate General, that the Community shall share its competence with the Member States unless there is "any indication to the contrary".[37] In other words, shared competence is the general principle, while exclusive Community competence is the exception.

According to the Court case-law, the Community's external competence may be regarded as exclusive in the following cases:[38]

Exclusive Community competence flows from the Treaty provisions from which the

[33] Opinion 1/94, *supra*, footnote 5, para. 88.

[34] Here it means internal powers concerned only.

[35] Opinion 1/94, *supra*, footnote 5, para. 90.

[36] Ibid., paras. 91 – 96.

[37] Opinion of Jacobs, A. G., in Case C – 316/91, *Parliament v. Council*, [1994] EcR 1 – 625, at para. 40.

[38] Macleod *et al.*, *supra*, footnote 19, pp. 56 – 61.

competence derives (exclusivity by the Treaty). For instance, in the EC Treaty, the Community's competence is exclusive, as the Court has made clear, under the Articles establishing the common commercial policy and the protection of fishery stocks. For the twelve Euro countries, the common monetary policy shall also fall within the EC's exclusive competence. It is, moreover, argued that the Treaty Articles on competition probably confer exclusive competence on the Community as well.[39]

Exclusive Community competence exists where internal powers can only be effectively exercised at the same time as external powers (exclusivity by nature). In Opinion 1/76, it would have been impossible to achieve the Community's objective-rationalizing of the inland waterways sector in the Rhine and Moselle basins-without involving a third country in the scheme envisaged. Therefore, "the conclusion of an international agreement is necessary in order to achieve Treaty objectives which cannot be attained by the adoption of autonomous rules."[40] Under these circumstances, the Community can acquire exclusive competence even in the absence of any internal measures being adopted beforehand.

In other cases, exclusive Community competence may only flow from the scope of measures adopted by the Community's institutions (exclusivity by measures adopted). According to the Court:

"... each time the Community, with a view to implementing a common policy envisaged in the Treaty, adopts provisions laying down common rules, whatever form these may take, the Member States no longer have the right, acting individually or even collectively, to undertake obligations which affect those rules."[41]

This constitutes the famous "AETR principle" which has brought about much debate.[42] It is notable that this principle is applicable even where Community legislation is not complete or "exhaustive".[43] For example, in the *International Labour Organization (ILO)* case, Part III of the Convention in question was considered within an area "which is already covered *to a large extent* by Community rules... adopted... with a view to achieving an ever greater degree of harmonization." (emphasis added).[44] The Court nevertheless ruled that the Community's competence in these matters was exclusive. Moreover, the principle is not confined to the "common policies" identified by that term in the EC Treaty, but applies "in all the areas corresponding to the objectives of the Treaty".[45]

As a special case of "exclusivity by measures adopted," exclusive Community competence may particularly arise from an express power in an internal act (exclusivity by acts). In Opinion 1/94, the Court stated that:

"... whenever the Community has included in its internal legislative acts provisions

---

[39] Macleod *et al.*, *supra*, footnote 19, pp. 56 – 57.

[40] Opinion 2/92, *supra*, footnote 10, para. 32.

[41] Case 22/70, *supra*, footnote 10, para. 17, regarding the Community's external competence regarding the European Agreement Concerning the Work of Crews ofVehicles Engaged in International Road Transport (AETR).

[42] Macleod *et al.*, *supra*, footnote 19, p. 58.

[43] Ibid.

[44] Opinion 2/91, *supra*, footnote 10, para. 25.

[45] Ibid., para. 10.

relating to the treatment of nationals of non-Member countries or expressly conferred on its institutions powers to negotiate with non-Member countries, it acquires exclusive competence in the sphere covered by those acts."[46]

However, the practice of this kind of exclusive competence is yet to be seen.

B. Exclusivity

Using the criteria explored above, this section examines in turn the exclusivity of the EC's external investment competence.

1. *Exclusivity by the Treaty*

The most likely means by which investment issues can become the exclusive competence of the EC under express provisions of the Treaty is by including them in the common commercial policy. However, as observed above, this would not be the case unless the Treaty were modified accordingly.

2. *Exclusivity by Nature*

This seems inapplicable to investment also, in accordance with the Court's Opinions 1/94 and 2/92. In the former Opinion, the Court said:

"That application of Opinion 1/76 to GATS cannot be accepted... Attainment of freedom of establishment and freedom to provide services for nationals of Member States is not inextricably linked to the treatment to be afforded in the Community to nationals of non-Member countries or in non-Member countries to nationals of Member States of the Community."[47]

In the latter, Opinion 2/92 on the National Treatment Instrument, the Court again held that "it is undisputed that that [a situation where the conclusion of an international agreement is necessary in order to achieve Treaty Objectives which cannot be attained by the adoption of autonomous rules] is not the case here."[48]

3. *Exclusivity by Measures Adopted and Exclusivity by Acts*

According to the Council Decision on agreements reached in the Uruguay Round negotiations, no act in Community law has been adopted on the basis of Article 57(ex Article 73c).[49] On the other hand, the Court observed, in its Opinion 2/92, that:

"... although the Community has adopted measures capable of serving as basis for an exclusive external competence in accordance with the aforesaid case-law and: fulling in particular within the scope of Articles 57(2), 75, 84 and 100a of the EC Treaty, it is undisputed that those measures do not cover all the fields of activity to which the Third Decision relates."[50]

Accordingly, the Court ruled out the Community's exclusive competence on it, though in general it upheld the existence of the EC's competence.[51] Therefore, the ex-

[46] Opinion 1/94, *supra*, footnote 5, para. 95.

[47] Ibid., at paras. 84 – 86.

[48] Opinion 2/92, *supra*, footnote 10, at para. 32.

[49] O. J. L 336/1, 23 December 1994.

[50] Opinion 2/92, *supra*, footnote 10, at para. 34.

[51] Ibid., at para. 35. It reads: "It follows that the Community is competent to participate in the Third Decision, but that such competence does not cover all the matters to which that Decision relates."

clusive Community competence on investment activities cannot flow from either an express power in an internal act or the scope of measures adopted by the Community institutions.

In summary, at present, the EC has not yet attained exclusive external competence on investment issues. What it has thereon is a kind of "shared competence" or "joint competence", which it shall share with the Member States. This is, as will be shown later on, confirmed by the practice of the Community.

Ⅲ. The European Community Practice on External Investment Relations

A. General Policy: from the 1972 Proposal to the 2000 Approach

The Community's interest in investment issues can be dated back to as early as 1972 when the Commission initiated a Proposal to the Council for a Regulation establishing a Community guarantee system for private investments in third countries (the 1972 Proposal).[52] Since then, the Commission has made persistent efforts on Community involvement in the protection and promotion of investments between the Community and third countries.

Based on the 1972 Proposal, the Commission made another Communication to the Council in 1978 on the "Need for Community Action to Encourage European Investment in Developing Countries and Guidelines for Such Action"[53] (the 1978 Communication). The change of the scope of application from "third countries" to "developing countries" did not make any significant difference, as the protection and promotion of FDI among developed countries had already been guaranteed by the Organisation for Economic Co-operation and Development's Codes of Liberalization of Capital Movements and Liberalization of Current Invisible Operations (the OECD Codes). In this Communication, the Commission argued that two categories of Community action were needed. The first involved the negotiation of agreements (or of clauses to be included in global agreements) between the Community and developing countries or groups of developing countries on basic rules relating to the treatment of foreign investment. The second involved specific projects selected on the ground of particular interests, the conclusion of specific protection agreements on a project-by-project basis, and the granting of guarantees and measures to promote investments.

In 1980, the Commission made a Report[54] to the Council (the 1980 Report) where it summarized the investment promotion and protection clauses in agreements reached between the Community and various categories of developing countries since 1978 and set forth the guidelines for joint action in the future. In the Report, the Commission concluded that the two categories of action proposed in the 1978 Communication were proved necessary and that certain guidelines had emerged from the Community's actions

---

[52] COM(72), 1461, Final. The European Parliament also produced a detailed Report on this proposal in 1973; see PE 33.931/fin(Document 208/73).

[53] COM(78), 23, Final.

[54] COM(80), 204, Final.

in this sphere. In particular they included:

the utility of raising the subject of investment with all partner developing countries;

the desirability of incorporating the basic rules on investment or other measures in an agreement distinct from the overall co-operation agreement;

the potential importance of the instrument comprising specific agreements for individual projects, preferably supplemented by financial guarantees; and

the Community's specific interest in negotiating investment clauses with groups of developing countries.[55]

In the 1980s and 1990s, the Community did not produce any new policy on investment, although it signed numerous co-operation agreements, partnership agreements or multilateral agreements including investment clauses. At the same time, the Community was very keen on the making of a world-wide multilateral investment agreement, either within the framework of the OECD or of the WTO. For instance, in the preparation for the Millennium Round negotiations, the Community very actively advocated a multilateral framework on investment under the aegis of the WTO.[56] To make the picture clearer, the Community's involvement in bilateral and multilateral agreements related to investment is explored below.

B. Bilateral Agreements Related to Investment Issues

So far, the Community has yet to successfully sign an agreement specialized in investment protection and promotion, despite its efforts as reflected in the 1978 Communication and the 1980 Report. In the late 1970s, the EC Member States had, surprisingly, reached a consensus within the framework of the Euro-Arab dialogue on a draft for a comprehensive investment protection agreement after their views on the principles had been co-ordinated with those on the Arab side. The document was "a fully worked-up and detailed legal text"[57] containing provisions on rights and obligations of the Member States of both the Arab League and the EC.[58] Unfortunately, this convention seemed to end without any outcome. In 1984, when the Community was to conclude a co-operation agreement with China,[59] the European Parliament proposed to sign another individual agreement with China on investment and intellectual property protection.[60] Again, it seems that nothing has been produced therefrom.

Nevertheless, the Community has managed to insert an investment clause, or sometimes even a section of investment clauses, into various framework agreements with third countries, mainly developing countries. These framework agreements include co-operation agreements, partnership agreements, free trade agreements, and so forth. Several examples of them are explored as follows.

---

[55] COM(80), 204, Final, p. 17.

[56] See *Seattle Conference Preparation: EC Approach to Trade and Investment*, at http://europa. eu. int/comm/ trade/2000 – round/1806ti. htm, 22 May 2000.

[57] COM(80), 204. Final, p. 2.

[58] Voss, *supra*, footnote 8, p. 364.

[59] O. J. L 250/1, 19 September 1985.

[60] See the European Parliament's resolution on economic and commercial relations between China and the EEC, O. J. C 127/210, 1984.

1. *Co-operation Agreements*

Co-operation agreements are the framework agreements most commonly used by the Community for developing general bilateral trade and economic relations with developing countries. Since the 1978 Communication, the Community has managed to insert a clause of investment protection into these co-operation agreements. For example, in the 1985 EC-China Co-operation Agreement,[61] Article 12 states that the two contracting parties agree "within the framework of their respective laws, rules and policies, to promote and encourage greater and mutually beneficial investment". The two parties also undertake "to improve the existing favorable investment climate in particular through encouraging the extension, by and to the Member States of the Community and by and to the People's Republic of China, of investment promotion and protection arrangements based on the principles of equity and reciprocity." Again, in the 1994 EC-India Co-operation Agreement, a clause on investment with similar content is included.[62] Other examples can be seen in the Community's co-operation agreements with Members of the Association of South-East Asian Nations, Yugoslavia, Brazil, etc.[63] Obviously, these investment clauses contain no substantial commitments, but an expression of political will which may, nevertheless, open the way for substantial co-operation in investment aspects in the future.

2. *The Lome Conventions and the EU-ACP Partnership Agreement*

The series of Lome Conventions between the EC and the African, Caribbean and Pacific States, which have been recently changed into a twenty-year Partnership Agreement,[64] have over time built up very substantial commitments on investment protection and promotion.[65]

Investment clauses were first embraced in the Second Lome Convention(Lome II), which entered into force in 1980. In the annexed Joint Declaration to the Convention, the ACP countries recognized that, as of the date of Lome II's ratification, investments from the EC(then EEC) Member States would not be subject to discriminatory treatment. This vague commitment was upgraded and detailed in the Third Lome Convention(Lome III), where the two sides agreed not only to accord generally "fair and equitable treatment" to investors,[66] but also to undertake certain specific commitments, including the exchange of information and a joint study of a joint ACP-EEC insurance and guarantee system.[67]

The Fourth Lome Convention(Lome IV), the last of the Lome Convention series, a-

---

[61] The official tide is the Agreement on Trade and Economic Co-operation between the European Economic Community and the People's Republic of China; see O. J. L 250/2, 19 September 1985.

[62] See O. J. L 223/23, 27 August 1994.

[63] COM(80), 204, Final, pp. 5 - 7.

[64] See *EU-ACP Negotiations*, at http://europa-eu.int/ comm/ development/ event/negotiation 10 - en. htm, 23 February 2000.

[65] For a detailed study on the investment clauses in earlier Lome Conventions, see Theresa I. Yard, *Promises, Promises-A Critical Analysis of Lome III's Private Investment Provisions,* Fordham International Law Journal, Vol. 9, 1986, pp. 634 - 679.

[66] Lome III, Article 240(b).

[67] Ibid., Articles 241 - 247.

chieved an even higher standard of investment protection and promotion. In this Convention, investment was treated with a whole Chapter-Chapter Ⅲ, which included sections of investment promotion, investment protection, investment financing, investment support, current payment and capital movements, qualification and treatment of business entities. The most significant of its advancements was, however, the inclusion of a special "non-discrimination" clause which, in fact, entitled all the contracting parties to the Convention to provisions in agreements negotiated between the ACP States or EU Member States concerned and any other State.[68] In other words, once an ACP(or an EU) country concluded a bilateral investment treaty(BIT) with any third country(the so-called "reference agreement"), all the EU(or ACP) Member States might enjoy the same protection as that provided for in the BIT by the ACP(or EU) country. Nonetheless, the application of this principle should not infringe the sovereignty of any contracting party and it can request a modification or adaptation of the "non-discrimination" treatment when international obligations or changed *de facto* circumstances so necessitate.[69]

It will be interesting to see the development of the new investment clauses in the new EU-ACP Partnership Agreement, which has not yet been published.

The experience of the Lome Conventions has demonstrated that the EC can enter into international agreements with substantial investment clauses. However, as said above, this kind of practice may not be used as evidence of the Community's competence on investment in general, owing to its special nature as an association agreement.

3. *The EC-Mexico Free Trade Agreement*

In early 2000, the EC and Mexico concluded a Free Trade Agreement which upgraded their bilateral relationship. Title III of the new Agreement deals with investment and related payments, where the Community, its Member States and Mexico "recall their international commitments with regard to investment, and especially the OECD Codes of Liberalization and the OECD National Treatment Instrument".[70] Therefore, by referring to the OECD instruments, this Treaty has put the EC-Mexico mutual investments under the highest level of international legal protection. Also, the Agreement is another mixed agreement jointly signed by both the Community and its Member States.

In short, the Community has managed to add investment clauses to various bilateral framework agreements with different developing countries, although it has not succeeded in concluding any bilateral agreement specifically devoted to investment protection and promotion. The above survey also suggests that signing international agreements involving investment issues does not fall within the Community's exclusive competence, but is shared competence between the Community and its Member States.

C. Multilateral Agreements Related To Investment Issues

The EC has been very active in multilateral investment law-making. This can be seen from its participation in the WTO Agreements, the Energy Charter Treaty, the Third

---

〔68〕 Lome IV, Article 261(2).

〔69〕 Ibid., Article 261(3) and(4).

〔70〕 See Title III, Article 34, of the EC-Mex ico Free Trade Agreement, at http://europa.eu.int/ comm/ trade/ bilateral/mexico/fta.htm, 19 August 2000.

Revised Decision of the Organisation for Economic Co-operation and Development on National Treatment(the Third Decision), and the OECD MAI negotiations.

1. *WTO Agreements*

By a broad definition of"trade", the WTO Agreements not only deal with what are clearly trade issues, but also deal with investment issues. In 1986, when the Uruguay Round negotiations were to be launched, three "new issues" were put onto the agenda, namely investment, services and intellectual property.[71] As a result, the WTO Agreements embrace three new agreements, two of which are closely investment-related, namely the Agreement on Trade-Related Investment Measures and the General Agreement on Trade in Services.

The TRIMs is within the Multilateral Agreements on Trade in Goods(MATG), which requires Members not to apply any "trade-related"[72] investment measures that are inconsistent with the principles of "national treatment"(Article 3, para. 4) and "general elimination of quantitative restrictions"(Article 11, para. 1) of GATT 1994.[73] To make matters clear, an illustrative list of those measures is annexed to the Agreement, including domestic content, import-export balancing and foreign exchange balancing requirements. Although the application scope is highly qualified, the significance of the inclusion of TRIMs within the world trading system cannot be overestimated. This was the first time that a world-wide agreement was reached on substantial issues of investment, and the follow-ups to the Agreement may lead to a full multilateral agreement on investment. It would thus be fair to conclude that TRIMs has marked a breakthrough in the history of international investment law-making.[74]

The GATS is another WTO Agreement dealing directly with investment issues.[75] According to the GATS, trade is defined to embrace investment,[76] since one of the four modes of trade in services is through "commercial presence", which includes "any type of business or professional establishment", no matter in form of a juridical person or a branch or a representative office.[77] Moreover, the GATS provisions on market access directly and specifically refer to joint ventures and limitations on the percentage of foreign ownership.[78] Therefore, it is sensible to consider the GATS as "Rules for Growth and

---

〔71〕 The "new issues" are in regards to GATS, TRIPS and TRIMs.

〔72〕 The phrase "trade-related" is about equal to having "trade restrictive and distorting effects"; see the Preamble of the TRIMs Agreement.

〔73〕 TRIMs Agreement, Article 2.

〔74〕 Wenhua Shan, *Comments on the International Investment Rules within the WTO Agreement* (in Chinese), CASS Journal of Law *(Faxue Yanjiu)*, No. 2, 1996.

〔75〕 The significance of GATS to FDI is in part due to the fact that the recent years have seen a much more rapid FDI growth in the services sector than in other sectors; see Thomas L. Brewer and Stephen Young, *The Multilateral Investment System and Multilateral Enterprises*, Oxford University Press, Oxford, 1998, p. 126. See also UNCTAD/World Bank, *World Investment Report* 1994*: Transitional Corporations, Employment and Workplace*, 1994, Tables 1. 8 and 1. 9, pp. 16 – 17.

〔76〕 Brewer and Young, ibid. , p. 126.

〔77〕 See GATS, Article XXVIII(d).

〔78〕 See GATS, Article 16, para. 2.

Investment". [79]

Additionally, other agreements, especially the Agreement on Trade-Related Aspects of Intellectual Property Rights(TRIPS), the Agreement on Subsidies and Countervailing Measures, the Dispute Settlement Understanding and the Trade Policy Review Mechanism are regarded as of continuous and direct relevance to FDI.[80] In fact, it could be argued that most of the WTO Agreements and their implementation measures are related to FDI since they influence the totality of the FDI business environment.

The EC was one of the leading players in the Uruguay Round negotiations and was one of the most active advocates to include the aforementioned "new issues" in the world trading system.[81] However, it was not clear how the EC should participate in this, whether the EC as an entity, the individual Member States, or the two jointly. As a matter of fact, the Punta del Este Declaration, which launched the negotiations, was approved by the Council and by the representatives of the governments of the Member States "to the extent concerned".[82] In order to ensure the maximum consistency, however, the Council decided that the Commission alone, on behalf of the Community and the Member States would conduct the negotiations.[83] The Council also stated, in the minutes of the meeting at which the Punta del Este Declaration was approved, that this decision "does not prejudice the question of the competence of the Community or the Member States on particular issues".[84]

Therefore, on 6 April 1994, some days before the WTO Agreements were to be signed, the Commission submitted to the Court a request for an Opinion on the exclusivity of the Community's competence to conclude all the WTO Agreements. In November of that year, the Court delivered its lengthy *Opinion 1/94* which confirmed the Community's exclusive competence to conclude the MATG, pursuant to Article 113(now Article 133) of the EC Treaty, but ruled that the Community had to share with its Member States the competence to conclude GATS and TRIPS.

Surprisingly, it seemed that the TRIMs was not called into any question at all during the proceedings. Nor did Opinion 1/94 even specifically mention the TRIMs. From the Opinion, a logical conclusion would be that the Community should have sole competence on TRIMs, as it is included in the MATG, which, as a whole, falls within the Community's exclusive competence.

However, this conclusion is ambiguous and could be dangerous. While it may be clear that those listed measures fall within the Community's sole competence, it would be doubtful whether the follow-up investment-related activities do the same. For example, does the Community have exclusive power to participate in the WTO reviews and negoti-

[79] World Trade Organization, *Trading into the Future*, second edition, july 1998, p. 21.

[80] See Brewer and Young, *supra*, footnote 75, p. 123.

[81] See *Trade and Investment, supra*, footnote 7.

[82] See Part Ill of Opinion 1/94, *supra* footnote 5, on the "Negotiation and Signature of the WTO Agreement"

[83] Ibid.

[84] Ibid.

ations on all investment-related matters[85] and, more disputably, can the Community alone take part in the possible negotiations on a multilateral investment agreement under the aegis of the WTO? If the answers are positive, it would be contradictory to the spirit expressed in Opinion 1/94, which actually rejected the broad interpretation of Article 133 on CCP to cover all trade-related economic issues. If the answers are negative, a finer line must be drawn on the scope of the TRIMs. Nevertheless, it should be clear that at least certain investment measures regulated by the TRIMs fall within the EC's exclusive competence.

As for the GATS, the Court said that only services provided through cross-border modes of supply were covered by Article 113(now Article 133) and therefore fell within the exclusive competence of the Community. Of other forms of services, including those supplied through "commercial presence", which fall outside the common commercial policy, it said that the Community did not have sole competence and had to share the power with its Member States.[86] This implies that the power to regulate direct investment in services sectors is a shared power rather than an exclusive one.

2. *The Energy Charter Treaty*

The Energy Charter Treaty[87] is a treaty establishing a legal regime to promote long-term co-operation in the energy field among the EU and many Eastern European countries. The ECT contains, as one of its two substantial parts, provisions on the protection and promotion of investment. The Community signed the ECT in December 1994 and is provisionally applying it to the extent that it has competence for matters governed by the Treaty.[88] Article 73(c) (now 57) was used, among other provisions, as the legal basis for the signature and provisional application.[89]

3. *The Third Revised Decision of the OECD on National Treatment*

The OECD has long been involved in activities concerning international investment and has laid down many legal instruments facilitating FDI flows, including the Codes of Liberalization on Capital Movement and Current Invisible Operations. Those instruments have led to the adoption of the "Strengthened National Treatment Instrument" which consists of two parts. One is the Revised Section on National Treatment in the Declaration of 1976 on International Investment and Multinational Enterprises(the Revised Declaration) and the other is the Third Decision.[90]

The Revised Declaration is not a legally binding instrument but a policy statement

---

[85] In fact, most of the reviews and negotiations scheduled for the early years of the WTO concerned investment issues, and several of them had the potential for significant expansion of the WTO's coverage of investment matters. Also, the 1996 Singapore Ministerial Conference created three new Working Groups, among which one was to investigate the relationship between trade and investment and the possibility to conclude a multilateral agreement on investment(MAI) within the WTO framework; see Brewer and Young, *supra*, footnote 75, p. 139. See also WTO, *supra*, footnote 79, p. 50.

[86] Opinion 1/94, *supra*, footnote 5, at paras. 36 – 53.

[87] For the text of the ECT, see O. J. L 380, 31 December 1994, pp. 24 – 49.

[88] Macleod *et al.*, *supra*, footnote 19, p. 388.

[89] Council Decision 94/998 [1994), O. J. L 380/1.

[90] Opinion 2/92, *supra*, footnote 10, Part 111. 1.

wherein the OECD Member countries express their intention to accord undertakings established in their territory and controlled by nationals of another Member country treatment no less favourable than that accorded in like situations to domestic undertakings, subject to certain exceptions and derogation.[91] However, the Decisions annexed to the Revised Declaration, including the Third Decision, are binding on Member countries. In the Third Decision, the Contracting Parties undertake, in particular, to comply with a procedure for notification and examination, within the framework of the OECD, of measures constituting exceptions to national treatment and of any other measures which have a bearing on national treatment.

Upon the Commission's recommendation, the Council authorized it in 1990 to negotiate a decision on national treatment within the OECD.[92] In November 1991, the Commission sent a Communication to the Council concerning the outcome of the negotiations, together with a proposal for a decision on participation by the Community in the Third Decision.[93] One month later, when the Third Decision was adopted by the Council of the OECD, the Commission representative stated that the Community intended to accede to the Third Decision, based on Articles 57 and 113 of the EC Treaty. At the same time, The Netherlands' representative expressed its concern that the Community Member States would be bound by it after the accession by the Community.[94] Hence, in December 1992, Belgium submitted its request to the Court for an Opinion on the legal basis of the EC's participation in the Third Decision.

The Court delivered its Opinion(Opinion 2/92) in March 1995, wherein it investigated both the relevant substantive rules in the Revised Declaration and the procedural rules in the Third Decision. In the Opinion, the Court held that neither Article 113(now Article 133) nor Opinion 1/76 applied to this case. It also said that, since the Community measures adopted so far did not cover "the fields of activity to which the Third Decision relates", the Community possessed only partial competence thereon.[95] In the end, it ruled that the Community was competent to participate in the Third Decision but must do it jointly with the Member States.

Since this was the first time that the Court gave an opinion on the EC's competence on a legal instrument especially devoted to investment issues, it meant a lot to the Community's competence on investment matters in general. It can be seen from the Opinion that, as a general rule, the Community has but non-exclusive competence on investment matters.

4. *The* OECD *MAI Proposal*

Soon after Opinion 2/92 was delivered, the Member countries of the OECD, including the EC Member States, decided to negotiate a binding Multilateral Agreement on

[91] See Article 11. 1 of the Revised Declaration.

[92] Opinion 2/92, *supra*, footnote 10, Part 111. 3.

[93] Ibid.

[94] Ibid.

[95] Ibid. , at paras. 28, 32 and 34.

Investment.[96] The MAI was a detailed, high standard agreement on investment protection and promotion. In order to co-ordinate actions of the Community and its Member States, a framework for co-operation was finally reached a year later. Adopted as a series of non-binding Council of Ministers' Decisions, the framework had four components:[97] the Community negotiated m areas of EC competence on the basis of directives from the Council and in consultation with appropriate Council committees; the negotiators for the Commission, Council and Member States met before each OECD negotiation session; a Working Group of government officials assisted the Commission and worked to ensure co-operation between the EC and the Member governments; and "modalities" structured participation and confirmed the obligation to co-operate in accordance with relevant treaties and Court case-law.

This framework turned out to be unsuccessful. In early 1998, when public opposition was mounting, a number of participating governments doubted the value of the Agreement and became concerned about the constraints it would impose on them.[98] Later, the French government first requested to suspend the talks for domestic consultation and then withdrew from them without formally consulting its Community negotiating partners.[99] This left the other EC Member States with the worst of both worlds. On the one hand, because the Community co-operation was characterized by "soft institution", they could not prevent the French withdrawal. On the other hand, since some aspects of the negotiations fell within the exclusive competence of the EC, other governments could not carry on the talks without France even if they wanted to.[100]

The failure of the MAI proposal within the OECD has demonstrated that the vaguely defined "shared competence" of the EC on investment issues cannot keep up with the needs of the ever-integrating Community and the fast-globalizing world economy.

In conclusion, the Community has successfully participated in several multilateral agreements especially devoted to or merely involved in investment issues, which shows that it has the corresponding competence. However, as Court *Opinions 1/94* and 2/92 made clear, such competence is, in general, not exclusive, but to be shared with Member States. Furthermore, the ill fate of the OECD MAI proposal has implied that something should be done to further clarify the power attribution between the Community and its Member States on investment matters.

IV. Conclusions: Towards a Common Community Invest-Ment Policy

From the preceding analysis, it can be concluded that both Community law, as interpreted by the Court, and Community practice have confirmed that the EC has competence on investment issues. However, this competence is generally regarded, at least for the time being, as a competence shared with the Member States rather than an exclusive

---

[96] Young, *supra*, footnote 8, pp. 108 – 111.

[97] Ibid.

[98] Ibid.

[99] Ibid.

[100] Young, *supra*, footnote 8, pp. 108 – 111.

competence. Moreover, the Community practice has also proven that the vaguely defined "shared competence" may put the Community as well as its Member States into awkward and difficult situations when negotiating international investment agreements.

In fact, the ambiguous division of competence between the Community and its Member States and the lack of a Community FDI policy not only slow deliberations, frustrate other countries and enable rivals like the United States and Japan to play off Member States against each other when the Community is entering into international negotiations.[101] They also result in problems and dilemmas when it deals with internal relations, such as relationships between different Community Directorates, between the Community and its Member States, and even between different Member States.[102] For instance, the Community's investment policies and policy-making are distributed at Directorate level, but there is no framework for ensuring a coherent approach to all relevant policies. Therefore, overlap, contradiction and gaps in policy coverage may happen frequently, which will probably affect the effectiveness and efficiency of administrative operations.

To the contrary, a common Community investment policy and a sole Community investment competence would, to a considerable extent, facilitate the efficient functioning of the EC and, at the same time, place the EU in a much more favourable position in future bilateral or multilateral investment law-making. Moreover, this could eventually secure equal treatment among European investors, both internally and externally. Last but not least, European multinational enterprises, the major investment players in Europe, now belonging to the Community rather than a single Member State, would benefit the most from this scheme.

To achieve this goal, it may be necessary, first of all, to co-ordinate and harmonize the laws and regulations existing in Member States on investment promotion and protection and to create a common Community policy thereon. In this regard, it would help for the EC to first establish an External Investment Unit under the Directorate-General for Trade of the Commission.[103] Its aims would be to facilitate information exchange between the Community and its Member States, to conduct research, to provide a forum for discussing internal and external investment issues and for furnishing an FDI input into the policies of the EC Directorates and, perhaps more specifically, to draft model investment agreements at the Community level, based on the co-ordination attained by the 1978 Communication and the 1980 Report.

Meanwhile, a Community programme on investment guarantees might also be established, to facilitate EC outward investment flow to third countries, especially to developing countries. Although by now many EU Member States have established their investment guarantee projects, it is preferable to have such a mechanism at the Community level, perhaps operated by the European Investment Bank (EIB), because of its larger

---

〔101〕 Brewer and Young, *supra*, footnote 8, p. 46.

〔102〕 For a detailed list of possible problems in different policy areas, see ibid., p. 45.

〔103〕 The Commission has recently established a Unit dealing with investment and other issues under Directorate F of the Directorate-General for Trade. However, in order to achieve this harmonization and coordination, it is probably necessary to have a Unit exclusively devoted to investment issues.

coverage, bigger size, higher credit and therefore higher efficiency. In this regard, the EIB could learn from the experience of the Multilateral Investment Guarantee Agency and the national investment insurers in the EU Member States.

When the time ripens, the EC could promulgate Community FDI guidelines to direct the internal harmonization and co-ordination of FDI-related laws and regulations, and these could be converted into a Community FDI Regulation based on Article 57(2) when the co-ordination and harmonization have been finally achieved.

In the end, it would be necessary and possible to clarify the common Community policy and competence, particularly its exclusive external competence on investment matters, in the EC Treaty, preferably by amending and extending the coverage of Article 133(ex Article 113).

In fact, during the Intergovernmental Conference 2000, a proposal was put forward by the European Parliament which simply changes the wording "the conclusion of tariff and trade agreements" in Article 133(1) into "the conclusion of tariff and trade agreements relating to trade in goods and services, investment and intellectual property" [104] As a result, however, in the Treaty of Nice this proposal has only been partly accepted. While it did extend the application of Article 133, paras. 1 – 4 to "the negotiation and conclusion of agreements in the fields of trade in services and the commercial aspects of intellectual property rights", [105] it did not accept that investment agreements should be treated in the same way.

Nevertheless, as the EU further integrates itself and intensifies its involvement in external investment issues, it is believed that, sooner or later, a Common Investment Policy of the European Community will be established.

---

[104] See Brok and Tsatsos, *supra*, footnote 22.

[105] Treaty of Nice, Article 2. 8, O. J. C 80/1, 10 March 2001.

The China – EU BIT: The Emerging "Global BIT 2. 0"? *

Ⅰ. Introduction

Since China and the European Union(EU) announced their decision to negotiate a bilateral investment treaty(BIT) at the 14th China – EU Summit in February 2012,[1] the two sides have engaged in two rounds of negotiations.[2] As the first standalone BIT that the EU has attempted to negotiate and a treaty between two of the world's largest economies, the China – EU BIT is bound to occupy a unique place in the world history of BIT negotiations.[3] This note attempts to assess the key issues that are likely to be involved in the negotiations of the BIT and its global implications. It concludes that, while there are many tough issues to tackle in the negotiations, a successful China – EU BIT is likely to become a symbol for the emerging ' Global BIT 2. 0' .[4]

Ⅱ. The China – Eu Bit: Major Issues

Although there are currently BIT arrangements between China and all but one Member State of the EU, the China—EU BIT negotiations would involve far more work than simply consolidating or streamlining ' the existing BITs between China and the EU

---

* *ICSID Review*, Volume 30 No. 1, 2015. the authors are Shan Wenhua and Wang Lu.

〔1〕 European Commission, ' Commission Proposes to Open Negotiations for an Investment Agreement with China' Press Relase(23 May 2013) <http://europa. eu/rapid/press-release_IP – 13 – 458_en. htm> accessed 7 April 2014.

〔2〕 European Commission, ' EU and China Hold Investment Talks Ahead of President Xi Jinping Visit to Brussels' Press Release(24 March 2014) <http://europa. eu/rapid/press-release_IP – 14 – 291_en. htm> accessed 7 April 2014.

〔3〕 Wenhua Shan and Sheng Zhang, ' The Potential EU-China BIT: Issues and Implications' in Marc Bungenberg and others(eds), EU and Investment Agreements: Open Questions and Remaining Challenges(Hart Publishing 2013) 118. See also Axel Berger, ' The Real Significance of a China-EU Investment Treaty' Caixin Online(15 October 2013) <http://english. caixin. com/2013 – 10 – 15/100591989. html> accessed 7 April 2014.

〔4〕 Wenhua Shan and Sheng Zhang, ' Market Access Provisions in the Potential EU Model BIT: Towards a "Global BIT 2. 0"?' [International Conference on The Anatomy of the(Invisible) EU Model BIT, Vienna, 25 – 26 November 2013](forthcoming in the Journal of World Investment and Trade).

Member States into a single and coherent text'.[5] Indeed, it can be expected that the two sides will seize this opportunity to update and upgrade their investment treaty arrangements, taking into account the recent world investment treaty practices in general and those of the two sides in particular.

Among other things, the following four aspects may be the key issues in the China-EU BIT negotiations and should be watched closely: (a) market access; (b) substantive provisions; (c) social clauses; and (d) dispute resolution.

A. Market Access

As well known, both China and the EU, including its Member States, used to follow the traditional 'European' approach to BITs, focusing on investment 'protection' without including concrete undertakings in investment market access or liberalization. However, this approach seems to have undergone drastic changes on both sides in recent years. The EU, on the one hand, has been very keen to promote investment market access as well as investment protection, as demon strated by the latest draft of the Comprehensive Economic and Trade Agreement (CETA) between the EU and Canada, which accepted pre-establishment national treatment on the basis of a negative list of reserved sectors.[6] In the context of the China – EU BIT talks, the EU Trade Commissioner De Gucht has made clear that 'the EU – China investment agreement is not about investment protection only, but also about market access for European companies'.[7] The European Parliament has likewise emphasized that the China – EU BIT negotiations would be opened only on condition that formal approval has been given by China for market access.[8] On the other hand, China seems to have also accepted market access obligations in BITs, as it has announced acceptance of pre-establishment national treatment obligations on the basis of a 'negative list' of reserved sectors and industries,[9] to the surprise of many observers and commentators.

Given the insistence of the EU on market access and China's recent move to accept

---

[5] For example, the EU has expressly stated that its objectives for this BIT are rather ambitious:

The main objectives of an agreement at EU level are to improve the protection of EU investments in China as well as Chinese investments in Europe, improving legal certainty regarding treatment of EU investors in China, reducing barriers to investing in China and, as a result, increasing bilateral investment flows. It should also, crucially, cover improved access to the Chinese market-addressing important issues like mandatory joint ventures.

See European Commission(n 3).

[6] Draft CETA Investment Text (21 November 2013) (CETA Draft) arts X. 7 and X. 14 <https://www.laquadrature.net/files/CETA-Draft-Investment-Text-Nov21-2013-203b-13.pdf> accessed 7 April 2014.

[7] European Commission, 'Investment deal with China: "Only under the condition that market access for European companies is granted"' News archive (18 October 2013) <http://trade.ec.europa.eu/doclib/press/index.cfm?id=976> accessed 7 April 2014.

[8] European Parliament, Resolution of 9 October 2013 on the EU-China negotiations for a bilateral investment agreement (2013/2674(RSP)) <http://www.europarl.europa.eu/sides/getDoc.do?pubRef=-%2F%2FEP%2F%2FTEXT%2BTA%2BP7-TA-2013-0411%2B0%2BDOC%2BXML%2BV0%2F%2FEN&language=EN> accessed 7 April 2014.

[9] Ministry of Commerce of the People's Republic of China (MOFCOM) Spokesman Shen Danyang, 'Comments on China and US to Promote Energetically Negotiations on Bilateral Investment Agreement' Spokesman's Remarks (16 July 2013) <http://english.mofcom.gov.cn/article/newsrelease/policyreleasing/201307/20130700200566.shtml> accessed 4 March 2014.

such obligations in BIT negotiations, it is likely that the China – EU BIT would contain concrete market access commitments. This is, nevertheless, much easier to be said than realized. This is primarily because both China and the EU have had little experience in making specific market access commitments in their investment treaty practice.[10] As a result, the preparations and negotiations for market access commitments are likely to take significant time, since both sides have to assess whether, and to what extent, each sector and each industry are internationally competitive and should be opened up to international investors.[11] In China, the laborious task might involve taking stock of non-conforming measures at both the central level and the local level. In the EU, further complexities are likely to arise due to the fact that the EU has only shared exclusive competence in concluding BITs covering both direct and indirect investments. It might be possible that the market access commitments from the EU side affect two levels, namely the EU level and the Member States level, with the latter then being further divided into central and local levels. Further complexities may also arise, in case of a breach of market access commitments, to determine which party—the EU or a Member State—shall be the respondent to answer the claims and possibly to pay compensation.[12] Working out solutions to such challenging and complex issues requires not only tremendous time, but also intelligence and perhaps innovations.

B. Substantive Rules

The existing BITs between China and the EU Member States have established substantive rules of investment protection, but they would have to be clarified and updated to reflect the latest developments in this respect. In other words, the substantive rules are likely to be 'recalibrated' by the China – EU BIT.[13] As a result, the traditional issuess—such as post-establishment national treatment, standards of compensation[14] and transfer—might cause little difficulty, as both sides have already adopted the fairly

〔10〕 Shan and Zhang(n 5) 102 – 4.

〔11〕 Ibid, p. 104.

〔12〕 The European Commission has proposed a regulation to deal with such matters, which has passed the first reading of the European Parliament with some amendments. But the outcome of the legislative process is yet to be determined, and it may translate into concrete terms in treaties, particularly in BITs. For the regulation proposal, see European Commission, Proposal for a Regulation of the European Parliament and of the Council establishing a framework for managing financial responsibility linked to investor – State dispute settlement tribunals established by international agreements to which the European Union is party, Brussels, 2012/0163 (COD) (21 June 2012) <http://trade.ec.europa.eu/doclib/docs/2012/june/tradoc_149567.pdf> accessed 15 December 2014. For details of the amendments after the first reading, see European Commission, Establishing a framework for managing financial responsibility linked to investor-state dispute settlement tribunals established by international agreements to which the EU is party: Amendments adopted by the European Parliament on 23 May 2013 on the proposal for a regulation of the European Parliament and of the Council establishing a framework for managing financial responsibility linked to investor-state dispute settlement tribunals established by international agreements to which the European Union is party(COM(2012)0335 – C7 – 0155/2012 – 2012/0163(COD)) <http://www.europarl.europa.eu/sides/getDoc.do?pubRef = -//EP//TEXT + TA + 20130523 + ITEMS + DOC + XML + V0//EN&language = EN#sdocta4> accessed 15 December 2014.

〔13〕 Christian Tams, 'An EU-China Investment Agreement?' EJIL Talk! (15 October 2013) <http://www.ejiltalk.org/an-eu-china-investment-agreement/> accessed 7 April 2014.

〔14〕 Wenhua Shan, The Legal Framework of EU-China Investment Relations: A Critical Appraisal(Hart Publishing 2005) 287 – 9.

standardized formats in their recent treaty practices.[15] It might nevertheless be unlikely to include express reference to the ‘Hull Formula’ in the BIT, given that China has been strongly opposed to it, and that the BIT would do just as well without such express reference.[16] The more controversial issues might be related to the specific ways of wording to be adopted to further define certain critical terms such as ‘investment’ (eg whether or not to include reference to the ‘characteristics of investment’ and if so, which characteristics should be included), ‘indirect expropriation’ (eg which guiding principles should be considered in its determination) and ‘fair and equitable treatment’ (eg which aspects should be specified to establish an irreducible core of the concept). Further, it remains to be seen whether there should be any reference to ‘customary international law’ or the ‘international minimum standard’ in defining Fair and Equitable Treatment (FET) given that it was absent from existing China – EU Member State BITs, but both sides have adopted it in certain recent investment treaty practices.[17] Moreover, it can be expected that certain generally applied exceptions would be included, given that both sides are keen to include a general exception, but it remains uncertain which specific exceptions might be included. Finally, it is unclear whether the issue of competitive neutrality would be addressed in the treaty, given the widely divided positions of the two parties on this point.[18] In short, the negotiations on investment protection might prove to be mostly focused on the certain important technical details, rather than on major issues of principle.

C. Social Clauses

As a way of rebalancing the investment treaties, ‘socialization’ has become part of

[15] See eg Agreement Between the Government of Canada and the Government of the People's Republic of China for the Promotion and Reciprocal Protection of Investments (signed 9 September 2012, entered into force 1 October 2014) (China-Canada BIT) arts 6, 10 and 12 <http://investmentpolicyhub.unctad.org/Download/TreatyFile/600> accessed 15 December 2014; CETA Draft (n 8) arts X.7, X.11 and X.12.

[16] Shan (n 16) 204; Shan and Zhang (n 5) 107.

[17] For EU practice, see eg CETA Draft (n 8) art 4. For Chinese practice, see Free Trade Agreement Between The Government of New Zealand And The Government of the People's Republic of China (signed 7 April 2008, entered into force 1 October 2008) (China-New Zealand FTA) art 143 <http://investmentpolicyhub.unctad.org/Download/TreatyFile/2564> accessed 15 December; Agreement Between The Government of The United Mexican States and The Government of The People's Republic of China on the Promotion and Reciprocal Protection of Investments (signed 11 July 2008, entered into force 6 June 2009) (China-Mexico BIT) art 5 <http://investmentpolicyhub.unctad.org/Download/TreatyFile/759> accessed 15 December 2014; China – Canada BIT (n 17) art 4; Free Trade Agreement Between The Government of The People's Republic of China and The Government of The Republic of Peru (signed 28 April 2009, entered into force 1 March 2010) (China-Peru FTA) art 132 <http://investmentpolicyhub.unctad.org/Download/TreatyFile/2586> accessed 15 December 2014. See also Norah Gallagher and Wenhua Shan, Chinese Investment Treaties: Policies and Practices (OUP 2009) 130.

[18] The European Parliament in particular has taken this treaty as a key opportunity to establish a level playing field for both State-run and private-sector companies. See European Parliament, Resolution of 9 October 2013 on the EU – China negotiations for a bilateral investment agreement (2013/2674 (RSP)) <http://www.europarl.europa.eu/sides/getDoc.do?pubRef=-%2F%2FEP%2F%2FTEXT%2BTA%2BP7-TA-2013-0411%2B0%2BDOC%2BXML%2BV0%2F%2FEN&language=EN> accessed 7 April 2014. On the other hand, it can be expected that China would forcefully resist the inclusion of such rules given the overwhelming significance of SOEs in her overseas investment activities.

a worldwide trend in investment treaty practice.[19] Since the EU and its Member States see themselves as champions in addressing social concerns in such treaties, it is not surprising the European Parliament has called ' new clauses' such as social, environmental and transparency rules to be included in the China – EU BIT.[20] China, on the other hand has traditionally rejected the inclusion of such provisions in its BITs. It might nevertheless be possible for the China – EU BIT to embrace provisions similar to the China – Canada BIT to address such social and environmental concerns of the EU. These provisions discourage waiving, relaxing or otherwise derogating from domestic health, safety or environmental measures to encourage investment; exclude in principle such measures from the scope of ' indirect compensation' ; and include some of them in the ' general exception' clause.[21] The China-Canada BIT also includes an extensive general exception of ' cultural industry' , which may well be adapted into the China – EU BIT given both sides are keen in protecting their own cultures and cultural industries.

D. Dispute Resolution

The above-mentioned ' recalibration' demanded for the China – EU BIT is aimed not only at substantive rules, but also at procedural rules. With a steep increase of investment treaty-based arbitration cases in the last decade, the investment dispute settlement regime has become a subject of wide and sharp criticism, which has led to a range of proposals for its reform.[22] As noted elsewhere, any investment dispute may involve, to different degrees, three dimensions of interests or concerns: economical, political and social. A ' matrix analysis' of such interests and concerns in such disputes may help to design(in the case of treaty drafting) or to locate(in the case of dispute resolution) the most appropriate method of dispute resolution. Such analysis also helps to explain most reform measures and proposals of reform of the investment dispute resolution system.[23]

In the context of the China – EU BIT negotiations, the European Parliament has suggested that the China – EU BIT should include effective State-to-State and investor-to-State dispute settlements mechanisms that are set within a suitable legal framework and subject to strict transparency criteria, in order to prevent frivolous claims leading to unjustified arbitration, and to ensure that all investors have access to a fair trial.[24]

Indeed, both the EU and China have been proactive in the reform of dispute resolu-

---

〔19〕 Wenhua Shan, ' Towards a Balanced Liberal Investment Regime: General Report on the Protection of Investment for the XVIIIth International Congress of Comparative Law 2010 Washington DC' (2010) 25(2) ICSID Rev—FILJ 421 – 97, 469.

〔20〕 European Parliament Resolution(n 20).

〔21〕 China – Canada BIT(n 17) arts 18, Annex B. 10 and Annex B. 33.

〔22〕 Anna Joubin-Bret and Jean E Kalicki, ' Introduction TDM Special issue on "Reform of Investor – State Dispute Settlement: In search of a Roadmap"' in Editorial(2014) 1 TDM Special Issue 1 – 32 <http://www.transnational-dispute-management.com/article.asp?key=2023> accessed 15 December 2014.

〔23〕 Wenhua Shan, ' A Matrix Analysis on ISDS Reform: Preliminary Considerations' (Ministerial Session of the 24th Meeting of the Energy Charter Conference 15 Years of Energy Investment Promotion and Protection under the Energy Charter Treaty, Cyprus, 5 – 6 December 2013) <http://www.encharter.org/fileadmin/user_upload/Conferences/2013_Dec_5 – 6/4 – 3_Shan.pdf> accessed 19 March 2014.

〔24〕 European Parliament Resolution(n 20).

tion mechanisms. From the EU's perspective, it has not only adopted the sophisticated and detailed approach to investment dispute resolution provisions, but also has attempted to make significant progresses and innovations on that basis. Progress has been made, for example, in the draft EU – Canada CETA which establishes ' the most progressive system' of investor – State dispute settlement(ISDS) especially by providing strong protections and full transparency while improving the control over frivolous claims.[25] The CETA Draft also provides for the possibility of establishing an appellate mechanism and encourages alternative dispute resolution by including explicit reference to mediation.[26] On the other hand, China has attempted to actively reform the ISDS in its recent BIT practice. The China-Canada BIT, for instance, explicitly provides that the legitimacy of financial prudential measures should be decided jointly by the financial service authorities of the contracting parties, or the State – State arbitral mechanism in case a joint decision could not be reached by the financial authorities.[27] This is, to a certain degree, an innovation. More progress may be expected from the negotiations of the China-USA BIT, even though it is unclear at this stage what direction it will take. In general, it seems that China and the EU share similar concerns and agree on the necessary measures in investment dispute settlement reform, such as refining the scope of the ISDS and State-to-State arbitration, and exploring the possibility of an appellate mechanism. Accordingly, it is likely that they might agree on an extensively and progressively reformed dispute settlement system in the China-EU BIT, which may in turn leave an important mark in the worldwide effort of investment dispute resolution reform. Such prospect is unlikely to be changed despite the current debate on ISDS within the Union in the context of the CETA ratification and the Transatlantic Trade and Investment Partnership (TTIP) negotiations.[28]

Ⅲ. The China-Eu Bit: The Emerging ' Global Bit 2. 0' ?

The BIT will undoubtedly ' benefit both the EU and China by ensuring an improved market access to investments in both directions and providing a simpler, secure and predictable legal framework to investors in the long term' .[29] However, its influence is likely to go well beyond the boundaries of the two economies.[30] Indeed, it can be ar-

---

〔25〕 European Commission, ' Investment Provisions in the EU – Canada free trade agreement(CETA)' (3 December 2013) < http: //trade. ec. europa. eu/doclib/docs/2013/november/tradoc_151918. pdf > accessed 7 April 2014.

〔26〕 Ibid.

〔27〕 China-Canada BIT(n 17) arts 20(2) (b) and 33(3) .

〔28〕 The European Commission launched a public consultation in March 2014 on ISDS in the Transatlantic Trade and Investment Partnership(TTIP) . See Eureopan Commisson, ' Preliminary Report: Online Public Consultation on Investment Protection and Investor-to-State Dispute Settlement(ISDS) in the Transatlantic Trade and Investment Partnership Agreement(TTIP) ' (July 2014) < http: //trade. ec. europa. eu/doclib/docs/2014/july/tradoc_152693. pdf > accessed 31 October 2014.

〔29〕 European Commission, ' EU and China Begin Investment Talks' Press Release(20 January 2014) < http: //europa. eu/rapid/press-release_IP – 14 – 33_en. htm > accessed 7 April 2014.

〔30〕 Shan and Zhang(n 5) 117.

gued that the China-EU BIT, once concluded, will become a symbol of the emerging new generation of global BIT practice, or the ‘Global BIT 2.0’.

Evidenced by the consensus achieved in some of the major investment treaties concluded or currently being negotiated, such as the Trans-Pacific Partnership Agreement (TPP), TTIP, CETA, and the China-USA BIT, it seems that a new generation of BITs of global import is taking shape. Such a ‘Global BIT 2.0’ features four main characteristics:[31] (a) concrete market access commitments, based on a combination of pre-establishment national treatment clauses and a negative list of reserved/protected sectors and industries(‘liberalization’);[32] (b) clarified and more balanced substantive provisions, such as the narrowing down of the definition of ‘investment’ by adding the ‘characteristics of investment’ requirement, establishing certain guiding principles, refining the details of ‘indirection expropriation’ and ‘fair and equitable treatment’ standards, and including certain exception clauses(‘balancing’);[33] (c) detailed and refined investment dispute settlement mechanisms, particularly the ISDS mechanism(‘refining’);[34] and

---

〔31〕 In the 2010 General Report on the Protection of Foreign Investment presented at the International Congress of Comparative Law in Washington DC, Wenhua Shan noted three main trends of foreign investment laws around the globe on the basis of the national/jurisdictional reports from 22 jurisdictions around the world. They are ‘liberalization’, ‘balancing’ and ‘socialization’. The new generation of global BITs can be regarded as the latest developments following these trends. In particular, consensus has been achieved by and large on how to ‘balance’ the rights of foreign investors against the right to regulate of the host States, in both substantive and procedural provisions. The trend of ‘liberalization’ has reached a new stage as the main stockholders are accepting the ‘protection + liberalization’ BIT model rather than the previously dominant ‘protection’ model. Also, more and more BITs and FTAs are including ‘social’ clauses to address health, safety, environmental and other issues of public concern. For the General Report, see Wenhua Shan, ‘General Report on the Protection of Foreign Investment’ in Wenhua Shan(ed), The Legal Protection of Foreign Investment: A Comparative Study(Hart Publishing 2011) 3 – 79.

〔32〕 See the leaked text of the TPP Investment Chapter(TPP Draft) arts 12.4 and 12.9 <http://www.citizenstrade.org/ctc/wp-content/uploads/2012/06/tppinvestment.pdf> accessed 11 April 2014; the leaked text of TTIP, EU Draft Proposal on Trade in Services Investment and E-Commerce(2 July 2013) (TTIP Draft) arts 4, 5 and 6 <http://www.transnational-dispute-management.com/legal-and-regulatory-detail.asp?key = 11330> accessed 11 April 2014; CETA Draft(n 8) arts X.7 and X.14; US Model BIT 2012 arts 3 and 14 <http://www.ustr.gov/sites/default/files/BIT%20text%20for%20ACIEP%20Meeting.pdf> accessed 11 April 2014. China has also agreed to negotiate with the US based on pre-establishment national treatment and a ‘negative list’ approach. See MOFCOM(n 11).

〔33〕 See ibid TPP Draft, arts 12.2, 12.6(2), 12.9, 12.12(1), 12.23(3) and Annexes 12 – C, 12 – D and 12.K, art XX.3; ibid TTIP Draft, arts 1.4(p), 12, 64 and Annex(X); CETA Draft(n 8) arts X.3, X.9, X.12, X.14, X.16 and Annex: Expropriation; ibid US Model BIT, arts 1, 5, 7(4), 8(3), 14, 18, 19, 20(2) and 21; Agreement among The Government of Japan, The Government of The Republic of Korea, and The Government of The People's Republic of China for the Promotion, Facilitation, and Protection of Investments(signed 12 May 2013, entered into force 17 May 2014) (China-Japan-Korea Trilateral Investment Agreement) arts 1, 5, 7, 10(2)(5), 13(3), 16, 18, 20, 21 and Protocol <http://investmentpolicyhub.unctad.org/Download/TreatyFile/2633> accessed 15 December 2014; China – Canada BIT(n 17) arts 8, 10(2), 12(3)(4), 14, 33 and Annexes B.8, B.10 and B.12; Agreement on Investment of the Framework Agreement on Comprehensive Economic Cooperation between The People's Republic of China and The Association of Southeast Asian Nations(signed 15 August 2009, entered into force 1 January 2010) (ASEAN-China Investment Agreement) arts 3(4), 5(4), 6, 7, 8(6), 10(3)(5), 16, 17 and 19(2) <http://investmentpolicyhub.unctad.org/IIA/country/42/treaty/3272> accessed 15 December 2014.

〔34〕 See TPP Draft(n 34) s B; Re: TTIP-Negotiations on Investor-State Dispute Settlement(Brussels, July 2013) in TTIP Draft(n 34); CETA Draft(n 8) s 6 and Annex X; US Model BIT(n 34) s B; ibid China – Japan – Korea Trilateral Investment Agreement, arts 4(3) and 15; China – Canada BIT(n 17) arts 5(3), 20 – 26 and Annex C.21; ibid China – ASEAN Investment Agreement, art 14.

(d) the inclusion of ‘linkage’ provisions addressing health, safety, environmental and other social concerns(‘socialisation’ or ‘linkage’).[35]

The China-EU BIT, analysed above, is very likely to include all four features, and it will not just be another major investment agreement following the emerging ‘Global BIT 2.0’ prototype, but a more definite signal of the emergence of the new generation of BITs worldwide.

This is because, on the one hand, the China-EU BIT would be the first BIT concluded between the EU and China, as the two most important economies in the world(other than the United States). Previously, all major investment treaties were negotiated with the US(eg. the TTIP and the China-US BIT), or with the US taking the leading role(eg. TPP). It might therefore be said that it was upon the US's insistence that these treaties exhibit such new features, which more or less was based on the US BIT experience. The China-EU BIT should represent the genuine will of the two sides, free from any direct influence from the US, the primary designer and advocate of the new generation BITs.

On the other hand, the BIT would not simply signal the voluntary transformation of the BIT practice of both the EU and China, but also the transformation of world BIT practice in general. First, the shift in EU's and China's policy already carries worldwide impact. As EU Member States have signed around a half(1400) of the BITs concluded worldwide, and China has the world's second largest BIT network(with over 130 BITs), together they easily make up the majority of the world's BITs. In other words, the EU's and China's shift towards the new generation BIT will have a direct impact on the majority of BITs worldwide. Second, the two parties enjoy tremendous influence on the BIT practice in the rest of the world, owing to historical, cultural, economical and political reasons. It has been well known that the European BIT prototype used to be the dominant BIT model. Most developing States(including China) and many other developed States have generally followed the conventional European approach. Also, as the largest and one of the most successful developing economies in the world, China— and with it, its BIT practice—carries considerable influence, particularly in other developing States. As a result, the shift of both the EU and China towards the new generation BIT is likely to significantly influence the BIT practice of other States and exhibit global implications. Finally, besides the European BIT model, an alternative BIT model adopted by many States was the North American model, which actually provided for the general framework of the new generation BIT, primarily by its combination of the investment protection and liberalization functions.

The voluntary shift of the EU and China(with their likely influence on other countries) can therefore be regarded as signalling the emergence of a global general consensus on the new generation BIT. In this sense, it would not be an exaggeration to say that a successful China-EU BIT is likely to become a more definitive symbol of the emerging ‘Global BIT 2.0’.

---

[35] TPP Draft(n 34) arts 12.15 and 12.15; TTIP Draft(n 34) art 1; CETA Draft(n 8) s 6 and Annex X; US Model BIT(n 34) arts 11, 12 and 13; China – Japan – Korea Trilateral Investment Agreement(n 35) art 23; China – Canada BIT(n 17) arts 18(3), 33 and Annex B.10; China – ASEAN Investment Agreement(n 35) art 14.

Market Access Provisions in the Potential EU Model BIT: Towards a "Global BIT 2. 0"? *

1 Introduction

The Treaty of Lisbon marked significant progress within the European Union(EU) on economic integration, particularly in the area of foreign direct investment(FDI) . However, the inclusion of ' foreign direct investment' in this Treaty is not an ideal solution for a comprehensive investment policy as it covers only foreign ' direct' investment, which has led to various interpretations concerning its exact meaning.[1] The legal implication of the EU's international investment competence after the Treaty of Lisbon on bilateral investment treaties(BITs) between EU Member States(intra-EU BITs) and BITs between EU Member States and third states(extra-EU BITs) has therefore been a carefully scrutinized subject and has resulted in diverse reactions from the Member States.[2] However, both the European Council and the European Commission support the development of a common investment policy which could establish a level-playing field for all EU investors in third countries and for investors from third countries. Indeed, the European Commission has already reached a political agreement with Canada on the key elements of the CETA, which include a substantive chapter on investment.[3]

Whereas there are still heated debates on whether the Treaty of Lisbon has granted full competence to the European Commission to negotiate BITs, an EU Model BIT,

---

* *The Journal of World Investment and Trade,* Volume 15, No. 3, 2014. the authors are Shan Wenhua and Zhang Shen.

[1] Wenhua Shan and Sheng Zhang, ' The Treaty of Lisbon: Half Way Toward a Common Investment Policy' (2010) 21 *Eur. J. Int' l* 1049, 1060 - 1065.

[2] Hungary, for example, indicated that the decision of whether or not to sign the amending BIT with Canada prior to Hungary's accession to the EU would rely on the entry into force of the forthcoming EU Regulation on the external investment protection agreements of its Member States and the conclusion of a Comprehensive Economic and Trade Agreement between the EU and Canada. Yet other Member States, such as Germany, Slovakia, Portugal, Latvia, Belgium, Spain and Lithuania, continue to conclude new BITs even after the Treaty of Lisbon. For details, *see* Wenhua Shan and Sheng Zhang, ' The Potential EU-China BIT: Issues and Implications' in M. Bungenberg, A. Reinisch and C. Tietje(eds.), *EU and Investment Agreements: Open Questions and Remaining Challenges* (Nomos 2013) 87, 97.

[3] European Commission, Press Release, *EU and Canada Strike Free Trade Deal, Brussels*, 18 October 2013 < trade. ec. europa. eu/doclib/press/index. cfm? id = 973 > (5 March 2014) .

as a non-binding instrument, could build a 'buffer zone' between the EU and its Member States on the potential conflict of their respective BIT practice and could help progressively complete the transition between the current Member State BITs and the future EU BITs. Also, an EU Model BIT could provide a pragmatic and realistic guideline for the updating of BITs concluded by the Member States. More generally, a well-crafted EU Model BIT could help promote the reform of the current international investment legal regime by offering a clear EU perspective. Even though the European Commission has indicated that a one-size-fits-all Model for investment agreements with third countries would be neither feasible nor desirable,[4] it has also admitted that the inclusion of standard polices and clauses is necessary.[5] In this sense, it is worth exploring the feasibility and possible contents of an EU Model BIT.

Against this background, this article discusses the possible market access provisions in a potential EU Model BIT.[6] Although repeated financial crises in the past two decades have demonstrated the 'darkness' of globalization, it was argued that bad policies, rather than openness, have been the culprit.[7] Increasingly, market access is becoming an important feature in contemporary international investment law.[8] Also, market access has a close connection to other clauses, such as the definition of investment, transparency, dispute settlement and performance requirements.[9]

The EU is the world's leading host and home economy of FDI. As a 'market leader,' the EU has benefited from its openness to the rest of the world, including in the area of investment.[10] This article firstly introduces the way the approach to market access has developed within the EU, and then follows with some observations on the current state of play of market access provisions in investment or trade agreements at both EU and Member State levels. Based on these international investment agreement(IIA) practices, it then analyses the more particular issues involved in the drafting of market

[4] European Commission, Communication, *Towards a Comprehensive European International Investment Policy*, com(2010) 343 final, Brussels, 7 July 2010, 6.

[5] IISD, *Towards a Comprehensive European International Investment Policy: An Interview with Tomas Baert, European Commission, Directorate General for Trade, Services and Investment*, 23 September 2010 < www. iisd. org/itn/2010/09/23/towards-a-comprehensive-european-international-investment-policy-an-interview-with-tomas-baert-european-commission-directorate-general-for-trade-services-and-investment > (5 March 2014).

[6] Even though the terms 'admission' 'establishment' or 'market access' are used interchangeably within international investment law, there are differences between them. The right of admission concerns the right of entry and the right of establishment deals the way the activity of the investors takes place over the duration of the investment and also with the protection of the type of presence that may be permitted. For more details, *see* Ignacio Gomez-Palacio and Peter Muchlinski, 'Admission and Establishment' in P. Muchlinski, F. Ortino and C. Schreuer(eds.), *The Oxford Handbook of International Investment Law* (oup 2008) 228 – 230. This article, however, will focus on market access from a broad perspective and will not look at the specific distinction between admission and establishment.

[7] Kenneth J. Vandevelde, 'Model Bilateral Investment Treaties: The Way Forward' (2011) 18 *Sw. J. Int'l L.* pp. 307, 314.

[8] unctad, *Bilateral Investment Treaties* 1995 – 2006*: Trends in Investment Rulemaking* (2007) 23 and 26 < unctad. org/en/docs/iteiia20065_en. pdf > (5 March 2014).

[9] unctad, *Admission and Establishment*, unctad Series on Issues in International Investment Agreements (2002) Executive Summary < unctad. org/en/docs/iteiit10v2_en. pdf > (5 March 2014).

[10] European Commission, *supra* note 4.

access provisions, including pre-or post-establishment national treatment (NT), the positive or negative list approaches and the way in which lists are compiled, performance requirements, senior management and boards of directors, the application of most-favoured-nation (MFN) clauses, and dispute resolution.

2 Policy Developments in Relation to Investment Market Access within the EU

2.1 Policy Developments before the Treaty of Lisbon

Before the Treaty of Lisbon, the EU did not have an exclusive but a shared competence in the area of international investment.[11] Since there were neither express treaty provisions nor measures adopted under such provisions covering the entire field of international investment, neither express nor implied exclusive competence could be established.[12] The European Court of Justice (ECJ) affirmed the EC's non-exclusive competence on international investment in its Opinion 2/92.[13] As a result, the then European Community (EC) and the Member States shared competences on matters relating to the liberalisation and protection of foreign investment.

2.1.1 Provisions in the Former EC Treaty

The legal basis which granted some competence to the EC with regard to the entry and operation of foreign investment before the Treaty of Lisbon was to be found in Article 56 (freedom of capital movement) and Article 43 (freedom of establishment) of the former EC Treaty (Treaty Establishing the European Community, Amsterdam Treaty).

As one of the four fundamental freedoms of European Law,[14] the freedom of capital movement was first introduced by the Treaty Establishing the European Economic Community (Treaty of Rome) and was significantly amended by the Amsterdam Treaty.[15] Article 56(1) of the EC Treaty provided that "all restrictions on the movement of capital between Member States and between Member States and third countries shall be prohibited" within the framework of the provisions set out in Chapter 4 (Capital and payment). It appeared that, under this provision, Member States and third countries received equal treatment. However, the following articles within Chapter 4 introduced a series of restrictions to give the European Community or its Member States the option to maintain or introduce restrictive measures.[16] Although the definition of 'the freedom of capital movement' was not specified in the EC Treaty, the European Commission summarised the material scope of Article 56 based on ECJ case law and pointed out that "direct in-

---

[11] Wenhua Shan, 'Towards a Common European Community Policy on Investment Issues' (2001) 2(3) *JWI*, pp. 603 – 625.

[12] Shan and Zhang, *supra* note 1, p. 1050.

[13] CJEU, Opinion C – 2/92, *OECD National Treatment Investment* [1995] ECR I – 521, para. 32.

[14] These four freedoms are the free movement of goods, the free movement of persons, the free movement of capital and the freedoms to provide service.

[15] For a detailed discussion of the evolution of the freedom of capital movement, *see* John A. Usher, 'The Evolution of the Free Movement of Capital' (2007) 31(5) *Fordham Int' l L. J.*, pp. 1533 – 1570; Rafael Leal-Arcas, 'Towards the Multilateralization of International Investment Law' (2010) 10 *JWIT* pp. 865, 882 – 885.

[16] Leal-Arcas, Ibid., p. 884.

vestment in the form of participation in an undertaking by means of a shareholding, or the acquisition of securities on the capital market, constitute capital movements for the purposes of Article 56 of the Treaty. "[17]

The provisions regarding the freedom of establishment within the EC Treaty were Articles 43 to 48. Article 43, in particular, prohibited "restrictions on the freedom of establishment of nationals of a Member State in the territory of another Member State" and "restrictions on the setting-up of agencies, branches or subsidiaries by national of any Member States established in the territory of any Member State. " Article 48 also provided that "companies or firms formed in accordance with the law of a Member State and having their registered office, central administration or principal place of business within the Community shall, for the purposes of this Chapter, be treated in the same way as natural persons who are nationals of Member States. " As explained by the European Commission, the freedom of establishment enables a person or a company to carry out an economic activity in a stable and continuous way in one or more Member States.[18] It should however be noted that Article 43 only applied to companies already established in an EU Member State, but not to companies from third states seeking market access in the EU. In other words, it did not apply to the establishment of foreign investment from third states, which was covered by Article 56 as discussed above. The case is the same for current Article 49 of the Treaty on European Union(TEU), successor to Article 43 of the EC Treaty.

2. 1. 2 The Minimum Platform on Investment for EU Free Trade Agreements (FTAS)

The Minimum Platform on Investment(MPoI) for EU FTAS, which was created by the Directorate-General for Trade(dg Trade) in the European Commission and adopted by the European Council on 27 November 2006,[19] was intended by the European Commission to form the basis on which ' an ambitious investment policy' was to be built. Even though the MPoI was only a negotiation template which has never been published, it represented the first formalised and systematic EU approach to international investment treatymaking.[20] The MPoI combined provisions on establishment in the services sector and establishment in other economic sectors to better serve EU interests. Chapter II(establishment) of the MPoI expressly provided that the minimum platform would "build on GATS provisions applicable to commercial presence in service sectors and extend them

---

[17] European Commission, Communication, *Intra-EU Investment in the Financial Services' Sector*. Official Journal C 293, 25 November 2005, 2. Indeed, the European Commission goes further to character the freedom of capital movement as foreign direct investment, real estate investments or purchases, securities investments, granting of loans and credits, and other operations with financial institutions when carried out on a cross-border basis. *See* European Commission, *Free Movement of Capital* < EC. europa. eu/internal_market/capital/overview_en. htm > (5 March 2014) .

[18] European Commission, *Freedom of Establishment* < ec. europa. eu/internal_market/ services/principles_en. htm > (5 March 2014) .

[19] Council of the European Union, 15375/06, 27 November 2006.

[20] Shan and Zhang, *supra* note 1, p. 1051. *See also* Niklas Maydell, ' The European Community's Minimum Platform of Investment or the Trojan Horse of Investment Competence' in Reinisch and C. Knahr(eds.), *International Investment Law in Context* (Eleven International Publishing 2007), pp. 73 – 92.

to establishment in non service sectors." Following Article XVII of the GATS, it provided that the national treatment for investors applied both to the pre-establishment and to the post-establishment phase. Furthermore, the platform included a list of commitments with respect to market access through establishment, comparable to the GATS-type ' positive list.'

Indeed, before the adoption of the MPoI, the European Commission issued a communication with the title ' Global Europe: Competing in the World,' in which the European Commission called for a comprehensive and ambitious free trade agreement scheme, "aiming at the highest possible degree of trade liberalization including far-reaching liberalization of services and investment."[21] Accordingly, these FTAS could build on WTO and other international rules by going further and faster in promoting openness and integration, by tackling issues which are not ready for multilateral discussion and by preparing the ground for the next level of multilateral liberalization. Many key issues, including investment, public procurement, competition, other regulatory issues and IPR enforcement, which remain outside the WTO at this time can be addressed through FTAS.[22]

2.2 Policy Developments after the Treaty of Lisbon

One of the most significant changes brought by the Treaty of Lisbon is the inclusion of foreign direct investment in the common commercial policy,[23] which conferred exclusive competence on FDI. Article 207(1) of the Treaty on the Functioning of the European Union(TFEU), in particular, provides that,

The common commercial policy shall be based on uniform principles, particularly with regard to changes in tariff rates, the conclusion of tariff and trade agreements relating to trade in goods and services, and the commercial aspects of intellectual property, foreign direct investment, the achievement of uniformity in measures of liberalisation, export policy and measures to protect trade such as those to be taken in the event of dumping or subsidies. The common commercial policy shall be conducted in the context of the principles and objectives of the Union's external action.

As discussed elsewhere, the competence for FDI should be interpreted as a comprehensive competence covering all FDI matters.[24] However, the heated debate on the interpretation of FDI among scholars was not treated as an extremely important issue from a practical policy perspective by the European Commission.[25] The European Commission, understandably, supports a broad interpretation of the inclusion of FDI by insisting that under the Treaty of Lisbon, investment policy will be developed and managed at the

---

〔21〕 European Commission, *Global Europe: Competing in the World* (2006) < trade. ec. europa. eu/doclib/docs/2006/october/tradoc_130376. pdf > (5 March 2014).

〔22〕 Ibid., p. 10.

〔23〕 Marc Bungenberg, ' Going Global? The EU Common Commercial Policy after Lisbon' in C. Herrmann and J. P. Terhechte(eds.), *Eur. Ybk. Int' l Econ. L.* 2010 (Springer 2010) 123, 151.

〔24〕 Shan and Zhang, *supra* note 1, p. 1065.

〔25〕 Ibid., *supra* note 5.

European level.[26] Considering that bilateral investment treaties typically cover not only foreign direct investment, but also portfolio investment,[27] the European Commission relies on Article 3 and the Chapter on capital and payments(Articles 63 – 66) of the TFEU to argue that the exclusive competence over international agreements on investment(including both FDI and portfolio investment) would be implied to the extent that such agreements affect the scope of the common rules set by the Chapter on capital and payments.[28]

In order to fulfill the progressive abolition of restrictions on foreign direct investment, the European Commission took the first step in July 2010 to issue a communication ' Towards a Comprehensive European International Investment Policy. '[29] The most important policy change stipulated in the communication was the shift from post-establishment to both pre-and postestablishment rights granted to foreign investors.[30] By embracing investment liberalisation and investment protection, the communication intends to better address investor interests throughout the lifecycle of an investment.[31] It was argued that such an approach would achieve broader EU policy goals, as stated, for example, in the Global Europe Policy of 2006.[32]

Together with the communication, the European Commission also brought forward a proposal for a regulation establishing transitional arrangements for BITs between Member States and third countries,[33] which offered guarantees on existing bilateral investment treaties concluded between EU and non-EU countries and those whose conclusion had been pending. It also established a framework and conditions for the Member States to

---

[26] European Commission, Press Release, *New EU Investment Package set to Boost Trade and Underpin Investor Rights*, 7 July 2010 < trade. ec. europa. eu/doclib/press/index. cfm? id =591 >(5 March 2014).

[27] Foreign direct investment is generally considered to include all foreign investment which serves to establish lasting and direct links with the undertaking to which capital is made available in order to carry out an economic activity. On the contrary, foreign investments where there is no intention of influencing the management and control of an undertaking are termed ' portfolio investments, ' European Commission, *supra* note 4, pp. 2 – 3.

[28] European Commission, *supra* note 4, Article 3. 2 of the TFEU provides that, "[t] he Union shall also have exclusive competence for the conclusion of an international agreement when its conclusion is provided for in a legislative act of the Union or is necessary to enable the Union to exercise its internal competence, or in so far as its conclusion may affect common rules or alter their scope."

[29] Ibid.

[30] Julien Chaisse, ' Promises and Pitfalls of the European Union Policy on Foreign Investment-How Will the New EU Competence on FDI Affect the Emerging Global Regimes?' (2012) 15(1) *J. Int' l Econ. L.* 19. As said in the communication, while Member States have focused on the promotion and protection of all forms of investment, the Commission elaborated a liberalisation agenda focused on market access for direct investment. In this respect, a clear and complementary division of labour in the field of investment has resulted in a rather large and atomised universe of investment agreements. European Commission, *supra* note 4, p. 11.

[31] European Commission, *supra* note 4, p. 5.

[32] Stephan Woolcock, *The EU Approach to International Investment Policy after the Lisbon Treaty*, European Parliament, Directorate-General for External Policies of the Union, Directorate B, Policy Department, Study, October 2010, EXPO/B/INTA/FWC/2009 – 01/Lot7/07 – 08 – 09 < www. europarl. europa. eu/RegData/etudes/etudes/join/2010/433854/EXPOINTA_ET(2010)433854_EN. pdf >(5 March 2014).

[33] European Commission, *Proposal for a Regulation of the European Parliament and of the Council, Establishing Transitional Arrangements for Bilateral Investment Agreements between Member States and Third Countries*, com (2010) 344 final, 2010/0197(cod) Brussels, 7 July 2010.

negotiate with the third countries in order to modify an existing bilateral agreement on investment.[34] In this proposal the European Commission considered the consistency of Member State agreements with not only the common commercial policy, but also "the common rules as laid down in Chapter 4 of Title IV of Part Three TFEU on the movement of capital between Member States and third countries, including in respect of capital movements involving investment."[35] This proposal was adopted by the European Parliament and Council of the European Union in December 2012.[36]

2.3 Summary

A close look at the policy developments demonstrates three main developments with respect to investment market access over the last decades. First, the competence over investment treaty-making by the EU has been significantly boosted by the Lisbon Treaty, although it remains essentially a competence to be shared with Member States when it comes to the negotiation and conclusion of comprehensive investment treaties covering both direct and portfolio investments. Second, the EU has started to actively promote the opening-up of market access for international investments. Third, with regard to the particular model of including pre-establishment investor rights in investment treaties, the GATS-style 'positive list' approach has been preferred, as reflected in the MPoI. These treaty practices are explored below.

3 The Current State of Play within the EU on Market Access

A closer look at EU and the Member State practice on market access in international investment agreements discloses two different scenarios: the EU has focused on market access and pre-establishment liberalisation while the Member States have committed to protect foreign investments once they are admitted. This is due to the shared competence between the EU and the Member States on foreign investment before the Treaty of Lisbon. This dual approach to international agreements by the EU and the Member States with regard to foreign investment is subject to changes after the entry into force of the Treaty of Lisbon.

3.1 EC Market Access Provisions in International Investment Agreements

Already the European Community has been very keen on concluding international agreements related to foreign investment both multilaterally and bilaterally.[37] However-

---

[34] European Commission, *Proposal for a Regulation of the European Parliament and of the Council, Establishing Transitional Arrangements for Bilateral Investment Agreements between Member States and Third Countries*, com (2010) 344 final, 2010/0197(cod) Brussels, 7 July 2010, p. 2.

[35] Ibid., p. 7.

[36] *Regulation(EU) No.* 1219/2012 *of the European Parliament and of the Council of* 12 *December* 2012 *establishing transitional arrangements for bilateral investment agreements between Member States and third countries*, Official Journal L 351, 20 December 2012, 40.

[37] For a detailed collection of the EU's bilateral trade and investment agreements, *see* European Commission, Memo, *The EU's Free Trade Agreements-Where Are We?*, Brussels, 3 December 2013 <trade.ec.europa.eu/doclib/html/150129.htm> (5 March 2014).

er, since it did not have exclusive competence over international agreements regarding international investment before the Treaty of Lisbon, the EC's practice mainly focused on investment in relation to trade. Recent years have witnessed the European Union's willingness to cover a broad range of investment liberalisation and protection provisions in its FTA practice.

3. 1. 1 Multilateral Agreements

3. 1. 1. 1 WTO Agreements

The EC was one of the leading players during the Uruguay Round negotiations which created the WTO.[38] With respect to the exclusivity of its competence to conclude all WTO agreements, the European Court of Justice(ECJ) delivered its Opinion 1/94. Opinion 1/94 confirmed that the European Community had the exclusive competence to conclude the Multilateral Agreement on Trade in Goods but decided that the Community had only shared competences with its Member States to conclude the General Agreement on Trade in Service(GATS) and the Agreement on Trade-Related Intellectual Property Rights(trips Agreement).[39] The GATS, in particular, covered the right of establishment. As one of the four modes of supply service provided in Article I(2) of GATS, 'commercial presence' is widely regarded as referring mainly to investment as it relates to the presence of a subsidiary or a branch. Under Article XVI of the GATS, where a WTO member makes specific commitments on market access, the member is prohibited to impose certain listed limitations on the supply of services, unless it expressly specifies that it retains such limitations. These limitations include measures that would affect the market access of foreign investment.[40] This approach is usually termed as a bottom-up or 'positive list' approach. Given that the ECJ's opinion stated that only cross-frontier supply falls within the exclusive competence of the then EC,[41] the EC shared the competence with the Member State on 'commercial presence' mode of service supply and accordingly on the market access of such investments.

3. 1. 1. 2 Negotiations on the Multilateral Agreement on Investment(MAI)

The draft consolidated text of the MAI, in the negotiations of which both the EC and the Member States participated, also includes provisions on market access. The preamble of the draft expressly states that the Contracting Parties wish to establish a broad multilateral framework for international investment with high standards for the liberalisation of investment regimes.[42] Article III 'Treatment of Investors and Investments' also accords national treatment and most-favoured-nation treatment at the pre-establishment and post-establishment stage. Different from the 'positive list' approach adopted by the GATS, the MAI draft adopted a 'negative list' approach according to which the pre-es-

---

[38] Wenhua Shan, *The Legal Framework of EU-China Investment Relations: A Critical Appraisal*(Hart Publishing 2005) 71.

[39] CJEU, Opinion 1/94, *WTO* [1994] ECR I-5267.

[40] Gomez-Palacio and Muchlinski, *supra* note 6, p. 246.

[41] CJEU, *supra* note 39, para. 46.

[42] OECD, *The Multilateral Agreement on Investment(Draft Consolidated Text)* DAFFE/MAI(98) 7/REV1, 22 April 1998.

tablishment obligations would apply to all economic sectors and laws of the host states, unless those sectors are specifically excluded in the annex or by virtue of one or more of the general exceptions to the proposed agreement.[43]

However, this approach seems to be problematic since the OECD members submitted an exorbitant number of exceptions to the proposed draft.[44] The need for guidelines to handle this matter was felt among delegates. However, this was not effectively achieved, which was believed to be one of the key reasons of the ultimate failure of the MAI negotiations.[45]

3. 1. 1. 3 The Third Revised Decision of the OECD concerning National Treatment(' the Third Decision')

The ' Third Decision' is a binding OECD instrument,[46] which concerns a procedure for notification and examination of measures relating to national treatment. In December 1991, when the Third Decision was adopted by the Council of the OECD, the Commission representative stated that the Community intended to accede to the Decision, on the legal basis of Articles 57 and 113 of the former EC Treaty.[47] With respect to this topic, the ECJ delivered its Opinion 2/92 ruling that the Community has the competence to participate in the Third Decision, but must do so jointly with the Member States, with respect to the matters covered by it that are already the subject of internal legislation containing provisions such as on the treatment to be accorded to foreign-controlled undertakings.[48] The ECJ also held in this Opinion that the Revised Section on National Treatment in the 1976 Declaration on International Investment and Multinational Enterprises, of which the Third Decision is a part, did not deal with the right of the Member States to regulate the entry of foreign investment.[49]

3. 1. 1. 4 The Energy Charter Treaty(ECT)

Based on the non-binding 1991 European Energy Charter, the ECT of 1994,[50] was originally intended to be a multilateral version of a bilateral investment treaty.[51] Both the EC and the Member States joined the ECT, and the ECT was the first treaty under which the EC undertook specific commitments with regard to investment protection.[52] A distinctive feature of the ECT is that pre-establishment obligations are mixed

---

〔43〕 Stefan D. Amarasinha and Juliane Kokott, ' Multilateral Investment Rules Revisited' in P. Muchlinski, F. Ortino and C. Schreuer(eds.), *The Oxford Handbook of International Investment Law* (oup 2008) 144.

〔44〕 Ibid.

〔45〕 Peter T. Muchlinski, ' The Rise and Fall of the Multilateral Agreement on Investment: Where Now?' (2000) 34 *The International Lawyer*, pp. 1033, 1042 – 1043.

〔46〕 OECD, *Third Revised Decision of the Council Concerning National Treatment* < acts. OECD. org/Instruments/ShowInstrumentView. aspx? InstrumentID = 232&InstrumentPID = 227&Lang = en&Book = > (5 March 2014).

〔47〕 Shan, *supra* note 38, pp. 72 – 73.

〔48〕 CJEU, *supra* note 13, paras. 33 – 35. *See also* Shan, *supra* note 38, p. 73.

〔49〕 CJEU, *supra* note 13, para. 22.

〔50〕 The Energy Charter Treaty, 1994 < www. encharter. org/index. php? id = 28 > (5 March 2014).

〔51〕 Sheng Zhang, ' The Energy Charter Treaty and China: Member or Bystander?' (2012) 13 *jwit* 597, 599.

〔52〕 Frank Hoffmeister and Günes Ünüvar, ' From BITs and Pieces Towards European Investment Agreements' in M. Bungenberg, A. Reinisch and C. Tietje(eds.), *EU and Investment Agreements: Open Questions and Remaining Challenges* (Nomos 2013), p. 57, 59.

with post-establishment obligations. Yet in contrast with the multilateral agreement mentioned above, the existing obligations at the pre-establishment stage are provided for in soft-law-like formulations, with the use of statements such as 'shall endeavor' when describing treaty obligations applying to the pre-establishment phase.[53] It is argued that pre-establishment obligations were covered in theory by the provisions on investor-state dispute settlement.[54] It is proposed that a Supplementary Treaty would be adopted to extend this obligation to ensure non-discriminatory treatment also in the pre-establishment phase.[55] However, this proposal remains under discussion among the Treaty's member states.[56]

3.1.2 Bilateral Agreements

Before the Treaty of Lisbon, the EC had managed to insert specific provisions or sometimes a whole chapter on investment into various legal instruments concluded with third countries, mainly in the developing world.[57] These framework agreements include, among others, co-operation agreements, partnership agreements, and free trade agreements.[58]

3.1.2.1 Co-Operation Agreements

Like the framework agreements commonly used by the European Community in order to develop general bilateral trade and economic relations with developing countries, co-operation agreements have managed to cover investment protection. However, their provisions on investment contain no substantial commitments, but are an expression of political will which may open the way for substantial co-operation in investment aspects.[59] Article 12 of the 1985 EC-China Co-operation Agreement,[60] for example, requires the two Contracting Parties to promote and encourage greater and mutually beneficial investment within the framework of their respective laws, rules and policies.

3.1.2.2 Economic Partnership Agreements(EPAs)

As trade and development agreements engaged in regional economic integration process, the EPAs between the EU and the African, Caribbean and Pacific(ACP) Group of States are more than conventional free trade agreements as they focus not only on improving the business environment, but also on the promotion of good economic govern-

---

[53] Paras. (1), (2) and(3) of Article 10 of the Energy Charter Treaty.

[54] Thomas W. Wälde, 'International Investment under the 1994 Energy Charter Treaty-Legal, Negotiating and Policy Implications for International Investors within Western and Commonwealth of Independent States/Eastern European Countries' (1995) 29(5) *J. W. T.* 23.

[55] Energy Charter Secretariat, *The Energy Charter Treaty and Related Documents, A Legal Framework for International Energy Cooperation* (2004) 14 <www.encharter.org/fileadmin/user_upload/document/EN.pdf> (5 March 2014).

[56] Zhang, *supra* note 51, p. 605.

[57] For a detailed analysis of investment provisions in EU FTAS, *see* S. Szepesi, 'Comparing EU Free Trade Agreements: Investment' (InBrief 6D), Maastricht: ecdpm, 2004 <www.ecdpm.org/Web_ECDPM/Web/Content/Navigation.nsf/index2?readform> and <www.ecdpm.org/Web_ECDPM/Web/Content/Content.nsf/0/5EEC2F714800B082C1256EED002C6980?OpenDocument> (5 March 2014).

[58] Shan, *supra* note 38, p. 71.

[59] Shan, *supra* note 11, p. 616.

[60] Agreement on Trade and Economic Cooperation between the European Economic Community and the People's Republic of China, signed 21 May 1985(entry into force 1 October 1985) <ec.europa.eu/enterprise/policies/international/files/f1748_en.pdf> (5 March 2014).

ance. Since the 2000 Cotonou Agreement,[61] the EU-ACP partnership agreements have created substantial commitments on the promotion and protection of foreign investment. The EU has signed a comprehensive EPA with 15 CARIFORUM countries.[62] Title II of the EU-CARIFORUM EPA on 'Investment, Trade in Services and E-Commerce' provides a relatively comprehensive framework for the promotion of mutual investment. Article 60 provides the objective of the treaty, which is the progressive, reciprocal and asymmetric liberalisation of investment.[63] With respect to market access commitments through commercial presence, the EU-CARIFORUM EPA has also adopted a GATS-type 'positive list' approach by setting out the sectors, including sub-sectors, where market access commitments and national treatment apply.[64]

3.1.2.3 FTAS

FTAS are the most common agreements used by the EU to encourage investment liberalisation. Since the EC did not have an exclusive competence in the field of foreign investment before the Treaty of Lisbon, the FTAS which were of mixed competence were a more feasible avenue for the EU to engage in investment issues. After the Treaty of Lisbon, the European Commission still suggests in a communication[65] that it would deal with investment in particular in the context of FTAS on the basis of an exclusive EU competence. This could help bypass the on-going debate on the scope of the EU competence on IIA issues, because according to the 'Pastis Principle,' where there is the slightest element of mixed competence in an agreement, the entire agreement will become mixed.[66]

In early 2000, the EC concluded an FTA with Mexico. Title III on 'Investment and Related Payments' under Chapter IV 'General Exceptions' of the FTA deals with investments and related payments, where the EU, the Member States and Mexico "recall their international commitments with regard to investment, and especially the OECD Codes of Liberalization and the OECD National Treatment Instrument." The EU-Chile Association Agreement of 2002 was the first agreement with a non-European country where full national treatment covering both the pre-and post-establishment stage for both natural and legal persons was granted in the sectors provided for in Annex X of this A-

[61] European Commission, The Cotonou Agreement, signed in Cotonou on 23 June 2000, revised in Luxembourg on 25 June 2005, revised in Quagadougou on 22 June 2010. The full text of the agreement is available at <ec.europa.eu/europeaid/where/acp/overview/ cotonou-agreement> (5 March 2014).

[62] Economic Partnership Agreement between the CARIFORUM States, of the one part, and the European Community and Its Member States, of the other part, signed 15 October 2008 (entry into force: provisional application: 29 December 2008), Official Journal L 289, 30 October 2008, 3. These 15 countries include Antigua and Barbuda, Bahamas, Barbados, Belize, Dominica, Dominican Republic, Grenada, Guyana, Haiti, Jamaica, St. Lucia, St. Vincent and the Grenadines, St. Kitts and Nevis, Suriname, Trinidad and Tobago.

[63] Ibid., Article 60.

[64] Ibid., Articles 66, 67, 68 and Annex IV. For a detailed analysis of the investment commitments in the EU-CARIFORUM EPA, *see* Thomas J. Westcott, 'Investment Provisions and Commitments in the CARIFORUM-EU EPA' (2008) 7(9) *Trade Negotiations Insights* <ictsdrg/i/news/tni/32972> (5 March 2014).

[65] European Commission, *supra* note 4.

[66] The 'Pastis Principle' is drawn from a comparison with the French alcoholic beverage that changes the colour of water. This principle is mentioned by Thomas Baert in an interview. *See* iisd, *supra* note 5.

greement.[67]

As the first FTA after the initiation of the MPoI, the EU-South Korea FTA[68] was believed to have significant legal implications for EU's other ongoing FTA negotiations with other Asian countries,[69] and some even argued that it could be a new model for post-NAFTA FTAS.[70] In the EU-South Korea FTA, the provisions on services and investment are merged into a single and integrated approach concerning establishment and national treatment.[71] One of the objectives set out in Chapter 7 on 'Trade in Services, Establishment and Electronic Commerce' is to improve the investment environment, and in particular the conditions of establishment between the Contracting Parties.[72] With respect to market access through establishment, the EU-South Korea FTA requires that national treatment should be accorded to "establishments and investors" of the other Party.[73] It also follows the GATS-type 'positive list' approach by securing binding market access and national treatment commitments on the economic activities specified in the list of commitments contained in Annex 7-A and subject to any reservations specified therein.[74]

Generally following the structure of the EU-South Korea FTA, the EU-Colombia-Peru FTA[75] and the drafts of other ongoing FTAS negotiations, namely those between the EU and Thailand[76] and the EU and Singapore,[77] adopt the GATS-type 'positive list' approach with respect to market access provisions and the national treatment.

However, the recently being negotiated ceta between the EU and Canada marks a breakthrough because unlike the FTAS discussed so far, it adopts a 'negative list' ap-

---

[67] Article 132 of the Agreement Establishing an Association between the European Community and Its Member States, of the one part, and the Republic of Chile, of the other part, signed 18 November 2002(entry into force 1 February 2003). *See* Hoffmeister and Ünüvar, *supra* note 52, p. 61.

[68] Free Trade Agreement between the European Union and Its Member States, of the one part, and the Republic of Korea, of the other part, signed 15 October 2009(entry into force 1 July 2011), Official Journal L 127, 14 May 2011, 6.

[69] See for example, Yonghyup Oh, 'The EU-Korea FTA: Challenges and Opportunities to China, Japan, Taiwan and South East Asia' 30 November 2011 <www. eias. org/documents/eias_20111130_Oh. pptx>(5 March 2014); also Anne Pollet-Fort, 'The EU-Korea FTA and its Implications for the Future EU-Singapore FTA' (2011)(4) *EU Centre in Singapore Background Brief* <www. eucentre. sg/wp-content/uploads/2013/06/BackgroundBrief-The-EU-Korea-FTA-and-its-Implications-for-the-Future-EU-Singapore-FTA. pdf>(5 March 2014).

[70] Dukgeun Ahn, 'Legal and Institutional Issues of Korea-EU FTA: New Model for Post-NAFTA FTAs?' (2010) *Sciences Po. and GEM Policy Brief* <gem. sciences-po. fr/content/ publications/pdf/ AHN_KOREU%20FTA%20201010. pdf>(5 March 2014).

[71] James Mathis and Eugenia Laurenza, 'Services and Investment in the EU-South Korea Free Trade Area: Implications of a New Approach for GATS V Agreements and for Bilateral Investment Treaties' (2012) 13 *JWIT* 157.

[72] Article 7. 1(1) of the EU-South Korea FTA, *supra* note 68.

[73] Ibid., Article 7. 11.

[74] Mathis and Laurenza, *supra* note 71, p. 168.

[75] Title IV 'Trade in Services, Establishment and Electronic Commerce' of the Trade Agreement between the European Union and Its Member States, of the one part, and Colombia and Peru, of the other part, signed 25 June 2012 (entry into force: Colombia: 1 August 2013; Peru: 1 March 2013), Official Journal L 354, 21 December 2012, 21.

[76] 2013 draft chapter on investment of the EU-Thailand FTA <www. bilaterals. org/spip. php? article 23972&lang=en>(5 March 2014).

[77] Chapter 8 'Service, Establishment and E-Commerce' of the Draft EU-Singapore FTA <trade. ec. europa. eu/doclib/docs/2013/september/tradoc_151743. pdf>(5 March 2014).

proach with respect to the establishment of investment.[78] Indeed, the EU-Canada ceta would be the first FTA with a comprehensive coverage of investment protection in addition to investment liberalisation and therefore it could become a benchmark for future EU investment negotiations.[79] Also different from the approach followed by Canada in its BIT practice, the EU-Canada ceta has a separate article on market access, which may establish absolute market access commitments in addition to pre-establishment national treatment. Article X. 4 on ' Market Access' of the EU-Canada ceta has two paragraphs. Based on Article XVI of the GATS, the first paragraph prohibits several limitations on market access of foreign investments. The second paragraph maintains the Contracting Parties' sovereign power to adopt measures concerning the development or use of land, fair competition in the fields of energy, transport and telecommunications, the concentration of ownership to ensure fair competition, sustainability of natural resources, the number of authorizations, and certain professions such as lawyers or accountants.

The EU draft negotiating mandate for the EU-USA FTA also indicates that the ' negative list' approach would be followed as it provides that,

> The aim of negotiations on investment will be to negotiate investment liberalisation and protection provisions including areas of mixed competence, such as portfolio investment, property and expropriation aspects, on the basis of the highest levels of liberalisation and highest standards of protection that both Parties have negotiated to date. The inclusion of investment protection and investor-to-state dispute settlement will depend on whether a satisfactory solution, meeting the EU interests concerning the issues covered by paragraph 22, is achieved.[80]

3. 1. 2. 4 BITs

So far the EU has not successfully concluded an agreement focusing exclusively on the liberalisation and protection of foreign investment, and a breakthrough may be brought about by the on-going investment negotiations between the EU and China. In October 2013, the Ministers of the Foreign Affairs Council adopted the mandate to allow the European Commission to negotiate the BIT with China, which would be the EU's first ever stand-alone investment agreement since FDI became the exclusive competence of the EU under the Treaty of Lisbon.[81] It should be pointed out that China recently agreed to negotiate a BIT with the US on the basis of a ' negative list' approach

---

[78] Nathalie Bernasconi-Osterwalder, ' The Draft Investment Chapter of the Canada-EU Comprehensive Economic and Trade Agreement: A Step Backwards for the EU and Canada?' *Investment Treaty News*, 26 June 2013 < www. iisd. org/itn/2013/06/26/the-draft-investment-chapter-of-canada-eu-comprehensive-economic-and-trade-agreement-a-step-back wards-for-the-eu-and-canada > (5 March 2014). The publicised text of the Investment Chapter(31 May 2013) may be found at < www. tradejustice. ca/? page_id = 2 > (5 March 2014).

[79] UNCTAD, *Investment Policy Monitor No.* 11, November 2013, 6 < unctad. org/en/Publications Library/ webdiaepcb2013d11_en. pdfY > (5 March 2014).

[80] Bilaterals. org, *EU Draft Negotiating Mandate for EU-USA FTA (5/2013)* < www. bilaterals. org/ spip. php? article23276&lang = en > (5 March 2014).

[81] Europe Commission, Press Release, *EU Investment Negotiations with China and asean*, 18 October 2013 < trade. ec. europa. eu/doclib/press/index. cfm? id = 975 > (5 March 2014).

concerning national treatment.[82] It at least suggests that China would agree to negotiate on market access with the EU in the future BIT. A consensus seems to have been reached in this respect because both the European Commission and the European Parliament have emphasised that the investment deal with China could be reached only on the condition that market access for European companies is granted.[83]

3.2 Member State Practice on Market Access of Foreign Investment

In contrast to the EU's progressively open attitude toward market access, the BITs of the Member States, such as Germany, the United Kingdom, France and Austria, seem to continue to follow the traditional approach of providing only investment protection and leave the regulation of admission to the host states.

In principle the admission of foreign investment is a matter of domestic jurisdiction, and a state may choose not to admit aliens or may impose conditions on their admission.[84] Most of the BITs concluded by the European countries do not grant a right of admission to foreign investors or investments,[85] and this approach is termed by UNCTAD as the investment control model.[86]

When defining the term 'investment,' most Model BITs of the Member States commonly require that investment should be made 'in accordance with national law.'[87] In the recently renegotiated BITs with Canada, Latvia, the Czech Republic and the Slovak Republic also refused to accept pre-establishment NT.[88] The reason Member

[82] mofcom, *mofcom's Spokesman Shen Danyang Comments on China and us to Promote Energetically Negotiations on Bilateral Investment Agreement*, 16 July 2013 < english. mofcom. gov. cn/ article/newsrelease/policyreleasing/201307/20130700200566. shtml > (5 March 2014).

[83] European Commission, Press Release, *Investment Deal with China 'Only under the Conditions that Market Access for European Companies is Granted,'* 18 October 2013 < trade. ec. europa. eu/ doclib/press/index. cfm? id = 976 > (5 March 2014); *European Parliament reso-lution of* 9 *October* 2013 *on the EU-China negotiations for a bilateral investment agreement(*2013/2674*(rsp))* < www. europarl. europa. eu/sides/getDoc. do? type = TA&language = EN&reference = P7 – TA – 2013 – 411 > (5 March 2014).

[84] James Crawford, *Brownlie's Principles of Public International Law* (oup 2012) 608.

[85] Rudolf Dolzer and Christoph Schreuer, *Principles of International Investment Law* (oup 2008) 81.

[86] With respect to admission and establishment, UNCTAD summarises the worldwide BITs and classifies them in the following five categories: the investment control model, the selective liberalisation model, the regional industrialisation programme model, the mutual national treatment model, and the combined NT and MFN model. *See* UNCTAD, *International Investment Agreements: Key Issues-Volume I*, UNCTAD/ITE/IIT/2004/10, 2004, 148 – 153 < unctad. org/en/docs/ iteiit200410_en. pdf > (5 March 2014).

[87] National Board of Trade, *Securing High Investment Protection for EU Investors: A Review of EU Member State's Model BITs*, May 2011, 14. As the total number of BITs between EU Member States and non-EU states is believed to exceed 1,300, a thorough study of all these BITs is neither possible nor realistic. Hence this article will focus on selective model BITs of the Member States.

[88] *See* Article 3(3) of the Agreement between the Government of Canada and the Government of the Republic of Latvia for the Promotion and Protection of Investments, signed 5 May 2009 (entry into force 24 November 2011) < unctad. org/sections/dite/iia/ docs/bits/canada_latvia. pdf > (5 March 2014); Article 3(4) of the Agreement between Canada and the Czech Republic for the Promotion and Protection of Investments, signed 6 May 2009 (entry into force 22 January 2012) < unctad. org/sections/dite/iia/docs/bits/ canada_czech% 20republic. pdf > (5 March 2014); and Article 3(4) of the Agreement between Canada and The Slovak Republic for the Promotion and Protection of Investments, signed 20 July 2010 (entry into force 14 March 2012) < unctad. org/sections/dite/ iia/docs/bits/Canada_slovakia_new. pdf > (5 March 2012).

States have adopted this approach is that market access issues within the EU are dealt with at the European Union level, rather than at Member State level. Some extra-EU BITs go further and provide MFN treatment that covers ' establishment. ' The Finland-China BIT(2003), for example, has such a stipulation.[89] Yet the requirement of ' in accordance with [host state] laws and regulations' is still present. This will, to a large extent, limit the effect of the extension of MFN treatment to the pre-establishment phase. Some other exceptions concern BITs concluded between the US and some Eastern European countries such as Bulgaria, the Czech Republic, Estonia, Latvia, Lithuania, Poland, Romania and Slovenia. These BITs have already embodied national treatment at the pre-establishment stage upon insistence on the part of the United States. The US-Czech Republic BIT of 1991, for example, contains such a national treatment provision in its Article II. 1:

1. Each Party shall permit and treat investment, and activities associated therewith, on a basis no less favorable than that accorded in like situations to investment or associated activities of its own nationals or companies, or of nationals or companies of any third country, whichever is the most favorable, subject to the right of each Party to make or maintain exceptions falling within one of the sectors or matters listed in the Annex to this Treaty. Each Party agrees to notify the other Party before or on the date of entry into force of this Treaty of all such laws and regulations of which it is aware concerning the sectors or matters listed in the Annex. Moreover, each Party agrees to notify the other of any future exception with respect to the sectors or matters listed in the Annex, and to limit such exceptions to a minimum. Any future exception by either Party shall not apply to investment existing in that sector or matter at the time the exception becomes effective. The treatment accorded pursuant to any exceptions shall, unless specified otherwise in the Annex, be not less favorable than that accorded in like situations to investments and associated activities of nationals or companies of any third country.

Clearly this is a typical us BIT of the early 1990s, with preestablishment national treatment accompanied by a negative list of sectoral exceptions. The existence of such BITs demonstrates the diversity of BIT practice within EU Member States.

3.3 Summary

It is clear that two layers of international practice with respect to FDI co-existed at EU and at Member State level. At EU level, the treaty practice on investment has been significantly transformed. First, there has been a change from an initial approach where concrete preestablishment obligations, namely national treatment, were not accepted; then, from a ' positive list' approach to a ' negative list' approach; and from cooperation agreements or EPAs to FTAS and BITs. Indeed, recent EU investment treaty practice has gone beyond its previously adopted policy, particularly on the acceptance of a ' negative list' approach.

At Member State level, whilst most states still stick to the traditional European ap-

---

[89] Article 3(3) of the Agreement between the Government of the Republic of Finland and the Government of the People's Republic of China on the Encouragement and Reciprocal Protection on Investments, signed 15 November 2004(entry into force 15 November 2006) < unctad. org/ sections/dite/iia/docs/bits/china_finland. pdf > (5 March 2014).

proach of not making concrete liberalisation commitments, some BITs have started to accept such obligations by extending MFN and/or national treatment obligations to the stage of investment admission. Hence, a 'mixed' picture is presented.

4 Issues of Market Access Provisions in the Potential Model BIT

To draft market access provisions, the following issues cannot be avoided:

(a) whether or not to accept concrete market access commitments by particularly adopting pre-establishment national treatment;

(b) whether to liberalise foreign investment, whether a 'negative list' or 'positive list' approach should be taken, and accordingly how the list might be drawn up, e. g., by the Union, the Member States or jointly;

(c) how to reconcile market access obligations with other typical treaty norms such as performance requirements, senior management and boards of directors, and MFN clauses; and

(d) whether or not to extend the investor-state dispute settlement(ISDS) mechanism to disputes over market access. The following is a discussion of those critical issues.

4.1 National Treatment in the Pre-Establishment Phase?

Essentially pre-establishment national treatment provisions in investment treaties aims at promoting transparency and stability of the legal framework for foreign investment. Even in countries where BITs require that foreign investment should be admitted in accordance with the domestic laws and regulations, the market access of foreign investment is guaranteed by law, albeit domestic law. Clearly including such provisions in investment treaties has the effect of lifting the protection and guarantee to the level of international law, hence it could significantly improve the stability and transparency of the commitments, as they can no longer be unilaterally changed.

In practice, the decision whether or not to accept pre-establishment NT commitments often relates to the balance between outbound and inbound FDI of an economy. It was observed that a US-styled BIT with provisions on market access would likely have more of an impact than other OECD BITs in promoting overall FDI,[90] because BITs including both investment liberalisation and investment protection could influence FDI flows by opening sectors previously closed to foreign investment.[91] This is particularly

[90] Jeswald W. Salacuse and Nicholas P. Sullivan, 'Do BITs Really Work? An Evaluation of Bilateral Investment Treaties and Their Grand Bargain' in K. P. Sauvant and L. E. Sachs(eds.), *The Effect of Treaties on Foreign Direct Investment: Bilateral Investment Treaties, Double Taxation Treaties and Investment Flows* (oup 2009), pp. 109, 154.

[91] Lisa E. Sachs and Karl P. Sauvant, 'BITs, DTTs, and FDI Flows: An Overview' in K. P. Sauvant and L. E. Sachs(eds.), *The Effect of Treaties on Foreign Direct Investment: Bilateral Investment Treaties, Double Taxation Treaties and Investment Flows* (oup 2009) xxvii, lvi. Through a comprehensive empirical analysis, Axel Berger and others argue that the extent to which international trade and investment agreements attract FDI from other parties depends on the inclusion and strength of key investment provisions in these agreements and they also claim that there is strong evidence that liberal admission rules promote bilateral FDI. *See* Axel Berger and others, 'Do Trade and Investment Agreements Lead to More FDI? Accounting for Key Provisions Inside the Black Box' (2013) 10(2) *International Economics and Economic Policy*, pp. 247, 268.

important for the Member States which are still struggling with the European debt crisis. In the long run, this could help enhance the competitiveness of the EU as a whole. More importantly, market access provisions could guarantee the EU and its Member States comparative advantages with regard to FDI. A high level of openness and transparency in EU Member States would make it much easier for foreign enterprises to start their undertaking. According to Doing Business 2013 of the World Bank, for example, most of the Member States are among the top 60 on the list of rankings in 185 economies.[92] German law, for example, provides foreign investors national treatment and no special legislation impacting FDI except some general restrictions.[93] However, foreign investment from the EU is subject to more restrictive entry requirements. The Business Confidence Survey 2013, published by the European Union Chamber of Commerce in China, for instance, reveals that 45% of European companies lost business opportunities due to market access and regulatory barriers.[94]

Even though most of the BITs signed by the Member States follow the investment control model, the selection of this approach was not due to significant reasons such as the protection of infant industries, natural resources, or even government and private monopolies,[95] but mainly because market access issues are dealt with at the European Union level. Indeed, the Member States do not reject market access. For instance, the EU Member States are members to the OECD Codes of Liberalization which include the Code of Liberalization of Capital Movement. The Code of Liberalization of Capital Movements, which includes the right of establishment and FDI, covers all long-and short-term capital movements between residents of OECD Member States.[96] Against this background, the difference between the EU and the Member States in the practice of market access is not as obvious as it appears. From a technical perspective, Member States are not faced with significant difficulties when it comes to implementing preestablishment national treatment for foreign investment. As mentioned above, the BITs between the US and some Eastern European countries have already adopted the ' negative list' approach on national treatment. Recent years also witnessed the EU's ambition to encourage market access provisions in its FTA negotiations. It can therefore be expected that the EU would continue the liberalisation approach on market access by adopting pre-establishment national treatment provisions in a model or in real investment treaties.

---

〔92〕 19 out of the 28 Member States are among the top 60 economies. For details, *see* World Bank, *Doing Business* 2013*: Smarter Regulations for Small and Medium-Sized Enterprises, International Bank for Reconstruction and Development and the World Bank* (2013) < www. doingbusiness. org/ ~/media/GIAWB/Doing% 20Business/Documents/Annual-Reports/ English/DB13 – full-report. pdf > (5 March 2014). According to the World Bank, research has repeatedly suggested that higher doing business rankings is associated with more foreign investment. Many factors taken into account concern market access, such as starting a business, permit and registration. For more details, *see* World Bank, Ibid.

〔93〕 The US Bureau of Economics and Business Affairs, 2013 *Investment Climate Statement*, April 2013 < www. state. gov/e/eb/rls/othr/ics/2013/204647. htm > (5 March 2014).

〔94〕 European Union Chamber of Commerce in China, *European Business in China: Business Confidence Survey* 2013, 2013 < www. europeanchamber. com. cn/en/publications-business-confidence-survey > (5 March 2014).

〔95〕 Gomez-Palacio and Muchlinski, *supra* note 6, p. 240.

〔96〕 Shan, *supra* note 38, p. 75.

4.2 'Positive List' Approach or 'Negative List' Approach?

As observed above, whilst most of the concluded or on-going FTAS adopt the GATS-type 'positive list' approach, the recently negotiated EU-Canada ceta adopts the 'negative list' approach and the same is likely to be adopted in the future EU-US FTA.

Theoretically, the 'positive list' approach and the 'negative list' approach are not as dramatically different as they appear. The choice between these two approaches is more a technical issue than one of principle. Both of them are methods to compile the list of sectors to demonstrate the level of openness of the investment market to foreign investors. The 'positive list' approach takes a so-called top-down approach which lists the sectors that are open to foreign investors and in which they enjoy national treatment. The 'negative list' approach, on the contrary, takes a bottom-up approach by listing the sectors that are closed in part or in full to foreign investment. By default, all other sectors are open to foreign investment and national treatment can be granted in their respect.

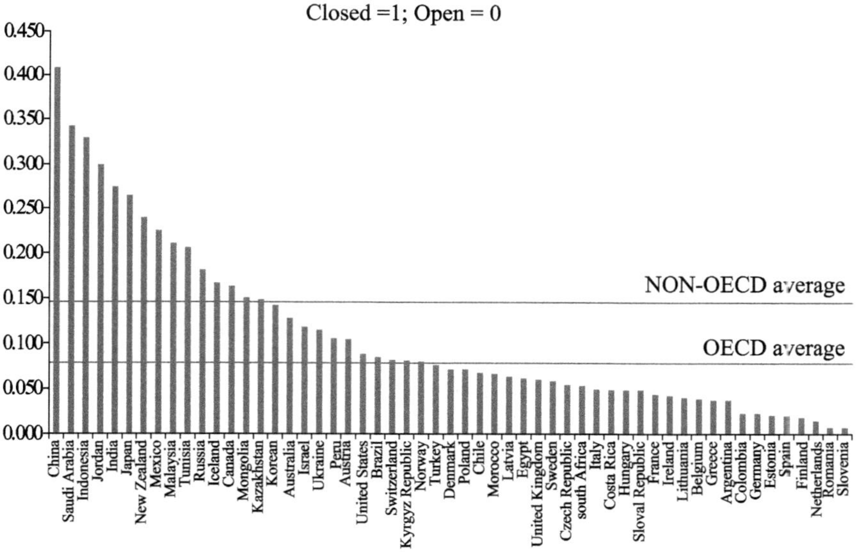

Source: OECD, *FDI Regulatory Restrictiveness Index* 2012 < www. oecd. org/daf/inv/ColumnChart-FDI_RR_Index_2012. pdf > (5 March 2014).

In theory, the positive list can be very open if it effectively lists most sectors, whilst the negative list can be very restrictive if it maintains an overly extensive list of sectors closed or limited to foreign investment. However, in practice, since people (treaty negotiators and compilers of the list) tend to adopt the method that is more 'energy-saving' (in the sense that they do not need to do too much work to draw up the list) and also 'good-looking' (in the sense that the list would not be too long suggesting the host economy is too conservative or restrictive), the 'negative list' approach does imply a more liberal attitude towards foreign investment. Furthermore, there is a more significant difference between the two methods: Under the 'positive list' approach, the host economy does not have to take a complete and thorough 'stick-check' of the competitiveness of each and every sector, as it can offer to open up to foreign investment only the sectors known to be competitive or otherwise appropriate to open up and there is no need to touch other sectors. Under a 'negative list' approach, in contrast, the host economy has to gauge the competitiveness of each and every sector and decide accordingly whether and to what extent such sectors should be opened up. In other words, the negative list requires a complete and thorough knowledge of the strengths and weaknesses of each and every sector of an economy, which requires much more work and much stronger ability on the part of the host economy. Such work and ability are not necessarily required for a 'positive list' approach. This factor is particularly significant for economies that are not familiar with or experienced in adopting such an approach, such as the EU and China. Finally, the 'negative list' approach has an effect of preventing the host economy from adopting measures that provide necessary incentives for domestic investors to promote an industry that may emerge in the future, as the list binds not only existing measures but also measures to be adopted in the future. Such a concern is particularly significant for emerging economies such as the bric countries. It can therefore be said that although the difference between the negative and positive list is a technical one, it is nonetheless a significant technical difference!

On the other hand, the merit of the 'negative list' approach lies in its greater transparency and predictability and, in most cases, higher level of openness. From the FDI regulatory restrictiveness index(see above), it can be concluded that most EU Member States are open to foreign investment. Yet some key strategic partners of the EU, such as China and India, still maintain a higher level of restrictive regulations. A BIT with a 'negative list' approach would therefore most likely create more opportunities for European investors.

As observed above, despite the fact that the GATS-type 'positive list' approach was very popular in investment talks in the WTO,[97] it seems clear that the EU has started to accept the North American-styled 'negative list' approach.[98] When adopting the communication on a comprehensive EU investment policy, for example, the European Council emphasised that, increasing access to non-EU markets and improving the level of protection of European investors should be the main criteria for assessing which option is the most appropriate. . . . It remains crucial that the main focus of international investment agreements should continue to be effective and ambitious investment protection and market access.[99]

Indeed, the 'negative list' approach is essential for the EU in order to exercise its influence on the development of future international investment law in an increasingly

---

〔97〕 International Centre for Trade and Sustainable Development, ' "Positive-List" Approach Popular at WTOI Investment Talks' (10 July 2002) 6: 26 *Bridges Weekly Trade News Digest*.

〔98〕 Chaisse, *supra* note 30, p. 19.

〔99〕 Council of the European Union, *Conclusions on a Comprehensive European International Investment Policy*, 3041st Foreign Affairs Council meeting, Luxembourg, 25 October 2010, p. 3 < www. consilium. europa. eu/uedocs/cms_data/docs/pressdata/EN/foraff/117328. pdf > (5 March 2014).

competitive world. The 'negative list' approach is gaining support worldwide and even major developing states such as China have agreed to negotiate a BIT with the US based on this approach, as already mentioned above.[100] When preparing for the EU-China BIT negotiations, the EU also insisted on the inclusion of pre-establishment national treatment on the basis of a negative list.[101] And the practice of the negative list seems to be that, although it is difficult to start with, once a country has started to adopt the negative list, it tends to stick to it as it does not require much further work but the country might obtain significant benefits out of it. Therefore, it would be a surprise if the EU would steer away from a 'negative list' approach in its investment treaty practice in the future real or Model BIT practice.

4.3 EU or MS Commitments?

Another specific question to be considered in the market access provisions is which party, the EU or the Member States, should be responsible for producing the negative list of non-confirming measures in the BIT. As it would be a BIT between the EU and a counterpart, it would be natural to expect that ultimately it should be the EU that makes commitments on the list as well as on other aspects. Article X. 14 'Reservations and Exceptions' of the EU-Canada ceta follows this approach by providing that both the EU and the Member States should maintain one Schedule in Annex II with respect to sectors, sub-sectors or activities. As a practical matter, however, it may be necessary for the EU to work closely with the Member States when drawing up the list. When necessary it should be possible to incorporate Member State specific exceptions in the negative list. Exactly how this should be done is a more technical matter that can be sorted out in the negotiation process.

4.4 Performance Requirements

Performance requirements could be imposed in connection with the establishment, acquisition, expansion, management, conduct or operation of an investment, or as a condition for the granting of some kind of advantage.[102] As a result, it is closely related to investment admission or market access of foreign investment. Even though performance requirements could be utilised to improve the quality of FDI and maximise its contribution to the development of the local economy, their usage declined during the past decade for reasons such as the need to comply with international commitments, notably the Trade-Related Investment Measures (TRIMs) Agreement, and an increasingly competitive environment for FDI.[103]

It has been argued that performance requirements are one of the most contentious

---

[100] It is believed that the China-US BIT, once concluded, could provide a template for a multilateral framework for investment. Karl P. Sauvant and Huiping chen, 'A China US Bilateral Investment Treaty A Template for a Multilateral Framework for Investment?' *Columbia FDI Perspective*, No. 85, 17 December 2012.

[101] Li Jiabao, 'China, EU Talking Investment' *China Daily usa*, 22 January 2014 <usa. chinadaily. com. cn/epaper/2014-01/22/content_17251011. htm> (5 March 2014).

[102] UNCTAD, *Foreign Direct Investment and Performance Requirements: New Evidence from Selected Countries* (2003) 2 <unctad. org/en/Docs/iteiia20037_en. pdf> (5 March 2014).

[103] Ibid., p. 33.

issues in the area of international investment agreements.[104] The inclusion of a performance requirements clause, as a result, is not a generalised practice worldwide and most performance requirements are already prohibited by the TRIMs Agreement. As with the pre-establishment NT obligation, the main advocates of the inclusion of extensive performance requirements are North American states, namely the us and Canada. Both the US and Canada go beyond the TRIMs Agreement by expanding the list of prohibited measures to include export, technology transfer and product mandating requirements.[105] The 2012 us Model BIT goes further yet by prohibiting local technology requirements.[106]

The EU seems to also have started to embrace such North American-styled performance requirements provisions. Restrictions on performance requirements, for instance, can be found in the EU FTAS signed with Mexico and Chile. They are also present in the BITs between some Eastern European countries and the US.[107] The EU-Canada ceta also includes performance requirements in Article X. 5, which is modeled after Article 7 ' Performance Requirements' of the 2004 Canadian Model BIT. Indeed the EU seems to have proposed the prohibition of some performance requirements that go beyond those of the Canadian Model BIT, e. g. , the requirements to export a given level or percent-age of goods or services, to transfer technology and the requirement for exclusive supply as conditions for the receipt or continued receipt of an advantage.[108]

It can therefore be expected that a performance requirements provision is likely to be included in the potential EU Model BIT. However, given that performance requirements are important policy tools used by the developing countries for the development of their economies,[109] a fine balance has to be maintained between such need of regulatory space and the need to effectively open foreign markets for international investors.

4.5 Senior Management and Boards of Directors

According to customary international law, states enjoy the freedom to adopt measures, such as those concerning visa requirements and the entry of natural persons.[110]

---

[104] Konrad von Moltke, ' A Model International Investment Agreements for the Promotion of Sustainable Development' (2004) *International Institute for Sustainable Development*, November 2004, 10.

[105] *See* Article 8 of the 2004 US Model BIT < www. state. gov/documents/organization/117601. pdf > (5 March 2014) and Article 7 of the 2004 Canada Model BIT < italaw. com/ documents/ Canadian2004 – FIPA-model-en. pdf > (5 March 2014).

[106] Article 8. 1. h of the 2012 US Model BIT < www. italaw. com/sites/default/files/archive/ ita1028. pdf > (5 March 2014).

[107] Article II. 5 of the Treaty between The United States of America and The Republic of Bulgaria concerning the Encouragement and Reciprocal Protection of Investment, signed 23 September 1992 (entry into force 2 June 1994) < unctad. org/sections/dite/iia/docs/bits/us_bulgaria. pdf > (5 March 2014) provides that, "[n] either Party shall impose performance requirements as a condition of establishment, expansion or maintenance of investments, which require or enforce commitments to export goods produced, or which specify that goods or services must be purchased locally, or which impose any other similar requirements."

[108] The publicised text of the Investment Chapter (31 May 2013) of the EU-Canada ceta may be found at < www. tradejustice. ca/? page_id = 2 > (5 March 2014).

[109] UNCTAD, *supra* note 102, p. 41.

[110] J. Anthony Vanduzer, Penelope Simons and Graham Mayeda, '*Integrating Sustainable Development into International Investment Agreements: A Guide for Developing Countries*' (Commonwealth Secretariat 2013) 219 – 220.

However, no investment can effectively be made without the involvement of personnel, *e.g.*, the senior management team and the members of the boards of directors. As a result traditional European BITs require that contracting parties facilitate the entry and stay of persons related to foreign investment, whilst the North American-styled BITs require the facilitation of entry and stay of members of the senior management and boards of directors.[111] The US and Canada adopt a special approach in their Model BITs by narrowing the general prohibition on nationality requirements by an exception permitting host states to require that a majority of the board of directors be of a particular nationality or residence provided that the requirement ' do not materially impair the ability of the investor to exercise control over its investment. '[112]

In the ceta with Canada, the EU accepts the prohibitions of nationality requirements for senior management but disallows nationality requirements for a majority of the investment's board of directors.[113] In the comments to this provision, the EU proposes not to include the exception or to make it a binding obligation against which reservations should be taken, or to omit this obligation as in any case such requirements would be covered under the national treatment. If the exception to allow the nationality requirements for a majority of the investment's board of directors is not included in the ceta, the EU proposes that the parties will list all requirements for nationality/residence relating to senior management and boards of directors. This practice is illustrative of how the EU may approach this issue in the potential Model BIT.

4.6 Applicability of MFN Clauses?

As a carve-out of market access commitments in the future EU BIT, the list of commitments in the Annexes would be carefully negotiated to reflect the economic situation of the contracting parties. There may be one situation where one sector specified in one EU BIT as an exception to the application of NT is not listed as such in a former EU BIT. In this respect, a question may arise whether foreign investors for the specific sector under the new BIT could claim national treatment of the old BIT by virtue of the MFN clause. US practice may provide one solution to this problem. In its Annex II ' Non-Confirming Measures for Service and Investment' of the US-South Korea FTA, the US proposes to reserve its right to adopt or maintain "any measure that accords different treatment to countries under any bilateral or multilateral international agreement in force or signed prior to the date of entry into force of this Agreement, " and to reserve "the right to adopt or maintain any measure that accords different treatment to countries under any bilateral or multilateral international agreement in force or signed after the date of entry into force of this Agreement involving aviation, fisheries or maritime matters including salvage. " The EU may need to consider whether similar reservations should be maintained in its Model or real BITs.

---

[111] Ibid., p. 220.

[112] See for instance, Article 6 ' Senior Management, Boards of Directors and Entry of Personnel' of the 2004 Canadian Model BIT.

[113] Article X.6 ' Senior Management and Boards of Directors' of the EU-Canada ceta.

4.7 Non-Application of ISDS to Pre-Establishment Commitments?

From the EU-Canada ceta, it appears that disputes with respect to pre-establishment commitments are not subject to ISDS.[114] When negotiating the ceta with Canada, the EU proposed that only claims arising out of the host states' breach of the chapter on investment protection may be subject to ISDS.[115] This is also the continuation of EU practice in this respect. Despite the fact that the EU has committed to market access in earlier FTAS, none of these allow disputes concerning market access to be solved under the ISDS mechanism. On the contrary, these disputes are subject to the state-to-state dispute settlement. As far as the Member States are concerned, as mentioned above, most of their bits do not have market access provisions; hence they also do not apply ISDS to the pre-establishment phase.[116] The European Council also considers that it is critical for the EU to ensure that ISDS does not apply to market access-related issues of investment.[117]

It can therefore be expected that the same approach will be adopted by the EU in its future real or Model BIT practice. However, whether there may be changes in this regard, particularly after the Transatlantic Trade and Investment Partnership(TTIP) negotiations with the us, remains to be seen.

5 Conclusion: Towards a ' Global BIT 2.0' ?

The EU investment treaty policy and practice have both developed towards acceptance of concrete pre-establishment obligations notably through the inclusion of pre-establishment national treatment together with a negative list of sectoral reservations and exceptions. The development is of tremendous significance, not only for the investment treaty-making of the EU, but also for the development of a sound investment regime worldwide.

For the EU, a comprehensive international investment treaty regime with market access commitments will provide European investors an open, sound and predictable business environment. The EU as a whole leads the world as the largest recipient and exporter of foreign investment. Comprehensive and transparent admission guarantees in

---

[114] Even though a detailed section on investor-state dispute settlement is not included in the publicised text, the latter specifies that the "scope of ISDS provision will include the non-application of ISDS to pre-establishment."

[115] The leaked document of the ISDS EU-Canada Compromised Table(17 May 2013) is avail able at < www. tradejustice. ca/? page_id = 2 > (5 March 2014). And from a report on the state of play of the EU-Canada ceta by the European Commission, it may be found both the EU and the Canada agreed on the non-application of the ISDS to pre-establishment.

[116] For a detailed analysis, see Nathalie Bernasconi-Osterwalder, *Commentary to the Draft Investment Chapter of the Canada-EU Comprehensive Economic and Trade Agreement(ceta)* (International Institute for Sustainable Development 2013).

[117] Council of the European Union, *Meeting Document from the European Commission to the Trade Policy Committee Concerning the EU Canada Comprehensive Economic and Trade Agreement-Landing zones*, Brussels, 6 November 2012 < lapresse. ca/html/1633/Document_UE_2. pdf > (5 March 2014).

the BITs could stimulate FDI flows.[118] Investment agreements with liberalisation provisions could enable investors from the EU to gain better access to the markets of the Union's strategic partners, in particular China, India and Russia.[119] When contributing to the economic development of these strategic partners, investment liberalization could positively and significantly contribute to the global competitiveness of EU enterprises, whilst preserving jobs at home.[120] Such a comprehensive investment policy will undoubtedly help to achieve the objectives of smart, sustainable and inclusive growth, as set out in the Europe 2020 Strategy.[121] As EU Trade Commissioner Karel De Gucht stated,

> [i]n the long run, a comprehensive investment policy will keep Europe as the world's number one player in the field of foreign direct investment, ensure the best deal for all European businesses, invigorate growth and create jobs at this crucial time.[122]

Beyond the EU, a comprehensive international investment agreement with market access commitments developed by the EU could significantly impact on the development of international investment law. Although most EU Member State BITs only grant post-establishment protection to foreign investment, the pre-establishment national treatment represents a new trend in investment agreements negotiations worldwide. It has been observed that more than 77 countries around the world have adopted such an approach.[123] A comprehensive European international investment agreement could facilitate a greater European influence over international investment agreements and guarantee the EU's leading position in shaping any potential multilateral investment treaty.

As noted above, whether or not to include provisions on investment liberalisation used to be the most significant distinction between European and the North American BITs. The recent practice of the EU and its Member States of accepting the North American-styled pre-establishment obligations is not only closing the gap between the respective investment policies of the two economies, but it also has significant wider implications. By aligning with the North American BITs on this and other significant aspects (such as the definition of indirect expropriation), the two 'worlds' of BITs are converging.

Considering that other major economies such as China, Japan, Canada and India are also moving toward the same direction, it can be argued that the world is moving towards an era of 'Global BIT 2.0,' that is, a new generation of BITs that combines investment protection with investment liberalisation.

Certainly there are still differences on fine details of different BITs concluded by

---

[118] Axel Berger, Matthias Busse, Peter Nunnenkamp and Martin Roy, 'More Stringent BITs, Less Ambiguous Effects on FDI? Not a Bit!' (2010) *Kiel Working Papers* 1621.

[119] European Commission, *supra* note 4, p. 7.

[120] European Commission, *Q&A: Commission Launches Comprehensive European International Investment Policy*, Brussels, 7 July 2010 <trade.ec.europa.eu/doclib/press/index.cfm?id=590> (5 March 2014).

[121] Ibid.

[122] European Commission, *supra* note 26.

[123] MOFCOM, *supra* note 82.

different states. The EU, China and the us, for example, may still have different preferences on how to clarify the meaning of the fair and equitable treatment and on whether ISDS covers pre-establishment obligations. A consensus seems to have been taking place, which is to construct an investment treaty regime that fairly balances the rights and obligations of the stake-holders, reforming the current regime(rather than leaving it intact or abandoning it altogether) in both substantive and procedural provisions. More specifically, on substantive rights, the world seems to have experienced two stages of reform: One is to more carefully define the meaning of the traditional provisions on investment protection; the other is to include concrete market access commitments as the EU and China are doing. On the procedural side, again two broader areas of reform can be identified: on the one hand, states are refining the scope of jurisdiction of investor-state dispute resolution; and on the other, the arbitration procedures are being modified to enhance account-ability of the adjudicators and the credibility of the system as a whole. As consensus is built on such substantive and procedural details in the reform process, the construction of a multilateral investment regime on the basis of a multilateral investment treaty(MIT) becomes all the more likely.

The EU certainly can and indeed should play a significant role in this process and an EU Model BIT would make a notable contribution in that direction. Whilst it is important to move forward to embrace preestablishment commitments, it is equally important to take a holistic approach to the introduction of such commitments. Pre-establishment commitments do not only concern one or two provisions of an investment treaty. Rather they concern an entire regime, ranging from definition to dispute resolution. It is therefore essential to not only pay great attention to the core market access provisions, but also to carefully assess the implications of the inclusion of such provisions on all other relevant provisions, making sure that they co-exist in harmony.

The Potential EU-China BIT: Issues and Implications*

Ⅰ. Introduction

As two of the largest, mutually complementary markets in the world, the European Union(EU) and the People's Republic of China (China) have everything to gain by strengthening their trade and investment ties.[1] Statistics show that the EU and China have become mutually most important partners not only on trade[2] but also on investment. Foreign direct investment(FDI) from the EU accounts for one fifth of total FDI in China, making the EU the largest foreign investor overtaking Taiwan, the US and Hong Kong.[3] Meanwhile both FDI inflows and stocks from China into the EU have been rapidly increasing particularly in recent years.[4] Yet there is still significant potential as EU investment in China represents less than 3% of the EU's total overseas FDI, whilst China's foreign investment in the EU accounts for 1% of the EU's inward

---

* In Marc Bungenberg, August Reinisch, and Christian Tietje (eds.), EU and Investment Agreements: Open Questions and Remaining Challenges, Hart Publishing, 2013. The authors are Shan Wenhua and Zhang Shen. The authors would like to thank the organisers Prof. Marc Bungenberg, Prof. August Reinisch and Prof. Christian Tietje of the International Conference on ' EU and Investment Agreements: Open Questions and Remaining Challenges' for the kind invitation and excellent organisation. They are also grateful to Dr. Michael Waibel for his very helpful comments and suggestions.

〔1〕 Shan Wenhua, *The Legal Framework of EU-China Jnvestment Relations: A Critical Appraisal* (Hart Publishing, 2005) 1.

〔2〕 Recent statistics illustrate that in 2011 China is the first import partner(17. 3%) and second export partner(8. 9%) for the EU, and the EU is the second import partner(13. 2%) and first export partner(20. 1%) for China in 2010. EU Directorate-General for Trade(DG Trade) 'statistics, EU Bilateral Trade and Trade with the World-China', 21 March 2012, available at http: //trade. ec. europa. eu/doclib/docs/2006/september/tradoc_113366. pdf.

〔3〕 DG Trade, Consultation on the future investment relationship between EU and China, Brussels, 2 May 2011, available at http: //trade. ec. europa. eu/doclib/docs/2011/may/tradoc_14786 6. pdf.

〔4〕 EU DG Trade Statistics, above(n. 2) . FDI from China in France, for example, increased five times in 2009 than in 2005. See DG for Trade, European Commission, Summary of contributions to the European Commission's public consultation on ' The future investment relationship between the EU and China' 15, available at http: //trade. ec. europa. eu/doclib/docs/20 11/december/tradoc_148394. pdf. According to this survey, 82% of the EU's respondents felt that FDI from China in their sector of operation was increasing.

FDI.[5] Both Chinese and EU investors are therefore keen on investing in the other side: Chinese investors believe that there could well be good commercial opportunities at a time of economic and financial crisis,[6] and most EU investors in China are optimistic about further growth within their sectors in China.[7]

In the absence of a global investment treaty, bilateral investment treaties(BITs) are the most important instrument for investment protection.[8] Yet there is no BIT between China and the EU itself, but 26 BITs signed between China and EU Member States. Such a fragmented legal framework lacks coordination and coherence and has resulted in an uneven playing field for the protection for both EU and Chinese investors.

A best solution is to have a BIT between the two sides and this view has been endorsed by both parties. Within the EU, the options for enhancing bilateral investment were first provided in the context of a summit meeting in April 2010, which was followed by the launch of a Joint EU-China Investment Task Force in summer 2010 exploring the scope for deeper cooperation on investment, including considerations of a possible standalone BIT.[9] In December 2010, the Investment Agreement Steering Group was set up under DG Trade to work on the impact assessment of the initiative of a new EU-China investment agreement.[10] The China-EU BIT negotiation was formally announced after the 25th meeting of a joint economic and trade commission between China and the EU held in 2011.[11] During the 14th China-EU summit held in February 2012, Chinese Premier Wen Jiaobao agreed with van Rompuy and Barroso that close attention should be paid to facilitating a two-way investment deal as soon as possible.[12] Indeed, it is

---

[5] DG Trade, above(n. 3).

[6] Ding Qingfen and Li Jiabao, 'Euro debt crisis creates opportunities', China Daily, 9 February 2012, available at http://www. chinadaily. com. cn/bizChina – 2012 – 02/09/content_14565938. htm. It is also reported that Europe for the first time became China's biggest region for overseas investment in 2011. See Liz Alderman, Foreign Investment in Europe Starts Anew, International Herald Tribune, 4 March 2012, available at http://www. nytimes. com/2012/03/05/business/global/in-europe-foreign-investment-starts-anew-gingerly. html? pagewanted = all.

[7] In the business confidence survey held by the EU Chamber of Commerce in China, 79% of the respondents give their positive answers when describing the business outlook in China. See European Union Chamber of Commerce in China, European Chamber Business Confidence Survey 2011, May 2011, 5, available at http://www. europeanchamber. com. cn/image s/documents/marketing_department/beijing/publications/2011/Business% 20Confidence% 2 0Survey% 202011_EN. pdf.

[8] UNCTAD, *Bilateral Jnvestment Treaties: 1995 – 2006: Trends in Jnvestment Rulemaking*(United Nations, 2007) 1.

[9] DG Trade, above(n. 3).

[10] DG Trade, 'Roadmap of EU-China investment relations', 21 March 2012, available at http://ec. europa. eu/governance/impact/planned_ia/docs/2012_trade_03_china_investment_agree ment_en. pdf.

[11] Xinhua News Agency, 'China-EU to seek bilateral investment treaty', 15 July 2011, available at http://english. peopledaily. com. cn/90001/90776/90883/7440924. html.

[12] Xinhua New Agency, 'China, EU seek stronger partnership amid Euro debt', 16 February 2012, China Daily, available at http://www. chinadaily. com. cn/bizchina/2012 – 02/16/content _14623589. htm. The full text of the Joint Press Communique of the 14th China-EU Summit may be found at http://news. xinhuanet. com/english/china/2012 – 02/14/c_131410070. htm.

possible that this BIT could be concluded before that of the China-US BIT[13], given that the current Chinese Model BIT is more comparable to the European than the US model.

Against this background, this article attempts to discuss the potential EU-China BIT, focusing on the key issues concerned. The paper first explores the current legal framework governing international investment between China and the EU, especially the developments after the Treaty of Lisbon. It then discusses the structural and specific issues likely to be involved in the potential BIT negotiation. The legal implications of the EU-China BIT are also analysed. It is submitted that the EU-China BIT will help improve EU-China bilateral investment relations, strengthen the legal framework of both China and the EU, and contribute to the development of international investment law.

Ⅱ. The Current Bilateral Legal Framework for China-EU Investment Relations: Key Components and Recent Developments

Currently the legal framework governing China-EU investment relations includes three levels of legal instruments: multilateral, bilateral and domestic[14]. A full discussion of all these three levels of legal framework can be found in an earlier book by Wenhua Shan[15]. This article will focus on the bilateral instruments, which are most closely related to the bilateral investment relationship and which have been under significant changes. They are mainly composed of the 26 BITs between China and EU Member States and the EC-China Cooperation Agreement of 1985.

1. BITs between China and EU Member States

As illustrated in Table 1, since its first BIT with Sweden signed in 1982, China has signed 26 BITs with EU Member States. Ireland is the only exception in this regard. As of April 2012, 23 out of the 26 BITs have entered into force[16]. These BITs can be roughly divided into two different categories reflecting three generations of Chi-

---

〔13〕 Michael S. Snarr, 'Will Europe Conclude A Bilateral Investment Treaty with China Before the United States Does?', China US Trade Law Blog, 22 February 2011, available at http: // www. chinaustradelawblog. com/ 2011/02/articles/investment/will-europe-conclude-a-bilate ral-investment-treaty-with-china-before-the-united-states-does/. On the matter of the conclusion of the China-US BIT, opinions were split in two directions. Some scholars, such as Cai Congyan, argued that a BIT between China and US will be concluded successfully because of China's recent americanised approach to investment treaties and the institutional support given by the China-US Strategic Economic Dialogue. See Cai Congyan, 'China-US BIT Negotiations and the Future of Investment Treaty Regime: A Grand Bilateral Bargain with Multilateral Implications', (2009) 12 Journal of International Economic Law 457. Some such as Axel Berger, however, believed that the future of the China-US BIT was rather bleak due to fundamental differences and the current political environment in the US. See Alex Berger, 'The Politics of China's Investment Treaty Making Program', in: Tomer Broude, Marc L. Busch, and Amelia Porges(eds), *The Politics of Jnternational Economic Law* (Cambridge University Press, 2011), 162 – 185.

〔14〕 Wenhua Shan, 'Towards a New Legal Framework for EU-China Investment Relations', (2000) 34 Journal of World Trade 137, 141. There are basically three investment-related conventions at the multilateral level, namely the WTO Agreement(especially the TRIMS), the ICSID Convention and the MIGA Convention. See *id.*

〔15〕 For a full view of the legal framework governing China-EU investment relations, especially the EU investment in China, see Shan, above(n. 1).

〔16〕 BITs with Cyprus, Latvia and Malta are just signed but not yet entered into force. The China-Czech Republic BIT(2005) has been signed but ratification is still pending, thus the BIT signed between China and the Czech Republic and Slovakia in 1992 is still effective with respect to the Czech Republic.

nese BITs.

Table 1 BITs between China and European Union Member States

Parties	Accession to the EU	BITs with China	Updated Version
Austria	1995	Signed on 12 Sep 1985, effective on 11 Oct 1986	
Belgium	1952	Signed on 4 Jun 1984, effective on 5 Oct 1986	New BIT signed on 6 Jun 2006, effective on 1 Dec 2009
Bulgaria	2007	Signed on 27 Jun 1989, effective on 21 Aug 1994	A protocol signed on 26 June 2007, effective on 10 Nov 2007
Cyprus	2004	Signed on 15 Jan 2001	
Czech	2004	Signed on 4 Dec 1991, effective on 1 Dec 1992	New BIT signed on 8 Dec 2005
Denmark	1973	Signed on 29 Apr 1985, effective on 29 Apr 1985	
Estonia	2004	Signed on 2 Sep 1993, effective on 1 Jun 1994	
Finland	1995	Signed on 4 Sep 1984, effective on 26 Jan 1986	New BIT signed on 15 Nov 2004, effective on 15 Nov 2006
France	1952	Signed on 30 May 1984, effective on 19 Mar 1985	New BIT signed on 26 Nov 2007, effective on 20 Aug 2010
Germany	1952	Signed on 7 Oct 1983, effective on 18 Mar. 1985	New BIT on 1 Dec 2003, effective on 11 Dec 2005
Greece	1981	Signed on 25 Jun 1992, effective on 21 Dec 1993	
Hungary	2004	Signed on 29 May 1991, effective on 1 Apr 1993	
Ireland	1973		
Italy	1952	Signed on 28 Jan 1985, effective on 28 Aug 1987	
Latvia	2004	Signed on 15 Apr 2004	
Parties	Accession to the EU	BITs with China	Updated Version
Lithuania	2004	Signed on 8 Nov 1993, effective on 1 Jun 1994	
Luxembourg	1952	Signed on 4 Jun 1984, effective on 5 Oct 1986	New BIT signed on 6 Jun 2006, effective on 1 Dec 2009

续表

Parties	Accession to the EU	BITs with China	Updated Version
Malta	2004	Signed on February 2009	
Netherlands	1952	Signed on 17 Jun 1985, effective on 1 Feb 1987	New BIT signed on 26 Nov 2001, effective on 1 Aug 2004
Poland	2004	Signed on 7 Jun 1988, effective on 8 Jan 1989	
Portugal	1986	Signed on 3 Feb 1992, effective on 1 Dec 1992	New BIT signed on 9 Dec 2005, effective on 26 Jul 2008
Romania	2007	Signed on 14 Jul 1994, effective on 1 Sep 1995	A protocol signed on 16 Apr 2007, effective on 1 Sep 2008
Slovakia	2004	Signed on 4 Dec 1991, effective on 1 Dec 1992	A protocol signed on 7 Dec 2005, effective on 25 May 2007
Slovenia	2004	Signed on 13 Sep 1993, effective on 1 Jan 1995	
Spain	1986	Signed on 6 Feb 1992, effective on 1 May 1993	New BIT signed on 24 Nov 2005, effective on 1 Jul 2008
Sweden	1995	Signed on 29 Mar 1982, effective on 29 Mar 1982	A protocol signed on 27 Sep 2004, effective on 27 Sep 2004
UK	1973	Signed on 15 May 1986, effective on 15 May 1986	

Source: compiled by the author on the basis of bilateral investment treaties published by the Ministry of Commerce of the Peoples' Republic of China(MOF COM): http://tfs.mofcom.gov.cn/aarticle/Nocategory/201111/20111107819474.html.

China was rather conservative in its BIT practice in its first and second generation of BITs(1979 – 1998):[17] only disputes concerning the amount of compensation could be submitted to international arbitration, whilst there was no commitment to substantial national treatment(NT).[18] These two generations reflect the Chinese FDI policy established since 1979, namely the ' three guiding principles' of international economic coop-

[17] The 1980s correspond to the first-generation of Chinese BITs; most of the 1990s to the second-generation BITs. BITs of both the first and second generations are very conservative, and the difference between the first and second generation lies in the fact that the latter have started to make unconditional reference to ICSID arbitration since China ratified the ICSID Convention on 7 January 1993.

[18] More details, see Norah Gallagher and Wenhua Shan, *Chinese Jnvestment Treaties: Policies and Practice* (OUP, 2009), 35 – 43. Stephan W. Schill, ' Tearing Down the Great Wall: the New Generation Investment Treaties of the People's Republic of China', (2007) 15 Cardozo Journal of International and Comparative Law, pp. 73, 77 – 83. Ling LI, ' Chinese BIT Practice and Challenges', Speech at the 2010 Chinese Society of International Economic Law Annual Conference, 16 October 2010, Nanjing, China, and Berger, above(n. 13), pp. 172 – 3.

eration and exchange: state sovereignty, equality and mutual benefit, and reference to international practice.[19] To promote the inflows of FDI from developed countries, Chinese BITs at this stage are mainly signed with major European countries.[20] China signed BITs with 23 Member States during these two generations. Though these BITs shared the same simple format and most substantial clauses, such as fair and equitable treatment (FET), most-favoured-nation(MFN) treatment, compensation against expropriation, subrogation, state-tostate dispute settlement, they varied in some aspects. For instance, only the BITs signed with the Czech Republic, Slovakia, Slovenia, Spain and the UK include NT clauses[21]. Also, with respect to investor-state dispute settlement, some BITs, such as the BITs with Germany, Finland, Italy, Denmark, Austria and Portugal, do not provide reference to ICSID arbitration, which could be found in the BITs with Romania, Estonia, Hungary, and Lithuania.[22] And the China-Sweden BIT(1982) does not include a clause on the settlement of investor-state disputes but only provides for a future supplementary agreement on ICSID arbitration.

The year 1998 witnessed the beginning of the third generation partly because the Chinese Government decided to implement a 'Going Abroad' strategy focusing on investing abroad.[23] As a result, a more liberal BIT regime was adopted by China, which notably included access to ICSID arbitration for all investor-state disputes and a substantial national treatment commitment.[24] Such changes can be seen not only in newly-signed BITs but also in re-negotiated BITs or their amending protocols. For example, BITs with the Belgium-Luxemburg Economic Union, Finland, France, Germany, the Netherlands,

---

[19] MeizhenYao, 'Legal Protection of International Investment', in *Selected Articles from Chinese Yearbook of Jnternational Law* (Zhongguo guo ji fa xue hui, 1983), pp. 169 – 186. See also Qingjiang Kong, 'Bilateral Investment Treaties: The Chinese Approach and Practice', (1998 – 1999) 8 Asian Yearbook of International Law, pp. 105, 110. See also Wenhua Shan, Norah Gallagher and Sheng Zhang, 'National Treatment for Foreign Investment in China: A Changing Landscape', (2012) 27 ICSID Review, p. 120.

[20] Admittedly China also signed BITs with other developing states and transition economies, but such BITs were signed more for diplomatic purposes than for investment protection since the Chinese economy was not strong enough to invest abroad. See for example the Chinese BITs with Romania(1983), Thailand(1985), Sri Lanka(1986) and Poland(1988). Ling Li, above(n. 18).

[21] See Article 3(2) of the China-Czechoslovakia BIT(1991) and Article 1 of its Protocol, Article 3(2) of the China-Slovenia BIT(1993), Article 3(4) of the China-Spain BIT(1992) and Article 3(3) of the China-UK BIT(1986). National treatment provisions in these BITs also vary. BITs with the UK and Slovenia take the same approach by providing that 'either Contracting Party shall to the extent possible, accord treatment in accordance with the stipulations of its laws and regulations to the investments of nationals or companies of the other Contracting Party the same as that accorded to its own nationals or companies'. The China-Spain BIT(1992) includes a provision saying that NT should be accorded in accordance with the laws and regulations of the host states. Article 2 of the Protocol to the China-Czechoslovakia BIT(1991) provides that 'it shall not be deemed' treatment less favourable' for either Contracting Party to accord discriminatory treatment, in accordance with its laws and regulations, to national and companies of the other Contracting Party, in case it is really necessary for the reasons of public order, national security, or sound development of national economy'.

[22] Article 9 of the China-Romania BIT(1994), Article 8(5) of the China-Estonia BIT(1994), Article 10(3) of the China-Hungary BIT(1993) and Article 8(3) of the China-Lithuania BIT(1993).

[23] See Cai Congyan, 'Outward Foreign Direct Investment Protection and the Effectiveness of Chinese BIT Practice', (2006) 7 The Journal of World Investment & Trade pp. 621, 627 – 631.

[24] Details can be found in Gallagher and Shan, above(n. 18), pp. 39 – 43.

Portugal, and Spain were renegotiated, whilst protocols were signed with Bulgaria, Romania, Slovakia and Sweden to supplement the BITs in force. Meanwhile, China signed BITs with Cyprus, Latvia and Malta. These BITs are more complicated and provide more comprehensive protection of FDI compared with the older generation ones, but they also vary in some details. The limitation of ' in accordance with its laws and regulations' , for instance, in the definition of ' investment' commonly found in Chinese BITs, was removed in the new China-Germany BIT(2003).[25] Whilst most BITs do not assume NT or MFN treatment for the pre-establishment stage, the China-Finland BIT(2004) extends MFN treatment to the pre-establishment stage.[26] Also, the ' cooling-off period' for investor-state dispute resolution differs: Six months are provided for in the BITs with Portugal and Spain,[27] while three months are required in the BIT with Finland and the 2004 Protocol to China-Sweden BIT.[28] Given that MFN treatment is provided in all Chinese BITs, investors from the EU or China might be able to rely on more favourable provisions in treaties with third states.[29] Accordingly, investors from Member States which only signed first or second generation BITs with China might be accorded the more comprehensive protection provided in the thirdgeneration BITs between other Member States and China by way of the MFN clause. Whilst the MFN clause helps level the protection of investments between China and the EU Member States, its effect is not always certain, particularly when it comes to the question of whether the MFN clause could cover investor-state dispute settlement. Arbitration practice has confirmed that it is possible to use the MFN clause to bypass purely procedural matters, for example, to shorten the cooling-off period from 18 months to three months as the *Maffezini* award decided. It would not however be safe to assume that, for instance, investors from the UK would be able to invoke the MFN clause to obtain the more favourable disputeresolution provisions provided in the China-Germany BIT(2003), which includes consent to ICSID arbitration as an option for all disputes.[30] In the first ICSID case concerning the interpretation of Chinese BITs, *Tza Yap Shum v. Peru,*[31] the tribunal rejected the claimant's attempt to rely on the MFN provision to extend the scope of the arbitration clause by invoking Article 12 of the Peru-Columbia BIT in order to enable the tribunal to decide on non-expropriation breaches of the treaty including notably breaches of FET and full protection obligations.[32]

---

[25] Article 1 of the China-Germany BIT(2003). It nevertheless maintains in Article 2(1) that each contracting party shall ' admit such investments in accordance with its laws and regulations' .

[26] Article 3(3) of the China-Finland BIT(2004).

[27] Article 9(2) of the China-Portugal BIT(2005) and Article 9(2) of the China-Spain BIT(2005).

[28] Article 9(2) of the China-Finland BIT(2004) and Article 1 of the 2004 Protocol to China-Sweden BIT.

[29] In the *MTD v. Chile* case, the tribunal held that the investor from Malaysia was able to rely on the MFN clause in the Malaysia-Chile BIT to benefit from the substantive protections in the Croatia-Chile and Denmark-Chile BITs to award permits to approved investments. See *MTD Equity Sdn. Bhd. and MTD Chile S. A. v. Chile*, ICSID Case No. ARB/01/7, Award, 25 May 2004.

[30] See also, Gallagher and Shan, above(n. 18) 156.

[31] *Tza Yap Shum v. Peru*, ICSID Case No. ARB/07/6.

[32] *Tza Yap Shum v Peru*, ICSID Case No. ARB/07/6, Decision on Jurisdiction and Competence, 19 June 2009.

2. The China-EC Cooperation Agreement

The 1985 China-EC Trade and Economic Cooperation Agreement[33] (China-EC Cooperation Agreement) is the framework agreement between China and the EU (then the EEC) on trade and economic cooperation. It replaced the China-EEC Trade Agreement signed in 1978. This Agreement has four chapters, Chapters 1, 3 and 4 relate to trade cooperation, a 'Joint Committee' and final provisions, and Chapter 2 defines various forms of economic cooperation.

The China-EC Cooperation Agreement is mainly aimed to promote and intensify trade and to encourage the steady expansion of economic cooperation in the mutual interest of both parties. Investment issues are addressed in Chapter 2. Article 12 requires the two parties to promote and encourage greater and mutually beneficial investment. The parties undertake to improve the existing favourable investment climate particularly through encouraging the extension of investment promotion and protection agreements based on the principles of equity and reciprocity.[34] Since this investment clause imposes no substantial obligation on the contracting parties, it has a more symbolic than practical value. Nevertheless it lays down a general legal basis for future cooperation in this field.[35] In 1994 and 2002 the Cooperation Agreement was supplemented by exchanges of letters establishing broader political dialogue between the two sides.

Currently, China and the EU are negotiating a Partnership and Cooperation Agreement (PCA) to replace the Cooperation Agreement. After being agreed upon during the 2006 EU-China Summit in Helsinki, negotiations on the PCA started in early 2007. In addition to updating the Cooperation Agreement, it will cover the political as well as the economic dimensions of EU-China relations. Understandably, trade and investment will form an important part of the agreement through the inclusion of technical barriers to trade, investment, competition, intellectual property rights (IPRs), and public procurement among other issues. Other issues, such as labour standards and environmental protection, might also be included as advocated by the EU.[36] A trade sustainability impact assessment (Trade SIA) was completed in 2007 for the negotiations of the PCA and the final report was presented in September 2008.[37] Different from the Cooperation Agreement, the PCA is intended to cover substantial provisions on both trade and investment. In this respect, one policy option proposed by the European Commission to fulfil the need of an EU-level investment liberalization and protection is to utilise the renegotia-

---

〔33〕 Officially the Agreement on Trade and Economic Co-operation between the European Community and the People's Republic of China, OJ L 250/2, 19. 9. 85.

〔34〕 Article 12 of the China-EC Cooperation Agreement, *id.*

〔35〕 Shan, above (n. 1) 94 – 95.

〔36〕 EU, Commission Paper on the 'Trade Sustainability Impact Assessment of the Negotiations of a Partnership and Cooperation Agreement between the EU and China', February 2009, available at http://trade.ec.europa.eu/doclib/docs/2009/february/tradoc_142373.pdf.

〔37〕 The final report is available at http://trade.ec.europa.eu/doclib/docs/2008/september/tradoc_140579.pdf.

tion of the PCA without the need to negotiate a new standalone investment agreement.[38] However, a standalone BIT would be preferred since the negotiation and conclusion of the PCA is a hard and time-consuming process due to its comprehensive coverage and the complexity involved in the process.[39]

3. The impact of the Treaty of Lisbon

The Treaty of Lisbon, which entered into force on 1 December 2009, has managed to include 'foreign direct investment' in the 'Common Commercial Policy' of the EU, thus vesting exclusive competence over FDI in the EU. However, the Treaty of Lisbon did not define FDI. As a result, different interpretations have been given to its scope.[40] The better view is that 'foreign direct investment' is different from 'foreign investment', as the latter includes short-term portfolio investment which is usually also covered by BITs.[41] This view has been confirmed by the EU in its 2010 Commission Communication.[42]

The Treaty of Lisbon bears significant implications for both intra-and extra-EU BITs.[43] For extra-EU BITs, of which Chinese BITs with EU Member States form a part, the first question is whether they need to be terminated or modified. Under either international law or EU law, the existing extra-EU BITs shall not be terminated or superseded. Under general international law, as spelt out in Article 30(4) of VCLT, 'a treaty between two parties will not be superseded by a subsequent treaty that one of the parties enters into with a third party'.[44] Under EU law, Article 351 of the Treaty of Lisbon(ex-Article

---

[38] DG Trade, above(n. 3). One participant in the public consultation, the Automobile Manufacturers' Association, supports that some key issues related to investment, such as environment protection can be achieved under the PCA. It favours the integration of sustainable development issues in the PCA, to ensure the cooperation on the environment is reflected in the EU-China partnership, see DG for Trade, above(n. 4) 4 – 5.

[39] Zeng Lingliang, 'A Preliminary Perspective of Negotiations of EU-China PCA: A New Bottle Carrying Old Wine or New Wine or Both?', (2009) 15 European Law Journal 121.

[40] Wenhua Shan and Sheng Zhang, 'The Treaty of Lisbon: Half Way toward a Common Investment Policy', (2010) 21 European Journal of International Law 1049, 1060 – 5.

[41] Wenhua Shan and Sheng Zhang, *id.*, 1050 – 7.

[42] The Commission Communication points out that '[t]his(FDI) contrasts with foreign investments where there is no intention to influence the management and control of an undertaking. Such investments, which are often of a more short-term and sometimes speculative nature, are commonly referred as "portfolio investments".' European Commission, Communication from the Commission to the European Parliament, the Council, the European Economic and Social Committee and the Committee of the Regions, 'Towards a comprehensive European international investment policy', COM(2010) 343 final, Brussels, 7 July 2010, 3, available at http://trade.ec.europa.eu/doclib/docs/2011/may/tradoc_147884.pdf.

[43] For more information about the legal implications of the Treaty of Lisbon on intra-EU BITs see, Shan and Zhang, above(n. 41), 1065 – 8. See also H. Wehland, 'Intra-EU investment agreements and arbitration: Is European Community law an obstacle', (2009) 58 International and Comparative Law Quarterly, 297, 297 – 320, and Armand De Mestral C. M., 'The Lisbon Treaty and the Expansion of EU Competence Over Foreign Direct Investment and the Implication for Investor-State Arbitration', in Karl P. Sauvant(ed) *Ybk Jnt'l Jnv. L. & Pol'y* 2009 – 2010 (OUP, 2011), 365 – 394.

[44] Article 30(4) of the VCLT states that: '4. When the parties to the later treaty do not include all the parties to the earlier one:

(a) as between States Parties to both treaties the same rule applies as in paragraph 3;

(b) as between a State party to both treaties and a State party to only one of the treaties, the treaty to which both States are parties governs their mutual rights and obligations.'

307 TEC) expressly states that rights and obligations arising from agreements between a Member State and a third state concluded before the entry into force of the present treaty shall not be affected by the provisions of the Treaties.[45] However, the Member States may be required by the European Commission to 'take appropriate steps to eliminate the incompatibilities established' between EC Law and the BITs with non-EU states.[46]

However, since the EU has obtained exclusive competence over FDI after the Treaty of Lisbon, its Member States could no longer negotiate BIT on their own. From an international law perspective, according to the rules of good faith laid down in Article 18 of the VCLT,[47] the Member States have the obligation to refrain from concluding new BITs which would defeat the object and purpose of the Treaty of Lisbon. From an EU law perspective, Article 2(1) of the Treaty of Lisbon provides that only the EU has the right to legislate and adopt legally binding acts where exclusive competence in a specific area is conferred on the EU, and the Member States can do so themselves only if so empowered by the EU or for the implementation of EU acts.[48] This general rule applies to international agreements insofar as the competence of the EU is exclusive.[49] The reactions of the Member States, however, have been diverse. When negotiating amendments of the BIT with Canada prior to its accession to the EU, Hungary indicated that the decision of whether or not to sign the BIT would rely on the entry into force of the forthcoming EU Regulation on the external investment protection agreements of its Member States and the conclusion of a Comprehensive Economic and Trade Agreement between the EU and Canada.[50] Other Member States, such as Germany, Slovakia, Portugal, Latvia, Belgium,

---

〔45〕 The Article states that:

'The rights and obligations arising from agreements concluded before 1 January 1958 or, for acceding States, before the date of their accession, between one or more Member States on the one hand, and one or more third countries on the other, shall not be affected by the provisions of the Treaties.

To the extent that such agreements are not compatible with the Treaties, the Member State or States concerned shall take all appropriate steps to eliminate the incompatibilities established. Member States shall, where necessary, assist each other to this end and shall, where appropriate, adopt a common attitude'.

〔46〕 Id. Indeed, the European Commission also made continuous efforts in practice to assert and expand its foreign investment competence, see Shan and Zhang, above(n. 41) 1052 – 1056.

〔47〕 Article 18 of the VCLT reads as follows:

'A State is obliged to refrain from acts which would defeat the object and purpose of a treaty when:

(a) it has signed the treaty or has exchanged instruments constituting the treaty subject to ratification, acceptance or approval, until it shall have made its intention clear not to become a party to the treaty; or

(b) it has expressed its consent to be bound by the treaty, pending the entry into force of the treaty and provided that such entry into force is not unduly delayed'.

〔48〕 Article 2(1) of TFEU.

〔49〕 Jan Asmus Bischoff, 'Just a Little of "Mixity"? The EU's Role in the Field of International Investment Protection Law', (2011) 48 Common Market Law Review, 1527, 1546.

〔50〕 Foreign Affairs and International Trade Canada, 'Background on the Canada-"EU 6" Foreign Investment Promotion and Protection Agreement(FIPA) Negotiations', available at http://www.international.gc.ca/trade-agreements-accords-commerciaux/agr-acc/fipa-apie/eu6-ue6.aspx?menu_id = 34&view = d. Among the six Member States (the Czech Republic, Hungary, Latvia, Poland, Romania and Slovakia) which acceded to the EU in 2004, Canada has signed amended treaties with Latvia(on 5 May 2009), the Czech Republic(on 6 May 2009), Romania(on 8 May 2009), and the Slovak Republic(on 20 July 2010). These treaties have now been ratified and are entering into force-Latvia(November 2011), the Czech Republic(January 2012), Romania(November 2011) and the Slovak Republic(March 2012).

Spain and Lithuania, continue to conclude new BITs even after the Treaty of Lisbon.[51] These new BITs, according to some scholars, are illegal.[52]

In order to address the conflict between the Treaty of Lisbon and the extra-EU BITs, the European Commission brought forward in July 2010 a proposal for a regulation establishing transitional arrangements for BITs between Member States and third countries.[53] The Regulation Proposal was accompanied by a communication with the goal of creating a ' comprehensive European international investment treaty' to situate the proposed regulation.[54] The aim of the Regulation Proposal is to clarify the status of extra-EU BITs, authorise the continued existence of all extra-EU BITs currently in force, and provide for an explicit guarantee of legal certainty as regards the conditions under which investments operate.[55] It obliges the Commission to review all current extra-EU BITs in force in order to assess their compliance with Union law.[56] Moreover, it provides the terms, conditions and procedures by which Member States may conclude or retain extra-EU BITs.[57] The Commission's Regulation Proposal was adopted by the European Parliament in May 2011.[58] Also, the Commission's Communication ' Towards a comprehen-

---

[51] The list of new BITs includes the Germany-Pakistan BIT(2009), Slovakia-Vietnam BIT(2009), Belgium-Montenegro BIT(2010), Latvia-India BIT(2010), Spain-Mozambique BIT(2010), Portugal-Senegal BIT(2011), Lithuania-FYR of Macedonia BIT(2011), Lithuania-India BIT(2011), Portugal-United Arab Emirates, Slovakia-Kenya BIT (2011). See UNCTAD, ' Investment Policy Monitor Series between December 2009 and January 2012', available at http://archive.unctad.org/Templates/Page.asp?intItemID=5237&lang=1.

[52] Julien Chaisse, ' Promises and Pitfalls of the European Union Policy on Foreign Investment-How Will the New EU Competence on FDI Affect the Emerging Global Regimes?', (2012) 15 Journal of International Economic Law 1, note 28, p. 4.

[53] European Commission, ' Proposal for a Regulation of the European Parliament and of the Council Establishing Transitional Arrangements for Bilateral Investment Agreements between Member States and Third Countries' (COM(2010) 344 final, 7 July 2010).

[54] European Commission, above(n. 42).

[55] European Commission, above(n. 53), Preamble.

[56] Id., Chapter II.

[57] Id., Chapter Ⅲ.

[58] European Parliament, European Parliament legislative resolution of 10 May 2011 ' On the proposal for a regulation of the European Parliament and of the Council establishing transitional arrangements for bilateral investment agreements between Member States and third countries' (COM(2010) 0344 - C7 - 0172/2010 - 2010/0197(COD)), 10 May 2011, Strasbourg, available at http://www.europarl.europa.eu/sides/getDoc.do?type=TA&language=EN&reference=P7-TA-2011-206. However, some argued that this proposal was ' poorly and incoherently drafted'. See Asmus Bischoff, above(n. 49), 1559. Julien Chaisse proposed a different option to map the transition phase, which consists of a progressive replacement of selected existing BITs with a country by a new agreement negotiated with the same partner country. According to his observation, he argued that this would be achieved by an inclusion of a clause in the chapter of ' investment' in a preferential trade agreement (PTA) saying that the termination of existing BITs when the new PTA comes into force, while the ' old' extra-BITs could be listed in a subsequent provision. However, he also admitted that this option could be achieved only in the case that the future EU investment agreement with a specific country ' has equivalent scope and provides for at least an equivalent treatment as' the former extra-EU BIT with the country in question. See Chaisse, above(n. 52), 30 - 1. Indeed, how to judge the term of ' equivalent' is a critical issue. Can we say, for example, that a new BIT focusing on the balance of investment protection and host state regulation provides ' equiv-alent treatment' as the ' old' BIT only addressing the promotion and protection of foreign investment? If the answer is ' no', the ' old' BIT could not be replaced by the new one because it is not compatible with the VCLT. On the other hand, the negotiation is not only up to EU or its Member States, but also up to the position of the third party.

sive European international investment law' was endorsed by the European Council in October 2010[59] and adopted by the European Parliament in April 2011.[60]

The existing extra-EU BITs will therefore continue to be effective before they are amended or replaced by the future EU investment treaty. It is pointed out in the Commission's Regulation Proposal that the procedure established must be regarded as an exceptional transitional procedure since the EU is exclusively competent for FDI and an EU investment policy will be gradually developed.[61] In its most recent document addressing investment and the EU economy, the EU said explicitly that it could negotiate on behalf of its 27 Member States on both the liberalisation and protection of investments.[62] It also pointed out that the EU would gradually replace the bilateral investment treaties concluded between EU Member States and third countries, which amount nearly to half of the worldwide total of BITs.[63]

4. Summary

The current bilateral legal framework between China and the EU covering mutual investment is primarily composed of the BITs between China and EU Member States and the Cooperation Agreement between China and the EU. Since the former is fragmented and the latter is outdated, the current bilateral legal framework is clearly insufficient for the purpose of mutual investment promotion and protection, particularly given the growing importance of the two parties, globally and between each other. Indeed, the need for an enhanced investment arrangement between the two sides has already been strongly felt. In the aforementioned European Commission's Communication entitled ' Towards a comprehensive European international investment policy', China was identified by the Commission as one of the key countries with which new investment agreements are particularly desirable.[64] The EU's public consultation on ' the future investment relationship between the EU and China' also confirms that China will be an increasingly strategic market for EU investors.[65] Most of the participants in the public consultation believe an EU-China agreement would contribute to clarifying the legal and operational framework for EU investors in China, thus reciprocally increasing efficiency and business confidence. They also believe that it would have a positive effect on employment and labour standards, environment and human rights.[66]

To address the EU-China investment relations, DG Trade issued a Roadmap in

---

[59] Council of the European Union, ' Conclusions on a comprehensive European international investment policy', 3014st Foreign Affairs Council Meetings, Luxembourg, 25 October 2010.

[60] European Parliament, above(n. 58).

[61] European Commission, above(n. 53), explanatory memorandum.

[62] European Union, ' Investment and the EU economy', available at http://trade. ec. europa. eu/doclib/docs/2012/april/tradoc_149332. pdf.

[63] Ibid.

[64] European Commission, above(n. 42)7.

[65] Sixty percent of the business respondents in this consultation foresaw China as a top-five destination for investment in their sector in 10 years' time. Meanwhile, 11 business respondents predict that China will become a more important destination for investment in their sector in 10 years' time than it is now. See DG for Trade European Commission, above(n. 4)4.

[66] Ibid., 4 – 5.

March 2012, which was expected to be adopted in October 2012,[67] but as of today it is still pending. Three policy options were provided in this Roadmap: the first option would be to leave the existing BITs between China and EU Member States untouched but only to continue the negotiations of the PCA; the second option would be to negotiate a standalone investment protection agreement to replace the existing 26 BITs but not include pre-establishment elements in such an agreement; the third option would be to negotiate a comprehensive investment agreement covering both pre-and post-establishment investment.[68] The third option is preferred by the EU's policymakers, since the first one would not improve the mutual investment climate and the second is 'unlikely to significantly help increase FDI flows between both partners'.[69] It is pointed out in the Roadmap that a comprehensive investment agreement would have considerable impact on investment flows, provide higher protection of European investors, guarantee market access and, most importantly, provide one single framework for the protection of FDI.[70] A large majority of the participants in the aforementioned public consultation also welcome one single investment agreement between China and EU.[71] This is furthermore echoed in the proposition made by the European Union Chamber of Commerce in China in its recent publication, 'European Business in China Position Paper 2011/2012'.[72]

Ⅲ. The EU-China BIT: Structural Issues

Traditionally, China's BITs were relatively simple and focused on only investment protection and promotion. Recent practice, however, has become more comprehensive and sophisticated. Examples include the China-Mexico BIT(2008), China-ASEAN investment agreement(2009) and China-Japan-Korea investment agreement(2012), and, most recently, the China-Canada BIT(2012).[73] The China-Canada BIT signed in September 2012, for instance, includes 35 articles and six annexes and is the most extensive bilateral investment agreement signed by China so far.[74]

Undoubtedly, the EU-China BIT will be based on the practice of China and the EU Member States. From a structural point of view, it is likely that issues such as investment liberalisation, investment protection, dispute resolution and sustainable development, will

[67] DG Trade, above(n. 10).

[68] Ibid.

[69] Ibid.

[70] Ibid.

[71] See DG for Trade European Commission, above(n. 4) 2.

[72] European Union Chamber of Commerce in China, 'European Business in China Position Paper 2011 – 2012, 2012', available at http://www.europeanchamber.com.cn/images/documents/pp_2011 – 2012/EN/PP%202011%20EN%20complete.pdf.

[73] Norah Gallagher and Wenhua Shan, 'Commentary on China's Model BIT', in Chester Brown and Devashish Krishan(eds.), *Commentaries on Selected Model Investment Treaties* (OUP, 2013)(forthcoming).

[74] MOFCOM, 'Interpretation of China-Canada Bilateral Investment Protection Agreement by An Official from the Department of Treaty and Law of MOFCOM', 13 September 2012, available at http://english.mofcom.gov.cn/aarticle/newsrelease/significantnews/201209/20120908359187.html. Full text of the China-Canada BIT is available at http://www.international.gc.ca/trade-agreements-accords-commerciaux/agr-acc/fipa-apie/china-text-chine.aspx?lang=en&view=d.

be discussed if not eventually included in the treaty. The following explores these issues in light of the existing practice of China, the EU and its Member States.

1. Investment Liberalisation

UNCTAD defines the concept of FDI liberalisation as relating to the avoidance of a series of discriminatory market-distorting measures.[75] Accordingly, the most significant element of investment liberalisation is to liberalise existing restrictions on entry and admission.[76] However, under customary international law states are not required to grant pre-establishment protection of foreign investment. And most BITs do not provide foreign investment with a right of establishment, though a growing number of treaties include pre-establishment protection and promotion.[77]

UNCTAD summarises the worldwide BITs and puts them into the following five models of establishment: the investment control model, the selective liberalisation model, the regional industrialisation programme model, the mutual national treatment model, and the combined NT and MFN model.[78] Generally, Chinese BITs follow the investment control model requiring all investment to be made ' in accordance with [host state] laws and regulations' in either the ' investment' definition or the admission clause or both.[79] In most cases, this qualification has not been further explained. However, an explanation could be found in the recent modification to the China-Cuba BIT.[80] The China-ASEAN investment agreement adds to the qualification with the word ' policies' and explains it in a footnote by stating that ' for great certainty, policies shall refer to those affecting investment that are endorsed and announced by the Government of a Party, and made publicly available in a written form' .[81] Moreover, the China-Finland BIT(2004), as mentioned above, goes a step further by extending MFN treatment to investment establishment,[82] in addition to the ' in accordance with its laws and regulations' requirement.[83] It is noted that the NT clause in this BIT does not refer to ' establishment' . Clearly, the ' establishment' was included here deliberately to widen the scope of the

---

〔75〕 UNCTAD, *World Jnvestment Report* 1994: *Transnational Corporations, Employment and the Workplace*, UNCTAD/DTCI/10(United Nations, 1994) 288 – 293.

〔76〕 Ibid., 286.

〔77〕 Howard Mann, ' Investment Liberalization: Some Key Elements and Issues in Today's Negotiating Context' , (International Institute for Sustainable Development, 2007).

〔78〕 UNCTAD, ' International Investment Agreements: Key Issues' , Volume I, UNCTAD/ITE/IIT/2004/10, 2004, 148 – 153.

〔79〕 Article 2 of the China-France BIT(2007).

〔80〕 One of the modifications of the China-Cuba BIT states that' [i] n reference to Article 1, Para-graph 1, the expression "pursuant to the latter's laws and regulations" shall mean that for any kind of invested asset to be considered as investment protected in this Agreement, it shall be in accordance with any of the foreign investment modalities defined by the legislation of the Contracting Party receiving the investment and registered as such in the correspondent registry. ' Indeed, the wording used in the original English version of the China-Cuba BIT(1995) is ' in accordance with the laws and regulations' . It is argued that it is unclear whether this explanation will create more clarity or confusion. See Gallagher and Shan, above(n. 18) 55.

〔81〕 Article 1.1.d of the China-ASEAN investment agreement.

〔82〕 Article 3(3) of the China-Finland BIT(2004).

〔83〕 Article 2(1) of the China-Finland BIT(2004).

MFN clause.[84] This has not been changed in the China-Canada BIT and it is unclear whether it would be changed as a result of the US-China BIT negotiations.

Like the Chinese BITs, extra-EU BITs do not grant a right of admission, although such a right does exist between EU Member States in accordance with the EC Treaty.[85] However, the EU has been pushing on market access and investment liberalisation through both multilateral and bilateral agreements at EU level. At the multilateral level, the General Agreement on Trade in Services(GATS), to which the EU is a party, has established a framework for services investment in the form of, most importantly, commercial presence. At the bilateral level, the EC-Chile Association Agreement, for example, grants full national treatment at the pre-and post-entry stages for both natural and legal persons from the other contracting party.[86] The EU-CARIFORUM Economic Partnership Agreement(EPA) signed in 2008 includes a chapter on liberalisation of investment based on a positive list, protection for current payments and capital movements related to FDI and some provisions on investor behaviour.[87] In February 2009, the EU and Canada published a joint report concerning the economic and trade relationship, in which investment rules might ' cover pre-and post-establishment in all sectors in order to improve market access and provide for non-discriminatory treatment of investors and investments, and to improve transparency. '[88] The EU-South Korea FTA, the first completed new generation FTA launched by the EU in 2007, also includes provisions on market access for investors and establishment.[89] In the recent 'statement on Shared Principles for International Investment', the EU and the US commit to establish an open and non-discriminatory investment climate by providing broad market access.[90] A similar approach could also be found in the July 2010 Communication.[91]

Indeed, the EU has long been pushing China to make further commitments on mar-

---

[84] Similar clauses could be found in Article 5(1) of the China-ASEAN Investment Agreement and the Article 139(1) of the China-New Zealand FTA. However, there are differences with respect to the exceptions of the application of MFN treatment in these two agreements. Article 5(2) of the China-ASEAN investment agreement reserves the right for the Contracting States to extend MEN treatment to future agreements or arrangements, while Article 139(3) of the China-New Zealand FTA includes a non-retroactive clause which provides that ' the Parties reserve the right to adopt or maintain any measure that accords differential treatment to third countries under any free trade agreement or multilateral international agreement in force or signed prior to the date of entry into force of this Agreement' .

[85] Dolzer and Schreuer, *Principles of International Investment Law* (OUP, 2008) 81. See also Article 2(1) of the German Model BIT(2005) and Article 2(1) of the UK Model BIT(2005).

[86] Agreement establishing an association between the European Community and its Member States, of the one part, and the Republic of Chile, of the other part, available at http://eur-le x. europa. eu/LexUriServ/LexUriServ. do? uri = OJ: L: 2002: 352: 0003: 1439: EN: PDF.

[87] Stephen Woolcock, ' The Treaty of Lisbon and the European Union as an actor in international trade' , ECIPE Working Paper, no. 1/2010, available at http://www. ecipe. org/the-treaty-of-li sbon-and-the-european-union-as-an-actor-in-international-trade, 10.

[88] ' Joint Report on the EU-Canada Scoping Exercise' , 5 March 2009 5 - 6, available at http://tr ade. ec. europa. eu/doclib/docs/2009/march/tradoc_142470. pdf.

[89] Section C Establishment of the EU-South Korea FTA, OJ L 127/27, 14 May 2011.

[90] Statement of the European Union and the United States on Shared Principles for International Investment' , April 2012, available at http://trade. ec. europa. eu/doclib/docs/2012/april/tradoc _149331. pdf.

[91] European Commission, above(n. 42).

ket access. Its 1998 strategy document 'Building a Comprehensive Partnership with China', for example, explicitly required China to improve the conditions for foreign companies, which includes 'removing all restrictions on the legal form of establishment(whether as a joint venture or a wholly-owned company), lifting geographic restrictions and those on the scope of permitted activity, and removing pre-establishment conditions'.[92] It also includes the removal of export performance requirements and export subsidies. Indeed, as reflected in the public consultation, many EU investors complained about pre-establishment barriers, including foreign ownership limitations, joint venture requirements, the length of licensing and regulatory approval procedures and its lack of regulatory transparency and predictability.[93] In its 'Roadmap for EU-China Relations', the EU explicitly expresses its will to sign an investment agreement integrating both investment liberalisation and protection to better address European investors' needs in an increasingly competitive investment environment.[94]

As mentioned above, China has traditionally rejected the liberal approach on investment admission. During the unsuccessful negotiation of a BIT with China from 1983 to 1987, the US proposed an NT provision covering investment admission, which was rejected by China.[95] In the current negotiations between China and the US launched in 2008, pre-establishment NT is still a most-disputed issue.[96] The China-Japan-South Korea investment agreement concluded in February 2012 does not include pre-establishment NT, mainly because China refused it by citing it has never done so in its investment treaties or free trade agreements with other countries.[97] The same is true for the China-Canada BIT. This is mainly because the Chinese economy is still in transition and its industrialisation is yet to be completed, which means that it is not sufficiently 'mature' for comprehensive investment liberalisation. Although China agreed to market access for investments in the services sector in connection with a positive list approach, the acceptance of market access for foreign investments in the services sector nevertheless confined to very limited sectors and industries and can be 'compensated' in other areas of the WTO agreements.[98]

The negotiation on investment liberalisation is therefore bound to be tough simply because both sides do not have experience in undertaking pre-establishment NT in BITs. China may be able to accept MFN on investment admission, as it did in the afore-

---

〔92〕 Commission of the European Communities, Communication from the Commission: Building a Comprehensive Partnership with China, Brussels, 25 March 1998, COM(1998)181 final, available at, http://eur-lex.europa.eu/LexUriServ/LexUriServ.do?uri = COM: 1998: 0181: FIN: EN: PDF.

〔93〕 DG for Trade European Commission, above(n. 4) 7. The following four investment barriers appear to be the most problematic for EU investors: licensing requirements/procedures, foreign ownership limitations, regulatory approval procedures, prohibition to invest/limited scope of business and joint venture requirements, *id.*, 8.

〔94〕 DG Trade, above(n. 10).

〔95〕 Timothy A. Steinert, 'If the BIT Fits: The Proposed Bilateral Investment Treaty between the United States and the People's Republic of China', (1988) 2 Journal of Chinese Law 405.

〔96〕 Berger, above(n. 13) 162 – 185.

〔97〕 Bilaterals.org, 'Korea, China, Japan to conclude investment pact after 5 years', 28 February 2012, available at http://www.bilaterals.org/spip.php?article21112.

〔98〕 Berger, above(n. 13) 182 – 3.

mentioned China-Finland BIT(2004), or accept 'positive list' pre-establishment NT, as it did in GATS.[99] Anything beyond these, e. g., a negative list approach, would take a long time to negotiate, if it would be possible at all. This is because both sides would have to work out which sector and industries they are ready and willing to open up to international investors. Indeed it would be a more demanding job for the EU, given that it is a unitary entity and will have to seek cooperation from the 27 Member State for the compilation of such a list. As a matter of fact, like China, all the EU Member States traditionally stick to the investment protection in BIT practice. Even in the recently concluded BITs with Canada, Latvia, the Czech and Slovak Republics, they also refused to accept pre-establishment NT.[100] At the moment, Chinese enterprises in Europe are highly concentrated in service activities, especially in less knowledge-intensive sectors.[101] However, China is keen on urging Europe to relax restrictions on high-tech exports to China.[102] Also, China would like the EU to recognise it as a market economy to counter the rising protectionism in trade and investment.[103] Treaty negotiation is a bargaining process. If investment liberalisation has to be included, it can be expected that China would raise these issues in the hope that they can be addressed. The EU itself might find it not such an easy job to satisfy China's need for investment admission.

Another element that adds to the difficulty in investment liberalisation is the MFN treatment. Because of the existence of the MFN provision in almost all BITs, any liberalisation achieved in the EU-China BIT is likely to be extended to investments from other countries with which China or the EU has concluded a BIT. This compound effect would have a profound impact on both sides, a fact which has to be seriously considered.

2. Investment Protection

Unlike the admission provisions, the investment protection clauses in the Member States' BITs are more or less similar to those in Chinese BITs, in particular more recent Chinese BITs. As mentioned above, China's new generation BITs have accepted higher standard of investment protection. A main reason behind this is the need to protect China's increasing outward direct investment(ODI). According to the MOFCOM, ODI from China has been increasing rapidly in the last nine years with an average growth rate of 49.9%. By the end of 2010, more than 13,000 domestic entities had established a-

---

[99] This will be fully discussed in Part IV. 3.

[100] See Article 3(3) of the Latvia-Canada BIT(2009), Article 3(4) of Czech Republic-Canada BIT(2009) and Article 3(4) of the Slovakia-Canada BIT(2010).

[101] Statistics reveal that 87% of China's OFDI in Europe is concentrated in less knowledge-intensive services. See Haiyan Zhang, Zhi Yang and Daniel Van Den, 'Euro-China Investment Report 2011 - 2012', the Antwerp Forum, 22 - 23 November 2011, available at http://www.theantwerpforum.be/documents/PPT-Presentation-of-The-Antwerp-Forum—China-OFDI-in-Europe_20111214142221.pdf.

[102] Chinese Premier Wen Jiabao clearly expressed his hope in this respect again during his visit to Europe in April 2012. See Esther Fung and Shen Hong, 'Wen Hints at Demands During European Tour', The Wall Street Journal, 24 April 2012.

[103] It seems that the EU was ready to grant China the status of market economy in 2009, but it gave up owing to objections from the US. See the Economist Intelligence Unit, 'Evaluating a potential US-China bilateral investment treaty: Background, context and implications', 30 March 2010, 29.

round 16,000 overseas enterprises, covering 178 countries/regions.[104]

Fair and Equitable Treatment: FET is a commonly-used standard of treatment in Chinese BITs. Most Chinese BITs do not make express reference to a particular body of law or other standards to further define it. Others refer to international law but tend to avoid referencing ' customary international law' or the ' international minimum standard', concepts with which China is not familiar and in whose formation China did not participate.[105] However, a separate more elaborate article on FET has been included in the China-New Zealand FTA[106] and the concept of ' minimum standard of treatment' was used in the China-Mexico BIT(2008)[107] and the China-Canada BIT(2012).[108] It has been noted that the term ' customary international law' has also been used in, e. g., the investment chapter of the China-Peru FTA[109]. Although it cannot be assumed that the same would necessarily be adopted in the EU-China BIT, such practice suggests that the possibility does exist.

Transfer: The monetary transfer provision is another important provision in any investment treaty, as it determines the level of freedom foreign investors may enjoy in the host state in making investment-related monetary transfers.[110] However, this freedom is not absolute. The European Commission has taken certainly Member States to the European Court of Justice(ECJ) for inconsistency of their BITs with EU law requirements particularly relating to possible restrictions on monetary transfers. In 2009, the ECJ sided with the European Commission judging that such clauses of the BITs concluded by three Member States-Austria, Sweden and Finland-with third countries before they acceded to the EU were incompatible with EU obligations and therefore should be amended[111]. Importantly, the ECJ explicitly held that its findings were ' not limited to the Member State which is the defendant in the present case'[112]. This appears to suggest that other extra-EU BITs may also be deemed to be violating the EU Treaties to the extent that they con-

---

[104] Ministry of Commerce, '2010 Statistical Bulletin of China's Outward Foreign Direct Investment', available at http://hzs.mofcom.gov.cn/accessory/201109/1316069658609.pdf.

[105] Gallagher and Shan, above(n. 18) 130.

[106] Article 143 of the China-New Zealand FTA.

[107] Article 5 of the China-Mexico BIT(2008).

[108] Article 4 of the China-Canada BIT(2012).

[109] Article 132 of the China-Peru FTA(2009).

[110] Gallagher and Shan, above(n. 18) 175.

[111] ECJ, 3. 3. 2009, Case C – 249/06 *Commission v. Sweden* [2009] ECR I – 1335; ECJ, 3. 3. 2009, Case C – 205/06 *Commission v. Austria* [2009] ECR I – 1301; ECJ, 19. 11. 2009, Case C – 118/07 *Commission v. Finland* [2009] ECR I – 10889. In the case of *EC Commission v. Finland*, a further unique question was raised with respect to the effect of a clause found in almost all the Finnish BITs(except the one with Russia):

'[E]very contracting party guarantees under all circumstances, within the limits authorized by its own laws and decrees and in conformity with international law, a reasonable and appropriate treatment of investments made by citizens or companies of the other Contracting Party'.

Finland argued there was no incompatibility with the Treaty of EC because any restrictive measures adopted by the Council, by virtue of the direct effect of Community law in Finland, formed part of Finnish law covered in the BIT clause. However, the ECJ concluded that the BIT clause at issue was not sufficient to ensure the compatibility of the agreement challenged by the Commission with Article 307 of the Treaty of EC.

[112] ECJ, 3. 3. 2009, Case C – 205/06 *Commission v. Austria* [2009] ECR I – 1301, para. 43.

tain similar free transfer provisions.[113] The new Germany-Pakistan BIT(2009) partly responds to these concerns by including a provision that allows the contracting states to prevent a transfer through the equitable, non-discriminatory and good faith application of its laws or to take safeguard measures in the event of a macro-economic imbalance,[114] even though explicit restrictions to the free transfer provision is not provided for in the German Model BIT.[115] In this regard, it should be noted that some Chinese BITs provide special provisions on temporal restrictions to transfer. The Protocol to the China-Slovakia BIT stipulates that the Contracting Parties may adopt or maintain measures relating to capital transfer in times of financial crisis.[116] Both the China-Mexico BIT(2008) and the China-Canada BIT (2012) include a balance of payments exception.[117] Hence this should advocate for the inclusion of the balance of payments exception to transfers.

The more sticky issue on transfer, nevertheless, would probably be related to China's restrictions on capital account transactions. Since the late 1990s, China has liberalised current account transactions but has maintained control on capital account transactions. Such control might have helped to stabilise the Chinese economy during both the Asian financial crisis in the 1990s and the more recent global financial crisis. Although China has expressed willingness to liberalise capital account transactions, it is unsure when this might actually happen. Until then the transfer provision in Chinese provisions would probably have to keep the 'Chinese characteristics', requiring monetary transfers to be subject to the 'formalities' maintained by the Chinese authorities.

Expropriation and Compensation: According to most Chinese BITs, expropriation is broadly defined to embrace 'nationalisation', 'expropriation' and measures having equivalent effects, which suggests 'indirect expropriation'. However, most Chinese BITs do not provide a definition of indirect expropriation, except for the China-India BIT (2006),[118] China-New Zealand FTA[119] and the China-Canada BIT(2012).[120] According to the provisions on direct and indirect expropriation, the determination of indirect expropriation requires a case-by-case, fact-based inquiry that considers not only the economic impact of measures, but also their 'character'. It also goes further to provide that a measure which is 'so severe in light of its purpose that it cannot be reasonably viewed as having been adopted and applied in good faith' is deemed as an expropriation.[121] Four conditions under which an expropriation may take place are included in Chinese BITs: public purpose, due process of law, non-discrimination, and against compensation. These four conditions may vary from BIT to BIT. For instance, most Chinese BITs refer to 'due

---

[113] Shan and Zhang, above(n. 40) 1054.

[114] Article 5(5) and(6) of the Germany-Pakistan BIT(2009).

[115] Article 5 of the German Model BIT(2008).

[116] Article 2 of the Protocol to the China-Slovakia BIT.

[117] Article 8 'Transfers' of the China-Mexico BIT(2008); Article 12 'Transfer' and Annex B. 12 of the China-Canada BIT(2012).

[118] Article 5 of the China-India BIT(2006) and its Protocol.

[119] Annex 13: Expropriation of the China-New Zealand FTA.

[120] Article 10 and Annex B. 10 of the China-Canada BIT(2012).

[121] Annex B. 10 of the China-Canada BIT(2012).

process of domestic law' or ' domestic procedures of law', but few to ' due process of law'.[122] As far as the standard of compensation is concerned, even though none of the Chinese BITs have referred to the ' Hull Formula' of ' adequate, prompt and effective' compensation, the specific provisions as well as the time and forms of the payment thereof show no significant deviation from general BIT practice.[123] There should therefore be no major difficulty in negotiating this provision.

3. Dispute Settlement

The dispute resolution provisions in BITs have been described as the ' ultimate' investor protection in modern investment treaties.[124] A comprehensive investor-state dispute settlement clause is common in recently signed Chinese BITs, with the China-Canada BIT being the most detailed with 14 articles on investor-state dispute resolution, far more detailed than a typical European-styled BIT.

As pointed out by the European Commission in the July 2010 Communication, the future EU BIT should also feature a strong investor-state dispute settlement clause.[125] However, a number of questions need to be addressed in order to achieve this goal.

First, the EU is not a party to the ICSID Convention, which is open to signature and ratification by state members of the Word Bank or party to the Statute of the International Court of Justice. In this respect, the European Commission argues that it would explore with interested parties the possibilities that the EU accedes to the ICSID Convention, as it already successfully acceded to a number of international agreements by negotiating an amendment.[126]

Second, with respect to international responsibility, the European Commission has stated that it would represent the European Union and defend all actions of EU institutions; it would also be a sole defendant regarding any measures taken by Member States which affect investments by third country nationals or companies falling within the scope of the agreement concerned.[127] However, it is unclear how an arbitral award might be enforced within the EU, in case foreign investors have won a case. For this purpose the EU Commission made a proposal entitled ' Proposal for a Regulation of the European Parliament and of the Council establishing a framework for managing financial responsibility linked to investor-state dispute settlement tribunals established by international agreements to which the European Union is party' in June 2012, which aims to establish a framework for managing the financial consequences of investor disputes that are conducted pursuant to investment agreements to which the EU is a party.

Third, the issue whether the MFN standard would extend to investor-state dispute settlement in the BITs will have to be determined. Most Chinese BITs are silent on this issue, which has been discussed in the first ICSID case concerning the interpretation of a

[122] For instance, Article 7(1)(c) of the China-Mexico BIT(2008).

[123] Shan, above(n. 1) 204.

[124] Gallagher and Shan, above(n. 18) 299.

[125] European Commission, above(n. 42) 10.

[126] Ibid.

[127] Ibid.

Chinese BIT, *Tza Yap Shum v. Peru,* as mentioned above. The China-New Zealand FTA, nevertheless, has an express exclusion confirming that the MFN does not ' encompass a requirement to extend to investors of the other Party dispute-resolution procedures other than those set out in this Chapter' .[128] A similar but slightly different provision is also provided in the China-Japan-South Korea investment agreement, which provides that MFN treatment does not include ' treatment accorded to investors of the third Contracting Party or any non-Contracting Party and to their investments provisions concerning the settlement of investment disputes between a Contracting Party and investors of the third Contracting Party or between a Contracting Party and investors of any non-Contracting Party that are provided for in other international agreements' .[129] The China-Canada BIT is more straightforward in providing that the MFN treatment does not encompass the dispute resolution mechanisms in other international investment treaties and trade agreements.[130] On the contrary, the UK Model BIT(2006) confirms that the NT and MFN treatment shall apply to ' the provisions of Article 1 to 11 of this Agreement' , which clearly include investor-state dispute settlement.[131]

4. Sustainable Development

Traditionally, BITs are treated by contracting parties as investment agreements, and focus on the promotion and protection of investment. Recent years have witnessed an international trend of ' balancing' investment protection and promotion in BITs with some ' social' clauses safeguarding health, safety, the environment and the core labour standards for the purposes of ensuring sustainable development.[132] This is also reflected in some recent Chinese BITs. The China-Canada BIT, for instance, recognises that ' it is inappropriate to encourage investment by waiving, relaxing, or otherwise derogating from domestic health, safety or environmental measures' ,[133] whilst stipulating that ' [e]xcept in rare circumstances, such as if a measure or series of measures is so severe in light of its purpose that it cannot be reasonably viewed as having been adopted and applied in good faith, a non-discriminatory measure or series of measures of a Contracting Party that is designed and applied to protect the legitimate public objectives for the well-being of citizens, such as health, safety and the environment, does not constitute indirect expropriation. '[134] A general exception clause is also included to protect such public policy objectives.[135]

---

[128] Article 139(2) of the China-New Zealand FTA. Similar provision may be found in Article 5(4) of the China-ASEAN investment agreement.

[129] Article 4(3) of the China-Japan-South Korea Investment Agreement. The trilateral investment agreement was signed on the 5th leaders' summit between China, Japan and South Korea held on 13 May 2012. The text of the investment agreement, yet to be ratified, may be found at http://www.mofa.go.jp/announce/announce/2012/5/0513_01.html.

[130] Article 5(3) of the China-Canada BIT(2012).

[131] Article 3 of the UK Model BIT(2005).

[132] UNCTAD, ' Bilateral Investment Treaties 1995 - 2006: Trends in Investment Rulemaking' , (United Nations, 2007) 92 - 3.

[133] Article 18 of the China-Canada BIT(2012).

[134] Annex B.10 of the China-Canada BIT(2012).

[135] Article 33 of the China-Canada BIT(2012).

The EU is a champion in the promotion of sustainable development. This is unsurprisingly reflected in investment agreement practice. In adopting the European Commission's July 2010 Communication, for example, the European Parliament calls on the Commission and its Member States to seize the opportunity to build an integrated and coherent investment policy which ' makes a positive contribution to worldwide economic progress and sustainable development' .[136]

However, the inclusion of provisions on sustainable development in investment agreements has not been welcome by some EU investors, who argued that the noninvestment issues, such as human rights and labour conditions, should not be introduced into the negotiations since the non-commercial issues are not dealt with in the existing EU Member States BITs and hence should not be part of a future EU agreement.[137] In its letter to the Trade Commissioner, the European Services Forum, for instance, insisted that non-commercial issues should not be included in the BIT negotiations since they would reduce existing protection and prolong the negotiating process.[138] Some scholars have also pointed out that the inclusion of clauses on non-economic values in EU-China BITs is a difficult aspiration.[139]

Nevertheless, given the policies and recent practice of both parties, it can be expected that social or sustainable development provisions will be seriously discussed in the BIT negotiation which is likely to lead to some concrete provisions included in the final BIT, although the specific contents are hard to predict.

Ⅳ. The EU-China BIT: Specific Issues

Whilst the existing BITs between China and the EU Member States have laid down good foundations for the future EU-China BIT, further controversies may arise over more specific issues such as the protection and regulation of state-owned enterprises(SOEs) , national security review, transparency and the exhaustion of local remedies.

1. State-owned Enterprises(SOEs)

SOEs as major international investors are a relatively new phenomenon. For China, the share of SOEs in China's outward foreign direct investment(OFDI) is relatively high. According to the MOFCOM, even though their share in OFDI stocks decreased in 2010, they still accounted for 66. 2% of the total stocks[140] . Like investors from other emerging economies, Chinese SOEs often encounter obstacles when investing in other countries. The national security reviews carried out by some countries were often seen to target China's OFDI especially after some eye-catching news such as China National Offshore

---

〔136〕 European Parliament, above(n. 58) .

〔137〕 DG for Trade European Commission, above(n. 4) 18.

〔138〕 European Services Forum, ' Letter sent to Commissioner De Gucht outlining the European services industry's views on EU Investment Policy towards China' , 3 October 2011, avail able at http: //www. esf. be/new/wp-content/uploads/2011/10/ESF2011 – 07 – Karel-De-Gucht-EU-China-Investment-Agreement-Final. pdf.

〔139〕 Bertram Boie, ' Chinese-European Investment Regulation: Progress in a Fragmented Area of Law' , available at http: //www. wti. org/fileadmin/user_upload/nccr-trade. ch/hi/Boie_slides. pdf.

〔140〕 MOFCOM, above(n. 104) , 18.

Oil Corporation(CNOOC) 's losing bid for Unocol in US and the failure of the Aluminium Corporation of China(Chinalco) in the Rio Tinto deal in Australia.[141]

As a result, China is very keen to make sure that her SOE investment is fully protected under her BITs including the potential EU-China BIT. This would include in particular her investment in the bonds issued by the European Governments.

Whilst such investments are typically protected under BITs, which tend to protect both private and public investments, it would help if it is clearly spelt out in the relevant BIT provisions such as the investment definition and dispute settlement provisions.

On the other hand, the EU has expressed certain concerns over SOE investments, including national security concerns, competition concerns, and concerns over governance and social and environmental standards.[142] The public consultation held by the European Commission illustrates that one third of the respondents expressed their concerns about the so-called unfair competition created by the differences in the situation of EU companies and Chinese SOEs, notably because of the subsidies received by the latter, which do not face the same strict competition/ state aid rules as companies in the EU. However, a majority of them replied that they see no particular issues.[143] With an increase of China's investment in Europe, the fear of China's ' scramble for Europe' is also rising.[144] The highway construction contract awarded to the Chinese SOE COVEC (Chinese Overseas Engineering Group) by the Polish government in 2009, for instance, raised a debate about unlawful dumping practices due to its bid of less than half of what the Polish government had budgeted.[145]

Alongside concerns over investment from China's SOEs, China's sovereign wealth funds(SWFs), mainly represented by China Investment Corporation have led to considerable concerns among experts in international economics and finance.[146] Though SWFs are different from SOEs in theory, the difference is not so obvious in reality.[147] China Investment Corporation, for instance, is also an SOE in China. However, there is consensus among states that SWFs should not be treated differently if they adhere to the Santiago Principles. A similar position has been announced by the EU in its joint statement with the US on' shared Principles for International Investment', in which they intend to

---

[141] Sheng Zhang, ' ECT and China: Member or Bystander?' (2012) 13 Journal of World Investment & Trade 597, 597 - 617.

[142] UNCTAD, *World Jnvestment Report* 2011, *Non-Equity Modes of Jnternational Production and Development*, UNCTAD/WIR/2011(United Nations, 2011), 28 - 38.

[143] DG for Trade European Commission, above(n. 4) 4.

[144] Francois Godement and Jonas Parello-Plesner, ' The Scramble for Europe', July 2011, available at http://www. ecfr. eu/page/ - /ECFR37_Scramble_For_Europe_AW_v 4. pdf.

[145] Id. However, this project was withdrawn by COVEC in 2011 after incurring heavy losses. See Bao Chang, ' COVEC stops Polish highway construction', China Daily, 18 June 2012, available at http://www. chinadaily. com. cn/bizchina/2011 - 06/18/content_12728120. htm.

[146] Julien Chaisse *et al.*, ' Emerging Sovereign Wealth Funds in the Making: Assessing the Economics Feasibility and Regulatory Strategies', (2011) 45 Journal of World Trade 837, 851.

[147] Larry C. Backer, ' sovereign Investing in Times of Crisis: Global Regulation of Sovereign Wealth Funds, State-Owned Enterprises, and the Chinese Experience', (2010) 19 Transnational Law and Contemporary Problems, 101.

ensure the so-called ' competitive neutrality' between SOEs and private commercial enterprises.[148] However, it has been observed that ' thus far the Chinese have been model actors, constraining their activities with stricter codes of conduct than that requested of them in the Santiago Principles. In addition to the suggested GAPP guidelines, the Chinese often accept limiting themselves to non-voting shares of stock and rarely purchase more than a ten-percent stake in target companies. '[149] As China has made efforts to implement these generally accepted principles and practice with respect to SWF investment, it seems that the EU should have little to worry about Chinese SOE investment.

2. National Security Review

National security review is now a common feature in the national foreign investment regime and of concern to mutual investors from both China and the EU. As a matter of fact, many states have established their own national security review system.[150] Under the terms of the Committee on Foreign Investment in the United States(CFIUS), for instance, all foreign investments into the US are reviewed in order to consider their national-security implications for the US. In the EU, a national security screening at the EU level is yet to be established and the power to screen foreign investment is delegated to national governments. Germany, for example, amended its Foreign Trade Act in 2009 to allow the government to review and prohibit investments by non-EU individuals/companies into German companies where the foreign investor obtains more than 25% of the voting rights in such companies. This approach, however, has been criticised for its failure to address pan-European national security risks and could ' permit room for protectionist abuse in the name of security' .[151]

As a newcomer to overseas investment, Chinese investors are particularly sensitive and vulnerable to national security reviews by host governments. President Obama, for instance, issued an order in September 2012 against Ralls Corporation, a US company owned by two executives of China-based Sany Group Co. , to dismantle its four wind farms in Oregon. This order has led to a court complaint against Obama and the CIFUS filed by Ralls Corporation in a US district court.[152] Besides, the CFIUS has already rejected a few bids by Chinese companies, including Huawei Technologies' bid for 3Com

[148] ' European Commission, EU and US adopt blueprint for open and stable investment climates', 10 April 2012, available at http://europa. eu/rapid/pressReleasesAction. do? reference = IP/12/356&format = HTML&aged = 0&language = EN&guiLanguage = en.

[149] See Jason Buhi, ' Negocio De China: Building Upon the Santiago Principles to Form an Effective International Approach to Sovereign Wealth Fund Regulation', (2009) 39 Hong Kong Law Journal 197 - 216.

[150] For a list of security-related investment control measuresby some EU Member States, see *id.*, 71.

[151] Thilo Hanemann and Daniel H. Rosen, ' China Investments in Europe: Patterns, Impacts and Policy Implications', Rhodium Group, June 2012, available at http://rhgroup. net/wp-content/uploads/2012/06/RHG_ChinaInvestsInEurope_June2012. pdf.

[152] The complaint filed by Ralls in a US district court for the District of Columbia is now available at http://online. wsj. com/public/resources/documents/RallsFiledAmendedComplaint. pdf. Even though it is believed that some of his arguments raise legitimate questions about how CFIUS operates and the suit could contribute to CFIUS becoming more trans-parent, it is commonly believed that the suit ' faces an uphill path' and the chance for Ralls to win is pretty slim, particularly given that presidential actions are not reviewable according to section 721 of the Defence Production Act.

in 2008 and CNOOCC's take-over of Unocal in 2005. As a result, Chinese investors are keen to make sure that national security review regimes in foreign states are transparent and predictable.

On the other hand, China has also established her own national security review mechanism, which has caused some concern to EU investors.[153] The establishment of the security review system to review merger and acquisition(M&A) activities by foreign investors is part of the Chinese Government's effort to ensure and improve the quality of foreign investment.[154] The concept of 'national security review' was first introduced in the 'Provisions on Guiding Foreign Investment' issued by the State Council in 2002, which prohibits foreign investment that may 'jeopardize national security'. Since then, a series of laws and regulations have been promulgated: 'Provisions on Mergers and Acquisitions of Domestic Enterprises by Foreign Investors' (issued by six ministries in 2006), an 'Anti-monopoly Law' (issued by the Standing Committee in 2007), 'Provisions on the Criteria for Reporting Concentration of Undertakings' (issued by the State Council in 2008), and the 'Notice of the General Office of the State Council concerning Security Review of Mergers and Acquisitions of Domestic Enterprises by Foreign Investors' (issued by the State Council in 2011), which is complemented by the 'Provisions on Implementing a Security Review System for Mergers and Acquisitions of Domestic Enterprises by Foreign Investors' (issued by the MOFCOM in 2011). After the entry into force of the 2011 MOFCOM Provisions in September 2011, China has formally established its security review system to review M&A activities by foreign investors.

Concerns over China's national security review system arose when the MOFCOM rejected Coca-Cola's bid for Huiyuan, a leading juice-maker in China. However, practice has proved that China does not use the national security review system to reject foreign investment or to practice protectionism. Statistics from the MOFCOM illustrate that 94% of the 194 cases of anti-monopoly application in 2011 were approved with no conditions attached.[155] Moreover, till now there has been no indication that Chinese investment has caused any damage to European national security.[156] In this respect, China and the EU could follow the approach taken by the EU and the US, by emphasising that 'governments should ensure their reviews, if any, of the national security implications of foreign investment focus exclusively on genuine national security risks'.[157] Still better perhaps, if a sentence could be added, would be to make sure that national security reviews are conducted as far as possible in a transparent and predictable manner. Meanwhile, it might be sensible to emphasise, as does the China-Canada BIT, that the outcome of the national

---

[153] European Chamber of Commerce in China, above(n. 7).

[154] With its undisputable and unprecedented success in attracting FDI, what concerns the Chinese Government now is no longer how to attract much more FDI but how to attract FDI of higher 'quality'. This change has been most clearly demonstrated in the eleventh Five-Year Plan(FYP) on the 'Utilization of Foreign Investments' published in 2006. For more, see Gallagher, Shan and Zhang, above(n. 19).

[155] MOFCOM, 'MOFCOM Press Release on Anti-Monopoly in 2011', 31 December 2011 http://english.mofcom.gov.cn/aarticle/newsrelease/significantnews/201112/20111207909353.html.

[156] Hanemann *et al.*, above(n. 151), 61.

[157] European Commission, above(n. 148).

security review of any investment shall not be subject to dispute settlement.[158]

3. Transparency

An open investment environment is very helpful to attract FDI. Traditionally, issues concerning transparency have been addressed in national law. However, increasingly transparency provisions have been included in BITs.[159] Some BITs include provisions which have been viewed as imposing a transparency obligation on host countries only, while some others include general transparency provisions imposing obligations on all stakeholders to the agreement, namely the host states, the home states and the foreign investors.[160] The transparency requirements may be provided under different titles. 'Transparency' requirements imposed on the contracting parties may be dealt with under the title of 'transparency', but transparency issues concerning corporate entities may be under some other headings, such as 'disclosure' or 'information requirements'.[161] The public consultation held by the EU showed that a BIT which would significantly increase transparency and legal certainty is welcomed.[162] The EU and US 'statement on Shared Principles for International Investment' also urges governments to maintain open, transparent and non-discriminatory investment climates.[163]

In Chinese BIT practice, an independent provision of 'transparency' is rare. However, the recent China-Japan-South Korea trilateral investment treaty marks a great step forward since this trilateral investment agreement includes transparency provisions imposing obligations upon both the contracting parties and the corporate entities. Obligations imposed on the contracting states are provided in Article 10, which requires the contracting parties to make information publicly available, provide a reasonable interval if introducing or changing laws or regulations, respond to specific questions and provide information, and provide an opportunity for public comments.[164] Meanwhile, Article 16 'special Formalities and Information Requirements' provides that the host state can require foreign investors to provide information concerning investments solely for informational or statistical purposes.[165] Another progress is made in the China-Canada BIT, which not only incorporates such provisions in the trilateral investment agreement, but also requires that all investor-state arbitral tribunal awards be made publicly available.[166] Further progress might be made as a result of the US-China BIT talks, if the transparency provisions in the new 2012 US model BIT are to be adopted. These could

---

[158] Annex D. 34 of the China-Canada BIT(2012).

[159] UNCTAD, 'Transparency', (2004) UNCTAD Series on Issues in International Investment Agreements, UNCTAD/ITE/IIT/2003/4.

[160] Ibid.

[161] Ibid.

[162] DG for Trade, above(n. 4) 3 and 7.

[163] Europe Commission, above(n. 148). The statement of the European Union and the United States on 'shared Principles for International Investment' can be found at http://trade.ec.europa.eu/doclib/docs/2012/april/tradoc_149331.pdf.

[164] Article 10 of the China-Japan-South Korea investment agreement.

[165] Article 16 of the China-Japan-South Korea investment agreement.

[166] Article 28(1) of the China-Canada BIT provides that '[a]ny Tribunal award under this Part shall be publicly available, subject to the redaction of confidential information [..]'.

serve as blueprint for a transparency provision in the EU-China BIT.

4. Exhaustion of Local Remedies

The rule of exhaustion of local remedies as customary international law has been confirmed by the International Court of Justice(ICJ) in the *Interhandel* case, in which the ICJ held that ' the rule that local remedies must be exhausted before international proceedings may be instituted is a well-established rule of customary international law' .[167] Hence, a claimant wishing to pursue an international claim had to have exhausted all domestic remedies.[168] The obligation to exhaust domestic remedies is a ' recognition of the judicial sovereignty of the state over issues that fall within its jurisdiction' .[169] In international investment law, the rule of exhaustion of local remedies had traditionally been embedded in the ' Calvo Doctrine' , which was first proclaimed by Latin American countries and then echoed by most developing countries.[170] However, this requirement has mostly been removed or more accurately superseded by modern BITs and arbitration.[171] Tribunals have confirmed that, despite the lack of an express waiver, the language of the dispute resolution provisions in current BITs gives an investor the option to elect for dispute mechanisms provided for in the treaty.[172] The ICSID Convention also makes it clear in Article 26 that the decision to arbitrate is to the exclusion of all other remedies including local remedies.[173]

A review of the EU Member States' Model BITs reveals that most of them do not require the investor to first resort to local remedies but treat international arbitration as an alternative means of settling disputes.[174] However, most Chinese BITs do require an investor to go through the appropriate domestic administrative review process before seeking to arbitrate. It is observed that even the third generation Chinese BITs impose a requirement on the investor to submit the dispute for domestic administrative review first.[175] On the other hand, it is interesting to find that the European Parliament has proposed to re-introduce the obligation to exhaust local judicial remedies in future European international investment treaties.[176] The Norwegian draft model BIT of 2007 also attempted to include the exhaustion of local remedies requirement prior to arbitration.[177] The Australian Government went even further to announce that it will no longer include provisions on investor-state dispute settlement in bilateral and regional trade agreements by referring to the principles of no greater rights for foreign investors and the

---

[167] ICJ, *Interhandel(Switz. v. U. S.)*, Preliminary Objections, 1959 ICJ REP. 6, 27.

[168] Ian Brownlie, *Principles of Public international law*, 6th edition(OUP, 2003) 472.

[169] M. Sornarajah, *The Jnternational Law on Foreign investment*, 2nd edition(CUP, 2004) 254.

[170] Cai Congyan, ' International Investment Treaties and the Formation, Application and Transformation of Customary International Law Rules' , (2008) 7 Chinese Journal of International Law 659, 677 – 8.

[171] Gallagher and Shan, above(n. 18) 364.

[172] Ibid.

[173] Ibid.

[174] Carolinn Hjalmroth, 'securing High Investment Protection for EU Investors: A Review of EU Member States' Model BITs'National Board of Trade, May 2011, 36.

[175] Gallagher and Shan, above(n. 18) 366.

[176] European Parliament, above(n. 58) .

[177] Article 15 of the Draft Norway Model BIT(2007) .

government's right to regulate to protect the public interest.[178]

It would therefore be very interesting to watch the outcome in the EU-China BIT negotiations with regard to local remedies. Most likely, China would insist on the local administrative review as a prerequisite procedure prior to international arbitration. This would actually be beneficial to and therefore welcomed by governments on both sides.

V. The EU-China BIT: Legal Implications

It can be foreseen that the EU-China BIT, a treaty between the largest developing country and the largest economic community, once achieved, will have profound legal implications from the perspective of its positive effect on the China-EU bilateral investment relations, from the perspective of its effect on the improvement of the Chinese and EU domestic legal frameworks, and from that of the reconstruction of the future international investment law.

Firstly, the level-playing field established by the EU-China BIT would stimulate the bilateral investment relations between China and the EU. On the one hand, the EU-China BIT would promote foreign investment from the EU into China. More recent studies concur that BITs do have a positive influence on FDI inflows from developed countries into developing countries.[179] Indeed, the importance of China as an increasingly strategic market, in particular after the recent global financial crisis, has been well-recognised.[180] Most transnational corporations treated China as the top destination for FDI.[181] A strong BIT would eliminate the concerns of EU investors and increase their business confidence. On the other hand, the EU-China BIT would improve the policy coherence, reduce asymmetries and uncertainties within the different provisions among the extra-EU BITs, and create an integrated and transparent EU for Chinese investors. Moreover, a level playing field would increase the attractiveness of the EU as an investment destination, which is of crucial importance when the EU seeks to attract foreign investment particularly at a time of a debt crisis.

Secondly, the China-EU BIT could improve the domestic legal frameworks of both China and the EU. Though China has made great effort to improve its domestic legal system, with her accession to the WTO and the reform of the governmental structure and the judicial reform, China's current FDI legal system is yet to be considered as a fully 'effective' legal system, let alone an ideal or a 'model' one[182]. In this respect, the regime set up by the international investment treaties, particularly the new generation BITs,

---

〔178〕 Kyla Tienhaara and Patricia Ranald, 'Australia's Rejection of Investor-State Dispute Settlement: Four Potential Contributing Factors', Investment Treaty News, 12 July 2011.

〔179〕 UNCTAD, 'The Role of International Investment Agreements in Attracting Foreign Direct Investment to Development Countries', (2009) UNCTAD Series on International Investment Policies for Development xiii.

〔180〕 European Union Chamber of Commerce in China, above(n. 7), 3. See also European Union Chamber of Commerce in China, 'European Chamber Business Confidence Survey 2010', June 2010, 3 – 4.

〔181〕 UNCTAD, *World Jnvestment Report* 2010: *Jnvesting in a Low-Carbon Economy*, (United Nations, 2010), 25.

〔182〕 Wenhua Shan and Sheng Zhang, 'FDI in China and the Role of Law: An Empirical Approach', (2011) 12 (4) Journal of World Investment & Trade 457.

would affect China's domestic institutions whilst benefiting foreign investors in China. This is due to the fact that China's international investment treaties exercise ' significant influences on the development of the domestic legal and economic structures in the host State. '[183] Besides, the contents of investment treaties should thus support the legal reform in China by contributing to good governance.[184] It is also believed that the investment treaties are ' likely to have spill-over effects on the domestic legal system' , by creating ' an incentive for China to promote liberal values on a broader basis by letting domestic economic factors benefit from the overall changes in the economic and legal system' .[185] For the EU, the conclusion of an EU-China BIT will help solve the ambiguities arising after the Treaty of Lisbon, especially with respect to the inclusion of FDI in the Common Commercial Policy, thus providing a transparent investment environment. A common investment policy is essential for the EU to deal with an increasingly competitive world.[186] It will also provide reference for the ongoing negotiations of BITs or FTAs pursued by the European Commission.

Thirdly, the successful conclusion of a BIT between China and the EU would represent a big accomplishment in international investment law. A treaty supporting sustainable development and the balance of interests will also enhance the global international investment treaties' network. On the one hand, with the development of international investment law, the general standards of treatment of foreign investment are largely harmonised. Although they are still subject to different interpretations between developed countries and developing countries, such differences in interpretation do not appear to show a north-south divide. On the contrary, the debate is now being shifted to the conflicting rights and interests of host states and foreign investors, which is essentially a ' private-public debate' .[187] The EU-China BIT will provide a general view of possible solutions to this ' privatepublic debate' . On the other hand, the EU-China BIT will help shape a global investment treaty. In fact, both China and the EU have been positively involved in the negotiations of a Multilateral Investment Agreement (MIA), within the OECD or the WTO. The EU is very proactive in concluding a MIA-type agreement within the WTO framework, and all its Member States, as OECD members, have participated in the three-year negotiations on the Multilateral Agreement on Investment(MAI). China, as the largest developing country, was closely watching these negotiations and was considering its own position and countermeasures.[188] Despite the attempts and failures

---

[183] Schill, above(n. 18) 116.

[184] Id. See also Rudolf Dolzer, ' The Impact of International Investment Treaties on Domestic Administrative Law' , (2005) 37 New York Journal of International Law and Politics 953, 954.

[185] Schill, above(n. 18) 117.

[186] Shan and Zhang, above(n. 40) 1071.

[187] Shan, ' Towards a Balanced Liberal Investment Regime: General Report on the Protection of Foreign Investment' , (2010) 25 ICSID Review, 42. See also Wenhua Shan, From "North-South Divide" to "Private-Public Debate": Revival of the Calvo Doctrine and the Changing Landscape in International Investment Law, (2007) 27 Northwest Journal of International Law and Business 631.

[188] China participated in both the negotiation on MAI and related discussions within the WTO, both as an observer. Shan, above(n. 1) 270 – 1.

of the negotiations of a MIA in both the OECD and the WTO, such a treaty is still necessary since the fragmentation and ' legitimacy crisis'[189] of bilateral and regional investment treaties have put the ' spaghetti bowl' of investment treaties under severe criticism.[190] There are renewed calls for a global investment regime in response to the rising investment protectionism since the financial crisis.[191] It is observed that the OECD MAI negotiation was not successful because the text was based on the US Model BIT and developing countries could not participate fully in the negotiation. The EU-China BIT is likely to help build up more consensus between developed and developing countries and further pave the way for a global investment agreement.

Ⅵ. Conclusion

Constructing an EU-China BIT is both desirable and feasible. Uneven protection and the lack of a level playing field in the current legal framework have demonstrated that an EU-China BIT is imperative. Although the current BITs between China and 26 EU Member States have provided a solid basis for such an EU-China BIT, a number of issues will have to be considered and tackled. These include structural issues such as investment liberalisation, investment protection, dispute settlement and sustainable development, as well as more specific issues such as SOE protection, national security reviews, transparency and exhaustion of local remedies. An EU-China BIT will not only enhance the strategic partnership between China and EU, but also help further strengthen the international investment regime driving it out of the ' legitimacy crisis' and the ' new regionalism'.

---

[189] Susan D. Franck, ' The Legitimacy Crisis in Investment Treaty Arbitration: Privatizing Public International Law Through Inconsistent Decisions', (2005) 73 Fordham Law Review, 1521.

[190] See also Shan and Zhang, above(n. 40) 1072.

[191] The OECD, for example, recently announced that it was considering the feasibility of a nonbinding "Model Investment Treaty" to avoid an escalation of investment restrictions. See Angel Gurria, ' The global economy and the global investment agenda-an OECD perspective', available at http: //www. oecd. org/document/0/0, 3343, en_2649_34529562_44775040_1_1_1_1, 00. html.

EU Enlargement and the Legal Framework of EU-China Investment Relations*

In May 2004, the European Union realized its fifth enlargement, the largest in its history.[1] Ten new Member States joined the Union, which made it a union of twenty-five States. The ten new Member States are Cyprus, the Czech Republic, Estonia, Hungary, Latvia, Lithuania, Malta, Poland, Slovakia and Slovenia (hereinafter collectively referred to as the EU 10; the EU Member States existing before May 2004 are collectively referred to as the EU 15).[2] Bulgaria and Romania are hoping to also join the Union in 2007, whilst another candidate country, Turkey, is not currently negotiating its membership. The 2004 EU enlargement successfully expanded the bound; try of the EU to embrace eight former communist countries with which China has had and maintained good relationships.

Whilst this enlargement may not tremendously increase the general volume of EU investment in China, it probably will significantly promote Chinese investment in the EU. The legal framework of EU-China investment relations will likewise be modified by the enlargement.[3] This article thus deals with the legal framework governing the investment relations between China and the EU 10 States. It first explores the trade and investment relations between China and the EU 10 States and the applicable legal framework. Then it takes a closer look at the bilateral investment treaties concluded between the two sides.

I. Trade and Investment Relations between China and the EU 10 States

China has a long trade and investment relationship with the EU 10 States, dating back to the 1950s soon after the People's Republic of China was established. China had,

---

* 6 *Journal of World Investment & Trade* 2, April 2005.

[1] For further details of the enlargement, see *Enlarging Europe*, available at: < news. bbc. co. uk/2/shared/spl/hi/europe/04/enlarging_europe/html/introduction. stm. (last visited 16 September 2004). See also information about enlargement at the European Union's official Website, at: < europa. eu. . int/comm/enlargement /Enlargement. htm > (last visited 10 September 2004).

[2] Further details of these new Member States are available at the BBC and EU Website, ibid.

[3] For a discussion of the legal framework governing Sino-EU 15 investment relations, see Wenhua Shan. *Towards a New Legal Framework for EU-China Investment Relations*, 34 Journal of World Trade 5, October 2000, pp. 137 – 179.

in particular, a close economic relationship with the eight former communist countries even before 1978, during the period when China was isolated from the Western world. For instance, the Chinese-Polish Joint Stock Shipping Company (CHIPOLBROK), established in 1951, was the very first joint-venture company that the People's Republic admitted.[4] This Section elaborates the investment relations between China and each of the EU 10 States in tum before giving an overview and comments on their implications.

A. Cyprus

China established diplomatic relations with Cyprus in December 1971.[5] The two sides have so far concluded a trade agreement(1981), a bilateral investment treaty(BIT) (2001)[6] and a bilateral double taxation treaty(DTT) (1990).[7] Whilst there are no specific statistics on bilateral investment, it is recorded that Sino-Cyprus trade nearly tripled between 1998 and 2002, from US $ 81.21million in 1998 to US $ 225.94 million in 2002.[8]

B. Czech Republic[9]

Sino-Czech trade relations date back to the 1950s.[10] Before 1991, bilateral trade was conducted in accordance with a clearing agreement and had reached an historic level of US $ 910 million in 1989.[11] Since 1991 when the clearing agreement was abolished, bilateral trade has decreased significantly.[12] Sino-Czech trade, however, has grown rapidly since 1999. In 2002, it reached US $ 962 million, a near three-fold increase since 1999.[13] By the end of 2002, the Czech Republic had made 248 investment project in China, with a total investment of US $ 64.68 million.[14] There are also some Chinese investment projects in the territory of the Czech Republic.[15]

In 1991, China singed a BIT with the Czech Republic(then the Federal Republic of Czechoslovakia).[16] China also entered into a DTT and a general economic and trade a-

[4] for more about the company. see *Brief introduction*, at its own Website, at: < www. chipolbrok. online. sh. cn/ e_gsjj. htm > (last visited 10 September 2004).

[5] For details about Sino-Cyprus relations. visit Chinas Ministry of Foreign Affairs(MFA)· Official Website: < www. fmprc. gov. cn/eng/wjb/zzjg/xos/gjlb/2808/default. htm > (last visited 13 March 2005).

[6] Ibid.

[7] Xin Zhang. The Law and practice of International taxation Treaties in China, Wildy. Simmonds ; and I lil, London, 2003. in Appendix1, "China's Double Tax Treaties and Arrangements", pp. 683 – 685.

[8] Ibid. See also General Information About Cyprus, at the MFA Website, at: < www. mfa. gov. cn/chn/wjb/zzjg/xos/gjlb/1404/1404x0 /default. htm > (last visited 10 September 2004)

[9] For further details. see *Sino-Czech Relations*, at the MFA website, at: < www. fmprc. gov. cn/eng/wjb/zzjg/xos/gjlb/3160/default. htm > (last visited 13 March 2005). See also Sino-Czech *Economic Relations*, at the website of the Ministry of Commerce of China(MOFCOM), at: < ozs. mofcom. gov. cn/article/200208/20020800037999_1. xml > (in Chinese) (last visited 24 August 2004).

[10] Sino-Czech Economic Relations, ibid.

[11] Ibid.

[12] Ibid.

[13] Ibid.

[14] Sino-Czech Relations, supra, footnote 9.

[15] Sin-Czech Economic Relations, supra, footnote 9.

[16] Sino-Czech Economic Relations, supra, footnote 9.

greement with Czech Republic in 1987 and 1993, respectively.[17]

C. Esionia[18]

Estonia established diplomatic link with China in 1991, and the two sides soon entered into three important economic agreements, namely an economic and trade agreement in 1992, a BIT in 1993 and a DTT in 1996.[19] Recent years have witnessed a dramatic surge in Sino-Estonia trade. It reached US $ 273 million in 2001, a near-twenty-fold increase in four years, from US $ 14.68 million in 1998.[20] There are by now fourteen Chinese-funded enterprises in Estonia, with a total investment of US $ 2 million. Most of them fall in the sectors of mobile phones, wholesale and retail trade, textile processing, and the entertainment and catering industries.[21]

D. Hungary[22]

Like the Czech Republic, Hungary started to trade with China in the 1950s and conducted trade in accordance with a bilateral clearing agreement until 1991.[23] As a result of the change of the trade arrangement, bilateral trade dropped in the early 1990s but soon revitalized.[24] In 2002, Sino-Hungary trade reached US $ 1.6 billion, which made Hungary the largest trade partner of China among Central and East European countries,[25] Statistics show that there are about 100 Chinese State-funded enterprises or representative offices in Hungary and about 1000 companies privately owned by Chinese residing in Hungary.[26] By 2002, China had invested in forty projects in Hungary, with a total investment of US $ 13 million.[27] Meanwhile, there were 424 Hungarian investment projects in China, contributing US $ 101 million of investment.[28] Hungary signed a BIT[29] and a DTT[30] with China in 1991 and 1992, respectively.

---

〔17〕 Sino-Czech Economic Relations, supra, footnote 9.

〔18〕 *Sino-Estonia Economic Relations,* at the MOFCOM official Website, at: < ozs. mofcom. gov. cn/article/200208/2(X)208(KKJ37919_ 1. xml > (in Chinese) (last visited 24 August 2004). For general Sino-Estonia relations (including trade relations), see *Sino-Estonia Relations,* at the Mfa Website, at: < www. fmprc. gov. cn/eng/ wjb/zzjg/xos/gjlb/3165/dcfault. htm(last visited 13 March 2005).

〔19〕 *Sino-Estonia Economic Relations, ibid.*

〔20〕 *Sino-Estonia Relations, supra, footnote* 18.

〔21〕 *Sino-Estonia Economic Relations, supra, footnote* 18.

〔22〕 See *Sino-Hungary Economic Relations,* at the MOFCOM official Website, at: < ozs. mofcom. gov. cn/ article/200208/20020800035951_1. xml > (in Chinese) (last visited 24 August 2004). See also *Sino-Hungary Relations, At* the MFA Website, at: < www. finprc. gov. cn/cng/wjb/zzjg/xos/gjlb/3175/dcfaulc. htm > (last visited 13 March 2005).

〔23〕 *Sino-Hungary Economic Relations, ibid.*

〔24〕 Ibid.

〔25〕 *Sino-Hungary Relations, supra, footnote* 22.

〔26〕 *Sino-Hungary Economic Relations, supra, footnote* 22.

〔27〕 *Sino-Hungary Relations, supra, footnote* 22.

〔28〕 Ibid.

〔29〕 Ministry of Foreign Trade and Economic Co-operation(now MOFCOM), *Collection of International investment Treaties,* Jingguan Jiaowu Press, Beijing(in Chinese and English), at 560 – 571.

〔30〕 Zhang, *supra, footnote* 7.

E. Latvia[31]

China established diplomatic relations with Latvia in 1991. Recent years have seen good progress in bilateral trade and investment relations.[32] According to the Chinese customs, Sino-Latvia trade reached US $ 72.75 million in 2002, a two-fold increase since 2000.[33] At present, there are eight Chinese-invested enterprises in Latvia, with a total investment of US $ 1.5 million.[34] Most of these are private investments.[35] Important bilateral economic treaties include an economic and trade agreement of 1994, a Dtt of 1996[36] and a BIT of 2004.[37]

F. Lithuania[38]

The Sino-Lithuania diplomatic relationship was established in September 1991. Soon after that, the two countries entered into an economic and trade agreement(1991), a BIT(1992) and a DTT(1993).[39] Recent years have seen a rapid increase in bilateral trade. According to the Chinese Customs, in 2002 bilateral trade reached US $ 110 million, a five-fold increase in five years' time.[40] Statistics of China's Ministry of Commerce(Mofcom) show that there are now about 200 Chinese companies or joint ventures in Lithuania, the total investment of which is US $ 12.5 million.[41]

G. Malta[42]

Sino-Malta trade started in the 1950s.[43] With the establishment of diplomatic relations in the 1970s, bilateral trade gradually increased.[44] Rapid growth of bilateral trade, however, did not come until the 1990s.[45] In 2001, bilateral trade reached US $ 150 million.[46] Recent years have also seen considerable growth of Maltese investment

---

[31] For more detail, see *Sino-Latvia Relations,* at the MFA Website, at: < www. fmprc. gov. cn/cng/wjb/zzjg/xos/gjlb/3190/default. htm > (last visited 13 March 2005). See also *Sino-Latvia Economic ReLations,* at the MOFCOM Website, at: < ozs. mofcom. gov. cn/article/200208/20020800035978_1 (in Chinese) (last visited 24 August 2004).

[32] *Sino-Estonia Relations, ibid.*

[33] Ibid.

[34] Ibid.

[35] Ibid.

[36] Ibid.

[37] The text of this BIT is available at the MOFCOM Website, at: < ozs. mofcom. gov. cn/article/ 200405/20040500218576_1. xml > (in Chinese) (last visited 10 September 2004).

[38] See *Sino-Lithuania Economic Relations, at the* MOFCOM Website, at: < ozs. mofcom. gov. cn/article/200208/20020800035979_1. xml > (in Chinese) (last visited 24 August 2004).

[39] Ibid.

[40] *Sino-Lithuania Relations, supra, footnote* 38.

[41] *Sino-Lithuania Economic Relations, supra, footnote* 38.

[42] *Sino-Malta Economic Relations,* at the Mofcom Website, at: < ozs. mofcom. gov. cn/article/200208/20020800036006_1. xml > (in Chinese) (last visited 24 August 2004). See also*Sino-Malta Relations,* at the Mfa Website, at: < www. fhiprc. gov. cn/cng/wjb/zzjg/xos/gjlb/3331/dcfault. html > (last visited 13 March 2005).

[43] *Sino-Malta Economic Relations, ibid.*

[44] Ibid.

[45] Ibid.

[46] *Sino-Malta Relations, supra, footnote* 42.

in China.[47] By September 2000, there were twenty-five Maltese investment projects in China, with a total investment of US $ 8.17 million.[48] There are also a few Chinese investment projects in Malta, including the Mediterranean Traditional Chinese Medical Center.[49] However, the Chinese government has provided, in four installments, US $ 147.1 million in aid to Malta since 1972.[50] Malta has not yet signed a BIT with China, but the two sides have concluded a Dtt(1993) and an economic and trade agreement (1997).[51]

H. Poland[52]

As did the Czech Republic and Hungary, Poland started to trade with China in the 1950s and conducted trade in accordance with a bilateral clearing agreement until 1991.[53] In 1989, bilateral trade reached US $ 910 million, a 161-fold increase since 1950.[54] The change of the trade arrangement in 1991 initially resulted in a sharp drop in bilateral trade,[55] which has gradually increased, however, since 1992. In 2002, Sino-Polish trade reached a new high of US $ 1.38 billion, making Poland one of the largest trade partners for China among Central and East European countries.[56]

As far as bilateral investment is concerned, the Chipolbrok, as aforementioned, was the first-ever Sino-foreign joint venture in the history of the People's Republic of China.[57] By 2002, Poland had invested US $ 43.35 million in China, which made it also one of the largest investors in China among Central and East European countries.[58] Meanwhile, there had been more than eighty Chinese-invested projects in Poland, with a total investment of US $ 45 million, which put China in the number 28th position in the Polish foreign investors' league table.[59] China signed a BIT and a Dtt with Poland in 1988 and a general economic and trade agreement in 1993.[60]

I. Slovakia[61]

Slovakia and the Czech Republic share the same historical trade links with China before 1993, as they were then both parts of the Federal Republic of Czechoslovakia. In 1994, Slovakia signed a general economic and trade agreement with China and formally

---

[47] *Sino-Malta Economic Relations, supra, footnote* 42.

[48] Ibid.

[49] Ibid.

[50] Ibid.

[51] Ibid.

[52] See Sino-*Poland Economic Relations, at the* MOFCOM Website, at: < ozs. mofcom. gov. cn/article/200208/20020800035940_1. xml > (in Chinese) (last visited 13 March 2005).

[53] *Sino-Poland Economic Relations, ibid.*

[54] Ibid.

[55] Ibid.

[56] Ibid.

[57] Ibid. See also *supra, footnote* 4.

[58] Ibid.

[59] *Sino-Poland Relations, supra, footnote* 52.

[60] *Sino-Poland Economic Relations, supra, footnote* 52.

[61] See *Sino-Slovakia Economic Relations, at the* MOFCOM Website, at: < ozs. mofcom. gov. cn/article/200208/20020800037924_1. xml > (in Chinese) (last visited 13 March 2005).

accepted that the BIT(1991) and DTT(1987), *inter alia*, concluded between China and the Federal Republic of Czechoslovakia continued to be effective between China and Slovakia.[62] According to the Slovakian Customs, bilateral trade reached US $ 344 million in 2002.[63] Also, Slovakia had committed to eighteen investment projects in China by 2002, realizing a total investment of US $ 14.63 million.[64]

J. Slovenia

China established diplomatic relations with slovenia in 1992 and a bilateral economic and trade agreement was concluded in the same year.[65] In the following years, the two governments entered into a BIT(1993) and a DTT(1995), among other agreements.[66]

China maintains good trade relations with Slovenia which date back to the former-Yugoslavia era.[67] According to Slovenian statistics, however, Sino-Slovenia trade remained rather low before Slovenia gained independence and dropped in the first few years immediately after independence.[68] Since 1999, bilateral trade has grown rapidly, from US $ 36.1 million in 1998 to US $ 125 million in 2002.[69] In 1999, the *Market Access Strategy of* Slovenia *Economy in China* was formulated by the Slovenian government.[70] Under such governmental support, Slovenian investors have become more active in exploring the Chinese market.[71] On the other hand, there is also some Chinese investment in Slovenia, mostly specializing in the trading and catering industries.[72]

K. Overview and Implications

Trade and investment relations between China and the EU 10 States are summarized in Table 1. It shows that total trade between China and these new Member States reached US $ 523.869 billion in 2002, which comprised 6.13 percent of the bilateral trade between China and the EU 15.[73] Considering that the combined gross domestic product of the 10 countries is less than 5 percent of that of the EU 15,[74] this result demonstrates that the EU 10 States have a particularly close trade relationship with Chi-

---

〔62〕 *Sino-Slovakia Economic Relations, ibid.*

〔63〕 Ibid.

〔64〕 *Sino-Slovakia Relations, supra, footnote* 61.

〔65〕 *Sino-Slovenia Economic Relations,* at the Mofcom Website, at: < ozs. mofcom. gov. cn/article/200208/20020800037923_1. xml > (in Chinese) (last visited 24 August 2004). See also*Sino-Malta Relations,* at the Mfa Website, at: < www. fhiprc. gov. cn/cng/wjb/zzjg/xos/gjlb/3230/default. html > (last visited 13 March 2005).

〔66〕 Ibid.

〔67〕 *Sino-Slovenia Economic Relations*, supra, footnote 65.

〔68〕 Ibid.

〔69〕 Ibid. See also *Sino-Slovenia Relations*, supra, footnote 65.

〔70〕 *Sino-Slovenia Economic Relations*, supra, footnote 65.

〔71〕 Ibid.

〔72〕 Ibid.

〔73〕 There are no direct statistics for EU-China bilateral trade for the whole year of 2002. but for the first eleven months the value of that trade was US $ 7,824.826 billion. The amount of bilateral trade in December was calculated according to the monthly average of the first eleven months' trade figures. For EU-China trade statistics in 2002 January-November), see the Website, at: < ozs. mofcom. gov. cn/article/200406/ 20040600237106_1. xml > (in Chinese) (last visited 15 September 2004).

〔74〕 See *Enlarging Europe, supra, footnote* 1.

na. Among the EU 10 States, Hungary is China's largest trading partner, followed by Poland and the Czech Republic. The EU enlargement has a perceivable impact on general EU-China trade. Indeed, this enlargement has readily put the EU in the second place in China's foreign trade partners' league table, and it is predicted that the enlarged EU will soon become China's largest trading partner.[75]

Table 1 China's Trade and Investment Relations with the EU 10 States 2002

New Member State	Bilateral Trade in 2002 (US $ millions)	Investment in China by 2002 (US $ millions)	Chinese Investmentby 2002 (US $ millions)	Trade Agreement	DTT	BIT
Cyprus	225. 94	n/a	n. /a	1981	1990	2001
Czech Republic	962. 00	64. 68	n/a	1993	1987	1991
Estonia	269. 00	n/a	2. 00	1992	1996	1993
Hungary	1, 600. 00	101. 00	13. 00	n/a	1992	1991
Latvia	72. 75	n/a	1. 50	1994	1996	2004
Lithuania	110. 00	n/a	12. 50	1991	1993	1992
Malta	150. 00 *	8. 17 * *	n/a	1997	1993	no
Poland	I, 380. 00	43. 35	45. 00	1993	1988	1988
Slovakia	344. 00	14. 63	n/a	1994	1987	1991
Slovenia	125. 00	n/a	n/a	1992	1995	1993
Total	5, 238. 69	231. 83	74. 00	9	10	9

Source: Compiled by the author from statistics of the Ministry of Economy of the People's Republic of China.

Note: * 2001 data.

* * As of 2000.

As far as foreign direct investment is concerned, whilst there is relatively small investment from the EU 10 States in China, there is a comparatively very large Chinese investment in the EU 10 countries. Table 1 shows that, on the one hand, a total amount of about US $ 231. 83 million of direct investment was made in China by these countries by 2002, which amounted to only 0. 68 percent of the EU 15's investment in China for the same period. Hungary again led the league table as the top investor in China from these countries, followed by the Czech Republic and Poland. The relatively small amount or investment of these countries in China suggests that the EU enlargement does not much change the general position of EU investment in China. However, on the other hand, it does change, to a considerable extent, the picture of Chinese investment in the EU. China had invested at least US $ 74 million in these countries by 2002, which a-

[75] See *EU Enlarged to be a Union of 25 Member States and the Largest Trade Partner of China*, available at: < www. qmgdaonews. com/contem/2004 - 04/28/content 3066496. htm > (in Chinese) (last visited 16 September 2004).

mounted to more than 19 percent of China's total direct investment in Europe(including Russia).[76] The historical links between China and these countries must be the major reason underlying such a significant investment. It can be anticipated that even more Chinese investment will be made in these countries following the enlargement in order to gain access to the huge, enlarged EU internal market.

It must be noted, however, that the EU enlargement might have a negative impact on the growth of bilateral trade and investment between China and the twenty-five EU Member States. In particular, "internal" trade and investment activities between the EU 15 and the EU 10 States will be significantly intensified as a result of the enlargement, which may have a negative effect on China's trade and investment exchange with both the EU 15 and the EU 10 States.[77] However, it is believed chat the positive effects of the enlargement should be able to offset the negative ones, particularly when viewing it from a long-term perspective.[78] One best way for the Chinese business community to counter the trade-transfer effect of enlargement may be to increase its investment in these new Member States and make full use of the common commercial policy of the EU.

With regard to bilateral investment and trade arrangements, an extensive bilateral treaty network has been established between China and the EU 10 States, including 9 BITs, 10 DTT and 9 trade(or economic and trade) agreements. This treaty network lays down a legal foundation for the development of bilateral trade and investment relations.

II. The Legal Framework of Investment Relations between China and the EU 10 States

Apart from the aforementioned bilateral treaties, particularly the BITs, the legal framework governing investment relations between China and the EU 10 States is composed of multilateral investment treaties to which both China and these States are contracting parties, as well as the domestic laws of China and the EU 10 States.

A. Multilateral Agreements to which China and the EU 10 States are Parties

The multilateral agreements governing investment relations between China and the EU 10 States are the International Convention on the Settlement of Investment Disputes (the ICSID Convention), the Convention Establishing the Multilateral Investment Guarantee Agency(the Mica Convention) and the World Trade Organization Agreements. As observed elsewhere, none of these agreements is a comprehensive treaty for investment protection, as each only touches upon certain specific aspects of international investment

---

[76] Chinese statistics show that by 2003 China had invested US $ 530 million in Europe(Russia included). They also show that US $ 150 million of investment was made in 2003. Thus, the total Chinese investment in Europe (including Russia) by 2002 should be US $ 380 million. For details of China's outward investment, *see* 2003 *China Outward Direct Investment Statistical Report,* at the Mofcom Website, at: < www. mofcom. gov. cn/ articlc/200409/ 20040900275569J. xnil > (in Chinese) (last visited 16 September 2004).

[77] See *EU Enlarged to be a Union of* 25 *Member States and the Largest Trade Partner of China,* supra, footnote 75.

[78] Luo, Xiaojun *How Will EU Enlargement Affect China,* available at: < www. nanfangdaily. com. cn/ southnews/sjjj/200405030319. asp > (in Chinese) (last visited 19 March 2005).

such as dispute settlement, investment insurance against political risks, and regulation of trade in goods and services.[79] The following elaborates some aspects of these agreements that are closely related to the investment relations between China and the EU 10 States.

1. The ICSID Convention

TheICSID Convention aims to set up a non-political international forum to settle investment disputes between host States and foreign investors by providing arBITration and conciliation facilities.[80] As Table 2 shows, China, together with nine of the ten new EU Member States, is a Contracting Party to the ICSID Convention. Poland is the only exception in this regard. However, it would also be possible to bring a case between China and Poland before the ICSID by resorting to that body's Additional Facility.[81] As will be seen below, most BITs concluded between China and these countries have referred to ICSID arbitration, which puts the ICSID in a prominent position in settling State—investor disputes between the two sides.

Table 2 *ICSID*, China and the EU 10 States

State	Signature	Deposit of Ratification	Entry into Force of the Convention
China	9 February 1990	7 January 1993	6 February 1993
Cyprus	9 March 1966	25 November 1966	25 December 1966
Czech Republic	23 March 1993	23 March 1993	22 April 1993
Estonia	23 June 1992	23 June 1992	23 July 1992
Hungary	1 October 1986	4 February 1987	6 March 1987
Latvia	8 August 1997	8 August 1997	7 September 1997
Lithuania	6 July 1992	6 July 1992	5 August 1992
Malta	24 April 2002	3 November 2003	3 December 2003
Slovakia	27 September 1993	27 May 1994	26 June 1994
Slovenia	7 March 1994	7 March 1994	6 April 1994

Source: *List of Contracting States and other Signatories of the Convention*(as of 3 November 2003); available at the ICSID Website, at: < www. worldbankgroup. org/icsid/constate/c-states-en. htm > (last visited 16 September 2004).

[79] Shan, *supra*, footnote 3, pp. 142 – 153.

[80] For further details of the ICSID Convention and its interaction with Sino-EU 15 investment relations, see ibid, pp. 142 – 145.

[81] The Additional Facility makes it possible for cases in which only one of the parties is a Contracting Party to the Convention to be heard by the ICSID, provided that both parties to the dispute consent to such a means of dispute resolution.

2. The MIGA Convention

The aim of the MIGA Convention is to promote international investment flow, particularly to developing countries, by providing guarantees against non-commercial risks which might not normally be insured by commercial insurance providers.[82] All the EU 10 States and China are Contracting Parties to the MIGA Convention.[83] Given that all of them are developing countries for the purposes of the MIGA Convention, mutual investments between China and the ten countries can all be guaranteed by the MIGA.[84] This might provide a special incentive for Chinese companies to invest in the EU 10 States, as compared with the EU 15 States, as Chinese investment in the EU 15 could not be insured by the MIGA.[85]

3. The WTO Agreements

The Agreement Establishing the World Trade Organization(the WTO Agreement) is relevant to investment issues, not only because it has some sub-agreements that deal with investment issues(such as the Agreement on Trade-Related Investment Measures and the General Agreement on Trade in Services), but also because the WTO has ongoing activities relevant to international investment law-making.[86] For example, the relationship between trade and investment has been one of the so-called "Singapore Issues" of negotiations and was included in the Doha Agenda, although the Cancun Ministerial Conference failed to formally launch negotiations on a multilateral investment agreement.[87] All ten countries and China are Member States of the WTO,[88] which means that both sides can mutually benefit from the reduction of customs tax and other concessions, including commitments on investment liberalization.

B. Bilateral Agreements between China and the EU 10 States

Among bilateral agreements and trade agreements, DTTs and BITs are the most important ones dealing with bilateral economic relations. As far as investment is concerned, BITs are the most important instruments, followed by the DTTs, which aim to avoid double taxation on foreign investors. Table 3 and 4, respectively, give further

---

[82] For further details of the MIGA Convention and its interaction with Sino-EU 15 investment relations, see Shan, *supra*, footnote 3, pp. 146 – 149.

[83] *MIGA Member States*, at the MIGA Website, at: <www. miga. org/screens/about/members/members. htm> (last visited 14 March 2005).

[84] MIGA only provides guarantees for investments made in developing countries, not for those made in developed or industrialized countries. Therefore, MIGA has classified its Member States into two categories: "Industrialized Countries" or "Developing Countries"; ee ibid

[85] All the EU 15 States are "Industrialized Countries" according to MIGA's classification, ibid.

[86] For further details of the WTO Agreement and its interaction with Sino-EU 15 investment relations, see Shan, *supra*, footnote 3, pp. 149 – 153.

[87] For more general work on the relationship between trade and investment within the WTO, see *Trade and investment*, at the WTO Website, at: < www. wto. org/english/tratop_c/invest_c/invest_e. htm > (last visited 18 March 2005). For the decision not to negotiate on the investment issue, see Article 1(g), para. 2 of the Decision Adopted by the General council on 1 August 2004(the Cancun Package), at: <www. wto. org/english/tratop_e/ dda_e/ draft_text_gc_dg 31july04_e. htm>(last visited 18 March 2005).

[88] *Members and Observers*, available at the WTO official Website, at: < www. wto. org/english/thewto_e/ whatis_e/tif_e/org6_e. htm>(last visited 16 September 2004).

details of the nine BITs and ten DTTs signed between China and the EU 10 States.

Details of the nineBITs will be explored below. A close discussion of these DTTs is, however, beyond the scope of this article.[89]

Table 3 Bilateral Investment Treaties between China and the EU 10 States

State	Date of Signature	Date of entry into force
Cyprus	15 January 2001	–
Czech Republic	4 December 1991	1 December 1992
Estonia	2 September 1993	1 June 1994
Hungary	29 May 1991	1 April 1993
Latvia	15 April 2004	–
Lithuania	8 November 1993	1 June 1994
Poland	7 June 1988	8 January 1989
Slovakia	4 December 1991	1 December 1992
Slovenia	13 September 1993	1 January 1995

Source: Compiled by the author in accordance with International Center for Settlement of Investment Disputes, *Bilateral investment Treaties,* available at: <www. worldbank. org/icsid/ treatics/china. htni> (last visited 18 March 2005); United Nations Conference on Trade and Development, *Total Number of Bilateral Investment Treaties Concluded, I January* 2003*(by China)*, available at: <stats. unctad. org/fdi/treatics/BITs/China. htm> (last visited 18 March 2005); and *Bilateral Investment Treaties*, available at the Website of the Ministry of Commerce of China at: <tfs. niofconi. gov. cn/h/h. html> (last visited 18 March 2005).

Table 4 Double Taxation Treaties between China and the EU 10 States

State	Date of Signature	Date of entry into force
Cyprus	25 October 1990	5 October 1991
Czech Republic	11June 1997	23 December 1987
Estonia	12 May 1998	8January 1999
Hungary	17June 1992	31 December 1992
Larvia	7 September 1996	27 January 1997
Lithuania	3June 1996	18October 1996

[89] DTTs deal with only one technical, albeit important, aspect of investment operation. For a good guide to China's DTT practice, see Zhang, supra, footnote 7.

续表

State	Date of Signature	Date of entry into force
Malta	2 February 1993	30 March 1994
Poland	7June 1988	7 January 1989
Slovakia	11June 1987	23 December 1987
Slovenia	13 February 1994	27 December 1995

Source: Xin Zhang, The *Law and Practice of International Taxation treaties in China*, Wildy, Simmonds and Hill. London, 2003, in Appendix 1, "China's Double Tax Treaties and Arrangements * *, pp. 683 – 685. See also United Nations Conference on Trade and Development, *Total Number of Double Taxation Treaties Concluded*, 1 *January* 2003*(by China)*, available at: < stats. unctad. org/ fdi/trcatics/dtts/China. htm > (last visited 18 March 2005).

C. Domestic Laws of China and the EU 10 States

Like China, the EU 10 States have extensive laws and regulations focused on international investment, particularly on inward direct investment. These laws and regulations, as well as the EU and Chinese laws on international investment, [90] constitute the domestic laws governing the investment relations between China and the EU 10 States. Whilst it would be interesting to investigate these domestic laws and regulations, it is beyond the scope of this article, where the focus is on the applicable international law. The Mofcom Website has provided very good information for the legal environment of investment in these European countries. [91]

D. Summary

The major components of the legal framework governing Sino-EU 10 investment relations include multilateral agreements, bilateral agreements and domestic laws. On the multilateral level, the ICSID Convention, the MIGA Convention and the WTO Agreements are most relevant, as China and most of the EU 10 States have now become Members of these treaties and institutions. On a bilateral level, there are bilateral trade agreements, DTTs and BITs. Domestic laws and regulations of the EU 10 States, in addition to EU and Chinese laws in regard to international investment, also play a significant role in protecting and promoting mutual investment flows. Since this article focuses oil the applicable international law and most elements of the multilateral treaties have already been dealt with elsewhere, the following Section only further investigates the BITs concluded between China and the EU 10 States.

---

[90] For further details of Chinese and EU FDI law in relation to Sino-EU 15 investment relations, *see* Shan, *supra*, footnote 3, pp. 158 – 165.

[91] *Sino-Europe Bilateral Economic and Trade Relations*, at the MOFCOM Website, at: < ozs. mofcom. gov. cn/article/ 200208/20020800036028_1. xml > (in Chinese) (last visited 18 March 2005).

Ⅲ. The Bilateral Investment Treaties between China and the EU 10 States

BITs are the most important legal instruments to protect mutual investment between China and the EU 10 States. As can be seen from Table 3, these BITs were mostly signed after the BITs between China and EU 15 States were signed, some as late as 2004. It will therefore be interesting to see whether and how these BITs are different from the earlier BITs concluded between China and the EU 15 States.[92] This Section elaborates these newer BITs and compares them with the earlier ones by comparing the provisions on important issues such as investment admission, standards of treatment, expropriation and compensation, subrogation and dispute settlement. The following discussions will be based on the nine BITs existing between China and the EU 10 States.[93]

A. Admission of Investments

The provisions for admission of investments in the BITs between China and the EU 10 States are similar to those found in the BITs between China and the EU 15 States. In other words, they all follow the European tradition of leaving the right to regulate the admission of foreign investments to the discretion of the host government.[94] Thus, all nine BITs provide that the admission of foreign direct investment should be conducted "in accordance with laws and regulations" of the host country. The recently signed Sino-Latvia BIT is not an exception in this regard(see Table 5). As with the Sino-Spain and Sino-Greece BITs,[95] eight of the nine BITs also require that the host country provide assistance and facilities when nationals from the other contracting party apply for visas or work permits in connection with the investment activities.

Table 5 Admission of Foreign Investments Under BITs between China and the EU 10 States

BIT	In accordance with legislation/laws and regulations	Assistance and facilities on visa and work permit applications
Sino-Cyprus BIT	Article 2. 1	Article 2. 2
Sino-Czech BIT	Article 2. 1	Articlc 2. 2
Sino-Estonia BIT	Article 2. 1	Articlc 2. 2

〔92〕 For discussions on Sino-EU 15 BITs, see Shan, *supra*, footnote 3, pp. 155 – 157. For further details, see Wenhua Shan, *the International Law of EU Investment in China*, 2 Chinese Journal of International Law 2, 2002, pp. 604 – 610.

〔93〕 In fact, it is only eight BITs, as the BITs with the Czech Republic and Slovakia are actually the same, i. e., the BIT signed between China and the former Federal Republic of Czechoslovakia, which was later divided into the current two countries, the Czech Republic and Slovakia.

〔94〕 For a detailed elaboration of these European BITs, see Rudolf Dolzer and Margrete Stevens. *Bilateral investment Treaties*, Martinus Nijhoff, 1995, pp. 50 – 56. See also Ibrahim F. I. Shihata, *Recent Treaties Relating to Entry of Foreign Direct investment*, 9 ICSID Rev. —F. I. L. J. (1994), pp. 55 – 56.

〔95〕 Sino-Spain BIT, Article 2. 2; Sino-Greece BIT, Article 2. 5.

续表

BIT	In accordance with legislation/laws and regulations	Assistance and facilities on visa and work permit applications
Sino-Hungary BIT	Articlc 2. 1	Article 2. 2
Sino-Latvia BIT	Article 2. 1	Articlc 2. 4
Sino-Lithuania BIT	Articlc 2. 1	Article 2. 2
Sino-Poland BIT	Article 2	–
Sino-Slovakia BIT	Article 2. 1	Article 2. 2
Sino-Slovenia BIT	Articlc 2. 1	Article 2. 2
Total(9)	9	8

B. Standards of Treatment

1. General Standards of Treatment

The provisions on the general standards of treatment of foreign investors in the nine BITs are, in general, similar to those in the thirteen BITs between China and the EU 15 States, although there are also some differences. Most-favoured-nation(MFN) treatment and "fair and equitable" treatment are established in almost all of the nine BITs, with MFN treatment being subject to normal exceptions such as customs union, border trade and taxation treaties. "Preservation of rights" clauses are common in these BITs, enabling foreign investors to enjoy the best possible treatment provided by the host government.

National treatment(NT) is used in five BITs with the EU 10 States, and in all of these its application is substantially qualified. In four of these, the application of NT shall not prejudice domestic laws and regulations, which is a standard qualification that China has adopted in its BIT practice. The application of NT is further limited in these BITs by phrases such as "to the extent possible"[96] and "sound development of national economy".[97] The Protocol to the Sino-Cyprus BIT, however, qualifies NT in China by attaching a "grandfather clause". Under this clause, the NT obligation does not apply to "any existing non-conforming measures" and their continuation within the territory of China. Such measures may also be amended, provided that such amendment does not increase their non-conformity with the NT obligation. It is undertaken, nonetheless, that "it will be endeavoured to progressively remove the non-conforming measures. . . "Thus, it can be said that the Sino-Cyprus BIT has moved a step forward by "freezing" the level of non-conformity to the NT principle in China at the level of that existing on the date

〔96〕 Anicle 3. 2, Sino-Slovenia BIT.

〔97〕 Point 1, Protocol to the Sino-Czechoslovakia BIT(now the Sino-Czech BIT and Sino-Slovakia BIT).

of the entry into force of the BIT. It is unclear, however, whether Cyprus can maintain similar measures, as Article 3, para. 4 of the BIT requires the application of the MFN and NT obligations on a reciprocal basis.

Non-discriminatory (ND) treatment is granted under two recently signed BITs, namely the Sino-Cyprus BIT and the Sino-Latvia BIT (signed in 2001 and 2004, respectively; both yet to be ratified). However, whilst such ND treatment is subject to the normal qualification in the Sino-Latvia BIT that its application shall not prejudice domestic laws and regulations, it is not qualified in the Sino-Cyrus BIT. Given the limitation there on the application of NT, such a failure to mention the normal qualification of ND treatment should not be regarded as a major advance in this regard.

Unlike other BITs which only loosely refer to "protection" of investment from the other contracting party, the Sino-Latvia BIT also has included a commitment to "constant protection and security". It can be argued, however, that such an addition does not add much more protection than that offered under "fair and equitable treatment, which is granted in most existing Chinese BITs.

It may be concluded, on the one hand, that the provisions on the standards of treatment of investment contained in the Sino-EU 10 BITs are generally similar to those in the Sino-EU 15 BITs, particularly in that MFN and "fair and equitable" treatment are provided and that the application of the NT obligation in China is substantially qualified. On the other hand, the Sino-EU 10 BITs do mark some progress in providing more favourable treatment to foreign investors. This is witnessed by, for example, the prohibition of further limitations on the application of NT and the inclusion of "constant protection and security treatment in the Sino-Latvia BIT. It can therefore be argued that the nine Sino-EU 10 BITs do add some more favourable treatment for EU 15 investors in China by the operation of the MFN clause. Details of these provisions are shown in Table 6.

Table 6 Treatment of Investments under BITs between China and the EU 10 States

BIT	Fair and Equitable Treatment	National Treatment	MFN Treatment	More favorable Treatment	Non-discriminatory treatment	Constant Protection and Security
Sino-Cyprus BIT	Article 3. 1	Grandfather clause * Article 3. 3 and Protocol	Article 3. 3	Article 10	Article 3. 2	–
Sino-Czech BIT	–	D. L. ** Article3. 2 and Protocol, Point 1	Article 3. 1	Article 10	–	–
Sino-Estonia BIT	Article 3. 1	–	Article 3. 2	Article 9	–	–

续表

BIT	Fair and Equitable Treatment	National Treatment	MFN Treatment	More favorable Treatment	Non-discri-minatory treatment	Constant Protection and Security
Sino-Hungary BIT	Article 3. 1	–	Article 3. 2	Article 11	–	–
Sino-Latvia BIT	Article 3. 1	D. L. * * Article3. 1	Article 3. 3	Article 11. 1	D. L. * * Article2. 3	Article2. 2
Sino-Lithuania BIT	Article 3. 1	–	Article 3. 2	Article 9	–	–
Sino-Poland BIT	Article 3. 1	–	Article 3. 2	–	–	–
Sino-Slovakia BIT	–	D. L. * * Article 3. 2 and Protocol, Point 1	Article 3. 1	Article 10	–	–
Sino-Siovenia BIT	Article 6. 1	D. L. * * Article 3. 2	Article 3. 3	Article 9	–	–
Total(9)	7	5(Grand-father * + D. L. *)	8	7	1(D. L. * *)	1

Source: Compiled by the author from the texts of the BITs.

Notes: * Grandfather means that national treatment is qualified by a grandfather clause that allows China to maintain(and even amend) existing non-conforming measures.

* * D. L. means that national treatment is granted only when it is not prejudicial to domestic laws and regulations.

2. Monetary Transfers

As shown in *Table* 7, the BITs between China and the EU 10 States guarantee free transfer of investments and returns without delay. Under these BITs, monetary transfers should be made in convertible currency at the official or prevailing market rate of exchange. However, in most of the nine BITs, such freedom is subject to the domestic laws and regulations of the host State. Even the Sino-Latvia BIT signed in 2004 follows this model. The Sino-Czech and Sino—Slovakia BITs(formerly the Sino-Czechoslovakia BIT) do not refer to "domestic laws and regulations" in the text but include a "China Clause" in the Protocol which effectively subjects monetary transfers to Chinese laws governing foreign exchange.

However, the Sino-Cyprus BIT may again mark a step forward in this regard. Although it also includes a restrictive "China clause, in this ease the clause refers to only" relevant formalities stipulated by the present Chinese laws and regulations relating to exchange control. This seems to imply that China may only maintain or introduce "procedural" restrictions("formalities") , rather than substantive ones. If this understanding is correct, then it is a substantial liberalization. It can be argued that, furthermore, the nine

BITs do provide further guarantees on the free transfer of investment and returns than the Sino-EU 15 BITs.

Table7 Monetary Transfers under BITs between China and the EU 10 States

BIT	(Free) trasfer without delay	domestic laws and regulations	Rate of exchange		In convertible currency
			Official/ prevailing	IMF	
Sino-Cyprus BIT	Article 6. 1	Special China clause * Protocol, Point2	Article 6. 2	–	Article 6. 2
Sino-Czech BIT	Article 6. 1	China clause * Protocol, Point3	Article 6. 1	–	Article 6. 1
Sino-Estonia BIT	Article 5. 1	Article 5. 1	Article 5. 2	–	Article 5. 2
Sino-Hungary BIT	Article 5. 1	Article 5. 1	Article 6. 1	–	–
Sino-Latvia BIT	Article 5. 1	Article 6. 1	Article 6. 3	–	Article 6. 3
Sino-Lithuania BIT	Article 5. 1	Article 5. 1	Article 5. 2	–	Article 5. 2
Sino-Poland BIT	Article 5. 1	Article 5. 1	Article 6	–	–
Sino-Slovakia BIT	Article 6. 1	China clause * Protocol, Point3	Article 6. 2	–	Article 6. 1
Sino-Siovenia BIT	Article 5. 1	Article 5. 1	Article 5. 2	–	–
Total(9)	9	7(3 with China clause *)	9	–	6

Source: Compiled by the author from the texts of the BITs.

Note: "China clause" normally refers to a special clause applicable to China which requires that all transfers be made from the foreign exchange accounts of the foreign-invested enterprise and that China guarantees the provision of foreign exchange in certain cases, as specifically prescribed, where the enterprise does not have sufficient foreign exchange in those accounts. See, for example, Point 3 of the Protocol of the Sino-Czech BIT. However, the Sino-Cyprus BIT has a "China clause" that refers to only the "formalities" of exchange control in China.

C. Expropriation and Compensation

The issues of expropriation are dealt with in BITs from three perspectives, namely its constitution, its conditions and compensation.

1. Constitution and Conditions

The nine BITs show striking uniformity in both the constitution and conditions of expropriation. All of them adopt a broad definition of expropriation which covers nationalization, expropriation and measures having equivalent effects. They all attach four conditions to expropriation-namely public interest, non-discrimination, due process of domestic law and compensation(see Table 8).[98] These are even stipulated in the same provisions of the BITs, Article 4, which suggests that they have followed a model BIT, probably one provided by China. These BITs are slightly different from the thirteen China—EU 15 BITs in that they unanimously adopt due process of "domestic law rather than merely due process of "law", which may include laws of other States and international law. This is probably another indication that the nine BITs followed the same model treaty. Also, this suggests that the EU 10 States, as developing States, share the same view China has on applicable law of "due process", that is, only the law of the host State.

Table 8 Conditions of Expropriation Under BITs between China and the EU10 States

BIT	conditions			
	Public interest	Non-discrimination	Due process of law	compensation
Sino-Cyprus BIT	Article 4. 1	Article 4. 1	Domestic law Article 4. 1	Article 4. 1
Sino-Czech BIT	Article 4. 1	Article 4. 1	Domestic law Article 4. 1	Article 4. 1
Sino-Estonia BIT	Article 4. 1	Article 4. 1	Domestic law Article 4. 1	Article 4. 1
Sino-Hungary BIT	Article 4. 1	Article 4. 1	Domestic law Article 4. 1	Article 4. 1
Sino-Latvia BIT	Article 4. 1	Article 4. 1	Domestic law Article 4. 1	Article 4. 1
Sino-Lithuania BIT	Article 4. 1	Article 4. 1	Domestic law Article 4. 1	Article 4. 1
Sino-Foland BIT	Article 4. 1	Article 4. 1	Domestic law Article 4. 1	Article 4. 1
Sino-Slovakia BIT	Article 4. 1	Article 4. 1	Domestic law Article 4. 1	Article 4. 1
Sino-Slovcnia BIT	Article 4. 1	Article 4. 1	Domestic law Article 4. 1	Article 4. 1
Total(9)	9	9	9	9

Source: Compiled by the author from the texts of the BITs.

2. Compensation

The provisions on the amount of compensation in the nineSino-EU 10 BITs are

---

[98] Most of these BITs state that contracting parties shall not expropriate foreign investments "unless the following conditions are met", However, the wording of the Sino—Czechoslovakia BIT(now the Sino-Czech BIT and the Sino—Slovakia BIT) suggests that "public interest' is the only prerequisite/condition of expropriation and the other three "conditions" are just what should be done after expropriation has taken place.

rather similar to those in the thirteen Sino-EU 15 BITs.[99] None of them refer to the "Hull formula" of "adequate, prompt and effective" compensation. None of the nine BITs even adopt an abstract standard of compensation, such as "appropriate" or "full" compensation. However, all of them guarantee that foreign investors will receive compensation, in case of expropriation, which shall be equivalent to the value of the expropriated investment(see *Table* 9). Seven BITs also expressly state that the amount of compensation must include interest. All nine BITs stipulate that the compensation should be paid without delay and be realizable and transferable.

Table 9 Compensation for Expropriation under BITs between China and the EU 10 States

BIT	Value of the expropriate investment	Adequate, effective and prompt	Without delay, realizable and transferable	Valuation of expropriated investment
Sino-Cyprus BIT	Plus interest Article 4. 2	–	Article 4. 2	
Sino-Czech BIT	Plus interest Article 4. 1	–	Article 4. 1	No method Subject to judicial review (Article 4. 2)
Sino-Estonia BIT	Article 4. 2	–	Article 4. 2	
Sino-Hungary BIT	Article 4. 2	–	Article 4. 2	
Sino-Latvia BIT	Plus interest Article 4. 2	–	Article 4. 2	Generally recognized principles (Article 4. 2)
Sino-Lithuania BIT	Plus interest Article 4. 2	–	Article 4. 2	
Sino-Poland BIT	Article 4. 2	–	Article 4. 2	No method Subject to judicial review (Article 4. 3)
Sino-Slovakia BIT	Plus interest Article 4. 21	–	Article 4. 1	No method Subject to judicial review
Sino-Slovenia BIT	Plus interest Article 4. 2 – 3	–	Article 4. 13	Market value, or generally recogni-zedprinciples and equitable
Total(9)	9(7 include interest)	0	9	

Source: Compiled by the author from the texts of the BITs.

[99] For a comparison of expropriation clauses in the Sino-EU 15 BITs, see Shan, *supra*, footnote 3, p. 156. See also Shan, *supra*, footnote 92, pp. 607 – 608.

Only two of the nine BITs have substantive rules on the evaluation of compensation. The 2004 Sino-Latvia BIT merely states that the determination of the value of the expropriated investment shall follow "generally recognized principles of valuation".[100] The Sino-Slovenia BIT goes a step further to adopt "market value" as the basis of valuation.[101] In case such a "market value" cannot be readily ascertained, the compensation shall be determined in accordance with "generally recognized principles of valuation and equitable principles, taking into account, *inter alia,* the capital invested, depreciation, capital already repatriated, replacement value and other relevant factors".[102] Whilst it is yet to be seen how it works in actual cases, this provision in the Sino-Slovenia BIT seems to have provided so far the most elaborate guidance on valuation of compensation in the twenty-one Sino-EU BITs. In addition, three BITs also provide for the possibility for the valuation of compensation to be reviewed by a judicial body or another independent body of the host country.[103]

D. Subrogation

The subrogation clauses in the Sino-EU 10 BITs are similar to each other and to those in the Sino-EU 15 BITs(see Table 10).[104] All these BITs require that a Contracting Party recognize the assignment of rights and claims from investors to the other Contracting Party if the latter Contracting Party has made any payment to its investor under a guarantee it has assumed in respect of an investment in the territory of the former Contracting Party. Accordingly, the Latter shall be entitled to assert such rights and claims to the same(or not to exceed the) extent as its predecessor(its investor) in title.[105] The Sino-Poland BIT further stipulates that any rights and counterclaims of the former shall also be taken into account.[106]

E. Dispute Settlement

Following general BIT practice, the nine Sino-EU 10 BITs deal with State-State disputes and State-investor disputes separately.

1. State-state Disputes

The State-State dispute settlement clauses are the same in all nine BITs. They all state that the parties shall endeavour to settle such disputes through diplomatic channels. However, if disputes cannot be resolved in six months, either of the two parties may

---

[100] Article 4. 2, Sino-Latvia BIT, supra, footnote 37.

[101] Article 4. 3, Sino-Slovenia BIT.

[102] Ibid.

[103] Article 4. 2, Sino-Czechoslovakia BIT(now the Sino-Czech BIT and the Sino-Slovakia BIT): and Article 4. 3, Sino-Poland BIT.

[104] For a comparison of subrogation provisions in the Sino-EU 15 BITs, see Shan, *supra,* footnote 3, pp. 155 – 157. See also Shan, *supra,* footnote 92, pp. 604 – 610.

[105] Article 7, Sino-Czech BIT; Article 6, Sino-Estonia BIT; Article 7, Sino-Hungary BIT; Article 7, Sino-Latvia BIT, *supra,* footnote 37; Article 6, Sino-Lithuania BIT; Article 7, Sino-Poland BIT; Article 7, Sino-Slovakia BIT; Article 6, Sino-Slovenia BIT.

[106] Article 7, Sino-Poland BIT.

submit the dispute to an *ad hoc* arbitration tribunal.[107] They also stipulate how the tribunal shall be set up and what procedural and substantive rules shall be followed (see Table 11).[108] In short, the State-State dispute settlement provisions are not different from these in the Sino-EU 15 BITs.[109]

Table 10 Subrogation under BITs between China and the EU 10 States

BIT	Rccognize the transfer and subrogation of rights and claims	Scope of subrogated rights				
		Same treatment as the guaranteed investor	Including litigation rights	Without prejudice to home State's right to invo ke State-Stat e arbitration	Shall not exceed the original rights	Can make countercla ims to the subrogated rights
Sino-Cyprus BIT	Article 7	–	–	–	–	–
Sino-Czech BIT	Article 7	–	–	–	Article 7	–
Sino-Estonia BIT	Article 6	–	–	–	Article 6	–
Sino-Hungary BIT	Article 7	–	–	–	Article 7	–
Sino-Latvia BIT	Article 7	–	–	–	–	–
Sino-Lithuania BIT	Article 6	Article 7	–	–	–	–
Sino-Poland BIT	Article 7	Article 6	–	–	–	–
Sino-Slovakia BIT	Article 7	Article 7	–	–	Article 7	Article 7
Sino-Siovenia BIT	Article 6	–	–	–	Article 6	–
Total(9)	9	3	0	0	5	1

Source: Compiled by the author from the texts of the BITs.

2. State-investor Disputes

Two important aspects of State-investor dispute settlement are commonly dealt with inBITs, namely the jurisdiction and the applicable law.

(a) Jurisdiction

The jurisdiction issue is essentially an issue of whether and to what extent the host-country accepts international arbitration as a venue to settle its disputes with foreign investors. In this regard, the provisions in the nine Sino-EU 10 BITs vary from each other. Although all nine BITs accept international arbitration, the degrees of acceptance

[107] Article 8, Sino-Czech BIT; Article 7, Sino-Estonia BIT; Article 9, Sino-Hungary BIT: Article 8, Sino-Latvia BIT, *supra*, footnote 37; Article 7, Sino-Lithuania BIT; Article 9, Sino-Poland BIT; Article 8, Sino-Slovakia BIT; and Article 7, Sino-Slovenia BIT.

[108] Ibid.

[109] For a comparison of provisions on State-State dispute settlement in the Sino-EU 15 BITs, see Shan, *supra*, footnote 3, pp. 155 – 157. See also Shan, *supra*, footnote 92, pp. 604 – 610.

Table 11 Dispute Settlement under BITs between China and the EU 10 States

BIT	State-State disputes: Negotiation/ consultation plus ad hoc international arbitration	State-investor disputes							
			jurisdiction			Applicable law			Future supplementary Agreement on ICSID arbitration
		Exclusive Domestic Jurisdiction	International Arbitration			Domestic Law(of the host country)	The Present Agreement	Principles of international law adopted by bothparties	
			Ad hoc		Submission to ICSID arBITration				
			No reference to ICSID procedures	Reference to ICSID procedures					
Sino-Cyprus BIT	Article 8	Shared with the ICSID and others Article 9.2	-	Article 9. 5	Article 9. 5 (any legal disputes)	Article 9. 7	Article 9. 7	Article 9. 7 (mutual adoption not required)	-
Sino-Czech BIT	Article 8	Article 9.2 (except AOC & Others *)	Article 9. 2 (except AOC & Others *)		-	-	-	-	-
Sino-Estonia BIT	Article7	Article 8.2-3 (exceptAOC *)	-	Article 8. 5 (AOC *)	-	Article 8. 7	Article 8. 7	Article 8. 7	-
Sino-Hungary BIT	Article 9	Article 10.1 (except AOC *)	-	Article 10. 3 (AOC *)	-	-	-	-	Protocol
Sino-Latvia BIT	Article 8	Shared with the ICSID	-		Article 9. 2 (all legal disputes)	Article 9. 3	Article 9. 3	Article 9.3(mutual adoption not required)	-
Sino-Lithuania BIT	Article 7	Article 8. 2 (except AOC & Others *)	-	Article 8. 4 (AOC & Others *)	Article 8. 2 (AOC & Others *)	Article 8. 7	Article 8. 7	Article 8. 7	-

续表

BIT	State-State disputes: Negotiation/ consultation plus ad hoc international arbitration	State-investor disputes							
		jurisdiction				Applicable law			Future supplementary Agreement on ICSID arbitration
		Exclusive Domestic Jurisdiction	International Arbitration			Domestic Law(of the host country)	The Present Agreement	Principles of international law adopted by bothparties	
			Ad hoc		Submission to ICSID arbitration				
			No referenceto ICSID procedures	Reference to ICSID procedures					
Sino-Poland BIT	Article 9	Article 10. 1 (exceptAOC *)	Article 10. 2 (AOC *)		-	-	-	-	-
Sino-Slovakia BIT	Article 8	Article 9. 2 (except AOC & Others *)	Article 9. 2 (AOC & Others *)		-	-	-	-	-
Sino-Siovenia BIT	Article7	Article 8. 2 - 3 (exceptAOC *)	-	Article 8. 2 - 5(AOC *)	-	Article 8. 6	Article 8. 6	Article 8. 6	-
Total(9)	9			5	3	5	5	5	-

Source: Compiled by the author from the texts of the BITs.

Notes: * AOC refers to "disputes concerning the amount of compensation".

AOC & Others refers to both AOC disputes and other disputes as agreed by both parties to the disputes(to submit them for international arbitration) .

are different. In four BITs, only disputes concerning the amount of compensation for expropriation(AOC cases) can be submitted to international arbitration, and the arbitration has to be *ad hoc* arbitration.[110] All other investment disputes fall exclusively within the domestic jurisdiction of the host country. The Sino-Czech and the Sino-Slovakia BITs concluded in December 1991 went a step further to allow investment disputes other than AOC cases to be submitted for *ad hoc* arbitration.[111] Another progress was achieved by the Sino-Lithuania BIT concluded in late 1993, under which AOC cases can be automatically submitted to the ICSID for arbitration.[112] Other investment disputes may also be submitted to ICSID arbitration, provided that both parties to the disputes so agree.[113] Interestingly, the Sino-Lithuania BIT provides for *ad hoc* arbitration for the settlement of these investment disputes in case both countries were not contracting parties to the ICSID Convention.[114] Among the eight BITs providing for *ad hoc* arbitration, five expressly state that the arbitration tribunal may refer to the ICSID arbitration Rules in establishing its arbitration procedures.[115]

A final breakthrough on jurisdiction came with the Sino-Cyprus BIT, which was followed and further strengthened by the Sino-Latvia BIT.[116] Both BITs were signed after 2000 and are yet to be ratified. In accordance with the Sino-Cyprus BIT, any State-investor dispute, if it cannot be settled after six months of consultation, may be submitted to either a competent court of the Contracting Party involved or to the ICSID or an *ad hoc* arbitration tribunal, "at the request of either party". The two choices are exclusive to each other. In other words, if an investor chooses to submit the case to a domestic court, it loses the right to submit the case to international arbitration. Further, the Contracting Party involved "may" require the investor concerned to exhaust the domestic administrative review procedure before submitting the dispute to international arbitration. The Sino-Latvia BIT maintains that all legal disputes concerning investment may be automatically (that is, without the need to seek the concerned Contracting Party's specific consent) submitted to the ICSID for arbitration.[117] Both BITs were signed after 2000 and are yet to be ratified. The Sino-Latvia BIT, nevertheless, includes in its Protocol a special requirement by China that investors exhaust local administrative review procedures before resorting to ICSID arbitration.[118] Such a local administrative review shall take a maxi-

---

[110] Article 8. 2 – 3, Sino-Estonia BIT; Article 10. 1, Sino-Hungary BIT; Article 10. 1, Sino-Poland BIT; Article 8. 2 – 3, Sino-Slovenia BIT.

[111] Article 9. 2, Sino-Czechoslovakia BIT(now the Sino-Czech BIT and the Sino-Slovakia BIT).

[112] Article 8. 2, Sino-Lithuania BIT.

[113] Ibid.

[114] Ibid., Article 8. 3 – 7.

[115] Article 8. 5, Sino-Estonia BIT; Article 10. 3, Sino-Hungary BIT; Article 8. 4, Sino-Lithuania BIT; and Article 8. 2 – 5, Sino-Slovenia BIT.

[116] The New Sino-Germany BIT signed in December 2003(pending ratification) similar provisions on the jurisdiction for State—investor disputes; see its Article 9. 1 – 3.

[117] It does not, however, provide the opportunity for *ad hoc* arbitration. Article 9. 1 – 2, Sino-Latvia BII, *supra*, footnote 37.

[118] This provision seems to be modelled on the New Sino-Germany BIT; see Point 6(re: Article 9), Protocol to the New Sino-Gcnnany BIT.

mum of three months.[119]

It can thus be anticipated that China will be exposed to a much greater extent tointernational arbitration, particularly ICSID arbitration, after these newly signed treaties enter into force. As it stands, only AOC eases can currently be submitted automatically to the ICSID and no other investment cases may be submitted to international arbitration unless the Chinese government so approves.

(b) Applicable law

Five of the nine BITs explicitly stipulate the law applicable to State-investor disputes. Three of them follow the normal route and accept laws of the host country, "the present BIT" and(generally recognized) principles of international law adopted by both parties.[120] Again, Sino-Cyprus BIT and the Sino-Latvia BIT, the newest ones among them, mark another breakthrough in that they accept generally recognized principles of international law, without the need for such principles to be specifically adopted by the contracting parties.[121] This provision obviously has followed the pattern of the Sino-Morocco BIT concluded in 1995.[122] Whilst it is still unclear what precisely these agreements mean by "principles of international law", they clearly demonstrate China's growing confidence in general international law.

F. Summary of Terms on BITs between China and the EU 10 States

The Sino-EU 10 BITs are, by and large, similar to the Sino-EU 15 BITs. They follow the general European BIT practice and leave the right to regulate investment admission in the hands of the host country. Under the Sino-EU 10 BITs, foreign investors enjoy fair and equitable treatment and most-favoured-nation treatment. To a limited extent, they also enjoy national treatment and non-discriminatory treatment. Monetary transfers in convertible currency at the official or prevailing market rate of exchange is guaranteed, but they are still subject to domestic laws and regulations, particularly in the case of foreign investment in China.

Expropriation is broadly defined and conditional on the fulfilment of four conditions: public interest; due process of domestic law; non-discrimination; and payment of compensation. As far as compensation is concerned, none of these BITs refer to a particular general standard of compensation such as "full" "appropriate" or "adequate, prompt and effective" compensation. They nonetheless all guarantee that compensation will be equivalent to the value of the expropriated investment and, in most of the BITs, plus interest. Whilst most Sino-EU 10 BITs do not define the methods of the valuation of compensation, the Sino-Slovenia BIT stipulates that valuation shall follow "generally recognized principles of valuation and equitable principles, taking into account, *inter alia*, the capital invested, depreciation, capital already repatriated, replacement value and other relevant factors". With regard to investment guarantees, all of the Sino-EU 10 BITs recognize the subrogation of rights and claims from guaranteed investors to the contrac-

[119] Protocol to the Sino-Latvia BIT, *supra*, footnote 37.

[120] Article 8. 7, Sino-Estonia BIT; Article 8. 7, Sino-Lithuania BIT and Article 8. 6, Sino-Slovenia BIT.

[121] Article 9 - 7, Sino-Cyprus BIT; Article 9. 3, Sino-Latvia BIT, *supra*, footnote 37.

[122] Article 10(4), Sino-Morocco BIT.

ting party providing such guarantees.

As it stands, only disputes between the host government and the foreign investor concerning the amount of compensation can be automatically submitted to the ICSID or an *ad hoc* international arbitration tribunal. Submission of other investment disputes still requires approval from the government concerned. However, once the Sino-Cyprus BIT or the Sino-Latvia BIT enters into force, all State-investor disputes may be automatically submitted to the ICSID for arbitration upon request of the foreign investor. In terms of the law applicable to State-investor disputes, a few BITs explicitly refer to not only the laws of the host country and "the present BIT" but also to "generally recognized principles of international law", which is sometimes qualified by "adopted by both parties".

On the whole, the nine Sino-EU 10 BITs have provided substantial protection for mutual investment between China and these nine new EU Member States. The nine BITs have also demonstrated the increased and increasing confidence of China in international arbitration and international law. However, the Sino-EU 10 BITs do not add much more protection for the EU 15 States, as they have already enjoyed an equivalent level of protection. The 2001 Sino-Cyprus BIT and the 2004 Sino-Latvia BIT will have the effect of significantly upgrading the protection level, notably by tightening up the restrictions on the application of national treatment and by granting foreign investors the right to bring all State-investor disputes to the ICSID for arbitration. However, it is yet to be known whether and when these BITs might enter into force.

IV. Conclusions

China has a long and close investment and trade relationship with the EU 10 States, mainly due to their shared past communist experience. A significant growth in trade and investment has been seen in recent years between the two sides. A notable feature of the bilateral economic relationships is that there has been significant Chinese investment in these EU 10 States and it is set to further increase in the future.

The current legal framework governing Sino-EU 10 investment relationships is mainly composed of multilateral agreements, bilateral agreements and domestic laws. Most importantly, the multilateral agreements include the ICSID Convention, to which China and nine of the EU 10 states are Contracting Parties, as well as the MIGA Convention and the WTO Agreement, to both of which China and all the EU 10 States are Members. The most important bilateral agreements are BITs and DTTs. So far, nine of the EU 10 States have concluded BITs with China and all of them also have DTT arrangements with China. Finally both China and the EU 10 States have extensive domestic laws and regulations on foreign investment.

A close examination of the Sino-EU 10 BITs shows that they do not differ significantly from the Sino-EU 15 BITs, as both sets of treaties follow the traditional European BIT practice. Under the Sino-EU 10 BITs, mutual investment is encouraged, but the right to regulate investment admission is still left in the hands of the host governments. Mutual investment is facilitated by the provision of equitable and fair treatment and most-favoured-nation treatment and, to a certain extent, national treatment and non-discriminatory treatment. Subject to domestic laws of foreign exchange control, the freedom of monetary transfers is also guaranteed.

Foreign investment is free from expropriation, unless such expropriation is conducted in the public interest, following due process of domestic law, in a non-discriminatory manner and accompanied with compensation. Such compensation will be equivalent to the value of the expropriated investment, plus necessary interest. Subrogation is recognized in all these BITs to facilitate the operation of government investment-guarantee schemes.

At the request of a foreign investor, it is now possible to directly submit State-investor disputes concerning the amount of compensation to the ICSID for international arbitration. Submission of other State-investor disputes is also possible, provided that such submission is approved by both parties to the dispute. After the Sino-Cyprus BIT or the Sino-Latvia BIT enters into force, it will be possible for all State-investor disputes to be automatically submitted to the ICSID for arbitration without the need to seek approval from the host country concerned. Some BITs make clear that the law applicable to such disputes is the domestic law of the host country, "the present BIT" and general principles of international law.

Although the Sino-EU 10BITs do not add much more protection for the existing EU 15 States, the enlargement of the EU does further enhance the bilateral investment and trade links between the two sides. Despite the trade-and investment-transfer effects the enlargement may have, the enlarged EU has become the second-largest trade partner of China and will likely soon lead China's trade partners' league table. EU-China investment relations will be likewise expanded, not only by increased EU investment in China but also by growing Chinese investment in the EU, particularly in the EU 10 States. Whilst the current legal framework does provide substantial protection for the development of mutual investment, and new BITs will foster such protection, it would still be better to have an investment arrangement with China at the EU level as envisaged elsewhere,[123] since such a new international legal framework between China and the EU would provide sufficient protection for all EU Member States, including those that have no BIT arrangements with China.

[123] In view of the deficiencies of the current legal framework governing EU-China investment relations, the author has proposed the establishment of a new international legal framework to promote and protect mutual investment in the form of a China-EU bilateral treaty or a multilateral agreement to which China and the EU would be parties: for further details, see Shan, *supra*, footnote 3. pp. 168 – 179.

The International Law of EU Investment in China*

Carefully EU investment in the People's Republic of China(hereinafter referred to as China[1]) has increased significantly in recent years. In the year 2000, the EU overtook Japan and the US, becoming the biggest "foreign" investor in China, excluding Hong Kong.[2] It is beyond doubt that the coming years will see an even more dramatic growth in EU direct investment in China, as a result of China's accession to the WTO. Indeed, as Mr. Perodi correctly pointed out, China's WTO accession "will provide substantial new market opportunities for European companies selling to China or investing there, and will create or secure many European jobs".[3]

However, what is the role of law in the development of EU investment in China? This question underlies a research programme in which this article represents some of the preliminary reflections. Although an outsider tends to discount the importance of law in the light of East Asian history particularly that of China after World War II, it was recently asserted that law has been among the most important factors in the Pacific economic boom.[4] In China's case, the great efforts that it has made to establish a favourable foreign direct investment(FDI) legal system have made a considerable contribution to

---

* *Chinese Journal of International Law*, Volume 1 No. 2, 2002.

The Author would like to thank Professor Sir Elihu Lauterpacht for his stimulating supervisions and particularly his insightful comments on an earlier draft of this article. He also wishes to thank Miss Alice Bianchi for her help and comments, and Trinity College, the Committee of Vice-Chancellors and Principals of the Universities of the United Kingdom(the CVCP) and the Cambridge Overseas Trust(the COT) for kindly sponsoring this research programme.

[1] Unless otherwise stated, "China" mainly refers to Mainland China, which does not cover Hong Kong, Macau and Taiwan where different economic and legal systems are in operation. Also, for clarity and at the risk of repetition, some abbreviations used herein are: "BIT" for "bilateral investment treaty"; "MC" for "Ministerial Conference"; "NPC" for "National People's Congress"; "PRC" for "People's Republic of China"; "SCNPC" for "the Standing Committee of the National People's Congress".

[2] The contracted and utilised EU FDIs were respectively US $ 8. 8 and US $ 4. 5. See Communication from the Commission to the Council and the European Parliament, EU Strategy towards China: Implementation of the 1998 Communication and future steps for a more effective policy, COM(2001) 265 final, 12.

[3] See <http: / /europa. eu. int/ comm/trade/bilateral/ china/prodi. htm > (07/06/2001).

[4] Nicholas Emilou and David O' Keeffe, The European Union and the World Trade Law: after the Uruguay Round, (1996), 363.

the success in attracting FDI to China.[5] According to a survey carried out by the author in 2001, when deciding to invest in China, most EU investors(82%) have considered law as an element of substantial importance(top, high or medium) (See Chart 1) and most of them have made an in-depth investigation of the legal regime.[6]

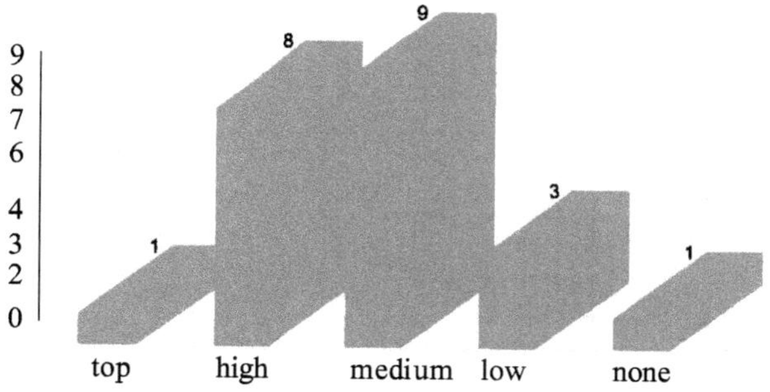

Chart 1 Relative Importance of Law in Investment Decision Making

Nevertheless, there are still deep concerns and worries among EU investors on the FDI legal environment in China. Some of the "old" ones who had suffered from the "retaliatory confiscation" or "hostage capitalism" may yet have to recover from the memories of bitter experiences. New investors may be frightened by political events or governmental interventions such as the "Beijing McDonald's" case[7] that had drawn wide and continuous international attentions. Indeed, as observed by Chew, the fact that China is in transition and under rapid change could lead to huge potential political risks.[8]

Unfortunately, so far there has been no specific study on the legal aspects of the EU-China investment relations, although there have been a few studies on the law and policy of the EC-China trade and economic relations in general.[9] As a result, EU investors' knowledge of the legal environment of EU investment in China has been fairly

---

[5] China has been the second biggest FDI recipient in the world and the single biggest among developing countries for several consecutive years. See e. g., Rubens Ricupero(Secretary General of UNCTAD), Recent Development In FDI Trends and Policies and Their Implications for Developing Counties, a paper submitted on the Forum on Direct Investment Strategies of the Multinational Corporations(Sept. 1998), Xiamen, 7.

[6] See Section 3. 1 of "The Report of Survey on Law and EU Investment in China"(the Survey Report), 40.

[7] In 1994, McDonald's Corporation's land lease on its flagship restaurant near Tiananmen Square was reportedly cancelled by a decision of Beijing municipal authorities. The city's position was that the location was needed as part of a larger redevelopment project funded by a Hong Kong investor. A settlement of the dispute, providing compensation to McDonald's, was reportedly reached between the parties in mid - 1996. McDonald's was also allowed to open at least two more outlets along a adjacent street. See U. S. and Foreign Commercial Service(US&FCS) (Telegraphic Report from the American Embassy In Beijing): China: Investment Climate Statement for 1997. See also Thomas L. Friedman, Fed Up, New York Times(04 - 12 - 1996), 29.

[8] Chew, a US scholar believes that despite the continuing increase of US investment in China, huge potential political risks persist and must not be overlooked. See Pat K. Chew, Political Risk and U. S. Investments In China: Chimera Of Protection And Predictability? Va. J. Intl. L. (1994), particularly part I. B and II. C.

[9] See e. g., Hu Yuanxiang, Legal and Policy Issues of the Trade and Economic Relations between China and the EEC, Kluwer(1991). Xiao Zhiyue, The EC and China, Butterworths(1993).

modest. For instance, the author's survey has shown that although most EU investors tried to investigate the governing national and international laws before they invested in China, less than 50% of them knew that there were bilateral investment treaties to be taken advantage of, and the knowledge of MIGA Convention and ICSID Convention was much worse(*less* than 20%) (Chart 2).[10] Unsurprisingly, such a lack of legal knowledge has prevented EU investors from taking full advantage of the market opportunities provided by China.[11]

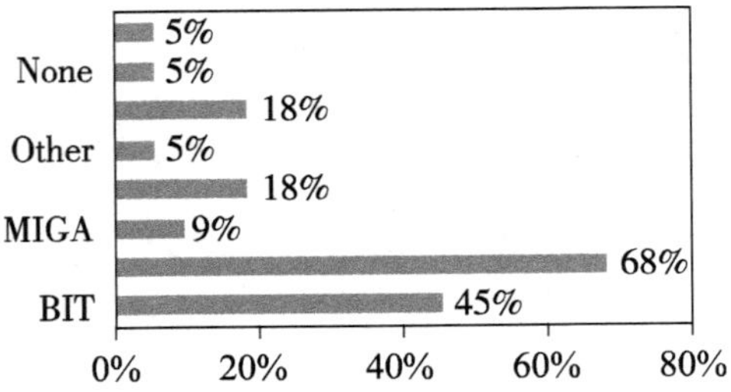

Chart 2 International Treaties Known when Making Investment Decisions

Against this background, this article aims to provide a survey of the applicable rules of international law governing EU investment in China. It is divided into four sections. Section I deals with the general relationship between Chinese law and international law. Section II investigates the multilateral legal framework while Section III looks at the legal regime on a bilateral level. Conclusions and comments are presented at the end of this article.

Ⅰ. EU Investment in China and International Law

1. Applicable International Law

International law plays an important role in the general legal framework of EU investment in China.[12] Within the context of the "Opening-up" policy, China has made great efforts to establish a sound international legal framework for protecting and attracting FDI. To this extent, the EU member states were among the first countries targeted by China with a view to concluding bilateral investment treaties. As early as 1982, China signed its very first bilateral investment treaty(BIT) with Sweden. Since then, China has signed 13 BIT with 14 EU member states. China has also concluded treaties of avoidance of double taxation(DTT) with most EU member states. In addition to the 1985 Coopera-

---

〔10〕 See Section 2. 2 of the Survey Report, 10, 11.

〔11〕 For example, EU investors have long been hesitant in taking the CJV form of investment, as a result of lack of knowledge on this form and the Chinese legal and business cultures in general. See e. g. , Hu Yuanxiang, above n. 10, 142 - 143.

〔12〕 According to the Author's Survey, about half of those who investigated the legal aspects before making the investment decisions studied applicable international treaties. See Section 2. 2 in the Survey Report, 10.

tion Agreement between the EU and China, the BITs and the DTTs constitute the bilateral network of international law that governs EU investment in China.

On the other hand, on a multilateral level, China also has participated in the major global agreements on investment. Among them, two multilateral agreements are devoted to specific aspects of investment, namely, the Conventions on the Settlement of Investment Disputes between States and Nationals of Other States(the ICSID Convention) and the Convention Establishing the Multilateral Investment Guarantee Agency(the MIGA Convention). Furthermore, the Agreement Establishing the World Trade Organisation (the WTO Agreement) is closely related to investment issues.

These bilateral and multilateral agreements constitute the international legal framework for EU investment in China, whose contents and implications on EU investment in China are explored in the following sections of this article.

2. International Treaties within the Chinese Legal System

Before investigating the substance of these applicable international treaties, it is necessary and indeed worthwhile to discuss the general role of international treaties within the Chinese legal system. To address this question, three interlinked aspects have to be examined, namely, the relationship between international treaties and domestic law, the integration of international treaties within Chinese law and their direct applicability by Chinese Courts.

2.1 The relationship between International Treaties and Municipal Law

As yet, no constitutional rules have been enacted to govern the relationship between international treaties and domestic law. The Chinese Constitution merely provides for general rules on treaty making and ratification[13] but is silent on their legal status within municipal legal systems.

However, laws and regulations in China provide that in cases of a conflict between international treaty and domestic law, international treaty provisions shall prevail. The General Principles of Civil Law(GPCL) stipulate that,

If an international treaty concluded or acceded to by the PRC contains provisions differing from those in the civil laws of the PRC, the provisions of the international treaty shall apply, unless the provisions are ones on which the PRC has made reservations thereon.[14]

Similar provisions can be found in as many as 70 laws and regulations, ranging from civil, civil procedure, administrative procedure, patent, wildlife preservation, to postal

---

[13] The Chinese Constitution provides that the State Council shall sign treaties and agreements with other countries, while the Standing Committee of the National People's Congress(SCNPC) shall decide to ratify or abolish these treaties and agreements, and the Head of the State shall approve or abolish these treaties and agreements in line with the decisions of the SCNPC. The treaty making procedure is similar to the procedure for domestic legislation. Such similarity suggests that international treaties have the same legal effect as domestic legislation. See Constitution of the PRC, Articles 89, 67 and 81. See also Wang Tieya, International Law, (1995), 33; Zeng Lingliang, Application of WTO Agreements in China and a Revolution of China's Legal Construction, Chinese Legal Science(Zhongguo Faxue), (2000, No. 6), 42.

[14] General Principles of Civil Law of the PRC, Article 142.

administration, etc.[15] In particular, the Regulations on Some Issues in Handling Foreign-related Cases, jointly promulgated in August 1987 by the Ministry of Foreign Affairs, the Supreme People's Court, the Supreme People's Procuratorate, the Ministry of Public Security, Ministry of State and the Ministry of justice, provide that,

When domestic legislation or internal regulations are in conflict with obligations undertaken by China under an international treaty, rules of the international treaty shall be applied. Provisions of domestic legislation shall not be invoked as justification for the refusal to perform the obligations undertaken by China under the international treaty.

Among Chinese scholars, several take these provisions as evidence to the effect that China has already accepted, as a general principle, the superiority of treaties over all municipal laws and regulations.[16] Others, however, believe that such provisions are merely an expression of China's willingness to accept the superiority of treaties within the legal hierarchy on specific areas, namely foreign-related civil and commercial, civil procedural and administrative procedural areas, rather than over the entirety of Chinese law.[17] It has been further pointed out that, given that the right to interpret rules on applicable laws rests in the hands of the Standing Committee of the National People's Congress (SCNPC), the general binding effect of the said Regulations is disputable.[18] As a result, it is unclear whether the overriding effect of international treaties over domestic law can be maintained in the absence of further constitutional clarification.

Accordingly, whether the aforementioned investment-related multilateral and bilateral agreements (hereinafter "investment treaties") override domestic law is still debatable. As a matter of fact, all major laws and regulations on foreign trade and FDI do not mention the status of international treaties *vis-a-vis* domestic law. Scholarly debates over the application of the WTO agreement in China have suggested that at least certain issues in the WTO Agreement relating to tariffs, anti-dumping, market access of financial services and trade-related investment measures are not subject to the principle of the superiority of international treaties over national law.[19]

The general status of the WTO Agreement within the Chinese legal system has also drawn special attentions. Some scholars argue that the place of WTO agreements shall be equal to laws made by the SCNPC, i. e., higher within the overall legal hierarchy than administrative regulations and local regulations but lower than constitutional and basic laws made by the National People's Congress (NPC).[20] Scholars have further argued that should conflicts arise between WTO agreements and laws, the principles of *lex poste-*

〔15〕 Chen Hanfeng, Zhou Weiguo and Jiang Hao, The Relationship between International Treaties and Municipal Law and the Practices of China, Political Science and Law Review (Zhengfa Luntan), (2000, No. 2), 122; Wang Tieya, above n. 14, 33.

〔16〕 He Xiaoyong, On the Application of WTO Agreements in Chinese Courts,]. Intl. Trade (Guoji Maoyi Wenti) (2001, No. 3), 50.

〔17〕 See e. g., id.; Wang Tieya, above n. 14, 33; Zeng Lingliang, above n. 14, 45; Chen Hanfeng et al., above n. 16, 122.

〔18〕 He Xiaoyong, above n. 17.

〔19〕 Ibid.

〔20〕 Above n. 17, 50 – 51.

rior derogate priori or *lex generalis non derogate legi speciali* shall apply.[21]

Indeed, under international law and as restated in the Vienna Convention of the Law of Treaties[22], China may not "invoke the provisions of its internal law as justification for its failure to carry out an international agreement".[23] In other words, China must guarantee that treaties and agreements it concludes or accedes to shall have binding force in China. Furthermore, as observed by Professor Judge Wang Tieya, the sheer fact that a series of laws covering a wide range of areas have adopted the principle of superiority of international treaties over domestic law, has indicated a clear legislative policy tendency and therefore, has made it possible for the principle to become a general principle of law in China.[24]

2.2 The Reception of International Treaties within Chinese Legal System

A survey of different countries' practices on the reception of international law reveals two basic approaches to give effect to international treaties within a given legal system: incorporation or transformation.[25] "Incorporation" implies a process of integration whereby international treaties become a part of the domestic legal system and as such can be directly applicable. This process may be achieved via enactment or amendment of constitutional provisions, the ratification and publication of treaties or via judicial means. "Transformation" implies that an international treaty will not be binding and applicable until domestic legislation is adopted to accept or absorb the contents of the treaty within national law.[26]

To this extent, the Chinese Constitution is silent, while its sub-constitutional legislation varies. So far Chinese legislative practices concerning international treaties may be classified as follows:

A. Numerous Chinese laws and regulations, as mentioned above, allow international treaties to take precedence over domestic law where a conflict arises between the two. This suggests international treaties will be directly applicable, regardless of the absence of legislation to give such treaties effect under Chinese law.

B. A few laws and regulations expressly provide that on certain specific issues international treaties shall be applied. For example, Article 263 of the Civil Procedure Law requires that, "Requesting or offering judicial assistance shall go through the channels provided for by international treaties that China concluded or acceded to; in the absence of such international treaties, diplomatic channels shall be adhered to".

C. Sometimes China also lays down specific regulations for the application of certain international treaties. For instance, China acceded to the Vienna Convention on Dip-

---

[21] Zeng Lingliang, above n. 14, 45; He Xiaoyong, ibid., p. 51.

[22] According to Chinese Ministry of Foreign Affairs, China deposited the protocol of accession on 3 September 1997, which took effect on 3 October 1997. See < http://www.fmprc.gov.cn/chn/premade/8275/duobian.htm > (visited4 December 2002).

[23] Vienna Convention on the Law of Treaties, Article 26.

[24] WangTieya, above n. 14, 33.

[25] Jiang Guoqin, Some Problems on International Law and International Treaties, at < http://www.people-daily.eom.cn/GB/shehui/212/3572/35 75/20001229/365132.html > (visited 5January 2001).

[26] Ibid.

lomatic Relations and the Vienna Convention on Consular Relations in 1975 and 1979 respectively. To implement them in China, China promulgated Regulations on Diplomatic Privileges and Immunities and Regulations on Consular Privileges and Immunities in 1986 and 1990.[27]

D. In some other cases, China promulgates municipal rules including contents of an international treaty as a preparatory step for formal accession to the treaty. For instance, in 1995, China enacted the "Civil Aviation Law", whose provisions reflect the rights of civil aircraft as they appear in the 1948 "Convention on the International Recognition of Rights in Aircraft". In October 1999, the SCNPC formally acceded to the Convention.[28]

It is therefore arguable that China has adopted a "mixed approach" towards the reception of international agreements: in the first two cases an "incorporation approach" is employed and in the latter two cases a "transformation approach" is used.[29]

On the reception of international trade and investment agreements, however, it has been made clear by a recent regulation stipulated by the Supreme People's Court (SPC),[30] that a "transformation approach" has been adopted. The regulation maintains that, in adjudicating administrative cases involving international trade, Chinese courts can only apply Chinese national and local laws and regulations.[31] The authority's explanations of the regulation clarify that this regulation applies to international investment administrative cases as well.[32] Further, it is said that such a regulation is compatible with the commitments that China made in the course of WTO accession negotiations.[33] Therefore, it is clear that, at least from a judicial point of view, international trade and investment agreements to which China has become a party must be transformed into Chinese law before they can be applied and implemented. Nevertheless, the regulation requires that the domestic laws and regulations implementing international trade and investment treaties be interpreted in a manner that is consistent with international treaties should there be more than one interpretations of any specific provision of those domestic laws and regulations.[34]

2.3 The Direct Applicability of International Treaties by Chinese Courts

The direct applicability of international treaties by local courts is closely linked to the approach that a country chooses to give effect to international treaties. If the "incorporation" method is used, international treaties have direct applicability without the need for extra legislation. In contrast, if a country adopts the "transformation" model, interna-

---

〔27〕 Chen Hanfeng et al., above n. 16, 121.

〔28〕 Ibid.

〔29〕 Similar argument can be seen in Zeng Lingliang, above n. 14, 42.

〔30〕 The Provisions on Some Issues on the Adjudication of Administrative Cases Concerning International Trade (The Trade Cases Provisions), promulgated by the SPC on 29 August 2002.

〔31〕 Article 7 and 8, The Trade Cases Provisions.

〔32〕 TianJi, Lin Zhi, Judicial Review of Administrative Actions Involving International Trade, People's Daily(overseas edition) (7 September, 2002), 3.

〔33〕 Ibid.

〔34〕 Article 9, The Trade Cases Provisions.

tional treaties cannot be directly applied but need to be "indirectly" applied via domestic legislation.[35]

In China, where there are no constitutional provisions as such, there is, again, no general rule on the direct applicability of international treaties before Chinese courts. However, as said above, the SPC's regulation has made clear that international trade and investment treaties are not directly applicable by Chinese courts.

2.4 Summary

China has not yet established a general rule or principle to deal with the relationship between international treaties and Chinese law. This results from a lack of relevant constitutional rules. However, numerous Chinese laws and regulations have either confirmed the direct applicability of international treaties or have expressly provided that international treaties take precedence over national law, which has shown China's willingness to accept the superiority of international treaties as a general principle of law.

Accordingly, China has not established a general rule on the reception of international treaties within Chinese legal system and the direct applicability of these treaties before Chinese courts. However, a recent judicial regulation has made clear that a transformation approach has been employed in implementing international trade and investment treaties in China and thus such treaties are not directly applicable by Chinese courts.

Ⅱ. EU Investment in China under Multilateral Agreements

1. The ICSID Convention

1.1 The ICSID Convention and EU Investment in China

The ICSID Convention, or the Washington Convention as it is sometimes referred to after its birthplace, was concluded in 1965 and entered into force in October 1966, under the auspices of the World Bank. Briefly speaking, the ICSID Convention provides an institutional and procedural mechanism for the settlement of investment disputes between governments and foreign investors, through conciliation and arbitration.[36] It establishes an International Centre for Settlement of Investment Disputes (ICSID or the Centre), which does not itself engage in conciliation or arbitration, but provides facilities for the conciliation commissions of arbitration tribunals constituted in accordance with the Convention to carry out these tasks.

The ICSID was established to satisfy the need for an apolitical mechanism to provide facilitates for the arbitration of investment disputes between developing states and foreign investors.[37] Traditionally, host countries would not accept the jurisdiction of

---

[35] Furthermore, the direct applicability of a specific international treaty may depend on its nature. For example, in the United States, domestic courts can only apply "self-executing" treaty provisions. Malcolm N. Shaw, International Law(4th ed. 1998), 118.

[36] ICSID Convention, Art. 1. For discussions of the Convention and the Center in Chinese please see CHEN An, A Commentary on the ICSID Convention (in Chinese) (hereinafter referred to as "ICSID Commentary") (1989).

[37] Kenneth Jacobs, Reinvigorating ICSID With a New Mission and With Renewed Respect for Party Autonomy(1992), 33.. Va. J. Intl L., 123.

conventional commercial arbitration institutions such as the International Chamber of Commerce(ICC) or the American Arbitration Association(AAA). On the other hand, "international" arbitration tribunals like the Permanent Court of Arbitration(PCA) were not open to private investors.[38] Therefore, there was a vacuum of a widely recognised and accepted arbitration tribunal which resulted in a variety of creative solutions.[39] The creation of ICSID is perhaps the most successful solution so far.

The ICSID Convention has drawn wide acceptance. As of October 1, 1999, 147 States had signed the ICSID Convention, 131 of which have already deposited their instruments of ratification.[40] Although not many disputes have been referred to the Centre, its caseload has increased significantly in recent years.[41] The fact that ICSID arbitration clauses are also commonly found in investment agreements between governments of member countries and investors from other member countries also suggests widespread adoption. Advance consents by governments to submit investment disputes to ICSID arbitration can be found in about 20 investment laws and in over 900 bilateral investment treaties.[42] Moreover, arbitration under the auspices of ICSID is one of the main mechanisms for the settlement of investment disputes under four recent regional trade and investment treaties, namely the North American Free Trade Agreement, the Energy Charter Treaty, the Cartagena Free Trade Agreement and the Colonia Investment Protocol of Mercosur.[43]

The ICSID Convention is an important multilateral legal instrument for EU investment in China since both China and all EU Member States are its signatories(See Table 1: China and EU member States as ICSID Signatories). Most EU countries signed the Convention in the 1960s and 70s while a few signed in the 1980s and 90s. After careful

---

〔38〕 William T. Ketcham, Arbitration between a State and a Foreign Private Party(1961), 405 – 406. However; since 1990s, the PCA has adopted optional rules, allowing private parties to make use of its arbitration and conciliation facilities when they have disputes with a State or an international organization. Details please see Permanent Court of Arbitration Optional Rules for Arbitrating Disputes between Two Parties of Which Only One Is a State(effective July 6, 1993), Permanent Court of Arbitration Optional Rules for Arbitration between International Organizations and Private Parties(Effective July I, 1996) and Permanent Court of Arbitration Optional Conciliation Rules(Effective July 1, 1996). All available at <http: / /pca-cpa. org/BD/ >(visited 3 December 2002).

〔39〕 For example, the World Bank and the President of the Bank have assisted in mediation or conciliation of some investment disputes, such as the nationalisation of Anglo-Iranian Oil Company's assets in 1951 and 1952, and the nationalisation by each of the Suez Canal in 1956. See Malcolm D. Rowat, Multilateral Approaches to improving the Investment Climate of Developing Country: The case of ICSID and MIGA, 33 Harv. Int'l. LJ. (1992), 106.

〔40〕 1999 ICSID: List of Contracting States, published on its website: <http: *I lwww.* worldbank. org/icsid/ about/ about. htm >.

〔41〕 So far ICSID has concluded 38 cases and 28 case are still in process. See ICSID Cases, at <http: / / www. worldbank. org/icsid/cases/cases. htm >. See also About ICSID, at <http: / /www. worldbank. org/icsid/about/about. htm >.

〔42〕 1999 ICSID: *About ICSID*, published on its website: <http: / /www. worldbank. org/ icsid/ about/about. htm >.

〔43〕 Ibid.

consideration[44], China signed the Convention in 1990 and ratified it in 1993.[45] Moreover, among the 13 BITs that China concluded with the EU Member States, most refer to the ICSID Convention.[46] Most of them provide that the arbitral tribunal established to settle a state-investor dispute shall determine its own procedures with references to the ICSID Convention,[47] while others require the negotiation of a supplementary agreement by the contracting parties on a binding system of dispute settlement within the framework of ICSID.[48]

Table 1 China and EU Member States as ICSID Signatories[49]

(As of October 1, 1999)

State	Signature	Deposit of Ratification	Entry into Force
China	Feb. 9, 1990	Jan. 7, 1993	Feb. 6, 1993
Austria	May 17, 1966	May25, 1971	June 24, 1971
Belgium	Dec. 15, 1965	Aug. 27, 1970	Sep. 26, 1970
Denmark	Oct. 11, 1965	Apr. 24, 1968	May 24, 1968
Finland	July 14, 1967	Jan. 9, 1969	Feb. 8, 1969
France	Dec. 22, 1965	Aug. 21, 1967	Sep. 20, 1967
Germany	Jan. 27, 1966	Apr. 18, 1969	May 18, 1969
Greece	Mar. 16, 1966	Apr. 21, 1969	May 21, 1969
Ireland	Aug. 30, 1966	Apr. 7, 1981	May 7, 1981
Italy	Nov. 18, 1965	Mar. 29, 1971	Apr. 28, 1971
Lux'g	Sep. 28, 1965	July 30, 1970	Aug. 29, 1970

[44] In 1986, Chinese publicists debated on the acceptance of the ICSID Convention by China, where very controversial views were presented. Some rejected immediate accession, as it would restrict Chinese sovereignty, while some others argued that China should join in as soon as possible to improve the investment environment and speed up the "opening up" process. A third voice purported that China investigate the ICSID mechanism thoroughly before making the decision. It seemed that the latter view had greater appeal as the Chinese government delayed accession to the Convention by 4 years.

[45] In January 1966, the Taiwanese Government signed the Convention and ratified it in 1968. However, its membership was revoked in October 1980 by the 14th Annual Meeting of the Administrative Council of ICSID, in the light of China's interest in joining in the Convention. See Chen An, International Investment Disputes Arbitration-A Study on the ICSID Mechanism (hereinafter referred to as "ICSID Mechanism") (2001), 21.

[46] Those include BITs between China and Sweden, Germany, France, Belgium-Luxembourg Economic Union, Finland, Italy, Austria and Denmark.

[47] See BITs between China and Germany, Belgium-Luxembourg Economic Union, Finland, Italy, Austria and Denmark.

[48] See Sino-France BIT and Sino-Sweden BIT.

[49] Compiled by the author according to List of Contracting States and other Signatories of the Convention; see: http://www.worldbank.org/icsid/constate/c-states-en.htm (visited 5 December 2002).

续表

State	Signature	Deposit of Ratification	Entry into Force
Neth'd	May 25, 1966	Sep. 14, 1966	Oct. 14, 1966
Portugal	Aug. 4, 1983	July 2, 1984	Aug. I, 1984
Spain	Mar. 21, 1994	Aug. 18, 1994	Sept. I 7, 1994
Sweden	Sep. 25, 1965	Dec. 29, 1966	Jan. 28, 1967
U. K.	May 26, 1965	Dec. 19, 1966	Jan. 18, 1967

So far, China has never called upon the ICSID. Nor has China been sued by any EU investor before the ICSID.

The paragraphs below analyse the Centre's mechanism, including its organisation, jurisdiction, applicable law and awards, particularly with reference to their application to China.

1.2 Organisation

The Centre has an Administrative Council and a Secretariat and maintains a Panel of Conciliators and a Panel of Arbitrators.[50] The Administrative Council is composed of one representative from each country, with the President of the World Bank as its *ex officio* Chairman.[51] The Administrative Council meets at least once every year and makes all the important administrative decisions of the Centre.[52] The Secretariat is headed by the Secretary General who is the legal representative of and the principal officer of the Centre.[53] The Secretary General is responsible for administration and performs the functions of registrar of the Centre.[54]

Contracting States and the Chairman have overall responsibility for the designation of the two panels of conciliators and arbitrators.[55]. Panelists are supposed to be persons of high moral character and of recognised competence in the fields of law, commerce, industry or finance, who may be relied upon to exercise independent judgment.[56] All EU member states have designated conciliators and arbitrators to the ICSID.[57] In 1993, China decided to designate 4 conciliators and arbitrators to the Centre. However, for some reason the process has not been finalised and no Chinese concili-

---

〔50〕 ICSID Convention, Art. 3.

〔51〕 Ibid., Art. 4(1).

〔52〕 Ibid., Art. 6 and 7.

〔53〕 Ibid., Art. ll.

〔54〕 Ibid.

〔55〕 Each Contracting State may designate 4 Conciliators and 4 arbitrators to the Panels, while the Chairman can designate 10 to each panel. Ibid., 13.

〔56〕 Ibid., Art. 14.

〔57〕 For details, see < http:/ /www. worldbank. org/icsid/pubs/icsid – 10/icsid-IO. htm > (01January, 2002).

ators or arbitrators have appeared in the two panels yet.[58]

The Centre itself does not engage in conciliation or arbitration, which are to be conducted by Conciliation Commissions(CCs) or Arbitration Tribunals(ATs) constituted according to the Convention. Parties to a specific dispute may appoint persons outside of the two panels as conciliators or arbitrators, provided they possess the quality required as panelists.[59]. However, in case the Chairman appoints conciliators or arbitrators, they shall be within the Panels.[60]

1.3 Jurisdiction[61]

The most important breakthrough that the ICSID has made lies in its jurisdiction provisions, which, for the first time in history, make it possible for an international institution to conciliate and arbitrate state-investor disputes that were previously exclusively reserved to domestic courts. According to Article 25(I) of the ICSID Convention,

The jurisdiction of the Centre shall extend to any legal disputes arising directly out of an investment, between a Contracting State(or any constituent subdivision or agency of a Contracting State designated to the Centre by that State) and a national of another Contracting State, which the parties to the dispute consent in writing to submit to the Centre. When the parties have given their consent, no party may withdraw its consent unilaterally.

Therefore, four conditions must be satisfied before the Centre can assume jurisdiction over a dispute:

Firstly, the dispute must involve a Contracting State and a national of another Contracting State. In other words, both the host and home states of an investor must have signed and ratified the Convention.[62] This limitation is in keeping with the purpose of the creation of the Centre as a new international forum for handling exclusively state-investor disputes, rather than state-state or private-private disputes that have already been dealt with by existing international courts and arbitration tribunals. The "Contracting State" here includes "any constituent subdivision or agency of a Contracting State designated to the Centre by that State", the consent of which shall be subject to the approval of that state until the State notifies otherwise.[63] "National of another Contracting State"

---

[58] Chen An, above n. 47, 70. Professor CHEN An was among the list of arbitrators designated by the Chinese Government.

[59] Ibid.

[60] Ibid., Art. 31 and 40.

[61] *As* noted by Aron Broches, the term "jurisdiction" here is open to objection, on the ground that the Centre is not a court but an administrative organ under whose auspices conciliation commission and arbitration tribunal may be established and proceedings conducted. However, he argues that precedent of this kind of usage could be found in the Hague Convention for the Pacific Settlement of International Disputes of 1907 which created the Permanent Court of Arbitration, an administrative framework to facilitate arbitral proceedings. See A. Broches, The Convention on the Settlement of Investment Disputes: Some Observations on Jurisdiction, in: Aron Broches(ed.), Selected Essays: World Bank, ICSID, and Other Subjects of Public and Private International Law(1995), 166.

[62] In 1978 the Centre added an "Additional Facility", which allowed recourse to the main Centre mechanism even if only one party met the requirement, provided that both parties had so agreed. See Elihu Lauterpacht, Foreword, in: The ICSID Convention: A Commentary(by Christoph H. Schreuer) (2001), xi.

[63] The ICSID Convention, Article 25(3).

could be a natural person or a juridical person having the nationality of a Contracting State other than the Contracting State party, on the date on which the parties consented to submit the dispute to the Centre.[64] In addition, a juridical person possessing the nationality of the Contracting State party can be qualified as a "national of another Contracting State" if the parties agree to treat it this way on grounds of foreign control.[65]

As a result, all EU investors in China, regardless of whether they are natural persons or juridical persons, are "nationals of another Contracting State" under the Convention and can make use of the ICSID regime to settle their investment disputes with the Chinese Government. Furthermore, foreign invested enterprises(FIEs) controlled by these EU investors may also be treated as "nationals of another contracting state" and may therefore be able to make use of the Centre mechanism, provided that both the FIE and the Chinese Government so agree.[66]

Secondly, the dispute must "arise directly out of an investment". There is no definition on "investment" within the ICSID regime. During the negotiations several definitions of "investment" were considered and rejected.[67] It was accepted in the end that a definition could be dispensed with "given the essential requirement of consent by the parties".[68] In other words, the requirement that investment disputes must arise out of "investment" can be inferred by a party's consent. Thus, the parties agreement that a dispute is an "investment dispute" will give great weight establishing the Centre's jurisdiction over a particular case, even though it might not be controlling.[69]

Thirdly, the dispute must be a "legal dispute"[70] Again, there is no definition of legal dispute in the Convention. According to the Executive Report, the term "legal dispute" indicates that while conflicts of rights would fall within the Centre's jurisdiction mere conflicts of interests would not. Furthermore, "the dispute must concern the existence or scope of a legal right or obligation, or the nature or extent of the reparation to be made for breach of a legal obligation".[71]

Finally and most importantly, both parties to the dispute must agree to submit the dispute to the Centre for conciliation or arbitration. "Consent" is regarded as the "cornerstone" of the jurisdiction of the Centre, which must be given by both parties and in writing.[72] As for the manner in which the consent may be given, the Executive Report offers a broad interpretation:

---

〔64〕 Ibid., Article 25(2). Broches believes that on this point, the parties should be given the widest possible latitude to agree on the meaning of "nationality" and that any stipulation of nationality made in connection with a conciliation or arbitration clause which is based on a reasonable criterion should be accepted.

〔65〕 Ibid.

〔66〕 According to Chinese FDI laws, most FIEs are "Chinese legal persons" and therefore are not *per se* "national of another contracting state".

〔67〕 A. Broches, above n. 62, 168.

〔68〕 See Report of the Executive Directors on the Convention on the Settlement of Investment Disputes between States and Nationals of Other States(Executive Report), ICSID Doe. 2, March 18, 1965, para. 27.

〔69〕 A. Broches, above n. 62, 168.

〔70〕 Ibid., para. 26.

〔71〕 Executive Report, above n. 69, para. 26.

〔72〕 Executive Report, above n. 69, para. 23.

Consent may be given, for example, in a clause included in an investment agreement, providing for the submission to the Centre of future disputes arising out of that agreement, or in a compromise regarding a dispute which has already arisen. Nor does the Convention require that the consent of both parties be expressed in a single instrument. This, a host State might in its promotion legislation offer to submit disputes arising out of certain classes of investments to the jurisdiction of the Centre, and the investor might give his consent by accepting the offer in writing.[73]

Moreover, Article 25(4) of the Convention provides that a Contracting State may, when or after ratifying, accepting or approving the Convention, notify the Centre of the class or classes of disputes that it would or would not consider submitting to the jurisdiction of the Centre, though such notification shall not constitute "consent", as required by the Convention.[74]

On acceding to the Convention, China declared, according to Article 25(4), that the Chinese government only agreed to refer disputes about the amount of compensation arising from expropriation or nationalization.[75] However, China is considering expanding the scope of disputes to be referred to the Centre and is enacting implementing regulations for the Convention.[76] In some newly signed BITs, China has agreed to refer to the Centre disputes other than those on the amount of compensation for expropriations, if both parties to the dispute so agree[77]. It can be argued that, according to the Most Favoured Nation[78] clause of the BITs between China and EU member states, EU investors shall also be able to refer non-compensation issues to the ICSID, if they obtain consent from the Chinese Government.

On the other hand, it may be worth mentioning here that the Convention also indicates that Conciliation Commissions and Arbitration Tribunals shall be the judges of their own competence. Hence if a case is brought before them, they can decide, *inter alia*, whether the specific dispute falls within the jurisdiction of the Centre.

ICSID jurisdiction is exclusive, i. e., parties consent to its jurisdiction excludes any other remedy, unless otherwise agreed to by the parties.[79] However, a Contracting State may require the exhaustion of local administrative and judicial remedies as a precondition of its consent to ICSID arbitration.[80] It may also provide for diplomatic protection or bring an international claim in respect of such a dispute when another Contracting

[73] Ibid., para. 24. However, it is unclear, in the third case, when the investor shall give the acceptance and in what form. For further discussion on this issue see A. Broches, above n. 62, 168 – 174.

[74] ICSID Convention, Art. 25(4).

[75] MU Zili, Chinese Government is to enact regulations to implement obligations under the ICSID Convention, Arbitration and Law Communication (Chinese International Economic and Trade Arbitration Commission-CIETAC), No. I 1997, 3 – 4.

[76] Ibid.

[77] See e. g., Article 9(3) of Sino-Korea BIT and Article 10(2) of Sino-Morocco BIT.

[78] Details of these BITs will be discussed in section 3 of this Article.

[79] ICSID Convention, Art. 26.

[80] ICSID Convention, Art. 26.

State has failed to abide by and comply with the award rendered therein.[81]

1.4 Applicable law

The provisions of applicable law[82] in the ICSID Convention is also distinctive. Article 42(1) of the Convention provides,

The tribunal shall decide a dispute in accordance with such rules of law as may be agreed by the parties. In the absence of such agreement, the Tribunal shall apply the law of the Contracting State party to the dispute(including its rules on the conflict of law) and such rule of international law as may be applicable.

This core provision on applicable law has two features: on the one hand, it allows parties to choose the governing "rules of law" rather than "the law". This may mean that the parties can submit different issues to rules of different legal systems, to submit disputes to rules common to more than one legal systems, to combine national and international legal systems, and to submit to laws of a nationalised system frozen on a set date.[83] On the other hand, if the parties fail to choose the applicable rules of law, the Convention requires the arbitration tribunal to apply "the law of the Contracting State party to the dispute(including its rules on conflict of laws) and such rules of international law as may be applicable".[84] Although this provision was regarded as a "considerate balance of interests between investors and host countries", it does not make clear the relationship between applicable domestic law and international law.[85] In theory, authoritative western commentators believe that international law not only fills the gaps left by domestic law, but also takes precedence over domestic law where the two are in conflict, although they disagree on the extent to which international law shall apply.[86] In practice, it also seems that in most ICSID cases the arbitrators tend to extend the application of international law and stress its precedence over national law.[87]

In Article 42(2), the Convention also ruled out the possibility of the tribunal bring-

---

[81] Id., Art. 27.

[82] The term "applicable law" should include both procedural law and substantive law as applicable. However, in this article, it means only applicable "substantive law". As for applicable procedural law, the Convention basically provides that it shall be autonomous. To be precise, unless the parties agree otherwise, the Conciliation Commission or the Arbitration Tribunal shall apply procedural rules of the Convention and the effective Conciliation Rules and the Arbitration Rules adopted by the Centre and shall decide the questions that are not covered by these rules mentioned. See ICSID Convention, Art. 33 and 44.

[83] I. F. I. Shihata and A. Parra, Applicable Substantive Law in Disputes between States and Private Foreign Parties: The case of Arbitration under the ICSID Convention, 9 ICSID Review-Foreign Investment Law Journal(1994), 189.

[84] ICSID Convention, Art. 42(1).

[85] See ZENG Huaqun, International Investment Law(in Chinese)(1999), 604 – 608.

[86] See e. g., A. Broches, above n. 62, 228 – 230; H. Lauterpacht, The World Bank Convention on International Dispute Settlement, in: Recueil detudes de droit international en hommage a Paul Guggenheim(1968), 642, 660 – 661.

[87] However, it is argued by some Chinese scholars that ICSID arbitration is dominated by western ideas since most arbitrators are from developed(capital exporting) countries, and the President of the Administrative Council tends to designate western scholars as Chairmen of arbitration tribunals and *ad hoc* committee members who could annul the awards. See ZENG Huaqun, above n. 86, 604 – 608. See also CHEN An, above n. 37, 125 – 126.

ing a finding of *non liquet* on grounds of silence or obscurity of the law.[88] Broches believes that this reflects the view that existing international law provides international judges or arbitrators sufficient elements for a legal decision of disputes, contrary to earlier positivist opinions purporting that the international legal order was incomplete. Leading Chinese scholars also consider this provision reasonable in both legal and economic terms.[89]

Finally, in Paragraph 3 of Article 42, the Convention empowers the tribunals to decide a dispute *ex aequo et bono* if the parties so agree.[90] This is held as, in the words of OConnell, "an authorisation to decide without reference to the rules of law".[91] However, as Hudson commented while speaking of same provisions in the Statute of the Permanent Court of Justice (PCU), "It cannot act capriciously and arbitrarily... It must proceed upon objective consideration of what is fair and just... The tribunal can not be justified in reaching a result which could not be explained on reasonable grounds".[92] In ICSID cases, the power to decide *ex aequo et bono* is based on agreement of the parties, and quite often, the tribunal will still take into account laws that might have been applicable. Issues that are decided purely *ex aequo et bono* normally are only issues about the evaluation of compensation of expropriation.[93]

1.5 Arbitral Award

ICSID awards are binding and final. They are not subject to any appeal or to any other remedy except as provided for in the Convention.[94] Every Contracting State must recognise an ICSID award in its courts as if it were a final judgement of that State.[95] Nevertheless, execution of an award is a matter for the law of the state in which execution is sought.[96] Moreover, Contracting States may claim sovereign immunity from execution of awards according to National law.[97]

1.6 Observations

Drawing from the preceding analysis, the ICSID Convention is a delicate compromise and balance of interests of both investors and the host countries.

On the one hand, the Convention reflects the interests of foreign investors and their home countries. Above all it proves satisfactory to investors as it successfully transferes the jurisdiction of state-investor disputes from host countries to an international forum-

---

[88] ICSID Convention, Art. 42(2).

[89] ZENG Huaqun, above n. 86, 608 – 609.

[90] ICSID Convention, Art. 42(3).

[91] OConnell, International Law(1970), 14.

[92] Manley 0. Hudson, The Permanent Court of International Justice, l920 – 1942(1943), 620.

[93] ZENG Huaqun, above n. 86, 611.

[94] ICSID Convention, Art. 53(1).

[95] Ibid., Art. 53(1), 54(1).

[96] Ibid., Art. 54(3).

[97] Immunity from jurisdiction must be distinguished from immunity from execution. Broches commented that this article had done no more than acknowledging State practice with regard to immunity from execution—so far only very few national courts have upheld absolute immunity from execution even in cases where state immunity from jurisdiction had either been waived or had been denied on the ground that the sovereign State had acted *jure gestionis*. See Broches, above n. 62, 238. See also ICSID Convention, Art. 55.

the Centre. It also ensures the application of international law to investment disputes, and avoids the uncertainty of whether international law will be applied in domestic courts of a host country. Finally, the finality and binding character of arbitral awards rendered by the ICSID tribunals guarantees the investors that the awards will be recognised and enforced in all Contracting States. In conclusion, the Convention provides, for the first time in history, a clear and unambiguous international legal basis for international investment disputes to be settled within an international forum. In fact, since the inauguration of the Centre, host governments have been almost exclusive "defendants" in ICSID cases.[98] This has been an extraordinary feature of the Centre, compared with other international arbitration agencies. In Broches's word, the Convention "gives investors almost all the assurance he could wish for, and all he could realistically expect".[99]

On the other hand, it also represents to some extent the interests of host countries. It may serve as an investment encouragement tool as membership to the Convention assures foreign investors and signals a positive and responsible attitude of the host country towards FDI. Technically, the Convention also takes into account the needs of host countries. For example, as far as jurisdiction is concerned, "consent" is the cornerstone, and as such enables the host states to control the pace and extent of the exposure to international jurisdiction. With regard to applicable law, it is clearly stated that, in the absence of any agreement on applicable law, the law(including law of conflicts) of the host country shall be applied first. Finally, host countries may still resort to state immunity from execution, to avoid the prejudicial effects of "forced execution".

At the same time, the ICSID Convention has been and will continue to be a very important tool to protect and encourage foreign companies to invest in China, especially EU investors who are used to running businesses on a rule of law basis. China's acceptance of this Convention is the result of careful investigation and consideration and demonstrates China's aspiration to be involved in the global economy and to attract FDI. Moreover, although the Centre has not yet been used to settle any investment dispute with China, the possibility that the Centre may play a role in settling investment disputes with China in the future should not be excluded, given that the mutual investment relations are becoming more and more frequent. In all events, the possibility for EU investors proposing to invest in China to resort to ICSID is of great assurance to them and is likely to attract greater EU FDI to China. Ultimately, such effect would be in line with China's goals and as such would be highly desirable.

2. The MIGA Convention

2.1 The MIGA Convention and EU Investment in China

As with the ICSID Convention, the MIGA Convention[100] (also known as the Seoul

[98] CHEN An, ICSID Mechanism, above n. 37 above, 16 – 17.

[99] Broches, above n. 62, 239.

[100] The MIGA Convention entered into force in April 12, 1988. Reprinted in 24 I. L. M. 1598. For an in-depth discussion of the Agency and the Convention, see lbrahim F. I. Shihata, MIGA and Foreign Investment(1988), and CHEN An(ed.), MIGA and China: Comments on the Multilateral Investment Guarantee Agency, (1995).

Convention) was concluded under the auspices of the World Bank. Signed in October 1985 and effected in 1988, it created the Multilateral Investment Guarantee Agency(MIGA or the Agency), whose core mission is to promote the flow of FDI to and among developing countries,[101] by providing insurance(including coinsurance and reinsurance) against political risks for investments made in a developing member country by another member country.[102] MIGA's aim is furthered by its complimentary investment promotion activities including provision of programs, dissemination of information on investment opportunities and technical assistance to enhance the capability of national investment promotion agencies.[103]

MIGA is legally and financially independent. It is composed of a Council of Governors, which is comprised of one representative for each member state and elects a Board of Directors responsible for the general operation of the MIGA and the election of the President.[104]

To a certain extent, MIGA's insurance programmes compliment national insurance programmes which generally contain strict eligibility requirements that exclude many investors and investments.[105] Firstly, MIGA may insure investments which may not qualify for insurance under national insurance programmes such as OPIC.[106] Secondly, it can eo-guaranty investments with national agencies via parallel or joint underwriting, and may provide re-insurance for these agencies.[107] Moreover, MIGA guarantees investments by investors originating from developing countries that do not have their own national insurance programs.[108]

MIGA has expanded significantly since its formation. Between fiscal years 1990 and 1998, MIGA issued a total of 348 guarantee contracts for \$4.2 billion in total coverage, facilitating an estimated \$25 billion in FDI.[109] By December 2, 1999, the number of member countries reached 151, and 15 countries were in the process of fulfilling membership requirements.

As the largest developing country and the greatest investment recipient in the devel-

---

[101] MIGA Convention, Art. 2.

[102] Ibid.

[103] Id., Art. 2 and Art. 23.

[104] MIGA Convention, Arts. 30 - 34.

[105] lbrahim F. l. Shihata, Factors Influencing the Flow of Foreign Investment and the Relevance of a Multilateral Investment Guarantee Scheme, 21 lntl. Law(1987), 671.

[106] Overseas Private Investment Corporation, a self-sustaining governmental agency of the U. S. See The Overseas Private Investment Corporation Act, 22 U. S. C. A. § § 2191 - 220b(1990 & Supp. 1995) For further discussion on OPIC, see Paul H. Vishny, Guide to International Commercial Law, § § 13. 13, 13. 14(1994). For Chinese research please see Chen An: Case Studies about the OPIC(in Chinese) (1986).

[107] MIGA Convention, Art. 2. For instance, in 1995, MIGA issued USS 45 million in reinsurance coverage to the Export Development Cmporation of Canada for CAMECO Corporations investment in the Kumtor Goldrnine in the Kyrgyz Republic. See MIGA Press Release(October 25 1995). See also Paul Comeaux & Stephen Kinsella, Protecting Foreign Investment under International Law: Legal Aspects of Political Risk(1997), 168.

[108] For example, in 1995, MIGA issued USS 13. 3 million of coverage to a Turkish beverage company(EFES Sinai Yatirim V. Tikaret), for its equity investment in Coca-Cola Almaty Bottlers in Kazakhstan. See Comeaux & Kinsella, ibid., p. l69.

[109] See Guarantees Issued During FY1999, <http: / /www. rniga. org/welcome. htm>.

oping world, China has taken a very positive attitude towards MIGA. As early as 1988, China signed and ratified the Convention. Since then China has became the fifth biggest shareholder of MIGA and the single largest one among developing countries, possessing more shares than most EU Member States.[110] In 1991, China and MIGA entered three Agreements concerning the local approval procedures, legal protection of MIGA Guaranteed foreign investments and the use of local currencies.[111]

MIGA has played, and will go on playing, an important role in encouraging and protecting investment in China. By the end of 1997, all EU Member States and China have became members of the MIGA Convention.[112] *As* EU members are developed countries and China is a developing country for the purposes of the Convention, all EU investments in China are in principle eligible to be guaranteed by MIGA.

So far MIGA has issued many guarantees for investments in China. The first guarantee was issued in fiscal year 1993.[113] By June 1998, MIGA had had US $ 131. 1 millions worth of outstanding guarantees in China, which accounted for 4. 6 percent of all guarantees issued by MIGA.[114] Most impressively, in fiscal year 1995, China hosted 9 of the 54 guarantees that MIGA issued in the year, valued at US $ 70. 6, accounting for 10. 5 percent of total MIGA guarantees. Quite a few of those MIGA guaranteed investments in China were from the EU. For example, among the 6 MIGA guaranteed investments in China in the fiscal year 1999, 2 were from the EU(See Table 2: MIGA Guarantees in China).

Table 2 MIGA Guarantees in China[115]

Fiscal Year	Guarantee Holder	Project Description	Maxim. wn Liability
1993	Non-Fluid Oil International	Glass Products	3. 96
1994	American Cyanamid Company	Medical Products	7
1994	Continental Enterprise Limited. (2 contracts)	Agriculture	4. 4
1994	China Capital Development Corporation	Copper Products	5. 4

[110] See MICA Capital Subscription Data, at <http: / /www. miga. org/welcome. htm> (visited on 10 December 1999).

[111] For details, see CHEN An, MIAG and China, above n. 101, 689 - 694.

[112] See MICA Capital Subscription Data, at <http: / /www. miga. org/welcome. htm> (visited on 10 December 1999).

[113] Lorin S. Weisenfeld, The Cooperation between MICA and China and its Potentials, in CHEN An, MIAG and China, above n. 101, 496.

[114] See MICA Guarantees Outstanding, MICA Annual Report 1998.

[115] Source: Compiled by the author according to Guarantees Issued in FY 1995, Guarantees Issued in FY 1996, Guarantees Issued in FY 1997, Guarantees Issued in FY 1998 and Guarantees Issued in FY 1999, all available at MIGA website: <http: / /www. miga. org/welcome. htrn> (29 October, 1999). The information of fiscal year 1993 and 1994 are based on Lorin S. Weisenfeld, The Cooperation between MIGA and China and its Potentials, in CHEN An, MIGA and China, above n. 101, 496 - 498.

续表

Fiscal Year	Guarantee Holder	Project Description	Maxim. wn Liability
1995	China Capital Development Corp.	Copper Products	2. 7
1995	Citibank N. A.	Banking	0. 5
1995	Honeywell Inc.	Petrochemicals	41. 4
1995	Sunnen Products Co.	Machine Tools	1
1995	Pepsi-Co Inc.	Silk Production	2. 7
1995	Ratti Technologies S. r. L.	Silk Production	C. 8
1995	Catalina Lightine: Inc.	Lighting Fixtures	C. 6
1995	Ingersoll-Rand China Ltd.	Machinery	14. 4
1995	Shinwha Textile Comoanv Ltd.	Silk Production	5. 9
1996	Finance B. V.	Diesel Power Plant	16. 7
1996	ING Bank N. V.	Silk Production	4
1997	Caribbean Mercantile Bank	Manufacturing	3. 83
1997	Philips Electronics N. V.	Banking	9
1997	Coastal Wuxi Power Ltd.	Manufacturing	27
1997	Coastal Wuxi Power, Ltd.	Infrastructure	4. 21
1997	Bank of Nova Scotia	Manufacturing	2. 1
1998	Andre & Cie, S. A. Banco Santander S. A. Sithe International Inc.	Agribusiness	1. 7
1998	Banff Resources Ltd.	Infrastructure	17. 7
1999	Coastal Nanjing Power Ltd. Cayman Islands	Infrastructure	20. 7
1999	BWF Untemehmensbeteiligungen GmbH (2 contracts} – Germany	Manufacturing	3. 8
1999	Schmalbach-Lubeca AGGermany	Manufacturing	5. 9
1999	Interface Asia Pacific Inc. – USA	Manufacturing	3. 2
1999	Coastal Guzu Heat and Power Ltd. – cayman Islands	Infrastructure	10 8
1999	Interface Asia Pacific Inc. – USA	Manufacturing	6. 3

Subsequent sections will deal with the main aspects of MIGA's operation, including its scope of covered risks, eligibility requirements, subrogation and dispute settlement. Special reference will again be given to their application to China.

2.2 Scope of Covered Risks

MIGA insurance covers the risks of currency transfer, expropriation and similar measures, war and civil disturbance and breach of contract loss.[116]

2.2.1 Currency Transfer Insurance

Currency transfer insurance covers currency transfer restrictions imposed by a host government on the transfer of local currency into a freely transferable currency or another currency acceptable to investors. It also covers the failure of the host government to act within a reasonable period after the submission of a transfer application.[117] Upon receipt of the blocked local currency from the holder of the guarantee, MIGA pays in the currency of its guaranty. Nonetheless, risks relating to devaluation and depreciation of currency are excluded from the scope of this insurance coverage, as they are considered as "normal business risks".[118]

In China, the foreign exchange(forex) regime has undergone rapid change, particularly in recent years. Since December 1996, China has formally accepted the obligations of Article VIII of the IMF Articles of Agreement, removing exchange restrictions on. current account transactions.[119] Although China still maintains some restrictions on capital accounts, they are compatible with WTO requirements, and will nevertheless be phased out eventually. Full convertibility of RMB is a set goal of the forex reform.[120] By August 2002, China had accumulated $ 253 billion in foreign reserve and a further $ 30 billion was expected to be achieved by the end of 2002.[121] Hence it can be said that it is very unlikely that FIEs in China will actually run into serious currency transfer risks.[122]

---

[116] ld., Art. ll.

[117] MIGA Convention, Art. ll(a) { i).

[118] Comeaux & Kinsella, above n. 108, 170.

[119] WTO, Reportof the Workingparty on the Accessionof China, WT/ACC/CHN/49 (I October 2001), 6 – 7.

[120] Tian Li, Our Foreign Reserve has Reached 212. 2 billion US Dollars, People's Daily(overseas edition), January 16, 2002, 1.

[121] State Statistics Bureau, Foreign Exchange Reserve will Reach S 280 Billion by the End of the Year. Source: <http: / /www. people. com. cn/GB/jinji/31 I 179/20021202/879382. html> (visited 3 December 2002).

[122] It has been observed that under the previous forex regime, there could be two occasions where currency transfer risks might occur. The SAFE may unduly delay in handling a FIE's application for approval to transfer capital out of China, thus breaking Article 1. 24 of the Operational Regulations of MIGA; Balance of payments(BOP) requirement on FIEs may also give rise to currency transfer risks. According to Article 75 of the previous Implementing Regulation of EJVL, if a Joint Venture fails to manage the balance of payments, due to reasons other than its failure to fulfil the Joint Venture contract, the "Department in Charge" shall be held responsible. Hence, should the Department fail to act, foreign joint venturers may be unable to remit their profits out of China in lines with the contract terms, thus generating currency transfer risks. However, since 1996, China has realised the free convertibility of RMB under current transaction. This significantly mitigates the first kind of risk. Moreover, since the recent modification of FDI laws and regulations, China has abandoned the BOP requirement for FIEs and, therefore, eliminated the second potential risk. See CHEN An, MIGA and China, above n. 101, 462 – 463. For a detailed discussion of the newly revised FDI laws and regulations, see Shan Wenhua, Towards a Level Playing Field for Foreign Investment in China, 3JWI(2002), 328 onwards.

2.2.2 Expropriation and Similar Measures Insurance

Expropriation and similar measures insurance covers any legislative or administrative action or omission attributable to a host government that deprives guarantee holders of their ownership, control of, or a substantial benefit from, their investment.[123] "Expropriation and similar measures" generally encompass nationalisation, confiscation, sequestration, seizure, attachment and assets freezing.[124] However, this insurance coverage excludes "non-discriminatory measures of general application which governments normally take for the purposes of regulating economic activity within their territories". According to the Commentary, such measures generally include taxation, environmental and labour legislation and normal measures for the maintenance of public safety.[125] This provision, nevertheless, is not to prejudice the rights of member countries or of investors under bilateral investment treaties.[126]

Upon assignment of the investor's interest in the expropriated investment, MIGA pays compensation. Compensation for total expropriation of equity investment includes the net book value of the insured investment. Where expropriation is partial, MIAG will compensate the insured portion of the expropriated fund or the net book value of the expropriated assets. As for loans and loan guaranties, MIGA insures the outstanding principal and any accrued and unpaid interest.[127]

Under the "opening up" policy, it is very unlikely that China will expropriate foreign investment as it did in its earlier years. However, risks may still arise and should not be overlooked,[128] particularly given that China has not completed its transition from a central planned economy to a "market economy" regulated by the rule of law. Also, inappropriate interventions from local authorities could cause serious problems on FIEs.[129] Moreover, unexpected changes of government policies and plans may also give rise to frustrations to foreign investors. For example, in 1994, McDonald's Corporation's land lease on its flagship restaurant near Tiananmen Square was reportedly cancelled by

---

[123] MIGA Convention, Art. 11(a)(ii).

[124] Commentary on the Convention Establishing the Multilateral Investment Guarantee Agency (MIGA Commentary), point 14, as reprinted in Shihata, MIGA and Foreign Investment, above n. 101, 391 – 416.

[125] Ibid.

[126] Ibid.

[127] Comeaux & Kinsella, above n. 108, 170.

[128] Chew, above n. 9.

[129] This probably happened more commonly in the earlier years of "opening-up", when local and central authorities were not so familiar with FDI. For instance, in 1986, a Sino-Japan joint venture fired two employees, which was an exercise of the JV's autonomy of management as provided by the EJVL. However, this action resulted in more than seven "investigation groups" investigating the JV. Investigating groups include the Party Disciplinary Committee of the Tourist Bureau of Tianjian Municipality. The venture's operation was deeply and adversely affected by these investigations and the planned enlargement was stalled. See Chen An, MIGA and China, above n. 101, 465.

a decision taken by Beijing municipal authorities.[130] Although it neither qualifies as a MIGA guaranteed investment, nor was it from the EU, this case aroused widespread international concern and has been cited as one of the most recent examples of expropriation.[131]

2.2.3 War and Civil Disturbance Insurance

War and civil disturbance insurance covers military action or civil disturbance occurring within the territory of a host country and includes revolutions, insurrections, *coups d etat* and similar political events, which are typically outside the control of the host government.[132] Acts of terrorism and similar activities specifically directed against an investor are, nevertheless, not be covered.[133]

If the investment is an equity investment, MIGA will compensate the investor's share of the least of the book value of the asset, replacement cost of the asset, or, for damaged assets, the cost of repair. In case of loans and loan guaranties, MIGA pays the insured portion of the principal and interest payments in default as a direct result of damage to the assets of the project caused by war or civil disturbance.[134]

From China's perspective, it is relatively unlikely that war or civil disturbance will break out in the near future. However, disputes over the South China Sea might give rise to future military action.[135] The Taiwan issue may also lead to civil disturbance. Since 1989, a few foreign investors temporarily withdrew from China. For example, all American staff in the Sino-American Shanghai Airplane Factory was extracted, and the cooperation was halted for 20 days. The America. . China Business Council(ACBC) also reported that at least 3 American companies pulled out their major engineers and announced *force majeure*.[136] While the Chinese Government admitted that it was a "riot" or"civil disturbance", they did not think it had constituted the "risk of civil disturbance" as stipulated in the MIGA Convention, as its impact on foreign investors was more psychologically than economically grounded.[137]

2.2.4 Breach of Contract Insurance

Breach of contract insurance covers breaches of contract by a host government with

---

〔130〕 The Municipality authorities held that the location was needed as part of a larger redevelopment project funded by a Hong Kong investor. A settlement of the dispute, providing compensation to McDonald's, was reportedly reached between the parties in mid – 1996. McDonald's was also allowed to open at least two more outlets along an adjacent street. See U. S. and Foreign Commercial Service(US&FCS), Telegraphic Report from the American Embassy In Beijing, China: Investment Climate Statement for 1997. See also Thomas L. Friedman, Fed up, New York Times, 4 December 1996, 29.

〔131〕 Claire A. Hill, How Investors React to Political Risk, Duke J. Comp. & lntl. L. (1998), 293 – 297.

〔132〕 MIGA Commentary, point 16.

〔133〕 Ibid.

〔134〕 Comeaux & Kinsella, above n. 108, 171.

〔135〕 In fact, in the 80s of the 20th century, China had been involved in few small military conflicts with Vietnam and, international analysts have considered the South China Sea one of the places where war will most likely break out. See CHEN An, MIGA and China, above n. 101, 467.

〔136〕 CHEN An, ibid., 469.

〔137〕 See Unifying Thoughts, Stabilising Situation and Making up the Damages, in Liao Wang Weekly(Chinese), No. 25 and 26, 1989. See also CHEN An, above n. 101, 469, 492.

a investor where the investor has no recourse to other forums, where a decision of the other forums is not available within a reasonable period, or where such a decision cannot been forced.[138]

The Chinese Government does not normally get involved in investment contracts and therefore does not acknowledge "state contracts". Even the joint exploitation contracts are signed between foreign investors and one of several state-run companies, rather than by the government itself. However, this does not exclude the possibility that the Chinese Government may explicitly undertake certain specific investment issues with foreign investors, such as convertibility of currency.[139] Moreover, the acceptance of the "Build-Operate-Transfer" investment model might have shown China's willingness to accept "state contracts".[140]

Except for the aforementioned insurances, MIGA insurance may also be written to cover certain other non-commercial risks, such as terrorism or investor-kidnapping or politically motivated strikes, upon a joint request of an investor and the host government and subject to approval by the Board of Directors of MIGA.[141]

2.3 Eligihility Requirements

Eligibility requirements define the scope of qualifying investors, investment projects and countries, as well the approvals required by the host country. Eligible investors of MIGA insurance must be nationals of a member county other than the host country, or juridical persons either incorporated in and having their principal places of business in a member country, or being majority-owned by nationals of member countries.[142] State-owned corporations are also eligible if they operate on a commercial basis.[143] Eligible investments are new investments that are "economically sound" and comply with declared development objectives as well as the laws and regulations of the host country.[144] The host country in turn must provide "fair and equitable treatment and legal protection for investment".[145] Moreover, only investment made in the territory of a developing member country as listed under Schedule A to the MIGA Convention may be guaranteed by MIGA.[146] Finally, the host government must approve the investment project before MIGA issues insurance coverage.[147]

This raises an important question: does China qualify itself as an eligible host country under MIGA Convention, in providing "fair and equitable treatment and legal protec-

---

[138] MIGA Convention, Art. 11(a)(iii).

[139] CHEN An, MIGA and China, above n. 101, 466.

[140] Xu Chongli, Lin Zhong, Chinese Foreign Investment Law(in Chinese)(1998), 184.

[141] MIGA Convention, Art. 11(b).

[142] Upon the joint application of both the investor and the host country, the Board may, by special majority, extend eligibility to a natural person who is a national of the host country, or a legal person who is either incorporated in and has its principal place of business in a member country, or is majority-owned by nationals of member countries, provided that the assets invested in are transferred outside the host country. Id., Art. 13.

[143] Id., Art. 13(a)(iii).

[144] Id., Art. 12(d).

[145] Ibid.

[146] Id., Art. 14.

[147] Id., Art. 15.

tion for investment", particularly in relation to EU investment? It does. Firstly, although so far no compromise has formally been reached upon the standards of treatment for FDI between developed countries and developing countries, the Operational Regulations of MIGA expressly state that investments can be regarded as being adequately protected if they come under the scope of a BIT between the host country and the home country of a investor[148]. That is to say, that with the exception of Ireland, investments from all EU Member States are adequately protected for the purposes of the MIGA Convention, as China has concluded BITs with these states. As far as Irish investment is concerned, it is up to the Agency to clarify whether the current Chinese legal treatment and protection conform with international standards of FDI protection.[149] In practice, the 1992 World Bank Guidelines on Treatment for Foreign Investment[150] (hereinafter the Guidelines) may be helpful in clarifying the standard of treatment that should be accorded. It has been observed that although China falls beneath the standards set forth in the Guidelines, China conforms to requirements set out in the MIGA Convention and its Operational Regulations.[151] As such, for the purposes of MIGA, it qualifies as an eligible host country. Finally, China and MIGA entered into an agreement by way of exchanges of notes in 1991, on the legal protection of foreign investments guaranteed by MIGA. This agreement reads as follows,

Considering the efforts this Agency has made in order to attain an agreement on the treatment of investments guaranteed by this Agency, your Government agrees to entitle this Agency to treatment no less favourable than that the PRC has given or will give in the future to any country or its investment guarantee agencies in an investment protection agreement. This treatment only applies to the rights this Agency subrogated as a subrogee of a compensated holder of a guarantee.[152]

This "most-favoured agency" provision actually enables MIGA to enjoy the best treatment available in China to member countries or their insurance agencies. Therefore, China fully qualifies as an "eligible host country" for the purposes of MIGA guarantees.

2.4 Subrogation

The most important provisions in the MIGA Convention is arguably the subrogation

---

[148] Operational Regulations of the Multilateral Investment Guarantee Agency, Art. 3. 16.

[149] It is provided that, "When there is no such treaty, adequate legal protection should be ascertained by the agency in the light of the consistency of the law and practice of the host country with international law." Id. Some developing country scholars argued that the "international law" standard was ambiguous and difficult to implement. See CHEN An, MIGA and China, above n. 101, 450.

[150] The Guidelines were drafted by a joint committee of experts from the World Bank and the International Monetary Fund (IMF), with a view to preparing "a set of Guidelines embodying commendable approaches which would not be legally binding as such but which could greatly influence the development of international law in this area..." Although it is clearly stated that it is not intended to be a binding legal instrument, it undeniably bears an influence on the operations of MIGA, a member of the World Bank Group. For details about the Guidelines, see Shihata, Legal Treatment of Foreign Investment: The World Bank Guidelines (1993), in particular, the Introductory Note to the Guidelines by I. F. I. Shihata.

[151] CHEN An, MIGA and China, above n. 101, 454.

[152] Agreement between China and MIGA on the Legal Protection of Foreign Investment Guaranteed by MIGA, Article 2, as reprinted in CHEN An, MIAG and China, above n. 101, 691.

clause. According to the clause, member countries agree that MIGA shall be subrogated to such rights or claims related to the guaranteed investment, as the holder of a guarantee may have against the host country and other obligors, as long as MIGA has paid or has agreed to pay compensation to the holder of a guarantee.[153] By subrogation, the MIGA Convention provides for the assignment of existing claims of the guaranteed investor to MIGA. As subrogee MIGA acquires the same rights as the investor had. The terms and conditions of subrogation are defined in the contracts of guarantee, which are particularly important for the investor since MIGA will only compensate investors for part of their losses.[154] According to Article 18(b), MIGA's right of subrogation is recognised by all members.

Besides, MIGA is entitled to be treated as favourably as the holder of the guarantee with respect to the use and transfer of local currency it received. Furthermore, it is authorised to use these currencies for the payment of its administrative expenditures or other costs and, where these currencies are not freely usable, to seek to enter into agreements with host countries on other currency uses.[155]

In order to facilitate MIGA's operation in China, MIGA and China signed three agreements in 1991, on the legal protection of MIGA guaranteed foreign investments, local approval procedures and the use of local currencies respectively. The first agreement enables the MIGA to enjoy "most-favoured agency" treatment. In the second agreement, the Chinese Government commits itself to respond to MIGA guarantee applications promptly and agrees that an approval will be inferred where no action has been taken by the Government within 45 days of the notification of the Chinese Director in MIGA. According to the third agreement, MIGA is entitled to acquire compensation paid with freely usable currencies, as the subrogee of the compensated holder of a MIGA guarantee. Moreover, China agrees that MIGA can make arrangements on the disposal of local currencies it may attain, as long as they are not done with organisations or individuals whom the Chinese law prohibited from dealing with Renminbi(RMB).[156] At the end, all three agreements provide that the Director-General of the Directorate-General of World Bank Affairs of the Ministry of Finance shall be responsible for MIGA issues.[157]

2.5 Dispute Settlement

The MIGA Convention has its own dispute settlement mechanism, which differentiates between disputes involving the Agency and its Members and disputes involving holders of a guarantee or reinsurance.[158] The latter class of disputes shall be settled through arbitration in accordance with the terms of the insurance contract, which in practice usually calls for arbitration under the ICSID rules.[159] For the former class of

---

[153] Id., Art. 18.

[154] MIGA Commentary, Point 26.

[155] MIGA Convention, Art. 18(c).

[156] The Chinese Currency.

[157] See the three agreement in CHEN An, MIGA and China, above n. 101, 689 – 694.

[158] Id., Arts. 56 – 58.

[159] Id., Art. 58; see also Comeaux & Kinsella, above n. 108, 176.

disputes, a separate Annex[160] is attached to the MIGA Convention, which refers to the ICSID rules of procedures to considerable extent.

2.6 Observations

MIGA and ICSID are "sister institutions" under in the World Bank Group.[161] They share similar objectives and are mutually complementary. Both of them aim to protect and guarantee foreign investments by alleviating and mitigating political risks through a system of international institutions. ICSID archives this by providing an international platform to conciliate and arbitrate investment disputes between states and nationals of other states, and safeguards investors against non-commercial risks via legal means, while MIGA archives this by directly underwriting such non-commercial risks, and thus protects investors via economic means. As MIGA Convention largely refers to the ICSID Convention in its dispute settlement mechanism, the links between the two should not, nevertheless, be underestimated.

Moreover, MIGA represents compromise and balance of interests between developing countries and developed countries, in the same way as the ICSID. This is evident from the Preamble, which states, on the one hand, that it is designed to "enhance the flow to developing countries of capital and technology of productive purposes under conditions consistent with their development needs, policies and objectives", while on the other hand, stressing that it shall be based on "fair and stable standards for the treatment of foreign investment". Another example is the voting arrangement, which is to "reflect the equal interest in the Agency of the two Categories of states listed under Schedule A of the Convention". The MIGA Convention further stipulates that supplementary votes may be allocated to either of the two Categories if at any time within the three years following this Convention's entry into force, the aggregate sum of membership and subscription votes of that Category is less than forty percent of the total voting power. It has been observed that in MIGA Convention, the interests of developing countries and developed countries have been better balanced than in the ICSID Convention.[162]

Consequently, China has taken a more active participation in the MIGA Convention than in the ICSID Convention. While China is an original member of the MIGA Convention, it did not sign the ICSID Convention until after it had been in force for more than three decades. Furthermore, China is the fifth biggest shareholder of the MIGA and is actively using the MIGA mechanism. Indeed, MIGA has already played an important role for protecting and promoting EU investment in China, as EU investors are keener in applying the MIGA mechanism compared with other investors in China. MIGA will undoubtedly become even more influential in China as more and more EU investors flockto China to seek the tremendous business opportunities brought about by China's WTO membership.

---

〔160〕 See Annex 11 to the MIGA Convention.

〔161〕 Both of them were established with World Bank's help, and are members of the Word Bank Group.

〔162〕 CHEN An, MIGA and China, above n. 101, 120.

3. The WTO Agreement

3.1 The WTO Agreement and EU Investment in China

In December 1994, the Uruguay Round trade negotiation drew to a conclusion and a comprehensive and powerful multilateral trading system was set up. The WTO Agreement lies at the heart of the whole system, and is embraced in the Final Act Embodying the Result of the Uruguay Round of Multilateral Trade Negotiations. The WTO Agreement is the *de facto* charter of the World Trade Organisation(WTO). It defines its legal status and lays down its institutional basis. The operational rules of the WTO Agreement, however, are contained in its four Annexes. Among these, three(Annex 1 - 111) are multilateral trade agreements[163] and one(Annex IV) includes 4 plurilateral trade agreements. Furthermore, WTO is not just a set of static rules, it is a dynamic system. It evolves and develops through its other roles, as a platform for multilateral trade negotiations, as a forum of trade dispute settlement and as a body of trade policy review.[164]

Initially, GATT did not deal with investment issues although the ill-fated Havana Charter[165] did encompass investment provisions. However, much effort has been made to include investment issues within the framework of the multilateral trade system, because of the close link between trade and investment.[166] In 1986, when investment was put on the agenda for the Uruguay Round negotiation, it was regarded as one of the several "new issues".[167] As a result, the WTO Agreement embraces an agreement called "Agreement on Trade-Related Investment Measures" (the TRIMs Agreement) within its multilateral agreements on trade in goods. Although narrowly defined, the TRIMs Agreement may be regarded as a break through in international investment law as it seeks to regulate investment explicitly and globally for the first time in history.[168] The General Agreement on Trade in Services(GATS) is another WTO agreement of significance on investment. It focuses mainly on the market access and national treatment of investment in service sectors. Other investment-related WTO agreements include the Agreement on Trade-related Intellectual Property Rights (TRIPS), the Agreement on Subsidies and Countervailing Measures(SCMs), the Dispute Settlement Understanding(DSU) and the

---

[163] They are: Annex I, which includes Agreements respectively on trade in good(GATT 1994), services (GATS) and trade-related property rights(TRIPS); Annex IT-Understanding on Rules and Procedures Governing the Settlement of Disputes(DSU) and Annex ill-Trade Policy Review Mechanism(TPRM).

[164] Article Ill, WTO Agreement.

[165] The Charter of International Trade Organisation(ITO), the underlying legal instrument of the CATT, which failed to enter into force and led to a plethora of 50 year long "provisional application".

[166] A simple but convincing indication of this link is the fact that approximately one-third of the total 6.1 trillion total for world trade in goods and services in 1995 was trade within companies—for example between subsidiaries in different countries or between subsidiaries and its headquarters. See WTO, Trading into the future(2d ed., 1998), 50.

[167] The "New Issues" are about CATS, TRIPS and TRIMs.

[168] On the contrary, it has been argued that this agreement is actually "retrogressive" because it narrowed down the scope of TRIMs that should be eliminated as required by the GATT. See Tomas L. Brewer & Stephen Young, The Multilateral Investment System and Multinational Enterprises, (1998), 124.

Trade Policy Review Mechanism(TPRM). These are regarded as having continuous and direct relevance to FDI.[169] In fact it could be argued that most of the WTO agreements and their implementation measures are related to FDI since they influence the FDI environment in its entirety. As such, the WTO Agreement as a whole is not only a breakthrough in the history of international trade law, but also a significant advance in international investment law.[170]

All EU Member Statesand the EC itself are original members of the WTO. On 11 December 2001, China finally became a member of the WTO, marking a successful conclusion to its 15 – year "long march" towards Geneva. Undoubtedly, China's entry into the WTO will significantly improve EU-China investment relations, and particularly the conditions for EU investment in China. In the Sino-US bilateral WTO Agreement done in November 1999, China made significant concessions in a large number of fields, notably in TRIMs measures and services sectors.[171] In addition, China offered further concessions in services sectors such as telecommunication, banking and insurance in the EU-China deal finished in May 2000, which undoubtedly "will provide substantial new market opportunities for European companies selling to China or investing there".[172]

The following is an analysis of the provisions of the WTO Agreement which are most closely related to investment, particularly EU investment in China. In turn it looks at the administration of trade regimes, the TRIMs Agreement and GATS.

3.2 The Administration of Trade Regimes

The manner in which a country administers its trade regime is crucial for effective implementation. The question of effective implementation of the WTO agreements in China raises particular concerns, as China's legal system has been criticised for its lack of touch with reality.[173]

The WTO Agreement itself does not specifically deal with the administration of trade regimes but requires each Member to ensure the conformity of its laws, regulations and administrative procedures with the undertakings provided in the annexed agreements.[174] In GATT 1947, Article X is entitled "publication and administration of trade regulations". It requires trade related laws, regulations, judicial decisions and administrative rulings of general application to be published promptly so as to enable governments and traders to become acquainted with them. International agreements are also to

[169] Tomas L. Brewer & Stephen Young, ibid., 123.

[170] SHAN Wenhua, Comments on the International Investment Rules within the WTO Agreement, CASS Journal of Law(Faxue Yanjiu)(1996, no. 2).

[171] For details of the Sino-US Bilateral WTO Agreement, see <http://www.uschina.org/>; for a summary of the Agreement, see <http://www.chinapntr.gov/bilatsumm.htm>.

[172] Statement on EU-China Trade Agreement by Romano Prodi, President of the European Commission, at <http://europa.eu.int/comm/trade/bilateral/china/prodi.htm> (22 May 2000). The Author's Survey also shows EU investors firmly believe that the WTO accession will significantly improve China's investment climate. See Section 3.1 of the Survey Report, 40.

[173] For an insightful discussion of the gap, see Peter Howard Come, Foreign investment in China: the Administrative Legal System(1997, Hong Kong University Press), 1 – 50.

[174] Article XVI:4 of the WTO Agreement.

be published. No new measures or amendments to existing measures shall be enforced prior to their publication. In general, each contracting party shall administer its laws, regulations, decisions and rulings affecting trade in a uniform, impartial and reasonable manner. Furthermore, each contracting party shall administer or institute as soon as practical, judicial, arbitral or administrative tribunals or procedures for the purpose, *inter alia*, of the prompt review and correction of administrative actions relating to custom matters.[175]

In the GATS, Article VI is devoted to "domestic regulation", which requires each member to ensure that all measures of general application affecting trade in services are administered in a reasonable, objective and impartial manner.[176] It also requires that members shall maintain or institute judicial, arbitral or administrative tribunals or procedures for prompt review of administrative decisions affecting trade in services.[177] Similar provisions can be found in Article 41 of the TRIPS Agreement.[178]

Accordingly, in the Protocol of China's accession to the WTO, special commitments are provided to ensure uniform administration and transparency, as well as judicial review of administrative decisions affecting trade.

3.2.1 Uniform Administration

One of the major concerns expressed by members while examining Chinese trade regime has been the uniformity of trade administration throughout China. China is such a huge country with several administrative levels and special economic areas (SEAs), namely, Special Economic Zones (EZs), border trade regions (BTRs), minority autonomous areas (MAAs), open coastal cities (OCCs), economic and technical development zones (ETDZs) and other areas where special regimes for tariff, taxes and regulations are established.[179] The Protocol maintains that:[180]

the provisions of the WTO agreement shall apply to the entirety of the Chinese custom territory, including in the SEAs. For this purpose, China shall notify to the WTO all the relevant laws, regulations and other measures relating to these SEAs by name and indicating the geographic boundaries that define them. Meanwhile China shall promptly notify any addition or modification to these SEAs, including related laws, regulations and other measures.

China shall apply and administer in a uniform, impartial and reasonable manner all its laws, regulations and other measures of the central governments as well as local regulations, rules and other measures issued or applied at the sub-national level pertaining to or affecting trade in goods, services, trade-related aspects of intellectual property rights (TRIPS) or the control of foreign exchange (collectively referred to as "trade-related

[175] Article X 1 - 3, WTO Agreement.

[176] Article VI: 1, GATS.

[177] Ibid., Article VI: 2.

[178] Article 41, TRIPS Agreement.

[179] WTO, Report of the Working Party on the Accession of China (WTO China Report), WT/ACC/CHN/49, 13 - 15.

[180] See Part 1: 2 of the Protocol on the Accession of the People's Republic of China (the China Accession Protocol or the Protocol), WT/ACC/CHN/49, 73 - 74.

measures"). Regulations, rules and other measures of local governments at the sub-national level shall conform to the obligations undertaken in the WTO Agreement and the Protocol.

A mechanism shall be established in China under which individuals and enterprises can bring cases of non-uniform application within the trade regime to the attention of the national authorities.

3.2.2 Transparency

The Protocol also provides concrete undertakings to increase the transparency of the Chinese trade regime, which has been widely criticised as one of the most significant barriers for doing business in China. China commits itself to:[181]

a) Only those trade-related measures that are punished and readily available to other WTO members, individuals and enterprises, shall be enforced. Moreover, China shall make available to WTO members, upon request, all these trade-related measures before they are implemented or enforced. In emergency situations, these trade related rules shall be made available at the latest when they are implemented or enforced.

b) China shall establish or designate an official journal for the publication of all those measures involving national security, specific measures setting forex rates or monetary policy and other measures the publication of which would impede law enforcement. This journal shall be published on a regular basis and copies of all its issues shall be readily available to individuals and enterprises.

c) China shall establish or designate an enquiry point providing information relating to publication requirements, upon request of any individual, enterprise or WTO members. Responses will be sent out within 30 days of receipt of a request and in exceptional cases within 45 days. Replies shall be complete, authoritative and notices of delay shall be provided with reasons in writing.

3.2.3 Judicial Review

In order to further ensure the uniform application of the WTO Agreement in China, a judicial review mechanism has been provided for in the Protocol. It requires China to establish or designate and maintain tribunals, contact points and procedures to review without undue delay all administrative actions relating to the implementation of laws, regulations, judicial decisions and administrative rulings of general application referred to in Article X: 1 of the GATT 1994, Article VI of the GATS and relevant provisions of the TRIPS Agreement.[182] Such tribunals shall be impartial and independent of the agency entrusted with administrative enforcement and shall have no substantial interest in the outcome of the matter.[183]

Review procedures shall include the opportunity for appeal, without penalty, by individuals or enterprises affected by any administrative action subject to review. If the initial right of appeal is to an administrative body, there shall in all cases be the opportu-

---

〔181〕 See Part 1: 2 of the Protocol on the Accession of the People's Republic of China(the China Accession Protocol or the Protocol), WT/ACC/CHN/49, 74 - 75.

〔182〕 Ibid., p. 75.

〔183〕 Ibid.

nity to choose to appeal the decision to a judicial body. Notice of the decision on appeal shall be given to the appellant and the reasons for such decision shall be provided in writing. The appellant shall also be informed of any right to further appeal.[184]

Undoubtedly China has taken concrete measures to guarantee the implementation of its WTO commitments. One of the most significant steps has been the establishment of three Directorate-Generals(DGs) devoted to WTO related issues under the Ministry of Foreign Trade and Economic Cooperation(MOFTEC). Among them the DG for WTO is in charge of the negotiations on behalf of China under the framework of the WTO; the DG for WTO Notification and Consultation of the Chinese Government deals with daily notification and consultation and trade policy review of China within the WTO; and the DG for Fair Trade of Import and Export undertakes work related to anti-dumping, countervailing and safeguard measures, as well as the direction and coordination of issues regarding the responses to foreign antidumping practices against China.[185] Another concrete measure is the newly adopted regulation on the adjudication of administrative cases involving international trade and investment issues, which enables all natural and legal persons the rights to file an administrative lawsuit against any specific administrative actions of any authority or individual with administrative competence.[186]

3.3 TRIMs Agreement

The TRIMs Agreement requires members not to apply any Trade-Related Investment Measures(TRIMs) that are inconsistent with the principles of "national treatment" (Art. 3 para. 4) and "general elimination of quantitative restrictions"(Art. 11 para. 1) of GATT 1994.[187] Under the Agreement, each member shall notify the Council of Trade in Goods of all their inconsistent TRIMs within 90 days of the entry into force of the Agreement, and eliminate them within a certain period of time.[188] To make matters clearer an illustrative list of those restrictive measures, which "are mandatory or enforceable under domestic law or under administrative rulings, or compliance with which is necessary to obtain an advantage", is annexed to the Agreement. These include:

A requirement of purchasing or using local products (Oocal content requirement);

A limitation on the purchase or use of imported goods to an amount related to its exportation(trade-balancing requirement);

A quantitative restriction of importation of products for local production in general or to an amount related to its exportation(general and trade-balancing importation restriction);

A quantitative restriction of importation by restricting its access to forex to an amount related to its forex contribution(forex balancing requirement);

---

[184] See Part 1:2 of the Protocol on the Accession of the People's Republic of China(the China Accession Protocol or the Protocol), WT/ACC/CHN/49, p. 75.

[185] Chen Gang, China Sets up Special Trade Departments to Deal with WTO Issues, People's Daily(Overseas Edition), November I, 2001, 2.

[186] Article 3, The Trade Cases Provisions.

[187] Art. 2 of the TRIMs Agreement.

[188] The transition period is two years for developed countries, five years developing countries or seven years for least-developed countries. Id., Art. 5, para. 1 – 2.

A quantitative restriction of exportation or sale for export (exportation restriction).[189]

While these existing rules on investment are very important, subsequent negotiations and reviews may be even more important for the future of investment issues in the WTO.[190] In 1996, the Singapore Ministerial Conference(MC) created three new working groups, among which one is to investigate the relationship between trade and investment.[191] Since then the working group has done extensive research on the relationship and the possibility to conclude a multilateral agreement on investment within the WTO framework. Despite the failure of the Seattle MC, the Doha MC held in November 2001, nevertheless, decided that negotiations for a multilateral framework on investment would take place in the next Session of the MC, on the basis of a decision to be taken then, by explicit consensus, on modalities of negotiations.[192]

According to the China Accession Protocol, China's offers on this point are probably more than satisfactory. Firstly, it undertakes to comply with the TRIMs Agreement upon accession, without any transitional arrangement.[193] Secondly, it not only commits itself to eliminating and ceasing to force trade and foreign exchange balancing requirements, as well as local content requirements as required by the TRIMs Agreement, but also undertakes to abolish export or performance requirements, which go beyond the TRIMs Agreement.[194] Moreover, China promises not to enforce provisions of contracts imposing such requirements.[195] China also agrees that the allocation, permission or rights for importation and investment will not be conditional on performance requirements set by national or sub-national authorities, or subject to secondary conditions covering, for example, the conduct of research, the provisions of offsets or other forms of industrial compensation including specific types or volumes of business opportunities, the use of local inputs or the transfer of technology. Permission to invest, import licenses, quotas and tariff rate quotas will be granted regardless of the existence of competing Chinese domestic suppliers.[196]

It is worth mentioning that China has already substantially modified its FDI laws and regulations, to ensure compatibility with the TRIMs Agreement.[197]

---

[189] See Annex: illustrative List, to the TRIMs Agreement.

[190] P. Sauve, A First Look at Investment in the Final Act of the Uruguay Round, 28. of World Trade(No. 5), 5 - 16. Id., Assessing the General Agreement on Trade in Services: Half Full or Half Empty?, 29J. of World Trade (No. 4), 125 - 145.

[191] WTO, Trading into the Future(1998, 2ncl ed.), 50.

[192] WTO Fourth Session of Ministerial Conference: Ministerial Declaration, WT/MIN(01)/DEC/W/1(14 Nov. 2001), 4 - 5.

[193] WTO, Report of the Working Party on the Accessionof China, WT/ACC/CHN/49(I October 2001)(01 - 4679), 40, 76.

[194] Ibid.

[195] Ibid.

[196] Ibid.

[197] For details please see Shan Wenhua, Towards a Level Playing Field of Foreign Investment in China, 3J. of World Investment I, 2002(forthcoming).

3.4 The GATS Agreement

GATS is another agreement in the WTO Agreement directly dealing with investment issues.[198] According to GATS, trade is defined to embrace investment,[199] since one of the four modes of trade in services is through "commercial presence", which includes "any type of business or professional establishment", either in form of a juridical person or a branch or a representative office.[200] Moreover, GATS's provisions on market access directly and specifically refer to joint ventures and limitations on the percentage of foreign ownership.[201] Therefore, as such, GATS can be considered as a set of "Rules for Growth and Investment" or "investor's agreement".[202]

In GATS, there are three parts of substantive rules. The first comprises the "general obligations and disciplines", which include MFN, transparency, a number of traditional GA1T-type exceptions, as well as competition, business practices and government procurement.[203]

The second part is entitled "specific commitments"[204] and establishes the framework for a schedule of commitments from each member. The "bottomup" approach is taken here, and as such, GATS applies only to the tabled or bound sectors established in the schedule and subject to the terms, conditions and limitations therein. Specifically, there are three categories of commitments, namely, limitations on market access, limitations on national treatment and additional commitments. Moreover, the commitments are listed by modes of supply outline in Article 1. 2 of the GATS[205] and are summarised as cross-border supply, consumption abroad, commercial presence and presence of natural persons.

The third part of substantive rules includes several articles on "progressive liberalisation",[206] which deal with approaches of future negotiations on the various specific commitments to be included in the schedules. It states clearly that in sectors where spe-

---

[198] The significance of GATS to FDI is in part due to the fact that in the recent years there has been rapid FDI growth in the services sector, more than in other sectors. See Tomas L. Brewer & Stephen Young, above n. 169, . 126. See also UNCTAD/WorldBank, World Investment Report 1994: Transitional Corporations, Employment and Workplace, Tables 1. 8 and 1. 9(1994), 16 – 17.

[199] Tomas L. Brewer & Stephen Young, ibid., 126.

[200] Any type of business or professional establishment, including through(i) the constitution, acquisition or maintenance of a juridical person, or(ii) the creation or maintenance of a branch or a representative office, within the territory of a Member for the purposes of supplying a service. See Art. XXVIII of GATS, item(d).

[201] See GATS Art. XVI, para. 2. (e) – (f).

[202] WTO, Trading into the Future, (July 1998, 2d. ed.), 21.

[203] Part IT, GATS: "General Obligations and Disciplines".

[204] Ibid., Part Ⅲ.

[205] GATS does not give a compact definition of"Trade in Services" but describes it as "the supply of a service:

from the territory of one Member into the territol) of any other Member;

in the territory of one member to the service consumer of any other Member;

by a service supplier of one Member, through commercial presence in the territory of any other Member;

by a service supplier of one Member, through presence of natural persons of a Member in the territory of any other Member".

[206] Part IV of GATS.

cific commitments are undertaken, the schedule shall specify,

terms, limitations and conditions on market access;

conditions and qualifications on national treatment;

undertakings relating to additional commitments;

where appropriate the time-frame for implementation of such commitments; and

the date of entry into force of such commitments.

Apparently, the second part, the "specific commitments" is of vital importance in defining members rights and obligations under the GATS.[207] However, GATS is only the framework agreement, and individual agreements have been entered into on specific industries of services, e. g. , maritime transport, financial services, telecommunication, basic telecommunication and air transport, etc.

In the Schedule of Specific Commitments on Services(hereafter the Service Schedule), as Part 11 of the Report of the Working Party on the Accession of China(The WPAC Report), China makes "horizontal commitments"(HCs) as well as "specific commitments"(SCs). HCs deal with commitments that apply to all sectors included in the schedule, while SCs only apply to the specific sectors or sub-sectors which they address. HCs specifically cover forms of investment, term limitations on land use as well as entry and stay of key personnel with a service presence in China.[208] Specific commitments cover professional services, computing and related services, real estate services, other business services, communication services, construction and related engineering services, distribution, educational services, environmental services, financial services, tourism and travel related services and transport services. Furthermore, there are several annexes on basic telecommunication, distribution services and insurance services.[209] Finally, according to the Working Party Report, the Chinese representative has made some further clarifications on issues such as service licensing, choice of partners, modification of the equity interests, prior experience requirements for establishment in insurance sectors, inspection services, market research, legal services and minority shareholder rights.[210] These clarifications are in line with the Part I Art. l(2) of the Protocol, integral parts of the WTO Agreement and are thus binding on China, as well as on other WTO members.[211]

3.5 Observations

The entry of China into WTO will significantly improve the legal environment for EU investment in China. First of all, as can be seen from the previous discussions, the specific commitments that China has made according to TRIMs Agreement and GATS

---

[207] John H. Jackson, The World Trading System: Law and Policy of International Economic Relations(1997, 2d ed.), 309.

[208] Schedule CUI-The People's Republic of China Part 11 – Schedule of Specific Commitments on Services, List of Article 11 MFN Exemptions(China's Service Schedule), WT/ACC/CHN/49/Add. 2, 2 – 4.

[209] Ibid., 5 – 48.

[210] WTO China Report, above n. 180, 63 – 68.

[211] China Accession Protocol, above n. 181, Part I(General Provisions), Art. I(2). This provision provides that, "This Protocol, which shall include the commitments referred to in paragraph 342 of the Working Party Report, shall be an integral part of the WTO Agreement".

will substantially improve the market access and treatment of the EU investors established and operating in China. Secondly, the general commitments that China made on the administration of trade and investment regime will upgrade the general legal environment of EU investment in China as they will increase the transparency, stability, and predictability of the legal system. Moreover, the constant trade policy review mecha nism[212] and the powerful dispute settlement system[213] guarantee that the Chinese Government will comply with its undertakings under the WTO Agreement and hence create a favourable and predictable political environment for EU investment in China. Finally, the WTO admission will inevitably speed up market-oriented reform and the opening-up process, which will in turn provide a general climate conducive to flourishing EU investment in China. In fact, in the services sector only, the US Embassy in Beijing has predicted a revenue growth of \$ 3 – 5 billion as a result of the removal of China's barriers to US suppliers.[214] Similarly the EU also stands to gain from the removal of barriers.[215]

4. Summary

Multilateral agreements to which the EU and China are members are bearing significant influence on EU-China investment relations, particularly in certain specific aspects or sectors. The ICSID Convention set up a unique multilateral investment dispute settlement mechanism which entitles private investors(e. g. , from the EU) to challenge sovereign states(e. g. , China) . The MIGA Convention establishes, on the other hand, a multilateral guarantee scheme to guarantee EU investments in China against non-commercial risks. It is evident that both of these mechanisms have the potential to facilitate and enhance mutual investment between the EU and China significantly and, particularly, EU investment in China. Besides, in the disguise of a trade agreement, the WTO Agreement contains a variety of rules on investment issues, and provides opportunities for future expansion and development. China's accession to the WTO will therefore significantly promote and strengthen EU-China investment relations.

However, it is equally clear that in the absence of a set of general principles and rules, these multilateral legal instruments and their specific provisions are incomplete, inconsistent and of limited application. To cite a few, these agreements failed to address various arguably crucial aspects, including the definition of "investment", general rules of admission, treatment standards, expropriation and compensation. Also, the

---

[212] This mechanism enables regular collective appreciation and evaluation of the full range of individual Members trade policies and practices and their impact on the functioning of the multilateral trading system. Article A of the Trade Policy Review Mechanism.

[213] Jackson regards the Dispute Settlement Understanding as "one of the great achievements of the Uruguay Round text". See Jackson, above n. 208, 124 – 127.

[214] Assessment of the Economic Effects on the United States of China's Accession to the WTO(China WTO on US) , US international trade Commission, Publication 3229, Set. 1999, xiv.

[215] The EU vigorously insists that it is relatively competitive in many services sectors. As a result of its bilateral WTO negotiations with China, further benefits for EU service suppliers have been secured. For details on the results of Sino-EU WTO negotiations, see Highlights of the EU-China Agreement on WTO, at <http: // europa. eu. int/ comm/trade/bilateral/ china/wto. htm >.

three sets of dispute settlement mechanism under the three agreements have not been harmonised. While investors can directly sue governments under the ICSID Convention, only members and not private parties are eligible to trade disputes before DSB of the WTO.[216] Therefore, these multilateral agreements are insufficient to adequately protect and promote EU investment in China. To achieve this goal, a general and substantive international legal framework between the EU and China may prove necessary.

Ⅲ. EU Investment in China under Bilateral Agreements

At a bilateral level, the framework for general EU-China economic relations is constituted by the 1985 Cooperation Agreement, which replaced the 1978 Trade Agreement. A sectoral agreement governing trade in textile products between the two sides, is also relevant. To date, China has concluded 13 bilateral investment treaties(BITs) with 14 Member States of the EU[217] (with the exception of Ireland, see Table 3: BITs between China and the EU Member States). Furthermore, 14 treaties have been signed between China and EU member states to avoid double taxation(DTTs).[218] However, only the Cooperation Agreement and the BITs between China and EU member states will be hereafter discussed, as both the Textile Agreement and the DTTs affect only sectoral or technical aspects of the investment climate.

Table 3 BITs between China and EU Member States[219]

Parties	Signature	Entry into Force
Austria	Sep. 12, 1985	Oct. 11, 1986
Bel'm-Lux'g	June 4, 1984	Oct. 5, 1986
Denmark	Sep. 4, 1984	Apr. 29, 1985
Finland	Apr. 29, 1985	Jan. 26, 1986
France	May 30, 1984	Mar. 19, 1985
Germany	Oct. 7, 1983	Mar. 18, 1985
Greece	June 25, 1992	Dec. 21, 1993
Italy	Jan. 28, 1985	Aug. 28, 1987
Netherlands	June 17, 1985	Feb. I, 1987

[216] This problem is beyond the scope of this article, as it could be the subject of a Ph. D. in its own right.

[217] One of those BITs is concluded between China and Belgium-Luxembourg Economic Union.

[218] So far China has concluded DTTs with 14 of the 15 member states of the-EU, with the exception of Greece. For details of these treaties, please see China International Tax Society, A Complete Collection of China's Taxation Agreements and Practices(1997). For updated information about these DTTs, please see: < http://www.ab-acn.com/csfg/index.php?lei = ssxd > (20 December 2001).

[219] Source: Compiled by the author in light of Bilateral investment Treaties, at ICSID Website: < http://www.worldbank.org/icsid/treaties/china.htm > (visited on 4 December 2002).

续表

Parties	Signature	Entry into Force
Portugal	Feb. 3, 1992	
Spain	Feb. 6, 1992	May 1, 1993
Sweden	Mar. 29, 1982	Mar. 29, 1982
U. K.	May 15, 1986	May 15, 1986

1. The Cooperation Agreement

The negotiations for a new agreement on trade and economic cooperation began in 1983 and were concluded in 1985. It replaced the 1978 Trade Agreement and is as yet the only framework agreement between China and the EU. The Cooperation Agreement[220] has four chapters. Chapter 1, 3 and 4 relate to trade cooperation, the Joint Committee and final provisions, and are essentially identical to the Trade Agreement. Chapter 2 is the only new chapter, which defines various forms of economic cooperation.

According to the Cooperation Agreement, Sino-EC economic cooperation is to be extended to every possible sphere,[221] particularly in the fields of industry and mining, agriculture(including agro-industry), science and technology, energy, transport and communication, environmental protection and cooperation in the third countries.[222] At the same time, both parties agreed to endeavour to promote and facilitate various forms of cooperation, including joint production and joint ventures; common exploitation; transfer of technology; cooperation between financial institutions; visits, contacts and activities designed to promote cooperation between individuals, delegations, and economic organisations; organisation of seminars and symposia; consultancy services; technical assistance, including the training of staff; and continuous exchange of information relevant to commercial and economic Cooperation.[223]

The Cooperation Agreement also takes into account the different level of development between the EC and China and requires that the EC be prepared to continue, step up and diversify its development activities in China, within the means at its disposal and in accordance with its rules.[224] This article purports that the EC is eager to grant China more development aid, despite the need to balance aids with reference to the need of the other developing regions, such as the ACP, the Mediterranean and the Eastern Europe countries.

Most significantly for the purposes of this research, the Cooperation Agreement addresses investment issues. Article 12 of the Cooperation Agreement requires the two par-

[220] Officially the Agreement on Trade and Economic Cooperation between the European Community and the People's Republic of China. See OJL 250(19/9/85).

[221] As long as they fall within the competence of the Community.

[222] Article 10 of the Cooperation Agreement.

[223] Id., Art. 11.

[224] Id., Art. 13.

ties to promote and encourage greater and mutually beneficial investment. Moreover, the parties undertake to further improve the investment climate, in particular, through encouraging the extension of BITs between China and the EC Member States.[225]

Article 12 follows the Community's model of cooperation agreements with non-associated countries and may have taken the mutual investment exchanges into account.[226] In fact, at the time the agreement was signed, there had been considerable EC investments in China and most EC Member States had signed BITs with China.[227] Since this investment clause imposes no substantial obligation on the contracting parties but rather expresses their intention for future cooperation, it has more symbolic than practical value. Nevertheless, it lays down a general legal basis for future cooperation in this field.

Last but not least, a joint Committee was set up under the Agreement, to monitor implementation of the agreement and to examine various means and opportunities of further developing economic cooperation. It may also make recommendations to further the objectives of the Agreement in areas of common interest. If deemed necessary the Joint Committee may also set up working parties.

It is worth mentioning that although the Community has exercised its power in concluding economic cooperation agreements for a substantial period of time, this power is not exclusive. In addition, Member States still hold the power to sign cooperation agreements with non-Member States. In order to decrease conflicts arising therefrom, the Council adopted the Decision 74/393.[228] The Decisions require Member States to hold prior consultation before the signing of any agreement of this kind and to inform the Commission of the agreement as well as the measures and commitments undertaken thereunder. As a matter of fact, most EC Member States have concluded economic cooperation agreements with China,[229] in parallel to the Cooperation Agreement on the Community level. Due to space constraints, these economic cooperation treaties are not to be discussed in this note.

2. BITs between China and EU Member States

As mentioned, so far China has concluded bilateral investment protection and promotion agreements with 14 of the 15 EU Member States. The first BIT was concluded with Sweden on March 29, 1982. This was followed by Germany, France, Belgium-Luxembourg Economic Union, Finland, Italy, Denmark, UK, the Netherlands, Austria, Portugal, Spain and Greece. As yet Ireland is the only member state not to have signed such a treaty with China but that is also under way. For the time being, BITs between China and the EU Member States are the most important international legal instruments for EU

[225] Id., Art. 12.

[226] See Hu Yuanxiang, above n. 10, 116.

[227] At that time, 7 of the 10 EC Members had concluded BITs with China. The other three were Greece, Ireland and the United Kingdom.

[228] See Council Decision 74/393, OJ L 203/23, 1974.

[229] For details of economic cooperation agreement between China and EC Member States, see Hu Yuanxiang, above n. 10, 79.

investment in China as they are the only legal instruments to provide general and substantial protection to EU investors.

The main purpose of these BITs is to promote and protect mutual investment, particularly investment in China. Therefore, all of them contain fundamental provisions relating to definitions, admission, treatment standards, expropriation and consequent compensation, war losses compensation, monetary transfers, subrogation, dispute setdement and so forth. Below is a thorough comparison of these provisions.

2.1 Scope of Application

The scope of application of these treaties is normally reflected in the definitions of "investment" and "investors". It sometimes also relates to the treaties retroactivity.

The term "investment" is almost unanimously defined as "every kind of asset",[230] which host countries permit investment in, particularly but not exclusively, as worded in the Sino-Sweden BIT.[231]

· Movable and immovable property as well as any other rights in rem, such as mortgage, lien, pledge, usufruct and similar rights;

· Shares or other kinds of interest in companies;

· Title to money or any performance having an economic value;

· Copyrights, industrial property rights, technical process, trade-names and good will; and

· Such business-concessions under public law or under contract, including concessions regarding the prospecting for, or the extraction or winning of natural resources,· as given to their holder a legal position of some duration.

The definitions of "investor", on the contrary, are not as universal. As far as natural persons are concerned, although most BITs use "nationality" as the defining criterion, others use "residence" as the only or additional criterion.[232] As far as juridical persons, partnership, or economic organisations are concerned, most BITs defines "investors" as those incorporated or established in accordance with the law of a contracting party and having their seat(residence, domicile, headquarter or registered head office) therein; other BIT define "investors" as those having a "major", [233] "predominant"[234] or "important"[235] interest or direct or indirect control over their investments.[236]

A few earlier BITs further require Chinese natural and juridical persons to obtain

---

[230] Only the Sino-Austria BIT uses the wording "all property", while all the other 12 BITs employ "every kind of asset". For details of these BITs between China and the EU member states, please see Oceana Publications, Investment Treaties(looseleaf) , Vol. 1 - 7; see also MOFTEC, Collection of Investment Treaties(Chinese and English) , Jing GuanJiaoyu Press, 1998.

[231] Article 1. (1) of the Sino-Sweden BIT.

[232] The Sino-Britain BIT(art. 1. 1) uses "right of abode in the UK and its territorial extension" as an additional requirement, while the Sino-Germany BITs(art 1. 3) uses "German resident" to define natural person investors. All other BITs use "nationality" to define natural person investors.

[233] Sino-Austria BIT, Article 1.

[234] Sino-Sweden BIT, Article 1. 2.

[235] Sino-Belgium Luxemburg BIT, Article 1. 1.

[236] Sino-France BIT, Article 1. 3.

prior authorization or registration and entitlement to cooperate with foreign countries on economic matters.[237]

Most of these BITs have retroactive effect, while only a few[238] do not. Some of them merely provide that they shall apply to investments made prior to the BITs coming into effect.[239] On the other hand, the Sino-Finland BIT expressly defines its application to all investment after July 1, 1979.[240]

2.2 Admission

All BITs provide that host countries shall admit investment in accordance to their laws, regulations and administrative practices.[241] The Sino-Belgium Luxemburg BIT further provides that host countries shall permit investors to sign and execute licensing agreements, business management agreements or technology assistance agreements.[242] In the Sino-Spain and Sino-Greece BITs,[243] host countries are required to offer assistance and facilities for obtaining visa and working permits, subject to its laws and regulations.

2.3 Standards of Treatment

The standards of treatment vary significantly from BIT to BIT. In general, the following standards of treatment apply:

· Fair and Equitable treatment is a quasi-universal standard of treatment in all these BITs,[244] despite slight changes of wording and in the absence of further definition.

· Most Favoured Nation(MFN) treatment is another common standard used, although exceptions include such areas as customs unions, free trade areas, frontier trade and avoidance of double taxation treaties.[245]

· National treatment can only be found in the Sino-Britain BIT and Sino-Spain BIT, which is limited to the extent possible and by host country's laws and regulations.[246]

· Non-discriminatory treatment shall be accorded under a few of these B1Ts.[247]

· International standard of treatment as contained in commonly accepted international rules and principles and as adopted by both parties, can be enjoyed by investors,

---

[237] Sino-Sweden BIT, Article 1. 2; Sino-Germany BIT, Article 1. 3.

[238] Including Sino-Sweden BIT, Sino-France BIT, Sino-Denmark BIT and Sino-Britain BIT.

[239] Sino-Germany BIT, Article 9; Sino-Bel gium and Luxemburg BIT, Article 13; Sino-Italy BIT, Article 10; Sino-Netherlands BIT, Article 10; Sino-Austria BIT, Article 9; Sino-Portugal BIT, Article 10; Sino-Spain BIT, Article 11; Sino-Greece BIT, Article 8.

[240] Sino-Finland BIT, Article 2. 2.

[241] See e. g. , Sino-Sweden BIT, Art. 2(1); Sino-Germany BIT, Art. 2; Sino-Finland BIT Art. 2. 1; Sino-Italy BIT, Art. 1; Sino-Netherl ands, Art. 2.

[242] Sino-Belgium Luxemburg BIT, Article 2. 2; Sino-Greece BIT, Article 2. 5.

[243] Sino-Britain BIT, Article 2. 2.

[244] See e. g. , Sino-Sweden BIT, Art. 2. (1); Sino-Germany Bit, Art. 2; Sino-France BIT, Art. 3; Sino-Netherl ands BIT, Art. 3. 1; Sino-Austria BIT, Art. 2. 2; Sino-Britain BIT, Art. 2. 2.

[245] See e. g. , Sino-Sweden BIT, Art. 2. (2); Sino-Germany BIT, Art. 3; Sino-France BIT, Art. 3; Sino-Netherlands BIT, Art. 3. 2 – 4; Sino-Austria BIT, Art. 3. 2 – 3; Sino-Britain BIT, Art. 3. 1 – 2.

[246] Sino-Britain BIT, Art. 3. 3; Sino-Spain BIT, Art. 3. 4.

[247] Sino-Spain BIT, Art. 3. 1; Sino-Britain BIT, Art. 2. 2; Sino-Austria BIT, Art. 3. 4; Sino-Denmark BIT, Art. 3. 4; Sino-Germany BIT, Art. 3. 4.

according to the Protocol to the Sino-Belgium Luxemburg BIT.[248]

· In most BITs, more favourable treatment based on domestic laws or international treaties is also acceptable.[249]

· The host country shall observe its obligations to investors as provided for in contracts.[250]

In conclusion, these BITs only define fair and equitable treatment and MFN treatment as accepted standards of investment treatment, while national treatment, non-discriminatory treatment and international treatment standards are but occasionally applied. Indeed, it is sometimes stressed that the host country may grant investors more favourable treatment on the basis of local or international law and that host countries shall observe their contract obligations with investors.

2.4 Expropriation and Compensation

All these BITS contain provisions on investment expropriation and compensation.[251]

· Rights of and conditions for expropriation: All these BITs provide that host countries may expropriate foreign investment, but must do so subject to the following criteria: a) public interest; b) legal procedure; c) against compensation and; d) non-discrimination.

· Compensation: There is no accepted general standard of compensation; rather a requirement that compensation be equivalent to the amount of expropriated investment plus interest.[252] Moreover, compensation shall be paid without undue delay, effectively realisable(in a convertible currency) and freely transferable.

· Under several BITs, investors may initiate Gudicial) review proceedings on expropriation cases and on the evaluation of their investment.[253]

2.5 Monetary Transfers

According to these BITs, each contracting party shall permit free transfer in convertible currency of any payment related to investment, at the prevailing rate of exchange, subject to its laws and regulations and, without undue delay.[254] A couple of

---

[248] Point 7 of the Protocol of Sino-Belgium Luxemburg BIT.

[249] See e. g. , Sino-Germany BIT, Art. 8. 1; Sino-France BIT, Art. 9; Sino-Netherlands BIT, Art. 10; Sino-Austria BIT, Art. 8; Sino-Spain BIT, Art. 10.

[250] See e. g. , Sino-France BIT, Art. 9; Sino-Denmark BIT, Article 3. 1; Sino-Britain BIT, Art. 2. 2. Sino-Greece BIT, Art. 2. 6; Sino-Spain BIT, Article 3. 1.

[251] See Sino-Sweden BIT, Art. 3; Sino-Germany BIT, Art. 4; Sino-France BIT, Art. 4; Sino-Belgium. Luxemburg BIT, Art. 4; Sino-Finland Bit, Art. 5; Sino-Italy Bit, Art. 4; Sino-Denmark BIT, Art. 4; Sino-Netherlands BIT, Art. 5 and 6; Sino-Austria BIT, Art. 4; Sino-Britain BIT, Art. 5; Sino-Portugal BIT, Art. 4; Sino-Spain BIT, Art. 4 and Sino-Greece BIT, Art. 4.

[252] Or the compensation shall be "to place the investor in the same financial position", or "amount to the(real) value of the investment expropriated", or be "equal to the(actual) value of the expropriated investment", etc. Id.

[253] Sino-Denmark BIT, Art. 4. 1; Sino-Britain BIT, Art. 5. 1 – 2 and Sino-Greece BIT, Art. 4. 2.

[254] See Sino-Sweden BIT, Art. 4; Sino-Gerrnany BIT, Art. 5 and 7; Sino-France BIT, Art. 5; Sino-Belgium Luxemburg BIT, Art. 5; Sino-Finland IT, Art. 6 – 7; Sino-Italy BIT, Art. 7; Sino-Denmark BIT, Art. 6; Sino-Netherlands BIT, Art. 4; Sino-Austria BIT, Art. 5 and 7; Sino-Britain BIT, Art. 6; Sino-Portugal BIT, Art. 5; Sino-Spain BIT, Art. 6 and Sino-Greece BIT, Art. 6.

BITs emphasis that the free transfer shall be conditional upon the payment of taxes and transfer fees,[255] while two BITs require an unrestricted transfer of investment related payments without reference to national laws or regulations.[256] More detailed rules are included in the Sino-Britain and Sino-Spain BITs, which, for example, provide a guarantee of 20% of returns transfer a year[257] and transfers no later than 6 months from the date of application respectively.[258]

2.6 Subrogation

It has been generally accepted that where a contracting party makes a payment to its investors under a guarantee it has given to its investors in respect of investments made in the territory of the other contracting party, the latter contacting party shall recognise the transfer of any right and title of the investor to the former contracting party and its subrogation to such right and title.[259] Nevertheless, such subrogated rights shall not exceed the original rights and, a few BITs allow counter-claims to be made.[260]

2.7 Dispute Settlement

Dispute settlement is an important element in all these BITs, which treat state-state disputes and state-investor disputes separately. Dispute over the amount of compensation is treated as a special case of state-investor dispute. These can be summarised as follows:[261]

· State-state disputes: Disputes concerning the interpretation and application of the BITs between contracting parties should be in so far as possible settled through diplomatic channels. Those failing to be settled in such a way in 6 months may be submitted to an *ad hoc* arbitral tribunal upon the request of a party.

· Normal state-investor disputes: Normal disputes between a host country and investors shall be settled within the jurisdiction of the host country, e. g., through conciliation or by a competent administrative authority or court of law of the host country.

· State-investor disputes over amounts of compensation: Disputes on amounts of compensation for expropriation can be, as an alternative to solutions within domestic jurisdiction, submitted to an international arbitral tribunal. The international arbitral tribunal shall determine the applicable arbitral procedures, with or without reference to the

---

[255] Sino-Belgium Luxemburg BIT, Art. 5 and Sino-Spain BIT, Art. 6. 5.

[256] Sino-Gerrnany BIT, Art. 5; Sino-Austria BIT, Art. 5.

[257] Sino-Britain BIT, Art. 6. 1 – 2.

[258] Sino-Spain BIT, Art. 6. 2 – 3.

[259] See Sino-Sweden BIT, Art. 5; Sino-Germany BIT, Art. 6; Sino-France BIT, Art. 6; Sino-Belgium Luxemburg BIT, Art. 7; Sino-Finland IT, Art. 8; Sino-Italy BIT, Art. 7; Sino-Denmark BIT, Art. 7; Sino-Netherlands BIT, Art. 8; Sino-Austria BIT, Art. 6; Sino-Britain BIT, Art. 9; Sino-Portugal BIT, Art. 6; Sino-Spain BIT, Art. 7 and Sino-Greece BIT, Art. 7.

[260] See e. g., Sino-Austria BIT, Art. 6.

[261] See Sino-Sweden BIT, Art. 6 and its Protocol; Sino-Germany BIT, Art. 10 and Protocol; Sino-France BIT, Art. 8, 9 and Protocol; Sino-Belgium Luxemburg BIT, Art. 12 and Protocol; Sino-Finland BIT, Art. 9 and Protocol; Sino-Italy BIT, Art. 11 and Protocol; Sino-Denmark BIT, Art. 8 and 9; Sino-Netherlands BIT, Art. 9 and 13; Sino-Austria BIT, Art. 4. 4, 10 and Protocol; Sino-Britain BIT, Art. 7, 8 and Exchange of Notes; Sino-Portugal BIT, Art. 7 and 8; Sino-Spain BIT, Art. 8, 9 and 12 and Sino-Greece BIT, Art. 9, 10 and 12.

ICSID rules.[262] The Protocol of the Sino-Sweden BIT and Article 10 of the Sino-Greece BIT advocate the establishment of a binding system for the settlement of state-investor disputes post China's ICSID accession. Several other BITs encourage further negotiations on supplementary agreements on the application of ICSID, upon China's accession to the ICSID Convention.[263]

3. Summary

Bilateral legal instruments are playing a more important and substantial role in current EU-China investment relations, when contrasted with the role played by multilateral legal instruments.[264] The 1985 Cooperation Agreement provides general legal framework governing economic relations between the EU and China, including investment relations. Although its provision on investment matters is not quite as spelled out as it might have been, it lays down general legal ground for future development. BITs between China and the EU Member States are instrumental in protecting and promoting investment. By determining the treatment, expropriation and compensation, dispute settlement and other crucial investment issues, they provide a solid legal basis for EU-China investment relations, particularly EU investment in China.

Nevertheless, it could be argued that both the Cooperation Agreement and the BITs are insufficient to protect mutual investment. On the one hand, the Cooperation Agreement is overly simplistic and fails to provide any concrete protection for investments. On the other hand, the BITs shortcomings can also be easily identified.

First of all, despite similarities, the BITs contain minor disparities between them. For instance, the Sino-Sweden BIT and Sino-Germany BIT require approval of the Chinese investors prior to investing abroad[265] while others do not uphold such restriction. Again, the Sino-Britain BIT's provision concerning national treatment[266] is unprecedented in the history of Chinese investment treaties. This provision is similarly adopted in the Sino-Spain BIT.[267] In respect of monetary transfers, most BITs subject them to local laws and regulations, while the BITs between China and Britain, Germany and Austria urge unrestricted transfers without reference to domestic laws and regulations.[268] Furthermore, as to the settlement of state-investor disputes, some BITs require contracting parties to conclude supplementary agreements on the utilisation of the ICSID mech-

---

[262] See e. g., Sino-Germany BIT, Protocol(4) c-d; Sino-France BIT, Art. 9 and Protocol. 4; Sino-Austria BIT, Art. 4. 4 and Protocol. 3; Sino-Denmark BIT, Art. 8; Sino-Italy BIT, Art. 5. 4 and Protocol(4).

[263] Sino-France BIT, Exchange of Letters dated May 30, 1984; Sino-Britain BIT, Exchange of Notes No. 1 – 2.

[264] This is confirmed by the Author's Survey, which shows that EU investors tend to pay much more attention on bilateral agreements than multilateral agreements. See Section 2. 2, the Survey Report, p. 11.

[265] See Sino-Sweden BIT, Art. 1. (2); Sino-Germany BIT, Art. 1. 3. This was because then China had not relaxed the restriction of companies to engage in foreign business.

[266] See Sino-Britain BIT, Art. 3. 3 – 4 and 4.

[267] See Sino-Spain BIT, Art. 3. 4.

[268] See Sino-Britain BIT, Art. 6. 1 – 2; Sino-Germany BIT, Art. 5; Sino-Austria BIT, Art. 5.

anism[269] while most of them do not. These factors discriminate among different EU investors from different Member States.[270] Moreover, transnational corporations with more than one EU nationality (or so-called European Companies) that want to invest in China are faced with the added complexity of identifying the applicable BIT. With the current trend in mergers, acquisitions and alliances among EU companies this complexity risks to become even more prominent. Ireland as yet presents unresolved issues. As Ireland has not concluded a BIT with China, Irish investment in China can by no means be effectively protected.

In the context of EU integration and China's transition to a market economy, further coordination, consolidation and strengthening of these investment provisions in the Cooperation Agreement and in these BITs is highly desirable, as it will contribute to a more mature international legal regime able to effectively protect and promote EU investment in China.

IV. General Conclusions

This Article outlines the international legal framework governing EU investment in China. Although China has not yet established general rules or principles to define the relationship between international treaties and Chinese law unequivocally, a great number of Chinese laws and regulations have either confirmed the direct applicability of international treaties or have expressly provided that international treaties take precedence over national law. To this extent, it might be argued that China is willing to accept precedence of international treaties as a general principle of law. Further, China has not yet established a general rule on the approach to implement international treaties and the direct applicability of them before Chinese courts. It is nevertheless clear that international trade and investment treaties must be transformed into Chinese law before they can be implemented and applied by Chinese courts.

The governing international law on EU investment in China includes mainly multilateral and bilateral agreements to which China and the EC and/or its member states are both contracting parties. On a multilateral level, the ICSID Convention, the MIGA Convention and the WTO Agreement are key instruments. While the first two conventions deal with dispute settlement and political risks guarantees respectively, the WTO Agreement mainly regulates TRIMs measures and investment in services sectors. On a bilateral level, the EC-China Cooperation Agreement provides for a general legal basis for investment exchange between the EU and China, while the BITs between China and EU Member States offer substantial international protection for investment between China and its EU contracting counterparts.

These investigations, however, have also shown that the existing international legal

[269] See Sino-Sweden BIT, Protocol; Sino-France BIT, Exchange of notes dated May 30, 1984; Sino-Britain BIT, Exchange of Notes No. 1 – 2.

[270] In theory, investors from the 14 EU Member States with which China has concluded BITs could enjoy the same protection and treatment because of the Most-Favoured-Nation provision included in all these BITs. However, as they stand, the BITs incongruities create a complete and uncertain environment for investment.

framework is not yet adequate in protecting and promoting EU investment in China because these legal instruments are incomplete, uncertain and at least partially contradictory. While the existing multilateral instruments are too specific to offer investment protection on a general level, the Cooperation Agreement is too vague to warrant any substantial commitment. Although the BITs between China and most EU Member States may be regarded as adequate in protecting investments between China and its counterparts, their limited application and the differences between them hinder the creation of a uniform framework for the protection of mutual investments between China and all EU Member States.

On the other hand, the uncertainty and ambiguity of the legal status of international law under Chinese law could generate confusion, hesitation and frustration and therefore, undermine the efforts that both China and the EU have made to create a favourable investment climate.

Further action is therefore needed to clarify the legal status of international law within the Chinese constitutional framework and strengthen the international legal instruments already in place. In order to achieve the latter, it would be best to negotiate and conclude a bilateral international treaty between the EU and China, or a multilateral investment agreement to which both the EU and China are parties.[271]

---

[271] The Author's Survey shows that an overwhelming majority(76%) of EU investors believe such a new international legal framework would be of substantial importance. See the Survey Report, 41. For further discussion on these potential legal arrangements, please see, Wenhua SHAN, Towards a New Legal Framework for EU-China Investment Relations, 34JWT(2000, No.5), 168 - 179.

Towards a New Legal Framework for EU-China Investment Relations*

Ⅰ. Introduction

As two of the biggest and mutually complementary markets in the world, China and the EU have everything to gain by strengthening their investment links. Since 1987, the EU investment in China has increased more than ten fold(see Table 1) and the EU has become the third biggest foreign investor in China(see Table 2). At the same time, more and more Chinese companies have realised the value of the European market and the Chinese investment in the EU is increasing rapidly as well(see Table 3).[1] Furthermore, EU-China investment is set to rise dramatically in the forthcoming years, with the eventual accession of China to the World Trade Organization (WTO)[2] and the construction of a Comprehensive Partnership between the EU and China.[3]

---

* 34 *Journal of World Trade 5*, October 2000.

The author would like to thank Mr. Daniel Bethlehem and Professor Alan Dashwood and Miss Noelle L' Hommedieu for their insightful comments on earlier drafts of this article.

[1] For instance, Eurostat figures indicate that although China accounted for only 1. 3 percent of extra-EU FDI average over 1992 – 94, it was running at 2. 4 percent or 507 million ECU by 1994—a five fold increase in two years. Eurostat Press Releases No. 7096(21 October 1996): *EU Direct Investment in the Rest-of-world*, see: < www. europa. eu. int/en/comm/eurostat/compres/en/7096/6207096a. htm >, 11 November 1999.

[2] So far China has finished bilateral negotiations with most WTO Members that want to negotiate with China, including the EU, US, Japan and other major trade partners of China. Also, the US House of Representatives has approved the establishment of a Permanent Normal Trading Relationship (PNTR) with China, while the US Congress is very likely to pass it eventually. See Jiang Liu, Xiaoming Hu, *US House of Representatives passed the PNTR with China Proposal*, People's Daily(Overseas Edition), 26 May 2000, p. 2.

[3] In March 1998, the Commission adopted a Communication called "Building a Comprehensive Partnership with China" which further upgraded and intensified the "Long Term Policy" adopted in 1995. See COM(1998) 181 Final and COM(95) 279 of 5 July 1995 respectively for details of the two documents.

Table 1 Eu Direct Investment in China(1987 V. 1997)

	Project number		Contractual value (10,000 US $)		Actual amount (10,000 US $)	
	1987	1997	1987	1997	1987	1997
Germany *	11	211	13,267	61,281	322	99,263
France	8	144	6,358	108,112	1,555	47,465
Italy	3	120	618	21,814	1,626	21,504
Netherlands		80		56,718	21	41,380
Belgium		21		1,999	754	3,326
United Kingdom	12	304	2,470	144,551	455	185,756
Denmark	3	20	57	6,486	242	1,681
Sweden	1	28	433	6,297	181	4,284
Austria	1	28	90	5,383	90	7,461
Greece		3		185	25	
Spain	1	38	19,000	1,863		3,881
Portugal * *		6		2,400		489
Ireland		3		83		30
Luxembourg		10		3,058		100
Finland		14		2,670		495
Total	40	1,030	42,293	422,900	5,271	417,115
Total FDI Inflow	2,233	21,001	370,884	5,100,353	231,353	4,525,704
Percentage	1.79	4.90	11.40	8.33	2.28	9.22

Source: Compiled by the author according to the *Chinese Foreign Economic and Trade Yearbook*(China Economy Press, 1988), pp. 592 – 596; (1998/1999), pp. 624 – 634.

Notes: * West Germany for figures of 1987.

* * Macao excluded.

Table 2 Foreign Direct Investment In China Unit: US $ 10000

Country/Region	1979 – 1998						1998					
	Projects	%	Contractual Amount	%	Actual Amount	%	Projects	%	Contractual Amount	%	Actual Amount	%
China Total	324, 667	100	57, 252, 434	100	26, 743, 125	100	19, 846	100	5, 213, 200	100	4, 558, 200	100
Hong Kong	178, 947	55. 12	29, 653, 085	51. 97	13, 871, 588	51. 87	78, 307, 830	39. 45	1, 651, 579	31. 68	1, 879, 027	41. 22
Japan	17, 592	5. 77	3, 249, 212	5. 68	2, 166, 984	8. 10	1, 188	5. 99	269, 855	5. 18	315, 778	6. 93
US	26, 651	8. 21	4, 632, 204	8. 09	2, 144, 651	8. 02	2, 215	11. 16	621, 221	11. 92	391, 241	8. 58
EU	9, 330	2. 87	3, 635, 040	6. 35	1, 741, 134	6. 51	997	5. 01	591, 138	11. 34	429, 896	9. 43
UK	2, 300	0. 71	1, 396, 398	2. 44	664, 206	2. 48	218	1. 10	168, 701	3. 24	127, 738	2. 80
Germany	1, 931	0. 59	839, 554	1. 47	368, 818	1. 38	207	1. 04	237, 360	4. 55	98, 687	2. 17
France	1, 472	0. 45	464, 230	0. 81	268, 338	1. 00	200	1. 01	48, 833	0. 94	70, 043	1. 54
Italy	1, 254	0. 39	213, 808	0. 37	142, 503	0. 53	124	0. 62	16, 655	0. 32	26, 442	0. 58
Netherlands	646	0. 20	339, 428	0. 59	164, 590	0. 62	97	0. 49	56, 267	1. 08	70, 559	1. 55
Belgium	2, 863	0. 09	43, 768	0. 08	27, 793	0. 10	22	0. 11	2, 375	0. 05	2, 827	0. 06
Sweden	334	0. 10	60, 491	0. 11	31, 700	0. 12	35	0. 18	16, 769	0. 32	13, 921	0. 03
Austria	368	0. 11	45, 127	0. 08	17, 697	0. 07	18	0. 09	2, 733	0. 05	2, 048	0. 04
Denmark	149	0. 05	101, 342	0. 18	21, 232	0. 08	13	0. 07	4, 922	0. 09	6, 016	0. 13
Spain	386	0. 12	61, 766	0. 11	17, 796	0. 07	32	0. 16	14, 088	0. 27	5, 528	0. 12
Finland	80	0. 02	33, 432	0. 06	8, 730	0. 03	10	0. 05	19, 331	0. 37	3, 953	0. 09
Luxembourg	45	0. 01	20, 549	0. 04	3, 779	0. 01	6	0. 03	1, 891	0. 04	1, 250	0. 03
Ireland	30	0. 01	8, 728	0. 02	1, 623	0. 01	5	0. 03	836	0. 02	…	…
Portugal	37	0. 01	4, 494	0. 01	2, 134	0. 01	5	0. 03	327	0. 01	854	0. 02
Greece	15	0. 00	1, 438	0. 00	213	0. 00	2	0. 01	50	0. 00	30	…

Source: *Yearbook of China Customs Statistics*, 1980 – 1999.

Table 3　China's Aproved Overseas Investment Enterprises

US $ 10, 000

Country/Region	Until 1997				1997			
	Enterprise Number	Total Investment	Chinese Contribution	Chinese Proportion	Enterprise Number	Total Investment	Chinese Contribution	Chinese Proportion
Total	2, 143	484, 328. 1	234, 861. 4	48. 5	158	32, 535. 1	19, 630. 2	60. 3
Hong Kong	172	35, 786. 2	21, 766. 6	60. 8	14	803. 1	566. 6	70. 5
Macao	37	9, 319. 2	4, 721. 3	50. 6	4	265. 3	264. 5	99. 7
USA	257	56, 657. 2	37, 541. 0	66. 3				
Japan	86	4, 447. 2	1, 648. 7	37. 1	4	179. 0	123. 8	69. 2
Russia	234	19, 417. 0	9, 707. 7	50. 0	7	161. 4	119. 2	73. 8
EU	109	10, 901. 9	4, 652. 3	47. 6	5	391. 8	165. 3	54. 5
Germany	30	1, 543. 2	932. 1	60. 4	1	83. 3	33. 3	40. 0
France	14	3, 059. 8	947. 7	31. 0				
Netherlands	12	816. 2	528. 9	64. 8	2	238. 5	92. 0	38. 6
Belgium	6	207. 0	162. 1	78. 3	1	20. 0	20. 0	100
Italy	6	1, 568. 5	298. 6	19. 0				
UK	10	1, 313. 1	675. 2	51. 4	1	50. 0	20. 0	40. 0

续表

Country/Region	Until 1997				1997			
	Enterprise Number	Total Investment	Chinese Contribution	Chinese Proportion	Enterprise Number	Total Investment	Chinese Contribution	Chinese Proportion
Luxembourg	1	40. 0	20. 0	50. 0				
Denmark	2	73. 9	34. 9	47. 2				
Finland	1	120. 0	23. 6	19. 7				
Sweden	5	318. 3	184. 1	48. 2				
Austria	7	369. 8	203. 9	55. 0				
Spain	12	1, 047. 1	411. 7	39. 3				
Portugal	3	425. 0	229. 5	54. 0				
Ireland								
Greece								

Source: Compiled by the author according to the *Chinese Foreign Economic and Trade Yearbook*, (China Economy Press, 1998/1999), pp. 739 – 744.

What is the role of law in these developments? This question underlies a research project of which this article presents some preliminary reflections.[4] Although an outside observer may tend to discount the importance of law in the light of East Asia history, especially that of China since World War II, it is recently asserted that law has been among the most important factors in the Pacific economic boom.[5] In fact, the Chinese success in attracting foreign direct investment(FDI)[6] has been, to a considerable extent, owing to the great efforts that China has made to establish a favourable FDI legal system. The promulgation of the first Chinese FDI law, the Law of Equity Joint Ventures(LEJV) in 1979 in fact signalled a new era of "Open-door" and economic reform. Recently, the Chinese government has been sorting out and reshaping its FDI laws and regulations, with a view to adapting to the requirements of the WTO.[7] On the other hand, the EU has expressed that improving the investment climate for European investment in China should be one of the EU's top objectives in building a comprehensive partnership with China.[8] Sir Leon Brittan, the EC's former Vice-President in charge of external trade issues, has further affirmed that:

"The biggest contribution that Europe can make is to provide consistent and vigorous support, as China seeks to build the institutions, rules and policies that makes it the first place investors want to come and the last place they wish to leave."[9]

With these points in mind, this article aims to study the existing legal framework governing the EU-China investment relations, particularly EU direct investments in China, with a view to exploring the direction of its future development. This article is therefore divided into three parts. Part II investigates in turn the multilateral, bilateral and "domestic" legal instruments of the current legal framework and their implications on the EU-China investment relations. Part III discusses the future agendas, with a view to constructing a new legal framework(s) for the enhanced and ever enhancing EU-China investment links.

---

[4] So far there has been no specific study on the legal aspects of the EU-China investment relations, while few studies have been conducted on the law and policy of the EC-China trade and economic relations in general. See e. g. , Hu Yuanxiang, *Legal and Policy Issues of the Trade and Economic Relations between China and the EEC*(Kluwer, 1991) , Xiao Zhiyue, *The EC and China*, (Butterworths, 1993) .

[5] Nicholas Emilou and David O' Keeffe, *The European Union and the World Trade Law: After the Uruguay Round* (John Wiley & Sons Ltd, 1996) , p. 363.

[6] China has been the second biggest FDI recipient in the world and the single biggest among developing countries for several consecutive years. See e. g. , Rubens Ricupero (Secretary General of UNCTAD) , "Recent Development in FDI Trends and Policies and Their Implications for Developing Counties", a paper submitted on the Forum on Direct Investment Strategies of the Multinational Corporations, (Xiamen, September 1998) , p. 7.

[7] Bin Lu, *et al.* , *American Asian Association Annual Enterprises Meeting Opened in Shanghai: Zhu Rongji Attended and Made Important Speech*, People's Daily(Overseas Edition) , 11 May 2000, p. 1. See also *China's Investment Climate will be Improved after its Accession to the WTO, as Concerning Departments are Sorting out FDI Laws and Policies*, People's Daily (Overseas Edition) , 25 November 1999.

[8] COM(1998) 181 Final.

[9] Sir Leon Brittan, "Opening Address at the EU-China Business Dialogue", (Beijing, 1998) .

Ⅱ. Existing Legal Framework for EU-China Investment Relations

Currently the general legal framework governing EU-China investment relations is mainly composed of three levels of legal instruments—multilateral, bilateral and "domestic".[10] At the multilateral level, there are basically three investment-related conventions to which both the EU (and/or all of its Member States) and China are or are likely to become members. They are the Convention on the Settlement of Investment Disputes between States and Nationals of Other States (the ICSID Convention), the Convention Establishing the Multilateral Investment Guarantee Agency (the MIGA Convention) and the WTO Agreement.

At the bilateral level, the framework agreement for general EU-China economic relationship is the 1985 Co-operation Agreement, which replaced the Trade Agreement made in 1978. Also, there is a sectoral agreement governing trade in textile products between the two sides, which was initially done in 1979.[11] Until now, China has concluded 13 bilateral investment treaties (BITs) with 14 Member States of the EU[12] (except Ireland, see Table 4).

At "domestic" level, on the one hand, China has developed an FDI law system governing the entry and operation of all FDIs in Mainland China. Hong Kong and Macao, as two Special Administrative Regions (SARs) of China, have their own FDI legal systems and are entitled to develop external investment relations with other countries or regions.[13] On the other hand, the EU and its Member States have their own laws and policies towards inward and outward FDI, although the distinction of power on FDI matters between them remains fairly vague.

Table 4 Bits between China and the EU Member States

Parties	Signature	Entry into Force
Austria	12 September 1985	11 October 1986
Belgium-Luxembourg	4 June 1984	5 October 1986
Denmark	29 April 1985	29 April 1985
Finland	4 September 1984	26 January 1986
France	30 May 1984	19 March 1985
Germany	7 October 1983	18 March 1985
Greece	25 June 1992	21 December 1993

[10] It is worth pointing out that only related international treaties are observed here, since other relevant international legal sources, such as the customary international law and UN Assembly Resolutions, are rather vague either in effect or in content.

[11] The Textile Agreement will not be discussed here as it is a sectoral agreement and does not affect the general picture of EU-China investment relationship.

[12] One of those BITs is concluded between China and Belgium-Luxembourg Economic Union.

[13] However, the legal frameworks of investment between the EU and Hong Kong, Macao are not to be discussed here due to space restraints.

续表

Parties	Signature	Entry into Force
Italy	28 January 1985	28 August 1987
Netherlands	17 June 1985	1 February 1987
Portugal	3 February 1992	
Spain	6 February 1992	1 May 1993
Sweden	29 March 1982	29 March 1982
United Kingdom	15 May 1986	15 May 1986

Source: Compiled by the author in light of Bilateral Investment Treaties, at ICSID Website: <www. worldbank. org/icsid/treaties/china. htm>, (10 December 1999).

A. EU-China Investment Relations Under Multilateral Agreements

1. *ICSID Convention*

In October 1966, the ICSID Convention came into force and the International Centre for Settlement of Investment Disputes(ICSID or the Centre) was established. The chief function of ICSID is to provide facilities for the conciliation and arbitration of disputes between member countries and investors as nationals of other member countries.[14] Accordingly, ICSID has adopted some administrative and operative rules.[15] Under ICSID Convention, the Centre can assume jurisdiction over a dispute when four conditions have been satisfied.[16] First, the dispute must involve a Contracting State[17] and a national of another Contracting State,[18] i. e. both the host and the home State of an investor must have signed and ratified the Convention. Second, both parties to a specific dispute must agree to submit the dispute to the Centre for conciliation or arbitration.[19] Third, the dispute must "arise di-

〔14〕 ICSID Convention, Art. 1. For discussions of the Convention and the Centre in Chinese please see Chen An, *Comments on ICSID*, (Lujiang Press, 1990).

〔15〕 For example, the Administrative and Financial Regulations, Rules of Procedure for the Institution of Conciliation and Arbitration Proceedings (Institution Rules), Rules of Procedure for Arbitration Proceedings(Arbitration Rules), and Rules of Procedure for Conciliation Proceedings(Conciliation Rules). For texts of the ICSID Convention and these Rules, see: <www. worldbank. org/icsid/basicdoc/basicdoc. htm>.

〔16〕 ICSID Convention, Art. 25.

〔17〕 "Contracting State" here includes "any constituent subdivision or agency of a Contracting State designated to the Centre by that State", the consent of which shall be subject to the approval of that State until the State notifies otherwise. As note 16, above, Art. 25.

〔18〕 "National of another Contracting State" could be a natural person or a juridical person having the nationality of a Contracting State other than the Contracting State party, on the date on which the parties consented to submit the dispute to the Centre. In addition, a juridical person possessing the nationality of the Contracting State party can be qualified as a "national of another Contracting State" if the parties agree to treat it this way on the ground of foreign control.

〔19〕 The consent shall be in writing and cannot be withdrawn unilaterally once it is made. The particular forms of consent are quite flexible and could vary from a formal "ICSID Arbitration Agreement" to a bilateral or even regional investment treaty, which includes a compulsory ICSID dispute resolution clause. For details of the forms in practice, see Huaqun Zeng, *International Investment Law*, (Peking University Press, 1999), pp. 588 – 589.

rectly out of an investment".[20] Finally, the dispute must be a "legal dispute".[21] ICSID jurisdiction is exclusive, unless otherwise agreed to by the parties. However, a Contracting State may require the exhaustion of local administrative and judicial remedies as a condition of its consent to ICSID arbitration.[22] It may also provide for diplomatic protection or bring an international claim in respect of such a dispute when another Contracting State has failed to abide by and comply with the award rendered therein.[23]

The system of applicable law in the ICSID Convention is distinctive in several ways. First, it allows parties to choose the governing "rules of law" rather than "the law". This may mean that the parties can submit different issues to rules of different legal systems, can submit disputes to rules common to more than one legal system, can combine national and international legal systems, and can submit to laws of a nationalised system frozen on a set date.[24] Second, if the parties fail to choose the applicable rules of law, the Convention requires the arbitration tribunal to apply: "the law of the Contracting State party to the dispute(including its rules on conflict of laws) and such rules of international law as may be applicable".[25] Although this provision was regarded as a "considerate balance of interests between investors and host countries", it is actually a mere mixture of conflicting arguments from developed countries and developing countries and does not make clear the relations between applicable domestic law and international law. That is to say, it leaves this question to the discretion of the arbitrators.[26] Third, it does not allow the tribunal to bring a finding of *non liquet* on the ground of silence or obscurity of the law.[27] Last but not least, it empowers the tribunal to decide a dispute *ex aequo et bono* if the parties so agree.[28]

ICSID awards are binding and final, i. e., not subject to any appeal except as provided for in the Convention.[29] Every Contracting State must recognise an ICSID award

---

[20] There is no definition within the ICSID regime on "investment". However, it is explained that the parties would define it when they consider referring to the Centre and therefore it is needless to do so in the Convention. See *Report of the Executive Directors on the Convention on the Settlement of Investment Disputes between States and Nationals of other States* (Executive's Report), (ICSID Doc. 2, 18 March 1965), at para. 27.

[21] The Executive's Report explains that "legal disputes" was intended to make it clear that while conflicts of rights would fall within the Centre's jurisdiction mere conflicts of interests would not. As note 20, above, at para. 26.

[22] ICSID Convention, Art. 26.

[23] As note 22, above, at Art. 27.

[24] I. F. I. Shihata and A. Parra, (1994) *Applicable Substantive Law in Disputes between States and Private Foreign Parties: The Case of Arbitration under the ICSID Convention*, 9 ICSID Review—Foreign Investment Law Journal, p. 189.

[25] ICSID Convention, Art. 42(1).

[26] In practice, most ICSID cases support many western commentators' argument that here international law not only fills the gap left by domestic law, but also precedes domestic law where the two are in conflict. However, it is argued by developing country scholars, that ICSID arbitration is dominated by western ideas since most arbitrators are from developed countries, and the President of the Administrative Council tends to designate western scholars as Chairmen of arbitration tribunals and *ad hoc* committee members who could annul the awards. See Huaqun Zeng, as note 19, above, pp. 604 – 608.

[27] ICSID Convention, at Art. 42(2).

[28] As note 27, above, at Art. 42(3).

[29] As note 27, above, at Art. 53(1).

in its courts as if it were a final judgement of that State.[30] Nevertheless, execution of an award is a matter for the law of the State in which execution is sought.[31] In some cases, the State in which the award was sought blocked the enforcement on the basis of sovereign immunity.[32]

The ICSID Convention is well accepted by both developed countries and developing countries. Although there have not been many disputes referred to the Centre, its caseload has increased significantly in recent years.[33] As of 1 October 1999, 147 States had signed the ICSID Convention, 131 of which have deposited their instruments of ratification.[34] ICSID arbitration clauses are also commonly found in investment agreements between governments of member countries and investors from other member countries. Advance consents by governments to submit investment disputes to ICSID arbitration are found in about 20 investment laws and in over 900 bilateral investment treaties.[35] Moreover, arbitration under the auspices of ICSID is one of the main mechanisms for the settlement of investment disputes under four recent regional trade and investment treaties, namely:

- the North American Free Trade Agreement;
- the Energy Charter Treaty;
- the Cartagena Free Trade Agreement; and
- the Colonia Investment Protocol of Mercosur.[36]

The ICSID Convention is an important multilateral legal instrument on EU-China investment relations since both China and all the EU Member States are its member countries (see Table 5). Most EU countries signed the Convention in the 1960s or 1970s while few did in the 1980s or 1990s. After prudent consideration, China signed the Convention in 1990 and ratified it in 1993. According to Article 25(4), China declared that the Chinese government only agreed to refer disputes about the amount of compensation arising from expropriation or nationalisation.[37] However, China is to expand the scope of disputes and to enact implementing regulations of the Convention.[38]

---

〔30〕 As note 27, above, at Arts. 53(1), 54(1).

〔31〕 As note 27, above, Art. 54(3).

〔32〕 See e. g., *Liberian Eastern Timber Corp. v. Republic of Liberia* and *Benvenuti and Bonfant v. The Republic of Congo*(1982) 21 ILM 740.

〔33〕 So far ICSID has concluded 38 cases and 28 cases are still in process. See "ICSID Cases", at <www. worldbank. org/icsid/cases/cases. htm>. See also "About ICSID", at <www. worldbank. org/icsid/about/about. htm>.

〔34〕 1999 ICSID, "List of Contracting States", published on its website: <www. worldbank. org/icsid/about/about. htm>.

〔35〕 1999 ICSID, "About ICSID", <www. worldbank. org/icsid/about/about. htm>.

〔36〕 As note 35, above.

〔37〕 Mu Zili, *Chinese Government is to enact regulations to implement obligations under the ICSID Convention*, Arbitration and Law Communication(Published by the Chinese International Economic and Trade Arbitration Commission-CIETAC, 1997), No. 1, pp. 3 – 4.

〔38〕 As note 27, above.

Table 5 Icsid, China and the EU(as of 1 October 1999)

State	Signature	Deposit of Ratification	Entry into Force of Convention
China	9 February 1990	7 January 1993	6 February 1993
Austria	17 May 1966	25 May 1971	24 June 1971
Belgium	15 December 1965	27 August 1970	26 September 1970
Denmark	11 October 1965	24 April 1968	24 May 1968
Finland	14 July 1967	9 January 1969	8 February 1969
France	22 December 1965	21 August 1967	20 September 1967
Germany	27 January 1966	18 April 1969	18 May 1969
Greece	16 March 1966	21 April 1969	21 May 1969
Ireland	30 August 1966	7 April 1981	7 May 1981
Italy	18 November 1965	29 March 1971	28 April 1971
Luxembourg	28 September 1965	30 July 1970	29 August 1970
Netherlands	25 May 1966	14 September 1966	14 October 1966
Portugal	4 August 1983	2 July 1984	1 August 1984
Spain	21 March 1994	18 August 1994	17 September 1994
Sweden	25 September 1965	29 December 1966	28 January 1967
United Kingdom	26 May 1965	19 December 1966	18 January 1967

Source: Compiled by the author according to List of Contracting States and other Signatories of the Convention, see: <www.worldbank.org/icsid/constate/c-states-en.htm>, (10 December 1999).

Among the 13 BITs that China concluded with the EU Member States, most refer to the ICSID Convention.[39] Some of them provide that the arbitral tribunal established to settle a State-investor dispute shall determine its own procedures with references to the ICSID Convention,[40] while few require that the Contracting Parties negotiate a supplementary agreement on a binding system of dispute settlement within the framework of the ICSID.[41] However, so far there has been no investment dispute involving China and the EU Member States that has been referred to the ICSID. Nevertheless, it is always an important precaution and an effective mechanism that both sides could use in the future.

〔39〕 Those include BITs between China and Sweden, Germany, France, Belgium-Luxembourg Economic Union, Finland, Italy, Austria and Denmark.

〔40〕 See BITs between China and Germany, Belgium-Luxembourg Economic Union, Finland, Italy, Austria and Denmark.

〔41〕 See Sino-France BIT and Sino-Sweden BIT.

2. *MIGA Convention*

The MIGA Convention,[42] signed in October 1985, created the Multilateral Investment Guarantee Agency(MIGA or the Agency). MIGA's operations are regulated by the Operational Regulations of the Multilateral Investment Guarantee Agency adopted in 1988.

The core mission of MIGA is to promote the flow of FDI to and among developing countries,[43] mainly by providing political risk insurance(including coinsurance and reinsurance) for investments in a developing member country that flow from another member country.[44] In addition, this purpose is accomplished by its complementary investment promotion activities such as provision of programmes, dissemination of information on investment opportunities, and technical assistance that enhances national investment promotion capabilities.[45]

MIGA insurance covers the risks of currency inconvertibility, expropriation and political violence. It also covers breach of contract loss as a separate class of risk coverage.[46] Eligible investors of MIGA insurance normally must be a national of a member country other than the host country, or a juridical person who is either incorporated in and has its principal place of business in a member country, or is majority-owned by nationals of member countries.[47] State-owned corporations are also eligible if they operate on a commercial basis.[48] Eligible investments must be new investments that are "economically sound" and compliant to the declared development objectives and the laws and regulations of the host country.[49] The host country must accord fair and equitable treatment and legal protection for investment.[50] Moreover, only investment made in the territory of a developing member country may be guaranteed by MIGA.[51] Finally, the host government must approve the investment project before MIGA issues insurance coverage.[52]

The most important clause in the MIGA Convention is the subrogation clause. According to the clause, member countries agree that MIGA shall be subrogated to such rights or claims related to the guaranteed investment as the holder of a guarantee may have against the host country and other obligators, as long as MIGA has paid or has a-

---

〔42〕 The MIGA Convention entered into force on 12 April 1988. See 24 ILM 1598. For detailed discussion of the Agency and the Convention, see Ibrahim F. I. Shihata, *MIGA and Foreign Investment*, (Martinus Nijhoff, 1988) and Chen An, *MIGA and China: Comments on the Multilateral Investment Guarantee Agency* (Fujian People's Press, 1995).

〔43〕 MIGA Convention, Art. 2.

〔44〕 As note 43, above.

〔45〕 As note 43, above, at Art. 2 and Art. 23.

〔46〕 As note 43, above, at Art. 11.

〔47〕 Upon the joint application of the investor and the host country, the Board, by special majority may extend eligibility to a natural person who is a national of the host country, or a juridical person who is either incorporated in and has its principal place of business in a member country, or is majority-owned by nationals of member countries, provided that the assets invested are transferred from outside the host country. As note 43, above, Art. 13.

〔48〕 As note 43, above, at Art. 13(a)(iii).

〔49〕 As note 43, above, at Art. 12(d).

〔50〕 As note 43, above.

〔51〕 As note 43, above, at Art. 14.

〔52〕 As note 43, above, at Art. 15.

greed to pay compensation to the holder of a guarantee.[53]

The MIGA Convention has its own dispute settlement mechanism, which differentiates between disputes between the Agency and Members and disputes involving holders of a guarantee or reinsurance. A separate annex[54] contains rules on the settlement of the former class of disputes, which to a considerable extent, refers to the ICSID rules of procedures.

MIGA has expanded significantly since its formation. Between fiscal year 1990 and 1998, MIGA issued a total 348 guarantee contracts for $4.2 billion in total coverage, facilitating an estimated $25 billion FDI.[55] By 2 December 1999, the number of member countries reached 151, and 15 countries were in the process of fulfilling membership requirements.

MIGA has played, and will go on playing, an important role in EU-China investment relations. By the end of 1997, all EU Member States and China had become members of the MIGA Convention(see Table 6). The EU members are all developed countries and China is a developing country for the purposes of the Convention, which means that all the EU investments in China are in principle eligible to be guaranteed by MIGA.

However, does China qualify itself as an eligible host country for MIGA guarantees, i.e., has China provided "fair and equitable treatment and legal protection for investment", or particularly for EU investment? This is apparently a very big question since so far no compromise has really been reached upon the standards of treatment for FDI between the developed countries and developing countries. Nevertheless, the operational regulations of MIGA have clarified that an investment could be regarded as being adequately protected if it is protected by a BIT between the host country and the home country of the investor.[56] That is to say, investments from all EU Member States except Ireland are adequately protected for the purposes of the MIGA Convention, as China has concluded BITs with these States. As to the eligibility of Irish investment in China to be guaranteed by MIGA, it is up to the Agency to make clear if Chinese investment laws and practices are in conformity with international law as to the protection of FDI.[57]

As the biggest developing country and the largest investment recipient in the world, China has taken a very positive attitude towards MIGA. As early as 1988, China signed and ratified the Convention. Since then China has became the fifth biggest shareholder of MIGA and the single biggest one among developing countries, with more shares than most EU Member States(see Table 6).

---

[53] As note 43, above, at Art. 18.

[54] See Annex II to the MIGA Convention.

[55] See "Guarantees Issued During FY 1999", <www.miga.org/welcome.htm>.

[56] Operational Regulations of the Multilateral Investment Guarantee Agency, Art. 3.16.

[57] As note 56, above. Some developing country scholars argued that the "international law" standard here was ambiguous and difficult to be implemented. See An Chen, as note 42, above, at p. 450.

Table 6　Miga, China and the Eu (as of 30 september 1999)

				Allocated Shares				Subscribed Shares		
				No. of Shares			Amount	No. of Shares		Amount
Date Signed	Date Ratified	Membership Date	Initial Capital	Capital Increase	Total	In US $	Initial Capital	Total	In US $	
China	04/28/88	04/30/88	04/30/88	3, 138	2, 392	5, 530	59, 834, 600	3, 138	3, 138	33, 953, 160
Austria	04/29/97	09/17/97	12/16/97	775	591	1, 366	14, 780, 120	775	775	8, 385, 500
Belgium	09/21/89	06/30/92	09/18/92	2, 030	1, 547	3, 577	38, 703, 140	2, 030	2, 030	21, 964, 600
Denmark	08/27/86	08/18/87	04/12/88	718	547	1, 265	13, 687, 300	718	718	7, 768, 760
Finland	05/13/88	12/28/88	12/28/88	600	457	1, 057	11, 436, 740	600	600	6, 492, 000
France	07/22/86	12/28/89	12/28/89	4, 860	3, 705	8, 565	92, 673, 300	4, 860	4, 860	52, 585, 200
Germany	07/24/86	10/06/87	04/12/88	5, 071	3, 865	8, 936	96, 687, 520	5, 071	5, 071	54, 868, 220
Greece	07/18/86	05/24/89	08/30/93	280	213	493	5, 334, 260	280	280	3, 029, 600
Ireland	09/18/86	07/05/89	10/27/89	369	281	650	7, 033, 000	369	369	3, 992, 580
Italy	02/19/86	04/29/88	04/29/88	2, 820	2, 150	4, 970	53, 775, 400	2, 820	2, 820	30, 512, 400
Luxembourg	09/24/90	06/04/91	08/29/91	116	88	204	2, 207, 280	116	116	1, 255, 120
Netherlands	02/03/86	10/09/87	04/12/88	2, 169	1, 653	3, 822	41, 354, 040	2, 169	2, 169	23, 468, 580
Portugal	10/01/87	06/06/88	06/06/88	382	291	673	7, 281, 860	382	382	4, 133, 240
Spain	04/27/88	04/29/88	04/29/88	1, 285	980	2, 265	24, 507, 300	1, 285	1, 285	13, 903, 700
Sweden	04/02/87	12/31/87	04/12/88	1, 049	800	1, 849	20, 006, 180	1, 049	1, 049	11, 350, 180
United										
Kingdom	04/09/86	04/12/88	04/12/88	4, 860	3, 705	8, 565	92, 673, 300	4, 860	4, 860	52, 585, 200

Source: Compiled by the author according to *MIGA Capital Subscription Data*, see: < www. miga. org/welcome. htm >, (1999 – 12 – 10).

In 1991, China and MIGA entered three Agreements concerning the local approval procedures, legal protection of MIGA Guarantees and the use of local currencies.[58] In the first agreement, the Chinese Government committed itself to answer MIGA guarantee applications promptly and, agreed that an approval could be regarded as having been given if no rejection has been made by the government within 45 days after the China Director in MIGA is notified. The second agreement entitles MIGA, in respect of the rights it subrogated from the holder of a guarantee, to enjoy treatment no less than those that the Chinese government has given or is going to give any country or its investment insurance agencies under a bilateral investment treaty. In the last agreement, the Chinese government recognises MIGA's rights, as subrogated from the compensated holder of a MIGA guarantee, to be compensated with freely usable currencies. Moreover, while foreign banks were not allowed to deal with *Renminbi* (RMB)[59] then, China agreed that MIGA could make arrangements on the disposal of local currencies it might attain therefor, to the extent that they were not done with organisations or individuals whom the Chinese law prohibited from dealing with RMB.

So far MIGA has issued many guarantees for investments in China. The first MIGA Guarantee in China was issued in fiscal year 1993.[60] By June 1998, MIGA had had US $ 131. 1 millions of outstanding guarantees in China, which amounted to 4. 6 percent of all guarantees by MIGA.[61] Most impressively, in fiscal year 1995, in the 54 guarantees that MIGA issued in the year, China hosted nine, which were valued at US $ 70. 6, accounting for 10. 5 percent of total MIGA guarantees. Many of those MIGA-guaranteed investments in China were from the EU. For example, among the six MIGA-guaranteed investments in China in the fiscal year 1999, two were from the EU(see Table 7).

3. ***WTO Agreement***

In December 1994, the Uruguay Round trade negotiation finally concluded and a powerful and comprehensive multilateral trading system was set up. At the heart of the whole system is the WTO Agreement, which is embraced in the Final Act Embodying the Result of the Uruguay Round of Multilateral Trade Negotiations. The WTO Agreement is the *de facto* charter of the World Trade Organization(WTO), defining its legal status and laying down its institutional basis. The operational rules of the WTO Agreement, however, are contained in its four Annexes, among which three(Annexes I – III) are multilateral trade agreements[62] and the other(Annex IV) includes four plurilateral trade agreements.

---

[58] For details, see An Chen, as note 42, above, pp. 689 – 694.

[59] The Chinese currency.

[60] Lorin S. Weisenfeld, *The Cooperation between MIGA and China and its Potentials*, in An Chen edited, as note 42, above, p. 496.

[61] See *MIGA Guarantees Outstanding*, MIGA Annual Report 1998.

[62] They are Annex I, which includes Agreements respectively on trade in goods(GATT 1994), services (GATS), and trade-related property rights (TRIPS), Annex II—Understanding on Rules and Procedures Governing the Settlement of Disputes(DSU) and Annex III—Trade Policy Review Mechanism(TPRM).

Table 7 Miga Guarantees in China (1995 – 1999)

Fiscal Year	Project number	Percentage of number *	Holder Liability (US $)	Percentage of Liability * *
1995	9	16. 7%	70. 6	10. 5%
1996	2	3. 0%	20. 7	2. 4%
1997	6	8. 6%	49. 8	8. 1%
1998	3	5. 5%	50. 0	6. 0%
1999	6	8. 3%	57. 9	4. 4%

Source: Compiled by the author according to *Guarantees Issued in FY* 1995, *Guarantees Issued in FY* 1996, *Guarantees Issued in FY* 1997, *Guarantees Issued in FY* 1998, *Guarantees Issued in FY* and *MIGA: The First Ten Years.* All available at MIGA website: <www. miga. org/welcome. htm>, (10/12/1999).

Notes: * As the proportion of MIGA-guaranteed projects in China in the total MIGA-guaranteed projects.

* * As the proportion of the value of MIGA guarantees in China in the total value of MIGA guarantees.

Traditionally, GATT did not deal with investment issues although the ill-fated Havana Charter[63] did have provisions on investment. However, much effort has been made to include investment issues in the framework of the multilateral trade system, on the grounds of the close link between trade and investment.[64] In 1986, when the investment issue was included in the agenda of the Uruguay Round negotiation, it was regarded as one of the several "new issues".[65] As a result, the WTO Agreement embraces an agreement called "Agreement on Trade-related Investment Measures"(the TRIMs Agreement) within the multilateral agreements on trade in goods. Although narrowly defined, the TRIMs Agreement may be regarded as a break-through in international investment law as it for the first time in history unambiguously and explicitly put the investment issue under global regulation.[66]

The TRIMs Agreement requires members not to apply any Trade-related Investment Measures(TRIMs) that are inconsistent with the principles of "national treatment"(Article 3 paragraph 4) and "general elimination of quantitative restrictions"(Article 11 para-

---

〔63〕 The Charter of International Trade Organisation(ITO), the underlying legal instrument for the GATT, which failed to enter into force and caused about 50 years of "Provisional Applications" of the latter.

〔64〕 A simple but convincing indication of this link is the fact that about one-third of the total 6. 1 trillion total for world trade in goods and services in 1995 was trade within companies—for example between subsidiaries in different countries or between subsidiaries and their headquarters. See World Trade Organization, *Trading into the Future* (2nd edn, 1998), p. 50.

〔65〕 The "New Issues" are about GATS, TRIPS and TRIMs.

〔66〕 Some people, on the contrary, argue that the agreement is actually "retrogressive" because the elimination of TRIMs that it requires has already been required under the GATT. See Tomas L. Brewer and Stephen Young, *The Multilateral Investment System and Multinational Enterprises* (OUP, 1998), p. 124.

graph 1) of GATT 1994.[67] To make matters clear an illustrative list of those measures is annexed to the Agreement, which includes domestic content, import-export balancing and foreign exchange balancing requirements. Under the Agreement, each member shall notify the Council of Trade in Goods of all their inconsistent TRIMs within 90 days of the entry into force of the Agreement, and eliminate them within a certain period of time.[68]

GATS is another agreement in the WTO Agreement directly dealing with investment issues.[69] According to GATS, trade is defined to embrace investment,[70] since one of the four modes of trade in services is through "commercial presence", which includes "any type of business or professional establishment", no matter in form of a juridical person or a branch or a representative office.[71] Moreover, GATS's provisions on market access directly and specifically refer to joint ventures and limitations on the percentage of foreign ownership.[72] Therefore, it is sensible to consider the GATS as "Rules for Growth and Investment".[73]

Additionally, other agreements, especially the Agreement on Trade-related Intellectual Property Rights(TRIPS), the Agreement on Subsidies and Countervailing Measures (SCMs), the Understanding of Dispute Settlement(DSU) and the Trade Policy Review Mechanism(TPRM) are regarded as of continuous and direct relevance to FDI.[74] In fact it could be argued that most of the WTO agreements and their implementation measures are related to FDI since they influence the totality of the FDI environment. Thus it is not exaggerating to say that the WTO Agreement as a whole is not only a breakthrough in the history of international trade law, but also a significant advance in international investment law.[75]

While these existing rules are quite important, the subsequent negotiations and reviews on those rules may be even more important for the future of investment issues in the WTO.[76] Most of the negotiation scheduled for the early years of the WTO concerned investment issues and several of them had the potential for significant expansion

---

〔67〕 Art. 2 of the TRIMs Agreement.

〔68〕 The transition period is two years for developed countries, five years for developing countries or seven years for least-developed countries. As note 57, above, at Art. 5, para. 1 – 2.

〔69〕 The significance of GATS to FDI is in part due to the fact that the recent years have seen a much more rapid FDI growth in the services sector than in other sectors. See Tomas L. Brewer and Stephen Young, as note 66, above, at p. 126. See also UNCTAD/World Bank, *World Investment Report* 1994*: Transitional Corporations, Employment and Workplace* (1994), Tables 1. 8 and 1. 9, pp. 16 – 17.

〔70〕 Tomas L. Brewer and Stephen Young, as note 66, above, at p. 126.

〔71〕 Any type of business or professional establishment, including through: (i) the constitution, acquisition or maintenance of a juridical person; or(ii) the creation or maintenance of a branch or a representative office, within the territory of a Member for the purposes of supplying a service. See Art. XXVIII of GATS, item(d).

〔72〕 See GATS Art. XVI, para. 2. (e) – (f).

〔73〕 World Trade Organization, *Trading into the Future* (2nd edn, July 1998), p. 21.

〔74〕 See Tomas L. Brewer and Stephen Young, as note 66, above, at p. 123.

〔75〕 Wenhua Shan, (1996) *Comments on the International Investment Rules within the WTO Agreement*, CASS Journal of Law (Faxue Yanjiu), No. 2.

〔76〕 See P. Sauvé, *A First Look at Investment in the Final Act of the Uruguay Round*, 28 J. W. T. 5, pp. 5 – 16. P. Sauvé, *Assessing the General Agreement on Trade in Services: Half Full or Half Empty*?, 29 J. W. T. 4, pp. 125 – 145.

of the WTO's coverage of investment matters.[77] Among them, the reviews of the TRIMs Agreement and GATS may be the most important ones.[78]

In 1996, the Singapore Ministerial Conference created three new working groups, among which one is to investigate the relationship between trade and investment.[79] Since then the working group has done much research on the relationship and the possibility to conclude a multilateral agreement on investment within the WTO framework. The suspension of the Seattle WTO Ministerial Conference, however, might have cast shadows over this prospect.

All the EU Member States and the EC itself are members of the WTO. China is not a member of the WTO although it has been one of the 23 original Contracting Parties of the GATT. In 1986 the Chinese government applied for the resumption of its original membership of the GATT. In late 1999, the United States concluded the bilateral trade negotiation about the Chinese accession to the WTO, which was widely regarded as great progress and paved the way for the eventual Chinese entry into the multilateral trading system. Recently the EU-China deal was made, removing the last major barrier for the Chinese accession. It is therefore anticipated that China may finally become a member of the WTO in late 2000 or early 2001.[80]

China's entry into the WTO will significantly improve the EU-China investment relations, especially the conditions for EU investment in China. In the Sino-US bilateral WTO Agreement, China has already made significant concessions in a large number of fields, notably in TRIMs measures and services sectors.[81] Moreover, China has offered further concessions in services sectors such as telecommunication, banking and insurance in the EU-China deal which "will provide substantial new market opportunities for European companies selling to China or investing there".[82]

4. ***Conclusion***

Multilateral agreements of which the EU and China are members are playing important roles in the EU-China investment relations in some specific aspects or sectors. The ICSID Convention set up a unique multilateral investment dispute settlement mechanism which entitles private investors (e. g., those from the EU) to challenge sovereign States (e. g., China). The MIGA Convention establishes, on the other hand, a multilateral guarantee scheme that can guarantee EU investments in China against non-commercial risks. It is evident that both of them could significantly facilitate and enhance mutual investment between the EU and China, notably EU investment in China. Besides, the WTO Agreement contains considerable rules on investment issues, with huge potential for fu-

---

[77] Tomas L. Brewer and Stephen Young, as note 66, above, p. 139.

[78] As note 66, above.

[79] World Trade Organization, *Trading into the Future* (2nd edn, 1998), p. 50.

[80] See the "Overview of China's Economic Reform and WTO negotiations", < www. europa. eu. int/comm/trade/bilateral/china/chr. htm >, 22 May 2000.

[81] For details of the Sino-US Bilateral WTO Agreement, see: < www. uschina. org/ >; for a summary of the agreement, see: < www. chinapntr. gov/bilatsumm. htm >.

[82] Statement on EU-China Trade Agreement by Romano Prodi, President of the European Commission, at < www. europa. eu. int/comm/trade/bilateral/china/prodi. htm >, 22 May 2000.

ture expansion and development, in the disguise of a trade agreement. China's accession to the WTO would therefore significantly promote and strengthen the EU-China investment relations.

However, it is equally evident that without a set of general principles and rules, these multilateral legal instruments and their specific provisions are incomplete and inconsistent. For example, there are many important conceptions and aspects that these agreements have not mentioned at all, such as the definition of "investment", general rules of admission, treatment standards, expropriation and its compensation. Also, the three sets of dispute settlement systems under the three agreements are quite different from each other: while investors can directly sue a government under the ICSID Convention, the WTO dispute settlement body (DSB) has a sort of compulsory jurisdiction over disputes arising within the WTO framework.[83] Therefore, they themselves are not sufficient to protect and promote investments between the two sides. To achieve this goal, a general and substantive international legal framework between the two sides is necessary.

B. EU-China Investment Relations Under Bilateral Agree Ments

1. *The Co-operation Agreement*

The negotiation for a new agreement on trade and economic co-operation was embarked on in 1983 and was finally concluded in 1985. It replaced the 1978 Trade Agreement and is still the only framework agreement between the two parties. The Co-operation Agreement[84] has four chapters. Chapters 1, 3 and 4 are about trade co-operation, Joint Committee and final provisions, which are virtually identical to the Trade Agreement, with slight modifications. The real change in the Co-operation Agreement is the inclusion of Chapter 3 about various forms of Economic Co-operation.

According to the Co-operation Agreement, the Sino-EC economic co-operation is extended to every possible sphere,[85] particularly in fields of: industrial and mining; agriculture including agro-industry; science and technology; energy; transport and communication; environmental protection; co-operation in the third countries.[86] At the same time, both parties agreed to endeavour to promote and facilitate various forms of co-operation, including joint production and joint ventures; common exploitation; transfer of technology; co-operation between financial institutions; visits, contacts and activities designed to promote co-operation between individuals, delegations, and economic organisations; organisation of seminars and symposia; consultancy services; technical assistance, including the training of staff; continuous exchange of information relevant to commercial

---

[83] This problem may well deserve a PhD dissertation and it is therefore beyond the scope of this article to discuss it in detail.

[84] The official name is the Agreement on Trade and Economic Co-operation between the European Community and the People's Republic of China. See [1985] OJ L250.

[85] As long as they fall within the competence of the Community.

[86] Article 10 of the Co-operation Agreement.

and economic co-operation, etc.[87]

The Co-operation Agreement also takes into account the different level of development between the EC and China and requires that the EC be prepared to continue, step up and diversify its development activities in China, within the means at its disposal and in accordance with its rules.[88] This article has shown the EC's willingness to grant China more development aid, though it had to balance it with the development needs of other developing regions, such as the ACP countries, the Mediterranean countries and the Eastern Europe countries.

Most significantly, the Co-operation Agreement contains a clause on investment. The investment clause requires the two parties to promote and encourage greater and mutually beneficial investment. Additionally, the parties undertake to improve the existing favourable investment climate in particular through encouraging the extension of BITs between China and the EC Member States.[89] This clause follows the Community's model set for this purpose in negotiations with non-associated countries,[90] and it may have been largely inspired by the fact that when the agreement was under negotiation there had been considerable EC investments in China and most EC Member States had signed BITs with China.[91] Since it imposes no substantial obligation for the Contracting Parties but expresses their intention for future co-operation, this provision is much more a symbolic declaration than a practical rule. Nevertheless, it lays down a general legal basis for future co-operation in this field.

Last but not least, a Joint Committee was set up under the Agreement, to monitor the functioning of the Agreement and to examine means and new opportunities of developing economic co-operation. It may also make recommendations that may help to attain the objectives of the Agreement in the areas of common interest. Where necessary the Joint Committee may set up working parties to assist it in its work.

It is worth mentioning that although the Community has exercised the power of concluding economic co-operation agreements for quite a long time, this power is not exclusive. At the same time, Member States still hold the power to sign agreements of this kind with non-Member States. In order to decrease conflicts therefrom, the Council adopted Decision 74/393. It requires the Member States in question to hold prior consultation before the signing of any agreement of this kind and to inform the Commission of the agreement and the measures and commitments undertaken thereunder.[92] However, those requirements restrain but do not exclude the Member States from the exercise of the power of concluding economic co-operation agreements. As a matter of fact, most EC

---

[87] As note 86, above, at Art. 11.

[88] As note 86, above, at Art. 13.

[89] As note 86, above, at Art. 12.

[90] See Hu Yuanxiang, as note 4, above, p. 116.

[91] At that time, seven of the ten EC Members had concluded BITs with China. The other three were Greece, Ireland and the United Kingdom, among which Greece and Britain, together with other subsequently acceded EC Members, have now signed BITs with China.

[92] See Council Decision 74/393, [1974] OJ L203/23.

Member States have concluded economic co-operation agreements with China,[93] parallel to the Co-operation Agreement on the Community level. Due to restraints of space and their lack of close relevance to investment issues, these economic co-operation treaties are not to be discussed in this article.

2. ***BITs between China and EU Member States***

As mentioned, so far China has concluded bilateral investment protection and promotion agreements with 13 of the 14 EU Member States. The first BIT among them was concluded with Sweden on 29 March 1982, followed by Germany, France, Belgium-Luxembourg Economic Union, Finland, Italy, Denmark, United Kingdom, the Netherlands, Austria, Portugal, Spain and Greece. Only Ireland has not signed such a treaty with China but it is in the process of doing so. For the time being, BITs between China and the EU Member States are the most important international legal instruments for EU-China investment relations since they are the only legal instruments that could offer European FDI with general and substantial protection.

The main purpose of these BITs, as they state, is to promote and protect mutual investment, particularly investment in China. Therefore all of them contain such fundamental provisions as definitions, admission, treatment standards, expropriation and its compensation, war losses compensation, monetary transfer, subrogation and dispute settlement and so forth. A comparison of those BITs identifies similar contents as follows:

– each contracting party shall encourage investors from the other contracting party to invest in its territory and shall permit such investment in accordance with its laws and regulations;[94]

– investments shall at all times be accorded fair and equitable treatment.[95] They shall also be treated no less favourably than investments from any third State(Most-Favoured-Nation—MFN treatment), with exceptions related to customs unions, free trade areas, frontier trade, avoidance of double taxation treaty, among others;[96]

– investments shall not be expropriated unless it is in the public interest, by process of law, non-discriminatory and with compensation. Compensation shall be equivalent to the value of the expropriated investment and shall be paid without undue delay and shall be effectively realisable and freely transferable;[97]

– investors of one contracting party whose investments in the other contracting party suffer losses due to war or other armed conflict, revolution, a state of national emergency, revolt or riot in the territory of latter contracting party shall be accorded MFN

---

[93] For details of economic co-operation agreements between China and EC Member States, see Hu Yuanxiang, as note 4, above, p. 79.

[94] See e. g. : Sino-Sweden BIT, Art. 2(1); Sino-Germany BIT, Art. 2; Sino-Finland BIT Art. 2. 1; Sino-Italy BIT, Art. 1; Sino-Netherlands BIT, Art. 2.

[95] See e. g. : Sino-Sweden BIT, Art. 2(1); Sino-Germany BIT, Art. 2; Sino-France BIT, Art. 3; Sino-Netherlands BIT, Art. 3. 1; Sino-Austria BIT, Art. 2. 2; Sino-Britain BIT, Art. 2. 2.

[96] See e. g. : Sino-Sweden BIT, Art. 2(2); Sino-Germany BIT, Art. 3; Sino-France BIT, Art. 3; Sino-Netherlands BIT, Art. 3. 2 – 4; Sino-Austria BIT, Art. 3. 2 – 3; Sino-Britain BIT, Art. 3. 1 – 2.

[97] See e. g. : Sino-Sweden BIT, Art. 3(1); Sino-Germany BIT, Art. 4. 1 – 2; Sino-France BIT, Art. 4. 2; Sino-Netherlands BIT, Art. 5. 1 – 2; Sino-Austria BIT, Art. 4. 1 – 2; Sino-Britain BIT, Art. 5. 1.

treatment;[98]

– subject to its laws and regulations, each contracting party shall permit without undue delay the free transfer in convertible currency of any payment related to investment;[99]

– if a contracting party makes a payment to its investors under a guarantee it has given to its investor in respect of an investment made in the territory of the other contracting party, the latter contacting party shall recognise the transfer of any right and title of the investor to the former contracting party and its subrogation to such right and title;[100]

– disputes concerning the interpretation and application of the BIT between contracting parties should be as far as possible settled through diplomatic channels. Those failing to be settled in this way in six months could be submitted to an *ad hoc* arbitral tribunal upon the request of a party;[101]

– normal disputes between the host country and an investor shall be settled by conciliation or in case of failure to settle it this way in six months, by a competent administrative authority or a competent court of law of the host country. As an exception, disputes on the amount of compensation for expropriation can be submitted to an international arbitral tribunal, which shall determine the arbitral procedure with or without reference to the ICSID rules.[102]

However, these BITs vary from each other in one way or another. For instance, early BITs like the Sino-Sweden BIT and Sino-Germany BIT require that the Chinese investors shall be approved before they make any investment abroad[103] while the later ones do not have this restriction. Again, the Sino-Britain BIT has a provision about national treatment,[104] which is unprecedented in the Chinese investment treaty history. The Sino-Spain BIT followed it and contained a similar provision.[105] In respect of monetary transfers, most BITs subject them to local laws and regulations, while the BITs between China and Britain, Germany and Austria claim unrestricted transfers without mentioning the limitation by domestic laws and regulations.[106] Finally, as to settlement of State-investor disputes, some BITs require that contracting parties shall conclude a supplementary a-

---

[98] See e. g. : Sino-Germany BIT, Art. 4. 3 – 4; Sino-France BIT, Art. 4. 3; Sino-Netherlands BIT, Art. 6; Sino-Austria BIT, Art. 4. 3 & 4. 6; Sino-Britain BIT, Art. 4. Sino-Denmark BIT, Art. 5; Sino-Italy BIT, Art. 4. 3 – 4.

[99] See e. g. : Sino-Sweden BIT, Art. 4; Sino-France BIT, Art. 5; Sino-Netherlands BIT, Art. 4; Sino-Denmark BIT, Art. 6; Sino-Italy BIT, Art. 8.

[100] See e. g. : Sino-Sweden BIT, Art. 5; Sino-Germany BIT, Art. 6; Sino-France BIT, Art. 6; Sino-Netherlands BIT, Art. 8; Sino-Austria BIT, Art. 6; Sino-Britain BIT, Art. 6; Sino-Denmark BIT, Art. 7; Sino-Italy BIT, Art. 7.

[101] See e. g. : Sino-Germany BIT, Art. 10; Sino-France BIT, Art. 8; Sino-Netherlands BIT, Art. 13; Sino-Austria BIT, Art. 10; Sino-Britain BIT, Art. 8; Sino-Denmark BIT, Art. 9; Sino-Italy BIT, Art. 11.

[102] See e. g. : Sino-Germany BIT, Protocol(4) c – d; Sino-France BIT, Art. 9 and Protocol 4; Sino-Austria BIT, Art. 4. 4 and Protocol 3; Sino-Denmark BIT, Art. 8; Sino-Italy BIT, Art. 5. 4 and Protocol(4).

[103] See Sino-Sweden BIT, Art. 1(2); Sino-Germany BIT, Art. 1. 3. This was because then China had not relaxed the restriction of companies to engage in foreign business.

[104] See Sino-Britain BIT, Art. 3. 3 – 4 and 4.

[105] See Sino-Spain BIT, Art. 3. 4.

[106] See Sino-Britain BIT, Art. 6. 1 – 2; Sino-Germany BIT, Art. 5; Sino-Austria BIT, Art. 5.

greement on the utilisation of the ICSID mechanism[107] while most of them do not.

3. ***Conclusion***

It can be seen that bilateral legal instruments are playing an even more important and substantial role in current EU-China investment relations in comparison with related multilateral legal instruments. The 1985 Co-operation Agreement acts as the general legal framework for all the economic relations between the EU and China, including investment relations. Although its provision on investment matters is quite simple and brief, it lays down a general legal ground for future development. In respect of the substantial protection and promotion of investment, BITs between China and the EU Member States are of the most significance. Through determining the treatment, expropriation and compensation, dispute settlement and other crucial investment issues, they provide a solid legal basis for EU-China investment relations, particularly EU investment in China.

Nevertheless, it could be argued that both the Co-operation Agreement and the BITs are insufficient to protect mutual investment. On the one hand, the Co-operation Agreement is too simple to provide any concrete protection for mutual investment. On the other hand, the BITs' shortcomings can easily be seen as well. First of all, as mentioned above, the BITs are different from each other despite their general similarities. This fact causes discrimination among different EU investors from different Member States.[108] Moreover, transnational corporations with more than one EU nationality (or so-called European Companies) that want to invest in China may face further problems of identifying the applicable BIT. This is very likely to happen now as mergers, acquisitions and alliances are more and more popular nowadays in EU countries. The last problem that shall be mentioned here is about Ireland. So far Ireland has not concluded a BIT with China, which means that the investment between Ireland and China can by no means be effectively protected.

These elements may further affirm the call for a new legal framework specialising in investment protection between the EU and China.

C. EU-China Investment Relations Under "Domestic" Laws

1. *FDI Regulations in the EU and its Member States*[109]

(a) EU's competence on FDI issues

After the Community attained exclusive competence in common commercial policy, it started to seek a uniform policy on the protection of the Community's private invest-

---

[107] See Sino-Sweden BIT, Protocol; Sino-France BIT, exchange of notes dated 30 May 1984; Sino-Britain BIT, Exchange of Notes No. 1 – 2.

[108] In theory, all the investors from the 14 EU Member States with which China has concluded BITs could enjoy the same protection and treatment because of the Most-Favoured-Nation provision included in all these BITs. It is, however, at least rather troublesome to check out all the Chinese BITs so as to find out the real picture of their legal status.

[109] For an early account of legal framework for FDI in the EEC, please see W. H. Balekjian, *Legal Aspects of Foreign Investment in the European Economic Community* (Manchester University Press, 1967). For recent research on FDI laws and policies in the EU and its Member States, see Stephen Young and Neil Hood, *Inward Investment Policy in the European Community in the* 1990*s* (Transnational Corporation, 1993), Vol. 2, No. 2; Tomas Brewer and Stephen Young, *European Union Policies and the Problems of Multinational Enterprises*, 29 J. W. T. 1.

ment in developing countries.[110] However, so far what it has achieved seems to be more symbolic than real. The EU Member States retain their full competence in concluding BITs with non-Member States whilst the Community has never managed to conclude a pure investment treaty by itself. Like that in the EU-China Co-operation Agreement, the normal practice for the EU in this respect is to insert one Article into the framework treaties with the developing counter parties, expressing their political willingness to promote and protect mutual investment in the future.[111]

A special example, however, is the Lome Convention, which may be the most substantial agreement the EU and its Member States have concluded in this field. In the fourth Lomé Convention, "Investment" has become the title of an individual Chapter that includes six sections and 17 articles.[112] This convention not only contains general rules such as fair and equitable treatment, national treatment, non-discriminatory treatment, but also includes specific commitments on investment financing and currency payment. Most significantly, it has a non-discrimination clause[113] which in fact entitles all the contracting parties to provisions in agreements negotiated between the ACP States or EU Member States concerned and another State. In other words, once an ACP country concludes a BIT with any third country (the so-called "reference agreement"), all the EU Member States may enjoy the same protection as that provided for in the BIT. Nonetheless, it is not a sole agreement signed by the EU, but a mixed association agreement signed jointly by the EU and its Member States.

When the WTO Agreement was to be ratified, the EU's competence in dealing with the "new issues" (GATS, TRIPS and TRIMs) was debated among the EU institutions and its Member States. The Commission requested the opinion of the Court of Justice of the European Communities (CJEC) under EC Treaty Article 300(6) (ex 228(5)) as to the exclusivity of the Community competence to conclude the Multilateral Agreements on Trade in Goods (the Goods Agreement), GATS and TRIPS Agreement. The Court held that concluding the Goods Agreement, which included the TRIMs Agreement was within the sole competence of the Community pursuant to Article 133 (ex Article 113) of the EC Treaty. However, the closely investment-related GATS, together with the TRIPS Agreement, were generally regarded to be outside the sole competence and the Community must sign this jointly with its Member States.

In the course of the OECD negotiations on the Multilateral Agreement on Investment (MAI), it was the Member States rather than the Community that participated in the negotiation, although they agreed on a framework of co-operation.[114] Nevertheless, this soft framework did not constitute binding effect. Later the French government with-

---

[110] Hu Yuanxiang, as note 4, above, p. 116.

[111] For instance, the EC-Yugoslavia Co-operation Agreement and the EC-Brazil Agreement, made in 1980. For details see [1980] OJ L130, and [1980] OJ C169, respectively.

[112] [1991] OJ L229/84.

[113] Article 261 of the Fourth Lome Convention.

[114] Alasdair R. Young (2000) *The Adaptation of European Foreign Economic Policy: From Rome to Seattle*, 38 Journal of Common Market Studies, No. 1, pp. 108 – 109.

drew from the talk without formally consulting its EU partners and the negotiation was suspended.[115]

In short, it is clear that the general authority on FDI issues still largely rests in the hands of Member States, although the division of competence between the EU and its Member States remains rather ambiguous.[116] Thus it is necessary to look at the regulations of this kind both at the Community level and Member States level to get a complete picture for EU regulations for FDI.

(b) FDI regulations at the Community level

At the Community level, although there is neither an established FDI policy nor Commission officials dealing 100 percent with FDI issues, many FDI-related Community rules exist and a range of EU Directorates handle various FDI matters.[117] Particularly, Articles 56 – 60(ex Article 73) of the EC Treaty may have the potential to be the general legal basis for a code on FDI or policy harmonisation.[118] Article 56 reads:

"1. Within the framework of the provisions set out in this Chapter, all restrictions on the movement of capital between Member States and between Member States and third countries shall be prohibited.

2. Within the framework of the provisions set out in this Chapter, all restrictions on the payment between Member States and between Member States and third countries shall be prohibited."

However, capital movement and payment are not treated exactly the same way as this Article appears. In fact, they are subject to several other qualifications as set forth in Articles 57, 58 and 59.

In implementing these Articles, some Member States were granted extensions to enable them to abolish exchange controls as required, with Greece being the last to liberalise in May 1994. At the same time, the Commission has tried to persuade Member States to remove the most blatant or discriminatory measures, such as the authorisation procedures for FDI in France and the 29.5 percent equity limitation on foreign ownership in British Aerospace plc and Rolls Royce plc in the UK.[119] In addition, Article 56 and Article 57(1)[120] taken together actually have the effect of prohibiting Member States from tightening direct investment regimes in force on 31 December 1993. Lastly, it may be worth pointing out that there is no notification procedure on inward FDI at EU level, except where State aid or regional aid is involved.[121]

Apart from the EC Treaty, a wide range of other rules and regulations at the EU level have implications for FDI, especially in the broad area of internal trade and factor

---

[115] As note 114, above.

[116] For studies on the EU's competence in external relations, see Alan Dashwood, *The Attribution of External Relations Competence*, forthcoming. For a general account, see Macleod, Hendry and Hyett, *The External Relations of the European Communities* (OUP, 1996).

[117] Tomas L. Brewer and Stephen Young, as note 109, above, at p. 41.

[118] Tomas L. Brewer and Stephen Young, as note 66, above, at p. 179.

[119] Tomas L. Brewer and Stephen Young, as note 109, above, at p. 41.

[120] Article 57(1) grandfathers all lawful restriction on such movement, which existed on 31 December 1993.

[121] As note 109, above, p. 40.

movement.[122] For example, regulations about mergers, acquisitions, and alliances (MAAs) and rules about corporate restructuring, government procurement, privatisation, have obvious implications for FDI. Likewise, other regulations on competition policy, trade and commercial policy, regional and social policy and industrial policy may have impact upon FDI in various ways.[123]

The EU has adopted measures to encourage Community investors to explore the developing markets. In 1988, the Community embarked on a "European Community Investment Partners" programme, which was enlarged in 1992 and further strengthened in 1995. The main purpose of this programme is to offer financial support for investment in Latin America, Asia and the Mediterranean Region. Also, the European Investment Bank (EIU) has extended its financial activities to funding overseas investments in Africa, Caribbean, Pacific and the Mediterranean Regions.[124] In 1996, the EU decided to grant Community guarantees to the EIU against losses from loans for projects in Latin America and Asian countries (including China) with which it had concluded co-operation agreements.[125] Accordingly, the EIU and the Chinese government signed a framework agreement for financing co-operation and the EIU soon offered a loan of 55 million to finance a China oil development programme.[126]

(c) FDI regulations in EU Member States

At Member State level, there are still a variety of controls, principally on inward FDI. These rules are permissible exemptions to the OECD Code of Liberalisation of Capital Movement and are mainly related to take-overs from outside the Country of the EU, or sectoral measures in regulated or sensitive industries (where additionally reciprocity requirements may prevail).[127] Restrictions on outward direct investment are very rare, except, for instance, notification or authorisation requirements in several countries and the 50 percent foreign-currency requirement in Greece.[128]

On the contrary, several Member States have developed schemes to promote and encourage outward investments, in addition to their efforts to conclude BITs with many developing countries. France, Germany, Britain and Sweden provide loan facilities for outward investments through various forms of developing financial corporations, such as "Caisse Centrale de Coopération Economique" in France, "German Finance Company for Investment in Developing Countries", the British "Commonwealth Development Corporation" and the "Swedish Fund for International Cooperation with Developing Coun-

---

[122] For a summary of these regulations and policies, see Tomas L. Brewer and Stephen Young, as note 109, above, pp. 39 – 40 (Table 1).

[123] As note 109, above.

[124] United Nations Department of Transitional Corporation and Investment, 1995 *World Investment Report*, (Chinese translation, Foreign Economic and Trade University Press, 1996), pp. 316 – 319. See also Zeng Huaqun, as note 19, above, p. 135.

[125] [1996] OJ L329, pp. 45 – 46.

[126] See 38th Annual Report of the European Investment Bank (1996).

[127] Tomas L. Brewer and Stephen Young, as note 109, above, p. 41.

[128] See *EU Member State Policies on FDI in 1980s* as reprinted in 29 J. W. T. 1, pp 42 – 43.

tries".[129] Additionally, Germany, France, Holland, Sweden, Britain and Denmark have established national political risk insurance schemes to encourage outward investment.[130]

2. ***Chinese Law for Foreign Investment***

(a) Chinese legal system for foreign investment

China has been very active in FDI law-making. In fact, the Chinese open-door policy started with the promulgation of the Law for Chinese-Foreign Joint Ventures in 1979, the first and most important law for FDI. In 1982, this practice of utilising FDI was "constitutionalised" when the Constitution was revised so as to "permit foreign enterprises, other foreign economic organisations and individual foreigners to invest in China and enter into various forms of economic co-operation with Chinese economic organisations".[131] From then on more and more laws and regulations on FDI were promulgated and the Chinese investment market was opened wider and wider. Now China has a comprehensive FDI law system,[132] which may be generally divided into three levels: the Constitutional rules, the national laws and regulations and the local regulations.

Among them, the six basic laws and regulations on FDI are most important. They are:

– Law of Chinese-Foreign Equity Joint Ventures(LEJV);

– Law of Chinese-Foreign Contractual Joint Ventures(LCJV);

– Law of Wholly Foreign Invested Enterprises(LWFE);

– Provisional Regulations on the Establishment of Stock Company with Foreign Investment(PRSCFI);

– Regulations on the Exploitation of Offshore Petroleum Resources in Co-operation with Foreign Enterprises(REOFF); and

– Regulations on the Exploitation of Onshore Petroleum Resources in Co-operation with Foreign Enterprises(REON).

In Order to implement or supplement these basic FDI laws and regulations, there are many other national rules governing FDI entry, registration, operation, employment, and tax and so forth in China. Among them, the three implementing regulations for the LEJV, LCJV and LWIE are the most important regulations as they specify the rules and principles set forth in the three basic laws. Accordingly, there are in general five forms of FDI in China: equity joint venture(EJV), contractual joint venture(CJV), wholly foreign invested enterprise(WFE), stock companies with foreign investment(SCFI) and joint exploitation(JE).

(b) Treatment of foreign investment under Chinese law

The treatment of FDI under Chinese law generally can be divided into three as-

---

[129] Huaqun Zeng, as note 19, above, pp. 134 – 135.

[130] As note 19, above, at pp. 141 – 143. See also Paul Comeaux, N. Stephan Kinsella, *Protecting Foreign Investment under International Law: Legal Aspects of Political Risks* (Oceana Publications Inc., 1997), pp. 179 – 181.

[131] The Constitution of the People's Republic of China, Art. 18, para. 1.

[132] Here it means merely the law system for inward FDI, while there are also several regulations on outward investment, which are not going to be discussed here owing to space restraints.

pects:

- management;
- protection; and
- promotion,

which are in turn summarised below.

Management of Foreign Investment under Chinese Law

The management of FDI can in general be classified in two stages: the admission stage and the operation stage.

China used to have no specific rules on the admission of FDI. Until the government approved the investment project, foreign investors had no clear idea which fields they should invest in and how their investment would be processed. In order to improve the transparency of FDI admission, the Chinese authority promulgated in 1995 the Provisional Regulations on the Direction Guide to FDI and the Guiding Catalogue of Industries for Foreign Investment. They classify the FDI into four categories: the encouraged, restricted and prohibited and permitted categories. They list the encouraged, restricted and prohibited industries. All the others are defaulted as permitted industries. FDIs in the encouraged category enjoy some special rights and preferences (mainly tax incentives), while FDIs in the restricted category are subject to certain restrictions, for example, local content, EJV form and so on. At the same time, they clarify the approval authorities and the distribution of the approval right of FDI projects between them. Recently, a Guiding Catalogue of High-tech Industries for Foreign Investment was promulgated.[133] Needless to say, these regulations are warmly welcomed by foreign investors. As to the specific procedures of setting up an FIE, foreign investors should refer to the corresponding implementing regulations of the form of FDI that they intend to establish.

Once an FIE is set up, it has the autonomy to manage the business, while the competent authorities from the Chinese government may guide, help and monitor them from different perspectives. From the beginning of 1997, an annual inspection on FIEs has been started.[134] Besides, there are some specific restrictions or performance requirements on FIEs under Chinese law, including local contents requirements, trade-balancing requirements, local employment requirements and so forth, some of which are prohibited by the TRIMs Agreement.[135] Since 1992, the Chinese government has embarked on gradually providing national treatment for FDI.[136] After the concluding of US-China WTO agreement, China started checking and reshaping its FDI laws and regulations, with a view to approximating to the WTO rules. Therefore a more liberal FDI legal system of FDI management might be expected in China in near future.

---

[133] People's Daily, (Overseas Edition), 16 February 2000, p. 1.

[134] See the "Experimental Arrangements on the Annual Inspection on Foreign Invested Enterprises"; see also Huaqun Zeng, as note 19, above, p. 81.

[135] Wenhua Shan, *National Treatment for Foreign Investment and its Implementing Conditions*, Social Sciences in China (1998), No. 5.

[136] Wenhua Shan, *Market Economy and National Treatment for Foreign Invested Enterprises in China* (Chinese Legal Science, 1995) No. 5.

Protection of Foreign Investment under Chinese Law

Generally, most foreign invested enterprises (FIEs) may gain the legal status as "Chinese legal person"[137] and foreign investors' investment, profit and other lawful earnings are all under the protection of Chinese law.[138] In principle, they are accorded the same treatment as other Chinese enterprises except certain special preferences (measures of FDI promotion) and restrictions (measures of FDI regulation/ management) otherwise provided for by the law. Specific protecting measures in Chinese law cover issues like nationalisation and its compensation, repatriation of investment and profits and stability of FDI laws.

According to Chinese investment laws, no-expropriation is generally promised for FIEs. When expropriation happens in special circumstances, in public interest, legal procedure shall be followed and corresponding compensation will be accorded.[139] Here "special circumstances" refers to emergencies such as war or threat of war and *force majeure* like severe natural disasters.[140] "Corresponding compensation" here means in a case where there is a binding BIT, compensation in accordance with the BIT provisions, and appropriate compensation in other cases.[141]

As to the repatriation of investments and profits, Chinese law guarantees that foreign investors can repatriate abroad profits lawfully earned from FIEs, as well as other lawful earnings and funds remaining after the enterprise is liquidated.[142] Also, wages, salaries and other legitimate income earned by foreign employees in an FIE may be remitted abroad after the payment of individual income tax in accordance with the law.[143] Furthermore, the 1996 Regulations on Foreign Exchange Control relaxed the foreign exchange regime and realised the convertibility of RMB in current transactions. Accordingly, the repatriation of foreign investors' profits, interest and earnings is no longer subject to approval by the foreign exchange authority.[144]

The Chinese Law of Foreign-related Economic Contracts (LFEC) has a general and extraordinary provision to safeguard the stability of the laws on FDI. It says that if new legal provisions are promulgated while contracts for EJVs, CJVs or JEs, which have been approved by the State, are being performed within the Chinese territory, the contract can still be carried out according to the terms of the contract.[145] In other words, the new law may not apply to these previously concluded contracts. Also, China uses the principle of

---

[137] All the EJVs and SCFIs are supposed to be "Chinese legal persons", while the CJVs and WFEs can also get the same status only if they are in conformity with the conditions of Chinese legal persons. See: Art. 2 of LEJV; Art. 2 of RESCFI; Art. 2(2) of LCJV; and Art. 8 of LWFE.

[138] See e. g. Art. 2 of LEJV and Art. 4 of LWFE.

[139] See e. g. Art. 2(3) of LEJV, Art. 5 of REON and Art. 5 of LWFE.

[140] Huaqun Zeng, as note 19, above, p. 36.

[141] As note 19, above. See also, Wenhua Shan, *The Development of the Theory and Practice of Nationalisation and the Chinese Countermeasures* (Legal Science, 1994) No. 5.

[142] Art. 10 of LEJV, Art. 23 of LCJV and Art. 19 of LWFE.

[143] Art. 11 of LEJV, Art. 23 of LCJV and Art. 19 of LWFE.

[144] Huaqun Zeng, as note 19, above, p. 36.

[145] Art. 40 of the LFEC. However, the newly published Law of Contract, which is to replace the LFEC, has abolished this Article, which may demonstrate that China is now confident of its legal stability.

"observing new laws or old ones when with more favourable arrangements" to deal with the changes of income tax laws, so as to guarantee that foreign investors are not to be harmed by those changes.[146] A similar principle is again applied in the new regulations about value-added tax (VAT), consumption tax, and business tax published in 1993.[147]

Promotion of Foreign Investment under Chinese Law

In order to attract FDI in China, the Chinese government adopted many investment incentives, most of which are tax incentives. For example, in the area of income tax, there are reduced tax rates in defined places, for defined trades and projects, for defined industries and projects in given times, for export-oriented and high-tech enterprises, for transfers of high-tech and tax incentives for expanding investment or re-investment.[148] In addition, there are some exemptions from tariff and VAT on machinery and other equipment imported by foreign investors investing in areas encouraged by the authority. In Special Economic Zones(SEZs) and other special economic areas, the central and local governments entitle the foreign investors to enjoy many other preferences and facilities.[149] Recently, new incentives have been adopted to encourage FDI in the vast West China.[150]

3. ***Conclusion***

From the preceding survey in this section, it can be concluded that in the EU FDI restrictions have been significantly liberalised. There are virtually no restrictions remaining on outward investment, either on the Member State level or on the Community level, while restrictions on inward investment are limited. Both the EU and its Member States have developed certain facilities for encouraging outward investment. As for the Chinese FDI law, it is very impressive that China has established a complex system for FDI in a short period. Foreign investments are generally guaranteed against expropriation; many attracting investment incentives and much progress in terms of its transparency and predictability have been made. The general "domestic" legal climate from both the EU and China's sides for mutual investment are favourable and promising.

However, there are also various problems existing on both sides. On the EU's side, the first problem is about its competence of and management on FDI matters. First of all, the range of interests in FDI matters in different Directorates may inevitably cause overlap, contradiction and gaps in policy coverage.[151] Moreover, the vague division of

---

[146] See the Income Tax Law of the PRC for Foreign Invested Enterprises and Foreign Enterprises (ITLF), Art. 27.

[147] See Decisions of the Standing Committee of the National People's Congress Regarding the Application of Provincial Regulations on Such Taxes as Value-added Tax, Consumption Tax and Business Tax to Foreign Invested Enterprises and Foreign Enterprises, Art. 2.

[148] For details of those incentives, see Faguang Cheng, "Foreign related Tax Regime and Its Tendency of Development", paper presented at Symposium on China's Foreign Investment Policies (Xiamen, China, September 1998).

[149] For details see LI Xuling(ed.), *Law of Special Economic Zones* (Law Publishing House, 1994).

[150] Dai Lan, *The Development of the West China is to Make a Substantial Move*, People's Daily(Overseas Edition), 19 May 2000, p. 1.

[151] Tomas L. Brewer and Stephen Young, as note 109, above, pp. 44 - 47.

competence between the EU and its Member States may result in further difficulties between the EU and its Member States, and among Member States themselves.[152] In fact, the experience of the ill-fated OECD MAI negotiations has proved that Member States instead of the Community participating in negotiations for a multilateral framework on investment must bring difficulties.[153] It at least slows deliberations, frustrates other countries and enables rivals like the United States and Japan to play off Member States against each other.[154] On the contrary, a uniform FDI policy in the EU and a clear division of competence between the EU and its Member States will not only facilitate the efficient functioning of the EC Directorates, but will also place the EU in a much more favourable position in future bilateral or multilateral investment law-making.

Another visible shortcoming on the EU's side is the lack of an investment guarantee scheme at the Community level. Although many EU Member States have established their investment guarantee projects, it is preferable to have such a mechanism at the Community level(e. g. , operated by the European Investment Bank-EIB) , because of its larger coverage, bigger size, higher credit and therefore higher efficiency. In this sense, the EIB could learn from various experiences of the MIGA and many national investment insurers in the EU Member States.

On the Chinese side, first, there is a structural problem with the FDI law system as well. Promulgated at different times and by different institutions, the six basic FDI laws are not so consistent with each other and with other laws and regulations. For example, LEJV, REON and LWFE have guarantees on expropriation and its compensation whilst other basic FDI laws keep silent on this issue. Again, almost all the six basic laws and regulations have detailed regulations on the approval and registration of investment projects, which do not fit the *Company Law* very well. Therefore China is seeking to consolidate its FDI laws and regulations. It is self-evident that a united FDI law would improve the coherence of the different basic laws and regulations. A possible solution could be a basic FDI law plus five implementation regulations.[155] To put it another way, a new general FDI law should be laid down so as to provide for basic rules for all the different forms of FDIs. At the same time, special implementation regulations based on the existing basic laws and regulations should be made to adapt the special needs and conditions of the five forms of Chinese FDI.

Second, while the Chinese government has made much progress in the transparency of its FDI law-making and law implementation, many "inside rules" still exist. Since these inside rules were promulgated by various governmental departments, sometimes even officials in charge feel confused by them, let alone the foreign investors. Now the government is struggling to sort them out, but since they are so many and they are so

〔152〕 As note 109, above.

〔153〕 As note 109, above. See also Alasdair R. Young, as note 114, above, at p. 109.

〔154〕 Tomas L. Brewer and Stephen Young, as note 109, above, p. 46.

〔155〕 According to the Minister of MOFTEC, China has been sorting out the FDI laws and Policies, so as to adjust related regulations and to establish a healthy legal system for FDI. See "News about Trade and Economy", < www. moftec. gov. cn >.

confusing, it is unlikely to be finished in a short time.

Third, although the investors enjoy tax concessions and may tolerate certain performance requirements, they would prefer equal treatment between them and Chinese investors. National treatment for FDI is something that could be expected in China but probably not in near future, due to constraints of the market economy construction and the limitation of general economic power in China.[156] Moreover, with the rapid development of FDI in China, some new forms of utilising FDI such as Built-Operate-Transfer (BOT), Merger and Acquisition (M&A) have emerged. Corresponding regulations are therefore needed. Last but not least, improving the implementation of FDI laws and regulations is crucial for improving the whole FDI legal environment, as it is often criticised that the well-made rules are distorted or even ignored by related authorities in the course of implementation.

After all, a common problem for both "domestic" laws is that they are only unilateral legislation and therefore may be altered unilaterally. To sufficiently guarantee mutual investment relations between the EU and China, a new international legal framework on FDI protection is in need.

D. General Conclusions

The investigations in this part have demonstrated the general picture of multilateral, bilateral and "domestic" legal instruments governing the EU-China investment relations. On the multilateral level, the ICSID Convention, the MIGA Convention and the WTO Agreement are the key instruments. While the first two conventions deal with dispute settlement and guarantee of political risks respectively, the WTO Agreement mainly regulates TRIMs measures and investment in services sectors. On the bilateral level, the EC-China Co-operation Agreement provides for a general legal basis for investment exchange between the EU and China, while the BITs between China and EU Member States offer substantial international protection for investment between China and its EU contracting counterparts. On "domestic" law level, the EU and its Member States have significantly relaxed restrictions on investment flow, especially on outward investment, while China has established a complex and generally favourable investment law system and is making progress towards an even better one.

The investigations, however, have also showed that the existing legal framework is not sufficient in protecting and promoting mutual investment because these legal instruments are incomplete, uncertain and at least partially contradictory. While the existing multilateral instruments are too specific to offer investment protection in a general sense, the Co-operation Agreement is too general to provide any substantial commitment. The BITs between China and most EU Member States are perhaps adequate for protection of investments between China and its counterparts, but the small coverage and their differences between each other prevent them from a sufficient BIT net for the protection of mutual investments between China and all EU Member States. In addition, the unilat-

---

[156] Wenhua Shan, *National Treatment for Foreign Investment and its Implementation* (Social Sciences in China, 1998), No. 5. See also Wenhua Shan, *The Reform of FDI Laws in the PRC* (Company Secretary, Feb. 2000), Vol. 10, No. 2.

eral character of "domestic" laws in both the EU and China preclude them from being reliable and stable legal instruments. Therefore, it would be best to establish a new legal framework specialised in investment protection between the two sides.

Ⅲ. Towards A New Legal Framework for EU-China Investment Relations

In fact, the European Parliament proposed an individual investment and intellectual property treaty at the Community level with China as early as 1984,[157] although no substantial progress has been achieved so far. However, today the time may be ripe to reconsider such an agreement because the political and economic climate has been changed significantly and favourably since then. In the EU, first, as observed above, with the establishment of the Single Market and the launch of Economic and Monetary Union, FDI laws and policies at both the Community level and Member States level have been significantly co-ordinated and further liberalised. At the same time, EU's competence on external relations has been expanded by the amendments to the EC Treaty and by decisions and opinions of the European Court of Justice(ECJ) . Second, in China, the establishment of a Market Economy is under way and the opening to the outside world is to be remarkably broadened and deepened by the forthcoming accession to the WTO. In particular, China is reshaping its FDI laws and regulations and reviewing its BIT programme, which means the negotiations of an EU-China investment treaty may have the possibility to affect the Chinese FDI legal environment as a whole. Furthermore, as pointed out, both the EU and China have been approaching each other quickly in recent years and have expressed extraordinary interest in furthering the bilateral investment relations, essentially facilitating EU investment in China. Third, on the world stage, the globalisation of economy, particularly the successful launching of the WTO has inspired more and more ambitious initiatives. Among them, a multilateral investment agreement has been discussed in several different fora. It could therefore safely be concluded that a new legal framework for EU-China investment relations is not only necessary but also possible.

The new legal framework could be in either of the two forms:

– a multilateral investment agreement MIA to which both the EU and China are contracting parties; or

– a bilateral investment treaty(BIT) between the EU and China.

Although they can serve the same purpose of facilitating EU-China FDI flows, they might be quite different simply because many more parties are involved in the former treaty. The two possible solutions are therefore explored below in turn.

A. An Mia to Which The Eu and China are Contracting Parties

Certainly, an MIA to which China and the EU are contracting parties is an inviting solution since it may provide uniform rules and therefore stability and predictability for

---

[157] See the European Parliament's Resolution on economic and commercial relations between China and the EEC, [1984] OJ C127/210.

FDI around the globe, not just between the EU and China. In fact, both China and the EU are deeply concerned about the negotiations of an MIA, no matter whether it is within the OECD or the WTO. The EU is one of the most active advocates of concluding an MIA within the WTO framework.[158] At the same time, all its Member States are OECD members and have participated in the three-year MIA negotiations. On the other hand, although not a member of either organisation, China, as the biggest developing country and the second largest FDI recipient in the world, is closely watching these negotiations and is considering its own position and countermeasures.[159] Furthermore, with the establishment of a market economy and the possible accession to the WTO in the near future, China will be more willing to take part in a multilateral legal framework on investment. Therefore, it is likely that in future MIA negotiations, both the EU and China will take a positive attitude as leaders from developed countries and developing countries respectively.

In considering an MIA, three aspects may be essential: the choice of forum, the full participation of interested countries and the balance of interests.

1. ***The Choice of Forum***

A prerequisite of concluding an MIA is to find an appropriate forum. The possibilities include mainly OECD, WTO, United Nations Conference on Trade and Development (UNCTAD) and World Bank(IBRD). Among them, the OECD is perhaps the most experienced organisation in analysis, discussions and negotiations on FDI issues, dating back to the 1960s. Some negotiations have led to formal agreements, such as the Codes of Liberalisation of Capital Movements and Current Invisible Operations.[160] On the contrary, the WTO may be preferable, owing to its approach to negotiation issues and its size and the nature of memberships, which could guarantee a real global negotiation with wide participation. UNCTAD also has long been involved in international investment issues and has planned to draft a multilateral framework on investment(MFI).[161] The advantage of UNCTAD as an MIA forum is that it is a UN institution that is experienced in organising multilateral negotiations and that may be able to balance the interests between developed countries and developing countries. The last option may be the World Bank. It has successfully organised the negotiation of the ICSID Convention and the MIGA Convention and has drafted influential Guidelines on the legal treatment of FDI. However, it

[158] See "EC Approach to Trade and Investment", <www.europa.eu.int/comm/dg01/1806ti.htm>, 11 November 1999. See also Sir Leon Brittan, *Investment Liberalisation: the Next Great Boost to the World Economy* (Transnational Corporations, April 1995), Vol. 4, No. 1.

[159] China participated in both the negotiation on MAI and related discussions within the WTO, as an observer. At the same time, many discussions on MAI have emerged recently in China, from both legal and economic perspectives. See e.g., Tong Lu(1999) *Comments on the Negotiation on the "Multilateral Agreement on Investment"* and Boming Sheng(1999) *The Negotiation of Multilateral Agreement on Investment and the Countermeasures of Developing Countries*, both in 7 World Economy(Chinese). See also Hong Zhao(1999) *Preliminary Comments on the "Multilateral Agreement on Investment"* and Huiping Chen(1999) *The Progress and Prospects of the Negotiation of the "Multilateral Agreement on Investment"*, both in Vol. 2, Journal of International Economic Law(Chinese).

[160] Tomas L. Brewer and Stephen Young, *Towards a Multilateral Framework for Foreign Direct Investment: Issues and Scenarios* (Transnational Corporations, April 1995), Vol. 4, No. 1, pp. 74–75.

[161] Huiping Chen, as note 158, above, p. 308.

has not so far initiated any proposal for making a formal MIA as such.

Keen on protecting their overseas investments, the EU and its Member States are very prudential in the forum selection and are generally in favour of an MIA either sponsored by the OECD or within the framework of the WTO.[162] Some scholars describe the possible scenarios of MIA negotiations, including discussion at the OECD and implementation at the WTO, negotiation at OECD and preparation for negotiations at WTO, negotiation of new agreements in both WTO and OECD, and creation of an entirely new legal framework and organisation for FDI.[163] They also argued that it was necessary to establish an Inter-agency Working Group on International Direct Investment, composed of the OECD, WTO, UNCTAD, World Bank and International Monetary Fund (IMF), to link their positions and facilitate further movement.[164] Sir Leon Brittan says that negotiations at OECD and WTO are not exclusive to each other and therefore can be done simultaneously.[165]

China does not object to the MAI within the OECD either, despite the fact that it is a club of rich countries. In fact, China has participated in some of its negotiations.[166] Many Chinese scholars, however, do not accept the MAI on the ground that its standard of investment protection is too high for a developing country to afford and its negotiating process virtually excludes any substantial participation by developing countries.[167] As for an MIA within the WTO regime, some Chinese commentators argue that the WTO might not be a proper forum for negotiating a global investment agreement since it is "neither democratic nor transparent",[168] while many others are not absolutely against it.[169] In addition, some argue that UNCTAD would be a better forum for such an MIA, with its experiences and development orientation.[170]

In short, all the aforementioned four avenues, with their different merits, have the possibility to become the forum(s) of a future MIA(s). However, the most likely two will be the OECD and WTO, as the World Bank has not yet developed an initiative thereon and the UNCTAD is not so popular among developed countries—the main driving force for such an MIA. Furthermore, the WTO may stand a better chance as compared with the OECD whose MIA proposal has failed to reach a consensus even among its member countries. No matter which venue the future MIA may take, however, it is essential to guarantee that most interested countries, developed countries and developing countries as well, are substantially involved in the negotiations and that their interests are fully reflected and balanced in the final act.

---

[162] Sir Leon Brittan, as note 157, above, p. 9.

[163] Tomas L. Brewer and Stephen Young, as note 159, above, pp. 74 – 75.

[164] As note 159, above.

[165] Sir Leon Brittan, as note 157, above, p. 9.

[166] Tong Lu, as note 159, above.

[167] See e. g. Hong Zhao and Huiping Chen, as note 158, above, pp. 286 – 293 and pp. 302 – 306.

[168] See e. g. Huiping Chen, as note 167, above, p. 307.

[169] See e. g. Hong Zhao, as note 158, above, p. 289.

[170] Huiping Chen, as note 158, above, p. 308.

2. ***The Full Participation of Interested Parties***

A truly global agreement must involve a sufficiently representative cross-section of the international community.[171] This does not only mean offering all interested parties a chance to sign the agreement as the OECD's MAI negotiations did, but more importantly, it means allowing them to fully participate in the entire process of negotiation.[172] The failure of the MAI in the OECD is partially attributed to the lack of substantial participation of developing countries. Although it allowed some countries to participate as observers and tried to publicise the progress of the negotiations, non-OECD countries could only give comments and could not directly affect the final outcome. Obviously, such a limited participation is not sufficient for a global investment agreement as it was designed to be. Besides, the participation of relevant international organisations is also valuable as the negotiation and implementation may therefore take full advantage of their legal and technical expertise on FDI-related matters.[173]

3. ***The Balance of Interests***

The balance of interests is probably the most important element among the three mentioned, because the other two elements are both for striking a good deal, a deal in which the interests of all participants in investment activities are well considered, reflected and balanced. In particular, there are two kinds of balance to be considered.

The one balance involves the interests between the host country and foreign investors. It is evident that international investments can establish sets of legal rights and obligations for governments and firms.[174] The balance of rights and obligations between the two sides has been a central issue in the contents of international investment agreements. It is observed, however, that the discussion has changed from an emphasis on firms' obligations and governments' rights to an emphasis on firms' rights and governments' obligations.[175] The abandonment of the United Nations' effort to develop a Code of Conduct on Transnational Corporations (TNC) and the dismantling of the United Nations Centre on Transnational Corporations(UNCTC) are outstanding evidence.

This shift is perhaps principally due to two reasons. On the one hand, most developing countries' attitude towards FDI has changed: now FDI is widely regarded as a scarce resource that no country can afford to drive away, instead of as a threat as it was perceived.[176] There has indeed been a competition for attracting FDI around the world, both in developing countries and developed countries. On the other hand, most of these new international legal instruments are sponsored and drafted by industrial countries without substantial participation by developing countries.

---

[171] Renato Ruggiero, *Foreign Direct Investment and the Multilateral Trading System* (Transnational Corporations, April 1996), Vol. 5, No. 1, p. 7.

[172] Similar ideas have been expressed in Hong Zhao, as note 158, above, pp. 289 – 290. See also Renato Ruggiero, as note 170, above, at p. 7; and Tomas L. Brewer and Stephen Young, as note 159, above, p. 80.

[173] Tomas L. Brewer and Stephen Young, as note 159, above.

[174] F. Fred Bergsten and Edward M. Graham, *Needed: New International Rules for Foreign Direct Investment*, International Trade Journal, 7, Fall 1992, pp. 15 – 44.

[175] Tomas L. Brewer and Stephen Young, as note 159, above, p. 70.

[176] Sir Leon Brittan, as note 157, above, p. 2.

However, future negotiations on a truly global MIA may refocus this discussion because developing countries have not given up their concerns about the conduct of transnational corporations(TNCs), especially on their restrictive business practices, transfer pricing, employment, environment protection, etc.[177] Whenever they can, they try to maintain their rights to use domestic laws and regulations to manage and regulate activities of foreign investors. For example, in the APEC statement of non-binding investment principles, they insisted on including that:

"Acceptance of foreign investment is facilitated only when foreign investors abide by the host economy's laws, regulations, administrative guidelines and policies, just as domestic investors should."[178]

In addition, the early draft of the Code of Conduct of Transnational Corporations, the OECD Guidelines for Multilateral Enterprises of 1976 and the OECD Declaration on International Investment and Multilateral Enterprises of 1994 may be used as a basis for the provisions on firms' conduct in the possible MIA.

The other balance involves the interests between developed countries and developing countries.[179] Although Renato Ruggiero has argued that the MIA issue shall not be "perceived as one of North/South relations, but as one of common interest",[180] it is an inevitable fact that the developed countries and developing countries are standing in different positions and therefore have different interests in FDI matters. In the world FDI market, developed countries are major investors and investment recipients as well, while developing countries are attracting more and more FDI inflows. For example, according to the *World Investment Report* 1999, developed countries accounted for 91.6 percent of FDI outflows and 71.5 percent of inflows in 1998, while developing countries made up only 8.1 percent of FDI outflows and 25.8 percent of FDI inflows.[181] These figures show that on the one hand most investment activities were carried out between developed countries and on the other hand, in investment relations between developed countries and developing countries, the former are generally capital-exporters while the latter are capital-importers. In fact, only a few developing countries are investing abroad, leaving most of them as pure investment recipients.[182] This situation is unlikely to change in a

---

[177] Tomas L. Brewer and Stephen Young, as note 159, above, pp. 70 – 71. See also Tomas L. Brewer and Stephen Young, *Investment Policies in Multilateral and Regional Agreement: a Comparative Analysis* (Transnational Corporations, April 1996), Vol. 5, No. 1, pp. 27 – 28.

[178] APEC Non-binding Investment Principles, "Investor behaviour" Section. Reprinted as annex in M Sornarajah, *Protection of Foreign Investment in the Asia Pacific Economic Cooperation Region* [1995] 29 J. W. T. 2 pp. 128 – 129.

[179] It is worth noting, however, those countries at similar development stage have conflicting interests which need to be balanced as well. For instance, during the OECD MAI negotiations, various disagreements existed and it was mainly these sorts of "internal conflict of interest" that led the whole project to break down. See Frans Engering, *The Multilateral Investment Agreement* (Transnational Corporations, 1996), Vol. 5, No. 3, p. 161.

[180] Renato Ruggiero, as note 171, above, p. 7.

[181] UNCTAD, *World Investment Report 1999: Foreign Direct Investment and the Challenge of Development*, p. 20, Table I. 3.

[182] UNCTAD, *World Investment Report 1999: Foreign Direct Investment and the Challenge of Development: Overview*, p. 19.

short period. Therefore, in the course of future global investment law-making fora, developed countries as representatives of international investors will go on seeking further liberalisation for FDI movement, while developing countries as host countries will struggle to defend their rights of regulating and managing FDI activities. Such a conflict of interest will inevitably continue to be reflected in any future North/South negotiation of investment treaties, whether in the form of a BIT or an MIA.

Admittedly, however, there are common interests in FDI issues between developed and developing countries as well: in the North countries there is plenty of surplus capital looking for overseas markets, while in the South countries there is a widespread hunger for capital for economic development. This common interest is actually the basis of all the BITs between the two State groups and is going to be the grounds of all North/South negotiations on any future MIA. Nevertheless, an MIA is to be a compromise of interests of all interested countries. Hence a fair balance of interests between the two groups of countries is crucial for an MIA's success.

To maintain such a balance, host countries must first be entitled to adopt laws and regulations to manage investment activities so as to make sure they are in conformity with their national plans and development objectives, in return for their providing a higher standard of protection for foreign investors. Second, the liberalisation of international investment should be done step by step, allowing countries in different development levels to have different transition periods and exemptions. Last but not least, in some sensitive aspects such as investment incentives and performance requirements where global consensus is unlikely to be attained at this stage, the "voluntary acceptance" principle may be used. In this sense, the WTO "plurilateral agreements" could be used as references.

To sum up, an MIA of which both the EU and China are members is a possible solution for a more effective protection of a mutual investment, provided that the agreement is negotiated with the full participation of all concerned countries and their interests are fully reflected and balanced. It could be anticipated that a fair and world-widely acceptable(global) investment agreement would be beneficial for both developed countries and developing countries and therefore would contribute to the peace and prosperity of the future world. However, the failures of MAI proposals in both the OECD and the WTO Seattle Conference have demonstrated that such an historical agreement cannot be achieved in a hurry. There is still a long way to go.

B. A BIT between the EU and China

A BIT between the EU and China, on the contrary, will be more practical an initiative at this stage as compared with an MIA. First, both sides are prepared to sign such a treaty because the bilateral political and economic links have been significantly improved and are ever improving. Second, because a bilateral treaty involves only two parties(the EU and its Member States as a whole) and therefore faces much less conflict of interest, it does not cost as much time and energy as would be the case with an MIA. Furthermore, a BIT, unlike an MIA, is widely regarded as a sort of pragmatic arrangement to attract and protect FDI, hence some historically controversial issues such as "Hull Rules" will not cause any serious problem. Also, the 13 BITs between China and

EU Member States have laid down a solid basis for the future negotiations of a BIT at Community level. Finally, the Joint Committee mechanism established under the Co-operation Agreement may serve as the preliminary vehicle of negotiating such a BIT, with its competence to "examine means and new opportunities of developing trade and economic co-operation" and to "make recommendations" in the areas of common interest.[183]

Nevertheless, there are also uncertain issues to be sorted out in discussing such a BIT. On the one hand, in respect of the legal form, at least two questions must be answered:

- is it a sole agreement that the EC itself can sign or a mixed agreement, which needs joint signature by both the Community and its Member States;
- what is its status in and relationship to the general legal framework for EU-China (economic) relations?

On the other hand, in respect of the substance of the treaty, although the old BITs have dealt with detail, many issues like the definitions, national treatment standard, compensation standard and its evaluation, transfer of funds and dispute settlement mechanism may either remain unclear or will need to be reconsidered.

1. ***A Sole Agreement or a Mixed Agreement*** ?

As discovered in preceding sections, the EU so far has not attained exclusive competence on FDI matters, therefore, it cannot yet sign any investment just in its own name, but must do it jointly with its Member States. In other words, it will be a mixed treaty rather than a sole treaty. It might be possible though in the future for the EC to start to sign agreements of this kind by itself, if the EU can successfully attain exclusive competence in this field.

2. ***The BIT and the General Legal Framework for EU-China Relationship***

An EU-China BIT could well fit in the current legal framework for the economic relationship between the EU and China. It could be a sub-agreement or a sectoral agreement under Article 12 the Co-operation Agreement. While in Article 12(2) the two sides undertake to extend the BITs by and to China and EU Member States, they also agree in Article 12(1) that the two "Contracting Parties" will "promote and encourage greater and mutually beneficial investment" within the framework of their respective laws, rules and policies. One may hesitate to say whether the EU may have the right to join the actions of BIT-making with its Member States, since this Article has only mentioned BITs between China and its Member States. However, I personally think this provision will not prevent the EU from taking a joint action as such, for the following reasons. First, Article 5(ex Article 3a) provides that the Community may take an action if and insofar as the objective of the proposed action cannot be sufficiently achieved by its Member States alone and therefore can be better achieved by the Community, by reasons of the scale or effect of the proposed action. Signing a mixed BIT with China will certainly fall within the sphere of such a Community "action" since it can better serve the Community's com-

[183] Article 15, para. 2, 3 of the Co-operation Agreement.

mon interest of protecting EU investment in China. It is self-evident that without the involvement of the Community, such a treaty will never be achieved by its Member States. Moreover, since the bargaining power of any Member State could not be comparable with that of the Community as a whole,[184] no Member State can expect a better BIT with China than that signed at the Community level. Second, in practice, the EU has signed mixed agreements with third countries that involve detailed investment protection provisions before. For example, as mentioned previously, the EU signed the Fourth Lome Convention, which had a lengthy chapter on investment matters. Finally, Article 12(1) might serve as a bilateral legal basis for the EU's involvement in such an agreement.

As an alternative to an individual BIT, it may adopt the form of a "built-in" chapter or section in the text of the Co-operation Agreement, like the one in the Fourth Lome Convention. In other words, the two sides may negotiate the revision of the agreement and then substantiate the section of investment with details of the potential BIT. This approach may be a bit more complicated as compared with the aforementioned one, since it requires a review of the whole framework treaty. Otherwise, it may look awkward to fit in the current Co-operation Agreement, as the current Co-operation Agreement is too slim to contain such a "big" investment section. It may be argued therefore that China could be "upgraded" as an association country of the EU and substantial investment rules may be included in the future association agreement. This idea, despite its creativeness, however, may be too good to be practical for the time being. Among others, China's human rights records in the EU's eyes may prove to be the biggest obstacle for such an association.

In short, an individual sub-agreement or sectoral agreement may be the most convenient choice of forms, while the model of a "built-in" investment section in the Co-operation Agreement or a possible association agreement may face many more difficulties, if it is ever viable.

3. ***The Substance of the BIT***

Although a bilateral instrument is supposed to be easier to strike than an MIA, the EU-China BIT may not prove so simple to conclude. There are many controversial issues on which both sides have very strong feelings. In addition, the leadership roles of both parties as developed countries and developing countries may further prevent them from deviating dramatically from traditional standpoints. While the timing of the negotiation may shift the focuses of concern, the following aspects may probably draw special attention:

(a) Admission of FDI

The admission of FDI, like many other FDI issues, used to be purely a question of domestic law, and so it was under all the existing BITs between EU Member States and China (existing BITs). However, it was recently brought to the international legal stage, mainly due to the insistence of the US government. Two of the central issues are the pre-establishment national treatment (PRENT) and the elimination of performance require-

[184] The results of the recently finalised EU-China WTO accession talk may well serve as a good example. It would be incredible that any single State of the EU can attain a "big deal" as such. For details, see < www. europa. eu. int/comm/trade/bilateral/china/hing. htm > 22 May 2000.

ments. These demands may be raised by the EU during the potential BIT talks since it now shares the same view with the United States. China, as a developing country and an economy still in transition, will definitely be reluctant to accept them. Possible compromises may be that China accepts a "bottom-up", "positive" list of fields where pre-establishment national treatment is applicable, and a flexible commitment on eliminating performance requirements.[185]

(b) Post-establishment treatment

In past BITs negotiations, China used to stick to fair and equitable treatment and MFN treatment. Post-establishment national treatment (POENT) has been scarcely used in existing BITs and when it is the case it is strictly limited by various qualifications, such as "to the extent possible"[186] or "in accordance with its laws and regulations"[187] and so forth. Surely the EU will ask for a larger POENT as it in fact lies at the centre of all its concerns. On the other side, China is striving for, at least partially because of the western pressures, providing national treatment for FDI. In fact, China has tried to provide national treatment without qualifications as mentioned above.[188] Therefore, a normal POENT may be possible in the future BIT, provided that both sides retain the right to regulate inward FDIs and make sure FDIs are in conformity with their respective development objectives.

(c) Expropriation and compensation

In respect of expropriation, attention may focus on the compensation standard and the valuation of compensation. Although China has agreed that compensation shall be "appropriate"[189] or "to place the investor in the same financial position",[190] it has never accepted such standards as "full compensation" or "adequate, prompt, effective compensation". As for the evaluation of compensation, China has already accepted the "real value"[191] or "actual value"[192] (of the expropriated property) standards, plus applicable interest, but not the so-called "anticipated profits" standard as some countries demanded (notably the United States again). Nevertheless, it may not be necessary to detail the valuation methods in the potential BIT.

(d) Transfer of property

It can be expected that the BIT will guarantee free transfer of funds, in convertible currency and without undue delay. However, these transfers may still be required to be subject to domestic laws and regulations, as China has not yet entirely liberalised foreign exchange controls. A much more relaxed foreign exchange regime might come about in China soon after its accession to the WTO, as China has made certain commitments

---

〔185〕 For example, the BIT may use such wording as Art. 2(6) of the US-Tunisia BIT: "Both Contracting Parties shall endeavour to avoid imposition of any performance requirements ..."

〔186〕 See Sino-Britain BIT, Article 3(3).

〔187〕 See Sino-Spain BIT, Article 3(4).

〔188〕 See e. g. Sino-Korea BIT, Article 3(2).

〔189〕 See e. g. Sino-France BIT, Article 4(2).

〔190〕 See e. g. Sino-Sweden BIT, Article 3(1).

〔191〕 See e. g. Sino-Britain BIT, Article 5(1).

〔192〕 See e. g. Sino-France BIT, Protocol(2).

thereon in the course of accession negotiations.

(e) Dispute settlement

China will accept international arbitration (including ICSID arbitration) as an option for settlement of disputes between investors and the host country, but probably not the compulsory jurisdiction of the ICSID over disputes of this kind as required in the OECD's MIA proposal. Nonetheless, agreeing to use the ICSID to solve investment disputes has already been a significant step forward for China, as the existing BITs between China and EU Member States have never gone that far.

(f) Other issues

Other issues may embrace some relatively new and fairly sensitive issues such as labour standard and environmental protection. While the EU may fancy them and put pressure on China, the Chinese government may be unwilling to accept them as it regards them as smokescreens that the developed countries are using to protect their comparatively disadvantaged industries against developing countries. Only "soft" or highly flexible obligations of these issues may be expected to be included in the BIT if any. An even more far-reaching and sensitive issue is that of human rights, which the Chinese government is frequently criticised for.[193] However, it is unlikely that human rights issues would be discussed in the BIT negotiations, given its nature of a sectoral agreement and the fact that the EU has decided not to link human rights issues with trade issues.

C. An EU-China BIT and Then an MIA?

Though this article addresses the initiatives of a BIT and an MIA individually, they are not necessarily exclusive. On the contrary, they are generally compatible with each other. In fact the co-existence of bilateral treaties and multilateral treaties on the same subject is not rare. It is particularly common when the bilateral treaties are concluded before the conclusion of the multilateral instrument, as they normally are.

For example, in the trade area, the GATT/WTO has lived with numerous bilateral trade agreements for decades.[194]

Nonetheless, the two agreements are very unlikely to be concluded simultaneously. As observed, the MIA may take quite a long time of preparation, while the BIT is almost readily at the hands of the two sides: the EU and its Member States as one, and the PRC as the other. It might therefore be the case that an EU-China BIT will be signed to satisfy the immediate need of investment protection, and then possibly (and hopefully) followed by the conclusion of an MIA in which both parties play important roles. In that case, the BIT may well serve as a sound basis for the MIA.

---

[193] Angela Ward, *Framework for Cooperation between the European Union and Third World: a Viable Matrix for Uniform Human Rights Standards*? 3 European Foreign Affairs Review, 505 – 536; Flinterman, (1997) *The European Union and China*, Maastricht Journal of European and Comparative Law, p. 217.

[194] However, an effective multilateral treaty may prevent the bilateral treaties of the same subject from further proliferation. For example, the old Friendship, Commerce and Navigation (FCN) agreement was no longer popular since the GATT was concluded.

單文華

国际法与比较法论集（下）

Wenhua Shan's Essays on International and Comparative Law

单文华 著
杜　娟 编

法律出版社
LAW PRESS · CHINA

目　录
Contents

上　　卷

第一编
国际法与比较法通论

第二编

欧洲联盟与中欧关系法

中　　卷

第三编

国际投资法

下　　卷

第四编

国际贸易法

第五编

"一带一路" 建设与国际能源法

下　　卷

第四编 国际贸易法

Part IV

923 -1181

加入 WTO 十五年:改变中国,重塑世界*

自 1986 年 7 月 10 日正式提出申请恢复《关税及贸易总协定》缔约方地位开始,经过 15 年的艰苦谈判,中国终于在 2001 年 12 月 11 日正式加入世界贸易组织(WTO),标志着我国的产业对外开放进入了一个全新的阶段。如今,中国加入 WTO 将近 15 年,过去十余年见证了中国经济的快速发展。今年 7 月 1 日,中国加入 WTO15 年保护期到期,引起一些媒体关于进口商品价格是否会大幅下降的关注。商务部表示,中国在 2001 年 12 月 11 日加入 WTO 以后,于 2002 年 1 月 1 日起开始全面下调关税,分 10 年逐步实施。其中,对绝大部分进口产品的降税承诺在 2005 年 1 月 1 日已经执行到位;到 2010 年 1 月 1 日,所有产品的降税承诺已经履行完毕。这意味着 7 月 1 日以后中国关税总水平仍会保持基本平稳。

"入世"给中国带来哪些重要变化?当前,世界经济格局变化将对 WTO 带来哪些影响?中国应该如何应对?面对这些问题,本报记者采访了西安交通大学法学院院长兼丝绸之路国际法与比较法研究所所长单文华教授。单文华表示,"入世"不仅深刻地改变了中国,而且事实上重塑了世界。中国经济得到"三维深化",即国际化、市场化和法治化。中国正以更加积极的姿态参与全球经济治理,"中国声音"和"中国方案"在一定程度上打破了发达国家对全球治理规则的"垄断",使这一套规则朝着更为公平、合理和更为均衡、和谐的方向发展。这既是全球经济持续健康发展的重要保障,也是"中国梦"和"世界梦"和谐共振的必然结果。

记者:中国"入世"15 年来主要有哪些变化?

单文华:中国"入世"15 年,不仅深刻地改变了中国,而且在事实上重塑了世界。

从中国的角度来看,"入世"15 年的成就突出表现在中国经济的"三维深化",即国际化、市场化和法治化。这三方面相互关联、深层互动。

---

* 本文发表在《法制日报》2015 年 7 月 14 日,第 10 版:环球法制,记者汪闽燕。

“国际化”是“入世”15 年最显著的成果，表现为中国经济深度融入世界经济的主流。就贸易而言，“入世”15 年，中国成为世界第一大出口国和第二大进口国；长期保持世界第二大吸收外资国的地位；同时也是世界上第三大对外投资国。在外汇储备方面，中国早已遥遥领先于世界各国，以接近 4 万亿美元的金额雄踞世界榜首。这些重要数据清楚表明中国不仅融入世界经济体系的主流，而且已经成为其中最重要的经济体之一。

“市场化”一直是中国改革的方向，“开放促改革”或“以外促内”是中国近三十年经济改革发展的基本路径，而入世则成为过去 15 年来中国市场化改革最重要的推进器。15 年来，中国一直认真履行相关承诺，逐年降低关税水平，截至 2010 年 1 月 1 日，中国加入世贸组织的关税减让承诺已经提前全部履行完毕。

市场经济是法治经济，中外皆然。“法治化”是中国经济“国际化”和“市场化”的必然要求。入世 15 年来，中国建立起了符合世贸规则和入世承诺的国内涉外经贸法律体制，进行了历史上最大的法律法规的清理工作，涉及 2300 多部法律法规和部门规章，19 万件地方性法规规章。与此同时，中国积极参与国际贸易规则的制定和国际贸易争端的法治化解决。中国是当前 WTO 争端解决机制的主要参加者。在缔约方面，一个重要的表征就是自由贸易区战略的实施。目前，中国已签署 14 个自贸协定，涉及 22 个国家和地区，自贸伙伴遍及亚洲、欧洲、大洋洲和拉美国家。

记者：中国入世对世界贸易格局产生了哪些影响？

单文华：从世界经济的角度来看，中国入世 15 年至少在两方面重塑了世界经济体系。

一方面，中国已经成为世界经济的一个主角和世界经济增长的主要引擎。入世以来，世界见证了中国经济发展最快的 15 年。这 15 年里，中国国内生产总值从 2001 年的 11 万亿元人民币增长到 2014 年的 64 万亿元人民币，增长约 6 倍，经济总量跃居世界第二。按照国际货币基金组织的购买力评价统计则为世界第一。这是中国经济史上的一件大事，也是当代世界经济史上的一件大事。

另一方面，中国的高速发展最有力地推动了全球经济的结构性转型。长期以来，世界经济由发达国家所主导乃至垄断。以中国为首的新兴经济体近 30 年特别是近 15 年的异军突起，使这一局面产生了重大变化。国际货币基金组织副总裁朱民直言，“30 年来，新兴经济体在全球 GDP 中的占比从 28% 上升至现在的 50%，社会财富从 22% 增长到 70%，贸易从 21% 发展到 50%，投资从 26% 增长到 65%，成为世界上最重要的经济群体之一”。新兴市场已经崛起，并将持续发展壮大。毫无疑问，中国是其中最大的贡献者。

记者：今年是WTO成立20周年，而当前区域及双边自贸协定谈判又如火如茶地进行，为什么会出现这种现象？

单文华：世界贸易组织的主要职能之一是制定多边贸易规则和组织多边贸易谈判等。但是，众所周知，多哈回合谈判自2001年开始后就长期停滞不前，使得世贸组织制定多边贸易规则和组织多边谈判这些主要职能搁浅。在这种情况下，各个国家开始尝试能够实现其利益诉求与经济发展的新途径。双边和区域自贸区谈判和建设便应运而生，且大有局部替代WTO多边贸易机制之势。这方面最突出的是一些大范围的区域性自贸区谈判，如《跨太平洋伙伴关系协定》(TPP)《跨大西洋贸易和投资伙伴关系协定》(TTIP)《区域全面经济伙伴关系协定》(RCEP)均大范围地分割了亚太、美欧、东盟与中、新、印等这些区域的市场，意图实现区域性的多边自由贸易。

世界贸易体系的变局既是挑战，也是机遇。对于像中国这样的崛起中大国而言，可以说是机遇大于挑战，原因在于既有的贸易体系虽曾令中国受益，但它并不完善，更非理想。正因如此，2014年11月15日在澳大利亚召开的G20峰会发言上，习近平主席指出，“今年是布雷顿森林会议70周年，各方都在总结布雷顿森林体系的经验，进一步完善全球经济治理。我们要以此为契机，建设公平公正、包容有序的国际金融体系，提高新兴市场国家和发展中国家的代表性和发言权，确保各国在国际经济合作中权利平等、机会平等、规则平等”。

记者：中国在当前国际经贸格局的背景下，可以发挥什么样的作用？

单文华：中国将更加积极主动地参与全球经济治理，并为此贡献中国智慧和中国方案。

首先，在国际贸易领域，RCEP和亚太自贸协定(APFTA)将是中国贡献全球经济法治的主战场。在“多哈回合”谈判陷入僵局后，中国也在积极寻求区域合作规则的不断完善。如今，中韩、中澳自贸协定已经结束；中国牵头推动的世界上最大的贸易协定之一的RCEP已经结束了多轮谈判。此外，在2014年亚太经合组织第一次高官会上，中国也提出了建设亚太自贸区的可行性研究倡议，这将是一项极具战略远见的“多赢”之举。

其次，中国对全球经济治理的制度贡献更有望通过“一带一路”的建设来实现。作为习近平主席立足中国对外开放和区域发展的新形势提出的伟大战略构想，“一带一路”建设体现出中国对外开放战略的重要调整与演进。总体而言，“一带一路”建设应该以区域经济一体化为目标，以经贸合作和文化交流为主要形式。其具体的建设内容涵盖基础建设、能源资源、贸易投资、货币金融、文化教育等诸多方面。而这些具体的合作目标需要通过凝聚政治共识进而缔结各种完善的条约规则来实现。通俗地说,就是要以“政治法律搭台、经济文化唱戏”。

最后,在国际投资领域,中国应该积极推动缔结一个全球性的多边投资协定。不论是中美投资协定谈判,还是中欧投资协定谈判,背后所体现的不仅是发展中国家与发达国家相关经济利益的综合考虑,更是对当前国际投资规则所面临的问题的正面回应。因此,这两个协定不管在内容上还是在形式上,都会对其他国家的投资协定产生重要影响。如果说中国已经错过了直接影响以 WTO 为主体的世界贸易规则创制的机会,我们必不能再错过参与乃至在一定程度上引领世界投资规则制定的机会。明年是中国首次作为 20 国集团的主席国。在这次会上提出世界多边或双边投资协定的议题,以推动世界范围内就此进行深入的研讨乃至谈判磋商,将是极为明智又极有分量的重大举措。作为世界上最大的发展中国家,“中国声音”和“中国方案”可在一定程度上打破发达国家对全球治理规则的“垄断”,使这一套规则朝着更为公平、合理和更为均衡、和谐的方向发展。可以说,中国以更加积极的姿态主动参与全球经济治理,并在与美欧等发达经济体的利益博弈中提出更为公平、合理的国际制度设计,既是全球经济持续健康发展的重要保障,也是“中国梦”和“世界梦”和谐共振的必然结果。

国际技术贸易法*

第一节　国际技术贸易法概说

一、技术

按世界知识产权组织出版的《发展中国家许可证贸易指南》与联合国贸易与发展会议制定的《国际技术转让行动守则(草案)》,"技术"指制造某种产品、实施某种工艺或提供某种服务的系统知识,不论这种知识是否体现为一项发明、外观设计、实用新型或一种动植物新品种,也不论它是否反映在技术情报、技能技巧中,或是反映在专家所提供的设计、安装、建立、维持一个工厂或管理一个工商企业而提供的服务或援助之中。这一定义是国际上比较一致的关于"技术"的界定。

从这一定义可以看出,"技术"具有如下三方面的特征。[1] 首先,技术是人们从事生产经营活动的知识、经验与技能,具有"生产性"。这里的"生产经营活动"包括制造产品、实施工艺与提供服务三大内容。正是这种"生产性"决定了技术的价值,决定了它的"商品"属性。其次,技术是一种无形的知识,具有无形性。技术固然可以用文字、数据、图表、公式和配方等有形形式记录下来,经验与技能也可以储存在人的头脑中,但这种知识与有形的商品仍有明显的质的区别。一台彩电,作为有形财产,其所有人行使权利出售、出借或出租它,标的均为该彩电本身;但一项专利技术,作为一种无形商品,当它的所有人行使权利转让它时,标的可能是使用制造该专利的产品的"制造权",或者是销售某种使用该专利的产品的"销售权",而不是专利技术本身。最后,技术还是系统的知识,具有系统性。

* 本文原载陈安主编:《国际经济法》(第2版)第5章,法律出版社2007年版。

〔1〕 沈金英:《国际技术贸易》,南京大学出版社1995年版,第1~2页。

这种系统性通常包括从产品设计、生产实施、生产管理乃至市场开拓、经营销售等各个环节的知识、经验与技能，而不仅仅为某一“点滴”的知识。根据知识的内容不同，可以把技术划分为产品技术与管理技术两大类。前者包括产品的原理和设计、制造方法和工艺、使用方法和维修等；后者指生产的组织和管理方法，包括产品发展的研究、生产计划的制定、各部门的协调以及质量管理、成本管理和经营销售等。

对技术的分类有多种多样，作为国际技术贸易的标的的“技术”，可以分为下列几种。

1. 专利技术。专利技术就是取得了专利的技术。它是可转让的技术的主要构成部分。按各国专利法，专利权人在法定的期限内，对制造、使用、销售（不少国家还包括进口该项专利产品或使用这一专利方法生产的产品）其专利产品，或使用其专利方法、享有专有权。其他人要实施上述行为，必须取得专利权人的同意，否则将构成侵权。专利技术具有专有性、时间性、地域性等特征。

2. 专有技术。“专有技术”（know-how）一般是指未向社会公开的技术、知识与经验，往往表现为可供实施的，关于产品设计、工艺程序、操作方法以及生产管理与商业经营方面的秘诀。实际上，不少专有技术是生产某种专利产品、实施某种具有专利权的生产方法所必需的最关键部分的技术，这使得专利技术与专有技术往往相伴而进行贸易与转让。

3. 计算机软件。计算机软件的许可是指许可方在被许可方支付使用费并满足其他一定条件的情况下，允许被许可方在一定时间与范围内使用其软件。计算机软件是一种新兴的高能技术，软件贸易已成为国际技术贸易的重要组成部分之一。

我们认为，商标不能算作是一种技术，因为商标本身不具有生产性，既不能直接用来制造商品、应用工艺，也不能直接用以提供服务。尽管商标的制作与经营不免有一定的技术成分与技术含量，但它本身仍只是一种产品或服务的标识，而不是制造这一产品、提供这一服务或应用某一工艺的知识、经验与技能，把它归为“技术”不免牵强。正因如此，《国际技术转让行动守则草案》规定，单纯的商标、服务标记和商号名称这三种工业产权的转让和使用许可并不能算作“技术贸易”。确认商标不是技术，并不是要否定商标权是国际技术贸易中可能涉及的标的或内容。如前所述，商标往往与技术一并被转让，在实践中，商标作为技术贸易的一部分标的的事例也不在少数。

二、技术贸易

根据《国际技术转让行动守则草案》第 1 章规定，技术贸易（早年多称为“技术转让”)大致包括下列内容:(1)各种形式的工业产权的转让、出售和使用许可,但不包括单纯的商标、服务标记和商号名称的转让与使用许可;(2)以可行性研究、计划、图表、模型、说明、手册、公式、基本或详细工程设计、培训方案和设备、技术咨询服务和管理人员服务以及人员培训等方式,提供专有技术和技术知识;(3)提供工厂和设备的安装、操作和运用以及交钥匙项目所需的技术知识;(4)对于将要或已经购买、租赁或依其他方式获得的机器、设备、中间产品和/或原材料,提供取得、安装和使用所需的技术知识;(5)提供工业和技术合作安排的技术内容。

可见,技术贸易是某些知识的有偿转移与传授,其内容是十分广泛的,包括制造技术、工艺规程、咨询、服务与管理经验等。

关于技术贸易的内容,我国立法中也有所体现。2002 年 1 月 1 日施行的《技术进出口管理条例》规定:本条例所称技术进出口,是指从中华人民共和国境外向中华人民共和国境内,或者从中华人民共和国境内向中华人民共和国境外,通过贸易、投资或者经济技术合作的方式转移技术的行为。前款规定的行为包括专利权转让、专利申请权转让、专利实施许可、技术秘密转让、技术服务和其他方式的技术转移。[2] 可见,我国立法中的“技术引进”包括工业产权的转让与许可、专有技术的许可与技术服务三种主要形式,这种解释与国际通行的解释是基本一致的。

与“技术”的特征相一致,“技术贸易”较之货物买卖,具有自己的特征:首先,技术贸易的标的是无形的知识,而货物买卖的标的则是有形的货物;其次,技术贸易多为技术使用权的让与,而不是技术所有权的转让,而在货物买卖中,通常是货物全部所有权的转移;最后,由于现代社会中高科技具有越来越重要的战略意义,所以,各国对技术贸易的控制与管理远较一般货物买卖严格,相关的法律措施也更为繁多周密。

技术贸易可以是单纯的技术知识交易,但它往往同时包含着技术知识的转让与相关设备转让,即软件(Soft Ware)与硬件(Hard Ware)结合起来交易。不过,单纯的硬件,即实施技术所需的机器设备等的买卖则不能算作技术贸易。

三、国际技术贸易

所谓的“国际”技术贸易,至少有三层含义:[3] (1)跨越一国国境的技术贸易;(2)受方与供方不居于同一国之中的技术贸易;(3)受方与供方虽居于同一国之

〔2〕《技术进出口管理条例》(2002 年 1 月 1 日施行)第 2 条。

〔3〕郑成思:《国际技术转让法通论》,中国展望出版社 1987 年版,第 10 页。

中，但其中有一方系外国公司的子公司、分公司或受到外国公司以其他方式控制的公司。在第(2)种情况下，如果受方取得技术的目的，仅仅在于把它交给自己设在供方所在国的分公司使用，则技术本身并未跨越国境。在第(3)种情况下，技术仅在一国境内转移，实质上完全不会跨越国境。

在联合国贸发会议起草《国际技术转让行动守则草案》时，发达国家组成的B组国家与由77国集团及前苏联东欧国家组成的D组国家针锋相对。作为国际技术贸易的主要供方，B组国家希望尽量缩小“国际技术转让”的范围，以回避有关国家的控制与管束，所以主张“国际技术转让”限于上述(1)、(2)两种情形。而由广大发展中国家及东欧集团国家组成的D组国家，作为多数情况下同属国际技术贸易的受方，则希望将“国际技术转让”的范围尽量扩大，以更可能广泛地将各种涉外技术贸易活动纳入本国法律的管辖与控制范围之内，所以，它仍主张上述三种情形都应算作“国际技术转让”。〔4〕我国的《技术进出口管理条例》规定“本条例所称技术进出口，是指从中华人民共和国境外向中华人民共和国境内，或者从中华人民共和国境内向中华人民共和国境外，通过贸易、投资或者经济技术合作的方式转移技术的行为”。〔5〕实际上我国只肯定了上述第(1)、(2)种形式的技术贸易为“国际”技术贸易。

现代国际技术贸易主要是第二次世界大战以后发展起来的。第二次世界大战以后，特别是近40年来，国际技术贸易发展速度惊人，技术贸易在国际贸易中所占的比重稳步上升，地位日见重要，技术贸易已与货物贸易及服务贸易鼎足而立，成为国际贸易的重要组成部分之一。目前，经合组织成员国出口中的1/4为技术贸易。〔6〕改革开放以来，我国的技术贸易得到了迅速发展。技术贸易缩短了我国与发达国家之间在科学技术与生产力水平上的差距，有效地推动了我国国民经济的发展与科技水平的提高。就引进外国技术的数量和规模来说，中国已居于发展中国家的前列。中国也因而跻身世界最大的技术引进国之列。仅1998年我国签订的技术引进和设备进口合同6254项，合同总金额达163.75亿美元，比上年增加2.48%。与此同时，中国的技术和成套设备出口发展很快，以技术带动成套设备出口已成为中国技术出口的主要形式。仅1998年，我国对外签订技术出口和设备出口合同2500项，合同金额66.87亿美元，比

〔4〕关于B组与D组国家的有关分歧与争论，参见郭寿康：《国际技术转让》，法律出版社1989年版，第2~4页。

〔5〕《技术进出口管理条例》(2002年1月1日施行)第2条。

〔6〕《经合组织报告认为——技术进出口改变世界贸易格局》，载《国际商报》1997年3月13日，第1版。

上年增加了 21.12%。[7]

四、国际技术贸易法

国际技术贸易法是规范国际技术贸易关系的法律规范的总称,由调整国际技术贸易关系的国际条约、国际惯例和国内立法所构成。

(一)国际条约

条约是国际技术贸易法的重要渊源。这些条约中,有的是专门针对国际技术贸易活动的,有的则是包含国际技术贸易方面的规则与规范的。

1. 关于国际技术贸易的专门条约

目前,世界上关于技术贸易方面的专门条约与协定并不多。已经正式签订的只有几个区域性的协定,如安第斯集团于 1970 年订立的《卡塔赫纳协定》和《欧洲经济共同体协定》及《共同体理事会第 17 号条例》。经互会关于技术贸易的共同条件,因其对经互会各成员国的外贸机构有强制性的规范作用,所以也可视为条约法规范。自 1974 年起,联合国贸易与发展会议(以下简称贸发会)就着手拟定一个国际技术贸易方面的全球性行为规范。1978 年 10 月,《国际技术转让行动守则草案》连同 3 个集团(发展中国家 77 国集团、发达国家 B 组集团与苏联东欧国家 D 组集团)的案文提交联合国讨论。由于各国政治经济利益的根本分歧与科技水平的重大差异,草案至今未获通过。目前,实际上并不存在一个国际技术贸易方面的世界性公约。尽管如此,几经波折的《国际技术转让行动守则草案》还是对各国立法具有一定的借鉴意义,其影响力不可忽视。

2. 与国际技术贸易有关的国际条约

与国际技术贸易直接相关的国际条约主要是工业产权保护方面的国际条约,如《保护工业产权巴黎公约》《专利合作公约》《保护植物新品种国际公约》《微生物备案取得国际承认布达佩斯协定》《专利国际分类条约》以及关贸总协定乌拉圭回合 1993 年达成的《与贸易有关的知识产权协议》。商标国际保护方面的一些国际公约,如《国际商标注册马德里协定》《商标注册条约》等也与技术贸易间接相关。

有些国际性政治或军事集团的成员国之间,以及这些成员国作为一个整体对外开展技术贸易过程中,也制定了一些制度进行控制。从技术贸易角度来看,这些控制性的规定也有一定的法律意义。例如,1950 年在巴黎成立的“巴黎统筹委

---

[7] 《中国对外经济贸易年鉴 1999/2000》,中国对外经济贸易出版社 1999 年版,第 72 页。

员会”[8]就是一个典型。此外,各国签订的有关技术贸易的双边贸易协定或其他协定对于当事国来说也具有条约法的意义。我国与外国签订的许多双边贸易协定就涉及技术贸易与知识产权保护问题。例如,1979年的《中华人民共和国和美利坚合众国贸易关系协定》第6条,就是关于双方根据各自的法律并考虑国际做法,给对方的知识产权以保护的规定。而我国与许多国家签订的双边投资保护协定与避免双重征税的协定也都与技术贸易问题密切相关。这些双边条约是我国处理同有关国家的双边技术贸易关系的重要国际法律规则。

(二)国际惯例

国际惯例作为国际技术贸易法的一项内容,与各国国内法及国际公约不同,它具有一定的伸缩性。它的作用是有一定的限度的,并不是对一切从事国际技术贸易活动的人都具有约束力。只有当某个具体的技术贸易活动的交易双方都承认并以某种方式明示或默示地采纳某一惯例时,这一惯例才对当事人双方有法律约束力,在这种情况下,惯例具有解释与补充当事人意思——合同的作用。而且,国际惯例的具体内容可以由交易活动的双方当事人协议增删或修改。此外,在某些国家,国际惯例除了作为解释与补充合同的工具之外,尚具有法律漏洞补充工具的法律意义。例如,我国《民法通则》第142条第3款规定“中华人民共和国法律和中华人民共和国缔结或者参加的国际条约没有规定的,可以适用国际惯例”。但是在国际技术贸易交易中,双方当事人适用国际惯例是有条件的,即中国法律与中国缔结或参加的有关国际条约没有相关规定,才可以适用国际惯例,同时适用国际惯例不得违背中国的社会公共利益。可以看出,在中国,国际惯例是作为中国法律的补充。[9] 在有些国家,如法国、瑞士等,由于承认国际惯例(现代商人法)为一种独立自治的法律体系,故当事人甚至可以选择“国际惯例”作为合同准据法。此时的“国际惯例”则不是可以补充法律而是可以取代传统实证意义上的法律,事实上成为一种真正的法律渊源,具有普遍的规范意义。

在国际技术贸易合同中不得订立限制性商业条款,是多数国家普遍接受的重要国际惯例。尽管发达国家与发展中国家对“限制性商业条款”的范围与含义见解尚有分歧,但有不少内容是一致的。在一些政府间及民间国际组织起草的建议性文件中,对国际技术贸易的许多常用术语的定义、技术提供的步骤、技术服务的

---

〔8〕 原名为“多国出口控制协调委员会”(coordinating committee for Multilateral Export Control,COCOM)。“巴统”不是根据任何条约成立的,它是一个非正式的自愿组织。随着前苏联、东欧的巨变,1994年3月,作为冷战产物的“巴统”也已宣布解散。

〔9〕 单文华:《国际贸易惯例的基本理论问题》,载梁慧星主编:《民商法论丛》(第7卷),法律出版社1997年版。

方式、提成费计算中的细节，如对“净销售值”的理解及许可证合同的范围等，均作了某些规定。其中有些规定在国际技术贸易实践中也常作为国际惯例而得以引用。

（三）国内法

目前，国际技术贸易法的主要法律渊源仍是各国的有关国内立法。这些国内立法中尤以工业产权法、反垄断法、涉外技术贸易法等法律与国际技术贸易活动关系至为密切。

此外，公司法、破产法、外商投资法、外汇管理法、银行法、税法等也直接、间接地与国际技术贸易活动相关联，也属国际技术贸易法的重要国内法渊源。

第二节　国际技术许可合同

从目前的实践来看，国际技术贸易大多是以独立或非独立的国际技术许可合同的方式来实现的。在采用交钥匙合同或合营企业等形式时，即使不单独订立非独立的技术许可合同，也必然在主合同中有相应的、与技术许可合同条款相似的条款。所以，国际技术许可合同是国际技术贸易最基本的法律形式，本节拟作集中介绍。

一、许可合同的种类

技术供方通过合同将自己的某项技术许可技术受方使用，从而获取一定的使用费或其他报酬，这种合同即为技术许可合同。按不同的标准，技术许可合同可以有许多不同的分类，如按技术标的的不同，可分为专利许可合同、软件许可合同与专有技术许可合同等。

但从其内容上看，许可合同基本上可分为四大类别。[10]

（一）普通许可合同（simple license contract）

普通许可合同是最常见的许可合同。按这种许可合同，供方许可受方在同一地域及同一时间使用该技术或与第三方签订类似许可合同而许可第三方使用这一技术。普通许可合同还可以细分为一般的普通许可合同与从属许可合同（或称分售许可合同）。后一种许可合同指的是受方经供方同意，自己以许可人身份再向第三方发出使用许可。

---

〔10〕 郑成思：《知识产权与国际贸易》，人民出版社 1995 年版，第 381～383 页

(二)独占许可合同(exclusive license contract)

独占许可合同是授权程度最高的许可合同。按这种许可合同,受方有权在指定的时间与地域内,排斥包括供方在内的一切人使用供方提供的技术。自然,供方也就不再有权在同一地域内向第三方发出使用该技术的许可。根据授权内容的不同,独占许可又可分为部分独占许可合同与完全独占许可合同。如许可合同规定受方不是在某国的全部领域,而只是在其中部分地区享有技术的独占权,或仅仅对使用该技术生产产品享有独占权,而对销售有关产品则不享有独占权,这种许可合同就是部分独占许可合同。

(三)独家许可合同(sole license contract)

独家许可合同的授权范围与独占许可合同基本相同,但受方无权排除供方自己在同一地域与同一时间内使用有关技术。换言之,在这种合同条件下,只有合同双方(供、受方)可以使用该技术,任何第三方(他方)均被排除使用,所以它又被称为“排他许可合同”。

(四)交叉许可合同(cross license contract)

交叉许可合同是指技术贸易双方当事人互为供方与受方,相互许可对方使用自己的技术时采用的许可合同形式。如果双方技术等价,则可互不支付费用;如不等价,则一方应向另一方支付一定的补偿费用。交叉许可合同最初为双边交叉,目前已发展为多个企业间的多边交叉,如美国汽车发动机方面形成了“专利同盟”,对同盟内的专利技术实施多边交叉许可,大大加速了汽车工业的技术进步。

上述四种许可合同,各有其利弊。在国际技术贸易中,究竟应采用何种形式许可,取决于多种因素,其中最重要的是市场销路与技术价格。一般来说,在市场广阔的情况下采用普通许可合同形式为多,而在市场较小的情况下不妨采用排他许可。独占许可因其价格过高,一般企业难以接受,所以在国际技术贸易中昌的比例较小,它多用于尖端技术与重大高新技术的国际转让之中。在西方,主要是高度垄断的工业部门使用独占许可合同形式。

值得一提的是,许可的不同类别反映的主要是法律问题,即责、权、利问题,而不是技术问题。供方并不会(也不应)由于受方需要的是非独占许可证就仅仅提供给他少于独占许可证的受方能得到的技术资料或技术服务,使他的生产达不到应有的效益。因此,受方完全不必在任何情况下都力争取得独占许可证。我国地域广阔,市场容量很大,许多产品即使多家采用同一先进技术生产,也未必能满足市场需求,所以,在多数情况下,我们没有必要浪费大量资金,去取得这种无实质经济效益的“独占许可”。

二、许可合同的基本内容

不同的许可合同，其具体内容自然各不相同，但总有一些基本的条款，是各类许可合同基本上都应具备的。这些通用性的基本条款，就构成许可合同的基本内容。在技术许可实践中，这些条款往往被分解为商务性、技术性与法律性条款三大类。[11] 这里为完整计，特按基本结构与主要条款的顺序予以介绍。

（一）许可合同的基本结构

一般来说，一份许可合同由开头语、鉴于条款、合同主要条款、签字及附件五部分组成。下面先简单介绍合同主要条款之外的四个部分。

1. 开头语。合同名称是开头语的一部分。合同名称要与合同内容相符。一般讲，名称写作“许可合同”或“技术贸易合同”，都能明确表示合同内容。有些以提供专有技术为主的合同也写作“Know-How 合同”，甚至只写作“合同”（agreement）。

开头语中最重要的是供方与受方的公司名称及主营业地（或总部所在地）的具体地址。在供方只是从属专利的所有人，或供方所提供的专有技术中有一部分要从第三方得到的情况下，在开头语中还可能提及第三方的名称。

开头语中双方的名称一定要用全称（如下文用简称，可在开头语中注明）。必要时，可到双方所在国的公司注册处核对其全称及准确的地址。开头语中在写明双方公司全称时，一般就写明了该公司的法人性质：是股份有限公司还是合伙企业（在英美国家，合伙也可称“公司”），是母公司、子公司还是分公司等。如果名称中表示不出，则应另有文字表示。

开头语中可以写明签合同的日期（也可以写在合同结尾）。开头语中一定要写明签合同的地点，这对于未规定“准据法”的合同尤为重要。按照国际私法中“合同成立地法”的原则，签合同的地点，可以成为日后产生合同争端时，法院（或仲裁庭）推定合同准据法的依据。

2. “鉴于”条款。“鉴于”是从英文“Whereas”译过来的。鉴于条款主要对合同起“导言”作用。在鉴于条款中，一般应写明下列内容：（1）当事人双方参加本技术贸易活动的背景；（2）双方签订合同的目的或愿望；（3）双方进行过的其他谈判活动；（4）双方曾签订的其他合同；（5）本合同涉及的知识产权或其他专有权；（6）本合同的签订对双方有何益处；（7）双方各自的原则立场。有的合同鉴于条款很简单，只有上述（1）、（2）、（5）3 项。

---

〔11〕 郭寿康：《国际技术转让》，法律出版社 1989 年版，第 77 ~ 102 页。

3. 签字。签字通常应在合同主要条款之后。签字页上应再次写明双方公司的名称,加盖双方公司通常在贸易活动中使用的印章。在为双方代表的手写签字留下的空白后面,要有该代表姓名的清晰的打印文字。

另外,合同的最后文本中如果有修改,在修改过的地方,均要有(在合同上签字的)双方代表以缩略语形式签上的自己的名字,以示该处系经双方同意后作的修改。

双方的签字代表必须是有权代表有关公司的人,而不是随意的任何人。

4. 附件。许可合同的附件至少要有技术附件与产品附件。技术附件中包括供方将提供的各种技术的名称、资料细目、向受方发送的步骤及具体日期等。产品附件中包括使用该技术生产的产品将在性能、功用、质量等方面达到怎样的指标。

在合同主要条款中,一般要有文字写明"本合同的附件系合同不可分割的一部分,与合同正文同样有效",以确保附件的法律效力。

(二)合同的主要条款

1. 定义条款。国际技术贸易的历史不很长,加上各国语言的不同、法律制度的不同,在许可合同中使用的一些关键性术语上,解释会各不相同,在国际上也还没有统一的必要。但作为一项具体的许可合同的当事双方,就必须有统一的解释。否则一是合同无法履行,二是发生了合同争端也将无法解决。因此,许多许可合同正式条款的第一条,就是"定义"条款,把双方同意的定义在这里写明。

也有的合同把定义分散在合同各条款中,而没有专门的"定义条款"。这样虽然并无不可,但毕竟不如集中规定在一个条款中那样能使人一目了然。

2. 授权范围条款。如果在"鉴于"条款中没有写明许可合同的标的,即供方提供的技术包括的那些项目含有哪些专有权,则要在授权范围条款中先写明这些专有权,然后才谈得上划定授权范围。

具体来说,"授权范围"有三方面含义。第一,划出许可的适用地域,也即其地域范围。这可以是整个国家境内,也可以是某一省、某一地区。第二,指明将专利权所含的哪些项目授予供方,也即权利范围。第三,规定授予受方独占许可、独家许可还是一般许可,受方有无权利进行从属许可。

此外,受方有无权利直接对侵犯专利权(或商标权)的行为起诉,有关专利权应由哪一方维持(交付年费等),也应有明确规定。

3. 不担保条款与担保条款。西方国家的出口技术的公司大都坚持在许可合同中订立"专利有效性不担保"条款,其原因有二。第一,所谓"专利",包括专利申请案,专利申请能否被批准,很难预言;最终被驳回的申请案,当然就是"无效专利”了。从这个角度讲，专利有效性很难担保。第二，许多西方国家规定了“专利复审制”，即在批准专利后专利期满前，任何人如果发现该专利本不应被批准，可向专利局请求复审；经复审而确认了请求人的意见，原专利将被判无效。专利权人不可能预知日后自己的专利是否会被判无效。从这个角度讲，也很难作出担保。

因此，受方对于专利效力不担保条款并不是完全不可接受的，不过，受方应坚持要求供方担保那些它应担保的内容，主要如：(1)保证向受方提供的技术是完整的、准确的、可靠的，按照该技术，能够生产出供方所生产的(或合同的产品附件中规定的)同样产品。(2)保证到合同签订之日为止，供方不知有任何可导致自己的专利被判无效的其他相同的现有技术。(3)保证实施自己的专利技术时，不会侵犯其他人的专利权；保证自己的专利不是“从属专利”，或虽然是“从属专利”，但自己已得到“基本专利”的权利人的有关许可。

4. 不弃权条款。供方对某些侵权行为未过问，并不暗示他放弃了专有权；供方对受方未按时支付的行为没有追究，也不暗示他放弃了取得使用费的权利等。

5. 质量控制条款。只有在供方许可受方使用其商标的情况下，才有权要求订立质量控制条款。因为产品质量的好坏，将影响供方的市场信誉。在质量控制条款中，大都是供方的权利。例如，有权定期检查受方产品的样品，有权因质量问题而中止合同等。

6. 技术服务条款。在这种条款中要规定供方从何日起、以何种方式、提供哪些专利与专有技术和实施专利及专有技术的其他必要资料；如何为受方培训人员作技术示范，以使受方能够掌握有关技术。在这种条款里，也会谈到一些支付问题，但它们与整个合同的使用费是两回事。

7. 保密条款。除了受方为供方的专有技术等秘密技术保密外，双方往往还有义务为对方的经营状况保密。当然，保密条款主要是规定双方如何对技术保密。

技术保密也不单纯是受方的义务。供方也必须保证不泄密。尤其是在独占许可的情况下，供方如将技术泄露给第三方，“独占”就无意义了。在有些许可合同中，供方的这项义务是订在“技术服务条款”中的。

8. 支付条款。支付条款是涉及受方单方义务的条款。过去技术许可的使用费，有多种支付方式：一次总付(Lump sum Payment)、按提成费(Royalty)支付、入门费(Initial Payment)与提成费结合支付等。目前为各国供受双方普遍接受的，是第三种方式。

入门费指的是受方在合同生效后一定时期(或收到首批技术资料后一定时期)内，向供方支付一笔“定金”性质的费用；待按照有关技术制作的产品销售(或生产出)之后,再按一定比例的提成费(一般是按许可年度)分批支付。许可合同中按净销售额计算提取的提成费,许多发展中国家都用法律规定了一定比例数不得超过之,以保护受方利益。我国有关法律没有规定具体百分比作为限制,以使技术引进方有谈判余地,并按实际情况作出决定。不过在技术贸易实践中,很少有受方同意支付超过净销售额5%的总支付费(包括入门费与提成费)。

9. 技术改进条款。是指许可合同的各方在改进了原有技术,因而取得了新的专有权之后,应当如何在优惠条件下向对方提供。对于供方来说,是如何继续提供技术援助;对于受方来说,是技术反馈或"回授"的问题。

10. 更改条款。在一些许可合同中并没有这个条款,因为合同的一方未取得另一方同意时,无权更改合同,这是不言而喻的。但有的合同当事人为避免某些误解,还是认为有必要订立这种条款。这种条款中一般都申明:合同生效后的任何修改,都必须通过双方的书面协议;双方任何时候的口头协议对于修改合同均无效力。

11. 不可抗力条款。虽然传统的英美法系国家与大陆法系国家分别使用着情势变迁与不可抗力两个术语,但近年来在许可合同中,已趋向于统一使用"不可抗力"这一术语。这个条款的目的,是事先规定万一发生了某些人力无法阻止的意外,使一方(或双方)无法按规定履行合同时,应当作何处理。

12. 合同有效期。许可合同的有效期一般不超过10年。有效期太长了,必然限制某一方当事人(或双方当事人)选择与其他人进行交易的自由。有些国家的技术贸易法还对许可合同的最长有效期作了规定。还有些国家以许可合同中包含的工业产权作为限制合同有效期的尺度,即不允许合同有效期长于合同中的工业产权(主要是专利权)的保护期。双方当事人按自己的需要规定保护期,是比较可取的。有长期合作意愿的双方,还可以规定:合同的"每届有效期"为若干年(如5年);在上一届有效期届满前若干日(如30日)内,如果任何一方均未向对方发出"不续展通知",则合同自动续展。这样,双方都有了使合同期或长或短的主动权。

13. 合同中止(Termination)条款。指当事人的一方行使中止权。在合同未履行完毕前中止合同,是对另一方未能履行(或按时履行)某些义务的一种制裁手段。中止条款有时并非一个独立的条款,而是分散在许多条款中,对于在何种情况下一方如何行使中止权,分别作出规定。对于规定了不得转让合同权利的许可合同来说,一方的公司(或企业)所有人变更,另一方也可提出中止合同。一方行使中止权,应在一定时间(如30日)之前通知另一方。

14. 通知形式条款。上面提到的合同一方对另一方的中止合同等通知,采取什么方式传递,通知的“提前期”从何起算,均要在合同中写明。通知一般均须以航空挂号信邮寄。至于“提前期”的计算日,英美法系国家习惯于从邮件发出之日算起(即“投邮主义”),大陆法系国家则从另一方收到邮件之日算起(即“到达主义”)。相隔遥远的两个公司,有时航空信从邮出到收悉要一周时间,如果“提前期”为30天,则实际上减少了1/4;况且,邮出的信件也有收不到的可能。所以,后一种计算法更显合理。

15. 合同权利让与条款。在西方传统的财产法中,一个合同的当事人参与订立合同并因此可得到的利益,也属于一种“无形财产权”,它与股票权、债权、知识产权等有类似之处。不同的是,合同的当事人是“双方”,如果一方当事人把他的合同权利转让给第三者,另一方的对于就变了,因此另一方未必同意。所以,在合同中必须规定双方各自有无权利转让自己的合同权利;如果有,在什么条件(前提)下方可以转让,以及转让哪些权利等。

16. 违约救济条款。总的说来,在许可合同条款中没有必要订“违约救济条款”。因为各国的合同法对违约救济都各有具体规定,合同中既有了“准据法”条款,救济条款也就暗含在内了。

一方从另一方那里取得赔偿或制止另一方的某些行为、强迫另一方必须作出某些行为,往往是诉诸法院或仲裁庭之后的事。在这些诉讼中的某些花费如何支付,则可能定在合同中。这种条款的标题叫做“执行成本”(Enforcement Costs)。

17. 政府批准条款。如供方国家对技术出口有法律上的限制,或受方国家对技术引进有法律上的限制,双方在签订许可合同时往往规定:如果合同生效日后一定时间内供方得不到政府的出口许可,或合同签字后一定时间内受方未能使合同被政府或上级主管部门批准(或仅仅部分被批准),另一方都有权退出合同,并且不负担任何赔偿。

18. 法律适用条款。许可合同的当事人双方一般都各自熟悉本国的法律,因此都会希望合同能选择自己所在国的法律为适用法,以便在发生合同争端时以自己国家的法律对合同作解释。大多数发达国家允许合同双方自由选择合同的适用法,不过身在这些国家的大公司,在它们的“格式合同”中,几乎无一例外地写明本国(或本州——美国,本省——加拿大)法律为适用法。一部分发展中国家规定技术引进合同必须适用引进国(即受方所在国)法律。我国对此未作硬性规定。从技术贸易的实践看,合同双方在适用法律条款上打破僵局的最后出路,往往是选择适用第三国法。但这也会遇到困难:有些发达国家(美国的某些州)虽然没规定只许适用某一方的法律,但却规定了不许适用第三国法。

订立准据法条款,不应忘记了知识产权的“地域性”特点——它们仅仅在自已依法产生的那个国家内有效。就我国的技术引进合同来讲,不论整个合同适用哪一国法,其中的专利与商标只能适用中国法。外国专利在中国不成其为专利;中国专利的内容、有效期等具体法律性质,均不可能用外国法来解释。因此,在技术引进的许可合同中,就会出现“准据法分割”现象,即一个合同适用几个不同国家的法律,其中一部分内容适用一个国家的法律,另一部分内容适用另一国的法律。

19. 争端解决条款。争端解决地点可以选择某国的法院或仲裁庭,也可以选择国际贸易合同经常选择的国际仲裁机构(如斯德哥尔摩商会仲裁院、苏黎世仲裁院、伦敦仲裁院等)。我国当事人参与的合同目前多在国际商会仲裁庭仲裁。另外,一般来说,如果选择了当事人双方中的一方所在国的法律为整个合同的准据法,则以选择该国的法院或仲裁庭解决争端为宜。

20. 合同文本条款。这是个容易被人忽视而又往往起重要作用的条款。许可合同谈判开始时,一般是占优势的一方拿出以本国文字书写的“格式合同”,但另一方要讨价还价,谈判中也可能拿出自己起草的合同。达成协议时,往往是双方合同的折中物,既有用供方国家的语言习惯表达的内容,也有以受方国家的语言习惯表达的内容。这种合同中最好写明:本合同以某两种文字写成,两种合同文本均须签字,并具有同等效力。

21. 其他条款。除上述条款外,一些许可合同还会有许多别的重要条款,如最惠方条款、对专利无争议条款、产品责任条款、代表权条款等。由于这些条款在多数许可合同中并不会出现,兹不赘述。[12]

三、许可合同双方的主要权利与义务

上述许可合同的内容其实就是合同双方权利义务的具体体现。为便于进一步理解,在此再对供方与受方的一般权利与义务略作归纳。

(一)供方的主要义务

供方的主要义务是提供合同标的技术和履行保证义务。

1. 提供合同标的技术。供方必须承担向受方提供有关专利、商标、计算机软件和专有技术的技术知识。如提供实施专利的有关技术说明和技术资料等;提供实施专有技术所必需的技术资料,包括为使用该技术,制造和销售产品所必需的设计、公式、计算、图纸、工艺、检验、标准、操作、维修、试验、包装运输等各种技术资料。供方有义务全部、完整、正确地提供这些资料。为使供方能履行这一义务,

---

〔12〕 郑成思:《国际技术转让法通论》,中国展望出版社 1987 年版,第 60 ~ 62 页。

一是要在合同中作出明确的规定；二是要在谈判中弄清供方掌握的专有技术所包含的整个内容，将其列出详细清单，作为合同的附件。供方提供的上述资料，应当是他拥有的最新资料。

供方对专有技术资料的提供，往往还不足以确保该专有技术的有效实施，即受方尚不能充分使用该项技术。所以，供方除了正确提供技术资料外，还要提供技术服务和进行技术培训。

如果供方提供技术实施的条件中包括技术实物（硬件），如机器和设备时，往往还要签订一个专门的货物供应合同。

如果供方不提供许可合同的标的技术，受方可终止合同和索回已支付的费用。如果供方延迟提供时，受方有权要求赔偿损失。

2. 供方的保证义务。供方的保证义务一般包括两个方面的内容：一是对技术的可实施性和可用性加以保证（技术保证）；二是对权利不足的保证（权利保证）。所谓技术上的可实施性是指可用现在已拥有的技术手段实施该项技术。例如，供方要保证其转让的专利技术可以实施，能够制造出产品。如无法实施，技术受方有权终止合同并要求供方退回已付的技术使用费。所谓技术上的可用性是指“发明必须达到它曾经达到的目标”，即使用该项技术可以达到合同规定的目标，制造出合格的产品。但是，在实践中的解释并不相同，有些供方不愿接受上述保证责任。因此，我国《技术进出口管理条例》第 25 条规定“技术进口合同的让与人应当保证所提供的技术完整、无误、有效，能够达到约定的技术目标”。〔13〕 我国对外谈判人员在技术引进谈判中，可利用我国法律的上述规定，力争在技术引进合同中订人供方的保证责任。如在引进的专利合同中订入“供方要保证专利技术的可实施性，如无法实施，则应终止合同并退回使用费”。在引进专有技术时，供方要保证受方在正确使用技术的条件下，能制造出达到合同规定的技术标准的产品。关于技术供方对产品性能的保证是通过合同中的考核与验收条款来规定的。如果经考核验收表明产品达不到合同规定的要求，且是由于供方的责任造成的，则受方有权终止合同，并请求供方赔偿有关损失。

供方对权利不足的保证，一般是指供方应对他提供的技术的合法性和有效性提供保证。

技术的合法性保证是指供方要保证自己是所提供技术的合法拥有者，或者保证自己有权转让或许可该项技术。例如分售许可就是如此。因此，专利技术供方还要保证不受第三方指控侵权和按规定缴纳维持专利的年费，以避免有关当局终

〔13〕《技术进出口管理条例》（2002 年 1 月 1 日施行）第 25 条。

止其专利权。

侵权是一个较为复杂的法律问题。这里所谓侵权有两种情况。一种情况是，由于专利权是一种独占权利，在专利法保护地域范围内未经专利权人许可，任何实施其专利的行为都是侵权行为。其中，如为非独占许可合同，受方一般要通知供方关于侵权的情况，由供方去处理；如为独占许可合同，一般是由受方根据有关法律向主管部门或司法机构请求追究第三方的侵权责任。另一种情况是，在专利法保护范围内，供方已将该项专利许可第三方独占使用，可是供方又许可受方在该地区使用。这样，受方在该地区制造和销售专利产品就构成对第三方的侵权。当然，供方如出让本不属于他的专利技术，就更有可能导致第三方的侵权指控。因此，我国《技术进出口管理条例》第 24 条规定“技术进口合同的让与人应当保证自己是所提供技术的合法拥有者或者有权转让、许可者。技术进口合同的受让人按照合同约定使用让与人提供的技术，被第三方指控侵权的，受让人应当立即通知让与人；让与人接到通知后，应当协助受让人排除妨碍。技术进口合同的受让人按照合同约定使用让与人提供的技术，侵害他人合法权益的，由让与人承担责任”。[14] 但在实践中，为避免使侵权问题复杂化，也可在合同中规定如下变通处理办法：如果供方许可的技术，发生第三方指控侵权，双方将共同与第三方交涉；如确系侵权行为必须修订许可合同的，或必须再与第三方签订专利使用许可合同的，则原合同总价应相应减少；如因侵权而无法履约时，受方有权终止合同，并要求退回全部费用和利息；与第三方交涉所发生的一切费用，应由供方承担。

此外，当我国引进的商标专用权被侵犯时，如果该外国商标已在我国注册，我国引进方可向县以上工商行政管理部门提出处理要求，或者向当地人民法院提出停止侵权行为的诉讼，并可请求赔偿损失。

至于专有技术的侵权问题，我国在专有技术引进的许可合同中，一般规定当发生第三方指控侵权时，由供方负责与第三方交涉并承担由此引起的一切法律上和经济上的责任。

供方对技术的有效性保证，主要指供方对其提供的专利权应当是有效的。因为对受方来说，引进过期的专利权、因不缴纳年费或被诉不符合《专利法》规定而已取消的专利权都是毫无意义的。有的供方为了逃避承担上述保证责任，一是迫使受方在合同中规定由受方缴纳维持专利的年费；二是在合同中规定不得对专利权的有效性提出异议(No-challenge)或称为不得反控条款(No-attack Clause)，即受方不仅自己不对专利权的有效性提出异议，也不协助第三方对该专利权的有效

---

〔14〕《技术进出口管理条例》(2002 年 1 月 1 日施行)第 24 条。

性提出异议。这是因为我国和外国的《专利法》一般都规定,专利权被授予以后,任何人认为该专利权的授予不符合有关专利法规定时,都可以请求有关专利当局宣告该专利权无效。而受方在使用专利过程中,很可能提出异议否定该项专利。不得反控条款是一种限制性条款,不符合我国《专利法》的规定,所以中方不应在合同中接受这种条款。

(二)受方的主要义务

受方的主要义务有两条:一是支付许可使用费;二是承担保密义务。

1. 支付许可使用费。支付许可使用费是技术受方的一项主要义务。许可使用费主要以货币支付,但也可采用实物支付形式,即以产品抵偿;或者以受方向供方提供其他技术知识的方式履行其支付使用费的义务,这实际上就构成了前面提到的“交叉许可”。

以货币支付时,可在合同中规定一次总付,或规定按提成支付,或规定入门费加提成支付。按提成支付时,受方可承担报账的义务,但是如双方无协议时,供方无权对受方的账得进行审查。

2. 承担保密义务。受方对许可合同中转让的技术秘密,要承担保密的义务。尤其是专有技术贸易合同更是如此。如前所述,专有技术是以其秘密为特征的,泄露其技术的秘密就等于使其丧失存在的基础。因此,在专有技术许可合同中一般都规定保密条款。对此,各国法律也是承认的。例如,我国《技术进出口管理条例》第26条规定“技术进口合同的受让人、让与人应当在合同约定的保密范围和保密期限内,对让与人提供的技术中尚未公开的秘密部分承担保密义务”。[15] 由此看来,我国法律主要肯定的是对技术的保密义务。实践中,正如前述,保密条款还应包括对商业、经营秘密的保密义务。

保密条款一般对保密范围、保密期限、保密措施和泄密责任作出规定。某种产品的制造往往需要多种技术和资料,因此受方承担保密的范围并不是全部技术和资料,而是机密资料和为公众和受方不知的技术知识和经验。对受方原已掌握的技术、为公众所知的资料或引进后供方和第三方公开了的技术,受方都不再承担保密义务。为了保密,受方应采取适当的措施,如由专人并指定专门地点保管、限制涉密人员,具体的安全措施也都要在合同中规定。如果泄密,一般规定供方有权收回资料,或要求赔偿损失。如果技术秘密是合同的基础,供方还可终止合同。保密期限通常为合同期限。供方往往要求合同期限届满后仍要受方承担保密义务,从合同关系来说这是不合理的,但实践中有延长保密期的趋势。

---

〔15〕《技术进出口管理条例》(2002年1月1日施行)第26条。

事实上，在技术贸易过程中，不仅涉及受方的保密问题，同样受方也可能将自己的某些技术秘密提供给供方，尤其是合同中规定了相互交换改进的技术时更是如此。所以，受方也可要求供方承担保密义务，并在合同中作出规定。

第三节　我国对技术进出口的管理

为了规范技术进出口管理，维护技术进出口秩序，促进国民经济和社会发展，根据《对外贸易法》及其他有关法律的有关规定，我国于 2001 年 10 月 31 日在国务院第 46 次常务会议上通过了《技术进出口管理条例》。根据该条例，2001 年 12 月 30 日，对外贸易经济合作部颁布了《技术进出口合同登记管理办法》。根据《对外贸易法》和《技术进出口管理条例》，对外贸易经济合作部、国家经济贸易委员会颁布了《禁止进口限制进口技术管理办法》，对外贸易经济合作部、科学技术部颁布了《禁止出口限制出口技术管理办法》。上述管理条例、管理办法于 2002 年 1 月 1 日起施行。这些条例、办法的制定和实施，构成了现行我国技术进出口管理工作的主要依据，进一步完善了我国技术进出口管理工作的体系。[16]

一、我国对技术进出口的管理范围和管理机构

根据《技术进出口管理条例》第 2 条规定，技术进出口是指从中华人民共和国境外向中华人民共和国境内，或者从中华人民共和国境内向中华人民共和国境外，通过贸易、投资或者经济技术合作的方式转移技术的行为，前款规定的行为包括专利权转让、专利申请权转让、专利实施许可、技术秘密转让、技术服务和其他方式的技术转移。前述行为都要接受国家的统一的管理制度。

国务院对外经济贸易主管部门（以下简称国务院外经贸主管部门）依照《对外贸易法》和《技术进出口管理条例》的规定，负责全国的技术进出口管理工作。省、自治区、直辖市人民政府外经贸主管部门根据国务院外经贸主管部门的授权，负责本行政区域内的技术进出口管理工作。国务院有关部门按照国务院的规定，履行技术进出口项目的有关管理职责。

二、我国对技术进出口的管理

1. 对进出口技术的分类

根据《技术进出口管理条例》第 8 条、第 17 条、第 31 条和第 39 条的规定，我

---

〔16〕 安丽：《国际技术转让法》，中国法制出版社 2003 年版，第 188 页。

国将对进出口的技术分为禁止进出口的技术、限制进出口的技术和自由进出口的技术。

《对外贸易法》第16、17条规定,国家基于下列原因,可以限制或者禁止有关技术的进口或者出口:(1)为维护国家安全、社会公共利益或者公共道德,需要限制或者禁止进口或者出口的;(2)为保护人的健康或者安全,保护动物、植物的生命或者健康,保护环境,需要限制或者禁止进口或者出口的;(3)为实施与黄金或者白银进出口有关的措施,需要限制或者禁止进口或者出口的;(4)国内供应短缺或者为有效保护可能用竭的自然资源,需要限制或者禁止出口的;(5)输往国家或者地区的市场容量有限,需要限制出口的;国际和平与安全,国家在货物、技术进出口方面可以采取任何必要的措施。

国家对限制和禁止进出口的技术实行目录管理,配额、许可证管理。未经许可,不得进出口。国务院外经贸主管部门会同国务院有关部门,制定、调整并公布禁止或者限制进出口的技术目录。2001年12月30日,外经贸部(现商务部)已颁布了第一批禁止进口限制进口技术目录。

不属于禁止进出口的技术和限制进出口的技术即为自由进出口的技术。

2. 对限制进出口技术合同的管理

根据《技术进出口管理条例》的规定,对属于限制进出口的技术,实行许可证管理;未经许可,不得进口。因此,我国对限制进出口技术的管理实行政府审批制。进口属于限制进口的技术,应当向国务院外经贸主管部门提出技术进口申请并附有关文件。技术进口项目须经有关部门批准的,还应当提交有关部门的批准文件。国务院外经贸主管部门收到技术进口申请后,应当会同国务院有关部门对申请进行审查,并自收到申请之日起30个工作日内作出批准或者不批准的决定。技术进口申请经批准的,由国务院外经贸主管部门发给技术进口许可意向书。进口经营者取得技术进口许可意向书后,可以对外签订技术进口合同。出口经营商取得技术出口许可意向书后,方可对外进行实质性谈判,签订技术出口合同。对没有取得技术出口许可意向书的限制出口技术项目,任何单位和个人都不得对外进行实质性谈判,不得作出有关技术出口的具有法律效力的承诺。进口经营者签订技术进口合同后,应当向国务院外经贸主管部门提交技术进口合同副本及有关文件,申请技术进口许可证。国务院外经贸主管部门对技术进口合同的真实性进行审查,并自收到前款规定的文件之日起10个工作日内,对技术进口作出许可或者不许可的决定。进口经营者在向国务院外经贸主管部门提出技术进口申请时,可以一并提交已经签订的技术进口合同副本。国务院外经贸主管部门应当依照《技术进出口条例》的规定对申请及其技术进口合同的真实性一并进行审查,并自收到前款规定的文件之日起 40 个工作日内,对技术进口作出许可或者不许可的决定。技术进口经许可的,由国务院外经贸主管部门颁发技术进口许可证。技术进口合同自技术进口许可证颁发之日起生效。申请人凭技术进口许可证或者技术进口合同登记证,办理外汇、银行、税务、海关等相关手续。经许可或者登记的技术进口合同,合同的主要内容发生变更的,应当重新办理许可或者登记手续。经许可或者登记的技术进口合同终止的,应当及时向国务院外经贸主管部门备案。此外,设立外商投资企业,外方以技术作为投资的,该技术的进口,应当按照外商投资企业设立审批的程序进行审查或者办理登记。

根据《禁止进口限制进口技术管理办法》规定,国务院外经贸主管部门自收到技术进口申请书之日起 30 个工作日内,会同国家经贸委分别对技术进口项目进行贸易审查和技术审查,并决定是否准予进口。限制进口技术的贸易审查应包括以下内容:是否符合我国对外贸易政策,有利于对外经济技术合作的发展;是否符合我国对外承诺的义务。限制进口技术的技术审查应包括以下内容:是否危及国家安全或社会公共利益;是否危害人的生命或健康;是否破坏生态环境;是否符合国家产业政策和经济社会发展战略,有利于促进我国技术进步和产业升级,有利于维护我国经济技术权益。

根据《禁止出口限制出口技术管理办法》的规定,国务院外经贸主管部门自收到技术出口申请书之日起 30 个工作日内,会同科学技术部分别对技术出口项目进行贸易审查和技术审查,并决定是否准予许可。限制出口技术的贸易审查应包括以下主要内容:是否符合我国对外贸易政策,并有利于促进外贸出口;是否符合我国产业出口政策,并有利于促进国民经济发展;是否符合我国对外承诺的义务。限制出口技术的技术审查应包括以下主要内容:是否危及国家安全;是否符合我国科技发展政策,并有利于科技进步;出口成熟的产业化技术是否符合我国的产业政策,并能带动大型和成套设备、高新技术产品的生产和经济技术合作;如果是实验室技术,鼓励首先在国内开发,转变为产业化技术后再出口,国内暂不具备条件转化应用的,则应在国家利益不受损害并取得知识产权有效保护的前提下方可出口;出口的技术是否成熟可靠并经过验收或鉴定,未经验收或鉴定但已经生产实践证明的,应由采用单位出具证明。

3. 对自由进出口技术合同的管理

《技术进出口管理条例》规定,对属于自由进出口的技术,实行合同登记管理。为规范自由进出口技术合同的管理,建立技术进出口信息管理制度,促进我国技术进出口的发展,根据《技术进出口管理条例》,外经贸部(现商务部)专门制定了《技术进出口合同登记管理办法》。

技术进出口合同包括专利权转让合同、专利申请权转让合同、专利实施许可合同、技术秘密许可合同、技术服务合同和含有技术进出口的其他合同。对自由进出口技术合同实行网上在线登记管理。外经贸主管部门是技术进出口合同的登记管理部门。自由进出口技术合同自依法成立时生效。

国务院外经贸主管部门负责对重大项目的技术进口合同进行登记管理。重大项目是指:项目资金来源中含有国家财政预算内资金、外国政府贷款、国际金融组织贷款的项目;国务院立项批准的项目。各省、自治区、直辖市和计划单列市外经贸委(厅、局)(以下简称地方外经贸主管部门)负责对重大项目以外的自由进出口技术合同进行登记管理。中央管理企业的自由进出口技术合同,按属地原则到地方外经贸主管部门办理登记。各省、自治区、直辖市和计划单列市外经贸委(厅、局)可授权下一级外经贸主管部门对自由进出口技术合同进行登记管理。技术进出口经营者在合同生效后,应在中国国际电子商务网上进行登记,并持技术进口合同登记申请书或技术出口合同申请书、合同副本和签约双方法律地作的证明文件,到地方外经贸主管部门或其授权机构履行登记手续。地方外经贸主管部门或其授权机构在收到上述文件起 3 个工作日内,对合同登记的内容进行核对,并向经营者颁发技术进口合同登记证或技术出口合同登记证。

中外合资、中外合作和外商独资企业成立时作为资本入股并作为合资章程附件的技术进口合同按外商投资企业有关法律规定办理相关手续。

第四节　联合国《国际技术转让行动守则草案》

国际技术贸易的发展促使各国纷纷制定管理国际技术贸易的法律规章,同时也推动着有关国际立法的发展。由于在国际技术贸易中地位的不平等性,发展中国家较之发达国家在这方面的要求尤见迫切。20 世纪 60 年代末,素有“南北对话的讲坛”之称的贸发会决定将技术贸易问题作为优先项目进行专门审议。1974 年 5 月,联大第六届特别会议通过决议,要求制定一项符合发展中国家普遍要求与条件的关于技术贸易的国际行动守则。次年,联合国大会(以下简称联大)第七届特别会议决议除重申上述主张外,还正式授权贸发会主持守则的起草工作。

为此,贸发会专门成立了“政府间国际技术转让行动守则专家组”(以下简称专家组),1976 年 11 月至 1978 年 7 月间,专家组在瑞士日内瓦先后举行了六次会议，专门研究守则草拟事宜。在会上，各国家集团，[17]尤其是发展中国家的77国集团和西方发达国家的B组集团意见分歧深刻，在诸如坚持守则的法律约束性问题、取消限制性条款问题、规定担保问题、制定和通过国家规章以便管制技术转让等重大问题上均持相反的立场。最后，只好将经过会议多次修改的守则的综合案文连同3个集团的案文一起提交即将召开的联合国关于守则的谈判大会，作为大会谈判的基础。

1978年10月16日，根据第32届联大通过的第32/188号决议，联合国国际技术转让行动守则谈判会议（以下简称谈判会议）在日内瓦万国宫举行。参加会议的有来自各国（包括观察员国家）、联合国各机构或专门机构及政府间或非政府间组织的代表。尽管工作组主席百般努力，每逢双方相持不下时，便提出主席文件作为折中案文来取代草案中的原有案文，以便推进谈判，但历经三周的谈判在许多实质性问题上仍未取得突破性的进展。

此后，根据联大各次决议，先后召开了关于守则谈判的第2届至第6届会议，终于对序言、第2章、第3章、第5章、第6章、第7章以及第1章与第8章的大部分条文取得了协议。但是，在一些重要问题上，意见仍严重对立。最后，终因在这些问题上的深刻分歧而导致谈判破裂，陷入僵局。第6届会议最后以通过一项提请联大就进一步的行动，包括有无可能就守则重新谈判问题采取必要措施的决议而告结束。

尽管如此，作为国际技术贸易领域唯一的全球性的统一规则，联合国《国际技术转让行动守则草案》（以下简称《守则草案》）仍旧有重大借鉴意义，在守则起草过程中体现出来的南北之间的激烈争执对于深入研究国际技术贸易法也颇具参考意义。因此，本章拟对守则草案的主要内容与守则草拟过程中的主要争论点略作介绍。

一、《守则草案》的主要内容

目前的《守则草案》包括序言和下列九章：(1)定义和适用范围；(2)目标和原则；(3)国家对技术转让交易的管制；(4)限制性惯例；(5)当事人各方的责任和义务；(6)对发展中国家的特殊待遇；(7)国际协作；(8)国际性体制机构；(9)适用的法律和争端的解决。

根据《守则草案》第1章第1.5款，守则普遍适用于一切国际技术转让交易，

---

[17] 长期以来，贸发会里形成了三个主要集团：77国集团，由广大发展中国家组成，现有127个国家参加；B组集团，是77国集团的主要谈判对手，由西方发达国家组成；D组集团，由前苏联、东欧国家及古巴、蒙古组成。我国自主地实施本国对外政策，不属于任何一个集团。

既适用于技术转让交易的所有当事方，也适用于所有国家和所有国家集团，而不论其经济和政治制度及其发展水平如何。相应地，《守则草案》的实质性条款可以分为两大类。一类是关于管理国际技术转让交易及其当事人各方行为的条款。它主要包括第4章中关于确立当事人各方应加以避免的惯例及其他做法的规范；第5章中关于确定和澄清当事人各方所承担的责任和义务的规范；以及第9章中关于适用法律和争端解决的规范。另一类是关于各国政府由于其本国政策或为了满足其对守则的承诺而采取的行动的条款。它主要包括第3章中有关说明各国在技术转让交易方面可能采取的措施及各国就此问题颁布本国立法时必须遵守的一般标准的规定；第6章中关于对发展中国家的特殊待遇及有关仅在技术接受国为发展中国家的情况下才适用的措施的规定；第7章中关于各国在双边、多边区域或区域间基础上进行国际合作的规定；以及第8章中有关在贸发会内设立一个负责实施和执行守则的国际性体制机构的条款。以下就《守则草案》的核心和重要内容略作介绍与分析。

（一）限制性惯例限制性惯例是指当事人各方有义务不在技术转让交易合同中规定的不合理的限制性条款或做法，《守则草案》惯例清单列举的限制性条款共有14项

1. 回授条款。要求取方（技术的受方）将取得技术后作出的改进部分，在由供方专享的基础上，无需供方给予补偿或承担互惠义务，或当转让或回受会使供方滥用其市场支配地位时，转让或回授给供方或供方指定的任何其他企业。

2. 对有效性的异议。要求取方对被转让的专利和其他保护发明的有效性，或对供方所要求或取得的其他此种权利的有效性，不表示异议。

3. 独家经营。限制取方就类似的或竞争性的技术或产品签订销售、代理或制造协定的自由，或取得竞争性技术的自由，而这类限制并非为确保取得合法利益所需，尤其不是为了确保所转让技术的机密性，或保证尽力履行经销或推销义务之所需。

4. 对研究的限制。限制取方从事旨在按当地情况吸收和更改所转让技术的研究和发展，或限制取方实施与新产品、新工艺、新设备有关的研究发展计划。

5. 对使用人员方面的限制。要求取方使用供方指定的人员（除非为保证转让和开始使用技术的传授阶段的效率之所需）；或其后已有经充分训练的当地人员时，仍继续作这种要求；或妨碍使用技术取方国家的人员。

6. 限定价格。管制取方对用所得技术制造的产品或提供的服务所定的价格。

7. 对技术更改的限制。禁止取方按当地情况更改进口技术，或在取方自行负责作出更改且不使用技术供方的名称、商标、服务标志、商品名称时，迫使取方在

设计或规格上作不愿要或不必要的变更(除非这种更改不适当地影响到这些产品或其他制造程序)。

8. 包销协定或独家代理协定。要求取方将包销权或独家代理权授予供方或供方指定的任何人(除非当事方在分包安排或制造安排中已同意,根据技术转让安排生产的全部或部分产品由供方或其指定的任何人销售)。

9. 附带条件的安排。强制取方接受其不愿要的额外技术、未来发明和改进部分、货物或服务,或限制技术、货物或服务的来源,作为取得所需技术的条件,而这样做并非为取方使用供方的商标、服务标志等时维持产品或服务的质量之所需,也非为履行所担保的特定效能方面的义务之所需。

10. 出口限制。施行地区或数量限制,或规定产品的出口或出口价格必须事先得到同意,或对用所供技术生产的可出口产品提高付款额,以这类限制方法禁止或严重妨碍出口(除非具有出于保护供方和任何取方的合法利益的充分理由,例如,为防止这类产品输往一方当事人的工业产权会因这类产品的输入而受到影响的国家,或输往已经被授予有关技术的专用许可证的国家,或已肯定而且明确地获得了特定选择权的国家)。

11. 共享专利或互授许可协定及其他安排。技术供应人之间的共享专利或互授许可协定或其他国际技术转让交流安排引起的、会不正当地限制取得新的技术发展或会造成滥行支配某一行业或市场的力量因而对技术转让产生不利影响的、对地区、数量、价格、顾客或市场的限制,但合作安排(例如合作研究安排)附带的适当限制不在此限。

12. 对宣传的限制。限制取方的广告或宣传的限制(除非因下列情况而可能需要限制这种宣传:由于广告或宣传提到供方的名称、商标或服务标志、商品名称等,以防止供方的商誉或名誉受到损害;或由于供方可能要对产品负赔偿责任,而有正当理由避免这种责任;或为了保障安全或保护消费者;或为了确保所转让技术的机密性)。

13. 工业产权期满后的付款和其他义务。对继续使用已失效、取消或期满的工业产权要求付款或承担其他义务,但承认任何其他问题,包括对技术的其他付款义务,应按照有关的适用法律和符合该法律的协定条款处理。

14. 在技术转让协议期满后的限制。在技术转让协议期满后,限制取方使用该项技术,包括因取方以外的行动而失去其机密性的诀窍,但不妨碍已议定的付款义务或现有的工业产权。

对上述许多限制性条款,发达国家(B集团)要求在相应的条款前加上“不合理地”或“不正当地”等词语,意指只有不合理和不正当的限制,才构成限制性条款。其弦外之音显然指除此之外的限制都是合理和正当的，因此并未与《守则草案》相抵触。

（二）当事人各方的责任和义务

这是《守则草案》规定的技术转让交易的各当事方在谈判阶段和合同阶段应共同承担的担保、责任和义务，它与前述限制性惯例共同构成守则草案的核心内容。

《守则草案》关于当事各方的责任和义务的规定适用于两个阶段：谈判阶段与合同阶段。

在谈判阶段，草案要求每一当事方应考虑到对方的要求。在技术和商业上实际可行的范围内：(1)尽可能利用当地可得资源，包括人才资源即由技术受方指派和提供的受过充分培训的当地人员（包括经理人员在内），以及包括由技术受方指明并提出的当地可得的材料、技术、技艺、顾问和工程服务在内的其他资源；(2)明确规定对所转让技术的应用和操作提供技术服务；(3)根据取方要求，供方应在实际可行的范围内就所转让技术的各个环节提供资料，以便作出充分的分项转让安排。

此外，当事人双方在谈判技术转让协定时，应配合当事人各方本国，特别是技术取方国家的经济和社会发展目标，遵守公道、诚实的商业惯例，以公平合理的条件，包括支付许可证费、特许权使用费和其他报酬等达成协定；互通情报；遵守一切法律义务或合同义务，将得自对方的一切机密资料予以保密；在任何一方认为无法达成满意的协定时，可停止谈判。

根据《守则草案》，取方应向供方及时提供取方国家在技术条件、官方经济和社会发展目标以及法规方面同谈判中技术转让和使用有关的现有具体资料。供方则：(1)应把他实际知道的，所供技术按合同条件使用时将不符合取方国家内他已经知道与该技术有关的，或已提请他特别注意的某些卫生、安全和环境规定的一切原因，以及供方已知道使用该技术和该技术产品可能引起的一切卫生、安全和环境方面的严重危险，及时地通知技术取方；(2)供方还应把他实际知道的、按合同规定授予权利或提供援助和服务的权力所受的任何限制，包括一切会直接不利地影响到转让权利的存在和有效性的未决官方程序或诉讼，通知技术取方；(3)尽可能考虑到取方的要求，在规定期限内，向取方供应供方所生产的，为使用被转让的技术所必需的附件、备件和部件，尤其在别无其他来源时。

在合同阶段，即合同有效期间，《守则草案》规定的当事人责任和义务包括：(1)当事各方在一定期间或合同有效期内，可获得所转让技术的改进技术；(2)对技术转让中得自对方的商业秘密、秘密诀窍和所有其他重大机密资料的范围、时限及使用均保守机密;(3)规定争端的解决和法律适用条款;(4)技术供方担保其技术符合技术转让合同所列的规格;(5)技术供方担保其技术如果遵照供方按合同提供的具体的操作规则使用,可适用于当事人各方所议定和协定所规定的货物制造或提供服务;(6)供方声明,在签订合同之日绝不知道按合同规定的用法使用技术会侵害第三方的有效专利权或类似的发明保障;(7)如果合同包括使用供方的商标、商品名称或类似的商誉标志,技术受方承诺,维持议定的质量水平,双方并承诺避免采取旨在或敌意损害另一方商誉或名声的行动;(8)应在合同中规定供方已同意担保的技术性能标准,包括规定达到这些标准的要求,详细说明如何确定性能是否已达标准,以及说明性能达不到标准的后果;(9)供方承诺将按合同正确、完整地及时提供为合同直接规定的特定目的所应提供的有关技术文件和其他数据;(10)遵照谈判的结果,适当地提供人员训练,供给附件、备件和部件;(11)应在合同中规定任何一方不履行技术转让合同所规定的责任而应负的赔偿责任,并包括损失、损坏或伤害的问题。

《守则草案》关于当事人各方责任和义务的大部分条款比较符合发展中国家技术受方的利益,尤其是关于当事人各方在进行技术转让时,除了遵守公道、诚实的商业惯例,还应配合当事方国家,尤其是技术受方国家的经济和社会发展目标的规定,及关于供方应提供对所提报价进行技术、体制和财务评价所需的各种资料,以便作出充分的分项转让安排的规定。这些都是广大发展中国家在谈判中长期坚持的结果。

(三)对发展中国家的特殊待遇根据《守则草案》规定,给予发展中国家的特殊待遇必须配合它们在不同经济社会发展阶段中的经济社会目标,必须特别注意最不发达国家的特殊问题和条件

具体来说,关于发达国家对发展中国家的特殊待遇的内容可分为三部分。

1. 第一部分。该部分要求发达国家通过一般的政府政策,由本国政府和本国企业或机构采取各种具体措施。比如:便利发展中国家取得可能有助于它们达到其经济社会发展目标的技术的供应情况、具体内容、所在地点以及可能时估计费用等现成的资料,让发展中国家有最自由、最充分的机会取得所需技术;尽量便利发展中国家取得科学和工业研究的现成数据,帮助发展中国家评价和更改现有技术及发展其本国技术;合作开发发展中国家的科技资源并培养其创新能力;通过创立和支援实验室、试验设施、训练机构、研究所等,帮助发展中国家加强其技术能力,特别是国民经济中基本部门的技术能力;合作建立或加强国际、区域或国家机构,包括技术转让中心,以帮助发展中国家发展并取得为建立、发展和提高其技术能力所必需的技术和技能,包括工厂的设计、建造和操作在内;鼓励更改研究发

展、工程和设计,以适合发展中国家的条件和具备的生产要素;在具体的双边或多边经济项目及其他发展项目中,更多地利用发展中国家人员和机构的管理、工程、设计和技术经验;鼓励训练发展中国家的人员。

2. 第二部分。该部分要求发达国家政府在进行发展援助与合作的计划时,为响应发展中国家的具体要求,所应采取的行动。主要包括:在发展援助计划和研究交流计划下提供专家,协助发展中国家发展本国技术;对发展中国家中从事发展本国技术或从事更改、利用被转让技术的研究人员、工程人员、设计人员和其他人员,提供训练;在拟订和执行便利技术转让的法律和规章方面提供协助与合作;支援发展中国家发展新技术和更改现有技术以适合发展中国家的特殊需要的项目;以优于通常商业贷款的条件给予信贷,给予已获批准、与技术转让交易有关的发展项目提供购买资本货物和中间货物的资金,以减抵项目费用,提高发展中国家所取得的技术的质量;在拟订和执行旨在避免技术及其产品危及卫生、安全和环境的法律规章方面提供协助和合作。

3. 第三部分。该部分要求发达国家政府鼓励并设法奖励本国企业和机构,在发展中国家内作出特别努力。包括:帮助发展中国家的企业发展其技术能力;从事发展适合发展中国家需要的技术;在发展中国家内从事对各该国有利的研究发展活动,并增进发达国家与发展中国家的企业和科技机构间的合作;对发展中国家的企业和机构发展新技术和更改现有技术以适合发展中国家的特殊需要和条件的项目,给予援助。

发达国家在技术转让贸易中给予发展中国家以特殊待遇,是联大多次决议的要求,也符合制定守则的初衷。此外,由于本部分的内容大都是一些政策性条文,故在谈判时障碍不大,较早达成了一致。不过,这些规定的真正实施,还有待于日后各国以更具体的方式采取进一步的行动。

(四)国际协作

首先,《守则草案》要求世界各国承认:各国政府、各政府机构、联合国系统内各组织和机构,包括依本守则建立的国际性体制机构,彼此间有必要进行适当的国际协作。继而,草案列举了一些通过国际协作,促进更多的国际技术交流,加强世界各国技术能力,并促使本守则条款得到执行的措施。包括:交换现有各种资料;协调各国技术转让法律和政策;促进平等对待技术供方、受方及双方政府的国际协定;促进寻求,获取和散播技术的共同计划;以及通过国际协定采取行动,尽可能避免对技术转让交易所产生的收益重复征税等。

(五)国际性体制机构

《守则草案》要求建立一个专门的国际性体制机构,来负责审议守则的法律约束力，更好地适用、执行守则的各项条款等。其中，已经达成协议的主要是关于该国际体制机构的职责部分，包括：作为场所和方式，供各国就有关本守则的问题，特别是其适用和协调的问题以及就业务方面取得的经验，进行协商、讨论和交换意见；定期进行和散发关于本守则各项规定的技术转让问题调查研究，以期增进经验交流，更好地适用和执行守则；针对有关守则的目标和原则的实现而采取适当步骤并向各国提出有关报告和建议；就本守则各项规定的适用主办座谈会，讲习班等；至少每年一次向贸发会提出工作报告。

此外，《守则草案》还明确规定，该国际性体制机构在执行其职责时，既不能起法庭的作用，也不能以其他方式对各国政府或各个当事方就某一项技术转让交易进行的活动或行为作出裁决。当某一项交易的当事方发生争端时，该国际性体制机构应避免卷入。

由于谈判各方意见分歧，对国际性体制机构仍有许多重要的内容，比如关于该体制机构的名称、结构、性质及其日后审查守则法律性质的程序等都还没有达成协议。

（六）法律适用与争端解决

关于适用法律的条款、解决争端的司法、行政及仲裁途径等问题，长期以来的谈判一直未能就此达成一致意见，所以，本章案文仍在审议之中。

二、《守则草案》中的主要争论点

守则起草谈判的过程是一个充满分歧与争论的过程。其中，有的分歧得以弥合，达成共识；有的则未能逾越，以致谈判最终陷入僵局。从根源上说，这些分歧所反映的是不同国家在技术转让交易中根本利益上的冲突。这种利益冲突在代表作为技术受方的广大发展中国家的 77 国集团与代表主要作为技术供方的西方发达国家的 B 组集团之间表现得尤其突出。本节就这些悬而未决的主要争论点逐个作一简单介绍。〔18〕

（一）守则的法律性质

所谓守则的法律性质即守则是不是一项国际性的具有正式约束力的法律文件的问题。这是守则制定过程中一个最先碰到、至今仍没有最后解决的问题。各区域集团的分歧在于：这项正在谈判、准备通过的守则是一项普遍的、按国际法对缔约国有正式约束力的多边公约，还是只是一个没有正式约束力，与联合国大会

---

〔18〕 郭寿康：《国际技术转让》，法律出版社 1989 年版，第 208 ~ 216 页；冯大同：《国际贸易法》，北京大学出版社 1995 年版，第 254 ~ 258 页；郑成思：《国际技术转让法通论》，中国展望出版社 1987 年版，第 296 ~ 304 页；沈金英：《国际技术贸易》，南京大学出版社 1995 年版，第 343 ~ 351 页。

决议效力类似的法律文件,其实施还有待于各国的立法来实现。

在历届谈判中,大多数发展中国家持前一种观点,他们深信这是“唯一能够有效地管理技术转让的方式”,“并有效地达到守则的目标,保证发展中国家在谈判中的地位及对进口技术的迫切需求”,B 组集团国家则持后一种观点。为了绕过这个障碍,1976 年贸发会决议规定,起草守则的政府专家组“应自由制定各项从强制性到任择性的条款草案,而不妨碍对守则法律性质的最后决定”。1979 年,在守则谈判第二届会议上,77 国集团作出让步。经过多次协商,各国同意把这个问题暂时搁置起来,先制定指导性文件,等到守则通过后若干年再审议。但是,对再审议的实质,各方仍持不同的立场。77 国集团认为再审议是为了“使本守则作为一份在法律上具有约束力的文件,获得普遍适用”;而 B 组国家则认为再审议是审查守则的各个方面,其中包括守则的法律性质,目前不便对审议结果先作出判断。D 组也主张再审议是对守则的法律性质作出最后决定。显然,B 组的“再审议”策略是为了坚持其“指导方针”的立场。而只要守则是指导方针式的,便难逃其“一纸空文”的命运。此案最后仍悬而未决。1985 年第 6 届会议的草案仍只是将各集团提议与会议主席提议作为附录,附在草案后面,以供进一步审议。

(二)守则的适用范围

在守则的适用范围问题上,各方都同意守则应平等、普遍地适用于各国政府和交易各当事方,而不论其有关国家的发展水平如何,以及它们的经济或政治制度如何。至于什么是“国际”技术转让,目前各方基本同意守则所规定的国际技术转让交易是指供方越过国境把技术转让给取方的交易。但是,对于跨国公司在海外的子公司在其所在国境内进行的技术转让交易是否适用守则这个问题,各国有重大分歧。77 国集团和 D 组国家都认为这些在所在国境内进行技术转让交易的子公司由外国实体控制,所以应属守则适用范围。而 B 组国家则坚持“越过国境”的定义,即国际技术转让交易就是越过国境转让技术的交易。而跨国公司子公司在其所在国境内的技术转让没有跨越国境,所以不属于守则适用的范围。但与此同时,又认为各国可以通过本国立法,使当事人各方在他们的国家境内进行的交易适用守则。很清楚,本案争议的实质在于是否对跨国公司的活动进行控制。长期以来,这些西方发达国家的跨国公司在发展中国家境内为所欲为,而今若是同意适用这种在管制技术转让交易方面比较有利于发展中国家的守则,则无异于自投罗网。所以,西方发达国家的代表是无论如何也不会对此作出让步的。为了绕过这一难题,在第 5 届会议上,会议主席曾提出回避性的案文,即“行动守则适用于国际技术转让”,意即各方对此案文可作出自己的理解。但这个提议仍未获得一致同意。《守则草案》第 4 章所讨论的是限制性条款问题。它的目的在于以规定不作为的义务的形式来规范技术转让交易的条件，确定交易各方之间的关系。毫无疑问，它是守则各章节中最重要的部分。也正因为如此，它成了历届谈判会议上讨论的中心，争论的焦点；同时也往往成为谈判破裂的导因。

整个第4章由标题和正文组成。正文内容包括导言部分（起段）和惯例清单两节。对此，无论是本章标题，还是正文内容，各国都存在着严重的分歧。在讨论中，曾出现三个不同的标题供各方审议：（1）“技术转让方面的惯例和安排的管制”；（2）“限制性商业惯例”；（3）“排除政治歧视和限制性商业惯例”。77国集团要求用“国际技术转让中惯例的管制”作为本章总标题，以强调对这些惯例实行管制；B组则坚持用“国际技术转让中的惯例”，使之保持中性，不带任何倾向；而D组则认为应该是“排除政治歧视和限制性商业惯例”。三个标题反映了各区域集团在惯例内容和范围上的争论。在第5届谈判会议上，中国代表提出用“国际技术转让中的限制性惯例”这个标题，明确地指出这些惯例是限制性的。D组同意中国的意见，认为这个标题既清楚，又结合本章的内容。后来77国集团也表示愿意放弃原来的提议，支持中国的意见。但B组固执己见，不同意中国的提议。所以，关于标题的案文至今没达成协议。草案中所列的还是那三个标题。

本章的分歧还集中在正文的起段部分，主要有以下三方面：（1）必须避免的惯例自古一般特性，即惯例的定义问题；（2）当事人各方或主管当局评价以致确定某一惯例是否为限制性惯例的标准问题；（3）本章条款是否对跨国公司母子公司间技术转让交易适用的问题。前两个问题实际上是密切相关的，它涉及对限制性惯例的基本看法问题。77国集团认为“本章的目标应是清除不利于有关国家特别是发展中国家的社会和经济发展的惯例”，所以，要求在起段部分中明确指出限制性惯例是不合理的，必须在技术转让交易中加以避免。至于在评价某一具体惯例是否应该避免时，应特别强调它是否对技术取方国家的经济技术发展产生不利影响，只有在不产生不利影响的个别情况下，才考虑接受。可见，77国集团对限制性惯例的总的态度是“基本否定，个别肯定”。而有关评定的标准则是“发展”的标准。与此立场截然不同的是B组国家的“基本肯定，个别否定”的观点。它们认为限制性惯例在多数情况下是合理的，可以接受的；只有在造成市场地位的滥用，并产生严重影响，且达到不合理程度时，才应当避免。所以，它们评价限制性条款的标准是“竞争”标准，并且搬出了以美国为典型代表的西方国家反托拉斯法的“合理规则”的概念，要求清单中每一惯例前都要冠以“不合理的”字样。对此，77国集团纷纷起来反对，认为“第4章的内容不应成为一种变相的反托拉斯法，因为后者的中心思想主要是保护竞争，而这远不是守则的主要着眼点”。至于在清单中的每一惯例前冠以“不合理”几个字的做法，发展中国家更是坚决反对。它们认为“不合理”这几个字意思含混,很容易产生由决策官员或当事各方自行任意解释的危险。与此相联系的是,77 国集团考虑到法律适用时应具有的灵活性,提议在本章中加个例外条款(也称豁免条款),意即在特殊情况下,取得技术国家的主管当局根据守则有权决定为本国公共利益而实施法律条文上所列的限制性惯例。当然,这种惯例不应对国家经济发展产生不良影响。D 组也赞成这一例外条款。但是这种主张也遭到了 B 组国家的反对。

在后来的一次谈判,即 1985 年第 6 届会议谈判中,中国代表团和 77 国集团出于尽快结束这无休止的谈判的动机,各自提出了新的案文。D 组和 E 组也都提出了自己的案文。这些新案文表明,除了 B 组外,其他的案文在某种程度上都设想了两种对限制性惯例进行评价的方法,即从这些惯例与取方国家的经济和技术发展的关系,以及从有关市场的普遍情况进行评价。中国代表团提出的案文强调发展和竞争的结合,并且措辞简洁,易于直接解释,受到工作组主席的好评,其中一部分被采用到主席提案中。而 B 组的案文只明确提到应考虑在有关市场进行竞争的情况,除此之外的则只字不提。会议主席根据大多数区域集团的意见拟出了一个可望达成协商一致的案文,并得到了中国、77 国集团及 D 组的同意,但 B 组仍不愿意接受,从而使各方代表渴望就此问题达成协议的希望再次幻灭。

在如何对待母子公司间限制性惯例的问题上,也存在着严重的分歧。B 组的立场是:为合理化目的或为在母子公司间合理分配职务而实施的限制,通常都是可以接受的。而 77 国集团则认为:如果子公司是完全独立的机构,即使它的产权属于母公司所有,它仍可以作为当事一方与母公司进行技术转让交易。这种交易显然属于守则的管辖范围。母子公司之间的限制性惯例同样也会对取方,特别是发展中国家的技术产生不良影响。这两种观点针锋相对,至今没有达成协议。

在本章正文的惯例清单部分的分歧主要集中在 1981 年草案的第 15 条至第 20 条这 6 条惯例上。在 1981 年 4 月会议上的草案曾列举了 20 条限制性惯例。而在 1983 年草案中,只列了 14 条,[19] 第 15 条至第 20 条则被删去。这 6 条内容是:(1)对引进技术所生产的产品的范围、数量和/或生产能力施加限制;(2)要求技术取方采用他所不愿意要的产品质量管理方法或质量标准(除非是为了满足产品质量担保的需要,或产品是使用技术供方的商标或服务标志时);(3)要求技术取方必须使用特定的商标、服务商标或商号名称;(4)迫使技术取方提供合股资本,或允许技术供方参加经营管理,并以此作为取得技术的条件;(5)技术转让协议的期限过长,或者根本不规定期限;(6)限制传播和扩大使用已进口的技术。

---

〔19〕 该 14 条参见本节第一目“守则草案的主要内容”。

B组认为这6条不具反竞争性质，均属不合理的做法，坚决不同意列入惯例清单。77国集团和D组虽不愿删去，但为了尽早达成协议，通过守则草案，不得不作出让步，同意目前暂时删掉，但要留下脚注，要求在将来的审查会议上重新来评价这几条的价值，从而最后确定是否删掉。

在前14条惯例中，目前存有分歧的主要是第10条，即出口限制问题。主要焦点是：77国集团认为对技术受方实行种种妨碍其出口的限制都不应采取。B组国家则认为一切出口限制都是合理的，除非技术供方严重地影响了受方的出口或者利用其控制的市场达到了滥用的程度时，才是不合理的。中国代表团基本同意77国集团的立场。但补充了一条例外情况，即技术供方已取得工业产权保护，或者已授予独占许可证的地区除外。这一立场得到了其他各集团的赞同。但后来B组国家又在主席案文中塞进“已保留”的措辞，这就不仅把授予独占许可证的地区，而且把将来可能授予独占许可证的国家也列为限制出口地区。B组的用意显然是想要维护其独占地位，达到垄断国际市场的目的。最后，B组也承认“已保留”几个字不妥，但仍坚持在这一惯例中要考虑供方一定的保留，同意另寻措辞来解决这一问题。目前此问题仍未最后解决。

（三）适用法律和争端的解决问题

本章所包含的问题有两个：第一，技术转让合同的法律适用问题；第二，关于解决争端的方法，主要指调解和仲裁的方法。

西方国家倚仗自己具有较完备的保护本国利益的立法，因而强烈主张“自由选择适用法律”，与此相关的还有“自由选择仲裁”及“自由选择仲裁庭”。而已经立法的发展中国家，特别是拉丁美洲国家，则坚持由技术受方国家的法律来管辖，尤其是在与国家主权和公共政策有关事项上，以维护其国家主权和利益。此外，许多尚未立法的非洲国家则希望由“公共政策”来管制技术转让交易。这种态度一直遭到西方国家的反对，在其他发展中国家也得不到赞同。所以，主要冲突是在77国集团与B组之间。

从目前情况来看，在关于调解和仲裁各条款方面，各方对会议主席在第六届会议期间提出的案文已有比较一致的意见。该案文指出：(1)技术交易当事各方应通过直接谈判或诉诸调解程序，以友好方式设法解决它们之间在交易方面可能发生的争端或分歧；(2)在可以根据当事各方的有关法律对争端进行仲裁时，当事各方经一致同意，可诉诸仲裁以解决技术转让交易引起的争端；(3)应鼓励当事各方使用国际上承认的仲裁规则，例如联合国国际贸易法委员会仲裁规则；(4)各国应按照其本国法规和它们已加入的有关国际协定，承认和执行仲裁裁决。但是，在法律选择条款方面，各区域集团仍存在着严重分歧。许多发展中国家认为,接受当事方的选择,实际上是接受强者的选择。后者总会强加一些对它最为有利的条款。看来,要想在法律选择适用条款上达成妥协,关键在于解决如何在权利与权限,即当事人各方自由选择法律的权利与国家有关法律的强制性规定的约束力之间取得应有的平衡的问题。目前,整个第9章都处于“尚在审议”阶段。在守则各章中,它是目前唯一未能编成案文的章次。

上述种种分歧长期悬而未决,对此广大发展中国家深感失望,它们指责代表西方发达国家的B组缺乏政治诚意,要求它们重新审查自己对整个守则及其悬而未决问题的立场。B组则辩解说:这是谈判中的正常现象,达成的协议越多,后面剩下的问题就越难;并以守则不是一个有约束力的条约来为自己的立场辩护。毫无疑问,77国集团和B组在上述问题上的分歧根源于双方在技术转让问题上根本看法的不同。因此,要想在双方间调和,并不是件轻而易举的事。不过,从整个发展趋势看,改革旧的国际经济秩序,提倡南北对话,乃是当今国际社会中一股不可抗拒的潮流;制定一套统一的关于国际技术转让的法律制度,是保证技术转让交易不断发展、扩大的客观需要。谈判各方若能清楚地认识到这些,互谅互让,进行更充分的磋商,最终达成一致,使守则顺利通过的可能性是完全存在的。如果真是这样,则正如一些发展中国家所憧憬的,国际技术贸易关系将进入新的阶段。守则必将在促进整个国际技术贸易,加速全人类的进步和发展方面,发挥出更重要的作用。

国际贸易管理法*

第一节　国际贸易管理法概说

一、国际贸易管理法的概念

完整意义上的国际贸易关系不仅包括平等的贸易商之间的交易关系,也包括政府对平等贸易商之间的交易进行管理和管制(包括鼓励、许可、限制、禁止、监督、奖励和促进等一系列活动)的关系。这后一种关系就是国际贸易管理(trade regulation)关系。国际贸易管理法则是调整这种国际贸易管理关系的法律规范的总和。

晚近全球经济一体化的飞速发展不仅使得国际贸易交易法得到进一步发展和统一化,更使国际贸易管理法得到了突飞猛进的发展。以世界贸易组织为首的世界多边贸易体制的建立,不仅标志着国际贸易法迈进了“世界贸易法”的新时代,也标志着整个国际经济法律体系乃至整个国际法律体系取得了重大突破。相应地,国际贸易管理法在国际经济法中的地位也日见彰显。

二、国际贸易管理法的体系

国际贸易管理法既包括有关贸易管理的国际法律规范,也包括相应的国内法律规范。国际贸易管理法就是有关贸易管理的国际与国内法律规范的总和。

从国内法上看,无论是在大陆法系国家还是在英美法系国家,其对外贸易管理法大都采用成文法或以成文法为基础。从法律渊源上看,各国一般都由立法机关制定对外贸易管理的基本法,及由政府或政府有关部门制定大量的管理对外贸易的法规、规章、决议、命令、公告。以美国为例,据统计,美国有关安全、环境保

---

* 本书原载陈安主编:《国际经济法》(第2版),第6章,法律出版社2007年版。

护、技术标准等一系列法规条文多达2000多个。在中国,则形成了以《对外贸易法》为龙头的外贸管理法律体系。

从国际法上看,各国在制定国内立法的同时,还同其他国家签订双边、区域性和多边贸易条约(如《世界贸易组织协定》《北美自由贸易协定》等),使本国的对外贸易管理立法与国际贸易条约的规则相互衔接、协调一致,形成了一个有机的整体。其中,《世界贸易组织协定》是国际贸易管理法律体系的核心。

本章将从中国的角度出发,扼要介绍中国外贸管理法、反倾销与反补贴法以及世界贸易组织的法律体系。

第二节　我国对外贸易管理基本制度

一、对外贸易体制改革与对外贸易管理立法

改革开放以来,我国外贸体制发生了深刻的变化。与外贸体制改革相适应,我国外贸法制建设也取得了突破性的进展。1994年5月12日通过,同年7月1日开始施行的《中华人民共和国对外贸易法》(以下简称"外贸法"或《对外贸易法》)是我国第一部比较全面、比较系统的对外贸易管理法。

在我国外贸管理法律体系中,《对外贸易法》居于核心地位,它是我国外贸管理方面的基本法,是我国45年外贸实践与国际贸易通行规则相结合的产物。《对外贸易法》实施的近10年里,中国对外贸易发展的状况和外部环境都发生了根本性的变化。外贸进出口额由1994年的2366亿美元,增加到2003年的8512亿美元,出口在全球的位次由1994年的第11位上升到2003年的第4位。[1] 中国真正成为对世界贸易有重大影响的贸易大国。贸易地位的变化对外贸法律提出了新的要求。2002年12月中国加入了世界贸易组织,根据世界贸易组织的规则享有权利、承担义务。根据世界贸易组织规则,中国应使其国内相关制度与世界贸易组织的要求相一致,这就要求对《对外贸易法》进行必要的修订,将中国根据世界贸易组织规则享有的权利和承担的义务转化到国内法中。其他国家的外贸制度也为中国完善《对外贸易法》提供了借鉴。根据这些情况,中国立法机关于2004年4月对《对外贸易法》进行了修订,使其更适应外贸发展和法律建设的需要。修订后的《对外贸易法》于2004年7月1日起实施。

这次《对外贸易法》的修订,一方面要落实中国根据世界贸易组织规则享有

---

〔1〕 郭寿康、韩立余:《国际贸易法》(第2版),中国人民大学出版社2005年版,第385页。

的权利和义务,另一方面要体现和保障中国可持续发展的需要。因而在修订的具体指导思想上,为对外开拓市场、对内保护国内产业利益提供法律机制,同时在中国外贸法律制度与世界贸易组织规则的要求相一致的前提下,借鉴其他国家的行之有效的外贸制度,制定相应的贸易规则,最终建立单边措施与多边措施相协调以及开拓、促进与防御相统一的外贸法律制度。[2]

这次修订,对原《对外贸易法》进行了增删、完善:删除了与《对外贸易法》的管理职能没有必要联系的条款,如外贸经营者应诚实信用等;增加了原《对外贸易法》没有调整的内容,如与对外贸易有关的知识产权、对外贸易中的垄断、对外贸易调查等;完善了原有的规定,如对外贸易经营者的资格、禁止或限制进出口的依据以及外贸救济制度等。修订后的《对外贸易法》,是一个结构比较合理、内容相对完善的法律,同时又为根据《对外贸易法》制定实施条例或细则提供了指导和依据。[3]

修订后的《对外贸易法》共 11 章 70 条。它规定了我国对外贸易基本制度与基本原则,确立了我国处理外贸关系的基本准则;明确了外贸经营主体的资格条件及其权利义务;规定了国家管理各类贸易,包括货物、技术进出口、国际服务贸易及与对外贸易有关的知识产权保护的基本方针、政策;规定了国家对外贸的促进措施、对外贸秩序的管理措施、对外贸易调查、对外贸易救济措施;最后,对违反外贸法的法律责任也作了明确规定。[4]

《对外贸易法》与 20 世纪 80 年代以来我国有关部门颁布、施行的一系列法律、法规,如《外汇管理法》《海关法》等,一同形成我国比较完整的外贸管理法律制度。

二、我国对外贸易法所确立的基本原则

根据《对外贸易法》,我国对外贸易法的基本原则大致可归纳为三项,即统一原则、平等互利原则和公平自由原则。三原则各有侧重,前者是就外贸制度而言,次者是就外贸关系而言,后者则是针对外贸秩序而设的。

(一)统一原则

《对外贸易法》第 4 条明确规定:"国家实行统一的对外贸易制度。"换言之,在外贸制度方面,我国要坚持统一原则。这里的"统一"主要指三个层次的制度的统一,即外贸方针、政策的统一,外贸法律法规的统一与外贸管理与促进措施的

---

〔2〕 郭寿康、韩立余:《国际贸易法》(第 2 版),中国人民大学出版社 2005 年版,第 385 页。
〔3〕 同上。
〔4〕 详见《对外贸易法》(2004 年 7 月 1 日开始施行)有关条款。

统一。统一的外贸制度不仅是国家整体经济利益的需要,也是承担国际贸易义务进而享受国际贸易权利的前提,它不是某个阶段的权宜之计,而是一项根本的制度与原则性的指针。

(二)平等互利原则

《对外贸易法》第5条规定:"中华人民共和国根据平等互利的原则,促进和发展同其他国家和地区的贸易关系。"由此确定了我国外贸关系上的一项基本原则,即平等互利原则。

平等互利原则所衍生出来的,还有对等互惠原则,这也是我国处理贸易关系的重要原则依据。我国《对外贸易法》第6条规定,中国在对外贸易方面根据其所缔结或参加的国际条约、协定,给予其他缔约方、参加方或根据互惠、对等原则给予对方最惠国待遇、国民待遇;第7条进而规定,任何国家或地区在贸易方面对中国采取歧视性的禁止、限制或者其他类似措施的,中国可以根据实际情况采取相应的措施。这些规定可以说是平等互利与对等互惠原则的具体体现。

(三)公平自由原则

《对外贸易法》第4条明确规定,国家依法维护公平、自由的对外贸易秩序。由此确立了我国外贸秩序方面的基本原则,即公平自由原则。

为建立公平自由的外贸秩序,《对外贸易法》第6章作了专门规定,其内容大体可分对内与对外两大方面。

就对内而言,《对外贸易法》第34条规定了外贸经营者必须遵守的若干重要行为准则。该条规定:"在对外贸易活动中,不得有下列行为:(一)伪造、变造进出口货物原产地标记,伪造、变造或者买卖进出口货物原产地证书、进出口许可证、进出口配额证明或者其他进出口证明文件;(二)骗取出口退税;(三)走私;(四)逃避法律、行政法规规定的认证、检验、检疫;(五)违反法律、行政法规规定的其他行为。"不仅如此,对于违反上述规定者,《对外贸易法》第10章还规定了其相应的法律责任,严重者得依照《刑法》有关规定处罚。足见其力度是很大的。就对外而言,《对外贸易法》主要针对外国的倾销、补贴等不正当竞争行为作出了相应规定。如《对外贸易法》第41条、第42条是关于反倾销的规定;第43条是关于反补贴的规定;第44条还对"保障措施"作了规定。

反倾销、反补贴与保障措施都是《世界贸易组织协定》允许的贸易保护措施。《对外贸易法》的上述有关规定与世贸组织的规则是一致的。

三、对外贸易经营者制度

(一)对外贸易经营者的概念

对外贸易经营者是我国参与国际贸易市场活动的经营主体。我国《对外贸易法》第 8 条规定:“本法所称对外贸易经营者,是指依法办理工商登记或者其他执业手续,依照本法和其他有关法律、行政法规的规定从事对外贸易经营活动的法人、其他组织或者个人。”

(二)对外贸易经营者

1.货物与技术进出口经营者

我国《对外贸易法》第 9 条规定:“从事货物进出口与技术进出口的对外贸易经营者,应当向国务院对外贸易主管部门或者其委托的机构办理备案登记;但是,法律、行政法规和国务院对外贸易主管部门规定不需要备案登记的除外。备案登记的具体办法由国务院对外贸易主管部门规定。对外贸易经营者未按照规定办理备案登记的,海关不予办理进出口货物的报关验放手续。”这一条实质上确立了我国技术与货物进出口经营资格的登记制度。至于外商投资企业,根据《中外合资经营企业法》《中外合作经营企业法》《外资企业法》等法律及其他有关法规,它们在设立时,即已取得企业自用的非生产物品以及生产所需的有关物资的进口权和企业生产的产品的出口权,而无须办理上述登记。

根据 2004 年 7 月 1 日起施行的《对外贸易经营者备案登记办法》第 3 条、第 4 条的规定,商务部是全国对外贸易经营者备案登记工作的主管部门。对外贸易经营者备案登记工作实行全国联网和属地化管理。

此外,依据《对外贸易法》第 11 条的规定,国家可以对部分货物的进出口实行国营贸易管理。实行国营贸易管理货物的进出口业务只能由经授权的企业经营;但是,国家允许部分数量的国营贸易管理货物的进出口业务由非授权企业经营的除外。实行国营贸易管理的货物和经授权经营企业的目录,由国务院对外贸易主管部门会同国务院其他有关部门确定、调整并公布。

2.对外服务贸易的经营者

我国《对外贸易法》第 10 条规定:“从事国际服务贸易,应当遵守本法和其他有关法律、行政法规的规定。从事对外工程承包或者对外劳务合作的单位,应当具备相应的资质或者资格。具体办法由国务院规定。”在我国,国际服务贸易涉及十几个行业。而我国实行的是各个部门分别管理的体制,各个行业都制定了各自不同的行业管理的法律、行政法规,其办法各不相同,一时尚难统一。因此,我国外贸法要求具体办法由国务院规定。

对外贸易经营者应当按照国务院对外贸易主管部门或者国务院其他有关部门依法作出的规定,向有关部门提交与其对外贸易经营活动有关的文件及资料。有关部门应当为提供者保守商业秘密。

(三)对外贸易代理制

1. 外贸代理的概念

我国的外贸代理是指对外贸易经营者接受他人的委托,在其对外贸易经营范围内代为办理所委托的对外贸易业务。

外贸代理有直接代理和间接代理两种。直接代理就是对外贸易经营者根据委托合同的规定,以委托人的名义,对外谈判签订合同,代为办理委托人的对外贸易业务。间接代理就是对外贸易经营者根据委托合同的规定,以自己的名义,对外谈判签订合同,代委托人办理其对外贸易业务。不管是直接代理还是间接代理,其受托人都必须是对外贸易经营者。目前,直接代理主要依据《民法通则》办理;间接代理则只能依据外经贸部(现商务部)1991 年颁布的《关于对外贸易代理制的暂行规定》(以下简称《暂行规定》)办理。显然,间接代理是我国外贸代理的主要形式。

2. 外贸代理的委托合同

《暂行规定》要求,外贸代理中的当事人双方依照《对外贸易法》的规定,应当签订委托合同。委托合同中应主要规定:委托人的名称、住址和受托人的名称、住址;委托的方式、委托的事项;费用和酬金;双方的权利和义务;合同的变更、终止和解除;违约责任;争议的解决方式;其他双方约定的事项。

外贸代理的委托合同一经签订即具有法律效力,任何一方当事人不能擅自违反合同的约定,否则应承担违约责任。如果双方在履约过程中发生争议,当事人可以通过协商或调解解决;不愿协商或调解解决的,可以依据委托合同中规定的仲裁条款或事后达成的书面仲裁协议向规定的仲裁机构申请仲裁;委托合同中没有仲裁条款且事后又未达成书面仲裁协议的,当事人可以向人民法院起诉,以诉讼方式解决。

四、货物进出口的管理制度

我国对货物的进出口实行统一的管理制度。《对外贸易法》把货物分为自由进出口的货物、限制进出口的货物与禁止进出口的货物。

1. 自由进出口货物

作为一般原则,国家准许货物的自由进出口。国务院对外贸易主管部门基于检测进出口情况的需要,可以对部分自由进出口的货物实行进出口自动许可并公布其目录。

实行自动许可的进出口货物,收货人、发货人在办理海关报关手续前提出自动许可申请的,国务院对外贸易主管部门或者其委托的机构应当予以许可;未办理自动许可手续的,海关不予放行。

2. 限制进出口和禁止进出口的货物作为货物自由进出口的例外,《对外贸易法》第16、17条规定,国家基于下列原因,可以限制或者禁止有关货物、技术的进口或者出口:(1)为维护国家安全、社会公共利益或者公共道德,需要限制或者禁止进口或者出口的;(2)为保护人的健康或者安全,保护动物、植物的生命或者健康,保护环境,需要限制或者禁止进口或者出口的;(3)为实施与黄金或者白银进出口有关的措施,需要限制或者禁止进口或者出口的;(4)国内供应短缺或者为有效保护可能用竭的自然资源,需要限制或者禁止出口的;(5)输往国家或者地区的市场容量有限,需要限制出口的;(6)出口经营秩序出现严重混乱,需要限制出口的;(7)为建立或者加快建立国内特定产业,需要限制进口的;(8)对任何形式的农业、牧业、渔业产品有必要限制进口的;(9)为保障国家国际金融地位和国际收支平衡,需要限制进口的;(10)依照法律、行政法规的规定,其他需要限制或者禁止进口或者出口的;(11)根据我国缔结或者参加的国际条约、协定的规定,其他需要限制或者禁止进口或者出口的;(12)国家对与裂变、聚变物质或者衍生此类物质的物质有关的货物、技术进出口,以及与武器、弹药或者其他军用物资有关的进出口,可以采取任何必要的措施,维护国家安全;(13)在战时或者为维护国际和平与安全,国家在货物、技术进出口方面可以采取任何必要的措施。

国家对限制和禁止进出口的货物实行目录管理和配额、许可证管理。此外,国家实行统一的商品合格评定制度,对进出口商品进行认证、检验、检疫,并对进出口货物进行原产地管理。

禁止进出口的货物目录由商务部会同国务院有关部门制定、调整并公布。经国务院批准,可以在《对外贸易法》规定的范围内,临时决定限制或者禁止目录以外的特定货物的进口或者出口。属于禁止进出口的货物不得进出口。进出口属于禁止进出口的货物的,由海关依照有关法律、行政法规的规定处理、处罚;构成犯罪的,依法追究刑事责任。

目前从2002年开始公布的禁止进口货物从第一批到第五批,禁止出口货物第一批和第二批,涉及的货物有保护生态环境的、我国参加国际条约履行的承诺、有关人身安全、生产安全和环境保护的商品等。

五、技术进出口的统一管理制度

技术进出口指通过贸易、投资或者经济合作的方式越境转移技术的行为,包括专利权转让、专利申请转让、专利实施许可、技术秘密转让、技术服务和其他方式的技术转移。国家对技术进出口实行统一的管理制度。

除法律、行政法规另有规定外，国家准许技术自由进出口。国家鼓励先进、适用的技术进口，鼓励成熟的产业化技术出口。与货物的进出口相同，我国也把技术分为自由进出口的技术，限制进出口的技术和禁止进出口的技术。

对于自由进出口的技术实行合同登记管理。合同自依法成立时生效，不以登记为合同生效的条件。合同的主要内容发生变更的，应重新办理登记手续。

对禁止、限制进口或出口的技术，通过技术目录管理。对限制进出口的技术，实施许可证管理。技术进出口合同，自技术进出口许可证颁发之日起生效。经许可的技术进出口合同，合同的主要内容发生变更的，应当重新办理许可手续。

我国目前限制进口技术目录主要有《中国禁止进口限制进口技术目录》。限制进口技术（第一批）共16项，涉及生物、化工、石油炼制、石油化工、生物化工技术领域。国家对限制进口的技术实行许可证管理，凡进口列入《中国禁止进口限制进口技术目录》中限制进口技术的，应履行进口许可手续。限制进口技术的进口许可由商务部管理。

我国目前限制出口技术目录主要有《中国禁止出口限制出口技术目录》和《敏感物项和技术出口许可证管理目录》。国家对列入《中国禁止出口限制出口技术目录》中的限制出口技术及相关产品实行许可证管理，凡出口国家限制出口技术及相关产品的，应当按规定履行出口许可手续。限制出口技术的出口许可由商务部会同科学技术部管理。依据国家有关出口管制法规，商务部会同海关总署联合发布了《敏感物项和技术出口许可证管理目录》。

目前，禁止进出口技术的目录时2002年颁布的《中国禁止出口限制出口技术目录》。该目录公布了第一批禁止进口技术，共25项，涉及钢铁冶金、有色金属冶金、化工、石油炼制、石油化工、消防、电工、轻工、印刷、医药、建筑材料生产技术领域。禁止出口部分的技术涉及测绘技术、地质技术、药品生产技术、农业技术等包括核技术在内的25个技术领域的31项技术。

进出口属于禁止进出口的技术的，依照有关法律、行政法规的规定处理、处罚；法律、行政法规没有规定的，由商务部责令改正，没收违法所得，并处罚款；构成犯罪的，依法追究刑事责任。

六、与对外贸易有关的知识产权保护

传统意义上的知识产权，其适用范围仅限于国内，对于在境外发生的侵犯本国知识产权的情况缺乏有效的救济。[5]《对外贸易法》专门处理对外贸易中知识

〔5〕 郭寿康、韩立余：《国际贸易法》（第2版），中国人民大学出版社2005年版，第386页。

产权问题的法律法规。它针对对外贸易中知识产权方面可能出现的问题,明确了基于对外贸易中我国在 TRIPS 项下享有的权利,对相应行为可以采取的措施及制裁的规定,其目的在于维护对外贸易秩序和社会公共利益。《对外贸易法》第 5 章是专门关于"与对外贸易有关的知识产权的保护"的规定。所谓"与对外贸易有关的知识产权的保护"是指针对在货物贸易、技术贸易和服务贸易中侵犯知识产权或者滥用知识产权专有专利,或者对知识产权保护给予歧视性待遇等损害我国对外贸易利益的行为,采取符合 WTO 规则的贸易保护措施。该章包括第 29 条、第 30 条和第 31 条。[6]

根据《对外贸易法》的规定,国家依照有关知识产权的法律、行政法规,保护与对外贸易有关的知识产权保护。进口货物侵犯知识产权,并危害对外贸易秩序的,国务院对外贸易主管部门可以采取在一定期限内禁止侵权人生产、销售的有关货物进口等措施。

知识产权权利人有阻止被许可人对许可合同中的知识产权的有效性提出质疑、进行强制性"一揽子"许可、在许可合同中规定排他性返授条件等行为之一,并危害对外贸易公平竞争秩序的,国务院对外贸易主管部门可以采取必要的措施消除危害。

其他国家或者地区在知识产权保护方面未给予中华人民共和国的法人、其他组织或者个人国民待遇,或者不能对来源于中华人民共和国的货物、技术或者服务提供充分有效的知识产权保护的,国务院对外贸易主管部门可以依照《对外贸易法》和其他有关法律、行政法规的规定,并根据中华人民共和国缔结或者参加的国际条约、协定,对与该国家或者该地区的贸易采取必要的措施。

七、对外贸易秩序

对外贸易秩序是指对外贸易经营者依照国家有关的法律、法规和规章制度展开经营活动,并做到有公平合理竞争而形成的有条理、不混乱的外贸经营局面与态势。[7]

《对外贸易法》第六章专门对对外贸易秩序进行了规定。其主要包括三部分内容。第一部分,规定了在维护对外贸易秩序中所禁止的以下行为:(1)违反有关反垄断的法律、行政法规的规定实施垄断行为;(2)以不正当的低价销售商品、串通投标、发布虚假广告、进行商业贿赂等不正当竞争行为;(3)伪造、变造进出口货物原产地标记,伪造、变造或者买卖进出口货物原产地证书、进出口许可证、进出口配额证明或者其他进出口证明文件;(4)骗取出口退税;(5)走私;(6)逃避

[6] 肖兵、何鹰:《国际经济法学》,科学出版社 2004 年版,第 181 页。
[7] 黄东黎、王振民:《中华人民共和国对外贸易法:条文精释及国际规则》,法律出版社 2004 年版,第 237 页。

法律、行政法规规定的认证、检验、检疫；(7)违反法律、行政法规规定的其他行为。第二部分，对外贸易经营者在对外贸易经营活动中，应当遵守国家有关外汇管理的规定。第三部分，授权国务院对外贸易主管部门向社会公布违反上述规定，危害对外贸易秩序的对外贸易经营者。

八、对外贸易调查

"对外贸易调查"一章为对外贸易主管机关严格执法提供了法律依据和执法手段，对相关利害关系方的利益提供了充分的保护。

为了维护对外贸易秩序，国务院对外贸易主管部门可以自行或者会同国务院其他有关部门，依照法律、行政法规的规定对下列事项进行调查：(1)货物进出口、技术进出口、国际服务贸易对国内产业及其竞争力的影响；(2)有关国家或者地区的贸易壁垒；(3)为确定是否应当依法采取反倾销、反补贴或者保障措施等对外贸易救济措施，需要调查的事项；(4)规避对外贸易救济措施的行为；(5)对外贸易中有关国家安全利益的事项；(6)其他国家针对中国的歧视性措施，侵犯知识产权、滥用知识产权或者未能对中国知识产权提供充分、有效的保护的事项；(7)其他影响对外贸易秩序，需要调查的事项。

第三节　反倾销法与反补贴法

倾销与补贴是两种常见的不公平贸易做法。相应地，反倾销与反补贴则是各国常用的"公平"贸易措施。然而，这两种措施在实践中又极易演变为贸易保护措施。近40年来，关税及贸易总协定以及世界贸易组织，为建立规范、统一、公平的国际反倾销、反补贴规则作出了不懈的努力。1997年，我国也建立了自己的反倾销与反补贴机制。

一、反倾销法

(一)倾销与反倾销法

20世纪初，雅各布·维勒(J. Viner)在其代表作《倾销：国际贸易中的问题》中，给倾销下了这样的定义：倾销指"同一商品在不同国家市场上以不同的价格销售"。他用边际成本[8]的概念解释倾销的三种形态。

---

〔8〕 边际成本(marginal cost)是指在原生产量的基础上，再增产1个单位产量时所增加的成本支出。参见《经济大辞典》(工业经济卷)，上海辞书出版社1983年版，第183页。

1. 偶发性倾销(sporadic dumping)。偶发性倾销边际成本等于零,是偶然清除存货的行为。倾销者可以不计成本将剩余品在国外市场廉价销售。这种销售为时甚短,而且,销售者没有掠夺国外市场的动机。

2. 间歇性倾销(intermittent dumping)。间歇性倾销边际成本高于边际收益。[9] 这类倾销是亏本的销售,一般说来,销售者存有掠夺他国市场甚至加以垄断的目的,故又称"掠夺性倾销"(predatory dumping)。销售者先以低于国内价格,甚至以低于成本的价格销售,在排除所有或大部分竞争者之后再提高价格,以享受垄断利润。

3. 长期性倾销(continuous dumping)。长期性倾销边际成本常等于或小于边际收益。当出口国厂商认为大量生产可以最大限度降低成本时,就会使用持续倾销的办法。过量生产会给出口国国内价格造成压力。出口国国内厂商希望采用在国外长期倾销的办法,保持其国内价格结构。只要买方支付的平均价格超过生产平均成本,企业的总销售就能保证持续不断地获得利润。如果企业打算把倾销的益处转给国内买主,那么,他就可以降低国内市场价格。但是,实际上企业都把在国外倾销所得的利润留给企业本身。政府或其他机构提供的出口补贴,也是造成长期性倾销的重要原因。

值得一提的是,以上分类所涉及的三种倾销均属于直接倾销,而近年来间接倾销与社会倾销已引起了国际社会的普遍关注。

间接倾销(indirect dumping),通常也指第三国倾销,是指 A 国的产品倾销至 B 国,再由 B 国销往 C 国,并对 C 国的有关产业造成损害。在这种情况下,虽然 B 国的出口商并无实施实际倾销行为,但 C 国相同产品生产商可依反倾销法申请对 B 国的生产商和出口商进行反倾销调查;也可请求 B 国对 A 国的产品采取反倾销措施。至于 B 国当局是否会根据 C 国的请求,对 A 国的倾销实施反倾销措施,则往往取决于 B 国和 C 国的政治与贸易关系。

社会倾销(social dumping),最初仅仅是指出口利用犯人廉价生产的产品,现在已扩大到对生产成本计算时必须考虑的其他因素。第二世界国家由于廉价劳动力和生产环境的低标准等种种因素,使其出口商品不单在国际市场价格偏低,在国内市场上的价格也偏低,因此不能按现有的法律定义确定其倾销。但由于这些廉价出口商品无疑对发达进口国的市场带来冲击,也可能损害其国内同类行

---

〔9〕 边际收益(marginal cost),指增售 1 个单位商品时所增的收益,如果增售这 1 单位商品得到的边际收益,小于增产这 1 单位商品的边际成本,就不合算;反之,则可继续增售,直到边际成本与边际收益相等为止。边际成本等于边际收益,是资本主义企业决定产量规模、价格等的重要依据。参见《经济大辞典》(工业经济卷),上海辞书出版社 1983 年版,第 183 页。

业，因此近年来，特别是欧盟的贸易保护主义者，一直在呼吁制止这种所谓的社会倾销。[10]

从反倾销立法的历史看，最初的国内立法旨在针对掠夺性倾销。

第二次世界大战结束后，由于西欧经济的复苏，国际竞争迅速加剧，倾销的作用大大增强，反倾销作为贸易保护措施的作用也有发展的趋势。于是，在1947年缔结《关税及贸易总协定》（以下简称《总协定》或GATT1947）时，缔约国就倾销与反倾销问题达成协定，形成了《关税及贸易总协定》第6条。第6条第1款规定："各缔约国确认，一国产品以低于该产品的正常价格销往另一国，如果它对该缔约国领土内建立的产业造成重大损害，或有重大损害的威胁，或严重阻碍某一国内产业的建立，应认为构成倾销。"

20世纪50年代末60年代初，许多西方国家以《关税及贸易总协定》第6条为模式，纷纷修订各自的反倾销法。60年代，反倾销法的作用日益增强，出现反倾销行动的贸易保护主义倾向。为此，肯尼迪回合多边贸易谈判，把如何最有效地控制国家滥用反倾销措施作为重要议题。25个国家和组织于1967年达成《关于实施关税及贸易总协定第6条的协议》，也即《关税及贸易总协定反倾销守则》（以下简称《总协定反倾销守则》）。制定该守则的目的是阐明总协定第6条的概念，填补第6条在反倾销调查程序上的欠缺，使所有的总协定成员国更规范地遵循第6条的规定。

《总协定反倾销守则》于1968年7月1日起生效，在1979年东京回合贸易谈判中又进行了修改，主要变化是，原则上规定在确定发展中国家的正常价格时，对发展中国家的特殊经济状况给予特殊的考虑。如果说，《总协定》第6条标志着反倾销法国际统一化的开始，那么，《总协定反倾销守则》则把反倾销法国际统一化进程迅速推向前进。

20世纪80年代以来，国际倾销与反倾销有增无减，尤其是反倾销措施频繁使用，保护色彩日显突出。为确保GATT目标的实现，乌拉圭回合仍将反倾销列为重要议题之一，并最终达成了《实施1994年关税及贸易总协定第6条的协定》（以下简称《反倾销协定》）。与原有守则相比，WTO的新协定更加系统与详细。相应地，欧盟与美国等许多国家的反倾销法也作了修改，使之与WTO《反倾销协定》相一致。

（二）总协定与世贸组织的反倾销规则

在东京回合多边贸易谈判中修订的《总协定反倾销守则》有三个部分，共16

---

〔10〕 姜圣复：《WTO法律制度：国际经济法学的新发展》，中华工商联合出版社2002年版，第405～406页。

条，于1980年1月1日起生效。1993年12月15日，总协定乌拉圭回合谈判结束。

在1994年4月摩洛哥马拉喀什会议上签署的乌拉圭回合《最后文件》包括26个协定，其中包括新的《反倾销协定》。新协定在原守则基础上，增加了以低于成本的价格出口、反规避措施等内容。这里对该协定的基本内容略作介绍。

1. 倾销的确定

根据前述《GATT1947》第6条第1款关于倾销的规定，倾销的成立有两个主要条件，一是有以低于正常价格出口的销售行为，二是对进口国某一产业造成实质损害。该规定较为笼统，又因为第6条属于《总协定》第二部分，约束力不强，因此，25个国家和组织于1967年达成协议，形成《总协定反倾销守则》，将《总协定》第6条关于倾销的定义分为倾销的确定和损害的确定两部分。

倾销的确定就是比较出口价格与正常价格之差额，出口价格低于正常价格的数额为倾销差额(margin of dumping)。

(1)正常价格

正常价格是指同类产品的正常价格。所谓"同类产品"应当是完全相同的产品，在各方面都和被控倾销的产品相同。在缺乏这种产品加以比较时，可采用另一种产品，这种产品和被控倾销的产品虽然在各方面不尽相同，但是在特征上十分相似。正常价格的确定有三个标准。

①出口国国内销售价格

出口国国内销售价格是指被控倾销的产品或与其相似的产品于调查期间，在出口国国内市场上实际支付或约定支付的价格。这种价格应当是在正常贸易过程中形成的，具有一定的交易量。

出口国国内销售价格是应当被首先选用的正常价格标准。《总协定》第6条在规定正常价格选用标准的同时，又在第6条附加注释中规定，在从"完全或实质上完全垄断其贸易，所有价格均由国家确定"的国家进口的情况下，和该国的国内价格作严格比较并不总是恰如其分的。但是，《总协定》第6条以及后来的《总协定反倾销守则》都没有对来自所谓"中央计划经济"国家的倾销作出特别规定，没有提出价格比较的选择办法，而留给各缔约国自行处理。这一授权为西方国家对社会主义国家的贸易歧视行为，提供了重要的法律依据。所谓"代用国"(surrogate country)在很大程度上是这一授权的产物。

②对第三国的出口价格

如果被控倾销的产品或与其相似的产品，在出口国没有销售或销售量太小，以致不能以国内销售价格作为正常价格，进口国可以选用出口国向第三国出口价格作为正常价格。

第三国的选择标准是:第一,向该第三国和向进口国出口的产品相司或最相似;第二,该第三国是出口国出口量最多的国家;第三,对该第三国和对进口国销售做法相似。

选用对第三国的出口价格作为正常价格,出口国对第三国的出口必须具有一定量的规模。

③推定价格(constructed value)

在没有国内销售价格作为正常价格标准时,可以选用对第三国的出口价格或推定价格(也称结构价格、构成价格)。所谓推定价格是指通过对被控倾销产品的生产成本加以估算,加上一定的管理和销售等费用以及合理的利润,从而推定出来的价格。所加利润不得超过原产地国国内市场上销售同类产品正常得到的利润。

(2)出口价格

出口价格一般指进口商实际支付或应支付的价格。如果没有出口价格,或反倾销机构担心,由于联合或进、出口商、第三方之间的协议,出口价格靠不住的情况下,出口价格可以以进口产品最初转售给独立的买方的价格为基础推定。

(3)价格调整为了在出口价格与正常价格间进行公平的比较,两种价格应以同一贸易标准,通常是以工厂交货价为标准并尽可能以同一时期的销售价格加以比较。在具体案件中,应当根据具体情况,对销售条件和状况的差异、征税的差异以及影响价格比较的其他差异作出适当的折让,因进口与转售而产生的关税、税捐花费等成本以及应计利润,也应当扣除。

(4)以低于成本的价格出口

美国首先在其《1974 年贸易法》中增加了低于成本销售规定,认为凡是价格低于平均总成本的销售都是不公平的竞争,属于不正常的贸易做法。乌拉圭回合新达成的《反倾销守则》认同了美国反倾销法的观点。该守则规定,当出口商在相当期间内以低于成本的价格销售,且数量可观,可以被认定为倾销,其正常价格按推定价格标准加以确定。

2. 损害的确定

只有在有关当局确定,倾销进口致使某一国内产业遭受实质损害或实质损害威胁,或严重阻碍某一国内产业的建立时,才可以作出损害裁决。损害的确定具体包括如下内容。

(1)国内产业的定义

国内产业(domestic industry)是指生产相似产品的全部生产商,或其产量占相似产品国内总产量大部分的生产商。但下列情况除外：

①当国内生产商与被控倾销产品的出口商或进口商有关，或他们本身就是被控倾销产品的进口商时，国内产业可以解释为其他的生产商。

②当进口国境内可能分成两个以上相互竞争的市场，其中任何一个市场的生产商在该市场内销售其全部或几乎全部有关产品，而且市场需求在很大程度上不是由境内其他市场的生产商提供的，如果倾销进口在这样一个独立的市场内集中销售，致使该市场内所有或几乎所有的生产商遭受损害，即使整个国内产业的大部分未受损害，也可以确定该市场内的产业遭受损害。

③当两个或更多的国家达到《总协定》第24条第8款第(1)项所指的一体化水平，使得区域经济具有单一和统一的市场特性，则整个一体化区域内的产业视为一般意义上的国内产业。

(2)损害的分类

①实质损害。国内产业已经实际上遭受相当程度的损害。

②实质损害威胁。损害威胁的确定应根据事实，而不能仅仅根据主张、推测或极小的可能性加以判断。倾销造成实质损害情况的变化，必须是显然可以预见的，并且是迫近的。对因倾销进口造成损害威胁的案件，应特别谨慎地研究和决定反倾销措施的适用。

③实质阻碍某一国内产业建立。国内某一新产业的实际建立受到阻碍，如建造产业，安装设备后，由于倾销进口，致使新建产业无法正常投产。

(3)判断损害的因素

①被控倾销产品无论是进口的绝对数量，还是相对进口国生产和消费的相对数量有巨大增长。

②与进口国相似产品的价格相比，倾销进口产品的价格大幅度削价，或者倾销进口大幅度压低了进口国相似产品的价格或阻止该价格上涨。

③倾销进口产品对国内生产相似产品的生产商造成影响。对国内产业影响的审查应包括对关系到产业状况的所有相关经济因素和指数的评估，如产量、销售、市场份额、利润、生产能力、投资回收、设备利用率、现金流量、库存、就业、工资、发展、筹资或投资能力。进口国主管当局在裁决损害时拥有相当大的自由裁量权。

(4)倾销与损害间的因果关系

1967年《总协定反倾销守则》规定，只有在确定倾销进口是致使某一国内产业遭受实质损害或实质损害威胁的主要原因，或严重阻碍某一国内产业建立的主要原因时，才可以作出损害裁决。1979年《总协定反倾销守则》在损害的确定上受美国等西方国家的影响，既不强调“实质”(material)损害，又不强调倾销进口必须是造成损害的“主要”(major)原因。应当说,相对于1967年《总协定反倾销守则》而言,1979年的修订本在这方面是大大退步了,从而增加了反倾销措施的贸易保护作用。世贸组织的《反倾销协议》对此未作修改。

世贸组织《反倾销协议》第3条第(5)款只是笼统规定,必须证明倾销进口的后果正在造成该守则范围内的损害。其他因素与此同时也可能正在对该产业造成损害,但其他因素造成的损害不应归咎于倾销进口。

3. 反倾销调查

反倾销案件是一种行政处罚案件,一般由进口国级别较高的行政机构负责审理。

(1)申诉与立案调查反倾销程序通常由受损害产业或其代表以书面提出申请而开始。申诉人应提供倾销、损害以及二者间因果关系的足够证据。

当主管机构认为申诉人缺乏足够证据,无理由立案调查时,应立即拒绝申请,终止调查;当倾销幅度或倾销进口产品的数量或损害被确认为微不足道(deminir-nis)或者可忽略不计(negligible)时,也应立即终止调查。[11]

当主管机构认为有足够的证据可以立案调查时,应通知案件当事人,并应发布公告,在反倾销调查的整个过程中,所有各方均有充分的机会为自己的利益进行抗辩。为检查有关资料或为取得更详细的资料,主管机构可以依要求在其他国家进行现场调查,但应取得有关公司的同意,通知有关国家的政府并征得其同意。

(2)裁决

对反倾销案件的审理分为初步裁决和最终裁决两个阶段。如果初步裁决确定了倾销和损害,可以对被控倾销产品采取临时反倾销措施,包括征收临时反倾销税或要求进口商交纳保证金,其金额应与临时反倾销税相同,但不得高于估计的倾销幅度。如果能够明确正常税和估计的反倾销税,也可以采取“扣缴估价”(appraisement be withheld)这种临时措施。临时措施的实施期限一般不得超过4个月,应当事人要求并经主管机构同意,最长不得超过6个月。

主管机构对案件进一步审理后作出最终裁决。如果确定倾销和损害成立,则由主管机构决定按倾销幅度全部或部分征收反倾销税。反倾销税数额不得超过已确定的倾销差额。

初步裁决、最终裁决的结果,以及裁决的撤销均应发布公告。反倾销诉讼不应妨碍进口清关程序。除特殊情况外,反倾销调查应在开始后的1年内结束。

---

〔11〕 在反倾销协议中,所谓微不足道指依出口价百分比计倾销差额不到2%;可忽略不计则一般指从特定国家的倾销进口数量占进口成员国相同产品的总进口量不到3%。

(3)价格保证(price undertakings)

如果由出口商作出令人满意的调整价格,或停止以倾销价格向有关地区出口的自愿保证,而且主管机构认为倾销的损害后果可以消除,则诉讼可以中止或终结,而无需采取临时措施或征收反倾销税。

出口商的价格保证被接受后,如果出口商希望完成调查,那么,关于损害的调查仍应进行。如果确定不存在损害,价格保证应自动失效。

因价格保证中止或终结反倾销调查的情况,应以官方形式发出通知并予公布。

4. 反倾销税的期限

在一般情况下,只有在确定倾销和损害的最终裁定生效后,才对倾销进口产品征收反倾销税。在下列情况时,可以对实施临时措施之前 90 天内的倾销产品征收反倾销税:

(1)有造成损害的倾销历史,或者进口商知道或理应知道出口商倾销而且会因此造成损害;

(2)在相当短期间内大量倾销进口产品,突发造成损害,为惩戒这类恶性行为,有必要对倾销进口产品追溯征收反倾销税。

如果必要的话,反倾销税(法令)将持续有效,以便抵销造成损害的倾销。

在利害关系人有正当理由,并提供准确的资料证实有复审需要时,主管机构可以复审是否应当继续征收反倾销税。主管机构也可以自行决定是否进行这种复审。

(三)我国的反倾销法

《反倾销条例》于 2001 年制定实施,于 2004 年 3 月修订。该条例将《对外贸易法》中有关反倾销的规定具体化、明确化,确立了反倾销调查和反倾销措施的要求和程序。根据该条例,进口产品以倾销方式进入我国市场,并对已经建立的国内产业造成实质损害或者产生实质损害威胁,或者对建立国内产业造成实质阻碍的,我国应依照反倾销条例进行调查,采取反倾销措施。进口产品存在倾销、对国内产业造成损害、二者之间有因果关系,是采取反倾销措施的必要条件。[12]

1. 倾销与损害的确定

确定倾销与损害是采取反倾销措施的基础。《反倾销条例》在这个方面的规定与国际上各种反倾销法基本相同。

(1)倾销。指在正常贸易过程中进口产品以低于其正常价值的出口价格进

---

〔12〕 郭寿康、韩立余:《国际贸易法》,中国人民大学出版社 2005 年版,第 394 页。

入中华人民共和国市场。确定正常价值的标准有三个:①进口产品的同类产品,在出口国(地区)国内市场的正常贸易过程中有可比价格的,以该可比价格为正常价值。②进口产品的同类产品,在出口国(地区)国内市场的正常贸易过程中没有销售的,或者该同类产品的价格、数量不能据以进行公平比较的,以该同类产品出口到一个适当第三国(地区)的可比价格或者以该同类产品在原产国(地区)的生产成本加合理费用、利润,为正常价值。③进口产品不直接来自原产国(地区)的,按照前述①的规定确定正常价值;但是,在产品仅通过出口国(地区)转运、产品在出口国(地区)无生产或者在出口国(地区)中不存在可比价格等情形下,可以以该同类产品在原产国(地区)的价格为正常价值。确定出口价格的标准有两个。①进口产品有实际支付或者应当支付的价格的,以该价格为出口价格。②进口产品没有出口价格或者其价格不可靠的,以根据该进口产品首次转售给独立购买人的价格推定的价格为出口价格;但是,该进口产品未转售给独立购买人或者未按进口时的状态转售的,可以以商务部根据合理基础推定的价格为出口价格。

进口产品的出口价格低于其正常价值的差额为倾销幅度。对进口产品的出口价格和正常价值应当考虑影响价格的各种可比性研究,按照公平合理的方式进行比较,确定倾销幅度。倾销幅度的确定,应当将加权平均正常价值与全部可比出口交易的加权平均价格进行比较,或者将正常价值与出口价格在逐笔交易的基础上进行比较;出口价格在不同的购买人、地区、时期之间存在很大差异,按照前款规定的方法难以比较的,可以将加权平均正常价值与单一出口交易的价格进行比较。

(2)损害。损害包括倾销对已经建立的国内产业造成实质损害或者产生实质损害的威胁,或者对建立国内产业造成实质阻碍。在确定损害时,应当审查倾销产品的数量、价格、对进口国国内产业的影响,以及倾销产品出口国的生产能力、出口能力和库存。

《反倾销条例》在确定损害方面有以下特点:①国内产业指中华人民共和国国内相同或者类似产品的全部生产者,或者其总产量占国内相同或类似产品全部总产量的主要的部分的生产者。所谓"主要的部分"没有界定比例。香港、澳门回归后,国内产业的内涵已随之发生重要变化。②规定反倾销调查涉及两个以上国家的进口产品的,可以对有关进口产品的影响进行累积评估。累积评估可以增加确定损害的可能性。

2. 反倾销调查

国内产业或者代表国内产业的自然人、法人或者有关组织,可按规定向商务部提出反倾销的书面申请并附具必要的证据。商务部收到申请后，应当进行审查，并决定立案调查或者不立案调查。遇有特殊情形，商务部有充分证据认为存在倾销和损害以及二者之间有因果关系的，可以自行决定立案调查。商务部应当将立案调查或者不立案调查的决定予以公告，并通知申请人、已知的出口经营者和进口经营者、出口国政府(地区)以及其他有利害关系的组织、个人。

决定立案调查后，商务部可以采用问卷、抽样、听证会、现场核查等方式向利害关系方了解情况，进行调查。商务部应当为有关利害关系方提供陈述意见和论据的机会。商务部认为必要时，可以派出工作人员赴有关国家(地区)进行调查；但是，有关国家(地区)提出异议的除外。商务部根据调查结果，就倾销、损害和二者之间的因果关系是否成立作出初裁决定，并予以公告。初裁决定确定倾销、损害以及二者之间的因果关系成立的，商务部应当对倾销及倾销幅度、损害及损害程度继续进行调查，并根据调查结果作出终裁决定，予以公告。只有初步裁定和最终裁定都认定存在倾销、损害，才能继续完成反倾销调查；否则，应当终止反倾销调查。申请人撤回申请；没有足够证据证明存在倾销、损害或者二者之间有因果关系的；倾销幅度低于2%的；倾销进口产品实际或者潜在的进口量或者损害属于可忽略不计的；商务部认为不适宜继续进行反倾销调查的，也应终止反倾销调查。

反倾销调查的期限，自立案调查决定公告之日起至最终裁定公告之日止为12个月，在特殊情况下可以延长至18个月。

3. 反倾销措施

(1)采取临时反倾销措施。初步裁定存在倾销、损害的，可以采取：①征收临时反倾销税；②要求提供现金保证金、保函或者其他形式的担保。临时反倾销税税额或提供的保证金、保函或者其他形式担保的金额，应当不超过初步裁定确定的倾销幅度。临时反倾销措施的期限，自临时反倾销措施决定公告之日起为4个月；遇有特殊情形，可以延长至9个月。

(2)出口经营者的价格承诺。如果倾销进口产品的出口经营者在反倾销调查期间作出价格承诺，商务部认为出口经营者作出的价格承诺能够接受并符合公共利益的，可以决定中止或者终止反倾销调查，不采取临时反倾销措施或者征收反倾销税。中止或者终止反倾销调查的决定由商务部予以公告。出口经营者违反其价格承诺的，商务部依照本条例的规定，可以立即决定恢复反倾销调查。上述承诺的期限为5年。

(3)征收反倾销税。最终裁定倾销存在并由此对国内产业造成损害的，可以征收反倾销税，征收反倾销税，由商务部提出建议，国务院关税税则委员会根据商务部的建议作出决定，由商务部予以公告。海关自公告规定实施之日起执行。反倾销税税额不得超过最终裁定确定的倾销幅度。已经采取临时反倾销措施的，反倾销税高于已付或者应付的临时反倾销税或者为担保目的而估计的金额的，差额部分不予收取；低于已付或者应付的临时反倾销税或者为担保目的而估计的金额的，差额部分应当根据具体情况予以退还或者重新计算税额。反倾销税的纳税人为倾销进口产品的进口经营者。

如果以下两种情形并存，可以对实施临时反倾销措施之日前90天内进口的产品追溯征收反倾销税，但立案调查前进口的产品除外：①倾销进口产品有对国内产业造成损害的倾销历史，或者该产品的进口经营者知道或者应当知道出口经营者实施倾销并且倾销对国内产业将造成损害的；②倾销进口产品在短期内大量进口，并且可能会严重破坏即将实施的反倾销税的补救效果的。

征收反倾销税的期限为5年。在此期限内，商务部可以自行或者应利害关系方的请求，对征收反倾销税的决定进行复审，根据复审结果，由商务部依照本条例的规定提出保留、修改或者取消反倾销税的建议，国务院关税税则委员会根据商务部的建议作出决定，由商务部予以公告；或者由商务部依照本条例的规定，作出保留、修改或者取消价格承诺的决定并予以公告。

另外，《反倾销条例》也涉及反规避行为。由于反规避行为与在进口国投资设立加工制造厂有密切关系，因此，该条例仅在第55条提及商务部可以采取适当措施，防止规避反倾销措施的行为。

二、反补贴法

（一）补贴与反补贴法

补贴是一国经济政策的重要内容，国内补贴比比皆是，出口补贴更是国家促进对外贸易发展的重要手段。补贴有双重作用：一方面，补贴的使用可以促进一国社会和经济政策目标的实现；另一方面，补贴的使用可能对其他国家的贸易和生产造成损害，破坏市场竞争秩序。因此，许多国家制定反补贴法，对造成损害的某些补贴采取征收反补贴税等救济措施，以抵销补贴所产生的不公平竞争。

鉴于反补贴法与反倾销法在确定损害、调查程序和采取救济措施等方面的规定相同或相近，因此，本节在相应内容上将予简略。

（二）《总协定》与世贸组织的反补贴规则

第二次世界大战以后，国际社会为了规范国际贸易秩序缓和贸易冲突，一直将补贴与反补贴纳入总协定法律制度加以调整。《总协定反补贴规则》规定在《总协定》第6条、第16条和第23条,其中第16条专为补贴而规定。该规则对于推动反补贴法的发展具有重要意义。在1979年东京回合多边贸易谈判中,有关国家在上述反补贴规则基础上,达成《关于解释与适用总协定第6条、第16条、第23条的协议》(亦即《总协定反补贴守则》)。1994年乌拉圭回合谈判在反补贴方面取得了重大进展,第一次确定了补贴定义,并对补贴进行分类调整,反补贴措施更加明确、具体。

1.《总协定》的有关条款

(1)第6条——反补贴税

《总协定》第6条是关于反倾销税和反补贴税的规定。由于二者具有许多相同之处,为了避免内容重复而于同一条文加以规定。这一体例为后来欧洲经济共同体反倾销和反补贴条例以及一些国家相关立法所采纳。

第6条有关反补贴税内容主要包括:

①反补贴税定义。由于补贴方式繁多,反补贴措施针对的补贴行为难于界定,因此,第6条只是规定,反补贴税是为了抵销对任何产品的制造、生产或出口所直接或间接给予的任何补贴或津贴而征收的一种特别关税。

②征收反补贴税的条件。只有在补贴对国内产业造成实质损害,或有实质损害威胁,或严重阻碍国内新产业建立的情况下,才能征收反补贴税。不得超过补贴数额征收反补贴税。对于同一倾销或补贴,进口国不得同时征收反倾销税和反补贴税。

③例外情况。进口国对产品于出口后退还,或因出口而免征的国内税,不得征收反补贴税。为稳定国内价格,对初级产品提供补贴,如其出口价格曾高于国内市场销售价格或不会导致刺激出口、损害他国利益,应推定其不致造成实质损害。

(2)第16条——补贴

《总协定》既没有确定补贴定义,也没有区别补贴类型,而仅规定,如果缔约国采取直接或间接的补贴措施,致使其出口增加或进口减少,应以书面形式将补贴的情形通知其他缔约国。一旦确定这种补贴对其他缔约国的利益造成实质损害或实质损害威胁,给予补贴的缔约国应在接到要求后同其他有关缔约国讨论限制这种补贴的可能性。这一规定显然限制性十分有限,难以产生抵制效果。第16条还规定,缔约国应当尽力避免对初级产品出口提供补贴。缔约国在实施这种补贴时,不应导致其产品在世界出口贸易中占有不合理的份额。缔约国不应对非初级产品出口给予任何形式的补贴,以使该产品的出口价格低于相似产品在国内市场销售时的可比价格。上述规定,将约束补贴的范围集中在出口贸易上,但原则上并不禁止出口补贴,要求缔约国不应再对非初级产品提供出口补贴,以出口价格低于国内市场价格(即正常价格)为限。这既容易将反倾销与反补贴措施混同起来,在很大程度上也放宽了对出口补贴的管制。

(3)第23条——争端的解决

第23条是《总协定》解决争端的一般规范。当某一缔约国不履行《总协定》义务时,受损害的国家可以向其提出解决问题的建议。如果缔约国无法自行解决争端,可以将争端提交缔约国大会,由专门委员会调查后,提出建议或作出裁决。如果大会认为情况严重,可以授权受损害的国家采取必要的救济措施。

2.《总协定反补贴守则》

为了确保反补贴措施作为公正手段,对受到补贴有害影响的生产者给予救济,有关国家在《总协定》第6条、第16条和第23条基础上,于1979年东京回合谈判中达成了《关于解释与适用总协定第6条、第16条、第23条的协议》。其主要内容如下。

(1)补贴的分类

一般将补贴分为国内补贴和出口补贴,并区别对待。

①国内补贴。《总协定反补贴守则》第11条确认出口补贴以外的补贴被广泛使用,以实现社会和经济政策目标。这是各国的权利,不应加以限制。

当国内补贴对其他缔约国国内产业可能造成损害或造成损害威胁,或严重妨碍其他缔约国的利益,或者可能抵销或减损其他缔约国依总协定所能享受的利益,尤其是对正常竞争条件造成不利影响时,缔约国应当避免使用补贴而造成上述影响。因国内补贴造成不利影响,有关国家应当按照《总协定》第16条的规定,寻求适当办法解决争端。

②出口补贴。该守则于附件中列举了12项出口补贴。除最后1项概括规定外,均不论出口补贴是否造成内外销价格差异。因此,明文列举的补贴实际上有11项。

第一,直接补贴。政府根据出口实绩对某一公司或工业企业提供的直接补贴。

第二,外汇留成计划或任何类似出口奖励的做法。

第三,为出口货物提供优于内销货物的国内运输及运费。

第四,为生产出口货物提供优于生产同类国内消费品的服务,其服务条件也比世界市场现有商业条件更为优惠。

第五，对出口产品已缴或应缴的直接税，[13]或社会福利费实行全部或部分免税、退税或缓付税款。

第六，在计算直接税基数时，给予出口产品或出口实绩的特别折扣高于给予内销品生产的折扣。

第七，对出口产品免除或退还的间接税，[14]超过内销品已缴或应缴的间接税。

第八，对出口产品免除、退还或缓付的优先分期累进间接税，[15]超过对同类内销品竞争、退还或缓缴的优先分期累进间接税。

第九，使用质量和性能部分相当于进口品的国产品代替进口品，而退还的进口税超过实际上已并入出口的进口品所征收的进口税。

第十，政府提供条件优惠的出口信贷担保或保险项目，以便不提高出口产品成本。

第十一，政府提供的出口信贷利率低于一般借贷利率，或为出口商、金融机构支付出口信贷费用。

《总协定反补贴守则》将出口补贴分为对初级产品的出口补贴和对非初级产品的出口补贴两种情形。除了发展中国家之外，该守则禁止对非初级产品提供出口补贴。给予初级产品出口补贴则不得因此使该产品在世界出口贸易中占有不合理的份额，或导致其价格远低于同一市场其他供应者的同类产品的价格。

(2)损害的确定

确定损害必须客观审查：①补贴进口的数量及其对国内市场同类产品价格的影响；②对国内同类产品生产者所带来的影响。

《总协定反补贴守则》所称的损害，是指补贴的进口产品正在造成损害。与此同时，损害国内产业可能有其他因素，而由其他因素造成的损害不应归咎于补贴的进口产品。与《反倾销守则》比较，这里所指的损害不包括"造成重大损害威胁"的情形，也不包括"累计评估"损害。除此之外，审议对国内产业影响的经济因素以及关于"国内产业"的定义，与《反倾销守则》的规定基本相同。

---

〔13〕 直接税包括对工资、利润、利息、租金、矿区使用费及其他各种收入所征收的税和占有不动产所征收的税。

〔14〕 间接税包括销售税、消费税、营业税、增值税、特许权税、印花税、流转税、仓储和设备税、边境税以及直接税和进口税以外的一切税收。

〔15〕 优先分期间接税指对直接或间接用于生产某项产品的货物或劳务所征收的间接税；累进间接税指对货物或劳务按一个生产阶段征收的税被用于生产的后续阶段则又没有征收以后税款的方法所征收的多级税。

(3)反补贴调查

受影响的产业部门或以受影响的产业部门名义的代理人,可以向国内反补贴机构提出书面要求发起反补贴调查。反补贴调查程序与反倾销调查程序基本相同。所不同的是,发起反补贴调查的要求被接受以后,无论如何要在调查开始之前,向产品受调查的签约国提供适当的机会进行磋商,以便澄清情况和寻找解决办法。在反补贴调查的整个过程中,也应继续进行这种磋商,以澄清事实真相和达成双方同意的解决办法。按照该守则附加的第 13 条注释,进口国反补贴机构未提供适当机会进行磋商,不得作出任何初步的或最后的肯定结论。

(4)反补贴措施

①临时措施和追溯效力。如果有关机构作出初步肯定的调查结论,认为存在补贴并有造成损害的足够证据,可以采取临时反补贴措施。临时措施可以采取临时反补贴税的形式,用现金、存款或相当于估计的补贴额的证券作担保。实施临时措施的期限一般不得超过 4 个月。如果最终确定的反补贴税税额高于已交的临时反补贴税金额,则不得征收其差额;如果最终确定的反补贴税税额地狱已交的临时反补贴税金额,则必须偿还其超额部分,或尽快发还抵押的证券。在紧急情况下,如果反补贴机构判定大量补贴的进口产品造成了难以补救的损害,为避免再发生这种损害,对那些实施临时措施之前 90 天进口的补贴产品,追溯补征确定的反补贴税。

②出口国或出口商的保证。如果出口国政府同意取消或限制补贴或采取有这种作用的其他措施,或者出口商同意修改其价格,使反补贴调查机构确信补贴的损害性影响已经消除,反补贴机构可以接受上述保证,在不采用临时措施或反补贴税的情况下,中止或终结调查。进口国有关机构可提议实行价格保证,但不得强迫出口商作出这种保证。作出保证以后,如果出口国希望继续调查损害,则还应完成调查损害的工作。如果确定不存在损害,则保证应自动失效。

③征收反补贴税。对进口产品征收反补贴税不得超过已查明的补贴额。如果征收较少的反补贴税足以消除补贴产品对国内产业的损害,则应当少于补贴总额征收反补贴税。

(5)关于发展中国家

按照该守则第 14 条规定,发展中国家在补贴与反补贴上享有特别待遇,签约国确认补贴是发展中国家经济发展计划不可缺少的部分,不禁止发展中国家采取出口补贴措施,关于禁止对非初级产品出口补贴的规定,不适用于发展中国家。

当某一发展中签约国承诺减少或消除出口补贴并且已经遵守其承诺后，其他签约国除按规定可以采取征收反补贴税和其他适当措施外，不得采取该守则第二部分和第六部分规定的反措施，例如将争端提交总协定调解委员会，经查明存在不利影响的性质和程度且调解无果后，允许撤销原对出口国承担的总协定的减让和义务。

(6)关于“非市场经济国家”

《总协定反补贴守则》第15条规定，如果发生了总协定“注释和补充规定”中所谓来自“非市场经济国家”的补贴进口产品造成损害，进口国可以根据该守则规定或总协定第6条的有关规定，采取行动和措施，也可用下列比较方法，计算倾销差额或估计补贴额：

①以出口价格与进口国以外的某一国家产品价或实际卖价相比较；

②以出口价格与进口国以外的某一国家同类产品的构成价值(以生产成本加合理的管理、销售及其他费用和利润所构成)相比较。

上述规定与《总协定反倾销守则》的规定无异，这是总协定多边贸易体制的重大缺陷，也反映了西方发达国家坚持对社会主义国家的歧视政策。

3. 世界贸易组织《补贴与反补贴措施协议》

1986年9月发起的GATT第8轮多边贸易谈判具有划时代的意义。乌拉圭回合的主要目标是进一步促进国际贸易自由化，进一步削减非关税壁垒。乌拉圭回合《最后文件》包括26个协议，其中包括《补贴与反补贴措施协议》(Agreement On Subsidies and countervailing Measures)。新达成的协议对《总协定反补贴守则》作了重大修改，主要有以下几点。

(1)第一次确定补贴的定义。乌拉圭回合达成的《补贴与反补贴措施协议》第一次对补贴下了定义：“缔约方境内的政府或任何公共机构(下称政府)提供，并由此而授予各种利益的财政资助措施或其他任何形式的收入或价格支持措施。”这个定义具有如下特点。

①明确界定补贴是由政府提供的。这里所谓“政府”为广义上的政府，包括政府及政府下属机构、政府资助或授权的其他团体、组织。

②补贴是一种财政性措施，而不是泛指一切优惠措施。出口国政府给予生产商、出口商现金补贴或财政上的优惠，使受补贴的产品在成本与价格上不公平地增加竞争力。

③所谓“补贴”是广义上的补贴。它不同于反倾销法中的“倾销”定义，非专指反补贴措施所针对的补贴行为，而是泛指一切补贴行为。

(2)把补贴分为“被禁止的补贴”“可申诉的补贴”和“不可申诉的补贴”三

类,并分别规定对于不同类别的补贴采取不同的救济措施。

①“被禁止的补贴”(prohibited subsidies)主要指产品出口或进口替代补贴。签约国不得采用这类补贴(发展中国家例外),否则,受影响方可适用世界贸易组织争端解决程序,由争端解决机构授权其采取反措施,例如授权中止其对于被诉方的减让或义务。

②“可申诉的补贴”(actionable subsidies)是指对其他缔约国实际造成不利影响的补贴,受影响方可以根据有关的反补贴法提出申诉,如果确定存在补贴并造成损害,即可对补贴进口产品采取反补贴措施。

③“不可申诉的补贴”(unactionable subsidies)实际上就是允许采取的补贴措施,例如对产品研究开发提供资助,对落后地区的经济援助、环境保护补贴等。如果其他签约国确定某种不可申诉的补贴对该国国内工业造成损害,可以通过磋商解决争端。

(3)对发展中国家的补贴作出新的规定,主要内容包括如下几点。

①“被禁止的补贴”自协议生效起8年内不适用于发展中国家。如果某一发展中国家认为8年期限届满后需要继续采用补贴做法,应于期限届满前1年与补贴与反补贴委员会磋商,并征得同意,发展中国家允诺在8年内逐步取消出口补贴,不应提高出口补贴水平。

②某些“可申诉的补贴”不适用于发展中国家,例如对上缴政府收入的补贴,但这种补贴必须与私有化计划有直接联系。

③在下列补贴比例情况下,反补贴调查应予终止:第一,总补贴额不超过产品金额的20%;第二,补贴产品不足同类产品进口额的4%;第三,所有发展中国家提供补贴的该种产品不足同类产品进口总额的9%。

(4)反规避规定。所谓“防止规避反补贴税法令”的目的是扩大被控补贴产品的范围。包含补贴的零部件出口到进口国组装成与被控补贴产品相同或类似的产品,在一定条件下,属于适用反补贴税法令范围。

(三)我国的反补贴法

2001年制定、2004年修订的我国《反补贴条例》规定:进口产品存在补贴,并对已经建立的国内产业造成实质损害或者产生实质损害威胁,或者对建立国内产业造成实质阻碍的,依照本条例的规定进行调查,采取反补贴措施。2004年4月修订的《对外贸易法》进一步明确了补贴的专向性,指“进口的产品直接或者间接地接受出口国家或者地区给予的任何形式的专向性补贴”。[16]

---

〔16〕 郭寿康、韩立余:《国际贸易法》,中国人民大学出版社2005年版,第397页。

1. 补贴

补贴是指出口国(地区)政府或者其任何公共机构提供的并为接受者带来利益的财政资助以及任何形式的收入或者价格支持。除收入或价格支持外,构成补贴须具备两个要素:财政资助和利益。

财政资助包括:(1)出口国(地区)政府以拨款、贷款、资本注入等形式直接提供资金,或者以贷款担保等形式潜在地直接转让资金或者债务;(2)出口国(地区)政府放弃或者不收缴应收收入;(3)出口国(地区)政府提供除一般基础设施以外的货物、服务,或者由出口国(地区)政府购买货物;(4)出口国(地区)政府通过向筹资机构付款,或者委托、指令私营机构履行上述职能。

根据反补贴条例进行调查、采取反补贴措施的补贴,必须具有专向性。下列补贴为专向补贴:(1)由出口国(地区)政府明确确定的某些企业、产业获得的补贴;(2)由出口国(地区)法律、法规明确规定的某些企业、产业获得的补贴;(3)指定特定区域内的企业、产业获得的补贴;(4)以出口实绩为条件获得的补贴,包括本条例所附出口补贴清单列举的各项补贴;(5)以使用本国(地区)产品替代进口产品为条件获得的补贴。在确定补贴专向性时,还应当考虑受补贴企业的数量和企业受补贴的数额、比例、时间以及给予补贴的方式等因素。

对补贴的调查和确定,由商务部负责。

2. 损害

损害,是指补贴对已经建立的国内产业造成实质损害或者产生实质损害威胁,或者对建立国内产业造成实质阻碍。对损害的调查和确定,由商务部负责;其中,涉及农产品的反补贴国内产业损害调查,由商务部会同农业部进行。

在确定补贴对国内产业造成的损害时,应当审查下列事项:(1)补贴可能对贸易造成的影响;(2)补贴进口产品的数量,包括补贴进口产品的绝对数量或者相对于国内同类产品生产或者消费的数量是否大量增加,或者补贴进口产品大量增加的可能性;(3)补贴进口产品的价格,包括补贴进口产品的价格削减或者对国内同类产品的价格产生大幅度抑制、压低等影响;(4)补贴进口产品对国内产业的相关经济因素和指标的影响;(5)补贴进口产品出口国(地区)、原产国(地区)的生产能力、出口能力,被调查产品的库存情况;创造成国内产业损害的其他因素。

3. 因果关系

补贴进口产品必须是造成国内产业损害的原因。对实质损害威胁的确定,应当依据事实,不得仅依据指控、推测或者极小的可能性。在确定补贴对国内产业造成的损害时,应当依据肯定性证据,不得将造成损害的非补贴因素归因于补贴。

4. 反补贴调查及反补贴措施

反补贴调查与反倾销调查的程序相同。反补贴措施与反倾销措施类似,包括临时反补贴措施、价格承诺及反补贴税。实施条件基本相同。在满足下列要求的情况下,必要时,可以对实施临时反补贴措施之日前90天进口的产品追溯征收反补贴税:补贴进口产品在较短的时间内大量增加;此种增加对国内产业造成难以补救的损害;此种产品得益于补贴。

第四节 世界贸易组织的法律体系

世界贸易组织是多边贸易体制的法律基础与组织基础,是国际贸易管理法领域最重要的多边国际条约与全球性国际组织。世界贸易组织的法律体系,目前主要是指《世界贸易组织协定》(Agreement Establishing the World Trade Organization,又译《关于建立世界贸易组织的协定》,以下简称《世贸组织协定》)。

一、《世界贸易组织协定》的主要内容

如前所述,《世贸组织协定》是乌拉圭回合谈判的产物,作为乌拉圭回合多边贸易谈判结果最后协议的根基,其正文仅有16条。它主要规定世贸组织的宗旨、地位、职能、范围、机构与运作,以及协议的接受、修改、退出、适用等内容,主要属于组织法的性质。此外,《世贸组织协定》还包括了4个附件,这4个附件内容极其广泛,是世贸组织规则的核心所在。

附件一是多边实体法部分(虽然各协议中也包含了个别的程序法规范),其中又包括了三个部分:第一部分是多边货物贸易协定,在这一部分中包括了1994年关贸总协定以及12个专门的多边货物贸易协议,其中1994年关贸总协定又是由4个部分构成的;第二部分是《服务贸易总协定》(GATS);第三部分是《与贸易有关的知识产权协议(TRIPS)。

附件二和附件三属于多边程序法。附件二是《关于争端解决规则与程序的谅解》(DSU),附件三是《贸易政策评审机制》(TPRM)。

附件四属于诸边协议,即可以自由选择参加的协议,目前由四个协议组成:《民用航空器协议》《政府采购协议》《国际奶制品协议》《国际牛肉协议》。诸边协议在世贸组织诸协议中具有相对的独立性,而且其成员的范围也比较有限。各协议仅对其成员适用(关于《世贸组织协定》的基本构成,参见下图)。

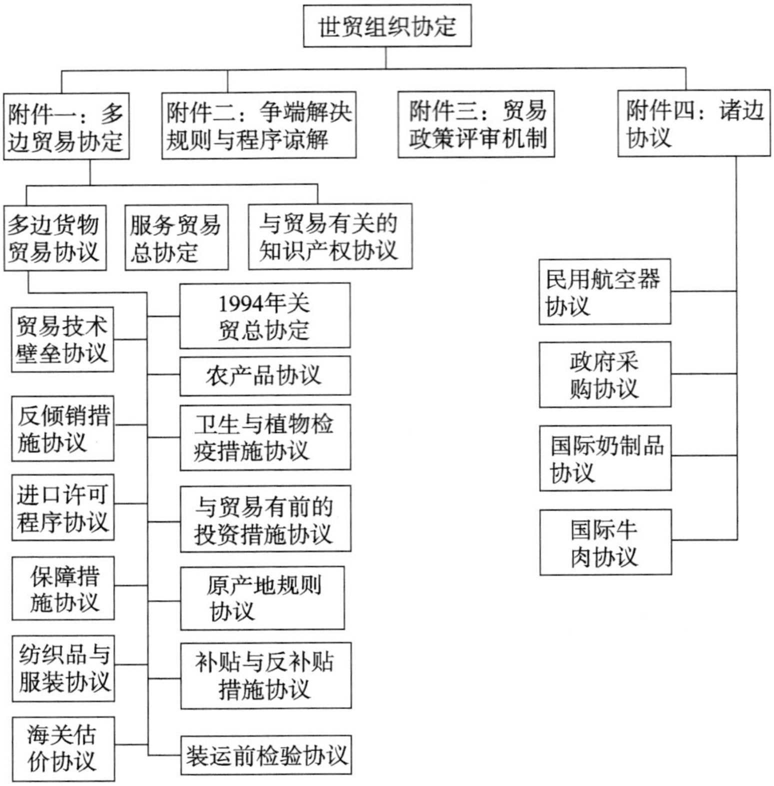

以上协议的构成并非是一成不变的。例如,根据有关规定,诸边协议可以从世贸组织协定中退出;在以后的谈判中,有些诸边协议也可能转化为多边协议;同时,新的诸边协议也可以加入世贸组织。在货物贸易、服务贸易、与贸易有关的知识产权领域,今后也必然还会有新的专门协议出现,而诸如《多边投资协议》(MAI)等新规则也可能出现在将来的世贸组织协定中。

除了正式的"协议"之外,根据《世贸组织协定》第 2 条第(2)款、第(3)款,与各"协议"有关联的所有"法律文件",均构成本协定不可分割的一部分,并对所有成员具有拘束力。因此,有关上述各协议的谅解、宣言、决定等法律文件同时也是《世贸组织协定》的有机组成部分。

此外,除非《世贸组织协定》和多边贸易协定另有规定,世贸组织应该接受1947 年关贸总协定缔约方全体以及 1947 年关贸总协定各机构所遵循的决定、程序和惯例的指导。据统计,这里所指的"决定、程序与惯例"多达 200 多件。[17]

---

〔17〕 赵维田:《最惠国与多边贸易体制》,中国社会科学出版社 1996 年版,第 13 页。

《世贸组织协定》内容之庞大复杂，于此可见一斑。

二、《世界贸易组织协定》的法律特征

乌拉圭回合所达成的世贸组织协定不仅内容庞大，而且特点鲜明，被认为是国际法领域的重要发展。大致说来，世贸组织协定至少有如下几个法律特征。

（一）《世贸组织协定》具有法律的权威性

作为一个正式的国际条约，世贸组织协定不仅强化了法律效力，还提高了法律层次。一方面，困扰关贸总协定的“祖父条款”被废除了。众所周知，关贸总协定的《临时适用议定书》第1条第b项规定各缔约方应在与现行立法不相抵触的条件下，最大限度地适用该协定第二部分。[18]

据此，各缔约方现有立法有如至尊的祖父，不仅不可撼动，更有优于总协定（第二部分的）条款的法律效力。因此，人们形象地称为“祖父条款”。

《世贸组织协定》则彻底解决了这一问题。协定第16条第4款明确规定“各个成员都要保证使其法律、规章与管理程序符合（本协定）所附各协定的义务。”极简短的一句话，扳倒了“现有立法”的“祖父”而赋予该协定以正式国际条约应有的法律效力与权威性。

与此同时，《世贸组织协定》作为一个完全意义上的国际条约，还一扫关贸总协定这一“临时适用”的“行政协定”的尴尬处境，获得了高于一般国内法的法律层次与地位，而且奠定了永久适用的法律基础。

此外，与一般国际条约不同，《世贸组织协定》采用“一揽子”接受的机制，一般不允许各成员作出保留。协定正文第16条第（5）款规定，“对本协定（指正文）的任何条款都不得有任何保留，对各多边贸易协议只有在该协议规定的范围内方可提出保留。而对各诸边贸易协议的保留，则必须按该协议的规定作出。”这显然进一步强化了协定的权威性。

（二）《世贸组织协定》具有较强的执行力

执行力是法律权威性的一种表征，但这一种权威性在国际法领域一般难以贯彻。在这方面，《世贸组织协定》比较特别，足以构成国际法的一个重大的发展。为监督与保障协定的执行，《世贸组织协定》建立了健全的机构，并制定了详备的规则，大大强化了其职能。其突出的表现，一为贸易政策评审机制，一为争端解决机制。其中，贸易政策评审机制旨在通过经常的、定期的贸易政策的评审，来督促各国更严格地遵守世贸组织规则与纪律，履行其义务。

---

〔18〕“第二部分”是关贸总协定的主要实体规则部分，主要规定关于非关税措施的纪律。

《世贸组织协定》执行力最有力的保证体现在其争端解决机制之中。与一般的国际争端解决机制不同,世贸组织的争端解决机制通过“全体一致才能否决”(negative consensus)规则的引入,使其拥有了准强制性的管辖权、准自动的裁判权与准自动授权救济的权力。[19] 尤为重要的是,世贸组织《争端解决规则与程序的谅解》(DSU)强调争端解决机构通过的建议或裁决应得到迅速执行。当事方如不主动执行,争端解决机构可以准自动地授权申诉方实施补偿、中止减让等救济。在中止减让义务方面,《世贸组织协定》还规定了所谓的“交叉报复”机制,使申诉方有权在广泛的领域寻求最有力的报复手段。尽管由于这种报复的力度最终仍取决于各国实力,但毕竟是提供了一种法律的可能,因而不失其进步意义。可以说,世贸组织协定的这种执行机制是国际经济贸易一体化的产物,也是国际法律机制的一大发展。

(三)《世贸组织协定》具有系统性

《世贸组织协定》是世界多边贸易体制的法律体系,具有系统性。这主要表现在三个方面。

首先,《世贸组织协定》具有层次性。在《世贸组织协定》庞大的法律体系中,《世贸组织协定》居于组织法的核心地位,其法律效力凌驾于其他附属协定之上,具有统率世贸组织法的作用。根据《世贸组织协定》第16条第(3)款规定,“如本协定中的某一规定,与任何多边贸易协定的某一规定发生冲突的,本协定的规定应在冲突的范围内优先适用”。

其次,《世贸组织协定》中既有实体法,又有程序法,还有冲突规范,具有完整性。如前所述,《多边贸易协定》与《诸边贸易协定》基本上是世贸组织协定中的实体法,而《贸易政策评审机制》与《争端解决规则与程序的谅解》则基本上是协定的程序法。与此同时,在一些实体与程序性协议中,又分别包括一些“冲突性”规范。实体法方面,例如,协定附件一(1)的解释性注释指出“当GATT 1994的某一规定与《世贸组织协定》的附件一(1)中另一协议的某一规定发生冲突时,该另一协议之规定在冲突的范围内应优先适用”。程序法方面,例如《争端解决规则与程序的谅解》第1条第(2)款规定,“如本谅解与其附录2中所列的专门的或补充的规则与程序之间出现冲突,则应以附录2中的专门的或补充的规则或程序为准。”这两个“冲突规则”都可以说是“特别法优于普通法”的国内法律冲突规则的体现。由此可见,世贸组织的规则虽然庞杂,但却各有所司,分工明确,可谓“自成体系”。

---

〔19〕 关于世贸组织争端解决程序,可参见陈安主编:《国际经济法》(第2版),第10章,第三节。

最后,《世贸组织协定》具有统一性。主要表现在如下三个方面。

第一,基本原则的一致性。尽管世贸组织协定各协议规则千差万别,但它们大都遵循着同样的法律原则,例如非歧视待遇原则、公平竞争原则、鼓励改革与经济发展原则等。

第二,争端解决机制的一致性。按《争端解决规则与程序谅解》(以下简称《争端解决谅解》),凡《世贸组织协定》范围内的所有争端,均应纳入统一的世贸组织争端解决机制来解决,即使是诸边贸易协议也不例外。

第三,管理机构的协调性。《世贸组织协定》不仅在法律上强化了世贸组织的国际组织地位,还从机构上作了充实与丰富,形成了一整套管理网络。使几乎每一个协议都有专门的管理与监督机构,它们又都由部长会议及常设的总理事会来统一领导。管理体制的协调统一对于《世贸组织协定》的统一也起到重要的作用。

此外,世贸组织协定的统一性还表现为其缔约资格与成员资格的一致性,各主要协议生效时间与接受期限的一致性等。[20]

(四)《世贸组织协定》允许互不适用

《建立世贸组织协定》第 13 条第(1)款规定,如果任何一方在成为成员时,任一成员与任何另一成员不同意在它们之间适用本协定及本协定附件一与附件二所含之多边贸易协定,则它们相互间可以互不适用。据此,世贸组织成员在接受《世贸组织协定》时,虽然必须“一揽子”接受所有的多边贸易协定,但却并不意味着他必须接受所有的成员。这种规定使世贸组织具备了一种灵活性。这种灵活性一方面使世贸组织具有更强的适应性与更多的成员,另一方面也为体制种下了某种不安定的因素。《世贸组织协定》对总协定这一规则的继承使其体制更具特色。

三、《世界贸易组织协定》的基本原则

在《世贸组织协定》各项规则之中,贯穿着一些共同的基本原则。这些原则是在总协定的基础上发展起来的,但却具有了更为广泛的内容,拓展了更新的领域。

(一)非歧视原则

非歧视原则一直是多边贸易体制中最为重要的原则,可以说是关贸总协定和世界贸易组织的一大基石。近 60 年来,关贸总协定的关键条文都确认,在各成员

---

〔20〕 曾令良:《世界贸易组织法》,武汉大学出版社 1996 年版,第 23 ~ 24 页。

之间以及在进口商品和本国制造商品之间进行歧视是非法的。而非歧视原则的主要体现就是最惠国待遇条款和国民待遇条款。

1. 最惠国待遇

根据《总协定》第1条"一般最惠国待遇"条款,各成员对于其他成员的产品必须给予不低于其给予任何其他国家的产品的优惠待遇。

与其他双边条约中的最惠国待遇条款相比,《总协定》的最惠国待遇条款主要具有以下几个特点。

(1)范围局限于货物贸易范围内。《总协定》的最惠国待遇义务是一定范围内的义务,它仅仅涉及货物在输出入时所享受的待遇,而没有包括服务贸易、投资等内容,其对象也不包括企业和个人。而在双边条约中,外国人的法律地位、对外国船舶的待遇等往往也是最惠国待遇所涉及的范围。

(2)《总协定》最惠国待遇具有多边性与自动性。双边经贸条约中所规定的最惠国待遇一般是由缔约双方互相给予的,但是《总协定》的最惠国待遇是在所有关贸总协定缔约方之间实施的,只要加入《总协定》和世界贸易组织,就可以自动地享受到这种待遇。

(3)《总协定》最惠国待遇使关税减让具有稳定性和主动性。与《总协定》第2条减让表相结合,最惠国待遇关税经常表现为约束关税,从而保证关税壁垒的不断下降。并且在关税问题上,多边的最惠国待遇使出口方不必等进口方对第三方作出减让后再享受利益,而是可以主动与主要进口国磋商,提出关税减让要求,从而可以获取最大的利益。

当然,最惠国待遇在《总协定》中也有一些例外,主要包括:(1)第20条"一般例外";(2)第21条"安全例外";(3)第24条"适用的领土范围——边境贸易——关税同盟和自由贸易区";(4)第5条"缔约国的联合行动"对义务方的豁免;(5)通过授权条款对发展中国家的例外(参见后文)。同时,反倾销与反补贴、保障条款、国际收支平衡例外等也可能构成最惠待遇的例外。

在《世界贸易组织协定》中,除了在1994年关贸总协定中规定了最惠国待遇条款之外,在其他协议中,如《与贸易有关的知识产权协议》(TRIPS)第4条、《服务贸易总协定》(GATS)第2条等也对最惠国待遇做了一些规定,这就使最惠国待遇从货物贸易领域扩展到了其他一些领域,而这正是乌拉圭回合谈判取得的重大成果之一。

2. 国民待遇

非歧视原则的第二种形式是"国民待遇"。传统的国民待遇,即《总协定》中的国民待遇,要求一旦货物已经进入某个市场,它们必须获得不低于相同的当地制造商品所获得的优惠待遇，我们不妨称为“国货待遇”。这主要体现在关贸总协定的第3条中。

国民待遇的实质是要求对外国货物与本国货物以同等的待遇。可以设想，如果商品能够享有国民待遇，在进口国内享有与进口国生产的商品同样的待遇，那么它就可以在比较公平的基础上与国产商品竞争。反之，如果它在进口国必须负担超重的税负，或者面临其他的壁垒，那么，即使进口国的关税很低，进口商品仍然不能顺利进入市场，从而使关税壁垒的降低变得毫无意义了。

但是，在《总协定》中的国民待遇要求其范围是有限的，它仅仅针对货物贸易而言，而不包括其他领域。而且，在关贸总协定中，对国民待遇还存在一些例外：包括“政府采购”例外、特殊补贴例外等。

在乌拉圭回合以前，关贸总协定的国民待遇仅仅涉及有关货物贸易的措施。但是，随着世界贸易组织的成立，多边体系规则所涉及的范围更广了，相应地，国民待遇也扩展到了这些新领域。〔21〕

无论最惠国待遇还是国民待遇，都是无歧视原则的体现。实际上，这两种待遇制度正是不歧视原则不可或缺的两翼。最惠国待遇旨在使外国货物、知识产权保护与服务之间所享受的待遇平等，国民待遇则使外国货物、知识产权保护与服务所享受的待遇与本国的平等，从而确保所有成员间的货物、服务与知识产权保护维持同一水准，做到货畅其流，人尽其才。然而，对于这种非歧视原则应该在何种程度上适用，不同的国家是有不同理解的。许多发展中国家，包括一些发达国家的有识之士认为，在不平等的基础上实行非歧视原则，本身就是一种不公平，正是因为这样，才有东京回合的授权条款，给予发展中国家以更优惠的待遇。所以，我们理解非歧视原则不应该孤立地，而应同其他原则，例如同鼓励发展和经济改革的原则结合起来理解。

（二）可预见和不断增长的市场准入原则

通过多边贸易体系，各国政府试图给投资者、雇主、雇员以及消费者提供某种商业环境以鼓励贸易和投资，并创造就业机会，为市场提供广泛的选择和低廉的价格。这样的一种环境需要稳定和可预见性，尤其是在企业准备投资和发展时，更是如此。因此，可预见与不断扩大的市场准入也成了世贸组织协定的一项基本原则。

可预见和不断增长的市场准入原则所包括的范围比较广泛。实际上，关税保护原则、关税约束和减让原则、一般禁止数量限制原则、按承诺开放服务贸易的原

〔21〕 单文华：《世界贸易组织协定中的国际投资规范评析》，载《法学研究》1996年第2期。

则、透明度原则等都可以纳入可预见和不断增长的市场准入原则。因为这些原则尽管表现形式不同，涉及的领域也不一样，但它们的目的都是一样的，就是使商品和服务享有稳定的、可预见的、不断改善的市场准入条件。这里择其要而略述之。

1. 数量限制的一般取消

数量限制在《总协定》和世界贸易组织中是被严格限制的。在一般情况下，世界贸易组织认为数量限制是非法的。1994 年 GATT 中有大量的篇幅与数量限制有关。其中，最核心的条款为第 11 条第 1 款："任何缔约方除征收税捐或其他费用以外，不得设立或维持配额、进出口许可证或其他措施以限制或禁止其他缔约方领土的产品的输入，或向其他缔约方领土输出或销售出口产品。"

尽管在世贸组织中，数量限制一般是非法的，但是世贸组织大量条款都旨在规定取消数量限制原则的例外情况，以及采取这些例外豁免的限制条件。

2. 关税保护与减让

在货物贸易中，可靠和可预见的市场准入机会的存在主要取决于关税的运用。配额在世贸组织中一般被视为非法，而关税在世贸组织中是合法的，它们被各国政府普遍运用以保护其国内产业（保护关税）并筹措财政收入（财政关税）。然而，关税的运用要符合规定——例如，它们对不同的进口不构成歧视——并且大部分关税要受到"约束"，即世贸组织成员对产品不征收高于该国减让表上规定的关税（1994 年 GATT 第 2 条），并且未经与其主要贸易伙伴的补偿谈判不得提高（1994 年 GATT 第 28 条）。

自从 1948 年《总协定》建立以来，通过七轮贸易谈判，平均关税水平逐步大幅度地下降。乌拉圭回合取得了更大的成功，大量地削减了关税，有的降到了零关税，同时大大提高了对关税的整体约束程度。在乌拉圭回合中，120 多个国家通过关税减让就市场准入作出的承诺，载入约 22，500 页的各国关税减让表中。[22] 与此同时，对农产品的所有非关税进口限制的"关税化"使农产品的市场可预测程度大大提高。

3. 服务贸易的逐步自由化

对于服务贸易虽然不存在边境上的关税，但同样需要贸易条件的可预见性。为了满足这种需要，各国政府承诺了一套初步义务，其范围包括影响各种服务活动的国内规章。这些承诺就像关税义务承诺一样，载入各国的约束承诺表中。实际上，各国通过承诺表所作出的承诺服务贸易开放的领域也就是其对服务贸易领

〔22〕 钟兴国、林忠、单文华：《世界贸易组织——国际贸易新体制》，北京大学出版社 1997 年版，第 4 ~ 5 页。

域实行国民待遇的领域。服务贸易的开放并没有像货物贸易一样规定统一的开放原则，各个成员对服务贸易开放到何种程度必须通过谈判来确定。

在《服务贸易总协定》第三部分"逐步自由化"中，对今后服务贸易领域的不断自由化作出了规定，在世贸组织协定生效之日起不迟于5年，为逐步实现更高水平的自由化，各成员应进行连续的谈判，并在以后定期举行。这种谈判的方向是减少或取消各项对服务贸易产生不利影响的措施，以此作为提供有效市场准入的一种方式。在这里，世贸组织作出的服务贸易不断自由化的规定实际上与货物贸易的关税减让原则的作用是一样的，都是为了改善市场准入的条件，促进贸易的自由化。

4. 透明度

贸易条件可预见性的关键往往在于国内法律、规章与措施的透明度。许多世贸组织协定都含有透明度条款，要求在国家层次上进行信息披露——例如通过在官方报刊登载或提供查询点——或在多边层次上通过向世贸组织正式通知的方式进行披露。世贸组织各机构的许多工作就是审查这些通知。

在乌拉圭回合谈判中，各成员达成了《关于通知程序的决定》，重申了1979年通过的《有关通知、磋商、争端解决和监督的谅解》。根据该决定设立了通知登记中心，并由货物贸易理事会负责《世贸组织协定》附件一(1)《多边货物贸易协议》项下有关通知事项的审查。

另外，通过贸易政策评审机制对各国贸易政策所进行的日常监督，为同时在国内及在多边层次上促进透明度提供了进一步的保障。

(三)促进公平竞争原则

世贸组织自己也认为：单是世贸组织允许关税以及在限定的条件下使用其他保护形式，就足以说明它不是一个人们所说的"自由贸易"机构。确切地说，它是一套致力于开放、公平、无扭曲竞争的规则体系。

其实，世贸组织的许多其他原则也与公平竞争原则是分不开的。例如，非歧视原则本身就是为了确保贸易条件的公平性，对发展中国家的一些特殊照顾是为了使发展中国家能够站在比较公平的地位来参与国际竞争。

在《世贸组织协定》中，当提到公平竞争规则的时候，经常指的是关于倾销和补贴的规则。以前的关贸总协定规则，为各国政府对这两种"不公平"竞争形式征收补偿性关税提供了法律依据，但在"东京回合"中达成的守则是"诸边"的，没有普遍约束力。现在这些规则在世贸组织各协议中得到了延伸和澄清，订立了《关于履行1994年关税与贸易总协定第6条的协议》(《反倾销协议》)以及《补贴与反补贴措施协议》，包含在"一揽子"接受的最后文本之中。

世贸组织正在讨论的一个新议题是竞争规则与竞争政策。例如:如何建立国内竞争法规,包括反垄断法规和其他的反不正当竞争法规;如何管制跨国公司的国际竞争行为,特别是限制性商业惯例;如何规范各国促进竞争的其他政策。这类问题对于建立一个公平的国际竞争环境具有十分重大的意义。另外,世贸组织《农产品协议》旨在给农业贸易提供更高的公平程度。《知识产权协议》将改善涉及智力成果和发明的竞争的条件,《服务贸易总协定》则将改善服务贸易竞争的条件。有关政府采购的诸边协议将在许多国家以千计的政府机构的采购活动中实行竞争规则。还有许多其他的世贸组织条款,它们都旨在促进公平的和非扭曲的竞争。

(四)鼓励发展和经济改革原则

3/4 以上的世贸组织成员是发展中国家以及正处于非市场经济改革进程中的国家。在乌拉圭回合 7 年的进程中,有 60 多个发展中国家和转型经济国家实施了贸易自由化计划。有的国家是作为其加入《总协定》的谈判的一部分,即以提出"入门费"的方式而实施的,有的则是在自愿基础上实施的。同时,发展中国家和转型经济国家在乌拉圭回合谈判中比以往任何一轮谈判都起到了更积极和更有影响力的作用。

按世贸组织秘书处的观点,发展中国家在世贸组织中起到的日益重要的作用逐渐消除了那种认为世界贸易体系是为发达国家而存在,是个"富人俱乐部"的看法。同时也改变了以前强调对发展中国家在特定的关贸总协定条款和协议上进行豁免的做法。随着乌拉圭回合的结束,发展中国家自身表明准备承担要求发达国家承担的大部分义务,但是以不超过其经济发展实际情况所能承担的义务为限。因此,关贸总协定原来包括的一系列照顾发展中国家的规定在世贸组织协定中仍然有效。这些规定包括如下几条。

1. 1994 年《总协定》第 18 条

1994 年《总协定》第 18 条即"政府对经济发展的援助"。该条款认为对于发展中国家来说,应该给予其在执行关贸总协定方面一定的便利和灵活性,这是关贸总协定最初文本中仅有的一条对发展中国家提供例外优惠的条文。

2. 1994 年《总协定》第四部分

1994 年《总协定》第四部分的标题是"贸易和发展",是 1994 年《总协定》中唯一有名称的一个部分,包括了在 1965 年制定的三个条款。

该条款作出的一个最为重要的规定是对发展中国家的"非互惠原则",作为"互惠原则"的例外。在第 36 条第 8 款规定"发达的缔约方对他们在贸易谈判中对发展中的缔约方的贸易所承诺的减少或撤除关税和其他壁垒的义务,不能希望得到互惠”。“非互惠原则”适应了新的世界形势，是发展中国家在20世纪五六十年代争取世界经济新秩序的斗争成果之一，与1964年第一届联合国贸发会议的召开有一定的联系。它打破了原来的一些国际经贸秩序原则在实际上的不公平，为发展中国家进一步争取改善经贸条件的努力开了一个好头。

3. 授权条款

在东京回合的谈判中，缔约方全体通过了《关于差别和更加优惠的待遇、互惠和发展中国家进一步参与的决定》，在该决定的第一段到第四段，规定了“授权条款”。“授权条款”的作用在于给发展中国家的优惠和差别、非互惠待遇提供法律基础。

“授权条款”第一段规定，缔约方可以背离关贸总协定第1条“一般最惠国待遇”条款，对发展中国家给予更加优惠的待遇，而不将此种待遇给予其他缔约方。

“授权条款”作为“东京回合”达成的协议，被世界贸易组织继承了下来，包括在1994年《总协定》中。

4. 乌拉圭回合的新内容

在乌拉圭回合谈判期间，许多国家纷纷进行改革，而且往往将改革与对外开放和贸易自由化结合起来，向市场经济体制转化。在意识到这种改革是有利于各国经济发展的同时，各谈判方也注意到了改革给经济转型国家在经济上和社会上造成的一些困难。在这种背景下，“乌拉圭回合”各协议增加了促进经济转型的内容。

在乌拉圭回合谈判达成的各个协议中，大多对发展中国家和经济转型国家规定了一定的特别和优惠的待遇，以鼓励经济发展和改革。这些优惠散见在各个协议之中。归纳起来，主要有以下几个方面。

(1)非对等优惠。《总协定》第四部分规定，发达成员对其给予发展中国家成员的减让，不能希望得到互惠。

(2)非歧视性原则的豁免优惠。东京回合通过的“授权条款”规定，给予发展中国家，特别是最不发达国家以及发展中国家之间互相给予的优惠待遇可以作为最惠国待遇的例外。

(3)过渡期优惠。对于发展中国家，可以给予较长的过渡期以使其实施世贸组织义务。

(4)差别义务优惠。在关税的削减、非关税的撤除等义务方面，发展中国家可以享受差别待遇，可以保持较高的壁垒或实施某些特定的措施。

(5)微量条款优惠。对于小规模的出口，特别是发展中国家的出口，可以在实施保障措施、反倾销措施、反补贴措施等方面，给予优惠。

(6)程序上的优惠。在通知程序、贸易政策评审程序、争端解决程序上对于发展中国家有更多的优惠。

另外,世贸组织还通过了《关于给予最不发达国家优惠措施的决定》,并继续寻求采取措施扩大最不发达国家的贸易机会。世贸组织通过贸易政策培训、建立咨询点、给予技术援助等方式以协助发展中国家履行其义务,与贸发会议合作通过国际贸易中心帮助发展中国家扩大其出口机会。

应该承认,这些对发展中国家与经济转型国家的优惠与照顾安排对发展中国家的经济发展与经济转型国家经济改革确实起到了一定的作用,但这种作用无疑是十分有限的。在1996年的新加坡会议上,中国代表龙永图就曾呼吁各成员给发展中国家以更多、更实际的关切,以实际行动来促进国际经济新秩序的建设与发展。显然,这需要广大发展中国家的共同努力,也有赖于发达国家的支持与合作,而这必将是一个任重而道远的漫长历程。

商事仲裁程序*

第一章　商事仲裁概述

第一节　商事仲裁的概念与种类

一、仲裁

仲裁是指纠纷当事人自愿达成仲裁协议,将纠纷提交非司法机构的第三人审理,并作出对纠纷当事人具有拘束力的裁决的争议解决方式或制度。[1]“仲”为居中,“裁”为裁判。对这种争端解决方法,过去我国曾经称为“公断”,现在则通称为“仲裁”。仲裁即由“第三人”居中裁断,但与诉讼不同,这个“第三人”不是国家设置的法官,而是双方意定的私人。

仲裁具有以下要素:(1)纠纷当事人自愿协商通过仲裁方式解决争端;(2)当事人选择由非司法机构的第三人解决争议;(3)当事人自愿接受第三人的裁决的约束。

依据仲裁组织存续时间的长短,可以将仲裁分为机构仲裁与临时仲裁。机构仲裁,是指当事人将其商事争议提交常设的仲裁机构而进行的仲裁。临时仲裁,是指当事人将其商事争议提交基于当事人的选择而临时组成的仲裁庭进行的仲裁。目前,机构仲裁占据主导地位。相对于机构仲裁,临时仲裁具有较强的灵活性,但其基本制度与机构仲裁相类似。本编主要论述机构仲裁的有关制度。

依据适用范围的不同,可以将仲裁分为国内仲裁与国际仲裁。

国内仲裁,通常是指纠纷当事人的住所或者惯常居所同在一国境内的仲裁。

---

* 本文原载齐树洁主编:《民事程序法》(第4版),第6部分,厦门大学出版社2006年版。

[1] 参见《牛津法律词典》对 arbitration(仲裁)的解释:The determination of a dispute by one or more independent third parties(the arbitrator) rather than by court. See Elizabeth A. Martin, Ox ford Dictionary of Law, Oxford University Press, 2002, p. 31.

国际仲裁则有广狭两种含义，狭义的国际仲裁仅指国家间为某一公法上的争端提请第三方解决的仲裁，属于国际公法范畴；广义的国际仲裁则不仅包括国家之间具有公法性质的仲裁，而且还包括对具有国际性的私法（商务）上的争端进行的仲裁（国际商事仲裁）。甚至兼具公法与私法一定特性的跨国仲裁。[2]

各国关于国内仲裁的规定与关于国际仲裁的规定存在不同程度的差别，但是在一些基本制度上国内仲裁与国际仲裁相趋同则是现代仲裁制度的发展趋势。因此，我们主要以国际商事仲裁为例对仲裁制度进行论述。

二、国际商事仲裁

国际商事仲裁是指国际商事纠纷当事人自愿达成仲裁协议，将其纠纷提交非司法机构的第三人审理，并作出对纠纷当事人具保留有拘束力的裁决的争议解决制度。国际商事仲裁是国际仲裁的一种。对于国际商事仲裁中“商事”与“国际”两个概念，国际公约、各国法律、仲裁规则的理解有所不同。

（一）“商事”一词的含义

1958年《承认及执行外国仲裁裁决公约》（以下简称《纽约公约》）规定，任何缔约国可以声明该国只对根据本国法律属于商事法律关系所引起的争执适用《纽约公约》。包括我国在内的许多国家对《纽约公约》等公约作了“商事保留”，规定只有具有“商事”性质的国际仲裁可以适用这些公约。各国对“商事”的认定标准各不相同，但是多数国家对“商事”一词都作了尽可能广义的解释。[3] 作为各国意志的折中反映，联合国国际贸易法委员会（UNCITRAL）1985年所制定的《国际商事仲裁示范法》（以下简称《示范法》）没有规定“商事”的含义，但是作了一个列举式的注释说明，认为“商事”一词应作广义解释，使其包括一切由于具有商事性质的关系，不论其是否为契约关系所发生的事实，商务性关系包括但不限于下列行为：任何提供或交换商品或劳务的贸易交易；销售协议；商事代表或代理；保付代理；租赁；咨询；设计；许可；投资；融资；银行业；保险；开采协议或特许权；合营企业或其他形式的工业或商业合作；客货的航空、海洋、铁路或公路运输。秘书处认为，像电力供应、液化气管道输送、商事关系中的损害赔偿等，虽未列入注释，但仍属“商事”范围。[4] 根据中国加入1958年《纽约公约》时作出的商事保留声

---

〔2〕 主要指一国国家与他国国民之间争端的仲裁，如解决投资争端国际中心——ICSID所进行的仲裁。ICSID所受理的案件多涉及国家主权和国际法的适用问题，其裁决不同于世界上任何一个仲裁机构的裁决，一国法院无权对该裁决进行任何形式的审查。因此，这种国际仲裁不同于本书所论述的国际商事仲裁。

〔3〕 韩健：《现代国际商事仲裁的理论与实践》，法律出版社2000年版，第15页。

〔4〕 Seventh Secretariat Note, A/CN. 9/264. 转引自朱克鹏：《国际商事仲裁的法律适用》，法律出版社1999年版，第13页。

明，我国仅就根据我国法律的规定属于契约或非契约性的商事关系[5]适用该公约。

我国《仲裁法》和有关仲裁规则所认定的“商事”既包括契约性关系，又包括非契约性关系，因而属于广义的理解。但是，“商事”的范围是有一定限制的。《仲裁法》第3条规定，婚姻、收养、监护、抚养、继承纠纷，及依法应当由行政机关处理的行政争议不能仲裁。

（二）“国际”一词的含义

许多国家法律对国际仲裁与国内仲裁作严格区分，分别对待，故应明确“国际”的含义。各国关于仲裁“国际性”的标准各不相同，但大致可以分为两类：一种是以实质性联结因素，如仲裁地、国籍、住、居所地、注册地、管理中心地等作为区分国际仲裁与国内仲裁的标准；另一种是抽象地以争端的国际性质作为认定标准。《示范法》做法实际上是将这两种标准结合在一起，形成一个综合标准。[6]根据《示范法》第1条的规定，符合下列条件之一的仲裁具有国际性：（1）仲裁合同当事人双方在缔结该合同时其营业地在不同国家境内。（2）下列地点之一位于双方当事人营业地共同所在的国家之外：①仲裁协议确定的或者依据仲裁协议确定的仲裁地；②商事关系主要义务履行地，或与争议的标的有最密切关系的地点。（3）当事人双方明示约定该仲裁协议的标的与一个以上的国家有关。根据2005年1月11日修订并通过的《中国国际经济贸易仲裁委员会仲裁规则》（以下简称《CIETAC仲裁规则2005》）第2条，“贸仲”可以受理下列争议案件：（1）国际的或涉外的争议案件；（2）涉及香港特别行政区、澳门特别行政区或台湾地区的争议案件；（3）国内争议案件。由此可见，新修订的《CIETA仲裁规则》对其受案范围作了进一步扩大解释，不仅包括所有国际性的争议，而且包括所有涉外的与涉港、澳、台的争议。其中，“涉外”一词也应作广义的解释。同时，在遵循当事人意思自治原则的情况下，“贸仲”还可以受理国内争议案件。2000年11月22日修订并通过的《中国海事仲裁委员会仲裁规则》（以下简称《CMAC仲裁规则2000》）第2条规定，“海仲”的受案范围为产生于远洋、近洋、沿海和与海相通的可航水域的运输、生产和航行等有关过程中所发生的契约性或非契约性的海事争议。

---

〔5〕 关于该“契约和非契约性商事法律关系”的具体含义，详见第七章。

〔6〕 韩健：《现代国际商事仲裁法的理论与实践》，法律出版社2000年版，第4~11页。

第二节　商事仲裁的性质

早在1973年,贝纳德(Albred Benard)就曾述及了关于国际商事仲裁性质的三种学说:第一种学说把仲裁协议与裁决分开,将裁决看作普通法院作出的判决;第二种学说把仲裁协议与裁决看做同一协议的两个方面,认为裁决具有契约性,不能看做判决;第三种学说则可以说是前两者的折中,它认为在裁决需要普通法院执行令的限度内,裁决才隶属于法院。贝纳德所描述的这三种学说现在分别被称为司法权说(jurisdictional theory)、契约说(contractual theory)与混合说(mixed or hybrid theory)。20世纪60年代中期以来又发展起来一种新学说,人们称为自治说(autonomous theory)。[7]

一、司法权说

司法权说认为,国家具有控制和管理在其管辖领域内所有仲裁的权力,除非国内法承认当事人有权提交仲裁,授权仲裁员裁定争议,并使仲裁员的判决具有强制性,否则仲裁是无意义和无的。质言之,仲裁的权限与效力源自国内法的让与。司法权说的实质在于强调法律的确定性,使裁决服从裁决作出地国的法律。其结果往往是仲裁必须适用仲裁地国的程序法与冲突规则。相应地,它使当事人和仲裁员自主权受到较大限制。

二、契约说

与司法权说相反,契约说则从仲裁的基础、仲裁庭的组成乃至仲裁的执行都有赖于当事人的合意这一事实发,认定仲裁具有契约性质。法国学者尼波耶特(Niboyet)提出,仲裁裁决具有契约性质,这是因为仲裁员权力的取得,不是来自法律或司法机构,而是来自当事人间的协议。仲裁员是按照当事人在协议中的意愿裁决争议的。当事人让仲裁员以公断人身份作出裁决是一种真正的委托,由此,裁决也被注入了契约性……如同所有协议一样,裁决必然具有法定效力,而且具有终审判决的权威。[8] 学者认为,商事仲裁是商人社会自律的产物,现代国际商事仲裁制度天生就具有契约,国际商事仲裁也离不开当事人之间的仲裁协议,

---

〔7〕 陈治东:《国际商事仲裁法》,法律出版社1998年版,第6~9页。
〔8〕 转引自韩健:《现代国际商事仲裁法的理论与实践》,法律出版社2000年版,第36~38页。

契约说学者抓住了仲裁的本质。[9] 契约说学者在强调仲裁的契约性的同时,否认国家对仲裁的影响。他们认为,仲裁裁决的拘束力及其强制执行力均源自其作为合同的效力,而不是源自判决或公共机构的授权。国家对仲裁的影响与干预等同于对所有其他合同的影响与干预。契约说的本质在于强调当事人在选择支配其关系的法律方面有着无限的自主权力。

三、混合说

作为司法权说与契约说折衷调协的产物,混合说在现代国际商事仲裁学界占有较大的优势,许多著名学者都倾向于这一理论。混合说学者认为,仲裁起始于当事人的私人协议,继之以民间性的程序,该程序极为尊重当事人的意愿;而仲裁的结果是作出具有拘束力的裁决,如果条件符合,绝大多数国家的法院将承认与执行该裁决。因此,这一民间程序具有了公共性效力,在各国法律确定的公共当局的支持下得以执行。[10] 因此,仲裁是一种混合的特殊司法制度,它起源于当事人的协议,并从民事法律中获得司法效力。在混合论者看来,尽管司法权说与契约说是相互对立的理论,但从仲裁实践来看,二者是可以协调的。现实是,仲裁既遵循了私法,又遵守了程序法,即仲裁既含有私法因素,又含有公法因素,契约和诉讼程序的特征在仲裁中兼而有之。就准据法的适用而言,混合说主张仲裁员应在仲裁地国际私法规则允许的范围内尊重与适用当事人选择的法律,在当事人没有明示选择的情况下,仲裁员可直接根据仲裁地国际私法规则确定准据法。[11]

四、自治说

自治论者把国际商事仲裁的发展归结为商人注重实效的结果,首先由商人在不顾及法律的情况下依其意思自治产生并发展了仲裁,而后仲裁才得到法律的确认。所以,当事人基于仲裁制度的实际需要自主决定仲裁适用的实体法与程序法。而只有使仲裁协议和仲裁裁决具有可执行性,才能保证国际商事关系顺利进行。自治说学者认为仲裁的性质不应与司法权与契约联系起来,他们既反对将仲裁制度定性为纯契约性或纯司法性,也反对混合说的观点。

自治说实质上是承认仲裁的非国内化以及当事人对仲裁的无限意思自治。由此,仲裁实质上具备了超国家的性质,当事人不仅可以选择国内法,也可以选择国际商法或有关贸易惯例,甚至可以选择一般公平原则等来裁定其关系。当事人

---

〔9〕 宋连斌:《国际商事仲裁管辖权研究》,法律出版社2000年版,第16~18页。

〔10〕 A. Redfern & M. Hunter, Law and Practice of International Commercial Arbitration, Sweet & Maxwell Limited, 1991, p. 8.

〔11〕 单文华主编:《国际贸易法学》,北京大学出版社2000年版,第903~904页。

未作明示选择时,仲裁员可以自主决定适用其认为适当的冲突规则,甚至可以直接适用有关的国际法或国际规则。[12] 表面看来,上述四种学说各有所重,甚至针锋相对,但究其实质,也仅仅是侧重点不同而已。司法权说并不否认仲裁具有意思自治与契约性的一面,契约说也不完全否认国内法院对仲裁干预的权力与事实。自治说虽然试图从根本上否定仲裁与国内法及内法院的联系,但也仅仅是一种理论预设,实践中并不多见,或者说至少未为仲裁实践的主流所接受。因此,至少在目前,混合说是最见全面的一种观点。但也有学者提出,与其将仲裁的性质简单地理解为司法性、契约性或自治性,不如全面地将之视为兼具契约性、自治性、民间性和准司法性的一种争议解决方式。这种综合理解更符合仲裁制度的发展历史及其本身的特质。[13]

第三节　商事仲裁制度的发展

仲裁作为争端解决方式,具有悠久的历史。早在古罗马时代,就开始了以仲裁方式解决商业往来中发生的纠纷。《十二表法》中就有关于仲裁的记载。中世纪时,在地中海等地的港口与集市,都设置了处理商事争议的行商法院(piepowder)。这种法院不同于现代意义的法院,它们的"法官"不只是商人自身,且每一争议的"陪审团"成员中有一半是本国商人,一半是外国商人,此种陪审团又称"双语陪审团"(half-tongue jury)。这些商人"法官"四处流动办案,既强调公正,也强调效率,要求审理案件像"弹去脚上的灰尘"那么快,或要求裁决在"潮汐之间"作出。这种"法院的程序也很不正规,其中诉可在无法院令状的情况下进行审理,并可不定期(de hora in horam)进行"。[14] 究其实质,这种争议解决方式与现代商事仲裁极为相近而与现代法院相去甚远。

14 世纪中叶,瑞典的某些地方性法规承认仲裁是解决纠纷的合法途径。1697 年,英国议会正式承认了仲裁制度,产生了第一个仲裁法案。此后,各国先后制定了有关仲裁的法律规定。但是,这一时期的仲裁主要是解决国内民商事纠纷的法律制度。商事仲裁在世界上得到普遍承认与广泛采用,则是 20 世纪的事

〔12〕 韩健:《现代国际商事仲裁法的理论与实践》,法律出版社 2000 年版,第 39~41 页。
〔13〕 黄进等:《仲裁法学》,中国政法大学出版社 1999 年版,第 5 页。
〔14〕 [英]施米托夫:《国际贸易论文选》,赵秀文译,中国大百科全书出版社 1993 年版,第 6~7 页。

情。[15] 仲裁的下述特点或者说优点，是它获得很快发展的重要因素：[16]

1. 仲裁自愿性。现代仲裁制度以当事人意思自治为首要原则，仲裁制度的内容充分体现了当事人意思自治原则。当事人可以自由协商是否将争议提交仲裁、向何机构或人员提交仲裁、仲裁庭如何组成、适用怎样的仲裁规则、争议实体的适用法律等事项。

2. 专业性。仲裁员往往从众多专业人士中选任。当事人可以事先了解各仲裁员的专业背景，选择具有相关专业背景的仲裁员审理案件、解决纠纷。民商事纠纷往往涉及具体而复杂的内容，具有较为突出的技术性。仲裁的专业性恰恰适应了民商事纠纷的专业需求，具有诉讼所无法替代的优势。

3. 保密性。仲裁一般以不公开审理为原则。对于不公开审理的案件，各国仲裁法及有关仲裁规则大都规定了相关人员的保密义务。《CITAC 仲裁规则 2005》第 33 条明确规定，不公开审理的案件，双方当事人及其仲裁代理人、证人、仲裁员、仲裁庭咨询的专家和指定的鉴定人、仲裁委员会秘书局的有关人员，均不得对外界透露案件实体和程序进行的情况。这与民事诉讼以公开审理为一般原则的情形不同，可以较好地为当事人保密，有利于维护当事人的商业形象。

4. 独立性。仲裁机构是民间机构，仲裁员是民间人士，不隶属于任何国家机关。仲裁机构相互之间、仲裁庭相互之间也不存在隶属关系。由此，仲裁庭对案件实体的审理不受仲裁机构和法院的干涉。我国仲裁法规定法院对于国际商事仲裁案件的实体审理不享有司法监督权。但是，现代仲裁制度仍然以国家法律为仲裁的依据，以国家司法机关的支持、监督为其后盾。

5. 快捷性、灵活性和经济性。仲裁一般实行一裁终局制度，各仲裁规则中均规定有审理时限，可以使当事人的纠纷在较短的时间内得到解决。仲裁可以不拘泥于仲裁地点、仲裁时间，可以根据当事人的意愿简化仲裁程序，体现了较强的灵活性。仲裁着重考虑当事人的意愿，其快捷性、灵活性可以使当事人节省大量的时间与金钱。这一经济性特征再次显现出仲裁相对于诉讼的优势。

6. 国家司法机关对于仲裁裁决的承认与执行。双方当事人地位平等、权利义务对等、裁决者中立的仲裁结构是仲裁公正性的保障。由于法院的判决是法院国的一种主权行为，所以只有在符合较为严格的条件的情况下，才能得到他国法院的承认与执行。相反，仲裁裁决系由民间机构作出，与主权无涉，故易于得到他国法院的承认与执行。例如，《德国民事诉讼法》第 328 条规定，对外国法院判决的

[15] 程德钧等编著：《国际惯例与涉外仲裁实务》，中国青年出版社 1993 年版，第 156 页。

[16] Hans Van Houtte, The Law of International Trade, Sweet & Maxwell, 1995, pp. 410 – 412.

承认与执行以互惠为条件,而按第1061条规定,对外国仲裁裁决的承认与执行则不以互惠为条件。世界上已有100多个国家加入了1958年《纽约公约》,使国际商事仲裁裁决在世界上绝大多数国家都能得到承认与执行。仲裁裁决与法院判决具有同等的强制执行性,有力地保证了当事人纠纷的最终解决。

诚然,仲裁也有它的短处。首先,仲裁不是一种能够完全自足的制度。这与仲裁的民间性不无关系。在当事人未自动履行仲裁裁决的情况下,裁决需求助于执行地法院的支持方能得到执行。这时,仲裁裁决及其程序就必须接受法院的审查。尽管这种审查是有限度的,但毕竟说明仲裁不是完全自足的一种制度,这可以说是它最大的不足。其次,仲裁协议是仲裁的前提条件,仲裁建立在契约基础之上,仲裁裁决只能拘束争端当事人双方,而不能约束第三人。最后,尽管在许多国家(如我国),仲裁费低于诉讼费,但是在一些国家,依据有关法律的规定,法官是国家公务人员,法院是国家审判职能机构,故当事人无须为法院与法官本身付费,而只需支付诉讼过程中的传唤费、受理费、法庭费、登记费等费用。但是在仲裁的情况下,当事人应当向仲裁员支付酬金。因而,仲裁费用可能会高于诉讼费用。[17]

第四节　商事仲裁的法律渊源

商事仲裁的正式法律渊源主要有两种:一种为国际条约;一种为国内立法。此外,国际商事仲裁还有一些非正式的法律渊源。

一、国际条约

关于商事仲裁的专门国际条约包括国际公约与双边条约,但以国际公约为主。国际公约可以分为两类:全球性国际公约和区域性国际公约。全球性国际公约主要包括国际联盟主持下的《仲裁条款议定书》《关于执行外国仲裁裁决公约》与联合国主持下的《纽约公约》。《仲裁条款议定书》是最早的全球性国际商事仲裁公约,1929年9月24日在国际联盟的主持下于日内瓦签署,共计8条。其主要内容包括:各缔约国承认仲裁协议的效力;仲裁程序包括仲裁庭的组成在内,应依当事人的意思与仲裁地国法律规定;缔约国保证由本国有权机关依照该国法律执行按公约规定在其境内作出的仲裁裁决。《关于执行外国仲裁裁决的公约》是对《仲裁条款议定书》的补充,1927年9月26日签订于日内瓦,共11条。1958年6

〔17〕 Hans Van Houtte, The Law of International Trade, Sweet & Maxwell, 1995, pp. 412 - 414.

月10日,在纽约召开的联合国国际商事仲裁会议上通过了《纽约公约》。公约共16条,比较详细地规定了缔约国对仲裁协议与仲裁条款的承认、仲裁裁决的约束力以及拒绝承认与执行外国仲裁裁决的条件。目前,《纽约公约》已在事实上取代了上述两个公约。成为世界上缔约国最多的公约之一。截至1998年8月,已有145个国家和地区加入该公约。[18] 我国已于1986年加入这一公约区域性国际公约主要指由一些区域性国际组织主持签订的国际商事仲裁公约,如《欧洲国际商事仲裁公约》《美洲国家国际商事仲裁公约》《阿拉伯国家商事仲裁公约》等。

除国际公约外,许多双边条约也涉及仲裁问题,例如中波(波兰)《关于民事与刑事司法协助的协定》第21条、中德《关于民事商事司法协助的协定》第25条均规定"缔约双方应根据1958年6月10日在纽约签订的关于承认与执行外国仲裁裁决的公约,相互承认与执行在对方境内作出的仲裁裁决"。1979年《中美贸易关系协定》第8条规定:"(1)缔约双方对两国的商号、公司和贸易组织间签订的合同所引起的或与其有关的任何争议,鼓励其通过友好协商、调解或其他双方均可接受的方式,迅速解决。(2)如果此类争议按上述方式之一不能迅速解决,争议双方可以根据合同规定的条款或仲裁协议,提请仲裁解决。此类仲裁可以由中华人民共和国、美利坚合众国或第三国的仲裁机构进行。仲裁采用各该仲裁机构的仲裁程序规则,也可以在争议双方和仲裁机构同意的情况下,采用联合国推荐的联合国国际贸易法委员会仲裁规则或其他仲裁规则。(3)缔约各方应设法保证由被申请执行仲裁裁决的国家主管当局,根据适用的法律和规章,承认与执行仲裁裁决。"目前,我国已经与包括欧盟在内的100多个国家和地区签订了此类贸易协定。[19]

二、国内法

就一国而言,仲裁分内国仲裁与外国仲裁。前者指在国内进行的仲裁;后者指在外国进行的仲裁,其中内国仲裁又可分为国内仲裁与国际仲裁(涉外仲裁),国内仲裁与涉外(国际)仲裁均须受本国仲裁法管辖,即便是外国仲裁,也可能因要在内国执行而受到内国仲裁法的影响。所以,各国关于仲裁的国内立法是国际商事仲裁的重要法律渊源。

自1697年的英国仲裁法案通过后,各国纷纷制定自己的仲裁法,到目前为止,世界上大多数国家都有自己的仲裁法,我国也不例外。1994年8月31日,八届人大常委会九次会议通过的《仲裁法》是我国第一部专门的仲裁立法。该法于

---

〔18〕 李虎:《国际商事仲裁裁决的强制执行》,法律出版社2000年版,第57页。

〔19〕 赵秀文:《21世纪中国国际仲裁法律制度现代化与国际化的发展方向》,载《河南省政法管理干部学院学报》2001年第3期。

1995 年 9 月 1 日起施行,适用于我国境内仲裁机构进行的所有仲裁。除《仲裁法》外,我国《民事诉讼法》《海事诉讼特别程序法》《合同法》等法律及有关法规、司法解释中也都有关于仲裁的规定。

三、非正式渊源

除有关国际条约与国内法外,尚有一些规则与仲裁制度密切相关,我们不妨笼统称为商事仲裁的非正式法律渊源。这些非正式渊源主要包括:

1. 示范法

示范法(model law)或称模范法、样板法。它既不是国际条约,也非国内立法,而是一种法的模式或样板。示范法通常由某一国际组织主持制定,然后由各主权国家采纳为国内法。在采纳示范法时,各国还可以对其进行修订或补充。示范法对于协调与统一各国国内法,具有重要意义。1985 年 UNCITRAL 制定的《示范法》,以促成各国仲裁立法的协调化与统一化发展为宗旨,对仲裁协议、仲裁庭的组成与管辖权、仲裁程序的进行、仲裁裁决的作出与程序的终止、对裁决的追诉以及承认与执行等方面作了较为系统而明确的规定。来自不同法律体系的 50 多个国家和 10 多个国际组织代表参加了《示范法》的起草工作,因而《示范法》具有广泛的代表性与重要的示范意义。许多国家与地区已经直接采纳了这一示范法。[20] 我国《仲裁法》也在相当程度上参考了示范法的有关规则。

2. 仲裁规则

仲裁规则是指国际组织或常设仲裁机构所制定的关于仲裁的程序规则。仲裁规则本身不是正式意义上的法律,但一经仲裁当事人采纳,即对该当事人及仲裁庭产生拘束力。世界各国的一些常设仲裁机构,如国际商会仲裁院、斯德哥尔摩商会仲裁院、伦敦国际仲裁院、中国国际经济贸易仲裁委员会、中国海事仲裁委员会等,均制定了自己的仲裁规则。这些仲裁规则一般都规定有仲裁庭的组成及权限、仲裁地、仲裁审理、仲裁裁决、仲裁语文及仲裁费用等内容。一些非仲裁机构的国际组织也制定了仲裁规则,以供选用。例如,UNCITRAL 于 1976 年制定了《仲裁规则》,供当事人双方约定将争议提交临时仲裁时选择使用。

---

〔20〕 如澳大利亚、百慕大、保加利亚、加拿大、塞浦路斯、埃及、荷兰、中国香港、墨西哥、尼日利亚、秘鲁、俄罗斯、突尼斯等国家和地区,以及美国的加州、康涅狄格、俄勒冈、得克萨斯等州都直接采纳了《示范法》。See Hans Van Houtte, The Law of International Trade. Sweet & Maxwell 1995, p. 318;陈治东:《国际商事仲裁法》,法律出版社 1998 年版,第 33 ~ 34 页。

第二章 仲裁协议

第一节 仲裁协议的概念

关于仲裁协议的概念,《仲裁法》未作规定。《CIETAC 仲裁规则 2005》第 5 条第 2 款仅规定,“仲裁协议系指当事人在合同中订明的仲裁条款,或者以其他方式达成的提交仲裁的书面协议”。一般而言,仲裁协议,是指双方当事人自愿将他们之间已经发生或者将来可能发生的商事争议提交仲裁解决的协议。仲裁协议具有以下特点:(1)仲裁协议是双方当事人之间仲裁合意的法律化形式,体现出双方当事人自愿以仲裁的方式解决纠纷。(2)仲裁协议当事人的权利与义务具有同一性,以仲裁方式解决争端是当事人权利与义务的全部内容。(3)仲裁协议具有广泛的约束力,双方当事人、法院、仲裁庭均受其约束。任何一方当事人不得就协议仲裁的争议事项提起诉讼;法院也不得受理约定以仲裁解决的争议案件;仲裁庭应当依据协议的授权通过仲裁解决纠纷。〔21〕

仲裁协议通常有仲裁条款与仲裁协议书两种类型。仲裁条款,是指争议发生之前,当事人在商事合同中订立的,约定将未来可能发生的商事争议提交仲裁解决的协议。仲裁条款是实践中最普遍采用的方式,一般以商事合同中的一个独立条款的形式存在。但是,实践中经常发生在商事合同不存在、无效、失效情况下,仲裁条款是否具有法律效力的争议。仲裁协议书,是指当事人在争议发生之前或之后单独订立的,约定将未来可能发生或者已经发生的商事争议提交仲裁解决的协议。仲裁协议书相对于仲裁条款来说,具有更为突出的独立性,可以不受当事人之间是否订有商事合同的约束。不论当事人之间发生的是契约性纠纷还是非契约性纠纷,当事人都可以根据仲裁协议书提交仲裁解决。此外,仲裁协议还可以是其他有关书面文件中包含的仲裁协议,以及当事人通过援引达成的仲裁协议。〔22〕

仲裁协议是仲裁的基础与前提。没有仲裁协议,仲裁机构就不能受理案件,当事人也就无法实现以仲裁解决争端的愿望。各国立法与各仲裁机构的仲裁规则均对此作出了明确的规定。例如我国《仲裁法》第 4 条规定:“当事人采用仲裁

〔21〕 乔欣:《仲裁权研究:仲裁程序公正与权利保障》,法律出版社 2001 年版,第 72 页

〔22〕 参见张斌生主编:《仲裁法新论》,厦门大学出版社 2004 年版,第四章“仲裁协议的效力”、第五章“仲裁协议的形式”。

方式解决纠纷,应当双方自愿,达成仲裁协议。没有仲裁协议,一方申请仲裁的,仲裁委员会不予受理。"《CIETAC 仲裁规则 2005》第 5 条第 1 款也明确规定:"仲裁委员会根据当事人在争议发生之前或者在争议发生之后达成的将争议提交仲裁委员会仲裁的仲裁协议和一方当事人的书面申请,受理案件。"

第二节　仲裁协议的有效要件

仲裁协议的有效要件,是指仲裁协议有效成立所必须具备的基本条件。仲裁协议的有效要件通常包括仲裁协议的形式、当事人的行为能力以及争议事项的可仲裁性三个方面。

一、仲裁协议的形式

尽管有少数国家(如瑞典与挪威)的仲裁法对于仲裁协议的形式未作要求,但是大多数国家的立法要求仲裁协议应当以书面形式订立。[23]

书面形式要求的法律效果有三种:第一种以此作为仲裁协议的有效要件,例如,1981 年《法国民事诉讼法》第 1443 条规定:"仲裁条款除非以书面在主合同中或在后者提及的文件中叙明,否则是无效的。"《纽约公约》第 2 条第 1 款也规定书面形式是仲裁协议有效并因此得到缔约国承认与执行的形式要件。第二种是作为协议存在的证明,如 1986 年的荷兰《仲裁法》第 1021 条规定,"仲裁协议应以文件证明"。第三种则仅要求以"书面"形式订立仲裁协议,而不具体言明其法律后果,如《美洲国家国际商事仲裁公约》第 10 条规定,仲裁协议"应该采用书面形式"订立。我国《仲裁法》第 16 条也作出相同的规定。[24] 要求仲裁协议采用书面形式,有利于证明当事人同意将争议效要提交仲裁的意愿。但是,随着社会的发展,书面形式如果局限于传统的纸面范畴,将会给商事实践和仲裁实践带来法律障碍。UNCITRAL 在制定《示范法》时,已经注意到了这一事实,采用扩大"书面形式"法律内涵的方式来解决书面形式所面临的问题。《示范法》第 7 条第 2 款规定:"仲裁协议如果包含在当事人签署的一个文件中,或者包含在记录该合同的信件、电传、电报或其他电讯通信的交换中,或包含在一方主张协议存在而他方并不否认的关于申诉与答辩的陈述的交换中,就是以书面作出的。"我国《合同法》第

---

〔23〕 李浩培:《国际民事程序法概论》,法律出版社 1996 年版,第 204 页

〔24〕 《仲裁法》第 16 条规定,"仲裁协议包括合同中订立的仲裁条款和以其他书面方式在纠纷发生前或者纠纷发生后达成的请求仲裁的协议"。

11 条规定，书面形式是指合同书、信件和数据电文（包括电报、电传、传真、电子数据交换和电子邮件）等可以有形地表现所载内容的形式。据此，应当肯定以数据电文的形式达成的仲裁协议的效力。

在内、外国关于仲裁协议形式要求的法律规定不相一致的情况下，一般应依内国的国际私法规则来决定协议形式的准据法。例如，德国 1896 年《民法施行法》第 11 条规定，“法律行为的方式，依构成该行为客体的那个法律关系应适用的法律规定，但遵守该行为作出地法律也已足够”。因此，只要符合行为客体适用法或者行为地法的规定，仲裁协议即属有效。

二、仲裁协议当事人的行为能力

当事人在订立仲裁协议时应当具有行为能力是仲裁协议的有效要件之一，这一点已为世界绝大多数国家法律所认同。[25] 我国《仲裁法》第 17 条规定，“无民事行为能力人或者限制民事行为能力人订立的仲裁协议”无效。这一要件也已得到《纽约公约》的肯定。[26] 然而《纽约公约》也并未规定判定当事人行为能力问题的准据法。因而，除了有关国际条约外，当事人行为能力将依法院地的冲突规则解决。

当事人的行为能力分自然人的行为能力与法人的行为能力两种。自然人的行为能力一般依其属人法，即本国法或住所地法。现在，大陆法国家多主张适用本国法，而英美法系国家多主张采用“住所地法”。[27] 除属人法外，许多国家主张可以选择适用当事人属人法或行为地法。例如德国 1896 年《民法施行法》第 7 条第 3 款规定：“外国人依本国法为无能力或限制能力，而依德国法为有能力者，就其在德国所为之法律行为视为有行为能力。”日本、瑞士、葡萄牙、希腊、泰国、意大利、匈牙利、波兰、捷克等国的法律也都有类似规定。英国与法国的实践也肯定了这一属人法与行为地法共同支配的原则。[28]

同自然人一样，大多数国家规定，法人的行为能力也依其属人法，即法人国籍国法。然而对于确立法人国籍的标准各国有所不同，如登记地标准、住所地标准、经济活动中心标准、资本控制标准等。登记地标准，即依法人成立地决定法人国籍的观点目前得到了英、美等国的采纳。住所地标准则得到了大陆法系国家的普遍支持，但其认定标准又各不相同。一种以管理中心地（董事会所在

---

〔25〕 韩健：《现代国际商事仲裁法的理论与实践》，法律出版社 2000 年版，第 62 ~ 63 页。

〔26〕 《纽约公约》第 5 条规定，当事人在订立仲裁协议时根据他们所适用的法律元行为能力的，被请求承认与执行仲裁裁决的主管机关可以据当事人的请求，拒绝承认执行有关裁决。

〔27〕 董立坤：《国际私法论》，法律出版社 2000 年版，第 211 页。

〔28〕 韩健：《现代国际商事仲裁法的理论与实践》，法律出版社 2000 年版，第 64 页

地)为国籍标志,如德、法、意、比、荷及瑞士;一种以营业中心所在地(矿场、工厂所在地)为国籍标志。资本控制标准,或称实际控制标准,是指以法人的控制者的国籍为法人的国籍。这一标准是登记地标准和住所地标准的辅助标准,“二战”后曾被各国普遍用以处理外国在内国的财产事宜。最高人民法院1988年《关于贯彻执行民法通则若干问题的意见》第184条指出“外国法人以其注册登记地国家的法律为其本国法,法人的民事行为能力依其本国法确定”。据此,我国采登记地标准。

三、争议事项的可仲裁性

争议事项的可仲裁性(arbitrability)也是仲裁协议的有效要件之一。争议事项的可仲裁性,是指对于当事人之间所发生的争议,一国法律是否允许以仲裁方式加以解决的问题。我国《仲裁法》第17条规定,“约定的仲裁事项超出法律规定的仲裁范围的”仲裁协议无效。

诚然,当事人只能将可以自行决定的事项提交仲裁,而不能将不能自行协商决定的权利纠纷提交仲裁。[29] 各国立法对可仲裁事项的范围作出了限定。这一做法也得到了国际公约的认可。可仲裁范围是法律的授权,具有强制性。当事人约定的争议事项不属于有关国家可仲裁范围的,不能提交仲裁,即便提交仲裁并作出裁决,该裁决也会被该国的法院撤销或者拒绝承认和执行。因此,即便是当事人可以自行决定的权利决定,仍应受到有关国家法律的约束。

国际公约及各国立法对于可仲裁性的规定经历了由严格到适当放宽的过程。如法国《民事诉讼法》规定,凡因当事人能自由规定的权利所引起的一切争议都可作为仲裁的内容,但反垄断、商标权等知识产权争议除外。而英国《1996年仲裁法》第1条则规定“当事人可以自由约定解决争议的方法,但以不违反公共利益为限”。《德国民事诉讼法》第1030条第1款规定“任何财产法上的请求都能成为仲裁协议的标的。关于非财产法上的请求的仲裁协议,以当事人就所争议的标的有权达成和解的为限,有法律效力”。因此,可仲裁性应当以当事人能够决定其权利为基础,以能够通过和解的方式解决争议为限制条件。当然,仍有许多国家认为涉及竞争法、反托拉斯法、婚姻地位及知识产权等问题的争议事项不能仲裁。

我国《仲裁法》第2条规定:“平等主体的公民、法人和其他组织之间发生的合同纠纷和其他财产权益纠纷,可以仲裁。”第3条又规定:“下列争议不能仲裁:(1)婚姻、收养、监护、抚养、继承纠纷;(2)依法应当由行政机关处理的行政争

---

〔29〕 K. H. Boeck Stìegel, Public Policy and Arbitrability, in ICCA series No. 3, Kluwer, 1987, p. 177.

议。”对于涉及侵权的合同争议能否仲裁，我国的司法实务在近十年里发生了从严到宽的变化。〔30〕 2000年，我国两大涉外仲裁机构修改其仲裁规则时，都将包括侵权行为在内的非契约性争议规定在可仲裁范围之内。〔31〕 我国台湾地区1998年修订的“仲裁法”参考德、日等国的立法，在第1条明确规定仲裁适用于一切可以以和解的方式解决的纠纷，包括侵权与违约竞合的纠纷。

对于争议事项可仲裁性问题的准据法，各国学者看法不一。有人主张应受法院地法制约，有人主张应根据仲裁协议准据法，还有人则主张重叠适用法院地法与协议准据法。在实践中，当事人往往还需考虑裁决执行地国的有关规定。〔32〕

第三节 仲裁条款的独立性

仲裁条款的独立性是指合同中的仲裁条款的效力是否独立于主合同，尤其是当主合同变更、解除、无效或终止时，合同中的仲裁条款的效力是否可以独立存在而不受主合同的影响。传统观点认为，仲裁条款与主合同不可分，主合同无效则仲裁条款无效；现代国际商事仲裁的理论与实践则普遍坚持仲裁条款独立性原则，主张仲裁条款与主合同是可以分割的，仲裁条款与主合同是两项分离的或独立的契约，主合同处理当事人双方的权利与义务，仲裁条款具有保障当事人通过救济实现商事权利的特殊性质与职能，专门处理双方因商事权利义务而产生的争执。〔33〕 因此，仲裁条款的效力独立于主合同的效力，其有效性不受主合同有效性的影响，即使主合同无效，仲裁条款仍然有效。〔34〕〔35〕 这一现代观点被称为“仲裁条款自治说”（doctrine of arbitration clause autonomy）。按此说，仲裁条款本身赋予仲裁庭行使对当事人之间争议的裁决权。因此，如果当事人对合同有效性提出异议，则此异议应由仲裁庭而不是法院解决。

20世纪60年代以来，仲裁条款的独立性已经得到世界各国的普遍承认。例如英国《1996年仲裁法》第7条、《德国民事诉讼法》第1040条均明确规定了仲裁条款独立原则。但是各国的承认程度并不一致，尤其是主合同自始无效或者不存

---

〔30〕 参见《最高人民法院公报》1989年第1期、1998年第3期。

〔31〕 《CIETAC仲裁规则2000》第2条；《CMAC仲裁规则2000》第2条。

〔32〕 韩健：《现代国际商事仲裁法的理论与实践》，法律出版社2000年版，第80～81页

〔33〕 A. Redfern & M. Hunter, Law and Practice of International Commercial Arbitration, Sweet & Maxwell, 1991, pp. 175－176.

〔34〕 宋连斌：《国际商事仲裁管辖权研究》，法律出版社2000年版，第106页。

〔35〕 韩健：《现代国际商事仲裁法的理论与实践》，法律出版社2000年版，第101页。

在的情况下，只有法国、美国、英国等国家及国际商会明确接受独立原则，其他国家的法律均只规定主合同元效并不导致仲裁条款无效，但是对主同自始无效或者不存在的情况下仲裁条款的效力问题却未置可否。

我国立法也采纳了仲裁条款自治说和仲裁条款独立原则。《仲裁法》第 4 条规定："仲裁协议独立存在，合同的变更、解除、终止或者无效，不影响仲裁协议的效力。"但是该法没有规定合同不存在的情况下仲裁条款是否有效的问题。《CIETAC 仲裁规则 2005》第 5 条的规定比较全面："合同中的仲裁条款应视为与合同其他条款分离地、独立地存在的条款，附属于合同的仲裁协议也应视为与合同其他条款分离地、独立地存在的一个部分；合同的变更、解除、终止、转让、失效、无效、未生效、被撤销以及成立与否，均不影响仲裁条款或仲裁协议的效力。"我国的司法实践也开始从认定因欺诈成立的合同（合同自始无效或者不存在）中仲裁条款无效，向肯定仲裁条款效力转变。[36]

一般认为，只要有初步证据表明合同是存在的，其中的仲裁条款是存在的，仲裁庭便可对管辖权异议行使管辖权，直至经审查该当事人之间的合同确实不存在为止。

仲裁条款的措词对其独立性也具重要影响。一些外国判例表明，"广义"的仲裁条款采用的如"因合同产生或与合同有关的争议"的措辞与"狭义"的仲裁条款采用的如"因合同产生的争议"的措辞之间的区别，往往成为法院判定仲裁条款是否具有独立性的主要标准。"因合同产生或与合同有关的争议"这样的措辞足以纳入合同是否有效这类争议。而"因合同产生的争议"的限制性措辞，则只可能使仲裁范围限于有关合同的解释或履行的争议事项，而不包括合同陈述说明中的欺诈问题和合同有效性问题等争议事项。

第四节　仲裁协议的基本内容

仲裁协议的基本内容，是指仲裁协议应当具有的内涵。仲裁协议的基本内容直接反映当事人是否具有提交仲裁的意愿，因而决定仲裁协议的效力、仲裁权的

〔36〕 赵秀文：《论仲裁条款独立原则》，载《法学研究》1997 年第 4 期；齐树洁、蔡从燕：《江苏轻纺公司诉香港裕亿公司等侵权纠纷上诉案评析——关于仲裁制度价值、争议事项可仲裁性及仲裁条款独立性问题》，载柳经纬主编：《厦门大学法律评论》（第 1 期），厦门大学出版社 2001 年版，第 189 ~ 205 页；涂晴：《仲裁条款独立原则与我国审判实践的发展对〈最高人民法院公报〉两个案例的评析》，载《法学》1999 年第 6 期。

取得与行使，是仲裁协议的核心。[37]

通常，仲裁协议应当包括寻求仲裁解决争议的意思表示、仲裁事项、仲裁地点、仲裁机构、仲裁员的指定、仲裁应适用的法律、仲裁语文、仲裁裁决的效力等内容。实践中，仲裁机构往往拟订了示范的仲裁协议条款，以使当事人订立的仲裁协议的内容符合有关法律的规定。例如，CIETAC 拟订的示范仲裁条款是“凡因本合同引起的或与本合同有关的任何争议，均应提交中国国际经济贸易仲裁委员会，按照申请仲裁时该会现行有效的仲裁规则进行仲裁。仲裁裁决是终局的，对双方均有约束力”。

一、寻求仲裁解决争议的意思表示

仲裁协议中应当有当事人自愿将争议提交仲裁的意思表示。这种仲裁合意是仲裁庭享有并行使管辖权的前提。当事人关于提交仲裁的意思表示应当是双方当事人本人共同的、真实的意思表示。非当事人的意思表示、仅为一方当事人的意思表示、不真实的意思表示都不视为仲裁合意，不能产生赋予仲裁庭管辖权的法律效果。

二、仲裁事项

仲裁协议中应当载明当事人提交仲裁解决的争议的范围和性质。例如载明提交“本合同产生的争议”“本合同项下租金数额的争议”“因本合同引起的或者与本合同有关的任何争议”等。明确仲裁事项的范围是仲裁庭受理与裁决的需要和限制范围。多数国家法律要求，仲裁协议须同当事人之间特定法律关系相联系，否则无效。当事人的申请与仲裁庭受理的争议事项均不得超过仲裁协议所约定的范围，否则，就越出部分所作裁决将为无效裁决，得不到承认与执行。

三、仲裁地点

仲裁地在仲裁协议中居于十分重要的地位。因为仲裁地往往决定仲裁所适用的程序法、仲裁裁决的国籍以及有关的司法协助条件。选择仲裁地时，应当有利于提高效率及便利当事人、仲裁员、代理律师及证人，同时还应考虑仲裁裁决的承认与执行等因素。我们认为，为了使仲裁裁决得到普遍承认与执行，最好选择《纽约公约》的成员国或成员地区为仲裁地。

---

〔37〕 乔欣：《仲裁权研究：仲裁程序公正与权利保障》，法律出版社 2001 年版，第 94 页。

四、仲裁机构

选择常设仲裁机构仲裁是最为普遍的做法。据统计,国际贸易中有95%的仲裁案都是在仲裁机构的主持下进行的。当事人可以选择的仲裁机构主要有三类;一为本国的常设仲裁机构,二为对方当事国的仲裁机构;三为第三国的仲裁机构。在当事人未作明确的不同约定的情况下,选择仲裁机构往往产生选择在该仲裁机构所在地进行仲裁的法律效果。但是单纯约定仲裁地点不能直接推知受理争议案件的仲裁机构,除非在该仲裁地只有唯一一家可以受理当事人争议的仲裁机构,而且当事人有着在该仲裁机构进行仲裁的默示意愿。[38]

值得一提的是,对仲裁机构的选择必须明确,不能模棱两可,否则,按有些国家的法律可能导致仲裁机构无法取得管辖权从而使当事人愿望落空。

五、仲裁员的指定

仲裁庭多由1人或3人组成。其中,独任仲裁员多由双方协商指定;三人仲裁庭的情况下,一般双方当事人各指定一名,而第三位仲裁员,即首席仲裁员,则多由当事人所指定的两位仲裁员协商指定,不能协商指定时,由第三人或中立的指定机关指定。仲裁员的具体指定方法可以订人仲裁协议。我国《仲裁法》第31条规定在三人仲裁庭情况下,当事人应各自选定或各自委托仲裁委员会主任指定一名仲裁员,第三名仲裁员由当事人共同选定或共同委托仲裁委员会主任指定,第三名为首席仲裁员。在国际经贸仲裁中,依据《CIETAC仲裁规则2005》的规定,双方当事人可以各自选定或者各自委托仲裁委员会主任指定仲裁员,可以共同选定或者共同委托仲裁委员会主任指定独任仲裁员或首席仲裁员。显然,《仲裁法》与《CIETAC仲裁规则2005》的有关规定既坚持了当事人意思自治,又兼顾了仲裁效率,具有科学性与可操作性。

六、仲裁应适用的法律

当事人应在仲裁协议中明确约定适用于争议实质性事项的准据法,即实体法。当事人没有选择的,仲裁庭很可能会依冲突法规则来确定准据法。在某些国家,也允许仲裁庭不依冲突法规则,而直接适用某国内实体法,或适用商人法(Lex Meratoria)等非国内法律规则。[39] 特别是在当事人在仲裁协议中明确授权仲裁庭依公平原则或作为“友好仲裁人”进行仲裁时尤其如此。

---

〔38〕 莫世健:《论〈仲裁法〉与仲裁协议的可执行性》,载《上海市政法管理干部学院学报》2000年第2期。

〔39〕 黄亚英:《论国际商事仲裁中实质事项的法律适用及其新发展》,载《政治与法律》1999年第3期。

在确立仲裁所依据的实体法的同时，当事人还可在仲裁协议中明確仲裁适用的程序法（仲裁法——Lex arbitri）。一般来说，当程序问题适用仲裁规则无法解决时，应适用仲裁程序法解决。如当事人未对仲裁程序法作出选择，一般情况下会导致仲裁地法的适用。不过，按欧洲近20多年来发展起来的“非国内化”（de-nationalised）国际商事仲裁体系理论，也可能导致对仲裁地之外的法律，如一般法律原则或商人法的适用。[40]

七、仲裁语文

当事人双方认为采用某种语文仲裁对他们较为方便时，一般可以在仲裁协议中作出约定。这一点已为《示范法》第22条第2款所确认。

八、仲裁裁决的效力

尽管各国仲裁法与各仲裁机构的仲裁规则一般都规定仲裁裁决是终局的，当事人不得就此向法院提出上诉，但当事人在仲裁协议中对此作进一步明确仍是有必要的。这样可以避免或减少引起复杂的上诉程序的可能性，也有助于在一方当事人不合作的情况下，尽快组成仲裁庭并行使其充分的权力，在特定条件下可以作出缺席裁决。

除此之外，仲裁协议还可包括仲裁时间表、仲裁费用、仲裁审理等方面的内容。按我国《仲裁法》第16条，仲裁协议必须具有三方面的内容：（1）请求仲裁的意思表示；（2）仲裁事项；（3）选定的仲裁委员会。《仲裁法》第18条进而明确，仲裁协议对仲裁事项或者仲裁委员会没有约定或者约定不明确的，当事人可以补充协议；达不成协议的，仲裁协议无效。

第五节　仲裁协议的效力

仲裁协议的效力，是指有效的仲裁协议对于当事人及有关机构的约束力。自从有仲裁法以来，各国都确认仲裁协议具有相应的法律效力。仲裁协议的效力主要表现在四个方面：

1. 约束仲裁协议当事人

无论是从合同法，还是从仲裁法的角度，仲裁协议对其当事人都具有直接的法律拘束力，具体表现为：

---

〔40〕 韩健：《现代国际商事仲裁法的理论与实践》，法律出版社2000年版，第205～210页。

第一,当事人负有依据仲裁协议的约定提交仲裁的义务。发生仲裁协议约定的仲裁事项后,当事人应当将争议提交仲裁协议所约定的仲裁机构或者临时仲裁庭进行仲裁。除达成新的仲裁协议外,当事人不能向非由协议约定的仲裁机构或者临时仲裁庭提交仲裁。

第二,当事人不能就协议仲裁的争议事项向法院提起诉讼。仲裁协议排除了当事人寻求仲裁以外的法律救济(诉讼)的权利。仲裁协议成立以后,除非当事人之间另有协议,否则当事人丧失了就协议约定的事项向法院提起诉讼的权利。相应地,如果一方当事人违背协议而就有关事项诉诸法院,另一方则有权依据仲裁协议要求法院中止诉讼程序,将争议交由仲裁处理。一方当事人诉诸法院,而另一方不及时提出异议,甚或前往应诉的,各国法律大多将此视为双方已就争议解决方式达成了新的协议,同意以诉讼解决纠纷,从而认定法院享有管辖权,另一方当事人因此丧失了以原仲裁协议排除诉讼管辖权的抗辩权。我国《仲裁法》第26条规定:"当事人达成仲裁协议,一方向人民法院起诉未声明有仲裁协议,人民法院受理后,另一方在首次开庭前提交仲裁协议的,人民法院应当驳回起诉,但仲裁协议无效的除外;另一方在首次开庭前未对人民法院受理该案提出异议的,视为放弃仲裁协议,人民法院应当继续审理。"

第三,当事人负有履行仲裁裁决的义务。因为仲裁协议既是接受仲裁这种争端解决方式的协议,也是接受其结果——仲裁裁决的协议。实际上,当事人同意交付仲裁解决,主要是为了得到一个双方信任的"裁决"。据此,当事人负有履行裁决之义务。

2. 赋予特定仲裁庭以管辖权

仲裁庭的管辖权源自当事人的仲裁合意。当事人的仲裁合意是对仲裁庭的授权。没有这种授权,仲裁庭的管辖权就无从谈起。这与法院的管辖权有明显区别。法院以管辖法定纠纷为天职,法律对法院管辖权制定了级别管辖、专属管辖、地域管辖等强制性的管辖原则。而仲裁庭的管辖权,则是因当事人之间的仲裁协议而产生的约(意)定管辖权。该管辖权不当然适用法律关于法院级别管辖、专属管辖、地域管辖的强制原则。例如《仲裁法》第4条规定:"当事人采用仲裁方式解决纠纷,应当双方自愿,达成仲裁协议。没有仲裁协议,一方申请仲裁的,仲裁委员会不予受理"。第6条进而规定:"仲裁委员会应当由当事人协议选定。仲裁不实行级别管辖与地域管辖。"

3. 排除法院的管辖权

仲裁已经成为一种独立的、具有终局性的争端解决方式,因此仲裁协议赋予仲裁机构以管辖权必然意味着排除法院对同一争议的管辖权。这实质上是一个问题的两个方面。对此,大多数国家的立法均予确认,即使是长期坚持“法院管辖权不容剥夺”的英国也不例外。英国《1996 年仲裁法》第 9 条第 1 款规定,仲裁协议一方当事人被诉(不论是本诉还是反诉)所涉及的事项如果属于根据仲裁协议应当提交仲裁的事项,则该当事人可以向受诉法院提出申请,要求中止就该事项提起的诉讼程序。[41] 根据申请,法院应当准许中止诉讼程序,除非仲裁协议无效、失效、不可操作或者不可执行。我国《仲裁法》第 5 条的规定在确认仲裁协议赋予仲裁机构以管辖权的同时,也明确了仲裁协议排除法院管辖的效力。

四、构成仲裁裁决执行力的法律前提

有效的仲裁协议是仲裁裁决具有强制执行力的重要条件,仲裁裁决的强制执行力是仲裁协议的最终效力表现。各国仲裁法一般都规定,如果一方当事人拒不履行仲裁裁决,另一方当事人可以向有关国家法院提交有效的仲裁协议和裁决书,申请强制执行。但是,如果当事人能够证明仲裁协议不存在或者是无效的或已经失效的,或者裁决事项超出仲裁协议的范围的,法院可以拒绝承认与执行基于该仲裁协议所作出的仲裁裁决。根据我国《仲裁法》第 63 条、第 58 条、第 71 条以及《民事诉讼法》第 217 条、第 260 条的规定,无论国内仲裁还是涉外仲裁,如果没有仲裁协议,或者裁决的事项不属于仲裁协议的范围,人民法院不仅可以裁定不予执行,而且可以撤销该仲裁裁决。

第三章　仲　裁　庭

第一节　仲裁庭的组成

仲裁庭是指依据当事人约定或者仲裁规则的规定,由仲裁员组成的审理仲裁案件的临时性组织。仲裁庭可以由一名或数名仲裁员组成。

关于仲裁庭的组成人数,一般可由当事人合意决定。选择由一名仲裁员组成仲裁庭的,该仲裁庭为独任制仲裁庭,该仲裁员为独任仲裁员,独立审理案件、作出裁决。选择由多名仲裁员组成仲裁庭的,该仲裁庭为合议制仲裁庭,通常设一名首席仲裁员,由首席仲裁员主持案件的仲裁。但是有些国家的法律强制规定应

---

[41] A party on an arbitration agreement against whom legal proceedings are brought (whether by way of claim or counterclaim) in respect of a matter which under the agreement is to be referred to arbitration (upon notice to the other party to the proceedings) apply to the court in which the proceedings have been brought to stay the proceedings so far as they concern that matter.

当由奇数仲裁员组成。[42] 多数国家的做法较为灵活，规定当仲裁协议约定的仲裁庭组成人员为偶数时，可以再补任一名仲裁员。[43] 依据《仲裁法》第30条的规定，在我国，仲裁庭可以由1名或3名仲裁员组成。在由3名仲裁员组成仲裁庭的情况下，应当设首席仲裁员。可见，我国也属于要求仲裁庭人数为奇数的国家，只是规定得更为具体明确。

当事人既没有约定仲裁庭的组成方法，也没有通过适用某一仲裁规则作出此种安排的，多数国家通过立法授权由法院决定仲裁庭的组成，如法国、[44] 美国、[45] 比利时[46] 以及一些拉美国家。少数国家的法律则认为这类仲裁协议无效。

值得一提的是，在一些国际商业组织或贸易协会内部的贸易仲裁中，仲裁庭往往由两名仲裁员组成。在这种体制下，争议发生后，先由双方各自指定一名富有经验的仲裁员组成贸易庭(trade tribunal)。如果该贸易庭不能就争议的解决达成一致意见，则将争议提交一名公断人(umpire)，由他像独任仲裁员一样进行仲裁。此时，原来的两名仲裁员将以各自当事人的辩护人(advocate)的身份参加后一阶段的仲裁，而不再具有仲裁员的身份。[47] 这种仲裁庭组成方法因其快速而不拘形式，在实践中颇见高效。

第二节　仲裁员的资格

担任仲裁员应当具有相应的资格，是体现仲裁专业性、独立性、公正性的内在要求。对于仲裁员资格的基本要求主要有三个方面。

第一，具有完全民事行为能力的要求。仲裁员必须具有完全民事行为能力，不能是无民事行为能力人或限制民事行为能力人。这是最基本的要求。有些国家的法律对此有明文规定，如法国、荷兰等国。

第二，国籍、职业等特定身份的要求。过去有许多国家(如葡萄牙、伊朗及拉美国家)的法律不允许外国人作为仲裁员。但是现在，为了适应现代国际商事仲

---

〔42〕 这类国家有意大利、西班牙、巴西、委内瑞拉、哥伦比亚、哥斯达黎加、伊拉克、厄瓜多尔、叙利亚、南斯拉夫等。

〔43〕 韩健：《现代国际商事仲裁法的理论与实践》，法律出版社2000年版，第153页。

〔44〕 参见法国《民事诉讼法》第1493条第2款。

〔45〕 参见美国《联邦统一仲裁法》第3条。

〔46〕 参见比利时《司法法典》(1995年修订本)第1684条。

〔47〕 A. Redfern & M. Hunter, Law and Practice of International Commercial Arbitration, Sweet & Maxwell, 1991, p. 199.

裁实践的需要,包括我国在内的绝大多数国家都允许外国人担任仲裁员。[48] 许多国家的法律禁止法官担任仲裁员(如奥地利),而有的国家(如美国与法国)则允许法官在某些条件下成为仲裁员。一些国际标准合同,特别是航运与商品交易方面的格式合同的仲裁条款规定只有"从事贸易的人"或"商人"才能被选为仲裁员。西班牙、葡萄牙、智利与厄瓜多尔等一些国家的法律规定,在当事人约定依法仲裁争议的情况下,只有律师才能被选为仲裁员。瑞士虽然不强求律师为仲裁员,但却规定不得排除律师的仲裁员资格。

第三,专业资历的要求。各国法律、有关仲裁机构的仲裁规则中,对于仲裁员专业资历也提出了程度不同的要求。我国《仲裁法》在这一方面的要求较高。《仲裁法》第13条规定:"仲裁委员会应当从公道正派的人员中聘任仲裁员。仲裁员应当符合下列条件之一:(1)从事仲裁工作满8年的;(2)从事律师工作满8年的;(3)曾任审判员满8年的;(4)从事法律研究、教学工作并具有高级职称的;(5)具有法律知识、从事经济贸易等专业工作并具有高级职称或者具有同等专业水平的。"

根据我国《仲裁法》第13条和多数仲裁机构仲裁规则的规定,仲裁委员会应当设有专门的仲裁员名册,只有列入名册的人才可能被指定为仲裁员。这一做法与国际商会仲裁院以及其他许多国家的做法不同。国际商会仲裁院、斯德哥尔摩商会仲裁院及美国仲裁协会等机构或者没有专门的仲裁员名册,或者即使有专门的仲裁员名册,也允许当事人在名册中或者名册外指定仲裁员。因此,有学者提出应当对这一制度进行改革。[49] 值得注意的是,《CIETAC 仲裁规则 2005》第21条第2款规定:"当事人约定在仲裁委员会仲裁员名册之外选定仲裁员的,当事人选定的或根据当事人之间的协议指定的人士经仲裁委员会主任依法确认后可以担任仲裁员、首席仲裁员或独任仲裁员。"

最后,需要说明的是,在仲裁员的资格方面,除法律有强制性规定外,各国一般都承认当事人的意思自治。例如《示范法》规定,被指定的仲裁员如不具备双方约定的资格,则构成对该仲裁员提出反对的理由、对仲裁庭提出无管辖权的理由,作为撤销仲裁裁决的理由以及拒绝承认与执行仲裁裁决的理由。[50]

---

〔48〕 有学者提出,我国应当重视仲裁员的国际化。在我国仲裁机构中增加海外仲裁员,可以带来国外仲裁制度发展的最新情况,以及发达的仲裁制度的有益经验,从而促进我国仲裁制度的发展以及与国际上的一般做法接轨,增加我国仲裁机构的可依赖性。参见肖永平、胡永庆:《加入 WTO 与我国仲裁法律制度改革》,载《中国法学》2001年第2期。

〔49〕 赵秀文:《21世纪中国国际仲裁法律制度现代化与国际化的发展向》,载《河南省政法管理干部学院学报》2001年第3期。

〔50〕 《示范法》第12条、第16条、第34条、第36条。

第三节　仲裁员的指定

在国际商事仲裁实践中，指定仲裁员的方式有多种，主要有当事人选定、仲裁机构指定、法院指定、贸易协会或专业机构指定、通过名册制度指定，以及由现有的仲裁员指定等。[51] 前三种指定方式最为常见。

一、当事人选定

当事人选定仲裁员，是指当事人预先或者在争议发生后共同选定某仲裁员独任仲裁或者担任首席仲裁员，或者分别选定仲裁员进行仲裁的方式。当事人选定仲裁员的方式体现了当事人的意思自治，因而得到了最为普遍的采用。当事人选定仲裁员涉及两个方面：一方面是当事人双方或一方自愿选择该仲裁员；另一方面是仲裁员接受当事人的选定。通常的做法是，在争议发生以后，各方当事人拟定3～4名他认为合适的人员名单(有时还附上其资历说明)。

实践中，当事人之间要达成选定独任仲裁员或首席仲裁员的协议较为困难，这两种仲裁员往往需要通过仲裁机构指定、法院指定等方法来确定。

二、仲裁机构指定

仲裁机构的仲裁规则中一般都规定仲裁机构在特定的情况下有指定仲裁的职权。《CIETAC仲裁规则2005》规定，仲裁委员会主任可以接受当事人的委托指定三人仲裁庭中的非首席仲裁员或接受双方当事人的共同委托指定独任仲裁员或三人仲裁庭中的首席仲裁员。当事人一方未能及时选定仲裁员或委托仲裁委员会主任指定仲裁员，或者双方当事人未能及时地共同指定或共同委托仲裁委员会主任指定首席仲裁员的，仲裁委员会主任有权代为指定。[52]

此外，有些仲裁机构还愿意为当事人提供指定仲裁员的服务。如国际商会便为不依其仲裁规则进行的仲裁提供此类服务，并酌收费用。[53]

三、法院指定

在当事人无法就仲裁员的选定达成协议，又未明示授权某仲裁机构或某人作

---

〔51〕 韩健：《现代国际商事仲裁法的理论与实践》，法律出版社2000年版，第157页。

〔52〕 《CIETAC仲裁规则2005》第22条至第24条。

〔53〕 A. Redfern & Hunter, Law and Practice OfInternational Commercial Arbitration, Sweet & Maxwell, 1991, p. 210.

出这一选定时,往往只能求助于有管辖权的国内法院来指定。有管辖权的法院一般是指仲裁地法院。大多数国家规定法院在当事人请求时有权指定仲裁员。《示范法》第11条也规定,在必要时,国内法院有权指定仲裁员。

我国采用的是当事人选定与仲裁委员会主任指定相结合的指定式。《仲裁法》第31、32条规定,当事人约定由3名仲裁员组的成仲裁庭的,应当各自选定或者各自委托仲裁委员会主任指定一名仲裁员,第三名仲裁员由当事人共同选定或者共同委托仲裁委员会主任指定。第三名仲裁员是首席仲裁员。当事人约定由1名仲裁员成立仲裁庭的,应当由当事人共同选定或者共同委托仲裁委员会主任指定仲裁员。当事人没有在仲裁规则规定的期限内约定仲裁庭的组成方式或者选定仲裁员的,由仲裁委员会主任指定。这一方式既体现当事人自治原则,也便于仲裁实务操作。但是我国没有法院指定的法律规定。有学者建议通过立法授予特定管辖法院或特定机构以协助组成仲裁庭的权力。[54] 公正地仲裁案件;(2)不得私自接触当事人及其代理人;(3)应当自觉披露可能有损公正审理的任何情况并予以回避;(4)谨慎履行职责;(5)严守仲裁秘密等。仲裁员违反上述行为规范的,应否承担责任,是理论界与实务界尚未明确的问题。主要观点有承担责任论、不应承担责任论、承担有限责任论三种。[55]

我国立法没有规定仲裁员责任制度。有学者认为,应当对此问题作出明确规定,以免仲裁员的责任处于不确定状态所可能造成的司法实践中无法可依、相互冲突的情况。[56] 根据《示范法》《纽约公约》和英国、新加坡等国仲裁法,仲裁员违反义务应承担的不利后果是:(1)仲裁员被仲裁机构或法院撤换或被裁定回避;(2)仲裁裁决被法院发回重审;(3)仲裁裁决被法院撤销;(4)法院不予执行仲裁裁决。此外,法院还可判令有过错的仲裁员返还全部或部分仲裁报酬。[57]

各国通常规定以对仲裁员提出异议和对仲裁员予以更换的方式来选择有相应资格的仲裁员审理案件,或者促使仲裁员正确地履行仲裁职责。

1. 对仲裁员的异议

各国大都规定,只要当事人有合理理由怀疑仲裁员的公正性与独立性,当事人就可以对仲裁员提出异议。《示范法》第12条(2)款规定,如果(1)存在着可使人合理地怀疑仲裁员的公正性与独立性的一些情况,例如,仲裁员与一方当事人

---

〔54〕 韩健:《现代国际商事仲裁法的理论与实践》,法律出版社2000年版,第164页。

〔55〕 黄进等:《仲裁法学》,中国政法大学出版社1999年版,第70~73页。

〔56〕 肖永平、胡永庆:《加入WTO与我国仲裁法律制度改革》,载《中国法学》2001年第2期。

〔57〕 王文英:《仲裁庭的权力、义务与责任研究》,载《仲裁与法律》2001年第6期。

有亲属关系,或曾为当事人的律师等;或者,(2)该仲裁员不具备当事人双方所约定应具备的资格,则当事人可以要求仲裁员回避。该条同时规定了异议的限制性条件,即如果当事人异议的仲裁员是当事人自己选定的,或是他曾参与选定的,则他只能根据指定后所知悉的原因提出回避要求,意即如果当事人在选定之前已经知悉该仲裁员应该回避而作出这种选定,则视为他已放弃以该回避理由提出异议的权利。除此以外,比利时、丹麦、瑞士等国家的仲裁法还要求异议应当在仲裁开始时提出或者在知悉回避事由后立即提出。

与当事人提出异议(申请回避)相对应的是仲裁员的"披露义务"及自行回避义务。各国立法与各仲裁机构的仲裁规则一般都明确规定,仲裁员有义务向当事人告知有损其公正性与独立性的任何情况。相应地,在被任命为仲裁员之前,将被任命为仲裁员的人可以以此自行回避,拒绝仲裁员的任命。

我国《仲裁法》对仲裁员的异议与回避作出了明确而严格的规定。根据该规定,仲裁员有下列情形之一的,必须回避,当事人也有权提出回避申请:(1)是本案当事人或当事人、代理人的近亲属;(2)与本案有利害关系;(3)与本案当事人、代理人有其他关系,可能影响公正仲裁的;(4)私自会见当事人、代理人,或接受当事人、代理人的请客送礼的。当事人申请回避时,应当说明理由,并在首次开庭前提出;如果回避事由在首次开庭后才知道的,则应在最后一次开庭前提出回避申请。仲裁员是否回避,由仲裁委员会主任决定,仲裁委员会主任担任仲裁员时,由仲裁委员会集体决定。

2. 仲裁员的更换

各国的法律大多规定,仲裁员由于某种原因未能完成仲裁任务时,原则上应当更换仲裁员,以完成仲裁。这就产生了仲裁员的更换问题。

仲裁员更换的具体原因有多种。《示范法》第 14 条将更换原因归为三类:一为事实上不能履行职能,如患重病、死亡等;二为法律上不能履行职能,如自行辞职(回避)或异议获准等;三为仲裁员未及时仲裁。

一般而言,更换仲裁员的程序与方法与选定或指定原仲裁员的程序与方法相同。《示范法》第 15 条规定,"应依指定被更换的仲裁员的规则,指定替代仲裁员"。我国《仲裁法》第 37 条也规定,仲裁员因回避或者其他原因不能履行职责的,应当依照本法规定重新选定或指定仲裁员。仲裁员更换后,当事人可以请求已经进行的仲裁程序重新进行,由仲裁庭作出是否准许该请求的决定。仲裁庭也可以自行决定已进行的仲裁程序是否重新进行。《CIETAC 仲裁规则 2005》第 26 条和第 27 条规定,由仲裁委员会决定仲裁员是否回避。在就此作出决定之前,被请求回避的仲裁员应当继续履行职责。仲裁员因回避或者由于死亡、除名等其他原因不能履行职责时,应按照原选定或指定该仲裁员的程序,重新选定或指定替代的仲裁员。仲裁员更换后,由仲裁庭决定以前进行过的全部或部分审理程序是否需要重新进行。

第四章　仲裁程序

第一节　仲裁程序规则的确定

仲裁程序,是指仲裁庭审理仲裁案件并作出仲裁裁决的过程。仲裁程序应当依据一定的仲裁程序规则进行。依据国际公约、各国国内立法、各仲裁机构仲裁规则的规定,应当首先依当事人的意思自治,即由当事人合意来确定仲裁程序规则;当事人没有或者不能合意决定的,则一般由仲裁庭或仲裁员决定。[58] 例如,1987 年瑞士《国际私法典》第 182 条规定:(1)当事人双方得直接地,或通过引用仲裁规则(而间接地)决定仲裁程序;他们也可以就仲裁程序服从其选择的程序法。(2)如当事人并未决定程序,仲裁庭应在必要的范围内,或者直接地通过引用国内法或仲裁规则,而决定程序。又如 1985 年伦敦国际仲裁院《国际仲裁规则》第 5 条规定:(1)当事人双方得决定仲裁程序,且鼓励双方作出这种决定。(2)如当事人双方未决定程序规则,且本规则中也没有这种规则,仲裁庭应在可能适用的法律许可的条件下享有最大限度的自由裁量权,以确保争端得到公正、迅速、经济与最终的解决。我国《仲裁法》的立法本意是规制常设仲裁机构的仲裁活动,当事人向某仲裁机构提交仲裁的行为表明其接受该仲裁机构的仲裁规则,因而没有规定当事人双方有决定仲裁程序的自由。但是从法律贵在严谨周密的角度来看,这种规定亦有不足——尽管当事人将争议提交某仲裁机构,在大多数情况下意味着接受该机构仲裁规则,但也不排除少数情况下,当事人接受某仲裁机构而反对其仲裁规则的可能;更何况在特设仲裁情况下,如不肯定当事人在仲裁程序规则方面的意思自治权,仲裁将无法进行。《CIETAC 仲裁规则 2005》第 4 条对此作了补充,凡当事人同意将争议提交该仲裁委员会仲裁的,均视为同意按照该仲裁规则进行仲裁。但当事人另有约定的,从其约定。这一规定符合仲裁实践的客观需要。

---

[58] 李浩培:《国际民事程序法概论》,法律出版社 1996 年版,第 216 页。

第二节　仲裁程序规则的基本内容

一般而言，仲裁程序规则应当包括仲裁地、仲裁形式、仲裁进程、语文、证据等基本内容。

一、仲裁地

如前所述，仲裁地对于仲裁来说是至关重要的。各国一般都承认当事人有选择仲裁地的自由。当事人在选择仲裁地，通常要考虑两方面的因素，即事实上的便利与法律上的便利。就前者而言，选择争端发生地便于物证的收集与证人的到庭，选择仲裁员居住地便于仲裁员出庭；选择仲裁设施完善地便于仲裁顺利进行。就后者而言，由于仲裁地法可能决定仲裁协议的成立与有效性、仲裁员的指定、仲裁程序的进行以及仲裁裁决的有效性，故选择一个其法律制度便于仲裁的国家作为仲裁地更显重要。此外，为使裁决得到承认与执行，选择一个与该国有相互承认与执行裁决关系的国家作为仲裁地也是很有必要的。

仲裁地不等于仲裁员的全部活动空间。正如《示范法》第20条第2款所规定的“除非当事人双方有相反决定，仲裁庭得在其认为适当的任何其他地方会合，以便互相商议、讯问证人、鉴定人、或当事人，或者检查商品、其他财产或文件”。但是，即使在并不存在实质性商议的书面仲裁的情况下，也应确定仲裁地，以便于决定仲裁裁决的国籍，从而使仲裁裁决得到相应国家的承认与执行。

二、仲裁形式

仲裁可以以口头审理、书面审理与混合审理三种形式进行。

口头审理又称“开庭审理”，是指在仲裁庭全体仲裁员、当事人及其代理人和其他有关人士，如证人、专家、鉴定人的参加下，听取当事人的口头陈述与辩论，对案件的事实与法律进行调查的审理活动。在仲裁实践中，开庭审理对于仲裁庭查清事实、适用法律、分清责任、公正裁决是至关重要的，因为在口头审理中，通过当事人面对面的交锋，通过证人、专家、鉴定人等的证言与专业意见，通过仲裁庭对当事人及证人、专家与鉴定人的询问，仲裁庭能够快捷地查明隐藏在各种错综复杂关系中的事实真相。由于当事人直接参与其中，这种审理方式能够得到当事人的高度信任。[59]

---

〔59〕 程德钧等：《国际惯例与涉外仲裁》，中国青年出版社1993年版，第219页。

书面审理，是指仲裁庭不举行开庭，只根据双方当事人提供的书面材料和证据材料（如仲裁申请书、答辩书、合同、往来函电等）以及证人、专家、鉴定人的书面证据材料，对争议案件进行审理。这种审理方式免除了当事人及证人到庭的麻烦，从而也节省了时间与费用。但是，由于当事人不到庭，可能有些关键性的事实与争点未能展开，从而不利于案件真相的查明。正因为如此，我国涉外仲裁规则均规定，未经双方当事人申请或经双方当事人同意，不能进行书面审理，而应开庭审理。

混合审理是口头审理与书面审理的结合。这种审理方式集中了上述两种方式的优点，因此也是国际贸易仲裁中常用的审理方式，对于较复杂的案件尤为适宜。其做法大体分三步：首先是仲裁庭根据双方当事人提供的书面材料进行书面审理，找出争点，并确定开庭审理的时间、地点及要点；其次，在书面审理的基础上开庭审理，以进一步查明争议事实；最后，如开庭尚未查明所有事实，仲裁庭可要求当事人在开庭之后限期向仲裁庭提交进一步的书面材料及证据，然后再依据这些书面材料，作进一步书面审理。〔60〕

三、仲裁进程

许多国家的法律规定，当事人对于仲裁的具体进程也可行使意思自治权利，即当事人可以与仲裁员协商确认仲裁的每个步骤，并详细说明每个步骤应做的工作。如果这些安排切合实际，它将成为一张有效的时间表，可以供当事人、仲裁员与代理律师在仲裁过程中共同参照执行。〔61〕

四、语文

依据《示范法》的规定，仲裁无须以仲裁地所使用的语文进行，当事人可以自由决定仲裁适用的语文。如双方不能决定，应由仲裁员决定。但是，仲裁员应选择最适合于该仲裁程序的语文，以便双方有完全的机会提出其所主张的案情。

为使仲裁程序便捷经济，除确有必要，仲裁应以一种语文为宜。该语文适用于一切口头与书面的陈述，以及仲裁裁决。不过，书证一般可以用原文提出，仲裁员如认为必要，可以令其将原文译成所定仲裁语文，并证明无误。〔62〕

五、证据

在仲裁过程中，当事人还可以与仲裁员协议决定或自行决定提出证据的方

---

〔60〕 郭寿康、赵秀文主编：《国际经济贸易仲裁法》，中国法制出版社 1995 年版，第 110～111 页。

〔61〕 关于当事人与仲裁员可以共同确定的具体环节，参见李浩培：《国际民事程序法概论》，法律出版社 1996 年版，第 218～219 页。

〔62〕 李浩培：《国际民事程序法概论》，法律出版社 1996 年版，第 218 页。

式,例如:当事人可以将其无争议的事实以及基本的文件,如契约、关键性报告、重要的通信等,提交仲裁员;当事人可以与仲裁员协议决定书证的提出方式,其证据的可接受性、相关性、重要性及证据力;当事人还可与仲裁员协议决定询问证人的方式(大陆法式或英美法式)及鉴定人的指定方式(当事人指定或仲裁员指定);当事人甚至可与仲裁员协议决定由一名仲裁员代表仲裁庭搜集证据。[63]

第三节 补充性的程序规则

当事人可能难以就所有的仲裁环节达成协议。事实上,除了上述一些基本内容外,其他的程序规则往往要借助各国仲裁法与仲裁机构的仲裁规则来补充。下面结合《示范法》的规定简单介绍一些常见的补充性程序规则。

一、仲裁程序的开始

依据《示范法》第21条的规定,除非双方当事人有相反约定,解决特定争议的仲裁程序自被诉人收到将该争端提交仲裁的请求之日起开始。

二、申诉、反诉与答辩

《示范法》第23条第2款第1款规定:"在双方当事人约定或在仲裁庭决定的时间里,申诉人应陈述支持其申诉的事实、争点及其所寻求的救济或补救,被诉人应陈述其关于这些事项的答辩,除非当事人双方就这些陈述所要求的各种因素另有约定。当事人双方可以随同其陈述提交其认为有关的一切文件或附加说明其拟提交的文件或其他证据。"同样,被诉人提起反诉时所应提出的支持事实、争点、寻求的救济与补救以及对方的答辩,也适用上款规定。

《示范法》第23条第2款还进一步规定,除非当事人另有约定,任何一方均可在仲裁程序中修改或补充其申诉或答辩,除非仲裁庭认为提出此要求已经太迟或者认为不宜许可此种修改。《示范法》的这些规定在《CIETAC仲裁规则2005》中也有所反映。

三、审理形式

依《示范法》第24条第1款的规定,在当事人双方对仲裁程序的形式没有特

---

〔63〕 详见张斌生主编:《仲裁法新论》,厦门大学出版社2004年版,第十一章"仲裁程序中的证据问题"。

别约定的情况下，仲裁庭可以自主决定仅采用口头审理程序或者仅采用书面审理程序，或者兼采这两种程序。但是，除非当事人双方约定不采用口头审理程序，否则，当事人一方请求举行口头审理时，仲裁庭必须举行口头审理，且该口头审理必须“在仲裁程序的适当阶段进行”。这里的规定与前述我国涉外仲裁的实践虽然有所不同，但强调口头审理（开庭审理）的精神却是一致的。

四、缺席仲裁

与各国国内法的简略规定相反，《示范法》关于缺席仲裁程序的规定可谓详尽而周密。依《示范法》第25条，如果：（1）当事人双方既未排除缺席（仲裁）程序，又未就一方缺席的情况订定特定的措施；（2）仲裁庭认为缺席的一方当事人并无“充分的理由”缺席（无效缺席），则可适用其缺席仲裁程序。

《示范法》第25条规定的缺席仲裁程序分四种情况：第一，申诉人向仲裁庭提起仲裁申请后，为了阻碍该仲裁庭的裁判管辖权，不向仲裁庭陈述支持其申诉的事实、争点及其所寻求的救济或补救。在这种情况下，仲裁庭应终止其仲裁程序。第二，被诉人未将其关于辩护的陈述及时地传达仲裁庭。在这种情况下，仲裁应继续进行，并可作出有拘束力的仲裁裁决，即使被诉人完全缺席。但是，被诉人的缺席不能被认为是对申诉人主张的事实上的承认；仲裁庭仍须对申诉人的证据与意见作出客观的评价。第三，申诉人或被诉人在举行口头审理时缺席。在这种情况下，如果仲裁庭认为缺席的一方并无足够的原因可以说明其缺席，它可以继续其仲裁程序，并依据向其提出的证据，作出仲裁裁决。但同样，一方的此种缺席不能被认为是对对方主张的承认。第四，申诉人或被诉人未提出书证。在这种情况下，仲裁庭可以请求有管辖权的法院命令该方提出证据，或者只是继续仲裁程序，并从该方的拒绝提供证据“作出不利的推断”。意即仲裁庭可以推断：文件既存在而拒不提出，必然含有对其不利的资料。可见，《示范法》所定义的缺席，不仅仅指开庭审理的未出席，也包括书面审理意义上的缺席，是一种广义的“缺席”。

在大多数法律体系中，缺席仲裁裁决较之缺席判决有更重要的影响。对于缺席判决尚可能有上诉的机会，而对缺席仲裁裁决则几乎无上诉机会。而且，缺席仲裁裁决作出后，仲裁员的裁决管辖权即告终止，而不能重新仲裁。因而，缺席仲裁裁决的威胁往往可以使本欲缺席的当事方改变态度，而与仲裁庭合作。〔64〕正是基于这种考虑，我国《仲裁法》第42条第2款规定：“被申请人经书面通知，无正当理由不到庭或未经仲裁庭许可中途退庭的，可以缺席裁决。”《CIETAC仲裁规

〔64〕 李浩培：《国际民事程序法概论》，法律出版社1996年版，第221～222页。

则2005》第34条第2款规定："被申请人无正当理由开庭时不到庭的，或在开庭审理时未经仲裁庭许可中途退庭的，仲裁庭可以进行缺席审理，并作出裁决；如果被申请人提出了反请求，可以视为撤回反请求。"可见，我国所界定的"缺席"只是开庭审理的缺席，而不包括书面审理意义上的"缺席"，是一种狭义的理解。其中，我国《仲裁法》所规定的席裁决程序仅适用于被诉人缺席，而不适用于申诉人缺席。对于申诉人缺席的情形，《仲裁法》规定"可以视为撤回仲裁申请"。

五、专家证据

当仲裁涉及复杂的技术问题时，往往需要依靠专家证据方能解决。在英美仲裁实践中，专家证据通常由当事人提出。按《示范法》，当事人也可提出专家证人。但是，提出专家证据的当事人必须将专家的报告传达给他方，以便后者有答辩的机会。仲裁庭在其认为必要时也可询问专家证人，而且，如仲裁庭认为当事人提出的专家证据不充分或混乱，它也可以自行指定专家证人。不过，按照《示范法》的规定，当事人可以约定而赋予仲裁庭以指定专家证人的权力。但从实践中看，如果当事人接受一个仲裁机构，该机构的仲裁规则又赋予了仲裁庭此种权力，则一般应认为当事人已承认了仲裁庭的这一权力。所以，《CIETAC仲裁规则2005》第38条规定，仲裁庭可以就案件中的专门问题向专家咨询或者指定鉴定人进行鉴定。

依《示范法》的规定，在请专家作证前，仲裁庭必须确定一些具体的争点，以便专家有针对性地提出报告。此外，仲裁庭可以要求当事人向专家提供有关资料，或向其出示或使其接近有关文件、商品或其他财产，以供检查。专家证据通常表现为书面报告。该报告应传达给当事人双方，以待对方举出反对意见。《示范法》也允许专家提供口头报告。在当事人请求或仲裁庭认为必要时，专家还必须参加开庭审理，在庭审过程中，当事人可以对报告予以质问、提出反对意见。对此，我国《仲裁法》第44条与《CIETAC仲裁规则2005》第38条均有类似规定。

六、法院协助取证

仲裁过程主要是当事人与仲裁庭自治的过程，但并不完全排除法院必要的协助。譬如，在取证方面，有时仲裁庭就必须借助法院的力量。《示范法》第27条规定，仲裁庭或当事人一方在仲裁庭许可下，可以请求仲裁地有管辖权的法院协助取得证据。该法院可以在其管辖权范围内依其取证规则执行该请求。

七、仲裁程序公正的基本标准

在仲裁中，当事人与仲裁员确定程序规则的自由并非绝对，而应受到公正程序的基本标准的制约。《示范法》归纳了各国的有关立法与实践，提出了仲裁程序公正的两项基本标准：一为当事人双方的平等和对他们的公正待遇，这就意味着仲裁员必须兼听当事人双方，不能偏听偏信；二为对席原则（principle of contradiction），即当事人一方所提出的一切主张与证据必须告知他方，并且给后者以答辩的机会。[65] 这两个基本原则可以说是《示范法》所确立的一切仲裁程序的基石。因此，该法关于仲裁程序的第18条明确指出："应对当事人双方平等对待，并且对每一方均应给予陈明案情的充分机会。"

第四节　我国《仲裁法》关于仲裁程序的基本规则

我国1994年颁布的《仲裁法》对仲裁程序作出了较详细的规定，兹概述如下：

一、开庭审理原则

仲裁原则上应以开庭审理的方式进行，但是，当事人协议不以这种方式进行时，仲裁也可以根据仲裁申请书以及其他材料作出裁决（书面审理）。

二、不公开原则

仲裁庭审理案件原则上不公开进行。不过，如当事人协议公开进行审理，且案件不涉及国家机密，也可以公开审理。

三、开庭通知

仲裁委员会应当在仲裁规则规定的期限内将开庭审理的日期通知当事人双方。当事人如有正当理由，可以在仲裁规则规定期限内请求延期开庭。是否延期由仲裁庭决定。

四、缺席处理

申请人经书面通知，无正当理由不到庭或未经仲裁庭许可中途退庭的，可以视为撤回仲裁申请；被申请人经书面通知，无正当理由不到庭或未经仲裁庭许可中途退庭的，可以缺席裁决。

五、证据及其保全

当事人应当为自己的主张提供证据，并在开庭时出示，当事人一方对他方提

〔65〕 李浩培：《国际民事程序法概论》，法律出版社1996年版，第224页。

出的证据可以质证。仲裁庭也可以自行搜集证据。在证据可能灭失或者以后难以取得的情况下,当事人可以申请证据保全。仲裁委员会应将当事人的这种申请提交证据所在地的基层人民法院处理。但是,如果涉外仲裁当事人申请证据保全,则仲裁委员会应将该项申请提交证据所在地的中级人民法院处理。

六、鉴定

仲裁庭认为专门性问题需要鉴定时,可以交由当事人约定的鉴定部门鉴定,也可以由仲裁庭指定的鉴定部门鉴定。根据当事人的请求或仲裁庭的要求,鉴定部门应派鉴定人参加开庭,当事人经仲裁庭许可,可以向鉴定人提问。

七、辩论

当事人在开庭审理过程中有权进行辩论。辩论终结时,首席仲裁员或独任仲裁员应当询问当事人的最后意见。

八、和解

当事人申请仲裁后,可以自行和解。如果达成和解协议,当事人可以请求仲裁庭根据和解协议作出裁决书,也可以撤回仲裁申请。当事人达成和解协议并撤回仲裁申请后及翻悔的,仍可以根据原仲裁协议再次申请仲裁。

九、调解

仲裁庭在裁决作出前,可以先行调解。当事人如自愿调解,仲裁庭应当进行调解。调解成功时,仲裁庭应当作成调解书,或者根据调解协议的结果作出裁决书。调解书与裁决书具有同等法律效力。调解书应写明仲裁请求与当事人协议的结果,由仲裁员签名,加盖仲裁委员会印章,并送达双方当事人。调解书经双方当事人签收后,即发生法律效力。在调解书签收前当事人翻悔,或调解不成时,仲裁庭应及时作出裁决。在仲裁程序中进行调解,称为“仲裁与调解相结合”的制度,是中国仲裁的一大特色。这种调解制度的实质是在查明案件事实、分清是非责任的基础上,促使双方当事人互谅互让,公平合理地自愿达成和解协议,以解决争端。它不仅有利于解决争端,而且有利于当事人发展友好合作关系,因而是一种有利无弊的制度。《CIETAC 仲裁规则 2005》第 40 条第 1 款规定:“当事人在仲裁委员会之外通过协商或调解达成和解协议的,可以凭当事人达成的由仲裁委员会仲裁的仲裁协议和他们的和解协议,请求仲裁委员会组成仲裁庭,按照和解协议的内容作出仲裁裁决。”第 2 款规定:“如果双方当事人有调解愿望,或一方当事人有调解愿望并经仲裁庭征得另一方当事人同意的,仲裁庭可以在仲裁程序进行过程中对其审理的案件进行调解。”据统计,在 CIETAC 的仲裁实践中,每年通过仲裁中的调解,可使占总数20% ~30%比例的案件以当事人和解撤案或者仲裁庭按和解协议裁决而结案。[66]

十、笔录

仲裁庭应当将开庭情况记入笔录。笔录由仲裁员、记录人员、当事人和其他仲裁参与人签名或盖章。当事人或其他仲裁参与人如认为笔录对自己的陈述有遗漏或错误,有权申请补正,如不予补正,也应记录该补正申请。

第五章 仲裁裁决

第一节 仲裁裁决的作出

一、仲裁裁决的种类

仲裁程序的结果,往往便是仲裁裁决的产生。大体上,仲裁裁决可分两大类,一类为临时裁决(provisional award),另一类为最终裁决(final award)。临时裁决只处理当事人之间争议中的部分问题,它又可具体分为初步裁决(preliminary award)、部分裁决(partial award)与中间裁决(interlocutory award)等。上述裁决形式均由仲裁庭自行作出,但在一定条件下,裁决也可能是在双方当事人协商一致的基础上作出的,这一种裁决一般被叫作"合意裁决"(consent award)。此外,在当事人一方缺席情况下作出的裁决,则称缺席裁决(default award)或一方当事人参加的裁决。

这里值得注意的是,中间裁决与部分裁决的区分。所谓中间裁决,是指对整个争议案已部分审理清楚,为了有利于进一步审理和作出最终裁决,仲裁庭在某一审理阶段所作出的某项暂时性裁决。部分裁决则指对整个争议中的某个或某几个问题已经审理清楚,为及时保护当事人合法权益或有利于继续审理其他问题,仲裁庭先行作出的对某一或某几个问题的终局性的裁决。这两种裁决都不是对整个案件的最后裁决。但二者还有区别的。就内容而言,中间裁决多是有关秩序问题与证据问题的裁决;而部分裁决一般会涉及实体问题;就效力而言,中间裁决不是终局的裁定,不具有强制执行力;而部分裁决却是终局性的,具有强制执行力。

当然,这并不意味着当事人可以无视中间裁决,当事人如拒不执行中间裁决,

[66] 王生长:《仲裁与调解相结合的理论与实务》,法律出版社2001年版,第83页。

即应承担一切相应的后果。[67] 我国法律与有关仲裁规则对这两种临时裁决也作了规定。我国《仲裁法》第55条规定，仲裁庭仲裁纠纷时，其中一部分事实已经清楚的，可以就该部分先行裁决。《CIETAC仲裁规则2005》第44条则规定："如果仲裁庭认为有必要或者当事人提出请求经仲裁庭同意时，仲裁庭可以在作出最终仲裁裁决之前的任何时候，就案件的任何问题作出中间裁决或部分裁决。任何一方当事人不履行中间裁决，不影响仲裁程序的继续进行，也不影响仲裁庭作出终局裁决。"

二、仲裁裁决的决定

如果是独任仲裁员仲裁，则仲裁裁决由其一人作出，自不待言。在多人仲裁庭的情况下，如果全体仲裁员不能达成一致意见，则通常依多数票规则与首席仲裁员决定规则决定。如《国际商会仲裁规则》第19条规定："仲裁院任命2名仲裁员时，裁决以多数票决定之。得不到多数时，应由仲裁庭主席单独决定。"我国《仲裁法》第53条规定，裁决应当按照多数仲裁员的意见作出，少数仲裁员的不同意见可以记入笔录。仲裁庭形不成多数意见时，裁决应当按照首席仲裁员的意见作出，《CIETAC仲裁规则2005》第43条也有类似规定。

三、仲裁裁决的形式与内容

仲裁裁决必须采用书面形式，这是世界各国有关立法与规则的共识。有的国家和地区，如西班牙、葡萄牙及美国有些州的法律甚至还要求仲裁裁决书须经过公证。[68] 我国《仲裁法》第54条也对仲裁裁决提出了书面形式的要求。

至于仲裁裁决的内容，一般包括仲裁机构名称与地址、仲裁员姓名与地址、双方当事人姓名、地址及代理人与其他参与人姓名，以及裁决作出的确切日期与地点；有关裁决背景的事实情况；仲裁庭对案件的评价以及对双方权利义务的处理结论；仲裁费用与仲裁员报酬；仲裁员鉴定。

仲裁裁决是否要说明理由，大陆法系与英美法系国家的立法有所不同。大陆法系国家提倡在裁决中附具理由，但如当事人有约定，也可不附具理由；在英美法系国家，仲裁裁决无须附具理由，但如当事人有附具理由的约定，则裁决应具明理由。不过，在实践上，两大法系都肯定，如当事人没有相关约定，则一般应在仲裁裁决中说明理由。我国《仲裁法》反映了这一国际趋势。《仲裁法》第54条规定，裁决书应写明仲裁请求、争议事实、裁决理由、裁决结果、仲裁费用的分担和裁决

〔67〕 程德钧等编著：《国际惯例与涉外仲裁实务》，中国青年出版社1993年版，第231页。
〔68〕 韩健：《现代国际商事仲裁法的理论与实践》，法律出版社2000年版，第335页。

日期。当事人协议不愿写明争议事实与裁决理由的,可以不写。裁决书由仲裁员签名、加盖仲裁委员会印章。对裁决持不同意见的仲裁员,可以签名,也可以不签名。

此外,大多数国家法律与仲裁规则规定,在下列两种情况下,当事人可以请求仲裁庭对仲裁裁决作出更正或补充,仲裁庭也可自行更正或补充:(1)裁决书有书写、打印、计算上的错误或其他类似性质的错误;(2)裁决书有当事人在仲裁程序中提出但在裁决书中遗漏的事项,或者有仲裁庭在其意见中陈述过但裁决中遗漏的应裁事项。不论是应申请作出还是仲裁庭自行作出的,仲裁庭的这种更正与补充均构成原裁决的一部分。[69] 我国《仲裁法》第 56 条也规定:"对裁决书中的文字、计算错误或者仲裁庭已经裁决但在裁决书中遗漏的事项,仲裁庭应当补正;当事人在收到裁决书之日起 30 日内,可以请求仲裁庭补正。"

第二节 仲裁裁决的撤销

一、撤销的可能

尽管仲裁裁决是"终局"的、"有拘束力"的,但这种终局性与拘束力并不是绝对的,而有赖于可适用的仲裁法的确认。事实上,各国在承认仲裁的终局性与拘束力的同时,总是力图维持对仲裁的一定程度的控制。允许当事人对仲裁裁决提出撤销申请(异议),便是这种控制的一种表现。对此,1958 年的《纽约公约》也已经予以了肯定。依该公约第 5 条第 1 款(e)项规定,"裁决对当事人尚未发生拘束力,或裁决已经由作出裁决的国家或裁决所依据法律的国家的主管机关撤销或暂停执行",构成法院拒绝承认与执行该外国仲裁裁决的一个理由。

二、撤销申请的管辖

撤销仲裁裁决的申请,应向有管辖权的法院提出。一般来说,该法院是裁决作出地国法院,但也可能是仲裁地以外的国家的法院,如上述《纽约公约》第 5 条第 1 款(e)项所提出的"裁决所依据法律的国家"的法院。事实上,也有的国家(如德国)立法确认,如某一裁决系依本国法作出的,即使作出地并不在本国,本国法院亦有权撤销该裁决。[70] 不过,实践中似乎并未出现这种情形。从我国立法的措辞来看,似乎只承认人民法院对在中国作出的裁决有申请撤销案的管

---

〔69〕 郭寿康、赵秀文主编:《国际经济贸易仲裁法》,中国法制出版社 1995 年版,第 133 ~ 134 页。

〔70〕 参见联邦德国 1961 年《关于 1958 年承认与执行外国仲裁裁决的法律》第 2 条。

辖权。[71]

三、申请撤销的理由

当事人申请撤销仲裁裁决的理由大致分为两大类：一类是实体问题，即裁决中的事实认定与法律适用方面问题；另一类是非实体问题，即仲裁管辖权与程序问题。目前，大多数国家的仲裁立法，都不允许当事人就仲裁裁决中的实体问题提出异议，但相当多的国家允许当事人对仲裁裁决的非实体问题，即仲裁庭管辖权与仲裁程序问题提出异议，要求撤销。例如，瑞典法禁止就裁决的是非曲直提出上诉，不管是关于事实的还是实体法的裁决，但却允许当事人就程序上或形式上的缺陷提出异议。[72] 德国、法国、日本、丹麦、比利时、匈牙利、波兰、南斯拉夫等均有类似规定。

至于申请撤销裁决的具体理由，各国国内法一般都有明确规定，归纳起来，主要可分为四类。第一类为裁决本身的问题，包括形式上与内容上的问题，如非书面形式、内容违法[73]等。第二类是管辖权问题。这是各国普遍承认的一条撤销裁决的理由。具体来说，这一问题又可分解为仲裁庭没有管辖权、仲裁庭超越管辖权与仲裁裁决未裁决当事人提交的全部问题（仲裁庭未充分行使管辖权）三种。在前两种情况下，法院一般都可以撤销该裁决或裁决中超越管辖权的那一部分（如果该裁决是可以分割的）。对于后一种情况，《示范法》指出了补充裁决的方法。第三类是程序问题。各国立法一般要求仲裁必须遵守前面述及的公正程序的最低标准。例如，给当事人以适当的开庭与听审通知，平等对待当事人，公平听证以及让双方享有充分与适当的机会申辩，等等。第四类是公共政策问题。这主要表现为仲裁必须遵守各国关于仲裁标的的可仲裁性的规定。否则，它既可能被撤销，还可能被拒绝承认与执行。

我国《仲裁法》关于申请撤销裁决的理由的规定对国内仲裁裁决与涉外仲裁裁决分别对待。对国内仲裁裁决，依其第58条，当事人举证证明有下列六种情形之一的，均可申请撤销：(1)没有仲裁协议的；(2)裁决的事项不属于仲裁协议的范围或者仲裁委员会无权仲裁的；(3)仲裁庭的组成或仲裁的程序违反法定程序的川的裁决所根据的证据是伪造的；(5)对方当事人隐瞒了足以影响公正裁决的

---

〔71〕 根据我国《仲裁法》第58条、第70条与《民事诉讼法》第260条的规定，我国国内裁决的申请撤销案的管辖法院为“仲裁委员会所在地的中级人民法院”，而可以在中国申请撤销的国际仲裁裁决只能是“中华人民共和国涉外仲裁机构作出的裁决”。

〔72〕 参见1999年《瑞典仲裁法》第33条、第34条，载《仲裁法律手册》，法律出版社2001年版，第392页。

〔73〕 显然，在对裁决不作实质审查的国家，自然就不存在以“内容违法”而撤销裁决的情况。

证据的刊的仲裁员在仲裁该案时有索贿受贿,徇私舞弊,枉法裁决行为的。此外,人民法院如认为该裁决违背社会公共利益的,应当裁定撤销。由此足见我国对国内仲裁裁决,既可以以程序性理由请求撤销,也可以以实体性理由(如伪证、枉法等)申请撤销,法院的监督是全面而有力的。然而,依我国《仲裁法》第70条与《民事诉讼法》第260条规定,我国涉外仲裁机构作出的涉外仲裁裁决只有在下列四种情形之一下,经人民法院审查核实,方可裁定撤销:(1)当事人在合同中没有订立仲裁条款或者事后没有达成书面仲裁协议;(2)被申请人没有得到指定仲裁员或者进行仲裁程序的通知,或者由于其他不属于被申请人负责的原因未能陈述意见的;(3)仲裁庭的组成或者仲裁程序与仲裁规则不符的沃的裁决的事项不属于仲裁协议的范围或仲裁机构无权仲裁的。可见,与国内仲裁不同,我国对涉外仲裁的司法审查仅限于仲裁管辖权与仲裁程序方面,而与仲裁裁决实体无涉。对此,学术界多有争议。

四、申请撤销的时限

为保证仲裁的效率,各国对当事人申请撤销裁决都规定了较短的时限。如瑞士为裁决通知当事人后30天;英国为裁决作出并告知当事人后21天;奥地利为裁决送达当事人后3个月。我国则为收到裁决书之日起6个月。比较起来,我国的时限是很宽松的。

第六章　仲裁裁决的承认与执行

仲裁裁决生效以后,就可能产生执行问题。实践表明,多数仲裁裁决都得到了当事人的自动履行,但也确有一些仲裁裁决,败诉方会拒绝履行。在这种情况下,胜诉方除依靠经济与心理影响力外,更重要的是要依靠国家的权力,向有关法院申请执行仲裁裁决。这种强制执行,便是我们通常所说的仲裁裁决的执行。

不过,确切地说,裁决承认与裁决执行是不同的。裁决承认是指司法机关根据当事人的申请依法确认仲裁裁决具有可予执行的法律效力;裁决执行则指司法机关应一方当事人的申请而强制裁决另一方当事人执行裁决事项。承认是执行的前提,裁决只有获得法院的承认才能取得法律上的强制执行力,执行裁决是承认裁决的自然结果。[74] 但承认并不必然导致执行。换言之,一项裁决可以被承认而不予执行,但一项裁决如得到了执行,必为实施执行的法院所承认。所以,实

〔74〕 程德钧等编著:《国际惯例与涉外仲裁实务》,中国青年出版社1993年版,第239页;谭兵主编:《中国仲裁制度研究》,法律出版社1995年版,第318页。

际上,其区别是“单纯承认”与“承认与执行”的区别。[75] “单纯承认”可以出现在这种情况下,如裁决作出后,败诉方就已裁决事项向法院起诉,此时,胜诉方以仲裁裁决具有既判力(res judicata)为由,反对法院受理此案。此时,胜诉方实际是要求法院“承认裁决”,而未要求“执行裁决”。可见,单纯的仲裁承认多表现为一种防御性程序;而裁决执行程序则往往表现为一种积极作为的程序。这里所要介绍的主要是后者即仲裁执行规则,或者确切地说,是仲裁的承认与执行规则,而不是单纯的防御性的仲裁承认规则。

在各国立法上,对国内仲裁裁决与外国仲裁裁决的承认规则往往不同,后者一般比前者更为严格。为使一国仲裁裁决能在其他国家得到顺利承认与执行,国际社会做出了巨大的努力。国际联盟主持制定了1923年《仲裁条款议定书》与1927年《关于执行外国仲裁裁决公约》。随后,在联合国的主持下,又在前二者的基础上制订了更完善的1958年《纽约公约》。统一了国际上关于承认与执行外国仲裁裁决的基本规则。本章以《纽约公约》为主体,对承认与执行外国仲裁裁决的国际制度及中国的特殊规则作简要介绍。

第一节　外国裁决的界定

所谓“外国裁决”的界定问题在《纽约公约》中表现为其适用范围的问题。关于这个问题,在公约起草过程中,曾有两种意见。一种意见主张采用“领域标准”,即裁决作出地国以外的国家领域内作出的裁决,方为外国裁决,方可适用本公约。[76] 另一种意见则主张采用更宽泛的“非国内裁决标准”,即凡被请求承认承认与执行国认为不属于其内国之裁决“均属外国裁决,可适用本公约”。[77] 最后,作为折中,两种标准纳入了公约文本。《纽约公约》第1条第1款规定:“由于自然人或法人间的争执而引起的仲裁裁决,在一个国家的领土内作成,而在另→个国家请求承认与执行时,适用本公约。在一个国家请求承认与执行一项这个国家不认为是其国内裁决的仲裁裁决时,也适用本公约。”

不过,需要注意的是,公约这里所采纳的两个标准并非并列关系,而是有主从关系的。一方面,从公约的措辞上可以看出,公约首先采用的是“领域标准”,其

---

〔75〕 韩健:《现代国际商事仲裁法的理论与实践》,法律出版社2000年版第371页。

〔76〕 参见联合国经社理事会(UNESCO)1955年拟定的《纽约公约》草案。U. N. Doc. E/2704, reprinted in G. Gaja ed. International Commercial Arbitration, New York Convention, at m. A. 1. 7. 1985.

〔77〕 参见意大利、法国、德国等八国提交的修正案。U. N. Doc. E/CONF. 26/L. 6.

次才规定符合“非内国裁决标准”的“也适用本公约”。另一方面，从公约的起草过程来看，工作组之所以同时采纳“非内国裁决标准”，主要是为了“使公约的适用范围更广一些。”两种标准的这种主从关系表明，当承认与执行地国与裁决作出地国不属于同一国家时，执行裁决可以适用该公约；当承认与执行地国与裁决作出地国同为一国时，如执行地国认为该在其领域内作出的裁决不是内国裁决，则依第二标准，也可适用公约。由此可见，第二标准（非内国裁决标准）仅适用于在承认与执行国领域内作出的裁决。[78]

第二节　承认与执行外国仲裁裁决的程序

《纽约公约》第3条规定：“各缔约国应承认仲裁裁决具有拘束力，并依援引裁决地之程序规则及下列各条所载条件执行之。承认或执行适用本公约之仲裁裁决时，不得较承认与执行内国仲裁裁决附加过苛之条件或征收过多之费用。”可见，公约规定了一个一般性的程序要求，即不得对外国裁决的承认与执行施以“过苛”限制或征收“过多”费用。至于具体的程序，则依“援引裁决地”，即执行裁决地的程序规则。

要使裁决得到顺利执行，执行裁决地的选择是十分重要的。从实用的角度来考虑，执行裁决地的选择将取决于仲裁败诉方的财产所在地。因为执行程序往往需要扣押或查封败诉方财产，故如在败诉方无财产地申请执行，并无实际意义。从法律的角度来看，选择执行地还应考虑可能执行的法院地与仲裁地的关系（如是否为《纽约公约》缔约国）与当地法院对执行外国仲裁裁决的态度。此外，在被执行者涉及一个国家或一个政府机构的情况下，还应考虑法院地国对国家豁免问题所持的立场与主张。

综观各国立法，可将其承认与执行外国仲裁裁决的程序规则

一、视同外国司法判决

许多国家除适用国际仲裁公约外，均将外国仲裁裁决视同外国判决。欧洲的意大利、西班牙、葡萄牙和东欧一些国家，以及埃及、伊朗、菲律宾、泰国和印度等国都采用这一规则。拉丁美洲的大多数国家也是如此。当然，这些国家关于执行的具体要求是有所不同的。不过，它们一般都要求在向执行地国提出申请执行裁

〔78〕　参见韩健：《现代国际商事仲裁法的理论与实践》，法律出版社2000年版，第380～382页。

决前，该裁决在其作出地国是可执行的，并要由裁决地国对该裁决予以确认，这些经确认的裁决在由执行地国法院审查后发给执行令予以执行。此外，除另有条款规定外，外国裁决一般不能依执行地国的简易程序（这种程序可能对内国仲裁适用）执行。

二、视同契约债务

在英美法系国家，通常把外国裁决看做是在“普通法仲裁”（Common Law Arbitration）中作出的裁决。对于这种裁决的执行，需由当事人基于此外国裁决提起普通民事诉讼（债权之诉），由法院依可适用的法律审查其有效性，然后作出新的判决。最后依执行内国判决的程序规则来执行该外国裁决。在这个债权之诉中，法院不审理当事人之间最初的争议，而只审查由该裁决所构成的所谓新“契约”的有效性与可执行性。质言之，只是对裁决的一种形式审查，而不是实质审查。[79] 因此，这种程序较之将外国裁决视同国外判决的做法更为简易。

三、视同本国裁决

在法国、德国、比利时、希腊、日本等国，一般把外国仲裁裁决视同本国裁决。

对于《纽约公约》缔约国作出的仲裁裁决（以下简称公约裁决）的承认与执行，有的国家还制订了有别于承认与执行普遍外国仲裁裁决的特别程序规则。例如，《美国法典》（United States Code）第 9 篇第 207 节规定，在美国执行公约裁决，当事人可在裁决作出后 3 年内向有管辖权的联邦法院申请执行许可书。裁决一经确认，即将作为美国判决而得到执行，而不需前述英美国家共通的重新起诉的繁琐程序。在丹麦，根据其 1973 年颁布的关于承认与执行外国仲裁裁决和国际商事仲裁的第 117 号政令第 2 条，对于公约裁决，可与本国裁决一样，向丹麦法院直接申请执行，而对于（外国）非公约裁决，则也必须经向丹麦法院重新起诉、判决后，作为内国判决而执行。

关于申请执行外国仲裁裁决的期限，《纽约公约》没有统一规定，而留待各国国内法决定。如在美国，期限为 3 年，在英国则为 6 年。[80] 依《纽约公约》第 6 条，如果被申请人已向主管机关提出撤销或暂停仲裁裁决效力的申请，被申请承认与执行仲裁裁决的机关可以依其自由裁量，延期作出执行仲裁裁决的裁定，并可以依申请执行人的请求，命令被申请人提供相当担保，以防止被申请人以申请撤销或停止裁决效力为幌子妨碍执行的实施。

---

〔79〕 赵承璧编著：《国际贸易法律》，中国对外经济贸易出版社 1986 年版，第 446 页。
〔80〕 程德钧等编著：《国际惯例与涉外仲裁实务》，中国青年出版社 1993 年版，第 246 页。

第三节　申请执行外国仲裁裁决的条件

关于申请执行外国仲裁裁决的条件,《纽约公约》第4条规定:

“一、申请承认及执行之一造,为取得前条所称之承认及执行,应于申请时提具:(甲)原裁决之正本或其正式副本;(乙)第二条所称协定之原本或其正式副本。

二、倘前述裁决或协定所用文字非为援引裁决地所在国之正式文字,申请承认及执行裁决之一造应备具该文件之此项文字译本。译本应由公设或宣誓之翻译员或外交或领事人员认证之。”

许多国家(如希腊、意大利、墨西哥等国)的司法判例也已确认,上述公约规定的条件是对当事人申请执行公约裁决的唯一要求。[81] 从某些国家的司法实践看来,在当事人未履行全部条件的情况下,法院往往并不是拒绝受理申请,而是允许申请人在提出申请后补充履行其未履行的条件。例如美国上诉法院就曾拒绝被诉人基于申请人未提供裁决的正式副本而提出驳回执行申请的请求,理由是申请人在被诉人提出驳回请求后已补充了所缺文件。这里,值得注意的是《纽约公约》并没有提及应依何国法律来认证裁决和仲裁协议的译本。不过,外国有许多判例认为,此认证可按裁决作出地或裁决执行地国的法律办理。[82]

第四节　拒绝承认与执行外国仲裁裁决的理由

依《纽约公约》第5条的规定,拒绝承认与执行外国仲裁裁决的理由可分两类:一类是必须由被申请人举证证明的拒绝执行理由;另一类是法院可以自行决定拒绝的拒绝执行理由。

一、必须由当事人举证证明的拒绝执行理由

依《纽约公约》第5条第(1)款的规定,此种理由有五种。它们有三个共同的特点:第一,这些理由是列举式的与穷尽的,仅在被申请人能证明所列的理由中之

---

〔81〕 U. S Court of Appeals (5th, Cir.), July 19, 1976, Imperial Ethiopian Government v. Baruch. Foster Corp., 2 Yearbook Commercial Arbitration, 1977, p. 252.

〔82〕 程德钧等编著:《国际惯例与涉外仲裁实务》,中国青年出版社1993年版,第246页。

一确实存在时,方可拒绝承认与执行该裁决;第二,不审查仲裁裁决的实体事项,因为仲裁裁决事实上或法律上的错误并非拒绝理由之一;第三,举证责任在被申请人,而非申请人。具体说来,此类理由包括:

1. 仲裁协议无效。指仲裁协议的当事人依对其适用的法律处于某种元行为能力的状态,或者该仲裁协议依当事人约定的法律是无效的,或者在未指明以什么法律为准时,依照裁决地所在国法律是无效。

2. 仲裁违反基本正当程序。指被申请人没有接到关于指定仲裁员或仲裁程序的适当通知,或者因为其他原因,被申请人未能申辩。

3. 仲裁员越权。指裁决所处理的争议不是提交仲裁的标的,或者不属于仲裁协议的范围。但是,如果裁决中现有部分是提交仲裁事项,又有部分是未提交仲裁事项,则如果提交仲裁事项与未提交仲裁事项是可分的话,裁决中关于提交仲裁事项的决定仍可承认与执行。

4. 仲裁庭的组成或仲裁程序不当。指仲裁庭的组成或仲裁程序与各当事人之间的协议不符,或者在没有这个方面的协议的情况下,与仲裁地所在国法律不符。

5. 裁决无约束力或已被撤销。指裁决对各当事人尚未发生拘束力,或者已被裁决所在地国或裁决所依据法律的国家法院撤销或暂停执行。

二、法院可以自行决定拒绝执行的拒绝执行理由

依《纽约公约》第5条第2款,执行地法院可以主动裁定不予执行仲裁裁决的理由有二:(1)依照执行地国的法律,争议事项是不能以仲裁解决的;(2)承认或执行裁决将违反执行地国的公共利益。学者一般都认为,关于争议的可仲裁性构成了公共秩序一般概念的部分。[83] 所以,这两个理由实质上均可归纳到“公共秩序保留”项下。

公共秩序是各国拒绝外国法适用的传统理由,也是拒绝承认与执行外国仲裁裁决的传统理由。一般来说,公共秩序的作用主要是用以保护“法院地的基本道德信念或政策”。

然而,迄今为止,尚无人能提出一个能为“公共秩序”下一个大家普遍接受的完整系统的定义。其原因在于各国所奉行的经济、法律、道德、政治、宗教、文化与社会标准相去甚远,各国对反映这些标准的公共秩序的理解也就大相径庭。正因如此,有学者批评道,对于申请执行裁决者来说,以公共政策抗辩,犹如一把高悬

---

〔83〕 P. Sanders, The New York Convention, in International Commercial Arbitration, Vol. 2, 1960, p. 323.

的达摩克利斯之剑，随时都可能有临头之险。[84] 不过，从目前的实践来看，将国内公共秩序与国际公共秩序区别开来似乎是大势所趋。例如，美国最高法院在 Fritz Scherk v. Alberto-Culver 一案中即认为，由国内合同产生的证券交易争议是不可仲裁的，但由国际合同所产生的证券交易争议则应是可以仲裁的。[85] 尽管如此，对何谓“国际公共秩序”，国际上也尚无一致的看法。实际内容的不确定性与含糊性仍是“公共政策的基本特征之一”。

第五节　仲裁裁决在我国的承认与执行

一、内国仲裁裁决的承认与执行

我国《仲裁法》第 62 条、63 条规定，一方当事人不履行裁决的，另一方当事人可以依民事诉讼法有关规定向人民法院申请执行。一方当事人申请执行，另一方当事人申请撤销裁决的，人民法院应当裁定中止执行。撤销裁决的申请被裁定驳回的，人民法院应当裁定恢复执行。上述规则是一般规则，对国内仲裁裁决与涉外仲裁裁决同样适用。但是，关于拒绝承认与执行仲裁裁决的理由，《仲裁法》却又对上述二者区别对待。对于国内仲裁裁决，当事人如能证明有下列情由，均可能导致不予执行：(1)当事人在合同中没有订立仲裁条款或者事后没有达成书面协议；(2)裁决的事项不属于仲裁协议的范围或者仲裁机构无权仲裁；(3)仲裁庭的组成或者仲裁的程序违反法定程序刊的认定事实的主要证据不足；(4)适用法律确有错误；(5)仲裁员在仲裁该案时有贪污受贿、徇私舞弊、枉法裁决行为。简言之，对国内仲裁裁决不仅可以程序性问题请求拒绝执行，还可以实体问题为由申请拒绝执行。对涉外仲裁裁决则不如此对待。按《仲裁法》第 71 条与《民事诉讼法》第 260 条的规定，拒绝承认及执行涉外仲裁裁决的理由与撤销仲裁裁决的理由一样。即同样地只因程序性问题，而不管实体的错误。对这种区别规定学者间有不同见解。[86]

二、外国裁决在我国的承认与执行

我国《民事诉讼法》第 269 条规定：“国外仲裁机构的裁决，需要中华人民共

---

〔84〕 G. Bernini. Enforcement of Foreign Arbitral Awards, Report to ICC Seminar on Techniques of International Commercial Arbitration ICC Doc. No. SEMAR 1/9. Paris, 1976. p. 2.

〔85〕 Scherk vs. Alberto-Culver Co. ,417 U. S. 506(1974), 1 Yearbook Commercial Arbitration 1975, p. 203.

〔86〕 参见陈安：《中国涉外仲裁监督机制评析》，载《中国社会科学》1995 年第 4 期；肖永平：《也谈我国法院对仲裁的监督范围——与陈安先生商榷》，载《法学评论》1998 年第 1 期；翁晓健：《两种意见四个焦点——再评中国仲裁司法监督制度》，载梁慧星主编：《民商法论丛》(第 19 卷)，金桥文化出版(香港)有限公司 2001 年版。

和国人民法院承认和执行的，应当由当事人直接向被执行人住所地或者其财产所在地的中级人民法院申请，人民法院应当依照中华人民共和国缔结或者参加的国际条约，或者按照互惠原则办理。”据此，外国仲裁裁决在我国的承认与执行可分为三种情况：

（一）在《纽约公约》缔约国作出的裁决

我国缔结或者参加的有关承认和执行外国仲裁裁决的公约中，最重要的就是1958年《纽约公约》。六届全国人大常委会第十八次会议于1986年12月2日决定我国加入1958年纽约公约。我国于1987年1月22日申请加入该公约。该公约于1987年4月22日起对我国生效。

我国加入该公约时提出互惠保留和商事保留。为了妥善地执行1958年《纽约公约》，最高人民法院于1987年4月10日就执行1958年《纽约公约》问题，发出了《关于执行我国加入的〈承认与执行外国仲裁裁决公约〉的通知》，“通知”指出以下几点：

1. 根据我国加入该公约时所作的互惠保留声明，我国对另一缔约国领土内作出的仲裁裁决的承认和执行适用该公约。该公约与我国《民事诉讼法》有不同规定的，按公约的规定办理。

对于在非缔约国领土内作出的仲裁裁决，需要我国法院承认和执行的，应按我国同申请人所在国缔结的其他条约或按互惠原则办理。

2. 根据我国加入该公约时所作的商事保留声明，我国仅对按照我国法律属于契约性和非契约性商事法律关系所引起的争议适用该公约。所谓“契约性和非契约性商事法律关系”，具体是指由于合同、侵权或者根据有关法律规定而产生的经济上的权利义务关系，例如，货物买卖、财产租赁、工程承包、加工承揽、技术转让、合资经营、合作经营、勘探开发自然资源、保险、信贷、劳务、代理、咨询服务和海上、民用航空、铁路、公路的客货运输，以及产品责任、环境污染、海上事故和所有权的争议等，但不包括外国投资者与东道国政府之间的争端。[87]

3. 根据1958年《纽约公约》第4条的规定，申请我国法院承认和执行在另一缔约国领土内作出的仲裁裁决，是由仲裁裁决一方当事人提出的。对于当事人的申请应由我国下列地点的中级人民法院受理：（1）被执行人为自然人的，为其户籍所在地或者居住地；（2）被执行人为法人的，为其主要办事机构所在地；（3）被

---

〔87〕 外国投资者与东道国政府之间的争端一般由1965年《关于解决各国和其他国家的国民之间投资争端的公约》（《华盛顿公约》）所设解决投资争端的国际中心解决。我国已于1992年批准加入1965年华盛顿公约。华盛顿公约规定每一缔约国都应承认依照该公约作出的裁决具有约束力，并在其领土内履行该裁决所确定的金钱上的义务，如同该裁决是该国法院的最后判决一样。

执行人在我国无住所、居所或者主要办事机构，但有财产在我国境内的，为其财产所在地。

4. 我国有管辖权的人民法院接到一方当事人的申请后，应对申请承认及执行的仲裁裁决进行审查，如果认为不具有1958年《纽约公约》第5条第1、2两款所列的情形，应当裁定承认其效力，并且按照民事诉讼法规定的程序执行；如果认定具有第5条第2款所列的情况之一的，或者根据被执行人提供的证据证明具有第5条第1款所列情形之一的，应当裁定驳回申请，拒绝承认及执行。

5. 申请我国法院承认及执行的仲裁裁决，仅限于1958年《纽约公约》对我国生效后在另一缔约国领土内作出的仲裁裁决。该项申请应当在民事诉讼法规定的申请执行期限内提出。依《民事诉讼法》第219条，双方或者一方当事人是公民的，其申请执行期限为1年；双方是法人或者其他组织的为6个月。

（二）在与我国订有双边条约的国家作出的外国裁决

在我国与一些国家订立的双边贸易、投资保护和司法协助的条约或协定中，规定有关于相互承认与执行对方国家的仲裁裁决的条文。对于在这些国家作出的仲裁裁决，可按双边条约的规定予以承认及执行。例如，1988年《中华人民共和国和法兰西共和国关于民商事司法协助的协定》第25条规定："缔约双方应根据1958年6月10日纽约关于承认与执行外国仲裁裁决的公约相互承认与执行在对方境内作出的仲裁裁决。"

（三）在与我国没有有关条约关系的其他国家作出的裁决

对于在《纽约公约》缔约国以及与我国订有双边条约国家以外的其他国家作出的仲裁裁决，需要在我国境内承认与执行的，应由申请人向我国法院提出申请，我国法院按互惠原则办理。如果外国裁决作出地国与我国有相互承认与执行仲裁裁决的互惠关系，并且裁决在形式上符合我国法律的规定，裁决的执行不违反我国法律的基本原则及国家主权、安全和社会公共利益的，法院裁定承认其效力，发出执行令，依照我国民事诉讼法规定的程序执行。

人民法院裁定执行仲裁裁决的，其执行措施应依我国《民事诉讼法》第22章"执行措施"的规定进行。在执行过程中，双方当事人也可以自行达成和解协议。仲裁裁决被人民法院裁定不予执行的，当事人可以根据双方达成的书面仲裁协议重新申请仲裁，也可以向人民法院起诉。

（四）我国承认与执行外国裁决制度的特点

从以上论述可以看出，我国承认与执行外国仲裁裁决的制度有三个突出特点。

第一，在审查承认和执行外国仲裁裁决的程序和条件方面，实行两种标准。

对于以我国所作保留为条件的属《纽约公约》范围的裁决,适用《纽约公约》。对于非公约缔约国的商事仲裁裁决或公约缔约国的非商事法律关系的仲裁裁决,则只能依我国民事诉讼法中的规定,按照互惠原则或按审查承认和执行外国判决的同样的程序和条件进行审查。

第二,对于向我国法院提出承认和执行外国仲裁裁决的申请,不论其情况是否相同均适用同一申请程序。在《纽约公约》缔约国领域内就商事法律关系争议作出的仲裁裁决以及在非缔约国领域内作出的仲裁裁决和在公约缔约国领域内作出的非商事法律关系的仲裁裁决,需要在我国承认和执行的,均应由当事人直接向被执行人住所地或其财产所在地的中级人民法院申请。

第三,对于经审查允许在我国执行的外国仲裁裁决,无论是在《纽约公约》缔约国领域内就商事法律关系争议作出的仲裁裁决,还是其他外国仲裁裁决,一律适用执行我国法院判决的同样程序予以执行。这一规定同许多国家的规定基本一致。一些有关承认和执行外国仲裁裁决的国际条约也有这样的规定,例如,1975 年《美洲国家国际商事仲裁公约》第 4 条规定:"根据适用的法律或程序规则不得上诉的仲裁决定或裁决,具有终局司法判决的效力,得以与本国或外国普通法院作出的判决相同方式,依执行地国的程序法以及国际条约的规定予以执行或承认。"

至于我国作出的仲裁裁决在外国的执行,《仲裁法》第 72 条规定:"涉外仲裁委员会作出的发生法律效力的仲裁裁决,当事人请求执行的,如果被执行人或者其财产不在中华人民共和国领域内,应当由当事人直接向有管辖权的外国法院申请承认与执行。"

我国已于 1987 年成为《纽约公约》的缔约国,因此,中国仲裁裁决在《纽约公约》100 多个缔约国境内获得承认与执行,一般不存在法律上的障碍。根据公约的规定,各缔约国相互承认外国仲裁裁决的拘束力并依照公约规定的各项条件予以执行。一般来说,我国涉外仲裁裁决的当事人可直接向被执行人住所地或者可供执行财产所在地的外国法院提出申请。目前,我国涉外仲裁裁决已在加拿大、美国、日本、新西兰、瑞士、意大利和泰国等国家及香港等地区得到承认与执行。

有些国家虽未参加《纽约公约》,但在同我国订立的双边贸易、投资保护条约或司法协助协定中有关于通过仲裁解决争议和承认与执行仲裁裁决的规定,我国涉外仲裁裁决的当事人可依照双边条约的规定到这些国家申请承认与执行。

除上述与我国有条约关系的国家外,我国涉外仲裁裁决如需在其他国家承认与执行,则只能依照执行地国国内法规定的条件和程序办理。

国际贸易惯例基本理论研究*

导　言

战后,国际贸易法[1]领域发生了历史性的变化。这一变化不仅表现为以《关税与贸易总协定》(GATT)为载体的世界多边贸易法律体制的创立,更表现为以国际贸易惯例为在要表现形式之一的商人法(Lex Mercatoria、Law Merchant)[2]的悄然复兴与迅速发展。

20世纪50年代末60年代初,东西方学者纷纷注意到商国际主义回归与商人自治法正迅速发展的世界性事实。1957年,施米托夫(C. M. Schmitthoff)教授在赫尔辛基大学演讲时指出,"我们正开始重新发现商法的国际性,国际法——国内法——国际法这个发展轮回已经完成,各地商法发展的总趋势是摆脱国内法的限制,朝着国际贸易法这个普遍性与国际性的概念发展",[3]随后,南斯拉夫的哥尔德斯坦(A. Gold stajn)写道:"尽管世界各国的政治、经济和法律制度不同,新的商人法却在国际贸易领域迅速发展着。现在是承认独立于国内法制度的商人自治法的存在的时候了"。[4] 1966年,联合国国际贸易法委员(UNCITRAL)的设立,

---

* 本文发表在梁慧星主编:《民商法论丛》(第7卷),1997年第1号。

〔1〕 这里的"国际贸易法"是指我国学者所一般理解的国际贸易法,即既包括传统的国际商法,也包括国家干预、管制国际商业贸易活动的法律。与本文中提及的许多西方学者所称的"国际贸易法"(一般仅限于传统国际商法范畴)是不同的。参见沈达明、冯大同编著:《国际贸易法新论》,法律出版社1989年版,第3~4页。

〔2〕 或译"商人习惯法"或"商法",指产生于中世纪西欧商人中间,调整他们彼此关系的一系列习惯与法律。参见[英]戴维·M.沃克编:《牛津法律大辞典》,北京社会与科技发展研究所译,光明日报出版社1988年版,第524页。"二战"后复兴的这种商人法则称为"现代商人法"(Modern Lex. Mercatoria New Law Merchant),其内容除商事惯例,一般尚包括国际公约、统一示范法、一般法律原则、国际商事仲裁裁决等。详见本文第二章第二节。

〔3〕 C. M. Schrnitthoff, "Modern Trends in English Commercial Law." in Chia-Jui Chenged. Clive M. Schmitthoff's Select Essays on International Trade Law, pp. 3 - 15.

〔4〕 A. Gold stajn. "The New L. aw Merchant", 1961, L. Bus. L. 12

正是这一时代趋势的产物;反过来说,它的成立与活动又大大地促进与加快了国际贸易惯例的编纂与现代商人法的统一化进程。到了80年代,这种统一化工作已达到了相当的广度与深度,以至于曾怀疑编纂全球性的国际贸易法典的现实可行性的施米托夫教授改变了看法,乐观地指出,"实现这一目标并非乌托邦式的幻想……"。[5] 考虑到现有的和计划中的统一规则,这是一项可行的建议。[6]

现代商人法的这一重大发展在改革开放的中国有着明确的积极回应。1985年,我国《涉外经济合同法》就明确规定:我国法律未作规定的,"可以适用国际惯例",[7]随后,《民法通则》则进一步明确,我国法律和我国缔结或参加的国际条约没有规定的,可以适用国际惯例。[8] 1992年通过的《海商法》,[9]1995年通过的《票据法》[10]与《民用航空法》[11]又一次重申了上述的立场。虽然,我国国内法把"国际惯例"置于"可补充适用"的地位。与此同时,全国上下不断反复强调,要"按国际惯例办事","与国际惯例接轨",足见改革开放以来,我国对"国际惯例"的重视程度。而这里所称的"国际惯例",恰如许多学者所指出的,主要是指国际贸易惯例,[12]此外,我国最近还强调提出,今后要"加强并发挥进出口商会的协调功能,逐步用行业组织的自律行为替代部分政府行为"。[13] 这一重大政策指针无疑将为国际贸易惯例在我国的编纂、发展与应用提供更为广阔的空间。

然而,究竟何为国际贸易惯例,其范围、分类与来源如何,其性质、效力与地位怎样,其解释与适用规则何在等,都是国外聚讼纷纭、因内尚乏深究的基本理论问题。即便是对上述有关国内立法中的"国际惯例"的含义、性质及其适用诸项,也鲜见集中深入的研究,更无准确统一的认识。在深化改革、扩大开放和与国际通行规则接轨的时代背景之下,这方面研究的缺陷事实上已经导致了理论上、立法上及实践上的许多混乱,并已引起了有关部门的高度重视。[14] 本文正由此出发,拟结合中外有关法律与实践,对上述问题作初步研究。

---

[5] C. M. Schmitthoff, Commercial Law in a Changing Economic Climate. 2nd ed. 1981, pp. 30–3, 1.

[6] C. M. Schmitthoff, "The Codification of The Law of International Trade", Jan. 1985. J. Bus. L. pp. 43–44.

[7] 参见《涉外经济合同法》第5条第3款。

[8] 参见《民法通则》第142条第3款。

[9] 参见《海商法》第268条第2款。

[10] 参见《票据法》第96条第2款。

[11] 参见《民用航空法》第184条第2款。

[12] 参见李双元主编:《国际私法》,北京大学出版社1991年版,第36页;浦伟良:《论〈民法通则〉中关于冲突法的总则性规定》,载《法学评论》1990年第5期。

[13] 《中华人民共和国国民经济和社会发展"九五"计划和2010年远景目标纲要》(以下简称《纲要》)第八部分第(二)点,载《中华人民共和国国务院公报》1996年第7号。

[14] 这一点,从国家最近把以往"与国际惯例接轨"的提法改为"按照国际通行规则"的提法这一事实即可看出。关于这一新提法,可参见《中华人民共和国国民经济和社会发展"九五"计划和2010年远景目标纲要》,载《国务院公报》1996年第7号。

第一章　国际贸易惯例的界定与沿革

第一节　习惯与惯例

要界定国际贸易惯例，首先有必要明确何为"惯例"。特别是要廓清它与"习惯"的区别与联系。由于在一般法律文献与日常生活中，"惯例"与"习惯"经常被交叉混用，歧异甚多，它们与英文"custom"及"usage"的对译也见仁见智、大相径庭 E 加之"custom"与"usage"本身的含义就混淆不清，要厘清此二者的关系，殊非易事。

一、关于习惯与惯例的区别的种种歧见

"惯例"与"习惯"是最常见的用以表达国际交往实践中逐渐自发形成的习惯性行为规范的两个概念。在我国国际法学、国际私法学与国际经济法学著作中，都把"国际惯例"或"国际习惯"作为其法源之一。[15] 然而，对于这种法源的理解，却因角度不同，而各有侧重、颇见歧异。如我国著名国际法学家王铁崖教授认为，应使用"国际习惯"一词称呼国际法的渊源；它是各种重复类似的行为而具有法律拘束力的结果，它必须具备"常例"（usus）与"法律确信"（opinio juris）主客观两方面的因素。"习惯"有别于"惯例"；狭义的"惯例"专指"习惯"，但广义的"惯例"则既包括习惯（狭义的"惯例"），也包括那些尚未取得法律拘束力的惯例，即《国际法院规约》第 38 条第 I 项（丑）款所指的"通例"。[16] 质言之，习惯与狭义的惯例同义，均指国际法上取得法律拘束力，作为国际法渊源之一的行为规范；而广义的"惯例"则涵盖很广，除习惯外，尚包括那些尚未被接受为法律的"通例"。著名国际私法学家韩德培教授则提出，国际惯例是在国际交往中逐渐形成的不成文的法律规范，它只有经过国家认可方有拘束力。在国际私法范围内，有两种不同的国际惯例，一种为强制性国际惯例，如"国家财产豁免"原则；另一种是任意性的实体法惯例，如《1932 年华沙—牛津规则》，等等。[17] 也就是说，应用"国际惯例"来称呼国际私法的这一不成文的法源，并将其细分为"强制性规范"与"任意

---

〔15〕 参见王铁崖主编：《国际法》，法律出版社 1995 年版，第 13 ~ 15 页；韩德培主编：《国际私法》，武汉大学出版社 1989 年版，第 27 ~ 28 页；陈安主编：《国际经济法总论》，法律出版社 1991 年版，第 136 ~ 137 页，尽管这里采用的是"国际经济惯例"的提法。

〔16〕 参见王铁崖主编：《国际法》，法律出版社 1935 年版，第 13 ~ 15 页。值得注意的是，该书的观点与王教授在其主编的 1981 年版的《国际法》的主张有所不同，后者曾提出，"狭义的国际惯例则仅指尚未取得法律拘束力的常例"，参见王铁崖主编：《国际法》，法律出版社 1981 年版，第 29 页。

〔17〕 参见韩德培主编：《国际私法》，武汉大学出版社 1989 年版 ，第 27 ~ 28 页。

性规范”两大类，同时强调国家的“认可”是惯例取得法律拘束力的必要前提。这无疑反映了国际私法上的国际惯例的特色——国际私法上的国际惯例主要是韩教授所说的“任意性规范”，即“只有经过当事人选择，才对他们具有拘束力的惯例”；而国际法上的国际惯例，无疑主要是“强制性规范”，因为它主要规范的是国家之间的公法关系，而不像国际私法上的国际惯例所规范的主要是私法关系。同理，我国国际经济法学者们对国际惯例这种法源的理解与国际私法学者基本一致。例如，在一篇专论中，陈安教授提出：对中国有关立法中的“国际惯例”应作广义理解，即既包括那些在国际社会中普遍认为具有拘束力的习惯或惯常做法，也包括那些尚未获得普遍承认，暂时还欠缺约束力的习惯或惯常做法。[18]

由此可以看出：一方面，尽管由于角度不同，在表述上各有侧重，但我国国际法、国际私法与国际经济法学者却一致认为，对“国际惯例”或“国际习惯”可以作广义的理解，既包括那些已获得普遍承认，具有当然的法律拘束力的习惯做法（韩教授所称的“强制性规范”），也包括那些目前尚未得到普遍承认，不具备当然的法律拘束力的习惯做法（韩教授所称的“任意性规范”）。另一方面，关于这两种习惯做法应称为“惯例”还是应称为“习惯”，则众说纷纭，相去甚远。按王铁崖教授原来的观点，[19]则“习惯”是有法律拘束力的，而“（狭义的）惯例”则没有。李双元教授[20]等也持同样看法；陈安教授[21]的主张则刚好相反，他认为，“惯例”是“由习惯而形成的规例”，应用“国际惯例”来称呼已取得法律拘束力的习惯或惯常做法（即《国际法院规约》所称的“international custom”），相应地，用“习惯”来称呼那些尚未取得法律拘束力的惯常做法。刘丁、[22]朱学山[23]及我国台湾地区学者雷崧生、[24]张镜影[25]等基本上也都是这种观点。与此同时，许多著名学者则只提“国际惯例”，或只提“国际习惯”，而不对“习惯”与“惯例”作对比区分。例如，韩德培教授、[26]周鲠生教授[27]及我国台湾地区学者何适、[28]张道行、[29]苏义雄[30]等只

〔18〕 参见陈安：《论适用国际惯例与有法必依的统一》，载《中国社会科学》1994 年第 4 期。
〔19〕 参见王铁崖主编：《国际法》，法律出版社 1981 年版，第 28 ~ 30 页。
〔20〕 参见李双元主编：《国际私法》，北京大学出版社 1991 年版，第 34 ~ 36 页。
〔21〕 参见陈安：《论适用国际惯例与有法必依的统一》，载《中国社会科学》1994 年第 4 期。
〔22〕 参见刘丁编著：《国际经济法》，中国人民大学出版社 1984 年版，第 13 页。
〔23〕 参见陈安主编：《国际经济法总论》，法律出版社 1991 年版，第 136 页。
〔24〕 参见雷崧生：《国际法概要》，汉林出版社 1982 年版，第 7 页。
〔25〕 参见何孝元主编：《云五社会科学大辞典》第 6 册，《法律学》，商务印书馆 1971 年版，第 302 页。
〔26〕 参见韩德培主编：《国际私法》，武汉大学出版社 1989 年版，第 27 ~ 28 页。
〔27〕 参见周鲠生：《国际法》（上册），商务印书馆 1976 年版，第 21 页。
〔28〕 参见何适：《国际公法》，商务印书馆 1980 年版，第 5 ~ 6 页。
〔29〕 参见张道行：《国际公法》，国立编译馆 1979 年版，第 4 页。
〔30〕 参见苏义雄：《平时国际法》，三民书局 1986 年版，第 30，35 页。

提及"国际惯例"这一概念;而梁西、[31]陈致中[32]及我国台湾地区学者邱宏达[33]等则只提"国际习惯"一词。"国际惯例"与"国际习惯"使用情形之纷乱,于此可见一斑。

这种分歧在很大程度上导源于国内学者们对英文"custom"与"usage",特别是对《国际法院规约》第38条第1款(丑)项提到的"international custom"一词的不同译法。大凡主张custom译成"习惯",将usage译成"惯例"的,一般都主张国际习惯有拘束力,而国际惯例没有拘束力;反之,凡主张将custom译成惯例,将usage译成"习惯"的,一般都主张国际惯例有法律拘束力,而国际习惯则没有。前者如王铁崖教授、[34]李双元教授[35]等;后者如陈安教授[36]等。同样,只提及"国际惯例"或"国际习惯"的学者也大都是因为他们将《国际法院规约》上述条款所称的custom分别译成了"惯例"或"习惯"。质言之,尽管国内学者对custom和usage的译法不同,但对于此二词的基本理解却是相同的,即custom是有法律拘束力的,而usage则尚未获得法律拘束力,custom是由usage发展而来的。

然而,在西方学者中间,关于custom与usage的法律效力与承继关系的理解却并不像我国学者那样一致,甚至可以说,这种理解上的混乱情形并不逊于我国学者对"惯例"与"习惯"二词的理解上的歧异。

诚然,大多数西方学者的理解与上述国内学者的理解是相同的。例如,新修订的《奥本海国际法》仍坚持认为"如果某一行为的明确而持续的惯行,是在这种行为按国际法为必须的和正当的这个法律信念的支配下形成的,则为custom;反之,如果某种行为的惯行的形成,并不是在按国际法为必须的和正当的这个信念的支配下进行的,则为usage"。[37] 换言之,custom同时具备物质因素与心理因素两个条件,是有法律拘束力的国际法渊源,而usage则因不具备心理因素—法律信念(opinio juris),故不能算作国际法的渊源,不具有法律拘束力。斯塔克(Starke)在其《国际法导论》中指出,custom与usage这两个术语经常交换使用。但严格说来,二者之间是有明显的技术性区别的:usage相当于custom不太明确的阶段,usage之终便是custom之始,usage是还未获得完全的法律确认的国际惯行(habit),usage可能互相冲突,而custom则是统一的和自相一致的。[38] 也就是说,custom

[31] 参见梁西主编:《国际法》,武汉大学出版社1993年版,第30~32页。
[32] 参见陈致中编著:《国际法教程》,中山大学出版社1989年版,第18~20页。
[33] 参见邱宏达主编:《现代国际法》,三民书局1986年版,第66~70页。
[34] 参见王铁崖主编:《国际法》,法律出版社1981年版,第29页;1995年版,第13~15页。
[35] 参见李双元主编:《国际私法》,北京大学出版社1991年版,第34~36页。
[36] 参见陈安:《论适用国际惯例与有法必依的统一》,载《中国社会科学》1991年第4期。
[37] Oppenheim's International Law, 9th ed. (1992). p. 27.
[38] J. G. Starke. An Introductíon to International Law, Lúndon, 1977. 8th ed. pp. 40 – 41.

源于 usage 而高于 usage；custom 有法律约束力，而 usage 则尚没有法律拘束力。

然而，并不是所有的西方学者都接受这种"主流派"的观点，有的学者的观点与此刚好相反。例如，霍尔（Hall）就曾说过："这种 custom 由此定型而成为一个确定的 usage"〔39〕换言之，usage 源于 custom 而高于 custom，usage 有法律拘束力，而 custom 则没有法律拘束力。

在这方面，《布莱克法学辞典》的立场看起来有点特别，这部权威的西方法学辞书将 custom 与 usage 含并起来立为一个条目（custom and usage），并统一解释为："人们通过普遍的采纳与默许，以及长期和无差别的惯行而形成的，具有强制力，从而在与之有关的场合或事项上具有法律拘束力的 usage 或 practice。它源自长期以来经常重复的一连串的行为，通过这种重复与未间断的默认，它获得了一种默示的和普遍的同意的效力。"〔40〕从这里看来，它似乎将 custom 与 usage 等而视之，不分轩轾，都看作狭义的有法律拘束力的习惯做法。不过，该辞典接下来却补充道："usage（辨义）是一种重复的行为；它不同于 custom，后者是此和重复行为所产生的法律或一般规则；可以有尚未形成 custom 的 usage，但如无 usage 伴行或先行，就不能形成 custom。"〔41〕也就是说，二者又有了质的区别。这种解释看似矛盾，实际上并不矛盾。前面合并立目，作同义解释，是指在日常的社会生活与语言实践中，甚或在一般法学学者（包括国际法学者）的论著中，对此二者的理解是基本相同的。正如陈安教授所指出的，"'custom'、'usage'和'pratice'，这三个名词实际上都具有习惯、惯例、惯常做法等多重含义，在辞典的名词字义注解中，常被用于互相交叉解释。可以说，在一定范围内，这三个单词实际上是字义互通的同义语"。〔42〕 后面辨义区分，是指在国际法学理论研究与实践操作的精微处，又需要对此二者作细致的法律区分。二者反映的是两者在不高层面上的区别与联系。

二、评价与主张

对于 custom 的法律含义及其与 usage 的关系，我们十分赞同国内学者的上述一致看法（并且十分庆幸这种一致观点的存在）。这不仅因为它为西方大多数学者所主张，更因为它得到许多权威的国际法律文献的肯定。例如，《国际法院规约》第 38 条第 1 款在规定国际法院可适用的国际法规范时，就在其（丑）项提到了

〔39〕 Oppenheím's International Law. 9th ed. Robert Jennings ed. 1992. p. 27, N. 9.

〔40〕 Black's Law Dictionary, 1979. 5th ed. p. 347.

〔41〕 B1ack's Law Dictionary. 1979. 5th ed. p. 347.

〔42〕 陈安：《论适用国际惯例与有法必依的统一》，载《中国社会科学》1994 年第 4 期。

"international custom as evidence of a general practice accepted as law"。[43] 这一事实上的国际法渊源条款无疑是认为 custom 是有拘束力的法律规范。反过来,1964 年的《国际货物买卖统一法》(以下统一用英文简称 ULIS)[44]与《国际货物买卖合同成立统一法》(以下统一用英文简称 ULFIS)[45]以及 1980 年的《联合国国际货物销售合同公约》(以下统一用英文简称 CISG)[46]中有关具有任意性质的国际贸易方面的惯例的条款,却一般用"usage"一词,而没有使用 custom,其隐含的意义无疑是:usage 一般是指尚未取得普遍法律效力的习惯做法。

在确立了 custom 与 usage 的含义之后,custom 与 usage 的中文对译实际上就完全取决于我们对"惯例"与"习惯"二词的法律意义与相互关系的理解。

我们认为,对于这两种国际实践中逐渐自发形成的习惯做法,称为"惯例"还是称为"习惯",这本身就是一个习惯问题,是学者们长期各自为用,在各自影响的范围内约定俗成的未能统一的结果。实际上,与西方社会对 custom 及 usage 的一般理解相似,在我国社会中,对"国际惯例"与"国际习惯"一般也不作严格区分。例如,《辞海》在解释"国际惯例"一词时,就说,它"也叫国际习惯,国际法的主要渊源之一,国际交往的不成文的行为规则。它是各国在交往过程中逐渐形成的先例,最初为某些周家长期反复使用,后来为各国所接受并承认其法律效力。"[47]也就是说,国际惯例等同于国际习惯,是对国际法中的这种不成文法律渊源的两种不同称呼,很明显,这里所称的"国际惯例"或"国际习惯"仅仅指狭义上的理解。对此,《法学辞典》也作同样解释,[48]在学者论著中,也有持这种看法的。例如我国台湾学者沈克勤在其编著的《国际法》教科书中,虽详细剖析了"惯"(custom)与"习尚"(usage)的区别与联系,却交叉使用"惯例"与"习惯"二字,未作任何区分,[49]其意与上述《辞海》的观点可谓不谋而合。

然而,如上所述,从法学理论研究与实务操作的精微处来看,对上述有法律拘束力的惯常做法与尚未取得法律拘束力的惯常做法还是有必要各设一个专门的称谓,以示区别,同时澄清混乱,方便使用。毫无疑问,启用新词很可能只会增加

---

[43] 中文本为"国际习惯,作为通例之证明而经接受为法律者",陈安教授将后者译为"有证据表明已被接受为法律的一般惯常做法"。该款在国外国际法学界也备受批评,例如波兰的马可斯基(J. Makowski)就曾尖锐地指出,"这条是写错了,因为不是习惯(custom)构成某一惯常做法(certain practice)的证据,而是昔日的惯常做法(univer. sal *practice*)构成习惯的证据"。哈德逊(Hudsonl)、施瓦曾伯格(G. Schwarzenberger)等也表述过类似的异议。详见 Karol Wolfke, Custom in Present International Law. 1993. 2nd ed. pp. 5 – 8.

[44] 参见 1964 年《国际货物买卖合同成立统一法》第 2、4、、5、6、11、13 等条款。

[45] 参见《国际货物买卖统一法》第 8、9、20 等条款。

[46] 参见《联合国国际货物销售合同公约》第 4、8、9 等条款。

[47] 《辞海》(缩印本),上海辞书出版社 1979 年版,第 769 页。

[48] 《法学辞典》(增订版),上海辞书出版社 1984 年版,第 527 ~ 528 页。

[49] 参见沈克勤编著:《国际法》,台湾学生书局 1980 年版,第 34、35 页。

混乱,倒不如在对“习惯”与“惯例”二词细加辨析之后,选择其中一种较妥帖的对应称谓方法。

在我国的社会语言实践中,“习惯”一词重在惯行的事实以及由此产生的惯性与趋势,而不强调其明确性与稳定性;“惯例”则似乎重在因惯成例,即不仅强调惯行的事实与趋势;更强调此种事实与趋势已经相对成型,形成了某种成例,其内容具有一定的明确性与稳定性;此外,它还暗示了“惯行”与“成例”之间的因果关系。例如,《现代汉语词典》对“习惯”的释义是,“在长时期里逐渐养成的、一时不易改变的行为、倾向或社会风尚”。〔50〕 显然,这里强调的是惯行与趋势。《辞海》对“惯例”的释义则为“亦称‘例’、‘成例’、‘通例’、‘旧例’,指法律上没有明文规定,但过去曾经施行,可以仿照办理的做法”。〔51〕 这里“惯例”既然是过去曾经施行,可以仿照办理的做法,则这种做法内容的相对明确性与稳定性是不言而喻的。而且,这里对“惯例”的解释一开始就直接与法律联系在一起,足见其法律意味是比较明显的。

由此可见,“惯例”一词的语义、语气、力度与法律意味,的确均强于“习惯”一词。〔52〕 所以,如果要对二者作精细的区分,则似以“惯例”(狭义的)称呼有法律拘束力的习惯做法,而以“习惯”称呼尚未取得法律拘束力的习惯做法为宜。

为行文方便,在本文中,对“惯例”与“习惯”一般也不作严格区分;但如遇必须对二者作对比区分的情形,则一般以“习惯”称呼已取得法律拘束力的习惯做法,而以“惯例”称呼尚未取得法律拘束力的习惯做法。这主要是基于三方面的现实考虑:首先,这主要是考虑到“国际贸易惯例”这一提法已为我国所长期使用与普遍接受,如改称“国际贸易习惯”很可能会造成新的混乱。其次,这也可与《国际法院规约》的中文本关于这种国际法渊源的法定用语“国际习惯”的提法相一致。最后,如前所述,我国有关立法中的“国际惯例”,按照大多数学者的理解,应指那些没有当然法律拘束力的任意性规范。这就意味着,以“惯例”称呼尚未获得法律拘束力的习惯做法,与我国学术界对国内有关立法中的“国际惯例”这一法定用语的理解也是相一致的。相应地,在本文中,如引用有关英文资料,则一般以“惯例”对译“usage”,以“习惯”对译“custom”。

---

〔50〕 参见《现代汉语词典》,商务印书馆 1978 年版,第 1221 页。

〔51〕 参见《辞海》(缩印本),上海辞书出版社 1984 年版,第 872 页。

〔52〕 参见陈安:《论适用国际惯例与有法必依的统一》,载《中国社会科学》1994 年第 4 期。

第二节 国际贸易惯例的初步界定

国际贸易惯例是指国际贸易领域中的国际惯例，它大致包括在国际合同、运输、保险、支付与仲裁等方面存在的国际惯例。各国对贸易习惯与贸易惯例的区分标准在理论上、立法上与实务界中间有所不同；而对贸易惯例的具体定义，学者的看法与各国立法也各有千秋。

一、贸易习惯与贸易惯例

在各国国内法与学者们的论著中，贸易习惯（trade custom）与贸易惯例（trade usage）是有区别的。一般来说，各国法律都肯定贸易习惯是法律的渊源。然而，由于在大多数国内法中，对贸易习惯的条件极高，[53] 因而事实上极少有符合全部条件的贸易习惯存在。这样，贸易惯例的意义更显突出。不过，贸易惯例似乎多不被认为是法律的正式渊源，而只是解释合同的工具之一。[54]

显然，这种区别是习惯与惯例的区别在贸易领域的体现。这方面，学者的观点与各国立法基本一致。不过，施米托夫曾提出的区分标准似乎又有些特别。他虽然也认为那些建立在重复行为基础上的商事惯例或商事惯常做法（commercial usage or practice）往往是商事习惯（commercial custom）的雏形（instatu nascendi），也即商事习惯的最初的、试验性阶段；商事习惯具有相当程度的肯定性，商事惯例则没有；因此，商事习惯是造法性渊源（law-creating source），而商事惯例则不是。[55] 但是，他是从国际组织制法的角度来作这种民分的，也即他所指的“商主要习惯”是指国际组织，如国际商会、联合国欧洲经济委员会等制定的文件；而不是由国际组织制定的则只能称之为商事惯例或商事惯常做法。[56] 在我们看来，这里施氏所指的“商事习惯”实际上只不过是贸易惯例中最为成熟、最具国际普遍性的部分，也即后面将提到的“跨国成文规则”，本质上它们仍属于不具备当然的法律拘束力的“惯例”的范畴. 而不能一般地算作造法性的渊源——“习惯”。

施氏的观点可能是受到了国际贸易实务界的影响。在国际贸易实务界中间，

---

〔53〕 例如，在英国，习惯必须是经常性的（const ant）、自发的（voluntary）、明确的（certain）、一贯的（constent）和合理的（reasonable），甚至还必须具备恒久性（im memoriality）。即必须是 1189 年，查理一世时代开始时就已经存在的。不过，在实践中这种要求已有所放松。参见 Filip DeLy，lnternational Business Law and Lex Mercatoria. 1992. p. 135。

〔54〕 lbid p. 158.

〔55〕 C. M. Shmitthoff，The Law of International Trade. Its Growth，Formulat：on and Operation，ìn Chia. Jui. Cheng ed. C. M. Schmitthoff's Select Essays on International Trade Law. 1988，p. 149.

〔56〕 C. M. Schmitthoff，The Law C）f International Trade. Its Growth，Formulation and Operattion，in Chia-Jui Chenged. C. M. Schmitthoff's Select Essays on International Trade Law. 1988，p. 149.

人们一般不对惯例与习惯作严格区分,而一律视为没有当然法律拘束力的惯常做法。例如国际商会编纂的《跟单信用证统一惯例》(UCP 500)与国际法协会编纂的《华沙—牛津规则》都同时使用了“惯例”与“习惯”两个概念。前者还同时使用了“惯常做法”(practice)这一概念,但它们显然都未被赋予当然的法律效力。[57]《国际贸易术语解释通则》(Incoterm,1990)虽然只使用了“惯例”与“惯常做法”两个概念,但其导言部分也明确表达了二者的契约性质,它们也不是有当然拘束力的法律规范。[58]

上述立法、学理与实务上的观点,无不反映了这样一个事实:在当今国际贸易中,严格意义上的贸易习惯是很鲜见的,大量存在并日见增多的是各种各样的贸易惯例。正是基于这一事实,上文提到的几个货物买卖方面的国际公约,如 ULIS、ULFIS 及 CISG 等的有关条款都只用“惯例”而不用“习惯”:也正因如此. 1980 年国际商会国际商事法律与实务研究所(The Institute of International Business Law and Practice)委托施米托夫进行一项专项研究时,也采用的是必国际贸易惯例(1nterna tional Trade Usages)的名称。[59]

严格说来,国际贸易惯例与国内贸易惯例(domestic trade usages)是不同的,各国立法机关与法院对待二者的态度也不一样,其实际效果也相差甚远。[60] 然而,在许多国家,特别是在发达的市场经济国家,如英国、美国、德国、奥地利、澳大利亚、意大利、西班牙、比利时、荷兰、瑞典、瑞士等国,对国际贸易惯例与国内贸易惯例并无明确的区分,原则上都适用同一标准,[61] 因而在其国内立法中,也多只用“贸易惯例”或“商事惯例”的名称,而不冠以“国际”二字。不过,在发展中国家,特别是在原计划经济国家,由于采取对内对外分立的两套法律体制,对国际贸易惯例或“国际惯例”一般都特别对待。例如南斯拉夫 1954 年制定了专门的《一般贸易惯例》,我国有关立法中则均采用“国际惯例”的提法,而将“国内惯例”排除在外。

二、国际贸易惯例的基本界定

要给国际贸易惯例下一个确切的定义显然不是件容易的事情。也正因如此,

---

〔57〕 参见《跟单信用证统一惯例》(UCP 500)第 1 条;《华沙—牛津规则》序文及第 1 条。

〔58〕 《国际贸易术语解释通则》(INCOTERMS 1990)序言最后规定,“愿意采用这些规则的商人现应在合同中规定,他们的合同受《INCOTERMS 1990》的约束”。这表明它不过是一种可供选择的契约安排. 而不是具有必然法律效力的法律规范。

〔59〕 C. M. Schmitthoff, International Trade Usages, as a special issue of NEWSLETTER of the Institute of Business Law and Practice. 1987, p. 10.

〔60〕 这一点在发达国家也不例外,第 10 页。

〔61〕 C. M. Schmitthoff. International Trade Usages, as a special issue of NEWSLETTER of the Institute of Business Law and Practice. 1987, p. 10.

大多数国家的有关立法与我国一样，只是提及惯例，而来给予明确定义。例如，《德国商法典》第 346 节规定："在解释商人之间的作为或不作为的意义与效果时，应充分考虑到商业交往中适用的惯例与习惯"，法国、西班牙、原东德等国也都如此。[62] 与此同时，许多国际贸易立法也都是采用这种"言及而不定义"的处理方式。如 CISG、ULIS、ULFLS 及《国际商事仲裁示范法》、联合国欧洲经济委员会制定的《关于民商事判决的管辖与执行公约》都提到了贸易惯例的作用，但也都未对它作哪怕是最简短的定义。[63]

美国《统一商法典》(UCC)可以说是少见的例外之一。该法典第 1 ~205 节第(2)款对"贸易惯例"下了一个定义，规定"贸易惯例是指任何习惯做法或交易方式，只要该做法或方式在某一地区、某一行业或某类贸易中得到了经常遵守，从而使人们有理由相信它在当前交易中也会得到遵守"(*A* usages of trade is any practice or method of dealing having such regularity of observance in a place, vocation or trade as to justify an expectation that it will be observed with respect to the transaction in question.)。该款的"正式评注"(Official Comment)指出，在这里，英国法关于习惯必须是"古老的"(ancient or immemorial)和"普遍的"(universal)等要求都被废弃了。这意味着该法典认可了所有的新惯例、目前为大多数交易商所遵守的惯例以及那些商人们协商一致采纳的惯例。[64] 同时，惯例的合理性也不再需要证明，接受惯例的事实本身就可构成其合理性的初步证据(prima facie)。[65] 可见，美国《统一商法典》对贸易惯例的界定是十分宽泛的，其基本要件，一是"经常遵守"，二是由此产生的"合理期望"(legitimate expectation)，所谓时间因素、地域因素与合理性因素，均不重要。除"贸易惯例"以外，美国《统一商法典》第 1 ~205 节(1)款还定义了"交易做法"(course of dealing)。即"特定交易的当事方在此交易之前做出的，可以合理地视为构成一种当事双方共同的认识基础，以解释他们的意图与其他行为的一连串行为。"可见，所谓"交易做法"实质上是仅适用于特定贸易中的交易双方的习惯做法，堪称适用面最窄、最不"普遍"的贸易惯例。按美国法，其判断标准与前述贸易惯例基本相同，即一为经常性的行为，一为合理预期。此外，按第 2 ~208 节规定，"履约做法"(course of performance)也具有同样的意义，其基本条件也完全一样。这几个条款实际上使贸易惯例的范围涵盖了从二人

---

〔62〕 C. M. Schmiuhoff. International Trade Usages, as a special issue of NEWSLETTER of the Institute of Business Law and Practice. 1987, pp. 11 - 12.

〔63〕 C. M. Schmiuhoff. International Trade Usages, as a special issue of NEWSLETTER of the Institute of Business Law and Practice. 1987, pp. 12 - 13.

〔64〕 Uniform Commercial Code. 1990 Official Text with Comments. 12th ed. p. 50.

〔65〕 Uniform Commercial Code. 1990 Official Text with Comments. 12th ed. p. 50.

之间到商业社会所有人之间所经常遵守并进而产生了合理期望的习惯做法,实在是广泛得无以复加了。不过,这里的"贸易惯例"及"交易做法"与"履约做法"主要是解释合同的工具,而不是正式的法律渊源。[66]

在其他国家,尽管不像美国这样以立法来明确定义贸易惯例,但从其判例及法学论著中可以看出,各国对于贸易惯例的基本含义的理解既有相通的一面,也有各自的特色和侧重。例如,英国一般认为,贸易惯例是"商业社会中从事某一行业的人所普遍接受的特定交易做法或行为规则"。[67] 这一表述可谓简洁明快。它也强调"普遍接受"这一事实,这一点与美国法类似,但它不要求有"合理期望",而与后者又略有不同。在德国,贸易惯例被定义为"在一段时间内得到普遍遵守并导致它们是可以适用的这样的一般信念的统一行为模式"。[68] 这里也强调普遍遵守,但同时强调的是可以适用的"一般信念",这与上述美国法的两个要件更为接近。

施米托夫在深入考察了各国有关立场的基础上得出结论,认为"贸易惯例是商业社会某一特定行业中普遍遵守,然而使从事该行业的人都认为其具有约束力的一种交易做法或行为方式"。[69] 这一定义无疑带有英美法的明显痕迹,但应该承认,这一定义确实比较全面地概括了国际贸易惯例的基本要点,具有相当的合理性与典型性。

在我国,虽然在法律中也只"言及而不定义",但许多学者论及了国际贸易惯例的定义。韩德培教授认为,国际贸易惯例是"在国际贸易中通行的有确定内容的一些规则";[70]冯大同教授提出:"国际贸易惯例是在国际贸易的长期实践过程中形成的"。[71] 赵承璧教授认为,"国际贸易惯例是在国际贸易实践中逐渐形成的一些通用的习惯做法和通例";[72]周忠海教授则认为,"国际贸易习惯……是指在国际贸易的长期实践中逐渐形成的一些通用的和普遍承认的做法与通例";[73]徐国建教授撰文指出,"国际贸易惯例法"是"体现在标准合同、标准合同条款和

---

〔66〕 Uniform Commercial Code. 1990 Official Text with Comments. 12th ed. p. 50.

〔67〕 C. M. Schmitthoff, International Trade Usages, as a special issue of NEWSLETTER of the Institute of Business Law and Practice, 1987, p. 14.

〔68〕 C. M. Schmitthoff, International Trade Usages, as a special issue of NEWSLETTER of the Institute of Business Law and Practice, 1987, p. 14.

〔69〕 C. M. Schmitthoff, International Trade Usages, as a special issue of NEWSLETTER of the Institute of Business Law and Practice, 1987, p. 14.

〔70〕 韩德培主编:《国际私法》,武汉大学出版社 1989 年修订版,第 196 页。

〔71〕 冯大同主编:《国际货物买卖法》,对外贸易教育出版社 1993 年版,第 18 页。

〔72〕 赵承璧编著:《国际贸易法律》,中国对外经济贸易出版社 1986 年版,第 48 页。

〔73〕 周忠海:《国际经济关系中的法律问题》,中国政法大学出版社 1993 年版,第 128 页。

一般交易条件中的，对当事人具有法律约束力的国际贸易原则、规则”；[74] 我国台湾地区学者张锦源认为，“所谓国际贸易惯例（customs &usages of international trade）是指具有规范国际贸易活动的功能，由权威机构所制定为条文或成文法化，而存于文献中，并为司法判决或仲裁判断所宣示或认可者”。[75] 如此等等，不一而足。

从上面的分析可以看出，尽管中外学者对国际贸易惯例含义的界定见仁见智、各有所重，但有如下几点是基本一致的。第一，国际贸易惯例是国际贸易实践中逐渐自发形成的惯常做法。与国家自觉制定的成文法不同，国际贸易惯例是在国际商业社会长期实践中所逐步自发形成的，其编纂也是由商业团体自发进行的，一般不受政府的控制与干预。因此，可以说，它具有形成过程上的自发性与渐进性特征。第二，国际贸易惯例是得到经常遵守并由此产生了应该得到遵守的合法期望的惯常做法。偶然的实践不能构成惯例，必须是经过多次重复一致的行为，才有可能成为惯例，而“因惯成例”的临界点正是使当事人（或广泛意义上的商人）产生了自己应该“照办”的义务感与对方也应该“照办”的合理期待心理的那一刻。可见心理因素对于判断惯例的成立与否是至关重要，尽管这在实践中，特别是举证上，可能是比较困难的。第三，国际贸易惯例的内容具有明确性与商业性。内容模糊的实践一定是发展的不够充分的实践，它不构成“惯行”，更谈不上“合理期望”，因而不能算是惯例。国际贸易惯例是国际商业贸易领域的惯例，其内容无疑是关于商事权利与商事义务的规则，因而具有商业性。第四，国际贸易惯例具有国际性与普遍性。这主要指两个方面，一是指其调整对象应是跨越国界的贸易关系，而不是国内商业关系；二是指其内容具有一定的国际统一性，即在国际上广为人知，并得到普遍接受。当然，这里的“普遍性”不应理解为人人都已经知道与接受，而只要从事同类贸易的大多数人都知道并接受，即可构成其普遍性，从而可以推定其他人“理应知道”这种惯例的存在——如同 CISG 所规定的那样。一般来说，仅适用于特定交易双方之间的“交易做法”或“履约做法”是不具备这种国际普遍性的，除非它们为大量其他的当事人所同样实践从而获得一定的普遍意义（如在某一地区、某行业或某类贸易中具有普遍意义）。第五，国际贸易惯例是任意性的规范。即一般来说只有当事人明示或默示同意采用，它们才对其有法律拘束力，如果当事人明示或默示排除，则不能将贸易惯例的义务强加给当事人。对此，本文第二章将详予论述。

---

〔74〕 徐国建：《现代商人法 · 论》，载《中国社会科学》1993 年第 3 期。

〔75〕 张锦源编著：《国际贸易法》，三民书局 1989 年版，第 33 页。

以上这五个方面的共通之处,也可以说是国际贸易惯例的基本特征。其中,第一、第二点最为本质。前者使之与国内法及国际条约相区别,后者则使之与一般性的实践相分离,从而体现了惯例的基本内核;第三、第四、第五点则是全面认识“国际贸易惯例”所必须把握的主要外部特征,也是国际贸易惯例这一概念的重要组成部分。

基于上述考察,我们不妨将国际贸易惯例初步界定为:国际贸易实践中逐渐、自发形成的,某一地区、某一行业或某类贸易中所经常遵守和普遍接受,并由此产生相应的义务感与合理期望的任意性行为规范。

第三节　国际贸易惯例的范围与分类

在对国际贸易惯例的内涵作了初步界定之后,尚须进一步探讨它的外延,即其范围与种类,这样才可能对“国际贸易惯例”这一概念有一个比较全面的理解。

一、国际贸易惯例的范围

应该承认,上节关于国际贸易惯例的定义实质上使它的范围十分广泛。可以说,它涵盖所有成文的与不成文的、世界性的与区域性、行业性的国际贸易惯例。它比把国际贸易惯例仅仅看作国际组织或贸易团体制定的成文惯例的范围理解广泛,但却比把仅仅适用于交易双方当事人的“交易做法”都纳入的范围界定狭窄。按这种界定,港口惯例虽不属国际组织或贸易协会制定的惯例,但也可纳入国际贸易惯例的范围;但如果是中国某公司与美国某公司之间在长期贸易实践中形成的一些习惯做法(交易做法),虽具备贸易惯例的某些基本特征,但由于缺乏普遍性,故一般不能算作国际贸易惯例。

与此同时,本文也不赞成把国际贸易领域的国际公约算作国际贸易惯例的说法。施米托夫在某一项研究报告中提出,国际公约一经国内立法所接受,就可成为国际贸易惯例的一种,即所谓的“规范性贸易惯例”(normative trade usages),例如由英国先后立法接受的《关于提单的海牙——维斯比规则》、1964 年的两个关于国际货物买卖的统一法,等等。〔76〕

诚然,国际贸易领域的许多公约(如 CISG)也是在总结国际贸易实践经验的基础上制定的;而且也具有任意性质,即当事人可以协议排除或修改其规定。另

〔76〕 C. M. Schmitthoff, International Trade Usages, as a special issue of NEWSLETTER of the Institute of Business Law and Practice, 1987, p. 28.

一方面，按照有些国家国内立法与某些国际公约的规定，国际贸易惯例的适用也不以当事人的明示同意为前提，甚至也不以当事人的确切知悉为前提。从这个意义上说，国际贸易公约与国际贸易惯例有共通之处。但是，从实证法的角度来看，国际贸易公约与国际贸易惯例又有明显的区别：国际贸易公约是国家参与制定的，具有制定法与国家意志的性质；而国际贸易惯例是国际贸易实践中自发形成，并由民间机构编纂而成的，具有自发性与自治性，一般与国家意志无涉。按许多国家〈如中国〉的法律，国际贸易公约一经签订，即直接获得优于国内法的法律效力；而国际贸易惯例的法律效力一般需通过国内立法认可或当事人同意采纳而间接获得，二者是不可等而视之的。不过，对于没有参加该公约的国家而言，国际贸易公约在一定意义上，也可以视为国际贸易惯例。同理，政府间国际组织制定的示范法，从一定意义上也可视为国际贸易惯例。但一般而言，它们都不能算是严格意义上的国际贸易惯例。

原经济互助委员会（CMEA）制定的《交货共同条件》（General Conditions for the Delivery of Goods）算不算国际贸易惯例，这也是有争议的。有些学者认为这一共同条件的形成是经互会外贸常设委员会的会员国代表，以政府名义批准的。其性质不是国际立法，也不是国际行政、外交公约，而是真正的商业习惯做法法典化的产物。因为社会主义国家的对外贸易是采用国家垄断与计划的方式进行，所以，其国际贸易惯例的编纂程序也自然以国家名义进行；[77] 反之，有些学者则认为，这种共同条件是由政府批准并直接领导参与制定的，所以是国际公约，应归于国家制定法之列，而不是商业社会的自然纯粹的贸易惯例。[78] 诚然，从立法形式来看，“否定说”言之有理，而“肯定说”则显得牵强，因为经互会的交货共同条件的最终形成显然不是商业社会自发的产物，而有着明显的政府干预因素。但是，从实质来看，该共同条件的内容是依据国际贸易惯例及实务经验所进行的统一立法，所以，在国际贸易惯例法源上仍有研究的必要，这一点持“否定说”者也都承认。[79] 更进一层来说，如果考虑到实行计划经济国家垄断外贸的特殊情况，则不妨认为国家实质上是这些计划经济国家商业团体的代言人，它代表商业团体所签订的这种共同条件，实质上还是应该算作国际贸易惯例的。《交货共同条件》与上述国际

---

〔77〕 J. Schapirs. Le Droit. International des Affaires, 1972. p. 39; M. Boyouslavski, “Les Confits de losic entre Pays Socialistes”, Rerue de droit contemporain. No. 1, June 1960. p. 268. 转引自柯泽东：《国际贸易法专论》，台大法学丛书之二十三，1981 年版，第 15 页。

〔78〕 如戈德曼（B. Goldman）及洛桑（Loussouarn）均持这种观点。其中，尤以戈氏反对最烈。参见柯泽东：《国际贸易法专论》，第 16 页及其注 20。

〔79〕 例如戈德曼在其 Droit du Commerce Intetnational Cours de Droit、1970－1971. 关于 Pays de l’Est 一节的说明中就曾指出这种研究的重要意义。参见柯泽东：《国际贸易法专论》，台大法学丛书之二十三，1981 年版，第 16 页。

公约的不同之处,也就在这里。不过,随着苏联东欧集团解体,该共同条件实质上已经不被使用,而只存在历史研究价值了。

国际商事仲裁裁决是否可构成国际贸易惯例?在许多西方学者看来,答案是肯定的。因为国际商事仲裁机构在适用法律方面,一般以国际商事惯例为主,而不以适用国内法或国际条约为主,[80]为此,国际商事仲裁可创造惯例。[81]国际仲裁创造惯例的最佳时机有三:其一为合同当事人在仲裁条款中未指定合同的准据法。据此,仲裁员可自主适用贸易惯例,形成一个习惯的判例。其二为当事人约定以和解(conciliation)或友好仲裁(Amiable Compositeur)为其争端解决方法此时,仲裁员可以运用公平(equity)原则。其三为合同当事人在仲裁条款中明示适用一般法律原则或国际贸易惯例,此时,仲裁员更可以最大限度地发挥其造法功能。[82] 从当代国际贸易惯例的发展现状来看,无疑,国际仲裁的意义十分重要。如果说贸易惯例是现代商人法的主要实体内容的话,国际仲裁无疑是其赖以生存发展的主要程序途径。正如哥尔德斯坦所指出的,现代商人法(国际贸易自治法〉作为尽可能独立于国内法规则的法规,是建立在合同自由与承认商事仲裁裁决这两项孪生原则的基础上的。[83] 仲裁裁决可以反映贸易惯例的实际应用情况,从而在一定意义上可以体现出贸易惯例的内容,这一点是不争的事实。然而,在大多数国家,仲裁裁决并不是法律的渊源,[84]而只是适用法律的结果,这也是事实。所以说,仲裁裁决创造法律的说法是难以接受的,相应地,它也就不能算作国际贸易惯例,只能看作实施国际贸易惯例的最佳程序途径。

一般法律原则(general principles of law)也不能算是国际贸易惯例。这主要是因为它不具备国际贸易惯例所必需的内容方面的明确性与商业性,同时,它也很难说是国际贸易实践中自发形成的。

从目前的国际实践来看,成文的国际贸易惯例的主要表现形式有两种:一种是非政府国际组织(如国际商会)制定的普遍适用的国际贸易惯例;另一种是各

---

〔80〕 Ph. Fouchard, L' Arbitrage Commercial International. 1965. No. 68 ets. 转引自柯泽东:《国际贸易法专论》,第27页。

〔81〕 参见柯泽东:《国际贸易法专论》,台大法学丛书之二十三,1981年版,第27页。

〔82〕 同上书,第31页。

〔83〕 A. Gold stajn:"International Conventions and Standard Contracts as Means of Escaping from theApplication of Municipal Law—I", in C. M. Schmitthoff ed. The sources of The Law of International Trade, p. 117.

〔84〕 例如,德国学者斯舒兹在考察仲裁裁决在德国的先例效力问题时就曾指出,一般来说,"一个仲裁裁决对其他裁决是没有实际先例效力的,而且至少在德国,仲裁裁决不会对法院产生影响,从狭义上说,它们也不是德国法的渊源"。参见罗夫·A.斯舒兹:《仲裁裁决的先例效力》,江波译,载《仲裁与法律通讯》1995年第5期。

类贸易协会(或称商业同业公会)专业团体以及某些国际经济组织制定的标准合同与标准合同条款。

非政府国际组织制定的贸易惯例具有适用普遍、影响广泛的特点。这些组织主要有国际商会、国际法协会与国际海事委员会,其中又以国际商会的贡献最为突出。

国际商会(ICC)是世界商事组织与商人的联盟,也是联合国经济与社会理事会的高级咨询机构。其成立于1919年,目前已扩展到100多个国家,由数万个具有国际影响的商业组织和企业组成,已在59个国家中成立了国家委员会或理事会,它们组织和协调国家范围内的商业活动。[85] 国际商会专门设有"国际商业惯例委员会""银行技术与惯例委员会""国际商事法律与实务研究所"等机构,分别从事贸易与银行惯例的编纂与研究工作。[86] 国际商会最杰出的贡献在于它编纂了《国际贸易术语解释通则》(以下简称INCOTERMS)与《跟单信用证统一惯例》(以下简称UCP)这两大贸易惯例。其中INCOTERMS制定于1936年,曾五度修订,目前适用的是1990年的修订本。该通则以简明的文字与代号,说明买卖双方在货物的交接方面所应承担的责任、风险和费用,不仅简化了谈判程序与时间,而且节约了费用,因而受到国际贸易界的普遍欢迎与采用,成为目前国际上应用最广、影响最大的国际贸易惯例。有些出口商.特别是欧洲大陆的公司,在其贸易的一般条款中规定,除非另有特别的约定,否则其所有合同均应受INCOTERMS的约束。[87] 在某些国家,如西班牙与伊拉克,INCOTERMS已被赋予了法定的效力。[88] 在一贯坚持采用其他术语(一般为《美国对外贸易定义》)的美国,INCOTERMS也得到推广使用。[89] 在法国与德国,某些权威学者认为INCOTERMS是贸易领域中的国际习惯(custom)。[90] UCP则是关于跟单信用证支付方式的国际惯例。它制定于1930年,也曾五度修订,目前采用的是1993年的修订本(UCP500)。UCP也得到了极为广泛的承认与使用,据统计,目前已有175个国家的银行通过银行协会加入或单独加入的方式采纳了这一惯例,其中包括英国、美国、前苏联及中国等。[91]

除INCOTERMS与UCP以外,国际商会编纂的贸易惯例还有:《托收统一规

[85] 参见程德钧、王生长、康明编著:《国际惯例与涉外仲裁》,中国青年出版社1993年版,第22、23页。
[86] 同上。
[87] C. M. Schmitthoff, Sc. hmitthoff's Export Trade: the Law and Practice of Internaítonal Trade. 9th ed. 1990, pp. 66 - 67.
[88] Ibid.
[89] Ibid.
[90] Ibid.
[91] Ibid.

则》(UCR1978)、《清洁提单问题》(1974)、《国际多边联运单据统一规则》(1975)、《合同担保统一规则》(1978)、《不可抗力与艰难情势规则》(1985)以及《国际商会调解与仲裁规则》等,其中《托收统一规则》的应用也十分广泛。[92]

国际法协会(ILA)原名为“改革与编纂国际法协会”,1873 年成立于布鲁塞尔,1895 年更名为国际法协会,现总部设于伦敦,[93]约在 50 个国家设有分会。国际法协会也是一个重要的国际贸易惯例编纂机构,它所制定的关于 CIF 合同的《华沙—牛津规则》至今仍被广泛使用。

国际海事委员会(IMC)成立于 1896 年,总部设在安特卫普,旨在统一海事私法。[94] 目前,由 33 个国家的国内海事委员会和一些终身个人会员组成。其主要贡献是 1974 年制定的《约克——安特卫普共同海损理算规则》,此外,它还与其他组织合作起草了海牙提单规则。

国际标准合同是国际贸易惯例的另一重要渊源。在商业实践中,“标准合同”一词有两种不同的含义:示范合同格式(model contract forms)和附合合同(contract of adhesion)。前者供律师和商人起草合同时参考并可对它进行修改,使之符合实际需要的合同格式;后者则是缔约一方当事人向另一方当事人提出的具有确定内容的格式,除无关紧要的具体细节外,一般不得加以改变,“要么接受、要么拒绝”(take it or leave it)。[95] 示范合同由于可以修改、补充,因而在经济上基本上是无害的、公平的,对其合同性质,无可置疑;附合合同则可以说是一方强加给另一方的合同,它在某种程度上对其真实性质深感困惑,甚至怀疑它究竟是不是合同。[96]

现代国际贸易中使用的标准合同属于示范合同,而不是附合合同。[97] 然而,即使是示范合同,其条款也总是倾向于维护经济强者的利益;[98]加之种种条件的限制,人们往往接受现成格式中的条款,[99]这就使其公平性并不总能得到很好的

---

〔92〕 C. M. Schmitthoff, Schmitthoff's Export Trade: the Law and Practice of Internaítonal Trade. 9th ed. 1990, pp. 66 – 67.

〔93〕 C. M. Schrnitthoff, Commercial Law ìn a Changing Economic Climate, 2nd ed. 1981, pp. 228 – 229.

〔94〕 Ibid.

〔95〕 C. M. Schmitthoff, “The Unification or Harmanisation of Standard Contract *and* General Conditions”, in Chia-jui Cheng ed. Clive M. Schmitthoff's Select Essays On Internatíonal Trade Law, 1988, p. 18.

〔96〕 Ibid., p. 189.

〔97〕 Ibid.

〔98〕 Ibid.

〔99〕 J. Vilus, Tipski Ugovori O Medunarodnoj Kupoprodaji(国际贸易中的标准合同格式), Bograd. 1963. p. 149.

维持。[100]

并不是所有的国际标准合同都能算是国际贸易惯例。只有那些经过长期实践,得到反复使用和广泛接受,从而产生了超出该合同的具体效力的某种一般性的效力,即产生前面提到的义务感与合理期望时,标准合同才能算是一种国际贸易惯例。一般而言,由国际商会、联合国欧洲经济委员会(UNECE)等国际组织与各重要贸易协会等商业团体制定的,长期使用的标准合同,大都具备国际贸易惯例的基本特征,是国际贸易惯例的重要组成部分之一。从实践的角度来看,国际标准合同对国际贸易惯例的发展具有重要意义,正如施米托夫所说的,"国际标准合同是国际商业社会制法活动的产物这一事实怎么强调都不过分。正是这一机制使得国际贸易法的协调与统一具备了特别的活力。商业社会的参与不仅创造了标准合同,更重要的是给统一活动带来了现实主义的新鲜空气,而这正是各国法学家们的类似活动中往往欠缺的"。[101] 正因如此,有些学者提出,以标准合同来统一国际贸易法会更见成效。[102] 而事实上,目前国际贸易惯例主要正是以用国际标准合同的形式在发展。

一般而言,国际标准合同可分为完全的示范合同格式和成套标准条件。二者的目的有所不同:完全的示范合同旨在实现全部标准化,即对合同的全部或大部分条款都作出规定,一般只空出当事人的名称,货物的规格与价金等部分,留待当事人填写,但当事人仍可斟酌取舍,通过协议自由地对合同条款作出修改。这种标准合同力图囊括"合同关系中的全部权利与义务,从合同的订立到合同的履行、解除和违反合同的救济"。[103] 各类国际贸易协会与联合国欧洲经济委员会制定的标准合同大都属于此类。另一标准合同只是将合同的一小部分标准化,即将那些典型的和经常使用的条款标准化,实质上只是标准条款而已。在这种情况下,当事人一般需要制定出他们自己的合同,并在合同中提及适用某一特定标准条款,以避免对这些条款作出不同解释。联合国欧洲经济委员会使用的一些比

[100] 关于标准合同中的公平与弱方利益保护问题,可参见 A. Boggiano, "International Standard Contract—The price of Fairness". 1992, pp. 141 – 150. C. M. Schmitthoff, "Standard Contract and The Protection of the Weaker Party in International Trade Relations", New Directions in International Trade Law, Vol. I, 1977, Oceana, p. 177 – 194.

[101] C. M. Schmittoff, "The Unification or Harmanisation of Law by Means of Standard Contract and General Conditions" in Chia-jui Chenged. Clive M. Schmitthoff's Select Essays On International Trade Law, 1988, pp. 191 – 192. .

[102] See eg. L. Kopelrnanas, "International Conventions and Standard Contracts as Means of Escaping from the Application of Municipal law", in The Sources of the Law of International Trade. Schmitthoff ed. 1964, pp. 118 – 126; Ole Lando, Standard Contracts, A Proposal and a Perspective (1966) in Scandinavian Studies in Law 129. p. 144.

[103] C. M. Schmitthoff "The Unification or Harmanisation of Law by Means of Standard Contract and General Conditions", in Chia-Jui Chenged. Clive M. Schrnitthoff's Select Essays on International Trade Law. 1988, pp. 192 – 193.

较完整的共同条件，就是由一系列标准条款组成的，当事人可以很方便地把这种简化了的条款纳入他们的合同之中。国际商会制定的上述《国际贸易术语解释通则》与《跟单信用证统一惯例》等惯例实质上也可算是一种标准合同条款集。〔104〕

国际标准合同在商品领域使用最为普遍，国际商品交易几乎无一例外地采用这种形式缔结。不过，目前，标准合同的使用已扩大到有关耐用消费品和工程产品等国际交易中。〔105〕

国际标准合同中最大量的部分是各类贸易协会制定的标准合同，其中，最主要的贸易协会有：英国羊毛联合会、伦敦可可协会、伦敦油籽油脂联合会、伦敦谷物贸易协会、国际毛纺织品组织、利物浦棉业协会、伦敦一般商品经纪人协会、伦敦黄麻协会、伦敦五金交易所、伦敦橡胶贸易协会、精糖协会、英国原木贸易联合会〔106〕以及荷兰谷物商协会、德国汉堡交易所谷物商协会，等等。这些标准合同多由同业公会邀请同业及专家学者共同研订印发，供当事人采用。其正面印有"主要条款"，供当事人协商后填入；背面印有标准的"一般条款"供双方当事人遵照执行。"由于这些合同格式已被广泛采用，在性质上，已渐具有被共同遵守的权威文书，并屡经仲裁院的确认，产生惯例的拘束力。"〔107〕

我国的各进出口公司、中国远洋运输公司、中国人民保险公司等也都分别制定了自己的格式合同、提单、保险单和保险条款。〔108〕这些标准合同虽行之有年，但往往失之简陋而欠细密严谨。为此，国家有关部门会同国外有关部门，开始研拟一种比较严密而实用的一般交易条款集。1992 年，在"中国对日贸易合同条款研究会"与"日本日中贸易合同条款研究委员会"的共同努力下，制定了《中日一般货物销售合同条款集》。〔109〕该条款集实质上就是一套标准合同条款，可以算是我国官方组织的标准合同与合同条款研拟工作的良好开端。目前，与其他国家的贸易合同条款也正在谈判研拟之中。显然，要取得惯例的效力，这种条款集也还有待于实践的检验与完善。

联合国欧洲经济委员会（UNECE）也制定了大量的示范合同（model con-

---

〔104〕 C. M. Schmitthoff "The Unification or Harmanisation of Law by Means of Standard Contract and General Conditíons", in Chia-Juí Chenged. Clive M. Schrnitthoff's Select Essays on lnternational Trade Law, 1988, pp. 192 – 193.

〔105〕 Ibid.

〔106〕 C. M. Schmitthoff, supra. Schmitthof f"s Export Tradc, p. 73.

〔107〕 参见张锦源编著：《国际贸易法》，三民书局 1989 年版，第 34 页。

〔108〕 参见韩健：《国际商事仲裁法的理论与实践》，法律出版社 1993 年版，第 250 页。

〔109〕 参见中国对日贸易合同条款研究会：《中日一般货物销售合同条款集》，中国经济出版社 1992 年版。

tracts)。它大致分为三类:谷物买卖合同、成套设备和耐用消费品合同以及其他合同(如国际柑橘买卖、固体燃料进出口及国际设备搬运等方面的一般条款),[110]其中,最重要的是成套设备与耐用消费品的示范合同格式。[111] 联合国欧洲经济委员会标准合同的主要优点在于它力图纠正合同强者与合同弱者双方之间经济上的种种不平衡,从而使标准合同建立在真正公平的基础之上。正因如此,它受到了极为广泛的欢迎,影响十分普遍。[112]

还有一类示范合同格式用于承建合同(construction contract)的,在海外安装工程和装配交易中,它们得到经常使用。[113]

在缺乏上述统一规则与标准合同的条件下,个别大的出口商所拟定的一般交易条款(general terms of business,如不可抗力条款、法律选择与仲裁条款、所有权留置条款等)[114] 在某种意义上也可以产生惯例的作用,但如果其缺乏惯例所必需的国际性与普遍性,则只能算是贸易惯例发展过程中的初级阶段,而不能算是贸

---

〔110〕 C. M. Schmitthoff,"The Unification or Harmanisation of Law by Means of Standard Contract and General Conditions ". in Chia-Jui Cheng ed. Clive M. Schmitthoff's Select Essays on International Trade Law. 1988,p. 196.

〔111〕 它们包括:

格式 188 用于供应成套设备和机器的出口;

格式 574 用于供应成套设备和机器的出口;

格式 188A 用于进出口成套设备和机器的供应与安装,格式 574A 用于进出口成套设备和机器的供应与安装。

格式 188B 在国外监督安装工程成套设备的附加条款,格式 574B 在国外监督安装工程成套设备的附加条款,格式 188D 在国外监督工程成套设备安装的附加条款,格式 730 用于耐用消费品及工程物资的出口。

上述格式中,格式 188 及其变式(188A、188B 与 188D)适用于自由市场经济的企业之间的贸易;格式 574 及其变式(574A 与 574B)适用于计划经济国家的企业之间的贸易及其与自由经济国家的企业之间的贸易;格式 730 则可用于任何经济体制的企业间的国际贸易. Sec C. M. Schmitthoff, Schmitthoff's Export Trade: the Law and Practice of International Trade. 9th ed. 1990,p. 74.

〔112〕 C. M. Schmitthoff,"The Unification or HarmaniSation of Law by Means of Standard Contract and General Conditions",in Chia-Jui Cheng ed. Clive M. Schmitthoff's Select Essays on International Trade Law,1988,pp. 196 - 197.

〔113〕 其中,最常用的有以下四种:

第一种是工厂土木工程承建合同条件(1987 年 3 月第 4 版),它们由国际工程咨询联合会(FIDIC)制定而成.

第二种是合同一般条件,由机械工程协会、电器工程协会和工程人员咨询协会推荐。主要格式有二:格式 B1 用于按 FOB、CIF 或 FOR 条件交货的合同(1981 年第 5 版);格式 B2 用于按 FOB、CIF,FOR 条件交货并包括监督安装的出口合同(1981 年第 5 版)。

第三种为世界银行贷款和国际开发协会信贷项下的采购行动守则(Guide Lines)(1985 年 3 月版。

第四种为由欧洲发展基金资助的公共工程和供货合同的一般条件,用于海外关联国家和地区的合同(1974 年 2 月 14 日版)。

此外,前述联合国欧洲经济委员会制定的标准合同格式也可用于国际承建工程。1988 年,联合国国际贸易法委员会还颁发了《关于起草工厂建造国际合同的法律指南》。它也可算作关于国际承建合同的一种惯例。See C. M. Schmitthoff's Export Trade: the Law and Practice of International Trade. 9th ed. 1990,pp,74 - 75.

〔114〕 C. M. Schmitthoffs Export Trade: the Law and Practice of International Trade,9th ed,1990,pp. 75 - 76.

易惯例本身。[115] 前述我国各进出口公司、中国远洋运输公司、中国人民保险公司的格式合同、提单、保险单和保险条款等基本上可归入这一类型。

此外，还有一些重要的国际贸易惯例是区域性的。1941 年修订的《美国对外贸易定义》就是其中一个突出的例子。它是通过美国商会、美国进出口理事会与全美对外贸易理事会组成的联合委员会于 1941 年修订而成的。其功能与 IINCO-TERMS 类似，但具体解释与后者相去甚远。《美国对外贸易定义》在南北美洲各国有很大的影响。[116]

二、国际贸易惯例的分类

在上文的分析过程中，实质上已经揭示了国际贸易惯例的某些一般性的分类。比如按适用的空间范围，可分为世界性贸易惯例（如 INCOTERMS 与 UCP）与区域性贸易惯例（如《1941 年修订的美国对外贸易定义》，经互会的《交货共同条件》）；按适用的行业范围，可以分为横向的国际贸易惯例（指适用于所有行业的国际贸易的惯例，如 INCOTERMS），和纵向的国际贸易惯例（指仅适用于特定行业的国际贸易惯例，如各种行业性的标准合同）：按其所涉贸易领域，又分为国际贸易术语（如 INCOTERMS、《华沙—牛津规则》及《美国对外贸易定义》）、国际运输惯例（如《约克—安特卫普共同海损理算规则》、《联运单据统一规则》）、国际保险惯例（如《伦敦保险协会货物保险条款》）、国际支付惯例［如《UCP500》《托收统一规则》（URC）］以及国际商事仲裁惯例（如联合国国际贸易法委员会制定的《国际商事仲裁示范法》及其《仲裁规则》与《调解规则》以及国际商会的《调解与仲裁规则》）。此外，按其存在形式，还可分为成文惯例（如 UCP）与不成文惯例（如某些港口惯例等）。

不过，在学术研究方面最有价值的分类，当属按其性质所作的分类。这方面各国的看法有所不同。[117] 法国与意大利法学界大都认为，国际贸易惯例应分规范性惯例（usagess de charactère impératif, usi normativi）与契约性惯例（usages conv-entionnels, usi negoziali）。西班牙法学界却认为应分为规范性贸易惯例与解释性贸易惯例，比利时学者们认为，国际贸易惯例应分事实性惯例（usages de fait）与专业性惯例（usages de droit on *à* la coutume）。

---

〔115〕 国际贸易惯例的发展是一个循序渐进的过程，它往往肇端于某些有影响的企业的商业活动过程而后成为建立在重复行为基础上的特定贸易中的一般做法（general practice）。然后发展为贸易惯例（trade usage）t 最终才可能取得稳定的规范的习惯（custom）的地位. 大公司所自订的一艘合同条款可以算是这一过程的最初阶段。参见［英］施米托夫书：《国际贸易法文选》，程家瑞编，赵秀文译，中国大百科全书出版社 1993 年版，第 205 ~ 206 页。

〔116〕 参见冯大同主编：《国际货物买卖法》，对外经济贸易出版社 1993 年版，第 22 页。

〔117〕 See C. M. Schmitthoff, supra, International Trade Usages, pp. 25 – 26.

据此,施米托夫提出一种“综合性的分类方法”(a comprehensive classification):[118]

- 国际贸易惯例
  - 规范性惯例(normative trade usages)
    - 法定惯例(statutory usages)
    - 普通惯例(universal usages)
  - 契约性贸易惯例(contractual usages)
    - 跨国成文规则(transnational formulations)
    - 其他契约性惯例(other contractual usages)
  - 事实性贸易惯例(factual usages)

其中,主要的两种分类,即规范性与契约性惯例之分,取自法国、意大利与西班牙,不过它们由第三类,即比利时提出的“事实性惯例”来补充。

所谓“规范性惯例”是指与其他法律规范一样,具有法律拘束力的惯例。又包括法定惯例与普遍惯例两种。[119] 法定惯例是指根据国内立法或授权立法而产生法律效力的惯例。其规范性特征十分显见。按施氏的观点,法定惯例又有两种形式。一种是由国内立法承认其效力的国际公约(international convention)。这在国际立法实践中屡见不鲜。例如,在英国,《关于提单的海牙—维斯比规则》就由其1971年的《海上货物运输法》赋予法律效力,《国际公路货物运输合同公约》(CMR)则由1965年的《公路货物运输法》予以确认。1964年的两个海牙统一货物买卖法的公约也通过1967年的《国际货物买卖法》而变成了法律。《关于承认与执行外仲裁的纽约公约》则由1975年《仲裁法》加以接受。显然,这里施氏把国际公约与国际惯例混为一谈了。如前所述,国际贸易公约与国际惯例尽管有许多接近之处,但其区别仍是明显的。所以,我们认为,国际贸易公约不能算作国际贸易惯例的一种形式,相应地,这种类型的法定惯例也就难以成立。施氏所指的另一种法定惯例是指由国内立法赋予法律效力的贸易惯例。例如,在西班牙,通过1979年9月14日的敕令,INCOTERMS被采纳为其进出口交易中法定的合同术语与条款。在伊拉克,INCOTERMS在对外贸易中也具有法定的效力。南斯拉夫1954年通过的《一般贸易惯例》是南斯拉夫商会制定的,从形式上看固不是制定法,但根据1978年的南斯拉夫《合同法典》,它也被认为具有规范性质。[120] 在

[118] See C. M. Schmitthoff, supra, International Trade Usages, p. 26.

[119] Ibid., p. 28.

[120] Ibid., p. 28.

原东德,《国际交易运输代理的一般条款》,通过 1976 年的法令,也具有法定的效力。同样的,经互会 1969 ~ 1975 年的《交货共同条件》也是经互会(CMEA)国家的法定贸易惯例。[121] 对于这种贸易惯例,就发生一个问题:惯例既"上升"而为法律,还可算是惯例吗? 我们认为,对这个问题分为二地看待。如果从狭义上看,这里的"惯例"显然本来是没有法律拘束力的习惯做法,与上升而为法律的"习惯法"有质的区别,固不可等而视之;但如果从广义来看,则"上升"为法律的习惯法本来就是惯例中的一种,仍称其为惯例,当不为过。

施氏这里所谓"普遍惯例"(universal usages)是指源自商人法(Lex Mercatoria)而为所有国家所普遍接受的规则(maxims)。实质上是指国际贸易中所抽象出来的一些法律原则,如"诚信"(good faith),"有约必守"(pacta sunt servanda)、"公平互利"(equilibrim of reciprocal undertakings)原则。[122] 对于商人法理论,本文后面将作专门介绍,兹不赘述。不过,如前所述,我们不赞成将抽象的一般法律原则视为贸易惯例的观点。因而这种贸易法的一般原则同样也不能算作贸易惯例。

"契约性贸易惯例"是指通过当事人行使意思自治权而纳入合同之中的那些惯例。这些惯例一经纳入,就取得与其他合同条款一样的效力,故称"契约性惯例"。契约性惯例中由国际组织,如国际商会及联合国欧洲经济委员会编纂的贸易惯例,因其由权威性国际机构制定,比一般契约性惯例(如各贸易协会制定的标准合同)具有更强的、更广泛的影响力与约束力,故称"跨国成文规则"。其中,最为重要的便是 INCOTERMS 与 UCP,如前所述,对这两种"跨国成文规则"各国都十分重视,有的则直接赋予其以法律的地位。此外,按施氏的观点,联合国贸法会制定的示范法也属于这一类。由于前面提到的原因,我们也不赞成这一提法。

其他民间组织,如贸易协会、专业机构、有关商业团体等所制定的文件都归入"其他契约性贸易惯例"一类。例如,伦敦谷物贸易协会制定的标准合同格式、FIDIC 合同条款,以及使用广泛的租约格式(charterparty forms),如纽约产品交易所的一般条款与格式,等等。[123] 不过,这一类标准合同并非不重要。实际上,如前所述,它们对国际贸易法的统一与协调具有重要意义。

"事实性惯例"是指上述两种惯例以外的贸易惯例。它们一般不具备太强的国际性,多为地方性惯例,仅适用于特定地域或行业。[124] 例如,英国的法院曾认

---

[121] C. M. Schmitthoff, supra, lnternational, Trade Usages. p. 28.
[122] Ibid., p. 29.
[123] Ibid., p. 29.
[124] Ibid., p. 27.

定:在石油行业中,存在 FOB 项下买方必须适时提醒卖方装船的贸易惯例;[125]而在集装箱行业中,则有这么一项贸易惯例,即如果集装箱所有人不适当地留置(retain)其集装箱的话,则他应负责办理清关手续。在法国,买方如指称货物有瑕疵,则他应在一个很短的迟延期内(dans un bref delai)起诉;而对于隐性瑕疵,该迟延(delai)的时间须由贸易惯例确定。[126] 再如,斯德哥尔摩的港口惯例规定,木制品如果是按"FOB 斯德哥尔摩"条件买卖的话,则意味着要按 FAS 条件交付[127]……这种例子可谓举不胜举,其程序法上共同的特点在于,它们的存在必须由作此主张的当事人依法举证证明。只有证明成立,它们才对当事人有拘束力。而契约性与规范性惯例由于已广为知晓并得到普遍接受,一般都不存在证明问题,尤其是在国际商事仲裁程序中,由于仲裁员多为业内专家,谙熟国际惯例,更不用作如是查证。[128]

基于上述考察,我们认为国际贸易惯例的基本分类为"契约性贸易惯例"与"事实性贸易惯例"两大类。其中,前者又可分为"跨国成文规则"与"其他契约性贸易惯例"两支。至于规范性贸易惯例,仅指那些由国内法予以认可了的贸易惯例(一般是跨国性成文规则,如 INCOTERMS,UCP 等)。由于规范性贸易惯例只是个别国家所认可的个别贸易惯例,而且这些惯例多已包括于契约性贸易惯例之中,故我们认为它不能算作一个独立的分类,而只能算作跨国成文规则的特殊表现形式。

第四节 国际贸易惯例的沿革

从完整意义上说,国际贸易惯例并非西方的专利,国际贸易惯例的历史自应包括东方国家与社会主义国家之间及其与西方贸易往来中的国际贸易惯例实践的历史。但由于东方国家及社会主义国家的国际贸易惯例及其发展史多未得到整理,又因为流行于现代国际贸易中的惯例多为在西方贸易发达国家之间发展起来的。所以,本节所介绍的国际贸易惯例的历史,主要指国际贸易惯例在近现代西方国家中的发展历史。

国际贸易惯例是近代西方国际商法与国际贸易法最初的表现形式,其历史可

[125] C. M. Schmitthoff, supra, lnternational, Trade Usages, p. 27.
[126] Ibid., p. 27.
[127] C. M. Schminhoff, supra, International Trade Usagos, p. 27.
[128] 关于国际贸易惯例的查证,详见本文第三章第四节。

谓源远流长。有学者指出，古罗马时代的万民法(*jus gentiunm*)中就包含有习惯规则，因而国际商法的历史渊源可以上溯至古罗马时代；[129] 多数学者则认为，国际商人法源自中世纪的商人法。[130] 本文采用通说，认为国际贸易惯例起源于中世纪商人法，并已经历了商人法国内化与现代商人法复苏两个阶段。

一、中世纪商人法

11 世纪晚期至 12 世纪，西欧农业生产迅速扩展，城市的规模和数量急剧扩大并增加。同时，还出现了一个新的职业商人阶层。它们在乡村与城市从事大规模的商业交易。[131] 然而，“无论是重新发现的罗马市民法，还是仅仅残存的罗马习惯法、包括万民法，都不足以应付在 11 世纪晚期与 12 世纪出现的各种国内和国际商业问题”。[132] 同时，商人们通过长期的实践，逐步自发地形成了一些习惯做法与规则。这种商业习惯做法与规则最初出现于威尼斯，后来随着航海贸易的发展，逐步扩展到西班牙、法国、德国及英国。其主要内容包括货物买卖合同的标准条款，两合公司、海上运输与保险、汇票以及破产程序等方面的规则。[133] 约 11 至 15 世纪间，地中海沿岸和北大西洋沿岸出现了各种商业行会。这些行会采用各种商业习惯做法来调整有关的贸易关系、解决贸易纷争。17 世纪中叶以前的这种“事实上支配那些往返于商业交易所在文明世界的各港口、集市之间的国际商人团体普遍适用的一整套国际习惯法规则”，就是中世纪商人法(拉丁文 lex mercatoria，英文为 law merchant)，或称旧商人法。可见，“中世纪商人法是为了弥补国家法律不完善而发展起来的”。[134]

商人法的形式多种多样，如商事法庭的判例汇编，无名法学家的论著摘编及各商业行会议定的规则，等等，其显著特点在于：“它是没有任何计划的，几乎是在

---

〔129〕 例如，戈德曼(B. Goldman)就主张古罗马万民法(jus gentium)是商人法的历史渊源，不过，他的有关论述比较简短，而且前后不一。最初，他把万民法视为罗马法的一部分。后来，他又说罗马万民法包含了一套适用于罗马与非罗马公民的习惯法规范，是独立于传统罗马法之外的。See Filip DeLy, Internatíonal Business Law and Lex Mercatoriat 1992. p. 9，伯尔曼(H. J. Bernan)则认为商人法形成于中世纪，但仍“得益于反映在新发现的查士丁尼法律文本中的罗马法”。参见伯尔曼：《法律与革命——西方法律传统的形成》，贺卫方等译，中国大百科全书出版社 1993 年版，第 413 页。

〔130〕 施米托夫、伯尔曼等人均作如是主张。参见[德]施米托夫：《国际贸易法文选》，程家瑞编，赵秀文译，中国大百科全书出版社 1993 年版，第 226 页；[美]哈罗德 · J. 伯尔曼：《法律与革命——西方法律传统的形成》，贺卫方等译，中国大百科全书出版社 1993 年版，第 413 页。

〔131〕 [美]哈罗德 · J. 伯尔曼：《法律与革命——西方法律传统的形成》，贺卫方等译，中国大百科全书出版社 1993 年版，第 407 页。

〔132〕 [美]哈罗德 · J. 伯尔曼：《法律与革命——西方法律传统的形成》，贺卫方等译，中国大百科全书出版社 1993 年版，第 414 页。

〔133〕 参见沈达明、冯大同编著：《国际贸易法新论》，法律出版社 1989 年版，第 2 页。

〔134〕 [德]施米托夫：《国际贸易法文选》，程家瑞编，赵秀文译，中国大百科全书出版社 1993 年版，第 85 页。

杂乱无章的情况下从习惯做法中发展而来的,并最终成为普遍接受的惯例。”[135]然而,这并不妨碍商人法具有与其他主要法律体系一样的客观性、普遍性、互惠性、参与裁判制、整体性以及发展性,[136]尤其是不妨碍商人法作为国际贸易惯例渊源所必须具有的普遍性,或者说国际性。这主要归功于四方面的原因。[137](1)集市法的统一。此时,“在各种各样的地方法中,各地大的集市法在本质上是相同的,该法几乎与教会法一样普遍”。[138] (2)海事惯例的统一。公元600至800年间,起源于腓尼基人与希腊人的海事法发展成为我们现在所说的《罗地海法》(Lex Rhodia),进而发展为《康索拉度海法》(Lex Consu lato),成为地中海沿岸的海事法典;1160年的《奥列隆惯例集》(Lex Oleron)成为英国海事法的基础;《维斯比海法》(Laws of Wisby)则适用于波罗的海和北海沿岸地区。[139] 此时的海事法虽然只适用于某一地区的若干城市,而且都是私人编纂而成的,[140]但其许多原则是共同的。[141] 例如,关于共同海损和船长为筹集必要的资金而有权卖掉货主的货物等项原则在上述各海事惯例中都是相通的。因此,沃姆瑟(Rene A. Wormser)在总结这些海事惯例的性质时指出,“显然,这种普遍性说明:海商法是商人们自己发展起来的,而不是各地王侯们的法律”。[142] (3)行商法院出现。此时,这些携带着货物往返于各港口、各集市的商人们有他们自己的解决争端的场所——行商法院(Piepowder)。通常,在行商法院中设有所谓的“双语陪审团”(halftongue jury),即在陪审团中,本地与外地的商人各占一半。这就使得陪审员的流动性很大。而且,其程序也不正规:申诉可在无法院令状的情况下进行审理:诉讼程序可不定期(de bora in horam)地进行。为此,库克(coke)形象地比喻说,按这种程序,行商法院审案的速度就像掸去脚上的灰尘一样快。[143] “行商法院”(Piepowder)

---

[135] [德]施米托夫:《国际贸易法文选》,程家瑞编,赵秀文译,中国大百科全书出版社1993年版,第10页。

[136] [美]哈罗德·J.伯尔曼:《法律与革命——西方法律传统的形成》,贺卫方等译,中国大百科全书出版社1993年版,第415页。

[137] [德]施米托夫:《国际贸易法文选》,程家瑞编,赵秀文译,中国大百科全书出版社1993年版,第5页。

[138] [德]施米托夫:《国际贸易法文选》,程家瑞编,赵秀文译,中国大百科全书出版社1993年版,第6页。

[139] 关于这几个海事法的中文译名,有多种方案,这里采用的是高等学校法学教材《海商法》中的译法,详见吴焕宁主编:《海商法》,法律出版社1989年版,第6页。

[140] 吴焕宁主编:《海商法》,法律出版社1989年版,第7页。

[141] [德]施米托夫:《国际贸易法文选》,程家瑞编,赵秀文译,中国大百科全书出版社1993年版,第6页。

[142] R. A. Wormsert, The Law(NewYork. 1949), p. 500;转引自[德]施米托夫:《国际贸易法文选》,程家瑞编,赵秀文译,中国大百科全书出版社1993年版,第6页。

[143] 参见[德]施米托夫:《国际贸易法文选》,程家瑞编,赵秀文译,中国大百科全书出版社1993年版,第6~7页。

一词源自法文中的"Prudhommes"意即"正直的人"(或行家)。这种行商法院无疑是统一的,具有现代调解与仲裁的性质,而不是严格意义上的法院。换用现代术语来表述的话,即它们具有常设国际仲裁庭的特征,在这里,非职业化的仲裁员被召集在一起,负责在各地解决争议。不论法院设在何处,地方惯例之间的差异,他们都明确适用相同的商事惯例。[144] (4)公证人的活动。自1326年起,位于法国香槟(champagne)地区的集市合同必须采用公证的形式:13世纪中叶,公证合同在意大利已普遍出现。据记载,马赛的一个公证员仅1245年一年就办理了上千件商事文书的公证,一个公证员在1天之内居然起草了近60件公证文件。当时的公证与现代不同,公证员是多方面的实务工作者,专司商事法律事务,其公证的许多合同显然就是我们现在所说的"标准合同",如租船合同(cartapartita)的雏形,或者只须略加修订。[145]

中世纪商人法的兴起对国际贸易惯例产生了重大的影响,当时使用的贸易用语,如商业票据、载货证券、租船运输及商业公司等在当代贸易惯例上仍旧沿用。[146]

二、商人法国内化

17世纪中叶至19世纪,随着资本主义在西欧的形成与发展,民族国家的兴起,中世纪的商人法被各主权国家先后纳入国内法制,形成各国商法,这就是所谓的"商人法国内化"时期。

不过,各国的商人法国内化并非按统一的方法进行的,而是基于不同的政治与社会背景,采用不同的实施方法。

在法国,全国性的法典编纂工作始于路易14时期的1673年《商事条例》(Ordinance Sur le commerce)和1681年科尔伯特(colbert)《海商条例》(Ordinance Sur le mar inc),这两个条例实际上就是把上述中世纪的海事惯例与商事惯例法典化了。1787年开始,人们即着手对这两项立法的修订,后来因法国大革命而中断,到19世纪初恢复,终于在1807年形成了拿破仑的《商法典》(code de commerce)。这是拿破仑法典的重要组成部分之一,它集中反映了法国大革命的政治观点与哲学,充分体现了合同自由与私有财产神圣不可侵犯的精神,被认为是第二等级(tiers état)的胜利,也就是商人和自由职业者的胜利,因此,我们可以说,法国商人

---

[144] [德]施米托夫:《国际贸易法文选》,程家瑞编,赵秀文译,中国大百科全书出版社1993年版,第7页。

[145] [德]施米托夫:《国际贸易法文选》,程家瑞编,赵秀文译,中国大百科全书出版社1993年版,第7页。

[146] 参见柯泽东:《国际贸易法专论》,三民书局1981年版,第6页。

法的国内化是政治运动胜利的最终标志。[147]

与法国不同，德国商法典的编纂是在一般民法的编纂之前进行的，是政治统一运动在法律上的反映。换言之，它试图通过统一法的编纂来推动政治上的统一。[148] 由于商法所固有的普遍性与统一性，选择商法作为首要的统一法目标是很自然的。1834 年，在德意志关税同盟(Zollverein)的主持下制定了德意志的《统一票据法》。1861 年公布了《统一商法典》，得到了包括奥地利与普鲁士在内的德意志联邦多数成员的采纳。1897 年德国又通过了新的《商法典》。德国商法的每一个编纂热潮都是其政治统一运动发展的产物，所以说，德国商人法的国内化与政治统一运动是密不可分的。

英国商人法国内化的背景与法、德均不同，它更多的是基于经济上的考虑，确切地说，是出于对海外贸易的高度重视。正如莫莉(Charles Molly)在其 1676 年法学著作《海事与航运法》(De Jure Maritimo et Navate)中所言："英伦此岛倘无对外贸易，将成为吾民禁锢之域，隐居之所，而与世隔绝；对外贸易使吾民获得财富、光荣及伟大，更使吾民得到美誉与举世之钦仰。"[149] 18 世纪中叶，商事法院衰落以后，对于普通法院而言，就要求当事人对商事惯例提出专门举证，这显然是很困难和不合时宜的。况且商事惯例的准确内容与普遍采纳情况很难确认。为革除这种弊端，在曼斯菲尔德(Mansfield)大法官的主持下，一方面制定了一套切合时需而且公正的实体商法，大大简化了商事程序；另一方面力图使商事惯例与普通法的各项原则协调一致，融为一体。事实证明，这一改革是成功的，得到了商人与法学家的普遍赞赏。

可见，商人法的国内化是时代政治、经济的必然产物，是与民族国家的兴起与中央集权的加强分不开的。显然，无论是欧洲大陆国家还是普通法国家，商人法国内化都是时代进步的标志之一。但其不断强化发展的结果，却使人怀疑，"从长远来看，不利因素是否超过了有利因素"。[150] 如童克(André Tunc)就曾指出，"把民族主义纳入法学领域，是法国的法典编纂与德国历史法学中令人遗憾的产物"，[151] 施莱辛格也注意到了"由于法典化所导致的各国法律相互孤立、难以沟通

---

〔147〕［德］施米托夫：《国际贸易法文选》，程家瑞编，赵秀文译，中国大百科全书出版社 1993 年版，第 9 页。

〔148〕参见［德］布鲁纳—海曼(Brunner-Heymann)：《德国法律史基础》德文第 7 版，第 276 页。转见［德］施米托夫：《国际贸易法文选》，程家瑞编，赵秀文译，中国大百科全书出版社 1993 年版，第 9 页。

〔149〕参见柯泽东：《国际贸易法专论》，三民书局 1981 年版，第 3 页。

〔150〕参见［德］施米托夫：《国际贸易法文选》，程家瑞编，赵秀文译，中国大百科全书出版社 1993 年版，第 10 页。

〔151〕A. Tunc, "English Lllw and COmmercial Law", 1961, J. Bus. L. 234, p. 237.

的状况”。[152]

然而,即使是在国内化时期,商人法也并未完全丧失其国际性。英国曼斯菲尔德大法官与波洛克(Frederick Pollock)等都承认商人法的国际性与世界性,德国的基尔克(J. Vow Gierke)教授也强调指出,由于国际商品交换是商法的核心内容,因而它的特征之一乃是国际性。[153] 从实践的角度来看,这一时期里,国际贸易惯例如 FOB、CIF 价格、银行信用贷款及进出口信用证付款方式等仍在商业社会中不断发展。[154]

与实体法国内化相伴而生的是国际私法(冲突法)的发展。因为商人法的国内法典化必然产生这样一个问题:即既然各实体法规定互异,一旦发生涉外诉讼,当依何国法律断案? 这时,一反中世纪普遍适用国际贸易惯例的传统,各国退而求诸其本国国际私法,依冲突法选择适用的法律。于是,国际私法应运而发展,国际公共秩序也常见引用。[155] 然而,通过国内法院解决国际贸易争端,依国际私法指示而适用法律,又兼有公共秩序的保留等项,实有迟缓、浪费而又不确定的缺点,[156] 这与日趋快捷的国际贸易现实很不相符。因此到了 20 世纪,乃有所谓商法“国际主义的回归”[157] 与现代商人法的兴起。

三、现代商人法

20 世纪初,随着以电力的发明与广泛应用为标志的第二次科技革命的完成,生产的社会化程度大幅度提高,进一步扩大与加强了世界各国的经济联系,形成了统一世界市场。这种世界市场不仅包括商品市场,而且包括金融市场、劳务市场等等。世界市场的形成与全面发展使世界经济进入现代化市场经济国际化发展的新阶段。[158] 这种国际化的世界经济必然要求有国际性的贸易规则。

如前所述. 传统的国际私法与内国民商法相结合的调整方法不仅迟缓、浪费,而且严重缺乏确定性与可预见性,这显然不能适应日趋频繁快捷的国际贸易发展的时代需要。因此,在各国谋求国际贸易统一立法的同时,国际商业社会再次发挥了其积极性与创造性,自发形成并编纂了大量的国际贸易惯例,同时又发展了

---

[152] R. B. Schlesinger, Comparativc Law 2nd ed. 1960, p. 185.

[153] 参见[德]施米托夫:《国际贸易法文选》,程家瑞编,赵秀文译,中国大百科全书出版社 1993 年版,第 11 页。

[154] 参见柯泽东:《国际贸易法专论》,台大法学丛书之二十三,1981 年版,第 7 页。

[155] 同上。

[156] 同上。

[157] 参见[德]施米托夫:《国际贸易法文选》,程家瑞编,赵秀文译,中国大百科全书出版社 1993 年版,第 12 页。

[158] 参见贾金思、俞坤一主编:《国际贸易通论》,群众出版社 1995 年版,第 39 页。

相应的程序制度——国际商事仲裁制度，为国际贸易的发展开拓出一条法律的新路。这种新型的国际贸易自治法律制度由于与中世纪国际主义的商人法有许多相似之处，被认为是国际贸易法领域中国际主义的回归与商人法的复兴。因而被称为“新商人法”(new Law merchant)或“现代商人法”(modern lex mercatoria)，有人甚至于脆直接沿用旧称“商人法”(1ex mercatoria)。正如施米托夫所鲜明指出的，“我们正在开始重新发现商法的国际性，国际法——国内法——国际法这个发展轮回已经自行完成；各地商法发展的总趋势是摆脱国内法的限制，朝着国际贸易法这个普遍性与国际性的概念发展”。[159]

现代商人法的兴起，在实践上的突出表现之一便是国际贸易惯例的大量涌现与广泛采用。20世纪以来，一些国际商业组织，特别是国际商会等掀起了编纂国际贸易惯例的热潮，它们将一些中世纪以来逐步形成的国际贸易惯例分门别类编纂成文，提供给国际贸易商自由采用。例如，1928～1932年，国际法协会制定了《华沙—牛津规则》；1933年，国际商会公布了《商业跟单信用证统一惯例》；1936年，国际商会制定了《国际贸易术语解释通则》。[160] 战后，世界爆发了以电子计算机、新能源、宇航、生物工程等发明与应用的第三次科技革命，使得国际分工与协作进一步深化，体现在资本、经济市场及资源配置等方面进一步国际化。世界市场不仅成形，而且已成为任何发展工业化、现代化国家赖以生存的经济环境。[161] 相应地，国际贸易惯例的编纂工作再掀高潮。旧的编纂机构，如国际商会不断更新原有惯例并制定新的惯例；新的编纂机构也不断涌现，如联合国欧洲经济委员会、各种贸易协会以及其他商业团体纷纷制定各式各样的标准合同与标准合同条件。联合国国际贸易法委员会则致力于一些国际公约与示范法的草拟工作及各种编纂机构之间的协调工作，直接间接地推动了国际贸易惯例的发展。

从总体上说，此时的国际贸易惯例固然与中世纪的贸易惯例有许多相似之处，但其特征与优点也是明显的。一方面，它不再是杂乱无章和任意形成的，而是由上述许多非政府的、具有一定权威性的国际组织与商业团体精心编纂而成的。这些国际组织在其制定的权威性文件中系统地阐述国际商业交往的规则，是现代商人法的显著特征。[162] 另一方面，它的国际性是真正意义上的“国”际性。由于中世纪并未形成民族意义上的近代国家，其商人法的“国际性”其实只能称为“普

〔159〕 C. M. Schmitthoff. “Modern Trands iu English Commercial Law”, in Chia-jui Cheng ed. Clive M. Schmitthoff's Select Essays on International Trade Law, 1988, pp. 3－15.

〔160〕 参见陈安主编：《国际经济法总论》，法律出版社1991年版，第41页。

〔161〕 参见贾金思、俞坤一主编：《国际贸易通论》，群众出版社1995年版，第39～41页。

〔162〕 参见[德]施米托夫：《国际贸易法文选》，程家瑞编，赵秀文译，中国大百科全书出版社1993年版，第231页。

遍性”;现代商人法则是超越自由市场经济国家与中央计划经济国家、普通法国家与大陆法国家的界限,而成为真正的“国际性”的规范。这种国际性还表现在它虽然不是国际立法,但它在各国的司法制度中得到适用,为各主权国家所允许,尽管这些国家可以公共秩序为由予以保留或限制。[163]

四、若干规律

从上述国际贸易惯例发展的大致脉络中,我们可以看出,国际贸易惯例的发展有如下一般规律:第一,国际贸易惯例是世界经济国际化的产物,并随着国际经济贸易的发展而发展。中世纪的商事惯例是地中海地区,商业贸易“国际化”的产物。商人法国内化时期,民族主义兴盛,贸易惯例发展缓慢,成果很少;20世纪以来,随着资本主义世界市场的形成与发展,国际贸易惯例迅速扩大,向深度与广度两个方向发展。第二,国际贸易惯例的发展主要归功于商人及商人社会自身的努力。正如伯尔曼所指出的,“商法最初的发展在很大程度上——虽不是全部——是由商人自身完成的,他们组织国际集市与国际市场,组建商事法院,并在雨后春笋般涌现于整个西欧的新的城市社区中建立商业事务所”。[164] 现代国际贸易惯例则主要是国际商业团体(如国际商会、各种贸易协会)编纂而成的。人们称以这种贸易惯例为主干的法律体系为自治的“商人”法,也正是基于这一客观事实。第三,国际贸易惯例的发展一般伴随着商事仲裁制度的发展。如前所述,中世纪的“行商法院”更接近于现代的商事仲裁庭,而不是真正的法院。现代国际贸易惯例更有许多是由国际商事仲裁所予以确认、宣示与发展的,商事仲裁对于贸易惯例的发展贡献极大。这是因为,自治的实体规则必然要借助自治的程序规则来实现其全部意义,贸易惯例与商事仲裁正如一对孪生兄弟,总是相伴而生,相伴而发展的。第四,海上运输惯例是国际贸易惯例最初的表现形式,后来逐步扩展到合同、保险、支付、仲裁等领域,这与国际贸易不断发展深化的过程是相一致的。

第二章　国际贸易惯例的性质与地位

第一节　国际贸易惯例的性质

国际贸易惯例是一种性质十分特殊的行为规范,这种规范特性主要表现为其

---

[163] 参见[德]施米托夫:《国际贸易法文选》,程家瑞编,赵秀文译,中国大百科全书出版社1993年版,第231页。

[164] 参见[美]哈罗德·J.伯尔曼:《法律与革命——西方法律传统的形成》,贺卫方等译,中国大百科全书出版社1993年版,第414页。

准法律性、跨国性、自治性与任意性四个方面。

一、国际贸易惯例的准法律性

国际贸易惯例究竟是不是法律？对于这个问题，向有肯定说与否定说两种观点。

否定说一般认为，国际贸易惯例不是法律，而只是一种贸易原则（principia metcatoria）。[165] 至于其理由，大致可分两类：第一类从实证法学的角度出发，或者认为国际贸易惯例的产生与发展不是国家意志的结果，[166]因而不是法；或者认为国际贸易惯例尚不具备法律所应有的某些实证要件，如认为它不具备可预见性（predictablity）、权威性（anthoritativcness）与一致性（consistency），更谈不上具有强制性（enforceability），[167]因而不能算是法律。另一种则从社会学的观点出发，认为惯例必须以某一共同体为依托，在时间与空间的制约下，方能成立。[168] 而现代世界的商业社会并未构成一个共同体，所以从法的观点来看，不存在所谓的国际惯例"。[169] 至于被称为国际贸易惯例的INCOTERMS与UCP，虽然是国际商会制定的，具有"国际性"，但实际上只不过将以英国为中心的海商贸易界的习惯予以成文化了而已，并非将各国共通的交易习惯予以成文化。因此，它们尚未获得各国商业界的共识，不能理解为肯定具有法律规范的效力。事实上，美国1941年修订的《对外贸易定义》即与INCOTERMS有若干重大差异。[170] 在此基础上，又有学者引入了"惯例圈"的概念，认为如果当事人一方不属于某惯例圈的话，不论是依"期待保护说"或"行为规范说"都不能将该惯例作为法的准则而强予适用。即使法庭地国承认惯例有一般法律的拘束力，如当事人属于不同惯例圈时，即不能遽然肯定该惯例具有法律上的拘束力。[171]

与否定说相反，持肯定说的学者们虽然也从实证法学及法社会学的角度出发，却得出了完全相反的结论——他们论证了国际贸易惯例是法律。这方面，又

---

[165] Cf. K. Highet. "The Enígima of the Lex Mercatoria", in Carbonneau ed. Lex Mercatoria and Arbitration, 1990, p. 108.

[166] 参见程德钧等编著:《国际惯例与涉外仲裁》,中国青年出版社1993年版.第7~8页。

[167] Cf. K. Highet, "The Enigima of thc Lex Mercatoria"、in Carhonneau ed. Lex Mercatoria and Arbitration, 1990, pp. 105 - 107。

[168] 参见张锦源:《贸易契约理论与实务》,三民书局1988年版,第55~56页。

[169] 例如,拉嘎德(P. Lagarde)就提出,根本不存在独立的国际商业社会,而只有许多"次社会"(sub-communities)在制定他们自己的规则;相应地,也不存在一个单独的'商人法',而只有许多"商人法群"(leges mercatotiae)并存着,而这种商人法群不能视同一个单一的法律体系。See Filip DeLy, International Business Law and Lex Mercato-ria, 1992, p. 228.

[170] 参见张锦源:《国际贸易法》,三民书局1989年版,第36页。

[171] 参见[日]坪田润二郎:《国际取引法の基本问题》,酒井书店1971年初版,第57~70页,转见张锦源:《国际贸易法》,三民书局1988年版,第37页。

以台湾学者柯泽东的分析最为透彻。[172] 柯氏指出，在实证法理学上，法律规范至少应具备三个基本条件，以区别于宗教、道德及其他一般社会规范，这三个条件是：第一，法律规范应具有一般性、普遍性，即法律规范的适用是抽象的、普遍的，而不是特殊的、个别的；第二，法律规范须有权威性，即由权威机构制定；第三，法律规范须具有制裁力，也即须具有强制执行效力。[173] 在柯氏看来，这三个条件国际贸易惯例都基本具备。

首先，国际贸易惯例具备法律规范的一般性与普遍性。[174] 国际商业团体所制定的标准合同虽然并不统一规范一切贸易合同，但它规范特定同类商品或专业的一切交易，因而具备一般性抽象的规范价值；交货共同条件（或条款）虽然也不是适用于一切合同，但对特定目的的商品交易来说，也具有专业上的普遍规范价值。所以，严格地说，标准合同、交货共同条件、贸易术语等国际贸易惯例，都具备法律规范的一般性与普遍性——至少从其外观形态与实践情况来看，它们条款明晰，普遍接受，适用于一般情况，“确合乎法律规范之精神”。诚然，这些惯例可依当事人明示的意思而予以排除，但这只能说明惯例的非强制性质，而不能借此否认其法律性质——如同民商法中的许多任意性规范一样。与此同时，国际贸易惯例的一般性还表现在其对合同的独特的解释功用。例如，在合同当事人既未明示约定不可抗力条款，又未指定合同应适用的法律，同时又难以确定最密切联系的内国法的情况下，仲裁员应适用何种法律规范来决定不可抗力问题？柯氏认为，这时最适当的法律依据是国际贸易惯例，如同类产品的标准合同中关于不可抗力的规定。这里适用惯例与适用内国法完全相似，而且从仲裁实践来看，这种方法的适当性也已得到证实——标准合同的上述法源常被用来解释及解决有关不可抗力、商品危险担保及合同成立等纠纷问题。此外，柯氏还引用现代贸易合同通用的关于正式合同签订以前的一切有关文字与口头约定均为无效的声明来证明贸易惯例的普遍及其对合同解释意义。

其次，国际贸易惯例具备权威性。[175] 这一方面是因为国际贸易惯例的绝大部分是由具有权威性的国际性商业机构（如国际商会）或专业团体所制定。这些组织历史悠久，领导人物实务经验丰富、专业知识渊博，“非纯司法或法学者或一般内国法律实务家可比拟”。因而，它具备权威与实际能力编定各种实用商业文

[172] 1976 年，柯泽东在《法治学刊》1996 年 1、2、3 期上发表了他的《国际贸易习惯法与国际贸易》一文，对国际贸易惯例与现代商人法的理论与实践作了深入的分析与精辟的论证，堪称我国关于商人法与贸易惯例研究的奠基之作。该文后来收入了台大法学丛书之（二十三）——《国际贸易法专论》（1981 年）之中。

[173] 参见柯泽东：《国际贸易法专论》台大法学丛书之二十三，1981 年版，第 31 ~ 32 页。

[174] 同上书，第 32 ~ 35 页。

[175] 同上书，第 35 ~ 37 页。

献，以供应各种商业活动实务上之需要。另一方面，由于现代国家肩负重要经济任务，为发展对外经济，已纷纷改变内国行政组织，使对外贸易机构升格成独立平行于财政或经济机关之地位，国家不仅干预贸易政策之厘定，还改变国内贸易机构组织形态，或参与私人企业，或以国营企业的方式参与外贸活动。[176] 所以，从逻辑上与实际需要上，国家必须承认这种商业组织团体的权威地位，而“容忍其创制习惯法的平行地位”。不过，柯氏承认这一与传统实证法理相者的现象“确难纯粹以法理分析之”，它只能算是国际法域与国内法域冲击的结果。换言之，这是“为求特殊内国利益与一般国际利益妥协、调和而不得不然耳”。因此，“倘若国家需要国际贸易，倘若国际贸易习惯确然存在，而倘若国际贸易发展与安全并不危害国家利益，则国家自然需要国际商业社会团体之合作，通过此等权威组织之研究，提供有利交易安全之方式，对外贸易活动庶可放开步伐，而不必全部囿于内国法以及因不信任外国法院等，致使国际贸易之开拓遭受限制。至此，国家乃不得不承认若干国际社会商业团体之权威地位，及其创造法律规范所具备之权威性”。柯氏进而指出，从历史法学派与社会法学派的观点出发，则权威机构制定并非法律规范的要件，但从法律的合法性与有效性出发，这一实证要素仍是惯例所必需的。但他认为，“习惯之普遍为司法判决或仲裁判断确认，习惯之被非公权力之有权威机构创制，复被普遍接受，而未被国家明示反对者，便应承认此习惯之具有权威性”。国家本身在其直接（如政府与外国私人企业订立交易生产、供应合同）或间接（经由公私合营公司与外国私法人或外国政府进行贸易）参与国际贸易时也使用贸易惯例，一方面自愿接受其约束，另一方面，在诉讼或仲裁时，也要担任原告或被告，这就构成对国际贸易惯例权威性与一般法律规范性质的默认。

第三，国际贸易惯例也具有制裁力。[177] 制裁力是实证法的基础。按实证法的观点，制裁力之有无是判断法与非法的标准。从表面上看，国际贸易惯例或者因为它不是强制性规范而不具强制适用的效力，或者因为仲裁裁决的执行须依法院的裁定而缺乏直接制裁力。然而，这并不说明它就不具有制裁力与强制力。因为国际贸易惯例的产生源自特殊商业社会的各种条件，因而它的制裁力方式及其有效性虽然从一般法律观点来看比较微弱，不如国内法。但从商业社会自治的角度来看，它的制裁除源自“法”的意义外，还包括经济与商业信誉的因素，后二者显然属于非“国家法”的因素。适用国际贸易惯例的仲裁裁决虽然有时不能立刻对“败诉方”产生直接有效的制裁，然而，这种裁决也可以形成直接或间接的社会

---

[176] 参见柯泽东：《国际贸易法专论》台大法学丛书之二十三，1981年版，第36页注64。

[177] 同上书，第37～41页。

影响,足以威胁败诉方的贸易信誉,进而影响其经济利益。仲裁之所以以秘密举行为原则,关键在于信誉上的考虑,而裁决之所以一般不说明理由,也是以商业秘密及商誉为主要原因,其不符合英美程序法只是次要原因。足见,经济利益及商业信誉为商业社会发展的原动力,也是该社会继续存在的基础。因而,源自这两方面的"制裁力"既是十分特殊的,也是十分有效的。在国际商务实践中,还会经常出现利用商情或其他重要报刊,或其他公示方式作为制裁手段,指责某国商人违背某商业规则,或不守信用;某专业团体或协会开除或警告其会员;某产品专业公会联合抵制(boycott,旧译"杯葛")违规的外国商人,等等;甚至有商业同业公会会章以罚款方式制裁违规会员等情形。[178] 更常见的是,在经济力量及行政组织方面已经相当强大健全的国际专业组织内,则进而规定买卖交易会员的加入,必须保证承认商业专业规则具有与其内国商业法规同等的效力,或者与国际公法原则具有同等效力,这一来,显然只能承认惯例的法律规范性质。况且,按《海牙统一国际商品买卖法》,在该统一法与惯例相抵触时,惯例应优于统一法的规定,由此可见,国际贸易惯例的制裁力虽然不完整,但却表现为另一种适应商业社会需要的形态,是"同时以法律、经济利益、心理(信誉)及商业道德为基础"的。[179] 至于仲裁裁决必要时须诉诸国家公权以为救济,也不能说明仲裁裁决因无直接执行力而属"非法",因为这只是不得已而为之,"并不即剥夺其亦为法律程序中的一种救济方法"。何况在实践中,绝大部分裁决能得到自愿执行,不需公权力救济。这说明借助公权力救济属于较少情形,并不影响仲裁规则及其判决的法律规范性。[180]

综合上述考察,柯氏得出结论:国际贸易惯例是法律工具之一,但却是尚未臻完全的法律体制,这种观点与戈德曼及我国学者徐国建等人的观点基本一致,足见其在肯定说中,有明显的典型性。

还有些学者则专从法社会学的角度出发论证国际贸易惯例等商人法的法律性。例如,法国学者卡恩(P. Kahn)就特别强调国际商法的社会学因素。他提出,按法社会学的观点,任何有组织的社会均可制定法律。因此,国际商业社会的自治规则,如惯例、一般条件、常用合同条款及一般法律原则等,也可以视为适用于国际商业社会或其分支部门的贸易活动的法律规范。[181] 卡恩专门研究了由买卖

---

〔178〕 参见柯泽东:《国际贸易法专论》,台大法学丛书之二十三,1981年版,第40页。

〔179〕 Pierre Mayer, Droit international Prive, 1977, pp. 18 – 20;转引自柯泽东:《国际贸易法专论》,第41页。

〔180〕 Cf. Ph. fouchard, L' arbitrage international, 1965, N. 619;转引自柯泽东:《国际贸易法专论》,第40页及其注49。

〔181〕 Cf. Filip De Ly, International Business Law and Lex Mercatoria, 1992, pp. 215 – 216.

双方所组成的、组织良好而且具有高度一致性与稳定性的国际商业社会。这种商业社会主要表现为欧债(Eurobond)市场上十分活跃的银行业社会,在其他市场上也屡见不鲜,且越来越多。[182] 比利时学者里高格斯(F. Rigaux)也是从法社会学中的这种“法律多元主义”(legal pluralism)的角度来解释国际贸易惯例等商人法的法律性质的。[183]

可见,对于国际贸易惯例的法律性,肯定说与否定说各执一词,而且针锋相对,否定说从实证法理学与社会学的传统理论出发,指出贸易惯例不具备法律所必备的基本实证要素与社会基础,因而不能算是法律;相反,肯定说虽也套用实证分析的方法,但着重从国际商业社会的特殊性以及从法社会学的观点出发,指出了贸易惯例的特殊性与规范性,从而论证其法律性。二者结论上的悬殊差别,主要是看问题的角度不同,侧重点互异的结果。

我们认为,对于国际贸易惯例的法律性质问题,应该从三个不同的层面分别予以考察。首先,从最狭义的法律的界定来看,“法律”仅指立法机关制定的规范性文件,[184] 即制定法或称成文法,是法律的“正式渊源”。[185] 从这个角度出发,则习惯与惯例都不是法律,国际贸易惯例自不例外。其次,从实证法学中一般意义上的法律定义来看,法律泛指法的一切法的外部表现形式,既包括制定法,也包括非制定法,即包括习惯法、判例法,等等。[186] 在这种情况下,国际贸易惯例可以成为“法律”。然而,它必须得到有权的国家机关的承认,才能够成为法律,即习惯法。[187] 在立法机关或法官赋予习惯与惯例以法律效力之前,它只是一种实在道德规则,[188] 而不是法律。

国家对惯例的承认,主要有立法承认与司法承认两种。[189] 显然,国家明示的立法承认是最为直接有效的认可途径。前面提到了西班牙与伊拉克对 INCOTERMS 的认可就是采用这种形式。此外,许多国家与地区(如瑞士、土耳其、泰国、阿根廷、奥地利及我国台湾)的民法典都赋予“惯例”或“习惯”以补充法律的地位。[190] 例如,《瑞士民法典》第 1 条规定,“如本法无相应规定的,法官应依据惯

---

[182] Cf. Filip De Ly, International Business Law and Lex Mercatoria, 1992, pp. 215 – 216.

[183] Cf. Filip De Ly, International Business Law and Lex Mercatoria, 1992, pp. 240 – 241.

[184] 参见孙国华主编:《法理学》,法律出版社 1995 年版,第 33 页。

[185] 孙国华主编:《法理学》,法律出版社 1995 年版,第 304、307 页。

[186] 孙国华主编:《法理学》,法律出版社 1995 年版,第 33 页。

[187] 孙国华主编:《法理学》,法律出版社 1995 年版,第 308 页。

[188] 参见[美]奥斯丁:《法理学范围之确定》,H. L. A. 哈特编,伦敦 1954. 第(30 – 33)163 ~ 164 页;转引自 E. 博登海默:《法理学——法哲学及其方法》,邓正来等译,华夏出版社 1983 年版,第 455 页。

[189] 参见张文显:《法学基本范畴研究》,中国政法大学出版社 1993 年版,第 45 页。

[190] 参见张坦:《论习惯在民法典中的地位》,载《河北法学》1996 年第 1 期。

例;无惯例时,依据自己作为立法者所提出的规则裁判,在前款情况下,法官应依据经过实践确定的学理和惯例"。我国台湾地区"民法"第1条也规定:"民事,法律所未规定者,依习惯;无习惯者,依法理。"我国《民法通则》第142条第3款则规定,"中华人民共和国法律和中华人民共和国缔结或者参加的国际条约没有规定的,可以适用国际惯例。"中外民法的这些规定是否可以理解为各国法律对各种"习惯"或"惯例"的法源地位"一揽子"立法承认呢?对此,有些学者是持肯定态度的。[191] 但多数学者则认为,上述规定中的"惯例"或"习惯"不过是"事实上的惯行",而非指已取得法律地位的习惯法。[192] 上述规定实质上是关于法律漏洞补充的规定,而不应理解为关于民事法律渊源的规定。[193] 法律漏洞的补充,在性质上,乃是"法律解释活动的继续",[194] 或者,"充其量只能说是一种造法的尝试,而非终局的法律之制定。由这种造法尝试所表现于判决先例中的法律见解,将来有可能转化为习惯法,亦可能迟早被抛弃"。[195] 换言之,这里的"习惯"或"惯例"与"学理"一样,只能视为补充法律漏洞的工具之一,而不能视为法律规范本身,因而也就不能说是一种法律渊源。所以说,各国民法上的这类规定不能算作各国对包括国际贸易惯例在内的所有"惯例"或"习惯"的"一揽子"承认。

同理,许多国家(如德国、瑞士、奥地利及美国、英国等)法律中关于惯例具有解释与补充合同的功能的规定,[196] 也只能理解为各国对惯例的作为意思表示(合同)解释工具之一的地位与功能的肯定,而不能算作对惯例的法律性质的承认。对《联合国国际货物销售合同公约》的有关规定也只能从这一角度进行解释。这样看来,国家对国际贸易惯例的法律性质的立法承认实在并不多见。

司法承认是另一种有效的惯例承认途径,这一点我国有关法理学著作也都持肯定态度。如孙国华教授在其主编的《法理学》中指出,"习惯和学说被作为断案的根据,正是国家权力认可它们有法律效力的表现"。[197] 张文显教授也持同样观点,他认为:"习惯法是根据需要,由国家立法机关赋予社会上早已存在的某些习惯、教义、礼仪等以法律的效力而产生的法律规范,或者是由法官对特殊的地方习惯的一般化。"[198]

然而,司法承认无论从大陆法还是从英美法的角度都存在着不确定性。在大

---

[191] 参见张坦:《论习惯在民法典中的地位》,载《河北法学》1996年第1期。
[192] 参见黄茂荣:《民法总则》,根植法学丛书编辑室,1982年增订版,第7页。
[193] 详见本文第四章的有关论述。
[194] 黄建辉:《法律漏洞、类推适用》,蔚理法律出版社1988年版,第71页。
[195] 黄茂荣:《法学方法与现代民法》,中国政法大学出版社1993年台湾繁体版,第378页。
[196] 可参见本章第二节。
[197] 参见孙国华主编:《法理学》,法律出版社1995年版,第335页。
[198] 参见张文显:《法学基本范畴研究》,第45页。

陆法系，这种不确定性主要是因为一些大陆法系国家要求“在法院将某习惯当作一种法律规则加以实施以前，这种习惯必须附有法律意见或必要意见”。[199] 这一要求意味着，如果社会成员坚信，某种惯例不具有法律拘束力而且不是强制性权利与义务的渊源，则该惯例便不能被承认为法律规范。简言之，在法院确定社会是否在事实上确信某种惯例具有法律拘束力之前，惯例的性质（即是否法律），往往是确定不了的。而要确定这种“社会法律信念”无疑是十分困难的。在英美法国家中，这一不确定性主要来自这样一种可能；即法院有权以某种惯例的不合理性为理由而拒绝赋予该习惯以法律效力。例如纽约州上诉法院就曾指出的，“合理乃是惯例的首要要素之一，所以不能确立一种不合理的或荒诞的习惯去影响当事人的法律权利”。[200] 晚近，英美法国家对惯例的“合理性”要求已经有所放松，而认为“惯例在商业上得到经常遵守的事实就构成其合理性的初步证据，而不必证明惯例自身的合理性。但在必要的时候，这一标准仍不可放弃”。[201] 可见，司法承认仍是一种很不确定，因而很难说可靠的惯例认可方式。对于国际贸易惯例而言，似乎也没有看到法院直接、明确地承认某惯例的法律效力的例子。

不过，我们或许可以从法院拒绝撤销根据贸易惯例作出的仲裁裁决的事实来“间接”推导出法院对贸易惯例的承认。例如，1989 年 7 月，法国巴黎上诉法院在“Compania Valenciana de Cementos Porthland S. A. v. Primary Coal Inc”一案中，就曾拒绝撤销一项由国际商会根据贸易惯例而作出的裁决。[202] 在 1988 年 12 月所作的关于该案的临时裁定中，仲裁员拒绝适用西班牙法、纽约法或英国法，而选择适用一套惯例（usages）。为此，有人根据《民事诉讼法》第 1502 条第 3 款，请求巴黎上诉法院撤销此项裁决，理由是仲裁员适用贸易惯例是超越了其权限范围的。法院驳回了这一起诉。法院认为，根据《国际商会仲裁规则》第 13 条第 3 款，仲裁员并不受任何国内冲突规则的约束。于是，法院得出结论，仲裁员对惯例的适用是与仲裁条款相一致的，因为仲裁员已经指出无论是西班牙法、纽约法还是英国法都会破坏当事人默示的意愿，他已适用了合同的自体法（proper law）。[203] 与此同时，法院还曾引用《民事诉讼法》第 1496 条以资佐证惯例是该案的自体法。[204] 由此可以看出，法国法院基本上是承认国际贸易惯例的法律性质的，而这与法国对

[199] 参见［美］E. 博登海默：《法理学——法哲学及其方法》，邓正来等译，华夏出版社 1983 年版，第 456 页。

[200] 参见［美］E. 博登海默：《法理学——法哲学及其方法》，邓正来等译，华夏出版社 1983 年版，第 457 页。

[201] Cf. Uniform Commercial Code, 1990 official Text with Comments. 12th ed. p. 50.

[202] Cf. Filip De Ly, International Business Law and Lex Mercatcria. 1992, p. 261

[203] 对“proper law”一词，我国学者有多种译法，这里采用的是韩德培先生的译法。关于其含义，也歧异甚多。详见韩德培主编：《中国冲突法研究》，武汉大学出版社 1993 年版，第 248 ~ 250、277 ~ 288 页。

[204] Cf. Filip De Ly, International Business: Law and Lex Mercatoria, 1992, p. 262.

现代商人法所持的一贯的肯定态度是分不开的。[205]

尽管有例可援，但在目前，各国这种有关的间接的司法承认的例子也尚不多见。因为，事实上，仲裁裁决大都能够得到自愿执行；不服而起诉到法院的情形本来就是不多的。

接下来的问题是，柯氏前面提到的国家直接间接地参与国际贸易，从而使用贸易惯例这一事实，是否可以视为国家对贸易惯例的“默认”？我们认为，一般来说，这种事实本身不构成国家对惯例法律效力的默认。

诚然，国家的承认可以有明示承认与默示承认（“默认”）两种，这一点从国家对新国家或新政府的承认中也可以看出[206]（尽管这种比照也许并不十分恰当）。然而国家的默认也须是国家通过以“主权者的身份”所作出的行为而体现的。上述柯氏提到的国家通过与外国私人企业订立交易生产与供应合同的“直接”方式，或通过经由公私合营公司与外国私法人或外国政府进行交易的“间接”方式参与国际贸易，而使用贸易惯例，一方面自愿接受惯例的约束，另一方面又甘当原告与被告的事实，在国际法上，只能算作是国家的“商业交易行为”（或称“私法行为”或“管理权行为”），而不是“主权行为”（或称“公法行为”“统治权行为”）。按现代国际法的一般观点与多数实践，国家这种“商业交易行为”属于不得援引国家豁免的行为。[207] 我国在实践上也主张国营公司或企业是具有独立法律人格的经济实体，不应享有国家豁免权。[208] 这主要就是因为国家的这种“商业交易行为”不是以“主权权利的主体资格”所作出的，而是以一个平等的市场主体的身份参与的，一般来说，不具有国家主权性质，也不具备国家意志性，事实上，如果肯定国家的这种行为中使用惯例是国家对惯例的默认的话，则所有实行对外贸易国家经营制度的国家（包括中国）都应该是承认国际贸易惯例是法律的——这显然与事实不符。众所周知，在中国的多数学者看来，贸易惯例不等于法律。[209]

基于这种分析，我们认为，国家参与国际贸易使用贸易惯例的事实一般不能构成国家对惯例法律性的默认。

此外，很显然，由于仲裁的民间性与自治性，仲裁裁决适用贸易惯例这一事实本身也不能视同国家对贸易惯例的默认。

可见，从实证法理学的角度出发，国际贸易惯例是不是“法律”，端赖国家的立法

---

〔205〕 事实上，法国在现代商人法的理论与实践两方面都是最为发达、最为激进的，关于各国适用商人法的理论与实践，详见本文第三章。

〔206〕 参见王铁崖主编：《国际法》，法律出版社 1995 年版，第 78、79 页。

〔207〕 王铁崖主编：《国际法》，第 133 页。

〔208〕 参见陈安主编：《国际经济法总论》，法律出版社 1991 年版，第 227 页。

〔209〕 参见沈达明、冯大同编著：《国际贸易法新论》，法律出版社 1989 年版，第 6 页。

或司法的承认。从目前的实践来看,明确承认某些惯例为法律的国家与被明确认可为法律的贸易惯例都是很有限的。绝大多数国家贸易惯例仍处在由“事实”向“法律”转变的过程之中。这一点就连自治商人法的积极倡导者也都毫不否认。例如戈德曼(B. Goldman)虽然鼓吹商人法是一种独立的法律体系,但它也不过是“形成中的法律”(droit en formation)。[210] 我国学者徐国建也认为“该法律远未完善。”[211] 因此,从实证法学来看,我们目前还不能一般地断定国际贸易惯例就是法律。尽管从总的发展趋势来看,它似乎正得到越来越多的承认与适用。

然而,假如我们换个角度,从更广阔法社会学的视野来理解“法律”的意义的话,则贸易惯例无疑是一种“行动中的法律”,是“活法”,尽管它不是“书本上的法律”。[212] 埃利希(E. Ehrlich)认为,“法律发展的重心不在立法,不在法学,也不在司法判决,而在社会本身”。他认为法有两类,一类是国家制定的法律,另一类是“活法”,即“支配生活本身的法,尽管这种法不曾制定为法律条文”“活法的科学意义,不限于对法律规范的内容发生影响,它还具有独立价值,它构成了人类社会的法律秩序的基础”[213] 在狄骥(L. Duguit)的著作中,这种“活法”被称为“客观法”,他说,对在社会中生活的人们必须有一种强迫服从的纪律,在整个社会团体之内人们势必要服从某种行为规则,“这些行为规则的总体形成客观法,因此客观法是人类社会所固有的”。这些规则具有拘束力,它并不是抽象的或超验的,而是基于生活事实。[214] 与“活法”概念相连的另一个重要的法社会学理论就是前面已提到的法律多元主义(legal pruralism)。这种理论认为,法是一种有强制力的,由特殊的机制所保证的行为规则,不仅国家制定的法律具有强制力,而且许多社会组织的行为规则,如行规、校规等也具有强制力,它们也都有特殊的机构来保证实施,因此,国家和这些社会组织的行为规则都具有法的属性。例如韦伯(M. Weber)曾说:“法是得到(身体的或心理的)强制力保证的,目的在于使人们服从或对违反它加以报复的,由为此目的而产生的特殊的工作人员而执行的秩序。”[215] 在他看来,大学生考试作弊受到教授的处罚是非法的,但交到学生司法委员会处理则是合法的;上级教士任意处罚下级教士是非法的,但是把他提交给宗教纪律会

---

[210] B. Goldrnan,“La Lex Mercatoria dans les Contrats et Larbitrage lnternationaux :Realite et Perspectives”, 106 Clunet(1979),pp. 475、502. 转引自徐国建:《现代商人法论》,载《中国社会科学》1993 年第 3 期。

[211] 参见徐国建:《现代商人法论》,载《中国社会科学》1993 年第 3 期。

[212] 参见孙国华主编:《法理学》,法律出版社 1995 年版,第 513 页。

[213] E. Ehrlich,Fundamental Principles of Sociology of Law,Cambridge,1936,pp. 23 - 24.

[214] L. Duguit,Law in the Modern State:New York,1970,pp. 70 - 71.

[215] Max Weber on Law in Economy and Society,A Clarion Book,1954,pp. 5 - 7. 转引自孙国华主编:《法理学》,法律出版社 1995 年版,第 515 页。

议处理则是合法的这些情况都属于法的范畴。[216] 同理，商会或行会惩戒委员会依照行规处理会员也是合法的，相应地，商事惯例，甚至于商会的章程，都属于“法”的范畴。

从前面的分析可以看出，国内外持“肯定说”的学者在论证国际贸易惯例的法律性的时候，或多或少都要求助于上述这种法社会学的理论基础。卡恩与里高格斯的观点就是其集中体现。此外，施米托夫也正是基于这种认识才提出，“我们应该把法的地位也赋予某一团体所普遍接受的惯例、行为守则、专业和准专业机构的行为指南、君子协定和被认为在法院没有强制执行力的其他规则”。[217] 德国霍恩(N. Horn)也认为，法律这一名称不仅指由一个或几个国家立法机关制定的客观的规范，而且还指当事人之间订立的，在他们之间有着法律约束力的合同在这方面，单个的合同以及典型而且广泛采用的合同格式也可以称为“合同法”(Lex contractus)。[218] 再者，从前面提到的柯氏对国际贸易惯例的“权威性”与“制裁力”的论述中，也可以清楚地看到法社会学理论的影子。

评判这几种法理学思想的优劣长短并作出取舍显然是困难而无益的。实际上，它们之所以能成真为法学流派，正是因为其对某一方面的侧重，质言之，即其“片面性”。片面的观点固然不是真理本身，但也正是这种片面的强调唤起了人们对以往被忽视的某一方面的注意，因而每一种学派的价值都是不可低估的。综合这种“片面”或许可以得到更接近“真理”的结论。我们认为，对于国际贸易惯例是不是“法”这样一个问题，我们不仅要看到其现状，也要看到其未来的发展；不仅要重视对贸易惯例的一般性分析实证，也要考虑到其客观的社会规范效果；不仅要考察在社会整体环境中的效力，也要重视它在商业社会中特殊的规范效力。从对法律规范的一般性的分析实证出发，显然，目前国际贸易惯例尚未被普遍接受为法律，不具备当然的、一般的法律拘束力；但同时，从对国际商业社会的特殊角度出发，则正如柯氏所揭示的，国际贸易惯例自有其一定的，尽管不完全的法律性质。据此，我们或许可以称为“准法律”规范，这种准法律规范不同于日常的、普通的实践，它具备相当的抽象性、普遍性与权威性，因而往往用来作为法律与合同的解释与补充；但它从总体上又尚未获得各国对其法源地位的普遍承认，因而在本质上还不能算是实证法学上的“法律”——“习惯法”，而只是一种“事实

---

〔216〕 孙国华主编:《法理学》,法律出版社 1995 年版,第 515 页。

〔217〕 C. M. Schmitthofft Commercial Law in 11 Changing Economic Climate, London, 1981, p. 1.

〔218〕 N. Horn, "Uniformity and Diversity in the Law of International Commercial Contracts", in N. Horn and C. M. Schrnitthoff ed. The Transnational Law of International Commercial Transaction, 1982, p. 13. 中译本参见《法学译丛》1985 年第 3 期。

上的惯行”,一种法律漏洞的补充工具。

二、国际贸易惯例的跨国性

众所周知,按传统的分类方法,法律可分为国内法与国际法。然而,随着国际交往的不断发展,调整各种性质与种类的国际关系的法律制度也相应地复杂化,出现了一种既不属于国内法也不是国际法的跨国法律制度,有学者称之为“第三法律秩序”(the third legal order)或“第三法律体系”(the third legal system),[219]有学者则索性称之为“跨国法”(transnational law)。[220]

然而,关于“跨国法”的概念,学者们的理解并不一样。霍恩指出,“跨国法”一词有三种不同的用法:(1)作为一种国际商事交易的法律制度的总称;(2)作为适用于国际商事交易的合同法,或在国际商业交易中使用的合同格式所具有的事实上的统一性与相似性的标志(3)商事法的国际渊源,即国际统一法原义。[221]

施米托夫看来是从国际统一法的原意来理解“跨国法”的。他指出,认为国际贸易法具有国际法或超国家法性质的看法都是错误的。因为国际贸易法的自治特征基于所有主权国家的同意或许可。它在性质上也不同于国际公法,因为它归根结底是建立在国内法基础上,但又是由国际商业界在与各主权国家无原则利害关系的领域发展起来的,阐明国际贸易法特征的最好方法是把它称为跨国法。[222] 显然,这里的“国际贸易法”是指以国际贸易惯例为主要载体的现代商人法。后来,他又明确提出,“跨国法是在与国家无原则性利害关系的任意性法律的范围内,在不同国家制度中发展起来的,调整平等当事人之间关系的统一法”。[223]

我们认为,与国际公法及国内法相比,国际贸易惯例确有其独特之处。[224] 它显然不是国际公法,因为它既不是主权国家签订的,一般也不涉及国家之间的关系。它也不同于一般意义上的国内法,因为它既不是国家制定的,它的调整对象也不是国内社会关系,而是国际贸易关系。尽管它的法律效力与最终执行有赖于国内法的支持,但这只意味着二者之间的一种特殊关系,而不意味着它就是国内

---

[219] P. Lalive,“Contacts between a State or a State Agenqy and Foreign Compans”,ICLQ,1964,p. 1008.

[220] “跨国法”这一概念最初是美国学者杰塞普提出来的。它泛指所有调整跨越一国国境的行为与事件的一切法律规范,不仅包括国际公法与国际私法,也不仅包括民法与刑法,而且还包括国内法中的其他公法与私法,甚至还包括难以归属于上述标准类别的其他各种法律规范。参见[美]杰塞普(P. Jessup):《跨国法》,1956 年英文版,第 1、2、106~107 页,转引自陈安主编:《国际经济法总论》,法律出版社 1991 年版,第 83 页。

[221] Cf. N. Horn, supra. p. 31.

[222] C. M. Schmitthoff, Commercial Law in a Changing Economic clirnate t London. 1981, p. 225.

[223] C. M. Schmitthoff,“Noture and Evolution of the Transnational Law of Commercial Transactions”, in The Transnational Law of International Commercial Transactions, 1982, p. 22.

[224] 陈安教授曾指出,国际商务惯例既不属于国际公法范畴,也不属于国际私法(冲突法)或各国经济法的范畴,而“自成一类”。详见陈安主编:《国际经济法学》,北京大学出版社 1994 年版,第 53~54 页。

法的一支,至少不是现存国内法体系中的任何一支。它是国际商业社会在与国家无原则性利害关系的任意性规范的领域中,自发地发展起来的一种调整国际商事交易的行为规范。这种行为规范已如前面所揭示的,尽管还未发展成为一种成熟的一般性的法律制度,但对国际商业社会而言,有着虽不完全但很特殊的法律约束力,因而,用"跨国法"这一有别于国内法与国际法的称谓不无可取之处。

不过,值得注意的是,这里的跨国法显然不是"超国法"(supranational law),而正是立足于主权国家的同意与承认的基础的。它也不是那种能够在全球普遍适用的"世界通用法"(universal Law)〔225〕。贸易惯例的适用一般只限于国际商业社会之中;而且,由于地理位置、历史发展等方面的原因,国际贸易也还远未真正实现全球化。区域性的贸易与相伴而生的区域性的贸易惯例仍占很大比重,不少惯例,如《美国对外贸易定义》等仅适用于某一或某些地区或某两个国家之间,并非都是全球通用的。而大量的国际标准合同与其他行业性的贸易惯例则更不能算是"世界普通法"。

三、国际贸易惯例的自治性

国际贸易惯例之所以被认为是有别于国际公法和国内法的"第三种法律秩序",或称"跨国法",其关键就在于它是一种自治性质的规范。

从前面述及的国际贸易惯例的历史沿革中,我们可以清楚看到国际贸易惯例本身就是挣脱国内法的束缚,而谋求一种切合己需的规范体系的产物。从实证的角度来分析,国际贸易惯例的自治性主要表现在如下三个方面:

首先,从制定程序来看,它既不是国家机关制定或颁布的,也不是外交会议上各国代表签署而后经过国内批准程序而生效的,它是在国际商业社会的贸易实践中自发形成,并经过商业团体予以条理化、系统化的产物。其过程主要是依赖商业社会自身的力量,而不是国家、政府的支持。

其次,从其内容来看,它是在与国家无原则利害关系的领域,即国家允许商业社会意思自治的领域发展起来的,反映国际贸易的一般规律,规范国际商事交易行为的规范;而不是国家强加给国际商业社会的法律规范。质言之,它直接反映的是国际商业社会的私人意志,而不是国家意志。就算国家意志通过法律的默认而得以体现,那也是一种间接的对既成事实的认可,更进一步来说,那反映的也只是国家对客观经济规律的认同与对国际贸易的需要。

最后,从国际贸易惯例的实施来看,国际贸易惯例最后固须借助国家公权力

---

〔225〕 Cf. A. F. Lowenfeld, "Lex Mercatoria: An Arbitrator's View", in Carbonneau ed. Lex Mercatoria and Arbitration, New York, 1990, pp. 51 – 52.

才能彻底实现，但大多数适用国际贸易惯例的仲裁裁决得到自愿执行的事实表明，上文柯氏所论述的国际商业社会所特有的经济利益与商誉驱动的经济制裁力是巨大的、有效的。从某种意义上讲，这种国际商业社会所特有的实施保证机制也体现出了国际贸易惯例的自治性质。

由此可见，国际贸易惯例是一种自治性规范。这种自治规范的理论基础有三：一为当事人意思自治原则，或称合同自由原则，这是各国法律都一致同意的一种国际通行的法律原则，也是国际贸易惯例存在与发展的法律前提与空间基础；二为有约必守(pacta sunt servanda)原则，即当事人意思自治所达成的合约是有法律效力的，除法定情形外，必须履行，否则构成违约，将受到各种形式的制裁，这是国际贸易惯例得以实现的法理基础；三为对国际商事仲裁的采纳。如前所述，国际商事仲裁是回避烦琐的国内法的适用程序，而实现国际贸易惯例的自治价值的最佳途径，是国际商业社会自身发展起来的一种切合己需的程序。质言之，它是国际贸易惯例自治性在程序上的必然表现。它们二者互为表里，相伴而生，比翼发展，相得益彰。

诚然，国际贸易惯例的自治性同样也不意味着国际贸易惯例是一种发展成熟的、完全独立于国内法律制度之外的规范体系。实际上，正如前面多次提到的，从实证的观点来说，国际贸易惯例既归因于国内法的认许而得以生存与发展，更有赖于国家公权力的支持而得以最终实施，完全摆脱国内法而彻底“独立”“自治”的国际贸易惯例或者商人法体系至少在目前是不存在的。所以说，国际贸易惯例的自治性是相对而言的，是对其规范特性的比较集中的表述，绝对化的理解不仅是不现实的，有时甚至会是十分危险的。

四、国际贸易惯例的任意性

一般来说，国际贸易惯例只是任意性的规范，即只在当事人明示或默示同意采用时，才对他们产生法律拘束力。换言之，惯例所规定的权利与义务通常不具有普遍的强制性，当事人可以采用，也可以不采用，还可以在采用时对其加以修改与补充。[226] 例如，《INCOTERMS1990》导言部分第22段就明确指出，“愿意采用这些规则的商人应在合同中规定，他们的合同受《1990年国际贸易术语解释通则》(INCOTERMS1990)的约束”。《UCP500》总则第1条也规定：“在《跟单信用证统一惯例》(1993年修订本，国际商会第500号出版物)被纳入信用证条款的情况下，它应适用于所有跟单信用证(在本惯例可适用的限度内，包括备用信用证)。

---

〔226〕 参见刘丁编著：《国际经济法》，中国人民大学出版社1984年版，第53页。

除非信用证另有明示规定，本惯例对所有各方均具有约束力。”前面提到的《中日一般货物销售合同条款集》的“序言”也明确指出，“各贸易公司在制订合同时，可以根据货物交易的性质，对本一般条款集中的条款加以修改，也可以增加新的条款”。《华沙—牛津规则》、1941 年修订的《美国对外贸易定义》等贸易惯例的序言部分也都有类似的规定。

然而，这并不意味着国际贸易惯例没有丝毫“强制性”。随着有关国内、国际立法与国际商事仲裁的发展，国际贸易惯例，特别是其中的“跨国成文规则”，已取得了一定的且越来越强的“强制性”效力。这种强制性主要表现在三个层面上：

第一，按某些国际公约与国内立法，国际贸易惯例的适用不再以当事人的明示同意为前提，而以当事人未明示排除为前提。换言之，对于那些众所周知的贸易惯例，“无声即为默许”，只要当事人没有相反的约定，便认为已被当事人默示采纳，因而可适用于他们之间的货物买卖合同之中。[227] 即便是当事人一方意欲排除某一惯例的适用，如果他不能证明另一方业已同意的话，该惯例仍应适用于他们的合同。[228] 在西方学者中间，以同意为前提的适用标准为“主观”（subjective）标准，反之，则为“客观”（objective）标准。目前，德、奥及美国等国的立法中，采用的是客观标准。[229] 我国的有关国内立法大抵也可算作此类。[230] 英国在实践上采用的也是这一标准，但理论上则仍要求参证当事人的意愿，在荷兰与瑞士，使用的是二者相加的“混合”标准。即惯例既可借以明确当事人意图，又可直接补充合同；只有法国与比利时等采用的仍旧是主观标准，但这种理论目前备受攻击。[231] 联合国《国际货物销售合同公约》（以下简称《公约》）第 9 条在肯定当事人应受他们业已同意的任何惯例的约束之后，进一步规定，除另有协议外，双方当事人应视为已默示同意受他们已经知道或理应知道的惯例的拘束。可见，从有关的国际、国内立法来看，客观标准是占有明显优势的，单纯以当事人为同意作为前提的主观适用标准似乎已经过时。

不仅如此，从上述《公约》中我们还可以推出第二层的强制性表现，即对于这些众所周知的惯例，甚至当事人的“知悉”（aware-ness）都不再是必要的，而只要他“理应知道”就够了。换言之，只要该惯例在国际贸易中是“广为人知”“并为有关

---

[227] 参见冯大同主编：《国际货物买卖法》，对外贸易教育出版社 1993 年版，第 29 页。

[228] C. M. Schmitthoff, lnternational Trade Usagess, 1987, pp. 15 – 16.

[229] Cf. Filip De Ly International Business Law and Lex Mercatoria, 1992, p. 239.

[230] 参见冯大同主编：《国际货物买卖法》，对外贸易教育出版社 1993 年版，第 19 页。

[231] Cf. Filip. De Ly, supra, p. 239.

特定贸易所涉同类合同的当事人所经常遵守”的，则该惯例就应对他适用。正如施氏所说的，“‘不知法者也不能免责’（ignorantia juris non excusat）原则看来对于贸易惯例也是适用的”。[232] 这一点在施氏前述研究所收到的许多国家的报告中都得到了强调，例如奥地利、原西德、西班牙、英国与美国。[233] 在德国，最高法院在几起判决中指出，个别商人对适用于他的交易的贸易惯例不了解这一事实并不能使其免责。[234] 不过，也有相反的意见，例如，瑞士的巴切尔（Bucher）教授在报告中提出，“一方不知的贸易惯例不构成合同的一部分”。他在报告中还提到了瑞典最高法院法官卡尔格林（Hjalmar Karlgren）的观点以资佐证。[235] 但是正如前面所提到的，多数国家采取的还是客观标准，而且这似乎是一种大势所趋。基于此，施氏进一步提出，即使是在缔结合同时，双方当事人都不知道某一惯例，该惯例仍然可能适用于该合同。[236] 事实上，一方不知与双方均不知并无质的区别，如果我们接受《公约》的观点，则对这一看似离奇的提法，也应能接受，只要他们“理应知道”或者说只要该惯例确是国际贸易中广为人知，并为特定贸易所涉同类合同所经常遵守的。

值得注意的是，《公约》所采用的这一标准与1964年海牙的两个《国际货物买卖统一法公约》的标准是有所不同的。后者关于当事人须受他的明示或默示同意的惯例或当事人之间业经确立的任何习惯做法的约束的规定与《公约》恰是基本一致的，但按ULFIS第13条第1款与ULLS第9条第2款规定，当事人还受一个通情达理的人（reasonable person）在同等条件下会认为可适用于他们的合同或其成立的惯例的约束。这与《公约》的惯例默示适用的条件是不一样的。显然，后者比前者更明确，也更严格。依前者，只要一个通情达理的人可能会认为其适用于他们的合同即为可适用，并未有进一步的具体要求；而依后者，默示适用的惯例必须符合两项附加条件，一是当事人必须知道或理应知道这些惯例，另一是这些惯例必须在国际贸易中，已为有关特定贸易所涉同类合同的当事人所广泛知道并为他们所经常遵守。前者主观性较强，后者则几乎是纯客观的要求，而避免了使用“通情达理的人”这样一个含混的概念。之所以出现这种区别，正是因为海牙的两个统一买卖法公约纯粹是发达国家之间的贸易公约，体现的是纯发达国家的法学观点；而后者则是在联合国贸法会主持下，发达国家与发展中国家所共同

〔232〕 C. M. Schmitthoff, International Trade Usages, 1987, p. 16.

〔233〕 Ibid.

〔234〕 BGH BB 1956, 572, BGH BB 1973. 635; RGZ 54, 182. 转引自［德］施米托夫：《国际贸易法文选》，程家瑞编，赵秀文译，中国大百科全书出版社1993年版，第10。

〔235〕 C. M. Schmitthoff, supra, p. 16.

〔236〕 Ibid., p. 17.

谈判制定的,体现的是二者的折中观点。正如伯奈尔(Bonell)所指出的,海牙统一买卖法的上述规定“对于来自发展中国家的当事人来说无疑是有害无益的”,[237] 事实上,由于现存于国际贸易中的大多数惯例是在主要发达国家的商品市场与交易中发展起来的,它们不仅在内容上是片面的,而且对于来自其他国家的商人来说,几乎是一无所知的。[238] 显然,采用一种较为明确严格与易于操作的规范对于广大发展中国家来说,是十分重要的。诚然,时至今日,发展中国家通过长期的参与,对许多国际贸易惯例已比较熟悉,然而这种差距与问题仍未完全消解,我们在认识、采用与适用国际贸易惯例时,对这一点应有清醒的认识与把握。与此同时,我们更应充分意识到,深入研究贸易惯例,积极发展与编纂自己的贸易惯例,不仅具有理论价值,更具有重大的现实意义。

国际贸易惯例的第三个层次的强制性表现是前面已经提到的由国内立法予以一般性地认可,从而赋以直接的法律拘束力的情形。如西班牙与伊拉克对 INCOTERMS 的认可。惯例既经国家认可,成为本身具有法律拘束力的“习惯法”,其效力即可获得国家公权力的有效支持,自然更可以得到强化,故置于第三层次的地位。

国际贸易惯例的这些强制性的表现是不是就意味着国际贸易惯例是强制性规范呢?我们认为,答案是否定的。这一结论建立在这样一个基本事实之上,即无论如何,当事人总可以通过协议排除一项贸易惯例对其合同的适用。[239] 这一点就是对于已获国家认可的贸易惯例也不例外,我们认为,像 INCOTERMS 这样的“跨国成文规则”,即使像在西班牙、伊拉克一样得到法律的承认而具有普遍性的法律效力,但仍不会改变其任意性规范的本质,如同我国《海商法》大量吸收了国际公约与惯例的内容,但其规范仍大都是任意性规范,当事人仍可以协议排除。正是考虑到国际贸易惯例规范效力的这二重表现,国内学者提出,国际贸易惯例是任意性与准强制性相结合的规范。[240] 这种提法无疑是比较全面、比较科学的。不过,这种“准强制性规范”本质上似乎仍只能算是任意性规范。

---

[237] Bianca-Bonell:Commentary on the International Sales Law. 1987, p. 105.

[238] Ibid.

[239] Cf. C. M. Schmitthoff, supra. p. 15.

[240] 参见韩德培主编:《国际私法》,武汉大学出版社 1989 年版,第 198 页;韩健:《现代国际商事仲裁法的理论与实践》,法律出版社 1993 年版,第 249 页。

第二节　国际贸易惯例的地位

上节关于国际贸易惯例性质的论述,实质上已经揭示了国际贸易惯例的基本法律定位,即它是一种有别于国际法与国内法的,具有准法律性、跨国性、自治性与任意性的国际贸易行为规范。然而,要进一步明确它在整个国际贸易法体系中的地位,尚有必要进一步考察它与有关国际贸易的国际与国内法律规范的法律关系特别是它们之间的效力层级关系。同时,由于贸易惯例在理论与实践上与现代商人法及合同的关系均十分密切,因而对这两重关系也有必要加以分析。

一、国际贸易惯例与国际贸易条约的关系

这里,"国际贸易条约"是指调整贸易关系的国际条约。这种国际条约大抵可分为两大类:第一大类是强制性的国际条约,这一大类似乎也可分为两种,一种是协调国家间贸易政策与法律的条约,如《关税及贸易总协定》《世界贸易组织协定》《北美自由贸易协定》以及大量的双边贸易条约与协定;另一类则是商事方面的某些具有强制性的国际立法,如《海牙规则》《汉堡规则》。强制性国际贸易条约与国际贸易惯例各有专司,一般互不相犯。前者调节的是国家利益与公共安全,大都属于公法范畴;后者调整的主要是私人之间的跨国交易关系,属私法范畴。两者一般不会发生交叉或冲突;万一发生冲突,则这种强制性国际贸易条约的效力当然优于国际贸易惯例。

与国际贸易惯例关系至为密切的是第二类的国际贸易立法,即任意性的国际贸易公约,主要指关于国际货物买卖的几个公约。如 1964 年的两个海牙国际货物买卖统一法公约,即《国际货物买卖统一法公约》和《国际货物买卖合同成立统一法公约》以及其后来发展合并而成的《联合国国际货物销售合同公约》。前两个统一法由于采用的是"示范法"的方式,即公约统一制定后由各国根据宪法程序纳入其国内法的方式,因此即使是符合适用该公约的条件,当事人也可以自由排除其约束。[241] 例如,英国在发布纳入了这两个公约的《国际货物买卖法》的命令中就规定,只有在合同当事人选择适用该买卖统一法公约时,该法才对他们有

[241]　Cf. C. M. Schrnitthoff, "Nature and Evolution of the Transnational Law of Commercial Transactions", in The Transnational law of International Commercial Transactions, 1982, p. 24.

约束力。[242] 换言之,只要当事人不选择适用该统一法,则可不受其约束。《联合国国际货物合同销售公约》则更加直接,其第6条明确规定,"双方当事人可以不适用本公约,或者在第12条的条件下,减损本公约的任何规定或改变其效力"。可见,这两个统一国际贸易合同及其成立规则的公约都是任意性的公约。

由于这种任意性,这种国际贸易条约与国际贸易惯例在效力性质上十分相似,而且它们都可算作现代商人法的重要组成部分。[243] 正如本文前面[244]所提到的,我们并不能据此认定这种国际公约也是国际贸易惯例的一种。在实证法学上,公约与惯例有着十分明显的区别。与此同时,上述三个任意性公约都十分重视贸易惯例的功能,并把贸易惯例置于比公约条款更高的法律地位。对此,ULFIS第2条与ULIS第9条第2款都有明确的规定。例如ULIS第9条第2款规定,"凡本法与惯例有抵触时,优先适用惯例"。CISG虽无明文规定,但也可认为是持同一态度的,[245]因为它是非强制性的公约,而且按其第4条(a)款规定,它也不涉及惯例的有效性问题.这就意味着,一旦贸易惯例与ULFIS、ULIS或CISG的规定不一致时,应优先适用惯例的规定。

二、国际贸易惯例与有关国内法的关系

如前所述,国际贸易惯例作为一种自发形成的跨国性自治规范,一方面,它超出了国内法的范畴,不是国内法的组成部分;另一方面,从实证法理学来看,它的法律效力又有赖于国内法明示与默示的承认,它的适用也多与国内法结合在一起,通过合同准据法而"间接"实现。[246] 这就是两者之间的一般法律关系,至于国内法的具体规范与国际贸易惯例规范之间的效力层级关系,各国大都认为,贸易惯例可以不符合国内法中的任意性规范(jus dispositivm),但不能超越法律的强制性规范(jus cogens)。[247] 例如,《法国民法典》的第1873条(该条现已废止)曾明确规定,在法典的有关部分中,贸易惯例应优于该法;瑞典的一些非强制性立法,如1915年的《合同法》、1905年的《货物买卖法》及《代理法》,都规定其条款应让位于"合同、习惯与惯例"。在美国,纽约州曾制定一项关于美国《统一商法典》的

---

[242] Cf. C. M. Schmitthoff, "Nature and Evolution of thc Transnational La w of Commercial Transactions", in The Transnational law of International Commercial Transactions, 1982, p. 24.

[243] 在施米托夫看来,这种国际公约即所谓的国际立法(international legislations)与国际商事惯例是国际商法——现代商人法的两大基本法律渊源。See eg, C. M. Schmitthoff, "lnternational Business Law: A New Law Merchant", in Chia-Jui Cheng ed. C. M. Schmitthoff's Select Essays on International Trade Law, 1988, p. 34.

[244] 参见本文第一章第二节。

[245] Cf. Filip De Ly, International Business Law and Lex Mercatorja, 1992, p. 161.

[246] 关于国际贸易惯例的适用理论与实践,详见本文第三章第二节。

[247] Cf. C. M. Schmitthoff. . International Trade Usages, as aspecial issue of thc NEWSLETTER of the Institute of International Business Law and Pratice, 1987, p. 18.

补充法案,其中规定:除非另有约定,只要根据信用证条款信用证应部分或全部受 UCP 的约束的话,《统一商法典》的第 5 编(关于信用证的)即不适用。换言之,UCP 的惯例优于 UCC 的立法。密苏里、亚利桑那、阿拉巴马等外也有类似的修订。南斯拉夫的哥尔德斯坦(Goldstajn)教授也指出,"……任何贸易惯例,在南斯拉夫国内法院都是允许的,除非它们与南斯拉夫的强制性规范,或有关社会制度和/或道德的宪法原则相背"。澳大利亚最高法院的一个判决也曾指出,关于汇票的贸易惯例不能改变具有强制性质(Zwingendes Recht)的法律,但可优于允许当事人作相反安排的法律(nachgiebiges Recht)。[248]

然而,对此也有不同的提法。有的国家并不是区分任意规范与强制规范,而只是规定国际贸易惯例可用来补充法律的规范性条款。例如,西班牙最高法院的几项判决指出,"商事习惯或惯例——法律的客观规则——对于法律规范具有补充意义"。意大利波卡(Pocar)教授所做的报告也提出贸易惯例的功能在于弥补法律的空白(la cunnae)。[249] 《涉外经济合同法》《民法通则》《海商法》《民用航空法》《票据法》的有关规定基本上也是持这种态度。从字面上看,这里国际贸易惯例被置于了"补充适用"的地位,从而即便是任意性规范,也似乎具有优于贸易惯例的效力。然而,一旦当事人明示或默示地将此惯例纳入其合同之中,则可成为合同的一部分,从而取得优于国内任意法的效力。如前所述,在许多国内法与国际公约中,那些"广为人知"并被"经常遵守"的国际贸易惯例往往不需当事人明示采用,甚至无须当事人知悉即可适用于其合同之中。因而,只要没有相反约定,这种惯例就可视为合同的当然组成部分之一,从而取得优于国内任意法的效力。可见,即使是视惯例为法律规范的补充,其效力往往也要优于国内法中的任意规范。所以说,贸易惯例的效力介于国内法中的任意规范与强制规范之间的论点基本上是可以成立的。各国立法强调惯例的"替补法律"地位,主要是出于补充法律漏洞,从而确保法律完整周延的考虑,[250] 而不应理解为对惯例这种应有效力的否定。

---

[248] Cf. C. M. Schmitthoff. . International Trade Usages, as aspecial issue of thc NEWSLETTER of the Institute of International Business Law and Pratice, 1987, pp. 17 - 18.

[249] Ibid. , pp. 18 - 19.

[250] 例如,我国《涉外经济合同法》关于我国法律未作规定的,可以适用"国际惯例"的规定主要就是考虑到当时"我国涉外经济法律还不够完备、处理合同争议适用我国法律时.有的可能找不到依据"。参见宋汝棼:《参加立法工作琐记》(上),中国法制出版社 1994 年版,第 60 页,关于法律漏洞补充及依习惯补充法律漏洞的方法,详见梁慧星:《法律漏洞及其补充方法》,载《民商法论丛》(第 1 卷),法律出版社 1994 年版,第 1 ~ 42 页。

三、国际贸易惯例与现代商人法的关系

关于“现代商人法”，无论是其名称、含义，还是其性质与渊源等，在国内外均无完全统一的看法。大致说来，所谓“商人法”（拉丁文为“Lex Mercatoria”，英文为“Law Merchant”或译“商法”“商人习惯法”等）是指从事国际贸易活动的各国商人在实践中所共同认可并遵守的、统一规范国际贸易活动的某些习惯和规则；而所谓“现代商人法”则是指“二战”以后，国际法学界的某些学者因不满于国际贸易合同受制于内容彼此相异的各主权国家国内法的状况而积极寻求的一种独立适用于日益发展变化着的国际贸易关系，并且能够反映国际贸易活动特征的法律制度。[251]

早在19世纪20年代末，法国的伦伯特（E. Lambert）就开始注意到这样一个事实：国际贸易不仅为国内法与国内法院所管辖，有关商业团体通过结合一般条款、贸易惯例及仲裁，在某种意义上已经制定了他们自己的法律。[252] 伦伯特称之为“国际共同法”（droit corporatif international）。他认为，在市场里的推动下，这种法律已经有效地实现了特定贸易与行业层面上的法律的统一，而且还将导致更普遍的法律统一化。[253] 虽然没有正式使用“现代商人法”的概念，但一般认为他的“国际共同法”理论为现代商人理论奠定了基础。1954年，英国的施米托夫提出了他的影响深远的“新商人法”（new Law Merchant）理论。施氏强调指出了国际立法（包括国际公约与国际统一示范法）与国际商事惯例这两大商人法渊源，[254]并认为现代商人法是由国际商业界在与各主权国家无利害关系的领域（即国家允许私法自治——当事人意思自治的任意性规范领域）中发展起来的自治性的跨国法。[255] 但是它归根结底建立在国内法基础之上，[256]“缺乏系统性，复杂多样，然而充满活力，现实主义与独创精神”。[257] 质言之，关于现代商人法的性质与地位，施氏并不认为它是一种完全独立于国内法之外的法律体系，而只是国际贸易领域一些自治性质的规范的总和（国际贸易自治法）；它不能完全摆脱国内法的控制，它的效力与执行等均有赖于国内法的支持，故而也不能完全“自治”，显然，施氏的观点体现了一种实务的态度与现实主义的精神，是对“商人法”在法律实践中的现状的比较客观的概括。

---

[251] 参见徐国建：《现代商人法论》，载《中国社会科学》1993年第3期。
[252] Filip De Ly, supra. p. 208.
[253] Ibid.
[254] See eg. C. M. Schmitthoff, “The Unification of thc Law of International Trade”. J. Bus. L. 1968. p. 109.
[255] Cf. C. M. Schmitthoff. Commercial Law in a Changing Economic Climate. 1982, 2nd ed. p. 225.
[256] Ibid.
[257] C. M. Schmitt hoff, “The Unification of the l. aw of International Trade”. J. Bus. L. 1968, p. 112.

与施氏的观点相反，法国的戈德曼(B. Goldman)在其1961年提出的商人法却持十分激进的态度。他认为，现代商人法不包括国际立法，它是由实体跨国规则(substantive transnational rules)、成文惯例、一般条款、一般法律原则、国际商事仲裁裁决以及关于国际公司的行动守则所组成的自治法律体系，是本身具有法律拘束力的正式法律渊源。因此，援引商人法规则的合同与适用商人法的仲裁裁决并非没有法律依据，而只是没有依据国内法而已。[258] 最初，戈氏也承认国内法对商人法的意义，但后来，他把商人法置于与外国法同等的地位，认为它可以通过当事人对商人法或实体跨国规则的选择而得以实现；而一旦选择了商人法，则可像选择了外国法一样，导致对法院地法的强制性规范的排除。尽管他也承认，适用商人法并不能违反法院地国的国际公共秩序，特别是其中的跨国公共秩序。[259]

20世纪70年代以来，我国学者开始注意到对现代商人法的研究。1976年，我国台湾地区学者柯泽东撰文率先作了这种研究。他称之为“国际贸易习惯法”，其法源限于标准合同与交货一般文件、贸易术语与跟单信用证统一惯例以及国际商事仲裁裁决三种。[260] 如前所述，柯氏从实证法理学与法社会学的角度，论证了国际贸易习惯法的法律性。同时他也承认，该法律体制“尚未臻完全”。可见，他的理论深受戈氏理论的影响，只是他对商人法外延的界定远较戈氏为窄。

我国大陆学者对商人法的专门研究起步甚晚。直到1993年，方有专论问世。在《现代商人法论》一文中，徐国建提出了他的商人法观点，他认为现代商人法法源包括国际公法、国际统一立法、一般法律原则、国际标准合同、合同标准条款、贸易惯例、国际组织制定的行为法典以及公开发表的国际商事仲裁裁决，等等。[261] 显然，这种法源界定较之上述任何一家均为广泛。至于商人法的性质与地位，徐氏认为商人法是具有跨国性与自律性的法律，是“混合法源”构成的“法律部门”，尽管“该法律远未完善”。[262] 笔者不很明白，他所指的“法律部门”是指国内法上的还是国际法上的法律部门，抑或这里“法律部门”指的就是“法律体系”？

大致在徐文发表的同时，韩健在其研究国际商事仲裁法的专著中，也专门探讨了商人法及其适用问题。他称之为“商法”，认为国际商法中得到世界公认且已发展成为具体明确规则的主要有国际条约、国际贸易惯例与标准格式合同三种。[263] 这种范围界定相对于徐文的界定来说狭窄得多，而与施氏的观点基本吻

---

[258] Cf. FiLip De Ly. supra. p. 214.

[259] Ibid. , p. 214 – 215.

[260] 参见柯泽东：《国际贸易法专论》，三民书局1981年版，第14～31页。

[261] 参见徐国建：《现代商人法论》，载《中国社会科学》1993年第3期。

[262] 参见徐国建：《现代商人法论》，载《中国社会科学》1993年第3期。

[263] 参见韩健：《现代国际商事仲裁法的理论与实践》，法律出版社1993年版，第243～250页。

合。此外，他还比较深入地研究了商人法在各国的适用概况。

由此看来，尽管学者们对于现代商人法的范围、性质及地位等众说纷纭，莫衷一是，但有一点是共通无疑的，那就是，学者们一致公认国际贸易惯例是现代商人法的基本组成部分之一。换言之，国际贸易惯例与现代商人法在外延上是包含与被包含的关系，这也就是二者之间基本的法律关系。从内涵上说，二者有着共同的历史背景与演进过程，有着基本相通的法律性质、地位与效力。因此，国内外学者关于国际贸易惯例的论述也多散见于他们对商人法的研究之中。所以，关于国际贸易惯例的理论基础与实践状况，也多只能从关于现代商人法的理论与实践中去发掘与推演。

至于国际贸易惯例与现代商人法的更为具体的关联，则因对现代商人法地位的不同理解而异。按戈氏的观点，现代商人法是一个独立的法律体系，则自有作为一个法律体系的整体功能与分工。据此，则国际贸易惯例可因其中的“实体跨国规则”而得到直接适用，又可据其“一般法律原则”而得到补充。但如按施氏的观点，现代商人法不过是一群同质规范的集合，并无“系统性”可言，不构成一个完全独立的法律体系，故不可能具备上述的整体功能与职能分工。

在我们看来，至少在目前，我们还不能认定现代商人法已经构成一个完全独立的法律体系。因为，从理论上说，正如许多学者所指出的，戈氏所理解的现代商人法的许多渊源是不是法律是一个很大的问题。[264] 例如，前已述及，从目前占统治地位的实证法理学的角度出发，国际贸易惯例的法律性就难予一般性地肯定。同时，从国际合同与商事仲裁的实践来看，合同当事人常常也并不笼统地选择“现代商人法”，而是明确地在其协议中规定适用诸如一般法律原则、贸易惯例等现代商人法的具体组成部分。[265] 足见在国际贸易实务界中间，现代商人法也并未被视为一个单独的“法律体系”，而不过是一些性质类似的具体规范的总和。所以，对于国际贸易惯例能否因商人法中所谓的“实体跨国规则”而得到直接适用，又能否依商人法中的一般法律原则而得到补充这些问题，目前仍是不能予以肯定作答的。

四、国际贸易惯例与合同的关系

国际贸易惯例与合同有着十分密切的关系。这种关系可从三个层次上进行分析：

---

〔264〕 例如，在荷兰学者 Filip De Ly 看来，戈氏所称的现代商人法的法源中，只有“一般法律原则”勉强可以算是真正的法律渊源。详见 Filip De Ly，supra. p，277 – 286.

〔265〕 参见徐国建：《现代商人法论》，载《中国社会科学》1993 年第 3 期。

首先,国际贸易惯例无论是作为标准合同还是作为标准合同条款、常常被纳入各种国际贸易合同之中,成为合同的一部分。例如,许多国际货物买卖合同的价格条款,往往采用"FOB"或"CIF"等 INCOTERMS 所定义的术语。在这种情况下,INCOTERMS 对有关术语的规定就构成了合同条款的一部分,从而取得合同法上的效力。

其次,即使未被合同所纳入,国际贸易惯例往往也用来解释合同。例如,在意大利、瑞士、南斯拉夫等国,虽然只承认 INCOTERMS 是契约性贸易惯例,但仍可作为解释合同的辅助工具之一。[266] 在1975年的一项判决中,联邦德国最高法院曾主张,买卖合同中的 FOB 条款应根据 INCOTERMS 第4条进行解释,即使当事人并未将其明示纳入合同之中。早在1957年慕尼黑的上诉法院也曾作出过类似判决。巴切尔(Bucher)在他的一份报告中对这一问题进行了深入的考察,得出的结论是:INCOTERMS 是可以采纳的推定"当事人可能意图的辅助依据与解释合同的补充手段"。[267] 在芬兰,大多数人认为,如果当事人采纳了 INCOTERMS 所定义的贸易术语,则除非有相反的表示,即使合同未曾具体引用 INCOTERMS,也应视为已经采纳了 INCOTERMS。[268]

事实上,贸易惯例对合同的解释功能正是各国民商法上"依习惯解释"的意思表示解释方式[269]的具体表现。对此,各国民商法大都有概括性规定。例如,《日本民法典》规定,"有与法令中无关公共秩序的规定相异的习惯,如果可以认定法律行为当事人有依该习惯的意思时,则从其习惯"。《德国民法典》也规定:"契约的解释应遵守诚实与信用的原则,并考虑交易上的习惯。"《法国民法典》则规定:"有歧义的文字依契约的订立地的习惯解释之""习惯上的条款,虽未载明于契约,解释时应用以补充之"。从这些原则性立法中可以看出,大陆法国家普遍认为,对于具体合同内容的解释应当考虑有关习惯;习惯即使未被纳入合同,也可对合同起补充解释作用。在英美法国家中,未明确纳入合同的贸易惯例对合同同样具有解释意义。例如,按照美国《统一商法典》第1~205(3)节规定,贸易惯例可"使合同条款产生特定含义,并对合同条款起补充与限制作用"。按照英国法,惯例也可用来补充合同条款或者解释合同,只要它是合理的,且不与合同的明示条款相排斥。此外,所有成立合同的市场、行为和地点盛行的有关惯例都被认为

---

[266] C. M. Schm itthoff, International Trade Usages, p. 34.

[267] Ibid.

[268] Ibid.

[269] 关于意思表示解释,可参见董安生:《民事法律行为——合同、遗嘱和婚姻行为的一般规律》,中国人民大学出版社1994年版,第236~252页。

是合同的默示条款,且这种条款不以当事人的知晓为前提。英国法把惯例当作合同的默示条款的理论基础在于惯例体现了当事人的推定意愿:“真相是:容许举证的原则,是当事人没有把它们的合同的全部条款记下来,他们只记载了在某些情况下需要的特别协议,这些特别协议可以有无穷无尽的不同规定,而余下普遍的、不变的事件,由默示的和不必说出的理解处理。在道理上,他们必然被视为愿意按惯例成立合同,除非他们明示排斥这些惯例。”[270]

贸易惯例的这种解释功能还得到一些国际公约与统一示范法的肯定与支持。按《国际货物买卖统一法》(ULIS)第5条第1款规定,当事人须受他们已明示或默示同意的惯例和当事人之间确立的任何习惯做法的约束《国际货物买卖合同成立统一法》(ULFIS)第2条有一相似条款,规定除非通过当事人之间业经建主的习惯做法表明适用其他规则外,适用该统一法。此外,ULFIS第13条第1款与ULIS第9条第2款还规定当事人尚须受一个通情达理的人在同等条件下会认为可适用于他们的合同或其成立的惯例的约束。可见,这两个统一法为惯例留下了广泛的效力空间,其解释功能是显而易见的。相应地,《联合国国际货物销售合同公约》也赋予惯例以解释功能。其第8条第3款规定,“在确定一方当事人的意旨或一个通情达理的人应有的理解时,应适当考虑到与事实有关的一切情况,包括谈判情况,当事人之间确立的任何习惯做法、惯例和当事人的其后任何行为”。不仅如此,第9条接着规定,“双方当事人业已同意的任何惯例和他们之间确立的任何习惯做法,对双方当事人均有约束力”,而且“除非另有协议,双方当事人应视为已默示同意对他们的合同或合同的成立,应适用双方当事人已经知道或理应知道的惯例”,只要“这种惯例,在国际贸易上,已为有关特定贸易所涉同类合同的当事人所广泛知道并为他们所经常遵守”。

值得注意的是,贸易惯例对合同的这种解释功能一般都包括两个方面:一方面,它可使合同中暧昧不明的内容得以明确,此即狭义的“解释”;另一方面,也包括对合同中不完整的内容加以补足,也即“补充”,是狭义的解释的延伸。例如,在上引美国《统一商法典》中,上述狭义的“解释”功能表现为贸易惯例可“使协议产生特定含义”,“补充”功能则表现为贸易惯例“对协议条款可起补充与限制作用”。

如前所述,关于贸易惯例对合同的解释的具体标准,向有“主观标准”与“客观标准”及“混合标准”之分,这种区别可以说是民法上意思表示解将理论中的意思主义理论与表示主义理论的一种反映。“主观标准”以探求当事人的“真意”为

---

〔270〕 何美欢:《香港合同法》(上册),北京大学出版社1995年版,第185页。

主旨，固惯例对合同的解释与补充一般须以当事人知悉惯例并同意用之解释为前提，法国与比利时[271]采用的是这一大陆传统的“意思主义”主张。“客观标准”则主张不问当事人意图如何，惯例可径直解释与补充合同，德国、奥地利[272]及英美法国家似乎多采用这一“表示主义”的标准；在此基础上，作为二者的折中，产生了一种“混合标准”。既主张惯例的功用在于探求当事人的“真意”，又允许采用惯例来补充合同，如瑞士、荷兰[273]就是这样。事实上，无论是主观标准还是客观标准在各国都不是绝对的，在大陆法国家民法中，往往都是采取折中主义立场，其区别仅在于偏重主观标准还是偏重客观标准。现代趋势似乎向客观标准或混合标准的方向发展。事实上，在法国与比利时，主观标准已准备受攻击，[274]而在上述几个国际公约中，显然都采纳了客观标准，或者更确切地说，是采用了“混合标准”。[275]

肯定贸易惯例为法律的学者们正是从贸易惯例往往可以不问当事人意图而径直解释与补充合同的客观标准立法出发，认为这体现出了贸易惯例的“规范性”(normative)效力，表明许多国家都承认了贸易惯例的法源地位。[276]但李(Filip De Ly)在深入分析了各国的有关立法后提出，各国的有关立法不过是将惯例作为解释合同的工具之一，并无意使之成为真正的法律渊源。[277]

贸易惯例与合同关系的最后一层表现在于：在效力上，合同明示条款优于且可排除未被纳入合同的贸易惯例。这是由前面论证的贸易惯例的任意性质所决定的。这一点中外皆然，毋庸赘述。对于已被纳入合同的贸易惯例，由于它已取得与其他合同明示条款同等的法律效力，因而不存在效力上孰先孰后的问题，而是合同条款自身的解释问题了。关于合同中的贸易惯例的解释，本文第三章第一节将予讨论。

---

〔271〕 Cf. Filip De Ly, International Business Law and Lex Mercatoria, 1992, pp. 145 - 158.

〔272〕 Ibid. at 138 - 141, 142 - 144.

〔273〕 Ibid. at 141 - 142, 144 - 145.

〔274〕 Ibid. at 145 - 158.

〔275〕 关于《联合国国际货物销售合同公约》所采用的合同解释标准，详见王贵国：《〈联合国国际货物销售合同公约〉的适用范围及其解释原则》，载《中国国际法年刊》1989年卷。

〔276〕 例如，王泽鉴提出，依据海牙统一买卖法公约，“通常合理之商事习惯，不待当事人约定，即可适用，其效力且优于本法规定。由此观之，此种商事习惯具有法源性质，实无疑义”。这里的“商事习惯”即为本文所指的“贸易惯例”，参见王泽鉴：《民法学说与判例研究》(第一册)，台大法学丛书(五)1978年第2版，第128页。

〔277〕 Filip De Ly, supra. at 158.

第三章　国际贸易惯例的解释与适用

第一节　国际标准合同的解释问题

“所谓解释，即系阐明当事人所做而不明白的意思表示。”[278] 由于语言本身及其传达工具的缺陷与障碍，法律与法律行为往往需要通过解释来明确其本意。[279] 国际贸易惯例无论是作为一种法律补充工具还是作为一种合同默示条款，都不可避免地存在一个解释问题。诚然，国际贸易惯例中发展最为成熟的部分，如 INCOTERMS，UCP 等本身已经是各种通行实践的统一解释，其解释上的问题不很突出。然而，国际贸易惯例中的国际标准合同与标准合同条款（一般契约条款），由予其形成过程与性质的特殊性，其解释也与国内标准合同[280] 一样，存在着不同于一般合同条款的解释的特殊问题，学者们对此也有所讨论。本节就标准合同解释上的一些共同性问题略作探讨。

一、标准合同解释方法上的特殊性

关于标准合同的基本解释方法，学者们的态度一般因其对标准合同性质的不同理解而异。[281] 有学者认为，标准合同条款具有“客观法”的性质，是法律的一种，因而其解释应依法规解释的方法进行；[282] 与此相反，有的学者则不认为标准合同条款具有客观法的性质，而不过是基于意思表示而成立的合同的内容，本质上仍是双方当事人的法律行为（意思表示行为）而形成的，故而其解释应依法律行为或合同的解释方法进行。[283] 换言之，在解释标准合同条款时，必须顾及个别交易当事人的具体的意见、真实的意思与当事人对于贸易惯例的理解情形等个别情况。此外，还有些学者虽然认为标准合同条款具有法律性，但认为应有其特殊

---

[278] 黄茂荣：《民法总则》，根植法学丛书编辑室，1982 年增订版。第 806 页。

[279] 同上。

[280] 严格地说，国际标准合同与国内标准合同之间，如同国际贸易惯例与国内贸易惯例之间，是存在区别的。国内标准合同更多见于日常生活之中，如水电、交通、通信等方面大量存在的服务性“大众契约”，而国际标准合同则多为买卖合同，前者往往更容易出现利益倾斜严重的“附合合同”的情况，而如前所述，现代国际标准合同多为示范性标准合同，而不是附合合同。关于“附合合同”，可参见黄越钦：《论附合契约》，载郑玉波主编：《民法债编论文选辑》（上），五南图书出版公司 1984 年版，第 288 ~ 404 页。

[281] 参见［日］米谷隆三：《约款法の理论》，有斐阁昭和 45 年初版，第 563 ~ 564 页；转引自刘春堂：《一般契约条款之解释》，载郑玉波主编：《民法债编论文选辑》（上），五南图书出版公司 1984 年初版，第 226 页及其注 11 至 14。

[282] 刘春堂：《一般契约条款之解释》，五南图书出版公司 1984 年初版，第 226 页。

[283] 同上。

的解释方法，即有别于一般的法律解释方法的方法。[284]

我们认为，一方面，作为国际贸易惯例的一种，国际标准合同与标准合同条款是一种广为人知并得到经常遵守的惯常做法或常用条款，具有相当的抽象性与普遍性．与变动不居而系偶然订入合同的“一次性”合同条款有着明显的差别；另一方面，从实证法的角度来看，前面已经证明，标准合同目前也很难说就是一种法律规范。它无疑是介于二者之间的一种特殊的社会行为规范。从其规范效力来看，显然它更接近于法律规范而与一般合同条款相去较远。基于此，我们认为，对国际标准合同的解释应采取类似于法律解释的方法，[285] 但同时，也须兼顾其特殊性，而辅以某些特殊的解释方法。

二、标准合同的解释原则

鉴于标准合同这种特殊性，我们认为，其解释应遵循客观解释、统一解释、限制解释与不利解释四大解释原则。传统法解释学一般认为，法律的解释与合同的解释在基本原则上完全对立：前者是客观的，旨在探求法律本身所具有的普遍的客观的意义；后者则是主观的，旨在寻求当事人主观上的真意。然而时至今日学者们大都认为法律的解释与合同的解释在本质上并无任何差异，二者都应该客观、合理地进行。[286] 标准合同作为一种特殊的行为规范，自然也应遵循客观解释的原则。也就是说，对标准合同的解释，应不受交易当事人个别的主观情事的影响，进而使其在不同的场合都有同样的理解，进而使其在未来不特定多数交易中具有统一的内容。不过，由于标准合同的产生、理论与价值判断等与国家制定法毕竟有所不同，因而两者虽然都遵循客观解释的方法，但其解释的基准却又有细微的区别：标准合同的解释应以该合同所通行的特定行业、特定地区或特定贸易中当事人的平均的、合理的理解可能性（Verstandnismoglichkeit）为基准，这与法律解释依据纯粹客观的解释方法是有所不同的。[287] 这主要是由于法律与标准合同在普遍性与抽象性程度方面的差异性使然：法律的效力一般及于域内的一切民众、一切地区；而标准合同往往仅存在于特定地区、特定行业或特定贸易。所以，对于海上保险合同条款、交易所的交易合同条款来说，因其一般适用于具有专门知识的商人（行家），应按该条款专业术语所含特殊意义来解释；而对于适用对象

---

[284] 刘春堂：《一般契约条款之解释》，五南图书出版公司1984年初版，第226页。

[285] 这种观点似乎也得到了许多国家的实践的支持。例如奥地利的一份权威性报告就说，人们经常会发现，在审判中，对贸易惯例解释采取的是与法律条文同样的规则，对于由国际组织编纂的贸易惯例，如INCOTERMS、UCP，更是如此。参见C. M. Schmitthoff, International Trade Usages. as a special issue of the NEWSLETTER of the Institute of lnternational Trade Law and. Practice, p. 33.

[286] 刘春堂：《一般契约条款之解释》，五南图书出版公司1984年初版，第227页.

[287] 同上。

范围为平民大众的人寿保险条款、一般住宅火灾保险条款来说,如其使用特殊的术语或文句(如医学上的用语),则只能按一般的日常用语的含义来解释。

国际商业社会编纂国际标准合同的全部目的,即在于避免分歧,促成统一。显然,对标准合同解释的不统一无疑是与编纂国际标准合同的初衷背道而驰的。为此,在解释国际标准合同时,尚须贯彻统一解释的原则。

显然,只有在解释权归于一个共同的法院,或者存在一个有权及时修订该规则的常设行政机构的情况下,像法律所要求的那样绝对统一的解释才有保障,〔288〕这对区域性国际公约,如《罗马条约》而言或许可以做到,但对国际标准合同来说无疑是不现实的。正如施米托夫所指出的,"就国际惯例而言,同……作为国际贸易自治法的一般标准相近就足够了"。〔289〕 这个一般标准也可以理解为上面提到的该标准合同所适用的特定地区、特定行业与特定贸易中的当事人的"平均的、合理的理解可能性"。

关于国际标准合同的解释上的歧异及其统一途径,马林托比(A. Malintoppi)做过比较深入的研究。他发现,国际标准合同在解释上的分歧,尽管从质上说是严重的,但从量上看却是有限的,可能仅仅涉及对其中一个或几个条款的解释。〔290〕 马氏进而探讨了防止分歧的种种方法,包括文本起草前、起草后以及文本修订的方法。其中,文本起草前的防止分歧方法包括定义(definitions)、解释性说明(explanatory statements)、会谈纪要(official minutes)及专家对译本的修订等。文本出台后的方法有互换资料(reciprocal imformation),批准前咨商(consultations preceding ratification)以及国内立法管制措施(control of municipal enactments)等。防止分歧的文本修订方法则指通过对原文本不适当与不清楚的条款进行修订,以有效防止未来分歧的发生。〔291〕

限制解释原则是指对标准合同的解释不能像对法律规范的解释一样,采用各种推理的解释方法,类推其他条款的规定而扩张其适用范围或补充其规定的欠缺,而只能以国家制定法或习惯法来补充,〔292〕也即应该有所限制。这主要是考虑到标准合同多导源于"交易强者"单方制定的定型化合同,往往片面维护交易强者的利益而有失均衡,与国家基于公平正义而制定的法律在内容上有所区别,如

---

〔288〕 Cf. C. M. Schmitthoff, The Law of Inte rnational Trade, It's Growth. Formulation and Operation", in Chia-Juì Cheng ed. C. M. Schmitthoff's Select Essays on International Trade Law, 1988, p. 155.

〔289〕 Cf. C. M. Schmitthoff, "The Law of International Trade, It's Growth, Formulation and Operation" in Chia-Jui Cheng ed. , C. M. Schmitthoff's Select Essays on International Trade Law, 1988, p. 155.

〔290〕 Cf. Antonio Malintoppi, "The Uniformity of Interpretation of International Conventions on Uniform Laws and of Standard Con tracts", in C. M. Schmitthoff ed. The Sources *of* the Law of International Trade, 1964, p. 128.

〔291〕 Ibid. pp. 130 – 137.

〔292〕 参见刘春堂:《一般契约条款之解释》,五南图书出版公司 1984 年初版,第 233 页.

允许对标准合同与法律解释一样作类推扩大解释,往往会违反合同的本来目的,而产生对交易弱者不利的结果,在合同为单方制成的情况下,后果将尤为严重。所以,如果海上保险条款有"基于船员过失之损害"之句,即应以解释为"船员过失"并不包括引水人的过失为宜。[293] 此外,限制解释还表现为同种限制或同一种限制原则(principle of ejusdem generis)。也就是说,当某一标准合同条款在列举某些具体事项之后,最后使用"其他"等等包括的文字予以概括规定时,对于这种包括的文句的含义,应解释为与前面所列举的具体事项属于同一种类。[294] 这种限制解释原则在解释风险责任条款时特别重要。

不利解释原则(contra proferenem)也是标准合同条款解释中常用的解释原则之一。罗马法上即有"有疑义应为表意者不利益之解释"的原则,在这里指在标准合同条款中,如有暧昧不清的文句或文字有疑义的时候,应从对提出该标准合同条款一方不利的角度出发来解释。这一原则自古以来即为许多国家的判例或学说所采纳,有的甚至视之为合同条款解释的特有原则。[295] 不过,晚近,不少学者提出对于这一原则的适用,不应绝对化,即只能在依其他一切解释方法都无法明了该有疑义用语的情况下,方可适用。[296] 质言之,它只能作为一种补充解释方法。因为合同条款因客观上不明了,或有双重意义,或有互相矛盾之处,以至于无法确定其意义时,如果依合同的一般原则,认定此为双方当事人的意思表示不合致(Dissens),从而应认定合同不成立或无效,显然会违背当事人的本意,对交易双方均为不利。所以,只能寻求一种使合同有效的解释方法。这正是不利解释原则的用武之地。[297] 进而,有学者甚至认为,即使在这种情况下,此原则也只能作补充适用,仅在下列条件下方有适用的余地:(1)这种不明了性对于法律确没有显著的妨害;(2)条款的混乱尚未达到无法辨认其合理意义的程度;(3)这种不明了处是附随的,并不影响契约的效力,或者依国家法律的补充仍无法使契约有效。[298]

此外,有人认为对不利解释原则不能一概而论,而应区别这种标准合同条款

[293] 刘春堂:《一般契约条款之解释》,五南图书出版公司1984年初版,第232页。
[294] 同上,第233页。
[295] 同上,第235页。
[296] 同上书,第235页。另见Antonio Boggiano,International Standard Contract,1991,p.88,N.188。
[297] 参见刘春堂:《一般契约条款之解释》,五南图书出版公司1984年初版,第235页及其注52。
[298] 刘春堂:《一般契约条款之解释》,五南图书出版公司1984年初版,第235~236页。

的形成形式，分别处理：对于“双方形成”[299]的标准合同条款，如有疑义，应归咎于双方，依解释合同的一般原则，解释为无效。[300] 也有人认为双方形成的标准合同条款与单方形成的并无质的差别，都是经济上占优势地位的当事方所设定、使用的。[301] 同样，对于“中立形成”的标准合同条款，也有这种对立的两种观点，理由也相同。[302] 有人还提出，标准合同条款的内容即使经过了行政机关认可，也可适用这一原则，因为行政机关的许可仅有公法上的意义，“并不含有拘束司法机关之意义”，因而司法机关如认为该标准合同条款仍有不明了或有矛盾的地方，自然可以依职权予以解释。[303]

不利解释原则在我国立法中也有所体现，如1995年通过的《保险法》的第30条就规定，“对于保险合同的条款. 保险人与投保人、被保险人或者受益人有争议时，人民法院或者仲裁机关应当作有利于被保险人和受益人的解释”。换言之，我国《保险法》中的不利解释原则是以“有利解释”的形式出现的。与此同时，我国有人也提出在这一原则的适用应以“应用其他解释原则不能正确解释”为前提。[304]

三、免责条款的解释问题

免责条款是标准合同中最容易产生利益倾斜与不公正的条款，也是争议最多的条款。为此，关于它的解释，有必要单独予以讨论。从理论上说，免责条款可分为两大类：[305]一类为合理的免责条款，即免除商业的合理经营所当然可以免除的责任的条款，如在通常火灾保险合同条款中的免除因地震或洪水所造成损害的赔偿责任的条款；另一类则是不合理的免责条款，即免除商业的合理经营所并非当然可以免除的法律上或契约上的责任的条款，如承运人在运输合同条款中设定的免除因其使用人的过失所造成的损害的责任的条款。合理的免责条款不仅符合商业经营的需要，也符合交易对方的“平均的合理的利益”，所以应确认其为有效——如果将地震、洪水所造成的火灾损害也包括在一般火灾保险责任范围之内，则势必扩大保险人的成本，使之难以发展；同时也会导致保险费的增加，而影

---

[299] 有学者提出，标准合同按其形成过程的不同，又可分成三类：由大企业或企业团体单方面所制定的为“一方形成”的标准合同；由交易双方协商制定的为“双方形成”的标准合同；由双方之外的公正第三方所制定的则为“中立形成”的标准合同，详见刘春堂：《一般契约条款之解释》，五南图书出版公司1984年初版，第222～223页。

[300] 刘春堂：《一般契约条款之解释》，五南图书出版公司1984年初版，第236页。

[301] 同上。

[302] 同上。

[303] 同上。

[304] 参见董开军主编：《〈中华人民共和国保险法〉释义》，中国计划出版社1995年版，第108～109页。

[305] 参见刘春堂：《一般契约条款之解释》，五南图书出版公司1984年初版，第237页。

响投保人的利益，最终导致对双方的不利。对于不合理的免责条款，学者们大都认为除非该免责条款已经违反了法律的强行规定，否则也不应一概否定其效力，只有当该条款使得双方的利益极不平衡时，方可否认。[306] 具体来说，在解释这种免责条款时，应根据其适用对象的专门知识水平与交涉能力等具体情况而区别对待。[307] 对于人寿保险或一般房屋火灾保险等标准保险合同条款，由于其适用对象为平民大众，不具备有关专门知识与交涉能力，固应从严解释，仅在其符合公众“平均的合理的利益”的情况下，才承认其效力；相反，对于海上保险、工厂火灾保险或海上运输保险等标准合同条款，由于其适用对象通常为具有专门知识的商人，他们对此条款比较熟悉，谈判能力较强，而且免责条款可能与其对低廉保险费或运费的需求也相符合，则自然应该从宽解释，不能随意否定其效力。[308] 显然，对于国际标准合同，属于后一种情况者居多，因多应作从宽解释。此外，学者们还主张，对于免责条款的解释，也不能因其形成形式的不同而区别对待，而只能根据其具体的免责内容，依上述原则判断其效力。[309]

四、对有关标准合同条款的仲裁裁决的司法审查问题

对仲裁裁决的实体部分不得进行司法审查，这是包括美国在内的许多国家都采用的一项原则，此原则并不因仲裁的标的物为对标准合同的解释还是“一次性”(one-off)的合同条款的解释而异。[310] 然而，英国的做法却与众不司。英国1979年的《仲裁法》规定，如果某标准合同是以英国法为准据法，则当事人只有在仲裁开始以后方可排除司法审查，而对其他国际合同则允许作这种事先排除。该条款的立法意旨据说在于保证这些标准合同的解释能得到统一。[311] 在英国看来，英国法是最先进、最适合国际贸易界需要的法律。从而，依据上述司法审查条款的规定，只要当事人选择了英国法，其标准合同的解释的国际统一化也就有了切实的保障。但连英国学者都承认，这种立法在实践上或许有效，但从法理上却实在是难以圆说的。[312]

五、标准合同解释的可上诉性问题

标准合同的解释是否可以上诉，即其是否具备可上诉性(revisibitity)，取决于

---

〔306〕 刘春堂：《一般契约条款之解释》，五南图书出版公司1984年初版，第237～238页。
〔307〕 同上。
〔308〕 同上。
〔309〕 刘春堂：《一般契约条款之解释》，五南图书出版公司1984年初版，第237～238页。
〔310〕 Cf. C. M. Schmitthoff, supra. International Trade Usages, p. 35.
〔311〕 Ibid., p. 35.
〔312〕 Ibid., p. 36.

对标准合同解释问题的性质的认定。按各国民事诉讼法,上诉审是法律审,只能针对法律问题提出。

如前所述,在各国法律中,那些适用于特定种类的交易的特定贸易惯例被认为是事实问题,不是法律问题,而因不可就此提起上诉。这一点对国际标准合同自然也是适用的。然而,这仅适用于标准合同的存在问题;对于标准合同的解释,学者们一般认为,那是法律问题,而不是事实问题。[313] 因为法律行为(合同)的解释旨在确定表示行为在社会上所应有的合理的意义,与确定某种自然事实是否存在不同,它本质上是依据解释的法则而对事实所作的法律的判断,即解释并非事实的确定,而是关于意义、价值、是非的判断,因而是法律问题,自可提起上诉。如前所述,标准合同的解释应类似于法律的解释,不仅在于探究当事人的真意,更要作客观的解释,进而谋求解释上的统一性,以确保交易的迅速与安全。如果这种解释不能客观统一地进行,而因审判法院的不同而有不同解释,以至于影响其效力,那必然与标准合同的作用与本质相背,而且有碍于法律秩序的安定。为此,更应确认标准合同的解释属于法律问题,是可以上诉的。[314]

第二节 国际贸易惯例的适用

"适用国际贸易惯例"这一提法,通常有两种含义:一种是指法院或仲裁庭运用国际贸易惯例调整、处理国际贸易关系的活动;另一种是指合同当事人在其合同中采纳某种贸易惯例的活动。在本节中,一般仅在前一种意义上使用这一提法。

国际贸易惯例的适用问题涉及面很广,甚至前面所论的解释问题也可纳入其中。本节只从各国理论与实践上对适用国际贸易惯例的态度、适用的具体途径、适用的条件与限制以及国际贸易惯例的查证等方面分别予以分析。

由于国际贸易惯例与现代商人法在各国的理论与实践上均密不可分,各国关于前者的理论与规定大都表现在对后者的研究与法律实践之中,所以,本节的许多有关讨论将把二者结合起来进行。

一、国际贸易惯例的可适用性

国际贸易惯例在审判与仲裁中究竟能否予以适用?也即国际贸易惯例究竟是否具备可适用性(applicability)?对于这一问题的态度,无论是从理论上还是从

[313] Cf. C. M. Schmitthoff, supra, at 19 - 20,

[314] 参见刘春堂:《一般契约条款之解释》,五南图书出版公司 1984 年初版,第 239 页。

法律实践上大都反映在各国对商人法的可适用性的态度之中。

从理论上看,对于这一问题,国外学术界大致有赞成说与反对说两种观点。反对说强调商人法的不完善性与不确定性。例如德国学者桑德洛克(O. Sandrock)认为,除少数领域外,目前还未从国际习惯,或为所有或多数国家所共有的法律原则中产生一套确定的规则,为解决国际贸易中出现的复杂问题提供明确的指导。因此,如果要求仲裁庭适用商人法的话,仲裁庭只能向别处寻找可适用的法律,即求助于各国的国内法律体系。而当各国国内法律体系存在矛盾冲突时,仲裁员就必须作出选择或发展新的方法。这就使依法律规则仲裁与依公允善良原则仲裁之间界限不明,依法仲裁的可预见性必将付之东流。因此,企业最好不要约定以现代商人法或其他不完善的规则作为合同准据法。[315] 与此同时,反对适用商人法的学者还从实证法学的角度出发,指出,商人法没有从任何国家权力机关中取得约束力,故不具备充分实在和有根据的制度,不能称其为一种法律秩序(legal order),因而也不宜作为解决争端的依据。曼(F. A. Mann)、马斯蒂尔(Mustill)与博伊德(Boyd)等人均持这种观点。[316]

相反,赞成说则提出商人法的约束力并不取决于国家权力机关制定和颁布的事实,而源自商业社会与国家权力机关承认它是一种自治形式的制度的事实。[317] 同时,他们实际上也并不否认国内法更具确定性,特别是当事人所协议选择的支配合同的某一特定国内法为仲裁员所熟悉时更是如此。他们强调指出,在许多案件中,如果当事人没有作出选择,而由仲裁员通过法律选择规则确定准据法的话,同样存在着许多问题。当仲裁员必须适用他并不熟悉的外国法律规则时,难度会更大,错误也会更多。反之,适用国际贸易惯例就可避免令人棘手的法律选择问题。[318] 赞成适用商人法的学者进而指出,即使仲裁员适用的是他所熟知的内国法,其裁决的不可预见性亦为难免。比如,有些国家的某些法律规则是专为调整国内关系而制定的,不适用于涉外案件。遇到这种情况,仲裁员势必在法律与公平之间进退两难,陷入窘境,远不如适用商人法更具确定性。[319]

事实上,持赞成说的理论又可分为两类,以戈德曼(B. Goldman)为代表的自治商人法理论认为,商人法是一种完全可以独立于国内法之外的自治的法律体

---

[315] Cf. Otto Sandrock, "Arbitration Between U. S. and West Germany Companies: An Example of Effective Dispute Resolution in International Busi ness Transactions" University of Pennsylvania Journal of International Business Law. Vol. 9, 1987, pp. 55 – 57.

[316] 参见韩健:《现代国际商事仲裁法的理论与实践》,法律出版社 1993 年版,第 251 页。

[317] Cf. Ole Lando, "The Lex Mercatoria in International Commercial Arbitration", 341. C. L. Q. (1985) p. 752.

[318] 参见韩健:《现代国际商事仲裁法的理论与实践》,法律出版社 1993 年版,第 251 ~ 252 页。

[319] Cf. Ole Lando, supra. pp. 753 – 754.

系。这种法律体系不仅有自己的实体法,而且发展了自己的冲突规则,即实体跨国规则(substantive transnational rules)。[320] 根据这种规则,商人法可以作为准据法而得到选择与直接适用。以施米托夫为代表的商人法理论则认为商人法不可能是独立的与完美的法律体系,它的存在不能完全独立于国内法体系之外,也不能完全排除选择国内法的必要性。[321] 质言之,他们主张将商人法的适用与国内法结合起来进行。

与这几种理论相应,在立法与实践上,各国关于商人法的适用,也主要有三种态度:

第一种最为激进,它允许当事人选择商人法,而不必参照任何国内法。这种做法显然是把商人法视为一种独立的法律体系,是戈德曼的自治商人法理论的反映,采取这种态度的典型国家是商人法理论最为发达的法国。法国 1981 年的《民事诉讼法典》第 1496 条规定,仲裁员必须按照当事人选择的"法律规则"裁决。如果当事人没有作出选择,则仲裁员应依其认为适当的法律规则裁决。该条文规定,在任何情况下,仲裁员都应考虑贸易惯例(usages ducommerce)。许多学者认为,法国法使用"法律规则"(rules of law)而没有使用"法律"(1aw)一词,其意义在于承认国内法以外的规则,如商人法等非国内法律规则具有法源地位。[322] 因此,多数学者认为,这一规定意味着法国法承认了商人法的适用。[323] 与此同时,法国法院的实践也表明,法国法承认依商人法或其他非国内法渊源所作出的仲裁裁决,即使是在当事人没有约定而是由仲裁庭直接适用这些规则的情况下也是如此。著名的 Norsolor 诉 Pabalk 一案就是很好的例证。1979 年,国际商会的仲裁庭裁决法国 Norsolor 公司违反了它与土耳其交易代理人 Pabalk Ticaret 公司之间的同,应清偿对方 80 万法郎。本案中,双方当事人既未选择适用的国内法,也未授权仲裁员按"公允及善良"原则裁决。结果仲裁庭既未适用法国法与土耳其法,也未适用奥地利《仲裁地》法。而是按照惯例与诚实信用原则作出了裁决。为此,Norsolor 向维也纳上诉法院起诉,请求撤销该裁决,理由是它只是按惯例与公平原则做出,而未适用任何国内法。Norsolor 指称"并不存在一种等同于法律体系的商人法。只有在可适用于有关代理协议的具体的法律规则没有排除适用商人法与善意原则时,才能适用这些原则"。维也纳上诉法院部分确认了 Norsolor 的

---

〔320〕 Filip De ly, International Business Law and Lex Mercatoria, 1992, pp. 210.

〔321〕 Ibid., pp. 209 – 210.

〔322〕 参见韩键:《现代国际商事仲裁法的理论与实践》,法律出版社 1993 年版,第 252 页及其注④。

〔323〕 See eg. Audit, "A National Codification of International commercial Arbitration", in Resolving Transnational Disputes, 1984, p. 133; David, Arbitration in International Trade, 1985, p. 342. Lando, supra. pp. 747 – 768.

上诉并判定仲裁员违反了《国际商会仲裁规则》第 13 条第 3 款，仲裁庭本应依冲突法确定可适用的国内法律来裁断，其按惯例来裁决是不许可的。由于仲裁员未能指出法国法与土耳其法在本案的主要问题上是一致的，上诉法院认为仲裁员有义务决定这两个国家的法律中哪一个应为准据法。然而奥地利最高法院却推翻了上诉法院的判决，而再次确认了原仲裁裁决，最高法院认为仲裁庭适用惯例裁决案件并未违反任何明确有效的强制性法律规则，仲裁庭也没有越权。[324] 法国巴黎地方法院不顾 Norsolor 的反对，签发了执行的命令。该院认为，仲裁员已适用了与《国际商会仲裁规则》第 13 条相一致的一种法律规则，因而不构成越权，也就不能拒绝其执行。[325] 可见，无论是法国法院还是奥地利的法院最后都承认贸易惯例的可适用性。同样，在前面提到的 Compania Valencia na de Cementos Port1and S. A. 诉 Primary Coal. Inc 一案中，法国巴黎上诉法院也拒绝撤销国际商会 1988 年根据贸易惯例而作出的裁决。除法国、奥地利以外，其他一些国家如丹麦、南斯拉夫等国的法律也允许当事人选择商人法或贸易惯例作为可适用的法律。[326]

第二种做法比较普遍，它是将贸易惯例或商人法与某一国内法体系结合起来适用的做法。这种做法可以算是施米托夫的商人法理论在各国的实践上的反映。如前所述，瑞士、土耳其、泰国、阿根廷、奥地利及我国台湾等地的民法典都赋予"习惯"或"惯例"以补充法律的作用。在其他许多国家，惯例则具有解释合同的作用。例如美国《统一商法典》第 1 ~ 205 节第（3）款规定，贸易惯例可赋赋予协议以特定的含义，对协议条款加以补充或限制。《法国民法典》第 1160 条规定："习惯上的条款，虽未载明于合同，解释时应补充之。"西班牙最高法院也曾提出："商事习惯或惯例——法律的客观规则——对于法律规范具有补充意义，即能反映缔约各方的意愿。"意大利的波卡（Pocar）教授的报告也指出，在意大利贸易惯例的功能在于弥补法律的漏洞。[327] 从我国有关立法来看，我国基本上也是采取国内法与惯例结合适用的方法。[328] 我国《涉外经济合同法》第 5 条与《民法通则》第 142 条分别规定了涉外经济合同与涉外合同的当事人"可以选择处理合同争议所适用的法律"，这种法律既可以是中国法，也可以是港澳地区法或外国法。至于是否可以选择适用商人法或国际贸易惯例，已如前述，法律与有关司法解释都没

---

[324] Berthold Goldman. The Applicable Law, ; General Principles of Law—the Lex Mercatoria in J. Lew de. Cont emporary Problems in International Arbitration, 1987, pp. 120 - 121.

[325] Filip De Ly. , Supra, pp. 256 - 257.

[326] 参见韩健：《现代国际商事仲裁法的理论与实践》，法律出版社 1993 年版，第 254 页及其注①。

[327] C. M. Schmitthoff, International Trade Usages, 1987, p. 19.

[328] 参见韩建：《现代国际商事仲裁法的理论与实践》，法律出版社 1993 年版，第 254 页。

有明定。在当事人没有选择适用的法律时,我国立法采取最密切联系原则确定合同准据法,在这种情况下显然是不可能指定商人法或国际贸易惯例为准据法的,因而也排除了单纯适用商人法或贸易惯例的可能。[329] 但是,我国立法并不完全否定国际贸易惯例与商人法的适用,承认它们可依中国法得到补充适用,即在合同准据法为中国法的情况下,如果我国法律与我国缔结或参加的国际条约没有有关规定时,可以适用"国际惯例"。[330]

第三种做法最为保守,它一般不承认依据商人法作出的裁决。采取这种方法的国家目前已十分鲜见。英国原来可以说是比较典型,但目前在实践上也已趋向灵活。传统上,英国法要求仲裁员按照支配争议的法律裁决争议,不论是英国法还是外国法。英国关于仲裁的法律不承认仲裁员依公约和善良原则或参照习惯商法作出的裁决。1978 年以前,英国曾多次撤销基于"公平"原则作出的裁决。1979 年的《仲裁法》颁布以后,英国法院对仲裁的司法审查权大大削弱,当事人可以通过书面协议排除法院司法审查其法律问题的权利。如果国际合同的当事人约定适用外国法,在争议发生前[331]也同样可预先订立排除英国法院审查的协议。不过,当事人是否可以直接选择商人法而且以同样的"排除协议"排除英国法院的审查呢? 这一点,英国法尚无明确的司法解释与判例。[332] 不过,近年无论是英国法学界的讨论还是司法部门的仲裁实践,也都表现出赞成采用公平裁决制度的倾向。[333] 一个突出的例证是,英国上诉法院 1978 年对于鹰星保险公司诉玉瓦尔保险公司(Eagle Star Insurance Co. Ltd. v. Yval Insurance Co. Ltd.)一案所作的判决一反过去的判例,使依据公平原则作出的外国裁决可以在英国得到承认与执行。[334] 近十年后,英国上诉法院 1987 年对于德国油井勘探与建筑有限公司诉卡玛国家石油公司(Dentsche Schachtbanund Tiefboargesell Schaft m. b. H. v. Ras AL Khaimah National Oil Co.)一案所作的判决使英国的司法实践向承认商人法的适用的方向又迈进了一步。[335] 上诉法院在该案判决中提出,完全以"国际上公认的法律原则"作出的外国仲裁并不违背英国的公共秩序,因而在英国可以得到承认

---

〔329〕 参见韩健:《现代国际商事仲裁法的理论与实践》,法律出版社 1993 年版,第 254 页。

〔330〕 关于"国际惯例"在我国的适用,详见本文第四章。

〔331〕 如前所述,这一点对标准合同不适用。对于标准合同,只能在仲裁开始后方可排除法院对其实体问题的司法审查。

〔332〕 关于英国的态度及其转变过程,详见韩健:《现代国际商事仲裁法的理论与实践》,法律出版社 1993 年版,第 254 ~ 255 页。

〔333〕 B. Goldman. The Applicable Law: General Principles of Law—the Lex Mercatoria in J. Lew ed. Contemporary Problems in International Arbitrationf, 1986, p. 118.

〔334〕 参见徐国建:《现代商人法论》,载《中国社会科学》1993 年第 3 期。

〔335〕 同上。

与执行。

看来,尽管各国有关立法与实践相去甚远,但总的趋势似乎是朝着接纳与承认商人法及国际贸易惯例的适用的大方向的。各国一致意识到,国际贸易中已形成与发展起一些具有特别性质的规则、惯例与习惯,乃是不可否认、不容忽视的客观事实,因而对它们的接纳与采用可能也只是一个时间与发展中的问题。显然,这方面的法律实践,商人法理论最发达的法国走在最前面,商人法作为一种自治的法律体系已得到了肯定与适用;英国法向来保守但亦已起步;大多数国家则尚停留在将其与国内法结合适用的阶段,既不排斥贸易惯例的适用,也不完全割断其与国内法的脐带,而一般使之处于补充国内法的地位。二者相对独立,但又联结在一起,总的趋势是逐步承认商人法与贸易惯例的可适用性与自治性。正如施米托夫在详细考察了各国报告人关于国际贸易法源的报告后所总结的,“在国际贸易法发展的现阶段,自治法与国内法相互补充,倾向赞成自治法者占有明显的优势”。[336]

二、国际贸易惯例的适用途径

与国际贸易惯例适用的理论与立法态度相应,在实践中,国际贸易惯例的具体适用途径主要有两种,一种是直接适用的途径,另一种是间接适用的途径。

所谓“间接适用”是指国际贸易惯例或现代商人法通过合同的准据法而间接获得适用。很显然,这种适用是前述将商人法与国内法结合起来适用的立场的具体体现,是视商人法为不完全脱离国内法体系的施米托夫的商人法理论的实践印证,同时也是目前世界上多数国家适用商人法与贸易惯例的现实途径。例如,按照我国《涉外经济合同法》及有关司法解释,当事人如选择了中国法律,而在中国法律没有有关规定的情况下,法院就可以适用国际惯例。又如前述,在美国、西班牙、意大利、日本等许多国家也都确立了国际贸易惯例在国内法体系中的这种可以“补充适用”的法律地位。这种间接适用在实践上十分普通,兹不赘述。

“直接适用”则指国际贸易惯例或现代商人法不通过合同的准据法而得到适用的情形。这种适用途径由于不需经过冲突法规则指向的某国国内法而直接获得适用,故称为“直接适用”途径。在理论上,这种适用一般以国家承认商人法为独立于国内法的自治法律体系为前提。如前所述,在实践中,已为法国、奥地利、丹麦、南斯拉夫等国家所承认。它又包括两大类,一类是依当事人选择而得到直接适用,另一类则是指根据合同自身的联络因素而得到适用。

---

[336] C. M. Schmitthoff, The Law of International Trade. Its Growth. Formulation and Operation, in Chia-Jui Cheng ed. Clive M. Schmitthoff's Select Essays on International Trade Law, 1988, p. 167.

所谓依选择直接适用是指在当事人明示或默示选择适用商人法或某贸易惯例的情况下,法院或仲裁庭适用商人法或该贸易惯例的情形。这种适用途径又包括两种情形:

第一种是当事人明示选择商人法或惯例作为合同的准据法。当事人既可以在合同缔结时,也可在合同缔结后,甚至还可以在合同争议发生以后、仲裁程序进行中间作出这样的选择。[337] 从国际合同与商事仲裁的实践来看,合同当事人常常并不笼统地选择"商人法",而是明确地在其协议中规定适用诸如一般法律原则、贸易惯例等商人法的具体组成部分。[338] 例如,国际商会第5904号仲裁裁决就是如此。该案当事人授权仲裁员根据通行于国际商事活动中的原则与惯例作出裁决。[339]

第二种依选择直接适用途径指当事人默示选择商人法作为合同准据法而得到适用的情形。这种情形的前提是当事人既未选择适用的国内法,也未明示选择适用商人法,而只是有意选择适用商人法。至于这种默示选择具体情形,学者们的理解宽窄不一,但一般不外乎如下三种:[340] (1)许多学者认为,当事人授权仲裁庭依"公平与善意"(ex a equo et bono)仲裁或作为"友好仲裁人"(amiable compositeurs)进行仲裁时,往往被认为是默示选择适用商人法。因为这种特别授权的仲裁与适用商人法是紧密联系的,甚至可以说公平或友好仲裁就意味着灵活适用商人法作出裁决。[341] 在国际仲裁实践中,不少仲裁裁决就是基于这种理由而依据商人法作出的,其中比较重要的有国际商会第1850(72)、3267(79)、3540(80)、3267(84)号仲裁裁决以及一临时仲裁庭于1977年11月3日所作的英国梅柯马公司诉比利时三M公司(Mechema Ltd. C. S. A. v. Mines, Minerais et Metaux)一案的仲裁裁决。(2)还有些学者甚至认为,当事人未议定某国际合同的法律适用问题却订有将合同争议提交国际仲裁的协议这一事实本身就意味着他们不愿使其合同受一国国内法的支配,实际上也就是默示选择商人法来支配他们之间的合同关系。不过,这种主张似乎未得到国际商事仲裁实践的支持。[342] 例如,在国际商会第1337(65)号仲裁案中,申诉人声称合同当事人缔结了将合同争议提交国际仲裁的协议便意味着排除了国内法的适用,但仲裁庭没有接受这一观点。[343]

---

[337] 参见徐国建:《现代商人法论》,载《中国社会科学》1993年第3期。

[338] 同上。

[339] Cf. Filip De Ly, supra. p. 254.

[340] 参见徐国建:《现代商人法论》,载《中国社会科学》1993年第3期。

[341] 同上。

[342] 同上。

[343] 同上。

(3)有学者甚至提出，当事人的“消极法律选择”(negative rechtswahl)可视为对商人法的默示选择。这里所谓均消极法律选择就是指当事人不在合同中明示选择合同的准据法。这种消极的不作为一般被认为当事人不愿使其合同受某一国内法律的支配，因而默示地选择了商人法。例如，在法国的Fougerolle诉黎巴嫩银行关于佣金一案的执行确认中，法国法院指出，本案仲裁员根据当事人在合同中的默示而适用跨国惯例是合法有效的，应予执行。随后，法国最高法院再次肯定其程序的合法性。[344] 此外，国际商会第1641(69)、4810(86)号仲裁裁决也是这种默示选择适用国际贸易惯例的例证。[345]

所谓依合同的联结因素而直接适用通常是在当事人未选择适用商人法或贸易惯例，而因为合同本身联结因素而得到适用的情形。它往往是在当事人来选择准据法，又无法确定适用某一国内法；或者由于有关不同国家国内法的适用将导致截然相反的结果而不可能予以适用的情况下而适用现代商人法或贸易惯例的。[346] 在施米托夫的一项调查研究中，比利时的范·赫特(Van Houtte)教授的书面报告称如果国际贸易惯例是与争议有最密切联系的法律环境中的法律的话，国际私法是允许仲裁员直接运用国际贸易惯例的。荷兰的报告也得出了同样的结论。[347] 在仲裁实践中，依合同联结因素而直接适用国际贸易惯例或商人法的案件也不乏其例，其中重要的包括国际商会第2291(75)、2375(75)、3131(79)、3572(80)、4338(84)、5065(86)、5321(87)号仲裁裁决。[348] 前文提到的Ncrsolor诉Pabalk一案也可以算是依合同联结因素(“国际性”)而适用贸易惯例的一例。[349]

从理论上说，这种依合同自身联络因素而直接适用的途径与依当事人默示选择而直接适用的途径是有区别的，前者所依据的是纯客观的标准来确定适用商人法或贸易惯例的，后者则主要根据当事人隐含在合同中的真实意图来确定适用商人法或贸易惯例的，采用的是主观标准。然而，在实践上，要划清二者的界限显然是困难的。比如前已述及，接某些学者的观点，当事人消极的法律选择即为对商人法或贸易惯例的默示选择。这样，在当事人未选择合同准据法的情况下，依默示选择的直接适用与依合同联结因素的直接适用就可能导致某种重叠或者竞合。不过，从仲裁实践的角度来看，对这两种直接适用方式作严格的区分似乎并没有多大意义。

---

[344] Cf. FiLip De Ly, supra. p. 255.
[345] 参见徐国建:《现代商人法论》,载《中国社会科学》1993年第3期。
[346] 同上。
[347] Cf. C. M. Schmitthoff, supra. International Trade Usages, p. 46.
[348] 参见徐国建:《现代商人法论》,载《中国社会科学》1993年第3期。
[349] 同上。

除了依国内法而“间接适用”与不经国内法而“直接适用”这两条正式的适用途径外，按一些国际商事仲裁立法与规则的规定，国际贸易惯例还可以由仲裁机关依职权“参考适用”。例如，1961 年《欧洲国际商事仲裁公约》第 7 条第 1 款规定，无论适用当事人指定的法律还是适用仲裁员确定的准据法，“仲裁员都应考虑到合同条款与贸易惯例”《联合国国际贸易法委员会仲裁规则》第 33 条第 3 款以及《国际商会仲裁规则》第 13 条第 5 款也都有类似规定。按这种规定，仲裁庭有权也有义务，“在任何时候”参照适用贸易惯例的有关规则而不需顾及当事人的意愿。参照适用与补充适用有明显的区别：参照适用时惯例仅供参考，不必完全遵守，而补充适用一旦确定适用，就应完全遵照惯例的规定办理，不能随意更改取舍；补充适用只在法律的正式渊源（法律与条约）没有规定时方可适用，而参考适用可在“任何时候”实施。从这一意义上讲，参照适用也可算作一种“直接适用”方法，尽管严格地说，这并不能算是一种独立的适用途径。

从目前已公开发表的国际商事仲裁裁决来看，国际贸易惯例与现代商人法的适用大多数是通过与国内法结合的间接途径得以适用的。例如，雷伊（Lew），在其 1981 年出版的《国际商事仲裁的适用法律》一书中总结道，“很少有仲裁裁决是完全依据无固定标准的商业习惯和贸易惯例而作出的”。[350] 德国学者洛伦兹（Lorenz）在分析了约 50 个国际商事仲裁裁决后也指出，大多数裁决是通过传统的冲突法的指引而适用国内法作出的。[351] 达泽（Dasser）在其博士论文中研究过 50 年国际商事仲裁裁决，发现其中只有一个是完全依据商人法作出的，而有 20 多个是同时以现代商人法与一个或多个国家的国内法或国际公约为依据而作出的。[352] 英国的马斯蒂尔（Mutill）的统计表明，到 1987 年为止，总共有 25 个国际商事仲裁是依据现代商人法作出的。[353] 尽管已发表的国际商事仲裁裁决数量有限，但上述关于商人法与贸易惯例适用的统计与前述各国对商人法及贸易惯例的态度与立场是基本吻合的。

三、对适用国际贸易惯例的限制

尽管各国越来越重视发挥国际贸易惯例的功能，在仲裁实践上国际贸易惯例的适用也日见频繁，但各国普遍认为，对国际贸易惯例的适用应施以必要的限制。

一般来说，对国际贸易惯例适用上的限制来自两个方面。一方面，国际贸易

---

〔350〕 J. Lew, Applicable Law in 1nternational Commercial Arbitration, 1978, p. 466.
〔351〕 参见徐国建：《当代商人法论》，载《中国社会科学》1993 年第 3 期。
〔352〕 同上。
〔353〕 同上。

惯例须受国内强行法的限制。如前所述,国际贸易惯例是在当事人意思自治的权限范围内发展起来的,而当事人的意思自治也只能在国家强行法以外的范围内进行。因此,国际贸易惯例不能与国家的强行法相抵触,否则无效。诚然,在国际贸易活动中,当事人可以根据意思自治原则,最大限度地将国际贸易惯例纳入其合同,而使后者受制于前者,但这仍不能完全排斥国内实证法的基本原则对其合同关系的制约,因为各国为确保标准合同等贸易惯例的公平合理,对它们的适用都各有严格的要求,国际贸易当事人只有使他们的合同关系符合国内实证法,方为合法有效。[354] 譬如,以毒品、武器为标的的合同,在许多国家的国内法上是无效的。[355] 依我国有关司法解释[356],不具备法定主体资格的合同当事人签订的合同,双方当事人恶意串通损害国家、集体或第三方利益的合同都是无效的。而 ULIS 第 8 条与 CISG 第 4 条则规定,公约不涉及国际贸易惯例的有效性问题,换言之,其最终是否合法有效,端视各国国内法的规定。当然,各国在规范国际贸易惯例时,有必要顾及国际贸易规则的一般标准,“按照国际通行规则”办事,从而确保它们在国际范围内得到统一适用,使国内经济更好地与世界经济对接。

另一方面,国际贸易惯例适用还须受公共秩序(public order)的限制。这又分两种情况:如果当事人之间的贸易合同受制于一外国法律,则贸易惯例不得与该国法律所规定的公共秩序相抵触;如果当事人之间的贸易合同受一般法律原则(或“商人法”)的支配,则国际贸易惯例的适用以不违反这种一般法律原则中的强制性原则以及公共秩序(即所谓的“跨国公共秩序”)为前提条件。[357] 不过,我国也有学者提出,以公共秩序排除国际惯例的立法在世界上是罕见的,因为各国一般认为运用惯例不会损害公共秩序,而一旦当事人选择了某一国际惯例,它就取得了高于国内法的效力,即使其适用有可能导致损害公共秩序的后果,也不能借国内立法限制适用。[358] 我们赞同国际贸易惯例一般不会危及公共秩序的提法,因为,如前所述,它是在与国家没有利害关系的领域中发展起来的。但如同这不能排除其有不合理的可能性一样,也不能因此而绝对否定其有损及公共秩序的可能。由于各国历史、文化及经济、社会的巨大差异性,在一地一时为合情、合理、

---

〔354〕 参见李双元主编:《市场经济与当代国际私法趋同化问题研究》,武汉大学出版社 1994 年版,第 66 页。

〔355〕 参见刘凤菊:《试析 1980 年维也纳公约关于贸易惯例效力的规定》,载《中南政法学院学报》1992 年第 3 期。

〔356〕 参见最高人民法院《关于适用〈涉外经济合同法〉若干问题的解答》中“关于无效涉外经济合同的确认问题”部分的规定。

〔357〕 参见李双元主编:《市场经济与当代国际私法趋同化问题研究》,武汉大学出版社 1994 年版,第 66 页。

〔358〕 参见胡振杰:《国际惯例立法修订的法律思考》,载《法学》1993 年第 2 期。

合法,成为“惯例”性的东西,到另一地另一时很可能是完全无法接受的。因而,我们认为,国际贸易惯例损害公共秩序的可能性是存在的。至于惯例一经选择即优于国内法的提法,笔者不敢苟同。诚然,经当事人协议采用后,贸易惯例自然可以取得优于国内任意法的效力,然而如前所述,贸易惯例不能与国内强行法相抵触,否则无效。显然国内强行法在效力上总是优于贸易惯例的,后者不可能高于前者。换言之,如果只针对国内任意法而言,此说则可以成立;若系针对所有国内法而言,此说则显然是难以成立的。

事实上,就是商人法理论的代表人物也都承认商人法的适用可能因主权国家的公共秩序而失效或受其限制。[359] 他们中有的还对公共秩序限制问题作了很细致深入的研究。他们首先提出了“国内公共秩序”与“国际公共秩序”的区别,认为,“国际公共秩序”仅限于有关国家真正根本性的法律秩序观念(really fundamental conceptions of legal order)问题。[360] 进而,有些学者提出了“第三种公共秩序”即“真正的国际公共秩序”或“跨国公共秩序”的概念。认为这种公共秩序的规则包括自然法则的规则、普遍的公平原则、国际公法中的强制性规定和为文明国家所取认的一般法律原则。[361] 在国际商事仲裁中,国际贸易惯例(商人法)的适用仅受“跨国公共秩序”的限制,而不受国内公共秩序甚至国际公共秩序的限制。[362] 在我们看来,他们所提出的这种公共秩序内容并不明确。实践上也没有什么国家去区别“国际公共秩序”与“真正的国际公共秩序”,更无国家根据1958年《纽约公约》作这种区分。[363] 而且所谓的“国际公共秩序”的根据仍是国内的,其成立与适用仍需国内法的认可或作出解释。[364] 所以,这种区分在目前似乎仍只有理论上的意义,在实践上很难实行。

除了国内强行法与公共秩序的一般限制外,按许多国家关于惯例或习惯可补充法律漏洞的立法规定,国际贸易惯例的适应还须受国内任意法的制约,即只有在国内任意法都没有相关规定的情况下,贸易惯例方得适用。

当然,对于这一立法,不应孤立地去理解,而应结合其他国内立法或国际公约

---

〔359〕 See eg. C. M. Schmitthoff, The Unification of the Law of International Trade, in Chia-Jui-Cheng ed. supra. p. 209.

〔360〕 P. Sanders, Trends in the Field of International Commercial Arbitration, Recueil des Cours de L Academic de droit international (《国际法学会讲演集》), Hague, 1975 I. p. 224. 转见韩健:《现代国际商事仲裁法的理论与实践》,武汉大学出版社1994年版,第347页。

〔361〕 例如戈德曼(B. Goldman)就作如是主张。参见韩健:《现代国际商事仲裁法的理论与实践》,武汉大学出版社1994年版,第348页及其注①。

〔362〕 Cf. Filip De Ly, supra, p. 215.

〔363〕 参见韩健:《现代国际商事仲裁法的理论与实践》,武汉大学出版社1994年版,第347、348页.

〔364〕 参见韩健:《现代国际商事仲裁法的理论与实践》,武汉大学出版社1994年版,第348页。

一并来考察。如果孤立地去理解,必然会得出在这些国家,所有的惯例必然在效力上低于国内任意法的错误结论。而这与事实往往不符。因为,如前所述,按许多国家国内立法及一些国际公约的规定,惯例可以用来解释甚至直接补充合同,而对当事人产生拘束力。[365] 例如,美国《统一商法典》,第1~205节第3款规定,贸易惯例可"使合同条款产生特定含义,并对合同起补充与限制作用"。《联合国国际货物销售合同公约》第8条则规定,在解释当事人意图时,应适当考虑到"当事人之间确立的任何习惯做法、惯例……"第9条则规定,有关特定贸易所涉同类合同的当事人所广泛知道并经常遵守的惯例,应视为已获得当事人的默示同意而可以直接适用于他们的合同或合同的成立,其补充功能更为明显。如果上述规定惯例或习惯可以补充法律漏洞的国家同时有关于惯例或习惯可以解释与补充合同的法律规定,或者他们已成为该公约的成员国的话,那么,在这些国家中,"惯例"就具有两种功能,一为补充法律,二为解释与补充合同。[366] 可解释与补充合同的惯例将获得优于国内任意法的效力而得到先期适用。只有不具备法定的条件,从而不能用来解释与补充合同的惯例才只能在国内任意法都没有相关规定的条件下得到适用。换言之,在具体合同争议中可以用来解释与补充合同的惯例实际上不必待到国内任意法都没有相关规定后方可适用,而是可能在国内任意法之前得到优先适用。这就从事实上将可能补充法律的惯例限制在那些不具备直接解释与补充合同条件,因而不构成合同条款的明示或默示的组成部分的惯例之内。

此外,由于惯例的任意性质,当事人在合同中已经明示排除的贸易惯例一般也不能适用于他们之间由该合同所引起的争议。

四、国际贸易惯例的证明问题

要适用国际贸易惯例,必须先确认国际贸易惯例的存在,这就涉及国际贸易惯例的"查明"或"证明"的问题。至于其证明途径,即由法官或仲裁员依职权(ex efficio)主动查明,还是由当事人举证证明,则一般取决于诉讼所在地的法律对国际贸易惯例的性质的认定——如果该贸易惯例被认定为"法律"(规范性贸易惯例),则法官可依职权(ex effjcio)主动查明,因为法官应知道法律(jura novit curia);反之,如果该贸易惯例仍停留在事实阶段(事实性贸易惯例),则当事人应举证证明其存在。据此,在西班牙与伊拉克,关于INCOTERMS的内容不必当事人举证,而可由法官径直查明,而关于中国或斯德哥尔摩的港口惯例,则通常由当事

〔365〕 详见本文第二章第二节。
〔366〕 在我国,"国际惯例"即具有这两种功能,详见本文第四章。

人证明。

那么，对于国际贸易惯例中大量存在的契约式贸易惯例，究竟应如何查证？我们认为，这种贸易惯例大都仍处在出事实性贸易惯例向规范性贸易惯例转化的过程之中，从本质上说，仍属于“事实”的范畴，而尚未上升至“法律”的高度。因而一般来说，当事人应负举证责任。正如Bonell考察了几个主要法系的做法后指出的采用第一种方法（指当事人证明方法），是世界上通用的。〔367〕美国《统一商法典》则明确规定，贸易惯例“是否存在及其适用范围，应作为事实问题加以证明”。〔368〕如果该惯例的存在为法官或仲裁员与双方当事人所已确知。则不一定要进行举证与审查。〔369〕特别是其中的跨国成文规则，不仅经过长期反复实践，而且经过了权威性商业组织的精心编纂，成为世界通行、众所周知的成文惯例，对此，法官或仲裁员适用时，当可免除当事人举证证明其存在的义务。当然，对于不成文的贸易惯例，当事人的举证证明其存在仍是有必要的。〔370〕与此同时，在多数大陆法国家，法官一般都可以主动查明有关惯例的存在。

至于具体的查证途径，各国的做法有所不同。在英美法系国家中，事实性贸易惯例通常由专家证人来证明。因此，如果在英国的法院发现像循环信用证是怎么回事这样的问题，劳氏银行（Llyd's Bank）的总裁就可能会作为专家证人而被召出庭，由他对法院解释银行业内的有关习惯做法。〔371〕在其他国家，这一程序就大不相同。常见的做法是，如果争议涉及事实性贸易惯例是否存在的问题，法院会征询有关的商会的意见。例如，瑞典法院常常敦请瑞典商会就当事人所指称的贸易惯例出具一份报告（res ponsum）。为此，商会还专门成立了一个“报告委员会”（Responsum Councíl），由一名法官及各个行业的专家组成。商会的这种报告往往具有相当的分量，尽管法院并不受其约束。类似的法院征询各商会的意见的做法在德国、芬兰与其他国家亦都存在。〔372〕

普通法系国家与大陆法系国家在事实性贸易惯例的查证方面还有一个重大的区别，那就是这么一个众所周知的事实：前者采用的是对抗制的程序而后者使用的是审问制的程序。

此外，意大利与德国的查证方式也许值得特别介绍，它们都大大简化了查证程序，提高了效率。按意大利1942年《民法典》序言部分第9条规定，除非有相反

---

〔367〕 Bianca-Bonell. supra. p. 111.

〔368〕 参见美国《统一商法典》，第1～205节第（2）款。

〔369〕 参见程德钧等编著：《国际惯例与涉外仲裁》，中国青年出版社1993年版，第13页。

〔370〕 参见程德钧等编著：《国际惯例与涉外仲裁》，中国青年出版社1993年版，第14页。

〔371〕 C. M. Schmitthoff, International Trade Usages, 1987, p. 20.

〔372〕 Id. p. 21.

的证据存在,公布在有关方面的主管机构的官方出版物上的惯例可以推定其存在。这些出版物是由工商部组建的常设委员会编辑出版的,在部里以及各省执行公共职能的商业、工业与农业商会处均可见到。这种正式公布的贸易惯例具有法定的证明力而不需当事人个别举证。反之,对于非经官方出版物正式承认的贸易惯例则只能通过一般证明程序予以查证。[373] 德国的商事法院一般由一名法官与两名陪审员组成。按德国《法院组织法》商事法院应根据经验与知识判断贸易惯例是否存在。然而,实践表明,作为一项规则,主审法官通常会向某一相应的商会征得一份报告,该报告将详细说明其结论的依据所在。法院经过审查这种报告后,也可以决定贸易惯例的存在与有效性。[374]

值得注意的是,法院与仲裁的查证程序往往也有所不同,因为如前所述,不少而且越来越多的仲裁立法与仲裁规则明确允许甚至要求仲裁员在进行裁决时,应考虑到有关贸易惯例。因此,仲裁员有更多责任了解、掌握与主动查明有关贸易惯例。因而往往不需要当事人证明贸易惯例的存在。这主要是因为各国际商事仲裁机构的仲裁员多为业内专家,对贸易惯例大都比较熟悉。但是,即使如此,对于那些仲裁员所不熟悉的,比较少见、比较偏僻的地方性与行业性的贸易惯例,则仍需当事人举证证明。

第四章　中国有关国际惯例立法评析

我国关于“国际惯例”的立法主要表现为《涉外经济合同法》等法律及有关司法解释。与此同时,由于我国已经批准了《联合国国际货物销售合同公约》(以下简称《公约》)而成为其缔约国,《公约》已成为中国法律的有机组成部分。[375] 因此,《公约》中有关惯例的规定也应视为我国的有关立法的一种表现形式。关于这些立法,本文前面已有所涉及,特别是对其中的《公约》已有较多评论。所以,这里主要就有关的国内立法,同时结合《公约》的规定,对“国际惯例”的内涵、性质及其适用问题略作评析。

一、有关“国际惯例”的国内法

迄今为止,我国关于“国际惯例”的国内立法主要为五部法律及两个司法解

---

〔373〕 C. M. Schmitthoff, International Trade Usages, 1987, pp. 21 – 22

〔374〕 ld. p. 22.

〔375〕 参见王贵国:《〈联合国国际货物销售合同公约〉的适用范围及解释原则》,载《中国国际法年刊》1989 年卷。

释。1985年,我国的《涉外经济合同法》第5条率先规定,“合同当事人可以选择处理合同争议所适用的法律。当事人没有选择的,适用与合同有最密切联系的国家的法律”“在中华人民共和国境内履行的中外合资经营企业合同、中外合作经营企业合同、中外合作勘探开采自然资源合同,适用中华人民共和国律”“中华人民共和国法律未作规定的,可以适用国际惯例”。次年,《民法通则》第8章第142条规定,“涉外民事关系的法律适用,依照本章的规定确定”“中华人民共和国缔结或者参加的国际条约同中华人民共和国的民事法律有不同规定的,适用国际条约的规定,但中华人民共和国声明保留的条款除外”“中华人民共和国法律和中华人民共和国缔结或者参加的国际条约没有规定的,可以适用国际惯例”。第150条进而规定,“依照本章规定适用外国法律或者国际惯例的,不得违背中华人民共和国的社会公共利益”。1992年的《海商法》第268、276条与1995年的《民用航空法》的第184、190条的规定与《民法通则》的上述两条规定几乎完全一样,只是少了《民法通则》第142条第1款的规定。1995年颁布的《票据法》第96条也有关于国际条约优先及国际惯例补缺的涉外法律适用规定,所不同的是:一方面,它所规定“适用国际惯例”的条件,是“本法”和中华人民共和国缔结或者参加的国际条约没有规定,而未采用通用的“中华人民共和国法律”这一措辞;另一方面,它也没有规定关于适用国际惯例时的公共秩序保留问题。

此外,我国还有两个最高人民法院的司法解释也规定了适用国际惯例问题,最高人民法院1987年10月19日发布的《关于适用〈涉外经济合同法〉若干问题的解答》之二(五)项规定,“当事人协议选择的或者人民法院按照最密切联系原则确定的处理合同争议所适用的法律,是指现行的实体法,而不包括冲突法规范和程序法”。其第(九)项规定,“在应当适用我国法律的情况下,如果我国法律对于合同争议的问题未作规定的,可以适用国际惯例”。最高人民法院同日发布的《关于审理涉港澳经济纠纷案件若干问题的解答》之三第(二)项规定,“审理涉港澳经济纠纷案件,在实体法方面,如果适用我国法律时,应按照民法通则的有关规定和涉外经济合同法、中外合资经营企业法及其实施条例、外资企业法等涉外的法律、行政法规办理。我国法律未作规定的,可以适用国际惯例”。

我国上述涉外法律与司法解释中关于可以适用“国际惯例”的规定受到了海内外“现代商人法”的倡导者们的热烈欢迎与充分肯定。我国台湾地区学者柯泽东称赞该规定做到了“国际化”“相当进步”;[376]德国的霍恩(N. Horn)则认为,这

---

〔376〕 参见柯泽东:《从国际私法方法论探讨契约准据法发展新趋势——并略评两岸现行法》,载《台大法学论丛》1996年第23卷第1期。

种规定不仅表明了中国立法者对于国际公认的法律意识的友好态度,而且也是中国在对于现代商人法这一概念的解释方面所作出的一项重要贡献。[377] 但国内学者则对这些规定深感困惑,聚讼纷纭。主要的问题有四:第一,这里的"国际惯例"的含义是什么,是冲突规则中的国际惯例,还是实体规则中的国际惯例?第二,这里的"国际惯例"的性质是什么,是国际法?国内法?还是别的什么规范?第三,这种国际惯例在我国适用时,应具备什么条件?以公共秩序排除国际惯例适用的立法究竟是否合理?第四,我国有关国际惯例立法与《公约》有关规定之间是什么样的关系?下面结合前文的论述,对这些问题逐一进行探讨。

二、"国际惯例"的含义

我国上述立法中的"国际惯例"的含义问题是我国民法学与国际私法、国际经济法学者争论最多的相关问题之一。有学者提出,这里的"国际惯例"只能是冲突法上的国际惯例;[378] 有学者则反之,认为它只能是实体法上的国际惯例;[379] 还有学者则认为二者兼有,即既包括冲突法上的国际惯例,也包括实体法上的国际惯例。[380] 我们赞成第二种观点,认为这里的"国际惯例"指的是实体"法"意义上的国际惯例。其理由有三:

第一,我国有关立法背景及司法解释表明,这里的"国际惯例"只能是实体法意义上的国际惯例。首先,我国最早的有关"国际惯例"的立法——《涉外经济合同法》的立法史表明,提出用"国际惯例"来补充法律主要是考虑到我国涉外经济法律尚不完备,在我国法被确定为合同准据法时可能出现"无法可依"的情况。再者,最高人民法院《关于适用〈涉外经济合同法〉若干问题的解答》之二[381](九)项也确认,"国际惯例"的适用以我国法为准据法,而我国法没有规定为前提。与此同时,依该解答之二(五)项规定,依选择或最密切联系原则所确定的合同争议准据法,"是指现行的实体法,而不包括冲突规范和程序法"。可见,这里作为准据法的补充而适用的国际惯例也只能是实体性规范,不包括程序法与冲突规范。换言之,《涉外经济合同法》中的"国际惯例"只可能是实体法意义上的国际惯例。

---

[377] 转引自徐国建:《现代商人法论》,载《中国社会科学》1993 年第 3 期。

[378] 参见李双元:《国际私法(冲突法篇)》,武汉大学出版社 1987 年版,第 42 页。作者指出我国《民法通则》中关于"国际惯例"的规定是在"涉外民事关系的法律适用"一章中作出的,"似应理解为是有关冲突法的国际惯例"。

[379] 参见佟柔主编:《〈中华人民共和国民法通则〉简论》,中国政法大学出版 1987 年版,第 287 页;浦伟良:《论〈民法通则〉中关于冲突法总则性规定》,载《法学评论》1990 年第 5 期。

[380] 参见王常营主编:《中国国际私法的理论与实践》,人民法院出版社 1993 年版,第 35 页。

[381] 参见《全国人大法律委员会对〈中华人民共和国涉外经济合同法(草案)〉审议结果的报告》(1985 年 3 月 13 日)之第一部分。

第二，根据法律体系的内在统一性原理，[382] 既然最初的《涉外经济合同法》中的“国际惯例”是指实体法意义上的国际惯例，则其他法律中的“国际惯例”也应为实体法意义上的国际惯例。上述的几部法律都属于我国涉外民商事(经济)立法的范畴，都是整个国内法律体系的构成部分，它们之间在概念、术语上应是协调统一的，这是作为一个统一的法律体系的基本要求。事实上，上述几部法律中的类似或相同规定是相互参照制定的。例如，《关于〈中华人民共和国票据法〉(草案)的说明》就明确指出，其关于涉外票据的法律适用一章是“根据民法通则的有关规定”而制定的。[383] 在这种情况下，这几部法律中的“国际惯例”在内涵上的一致性应无疑义。换言之，它们都应该指的是实体法意义上的“国际惯例”。那种主张《涉外经济合同法》的“国际惯例”是指实体法，而《民法通则》中的“国际惯例”是指冲突法的观点[384] 比较令人费解。

第三，从实践上考察，各国普遍认为，目前世界上只有冲突规范的国际条约，而不存在冲突规范的国际惯例。[385] 尽管随着国际民事经济生活的发展，各国国内法和若干国际条约常有一些共同采用的冲突规则，但多数学者都不承认在法律适用上存在有某种私法关系上必须适用某国法律的国际惯例，充其量只能说有了一些国际上比较普遍的实践或习惯做法。[386] 相反，实体法领域中的国际惯例却大量存在。可见，我国有关立法中的“国际惯例”只能是指实体法意义上的国际惯例。而这种国际惯例的主体部分，正是本文所探讨的国际贸易惯例。

值得一提的是，这里，通行的“实体法国际惯例”的提法并不妥当。因为，正如本文前面曾探讨而且将要接着讨论的，国际经济贸易领域中的这种“国际惯例”多为本身不具备法律拘束力的习惯做法，本质上尚不是“法律”，所以也就不能称之为“实体法”或“实体法国际惯例”。为区别计，不妨称“实体性国际惯例”。

那么，这种实体性国际惯例究竟包括哪些？显然，这里不可能也没必要一一加以罗列。但学者多同意，对这里的“国际惯例”应作广义理解，即不单单包括那些严格意义上的，具有任意性、自发性与明确性的国际惯例，如本文所研究的INCOTERMS、UCP等国际贸易惯例。对于那些中国没有缔结或尚未参加的国际公约，甚至于国外先进的立法通例，或体现在各国法律与国际立法中的具有进步意义的一般法律原则，等等，只要经过深入的研究和认真的鉴别，确认它们不致违反

---

〔382〕 参见孙国华主编：《法理学》，法律出版社1995年版，第288～290页。

〔383〕 参见国务院法制局财政金融法规司：《〈中华人民共和国票据法〉讲解》，法律出版社1995年版，第284页。

〔384〕 参见李双元：《国际私法(冲突法篇)》，武汉大学出版社1987年版，第42页。

〔385〕 参见浦伟良：《论〈民法通则〉中关于冲突法总则性规定》，载《法学评论》1990年第5期。

〔386〕 参见李双元主编：《中国与国际私法统一化进程》，武汉大学出版社1993年版.第57页。

我国强制性立法与我国的社会公共利益，而又确实为我国司法实践所需要，也可以视为“国际惯例”而“拿来”适用，以补足我国有关立法的漏洞与不足。[387] 从这一意义上看，霍恩（N. Horn）对我国立法中的“国际惯例”内容的理解[388]是有一定道理的。然而，从现代商人法的发展现状与我国的实际认识程度来看，将我国上述立法中的“国际惯例”等同于西方学者所主张的“现代商人法”，至少在目前是我们所难以接受的。

三、“国际惯例”的性质

关于我国立法中的“国际惯例”的性质，主要有两种观点：一种认为这里的“国际惯例”“显然就是我国公法学家们所称的‘国际惯例’”；[389] 质言之，这里的“国际惯例”属于国际公法的范畴；另一种观点认为，上述国际惯例可以补充我国法律的规定意味着我国对国际惯例效力的立法承认，因此，这里的“国际惯例”是我国法律的渊源之一。[390] 我们认为，这两种观点都是值得商榷的。

首先，这里的“国际惯例”不可能是作为国际法渊源之一的“国际惯例”（International Custom）。道理很简单，如果这里的国际惯例已上升为国际法，则按国际法优先的原则，“国际惯例”应先于国内法而得到适用，而且是必须得到适用，决不至于等到在国内法中找不到规定以后，才“可以适用”同时，从事实上说，正如我国国际私法与国际经济法学者们所公认的，在国际经济贸易领域，像“国家主权豁免”这样的强制性国际惯例很少，而大量存在的是任意性的国际惯例。[391]

与此同时，在我们看来，这里的规定似乎也不宜理解为我国对国际惯例的立法承认，从而也不能据此认定“国际惯例”为我国法律的正式渊源之一。因为，首先，国际惯例是一个内容十分庞杂，发展程度各异的习惯性规范群体，这里面有世界性惯例、地区性惯例，还有行业性的惯例，甚至还包括某特定双方当事人之间的“交易做法”与“履约做法”。而且每项惯例的确切内容、适用范围、被接受程度等等也相去甚远。由一项立法统一予以承认既不现实，也不可取。其次，从国际惯

---

〔387〕 例如，陈安教授就认为，对我国有关立法中的国际惯例，“似宜作广义理解”“举凡中国并未缔结或参加的国际条约一切外国的法律、一切国际民间团体编纂的规则，其中所包含的国际经贸行为规范或行为准则，都可以视为‘国际惯例’，只要它确实有利于促进我国社会主义市场经济体制的建立，就应当奉行‘拿来主义’，尽可能地博采众长，大应采用”，参见陈安：《论适用国际惯例与有法必依的统一》，载《中国社会科学》1994 年第 4 期。

〔388〕 霍恩（N. Horn）曾提出，我国《涉外经济合同法》中的“国际惯例”实质上就是指以调整国际贸易和经济关系的统一的法律基本原则为指导思想和全部内容的‘现代商人法’，它既包括法律规范（以国际条约为基础的统一立法或习惯法），也包括对合同和法律规范的解释起帮助作用的实际行动的规范和习惯。转见徐国建：《现代商人法论》，载《中国社会科学》1993 年第 3 期。

〔389〕 参见李双元主编：《中国与国际私法统一化进程》，武汉大学出版社 1993 年版，第 108 页。

〔390〕 例见张坦：《论习惯在民法典中的地位》，载《河北法学》1996 年第 1 期。

〔391〕 参见韩德培主编：《国际私法》，武汉大学出版社 1989 年版，第 28 页。

例的发展历史来看,国际经济贸易领域的惯例主要是西方国家贸易实践经验的总结与提炼,其内容不仅为发展中国家所不熟悉,而且不免带有维护其贸易优势地位的倾向。这一点西方学者也不否认,例如,伯奈尔(Bonell)就曾指出,“事实上,由于现存于国际贸易中的大多数惯例是在主要发达国家的商品市场与交易中发展起来的,它们不仅在内容上是片面的,而且对于来自其他国家的商人来说,几乎是一无所知”。[392] 诚然,前已述及,经过发展中国家的不断学习与不懈斗争,这种片面性与一无所知的状况已有所改变,但根本改观在短期中无疑是不可能完成的。所以,迄今为止,发展中国家(包括中国)对这些惯例的掌握仍不能说是很全面与熟练,而这种利益上的片面性也未能完全纠正过来。在这种背景之下,如果我们不问良莠,一律予以承认,奉之为“法律”无异于自投罗网,作茧自缚。不仅难以达到促进“对外开放”的初衷,反而会束缚我国外经贸当事人的手脚,对我国的改革开放事业造成不可忽视的负面影响。最后,从各国的实践来看,目前似乎也没有任何一个国家曾经“一揽子”式地承认所有的“国际惯例”,伊拉克与西班牙对 INCOTERMS 的承认都是鲜见的例子,而且是对个别惯例的具体承认。而许多国家民法典中对“惯例”或“习惯”补充法律功能的确认,已如前述,一般也被认为是国家对“惯例”或“习惯”作为法律漏洞的补充工具的功能的承认,而不是对其“法律”地位的一般认可。事实上,正如前面已经提到的,许多发达国家至今仍在为贸易惯例是不是法律、构不构成法律的真正渊源的问题争论不休。国际商会作为最具权威性的国际贸易惯例编纂机构,也曾特别警告说,它所制定的这些惯例仅仅是私人机构所制定的,只有在当事人直接或间接采用时,采对他们有拘束力。不可轻率地肯定其具有法源地位或法律拘束力。[393] 在这种情况下,如认为我国已经笼统地承认所有由这些发达国家所发展起来的、片面而为我们所不熟悉的“国际惯例”,则不仅是不合理的,简直可以说是荒唐的!

基于上述理由,我们认为,我国有关立法中的“国际惯例”的规定不应理解为对“国际惯例”的效力及其法源地位的普通立法承认。那么,究竟该怎么理解呢?我们认为,实质上,我国的有关国内立法赋予“国际惯例”的只是作为我国法律漏洞补充工具的性质与地位。

任何法律皆有漏洞,这是当今判例学说所公认的事实。[394] 所谓法律漏洞,是

---

[392] Bianca-Bonell, Commentary on the International Sales Law—the 1980 Vienna Sales Convention, 1987, p. 105.

[393] 参见张锦源:《贸易契约理论与实务》,三民书局 1988 年版,第 55 ~ 56 页。

[394] 参见王泽鉴:《民法学说与判例研究》(第一册),《台大法学丛书》(十六)第 303 页。

指现行法律体系上存在影响法律功能,且违反立法意旨的不完全性。[395] 这种漏洞的产生,或者因为立法者考虑不周,根本未考虑到,或虽考虑到但不质详,或者由于情事发生变化,或者由于立法者自觉其对所要规范的情形了解不够,而不加规范。[396] 但是无论其因何而生,有漏洞就应予补充,这样才能实现法律维护公平正义及法律秩序的目的,同时确保法律体系的完整与协调。[397]

关于法律漏洞补充的性质,有两种观点:一种观点认为,法律漏洞的补充是法律解释活动的继续。法院审理具体案件的第一步,就是找寻所应适用的法律规范,即进行“三段论”推理中的大前提,称“找法活动”,找法活动又可区分为法律解释与漏洞补充两个阶段。区分二者的分界线在于法条可能的文义。在可能的文义内找法,为法律解释;在可能文义之外找法,即为漏洞补充。但通说又认为二者不能截然分开,有相互交叉地带,即所谓的法内漏洞的补充。因为法内漏洞的补充,既可以算是在法条可能文义范围之内,也可说是在可能文义范围之外。[398] 但是一般来说,法律漏洞补充是在法律解释活动不足以解决的可能文义范围之外的问题时,才发挥其功能,即法律漏洞是法律解释活动的继续。[399] 另一种观点则认为法律漏洞补充是造法的尝试,而不是立法活动。因为,首先,法律漏洞补充是针对一件待决案件,取向于法律体系与价值而采取一个法律见解,将其作为裁判依据,并在裁判中表现出来。因此,它只是作为一个裁判,属于行使司法权的活动,而不是针对某一类案件补充地制定一般性规范的活动。其次,虽然作为判决先例在事实上有类似法律的效力,但事实上的效力毕竟不同于法律的规范效力。因此,判决先例并不构成法源,违反判例也不构成违法。再次,法院对既存判决先例无遵守的义务,仅有斟酌的义务。由此产生法院对于采纳或不采纳判决先例中的法律见解负有说理义务。[400] 可见法院的法律漏洞补充活动,在性质上充其量只能说是一种“造法的尝试”,而非终局的法律制定。由这种造法活动所表现于判决先例中的法律见解,将来有可能转化为习惯法,也可能迟早被抛弃。[401]

总而言之,无论是作为法律解释的继续,还是作为适法的尝试,法律漏洞补充都不是国家的立法活动,而是司法机关具体适用法律的活动。相应地,补充法律漏洞的依据或工具,也就不能视为法律,不属于法律渊源的范畴。

---

[395] 参见梁慧星:《法律漏洞及其补充方法》,载梁慧星主编:《民商法论丛》(第1卷),法律出版社1994年版,第7页。

[396] 参见黄茂荣:《法学方法与现代民法》,中国政法大学出版社,1993年台湾繁体版,第353页。

[397] 参见梁慧星:《法律漏洞及其补充方法》,载《民商法论丛》第1卷,法律出版社1994年版,第19页。

[398] 参见黄茂荣:《法学方法与现代民法》,中国政法大学出版社,1993年,第370~371页。

[399] 参见黄建辉:《法律漏洞、类推适用》,蔚理法律出版社1988年版,第69~70页。

[400] 参见黄茂荣:《法学方法与现代民法》,中国政法大学出版社,1993年,第373~375页。

[401] 同上书,第378页。

法律漏洞的补充方法大致有三种，一种就是依习惯补充，另外两种为依法理补充与依判例补充。[402]

依习惯补充法律漏洞，其根据通常在于各国民法均以明文规定，在一定条件下习惯有与法律同一的效力。[403] 例如，《瑞士民法典》第 1 条规定，“如本法无相应规定时，法官应依据惯例；无惯例时，依据自己作为立法者所提出的规则裁判”。此外，土耳其、泰国、阿根廷、奥地利等国的民法也都有类似的规定。[404] 我国清末的民法草案也曾采用这一外国立法例。这种立法迄今在我国台湾地区“民法”中仍得以维持。现行我国台湾地区“民法”第 1 条规定，“民事，法律所未规定者，依习惯；无习惯者，依法理”。[405] 依我国台湾地区权威学者的解释，这里的“习惯”乃指“事实上的惯行”，而不是已经上升为法律的“习惯法”。[406]

我国《民法通则》虽然没有一般性地赋予“习惯”或“惯例”以补充法律漏洞的功能，但《民法通则》第 142 条第 3 款及《涉外经济合同法》等涉外立法的有关规定，却显然是承认了“国际惯例”才我国涉外民商事法律漏洞的补充意义。换言之，我国法律只是不承认“国内惯例”对法律漏洞具有补充功能，对于“国际惯例”的补充功能则是承认的。这一点如果说仅仅从法条本身还难以明确的话，从有关的立法背景与司法解释中则可以找到明确的肯定的证据。回顾我国最早的关于“国际惯例”的立法——《涉外经济合同法》的立法史，就可以知道，“中华人民共和国法律没有规定时，可以适用国际惯例”这一款的提出，乃是有关部门考虑到“目前我国涉外经济法律还不够完备，处理合同争议适用我国法律时，有的可能找不到依据”而建议增写的。[407] 随后，前面提到的最高人民法院《关于适用〈涉外经济合同法〉若干问题的解答》之二第（九）项再次明确，上款的意思在于在应当适用我国法律的情况下，如果我国法律对于合同争议的问题未作规定的，可以适用国际惯例。可见，无论是“立法者”还是司法机构都把“国际惯例”当作补充我国涉外法律漏洞（法律不够完备即谓存在法律漏洞）的具体“依据”，而并无意使之统统成为有当然法律约束力的“法律”和正式的法源。霍恩（N. Horn）显然也意识到了这一点，他提出，中国法律实际上是承认了国际惯例（他所理解的“现代商人法”）是本国涉外经济合同法的一个“替补渊源”[408]——“替补渊源”显然不是法

---

〔402〕 参见梁慧星：《法律漏洞及其补充方法》，载《民商法论丛》第 1 卷，法律出版社 1994 年版，第 23 页。

〔403〕 同上。

〔404〕 参见张坦：《论习惯在民法典中的地位》，载《河北法学》1996 年第 1 期。

〔405〕 同上。

〔406〕 参见黄茂荣：《民法总则》，根植法学丛书编辑室，1982 年增订版，第 7 页。

〔407〕 参见《全国人大法律委员会对〈中华人民共和国涉外经济合同法〉草案审议结果的报告》，载宋汝棼：《参加立法工作项记》，中国法制出版社 1994 年版，第 60 页。

〔408〕 转引自徐国建：《现代商人法论》，载《中国社会科学》1993 年第 3 期。

律的正式渊源,而只是正式法律渊源的补充,确言之,是正式法律渊源中的法律漏洞的补充工具。

作为法律漏洞补充工具的国际惯例与作为法律的国际惯例是有明显区别的,前者可能只有个别意义,即可能只在个案中偶尔得到采用,不能必然地适用于所有同类案件;后者则具有普遍意义,对于同类情况均有规范效力。前者是有条件的,附从的,即只有在法律没有规定,“无法可依”的条件下,方可适用,它服从于法律或者整个法律秩序的目的,而不具备独立的法律性格;后者则一般是无条件的、主动的和独立的,基于自身的法律价值而存在,而不必然地服从于某一或某类法律的目的与价值。质言之,后者是法,所以具有法律的全部普遍性、规范性、抽象性;前者不是法,而只是一种“事实上惯行”,本质上仍是“事实”,故不具有法的一般抽象性与普遍规范力。

值得一提的是,“国际惯例”或“习惯”作为法律漏洞的补充工具之一,与学理、判例等其他补充工具又是有区别的。如前所述,“习惯”特别是“国际(贸易)惯例”是特殊的社会机制所形成的一种具有事实上的约束力的社会行为规范,其中不少已为国际(商业)社会所“广泛知悉”并“经常遵守”,其规范效力与学理、判例等是不可同日而语的。正因如此,在上述各国的民法典中,习惯居于优先补充的地位。也正是因为这一点,才使人们误认为我国立法中的上述有关规定实质上就是对其法律效力与法源地位的承认。然而,从本质上说,“国际惯例”对我国法律的补充意义与“习惯”“学理”“判例”等对上述其他国家法律的补充意义是没有区别的。

确立“国际惯例”的法律漏洞补充工具性质与地位在理论上与实践上都颇有意义。在理论上,它可以比较圆满地解将我国既然普遍不承认国际惯例是法律又何以规定“可以适用国际惯例”这一看似矛盾的现象,有利于澄清种种观念上、思想上的模糊与混乱;在实践上,则不仅有利于我国外经贸事业的开展,也有利于司法活动中对“国际惯例”的科学、准确适用,避免将“适用国际惯例”凌驾于“有法必依”之上的错误做法。实际上,目前我国官方采用“按照国际通行规则”取代以往“与国际惯例接轨”的提法这一事实就表明我国决策层已经意识到“国际惯例”的任意性质与补充地位,在认识上已向前迈进了一大步。

四、“国际惯例”适用的条件

从上面的分析可以看出,在我国,国际惯例要得到适用必须同时具备六个条件:第一,该争议问题的准据法是中国法;第二,中国法律和中国缔结或参加的国际条约对该争议问题没有规定;第三,对于该争议问题存在着国际惯例;第四,该惯例未为当事人所明示排除；第五，该国际惯例的适用不会违反中国的社会公共利益；第六，中国的司法机关决定适用该国际惯例来补充法律。

第一，国际惯例在我国的适用须以我国法为争议问题的准据法为前提。如果该争议的准据法为外国法，或者港澳地区的法律，则“国际惯例”之能适用与否须视该准据法的规定。如果该准据法允许适用国际惯例，国际惯例方有可能得到适用，反之，则不能适用。与此同时，依我国《涉外经济合同法》《民法通则》及其司法解释，涉外经济合同与涉外合同当事人均可以选择处理合同争议所适用的法律，这种法律“可以是中国法，也可以是港澳地区的法律或外国法”，[409]而未提及“国际惯例”。但是从我国对“国际惯例”性质的一般认定及我国立法对其法律漏洞补充地位的确定来看，我国似乎是不太可能同意当事人选择适用“国际惯例”的。至于依据“最密切联系原则”所确立的准据法，则更不可能是“国际惯例”，[410]因为《民法通则》与《涉外经济合同法》都明确规定，合同当事人没有选择时，适用的是与合同有最密切联系的“国家的法律”。换言之，这里明确肯定所适用的只能是内国法，而不包括不归属于任何国家的“国际惯例”。

第二，国际惯例在我国的适用须以我国法律与我国缔结或参加的国际条约对争议问题没有规定为条件。这显然是由“国际惯例”在我国法律中的补充适用地位所决定的。由于香港、澳门是独立的两个法域，这里的中国法律应不包括香港法与澳门法。而这里的“没有规定”应指无论是中国法中的强制性规范还是任意性规范都没有相应的规定。[411]

第三，适用“国际惯例”固须以相关领域国际惯例的存在为前提。显然，这里就存在“国际惯例”的查明问题，其具体方法大致可参考本文前面论及的国际贸易惯例的证明方法。不过，对于我国未缔结或参加的国际公约、国际统一示范法等国际立法规范，如若也视同国际惯例而予以适用，一般来说就不存在上述查明或证明问题了，至于在查明不存在适用的国际惯例的情况下，该依据什么判决的

---

[409] 参见最高人民法院《关于适用〈涉外经济合同法〉若干问题的解答》之二（二）项。

[410] 韩健也持同样观点，参见韩建：《现代国际商事仲裁法的理论与实践》，法律出版社 1993 年版，第 254 页。

[411] 日本学者石田穰先生将习惯区分为三种情形而论其效力。其一，既不违反法律强行规定，也不违反任意规定的习惯，有与法律同一之效力；其二，不违反法律强行规定，而违反任意规定的习惯，以当事人认同为条件，有与法律同一之效力；其三，违反法律强行规定的习惯，无与法律同一之效力。因此，他总结道，依习惯补充法律漏洞，须以该习惯不违反法律强行性规定及任意性规定为条件。参见［日］石田穰：《法解释学的方法》，青林书院新社 1980 年版，第 34 页，转引自梁慧星：《法律漏洞及其补充方法》，载梁慧星主编：《民商法论丛》（第 1 卷），法律出版社 1994 年版，第 24 页。

问题，似乎已超出本文的范围，兹不赘述。[412]

第四，国际惯例的适用还应以该惯例未被当事人所明示排除为前提。这主要是由这里的“国际惯例”的任意性质使然。如前所述，各国普遍认为，国际（贸易）惯例属于当事人意思自治的范畴，如当事人在合同中已明示排除某惯例的适用，则无论该惯例如何广为人知且被普遍遵守，均不可拘束此合同的当事人。[413] 我国法律既承认合同自由，对此当无异议。故在考虑补充适用国际惯例时，如可适用的惯例已为当事人所明示排除，则该惯例不应得到适用。

第五，按我国《民法通则》等立法规定，适用的国际惯例还不得与我国的社会公共利益相违背，否则应予排除。这一公共秩序保留条款在国内似乎备受攻击，认为稀世所罕见。[414] 因为各国一般认为适用国际惯例不会损害公共秩序；而一旦当事人选择了某一国际惯例，就取得了高于国内法的效力，即使其适用有可能导致损害公共秩序的后果，也不能因国内立法限制其适用。[415] 我们认为这种看法颇值商榷。诚然，国际（贸易）惯例由于一般是在与国家没有原则性利害关系的领域内自发形成的，一般不会危及公共秩序。然而，并不能因而绝对排除其有危害公共秩序的可能。如前所述，由于各国历史、文化及经济、社会的巨大差别性，在一时一地为合理合法，成为“惯例”的东西，到另一地另一时很可能是完全无法接受的。特别是许多由发达国家提出的所谓的“国际惯例”，往往带有浓厚的霸权主义气息，为发展中国家所无法接受。例如，某些发达国家坚持对固有化实行“及时、充分、有效”的补偿是“国际惯例”，而这一所谓的国际惯例不仅仅是索价甚高，几近敲诈勒索，实际上大大限制，甚至无异于完全剥夺了贫弱的发展中国家征用境内外资的主权权利。[416] 对于这样的“国际惯例”我们显然不能不分青红皂白地照单全收，而应充分意识到其危害性，运用公共秩序保留予以坚决的抵制。实际上，在西方国家，也并未放弃公共秩序保留的权利。例如，施米托夫与哥尔德斯坦均认为，现代商人法可能因主权国家的公共秩序而失效，也可能因公共秩序而受到限制。[417] 就连自治商人法理论的积极鼓吹者戈德曼（B. Goldman）也

---

〔412〕 有人曾提出可以依“政策”来补充国际惯例，参见浦伟良：《论〈民法通则〉中关于冲突法总则性规定》，载《法学评论》1990 年第 5 期。我们认为，也不妨以法理及判例来补充。关于依法理及判例的和补充，可参见梁慧星：《法律漏洞及其补充方法》，载梁慧星主编：《民商法论丛》（第 1 卷），法律出版社 1994 年版；另见徐国栋：《民法基本原则解释——成文法局限性之克服》，中国政法大学出版社 1992 年版。

〔413〕 Cf. C. M. Schmitthoff, lntemational Trade Usages, 1987, p. 15.

〔414〕 参见胡振杰：《国际惯例立法修订的法律思考》，载《法学》1993 年第 2 期；另见李双元主编：《中国与国际私法统一化进程》，武汉大学出版社 1993 年版，第 123 页.

〔415〕 胡振杰：《国际惯例立法修订的法律思考》，载《法学》1993 年第 2 期。

〔416〕 参见陈安：《论适用国际惯例与有法必依的统一》，载《中国社会科学》1994 年第 4 期。

〔417〕 Cf. C. M. Schmitthoff, The Unification of the Law of International Trade, in Chia-Jui Cheng ed. Clive M. Schmitthoff's Select Essags On International Trade Law, 1988, p. 209.

认为商人法的适用应受公共秩序的限制，尽管他使用的是所谓的“跨国公共秩序”的概念。[418] 至于国际惯例一经选择即取得优于国内法的效力的提法，我们更不敢苟同。如前所述，国际惯例多为任意性的规范，即使经当事人采用，也只取得优于任意法的效力，而无论如何应受强行法的约束。换言之，如果此说只是对任意法而言，则可以成立；如果系针对所有国内法而言，则显然是不能成立的。我们认为，既然对国际惯例的公共秩序保留为世所公认，则我国有关立法的合理性应无疑问，即便是这种规定真的是“世所罕见”。

第六，国际惯例的适用还取决于司法机关对补充适用国际惯例的选择。这一点往往为人们所忽视。实际上，我国所有有关立法，无不是规定“可以适用”国际惯例。换言之，也可以不予适用——事实上，基于公共秩序原因而不适用即其表现之一。“用与不用，悉听司法、执法者的自由裁断。”[419] 在我们看来，这也可以用“三个有利于”标准来衡量取舍，凡是有利于发展社会生产力，有利于改革开放，有利于建设社会主义市场经济的“国际惯例”我们就应大胆拿来，取长补短；反之，凡是不利于发展社会生产力，不利于改革开放，不利于建设社会主义市场经济，甚至于会违反我国社会公共利益的“国际惯例”，我们则应弃之如敝屣，毫不足惜。有“惯例”而不予适用固然可能导致司法过程复杂化，但不加区别地盲目适用那些不合时宜、甚至严重损害国家主权与社会公益的所谓的“国际惯例”无疑会危害更大。诚然，我们要与“国际通行规则”接轨，但我们不可能不顾中国的具体国情，不惜一切代价，更不可能为此而完全抛弃我们作为一个有中国特色的社会主义国家的基本社会制度与基本价值观念！

五、我国关于“国际惯例”的国内立法与《联合国国际货物销售合同公约》的有关规定之间的关系

《联合国国际货物销售合同公约》（以下简称《公约》）主要有三个条款与国际惯例直接相关。《公约》第 4 条规定，本公约除非另有明文规定外，与任何合同、任何条款或任何惯例的有效性问题无关。换言之，合同、合同条款或惯例是否合法、有效，《公约》并无意作统一规定，而留待各国国内法具体解决。这一条实质上使得惯例必须受国内强行法以及公共秩序的制约。例如，按照我国《涉外经济合同法》第 9 条的规定，违反中华人民共和国法律或者社会公共利益的合同无效。显然，这里的“法律”指的是强制性法律，而不包括任意性法律。

《公约》第 8 条、第 9 条是关于合同的解释与补充规则的规定。其中，第 8 条

---

[418] Cf. Filip De Ly, International Business Law and Lex Mercatoria, 1992, p. 215.

[419] 陈安：《论适用国际惯例与有法必依的统一》，载《中国社会科学》1994 年第 4 期。

第3款规定在解释合同时,"应适当地考虑到与事实有关的一切情况",其中应包括当事人之间确立的任何习惯做法或惯例。也就是说,该款规定"惯例"是解释合同的重要因素之一。《公约》第9条实质上是关于惯例对合同的补充功能的规定。由于合同补充也可以说是解释的延长,故总体上仍属于合同解释的范畴。该条第1款规定,当事人之间业已同意的任何惯例和他们之间确立的任何习惯做法,对双方当事人均有约束力。第2款则规定除非另有协议,双方当事人应视为已默示地同意对他们的合同或其成立适用双方当事人已经知道或理应知道的惯例,条件是这种惯例必须是在国际贸易上已为有关特定贸易所涉同类合同的当事人所广泛知道并为他们经常遵守。质言之,双方当事人明示或默示同意纳入其合同的惯例均构成合同的一部分,从而对合同具有补充的功能。而这种"默示同意"的判断标准便是这种惯例必须是在国际贸易中被广泛使用,并被认为是约定俗成的习惯做法。[420] INCOTERMS 以及 UCP 就是这样的惯例。这里的"经常遵守"条件是继承了《国际货物买卖统一法》第9条第2款的规定,而"广泛知道"条件则是《公约》的创新。其意旨在于避免原限于国内使用的惯例被任意推广适用于与外国贸易商的交易之中。[421] 这样一来,英国的设备出口商在与印度商人交易时,就不能援用英国国内设备买卖中的惯例,即使该惯例在英国是尽人皆知以至于外方当事人"已经知道"或者至少"理应知道"这些惯例。[422]

不过,也有学者提出《公约》这一条款也并不排除在某些情况下,地方或国内惯例适用于与外国交易的可能。例如,某些商品交易所、贸易洽谈会中的惯例,如果在与外国人的交易中也得到经常遵守,也可以在同类国际贸易当事人之间产生约束力。又如,某外商曾与一国当事人签订过大量同类合同,则有关该类合同的既定惯例对于该外商也是有约束力的。[423] 但无论如何,《公约》"只给了地方性惯例以非常有限的承认"。[424]

值得注意的是,"广泛知道"与"经常遵守"不仅仅是推定当事人"理应知道"的客观标准,在当事人"已经知道"某惯例的情况下,它也必须同时具备这两个条件。这一点从上文关于英国设备买卖国内惯例一般不能约束国外的当事人(即使他们已经知道该惯例)的例子足以证明。显然,《公约》的这一规定对来自发展中

---

[420] 参见王贵国:《〈联合国国际货物销售合同公约〉的适用原则及解释原则》,载《中国国际法年刊》1989年卷。

[421] Bianca-Bonell, Commentary On the International Sales Law—the 1980 Vienna Sales Convention, 1987, p. 109.

[422] Ibid.

[423] Ibid.

[424] Ibid.

国家的贸易新手来说是十分有利也十分必要的。也正因如此,它才成了包括中国在内的许多发展中国家积极参加的一个公约。

《公约》关于惯例的这些规定与我国国内法上的有关“国际惯例”的规定既互相区别,又相互联系、互相补充。《公约》的规定是对特定惯例、对合同的解释与补充功能的确认,本质上属于合同解释的范畴;我国国内法的有关“国际惯例”的规定是关于国际惯例对我国法律的补充的功能,本质上属于法律解释的范畴。二者属于不同的法律层面。但同时这两种规定又是互相联系、互相补充的。《公约》关于特定惯例的补充功能的规定使国际惯例中的一部分可作为合同的默示条款而直接补充合同的内容,从而取得优于《公约》及国内任意法律规范的法律效力。而我国国内法的规定则使所有未依《公约》而明示或默示地纳入合同,且不违反我国社会公共利益的“国际惯例”可以用来补充国内法的不足。对于某一具体惯例而言,一旦它符合《公约》规定的条件而构成某合同的一部分,则通常不会再被用作该合同争议的法律补充工具,因为它已经在合同解释与补充中得到了先期适用,从而实现了其规范功能,自不必待到无法可依后再行适用;但如果它不符合《公约》规定的条件,不能直接补充该合同,不构成该合同的一部分,则它只能在“无法可依”的情况下,才可能得到适用。但对于某一类合同中所有惯例而言,只有那些符合《公约》规定条件的国际惯例构成该类合同的一部分,可对合同内容进行直接补充;而不符合《公约》规定条件,不构成该类合同的一部分的国际惯例在我国法律不敷适用时,则可以用来补充法律的不足而适用于该类合同争议。换言之《公约》与我国国内法的结合,实质上使“国际惯例”分割成两大部分,符合《公约》条件的部分可直接补充合同,构成合同的组成部分而先期得到适用;不符合《公约》规定条件的国际惯例则只能作为漏洞补充的工具而得到补充适用。这也就意味着,事实上,对法律起补充作用的“国际惯例”不仅仅因没有被吸收进入我国的国内法或上升而为我国缔结或参加的国际条约,而且因没有根据《公约》的规定而被纳入合同,成为合同明示或默示条款。这无疑是对补充适用的国际惯例的一种事实上的限制。

基于上述分析,我们认为,“国际惯例”与《公约》及我国国内法三者之间的效力等级与适用顺次大致可归纳如下,即先后依次是:我国法的强制性规定——依《公约》规定而成为合同明示或默示条款的惯例——《公约》的规定[425]——我国法中的任意性规定——依《公约》规定不构成合阐明示或默示条款的国际惯例。

由此可见,《公约》有关惯例的规定与我国有关国际惯例的国内立法相结合

---

[425] 这里,需注意的是,《公约》中我国已作出保留的部分将不对我国产生《公约》的约束力。

实际上使国际贸易惯例在我国涉外民商事(特别是合同)法律适用过程中据有十分重要的地位。而这,也正是本文的现实意义之所在。

六、结论

综上所论,我们认为,我国有关国内立法中的“国际惯例”当仅指实体意义上的国际惯例:它既不属国际法,也不属国内法,而只是国际法与国内法的补充,是法律漏洞补充的工具;国际惯例在我国的适用以我国法为准据法而我国有关国内法与国际条约未作规定,且以当事人未明示排除作为适用前提,同时,国际惯例的适用并不违反我国的社会公共利益;此外,我国所参加的《联合国国际货物销售合同合约》的有关规定则赋予了“惯例”以解释与补充合同的法律意义,这使得国际惯例中我国对外经济交往中具备了更重要的法律意义。

进而言之,我国现行有关“国际惯例”的立法是否真如某些学者所主张的,需要作根本性的修改呢?在我们看来,我国现行有关立法既体现了尊重国际惯例的时代精神,也适应与国际通行规则接轨,弥补国内法律不足的现实需要,是必要的,也是合理的,无须作大的修改。不过,考虑到理论与实践中存在的种种歧异,我们似有必要对其作出科学、权威的法律解释,以明确其含义、性质、适用条件等诸项,从而统一认识,使相关法学理论研究与立法司法实践得以明确化、深层化与科学化。

经济技术开发区法律制度*

第一节 经济技术开发区的概念与立法概况

一、经济技术开发区的概念

关于经济技术开发区的概念,各地的开发区条例并无统一的规定。例如,《广州经济技术开发区条例》第3条规定,开发区是在广州市人民政府领导下实行国家优惠政策的经济技术区域。《宁波市经济技术开发区暂行条例》第2条则规定,宁波市经济技术开发区是在宁波市人民政府领导下,以兴办技术密集型、生产型、出口创汇型项目为主的,实行经济特区某些政策的经济技术开发区。可见,各地对开发区的界定各有侧重,并不完全一致,但其基本内容却又是相对统一的。据此,再结合各地开发区的实践,我们可以对经济技术开发区作如下界定:经济技术开发区是国家在开放城市中划出的,有特定地域范围,并在该市人民政府领导下的相对独立的特别经济区域。在这种特别经济区内,实行我国经济特区的某些特殊政策,主要兴办生产性企业和科研事业,以开发新技术、新产品和发展新兴产业。

1984年春,国务院召开了进一步对外开放沿海14个城市的座谈会,会议为我国进一步对外开放作出了重大决策。随后,国务院在1984、1985年两年内,先后批准在大连、秦皇岛、天津、烟台、青岛、连云港、南通、宁波、福州、广州、湛江等11个沿海开放城市兴办经济技术开发区。1986年8月和1988年6月,国务院先后批准了上海的闵行、虹桥和漕河泾经济技术开发区。1992年,国务院批准了温州、昆山、营口、威海以及福建的融侨和东山经济技术开发区。1993年3月,国务院又批准了沿江和内陆省会城市沈阳、哈尔滨、长春、杭州、武汉、重庆、芜湖7个经济技术开发区。加上1994年批准的北京与乌鲁木齐两个经济技术开发区,总计全国已有32个国家级的经济技术开发区(以下简称开发区)。

---

* 本文原载黎学玲主编:《特别经济区法》第11章,法律出版社1997年版。

国家设立经济技术开发区的主旨大都在于依托与发挥所在城市的优势,促进经济结构的调整,推动科技进步,扩大出口贸易,发展对外经济合作和技术交流。少数则另有特定的发展目标,或是拓展对外经贸业务,或是以发展高新技术产业为主,或是发展现代的创汇农业,或是进行地区经济综合开发,等等。

32个开发区中,1988年以前批准的14个以及在正式批准前已开发建设多年的昆山、温州两个开发区一共16个,都已经取得了显著实际,具有相当的产业规模,走上了经济结构以外商投资企业为主、产业机构以现代工业为主、产品销售以出口为主,致力于引进与开发先进技术的发展道路,显示了速度、效益同步增长的好势头。据统计,上述16个开发区1993年共批准外商投资项目2496个,协议外资金额41亿美元,实际利用外资15.4亿美元,都比上年有较大幅度的增长。1993年平均单项外商投资额为272万美元,高出全国平均水平一倍以上。上海闵行开发区、广州开发区平均单项外商投资额更分别高达840万美元与630万美元。[1] 目前,各开发区正按照中共十四届三中全会提出的"统筹规划,认真办好"的要求,致力于产业合理化、技术先进化、市场国际化、服务优质化、功能完善化、抓机遇、上水平、争效益,向更高的水平迈进。

二、经济技术开发区的性质与特征

经济技术开发区是一种特别经济区,它既不是一级独立的行政区域,也有别于经济特区。它是一种依托开放城市但又相对独立的,实施某些特殊经济政策,执行特定的经济功能的特别经济区。其主要特征是:

1.经济技术开发区不是独立的行政区域。国家设立经济技术开发区,为的是促进对外经济技术合作与开发,并不是要实施特殊的政治、行政体制,或者增加一层特别的行政层级。从我国的实践来看,各开发区虽然都设立了相应的管理机构,但它仍由所在市人民政府领导。开发区管理机构一般只是所在市人民政府的派出机构,它经市政府授权,代表市政府进行管理。

2.经济技术开发区不同于经济特区。这主要表现在两个方面:首先,在经济结构上,经济特区是以工业为主,工贸结合的外向型的综合性经济;开发区则以发展生产性企业和科研事业为主,第三产业主要依托所在城市,必要时,也可在区内设立外贸、金融、商业、仓储、运输、生活设施,但这主要是为本区域生产、经营、生活提供服务。其次,在政策优惠方面,开发区内仅执行经济特区的某些特殊政策。例如,经济特区的外商投资企业不论是生产性的还是非生产性的,一律按15%的

---

〔1〕 参见李岚清主编:《中国利用外资基础知识》,中共中央党校出版社、中国对外经济贸易出版社1995年版,第291页。

税率征收企业所得税;而在开发区内,则只有生产性外商投资企业才能享受这一优惠待遇。开发区与经济特区的这些区别表明开发区是继经济特区之后的,对外开放的另一个层次。

3. 经济技术开发区的经济功能是促进对外经济合作与技术开发。兴办开发区的宗旨,在于引进外资,引进先进的科学技术和科学的管理技术,集中举办生产性外商投资企业和中外合作的科研机构,发展合作生产、合作研究设计,开发新产品、新技术,发展新产业。所以,开发区必须是一个技术与知识密集的生产性与科研性区域。它的经济结构以生产性企业和科研事业为主。正式这一经济功能的特征使之与经济特区、保税区、高新技术产业开发区、边境经济合作区、旅游度假区等其他特别经济区内在地区别开来。

4. 经济技术开发区实行特殊的政策。经济开发区作为执行特定经济功能的一种特别经济区,作为国家对外开放与引进外资的重点区域,必然要给予其特殊的政策,这种政策的特殊性目前主要表现为税收优惠,同时也表现为管理体制上的某些特殊性,具体内容后面将各设专节介绍。

三、经济技术开发区的立法概况

引进外资是我国设立经济技术开发区的首要目标。然而,世界各国的实践表明,一个开发区对外资的新引力,在很大程度上取决于该区的法律环境。良好的法律环境不仅可以保护投资者的合法权益,促进外资流入,还可以调整区内各种复杂的经济关系,保障开发区经济的稳定、健康、快速地发展。

我国的开发区建立以来,就比较重视法制建设,经过十多年的努力,已制订了一系列的法规与规章,初步形成了我国的经济技术开发区法规体系,有效地规范与引导了开发区的各种经济行为。

大致说来,我国有关开发区的立法分两个层次:一是国务院和中央各部门制定的法规和规章,如国务院《关于经济特区和沿海十四个港口城市减征、免征企业所得税和工商统一税的暂行规定》(1984 年 11 月),国务院《关于鼓励外商投资的规定》(1986 年 10 月)、财政部《贯彻国务院〈关于鼓励外商投资的额规定〉中的税收优惠条款的实施办法》(1987 年 11 月)和海关总署、财政部与对外经济贸易部联合发布的《关于中外合资企业进出口货物的监管和征免税规定》(1984 年 4 月)及海关总署《对经济技术开发区进出口货物管理规定》(1984 年 4 月),等等。这些法规与规章虽然不全是专门针对开发区的,但均设计了开发区这一特别经济区。这些相关法规与规章实质上成了各地具体制定投资优惠、企业等级、劳动工资、土地、财务、合同、技术引进等方面的地方性法规与规章的法律依据。

第二个层次是省(直辖市)人民代表大会和政府制定的有关法规和规章,以及各开发区所在市人民政府制定的一些规定与办法,后者一般比较具体,涉及企业登记、劳动工资、土地使用等具体领域。

在实践中,各开发区一般在管委会或总公司里设置了专门从事规章调研、草拟的部门,如广州开发区在管委会里设了条法处,宁波开发区在管委会中设政策研究室。这些部门的设立是的各开发区的立法工作发展较快。

开发区创建以来,上海、天津、广东、辽宁、浙江、江苏、福建、山东等省、市人大常委会根据自身的职权,都相应地制订了其经济技术开发区条例。各开发区所在地的市人民政府还相继发布了许多规章或规范性文件。开发区的立法主要设计如下几个方面:

1. 经济技术开发区条例。有的成为经济技术开发区管理条例(如天津)。各开发区条例一般都对立法根据、开发区的总体目标、行政管理、投资优惠、注册经营、劳动管理、土地管理及环境保护等作原则性的规定。开发区条例是知道开发区各项活动的准则,也是建立开发区其他规章制度的依据。

2. 有关开发区制定规范性文件的规定。如开发区规范性文件的制定、修改及废止办法等。这类规定对开发区规范性文件的名称、拟定、送审、批准制定、颁布、解释、修改、补充和废止等程序及其职掌机关、适用原则等都作了具体规定。

3. 有关项目引进、管理方面的规定。如开发区鼓励技术引进、技术开发的规定、开发区企业登记管理规定、开发区外资企业申请和审批程序规定、开发区内联企业的申请、审批程序的规定、开发区企业经济合同管理规定等,这些规定对开发区技术引进的内容、方式、优惠待遇,技术引进的项目管理,内联与外资企业申请、审批、登记注册程序,合同订立和合同纠纷处理等作了具体规定。

4. 有关税费管理方面的规定。如开发区涉外税收实施办法、内联企业征税办法、开发区各类收费标准等。这些规定对在区内征收工商统一税、企业所得税、城市房产税、车船使用牌照税、个人所得税及其他各类费用的征收标准、减免税费条件、违反规定的罚则等作了详细规定。

5. 有关土地管理方面的规定。如开发区土地使用管理办法、开发区土地使用费收取办法等,对开发区土地使用的申请、批准,土地使用年限、土地的合理利用,土地费用的收取标准等作了具体规定。目前,上海、天津、广州等开发区都陆续颁布了开发区土地使用权有偿出让和转让办法,使开发区土地使用迈入了从收取土地费向有偿转让土地使用权过度的第一步。这些办法对土地使用权出让的形式,各类形式出让的程序、土地使用权的抵押和转让、价格和费用,土地使用权的回收及违反土地使用规定的法律责任等作了具体规定。

6. 有关劳动人事管理方面的规定。如开发区企业劳动工资管理办法、引进招聘人才优惠待遇的规定、开发区实行干部聘任制的办法、开发区社会劳动保险办法等，这些规定对开发区劳动管理机构及其职能、职工待遇、劳动保险、职工调配、人才引进、干部的管理和聘用等作了具体规定。

此外，有的开发区还对区内的环境管理、能源管理、消防管理、道路管理、建设规划、市政设施、外汇留成、施工现场管理、商品厂房管理等一系列问题制定了具体办法和规定。

这些条例、规定、办法的制定与执行，基本上将开发区各项经济活动纳入了法律调整的范围，使之有法可依，从而有效保障了投资者的合法权益，对开发区招商引资，加快技术进步与经济发展，完善投资环境，进而带动相邻地区的经济技术发展，起到了积极的作用。

第二节　经济技术开发区的投资待遇

一、经济技术开发区的外商投资待遇

吸引外资是开发区的首要任务，为此，中央及地方政府制订了一系列特殊的优惠待遇，以确保开发区目标的全面实现。这些优惠待遇主要包括税收、土地使用、货物进出境及信贷、外汇等方面。

（一）税收优惠

1. 所得税

对在开发区内开办的生产性、科技性外商投资企业（以下简称开发区企业），其所得税减按 15% 的税率计征。其中，经营期在 10 年以上的，经批准从开始获利年度起可以免征 2 年，减半征收 3 年所得税。从 1986 年 10 月起，开发区内的产品出口企业，按照国家规定减免企业所得税期满后，凡当年出口产品产值达到当年企业产品产值 70% 以上的，减按 10% 的税率缴纳企业所得税。对开发区企业征收的地方所得税，需要给予减征、免征优惠的，由所在市人民政府决定。

对开发区内中外合资经营企业的外商免征汇出利润所得税。外商在中国境内没有设立机构而有来源于开发区的股息、利息、租金、特许权使用费和其他所得的，除依法免征所得税的外，减按 10% 的税率征收。其中，提供资金、设备的条件优惠，或者转让的技术先进，需要给予更多减征、免征优惠的，也由所在市人民政府决定。

2. 流转税

对外商投资企业和外国企业产品销售收入等流转环节的征税，在 1994 年 1 月 1 日前为工商统一税。为贯彻税收优惠政策，国家规定，开发区企业进口自用的建筑材料、生产设备、原材料、零部件、元器件、交通工具、办公用品，免征工商统一税。开发区企业生产的出口产品，除国家限制出口的产品意外，免征工商统一税，内销产品，则同样须照章纳税。

随着税制改革的神话，从 1994 年 1 月 1 日起，流转税由增值税、消费税、营业税组成，并统一适用于内资企业与外商投资企业和外国企业，取消了对外商投资企业和外国企业的工商统一税。

3. 关税与进口环节税

在开发区建设指出，国家为扶持其启动与发展，在关税与进口环节税方面也给开发区以特殊优惠待遇。

按照海关总署 1988 年 4 月发布的《海关对经济技术开发区进出境货物管理规定》，开发区内的企业机构，经批准进口供本开发区内使用的货物，其关税、进口调节税和工商统一税（产品税或增值税），按一下规定办理：

（1）开发区基础设施建设所需进口的机器、设备和其他基建物资，予以免税。此项规定原定自批准之日起 5 年内实行，后来延长到 1993 年。

（2）区内企业进口自用的建筑材料、生产和管理设备、生产用燃料、合理数量的生产用车辆、交通工具、办公用品及上述机器设备、车辆所需进口的维修零配件，予以免税。

（3）开发区内的行政机关、事业单位等机构进口自用合理数量的建筑材料、交通工具、办公用品、管理设备，比照上项的规定办理。

（4）区内企业进口专为生产出口产品所实际耗用的原材料、零配件、元器件、包装物料、旅游餐饮业营业用的餐料，利用外资养殖出口产品所需进口的饲料，予以免税。

上述进口的减免税货物原则上限在本区内使用，经批准内销时，须补办进口手续和补征税款。

开发区进口上述 1、2、3、4 项规定范围以外的其他货物，则须照章纳税。

值得注意的是，1995 年年底，国务院发布了《关于改革和调整进口税收政策的通知》（以下简称《通知》）。《通知》规定，从 1996 年 4 月 1 日起，全国各类特定区域（包括经济技术开发区）进口各类物资，一律按法定税率征收关税和进口环节税。

至于开发区出口产品，则仍按一下规定办理：

(1)开发区内企业出口开发区生产的产品,免征出口关税。

(2)使用内地料件或半成品,在开发区内加工出口应征出口关税的产品,已经实质性加工,增值20%以上的,可视为开发区产品,海关凭有关证明文件免征出口关税。

开发区企业代理或收购区外产品出口,应按国家有关规定办理;出口应征出口税的产品,照章征收出口关税。

(二)土地使用方面

为吸引外商投资,各开发区还在土地使用方面提供了一些优惠措施。例如,根据《广州经济技术开发区土地管理试行办法》,广州开发区的场地使用费包括土地开发费和土地使用费,其收费标准视企业类别而定。其中,产品出口企业和先进技术企业的土地开发费和使用费,如综合计收的,可减按每平方米5元人民币收取(即国家所允许的最低地价);开发费一次技术或企业自行开发场地的,经批准可以给予更多优惠。还有一种租赁土地费,租期分别为半年、一年和两年,租期较长则收费略低,租期较短则收费略高,比较灵活,也比较合理。

(三)其他方面

对开发区的建设所需投资,国家给予信贷资金的支持,并对部分开发性贷款给予利息;开发区范围内新政家的财政收入在一定期限内免除上缴任务、留给开发区作为发展之用,后者原定自批准之日起5年内实行,后亿决定延长到1993年。

此外,开发区企业还可享受国务院《关于鼓励外商投资的规定》等一系列涉外经济法规所确定的优惠措施。

应该承认,我国给予经济技术开发区的各项优惠对促成开发区的迅速启动与发展起到了重要的作用。然而,优惠措施仅仅是引进外资的手段,而不是目的。目前,我国有的开发区除减免地方所得税(10%)外,还竞相压低土地使用费,以期通过优惠竞争来吸引外资入区。有的开发区甚至违背国际惯例及《中外合资经营企业法》的规定,先分给外商10%红利,再按投资比例分红。这种畸形的、片面的减税让利的做法势必影响开发区乃至国家的总体经济效益,同时也会使外商产生误解。况且,过分强调减税让利往往导致护士对外资流向的引导,这些无论对外资的引进还是对产业结构的调整都是不利的。特别是在党和国家已经提出,要创造条件,逐步对外商投资企业实行国民待遇的新形势下,我们确有必要对这种优惠措施予以重新审视。

尽管税收优惠通常被认为是吸引外资最为直接有效的方法。但当代脱机投资流动的实践却反复证明,税收优惠的作用是十分有限的,特别是对于实行税收饶让政策国家的外商,这种优惠的吸引力根本不存在。同时,作为当代国际投资的主导力量,跨国公司在投资时更看重的是一个稳定的、可预见的、有保障的投资环境,而不是片面的税收减免优惠——这种反应,在近几年的《世界投资报告》中几乎年年都出现过,而且越来越强烈。

与此相应,当代世界各国,尤其是发展中国家,也越来越意识到公平竞争的投资环境的重要性,纷纷调整外资政策,走上了国民待遇的道路。换言之,各国正着力于塑造一个公平、公正、公开的投资与竞争环境,而太低曾经盛行的国际优惠攀比。

中国已经选择了市场经济的发展道路,同时,中国正在争取加入世界贸易组织,这些客观上都要求我们按市场经济的一般规律与投资管理的国际通例来重塑我国的外资立法,所以,党中央在1993年年底正式提出了要创造条件,对外商投资企业实行国民待遇。

这一决策一方面意味着我国将逐步减少对外资的种种歧视与限制,另一方面,也意味着要淡化与缩小对外资的过多、过杂的优惠措施。事实上,中国政府已经明确,自1996年4月1日起对新批准成立的外商投资企业总额内进口的设备和原材料,将一律按法定税率征收关税和进口调节税,不再减免,经济开发区也不例外。与此同时,大幅度地下调进口关税,这正是这一改革进程的重要一环。

然而,这也不当然意味着所有的优惠均需"一揽子"同时取缔。在现阶段,可以认为,经济技术开发区的历史使命并未完成,其作为具有特定经济功能的特别经济区仍具有存在价值,为确保这种经济功能的实现,维持一定的优惠,是必要的,也是可行的。

为此,应该分部门、有选择、有重点地给予外资优惠。对现有的各种优惠条款,特别是税收优惠条款应加以清理。对在诱导外资投向中相互矛盾的条款、对有损宏观经济利益的地方性攀比优惠条款,对造成企业在相互经济活动不平等税负的条款要加以修改、调整,以立法形式对不同外商投资企业在原材料供应、职工的招聘、税收的优惠、地价的高低、产品的销售等方面给予不同的优惠待遇,将外资真正引向技术先进型和产品出口型企业,实现外资的最优配置,使开发区的产业结构趋于合理,开发区的经济功能趋于实现。与此同时,优惠政策还应注意与国内投资政策相衔接,给予国内投资者以适当的优惠。

二、经济技术开发区内资企业的投资待遇

(一)经济技术开发区内资企业概述

开发区的企业按投资来源,可分为两大类:一类是外商投资企业;另一类即是内资企业,即国内事业单位和机关在开发区独立或联合举办的企业,其投资全部来源于国内。内资企业可分为国内独资企业与国内联合投资企业,简称内资企业与内联企业。

在开发区内设立内资企业首先是开发区创建投资“硬环境”的需要。开发区多设在离母城一定距离的地方,一般不具备工业发展的条件,需投入大量的人力、物力、财力从事通电、通水、通气、通路等基础设施建设和地上建筑工作。开发区开创初期,这种投资“硬环境”的建设工作多由内资企业进行。其次,内资企业是完善开发区投资环境的需要。由于开发区的外商投资企业多为生产性企业,必须有相应地配套服务性行业来保证生产的顺利开展和满足日常生活的需要,所以,饮食、旅馆、商场等服务型内资企业就成为一个完成的开发区投资环境所不可或缺的组成部分。最后,内资企业还可以繁荣经济、增加区内的财政收入,缓解资金紧张状况,为开发区的进一步发展积累资金。

开发区内资企业的形式多种多样,但大体可分6种:即国内一家企业单独投资、两家或两家以上企事业单位联合投资、国内企事业单位与开发区直属企业联合投资、划片开发、联合开发以及组建企业集团等。其中,划片开发指实力强大的大公司经过开发区管委会的同意,在区内划出一定区域,自行投资,自行开发,自行组织兴办外资企业和内联企业,如天津开发区划出0.77平方公里,包给中国国际信托投资公司投资开发,就是这种划片开发的成功典范。

各开发区都在建区初期就开始创立内资企业。大致来说,开发区的内资企业的发展经历了三个阶段:第一,基础开发阶段,主要投资者是建筑施工企业,投资方向主要是基础设施、基本建设等的建设;第二,生活环境完善阶段,内资企业开始向商业、饮食业等服务行业发展,以适应开发区工业发展的需要;第三,工业发展阶段,内资企业转向工业投资。目前,各开发区以商业、工业、服务业、建筑业的内资企业为多,尤其是商业和服务业约占内资企业的50%;同时,工业企业在企业数量、投资额、创造产值和就业人数方面也达到一定规模。以天津开发区为例,到1989年底,内资企业就已有135家,约占开发区企业总数的1/2,投资总额约2.5亿元,1989年社会总产值为1.7亿元,约占全区1/4;实现利润3641万元,占全区利润23%;税金1952万元,约占全区税收的30%;出口创汇520万美元,占开发区出口总额的34%,可见,内资企业在开发区分量还是很大的。

经济技术开发区内资企业的优惠原则各开发区基本上都对内资企业实行优惠,优惠的目的在于吸引国内厂家到开发区来兴办产业。但这种鼓励与优惠带有指导性,是有所侧重的,具体来说有下列几个方面:

第一,合资导向。引进内资的一个目的是增加开发区的经济市立,以利于吸引外资,因而开发区比较欢迎有与外商合作前景的内资企业,作为开发区发展的预备力量。有合作前景通常是指行业符合国际产业结构变化形势,技术人员和工人具备较好素质,商品在市场上有竞争力。

第二,出口导向。开发区对技术水平较高或工艺独特,产品外销可能性较大的企业是鼓励和优惠的。因为利用国内资源,加工成成品出口,或进口原料,加工增值后再出口,符合开发区和国家扩大出口、多创汇的目的。另外对生产的产品可用于进口替代的企业,开发区也予以鼓励。

第三,技术导向。开发区鼓励高技术水平的企业尤其是技术密集型、知识密集型企业进区。这两类企业同开发区的优势及有利条件结合,会对开发区产生深远的影响。

第四,规模导向。即鼓励以名牌产品为龙头,组织同一行业和相关行业的企业,形成共产销,科研、设计、开发、教育相结合的外向型企业集团,即一条龙式的强大的出口规模生产体系。

第五,产业导向。即只对某些行业进行鼓励,具体行业依据国际经济发展趋势、开发区产业政策和出口商品结构确定,通常鼓励的行业有电子、建材、石油化工、食品、轻纺等。

第六,开发导向。即对来开发区划片开发的企业、公司持欢迎态度。这种开发使开发区区域开发力量大为增强。

此外,开发区还依据投资期限的长短、工业、建筑业、商业等行业的不同,分别给以不同的优惠措施,鼓励投资期限长的企业,鼓励工业项目的内资企业。

由此可知,并非所有内资企业均可进入开发区经营,未列入鼓励范围的投资将在审批时受到限制,即使对进区的内资企业也并非采取同样的待遇,而是依据开发区的发展需要确定不同的优惠措施,实现优惠的指导和推动作用。

(二)经济技术开发区对内资企业的优惠措施

开发区对内资企业采用的优惠措施通常以地方性法规、规章的形式加以规定,这些优惠措施涉及许多方面,是吸引国内企业到开发区投资的主要因素之一。这些措施如下:

1. 税收优惠

这是各开发区普遍采用的优惠办法,包括所得税减免,进口税和出口税的减免。

所得税的减免:开发区均对内资企业实行一定期限内减免所得税的优惠。一般是按国有企业所得税率进行征收,再比照开发区“外商投资”企业待遇给予一定退让,这种优惠还依据行业的不同有所区别,如对商业、旅游业的优惠要比对工业企业的优惠少一些。

进口税减免:设在开发区的内资企业其进口自用的机器设备、仪器仪表、交通工具、办公用品、建筑材料等,免征进口税和工商统一税。企业为出口而进口的零配件、元器件、原材料、包装材料等,免征进口税,以鼓励企业从事出口加工(同样,随着我国进口税收政策的调整,这种减免也已经不复存在)。

出口产品税减免:为鼓励出口,对内资企业的出口产品免征出口产品税和增值税。

此外,税收方面的优惠还有税前还贷,加速折旧,免征建筑税等。

2. 外汇方面的优惠

开发区对于有出口业务的内资企业,通常允许设立外汇账户,所得外汇可按开发区的规定全部留成或以较高的比例留成,并允许自由汇出区外。

3. 场地使用费的优惠

场地使用费分为土地开发费和土地使用费。对技术先进的,出口产值高的或经营期限长的内资企业,分别不同情况给以不同的优惠。通常是征收较低的场地使用费或给以一定比例的减征或一定期限的免征。对一次性交纳场地使用费有困难的,则允许后交或免交。

4. 用人自主权

内资企业有权公开招聘人员,开发区不予干涉。对技术先进型或产品出口型企业还允许比照合资企业确定其工资标准和福利待遇。

5. 贷款优惠

对内资企业固定资产或自有资金不足部分,开发区银行可提供贷款或优先提供贷款予以扶持。特别是对划片开发的企业集团,优惠更多,除享受上述优惠外,还在其开发片内拥有下述权力:审批一定限额以下的外商投资企业或内资企业;批准企业人员的组团出国;经批准后,对其所开发的土地可以保值抵押,有偿转让使用权;产品出口达一定规模,经批准后可组成以产品为龙头的工业公司,给予外贸经营权。

上述优惠措施由各开发区依据其具体情况确定,各区的优惠措施大致相同。由于上述优惠措施是对内地企业权限的较大突破,因而在吸引内资方面起了较大的推动作用。当然,在我国对外经贸政策大幅调整的大前提下,这种内资企业的地区差别待遇也有待于进一步合理化与完善化。

第三节 经济技术开发区的行政管理体制

经济技术开发区经过10年多的建设与发展，已取得较显著的经济效益。目前，开发区正面临着政策优惠优势逐渐削弱，体制改革的迫切性加强，体制作用越来越明显的状况。这是因为随着我国对外开放向纵深发展，许多优惠政策已非开发区所独有。同时，由于开发区投资环境尚不尽如人意，这就使开发区的吸引力有所降低。为使开发区得以进一步发展，就必须"增创新优势，更上一层楼"。管理体制作为整个开发区经济活动的保障，是一个重要的突破口。

经济技术开发区的管理体制包括两个方面，即开发区的行政管理体制与经济管理体制。前者指开发区内管理机构的设置组织与权限分工；后者则指开发区对区内经济活动的宏观管理与调控行为。

经济技术开发区的经济活动与管理具有相当程度的市场化与国际化的特性，但现行的管理体制却在一定程度上束缚着开发区经济的发展，这就在客观上要求尽快进行管理体制的改革，以形式与开发区的经济功能和区位特征相适应的管理体制，为全国的体制改革起到示范与"窗口"的作用。

一、经济技术开发区行政管理体制的现状与问题

采用什么样的行政管理模式更为有效，这一直是各开发区探索的重点。10年来，各开发区都在适时地调整组织机构的设置和完善管理职能。从现状来看，各开发区的管理体制可归结为三种模式：

（一）政企合一型

这种管理模式的中心是管理体制的高度集中和统一。其机构设置主要是管委会本身机构，包括负责决策及职能管理的各个部门和服务性机构。目前许多开发区还设立了海关、商检等政府派驻机构。另外，在区内设立发展总公司，负责开发区的基础设施建设，一般总公司是行政公司，即使有的是经济实体，但管理行为仍然是行政性的。管委会和总公司相互混合，主任及总经理互兼，即通常说的"两块牌子，一套班子"，形成统一的集权式管理。在这种体制下，政府的管理具有双重性，不仅行使审批，规划等行政职权，同时还负责资金筹措，建设开发等具体经营事务。管委会管理的最大特征是具有统一性和权威性，而开发区总公司和专业公司基本没有自我决策权。这种集权式，以行政管理为主的管理模式在开发区建立初期对开发区建设起了推动作用。但随着开发区进

一步发展,其弊端也较明显地暴露出来。在开发区初建时期,我国数个开发区采用这种模式,如天津、南通等。目前,连云港仍实行这一模式。

这一模式的弊病在于:(1)管委会权力过于集中,不仅负责决策,而且从事一般经营管理,尤其是开发区从开发阶段进入项目引进阶段后,从项目审批到建成投产等一系列活动均由管委会管理,使管委会陷入一般具体事务中,分散了对开发区进行重大决策的精力。另外,管委会既无资金,也无管理具体经营活动的能力,结果只能是管理机构的不断膨胀。(2)在这种模式下,政企不分容易造成对行政手段的过分依赖,公司缺少活力,形成呆板僵化的机制。

(二)政企分开型

目前这一模式为大多数开发区采用。管委会作为地方政府的派出机构行使政府的管理职权,而开发区的所有公司(包括总公司和各专业公司)作为企业法人,实行企业内部自我管理,这样使政府的行政与企业的经营权分离。其次,管委会的管理职权基本上包括了对区内各项经济活动的监督、管理和协调。当然,各开发区的管理权限也存在一定差异。有些开发区,如广州开发区,管理的范围较广,无论规划、立法、项目管理,还是文教、卫生都由管委会负责,基本上相当于一级政府的权力;但也有些开发区,如南通开发区,其管委会的职权范围相对较小,管委会只负责开发区的经济管理。

这种管理模式虽不直接运用行政手段干预企业活动,但在目前开发区配套机制不完善,管理手段不充分的情况下,对区内经济发展和布局在管理上仍有相当难度,仍无法摆脱旧体制的束缚。另外,在我国整个经济管理体制条块分割的情况下,开发区管委会同政府各部门,如同计经委、外经委,甚至规划、环保等部门容易产生矛盾,尤其在级别相当的部门之间,要么相互推诿,要么分庭抗礼,在有些开发区还出现了权力不能落实的情况。例如,政府授予开发区的项目审批权,因没有资金、物资权,使审批权形同虚设;一些较大的项目都需供水、供热、供电、中方配套资金等。但有的开发区虽有相当于市级的项目审批权,即无审批电力、规划等其他配套设施权,使项目审批权无法落实。

目前这种政企分开的管理模式又可分为三种类型:

1. 管委会与总公司并存型:开发区既设有管委会,又设有开发总公司。管委会负责宏观决策,监督与协调以及审批项目;总公司负责开发及项目引进,经营各种基础设施。总公司是一个经济实体。但也有些管委会授予总公司部分管理权限。目前广州开发区和天津开发区都属这一类型。

2. 管委会与专业公司并存型:开发区设立管委会,同时又设立各种专业公司(或名义上叫总公司,实质上是专业公司),由各专业公司负责各项基础设施的开发和经营。如福州马尾开发区。

3. 管委会与联合公司并存型:这种类型是宁波开发区的一个创新。管委会作为政府派出机构行使管理职权,而负责开发建设及项目引进的总公司是由开发区管委会、中国五金矿产进出口总公司、中国机械进出口总公司共同出资成立的股份制企业。在"小政府、大企业"的原则下,由联合公司负责开发区的规划、建设、经营和管理,充分体现了政企分开的原则。创办这种内联型的股份制公司,是开发区建设的一个新的尝试,可以充分利用大集团、大企业雄厚的资金,先进的技术及管理经验来弥补开发区自身的不足。

以上两种模式都设有管委会,它作为政府的派出机构行政职权。目前全国有11个开发区设有管委会。

(三)无管委会模式

上海的闵行、虹桥两个开发区以及1988年成立的漕河泾微电子高技术开发区都具有面积小,离市区远的特点,且三个开发区分工明确。管理模式也更具特色。闵行、虹桥开发区建立后,由闵虹公司同香港合资建立的闵行虹桥联合发展有限公司负责区内的基础设施建设及项目引进。公司作为经济法人组织区内的经济活动,并承担了政府职权中部分协调的职能。随着开发区的发展,仅有的协调权已远远不能满足对开发区的管理需要。开发区的规划、对区内的企业的管理等均需有专门机构来统一管理,而开发公司本身是一个经济实体,并不具有政府职能,因此提出了管理机构重新设置的三套方案:一种是设管委会,但根据各开发区的经验,认为管委会虽有利于协调区内事务,但作为新的权力机构很难处理与其他政府部门的关系。第二种是把管理机构挂在某一部门(如经贸委、经委等)的一个处室,但也同样很难解决条块之间的矛盾。经过反复论证,提出了第三种方案,也是目前正在实施的,即由上海市专门管理外资的外国投资事务工作委员会来管理开发区。通过实践证明,这样的管理模式可以使政企完全分开,开发公司只负责内部的经营管理,而外资委作为专门管理外资的机构,一方面便于全面领导,协调开发区同区外的工作,把开发区的规划纳入地方发展战略之中;另一方面,外资委直属市长领导,具有较强的权威性和协调性,既可以处理区内经济事务,也有利于协调同区外其他各方的关系。另外,外资委仅负责从项目审批到营运的经济事务,而区内的其他社会事务则由原行政区管理,这样可以使管理工作实现集中化和专业化。

但是,这种无管委会的模式同样也存在一些问题,作为专门管理外资的机构不仅要管理开发区,还要管区外的外资食物,这样势必对开发区的管理有一定影响。其次,开发区的管理由政府原有部门负责,如外资委分管经济事务,开发区所在行政区政府分管社会事务，在现有的管理体制下，很容易使管理手段和方法陷入老框框。用老办法对待新事物，这与开发区国际化的要求是矛盾的。例如，环卫工作本应由行政区环卫部门负责管理。但环卫部门认为整个开发区是由联合公司开发，而且按我国的管理方法，一般的国营企业都需承担一定的社会职能，如自管环境卫生，自办托幼、教育，他们也把同样的观点用于开发区，使开发区目前还存在区内交通、环境卫生等方面无人管理的问题。

从上述开发区的集中管理模式来看，各开发区的管理体制有其产生的历史背景，很难简单地给某一模式下一个结论。各种模式虽然都在不断调整、吸收好的经验，但无论哪种都未能摆脱中国传统条块管理体制的束缚，只是程度不同地对旧的管理体制进行改良，还没有建立起一套全新的管理体制，没有运用外向型的管理方法来管理外向型的经济区域。我国开发区政府管理体制主要存在这样几个问题：

1. 传统束缚力强。在我国整个经济管理体制仍是一种计划性较强的集权式管理体制下，开发区的管理模式也难以摆脱旧体制的束缚，传统势力和习惯势力仍在起着重要作用，机构设置仍未能摆脱原有的框框和条块分割局面，因此，多数开发区只能在旧体制中寻求改良方式，以使管理体制趋于比较合理。

2. 政企分开不彻底。一些开发区管委会与总公司名义上分开，但实际上机构仍有交叉，政府对企业的侵权行为屡有发生，而企业内在动力和自我约束机制仍未形成，这种管理形式与开发区发展外向型经济及多种经济成分并存的要求相距较远。

3. 管理手段未能充分运用。目前，开发区政府管理体制受传统束缚力强，管理方法也受传统影响，行政手段运用仍然较多，有时仍采用对待国营企业的管理方法来对待外商投资企业；经济管理手段已开始应用，但不够充分；而立法、执法不够完善，咨询管理的运用几乎没有或者极少。

4. 管理机构效率比较低。在机构设置方面，开发区的管理机构一般要十人甚至上百人，有的达几百人，人员庞杂，人浮于事的现象比较普遍。有的开发区还没有建立"一条龙"式的项目审批服务，使项目的引入和运营要"过五关斩六将"，工作效率很低。

二、境外出口加工区的行政管理模式及其借鉴

上述问题的出现，说明开发区在管理方面仍未能找出合适的管理体制，有必要借鉴一下国外及境外出口加工区的政府管理模式和经验。目前，亚洲较成功的出口加工区主要有我国台湾地区的高雄、南梓、台中，韩国的马山出口加工区，以

及菲律宾的巴丹出口加工区。我国的开发区与出口加工区虽然在设区目标上不尽相同,但基本内容仍然十分相似。我国的开发区设区目标具有双重性,即出口创汇与引进高技术兵种,而一般的出口加工区则以出口创汇为主要目标,对高技术另行设区,如台湾的新竹科学工业园区就是这样。但无论开发区还是出口加工区都是在一定区域内实行特殊政策来吸收外资,出口创汇的。因此了解各出口加工区的政府管理模式,对开发区的管理体制创新具有借鉴意义。

通过管理体制比较分析表(见附表),我们可以看出出口加工区主要存在两种管理模式:

(一)企业型模式

这是由企业型的法人组织或企业集团来开发、管理、经营区内的一切事务。公司具有企业性质,同时又具有政府职能。如菲律宾的巴丹出口加工区,管理权限较大,管理方式也比较灵活。

技术经济开发区与各(地区)出口加工区管理体制的比较表

	菲律宾巴丹出口加工区	韩国马山加工区	斯里兰卡大科伦坡投资促进区	我国台湾地区出口加工区	印度坎德拉加工区	中国经济技术开发区
机构性质	总统领导下具有一切法人权力的国营公司	工商部领导下的一个管理集团,不受政府管理机构约束	直属总统领导的法人团体	"经济部"领导下的一个管理部门	在两个机构领导下的管理厅	直属市政府领导
领导层次	2	2	2	2	3	
权限	被赋予相当广泛的权力,可批准外资企业的投资申请,决定加工区各种公用事业及服务行业的收费标准,拥有警察及治安职权	可批准投资,申请外汇结存,颁发进出口许可证,建筑许可证、入境居留许可证;对设在区内的各种管理机构拥有监督管理的权力	拥有在科伦坡以北的一片4.16平方公里的全权管辖区,全权处理外商投资事宜,不受国内法律的约束,可修订某些法律适用范围	管理部门作为区内海关、港务、警察、外汇汇兑等一切方面的总负责机关,使出口加工区的经营管理工作一元化	管理体制由三级组成,出口加工厅在两个机构的领导下,区内工作要与60个左右机构打交道,手续繁杂,行政工作效率低	各开发区管理权限不完全相同,一般包括:项目审批,土地规划及管理,以及财政、税收、监督、检查等职能,有的开发区还有教育、公安等社会职能

资料来源:《特区经济资料》1983年第21期。

（二）政府管理机构模式

这是由中央直属部门中的一个管理层或管理集团管理，但政府行政机构对其约束力较小。如韩国的马山出口加工区是由工商部领导下的管理集团进行管理，台湾的出口加工区亦属此类，具有更大权限，统管区内的一切事务。

出口加工区无论哪种模式，其成功的经验主要有这样几点：

1. 出口加工区的管理机构不管是哪种类型，都必须具有企业的性质，这是联合国工业发展组织在总结了世界出口加工区的经验后提出的观点，其根据是出口加工区涉外性强并与国际市场紧密相连，随时要对变化莫测的世界市场作出判断，要有较强的应变能力，同时也要有冒险性，这对于一般性政府机构是很难做到的。因此，出口加工区的政府管理必须突破政府计划管理模式。这为我国开发区体制建设提供了一个新思路。

2. 层次少、级别高、权限大，这是几个成功的出口加工区的共同点。许多出口加工区直属国家元首领导，如巴丹出口建工区属总统领导，理事会由部长和银行、投资局的最高官员组成，对区内各项事务拥有领导权，甚至有立法权，如科伦坡管理机构可不受国内法律约束或可修订某些法律适用范围，从而对加工区进行有效的统一管理。

3. 人员精干，工作效率高。成功的出口加工区都离不开高级管理人员，如巴丹加工区理事会仅有 6 人组成，科伦坡经济委员会仅有 5 人，在人员精干、管理层次少的条件下，多数出口加工区实行了集中式服务管理，“一条龙”式办公，工作效率很高。

在对出口加工管理模式进行比较之后，我们可以发现，出口加工区与开发区的管理是不应完全相同的，出口加工区的外部条件好，市场发育完善，加之其高效、统一、灵活的领导特色，容易取得较大的成功；而开发区本身市场条件不完善，管理权限相对较小，所以出口加工区的有些经验值得开发区借鉴。对开发区来说同样需要兼顾两方面，即既要加强政府控制管理，又要具有管理机动权。目前，我国的开发区面积较大，数量较多，在全国管理体制计划性较强的情况下，较难采用企业式的管理形式，而设置政府管理机构的管理模式与我国情况较接近。因此，出口加工区政府管理机构的机构设置、职权范围及管理特点等仍可为我们探索新的开发区管理模式提供一些有益的参考。

三、经济技术开发区管理机构的职能

从目前来看，我国开发区的管理结构大都具有比较广泛的管理职能。以大连开发区为例，其职能包括：

1. 编制开发区的总体规划和经济、社会发展规划，经批准后组织实施；
2. 依据国家的法律法规，制定开发区的各项行政管理规定；
3. 管理开发区内的土地和各项基础设施、公共设施；
4. 按规定权限审批或审核在开发区内的投资项目；
5. 依法管理开发区的财政、税收、劳动人事和工商行政；
6. 管理开发区的进出口业务；
7. 处理开发区的涉外业务；
8. 兴办和管理开发区的教育科技、文化、卫生、体育和其他事业；
9. 对开发区内的企业、事业单位进行指导和监督；
10. 监督、管理市政府各部门设在开发区的分支机构的工作；
11. 大连市人民政府授予的其他职权。

第四节　经济技术开发区的经营管理制度

经济技术开发区的经营管理主要包括投资管理、技术引进管理、土地管理与劳动管理四大方面。对此，各开发区条例一般都作了原则性的规定，具体的规定则多散见于各开发区颁布的有关专门规章之中。

一、经济技术开发区的投资管理

吸收投资，促进开发是开发区的基本发展途径，相应地，对国外投资的管理也就构成开发区经济管理的首要内容。开发区的投资管理措施主要包括有关投资条件、投资方式、审批程序等方面的规定。这些规定一般的都由各开发区的开发区条例作出。

(一) 投资条件

各开发区一般都结合办区宗旨，对前来开发区的国内外投资项目作出了某些条件限制。多数开发区规定了投资的积极条件，如大连开发区要求重点兴办符合下列条件之一的生产性项目：

1. 生产工艺和制造技术属国际先进或国内急需的；
2. 产品以外销为主的；
3. 产品能替代进口的。

有的开发区则同时规定了投资的消极条件，如天津、大连都规定开发区内不得开办下列生产项目：

1. 技术落后或设备陈旧的；

2. 污染环境无切实治理措施的；

3. 产品属于我国政府禁止、限制生产的。

（二）投资方式

各开发区一般都允许投资者采用灵活多样的投资方式。例如，大连明确规定在开发区投资和经营可以采取中外合资、中外合作、外商独资、国内独资、国内联营、补偿贸易、租赁及中国法律允许的任何其他投资方式。

（三）投资审批

在开发区兴办企业、事业，一般应向开发区管理机构提出申请，经批准后分别办理土地使用证、营业执照、税务登记等手续。

经批准兴办的企业、事业，须按规定的期限投入资本、动工兴建。如不能按期投入资本、动工兴建的，应申请延期；无故拖延的，缴销营业执照和土地使用证书。

开发区内企业经营期满或中途歇业，一般应向原批准机关申报。经批准，清理企业的税务、债务和财产，提出清算报告，缴销营业执照后，投资者的资产可以转让，外商的资金可以按外汇管理的规定汇出。

（四）其他投资管理措施

各开发区一般都保障开发区企业的自主经营权。外商投资企业有权自行制定生产经营计划，筹措、运用资金，采购生产资料，销售产品；自行确定工资水平、工资标准、工资形式、奖励、津贴制度；自行确定机构设置和人员编制，聘用或辞退高级管理人员，增加或辞退职工。

开发区企业一般应在开发区设立会计账簿，进行独立核算，按规定向开发区财政、税务、外汇管理等有关部门和银行报送会计报表，并接受监督。外商投资企业的年度会计报表应经中国注册的会计师验证并出具证明。

外商投资企业一般应在开发区的中国银行或经外汇管理部门指定的其他银行开户。开发区内的中国银行或经中国人民银行批准的其他银行，可以对外商投资企业开办现汇抵押业务，贷放人民币资金。外商投资企业的各项保险，应向开发区内的中国人民保险公司或中国其他地区的保险公司投保。

开发区外商投资企业之间、内联企业之间，可以在外汇管理部门的监督下调剂外汇余缺。

开发区企业还应严格执行国家有关环境保护的法律法规，污染物的排放与处理必须符合国家和地区规定的标准。

二、经济技术开发区的技术引进管理

引进先进技术是开发区的另一主要目的。为此，有些开发区制定了专门的规章,以规范区内的技术引进活动。例如,广州开发区就于 1985 年颁布了《广州经济技术开发区技术引进暂行规定》,对引进技术的内容、方式、优惠、技术转让合同、当事人的权利与义务及引进技术的审批等项作了较详细的规定。

（一）引进技术的内容

引进技术的内容包括引进技术的范围与引进技术的条件两个方面。关于引进技术的范围,广州开发区作了广义的界定,及既包括已取得有效专利权的技术,也包括尚未取得有效专利权但正在申请专利的技术,还包括专有技术(know-how)与其他先进技术软件。同时,广州开发区明确规定鼓励引进下列技术:

1. 以微电子为基础的信息产业和家用电器工业;

2. 以生物工程为基础的心形食品工业、医药工业;

3. 以新材料技术为基础的新兴原材料工业;

4. 能源工业;

5. 与微电子技术和节能技术相结合的新兴的机电工业。

其中,供方向受方转让已取得专利权的技术,必须提供该专利的说明书和专利证书;有专利权转让证明的,应同时提供该证明。供方向受方转让正在申请专利的技术,必须提供请求书、说明书及其摘要、权利要求书等专利申请文件及申请的进展情况;有专利权和专利权转让证明的,应同时提供该证明。供方向受方转让专有技术的,必须提供有关的设计图纸、工艺规程和示意图、技术数据、配方、公式、关键设备、模型、样品、材料清单和说明书、操作方法说明、产品质量控制和检验方法、维修方法和设备以及有关的商业情报等。

至于引进技术所必须具备的条件,广州开发区要求所引进的技术必须是现金的、适用的和具有明显经济效益的。简言之,即必须具备先进性、适用性与效益性三大要件。这里,所谓"先进性",是指比国内同类技术先进、并且是当前发达的工业国家正在采用的,或尚在开发中的,或者有利于我国、广东省、广州市某个行业、某种产品赶上世界先进水平的。"适用性"则是指在开发区能够研制、可促进广州市、广东省和内地企业技术改造以及适合我国实际情况的。"效益性"是指符合下列一项或数项要求:

1. 能提供广州市、广东省或我国重点发展的新兴技术、新兴产品、新兴材料的;

2. 能提高产品质量和性能,降低生产成本,节约能源和材料的;

3. 有利于充分利用我国资源的;

4. 产品能开拓外销市场和替代进口的;

5. 能提供国内紧缺、需要大量进口的产品的;

6. 有利于环境保护的；

7. 有利于改善经营管理的；

8. 生产工艺和制造技术是国内特别需要的。

(二)引进技术的方式

在广州开发区，技术引进可以采用下列方式中的任何一种：

1. 供方提供技术或提供专用设备及其有关技术，同受方合作经营；

2. 供方以技术作投资股本与受方合资经营；

3. 许可证贸易；

4. 补偿贸易；

5. 供方向受方提供技术咨询或技术服务。

同时，供方以技术作投资股本与受方合资经营的，其技术股本的比例一般不超过合资企业注册资本的20%，同时应以等值以上的现金或实物作投资资本。

(三)引进技术的优惠待遇

在广州开发区，引进的技术按先进性、适用性、经济效益的不同情况，经开发区管理委员会(以下简称开发区管委会)批准，可以享受下列一种或一种以上优惠待遇：

1. 按《广州经济技术开发区工商税收实施(试行)办法》的有关优惠规定征税；

2. 减交或免交土地使用费；

3. 在开发区需要进口的商品中，在价格质量相同的条件下，供方提供的商品可享受优先权；

4. 扩大产品内销比例；

5. 延长合同期限；

6. 缩短固定资产折旧期限；

7. 安排一定数量的供方国内亲属就业；

8. 允许供方国内亲属作为供方代表参加企业管理。

(四)技术转让合同

技术转让合同一般应当包括下列主要内容：

1. 项目名称、双方当事人的法定名称、注册国家、法定地址及授权代表的姓名和职务；

2. 关键词定义；

3. 技术的内容和范围、技术资料清单和交付日期，其中涉及专利的，清单应包括该规定第八条、第九条列举的文件；

4. 商标的使用；

5. 应达到的技术目标及实现技术目标的期限和措施，实施的计划、进度和技术服务、技术培训；

6. 技术的保证和验收；

7. 保密；

8. 双方对改进技术的权利和义务；

9. 技术酬金的计算和支付方法；

10. 违约责任和索赔；

11. 不可抗力；

12. 仲裁协议或其他解决纠纷的方法；

13. 旅行的期限、地点和方式；

14. 签订的日期和地点；

15. 双方认为必要的其他事项。

合同附件是合同整体不可分割的组成部分，与合同文本有同等法律效力。合同附件一般应包括转让技术的具体内容和技术参数、指标，提供技术资料的具体内容清单、数量、交付时间和教父办法；技术考核验收方法，供方派遣人员规定，供方培训受方人员规定，双方银行保证函格式等。

合同的期限应与受方掌握引进技术所需要的时间相适应，一般不超过10年。但经双方统一并报开发区管委会批准可以适当延长。延长合同期限的申请，应在合同期满6个月前提出，开发区管委会在接到申请报告之日起1个月内批复。转让专利技术合同的终止日期不得超过该项专利权终止日期。合同自批准之日起6个月内未实施的，开发区管委会可予撤销，但如有正当理由，经开发区管委会批准可以延长，但延续其不得超过3个月。延长实施期限的申请，应在期限届满前提出。合同的期限，自批准之日起计算，申请延长实施的期限，自批准延期之日起计算。

（五）双方当事人的权利和义务

技术引进双方当事人的权利与义务必须对等。合同不得订有使任何一方受到不合理的限制或对任何一方不公平的条款。具体来说，合同一般不应含有下列限制性条款：

1. 要求受方接受与引进技术无关的附带条件的；

2. 非技术上原因而规定受方职能向供方指定的第三方购买原材料、零部件和设备的；

3. 限制受方发展和改进引进的技术的；

4. 限制受方从其他来源获得类似技术或与之竞争的同类技术的；

5. 双方交换改进技术的条件不对等的；

6. 限制受方引进金属所生产的数量、品种和销售价格的；

7. 不合理地限制受方的销售渠道或出口市场的；

8. 合同期满后，禁止受方继续使用引进技术或要求受方继续支付费用的；

9. 要求受方为不使用的或失效的专利支付报酬或承担义务的。

在合同有效期内，一方当事人未经另一个方当事人统一，擅自将合同的权力与义务全部或部分转让他人的，或将已作为股本投资的技术转让他人的，应承担违约责任。在签订合同以前，供方将同一技术转让给他人的，应将原技术转让合同的副本提交受方。供方应保证自己是所提供技术的合法拥有者，由第三方指控侵犯专利权而引起的一切经济损失，由供方负责赔偿。专利权中途失效或专利申请被拒绝，受方有权提出修改或终止合同；对造成损失的，供方应赔偿损失。供方应保证所提供的技术完整、无误、有效，并保证在合同规定的期限内使受方掌握全部转让的技术，达到合同规定的目标；由于供方原因，引进的技术没有达到合同规定的目标，供方应承担责任，赔偿损失。供方转让的技术，向专利局申请专利权并经审定公布的，受《专利法》的保护。受方应严格遵守合同的规定，切实尊重供方的技术专利权。对引进技术中的秘密部分，受方应按照合同规定的范围和期限承担保密义务。受方违约泄密造成供方损失的，应按合同规定赔偿损失。受方有关人员应承担保密义务，对泄密者应追究法律责任，令其赔偿损失。

(六)引进技术的审批

申请引进技术的当事人，应依次办理以下申请和报批手续：

1. 向开发区管委会提交申请意向书和可行性研究报告；

2. 前项申请由开发区有关部门审核并经开发区管委会同意后，领取技术转让申请书；

3. 签订合同；

4. 将合同中文本、英文本或双方商定的其他外文本一式三份报请开发区管委会及其授权的部门审批，并附下列证件：

(1)技术转让申请书一式三份；

(2)供方合同身份证明副本一式三份(法人代表或委托他人代理的，应付供方的授权书或委托书正本一份，副本一式两份)；

(3)受方的营业证书一式三份(正在申请建立企业或在技术转让合同批准后建立企业的，应附具体企业的章程副本一式三份)。

开发区管委会于合同报批之日起 40 天内将批准、不批准或要求修改的决定通知申请人。经批准的合同,开发区管委会发给批准通知书。要求修改的合同,受方与供方应重新协商,修改后再报批。合同自开发区管委会批准之日起生效。合同当事人应按开发区有关规定将合同副本送开发区工商行政办事处登记注册,并向开发区税务机关登记。

三、经济技术开发区的土地管理

土地是开发区的基本资源之一,对土地的管理是开发区宏观经济管理的重要组成部分。所以,各开发区一般都依据国家有关法律法规,结合各区实际,对这一问题作了专门的规定。

(一)土地管理机构

开发区内的土地和自愿一般来说均为国有。并由各开发区管理机构实施统一管理。任何单位或个人都必须遵守、执行开发区建设的总体规划和详细规划;未经批准,不得随意改变开发区范围内的地形、地貌,不得私自占用土地或者建设、拆除各种建筑物、构筑物。

(二)土地的使用管理

单位和个人需要使用开发区内的土地,须向开发区管理机构申请,凭开发区管理机构批准的文件和合同、协议向开发区规划管理部门办理用地的手续,领取土地使用证书后,方可使用。

经批准使用土地的单位和个人,对其所使用的土地只有使用权;不得开采、动用或者破坏地下资源和其他资源。使用土地的单位和个人,应自签发土地使用证书之日起的6个月内,向开发区规划管理部门提交施工和投产计划,9个月内开始施工,否则,吊销其土地使用证书,但如有正当理由并出具证明文件,经开发区管理机构批准后,可适当推迟提交施工和投产计划以及开始施工时间。使用土地的单位和个人完成合同、协议所规定的工程建设要求后,须经开发区规划管理部门检验,符合中华人民共和国有关建筑规范和安全规定,方可正式使用。凡擅自投产使用的,一经发现,应立即停止适用,并补办检验手续;导致发生事故,还应赔偿损失并承担责任。使用土地的单位和个人需要扩大用地范围,应办理扩大用地的申请和批准手续。

开发区内单位和个人使用土地年限,由开发区管委会根据经营项目的实际需要确定。需要延长使用土地年限,应当办理延期使用手续。任何单位和个人使用开发区的土地,都应缴纳土地使用费。各开发区一般都专门制订了区内土地使用费的标准和收取办法。一般来说,在开发区内开办教育、文化、科学技术、卫生和其他不以营利为目的的社会公益事业以及技术特别先进项目,经开发区管理机构批准,可减收或者免收土地使用费。同时,在开发区内投资兴建和经营供水、供气、供热、排水、道路以及其他基础设施,5~10 年内可以减收或者免收土地使用费。

(三)公共设施建设

按各开发区的有关规定,使用土地的单位和个人,其用地范围内按合同或者协议规定应承担的基础设施建设,须按城市规划要求修建。其用地范围内的上水、下水、电力、热力、煤气、道路、通信以及其他工程设施,应自行修建。此外,使用土地的单位和个人在用地范围内"三废"的排放与处理,还必须按照我国规定的排放标准和处理要求处理,并接受有关部门的检查与监督,按规定缴纳排污费。

四、经济技术开发区的劳动管理

劳动管理也是开发区经济管理的一个重要方面,各开发区也都有相应的专门规定。

(一)职工的录用

开发区企业职工的录用,通常有三种方式:即既可以由开发区劳动服务公司介绍,又可委托开发区劳动服务公司招聘,还可经开发区管理机构批准自行招聘。开发区企业录用的职工,应在 16 周岁以上,具有一定的文化水平。开发区企业所需职工,要经过考核、体格检查,择优录取,并签订劳动合同。

(二)劳动合同制

开发区职工一般都是实行劳动合同制。劳动合同可由企业同职工集体签订,也可由企业同职工个别签订。

劳动合同一般包括以下内容:职工的录用、解雇和辞职,合同期限和试用期,生产和工作任务,工资和奖惩,工作时间和假期,劳动保护、劳动保险和生活福利、劳动纪律以及合同变更。劳动合同中不得有对职工的歧视性条款,职工试用期不得超过 6 个月。

劳动合同由开发区劳动管理部门审核、批准。

(三)工资与待遇

开发区企业雇用的职工,应按人支付工资。企业职工最低工资水平,由开发区管理机构规定。开发区企业职工的工资待遇、工资形式以及奖励和津贴制度,由企业自行决定,报开发区劳动管理部门备案。每个职工的工资标准,应按照工作岗位、技术熟练程度和劳动强度大小由企业自行确定。工资应根据职工劳动技术熟练程度和企业盈利情况,每年有所增加。每年递增的百分比,由企业与工会协商确定。

开发区企业应当按月向开发区劳动服务公司缴纳社会劳动保险基金，社会劳动保险几斤的适用范围和办法，由开发区管理机构制定。

开发区企业职工的工作时间，每周不得多于6日，每日不得多于8小时，必须连续作业的作业，每周工作时间不得超过48小时。因生产需要职工必须加班，应征得本企业工会的同意。在公休日或者8小时工作时间以外加班，应发给不少于日标准工资额的加班费；在法定节日、假日加班，应发给不少于日标准工资额200%的加班费。开发区企业职工享受我国政府规定的公休日、节日、假日和休假制度。

开发区企业必须执行我国与开发区所在城市有关劳动保护的规定，实行安全生产和文明生产，有关主管机关有权检查、监督。开发区企业应按照我国和所在市有关女工保护的规定，对女工实行特殊保健。开发区企业的职工，患职业病或者因工负伤、致残、死亡的保健待遇、经济补助、抚恤金标准和办法，由开发区管理机构根据我国有关规定制定。

开发区企业对录用的职工，根据合同规定和本企业经营需要进行管理。对违反企业规章制度，并造成不良后果的职工，企业可根据情节给予处分，直至开除。开除职工应征求本企业工会意见，并报开发区劳动管理部门备案。

（四）辞退与辞职

开发区企业对因生产、技术条件发生变化而多余的职工，或者经过培训不能适应要求、也不宜改变工种的职工，可以辞退。辞退职工应报开发区劳动管理部门备案。职工因工伤和患职业病进行治疗或者疗养期间，因病或者非因工负伤住院治疗期间，女职工怀孕6个月以上和产假期间，不得辞退。企业辞退职工，应按职工在本企业工作年限发给一定数额的辞退补偿金。

开发区企业的职工，可以按照合同规定提出辞职申请。辞职申请应于一个月前提出，企业应予照准。职业经企业培训3个月以上，培训结业后一年内辞职或者擅自离职，应向企业偿付培训费。培训费应按培训期间用于职工本身的支出额计算。

（五）劳动服务公司与工会

各开发区一般都设立了劳动服务公司，以协助开发区企业招聘和培训职工，指导职工与企业签订劳动合同，辅导职工就业，收到、发放和管理社会劳动保险几斤。与此同时，开发区企业职工有权依法建立工会组织，开展工会活动。企业应支持工会的工作，工会应支持企业的正常经营活动。

（六）争议的解决

开发区企业发生劳动争议时，一般应尽量协商解决。协商不成的，一般可向开发区劳动管理部门请求调解。调解不成，当事人可向有关劳动争议仲裁机构申请仲裁。当事人也可不经调解而直接申请仲裁。对仲裁不服的，可以向人民法院起诉。

边境经济合作区法律问题*

第一节　边境经济合作区的概念与立法概况

一、边境经济合作区的概念

在我国,“边境经济合作区”一词首见于1992年3月9日国务院发布的《关于进一步对外开放黑河等四个边境城市的通知》(以下简称《通知》),该《通知》提出,黑河绥芬河、珲春、满洲里四个边境城市,“可在本市范围内划出一定区域,兴办边境经济合作区,以吸引内地企业投资为主,举办对独联体国家出口的加工工业和相应的第三产业”,其目的在于“积极扩大对和罗斯和独联体其他国家的边境贸易和地方贸易,发展投资合作、技术交流、劳务合作等多种形式的经济合作,合理利用当地的优势发展加工制造业和第三产业,促进边境地区的繁荣与稳定”。同年6月9日,国务院在其《关于进一步开放南宁、昆明市及凭祥等五个边境城镇的通知》中指出,凭祥、东兴、畹町、瑞丽和河口五个市(县、镇),具备条件的,允许“兴办边境经济合作区,举办出口加工企业和相应的第三产业”。国务院同时作出的《关于进一步开放二连浩特市的通知》则采用援引上述黑河等四个边境开放城市政策的方式规定了其基本政策与待遇。

可见,对于边境经济开发区,我国最早的,也是目前最重要的法律规范便是上称《通知》,而根据该《通知》的精神可以认为,所谓边境经济合作区,指的是国家为促进边境地区年乃至全国的经济发展,而在边境城市所划出的实行特殊的经济政策与管理体制,以集中发展出口加工工业和第三产业的特别经济区域。

1992年,按照邓小平同志视察南方重要谈话精神,为繁荣内陆边境和少数民族地区经济,发展同周边国家的经济技术合作,国务院先后批准了黑河、绥芬河、珲春、满洲里、伊宁、博乐、塔城、凭祥、东兴、畹町、瑞丽、河口、二连浩特、丹东等

---

* 本书系黎学玲主编:《特别经济区法》第15章,法律出版社1997年版。

14 大边境开放城市各举办一个边境经济合作区。这 14 个边境经济合作区的规划总面积为 78.45 平方公里。

兴办边境经济合作区,旨在利用边境开放城市的特殊条件,外引内联,广泛吸引国内外投资,在合作区内举办一些面向周边国家市场的出口加工工业,加速沿边地区的工业化进程,带动真哥哥边境开放城市的经济发展,进而增强与毗邻国家发展经济交往的能力。几年的实践证明,国家举办边境经济合作区的决策是正确的。据统计,截至 1993 年年底,在不到两年的时间里,我国各边境经济合作区已与国内外企业达成意向性投资协议近 2000 项,协议金额上百亿元,已有相当一批项目开始动工建设,其中相当一部分为生产性企业。[1]

二、边境经济开发区的特征

从上述初步界定可以看出,边境经济合作区具有如下几个方面的特征。

1. 边境经济合作区是我国边境对外开放政策的产物,是以边境城市为依托的一种特别经济区。按上述《通知》的精神,边境经济合作区是边境城市的不可分割的一部分,是在边境开放城市内划出一定地狱而兴办的特别经济区。这一点与经济特区不同,与经济技术开发区也不尽相同。经济特区是一个新型的独立区域,后来则发展成为一个新兴的城市,它不是某一城市的下属区域;经济技术开发区虽然也是依托开放城市,但它们所依托的一般是沿海、沿江开放城市,这些城市基础大都比较雄厚,综合经济力量较强,而合作区所依托的一般都是边陲小城镇,其经济总量与城市功能远较开发区的母城为低。

2. 边境经济合作区执行特殊的经济功能。这种经济功能便是大力吸收国内外投资,发展出口加工工业和相应的第三产业,从而加速沿边地区工业化进程,带动整个边境开放城市经济的发展,进而增强与毗邻国家发展经济交往的能力。具体来说,与经济特区及经济技术开发区相比,边境经济合作区的经济功能有如下特征:首先,它不像特区与开发区以吸引外资为主;其次是侧重于吸引内地投资;再次,它着重发展出口加工工业和第三产业,这与经济特区的综合性经济结构及开发区的纯科技与出口导向的经济结构是有所区别的;最后,边境经济合作区的宏观经济功能在于“兴边”与“睦邻”,与特区、开发区的“基地”“窗口”“试验场”等宏观经济功能也不一样。

3. 边境经济合作区实行特殊的经济政策与管理体制。其优惠措施主要表现为国家在税收、财政上所给予的必要的扶持与引导。但总的来讲,其优惠待遇

---

〔1〕 参见李岚清主编:《中国利用外资基础知识》,中共中央党校出版社、中国对外经济贸易出版社 1995 年版,第 302 页。

较特区与开发区为低。边境经济合作区管理体制建设的目标则在于建立一个高效高能的新型管理模式，以有效指挥与管理合作区各项建设事业的迅速、稳定发展。

三、边境经济合作区的立法

(一)边境经济合作区的立法现状

边境经济合作区是在我国《宪法》、法律与国家对外开放政策及各地的具体法规、规章的指导、规范下兴办与运作的。它一刻也离不开国家法律、法规、规章与政策的调整。从另一个角度来说，法律环境又是边境经济合作区整个投资环境的重要的、基础性的组成部分。

有关合作区的国家专门立法目前尚不存在。中央一级的规范目前主要表现为国务院关于开放沿边城市的一系列通知与决定。其中，最重要的就是上述四个通知。此外，1992 年6 月9 日，国务院发布的《关于进一步积极发展与原苏联各国经贸关系的通知》，经贸部发布的《关于积极发展边境贸易和经济合作促进边疆繁荣的意见》(1992 年 4 月 14 日)及经贸部和国家商检局联合发出的关于“边贸要走以质取胜之路”的通知，等等，也都可算是关于合作区的重要规范性文件。

合作区的规范化管理更多地表现为地方性的政策规定。这里又分为两个层次。第一层是地方政策，即黑龙江、新疆、云南、内蒙古、广西等省、自治区的有关政策。例如，中共黑龙江省委、黑龙江省人民政府《关于进一步扩大开放，加快发展外向型经济的决定》《新疆维吾尔自治区进一步扩大开放，鼓励投资的优惠政策》《云南省人民政府关于发展边境贸易的若干补充规定》等。第二层则是各边境开放城市所制定的一些具体的行政性规定与办法。从目前来看，各边境城市所制定的这种规定与办法主要涉及土地有偿使用、房屋开发管理、企业兼并、税收优惠、户口管理、金融市场发展规划、股份制筹资等许多方面，各城市均有所侧重，并不完全一律。其中，关于优惠政策的规定是最常见的，上述边境开放城市几乎均有有关优惠政策的规定，尽管有的并不是直接采用“优惠规定”之名称。

值得一提的是，目前全国上没有一部专门规定边境经济合作区的法律，甚至连中央和地方有关的政策也大都不是专门针对边境经济合作区。在各边境城市的有关规章中，也只有《凭祥市边境经济合作区优惠政策》和《伊宁市边境经济合作区投资环境与优惠政策》两项政策性文件，是关于合作区的专门性规章。这反映出合作区起步较晚，法制建设较为迟滞的事实。

(二)关于制定“边境经济合作区条例”

为加强边境经济合作区的法制建设，改善其投资环境，有必要制定全国统一的“边境经济合作区条例”。该条例的基本意义在于根据我国《宪法》和法律以及国家对外开放总体战略和沿边对外开放战略，确立我国边境经济合作区的性质与法律地位及其他基本制度，如合作区建设的原则，管理体制，合作区设立的条件、程序和任务；合作区的管理机构、企事业单位、社会组织及相互之间的权利义务关系以及合作区与所在开放城市之间的关系等。“边境经济合作区条例”应是关于全国各合作区的统一的、专门的立法，是合作区其他具体法规、规章的基础与依据。

然而，如果从对各种特别经济区统一立法的角度出发，也可以考虑在统一的“特别经济区法”中对合作区作专章规定，纳入上述基本内容，从而起到同样的立法功用。当然，还可以并用这两种方式，即在统一的“特别经济区法”中确立合作区的法律地位、基本功能与优惠导向；在“边境经济合作区条例”中则进一步将“特别经济区法”中的各项原则规定具体化，明确化。二者的关系应是两个层次的法律规范的关系，“边境经济合作区条例”应以“特别经济区法”为依据，并不得与之抵触，否则无效。

（三）关于边境经济合作区目前的立法重点

合作区目前尚处在起步阶段，首先要解决的便是奠定物质基础与吸引内、外投资与技术的问题。为此，必须加强合作区投资环境中这两个方面的立法，尽早、切实地解决这两个“瓶颈”问题。

其一，应当根据国家产业政策所赋予合作区的特殊优惠政策，从合作区的实际出发，按基础设施的分类，分别制定调整各种基础设施建设关系的法律规范。例如，合作区水资源开发、利用和保护办法，电子、能源开发供应办法，道路建设及管理和邮电通讯投资等法律规范，等等。在建立、健全调整合作区基础设施建设的法律制度时，应当强调以下几点：(1)贯彻投资优惠政策中的行业倾斜原则，吸引内资、外资，把资金、技术投向水、电、能源的开发、利用以及交通运输、邮电通信等薄弱环节，以及改变合作区及其开放母城基础设施的严重落后状况。(2)合作区的基础设施，应当采取公用事业大家办的原则，动员社会大力筹集社会资金，缓解资金紧缺问题；对于进入合作区的企业和经济组织积极投资进行基础设施建设的，给予利用基础设施的便利与优惠。(3)合作区的基础设施实行有偿使用的原则，其获得的使用费一方面要用于清偿基础设施建和的借款，支付基础设施管理和维护的费用；另一方面要用于基础设施的再投资，以形成基础设施建设的良性循环。

其二，应根据边境经济合作区发展战略目标，建立、健全外引内联、南联北开的法律制度，促进合作区投资软环境的优化与完善。根据国务院关于沿边区开放的基本精神，一方面应当制定合作区关于国内企业、组织或个人的投资管理办法，以吸引内地企业投资；另一方面，还应当制定合作区关于外商投资的管理办法，以吸引周边国家或其他周边的外资。建立、健全内、外投资的管理制度，旨在使合作区享有的各项投资优惠政策制度化、法律化，同时，对投资原则、形式、程序以及投资人的权利、义务及其保护加以明确，而不是擅自扩大优惠面与优惠幅度，搞“优惠大战”。在完善投资立法的同时，还要特别注意对技术引进的立法导引与促进。可以考虑根据国家有关法律与政策，具体规定对于重大的技术引进项目和先进适用技术的引进项目的优惠与奖励办法；同时还要加强对技术引进的管理，力求避免重复引进和非先进技术的引进。

在建立健全关于基础设施建设及吸引投资等基础性法规与规章的同时，边境经济合作区还应健全和完善合作区的其他各项经济管理法规、规章与规则。例如，企业登记管理制度，进出口商品管理制度，企业工商税收制度，海关报关、验关、放关制度，外汇管理制度，劳动工资管理制度等。这些经济管理规章与规则首先应体现政策从优、体制创新与限制放宽的特点，贯彻程序简化、手续简单的原则，以提高管理效率，增进经济、社会效益；同时，这些规章与规则应具有广泛的透明度与可操作性，改变那种“内部规定”内部掌握的现象，使投资者做到心中有数，同时也可杜绝政府工作人员的徇私舞弊行为。

第二节　边境经济合作区的优惠待遇

一、边境经济合作区的优惠措施

作为一种特别经济区，合作区执行特别的经济功能。为保证这种特别经济功能的实现，国家提供了相应的优惠与奖励措施（可以说，特殊的功能与特殊的政策是各种特别经济区赖以存在的基础前提，也是它们的基本特征。边境经济合作区也不例外）。这种优惠措施主要包括：

1. 合作区内的基础设施建设所需进口的机器设备和其他物资以及合理数量内的办公用品，免征进口关税和产品税（或增值税）1996 年 4 月 1 日起不再免征。

2. “八五”期间，合作区的新增财政收入留在当地，用于基础设施建设。

3. 对合作区内以出口为主的生产性内敛产业，其生产出口规模达到一定额度的，经经贸部批准，给予对毗邻国家进出口经营权。内敛企业的企业所得税在当地减按 24% 的税率征收，如内敛投资者将企业所得利润解回内地，则由投资方所在地加征 9% 的所得税。“八五”期间免征投资方向调节税。

4. 合作区内的内联企业和外商投资企业在毗邻国家易货所得，允许自行销售，进口时减半征收关税和工商统一税（1992 年以后改征增值税、消费税、营业税）。属于国家限制进口的商品，要按国家有关规定办理进口审批手续。

5. “八五”期间，人民银行每年专项安排一定数量的固定资产贷款，用于边境开放城市和边境经济合作区的建设，纳入国家信贷和投资计划。

6. 合作区内的外商投资企业，按照国家给予其母城的待遇标准，其企业所得税减按 25% 的税率征收。同时允许毗邻国际投资者在其投资总额内用生产资料或其他物资、器材等实物作为投资资本。这部分货物可按我国边境贸易的有关规定销售，并减半征收进口关税和工商统一税。

除了上述国家统一的优惠措施外，各地还颁布了大量的地方性优惠措施。以凭祥合作区为例，按照《凭祥边境经济合作区优惠政策》，合作区还可进一步享有下列优惠待遇：

1. 合作区内的内敛企业生产规模达到一定额度的，可报经贸部批准，给予对毗邻国家进出口经营权。在未获批准之前，可委托凭祥合作区实业开发总公司代理进出口，征收 1% 的代理费。

2. 合作区内敛企业的企业所得税，在当地减按 15% 的税率征收。

3. 合作区内的生产性外商投资企业，其所得税减按 15% 计征。其中，凡出口产值达到当年企业产品产值 50% 以上的，实际缴纳所得税税率高于 10% 以上部分由当地财政返还企业；设置贸易机构从事进口和转口贸易，国内商品进入合作区保税仓库即视为出口，实行退税政策；在合作区内使用的合理数量的产品、设备及其他物资，可以享受出口产品有关的退税政策。

4. 合作区实行优惠的土地出租，转让价格在合作区内使用土地，按当年规定的土地出租、还让价格根据所用土地的区域、位置、产业结构、投资额度等给予 20% 到 40% 的优惠；外商从事成片开发经营土地，按用地所在地段的出让金标准，给予 50% 优惠；开发建设期免征土地使用费；土地使用年限分别为：商业用地 40 年，工业用地 50 年，居住用地 70 年，其他用地 50 年。

凭祥合作区知识一个典型的例子，类似的优惠与见面在各合作区及其开放母城几乎全部同样地存在，只是措辞略有不同。例如黑河行署 1992 年 5 月 3 日颁布的《边境开放城市优惠政策》规定：设在合作区内的生产性外商投资企业，经批准可以由当地财政退还已缴纳税金的一部分，企业实际缴纳的所得税最低可按 15% 税率计征；产品出口企业，按照国家规定减免企业所得税期满后，当年企业出口产品产值达到当年企业产值 50% 以上的，可以按照国家规定的税率，减半缴纳所得税；对于合作区内的生产性内联企业，则仍减按 24% 征收企业所得税。换言之，凭祥合作区的政策，较之黑河更为优惠，这是由于黑河开放在先的缘故，从中可以看出各合作区“优惠大战”的影子。

二、边境经济合作区优惠待遇的调整

从上面的分析可以看出，对于边境经济合作区这种特别经济区，国家所给予的优惠政策是较为慎重的，这从内联与外商投资企业的企业所得税率都可以看出。从总体看来，合作区虽然是开放得比较晚的，但其“优惠总水平”尚不及经济特区与经济技术开发区。这主要是因为边境经济区所处的地理位置十分特殊，与地缘政治及国家主权关系十分密切，国家不便过分放开。但国际经济一体化的大趋势与边境贸易日益繁荣的事实又使国家不得不重视边区的开发、建设与发展。这一情况，导致了前面提到的沿边开放的重大决策，进而导致了沿边开放城市及其合作区采取较为谨慎的开放与有限度的优惠的中央政策。这一政策与政策无疑有其合理性。

然而地方的出发点却有所不同。一些边境经济合作区所在地政府认为，鉴于国家向来对边区建设投入太少及边区经济技术与文化教育落后的现实，国家应给予边境地区，尤其是边境开放城市及其经济合作区以更为优惠的政策措施。现行的优惠政策不仅比不上经济特区与经济技术开发区的优惠，也赶不上俄罗斯联邦赋予其西伯利亚和远东自由经济区的政策优惠，因而是不够的，很难产生“外引内联，南联北开”的吸引力。所以，要求国家对沿海、沿边、沿江的对外开放进行综合研究，正确确定赋予边境经济合作区优惠政策的最佳幅度：国家应当赋予边境经济合作区对内资、外资具有足够吸引力的优惠政策；并且这种优惠政策既要同国内经济特区、开发区的优惠政策相平衡，又要同周边国家经济性特区的优惠政策相呼应。具体来说，赋予边境经济合作区对外开放的优惠政策，应当注意四点：一是对内资、外资的投资所得税税收优惠，应比照经济特区的规定办理；二是对内、外投资者取得的土地使用权，可以根据国家产业政策分别规定一定的无偿使用期限（限制项目除外），例如 15 年、10 年、5 年无偿使用期；三是对于投资现金、适用技术项目，能够生产进口替代产品的外引内联的企业，可以适当让出边疆省、自治区，甚至国内的一定范围的市场；四是外汇管理制度应当能够保证外国投资者合法收益的自由汇出，实现投资收益的目的。[2]

地方的这种论点有一定的道理。去的优惠政策特别是关于合作区优惠措施应与国内外经济性特区的优惠政策相呼应、相平衡的提法是颇为有力的，值得有

---

〔2〕 参见梁茂邦等：《中俄边贸法论》，黑龙江人民出版社 1993 年版，第 278 ~ 279 页。

关方面重视。但问题是，有关地方政策在未获得国家同意之前，擅自“突破”国家政策、法规界限，降低企业所得税率与土地使用费率的做法是十分有害的。税收政策是国家宏观调控的基本工具之一，土地所有权一般也属于国家，二者都应是只有中央政府才能处分的权益。各地的这种“优惠攀比”的做法严重破坏了国家政策、法规的严肃性与统一性，不仅不利于外引内联、发展边贸，反而会破坏我国整体的投资环境，从而影响国内外投资者的信心与积极性。国际投资的历史一再证明，优惠只是初级阶段的投资吸引策略，要引进有质量、能产生长期效益的投资，更重要的是要靠一个稳定和可预见的投资环境——然而，这种混乱的地方性“优惠大战”无疑只会破坏我国投资环境中现有统一、稳定与可预见的优势。

因此，根本途径仍在于调整国家对边境经济合作区的政策。这种调整应与对国内其他各种类型的特别经济区的政策与立法结合起来进行。大体上说，国内各种类型的特别经济区的优惠政策，今后一定要向功能型导向的优惠发展。即一方面，各种特别经济区的优惠一定要与其特定的经济功能结合起来。优惠一定是为了促成这种功能早日实现和尽量发挥。那种一揽子，不分产业统统优惠的做法不应继续维持，而功能导向、产业导向、地区发展导向的优惠则不仅应得到维持，还可以有一定的发展。正如前面所体现的，特别经济区之所“特”，首先在于其特殊的经济功能与宏观使命，同时，为保证这种功能的实现与使命的完成，一定的特殊政策（主要是以优惠为表现形式）是十分有必要的。

第三节　边境经济合作区的行政管理体制

一、边境经济合作区行政管理体制的建立

边境经济合作区的建设离不开一个高效的管理体制，在合作区起步较晚、基础较差的前提下，一个高效高能的新型管理体制显得尤为重要。

目前，国家尚无统一的边境经济合作区法，因而关于合作区的行政管理体系，还没有一个全国统一的模式，各地均处于探索之中。从现状来看，管理体制不健全，管理关系没有理顺，是一个比较突出的问题。以最先开放的黑河市为例，直接管理黑河边境经济合作区的三个“政府”，即黑河行署（目前国家已决定撤销黑河地区）、黑河市政府和黑河边境经济合作区管理委员会，外加一个“红太阳”，即由黑河地委，黑河市委主要负责同志组成的边境经济合作区领导小组。这四者之间没有明确的层级体系与职能分工，导致管理上的混乱，行政效能低下。这种层次繁多、手续复杂、效率低下的管理体制，显然不符合合作区建设

与发展的需要。许多沿海与内地的投资和纷纷反映,“开放不放(权),特事不特(办),办事太难”。这从反面说明,能否建立起一个高效高能的管理体制,促进各种优惠政策的有效实施,增强对内、外投资者的吸引力,对边境经济合作区的建设与发展至关重要。

建立边境经济合作区的行政管理体制,我们既要考虑到我国特别经济区的一般情况,也要考虑靠边境经济合作区的特殊需要。与特别经济区一样,须收到中央、省及边境城市三层领导,同时还要建立自身的管理机构。然而,边境经济合作区特殊的地理位置决定了我们在设计管理体制时应采取的谨慎立场。从我国设立边境经济合作区的主旨出发,结合各合作区的实际情况,确立中央与地方两级管理比较现实,其中,地方级的管理又可细分为省、市及区三个层次,各有其明确的职权范围与分工。这种体制模式,不妨简称为“两级四层”的行政管理模式。

具体来说,中央的管理通常由国务院及其特区办具体设施,主要解决对各合作区的宏观规划与大政方针的决策问题。省级政府及其主管部门对边境经济合作区的管理也应转换职能,减少对合作区的微观活动的直接管理,加强宏观调控职能,发挥其规划、指导、组织、协调、综合、服务、检查、监督等作用。合作区应是其所在省、自治区对外经贸这盘棋中的“眼”,做活这个“眼”,可以带动沿边设和发展纳入自己的总体规划之中,协调合作区与开放城市、与其他地区的关系;并且,在组织实施自己的规划中,进行指导、检查、服务、监督;对于合作区建设中的问题,尤其是合作区自身难以解决的各种重大问题,应切实帮助解决。边疆省级政府是上承中央,下启合作区的关键环节,应当特别重视方针政策的管理,即依据中央赋予边疆省、自治区以及合作区的特殊政策和有关法律、法规,创造性地制定具体的实施措施,并使之制度化、规范化,保证放活微观,管好宏观,充分发挥政策法律的效能与效益。

边境经济合作区是以边境开放城市为依托所建立的特别经济区,所以,合作区的建设与发展,离不开开放母城的基础设施及经济与社会服务机构,更离不开母城的指导与管理。另外,边境开放母城的主要职责应是对以合作区为核心的母城进行全面规划、组织、协调、指导、检查、服务与监督。其管理重点在于母城的整体投资环境建设,包括投资硬环境建设及软环境就爰难舍,前者主要指基础设施建设,后者则主要指法律环境及社会经纪服务体系的建设。鉴于合作区管理层次过多,可以考虑确定边境开放城市的省辖市资格,同时还可考虑撤销原设于开放母城之上的专员行署,其职能改由开放母城职掌。对于开放母城原由省辖市管辖的,也可考虑另建省辖市,并对相邻市、县适当重新归并。这样,边境经济合作区的母城就有了更大的范围可供规划、组织与协调，从而有利于对合作区管理与服务目标的全面实现。

在上述三个行政层级之下，边境经济合作区还应设立一个专门的、日常性的管理机构，如合作区管理委员会。这是整个合作区的行政管理体制中的基础环节，也是最具体、最重要的管理层级。援引经济技术开发区的通利，合作区的管委会也不妨作为边境开放母城政府的派出机构。这样，它就可以享有边境开放母城对合作区行政事务的全部管理权力。不仅如此，对省级政府转变职能后下放给边境开放母城政府的权力，只要是属于合作区内行政事务的，也均应由合作区管委会行使。例如，按照黑龙江省省委和省政府《关于进一步扩大开放，加快发展外向型经济的决定》，赋予黑河、绥芬河两市在边境贸易和经济合作方面以相当于省级的管理权限。在这种情况下，黑河与绥芬河两个合作区的管委会作为两市政府的派出机构，对合作区内的有关事项，当然可以具有同样的，或者是相应的管理权。

二、边境经济合作区管委会的职权

为确保合作区管委会能科学、高效地实施管理，一般享有下列职权：

1. 规划制定权。管委会负责制定合作区发展战略、建设总体规划和产业政策，报请开放母城政府批准后组织实施。

2. 基本建设管理权。合作区内的土地，在报经市政府批准的总体规划之下，各类建设工程的规划、设计、报建、施工组织、工程验收、发放房地产权证书等行政事务，由管委会审批办理。

3. 项目审批权。对合作区内外引内联的投资项目，设置的企业和办事机构，管委会统一审批，市政府主管部门凭管委会的批准文件颁发批准证书。

4. 人事管理权。合作区根据自己的发展规划，在服从全市统一计划的前提下，管委会可采取相对灵活的方式管理。

5. 体制改革权。管委会可以根据合作区建设中出现的新情况、新问题，按新事新办、特事特办的原则，提出改革方案，报市政府审批并组织实施。

6. "一站式"管理权，在管委会的统一协调下，海关、边检、工商、公安、税务等部门，在合作区内设立办事机构，集中办公，统一办理各有关业务。[3]

此外，合作区的管理体制还牵涉合作区管委会下属的各种投资公司、开发公司。例如，合作区内以国家预算拨款、地方预算拨款以及吸收国际组织或者外国

---

〔3〕 参见梁茂邦等：《中俄边贸法论》，黑龙江人民出版社1993年版，第286页。

国家贷款，通过其他各种形式筹集的资金建立起来的水、电、路，交通运输，邮电通信等各种公用事业公司，土地投资开发公司，等等。这类公司的职能有两个方面：一方面，它要按照边境经济合作区管委会的整体规划，实施对市政府公用设施、地产物业的管理；另一方面，它又应实行企业化经营，其收入部分用于保证合作区管理机构的行政开支，大部分则用于合作区市政公用设施、基础设施的管理，维护和开发、建设。因此，这类公司虽然在一定程度上承担着合作区社会经济管理职能，但其主要职责仍在于经营，在经营中实现管理，故它对于合作区管委会，仍具有相对的独立性。

跨国特别经济区的基本法律问题初探*

近十几年来,特别经济区日益成为超越社会政治制度和生产力水平的世界性经济现象,其影响面越来越广,功能与方式也不断推陈出新。跨国化就是世界特别经济区的重要发展方向之一。1988年,欧洲设立了第一个跨越边界的开发区,此后,东南亚出现了一批“增长三角”,其中的“黄金四角”与东北亚筹建中的图们江经济开发区等则与我国直接相关。这种小区域[1]的国际经济合作牵涉面十分广泛。其中,法律方面的因素无疑是十分关键的。可以说,这种跨国特别经济区的每一步实质性的进展,都必然表现为某种国际条约、协议或国内立法的诞生。本文拟在简析跨国特别经济区的概念与特征的基础上,对其法律性质、国内立法与政策的国际协调等基本法律问题作初步的分析与探讨。

一

跨国特别经济区是各种跨越国界,实施特殊经济政策与管理体制的特定区域的总称。它一般是由地理位置上相互邻近的国家或地区,基于某种共同的发展目标,或生产要素的客观互补性,而相互协调政策,达成协议,采取某种特殊优惠与便利,以联合开发特定相邻区域,达到优势互补、资源共享共同发展的目的。

跨国特别经济区具有下列特征:

第一,跨国特别经济区具有跨国性。它一般是相邻或相向的国家或地区之间协商一致的结果,其具体开发与经营也都有赖于多国或多地区的共同努力与团结协作,方能发挥各自的比较优势,创造更新、更大的竞争优势。然而,这种区域又不同于贸易集团意义上的“区域”(如亚大、北美、欧盟之类)或“次区域”(如东盟等),而仅仅是一种“小区域”的国际经济合作形式。

---

* 本文发表在《国际贸易问题》1996年第6期。

〔1〕“小区域”不等于“次区域”,二者的重要区别在于:前者(如东盟自由贸易区)是个由数国组成的贸易集团,而后者只是一个小型的国际经济开发区,并不构成个贸易集团。详见后文。

第二,跨国特别经济区一般都以区域经济开发为目的。它不是特别行政区,也不具有独立的政治权利与利益,而只是有关各国政府在遵守共同的国际协调规则的前提下,各自或联合管理下的特别经济区域,即便是实行联合管理,也毫不意味着领土主权的让渡,而仍将充分体现主权国家的意志。

第三,跨国特别经济区内一般执行有别于有关国家或地区的其他地区的特殊的经济政策与管理体制。这种特殊的政策往往表现为关税减免及外汇、金融、房产、交通、通讯等方面政策的优惠与协调。其管理体制上的特殊性则表现为跨国特别经济区一般都要建立一定形式的国际协调机构,条件成熟的则可能成立联合管理委员会之类的集中统一的管理机构。

第四,跨国特别经济区具有发展性与增长性。如同特别经济区是一国经济发展的增长点与发动机一样,跨国特别经济区也是有关各国地区经济发展的新机与国民经济增长的新节点。所不同的只是,其增长效应不仅及于一国、一地区,而且及于数个国家或地区,成为区域经济中的增长节点,因而具有更大的牵引力与更强的发展性。

第五,跨国特别经济区具有开放性和外向性。跨国特别经济区以发展外向型经济为主,具有明显的开放性。各跨国特别经济区一般都是一个开放结构,没有排他性,各种要素的获得和其他经济机会不仅对区内平等,而且对国际市场开放。例如其资金与技术,可以来自国内、区内,也可以来自国外、区外。特别是在有关各国经济互补性不强、内部市场容量有限的情况下,这种开放性与外向性尤见关键只有对外开放,发展外向型经济,跨国特别经济区才能获得外来的生产要素与外部市场,才可能进而强化有关各国的集体国际竞争力。

跨国特别经济区目前最主要的表现形式便是亚洲近年来涌现的"增长三角"(或称"成长三角"),1989 年 12 月,新加坡副总理吴作栋提出在新加坡、马来西亚的柔佛州和印尼的廖内群岛之间的三角地带建立经济开发区,以达到共同发展的目的并称这种跨国三角经济开发区为"增长三角"(Growth Triangle)。此后"增长三角"作为一个新的经济术语流行于世。然而,关于"增长三角"的确切定义却并无统一的界定。1993 年 2 月,亚洲开发银行和日本国际大学联合发起了"亚洲增长三角"的国际研讨会。会上,亚洲开发银行学者将这一概念定义为:"利用不同国家在地理邻近地区的互补性,谋求在出口增长方面获得更大的竞争优势,为投资提供资本的私有成分和通过发展基础设施,提供财政鼓励或精简现有行政程序而使之提高效益的公有成分之间的合作,以利以充分地利用这些互补性。"[2]这

〔2〕 参见汤敏、缪·塞:《增长三角:概念与动作问题》,陈德照译,载《世界经济译丛》1993 年第 7 期。

一界定指明了增长三角的基本特点与性质,颇具启迪意义。

目前在亚洲,除上述“新—柔—廖增长三角”外,已经在实施中的还有东北亚的图们江三角洲增长三角,参加方有中国吉林省、俄罗斯远东地区及朝鲜,合作国家则还有韩国、日本与蒙古国。此外,正在构想中的增长三角还有:(1)中南半岛的“澜沧江—循公河”增长三角,又称“黄金四角”或“金四角”,包括中国云南省的西南部及缅甸、老挝、泰国与之接壤的边境地区;(2)东盟北部地区增长三角(简称“北三角”,包括马来西亚北部几个州、印尼的苏门答腊及泰国南部地区;(3)东盟东部地区增长三角(简称“东三角”),包括菲律宾的达澳、印尼苏拉威西岛的万鸦老及东马来西亚的山打根;(4)黄海增长三角,包括中国渤海湾、韩国西海岸、日本的九州等。亚洲开发银行的专家把一华南经济圈也视为一个已经实施并取得成功的增长三角——“华南增长三角”,[3]包括中国广东省、福建省、台湾地区和香港地区。还有学者则将构想中的“环日本海经济圈”也列入亚洲可能出现的增长三角之列,内容包括日本西部、俄罗斯远东地区、中国东北及朝鲜、韩国的部分地区。[4]

二

从跨国特别经济区的上述特征可以看出,跨国特别经济区既不是一种新的、特殊的国际政治区域,也不是区域性的贸易集团或经济集团,它只是地理位置相邻或相向的国家之间的一种小区域的国际经济开发区。这就是跨国特别经济区的基本法律性质之所在。

首先,跨国特别经济区不是跨国特别行政区。设区各国的主权权利是完整无缺的:其所设立的多边协调机构或联合管理组织本身并不具备独立的主权权利与外交地位,而不过是各主权国家意志的间接表现形式。跨国特别经济区的设立,其根本的动机与目的是发挥经济互补优势,发展外向型经济,形成本国本区经济的新的增长点,从而带动一片,壮大国家总体经济实若一其政治与外交意义是次要的和不明显的。

其次,跨国特别经济区不是区域性的贸易集团。区域性贸易集团(如欧盟、北美等)是某些地理位置邻近、经济发展水平相当或经济上互补的国家,通过建立关税同盟等特殊的国际法途径,而实现区域内投资、贸易等方面的自由化的贸易集团,其与跨国特别经济区的区别主要在于:一方面,贸易集团是国家的联盟,各国

---

〔3〕 参见[亚洲开发银行]汤敏、缪·塞:《增长三角:概念与动作问题》陈德照译,载《世界经济译丛》1993年第7期。

〔4〕 参见《中朝俄韩蒙签署开发图们江地区协定》,载《国际商报》1995年12月8日第1版。

提供的合作区域及于整个国家,跨国特别经济区一般仅及于一国的部分区域。虽然后者也不排除在特定情况下个别国家将其整体纳入该特区的可能性,如“新—柔—廖”,增长三角中的新加坡,但这种情况毕竟极为鲜见。另一方面,至少到目前为止,各跨国特别经济区尚未出现像《北美自由贸易协定》那样宏大而周详的国际条约的硬性约束,其有关各方更多地通过协调机构或联合管理组织进行区内立法与政策的协调与统一,一般不形成刚性而具体的国际法约束。

最后,由于同样的原因,跨国经济特别区也不同于象“东盟”这样的次区域经济合作形式,其合作区域、合作内容与合作程度均明显较小、较低。

三

跨国特别经济区首先是有关各方协商一致的产物。否则,它就只能是一国的特别经济区,而不能认为其具有“跨国性”。跨国特别经济区建成以后,更需要有关各国就有关立法与政策进行经常性的磋商、谈判与协调,为此,成立一个由有关各国组成的多边协调机构是完全有必要的。1995 年 12 月 6 日,中、朝、俄三国代表签署了《关于建立图们江地区开发协调委员会的协定》,至此图们江地区第一次出现了政府间经济合作组织,它将促进图们江经济开发区的铁路、公路、港口、电力、工业区和其他基础设施的建设,以确保这一个地区的潜力得到充分的开发[5]。“新—柔—廖”三角区原本也打算组建三方政府的官方联合机构,以共同协调本地区的开发计划,但至今三边合作机构尚未设立,而以双边协调形式进行的联合开发计划则正在进行之中。今后如果条件成熟,则还可以在这种多边或双边协调机构的基础上成立特区的联合管理机构,使之具有一定的自主经营管理权。按联合国开发计划署的计划,图们江经济开发区的一体化目标模式就是这种具有一定自治权的联合管理模式。

至于跨国特别经济区的立法与政策国际协调的具体内容,则须视不同特区的具体情况而定。从目前来看,关税、外汇、出入境管理、金融、投资、贸易等基本方面的政策是最需要国际协调的。以“新—柔—廖”增长三角为例,1990 年 8 月,印尼与新加坡签订合作开发廖内群岛的协议,成立了联合开发委员会,双方决定简化人员来往和产品进出口的手续,共同开发旅游业。次年,双方又签订了 50 年的供水协议,减少新对马来西亚淡水供应的依赖程度。印度尼西亚方面还放宽了对外资的限制,允许外资拥有 100% 的股权,并同意由私人建立工业园区。在“黄金

---

〔5〕 参见《图们江贸易区开发取得新进展,中俄朝韩蒙成立两个多边机构》,载《参考消息》1995 年 12 月 8 日,第 1 版。

四角”，四国一致同意优先发展交通和旅游业方面的合作，以此带动其他领域的合作。与此同时，中国方面已开设了磨憨、勐腊两个国家级口岸和打洛、景洪、思茅3个省级口岸；老挝在泰老边境开设了12个对泰通商口岸；泰方则批准削减29%的对老商品出口税，过去的禁控商品也有所放松。

在图们江跨国经济区，有关各国经协商一致，都加快了有关地区的开放步伐。1992年，中国批准珲春为沿边开放城市，享有沿海开放城市的政策与待遇，同时着重加强基础设施的建设，如为促进三国毗邻的防川—敬信地区的开发，加快延吉—图们公路的改造，新建了图们—珲春铁路，修筑了图们—珲春九级公路；俄罗斯在联合国工业发展组织的协助下，提出了海参崴自由经济区发展计划，设立了符拉迪沃斯托克、纳霍德卡和哈桑3个开发区；朝鲜方面也在邻近地区建立了罗津—先锋自由经济贸易区，同时公布了罗津—先锋自由经济贸易区的招商投资项目，颁布了外商进入该区的21点详细规定，给予外商出人以宽松政策。

尽管如此，边境地区的政治、历史敏感性与各国经济、文化与法律制度等方面的巨大差异性与复杂性，使各国关于跨国特别经济区的立法与政策的国际协调远非易事。设立一两个多边协调机构虽然可以有效促进这种国际协调的进展，但并不能解决所有的问题。跨国特别经济区的发展应该是循序渐进的，不可能一蹴而就。随着跨国特别经济区的不断向前发展，其吸收与辐射功能将不断增强。相应地，各国有关跨国特别经济区的立法与政策也将渐趋完善。其国际协调性与统一性也必将逐渐提高。

第五编 “一带一路”建设与国际能源法 Part V

1083 -1262

“一带一路”建设背景下中国加入《能源宪章条约》的成本收益分析*

能源合作是“一带一路”建设的重中之重。习近平主席在2015年博鳌论坛主题演讲指出“能源安全等非传统安全和全球性挑战不断增多,南北发展差距依然很大”“要推进建设亚洲能源资源合作机制,保障能源资源安全”。[1]《推动共建丝绸之路经济带和21世纪海上丝绸之路的愿景与行动》(以下简称《“一带一路”愿景和行动》)将能源合作列为“一带一路”建设的“合作重点部分”。[2]

倡导依托既有合作平台拓宽国际互利合作,“强化多边合作机制作用,让更多国家和地区参与一带一路建设”。亚欧大陆上的能源合作并不是制度洼地,传统上由欧洲国家主导的、成员国涵盖欧洲和苏联加盟共和国的能源宪章体系[3]是国际能源领域最重要的多边法律治理机制。转型中的能源宪章体系

---

* 本文发表在《国际法研究》2016年第1期。作者单文华、王鹏、王晗。本文系教育部哲学社会科学研究重大课题攻关项目“推进丝绸之路经济带建设研究”(项目编号14JZD022)和陕西省社会科学基金重点项目“丝绸之路经济带贸易投资便利化法律框架研究”(项目编号13SC032)的阶段性成果之一。本文在2015年5月《国际能源宪章》签署之前写就,并在此后略作修改。

〔1〕《习近平:迈向命运共同体开创亚洲新未来》,载http://news.xinhuanet.com/politics/2015-03/28/c_1114794507.htm,2015年12月18日访问。

〔2〕《“一带一路”愿景和行动》在合作重点部分指出,“加强能源基础设施互联互通合作,共同维护输油、输气管道等运输通道安全,推进跨境电力与输电通道建设,积极开展区域电网升级改造合作;加快投资便利化进程……消除投资壁垒,加强双边投资保护协定、避免双重征税协定磋商,保护投资者的合法权益。……加大煤炭、油气、金属矿产等传统能源资源勘探开发合作,积极推动水电、核电、风电、太阳能等清洁、可再生能源合作,推进能源资源就地就近加工转化合作,形成能源资源合作上下游一体化产业链;加强能源资源深加工技术、装备与工程服务合作”。参见国家发展改革委、外交部、商务部:《推动共建丝绸之路经济带和21世纪海上丝绸之路的愿景与行动》,载http://www.sdpc.gov.cn/xwzx/xwfb/201503/t20150328_669089.html,2015年5月10日访问。

〔3〕关于术语,在本文中,“能源宪章条约”指代1994年开放签署的、规定了具体的国际法律权利和义务的《能源宪章条约》(Energy Charter Treaty),“能源宪章组织”泛指依照1991年《欧洲能源宪章》(European Energy Charter)政治宣言和1994年《能源宪章条约》等国际法文件而建立的常设性国际组织,其秘书处设在欧盟总部所在地比利时的布鲁塞尔。“能源宪章”或“能源宪章体系”在本文中泛指以1994年《能源宪章条约》为主体、以多种后续补充法律文件为辅助的法律框架体系以及据此建立的国际组织。

和我国的“一带一路”建设在地理范围上重叠，在政策议题上兼容，极有可能构成“一带一路”能源合作所依托的制度平台。在能源宪章体系转型和中国大力推动“一带一路”的背景下，中国是否应该加入能源宪章体系成为一个需要严肃审视和仔细考量的学术命题。[4] 由此，本研究首先讨论能源宪章改革面临的挑战及其为中国深度参与国际能源治理带来的机遇，其次从成本和潜在收益两方面详细讨论中国参与能源宪章体系的前景。

一、十字路口的能源宪章与中国

（一）历史上的《欧洲能源宪章》

能源宪章体系是以 1994 年签署的《能源宪章条约》为核心的国际能源法律治理体系。它以能源贸易、能源投资、能源过境运输为主，兼顾能源效率、竞争政策、金融、税收、保险、环保、人员往来、政策透明度等广泛议题，是一个综合性的能源规制体系。

能源宪章体系可以追溯到 20 世纪 90 年代欧洲国家提出的整合东西欧洲能源资源合作框架的政治动议。“冷战”结束后，欧亚大陆——尤其是东西欧洲合作的政策优先点是建立一个更紧密的能源合作机制。能源宪章体系在此背景下构建，它以 1911 年《欧洲能源宪章》（*European Energy Charter*）政治宣言为龙头，以 1944 年《能源宪章条约》（*Energy Charter Treaty*）为主体，以《关于能源效率和相关环境议题的能源宪章议定书》（*Energy Charter Protocol on Energy Efficiency and Related Environmental Aspects*）和《能源宪章条约贸易修正案》（*Trade Amendment to the Treaty*）等诸多后续法律文件为补充，共同构成了一个以能源规制为核心的多层级的政治和法律框架体系。能源宪章组织的成员国[5]传统上以欧洲和苏联加盟共和国为主，逐渐吸收了部分亚洲国家。

（二）《能源宪章条约》的主要实体规则

《能源宪章条约》是能源宪章体系下法律拘束力最强、涵盖议题最广的国际条约。条约包括 50 条正文和 14 个附件，详细规定了成员方在能源贸易、能源投

---

〔4〕 关于中国加入《能源宪章条约》的分析，参见白中红、潘远征：《中国加入〈能源宪章条约〉的利弊论》，载《生态经济》2010 年第 10 期；Sheng Zhang, “The Energy Charter Treaty and China: Member or Bystander?”, (2012) 13 *The Journal of World Investment & Trade* 597; Wenhua Shan, *Report on the Compatibility of Chinese Laws and Regulations with the Energy Charter Treaty*, November 2015, Energy Charter, http://www.energycharter.org/fileadmin/DocumentsMedia/CONEXO/20151127 - Compatibility_of_Chinese_Laws_and_Regulations_with_ECT_Report.pdf (last visited December 18, 2015).

〔5〕 “Members of the Energy Charter Conference”, available at http://www.energycharter.org/who-we-are/members-observers/ (last visited December 18, 2015).

资、能源过境运输等方面承担的法律义务,规定了详细的争端解决程序。[6]

在能源贸易方面,能源宪章体系与世界贸易组织体系相衔接,并细化了在竞争政策、技术转移和金融领域等方面的规定。在能源投资方面,《能源宪章条约》与一般国际投资协定类似,规定了较为具体的投资保护和促进义务。但是,《能源宪章条约》所规定的条约义务较高,包括全部的准入后待遇和全面的"投资者—国家争端解决机制",总体上高于中国与《能源宪章条约》缔约方签订的双边投资协定。在能源过境运输方面,《能源宪章条约》规定缔约方应采取必要措施,以便利能源运输设施的开放和能源运输的进行,并规定了以能源宪章秘书长任命的调解员(conciliator)为主要裁断方式的争端解决机制。[7]

(三)结构转型、制度升级、领袖缺位——能源宪章的挑战与机遇

能源宪章的出现与20世纪90年代初苏联解体后东西欧洲紧张的地缘环境密切相关。为了稳定东欧国家的政局和对西欧国家的能源供给,在当时的历史条件下,迅速形成促进西欧充裕资本、技术与东欧能源资源禀赋相互融合,并以此为核心优势的能源宪章制度框架,且成为稳定欧洲地区局势、促进经济一体化的重要政策工具。[8]

然而伴随欧洲一体化的顺利推进,能源宪章初始的制度优势显著下降。欧洲政局稳定,不断出现的一体化程度更高的欧洲区域组织分散了欧洲各国对能源宪章体系的政治注意力。虽然能源国际合作仍是欧盟对外政策的重要一环,但其政策优先级不断下降。由于《能源宪章条约》项下义务与其国内能源规制体系的差异,加之"尤科斯案件"[9]裁决的影响,俄罗斯于2009年停止了《能源宪章条约》的临时适用(provisional application),《能源宪章条约》进一步促进欧洲能源合作

[6] 关于能源宪章争端解决机制的具体研究,参见白中红:《能源宪章条约的争端解决机制研究》,载《外交评论》2011年第3期。

[7] 关于能源运输争端解决机制的更具体研究,参见杨泽伟:《跨国能源管道运输的争议解决机制》,载《法学》2007年第12期。

[8] 也正因为能源宪章的促进地区政局问题、密切能源合作的功能,有学者指出东亚也应建立类似的能源合作组织,参见杨泽伟:《"东北亚能源共同体"法律框架初探》,载《法学》2006年第4期;舒小昀:《东亚能源共同体建设的背景、进程与前景——基于〈能源宪章条约〉的讨论》,载《世界经济与政治论坛》2010年第3期。

[9] 尤科斯公司(OAO Yukos Oil Company)曾是俄罗斯最大的石油公司,后因俄罗斯对其公司展开的一系列刑事和民事调查而导致该公司运营不善、最终破产,其大部分资产被俄罗斯国有企业收购。尤科斯公司的三个控股股东根据《能源宪章条约》向海牙常设仲裁庭提起仲裁,起诉俄罗斯。俄罗斯被仲裁庭认定违反了《能源宪章条约》第13(1)条,因而需向尤科斯支付上百亿美元的巨额赔偿。具体案情事实和仲裁裁决,参见*Yukos Universal Limited (Isle of Man) v. The Russian Federation*, Final Award. PCA Case No. AA 227, 18 July 2014。

和治理的功能遭遇重大挫折。[10] 为扭转局面,2010 年 11 月,能源宪章组织成员方通过了《能源宪章进程现代化路线图》(*Road Map for the Modernisation of the Energy Charter Process*),能源宪章体系开始了其历史上的最大转型——致力于重塑制度优势和拓宽地理版图。2015 年 5 月,《国际能源宪章》(*International Energy Charter*)在荷兰海牙举行的能源宪章部长级会议上得以签署,这是能源宪章现代化升级和全球化战略的最新动向,标志着能源宪章进入了 2.0 时代。

在目前能源宪章现代化进程中,结构转型和制度升级是其两条生命线。结构转型表现为能源宪章组织正推行去欧洲化的国际化和全球化战略,能源宪章组织希望借助结构转型吸引更多国家(尤其是新兴经济体国家)参与到能源宪章体系中,在地理版图上实现扩张,并以此激活既有成员国对能源宪章的政治热情,增强能源宪章对潜在成员国的吸引力。制度升级则是试图重塑能源宪章的制度优势,使其更加适应不同国家在新形势下的能源需求,在更大范围内、更好地发挥以能源投资、能源贸易和能源过境运输为核心的制度优势。

能源宪章的现代化进程却面临"领袖缺位"困境。同所有国际组织一样,能源宪章组织是一个"成员国驱动"的体系。因此,其秘书处与秘书长虽然能够发挥重要作用,但决定性的力量仍然保留在成员国之手。对能源宪章组织态度积极并有能力大力推动能源宪章体系现代化的成员国是推动能源宪章全球化战略的主导力量。欧盟成员国传统上对能源宪章影响最大,但目前德、法、英等欧洲大国普遍对其热情不高,主要认为其目前的"剩余价值"有限。荷兰和波兰等国家比较有兴趣但推动力不足。俄罗斯虽对能源宪章现代化表示了兴趣,但缺乏明确表态,同时当前俄欧关系也对其参与具有一定的消极影响。美国已经签署 2015 年 5 月的《国际能源宪章》政治性宣言,但对《能源宪章条约》尚未表态。历史上美国曾经积极参与了规则的制订但是最后没有签署《能源宪章条约》,主要因为条约的投资保护水平不及其双边投资协定的保护水平。还有一些地区大国如加拿大、澳大利亚则仍在观望。伊朗参加了 2015 年 5 月在海牙举行的宪章大会,这是石油输出国组织成员首次参加能源宪章的重要会议,加之伊朗在石油输出国组织中分量很重,因此其潜在意义较大。但鉴于伊朗目前只是采纳了《国际能源宪章》政治宣言,其未来影响力尚难估测。此外还有智利、哥伦比亚等拉美国家和一些非洲国家也已经签署《国际能源宪章》政治宣言。可以说,能源宪章已经吸引了世界能源界的高度关注,但主要能源大国仍在观望,形成了"领袖缺位"的状态。

---

〔10〕 更多讨论,参见 Anna Aseeva,"EU-Russia Energy Relations: the Role of International Law from Energy Investment and Transit Perspective",Institut Europeen de l'Universite de Gnenve,2010,at http://www.isn.ethz.ch/Digital-Library/Publications/Detail/? id = 126492&lng = en(last visited December 18,2015)。

“领袖缺位”的现状反映了能源宪章现代化的权力困境。如何提供一套具有比较制度优势的国际能源治理体系，以保持既有成员国的政治热情并吸引更多国家——尤其是新兴经济体国家的参与，并有效推进能源宪章体系的全球扩张，是能源宪章组织目前所面临的最大挑战。不过，这对中国则很可能意味着一个巨大的机遇。

（四）中国与能源宪章：国际法律关系的现状与未来

在能源宪章所涵盖的能源贸易、能源投资等主要领域，中国已经与能源宪章组织成员国建立了一定的国际法律关系。在《能源宪章条约》所有54个缔约方中，44个缔约方是世界贸易组织的成员方，5个缔约方是世界贸易组织的观察员，3个缔约方没有参加世界贸易组织。中国与50个《能源宪章条约》缔约方签订有双边投资协定，与欧盟正在进行双边投资协定谈判，与2个缔约国（阿富汗、列支敦士登）未签订双边投资协定。[11]

中国与《能源宪章条约》缔约方签订双边投资协定的时间较早，多数处在20世纪80年代或90年代，仅有14个双边投资协定是2000年以后签订或修订的。20世纪80年代或90年代签订的双边投资协定内容较为简略，条约范围和义务程度较低，多不具有全面“投资者—国家争端解决机制”，[12]未给予投资者充分的准入后待遇，特别是国民待遇，因而与《能源宪章条约》项下投资规制体系的差距较大。

能源宪章体系希望借助结构转型吸引更多国家参与到能源宪章体系中，在地理版图上实现扩张，其扩张的重点正是亚洲、非洲和拉丁美洲等新兴国家。[13] 现有的成员版图与我国的“丝绸之路经济带”规划基本吻合，其扩大的方向则和我国“21世纪海上丝绸之路”的方向大体一致。[14] 在这个意义上，能源宪章的发展方向和我国的“一带一路”建设不谋而合。三者合力，完全有可能成功打造一个具有全球影响的“丝绸之路能源带”。

---

〔11〕 参见本文附表1：中国与《能源宪章条约》缔约方的国际法律关系一览。

〔12〕 更多讨论，参见单文华：《外资国民待遇与陕西的外资政策研究》，载《西安交通大学学报》（社会科学版）2013年第2期；单文华主编：《中国对外能源投资的国际法保护：基于实证和区域的制度研究》，清华大学出版社2014年版。

〔13〕 关于能源宪章体系的升级计划的简介，参见“Frequently Asked Question about the Energy Charter Process”, Energy Charter, at http://www.energycharter.org/process/frequently-asked-questions/ (last visited December 18, 2015)。

〔14〕 参见《“一带一路”愿景和行动》。

二、中国加入能源宪章体系的可能成本

(一)经济成本

中国加入能源宪章体系的经济成本较低。首先,《能源宪章条约》对国内公共政策的挤压效应并不明显,《能源宪章条约》项下的能源贸易和能源投资义务并未超出中国在世界贸易组织和国际投资协定体系下的条约义务。《能源宪章条约》项下较为独特的能源运输义务规定以中立和自由的能源运输为政策取向,政治争议较小,反而有助于中国国际能源贸易和运输,保障中国能源需求的有效、稳定供给。

其次,《能源宪章条约》并不会显著增加中国在国际投资仲裁下的被诉风险。原因有二:其一,由于中国与《能源宪章条约》缔约方基本都签订有双边投资协定,且《能源宪章条约》项下的投资保护义务并未超出2012年签署的《中华人民共和国政府和加拿大政府关于促进和相互保护投资的协定》和《中华人民共和国政府、日本国政府及大再民国政府关于促进、便利和保护投资的协定》,因此中国因签署《能源宪章条约》而被投资者起诉的可能性较小。[15] 其二,中国能源行业吸引外商投资的数量小、比重低,[16] 外国技资者利用《能源宪章条约》提起投资仲裁的可能性亦不高。

最后,能源宪章秘书处的规模相对较小,成员国的会费压力不大。能源宪章组织会费以联合国会费分担为蓝本,佐以成员国自愿捐助。[17] 如果中国加入能源宪章体系,中国承担的相对会费比例虽然较高,例如中国有可能因国内生产总值而成为能源宪章体系最大的会费缴纳国(国内生产总值不是唯一的衡量因

---

[15] 参见本文附表2:《能源宪章条约》下投资仲裁案件一览。

[16] 长期以来,中国能源行业所吸引外商投资占中国吸引外商投资总额(实际使用金额)的比例不足1%。以下数据由笔者根据中国国家统计局网站的相关统计整理而来。统计科目指标为"对外经济贸易—按行业分外商直接投资额—实际使用金额",搜索关键词为"外商直接投资",载 http://data. stats. gov. cn/easyquery. htm? cn = C01&zb = A060G01&sj = 2013,2015年12月18日访问。

(单位:元)

年份 / 中国实际利用外商直接投资金额	2008	2009	2010	2011	2012	2013
采矿业	57, 283	50, 059	68, 440	61, 279	77, 046	36, 495
总计	9, 239, 500	9, 003, 300	10, 573, 000	11, 601, 100	11, 171, 600	11, 758, 600
采矿业所占比例(%)	0.69	0.56	0.65	0.53	0.69	0.31

[17] 参见《能源宪章条约》第37条。

素），但中国缴纳的会费的绝对数额小。[18] 中国的较大或最大会费缴纳国的身份无疑会对能源宪章秘书处的日常运作产生正式的或非正式的影响，从而能够影响能源宪章体系的总体走向。换言之，中国的能源宪章会员缴费的技人产出比高，杠杆效应明显。

（二）法律成本

中国加入能源宪章体系所引致的法律成本不高。首先，中国为履行条约义务而改革国内立法体系的法律转轨成本较低。中国虽然仍未出台综合性的能源法，但中国已经制定了多部相关能源立法，[19] 内容涵盖自然资源、煤炭、电力、石油天然气、核电、节能和可再生能源、环境保护等多个方面。尽管《能源宪章条约》涉及了诸如市场经济、金融、税收、环境保护国有企业等多个政策框架，但对于中国而言，在加入世界贸易组织后，中国以市场经济为基础的现代法律体系基本建立，[20] 中国国内能源立法体系与能源宪章体系的总体差距不大。如果中国需要为履行《能源宪章条约》义务而整合国内分散立法，那么，这种整合在很大程度上是在推动本应推进的国内立法，应当视为中国加入能源宪章体系的政策红利，而不是法律成本。[21]

其次，《能源宪章条约》缔约方多数都是世界贸易组织成员方，[22] 且中国与绝大多数《能源宪章条约》缔约方签订有双边投资协定。中国在世界贸易组织和新近签订的国际投资条约中所承担的国际法律义务水平实际上已经超出《能源宪章条约》，[23] 因此中国签署《能源宪章条约》并不会明显增加中国已承担的国际法律

---

〔18〕 据能源宪章秘书处初步估算，以联合国现有会费分担比例为基准，中国应承担的能源宪章会费数额约为 43 万欧元。2016 年联合国会费分担比例调整后，中国承担的能源宪章会费大约在 50 万到 100 万欧元之间。

〔19〕 关于中国能源立法的简介及中国起草能源法草案的背景，参见清华大学环境资源与能源法研究中心：《清华大学〈能源法（草案）〉专家建议稿立法理由书》（2007 年 11 月），载 http://erelaw.tsinghua.edu.cn/news_view.asp? newsid = 640，2015 年 12 月 18 日访问。

〔20〕 国务院新闻办公室：《中国特色社会主义法律体系》（白皮书），载 http://www.gov.cn/jrzg/2011 - 10/27/content_1979498.htm，2015 年 12 月 18 日访问。该白皮书指出"截至 2011 年 8 月底……涵盖社会关系各个方面的法律部门已经齐全……中国特色社会主义法律体系已经形成"。

〔21〕 参见本文附表 3：《国内能源相关立法及规定一览表》。

〔22〕 关于世界贸易组织与能源宪章体系的关系的讨论，参见 Joost Pauwelyn (eds.), *Global Challenges at the Intersection of Trade, Energy and The Environment*, (Geneva: Centre for Economic Policy Research, 2010); Energy Charter Secretariat, "Trade in Energy: WTO Rules Applying under The Energy Charter Treaty", at http://www.energycharter.org/fileadmin/DocumentsMedia/Thematic/WTO_Rules_applying_to_the_ECT_2002_en.pdf (last visited December 18, 2015); Rafael Leal-Arcas, Costantino Grasso and Juan Alemany Rios, "Multilateral, Regional and Bilateral Energy Trade Governance", (2015) 6(1) *Renewable Energy Law and Policy Review* 38; Pamela Ugaz, "Prospects for a Transit Regime on Energy in the WTO", (2011) 29 *Agenda International* 247。

〔23〕 中国 2012 年签署的中日韩投资协定和正在谈判中的中美双边投资协定所规定的投资保护和投资自由化的程度，已经高于《能源宪章条约》。关于中美双边投资协定及美国 2012 年 BIT 范本的可接受性分析，参见单文华：《美国投资条约新范本及其可接受性问题研究》，载《现代法学》2013 年第 5 期。

义务负担。

(三)政治成本

中国参与能源宪章体系的政治成本较小,占用的政策资源较少,且与中国积极主导的"一带一路"战略在地理范围上兼容。首先,《能源宪章条约》现有缔约方涵盖欧洲和苏联加盟共和国,在地里区位上与"丝绸之路经济带"相衔接,在政策导向上与中国倡导的国际关系民主化与法治化理念相一致,在制度建设上与上海合作组织、亚洲基础设施技资银行、亚洲相互协作与信任措施会议等"丝绸之路经济带"建设制度框架兼容。其次,《能源宪章条约》潜在缔约方涵盖非洲、拉丁美洲中的发展中国家,与"21 世纪海上丝绸之路"规划契合度较高。最后,能源宪章体系是较为成熟的能源治理机制,组织框架较为完善,虽然正处在体系转型期,但并非"一穷二白、白手起家",如果中国意欲参与能源宪章体系并试图推动其全球化战略进程,中国所面临的制度建构难度将低于"另起炉灶"的全新国际制度。

三、中国加入能源宪章体系的可能收益

(一)经济收益

能源宪章体系与世界贸易组织体系兼容,因而《能源宪章条约》对国际贸易影响较小,其经济收益主要体现在保护和促进我国对外投资和外国对华投资方面。

1. 保护中国在《能源宪章条约》缔约方的直接投资

(1)保护与促进中国在《能源宪章条约》现有缔约方的直接投资

《能源宪章条约》现有缔约方主要包括欧洲国家、苏联加盟共和国和部分亚洲国家和地区,中国对现有《能源宪章条约》缔约方的投资集中于西欧主要国家和日本。中国对《能源宪章条约》缔约方的直接投资占中国当年对外直接投资总量的比率大致在10% ~20%,且呈现逐渐上升趋势,如图1 和图2 所示。这与中国不断增长的对外直接投资趋势相同,但增长比例略低于中国总体对外直接投资的增长率。可以说,中国对《能源宪章条约》成员方投资的增长潜力巨大。[24]

---

〔24〕 参见本文附表4:中国对《能源宪章条约》缔约方直接投资流量。

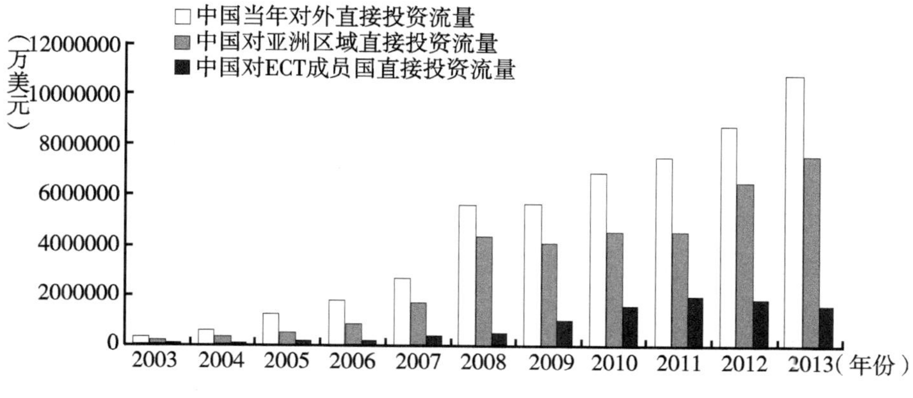

图 1　中国对《能源宪章条约》缔约方投资增长流量[25]

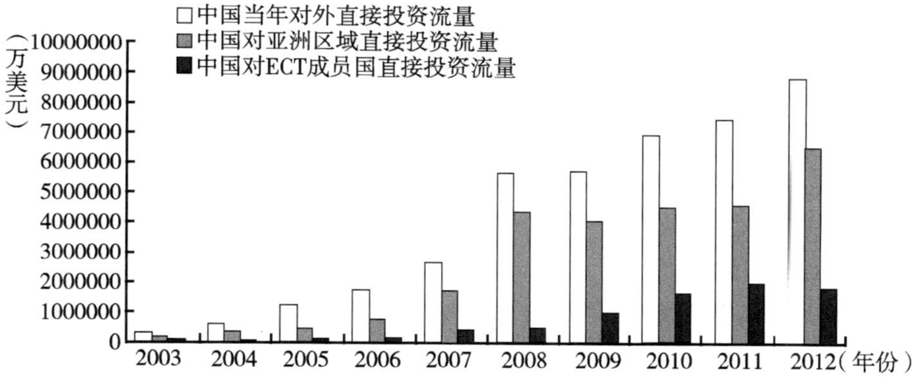

图 2　中国对《能源宪章条约》缔约方直接投资存量

值得强调的是,中国签署《能源宪章条约》可以在相当程度上提高对中国在《能源宪章条约》缔约方直接投资的保护水准。目前我国和《能源宪章条约》缔约方签订的投资条约大多数属于我国投资条约在 20 世纪 80 年代或 90 年代的版本,保护范围较窄,保护力度较弱,如往往没有提供实质性的国民待遇,投资者可以起诉东道国的争端范围也仅限于征收补偿数额一项等。[26]《能源宪章条约》相

〔25〕 图 1、图 2、图 3、图 4 由笔者根据《中国商务年鉴》(2014 年)数据整理得出,具体数据参见本文的附表 4。《中国商务年鉴》编辑委员会:《中国商务年鉴 2014》,中国商务出版社 2015 年版,第 179 ~ 192 页。《中国统计年鉴》也能提供一些中国对主要国别(地区)的对外直接投资数据,载 http://www.stats.gov.cn/tjsj/ndsj/,2015 年 12 月 20 日访问。

〔26〕 Alex Berger, "The Politics of China's Investment Treaty Making Program", in Tomer Broude, Marc L. Busch and Amelia Porges (eds.), *The Politics of International Economic Law* (Cambridge: Cambridge University Press, 2011), p. 174.

对发达的投资保护机制将构成对既有双边技资协定的重要补充，就此而言，《能源宪章条约》对增强中国境外投资的法律保护的作用将较为显著。

(2)保护和促进中国在《能源宪章条约》潜在缔约方的直接投资

中国加入能源宪章体系的潜在经济收益不容小觑，因为《能源宪章条约》可以有效改善中国在拉丁美洲、非洲等《能源宪章条约》潜在缔约方的直接投资保护。关于能源宪章体系全球化战略，拉美、非洲等国反应正面，伊朗等海湾国家态度积极。非洲和拉丁美洲的国家是中国对外能源投资较为集中的目的地国家。中国与这些国家签订的投资条约也大多属于保护水准较低的早期版本，加之这些国家多为发展中国家，政治的稳定性与法制的健全程度都有待完善。[27]

如果中国加入能源宪章体系，这些非洲和拉美国家很有可能跟随中国加入到能源宪章体系，而此举无疑将会大大增强中国在这些国家的直接投资保护力度。如图3和图4所示，就绝对数量而言，2000年以来中国对这两个地区的投资无论是存量还是流量都增长明显。但是相对于中国对外投资总体流量和存量而言，中国对这两个地区的投资增长并不突出。可以说，其增长潜力同样巨大。尤其是近几年来，我国主要领导人高度重视与非洲和拉丁美洲国家的合作，频频访问相关国家，鼓励中国企业对这两个地区开展投资合作。[28] 无疑，中国加入《能源宪章条约》将对这一战略的实施产生积极的推动作用。

2. 保护和促进《能源宪章条约》缔约方投资者来华投资

中国加入能源宪章体系另一可能经济收益是促进《能源宪章条约》缔约方对中国的直接投资。《能源宪章条约》缔约国中的日本、德国、法国、英国、荷兰、瑞士等国，长期位列于对华投资前十位的国家或地区。来自《能源宪章条约》缔约方的直接投资占中国当年吸引的外商投资总量的比例基本维持在10%左右。[29] 加入能源宪章体系有助于进一步促进和保护《能源宪章条约》缔约方的在华投资。

---

〔27〕 “Investment Climate Statements 2014”，U. S. Department of State，at http://www.state.gov/e/eb/rls/othr/ics/2014/index.htm(last visited May 10，2015).

〔28〕 据美国有线电视新闻网报道，2014年在非洲的投资将达到2460亿美元，中国在非洲的投资大约以每年16%的速度增长。另据新华社报道，作为拉丁美洲第二大贸易伙伴，中国已经在当地投资了超过800亿美元，是中国对外直接投资的13%。与此同时，中国与拉丁美洲之间的贸易额在2013年上升到2616亿美元，是2000年时的20倍。2015年1月，习近平在出席中拉合作论坛时则表示，未来10年，中国将在拉美地区投资2500亿美元。参见《CNN：中国在非洲的投资远超美国》，载 http://finance.sina.com.cn/stock/usstock/c/20140806/175719932066.shtml，2015年5月10日访问；《港媒：习近平表示未来10年中国将向拉美投资2500亿美元》，http://finance.ifeng.com/a/20150108/13415612_0.shtml，2015年5月10日访问。

〔29〕 参见本文附表5来自《能源宪章条约》主要缔约方的投资占中国当年实际吸引外资总额的比重。

(二)法律收益

中国加入能源宪章体系的法律收益明显。从国内看,中国签署以能源行业为核心内容的《能源宪章条约》将为整合国内能源立法提供政策契机,并推动以市场经济体系为基础的国内现代治理体系建设。从国际看加入能源宪章体系将使中国有机会深度参与既有国际经济治理制度的改革,积累参与国际组织日常运作的一手经验,为中国更加深入、更负责任、更具建设性地参与和积极改变已有国际法律制度和组织提供"制度实验场"。

1. 国内法律制度改革收益

(1)整合国内能源相关立法

中国至今尚无综合性的专门能源立法。2007年的《能源法(征求意见稿)》迄今公布已有6年,[30]但至今仍未能进入人大立法审议程序。核心原因之一在于其与能源相关的基本立法关系仍未理顺,相关政府部门推动能源立法的政策动力不足,政策窗口有限。[31] 中国加入能源宪章体系将为推动国内能源法的出台提供政策机遇,进一步理顺有限政府原则[32]下的国内能源治理体系。

(2)推动国内现代治理体系综合改革

中国加入能源宪章体系也是中国"以开放促改革"的国内综合治理体系改革战略的重要组成部分,为拟定政府权力清单、深化国有企业改革提供了政策契机。能源产业一直是国有企业改革的重点,加入能源宪章体系有助于进一步完善国有企业的公司治理体系,明确政府监管权限,并以能源产业改革为核心推动国内现代治理体系的综合改革。

2. 国际法律制度改革收益

(1)参与既有国际制度的立法过程

欧盟主导的能源宪章体系是西方发达国家设计、主导的国际经济治理制度的典型代表。中国可以通过参与能源宪章体系深入观察、了解、学习西方国家主导设计的国际法律制度的运作机理,熟悉正式的和非正式的国际制度运作模式,包括议程设定、国际组织日常运作、政治话语、非正式谈判等国际法律技巧,为中国

---

〔30〕 国务院:《〈能源法〉征求意见稿面向社会征集意见(全文)》,载 http://www.gov.cn/gzdt/2007-12/04/content_824569.htm,2015年5月10日访问。

〔31〕 See Xin Qiu & Honglin Li, "Energy Regulation and legislation in China", (2012) 42 *Environmental Law Report* 10678, p. 10683.

〔32〕 《中共中央关于全面推进依法治国若干重大问题的决定》第三部分《深入推进依法行政,加快建设法治政府》明确提出:"行政机关不得法外设定权力,没有法律法规依据不得作出减损公民、法人和其他组织合法权益或者增加其义务的决定。推行政府权力清单制度,坚决消除权力设租寻租空间。",参见《中共中央关于全面推进依法治国若干重大问题的决定》,载 http://news.xinhuanet.com/politics/2014-10/28/c_1113015330.htm,2015年5月10日访问。

以后参与和建立国际制度积累经验。

中国参与能源宪章体系的经验具有可移植性。中国从参与能源宪章体系所获得的经验，尤其是推动能源宪章体系全球化转型所获得的制度性知识将有利于中国深度参与、影响和改变既有布雷顿森林体系下的其他国际经济治理框架，例如世界银行、国际货币基金组织和世界贸易组织等制度。

(2)介入并主导国际组织的日常运作

常设国际机构对国际法律体系的运作和发展具有重要作用。作为常设机构，能源宪章秘书处对能源宪章体系的正常运作和改革发展都发挥着至关重要的作用，能源宪章的改革议程往往由秘书处首先提出并负责具体操作。能源宪章组织处于领袖缺位期，中国有机会成为能源宪章体系的主导国，将其改造成更加包容、更为公平的国际组织。此外，加入能源宪章体系也能为中国积累运作国际组织的经验，培训具有国际组织工作经验和视野的实务人才。

(三)政治收益

中国参与能源宪章体系的政治收益十分可观，在多个层次上与中国近期对外政策相契合。中国加入能源宪章体系有利于建立符合中国利益的国际能源治理框架，搭建"丝绸之路能源带"的战略平台，推进以能源产业为核心的综合性国际经济治理体系改革的战略。

1. 改善国际能源治理框架

能源安全对崛起中的中国的重要性是显而易见的。国际能源合作与治理显然是中国对外政策的重要组成部分，中国对外直接投资相当部分集中在能源资源领域。一个中立、公平、高效的国际能源治理体系对经济快速发展、能源需求旺盛的中国是一个利好消息，而一个充分反映我国利益诉求并有广泛国家参与的国际能源治理框架对中国而言将是最佳的政策选项。[33] 能源宪章体系正是这种国际能源治理框架的雏形。能源宪章体系以能源产业为核心、基本涉及与能源相关的所有政策维度和侧面，基本具备多边综合性国际能源治理框架雏形。

2. 搭建"丝绸之路能源带"的战略平台

能源宪章体系可能构成"丝绸之路经济带"总体外交战略的重要组成。其一，《能源宪章条约》现有缔约方以欧洲和亚洲国家为主，地理上与"丝绸之路经济带"相互契合，呈梯次展开趋势；《能源宪章条约》潜在缔约方覆盖西亚、非洲、拉丁美洲等能源禀赋丰富的地区，与"21 世纪海上丝绸之路"相衔接。其二，能源

---

〔33〕 相关典型研究，参见国家发展和改革委员会能源研究所、英国帝国理工大学葛量洪研究所：《全球能源治理改革与中国的参与(征求意见报告)》(2014 年 11 月)，载 http://www.eri.org.cn/uploadfile/Consultation%20report%20(CN).pdf，2015 年 12 月 18 日访问。

宪章体系在制度框架上具备综合性能源合作的架构,可能构成"丝绸之路能源带"的制度基础,与以亚洲相互协作与信任措施会议、上海合作组织为主体的"丝绸之路安全带"、以亚洲基础设施投资银行为主体的"丝绸之路技资带"、以丝路开发银行为主体的"丝绸之路金融带"相配合,构成"丝绸之路经济带"建设的"四驾马车"。[34]

3. 推进以能源产业为核心的综合性国际经济治理体系改革的战略

加入能源宪章体系将使中国有机会整合能源宪章体系的制度优势与中国作为新兴经济体国家的比较优势,创造中国推进新一轮国际经济治理体系改革的契机。其一,中国的加入将使能源宪章体系的西方国家背景与中国等新兴经济体国家角色相结合,使得中国建构国际能源治理体系的政策更具有代表性。其二,能源宪章体系对成员国的国内治理体系具有广泛的社会嵌入性,对以贸易、投资、金融为行业划分的现有国际经济治理体系的关联效应明显。因此,加入能源宪章体系并促进乃至主导其改革更有利于中国以点带线、以线促面地促进综合性的国际经济治理体系改革。

四、结论

能源宪章体系的现状与发展方向与我国"一带一路"建设规划不谋而合。能源宪章体系是以国际能源合作和监管为核心的多边治理框架,但目前正在经历结构转型和制度升级。能源宪章体系的全球化战略面临"领袖缺位"的困境,而这为中国建设性参与全球能源治理、重塑国际经济新秩序提供了重要的战略机遇。2015 年 5 月 20 日召开的能源宪章部长级会议是能源宪章体系转折更生的一次历史性会议,也是中国积极参与并谋求主导全球能源有效治理的一个重要机遇。中国加入能源宪章体系,成本较小,收益较大,战略意义可望巨大而深远。鉴此,建议中国应该积极参与能源宪章进程现代化升级,谋求在能源宪章决策和运行机制中发挥重要甚至主导作用,使能源宪章进程与"一带一路"建设良性互动、优势互补;中国还应在进一步研究的基础上,考虑签署《能源宪章条约》,以核心缔约国身份推动其升级改造,以确保我国在国际能源合作中的合理诉求和平等利益。

---

〔34〕 关于能源宪章体系与保护中国在中亚的能源投资保护的问题,参见 Zhuwei Wang, Securing Energy Flows from Central Asia to China and the Relevance of the Energy Charter Treaty to China, Energy Charter Secretariat, 2015, at http://www.energycharter.org/what-we-do/trade-and-transit/trade-and-transit-thematic-reports/securing-energy-flows-from-central-asia-to-china-and-the-relevance-of-the-energy-charter-treaty-to-china-2015/ (last visited December 18, 2015)。

附　表

表1　中国与《能源宪章条约》缔约方的国际法律关系一览[35]

《能源宪章条约》缔约方	签署《能源宪章条约》(1994)时间	是否世界贸易组织成员方/加入的时间	是否与中国签订有双边投资协定/签订的时间
阿富汗	19/01/2013	否	否
阿尔巴尼亚	17/12/1994	8/09/2000	13/02/1993
亚美尼亚	17/12/1994	5/02/2003	04/07/1992
澳大利亚	17/12/1994 (尚未批准)	1/01/1995	11/07/1988
奥地利	17/12/1994	1/01/1995	12/09/1985
阿塞拜疆	17/12/1994	观察员	08/03/1994
白俄罗斯	17/12/1994 (临时适用)	观察员	11/01/1993
比利时	17/12/1994	1/01/1995	04/06/1984,06/06/2005
波黑	14/06/1995	观察员	26/06/2002
保加利亚	17/12/1994	1/12/1996	27/06/1989
克罗地亚	17/12/1994	30/11/2000	07/06/1993
塞浦路斯	17/12/1994	30/07/1995	17/01/2001
捷克	08/06/1995	1/01/1995	08/12/2005
丹麦	17/12/1994	1/01/1995	29/04/1985
爱沙尼亚	17/12/1994	13/11/1999	02/09/1993
芬兰	17/12/1994	1/01/1995	04/09/1984
法国	17/12/1994	1/01/1995	30/05/1984
格鲁吉亚	17/12/1994	14/06/2000	03/06/1993
德国	17/12/1994	1/01/1995	07/10/1983,01/12/2003
希腊	17/12/1994	1/01/1995	25/06/1992
匈牙利	27/02/1995	1/01/1995	29/05/1991

〔35〕本表数据由笔者根据能源宪章网站信息、中国商务部网站信息和世界贸易组织网站信息整理而来。详见,"Members of the Energy Charter Conference",Energy Charter,at http://www.energycharter.org/who-we-are/members-observers/ (last visited December 20,2015);商务部条约法律司:《我国对外签订双边投资协定一览表》,载 http://tfs.mofcom.gov.cn/article/Nocategory/201111/20111107819474.shtml,2015 年 12 月 20 日访问。

续表

《能源宪章条约》缔约方	签署《能源宪章条约》(1994)时间	是否世界贸易组织成员方/加入的时间	是否与中国签订有双边投资协定/签订的时间
冰岛	17/12/1994	1/01/1995	31/03/1994
爱尔兰	17/12/1994	1/01/1995	19/4/2000
意大利	17/12/1994	1/01/1995	28/01/1985
日本	16/06/1995	1/01/1995	27/08/1988
哈萨克斯坦	17/12/1994	观察员	10/08/1992
吉尔吉斯斯坦	17/12/1994	20/12/1998	14/05/1992
拉脱维亚	17/12/1994	10/02/1999	15/04/2004
列支敦士登[36]	17/12/1994	1/09/1995	否
立陶宛	05/04/1995	31/05/2001	08/11/1993
卢森堡	17/12/1994	1/01/1995	04/06/1984,06/06/2005
马耳他	17/12/1994	1/01/1995	22/02/2009
萨尔多瓦	17/12/1994	26/07/2001	06/11/1992
蒙古国	21/07/1999	29/01/1997	25/08/1991
荷兰	17/12/1994	1/01/1995	17/06/1985,26/11/2001
挪威	16/06/1995(尚未批准)	1/01/1995	21/11/1984
波兰	17/12/1994	1/07/1995	07/06/1988
葡萄牙	17/12/1994	1/07/1995	03/02/1992
罗马尼亚	17/12/1994	1/07/1995	12/07/1994
俄罗斯	17/12/1994(2009 年 10 月 18 日停止临时适用)	22/08/2012	21/07/1990,09/11/2006
斯洛伐克	17/12/1994	1/01/1995	04/12/1991
斯洛文尼亚	17/12/1994	30/07/1995	13/09/1993
西班牙	17/12/1994	1/01/1995	06/02/1992,14/11/2005
瑞典	17/12/1994	1/01/1995	29/03/1982

〔36〕 但中国与列支敦士登于 2014 年 1 月 27 日签订有《中华人民共和国政府和列支敦士登公国政府关于税收情报交换的协定》。

续表

《能源宪章条约》缔约方	签署《能源宪章条约》(1994)时间	是否世界贸易组织成员方/加入的时间	是否与中国签订有双边投资协定/签订的时间
瑞士	17/12/1994	1 /07/1995	12/11/1986,27/01/2009
塔吉克斯坦	17/12/1994	2/03/2013	09/03/1993
马其顿	26/03/1998	31/05/1995	09/06/1997
土耳其	17/12/1994	26/03/1995	13/11/1990
土库曼斯坦	17/12/1994	否	21/11/1992
乌克兰	17/12/1994	16/05/2008	31/10/1992
英国	17/12/1994	1/01/1995	15/05/1986
乌兹别克斯坦	05/04/1995	观察员	13/03/1992,19/04/2011

表 2 《能源宪章条约》下投资仲裁案件一览(截至 2015 年 5 月 10 日)[37]

	投资者	母国	注册时间	被告国	仲裁机构	争议事项
1	AES Summit Generation Ltd.	英国、美国	2001	匈牙利	ICSID	电力销售合同
2	NykombSynergetics Technology Holding AB	瑞典	2001	拉脱维亚	SCC	电力销售合同
3	Plama Consortium Ltd	塞浦路斯	2003	保加利亚	ICSID	炼油厂投资
4	Petrobart	英国—直布罗陀	2003	吉尔吉斯斯坦	SCC	天然气交付合同
5	Alstom Power Italia SpA,Alstom SpA	意大利	2004	蒙古国	ICSID	热能工程、锅炉改造
6	Yukos Universal Ltd	英国—曼岛	2005	俄罗斯	UNCITRAL(PCA)	歧视措施和投资征收

〔37〕 本表数据由笔者根据网上公开信息和能源宪章秘书处公开资料搜集而来,截至 2015 年 5 月 10 日。ITALAW 网站是最常用的国际投资仲裁案例搜索网站,读者可以根据准据法、投资者、东道国等多项指标搜索相关仲裁案例,并跟踪仲裁进程。另外,本表为便于读者准确搜索仲裁案件,保留了投资者的英文名称(作者注);表格中仲裁机构一列英文简写含义为:ICSID(国际投资争端解决中心)、SCC(斯德哥尔摩商会仲裁院)、UNCTIRAL(联合国国际贸易法委员会)、PCA(常设仲裁法院)、ad hoc(临时性)。参见 http://www.italaw.com/search/site,ZnvestorState Law Guide(last visited December 20,2015)。虽然不是秘书处的法定义务和功能,但能源宪章秘书处网站也定期搜集和整理依据《能源宪章条约》挺起的国际投资仲裁,详见"Investment Dispute Settlement Cases", at http://www.energycharter.org/what-we-do/dispute-settlement/investment-dispute-settlement-cases/(last visited December 20,2015)。

续表

	投资者	母国	注册时间	被告国	仲裁机构	争议事项
7	Hulley Enterprises Ltd	塞浦路斯	2005	俄罗斯	UNCITRAL (PCA)	歧视措施和投资征收
8	Veteran Petroleum Trust	塞浦路斯	2005	俄罗斯	UNCITRAL (PCA)	歧视措施和投资征收
9	IoannisKardassopoulos	希腊	2005	格鲁吉亚	ICSID	石油天然气运输企业
10	Amto	拉脱维亚	2005	乌克兰	SCC	核电厂
11	HrvatskaElektro-privedad. d. (HEP)	克罗地亚	2005	斯洛文尼亚	ICSID	核电厂
12	Libananco Holdings Co. Limited	塞浦路斯	2006	土耳其	ICSID	电力生产和分销特许(征收)
13	Azpetrol International Holdings B. V. , Azpetrol Group B. V. and Azpetrol Oil services Group B. V.	荷兰	2006	阿塞拜疆	ICSID	石油天然气分销、贸易、存储和运输企业
14	Barmek Holding A. S.	土耳其	2006	阿塞拜疆	ICSID	电力特许
15	Cementownia "NowaHuta" S. A.	波兰	2006	土耳其	ICSID	电力特许
16	Europe Cement Investment and Trade	波兰	2007	土耳其	ICSID	电力特许
17	Liman Caspian Oil B. V/ NCL Dutch Investment B. V.	荷兰	2007	哈萨克斯坦	ICSID	烃类探测和开发
18	Electrabel S. A.	比利时	2007	匈牙利	ICSID	电力生产和分销特许(征收)
19	AES Summit Generation Ltd. / AES-Tisza EromüKft.	英国	2007	匈牙利	ICSID	电力生产
20	Mohammad Ammar Al-Bahloul	奥地利	2008	塔吉克斯坦	SCC	油气探测许可
21	Mercuria Energy Group Ltd	塞浦路斯	2008	波兰	SCC	强制性燃料储备
22	AlapliElektrik B. V.	荷兰	2008	土耳其	ICSID	电力特许
23	Remington Worldwide Ltd	英国—直布罗陀	2008	乌克兰	SCC	核能

续表

	投资者	母国	注册时间	被告国	仲裁机构	争议事项
24	Vattenfall AB, Vattenfall Europe AG, Vattenfall Europe Generation AG & Co. KG	瑞典	2009	德国	ICSID	燃煤电厂建设和环境保护措施(征收)
25	EDF International S. A.	法国	2009	匈牙利	UNCITRAL	长期电力购买合同的终止
26	EVN AG	奥地利	2009	马其顿	ICSID	电力分销(征收)
27	AES Corporation and tau Power B. V	荷兰	2010	哈萨克斯坦	ICSID	电力设施和贸易公司
28	Anatolie Stati, Gabriel Stati, Ascom S. A., Terra Raf Trans Traiding Ltd	罗马尼亚、马耳他、直布罗陀	2010	哈萨克斯坦	SCC	油田
29	Khan Resources B. V	荷兰	2011	蒙古国	UNCITRAL	铀采矿项目
30	TürkiyePetrolleri AnonimOrtakligi	土耳其	2011	哈萨克斯坦	ICSID	石油勘探和生产的合资企业
31	The PV Investors	德国	2011	西班牙	UNCITRAL	太阳能光伏产业关税制度改变
32	Slovak Gas Holding BV	荷兰	2012	斯洛伐克	ICSID	天然气服务
33	Vattenfall AB	瑞典	2012	德国	ICSID	核电厂
34	Charanne and Constructions Investments	荷兰、卢森堡	2013	西班牙	SCC	太阳能光伏产业关税制度改变
35	CËZ	捷克	2013	阿尔巴尼亚	UNCITRAL ad hoc	阿尔巴尼亚监管当局对 CËZ Shperndje 许可的撤销决定

续表

	投资者	母国	注册时间	被告国	仲裁机构	争议事项
36	Antaris Solar GmbH et al	德国、卢森堡、英国	2013	捷克	UNCITRAL	对享有政府奖励措施的太阳能发电厂的利润施加26%的溯及既往税
37	EVN AG	奥地利	2013	保加利亚	ICSID	与可再生能源相关的电力价格和公共义务赔偿的变化
38	Isolux Infrastructure Netherlands B. V.	荷兰	2013	西班牙	SCC	影响可再生能源产业的法律制度改革
39	CSP Equity Investment S. a. r. l.	卢森堡	2013	西班牙	SCC	影响可再生能源产业的法律制度改革
40	EF Infrastructure (G. P.) Limited and RREEF Pan-European Infrastructure Two Lux S. à. r. l.	泽西岛、卢森堡	2013	西班牙	ICSID	影响可再生能源产业的法律制度改革
41	Antin Infrastructure Services Luxembourg S. à. r. l. and AntinEnergiaTermosolar B. V.	卢森堡、荷兰	2013	西班牙	ICSID	影响可再生能源产业的法律制度改革
42	MOL Nyrt.	匈牙利	2013	克罗地亚	ICSID	天然气定价和分销
43	Eiser Infrastructure Limited and Energia Solar Luxembourg S. a. r. l.	卢森堡	2013	西班牙	ICSID	影响可再生能源产业的法律制度改革

续表

	投资者	母国	注册时间	被告国	仲裁机构	争议事项
44	Natland Investment Group NV, Natland Group Limited, G. I. H. G. Limited, and Radiance Energy Holding S. A. R. L.	荷兰、卢森堡	2013	捷克	UNCITRAL	对光伏产业的监管
45	Voltaic Network GmbH	德国	2013	捷克	UNCITRAL	对光伏产业的监管
46	ICW Europe Investments Limited	英国	2013	捷克	UNCITRAL	对光伏产业的监管
47	Photovoltaik Knopf Betriebs-GmbH	德国	2013	捷克	UNCITRAL	对光伏产业的监管
48	WA Investments-Europa Nova Limited	塞浦路斯	2013	捷克	UNCITRAL	对光伏产业的监管
49	Mr. Jürgen Wirtgen, Mr. Stefan Wirtgen, and JSW Solar (zwei)	德国、捷克	2013	捷克	UNCITRAL	对光伏产业的监管
50	Masdar Solar & Wind Cooperatief U. A.	阿布达比酋长国	2014	西班牙	ICSID	影响可再生能源产业的法律制度改革
51	Blusun S. A., Jean-Pierre Lecorcier and Michael Stein	法国	2014	意大利	ICSID	光伏发电项目
52	NextEra Energy Global Holdings B. V. and NextEra Energy Spain Holdings B. V.	荷兰	2014	西班牙	ICSID	影响可再生能源产业的法律制度改革
53	Infrared UK	英国	2014	西班牙	ICSID	影响可再生能源产业的法律制度改革

续表

	投资者	母国	注册时间	被告国	仲裁机构	争议事项
54	Elektrogospodarstvo Slovenije-razvojinin zeniringd. o. o.	斯洛文尼亚	2014	波黑	ICSID	火电厂建设项目
55	Energoalians SARL	乌克兰	2010	摩尔瓦多	UNCITRAL ad hoc	电力供应
56	State Enterprise Energorynok	乌克兰	2012	摩尔瓦多	SCC	电力供应
57	CemUzan	土耳其	2014	土耳其	SCC	电力生产和分销特许
58	RENERGY S. à. r. l.	卢森堡	2014	西班牙	ICSID	影响可再生能源产业的法律制度改革
59	ALPIQ	瑞士	2014	罗马尼亚	ICSID	长期能源供应合同的终止
60	RWE Innogy GmbH and RWE InnogyAersa S. A.	德国、西班牙	2014	西班牙	ICSID	影响可再生能源产业的法律制度改革
61	Stadtwerke Munchen GmbH, RWE Innogy GmbH et al.	德国、西班牙	2015	西班牙	ICSID	影响可再生能源产业的法律制度改革
62	STEAG GmbH	未公布	2015	西班牙	ICSID	影响可再生能源产业的法律制度改革
63	JKX Oil & Gas, et. al.	英国	2015	乌克兰	SCC	该国石油和天然气生产相关的租费的报销问题
64	Albaniabeg Ambient Sh. p. k. , M. Angelo Novelli and Construzioni S. r. l.	阿尔巴尼亚	2014	阿尔巴尼亚、意大利	ICSID	废物处理和可再生能源生产项目

续表

	投资者	母国	注册时间	被告国	仲裁机构	争议事项
65	Aktau Petrol Ticaret A. Ş. and Som Petrol Ticaret A. Ş.	哈萨克斯坦	2015	未公开	ICSID	石油运输和海运
66	Mamidoil Jetoil Greek Petroleum Products Societe Anonyme S. A. (Greek)	阿尔巴尼亚	2011	希腊	ICSID	石油存储和分销工程
67	9REN Holding S. a. r. l	西班牙	2015	未公开	ICSID	影响可再生能源产业的法律制度改革

表 3　国内能源相关立法及规定一览[38]

《能源宪章条约》主要规定	中国国内立法及规定相关状况
第 3 条、第 4 条和第 29 条 国际市场和贸易	《中华人民共和国能源法(征求意见稿)》
	《中华人民共和国对外贸易法》
	《中华人民共和国电力法》
	《中华人民共和国煤炭法》
	《中华人民共和国节约能源法》
	《中华人民共和国可再生能源法》
	《中华人民共和国海关法》
	《中华人民共和国进出口关税条例》
	《中华人民共和国海关进出口货物征税管理办法》
第 6 条　竞争	《中华人民共和国反不正当竞争法》
	《中华人民共和国反垄断法》
	《中华人民共和国国家安全法》
	《中华人民共和国外国投资法(草案征求意见稿)》
第 7 条　跨境运输	《石油天然气管道保护法》
	《中华人民共和国核材料管制条例》
	《电力设施保护条例》
	《中华人民共和国环境影响评价法》
	《建设项目环境保护管理条例》
	《建设项目环境影响评价资质管理办法》

〔38〕 本表由笔者根据主要政府职能部门网捕搜集的数据整理所得。

续表

《能源宪章条约》主要规定	中国国内立法及规定相关状况
第8条　技术转移	《中华人民共和国著作权法》
	《中华人民共和国专利法》
	《中华人民共和国商标法》
	《中华人民共和国进出口货物原产地条例》
	《实施国际著作权条约的规定》
	《商务部关于印发〈境外企业知识产权指南(试行)〉的通知》
第9条　融资渠道	《中华人民共和国商业银行法》
	《中华人民共和国银行业监督管理法》
	《中华人民共和国票据法》
	《中华人民共和国保险法》
	《中华人民共和国行政许可法》
	《中华人民共和国证券法》
	《中华人民共和国证券投资基金法》
	《中华人民共和国外资银行管理条例》
	《中华人民共和国外资金融机构管理条例》
第10条　投资	《中华人民共和国外国投资法(草案征求意见稿)》
	《中华人民共和国中外合资经营企业法》
	《中华人民共和国民法通则》
	《中华人民共和国外资企业法》
	《中华人民共和国中外合作经营企业法》
	《中华人民共和国公司法》
	《中华人民共和国台湾同胞投资保护法》
	《指导外商投资方向规定》
第11条　关键人员	《中华人民共和国出境入境管理法》
	《中华人民共和国外国人入境出境管理条例》
	《外国人入境完成短期工作任务的相关办理程序(试行)》
	《外交部关于进一步简化外籍专业人才来华手续的规定》
	《外国人在中国永久居留审批管理办法》
	《外国人在中国就业管理规定》
第12条和第13条　损失补偿、征收	《中华人民共和国宪法》
	《中华人民共和国物权法》
	《中华人民共和国外国投资法(草案征求意见稿)》
	《中华人民共和国国家赔偿法》
	《国有土地上房屋征收与补偿条例》

续表

《能源宪章条约》主要规定	中国国内立法及规定相关状况
第 12 条和第 13 条　损失补偿、征收	《中华人民共和国土地管理法》
	《中华人民共和国行政处罚法》
	《中华人民共和国行政复议法》
第 14 条　转移	《中华人民共和国外汇管理条例》
	《外商直接投资人民币结算业务管理办法》
	《国家外汇管理局关于进一步简化和改进直接投资外汇管理政策的通知》
	《合格境外机构投资者境内证券投资管理办法》
第 15 条　代位	《中华人民共和国保险法》
	最高人民法院《关于审理海上保险纠纷案件若干问题的规定》
	最高人民法院《关于适用〈中华人民共和国保险法〉若干问题的解释(一)》
	最高人民法院《关于适用〈中华人民共和国保险法〉若干问题的解释(二)》
	最高人民法院《关于海上保险合同的保险人行使代位请求赔偿权利的诉讼》
	《时效期间起算日的批复》
第 18 条　自然资源主权	《中华人民共和国矿产资源法》
	《外商投资矿产勘查企业管理办法》
	《产业结构调整指导目录》
	《外国的组织或者个人来华测绘管理暂行办法》
	《探矿权采矿权转让管理办法》
第 19 条　环境问题	《中华人民共和国环境保护法》
	《中华人民共和国海洋环境保护法》
	《中华人民共和国清洁生产促进法》
	《中华人民共和国环境影响评价法》
	《中华人民共和国节约能源法》
	《中华人民共和国清洁生产促进法》
	《中华人民共和国大气污染防治法》
	《中华人民共和国煤炭法》
第 20 条　透明度	《中华人民共和国政府信息公开条例》(2007)
	《国务院法制办公室法律法规草案公开征求意见暂行办法》
	《中华人民共和国保守国家秘密法实施条例》
	《中华人民共和国行政许可法》
	《关于推进司法公开三大平台建设的若干意见》
	《关于人民法院在互联网公布裁判文书的规定》

续表

《能源宪章条约》主要规定	中国国内立法及规定相关状况
第 20 条　透明度	《关于人民法院执行流程公开的若干意见》
	《中华人民共和国政府采购法》
第 21 条　税收	《一般反避税管理办法(试行)》
	《中华人民共和国个人所得税法》
	《中华人民共和国审计法》
	《中华人民共和国反洗钱法》
	《中华人民共和国企业所得税法》
	《中华人民共和国个人所得税法》
第 22 条　国家和特权企业	《中华人民共和国全民所有制工业企业法》
	《中华人民共和国企业国有资产法》
	《外商投资产业指导目录》
	《基础设施和公用事业特许经营管理办法(征求意见稿)》
	《政府核准投资项目管理办法》
	《外商投资项目核准和备案管理办法》
	《西部地区鼓励类产业目录》
	《关于 2009 年深化经济体制改革工作的意见》

表 4　中国对《能源宪章条约》缔约方直接投资流量(2003 ~ 2013 年)[39]

单位:万美元

缔约方	2003 年	2004 年	2005 年	2006 年	2007 年	2008 年	2009 年	2010 年	2011 年	2012 年	2013 年
阿富汗	30	0	0	25	10	11391	1639	191	29554	1761	- 122
阿尔巴尼亚	0	0	0	1	0	0	0	8	0	0	56
亚美尼亚	N/A	N/A	N/A	N/A	N/A	N/A	N/A	N/A	N/A	N/A	N/A
澳大利亚	3039	12, 495	19, 307	8760	53, 159	189, 215	243, 643	170, 170	316, 529	217, 298	345, 798
奥地利	40	0	0	4	8	0	0	46	2022	5343	15
阿塞拜疆	35	20	0	394	- 115	- 66	173	37	1768	34	- 443
白俄罗斯						210	210	1922	867	4350	2718

〔39〕 本表由作者根据《中国商务年鉴(2014 年)》数据整理而来,因为统计口径的原因,相关国家的数据在《中国商务年鉴》中没有统计或收录,在表中用“*N/A*”予以标示。参见《中国商务年鉴》编辑委员会:《中国商务年鉴 2014》,中国商务出版社 2015 年版,第 179 ~ 192 页。需要明确,由于欧盟和欧洲原子能共同体也是《能源宪章条约》的缔约方,因此中国对《能源宪章条约》成员方的投资总量的统计存在部分重复。《中国统计年鉴》也能提供一些中国对主要国别(地区)的对外直接投资数据,详见 http://www.stats.gov.cn/tjsj/ndsj/,2015 年 12 月 20 日访问。

续表

缔约方	2003 年	2004 年	2005 年	2006 年	2007 年	2008 年	2009 年	2010 年	2011 年	2012 年	2013 年
比利时	30	5	0	13	491	0	2362	4533	3590	9840	2578
波黑	146	0	0	0	0	0	151	6	4	6	N/A
保加利亚	35	35	172	0	0	0	-243	1629	5390	5417	2069
克罗地亚	0	0	0	0	120	0	26	3	5	5	N/A
塞浦路斯	0	0	0	0	30	0	0	0	8954	348	7634
捷克	0	46	0	910	497	1279	1560	211	884	1802	1784
丹麦	7388	-778	1079	-5891	27	133	264	161	589	514	2739
爱沙尼亚	N/A	N/A	N/A	N/A	N/A	N/A	N/A	N/A	N/A	N/A	N/A
欧盟(EU)和欧洲原子能共同体(Euratom)	14, 503	15, 721	39, 549	59, 771	154, 043	87, 579	335, 272	676, 019	825, 108	703, 509	594, 853
芬兰	0	0	0	0	1	266	111	1804	156	136	852
法国	45	1031	609	560	962	3105	4519	2641	348, 232	15, 393	26, 044
格鲁吉亚	0	484	0	994	821	1000	778	4057	80	6874	10, 962
德国	2506	2750	12, 874	7672	23, 866	18, 341	17, 921	41, 235	51, 238	79, 933	91, 081
希腊	0	20	0	0	3	12	0	0	43	88	190
匈牙利	118	10	65	37	863	215	821	37, 010	1161	4140	2567
冰岛	0	0	0	0	0	0	0	-5	0	0	0
爱尔兰	14	0	0	2529	20	4233	-95	3288	1693	4888	11, 702
意大利	29	310	746	763	810	500	4605	1327	22, 483	11, 858	3126
日本	737	1530	1717	3949	3903	5862	8410	33, 799	14, 942	21, 065	43, 405
哈萨克斯坦	294	231	9493	4600	27, 992	49, 643	6681	3606	58, 160	299, 599	81, 149
吉尔吉斯斯坦	244	533	1374	2764	1499	706	13, 691	8247	14, 507	16, 140	20, 339
拉脱维亚	158	0	0	0	-174	0	-3	0	0	0	0
列支敦士登	0	0	0	0	28	0	7	355	0	0	0
立陶宛	0	0	0	0	0	0	0	0	0	100	551
卢森堡	0	0	0	0	419	4213	227, 049	320, 719	126, 500	113, 301	127, 521
马耳他	0	37	0	10	-10	47	22	-237	27	0	12
摩尔瓦多	N/A	N/A	N/A	N/A	N/A	N/A	N/A	N/A	N/A	N/A	N/A
蒙古国	443	4016	5234	8239	19, 627	23, 861	27, 654	19, 386	45, 104	90, 403	38, 879
荷兰	447	191	384	531	10, 675	9097	10, 145	6453	16, 786	44, 245	23, 842

续表

缔约方	2003 年	2004 年	2005 年	2006 年	2007 年	2008 年	2009 年	2010 年	2011 年	2012 年	2013 年
挪威	0	0	0	14	360	9	360	13473	1857	849	19, 629
波兰	155	10	13	0	1175	1070	1037	1674	4866	750	1834
葡萄牙	0	0	0	0	0	0	0	0	0	515	1494
罗马尼亚	61	268	287	963	680	1198	529	1084	30	2541	217
俄罗斯	3062	7731	20, 333	45, 211	47, 761	39, 523	34, 822	56, 772	71, 581	78, 462	102, 225
斯洛伐克	0	0	0	0	0	0	26	46	594	219	33
斯洛文尼亚	N/A	N/A	N/A	N/A	N/A	N/A	N/A	N/A	N/A	N/A	N/A
西班牙	0	170	147	730	609	116	5986	2926	13, 974	4624	-14, 575
瑞典	17	264	100	530	6806	1066	810	136, 723	4901	28, 522	17, 082
瑞士	0	58	59	101	121	1	2099	2725	1719	864	12, 826
塔吉克斯坦	0	499	77	698	6793	2658	1667	1542	2210	23, 411	7233
马其顿	N/A	N/A	N/A	N/A	N/A	N/A	N/A	N/A	N/A	N/A	N/A
土耳其	153	158	24	115	161	910	29, 326	782	1350	10, 895	17, 855
土库曼斯坦	0	0	0	-4	126	8671	11, 968	45, 051	-38, 304	1234	-3243
乌克兰	6	120	203	183	565	241	3	150	77	207	1014
中国对缔约方直接投资流量	33, 735	47, 965	113, 846	145, 176	364, 732	466, 305	996, 006	1, 601, 569	1, 961, 231	1, 811, 489	1, 605, 525
中国当年对外直接投资流量	285, 465	549, 799	1, 226, 117	1, 763, 397	2, 650, 609	5, 590, 717	5, 652, 899	6, 881, 131	7, 465, 404	8, 780, 353	10, 784, 371
中国对亚洲区域直接投资流量	150, 503	301, 399	448, 417	766, 325	1, 659, 315	4, 354, 750	4, 040, 759	4, 489, 046	4, 549, 445	6, 478, 494	7, 560, 426

表5　来自《能源宪章条约》主要缔约方的投资占中国大陆当年实际吸引外资总额的比重(2008～2014年)〔40〕

单位:亿美元

对中国大陆投资前十位国家/地区	2008年	2009年	2010年	2011年	2012年	2013年	2014年
1	中国香港地区(410.36)	中国香港地区(539.93)	中国香港地区(674.74)	中国香港地区(770.11)	中国香港地区(712.89)	中国香港地区(783.02)	中国香港地区(857.4)
2	英属维尔京群岛(159.54)	中国台湾地区(65.63)	中国台湾地区(67.01)	中国台湾地区(67.27)	日本(73.8)	新加坡(73.27)	新加坡(59.3)
3	新加坡(44.35)	日本(41.17)	新加坡(56.57)	日本(63.48)	新加坡(65.39)	日本(70.64)	中国台湾地区(51.8)
4	日本(36.52)	新加坡(38.86)	日本(42.42)	新加坡(63.28)	中国台湾地区(61.83)	中国台湾地区(52.46)	日本(43.3)
5	开曼群岛(31.45)	美国(35.76)	美国(40.52)	美国(29.95)	美国(31.3)	美国(33.53)	韩国(39.7)
6	韩国(31.35)	韩国(27.03)	韩国(26.93)	韩国(25.51)	韩国(30.66)	韩国(30.59)	美国(26.7)
7	美国(29.44)	英国(14.69)	英国(16.42)	英国(16.1)	德国(14.71)	德国(20.95)	德国(20.7)
8	萨摩亚(25.5)	德国(12.27)	法国(12.39)	德国(11.36)	荷兰(11.44)	荷兰(12.81)	英国(13.5)
9	中国台湾地区(18.99)	澳门(10)	荷兰(9.52)	法国(8.02)	英国(10.31)	英国(10.39)	法国(7.1)
10	毛里求斯(14.94)	加拿大(9.59)	德国(9.33)	荷兰(7.67)	瑞士(8.78)	法国(7.62)	荷兰(6.4)

〔40〕 表中日本、德国、法国、英国、荷兰、瑞士等国为《能源宪章条约》的缔约国。《2014年1～12月全国吸收外商直接投资情况》,载http://www.mofcom.gov.cn/article/tongjiziliao/v/201501/20150100880913.shtml,2015年5月10日访问。

续表

对中国大陆投资前十位国家/地区	2008 年	2009 年	2010 年	2011 年	2012 年	2013 年	2014 年
当年实际吸引外资总额	923. 95	900. 33	1057. 35	1160. 11	1117. 16	1175. 86	1195. 6
前十位百分比	86. 85	88. 3	90. 1	91. 61	91. 4	93	94. 2
缔约方所占比例	3. 95	7. 57	7. 58	9. 19	10. 65	10. 33	7. 61

中国海外资源能源投资法律问题调查报告*

引言

近年来，随着海外经济利益持续拓展，我国对外投资高速增长，年均增幅达70%以上，其中比重最大、最为引人注目的是资源和能源领域的投资。据不完全统计，2008年至2009年间，以中国企业为买方的跨国并购，目标领域为能源产业的有13宗，交易金额277.54亿美元，占1亿美元以上并购案交易总额的48.6%；矿业15宗，交易金额262.34亿美元，占交易总额的45.9%。[1] 海外资源能源投资不仅涉及重大商业利益，更关乎国家能源安全，其在国家政治经济和社会生活中的分量不言而喻。

然而，在对外投资高速增长的同时，我国"走出去"的企业特别是资源能源企业所面临的政治与法律风险也加速显现。一段时间以来，中石油、中铝海外并购屡屡受阻，中国商人黄怒波冰岛购地申请被拒——越来越多的事件表明，中国企业"走出去"的努力正在遭遇全球投资保护的寒冬。特别是2011年中东、北非的政治动荡，更给我国在这些地区的投资带来了巨大的损失。[2] "风险控制"顿时成为2011年中国企业"走出去"的一个关键词。在这个背景之下，

---

* 本文发表在《国际经济法学刊》2012年第19卷第2期。作者为单文华及课题组。

本调研系单文华主持的2008年司法部国家法治与法学理论研究课题"中国对外能源投资合作法律问题研究"和2009年度国家社会科学基金重大招标项目"促进与保护我国海外投资的法律体制研究"（总主持人：曾华群、余劲松）子课题六《中国海外资源类投资的法律问题研究》的重要组成部分之一。由于篇幅所限，本报告在发表时由编辑部作了删减。

本调研课题组由单文华牵头，主要成员包括任翔、贺艳、王玉苹、贾艳等。王朝恩、张生、王鹏、王钊、马俊飞、马莎、冷帅等也有贡献。同时，课题调研得到了许多中央和地方政府部门、涉外律师事务所、会计师事务所以及广大对外投资企业的支持和帮助，在此谨致诚挚谢忱（尽管由于保密原因不能一一署名致谢）！

[1] 《海外投资猛增，中国企业"走出去"风险加剧》，载《经济参考报》2011年3月23日。

[2] 新华网：《中东乱局考验中国"走出去"战略》，载 http://news.xinhuanet.com/world/2011-05/02/c_121369653_4.htm，2012年5月30日访问；郭丽琴、孟李洋：《风险控制：2011企业走出去又一关键词》，载 http://finance.sina.com.cn/roll/20110302/01299453621.shtml，2012年5月30日访问。

针对我国资源能源领域的海外投资企业，我们开展了一项问卷调查，旨在厘清我国海外资源能源投资所切实面临的政治风险和主要法律障碍，并在此基础上探讨改善我国海外投资法律保护的方法和途径。本调查问卷涵盖政治风险、准入限制、一般待遇、具体制度、法律纠纷、法治状况、其他因素以及改善措施等八大方面的问题。调研对象包括从事海外资源能源投资（包括石油天然气、电力、煤炭、黑色金属、有色金属等）的中国企业、管理海外资源能源投资的政府部门以及提供相关法律和会计服务的律师事务所和会计师事务所。

本调查报告共分十一章。第一章简述了本次调查背景、调查对象、问卷设计、问卷反馈以及数据处理；第二章宏观勾勒中国投资面临的政治风险总体情况；从第三章起至第八章，分述了中国投资准入限制、享受一般待遇情况、享受具体待遇情况、东道国法治状况、投资争端解决以及贸易壁垒和环境问题等投资的其他影响因素；第九章则从我国五个主要海外投资区的角度对我国投资遭遇政治风险与法律问题的情况进行了分析；第十章提出了改善我国海外投资环境的法律与政策建议；第十一章则是整份报告的最后总结。

第一章　调查概述[3]

一、调查背景

资源和能源是经济发展的血脉。对外资源能源投资[4]事关国家资源能源安全，是我国对外直接投资的重要组成部分。以采矿业为例，2009 年末中国对外直接投资在采矿业的存量为 405.8 亿美元，主要分布在石油天然气开采、有色金属开采、黑色金属矿采选业。中国在采矿领域的巨大投资使采矿业成为继租赁和商务服务业以及金融业之后，对外直接投资流向的第三大行业。

然而，资源能源投资具有投资金额大、回收周期长等特点，这些都使得资源能源投资与一般投资相比面临着更大的风险。同时，我国主要资源能源投资区的市场大多尚欠完善，法律环境亟待改进，政治不够稳定，这些都构成我国企业进行海外资源能源投资的种种障碍。本研究即旨在切实调研我国海外资源能源投资（以下简称“中国投资”或“我国投资”）企业所面临的政治法律风险与障碍，并在此基

〔3〕 为尽量以原风貌呈现，本调查报告在体例上并未完全遵从本刊一般习惯，特此说明。另外，由于篇幅所限，编者对原调查报告的大量图表有所删减。——编者注

〔4〕 除非特别说明，本报告中“投资”均指“中国海外资源能源投资”，“投资者”均指“中国海外资源能源投资者”。“受访者”指参与此次问卷调查或调查回访的人，包括来自中国投资企业、相关政府主管部门以及涉外律师事务所和会计师事务所中所有对调研作出有效回复的人。

础上探讨国家所可能采取的相应的法律与政策对策。

二、调查对象

本问卷调查的对象是从事海外资源能源投资(包括石油天然气、电力、煤炭、黑色金属、有色金属等)的中国企业、管理海外资源能源投资的政府部门,以及从事相关服务的律师事务所和会计师事务所("两所")。

根据商务部《境外投资企业(机构)名录》,[5]我国共有海外资源能源投资企业787家。这些企业在海外设立企业或机构的区域分布情况为:大洋洲51家,拉丁美洲33家,北美79家,非洲97家,东南亚163家,中亚149家,西亚27家,港澳92家,南亚16家,欧洲29家,东亚51家。本次调研选择了在五个主要资源能源投资区(大洋洲、拉丁美洲、非洲、东南亚、中亚)中的21个国家[6]设有企业或机构的中国企业投资者。入选企业的经营范围中至少有一项涉及能源投资。对于在多个国家或地区都设有企业或分支机构的境内投资主体则只保留一个。在剔除重复出现的"境内投资主体"时所采用的原则是:在"经营范围"条目下,矿产、能源投资的较其他相关领域优先保留;"境外投资企业(机构)"条目下,"公司"较"办事处"优先保留;两者相差不大时,则考虑各地区企业数目分布的平衡。经过首选和有效性筛选,调研对象总计300个,占《境外投资企业(机构)名录》中全部海外资源能源投资企业的50.68%。我们希望并相信这个样本基数能够大体上反映我国海外投资法律问题的概貌。

三、问卷设计

在可能遭遇的风险方面,Rubins和Kinsella将国际投资中的政治风险分类为直接征收、行政性干涉、汇兑风险、内乱、违反国家合同、腐败、贸易管制等七种。[7] 在获得保护方面,Dolzer将保护国际投资的标准分由公平与公正待遇、充分保护与安全、保护伞条款、司法救济保证、正当程序、司法拒绝、紧急情况,必要情形、武装冲突、不可抗力、权利保留、随意的或歧视性的措施、国民待遇、最惠国待遇,以及国际间财产转移等方面进行了详尽的论述。[8] 此外,其他一些非经济

---

[5] 商务部:《境外投资企业(机构)名录》,载 http://wszw.hzs.mofcom.gov.cn/fecp/fem/corp/fem_cert_stat_view_list.jsp,2012年5月30日访问。

[6] 这21个国家为:(大洋洲)澳大利亚、新西兰、巴布亚新几内亚;(拉美)委内瑞拉、巴西、阿根廷、智利、秘鲁;(非洲)苏丹、刚果、利比亚、尼日利亚;(东南亚)缅甸、马来西亚、印度尼西亚;(中亚)俄罗斯、哈萨克斯坦、土库曼斯坦、吉尔吉斯斯坦、乌兹别克斯坦、蒙古。

[7] Noah Rubins, Stephan Kinsella, International Investment, Political Risk and Dispute Resolution: A Practitioner's Guide, Ocean Publications, 2005, pp. 5 – 24.

[8] Rudolf Dolzer, Christoph Schreuer, Principles of International Investment Law, Oxford University Press, 2008, pp. 119 – 194.

因素包括人权、环境的可持续性和气候变化也对国际投资活动产生着不可忽视的影响。由于资源投资的期限长,中国对外资源投资也经受着这些非经济因素的考验。又由于这类投资是在自然环境中直接掘取资源和能源,环保问题在此也就比在其他种类的国际投资活动中而更显突出。

《能源宪章条约》(Energy Charter Treaty,ECT)是现有的唯一一个规范能源投资保护的重要多边条约。因此,本研究选择了《能源宪章条约》为本次实证考察框架设计的实践基础。问卷设计前期,在理论资料准备的同时,本研究总结了《能源宪章条约》下所有可得的已裁案例的争议焦点,并以此作为国际资源能源法律问题的基本实践依据。

基于上述两方面的考察,本课题最终将实证调研的范围确定为政治风险总体情况、准入限制(业绩要求)、享受一般待遇情况(包括国民待遇、公平与公正待遇、充分安全与保障)、享受具体待遇情况(包括国有化措施、政治动乱、投资合同、财产转移)、东道国法制状况(包括司法公正、法律稳定性、官员腐败)、投资争端解决(包括投资争端情况、救济措施选择)以及其他影响因素(包括贸易壁垒、环境问题)等方面,在此基础上设计了问卷。

四、问卷反馈

调研问卷初次发放至回收时间为2010年10月至2011年4月。本次调研问卷的回收率为15.33%。调研对象的构成及问卷反馈的具体情况如表1.1所示。

表1.1 调研对象采选及问卷反馈情况

		初选调研对象数	回复数	回复率
企业答卷者	大洋洲	60	18	30%
	拉丁美洲	30	6	20%
	非洲	60	10	16.67%
	东南亚	60	10	11.11%
	中亚	30	6	10%
	企业小计(不重复计算)	240	38	12.67%
政府部门答卷者		20	3	15%
律师事务所和会计师事务所答卷者		40	5	12.5%
总计		300	46	15.33%

注:若某企业投资者在两个或以上区域均有投资,除非答卷者作出特别说明,在分区域统计时同一份问卷会在统计这些区域中被重复计算。

本次调研的问卷调查把握程度设为100%、80%及60%三个等级。答卷者中有21.74%的人对其回答准确性的把握程度为60%,有58.70%的人对其回答准确性的把握程度为80%。对其回答准确性的把握程度在80%以上的答卷者占78.27%。

五、数据处理

所有有效答卷依照所设计的22个问题逐一统计。进而,为了反映投资活动中不同利益攸关方对同一问题可能不同的看法,本研究将答卷者划分为企业答卷者、政府部门答卷者、"两所"答卷者(律师事务所和会计师事务所答卷者),并从他们各自的角度对反馈信息进行了统计和分析。同时,本研究将参与调研的企业答卷者按照大洋洲投资区、东南亚投资区、中亚投资区、非洲投资区和拉丁美洲投资区等五个主要的资源能源投资区域进行分类,分别统计其反馈的信息,以此体现中国投资者在不同区域进行资源能源投资的情况。

为更清晰地体现这些法律问题在各个投资区发生的情况,本研究将问卷问题按照封闭式和开放式予以分类,并对所有封闭式问题的答案进行统计学编码,将"从来没有、极少、有时、经常、总是如此"作为预设法律问题的发生情况,按照发生频度大小依次编码为"从来没有=0,极少=1,有时=2,经常=3,总是如此=4"。"不知道"则作为无效回答处理。按照不同受访主体和不同投资区域将答卷者对反馈信息进行分别统计,并分别计算每个法律问题发生频度的均值。[9] 虽然由此得出的各个法律问题的均值并不等于这些法律问题在中国海外资源能源投资活动中的实际发生情况,但在其产生的编码体系内,这些均值数据应被认为能够反映出这些法律问题发生频度高低的相对情况。同时,由于均值的计算容纳了就每一具体法律问题的答卷者作答的程度和人数,故每一均值应被理解为是相应法律问题(风险)发生的频繁程度和涉及人数广度的综合性反映。

在对这些均值进行定量分析时,我们参考世界银行等国际开发援助机构所确立的"理想制度范式"(Ideal Institutional Paradigm)[10] 以及 Perry 应用这个范

[9] 由于考察"国民待遇""公平与公正待遇"和"充分安全与保障"的在问卷中以积极描述设计,故所得数据为投资者享受这些待遇的情况。为与其他负面描述问题相统一以便比较,这三个问题的均值结果均被频度最高情况(即4)相减,最终数据表示未能享受到这些待遇的情况。

[10] World Bank, Governance and Development, Washington DC: World Bank, 1992, at 4.

式所作的实证研究,[11]确定以 0.8 为达标基准线,并以 0.8 为级差。[12] 换言之,问题均值为 0.8 及以下为“达标”(≦0.8),0.8 以上均属于“超标”状态;依其严重程度,又依次细分为“轻度超标”(>0.8 且≦1.6)、“明显超标”(>1.6 且≦2.4)、“严重超标”(>2.4 且≦3.2)和“根本超标”(>3.2 且≦4)。我们希望这样的定量分析能够更加清晰准确地揭示相关法律问题存在的程度。

第二章　政治风险总体情况

一、中国投资遭遇政治风险的总体情况

政治风险是基于政府行为,或者市场中经济状况变化以外的原因,而产生的对于投资项目盈利能力的消极影响或威胁。[13] 这里的政府行为指投资东道国政府通过作为或者不作为的方式,导致减损投资者实现其投资的预期收益能力的行为。[14] 本研究以一个独立问题询问答卷者中国的海外投资有没有因为政治因素而受阻或受损的情况,以便了解答卷者对于中国投资在海外经历政治风险的总体情况。

从总体情况看,有约三成答卷者表示中国投资从未遇过政治风险。其余答卷者中,有四成表示政治风险导致中国投资受损或受阻的情况有时发生,另有近一成答卷者认为这种情况经常或总是存在。两项相加表明有半数答卷者认为中国资源能源投资面临着某种程度的政治风险,总体均值为 1.31,处于“轻度超标”状态。

二、分类答卷者反映中国投资遭遇政治风险的情况

半数企业答卷者表示其投资从未或极少受到由政治风险转化而来的损失。36.84% 的企业答卷者表示其投资有时会遭受这种损失;但表示经常或总是会遭受这种损失的则占 10.52%,其均值为 1.24,处于“轻度超标”状态。政府主管部

---

〔11〕 Amanda Perry, Effective Legal Systems and Foreign Direct Investment: In Search of the Evidence, International and Comparative Law Quarterly, 2000, Vol. 49, No. 4, pp. 779 – 799. See also Shan Wenhua, The Legal-Framework of EU-China Investment Relations: A Critical Appraisal, Hart Publication, 2005, p. 253.

〔12〕 在 Perry 应用世界银行“理想制度范式”的研究中,她将调查结果按照正向符合此理想制度范式的程度以 5 分为满分赋值,并以 4 分为“有效”制度的基准线,以 1 分为等差。故其结果等级依次为“有效”(≦4)、“无效”(≥2 且<3)和“严重无效”(<2)。相应地,本研究按反向不符合(即在何种程度上不符合理想制度范式从而构成法律风险可导致投资损失)为量值处理,并以 4 分为满分赋值,则其达标线应为 0.8,且其等差亦为 0.8。Amanda Perry,同注[10]引文。

〔13〕 Thedore H. Moran, Political and Regulatory Risk in Infrastructure Investment in Develo-ping Countries: Introduction and Overview, CEPMLP Journal, Vol. 5 – 6a, p. 3 (citing Harvard Professor Louis Wells, Jr.). Also see Noah Rubins, Stephan Kinsella, *supra* note 6, pp. 2 – 3.

〔14〕 Noah Rubins, Stephan Kinsella, *supra* note 6, pp. 2 – 3.

门的答卷者对中国投资在海外遭遇政治风险情况的看法较为统一，认为政治风险“有时”会影响中国投资，其均值为2.00，处于“明显超标”状态。涉外律师事务所和会计师事务所基于为中国投资企业提供法律和会计服务的经验，也对中国投资遭遇政治风险的情况予以反馈。其中有60%的“两所”答卷者认为中国投资因政治风险受损或受阻的情况极少发生，另有40%的答卷者认为这种情况有时会发生，均值为1.40，处于“轻度超标”状态。

比较而言，企业答卷者所感受的政治风险程度最低，“两所”答卷者的认识与企业答卷者相比略高但比较接近，而政府部门答卷者所感受政治风险程度则最为突出。表面看起来，这似乎意味着我国海外资源能源投资企业事实上所面临的政治风险并不像相关政府部门所担心的那么突出。另一种解释也许是因为政府部门的观察往往着眼宏观，对政治风险的存在与影响较之投资企业更加敏感。无论如何，约四成企业答卷者认为其投资在某种程度上会因政治风险而受损或受阻这一事实表明政治风险对中国海外资源能源投资已经产生了不可忽视的负面影响。

三、中国投资在不同区域遭遇政治风险的情况

除中亚投资区外，其余四个投资区各有三成至四成的答卷者表示其投资从未遭遇过政治风险。在五个投资区中，拉丁美洲投资区有2/3的答卷者反映其投资从未或极少遭遇政治风险，是答卷者反映政治风险发生频度最低的投资区，均值为1，属于接近达标的“轻度超标”状态。中亚投资区的所有答卷者都表示其投资在不同程度上遭遇过政治风险，且在该投资区有16.67%的答卷者表示其投资总是会遭遇政治风险并因此受损或受阻，使其成为五个投资区中政治风险发生频度最高的投资区，其均值为2.17，属于“明显超标”状态。

四、小结

从总体情况上看，约有一半答卷者认为海外资源能源投资经常或者不时因为政治风险受到损失或者遭受阻碍，处于“轻度超标”状态。显然，这种风险不可忽视。从不同受访主体的角度看，政府部门较之企业与“两所”更担心我国海外资源能源投资所面临的政治风险。从不同投资区域的角度来看，我国在中亚投资区资源能源投资的政治风险最高，而拉丁美洲地区则为最低。

第三章　准入限制（业绩要求）

一、中国投资被附加业绩要求的总体情况

在国际直接投资中，东道国政府往往规定外国投资者应该作出某些承诺或承

担一定义务，以作为投资者获得投资准入或享受某些特殊优惠或特权的前提条件。这些条件被称为“业绩要求”。[15] 因此，本研究设计了开放式问题询问答卷者中国资源能源投资被附加各种业绩要求的情况。

结果表明，在所考察的业绩要求中，当地雇佣要求是中国投资者最常见的业绩要求（67%）；位居其次的是当地股权要求（43%）。其余四项所考察的业绩要求被附加的较少，按答卷者选择的多少依次为：当地成分要求、技术转让要求、外汇平衡要求、出口实际要求。此外，另有少数答卷者表示中国投资曾被附加过这些义务以外的其他业绩要求，例如安全环保要求、原油分成要求、承接该国其他工程要求、提供赞助，等等。

二、分类答卷者反映中国投资被附加业绩要求的情况

从不同答卷者反馈的信息来看，当地雇佣要求仍是企业答卷者表示最常被附加的业绩要求，其次是当地股权要求。政府部门则认为当地雇佣要求是中国投资被附加最多的义务。涉外的律师事务所和会计师事务所基于所提供法律和会计服务的经验同样认为当地雇佣要求是中国投资被附加最多的义务，当地股权要求和当地成分要求在准入阶段也是中国投资被附加的重要业绩要求。这说明各类答卷者普遍认为当地雇佣要求是东道国在准入阶段最经常要求中国投资承担的一项义务，尽管他们对其他业绩要求的附加情况的认知并不完全一致。

三、中国投资在不同区域被附加业绩要求的情况

根据本次调研所得数据显示，当地雇佣要求在五个投资区都是最多答卷者认为曾被施加的业绩要求，在这五个资源能源投资区中分别占到七到八成。这说明当地雇佣要求是中国投资在各区域投资普遍会被附加的准入义务。

当地股权要求是继当地雇佣要求之后答卷者反映最多的业绩要求，五个资源能源投资区的答卷者中分别有五到七成不等的答卷者反映中国投资曾被附加这一要求。在东南亚投资区的答卷者认为，当地股权要求与当地雇佣要求一样是在该区域投资最为常见的业绩要求。紧居其后的是当地成分要求，五个投资区中分别有三到六成的答卷者反映其投资曾被附加这一业绩要求。拉丁美洲和非洲投资区的东道国附加当地成分要求的情况要略高于中亚、东南亚和大洋洲投资区。

在非洲进行投资中的答卷者中半数以上反映曾被附加过技术转让要求，是五

[15] 单文华：《欧盟对华投资的法律框架：解构与建构》，蔡从燕译，北京大学出版社2007版，第123页。

个投资区中最高的。这说明先进技术是在非洲区域投资资源能源的重要因素。外汇平衡要求在拉丁美洲区域、非洲区域和东南亚区域的重要程度要略高于其在中亚区域和大洋洲区域的情况，说明拉丁美洲、非洲和东南亚区域的东道国对外汇管制相对更为严格。出口实际要求则是答卷者最少提及的业绩要求，说明东道国对资源能源投资中产品的销售大多未作特殊要求。可见，不同区域政府对我国资源能源投资企业的业绩要求大体趋同，但也各有所侧重。

四、小结

在投资的准入阶段，我国海外资源能源投资往往被附加各种业绩要求。其中当地雇佣要求是中国在海外进行资源能源投资时最经常被附加的业绩要求；其次是当地股权要求和当地成分要求。就区域特点而言，在非洲的投资常常被要求承担技术转让义务；而在拉丁美洲、东南亚和非洲投资区则常有外汇平衡要求。

第四章　享受一般待遇情况

在调查中国企业在从事资源能源投资的过程中享受一般待遇情况时，答卷者被问及三个问题：一是其在投资东道国是否享受到了与当地的本土企业以及其他外国企业同等的待遇（即“国民待遇”）；二是作为投资者，其认为自己在东道国享受到的待遇是否公平与公正（即“公平与公正待遇”）；三是东道国的法律是否为投资活动提供了充分的安全与保障。

一、国民待遇

就国民待遇问题，有43.48%的答卷者表示中国投资经常或总是能享受国民待遇；21.74%的答卷者认为其投资有时能享受国民待遇；少数答卷者（6.52%）认为中国投资从来没有或极少能享受国民待遇。此外值得注意的是，有28.26%的答卷者表示对投资是否享有国民待遇不甚清楚，因而未对问卷中的相应问题作出正面回答。从正面答卷来看，大部分答卷者认为中国投资享受国民待遇，但仍有相当比例的答卷者表示我国投资未能享受稳定的国民待遇，其问题均值为1.21，属于“轻度超标”。

（一）分类答卷者反映中国投资享受国民待遇的情况

从不同答卷者的角度来看，企业答卷者中有近半数（44.74%）认为其投资经常或总是能够享受国民待遇，仅有极少数企业答卷者认为其投资享受国民待遇的状况不佳,从来没有或者只在极少情况下可以享受国民待遇,均值为1.15。对于同一问题,政府部门答卷者有2/3认为经常能享受到国民待遇,"两所"的答卷者中2/3的多数则出现在"有时",其各自均值为1.33和1.50。这说明"两所"答卷者对中国投资享受国民待遇的情况最为担忧,其次是政府部门答卷者,最后是投资企业答卷者。不能忽视的是,企业答卷者中有约三成答卷者选择"不知道"选项,不能对其投资享受国民待遇的情况作出判断,这说明有相当数量的中国投资企业对自己是否享受国民待遇的情况缺乏了解。

(二)中国投资在不同区域享受国民待遇的情况

东南亚和中亚区域的绝大多数中国投资经常或总是能够享受国民待遇,是五个投资区中中国投资享受国民待遇情况最为良好的,问题均值分别为0.71和0.83,达到或很接近"达标"状态。同时,来自中亚投资区的答卷者对此问题全部作以正面回答,没有答卷者选择"不知道"项,说明中亚区域的答卷者对投资享受国民待遇的状况了解情况最好。

与此相反,其他投资区反馈的问题均值则均在1.2到1.3之间,属于"轻度超标"。其中,大洋洲区域的答卷者中,有四成反映其对投资享受国民待遇的情况不甚了解,其余的答卷者则较为平均地表示投资在大洋洲享受国民待遇的情况有时、经常或总是如此的。这说明在大洋洲的答卷者对中国投资是否享受国民待遇不甚了解,对于投资享受国民待遇状况的看法也较为分散。此外,东南亚、非洲和拉丁美洲的答卷者反映投资享受国民待遇的情况也较为分散。这说明这些区域为中国投资提供国民待遇的情况参差不齐。

二、公平与公正待遇

当询问中国投资在东道国享受到的待遇是否公平与公正时,过半数答卷者(52.17%)表示其所受待遇经常或总是公平并公正的。21.74%的答卷者表示其投资所享待遇有时公平与公正。表示中国在海外投资资源能源极少受到公平与公正待遇的答卷者仅为极少数(4.35%)。这说明多数中国投资在海外享受了公平与公正待遇的同时,仍有一定比重的中国投资未能享受稳定的公平与公正待遇,其问题均值为1.11,与国民待遇问题一样处于"轻度超标"状态,但相对后者略低。

(一)分类答卷者反映中国投资享受公平与公正待遇的情况

对于中国投资在海外享受公平与公正待遇的情况,过半数企业答卷者(55.27%)认为其投资所享受的待遇经常或总是公平与公正的,问题均值为1.00。从管理者的角度来看,政府部门中有2/3的答卷者认为中国投资所受待遇经常是公平与公正的,但并不总是如此,其问题均值为1.33。律师事务所和会计师事务所中仅有20%的答卷者认为中国投资经常能享受公平与公正待遇,大部分答卷者认为仅有时公平与公正,其问题均值为1.75,属于“明显超标”的状态。这表明,“两所”答卷者对投资享受公平与公正待遇情况的评价最低,其次是政府部门答卷者和投资企业答卷者。值得注意的是,有23.68%的企业答卷者表示对此问题不能判断,说明他们对于投资是否享受公平与公正待遇的情况缺乏了解。

(二)中国投资在不同区域享受公平与公正待遇的情况

大洋洲、东南亚、中亚和拉丁美洲投资区中,大部分的答卷者都表示其投资经常或总是能够享受公平与公正的待遇;仅小部分答卷者表示极少或有时能够享受公平与公正待遇,其问题均值均在0.85以下,达到或接近“达标”状态。而在非洲投资区的投资享有公平与公正的待遇的水平则明显低于其他四个投资区,问题均值达到1.22,处于“轻度超标”状态。此外,大洋洲投资区和东南亚投资区中有相当比例的答卷者表示不能作答,说明这两个投资区的投资者对其是否享受公平与公正待遇的情况欠缺了解。

三、充分安全与保障

几乎所有的投资条约都把为外国投资提供充分的安全与保障列为东道国的义务之一,[16]这使东道国负有保护外国投资不致受到有害影响的积极作为的责任。当然,对投资产生的有害影响可以来自东道国的政府机构,也可以来自任何第三方。[17]

总体上看,大部分答卷者(54.35%)表示中国投资经常或总是能够得到东道国的充分保障和保护;21.74%的答卷者表示中国投资有时能够得到这种保护;少数答卷者(6.52%)认为东道国极少给其投资提供充分的保障和保护。可见,大多数答卷者对中国投资在海外享有东道国所提供保障和保护的反应良好,但也有相当比重的答卷者反映我国投资未能享受稳定的安全保障,其问题均值为1.21,与国民待遇相同,较公平与公正待遇问题略高,同样处于“轻度超标”状态。

(一)分类答卷者反映中国投资享受东道国充分保障和保护的情况

从不同答卷者的角度来看,企业答卷者中,有60.52%的人表示中国投资经常或总是能够受到东道国的充分保障与保护。但同时,仍有小部分答卷者(7.89%)表示这种保护是极少的。政府部门中有2/3的答卷者认为这样的保护有时才能获得,而东道国总能够为中国投资提供保障和保护是难以实现的。据来自律师事务所和会计师事务所的反馈信息显示,60%的受访从业人员认为有时能

〔16〕 Noah Rubins, Stephan Kinsella, *supra* note 6, p. 217.

〔17〕 Rudolf Dolzer, Christoph Schreuer, *supra* note 7, p. 149.

受到充分的保障和保护,有时则不能。三类答卷者反馈数据的问题均值分别为1.10、1.67和1.75。不难看出,企业答卷者对于中国投资受到东道国政府充分保障和保护的程度的评价相对较高(属于“轻度超标”),政府部门答卷者对此的评价相对较低,而“两所”答卷者评价则为最低(均处于“明显超标”状态)。

(二)中国投资在不同区域享受东道国充分保障和保护的情况

从不同投资区的角度来看,五个投资区都有大部分的答卷者表示中国投资经常或总是能够得到东道国的充分保障和保护。相当而言,大洋洲和拉丁美洲投资区的保护情况反馈较好,其问题均值为1或以下,与“达标”线较为接近;东南亚、中亚和非洲投资区较差,其均值均在1.22或以上,处于较明显的“轻度超标”状态。其中,中亚区域的答卷者中没有人认为总是能够得到这种保护;在非洲和东南亚区域的答卷者中各有20%表示东道国极少为其提供充分保障和保护。此外,中亚和非洲投资区有占相当比例(20%以上)的答卷者对于东道国实施充分保障和保护的情况不甚了解,因而不能作出判断。

四、小结

总体上看,中国投资在海外享有一般待遇状况不佳。在东道国提供的国民待遇、公平与公正待遇或充分安全与保障三个核心方面,其问题均值均在“轻度超标”范畴。

从不同种类答卷者的角度来看,企业答卷者对中国投资享有一般待遇的评价情况要略高于其他两类答卷者的评价。从不同区域的角度来看,中国投资在东南亚和中亚区域能享受比较好的国民待遇(达到或很接近“达标”状态),而在大洋洲、非洲和拉丁美洲区域则国民待遇状态相对较差(“轻度超标”);除非洲(“轻度超标”)以外,中国投资在各东道国能享受到大体“达标”的公平与公正待遇;而在东道国提供的充分安全与保障方面,答卷者反映大洋洲和拉丁美洲的东道国表现相对较好,其他区域较差。此外,不容忽视的是有相当比例的答卷者表示不知道中国投资在海外享有一般待遇的状况,因而不能进行判断。这说明中国海外投资活动的参与者仍需加强对投资所能享有的各种一般待遇情况的关注,以更好地保护投资应享有的权益并实现投资利益。

第五章　享受具体待遇情况

本章对中国海外资源能源投资享受具体待遇的情况进行考察,具体包括中国海外资源能源投资遭遇国有化措施的情况、因政治动乱受损受阻的情况、投资合同遭东道国政府违反的情况以及投资中财产转移是否顺利的情况几个方面。

一、国有化措施

数据显示,超过半数答卷者(58.70%)表示他们的投资项目从来没有因为东道国政府的直接或间接的征收、征用或国有化措施而遭受损失;有17%的答卷者表示这种征收或国有化措施极少发生,另有共约15%的答卷者则认为这类措施有时、经常或者总是会发生,其问题均值为0.62,处于“达标”状态。在补偿方面,只有不到三成的答卷者表示征收得到了“及时、充分、有效的补偿”,有一半以上的答卷者从来没有或极少会有得到这种补偿,另有20%的答卷者表示不了解情况,其问题均值为3.06,处于“严重超标”状态。由此可见,尽管绝大多数答卷者未曾遭受征收或国有化措施,但一旦遭受这种情形,其所获赔偿往往达不到“及时、充分、有效”补偿的标准。

(一)分类答卷者反映中国投资遭受国有化措施及获得补偿的情况

从不同答卷者的角度来看,多数企业答卷者(63.16%)表示其投资从未受东道国政府任何形式的征收、征用或国有化措施。有28.94%的企业答卷者表示其投资曾在不同频度上遭遇过此类措施。企业、政府和“两所”答卷者对此问题反馈数据的均值分别为0.60、1.00和0.50,相比之下可见,政府部门答卷者对投资遭受国有化措施的情况比较忧虑,而企业答卷者和“两所”答卷者的反应则相对平和。

在获得补偿方面,曾受过东道国征收、征用或国有化措施的企业答卷者中有63.63%从未能或极少能获得及时、充分、有效的补偿。“两所”的答卷者中认为中国投资从未能获得补偿和有时能获得此标准补偿的各占一半。政府部门答卷者则普遍认为这种补偿有时能够实现,有时则不能。

(二)中国投资在不同区域遭受国有化措施及获得补偿情况

五个投资区都有过半数的答卷者表示其投资从来没有或极少遭遇任何形式的征收、征用或国有化措施。相当而言,东南亚、拉丁美洲情况最好(均值均为0.33),大洋洲与非洲次之(均值均在0.7以下),中亚最差(均值1.33)。这说明虽然中国投资遭遇国有化措施的总体情况并不严重,但在有些地区问题比较突出。

与此同时,几乎所有遭受过国有化措施的答卷者表示其损失从来没有或极少能够获得补偿,彰显了问题的严重性。

二、政治动乱

政治动乱,指的是在东道国境内发生的军事行动或者内乱,包括革命、骚乱、军事政变及其他政治事件,东道国政府通常已经失去对这些事件的控制。[18] 当询问答卷者中国海外资源能源投资是否曾发生过投资因为骚乱、暴动或者战争等而受损的情况时,约有七成答卷者表示到目前为止,从未或极少发生因政治动乱受损的情况,但同时也有超过两成答卷者表示这种情况时有发生,另有约4%的答卷者表示总是如此或经常发生。其问题均值为0.73,与上述征收的频率接近但略高,仍处于"达标"状态。在肯定答卷者中,有近半数(44.45%)表示中国投资的损失从未或极少能获得及时、充分、有效的补偿,27.78%的答卷者认为有时可以得到这种标准的补偿,另有约11%的答卷者表示经常或总是可以得到充分补充。其问题均值为2.58,与上述征收补充情况类似但略高,同样处于"严重超标"状态。

(一)分类答卷者反映中国投资因政治动乱受损及获得补偿的情况

企业答卷者和"两所"答卷者中各有六成表示中国投资从未因骚乱、暴动或战争等而遭受损失。但同时,这两类答卷者中有的也认为中国投资曾经在不同频度上因骚乱、暴动或战争等而遭受损失。政府部门的答卷者普遍认为骚乱、暴动或战争等曾给中国投资造成损失,其中2/3认为其职务所涉的中国投资有时会遭遇这种情况。企业投资者、政府部门以及"两所"答卷者就此问题反馈数据的均值分别为0.68、1.67和0.50。由此不难看出,政府部门答卷者反映中国投资遭遇政治动乱等受损的情况比企业答卷者和"两所"答卷者的反映更为严重。在获得补偿方面,曾因政治动乱受损的企业答卷者中有三成从未或极少能获得"及时、充分、有效"的补偿,仅少数表示有时能获得这样的补偿,认为经常或总是能获得这样补偿的企业答卷者则更是少之又少。受访的政府部门答卷者都认为因政治动乱受损的中国投资有时能获得及时、充分、有效的补偿,而来自"两所"的答卷者普遍认为这种补偿极少能够实现。这说明中国投资因政治动乱受损后获得补偿的情况很不理想。

(二)中国投资在不同区域因政治动乱受损及获得补偿情况

从反映中国投资在不同区域因政治动乱受损及获得补偿情况来自,大洋洲情况最好,绝大部分答卷者从未遇到政治动乱或因此受损(问题均值仅0.24),这说明大洋洲投资区政治环境平稳,投资环境非常安全。最差的是拉丁美洲投资区,有17%的答卷表示经常会遇到政治风险并受损,另有半数答卷者反映这种情况时有发生,其问题均值达1.67,属于"明显超标"状态。其他依次为非洲(1.33)、东南亚(1.20)和中亚(1.17),属于"轻度超标"。在东南亚投资区,有四成答卷者

[18] 单文华:《欧盟对华投资的法律框架:解构与建构》,蔡从燕译,北京大学出版社2007年版,第398页。

表示从未遇到政治风险并因此受损，但同时有同样比例的答卷者表示有时会遇到政治风险并因此受损，这说明东南亚区域各国作为资源能源投资的东道国，有些国家政治平稳，而有些国家时有政治动乱发生。中亚投资区也有半数答卷者表示其投资有时会因为遭遇政治风险受到损失，说明这些区域政治环境不太稳定，不时会使中国投资遭受损失。

就投资受损后获得补偿的情况而言，在大洋洲区域、东南亚区域和中亚区域表示曾经受到政治风险损害的答卷者中大部分都表示其投资从未或极少获得"及时、充分、有效"的补偿。非洲和拉丁美洲区域曾经因政治风险受损的答卷者中，分别有四成表示有时或经常可以获得这样的补偿，说明中国投资在这两个投资区较之在另外三个投资区所获得政治风险损失补偿的情况更好。此外值得注意的是，中亚和拉丁美洲区域的答卷者中各有相当比例的人表示对受损投资获得补偿的情况不清楚，说明这两个区域的答卷者对投资因政治风险受损获得补偿的情况了解欠佳。

三、投资合同

在本次问卷调查中，答卷者同样被问及是否曾遇到东道国政府不遵守其与投资者所签订的投资合同的情况。对于这一问题，过半数的答卷者（54.35%）表示东道国政府违反投资合同的情况尚未发生过，其余答卷者中有13.04%表示极少遇到东道国政府违反投资合同的情况，问题均值为0.76，属于"达标"状态。这说明东道国政府违反投资合同使投资利益受损的情况在中国海外资源能源投资中并不常见。

（一）分类答卷者反映中国投资遭遇东道国政府不遵守投资合同的情况

从不同答卷者的角度来看，大多数企业答卷者认为其投资不曾遇到东道国政府不遵守其与投资者所签订的投资合同的情况。政府部门答卷者中的大多数也认为这种状况极少发生。而对于同一问题，大部分的"两所"答卷者则认为这种风险时有发生，并且其中有20%的答卷者认为经常会出现这种情况。这说明就东道国政府违反投资合同风险发生的频度，政府部门答卷者比企业答卷者认为更高，而"两所"答卷者评价的频度更高于政府部门的答卷者。这种差异可能是由于不同答卷者掌握信息情况的不同，也可能是不同答卷者对风险的评估不同而造成的。

（二）中国投资在不同区域遭遇东道国政府不遵守投资合同的情况

五个投资区中，大洋洲东道国政府遵守投资合同状况最为良好，有83%的答卷者表示不遵守的情形从未出现，均值仅为0.18，属于非常好的"达标"状态。其次是东南亚，有六成答卷者表示从未出现违约情况，均值为0.38，也处于良好的

"达标"状态。其他三个区域均处于"轻度超标"状态。其中在拉丁美洲和中亚有一半答卷者表示从未发生,其均值均为1;而最严重的是非洲,答卷者认为这种风险有时发生的占半数,另有一成答卷者认为违约情况经常发生,其均值达到1.4。

四、财产转移

国际投资中的财产转移自由主要包括投资原本及利润的转移自由和资金兑换汇率的稳定两个方面。中国企业在海外进行资源能源投资的过程中,在财产转移这部分,同样面临转移困难和汇率波动两方面的风险。

(一)转移困难

在财产转移风险方面,大部分答卷者(63.04%)表示他们从投资项目运营之始至今,从未或极少在将投资原本和利润汇出东道国境外时遇到过困难。与此同时,答卷者中有10.87%的答卷者反映经常会遇到这类财产转移的困难,另有一成以上的答卷者认为这类困难时有发生。其问题均值为0.98,属于"轻度超标"状态,表明这方面的问题确实存在但并不很严重。根据调研员进一步回访的了解,多数答卷者在此方面尚未遇到困难的原因主要有两种:其一在于他们的投资项目未曾遭受东道国政府在财产转移上施加的管制措施;其二在于资源能源投资项目一般周期较长,这些答卷者的投资项目处于前期开发阶段,尚未盈利。因为没有将利润汇回母国的资金转移活动,因而未曾遇到过财产转移方面的困难。

1. 分类答卷者反映中国投资遭遇财产转移困难的情况

从不同受访者的角度来看,企业、政府部门和"两所"的受访者的大多数都认为中国投资从未或极少会遭遇转移困难的情况。可以说中国投资所涉的东道国大都允许投资项下的国际间财产自由转移。

但不容忽视的是,三类受访主体中都有少数表示中国投资有时或经常会遇到国际间财产转移的困难。这说明虽然中国投资进行国际间财产转移通常顺利,但在有些地区仍会遇到东道国政府的管制。

2. 中国投资在不同区域遭遇财产转移困难的情况

就区域比较,非洲和中亚这两个区域企业答卷者表示经常存在转移困难的答卷者达30%,问题均值分别为1.4和1.3。其他区域相对较好,均值均在1.15以下。这说明虽然五个投资区中转移困难时有发生,但部分国家和地区的国际间财产转移困难表现得比较明显。

(二)汇率波动

在汇率风险方面,调查数据显示绝大多数的答卷者(86.95%)都遭受过汇率风险带来的损失,而表示这种风险"有时"发生的答卷者占最多数(47.83%)。仅有极少数答卷者(8.70%)表示其海外资源能源投资从未因汇率波动受损。该问题均值为1.98,属于偏严重的“明显超标”状态。

1.分类答卷者反映中国投资因汇率波动受损的情况

从不同受访者的角度来看,企业受访者中仅有10.53%认为其投资从来没有因为汇率波动遭受损失。84.21%的投资者表示在其从事海外资源能源投资的过程中都曾经在不同频度上受到汇率波动带来的损失。

对于同一问题,政府部门受访者和“两所”的受访者都普遍认为中国投资因为汇率波动受到损失,只是因此受损的频度有所不同。

2.中国投资在不同区域因汇率波动受损的情况

五个投资区中,中亚和拉丁美洲投资区中表示投资经常或有时遭遇转移困难的答卷者比例较高(均值分别高达2.4和2.17),说明这两个投资区中转移困难的发生较其他投资区而言更为常见。其次是非洲和大洋洲投资区,均值分别为2和1.94。东南亚投资区情况最好,但其均值也达到了1.8。这说明中国投资所遇到汇率波动问题普遍比较突出。

五、小结

从上面对影响国际资源能源投资的几项具体制度的考察可以看出,总体上说,我国投资受国有化与征收、政治动乱以及政府违约的影响较小(处于“达标”状态),但受国际财产转移限制的影响较大(处于“轻度超标”状态),尤以汇率波动的影响甚为突出(处于“明显超标”状态)。

具体来说,就国有化与征收问题而言,虽然我国投资目前很少遇到这种情形,但一旦产生,其补偿往往大打折扣,普遍达不到“充分、及时、有效”的标准(处于“严重超标”状态)。就区域而言,中亚的征收风险最严重,拉丁美洲和东南亚则最为少见。政治动乱及其补偿的总体情况与征收类似,但频率略高,补偿状况也略好。就区域而言,拉丁美洲政治动乱的频率最为突出,大洋洲则属最好。

从投资合同的遵守情况来看,我国投资所遇到的问题总体上不很突出,但区域差异很大。其中大洋洲和东南亚状况良好(处于良好“达标”状态),而非洲这个方面问题最为突出(“轻度超标”)。

财产转移问题是中国海外资源能源投资所遇到的比较严重的问题,尤其是在中亚和非洲。但更突出的是,汇率波动给中国投资造成损失的情形颇为常见。从区域角度看,汇率波动问题在中亚和拉丁美洲投资区最为显著,在东南亚投资区则最为轻微,但总体上均处于较为严重的“明显超标”状态。

第六章　东道国法制状况

在考察投资东道国的投资法制环境时，本研究从司法、立法、行政三个角度分别考察东道国司法执行的公正程度、立法中的法律稳定性以及行政中政府执法的廉洁程度这三个重要指标。

一、司法公正

从总体上看，半数投资者反映在东道国尚未在司法活动中遇到过不公对待的情况。但与此同时，仍有超过四成受访者反映曾在不同程度上遭遇过司法不公的情况，而其中多数认为此情况为“有时”发生。

中国投资遭遇司法不公的总体均值为0.9，属于“轻度超标”，问题总体不算突出，但不同类型和区域答卷者的反馈差异很大。其中，企业答卷者和政府部门的答卷者中各有约六成人表示中国投资从来没有或极少遭遇过司法不公的情况，另各有约三成人表示司法不公的情况有时发生。“两所”答卷者中认为司法不公从未或极少发生的所占比例则明显低于持相同看法的答卷者在其他两类受访主体中所占的比例。例如，“两所”答卷者中有20%的人表示司法不公经常发生，远远高于持相同看法的答卷者在其他两类受访主体中所占的比例。这说明“两所”的答卷者从提供专业服务的角度，认为中国投资遭遇司法不公的情况较其他两类受访主体而更为严重。

从区域来看，东南亚投资区有七成的答卷者表示投资从来没有遇到司法不公的情况，并且认为投资有时或经常遇到司法不公的答卷者也很少，其问题均值为0.56（“达标”），是五个所考察的投资区中答卷者反映司法公正程度最高的投资区。其次是大洋洲，有一半表示从未发生，另有一成表示极少发生，均值为0.73（“达标”）。反之，在中亚投资区，除了表示对此问题“不知道”的答卷者外，所有答卷者都表示司法不公的情况时有发生，均值高达2，处于“明显超标”状态。这使得中亚投资区成为五个投资区中司法不公情况最为严重的区域。非洲有一半答卷者表示司法不公时有发生，另有一成答卷者认为这种现象经常发生，均值达到1.4（“轻度超标”），是司法不公问题第二严重的区域。拉丁美洲均值为1，但也有半数答卷者表示司法不公时有发生，值得关注。

二、法律稳定性

总体上，受访者就投资因东道国法律不稳定而遭受损失或阻碍的反映与对司法不公的反映类似，半数受访者尚未遭受过此类损失，但表示曾在不同程度上因此受损的反馈则比因司法不公受损的比例更高(45.66%),均值为0.88,也处于"轻度超标"。

我国投资遭遇法律变动的问题在不同类型和区域答卷者的反馈同样差异很大。总体上企业答卷者中有超过半数的答卷者(55.26%)认为其投资从来没有因为东道国法律变动而受损。来自政府部门的答卷者中,有2/3表示中国投资因为东道国法律变动而受损极少发生。此外,这两类受访主体中仍有占相当比例(20%以上)的答卷者表示这种损失时有发生。比较而言,"两所"答卷者反馈的情况则严重得多,其中有60%的答卷者表示有时会遇到这种情况。这可能是因为企业答卷者以运营投资项目为主要工作内容,相关政府部门更专注于对中国海外投资的管理,二者对于各个投资东道国法律的变化不是很敏感。而提供专业服务的"两所"——尤其是律师事务所——对法律问题关注更多,能更好地知悉东道国法律变动为投资带来的损害。

大多数在大洋洲和东南亚区域进行投资的答卷者都从来没有遇到投资因为东道国法律变化而受损或受阻的情况,其均值为0.5,处于较好的"达标"状态。这说明这两个区域内投资东道国的法律稳定性良好。中亚投资区中有约八成的答卷者都表示投资曾经因为法律变动受损,均值为1.67(达到"明显超标"状态),是答卷者反映的东道国法律稳定性最为欠缺的投资区。此外,该区域有三成答卷者表示法律变动引起投资损失经常发生,说明该区域除了法律变化较为常见以外,其中某些地区法律变动的频度也较高。拉丁美洲投资区有少数答卷者表示投资有时或经常受到法律变动带来的损失,这可能是由于该区域内某些东道国或行业领域(如石油天然气行业)法律变化较多的原因缘故。非洲区域有答卷者表示投资极少(20%)或有时(30%)会遭受这种损失,表明该区域法律变动的频度虽然不高,但因此受损的中国投资也不少。

三、官员腐败

与对司法不公和法律不稳定的反映有所不同,过半数的受访者(54.35%)表示投资曾在不同程度上因东道国官员腐败而受损或受阻。其中,三成受访者表示这种损失"有时"发生,均值达1.41,处于比较明显的"轻度超标"。

从三类答卷者角度来看,企业答卷者中有近半数的答卷者表示曾经在不同频度上因为东道国官员腐败而受损。来自政府部门的答卷者普遍认为东道国官员腐败而使投资受损的情况有时会发生。"两所"答卷者中也有八成表示曾经遇到这种情况。这说明三类答卷主体都认为东道国官员腐败是中国投资在海外受损的一个常见因素。

有约六成答卷者表示中国在大洋洲投资区从未因东道国官员腐败受损,均值为0.36,处于良好“达标”状态,是五大投资区中官员腐败导致投资受损最少的区域。反过来,其他四个投资区这方面问题均较严重,尤以非洲、拉丁美洲和中亚为最。其中,非洲投资区所有正面答卷者均表示这种情况总是存在(20%)或时有发生(60%),问题均值高达2.5,处于“严重超标”状态。拉丁美洲投资区有超过八成的答卷者反映曾遭受官员腐败引发的损失,更值得注意的是该区域反映此种损失经常或总是发生的答卷者所占比例远高于其他四个投资区(50%),表明该区域官员腐败使投资受损的情况频度很高。而中亚投资区中所有答卷者都表示其投资曾受官员腐败的不利影响,问题之普遍,亦可见一斑。

四、小结

从本章数据可以看出,我国海外投资东道国法制状况总体欠佳,且区域差异很大。相对而言,官员腐败问题比较突出,司法不公与法律稳定性问题也在一定程度上存在,三者均未“达标”。其中,司法不公在中亚和非洲区域比较严重,而在东南亚和大洋洲区域则鲜有发生。同时,大洋洲和东南亚区域的法律也较为稳定,相比之下中亚区域的法律稳定性最差,往往给中国投资带来损失。非洲、拉丁美洲和中亚区域官员腐败致使中国投资受损的情况颇为常见,而在大洋洲这种现象则很少发生。总体而言,大洋洲的法制状况最好,东南亚次之,非洲、中亚和拉丁美洲的法制问题则比较严重。

第七章　投资争端解决

一、投资争端情况

实践中东道国与投资者的争端多因东道国行使国家权力或发生其他政治事件致使投资遭受损失而发生,主要包括:国有化引起的争议;东道国管理行为引起的争议(外汇管制、增加税收、干预企业经营活动等引起的争议);东道国国内政治动乱、革命、战争等事件引起的争议。[19] 在本次实证考察中,中国海外资源能源投资者与投资东道国政府发生法律纠纷的情况如图7.1所示。

〔19〕 姚梅镇:《比较外资法》,武汉大学出版社1993年版,第939页。

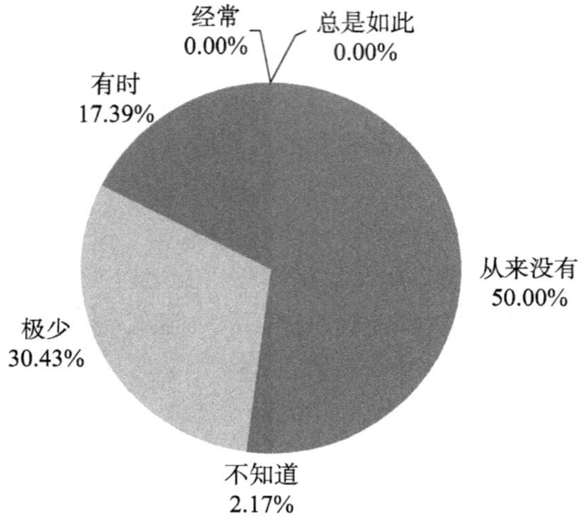

图 7.1　中国投资遭遇法律争端的总体情况

可以看出,半数答卷者表示在其投资过程中从未与东道国政府发生过法律纠纷。另有 30.43% 的答卷者表示与东道国政府发生纠纷的情况极少出现,均值为 0.67,属于"达标"状态。这说明国家与投资者纠纷在中国海外资源能源投资中鲜有发生。就此问题,企业投资者、政府部门和"两所"答卷者反馈数据的均值分别为 0.55、2.00 和 0.75,说明政府部门所了解到的投资法律纠纷最多,其次是"两所",对投资法律纠纷接触最少的是企业投资者。

二、救济措施选择

(一)自力救济——保险

海外投资保险可以对海外投资中东道国可能发生的政治风险进行承保,在政治风险发生后减轻投资的损失。如图 7.2 所示,在询问我国海外资源能源投资购买国际投资保险的时候,47.83% 的答卷者表示从未或极少为其在海外的投资购买保险,23.91% 的答卷者表示有时会购买保险以降低投资风险。经常或总是会为其海外资源能源投资购买保险的答卷者仅占 10.87%。这说明海外投资保险在中国海外资源能源投资中虽然尚未成为主流,但也发挥了一定的作用。

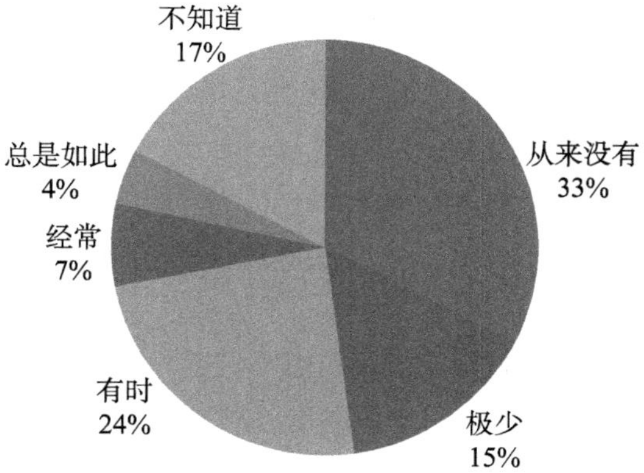

图 7.2　中国投资购买保险的情况

(二)公力救济——法律解决

在发生了法律纠纷后的纠纷解决方式的选择上,如图 7.3 所示,绝大多数答卷者表示会首先选择通过协商谈判的方式处理纠纷。有半数答卷者表示除协商谈判外,最倾向于通过当地法院寻求救济,其次是通过向当地仲裁寻求救济。相比之下,仅有少数答卷者愿意通过国际司法途径(如 ICSID、专设国际仲裁)寻求保护。

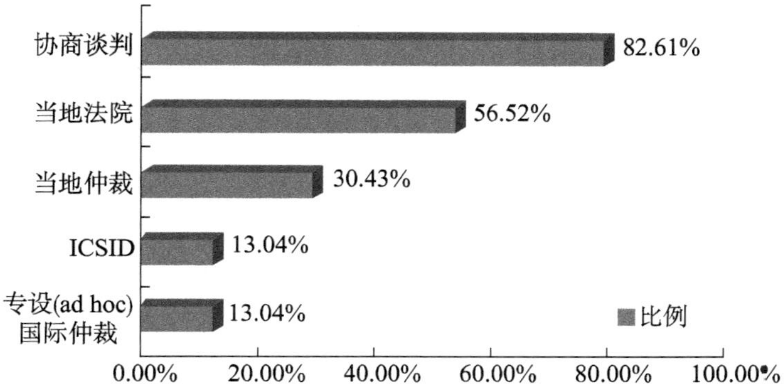

图 7.3　中国投资者选择纠纷解决方式的情况

由此可以看出,东道国国内救济(当地法院或当地仲裁)是继协商谈判之后最受中国投资者青睐的纠纷解决方式。相比之下,国际仲裁的纠纷解决方式则较受冷落。究其原因或许是因为我国早期签订的投资协定规定了只有涉及征收补偿数额的纠纷可以提交国际仲裁,而其他纠纷只能通过国内途径解决。另一个原因则很可能是由于中国投资者在国际投资仲裁知识、经验和人力资源上的欠缺。

三、小结

中国投资在海外很少与东道国政府发生法律纠纷。相对而言,在大洋洲、东南亚的投资纠纷较少,而在中亚和非洲的投资纠纷较多。投资保险虽然尚未成为中国投资者减小投资政治风险的主流方式,但也已经发挥了一定的作用。一旦与东道国政府发生纠纷,中国投资者往往倾向于通过东道国国内的司法或仲裁方式寻求救济,而不是选择国际仲裁。这表明中国投资者对国际仲裁认识不足,重视不够,亟须加强。

第八章　其他影响因素

外国直接投资的政治风险不仅来源于投资措施,也来源于贸易措施。意料之外的贸易管制可能对投资者造成负面影响,也可能对直接参与相关产品或服务贸易的人产生影响。[20] 同时,投资者在另一国开展资源能源投资活动,对当地自然环境和居民产生直接影响,可能导致生态环境破坏、原住民安置、土地资源纠纷等等问题。[21] 因此,投资过程中的环保问题也可能是引起资源能源投资受损的重要政治风险之一。鉴于此,本研究还考察了上述这两个重要非投资因素对中国投资的影响。

一、贸易壁垒

在被问及是否曾遇到过投资项目因为贸易壁垒受损或受阻的情况时,四成答卷者表示他们从未遇到过这种情况,另有 23.91% 的答卷者表示其海外资源能源投资项目有时因为东道国施加贸易壁垒而遭受损失,均值为 0.86,临近“达标”水平。这表明中国投资不时会受国际贸易的影响,在有些地区还会因为东道国施加的贸易壁垒而遭受损失。

(一)分类答卷者反映中国投资因东道国贸易壁垒受损的情况

企业答卷者中有近半数(47.37%)表示从来没有因东道国贸易壁垒受损,同时也有少数答卷者表示贸易壁垒带来的损失极少发生或有时发生,其

〔20〕 Noah Rubins, Stephan Kinsella, *supra* note 6, p. 23.

〔21〕 Peter D. Cameron, International Energy Investment: The Pursuit of Stability, Oxford Uni-versity Press, 2010, p. 336.

反馈数据均值为0.63。政府部门的答卷者则普遍认为中国投资因东道国贸易壁垒受损有时发生，均值为2.00。而“两所”答卷者中有八成表示中国投资曾经因东道国贸易壁垒受损，但其中有半数（40%）认为这只是极少的情况，这种损失发生的频度并不高，反馈数据均值为1.75。相比之下，政府部门对投资因为贸易壁垒受损或受阻最为担忧，其次是“两所”，最后是企业答卷者。

（二）在不同区域中国投资因东道国贸易壁垒受损的情况

从不同投资区的角度来看，六成大洋洲答卷者从来没有遇到其投资因东道国贸易壁垒受损的情况，均值为0.53，处于“达标”状态，是最少出现投资因贸易壁垒受损的区域。在东南亚区域，六成答卷者表示从未或极少遇到投资因贸易壁垒受损或受阻的情况。但值得注意的是，这两个投资区中仍有少数答卷者反映因贸易壁垒产生的损失有时发生。这说明这两个区域的某些地区或个别领域的投资仍会受到贸易壁垒的不利影响。非洲投资区中有半数答卷者表示投资有时会因为贸易壁垒受损，均值为1.22（边界状态），是五个投资区中答卷者反映贸易影响投资最为频繁的。中亚投资区有半数答卷者表示不知道贸易壁垒是否影响到其投资，说明该区域的投资者对贸易壁垒引起的损失关注程度偏低。

二、环境问题

对于中国海外资源能源投资遭遇此种政治风险的情况，有67.39%的受访答卷者表示其投资项目曾经或多或少因为人权或环保问题受损或受阻，均值为1.39，处于“轻度超标”状态。在统计这一问题时，峰值出现在“有时”这一选项上（41.30%），说明多数答卷者的投资活动曾因环境保护问题受损或受阻。另外有部分答卷者（28.26%）表示其投资尚未遭遇过这种政治风险的损害。其中有答卷者表示，其资源能源投资项目是由当地公司进行施工的，他们通过这种雇佣当地企业的办法来缓冲与当地居民（原住民）的冲突。

（一）分类答卷者反映中国投资因环保问题受损或受阻的情况

三成企业答卷者表示尚未遇到因环保问题受损或受阻的情况，但同时却有约四成答卷者表示有时会发生这种损失，均值为1.24。政府部门的答卷考中有六成认为中国投资因环保问题受损或受阻的情况曾经发生，均值为1.50，高于企业答卷者对环保问题减损投资的反映。而“两所”答卷者就环保问题对投资产生的不利影响所做反应的均值为2.40，大大高出另两类答卷者的反馈情况，其工作的专业性质可能是导致这种高值反馈的主要原因。

(二)中国投资在不同区域因环保问题受损或受阻的情况

五个投资区中都有少数答卷者表示尚未遇到环保问题是投资受损或受阻的情况。但不能忽视的是,五个投资区都有占更大比例的答卷者表示中国投资有时会遭受这种损失。这表明虽然有些地区的答卷者尚未遇到环保问题减损投资的情况,但在某些地区中环保问题对中国投资的不利影响已经突显出来。

将五个投资区的数据相互比较后不难发现,东南亚和中亚投资区表示遇到环保问题所致损失的答卷者最多,均值分别为 1.78 和 1.67,达到了“明显超标”程度。这说明在这两个区域的中国投资因环境保护问题受损或受阻的情况较其他区域(“轻度超标”)而更为常见。

三、小结

本节数据分析显示,在与资源能源投资活动密切相关的两个法律问题中,贸易壁垒对中国投资产生的不利影响相对较低。进行区域间比较后发现,非洲区域的投资受贸易壁垒的不利影响要明显大于投资在其余区域受贸易壁垒的影响,而大洋洲则是受影响最小的区域。

值得关注的是,环境保护问题对中国投资的影响比较严重。中国在五大区域的投资均在较大程度上因此受阻或受损,但其中最为严重的区域则是东南亚和中亚,这应当引起海外投资者和有关方面的高度重视。

第九章　区域性特征

如第一章中所述,为更清晰地体现这些法律问题在各个投资区发生的情况,本研究将问卷问题按照封闭式和开放式两种予以分类,并对所有封闭式问题的答案进行统计学编码,按照不同的投资区域将答卷者的反馈信息进行分别统计,并分别计算每个法律问题发生频度的均值,得出如下均值表 9.1。

关于各个方面的统计分析已如前述。下面将从不同区域的角度对五个投资区中法律问题发生的特点进行简要总结。

表 9.1　中国资源能源投资在各区域遭遇法律问题情况均值表

法律问题 \ 发生频度			总体[22]	大洋洲	东南亚	中亚	非洲	拉丁美洲
政治风险总体情况[23]			1.31	1.29	1.20	2.17	1.30	1.00
准入限制(业绩要求)			—	—	—	—	—	—
一般待遇[24]	国民待遇		1.21	1.30	0.71	0.83	1.22	1.20
	公平与公正待遇		1.11	0.85	0.71	0.83	1.22	0.80
	充分安全与保障		1.21	0.93	1.33	1.25	1.22	1.00
具体制度	国有化措施		0.62	0.67	0.33	1.33	0.60	0.33
	政治动乱		0.73	0.24	1.20	1.17	1.33	1.67
	投资合同违反		0.76	0.18	0.38	1.00	1.40	1.00
	财产转移	转移困难	0.98	1.13	1.11	1.40	1.30	1.00
		汇率波动	1.98	1.94	1.80	2.40	2.00	2.17
法制状况	司法不公		0.90	0.73	0.56	2.00	1.40	1.00
	法律不稳定		0.88	0.50	0.50	1.67	0.89	1.00
	官员腐败		1.41	0.36	1.75	2.00	2.50	2.33
争端解决	遭遇法律纠纷		0.67	0.29	0.50	1.17	1.00	0.67
	救济措施选择		—	—	—	—	—	—
其他因素对中国投资的影响	贸易壁垒		0.86	0.53	0.88	1.00	1.22	1.00
	环境问题		1.39	1.44	1.78	1.67	1.44	1.33

一、大洋洲投资区

我国投资在大洋洲投资区的总体政治风险均值为1.29,略低于我国投资的总体政治风险均值。就本次调研所考察的这5类14个具体法律问题(见图9.1)而言,大洋洲在多数方面(包括国有化、政治动乱、政府违约、法律纠纷、司法不公、法律不稳定、官员腐败、贸易壁垒8个方面)的问题均值都在0.8以下,属于"达

〔22〕 每个法律问题(风险)的总体均值是全体受访者(包括企业受访者、政府部门受访者和"两所"受访者)就每个独立问题反映的均值。各个投资区域下各法律问题的均值仅体现该区域内企业受访者的反映情况。

〔23〕 本组均值所对应的是个独立的问题,询问受访者中国投资遭遇政治风险的总体情况,而非所有法律问题均值的平均数。

〔24〕 分别考察"国民待遇""公平与公正待遇"和"充分安全与保障"的问题在问卷中以积极描述设计,故所得数据为投资者享有这些待遇的情况。为与其他负面描述问题相统一以便比较,这三个问题的均值结果均被频度最高情况(即4)相减,最终数据表示未能享受到这些待遇的情况。

标”状态。其中,尤其是在政治动乱、政府违约、法律纠纷、官员腐败等方面表现良好,总体表现是五个投资区域中投资法律环境最佳的区域。

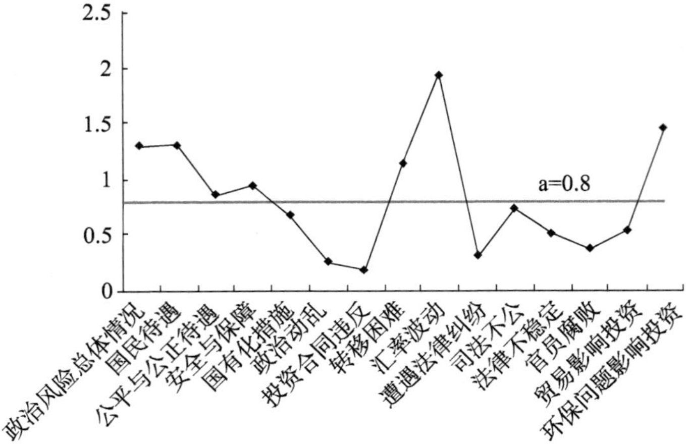

图 9.1　中国投资在大洋洲投资区遭遇各法律问题均值图

注:直线 a = 0.8,系“达标”线。

当然,中国投资在大洋洲也遇到了不少法律问题,具体表现在政治风险、国民待遇、公平与公正待遇、安全保障、转移困难、汇率波动以及环境问题七个方面仍处于超标状态。其中,尤以汇率波动、环境问题、国民待遇等问题较为突出,值得引起重视。

进一步考察可发现,在上述三个问题中,投资在大洋洲遭遇汇率波动的均值小于中国投资汇率波动发生的均值,而遭遇国民待遇和环境保护法律问题所致的风险均值却大于中国投资遇此风险的总体平均水平。说明在大洋洲答卷者反映较为突出的三个法律问题中,国民待遇和环境保护问题对中国投资的影响最大。这是在该区域进行资源能源投资的中国企业应予以特别关注的。

基于此,中国在大洋洲的资源能源投资者应特别加强防范国民待遇法律问题、环境保护法律问题和汇率法律问题可能引发投资损失的风险,或可未雨绸缪,以在风险最终发生时尽量减小其带来的损失。

二、东南亚投资区

东南亚投资区是五个投资区中总体法律环境次优的区域。其政治风险均值为 1.20,比大洋洲略低。如图 9.2 所示,在 14 项指标中,本区有 7 项处于“达标”状态,包括国民待遇、公平与公正待遇、国有化、政府违约、法律纠纷、司法不公、法律不稳定在内,尤以国有化、政府违约两方面表现最好。反过来,该区域在安全保障、政治动乱、转移困难、汇率波动、官员腐败、贸易壁垒以及环境问题七个方面均超标,尤以汇率波动、官员腐败和环境问题为最。

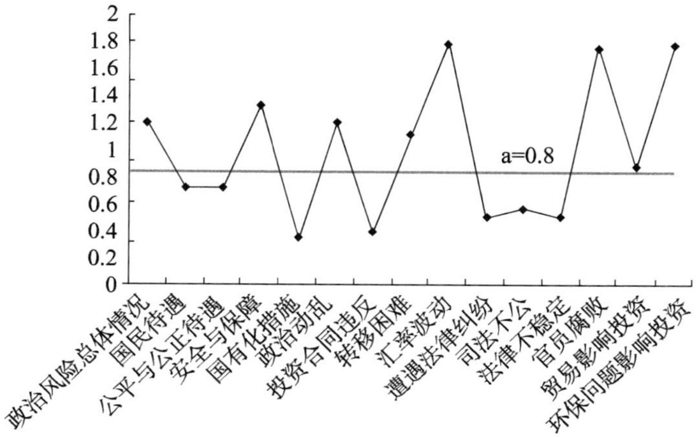

图 9.2　中国投资在东南亚投资区遭遇各法律问题均值图

注:直线 a = 0.8,系“达标”线。

具体来说,在一般待遇方面,中国投资在东南亚投资区享受国民待遇和公平与公正待遇的情况良好,是几个投资区中情况最好的。但同时,中国投资在该区域享有东道国提供充分安全与保障的情况较差,是在几个投资区中情况最为欠佳的,其风险程度也高于中国投资享有充分安全与保障待遇的总体风险程度。中国投资在该投资区很少遇到东道国政府施加国有化措施或者因东道国政府违反投资合同而受损或受阻的情况。汇率波动问题是该区域中对中国投资影响最为显著的具体制度因素,紧随其后的是政治动乱和财产国际间转移方面的困难。在东南亚区域,中国投资与东道国政府之间的法律纠纷并不多见,但答卷者认为该区域内官员腐败对投资产生的不利影响较大。在影响投资的其他因素中,贸易壁垒的影响显得温和。相比之下,环境保护问题的影响决不能忽视,其致使中国投资受损或受阻的情况比其他任何一个投资区都要多,而且其发生频度的均值也高于环保问题对中国投资总体影响的均值。因此,投资者可以在投资活动中对此多加关注,以更好地实现投资利益。

三、中亚投资区

中亚投资区政治风险发生总体情况的均值(2.17)在五个投资区中是最高的,

大于拉丁美洲投资区同类均值(1.00)的一倍多,也大于所有答卷者反映的政治风险发生的总体情况的均值(1.31)。这使中亚投资区成为所考察的投资区中政治风险发生最为常见也最频繁的区域。中亚投资区法律问题发生状况的均值如图9.3所示。不难看出,在所有14项指标上中亚均未能“达标”,足见其法律环境属于海外投资最不理想的区域之一。

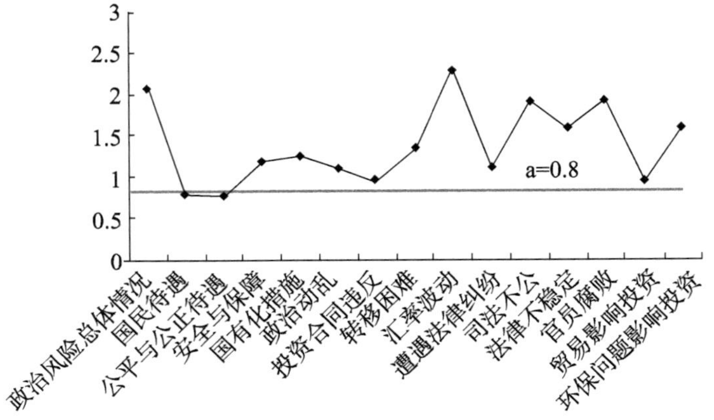

图9.3　中国投资在中亚投资区遭遇各法律问题均值图

注:直线a=0.8,系“达标”线。

在具体制度方面,中国投资在中亚区域遭遇五种法律问题的状况较之于其他区域也更为严重。具体表现为,汇率波动是五个区域中减损中国投资最为严重的;中国投资遭遇东道国国有化措施、因政治动乱受损或受阻、遭东道国政府违约,以及曾经遇到的财产转移中的困难,都比中国投资总体遭遇这些法律风险更为普遍和频繁。尤其是遭遇东道国国有化措施方面,中亚答卷者就此问题反应的均值更是高达答卷者总体反映均值的两倍。这说明以上几种法律风险在中亚区域都较为常见,中国资源能源投资者应予以重视。

中亚区域的答卷者反映与东道国政府发生的法律纠纷是最多的,并且该问题在中亚区域的均值(1.17)也远远高于全体答卷者就同一问题反应的均值(0.67),说明中国投资在该区域更有可能与东道国政府发生法律纠纷。就中亚区域的法治状况,在该区域投资的答卷者作出的评价同样相对较低。答卷者反映在投资过程中遭遇司法不公,或因法律变动受损,或因东道国官员腐败受损的程度几乎都是中国投资总体遭遇同样问题的两倍。这说明中亚区域的投资法治环境相对而言明显欠佳。

四、非洲投资区

从政治风险总体发生情况的均值可以判断，非洲投资区较少发生政治风险，并且其政治风险发生的总体水平与中国投资总体政治风险发生的水平基本一致。非洲投资区各个法律问题发生的情况如图 9.4 所示，除国有化一项以外，在所有具体制度方面，非洲所存在的法律问题均值均未能“达标”，其中尤以官员腐败和汇率波动问题最为突出。

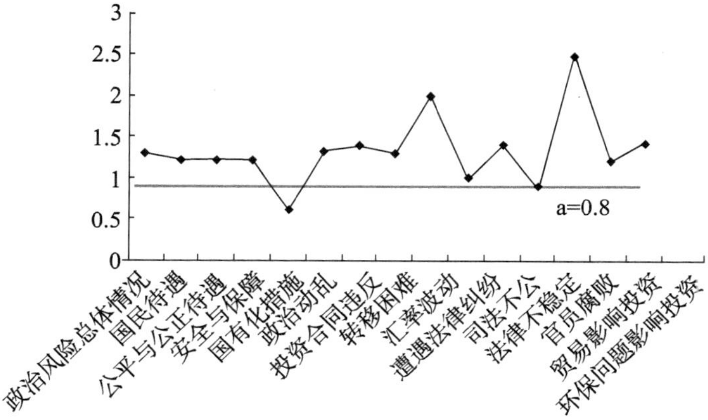

图 9.4　中国投资在非洲投资区遭遇各法律问题均值图

注：直线 a =0.8，系“达标”线。

就一般待遇享受情况而言，可以看出中国投资在非洲未能享受这些待遇的情况略高于中国投资未能享受这些一般待遇标准的总体均值，与其他四个投资区相比该风险在非洲也略显突出。

在具体制度方面，根据非洲区域投资者的反映，东道国的政治动乱导致损失、东道国政府违约和国际间财产转移中的转移困难等三个法律问题发生的均值都略大于全体答卷者均值。这表明这三个问题在非洲投资区较总体水平而言更为常见，是该区域内对中国投资影响最大的法律问题。

在遭遇法律纠纷方面，非洲区域的均值（1.00）大于同一问题在大洋洲、东南亚及拉丁美洲投资区的均值，也大于全体答卷者对该问题总体反应的均值，说明这个问题也比较突出。在评价非洲区域的法治环境时，答卷者对司法不公和官员腐败这两方面的反映较为剧烈。答卷者表示投资因这两个因素受损的均值几乎为全体答卷者反映同样问题均值的 1.5 倍。因此，可以推断非洲投资区的法治环境较差，司法不公和官员腐败给中国投资造成损失的可能性较大。

此外,在非洲区域投资值得注意的是贸易壁垒以及环境问题对投资的影响。据调查显示,非洲投资区内贸易壁垒给中国投资造成的不利影响要比其他任何一个投资区内都要严重,该区域内答卷者对此问题反映的均值也高于全体答卷者对中国投资因贸易壁垒受损或受阻反映的均值。而非洲的环境问题风险也高于拉丁美洲投资区,而与大洋洲持平,表明这一问题同样不容忽视。

五、拉丁美洲投资区

拉丁美洲投资区政治风险总体情况的均值(1.00)小于全体答卷者对同一问题反映的均值,也小于其他投资区的答卷者对同一问题反映的均值,说明总体上拉丁美洲投资区政治风险最少发生,政治环境较好。拉丁美洲投资区中法律风险发生的具体情况如图 9.5 所示。

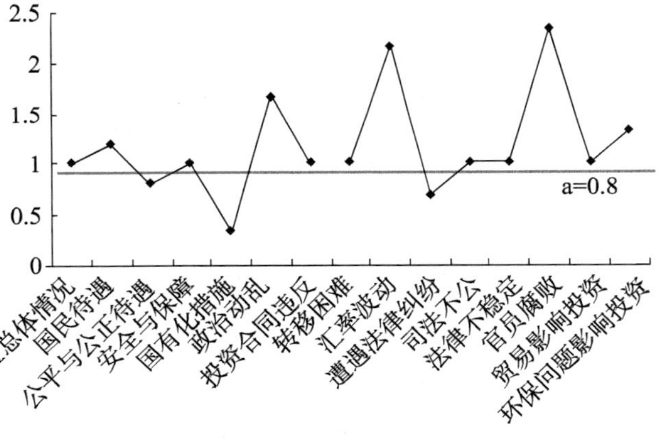

图 9.5　中国投资在拉丁美洲投资区遭遇各法律问题均值图

注:直线 a = 0.8,系“达标”线。

从图 9.5 可以看出,在被问及具体法律风险发生的情况时,答卷者仅对国有化、法律纠纷以及公平与公正待遇三方面比较满意(“达标”),而对政治动乱、汇率波动、东道国官员腐败以及环境保护问题给投资带来的损失或阻碍反应较为强烈。其中,政治动乱、汇率波动和官员腐败三个问题的均值不仅超过了全体答卷者对相同问题反应的均值水平,也是五大投资区答卷者中对相同问题反映较为强烈的。这说明,这三方面问题是对在拉丁美洲区域的中国投资产生较为严重影响的法律问题,也是该区域的中国投资者应当着力防范的法律风险。

此外,答卷者反映与东道国政府发生法律纠纷的情况与中国投资就同样问题的总体情况基本处于同一程度。但在评价拉丁美洲内投资东道国的法治状况时，答卷者反映遭遇司法不公或是因法律不稳定而受损的情况略高于中国投资的总体水平。

六、小结

各投资区基于不同的政治、法制、地理环境，在处理外国的资源能源投资时展现出了不同的特点，也存在各自的问题。总体而言，大洋洲的投资法律环境相对最好，其次是东南亚，再次是拉丁美洲、非洲，最差的是中亚。

具体而言，在大洋洲的中国投资比较容易受到国民待遇、汇率波动和环保问题的影响。中国投资在东南亚享有东道国充分保障和保护的情况欠佳，同时汇率波动、环境保护以及官员腐败问题对投资的不利影响较大。中亚投资区政治风险发生的程度相对较高，东道国为投资提供充分安全与保障的情况欠佳，该区域的投资者应多留意国有化措施、国际间财产转移困难以及法制环境欠佳对投资带来较大的不利影响。

在非洲投资区，政府违反投资合同、汇率波动、司法不公和官员腐败是对中国投资产生不利影响较多的法律问题。而拉丁美洲投资区中对中国投资影响较大的是政治动乱、汇率波动和官员腐败等法律问题。中国投资者需根据投资所在的不同区域对这些法律问题给予有针对性的关注。

第十章　法律与政策建议

本章对答卷者就中国海外资源能源投资环境的法律与政策建议的调查反馈进行分析评论，具体包括中国海外资源能源投资在遭遇困难时获得中国政府支持与保护的情况，答卷者对海外投资保护和海外投资促进方式选择，以及关于中国海外投资保护的意见和建议等四个方面。

一、政府支持情况

当问及答卷者在遭遇困难时，是否得到了中国政府及时有效的支持和保护时，其反映情况如图 10.1 所示。

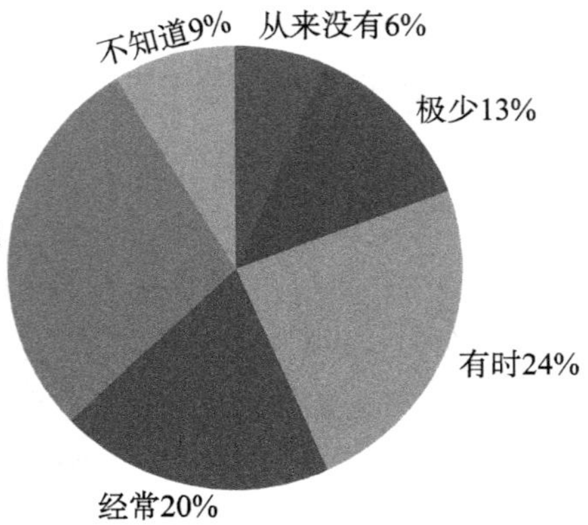

图 10.1　中国投资获得中国政府支持与保护的情况

近半数答卷者(47.83%)表示经常或总是能获得中国政府的支持和保护。而根据研究员回访的结果,从来没有或极少获得中国政府支持与保护的答卷者也大多作说明为投资尚未遇到特别的困难,暂时还没有向中国政府寻求保护的经历。这说明中国答卷者普遍认为中国政府能够在投资遭遇困难时为其提供支持和保护。

二、海外投资保护

本问卷调查以多选题的形式询问答卷者眼中中国海外投资最有效的安全保障方式,所得反馈信息如图 10.2 所示。

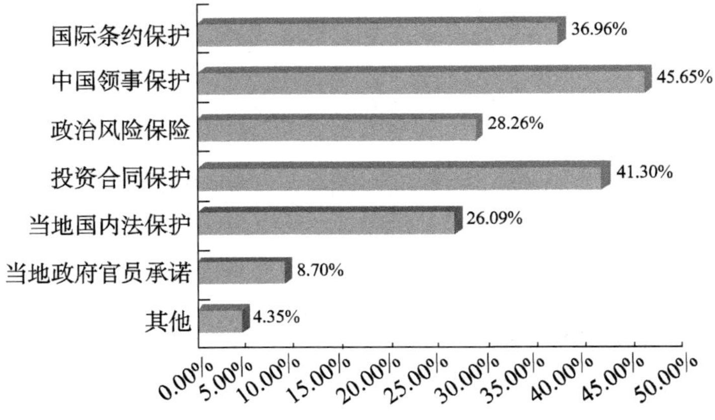

图 10.2　中国投资者认为最有效的安全保障

中国领事保护是现阶段答卷者认为最为有效的安全保障方式,其次是投资合同的保护。国际条约保护也是有较多答卷者选择的有效地保护投资的方式之一,相比之下选择政治风险保险保护投资的答卷者则相对较少。值得注意的是,虽然在之前第七章的考察中,当地国内救济是答卷者在遭遇纠纷时首选的救济方式,但此处数据则显示出仅有少数答卷者信赖当地国内法保护是中国海外投资有效的安全保障方式。这表明中国投资比较重视国际法对海外投资的保护作用,尽管他们对国际救济方式尚缺乏了解。此外,有少数答卷者在问卷预设选项外提出了其他可以保障投资安全的方式,具体如仲裁以及东道国当地政局稳定,等等。

三、海外投资促进

如图10.3所示,大多数答卷者都认为缔结双边条约是促进中国企业进行海外投资的积极性最为有效的方式。并且,期待强化海外投资担保的答卷者已经多于期待政府制定财政税收激励措施的答卷者,而期待以加强海外领事保护的方式来促进中国企业进行海外投资的答卷者则相对较少。这表明在现今的中国海外投资中,相比依靠传统的外交方式获得保护,投资者已经逐渐意识到法律对于保护投资的重要作用。

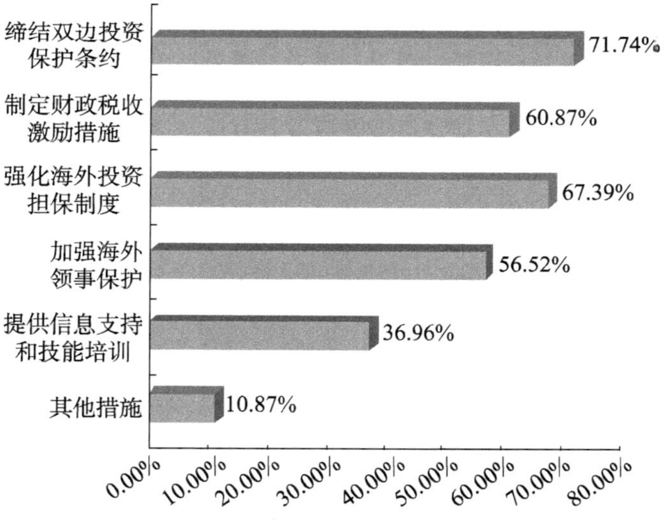

图10.3　有效促进中国企业进行海外投资积极性的措施

注:其他措施包括驻外人员安全、提供当地翻译、给予优惠的保险条件、政府组织商务拜访活动、简化和放宽审批手续等。

四、其他意见和建议

除了本研究已经显示的数据,答卷者还就中国海外投资保护提出了丰富的意见或建议,经分类整理后如下所列:

(1)兼顾战略和投资回报选择市场。答卷者反映国资背景的企业,海外投资遭遇复杂,而且出于战略需要会不可避免地选择一些不成熟的市场,如非洲和南美一些国家。建议民营企业选择成熟的市场,如澳洲等。有条件的企业要有战略考虑,不计较短期回报,以实现长远的投资收益。

(2)为海外投资配备专业人员。答卷者提出可以培养海外投资企业负责人的风险意识和全球视野。此外,建议国家考虑制定引进具有全球化管理经验的经理人的企业税费优惠措施。

(3)国家给予经济性的支持。答卷者表示国家可以在条件允许的情况下加强对战略资源能源类海外投资的资金奖励和外汇支持,或者对进口投资产出的资源能源产品(如矿产品)给予更多的优惠政策,尤其是税收方面的优惠政策。

(4)建立健全保障制度。答卷者建议国家可以主动为海外投资设立各种保障。要求投资企业为海外投资项目和其中的工作人员强制投保,并在条件允许的情况下由国家承担一定比例的保险费用。同时需要中国政府加大在东道国对其海外投资的保护。

(5)简化审批手续。答卷者提出非央企出身的企业在走出去时需要向各级发改委、商务部等行政机构层层报批,由于审批时间的拖延导致错过许多机会。因此项目报批流程亟待简化,审批时间亟待缩短。

主管政府部门可以加强指导,正确引导。

五、小结

根据答卷者的反映,中国投资在遭遇困难时普遍能够获得中国政府的支持和保护。就海外投资保障方式而言,领事保护仍然是目前最为有效的安全保障方式,但投资合同以及国际条约的保护作用也正日渐彰显。在投资促进方式上,双边投资条约已成为最受我国投资者期待的促进中国海外投资的措施。此外,海外投资担保制度的重要作用也已逐渐凸显,答卷者对此的期待甚至超过了对财政税收激励措施和外交领事保护的期待。由此可见,我国投资者对国际投资法的需求正与日俱增。

第十一章 结 论

在中国经济发展过程中,资源与能源安全占有举足轻重的地位。加强海外资源能源的投资是维护中国资源能源安全的重要措施。为此,在国家实行"走出去”战略过程中,强化以获取稳定的海外资源能源保障为目的的资源能源投资显得尤为重要。本研究对从事海外资源能源投资的中国企业、管理海外资源能源投资的政府部门,以及提供相关法律和会计服务的律师事务所和会计师事务所进行了问卷调查,切实考察了中国海外资源投资面临各种法律问题和风险的实际情况,并对突出的法律问题及其对策进行分析。通过本次调查,我们得出主要结论如下:

(1)总体而言,我国海外资源能源投资总体法律环境比较严峻。如图11.1所示,一方面,我国投资总体政治风险水平均值处于“超标”状态,需要密切关注并实施风险防控;另一方面,在本调查所考察的14项具体指标中,绝大多数(10项)出于“超标”甚至“明显超标”和“严重超标”状态;同时“达标”的四项的均值也都属于不太理想的达标状态。

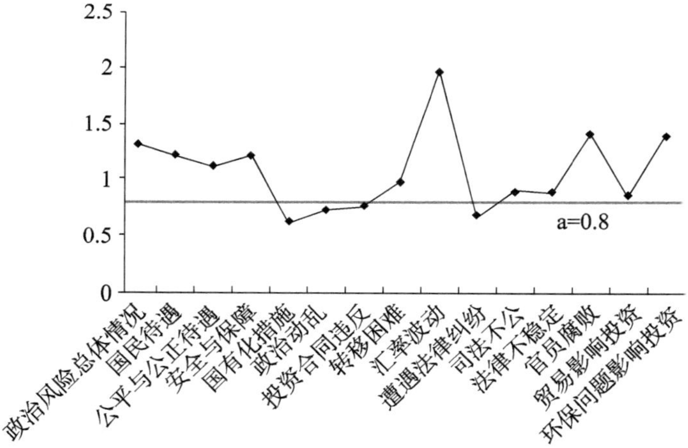

图11.1 中国投资面临法律风险总体均值图

注:直线a=0.8,系“达标”线。

(2)就准入条件而言,我国海外资源能源投资往往被附加各种业绩要求。其中当地雇佣要求是中国在海外进行资源能源投资时最经常被附加的业绩要求,其次是当地股权要求和当地成分要求。

(3)我国投资在海外享有一般待遇状况较差。在东道国提供的国民待遇、公平与公正待遇或充分的安全与保障三个核心方面,其问题均值均在“超标”范畴。

(4)就具体制度而言,我国投资受国有化与征收、政治动乱以及政府违约的影响较小(处于“达标”状态),但受国际财产转移限制的影响较大(处于“轻度超标”状态),尤以汇率波动的影响最为显著(处于比较严重的“明显超标”状态)。

其中,虽然我国投资目前很少遇到国有化与征收问题,但一旦产生,其补偿往往达不到“充分、及时、有效”的标准(处于“严重超标”状态)。

(5)我国海外投资东道国法制状况欠佳,且区域差异很大。相对而言,官员腐败问题比较突出,司法不公与法律稳定性问题也在一定程度上存在,三者均未能“达标”。

(6)中国投资在海外很少与东道国政府发生法律纠纷。投资保险尚未成为中国投资者减小投资政治风险的主流方式,但也已经发挥了一定的作用。一旦与东道国政府发生纠纷,中国投资者往往倾向于通过东道国国内的司法或仲裁方式寻求救济,而不是选择国际仲裁。对国际投资仲裁的重视亟待加强。

(7)在与资源能源投资活动密切相关的两个法律问题中,贸易壁垒对中国投资产生的不利影响相对较低,环境保护问题对中国投资的影响相对较重。

(8)就区域总体状况而言,目前大洋洲投资区的法律环境相对最好,其次是东南亚投资区,最后是拉丁美洲、非洲投资区,最不理想的是中亚投资区。

(9)就区域具体特征而言,在大洋洲的中国投资比较容易受到国民待遇、汇率波动和环保问题的影响。在东南亚的投资享受东道国充分保障和保护的情况欠佳,同时汇率波动、环境保护以及官员腐败问题对投资的不利影响较大。中亚投资区政治风险发生的程度相对较高,东道国为投资提供安全保障的情况欠佳,该区域的投资者应多留意国有化措施、国际间财产转移困难以及法制环境欠佳对投资带来较大的不利影响。在非洲投资区,政府违反投资合同、汇率波动、司法不公和官员腐败是对中国投资产生不利影响较多的法律问题。而拉丁美洲投资区中对中国投资影响较大的是政治动乱、汇率波动和官员腐败三个方面的法律问题。建议我国投资者根据投资所在的不同区域对这些法律问题给予有针对性的关注。

(10)我国投资在遭遇困难时往往能够获得中国政府的支持和保护。就海外投资保障方式而言,领事保护被认为是目前最为有效的安全保障方式,但投资合同以及国际条约的保护作用也正日渐彰显。在投资促进方式上,双边投资条约已成为最受我国投资者期待的促进中国海外投资的措施。此外,海外投资担保制度的重要作用也已逐渐凸显,投资者对其的期待已经超过了对财政税收激励措施和外交领事保护的期待。这些都表明我国对外投资者对国际投资法律保护的需求正日趋强劲。

深度参与新能源宪章搭建“丝路能源带”*

受荷兰政府邀请，中国国家能源局局长努尔·白克力不久前率团出席在荷兰海牙举办的能源宪章部长级会议，并代表中国签署了新的《国际能源宪章宣言》。中国自2001年12月成为能源宪章受邀观察员国以来，双方通过人员互访、召开研讨会和信息交流等方式开展了大量合作。国家发改委强调，本次签署国际能源宪章宣言，标志着中国由受邀观察员国变为签约观察员国，在国际能源治理的道路上迈出了新的一步。

从欧洲能源宪章到国际能源宪章

能源宪章是欧洲国家发起设立的、成员国覆盖欧亚大陆的多边性国际能源法律治理体系，以1991年《欧洲能源宪章宣言》为龙头，以1994年《能源宪章条约》为主体，规制内容以能源投资、贸易、运输为主，兼及能源效率、竞争政策、金融、税收、保险、环保、人员往来、政策透明度等广泛议题。2010年11月，能源宪章成员方通过了“能源宪章进程现代化路线图”，启动全球化战略，力图扩大成员国的地理覆盖范围，并重塑以能源贸易、能源投资和能源运输为核心的制度优势。

2015年5月在荷兰海牙举行的能源宪章部长级会议上签署的《国际能源宪章宣言》，是能源宪章体系现代化进程的最新也是最重要的事件，宣告了能源宪章体系从欧洲能源宪章到国际能源宪章的华丽转身。结构转型和制度升级是决定能源宪章转型成败的两条生命线。其中，制度升级试图重塑能源宪章体系的制度优势，凝聚以能源贸易、能源投资和能源运输为核心的制度设定，并以此激活既有成员国对能源宪章的政治热情，并加强其对非成员方的吸引力。结构转型则表现为能源宪章目前正在推行的全球化战略。能源宪章体系希望借助结构转型吸引更多国家参与到能源宪章体系中，在地理版图上实现全球化，其扩张的重点，正是

---

* 本文发表在《法制日报》2015年6月23日，第10版：环球法治。

亚洲、非洲和拉美等新兴国家。

能源宪章全球化战略和我国“一带一路”建设在地理范围上重合，在政策议题上兼容，两者殊途同归，不谋而合。能源宪章现有成员版图刚好和我国的“丝绸之路经济带”规划基本吻合，其扩大的方向以亚洲、非洲和拉美等新兴国家为重点，与我国“21 世纪海上丝绸之路”的方向大体一致。在这个意义上，二者合力，完全有望成功打造一个有全球影响的“丝绸之路能源带”。

能源宪章与“一带一路”能源合作

博鳌亚洲论坛之后，“一带一路”建设进入新阶段。2015 年 3 月 28 日，习近平主席在博鳌论坛发表《迈向命运共同体、开创亚洲新未来》的主题演讲，指出：“国际形势继续发生深刻复杂变化，国际格局和国际秩序加速调整演变；能源安全等非传统安全和全球性挑战不断增多，南北发展差距依然很大”；“一带一路”合作倡议契合中国、沿线国家和本地区发展需要，符合有关各方共同利益，顺应了地区和全球合作潮流。

习近平主席强调“一带一路”建设“要推进建设亚洲能源资源合作机制，保障能源资源安全”。紧随习近平主席博鳌演讲，国家发改委、外交部、商务部经国务院授权联合发布了《推动共建丝绸之路经济带和 21 世纪海上丝绸之路的愿景与行动》（以下简称《“一带一路”愿景和行动》），细化“一带一路”建设路线图，明确中国推进“一带一路”建设的共建原则、框架思路、合作重点和合作机制。而能源合作是“一带一路”建设的重中之重。

《“一带一路”愿景和行动》倡导依托既有合作平台拓宽国际互利合作，强化多边合作机制作用，让更多国家和地区参与“一带一路”建设。需要指出的是，亚欧大陆上的能源合作并不是制度洼地，转型中的能源宪章体系极有可能构成“一带一路”能源合作所依托的制度平台。中国参与能源宪章在多个层次上与中国优先对外政策高度契合，有利于中国建立符合中国利益的国际能源治理框架，搭建“丝绸之路能源带”的战略平台，形成撬动以能源产业为核心的综合性国际经济治理体系改革的战略支点，而且有助于树立中国建设性地、负责任地参与国际治理的国际形象。

中国应深度参与能源宪章进程

签署《国际能源宪章宣言》是中国参与能源宪章体系转型进程的第一步。作为政治性宣言，宣言明确了能源宪章转型的重点，昭示了缔约国在能源领域进行合作的姿态。然而，宣言并不具有法律拘束力，任何接受这些原则的国家都可以签署。更实质性参与能源宪章体系的一步是签署具备法律拘束力、处在能源宪章体系核心的 1994 年《能源宪章条约》,并推动其核心条款修改,致力于达成新的《国际能源宪章条约》。

从短期来看,中国应考虑签署《能源宪章条约》。中国加入《能源宪章条约》的成本较低、收益较大。一方面,《能源宪章条约》项下的法律义务要求与中国在世界贸易组织和新一代国际投资协定下已承担的国际义务大体相当;国内能源立法体系与能源宪章条约的衔接度高,而且加入《能源宪章条约》有助于整合国内碎片化的零散能源立法。另一方面,作为相对发达的投资条约,《能源宪章条约》可以弥补我国与《能源宪章条约》缔约国签署的早期投资条约保护范围有限、保护程度不足的缺点,提高对中国在《能源宪章条约》缔约国直接投资的保护水准。而且,签署《能源宪章条约》与中国最近优先推进的"一带一路"战略高度契合,也使我国有机会积累参与乃至引领国际制度改革的一手经验,为中国更加深入、更负责任、更具建设性地参与乃至引领现有国际经济制度的建构改造提供一个最佳的"制度练车场"。

从长期来看,中国应积极推动修订《能源宪章条约》,引领能源宪章体系的 2.0 升级。出席今年 5 月举行的能源宪章部长会议并签署《国际能源宪章宣言》已经昭示了中国积极参与并谋求主导全球能源有效治理的姿态。中国应继续在签署《能源宪章条约》的基础上推动条约机制升级,打造更加平衡、更加高效、更能回应跨国投资监管政策需求的新一代多边投资条约,并纳入更广泛的能源合作议题。中国应该积极谋求在能源宪章决策和运行机制中发挥重要甚至主导作用,使能源宪章进程与"一带一路"建设良性互动、优势互补,着力打造以我为主、于我有利并惠及全球的"丝绸之路能源带"。

构建“丝绸之路学术带”*

作为中国西部高等教育的“排头兵”，西安交通大学积极响应国家“一带一路”战略，于今年1月成立了“丝绸之路经济带研究协同创新中心”。日前，西安交通大学法学院院长、丝绸之路经济带研究协同创新中心召集人单文华教授接受了本报专访，揭开了中心的“神秘面纱”。

主动融入“一带一路”战略

问：西安交通大学创办“丝绸之路经济带研究协同创新中心”的初衷是什么？

单文华：西安交大2006年成立了“丝绸之路国际法研究所”，致力于研究攸关丝路的一般性和特殊性国际法律问题。之所以聚焦“丝绸之路”，我们有三方面的考虑：第一，丝绸之路是和平之路、发展之路，也是法治之路。我们创办的国际法研究所要彰显丝路精神，最终引领国际法发展的正确方向；第二，西安是古丝绸

---

* 本文发表在《人民日报海外版》2015年7月3日，第5版：丝路特刊，记者吴绍礼。

之路的起点，拥有得天独厚的地理优势；第三，丝绸之路作为国际上最重要的贸易通道之一，对于其贸易投资法制、规则的研究较少，我们有义务加强研究，弥补空缺。

2008 年，研究所更名为“丝绸之路国际法与比较法研究所”，更加明确了以推动世界特别是丝路法治为己任的研究目标。2013 年，习总书记提出“一带一路”战略构想。学校高度重视，经过统筹谋划，协同外交部、商务部、中国社会科学院共建“丝绸之路经济带研究协同创新中心”，并于今年 1 月正式揭牌。该中心以建成世界一流智库为目标，致力于发展丝绸之路经济带建设的法律、政治、社会和文化层面合作与创新研究。年初，中心启动了“中国法与国际商法”法律硕士项目。借助于 5 月刚刚成立的“新丝绸之路大学联盟”，西安交大将与哈萨克斯坦国立欧亚大学、印度德里大学等丝路沿线著名的高等学府和其他世界领先学府开展实质性的教育合作，竭尽全力为建设“丝绸之路经济带”培养精英人才和领军人才，助力中华文化“走出去”。

建设世界一流智库

问：中心成立以来，围绕丝绸之路经济带建设做了哪些事？

单文华：中心的工作可以概括为“一体两翼”，以创新研究为主体，以高端人才培养和社会服务为双翼。

我们与剑桥大学合作签署了“丝绸之路学者项目”，和牛津大学出版社合作创办了英文国际期刊《中国比较法学刊》，还创办了教育部和国家外专局特色外专项目“丝绸之路国际经济法高级国际研讨班和圆桌讨论会系列”。其中，与剑桥的合作已经持续了 5 年，送出了 5 名优秀学生学者，其中有的已经成为我校的“青年拔尖人才”。在牛津出版的学刊是国际比较法科学院支持出版的唯一学术期刊，已经出版了 3 年，在国际上已经产生良好反响，正在成为一条“中国法学学术对外交流的丝绸之路”。研讨班已经培训了 3 批国际经济法的优秀人才。

在协同创新研究方面，我们承接了国家教育部“推进丝绸之路经济带建设研究”的重大课题攻关项目，这是教育部目前唯一的关于丝绸之路经济带的重大项目，也是全国仅有的几个关于“一带一路”的重大课题之一。课题组协同国家商务部、陕西师范大学中亚所、厦门大学国际经济法研究所，以及国内外校内外法律、政治、经济、能源和文化等领域顶级专家，从区域治理、产业结构、投资贸易便利化和一体化、能源合作以及文化 5 个方面开展实质性研究。

近日，应能源宪章秘书处的邀请，我主持了作为中国加入能源宪章的可行性研究重要组成部分之一的“中国法与能源宪章条约的兼容性研究报告”的研究工作,并就此做了大会报告。能源宪章体系的发展方向与我国“一带一路”建设规划不谋而合,我国与能源宪章合力,完全有望打造惠及全球的“丝绸之路能源带”。根据此项专题研究,协同创新中心已向国家能源局等有关部门递交了《中国加入能源宪章条约的成本收益分析》的政策研究报告,为我国签署《国际能源宪章》政治宣言提供了直接的学术支持。

协同沿线各国力量共建

问:“丝绸之路学术带”由西安交大首倡,如何理解这一构想?作为学者,您对“丝绸之路经济带”建设有何建议和期望?

单文华:在协同创新中心成立之际,我校同时举办了高端国际论坛,首次提出“丝绸之路学术带”这一学术概念。作为一所负责任的大学,西安交大牵头发起“新丝绸之路大学联盟”,编织了丝路沿线国家的教育纽带;作为一个有前瞻性的协同创新中心,我们不仅要发挥自身的力量,更要将沿线各国的力量协同起来,构建“丝绸之路学术带”,服务于“一带一路”建设发展。

我认为,“丝绸之路经济带”的建设路径概括起来应该是三句话,即“政治法律搭台,经济文化唱戏,交通通信奠基”。

“政治法律搭台”,首先要努力凝聚沿线国家政治共识,缔造相关法律体制,尽快改进完善对外投资保护、贸易保护、通关便利化的法律规则,保障丝路建设中的投资者贸易商的安全与利益。我们要做到与别的国家贸易畅通,货币流通,百姓民心相通,这其中最强有力的纽带就是法律制度尤其是国际法律制度。所以丝路建设急需“立制”,确立相应的国际制度和体制机制的框架。其次是“经济文化唱戏”。经济必然是丝路建设的主要抓手,商业力量的驱动无疑应该是实质意义上的基本动力。同时,文化建设也要同步跟进,起到贯穿始终的作用。丝绸之路是和平发展、合作共赢之路,我们的研究不仅着眼于政治法律等上层建筑,也将关注经济基础和文化交流,努力实现多层次多方面的一体化研究服务。丝路建设还有一个基础性的工作就是确保“交通通信奠基”。协同中心准备结合校内外交通工程与管理学科的优势,开展铁路、公路、航空、管道、网络的互通互联方面的研究,为丝路经济建设奠定扎实的物质基础。

西安交大丝绸之路经济带研究协同创新中心将以“世界视野、丝路重心、中国特色”为主旨,在创新研究、精英培养、决策咨询、专业服务、争端解决 5 个方面服务“一带一路”,为丝绸之路经济带建设提供最优质的学术和教育支持。

丝路建设亟须“立制”*

陕西省省长娄勤俭出席座谈会

习近平主席提出丝绸之路经济带建设，至7日已整一年。对于如何更快更好地推进经济带建设，有专家呼吁，当务之急是要突出强调法律制度的稳定、规范和先导作用。

西安交通大学法学院院长、博士生导师单文华，昨日在出席“陕西省建设丝绸之路经济带新起点座谈会”时呼吁——在区域内各国已经形成高度政治共识的今天，当务之急是要将政治共识，凝固成强有力的法律框架，并在这个框架的基础上展开各项具体的工作。

* 本文发表在《大公报》2014年9月6日，记者雷永刚。

陕西省委常委、宣传部部长景俊海主持会议

他建议,首先应锚定丝绸之路经济带建设的目标基石。综观世界,区域合作方兴未艾,既有像欧盟这样的高度宪政化的区域一体化组织,也有像欧安组织这样的区域安全合作机制和像《北美自由贸易协定》(NAFTA)这样的区域经济合作机制,还有以TPP和TTIP为代表的高标准的新型区域合作形式。结合丝绸之路经济带的发展现状,先期宜以打造一个可与TPP和TTIP相媲美的、涵盖经贸合作诸领域的《丝绸之路经济带自由贸易协定》为目标。

西安交通大学法学院院长单文华吁为丝路"立制"

其次,围绕先期目标,要明确丝绸之路经济带建设的总体框架和具体任务。

尽快将各方共识凝聚成有一定效力的国际法律文件,使之成为丝绸之路经济带建设强有力的法律纽带。如以《原则宣言》、《各方共识》或《框架协定》等国际法律文件形式明确丝绸之路经济带建设的原则精神、目标模式、体制机制和时间安排等问题。同时辅以一系列协定或议定书以具体细化有关任务。特别是围绕政策沟通、道路联通、贸易畅通、货币流通、民心相通的“五通”目标制定相应的法律规则。

同时,要建立相应的工作机制。如国际层面上的国家领导人定期会晤机制、特设工作组机制、信息交换机制;国内层面的联络点机制、专人负责制等等。通过这些工作机制,推动丝绸之路经济带建设的稳步开展。

陕西省建设丝绸之路经济带新起点座谈会于9月5日下午举行

在创新丝绸之路经济带建设路径方面,在合作区域、合作产业、制度建设、推动方法上,宜采取先易后难、由小到大的方式,逐步扩大成果。

另外,还应加强官、产、学、研的合作交流。因为丝绸之路经济带建设,是一项复杂的系统工程,涉及方方面面的利益,需要集思广益。这种交流合作既包括一国之内的纵向交流,也要包括国与国之间的横向交流。特别在当前起步时期,应当重视这种交流对形成良好共识和舆论氛围的作用。单教授建议,应尽快设立“中国丝绸之路经济带研究院”,而努力打造“丝绸之路经济带”新起点和桥头堡的陕西,应该是极佳的落户地点。

“丝路”战略促陕快速发展*

2013 年 9 月 7 日，习近平主席在哈萨克斯坦纳扎尔巴耶夫大学演讲时首次提出了“丝绸之路经济带”的概念，并为此提出加强政策沟通、道路联通、贸易畅通、货币流通、民心相同的“五通”举措，皆在逐步加强区域合作，用创新合作模式共同建设“丝绸之路经济带”。

在此背景下，陕西作为古丝绸之路的起点，应采取怎样的举措去承担“丝绸之路经济带”新起点的责任？让古长安的繁荣景象再现？记者联系西安交通大学多位学者，以他们不同的研究领域，解读起点陕西。

记者：陕西是“丝绸之路经济带”的新起点，您认为这个战略构想，将会给陕西带来哪些实际的发展机遇？

单文华：丝绸之路经济带战略构想是国家最高层在新的历史时期谋划“以我为主、于我有利”的世界格局的重大战略构想之一。它的实施不仅将能够大力改善和优化中国新时期对外开放和对内改革的宏观国际环境，也将极大巩固和加强中国与相关国家在政治、经济、文化、科技、社会等方面的具体交流与合作，将会有力推动经济带地区的稳定与和谐发展。作为丝绸之路经济带的新起点，这一战略构想的提出无疑为陕西的发展开辟了一片新天地，将成为未来 5 到 10 年引领陕西快速发展的一个最重要的战略契机。

首先，建设丝绸之路经济带作为我国向西开放战略的重要举措，将会进一步密切中国与中亚乃至西亚、中东甚至是东欧、西欧与北非的经贸合作与交流。围绕丝绸之路经济带建设的目标，各国间将会进一步加深政策沟通与协调，加强有利于区域合作的体制建设；进一步消除投资、贸易壁垒，加强投资贸易自由化的制度安排建设，改善投资、贸易环境；进一步加强道路交通和运输管网建设，为区域合作提供便利的物流机制；进一步深化区域内的金融合作，便利货币结算、融投

---

* 本文发表在《文汇报》2014 年 6 月 27 日，记者黄帅。

资；进一步加强文化交流合作，为开展区域合作奠定坚实民意基础和社会基础。可以说，丝绸之路经济带建设将会在区域层面不断创新机制，促进区域活力，而一个充满活力、交流密切、沟通顺畅的广大区域，将会为陕西更好地融入区域发展、融入全球经济贸易体制创造更加有利的机遇。

其次，构建丝绸之路经济带也是我国促进西部地区发展和西部大开发的现实需要。相信围绕丝绸之路经济带建设构想的落实，国家也将进一步推出有利于西部地区参与丝绸之路经济带建设的政策、措施和配套法律法规机制，促进西部地区的对外开放水平和经济社会发展活力。陕西作为西部地区的龙头，理应抓住这一历史机遇期，实现率先启动、领先发展，全面参与并领跑丝绸之路经济带建设和西部大开发进程。

再者，丝绸之路经济带构想的提出，更加明确了国家对外开放的东西平衡发展战略布局。作为面向东方、面向海洋开放的沿海地区和面向西部、面向欧亚大陆开放的西部地区的重要战略连接点，陕西承接东部产业转移、承担西向开放窗口的地位更加突出，对外开放的全方位格局更加清晰，发展优势也更加明显。可以说，随着丝绸之路经济带建设的进一步深入，陕西将会迎来更加有利的发展前景。

最后，丝绸之路经济带的建设将有力带动经济带沿线重要城市的大发展大繁荣，从而极大推动西安的国际化大都市建设。丝绸之路经济带的建设将以点带面逐步推进，建设若干作为主要支点的战略性城市无疑将成为其中的关键节点。作为国家重点建设的国际化大都市，西安无疑应该成为其中最关键的节点和最闪亮的亮点，成为新丝路桂冠上的一颗最耀眼“明珠”。

可以预见，随着丝绸之路经济带的建设和深化发展，西安市的各项建设及其区域引领作用，乃至于其世界性地位和影响将不断彰显。这是西安的历史机遇，显然也是陕西的历史机遇。

记者：从您研究的角度看，陕西与中亚国家合作的优势有哪些？投资价值在哪？

单文华：陕西参与对中亚的合作具有得天独厚的优势。这种优势首先是区位优势，一方面陕西是承接东西部的连接点，是东部生产力向中亚、中东乃至欧洲、非洲出口的必经之路，也可以作为进口西来物资在我国境内的分配集散点，有利于发展大规模贸易和物流业，实现欧亚大陆尺度上的物资交汇和交易。另一方面，陕西也是丝绸之路经济带上发展最好、经济活力最高的地区之一，拥有良好的吸纳外来投资的空间，可以成为外来投资参与丝绸之路经济带的发展平台，从而带动整个丝绸之路经济带的经济发展。

其次，陕西还具有得天独厚的人才和知识优势，作为丝绸之路经济带科研院校最密集的地区，陕西每年能为丝绸之路经济带建设提供数以万计的人才，有利于带动丝绸之路经济带的高科技产业发展和科技创新。

此外，陕西还有着独特的文化优势，散布境内的古丝绸之路文明遗存为加强与中亚国家的旅游和文化合作提供了便利，为打造丝绸之路旅游线路和拓展电影、电视、艺术等为载体的文化产业发展提供了丰富素材和现实载体。

第六编 法学教育 Part VI

1263－1311

Legal Education in China: The New "Outstanding Legal Personnel Education Scheme"*

INTRODUCTION

The handover of power which took place in late 2012 significantly raised the expectation for the rule of law in China. In the Central Committee's Report to the ruling Chinese Communist Party(CPC) 18th National Congress, the Party for the first time placed the "rule of law"(Fazhi) as "the fundamental means of governance" and urged "a government under the rule of law"(Fazhi Zhengfu) to be established by 2020.[1] This is further affirmed by the new leader Xi Jinping, Secretary-General of the Chinese Communist Party(CPC), when he urged the establishment of "China under the Rule of Law" (Fazhi Zhongguo) in a more recent speech.[2]

Such a significantly raised expectation on the rule of law, undoubtedly, would not be possible without a significantly strengthened legal education system. Indeed, much has been debated among China's legal educators as to how legal education should education institutes were then set up. For instance, the Department of Law was created to teach law at Renmin University of China in 1950, followed by other legal institutes such as Beijing University Department of Law, Beijing College of Political Science and Law (currently China University of Political Science and Law), and Fudan University School of Law. In the 1950s, the Central Government adjusted and remodelled the Law Departments of those Universities and reduced the number of them from thirty-four to six,[3] with a view to optimising the distribution of legal institutes in the country.

The"Cultural Revolution"(1966 – 1976) marked a disastrous turn to legal respond to the changed and changing circumstances within and beyond China. The most significant move so far has been the "Outstanding Legal Personnel Education Scheme" (the "Outstanding Scheme"). This article therefore explores the history, the main aspects and

* *Legal Information Management*, Vol. 13, No. 1, Cambridge University Press, 2013.

[1] Hu Jintao, Report to the 18th CPC National Congress(8 November 2012), available at: < http: //www. xj. xinhuanet. com/2012- 11/19/c_113722546. htm >, access 30 January 2013.

[2] Xi Jinping Speaks on How to Improve the Political and Legal Works under the New Circumstances(7 January 2013), available at < http: //news. xinhuanet. com/politics/2013-01/07/c_114284339. htm >, accessed 30 January 2013.

[3] Xiangde Ji(2008), New Development of Legal Studies, China Social Sciences Press, p. 6.

Wenhua Shan

the issues of the current legal education system, before examining the contents and implications of the new "Outstanding Scheme". It concludes that the new scheme will significantly improve the structure, contents and methods of Chinese legal education, and will forcefully boost the cooperation between the law schools and the legal practice sectors. However, further measures are needed to achieve the desired results of the scheme and to place the Chinese legal education into an internationally competitive position.

Ⅰ. LEGAL EDUCATION IN CHINA: A BRIEF HISTORY

A brief review of the history helps to put the current reform in historical context, against which the reform might be better understood. The 60 years or more of Chinese legal education can be roughly divided into two broad periods with the adoption of the Reform and Opening-up policy in 1978 as the watershed. Generally, the first 30 years were the period when Chinese legal education was established and then effectively abandoned, whilst the latter 30 years had witnessed its resumption and rapid development.

1. The Pre-Reform period(1949 – 1978)

After the founding of People's Republic of China in 1949, the Government determined to abolish the previous legal system and legal education, and instead introduced a new legal system and legal education in China, with Marxism theory as the guiding light. In practice, China modelled on the experiences of the Soviet Union. Russian educators were, therefore, imported to China in the early 1950s, whilst teaching materials were translated from Russian into Chinese, as well as Soviet pedagogical techniques being adopted as teaching methods.[4] A few legal education in China, which effectively abandoned legal education altogether. Most law departments and institutes were closed down with the exception of one university and one institute, which also stopped admitting

〔4〕 Han Depei and Stephen Kanter, "Legal Education in China", American Journal of Comparative Law, Vol. 32 No. 3(1984), p. 545.

students.[5] Many of the law professors had to seek non-legal careers. China's legal education therefore fell into paralysis during the ten-year "Cultural Revolution".

2. The Post-Reform period(1978-present)

The Third Plenary Session of the Eleventh Central Committee of the Communist Party of China of 1978, which embarked on the policy of Reforms and Opening-up, signalled a revival of legal education in China. In order to support economic reform and opening-up to the outside world, China decided to resume legal education and the construction of legal infrastructures. Since then, legal education has flourished throughout the country.

In 1978, six legal institutes were successively restored and started to recruit students. They included Beijing University Department of Law, Renmin University of China Department of Law, Beijing College of Political Science and Law(currently China University of Political Science and Law), Southwest College of Political Science and Law (currently Southwest University of Political Science and Law), East China College of Political Science and Law(currently East China University of Political Science and Law), Northwest College of Political Science and Law(currently Northwest University of Politics and Law)[6] The size of legal education in China reached the level of pre-Cultural Revolution stage. Rapid growth was seen in the 1980s, when almost all comprehensive universities and some specialised colleges set up law departments or schools. The number of law schools/departments reached 106 in 1988, an 18 times' increase within ten years. This number was doubled in 1998 to reach 214, which was again tripled by the end of 2007 reaching 615.[7] In short, there had been a 100 times' increase in law school/departments within 30 years, a spectacular development in the legal education landscape in China. As of 2012, there are 624 legal education institutes in the country, according to statistics frm the Ministry of Education.[8] (Chart 1)

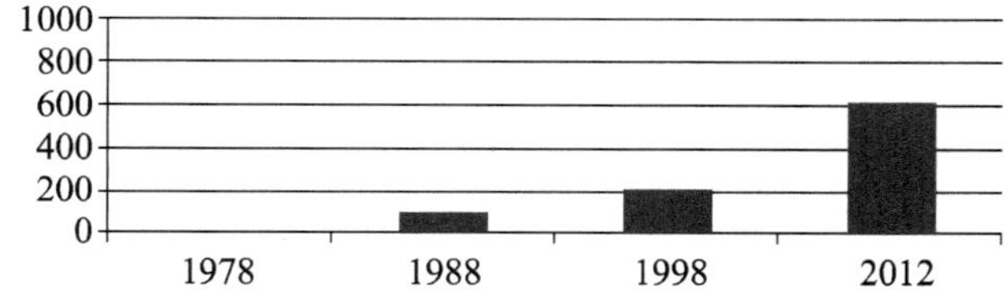

Chart 1 Number of Legal Education Institutes in China 1978 – 2012

Likewise, the undergraduate law student population has been dramatically increased

[5] Han Depei and Stephen Kanter, supra n. 3, p. 554.

[6] Xiangde Ji(2008), supra n. 4, p. 7.

[7] Xiangde Ji(2010), Modal of Legal Education in China, China Social Sciences Press, p. 2.

[8] Source: Legal Daily(9 October 2012), available at: < http://www.chinalegaleducation.com/article/show.asp?id=290 > (last visited 17January 2013).

during the same period.[9] In 1978, 1299 undergraduate law students were recruited by the six universities and colleges. This number reached 28, 325 in 1988, 87, 977 in 1998, and over 300, 000 at the end of 2007[10]. In 2012, there were over 450, 000 undergraduate law students enrolled in Chinese universities and colleges. (Chart 2)

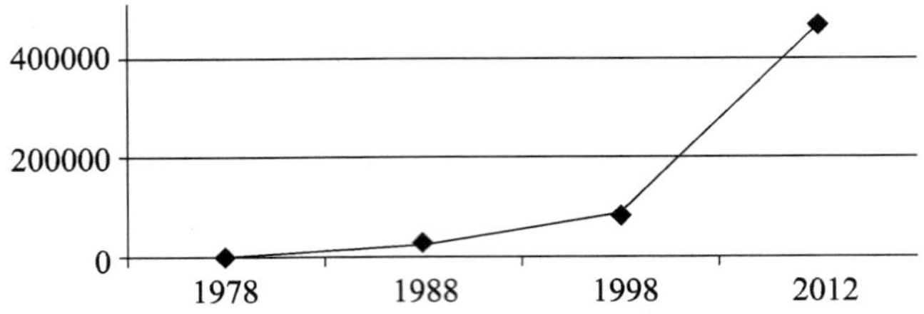

Chart 2 Number of Undergraduate Law Students in China 1978 – 2012

If the rapid increase of law schools and students in the 1980s and 1990s were correspondent to the economic development of the country, the sharp growth in the first decade of the 21st century was mainly due to the dramatic overall expansion of higher education that took place then. Law experienced a more dramatic expansion compared with other subjects, mainly because it appealed to students and it was less expensive to set up and operate. Yet such expansion proved to be too rapid for the economy and society to absorb. As a result, low employment rate and uneven quality of education have become more and more visible issues. Those, and other, issues are to be discussed below.

Also, it is noted that the approach towards legal education had experienced some changes during this period.[11] Since 1978, through the 1980s, the Soviet approach of legal education, adopted in the pre-reform period emphasising political attainment, was abandoned. Instead Chinese law schools generally followed the continental European approach, emphasising the overall development of their law students rather than the training of professional legal skills. Such an approach, however, was somehow changed again since the 1990s after the socialist market economy concept was accepted in China. An Anglo-American approach was introduced into Chinese legal education, with the Socratic approach and legal clinic being practiced in some law schools. However, the continental educational approach remains dominant, and the Anglo-American methods are used only as supplementary techniques.

Ⅱ. LEGAL EDUCATION IN CHINA: MAIN ASPECTS

1. Legal Education Providers

On the basis of educational objectives, current legal education can be classified in-

[9] A statistical analysis can be found in Weidong Ji, "Legal Education in China: A Great Leap Forward of Professionalism", www. law. kobe-u. ac. jp/lawrev/2005ji. pdf(last visited 7 December 2012).

[10] Xiangde Ji(2010), supra n. 7, p. 3.

[11] Xiangde Ji(2011), The Formation of a Chinese Model of Legal Education, Legal Forum(Faxue Luntan, in Chinese), Vol 26, No. 5, p. 77.

to two categories.[12] One is for academic qualifications, which is normally provided by universities or schools of law. This is the core of legal education which offers all degree programmes ranging from LLB to PhD. The other is for vocational education, namely professional training for judges, procurators, and lawyers.[13] This kind of education is usually provided by colleges of judges, prosecutors and lawyers.[14]

As the main providers of legal education, law schools and universities were divided into three categories before 1998, on the basis of their nature and level. Firstly, there were law colleges and universities under the jurisdiction of Ministry of Justice. They included five universities: China University of Political Science and Law, Southwest University of Political Science and Law, Northwest College of Political Science and Law, Zhongnan College of Political Science and Law, East China College of Political Science and Law. Secondly, there were universities directly under the jurisdiction of Ministry of Education, such as Beijing University, Tsinghua University, Renmin University, Jilin University, et al. Finally, there were universities subject to local authorities, which had law departments. They were necessary supplements to the above two categories of national legal education institutes. Since 2000, however, all of those five law colleges and universities were detached from the Ministry of Justice. Most of them became subject to relevant provincial authorities, except China University of Political Science and Law and the Zhongnan University of Economics and Law, which became universities under the direct administration of the Ministry of Education.[15]

2. Academic legal education

As mentioned above, academic legal education offers degrees of various levels, from bachelor to doctorate.

LLB. The first degree is at Bachelor level, which is called Bachelors of Law(LLB). After graduation from the senior high school and successfully passing the National College Entrance Exam, students apply to a law school or university to study for their first degree in law. After successfully completing their four year studies they are awarded a LLB degree, with which they may take the National Entrance Exam for Graduate Students if they wish to purse a higher degree, e. g. a masters' degree. They may also take the National Judicial Exam(NJE) if they wish to become a judge, prosecutor or a lawyer.[16]

LLM. Unlike the LLM programme in most western countries which normally takes only one year, a LLM degree in China takes two or three years of full-time study. Typi-

---

[12] One could perhaps add a third category of legal education, which is has been organized by the justice departments of all levelsin the country, with a view to improving the general consciousness and basic knowledge of law among the general public. Since 1986, five rounds of such mass legal education have been conducted. For further details, see Xiangde Ji, ibid, pp. 78 – 79.

[13] Ibid, p. 81.

[14] Jun Zhao, Ming Hu, "A Comparative Study of the Legal Education System in the United States and China and the Reform of Legal Education in China", Suffolk Transnational Law Review, Summer, 2012, p. 335.

[15] Xiangde Ji(2008), supra n. 4, pp. 8 – 9.

[16] Previously, National Judicial Exam is only available for those who have already obtained a bachelor's degree. This was changed in 2008, when students of their third year in law schools were also allowed to take this Exam.

cally, each student is allocated a supervisor to guide his or her study and research. Apart from taking courses, students are required to write a dissertation of certain length(normally around 30-thousand-words), which has to be defended in an oral examination. Indeed, it would be closer to an MPhil or MA in an AngloAmerican university.

JM. Since 1995, China has established a new legal education programme, the Jurist Master or J. M. Modeled on JD program common in the USA,[17] this programme used to admit only candidates from a non-legal background. In other words, applicants have to have a first degree in a subject other than law. Recently, this was changed and law graduates are also allowed to attend JM courses. The JM program is more practice-oriented hence incorporates more practice-related components such as legal writing, model court, internship, et al. They are also required to write a dissertation under supervision by a staff.

PhD. China did not start formal PhD education until the early 1980s. Hence the PhD education history in China has been relatively short. In 1981, 151 universities were selected by the State Council to confer PhD degrees, among which only three universities were entitled to confer the degree of PhD in law. Now the number of the universities and institutes that could confer PhDs in law has reached 37.[18] Some universities also offer interdisciplinary law PhD degrees. The Law and Governance PhD programme, for example, is a unique(XJTU) PhD programme created by the Xi' an Jiaotong University aiming at promoting interdisciplinary research between legal and management studies.

A PhD in law normally takes three or four years of full time study. Candidates are expected to attend a few courses and write a dissertation under the supervision of a senior member of staff which normally would be a full professor. The dissertation will be defended at a viva. The dissertation shall be within 100,000 Chinese characters and is expected to make a significant contribution to learning. Many universities require that they shall publish a certain number of articles in a certain level of journals before they can apply for a viva. Most PhD graduates go to higher education institutes for teaching and research. Others go to a variety of other sectors including judicial institutions, governmental departments, law firms and private companies.

It is also possible to do a PhD on a part-time basis, which is the so-called "thesis-based PhD". They are not expected to attend regular classes but are expected to submit coursework, or any other means of assessments for the compulsory courses. The thesis requirement is the same as for full time PhD candidates. However, some universities attach extra requirements for their graduation. For example, XJTU requires part-time PhD students to have received an award of provincial or above level for research excellence. The LLM can likewise be done on a part time basis and there is a special category of JM programme that are open only for part-time candidates. It is however normally impossible to obtain a LLB through part-time studies at a university.

All law degree programmes may accept foreign students. In the XJTU Law School,

---

〔17〕 Zuo Haicong, "Legal Education in China: Present and Future", Oklahoma City University Law Review, Spring, 2009, p. 53.

〔18〕 Xiangde Ji(2010), supra n. 7, p. 215.

for instance, there are foreign students at the LLB, LLM and PhD levels. The admission procedures for foreign students are separated from domestic applicants. At XJTU, the application is made through the School of International Education although the academic decision is made by the law school. It might also be possible for foreign students to apply for scholarship provided by the China Scholarships Council(CSC), which might cover the full cost of the entire degree programme including tuition fees, accommodation and maintenance.

Moreover, China has established the post-doctorate research system since 1985.[19] It is not a degree programme but an opportunity to conduct research work on the basis of one's PhD dissertation, with some guidance from a designated contact at the host institute. Such post-doc programs, as well as the PhD programs, are normally selected and approved by the central governmental authorities. In 1997, the number of the post-doctorate research centres in law was 11, which reached 19 in 2010.[20]

3. Judicial Exam and Vocational Legal Education

To become a qualified legal professional such as a judge, prosecutor or a lawyer, one has to pass the NJE. China's NJE was firstly held on 30 – 31 March 2002, with a predetermined pass rate of 7%.[21] The competitiveness of this exam has rendered it a name as the "No. 1 Exam in China". Before 2002, there were separate exams for lawyers, judges and prosecutors.[22]

Judges or procurators who had already been inservice in their early years without a bachelor degree or without passing the NJE, are required to attend professional training to meet the relevant qualification requirements. For that purpose the State Judges' College and the State Procurators' College were respectively set up in 1997 and 1998. Similar colleges or institutes have since then been set up at provincial and lower levels. Originally the State Judges' College was set up as a parttime professional training institute. It became a regular college in December 2001.[23] The training contents for judges and procurators include legal knowledge, practical skills, political theories and professional ethics.[24] Also, newcomers to the judiciary must attend a certain period of professional training at a judges' college at appropriate level before they can serve in a court.

The vocational education for lawyers in China comprises two parts: one is the education for apprentice lawyers, and the other is that for practicing lawyers.[25] Under the Lawyers Law, the China Bar Association is responsible for organising professional training for lawyers. According to a regulation promulgated by the Ministry of Justice in 1997, all lawyers are required to take training courses each year of no less than 40 class

---

[19] Zeng Xianyi, "Legal Education in China", South Texas Law Review, Spring 2002, p. 713.

[20] Xiangde Ji(2010), supra n. 7, p. 256.

[21] Weidong Ji, supra n. 9.

[22] For example, the National Lawyers Exam was started as early as 1986.

[23] Xiangde Ji(2010), supra n. 7, pp. 394, 418; Weidong Ji, supra n. 9.

[24] Xiangde Ji, ibid, pp. 397, 424.

[25] Xiangde Ji(2008), supra n. 4, p. 101.

hours.[26] However, unlike the continuing education of judges and prosecutors, for a long time the continued professional training for lawyers has not been institutionalised. Most of such trainings were done by temporary agencies or training organisations. In November 2012, the National Lawyers' College was officially established in Hebei Province to fill the gap.[27]

4. Curriculum

Different levels of education have different curriculums. Indeed, institutes vary significantly from each other in the specific courses offered, particularly at postgraduate levels. However, in order to guarantee that all LLB graduates have a solid grasp of legal knowledge, the Ministry of Education has prescribed 16 core courses that must be offered in each institute offering LLB programmes. Such courses include: Jurisprudence, Chinese Legal History, Chinese Constitution Law, Administrative Law and Administrative Procedural Law, Civil Law, Commercial Law, Intellectual Property Law, Economic Law, Criminal Law, Civil Procedural Law, Criminal Procedural Law, International Law, Private International Law, International Economic Law, Environmental and Resources Law, and Labour and Social Security. These core courses are all compulsive ones. Among them, the first fourteen were determined in 1998, and the remaining two were added in 2007.[28]

Undergraduate legal education in China is designed as general legal education. In other words, undergraduate students are not specialised in any specific area of law, but in the general subject area of law. This explains why Chinese LLB students are expected to take such a wide range of core modules. The idea is that law undergraduates should be offered basic training in legal concepts and skills. More specifically, undergraduates should have learned upon graduation the basic theory and knowledge of every branch of law, the basic methods and skills for legal analysis, the new trends in legal theory; practical skills to handle problems, document research and basic methods of gathering materials, and the fundamental ability to do theoretical research.[29]

At postgraduate level, the curriculum is more specialised and varied. For LLM programmes, for instance, both common curriculum and speciality courses are offered. Common curriculum, most of which are compulsory, mainly refer to political and foreign language courses. Speciality courses are offered as either compulsory or elective courses. Students in the LLM programme may take different courses depending on their specific subject areas of research. This also applies to the PhD programme, which has far less in terms of taught courses but a much heavier workload for the dissertation.

The JM curriculum is different from the LLM as it is generally the first law degree

---

[26] The Notification by Ministry of Justice, available at http: //www. lawyee. net/act/act_display. asp? rid = 37149(last visited 15 January 2013).

[27] Available at: < http: //www. legalinfo. gov. cn/index/content/2012 - 12/21/content_4074659. htm? node = 25329 > (last visited 15 January 2013).

[28] Zuo Haicong, supra n. 17, p. 55.

[29] Kara Abramson, "Paradigms in the Cultivation of China's Future Legal Elite: A Case Study of Legal Education in Western China", Journal of Asian-Pacific Law & Policy, Vol. 7, Issue 2, Summer 2006, p. 328.

education. A solid and wide basic knowledge base is therefore crucial. Essentially they cover the same core courses of the LLB although the way they are taught should be different-they should be more practice-based. In addition, a number of compulsory practical courses are included, such as legal writing, moot court, and legal negotiation skills, as mentioned above. The JM students are also expected to do a dissertation, which is much shorter than the LLM dissertation.

5. Teaching methods

Lectures are the main method of teaching in Chinese law schools, particularly for undergraduate courses, although other methods are increasingly used particularly in postgraduate teaching. In a typical law classroom, teachers fill most of the class time with systematic lecturing, going through the specific theory or rules as detailed in the textbook. Some teachers use PPT slides or handouts in lectures but other do not. Seminar, class or group discussions are rarely used.[30]

However, as mentioned above, there is a trend in recent years of importing US pedagogies into Chinese classrooms with the case-centred teaching style and practice-oriented pedagogy. Some law schools have started to introduce more "unconventional" teaching methods such as moot court and legal clinic. In reality, nevertheless, case study was only occasionally used, as examples to explain legal theories. In other words, they act only as teaching aids, not the main teaching method.[31] Moot court and legal clinic are offered only in a few schools and are yet to be used in a structured and systematic manner.

To summarise, China has established a comprehensive and complex legal education system consisting of both academic and vocational education. In academic legal education, there are law degree programmes of all levels ranging from LLB, to LLM and PhD. More recently, JM has been introduced to China to enhance practiceoriented and interdisciplinary education, modelled on the JD programme from the United States. Some elite universities have started to accept international students for their degree programmes, some of which have obtained scholarship provided by the Chinese government. Vocational legal education is mainly provided by vocational training institutes such as the Judges' College, the Prosecutors' College and the Lawyers' College at national and local levels.

Whilst the general approach is closer to the continental European legal education, more recently elements of the Anglo-American legal education have also been imported and practiced. Indeed one may call this, "a legal education system with Chinese characteristics" or a "Chinese Model".[32] Such a system or model has nevertheless been sub-

[30] Kara Abramson, "Paradigms in the Cultivation of China's Future Legal Elite: A Case Study of Legal Education in Western China", Journal of Asian-Pacific Law & Policy, Vol. 7, Issue 2, Summer 2006, p. 335.

[31] Zuo Haicong, supra n. 17, p. 54.

[32] Xiangde Ji, supra n. 11.

ject to increasing criticism particularly among the elite educators in the country.[33] An analysis of the key issues of the Chinese legal education follows.

Ⅲ. LEGAL EDUCATION IN CHINA: KEY ISSUES

Many issues have been touched upon in the current debate on the reform of the Chinese legal education. Among them, the focuses have been on the following five aspects: quality assurance; professional skills; internationalisation demands; outdated curriculum; and regional imbalance.

1. Quality assurance

As mentioned above, the last 30 years have witnessed a dramatic expansion of Chinese legal education, with over 100 times of increase in law schools and over 300 times of increase in undergraduate student population.[34] This development is pleasing and problematic at the same time. One the one hand, the expansion helps to produce legal personnel that are much needed in contemporary China in her endeavour to set up a rule of law system to tackle the increasingly common and pressing social, economic and political challenges. On the other hand, the expansion has been too rapid for the state and society to absorb. As a result, the employment rate of law graduates, which was once among the highest, has become one of the lowest in the country, as compared with graduates from other subjects.[35] Compared with legal education in the USA, China has a much higher percentage of universities that offer first law degree education. In the US statistics show that there are 202 ABA-accredited law schools,[36] out of 2968 universities offering bachelor degree education, or over 1700 universities[37] offering postgraduate degree education.[38] In other words, less than 7% of bachelor universities, or less than 12% of graduate universities offer first law degree(JD) education. In China the percentage is

---

[33] Wenxian Zhang, China's WTO Accession and the Reform of Legal Education; Xianming Xu, Recent Trends in the Development of Legal Education and its Reform; Jin Huang, Improving the Quality of Legal Education to Cultivate Outstanding Legal Personnel; Limin Wang, Suggestions to the Current Reform of Legal Education and Teaching; Qinhua He, Promoting Concerted Innovation to Improve the Quality of Legal Education; Zhenmin Wang, Legal Education Should Pursue Value not Technicality. All of them are in Chinese and are available at the website of the China Society of legal Education: <http: //www. chinalegaleduca- tion. org/article/list. asp? classid = 8 >(accessed on 31 January 2013). Other important discussions include Li Su, Challenges and Opportunities to Contemporary Legal Education in China, Legal Science(Fa Xue) 2006 No. 2; Dayuan Han, Challenges to Chinese Legal Education in the Context of Globalization, Law Magazine(Faxue Zazhi), 2011 No. 3.

[34] Chen Xueli, The Lowest Employment Rate for Law Graduates and 100 Times Increase for Law Schools in 30 Years, available at <http: // www. chinanews. com. cn/edu/qzjy/news/2009/03-09/1593950. shtml >(last visited 12 December 2012)

[35] Chen Xueli, ibid.

[36] Source: ABA, available at < http: //www. americanbar. org/groups/legal_education/resources/aba_approved_law_schools. html >(accessed 31January 2013).

[37] Source: Fulbright Commission: Choosing a Degree Program, available at: <http: //www. fulbright. org. uk/study-in-the-usa/postgradu- ate-study/choosing-a-degree-programme >(accessed 31 January 2013).

[38] Source: US National Centre for Educational Statistic, available at < http: //nces. ed. gov/programs/digest/d12/tables/dt12_279. asp >(accessed31 January 2013).

56% (624 out of 1112 universities offering bachelor degree education[39]), which is 8 or 5 times of that in the USA. This shows that law subject has been much more common a subject in Chinese universities than in US universities. Chinese legal education, in general, appears to have become a kind of "mass education", rather than an "elite education", as many educational elites might like it to be.[40] Such assessment would be more valid considering that many law programmes started only a few years ago and are rather poorly resourced in terms of staffing, accommodation, libraries and other resources.

Various proposals have been made to improve the employment situation. For instance, one proposal has been to "cut" some of the law programmes that fall short of the minimum standard of quality assurance.[41] Indeed attempts had been made by the education authority to conduct an evaluation of certain law schools and departments.[42] However, it has not been implemented nationally as it was deemed premature at this stage.

Indeed, forcing some of the institutions out of legal education by administrative measures might not be preferable. Ultimately it should be the "market", rather than the "ministers", that should decide the size of Chinese legal education. If, for instance most graduates from certain law schools could not find a job after graduation, then they will attract fewer and fewer students.[43] Eventually, such law schools will phase out.

China is a big country. Considering that China has a population that is more than five times that of the United States, it is not impossible to accommodate 624 law schools. Indeed the number of LLB students in China is just about 3 times the number of the US JD student population.[44] The real question, or problem, is quality; are they good enough to undertake the tasks of legal construction and development in the country? And if not, how can they be improved to the desired standard? This is where the government could play a crucial role, by designing a set of standards against which law schools and universities might be assessed and supported. Clearly, given the size of the country, legal education providers might not necessarily have to be the same but could, and indeed should be, diversified, horizontally into different categories and, vertically into different levels. But as they all produce bachelors in law(LLB), they should at least meet the minimum standards. It is on the basis of such standards that they might be diversified to developing their own characters. Also, professional bodies such as bar associations could play a significant role, for instance, in providing accreditation similar to that of the USA.

---

[39] Source: Legal Daily (9 October 2012), available at < http://www.chinalegaleducation.com/article/show.asp?id=290 > (last visited 17January 2013).

[40] See e.g., Xianming Xu, supra n. 33.

[41] Li Su, supra n. 33, at 11.

[42] Ibid.

[43] Zuo Haicong, supra n. 17, p. 58.

[44] ABA statistics show that in 2011 - 2012 the total enrollment of JD student in the USA is 146, 288. For further details see ABA, "Enrollment and Degrees Awarded 1963 - 2011", available at < http://www.americanbar.org/groups/legal_education/resources/stat- istics.html > (accessed 31 January 2013).

2. Professional skills

The separation between legal education and legal practice has often been criticised, but the problem is yet to be resolved. There are two main reasons. The first reason is institutional. There is no smooth channel for Chinese law graduates to enter into the legal profession. Like graduates from other disciplines, law graduates have to pass two national exams, namely the NJE and the National Public Services Exam(NPSE), to enter the judicial institutions. There are two problems here. On the one hand, the NJE is already very difficult with a pre-set 7% of passing rate, but the NPSE creates another hurdle and makes it even more difficult for law graduates to enter the judicial institutions. On the other hand, since law graduates also have to take the NJE in the same way as graduates from other disciplines, it is felt that their four year legal education has not been sufficiently recognised. In the UK, for instance, the legal profession represented by the Law Society and the Bar Council work closely with law schools to monitor the quality of legal education. As a result, qualified law graduates are automatically permitted to become an intern of law firms, whilst graduates from other disciplines have to take an intensive conversion course before they may enter into the legal profession. No such close cooperation exists between Chinese law schools and the legal profession at the moment.

The second reason is to do with the historical background against which Chinese legal education was restored. Since legal institutions were abandoned during the Cultural Revolution, when legal education was resumed in 1978 it was not possible for law professors to make use of existing cases or other practices of the legal profession. Also, because China generally adopts the continental legal system, it was only natural that the continental legal education approach was also adopted.

As a result, Chinese legal education places significant emphasis on legal theories and knowledge, with little attention paid to practical professional skills. The mission of most, if not all, law schools seems to be training legal academics, not to train practitioners.[45] Most law courses in China focus on "the studying of legal theories, concepts and statutes" and lecturers pay little attention to the process of reasoning or to the training of professional skills.[46]

For a long time the legal educators have been debating whether legal education should be academic education or vocational education.[47] As indicated above, most if not all law schools have actually long followed the route of academic education. As Xu observed, this is partly due to the fact that Chinese law schools have to cultivate academic strength in order to earn appropriate status within the country.[48] For instance, much of the attention of the Deans of law schools is directed by the state authorities in

---

〔45〕 Hou Xinyi, "Modern Legal Education in China", Address at Okla. City Univ. L. Sch. (Aug. 25, 2005) in 31 Okla. City U. L. Rev. 293(2006).

〔46〕 Ibid.

〔47〕 See e. g., Yuan Ming, "The Aim of Legal Education and Its Approach", available at http://www.chinalawinfo.com/fxyluntan/gf3.html(last visited 14 December 2012); Qilin Ma, "Legal Education of Today's China: Problems and Suggestions", 2012, http://works.bepress.com/qilin_ma/1(last visited 13 December 2012).

〔48〕 Xu, supra n 33.

the application for LLM, PhD programs or State Key Disciplines, leaving little time for them to think about what would be the best approaches of teaching for students.

Now it seems a consensus has emerged among educators that professionalisation should be a way forward.[49] Accordingly, more practice-oriented teaching methods have been introduced by some law schools and universities, such as legal clinic and moot court, aiming at training practical skills. However, there are a few hurdles preventing such teaching methods to be widely and regularly used. First, things like moot court and legal clinic require considerable resources including accommodation, equipment and their maintenance. Second, there is a shortage of experienced staff who can effectively coach such practical courses. Again, to recruit new competent staff or to train existing staff for this purpose would require further financial support. Third, given the "publish or peril" culture in universities including law schools, it is a constant challenge to make sure that there are competent staff that are committed and devoted to such courses.[50] Finally, since seminars have not become a common method of teaching, to take this on board as a regular method of legal teaching requires a change of the overall curriculum in universities, which is often difficult.

3. Internationalisation demands

Although law is primarily a local knowledge, it is also an international phenomenon. Modern Chinese law has essentially been an outcome of the functioning of comparative and international law, and it has also started to influence the development of laws in other countries.[51]

As China emerges as a major power in the world, the demands for internationalised Chinese lawyers have been intensified. For instance, there is a shortage of Chinese lawyers that are able to participate in discussions at various international organisations such as the United Nations and the World Bank, or to appear before international courts and tribunals such as the International Court of Justice and the dispute settlement body of the World Trade Organisation. Increasingly, there are stronger and stronger demands for Chinese legal scholars to present papers at major academic conferences and seminars. Also, the implementation of China's "going global" strategy requires more and more internationalised Chinese lawyers to provide quality legal support. Clearly, there is a very strong demand for the education of internationalised Chinese lawyers.

On the supply side, the shortage is obvious. Most Chinese law schools are not sufficiently resourced to train such internationalised lawyers. Therefore the conventional method of internationalisation of legal education has been to send students to overseas institutes for exchange. Recently, attempts have been made by some law schools to strengthen "in-house provision" of internationalised legal education, by recruiting internationalised staff and establishing internationalised curriculum and educational projects. In XJTU Law School, a series of measures have been taken to internationalise legal edu-

---

[49] Xu, supra n 33.

[50] Zuo Haicong, supra n. 17, p. 57.

[51] Wenhua Shan, Editorial, The Chinese Journal of Comparative Law(OUP), Vol. 1 No. 1.

cation. First, the school recruited a number of new staff graduated from leading overseas universities, some of which previously held senior academic posts. Secondly, agreements have been entered into with institutes such as the Lauterpacht Centre for International Law at the University of Cambridge, to foster cooperation in legal education. Thirdly, it has implemented the "Silk Road International Workshop and Roundtable Series on International Economic Law", which is sponsored by the Ministry of Education and has attracted leading scholars from the world to give a series of lectures to young faculty members and research students from home and abroad. Similar measures have also been adopted by other institutes. Notably, Xiamen University has established the Xiamen Academy of International Law, which offers a summer programme on annual basis, in a similar way to the Hague Academy of International Law.

These are nonetheless the exceptions rather than the norm, and even in those schools, internationalisation is yet to be further strengthened and systematised.

4. Outdated curriculum

It has been argued that China's undergraduate law curriculum is short of interdisciplinary, comparative and cutting-edge courses.[52] First, it is thought that "Chinese law school must cultivate interdisciplinary talents by breaking the boundaries between different disciplines",[53] and that law schools should "offer more interdisciplinary courses such as 'Law and Economics' 'Law and Engineering' or 'Psychological Analysis of Judicial Process'.[54] Second, "the more profound proposal for increasing global content in law schools is that international, comparative and transnational legal study should not be compartmentalised and taught separately".[55] Rather, those dimensions of legal study should be "integrated into the traditionally domestic core of law school curriculum".[56] Third, Chinese law schools should provide cutting-edge law courses such as "Law and, Biotechnology" and "E-Intellectual Property Law" and "the teaching of law could be integrated with research activities at research institutes".[57]

On the other hand, some of the existing courses have been viewed as "unrelated to the study of law but still enjoy a very high proportion of credits",[58] such as the Basic Theory of Marxism, Introduction to Mao Zedong Thoughts, Deng Xiaoping Theory, the History of Communist Party of China. These courses, however, formulate the "Chinese characteristics" of legal education, which may not be changed by the law schools.

5. Regional imbalance

The gap in wealth between the eastern and western parts of China is well known to the world. Little is known that such a gap also exists in legal education. Whilst law grad-

---

[52] Jun Zhao, Ming Hu, supra n. 14, pp. 356 – 358.

[53] Ibid, p. 356.

[54] Ibid.

[55] Adelle Blackett, "Globalization and its Ambiguities: Implications for Law School Curricular Reform", 37 Colum. J. Transnat'l L. 57, 68(1998).

[56] Jun Zhao, Ming Hu, supra n. 14, p. 357.

[57] Ibid.

[58] Qilin Ma, supra n. p. 47.

uates in the eastern regions find it more and more difficult to find a job, many counties in the western regions have had difficulty in finding an eligible person to fill a judge's post.[59] Another example is that until 2011 when XJTU established the first PhD programme in Law and Governance, there had been no PhD programme in law in the vast north-western region, which accounts for one third of the land territory of the entire country.

In short, the key issues relating to China's legal education concerns quality assurance, professional skills, internationalisation demands, outdated curriculum and regional imbalance. However, the central concern has been the overall quality of legal education. The other four elements are all important aspects of the overall quality issue. The key question facing the current Chinese legal education is therefore how to improve the quality of education, in the aftermath of the dramatic expansion in quantity, against great domestic expectation and fierce international competition. And the government's answer is the newly enacted "Outstanding Legal Personnel Education Scheme", which is elaborated below.

Ⅳ. LEGAL EDUCATION IN CHINA: THE NEW "OUTSTANDING LEGAL PERSONNEL EDUCATION SCHEME"

To take up the challenges facing Chinese legal education in the 21st century, particularly those discussed above, China formally launched the "Outstanding Legal Personnel Education Scheme" on 26 May 2012.[60] The scheme was jointly enacted by the Ministry of Education and the CPC Central Political and Legal Affairs Committee on 23 December 2011,[61] and provided guidelines for China's most important legal education in the decade to come. The main contents of the scheme are summarised as follows.[62]

1. Overall objectives

This scheme aims at: formulating a scientific and advanced legal educational ideology with Chinese characteristics, establishing an open and diversified legal education system that fits the conditions of China; and cultivating groups of high quality legal personnel with firm belief, high moral standing, rich knowledge and strong practical skills, within a decade.

2. Specific tasks

To achieve the overall objectives specified above, five more specific tasks are identified. They include:

---

〔59〕 Dayuan Han, supra n. 33, pp. 18 – 19.

〔60〕 China launches Outstanding Legal Personnel Education Scheme", China Education Daily(28 May 2012), available at < http: // www. edu. cn/xin_wen_dong_tai_890/20120528/t20120528_781905. shtml > (accessed 1 February 2012).

〔61〕 The full name of the document is "Several Opinions on the Implementation of the Scheme on Education and Cultivation ofOutstanding Legal Personnel", which was jointly enacted by Ministry of Education and the CPC Central Political and Legal Affairs Committee, on 23 December 2011, available at < http: //www. moe. gov. cn/publicfiles/business/htmlfiles/moe/s3875/ 201204/xxgk_134451. html > (last visited 8 December 2012).

〔62〕 Unless otherwise specified, all the contents of scheme are based on the above-mentioned document. Ibid.

(1) To classify the education for outstanding legal personnel on the basis of their different educational objectives.

Three categories of outstanding legal personnel are identified here. Firstly, the education and training of practice-oriented and inter-disciplinary legal professionals is the main focus of the scheme. The purposes are to enhance the education of legal professional ethics, strengthen the training of practical skills, to improve students' ability to apply knowledge of law and other disciplines to solve practical legal problems, and to promote deep coordination between legal education and the legal profession. This category of legal personnel is apparently designed to address the second issues discussed above, namely the "practical skills" issue.

Secondly, a category to cultivate groups of outstanding foreign related legal personnel with world vision, sound knowledge of international rules and ability to participate in international legal affairs and to protect the national interests of China, so as to meet the needs of the political multi-polarisation and economic globalisation of the world and the opening-up of China. This category of legal personnel is in turn designed to address the third issue discussed above, i. e. , the "internationalisation demands" issue.

Thirdly, to train groups of legal personnel with strong commitment and competent practical skills to serve the legal institutions at grassroots level in the western region of the country. This category is, in turn, designed to address the above mentioned fifth issue, namely the "regional imbalance" issue.

(2) To make innovations on China's legal education system.

Two particular innovative mechanisms are mentioned here. One is a joint education mechanism between universities and practical sectors, under which universities works jointly with the practical sectors to set the aims of education, to design curriculum, to development quality textbooks, to formulate teaching teams, to establish internship centres, so as to explore a regular and institutionalised mechanism for outstanding legal education.

The other is a joint education mechanism between domestic and overseas legal institutes. The purposes are to strengthen exchange and cooperation between domestic and good overseas law schools, to promote exchange of staff and students, as well as mutual recognition of academic credits and joint degree arrangements, so as to make good use of quality overseas legal educational recourses and build up a mutually complementary legal education mechanism.

(3) To promote the education on socialist legal ideology.

The main purpose of this task is to enhance education on students' professional consciousness and professional ethics, and to strengthen their commitment to serve the construction of a socialist state under the rule of law.

(4) To strengthen practical legal education.

It is emphasised that the portion of practical education should be increased, making sure that the credit for practical education counts for no less than 15% of the total credits. The encouraged practical education methods include legal methods, case study, moot court, legal clinic, among others. Meanwhile, law schools are encouraged to set up internship centres at professional institutions and make full use of their facilities, so as to improve their ability in legal interpretation, legal reasoning, legal argumentation and legal fact finding.

(5) To enhance the quality of the faculty members.

Two measures are mentioned in the scheme. One is to explore a mutual appointment system between law schools and practical sectors, thereby encouraging experienced experts from the practical sectors to teach at law schools, whilst encouraging staff of law schools to be seconded to legal professional institutions. In the end, the purpose is to establish a body of law faculty members that combines legal academics and practitioners.

The other measure is to encourage key staff members to go to overseas institutes to study and conduct research, thereby improving their professional level and teaching ability. At the same time, it is also encouraged to actively recruit high level legal talents including world class scholars from overseas to teach and conduct research in China.

3. Implementing measures

To carry out this scheme, more specific measures have been spelt out. They include:

(1) To establish outstanding legal personnel education centres. More specifically, around 80 "Practice. Oriented and Interdisciplinary Legal Professional Personnel Education Centres", around 20 "Foreign. related Legal Personnel Education Centres" and around 20 "Western Grassroots Legal Personnel Education Centres" are to be established.

(2) To implement a "Double-1000" scheme between universities and practical sectors. Accordingly, 1000 excellent law teachers shall be elected and seconded to professional organisations such as courts or other judicial organs for one to two years. At the same time, 1000 staff with abundant practical experiences from these practical organizations shall be selected to teach in universities for one to two years.

(3) To set up legal practice education centres. On the basis of the "Bachelors Teaching Project", 100 "Model Legal Practice Education Centres" are supported to be established through the cooperation between universities and practical sectors. Meanwhile universities are encouraged to establish such centres taking into account the conditions of their localities.

(4) To conduct international exchange and cooperation in legal education. With the support of the China Scholarship Council, law students are strongly encouraged to further their studies abroad, and for key teaching staff in universities to study or conduct research in overseas institutes.

(5) To build up high level textbooks. Key law textbooks should be compiled and put in use. Based on China's legal practice, case materials combining both theory and practice should be compiled. Moreover, high quality overseas legal textbooks may also be introduced on a selective basis.

(6) To lay down standards for outstanding legal personnel education. Each participating university shall formulate its own standards on outstanding legal personnel education, in accordance with the educational categories and the need of practical sectors. On the basis of those standards, Ministry of Education and CPC Central Political and Legal Affairs Committee will then establish the national standards on outstanding legal person-

nel education.

4. Preliminary implementation

In November 2012, Ministry of Education and CPC Central Political and Legal Affairs Committee announced the completion of the first round of selection of the "Outstanding Legal Personnel Education Centres". As a result, 58 universities were granted "Practice-Oriented and Interdisciplinary Legal Professional Personnel Education Centres", 22 universities "Foreign-related Legal Personnel Education Centres" and 12 universities "WesternGrassrootsLegalPersonnelEducation Centres". A list of the selected universities for the three categories of centres is attached in Annexes A-C. At the time of writing this paper, the selected universities are drafting their implementation plans, in accordance with the national scheme detailed above.

Meanwhile, some professional organisations have started to implement the "Double-1000" plan. In Shaanxi Province, for example, Xi' an City Intermediate People's Procuratorate has entered into agreements with XJTU and another two universities, under which each year three or more members of teaching staff from those universities are selected to be seconded to the procuratorates of different districts in Xi' an, serving as Associate or Assistant Prosecutors for a year. Meanwhile, XJTU law school carries on with the practice of sending members of staff or PhD students to work at the Ministry of Commerce (MOFCOM) or the Ministry of Foreign Affairs(MFA) for a few months or a year. In Jiangsu Province, the Jiangsu Higher People's Court also launched cooperation with six law schools as an implementation of the national "Outstanding Scheme".[63]

5. Implications

Given that the scheme is still at its earliest stage of implementation, it is too early to give a definitive assessment of its implications. It might nevertheless be possible make some preliminary evaluation on the basis of the actual and planned implementation measures. On the whole, it can be expected that the quality of legal education in China particularly in the selected universities would be significantly improved. More specifically, the scheme will have a tremendous impact on the structure, the contents and methods of Chinese legal education, as well as its interaction with the practice sectors.

First of all, the scheme is changing the structure of legal education in China, with the emergence of a "5 + 15" structure of outstanding legal education centres. A close look at the three lists can find out that only 20 universities were awarded both the first ("practice-oriented and interdisciplinary") and second("foreign-related") categories of centres, which were centres of general significance. Those universities can accordingly be considered as the most significant institutes for legal education. Among them, the 5 universities mainly specialised in law(the law universities) are all conferred two centres, which proves the overall strength of those university in legal education. Among the remaining 15 institutes, 13 are comprehensive "985" universities, which are the most important universities in China. Two are "211" universities that focused on business and

---

[63] Source: Legal Daily(1 November 2012), available at < http://www.legaldaily.com.cn/index/content/2012-11/01/content_3953745.htm?node=20908 > (accessed 2 February 2013).

finance subjects, which demonstrates the close link between law and business (the Zhongnan University of Economics and Law is actually also a business university at the same time as it is a law university) . This new "5 + 15" structure(see Chart 3) is set to lead the Chinese legal education and its reform in the decade to come.

Chart 3 The New "5 + 15" Structure of China's Outstanding Legal Education

Region	City	5 Law Universities	15 Law Schools
Northern China	Beijing	China University of Political Science and Law	Beijing University; Remin University; China Tsinghua University; Beijing Normal University; University of International Business and Economics; Central University of Finance and Economics
North-Eastern	Changchun		Jilin University
Eastern China	Shanghai Nanjing Hangzhou Xiamen Jinan	East China University of Political Science and Law	Fudan University; Shanghai Jiaotong University; Nanjing University; Zhejiang University; Xiamen University; Shandong University
Central Southern	Wuhan	Zhongnan University of Economics and Law	Wuhan University
South-Western	Chongqing	South-West University of Political Science and Law	
North-Western	Xi' an	North-West University of Political Science and Law	Xi' an Jiaotong University

Geographically, seven of the institutes with two centres are located in Beijing, confirming the unrivalled strength of the capital in legal education. This is followed by Shanghai with three institutes and then by Wuhan and Xi' an with two institutes awarded both centres. The fact that Xi' an has two institutes awarded two centres is particularly pleasing given the aforementioned need to redress the imbalance between the eastern and western regions.

Secondly, the contents or curriculums of Chinese legal education will be changed, with an emphasis on practical, interdisciplinary and internationalised courses. In XJTU, for example, we have already redesigned our curriculum, to make room or preparation for interdisciplinary and internationalised education. Unlike other law schools, undergraduate students in our law schools do not attend general university English classes but the English classes offered to students of the School of Foreign Language, specialising in English. In other words, they receive professional English training rather than general university English education. As a result our undergraduate students are well prepared for internationalised studies. Also, most international and comparative law modules, particularly those for postgraduate students, are taught either in English or bilingually combining both Chinese and English. Some of them are taught by distinguished visiting professors from leading overseas universities. On the other hand, in order to promote interdisciplinary studies, we have launched a "2 + 4" interdisciplinary education programme, under which law undergraduate students after admission to XJTU are placed in schools of other disciplines to study for 2 years, before they return to the law school for another 4 years of legal education. Successful students can obtain a LLB and a LLM, and possibly also a second bachelors degree in their disciplines of their first 2 years of studies. Furthermore, in the Law and Governance PhD program, we have included coursed offered by staff from other schools such as the School of Public Administration and the School of Management.

In our plan to implement the "Outstanding Scheme" at our school, we will set out two "Outstanding Classes", one for interdisciplinary legal studies and the other for foreign-related legal studies. The interdisciplinary class will follow the "2 + 4" pathway but increase the practical skill components, e. g. , by sending them to practical sectors such as local courts or legal departments of local governments for 6 months to one year internship. The foreign-related class will receive the intensive professional English training at the Foreign Language School mentioned above, and will have most of their courses taught bilingually or in English. Also, agreements have been signed with good overseas law schools to make sure that all or most of them could study abroad to get international experience or/and an academic degree. Such practice would become more and more common in Chinese law schools, particularly in "5 + 15" institutes.

Third, there will be changes in methods of legal teaching. Seminars, which are commonly regarded as very useful in promoting practice-oriented legal thinking, will become more and more widely adopted. More specialised courses to train professional skills such as case studies, moot court, and legal clinics, will also be more widely practiced. At XJTU Law School, a Falv Fang(Legal Workshop) has been established, which combines accommodation and equipment for moot court, moot arbitration tribunal and legal clinic.

Last, but not least, the cooperation between law schools and practical sectors will be significantly enhanced. In particular, the implementation of the "Double 1000" plan and the joint education mechanism between the schools and the practical sectors will boost tremendously the cooperation between the two sides. As a result, practical sectors will benefit from the expertise of law staff from leading universities. This would be particularly helpful in some western regions where qualified judges and prosecutors are in short supply. On the other hand, law schools will benefit from the teaching provided by experts from the legal profession, and their input in activities such as joint course/curriculum design and joint textbook compilation. Law school can also benefit from the enhanced practical knowledge and skills of their staff seconded to work at the practice sectors. Eventually law students will receive a more balanced education combining both advanced legal knowledge and professional legal skills. This would therefore be a win-win situation, which will help in the construction of a solid "legal professional community" in China that share the same knowledge, skills and values.

However, whilst the scheme is a great scheme that is poised to significantly boost the quality of Chinese legal education, there are uncertainties as to how much a difference it may make. Three points can be made here.

First, whilst the scheme has detailed the measures to be taken to implement it, it has not detailed how such universities and practical sectors will be funded to support such reform measures. The scheme only mentions that participating universities will be funded through the "Undergraduate Teaching Project". However, since some participating universities are not included in the project, it is unclear whether, and how, those universities will be funded. Whilst the scheme also mentions that local governments should provide financial support to participating universities, nothing has happened so far. As an important national scheme, the central government should provide strong financial support to guarantee its success. This is particularly true given that the central government is in a much better financial position than the local government at the moment. If the participating universities are expected to carry out the scheme on the basis of self-funding, the actual effect of such a grand scheme will certainly be thwarted.

Second, whilst the scheme will certainly boost the quality of legal education in the participating universities, it is unclear how it might impact the non-participating universities, which account for the vast majority of Chinese law schools. Obviously some of them might still hope for a chance to get in the scheme given that there may be other rounds to select the remaining 22 centres for practice-oriented and interdisciplinary legal personnel and 8 centres for the Western Grassroot legal personnel. The bulk of them cannot expect it. For those law schools it is uncertain what prospect is awaiting them. The heads of some of those law schools have already started to worry whether their schools will survive. Although the scheme helps in pointing out the direction of the development of Chinese legal education, it is certainly impossible for all of 624 schools to become "outstanding" legal education providers. How to treat such law schools remains unclear as a national policy. As said above, the preferred approach would be for the government to set up minimum standards to guarantee the quality of legal education, so that those schools could plan their future accordingly.

Last, but not least, the scheme does not touch the institutional problem of the "double-exams" for law graduates to enter into the judicial institutions. As said above, this creates a significant hurdle to law graduates in their job-seeking efforts. In this regard, the British approach might be used as a reference. Thus the legal professional bodies should work together with the legal educators to set up and monitor the standards of legal education. Accordingly, graduates from such accredited law schools who have successfully completed all the qualifying law courses should be waived the NJE and could directly enter into the professional institutions. The NJE should be required only for other graduates. Also, the NPSE should only be required for such law graduates when they apply for non-legal public services posts.

5. CONCLUSIONS

Legal education is the fundamental and fore-running component of a sound and strong legal system. Since the Reform and Opening up policy adopted in 1978 particularly in the last two decades, Chinese legal education experienced a dramatic increased in the number of law schools and law students. As the quantity sharply grows, the quality issue has emerged and became more and more prominent. This has damaged not only the employment prospect of law graduates but also the general reputation of Chinese legal education.

The"Outstanding Legal Personnel Education Scheme" came at the right time with the right measures and promises to be a great landmark in China's legal education reform in the decade to come. It will significantly change the structure, contents and methods of Chinese legal education, particularly legal education in the participated universities. Also it will forcefully boost the cooperation between legal academia and practical sectors. Nevertheless, further measures need to be taken to solve the financial issue of the scheme, to set standards for legal education applying to the non-participating institutes, and to establish a smooth channel for qualified law graduates to enter into the legal profession.

If the scheme is fully implemented and the other issues also effectively addressed, it can be expected that not only the current problems now facing the legal education system will gradually be eased off; Chinese law schools may soon become one of the leading legal education forces in the world.

Annex Lists of Universities Selected in 2012 to Establish National Centers under the "Outstanding Legal Personnel Education Scheme"

A. Practice-Oriented and Inter-disciplinary Legal Professional Personnel Education Centres(58)		
Beijing University	Renmin University of China	Tsinghua University
Beijing Normal University	University of International Business and Economics	Central University of Finance and Economics
China University of Political Science and Law	Minzu University of China	Chinese People's Public Security University
Beijing University of Aeronautics & Astronautics	China Youth University for Political Sciences	Nankai University
Xi' an Jiaotong University	Hebei University	Shanxi University
Dalian Maritime University	Liaoning University	Shenyang Normal University
Jilin University	Jilin University of Finance and Economics	Heilongjiang University
Fudan University	Tongji University	Shanghai Jiaotong University
Shanghai University of Finance & Economics	East China University of Political Science and Law	Nanjing University
Soochow University	Nanjing Normal University	Zhejiang University
Zhejiang Gongshang University	Anhui University	Xiamen University
Jiangxi University of Finance and Economics	Shandong University	Lanzhou University

Yantai University	Zhengzhou University	Henan University
Wuhan University	Zhongnan University of Economics and Law	Central South University
Hunan University	Xiangtan University	Hunan Normal University
Sun Yat-Sen University	South China University of Technology	Jinan University
Guangdong University of Business	Guangxi University	Hainan University
Studies		
Chongqing University	Southwest University of Political Science and Law	Sichuan University
Southwestern University of Finance and Economics	Guizhou University	Yunnan University
Northwest University of Politics and Law		

B. Foreign-related Legal Personnel Education Centers(22)		
Peking University, Renmin University of China	Tsinghua University	
Beijing Normal University, Beijing Foreign Studies University	University of International Business and Economics	
Central University of Finance and Economics, China University of Political Science and Law	China Foreign Affairs University	
Jilin University, Fudan University	Shanghai Jiao Tong University	
East China University of Political Science and Law, Nanjing University	Zhejiang University	
Xiamen University, Shandong University	Wuhan University	

续表

Zhongnan University of Economics and Law, Southwest University of Political Science and Law	Xi' an Jiaotong University	
Northwest University of Politics and Law		

C. Western Grassroots Legal Personnel Education Centers(12)		
China University of PoliticalInner Mongolia University Science and Law	East China University of Political Science and Law	
Zhongnan University of Economics and Law, Southwestern University of Political Science and Law	Sichuan University	
Southwestern University for Yunnan University of Nationalities Nationalities	Northwestern University of Politics and Law	
Gansu Political Science and Qinghai Nationalities University Law Institute	Xinjiang University	

Acknowledgements

The author would like to thank his research assistants, Miss Juan Du for her assistance in preparing the first draft, and Miss Luella Wang for proofreading the final draft.

Biography

Professor Wenhua Shan has PhDs from Cambridge and Xiamen. He was the Founding Dean and Ministry of Education Changjiang Chair Professor of Law, Xi' an Jiaotong University School of Law; Professor of Law, Oxford Brookes University; Editor-in-Chief, The Chinese Journal of Comparative Law(OUP).

大学精神论纲

——英国经验与国际共识*

自从17岁考上中山大学以来,我就再没有离开过大学,不是在念书,就是在教书,有时也承担一些管理工作。我在英国的大学里前后待了16年。这期间,我在剑桥大学这所老牌大学做过访问学者,读过博士学位;也在牛津布鲁克斯大学这所新派大学任过教职,从讲师开始,一直做到教授;还在伦敦、利物浦等"红砖大学"兼职从事过教学研究工作。现在虽然已经全职回国,但在剑桥仍然保留着一份资深研究员的兼差,因此对英国的大学可以说有一定的经历和了解。

在我看来,英国的大学精神,就是大学作为一个由学者、学生组成的学术共同体的独立和自由的精神。[1] 这种精神,又可分为内外两个层面:对外,是大学治理的独立自主,简称"大学自治";在内,是学术探索的无界自由,也即"学术自由"。

大学自治

大学自治是英国大学的历史传统,也是英国大学的基本现实。英国关于大学自治的传奇故事可谓层出不穷。其中,牛津大学拒绝授予撒切尔夫人名誉博士学位一事堪称经典。1985年1月30日,牛津大学的议事厅里人声鼎沸,1000多名教师和学生代表正在激烈地辩论要不要授予他们的校友、当朝首相撒切尔夫人荣誉法学博士学位。经过两个多小时的激辩,大学以738票反对、319票赞成的压倒性多数否决了给予撒切尔名誉博士的提案。这是一个艰难的决定,因为自"二战"以来,授予担任英国首相的校友以荣誉博士学位已经成了牛津的惯例,从无例外。但是,在牛津的绝大多数师生看来,这又是一个必然的结果:他们认为,"即使

---

* 本文发表在《中山大学法律评论》2014年第3期。

[1] 毫无疑问,这种精神与中大先师陈寅恪所倡导的"独立之精神,自由之思想"是一脉相承的。

是王国最高长官,也不能期待我们授予她荣誉,而忽略她所推行的政策对我们学人所毕生信奉的价值以及所从事的工作的影响”。究其根源,在于“铁娘子”政府对教育经费的大幅缩减,使英国曾经长期领先世界优势的高等教育陷于严重困难的境地。“如果授予撒切尔名誉学位,那将是对公立教育部门每一个人的沉重打击。”30 年过去了,当年决定的对错已经不再重要。重要的是,牛津顶住了政治和舆论的巨大压力,坚持了自己的价值判断,展示了数百年名校傲世独立的风范。所谓大学自治,简单地说就是大学的事务由大学自己做主,不受政治、经济等外在因素的不当干扰。正如欧洲大学协会 2011 年发布的“大学自治排行榜”所揭示的,大学自治具体来说又可细分为组织自治、财务自治、师资自治和学术自治等方面。在所有这些方面,英国大学均高居欧洲教育大国中的最高位置。英国大学的高度自治,于此可见一斑。

英国的大学始于牛津和剑桥。和欧洲大陆的其他中世纪大学一样,它们一开始就是一个由学者和学生组成的行业性共同体。由于得到教会与王室的庇护,它们不仅拥有高度的自治,而且还享有诸多特权(例如可以免税、可以罢工),有“国中之国”的地位。19 世纪以来,牛津剑桥的教育垄断被打破,伦敦大学等大学陆续设立,但大学仍长期游离于英国公共事业体系之外,英国政府并没有对大学进行系统的财政支持。1918 年,面对“一战”过程中大学的财务困境,英国成立了大学拨款委员会,作为政府为大学提供拨款的咨询建议机构。1988 年《教育改革法》通过以后,英国成立了大学基金委员会以取代原有的大学拨款委员会,增加了社会产业界人士的比重。随后,英国根据 1992 年《继续和高等教育法》组建了新的高等教育基金委员会以取代原有的大学基金委员会,但基本延续了大学基金委员会改革的思路,继续扩大委员会中的产业界代表比例,进一步加强大学与社会产业界的联系,同时建立更加严格的质量监督和评价体制,以财政拨款为媒介,加强政府的宏观调控。即使如此,英国政府对于大学的调控以及产业对大学的介入依然遵循法治和间接的原则进行,大学的办学自主权并没有受到根本性的影响。正因如此,英国才能继续以大学的高度自治岸然立世,英国的高等教育也才能继续保持世界领先的卓越地位。

学术自由

如果说大学自治是大学精神的七级浮屠,那么学术自由就是这座浮屠塔里所供奉的佛骨舍利。大学是学问与知识生产、传承与养护的场所,而学问、知识得以生产与传承、养护的前提,就是有一片能够滋养知识与学问的自由与宽松的土壤。如同在钢筋混凝土里开不出鲜花一样,在没有自由的地方不可能产生真正的、有生命力的学问。

作为培养了世界上最多诺贝尔奖得主的大学，剑桥无疑是世界科学与学术的重镇。然而，当莱谢克·博里塞维奇校长在谈到剑桥科研环境的优点时，并没有列举有多少先进的实验设备，而是指出其提供了充分的学术自由，让科研人员有根据个人兴趣开展研究的时间和空间。剑桥明文列出的核心价值观第一条就是“思想与表达的自由”。这就可以解释为什么曾在剑桥念神学的达尔文，后来却可以冲破神学观念和英国基督教环境的束缚，提出与“上帝造人说”完全对立的进化论。如果他的大学当初不曾给予这种自由思想的空间，就难以想象他能够取得这样的成就。

在英国做研究很少受到干扰，想研究什么领域，召开哪个主题的学术会议，如果不用申请经费，从来不需要经过任何审批，也从不会有人以会议议题或所发表言语“离经叛道”而横加干预。刚到剑桥时，我脑子里面更多的是国内几年研究积累的观念、知识和经验，不少带有比较浓厚的意识形态色彩，用导师们的话来说，就是有点教条。比方说，谈到外国投资的征收补偿标准，往往就觉得要求充分补偿只是资产阶级贪得无厌的表现，不存在任何法律乃至道义的正当性。我时不时还会引用国内老先生们所确立的论据来和导师们“据理力争”，不情面红耳赤。导师们不仅没有生气，反而觉得我认真得可爱——只是他们会很温和地指出我需要看到硬币的另外一面。我在剑桥做的博士论文提出欧盟和中国应该签订双边投资协定，当时不少人都觉得这个主张有点太超前，因为欧盟当时根本就不具备缔结这种条约的法律权能。但是，导师们不但没有反对，反而特别支持甚至鼓励我做这个选题。事实证明，他们是对的：10 多年以后的今天，欧盟不仅取得了这个法律权能，而且也正在和中国谈判这样一个条约。而这两方面，正是我的论文首次提出的两个核心观点。

事实上，在剑桥，就像在英国其他大学一样，师生平等对话、唯学是问的故事比比皆是。而我的故事要是和维特根斯坦（和罗素一样也是我在剑桥学院圣三一学院的院友）的相比只能算是平淡得不能再平淡的了。故事里说，维特根斯坦的剑桥博士论文是在第一次世界大战期间的战营里写就的，叫《逻辑哲学导论》。当时没有人能够读懂他的这部天书，因此出版商找到他的老师罗素。罗素自告奋勇，为这部书写了一篇洋洋洒洒的序言，并为这部书的出版费尽心机。书出版了，但维特根斯坦并不领情，还说罗素根本就没有读懂他的论文！罗素不以为忤，反以为豪，因为他知道天才人物往往有个性，而他作为老师，剑桥作为一所大学，所能做得最好的事情，就是为这样的人才提供一片任其驰骋的广袤天空。

国 际 共 识

大学自治与学术自由是在英国大学最为彰显的大学精神，但并不是只“属于”英国的大学精神。事实上，英国的大学最初效仿的是欧洲的大学，而英国和欧洲的大学又影响了整个世界的大学发展。其结果是，在世界上比较有影响的大学，都遵循大体一致的大学精神。一个最为显著的表现，就是来自世界上 80 多个国家的 700 多所知名大学对于 1988 年《大学大宪章》（*Magna Charta Universitatum*）的共同拥戴。其中就包括两所中国的大学：北京大学和武汉大学。

《大学大宪章》由世界上最早的大学意大利博洛尼亚大学所首倡，并于 1988 年在该大学 900 周年诞辰之际，由来自世界各国的 430 所大学的校长们所共同签订。而该大宪章所确立的四个基本原则中，最根本的两个原则，正是“大学自治”和“学术自由”。其中，“大学自治”是大宪章所确立的首要原则。它开宗明义“大学是自治的机构……大学的研究和教学必须从道义上和智识上均独立于所有的政治权威或者经济力量”。而关于“学术自由”，大宪章指出“研究与教学的自由是大学的根本原则；政府与大学必须尽其所能确保对这种自由的尊重”。毫无疑问，这些表述正是大学精神的最好阐释。

千 秋 基 业

大学之所以需要独立于政治与经济之外实行自治并享受学术自由，有其必要性和必然性。在现实的世界里推动社会的发展演进主要有三种力量：政治、经济和教育。它们各有其主体与载体。其中，政治的主体主要是政客和官僚，其载体主要是各种权力机关及其所掌握的各种权力资源；经济主要以商人与企业为主体，并以金钱以及其所能支配的广泛资源为载体；而教育的主体则主要是受过教育的人群即学者或学生，其主要载体则为以大学为代表的学校以及其所孕育传承的知识、思想、学识与学问。

这三支力量之间既相互联系、互相支持配合，又相对独立、互相监督制约。其中，一方面，大学与教育亟须政治力量的保护与经济力量的支持，否则其生产与发展均将难以为继。古今中外的经验表明，成功的大学往往得益于政权的呵护和商界的扶持。另一方面，大学与教育又必须保持相对于政治与经济力量的独立性。否则它不可能开展其赖以生存的独立自主的思考以及建立在此基础上的知识创新与文明传承，也就不可能为另外两个部门提供必要的人才供给和智力支持。可以说，对于政治与经济而言，大学与教育的独立自主和自由生发最符合其最大、最长远的利益。而在历史的长河中，往往是，政治和经济的成就可能倏忽间烟消云散，而大学和教育的成果却可以历久弥新，它们可以更深刻、更久远地定义并滋养着一个民族、一种文明。从这个意义上讲,维护大学的独立自主与学术自由不仅仅是政治、经济和教育部门共同的事业,而且是它们共同的千秋万代的基业。

撒切尔曾经断言:"中国不可能成为超级大国,因为中国只能出口电视机,出口不了创新的理念。"话粗理不粗。中国应该如何重拾大学精神,破解"撒切尔魔咒",值得政治、经济和教育部门的远见丰识和深思慎对。

聚焦当下的中国法学教育*

李挚萍教授：有问题在，就有解决问题的方法在，关键在于我们怎么寻找

很荣幸能请到各位法学院院长和法学专家来中山大学为我们传经送宝，在座不仅是法学学术领域的专家，更是法学教育管理领域的专家，因此我们能听到很多关于教育和教育管理的真知灼见。我们的讨论将涵盖以下议题：关于法学本科教育的经验、问题和对策；关于法学研究生教育的经验、问题和对策；关于法律硕士培养的经验、问题和对策；关于新增法律硕士（法学）专业的培养方式；关于法律实践教学的经验和方法；关于法学对外合作办学的合作和方法。在展开讨论前，我们想把中山大学法学院的困惑和做法先提出来，希望得到大家的指教。这几年来，中山大学在本科生层次和研究生层次都进行了一些新的尝试，比如，在本科教学方面，我们进行了学期制改革，将两学期制改为三学期制，目的是通过新增的小学期增强跨学科教育、通识教育和实践课程；研究生教育方面，我们对传统法学研究生教育进行压缩和优化，另外不断扩大专业型学位的招生和培养，不过目前让我们困惑较多的是新增法律硕士（法学）专业的培养方式问题；法律实践教学方面，我们不仅要加强研究生实践教学的力度，也要设置本科生实践教育课程；在对外合作办学方面，教育部最近给予广东在对外合作办学方面先行先试的新政策，如“2＋2”项目，广东省可以自己审批，这也是一个新的契机。我们可以结合当前的情况，从法学教育的培养理念、培养模式、培养方案等层面共

---

* 本文发表在《中山大学法律评论》2010年第1期。作者分别为中山大学法学院副院长李挚萍教授、吉林大学法学院院长姚建宗教授、中南财经政法大学法学院院长刘仁山教授、苏州大学法学院常务副院长胡玉鸿教授、西安交通大学法学院院长单文华教授、山东大学法学院副院长周长军教授、深圳大学法学院院长黄亚英教授、厦门大学法学院党委书记侯利标教授、武汉大学法学院党委书记侯振发教授、中国诊所法律教育专业委员会副主任暨中山大学法学院蔡彦敏教授以及中山大学法学院法律诊所学生们。感谢教授们和同学们对当下中国法学教育的关注和贡献他们的精辟见解。

本文汇集了来自国内诸多法学院院长和法学教授关于当下中国法学教育的观点，这些观点来自于两个论坛，一是2009年11月中山大学法学院复办30周年庆典“中国法学教育院长论坛”；二是2006年11月在科尔多瓦举办的GAJE年会上关于“在社会变革背景下的社会正义教育”的主题研讨以及中山大学法律诊所师生们关于法学教育的探讨。

同探讨、分享经验。我想，有问题在，就有解决问题的方法在，关键在于我们如何寻找。

姚建宗教授：关键在于打好知识、方法和人格的基础

对于本科生的法学教育，吉林大学法学院相当重视，也一直在考虑和探索如何提升本科教学质量。目前本科生教学工作中的确有一些困难。一方面，近年来许多高等院校大规模扩招，本科生的质量水平却不容乐观，这不仅影响法学的专业教育质量，同时也因为没有切实可行的措施而将法学教育置于一个尴尬的境地。虽然教育部对此有一个教学质量工程，但其中能够落实的确实很少。另一方面，法学教育到目前为止并没有一个可靠的质量监控体系，仅仅依靠教授的个人良心，这是应该的；但问题是缺乏制度保障，这就为教学质量水平的保证增加了许多不确定性。例如，由于本科教学与研究生教学方式不同，有的教授可能会有一些功利想法，会在一定程度上对教学质量产生负面影响。我一直相信"本科生是基础"，所以这几年吉林大学法学院也在做一些努力。对于法律学习，我认为首先要做好基础知识的传授，另一方面思维方式的培养也是重点，但人格的养成这个更关键。我做普通教师的时候，感觉到"英雄主义"是行不通的。大一的时候，我可以通过鼓励和长时间的宣扬来提高学生的兴趣和职业荣誉感，但大三大四时可能由于其他教授不同的教学模式而中断这种教育。效果当然不好。这说明教师队伍这个方面还是需要一个制度来发挥作用的。与博士生、研究生教育注重质量不同，我觉得本科教育更注重基础知识的学习，关键在于打好基础——知识基础、方法基础、人格基础。

因此，我们今年尝试了一些方法。第一，实行团队教学。我们要求由一个高职教授为主导，对教学工作提前提出设想、计划及要求，并且在教学计划的实施过程实行有效的监控；三个以上教师相互合作，能够对教学工作投入更多的精力；同时使学生有机会接触到不同类型的教师及教学风格，从而也提高学习兴趣和新鲜感。第二，重视师资梯队的培养，使学生通过过硬的基础理论的学习，能够有良好的自学能力和思维方式。这可能与教育部提倡开设公选课矛盾，但只要学生可以掌握基本的知识，基本的方法，完全有能力自己完成；强调公选课只是主观臆断，打好基础才是重中之重。第三，注重对学生的人格培养。毕竟大学生活不同于高中，学生脱离了受保护的状态来到了大学，其实在许多方面是需要我们给学生以必要的引导。老师都要把对学生世界观、人生观以及人格培养的引导作为重任，帮助学生培养良好的人格。当然这些举措的效果还不明显，但我在与学生的交流中，一直谈到过以往我为本科新生所作的几次演讲，分别是《在吉林大学涵养知识分子品格》《以感恩的心对待生活》《坚守法律人的底线》和《抱着一种理想的职业生活情怀》。总的来说，我希望在专业学习的过程中同学们能够实现人格养成，学会感恩，坚守底线，成为一个专业素质过硬、职业道德良好的法律人。近来在司法界，出现了许多高官落马的事情，因此同学们要知道什么坚决不能去做，什么必须要做。

刘仁山教授：法学教育的繁荣、忧虑、光荣和梦想

中山大学法学院庆典上当我听到学生代表的那句话“今天是中大法学院的生日”，我觉得特别感动。在此，我代表中南财经政法大学6000多名师生对中山大学法学院表示衷心的祝贺和美好的祝愿。对于中国法学院的发展现状，我有四个词语可以概括我的心得：繁荣、忧虑、光荣、梦想。首先，繁荣是近年来法学发展的写照。元论是在校学生数量还是师资队伍，中国现在已经有了一个相当庞大的法学专业人员队伍，规模发展迅速，全国有630多所高校开设法学专业，在校学生约30万人。因此可以肯定地说，我们现在处于法学教育的盛世，可以看到法学教育的繁荣。其次，从理性的角度来看，则是忧虑。培养法律研究者对于我国目前的法学本科教育来说并不现实，因此培养法律工作者更为重要。然而现实中却存在很多问题。例如，对于中国司法考试，法学本科教育应该迎合、忽视或者居于其间，这是一直困扰的问题；中国法学教育队伍的庞大与就业率不高这一现实矛盾，使许多同学对于工作前景感到迷茫；教师和学生联系的淡化也对法学教育产生了不利的影响；等等。因此，如何给高校法学院以更多的自主权来主导法学教育，如何给学生创造更为理想的环境，如何给教师“减负”，都是我们应该深入思考理性对待的问题。最后，对于法学教育的发展，我们应该怀着光荣和梦想。新中国的宪法向全世界庄严宣布“努力建设成为社会主义法治国家”，这如今成为我们肩上的光荣的任务和责任。尽管我们面对着非常严峻的就业形势，尽管我们承受着非常大的压力和挑战，尽管我们现在的法学教育的竞争的态势非常激烈；我们仍要放飞法治的理想，高唱法治的战歌。无论何时都应当坚信，我们今天所有的行为，都将为中国的民主法治进程贡献出自己的一份力量，为中国的民主法治建设锦上添花！

胡玉鸿教授：法学教育的定位、任务和应有的环节

这是很有意义的话题，法学教育是每一法学教育工作者和法学学生关注的。我想结合苏州大学法学院的情况，主要谈三个方面：

第一，法学教育的定位。有关法学教育的定位争论了很长时间，我认为法学教育仍是一种职业教育。职业教育是从培养人才的知识结构，面向社会服务的层面来讲的,毕竟我们绝大部分学生要到司法实践部门,充任法律职业者。这是法学院办学的基本目标,因此我们的教育模式也应当围绕法律职业教育展开。有些人可能会误解,认为职业教育和素质教育是完全对立的,我认为并不如此。因为工匠式的教育可能不会关注人格和理想;但法律教育不一样,它毕竟是解决人际纠纷,调整人际关系所制定的规则,脱离社会也就没有法学教育。因此,法学教育的职业性和素质培养可以完整结合。法律职业教育涵盖三方面内容:其一为职业思维。老师教给学生的不应只是知识,而是方法或思维。同质的法律共同体首先在思维上是同质的,我们对法律问题有相似的看法,对法律有基本相似的信念和理想。法律思维有四类,一是规则思维,任何一个法律职业者包括法学院学生都应有这样的意识——要尊重规则,此规则指法律要素的规则,“禁止向一般条款逃逸”,这要求我们审视任何法律问题都要结合具体规则进行,而不是跳出规则考虑所谓的民意或情理,这是法科学生应有的思维态势;二是逻辑思维,杨仁寿先生的《法学方法论》和拉伦茨的《法学方法论》都很注重逻辑能力的培养,法律在很大程度上需要逻辑的推导;三是类型思维,它更多指的是对法律当中某一本质固定或能涵盖其他情况的情况进行分析和归纳;四是情理思维,只有在规则、逻辑和类型都不适用时,才能考虑情理。其二为职业知识,这是我们课堂上教授的。其三为职业人格,这是法学教育不能缺乏的。

第二,法律教育的任务。我认为重在能力的培养,而不是知识的灌输。法科学生必须具备三种能力:一是概括能力。对自己思想和对别人思想的概括。现在中外法学资料非常多,我们怎样从中发现区别,概括出法学发展的趋势,非常重要。同时,我们也要清晰有层次地概括出自己的想法。二是分析能力。我们需要从法律条文中分析出字词句中隐含的意义,从事实的蛛丝马迹中提炼案件的脉络,通过案例分析法律关系的属性,涉及的当事人。三是表达能力。法律人终身与语言文字打交道,所以说良好的语言表达能力或文字表达能力非常重要。现在中国学生外语越来越好,中文越来越差,这让我们忧虑。梳理思想,表达观点。法律文书本身就是语言文字综合能力的概括,法庭论辩需要能够打动人的口才。

第三,法律教育的环节。近几年,国内法学界法学方法和法学技术的研究非常热门。我们的教学中缺乏了这块内容。法理学由三方面构成:知识、原理、技术。技术除了法律解释和法律推理,其他的谈之甚少。技术主要分为三个方面:一是文本分析技术。一个法科学生能看懂法条,这是基本能力。假设我们将一部新颁布的法律发给高年级的学生,它的主要概念能不能概括,它的总则和分则之间有没有矛盾、同一个概念在不同场合是否保持同样的意思等,这种能力是正确解读法条的基础。现有教材中对此并不注重。比如刚才提到的类型思维是德国法学的概念，他们认为类型和概念不一样，有些法律名词是法律概念，有些只能称为法律类型。如“抢劫”，并不是一个概念，只应称为类型；因为它没法在内涵明确外延清晰的情况下作出完整准确的定位，只能作出这样的描述——“使用暴力、胁迫或者其他方法”——“其他方式”意味着只要达到暴力、胁迫相似效果的方式都可以归类为抢劫。这就是一个类型的问题。因此，文本分析技术很重要。二是事实发现技术。从法律技术规则角度讲事实，如何判断事实、如何确定事实，尤其是法律事实和客观真实之间存在的差异。比如证据的合法性可能无法涵盖证据的本质特征，应该以伦理性作为证据更本质的内容。因为，如果我们把刑讯逼供也规定在法律当中，它自然就合法了。可是证据之所以会排除某些事实，是因为这些事实是以损害了人的尊严的方式获得的，如侵犯了他人的隐私权、刑讯逼供；或者现在经常提到的钓鱼执法，利用了人性的缺陷，也不能成为证据。因此，证据需要去厘清一套事实发现的技术规则。三是法律适用技术，包括法律渊源的识别技术。对法官而言，他究竟应适用哪个法律文件、哪种法律规范、哪个法条、哪个规则来解决案子，这就存在选择和识别的问题。还有我们经常提到的法律解释、法律推理、利益衡量、漏洞填充、判决说理等，这些都应有一整套规则。因此，这方面也应逐步纳入法学本科教育内容当中，从而为培养合格的法律职业者提供知识上的支撑。

单文华教授：让我们的法学教育富有特色，符合需要

我是中山大学法律系毕业生，后来去英国剑桥大学等留学和任教，回来又在西安交通大学法学院任教。先后在中国和英国学习和任教，应该说对两国法学教育都有较全面了解。我一直在思考，如何让我们的法学教育有特色，符合同学们和社会的需要。我认为法学教育是培养知识、方法、人格三位一体。比较中英两国，知识方面都一样，但方法和人格两方面区别很大。在方法方面，本科教育中我借鉴了小班研讨这一形式，每节课对问题进行讨论，学期初给学生一个单子，告诉他们具体的教学安排和数目，讨论的题目分两种，一类是知识，另一类是案例分析。本科阶段使用这种教学方式，可以培养学生们较早地用法律人的思维思考问题、解决问题。当然，小班教学在实践方面存在困难，但我相信这些困难都是可以克服的。从人格培养角度，我们借鉴了导师制。牛津和剑桥大学实行的是双导师制，一个是负责指导大学生生活的导师（Tutor），其指导非常全面，从读书到日常生活细节，如住宿、奖学金、感情；另一个是负责课业的导师（Supervisor），他在自己的专业范围内为学生进行辅导。这种双导师制对学生人格成长非常关键，从生活和学业两方面培养学生人格的养成。但双导师制很奢侈，实践起来很困难。但我们已决定实行这种导师制，每位导师负责 10 个学生左右，每个老师学期初必须和学生见面，帮同学解惑，明确学习生活方向；平时老师须公布固定的工作时间，学生可以去找他讨论学习生活中遇到的问题。另外，在英国，L. L. M.（Master of Law）只有 1 年，可借鉴性不强。Ph. D.（Doctor of Philosophy）则与国内的博士培养模式区别很大，第一，在课程设置上国内要上很多课，英国只有一门研究方法课，各科教授系统地介绍各科的具体研究方法，作为一个研究型学位，给学生大量时间自己做研究；第二，在标准上要求有原创性的贡献，没有国别要求（主要是英语世界），因此其成果是在国际上有影响的。当然，最后，我想说，现在同学们的条件比我们好很多，如果我做到了什么，你们也一定能够做到，谨以此与大家共勉。

周长军教授：融通教育模式，立足于将法学教育定位为职业教育

我想介绍山东大学法学院今年开始开展的“4 + 2”法学 6 年融贯式教育。

这种模式的设置思路是：前 4 年进行本科教育，主要是法学知识方面的教育；后 2 年相当于研究生教育，主要是实习和法学职业教育（包括司法考试的课程）。这种培养模式的导向，立足于将法学教育定位为职业教育。这种模式开始于徐显明校长在中国政法大学的研究课题，这个课题在考察了美国、英国、德国、法国、日本、韩国的法学教育后得出三点结论：第一，这些国家基本上都将法学教育定位为职业教育。第二，法学教育基本上分为两块，专业学习和职业教育（实习），美国是学士后教育；英国是 3 年本科加 1 年职业培训和 2 年特定机构实习，基本上是 6 年；日本由法学院和法科大学院构成，法学院相当于本科，法科大学院相当于研究生，大概是 6 年或 6. 5 年；韩国进行了美国式的改革；德国是 4 年本科，进行第一次司法考试，然后进行职业方面的培训，接着是第二次司法考试，大概也是 6 年。第三，这些国家普遍将法律实务部门（法院、检察院）纳入到法学教育体系中，在法学教育中占很大比例，如实习、培训。中国法学教育的问题有：其一，重知识教育，轻职业技能教育和职业伦理教育。其二，法科学生的培养是学术化培养，法理很深，但案例不够。学生更多的是考虑就业，教学内容与学习意愿脱节。其三，法学培养层次很多，人才培养质量不高，且司法考试没有门槛限制，出现法学学生考不过非法学学生的现象。针对这些问题，我们提出了“4 + 2”6 年贯通教育模式。这次实验班是从 150 多名学生中选取了 30 名较优秀的学生，这些学生毕业后拿的是专业学位。可能有些人认为还是法学硕士学位高一些，但我们的培养目标是为这些同学进入“公检法司”做努力。与此制度相配套的，也是未来高等法学教育改革和司法考试改革所希望的提高法律职业门槛。这种模式前 4 年是法律知识的学习，然后拿出 1 年时间，在专门的实习基地实习。另外，我们也实行双导师制。与单文华院长所讲的不同,我们的双导师制是在学校给学生安排一位学校的老师,在实习以后再给他安排一位实务老师,两个老师的指导内容各不相同。

黄亚英教授:成本很高,但为提高培养的人才的水平,是必要的

反观近20多年来我国的法学教育,我认为主要有三个不够:法学办学的特色和个性化不够;创新人才的培养机制不够;法律职业技能和门槛的高度不够。为此,在法学本科教育中,深圳大学法学院采取了一些做法,例如,其一,设立教学指导委员会。教学指导委员会由30位成员组成,有教师代表、学生代表、家长代表、校友代表、公检法业务骨干、领导代表,委员会的成员们在开学期间可以随机监督课程设置,可以随堂听课和抽查。经过实践的检验,教学指导委员会取得了较佳效果。其二,是关于法学专业技能的培养。这主要是考虑到实践环节,专门有教学实践经费,在学生到司法实务部门实习以外,特地举办法律事务精英论坛,邀请来自司法领域各个方面的精英来给学生讲授,把讲座课程化,这是"请进来"与"走出去"的很好结合,弥补了单纯实习的不足。其三,法学是个经验的课程,应用法学即法律硕士,可以分为三类,即全日制法硕、在职法硕和法学法硕。对于他们的培养,主要通过给每类的法律硕士配备双导师,即为一个院内导师,另外聘请一个院外的公检法业务骨干作为导师。当然,这成本很高,但为提高培养的人才的水平,是必要的。此外,对法硕的授课,提倡一门课由多个老师授课,实现了团队教学,使学生博采众长。

侯利标教授:本科,有条件的,可以采取"圈养"的状态

法学教育本科是基础,打好基础是非常重要的。本科,有条件的,可以采取"圈养"的状态。本科学习,从专业知识方面,主要做好培养三种能力,第一是学习能力的培养,不在于单纯知识的传授,重要的是学习方法的传授。第二是实践能力的培养,职业化、实践技能的培养。第三是创新意识的培养,有意识才会有转化为具体应用的可能。厦门大学法学院的本科教育主要落实好了以下几个方面:一是针对新生迷茫问题的解决。为了让刚入学的学生尽快适应新生活、新学习,开设学科入门讲座这门新课,由公认的名师介绍相关学科基本概况和学习方法。二是本科生导师制。辅导员解决日常事务管理和政治思想工作方面的管理,导师是专任教师,解决学习问题、选课、教学等问题。三是学长辅助计划,带动低学年的学生学习和发展。四是职业生涯规划课程的开设,让新生一进校门就有个规划的认识,请老师和实务工作部门的校友等来传授。在专业知识传授方面,一是充实本科一线的教学力量,要求教授上本科的课,为其配备教学助理,从研究生中聘请,并培养年轻教师;二是增加讲座的数量,借助内外的力量;三是校园文化的建设，通过多些开展学术讲座把知识的传播、知识的理解和知识的巩固这三个环节串联起来。最后，在实践方面，注意建设教育实践基地，与公检法等实务部门联合，使学生定期接受培训与训练；另外聘请法官等优秀实务部门人才承担课程的教学和开设讲座，探讨典型案件和法律问题。

侯振发教授：在和国外的法学教育交流交融交锋中继续向前推进

武汉大学法学院和中大法学院都有很密切的联系，我们都有着共同的感受。作为法学院书记，我主管的比较宏观，就法学教育简单讲几点：首先，在法学本科教育方面，我们的一个做法是推行法语法学和德语法学，准备将其推广到本硕博等各阶段。其次，在研究生教育方面，我们是少数进行研究生培养机制改革的高校。关于新增的法律（法学）硕士专业，我们透过现象看本质，按照法学硕士来培养。最后，我想强调的是，中国法学教育的趋势必然是在和国外的法学教育交流交融交锋中继续向前推进。

蔡彦敏教授：诊所法律教育促使我们思考并付诸行动，使法学院培养出来的不是法律的工匠，而是具备更高的道德目标的法律人

当世纪之交我和我的同事一起探讨建立法律诊所项目时，法律诊所对我们来讲是既新鲜又朦胧。当时的动因实际上并不复杂，我们只是觉得传统的法学教育模式的缺陷令人缺乏成就感，不能满足培养优秀法学院学生的需要，也不能适应社会的需要，希望能够做些什么以改变这种状况。时光荏苒，在诊所教育实践多年以后，那些触动心扉的情景时常历历在目，一次次的课程让我对诊所法律教育与中国传统法学院课堂教学模式的不同有了直观的感受；一批又一批成长的诊所学生，令我们渐深感悟诊所法律教育的真谛，开始思考法学教育与社会责任的关系。

今天，法律诊所教育犹如星星之火在全国越来越多的高校孕育、诞生和成长。据统计，至 2009 年 10 月，中国诊所法律教育专业委员会（CCCLE）已有成员 115 个；有 76 所院校开设了法律诊所课程，共有诊所 101 个；不同院校的法律诊所各具特色，形成了各个专门性法律诊所，如劳动者权益保护诊所、公益法诊所、弱者权利保护诊所、妇女权益保护诊所、公民权利保护诊所、刑事法律诊所、环境法诊所、诉讼诊所、立法诊所等；全国已有 553 名法律诊所教师，其中校外教师 84 名（包括律师、法官、检察官等）；培养了 17,063 名法律诊所学生；承办法律援助案件 3432 起；提供免费法律咨询等服务 27,248 起。诊所法律教育诞生与蓬勃发展的景象，是中国内生性需求因素和外生性支援因素互相积极作用的结果。过去 10 年中，中国的法学教育者中的一批先知们在传统法学教育的背景下开始了法学教育改革的积极探索,将诊所法律教育引入中国,复旦大学、华东政法大学、武汉大学、中南财经政法大学、北京大学、清华大学、中国人民大学、中山大学、西北政法大学、四川大学等中国著名高校成为我国较早启动诊所法律教育的高校;同时,美国福特基金会、岭南基金会和一些大学等机构为诊所法律教青的建设与发展提供了强有力的资金和资源方面的支持;而来自美国和世界其他一些国家的一批诊所教师为中国诊所法律教育的建设和发展倾注了他们真挚的诚意和勤勉的努力。

2008 年夏季,美国法律纪实文学《法庭风暴——美国耶鲁师生诉战总统》一书中文版发行。该书是 CCCLE 向中国法律院校师生重点推荐的著作,其故事是在耶鲁法学院及其诊所法律教育的背景下渐次展开的,它生动地传达了诊所法律教育"在实践中学习"和"通过公益服务而学习"的双元价值理念以及以培养兼具法律实践能力与社会责任感的法学院学生的法学教育目标。作为该书的译者,我在翻译中深为耶鲁诊所师生的故事所震撼,同时也更为深切地认识到,法学教育的价值目标问题,实际上不仅是美国法学院所面对的问题,同样也是中国法学院所面对的问题;而且,对于正处于从传统走向现代化过程之中的中国法学教育而言,对该问题恰当回应的紧迫性更为凸显。诊所法律教育促使我们思考并付诸行动,将法学教育与社会责任紧密联系;使法学院培养出来的不是法律的工匠,而是具备更高的道德目标的法律人。

作为中国法律诊所教育的践行者和推动者,10 年的亲身经历令我们深谙,历经着迅速的经济发展与社会转型的中国,亟须对社会弱势群体、公共利益以及法律人职业能力与职业道德等问题给予高度关注。中国法学教育的品质决定着中国法律职业以及法治社会建设的品质,而诊所法律教育对于塑造和提升中国法律职业共同体的品质具有不可代替、不可或缺的重要意义。她为中国法学教育从传统的单纯法学知识与理论的传输模式到更具社会适应性的法律职业教育模式转化提供了一种具体的路径和实施的平台,并使法学教育在培养学生法学理论和职业技能的同时,注重对其职业道德和社会责任感的培育。相信这一观点会得到越来越多的法学教育同行们的认同,相信中国的法律诊所教育方兴未艾,任重道远。

附:中山大学法律诊所学生们眼中的法学教育

汪同学:诊所法律教育的魅力就在于,它在把学生推向复杂甚或残酷的社会现实的同时,也在引导学生学会如何从中获取积极正面的力量。诊所课程使我一方面有机会在踏入社会之前就对其不完美有了充分的心理准备,另一方面也激励我在这个不完美的社会工作中继续保持对法律的信心和对正义的信仰。

严同学:参加法律诊所的经历是我的研究生生活的一个亮点。外来打工者在咨询过程中表现出来的对自己境况的无奈,极大地触动了我。他们不仅让我了解到许多社会问题,也让我意识到个人的努力尽管渺小,但却有可能帮助甚至改变一些人、哪怕一个人。

陈同学:诊所课程令我最难忘的是我第一次代理我的当事人出庭的经历。虽然庭前进行了充分准备,但刚一站在法庭上时,我的双腿止不住地颤抖。而当我真的开始向法庭陈述案件时,紧张感一下子消失了——当我后来作为一名检察官单独出庭时,诊所学习与办案的经历,使我感到从容和自信多了。

潘同学:法律诊所让我提早进入了社会、遭遇了挫折;但在关键时刻,诊所的老师把我从现实的黑暗中重新拉回到理想的光明。对我而言,法律诊所不仅是实践的洗练平台,还是法律职业理想的涤荡熔炉以及法学研究之路的起点。

肖同学:是法律诊所教育的经历令我做出并践行了赴西北做法律援助志愿者的决定,我一直认为诊所法律教育和西部法律援助的经历是我人生无比珍贵的财富。现在虽然我是一名商务律师,但我依然特别关注公益服务领域,也一直在自己的职业发展中寻找与公益服务的新的契合点。

汪同学:虽然在法律诊所主要是培养我们以准律师的身份为维护当事人的权利而努力;而检察官更经常是代表公权并以依法行使权力为主要职责。但两者都是法律职业,有根本性的共通点,那就是法律人的职业道德和社会使命。不论在怎样的工作岗位上,我始终不会忘记对现行法律和司法制度保持一种批判性敬畏——敬畏乃是出于对法与司法权威的坚定信仰,而带着批判的眼光则是基于对司法正义的不懈追求。

我国法学本科教育若干问题探讨*

法学本科教育在我国整个法学教育体系中居于举足轻重的地位。然而，我国现行的法学本科教育在许多方面都有待于改进与完善。事实上，我国有关方面近年来已经着手开展这项工作。鉴于此，本文拟对我国法学本科教育中的几个基本问题，包括培养目标、专业设置、课程体系与教学方法等问题作初步分析探讨。

一、培养目标问题

确立一个明确而适当的培养目标对于法学本科教育来说是至关重要的，因为培养目标在很大程度上将决定培养模式。通常，我们把法律人才分为两类：一类是学术型法律人才，或称“法学家”，主要指大学法学教授与研究机构研究员；另一类是应用型法律人才，或称“法律家”“法律匠”，主要指律师、法官、检察官、公证人、企业法律顾问等。[1] 尽管有许多法学院系喜欢自称为“法学家的摇篮”，但是应该承认，法学本科毕业生离法学家距离尚十分遥远。法学家的成就是一个长期积累的过程，仅仅凭借法学院系的本科教育就能够成为法学家，这是一个从没有实现也不太可能实现的梦想。[2] 正如美国大法官霍尔姆斯在题为“法学院的作用”的演讲中所说过的：“大师不是靠教育创制的，而是凭天赋自我造就的。自学之外的教育应注重让学生产生兴趣、形成目标。”[3] 从现实的角度来看，目前我国大多数的法学本科毕业生的主要流向也是法律实务部门，如律师事务所、法院、检察院、公司、政府部门等。国外的情况也大致如此。因此，我国多数学者认为，我国法学本科教育的主要培养目标应该定位为职业教育，即应用型法律人才的教育，而不是学术型法律人才的教育。[4]

---

* 本文发表在《社会科学研究》1998 年第 5 期。

〔1〕《为建设社会主义法制国家奠定基石》，法律出版社 1996 年版，第 268 页。

〔2〕方流芳：《中国法学教育观察》，载《比较法研究》1996 年第 2 期。

〔3〕Joel Seligaman ,The High Citadel: The Ingluence of Harvard Lan school. 215(1978).

〔4〕方流芳：《中国法学教育观察》，载《比较法研究》1996 年第 2 期。

当然,这并不意味着在大学法学本科教育中,可以忽视理论教育与学术能力的培养。这是因为,一方面,尽管法学本科教育的主要产品是应用型法律人才,但是,法学本科教育又是中国法学的总体教育体系中的一个组成部分,它必须为法学的硕士教育和博士教育提供人才。质言之,法学本科教育必须源源不断地为法学研究的高级人才、法学教师提供后备力量,特别重要的是为培养出中国自己的法学家奠定基础。这就需要保持一定的有质量的法学理论教育。另一方面,就我国法律教育的现状来看,法学本科教育相对于成人教育、自学考试、电大教育而言,具有理论、学术力量上的优势,这就决定了法学本科教育不能目光短浅,将自己仅仅限定为一般的法律职业培训,从而等同于其他类型的法学教育。

对于应用型法律人才的培养,在世界各国也各有侧重。其中,以美国和德国最为典型。美国的法学教育特别侧重于对律师的培养,只有资深、出色的律师才有可能被选为法官;同时,那些有成就的律师、检察官和法官也往往被聘为法学院的教授,其中对教育深感兴趣并学业不凡的,或许会就此投入专任教授的队伍。[5] 德国则刚好相反,依德国法律,所有的法律职业者都必须经过两次国家考试,首先取得法官的职务资格,而后才能担任律师。[6] 法国、日本等国家的法学教育体制与德国的体制相似,只是其侧重点不像德国那么明显。不同的培养目标必然导致不同的教学模式。例如,在美国,法科学生从一开始就要接受律师思维模式的训练;而在德国,法科大学生的培养则是从头到尾按照法官的行为举止要求进行的。对此,本文将在后面作进一步讨论。

我国目前的法律人才培养机制与日本模式比较类似。按我国现行有关法律,大学本科毕业生经过一段时间的见习,通过相应的资格考试,可以取得律师、法官、检察官的任职资格。有些学者基于社会对律师的巨大需求,提出在未来的若干年中,我国法学本科教育应以培养律师作为重点。我们认为,这种观点虽然有一定合理性,但是容易导致法学本科教育导向性的错误。法学本科教育应该培养律师,诚属责无旁贷,律师是法学本科毕业生的主要流向且社会迫切需要大量的律师,这也是事实。但是,这些都并不意味着法学本科教育重点就应该放在培养律师上。因为正规法学本科教育周期比较长,招生的计划性也比较强,所以,与其他社会力量所开办的各种短期培训班相比,用高校十分有限的教育资源来急功近利式地培训律师的做法是不可取的。[7] 而且,就我国的法治现状而言,法院、检察院等执法部门也需要甚至是更需要有大量法学本科毕业生去充实。因此,正规

〔5〕《为建设社会主义法制国家奠定基石》,法律出版社 1996 年版,第 269 页。
〔6〕同上书,第 268 页。
〔7〕孙东东:《市场经济体制下高等法学本科教育课程结构之我见》,载《中外法学》1995 年第 4 期。

的法学本科教育应该充分发挥自己的优势，把培养律师与培养法官、检察官等各方面的法律人才同时并重，即应旨培养“法律通才”，而不可偏废任何一个方面。

二、专业设置问题

当前，我国高等法学本科教育一般设四个专业：(1)法学专业；(2)国际法专业；(3)经济法专业；(4)国际经济法专业。这种设置对培养各类法律专门人才曾起到一定的积极作用。但是随着改革开放的深入进行，特别是社会主义市场经济体制的确立和逐步发展，这种专业划分越来越不适应新的社会需求，产生出越来越多的弊端。[8] 首先，过分强调“专”的一面，不利于学生完整地掌握法律知识，而且，这种硬性摊派专业的做法伤害了学生学习的积极性，也造成学生毕业就职难的现象；其次，专业设置被教研室的行政设置所巩固，不利于教师跨室、跨专业开课的积极性的发挥，从而造成人力资源的严重浪费；再次，有的专业由于明显失去人才市场需求而形同虚设，乏人问津；最后，“双专业”的做法虽然能调动学生学习的主动性，但是却使学生课程负担大大加重，忙于应付考试，知识难以消化，因而也很难达到预期的目的。因此，取消专业成了共同的呼声。

但是，在我国目前的这种高等教育体制下，取消法学专业设置条件尚未成熟，“专业”对于各法律院系来说还具有重要意义。首先，专业意味着分享“计划内招生”配额的资格。按我国体制，国家教委按一定比例确定每一种专业的计划内招生人数，然后按专业确定每一所院校的招生人数。只有国家教委许可设立某一专业的院校，才能分得该专业的招生配额。因此，一所院校设立新的专业或者将原有的专业拆细，意味着该校招生配额的增加或者该校内部分享招生配额的渠道增加。其次，专业意味着院校内部机构设置。各院校按照专业来设置系、研究所、教研室等机构。每一专业通常有一个机构为代表，专业与机构按同样的比例和速度增加。无论是一个法学系分解为若干个系(所)，还是一个教研室扩展为系(所)，都可以从原班人马中产生出更多的“系主任”“副系主任”“教研室主任”。这显然能给在其位而谋其政的人带来实惠。最后，专业同时还是一种学位授予权的特许制度。国家教委直接决定一个院校能授予何种学科、何种等级的学位，国家教委许可的“学士点”“硕士点”“博士点”一律按专业分类设立。

因此，除了3年制的大专之外，每一专业都是一个本科项目或者研究生项目。最后，专业还是一种教授聘任权的特许制度。一所学校要获得教授聘任权，必须先后得到地方教委和国家教委单项许可，即没有一所院校能够获得通用的教授聘任

---

[8] 武树臣：《淡化专业与课程体系的调整》，载《中外法学》1996年第2期。

权，而只能就某一学科、某一专业的教授聘任权申请专项许可。但是，这种申请很难得到批准，因为一旦学校获得教授聘任权，就意味着教委失去了这项权力。[9]

因此，目前比较现实的做法是淡化专业。淡化专业是为取消专业作准备的，是一种过渡措施。淡化专业无论对于社会、对学生还是对教师来说，都具有积极意义。从社会的角度来看，淡化专业能够更好地培养法律通才，培养为当今市场经济和法治社会所迫切需要的、合格的法律人才。从学生的角度来看，淡化专业能够调动学生自主学习的积极性，为他们将来自主择业和就职后自我更新知识与能力打下良好的基础。从教师的角度来看，淡化专业能够调动教师的教学积极性，实现一专多能，完善教师的知识结构与更新教师的知识，改变因人设课的现象，改变教研室之间人为阻隔与重复浪费的现象，从而降低教学成本，提高办学效率。因此，淡化专业可以说是势在必行。事实上，一些法律院系已经开始进行这种探索。例如，厦门大学法律系自 1997 年以来，就开始实行按系招生，而不再分专业招生。学生到了第三年级的时候再开始考虑专业的选择问题。我们认为，这是一种比较合适可行的过渡办法。当然，这只是一种临时措施，待条件成熟后，尚应进一步取消本科的专业划分。为此，我们建议，国家教育行政部门与其他部门应协调行动，俾使全国所有的法律院系统一行动，同时取消大学本科的专业划分，以免先行采取这种措施的院系的利益受到损害。

三、课程体系问题

课程体系的改革应该是法学本科教学改革的核心。在 1996 年 1 月召开的高等法学教育改革研讨会上，专家们一致认为，我国目前的法学本科课程设置至少存在着以下几个方面的主要问题：[10] 第一，一些不必要的课程占据了宝贵的学习时间。第二，课时交叉、重复现象在各校都存在。由于教研室的设置，把教师限定在一个相对狭小的理论领域，妨碍了多学科的交流和探讨。第三，课程设置的先后顺序缺乏科学性，忽视了知识的循序渐进的特点。例如，法理学现在作为基础课，一般是在第一个学期上，一年级学生很难接受。第四，课程设置混乱，甚至有颁布一部法就开设一门课的现象。为此，专家们建议：首先，国家教委应组织专家对法学课程体系作出科学的论证，只有那些以系统理论为基础的法律，才能作为一门课开设；同时，还应论证学生需要的基础知识。其次，应在课程体系中加入职业道德教育课程。因为法律职业的道德问题十分重要。最后，关于实习问题，目前各校的做法不一，有的时间长些，如一学期，有的时间短些，如两个月；有的比较

---

〔9〕 方流芳：《中国法学教育观察》，载《比较法研究》1996 年第 2 期。

〔10〕《高等法学教育改革研讨会会议纪要》，载《中外法学》1996 年第 2 期。

重视,有的只流于形式。因此,一种意见认为,应把实习纳入总体的教育制度改革来考虑,在适当的时候取消实习。理由是:学生在学校学习时间有限,实习占去了3~5门课的学习时间,今后学校改为收费上学,学生不会花钱不上课而去实习的,所以对实习问题应重新考虑。〔11〕

对于课程体系问题,不少专家还专门撰文提出了自己的看法。许多专家认为,应该适当减少必修课门数。例如,苏力教授提出,应在规定法学本科必需修满的法学课程总时数的前提下,重新确定一般法学基础教育的必修课程,将其减少至20门左右。这20门课大致是:中国司法制度、刑法、刑事诉讼法、民法通论、民事诉讼法、公司企业法、合同法、反不正当竞争法和反垄断法、税法、侵权法(消费者权益保护法)、知识产权保护法、法理学和法律社会学(或法律经济学分析)、票据法、法律公文写作和模拟法庭、不动产法、国际私法、国际贸易法或国际商法、中国宪法和行政法、法律职业道德。〔12〕 而武树臣教授则认为,法学本科的必修课程应该减至11门,即中国当代社会与现行法律制度、法律专业语文、法理学、宪法、民法、民事诉讼法、刑法、刑事诉讼法、行政法与行政诉讼法、中国法史(二选一)、外国法史(二选一)。武树臣教授进而提出,在必修课程之外应该建立专业课程群,作为指导性的课程体系,并以它来取代原先的专业设置。专业课程群应分四种:

(1)理论法学课程群——培养法学理论研究人才、公务员;(2)公法(国家法)课程群——培养公务员、律师、司法人员;(3)民商法课程群——培养律师、法官、经济管理人才;(4)刑事法课程群——培养律师、法官、检察官、公务员。与此同时,他还为不同的课程群拟就了具体的课程。〔13〕

1997年10月,国家教委法学教育指导委员会在广州召开会议,初步拟定了法学类本科专业核心(基础)课程体系方案。它们包括宪法、法理学、民法、刑法、行政法与行政诉讼法、刑事诉讼法、民事诉讼法、国际法、国际私法、国际经济法、经济法、知识产权法、商法、中国法制史,一共14门。这个方案涵盖了目前我国法学的几乎所有的部门,而且十分精简,无疑有着相当的合理性。但是,它仍然有值得完善的地方:一方面,有些十分重要的课程没有列入这个方案中,例如法律逻辑学、法律语文、法律职业道德以及经济学等课程。法律逻辑学对于培养法科学生的逻辑思维能力来说具有十分重要的意义;法律语文对于培养学生的法律语言表达能力和书面表达能力来说更是十分关键;法律职业道德对于法科学生和法律职业人员的重要意义已如前述;在当今国际与国内环境下,法科本科生有必要掌握

〔11〕《高等法学教育改革研讨会会议纪要》,载《中外法学》1996年第2期。
〔12〕苏力:《法学本科教育研究和思考》,载《比较法研究》1996年第2期。
〔13〕武树臣:《淡化专业与课程体系的调整》,载《中外法学》1996年第2期。

一定的经济学知识和经济学的分析方法，因此有必要设立经济学这一门必修课程（当然，在少数学校，经济学是作为全设公共必修课来开的，自应另当别论）。另一方面，这个方案虽然提出了有关的课程名称但尚未提出它们的学分与教学安排。这就使有关课程的落实仍然取决于各校自主安排。如果国家教委能够提供一个指导性的教学计划方案，必然有助于全国法学本科教学工作的改善。

以厦门大学法律系为例。适应淡化专业的需要，厦门大学法律系调整了本科教学计划。在新的教学计划中，除了全校性的公共必修课，如中国革命史、政治经济学、哲学、军事理论、英语、体育、计算机应用技术等之外，法科本科生的“公共”（基础）必修课包括法学基础理论、宪法学、刑法学、国际公法、中国法律史、刑事诉讼法、民事诉讼法、行政法原理、国际私法、外国法律史、法律文书、国际经济法导（概）论、民法总论、物权法、婚姻家庭法、债权法。与上述国家教委的方案相比，该计划中的必修课多了法律文书一门，少了经济法、商法与知识产权法三门，而将民法学细分为四门课程，包括民法总论、物权法、债权法及婚姻家庭法，体现了强化民法基础的倾向。在必修课中增加法律文书一门有其必要性与合理性，其理由已如前述。将民法扩开作为四门课来上，也有它的合理性。但是，作为重要法律与法学分支的经济法、商法与知识产权法等却未被列入必修（基础）课程之内，未免有失偏颇。

除法学公共的必修课以外，该教学计划还为各个不同的专业设置了不同的专业必修课。例如，国际经济法专业的专业必修课有商法概论、国际贸易法、国际投资法、国际货币金融法等；法学专业则有经济法概论、公司法、知识产权法、海商法、劳动法等。必修课之外，是大量的选修课，各专业所开列的选修课有所不同，有的多一些，有的少一些。其中，国际经济法专业的选修课最多，有 25 门。从中我们可以看出，作为取消专业的过渡阶段安排，该教学计划确实反映了淡化专业的总体取向，尽管在具体的课程设置上仍不无修改完善的余地。

四、教学方法问题

不同的培养目的与法律传统往往决定了不同的教学方法。例如，在旨在培养法官的德国与旨在培养律师的美国在法学的教学方法上就存在重大差别。美国所提倡的是案例教学法；而德国仍旧采取的是比较传统的教学方法。在德国，典型的情况是，由法学教授对教学内容进行处置、摘要和阐述，学生不需要去准备或重新组织所学的内容，甚至也不需要去听课，学生往往被设置在某种特设的事实情境中，且往往会按照传授法律观念的方式教学，其目的是使学生能合理利用各种法律、法规来理解各种事实背景。与美国法学院强调让学生进行争辩和辩论不同，德国法学院的学生往往被要求作出对“法律背景”的公正的意见。换言之,它是按照对法官的行为举止的要求,而不是按照对辩护人或开业律师要求来训练的。[14]

流行的案例教学法,又称哈佛教学法,一般认为起源于1871年,是由哈佛大学法学院的教授兰代尔所首创。案例教学法运用具体的案件来分析基本的法律概念和原则,它是将法律专业理论与律师办案实践相结合的教学方法。它的一般做法是教师选取有代表性的案例,编纂成各种案例集作为教材分发给学生学习。这些案例常常是一个已确立的法律理论的代表,同时也是法律原则的总结。这些案件事实常常含有疑难的法律上的争议点,如订立合同的诸条件是否合理?杀人者是否具备杀人罪所必需的精神上的能力和故意?一个妇女宪法上的权利是否被雇主剥夺?等等。他们认为这些案例所提供的良好的法律推理模式,同提出一个正确的法律结论具有同等价值。

案例教学法的基本方式是问答式或讨论式,或称苏格拉底式。教师上课不是采用课堂讲授的方法,一般不讲序言、概论、定义之类的抽象的东西,一上课就开门见山组织引导学生分析案例,提出问题和学生共同讨论,即使几百人的大课也不例外。案例教学法要求学生事前准备,阅读有关案例的大量的参考书,在课堂上阐述、分析、评论、比较具体案例的实际情况,像律师和法官那样运用原始材料,概括提炼自己的基本意见。在课堂上,不仅教师可以提问学生,也容许学生提问,还允许学生发表与教师不同的看法,允许学生打断教师的讲述进行争论。如果学生在课堂上不爱提问、不爱发言,他的分数反而会受到影响。美国法学院实施案例教学法的主要原因在于:一方面,美国是一个普通法国家,判例在其法律体系中占据非常重要的地位。另一方面,案例教学法也确实有助于培养学生的法律推理和表达能力。它的优点是:理论用实际案例来印证,易懂易记、形象生动、印象深刻;通过真实案例教学,有助于增强学生处理实际问题的能力;有利于变教师讲学生听的单项灌输,为教与学的双向交流,促使学生学得更主动。[15]

我国法学的教学方法通常是以解释法律概念为中心的课堂讲授,主要是灌输现成的理论,而忽视探索理论产生的背景和原因。常见的情况是教师讲知识,学生记笔记,考试时背笔记。这种教学方法虽说源自德日,但比后者更见呆板。为此,不少人提出要改变这种课堂上以教师为主的习惯,强调学生的主动性和参与性;鼓励学生课下阅读,甚至对个别概念和词语都要仔细琢磨;课堂上教员提问,学生回答,并可以相互讨论。要教给学生分析问题和解决问题的方法,而不是问题的结论。[16]

---

〔14〕《为建设社会主义法制国家奠定基石》,法律出版社1996年版,第309页。

〔15〕同上书,第284页。

〔16〕《高等法学教育改革研讨会会议纪要》,载《中外法学》1996年第2期。

在这方面,不少学者都提到了案例教学法;并强调,应对司法审判中的案例,而不是虚构的案例进行分析,要运用模拟法庭等教学手段。过去习惯于用案例说明法律问题、条文和定义,但很少用案例作为一种思考、一种方法和一种能力。这种情况应有所改变。显然,这方面,美国的案例教学法值得认真研究借鉴。需要注意的是,这种借鉴不等于生搬硬套。这不仅因为我国与美国的法律背景之间存在巨大的差异,更因为案例教学法本身也不是完美无缺的。事实上,近年来,美国反对这种教学法的意见也不少,主要是一些教师不善于运用这种方法,有些学生课前不预习,以致上课听不懂,不能与教师有机配合。〔17〕 可见,对案例教学法的理解与借鉴不应该简单化,而有必要深入研究,从而探索出适合中国实际的案例教学法来。

与案例教学法相关的一个重要的问题就是有关案例的编写。目前我国之所以没有在法学教学中普及案例教学法,一个很重要的原因便是没有适当的案例,这有待于法律教育工作者与法律实务部门共同努力、积极配合。目前,有的政法院校已经就这方面作出尝试。如西南政法大学已尝试将刑诉教材分为两本,第一本是刑事诉讼法的基本原理,包括介绍外国的理论、我国已取得的成果;第二本是刑事诉讼法案例教材。〔18〕 显然,这是一种有益的尝试,值得加以推广、完善。

---

〔17〕《为建设社会主义法制国家奠定基石》,法律出版社 1996 年版,第 284 页。

〔18〕《高等法学教育改革研讨会会议纪要》,载《中外法学》1996 年第 2 期。

第七编 仲裁实践 Part VII

1313 -1378

关于×××投资有限公司与×××国投资条约仲裁案的专家意见书（提交新加坡高等法院）*

In the Matter of Section 10 of the International Arbitration Act(Cap. 143A)
And
In the Matter of Order 69A of the Rules of Court(Cap. 322, R 5, 2006 Rev Ed)
Between
THE GOVERNMENT OF THE LAO PEOPLE'S DEMOCRA TIC REPUBLIC
(No ID exists)
. ...Plaintiff
And
×××× INVESTMENTS LIMITED (hereinafter as A)
(ID No. not known)
...Defendant

AFFIDAVIT OF WENHUA SHAN

I, Wenhua Shan of 28 Xianning West Road, Xi'an 710049, Shaanxi Province, People's Republic of China, do solemnly and sincerely make oath/affirm and say as follows:

1. I am the founding Dean and University Chair Professor of International Law at Xi'an Jiaotong University, People's Republic of China ("PRC"), and a Senior Fellow of the Lauterpacht Centre for International Law at the University of Cambridge. I am a "State Specially Recruited Expert", which is "the highest title of honour established by the PRC for the high level experts introduced from overseas". I am also a "Yangtze River Chair Professor", "State Council Special Allowance Expert' Arbitrator of China International Economic and Trade Arbitration Commission (CIETAC), and Legal Advisor of the People's Government of Shaanxi Province.

2. I have been lecturing in and teaching international law since 1996, with a parti-

* In Wang Gungwu and Zheng Yongnian (eds.), China and the New International Order, Part I, Routledge, 2008. Originating Summons No. xx of 2014 Summons No. xxx of 2014.

cular focus on international investment, trade and arbitration law. At the same time, I have been practising Chinese and international law since 1994 when I became a fully licensed Attorney-at-Law in the PRC. I am now practising as a Senior Counsel at Beijing Kangda Law Firm(Xi'an Branch). Copies of my *curriculum vitae* and practising certificate are exhibited at Annex 1 and Annex 2 to "WS-l", respectively.

3. I have been engaged by the Defendant to prepare an expert report for the purpose of these proceedings. A copy of my report is now shown to me and exhibited as "WS - 1"("Report").

4. I confirm that I prepared the Report exhibited as "WS-l" in my personal capacity as a specialist in the field and I accept fully responsibility for the Report. For the reasons explained in the Report, I believe that my opinions stated therein are correct.

5. I have read and understood the duties of an expert witness set out in Order 40A of the Rul es of Court, Singapore. I understand that it is my duty to assist the Court on matters within my expertise, and that this duty overrides any obl igation to the person from whom I have received instructions or by whom I am paid. I understand that in giving this Report, my duty is to the Court and I confirm that I have compl ied with this duty.

AFFIRMED/SWORN by the above named

Wenhua Shan

this 18th day of March 2014

This affidavit is fil ed on behal f of the Defendant.

TO ALL TO WHOM THESE PRESENTS SHALL COME, I xxxx of the City of London NOTARY PUBLIC by royal authority duly admitted and sworn and authorised to practise throughout England and Wales DO HEREBY CERTIFY that on the day of the date hereof in Abingdon, Oxford shire, England before me personally came and appeared WENHUA SHAN, holder of Chinese passport number xxxxxxxx and whose personal identity I attest, the (General Notary) deponent named and described in the foregoing affidavit, WHO in my presence by solemn affirmation by him taken in due form of law did solemnly and sincerely affirm and depose to the truth of the several matters and things mentioned and contained in the said affidavit.

IN WINTNESS WHEREOF I have hereunto set my hand and seal of office at London, England this eighteenth day of March two thousand and fourteen.

THIS IS THE EXHIBIT MARKED"WS - 1" REFERREDTO IN THE AFFIDAVIT OF WENHUASHAN AFFIRMED THIS 18th DAY OF MARCH 2014

BEFORE ME

Notary Public London, England (× × × × × ×)

A NOTARY PUBLIC

Notary Public London England
(Christopher G. Higgins)

SAVILLE & Co
NOTARIES PUBLIC
One Carey Lane
London EC2V 8AE
Telephone: +44 (0)20 7920 0000
Facsimile: +44 (0)20 7920 0088
www.savillenotaries.com

EXPERT REPORT OF PROFESSOR WENHUA SHAN

Ⅰ. INTRODUCTION

1. I, Wenhua Shan, am the founding Dean and University Chair Professor of International Law at the Law School of Xi'an Jiaotong University, People's Republic of China ("PRC"), and a Senior Fellow of the Lauterpacht Centre for International Law("LCIL") at the University of Cambridge. I am a "State Specially Recruited Expert", which is "the highest title of honour established by the PRC for the high level experts introduced from overseas", and the "Yangtze River Chair Professor", which is regarded as "the highest academic honour given by the People's Republic of China" in the legal field.

2. I am a "State Council Special Allowance Expert" awarded by the PRC Government, an arbitrator of the China International Economic and Trade Arbitration Commission("CIETAC"), and Legal Advisor to the People's Government of Shaanxi Province.

3. As described in further detail below, I have been teaching international law since 1996, with a particular focus on international investment, trade and arbitration law. At the same time, I have been practising Chinese and international law since 1994 when I became a fully licensed Attorney-at-Law in the PRC. I am now practising as a Senior Counsel of Beijing Kangda Law Firm(Xi'an Branch). Copies of my detailed curriculum

vitae and practising certificate are annexed hereto as "Annex 1" and "Annex 2", respectively.

4. I have been approached by the Defendant to act as an expert witness to provide my opinion on certain issues of PRC and international law arising out of Originating Summons 24 of 2014("OS 24").

5. For the reasons stated herein, I have specific expertise in the issues on which I was asked to opine, and I believe that my opinion is correct.

6. I have read Order 40A of the Rules of Court, Singapore. I understand that it is my duty to assist this Honourable Court on matters within my expertise, and that this duty overrides any obligation to the person from whom I have received instructions or by whom I am paid. I understand that, in giving this report, my duty is to the Honourable Court and I confirm that I have complied with that duty.

Ⅱ. PROFESSIONAL EXPERIENCE AND QUALIFICATIONS

7. I received my first law degree in 1991 from Zhongshan(Sun Yet-Sen) University. I then received a Masters of Economics from Jinan University in 1994, and a Ph. D. in Law from Xiamen University in 1996. In 2004, I received my second Ph. D. From Trinity College, University of Cambridge.

After I completed my first Ph. D. at Xiamen, I started to teach as a Lecturer and then Associate Professor of Law at Xiamen University School of Law. During 1998 and 1999, I was a Visiting Fellow at LCIL at the University of Cambridge, before I embarked on a second Ph. D. at Cambridge in September 1999.

8. I taught at Oxford Brookes University in England, as a Lecturer, Senior Lecturer, Reader and Professor of International Law from 2002 till 2013, when I took up a Senior Fellowship from the LCIL. From 2005 till 2008, I worked at Xi'an Jiaotong University, on secondment from Oxford Brookes, as the Dean of the College of Humanities and Social Sciences and the University Tengfei Chair Professor of International Law. In 2008, I started to work on a full time basis as the founding Dean of the School of Law at Xi'an Jiaoto University. Meanwhile I retained my job at England on a part time basis.

9. I have been practising Chinese and international law since 1994 when I received a full licence as a PRC attorney. Over the years I have practiced at law firms based in Guangzhou, Xiamen and Shanghai, and I am now practising at Beijing Kangda Law Firm (Xi'an Branch) as a Senior Counsel. I am an appointed arbitrator at CIETAC and the South China International Economic and Trade Arbitration Commission(SCIA)/Shenzhen Court of International Arbitration, among others. I am also Legal Advisor to the People's Government of Shaanxi Province.

10. I have published more than ten books in international and comparative law by English and PRC publishers, and numerous articles in journals such the European Journal of International Law and the American Journal of Comparative Law. I am the founding Editor-in-Chief of The Chinese Journal of Comparative Law published by the Oxford University Press and Editor-in-General of the "China and International Economic Law Series" and "Silk Road Series on International and Comparative Law".

11. Many of my books and articles concern the PRC and its bilateral investment treaty regime, including "Chinese Investment Treaties: Policy and Practice (OUP 2009)", which I co-authored with Professor Norah Gallagher, formerly Director of the Investment Treaty Forum at the British Institute for International and Comparative Law. I have also given testimony on the EU-China investment treaty before the European Parliament and taught at the UNCTAD-APEC Regional Training Course on Core Elements of International Investment Agreements in the APEC Region.

12. As a "State Specially Recruited Expert" and "State Council Special Allowance Expert", I have led a team of experts to advise and support the PRC Government on certain key investment treaty negotiations, and have personally participated in some of the negotiations. More generally, I have advised foreign governments, international organizations, and transnational corporations on international investment, trade, arbitration and other legal matters. I should emphasize, however, that I submit this expert report in my personal capacity as an expert in PRC and international law, independent from the PRC or foreign governments to which I have provided professional services.

Ⅲ. FACTS AND ISSUES

14. I understand that the present proceedings arise out of an investor-state dispute between the Government of the Lao People's Democratic Republic ("Laos") and A Investments Limited an entity incorporated in the Macau Special Administrative Region ("Macau SAR"). This dispute has been referred to arbitration in PCA Case No. 2013 – 13 ("PCA Arbitration") and an award on jurisdiction was issued on 13 December 2013 ("Award" attached as "Annex 3"). In the Award, the international tribunal ruled that it had jurisdiction to arbitrate A's expropriation claims under Article 8(3) of the Agreement between the Government of the People's Republic of China and the Government of the Lao People's Democratic Republic Concerning the Encouragement and Reciprocal Protection of 1nvestments dated 31 January 1993 ("PRC-Laos Treaty"). The tribunal also ruled that the PRC-Laos Treaty extends to Macau SAR such that the tribunal has jurisdiction over Macau investors such as A under the PRC-Laos Treaty.

15. I further understand that Laos now appeals against part of the Award, arguing that the tribunal erred in ruling that it has jurisdiction over A's expropriation claims. Laos also takes the position that the PRC-Laos Treaty does not extend to Macau SAR. A, on the other hand, takes the position that the international tribunal was correct and that the PRC-Laos Treaty applies to Macau SAR and the tribunal has jurisdiction over A's claims.

16. I understand that after the tribunal issued its Award rejecting Laos's jurisdictional objections, Laos claimed that it wrote a letter to the Embassy of the PRC based in Vientiane, Laos (the "PRC Embassy"). In the present appeal, I understand that Laos seeks to admit this correspondence allegedly between the PRC Embassy and Laos, namely:

a) A letter in English allegedly from the Ministry of Foreign Affairs of Laos to the PRC Embassy of the PRC dated 7 January 2014; ("Laos Request" attached as "Annex

4") and

b) A letter in Chinese allegedly from the PRC Embassy to the Ministry of Foreign Affairs of Laos dated 9 January 2014("Embassy Letter" attached as "Annex 5").

(collectively, "the Embassy-Laos Correspondence").

17. I have been asked to provide my opinion on the following issues:

a) Whether the Embassy Letter represents formal decision or an authoritative interpretation of the PRC Government on the question of whether the PRC-Laos Treaty applies to Macau SAR under PRC domestic law; and

b) Whether the Embassy Letter is relevant to the question of the interpretation of the PRC-Laos Treaty under international law.

(collectively, the "Issues").

IV. DOCUMENTS REVIEWED

18. For the purposes of preparing my report, I have reviewed the following documents:

a) The Embassy-Laos Correspondence

b) The Award

c) Originating Summons 24 of 2014

d) OS 24

e) 1st Affidavit of Chin-Puar Yow Hoy

2nd Affidavit of Outakeo Keodouangsinh

19. I have also reviewed the relevant legal authorities cited for the purposes of preparing my report.

V. SUMMARY OF CONCLUSIONS

20. The Embassy Letter represents neither a formal decision nor an authoritative interpretation of the Central People's Government("CPG") on the territorial scope of the PRC-Laos Treaty and thus has no legally binding force under PRC domestic law. The discussion of domestic law in the Embassy Letter bears no legal effect on the interpretation of the territorial scope of the PRC-Laos Treaty, and the Embassy Letter should not be given retroactive effect under international law.

VI. OPINION

21. Set out below is my detailed opinion on the Issues. I shall deal first with the PRC domestic law issue, then the issue under international law.

A. The Embassy Letter Represents Neither a Formal Decision Nor an Authoritative Interpretation Taken by the PRC Government As a Matter of PRC Domestic Law

1. The Embassy Letter Does Not Constitute A Formal Decision of the PRC Government Regarding the Question of whether the PRC-Laos Treaty Applies to Macau SAR under PRC Domestic Law

22. It is possible for the CPG to make a decision on whether or not a particular international agreement concluded by the PRC applies to Macau SAR, on the basis of paragraph 1 of Article 138 of the Macau Basic Law, which stipulates that:

The Central People's Government may, in accordance with the circumstance and needs of the Macau SAR, and after consultation with the government of the Macau SAR, decide whether or not an international agreement(s) entered into by the People's Republic of China applies to the Macau SAR.[2]

23. However, the Embassy Letter may not be considered as representing a formal decision taken by the CPG under this paragraph, for the following three reasons.

24. *First*, the Embassy Letter does not indicate that a formal decision has been made by the CPG and that the letter is based on such a decision. Rather, it bases its reply on an interpretation of relevant provisions of the Basic Law of Macau SAR. Specifically, the Embassy Letter states, in relevant part, that:

> According to the Basic Law of the Macao Special Administrative Region (Macau SAR), subject to specific authorization by the Central People's Government, the government of the Macau SAR may by itself enter into and fulfil investment agreements with foreign and regional entities; bilateral investment agreements entered into by the Central People's Government are in principle not applicable to the Macau SAR save where otherwise arranged after consultation with the government of the Macau SAR and negotiations with the parties to the agreement.[3]

25. Had there been a formal decision made by the CPG, it would have been more straightforward to have referred to such a decision as the legal basis of the Embassy Letter.

26. *Second*, the making of such a decision by the CPG is dependent on the fulfilment of a procedural condition, that is, "after consultation with the government of the Macau SAR", which does not seem to have been met. A careful reading of the paragraph in the original Chinese version reveals that such a procedural condition has to be met in both cases of the CPG deciding "whether or not" *(shì fou)* a particular treaty applies to Macau SAR. In other words, for the CPG to effectively make such a decision, whether it is *for or against* the application of a particular treaty to Macau SAR, it has to consult the SAR Government.

27. As noted by the tribunal when citing a statement made by the Respondenet,[4] no such consultation between the CPG and the SAR Government had actually taken place. Also, it is noted that, the Embassy Letter is dated just two days after Laos's Request was submitted in English. It is therefore highly unlikely that such consultation had actually taken place before the Embassy Letter was issued.

28. *Third*, had a formal decision been taken by the CPG on this matter, it would be expected that the decision should be made public in good time, given the significance of

---

[2] Basic Law of the Macao Special Administrative Region of the People's Republic of China, adopted by the Eighth National People's Congress at its First Session on 31 March 1993 (Macau SAR Basic Law), Art. 138(1) (emphasis added) ("Annex 6").

[3] Embassy Letter ("Annex 5").

[4] Award, 260 ("Annex 3").

the decision. The significance lies in the fact that such a decision would impact on not only the interests of international investors in Macau SAR, but also those in Hong Kong, which itself is the world's third largest capital importer and fourth largest exporter[5].

29. Indeed, such publication is required under Article 9 of the 2007 Provisions of the People's Republic of China on the Disclosure of Government Information ("Provisions")[6], which requires administrative organs to disclose on their own initiative government information that involves "immediate interests of citizens, legal persons or other organizations". For international investors in the PRC SARs, whether or not they can benefit from the protection and promotion of the PRC BIT network, which is the second largest such network in the world, should be considered a matter of "immediate interests".

30. Consequently, if any decision on such matters had been made by the executive branch of the CPG in or before early January of this year, one would expect it to have already been made public in accordance with the Regulations[7]. However, so far there has been no evidence or indication that such a decision has been publicised.

31. It can therefore be concluded that no formal decision has been made by the CPG on the application or non-application of the PRC-Laos Treaty to the Macau SAR and consequently the Embassy Letter cannot be viewed as representing a formal decision of the CPG under PRC domestic law.

2. The Embassy Letter Is Not An Authoritative Interpretation of the Basic Law

32. As noted above, the Embassy Letter appears to have intended to provide an interpretation of the Macau Basic Law on the question of whether or not the PRC-Laos Treaty applies to the Macau SAR. However, it does not and cannot represent an authoritative interpretation of the Macau Basic Law under PRC domestic law.

33. *First of all*, Article 143 of the Basic Law is clear on this point: Authority to issue interpretations of the Law rests exclusively with the Standing Committee of the National People's Congress of the PRC("Standing Committee"):

The power of interpretation of this Law shall be vested in the Standing Committee of the National People 's Congress. The Standing Committee of the National People's Congress shall authorize the courts of the Macau Special Administrative Region to interpret on their own, in adjudicating cases, the provisions of this Law which are within the limits of the autonomy of the Region... However, if the courts of the Region, in adjudicating cases, need to interpret the provisions of this Law concerning affairs which are the responsibility of the Central People 's Government, or concerning the relationship between the Central Authorities and the Region, and if such interpretation will affect the

---

[5] UNCTAD, WORLD INVESTMENT REPORT 2013, at xiv-xv, *available at* http://unctad.org/e n/pages/Publication Webflyer.aspx?publicationid=588(figures 2 and 3).

[6] The Provisions were adopted by the State Council on January 17, 2007, and took effect on May 1, 2008. Order of the People's Republic of China State Council(No. 492).

[7] According to Article 18 of the Provisions, information falling within Article 9 shall be disclosed within 20 working days.

judgments in the cases, the courts of the Region shall, making their final judgments which are not appealable, seek an Interpretation of the relevant provisions from the standing Committee of the National People'sCongress through the Court cf Final Appeal of the Region. when the Standing Committee makes an interpretation of the provisions concerned, the courts of the Region, in applying those provisions, shall follow the interpretation of the Standing Committee. However, judgments previously rendered shall not be affected. The Standing Committee of the National People's Congress shall consult its Committee for the Basic Law of the Macau Special Administrative Region before giving an interpretation of this Law.[8]

34. Article 143 exists because under Article 67(4) of the Constitution of the PRC, the authority to interpret PRC law belongs excl usively to the Standing Committee. Article 67(4) provides:

> The Standing Committee of the National People's Congress exercises the following functions and powers:
>
> [...]
>
> (4) to interpret laws[.][9]

35. As a matter of fact, the Standing Committee has, on a number of occasions, issued interpretations of the Basic Laws of both Macau and Hong Kong Chinese SARs.[10] However, there is no record of any interpretation issued by the Standing Committee on the question of whether PRC BITs apply to the Macau or Hong Kong SARs. Accordingly, the Embassy Letter cannot purport to set forth the position of the Standing Committee as an authoritative interpretation of the Basic Law of Macau SAR on this matter.

36. *Moreover*, the Embassy Letter, in its interpretation of the Macau Basic Law, errs in that it presumes that the PRC-Laos Treaty, in principle, does not apply to Macau SAR, unless certain procedural conditions have been met. In other words, it considers that the Macau Basic Law has established a default position of non-application, and that a decision of the CPG is required only when the CPG intends to extend it to the Macau SAR.

37. The presumption that such PRC treaties do not apply to the Macau SAR is not supported by the language adopted by Article 138 of the Macau Basic Law, particularly in the original Chinese version. A careful reading of the Article demonstrates that: a) the

---

[8] *Macau SAR Basic Law*, Art. 143.

[9] Constitution of the People's Republic of China(adopted at the Fifth Session of the Fifth National People's Congress and promulgated for implementation by the Proclamation of the National People's Congress on December 4, 1982, and amended in accordance with the amendments to the Constitution of the People's Republic of China adopted at the First Session of the Seventh National People's Congress on April12, 1988, at the First Session of the Eighth National People's Congress on March 29, 1993, at the Second Session of the Ninth National People's Congress on March 15, 1999, and at the Second Session of the 10th National People's Congress on March 14, 2004), Art. 67.

[10] An example of such interpretations on Hong Kong SAR Basic Law can be found at the official website of the Hong Kong SAR Government: < httP://www. Legisl ation. gov. hk/blis ind. nsf/cura llengdoc/77E7FBB936DE3D7 14 82575EEOOO DF 62E? Open Document > (accessed on 16 March 2014). Also, an example of the interpretation of the Macau SAR Basic Law is reported by the China Daily, available at http.//europe. chinadaily. com. cnchina/2011 - 12/31/content 14366802. htm > (accessed on 16 March 2014).

CPG may or may not make a decision on such an issue of application or non-application; and b) in case the CPG intends to make such a decision, either *for or against(shì fou)* such application of an international agreement concluded by the CPG to the Macau SAR, the SAR Government must be consulted in advance. Until a decision has been thus made the matter is undecided as a matter of PRC domestic law.

38. Such a presumption is also not supported by the stated purposes of the Basic Law of the Macau SAR. The Preamble of the Basic Law stipulates that:

> Upholding national unity and territorial integrity, contributing to social stability and economic development and taking account of its history and realities, the People's Republic of China has decided that upon China's resumption of the exercise of sovereignty over Macau, a Macau Special Administrative Region will be established in accordance with the provisions of Article 31 of the Constitution of the People's Republic of China, and that under the principle of "one country, two systems", the socialist system and policies will not be practiced in Macau.[11]

39. It can be seen that the fundamental purposes of the Macau Basic Law are to uphold national unity and territorial integrity on the one hand, and to contribute to social stability and economic development on the other. It would indeed be difficult to see how excluding the Macau(and potentially Hong Kong) SAR form the territorial scope of the PRC-Laos Treaty(and potentially all PRC BITs) in principle might help to maintain the national unity and territorial integrity of China, or to promote social stability or economic development of either the SAR or the country as a whole. The opposite seems to be more likely: By depriving foreign investors in Macau(and potentially Hong Kong) the protection offered by the PRC BITs, this interpretation has the potential to undermine both the national unity and territorial integrity of PRC and the social stability and economic development of Macau SAR.

40. In sum, for the reasons stated above, the Embassy Letter represents neither a formal decision nor an authoritative interpretation on the territorial scope of the PRC-Laos Treaty, and is therefore not legally binding under PRC domestic law. Consequently the question of whether the PRC-Laos Treaty applies to Macau SAR remains undecided as a matter of PRC domestic law.

B. The Relevance of the Embassy Letter To The Question of Interpretation of the PRC-Laos Treaty As A Matter of International Law

1. The Embassy Letter's Discussion of Domestic Law Is Irrelevant to the Territorial Scope of the Treaty Under International Law

41. It is of course the case that the question before the tribunal was one of interpretation of the PRC-Laos Treaty, which is governed by international law, not domestic law in the form of PRC law.

42. The relevant international law provisions governing the territorial scope of a treaty are Article 15 of the 1978 Vienna Convention on Succession of States in respect

[11] Macau SAR Basic Law, Preamble.

of Treaties("VCST") (attached as "Annex 7") and Article 29 of the 1969 Vienna Convention on the Law of Treaties("VCLT") (attached as "Annex 8") . Those provisions dictate that a treaty applies to the entire sovereign territory of a State "[u] nless a different intention appears from the treaty or is otherwise established"(Art. 29) or "unless it appears from the treaty or is otherwise established that the application of the treaty to that territory would be incompatible with the object and purpose of the treaty or would radically change the conditions for its operation"(Art. 15) . These provisions are referred to as the "moving treaty frontiers" rule of international law.

43. In other words, the default position under international law is that the PRC-Laos Treaty shall apply to the Macau SAR since it was handed over to China in 1999. There are two types of exception to such a norm. The first type is an "explicit exception" found in the treaty text. The second type is an "implied exception", which has to be "otherwise established".

44. The Embassy Letter is entirely without legal effect on this question of the territorial scope of the Treaty as a matter of international law, for the simple reason that it purports to relate only to the status of the Treaty under domestic PRC law and not under international law. Article 27 of the VCLT, which codifies a well established principle of customary International law, stipulates that "[a] party may not invoke the provisions of its internal law as justification for its failure to perform a treaty". The tribunal also noted in the Award that "[i] t is well known that "the binding character of treaties is determined by international law, which on this point takes precedence over internal law. "[12] On this basis alone, the Embassy Letter has no relevance to the question of jurisdiction before the tribunal or this Honourable Court.

45. In any event, the Embassy Letter also cannot satisfy the "explicit exception" under either Article 29 of the VCLT or Article 15 of the VCST or the "implied exception" under Article 15 of the VCST. The PRC-Laos Treaty is silent on this matter. Neither does the Embassy Letter purport to interpret the terms of the PRC-Laos Treaty.

46. In addition, the implied exception established under Article 15 of the VCST provides for objective tests: is the application of the PRC-Laos Treaty to Macau SAR incompatible with the object and purpose of the treaty or would it radically change the conditions for its operation? The PRC's subjective intent with regard to the territorial scope of the Treaty is irrelevant to these questions. The International Law Commission, which drafted the VCST, described the implied exception in its Commentary on the Treaty as follows: "by such a formula, the Commission intends to lay down an international objective legal test of compatibility which, if applied in good faith, should provide a reasonable, flexible and practical rule. "[13]

47. It therefore follows that the Embassy Letter is irrelevant to the question of the Treaty's interpretation as a matter of international law(including with respect to attempting to establish an exception to the general rule of territorial scope of treaty applica-

---

〔12〕 Award, 257.

〔13〕 2 YEARBOOK OF THE INTERNATIONAL LAW COMMISSION 1974, 210 (United Nations, 1975) , Vol. 2 Part 1, at 210(emphasis in original) (internal quotation omitted) ("Annex 9") .

tion). As a result, the PRC-Laos Treaty should follow the general rule and apply to the entire territory of the PRC, including Macau SAR.

2. The Embassy Letter Does Not Apply Retroactively To Establish the PRC's Intent With Respect to the PRC-Laos Treaty Under International Law

48. Even if the Embassy Letter could be construed as a statement of PRC intent regarding the territorial scope of the Treaty for the purposes of Article 29 of the VCLT, it does not purport to be a statement of the PRC's intent at the time of the handover of Macau SAR.

49. To the extent that the Embassy Letter purports to establish the PRC's intent today, it is irrelevant. Because no contrary statement of intent was issued at the time of the handover, the Treaty automatically extended to Macau SAR as a matter of customary international law. Therefore, when A first invested in Laos in 2007, Macau SAR was included within the territorial scope of the PRC.

50. There are no grounds for granting the statement in the Embassy Letter retroactive effect. Basic considerations of fairness and due process dictate against such a conclusion, especially where Laos took steps to solicit the Embassy Letter in order to assist its attempt to defeat jurisdiction before this Honourable Court after the tribunal has made its ruling in the Award. As international law scholars Rudolf Dolzer and Christoph Schreuer have observed:

> [A] mechanism whereby a party to a dispute is able to infl uence the outcome of judicial proceedings—by issuing an official interpretation to the detriment of the other party—is incompatible with the principles of fair procedure and is hence undesirable.[14]

51. Indeed, since the Embassy Letter expresses an intent that would deprive international investors in Macau SAR of the protection of the PRC-Laos Treaty that they otherwise would enjoy, it amounts to an amendment of the existing treaty language. Such an amendment to a treaty, even if it is agreed between the contracting parties, does not have retroactive effect.[15] In more than one treaty-based investment arbitration case, tribunals have held that such interpretations given to a treaty provision after the treaty has been signed and entered into force do not necessarily govern the treaty.[16] The *Enron* v *Argentina* tribunal, for instance, succinctly ruled that:

Not even if this was the interpretation given to the clause today by the United States would this necessarily mean that such interpretation governs the Treaty. What

---

[14] Rudolf Dolzer & Christoph Schreuer, PRINCIPLES OFINTERNATIONA INVESTMENTLAW, 35(2nd ed. 2012) (internal citations omitted) (quoting the United States Model BIT of 2004) ("Annex 10").

[15] Mark E. Villiger, COMMENTARY ON THE 1969 VIENNA CONVENTION ON THE LA W OF TREATIES, 513(2009) ("Annex 11").

[16] *See e. g.*, *Enron v. Argentina*, ICSID Case No. *ARB/*01/3, Award, 337 – 38(May 22, 2007) ("Annex 12"); *Sempra v. Argentina*, ICSID Case No. *ARB/*021l6, Award, 382 – 87(Sep. 28 2007) ("Annex 13"). Other discussions on the legal effect of interpretation given by contracting parties can be seen in*Aguas del Tunari*v. *Bolivia*, Decision on Respondent's Objections to Jurisdiction, 47, 249 – 63(Oct. 21, 2005) ("Annex 14"), and*National Grid*v. *Argentina*, UNCITRAL, Decision on Jurisdiction, (June 20, 2006) ("Annex 15") (noting that the intent of both parties is necessary to interpret a treaty).

is relevant is the intention the parties had in signing the Treaty and this does not confirm the self-judging interpretation. Even if this interpretation were shared today by both parties to the Treaty, it would still not result in a change of its terms. States are of course free to amend the Treaty by consenting to another text, but this would not affect rights acquired under the Treaty by investors or other beneficiaries.[17]

52. For the aforementioned reasons, and given the circumstances under which the Embassy Letter was issued and its shaky foundation under PRC domestic law, as observed above, it is beyond doubt that no retroactive effect should be given to the interpretation contained in the Embassy Letter.

Ⅶ. CONCLUSION

53. Based on the reasons stated above, it is my considered view that the Embassy Letter does not represent competent evidence under either PRC or international law for overturning the tribunal's decision with respect to the application of the Laos-PRC Treaty to Macau SAR.

Dated: 18th March 2014

Professor Wenhua Shan

---

〔17〕 *Enron v. Argentina*, *supra* note 16, 337("Annex 12").

华南国际经济贸易仲裁委员会关于审理广州×××公司与×××(外国)公司贸易合同仲裁案裁决书

申　请　人:
地　　　址:
法定代表人:
代　理　人:
被 申 请 人:
地　　　址:
授权代表人:

深　圳

二〇一五年　月　日

裁　决　书

华南国仲深裁〔2015〕号

华南国际经济贸易仲裁委员会(以下简称"本会")根据申请人与 被申请人于×年×月×日签订的《还款协议(Repayment Agreement)》中的仲裁条款和申请人于×年×月×日向本会提交的书面仲裁申请受理了本仲裁案。

本案仲裁程序适用自2012年12月1日起施行的《华南国际经济贸易仲裁委员会仲裁规则》(以下简称《仲裁规则》)。

2014年10月16日,本会秘书处以中国邮政特快专递(EMS)方式向申请人提供的被申请人地址发出仲裁通知,并随函附送了《仲裁规则》、《仲裁员名册》及申请人提交的仲裁申请书及证据材料。相关文件也一并向申请人寄送。经查,寄送给双方当事人的邮件均已妥投。

依据《仲裁规则》的规定,申请人选定A先生作为本案仲裁员,因被申请人未在规定的期限内选定或委托本会主任指定仲裁员而由本会主任为被申请人指定B先生作为本案仲裁员,因双方未在规定的期限内共同选定或共同委托本会主任指定首席仲裁员而由本会主任指定C先生作为本案首席仲裁员,以上三名仲裁员于2014年11月24日组成仲裁庭审理本案。

仲裁庭确定于2014年12月15日十四时三十分在本会所在地开庭审理本案。本会秘书处于2014年11月24日以中国邮政特快专递(EMS)方式向双方当事人邮寄了《仲裁庭组成通知》及附件、《开庭通知书》。同日,本会秘书处向申请人提供的被申请人的邮箱、传真再次发送了仲裁通知、《仲裁庭组成通知》及附件、《开庭通知书》等仲裁文件。经查,上述仲裁文件均已妥投。

本案于2014年12月15日在本会所在地开庭审理,申请人和被申请人的代理人均出席了庭审。申请人的代理人出席了庭审,被申请人未出庭。根据《仲裁规则》第三十九条第二款的规定,仲裁庭对本案进行了缺席审理。仲裁庭听取了申请人的陈述,核对了申请人提交的证据原件并就案件有关问题询问了申请人代理人。

同日,本会秘书处以中国邮政特快专递(EMS)方式向被申请人发出华南国仲深发〔2014〕××××号函,将缺席审理的情况书面通知了被申请人,明确告知被申请人若其就本案申请人的证据有任何质证意见或代理意见,应于收到该函之日起5日内以书面方式一式五份提交本会秘书处,逾期不作答复,仲裁庭将择日作出裁决。经查,邮寄给被申请人的上述邮件已经于2014年12月28日妥投。

庭后,申请人提交了补充证据等材料,本会秘书处已将申请人提交的材料邮寄给被申请人和仲裁庭。经查,上述邮件均已妥投。

本案现已审理终结。仲裁庭根据现有文件以及庭审所查清的事实和查证的证据作出本裁决。

现将本案案情、仲裁庭意见以及裁决内容分述如下。

一、案情

(一)申请人的仲裁请求及依据

申请人诉称:

申请人是生产日化原料的公司,自2009年至2012年,被申请人向申请人采购了乙内酰脲(TC-DMDMH)、卡波姆(TC-Carbomer340)、椰油酰胺丙基甜菜碱

(TC-CAB35)等产品，申请人已履行完毕全部交货义务，但被申请人没有按约定付款。截至2013年11月11日，双方签订《还款协议》确认，被申请人尚拖欠申请人货款余额共计417,166.50美元。

按照双方签订的《还款协议》约定，被申请人应于2014年1月30日前以转账方式一次性向甲方支付第一期欠款25,000.00美元；剩余欠款225,000.00美元，自2014年1月1日起，每月10日前以转账方式支付欠款8000.00美元，直至申请人收齐全部全部款项为止。且双方还约定，若被申请人能按上述约定偿还拖欠货款，申请人同意给予被申请人167,166.50美元的折让，折让后欠款余额为250,000.00美元。但至今被申请人从未履行过还款义务，按照《还款协议》的约定，折让予以取消，被申请人仍需向申请人全额支付欠款共计417,166.50美元，同时，根据《还款协议》约定，被申请人还应按照欠款总额417,166.50美元的1%/天支付逾期付款违约金。

对于被申请人拖欠的上述款项，申请人已多次催讨，但被申请人一直没能支付。被申请人的行为，已经给申请人造成较大的经济损失，为维护自身的合法财产权益，特具状仲裁。

依上述事实和理由，申请人提出如下的仲裁请求：

1. 判令被申请人支付申请人拖欠的货款共计417,166.50美元，并按《还款协议》约定条款支付逾期付款违约金（按逾期付款总额417,166.50美元的日1%计算，自2014年1月31日计至实际给付之日）。

2. 由被申请人承担本案的全部仲裁费用。

（二）申请人提交的证据

申请人提交了以下证据：

1.《还款协议》，申请人以此证明被申请人拖欠申请人货款。

2. 双方往来邮件，申请人以此证明被申请人拖欠申请人货款。

3. 编号为TC-2010102的合同交易、编号为TC-2010102(2)的合同交易、编号为TC-2010103的合同交易、编号为TC-2010110的合同交易、编号为TC-2011290的合同交易，每一合同交易均提供了相应的合同、发票、提单、报关单、原产地证明，申请人以此证明申请人与被申请人之间的交易情况。

4. 部分货款支付凭证付款凭证被申请人支付部分货款。

5. 服务合同—逾期账款管理服务、订单委托书，证明申请人委托第三方催收货款；收回货款凭证及支付服务费用凭证、发票，证明第三方收回部分欠款的事实。

6. 现业务员D与被申请人的授权代表人E沟通邮件公证书及翻译，证明协议签署前，申请人向被申请人催收货款，沟通《还款协议》的过程，申请人提起仲裁后,被申请人邮件确认欠款事实,并确认已收到仲裁资料,希望推迟还款。

7. 业务员证人证言、业务员 D 往返约旦的机票,证明 D 与被申请人协商还款及《还款协议》签署的情况;E 名片,证明 E 身份。

8. 业务沟通邮件及翻译(部分邮件由于业务员均已离职,无法取得联系,也无法进行公证,供仲裁庭参考),证明双方业务往来情况。

(三)被申请人未提交任何书面答辩意见和证据材料,也没有参加庭审

(四)仲裁庭查明的事实

仲裁庭听取了申请人在庭审中的陈述,并仔细审阅了其提交的全部书面材料,查明如下事实:

1. 至少自 2010 年 3 月始,申请人作为卖方向被申请人供应,被申请人作为买方从申请人处采购乙内酰脲(TC-DMDMH)、卡波姆(TC-Carbomer340)、椰油酰胺丙基甜菜碱(TC-CAB35)等产品;

2. 经过申请人多次催收和双方多次沟通,申请人和被申请人在 2013 年 11 月 11 日签署了"还款协议",协议确定了,截至 2013 年 10 月 23 日,被申请人拖欠申请人货款余额为 417,166.50 美元,并约定还款计划为:

——如(被申请人)按本协议约定履行相应义务,(申请人)同意就上述欠款金额给予(被申请人)167,166.50 美元的折让。双方确认,折让之后,(被申请人)拖欠(申请人)的欠款余额为 250,000 美元;

——双方同意,本协议签订生效后,(被申请人)按以下期限和方式向(申请人)分期支付欠款 250,000 美元;

——如(被申请人)不能按照本协议第二条约定的期限和/或金额支付任何一期款项的,双方同意取消本协议第一条约定的折让 167,166.50 美元,即(被申请人)仍需向(申请人)全额支付上述欠款余额 417,166.50 美元;

——本协议签署后,若(被申请人)逾期付款,每逾期一天,(被申请人)应按到期应付款项总额的 1% 向(申请人)支付违约金。

——本协议以中、英文写成,但中文条款和英文条款存在冲突的,以英文条款为准。

二、仲裁庭意见

就本案争议,仲裁庭意见如下:

(一)关于合同的有效性和法律适用问题

经查,申请人与被申请人于 2013 年 11 月 11 日签署了《还款协议》,《还款协议》第六条约定,"本协议适用中华人民共和国法律"。本案一方当事人位于国

外，还款协议属于具有涉外因素的合同。涉外合同当事人不仅可以商定双方的权利义务，也可以协商选择处理合同争议所适用的法律。无论是还款协议，还是还款协议所涉及的买卖合同，本仲裁庭均没有了解到有法律规定不能选择适用法律的情形。

此外，还款协议是经过双方当事人数次邮件往来后自行签署，没有证据表明本还款协议的缔结有胁迫，或其他未反映当事人真实意思，也没有违反法律的强制性规定的情形。为谨慎起见，应仲裁庭要求，申请人还提供了 2010 年至 2011 年编号为 TC-2010102，TC-2010102（2）、TC2010103、TC2010110 和 TC2011290 的合同以及部分支持性文件，以表明双方确实存在业务往来和钱款给付，该还款协议是有真实的货物买卖作为依据而存在的。

根据中华人民共和国合同法第 44 条，"依法成立的合同自成立时生效"，仲裁庭没有了解到本合同存在需要根据法律或行政法规应当办理批准、登记等生效手续情形；也没有注意到合同中订有附生效条件生效之内容；更没有了解到，任何致使本合同无效的情形或事件存在。

因此，本案"还款协议"合法有效，构成约束双方权利义务的合同，并适用包括中华人民共和国合同法在内的中华人民共和国法律。

（二）关于仲裁语言问题

经查，《还款协议》第五条约定，"本协议以中英文写成，但中文条款和英文条款存在冲突的，以英文条款为准"。

首先，仲裁庭经过比对中英文条款，没有发现还款协议中各个条款之中英文内容存在矛盾之处，特别是还款协议的正文部分；

其次，在庭审过程中，仲裁庭注意到申请人代理人均为中华人民共和国国籍，中文为其母语，经询问和征得申请人同意，确定整个庭审以中文进行，裁决书以中文书就，辅以英文译文；

最后，根据本会现行有效仲裁规则，使用中文作为仲裁语言亦符合规则之规定。

（三）被申请人拖欠货款的本金

经查，申请人提供了还款协议，以及为证明还款协议下内容的真实性，还提供了五份买卖合同及合同履行文件，货款支付凭证、委托第三方催收货款的逾期账款管理服务合同、经过公证的多封双方往来邮件、申请人方面业务人员证人证言、被申请人联络人名片以及多封双方业务往来邮件。

以上这些证据构成了一个完整的证据链，足以证明被申请人欠款事实，以及拖欠货款的本金数额为 417，166.50 美元。因为自双方签署协议后，被申请人没有给付任何款项，故《还款协议》下第一条关于折让的条款不适用，即被申请人拖欠申请人的货款本金数额为417,166.50美元。

（四）拖欠货款之逾期违约金

仲裁庭同时认为，被申请人未按期支付租金的行为，已构成违约，根据《中华人民共和国合同法》的规定，合同约定违约责任的，违约人应当按合同约定承担违约责任。仲裁庭注意到，双方当事人对违约责任有约定，《还款协议》第4条约定"若（被申请人）逾期付款，每逾期一天，（被申请人）应按到期应付款项总额的1%向（申请人）支付违约金"。

《中华人民共和国合同法》第114条规定，当事人可以约定一方违约时应当根据违约情况向对方支付一定数额的违约金，也可以约定因违约产生的损失赔偿额的计算方法。约定的违约金低于造成的损失的，当事人可以请求人民法院或者仲裁机构予以增加；约定的违约金过分高于造成的损失的，当事人可以请求人民法院或者仲裁机构予以适当减少。

中华人民共和国最高人民法院《关于适用〈中华人民共和国合同法〉若干问题的解释（二）》第29条规定，当事人主张约定的违约金过高请求予以适当减少的，人民法院应当以实际损失为基础，兼顾合同的履行情况、当事人的过错程度以及预期利益等综合因素，根据公平原则和诚实信用原则予以衡量，并作出裁决；当事人约定的违约金超过造成损失的百分之三十的，一般可以认定为《合同法》第114条第二款规定的"过分高于造成的损失"。

仲裁庭同时还注意到最高人民法院于2009年7月7日发布的《关于当前形势下审理民商事合同纠纷案件若干问题的指导意见》第二条的规定。仲裁庭特别注意到，在该意见中，最高人民法院指出："6.在当前企业经营状况普遍较为困难的情况下，对于违约金数额过分高于违约造成损失的，应当根据合同法规定的诚实信用原则、公平原则，坚持以补偿性为主、以惩罚性为辅的违约金性质，合理调整裁量幅度，切实防止以意思自治为由而完全放任当事人约定过高的违约金。"

本案被申请人未陈述意见，未主动提出调整违约金的请求。但仲裁庭认为，过高违约金应予调整的精神在仲裁中可予适用。仲裁庭认为，在认定被申请人违约且适用违约金条款的同时，应当根据前述《中华人民共和国合同法》第114条的规定，并参照前述中华人民共和国最高人民法院《关于适用〈中华人民共和国合同法〉若干问题的解释（二）》的规定，同时注意到最高人民法院有关违约金的指导意见，对在本案中所约定的计算标准是否合适作出考量。

仲裁庭认为，当事人的约定并不能完全排除仲裁庭根据法律所确立的公平原则，参照有关的司法解释，并根据有关事实就违约金的标准或数额作出其认为更为合理的判断和认定。考虑到本案合同的履行情况以及未如约支付可能产生的损失,并根据公平原则,仲裁庭认为,合同中约定的到期应付款项总额每日1%的违约金显然过分高于给申请人造成的损失,也未能完全体现补偿性为主、惩罚性为辅的违约金性质。

综合上述,仲裁庭裁量认定,违约金按到期应付款项总额的每年30%计算,不足一年部分按照每年365日计算至本裁决作出之日。

(五)关于申请人的仲裁费用

申请人要求被申请人支付仲裁费。仲裁庭认为:依据《仲裁规则》第46条第(一)款,仲裁庭裁定本案仲裁费应由被申请人承担。

三、裁决

根据上述事实和仲裁庭意见,仲裁庭对本案作出裁决如下:

(1)裁决被申请人向申请人支付货物欠款本金417,166.50美元;

(2)裁决被申请人向申请人支付货物欠款违约金,该违约金自2013年1月31日起,按照单利年利率30%,不足一年的按照每年365天比例计算至本实际给付之日。

(3)本案仲裁费用人民币【】元,全部由被申请人承担,申请人预缴的仲裁费人民币【】元抵作本案仲裁费,被申请人应将申请人代其垫付的仲裁费人民币【】元径付给申请人。

上述全部支付义务,被申请人应于本裁决作出之日起15日内履行完毕。

本裁决为终局裁决,自作出之日起生效。

华南国际经济贸易仲裁委员会关于审理申请人×××与被申请人×××等三人股份转让协议仲裁案裁决书

申　　请　　人：
公民身份号码：
身份证住址：
代　　理　　人：

第一被申请人：
公民身份号码：
地　　　　址：
代　　理　　人：

第二被申请人：
公民身份号码：
地　　　　址：
代　　理　　人：

第三被申请人：
公民身份号码：
地　　　　址：
代　　理　　人：

深　圳

二〇一六年　月　日

裁 决 书

华南国仲深裁〔2016〕155号

华南国际经济贸易仲裁委员会(下称“本会”或“仲裁委员会”)根据A(下称“申请人”)与B(下称“第一被申请人”)、C(下称“第二被申请人”)、D(下称“第三被申请人”,除特别指明,第一、第二、第三被申请人以下合称为“被申请人”)于×年×月×日签订的《股份转让协议》(下称“《协议》”)、同日签订的《股份转让补充协议》(下称“《补充协议》”)中的仲裁条款,以及申请人于×年×月×日提交的《仲裁申请书》,于2015年11月18日受理了本案。

本案仲裁程序适用自2012年12月1日起施行的《华南国际经济贸易仲裁委员会仲裁规则》(下称“《仲裁规则》”)。

2015年10月15日,本会秘书处按照申请人提供的送达地址,以中国邮政特快专递(EMS)方式向各方当事人寄送了《仲裁通知》、《仲裁规则》和《仲裁员名册》,并同时向各被申请人附寄了申请人提交的《仲裁申请书》及证据材料。经查,寄送给申请人及被申请人的邮件均已妥投。

根据《仲裁规则》第二十九条的规定,申请人选定甲先生作为本案仲裁员,被申请人共同选定乙先生作为本案仲裁员,因双方未在规定的期限内共同选定或共同委托本会主任指定首席仲裁员,本会主任指定丙先生作为本案首席仲裁员,以上三名仲裁员于2016年1月27日组成仲裁庭审理本案。

仲裁庭定于2016年3月3日上午九时三十分在本会所在地开庭审理本案。本会秘书处于2016年1月27日以中国邮政特快专递(EMS)的方式将《仲裁庭组成通知》、《开庭通知书》及附件邮寄给双方当事人。经查,上述文件均已妥投。

本会秘书处向各被申请人发出的包括但不限于《仲裁通知》、《仲裁庭组成通知》、《开庭通知书》、其他当事人的材料等在内的所有仲裁文书,按照《仲裁规则》第五条的规定,均已实际送达。

2016年×月×日,仲裁庭在本会所在地开庭审理了本案。申请人及其代理人、第一被申请人的代理人、第二被申请人的代理人、第三被申请人的代理人出席了庭审。庭审中,申请人及其代理人和第一、第二、第三被申请人的代理人分别就仲裁请求作了陈述和答辩,各方分别对对方提交的证据进行质证,并就本案的事实和法律问题进行了辩论,回答了仲裁庭的调查询问,各方充分发表了意见。在庭审结束前,仲裁庭经征求双方当事人的意见对本案进行了调解,双方和解方案差距较大，无法达成一致意见。各方进行了最后陈述。

庭审结束后，申请人和被申请人在规定的期限内提交了代理词和补充证据，有关材料均已送达双方当事人。2016年4月25日，申请人向仲裁庭提交《变更仲裁请求申请书》，鉴于该申请已经超过了仲裁庭规定的补充证据和书面意见的期限，仲裁庭无法重新审理，决定不予以采纳。

本案现已审理终结，仲裁庭根据认定的证据和查清的事实依法作出裁决。

现将本案案情、仲裁庭的意见以及裁决内容分述如下：

一、案情

(一)申请人的仲裁请求及事实、理由

申请人提出以下仲裁请求：

1. 裁决第一被申请人向申请人支付股权回购款人民币46,800,000元；

2. 裁决第一被申请人向申请人支付至实际支付之日为止的违约金人民币(暂计至2015年10月21日，违约金为人民币953,950元)；

3. 裁决第一被申请人向申请人支付保全费人民币5000元、担保费人民币327,600元和律师费人民币450,000元；

4. 裁决第二被申请人和第三被申请人就上述支付股权回购款、违约金义务和赔偿申请人维护自己权益产生的费用承担连带担保责任；

5. 裁决由三被申请人承担本案的全部仲裁费。

庭审过程中，申请人承认第二被申请人已经于2015年11月17日、18日分别向申请人归还人民币500万元和港币399万元的事实，同意将该金额从回购款中扣除。

申请人提出以下事实与理由：

2014年12月17日，申请人与第一被申请人签署了《协议》。《协议》中约定“转让方(即第一被申请人)同意将其持有的E公司【肆佰伍拾万】股的股份转让给受让方(即申请人)，受让方同意受让上述股份”，“转让方和受让方共同约定：上述股权转让的总价款为人民币【36,000,000.00】元”，并约定“双方因本协议的签订、履行而产生的任何争议应通过友好协商解决。若争议发生后30天内协商解决不成的，任何一方有权应向华南国际经济贸易仲裁委员会(深圳国际仲裁院)申请仲裁”。

2014年12月17日，申请人与第一、第二、第三被申请人签署了《补充协议》。《补充协议》第二条第2款中第一被申请人向申请人保证并承诺“E公司(或其实际控制人及其他股东)最迟于本协议签署之日起四个月内完成公司上市程序或与上市公司签署整体收购的协议报证监会审核，且收购价格不低于每股 12 元，受让方（即申请人）所持有的 E 公司股份有限公司（下称‘E 公司’）能够置换为该上市公司的【肆佰伍拾万】股股份”。

《协议》和《补充协议》生效后，申请人已经按约定履行《协议》和《补充协议》中所约定的义务，但至今 E 公司（或其实际控制人及其他股东）未能实现第一被申请人承诺的“于本协议签署之日起四个月内完成公司上市程序或与上市公司签署整体收购的协议报证监会审核，且收购价格不低于每股 12 元，受让方（即申请人）所持有的 E 公司股份能够置换为该上市公司的【肆佰伍拾万】股股份”。根据补充协议的回购条款约定“如果转让方（即第一被申请人）上述承诺不能按时兑现，则受让方有权要求转让方按照人民币【46,800,000.00】元回购受让方所持有的【肆佰伍拾万】股 E 公司股份”；“上述回购应该在受让方提出回购要求之日起十日完成，且转让方应当足额在该期限内向受让方支付上述回购款项（即使回购股份的工商变更登记没有完成，转让方也需在该期限内支付上述回购款项），否则每延期一日应按应付款项的千分之三支付违约金”，第一被申请人应按照人民币 46,800,000 元回购申请人所持有的【肆佰伍拾万】股 E 公司。另外，申请人于 2015 年 8 月 30 日向第一被申请人发出要求其在 2015 年 9 月 20 日前回购的通知，根据各方约定，第一被申请人每延期一日还应按应付款项的千分之三支付违约金，暂计止至 2015 年 10 月 21 日，第一被申请人还应向申请人支付违约金人民币 433 万元，但申请人考虑到违约金计算标准比较高，主动调低按照每日万分之六点五八的标准计算，暂计至 2015 年 10 月 21 日，第一被申请人应向申请人支付违约金为人民币 953,950 元。

第一被申请人直到 2015 年 10 月 21 日都未履行合约，且由于情况紧急，为防止三被申请人转移财产，申请人向深圳市中级人民法院对三被申请人名下财产进行保全，并因此向深圳市 F 创融资担保有限公司支付担保费人民币 327,600 元和向中级人民法院支付保全费人民币 5000 元。为维护自己权益，申请人聘请 G 律师事务所支出律师费人民币 450,000 元。

另外《补充协议》第四条担保条款约定“担保人 1（即第二被申请人）与担保人 2（即第三被申请人）愿意对于转让方在《协议》及本协议中所产生的所有责任、义务承担无限连带责任担保，担保期限为本协议签署之日起五年止”。第二被申请人和第三被申请人作为连带保证人，应对第一被申请人向申请人应承担的包括但不限于支付回购款的义务、违约责任和赔偿申请人为维护自己权益所花费的费用等所有责任、义务承担连带保证责任。

（二）第一被申请人对于本案的意见

第一被申请人没有提交书面答辩意见。庭审过程中其代理人口头答辩，对案件的主要事实没有异议。但其代理人称，由于公司搬家，第一被申请人没有收到申请人在2015年8月30日发出的回购通知。另外，第一被申请人代理人表示，第一被申请人没有收到股份转让款，股份转让款实际全部打入E公司的公司账户，但承认，申请人是按照第一被申请人的指示将股份转让款转入公司账户。

（三）第二被申请人对于本案的意见

第二被申请人的代理人在庭审答辩中发表了对于本案的意见，并在庭后提交书面意见，其意见如下：

1. 申请人和第二被申请人之间是借款关系，申请人所出借的人民币3500万元实际由E公司使用，但E公司与申请人没有签订任何协议，属于不当得利，应当返还申请人和第二被申请人。

2. 申请人与第一被申请人签订的《协议》有效，但《补充协议》的部分条款无效，特别是约定将申请人出借的人民币3500万元转为股份转让款的约定无效，因为该约定没有经过E公司的同意和追认，损害了E公司及其股东的利益。

3.《补充协议》关于人民币3500万元借款转为股份转让对价的条款无效，因此申请人尚未履行《协议》中的付款义务，第二被申请人的担保义务尚未产生。

4. 因为申请人与第二被申请人之间是借款关系，关于人民币3500万元借款的归还、利息计算、争议解决等，应当以申请人和第二被申请人之间于2014年12月16日签订的《借款协议》为准，第二被申请人没有保留该协议的文本，第二被申请人请求申请人向仲裁庭出示该协议文本，并认为该借款纠纷应当另案处理。

5. 第二被申请人已经向申请人支付了人民币500万元和港币399万元，这两笔钱应从E公司的不当得利款中扣除。第二被申请人也是E公司不当得利的受害人，但第二被申请人和申请人签了借款合同，又是老乡，所以先替E公司偿还了部分不当得利。

（四）第三被申请人对于本案的意见

第三被申请人的代理人在庭审答辩中进行了答辩，发表了对于本案的意见，其意见如下：

1.《补充协议》的第四条担保条款约定，担保人1（即本案第二被申请人——仲裁庭注，下同）、担保人2（即本案第三被申请人——仲裁庭注，下同）愿意为合同的所有义务承担无限连带责任担保，根据相关法律法规规定，保证期限应该是二年，该条款约定保证期限五年，与法律规定有冲突，可以视为约定不明，在约定不明的情况下，担保责任应该是半年。申请人主张保证责任的时间已经超出半年期限。

2.《补充协议》没有规定保证人应当承担申请人追索债权产生的费用。申请人主张的律师费保全费不属于被申请人保证责任范围,保证人不应当承担。

3. 申请人主张的违约责任过高,申请人仅应就其损失主张赔偿,而其损失是借出人民币 3500 万元的利息损失。

4. 申请人与被申请人之间签订的《协议》和《补充协议》的回购条款,实质是对赌条款,显失公平。申请人付出人民币 3600 万元购买相应的股权,在满足相应的条件以后,要求回购,其回购的数额远远超出了一般意义上的利润范畴。

二、仲裁庭意见

依据当事人提交的证据以及仲裁庭的庭审调查,仲裁庭对于本案作如下分析和认定:

(一)基本事实认定

1. 股份转让还是借款

本案各方当事人对《协议》以及《补充协议》的真实性没有异议,根据这两份协议的相关条款,仲裁庭不难对交易的性质作出认定。《补充协议》的第一条"股份转让款的支付"是这样描述交易的演变过程的:

(1)2014 年 12 月 16 日,担保人 1(即第二被申请人——仲裁庭注)与受让人(即申请人—仲裁庭注)签署了《借款合同》,约定担保人 1 向受让人借款人民币叁仟伍佰万元(¥3500 万元),该款项根据担保人 1 的指令转入了 E 公司股份有限公司(以下简称 E 公司)的收款账户,用于偿还 E 公司的银行贷款。

(2)担保人与转让方(即第一被申请人——仲裁庭注,下同)系关联关系,担保人 1 与转让方发生上述借款实际为替转让方进行的融资。

(3)根据转让方的要求,受让方愿意将该借款转为按照《股份转让协议》应支付的股份转让款。剩余的壹佰万元股份转让款受让方应当在股份转让变更登记完成后十日内支付到转让方指定的以下收款账户。

由此可见,尽管第二被申请人对本案交易的实质有所争议,但上述条款十分清楚的记录了交易的过程。即 2014 年 12 月 16 日第二被申请人先与申请人签订了《借款协议》,向申请人借款人民币 3500 万元,并要求申请人将款项转入 E 公司银行账户,用于 E 公司归还银行贷款。2014 年 12 月 17 日,申请人和第一被申请人达成股份转让协议,申请人向第一被申请人购买 E 公司 450 万股股份,购买总价款为人民币 3600 万元,申请人同意将前述人民币 3500 万元借款转为股份转让款,剩余的人民币 100 万元在股权变更登记完成后也支付。申请人、第一被申请人和第二被申请人之间同意将借款转为股份转让款的行为,属于合同当事人之间的合同变更行为,尽管第二被申请人的代理人主张该行为无效,但仲裁庭不认为该变更行为属于违反国家法律法规、侵犯第三人利益或其他可能导致合同无效的行为。

《协议》第二条也作出类似规定,要求申请人将人民币3600万元合同价款支付给E公司的同一银行账户。庭审过程中,申请人和被申请人各方的当庭陈述也和上述规定相吻合。

庭审中,申请人确认股份转让已经完成,E公司已经完成股份转让的登记变更手续,将申请人登记为其股东,持有450万股股份。

仲裁庭据此确认申请人与被申请人之间的股份转让关系成立。交易过程中,申请人将借贷给第二被申请人的人民币3500万借款转为股份转让款,该行为明确记载在《补充协议》中,经申请人、第一被申请人、第二被申请人以及第三被申请人签字确认,没有出现法律规定的可能导致合同无效或不生效的情形。

第二被申请人在答辩中提及的借款合同关系,不属于本仲裁审理范围,而且当事人都没有提交借款合同文本,仲裁庭无法审理。因此仲裁庭不认可第二被申请人关于本案所涉及的争议是借款合同关系的说法。如果有必要,第二被申请人可以就其主张的借款合同关系另行起诉或申请仲裁。

2. 付款金额和性质

申请人提交了银行付款凭证、第一被申请人在2014年12月16日出具的人民币3500万元的收款收据(申请人在2014年12月31日另行向第一被申请人支付人民币100万元)。上述证据显示申请人总共支付了人民币3600万元的价款。其中人民币3500万元转入E公司账户,按照《补充协议》的规定,该部分支付款转为申请人支付给第一被申请人的股权转让款。

据此,仲裁庭认定申请人按照合同规定,足额支付了人民币3600万元的股份转让款。第二被申请人认为,上述价款实际为E公司所使用,是不当得利,E公司应该返还。该主张不属于本案审理范围,第二被申请人如果认为有必要,可以另行起诉或者申请仲裁主张其权利。

(二)第一被申请人的回购义务

根据《补充协议》,"如果转让方(即第一被申请人)上述承诺之一不能按时兑现,则受让方(即申请人)有权要求转让方按照人民币【46,800,000】元回购受让方所持有的【肆佰伍拾万】股E公司股份"。第一被申请人对该项义务没有提出明确异议,没有否认E公司未能在规定期限内申请公开发行上市或与上市公司进行整体并购的事实。申请人出示的微信或短信沟通记录也显示,申请人和第一被申请人之间进行了多次沟通,各方同意第一被申请人应该在2015年9月20日之前按照人民币4680万元的价格回购申请人持有的450万股E公司的股份。

基于以上事实,仲裁庭认定,按照《补充协议》的规定,第一被申请人回购申请人所持有的股份义务成立。

(三)第二被申请人和第三被申请人的保证义务

《补充协议》第四条规定"担保人1(即第二被申请人—仲裁庭注)与担保人2(即第三被申请人—仲裁庭注)愿意对于转让方在《协议》及本协议中所产生的所有责任、义务承担无限连带责任担保,担保期限为本协议签署之日起五年止"。各被申请人对于该规定没有提出异议。针对第二被申请人和第三被申请人在庭审过程中提出一些答辩意见,仲裁庭根据经审理采纳的事实和证据,作出如下认定:

1. 仲裁庭已经认定本案股份转让及其价款支付关系成立,第二被申请人主张的借款关系和不当得利不属于本案审理范围。因此,仲裁庭不采纳第二被申请人认为申请人支付的人民币3600万元是借款,本案是借款关系的主张。

2. 同理,仲裁庭不采纳第二被申请人的以下主张:人民币3500万元借款转为股份转让对价的条款无效、申请人尚未履行《协议》中的付款义务、被申请人的担保义务尚未产生。

3. 第三被申请人主张根据相关法律法规规定,保证期限应该是二年,该条款约定保证期限五年,与法律规定有冲突,可以视为约定不明,在约定不明的情况下,担保责任应该是半年。仲裁庭认为,该主张没有法律依据,与我国《担保法》有关保证期限的规定不符。

4. 第三被申请人还主张申请人主张的律师费保全费不属于被申请人保证责任范围,被申请人不应当承担。仲裁庭注意到《补充协议》关于保证责任的原文是第二被申请人和三对"《协议》及本协议中所产生的所有责任、义务承担无限连带责任担保",仲裁庭认为,所有的责任、义务应当包括申请人主张债权而发生的合理费用。

5. 第三被申请人还主张,申请人要求的回购款金额人民币4680万元明显过高,显失公平。仲裁庭认为,4680万元回购款是《协议》和《补充协议》规定的金额,不论是仲裁庭,还是协议当事人都应该首先尊重当事人之间的约定。仲裁庭认为,对于合同约定的金额是否显失公平或是否过高,应该结合合同签订时的具体情形进行分析,被申请人具有完全行为能力,应该对自己签订的合同负责,不能在出现纠纷后随意否定自己签订的合同效力。在股份转让交易中,申请人与第一被申请人签订的股权转让合同时的期望值是,E公司可以在较短时间内上市,申请人可以获取高额收益。而且,上市或被上市公司并购是第一被申请人邀约申请人进入交易的主要承诺之一。对这一交易背景,被申请人各方是十分清楚的。在这一前提下,仲裁庭无法按照一般的借款利率来认定人民币 4680 万元的回购款是否过高或显示公平。如果被申请人认为该金额显失公平或者有其他不当之处,应当承担举证责任。遗憾的是,被申请人没有提出令人信服的法律或事实上的证据,证明该金额显失公平。

（四）关于申请人的仲裁请求

基于上述认定的事实,仲裁庭认为被申请人违反了《协议》和《补充协议》的规定,有义务按照申请人的请求,以人民币 4680 万元的价格回购申请人持有的 E 公司的 450 万股股份。回购的起算时间应当从 2015 年 9 月 20 日起算。第二被申请人已经在 2015 年 11 月 17 日和 2015 年 18 日向申请人支付了人民币 500 万元和港币 399 万元,应该予以扣除。按照中国人民银行公布的 2015 年 11 月 18 日港币和人民币汇率中间价,港币 399 万元相当于人民币 3, 292, 359 元。因此被申请人共已经支付人民币 8, 292, 359 元,还应支付回购款人民币 38, 507, 641 元。

《补充协议》约定,如果被申请人没有在规定期限内支付回购款,每延期一日应当按照应付款项的千分之三支付违约金。申请人自己认为每日千分之三的违约金过高,主动调整为每日万分之六点五八的利率。仲裁庭认为,申请人在 2014 年 12 月实际支付的投资款本金总额为人民币 3600 万元,协议规定的回购款人民币 4680 万元超过本金人民币 1080 万元,超过部分已经是申请人获得的收益。在人民币 4680 万元的基础上按照每日万分之六点五八计算违约金,仍然过高,而且在超过本金的部分基础上计算违约金,有重复计算之嫌。为公平合理起见,仲裁庭酌情裁定,按照每日万分之五计算迟延部分金额的违约金。其中:

1. 自 2015 年 9 月 20 日起按照人民币 4680 万元,每日万分之五计算违约金,计算至 2015 年 11 月 18 日止,共 59 天,应计违约金人民币 1, 380, 600 元。

2. 自 2015 年 11 月 18 日起,人民币 4680 万元应当扣除被申请人二向申请人支付的人民币 500 万元和港币 399 万元,合人民币 8, 292, 359 元。未付款金额为人民币 38, 507, 641,以此为基础按每日万分之五的比例计算违约金。计算至被申请人实际支付回购款和违约金之日止,暂计至 2016 年 4 月 30 日,共计 164 天,应计违约金人民币 3, 157, 626. 56 元。

3. 以上两项,暂计至 2016 年 4 月 30 日,违约金总额为人民币 4, 538, 226. 56 元。

鉴于仲裁庭认定第一被申请人应当承担的违约责任,仲裁庭认为第一被申请人应当承担申请人因本案发生的律师费、保全费和因保全发生的第三方担保费。申请人提交了相关合同和发票证明其发生的上述费用及金额,第一被申请人没有对这些费用提出明确异议,或虽然提出异议但没有举证证明这些费用与本案无关或存在不合理之处,因此,仲裁庭支持申请人的请求。

鉴于仲裁庭支持了申请人的绝大部分仲裁请求,第一被申请人应当承担本案的全部仲裁费用。

三、裁决

综上,仲裁庭对本案作出裁决如下:

(一)第一被申请人应向申请人支付人民币38,507,641元的股权回购款,回购申请人持有的E公司股份有限公司的股权。

(二)第一被申请人应按每日万分之五的利率承担至实际支付之日为止的迟延付款金额的违约金。暂计至2016年4月30日,违约金总额为人民币4,538,226.56元。

(三)第一被申请人向申请人支付保全费人民币5000元、担保费人民币327,600元和律师费人民币450,000元。

(四)本案仲裁费人民币605,366元,由第一被申请人承担。鉴于申请人已经支付该仲裁费,第一被申请人应直接向申请人支付上述仲裁费。

本案仲裁员实际开支费用人民币4357.50元,由第一被申请人承担,鉴于申请人与被申请人分别预缴了人民币7500元,冲抵本案仲裁员实际开支费后仍结余人民币10,642.50元,将由本会分别退还申请人人民币7500元、被申请人人民币3142.50元。

(五)第二被申请人和第三被申请人对第一被申请人应当向申请人支付的上述股份回购款、违约金和各项费用承担连带担保责任。

以上被申请人应支付的款项应在本裁决书作出之日起15日内履行完毕。

本裁决为终局裁决,自作出之日起生效。

首席仲裁员:

仲　裁　员:

仲　裁　员:

二〇一六年五月二十五日于深圳

Commentary on Maffezini v. Spain, Decision on objections to jurisdiction: , ICSID Case No. ARB/97/7 , IIC 85 (2000) *

Maffezini v Spain, Decision on objections to jurisdiction, ICSID Case no ARB/97/7, (2001) 16 ICSID Rev-FILJ 212, (2002) 5 ICSID Rep 396, (2003)

124 ILR 9, (2001) 40 ILM 1129, IIC 85(2000), 25th January 2000, International Centre for Settlement of Investment Disputes [ICSID]

Date: 25 January 2000

Content type: Arbitral Decisions Jurisdiction: International Centre for Settlement of Investment Disputes [ICSID]

Citation(s): ICSID Case no ARB/97/7(Official Case No)

(2001) 16 ICSID Rev-FILJ 212(Official Citation)

(2002) 5 ICSID Rep 396(Other Reference)

(2003) 124 ILR 9(Other Reference)

(2001) 40 ILM 1129(Other Reference)

IIC 85(2000) (OUP reference)

Product: Investment Claims [IC]

Module: International Investment Claims [IIC]

Parties: Emilio Agustín Maffezini(Argentina [ar]) Spain

Judges/Arbitrators: Francisco Orrego Vicuña (President); Thomas Buergenthal (Claimant appointment); Maurice Wolf(Respondent appointment)

Counsel for Party One: Dr Raúl Emilio Vinuesa(Estudio Vinuesa y Asociados, Buenos Aires, Argentina)

Counsel for Party Two: Mr Rafael Andrés León Cavero(State Attorney, Ministry of Justice, Madrid, Spain)

Procedural Stage: Decision on objections to jurisdiction

Previous Procedural Stage(s):

Procedural order no 1; *Maffezini v Spain*, ICSID Case no ARB/97/7, 21 August 1998

Procedural order no 2; *Maffezini v Spain*, ICSID Case no ARB/97/7, IIC 84 (1999), 28 October 1999

---

* Oxford University Press, Nov. 2013.

Subsequent Development(s):

Award; *Maffezini v Spain*, ICSID Case no ARB/97/7, IIC 86(2000), 11 November 2000

Rectification of the Award; *Maffezini v Spain*, ICSID Case no ARB/97/7, IIC 87 (2001), 31 January 2001

Arbitral Rules: Convention on the Settlement of Investment Disputes Between States and Nationals of Other States(18 March 1965) 575 UNTS 159, entered into force 14 October 1966

Governing Law: Agreement between the Government of the Argentine Republic and the Kingdom of Spain for the Promotion and Reciprocal Protection of Investments, (03 October 1991), IC-BT 1051(1992), entered into force 28 September 1992; Agreement between the Kingdom of Spain and the Republic of Chile on the Reciprocal Protection and Promotion of Investments, (2 October 1991), BOE 1994 no 67 9149; BOE 1994 no 107 13801; 1774 UNTS 15; I-30883, entered into force 28 March 1994

1774 UNTS 15, entered into force 28 March 1994

Subject(s):

Exhaustion of local remedies—Jurisdiction of arbitral tribunals—Jus standi—Most-favoured-nation(MFN), jurisdictional matters—Most-favoured-nation(MFN), procedural matters—State entities and attribution.

Core Issue(s):

Whether resort to local remedies was required before a case could be submitted to the arbitration of the International Centre for the Settlement of Investment Disputes under the Agreement between the Government of the Argentine Republic and the Kingdom of Spain for the Promotion and Reciprocal Protection of Investments('Argentina-Spain BIT').

Whether the MFN clause included in the Argentina-Spain BIT covered procedural and jurisdictional provisions of the treaty.

Whether the claimant was qualified as an investor within the meaning of Article 25 (1) of the Convention on the Settlement of Investment Disputes Between States and Nationals of Other States.

Whether the conduct of the claimant's business partner was attributable to Spain. Whether the dispute was eligible for the protection of the Argentina-Spain BIT.

Facts

F1 In 1989, Mr Maffezini set up Emilio A Maffezini SS('EAMSA') to produce and distribute chemical products in Galicia, Spain, jointly with Sociedad para el Desarrollo Industrial de Galicia('SODIGA'). Maffezini contributed 70% of the capital for the EAMSA, while SODIGA contributed 30%. SODIGA also granted a loan of ESP 40 million to EAMSA. Various subsidies were requested from and approved by the Spanish Ministry of Finance and the *Xunta de Galicia*.

F2 During the preparation for the establishment of the enterprise, EAMSA began to experience financial difficulties. Measures were taken to cope with the difficulties, and a transfer of ESP 30 million was made from a personal account of Maffezini to EAMSA.

F3 In early March 1992, Maffezini ordered the construction to stop and the dismissal of EAMSA employees. In June 1994, an attorney working for Maffezini approached SODIGA with an offer inviting them to cancel all outstanding debts owed to it by EAMSA and Maffezini in exchange for EAMSA's assets. SODIGA did not express acceptance of the offer until 13 June 1996. Maffezini did not follow up on SODIGA's delayed acceptance.

F4 On 18 July 1997, Maffezini filed a request for arbitration proceedings against Spain, on the basis of the Agreement between the Government of the Argentine Republic and the Kingdom of Spain for the Promotion and Reciprocal Protection of Investments, (3 October 1991), IC-BT 1051(1992), entered into force 28 September 1992('Argentina-Spain BIT'). Maffezini submitted first that because of SODIGA's status as a public entity, all of its acts and omissions were attributable to Spain. Second, that the project failed because of the wrong advice given by SODIGA with regard to the costs of the project, which had turned out to be significantly higher than originally estimated. Third, that SODIGA was also responsible for the additional costs resulting from the EIA since EAMSA was pressured to make the investment before the EIA process was finalized and before its implications were known. Fourth, that Maffezini had not agreed to a loan to EAMSA for ESP 30 million and that the transfer of this amount from his personal account to EAMSA was irregular.

F5 Spain challenged the jurisdiction and competence of the Tribunal on the grounds that Maffezini had failed to comply with the requirements of Article X of the Argentina-Spain BIT, particularly Article X(3)(a) requiring the exhaustion of certain domestic remedies in Spain, and Article X(2), which required Maffezini to submit the case to the Spanish courts before referring it to international arbitration.

F6 Spain further challenged Maffezini's alternative argument that through the operation of the MFN clause under the Argentina-Spain BIT, he was entitled to the more advantageous provisions under the Agreement between the Kingdom of Spain and the Republic of Chile on the Reciprocal Protection and Promotion of Investments(2 October 1991), BOE 1994 no 67 9149; BOE 1994 no 107 13801; 1774 UNTS 15; I-30883, entered into force 28 March 1994 1774 UNTS 15, entered into force 28 March 1994('Chile-Spain BIT') and could therefore bypass the local remedies procedure. Spain stated that treaties made by Spain with third countries were—in respect of Argentina—*res inter alios acta* and consequently could not be invoked by Manffez ini. Spain also argued that under the principle *ejusdem generis* the MFN clause could only operate in respect of the same matter, which—in the context of the Argentina-Spain BIT—meant 'substantive matters or material aspects of the treatment granted to investors and not to procedural or jurisdictional questions'. Only if it could be established that resort to domestic tribunals would produce objective disadvantages for the investor would it have been possible to argue material effects on the treatment owed.

F7 The third challenge brought by Spain was that the claimant lacked standing to file this request for arbitration because EAMSA was a Spanish juridical entity and had a juridical personality separate and distinct from its shareholders. Spain contended that as long as the company continued to exist qua company, a shareholder had no standing to seek to lift the corporate veil and sue in his personal capacity for damages sustained by the company. Maffezini emphasiz ed that he was not bringing this case on behalf of EAMSA, but in his personal capacity as a foreign—Argentine—investor.

F8 Fourth, Spain contended that the dispute was between Maffezini and a private corporation—SODIGA—not the Kingdom of Spain.

Held

H1 Maffezini's interpretation of Article X was rejected. The article was intended to ' give their respective courts the opportunity, within the specific period of 18 months, to resolve the dispute before it could be taken to international arbitration' . Article X(3)(a) was not a strict exhaustion of domestic remedies requirement because it failed to require the exhaustion of all available domestic remedies. (paragraphs 21 – 37)

H2 The MFN clause in the Argentina-Spain BIT had not embraced the dispute settlement provisions of the treaty. Maffrzini was entitled to submit the case to international arbitration without first accessing the Spanish courts, relying on the relevant provisions in the Chile-Spain BIT.

H3 In arriving at the above conclusion, relevant previous cases were examined, and the analyses were founded—in particular—on the findings of the International Court of Justice in *Award of the Commission of Arbitration established for the Ambatielos claim between Greece and the United Kingdom* 6 March 1956(' *Ambatielos* '), which concluded that administration of justice might not necessarily be excluded from the field of application of the MFN clause, and that the question could ' only be determined in accordance with the intention of the contracting parties as deduced from a reasonable interpretation of the Treaty' .

H4 The ' fundamental question of public policy' was answered in favour of investors, as ' today dispute settlement arrangements are inextricably related to the protection of foreign investors, as they are also related to the protection of rights of traders under treaties of commerce' , so much so that:

such arrangements, even if not strictly a part of the material aspect of the trade and investment policy pursued by treaties of commerce and navigation, were essential for the adequate protection of the rights they sought to guarantee.

In support, the context of the treaty, the negotiations relating to it, other legal arrangements and the subsequent practice of the parties were also examined. (paragraphs 43 – 64)

H5 A number of scenarios in which the MFN clause may not have worked were stated.

(paragraphs 62 – 63) Nevertheless ' some important limits' resulted from ' public policy considerations that the contracting parties might have envisaged as fundamental conditions for their acceptance of the agreement in question' . There were a number of scenarios in which the MFN clause might not have worked.

a) First, if a contracting party had conditioned its consent to arbitration on the ' exhaustion of local remedies', this requirement could not be bypassed by invoking the MFN clause in relation to a third party agreement that did not contain this element;

b) Second, if the parties had agreed to a ' fork in the road' dispute arrangement, this stipulation could have been bypassed by invoking the clause.

c) Third, if the agreement provided for a particular arbitration forum—such as ICSID, for example—this option could not have been changed by invoking the clause.

d) Finally, if the parties had agreed to a highly institutionalized system of arbitration that incorporated precise rules of procedure—as in the case of the North American Free Trade Agreement(17 December 1992) US Gov't Printing Office(1992), entered into force 1 January 1994—such mechanisms could have been altered by the operation of the clause.

e) To conclude:

it is clear, in any event, that a distinction has to be made between the legitimate extension of rights and benefits by means of the operation of the clause, on the one hand, and disruptive treaty-shopping that would play havoc with the policy objectives of underlying specific treaty provisions, on the other hand. (paragraphs 62 – 63)

H6 Maffezini had made out a *prima facie* case that he had standing to file the case as an Argentine investor in a Spanish company. (paragraphs 67 – 70)

H7 Maffezini had made out a *prima facie* case that SODIGA was a state entity acting on behalf of Spain. (paragraphs 74 – 89)

H8 The dispute was covered by both the Argentina-Spain BIT and the Chile-Spain BIT, since in technical and legal senses it began to take shape in 1994, after the two BITs had entered into force. (paragraphs 94-98)

H9 The dispute fell within the jurisdiction of the International Centre for the Settlement of Investment Disputes and the competence of the Tribunal. (paragraph 99)

Date of Report: 14 November 2013

Reporter(s): Wenhua Shan

Analysis

A1 The *Maffezini* case was the first case in which an investment arbitration tribunal closely looked into the potential jurisdictional application of an MFN clause in an investment treaty.

A2 The *Maffezini* decision was followed and further strengthened by *Siemens AG v Argentina*, Decision on jurisdiction, ICSID Case no ARB/02/8; (2005) 44 ILM 138; IIC 226(2004), 3rd August 2004, particularly paragraphs 102-120. In this case, the MFN clause in the basic agreement, Treaty between the Federal Republic of Germany and the Argentine Republic on the Encouragement and Reciprocal Protection of Investments, (9 April 1991), ICBT-029(1991), entered into force 8 November 1993(' Argentina-Germany BIT'), did not have the opening words of that in Art IV(2) of the Argentina-Spain BIT(' [I]n all matters subject to this agreement...'). The Tribunal nevertheless accepted the incorporation of the relevant dispute settlement provisions from the Argentina-Chile BIT.

A3 Maffezini's approach was criticized and rejected by *Salini Costruttori SpA and Italstrade SpA v Jordan*, Decision on jurisdiction, ICSID Case no ARB/02/13, (2005) 20 ICSID Rev—FILJ 148; (2005) 44 ILM 569; IIC 207 (2004), 29th November 2004 ('*Salini*'), *Plama Consortium Limited v Bulgaria*, Decision on jurisdiction, ICSID Case no ARB/03/24; (2005) 20 ICSID Rev—FILJ 262; (2005) 44 ILM 721; IIC 189(2005), 8th February 2005('*Plama*'), and Telenor Mobile Communications AS v Hungary, Award, ICSID Case no ARB/04/15, (2006) 21 ICSID Rev—FILJ 603, IIC 248(2006), 13th

September 2006('*Telenor*'). In *Salini*, the Tribunal first examined the decision in *Ambatielos* and concluded that the solution adopted in *Ambatielos* could not be directly transposed into the case before it. (*Salini*, para 112) The Tribunal proceeded to examine the *Maffezini* decision, and expressed considerable concern about the approach adopted in that case. In particular, it commented that the public policy-based exceptions to the general rule allowing extension of an MFN clause to dispute resolution procedures might be difficult to apply, thus increasing the risk of 'treaty shopping' by claimants. (*Salini*, para 115)

A4 In *Plama*, the Tribunal likewise rejected the claimant's argument that the MFN provision in the Agreement between The Government of the people's Republic of Bulgaria and The Government of the Republic of Cyprus on Mutual Encouragement and Protection of Investments, (12 November 1987), entered into force 18 May 1988('Bulgaria-Cyprus BIT') only could be used as a means of incorporating more favourable dispute settlement provisions from Bulgaria's other BITs. The Tribunal based its decision on a well-established principle in both domestic and international laws that an agreement to arbitrate must be 'clear and unambiguous' (*Plama*, para 198), and as such:

[C]ontracting states cannot be presumed to have agreed that those provisions can be enlarged by incorporating dispute resolution provisions from other treaties negotiated in an entirely different context. (*Plama*, para 207)

The *Plama* Tribunal flatly rejected the general approach adopted by the *Maffezini* Tribunal that: ' the principle with multiple exceptions as stated by the tribunal in the *Maffezini* case should instead be a different principle with one, single exception: an MFN provision in a basic treaty does not incorporate by reference dispute settlement provisions in whole or in part set forth in another treaty, unless the MFN provision in the basic treaty leaves no doubt that the Contracting Parties intended to incorporate them. (*Plama*, para 223)

A5 The *Plama* principle was 'wholeheartedly' endorsed by the *Telenor* Tribunal. (*Telenor*, para 90), which ruled that the MFN clause(Article IV) in the basic treaty(Agreement between the Government of the Republic of Hungary and the Government of the Kingdom of Norway on the Promotion and Reciprocal Protection of Investments(8 April 1991) IC-BT 1564(1991), entered into force 4 December 1992('Norway-Hungary BIT')) could not be used 'to extend the Tribunal's jurisdiction to categories of claim' other than that specified in Article XI of the basic treaty(expropriation), 'for this would subvert the common intention of Hungary and Norway in entering into the BIT in question'. (*Telenor*, para 100) In supporting this conclusion, the Tribunal gave several 'compelling reasons': (1) MFN clauses should normally cover only 'substantive' rights, not 'procedural' rights; (2) problems of treaty shopping, uncertainty, and instability that an expansive interpretation of the MFN clause might generate; (3) the treaty practice of both Hungary and Norway did not warrant an extensive reading of the clause. (*Telenor*, paras 91 – 97)

A6 The *Maffezini* decision has also resulted in concerns and reactions among host states, and has led to specific negotiation of MFN clauses in investment treaties such as the North American Free Trade Agreement(JW Bocariol and OE Silva, 'The Didening of the MFN Obligation and its Impact on Investor Protection' Int TLR 2005, 11(2), 61 – 67, at 66) and the UK Model BIT, which says in the third paragraph of the MFN clause that, '[F]or avoidance of doubt it is confirmed that the treatment provided for in paragraphs(1) and(2) above shall apply to the provisions of Articles 1 to 11 of this Agreement'.

A7 The reactions to the *Maffezini* decision have demonstrated that its rationale is dissatisfactory, if not completely wrong. The Tribunal might be right in answering the question in the affirmative in the present case, given the opening wording of the MFN clause concerned, the negotiation history of the BIT concerned, and the practice of Spain, as identified by the Tribunal in the case. However, the same answer cannot be given as a general rule. On the contrary, the approach adopted by the *Plama* Tribunal could reasonably be preferred for two main reasons.

A8 First, the *Plama* approach takes into account sovereign interests as part of its public policy analysis. The Tribunal in *El Paso Energy International Company v Argentine Republic*, Decision on jurisdiction, ICSID Case no ARB/03/15; IIC 83(2006), 27 April 2006('*El Paso*'), balancing both approaches, required that a tribunal take into account:

both state sovereignty and the state's responsibility to create an adapted and evolutionary framework for the development of economic activities, and the necessity to protect foreign investment and its continuing flow. (*El Paso*, para 70).

A9 Second, the use of the *Ambatielos* decision in *Maffezini* has significant weaknesses. A close read of the decision can find that, the *Ambatielos* Tribunal, although it considered that 'administration of justice' could be covered by an MFN clause, it considered this as an 'exception', rather than a 'principle'.

Date of Analysis: 14 November 2013 Analysis by: Wenhua Shan

Further analysis:

E Gaillard, 'Establishing Jurisdiction through a Most-Favoured-Nation Clause', New York Law Journal Vol 233, No 105(2 June 2005)

S Fietta, 'Most Favoured Nation Treatment and Dispute Resolution unde Bilateral Investment Treaties: A Turning Point?' [2005] International Arbitration Law Review, 131 – 138

JW Boscariol and OE Silva, ' The Widening of the Obligation and its Impact on Investor Protection' , 2005 International Trade Law and Regulation, 11(2), 61 – 67

R Dolzer and T Myers, ' After *Tecmed*: Most Favoured-Nation Clauses in Investment Protection Agreement' 19 ICSID Review—Foreign Investment Law Journal 49(2004)

OECD: ' Most-Favoured-Nation Treatment in International Investment Law' OECD Working Paper on International Investment, no 2004/2, September 2004

Instruments cited in the full text of this decision:

International

Convention on the Settlement of Investment Disputes Between States and Nationals of Other States(18 March 1965) 575 UNTS 159, entered into force 14 October 1966, Articles 25(1), 26

Agreement between the Government of the Republic of Hungary and the Government of the Kingdom of Norway on the Promotion and Reciprocal Protection of Investments, (8 April 1991) IC-BT 1564(1991), entered into force 4 December 1992

Agreement between the Government of the Argentine Republic and the Kingdom of Spain for the Promotion and Reciprocal Protection of Investments, (3 October 1991), IC-BT 1051(1992), entered into force 28 September 1992, Article X

Agreement between the Kingdom of Spain and the Republic of Chile on the Reciprocal Protection and Promotion of Investments(2 October 1991), BOE 1994 no 67 9149; BOE 1994 no 107 13801;

1774 UNTS 15; I-30883, entered into force 28 March 1994

North American Free Trade Agreement(17 December 1992) US Gov't Printing Office(1992), entered into force 1 January 1994

Cases cited in the full text of this decision:

Award of the Commission of Arbitration established for the Ambatielos claim between Greece and the United Kingdom 6 March 1956

To access full citation information for this document, see the Oxford Law Citator record

Commentary on Tza Yap Shum v Peru: Decision on jurisdiction and competence, ICSID Case no ARB/07/6, IIC 382 (2009) *

Shum v Peru, Decision on jurisdiction and competence, ICSID Case no ARB/07/6, IIC 382(2009), despatched 19th June 2009, International Centre for Settlement of Investment Disputes [ICSID]

Despatched: 19 June 2009

Content type: Arbitral Decisions Jurisdiction: International Centre for Settlement of Investment Disputes [ICSID]

Citation(s): ICSID Case no ARB/07/6(Official Case No)

IIC 382(2009) (OUP reference)

Product: Investment Claims [IC]

Module: International Investment Claims [IIC]

Parties: Tza Yap Shum(China [cn]) Peru

Judges/Arbitrators: Judd L Kessler(President); Hernando Otero(Claimant appointment); Professor Juan Fernández-Armesto(Respondent appointment)

Counsel for Party One: Mr Orlando Siu(Estudio Paitán & Abogados, Lima, Peru); Mr Carlos Paitán(Estudio Paitán & Abogados, Lima, Peru); Mr Christian Carvajal (; Estudio Paitán & Abogados, Lima, Peru)

Counsel for Party Two: Mr Louis B Kimmelman(Allen & Overy LLP, New York, United States); Mr Stephen Jagusch(Allen & Overy LLP, New York, United States); Ms Nicole R Duclos(Allen & Overy LLP, New York, United States); Mr Anthony Sinclair (Allen & Overy LLP, New York, United States)

Procedural Stage: Decision on jurisdiction and competence

Arbitral Rules: Convention on the Settlement of Investment Disputes Between States and Nationals of Other States(18 March 1965) 575 UNTS 159, entered into force 14 October 1966

Governing Law: Agreement between the People's Republic of China and the Government of the Republic of Peru concerning the Encouragement and Reciprocal Protection of Investments(China/Peru BIT) (9 June 1994) MOFCOM, Collection of International Investment Treaties(Jingguan Jiaoyu Press 1998) 929 – 941; IC – BT 457(1994), entered into force 1 February 1995; International law

---

* Oxford University Press, Sep. 2012.

Subject(s):

Consent to jurisdiction(express)—Consent to jurisdiction(implicit)—Expropriation—Investment defined in treaties—Fair and equitable treatment standard—Most-favoured-nation(MFN), jurisdictional matters

Core Issue(s):

Whether the claimant was an investor under the Agreement between the People's Republic of China and the Government of the Republic of Peru concerning the Encouragement and Reciprocal Protection of Investments('China/Peru BIT').

Whether the claimant made an investment protected by the China/Peru BIT.

Whether the International Centre for the Settlement of Investment Disputes('Tribunal') had jurisdiction over the question whether expropriation had actually taken place.

Whether the Tribunal could hear disputes other than those involving expropriation.

Facts

F1 The dispute arose from tax actions imposed by the Peruvian Tax Administration('SUNAT') on the TSG Peru SAC. ('TSG'), a Peruvian company in the business of producing fish based food products and exporting them to Asian markets. Mr Tz a Yap Shum—a Chinese national residing in Hong Kong—was the majority shareholder of TSG.

F2 In December 2001, TSG was incorporated in the Republic of Peru and mainly engaged in the production and manufacturing of fish flavour. In 2002, Linkvest—a company incorporated in the British Virgin Islands and wholly controlled by Shum—purchased 90% of TSG shares. In May 2004, the SUNAT commenced an audit on TSG, which resulted in a tax lien with a bank account garnishment against TSG. In February 2005, Shum became the majority shareholder of TSG on behalf of Linkvest.

F3 On 14 September 2006, Shum and TSG filed with ICSID a request for arbitration against Peru, alleging that the unlawful and arbitrary tax lien had the effect of destroying TSG business operations and economic viability. It was also pointed out that Peru violated the following obligations of the Agreement between the People's Republic of China and the Government of the Republic of Peru concerning the Encouragement and Reciprocal Protection of Investments(China/Peru BIT)(9 June 1994) MOFCOM, Collection of International Investment Treaties(Jingguan Jiaoyu Press 1998) 929 – 941; IC – BT 457(1994), entered into force 1 February 1995('China/Peru BIT'): (a) the obligation to accord fair and equitable treatment; (b) the obligation to give full protection and security; (c) the obligation to provide compensation against expropriation; and, (d) the obligation to guarantee the free transfer of investment and returns. Because TSG was a company incorporated in Peru, it was not qualified to be a 'foreign' investor in Peru. In January 2007, the request by TSG was withdrawn.

F4 Correspondingly, Peru denied Shum's allegation and made four objections to the jurisdiction of the International Centre for the Settlement of Investment Disputes

(' Tribunal'): (a) Shum had not proved his Chinese nationality and thus could not qualify as a ' foreign' investor under the China/Peru BIT or even if Shum proved his Chinese nationality, he did not have recourse to the China/Peru BIT because he resided in the Hong Kong Special Administrative Region; (b) Shum made indirect investment in TSG through Linkvest when the dispute arose, and the China/Peru BIT did not protect indirect investments; (c) Shum had not filed a *prima facie* claim that qualified as an expropriation under the China/Peru BIT; and (d) Shum's claims regarding expropriation were not covered within the investor-state dispute settlement clause of the China/Peru BIT, and only disputes involving the amount of compensation for expropriation could be submitted to international arbitration under the China/Peru BIT.

Held

H1 The Tribunal had jurisdiction to hear the expropriation claim of Shum. (paragraph 221)

H2 Most of Peru's objections to jurisdiction were rejected. Considering the specific wording of Article 8 China/Peru BIT regarding the settlement of investor-state dispute, many of Shum's claims were out of the scope of that provision, and therefore had to be dismissed. (paragraph 216)

H3 Shum could be considered a Chinese national and protected by the China/Peru BIT. The Chinese passport and the identity document produced by Shum was sufficient to prove his Chinese nationality. (paragraph 58)

H4 The nationality conferred by a state to a person under its laws had a strong presumption of validity, which Peru failed to challenge. (paragraph 63)

H5 Neither the Convention on the Settlement of Investment Disputes Between States and Nationals of Other States(18 March 1965) 575 UNTS 159, entered into force 14 October 1966(' ICSID Convention') nor the China/Peru BIT stipulated explicit limitation to the right of Chinese nationals with residence in Hong Kong. (paragraph 77)

H6 Shum did have an investment in Peru as early as 2001, which was earlier than the SUNAT audit started. (paragraph 88) either the ICSID Convention nor international investment law provided that indirect investments were excluded or forbidden. The China/Peru BIT did protect indirect investments of natural persons of Chinese nationality in Peruvian territory. (paragraph 111)

H7 With respect to the *prima facie* claim, in the procedural stage it was not appropriate to take a definitive position on the alleged facts in connection with Article 4 (expropriation) of the China/Peru BIT(paragraph 127), and the Tribunal only needed to study the evidence that could meet the minimal requirements of jurisdiction required by the ICSID Convention and the China/Peru BIT. (paragraph 126) In this respect, Shum had filed a *prima facie* expropriation claim. (paragraph 128)

H8 The Tribunal had jurisdiction to decide the merits of the expropriation claims filed by Shum. (paragraph 188) The China/Peru BIT stipulated that only a dispute involving the amount of compensation agreed to in its text and any others consented to by the parties to the dispute could be submitted to the Tribunal. Peru argued that the interpretation of this clause should be based on a strict and literal ground, (paragraphs 129 – 131) which meant that only disputes involving the agreed amount of compensation could be settled through arbitration of the Tribunal when the occurrence of an illegal expropriation had been determined by the local court. (paragraph 134) On the contrary, after interpreting this clause in accordance with Articles 31 and 32 of the Vienna Convention on the Law of Treaties (23 May 1969) 1155 UNTS 331; 8 ILM 679 (1969); 63 AJIL 875 (1969), entered into force 27 January 1980 and taking into account other arbitral practice, the word ' involving' was to be interpreted broadly, to include not only the mere determination of the amount but also any other issues inherent to an expropriation, including whether the expropriation occurred and the amount of compensation due. Further, a strict interpretation of the word ' involving' would preclude the provision related to the Tribunal's arbitration. Consequently, the Tribunal was competent to hear the expropriation claims. (paragraph 188)

H9 However, the most favoured nation clause of the China/Peru BIT could not be used to broaden the scope of the Tribunal's arbitration. The claims, other than the one concerning expropriation, were rejected, based on the consideration that it was not appropriate to interpret the China/Peru BIT dispute settlement clause together with the most favoured nation clause contained in Article 3 of the China/Peru BIT to rely on such dispute settlement clause in the Agreement between the Government of the Republic of Colombia and the Government of the Republic of Peru concerning the Promotion and Reciprocal Protection of Investments (26 April 1994), entered into force 2003. The latter stipulated that any dispute between a foreign investor and the host state could be submitted to The Tribunal. The specific wording of Article 8(3) of the China/Peru BIT:

[a]ny disputes concerning other matters between an investor of either Contracting Party and the other Contracting Party may be submitted to the Centre if the parties to the dispute so agree.

prevailed any general wording of the most favoured nation clause. Accordingly Shum's first, second, and fourth claims were dismissed. (paragraph 216)

Date of Report: 28 September 2012

Reporter(s): Wenhua Shan, Jerry Sheng Zhang, Yuting Hua

Analysis

A1 The *Tza Yap Shum* jurisdiction decision is significant in many ways. First of all, it is the first case involving a Chinese investment treaty. Given that China is now both an important recipient and source of foreign investment and that it has one of the most extensive BIT networks in the world, the interpretations given in this case bear significant implications for existing and future investors in China as well as Chinese investors investing abroad. It is therefore not surprising that the case has drawn wide attention from business and legal communities.

A2 Second, the Tribunal's interpretation concerning the scope of the dispute settlement provision has significant implications for foreign investors covered by traditional Chinese BITs. These traditional BIT's containing such narrow dispute settlement clauses as those in the China/Peru BIT account for the vast majority of China's BITs clauses (which also appear in many Soviet-era Russian and Eastern European BITs), and typically permit arbitration of only disputes concerning the amount of compensation for expropriation. As noted by the *Tza Yap Shum* Tribunal, some previous tribunals had read such BITs as not allowing for arbitration of the question of whether expropriation had actually occurred. This decision, however, sides with other tribunals—such as the one in *Renta 4 SVSA and ors v Russian Federation*, Award on preliminary objections, SCC Case no 24/2007; IIC 369(2009), 20 March 2009—that have taken a more expansive view of such BITs, suggesting that foreign investors in China may be able to directly rely on protections provided under those traditional BITs to protect their investments against expropriatory government measures. (paragraphs 167 – 169)

A3 Thirdly, the decision contributes further to the ongoing debate concerning the legal effects of most-favoured-nation('MFN') clauses in BITs. Some tribunals—such as the one in *RosInvest Co UK Ltd v Russian Federation*, Jurisdiction award, SCC Case no V079/2005; IIC 315(2007), 5 October 2007—have interpreted a BIT's MFN clause as allowing for the arbitration of claims otherwise falling outside the scope of the BIT's dispute settlement clause. This Tribunal, however, follows the approach of other tribunals—such as *Plama Consortium Limited v Bulgaria*, Decision on jurisdiction, ICSID Case no ARB/03/24; IIC 189(2005), 8 February 2005—in holding that such clauses cannot be used to extend the scope of dispute settlement provisions to substantive claims not specifically referenced in those provisions. The main reason given in the decision is, however, somewhat unique. It appears to have based its decision on the principle of 'special rules prevail over general rules', concluding that the express specific requirement of party consent contained in Article 8(3) for submission of non-expropriatory measures to arbitration prevails over the general wording of the MFN clause. Whilst this might be the correct reading of what has been intended under Article 8(3), it does not answer the question whether other—ie, non-expropriatory—measures might be submitted to arbitration absent such specific requirement. Indeed, most Chinese BITs have followed this prototype. (paragraphs 210 – 211)

A4 Finally, the decision is noteworthy in that it is the first case involving an investor from Hong Kong SAR. It therefore provides a first opportunity to look into a somehow unique Chinese question of whether a Hong Kong investor is qualified as a Chinese investor and consequently protected by Chinese BITs, given the high degree of autonomy enjoyed by Hong Kong in external economic relations, including its competence to conclude BITs in its own name. The Tribunal answered the question in the positive, which would have the effect of encouraging Hong Kong investors to invest abroad making use of the extensive BIT network of China. The same view has been expressed in Norah Gallagher and Wenhua Shan, *Chinese Investment Treaties: Policies and Practice*, Oxford University Press 2009, pp. 93 – 96.

A5 It should be noted that China signed the China-Peru Free Trade Agreement (CPFTA) (28 April 2009), entered into force 1 March 2010. Article 139 of this Agreement stipulates that any investor-state dispute can be submitted to international arbitration after the exhaustion of the local administrative review procedure. Though this Agreement has not yet entered into force, it provides another example of the open attitude that the Chinese authorities have taken in dealing with investment treaty-based arbitration.

Date of Analysis: 28 September 2012

Analysis by: Wenhua Shan, Jerry Sheng Zhang, Yuting Hua

Further analysis:

Norah Gallagher, Wenhua Shan , *Chinese Investment Treaties: Policies and Practice*, Oxford University Press, pp. 93 – 96, (2009)

Andrew Newcombe, ' Another misapplication of MFN? Tz a Yap Shum v The Republic of Peru' , available at http://kluwerarbitrationblog.com/blog/2009/10/21/another-misapplication-of-mfn-tz a-yap-shum-v-the-republic-of-peru/

An Chen, *Could China-Peru BIT* 1994 *Be Applied to Hong Kong Special Administration Region under "One Country, Two System"?*—A Jurisprudential Analysis on the Case of Tza Yap Shum v Republic of Peru, *Commentaries by An Chen on international economic law, Vol.* 3, *pp* 1147 – 1196*(*2008*)*

Ko-Yung Tung, Rafael Cox-Alomar, ' The New Generation of China BITs in Light of Tz a Yap Shum v Republic of Peru' , 17 *Am Rev Int'l Arb* 461*(*2006*)*

Instruments cited in the full text of this decision:

*Convention on the Settlement of Investment Disputes Between States and Nationals of Other States(*18 *March* 1965*)*575 *UNTS* 159, *entered into force* 14 *October* 1966 *Article* 25

*Agreement between the People's Republic of China and the Government of the Republic of Peru concerning the Encouragement and Reciprocal Protection of Investments(*9 *June* 1994*), entered into force* 01 *February* 1995 *Articles* 3, 4, 8, 8*(*3*)*, 12

*Agreement between the Government of the Republic of Colombia and the Government of the Republic of Peru concerning the Promotion and Reciprocal Protection of Investments (*26 *April* 1994*), entered into force* 2003

Cases cited in the full text of this decision:

Maffezini v Spain, *Award on jurisdiction, ICSID Case no ARB/97/7; (Argentina/Spain BIT)*, 25 *January* 2000

Siemens AG v Argentina, *Decision on jurisdiction, ICSID Case no ARB/02/8; IIC* 226*(*2004*)*, 3 *August* 2004

Salini Costruttori SpA and Italstrade SpA v Jordan, *Decision on jurisdiction, ICSID Case no ARB/02/13; IIC* 207*(*2004*)*, 15 *November* 2004

Plama Consortium Limited v Bulgaria, *Decision on jurisdiction, ICSID Case no ARB/03/24; IIC* 189*(*2005*)*, 8 *February* 2005

RosInvest Co UK Ltd v Russian Federation, *Jurisdiction award, SCC Case no V079/2005; IIC* 315*(*2007*)*, 5 *October* 2007

To access full citation information for this document, see the Oxford Law Citator record

Commentary on Metalclad Corp v Mexico, Award, Ad hoc – ICSID Additional Facility Rules; ICSID Case No ARB(AF)/97/1, IIC 161 (2000) *

Metalclad Corporation v Mexico, Award, ICSID Case No ARB(AF)/97/1, (2001) 16 ICSID Rev – FILJ 168,

(2001) 40 ILM 36, (2001) 26 YB Com Arb 99, (2002)

119 ILR 618, (2002) 5 ICSID Rep 212, (2001) 13(1)

World Trade and Arb Mat 45, IIC 161(2000), 25th August 2000, despatched 30th August 2000, International Centre for Settlement of Investment Disputes [ICSID]

Date: 25 August 2000

Citation(s): ICSID Case No ARB(AF)/97/1(Official Case No)

(2001) 16 ICSID Rev-FILJ 168(Other

Reference)

(2001) 40 ILM 36(Other Reference)

(2001) 26 YB Com Arb 99(Other Reference)

(2002) 119 ILR 618(Other Reference)

(2002) 5 ICSID Rep 212(Other Reference)

(2001) 13(1) World Trade and Arb Mat 45(Other Reference)

IIC 161(2000) (OUP reference)

Product: Investment Claims [IC]

Module: International Investment Claims [IIC]

Despatched: 30 August 2000 Content type: Arbitral Awards Jurisdiction: International Centre for Settlement of Investment Disputes [ICSID]

Parties: Metalclad Corporation(Delaware) Mexico

Judges/Arbitrators: Sir Elihu Lauterpacht, QC, CBE (President); Benjamin R Civiletti(Claimant appointment); José Luis Siqueiros(Respondent appointment)

Counsel for Party One: Clyde C Pearce, Esq(Law offices of Clyde C Pearce, Cali-

* Oxford University Press, Jul. 2007.

fornia, US)

Counsel for Party Two: Hugo Perezcano Díaz(Consultor Juridico, Subsecretaria de Negociaciones Comerciales Internacionales Direccion General de Consultoria Juridica de Negociaciones Secretaria de Comercio y Fomento Industrial, Mexico)

Procedural Stage: Award

Subsequent Development(s):

Judicial review; *Metalclad Corp v Mexico*, 2001 BCSC 664; IIC 162(2001); (2001) 14 BLR(3d) 285;

(2001) 89 BCLR(3d) 359, 2 May 2001 Supplementary Reasons for Judgment; *Metalclad Corp v Mexico*,

2001 BCSC 1529; IIC 163(2001), 31 October 2001

Arbitral Rules: Additional Facility Rules, Doc ICSID/11, International Centre for Settlement of Investment Disputes, June 1979

Governing Law: North American Free Trade Agreement(12 December 1992) US Gov't Printing Office(1992), entered into force 1 January 1994('NAFTA'); International law

Subject(s):

Jurisdiction of arbitral tribunals—Indirect expropriation—Fair and equitable treatment standard—Legitimate expectations—Transparency—Actions of political subdivisions and attribution—Treaties, interpretation—Incidental & additional claims—Discounted cash flow(DCF), anticipated future profits—Valuation

Core Issue(s):

Whether Mexico breached Articles 1105(fair and equitable treatment) and Article 1110(expropriation) of the North American Free Trade Agreement when, despite the fact that the Federal Government had granted a permit for the construction of the investor's hazardous waste disposal landfill and represented that no further license would be required, the municipal authorities declined a second permit and declared the area to be an ecological preserve.

Facts

F1 The dispute arose from the construction of a hazardous waste landfill in Guadalcaz ar, in the State of San Luís Potosí('SLP'), México, by Confinamiento Tecnico de Residuos Industriales, SA de CV('COTERIN'), which was a Mexican company that was later bought up by a US corporation, Metalclad. In 1990, the federal government of Mexico granted a permit to COTERIN to construct and operate a hazardous waste transfer station on the site. [paragraph 1] In the same year, COTERIN applied for, and was denied, a municipal permit to construct a hazardous waste landfill.

F2 In 1993, COTERIN obtained permits to build a haz ardous waste landfill from the federal National Ecological Institute('INE'). Shortly thereafter, Metalclad contracted for a six-month option to buy COTERIN and its permits. The option agreement was subject to the condition that COTERIN obtain either a municipal building permit or a definitive judgment from the Mexican courts that a building permit was not necessary.

[paragraphs 29 – 30]

F3 In May 1993 SLP issued a state land use permit to construct the landfill, subject to certain conditions. Metalclad then met with the governor of SLP, and believed it had obtained his support for the project. Metalclad also secured assurances from the president of the INE and the general director of the Mexican Secretariat of Urban Development and Ecology(' SEDUE') that all the permits necessary for the landfill had been issued except a federal permit for operation of the landfill, and that the federal government would obtain support for the project from Guadalcazar and SLP. The federal permit was then issued by INE in August 1993, and one month later Metalclad exercised its option to purchase COTERIN, the landfill site, and the permits. [paragraphs 31 – 5]

F4 Shortly after the purchase, the governor of SLP began to denounce the landfill project. Metalclad then tried to negotiate with SLP, and believed that it had secured SLP 's support. It then began construction. About six months later, in October 1994, however, Guadalcazar issued a stop work order on the ground that Metalclad had not obtained a municipal building permit for the construction. Metalclad complained to federal officials, who again assured Metalclad that it had all the necessary permits to construct and operate the landfill and that the municipality had no basis for denying a construction permit. The federal officials nevertheless suggested that Metalclad go through the formality of applying for the building permit in order to appease the municipality. Metalclad did apply for the permit, and resumed construction, completing the landfill in March 1995. [paragraphs 37 – 45, 87 – 9]

F5 The landfill's opening was impeded by demonstrations staged by facility opponents and further negotiations ensued. In November 1995, Metalclad concluded an agreement with the Federal Authorities(the INE and the Mexican Federal Attorney's Office for the Protection of the Environment or ' PROFEPA') . This agreement, referred to as the *Convenio*, set forth the conditions under which the landfill could operate.

F6 In December 1995, the municipality of Guadalcaz ar officially denied Metalclad's application for the construction permit which had been requested 13 months earlier; and challenged the *Convenio* by first making an administrative complaint to the Secretariat of the Environment, which was denied. It then filed an *amparo* proceeding with the Federal Court in January 1996, by which an injunction was issued barring Metalclad from conducting any haz ardous waste landfill operations. The *amparo* was dismissed and the injunction lifted in May 1999. In contrast, the INE granted in February 1996 an additional permit authorising a 10 times expansion of the landfill capacity. [paragraphs 55 – 6]

F7 After failed attempts to negotiate a solution, Metalclad filed a claim under Chapter 11 of the North American Free Trade Agreement(12 December 1992) US Gov't Printing Office(1992) , entered into force 1 January 1994 in January 1997, alleging that Mexico violated Articles 1105(fair and equitable treatment) and 1110(expropriation) . [paragraphs 58, 72]

F8 While the claim was pending and just before he was to leave office, the governor of SLP issued an Ecological Decree declaring a natural area for the protection of rare cacti that encompassed the landfill site, which, according to Mexican media, had the effect of preventing operation of the landfill. [paragraphs 59 - 61] Mexico objected to the jurisdiction of the Tribunal on the consideration of the Ecological Decree as it was enacted after the filing of the Notice of Intent of Arbitration.

Held

H1 The actions of the Mexican Government and its municipalities amounted to a breach of Mexico's obligation to afford Metalclad's investment treatment in accordance with international law, including fair and equitable treatment, under Article 1105 of the NAFTA. Mexico's measures were an expropriation under Article 1110 of the NAFTA, that required compensation.

H2 Mexico was internationally responsible for the acts of SLP and Guadacazar. [paragraph 73]

H3 Mexico had violated Article 1105, which was intended to promote 'transparency', or the idea 'that all relevant legal requirements for the purposes of initiating, completing and successfully operating investments made, or intended to be made... should be capable of being readily known to all affected investors'. It was up to 'the central government of any Party' to ensure that there was no confusion as to the meaning of 'transparency'. [paragraph 76]

H4 Metalclad was entitled to rely upon the representations of the Federal Government that no local construction permit was necessary, and that the municipality would have no legal basis for denying the permit. Even if a municipal permit had been required under Mexican law, the municipality only had authority over matters related to physical construction or defects in the site. [paragraph 86]

H5 The impropriety of the municipality's denial of the permit, coupled with Metalclad's reasonable reliance on the Federal Government's representations and the 'absence of a clear rule as to the requirement or not of a municipal construction permit, as well as the absence of any established practice or procedure as to the manner of handling applications for a municipal construction permit' amounted to a failure to 'ensure a transparent and predictable framework' and demonstrated 'a lack of orderly process and timely disposition' in relation to an investor who acted in the expectation of fair and just treatment under NAFTA. [paragraphs 88 - 99]

H6 Mexico's actions violated Article 1105(1) of the NAFTA on fair and equitable treatment, 'particularly in light of the governing principle that internal law (such as the Municipality's stated permit requirements) [did] not justify failure to perform a treaty.' [paragraph 100]

H7 Mexico's actions violated the expropriation provision of the NAFTA, which prohibited 'not only open, deliberate and acknowledged takings of property, such as outright seizure or formal or obligatory transfer of title in favour of the host State, but also covert or incidental interference with the use of property which has the effect of depriving the owner, in whole or in significant part, of the use or reasonably-to-be-expected economic benefit of property even if not necessarily to the obvious benefit of the host state.' [paragraph 103]

H8 Mexico's measures were tantamount to expropriation in violation of NAFTA Article 1110(1), ' by permitting or tolerating the conduct of Guadalcazar ... and by thus participating or acquiescing in the denial to Metalclad of the right to operate the landfill, notwithstanding the fact that the project was fully approved and endorsed by the federal government. ' [paragraph 104]

H9 Mexico's measures amounted to an ' indirect expropriation', largely due to Mexico's representations regarding the viability of the project, on which Metalclad relied. [paragraphs 105 – 7]

H10 Considerations on the Ecological Decree fell within the Tribunal's jurisdiction, though ' controlling importance' did not attach to it. The Ecological Decree had effectively ' barred forever the operation of the landfill' and therefore constituted an act tantamount to expropriation. [paragraphs 64 – 9, 109 – 11]

H11 Compensation for the violation of Article 1105 and for the expropriation were the same because both violations negated the possibility of any ' meaningful' return on Metalclad's investment. Metalclad's actual investment was used as the basis of valuation. Metalclad was awarded US $ 16.7 million, plus interest, after taking away costs occurred prior to the purchase, bundling costs, and costs for the remediation of the site. [paragraphs 113 – 31]

Date of Report: 09 July 2007

Reporter(s): Wenhua Shan

Analysis

A1 The *Metalclad* Award was the first decision to find a violation of the expropriation obligation under Article 1110 of NAFTA. In particular, the Tribunal's definition of ' expropriation' has been controversial, namely regarding the line between compensable expropriation and regulatory takings under customary international law.

A2 The Tribunal departed from the customary approach to the concept of expropriation, adopting an open-ended definition of indirect expropriation, considering that the form of the host State measure was not relevant. The Tribunal considered that expropriation may occur irrespective of whether the State measure might also be labelled as a regulatory act, without resolving the issue of whether a bona fide environmental regulation may amount to a taking under Chapter 11 of NAFTA. Outside the scope of Chapter 11, the decision in *Compañía del Desarrollo de Santa Elena, SA v Costa Rica*, Award, ICSID No ARB/96/1 [192] considered that whenever ' property is expropriated, even for environmental purposes ... the state's obligation to pay compensation remains' . This statement was quoted and followed in *Tecnicas Medioambientales Tecmed SA v Mexico*, Award, ICSID No ARB(AF)/00/2 [121]; IIC 247(2003).

A3 The border between environmental regulation and expropriation depends on the impact the host State measure has on the investment; but in applying the effects-based test tribunals have acknowledged the right of States to adopt measures having social or general welfare purpose. These measures should be accepted without any responsibility of the host State, unless they were disproportionate or unnecessary for a legitimate purpose(See *LG&E v Argentina*, Award on Liability, ICSID No ARB 02/1 [190 - 5]; IIC 295(2007).

A4 The right of States to regulate on environmental matters was acknowledged by the United States during the Metalclad proceedings, advocating for a narrow definition of indirect expropriation. Thus, the United States had made a Submission to the Tribunal on 10 November 1999 explaining that the expression ' tantamount to expropriation' referred to ' indirect' expropriation and did not create a new category of expropriation beyond that encompassed in customary international law.

A5 Further efforts have been made by NAFTA parties, particularly the United States and Canada, to clarify and limit the scope of application of the expropriation clauses under investment treaties. For instance, both the US Model BIT and the Canadian Model BIT adopted in 2004 included annexes specifying guidelines and criteria to determine whether in a particular situation an indirect expropriation has in fact taken place. They clarified that an adverse effect on the economic value of an investment, standing alone, did not establish that an indirect expropriation had occurred. They further stated that, except in rare circumstances, non-discriminatory regulatory actions by a Party aimed at protecting legitimate public welfare objectives, such as public health, safety, and the environment, did not constitute indirect expropriations(Annex B, US Model BIT 2004, Annex B 13(1), Canadian Model BIT 2004). Whilst these measures may have been useful in clarifying the view points of the States concerned, it remained unclear where to draw the general line between expropriation and regulation under international law.

A6 Another criticism of the *Metalclad* case related to the Tribunal's reasoning on Mexico's violation of Article 1105(1) (fair and equitable treatment standard). The Tribunal largely relied on the transparency standard, which was outside NAFTA Chapter 11. Mexico sought to challenge the Award before the Supreme Court of British Columbia (' BCSC'), the seat of the arbitration, and the BCSC confirmed that by relying on the ' imported' principle of ' transparency', the arbitral Tribunal had exceeded the scope of the matters submitted to it for arbitration. The Judge indicated that his conclusion might have been different had the Tribunal relied on the concept of fair and equitable treatment under Article 1105. (see *Metalclad*, Supplementary Reasons for Judgment, 2001 BCSC 1529 [66 - 9])

A7 The interpretation of the fair and equitable treatment standard—including the *Metalclad* Tribunal's approach to Article 1105—has been the subject of an intensive debate. It was clear that under the heading ' Minimum Standard of Treatment', Article 1105(1) followed the minimum standard of protection in accordance with general international law. In *SD Myers Inc v Canada*, First Partial Award, IIC 249(2000), 13 November 2000, the Tribunal stated that a breach of the above mentioned international minimum standard occurred only when it was shown that an investor had been treated in such an unjust and arbitrary manner that the treatment rose to a level that was unacceptable from the international perspective. This would occur when it amounted to ' an outrage, to bad faith, to willful neglect of duty, or to an insufficiency of governmental action so far short of international standards that every reasonable and impartial man would readily recognize its insufficiency' (see JC Thomas, 'Reflections on Article 1105 of NAFTA: History, State Practice and the Influence of Commentators' 17 ICSID Rev—Financial Investment L J 31, citing *United States(LF Neer) v Mexico* (1926) RIAA iv 60, 61 - 2).

A8 However, the *Metalclad* Tribunal was not alone in adopting an expansive reading of Article 1105. In *Pope & Talbot Inc v Canada*, Award, IIC 193(2001), 10 April 2001 [110 - 13], for example, the Tribunal concluded that 'investors under NAFTA are entitled to the international law minimum, plus the fairness elements'. In *SD Myers*, Separate Opinion by Dr Bryan Schwartz [256], Arbitrator Schwartz expressed the view that Article 1105 could have been interpreted in an expansive manner to include norms that had not yet technically passed into customary international law, such as the principle of 'transparency' and 'procedural fairness'.

A9 In July 2001, the NAFTA Free Trade Commission adopted its 'Notes of Interpretation of Certain Chapter 11 Provisions' [http://www. dfait-maeci. gc. ca/tna-nac/NAFTA-Interpr-en. asp], which confirmed that the concepts of 'fair and equitable treatment' and 'full protection and security' under Article 1105(1) 'do not require treatment in addition to or beyond that which is required by the customary international law minimum standard of treatment of aliens'.

A10 Hence it may be unlikely that NAFTA arbitration tribunals would take an expansive approach to the interpretation of Article 1105. However, this does not mean the end of any ambiguity or uncertainty with regard to the fair and equitable standard. Beyond NAFTA, the standard may still be subject to broad interpretation by tribunals.

Date of Analysis: 09 July 2007

Further analysis:

J Williams, 'Regulating Multinational Polluters in a PostNAFTA Trade Regime: The Lessons of Metalclad V. Mexico and the Case For A "Takings" Standard' (2003) 8 UCLA J Int'l L & Foreign Aff 473

LE Godshall, 'In the Cold Shadow of Metalclad: The Potential for Change to NAFTA's Chapter Eleven' (2002) 11 NYU Envtl LJ 264

J Harbine, 'NAFTA Chapter 11 Arbitration: Deciding the Price of Free Trade' (2002) 29 Ecology LQ 371

C Tollefson, 'Metalclad v United Mexican States Revisited: Judicial Oversight of NAFTA's Chapter

Eleven Investor-State Claim Process' (2002) 11 Minn J Global Trade 183

M Ewing-Chow, 'Investor Protection in Free Trade Agreements: Lessons from North America' (2001) 5 Sing J Int'l & Comp L 748

LJ Dhooge, 'The North American Free Trade Agreement and the Environment: The Lessons of Metalclad Corporation v United Mexican States' (2001) 10 Minn J Global Trade 209

JC Thomas, 'Reflections on Article 1105 of NAFTA: History, State Practice and the Influence of Commentators' 17 ICSID Rev—Financial Investment L J 31

Instruments cited in the full text of this decision:

International

Vienna Convention on the Law of Treaties(23 May 1969) 1155 UNTS 331; 8 ILM 679(1969); 63 AJIL

875(1969), entered into force 27 January 1980, Articles 26, 27, 31(1), 31(2)(a), 31(3)

Additional Facility Rules, Doc ICSID/11, International Centre for Settlement of Investment Disputes, June 1979 Articles 4(2), 21, 28, 48, 48(1), 48(2)

North American Free Trade Agreement(12 December 1992) US Gov't Printing Office(1992), entered into force 1 January 1994, Chapter 11, Articles 102(1), 102(1)(c), 102(2), 105, 201(1),

201(2), 1105, 1105(1), 1108(1), 1110, 1110(1), 1110(2), 1114, 1117, 1118, 1119, 1120, 1120(2),

1121, 1131(1), 1134, 1135(1)(a), 1135(2)(b), 1135(2)(c), 1802.1

Domestic

Constitution, Mexico, Article 115, Fraction V

General Ecology Law, 1988(Mexico), Articles 5, 7, 8

Cases cited in the full text of this decision:

International Centre for the Settlement of Investment Disputes

AGIP SPA v Congo, 1 ICSID Rep 306; 21 ILM 737

Benvenuti and Bonfant Srl v Congo, 1 ICSID Rep 330; 21 ILM 758 Asian Agricultural Products v Sri Lanka, 4 ICSID Rep 245

Iran-United States Claims Tribunal

Phelps Dodge Corp v Iran, (1986) 10 Iran-USCTR 121

Sola Tiles, Inc v Iran, (1987) 14 IranUSCTR 224; 83 ILR 460

Permanent Court of International Justice

Chorzow Factory Case, Germany v Poland, Claim for Indemnity, Merits(1928) PCIJ Series A no 17

Miscellaneous

Biloune and ors v Ghana Investment Centre and ors, (1993) 95 ILR 183

To access full citation information for this document, see the Oxford Law Citator record

Commentary on Metalclad Corp v Mexico, Review by the supreme court of British Columbia, ICSID Case No ARB(AF)/97/1, IIC 162 (2001) *

Metalclad Corporation v Mexico, Review by the Supreme Court of British Columbia, ICSID Case No ARB(AF)/97/1, IIC 162(2001), 2nd May 2001, Supreme Court [BCSC]

Date: 02 May 2001

Content type: Arbitral Decisions

Jurisdiction: Supreme Court [BCSC]

Citation(s): ICSID Case No ARB(AF)/97/1(Official Case No)

IIC 162(2001)(OUP reference)

Product: Investment Claims [IC]

Module: International Investment Claims [IIC]

Parties: Metalclad Corp(United States [us]) Mexico

Judges/Arbitrators: Honourable Mr Justice Tysoe

Counsel for Party One: Patrick G Foy QC; J Christopher Thomas; Robert JC Deane

Counsel for Party Two: D Geoffrey Cowper QC; Henri CA Alvarez; BJ Greenberg; MD Parrish

Procedural Stage: Review by the supreme court of British Columbia

Subsequent Development(s):

Supplementary reasons for judgment; *Metalclad Corporation v Mexico*, 2001 BCSC 1529; IIC 163(2001), 31 October 2001

Governing Law: North American Free Trade Agreement(12 December 1992) US Gov't Printing Office(1992), entered into force 1 January 1994; Law of Canada

Subject(s):

Standard of review—Indirect expropriation—International minimum standard—Transparency—Treaties, interpretation—Applicable law—Public policy(Canada, Standard of Review)

---

* Oxford University Press, Jul. 2007.

Core Issue(s):

Whether the dispute was a ' commercial' dispute that was governed by the International Commercial Arbitration Act.

Whether the Court should have taken the ' pragmatic and functional approach' of the Supreme Court of Canada to determine the proper standard of review.

Whether and to what extent the Arbitral Tribunal rendered an Award beyond the scope of its authority.

Facts

F1 In *Metalclad Corporation v Mexico,* Award, ICSID Case No ARB(AF)/97/1; IIC 161(2000), (2001) 16 ICSID Rev—FILJ 168; (2001) 40 ILM 36; (2001) 26 Ybk Com Arb 99(excerpts); (2002) 119 ILR

618; (2002) 5 ICSID Rep 212; (2002) 129 Journal du Droit International Clunet 233(excerpts), 30 August 2000(the ' Award'), the dispute concerned the construction of haz ardous waste disposal plant in Mexico. Metalclad, a United States company in the waste management business purchased a Mexican waste management company that operated a waste transfer station in the municipality of Guadalcaz ar, with the intention to build and operate a haz ardous waste landfill on that location.

F2 The Federal Government granted Metalclad a permit for the construction of the landfill. Metalclad was never granted a local permit, but the Federal Government assured no permit other than a Federal licence was required for the construction of the plant. Metalclad initiated the construction of the project without a local permit and continued until the municipal authorities ordered Metalclad to cease operations. Subsequently, the municipal authorities declined a second permit and declared the area to be an ecological preserve.

F3 The Tribunal of the International Centre for Settlement of Investment Disputes (' ICSID') rendered an Award on 30 August, 2000 finding that the Mexican authorities violated two investor rights protected by the North American Free Trade Agreement(12 December 1992) US Gov't Printing Office(1992), entered into force 1 January 1994 (' NAFTA'): Article 1110 on expropriation and Article 1105 on minimum treatment under international law. For these two violations, the Tribunal found that Metalclad was entitled to compensation in the amount of $16.9 million.

F4 The present case concerned the petition by Mexico to set aside the Award. The petition was based on its allegation that the Tribunal had exceeded its jurisdiction; that the Tribunal failed to explicitly address two categories of improper acts on the part of Metalclad, which would render the Award in conflict with the pubic policy in British Columbia; and that the Tribunal failed to answer all the questions raised by it. (paragraphs 55, 106, 119)

F5 Mexico contended that arbitration under Chapter 11 of the NAFTA was not a ' commercial arbitration' as one between parties with privity of contract relating to a particular commercial arrangement. Mexico argued that as it was not in a ' commercial' relationship with Metalclad, the review by the Court was not subject to the limits imposed by the International Commercial Arbitration Act 1996, RSBC 1996, c 233, 1996(Canada) (' ICAA') . (paragraph 44)

F6 Mexico also argued that the court could review the award on the basis of the domestic standard for ' patently unreasonable error' , and that the court should have used the ' pragmatic and functional approach' to determine the appropriate standard of review under the ICAA and the Commercial Arbitration Act 1996, RSBC 1996, c 55, 1996 (Canada) (' CAA') . (paragraphs 52, 53) Mexico identified 19 areas in respect of which the tribunal failed to consider relevant evidence and thereby made ' patently unreasonable finding' , which amounted to an excess of jurisdiction. (paragraphs 92, 98)

F7 Metalclad contended that Mexico should not have been entitled to challenge the Tribunal's excess of jurisdiction because it did not comply with section 16(3) of the ICAA, which provided that a plea that a tribunal was exceeding the scope of its authority should be raised as soon as the matter alleged to be beyond the scope of its authority was raised during that arbitration. (paragraph 75)

F8 Mexico submitted that the Tribunal failed to address two categories of improper acts that Metalclad conducted, which would render the Ward in conflict with the public policy in British Colombia, namely corruption of a former federal officer Mr Rodarte and the excess damage claim made by Metalclad. (paragraphs 106 – 116)

F9 Mexico contended that the Tribunal also failed to answer all questions it raised which could have affected the result, such as questions relating to the breach of Article 1105, the question of whether Metalclad acted in bad faith, the question of deception in Metalclad's memorial, and the question of calculation of damages to which Metalclad was entitled. Mexico relied on three ICSID annulment decisions to support its view that such failure to address all arguments made by the parties which would have changed the outcome of the award. (paragraphs 119 – 120)

Held

H1 The Supreme Court of British Colombia(the ' Court') held that the review of the Award was governed by the provisions of the ICAA. The Court reasoned that the ICAA applied to international commercial arbitrations. There was no dispute that the arbitration between Mexico and Metalclad was an international arbitration. Whether the arbitration was a commercial arbitration depended on section 1(6) of the ICAA which provided that ' ...an arbitration [wa] s commercial if it a[rose] out of a relationship of a commercial nature including, but not limited to...(d) an exploitation agreement or concession...' ; or a relationship of investing. The dispute was essentially a ' commercial' dispute subject to the ICAA because ' the primary relationship between Metalclad and Mexico was one of investing and the exercise of a regulatory function by the Municipality was incidental to that primary relationship' . (paragraphs 44 – 49)

H2 The Court held that the extent to which the Court could interfere with an international commercial award was limited by the provisions of the ICAA; and that the standard of review in the present case was set out in sections 5 and 34 of the ICAA. Section 5(1) stated that ' ...a court must not intervene unless so provided in this Act...' ; and section 34(2) listed the grounds on which an award could have been set aside. Therefore, the Court treated the ICAA as an Act which established not only the Court's powers, but also the scope and standard of review. Accordingly, the Court refrained from applying the emerging jurisprudence of Supreme Court of Canada in what might be called the common law of administrative review, which applied a ' pragmatic and functional' approach, rejecting Mexico's arguments with regard to the standard of review. (paragraphs 52 – 54)

H3 The Court held that the arbitral tribunal's interpretation of ' international law' in Article 1105 of the NAFTA went beyond the established meaning of ' international law' without an adequate basis to do so, and wrongly imported into Chapter 11 of the NAFTA an obligation of transparency, thus exceeding the scope of the submission to arbitration. The Court reasoned that Mexico was entitled to challenge the Tribunal's excess of jurisdiction, because it raised a sufficient objection during the arbitration. It submitted in its counter memorial that there was no authority for interpreting Article 1105 to extend to transparency requirements and it pointed out that transparency matters were addressed in Chapter 18 of the NAFTA. (paragraph 75)

H4 The Tribunal decided on a matter beyond the scope of submission to arbitration in connection with its finding that there was a failure of transparency, because the concept of transparency was not resulted from proper interpretation of Article 1105, but was imported from chapters other than Chapter 11 of the NAFTA, namely Article 1802 in Chapter 18 and Article 102. (paragraphs 67 – 77)

H5 The Tribunal's analysis of Article 1105 of the NAFTA ' infected' its analysis of Article 1110. In relying on the concept of transparency, at least in part, to conclude that there had been an expropriation within the meaning of Article 1110, the Tribunal again decided a matter beyond the scope of the submission to arbitration. (paragraphs 77 – 80)

H6 The Tribunal's consideration on the Ecological Decree, 20 September 1997 (' the ' Decree') was correct and independent from other findings of breach of the NAFTA, and therefore should not have been set aside. The Tribunal gave an extremely broad definition of expropriation for the purposes of Article 1110, which was a question of law with which this Court was not entitled to interfere. (paragraphs 81 – 105)

H7 It had not been established that there were any improper acts such as corruption or excess damage claim on behalf of Metalclad which put the Award in conflict with the public policy in British Columbia. (paragraphs 106 – 118)

H8 The Tribunal had adequately dealt with the principal issues before it and its failure to explicitly deal with all of Mexico's arguments was not sufficiently serious to justify the setting aside the Award. (paragraphs 119 – 132)

H9 As a result, the Award should have been partially set aside, because Mexico succeeded in challenging the first two of the Tribunal's findings of breaches of Articles 1105 and 1110, but failed on the remaining points. Accordingly, the Award was set aside to the extent that it included interest prior to 20 September 1997—and any consequential compounding effects. If Metalclad wanted to pursue the portion of the interest that was set aside, by establishing a breach of Article 1105 or Article 1110 prior to the issuance of the Decree without regard to the concept of transparency, the matter was remitted to the Tribunal. (paragraphs 133 - 137)

Date of Report: 01 July 2007

Reporter(s): Wenhua Shan

Analysis

A1 The judgment of the Court reviewing the Metalclad Award was a landmark decision and was one of first impression in many respects: It was the first ever judicial review of an award made under the Additional Facility Rules, Doc ICSID/11. International Centre for Settlement of Investment Disputes, June 1979 ('ICSID Additional Facility Rules'); it was the first review of a NAFTA investor-state arbitral award; and it was the first national court review of an investor-state arbitral award. It was unsurprising that the case attracted considerable attention and resulted in extensive literature, some of which are listed below.

A2 On the one hand, the decision was fiercely criticised by some international lawyers. Brower—CH Brower II, 'Investor-State Disputes Under NAFTA: The Empire Strikes Back', 40 Colum J Transnat'l L 43(2002), 47, 68('Brower')—for example, attacked that the judgement was an example of 'heightened judicial review' of Chapter 11 awards and that such reviews constituted 'an independent violation of Chapter 11'.

A3 In particular, Brower identified at least four elements of heightened review in Court's partial annulment of the Award. Firstly, the court failed to apply the 'powerful presumption' that the tribunal acted within its jurisdiction, which arguably could have sustained the argument that the tribunal merely interpreted Article 1105 to include principles of transparency. Secondly, the court 'implied' that it could not accept such a broad interpretation of Article 1105 on the ground that principles of transparency fell outside Chapter 11. Thirdly, the court overruled the tribunal's interpretation of Article 102(1), which would have included transparency among the NAFTA's animating principles. Fourthly, the court rejected the tribunal's interpretation of *Biloune v Ghana Investments Centre*, (1990) 95 ILR 183, although it could have sustained the tribunal's first finding of expropriation based there.

A4 NAFTA Parties, on the other hand, welcomed the decision, and cited it with approval in later proceedings. The US, for example, cited it in *Methanex Corporation v United States,* Final award on jurisdiction and merits, Ad hoc—UNCITRAL Arbitration Rules; IIC 167(2005), 3 August 2005, as have the other NAFTA Parties in other proceedings—see JC Thomas, 'A Reply to Professor Brower', (2002) 40 Colum J Transnat'l L 433, 434('Thomas').

A5 The decision served as a guideline for future tribunals to avoid importing Chapter 18 concepts of transparency for the interpretation of fair and equitable treatment under Article 1105. Instead, Chapter 11 Tribunals should have relied on the NAFTA Free Trade Commission's official interpretation of the 'minimum standard of treatment under international law.' In July 2001, the Free Trade Commission adopted its Notes of

Interpretation of Certain Chapter 11 Provisions(NAFTA Free Trade Commission), 31 July 2001, which stated that the concepts of ' fair and equitable treatment' and ' full protection and security' under Article 1105(1) ' d[id] not require treatment in addition to or beyond that which [wa]s required by the customary international law minimum standard of treatment of aliens'.

A6 Clearly the Court's decision could not be characterised as ' a model of deference' of international arbitration awards—see Brower. It would not be fair, however, to classify the Metalclad judgement as simply one-sided or abusive. Clearly efforts had been made to balance the need to address concerns of state parties, with the need to respect decisions made by international arbitration tribunals. Thus, it ruled that the governing law should be the ICAA, rather than the CAA, which would have entailed more aggressive review, including points of law.

A7 It also rejected the more intrusive standards of review proposed by Mexico, such as the ' patently unreasonable' test and the ' pragmatic and functional approach'. Its substantive decisions, moreover, arguably reflected such efforts: rather than annulling the entire award, it set aside only part of it. Finally, such efforts could be seen in the fact that, the resulting adjustment of damage did not substantially change the amount of damage granted by the Tribunal. Having said that, however, the Court did appear to have taken more points from Mexico than from Metalclad in *Metalclad Corporation v Mexico;* Supplementary reasons for judgment, 2001 BCSC 1529; IIC 163(2001), 31 October 2001, somehow a reversal to the approach taken by the Tribunal in the Award.

A8 Although the appeals were eventually abandoned as part of the settlement the parties arrived on 26 October 2001—see Thomas—the case opened the door for domestic courts to check and control awards of international investment arbitration tribunals, challenging the finality and authority of investment treaty based arbitration. Whilst the decision did not directly affect proper ICSID arbitration, which did not allow judicial review by domestic courts, it might have had the effect of encouraging ICSID annulment proceedings, which were apparently on the rise.

A9 Perhaps, it is now time to consider, on global level and in a systematic manner, a mechanism that can not only maintain efficiency and effectiveness in resolving state-investor disputes, but also guarantee consistency and credibility in the decisions it renders. In this connection, it is noted that various initiatives, such as an appeal mechanism, have been contemplated or devised in recent prototypes of international investment and free trade agreements; and were part of the discussion regarding the revision of the ICSID Additional Facility Rules and UNCITRAL Arbitration Rules, UN Doc A/31/98; 31st Session Supp No 17, UN General Assembly, 1976.

Date of Analysis: 01 July 2007 Analysis by: Wenhua Shan

Further analysis:

J Williams, ' Regulating Multinational Polluters in a Post-NAFTA Trade Regime: The Lessons of Metalclad v Mexico and the Case For a "Takings" Standard' 8 UCLA J Intl L & Foreign Aff 473 , Fall\Winter 2003

JC Thomas, ' A Reply to Professor Brower' , (2002) 40 Colum J Transnat'l L 433, 434

CH Brower II, ' Beware The Jabberwock: A Reply To Mr. Thomas' , 40 Colum J Transnat'l L 465(2002)

CH Brower II, ' Investor-State Disputes Under NAFTA: The Empire Strikes Back' , 40 Colum J Transnat'l L 43(2002), 47, 68

H Olasolo, ' Have Public Interests Been Forgotten in NAFTA Chapter 11 Foreign Investor/Host State Arbitration? Some Conclusions from the Judgment of the Supreme Court of British Columbia on the Case of Mexico v Metalclad' , Land Business Rev of the Americas, Winter/Spring, 2002

J Harbine, ' NAFTA Chapter 11 Arbitration: Deciding the Price of Free Trade' , 29 Ecology L Q 371(2002)

C N Seymour, ' The NAFTA Metalclad Appeal—Subsequent Impact or Inconsequential Error? ... Only Time Will Tell' , 34 U Miami Inter-Am L Rev 189, Winter 2002

Instruments cited in the full text of this decision:

International

Convention on the Settlement of Investment Disputes Between States and Nationals of Other States(18 March 1965) 575 UNTS 159, entered into force 14 October 1966, Articles 48, 52

Vienna Convention on the Law of Treaties(23 May 1969) 1155 UNTS 331; 8 ILM 679(1969); 63 AJIL 875(1969), entered into force 27 January 1980, Articles 28, 31

North American Free Trade Agreement(12 December 1992) US Gov't Printing Office(1992), entered into force 1 January 1994, Articles 1105, 1110, 1119, 1120, 1116, 1503, 1101, 1102, 1103, 1104, 1105, 1106, 1107, 1108, 1109, 1110, 1111, 1113, 1114, 201, 102, 1131, 1801, 1802, 1803, 1115, 1122, 1102, 1103, 1120

Additional Facility Rules, Doc ICSID/11, International Centre for Settlement of Investment Disputes, June 1979, Articles 48, 53, 3, 49, 58

Domestic

International Commercial Arbitration Act 1996, RSBC 1996, c 233, 1996(Canada)

Commercial Arbitration Act 1996, RSBC 1996, c 55, 1996(Canada)

Cases cited in the full text of this decision:

Ad hoc

Shalansky v Regina Pasqua Hosp Bd of Gov, (1983), 83 CLLC 14, 026, 145 DLR (3d) 413, 22 Sask R

153, 47 NR 76(SCC)

Blanchard v Control Data Canada Ltd, (1984) 2 SCR 476

Mitsubishi Motors Corp v Soler Chrysler-Plymouth Inc, 473 US 614(1985)

Navigation Sonamar Inc v Algoma Steamships Ltd, (1987) RJQ 1346; (1995), 1 MALQR 1(Que SC)

UES, Local 298 *v Bibeault*, (1988) 2 SCR 1048

Transport de Cargaison(Cargo Carriers)(Kasc-Co) Ltd v Industrial Bulk Carriers, (1990) RDJ 418(Que CA)

Biloune v Ghana Investments Centre, (1990) 95 ILR 183

Quintette Coal Limited v Nippon Steel Corporation, (1991) 1 WWR 219(BCCA)

Société European Gas Turbines SA v Westman International Ltd, 2 Revue de l'arbitrage 359(1994)(Paris CA)

Food Services of America Inc v Pan Pacific Specialities Ltd, (1997) 32 BCLR(3d) 225

Pushpanathan v Canada, (1998) 1 SCR 982

Corporacion Transnacional de Inversiones SA de CV v STET International SpA, (1999), 45 OR(3d) 183(Ont SCJ); affirmed(2000), 49 OR(3d) 414

DLT Holdings Inc v Grow Biz International Inc, (2000), 194 Nfld & PEIR 206

SD Myers Inc v Canada, First partial award and separate opinion, Ad hoc—UNCITRAL Arbitration Rules; IIC 249(2000), 13 November 2000

Pope & Talbot Inc v Canada, Award on the merits of phase 2, Ad hoc—UNCITRAL Arbitration Rules; IIC 193(2001), 10 April 2001

International Centre for Settlement of Investment Disputes

Klöckner Industrie—Anlagen GmbH and ors v Cameroon, Decision on annulment, Case No ARB/81/2, 3 May 1985

Amco v Indonesia, 1 ICSID Rep 508, 16 May 1986

Maritime International Nominees Establishment('MINE') v Guinea, Decision partially annulling the award, ICSID Case No ARB/84/4; (1990) 5 ICSID Rev—FILJ 95; (1990) 5 Int'l Arb Rep No 2, Section E;

(1997) 16 Ybk Com Arb 40; (1997) 4 ICSID Rep 79; (1991) 118 Journal du Droit International Clunet 166(excerpts), 22 December 1989

To access full citation information for this document, see the Oxford Law Citator record

Commentary on Metalclad Corp v Mexico, Supplementary reasons for judgment, 2001 BCSC 1529, IIC 163 (2001) *

Metalclad Corporation v Mexico, Supplementary reasons for judgment, 2001 BCSC 1529, (2001) 95

BCLR(3d) 169, IIC 163 (2001), despatched 31st October 2001, Supreme Court [BCSC]

Despatched: 31 October 2001

Content type: Arbitral Decisions

Jurisdiction: Supreme Court [BCSC]

Citation(s): 2001 BCSC 1529 (Official Case No) (2001) 95 BCLR(3d) 169 (Other Reference)

IIC 163 (2001) (OUP reference)

Product: Investment Claims [IC]

Module: International Investment Claims [IIC]

Parties: Metalclad Corporation (United States [us]) Mexico

Judges/Arbitrators: Honourable Mr Justice Tysoe

Counsel for Party One: Patrick G Foy, Q C; J Christopher Thomas; Robert JC Deane

Counsel for Party Two: D Geoffrey Cowper, Q C; Henri CA Alvarez; BJ Greenberg; MD Parrish

Procedural Stage: Supplementary reasons for judgment

Previous Procedural Stage(s):

Review by the Supreme Court of British Columbia; *Metalclad Corporation v Mexico*, ICSID Case No ARB(AF)/97/1; IIC 162(2001), 2 May 2001

Governing Law: Law of Canada

Subject(s):

International investment law—Appeal from award

Core Issue(s):

Whether the Supreme Court of British Columbia may have adjourned the proceed-

* Oxford University Press, Mar. 2008.

ings in order to give the Tribunal an opportunity to resume the arbitral proceedings for the purpose of determining whether there was a breach of Article 1105 or 1110 of the North American Free Trade Agreement prior to the issuance of the Ecological Decree without regard to the concept of transparency and thereby determining whether Metalclad was entitled to interest prior to 20 September 1997.

Facts

F1 The Supreme Court of British Columbia('BCSC') rendered its Reasons for judgment—*Metalclad Corporation v Mexico,* Review by the Supreme Court of British Columbia, ICSID Case No ARB(AF)/97/1; IIC 162(2001), 2 May 2001—on May 2, 2001, setting aside in part the Award of the Tribunal of the International Centre for the Settlement of Investment Disputes—*Metalclad Corporation v Mexico*, Award, ICSID Case No ARB(AF)/97/1, IIC 161(2000), 30 August 2000—, namely the first two breaches which were based on a concept of transparency, and accordingly the interest from 5 December 1995 to 20 September 1997 granted by the Tribunal. The BCSC also decided that if Metalclad wished to pursue the portion of the interest contained in the Award that it had set aside, by establishing a breach of Article 1105 or 1110 of the North American Free Trade Agreement(12 December 1992) US Gov't Printing Office(1992), entered into force 1 January 1994('NAFTA'), prior to the issuance of the Ecological Decree without regard to the concept of transparency, the matter was remitted to the Tribunal. (paragraphs 1 – 4)

F2 Mexico appealed the BCSC's refusal to set aside the entire Award. Metalclad cross-appealed the referral back to the Tribunal based on the BCSC's conclusions with respect to the first two findings of breaches of Articles 1105 and 1110 of the NAFTA.

F3 By notice of motion dated 1 October 2001, Metalclad made application(i) for directions respecting the reference to the Tribunal contemplated in paras 135 and 136 of *Metalclad Corporation v Mexico,* Reasons for judgment(ii) to settle the form of Order flowing from the Reasons for Judgment and(iii) for an Order adjourning these proceedings generally or to a specified date to provide the Tribunal opportunity to resume the arbitral proceedings in accordance with the Reasons for Judgment and directions of the BCSC or to take such other action as in the Tribunal's opinion would eliminate the grounds upon which the BCSC had set aside the Award in part. (paragraph 7)

F4 Mexico contended that the BCSC should not have entertained Metalclad's application and should have left the matter to the Court of Appeal. Mexico alternatively argued that the Award ought to have been set aside in its entirety or that these proceedings should have been adjourned in order to allow the Tribunal to resume the arbitral proceedings in respect of the Ecological Decree. (paragraphs 12, 16)

Held

H1 The BCSC partially set aside the Award and suggested that the matter be remitted to the arbitral tribunal if the parties were unable to agree on the issue at stake. The applicable statute, however, provided for remission only if the setting aside proceedings were adjourned and if the court determined a time period for the tribunal to complete its task.

H2 The BCSC rejected Mexico's view that the Award should have been set aside in its entirety. The BCSC admitted that it was inappropriate to have followed the usual common law approach of partially setting the Award aside and remitting the matter to the Tribunal.

H3 The BCSC adjourned the proceedings for 18 months to give the arbitral tribunal the opportunity to resume the arbitral proceedings to determine whether there was a breach of Article 1105 or 1110 of the NAFTA prior to the issuance of the Ecological Decree, without regard to the concept of transparency, giving the arbitral tribunal a period of time to decide whether Metalclad was entitled to interest prior to 20 September 1997.

Date of Report: 18 March 2008

Reporter(s): Wenhua Shan

Analysis

A1 Although a technical decision on the face, the Supplementary Reasons for Judgement may be regarded as a further effort by the BCSC to show its deference to international arbitration tribunals.

A2 It should be noted that, shortly before the delivery of the Supplementary Reasons for Judgement, the dispute was settled on 26 October 2001, and both parties abandoned their appeals

—see JC Thomas, 'A Reply to Professor Brower', 40 Colum J Transnat'l L 433 (2002), 435, fn 11.

A3 For further comments on the Award and the original review decision, see the Commentary to the Award, and the Commentary on the Reasons for Judgement in Review by the Supreme Court of British Columbia respectively.

Date of Analysis: 18 March 2008 Analysis by: Wenhua Shan

Further analysis:

JC Thomas, 'A Reply to Professor Brower', 40 Colum J Transnat'l L 433(2002), 435, fn 11

Instruments cited in the full text of this decision:

International

Additional Facility Rules, Doc ICSID/11, International Centre for Settlement of Investment Disputes, June 1979, Article 36

North American Free Trade Agreement(12 December 1992) US Gov't Printing Office(1992), entered into force 1 January 1994, Articles 1105, 1110

UNCITRAL Model Law, Article 34

Domestic

Ecological Decree

Cases cited in the full text of this decision:

Canadian domestic courts

Sharp Electronics of Canada Ltd v Ono, (1982) BCJ No 470(QL)

Liu v Hansen, (1995), 38 CPC(3d) 398(BCSC)

Constantinescu v Barriault, (1996) BCJ No 2105(QL) *Coughlin v Kuntz*, (1997), 43 BCLR(3d) 360(SC) *Hellinckx v Large*, (1998) BCJ No 3072(QL)

Metalclad Corporation v Mexico, Award, ICSID Case No ARB(AF)/97/1, IIC 161 (2000), 30 August 2000

Metalclad Corporation v Mexico, Reasons for judgment

To access full citation information for this document, see the Oxford Law Citator record

第八编

人物专访 Part VIII

1379－1403

“千人计划”专家单文华：努力创建引领型的一流法学院*

导　读

教育是立国之本，民族之魂，强国之基础；教育是以生命影响生命；教育是一棵树摇动另一棵树，一朵云推动另一朵云，一个灵魂唤醒另一个灵魂。百年大计，教育为先；国富民强，教育为要！今天，就让千人计划网小编带您一起走近国家“千人计划”特聘专家、西安交通大学法学院院长单文华教授，听他讲述创建引领型一流法学院的故事。

专家小传

单文华，西安交通大学法学院院长、国家“千人计划”特聘专家、教育部“长江学者”讲座教授、牛津《中国比较法学刊》主编、剑桥大学劳特派特国际法研究中心资深研究员。

“渌田农村走出的‘世界名人’”

在单文华的老家湖南攸县渌田镇，他的名字在当地被老师用来激励学生——“渌田农村走出的‘世界名人’”。

单文华听到这里哈哈大笑，说这样的说法源自老家湖南攸县电视台的一个采访。那时候刚刚入选《马基士世界名人录》，媒体为了突出前后反差，彰显励志效果，就用了“攸县走出的世界名人”的标题。后来有渌田乡党转发此文，标题就改成了“渌田农村走出的‘世界名人’”。用现在的话来说，这个提法有点“标题党”。

无疑，单文华是家乡的骄傲。1987年，他是湖南株洲市的高考文科状元。不过，他说这也不算什么，要说一个市一个状元，光湖南就有多少状元，还不要说全

* 本文载千人计划网，http://www.1000plan.org/qrjh/qrticle/61231，2015年4月10日访问，作者张星利。

国。但这事还是引起了轰动,因为单文华所在的攸县六中在单文华之前就没有文科生考上过本科的,单文华不仅实现了本科零的突破,而且还上了重点大学,成了全市状元,不由得人们不刮目相看。当株洲日报在醒目位置报道了攸县六中出状元的新闻之后,人们都很惊讶,觉得不可思议,是一个奇迹!市长亲自前往视察,人们捕风捉影的传说形容县教育局的楼板都差点给震塌了!

在英国讲授国际法的中国人

2002 年 9 月,单文华在剑桥大学攻读博士学位期间,开始受聘英国牛津布鲁克斯大学讲师,主讲国际法。中国人在英国这个国际法重镇讲国际法,这在新中国成立以来还是破天荒的头一次。

尽管过去了 12 年之久,但单文华讲起这段经历还是有点激动。毕竟是人生第一讲,多少还是有些紧张。做学生时,在台下听,只是信息的输入,而做老师就要从输出的这个角度来考虑,讲什么,怎么讲,都要胸有成竹。何况还有台下无数的挑剔的眼光在等着挑刺呢。

单文华形容那段时间非常艰难、压力很大,不仅要作为全职讲师上很多的课,要继续完成剑桥的博士学位论文,同时还要系统学习英国大学的教学方法。更有难度的是,要他上的课有的还是他自己都没有学过的,需要从头学起,"现学现卖"。那时候,单文华每天要靠喝咖啡来提神,每天都要喝 10 杯以上。因为那段时间喝得太多,单文华说他此后再也不想喝咖啡了。

不过,单文华坦言,压力大收获也大,所有的挑战都是全新的,一旦挺过来收获却是最大的。因为语言环境、文化背景、教学方法等都构成极大的挑战,一般人不敢接受,而单文华做到了。因此,对于这段经历,他十分感念。他说:"如果没有在海内外这么长时间的教学历练,我或许还仅仅是个学生,对西方的学术保持着习惯性的仰角。我特别庆幸自己有过比较长时间在英国教授和研究国际法的经历,使自己能够平和淡定地对待西方学术和学者。"

单文华认为小到学术交往,大到国际关系,都存在三个不同的境界。第一境界是"学习",你是"学生",仰视着你的"老师",从他或她那里学到先进知识和技能;第二境界是"对话",你是一个"同事",和别人各有所长,平起平坐,是"平视"的关系;第三境界是"引领",你成了"老师",掌握先进知识技能,具有"俯视"全场和引领群伦的能力和威望,别人向你学习求教。我们的学术研究目前大体处于从"学习"向"对话"转变的阶段,简单地说也就是 1.5 版本时代。而我们时代的需求却大体在 2.5 版本的层面。足见我们的学术研究还远远落后于时代的需要。

单文华认为,我国的对外能力建设供求现状也大抵如此。在现代化的漫漫征途中,中国长期以来就是一个“学生”。做学生有做学生的好处,不仅可以学习,还不用承担多大责任。但是学生总会有毕业的时候,而且越是优秀的学生会毕业的越快。中国改革开放30年,实际上就是在学多方面向西方先进国家学习了30年。中国是很优秀的学生。30年的学习不仅让我国成功地融入了世界体系,而且让我们具备了在其中发挥重大影响的某些实力。越来越多地,世界不仅不再也不能继续俯视或者忽视我们,反而会仰望我们,期待我们能够提供各种各样的支持和帮助。因此,不仅仅是我们自己不能满足于做学生,世界的现实也越来越期待我们做出更大、更积极的贡献。在许多方面,我们还是需要继续当好学生,但是在更多方面和场合,我们需要成为世界各国的“同事”,甚至在越来越多的方面,不少国家还期待我们能够成为它们的“老师”。我们的视角正在从“仰视”变成“平视”甚至某种积极意义上的“俯视”,因为我们的角色正在从“学生”变成“同事”甚至“老师”。

“不管你愿不愿意,准备没准备好,中国的崛起是一个既成事实。我们不仅需要平等参与和对话,还需要发挥引领作用,做引领型国家。特别是对于许多发展中国家而言,我的经验对于他们的市场化现代化很有借鉴意义,它们也很希望向我们学习借鉴。对此,我们既不能妄自尊大,也不应妄自菲薄。”

单文华向我们展示了一本由他主编并由牛津大学出版社出版的英文国际期刊《中国比较法学科》,并表示:“这本刊物的宗旨是‘世界视野、中国重心’,就是要让世界法学优秀成果服务中国,让中国法学先进成果走向世界,努力打造新时代中国法学国际学术交流的丝绸之路!”

站在丝绸之路的新起点

2005年单文华受聘西安交通大学。来到西部,他有一个梦想,就是要把西部法学做大做强。

经过不懈努力,2008年西安交通大学法学院从无到有,已然成型。伴随学院架构的搭建起来,交大法学逐步走进了发展的“快车道”,先后取得了一系列不凡成绩。2011年,法学成为西安交通大学“985”三期重点建设学科,其中国际经济法与比较法学科被确定为拟建世界一流学科;2012年,法学学科首批获得由教育部和中央政法委员会联合评审批准的两个国家级卓越法律人才教育培养基地——“应用型、复合型法律职业人才教育培养基地”和“涉外法律人才教育培养基地”。学院现已形成“法律治理学”(Law and Governance)交叉学科博士点、法学硕士(一级学科硕士点)和法学本科的完整法学人才培养体系,并取得了法律硕士(J. M.)专业学位授予权,目前在校学生(包括博士生、硕士生、本硕连读生和本科生)400 余人,是我国最重要的法学人才培养基地之一。有了博士点、卓越基地,西部法学的前景就更加清晰起来,与此同时,把西安交大法学院建设成为“高起点、国际化、研究型”的国际一流法学院的目标也正在陆续实现。

虽然身处西部,交大法学院一开始就强调要有国际化的视野,争取发挥引领作用,努力建设成为一所国际一流的法学院。早在 2006 年,地处丝绸之路起点的西安交大就筹建了丝绸之路国际法与比较法研究所,聘请一批国际国内知名学者担任“马可波罗”研究员和“郑和”研究员,发扬丝路精神,沟通中西法学。单文华认为,丝绸之路不仅是一个文化符号、一个交通脉络、一个贸易通道,而且是一个承载着历史和现实的政治、经济、文化、制度交流沟通的平台。随着丝绸之路经济带概念的提出,未来丝绸之路的地位将更加显现。如果说古代丝绸之路是沟通中西的贸易通道的话,在某种意义上,今天的丝绸之路将不仅是贸易通道而且是我们重构国际关系的重要杠杆。而丝绸之路沿线法律的比较和整合将成为这一杠杆的重要推手。通过丝绸之路经济带法律建设,凝聚政治共识,凝结成一个法律框架,进而希望能够建立丝绸之路经济带的自由贸易区乃至进一步整合,就能更好地发挥杠杆作用。

围绕丝绸之路经济带法律制度建设这一关键点,近年来,以单文华为首的交大法学团队先后获得教育部重大攻关课题、国家社科基金重点课题以及陕西省重点项目的重点支持。西安交大丝绸之路国际法与比较法研究所已然成为全国丝绸之路经济带研究上的一支重要生力军。

“丝绸之路是贸易之路,和平之路,更是发展之路。丝绸之路经济带建设过程中最为有力和可靠的纽带是法律纽带。这是世界区域一体化的一般经验,也是建设成功的丝绸之路经济带的必由之路。”单文华如是说。

单文华访谈录*

1970年2月生，湖南株洲人。西安交通大学法学院院长、腾飞学者特聘教授、博士生导师；牛津布鲁克斯大学国际法教授；教育部长江学者讲座教授；英国剑桥大学圣三一学院法学博士；欧盟对华框架条约咨询专家、英国政府国家安全战略咨询专家与经济与社会研究基金委员会（ESRC）项目评审专家、享受国务院政府特殊津贴专家、中国欧洲法研究会副会长；牛津哈特出版社“中国与国际经济法系列专著”和北京大学出版社《海外法学学子文库》主编；上海昊理文律师事务所高级顾问（中国执业律师）。曾任剑桥大学中国学生学者联谊会主席、全英中国法学会（UKCLA）首任理事长、剑桥大学劳特派特国际法中心客座研究员。

主要著作有：《欧盟对华投资的法律框架：解构与建构》、《欧盟商法》（合译）、《国际贸易法学》（主编）等。主要论文有：《外资国民待遇及其实施条件》、《中国国际经济法学的创立于发展》（合作）、《电子贸易的法律问题》、《中国有关国际惯例的立法评析》、《国际贸易惯例基本理论问题研究》、《世界贸易组织协定中的国际投资规范评析》、《我国外资国民待遇制度的发展与完善》、《市场经济与外商投

* 本文原载何勤华主编：《中国法学家访谈录》（第十卷），北京大学出版社2014年版。

点小钱,也是有意义的锻炼。其他还有一些有趣的同学,我就不一一说了。

可以说是陈安老师真正把我带入了国际经济法的核心地带,为此我对他一直十分感念。

记:您现在从事国际经济法研究,研究兴趣是何时产生的?

单:我在中大读书的时候就有兴趣了。从精神角度而言,对我影响最大的可能要算端木正老师了。我没上过他的课,只听过他的讲座。经常看到他从法律系旁边一条小道上走向系里。他人很高大,拄着拐杖或者让人搀扶着走来,感觉就像一尊宝塔巍巍而来,特别能给人高山仰止的感觉。这是精神方面的影响。学术上对我影响较大的黎学玲教授。他讲授涉外经济法,还是我本科论文的指导老师,讲课辅导时带着一口浓重的湖南口音。我至今记得他在讲对外国投资者保护的国民待遇标准时,说要给予外商"同等的保护",他的发音有点像是"统统的保护"。我学术兴趣的萌芽,恐怕就是始于这"统统的保护"(笑),因为国民待遇是我在国际经济法方面认真研究的第一个课题。我的第一篇比较像样的文章也是关于国民待遇的,于 1994 年发表于《中国法学》。后来又在《法学研究》和《中国社会科学》上各发表了一篇相关文章。我这三篇文章发表得比较早,后来有学者研究国民待遇问题时,往往会对它们有所参考。

我写毕业论文的时候,法学教育恢复不久,还没有讲"依法治国",而讲"依法治厂"。所以,我写的毕业论文是《厂长/经理的法律意识初探》。黎老师主张实证研究,所以为了写好毕业论文,我特地到佛山的一些企业进行问卷调研。毕竟,纸上得来终觉浅。后来在剑桥的时候,剑桥的导师也建议做问卷、做访谈,走的也是实证研究的路子。黎老师对我的论文抓得比较紧,我论文后来得了优,因此我在学术上获得了一点小小的信心,接着便"斗胆"考研了。不过,那时我懵懵懂懂,在考试报名截至前一天才知道消息。我马上打电话联系我哥哥,我哥鼓励我去考。那年是 1991 年,由于本校不招经济法专业的硕士研究生,我就只好考虑报考外校。因为我对广州怀着强烈的感情,所以我就决定报考同在广州的暨南大学。

记:考上暨南后,研究生的学习生活大体是怎么样的呢?

单:很愉快,我的老师特别好,主要是张增强教授和王河教授。张老师课讲得好,人也特别宽厚,学风严谨,写字一丝不苟,特别工整。不仅教会我怎么严谨地做学问,做人方面也给了我很大的启发。王河老师非常善于在业务上开拓,不管是律师业务还是学术业务。学术上,他在包括《法学研究》《中国法学》在内的很多刊物上都发过文章,这在当时南方的学校里是很少见的。我们特别想请教他怎么写文章怎么发表,他说没什么诀窍,要靠自己摸索,我至今深以为然。

我在读研究生的时候发表过几篇文章。因为我发表的几篇论文,使我在同学中显得比较突出。三年的研究生,我只用了两年时间就念完了,还拿过省里的“南粤优秀研究生二等奖”,当时算是最高奖项了。我在读研期间,社会工作参加过一些,在研究生会也工作过,还担任过研究生报的主编。相比之下,我觉得暨南大学的研究生生活比较活跃,中大的生活就似乎显得有些刻板了。另外,暨南的老师、同学都有比较强烈的接触社会的愿望。比如老师会把上课的机会介绍给学生。我就在好几个地方兼过课,又一次去增城讲授法律,全程还是用粤语讲的。我感觉比后来在英国用英语讲课还难(笑)。因为粤语我日常会话使用得比较多,专业术语的讲法就不太熟悉了。不过,讲了好几个小时,效果似乎还不错。总的来说,我在暨南的生活是很愉快的。

记:您能回忆一下当年考博的情形吗?

单:我在暨南大学读书的时候,认识了一位会计系的师兄,他读了两年书后就到厦大读了博士。我问导师自己能不能也效仿一下师兄,读两年就到厦大读博。因为我当时的课程已经都学完了,成绩也还不错,于是导师便同意了,而且给我写了很好的推荐信。在暨南的时候,我读的虽然是经济法,但挂靠的学科是企业管理。

打定主意考博以后,我决定报考厦门大学陈安教授的博士,但是我却错过了报考的时间。正当我急得不知如何是好的时候,有一位工作人员告诉我说不妨前去厦门拜访一下陈先生。于是那年“五一”我坐轮船到了厦门。不过,陈安老师并没有让我去他家拜访,而只是和我通了个一两个小时的电话,相当于一次电话interview。后来我才知道陈老师素以严格出名,有的副省长、副市长级别的人物报考陈老师的博士,只要陈老师一听说对方有“通路子”的行为,马上就不让报考,一点通融的余地都没有。同时,他为人很是循规蹈矩,他希望报考他博士的人是正正规规法学专业三年硕士出身,而我恐怕是“三突破”了他的标准,硕士挂的是企业管理,不是法学;又只读了两年,而不是三年;然后报考的时间又延迟了。所以,陈安老师对我的报考可以说是满腹狐疑,问得很是仔细,包括我以前读硕士期间学过些什么课、老师是谁,以及写过什么文章等。我记得打电话的时候我正在感冒,打完电话,只觉得后背出了一身的大汗,感冒似乎也好了(大笑)。

陈老师治学极其严谨,他恐怕是我接触过的最严谨的学者之一了。他常说:“板凳宁坐十年冷,文章不写半句空。”他的身教和言教对我而言都同样重要。这样一位活生生的大家在我面前,并最直观地让我接触他活生生的大作从粗胚到成品的过程,让我强烈感到,我和老先生的差距是巨大的,老先生就像一座高标，虽然高，但我至少还能够看得见，心向往之，于是在读博期间"斗胆"在《中国法学》《法学研究》发表了两篇文章，这同老先生的鼓舞是分不开的。在陈先生的带领下，我们博士生也养成了非常严谨的学风。老先生可以说是用"铁腕手段"打造了一支学术团队。国际经济法这个学科那时人才稀缺、博士点很少，老先生每年招的人很有限。先生精心栽培，许多都送出国去学习，多数回来了，也有的就没有回来。老先生对送出去不回来的学生比较生气，认为那些人可以说是"反面教材"。有的人说老先生要求博士生留校是"近亲繁殖"，而陈老先生对我们说，他这不是"近亲繁殖"，如果不这么做，他就要"断子绝孙"。我现在做院长，也很有感触。陈老师不只是个人写写文章，独善其身，而是要带领一支团队，在国际法学科上拼出一条血路。韩德培先生以前就对我说过，他很早就认为，陈安老师是一个"帅才"。可以说，是陈安老师真正把我带入了国际经济法的核心地带，为此我对他一直十分感念。

剑桥就是这样一种环境，她能够养得起学者的骄傲、对学术至高无上的钟情。这样一个氛围，我认为就是理想的学术氛围。

记：您觉得您在自己的领域内，有哪些主要的学术成果？

单：这么多年来，我写过不少文章，每篇文章里都有自己的观点。比如我在厦大的博士论文写的是国际贸易惯例，对国际贸易惯例的性质、功能与用途作了一些有开拓性的探讨。韩德培老师是我博士论文的评阅人和答辩委员会主席，他对我论文的评语是："这是一篇比较优秀的博士学位论文。"这个评价让我有点受宠若惊。再比如说电子商务法，我可以说是最早比较系统研究电子商务法的学者。周汉民老师在国内回顾国际经济法的成果时，还特别提到我这方面的研究，给了比较高的评价。我主编的《国际贸易法学》这本书，两卷本84万字，可能是当时国内同类专著中规模最大的一本。这本书属于陈先生主持的国际贸易法学系列专著第二套，是这个系列里最重要的一本书之一。编这套书的时候我刚博士毕业，还是讲师。能够让我主编，这又体现了陈先生的一个有点：有魄力，敢于起用年轻人。

在国外的研究成果，首先是我的博士论文，是关于中国与欧盟投资关系中法律关系的论述，后来由牛津哈特出版社出版，是这方面的第一本专著。近年来中国和欧盟在谈判伙伴关系协定，这是双方最重要的一份条约，将奠定双边关系的法律基石。欧盟方面聘我为高级顾问，专门研究起草该条约中的投资部分。其中涉及的问题比较多，比如牵涉欧盟对外投资签约的能力问题。一段时间以来，欧盟并没有签约的能力，双边投资协定都是以成员国的名义签的。我觉得无论从经济角度还是理性角度而言,让欧盟具有签约的权能无疑是更好的。这一点现在在《里斯本条约》里也实现了,可以说是直接源于我的建议。我觉得这一点是很有意义的。近几年来,我主要在钻研中国对外投资条约。我写的 Chinese Investment Treaties:Policies and Practice 这本书是牛津大学出版社出版的。应该说,非英语国家的学者在牛津出书是很少的,中国人就更少了。写这本书光论证过程就花了两年,由七名专家对书的 Proposal 进行论证,每个人都有修改意见,总体上是肯定的,但还是改了好多回。从国别角度写双边投资协定,我这本书可能是第一次尝试。此外,我还比较关注国际法特别是国际经济法中的一些结构性问题,如经济全球化背景下的国家主权界定问题。2007 年我就此主办了一个国际研讨会,请来了世界顶级的国际经济法和国际公法学者来探讨这个问题。会议很成功,论文后来还结集出版了。目前,我在主持国际比较法科学院(IACL)的一个全球性研究项目,有 IACL 指定的 20 多个国家的专家参与,目的是要对世界上主要国家和地区的外国投资条约和法律作一个系统化的比较研究。各国的国别研究报告和我的总报告,都会在四年一度的国际比较法大会上宣读,并最后由牛津哈特出版社出版。

剑桥博士毕业照

记:*放眼当下学术环境的建设,您认为在年轻学者当中,是否存在着一种浮躁的情绪?*

单:当然是存在的,因为大环境如此。我们的评价机制还在完善过程当中,现在这种量化的考核指标应当是造成这种浮躁的一个重要原因。评职称的压力,使得大家有时不得不去做一些不那么符合规范的事情。而剑桥的学术环境就非常让人羡慕。在剑桥,写文章和出版的压力也是存在的,毕竟要想往上晋升,不发文

西安交大法学院的国际范*

在中国法学界，当“长江学者”和“千人计划”两项国家特聘专家学术荣誉相遇于一身时，我们不难找到一个唯一的名字——单文华。从2005年开始，这位国际法与比较法领域的国际著名学者就与西安交大结下不解之缘。

2005年，作为我国海外学子中首位在英国高校执教的国际法学教授，当时受聘于牛津布鲁克斯大学法律系的单文华作出一个让人难以理解的决定：放弃国外优越的工作环境和舒适生活，回到古城西安，受聘于西安交大，带领这所大学的法学院开始了一段“追梦”之旅。

唱响法学国际风

当年仅35岁的单文华人生第一次踏上西北这片广袤而陌生的土地时，恰逢西安交大恢复法学专业20年。当时的法学系还归属人文学院。单文华带着最初的梦想“空降”就任人文学院院长，作为当时西安交大最年轻的院长，他顶着各种“拭目以待”，一切从头开始。

2008年，西安交大正式成立法学院，单文华转任法学院院长。年轻而朝气蓬勃的法学院让单文华很快给自己的梦想找到了一个现实定位：要将它建设成为一所“高起点、国际化、研究型”的国际一流法学院。他的目标越来越清晰，法学院的发展要让国际经济法与比较法快速达到世界先进水平，并带动知识产权与科技法、信息安全与政府规制等建成国内一流学科方向，让中国在国际法学领域产生一定的影响和学术引领，发出属于中国人的声音，维护中国人的国际话语权。

借助于单文华及其团队多年厚积薄发的国际合作平台和国际影响力，西安交大法学院被完全置于世界图景下，先后与英国剑桥大学、英国国际法与比较法研究院等多所国际一流法学院建立了密切的学术交流与合作关系，这让法学院的发

* 本文发表在《中国科学报》2013年11月7日第6版：动态，记者谢霞宇。

展从一开始就颇具“国际范”。

如今,西安交大法学院已形成全球首个“法律治理学”交叉学科博士点,与一级学科硕士点法学硕士、法学本科共同构成了完整的法学人才培养体系,取得了法律硕士专业学位授予权,同时进入国家首批卓越法律人才教育培养基地。法学院已成为我国最重要的法学人才培养基地之一。

凝练法学人才链

时至今日,单文华扎根西部已有八年,他的梦想也在这片土地上生根发芽。在他的领导下,“国际化”成为法学院人才培养和引进的一个核心主题词。该院也构建了“高起点、国际化、研究型、重实践”的创新型法学人才培养体系,并将“国际化”融入到人才培养的整个过程。

2011 年,法学院与剑桥大学劳特派特国际法中心正式签署人才联合培养协议——剑桥“丝绸之路学者”项目,该项目也成为与美国以外的第一个海外机构签订的常设性人才联合培养项目。基于法学院与英国剑桥大学劳特派特国际法中心、英国格拉斯哥大学、澳大利亚莫纳什大学等学术机构建立的联合培养机制,2012 年,法学院成功入选国家首批 22 所“涉外法律人才教育培养基地”,获批“应用型复合型法律职业人才教育培养基地”和“涉外型法律人才教育培养基地”两个卓越法律人才教育培养基地。2013 年,法学院因此特设“法学复合型卓越班”,按照“2 +4 + X”模式培养,其中优秀的法学本科生、博士生可与国外著名大学进行联合培养。

在法学院的发展历程中,国际化学术交流活动显得尤为活跃。从 2011 年开始,法学院连续三年举办教育部、国家外专局“学校特色项目”丝绸之路国际经济法高级国际研讨班系列,聘请多位国际一流学者前来讲学。

法学院和丝绸之路国际法与比较法研究所已形成一定的海内外影响力,对学院的学科发展和学术提升产生了较大的影响,由国际比较法研究院指导、牛津大学出版社出版的《中国比较法学刊》也顺利出版。一批英文研究成果也在牛津大学出版社、牛津哈特出版社等国际一流出版社出版,相关理论研究成果还登上了《美国国际法杂志》《美国比较法杂志》《欧洲国际法杂志》等国际一流法学期刊。

引入法学精英群

频繁的国际学术交流让法学院的发展机遇与挑战并存,成为中国海外法学学子乃至国际法学专家学者加盟西安交大的首选。其中,既有毕业于剑桥、牛津等世界知名学府的青年才俊,也不乏“千人计划”、长江学者等高端国际化法学人才。

为加快“高起点、国际化、研究型”国际一流法学院的建设步伐，进一步提升师资队伍的国际化程度和教学科研水平，法学院面向全球招聘外籍教师。近日，4 位国外学者从来自亚洲、欧洲、北美洲、拉丁美洲、大洋洲、非洲的 50 多位全球应聘者中脱颖而出，成为法学院全职外籍教师。值得一提的是，在本次招聘中，外国应聘者和国内应聘者适用同样的应聘程序和同样的薪资待遇，这在西安交大尚属首例，在国内高校招聘中也极为少见。

这些只是西安交大法学院国际化建设的一个缩影。近日，世界国际法顶尖权威学者、剑桥大学法学院惠威尔教授詹姆斯·克劳福德（James Crawford）已通过全国评审成为西安交大法学院的“长江学者”讲座教授。同时，国际经济法权威学者、新加坡国立大学教授索纳冉加（M. Sornarajah）也已登陆西安交大首个夏季小学期，为法学本科生传道授业。

在大西北这片广袤的土地上，如何炼成一个国际一流法学院？单文华认为首先要坚持学术研究的全球视野、世界眼光，这也是维护中国的国际利益的必然要求，“要让中国的学术和理论国际化，并在法律领域让中国人真正起到学术引领作用，我们一方面要面向世界，广纳世界学术成果为我所用；另一方面要立足中国，坚持学术自信和理论自觉，让中国法学学术走向世界并逐步引领世界学术，这样才能让中华法学文明巍然屹立于世界文明之林”。

单文华:一个国际法学者的中国梦*

单文华,英国剑桥大学法学博士,现任西安交通大学学术委员会副主任、法学院院长兼丝绸之路国际法与比较法研究所所长、博士生导师;“千人计划”国家特聘专家、长江学者讲座教授;兼任剑桥大学劳特派特国际法中心资深研究员,是中心聘请的7位资深研究员中唯一一位亚洲学者。主要研究领域为国际法与比较法(特别是投资、贸易、商事与仲裁法),是该领域的国际著名学者。2011年被推选为世界比较法权威学术团体国际比较法科学院(IACL)荣誉院士(Titu-larMember),是该科学院全球80名荣誉院士中第一位来自中国大陆的荣誉院士。

带着梦想

八年前,年仅35岁的单文华回到祖国母亲的怀抱,这是他人生第一次踏上西北这片广袤而陌生的土地。2005年也恰逢西安交大恢复法学专业20年,法学系当时归属人文学院。“想做点事情,想把西部法学做起来”,单文华带着最初的梦

* 本文发表在《法制日报》2013年11月5日第10版:环球法治,记者汪闽燕。

单文华:从做强中国法学的角度,特别是加强中国法学在世界的影响力来说,我们已经做了不少工作。从我个人而言,我曾作为第一位中国学者在国际比较法大会、ASIL 年会、SIEL 双年会、ITF 等本专业最重要的国际学术会议上作总报告、专题主持人或主题报告人。

又比如,我们创办并主编了由牛津大学出版社出版,并由 IACL 指导的英文国际期刊《中国比较法学刊》,目的就是要以"世界视野、中国重心"为宗旨,大力推动中外法学交流互动,从而在世界法学特别是比较法学的发展演进过程中发出中国声音,扩大中国影响。但是,总体而言,我们在这方面的工作还做得很不够,距离引领世界法学发展的时代需求差距还很大。这是我们所面临的问题和挑战,也是中国法律学人重大的历史机遇和历史使命!

记者:现在,我们经常提"中国的话语权",作为一名国际法教授,您认为我们应该如何提升我们的话语权?

单文华:在展现"中国话语权"的层面,我们的能力建设尚需大大加强。但是,国家目前对此非常重视,"千人计划""长江学者奖励计划""新世纪人才计划"等重要人才计划的实施为这方面的人才队伍建设奠定了一定的基础。同时,教育部卓越法律人才计划的实施,特别是"涉外型法律人才教育培养基地"的布点建设,从长远来看,也将有力推动这方面的能力建设工作。不少领先型的法学院已经把高端国际化人才的培养作为其人才培养的重中之重。可以预见,在未来的几年里,将迎来国内先进法学院国际化的一个热潮。

感受剑桥*

剑桥无疑是世界上最出色的大学之一，而三一学院又是剑桥最富有的学院，据称其财产在英国仅次于王室。坐在学院那修道院式的古老饭厅里，吃着法学院单文华博士招待的午饭，环顾墙上一幅幅著名人物的画像，一种肃然起敬之情油然而生。

坐在我对面的单文华今年31岁，出身于湖南株洲攸县农家，17岁作为株洲地区文科状元考入中山大学学习法律，21岁进入厦门大学念研究生，26岁拿到博士学位并留校任教，一年后破格提升为法学院副教授，为厦大历史上最年轻的副教授。

吃过午饭，单文华带我来到剑桥著名的果园茶屋（Orchard）。在罗素等不少名人高谈阔论过的地方，他同我聊起在剑桥的所见所闻所感：

老早就知道剑桥，一直想来这里。上网看了看，按程序填了表寄过去。当时我同时申请了合作研究和人员交流两项，结果大出意料，两项申请都被批准了。

1998年9月15日，我第一次来到剑桥，这也是我第一次出国。坐在从伦敦到剑桥的火车上，看着夜色中华灯初放，想象着剑桥的样子。到了剑桥，一看是这么简单的一个小站——简直都看不出来是火车站，忍不住有点失望。

刚到的时候最大的问题是语言。以前学的都是美式英语，听不惯英国人说话，经常有交流障碍。而且刚开始容易没信心，跟人说话时，人家听不懂，"pardon"（请再说一遍）一声，就老觉得是自己的错。

人到了外国，就像第二次人生的开始，只是过程更短。比如首先要学会找吃的，其次要学会交流，学语言。开始时，老外因为你是新来的，会对你很客气、很好，但总归不是在一个平等的地位上，因此感觉容易拘束、压抑。也不认

* 本文发表在《参考消息》2001年4月26日第16版，新华社驻伦敦记者王艳红。

识几个中国人，即使认识几个，人家也挺忙的，不会总有时间跟你谈心。当时是9月份，我住处的窗外有一朵很大的玫瑰花，不过已经残败了。我就给爱人写信，诉说日子多艰苦，好容易找到吃的东西，又这么贵，说看着这英格兰最后的一朵玫瑰感觉很伤心。她接到信读着读着就哭了。

适应了这边的食物、语言之后，就要考虑做点事——你到这边来是做研究的呀！很多访问学者出来很容易陷入一个孤立的范围里，仍在中国人的圈子里打转，没进入学术的主流世界。最后，一年下来只是看过人家几本外文书，这就跟在国内没什么区别，甚至更糟，因为心理状态跟在国内完全不一样。本来觉得来这里待一段时间应该是学到不少东西的，结果适得其反。

对刚来的人来说，中外朋友都需要。刚来的时候，交流本领达不到那个水平，深层的社会需要就肯定得往熟悉的乡情里去找。但必须意识到，来这里的目的是要看外面、学人家的东西，而不是为了回顾，回顾很容易形成一种消极或片面的状态。有的人刚来时很积极，选很多课，参加各种讲座，但毕竟语言方面有困难，可能一星期之后就懈怠了……贵在坚持。我来时很多活动都积极参加，慢慢跟外国同行熟了，感觉就是其中一员，他们也不把你当外人。

来英国的目的，是体验一下西方社会和法学教育，并做一点合作研究。在劳特派特中心做完欧盟外资法的研究后，觉得一年时间所学的还是不够，于是我就申请读博士，拿到了三一学院的全额奖学金。学费和学院费都不用自己操心，每年有几千英镑的生活费，住的是学院提供的一套房子，房租比较便宜。

剑桥所谓的导师跟中国的理解不太一样，相当于中国的辅导员，给你生活上的照料，并不管具体学业。我在国内教书时感觉到，大学生刚进学校时面临一个心理断乳期，突然离开家庭是一方面，学业又是一方面，心境落差特别大，感觉特别迷惘。剑桥的学院有一个庞大的辅导员队伍，具体照顾学生的生活起居，事无巨细。例如跟老师斗气啦，音乐放得太吵啦，要做什么研究项目需要资金啦，辅导员都会帮你解决。如果你有兴趣，还可以参加各种各样的俱乐部，这都是受学院补贴的。这种体制，对学生来说更有利。

从老师这方面来看，学院制也是有意义的。学院养院士(fellow)，并没有具体任务规定，比如要发表几篇论文之类的，只是看中你这个人。

在聘任期间，你可享受各种待遇。这里的人都是很杰出的，彼此竞争非常激烈，表面上没有任何压力，其实压力很大。我跟许多学生聊过，他们都觉得压力很大。英国大学里自杀率挺高的,就因为压力实在太大了。剑桥的自然环境固然能给人以温馨的感觉,在草地上一躺下就不想起来,但有几个人能真的躺得下去?而且中国人在这里往往又要花成倍的努力才能获得同等待遇。就算你在同辈里已经“独孤求败”了,还有学院和剑桥本身的压力,比如三一学院出过三十几个诺贝尔奖得主,他们摆在那里,你永远都会有压力。

此外,在剑桥有机会听到各种各样的高谈阔论或奇谈怪论,每周不来几个世界名人就好像白过了似的,这可以让人思维开阔。剑桥国际法研究中心每周五都有一个讲座,时间只有一个小时,但来的人都是这一领域的重量级人物。他们能对世界上发生的事情作出即时、敏锐的反应,接触这些人对开阔视野、培养独立思考能力是挺有帮助的。

在这里,要熟悉他们的学术套路、研究模式,在具体搞研究、创作的时候要考虑他们的程式,研究过程中的方法,要学习写东西的体例,这也是另外一次学术的再生。

平常除了用功之外,喜欢来 orchard,经常是周末来,带点报纸,要一壶茶,或者再要一块点心,把凳子一放,就着温情的阳光,蓝天白云,可以消磨一个上午,或一个黄昏。脑子里似乎就又澄清了,回去又可以从头开始。

周末我有时也去朋友家,聚餐、打扑克牌和唱卡拉 OK。有时候还会去老外同事家里,他们喜欢烤肉,比较简单,但大家可以聊聊天。

我从去年 10 月开始当剑桥中国学生学者联谊会主席。我们学联在学校网站上办了一个正式的网页,还创办了文学杂志《剑河风》,可以让大家业余时自娱自乐,体会中文的光荣,回味乡音。

学联有些固定的活动,特别对那些初来乍到的人,感觉就像找到了“组织”。大家互相聊天,看看中国影片,读读中国杂志。每两周还有一个学术论坛,讨论与中国相关的问题。

我同单文华谈了良久,意犹未尽,果园茶屋要打烊了。下着毛毛细雨的黄昏,实在并不是欣赏果园和剑河的好时候。不过,“周末的早上,一觉醒来,划一条船,溯河而上,到这里弃舟登岸……”他的这番描述还是让人动心的,不由得也想到剑桥来读两年书。当然,真要实现这打算的话,是需要足够勇气和实力的。剑桥可读的并不仅是这“温情脉脉”的自然环境,更是那 800 年积淀下来的深厚的历史。

图书在版编目(CIP)数据

单文华国际法与比较法论集：全3册：汉、英／单文华著；杜娟编．-- 北京：法律出版社，2016.11(2018.6重印)
ISBN 978-7-5197-0216-8

Ⅰ．①单… Ⅱ．①单… ②杜… Ⅲ．①国际法-比较法-文集-汉、英 Ⅳ．①D99-53

中国版本图书馆CIP数据核字(2016)第253480号

单文华国际法与比较法论集
SHANWENHUA GUOJIFA YU BIJIAOFA LUNJI

单文华 著
杜 娟 编

责任编辑 黄倩倩
装帧设计 李 瞻

出版 法律出版社
总发行 中国法律图书有限公司
经销 新华书店
印刷 北京虎彩文化传播有限公司
责任校对 王沁陶
责任印制 陶 松

编辑统筹 学术·对外出版分社
开本 720毫米×960毫米 1/16
印张 89.5
字数 1574千
版本 2016年11月第1版
印次 2018年6月第2次印刷

法律出版社／北京市丰台区莲花池西里7号(100073)
网址／www.lawpress.com.cn
投稿邮箱／info@lawpress.com.cn
举报维权邮箱／jbwq@lawpress.com.cn
销售热线／010-63939792
咨询电话／010-63939796

中国法律图书有限公司／北京市丰台区莲花池西里7号(100073)
全国各地中法图分、子公司销售电话：
统一销售客服／400-660-6393
第一法律书店／010-63939781/9782
西安分公司／029-85330678
重庆分公司／023-67453036
上海分公司／021-62071639/1636
深圳分公司／0755-83072995

书号：ISBN 978-7-5197-0216-8
定价(三卷本)：238.00元
(如有缺页或倒装，中国法律图书有限公司负责退换)

單文華

国际法与比较法论集（中）

Wenhua Shan's Essays on International and Comparative Law

单文华 著

杜　娟 编

法律出版社

LAW PRESS·CHINA

目 录
Contents

上 卷

第一编
国际法与比较法通论

中　卷

第三编

国际投资法

下 卷

中　　卷

第三编

国际投资法 Part III

287 -919

Toward a Multilateral or Plurilateral Framework on Investment*

Introduction

The need for a multilateral framework on investment (MFI) has long been felt, but never as strong as it is today. The global network of international investment agreements (IIAs) continues to grow, and three mega-regional agreements are being actively negotiated — the Trans-Pacific Partnership Agreement (TPP), the Transatlantic Trade and Investment Partnership Agreement (TTIP), and the Regional Comprehensive Economic Partnership Agreement (RCEP). Meanwhile, new campaigns against the Investor-State Dispute Settlement (ISDS) feature of IIA regimes are emerging, particularly in the European Union (EU). The European Parliament just voted in favour of the TTIP in general, but on the condition that its ISDS mechanism will be modified.[1] Beyond Europe, similar reactions have been seen in the United States (US) (where objections to ISDS were part of the debate over fast track authorisation); Australia (where ISDS was rejected in some IIAs but not in the recent ones with South Korea and China);[2] Brazil (where three new bilateral investment treaties (BITs) have been signed after a decade of silence);[3] and India (where a more conservative model BIT has just been adopted).[4] Undoubtedly, the challenges for IIA regimes have reached global dimensions, which require an answer of global scale.

---

* E15 Initiative Thinkpiece, Geneva: International Centre for Trade and Sustainable Development (ICTSD) and World Economic Forum, 2015.

[1] Members of the European Parliament insisted a new ISDS system should be run by publicly appointed judges instead of a private arbitration. See European Parliament, Plenary highlights: Greece, TTIP, emission trading reform, 10 July 2015, available at, < http://www.europarl.europa.eu/news/en/news-room/content/20150706STO74853/html/Plenary-highlights-Greece-TTIP-emissions-trading-reform > (accessed on 19 July 2015).

[2] For instance, the IIAs without ISDS provisions are the Australia-United States FTA (2004) and the Australia-Malaysia FTA (2011), while the IIAs with ISDS provisions are Australia-South Korea FTA (2013) and Australia-China FTA (2015).

[3] Brazil recently signed three BITs separately with Mexico, Angola, and Mozambique, for analysis, see Pedro Martini, Brazil's New Investment Treaties: Outside Looking ...out?, Kluwer Arbitration Blog, 16 June 2015, available at, < http://kluwerarbitrationblog.com/blog/2015/06/16/brazils-new-investment-treaties-outside-looking-out-2/ > (accessed on 19 July 2015).

[4] The text of the new Indian Model BIT is available at, < https://mygov.in/sites/default/files/master_image/Model%20Text%20for%20the%20Indian%20Bilateral%20Investment%20Treaty.pdf > (accessed on 19 July 2015).

This think piece attempts to answer three fundamental questions related to an MFI: why now, what, and how? It first explores why a multilateral or plurilateral framework on investment (MFI/PFI) should be considered now, before analysing what kind of policy goals should be achieved and what kind of provisions should be included. It then discusses possible steps toward an MFI, proposing a PFI as a stepping stone. Finally, it assesses the possible venues for an MFI/PFI to be negotiated.

It concludes that the time is ripe to seriously consider an MFI, perhaps starting with a transitional PFI. The contents of the MFI or PFI should be based on a systematic reform of the IIA regime "from root to rules," reflecting the fundamental shift of tension "from North-South divide to private-public debate."[5] The goal of the reform should be a balanced and liberal investment regime rectifying the deficiencies in current IIAs, from the preamble to definitions, from substantive to procedural rules, and from investment norms to relevant social clauses. The 2016 G20 Summit would provide a good opportunity for the proposals related to an MFI/PFI to be brought for consideration by world leaders. The World Trade Organization (WTO) remains the best venue to negotiate an MFI/PFI, while a trilateral investment or free-trade agreement between the US, the EU, and China would provide a solid stepping stone. The International Centre for Settlement of Investment Disputes (ICSID) could make a significant contribution toward ISDS reform by establishing an appeal mechanism and perhaps a permanent court. Other venues, such as the United Nations (UN), the Organisation for Economic Co-operation and Development (OECD), the International Energy Charter (IEC) and the Asian Infrastructure Investment Bank (AIIB) may also have significant roles to play in this process.

A Better Time for an MFI

Investment and trade have been driving forces for world economic growth and development, with investment playing a rapidly rising role. Between 1970 and 2013, the ratio of foreign direct investment (FDI) stocks to global GDP rose from 6 percent to 34 percent, while the ratio of exports (goods and services) to global gross domestic product (GDP) rose from 14 percent to 29 percent.[6] The role of international investment is set to further increase as a conduit for improved technology and as the demand for infrastructure in OECD countries plus Brazil, Russia, China, and India requires about US $1 trillion each year over the next 15 years.[7]

One defining feature of contemporary international investment is that it is often in-

---

[5] Shan Wenhua, "From 'North-South Divide' to 'Private-Public Debate': Revival of the Calvo Doctrine and the Changing Landscape, International Investment Law," Northwestern Journal of International Law and Business, 2007, 27(3): 631 – 664.

[6] Hufbauer, Gary and Tyler Moran, Investment and Trade Regimes Conjoined: Economic Facts & Regulatory Frameworks, E15 TFM1 Thinkpiece, 23 – 24 March 2015, p. 3.

[7] The global spending on basic infrastructure currently amounts to $2.7 trillion a year when it ought to be $3.7 trillion. See Economist, The Trillion-dollar Gap, 22nd March 2014, available at, <http://www.economist.com/news/leaders/21599358-how-get-more-worlds-savings-pay-new-roads-airports-and-electricity> (accessed on 19 July 2015).

tertwined with international trade to create global value chains (GVCs).[8] FDI by multinational enterprises (MNEs) determines to a significant extent the patterns of value added in GVCs.[9] If the older pattern of the international economy featured "made here and sold there," the current pattern features "made here and there and sold everywhere."[10]

The critical and growing importance of international investment in the global economy requires a sound global legal framework to guarantee secure and harmonious international relations. The emergence of GVCs makes the task more pressing. Yet, the global investment regime is far from satisfactory. Unlike trade, which has the world trading system led by the WTO and a large set of multilateral agreements, global investment is regulated by a "spaghetti bowl" of over 3000 IIAs.[11] Such a "spaghetti bowl" of bilateral and small regional IIAs provides protection to a considerable portion of international investment relationships, but it offers far less than comprehensive global coverage, and its rules are far from consistent, or consistently interpreted and applied by the hundreds of different arbitral tribunals specifically constituted for each case. Indeed, the challenges to the current international investment treaty regime, including its dispute settlement system have been so severe that it is sometimes termed a "legitimacy crisis."[12] The solution to such a crisis cannot be just piecemeal, mending on bilateral or regional basis. Investment protection is a global issue, which requires a global solution.

Unfortunately, no multilateral agreement on investment is in place despite a major effort in the OECD and a stillborn attempt in the WTO. The failure of the OECD in negotiating a Multilateral Agreement on Investment (MAI) in the late 1990s was attributable to several factors. On the one hand, the negotiating parties had conflicting interests on some issues that could not be solved, owing to lack of high-level political support. On the other hand, non-governmental organizations (NGOs) successfully waged a campaign against the MAI as a threat to the environment and other public policy goals.[13] The failure of the WTO in negotiating a similar investment agreement at the Cancun Ministerial Conference in 2003 was mainly due to the differing interests and priorities of

---

[8] OECD, WTO and UNCTAD, *Implications of Global Value Chains for Trade, Investment, Development and Jobs*, 6 August 2013, p. 8, available at, <www.oecd.org/trade/G20-Global-Value-Chains-2013.pdf> (accessed on 19 July 2015). See also Gary Hufbauer and Tyler Moran, Investment and Trade Regimes Conjoined: Economic Facts and Regulatory Frameworks, E15 Investment Task Force, 14 May 2015.

[9] OECD, Interconnected Economies: Benefiting from Global Value Chains, 2013, p. 118.

[10] Gary Hufbauer and Tyler Moran, ibid.

[11] Until the end of 2014, there were 3271 , including 2926 BITs and 345 other IIAs. See UNCTAD, World Investment Report 2015: Reforming International Investment Governance, United Nations: New York and Geneva, June 2015, p. 106.

[12] Franck, Susan D., "The Legitimacy Crisis in Investment Treaty Arbitration: Privatizing Public International Law Through Inconsistent Decisions", *Fordham Law Review*, 2005, 73(4): 1521 – 1625.

[13] PIIE: The MAI and the Politics of Failure: Who Killed the Dog? Available at: <http://www.piie.com/publications/chapters_preview/91/2iie2725.pdf> (accessed on 31 October 2015). See also Eric Neumayer, Multilateral agreement on investment: lessons for the WTO from the failed OECD-negotiations. Wirtschaftspolitische Blatter, (1999) 46 (6). pp. 618 – 628.

the developed and developing states.[14]

However, a multilateral legal framework becomes even more desirable at the present stage, particularly given the economic downturn the world is currently experiencing and the interconnected nature of trade and investment in GVCs. As the OECD pointed out, "[M] ultilateral co-operation and co-ordination are needed to maintain the open and predictable international investment climate that has supported investment in GVCs."[15] And, the atmosphere for seriously reconsidering an MFI is now far better than it was 10 or 20 years ago mainly for three reasons.

First, the players in international investment have become much more mixed than before. International investment used to be dominated by advanced western states, which accounted for the vast majority of both inward and outward FDI. Now, the picture has significantly changed. Developing states not only attract more than half (55percent) of the world investment inflow (Figure 1), but also they represent one-third of the world investment outflow (Figure 4). This is a sharp contrast to 2002, the year before the WTO Cancun conference took place, when the developing states attracted less than a quarter of world FDI inflows and less than 20 percent of world FDI outflows.[16] The rise of developing states in international investment, particularly in outward FDI, implies that they are starting to view the international investment regime from not only a capital importing or host state perspective, but also from a capital exporting or home state perspective. At the same time, advanced economies, including the US and the EU, have started to consider their defensive interests as recipients of inward FDI in addition to their offensive interests as suppliers of outward FDI, particularly in light of the ISDS cases filed against the US and the EU member states. Such significant changes in the roles of both advanced and developing states mean that the two traditionally divided camps now find more common ground in the international investment regime.[17] This should, in particular, significantly help address the issue of the "north-south divide" that led to the collapse of the investment talks within the WTO at Cancun.

---

〔14〕 For further details, see Smythe, Elizabeth. From Singapore to Cancún: Knowledge, Power and Hegemony in the Negotiation of Investment Rules at the WTO (Paper presented at the annual meeting of the International Studies Association, Montreal, Quebec, March 18, 2004.

〔15〕 OECD. Trade Policy Implications of Global Value Chains, 2013. Available at, <www.oecd.org/sti/ind/Trade_Policy_Implicatipns_May_2013.pdf> (accessed on 19 July 2015).

〔16〕 United Nations Conference on Trade and Development, World Investment Report, United Nations, 2003, pp. 7, 9.

〔17〕 Shan Wenhua, "Towards a Balanced Liberal Investment Regime: General Report on the Protection of Investment for the XVIIIth International Congress of Comparative Law" 2010 Washington DC, ICSID Review: Foreign Investment Law Journal, 2010, 25(2): 421 – 497.

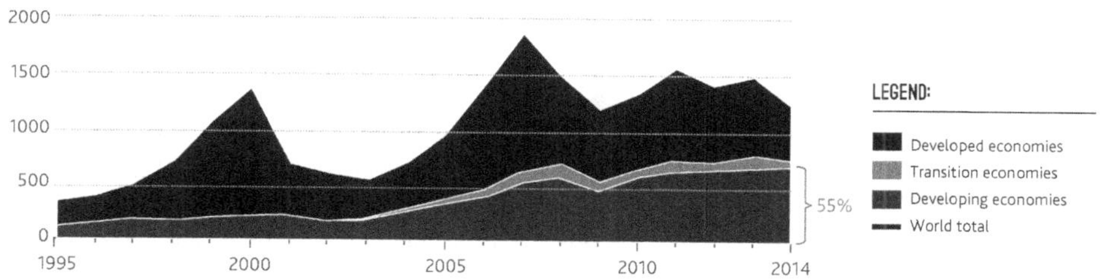

Figure 1　FDI inflows, Global and by Group of Economies, 1995 – 2014 (Billions of Dollars)

Source: UNCRAD, FDI/MNE database (www.uncrad.org/fdistatistics).

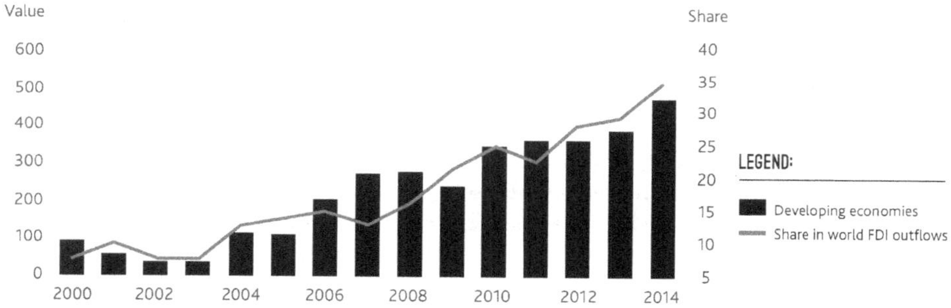

Figure 2　Developing Economies: FDI Outflows and Their Share in Total World Outflows, 2000 – 14 (Billions of dollars and percent)

Source: UNCTAD, FDI/MNE database (www.unctad.org/fdistatistics).

Note: Excludes Caribbean offshore financial centers.

Second, the mixed roles of advanced and developing states have led to converging IIA practice, demonstrated by four general features:[18]

- Typically, the new-generation IIAs embrace investment liberalisation as well as investment protection.
- They adopt more clarified and balanced terms on key substantive provisions, such as investment definition, indirect expropriation, and fair and equitable treatment (FET).
- The dispute settlement provisions (ISDS) are more detailed and refined than before.

---

[18] Shan Wenhua and Lu Wang, "The China – EU BIT and the Emerging, "Global BIT 2.0", ICSID Review, Vol. 30, No. 1 (2015), pp. 260 – 267; Shan Wenhua and Sheng Zhang, "Market Access Provisions in the Potential EU Model BIT: Towards a "Global BIT 2.0"? *Journal of World Investment and Trade*, 2014, 15(3): 422 – 453, p. 453. See also UNCTAD, supra note 11, p 110 – 112; Cross Karen H, "Converging Trends in Investment Treaty Practice," 38 *N. C. J. Int'l & Com. Reg.* 151 (2012); Feldman Mark. The emerging harmonisation of the international investment law regime, E15 Blog, August 2015. Available at: <http://e15initiative.org/blogs/the-emerging-harmonisation-of-the-international-investment-law-regime/> (accessed 21 August 2015).

- Finally, certain social clauses addressing environmental, labour, and other concerns are included.

Such features suggest that a "global BIT 2.0"[19] is taking shape, which helps pave the way for a MFI. As a more balanced and more society-friendly IIA model, it should to a certain degree also help address the concerns of NGOs expressed during and after the MAI negotiations.

The third and final reason for suggesting that an auspicious MFI moment may be at hand is that the current IIA regime has now attracted global attention. Many governments, NGOs, scholars, and practitioners are debating the IIA regime, in particular its ISDS mechanism. As mentioned, the regime is somehow experiencing a "legitimacy crisis." However a crisis suggests opportunity as well as challenge. While some of the extreme criticisms might exert a negative impact on the future development of a MFI, the attention the debate has generated helps create the political and social momentum necessary for a MFI. For example, more and more voices are heard on the desirability of a permanent appeal mechanism for ISDS awards,[20] which affirms the need for a MFI, as it would not be reasonable to expect a separate mechanism to be set up for each of the more than 3000 IIAs. Indeed, IIAs have often become topics of addresses by — and conversations among — top leaders of the world, which helps to build up high-level political support for a sound global investment regime — something that was lacking in the MAI negotiations.

The aforementioned three changes, taken together, constitute a fundamental change in present circumstances compared with those of the late 1990s or early 2000s, when the OECD and the WTO made similar attempts. The key to a successful MFI, nevertheless, is of course to design an instrument that reflects the interests of and therefore appeals to all stakeholders concerned. The question then arises: what would such an MFI look like?

The Need for a Balanced and Liberal Regime

A balanced and liberal MFI would best serve the interests of all stakeholders.[21] The regime has to pursue investment liberalisation to meet the needs of GVCs. As noted above, FDI plays a critical role in supporting GVCs, which in turn are essential for world economic growth and development. Accordingly, the general policy of an MFI should be geared toward investment liberalisation, rather than investment restriction. This is confirmed by the fact that states around the world are still adopting more liberal

---

[19] Shan and Wang, ibid; Shan and Zhang, ibid.

[20] In a recent concept paper sent to the European Parliament and to the Council, Commissioner Cecilia Malmstr. m of the European Commission proposed creating a permanent investment court to replace the ISDS mechanism. The concept paper further considered an appeal body with permanent members directly within the TTIP as a medium step toward a permanent multilateral court. See European Commission. Concept Paper: Investment in TTIP and beyond—the path for reform. Available at: < http://trade. ec. europa. eu/doclib/docs/2015/may/tradoc_153408. PDF > (accessed on 19 July 2015).

[21] Shan Wenhua, supra note 17.

investment measures than restrictive ones, as Figure 9 illustrates. Some 31 additional IIAs were signed in 2014, while nearly 90 countries are involved in the five ongoing regional IIA negotiations, including the TPP, the TTIP, and the RCEP.[22] Clearly the world is generally following a path of investment liberalisation, rather than the other way around.

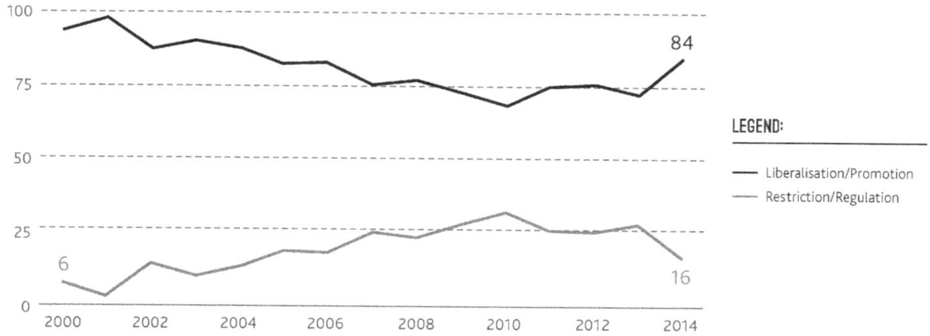

Figure 3 Changes in National Investment Policies, 2000 – 2014

Source: UNCTAD, Investment Policy Monitor.

However, the generally liberal path does not mean the current IIA regime is almost perfect. On the contrary, the current IIA regime is undergoing significant reform. And, the general theme of reform is "balancing." The original template for the IIA regime was "unbalanced," in the sense that it emphasised investment protection and promotion against the background of the "North-South divide," with little regard for preserving the regulatory space of the host state. For example, in an editorial published in 1960 on the Draft Convention on Investments Abroad, the first global investment pact proposed, the background of the draft convention was explained as follows:

> "Since it is now widely recognised that major steps must be taken to buttress the economic position of the free-world nations, both as a measure against Soviet moves and as a means of resolving some of the demands being made by the peoples of the underdeveloped nations of the world, the notion of greater protection under international law takes on added importance."[23]

Vandevelde, in his monograph on US investment treaties, wrote this about the background of the US BIT programme:

> "The BIT Program began in 1977 as a reaction to a large number of expropriations of foreign investment that had occurred in the post-war world and to the growing number of states that questioned whether customary international law required payment of full compensation for expropriated foreign investment... The United States hoped to provide treaty protection beyond that ac-

[22] UNCTAD. *World Investment Report* 2015: *Overview*, United Nations: New York and Geneva, June.

[23] The Editors, *The Proposed Convention to Protect Private Foreign Investment: A Roundtable*, *Journal of Public Law*, 1960, 6: 115 – 124, p. 115.

corded by customary international law, to develop a body of state practice in support of protection of foreign investment, and to establish a mechanism whereby its investors could obtain compensation from host states for unlawfully injured investment, without the involvement of the U. S. government."[24]

These authoritative accounts clearly demonstrate that investment treaties were originally designed as "swords" of the advanced capital exporting states in the "North-South struggle" that took place after the Second World War. Their purpose was to safeguard the interests of the capital exporting states and their investors by strengthening their positions under international law (both treaty and customary law) and by creating a depoliticised ISDS mechanism. This was part of the reaction of the advanced world to the New International Economic Order (NIEO) movement that was crystallised by the adoption of UN General Assembly Resolution 1803 (Permanent Sovereignty over Natural Resources, adopted in 1962) and Resolution 3281 (Charter of Economic Rights and Duties of States, adopted in 1974). These resolutions, particularly Resolution 3281, essentially denied the legitimacy of an international minimum standard espoused by advanced countries, especially regarding the standard of compensation in the event of expropriation.[25]

Hence, it can be said the NIEO was a thick "shield" erected by developing nations (together with Soviet countries) to protect state sovereignty in regulating foreign investment and multinational enterprises, while the IIAs were sharp "swords" to safeguarding the interests of advanced countries and their investors abroad. Effectively, the NIEO instruments constituted the "counterbalance" of the IIAs. Taken separately, neither of them would be balanced, as the IIAs ignore the regulatory space of the host states, while the NIEO resolutions deny international minimum standards. Taken together, however, they maintain a balance of the system of the international investment regime as a whole.

This background powerfully explains why the original investment treaties were so unbalanced as to the rights and obligations of host states and foreign investors: the lack of express reference to host states' right to regulate foreign investment in the preamble; the widest possible definition of "investment" to cover "every kind of assets" regardless of the "characters of investment;" the undefined and unqualified FET standard; the "adequate, prompt and effective compensation" requirement for expropriation or any act of expropriation, direct or indirect; and finally the widest possible access to an international tribunal initiated only by the foreign investor. IIAs were intentionally designed as one-sided instruments, protecting the interests of foreign investors, with little or no attention paid to the regulatory rights of host states. To uphold their regulatory rights, host states had to resort to the NIEO instruments, which many developing states asserted

---

[24] Vandevelde, Kenneth J. *US International Investment Agreements*, Oxford University Press, 2009, p. 1.

[25] Article 2. 2(c) of Resolution 3281 provides that (each state has the right) "To nationalize, expropriate or transfer ownership of foreign property, in which case appropriate compensation should be paid by the State adopting such measures, taking into account its relevant laws and regulations and all circumstances that the State considers pertinent."

as reflecting new customary international law.[26] The original imbalance in the IIAs can be termed a "birth defect" of the IIA system, which still impacts IIA treaty-making and interpretation today.

Since NIEO instruments provide the counterbalance to the IIAs, it might seem legitimate to take the NIEO instruments into account when interpreting IIAs. This implies that, in case of doubt or ambiguity, IIA provisions should be interpreted in favour of the host state, because, as a default rule, the host state is entitled to regulate foreign investment.[27] In practice, Resolutions 1803 and 3281 were referred to in at least one case in support of the tribunal's determination of the position of the host states.[28]

However, foreign investors might continue to argue for a pro-investor presumption in case of doubt or ambiguity on the ground that the purposes of the treaties are expressed in preambles, sometimes in combination with treaty titles. This view has been accepted by some tribunals.[29]

It is difficult to offer an absolute answer to such questions of treaty interpretation. Instead, they have to be answered on a case-by-case basis in accordance with the treaty language and the surrounding circumstances. In general, it seems reasonable to argue that rules contained in the IIAs ("internal rules") should carry more weight than rules contained in other albeit closely related instruments ("external rules"). In other words, host states might not find much support of their positions by referring to the NIEO instruments when defending their cases against foreign investors. This, in turn, confirms the need for an investment regime that is internally balanced.

Indeed, much of the effort at reforming the current IIA regime goes in the direction of internal "self-rebalancing": the narrowing down of the "investment" definition; the restrictive definition of key terms, such as FET and "indirect expropriation"; the exclusion of most-favoured nation (MFN) from jurisdictional or procedural rights; to name the most important. On the surface, this appears to have happened because western capital exporting countries suddenly discovered that the BITs, or the investment chapters in FTAs, were "double-edged": they can "bite" advanced countries in the same way they "bite" developing states. The deeper reason was the fundamental shift of tension and attention in international investment law that has taking place since 1990s, from "North-South divide" to "private-public debate."[30]

---

[26] Some also argued that the NIEO may bring about the development of new rules of customary international law. See Joyner Christopher C. (ed.), *The United Nations and International Law*, Cambridge University Press, 1997, p. 263.

[27] Indeed on occasion the World Court has referred to sovereign rights as a basis for a restrictive interpretation of treaty obligations. See e. g., Wimbledon (1923) PCIJ Ser A No. 1, 24. See also Crawford, James. *Brownlie's Principles of Public International Law*, 8th Edition, Oxford University Press, p. 450.

[28] There is at least one investment treaty arbitration case in which the tribunal has referred to the NIEO resolution to ascertain the general positions of the host state concerned on investment protection. *See Yaung Chi Oo Trading PTE Ltd. v. Government of the Union of Myanmar*, ASEAN I. D. Case No. ARB/01/1, Award, 31 March 2003, para. 21.

[29] *Tradax Hellas SA v Albania* (1996) 5 ICSID Reports 43, 68 – 9; *Frapport AG Frankfurt Airport Services Worldwide v Republic of the Philippines*, Award, 16 August 2007, para. 80.

[30] Shan Wenhua, *supra* note 5.

In the 1990s, when neo-liberalism ruled the world, almost all countries embraced FDI and IIAs, including even Latin American states, home of the Calvo Doctrine.[31] States entered into IIAs not only with countries of the other camp, i. e., North-South IIAs, but also with countries from the same camp, i. e., South-South or North-North IIAs. No longer were there debates on the standard of compensation in the event of expropriation, as most BITs explicitly or implicitly followed the same prototype requiring "adequate, effective, and prompt" compensation. Evidently, the North-South divide became blurred.

Instead, the world's attention shifted towards the balance of the rights and obligations of the two key stakeholders in an IIA, the foreign investor and the host state. Not only developing states pay attention to the preservation of the regulatory space under IIAs; advanced countries also have started to do so, particularly after they were sued under the North American Free-Trade Agreement (NAFTA) or other IIAs. Meanwhile, some developing states, such as China, Russia, Singapore, and South Korea have become keen on protecting their investors abroad as their overseas investments gained more significance. The mixed roles of both leading advanced and developing states in international investment, as noted above, has led to converging IIA practices, concentrating on balancing rights and interests between foreign investors and the host state. To a certain extent, this helps to pave the way toward a balanced and liberal MFI.

Towards A Balanced And Liberal MFI: Basic Content

The negotiation of an MFI provides a perfect opportunity for a systematic review and reform of the IIA regime "from root to rules." The "root" refers to the underlying spirit of the investment regime: no longer should it be a "one-sided" instrument ("sword") focused on the interests of foreign investors and the capital exporting countries with little or no regard to the regulatory space of the host state; rather, it should be a self-balanced system ("scale") that more evenly and proportionately serves the interests of both foreign investors and host states, or both capital exporting and importing countries.

The new spirit should be reflected in the preambular language of the MFI and guide the crafting of each and every provision of the treaty, including scope of coverage, investment liberalisation, substantive protections, social clauses, and dispute settlement. Below is a sketchy discussion of how the contents of the treaty might be formulated. In fact, many of the proposed changes to be included in the MFI have already been achieved in recent IIAs. Still, it is necessary to take a more systematic approach toward the needed reforms.

Preambular Language

The importance of preambular language cannot be underestimated, as the words stipulate the object and purpose of the treaty, providing important assistance in treaty

[31] Shan Wenhua, "Is Calvo Dead?" American Journal of Comparative Law, 2007, 55(1): 123 - 163, pp. 130 - 142.

interpretation. The fundamental rule of treaty interpretation, as codified in Article 31.1 of the Vienna Convention on the Law of Treaties, requires that a treaty shall be interpreted in good faith in accordance with the ordinary meaning of the terms in their context and "in the light of its object and purpose."

To achieve a balanced and liberal investment regime, the preamble of the MFI should continue to highlight the critical role of foreign investment in promoting economic growth and development, as well as the importance of a sound legal framework for the promotion and protection of such investment. At the same time, it should also highlight the host state's inherent right to regulate foreign investment unless overriding commitments are undertaken by the host state under international law. Arguably, this is a default rule of international law and need not to be expressly stated. However, given the historical background of IIAs, as discussed above, and the fact that many arbitrators in ISDS arbitration come from non-public international law backgrounds,[32] it is necessary to highlight the customary rule in the preamble to prevent misguided interpretation.

In addition, the preamble should address social concerns, making sure that the MFI will not negatively affect the promotion of environmental (and perhaps also labour) standards. As well, it might encourage foreign investors to become "responsible investors" by embracing corporate social responsibility (CSR). Equally important, the fundamental political and economic systems chosen by the host state should not be negatively affected by the investment agreement. Finally, as a multilateral instrument, the MFI needs to appreciate the special needs of least-developed states and give them greater room to adapt to the multilateral investment system.

Scope of Coverage

To begin with, the MFI should protect only proper investments, rather than assets that do not possess the characteristics of investments. The characteristics should include, for example, the contribution of capital, the expectation of return, and the assumption of risk.

Second, all covered investments should be equally protected without discrimination. It does more harm than good to create separate rules for different categories of investment, such as hedge funds or investments by state-owned enterprises (SOEs) or sovereign wealth funds (SWFs). The latter approach would not only further fragment the investment regime; but also it could prevent constructive dialogue between major players for a more desirable investment regime. A better approach to address concerns related to certain categories of investment is to establish generally applied rules for all investors to observe. For instance, for SWF investment, the "Santiago principles" prove to be rather useful rules.

Finally, a "denial of benefits" rule might be included, particularly if the definition of covered investment does not require substantial business connections of the investor with the home state.

---

[32] Roberts Anthea, "Power and Persuasion in Investment Treaty Interpretation: The Dual Role of States," *American Journal of International Law*, 2010, 104(2): 179-225, p. 207, note 134.

Investment Liberalisation

Investment liberalisation should be included in the MFI, not only because it conforms to the worldwide trend of investment liberalisation as a critical component of economic globalization, but also because it provides a crucial incentive for countries (especially capital exporting states) to enter into IIAs, including the MFI, particularly after investment rules have become more balanced or "neutralised." As states become increasingly interdependent, continuous investment liberalisation should be encouraged. This becomes ever more important at a time of global economic downturn. Studies indicate that treaties with market access provisions result in more FDI inflows.[33] The proposed MFI should play a significant role in facilitating investment access.

Investment liberalisation might be achieved by either the "negative" or the "positive" list approach. Both approaches seek to promote transparency and predictability in investment access, features which should be welcomed. The difference between the two is technical, depending primarily on the degree of openness in the investment market and resources for its governance. Admittedly, the first time a list is compiled, either negative of positive, the country may require technical assistance from a neutral international organisation (such as an "investment advisory centre").[34] But, it is not "mission impossible" for most countries to prepare such a list. Also, it might be desirable to give developing states or at least the LDCs more leeway, by for instance allowing them to use a positive list on market access to start with. An example in point is the market access commitments on trade in services between China and Australia, in which Australia adopted a negative list while China adopted a positive list.[35]

Substantive Protections

Much has been written on the reform of the substantive protections for investment protection, and many reform measures have already been implemented in IIA practice.[36] For example, the FET standard has been clarified under the NAFTA, and the clarification has been accepted in most recent IIAs. This standard has been further narrowed in the recently signed Comprehensive Economic and Trade Agreement (CETA) between the EU and Canada.[37] As a result, it can be said that most of the substantive

---

[33] Saches, Lisa E. and Karl P. Sauvant, 'BITs, DTTs, and FDI Flows: An Overview', in *The Effect of Treaties on Foreign Direct Investment: Bilateral Investment Treaties, Double Taxation Treaties and Investment Flows*, edited by Sauvant Karl P. and Lisa E. Sachs (OUP, Oxford 2009): xxvii- lxii, lvi. See also Berger, Axel, et. al. "Do trade and investment agreements lead to more FDI? Accounting for key provisions inside the black box,", *International Economics and Economic Policy*, 2013, 10(2): 247 – 275, 268.

[34] For a proposal for such a centre, see e. g., Joubin-Bret, Anna. Establishing an International Advisory Center on Investment Disputes, Thinkpiece for the Second Task Force Workshop on Investment Policy, 9 – 10 June 2015. Although it mainly target on ISDS support, it can also provide other technical supports.

[35] See Chapter 8 "Trade in Service" of the 2015 China-Australia FTA, available at, < http://fta.mofcom.gov.cn/Australia/annex/xdwb_08_en.pdf > (accessed on 19 July 2015).

[36] See e. g., Sauvant, Karl P. and Federico Ortino, Improving the International Investment Law and Policy Regime: Options for the Future, published by the Finnish Ministry of Foreign Affairs, particularly part 3, pp. 65 – 73. See also, Ortino Federico. Substantive Provisions in IIAs and Future Treaty making: Addressing Three Challenges, First Task Force Workshop Thinkpiece 23 – 24 march 2015.

[37] Article X. 9 "Treatment of Investors and of Covered Investments" of the 2014 EU-Canada CETA.

provisions under IIAs have already been reformulated to achieve a better balance between the needs of investment protection and the needs of regulation.

What is needed is a more systematic review of all the patchy measures of reform to establish a coherent set of rules for substantive investment protection. Key questions include, for example, what would be the best approach to express abstract standards, such as FET and the international minimum standard? More precisely, how can a balance be achieved between predictability and flexibility in the standard? Should general exceptions be included, and if so, what is the best wayto ensure they work well with other terms of the treaty? How should amplifying provisions, such as the MFN clause and the umbrella clause, be reformulated or replaced to exclude an unnecessary expansion of treaty obligations? These are all important questions, the answers to which require further more comprehensive studies.

Social Clauses

It is now almost impossible to conclude an IIA without addressing social concerns, notably environment and labour protection, given the increasingly loud voices from NGOs. And, it is legitimate that the MFI should address such issues, as they have become part and parcel of global public goods. It is also reasonable to require foreign investors to become good corporate citizens in the host state, embracing the norm of corporate social responsibility.

However, social clauses should be treated with caution and proportionality in IIAs. While such matters can and should be addressed in any IIA, they should not be the main purpose of such treaties. After all, IIAs are "investment" treaties, and their primary task is for investment protection and promotion. True, IIAs should not promote investment at the expense of fundamental environment, labour or other standards. But, equally, they cannot be expected to undertake the tasks of proper environment or labour agreements. Social issues are better dealt with by local rules. Investment treaties can certainly help to promote social standards in general terms, but they are not the best forum to provide concrete rules. Accordingly, the principle of complementarity should be observed when drafting an MFI or IIA. Social clauses should be necessary complements to the main body of obligations and rights embodied in the investment treaties, rather than parallel provisions.

Dispute Settlement

Dispute settlement, particularly the ISDS system, is now the hottest topic in international investment law. Much has been written on it,[38] and there is no need or possibility to provide a comprehensive review here. Rather, it is useful to highlight two systemic implications.

---

[38] UNCTAD, Reform of the IIA Regime: Four Paths of Action and a Way Forward, IIA Issue Note, No 3, United Nations: New York and Geneva, 2014; A. Joubin-Bret and J. E. Kalickied., TDM Special issue on "Reform of Investor-State Dispute Settlement: In search of a Roadmap", TDM 1 (2014), Available at, <http://www.transnational-dispute-management.com/journal-browse-issues-toc.asp?key = 52> (accessed on 19 July 2015); Stephen Shill, Improving Investor-State Dispute Settlement (ISDS): Conceptual Framework and Options for the Way Forward, Thinkpiece for the Second Task Force Workshop on Investment Policy, 9 – 10 2015.

Table 1 Matrix Analysis of Investor-state Disputes and Their Settlements

Disputes (Political / Social)	High	Low
High	Red Zone (for both politically sensitive and socially influential disputes) →No ISDS (Local remedy or State-State DS)	Blue Zone (for socially influential but politically less sensitive disputes) →Local remedy or socially monitored ISDS
Low	Yellow Zone (for politically sensitive but socially less influential disputes) →State Controlled ISDS or State-State DS	(Green Zone, for low political and social sensitivity disputes) →ISDS

First, it is necessary to take a systematic view of the dispute settlement (DS) system as a whole, rather than focusing on the ISDS mechanism only. For this purpose, it is helpful when drafting such provisions to introduce a matrix analytical framework (MAF) to ascertain which DS method, ISDS, state-state arbitration, or local remedies, are best fit for each category of investment disputes. The framework is based on the assumption that each investment dispute potentially involves three main dimensions: economic, political, and social. Every investment dispute has to have economic implications to establish a case, so the matrix analyses only the political and social dimensions of disputes.

As the matrix below shows, if the dispute involves few political or social complications — in other words, if it is not a politically or socially sensitive dispute — such as a case involving an individual act of direct expropriation ("Green Zone" cases), the case is suitable for a conventional ISDS mechanism. However, if the dispute is both politically and socially sensitive, involving essential security or national emergency rules ("Red Zone" cases), it makes more sense to exclude it from ISDS and leave it to other venues, such as local remedies or state-state dispute resolution mechanisms under investment treaties or general international law. For disputes that are politically highly sensitive, but socially insensitive, such as individual taxation measures or prudential measures of financial regulation ("Yellow Zone" cases), they might be subject to stronger state control by relying on state-state dispute settlement rather than ISDS. The last category encompasses cases that are socially but not politically sensitive, such as cases involving environmental or human health measures ("Blue Zone" cases). Such cases are better dealt with through local remedies or by introducing stronger social monitoring in the ISDS system. Social monitoring measures might include transparency requirements, amicus curie briefs, etc.[39]

Second, it is crucial to "de-commercialize" the ISDS mechanism to enhance its legitimacy under public law, since almost all investment cases question, to some degree, public authority. Perhaps one clear exception is a pure commercial contract between the host state government and a foreign investor covered by the "umbrella clause" under an IIA. Another exception may be the determination of the amount of compensation in case of expropriation, as stipulated in many earlier Chinese BITs.[40] However, even in an expropriation case a tribunal may decide that it has the competence to look into the question whether there is an expropriation at the first place,[41] which is clearly an issue of public law. Since most ISDS cases involve public law matters, the ISDS process should be conducted in a way that meets fundamental public law requirements, such as accountability, openness, coherence, and independence.[42] Reform measures adopted in some recent IIAs, such as qualification requirements, roster systems, codes of conduct for arbitrators, transparency rules, detailed procedural rules, appeal mechanisms, and suggestions for a permanent court for international investment all point in a public law direction. Among them, the appeal mechanism and permanent court proposals are most significant and would require a multilateral platform to guarantee its effectiveness and efficiency.

Towards A Balanced and Liberal MFI/PFI: A PFI Then An MFI?

Although the desirability of an MFI is beyond doubt and its feasibility has significantly increased over the past decade, an MFI of global reach might not be realistic in one go. Instead, a PFI might provide an essential stepping stone toward the ultimate MFI.

Undoubtedly, the mega-regional pacts, the TPP, the TTIP, and the RCEP, along with the super-bilaterals such as the CETA, and the Chinese BITs with the US and EU currently under negotiation, will play significant roles in the development of the PFI and ultimately the MFI. A PFI might start with a tripartite investment agreement between the "big-three," namely the US, the EU, and China. Currently, the three parties are separately negotiating bilateral investment (and trade in the case of the TTIP between the US and the EU) agreements with each other. It would make sense to consolidate such divided efforts to negotiate a trilateral agreement on investment (or better still on both investment and trade). The three economies represent not only developed and developing countries, but also more than half of world GDP. Such an agreement would be a like a "super NAFTA", involving two advanced economies

---

[39] For further details, see Shan Wenhua. A Matrix Analysis on ISDS Reform: Preliminary Considerations, paper presented at the 24th Energy Charter Ministerial Conference held at Cyprus in December 2013, available at, <http://www.encharter.org/fileadmin/user_upload/Conferences/2013_Dec_5-6/4-3_Shan.pdf> (accessed on 19 July 2015).

[40] Norah Gallagher and Wenhua Shan, Chinese Investment Treaties: Policies and Practice, OUP, 2009, pp. 253-298.

[41] See, for instance, Tza Yap Shum v. Republic of Peru, ICSID Case No. ARB/07/6, July 7, 2011.

[42] Gus van Harten, Investment Treaty Arbitration and Public Law, OUP, 2007, pp. 153-174.

and one developing economy, even more so if the treaty covers non-investment matters, like the NAFTA. Such a trilateral investment agreement (TIA) or trilateral free-trade agreement (TFTA) would quickly become the blueprint for a global MFI or FTA. Given that the three parties are coming closer to each other in general investment treaty practice,[43] concluding such an agreement is not only desirable, but also possible.

A more representative PFI might be negotiated among the top five capital exporting and importing states in the world, which together accounted for 53.2 percent of world FDI inflow and 76.1 percent of outflow, as well 66.3percent of total world GDP in 2014.[44] A survey of the recent treaty practices by these countries reveals a general convergence, exhibiting features of the "Global BIT 2.0" mentioned above. (Table 2) This confirms that a PFI is indeed not too far away.

Table 2 Converging Treaty Practices of Top Five Investor and Host Economies

Representative Investment Agreements	2015 TPP Investment Chapter (US, Japan, Singapore)	2015 China-Australia FTA (China)	2014 EU-Canada CETA (EU)
Refined definition of investment	Yes (Art 9.1)	Yes (Art 9.1)	Yes (Art X.3)
Market Access or Pre-establishment NT	Yes (Art 9.4)	Yes* (Art.9.3(1))	Yes (Art X.4 & 6)
FET standard clarified by reference to CIL or a list of factors	Yes (Art 9.6)	(to be negotiated) Yes	(Art X.9)
Exclusions of dispute settlement from the MFN clause	Yes (Art 9.5(3))	Yes (Art 9.4(2))	Yes (Art X.7)
Clarification on the constitution of indirect expropriation	Yes (Art 9.7 & Annex 9-B)	(to be negotiated)	Yes (Art X.11 & Annex X.11)

[43] Shan and Wang, ibid, note 18 above, pp. 260–267; Shan and Zhang, note 18 above, p. 453.

[44] According to *World Investment Report* 2015, the top five investor economies include the US; Hong Kong, China; China; Japan; and Germany, while the top five home economies are China; Hong Kong, China; the US; the UK; and Singapore. As Germany and the UK can be represented by the EU, Hong Kong can be represented by China, the top five investor and home economies group can actually be represented by five economies, namely the US, the EU, China, Japan, and Singapore. Together they accounted for 53.2 percent of world FDI inflow and 76.1 percent of outflow, as well 66.3 percent of total world GDP in 2014.

续表

Representative Investment Agreements	2015 TPP Investment Chapter (US, Japan, Singapore)	2015 China-Australia FTA (China)	2014 EU-Canada CETA (EU)
A carve-out for prudential measures	Yes (Art. 9. 3(3 (3))	Yes (Annex 8-B)	Yes (Art X. 12 and Chapter 15)
Performance Requirements	Yes (Art. 9. 9)	(to be negotiated)	Yes (Art X. 5)
Denial of Benefits	Yes (Art 9. 14)	Yes (Art 9. 6)	Yes (Art X. 15)
Omission of Umbrella Clause	Yes	Yes	Yes
Senior Management	Yes (Art 9. 10)	(to be negotiated)	Yes (Art X. 8)
Public Policy Exceptions	Yes (Preamble & Art 9. 15)	Yes (Arts 9. 8 & Art. 9. 11(4))	Yes (Preamble & Annex X. 43. 1)
Elaborate rules on ISDS	Yes (Section B)	Yes (Section B)	Yes (Section 6)
Disposing 'frivolous' claims	Yes (Arts 22 & 28 (4))	Yes (Arts 9. 11 – 14)	Yes (Art X. 29)
Consolidation of claims	Yes (Art 9. 27)	Yes (Art 9. 21)	Yes (Art X. 41)
Transparency of Arbitral Proceedings	Yes (Art 9. 23)	Yes (Art 9. 17)	Yes (Art X. 33)
Joint interpretation	Yes (Art 9. 25)	Yes (Arts 9. 7(3) & 9. 18)	Yes (Art X. 27)
Appellate mechanism	Yes (Art . 22(11))	Yes (Art 9. 23)	Yes (Art X. 42)

* According to the China-Australia FTA, pre-establishment obligation is only imposed on Australia for now, but it can be extended to China in the future.

Towards A Balanced and Liberal MFI/PFI: Possible Venues

The MFI or PFI could not succeed without a proper venue. There are two broad possibilities: launch a stand-alone negotiating process for an MFI/PFI, or make use of an existing multilateral mechanism, such as the OECD or the WTO to conduct studies and perhaps negotiations.

A Stand-Alone Process

A stand-alone process is appealing, given the failure of multilateral investment initiatives in both the OECD and the WTO. Similar international stand-alone negotiations serve as useful precedents.[45] For instance, when the UN General Assembly established in 1990 the Intergovernmental Negotiating Committee for a Framework Convention on Climate Change and adopted the Convention in May 1992, the negotiations were serviced by an independent interim secretariat that was not part of the UN structure. Also, the Convention on the Prohibition of the Use, Stockpiling, Production and Transfer of Anti-Personnel Mines and on their Destruction was originally launched by a group of countries. Dissatisfied with the lack of progress in the Geneva-based Conference on Disarmament, they established in 1996 a negotiating process on the convention, independent from the Conference on Disarmament. A more recent example is the Trade in Services Agreement (TiSA), which involves a process independent from the WTO. A conditional plurilateral agreement is being negotiated by interested parties that would be open for future accessions by other states. Obviously, a stand-alone process requires leadership to provide momentum. In this respect, the G20 could play a significant role, as discussed below.

Existing Organisations and Mechanisms

Although similar attempts have failed in the OECD and the WTO, it remains possible for an MFI or PFI to be negotiated and concluded under the framework or with the support of existing institutions. Such institutions and mechanisms include the G20, the WTO, the World Bank, the UN, the OECD, the IEC, and the AIIB, which are briefly discussed in turn below.

1. G20

The G20 is now the premier forum for global economic cooperation and decision-making. It represents a wide spectrum of large countries. The Group has paid close attention to international investment matters. For example, the first G20 Trade and Investment Promotion Summit held in November 2012 concluded that participants "agreed to establish a platform for the regular exchange of experiences and good practices in trade investment promotion and policy advocacy."[46]

The G20 could initiate an exploratory process for a plurilateral/multilateral framework on investment, assessing its desirability and feasibility. It could go further and give overall political guidelines: for example, it could indicate the purposes that IIAs should serve; and it could confirm certain core principles, such as the importance of protection, the right to regulate, the need for responsible business conduct, and the need to

---

〔45〕 Sauvant Karl P and Federico Ortino, supra note 40, p. 134, note 335.

〔46〕 UNCTAD, G20 Fosters Synergies Between Trade and Investment Promotion, November 12, 2012, available at, <http://unctad.org/en/pages/newsdetails.aspx?OriginalVersionID=351> (accessed on 19 July 2015). See also UNCTAD, Joint UNCTAD-OECD Reports on G20 Investment Measures, available at, <http://unctad.org/en/Pages/DIAE/G20/UNCTAD-OECD-reports.aspx> (accessed on 19 July 2015).

have adequate dispute-settlement.[47]

In short, although not an organisation itself, the G20 could certainly play an important role in launching the MFI/PFI process, particularly if it takes the stand-alone approach. Given the time is now ripe for the consideration of an MFI or PFI, it would be a great idea if China could table the MFI/PFI initiative on the G20 2016 agenda when she chairs the G20 summit.[48]

2. WTO

Despite the failure to launch investment negotiations at the Cancun Ministerial Conference, the WTO remains the best forum for MFI/PFI talks, given its global membership and its successful dispute settlement mechanism.[49] Also, with its broad mandate over trade and investment matters, the WTO offers a forum that is more conducive than others for discussions on those topics.[50] The successful conclusion of the General Agreement on Trade in Services (GATS) and the Agreement on Trade-Related Investment Measures (TRIMS) suggests that such an MFI can be achieved within the WTO.

Indeed, the WTO offers the best platform for trade and investment regimes to be combined and consolidated, as a unified system providing systematic legal and institutional support for the future growth of GVCs. Thus, the substantive investment rules could be negotiated and included as a new multilateral agreement of the WTO, perhaps with some adjustments on the existing investment-related agreements, most notably the TRIMs and the GATS. Indeed, the current TRIMs could be replaced, since its contents are most likely to be covered by the performance requirements provisions under the investment agreement. Likewise, mode 3 "commercial presence" might be removed from the GATS to avoid duplication with the new investment agreement (the schedule of commitments should be modified accordingly). Investment disputes could be settled in accordance with the current Dispute Settlement Understanding (DSU) or under a parallel ISDS regime to be negotiated and accepted by like-minded WTO members as a plurilateral arrangement. It would also be possible and indeed more appealing if the DSU could be reformed by combining the strengths of both the DSU in the WTO and the ISDS under investment treaties, so that private traders might directly access the dispute settlement system, while all cases, including investor-state cases, could be heard by a permanent appellate body to maintain consistency and predictability.[51] A less ambitious but

---

〔47〕 Sauvant, Karl P. and Federico Ortino, *supra* note 40, pp. 135 – 136.

〔48〕 See e. g., Shan Wenhua. "China in WTO at 15th: Changing China whilst Reshaping the World," *Legal Daily*, 14 July 2015, p. 10. Available at, < http://epaper. legaldaily. com. cn/fzrb/content/20150714/Articel10001GN. htm > (accessed on 19 July 2015). See also Yifu Lin, Justin. China's G-20 agenda: Call for a multilateral investment framework for development, July 2015. Available atat, < http://e15initiative. org/blogs/chinas-g-20-agenda-call-for-a-multilateral-investment-framework-for-development/ > (accessed on 19 July 2015).

〔49〕 González, Anabel. Executive Summary, in World Economy Forum, Foreign Direct Investment as Key Driver for Trade, Growth and Prosperity: The Case for a Multilateral Agreement on Investment, 2013, p. 8.

〔50〕 Dattu Riyaz. "A Journey from Havana to Paris: The Fifty-Year Quest for the Elusive Multilateral Agreement on Investment," *Fordham International Law Journal*, 2000, 24(1): 275 – 316, p. 203.

〔51〕 See e. g., Hufbauer, Gary and Tyler Moran. Investment and Trade Regimes Conjoined: Economic Facts & Regulatory Frameworks, E15 TFM1 Thinkpiece, 23 – 24 March 2015.

easier alternative would be to negotiate a separate investment agreement within the WTO with distinct substantive and procedural norms, operating in parallel to the existing trade rules.

However, the weakness of the WTO system is the converse of its strength. Its global membership combined with a consensus decision-making practice makes it difficult for the WTO to move quickly to adapt to the rapidly changing world. As a result, it is hard to make progress even on traditional trade matters, as shown by the continuous delay of Doha round negotiations. Perhaps, it is unrealistic to expect the WTO to take up the MFI/PFI initiative in the very near future. Nevertheless, it might be possible for the WTO to foster a PFI negotiation in Geneva in a manner similar to the TiSA talks mentioned above.

3. World Bank

The World Bank has historically played a key role in global investment institutions, most notably by establishing the Multilateral Investment Guarantee Agency (MIGA) and the ICSID. The ICSID, in particular, has served as the central forum for international investment dispute resolution, as it handles over half the investment cases worldwide.[52]

It is, therefore, natural to expect that the Bank to play a significant role in the negotiation of an MFI/PFI. The Bank might initiate MFI/PFI negotiations, as it did for the ICSID Convention and the MIGA Convention. It could also, perhaps more realistically, lead the reform of the world ISDS system by updating the ICSID Convention to better serve foreign investors and host states alike, particularly by establishing an appeal mechanism or a permanent court system. However, to do this, the Bank probably would have to adjust itself to the changed world, particularly by giving the emerging countries a larger say in its decision processes. Otherwise, it would be difficult to find favour for the Bank's initiative from the developing world.

4. United Nations

As the most representative international organisation in the world, the UN certainly has a role to play in the MFI/PFI process. Indeed, the United Nations Conference on Trade and Development (UNCTAD) has done tremendous work in the field, particularly by compiling databases on investment and relevant rules and by providing monitoring and analytic services. Recently it has tried to establish a multilateral mechanism on investment policy-making.[53] Modelled on the Investment Policy Framework for Sustainable Development launched in 2012, UNCTAD is seeking to develop a potential multilateral consensus-building institution on foreign investment. Also, the United Nations Commission on International Trade Law (UNCITRAL) has successfully concluded a conven-

---

[52] As of 2014, there were 608 known ISDS cases, and more than 300 were solved through ICSID . See UNCTAD, Investor-State Dispute Settlement: Review of Development in 2014, IIA Issue Note, No. 2, May 2015, available at, < http://investmentpolicyhub. unctad. org/Upload/Documents/UNCTAD_WEB_DIAE_PCB_2015_%202%20IIA%20ISSUES%20NOTES%2013MAY%20. pdf > (accessed on 19 July 2015).

[53] UNCTAD, Towards A New Generation of International Investment Policies: UNTAD's Fresh Approach to Multilateral Investment Policy-Making, United Nations: New York and Geneva, April 2013.

tion on transparency in ISDS arbitration. The International Law Commission (ILC) has also done notable work on relevant issues, including in particular the Vienna Convention on the Law of Treaties and the ILC Draft Article on State Responsibility.

However, since the function of UNCTAD mainly focuses on policy commentary, advisory reports, and technical assistance, it lacks the mandate to push forward a binding multilateral investment agreement. It may also be difficult to reach consensus among such a huge membership. As a way forward, the UNCTAD, the ILC, and UNCITRA might work together to set up a joint task force on an MFI/PFI, and open a draft agreement for signature when a broader consensus has been established.

5. OECD

The OECD has long been committed to investment liberalisation and has achieved significant outcomes, notably the Draft Convention on the Protection of Private Investment, the Code of Liberalisation of Capital Movements, and the Code of Liberalisation of Current Invisible Operations. In 1995, the OECD initiated unsuccessful negotiations on the MAI. In recent years, it has generated a wealth of working papers and other studies in the investment field.

The OECD could restart a negotiation on a renamed MAI; but, to succeed it would have to open the negotiations to non-member states, making sure that their voices are heard and interests reflected in the final outcome.

International Energy Charter

The IEC Treaty established a multilateral framework for energy, albeit with a limited geographical reach. Recent statistics confirm the significance of the Charter, as the most cited investment treaty in international investment arbitration. In May 2015, the Charter moved to a second phase of modernisation and globalisation.[54] A few new countries, including China, signed the new political Charter. Iran, an important member of the Organization of the Petroleum Exporting Countries (OPEC), attended the IEC conference.

If successful, the IEC could become a genuinely global and modern system of energy governance, which could inform and inspire the MFI/PFI. However, its industrial limits might prevent it from playing a wider role in global investment governance.

6. AIIB

The AIIB is an international financial institution focused on supporting infrastructure construction in the Asia-Pacific region. The bank was proposed by China in 2013, and the Articles of Agreement were signed by 51 Prospective Founding Members (PFMs), including Brazil, France, Germany, Russia, and the United Kingdom.

Although its name suggests a regional scope, its membership actually has a global reach with representatives from both developing countries and advanced countries. On this basis and given its mandate as an investment bank, it has the potential to provide a

---

[54] After many years of planning, discussion, diplomatic efforts and negotiations, the International Energy Charter was adopted at a High-level Ministerial Conference in May 2015. European Commission, New International Energy Charter adopted, 21 May 2015, available at, <https://ec.europa.eu/energy/en/news/new-international-energy-charter-adopted> (accessed on 19 July 2015).

platform for the negotiation of an MFI/PFI. However, given that it is still in an early stage of development, it cannot be expected to launch such a major project in the near future.

Conclusion

The prominence of investment in the global economy requires a global legal framework that provides an opportunity for systemically reviewing and reforming the current IIA regime. The mixed role of major economies and the converging treaty practices have paved the way for an MFI, while the global debate on the IIA regime helps build political and social momentum for its launch.

Given the "birth defect" or the unbalanced origin of IIAs, the reform of the IIA regime has to take a thorough "from root to rules" approach, reflecting the fundamental shift of tension from a "North-South divide" to a "private-public debate." The key to improving the substantive provisions is to rebalance private-public interests, while the key to ISDS reform is to restructure investment dispute settlement mechanisms and decommercialise the current ISDS system. Certain social clauses may be included to address social concerns, but only on a complementary basis, to ensure that the regime is viable and focused, while paying due deference to local authorities and local norms.

To restructure the currently fragmented IIA system, a PFI represents the best first step forward. A PFI could bring together top players in international investment to achieve a reasonably high-standard agreement. To this end, it would be most effective to consider a trilateral investment agreement between the US, the EU and China, which could provide a significant stepping stone toward an MFI/PFI. The WTO is best positioned to start a PFI negotiation, while the G20 could build a political consensus for this venture. An appeal mechanism or a permanent court might be established within the ICSID regime, which would significantly enhance the legitimacy of the ISDS system. Other venues such as the UN, the OECD, the IEC, and the AIIB also have the potential to play roles in this process, particularly when a wider consensus matures.

Comments by Gary Hufbauer & Tyler Moran

Professor Wenhua Shan covers a large swath of investment territory in his fine essay. We agree with a substantial majority of his themes. In this short Comment, however, we highlight areas of disagreement, both because those will be of greatest interest to readers and because clear differences are more informative than fuzzy compromises.

Professor Wenhua Shan describes why advanced capital-exporting countries pursued international investment agreements (IIAs) after a surge in expropriations during the first two decades following the Second World War. The US and Western European nations sought to protect their firms that invested abroad. But, for North-South IIAs, that is only half the story. During the 1960s and 1970s, many developing countries were either non-aligned in the geopolitical contest known as the Cold War, or aligned themselves with the Soviet Union. In short, developing countries were perfectly able to pursue their own political and economic fates, and ignore the entreaties of advanced nations.

The fact that many North-South IIAs were signed in those decades and since proves, we think, that the agreements were not onesided, or as Professor Wenhua puts the matter, "unbalanced." If 20th century IIAs were simply a "sword," to use Professor Wenhua's description, no one could have expected that more than 3000 would be in existence today. Even small developing countries don't willingly create weapons for advanced powers to use against them.

In our view, developing country signatories were eager to attract FDI, and national leaders realised the reputations of their local institutions gave multinational corporations (MNCs) ample reasons to invest elsewhere. BITs and investment chapters in FTAs accordingly served as quick "reputation enhancers".

A country might instead have built investor confidence over time by not expropriating and by giving fair treatment to MNCs. But, that's a slow process. Projects, such as mines, power plants, auto factories, and even banks can take more than a decade to cover their upfront costs, so a few years of good behaviour may not prove sufficient to ease the fears of foreign investors. IIAs, therefore, can serve as shortcuts. For this reason, we contend that twentieth century IIAs were "balanced."

Accordingly, we reject the proposition that UN General Assembly Resolutions 1803 and 3281 — products of the NIEO era — were needed as "shields." To be sure, the resolutions expressed the ideological views of their proponents, but they were not needed to defend against oppressive IIAs. The fact that, in the 21st century, new provisions are finding their way into IIAs reflects a reaction against certain arbitral awards and, probably more important, extensive, but as yet undecided, claims of some MNCs. The most important new provisions ensure that regulations to protect health, safety, and the environment cannot be challenged unless they outrageously discriminate against foreign firms. Moreover, the total magnitude of actual awards from the 600odd decided and settled cases handled by ICSID is very likely less than US $ 50 billion, a sum that is trivial compared with the US $ 26 trillion of global FDI stock.

Under customary international law, countries have nearly complete sovereignty over investment within their borders. The vast majority of investment disputes are litigated under IIAs that were freely negotiated, ensuring investor protection beyond the norms of customary international law. NIEO doctrines of the 1970s are largely forgotten today, because rejecting international investment is poor economic policy. MNCs have no desire to pump billions of dollars into a country that proudly proclaims it will treat foreign investors however it pleases.

Like Professor Wenhua Shan, we welcome greater transparency in ISDS deliberations and decisions, along with the possibility of creating ad hoc appellate mechanisms and even a permanent international court. However, it may be no easier today to create multilateral oversight of international investment than it was in Havana in 1948 or in the OECD in 1998. We agree that conditions could be auspicious for a fresh attempt, owing to the more balanced configuration of inward and outward FDI as between advanced and developing countries. We further agree that, in the near term, a plurilateral agreement seems far more likely than a multilateral agreement. Finally, in our opinion, the WTO is the right forum for a fresh attempt.

But, we offer three notes of caution. First, in the foreseeable decade of lethargic growth, poor productivity, and enormous unmet infrastructure requirements, the overwhelming need in the world economy is more FDI, not less. In 2014, FDI was only US $ 1.4 trillion, barely 60 percent of its peak in 2007, some US $ 2.2 trillion. The world needs at least US $ 3 trillion of FDI annually over the next decade. Any multilateral or plurilateral framework on investment (MFI or PFI) should be framed with the overriding goal of boosting investment flows, not retarding them.

Second, given the existence of more than 3000 IIAs, any MFI or PFI should supplement, not override the existing IIAs. To be sure, new conventions (perhaps as part of a PFI) might fill gaps in existing agreements, such as procedural transparency (in the spirit of the 2014 UNCITRAL Mauritius Convention) or an optional appellate mechanism under ICSID auspices. But, care should be taken not to excite opposition to a PFI by seeming to indirectly override existing IIAs. And a PFI should stay far away from contentious international tax issues of the sort raised by the OECD in its project on "Base Erosion and Profit Shifting."

Third and finally, we think a PFI should be launched with a small number — perhaps not more than a dozen — WTO members that are both large home countries for outward FDI and large host countries for inward FDI. A small group of this nature is more likely to reach agreement, while fairly representing the interests of host countries, home countries, and MNCs.

Towards a Balanced Liberal Investment Regime: General Report on the Protection of Foreign Investment*

Introduction

The law of foreign investment is at a crossroad, in the wake of an unprecedented global financial crisis leading to a sharp decrease in global investment flows (Chart 1) and a dramatic surge of investment treaty arbitration cases (Chart 2). Scholars and government officials from both developed and developing countries have been debating whether and to what extent the previously neo-liberalist approach represented by liberal BITs should be reformed to fit the new reality of the current world. This study presents an updated account of the *status quo* of the legal protection of foreign investment in the world, on the basis of a comparative study of reports on the subject from 22 representative jurisdictions, taking into account other relevant recent studies such as those conduced by UNCTAD and OECD.

The main purpose of this report is to identify major differences, similarities and trends in the law of foreign investment protection in different jurisdictions, and to make suggestions for future actions to be taken at global and/or jurisdictional levels. The surveyed laws cover both domestic law and applicable international treaties. Wherever possible, it also investigates how they have been implemented and interpreted in practice.

This report is primarily based on 22 original jurisdictional reports[1] produced by leading scholars from the corresponding jurisdictions, including Argentina, Australia, Canada, China, Croatia, Czech Republic, Ethiopia, France, Germany, Greece, Italy, Ja-

---

* *ICSID Review: Foreign Investment Law Journal*, 2010, 25(2).

This report will be published, together with the national/jurisdictional reports, in an edited collection entitled *Legal Protection of Foreign Investment: A Comparative Study* (W. Shan ed., Hart Publishing Oxford, 2011 forthcoming). The author would like to thank ICSID and Hart Publishing for kindly agreeing on this publication arrangement. He would also like to thank Mr. Sheng Zhang (Jerry) for his excellent assistance in preparing this report, and all participants of the "Protection of Foreign Investment" Session of the IACL 2010 Congress, particularly the Chair, Ms. Meg Kinnear, as well as all National/Jurisdictional Reporters, for their insightful comments on its earlier drafts.

[1] The commonly used term is "national report." However, the term "jurisdictional report" is used here as it is more appropriate to also cover the report of Macau, which is not a "national report."

pan, South Korea, Macau, Peru, Portugal, Russia, Singapore, Slovenia, Turkey, the uk and the US.[2] They cover all of the five continents, and three major categories of economies, namely developed, developing and transition economies. They not only include 7 of the top 10 foreign direct investment (FDI) recipients in the world, but also 8 of the top 10 capital-exporting countries (Chart 3). Six of the reported economies are also among the top ten signatories of BITs up to the end of 2008 (Chart 4). It can therefore be said that, to a considerable extent, this study illustrates the *status quo* of legal protection of foreign investment in the world.

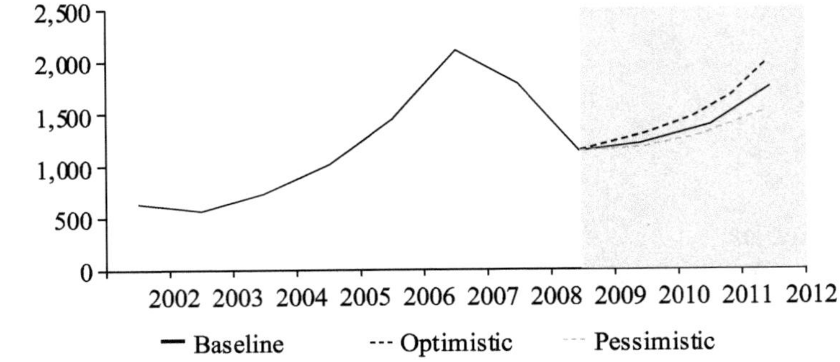

Chart 1 Global FDI Flows 2002 – 2009 with Predictions for 2010 – 2012 (US $ Billion)

Source: UNCTAD, *World Investment Report* 2010.

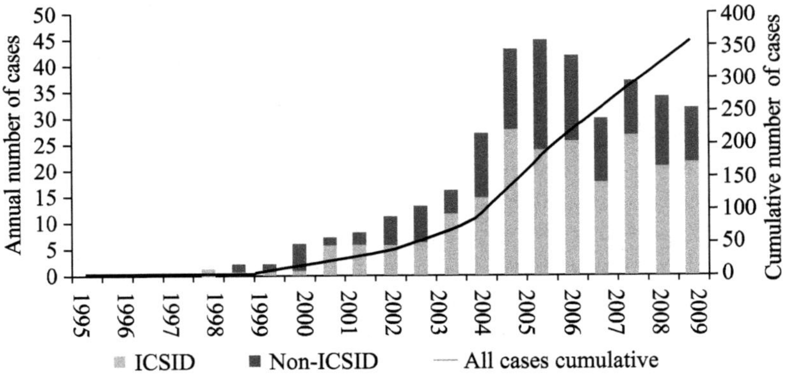

Chart 2 Known Investment Treaty Arbitration Cases (Cumulative and New Cases) 1989 – 2009

Source: UNCTAD, *World Investment Report* 2010.

[2] Jurisdictional Reporters are approved by the IACL upon nominations by either the national committee of the IACL or the general reporter.

As do the jurisdictional reports, this general report will follow the questionnaire designed by the general reporter for this study. It intends to cover the most important aspects concerning the protection of foreign investment, ranging from admission regimes to post-admission standards of treatment, and from protection against expropriation and guarantee of free transfer to settlement of investment disputes. It starts with a comparison of the overall legal framework for foreign investment and concludes with an outlook at the future regime on international investment.

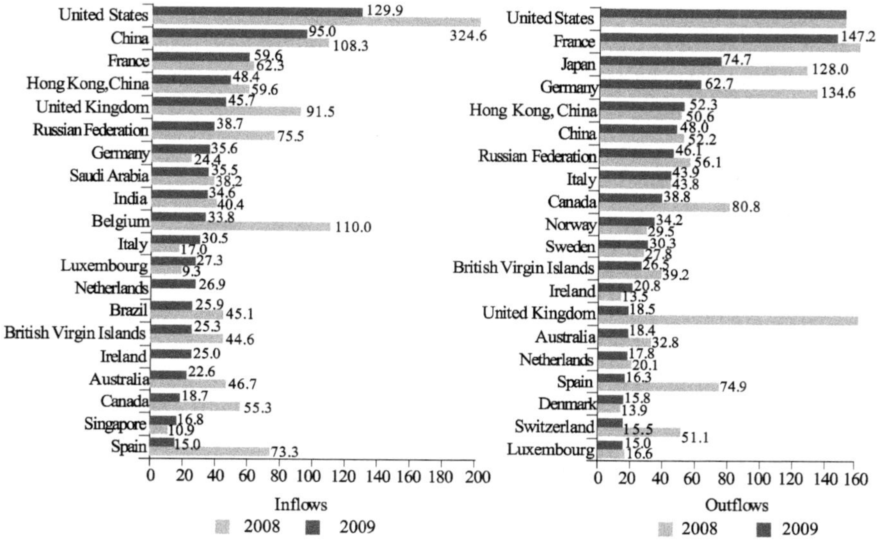

Chart 3 Top 20 FDI Importers and Exporters 2008 – 2009 (Billion US $)

Source: UNCTAD, *World Investment Report* 2010.

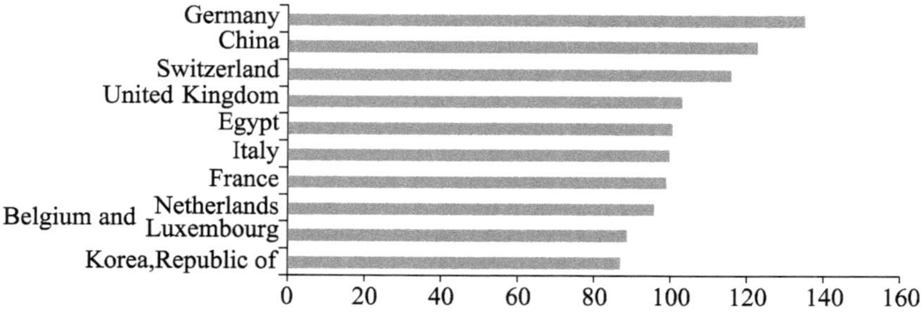

Chart 4 Top Ten Signatories of BITs by 2008

Source: UNCTAD (www. unctad. org/iia).

The study has identified three main themes of recent development in foreign investment protection, namely "harmonisation," "balancing" and "socialisation." It concludes that the paradigm of international investment law has been shifting from "North-

South Divide" to "Private-Public Debate," and that the future development of international investment law will most likely lead to a multilateral investment agreement (MIA) effectuating a "balanced liberal" investment regime.

1. Legal Framework Governing Foreign Investment

To compare foreign investment laws and treaties it is important to understand how they fit together and interact with each other. In other words, it is important first of all to establish the general legal framework that governs foreign investment in a given jurisdiction including both domestic and international laws. The relationship between domestic and international laws should also be discussed to ascertain any hierarchy between them. The issue of transparency is also addressed, as a subject of growing importance.

a) The Legal Framework

Domestic Laws and Regulations

Protection of foreign investors and investments is often provided in the constitutions[3] of the host economies. Many of the constitutions stipulate that foreign investments and investors are protected in the same way as native investments and investors (national treatment).[4] Also, they tend to provide protection of property, as well as guarantees against impairment of contractual rights.[5]

Protection of foreign investments can also be found in forms of domestic law other than the constitution, such as the laws, regulations and administrative decrees. As Table 1 demonstrates, 11 of the 22 jurisdictions have special laws regulating foreign investment, whilst others do not. Australia, Canada, China, Russia and Turkey are among those having special foreign investment laws. In Australia, the Foreign Acquisitions and Takeovers Act 1975 (FATA) and its implementing regulations have been promulgated to regulate foreign acquisition and takeovers of Australian companies.[6] In Canada, the law governing foreign direct investment activities is the Investment Canada Act.[7] Foreign investment in China is primarily governed by the Sino-Foreign Equity Joint Venture Law, the Sino-Foreign Contractual Joint Venture Law and the Wholly Foreign Owned Enterprises Law.[8] In Russia, the two basic laws governing foreign investment are the

---

[3] In the case of Macau, the "Constitution" is the Basic Law of Macau Special Administrative Region of the People's Republic of China.

[4] For example, the Peruvian Constitution states that "National and foreign investments are subject to the same terms." The US Constitution prohibits state and local governments from discriminating against resident aliens, except in the case of the exercise of political rights or employment as a public officer. See Article 63 of the Peruvian Constitution; US Report, Section on "General standard of treatment of foreign investment and investors."

[5] The Charter of Fundamental Rights and Freedoms of Czech Republic, for example, guarantees the right to property for everyone including foreign investors. On the other hand, the "Contracts Clause" in the US Constitution prohibits the state or local government from impairing the obligation of contracts. See Czech Report, Section 1 (on the Framework and hierarchy of foreign investment laws and treaties); US Report, Section on "Investment Contracts" (citing Article 1, Section 10 of the US Constitution).

[6] Australia Report, Section 1.

[7] Canada Report, Section 1.

[8] China Report, Section 1.

Federal Law on Foreign Investment in the Russian Federation and the Federal Law on Investment Activity in the Russian Federation.[9] In Turkey, foreign direct investment is governed by the Foreign Direct Investment Law[10] (Table 1). It can be seen that not only developing states have adopted special regimes for foreign investment; developed states such as Australia, Canada and Greece have taken the same course of action. There seems to be no clear-cut distinction between developed and developing states in this regard.

Applicable International Treaties

So far there is no comprehensive agreement on a global scale on foreign investment, a sharp contrast to the area of international trade where the World Trade Organisation (WTO) Agreements provide the general legal framework for world trade regulation. There are nevertheless some specialised multilateral investment treaties, such as the ICSID Convention and the MIGA Convention, which focus on certain aspects of investment protection. The General Agreement on Trade in Service (GATS) and the Trade-Related Investment Measures Agreements (TRIMs) under the regime of the WTO, and the New york Convention are also very important for protection of foreign investments. Among the 22 jurisdictions, 20 are WTO members (excluding Ethiopia and Russia); 20 ratified the ICSID Convention (except Canada and Ethiopia); 21 are parties to the New york Convention (excluding Ethiopia); and 22 are MIGA member states. In other words, these multilateral agreements are playing important roles in regulating and facilitating foreign investment in these jurisdictions, as they do in the rest of the world (Table 1).

However, the most important instruments for investment protection continue to be bilateral investment treaties (BITs).[11] It is unsurprising that the 22 jurisdictions have concluded 1,355 BITs, nearly half of the total BITs in the world (Table 1). Six of them are among the top ten signatories of the world.[12] Germany is leading the league table, followed by China (2nd), the UK (4th), Italy (6th), France (7th) and South Korea (10th).[13] Other international investment-related agreements ("other IIAs" as termed by the UNCTAD reports), such as free trade agreements (FTAs), have gained significance in investment protection.[14] For example, Canada, China, France, Germany, the UK, the US and South Korea all concluded at least one new IIA between November 2009 and May 2010.[15] It should nevertheless be noted that such IIAs tend to focus on investment liberalisation and investment promotion, rather than providing a full set of in-

---

[9] Russia Report, Section 1.

[10] Turkey Report, Section 1.

[11] According to the statistics of UNCTAD, the total number of BITs rose to 2, 750 at the end of 2009. See UNCTAD, World Investment Report 2010, at 81.

[12] See UNCTAD/WEB/DLAE/IA/2009/8, Recent Developments in International Investment Agreements (2008 – June 2009), IIA Monitor No. 3 (2009), available at: http://www.unctad.org/en/docs/webdiaeia20098_en.pdf.

[13] Id.

[14] UNCTAD statistics show that by the end of 2009, 2, 894 double taxation treaties (DTTs) and 295 other IIAs have been concluded, making the total number of IIAs reaching 5, 939. See UNCTAD, World Investment Report 2010, at 81.

[15] UNCTAD and OECD, Third Report on G20 Investment Measures (Geneva and Paris, 14 June 2010), at 7.

vestment protection provisions typically found in BITs.[16] They therefore tend to be complimentary to, rather than substitutes for, BITs.

b) The Relationship between International Treaties and Domestic Laws

To establish the legal framework for foreign investment protection, it is necessary to investigate the relationship between domestic and international norms existing within the framework. Without indulging in a lengthy discussion on relevant theories, suffice it to say that there are different theories on the relationship, including dualism, monism and ' a third approach, being somewhat a modification of the dualist position. '[17] Another classification is between "transformation" and "incorporation" approaches. In practice, it is not always so easy to classify a jurisdiction as falling squarely within one of the categories. Whilst the dualist theory may still represent the legal reality of the world, the kelsenian monist theory seems to have been gaining ground with international law, making more and more significant inroads into domestic legal systems.[18] In this regard international investment law provides a significant example, as it is increasingly impacting domestic law and policy-making.

Most of the 22 jurisdictions have some express rules on the relationship between international law and domestic law in their constitutions, except China, Japan and the UK, which do not have such written constitutional rules nor written constitutions altogether. With respect to the hierarchy between international treaties and domestic laws, most of the constitutions recognize the supremacy of the constitution. In general, the legal hierarchy goes from higher to lower as follows: the Constitution, international treaties, and national laws.[19] However, there are exceptions and complications. The Supreme Court of Japan, for instance, considers that certain types of treaties such as the peace treaties and treaties modifying territories are superior to the Constitution.[20] The Constitution of Argentina gives primacy to integration and human rights treaties over other treaties.[21] Under the Peruvian laws, the hierarchy of international treaties depends on the status of the legal entity approving the treaties.[22] Consequently, the hierarchy of the laws goes from higher to lower as follows: Constitution, international treaties approved by congress, national law, and international treaties approved by the President.[23] In cases of conflict between international treaties and domestic laws, most states provide that international treaties shall prevail. However, in the US a treaty has the same status as a federal law, and a subsequently enacted federal law can supersede a treaty for domestic purposes, e-

---

〔16〕 It is, however, noted that most of Canada's FTAs (e. g., NAFTA and FTA with Chile, Jordan but not EFTA and the Costa Rica FTA) include investment chapters that are just like Canada's BITs.

〔17〕 See e. g., Malcolm N. Shaw, *International Law* (5th ed., Cambridge University Press 2003), at 121 – 124.

〔18〕 Antonio Cassese, *International Law* (2nd ed., Oxford University Press 2005), at 216 – 217.

〔19〕 In Argentina, for instance, treaties prevail over internal laws, but not provisions of the Federal Constitution. See Argentina Report, Section 1.

〔20〕 Japan Report, Section 1.

〔21〕 Argentina Report, Section 1.

〔22〕 Peru Report, Section 1.

〔23〕 Id.

ven though the treaty may still be binding as a matter of international law. The same applies to Germany where international treaties are conceived as federal statutes within the domestic hierarchy. International treaties may be abrogated or amended by subsequent federal statutes, even though it might trigger international responsibility from an international law perspective. The German Constitution nevertheless requires that subsequent statutes be interpreted and applied in utmost conformity with previous international treaties, unless the legislator's intention to deviate from a previous treaty is explicit and unquestionable.

As Table 1 shows, many jurisdictions do not recognize "direct effect" of international treaties within the domestic legal system. Thus in states such as the UK, Germany, China, Australia, Canada and Greece, foreign investors cannot directly invoke international treaties before local courts.[24] However, exceptions do exist. For example, Articles 2 and 9(2)(a) of the Singapore-Slovakia BIT confer jurisdiction on Singapore courts to adjudicate a qualifying dispute between a Slovakian investor and the Singapore Government by applying the provisions of the treaty.[25] On the other hand, international law may still play a significant indirect role in the domestic courts of these jurisdictions. In Australia, for example, the highest court confirmed in the *Toeh* case that:

Apart from influencing the construction of a statute or subordinate legislation, an international convention may play a part in the development by the courts of the common law. The provisions of an international convention to which Australia is a party, especially one which declares universal fundamental rights, may be used by the courts as a legitimate guide in developing the common law.[26]

In the US and Japan, whether an international treaty can be directly invoked depends on the nature of the particular case. Only "self-executing" treaties can be directly invoked whilst others cannot.[27] To some extent the Czech Republic and Slovenia seem to have adopted the same line.[28] Some jurisdictions such as Germany, however, accept direct application of customary international law and general principles of international law.[29] Canada also admits the automatic incorporation of customary international law into its domestic laws, but this does not apply to the extent that it conflicts with existing Canadian laws or common laws.[30]

In other jurisdictions, however, international treaties automatically become part of the domestic law. Thus, a treaty ratified by the federal Parliament of Ethiopia automati-

---

[24] See the relevant sections of the countries' jurisdictional reports.

[25] See Singapore Report, Section 3.

[26] *Minister for Immigration and Ethnic Affairs v Teoh* (1995) 183 CLR 273 per Mason CJ and Deane J at 288 (citing *Mabo v Queensland (No 2)* (1992) 175 CLR 1, 42 per Brennan J (with whom Mason CJ and McHugh agreed); *Dietrich v The Queen* (1992) 177 CLR 292, 321 per Brennan J, 360 per Toohey J; *Jago v District Court of New South Wales* (1988) 12 NSWLR 558, 569 per kirby P).

[27] See Section 1 of the US and Japan Reports.

[28] See Section 1 of the Czech and Slovenia Reports.

[29] See Germany Report, Section 2.

[30] A very similar position is taken in the UK. See e. g., *Trendtex Trading Corporation v Central Bank of Nigeria* [1977] QB 529.

cally becomes an enforceable law the same as other domestic legislation. Courts of appropriate jurisdictions are therefore empowered to apply the law should the need arise. Accordingly, foreign investors are able to rely on these laws either before domestic courts or international tribunals.〔31〕 The same applies to Peru and South korea. Moreover, in EU Member States such as the UK, Germany, France, Italy, Greece and Slovenia, EU Law can be directly invoked by EU investors before domestic courts, as established by the European Court of Justice (ECJ) in the *Van Gend* case.〔32〕

A unique problem for the EU Member States is the overlap between the BITs they have signed and the European Community (EC) law. Traditionally, the Member States enjoy the power to enter into BITs, whilst the EU also has certain powers over foreign investment, e. g., on monetary transfer. Such overlap of competence has led to some cases before European courts〔33〕 and international arbitration tribunals.〔34〕 In the European court cases, the supremacy of EC law was upheld and the relevant Member States were ordered to modify their BITs to comply with the EC law requirements.〔35〕 In some investment treaty arbitration cases, several EU Member States were ordered to honor BIT commitments, notwithstanding the conflicting EC law requirements.〔36〕 The inclusion of foreign direct investment (FDI) in the Common Commercial Policy under the 2009 Treaty of Lisbon might not have completely cured the problem. At least portfolio investment is not yet brought under the express exclusive competence of the EU. It is therefore only halfway towards a complete "common investment competence."〔37〕 Recently, the EU has launched an investment package, which comprises two documents: a policy paper entitled "Towards a comprehensive European international investment policy," and a proposal for a Regulation that would establish transitional arrangements regarding BITs concluded by EU Member States and third states before the Lisbon Treaty.〔38〕 It is in-

---

〔31〕 See e. g., *Salini Costrutorri S. p. A and Italstrade S. p. A v. The Federal Republic of Ethiopia, Addis Ababa Water and Sewerage Authority*, Award regarding the suspension of proceedings and jurisdiction, ICC Case No. 10623/AER/ACS (December 7, 2001), also available at: http://www.asil.org/ilib0616.cfm#j2 (accessed 17 September, 2009). See Section 1 of the Ethiopia Report.

〔32〕 See *Case 26/62, Van Gend en Loss v Nederlanse Administratie der Belsatingen*, ECR1 (1963).

〔33〕 In 2004, the European Commission filed cases against Austria, Finland, Sweden and Denmark before the European Court of Justice (ECJ), alleging that some of their pre-accession BITs with non-EU countries may be in conflict with the EC Law. According to the Commission, the BITs signed between these four Member States and non-EU states do not include exceptions allowing for possibility of EU controls on capital flows in exceptional circumstances.

〔34〕 See, for instance, *Eastern Sugar BV (Netherlands) v The Czech Republic* (*Eastern Sugar v Czech*), SCC No. 088/2004. The Award is available at: http://ita.law.uvic.ca/documents/EasternSugar.pdf.

〔35〕 In March 2009, the ECJ held that Austria and Sweden were both in breach of Article 307 of the EC Law as regards their failure to revise BITs with certain non-EU countries. On 19 November 2009, in *Commission v Finland* (Case C 118/07), the ECJ held that Finland also failed to take the appropriate steps to eliminate incompatibilities with EC Law with regard to transfer of capital contained in the BITs at issue. See PLC Arbitration, ECJ finds Finland's BITs breach article 307 of the EC Treaty, available at: http://arbitration.practicallaw.com/1-500-8076.

〔36〕 See e. g., *Eastern Sugar v Czech, supra* footnote 34.

〔37〕 Further details and analysis can be found in e. g., Wenhua Shan & Sheng Zhang, "The Lisbon Treaty: Halfway Towards a Common Investment Policy of the EU," *European Journal of International Law*, No. 4, 2010.

〔38〕 The two documents can be found at: http://trade.ec.europa.eu/doclib/docs/2010/july/tradoc_146308.pdf (last visited on 10 July 2010).

tended to provide legal security for European and foreign investors, without hampering the EU's ability to negotiate new investment treaties at the EU level. Whether or not it will succeed remains to be seen.

c) Hierarchy in Domestic Laws and Regulations

Generally speaking, the hierarchy goes from higher to lower as follows: constitution, national law and local law.[39] At the national law level, formal laws prevail over administrative regulations, which in turn prevail over ministerial orders. It shall be noted, however, that in small countries such as Singapore there is no hierarchy of domestic laws because all domestic legislation is national legislation.[40]

d) Transparency

Almost all 22 jurisdictions[41] have reported certain mechanisms to ensure transparency of foreign investment law and policies. This requirement is stipulated in domestic laws and/or international treaties. Article 52 of the Czech Constitution, for example, provides that publication is required as a condition for validity of such laws and policies.[42] Canada has issued many acts concerning access to public information, including the federal Access to Information Act and Privacy Act.[43] On the other hand, the Sino-New Zealand FTA[44] and the Sino-Australia BIT[45] are examples of BITs that contain transparency provisions.[46] The North American Free Trade Agreement (NAFTA) also requires the member states to ensure that all laws, regulations, procedures and administrative rulings of general application are published promptly or made available to interested persons.[47] In practice, the relevant laws and regulations are published in the official *Gazette*, and can also be accessed online. In Australia, there is a designated organization, namely the

---

[39] It is noted that under federal structure such as that in Canada, the provincial governments have exclusive (or shared) jurisdiction over many matters relevant to commercial regulation, such as environmental protection. See Canada Report for further details.

[40] See e. g., Singapore Report, Section 3.

[41] Some Jurisdictional Reports, such as the US and Peru Reports, did not provide complete information on this.

[42] Czech Report, Section 1.

[43] Canada Report, Section 1.

[44] According to this FTA, Committee of Investment established by Contracting Parties will consider to develop procedures that can enhance the transparency of non-confirming measures.

[45] Article 6 'transparency of laws' of the Sino-Australia BIT provides that:

Each Contracting Party shall, with a view to promoting the understanding of its laws and policies that pertain to or affect investments in its territory of nationals of the other Contracting Party:

(a) make such laws and policies public and readily accessible;

(b) if requested, provide copies of specified laws and policies to the other Contracting Party; and

(c) if requested, consult with the other Contracting Party with a view to explaining specified laws and policies.

[46] China Report, Section 1.

[47] Article 1802 'publication' of NAFTA provides that:

Each Party shall ensure that its laws, regulations, procedures and administrative rulings of general application respecting any matter covered by this Agreement are promptly published or otherwise made available in such a manner as to enable interested persons and Parties to become acquainted with them.

To the extent possible, each Party shall:

publish in advance any such measure that it proposes to adopt; and

provide interested persons and Parties a reasonable opportunity to comment on such proposed measures.

Australian Legal Information Institute, which provides free and comprehensive online access to Australian legal materials.[48] In Argentina, all congressional debates are published and the general public can readily access them.[49] In Singapore, an online database is provided by the Ministry of Trade and Industry.[50]

In addition, some jurisdictions provide for public consultation procedures in relation to foreign investment laws and regulations. In Japan, comments from the public have to be sought when an administrative organ intends to lay down an administrative order.[51] Chinese law also requires that opinions from relevant organs, organizations and citizens be solicited when drafting administrative regulations.[52] The solicitation of opinions may be conducted in such forms as meetings, seminars and public hearings. In Argentina, a public hearing is required before any change of tariffs or other substantial changes can be implemented by the Controlling Bodies in the system of privatized public services. Non-governmental organizations (NGOs) and the general public can participate in these hearings to discuss any amendment to the system of tariffs or any procedures that may affect consumers.[53] Similar hearings are required when there are important changes in federal environmental matters affecting regulated industries. Such mechanisms help to alert the public and investors of any regulatory changes that may adversely affect their interests.[54] In Italy, a number of general principles are provided in local statues with regard to access to the documents of the procedure, the right to participate and submit (written) observations, the duty to motivate any decision of the public administration, and the duty to adopt a final decision when the procedure is obligatorily initiated upon request of an interested party.[55] An impact assessment may also be carried out to assess the potential effects of any administrative or regulatory act on foreign investment.[56]

2. General Standards of Treatment

The general standards of treatment determine the general status of foreign investment in a given host state. They are often stipulated in a separate provision in investment treaties. Other common BIT provisions, such as those for expropriation and compensation, monetary transfer, and subrogation, also set forth standards of treatment but on more confined, albeit important, issues. As Table 2 shows, on the one hand, the most common general standards of treatment under international investment treaties are non-discriminatory treatment, including national treatment and MFN treatment, and fair and equitable treatment, complimented by the international law minimum standard of

---

[48] Australia Report, Section 1.
[49] Argentina Report, Section 1.
[50] Singapore Report, Section 3.
[51] Japan Report, Section 1.
[52] Article 58 of Chinese Law on Legislation 2000.
[53] Argentina Report, Section 1.
[54] Argentina Report, Section 1.
[55] Italy Report, Section 1.
[56] Id.

treatment and constant protection and security. On the other hand, domestic law tends to focus on the implementation of (or the deviation from) national treatment.

a) Standards of Treatment under International Treaties

Under international treaties, some general standards of treatment have been established. The most common standards of treatment under investment treaties are non-discriminatory treatment, including national treatment and most-favoured-nation treatment, and fair and equitable treatment. In some cases investment treaties also require international law minimum standard of treatment and constant protection and security. Such standards are nevertheless subject to variations in detail and may also be interpreted in different ways by arbitration tribunals. The following discusses the three most common standards.

Non-discriminatory Treatment

The non-discrimination principle is one of the fundamental principles underpinning international investment treaties. Its most common manifestations are the most-favored-nation (MFN) clause and the national treatment (NT) clause.[57] Lorz noted in his German Report that the two standards appeared to be central to German BIT policy and have been characterized as ' *sine qua non conditions*' for the conclusion of an investment treaty by Germany.[58] Indeed, they are standards that have now been accepted by all of the 22 jurisdictions (Table 2) .

MFN Treatment

The MFN standard of treatment is the most commonly adopted standard in international investment treaties. Under such a standard, the relevant parties undertake to treat each other in a manner that is at least as favorable as they treat third parties. The purpose of this standard therefore is to create a level playing field among different foreign states by prohibiting discrimination on the basis of different foreign nationalities.[59] The MFN treatment in most of the BITs and FTAs is restricted to the post-establishment phase of an investment. However, in the recent BIT practice by the US, Canada and Japan, this treatment is extended to cover the establishment stage of foreign investment.[60]

The most controversial question concerning MFN treatment is whether it would cover

---

[57] Norah Gallagher & Wenhua Shan, *Chinese Investment Treaties: Policy and Practice* (Oxford University Press 2009) , at 139.

[58] Germany Report, Section 2.

[59] Gallagher & Shan, *supra* footnote 57, at 140.

[60] Article 2. 2 of the Japan-Republic of korea BIT provides that: ' Each Contracting Party shall in its territory accord to investors of the other Contracting Party and to their investments treatment no less favorable than the treatment it accords in like circumstances to investors of any third country and to their investments (hereinafter referred to as ' most-favored-nation treatment') with respect to investment and business activities. ' Article 2. 1 of this BIT provides that ' investment and business activities' refer to ' the establishment, acquisition, expansion, operation, management, maintenance, use, enjoyment, and sale or other disposal of investments. ' Article 4 ' most-favored-nation treatment' of the US Model BIT 2004 provides that ' Each Party shall accord to investors of the other Party treatment no less favorable than it accords, in like circumstances, to investors of any non-Party with respect to the establishment, acquisition, expansion, management, conduct, operation, and sale or other disposition of investments in its territory. ' Article 4 of the Canada Model BIT 2004 has almost the same stipulation with that of the USA.

dispute-resolution provisions. On the one hand, the MFN clause has been used to effectively bypass purely procedural matters, such as the requirement of a minimum time period before submission to international arbitration.[61] On the other hand, it may be relied on to broaden the tribunal's jurisdiction.[62] To avoid such extension, a good practice is to include an express provision precluding the MFN from applying to dispute resolution. The Japan-Peru BIT and the Japan-Switzerland Economic Partnership Agreement (EPA) explicitly exclude clauses on dispute settlement from the scope of the MFN.[63] According to the Czech Report, the Czech doctrine and practice share the view that MFN applies only to substantive law provisions of the BIT and not to the arbitration clause.[64] The investment chapter in the Sino-New Zealand FTA also clarifies that 'for greater certainty, the obligation in this Article does not encompass a requirement to extend to investors of the other Party resolution procedures other than those set out in this chapter.'[65]

In most of the BITs and FTAs there are also some general exceptions to the MFN clause. These exceptions include regional economic integration, taxation treaties and frontier trade. Several of the most recent Chinese BITs contain a 'grandfather clause' exempting existing non-conforming measures or changes thereto from the reach of the MFN clause.[66] The Canadian Model BIT contains GATT-like general exceptions allowing parties to take measures necessary to (a) protect human, animal, or plant life or health; (b) ensure compliance with laws and regulations that are not inconsistent with the provisions of the Agreement; and (c) conserve living or non-living exhaustible natural resources.[67] These general exceptions, of course, apply to the MFN treatment.

National Treatment

National treatment (NT) is the other main standard that underpins the principle of non-discrimination under investment treaties.[68] The purpose of this clause is to oblige a host state to make no negative differentiation between foreign and national investors.[69] However, the NT clause is not as common as the MFN clause in BITs. In

---

[61] Such as the case *Emilio Agustín Maffezini v. Kingdom of Spain* (ICSID Case No. ARB/97/7).

[62] Such as the case *RosInvest Co UK Ltd v Russian Federation*, Jurisdiction award, SCC Case No V079/2005, 5 October 2007 (became public in 2008).

[63] Japan Report, Section 2.

[64] Czech Report, Section 2.

[65] China Report, Section 2.

[66] Such as Article 3. 3 of the Sino-Czech Republic BIT, which provides that the obligation to ensure MFN treatment to investors shall not apply in respect of the People's Republic of China to:

(d) Any existing non-confirming measures maintained within its territory;

(e) The continuation of any non-confirming measure referred to in subparagraph a);

(f) An amendment to any non-confirming measure referred to in subparagraph a) to the extent that the amendment does not increase the non-conformity of the measure, as it existed immediately before the amendment, with those obligations.

China nevertheless undertakes to take all appropriate steps in order to progressively remove the non-confirming measures. See China Report.

[67] Canada Model BIT 2004, Article 10. See Canada Report, Section 2.

[68] Gallagher & Shan, *supra* footnote 57, at 157.

[69] Rudolf Dolzer & Christoph Schreuer, *Principles of International Investment Law* (Oxford University Press 2008), at 178.

China's more than 120 BITs, for example, less than half of them have an NT provision. However, given that all of the Chinese BITs contain an MFN clause, the investors and investments covered by a BIT without an NT clause may be entitled to NT by virtue of the MFN clause.[70] Likewise, not every Singaporean BIT has an NT clause.[71] In most BITs, including those concluded by EU Member States, China, Russia and the Latin American states, the NT clause only applies to the post-establishment phase.[72] This is contrasted to the BIT practice of the US, Canada and Japan, which tend to permit the NT clause to cover both market access and pre-establishment rights.[73]

In most BITs the NT obligation is subject to qualifications and exceptions. The UK-USSR BIT for instance provides for national treatment 'to the extent possible' and 'in accordance with its laws and regulations.'[74] The UK-Papua New Guinea BIT provides that 'special incentives granted by one contracting Party only to its nationals in order to stimulate the creation of local industries are considered compatible with this Article provided they do not substantially impair the investments and activities of nationals and companies of the other Contracting Party in connection with an investment.'[75] NAFTA also provides exceptions from the NT obligations for measures relating to the allocation of government procurement and subsidies and grants.[76] In the Canadian Model BIT, the above-mentioned general exceptions also apply to the NT clause.[77] In Chinese investment treaties, six different approaches to NT provisions can be identified, and most of them are subject to certain exceptions.[78] The Singapore-Turkey BIT contains a peculiar provision precluding foreign investors from bringing an arbitration claim against the host state on the ground that they have received less favorable treatment than native investors.[79]

Fair and Equitable Treatment

Fair and equitable treatment (FET) is an absolute standard of treatment, whilst the MFN and NT are relative standards of treatment. FET has been the most commonly used standard of treatment under BITs (Table 2), and is the most frequently invoked standard in investment disputes.[80] This is because in BITs there is normally no further defini-

---

[70] Gallagher & Shan, *supra* footnote 57, at 157.

[71] Singapore Report, Section 3.

[72] See Section 2 of these respective jurisdictional reports.

[73] See Section 2 of these respective jurisdictional reports.

[74] UK Report, Section 2.

[75] Id.

[76] Article 1108.7 provides that:

Articles 1102 (national treatment), 1103 (most-favored-nation treatment) and 1107 do not apply to:

(a) procurement by a Party or a state enterprise; or

(b) subsidies or grants provided by a Party or a state enterprise, including government supported loans, guarantees and insurance.

[77] Canada Report, Section 2.

[78] Gallagher & Shan, *supra* footnote 57, at 166-171.

[79] Singapore Report, Section 3.

[80] Dolzer & Schreuer, *supra* footnote 69, at 119.

tion for this standard. Most BITs, including those signed by the UK,[81] Germany, and China, typically simply prescribe fair and equitable treatment without any further explanation.[82] NAFTA Article 1105, however, links the FET standard with the standard required under general international law. It reads, "[e]ach Party shall accord to investments of investors of another Party treatment in accordance with international law, including fair and equitable treatment and full protection and security."

However, this does not seem to have provided sufficient clarity. A few earlier arbitration cases have led to unwanted interpretations of this provision by tribunals. As a result, in 2001 the Free Trade Commission (FTC) of NAFTA adopted an official interpretation. It stipulates that the FET standard reflects the customary international law minimum standard and does not require treatment in addition to or beyond that standard. Also, the determination that there has been a breach of another provision of the NAFTA, or of a separate international agreement, does not establish that there has been a breach of FET. The interpretation has been followed by the US and Canada in their subsequent BIT practice and their Model BITs.

Recent BIT practice has witnessed a wider acceptance of the FTC's interpretation of FET beyond North America. Article 3(1) of the UK-Mexico BIT, for example, provides that: "Investments of investors of each Contracting Party shall at all times be accorded treatment in accordance with customary international law, including fair and equitable treatment ... in the territory of the other contracting party."[83] Article 5 'Minimum Standard of Treatment' further defines the standard of treatment as follows:

1. Each Contracting Party shall accord to investments of investors of the other Contracting Party treatment in accordance with international law, including fair and equitable treatment and full protection and security.

2. For greater certainty, this Article prescribes the international law minimum standard of treatment of aliens as the minimum standard of treatment to be afforded to investments of investors of the other Contracting Party. The concepts of "fair and equitable treatment" and "full protection and security" do not require treatment in addition to or beyond that which is required by the international law minimum standard of treatment of aliens as evidence of State practice and *opinio juris*. A determination that there has been a breach of another provision of this Agreement, or of a separate international agreement, does not establish that there has been a breach of this Article.

Clearly this is almost the same as the NAFTA and FTC language, except with the addition of "as evidence of State practice and *opinio juris*" as a qualification on the international law minimum standard. This addition seems to suggest an equation between the customary international law standard and the international law minimum standard.

Some recent Japanese BITs and Economic Partnership Agreements (EPAs) also in-

---

[81] In some cases concerning the UK BITs with other states, such as *Biwater Gauff Ltd v Tanzania* and *National Grid PLC v Argentina*, both tribunals took the view that fair and equitable treatment is an autonomous treatment standard, which is different from customary international law. See Section 2 of the UK Report.

[82] See Section 2 of the UK, Germany and China Reports respectively.

[83] UK Report, Section 2.

clude notes similar to the FTC interpretation.[84] For instance, the Japan-Brunei EPA notes that FET "[does] not require treatment in addition to or beyond that which is required by customary international law minimum standard of treatment of aliens." (Art. 59)[85] Also, some BITs/EPAs note that "a determination that there has been a breach of another provision of this Agreement, or of a separate international agreement, does not establish that there has been a breach of this Article" (with slight differences in the terms: Japan-Mexico EPA (Art. 60 Note), Japan-Philippines EPA (Art. 91 Note), Japan-Thailand EPA (Art. 95 Note) and Japan-Laos BIT (Art. 5(1) Note 1)).[86] Further, some EPAs add further clarifications. For example, the Japan-Peru EPA stipulates that

'[f]air and equitable treatment' includes the obligation of the Contracting Party not to deny justice in criminal, civil, or administrative adjudicatory proceedings in accordance with the principle of due process of law. Each Contracting Party shall accord to investors of the other Contracting Party, non-discriminatory treatment with regard to access to the courts of justice and administrative tribunals and agencies of the former Contracting Party in pursuit and in defence of rights of such investors (Art. 5 (2) Note).[87]

According to the Peruvian Report, fair and equitable treatment must be understood as the protection of legitimate expectations, good faith, transparency, consistency, and non-discrimination. Moreover, the Peru-Japan BIT stipulates that the FET standard includes the obligation of "due process of law."[88]

Another approach can be found in some Russian and Chinese BITs, which link the FET standard with the MFN and NT standards. For instance, Article 3 of the Sino-Qatar BIT reads:

1. Investments and activities associated with investments of investors of either Contracting Party shall be accorded fair and equitable treatment and shall enjoy protection in the territory of the other Contracting Party.

2. The treatment and protection referred to Paragraph 1 of this Article shall not be less favorable than that accorded to investments and activities associated with such investments of investors of a third State.

This linkage helps in providing at least further criteria for the assessment of the FET standard. Thus the fair and equitable standard provides a fixed reference point, a definite standard that will not vary according to external considerations, because its content turns on what is fair and reasonable in the circumstances. It also prevents discrimination against the beneficiary of the standard, where discrimination would amount to unfairness or inequity in the circumstances.[89] However, such further criteria, namely the

[84] Japan Report, Section 2.

[85] Japan Report, Section 2.

[86] Id.

[87] Japan Report, Section 2.

[88] Peru Report, Section 2.

[89] UNCTAD, Fair and Equitable Treatment, UNCTAD Series on issues in international investment agreements, UNCTAD/ITE/IIT/11(Vol. 3).

MFN and NT standards, are serving as merely minimum requirements for the FET standard. How much higher the FET standard may lie above them is still an open question.

b) Standards of Treatment under Domestic Law

It is common in the 22 jurisdictions that foreign investors and investments are accorded national treatment under domestic laws (Table 2). Such treatment is often affirmed in the national constitution. The US Constitution, for example, prohibits state and local governments from discriminating against resident aliens.[90] However, the concept of national treatment seems to vary among the 22 jurisdictions. Under Argentine law, the state does not give foreigners greater rights than those enjoyed by its citizens.[91] This could be regarded as a demonstration of the Calvo Doctrine.[92] In Portugal, particularly complex investments with high national interest, Special Projects of National Interest, or "PINs," may be granted a special status with advantages for the investor.[93] In China, foreign investors used to enjoy 'superior' national treatment in some respects; while in other respects may have been subject to 'inferior' national treatment. However, such superior or inferior treatment has been significantly decreased with China's rapid economic growth coupled with continuous reform and opening-up to the outside world.[94] In Italy, the national treatment of foreign citizens is subject to the condition of reciprocity.[95]

Deviation from the national treatment is also possible under the domestic laws of some jurisdictions. Thus in Russia restrictive measures may be adopted against foreign investments by the federal law, for the protection of the constitutional system, morals, health, rights, and lawful interests of others, national defense and state security. Other exceptions to the NT relate to admission and ownership of property, which will be discussed in detail below.

To summarise, the general standards of treatment for foreign investment under international treaties have been largely standardized. This can be seen from the fact that almost all BITs have included such common standards as FET, MFN and NT. However, variations remain in different states. Thus the NT standard applies to both admission and operation stages of foreign investment under investment treaties signed by the US, Canada and Japan, whilst it applies to only the operation stage under investment treaties in other jurisdictions. Moreover, China has long been reluctant in accepting this standard due to its planned-economy legacy. It is now implementing the standard in more recent BITs but still subjecting it to significant reservations. Under the domestic laws of these jurisdictions, NT is generally upheld but also subject to variations in its implementation. Thus in Latin American states such as Argentina it is emphasized that foreign investors should not be granted better treatment than domestic investors. In contrast, preferential treatment can be granted to foreign investors in states such as Portugal or Croatia if they

[90] US Report, Section 2.

[91] Argentina Report, Section 2.

[92] See Wenhua Shan, "Is Calvo Dead?", *American Journal of Comparative Law*, 55(1), 2007.

[93] Portugal Report, Section 2.

[94] China Report, Section 2.

[95] Italy Report, Section 2.

invest in PIN projects, or in certain regions or industries. For reasons mentioned above, China was not able to implement the NT standard but had to offer foreign investors a combination of both "superior" and "inferior" national treatments.

3. Admission and Entry Requirements

a) The Admission Regime and Areas Open to Foreign Investment

The first step in any foreign investment process is the admission, entry, or establishment of the investment. Unless there are overriding treaty obligations, the host state has the discretion in deciding whether and on what conditions a foreign investment project may be accepted in its territory.[96] In most investment treaties, BITs or otherwise, states do not undertake any substantial obligation with regard to investment admission. Thus BITs concluded by European countries (such as the UK, Germany, France, Italy, Czech Republic, and Slovenia), China and Australia have affirmed such a right of the host state concerning admission.[97] A typical clause provides that each contracting state shall in its territory promote as far as possible investments by investors of the other contracting state and admit such investments in accordance with its legislation.[98] This type of admission clause exposes the host state to no obligation to revise its domestic laws of admission after the ratification of the BIT.[99]

However, the US, Canada and Japan take a different approach.[100] The BITs negotiated by these states, to some extent, impose market access obligations. Under these BITs, a right of admission is established on the basis of NT and MFN treatment[101] (Table 2). The US Model BIT (2004), for example, provides in its Article 3.1 (National Treatment) that, "[e]ach Party shall accord to investors of the other Party treatment no less favorable than that it accords, in like circumstances, to its own investors with respect to establishment, acquisition, expansion, management, conduct, operation, and sale or other disposition of investments in its territory."

Likewise, Article 4.1 (Most-Favored-Nation Treatment) of the US Model BIT reads: "Each Party shall accord to investors of the other Party treatment no less favorable than that it accords, in like circumstances, to investors of any non-Party with respect to the establishment, acquisition, expansion, management, conduct, operation, and sale or other disposition of investments in its territory."

The extension of MFN and NT obligations to cover "establishment, acquisition, expansion" of foreign investment clearly imposes obligation regarding investment admission. On the other hand, exceptions are also provided in the Model BIT in a 'negative-list approach' listing the sectors, sub-sectors and activities to which the non-discrimination treatments do not apply.

Under the domestic laws of these jurisdictions, investment admission regimes are

---

[96] Dolzer & Schreuer, *supra* footnote 69, at 79–80.

[97] See the Admission section of the respective jurisdictional reports.

[98] Article 2.1 of the German Model BIT (2005).

[99] Dolzer & Schreuer, *supra* footnote 69, at 81.

[100] Section 3 of the US, Canada and Japan Reports respectively.

[101] Id.

generally liberal but varied. Most of the 22 jurisdictions (such as Argentina, Australia, Czech Republic, Germany, Italy, Japan, Macau, Peru, Portugal, Singapore, Slovenia, the UK and the US) do not attach special conditions other than those required for domestic investors. In other words, national treatment on admission is generally upheld.[102] Other jurisdictions have either special registration/notification or approval/authorization requirements as the general admission regime. Thus in Canada, France, Russia, Singapore, Italy, South korea and Turkey, a registration system for foreign investments is in place.[103] China, on the other hand, is a representative of an authorization system by which all foreign investment projects are subject to governmental approval/authorization.[104] Ethiopia and Greece seem to also follow this approach (Table 3).

On the whole, it can be seen that again there is no clear gap in the level of liberalization in admission regimes: some developing and transition economies (such as Argentina, Czech Republic and Peru) are implementing the most liberal regime imposing no additional requirements for foreign investment admission, whilst a few developed economies (such as Canada and France) are actually practicing a less liberal admission mechanism requiring notification and authorization for foreign investment.[105] There is no longer any clear sign of a "North-South divide." States regulate investment admission wherever they deem necessary, regardless of their level of economic development.

With regard to the specific areas open for foreign investment, no state grants unlimited access.[106] A 'negative-list' approach is favored by most of the 22 jurisdictions (Table 3). In the US, for example, ownership is only limited to US citizens and corporations in some sensitive industries, or the magnitude of foreign holdings is limited. These industries include airlines, telecommunication and others deemed to affect national security. Meanwhile, political reaction to certain proposed foreign investments may also have an adverse effect on the prospects for the investment.[107] In Italy, special authorizations are needed if foreign investors want to invest in areas such as civil flights.[108] In Peru, restrictions of foreign investments can be found in areas such as radio and television, commercial airline transportation and marine merchant activities.[109] In Japan, investments in certain areas, such as those in the defense industry, agriculture, forestry, mining, infrastructure and telecommunication industries, are required to be reported in ad-

[102] Some of these jurisdictions nevertheless have registration or approval requirements for foreign investment in some sectors or industries. For example, registration or authorization is required for foreign investment in few economic areas. See Table 3 and the US Report for further details.

[103] Some of them require approval/authorization for some foreign investment projects. Thus, in Canada, review and approval are required for large, cultural and national security investments. See Table 3 and Canada Report for further details.

[104] China requires that every foreign investment project be approved by the relevant authorities. It is pointed out that foreign investment projects, as a rule, are either approved by various development and reform authorities or the authorities in charge of commerce, while contract of foreign investment projects and articles of association are approved by development and reform authorities.

[105] See Section 3 of the jurisdictional reports of these jurisdictions respectively.

[106] Dolzer & Schreuer, *supra* footnote 69, at 81.

[107] US Report, Section 3.

[108] Italy Report, Section 3.

[109] Peru Report, Section 3.

vance to the competent ministries. The ministries may order foreign investors to change or discontinue their investments, if the investments are considered to impair national security, to disturb the maintenance of public order, to hinder the protection of public safety, or to bring significant adverse effect to the smooth management of the Japanese economy.[110] Also, only Japanese nationals are qualified to hold mining rights or radio licenses.[111] The German Foreign Trade and Payments Act also empowers the government to control or restrict investments and trade for reasons of foreign policy and national security.[112] In Portugal, private enterprise is not allowed in certain areas of activity, including rail transport in the public interest, communications by mail, the exploitation of seaports, and the collection, treatment and distribution of water for public consumption.[113] Although the UK does not require authorization for foreign investments admission, the government retains some statutory powers to block acquisitions of companies by foreign investors in certain circumstances.[114] For instance, it could prohibit the change of control of an important manufacturing undertaking, on the ground of national interests.[115] It also can refer a merger to the Office of Fair Trading on the grounds that the merger raises issues of public interest, including national security and the stability of the financial system.[116] Finally, it may regulate the control of certain privatized companies through the insertion of certain clauses such as those limiting the ability of any individual or corporation to control a certain percentage of shares.[117]

An obvious trend in this respect is that the monitoring of Sovereign Wealth Funds (SWFs) is becoming more and more common. In Australia, all proposed investments by foreign governments and their agencies are subject to notification and screening requirements, irrespective of the size of the proposal.[118] In 2007, the Minister of Industry of Canada issued guidelines regarding the approach to be taken for reviewing acquisitions by state-owned enterprises (SOEs) to determine if the net benefit test is met.[119] The guidelines indicate that the Minister will examine whether the SOE adheres to Canadian standards of corporate governance and to Canadian laws and practices. This trend demonstrates a growing caution of some states to SWFs investments.

b) Competition Policy and Antitrust Law

Most of the 22 jurisdictions monitor foreign investments by virtue of competition policy and antitrust law, which take the form of either a special legislation or provisions within a more general legislation such as the enterprise law, commercial law or trade law.

In the US, an investment or acquisition may trigger an antitrust review, if its effect

---

[110] Japan Report, Section 3.

[111] Id.

[112] Germany Report, Section 2.

[113] Portugal Report, Section 3.

[114] UK Report, Section 3.

[115] UK Report, Section 3.

[116] Id.

[117] For further details see the respective jurisdictional reports.

[118] Some other foreign investment proposals are subject to notification and vetting requirements if they are above a certain prescribed value. See the Australia Report, Section 3.

[119] See Canada Report, Section 3.

would be to create a monopoly or a restraint on trade.[120] Japan maintains an Act on Prohibition of Private Monopolization and Maintenance of Fair Trade to monitor investments which may substantially restrain competition.[121] Within the EU, some Member States have promulgated their own competition policy or antitrust law,[122] though they should be in conformity with the EU Law, which has established a Community mechanism in this area. China's Anti-monopoly Law was passed in 2007, which also applies to foreign-invested enterprises.[123] The main piece of federal legislation protecting competition in Canada is the Competition Act, which contains provisions relating to anti-competitive behavior including agreements among competitors to fix prices, and abusive behavior by a dominant firm that reduces competition.[124]

4. Investment Contracts

Investment contracts are often used when conducting international investment. In a broader sense, they include all kinds of contracts for making a foreign investment, such as various joint venture contracts between private parties. In a narrow sense, they only refer to state contracts, in which the host state government is a party. The dual role of the host government in such contracts, namely a contracting party and a regulatory authority, has led to significant complications and controversies. As a result, they are often subject to stricter rules than normal commercial contracts. For instance, they are often subject to local law and local jurisdiction whilst in normal commercial contracts party autonomy in those aspects is usually guaranteed.

None of the 22 jurisdictions have maintained strict requirements on the form of investment contracts (Table 4). In practice, the most common forms of such contracts seem to include public-private partnership (PPP), build-operate-transfer (BOT), economic development contracts, concession agreements and licensing, and joint venture contracts. PPP is most common in Australia, Canada, Greece and Slovenia.[125] In France, investment contracts include BOT contracts, joint-venture contracts and contracts for the exploration of natural resources.[126] In Italy, investment contracts may take such forms as BOT, sponsoring contracts, leasing, outsourcing and urban concessions.[127] In the US, investment contracts are sometimes used by a state or local government or its subsidiary economic development agency to encourage businesses to locate in a particular city or region by offering the investor a special benefit or concession.[128] In Peru, the

---

[120] US Report, Section 3.

[121] Japan Report, Section 3.

[122] Germany, for example, has its German Law Against Restraints on Competition.

[123] China Report, Section 3.

[124] Canada Report, Section 3.

[125] See Section 4 of the jurisdictional reports of Australia, Canada and Slovenia, and Section 3 of the Greece Report.

[126] France Report, Section 4.

[127] Italy Report, Section 4.

[128] The incentives can include assistance in acquiring suitable parcels of land for the enterprise, provision of infrastructure development, and tax incentives. However, the economic development contracts can contain performance requirements, such as local employee requirement. See US Report, Section 4.

Constitution provides for a 'law contracts' regime by which the state provides guarantees that cannot be unilaterally modified. They nevertheless can be modified if the state and the other party agree to do so.[129]

As a matter of practice, state contracts tend to be governed by domestic laws and are subject to the jurisdiction of local courts. However, only a minority of the 22 jurisdictions maintain explicit local law and local jurisdiction requirements as a matter of law (Table 4). Thus in Argentina, all contracts between the Government and Argentine companies controlled by foreign investors are subject to Argentina's internal laws and shall be submitted to Argentina's courts.[130] Article 126 of the Chinese Contract Law also provides that 'for contracts fulfilled in the territory of the People's Republic of China on Chinese-foreign equity joint ventures, on Chinese-foreign contractual joint ventures and on Chinese-foreign cooperation in exploring and exploiting natural resources, the laws of the People's Republic of China shall apply.'[131] In Australia, if the contract is for the purchase of interests in real estate, the governing law is the law of Australia.[132] In Japan, although there is no specific provision on the governing law in investment contracts, these contracts will usually be governed by Japanese law according to the Act on General Rule for Application of Laws, and it will usually be the Japanese courts that have jurisdiction over such disputes.[133] Here again there seems to be no clear gap between developed and developing states in the way they treat investment contracts. There are developed states such as Japan, Greece, Portugal and the US that are imposing local law requirement, whilst most reported developing states do not have such a requirement.

An additional aspect that should be noted here is the 'umbrella clause,' which can be found in more than half of the BITs. It typically appears as follows: "Each contracting party State shall observe any other obligation it has assumed with regard to investments in its territory by investors of the other Contracting State."

This clause has been put into BIT practice by most states, including the UK, France, Australia, Argentina, Greek, Germany, the US, China, Japan and South Korea.[134] The exact legal effect of such a clause is still subject to vigorous debate due to inconsistent arbitral interpretation.[135] However, at least some of the relevant arbitration awards have confirmed that it may elevate the disputes arising out of investment contracts subject to domestic court and domestic law, to the international level and allow for review by an international tribunal applying international law. It can therefore be concluded that freedom of contract is generally upheld in domestic laws, whilst investment treaties tend to offer further protection on foreign investors' contractual rights.

---

[129] Peru Report, Section 4.

[130] Argentina Report, Section 4.

[131] China Report, Section 4.

[132] Australia Report, Section 4.

[133] Japan Report, Section 4.

[134] OECD Working Papers on International Investment, Interpretation of the Umbrella Clause in Investment Agreements, October 2006, available at: http://www.oecd.org/dataoecd/3/20/37579220.pdf.

[135] Id. See also Dolzer & Schreuer, *supra* footnote 69, at 152.

5. Performance Requirements

Performance requirements refer to measures adopted by the host state requiring foreign investors to fulfill certain requirements as a condition of either investment approval, or as a condition for the enjoyment of certain advantages. Since some of such requirements have the effect of distorting international trade and/or investment, efforts have been made to regulate such measures. At the global level, the WTO Agreement on Trade-Related Investment Measures (TRIMs) is an agreement regulating certain performance requirements. As noted above, 20 out of the 22 jurisdictions are members of the WTO, so most of them are subject to obligations set forth by the TRIMs Agreement. Similar regulations can also be found in some EPAs and/or BITs. Some of Japan's EPAs, such as the Japan-Brunei EPA, Japan-Malaysia EPA and the Japan-Switzerland EPA, incorporate TRIMs' prohibitions of performance requirements by reference.[136] Article 8 of the 2004 US Model BIT, for example, also prohibits certain categories of performance requirements. In addition, some performance requirements are found in domestic laws, either as conditions for authorization or as conditions for investment incentives.

a) Performance Requirements as Conditions for Authorization

Most performance requirements as a condition for authorization are industry-specific, whilst others are more general by nature. In Italy, the incorporation of a limited partnership is subject to a minimum capital requirement, thus 25% of the minimum capital must be deposited in a bank account prior to the registration of the company before a public notary.[137] In Peru, for instance, performance requirements are reserved when investment is related to hygiene and industrial security, environmental conservation and health.[138] In Japan, a Japanese ship may be possessed by a foreign company on the condition that all of its representatives are Japanese nationals.[139] In France, according to the French Monetary and Financial Code, foreign investors might be required to have the ability to guarantee the security of the supply, to preserve the durability of its activity, and to execute its contractual obligations arising from public procurements or contracts relating to public security, national defense or research interests, production or business of arms, munitions, gunpowder or explosive substances.[140] In Argentina, performance requirements function as conditions of approval for investments in some industries, such as the automobile industry. Such requirements include capital-investment requirements and export-commitment requirements.[141] In Australia, specifications regarding the time for completion of development activities or environmental requirements are examples of conditions which may be imposed when approving a particular foreign investment project.[142] According to the Investment Canada Act, performance requirements may be imposed as conditions for

[136] Japan Report, Section 5.
[137] Italy Report, Section 3.
[138] Peru Report, Section 5.
[139] Japan Report, Section 5.
[140] France Report, Section 5.
[141] Argentina Report, Section 5.
[142] Canada Report, Section 5.

approval of an investment.[143] In Ethiopia, foreign investors are encouraged to transfer technology to the local partner.[144]

It should be noted that some performance requirements are performed after the admission of an investment has been authorized. According to Article 54 of the Slovenian Companies Act 2009, all companies and sole traders must keep the books of account and make year-end accountings once a year in accordance with the Slovenian Accounting Standards or the International Financial Reporting Standards, unless otherwise stipulated by the law.[145] There are also financial reporting and auditing requirements in respect of all enterprises doing business in Macau, which apply to foreign investments.[146]

b) Performance Requirements as Conditions for Incentives

In most circumstances, performance requirements are imposed as non-mandatory conditions for enjoyment of certain incentives. Such requirements exist in almost all of the 22 jurisdictions.

In the US, the economic development agreements signed between state or local development agencies and foreign investors may contain some kinds of performance requirements such as the requirement of creation of jobs in the local market.[147] The "new generation" BITs/EPAs of Japan normally permit certain performance requirements only in exchange for certain advantages conferred by the host state. Such performance requirements include: technology transfer, location of headquarters, achieving research and development within the host state and destination of export.[148] In Portugal, the cre-

---

[143] Where an investment is subject to review under the Investment Canada Act, the investor's plans regarding employment, resource processing, domestic content, exports, technology development or transfer and the other relevant factors are examined by Investment Canada. See Canada Report, Section 5.

[144] Ethiopia Report, Section 5.

[145] Slovenia Report, Section 5.

[146] Macau Report, Section 5.

[147] US Report, Section 4.

[148] Article 4 of the Japan-Vietnam BIT, for example, reads as follows:

1. Neither Contracting Party shall impose or enforce, as a condition for investment activities in its Area of an investor of the other Contracting Party, any of the following requirements:

(a) to export a given level or percentage of goods or services;

(b) to achieve a given level or percentage of domestic content;

(c) to purchase, use or accord a preference to goods produced or services provided in its Area, or to purchase goods or services from natural or legal persons or any other entity in its Area;

(d) to relate the volume or value of imports to the volume or value of exports or to the amount of foreign exchange inflows associated with investments of that investor;

(e) to restrict sales of goods or services in its Area that investments of that investor produces or provides by relating such sales to the volume or value of its exports or foreign exchange earnings;

(f) to appoint, as executives, managers or members of boards of directors, individuals of any particular nationality;

(g) to transfer technology, a production process or other proprietary knowledge to a natural or legal person or any other entity in its Area, except when the requirement (i) is imposed or enforced by a court, administrative tribunal or competition authority to remedy an alleged violation of competition laws; or (ii) concerns the transfer of intellectual property rights which is undertaken in a manner not inconsistent with the Agreement on Trade-Related Aspects of Intellectual Property Rights, Annex 1C of the Marrakesh Agreement Establishing the World Trade Organization;

(h) to locate the headquarters of that investor for a specific region or the world market in its Area;

(i) to achieve a given level or value of research and development in its Area; or

(j) to supply one or more of the goods that the investor produces or the services that the investor provides to a specific region or the world market, exclusively from the Area of the former Contracting Party.

2. The provisions of paragraph 1 above do not preclude either Contracting Party from conditioning the receipt or continued receipt of an advantage, in connection with investment activities in its Area of an investor of the other Contracting Party, on compliance with any of the requirements set forth in paragraph 1 (f) through (j) above.

See Section 5 of the Japan Report.

ation of local employment, the obligation to transfer technology and other requirements may be part of the requirements for the granting of certain benefits or advantages to the investor concerned.[149] There are also performance requirements in the Czech Republic which must be fulfilled in order to enjoy some tax incentives, such as technology-transfer requirements, local employment requirements and local content requirements.[150] In Greece, performance requirements are imposed as conditions for incentives. These include tax exceptions, grants and subsidized loans to stimulate regional development, job creation, competitiveness, industrial restructuring, environmental protection and energy saving.[151]

Singapore is an exception in this respect. The local employment quotas are defined by the Singapore Ministry of Manpower and they differ from industry to industry. In some industries, the quotas are very high. For instance, 35% is required in the manufacturing sector while 50% is required in the service sector. However, quite interestingly, this kind of local requirement is imposed neither as a condition for admission nor as a condition for enjoying some kind of benefit or advantage. It is carried out in the form of sanctions the employer may be subject to if otherwise breached.[152]

6. Tax Regime and Incentives

a) General Tax Regime

Most of the domestic legislations in the 22 jurisdictions uphold the principle of equality of treatment with regard to their tax regimes. Article 51 of the Croatian Constitution for instance states that everyone needs to participate in the defrayment of public expenses in accordance with his or her economic capabilities and that the system of taxation shall be based on the principles of equality and equity.[153]

b) Special Tax Regimes for Foreign Investors?

Many states, particularly the developing ones, adopt special tax regimes to attract foreign investment, usually in the form of tax reductions or exemptions. Some reductions or exemptions may apply to all foreign investment, but the majority of them target certain industries or regions. In Ethiopia, for example, foreign investors enjoy income tax exemption for up to five years provided that they are able to export at the required level. Further income tax exemptions are provided for investors engaged in least developed regions of the country such as the Somali, Afar and Gambella regional states.[154] Such incentives

---

[149] Portugal Report, Section 5.

[150] Czech Report, Section 5.

[151] Greece Report, Section 3.

[152] Singapore Report, Section 2.

[153] Croatia Report, Section 5.

[154] See Section 6 of the Ethiopia Report. In China, tax incentives used to be a major tool to attract foreign investment. Tax incentives are provided in the EJV Tax Law 1980 and the Foreign Enterprise Income Tax Law 1981. Furthermore, local governments were authorized to provide more tax incentives in the FIEs Income Tax Law 1991. However, with the improvement of the investment environment in China, the tax incentives are removed by and large. In 2007, the Enterprise Income Tax Law was issued, repealed the abovementioned two laws. Article 4 of this Law provides that ' the rate of enterprise income tax shall be 25%. ' This law constitutes a fundamental step for China to build a neutral investment regime without differentiating domestic investors and foreign investors through a unified tax burden. See Section 6 of the China Report.

can also be regarded as performance requirements.

Croatia has issued a series of laws to regulate the performance of business activities in respective areas, and they also include tax relief and exemptions. The laws include: Reconstruction and Development of the Town of Vukovar Act, Areas of Special State Concern Act, Hill and Mountain Areas Act, Free Zones Act and Investment Promotion Act.[155] According to these laws, taxpayers that do business in the given areas can enjoy tax relief and exemptions.[156] In order to improve living conditions and development of certain Peruvian regions, Peru also provides tax incentives for investment in areas such as the Amazonian region and certain high Andean territories.[157]

Free trade zones in Slovenia are regulated by the Economic Zones Act 1998.[158] Currently there are only two special economic zones in Slovenia—the koper economic zone, which is located in the port of koper on the Slovenian Adriatic coastline, and the Maribor economic zone, Maribor being the second largest city of Slovenia. A company operating in an economic zone may claim tax concessions.[159]

As mentioned above, in some jurisdictions tax reductions and exemptions may be granted to foreign investments in certain industries. They exist in both developed and developing countries. In Canada, for example, the use of tax measures as instruments to encourage investment in Canada can be traced back to the early 1970s, when Canada introduced tax credits measures and the Accelerated Capital Cost Allowance to encourage investments in manufacturing, processing and primary industries, such as agriculture, food processing, and forest products.[160] More recently, the Government has implemented a number of tax incentive programmes to attract foreign investments in sectors such as research and development, natural resources and film production.[161] Most of these incentives are available only to foreign investors that have established a corporation in Canada, which qualifies them as residents under Canadian tax law.[162] In Peru, there are advantageous tax and labour regimes applicable to investments made in certain industries such as agriculture and aquaculture.[163] In Greece, more favorable treatment for the shipping industry was offered by special legislation.[164] Under the Law on Encouragement of Tourism, Turkey also uses tax incentives to promote the development of tourism.[165]

c) Double-Taxation Treaties (DTTs)

A potential significant problem for international investors is the problem of double taxation. To a large extent, the problem of double taxation is solved through international

---

[155] Croatia Report, Section 5.
[156] Id.
[157] Peru Report, Section 6.
[158] Slovenia Report, Section 6.
[159] Id.
[160] Canada Report, Section 6.
[161] Id.
[162] Id.
[163] Peru Report, Section 6.
[164] Greece Report, Section 3.
[165] Turkey Report, Section 6.

treaties. All 22 jurisdictions have concluded double-taxation treaties. However, the number of these DTTs in each jurisdiction varies. Among them, China has the most DTTs with 90, whilst Macau only has two.[166] The double taxation issue is also addressed in domestic law. The UK, for example, provides unilateral tax credit relief under certain circumstances.[167] To a certain extent Peruvian law allows companies registered in Peru to deduct from their gross revenue income tax paid abroad.

d) Other Incentives

Apart from the various tax incentives, some jurisdictions offer a number of other incentives to attract foreign investments. In Macau, the Government provides support to private companies in the form of interest subsidies for their bank loans. There are also employment subsidies and export-diversification incentives available.[168] The European Union also plays a great role in providing incentives for foreign investment. It provides incentives for investments through the European Social Fund as well as the European Regional Development Fund. In Germany, there are not only "investment incentives" aimed at covering investment costs, but also "operational incentives" supporting investors after their investment has been realized by subsidizing operating costs. Such incentives, for example, may be in the form of cash incentives, interest-reduced public loans, or public guarantees.[169] In addition to tax incentives, the Canadian Government offers a number of assistance programmes to stimulate economic activities, which apply to foreign investment.[170] Under these programmes, financial support, technical assistance, loan guarantees, equity financing, and advisory assistance are provided.[171] In Italy, agencies at the national and regional level provide support for companies willing to invest in Italy.[172] Foreign companies investing in Italy may receive technical or financial support.[173] The Peruvian Investment Law provides four basic types of incentives: (a) capital aids in the form of cash grants; (b) leasing subsidies, which cover partial payment by the state of the installments relating to a lease which has been entered into for the use of new mechanical and other equipment; (c) tax-free reserves; and (d) subsidies for the expenses of wages relating to the employment created by the investment.[174]

7. Property Rights, Expropriation and Compensation

Security of investment is the most fundamental concern to any foreign investors. The protection of property right, particularly in case of expropriation, is therefore the most important aspect in foreign investment law. Such protection is typically offered by

[166] One is signed with China and the other with Portugal.
[167] Income and Corporation Taxes Act 1988 s 790. See Section 6 of the UK Report.
[168] Macau Report, Section 6.
[169] Germany Report, Section 2.
[170] Canada Report, Section 6.
[171] Id.
[172] Italy Report, Section 6
[173] Id.
[174] Peru Report, Section 6.

domestic laws, but more importantly, by international treaties.

a) General Protection of Property Rights

Protection of property rights is offered by domestic law in almost all of the 22 jurisdictions, which tend to guarantee national treatment (Table 5). Often, a right to property for foreigners (and nationals) is provided by the constitution as a fundamental right. The property of foreign investors is thus guaranteed at the highest level of the domestic legal system. Article 13 of the Chinese Constitution 2004, for example, stipulates that "[t]he State protects the right of citizens to own lawfully earned income, savings, houses and other lawful property." The Canadian Constitution, however, does not contain express provisions on the protection of property rights. In the UK, there is no written constitution, but property protection is covered by the Human Rights Act 1998.

b) Protection of Intellectual Property Rights

With respect to the protection of intellectual property rights, the domestic laws of many jurisdictions, including China, the US, Peru, Japan, Germany, France, Italy, Singapore and Argentina, provide the protection of intellectual property rights regardless of the nationality of the beneficiary.[175] The BITs and EPAs concluded by most of the jurisdictions contain a clause explicitly including intellectual property rights in the definition of investments.

c) Right to Expropriate

It is recognized by customary international law that a state enjoys the right to expropriate property of foreign investors located within its territory.[176] Such sovereign right is sometimes ensured in the constitution of some states. Article 29 of the Japanese Constitution, for instance, explicitly provides that private property may be expropriated.[177] Article 13 of China's 2004 Constitution stipulates that: "The state may, for the public interest, expropriate or take over private property of citizens for public use, and pay compensation in the accordance with law."[178] Pursuant to Article 17 of Argentina's Constitution, expropriation is permitted when conducted in the public interest and under the conditions provided by law.[179] Article 42 of the Italian Constitution provides that in cases defined by the law, and provided that compensation is paid to the owner, property can be expropriated for reasons of general interest.[180] According to the local statue in Singapore, the Government may acquire land for any public purpose or any residential, commercial or industrial purposes.[181]

The right to expropriate by host states is also affirmed by international treaty law. Almost every BIT contains an article on expropriation. Whilst it typically details the conditions and standards of compensation for expropriation, it implicitly affirms the host

---

[175] See the relevant section of the jurisdictional reports of these jurisdictions respectively.

[176] Dolzer & Schreuer, *supra* footnote 69, at 89.

[177] Japan Report, Section 7.

[178] China Report, Section 7.

[179] Argentina Report, Section 7.

[180] Italy Report, Section 7.

[181] Singapore Report, Section 2.

state's right to expropriate aliens' property.

d) Definition of Expropriation

Direct expropriation or outright nationalization of an asset is generally easier to establish as there is a physical taking by the states of the relevant assets.[182] However, indirect expropriation or measures equivalent to expropriation are much more difficult to define.

Argentina is one of the few states that has defined direct and indirect expropriation in its domestic law.[183] According to its domestic laws and regulations, direct expropriation is resorted to when the Government as guarantor of public interest needs certain property in order to satisfy a general and collective community interest and therefore has to take or use property owned by a person. Indirect or irregular expropriation takes place when (i) there is a law declaring the public interest of certain goods and the state takes it without previous compensation; (ii) the good declared to be of public interest by law cannot be disposed of in normal conditions; and (iii) the state imposes an unlawful restriction upon private property. In all of these cases, the affected owner may take the matter to court in which a judge may declare whether indirect expropriation actually has taken place.[184] It is therefore clear that irregular/indirect expropriation under Argentine domestic law differs from indirect or creeping expropriation as understood in international law. Under international law, indirect expropriation deals with state measures which substantially deprive investors of their private property. These kinds of measures do not generally qualify as expropriation under Argentine domestic law. Rather, the deprived owner should seek compensation through the broader concept of state responsibility.[185]

In Germany, Article 14(3) of the Basic Law sets forth specific criteria for the constitutionality of an expropriation. According to this Article, four elements should be fulfilled: every expropriation must be based on a statutory law passed by the legislation; the intent of an expropriation should be to promote a common good or further national welfare; expropriations need to meet the principle of proportionality; and expropriations should be executed in exchange for reasonable compensation.[186] In France, four conditions[187] must be met to qualify as an indirect expropriation, and the foreign investor has to prove all the criteria in case of an indirect expropriation.[188]

---

[182] Gallagher & Shan, *supra* footnote 57, at 257.

[183] Argentina Report, Section 7.

[184] Id.

[185] Id.

[186] Germany Report, Section 2.

[187] According to Section 7 of the France Report, the four conditions include: (1) the possession must be irregular and must have arisen at the occasion of an ordinary and regular operation (such as an operation of public work) or must have become irregular when the transfer of property was later declared void; (2) the possession must be maintained by the public authority for reasons of public necessity; (3) the beneficiary of the indirect expropriation must not provoke direct expropriation or agree with the owner of the property to pay it/him a periodical indemnity for the occupation of the property; and (4) the owner of the property must ask the judge of the French civil court of justice, the Tribunal de Grande Instance, to declare the transfer of property and to fix the amount of the indemnity which must be accompanied by a dispossession indemnity.

[188] Id.

Although an expropriation clause can be found in every BIT, most of them do not contain a definition of the concept of indirect expropriation. However, some BITs do attempt to give a definition. Article 5 of the Slovenia-kuwait BIT provides that for the purposes of the agreement, the term "expropriation" also includes interferences or regulatory measures, which have a *de facto* expropriatory effect, because of which the investor is dispossessed of his property rights, control or substantial benefits related to his investment; or his investment is deprived of its economic value or suffers substantial damage. Examples of these interferences include the freezing or blockage of the investment, introduction of arbitrary or disproportionate taxes, forced sale of the whole investment or its part, and other comparable measures.[189]

Some recent BITs include what may be called "public welfare or exceptions" to ensure that public welfare/interest measures by the host state are not caught by the expropriation clause. Thus the 2004 US Model BIT stipulates that: "Except in rare circumstances, non-discriminatory regulatory actions by a Party that are designed and applied to protect legitimate public welfare objectives, such as public health, safety, and the environment, do not constitute indirect expropriations."[190]

A similar provision can be found in Article 17 of the Japan-Uzbekistan BIT, which states that: "[N]othing in this Agreement [...] shall be construed to prevent a Contracting Party from adopting or enforcing measures: (a) necessary to protect human, animal or plant life or health; (b) necessary to protect public morals or to maintain public order."

An explanatory note was added to this provision: "The public order exception may be invoked only where a genuine and sufficiently serious threat is posed to one of the fundamental interests of society." This should help to avoid abuse of this exception.[191]

The FTAs signed between Australia and other states, such as the Australia-United States Free Trade Agreement (AUSFTA) and the Australia-New Zealand Free Trade Area (AANZFTA), include an Annex on Expropriation to clarify the parties' mutual understanding on the constitution of expropriation. The Annexes make clear that an action or a series of actions by a government cannot constitute an expropriation unless "it interferes with a tangible or intangible property right or property interest in an investment."

e) Conditions of Expropriation

Conditions of expropriation are provided in both domestic laws and international treaties. However, the latter is more comprehensive than the former. According to US domestic laws, the usual standard is that expropriations can only be undertaken for public purposes and that the compensation should be 'prompt, adequate and effective.' Article 70 of the Peruvian Constitution grants the necessity guarantees required in case of expropriation. Only for national security or public purposes, declared by law and accompanied

[189] Slovenia Report, Section 7.

[190] 2004 US Model BIT, Annex B (Expropriation) point 4(b).

[191] Japan Report, Section 7.

with cash payment of the appraised value, can expropriations be legally justified. The Japanese Constitution also provides that '[p]rivate property may be taken for public use upon just compensation.' Accordingly, public purpose and compensation are the two key elements enshrined in domestic laws and regulations.

In most BITs/FTAs, four conditions are required to qualify for a lawful expropriation: (1) for a public purpose; (2) on a non-discriminatory basis; (3) in accordance with due process of law; and (4) upon payment of prompt, adequate and effective compensation. However, this formula has not always been closely followed. Chinese investment treaties, for example, although generally following the prototype in requiring the four substantive requirements, do not expressly accept the "prompt, adequate and effective" standard of compensation.[192] This is because China has traditionally supported the developing states' position that in case of expropriation, it is "appropriate compensation," rather than the "Hull Formula" of "prompt, adequate and effective" compensation, that is required.[193] They nevertheless accept the common methods of valuation, such as 'market value' or 'fair market value' or 'genuine value' of the taken assets.[194] Acceptance of these concepts, particularly the concept of "market value" suggests that the actual standard of compensation available under Chinese BITs does not materially differ from BIT practice of the rest of the world (Table 5).

It can be observed that international investment treaties tend to attach more stringent conditions on the exercise of the right of expropriation than what is required under domestic laws. Thus two more conditions are added, namely the due process of law and non-discrimination requirements. One might argue that since most states tend to guarantee the two aspects either in their constitutions or other laws, they are implicitly included as conditions of expropriation. However, the explicit inclusion of them in investment treaties suggests that such assumption might not always be valid—otherwise there should be no such need as to explicitly incorporate them in the treaties. Thus the treaty standard here is clearer, and in some cases perhaps higher, than the domestic law standard.

f) Compensation for Expropriation

As indicated above, the most widely used standard of compensation under investment treaties seems to be the so-called 'Hull Formula' requiring "prompt, adequate and effective" compensation. However, there are states that persistently refuse to include the formula in their BITs. China is an example. So far no Chinese BIT has explicitly accepted the three-term formula, even though, as mentioned above, the actual standard of compensation provided under Chinese BITs might not be materially different from the Hull formula requirements.

Under domestic laws, terms used for the standard of compensation vary. The US and Japan tend touse 'just compensation' in their domestic laws, whilst France often uses

---

[192] China Report, Section 7.

[193] Id.

[194] Id.

' fair compensation. '[195] Other terms such as "full and just compensation" (Argentina), "appropriate compensation" (China), "reasonable compensation" (Germany), and "due compensation" (Macau) are also used. Whilst "just compensation" is often interpreted to mean the same as the "Hull formula" in the US, this interpretation is certainly not the uniform interpretation accepted in all other states. The European Court of Human Rights has held that ' Article 1 does not ... guarantee a right to full compensation in all circumstances, since legitimate objectives of "public interest" may call for less than reimbursement of the full market value. '[196] Although Argentina adopts "full and just compensation" as the standard of compensation, it excludes any loss of future profit from its calculation[197] (Table 5). To summarize, whilst the standard of compensation is largely standardized under investment treaties, varied terms are used under domestic laws. Again the treaty standard appears clearer, and perhaps in some cases higher, than the domestic law standards.

Most BITs do not have express provisions on the valuation methods for compensation. Many BITs/FTAs simply provide that compensation should be paid without delay, and the compensation should be equivalent to the fair market value of the expropriated investment immediately before the expropriation took place. They also provide that the compensation should not reflect any change in value as a result of the intended expropriation becoming publicly known. In addition, most BITs stipulate that interest from the date of expropriation to the date of payment should be included in the compensation. Finally, some BITs, such as the Sino-Germany BIT, emphasize that the MFN principle applies to the expropriation provisions.[198]

8. Monetary Transfer

a) Transferable Assets

Most investors expect to be able to transfer any profits made from their investments back to their home states. Such expectation is protected under most BITs. Article 8(2) of the UK-Mexico BIT, for example, sets out a much more detailed list of transfers coved by the provision of transfer:

(a) Profits, dividends, interests, capital gains, royalty payments, management fees, technical assistance and other fees and amounts derived from the investment;

(b) Proceeds from the sale of all or any part of the investment, or from the partial or complete liquidation of the investment;

(c) Payments arising from compensation from expropriation;

(d) Payments pursuant to the application of provisions relating to the settlement of disputes;

---

[195] See Section 7 of the Jurisdictional Reports of these Jurisdictions respectively.

[196] *Holy Monasteries v Greece* (Judgment of 9 December 1994) (1995) 20 EHRR 1, para 71.

[197] Argentina Report, Section 7.

[198] Article 4 (3) of the Sino-Germany BIT, for example, reads:

"Investors of either Contracting Party shall enjoy most-favoured-nation treatment in the territory of the other Contracting Party in respect of the matters provided for in this Article."

(e) Payments arising from the compensation and losses under Article 6 of this Agreement.

Likewise, most of China's BITs also include such an open definition, and provide that the list is non-exhaustive.[199]

b) Restrictions to Transfer

The transfer or repatriation of funds provision in BITs is at the heart of the object and the purpose of an investment treaty.[200] Most jurisdictions thus guarantee free transfer with only few exceptions/restrictions. The UK Model BIT, for instance, prescribes that the contracting parties shall guarantee the unrestricted transfer of any investment which falls within the treaty regime and any returns on such investments. The Model BIT does not include any general exceptions.[201] In the US, there are no restrictions on the transfer of money to or from the US through the usual banking channels.[202] There are no restrictions in Macau on the transfer of investment assets.[203]

However, restrictions do exist. They can be summarized as follows:

· Situations of exceptional balance of payment difficulties. For instance the UK-Singapore BIT provides that the monetary transfer should be subject to 'the right of each Contracting Party in exceptional financial or economic circumstances to exercise equitably and good faith powers conferred by laws.'[204] Article 59 of the European Community Treaty states that in case of exceptional circumstances for which transfer of assets from or to foreign countries cause or threaten to cause serious difficulties for the functioning of the economic and monetary union, the institutions of the European Union can take protective measures for a period not exceeding 6 months.

· Anti-money laundering and anti-terrorism. Transport of cash in excess of US $ 10, 000 across the borders is subject to reporting in the US in order to prevent money laundering.[205] Australia also has an extensive asset freezing regime as part of its anti-terrorism and anti-money laundering exercise. The Government of Canada also has strengthened its anti-money laundering regime to deal with terrorism and money laundering that threaten the security of the state.[206]

· Registration or report. In Germany, there is an obligation to register certain monetary transactions with the German Central Bank for the sake of statistical reports.[207] Australia also requires that the export from, or import to, Australia of any currency in excess of A $ 10, 000 in value must be reported to the Australian Financial Transaction Reports and Analysis Centre.[208]

---

[199] China Report, Section 8.

[200] See Gallagher & Shan, *supra* footnote 57, at 175.

[201] UK Report, Section 8.

[202] US Report, Section 8.

[203] Macau Report, Section 8.

[204] UK Report, Section 8.

[205] US Report, Section 8.

[206] Canada Report, Section 8.

[207] Germany Report, Section 2.

[208] Australia Report, Section 8.

In recent BIT practice, the exceptions to monetary transfer have become more sophisticated. Again, the UK-Mexico BIT is a example. Its Article 8(3) contains a broader list of exceptions which allow a Contracting Party to prevent a transfer in cases of:

(h) bankruptcy, insolvency, or the protection of rights of creditors;

(i) issuing, trading or dealing in securities;

(j) criminal or administrative violations;

(k) reports of transfers of currency or other monetary instruments; and

(l) ensuring the satisfaction of judgments in adjudicatory proceedings.

Among the 22 jurisdictions, Argentina and Ethiopia seem to have a more restrictive regime on monetary transfer. Since early 2002 the Central Bank of Argentina has tightened its control over foreign currency exchange transactions in an effort to mitigate the volatility of foreign currency exchange rates against the Argentine peso as a consequence of the current international financial crisis.[209] Monetary transactions require authorization in accordance with foreign exchange regulations. Prior registration is required, and exchange transactions must be documented in an exchange contract to be executed with the authorized foreign exchange entity.[210] Moreover, all foreign currency transfers into Argentina have to be translated into local currency.[211] In Ethiopia, payments and transfers are subject to a stringent supervision and control by the National Bank of Ethiopia (NBE), which enjoys a monopoly over all sorts of foreign currency transactions. Foreign investors are entitled to open and operate a foreign currency account in Ethiopia, although not more than US $ 50,000. There is a full set of regulations concerning the exchange currency rates.[212]

c) Currency Exchange

Most of the states provide that the currency exchange should use ‘freely convertible currency’ or ‘freely usable currency.’ The UK Model BIT additionally guarantees the right to have the transfer made in the currency in which the capital was originally invested.[213] In Argentina, the exchange transaction must be executed by the authorized foreign exchange entity. And the operator will convert the foreign currency into local currency, then change it into the desired currency, and finally make the transfer.[214] In Ethiopia, currency exchange rates are determined and fully regulated by the National Bank of Ethiopia.[215]

9. Dispute Settlement

The greatest breakthrough in the area of international investment law is the creation of an investor-state dispute settlement mechanism enabling foreign investors to sue the

---

[209] Argentina Report, Section 8.

[210] Id.

[211] Id.

[212] Ethiopia Report, Section 8.

[213] UK Report, Section 8.

[214] Argentina Report, Section 8.

[215] Ethiopia Report, Section 8.

host government. Most of the 22 jurisdictions have been involved in investor-state disputes. According to the statistics of the UNCTAD, Argentina leads the table of known investment treaty claims (as defendant) with 51 cases. The Czech Republic ranked third with 16 cases. Both the US and Canada have 14 cases each. Turkey and Russia both have 8 cases. Slovenia and Germany have 2 cases. The UK, Portugal, France and Croatia all have been involved in one case, while China, Italy and Singapore have not been exposed to any international arbitration cases.[216]

a) Domestic Jurisdiction

By default, all foreign investment disputes are subject to the jurisdiction of the domestic courts and tribunals of the host state, unless there is an overriding international law arrangement. As can be seen in Table 6, none of the 22 jurisdictions have established special rules or mechanisms for the settlement of foreign investment disputes. Rather, such disputes are subject to the general rules and mechanisms of dispute settlement, available in the host jurisdiction. In other words, national treatment is guaranteed in this regard.

In some jurisdictions, exhaustion of local remedies is required as a condition to submit investment disputes to international arbitration. According to the US Report, for example, the US requires that a foreign investor must exhaust available local remedies before turning to international arbitration.[217] Article 10 of the Germany-Argentina BIT also provides that an investor-state dispute must be submitted to the national courts of the host state first.[218] Older generation Chinese BITs (before 1997) reserve all foreign investment disputes other than those concerning the amount of compensation to be submitted to local courts.[219] Since 1998, China has embarked on a new generation of BITs allowing all foreign investment disputes to be submitted to international arbitration, including ICSID arbitration.[220] China nevertheless requires resort to local administrative review before submission to international arbitration. Another technique to uphold national jurisdiction is through the so-called 'fork-in-the-road' clause, which aims to preclude an investor from commencing international arbitration after having chosen local remedies.[221]

It is noted that without a 'fork-in-the-road' clause and the 'exhaustion of local remedies' requirements, there would likely be parallel proceedings and conflicts. The duplication of international and domestic proceedings is an unresolved problem to date. This makes the state run the risk of multiple liabilities, and threatens the authority and efficacy of both judicial systems. The international and national dispute settlement mechanisms will be severely damaged if conflicting decisions are rendered on the same for-

---

[216] UNCTAD, Latest Developments in Investor-State Dispute Settlement, IIA Issues Note No. 1 (2010), at 13.

[217] US Report, Section 9.

[218] Argentina Report, Section 9.

[219] China Report, Section 9.

[220] Id.

[221] It is noted that some investment agreements, such as NAFTA and other Canadian agreements, require the investor to waive claims for financial relief as a condition of making an investor-state claim.

eign investment case.[222]

b) International Arbitration

The charm of international investment law lies in its investor-state arbitration system though it is not provided in every investment treaty.[223] International investment arbitration cases have been on rapid surge in the first decade of the new century, with ICSID playing a prominent role.[224] Among the 22 jurisdictions, 20 are members of ICSID. Canada and Ethiopia are the only exceptions (Table 6). Of the 20 Member States, China made a notification when it ratified the ICSID Convention, allowing only disputes concerning compensation for expropriation to be submitted to ICSID. However, this notification was effectively changed in 1998 when the Sino-Barbados BIT was concluded to provide that any investment dispute may be submitted to ICSID, or *ad hoc* arbitration under the UNCITRAL Arbitration Rules.

The earlier BITs concluded by some states only provide for ICSID arbitration. Most UK BITs concluded before February 1982 for example contained a dispute settlement clause that allowed an investor to submit a dispute only to ICSID conciliation or arbitration.[225] Earlier Japanese BITs also did not mention arbitration mechanisms other than ICSID.[226] However, other arbitration mechanisms are becoming more and more common in BITs and FTAs. They include the ICSID Additional Facility, UNCITRAL arbitration, ICC arbitration and *ad hoc* arbitration. The MIGA arbitration mechanism was also recently used in some cases against Argentina[227] (Table 6).

For non-ICSID arbitration, the New York Convention is of vital importance in guaranteeing enforcement. Most of the 22 jurisdictions are members to the New york Convention. Article V of the New York Convention sets forth the grounds upon which a state

---

[222] Germany Report, Section 3.

[223] However, not every BIT contains an investor-state dispute resolution clause. The Germany-Somali BIT, for example, does not contain the consent to investor-state arbitration. See Section 2 of the Germany Report. Also, the BITs signed by Singapore with the US and Switzerland only provide for state-state arbitration mechanism. See Section 3 of the Singapore Report.

[224] According to the Statistics of UNCTAD, of the total 357 known disputes until the end of 2008, 225 were filed with the International Centre for Settlement of Investment Disputes (ICSID) or under the ICSID Additional Facility, 91 under the United Nations Commission on International Trade Law (UNCITRAL) rules, 19 with the Stockholm Chamber of Commerce, eight were administered by the Permanent Court of Arbitration in the Hague, five with the International Chamber of Commerce (ICC) and four are *ad hoc* cases. One further case was filed with the Cairo Regional Centre for International Commercial Arbitration. In four cases the applicable rules are unknown so far. See UNCTAD, Latest Developments in Investor-State Dispute Settlement, IIA Issues Note No. 1 (2010), at 2.

[225] UK Report, Section 9.

[226] Japan Report, Section 9.

[227] In 2006, MIGA was actively seeking to solve three pending claims involving issues of expropriation between Argentina and the kyrgyz Republic. At that time, MIGA was also closely monitoring and actively working to resolve the problems of eight other disputes relating to investments guaranteed by the Agency in Argentina, Guatemala, the kyrgyz Republic, Mauritania, Nicaragua, Senegal, and Venezuela. Four of these involve issues related to expropriation; three involve breach of contract; and two involve transfer convertibility issues. See Argentina Report.

might refuse the recognition and enforcement of an arbitration award.[228] In addition, there tend to be detailed rules in each jurisdiction setting forth certain domestic control mechanisms for international arbitration. In the UK, for instance, an arbitral award may be challenged on the ground that the tribunal did not have substantive jurisdiction.[229] Also, an arbitration award may be challenged on the basis of a serious irregularity affecting the tribunal, the proceedings, or the award. In this respect, it is also necessary to show that the serious irregularity has caused or will cause a substantial injustice to the applicants. Japan's Arbitration Act sets forth two conditions of arbitrability: an arbitrable dispute must be a "civil dispute" that "may be resolved by settlement between the parties."[230]

For ICSID arbitration, the situation is rather different. According to Article 26 of the ICSID Convention, ICSID arbitral awards will be automatically recognized and enforced in most of the cases.[231] However, the solution provided in the ICSID Convention was severely criticized by some Argentine scholars who consider it to be unconstitutional.[232] Although the Argentine Government has declared that it would subject ICSID awards to the review of local courts, it is yet to happen in practice.[233] ICSID arbitration awards may also be subject to constitutional review in Japan (Table 6). The UK main-

[228] 228The Article reads:

1. Recognition and enforcement of the award may be refused, at the request of the party against whom it is invoked, only if that party furnishes to the competent authority where the recognition and enforcement is sought, proof that:

(a) The parties to the agreement referred to in article II were, under the law applicable to them, under some incapacity, or the said agreement is not valid under the law to which the parties have subjected it or, failing any indication thereon, under the law of the country where the award was made; or

(b) The party against whom the award is invoked was not given proper notice of the appointment of the arbitrator or of the arbitration proceedings or was otherwise unable to present his case; or

(c) The award deals with a difference not contemplated by or not falling within the terms of the submission to arbitration, or it contains decisions on matters beyond the scope of the submission to arbitration, provided that, if the decisions on matters submitted to arbitration can be separated from those not so submitted, that part of the award which contains decisions on matters submitted to arbitration may be recognized and enforced; or

(d) The composition of the arbitral authority or the arbitral procedure was not in accordance with the agreement of the parties, or, failing such agreement, was not in accordance with the law of the country where the arbitration took place; or

(e) The award has not yet become binding, on the parties, or has been set aside or suspended by a competent authority of the country in which, or under the law of which, that award was made.

2. Recognition and enforcement of an arbitral award may also be refused if the competent authority in the country where recognition and enforcement is sought finds that:

(a) The subject matter of the difference is not capable of settlement by arbitration under the law of that country; or

(b) The recognition or enforcement of the award would be contrary to the public policy of that country.

See Article V of the New York Convention.

[229] UK Report, Section 9.

[230] Japan Report, Section 9.

[231] In states such as Singapore, a special statute has been enacted for the purpose of ratifying and implementing the ICSID Convention. See Singapore Report, Section 3.

[232] Argentina Report, Section 9.

[233] Id.

tains a registration requirement for ICSID awards to be enforceable in the country.[234]

In short, national treatment is commonly guaranteed under domestic laws with regard to the resolution of foreign investment disputes. Under treaty law, international investor-state arbitration is provided in almost all investment treaties, and in some states is subject to restrictions on the scope of disputes that may be submitted. Most of the reported jurisdictions have accepted ICSID arbitration. Decisions rendered out of ICSID arbitration may nevertheless be subject to constitutional review in some states such as Argentina and Japan.

10. FDI Statistics, Policies and Authorities

Recent decades have seen a significant rise in outward and inward flows of investment in most of the 22 jurisdictions. This is at least partly due to the improvement of the foreign investment environment and the liberal approaches taken by these jurisdictions. FDI is playing a more and more significant role in economic development. The only exception seems to be Argentina. FDI in Argentina can be divided into two periods. The first, from 1990 to 2001, was characterized by strong foreign and local investment due to free trade and open market policies and the whim of foreign exchange controls. The second period started with the national crisis that reached its critical point between December 2001 and January 2002 and is demonstrative of constant capital flight from Argentina.[235]

All of the economic groupings, including developed countries, developing countries and the Commonwealth of Independent States, suffered losses when the financial crisis exploded in 2008. However, it is noted that whilst FDI inflows fell in developed countries in 2008, in developing and transition economies they actually continued to increase.[236] According to the World Investment Report 2010, "FDI inflows plummeted in 2009 in all three major groupings—developed, developing and transition economies ... After six years of uninterrupted growth, FDI flows to developing countries declined by 24 per cent in 2009."[237] However, it also predicts that "[t]he recovery of FDI in-flows in 2010—if modest in global terms—is expected to be stronger in developing countries than in developed ones."[238]

In order to attract FDI, some states have taken measures to promote investments. Portugal for example has established some institutions to promote investments. These institutions include the Agency for Investment and Foreign Trade (AICEP), the Institute of Support to Small and Medium Industrial Enterprises (IAPMEI) and the Instituto de Turismo de Portugal.[239] In contrast, some jurisdictions have tightened up the foreign in-

---

[234] UK Report, Section 9.

[235] Argentina Report, Section 10.

[236] UNCTAD, World Investment Report 2009, Transnational Corporations, Agricultural Production and Development, available at: http://www.unctad.org/templates/webflyer.asp?docid=11904&intItemID=1397.

[237] World Investment Report 2010, p. 3.

[238] Id.

[239] Portugal Report, Section 10.

vestment review procedures. For instance, the Investment Canada Act was amended in 2009, introducing a process for national security reviews.[240] The federal Cabinet acting on a recommendation of the Minister can require such a review where deemed necessary regardless of the size of the transaction.[241]

11. Trends in Foreign Investment Laws

It is difficult to identify the trends of development in foreign investment law out of reports from 22 distinctive jurisdictions covering such a wide range of issues. It is however a "must" for a general report. Nevertheless it seems that three trends of the law of foreign investment protection have emerged, namely "harmonization", "balancing" and "socialization."

a) "Harmonization"

The first and perhaps also the most significant finding is that the core legal principles of foreign investment protection in different jurisdictions have been, by and large, harmonized. This is largely due to the proliferation of BITs and other investment treaties such as FTAs and EPAs. Since such instruments have adopted largely the same or at least similar language on some of the core aspects (such as standards of treatment, expropriation and compensation, freedom of transfer and international arbitration to resolve investment disputes), the general principles or norms of foreign investment protection in different jurisdictions have essentially been "harmonized." Obviously different variations exist and in some cases such variations are material. For example, the US, Canada and Japan tend to extend national treatment obligations to the stage of investment admission, whilst other BITs normally leave investment admission to the complete discretion of the host state authorities. Another example is perhaps China's long resistance to the national treatment standard, which has not been a problem in most other jurisdictions. Such variations, however, have not prevented those jurisdictions from consenting to the core principles of investment protection in the form of international treaties.

Understandably the languages adopted in the domestic laws of different jurisdictions are less unified. yet they also seem to uphold the same or similar principles, such as national treatment to foreign investors. Even in the area of investment admission, which is traditionally left to the discretion of the host states, there is now significant convergence between developed and developing states, as observed above. This further confirms that the past two decades of investment liberalization have indeed resulted in a generally level playing field for foreign investment, in the forms of both international treaties and domestic laws.

However, it should be pointed out that the harmonization of core principles is not the end of the story. Rather, harmonization is still an ongoing process. This is because whilst the principles are harmonized, the detailed meanings of such principles are subject to the often varied implementations and interpretations by domestic authorities of

[240] Canada Report, Section 10.

[241] Id.

different jurisdictions and different international arbitration tribunals. For instance, whilst the NT standard is equally upheld in different jurisdictions, as observed above, different jurisdictions actually have different understandings on the standard. The same applies to the standard of compensation for expropriation where a number of different terms are used under domestic laws of different states. To make it worse, international arbitration tribunals often offer varied interpretations of such principles. The aforementioned diverse interpretations by different arbitration tribunals on the principles of FET, MFN and umbrella clauses are telling examples. The harmonization process therefore still has a long way to go to build up a more solid consensus in international investment protection. As discussed below, much effort has been made in recent investment treaties to clarify the meanings of some of the core principles with a view to preventing farfetched interpretations. Also, domestic laws are to be further harmonized as more and more liberalization measures continue to be adopted by states in recent years, as demonstrated in Chart 5. Hence harmonization of foreign investment laws is not a done business, but an ongoing process and a current trend of development.

b) "Balancing"

Second, there seems to be an emerging trend among states to pursue an investment regime that is more "balanced" in the rights and obligations of the host state and the foreign investors, revising the previously "one-sided" regime committed to unfettered investment protection and liberalization. Thus, as noted above, the FTC of the NAFTA Parties has adopted interpretations on such core principles as FET and expropriation, with a view to preserving necessary regulatory powers of host states, which have been incorporated into the new model BITs of both the US and Canada, as well as BITs concluded by some other states. This is confirmed by the recently released World Investment Report 2010, which has noted that many of the recent BITs demonstrate governments' efforts to "seek to formulate agreements more precisely, paying greater attention to ensuring that the treaty language reflects their domestic policy objectives, reaffirming and strengthening States' right to regulate in the public interest, and trying to enhance the legitimacy of the ISDS processes."[242] In particular, it has noted five broad developments in these IIAs, namely: the clarification of the scope of the treaty; the introduction of general and security exceptions that allow more room for regulation by host states; the clarification of the scope and meaning of specific obligations; the addition of environmental clauses; and the inclusion of corporate social responsibility clauses.[243] Among them, three developments are directly targeted at increasing the policy space of the host state, whilst the other two (the clarifications of relevant scope and terms) indirectly have the same effect. The balancing trend is thus highly visible in investment treaty practice, which seems to have also had an impact on investment arbitration practice, as more and more tribunals

---

[242] UNCTAD, World Investment Report 2010, at 87.

[243] UNCTAD, World Investment Report 2010, at 87 - 88.

have opted for a "balanced" approach to treaty interpretation.[244]

The balancing trend is also evident in domestic legal changes. This is witnessed by the recent measures taken by, for instance, the Canadian Government. Canada recently created a highly unpredictable national security review process and adopted special guidelines for the application of the net benefit test to state-owned enterprises (SOEs), which suggests a new emphasis of Canada to regulate foreign investment with the goal of ensuring that Canadian national interests are protected.[245] The Slovenian Report also points out that the general direction of development of its national legislation is towards a balanced approach.[246] In general, as Chart 5 shows, although states continue to adopt more favorable than restrictive measures on foreign investment, the portion of restrictive regulatory changes has increased rapidly in recent years with an annual 3% increase since 2000. In 2009, restrictive changes reached 30% of the total changes (Chart 5). If this trend continues, within 8 years time the world will see more restrictive measures adopted than favorable ones. By then there should be a better chance to strike a balanced investment regime in states around the world.

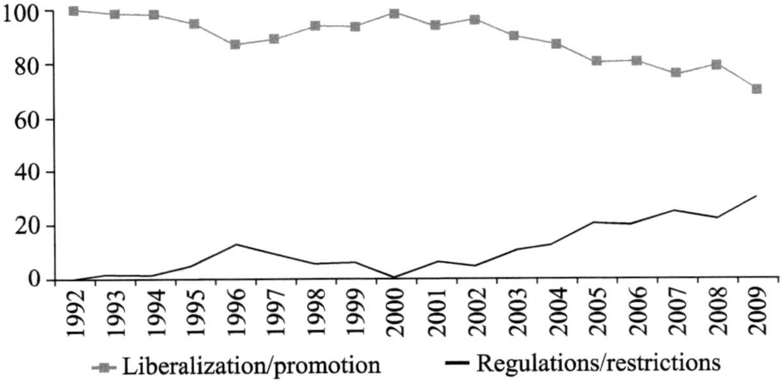

Chart 5 National Investment Policy Changes 1992 – 2009

Source: UNCTAD, *World Investment Report* 2010.

From a historical perspective, the current balancing trend can be viewed as a necessary balance between the generally nationalistic trend on foreign investment experienced in the 1960s and 1970s, and the liberalist trend commenced in the late 1980s (Table 7). Both trends had their historical value: the nationalistic campaign

---

[244] In *Noble Ventures, Inc. v Romania*, for instance, the tribunal pointed out that "it is not permissible, as is too often done regarding BITs, to interpret clauses exclusively in favor of investors." Also, the *El Paso* decision on jurisdiction is noted for its "balanced interpretation." The relevant sentence goes as follows:

"The tribunal considers that a balanced interpretation is needed, taking into account both State sovereignty and State responsibility to create an adapted and evolutionary framework for the development of economic activities, and the necessity to protect foreign investment and its continuing flows."

See *Noble Ventures, Inc. v. Romania*, ICSID Case No. ARB/01/11, Award, 12 October 2005, para. 52; *El Paso Energy International Company v. The Argentine Republic*, ICSID Case No. ARB/03/15, Decision on Jurisdiction, 27 April 2006, at para 70.

[245] Canada Report, Section 11.

[246] Slovenia Report, Section 11.

helped the nation-building process of numerous states which emerged during the decolonization process whilst the liberalistic movement contributed to the economic development of those states as well as other ones. However, as a legal system, both the nationalist and liberalist regimes were biased towards one side and failed to strike a balance between the rights and obligations of the host states and foreign investors. A balanced investment regime will certainly be a more sustainable regime.

c) "Socialization"

Last but not least, the "social dimensions" of the investment regime have been increasingly stressed. There are two sides of the coin. On the one side, more and more model BITs and actual BITs have expressly carved out regulations in the areas of key social concern such as health, safety, and environment as exceptions to the expropriation rules or the treaty regime in general. For example, the US Model BIT 2004 excludes "non-discriminatory regulatory actions by a Party that are designed and applied to protect legitimate public welfare objectives, such as public health, safety, and the environment" from the scope of "indirect expropriations."[247] The Canadian Model BIT contains similar provisions in Annex B. 13(1), in addition to the "general exceptions" provided in Article 10 relating to health and the protection of the environment. Another example can be found in Article 17 of the Japan-Uzbekistan BIT. On the other side, some recent investment treaties have started to emphasize social responsibilities of foreign investors. For instance, an attempt has been made in the 2007 Norwegian Model BIT draft to include a "best effort" provision promoting "corporate social responsibility."[248] Such efforts, including both sides of the coin, actually serve to improve the balance of the investment regime, by affirming the host state's right on the one hand and promoting the social obligations of foreign investors on the other.

The trend of "socialization" also fits well in the above historical analysis. The nationalist approach before the 1980s was used mainly to serve the "political" needs of the time; the newly emerged states solidly established themselves by exercising their newly found sovereign powers to nationalize foreign investments that controlled their economies. The liberalist approach prevalent in the 1990s served primarily the "economic" needs of the time when almost every state around the world was committed to economic development after each nation's state sovereignty had been solidly established. The current "socialization" campaign adds to the dialogue a third dimension, the "social" dimension of the investment regime. In so doing it aims to establish an investment regime in which the political, economic and social rights and interests of all stakeholders (including not only host states, foreign investors and home states, but also other parties such as local, and indeed, foreign citizens who might have a direct or indirect interest in the regime) are equally respected, promoted and protected (Table 7).

---

[247] US Model BIT 2004, Annex B on Expropriation, point 4(b).

[248] The article reads as follows:

Article [32] corporate social responsibility

The Parties agree to encourage investors to conduct their investment activities in compliance with the OECD Guidelines for Multinational Enterprises and to participate in the United Nations Global Compact.

See Norway Model BIT draft 2007, Article 32. The draft, however, has been shelved by the government in 2009. See Damon Vis-Dunbar, "Norway shelves its draft model bilateral investment treaty," *Investment Treaty News*, 8 June 2009, available at: http://www.investmenttreatynews.org/cms/news/archive/2009/06/08/norway-shelves-its-proposed-model-bilateral-investment-treaty.aspx (last visit on 19 July 2010).

12. General Conclusions

Without repeating the specific findings of this comparative study, several general conclusions might be drawn.

a) The Need for Comparative Analyses Based on In-depth Country-Specific Studies

The importance of comparative analyses based on in-depth country-specific studies should be stressed. International investment law is at a crossroads and demands detailed study. Existing studies tend to be general studies on the subject as a whole. yet with the MFN provisions found in almost every investment treaty, one could not really obtain a thorough understanding of the international and domestic rules applicable to any given case, without in-depth comprehensive country-specific studies. Comparative studies on the basis of such country-specific data could serve as invaluable guides to governmental officials, legal professionals and academics alike. This study is a first attempt towards this direction.

b) The Shift of Paradigm: From "North-South Divide" to "Private-Public Debate"

The study confirms that the primary tension or paradigm of international investment law is shifting from "North-South divide" to "private-public debate," as the investment protection gap between developed and developing states has been significantly closed, whilst the remaining theme of reform and controversy is focused on the balance of rights and obligations of private investors on the one hand and host governments on the other.[249] Thus, not only have developing states adopted special laws to deal with foreign investment, developed states such as Canada, Australia and Greece have done the same. In the traditionally domestic law area of investment admission, many developing states adopted a complete national treatment approach whilst a few developed states are implementing special regimes scrutinizing foreign investment. Hence there is no longer a clear-cut distinction between the approaches adopted in developed and developing states toward foreign investment under domestic laws. Under international treaties, the general standards of treatment of foreign investment are largely harmonized. Although they are still subject to different interpretations, such differences in interpretation do not appear to show a "North-South divide." On the contrary, the debate is now being shifted to the conflicting rights and interests of host states and foreign investors, which is essentially a "private-public debate."[250]

---

[249] For further discussion on the shift of focus, see Wenhua Shan, "From ' North-South Divide' to ' Private-Public Debate,' " *Northwestern Journal of International Law and Business*, 27(3), 2007.

[250] In this connection, it is noted that the Australian Government seems to have adopted a practice to differentiate developed and developing states in their BITs: It includes investor-state dispute settlement (ISDS) with third-party arbitration in agreements with developing countries (e.g. the Australia-Thailand Free Trade Agreement), whilst not including it with developed countries such as the US. However, this practice does not seem to be exceptional and has not been followed by other states. Indeed, the fact that developed states have started to negotiate investment treaties between them is proof of the closing gap between the developed and developing states: Investment treaties are no longer viewed as a tool to open markets of developing states and to provide essential protections, they are becoming a tool of investment promotion and protection universally used to both developed and developing economies. Moreover, it is noted that although the US-Australia FTA does not contain an ISDS provision, it does not completely rule out investor-state dispute settlement. Article 11.16 of the agreement does provide for the possibility of future consultations on the question of investor-state arbitration, including on the development of appropriate procedures for such arbitration. The difference is therefore not so significant as it appears. See Australia Report, Section 9.

Indeed, the three trends identified above all help to confirm that this shift is taking place. "Harmonization" helps to close the gap between the investment regimes of developed and developing states, whilst both "balancing" and "socialization" aim at ensuring the balance of rights and interests of the two primary parties in international investment, namely host states and foreign investors.

Many factors might have contributed to this shift. The most fundamental factor is that "private-public" tension is actually the basic tension underlying the international investment regimes. On the surface, however, the most significant factor is perhaps the change of roles, or the understanding of the roles, of both the developed and developing states in international investment. Facing a considerable number of investment claims, many developed states have now realized that as large recipients of investment they could also be "bitten" by the liberal investment regime they established. They therefore have an equally important interest in protecting the rights of the host state in investment treaties, much as their interest in protecting their investment abroad. On the other hand, some previously pure capital-importing states, such as China, have become noticeable capital exporters.[251] This change of role helps push them to abandon their previously conservative approach and to accept a more liberal international investment regime. Increasingly the two trends, namely the conservative trend of developed states and the liberalist trend of developing states, are converging with each other and, as a result, the previous "North-South divide" is giving way to the current "private-public debate."

c) Future Investment Regime: Liberalist or Protectionist?

It is believed that states will continue to liberalize their investment regimes, but will also try to balance their regimes by asserting, or when necessary strengthening, the regulatory power of the state. In other words, a "balanced liberal regime" might be the outcome of the development. On the one hand, investment liberalization will continue to be pursued by states, given the increasing interdependence of states resulting from the irreversible globalization process. Therefore, new domestic measures will continue to be adopted by states to open their markets, facilitate investment entry and operation. Meanwhile BITs and other IIAs will also increasingly provide protection and promotion of international investment. On the other hand, states will also be more and more ready to exercise their sovereign rights to regulate foreign investments and make sure that the host state benefits from the investment. Accordingly they will be more and more assertive in retaining their regulatory discretion when negotiating or re-negotiating BITs or other IIAs. The surge of investment arbitration cases and the global financial crisis might have significantly contributed to this process.

Both trends can be clearly seen from the data on national regulatory changes recorded by the UNCTAD. On the one hand, the vast majority of regulatory changes continue to be in favor of foreign investors. For example, in 2009, 102 regulatory changes were adopted in the world, of which 71 were favorable to investors. On the other hand, as mentioned above, restrictive legal changes have increased more rapidly, particularly since the beginning of the 21st century.

---

[251] According to UNCTAD, China ranked 13th in the world FDI supplier league table, with an increase of 132% in 2008. This does not take into account FDI outflow from Hong kong, which itself ranked in 10th place in the world. Much of such outward investment from Hong kong is believed to be ultimately originated from mainland China. See World Investment Report 2009: Overview (UNCTAD, 2009), at 6.

The same can also be seen from the most recent developments in investment treaty practice. As Chart 6 demonstrates, on the one hand, states continue to enter into international investment treaties promoting and protecting foreign investments. On the other hand, as mentioned above, states are revising or renegotiating their actual and model investment treaties with a view to preserving their necessary power to regulate foreign investment. It can therefore be argued that the current dual trends of liberalization and balancing will carry on until a "balanced liberal" investment regime is finally achieved.

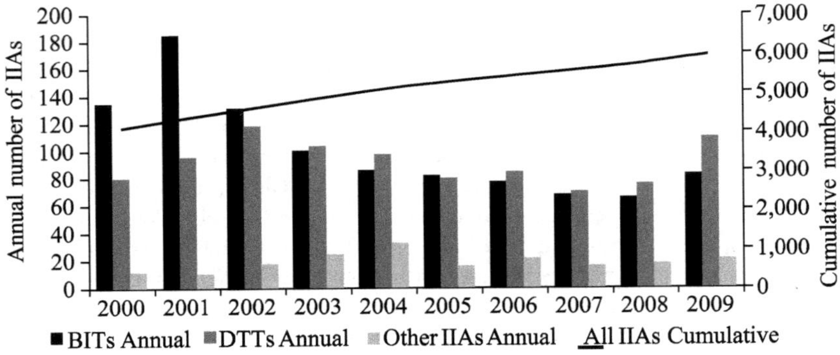

Chart 6 Trends of BITs, DTTs and Other IIAs 2000 – 2009

Source: UNCTAD, *World Investment Report* 2010.

d) Towards a Multilateral Investment Agreement

The current state of the international treaty network for investment protection is commonly and vividly described as a "spaghetti bowl." It can be anticipated that, in the years to come, with more BITs being concluded, the bowl will become larger and larger. But the question is whether such expansion will eventually lead to a multilateral investment agreement (MIA), or merely a larger "spaghetti bowl."

The collapse of multilateral agreement on investment (MAI) negotiations and the stalemate in the Doha Round have led some countries, such as Japan, to partially abandon its "multilateral belief" and promote bilateral or regional free trade agreements instead.[252] However, it is believed that an MIA is a desirable outcome[253] and will be achieved eventually. It is desirable first because it can bring uniformity in the substantive and procedural rules of foreign investment in the world. As observed above, international investment rules have now been harmonized with a set of core obligations being established in the network of BITs. However, beyond that core, there are numerous variations, some of which are rather significant, such as the North American preference for concrete obligations on investment admission and the complete abandonment of dispute resolution provisions in some BITs. An MIA would establish universal rules of foreign investment, which would build a level playing field for foreign investors around the

[252] Japan Report, Section 11.

[253] See e. g., Slovenia Report, Section 11.

globe. Second, an MIA would also be more cost effective in that it could save the resources invested in the negotiation and implementation of the large number of BITs. Third, as the WTO regime demonstrates, less developed states, particularly the least developed states, would be better off relying on a multilateral system. Finally, an MIA would be more comprehensive in coverage so that important players currently left out of the existing system might be attracted to the MIA system because the potential loss would be too large to afford.

The possibility of an MIA has been increased thanks to the following factors. First, the global financial crisis has passed its worst stage and the global economy is on its way to a full recovery, which promises a better economic foundation for a multilateral regime on investment. Second, as demonstrated by the G20 declarations, leaders from the major economies in the world are mindful of the harm of investment protectionism and are committed to investment liberalization. This provides a sound political and institutional foundation for a global pact on investment. Third, international BIT practices have been continuously harmonized. One recent example is the wider acceptance of the FTC interpretation on the meaning of FET standards by states beyond North America. So the legal foundation for such an MIA is becoming more and more solid. Obviously there are still many legal disagreements on which compromises are needed. But it is clear that with the proliferation of BITs and the continuous liberalization of domestic investment regimes, the world is technically much more prepared for an MIA, than say, twenty years ago. Fourth, some major players, particularly the EU and OECD, have announced plans to draft their new model BITs, which could serve as stepping stones toward a global MIA.[254] Finally, since the EU is a major advocate for an MIA, its newly acquired exclusive competence on FDI matters will certainly increase the momentum for the potential MIA.

To achieve such an MIA, three main aspects merit thorough consideration. First, the forum needs to be carefully selected, be it the WTO, OECD, UNCTAD or the World Bank. Second, the interested parties, particularly the main stakeholders, must have a chance to fully participate in the negotiations. An MAI-type of "closed-door" negotiation excluding the majority of the world will not work. Third, again, various interests must be carefully balanced, particularly the interests of the foreign investors on the one hand and the host governments on the other. A one-sided agreement will not be accepted by the world.[255]

Certainly there are details that need to be worked out, which deserve at least another dissertation. But in a globalizing world with international investment serving as life blood, there is every reason to be optimistic about the prospect of an MIA.[256]

---

[254] In a recent conference held in Washington in March 2010, Angel Gurría, the OECD Secretary-General, said that OECD was considering the feasibility of a non-binding "Model Investment Treaty" to avoid an escalation of investment restrictions. See Angel Gurría, The global economy and the global investment agenda—an OECD perspective, available at: http://www.oecd.org/document/0/0,3343,en_2649_34529562_44775040_1_1_1_1,00.html.

[255] For further details of these considerations, see Wenhua Shan, *The Legal Framework of EU-China Investment Relations: A Critical Appraisal* (Hart Publishing 2005), at 270 – 276.

[256] It is interesting to see that the newly published World Investment Report 2010 seems to share the same view, when it notes that development in IIAs in 2009 indicate that "the landscape of the IIA system is consolidating in different respects," "from a rapid expansion of IIAs at the bilateral level to a more integrated, inclusive and elaborate approach." UNCTAD, World Investment Report 2010, at 83 – 85.

Table 1 Legal Framework

Jurisdiction	Special FI Law	International treaties		International treaties vs. domestic law			Transparency	
		BITs	*Multilateral Agreements*	*Transformation*	*Incorporation*	*Partial Incorporation*	*Public Access*	*Public Consultation*
Argentina	(Foreign Investment Law, Law 21382 of 1976)	59	ICSID, New York Convention, MIGA, WTO		√		(Official Ga-zette, Congress's website)	(public hear-ings and comments)
Australia	Foreign Acquisitions and Takeovers Act 1975 (Cth) (the FATA)	23	ICSID, New York Convention, MIGA, WTO	√			(Australasian Legal Informa-tion Institute)	(Parliamen-tary committee system at federal and state levels)
Canada	√ (Investment Canada Act)	28	New York Convention, MIGA, WTO, NAFTA	√		(Customary IL automatically incorporated)	(Access to Informa-tion Act, Privacy Act, Of-ficial Gazette)	(public hear-ing, consultation, and Parliamen-tary committee system at federal and state levels)
China	(EJCL, CJVL, WFEL, etc)	130	ICSID, New York Convention, MIGA, WTO	√			(State Council Gazettes, Official Websites)	(public hear-ing, expert consultation and congress discussions)
Croatia		59	ICSID, New York Convention, MIGA, WTO		√		(Official Ga-zette)	√
Czech Republic		83	ICSID, New York Convention, MIGA, WTO, and the ECT		√		(Law on free access to infor-mation)	/
Ethiopia	(Invest-ment Proc-lamation, etc.)	30	MIGA, COMESA, IGAD		√		(National Gazette, EIA website)	/
France		102	ICSID, New York Convention, MIGA, WTO, and the ECT			EU law has direct effect	√	√

续表

Jurisdiction	Special FI Law	International treaties		International treaties vs. domestic law			Transparency	
		BITs	*Multilateral Agreements*	*Transformation*	*Incorporation*	*Partial Incorporation*	*Public Access*	*Public Consultation*
Germany		139	ICSID, New York Convention, MIGA, WTO, ECT	√		(customary law and general principles of public interna-tional law)	(Official Ga-zette)	(public hearings, expert consultation, etc.)
Greece	√ Legislative Decree 2687/1953	44	ICSID, New York Convention, MIGA, WTO, ECT	√		EU law has direct effect	(Government Gazette, Efimerida tis kyvrniseos)	/
Italy		95	ICSID, New York Convention, MIGA, WTO, ECT	√		EU law has direct effect	(the national Official Journal, etc.)	√
Japan		16	ICSID, New York Convention, MIGA, WTO, ECT			(Self-executing treaties directly applicable)	(government's website)	√
South Korea	(Foreign Investment Promotion Act)	94	ICSID, New York Convention, MIGA, WTO		√		(Official Gazette, internet)	√
Macau		2	ICSID, WTO, MIGA, New York Convention			(direct effect depends on the treaty)	(Official Bulletin)	√
Peru	√ (Legislative Decree No 662 and Decree No 757)	29	WTO, ICSID, MIGA, New York Conventions		√		(official gazette)	/
Portugal		51	ICSID, New York Convention, MIGA, WTO, ECT		√		(publication as a condition for validity)	√

续表

Jurisdiction	Special FI Law	International treaties		International treaties vs. domestic law			Transparency	
		BITs	*Multilateral Agreements*	*Transformation*	*Incorporation*	*Partial Incorporation*	*Public Access*	*Public Consultation*
Russia	(The Law on Investment Activity and the Law on Foreign In-vestments)	67	ICSID, New York Convention, MIGA		√		(Official Gazette, internet)	√
Singapore		41	ICSID, New York Convention, MIGA, WTO		√		(Government Gazette and database)	√
Slovenia	√ (Promotion of Foreign Direct Investment and Interna-tionalisation of Enter-prises Act)	38	ICSID, New York Convention, MIGA, WTO, ECT		√		(Official Gazette, internet)	√
Turkey	(Foreign Direct Investment Law)	80	ICSID, New York Convention, WTO, GATS		√		(Official Gazette and internet)	√
UK		105	ICSID, New York Convention, MIGA, WTO, and the ECT	√		EU law has direct effect.	(Official Gazette and internet)	(a comprehensive system)
USA		40	ICSID, New York Convention, MIGA, WTO			(self-executive directly applicable)	/	/
Total	11	1355		7	11	3		

Table 2　Standards of Treatment

Jurisdiction	Treatment under international treaties						Treatment under domestic law	
	Fair and Equitable Treatment	*National Treatment*	*MFN Treatment*	*International Law Minimum Standard*	*Constant Protection and Security*	*Other Standards*	*National Treatment*	*Other Standards*
Argentina	√	√	√	√	√	/	√	/
Australia	√	√	√	√	√	transparency	√	/
Canada	√	(+ admission)	(+ admission)	√	√	transparency, limitations on performance requirements, nationality requirements for senior officers.	(on property interests under the Citizenship Act)	/
China	√	(recent treaties)	√	√	√	/	√	/
Croatia	√	√	√	√	√	/	√	region and industry-specific incentives
Czech Republic	√	√	√	√	√	/	√	/
Ethiopia	√	√	√	√	√		/	/
France	√	√	√	√	√	/	√	/
Germany	√	√	√	√	√	/	√	/
Greece	√	√	√	√	√	/	√	/
Italy	√	√	√	√	/	/	√	/
Japan	√	(+ admission)	(+ admission)	√	√		√	/

续表

Jurisdiction	Treatment under international treaties						Treatment under domestic law	
	Fair and Equitable Treatment	*National Treatment*	*MFN Treatment*	*International Law Minimum Standard*	*Constant Protection and Security*	*Other Standards*	*National Treatment*	*Other Standards*
South Korea	√	√	√	√	√	/	√	/
Macau	√	√	√	√	√		√	/
Peru	√	√	√	√	√		√	/
Portugal	√	√	√	√	√	/	√	preferential treatment (PIN)
Russia	√	√	√	√	√	/	√	/
Singapore	√	(some)	√	√	√	/	√	/
Slovenia	√	√	√	√	√	/	√	/
Turkey	√	√	√	√	√	/	√	/
UK	√	√	√	√	√	reasonable treatment	√	/
US	√	(+ admission)	(+ admission)	√	√	/	√	/
Total	22	22 (3 + admission)	22 (3 + admission)	22	21	/	21	/

Table 3 Admission and Entry

Jurisdiction	Admission regime		Areas of investment		
	No Special Formality	*Registration/Notification*	*Approval/Authorisation*	*Negative List*	*Positive List*
Argentina	√		"national interest" investments	(Selective/restrictive for investments in certain types of industry and its specific location, particularly in mining, forestry, and the automobile industry.)	
Australia	√		Notification and approval required for defined investments	(defined by FATA and its regulations, including large, sensitive, and urban land projects.)	
Canada		√	Review and approval required for large, cultural and national security investments	(National security investments. Also ownership restrictions in sensitive industries as required by relevant laws.)	
China			√	(All are "Permitted" FI projects unless they fall within the "encouraged," "prohibited" or "restricted" categories stipulated in the Investment Catalogue.)	
Croatia	/	/	Approval required in certain sectors such as banking, insurance, energy, etc.	√	/
Czech Republic	(registering in the Commercial Register for a Trade License)			(Only few areas reserved to protect state interest and individuals.)	
Ethiopia			(licensing)	(By Proclamation 280/2002 and Council Regulation 84/2003.)	

续表

Jurisdiction	Admission regime		Areas of investment		
	No Special Formality	*Registration/Notification*	*Approval/Authorisation*	*Negative List*	*Positive List*
France		(1. a statistical registration with the Banque de France so as to make out the French balance of payments; or 2. a registration with the French minister of economy and finances for the finances department.)		(Some specific strategic areas, listed in article R. 153 – 2 of the French Monetary and Financial Code. A prior authorization from the minister of economy and finance required for such investment.)	
Germany	√	Registration of certain monetary transactions with the German Central Bank (*Deutsche Bundesbank*) for the sake of statistical reports.	Acquisitions of 25% or more of a German enterprise by a foreign undertaking are now subject to scrutiny.	/	/
Greece	/	/	(Approval required by Greek foreign investment law Legislative Decree 2687/1953.)	/	/
Italy	√		Exceptional, only for particular protection purposes such as the field of civil flights.	(Intense controls by national authorities, particularly in regulated industries.)	/
Japan	√		Exceptional, only for investments likely to impair national security, public order, public safety or to bring significant adverse effect to the smooth management of the Japanese economy.	(Areas specified in the Public Notice of the Prime Minister's Office, etc.)	
South Korea		(Notification at Invest Korea (Kotra), etc.)		/	

续表

Jurisdiction	Admission regime			Areas of investment	
	No Special Formality	*Registration/Notification*	*Approval/Authorisation*	*Negative List*	*Positive List*
Macau	√			/	/
Peru	(Registration with PROINVERSION) (na – tional treatment)			(Only few restrictions in fields such as ra-dio andtelevision, commercial airline transportation and marine merchant activi-ties.)	
Portugal	(National treatment)			/	/
Russia		√	The authorization regime was enacted only for enti-ties that have strategic im-portance for ensuring the country's defense capacity and state security.	(The Federal Law of April 29, 2008 N. 57 – FZenumerates 42 kinds of activity.)	
Singapore		(registration pursuant to the Business Registration Act)		(business which is unlawful or prejudicial to public welfare or national security is not allowed)	
Slovenia	(Generally national treatment.)	some forms of foreign invest-ments are subject to registration	Some business activities need authorisation.	√	
Turkey		√		/	/
UK	√		Exceptional	(As stipulated by law such as Industry Act 1975, Enterprise Act 2002.)	
US	√	Registration required for invest-ment in agricultural land	Exceptional	(Industries such as airlines, telecommuni-cation, and other industries deemed to af-fect national security.)	
Total	12	7	3	16	0

Table 4 Investment Contracts under Domestic Law

Jurisdiction	Forms required		Domestic law requirement		Domestic jurisdiction requirement	
	Yes	*No*	*Yes*	*No*	*Yes*	*No*
Argentina		(BOT)	√		√	
Australia		(PPP)	Real estate contracts	√		√
Canada		√	Real estate contracts	√		√
China		(BOT)	√		√	
Croatia		√		√	/	/
Czech Republic		√		√		√
Ethiopia		√		√		√
France		(BOT)		√		√
Germany	/	/	/	/	/	/
Greece		(PPP)	√			√
Italy		√		√		√
Japan		√	√		√	
South Korea		√	/	/	/	/
Macau		√(concession agreement or licensing)	√		√	
Peru		(law contract)	√		/	/
Portugal		√		√		√
Russia	/	/	/	/	/	/
Singapore		√		√		√
Slovenia		(PPP)	(Public-Private Partnership Act 2006)			√
Turkey		(BOT)	/	/		√
UK		√		√		√
US		(economic development contracts)	√			√
Total		20	8	10	4	13

Table 5 Property and Expropriation

Jurisdiction	Protection of property		Conditions for expropriation				Standards for compensation	
	National Treatment	*Other Standards*	*Public Purpose*	*Non-discrimination*	*Due Process of Law*	*Compensation*	*Hull Formula*	*Other Standards*
Argentina	√		√	√	√	√		lost profit excluded
Australia	√		√	√	√	√	√	
Canada	√	BITs offer higher treatment	√	√	√	√	√	‘special economic advantage’ might be added
China	√	Higer treatment under BITs	√	√	√	√		“appropriate compensation” but not materiallydifferent from Hull formula
Croatia	√		√	/	/	√	/	Fair market value
Czech Republic	√		√	√	√	√	√	
Ethiopia	/	/	√	√	√	√	√	
France	√		√	√	√	√	/	Fair compensation under domestic law
Germany	√		√	√	√	√	√	Reasonable compensation under domestic law
Greece	/	/	√	√	√	√	√	
Italy	√		√	√	√	√	/	/
Japan	√		√	√	√	√	√	
South Korea	/	/	/	/	/	/	/	/

续表

Jurisdiction	Protection of property		Conditions for expropriation				Standards for compensation	
	National Treatment	*Other Standards*	*Public Purpose*	*Non-discrimination*	*Due Process of Law*	*Compensation*	*Hull Formula*	*Other Standards*
Macau	√		√	√	√	√		Due compensation
Peru	√		√	√	√	√	√	
Portugal	√		√	/	/	√	/	Just compensation under domestic law
Russia	/	/	/	/	/	/	/	/
Singapore	√	/	√	√	√	√		Compensation shall be valued prior to expropriation
Slovenia	(reciprocal)		√	√	√	√	√	Just compensation
Turkey	√		√	√	√	√	/	(Full and prompt compensation)
UK	√		√	√	√	√	√	" Appropriate compensation " under ECHR
US	√		√	√	√	√	√	"just compensation"
Total	18		20	18	18	20	11	

Table 6 Dispute Settlement

Jurisdiction	National jurisdiction		ICSID Arbitration		Non-ICSID arbitration		National control	
	Special Rules	*General Rules*	*ICSID Membership*	*ICSID Reservations*	*UNCITRAL*	*Others*	*On ICSID Arbitration*	*On other Arbitrations*
Argentina	x	√	√	x	√	(MIGA, ICC)	(constitutionality)	√
Australia	x	√	√	x	√	/	x	√
Canada	x	√	x	x	√	(ICSIDAdditional Facility)	x	√
China	x	√	√	√(notification)	√	(ICC, ICSIDAdditional Facility)	x	√
Croatia	x	√	√	x	√	(MIGA, ICC)	/	√
Czech Republic	x	√	√	x	√	(ICC)	/	/
Ethiopia	x	√	x	x	√	(MIGA, ICC)	/	/
France	x	√	√	x	√	(ICC)	/	/
Germany	x	√	√	x	/	/	x	√
Greece	x	√	√	x	√	/	/	/
Italy	x	√	√	x	√	(MIGA, ICC)		
Japan	x	√	√	x	√	√	(constitutionality)	√
South Korea	/	/	√	/	/	/	/	/
Macau	x	√	√	√(notification)	/	/		√
Peru	x	√	√	x	/	/	/	√
Portugal	x	√	√	/	/	/	/	/
Russia	/	/	√	/	/	/	/	/
Singapore	x	√	√	x	√	(ICC)		
Slovenia	x	√	√	x	√	√		√
Turkey	x	√	√	x	/	/	/	√
UK	x	√	√	x	√	(PCA)	(Registration)	√
US	x	√	√	x	√	√		√
Total	x (20)	√ (20)	√ (20)	x (17)	√ (15)	√ (12)	√ (2)	√ (13)

Table 7 Three Generations of International Investment Regimes: A Comparison

Generation	Principal Feature	Primary Need Served
First Generation (1945 – 1970)	Nationalisation	Political need
Second Generation (1980 – 1990)	Liberalisation	Economic need
Third Generation (2000 –)	Balancing/Socialisation	Social need

Is Calvo Dead? *

The "death" of the Calvo Doctrine is not at all a new topic. As early as 1955, Shea had pronounced its death because the Doctrine "failed to receive recognition as a principle of international law," by which he meant recognition by Western Countries.[1] In the mid1990s, the "imminent death" of this doctrine was again declared due to changing attitudes in Latin American states towards foreign investment as witnessed in their international and domestic law making practice.[2] Now that ten years have passed, have the predictions of "imminent death" come true? This study shows that Calvo is not completely dead, even though it has been, by and large, deactivated.

The article has four Parts. Part I explores the essence and elements of the doctrine, thus setting forth the criteria for assessment; Part II introduces the broader background of the attitude changes in Latin America towards foreign investment and arbitration since the 1980s. Parts III and IV examine international treaty practices and domestic legislation, with a view toward assessing whether and to what extent the Calvo Doctrine is dead. Part V summarizes and concludes the article.

I. CALVO DOCTRINE: ESSENCE AND ELEMENTS

A. The Essence of the Calvo Doctrine

It is often said that the essence of the Calvo Doctrine is "equal treatment/national treatment" or "equality." For example, Donald Shea, probably the most eminent researcher on this theory, has asserted that "these two concepts of non-intervention and absolute equality of foreigners with nationals are the essence of the Calvo Doctrine."[3] Manning-Cabrol, a more recent writer on this principle, has also maintained that "equality is the central tenet of the Calvo Doctrine."[4] Yet while "equality of states," in conjunction with state sovereignty, has provided the legal foundation of the Calvo Doctrine, it in

---

* 55 *American Journal of Comparative Law* 123, 2007 *June-August Issue*.

[1] Donald Shea, The Calvo Clause: A Problem of Inter-American and International Law and Diplomacy 20 (1955).

[2] Denise Manning-Cabrol, *The Imminent Death of the Calvo Clause and the Rebirth of the Calvo Principle: Equality of Foreign and National Investors*, 26 LAw & PoL'Y INT'L Bus. 1169(1995).

[3] SHEA, *supra* note 1, at 19 – 20.

[4] It is noted that the doctrine embraced two levels of equality, namely "equality of nation-states or the equal treatment of nationals and foreigners." *See* ManningCabrol, *supra* note 2, at 1172.

itself does not fundamentally characterize Calvo. Instead of emphasizing "absolute equality" between states or between nationals and foreigners, the Calvo Doctrine actually emphasizes rejection of superiority or imperial prerogatives of powerful states and their nationals. In other words, the Calvo Doctrine is essentially "anti-superstate" or "anti-super-national-treatment," focusing on the opposition and rejection of any discriminatory treatment by western powers against weak, developing host states and their nationals, as compared to the treatment those western power accord each other and demand for their citizens in these host states. Unlike "equal/national treatment," "anti-super-national-treatment" does not deny or reject the special privileges that host countries often grant or reserve to their own nationals. A close reading of Calvo's writing supports this distinction: though he did use equality of states and individuals as the legal basis of his arguments, what he specifically rejected was special privileges enjoyed by foreign states and their nationals, not the privileges that a national might enjoy in his or her home state based on citizenship. For instance, he wrote,

The rule that in more than one case it has been attempted to impose on American states is that foreigners merit *more regard and privileges more marked and extended* than those accorded even to the nationals of the country where they reside. This principle is intrinsically contrary to the law of equality of nations... To admit that in the present case governmental responsibility, that is the principle of an indemnity, is to create *an exorbitant and fatal privilege, essentially favorable to the powerful states and injurious to the weaker nations,* establishing an unjustifiable inequality between nationals and foreigners.[5]

He then concluded that "the responsibility of governments towards foreigners cannot be *greater* than that which these governments have towards their own citizens."[6]

Calvo's "anti-super-state" or "anti-super-national-treatment" approach is reified in the widely used "Calvo Clauses" in domestic constitutions and laws, and in bilateral and regional treaties; such lauses often highlight that the treatment of foreigners and foreign investors should be "no more favorable than" that accorded to national and national investors, as we will see below in Section I. C. The "anti-super-national-treatment" approach of Calvo can be explained by the specific background against which this theory was developed. *As* Shea pointed out, the Calvo Doctrine was born at a time when "strong logical, moral and legal defenses" were badly needed in Latin American countries, which then were facing "real or imagined abuses of either diplomatic protection of aliens living within their territories or armed intervention in behalf of their foreign creditors" and which were unable to resist by force.[7]

Characterizing the Calvo Doctrine as supportive of "anti-superstate" and "anti-super-national-treatment" rather than of "equality" or "national treatment" not only more accurately reveals the focus of this theory, but also distinguishes Calvo from the "national treatment" standard frequently used in Bilateral Investment Treaties (BITs). Indeed,

---

[5] SHEA, *supra* note 1, at 18.

[6] Id., at 19.

[7] Id., at 14.

although both standards highlight the value of "equality" and therefore are often confused by commentators,[8] the "anti-super-national-treatment" under the Calvo Doctrine and the "national treatment" under BITs actually represent the two extremes of the spectrum of "equality": while the former focuses on the elimination of discrimination against host states and their nationals, the latter emphasizes the abandonment of discrimination against foreigners.[9] The distinct character of the "national treatment" principle in BITs is evidenced by the use of the expression "treatment *no less favorable than* that accorded to national investors" in most BITs, provisions which might better be characterized as "anti-inferior-national-treatment." Nevertheless, these two distinctive principles might converge and unite as one principle under the umbrella of the principle of "equality" or "national treatment." This is particularly the case when the phrase "the same treatment" is used; as will be discussed below, this appears to be what happened in the 1990s in Latin America.

B. Key Elements of the Calvo Doctrine

The essence of the Calvo Doctrine may be broken down into two key elements: a substantive sense and a procedural sense.[10] In the substantive sense, the Calvo Doctrine emphasizes that host states shall not grant foreigners any rights or benefits greater than those they accord to their own nationals. This carries both specific and abstract implications: on a specific or practical level, it prohibits the provision of any special privileges or incentives to foreigners and foreign investors by a host state; on an abstract or theoretical level, it rejects the so-called "international minimum standard" as a standard of law applicable to the treatment of foreigners including foreign investors. In the procedural sense, the Calvo Doctrine emphasizes that foreigners shall not be entitled to any remedies other than those available to nationals of a host state. It therefore implies a rejection of both non-local remedies (i. e., foreign or international remedies including diplomatic protection or military intervention) and non-local laws (i. e., foreign or international law) as applicable laws. *As* a procedural requirement, the rejection of non-local laws echoes and coincides with the substantive law requirement of rejection of an "international minimum standard." The two requirements may therefore be regarded as one element. It can thus be seen that the Calvo Doctrine indeed takes a very classic, state-centric view of international law, based on an absolutist view of state sovereignty and equality of states.

---

[8] For example, Manning-Cabrol considers national treatment in international investment treaties to be the same as the "equal/national treatment" principle enshrined in the Calvo Doctrine, and argues that Calvo found new life in such treaties (as well as in domestic legislation). *See* Manning-Cabrol, *supra* note 2, p. 1195.

[9] Zamora also noted such a distinction between the two principles and has pointed out that, "[U]nlike concepts of national treatment, however, the Calvo Doctrine was created to address the perceived favoritism granted to foreigners, rather than discrimination against them. In other words, the purpose of the Calvo Doctrine is to bring foreigners down to the level of nationals, while the purpose of national treatment is to raise them up to the level of nationals." *See* Stephen Zamora, *Allocating Legislative Competence in The Americas: The Early Experience under NAFTA and the Challenge of Hemispheric Integration*, 19 Haus. J. INT'L L. 615, 622 (1997).

[10] Kenneth J. Vandevelde, *Sustainable Liberalism and the International Investment Regime*, 19 MrcH. J. INT'L L. 373, 379 (1998).

In short, the Calvo Doctrine effectively means, on the one hand, a rejection of special substantive privileges to foreigners and foreign investors ("no super-national treatment"), including specific incentives and benefits and in an abstract sense the "international minimum standard" of treatment they allegedly may enjoy; and, on the other hand, a rejection of any special procedural privileges to foreigners, including recourse to non-local remedies and the applicability of non-local laws. More specifically, the rejection of special substantive and procedural privileges for foreigners may be described in three basic elements, namely the "anti-super-national-treatment" standard, exclusive local jurisdiction, and exclusion of diplomatic protection,[11] with the first being the substantive requirement, and the latter two the procedural requirements. As the substantive standard for the doctrine, the "anti-super-national-treatment" standard may thus be regarded as the body of the norm, while "exclusive local jurisdiction" and "exclusion of diplomatic protection" may be regarded as the legs on which the body stand, or the arms without which the body could not effectively operate. In a sense, the procedural aspects of the Calvo Doctrine, namely "exclusive local jurisdiction" and "exclusion of diplomatic protection," are actually more important than the substantive aspect, the "anti-super-national-treatment" standard.

C. The Calvo Doctrine and Calvo Clause

The Calvo Doctrine understandably did not win acceptance by European and U. S. governments and lawyers, as it not only eliminates the possibility of abusing diplomatic protection, but also "[e] liminate[s] the institution itself, without substituting an acceptable alternative."[12] Latin American states, on the other hand, "enthusiastically received" this doctrine and, as a countermeasure to the rejection of the doctrine by western powers, they resorted to "Calvo Clauses" to enforce it.[13] Calvo Clauses typically can be found in constitutions, domestic legislation, international treaties and contracts signed between foreign investors and Latin American governments.[14] The 1933 constitution of Peru, for example, included the following article:

Article 31. Property, whoever maybe the owner, is governed exclusively by the laws of the Republic and is subject to the taxes, charges, and limitations established in the laws themselves.

The same provision regarding property applies to aliens as well as Peruvians, except

---

[11] Such factors are also the three key elements of the Calvo Clause, see Manning-Cabrol, *supra* note 2, at 1173. However, according to Lipstein, the Calvo Clause has five elements: "submission to local jurisdiction, free choice oflaw, sphere of application, waiver of protection by home state and surrender of rights under international law." *See* Kurt Lipstein, *The Place of the Calvo Clause in International Law*, 22 BRIT. Y. B. INT'L L. 130, 131 – 33 (1945). Wesley likewise observes that there are five common provisions in the clause: "(1) Submission to local jurisdiction; (2) application oflocal law; (3) assimilation of foreigners for purposes oflocal contractual arrangements; (4) waiver of diplomatic protection by the foreigner's home state; and (5) surrender of rights arising under international law." Roger C. Wesley, *The Procedural Malaise of Foreign Investment Disputes in Latin America: From Local Tribunals to Fact-finding*, 7 LAw & PoL'Y INT'L Bus. 813, 818 (1975).

[12] SHEA, *supra* note 1, at 20.

[13] Id. at 21.

[14] Id. at 21 – 32.

that in no case may the said aliens make use of their exceptional position or resort to diplomatic appeals.[15]

A piece of Ecuadorian legislation from 1938 likewise stipulated that:

[f]oreigners, by the act of coming to the country, subject themselves to the Ecuadorian laws without any exception. They are consequently subject to the Constitution, laws, jurisdiction and police of the Republic, and may in no case, nor for any reason, avail themselves of their status as foreigners against the said conditions, jurisdiction, and police.[16]

As an example of a "Calvo Clause" implemented by contract, the contract between Mexico and the North American Dredging Company of Texas contained the following provision:

Article 18: The Contractor and all persons, who as employees or in any capacity may be engaged in the execution of the work under this contract either directly or indirectly, shall be considered as Mexicans in all matters, within the Republic of Mexico, concerning the execution of such work and the fulfillment of this contract. *They shall not claim, nor shall they have, wither regard to the interests and the business connected with this contract, any other rights or means to enforce the same than those granted by the laws of the Republic of Mexicans, nor shall they enjoy any other rights than those established in favor of Mexicans. They are consequently deprived of any rights as aliens, and under no conditions shall the intervention of foreign diplomatic agents be permitted, in any matter related to this contract.*[17]

The Calvo Doctrine was also fully embodied in international treaties,[18] particularly in regional integration arrangements within Latin America. For example, Decision 24, the first foreign investment code of the Andean Pact countries, forbade Andean Community member countries from "granting to foreign investors any treatment more favorable than that granted to national investors"[19] and required that "in no instrument relating to investments or the transfer of technology shall there be clauses that remove possible conflicts or controversies from the national jurisdiction and competence of the recipient country or allow the subrogation by States to the rights and actions of their national investors."[20]

The Calvo Doctrine was first embraced in Latin America, but its influence has gone well beyond that quarter of the world, particularly after World War II when a number of new states emerged in Asia and Africa as the result of the decolonization process. These newly independent states, like Latin American states, were more than ready to embrace

---

[15] *Constitution of* 9 *April* 1933, *in* CONSTITUTIONS OF THE AMERICAS 670 – 71 (Russell H. Fitzgibbon ed., 1948), as cited in *id.* at 24.

[16] SHEA, *supra* note 1, at 26 and n. 56 (with sources for further examples of such constitutional provisions).

[17] SHEA, *supra* note 1, at 29 (emphasis added).

[18] For an extensive list of such treaties, see *id.* at 23 and n. 44.

[19] Art. 50, Decision 24. Andean Commission: Decision 24, Common Regime of Treatment of Foreign Capital and of Trademarks, Patents, Licenses, and Royalties, art. 50, Nov. 30, 1976, 16 I. L. M. 138, at 153 (1977) [hereinafter Decision 24).

[20] Art. 51, Decision 24.

this state-centric or absolutist international law theory that they believed would help safeguard their state interest, particularly by taking back control over natural resources within their territories that were previously controlled by developed western powers. Meanwhile, communist governments that formed the Soviet block also found this theory appealing, as it would help them expel and exclude the presence and influence of Western capitalists. As a result, "Calvo Clauses" have been embedded in the domestic laws of developing states beyond Latin America, especially in Asian and African states. For example, Chinese law dealing with foreign related contracts, since 1986 and as stands today, has a "Calvo Clause," which provides that all Sino-foreign equity joint venture contracts, Sino-foreign cooperative joint venture contracts and Sino-foreign contracts for the joint exploration and development of natural resources, shall be governed by Chinese law and subject to the exclusive jurisdiction of Chinese courts.[21] Furthermore, a Calvo Clause was also included in United Nations General Assembly (UNGA) resolutions when the New International Economic Order (NIEO) movement reached its summit, when the aforementioned two forces, namely the newly emerged states and the soviet block, formed a united front in the 1960s with a vast majority in the U. N.[22] Article 2 (2) of UNGA Resolution 3281confirms, on the one hand, states' rights to regulate foreign investment in accordance with their respective laws and regulations and to reject the granting of preferential treatment to foreign investment. On the other hand, it stipulates that in case of expropriation, compensation should be paid by the state adopting such measures, "taking into account its relevant laws." Resolution 3281 might therefore be *regarded as a global version of a "Calvo Clause"*.[23] The Calvo Doctrine thus reached its historical high in this Resolution.

However, the acceptance by an overwhelming majority of U. N. members in Resolution 3281 did seem to have secured a permanent international footing for this principle. Not long after the Resolution was adopted, the world was swept by the tides of economic liberalization and globalization. The Calvo Doctrine faced severe challenges ahead, which brought it to the brink of death.

II. INVESTMENT LIBERALIZATION AND LATIN AMERICAN STATES

Investment liberalization, as a manifestation of economic liberalization and globalization, started to sweep the developing world in the 1980s and reached its peak in the

[21] See art. 126 of the Contract Law of the People's Republic of China (stating that such contracts should be governed only by Chinese law) and art. 246 of the Civil Procedural Law of the People's Republic of China (stating that any disputes arising out of such contracts should only be subject to the jurisdiction of Chinese courts).

[22] Vandevelde, *supra* note 10, at 384.

[23] Lillich noted that Latin American efforts on the Charter were "no more than a thinly-disguised attempt to endow the Calvo Doctrine." *See* Richard Lillich, *The Diplomatic Protection of Nationals Abroad: An Elementary Principle of International Law Under Attack*, 69 AM. J. INT'L L. 359, 361 (1975). Schneiderman considers that the Calvo Doctrine was "a central plank of the new International Economic Order (UNGA 3171 of the 1973) and the UN Charter of Economic Rights and Duties of States (1974)"; David Schneiderman, *Investment Rules and The New Constitutionalism*, 25 LAw & Soc. INQUIRY 757, 766 (2000).

1990s. A number of factors contributed to this phenomenon, the most important among which were believed to be the debt crises of developing states since early 1980s (hence a further hunger for foreign direct investment, or "FDI"), the collapse of the Soviet block in the 1990s (hence a further boost of market oriented economic reform in the former USSR and Eastern European countries), and the success stories of "Asian Tigers" characterized by private investment and export trade.[24]

One of the most important elements of investment liberalization is the liberalization of regulatory regimes of foreign investment. According to the World Investment Report 2005, since 1991, an average of 64 states per year made changes to their FDI laws and regulations. Among the 2, 156 changes during that period, 2, 006 were changes for more liberal investment regimes, accounting for 93 percent of the total changes.[25] (Table 1) Another element of investment liberalization has been the sharp rise of BITs. UNCTAD statistics show that by the end of 2004, the number of BITs worldwide had reached 2, 392, of which 2, 010 were concluded in the 1990s, with 1996 being the peak year in terms of the number of new BITs.[26] (Tables 2 - 3) Meanwhile, states have been very active in entering into bilateral, regional and trans-regional preferential trade and investment agreements (PTIAs). By April 2005, 212 such agreements had also been coneluded, of which about 87 percent were signed in the 1990s.[27] These PTIAs differ from BITs in their coverage, yet they resemble the latter in their content on investment protection and liberalization. They almost invariably guarantee national and most favored nation (MFN) treatment, free transfer of funds and profits, compensation for expropriation, and resort to international arbitration tribunals in case of disputes between a foreign investor and the host state. In other words, these bilateral, regional and multilateral treaties aim to set standards at the international level and to guarantee access to international dispute settlement platforms, both of which run in the opposite direction of the Calvo Doctrine.

Table 1 Changes in Domestic Legislations (1991 - 2004)

Year	Number of countries changed FDI laws	Number of changes made to FDI laws	Changes in favor offoreign investors	Changes detrimental to foreign investors
1991	35	82	80	2
1992	43	79	79	0
1993	57	102	101	1
1994	49	110	108	2
1995	64	112	106	6

[24] Vandevelde, *supra* note 10, at 386 - 91.

[25] UNCTAD, *World Investment Report* 2005, UNCTAD/WIR/2005, at 26.

[26] Ibid., at 28.

[27] Id.

续表

Year	Number of countries changed FDI laws	Number of changes made to FDI laws	Changes in favor offoreign investors	Changes detrimental to foreign investors
1996	65	114	98	16
1997	76	151	135	16
1998	60	145	136	9
1999	63	140	131	9
2000	69	150	147	3
2001	71	208	194	14
2002	70	248	236	12
2003	82	244	220	24
2004	102	271	235	36

Source: *UNCTAD World Investment Report* 2005, p. 26.

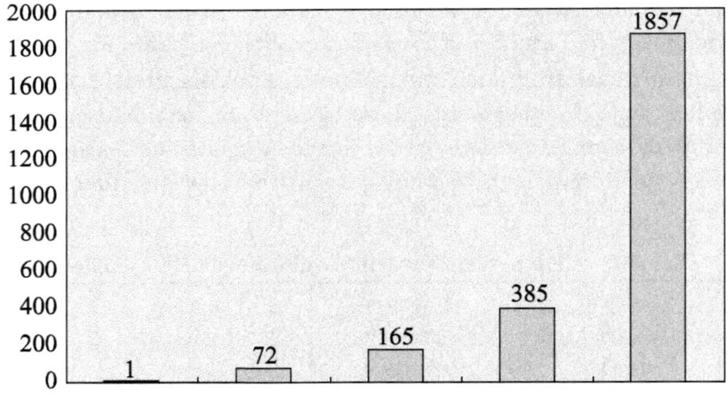

Chart 1 INCREASE IN BITs (1959 – 1999)

Source: *UNCTAD: Bilateral Investment Treaties (*1959 – 1999*)*, UNCTAD/ITE/IW2 (2000), p. 1.

It is not a surprise that Latin American states had initially resisted investment liberalization and such treaties. However, economic events in the 1980s, principally the Latin American debt crisis, forced many Latin American countries to shift their attention from commercial loans back to foreign direct investment (FDI). The debt crisis caused "drastic reductions in net voluntary commercial bank lending to LDCs."〔28〕〔29〕 These reductions

〔28〕 LDC here stands for Less Developed Countries.

〔29〕 *See* Stijn Claessens, *Alternative Forms of External Finance* (World Bank, Working Paper No. 812, 1991).

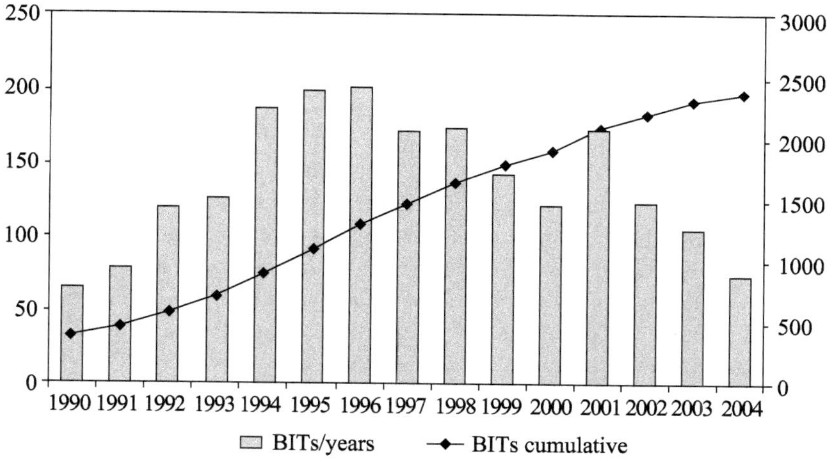

Chart 2 BITs (1990 – 2004)

Source: *World Investment Report* 2005, p. 27.

forced the LDCs to correct their external balances and seek alternative forms of external financing, most notably FDI.[30] Meanwhile, the worldwide trend of investment liberalization rendered the Latin American state no choice but to open up their markets and adopt higher standards of treatment for foreign investors to attract foreign investment.[31] Consequently, many Latin American countries began to conclude international investment treaties in the late 1980s, while modifying their domestic legislation to accommodate international arbitration and international standards of treatment for foreign investment. A close look follows in the next two Parts, examining these international treaties and domestic laws respectively.

III. INTERNATIONAL INVESTMENT TREATIES BY LATIN AMERICAN STATES

In the last couple of decades, Latin American states have been active in entering into international investment treaties at all levels: bilateral, regional and global. The following explores the three levels of treaties in turn and assess how far they have deviated from the Calvo Doctrine.

A. Bilateral Investment Treaties (BITs)

UNCTAD Statistics show that Latin American states did not engage in BITs until

---

[30] The term "alternative finance" refers to "all forms of external financing outside the public sector… [Alternative finance] thus includes FDI, project lending, portfolio investment, closed-end equity funds, private non-guaranteed debt, licensing, joint ventures, quasi-equity contracts, and other forms of private-to-private lending." Id.

[31] Some economists considered that such a change marked a rejection of the import substitution model of the 1950s, 1960s, and 1970s, and the emergence of a development model. *See generally,* THE MACROECONOMICS OF POPULISM IN LATIN AMERICA (Rudiger Dornbusch & Sebastian Edwards eds., 1991), and VICTOR BULMER-THOMAS, THE ECONOMIC HISTORY OF LATIN AMERICA SINCE INDEPENDENCE (1994).

the late 1980s.[32] By the end of the 1990s, Latin American states had entered into a total of 300 BITs, of which 93 percent were signed in the 1990s.[33] With the exception of Brazil and Colombia, all Latin American states have ratified some BITs; Argentina lead the field with 43 ratified BITs, followed by Peru with 24 BITs, Chile (22), Cuba (19), Ecuador (18), Venezuela (17), Bolivia (15), Paraguay (15), Uruguay (13), and El Salvador (10).[34] The remaining states have also ratified BITs, including Panama (9), Mexico (3), Honduras (3), Nicaragua (3), Belize (2), Costa Rica (3), Guiana (2) and Dominica Republic (1).[35] Like all other BITs, BITs by Latin American states contain two categories of provisions: substantively, they accept general standards of treatment such as fair and equitable treatment, national treatment and MFN treatment, free transfer of funds and guarantee of compensation in case of expropriation; procedurally, they accept the jurisdiction of international arbitration tribunals.[36]

It has been observed that the early BITs by Latin American states still had elements influenced by Calvo, requiring certain conditions to be fulfilled before recourse to international arbitration.[37] For example, earlier Argentine BITs required that submission to international arbitration might not be initiated until the issue had been submitted to a local court, and either the local court decided the issue, or the issue did not receive a verdict from the local court after the lapse of certain period of time.[38] In other words, resorting to local remedies was the prerequisite for launching international arbitration. Such local remedies requirements, however, were abandoned in later BIT practice. The Argentina-U.

---

〔32〕 UNCTAD, *Bilateral Investment Treaties* 1959 – 1999, UNCTAD/ITE/IIA/2, at 15 (2000). According to UNCTAD, however, the total number of BITs concluded by Latin American and Caribbean States reached 451 by the end of 2004. *See* UNCTAD: *Recent Developments in International Investment Agreements,* IIA MONITOR No. 2 (Aug. 30, 2005) UNCTAD/WEB/ITE/IIT/2005/1, at 2.

〔33〕 UNCTAD, *Bilateral Investment Treaties* 1959 – 1999, UNCTAD/ITE/IIA/2, at 15 (2000).

〔34〕 UNCTAD, *Bilateral Investment Treaties* 1959 – 1999, *supra* note 32, at 7 – 14.

〔35〕 Some countries have signed some BITs without ratifying any of them. For example, Brazil and Colombia have signed 14 and 6 BITs respectively, but neither of them has ratified any of them. UNCTAD, *Country-specific Lists of BITs, available at* http://www.unctad.orgfl'emplates/Page.asp?intltemlD = 2344&lang = l (last visited June 14, 2006). For an analysis on the legal effects of such un-ratified BITs, see UNCTAD: *Recent Developments in International Investment Agreements, supra* note 32, at 8. For a more elaborate discussion on its implication on the consent to international arbitration, see Ceskoslovenska Obchodni Banka, A. S. v. The Slovak Republic (ICSID Case No. ARB/97/4), Decision on the Further and Partial Objection to Jurisdiction (Dec. 1, 2000), paras. 33 – 59. The text of this Decision is published online as it appears in Vol. 15, No. 2 issue of ICSID Review-Foreign Investment Law Journal (2000): http://www.worldbank.org/icsid/cases/csob.pdf (last visited Feb. 5, 2007). In this case, the relevant BIT was signed but not ratified, and the Arbitration Tribunal held that state consent to submission to ICSID arbitration could not be established on the basis of the BIT. The Tribunal nevertheless found such consent was given by the Czech Government by way of the Consolidation Agreement entered into between the parties expressing that the Agreement should be governed by domestic laws and the BIT.

〔36〕 Jeswald W. Salacuse, *BIT by BIT: The Growth of Bilateral Investment Treaties and Their Impact on Foreign Investment in Developing Countries,* 24 INT'L LAw. 655, 664 – 73 (1990).

〔37〕 In a recent article, Scheurer called this one of "Calvo's grandchildren." Christoph Scheurer, *Calvo's Grandchildren: The Return of Local Remedies in Investment Arbitration,* 4 LAW AND PRACTICE OF INTERNATIONAL COURTS AND TRIBUNALS 1, at 3 – 5 (2005).

〔38〕 Bernardo M. Cremades, *Disputes Arising out of Foreign Direct Investment in Latin America: A New Look at the Calvo Doctrine and Other Jurisdictional Issues,* 59 DISPUTE RESOLUTION JOURNAL 78, 80 (2004).

S. A. BIT of 1991, for example, does not require exhaustion of local remedies as a prerequisite.[39] One commentator concluded, therefore, that this BIT signaled "the abandonment, by Argentina, of the Calvo Doctrine which has governed for more than a century investments from abroad."[40]

In the other 11 BITs entered into between the U. S. and the Latin American states, including Bolivia, Ecuador, El Salvador, Grenada, Haiti, Honduras, Jamaica, Nicaragua, Panama, Trinidad and Tobago and Uruguay (See Table 4), submission to international arbitration is not conditioned on prior recourse to local remedies.[41] With regard to applicable law, although most of these BITs do not refer to specific applicable laws, they generally require the BITs not prejudicing legal effects of domestic laws of the host state, any investment agreement or investment licenses, as well as any "international legal obligations."[42] The Uruguay-U. S. A. BIT signed in 2004 (the first U. S. BIT since its 2004 model was released) went further, stipulating in Articles 3 to 10 that the current BIT itself, as well as applicable rules of international law, will be the applicable law in case of alleged violation of the substantive obligations contained in the BIT; if the claim involves violation of an investment agreement or investment authorization, then the applicable law will be the "rules of law" specified in the pertinent investment agreement or investment authorization, or the rules of law to which the disputing parties may otherwise agree. If such rules of law have not been specified or otherwise agreed, then the applicable law will be "(i) the law of the respondent, including its rules on the conflict of laws; and (ii) such rules of international law as may be applicable."[43] In other words, applicable international law is one of the default rules of law to be applied, unless the dispute involves an investment agreement or investment authorization, in which case the rules of law are otherwise specified or agreed upon.

The previous survey of BITs concluded by Latin American states shows that, while earlier BITs were somewhat influenced by the Calvo principle (requiring resort to local remedies as a prerequisite to international arbitration), recent BITs have generally accepted nonlocal remedies and general international law as the governing norms, departing significantly from the Calvo principle. Indeed, a "silent revolution" has taken place, particularly in the sense that some BITs accept international arbitration for state-investor disputes.[44]

---

[39] Art. 7, Argentina-U. S. BIT.

[40] Heribert Golsong, Introduction to Treaty Concerning the Reciprocal Encouragement and Protection of Investment between Argentina and the USA, Nov. 14, 1991, 31 I. L. M. 124 (1991).

[41] See art. 9, Bolivia-U. S. BIT; art. 6, Ecuador-U. S. BIT; art. 9, El Salvador-U. S. BIT; art. 6, Grenada-U. S. BIT; art. 7, Haiti-U. S. BIT; art. 9, Honduras-U. S. BIT; art. 6, Jamaica-U. S. BIT; art. 7, Nicaragua-U. S. BIT; art. 1, 2000 Amending Protocol to Paraguay-U. S. BIT; art. 9, Trinidad and Tobago-U. S. BIT; and art. 24, Uruguay-U. S. BIT.

[42] *See, e. g.*, art. 10, Argentina-U. S. BIT.

[43] Art. 30, Uruguay-US BIT.

[44] Nigel Blackaby et al., *Overview of Regional Developments, in* INTERNATIONAL ARBITRATION IN LATIN AMERICA, at 10 (Nigel Blackaby et al. eds., 2002).

Table 2 U. S. BITs WITH LATIN AMERICAN STATES

Partner	Date of Signature	Date of entry into force
Argentina	14 – Nov – 91	28 – 0ct – 94
Bolivia	17 – Apr – 98	6 – Jun – 01
Ecuador	27 – Aug – 93	11 – May – 97
El Salvador	10 – Mar – 99	
Grenada	2 – May – 86	3 – Mar – 89
Haiti	13 – Dec – 83	
Honduras	1 – Jul – 95	11 – Jul – 01
Jamaica	4 – Feb – 94	7 – Mar – 97
Nicaragua	1 – Jul – 95	
Panama	27 – 0ct – 82	30 – May – 91
Trinidad and Tobago	26 – Sep – 94	26 – Dec – 96
Uruguay	4 – Nov – 05	

Source: *UNCTAD: Total number of Bilateral Investment Agreements concluded by United States, June* 1, 2005, *available at: http://www.unctad.org/Templates/Page.asp*? intltemID = 2344& lang = l(last visited May 27, 2006).

B. Regional Arrangements

Regional integration in Latin America dates back to the 1960s when some Latin American states entered into the Andean Pact.[45] However, the liberalization movement in Latin American states has resulted in some changes to the Andean Pact since the late 1980s. Decision 24, the original FDI code of the Andean Pact, as mentioned above, had two distinctive "Calvo Clauses" (Articles 50 and 51) prohibiting the provision of "supernational treatment" to foreign investors and recourse to remedies of foreign jurisdiction. However, these two clauses were gradually changed in the late 1980s and early 1990s. In 1987, the Andean Group modified its FDI code and replaced it with Decision 220, which maintained the "anti-super-nationaltreatment" provision[46] but loosened the strict nation-

〔45〕 The recent wave of regional integration within that region, however, demonstrated a marked difference from the original Andean Pact movement, in that it no longer sticks to the nationalistic approach and import substitution policies but places the emphases on market forces. Sebastian Edwards, *Latin American Economic Integration: A New Perspective on an Old Dream*, 16 WORLD ECONOMY 317 (1993).

〔46〕 Art. 33 of Decision 220 provided that "member countries could not grant foreign investors more favorable treatment than that granted to national investors." It is noted that although art. 33's text differed slightly from that of art. 50, the effects were identical: foreign investors were not to be granted rights greater than those granted to nationals. *See* Eduardo A. Wiesner, *ANCOM: A New Attitude toward Foreign Investment*?, U. MIAMI INTER-AM. L. REV. 435, 447 (1993).

al jurisdiction requirement. Article 34 of Decision 220 provided that, "[f] or the settlement of disputes or conflicts deriving from direct foreign investments or from the transfer of foreign technology, Member Countries shall apply the provisions established in their local legislation."[47] It thus left member states discretion to stick to or derogate from the Calvo Doctrine. This, nevertheless, leaves doubt as to whether investors in the Andean Pact countries are still limited to taking recourse in national law and tribunals, given that "anti-super-national-treatment" provision survived.[48]

The Andean Group's alleged shift in attitude toward foreign investment occurred in 1991 when Decision 291,[49] the latest and most liberal FDI code, was adopted. In an attempt to stimulate foreign capital and technology flows into sub-regions of the Andean Community (ANCOM), the Andean Group relaxed the "anti-super-national-treatment" provision in the previous FDI codes.[50] Article 2 of Decision 291 provides that "foreign investors shall have the same rights and obligations as pertain to national investors, except as otherwise provided in the legislation of each Member Country."[51] Apart from allowing member countries discretion in deciding the treatment of foreign investors, this provision also marked a subtle change of emphasis from "anti-super-national-treatment" towards "equal treatment" or "national treatment," which are closer to the national treatment standards embedded in most BITs. Hence it might be an example of the said "convergence" of the two originally distinct standards of "equal" and "national" treatment. Decision 220 and Decision 291 thus opened the possibility for ANCOM member countries to accept international standards of treatment and the jurisdiction of international arbitration tribunals. It is therefore essential to look into the domestic legislation of member states to ascertain the extent of such change of attitude, which will follow in Part IV.

Another example of regional integration is MERCOSUR, the Common Market of the South created in 1991 by four countries in Latin America: Argentina, Brazil, Paraguay and Uruguay.[52] MERCOSUR adopted two Protocols that use more or less the same lan-

---

[47] Art. 34, the Common Foreign Investment and Technology Licensing Code, Decision 220 of May 11, 1987, Commission of the Cartagena Agreement, *reprinted in* 27 I. L. M. 974 (1988) [hereinafter Decision 220].

[48] One commentator argued that, while Decision 220 did not completely denounce the Calvo principle, it nevertheless denied "an ANCOM passport to roam the Andes at will." However, another commentator argued that, "[I] f, as this article argues, national laws only permit the settlement of disputes before local courts and under local laws, then Calvo's other principle that there is no right to diplomatic protection must also survive." *See* Ewell E. Murphy, Jr., *The Andean Decisions on Foreign Investment: An International Matrix of National Law*, 24 INT'L LAW 643, 653 (1990); and Wiesner, *supra* note 46, at 448 – 49.

[49] Commission of the Cartagena Agreement: Decision 291, Common Code for the Treatment of Foreign Capital and Trademarks, Patents, Licenses, and Royalties, Mar. 21, 1991, *reprinted in* 30 I. L. M. 1283 (1991) [hereinafter Decision 291].

[50] Art. 2, Decision 291.

[51] Id.

[52] For the basic treaty of Mercosur, see Treaty Establishing a Common Market between the Argentine Republic, the Federal Republic of Brazil, the Republic of Paraguay and the Eastern Republic of Uruguay, *available at* http:/164.233.183.104/search? q = cache: lrC6UFek7KAJ: www.sice.oas.org/trade/mrcsr/mrcsrtoc.aspercosur&hl = zh-CN&ct = clnk&cd = 7 (last visited June 16, 2006).

guage, regulating investment between member states and from non member states: respectively, the Buenos Aires Protocol (extrabloc) and the Colonia Protocol (intrabloc). The Protocol regulating investments from non-member states (the Buenos Aires Protocol)[53] provides in Article 2(c) for national treatment, MFN treatment and "just and equitable treatment" for foreign investment. The terms "national treatment" and "MFN treatment" are typical BIT language, meaning, respectively, treatment "no less favorable" than that granted to national investors or investors from other non-member states.[54] With regard to state-investor dispute resolution, Article 2(h) of the Protocol provides a "fork in the road" clause, which avails investors of choosing between two options: either competent courts of the host state, or an international arbitration tribunal, which may be either an ad hoe or an institutional tribunal.[55] Since the Protocol uses local remedies only as a conclusive alternative to international arbitration, it differs significant from the Calvo principle of "exclusive local remedies." The Protocol goes on to stipulate that the governing law of such disputes must include the terms of the present Protocol, the laws of the host state including its rules on conflicts of law, the terms of any agreements between the investor and the host state, and "principles of international law."[56] Clearly this Protocol, although yet to take effect, generally follows a liberal BIT approach rather than the Calvo principle.

Finally, although negotiation of the Free Trade Agreement of the Americas has been suspended, the latest negotiation draft suggests acceptance of international standards of treatment and the jurisdiction of international arbitration tribunals.[57] It therefore might be regarded as another attempted departure from the Calvo Doctrine in the form of regional integration instruments.

C. Global Conventions

Although so far there is no comprehensive global agreement on investment protection, there are a few global conventions that bear significant implications for international investment. Most important among these global conventions are two World Banks initiatives: the Convention on the Settlement of Investment Disputes between States and Nationals of Other States (ICSID Convention),[58] and the Convention Establishing the Multilateral Investment Guarantee Agency (MIGA Convention).[59] The New York Convention on the Recognition and Enforcement of Foreign Awards[60] is also important in

---

[53] Protocol on Promotion and Protection of Investment Proceeding from Non-Member Countries of the MERCOSUL, *available at* http://www.cvm.gov.br/ingl/inter/mercosul/buenos-e.asp (last visited June 15, 2006).

[54] Id. art 2 (c).

[55] Id. art 2 (h).

[56] Id. art 2 (h)(4).

[57] Subsection C. 2. b, Chapter XVII Investment, of the Free Trade Area of the Americas (Draft Agreement) (Derestricted, FTAA. TNC/w/133/Rev. 3, Nov. 21, 2003), particularly arts. 29 & 41.

[58] The Convention is *available at* http://www.worldbank.org/icsid/basicdod basicdoc.htm (last visited June 15, 2006).

[59] The Convention is *available at* http://www.miga.org/sitelevel2/level2.cfm?id = 1107 (last visited June 15, 2006).

[60] The full text of the Convention is *available at* http://www.jus.uio.no/lm/un.arbitration.recognition.and.enforcement.convention.new.york.1958/doc (last visited June 16, 2006).

the context of investment dispute settlement.

As an important companion to BITs, the ICSID Convention aims at providing an international mechanism for the settlement of state-investor disputes, particularly by facilitating international arbitration and conciliation. This mechanism appears to go against the Calvo Doctrine, which advocates exclusive national jurisdiction and local remedies. It is therefore unsurprising that Latin American states boycotted this convention in 1964 even after the drafters made efforts to revise some of the provisions to address Latin American states' concerns.[61] Before 1980, only a few small Latin American and Caribbean states (Jamaica and Trinidad and Tobago) had joined in the convention. But now most Latin American states have become members of the Convention (with the notable exceptions of Brazil and Mexico), and most of these states realized their membership in the 1990s. (Table 5) This again confirms that the investment liberalization took place most dramatically in the 1990s.

Meanwhile, Latin American states also dropped their rejection to the New York Convention facilitating the enforcement of arbitration awards made in other states.[62] Now almost all Latin American states, even Brazil and Mexico, have become members of the Convention. This demonstrates that Latin American states have made a Uturn in their attitudes towards international arbitration, from utter rejection to general acceptance and recognition.

Table 3 Latin American Members of the ICSID Convention (As of January 25, 2006)

Contracting State	Date of Signature	Date of Ratification	Date of Entry into Force
Argentina	21/05/1991	19/10/1994	18/1111994
Bahamas	19/10/1995	19/10/1995	18/1111995
Bolivia	03/05/1991	23/06/1995	23/07/1995
Colombia	18/05/1993	15/07/1997	14/08/1997
Costa Rica	29/09/1981	27/04/1993	27/05/1993
Dominican Republic	20/05/2000		
Ecuador	15/01/1986	15/01/1986	14/02/1986
El Salvador	09/06/1982	06/03/1984	05/04/1984
Grenada	24/05/1991	24/05/1991	23/06/1991

[61] Gonzalo Biggs, *The Latin American Treatment of International Arbitration and Foreign Investments and the Chile-U. S. Free Trade Agreement*, 19 ICSID REVIEWFOREIGN INVESTMENT LAW JOURNAL 68 (2004).

[62] Latin American states had long been hostile to the New York Convention, and were, in general, among the last countries to accept it. For example, Brazil did not accept it until 2002. *See* Gonzalo Biggs, id. at 63.

续表

Contracting State	Date of Signature	Date of Ratification	Date of Entry into Force
Guatemala	09/1111995	21101/2003	20/02/2003
Haiti	30/01/1985		
Honduras	28/05/1986	14/02/1989	16/03/1989
Jamaica	23/06/1965	09/09/1966	14/10/1966
Nicaragua	04/02/1994	20/03/1995	19/04/1995
Panama	22/11/1995	08/04/1996	08/05/1996
Paraguay	27/07/1981	07/01/1983	06/02/1983
Peru	04/09/1991	09/08/1993	08/09/1993
Trinidad and Tobago	05/10/1966	03/0111967	02/02/1967
Uruguay	28/05/1992	09/08/2000	08/09/2000
Venezuela	18/08/1993	02/05/1995	01106/1995

Source: *ICSID: List of Contracting States and other Signatories of the Convention* (*as of Jan.* 25, 2006), *available at http://www. worldbank. org/icsid lconstatel c-states-en. htm* (*last visited May* 19, 2006).

Latin American states have finally also accepted the MIGA Convention, aimed at providing guarantees for international investment.[63] Since the MIGA mechanism is based on host states' recognition of the subrogation of rights of investors by the MIGA, the states' acceptance again evidences derogation from the Calvo Doctrine by Latin American states.

D. Observations

The preceding survey suggest that since the 1980s, Latin American states have generally deviated from the Calvo Doctrine in their international investment treaty practice, as most of them have entered into BITs that guarantee international standards of treatment and access to international arbitration. At the regional level, MERCOSUR follows the BIT approach, and the Andean Pack has been revised to accommodate the member states' need of flexibility in departing from the Calvo Clause. Most of the Latin American states have also accepted the ICSID Convention providing an international platform for arbitration of state-investor disputes, the MIGA Convention recognizing rights of subroga-

[63] According to the MIGA website, MIGA members from Latin America and the Caribbean include: Antigua and Barbuda, Argentina, Bahamas, Barbados, Belize, Bolivia, Brazil, Chile, Colombia, Costa Rica, Dominica, Dominican Republic, Ecuador, El Salvador, Grenada, Guatemala, Guyana, Haiti, Honduras, Jamaica, Nicaragua, Paraguay, Panama, Peru, St. Kitts & Nevis, St. Lucia, St. Vincent, Suriname, Trinidad & Tobago, Uruguay and Venezuela. See MIGA: *MIGA Member Countries* (Last updated: Oct. 27, 2005), *available at* http://www. miga. org/sitelevel2/level2. cfm? id = 1l52 (last visited May 28, 2006).

tion, and the New York Convention facilitating world wide enforcement of arbitration awards.

It may still, however, be a step too far to conclude that all Latin American states have completely abandoned Calvo in their treaty practice. There are three main reasons supporting this argum ent. First of all, there are significant exceptions to such general treaty practice. For instance, Brazil, the largest state and FDI recipient[64] in the region, has not yet ratified any BITs (although has concluded a few of them) or the MERCOSUR Protocols,[65] nor has it accepted the ICSID regime. Furthermore, it seems unlikely that Brazil will change its approach in the near future, as it is doing enormously well as a magnet for foreign investment.[66] Colombia also has not ratified any BITs despite the fact that it has signed six of them.[67] Moreover, Mexico, another important state in the region, also has not signed the ICSID Convention, although it joined the North America Free Trade Agreement (NAFTA) and concluded a number of BITs. Secondly, some investment treaties contain significant reservations to the acceptance of international standards and international arbitration. Using Schuruer's language, some of the treaty provisions are actually "Calvo's Grandchildren." Early BITs by Latin American states, for example, often make local remedies a prerequisite for international arbitration. Given the uncertainty about the applicability of MFN to procedural aspects following recent arbitration cases such as *Salini v. Jordan*[68] and *Plama v. Bulgaria*[69] cases, such reservations should not be ignored. Also, the Andean FDI code still, as a general principle, requires "equal treatment" between domestic and foreign investors and leaves member states the discretion to adopt higher standards of treatment or access to international arbitration, not "requiring" them to do so. It is therefore essential to look into domestic legislation in the region to establish whether the Calvo Doctrine has actually been abandoned in the Andean Community. Thirdly, it has been argued and has increasingly been recognized that developing countries including Latin American states enter into BITs and other investment treaties mainly for economic considerations,[70] rather than because of a genu-

---

[64] UNCTAD Press Release, UNCTAD Doc. UNCTAD/PRESS/EB/2004/007 (Mar. 5, 2004).

[65] Inter-American Development Bank (IADB), *Legislation for Foreign Investment Statutes in Countries in the Americas, Comparative Study-Brazil* (2006), http://alca-ftaa.iadb.org/eng/invest/BRA - 1. HTM (May 16, 2006).

[66] Cremades, *supra* note 38, at 81.

[67] UNCTAD, *Country-specific Lists of* BITs, *supra* note 35.

[68] Salini Construttori S. p. A. and Italstrade S. p. A. v. the Hashemite Kingdom of Jordan (Case No. ARB/02/13), Decision of the Tribunal on Jurisdiction, Nov. 29, 2004. This case and the following case, Plama v. Bulgaria, basically decided that MFN clauses in BITs do not generally extend privileges under procedural provisions, which marks a reversal of the view as held in earlier cases, notably the Emilio Agustin Maffezini v. Kingdom of Spain (Case No. ARB/9717), Decision on Objections to Jurisdiction, Jan. 25, 2000 (Maffezini v. Spain), and Siemens A. G. v. Argentine Republic (Case No. ARB/02/8), Decision on Jurisdiction of Aug. 3, 2004 (Siemens v. Argentina), para. 103.

[69] Plama Consortium Limited v. Republic of Bulgaria (Case No. ARB/03/24), Decision on Jurisdiction of Feb. 8, 2005.

[70] *See e. g.*, Rudolf Dolzer, *New Foundations of the Law of Expropriation of Alien Property*, 75 AM. J. INT'L L. 553, 583 - 89 (1981); Oscar Schachter, *Compensation for Expropriation, Editorial Comment*, 78 AM. J. INT'L L. 121, 127 (1984); Andrew T. Guzman, *Explaining the Popularity of Bilateral Investment Treaties: Why LDCs Sign Treaties that Hurt Them?* (Harvard, Jean Monnet Working Paper No. 12/97, at 72, 1997).

ine belief in the norms embedded therein. In other words, the departure from or even rejection of the Calvo Doctrine represents only a change in technique, not a change in principle. This is supported by the following examination of the domestic constitutions and laws.

IV. Domestic Legislations in Latin American States

Compared with international treaties, domestic legislation better reveals the real attitude of Latin American states towards the Calvo Doctrine, as domestic legislation more accurately reflects the unilateral wills of the host states, unlike international treaties, in which the host state must compromise with other states. Also, the Andean Pack FDI code refers to domestic laws to determine the treatment and methods of dispute settlement for foreign investment. It is therefore crucial to look into domestic laws and regulations to ascertain whether Latin American states have shifted their attitudes towards foreign investment. This section intends to do so by exploring and comparing domestic legislation, particularly the rules on standards of treatment and the investment dispute settlement, in nine major Latin American states, namely Argentina, Bolivia, Brazil, Chile, Colombia, Ecuador, Mexico, Peru and Venezuela.

A. Argentina

Argentina has been lauded as having "probably the most probusiness" FDI legislation in the world.[71] The general standard of treatment of foreigners and foreign investors is laid down in the national constitution and laws.[72] Article 20 of the Argentine Constitution establishes the principle of "equal treatment" of foreigners and nationals, stating that:

[f]oreigners enjoy in the territory of the Nation all the civil rights of a citizen; they may engage in their industry, commerce or profession; own real property, purchase it and alienate it.[73]

Accordingly, the Foreign Investment Law of 1993 (No. 21, 382) grants foreign inves-

---

〔71〕 One Argentine website highlights the main aspects of investment liberalization as follows: (1) Foreign investments are warmly welcomed and virtually unrestricted, with no sector restrictions-investments are allowed even in sensitive areas such as oil, mass media (broadcasting, cable, newspapers and magazines), nuclear power generation and nuclear mineral mining; (2) No approvals or paperwork of any kind are required to materialize foreign investments-there is absolutely no red tape; (3) No registration of investments is ever required: complete confidentiality assured; (4) Foreign investors are entitled, without approvals or formalities, to repatriate capital and remit profits abroad at any time-no waiting periods whatsoever; (5) Unrestricted access to foreign exchange markets-absolutely no approvals or formalities for making transfers abroad; (6) No discrimination against foreign investors: foreign and domestic companies are treated equally under the law, including access to domestic or foreign currency financing in the local market and full eligibility for economic development incentive programs; (7) No performance requirements to be met by foreign investors; and (8) International law protection: most capital-exporting countries covered by a valid bilateral investment treaty. *See* Hacienda Virtual Realty Argentina-HVRA, Legal Reforms and the Foreign Investor, *available at* http://www.hvra.com.ar/enforinv.htm (May 20, 2006).

〔72〕 IADB: *Legislation for Foreign Investment Statutes in Countries in the Americas, Comparative Study-Argentina* (2006), http://alca-ftaa.iadb.org/eng/invest/ARG – 1. HTM (May 16, 2006) [hereinafter IADB: *Argentina*], sec. 1.

〔73〕 Art. 20, Argentine Constitution.

tors rights equal to those of local investors in all fields, while liberalizing the entry and outflow of capital.[74] The legal and tax treatment is virtually the same for Argentine citizens and foreigners.[75] Decree 1853/93 of September 1993, which combines in one piece of legislation the liberalization measures contained in the Economic Emergency and State Reform Acts of 1989 and the above mentioned Foreign Investment Law,[76] confirms in Article 2 that "foreign investors may invest in the country without any prior approval, on the same terms as investors domiciled in the country." Thus it is clear that Argentina enshrines national treatment as the cardinal principle of treatment for foreign investors.

On the settlement of state-investor disputes, Argentina also insists on the equal treatment principle. Foreign investors are therefore entitled to "exactly the same recourse" available to local investors.[77]

It can thus be concluded that, within its domestic legislation, Argentina loyally adheres to the cardinal Calvo principle of equal/national treatment for foreign investors. Such national treatment, however, seems to subtly differ from Calvo, as it emphasizes absolute equality between foreigners and nationals, and does not have the classical "Calvo stress" emphasizing the non-discrimination against nationals, i. e., the prohibition of special favor to foreigners.

On the other hand, it must be noted that Argentina has been very active in entering into investment promotion and protection treaties. So far it has signed the ICSID Convention, the MIGA Convention,[78] the New York Convention, the Inter-American Convention on International Commercial Arbitration (the Panama Convention),[79][80] and at least 58 BITs, of which 53 have entered into force. so It has also signed on to some regional treaties, including the two MERCOSUR Protocols on investment protection (namely the Colonia Protocol and the Buenos Aires Protocol) and a few arbitration conventions.[81]

Such treaties have effectively raised the standards of treatment for foreign investors well beyond the standards of treatment for national investors, most notably by allowing foreign investors to resort to international arbitration mechanisms such as the ICSID, and by accepting the applicability of general principles of international law. These treaties thus raise a question of constitutionality: since international treaties are subordinate to the Constitution in Argentina,[82] does it constitute a breach of the constitutional requirement of absolute equality of treatment between national and foreign investors to grant foreign investors higher treatment than that given to domestic investors? Such an unconstitutionality challenge has already been raised by the Argentine government in the pro-

---

[74] IADB: *Argentina, supra* note 72, at sec. 1.2.

[75] Id.

[76] HVRA, Legal Reforms and the Foreign Investor, *supra* note 71.

[77] IADB: *Argentina, supra* note 72, at sec. 5.1.

[78] Alessandro Spinillo & Emilio Vogelius, *Argentina, in* INTERNATIONAL ARBITRATION IN LATIN AMERICA, *supra* note 44, at 19.

[79] Id. at 439.

[80] UNCTAD, *Country-specific Lists of BITs, supra* note 35.

[81] For details of such regional arbitration conventions, see Spinillo & Vogelius, *supra* note 78, at 20, 25 – 26.

[82] IADB: *Argentina, supra* note 72, at sec. 5.4.

ceedings of some of the investment arbitration cases against the country.[83] The Argentine prosecutor, for example, argued in a hearing in the *CMS Gas Transmission Company v. Republica Argentina* case[84] that bilateral treaties do not supersede the National Constitution and that a company therefore cannot invoke such a treaty to avoid trying the case in *AI* gentina before local courts.[85] The Aigentine judiciary has also recently echoed the government's position by deciding in a landmark case (*Jose Cartellone Construcciones v. Hid roelectrica Norpatagonica S. A.*) that, as far as matters of public policy are involved, the Aigentine courts may review the reasonability, fairness and constitutionality (i. e., the merits) of an arbitration award.[86] Further developments down this line include a new decree passed in 2003 to terminate a decision made in 1996 authorizing the submission of disputes between Aigentine Government and a foreign investor, Bulgheroni Group, to international arbitration tribunals,[87] and a reportedly proposed bill aimed at limiting the intervention of national or international arbitral tribunals in cases involving the State, State agencies or enterprises.[88] Indeed, such anti-BIT and investment arbitration moves in Aigentina, together with similar moves in other Latin American states, have been regarded as signals of the "resurgence of the Calvo Doctrine."[89]

---

[83] Carlos E. Alfaro & Pedro M. Lorenti, *The Growing Opposition of Argentina to ICSID Arbitral Tribunals: A Confiict between International and Domestic Law*?6 JOURNAL OF WORLD INVESTMENT & TRADE, at 426 - 27, 428 - 30 (2005).

[84] ICSID: CMS Gas Transmission Company v. The Republic of Argentina (Case No. ARB/01/8) Decision of the Tribunal on Objections to Jurisdiction, July 17, 2003, *reprinted as* 42 ILM 788 (2003).

[85] Carlos E. Alfaro, *The Battle of the Century: Argentina Against the ICSID Arbitration and the BITs*, 31 WORLD LAw GROUP E-NEWS (Nov. 2004), *available at* http://www.imakenews.com/bcastro/e_Art00033231 8.cfm?x = Bl, O, w (last visited July 9, 2006).

[86] Carlos E. Alfaro, ICSID Arbitration and BITs Challenged by the Argentine Government (Dec. 21, 2004), *available at* http://www.alfarolaw.com/ima/tapa/alfaro3.htm (last visited July 9, 2006).

[87] Laurence Norman, Government Reopens 7 - Year-Old Case Vs Oil Group, Dow JoNEs NEWSWIRES, Oct. 28, 2003, 15 - 16.

[88] The proposed bill prohibits access to international arbitration in such cases unless: a) an appeal of their decision before Argentine federal courts is provided, or b) the State's counterparty in the dispute is a foreign State (State-State disputes); or c) the Congress has provided for an exception in the case through a specific statute. The bill also requests the Executive to inform the appropriate authorities of Argentina's repeal of any treaty by means of which Argentina has accepted such jurisdiction; and, meanwhile, demands the Executive, its agencies and enterprises to issue necessary orders or decisions in order to annul prior agreements or decisions contrary to such provisions. Since the bill generally requires all state-investor arbitration cases to be subject to the ultimate control of national courts, it would effectively abolish the finality, and hence the autonomy, of arbitration. In this sense, it can be said that it will mean that the Calvo Doctrine finally returns to its birthplace. It remains to be seen, however, whether this is mere rhetoric or will lead to concrete steps towards its adoption. For details of the proposed bill, see Guido Santiago Tawil, *Is Calvo Finally Back*?3 TRANSNATIONAL DISPUTE MANAGEMENT (2005), in part, *available at* http://www.transnational-dispute-management.com/news/tdm2 - 2005_5.htm (last visited Feb. 18, 2006).

[89] Similar recent events in other Latin American States include Brazil's 2004 Private Public Partnership Act prohibiting international arbitration, and Venezuela's constitutionality challenge against international arbitration, which will be discussed below. Indeed, a seminar was organized in order to look into the issue of the resurgence of Calvo and its implications on international arbitration. *See* D. C. Bar Luncheon Program: The Resurgence of the Calvo Doctrine?, *available at* http://www.bgconsulting.com/docs/calvo_program.jpg (last visited July 11, 2006). *See also* Cremades, *supra* note 38, esp. 81 - 82. For further details of such events in and beyond Latin America and its implications in international investment law, see Wenhua Shan, *From "North-South Divide" to "Private-Public Debate": Revival of Calvo Doctrine and the Changing Land scape in International Investment Law*, 27 Nw. J. INT'L L. & Bus., No. 3 (Spring 2007, forthcoming).

The constitutionality of BITs and treaty-based investment arbitration, as we will see below, is an issue existing in many Latin American countries that has already been tested before local courts in these countries, notably in Colombia.

B. Bolivia

The standard of treatment for foreign investors in Bolivia is governed by Bolivian Foreign Investment Law (Law No. 1182).[90] Article 2 of the law expressly adopts the national treatment standard by providing that:

[e]xcept where otherwise established by law, foreign investors and the entities or companies in which they take part, have the same rights, duties and guarantees that the laws and regulations give to national investors.[91]

With regard to investment dispute settlement, Article 24 of the Constitution of Bolivia expressly denies foreigners the right to diplomatic protection by stating:

[f]oreign subjects and enterprises are subject to Bolivian laws, and in no case may they invoke exceptional positions or have recourse to diplomatic claims.[92]

Article 10 of the Foreign Investment Law of Bolivia nevertheless permits investors to agree to settle their disputes in courts of arbitration.[93] Accordingly, cases involving technical disputes may be referred to international arbitration panels governed by international arbitration rules.[94] In 1997, Bolivia passed Law No. 1770, a legal framework for dispute settlement and arbitration to which the parties may resort before bringing their disputes before the courts.[95] In this context, it is noted that Bolivia has entered into 22 BITs[96] and is a member of the ICSID Convention, the MIGA Convention, the New York Convention and the Inter-American Convention on International Commercial Arbitration.[97]

Like Argentina, Bolivia enshrines equal/national treatment as the cardinal standard of treatment for foreign investors. Bolivia appears, however, to be more loyal to the Calvo Doctrine than Argentina, in that Bolivia's Constitution still explicitly renounces diplomatic protection. Nevertheless, technical disputes are allowed to be submitted to international arbitration.

C. Brazil

Brazilian laws also embrace equal/national treatment for foreign investors. Article 5

---

〔90〕 92. *Ley de Sept.* 17, 1990, *Inversiones No.* 1182, *Gaceta Oficial de Bolivia, Sept.* 26, 1990. *See also* IADB (2006): *Legislation for Foreign Investment Statutes in Countries in the Americas, Comparative Study-Bolivia,* http://alca-ftaa.iadb.org/eng/invest/BOL-1.HTM (05/16/06) [hereinafter IADB: *Bolivia*], sec. 1.2.

〔91〕 *Art.* 2, *Ley de Sept.* 17, 1990, *Inversiones No.* 1182, *Gaceta Oficial de Bolivia, Sept.* 26, 1990.

〔92〕 Art. 24, The Constitution of Bolivia (as amended by No. 2410, Aug. 8, 2002), *in* CONSTITUTIONS OF THE COUNTRIES OF THE WORLD (Albert P. Blaustein & Gisbert H. Flanz eds.) Doose-leaf], (20 Vols., Oceana Publications, 1971) [hereinafter WORLD CONSTITUTIONS).

〔93〕 IADB: *Bolivia, supra* note 90, sec. 5.

〔94〕 Wiesner, *supra* note 46, at 460.

〔95〕 WTO, *Trade Policy Review-Bolivia: Secretariat's Report* 18, WT/TPR/154/Rev. 1 (2005).

〔96〕 UNCTAD, *Country-specific Lists of BITs, supra* note 35.

〔97〕 IADB: *Bolivia, supra* note 90, sec. 5.2.

of Brazilian Constitution (as amended) states:

[A]ll persons are equal before the law, without any distinction whatsoever, Brazilians and foreigners residing in the country being ensured of inviolability of the right to life, to liberty, to equality, to security and to property...[98]

This marks a significant change from the 1988 Constitution, which differentiated "Brazilian Company of National Capital" and "Brazilian Company of Foreign Capital" and treated them differently.[99] Law No. 4131 stipulates in Article 2 that "the same legal treatment dispensed to national capital shall, under the same circumstances, be dispensed to the foreign capital invested in the country, any and all forms of discrimination not foreseen in this present law being prohibited."[100] This article is repeated in Article 2 of the Decree No. 55762 that sets down implementing regulations with regard to Law No. 4131 (as amended).[101]

With regard to settlement of investment disputes, Brazil also adheres to the aforementioned national treatment principle. Foreign investors are therefore able to resort to the same procedures as the national investors do and there is no special form of recourse for foreign investors.[102] It is important to note, however, that Brazil did not accept arbitration until the Arbitration Act was passed in 1996. Yet the constitutionality of the Act was immediately challenged in the case *MBV u. Resil* before the Brazilian Federal Supreme Court soon after it was promulgated.[103] Although the Act was declared constitutional in the end, the lengthy deliberation on the case (more than five years) and the substantial portion of dissenting judges (four out of eleven including the reporting judge) has clearly demonstrated the country's hesitation and substantial resistance to arbitration, particularly to international arbitration.[104] A year later, on December 30, 2004, Brazil adopted Federal Law No. 11079, establishing a legal framework for Brazil-

[98] The Constitution of Brazil (including amendments until Constitutional Amendment 52, enacted on Mar. 8, 2006), *available at* http://www.v-brazil.com/gov ernmentllaws/constitution.html (last visited June 16, 2006).

[99] Pedro Da Motta Veiga, FOREIGN DIRECT INVESTMENT IN BRAZIL: REGULATION, FLOWS AND CONTRIBUTION TO DEVELOPMENT 3-4 (2004), *available at* http://www.iisd.org/pdf72004/investment_country_report_brazil.pdf (last visited May 20, 2006).

[100] Law No. 4131, Sept. 3, 1962, which regulates the investment of foreign capital and remittance of funds abroad, *in* ICSID: INVESTMENT LAWS OF THE WORLD, [loose-leaf] [hereinafter INVESTMENT LAWS OF THE WORLD]; *see also* IADB: *Legislation for Foreign Investment Statutes in Countries in the Americas, Comparative Study-Brazil*, http://alca-ftaa.iadb.org/eng/invest/BRA-1.HTM (May 16, 2006) [hereinafter IADB: *Brazil*], sec. 3.1.b.

[101] Decree No. 55,762 of Feb. 17, 1965, which sets out regulations for implementation of Law No. 4131, Sept. 3, 1962, as amended, in INVESTMENT LAWS OF THE WORLD, *supra* note 100.

[102] IADB: *Brazil*, *supra* note 100, sec. 5.

[103] For details of the case, see Joao Bosco Lee, *Brazil*, *in* INTERNATIONAL ARBITRATION IN LATIN AMERICA, *supra* note 44, at 63-66; Guido Santiago Tawil, THE ROLE OF ARBITRATION AND INTERNATIONAL, REGIONAL, SUBREGIONAL AND BILATERAL TREATIES IN LATIN AMERICA, *available at* http://66.249.93.104/search?q::cache:xjw8Vj40l7wJ: www.bomchilgroup.org/argdec02.html + Brazilratifiedcolonialprotocolercosur&hl=zhCN&ct=clnk&cd==9 (May 22, 2006).

[104] Tawil, *supra* note 103.

ian public-private partnerships (the PPP Law).[105] The PPP Law permits parties to choose arbitration as a means to settle any disputes arising from PPP contracts,[106] but requires that the seat of the arbitration be in Brazil and the proceedings be conducted in the Portuguese language.[107] Also, it only accepts domestic arbitration and expressly prohibits international arbitration. It thus demonstrates the reluctance of the Brazilian government to subject cases involving public entities, such as state-investor disputes, to international arbitration.[108]

This is confirmed by the fact that although Brazil has signed 14 BITs[109] and two MERCOSUR Protocols, it has ratified none of these agreements and protocols.[110] Indeed, the government decided to withdraw these agreements from the consideration of the Brazilian Parliament, because some elements of their texts were considered by members of Parliament to be incompatible with the Brazilian Constitution.[111]

Brazil can therefore be regarded as a country that unreservedly upholds the absolute "national/equal treatment" principle in dealing with foreign investors. It does so not only through its domestic laws, but also by rejecting international treaties that would have the effect of granting more favorable treatment to foreign investors.

D. Chile

The Chilean Constitution establishes national treatment for both national and foreign investors.[112] Article 9 of the Foreign Investment Statute establishes that foreign investment and the enterprises participating in it shall also be subject to the regular legal regime that applies to national investment, and may not be discriminated against either directly or indirectly.[113] The law further clarifies that any legal or regulatory provisions applicable to most of a particular productive activity and that exclude foreign investment

---

[105] The law is posted at the Brazilian Ministry of Planning, Budget and Management website, https://www.planalto.gov.br/ccivil_03/_Ato2004-2006/2004/Lei/Ll 1079.htm (last visited June 22, 2006). An English version is also *available at* http://www.planejamento.gov.br/arquivos_down/ppp/legislacao/lei_1 1079_301204_eng.pdf (last visited June 22, 2006).

[106] Art. 11 III, THE PPP LAw, id.

[107] Id.

[108] As noted by Rubins, the only path towards international arbitration recognized in Brazil is the carefully drafted arbitration clause in contracts between a foreign investor and the Brazilian Government, as, "Brazil lacks the legal infrastructure that [exists] in many other countries in Latin America give[ing] foreign investors explicit guarantees of equitable treatment and access to international arbitration." *See* Noah D. Rubins, *Investment Arbitration in Brazil, in* 4 J. WORLD INVESTMENT & TRADE, at 1080-81, 1091 (2003).

[109] Namely, BITs with Belgium, Chile, Cuba, Denmark, Finland, France, Germany, Italy, the Republic of Korea, the Netherlands, Portugal, Switzerland, the United Kingdom and Venezuela. *See* UNCTAD, *Country-specific Lists of BITs, supra* note 35. *See also* Rubins, *supra* note 108, at 1979, 1088-90.

[110] WTO: *Trade Policy Review-Brazil: Secretariat's Report* 24, WT/TPR/S/140(Nov. 1, 2004).

[111] Id.

[112] IADB: *Legislation for Foreign Investment Statutes in Countries in the Americas, Comparative Study-Chile,* http://alca-ftaa.iadb.org/eng/invesUCHI-l.HTM (May 16, 2006) [hereinafter IADB: *Chile*], sec. 4.1.

[113] Art. 9, Foreign Investment Statute, *in* INVESTMENT LAWS OF THE WORLD, *supra* note 100. *See also* IADB: *Chile, supra* note 112, sec. 4.1.

shall be deemed discriminatory.[114] Similarly, rules that establish sectoral or zonal exception regimes are discriminatory if foreign investment does not have access to them.[115]

According to Chilean law, foreign investors have the same procedural recourse as local investors.[116] Article 10 of the Statute, furthermore, prescribes that in the event that legal provisions are issued which foreign investors or enterprises with foreign capital may consider to be discriminatory, the investors or enterprises may request the Foreign Investment Committee to eliminate the discrimination, provided that no more than one year has lapsed since the provision was issued.[117] Besides its purely domestic law, Chile is an ICSID signatory, as well as a signatory to the MIGA Convention, the New York Convention and the Panama Convention.[118] Chile has also signed at least 51 BITs, 15 of which were yet to enter into force.[119]

It can thus be said that Chile seriously upholds the national treatment principle, with an emphasis on the elimination of discriminatory measures against foreign investors. Meanwhile, Chile is active in signing investment treaties that have the effect of upgrading the standard of treatment and protection afforded to foreign investors, well beyond those accorded to national investors; this may, in turn, result in the "constitutionality" issue elaborated above in Argentina's case. The general attitude of the country seems to be moving away from the Calvo Doctrine towards a more liberal investment regime.

E. Colombia

The Colombian Constitution generally grants national treatment to foreigners in Colombia, subject to exceptions maintained by the Constitution and the laws.[120] According-

---

[114] Art. 9, Foreign Investment Statute, *in* INVESTMENT LAWS OF THE WORLD, *supra* note 100. *See also* IADB: *Chile, supra* note 112, sec. 4. 1.

[115] Id.

[116] IADB: *Chile, supra* note 112, sec. 5. 1.

[117] Art. 10, Foreign Investment Statute, *in* INVESTMENT LAWS OF THE WORLD, *supra* note 100. *See also* IADB: *Chile, supra* note 112, sec. 5. 1.

[118] Carlos E. Jorquiera et al., *Chile, in* INTERNATIONAL ARBITRATION IN LATIN AMERICA, *supra* note 44, at 91 – 92.

[119] Chile has effective BITs with Argentina, Australia, Austria, Belgium, Bolivia, China, Costa Rica, Croatia, Cuba, the Czech Republic, Denmark, Ecuador, El Salvador, Finland, France, Germany, Greece, Guatemala, Honduras, Italy, Indonesia, Lebanon, Malaysia, Nicaragua, Norway, Panama, Paraguay, Peru, the Philippines, Poland, Portugal, Romania, Spain, Sweden, Switzerland, Ukraine, the United Kingdom, Uruguay and Venezuela. Further bilateral investment agreements have been, or are being negotiated, with Brazil, Colombia, the Dominican Republic, Egypt, Greece, Hungary, the Netherlands, New Zealand, South Africa, Tunisia, Turkey and Viet Nam; those were not yet in force in May 2003. WTO, *Trade Policy Review-Chile: Secretariat's Report* 18, WT/TPR/S/124 (2003). For more updated information, see UNCTAD, *Country-specific Lists of BITs, supra* note 35.

[120] Art. 100 of the Colombian Constitution stipulates that, "[F]oreigners in Colombia enjoy the same civil rights that are granted to the Colombians. Nevertheless, for reasons of public order, the law may subject foreigners to special conditions or deny their exercise of certain civil rights. Also, foreigners enjoy, in the territory of the Republic, the guarantees granted to the nationals, save the limitations established by the Constitution or the law." *See Constitución de* 1991 *con reformas hasta* 2005 [Political Constitution of 1991 through 2005 reforms], *available at* http://pdba.georgetown.edu/Constitutions/Colombia/col91.html (June 16, 2006).

ingly, Article 3 of Resolution 51 (issued by the National Economic and Social Policy Council of Colombia (CONPES) pursuant to Law No. 9 of 1991 regulating foreign investment and foreign exchange in Colombia[121]) further elaborates the national treatment standard for foreign investment:

Subject to Article 100 of the Constitution of Columbia, and to Article 15 of Law 9 of 1991, and except for those matters relating to the transfer of funds abroad, the investment in Colombia of foreign capital will be treated, for all effects and purposes, in the same way as are the investments of residents in Colombia. Consequently, and without prejudice to the provisions set forth in special regulations or regimes, *no discriminatory conditions or treatments may be imposed on those who invest foreign capital vis-a-vis national private resident investors, nor may investors of foreign capital be given a more favorable treatment than that granted to national private resident investors.* (emphasis added)[122]

Thus, Colombian law unambiguously states its absolute equal/national treatment principle, which means a prohibition of any sort of discrimination between foreign and domestic investors, subject to express exceptions. Columbian law distinguishes itself from other Latin American legislation in that it still explicitly declares its prohibition of discrimination against domestic investors, i. e., special privileges for foreign investors.

The most important provision related to investment dispute resolution is Article 23 of Resolution 51, which states:

Except as provided by in international treaties and conventions in force, the provisions set forth in Colombian law shall be applied to the resolution of controversies or conflicts derived from the application of the Regime of Investments of Foreign Capital [the Statute]. International arbitration will be subject to the provisions of Decree 2279 of 1989 as well as the norms and regulations that amend or supplement it.

With the same exception established in the preceding paragraph and without prejudice to actions that may be brought before foreign jurisdictions, all matters pertaining to the investment of capital from abroad will also be subject to the jurisdiction of Colombian courts as well as to Colombian arbitration rules.[123]

Article 23 thus establishes that, as a general principle, foreign investment disputes are subject to the jurisdiction of Colombian courts and tribunals applying local laws, including local arbitration rules. However, if an effective international treaty or convention to which Colombia is a party gives foreign investors the right to submit investment-related disputes to the jurisdiction of a non-Colombian court and/or to apply non-Colombian laws, then the above-quoted local jurisdiction and local law requirements may be waived. Paragraph 2 of Article 23 also suggests that in certain cases it is possible to bring a suit in a foreign jurisdiction, in which case the parties are not required to subject

---

[121] IADB: *Legislation for Foreign Investment Statutes in Countries in the Americas, Comparative Study-Colombia*, http://alca-ftaa.iadb.org/eng/invest/COL-1.HTM (May 16, 2006) [hereinafter IADB: *Colombia*], sec. 3.1 and 4.1.

[122] Art. 3 of Statute of Foreign Investment (Resolution 51 as amended), *in* THE INVESTMENT LAWS OF THE WORLD, *supra* note 100. *See also* IADB: *Colombia, supra* note 121, sec. 3.1 b.

[123] Art. 23 of Statute of Foreign Investment (Resolution 51 as amended), *in* INVESTMENT LAWS OF THE WORLD, *supra* note 100. *See also* IADB: *Colombia, supra* note 121, sec. 5.1.

the dispute to Colombian jurisdiction and Colombian arbitration rules. Article 23 therefore opened the door for Colombia to enter into international treaties that accept international arbitration and international law. In this vein, it should be noted that, although Colombia has joined in the ICSID Convention, MIGA Convention and the New York Convention, it has so far, like Brazil, not ratified any BITs even though it has signed six of them.[124]

Two constitutionality challenges might have contributed to such a conservative approach towards BIT ratification. The first was a 1995 case against the 1994 BIT with the U. K. The 1994 Colombian U. K. BIT contains such normal BIT provisions as national treatment, MFN treatment, and expropriations and their compensation. In particular, expropriation is prohibited unless it is for a public purpose, non-discriminatory, and accompanied by the payment of "prompt, adequate and effective compensation."[125] As required by the Constitution,[126] the BIT (as enacted by Law 246/95) was presented to the Colombian Constitutional Court for its certification. The Court ruled by a six to three majority that the BIT was contrary to the Colombian Constitution, particularly in two respects.[127] First, the BIT would effectively deactivate such provisions of the Colombian Constitution as the provision on expropriation without the payment of compensation in the interests of equity.[128] It was held that the government could not waive the exercise of a power delegated to it by the Constitution by conceding the payment of "prompt, adequate, and effective compensation" in case of all expropriation. Second, the investment treaty runs against the equal/national treatment provisions of the Constitution by granting British investors more favorable treatment with respect to expropriations than that available to Colombian nationals. The Constitutional Court rendered a similar decision in a later case with regard to a Cuba-Colombia BIT.[129] It is notable that despite the removal of the expropriation without compensation in case of equity provision after the 1999 amendment to the Constitution, the Colombian government still has not ratified any BITs.

It can thus be concluded that, on the one hand, Colombian laws uphold the Calvo Doctrine by adhering to the principle of equal/national treatment for foreign investment in an absolute sense, prohibiting discrimination against either foreign or domestic investors. On the other hand, Colombian laws deviate from the Doctrine in that they opened the door through domestic legislation to accept non-national jurisdiction and the application of non-national law based on international treaties. However, the constitutionality challenge to and the non-ratification of the signed BITs suggest that strong resistance

---

[124] UNCTAD, *Country-specific Lists of BITs*, *supra* note 35.

[125] David Schneiderman, *Constitutional Approaches to Privatization: An Inquiry into the Magnitude of Neo-Liberal Constitutionalism*, 63 LAW & CONTEMP. PROSS. 83, at 107 (2000).

[126] Art. 241, Colombian Constitution of 1994.

[127] Colombian Constitutional Court Decision No. C – 358/96, *as cited in* Schneiderman, *supra* note 125, at 107 and n. 176.

[128] Art. 58, Colombian Constitution as of 1994.

[129] Colombian Constitutional Court Decision No. C – 379/96, *as cited in* Schneiderman, *supra* note 125, at 107 and n. 178.

still exists in Columbia towards such deviation from Calvo principles.

F. Ecuador

Ecuador also sets forth national treatment as the cardinal standard for foreign investment. This stems from Article 13 of the Ecuadorian Constitution, which stipulates that, with the exception of limitations established in the Constitution and by law, foreigners generally enjoy the same rights as do Ecuadorians.[130] Under the Constitution, the Law on Investment Promotion and Guarantees and its implementing regulations and the Foreign Trade and Investment Law are the key instruments governing foreign investments in Ecuador.[131] Article 13 of the Law on Investment Promotion and Guarantees confirms that foreign investments enjoy the same conditions as those provided for investments by Ecuadorian natural and legal persons.[132] However, the Law on Investment Promotion and Guarantees allows discriminatory treatment between domestic and foreign investors in "strategic" areas, including fisheries, mining and hydrocarbons.[133] The Constitution restricts the purchase, for economic purposes, of land or concessions in national security areas by foreigners.[134] Thus, the national treatment principle is provided to foreign investors but with important reservations.

With regard to settlement of disputes, the Ecuadorian Constitution used to reject diplomatic protection and foreign jurisdiction in foreign investment contract disputes.[135] The current Constitution modifies this provision, establishing an exception to the exclusive local jurisdiction requirement in cases where foreign jurisdiction was established in accordance with an international treaty. Article 14 of the 1998 Constitution reads:

[C]ontracts executed between the Government, or between Public Entities and natural or legal foreign persons, will implicitly entail the waiver of any diplomatic protection; it is not allowed to agree to submit the aforementioned contracts to a foreign jurisdiction if they are executed in the territory of the Republic of Ecuador, unless it is provided for in an international agreement.[136]

Accordingly, the Law on Investment Promotion and Guarantees affirms, "[B]oth the State and foreign investors shall be able to submit any dispute arising from the application of this law to any Arbitration Court constituted under the terms of international treaties of which Ecuador is a member, as well as to the procedures specifically agreed upon or set forth in bilateral or multilateral agreement executed and ratified by Ecuador."[137] In this context, Ecuador has signed 29 and ratified 22 BITs, mostly in the 1990s.[138] Ec-

---

[130] It was art. 14 in the 1979 Constitution. In the current Constitution, the Constitution of 1998, it is retained but renumbered as art. 13.

[131] WTO: *Trade Policy Review-Ecuador: Secretariat's Report* 18, WT/TPR/S/Rev. 1 (2005).

[132] Id.

[133] Id.

[134] Art. 15, The Political Constitution of the Republic of Ecuador 1998.

[135] Art. 16, The Political Constitution of the Republic of Ecuador 1979.

[136] Art. 14, The Political Constitution of the Republic of Ecuador 1998.

[137] Art. 32, The Law on Investment Promotion and Guarantees, *in* INVESTMENT LAWS OF THE WORLD, *supra* note 100.

[138] UNCTAD, *Country-specific Lists of BITs*, *supra* note 35.

uador also accepted ICSIDConvention, MIGA Convention and New York Convention.[139]

Ecuador thus serves as another example of a Latin American state that generally still insists on the Calvo Doctrine but has modified it so as to allow the flexibility provided for in international treaties.

G. Mexico

In general, Mexico grants national treatment to foreigners and foreign investors. This stems from Article 33 of the Mexican Constitution, which entitles them the guarantees granted by Chapter I Title I of the Constitution. In terms of property rights, Article 27 contains a well known Calvo provision:

Only Mexicans by birth or naturalization and Mexican companies have the right to acquire ownership of lands, waters, and their appurtenances or to obtain concessions for the exploitation of mines or waters. The State may grant the same right to foreigners, provided they agree before the Ministry of Foreign Affairs to consider themselves as nationals in respect to such property, and bind themselves not to invoke the protection of their governments in matters relating thereto; under penalty, in case of non-compliance with this agreement, of forfeiture of the acquired property to the Nation.[140]

This provision clearly upholds the national treatment principle and at the same time denounces diplomatic protection. It was reiterated and implemented in Mexico's previous FDI law and regulations, namely the Foreign Investment Law of 1973[141] and Foreign Investment Regulations of 1989.[142] It was, however, deleted from the current FDI legal regime, which consisted mainly of the Foreign Investment Law of 1993 and the Foreign Investment Regulations 1998, a sign of a more liberal approach taken by the authorities. Despite such deletions, however, Mexico's general adherence to the Calvo principle elaborated above remains valid, as the constitutional provision remains unchanged.

With regard to dispute settlement, foreign investors generally have the same proce-

[139] Ramiro S. Cordero, *Ecuador, in* INTERNATIONAL ARBITRATION IN LATIN AMERICA, *supra* note 44, at 135.

[140] Art. 27, Mexican Constitution.

[141] 1973 *Law to Promote Mexican Investment and to Regulate Foreign Investment,* OFFICIAL GAZETIE, Mar. 9, 1973. Art. 3 of this law provided:

Foreigners who acquire properties of any kind in the Mexican Republic agree, because of such action, to consider themselves as Mexican nationals with regard to these properties and not to invoke the protection of their governments with respect to such properties, under penalty, in case of violations, of forfeiting to the Mexican Government the properties thus acquired.

[142] Regulations of the Law to Promote Mexican Investment and to Regulate Foreign Investment (as amendments), *Diario Oficial de la Federaci6n* (Mexico), May 16, 1989. It stipulated in art. 31:

When the "foreigners exclusion clause" is not in the company by-laws, the express agreement or covenant, which is an integral part of the company bylaws, whereby the present or future foreign partners of the companies in question shall be obligated to formally agree with the Secretary of Foreign Relations to be considered as nationals with respect to shares of said companies which they acquire or of which they are holders, as well as of the assets, rights, concessions, participation or interest which they hold in such companies, or else of the rights and obligations which they derive from the contracts in which the same companies are party to with the Mexican authorities, and to not invoke, for that purpose, the protection of their Governments, under the penalty, otherwise, of losing their equity interests in favor of the Nation.

dural recourse as national investors.[143] In this regard, it is notable that relevant local laws, such as the Federal Code of Civil Procedure and the Code of Civil Procedure of the Federal District, have established the exclusive competence of the national courts on certain matters, including matters relating to land and water, resources of exclusive economic zones, acts of authorities, criminal liability, most family matters, tax matters, employment matters and certain agricultural matters.[144]

Special recourse for foreign investors, however, is envisaged only in the dispute settlement sections of free trade treaties or BITs to which Mexico is a party.[145] In this context, it must be noted that in 1992 Mexico ratified the North America Free Trade Agreement (NAFTA), the Chapter 11of which contains a very liberal investment regime. Since NAFTA, Mexico has concluded several BITs, of which 12 have entered into force.[146] Mexico is a member of the New York Contention and the Inter-America Convention for Commercial Arbitration, but notably has not joined with ICSID Convention or MIGA Convention.

Here again, it appears to be an issue of the constitutionality of these international treaties because Mexican nationals are not entitled to such standards and access to international remedies as are provided for in these treaties. In an effort to address this issue, the Mexican government passed the Law Regarding the Making of Treaties in 1992,[147] which authorizes the state to negotiate international treaties with enforceable dispute settlement mechanisms.[148] Some commentators believe that this law has cleared "any doubts about the scope of the Calvo Clause in the Constitution."[149] However, given that the Law Regarding the Making of Treaties is law subordinate to the Constitution, one has to doubt whether such a statement is overoptimistic. Besides, the Law also requires such dispute settlement mechanisms to render equal treatment to Mexicans and foreigners.[150]

H. Peru

The Peruvian Constitution of 1993 (as amended) established the principle of equal treatment for foreign and national investment with an exception to ensure reciprocity.[151] Article 63 of the Constitution states:

Domestic and foreign investments are subject to the same conditions... If another

---

[143] IADB: *Legislation for Foreign Investment Statutes in Countries in the Americas, Comparative Study-Mexico,* http://alca-ftaa.iadb.org/eng/invest/MEX - 1. HTM (May 16, 2006) [hereinafter IADB: *Mexico*], sec. 5. 1.

[144] Claus von Wobeser, *Mexico, in* INTERNATIONAL ARBITRATION IN LATIN AMERICA, *supra* note 44, at 160 - 62.

[145] Id.

[146] UNCTAD, *Country-specific Lists of BITs, supra* note 35.

[147] Law Regarding the Making of Treaties, Dec. 21, 1991, Mex., 31 l. L. M. 390 (1992). The official text of the law appears in CDLX *Diario Oficial de la Federación*, Jan. 2, 1992 at 2.

[148] Antonio Garza Canovas, Introductory Note to the Law Regarding the Making of Treaties, 31 I. L. M. 390, 391 (1992).

[149] *See id.* at 391. *See also* Justine Daly, *Has Mexico Crossed the Border on State Responsibility for Economic Injury to Aliens? - Foreign Investment and the Calvo Clause in Mexico after NAFTA,* 25 ST. *MAR's* L. J. 1147, at 1189 (1994); Schneiderman, *supra* note 23.

[150] Garza Ca. novas, *supra* note 148, at 391.

[151] WTO: *Trade Policy Review-Peru: Secretariat's Report* 17, WTTRPR/S/69 (2000).

country or countries adopt protectionist or discriminatory measures that prejudice the national interest, the State may, in defense of the latter, adopt similar measure.[152]

This national treatment standard is reflected in Legislative Decree No. 662 of August 29, 1991 on foreign investment promotion.[153] Decree 662 sets as its objective the removal of "[o]bstacles and restraints to foreign investors in order to guarantee the equality of rights and duties applicable to foreign and national investors..."[154] and establishes in Article 2 the national treatment standard by providing that, except for constitutional and decree limitations, foreign investors and their companies have "the same rights and obligations as those of national investors and companies." It goes further by requiring, in absolute terms, that "the national laws shall, in no event, discriminate against investors or companies on the basis of national or foreign investors participating therein."[155] In particular, Decree 662 announces that "all laws limiting or restricting in any manner foreign investments in any economic activity are hereby revoked as from the effective date thereof."[156] It is therefore clear that the national treatment standard established in Peruvian law emphasizes the prohibition of discrimination against foreign investors in an attempt to attract FDI.

With regard to dispute settlement, Peruvian Constitution contains the following provision:

In all State contracts and those of public officials with resident aliens, submission of latter to the laws and competent authorities of the Republic and their renunciation to all diplomatic claims are in order. Contracts of financial nature may be exempted from the national jurisdiction.

The State and other persona of public law may submit disagreements stemming from contractual relations to courts established by virtue of treaties in force. They may also submit to domestic or international arbitration in the form provided by law.[157]

This constitutional provision might be regarded as a moderated "Calvo Clause." It is essentially a Calvo Clause in that it absolutely denounces diplomatic protection and generally upholds the exclusive use of domestic law and domestic jurisdiction. It is moderated by allowing two exceptions: one is for contracts of a financial nature, which are allowed to resort to non-national jurisdiction; the other is for treaty-based arrangements on jurisdiction and applicable law. One commentator maintains that there is a presumption in favor of investment-dispute settlement before Peruvian courts and under Peruvian law, since although Article 16 of Decree 662 permits the State to submit disputes to arbitration tribunals based on international treaties, foreign investors can never be certain if

---

[152] Art. 63, paras. 1 – 2, The Political Constitution of the Republic of Peru 1993 (as amended to 2005), *in* WORLD CONSTITUTIONS, *supra* note 92.

[153] *Supra* note 151.

[154] Preamble and Art. 2 respectively, Legislative Decree No. 662 of 29 Aug. 1991, *as in* INVESTMENT LAWS OF THE WORLD, *supra* note 100.

[155] Id. art. 2.

[156] Id. art. 31.

[157] Art. 63, The Political Constitution of the Republic of Peru 1993 (as amended to 2005), *in* WORLD CONSTITUTIONS, *supra* note 92.

the Peruvian government will actually agree to do so.[158] Nevertheless, this exception at least makes it constitutionally possible for the government to enter into international agreements on the solution of investment disputes. Indeed, Peru has signed 29 and ratified 26 BITs.[159] Peru is also a member of ICSID Convention, MIGA Convention, New York Convention and the Panama Arbitration.[160]

I. Venezuela

In accordance with the 1999 Venezuelan Constitution, foreigners and foreign investors enjoy national Vequal treatment. Article 301 of the Constitution states:

[B] usiness enterprises, organs or persons of foreign nationality shall not be granted with regimes more advantageous than those established for Venezuelan nationals. Foreign investment is subject to the same conditions as domestic investment.[161]

The Investment Protection and Promotion Law of 1999[162] affirms such a principle by stating in Article 7 that, in similar circumstances, foreign investors and their investments are subject to the same rights and obligation as national investors and their investments, except for measures provided for in special laws and the limitations contained in the present law.[163] The law also provides in Article 6 "fair and equitable treatment" for foreign investment in accordance with international law, and guarantees that foreign investors will not be subject to "arbitrary or discriminatory measures affecting the maintaining, management, use, enjoyment, expansion, sale or liquidation" of their investment.[164] Article 9 goes further, allowing foreign investors to enjoy the more favorable of the two treatment standards established by Articles 6 and 7, i. e., between national treatment and fair and equitable treatment.[165] Article 8 establishes MFN treatment for foreign investment.[166] While the preceding four articles seem to have, distinctively, adopted BIT language guaranteeing the best standards of treatment for foreign investors, Article 10 turns the attention to national investors and assures that, in similar circumstances, they will be not be treated in a way that is "less favorable" than the treatment accorded to foreign investors.[167] Thus, the Investment Protection and Promotion Law establishes high standards of treatment for all investors and their investments.

On dispute settlement, the 1999 Venezuelan Constitution includes an unambiguous "Calvo Clause" that says:

---

[158] Wiesner, *supra* note 46, at 463.

[159] UNCTAD, *Country-specific Lists of BITs, supra* note 35.

[160] Pelipe 0. Parodi, *Peru and Annex 1: Table of Adherence to the New York Convention, Panama Convention and Washington Convention, in* INTERNATIONAL ARBITRATION IN LATIN AMERICA, *supra* note 44, at 194 and 439.

[161] Art. 301, The Constitution of the Bolivarian Republic of Venezuela (adopted at the referendum of Dec. 15, 1999), *as in* WORLD CONSTITUTIONS, *supra* note 92.

[162] *Ley de Promoción y Protección de Inversiones (Decreto N°* 356, 3 *de octubre de* 1999*), Gaceta Oficial N°* 5. 390 *Extraordinario de fecha* 22 *de octubre de* 1999 [hereinafter Investment Protection and Promotion Law].

[163] Id. art. 7.

[164] Id. art. 6.

[165] Id. art. 9.

[166] Id. art. 8.

[167] Id. art. 10.

Article 151: In the public interest contracts, unless inapplicable by reason of the nature of such contracts, a clause shall be deemed included even if not expressed, whereby any doubts and controversies which may raise concerning such contracts and which cannot be resolved amicably by the contracting parties, shall be decided by the competent courts of the Republic, in accordance with its laws and shall not on any grounds or for any reason give rise to foreign claims.[168]

The Constitution thus not only renounces diplomatic protection, but also unreservedly upholds the exclusive jurisdiction of national courts and national law on public interest contracts. In this regard, it appears that Article 155 of the Constitution would not be of relevance, as it seems to cover treaties between state parties, but not contracts made by the state as governed in Article 151. Article 155 essentially establishes that if there is any international agreement entered into by the Venezuelan government and a foreign party, any disputes arising between the parties in connection with the interpretation or implementation of the agreement should be resolved by "peaceful means recognized under international law or agreed upon between them in advance."[169]

Such a Calvo position does not, however, seem to have been taken in the Investment Protection and Promotion Law, which effectively adopts a very liberal, BIT-style approach toward the settlement of international investment disputes.[170] Articles 21 through to 23 of the Law deal with such issues. Article 23 sets forth the rule for the resolution of disputes relating to the application of the present law. It provides that investors (presumably national or foreign) may choose to submit the dispute to a local court or a local arbitration tribunal after having exhausted all administrative remedies.[171] If a dispute involves an "international investor," special channels will apply as provided for in Articles 21 and 22. Article 22 deals with situations where a dispute arises between Venezuela and an international investor whose home state has an investment treaty arrangement with Venezuela, or where provisions of the ICSID Convention or MIGA Convention are applicable to the dispute.[172] In such cases, arbitration under the terms of the relevant treaty or agreement would apply.[173] Alternatively, the international investor may opt to institute proceedings in Venezuela.[174] Related to these policies, Venezuela has signed 25 and ratified 21 BITs[175] and is a member of the ICSID Convention, MIGA Convention, New York Convention and the Panama Convention.[176]

---

[168] Art. 151, The Constitution of the Bolivarian Republic of Venezuela (adopted at the referendum of Dec. 15, 1999), *as in* WORLD CONSTITUTIONS, *supra* note 92.

[169] Id. art. 155.

[170] Art. 21 – 23, Investment Promotion and Protection Law, *supra* note 161.

[171] Id. art. 23.

[172] Id. art. 22.

[173] Id.

[174] Id.

[175] UNCTAD, *Country-specific Lists of BITs, supra* note 35.

[176] Bernardo Weininger & David M. Lindsey, *Venezuela and Annex 1: Table of Adherence to the New York Convention, Panama Convention and the Washington Convention, supra* note 44, *in* INTERNATIONAL ARBITRATION IN LATIN AMERICA, at 227 and 439.

In such disputes, where the disputant international investor is a national of a state with which Venezuela does not have an investment treaty and the dispute is related to "the interpretation and application of the rules provided for in the present Law," then the international investor may assign the dispute to its home state, which may then submit the case to international arbitration once diplomatic channels are exhausted.[177] In that case, the composition, method of selection, procedure and treatment of costs of the arbitration are to be determined by mutual agreement of the investor's home state and Venezuela.[178] Alternatively, the international investor may opt to take the domestic remedies established in Article 23.[179]

Two major conflicts between the Constitution and the FDI Law may be observed here. First, the diplomatic protection envisaged in Article 21 conflicts with the denunciation of diplomatic claims stipulated in Article 151 of the Constitution, as it could well the case that the dispute also involves a public interest contract. Secondly, for the same reason, the international remedies for disputes involving international investors provided for in Articles 21 and 22 also seem to breach of the exclusive national jurisdiction requirement in the same constitutional provision.

In this regard, it would be useful to recall that the Venezuelan government had already been challenged by local citizens for violation of Article 151 on its agreement to submit disputes arising out of oil concession agreements to international arbitration. In the socalled "Exploration Round Case," a group of Venezuelan citizens filed a petition in December 1995 with the Venezuelan Supreme Court asking for a ruling on the constitutionality of arbitration provisions in the Congressional Accord approving the 1995 Exploration Bidding Round, which included a provision (Condition 17) requiring all disputes arising from Association Agreements (i. e., oil exploration agreements with investors concluded following the bid) be resolved by binding arbitration.[180] Although the case was resolved in favor of arbitration and foreign investors, the uncertainty of the constitutionality of arbitration has not been eradicated because the Supreme Court did not do much to clarify the ambiguity surrounding the "nature of the contract" exception. This ambiguity was not helped by the new Constitution adopted in 1999 after the case was settled, which the kept contested provision (Article 127 in the previous Constitution) but merely renumbered it as Article 151. Further, in March 2001 the President of Venezuela issued Instructive Order No. 4 "[t]o regulate the internal review mechanisms for public interest contracts to be executed by the Republic, particularly, in connection with the inclusion of international arbitration clauses."[181] According to the Order, contracts concerning public interests must be submitted to the Attorney General of the Republic for an opinion on the legality of the arbitration clause in light of the Article 151

[177] Art. 21, Investment Promotion and Protection Law, *supra* note 161.

[178] Id.

[179] Id.

[180] Elisabeth E. Elijuri, *Oil Opening: A Constitutional Challenge, available at* http://www.natlaw.com/pubs/spveenl.htm (last visited Feb. 12, 2006).

[181] Werninger & Lindsey, *Venezuela, supra* note 176, at 235.

of the new Constitution.[182] In a more recent case, the *Minera Ias Cristinas, C. A. (MINCA) v. Corporacion Venezuelana de Guyana (CVG) case* (the *MINCA Case*),[183] the Supreme Court dismissed MINCA's petition on the ground that the subject matter concerned state assets and therefore could not be subject to arbitration.[184] The Court founded its decision on, *inter alia*, the aforementioned Article 151 of the Constitution, which generally subjects public interests contracts to the exclusive jurisdiction of local courts.[185] It thus restarted the uncertainty of Venezuela's position towards international arbitration.

Venezuelan law is therefore characterized by, on the one hand, the rather traditional provisions in the Constitution that adopt a Calvo approach, and, on the other hand, the very liberal provisions in the FDI law that adopt BIT-style standards of treatment and dispute settlement methods. Venezuelan law thus displays significant disparities between the two levels of laws, particularly on dispute settlement. The constitutionality of governmental actions has already been challenged again and again before Venezuelan courts.

J. Observations

Despite differences in detail, four general observations might be extracted from the preceding survey on the domestic laws in the nine major Latin American states.

First of all, all the countries considered subscribe to the national/equal treatment standard. In most of the countries, the national/equal treatment standard is guaranteed in the national constitutions and reaffirmed in relevant FDI laws. Though this generally demonstrates the continued existence and validity of the Calvo principle, it must be noted that there has been a shift of emphasis, from non-discrimination against nationals and national investors, toward a general requirement of non-discrimination based on nationality. Thus, in the constitutions of most countries, foreigners and foreign investors are guaranteed the "same rights and obligation" as nationals and national investors. In some countries, such as Colombia and Venezuela, emphasis has been explicitly placed on both ends of the national treatment standard: the non-discrimination against foreign investors on one end and non-discrimination against national investors on the other. Clearly such legislation reflects the influence of BITs; the recent Venezuelan FDI law effectively copies BIT standards. It might be said that Calvo and BIT approaches, the two traditionally distinct and opposing approaches towards national treatment, have both been transformed and have converged here to formulate a standard of national treatment that pursues genuine equality: equality of treatment regardless of nationality. Nevertheless, such transformation and convergence may still be regarded as changes within the Calvo paradigm of national treatment, a paradigm based on the equality of states and the equality of individuals.

Second, apart from Brazil (and, to a lesser degree, Colombia,) all countries have accepted international investment treaty-based arbitration, by explicit domestic provi-

[182] Werninger & Lindsey, *Venezuela, supra* note 176, at 235.

[183] Decision No. 0083 of the Political Administrative Chamber of the Supreme Court of July 15, 2004.

[184] Id.

[185] Id.

sions and/or by actively entering into investment treaties. However, the degree of such acceptance varies. Thus in Bolivia only "technical disputes" might be referred to international arbitration, while in Venezuela, foreign investment disputes can be submitted for international arbitration even though there is no treaty obligation specifically providing for such submissions. Needless to say, international investment treaty-based arbitration is simply inaccessible to foreign investors in Brazil. The access of different foreign investors to international arbitration varies, depending on whether there is a valid BIT between their home states and the host country, and on the specific provisions on dispute settlement contained in such BITs. Nonetheless, despite the potential issue of constitutionality in some countries and apart from Brazil, it is clear that Latin American states have generally moved away from absolute exclusive national jurisdiction and have accepted general international law as applicable law. In this sense, one may say that Calvo has been substantially eroded and generally discarded, albeit with certain important exceptions and reservations highlighted in the end of Part Ill.

Third, diplomatic protection is still expressly denounced in the constitutions of most countries, namely Bolivia, Colombia, Ecuador, Mexico, Peru and Venezuela, particularly in relation to public interest contracts. In this regard, it might be said that Calvo is still very much alive.

Finally, recent years seem to have seen a "resurgence" of Calvo, witnessed most notably by constitutionality challenges in Argentina, Colombia and Venezuela against BITs and investment arbitration, and Brazil's PPP Law prohibiting international arbitration.

V. Conclusion: Calvo is Not Dead but Deactivated

The preceding survey of domestic laws and international treaties by Latin American States shows that Calvo is still alive with regard to diplomatic protection, alive but transformed and melded with BITs on the national treatment standard, and greatly eroded and largely discarded on the exclusive national jurisdiction and national law requirement. Admittedly, the last element, the exclusive national jurisdiction and national law requirement, constitutes the core of the whole doctrine. Even on this point, as discussed above, Calvo is not completely dead, as there are still important exceptions and reservations. It would therefore only be fair to conclude that Calvo has been significantly changed, or substantially "disfigured," or generally "deactivated," but not yet completely "dead." When political and economic climates are "right," it could be re-activated again and "resurge," as what seems to be happening.

“卡尔沃主义”死了吗？*

卡尔沃主义的“死亡”问题并不是一个新问题。早在1955年，Shea教授就已经宣布它的死亡，理由是卡尔沃主义“不能赢得作为一项国际法原则所必须获得的认可”，她这里所指的认可自然是指西方国家的认可。[1] 在20世纪90年代中期，有学者基于拉美国家在国际与国内的立法实践中改变了对外国投资的态度的事实，再次宣称卡尔沃主义“行将就木”（imminent death）。[2] 十多年后的今天，卡尔沃主义“行将就木”的预言真的应验了吗？笔者认为卡尔沃主义并没有完全死亡，而只是暂时搁浅了。

本文分为五个部分。第一部分探讨卡尔沃主义的本质与要素，以确定评判的标准。第二部分介绍自20世纪90年代以来拉美国家对外国投资的态度发生转变的大背景。第三、四部分通过对拉美国家国际条约和国内立法实践进行分析来验证卡尔沃主义是否以及在何种程度上已经死亡。第五部分对本文进行概括和总结。

一、卡尔沃主义：本质与要素

（一）卡尔沃主义的本质

一般认为，卡尔沃主义的本质在于“平等待遇”/“国民待遇”或“平等”。例如，研究该理论的最有影响的学者Donald Shea认为“不干预和外国人与本国人的绝对平等这两个概念是卡尔沃主义的本质”。[3] Manning-Cabrol在其不久前发表

---

* 本文发表在《国际经济法学刊》（第15卷）2008年第2期。作者单文华，译者张生、劳志健。

英文原文曾在《美国比较法学刊》（American Journal of Comparative Law, Vol. 55, No. 3, 2007）上发表。本文作者关于本问题的早期研究成果曾以《卡尔沃主义的“死亡”与“再生”》为题，发表在《国际经济法学刊》第13卷第1期（北京大学出版社2006年版）上，谨此说明。

〔1〕 Donald Shea, The Calvo Clause: A Problem of Inter-American and International Law and Diplomacy, Minnesota University Press, 1956, p. 20.

〔2〕 Denise Manning-Cabrol, The Imminent Death of the Calvo Clause and the Rebirth of the Calvo Principle: Equality of Foreign and National Investors, 26 Law & Pol'y Int'l Bus. 1169 (1995).

〔3〕 Shea, *supra* note 1, at 19 – 20.

的论文中也认为“平等是卡尔沃主义的核心”。[4] 然而，虽然“国家平等”与国家主权构成了卡尔沃主义的法理基础，“平等”本身并非卡尔沃主义的根本本质。卡尔沃主义所强调的不是国家间或外国人与本国人之间的“绝对平等”，而是拒绝大国及其国民享有的优越性和帝国特权。也就是说，卡尔沃主义的本质在于“反超级国家待遇”或“反超国民待遇”，它着重于反对和摒弃西方强权针对弱小国家、欠发达东道国及其国民的任何歧视性待遇，这种歧视性待遇是相对于西方各大势力之间以及他们要求上述东道国给予其国民的待遇而言的。与“平等/国民待遇”不同，“反超国民待遇”并不否认和拒绝东道国经常给予其本国国民的一些特权。对卡尔沃的著作进行深入解读，可以发现他也主张这种区别：虽然该主义确实采用了国家间和国民间的平等作为法理基础，但其反对的不是个人基于公民身份在其母国得到的特权，而是外国及其国民在东道国享有的特权。例如，他写道：“一次又一次，拉丁美洲国家被要求接受这样一个原则，那就是外国人应享有比本国人更多的敬重和更广泛更突出的特权。这一原则是内在地与国家平等原则背道而驰的……如果在当前案件中适用这一原则作为确立国家责任的原则，就会创制一种过分的致命的对大国有利而对弱国有害的特权，从而造成内国国民与外国国民之间的一种不合理的不平等。”[5]

因此，他得出结论：“政府对外国人所担负的责任不能超过对本国国民所担负的责任。”[6]

卡尔沃的“反超级国家”或者“反超国民待遇”的主张具体表现在国内宪法与法律、双边和区域的条约中广泛运用的“卡尔沃条款”上。这些条款经常强调外国人与外国投资者受到的待遇应“不优于”本国人和本国投资者所享有的待遇，有关内容将在本部分的第三项中进一步探讨。卡尔沃的“反超国民待遇”观点可以从其产生与发展的具体背景中得到解释。正如 Shea 所指出，卡尔沃主义是产生于这样的时代背景，当时，拉美国家急需“强有力的逻辑上、道德上以及法律上的抵御工具”，来抵御它们面临着“（西方大国）现实或想象中的欺凌，它们动辄为本国在外侨民提起外交保护，甚至不惜兴兵索债”。而这种种欺凌是积贫积弱的拉美国家无力用武力来抗拒的。[7]

把卡尔沃主义阐述成“反超级大国”或者“反超国民待遇”而不是“平等”本身

---

〔4〕 卡尔沃主义中的平等包含两层意思：“国家间的平等和本国人与外国人间的平等。” *See* Manning-Cabrol, *supra* note 2, at 1172.

〔5〕 Shea, *supra* note 1, at 18.

〔6〕 Id., at 19.

〔7〕 Id., at 14.

或“国民待遇”不但是为了准确阐明该理论的核心,更是为了把卡尔沃主义与双边投资协定(BITs)中经常运用到的“国民待遇标准”加以区别。事实上,虽然以上两种标准都强调“平等”的价值追求,以致被评论学者所混淆,[8]但是卡尔沃主义下的“反超国民待遇”和双边投资协定下的“国民待遇”实际上反映的是“平等”的两个极端维度:前者强调消除对东道国及其国民的歧视性待遇,而后者则强调消除对外国人的歧视性待遇。[9] 多数双边投资协定将“国民待遇”表述为“不应低于给予本国投资者的待遇”,因此称之为“非次国民待遇”更显确切。诚然,这两个不同的原则可能在“平等”与“国民待遇”的大原则下交汇、融合,尤其是在“同等待遇”表述得以应用的情况下。这似乎正是20世纪90年代拉丁美洲所发生的情况,正如下文所述的那样。

(二)卡尔沃主义的关键要素

卡尔沃主义的本质包含了两方面的关键要素:实体上的和程序上的。[10] 从实体上来看,卡尔沃主义强调外国国民不能享有优于东道国给予其本国国民的任何权利和利益的待遇。这又有着具体的和抽象的两重含义:就具体的或者实践的层次而言,其禁止东道国给予外国以及外国投资者任何特权或激励;就抽象或者理论的层次而言,其反对把所谓的“国际最低标准”作为衡量包括外国投资者在内的外国国民的待遇的法律标准。从程序上来看,卡尔沃主义强调外国国民除了东道国给予本国国民的救济外,不应该被赋予任何额外的救济。因此,其暗示了对非本国救济(如包括外交保护或军事干预在内的外国或者国际救济)与非本国法(外国或者国际法)的排除适用。作为程序上的要求,排除非国内法适用反映和融合了反对“国际最低标准”的实体上的要求,因此两者可被视为一个要素。由此可见,卡尔沃主义所体现的是一种建立在绝对的国家主权和国家平等观基础上的传统的国家中心国际法观。

概括起来,卡尔沃主义事实上意味着:一方面,拒绝给予外国人和外国投资者任何实体上的特权(“反超国民待遇”),包括具体的激励和利益,以及抽象层面上

---

[8] 例如,Manning-Cabrol 认为国际投资条约中的国民待遇与卡尔沃主义坚持的“平等(国民)待遇”原则相同,并且认为卡尔沃主义在这些条约中获了新生(在国内立法也同样如此)。*See* Manning-Cabrol, supra note 2, at 1195.

[9] Zamora 也注意到了两原则间这样的区别,并指出:“然而,与国民待遇不同的是,卡尔沃主义是为了应对对外国国民的优惠而诞生的,而不是为了应对对外国国民的歧视。换言之,卡尔沃主义的目的是将外国国民降到与内国国民相同的层次,而国民待遇的目的则是将外国国民上升到与内国国民相同的层次。”See Stephen Zamora, Allocating Legislative Competence in The Americas: The Early Experience under NAFTA and the Challenge of Hemispheric Integration, 19 Hous. J. Int'l L. 615, 622(1997).

[10] Kenneth J. Vandevelde, Sustainable Liberalism and the International Investment Regime, 19 *Mich. J. Int'l L.* 373, 379(1998).

的"国际最低标准"待遇。另一方面,拒绝给予外国人任何程序上的特权,包括求助于非本国救济和适用非国内法。更具体地说,拒绝给予外国人实体上与程序上的特权包括了以下三个基本要素:就是"反超国民待遇"标准、排他性的当地救济和排除外交保护。[11] 其中,第一个要素是实体性的要求,后两个则是程序性的要求。作为卡尔沃主义的实体性标准,"反超国民待遇"标准可比喻成该主义的身躯主干,而"排他性的当地救济"和"排除外交保护"则可比喻成身躯靠之站立的双脚或身躯上的双手。缺了双脚或双手,身躯就难以有效地运作,从某种意义上讲,"排他性的当地救济"和"排除外交保护"比"反超国民待遇"标准事实上更重要。

(三)卡尔沃主义与卡尔沃条款

卡尔沃主义不但阻止了外交保护的槛用,并且也"否定了该制度自身而又没有提供一个可接受的替代制度",因此不难理解它不能为欧洲与美国政府以及法律界所接受。[12] 反过来,拉美国家则"怀着极大的热情拥抱"了卡尔沃主义,并且通过"卡尔沃条款"来实施卡尔沃主义,以此应付反对卡尔沃主义的西方势力。[13] 卡尔沃条款一般存在于宪法、国内法律、国际条约和外国投资者与拉美国家政府签订的契约里。[14] 例如,1933 年秘鲁《宪法》就包含以下条款:

"第 31 条:任何人的财产均排他地受秘鲁法律的管辖,同时在税收、费用及限制上受该法律相关规定的约束。在财产方面,调整外国人的法律条文与本国人相同,外国人在任何时候都不能有所例外或诉诸外交保护。"[15]

厄瓜多尔 1938 年的一项国内立法也作出了同样的规定:外国人,一旦来到本国境内,即自觉接受厄瓜多尔法律约束,没有例外。外国人需遵守宪法、法律、判例和国家政策,无论何种原因,何种情况,都不可违反既有的待遇、判例和政策。[16] 作为"卡尔沃条款"体现在合同中的一个例子,墨西哥与堪萨斯北美挖掘机公司签订的合同中规定有以下条款:

---

〔11〕 这些要素同样是卡尔沃主义的三主要要素,see Manning-Cabrol, *supra* note 2, at 11730。然而,Lipstein 认为卡尔沃主义有五要素:"当地管辖、法律选择自由、法律适用范围、拒绝母国外交保护和国际法下的权利放弃。"See Kurt Lipstein, The Place of the Calvo Clause in International Law, 22 *Brit. Y. B. Int'l* L. 130, 131 – 33 (1945). Wesley 同样认为卡尔沃主义有五要素:(1)当地管辖;(2)本国法适用;(3)外国人享有基于契约安排的相同待遇;(4)拒绝母国外交保护;(5)国际法下的权利放弃。See Roger C. Wesley, The Procedural Malaise of Foreign Investment Disputes in Latin America: From Local Tribunals to Fact-finding, 7 *Law & Pol'y Int'l Bus.* 813, 818 (1975).

〔12〕 Shea, *supra* note 1, at 20.

〔13〕 Id., at 21.

〔14〕 Id., at 21 – 32.

〔15〕 1993 年 4 月 9 日通过的《宪法》, See Russell H. Fitzgibbon (ed.) *Constitutions of the Ameri-cas*, The University of Chicago Press, 1948, pp. 670 – 71, as cited in*id.*, at 24.

〔16〕 Shea, *supra* note 1, at 26 and n. 56.

"第18条:合同双方及其雇员以及直接或间接地执行该合同的其他人,在墨西哥共和国境内,在执行有关工作与履行该项合同过程中,在任何情况下必须被视为墨西哥公民,关于与合同有关的利益和交易,其不能主张,也不能拥有墨西哥共和国法律没有赋予的任何其他权利和手段,也不能享有比墨西哥国民更优惠的权利。其被剥夺了作为外国国民所享有的任何特殊权利,在与合同有关的任何事务中,在任何情况下,外国外交机构的干预都是不允许的。"[17]

卡尔沃主义在国际条约上也得到充分的体现,[18]特别是在拉丁美洲区域一体化议定书文件中。例如,安第斯条约组织的第一部《外国投资法典》(即安第斯委员会第24决议)禁止成员国"给予外国投资者优越于本国投资者的待遇"[19]和要求在任何有关投资和技术转让的合约文书中,均不得有排除东道国本国对有关冲突和纠纷的管辖权或允许投资者母国代位求偿的规定。[20]

卡尔沃主义首现于拉美国家,但它的影响已经不局限于仅占世界1/4的拉美,特别是"二战"后,随着反殖民主义运动的兴起与发展,亚非建立了大量的新国家,卡尔沃主义也随之在这些国家间传播。这些新独立国家,就像拉美国家一样,更热衷于接受这个以国家为中心或称绝对主义的国际法理论。因为他们认为该理论能帮助维护他们国家的利益,特别是取回之前被西方发达国家控制的国内自然资源的控制权。同时,组成苏维埃共同体的共产主义政府也十分赞许卡尔沃主义,因为该理论可以阻止和排除西方资本主义的渗透与影响。正因如此,卡尔沃主义已深深渗透到了拉美国家以及广大亚非发展中国家的国内立法中。例如,中国从1986年以来所有调整涉外合同的法律都同样规定了"卡尔沃条款"中国境内的中外合资经营企业合同、中外合作经营企业合同、中外合作勘探开发自然资源合同,需适用中国法律和由中国法院管辖。[21] 此外,20世纪60年代,卡尔沃条款在联合国大会的决议上也得到体现,当时正值国际经济新秩序运动达到顶峰,新兴国家与苏维埃共同体在联合国组成联合阵线且在联合国占据了多数。[22] 联合国大会第3281号决议第二节第2款一方面强调国家有权根据其本国法律规定对外国投资进行管理并拒绝给予外国投资以优惠待遇。另一方面又规定在对外

---

〔17〕 Shea, *supra* note 1, at 29 and n. 56, at 29.

〔18〕 参见此类条约的详细列表。

〔19〕 Art. 50, Decision 24. Andean Commísison: Decision 24, Common Regime of Treatment of Foreign Capital and of Trademarks, Patents, Licenses, and Royalties, art. 50, Nov. 30, 1976, 161. L. *M.* 138, at 153 (1977) [hereinafter Decision 24].

〔20〕 Art. 51, Decision 24.

〔21〕 参见《中华人民共和国合同法》第126条(规定此类合同应当适用中国法律)和《中华人民共和国民事诉讼法》第246条(规定此类合同引起的任何纠纷应由中国法院管辖)。

〔22〕 Vandevelde, *supra* note 10, at 384.

国投资收归国有、征收或转移时，应由采取此种措施的国家“考虑到相关立法”给予赔偿。以致第3281号决议被认为是世界性版本的“卡尔沃条款”。[23] 由此，此决议标志着卡尔沃主义达到历史高峰。

联合国大会上以压倒性多数票通过的第3281号决议保证了卡尔沃主义的永久国际地位。然而，在第3281号决议通过后不久，经济自由化与全球化的浪潮席卷了世界。卡尔沃主义面临着严峻的挑战，被推到了死亡的边缘。

二、投资自由化与拉美国家

作为经济自由化与全球化的重要表现，投资自由化于20世纪80年代开始席卷广大发展中国家，并于20世纪90年代达到巅峰。导致此现象的原因是多重的，其中最重要的原因包括20世纪80年代初期开始的发展中国家的外债危机，20世纪90年代初期苏联东欧社会主义集团的解体，以及以私人投资和出口贸易为特征的“亚洲四小龙”的成功范例等因素的综合作用。这些因素导致了20世纪80年代以来国际投资自由化的蓬勃发展，并在90年代形成世界性的浪潮，席卷了几乎所有的发展中国家。[24]

投资自由化的最重要表现之一是外国投资监管体制自由化。联合国贸发会(UNCTAD)发布的《2005年世界投资报告》表明，自1991年以来，每年平均有64个国家对外国直接投资的法律和法规作出修改。

在这一时期所做出的2156个修订中，促进投资自由化的修订就有2006个，占了总数的93%[25]（见表1）。投资自由化的另一个重要因素是双边投资协定(BITs)的大量签订。UNCTAD的统计数据显示，截至2004年年底，世界范围内BIT的数量达到了2392个，[26]其中有2010个在20世纪90年代签订，而1996年是BIT签订数量最多的年份[27]（见图1、图2）。同时，大部分国家热衷于加入双边的、区域的和跨区域的贸易与投资的协定(PTIAs)。截至2005年4月，这类的协定

---

〔23〕 Lillich认为拉美国家在该宪章上的努力对于推动卡尔沃主义是杯水车薪。See Rich-ard Lillich, The Diplomatic Protection of Nationals Abroad: An Elementary Principle of International Law Under Attack, 69 *Am. j. Int'l*L. 359, 361(1975). Schneiderman认为卡尔沃主义是“国际经济新秩序(1973年联合国大会的第3171号决议)和联合国《各国经济权利与义务宪章》的中流砥柱”。See David Schneiderman, Investment Rules and The New Constitutionalism, 25 *Law & Soc.* In*quiry*757, 766(20).

〔24〕 Vandevelde, *supra* note 10, at 386 - 91.

〔25〕 Id. , at 386 - 91.

〔26〕 实际上截至2006年年底，世界范围内BIT的数量已达到2573个。参见UNCTALD, *World Investment Report* 2007, *UNCTAD/WIR/*2007, at 46。

〔27〕 UNCTAD, *World Investment Report* 2005, UNCTAD/WIRI2005, at 28.

已达212个,[28]其中87%是在20世纪90年代签署的。[29] 这类协定在涵盖的内容上与BITs有所不同,但它在保护投资和促进自由化上与BITs有着异曲同工之处。两者都承诺给予外国投资者国民待遇与最惠国待遇、保证资本与利润的自由转移、对国有化给予补偿、在解决外国投资者与东道国之间的投资纠纷时接受国际仲裁庭的管辖权。也就是说,这些双边的、区域的和多边的协定目的在于建立国际水准的标准和提供国际投资争端解决平台,而这两方面都是有违卡尔沃主义的。

表1 国内投资立法的修订(1991年至2004年)

(单位:个)

年份	修订FDI法律的国家数	FDI法律的修订数量	有利于外国投资者的法律修订数量	不利于外国投资者的法律修订数量
1991	35	82	80	2
1992	43	79	79	
1993	57	102	101	1
1994	49	110	108	2
1995	64	112	106	6
1996	65	114	98	16
1997	76	151	135	16
1998	60	145	136	9
1999	63	140	131	9
2000	69	150	147	3
2001	71	208	194	14
2002	70	248	236	12
2003	82	244	220	24
2004	102	271	235	36

资料来源:联合国贸发会:《2005年世界投资报告》,第26页。

〔28〕 截至2006年年底,这类协定共有241个。参见UNCTALD, *World Investment Report* 2007, UNCTAD/WIR I2007, at 46。

〔29〕 Ibid.

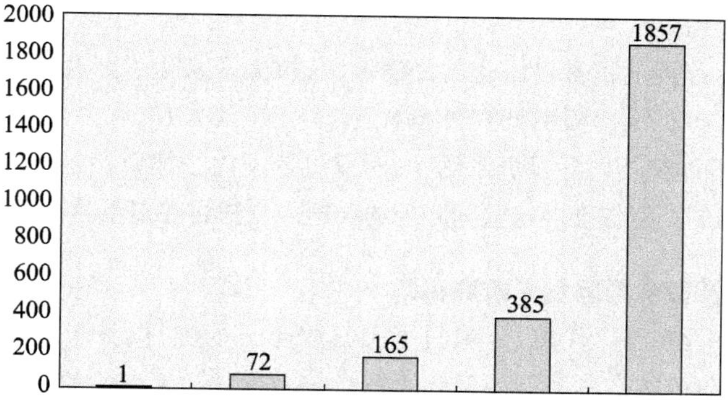

图 1　BITs 的增量(1959 年至 1999 年)　　(单位:个)

资料来源:联合国贸发会:《双边投资协定》(1959 年至 1999 年)(2000 年),第 1 页。

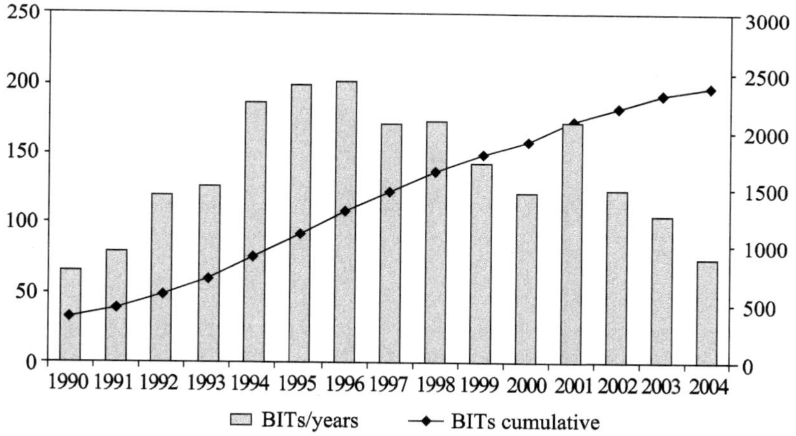

图 2　BITs 的年存量(1990 年至 2004 年)　　(单位:个)

资料来源:联合国贸发会:《2005 世界投资报告》,第 27 页。

拉美国家最初抵制投资自由化和此类协定是不足为奇的。然而,20 世纪 90 年代发生的经济事件,主要是拉美的债务危机,促使拉美国家不得不将其注意力从依靠商业贷款转移到吸引外国直接投资上来。债务危机使得"商业银行向欠发达国家(LDCs)[30]发放的自愿性贷款剧减"。[31] 外国商业贷款的剧减迫使欠发达国家采取措施平衡国际收支并寻找国外商业贷款的替代形式,最显然的选择就是

〔30〕 LDC 意为 Less Development Country(欠发达国家)。

〔31〕 *See* Stijn Claessens, *Alternative Forms of External Finance*, World Bank, Working Paper No. 812, 1991.

外国直接投资(FDI)。[32]

面对世界范围的投资自由化的汹涌浪潮,拉美国家除了开放本国市场和采取更高的投资保护标准以阪引外资外别无选择。[33] 结果是,许多拉美国家于20世纪80年代末开始缔结国际投资条约,同时修订其国内法律以接纳国际仲裁和采纳外国投资待遇的国际标准。这些国际条约和国内立法将在以下的两部分分别探讨。

三、拉美国家的国际投资条约实践

到了20世纪80年代末,拉美国家大都放弃了抵抗,投身于投资自由化的国际洪流之中,积极签订各类型的国际投资协定:双边的、区域性的和全球性的。以下将对这三类协定逐一分析,判断其多大程度上背离了卡尔沃主义。

(一)双边投资协定

UNCTAD的数据显示,拉美国家自20世纪80年代末才开始签订双边投资协定。[34] 到20世纪90年代末期,拉美国家共签订了300个BITs,其中93%是20世纪90年代签订的。[35] 其中,除了巴西和哥伦比亚外,绝大多数国家都已经批准了一些双边投资协定,例如,阿根廷批准了43个,秘鲁24个,智利22个,古巴19个,厄瓜多尔18个,委内瑞拉17个,玻利维亚15个,巴拉圭15个,乌拉圭13个,萨尔瓦多10个。[36] 此外,巴拿马批准了9个,墨西哥3个,洪都拉斯3个,尼加拉瓜3个,伯利兹2个,哥斯达黎加2个,圭亚那2个,多米尼加共和国1个。[37] 与其他BITs一样,

---

〔32〕“替代性金融”是指“公共资产外的各种外部资金形式……(替代性金融)包括FDI、项目融资、证券投资、封闭股权基金、私人贷款、租赁、合资、类股权合同初其他私人间贷款形式”。Ibid.

〔33〕一些经济学家认为该转变是对20世纪50年代、60年代和70年代的重要替代模式的否定,是新的发展模式的呈现。See generally, Rudiger Dombusch & Sebastian Edwards(eds.)The Macro economic. of Populism In Latin America, University of Chicago Press, 1991, and Victor Bulmer-Thomas, The Economic History of Latin America Since Independence, Cambridge University Press, 1995.

〔34〕UNCTAD. *Bilateral Investment Treaties* 1959 - 1999. UNCTAD/ITE/I1A/2. at 15(2000). UNCTAD统计数据表明,截至2004年年底,拉美和加勒比海地区国家的BIT为451个。*See* UNCTAD: Recent Developments in International Investment Agreements. Ⅱ*A Monitor* No. 2(Aug. 30. 2005). UNCTAD/WEB/ITE/IIT/2005/1. at 2.

〔35〕Ibid.

〔36〕UNCTAD, *Bilateral Investment Treaties* 1959 - 1999, *supra* note 34, at 7 - 14.

〔37〕以上是2005年统计数据,实际上根据最新统计的数据,巴西是唯一一个签订了部分BIT(14个)而没有批准一个的国家。除此之外,阿根廷批准了54个,伯利兹6个,玻利维亚19个,智利39个,哥伦比亚1个,哥斯达黎加13个,古巴39个,厄瓜多尔12个,圭亚那3个,墨西哥19个,尼加拉瓜12个,巴拿马17个,巴拉圭21个,秘鲁28个,乌拉圭26个,委内瑞拉24个,萨尔瓦多20个。UNCTAD, Country-specific List of BITs., available at http://www.unctad.org/Templates/Page.asp? intitemID = 2344&lang = 1(last visited Mar. 28, 2008). 对这类的未获批准的BITs的分析材料,可参见UNCTAD: Recent in lntemalwnal lnvestment Agreements, *supra* note 9, a\8. 关于国际仲裁的适用的进一步讨论可参见。Ceskoslovenska Obchooni Banka, A. S. v. The Slovak Republic(ICSID Case No. ARB/97/4), Decision on the Further and Partial Objection \0 Jurisdiction(Dec. 1, 2000), paras. 33 - 59. The text of this Decision is published online as it appears in Vol. 15, NG2 issue of ICSID Review-Foreign Investment Law Journal (2000), available at http://www.worldbank.org/icsidlcaseslCSGb.pdf(last visited Feb. 5, 2007). 此案中,该BIT是签订但没获得批准,仲裁机构认为国家不能基于该BIT把此争端提交给ICSID处理。仲裁机构认为捷克政府不能根据所签订的联合协定中规定的该协定由国内法和BIT调整的规定来把此争端提交给ICSID处理。

这时期拉美国家签订的BITs都包含了两类条款：一是在实体上接受有关外国投资者待遇的国际标准，如公平待遇、国民待遇和最惠国待遇、资本与利润的自由转移及国有化的补偿保证；二是在程序上接受国际仲裁庭的管辖权。[38]

在拉美国家早期签订的BITs中，往往还有一点卡尔沃主义的痕迹，强调将投资纠纷提交国际仲裁必须满足一定的条件。[39] 例如，早期阿根廷缔结的BITs往往要求满足如下条件：在提交国际仲裁之前该争端必须首先提交国内法院，同时要么国内法院已经就此作出裁决；要么争议已提交国内法院且已过一定时日但未能得出裁决。[40] 换言之，用尽当地救济是提交国际仲裁的必要前提条件。然而，在一些较晚近的BITs中，上述前提条件已被废弃。例如，在阿根廷与美国签订的BIT中，用尽当地救济不再是提交国际仲裁的必要前提条件。[41] 据此，有人认为，阿根廷与美国签订的BIT标志着"阿根廷对管制外国投资达一个多世纪之久的卡尔沃主义的弃绝"。[42]

其他11个拉美国家（包括玻利维亚、厄瓜多尔、萨尔瓦多、格林纳达、海地、洪都拉斯、牙买加、尼加拉瓜、巴拿马、特立尼达与多巴哥以及乌拉圭）（见表2）与美国签订的BIT也都没有规定将争端提交国际仲裁要以寻求当地救济为前提。[43] 就准据法而言，尽管上述协定大都并不规定争端解决的具体准据法，但它们一般都规定投资协定不得影响东道国国内法、投资协议与投资许可，以及"国际法律义务"[44]的法律效力。2004年签订的乌拉圭与美国BIT（美国自颁布其2004年投资条约范本后签订的第一个BIT）第3条至第10条则明确规定，东道国与投资者之间的争议，如果是由于对本协定项下的实体法律义务（第3条至第10条义务）的违反，则应适用本条约规定和使用的国际法律规则；如果是出于对投资许可或投资协议的违反，则适用投资许可或投资协议规定的"法律规则"或者双方约定的法律，如果这种法律规则不具体或者当事双方没有约定，则应适用：（1）东道国的法律包括

---

[38] Jeswald W. Salacuse, BIT by BIT: The Growth of Bilateral Investment Treaties and Their Impact on Foreign Investment in Developing Countries, 24 *lnt'l Law*. 655, 664 - 73(1990).

[39] 在最近的一篇文章里，Scheurer把这样的条约条款视为"卡尔沃主义的孙儿"。See Christoph Scheurer, Calvo's Grandchildren: The Return of Local Remedies in Investment Arbitration, 4 *Law and Practice of International Courts and Tribunals*1, at 3 - 5(2005).

[40] Bernardo M. Cremades, Disputes Arising oul of Foreign Direcl Investm enl in Latin Ameri-ca: A New Look at the Calvo Doctrine and Other Jurisdictional Issues, 59 *Dispute Resolution journal* 78, 80(2004).

[41] Art. 7, Argentina-U. S. BIT.

[42] Heribert Golsong, Introduction to Treaty Concerning the Reciprocal Encouragement and Protection of Investment between Argentina and the USA, Nov. 14, 1991, 31 I. L. M. 124(1991).

[43] See art. 9, Bolivia-U. S. Bπ; art. 6, Ecuador-U. S. BIT; art. 9, El Salvador-U. S. BIT; art. 6, Grenada-U. S. BIT; art. 7, Haiti-U. S. BIT; art. 9, Honduras-U. S. BIT; art. 7, Nicaragua-U. S. BIT; art. 1, 2000 Amending Protocol to Paraguay-U. S. BIT; art. 9, Trinidad and Tobago-U. S. BIT; and art. 24, Uruguay-U. S. BIT.

[44] See, e. g., art. 10, Argentina-US BIT.

其冲突法,以及(2)可适用的国际法律规范。[45] 换言之,在确立可适用的法律规则时应包括可适用的国际法,除非争端涉及一项投资协议或许可,而投资协议或投资许可已对可适用的法律规则作出具体规定或者当事方另有约定。

以上关于拉美国家所签订的 BITs 的概况分析表明,拉美国家早期签订的 BITs 中,往往还有一点卡尔沃主义的痕迹(强调将投资纠纷提交国际仲裁必须满足一定的条件),但晚近拉美国家的双边投资条约充分接受了非东道国管辖权和非东道国法的适用,与其过去坚守的卡尔沃主义可以说是渐行渐远。事实上,在 BITs 接受国际仲裁解决国家与投资者争端方面,可以说一场"悄无声息的革命"已经发生。[46]

表 2　美国与拉美国家间的 BITs 概况

缔约方	签订日期	生效日期
阿根廷	14 - 11 - 1991	28 - 10 - 1994
玻利维亚	17 - 04 - 1998	06 - 06 - 2001
厄瓜多尔	27 - 08 - 1993	11 - 05 - 1997
萨尔瓦多	10 - 03 - 1999	
格林纳达	02 - 05 - 1986	03 - 03 - 1989
海地	13 - 12 - 1983	
洪都拉斯	01 - 07 - 1995	01 - 07 - 2001
牙买加	04 - 02 - 1994	07 - 03 - 1997
尼加拉瓜	01 - 07 - 1995	
巴拿马	27 - 10 - 1982	30 - 05 - 1991
特立尼达与多巴哥	26 - 09 - 1994	26 - 12 - 1996
乌拉圭	04 - 11 - 2005	

资料来源:联合国贸发会:截至 2005 年 6 月 1 日,拉美国家与美国签订的双边投资协定总量,载 http://www.unctad.org/Templates/Page.asp? intItemID = 2344&lang = 1,2008 年 3 月 28 日访问。

(二)区域性投资贸易协定

早在 20 世纪 60 年代,拉丁美洲区域经济一体化运动就已开始,一些拉美国

---

〔45〕 Art. 30, Uruguay-US BIT.

〔46〕 Nigel Blackaby et al., Overview of Regional Developments, *in International Arbitration in* Latin *America*, at 10(Nigel Blackaby et al. eds., 2002)

家成立了安第斯条约组织。[47] 然而,拉美国家自20世纪80年代末开始的自由化浪潮导致了安第斯条约内容发生了改变。在上文提及的该组织的原《外国直接投资法典》(安第斯委员会第24号决议)中,有两项著名的"卡尔沃条款"(第50条与第51条):一方面禁止给予外国投资者"超国民待遇";另一方面,禁止把争端诉诸外国法院。不过这两个条款在20世纪80年代末和90年代初被逐渐修订了。1987年,安第斯条约组织修改了其先前的《外国直接投资法典》,代之以第220号决议,该决议保留了"反超国民待遇"的条款,[48]但放松了严格的国内管辖权要求。该决议第34条规定"直接投资和技术转让的争端解决,各成员国应依据其本国法的规定来处理。[49] 换言之,它让各成员国自主决定是坚持还是背离卡尔沃主义。这就产生了一个疑问:既然"反超国民待遇"条款仍然存在,那么安第斯条约成员国内的外国投资者是否仍然必须像东道国技资者一样,只适用东道国国内法和诉诸国内法院?[50]

安第斯条约组织对外国投资态度的更大转变发生在1991年,最新的与最自由的《外国直接投资法典》即第291号决议在该年获得通过。[51] 为了促进外国资本与技术流入安第斯共同市场(ANCOM),该法典进一步在"反超国民待遇"方面有所放松。[52] 第291号决议第2条规定"原则上外国投资者应享有与本国投资者同样的权利和义务,除非成员国国内法另有规定"。[53] 该条款不但赋予成员国在决定外国投资者待遇上的自主性,还标志着从强调"反超国民待遇"向强调"平等待遇"或"国民待遇"的微妙转变,这样更接近多数BITs中规定的国民待遇原则。因此这可作为"平等待遇"与"国民待遇"这两个原本不同的待遇标准达到

---

〔47〕 在拉美最近的区域一体化浪潮中,出现了与《安第斯条约》规定的不一致情况,不再坚持当地救济和重要的替代政策而是把重点放在市场的作用上。Seba Stian Edwards, Latin American Economic Integration: A New Perspective on an Old Dream, 16 *World Economy* 317 (1993).

〔48〕 第220号决议第33条规定"成员国不得给予外国人比本国国民更高的待遇"。虽然第33条与第50条在行文上有个别差异,但目的还是一样即外国人不能享有比本国国民更高的待遇。*See* Eduardo A. Wiesner, ANCOM: A New Attitude toward Foreign Investment? *U Miami Inter-am.* 435, 447 (1993).

〔49〕 Art. 34, the Common Foreign Investment and Technology Licensing Code, Decision 220 of May 11, 1987, Commit tion of the Cartagena Agreement, *reprinted in* 271. L. *M.* 974 (1988) [hereinafter Decision 220].

〔50〕 有学者认为,虽然第220号决议并没有完全否定卡尔沃主义,但它没有否认"安第斯共同市场正使得整个安第斯集团更加自由"。但另有学者认为"正如此条款所规定,如果国内法只允许争端由国内法院管辖和适用国内法的话,那么卡尔沃主义的其他原则必须也有规定,如拒绝外交保护原则"。*See* Ewell E. Murphy, Jr., The Andean Decisions on Foreign Investment: An International Matrix of National Law, 24 Int'l Law 643, 653 (1990).

〔51〕 Commission of the Cartagena Agreement: Decision 291, Common Code for the Treatment of Foreign Capital and Trademarks, Patents, Licenses, and Royalties, Mar. 21, 1991, reprinted*in* 30 *I. L. M.* 1283 (1991) [hereinafter Decision 291].

〔52〕 Art. 2, Decision 291.

〔53〕 Id.

"融合"的一个例证。第220号与第291号决议为安第斯共同市场的成员国接受国际待遇标准和国际仲裁庭管辖提供了可能性。因此对该共同体成员国国内立法进行考察以确认这种态度上转变的程度是十分必要的。本文第四部分将对此展开论述。

拉美区域一体化的另一个例子就是南锥体共同市场(MERCO-SUR),该共同市场是由阿根廷、巴西、乌拉圭及巴拉圭在1991年共同成立的。[54] 南锥体共同市场在规制来自其成员国和非成员国的投资方面通过了两个内容基本相同的议定书:一个是管辖成员国之间投资的《科洛尼亚议定书》;另一个是管辖成员国与共同市场外国家之间的投资的《布宜诺斯艾利斯议定书》。[55]《布宜诺斯艾利斯议定书》第2条第3项规定了对外国投资者实施国民待遇、最惠国待遇和"公正与平等待遇"。关于国民待遇、最惠国待遇的条款采用的是典型的BIT用语,即"不应低于"给予该缔约一方国民和公司的待遇或不应低于给予第三国国民和公司的待遇。[56] 关于东道国与外国技资者投资争端的解决,《布宜诺斯艾利斯议定书》第2条第8项规定了"岔路口"条款,投资者要么将争端提交东道国适格的法院审理要么将其提交国际常设仲裁机构或特设仲裁机构仲裁。[57]《布宜诺斯艾利斯议定书》只把当地救济规定为国际仲裁的可替代途径,这与卡尔沃主义的"绝对当地救济"原则相去在埠。《布宜诺斯艾利斯议定书》继而规定了争端解决的准据法应该包括本议定书、东道国处理投资争端的法律、东道国与外国投资者签订的契约以及"国际法律原则"。[58] 十分明显,虽然这两个议定书尚未生效,但总体上遵循的是自由化的BIT语言模式而非卡尔沃主义模式。

最后,虽然美洲自由贸易协定谈判搁浅了,但新近的谈判草案建议接受国际待遇标准和国际仲裁机构的管辖。[59] 这可以看作为以区域一体化文件的方式对卡尔沃主义的又一次背离。

---

〔54〕 南锥体共同市场的基本条约可参见 Treaty Establishing a Common Market between the Argentine Re-public, the Federal Republi c of Brazil, the Republic of Paragua y and the Eastern Re-public of Uruguay, *available at* http://64. 233. 183. 104/search? q = cache; lrC6UFek7KAJ, www. sice. 088. org/trade/mrcsr/mrcsrtoc. asp? ercosur&hl = zh-CN&c! = clnk&cd = 7(Iast visited June 16, 2006)。

〔55〕《布宜诺斯艾利斯议定书》,载 http://www. cvm. gov. br/ingllinter/mercosullbuenos-e. asp,2006年6月15日访问。

〔56〕 Id. , art 2(c).

〔57〕 ld. , art 2(h).

〔58〕 Id. , art 2(h)(4).

〔59〕 Subsection C. 2. b, Chapter XVII Investment, of the Free Trade Area of the Americas(Draft Agreement) (Derestricted, FTAA. TNC/w/133/Rev. 3, Nov. 21, 2003), particularly arts. 29 & 41.

(三)世界性投资协定

虽然到目前为止,还没有一项关于投资保护的综合性的全球公约,但一些公约在国际投资上还是有着重要的实用价值。其中最重要的两个是世界银行主持创立的《解决国家与他国国民间投资争端公约》(《ICSID 公约》)[60]和《建立多边投资担保机构公约(《MIGA 公约》)。[61]《承认及执行外国仲裁裁决公约》(《纽约公约》)[62]在投资争端解决方面同样有着重要的作用。

作为 BITs 的重要补充,《ICSID 公约》致力于提供国家与他国国民间投资争端的国际解决机制,特别是为国际仲裁和调解提供便利。该机制似乎与主张绝对的国内管辖与当地救济的卡尔沃主义背道而驰。所以,即使公约起草者试图修改个别条款来吸引拉美国家,拉美国家仍然大力抵制该 1964 年签订的公约就不足为怪了。[63] 20 世纪 80 年代以前,只有个别拉美小国如牙买加和特立尼达与多巴哥加入了该公约。但现在大多数拉美国家(巴西和墨西哥除外)都成为了《ICSID 公约》的缔约国,其中大部分是在 20 世纪 90 年代加入的(见表 3)。这进一步表明了 20 世纪 90 年代的投资自由化浪潮是何等的汹涌澎湃。

表 3 《ICSID 公约》的拉美成员国(截至 2007 年 11 月 4 日)

签署国	签署日期	批准日期	生效日期
阿根廷	21/05/1991	19/10/1994	18/11/1994
巴哈马	19/10/1995	19/10/1995	18/11/1995
伯利兹	19/12/1986		
智利	25/01/1991	24/9/1991	24/10/1991
哥伦比亚	18/05/1993	15/07/1997	14/08/1997
哥斯达黎加	29/09/1981	27/04/1993	27/05/1993
多米尼加共和国	20/05/2000		
厄瓜多尔	15/01/1986	15/01/1986	14/02/1986
萨尔瓦多	09/06/1982	06/03/1984	05/04/1984

---

〔60〕 该公约约文可见于 http://www.worldbank.org/icsid/basicdoc/basicdhtm,2008 年 3 月 28 日访问。

〔61〕 该公约约文可见于 http://www.miga.org/sitelevel2/level2.cfm? Id = 1107,2008 年 3 月 28 日访问。

〔62〕 该公约约文可见于 http://www.jus.uio.no/lm/un.arbitration recognition and enforcement convention.new-york.1958/doc,2008 年 3 月 28 日访问。

〔63〕 Gonzalo Biggs, The Latin American Treatment of International Arbitration and Foreign In-vestments and the Chile-U.S. Free Trade Agreement, 191 *CSID Review Foreign Investment* Law *journal* 68(2004).

续表

签署国	签署日期	批准日期	生效日期
格林纳达	24/05/1991	24/05/1991	23/06/1991
危地马拉	09/11/1995	21/01/2003	20/02/2003
海地	30/01/1985		
洪都拉斯	28/05/1986	14/02/1989	16/03/1989
牙买加	23/06/1965	09/09/1966	14/10/1966
尼加拉瓜	04/02/1994	20/03/1995	19/04/1995
巴拿马	22/11/1995	08/04/1996	08/05/1996
巴拉圭	27/07/1981	07/01/1983	06/02/1983
秘鲁	04/09/1991	09/08/1993	08/09/1993
特立尼达与多巴哥	05/10/1966	03/01/1967	02/2/1967
乌拉圭	28/05/1992	09/08/2000	08/09/2000
委内瑞拉	18/08/1993	02/05/1995	01/06/1995

资料来源:《ICSID 公约》缔约国和其他公约签订国列表(截至 2006 年 1 月 25 日),载 http://www. worldbank. org/icsid/constate/c-states-en. htm,2008 年 3 月 28 日访问。

与此同时,拉美国家还一改过去对《纽约公约》的抵制与反对态度,[64]纷纷签订并批准了该公约,在这一点上,连相对保守的巴西与墨西哥也不例外。这一事实表明,拉美国家对国际仲裁的态度从总体上已发生了 180 度的大转弯:从完全的反对转向普遍的认可与接受。

此外,绝大多数拉美国家还接受了旨在为国际投资提供担保的《建立多边投资担保机构公约》。[65] 由于多边投资担保机构机制以承认多边投资担保机构代位行使投资者的权利为基础,拉美国家对《MIGA 公约》的接纳再一次表明了他们对卡尔沃主义的背离。

〔64〕 拉美国家长期反对《纽约公约》,基本上是最后才加入此项公约。例如,巴西直到 2002 年才加入该公约。

〔65〕 According to the MIGA website, MIGA members from Latin America and the Caribbean include: Antigua and Barbuda, Argentina, Bahamas, Barbados, Belize, Bolivia, Brazil, Chile, Co-lombia, Costa Rica, Dominica, Dominican Republic. Ecuador, El Salvador, Grenada, Guatemala, Guyana, Haiti, Honduras, Jamaica, Nicaragua, Paraguay, Panama, Peru, St. Kitts & Nevis, St. Lucia, St. Vincent, Suriname, Trinidad & Tobago, Uruguay and Venezuela. See MIGA: *MIGA Member Countries* (Last updated: Oct. 27, 2005), *available at* http://www. miga. org/siteleve12/leve12. cfm? id = 1152 (last visited May 28, 2006).

（四）结论

以上考察表明自20世纪80年代以来，拉美国家在国际投资条约实践中基本上已经背离了卡尔沃主义。因为大多数拉美国家已经与外国签订含有保证国际标准待遇和接受国际仲裁条款的BITs。在区域层面上，南锥共同体采取了BITs的语言模式，而修改后的安第斯条约也体现出足够的灵活性，使成员国可以不必恪守卡尔沃条款。大多数拉美国家都接受了《ICSID公约》（为通过仲裁方式解决国家与投资者之间的争端提供国际平台）、《MIGA公约》（承认成员方享有代位的权利）及《纽约公约》（为在世界范围内执行仲裁裁决提供便利）。

然而，认为所有拉美国家在条约实践中已完全抛弃卡尔沃主义还是言之过早。主要理由有三。首先，这些条约实践存在着重大的例外。例如，拉美国土最大且吸收外国直接投资最多的，[66]巴西还尚未批准一个BIT（尽管达成了个别协议）和南锥体共同体议定书，[67]更未签署《ICSID公约》。更重要的是，巴西在可预见的将来似乎也不会改变政策，因为现在它的做法足以吸引巨大的外国投资。[68]哥伦比亚尽管已签署了8个BITs，但至今只批准其中一个。[69]此外，作为拉美的另一个重要的国家，墨西哥虽然已加入《北美自由贸易协定》（NAFTA）和签署了部分BITs，但它仍然没有签署《CSID公约》。其次，有些投资条约对采取国际标准待遇和接受国际仲裁做出了保留。如Schuruer所说的，部分条约条款事实上是“卡尔沃主义的子孙”。拉美国家早期签订的BITs经常规定用尽当地救济是国际仲裁的必要条件。虽然在*Salini v. J ordan*[70]和*Plama. v. Bulgaria*[71]两仲裁案中，最惠国待遇是否适用于程序规则尚难确定，但以上提及到的保留做法的重要性是不能忽视的。此外，安第斯组织的《外国直接投资法典》仍以以下规定作为一项基本原则：即规定内国与外国投资者的“平等待遇”和东道国有给予外国投资者更优的待遇或诉诸国际仲裁的自主性，但该法典对此并不做强制要求。所以要明确

[66] UNCTAD Press Release, UNCTAD Doc. UNCTAD/PRESS/EB/2004//007 (Mar. 5, 2004).

[67] Inter-American Development Bank (*Legislation for Foreign Investment statutes in Countries in the American*, *Comparative Study-Brazil* (2006), *available at* http://alca-ftaa.iadb.org/eng/invest/BRA-L HTM (May 16, 2006).

[68] Cremades, *supra* note 10, at 81.

[69] UNCTAD, *Country-specific Lists of* BITS, *supra* note 8.

[70] Salini Construttori S. p. A. and Italstrade S. p. A. v. the Hashemite Kingdom of Jordan (Case No. ARB/02/13), Decision of the Tribunal on Jurisdiction, Nov. 29, 2004. 此案与Plama v. Bulgaria一案基本说明了BIT中最惠国苛遇条款不会扩大到有关程序条款，这与之前案例所持的观点相反，如notably the Emilio Agustin Maffezini v. Kingdom of Spain (Case No. ARB/97/7), Decision on Objections 10 Jurisdiction, Jan. 25, 2000 (Maffezini v. Spain), and Siemens A. G. v. rgentine Republic (Case No. ARB/02/8), Decision on Jurisdiction of Aug. 3, 2004 (Siemens v. Argentin a), para. 103.

[71] Plama Consortium Limited v. Republic of Bulgaria (Case No. ARB/03124), Decision on Jurisdiction of Feb. 8, 2005.

卡尔沃主义是否在安第斯共同体中已被完全抛弃,有赖于对拉美国家的国内立法进一步分析。最后,通常认为,包括拉美国家在内的发展中国家签署 BITs 和其他投资条约是出于经济上的考虑,[72] 并不是因为他们对条约中条款的法律确信,这一观点逐渐得到认同。也就是说,拉美国家对卡尔沃主义的背离甚至抛弃只是技术层面上的,在原则层面上态度并没有改变。这一点在以下对拉美国家国内宪法与法律状况的分析中可以看出。

四、拉美国家的有关国内立法实践

与国际条约相比,国内立法更能反映拉美国家对卡尔沃主义的真实态度,因为国内立法更准确反映东道国的单方意志,而不像国际条约那样,东道国还要与其他国家达成意志的妥协。此外,安第斯条约组织的《外国直接投资法典》则规定确立外国投资者待遇与争端解决方法的依据是各国的国内法律。这样,对拉美国家的国内法律和法规进行分析以判定拉美国家对外国投资的态度是否已发生根本改变尤为重要。以下将对拉美主要的九个国家(分别是阿根廷、玻利维亚、巴西、智利、哥伦比亚、厄瓜多尔、墨西哥、秘鲁、委内瑞拉)的国内立法,特别是对有关待遇标准与争端解决的法规,进行探讨与比较分析,以期达到上述目的。

(一)阿根廷

阿根廷被认为是拥有世界上"最超前"的外国直接投资立法的国家,[73] 其国内宪法与法律规定了外国和外国投资者的一般待遇标准。[74] 该国《宪法》第 20 条规定了外国人与国民的"平等待遇"原则外国人在阿根廷领土上享有本国公民所享有的一切民事权利;他们可以从事工业、商业和其他职业;拥有、购买和转让不动产……[75]

---

〔72〕 See e. g. , Rudolf Dolzer, New Foundations of the Law of Expropriation of Alien Property, 75 *AM.* J. *INT'LL.* 553, 583 - 89(1981); Oscsr Schachter, Compensation for Expropriation, Editorial Comment, 78*AM.* J. *INT'LL.* 121, 127 (1984); Andrew T. Guzman, *Explaining the Popularity of Bilateral Investment Treaties: Why LDCs Sign Treaties that Hurt Them?* (Harvad, Jean Monnet Working Paper No. 12/97, at 72, 1997.)

〔73〕 一阿根廷网站强调投资自由化的主要方面为:(1)外资深受欢迎和事实上不受限制,不存在行业限制,甚至允许外资进入如石油、大众媒体(广播、网络、报纸与杂志)、核电站和核矿产开发等敏感行业;(2)对于外国投资来说,不存在任何许可或类似的书面文件要求,绝对没有禁区;(3)外资不需登记,机密得到完全保证;(4)外国投资者不需任何批准可随时把资本和利润转回母国,没有"等待期限"限制;(5)自由进入外汇市场,汇兑自由;(6)禁止对外国投资者作出歧视对待,法律面前国内外投资者一律平等,在国内市场融资上和在经济发展促进计划的资格上也需平等;(7)对外国投资者不存在任何业绩要求沃的国际法保护:多数资本输出国受到有效的双边投资条约保护。*See* Hacienda Virtual Realty Argentina - *HYRA*, *Legal Reforms* and the Foreign Investor, *available at http://www. hvra. com. ar/enforinv. htm*(*May* 20. 2006).

〔74〕 IADB: *Legislation for Foreign Investment Statutes in Countries in the Americas*, *Comparative Study-Argentina*(2006), available at http: 1lalca-flaa. Iadb. orgleng/invest/ARG - 1. HTM(May 16. 2006)[hereinafter IADB: Argentina] sec. 1.

〔75〕 Art. 20. Argentine Constitution.

相应地,1993 年的《外国投资法》(第 21382 号)授予外国投资者在全部领域内享有与国内投资者一样的权利,同时规定资本可以自由流出和流入。[76] 外国投资者所享受的法律上与税收上的待遇几乎与阿根廷公民完全相同。[77] 1993 年 9 月的 1853/93 号法令第 2 条整合了 1989 年《紧急状态与国家改革法案》和以上谈到的《外国投资法》[78] 中包含的自由化措施,规定"外国投资者与国内投资者一样无须事先征得许可即可在阿根廷投资"。可见,阿根廷把国民待遇奉为外国投资者待遇的金科玉律。

在国家与外国投资者间的投资争端解决上,阿根廷同样坚持平等待遇原则。外国投资者与国内投资者享有"完全一致的救济措施"。[79] 由此可见,阿根廷国内法坚持内外国投资者"平等/国民待遇"[80] 这一重要的卡尔沃原则。不过,这里的国民待遇与卡尔沃主义略有出入。它强调的是内外国国民之间的绝对平等,而卡尔沃主义强调的是对国民的非歧视待遇,即禁止外国人享有特权。

另外,应注意到阿根廷热衷于加入有关投资促进与保护的条约。目前为止,阿根廷已加入《ICSID 公约》、《MIGA 公约》、《纽约公约》、《美洲国际商事仲裁公约》(《巴拿马公约》)[81] 以及缔结了至少 58 个 BITs(其中 54 个已经生效)。[82] 阿根廷也签订了一些区域协议,包括南锥体共同市场的两个有关投资保护协议(《科洛尼亚议定书》和《布宜诺斯艾利斯议定书》)和少量仲裁公约。[83]

以上条约有效地提高了外国投资者的待遇标准,远远超过了本国国民所享有的待遇标准。特别是这些条约允许外国投资者可以诉诸如《ICSID 公约》的国际仲裁机制和接受国际法一般原则的适用。因此,这样的条约引发了一个合宪性问题:既然在阿根廷国际条约是从属于宪法的,[84] 那么这些条约给予外国投资者比本国国民更高的待遇标准是否与宪法规定的内外国国民之间待遇要绝对平等的要求相违背?在部分针对阿根廷的投资仲裁案件中,这样的违宪性抗辩

---

〔76〕 IADB:*Argentina. supra* note 74. at sec. 1. 2

〔77〕 *Supra* note 76.

〔78〕 HVR A, Legal Reforms and the Foreign Investor, *supra* note 73.

〔79〕 IADB:*Argentina*, *supra* note 74, at sec. 5. 1.

〔80〕 Alessandro Spinillo & Emilio Vogelius, Argentina, in International Arbitration In Latin America, *supra* note 46, at 19.

〔81〕 ld. , at 439.

〔82〕 UNCTAD, Country-specific Lists 0/8fTs, *supra* note 37.

〔83〕 For details of such regional arbitration conventions, see Spinillo & Vogelius, at 20, 25 – 26.

〔84〕 IADB:*Argentina*, *supra* note 74, at sec. 5. 4.

已被阿根廷政府提出。[85] 如在 *CMS Gas Transmission Company v. Republic Argentina* 一案[86]中,阿根廷检察官在法庭辩论上认为,双边条约不能优先于国家宪法,所以,一公司不能直接引用条约来规避阿根廷国内法院的管辖。[87] 阿根廷法院最近在一个具有里程碑意义的案子判决中(*Jose Cartellone Construcciones v. Hidro-electricaNorpatagonica S. A.*)也响应了阿根廷政府的立场,判决认为只要某一仲裁裁决涉及公共政策事项,就应考察其合理性、公平性及合宪性(即其实体内容)。[88] 进一步地,阿根廷政府于2003年通过新的法令废除了1996年颁布的一项有关阿根廷政府与保格罗尼集团公司(Bulgheroni Group)之间的争议可提交国际仲裁庭解决的命令,[89]以及一项旨在限制把牵涉到国家、国家代理人或国有企业[90]的案件提交给国内或国际仲裁解决的公开立法建议案。实际上,阿根廷与其他拉美国家的这些针对 BIT 和投资仲裁措施被看作"卡尔沃主义复苏"的象征。[91]

如我们以下将看到的,BITs 与基于条约的投资仲裁的合宪性问题存在于许多拉美国家,并在有的国家已经被诉诸法院进行审查,哥伦比亚就是一个突出的例子。

(二)玻利维亚

《玻利维亚外国投资法》(第1182号法令)规定了外国投资者的待遇标准,[92]该法第2条明文规定了国民待遇标准:除非法律另有规定,外国投资者及其参与的企业或公司与国内投资者拥有法律及法规所赋予的相同权利、义务和保证。[93]

---

〔85〕 Carlos E. AIfaro & Pedro M. Lorenti, The Growing Opposition of Argentina to ICSID Arbitral Tribunals: A Conflict between International and Domestic Law? *journal Of World Investment & Trade*, at 426 - 27, 428 - 30(2005)

〔86〕 ICSID: CMS Gas Transmission Company v. The Republic of Argentina (Case No. ARB/01/8) Decision of the Tribunal on Objections to Jurisdiction, July 17, 2003, *reprinted* 42 ILM 788(2003).

〔87〕 Carlos E. Alfaro, The Battle of the Century: Argentina Against the ICSID Arbitration and the BITs, 31 *World Law Group E-News*(Nov. 2004), *available at* http://www.imakenews.com/*bcastro*/*e*Art 0332318.cfm? x = Blow(last visited July 9, 2006).

〔88〕 Carlos E. A Ifaro, *ICSID Arbitration and BITs Challenged by the Argentine Government*(Dec. 21. 2004), *a-vailable at* http://www.alfarolaw.com/imaltapalalfaro3.htm(last visited July 9, 2006).

〔89〕 Laurence Norman, Government Reopens 7 - Year-Old Case vs Oil Group, *Dow Jones News* Wires, Oct. 28, 2003, 15 - 16.

〔90〕 该法案禁止国际仲裁,除非:(a)得到阿根廷联邦法院的允许,或者(b)纠纷的对方是外国政府,即属于国与国之间的纠纷,或者(c)议会以特别法令批准。

〔91〕 同样的情况在其他拉美国家也有所发生,包括2004年巴西《公私合伙法》禁止国际仲裁,和委内瑞拉对国际仲裁的合宪性质疑,这都将在下文得到分析。事实上,已有研讨会对卡尔沃主义的重生和它在国际仲裁上的运用等问题进行了探讨。*See* D. C. Bar Luncheon Program: The *Resurgence of the Calvo Doctrine*? *a-vailable at* http://www.bgconsulting.com/docs/cal-vo_program.jpg(last visited July 11, 2006).

〔92〕 Ley de Sept. 17, 1990, Inversiones No. 1182, Gaceta Oficial de Bolivia, Sept. 26, 1990. See also IADB (2006): *Legislation for Foreign Investment Statutes in Countriesin the American*, *Comparative Study-Bolivia*, *available at* http://alca-ftaa.iadb.orglenglinve8vBOL-I.HTM(05/16/06)[hereinafter IADB: Bolivia], 8ec. 1.2.

〔93〕 Art. 2, Ley de Sept. 17, 1990, Inversiones No. 1182" Gaceta Oficial de Bolivia, Sept 26, 1990.

关于投资争端解决,该法第24条明文否定了外国人的外交保护权,即外国人及其企业受玻利维亚法律调整,任何时候都不能享有特权或求助于外交保护。[94]

然而,《玻利维亚外国投资法》第10条允许投资者协商将争端提交仲裁。[95]相应地,有关技术争端的案子则可以提交依据国际仲裁规则设立的国际仲裁庭处理。[96] 1997年玻利维亚颁布了第1770号法令,提供了争端解决的法律框架,规定在诉诸法院之前,双方可以把争端提交仲裁。[97][98] 在这种环境下,玻利维亚与外国签订了22个BITs,加入《ICSID公约》、《MIGA公约》、《纽约公约》和《巴拿马公约》。[99]

与阿根廷一样,玻利维亚同样把平等待遇(国民待遇)视为外资投资待遇的基本标准。相比之下,玻利维亚比阿根廷更忠诚于卡尔沃主义,因为它在宪法中仍然拒绝外交保护。当然,技术性的争端则允许提交国际仲裁。

(三)巴西

巴西的法律同样规定了外资的平等待遇(国民待遇)。巴西现行《宪法》第5条规定:法律面前人人平等,不存在任何差别,巴西公民与定居在巴西的外国人具有神圣不可侵犯的生存权、自由权、平等权、安全权和财产权……[100]

这与巴西1988年《宪法》有着很大的差别,1988年《宪法》区分"巴西内资公司"与"巴西外资公司"并区别对待。[101] 第4131号法令第2条规定"在同等条件下,国内资本得到的待遇应同时赋予外国资本,禁止现有法律没有规定的任何形式的歧视对待"。[102] 落实第4131号法令(修订)的第55762号命令在第2条也重

[94] Art. 24, The Constitution of Bolivia (as amended by No. 2410, Aug. 8, 2002), *in Constitutions of the Countries of the World* (Albert P. Blaustein & Gisbert H. Flanz eds.) [loose-leaf], (20 Vols., Oceana Publications, 1971) [hereinafter WORLD CONSTITUTIONS].

[95] IADB: Bolivia, *supra* note 92, sec. 5.

[96] Wiesner, *supra* note 48, 81460.

[97] WTO, Trade Policy Review-Bolivia: Secretariat's Report 18, WT/TPR/154/Rev. 1 (2005).

[98] UNCTAD, *Country* - specific *List of BITs*, *supra* note 37.

[99] IADB: *Bolivia*, *supra* note 92, sec. 5. 2.

[100] The Constitution of Brazil (including amendments until Constitutional Amendment 52, enacted on Mar. 8, 2006), *available at* http://www.vbrazil.com/government/laws/constitution.html (last visited June 16, 2006).

[101] Pedro Da Motta Veiga, *Foreign Direct Investment In Brazil: Regulation, Flow. And Contribution To Development* 3 - 4 (2004), *available at http://www.* iisd.org/pdf/2004/investment country_report_brazil.pdf (last visited May 20, 2006).

[102] Law No. 4131, Sept. 3, 1962, which regulates the investment of foreign capital and remittance of funds abroad, in *ICSID: Investment* Laws *of the World* [looseleaf] [hereinafter Investment Laws of the World]; *see also* IADB: *Legislation for Foreign Investment Statutes in* Countries in Americas, *Comparative Study-Brazil*, available at http: alca - . ftaa. iadb. Org/eng/invest/BRA - 1. HTM (May 16, 2 6) [hereinafter IADB: *Brazil*], sec3. 1. b.

申了上述内容。[103]

在投资争端解决方面,巴西同样采用了上述所说的国民待遇原则。因此,外国投资者与国内投资者享有同样的救济途径,外国投资者不享有任何特殊形式的救济。[104] 值得注意的是,直到1996年通过《仲裁法案》,巴西才接受仲裁方式。然而,在该法案颁布后不久,在巴西联邦高等法院审理的 *MBV v. Resil* 一案中,关于该法案的合宪性问题就被提了出来。[105] 虽然判决最后认定该法案没有违宪,但该案漫长的审理(超过5年)和较多的反对意见(包括主审法官在内的11个中有4个表示有异议)充分表明了巴西人对仲裁特别是国际仲裁的犹豫和抵制情绪。[106] 2004年12月30日,巴西政府批准了第11079号联邦法令,该法案确立了调整公私合作关系的法律框架。[107] 该法允许双方把基于公私合作合同产生[108]的纠纷提交仲裁处理,但前提是该仲裁机构只能在巴西境内,并且采用葡萄牙语审理。[109] 换言之,巴西只接受国内仲裁并明确拒绝国际仲裁。这反映了巴西政府不愿意把涉及公共主体的争端(如国家和投资者之间的争端)提交国际仲裁。[110]

这也可以通过以下事实得到印证:尽管巴西已经签订了14个BITs[111]和两个南锥体共同市场议定书,但这些条约与议定书都没有得到国会的正式批准。[112] 实际上,巴西政府已经决定不再将这些提案提交国会讨论,因为巴西国会议员认为这些条约中的一些条款违反了巴西宪法。[113] 合宪性问题在此又一次浮出水面。

在外国投资者待遇上,巴西可以说是毫无保留地坚守"国民待遇(平等待

---

[103] Decree No. 55,762 of Feb. 17, 1965, which regulations for implementation of Law No. 4131, Sept. 3, 1962, as amended, in *Investment Laws of the World*, *supra* note 102.

[104] IADB: *Brazil*, *supra* note 102, sec. 5.

[105] For details of the case, see Joao Lee, Brazil, in International Arbitration In Latin America, at 63 – 66; Guido Santiago, Tawil, The Role of Arbitration And International, Regional, Subregional And Bilateral Treaties In Latin America, available at http://66. 249. 93. 104/search ? q = cache: xjw8 Vj4017wJ: www. bomchilgroup. Org/argdec02. html + Brazilratifiedcolonia-protocol? ercosur&hl = zh. CN&ct = clnk&cd = 9(May 22, 2006).

[106] Tawil, *supra* note 105.

[107] The law is posted at the Brazilian Ministry of Plannig, Budget and Management website, https://www.planalto. gov. br/ccivil_03/_Ato2004 – 2006/2004/Lei/Ll 1079. htm. An English version is also *available at* http://www. planejamento. gov. br/arquivos down/ppp/legislacao/lei_11079_301204_eng. pdf(last visited June 22, 2 6).

[108] Art. 11 III, THE PPP LAW, Ibid.

[109] Ibid.

[110] Rubins 认为在巴西把纠纷诉诸国际仲裁的唯一途径是在巴西政府与外国投资者之间签订详细的仲裁条款,因为"巴西缺乏其他拉美国家明确保证外国投资者可把纠纷提交国际仲裁的法律制度"。See Noah D. Rubins, Investment Arbitration in Brazil, in 4 J. World Investment & Trade, at 1080 – 81, 1091(2003).

[111] Namely, Brr. with Belgium, Chile, Cuba, Denmark, Finland, France, Germany, Italy, the Republic of Korea, the Netherlands, Portugal, Switzerland, the United Kingdom and Venezuela. See UNCTAD, Country-specific Lists 01 8lT. , *supra* note 37.

[112] WTO: Trade Policy Review-Brazil: Secretariat's Report 24, WT/TPR/S/140(Nov. 1, 2004).

[113] lbid.

遇)”的。这不但可以通过其国内法看出,更可通过其对可能赋予外国投资者更优越待遇的国际条约的抵制中看出。

(四)智利

智利《宪法》规定国内外投资者都享有国民待遇。[114] 其《外国投资法》第9条规定外国投资者及其企业与国内投资受同样的法律调整,不受直接的或间接的歧视。[115] 该法进一步明确了任何监管法规若只适用于特定的生产活动或排除外国投资即可视为歧视。[116] 同样,规定部门和地区例外,不允许外资进入也是歧视。[117]

根据智利法律,外国投资者与国内投资者享有同样的程序性救济手段。[118]《外国投资法》第10条进一步规定,当外国投资者及其企业认为某项法律条文存在歧视,该投资者及其企业可以在该法律条文颁布后的一年内向外国投资委员会提出申请,请求取消歧视。[119] 除了国内法的相关规定,智利还是《ICSID公约》、《MIGA公约》、《纽约公约》和《巴拿马公约》的签约国。[120] 智利还签订了52个BITs(13个仍未生效)。[121]

从智利消除对外资的歧视的有力措施可以看出,智利严格坚守国民待遇原则。同时,智利也积极参与赋予外国投资者以相对于本国投资者而言更高待遇、更多保护的国际条约。显然,在也可能导致类似阿根廷的“合宪性”问题。不过,同阿根廷一样,该国对外资的总体态度是趋向于投资自由化,而偏离卡尔沃主义的。

---

[114] IADB:Legislation for Foreign Investment Statutes in Countries in the Americas,Comparative Study-Chile, http://alca-flaa. iadb. org/eng/invest/CHI-I. HTM(May 16,2006)[hereinafter IADB:Chile],sec. 4. 1

[115] Art. 9,Foreign Investment Statute,in Investment Laws 01 the World,*supra* note 100. See also IADB:Chile,supra note 112,sec. 4. 1.

[116] Ibid.

[117] Ibid.

[118] IADB:Chile,*supra* note 112,sec. 5. 1.

[119] Art. 10,Foreign Investment Statute,in Investment Laws of the World,*supra* note 100. See also IADB:Chile,*supra* note 112,8ec. 5. 1.

[120] Carlos E. Jorquiera et al. ,Chile,in International Arbitration In Latin America,*supra* note 46,at 91 -92.

[121] Chile has effective BITs with Argentina,Australia,Austria,Belgium,Bolivia,China,Costa Rica,Croatia,Cuba,the Czech Republic,Denmark,Ecuador,El Salvador,Finland,France,Germany,Greece,Guatemala,Honduras. Italy,Indonesia,Lebanon,Malaysia,Nicaragua,Norway,Panama,Paraguay,Peru,the Philippines,Poland,Portugal,Romania,Spain,Sweden,Switzerland,Ukraine,the United Kingdom,Uruguay and Venezuela. Further bilateral investment agreements have been,orare being negotiated,with Brazil,Colombia,the Dominican Republic,Egypt,Greece,Hungary,the Netherlands,New Zealand,South Africa,Tunisia,Turkey and Vietnam;those were not yet in force in May 2003. WTO,Trade Policy Review-Chile:Secretariat's Report 18,WT/TPR/S/124(2 3). For more updated information,see UNCTAD,Country-specific Lists of BITs,*supra* note 37.

（五）哥伦比亚

哥伦比亚的宪法普遍赋予外国人以国民待遇，除非宪法与法律有例外规定。[122] 于是，第 51 号决议第 3 条（由哥伦比亚国家经济与社会政策委员会根据 1991 年规制外资和外汇的第 9 号法令提出[123]）进一步落实了对外资的国民待遇：根据《宪法》第 100 条和 1991 年第 9 号法令第 15 条，除涉及基金的海外转移外，在哥伦比亚的外资与内资将享有同等的待遇。因此，除非法规和管理制度有特殊规定，不得对进行投资的外国投资者施加与内国私人投资者不同的歧视性条件和待遇。同时，也不得赋予外国投资者比本国投资者更优越的待遇。[124]

因此，哥伦比亚明确坚持平等待遇（国民待遇）原则，禁止内外资间任何形式的歧视，除非有其他明文规定。哥伦比亚与多数拉美国家在立法上不同的是，它同时明确禁止对内国投资者的歧视，即反对让外国投资者享有特权。

关于投资争端解决的最重要条款是第 51 号决议第 23 条：除生效的国际条约与公约另有规定外，在解决因外资法令所产生的争端和冲突时应适用哥伦比亚法律。国际仲裁则应受 1989 年颁布的第 2279 号法令及其修订和补充案的约束。除生效的国际条约与公约另有规定以及允许提交给外国法庭管辖的情形外，所有涉及外资的事项都受哥伦比亚当地法庭管辖或受哥伦比亚仲裁规则制约。[125]

第 51 号决议第 23 条就此确立了一项一般原则，即外资争端需提交给哥伦比亚国内法院或仲裁机构处理，且必须适用当地法律，包括当地仲裁规则。然而，如果哥伦比亚签订的有效的国际条约或公约规定外国技资者有权把技资争端提交给非哥伦比亚法院处理或适用非哥伦比亚法律之时，那么上述当地管辖和当地法律适用要求就可以排除。第 23 条第 2 款则表明在特定情况下还可以将案件交由外国管辖，而不必将争端提交给哥伦比亚法院或适用哥伦比亚仲裁规则。因此，第 23 条为哥伦比亚订立接受国际仲裁与国际法律的国际条约打开了方便之门。这里值得注意的是，哥伦比亚已经加入《ICSID 公约》、《MIGA 公约》和《纽约公

---

[122] 哥伦比亚《宪法》第 100 条规定哥伦比亚境内的外国人与哥伦比亚国民享有同样的权利。但在为了公共利益，法律可以对外国人作出限制或取消部分现有的权利。境内的外国人也享有赋予本国国民同样的保证和受宪法或法律规定的约束。*See* Constituci on *de* 1991 *con*reforms *hasta* 2005 [Political Constitution of 1991 through 2005 reforms], *available at http*://pdba. georgetown. edu/Constitutions/Colombia/col91. html(June 16. 2006).

[123] IADB: Legislation for Foreign Investment Statutes in Countries in the Americas. Comparative Study-Colombia, *available at* http://alca-ftaa. iadb. Org/eng/invest/COLI. HTM(May 16. 2006) [hereinafter IADB: Colombia]. sec. 3. 1 and 4. 1.

[124] Art. 3 of Statute of Foreign Investment (Resolution 51 as amended). in The Investment Laws of the World, *supra* note 100. See also IADB: Colombia. *supra* note 121. sec. 3. 1 b.

[125] Art. 23 of Statute of Foreign Investment (Resolution 51 a8 amended), in Investment Laws of the World, *supra* note 100. See also IADB: Colombia. *supra* note 121. sec. 5. 1.

约》。但到目前为止,哥伦比亚只批准了一个 BIT(已签订了 8 个)。[126]

两个挑战 BIT 合宪性的案件或许部分解释为什么哥伦比亚对批准 BIT 采取保守态度。第一个是 1995 年发生的有关 1994 年签订的哥伦比亚与英国 BIT 的案子。该 BIT 含有国民待遇、最惠国待遇、国有化补偿等典型条款。其中,特别规定国有化只有在为了公共利益且不存在歧视的情况下才能做出,并且补偿要采用"充分、及时、有效"原则。[127] 根据哥伦比亚宪法的规定,[128] 该 BIT(根据第 246/95 号法令签订的)被提交给哥伦比亚宪法法院审查。宪法法院以 6 票比 3 票的结果判决该 BIT 违反了哥伦比亚宪法,特别是在以下两个方面:[129] 第一,该 BIT 违反了哥伦比亚宪法关于国有化不需给予股权投资以任何补偿的规定。[130] 宪法法院认为政府不能滥用宪法赋予的权利而承认所有征收都可以得到"充分、及时、有效"的补偿。第二,该投资条约赋予了英国投资者在国有化补偿上比国内投资者更优越的待遇,这违背了宪法中规定的平等待遇(国民待遇)。在哥伦比亚与古巴签订的 BIT 违宪审查案中,宪法法院也作出了同样的判决。[131] 应该注意到,尽管 1999 年哥伦比亚宪法修正案删除了国有化时对股权投资不必支付补偿的规定,但哥伦比亚政府仍然没有批准任何 BITs。

由此可见,一方面,哥伦比亚法律通过为外资确立绝对的平等待遇(国民待遇)原则和禁止对国内外投资间的任何歧视来支持卡尔沃主义。另一方面,哥伦比亚法律在某些方面是背离卡尔沃主义的,如在国际条约里接受外国法院管辖和援用非国内法。但是,对 BIT 违宪审查案与对已签 BITs 的拒绝批准表明:该国对偏离卡尔沃主义走向自由化仍然存在着强烈的抵触情绪。

(六)厄瓜多尔

厄瓜多尔同样把国民待遇作为外资的基本待遇标准。厄瓜多尔《宪法》第 13 条规定:除《宪法》或法律另有规定外,外国人享有和厄瓜多尔公民一样的权利。[132] 除了《宪法》,厄瓜多尔调整外国投资的主要法律有《投资促进与担保法》

---

[126] UNCTAD, *Country - specific Lists of BITs*, *supra* note 37.

[127] David Schneiderman, Constitutional Approaches to Privatization: An Inquiry into the Magnitude of Neo-Liberal Constitutionalism, 63 Law & Contemp. Probs. 83, at 107(2000).

[128] Art. 241, Colombian Constitution as of 1994.

[129] Colombian Constitutional Court Decision No. C - 358/96, *as cited* in Schneiderman, *supra* note 125, at 107 and n. 176.

[130] Art. 58, Colombian Constitution as of 1994.

[131] Colombian Constitutional Court Decision No. C - 379/96, *as cited* in Schneiderman, *supra* note 125, at 107 and n. 178.

[132] It was art. 14 in the 1979 Constitution. In the current Constitution, the Constitution of 1998, it is retained but renumbered as art. 13.

及其实施条例和《对外贸易与投资法》。[133] 《投资促进与担保法》第 13 条规定外资享有与厄瓜多尔自然人与法人相同的待遇。[134] 然而,《投资促进与担保法》允许在包括渔业、采矿业和化工业等“战略性”领域上对内外资区别对待。[135] 厄瓜多尔宪法禁止外国人为了经济目的而购买土地或取得涉及国家安全的特许经营权。[136] 由此,厄瓜多尔的国民待遇原则是存在重要保留的。

关于投资争端解决,厄瓜多尔原《宪法》拒绝外交保护和外国投资合同纠纷的国外管辖权。[137] 厄瓜多尔现行《宪法》对此条款内容作了修订,规定如果国际条约规定了非国内法院管辖,就可排除当地法院管辖。1998 年厄瓜多尔《宪法》第 14 条规定:政府间的契约或公有主体与外国自然人及法人之间的契约排除任何外交保护;如果以上契约是在厄瓜多尔境内履行的话,不允许将有关纠纷提交外国法院管辖,除非国际条约另有规定。[138]

由此,《投资促进与担保法》规定“国家与外国投资者都可以将任何由适用本法所产生的纠纷提交给根据厄瓜多尔所参加的国际条约的规定所组成的仲裁庭解决,或者适用任何厄瓜多尔批准并执行的双边或多边协定中所同意或规定的程序解决”。[139] 相应地,厄瓜多尔签订了 28 个 BITs(其中批准了 23 个),主要集中在 20 世纪 90 年代。[140] 厄瓜多尔还加入了《ICSID 公约》、《MIGA 公约》和《纽约公约》。[141]

厄瓜多尔可被视为拉美国家中又一个仍然坚持卡尔沃主义,但是对该主义做出了修正以适应国际条约所要求的灵活性的例子。

(七)墨西哥

墨西哥《宪法》第 33 条规定了外国人及外国投资者享有国民待遇,这使得外国投资者可以享有宪法第一章第一节作出的保证。在财产权方面,第 27 条包含了一个著名的“卡尔沃条款”。其规定只有墨西哥自然人或法人才有权拥有对土地、水域及其孳息的所有权和矿藏及水资源开采的特许经营权。上述财产权也可以同样地赋予外国人,条件是该外国人要在外交部表示同意在这方面把他们视为

---

[133] WTO: *Trade Policy Review-Ecuador: Secretariat's Report*18, WT/TPR/S/rev. 1(2005).

[134] Ibid.

[135] Ibid.

[136] Art. 15, The Political Constitution of the Republic of Ecuador 1998.

[137] Art. 16, The Political Constitution of the Republic of Ecuador 1979.

[138] Art. 14, The Political Constitution of the Republic of Ecuador 1998.

[139] Art. 32, The Law on Investment Promotion and Guarantees, *in* Investment Laws of The World, *supra* note 100.

[140] UNCTAD, *Country-specific* List of BITs, *supra* note 37.

[141] Ramiro S. Cordero, *Ecuador*, *in International Arbitration in* Latin *America*, *supra* note 46, at 135.

本国人，在事关以上财产权事项上不求助母国政府的外交保护，并且在不遵守以上承诺时接受将所得财产收归国有的惩罚。[142]

可见，该宪法条款明确坚持国民待遇原则和拒绝外交保护。这在墨西哥前期的外国直接投资法律与法规（1973 年《外国投资法》[143] 和 1989 年的《外国投资监管条例》）中得到重申和运用。[144] 但现在的外国直接投资法规（即 1993 年《外国投资法》和 1998 年《外国投资监管条例》）已经把这样的规定删除了。这表明了墨西哥当局倾向于采取更自由的政策。即使作出了这样的删除，正如上文所阐述的，墨西哥对卡尔沃主义的一贯坚持的态度并没有改变，因为墨西哥宪法的上述"卡尔沃条款"仍然没变。

关于争端解决，墨西哥的外国投资者通常有着与国内投资者相同的程序救济。[145] 在这方面值得注意的是，墨西哥的相关国内法律，如《联邦民事诉讼法典》和《联邦特区民事诉讼法典》，已经规定了国内法院对特定事项的排他管辖权，包括土地与水资源、专属经济区、授权行为、刑事责任、多数家庭纠纷、税收征纳、雇员纠纷和个别农业纠纷等事项。[146]

外国投资者的特殊救济途径只在墨西哥签订的自由贸易协定或双边投资协定的争端解决部分作出了规定。[147] 这里必须要提及的是 1993 年墨西哥批准了《北美自由贸易协定》（NAFTA），其中第 11 章规定了一个非常自由化的投资制度。自 NAFTA 后，墨西哥已经签订了多个 BITs，其中 19 个已生效。[148] 墨西哥是《纽约公约》与《美洲国际商事仲裁公约》的成员国，但还没加入《ICSID 公约》与《MIGA 公约》。

这里，又产生了一个国际条约的合宪性问题，因为墨西哥公民并没有享有条

---

[142] Art. 27, Mexican Constitution.

[143] 1973 Law to Promote Mexican Investment and to Regulate Foreign Investment, *Offcial Gazette*, Mar. 9, 1973. Art. 3 of this law provided：如果外国人同意在事关财产权时把他们视为本国人；在事关以上财产权上不求助该国政府的外交保护；在不遵守以上承诺时接受其财产被收归国有的惩罚的话，外国人可以享有以上财产权利。

[144] Regulations of the Law to Promote Mexican Investment and to Regulate Foreign Investment (as amendment.), *Diario Oficial de la Federaci' on* (Mexico), May 16, 1989. 11 stipulated in art. 31："……如果公司章程中没有包含"排除外国国民的条款"，那么一个明确的协议或约定必须是该公司章程的一个必不可少的部分，即该公司现在或将来的外国投资者有义务与外交部达成正式协议将其就其所取得的该公司的股份，以及其在该公司所持有的其他资产、权利、许可、参与或利益，或其从该公司与墨西哥政府所签订的合同中所取得的其他权利义务而言，将其视为内国国民，并不得向其本国政府提起外交保护的请求，如有违反，则必须接受为了国家利益没收其取得的利益。"

[145] IADB：*Legislation for Foreign Investment Statutes in Countries in the Americas*, *Comparative Study-Mexico*, *available at* http://alca-ftaa.iadb.Org/eng/invest/MEX－1.HTM (May 16, 2006) [hereinafter IADB：Mexico] sec. 5.1.

[146] Claus von Wobeser, *Mexicao*, *supra* note 46, *at* 160－62.

[147] Ibid.

[148] UNCTAD, *Country-specific list of BITs*, *supra* note 37.

约中规定的如此高的待遇标准和国际救济。为解决该问题,墨西哥政府于 1992 年通过了《条约签订法》,〔149〕授权政府可协商缔结包含可执行的争端解决机制的国际条约。〔150〕 一些学者认为,这部法律已经排除了有关“《宪法》中的卡尔沃条款的适用范围的所有疑问”。〔151〕 然而,由于《条约签订法》是《宪法》的下位法,人们有理由怀疑这种说法其实过于乐观。〔152〕

(八)秘鲁

秘鲁《1993 年宪法》(修订版)规定除为实现互惠例外之外,外国投资与国内投资享有平等待遇。〔153〕 其第 63 条规定:国内与外国投资享有同等待遇……如果另一国或另一些国家采取侵害本国利益的保护性或歧视性的措施,本国出于防卫目的可采取相似措施。〔154〕

秘鲁的国民待遇标准体现在关于促进外国投资的 1991 年第 662 号法令中。〔155〕 该法令目的在于清除“外国投资的障碍与限制以保证外国与本国投资的权利与义务平等……”,〔156〕以及确立国民待遇标准(第 2 条),规定除宪法与法律另有规定外,外国投资者及其企业拥有“与国内投资者及其企业相同的权利与义务”。该法进一步明确规定“国内法律一概不得依据国籍来区别对待投资者及其企业”。〔157〕 该法令特别规定“所有对外国投资的经济活动作出限制或约束的法律在本法生效后自然失效”。〔158〕 由此可见秘鲁法律所规定的国民待遇标准强调的是禁止对外国投资者的歧视行为。

在争端的解决方面,秘鲁宪法包含以下规定:所有国家契约和公共部门与定居在国内的外国人之间的契约都必须受本国法律约束,由本国法院管辖,并放弃外交保护。金融性契约可免除国内法院管辖要求。国家与其他公法实体可以把由契约关系引起的争议提交给按照生效条约设立的法院解决。也可以按法律规

---

〔149〕 Law Regarding the Making of Treaties, Dec. 21, 1991, Mex., 31 I. L. M. 390 (1992). The official text of the law appears in CDLX *Diario Oficial de la Federaci' on*, Jan. 2, 1992 at 2.

〔150〕 Anlonio Garza C'anovas, Introductory Note to the Law Regarding the Making of Treaties, 31 *I. L. M.* 390, 391 (1992).

〔151〕 See Ibid. At 391. See also Justine Daly, Has Mexico Crossed the Border on State Responsibility for Economic Injury to Aliens? – Foreign Investment and the Calvo Clause in Mexico after NAFTA, 25*St. Mary's L.* J. 1147, at 1189 (1994); Schneiderman, *supra* note 23.

〔152〕 Garza C'anovas, *supra* note 148, at 39 1.

〔153〕 WTO: *Trade Policy Review-Peru: Secretariat's Report*17, WT/TPR/S/69 (2000).

〔154〕 Art. 63, paras. 1 – 2, The Political Constitution of the Republic of Peru 1993 (as amended to 2005), *in World Con*stitutions., *supra* note 92.

〔155〕 *Supra* note 150.

〔156〕 Preamble and Art. 2 respectively, Legislative Decree No. 662 of 29 Aug. 1991, *as in* Investment Laws of the World, *supra* note 100.

〔157〕 Ibid., art. 2.

〔158〕 *Supra* note 157, art 31.

定的形式提交国内或国际仲裁解决。[159]

该宪法条款可看作为一个温和的卡尔沃条款。在实质上,它是一个卡尔沃条款,因为它绝对拒绝外交保护和一贯坚持国内法与国内法院的排他适用。同时,它又是一个温和的卡尔沃条款,因为它允许两个例外:一是金融性契约可以诉诸非国内法院解决;二是可适用条约规定的管辖方式与准据法。有论者认为该条款包含一个将投资争端提交秘鲁法院解决并适用秘鲁法律的倾向,因为虽然第662号法令第16条允许国家根据国际条约将争端提交给国际仲裁庭解决,外国投资者仍无法确定秘鲁政府实际上是否会同意这么做。[160] 不过,该例外至少扫清了秘鲁加入有关投资争端解决的国际协定的合宪性障碍。事实上,秘鲁已经签订了31个BITs,并批准了其中28个。[161] 秘鲁还是《ICSID公约》《MIGA公约》《纽约公约》《巴拿马公约》的成员国。[162]

(九)委内瑞拉

根据1999年委内瑞拉《宪法》规定,外国人与外国投资者享有国民(平等)待遇,该《宪法》第301条规定:外国企业、机构或外国人的待遇不应高于给予委内瑞拉国民和公司的待遇。外国投资与国内投资享受同等条件。[163]

1999年《投资保护与促进法》[164]强调了这一原则,该法第7条规定除特别法和现行法律有特殊规定外,在同等条件下,外国投资者及其投资与国内投资者及其投资享有同等的权利与义务。[165] 该法第6条同时规定按照国际法给予外国投资者"公正和平等的待遇",保证外国投资的运作、管理、用途、收益、扩建、销售和清算不受武断和歧视的对待。[166] 该法第9条进一步允许外国投资者在第6、7条规定的两种待遇标准,即国民待遇与公平和平等待遇间,享有更优惠的待遇。[167] 该法第8条赋予了外国投资最惠国待遇。[168] 显然,以上四个条款采用了BIT语言保证给予外国投资者最优惠的待遇。然而,该法第10条却将注意力转向国内

[159] Art. 63, The Political Constitution of the Republic of Peru 1993 (as amended to 2005), in *World Constitutions*, *supra* note 94.

[160] Wiesner, *supra* note 48, at 463.

[161] UNCTAD, *Countries-specific list of BIT.*, *supra* note 37.

[162] Pelipe O. Parodi, Peru and Annex: 1: Table of Adherence to the New York Convention, Panama Convention and Washington Convention, *supra* note 46, at 194 and 439.

[163] Art. 301, The Constitution of the Bolivian Republic of Venezuela (adopted at the refrendum of Dec. 15, 1999), as in World Constitutions, *supra* note 94.

[164] Ley de Promoci'on y Prolecci'on de lnversiones (Decrelo N. 356, 3 de oclubre de 1999), Gaceta Oficial N. 5.390 Extraordinario de fecha 22 de octubre de 1999 [hereinafter Investment Protection and Promotion Law].

[165] ld., art. 7.

[166] ld., art. 6.

[167] ld., art. 9.

[168] ld., art. 8.

投资者,规定"在同等条件下,国内投资者享有的待遇不应低于外国投资者"。[169] 可见,该《投资保护与促进法》的高标准待遇适用于全部投资者及其投资。

关于争端解决,1999 年委内瑞拉《宪法》第 151 条规定了一个明确的"卡尔沃条款"在涉及公共利益的合同中,除依合同的性质无法适用该项法律,应视为内含了这样的一个条款(即使该条款并未被明确规定在合同中):即有关这类合同的任何疑问或纠纷,如不能由合同双方协商解决,则应该由委内瑞拉有管辖权的法院,根据其法律来解决,而不得诉诸国际求偿。[170]

该宪法不但拒绝外交保护,而且在公共利益契约上毫无保留地坚持国内法院的排他管辖和适用国内法。在这方面,该《宪法》第 155 条似乎与该条款无关,因为它并不调整第 151 条所规定的国家契约,而只是调整国家间的条约。第 155 条实质上规定:由任何委内瑞拉政府与他国签订的国际协议的解释与适用所产生的纠纷需要通过"国际法所认可的和平方式或双方事先同意的方式"解决。[171]

然而,《投资保护与促进法》却似乎并未采纳卡尔沃立场,而是采用了十分自由的 BIT 模式来规定国际投资争端。[172] 该法第 21 条至第 23 条对此作出了规定。第 23 条规定了解决适用该法所产生争议的解决规则,它允许投资者(国内或国外)在穷尽行政救济的情况下可以把争端提交给当地法院或仲裁机构处理。[173] 如果争端牵涉"外国投资者",则适用第 21 条与第 22 条规定的特殊解决渠道。当委内瑞拉国内主体与外国投资者发生争端,且该外国投资者母国与委内瑞拉签有投资协定时,或者该争端适用《ICSID 公约》或《MIGA 公约》时,[174] 适用第 22 条。在这样的情况下,相关争端由相关条约或协定所规定的仲裁方式来解决。[175] 同样,该外国投资者也可以诉诸委内瑞拉的国内争端解决程序。[176] 为落实以上政策,委内瑞拉已经签订了 26 个 BITs,并批准了其中 24 个,[177] 同时它还加入了《ICSID 公约》、《MIGA 公约》、《纽约公约》和《巴拿马公约》。[178]

---

[169] Ley de Promoci'on y Prolecci'on de lnversiones(Decrelo N. 356,3 de oclubre de 1999),Gaceta Oficial N. 5. 390 Extraordinario de fecha 22 de octubre de 1999 [hereinafter Investment Protection and Promotion Law],art. 10.

[170] Art. 151,The Constitution of the Bolivian Republic of Venezuela(adopted at the referen-dum of Dec. 15, 1999),*in World Constitutions*,*supra* note 94.

[171] *Supra* note 170,art. 155

[172] Art. 21 – 23,Investment Promotion and Protection Law,*supra* note 161.

[173] ld. ,art. 23.

[174] lbid. ,art. 22.

[175] lbid.

[176] lbid.

[177] UNCTAD,*Countries-specific list of BITs*,*supra* note 37.

[178] Bemardo Weininger & David M. Lindsey,Venezuela and Annex 1:Table of Adherence to the New York Convention,Panama Conventfon and the Washington Convention,*supra* note 46,at 227 and 439.

当争端所涉外国投资者的母国与委内瑞拉并没有签订任何投资协定，并且争端涉及“本法的理解与适用时”，该国际投资者可将该争端提交给其母国，而母国在穷尽外交救济的情况下可将该争端交由国际仲裁解决。[179] 在这种情况下，仲裁人员的组成、选择方法、程序及费用分担将由投资者母国与委内瑞拉协商一致达成。[180] 与此同时，外国投资者也可选择求助于第 23 条所规定的国内救济手段。[181]

比较起来可以看出，在委内瑞拉宪法与外资法之间存在着两个主要矛盾。一是允许外交保护的《投资保护与促进法》第 21 条与拒绝外交保护（特别是涉及公共利益契约的情况下）的《宪法》第 151 条相矛盾。二是允许国际投资争端可请求国际救济的《投资保护与促进法》第 21 条与第 22 条同样与规定争端的由国内法院排他管辖的《宪法》第 151 条也相矛盾。

这里有必要提及的是，委内瑞拉政府同意将由石油许可协议所产生的纠纷交由国际仲裁解决的做法已经受到来自本国公民的挑战，理由是该规定违反《宪法》第 151 条。在所谓的“勘探回合案”（*Exploration Round Case*）中，一群委内瑞拉公民在 1995 年 12 月向委内瑞拉最高法院提起诉讼，质疑 1995 年 7 月 4 日委内瑞拉国会的一项批件（Congressional Accord）中的仲裁条款的合宪性。该批件批准了该国 1995 年的一项石油勘探招标安排。其中一个条款（第 17 个条件）规定所有由附属协议所产生的争端（例如，招标后与投资者所达成的石油开发的协议）可通过有拘束力的仲裁来解决。[182] 尽管该案的最终裁决有利于仲裁和外国投资者，关于仲裁的合宪性问题并没有根本解决，因为最高法院并没有对模糊的“合同性质”例外作出澄清。而在该案审理完结后于 1999 年通过的新《宪法》也未能解决该问题。新《宪法》保留了原《宪法》备受争议的条款（即第 127 条），只是重新将其编号为第 151 条。此外，2001 年 3 月委内瑞拉总统颁布了第 4 号指令，规定了“对由共和国履行的涉及公共利益的合同特别是其中包含的国际仲裁条款的国内审查机制”。[183] 根据此项指令，涉及公共利益的契约必须提交给共和国的司法部长，由他依据新《宪法》第 151 条对契约中的仲裁条款的合法性提出意见。[184] 在最近的案件中，即在 *Minera Ias Cristinas*, C. A. (*MINCA*) *v. Corporacion Venezuelana de Guyana*（*CVG*）案（the MINCA 案）中，[185]最高法院驳回了 MINCA 公

[179] Art. 21, Investment Promotion and Protection Law, *supra* note 161.

[180] lbid.

[181] *Supra* note 180.

[182] Elisabeth E. Elijuri, *Oil Opening: A Constitutional Challenge*, *available at* http://www.natlaw.com/pubs/spveenl.htm (last visited Feb. 12, 2006).

[183] Werninger & Lindsey, *Venezuela*, *supra* note 176, at 235.

[184] lbid.

[185] Decision No. 0083 of the Political Administrative Chamber of the Supreme Court of July 15, 2004.

司的起诉,理由之一是涉及国家财产的争端不能提交仲裁。[186] 法院这一判决的主要依据就是新《宪法》第 151 条关于公共利益契约受国内法院的排他性管辖的规定。[187] 此案反映了委内瑞拉对国际仲裁立场的不确定。

总而言之,委内瑞拉国内法律的特征表现为两个方面:一方面是在宪法中规定相当典型的卡尔沃条款;另一方面是在外国直接投资法中规定非常自由化的条款,包括 BIT 式的标准和争端解决方式。可以说委内瑞拉国内法在以上两方面(特别是在争端解决上)显得十分不协调。其政府行为经常在法院受到合宪性质疑也就不足为奇了。

(十)结论

尽管在细节上存在差异,但通过以上对九个拉美主要国家的国内法分析可得出以下四个结论:

首先,所有拉美国家都规定了国民待遇(平等待遇)。多数国家都在宪法中规定了国民待遇,同时在外资法律中进一步明确。这虽然表明了卡尔沃主义还继续存在且仍然有效,但值得注意的是其重心已有所转移,由强调对东道国国民及其投资的非歧视转到强调不得依国籍来区别对待。所以,在多数拉美国家的宪法中都规定外国人和外国投资者都享有与本国人和本国投资者"相同的权利与义务"。在一些国家,如哥伦比亚和委内瑞拉,则对国民待遇的两个极端都作了明确规定:即既禁止对外国投资者的歧视待遇,也禁止对本国投资者的歧视待遇。这种立法显然是受了 BITs 的影响,其中委内瑞拉最近的外资法则完全复制了 BIT 的标准条款。可以这样说,卡尔沃与 BIT 这两种在传统上各有侧重甚至相互对抗的国民待遇条款在这里已被转化并趋于融合,形成了一个真正平等的国民待遇——即不考虑投资者国籍的平等待遇的追求。当然,这样一种转化与融合仍然可以看作是在卡尔沃原则范畴内所发生的变化,因为卡尔沃主义本是一个建立在国家平等与国民平等基础上的理论。

其次,除巴西(及较低程度上的哥伦比亚)以外的所有拉美国家都通过明确的国内法条款并且/或者通过加入投资条约的行为接受了基于国际条约的国际仲裁。当然,接受的程度因国而异。例如,玻利维亚规定只有"技术性纠纷"才可以提交国际仲裁解决,而委内瑞拉则规定即使没有条约的明确规定外国投资争端也可以提交给国际仲裁解决。何况,在巴西的外国投资者则根本无缘求助于国际投资条约仲裁来解决投资争端。并非所有外国投资者都可以就投资争端提起国际仲

[186] *Supra* note 185.

[187] Ibid.

裁,这取决于其母国与东道国之间是否存在一个有效的 BIT,以及该 BIT 中争端解决条款的具体规定。但是,尽管 BITs 在一些国家受到了违宪审查,尽管有巴西的例外,拉美国家从总体上说已经明显地远离国内法院排他管辖的原则,而且已经普遍接受了国际法作为可适用的法律。从这个意义上讲,可以说卡尔沃主义已经被侵蚀殆尽并被弃置一旁,尽管还存在上文所强调的某些重要的例外与保留。

再次,大多数拉美国家仍然在宪法中明确反对外交保护,这一点在公共利益契约方面尤显突出。这些国家包括玻利维亚、哥伦比亚、厄瓜多尔、墨西哥、秘鲁和委内瑞拉六国。可以认为,在这方面卡尔沃主义仍然存在。

最后,从最近在阿根廷、哥伦比亚和委内瑞拉所发生的对投资条约违宪审查案和巴西《公私合伙法》对国际仲裁的禁止等事件看来,近年来卡尔沃主义有“复苏”的趋势。

五、概括和总结:卡尔沃主义并没有死亡而只是搁浅了

以上对拉美国家国内法和国际条约的认真分析表明,卡尔沃主义在排斥外交保护上依然存在;在外资待遇上实现了转型,与 BIT 达成了融合;在国内法院排他管辖和国内法排他适用问题上被大大弱化和搁置起来了。国内法院排他管辖和国内法排他适用可以被认为是卡尔沃主义的核心所在。但即使在这点上,正如上文所论,卡尔沃主义也并没有完全“死亡”,因为现今还存在大量的重要例外条款和保留条款。所以,只能说卡尔沃主义在当代已经发生了重大的变化,已经“变形”了或被“搁浅”了,而不能说它已经完全“死”了。当世界政治与经济气候趋向适宜时,卡尔沃主义有可能获得“复苏”——这一 切似乎正在发生。

From "North-South Divide" to "Private-Public Debate": The Revival of Calvo and the Changing Landscape in International Investment Law*

After dominating Latin American states for over a century, the Calvo Doctrine has been widely described as "dead,"〔1〕 particularly since the 1990s, in the wake of global tides of economic liberalisation. However, some recent moves within and beyond Latin America suggest that this principle is not dead, but on the resurgence. The "Revival of Calvo" phenomenon signals a change of direction in international investment law: neo-liberalism no longer dominates international investment law-making, and a more balanced, and perhaps also a more conservative and nationalistic approach, is gaining ground.

This essay explores these recent events and analyzes to what extent the Calvo Doctrine is returning, as well as how the ideology of international investment law is changing. The essay proceeds in four parts. Parts I and II examine the events signaling the revival of the Calvo Doctrine within Latin America and the changing trend in international investment law beyond. Part III explores the future of the international investment regime by critically examining both the Calvo Doctrine and the neo-liberalist investment regime. Part IV concludes by arguing that the main theme in international investment law-making is being shifted from a "North-South Divide" towards a "Private-Public Debate."

---

* *Northwestern Journal of International Law and Business, Volume* 27 *Issue* 3, *Spring* 2007.

The article is based on a lecture given at Beijing University Law School in April. The author would like to thank participants of the lecture for their valuable feedback.

〔1〕 As early as 1955 Shea pronounced the Calvo Doctrine's death in light of its rejection by European and North American States. *See* DONALD SHEA, THE CALVO CLAUSE: A PROBLEM OF INTER-AMERICAN AND INTERNATIONAL LAW AND DIPLOMACY 20 (UNIV. OF MINN. PRESS, 1955). More recently, Giesze wrote that, "[a]s a practical matter, the Calvo doctrine is a dead letter in the overwhelming majority of Latin American countries." Craig R. Giesze, *Helms-Burton In Light Of The Common Law And Civil Law Legal Traditions: Is Legal Analysis Alone Sufficient To Settle Controversies Arising Under International Law On The Eve Of The Second Summit Of The Americas?*, 32 INT' L LAWYER 51, 77 (1998) (emphasis added). Shihata also considers the Calvo Doctrine less relevant in the current world. *See* Ibrahim F. I. Shihata, *Towards a Greater Depoliticization of Investment Disputes: The Roles of ICSID and MIGA*, 1 ICSID REV. —FOREIGN INV. L. J. 1, 24 (1986). In an article published in 1995, Manning-Cabrol pronounced the "imminent death" of Calvo Clause. *See* Denise Manning-Cabrol, *The Imminent Death of the Calvo Clause and the Rebirth of the Calvo Principle: Equality of Foreign and National Investors*, 26 LAW & POL' Y INT' L BUS. 1169, 1169 (1995).

Ⅰ. Revival of the Calvo Doctrine: Within Latin America

For over a hundred years, Latin American states adhered to the Calvo Doctrine, named after Carlos Calvo, a nineteenth century Argentine international lawyer and diplomat. The Doctrine essentially asserts "two concepts of non-intervention and absolute equality of foreigners with nationals,"[2] with emphasis placed on the rejection of the superiority or imperial prerogatives of powerful states and their nationals. The Doctrine can be further decomposed into three key elements, namely an "anti-super-national-treatment" standard, exclusive local jurisdiction, and the exclusion of diplomatic protection.[3] The Latin American states "enthusiastically received" this doctrine and implemented it in their constitutions, domestic legislation, international treaties and contracts signed between foreign investors and Latin American governments,[4] even though its validity was denied in Europe and North America.[5] The early influence of the Calvo Doctrine went well beyond Latin America and won wide support in the developing world, particularly in the new states emerging in Asia and Africa during the decolonisation process. It was even incorporated into United Nations General Assembly (UNGA) resolutions when the New International Economic Order (NIEO) movement reached its peak.[6]

The influence of the Calvo Doctrine was severely challenged by the global wave of economic liberalisation, which reached its height in 1990s. As a result, some commentators assumed or predicted that the Doctrine was already dead.[7] The challenges to Calvo came primarily from the proliferation of international investment treaties, especially the bilateral investment treaties (BITs) entered into by Latin American states. The U.N. Conference on Trade and Development (UNCTAD) Statistics show that Latin American states did not engage in BITs until the late 1980s.[8] By the end of 1990s, Latin

---

[2] *See* SHEA, *supra* note 1, at 19 – 20.

[3] *See* Wenhua Shan, *Is Calvo Dead?*, 54 AM. J. COMP. L. (forthcoming 2007), Section I. 1; *see also* Manning-Cabrol, *supra note* 1, at 1173.

[4] *See* SHEA, *supra* note 1, at 21 – 32.

[5] The Calvo Doctrine failed to gain the support of international lawyers in Europe and the United States in part because acceptance of the Doctrine "would eliminate the abuses of diplomatic protection, [but] it would also eliminate the institution itself, without substituting an acceptable alternative." SHEA, *supra* note 1, at 20.

[6] Lillich noted that Latin American efforts on the Charter were "no more than a thinly-disguised attempt to endow the Calvo Doctrine." Richard Lillich, *The Diplomatic Protection of Nationals Abroad: An Elementary Principle of International Law Under Attack*, 69 Am. J. INT' L L. 359, 361 (1975). Other commentators considered the Calvo doctrine "a central plank of the new International Economic Order (UNGA 3171 of the 1973) and the UN Charter of Economic Rights and Duties of States (1974)." David Schneiderman, *Investment Rules and The New Constitutionalism*, 25 LAW & SOC. INQUIRY 757, 766 (Summer 2000); *see also* Kenneth J. Vandevelde, *Sustainable Liberalism and the International Investment Regime*, 19 MICH. J. INT' L L. 373, 384 (1998) (noting the UN's adoption of Resolution 3201, which contained "a Declaration on the Establishment of a New International Economic Order").

[7] *See supra* note 1.

[8] U. N. Conf. on Trade and Dev. [UNCTAD], *Bilateral Investment Treaties* 1959 – 1999, 15, UNCTAD/ITE/IIA/2(2000) (*prepared by* Abraham Negash), *availableat* http://www.unctad.org/en/docs/poiteiiad2.en.pdf, last accessed on March 27, 2007. According to UNCTAD, however, the total number of BITs concluded by Latin American and Caribbean states reached 451 by the end of 2004. UNCTAD, *Recent Developments in International Investment Agreements*, 2, IIA MONITOR No. 2, UNCTAD/WEB/ITE/IIT/2005/1 (August 30, 2005), *available at* http://www.unctad.org/en/docs/webiteiit20051_en.pdf, last accessed on March 27, 2007.

American states had entered into a total of 300 BITs, among which 93% were signed in the 1990s.[9] At a regional level, Mercosur followed the BIT approach[10] and the Andean Pact has been revised to accommodate member states' need of flexibility in departing from the Calvo Doctrine.[11] Most Latin American states also accepted the Convention for the Settlement of Investment Disputes between States and Nationals of other States ("the ICSID Convention"), providing an international platform for arbitration of state-investor disputes, the Convention Establishing the Multilateral Investment Guarantee Agency ("the MIGA Convention"), recognizing rights of subrogation, and the New York Convention for the Recognition and Enforcement of Foreign Arbitration Awards ("the New York Convention"), facilitating world-wide enforcement of arbitration awards.[12] Meanwhile, domestic laws and regulations in Latin American states have generally been relaxed to accept international standards and international dispute settlement mechanisms in order to protect and promote foreign investment.[13] Although it might be incorrect to assert that Calvo is completely "dead", it can be argued that it had been, by and

[9] UNCTAD, *Bilateral Investment Treaties* 1959 - 1999, *supra* note 8.

[10] Mercosur is the Common Market of the South created in 1991 by four countries in Latin America, namely Argentina, Brazil, Paraguay and Uruguay. Mercosur adopted two Protocols regulating investment between member states and from non member states respectively [the Buenos Aires Protocol (extrabloc) and the Colonia Protocol (intrabloc)], with similar language. Article 2(c) of the Protocol regulating investments from non-member states (the Buenos Aires Protocol) provides for national treatment, MFN treatment and "just and equitable treatment" for foreign investment. The wording for "national treatment" and MFN treatment is in typical BIT language, which means treatment "no less favourable" than that granted to national investors or investors from other non-member states. With regard to state-investor dispute resolution, Article 2(h) of the Protocol provides a "fork in the road" clause, which avails investors to choose between two options: either competent courts of the host state, or an international arbitration tribunal, which could be either an ad hoc or an institutional tribunal. Since it uses local remedies only as a conclusive alternative to international arbitration, it differs significantly from the Calvo principle of "exclusive local remedies." *See* Protocol on Promotion and Protection of Investment Proceeding from Non-Member Countries of the MERCOSUL, March 26, 1991, *available at* http://www.cvm.gov.br/ingl/inter/mercosul/buenos-e.asp.

[11] The revision was reflected in Decision 220 and Decision 291, which respectively abandoned the stiff "Calvo Clause" in the previous investment code embodied in Decision 24, and opened the possibility for ANCOM member countries to accept international standards of treatment and jurisdiction of international arbitration tribunals. *See* Commission Decision 220 Replacing Decision 24, The Common Foreign Investment and Technology Licensing Code, May 11, 1987, 27 I. L. M. 974 (1988); *see also* Commission Decision 291—Common Code for the Treatment of Foreign Capital and on Trademarks, Patents, Licenses and Royalties, Mar. 21, 1991, 30 I. L. M. 1283 (1991). Article 34 of Decision 220 provided that, "[f]or the settlement of disputes or conflicts deriving from direct foreign investments or from the transfer of foreign technology, Member Countries shall apply the provisions established in their local legislation." Commission Decision 220 Replacing Decision 24, *supra*. Article 2 of Decision 291 provides that "foreign investors shall have the same rights and obligations as pertain to national investors, except as otherwise provided in the legislation of each Member Country." Commission Decision 291, *supra*.

[12] Those international treaties, particularly BITs, have generally accepted non-local remedies and general international law as the governing norms, which depart significantly from the Calvo principle. It can indeed be argued that a "silent revolution" has taken place in Latin America, particularly in the sense of accepting international arbitration for state-investor disputes. *See* Nigel Blackaby, David M. Lindse & Andrew Spinillo, *Overview of Regional Developments*, *in* INTERNATIONAL ARBITRATION IN LATIN AMERICA 10 (Nigel Blackaby, David M. Lindse & Andrew Spinillo. eds., 2002).

[13] *See* Wenhua Shan, *Is Calvo Dead?*, 54 AM. J. COMP. L. (forthcoming 2007), Section IV; *see also* Manning-Cabriel, *supra* note 1, at 1181 - 1190; Eduardo A. Wiesner, *ANCOM: A New Attitude toward Foreign Investment?*, 24 U. MIAMI INTER-AM. L. REV. 435, 449 - 464 (1993).

large, "deactivated" by the network of investment treaties providing an international platform for investment dispute settlement since the 1990s.[14]

The tide of investment liberalisation, however, seems to have reversed itself in recent years. As a result the Calvo Doctrine has returned to the world stage, particularly to Latin America. The chief indicator of the Calvo Doctrine's revival is the dramatic increase of investment treaty-based arbitration cases, which have forced states worldwide, particularly in Latin America, to rethink their approach towards investment liberalisation in general and the acceptance of international arbitration in particular. According to UNCTAD there were 219 investment treaty-based arbitration cases by November 2005, more than two-thirds initiated since 2002.[15] In other words, an average of more than 30 cases have been initiated in each of the last four years. Almost all of these cases have been brought by investors against states.[16] Most defendant states were developing states (47 out of 61), most frequently Latin American.[17] Argentina topped the list with 42 cases, which accounted for nearly 20% of the total caseload.[18] Mexico followed with 17 cases.[19] Ninety-four percent of the states that had been sued two or more times were developing states, including three more Latin American states: Ecuador (7), Chile (4) and Venezuela (3). Statistics from the ICSID shows that of 72 cases pending before ICSID in April 2004, 41 were against Latin American states, nearly 60% of the total number.[20]

The surge of investment treaty arbitration cases demonstrates the teeth of BITs and puts governments across the world on notice. Latin American states, the states with the strongest Calvo tradition, have naturally adopted, or are contemplating adopting, measures to limit investment treaty arbitrations and bring them under national control. This new trend is most perceptible in Argentina, Brazil and Venezuela.

1. *Argentina*

Argentina is the home country of Carlos Calvo, the father of the Calvo Doctrine. However, it was also among the most enthusiastic Latin American countries in departing from that Doctrine by entering into BITs. Indeed, Argentina signed at least 58 BITs,

---

[14] The author's survey of 9 major Latin American states' laws and regulations shows that most of the states still stick to the Calvo principles of excluding diplomatic protection and equal national treatment. Hence it would be incorrect to say that the Calvo Doctrine is completely dead. However, as most Latin American states have entered into international agreements subjecting state-investor disputes to international arbitration, the exclusion of foreign and international remedies has been largely discarded. This supports the argument that the Calvo Doctrine is not completely "dead," but only "deactivated." *See* SHAN, supra note 1313, Section V.

[15] UNCTAD, *Latest Developments in Investor-State Disputes Settlement*, 1 – 2, IIA Monitor No. 4, (UNCTAD/WEB/ITE/IIT/2005/2).

[16] Id.

[17] Id. at 3.

[18] In UNCTAD statistics, there are 14 developed defendant states, 37 developing states and 10 Southeast European and the Commonwealth of Independent States (CIS). As Southeast European and CIS states are generally developing states, the number of developing states might be counted as 47. Id. at 1 – 2.

[19] Id.

[20] *See* Bernardo M. Cremades, *Disputes Arising out of Foreign Direct Investment in Latin America: A New Look at the Calvo Doctrine and Other Jurisdictional Issues*, 59 DISP. RESOL. J. 78, 81 n. . 8 (2004).

leading the BIT league table in Latin America.[21] The recent dramatic rise of BIT-based arbitration cases against Argentina was triggered by Argentina's Emergency Law No. 25561, adopted in January 2002. The law, responding to an economic crisis, declared a public emergency until December 10, 2003, froze local tariffs, and abolished the one-to-one US Dollar-Peso convertibility.[22] Such measures had a significant negative impact on foreign investors who had stakes in privatised state-owned enterprises. One commentator observed that the net consequence of these measure for the utility companies was "a roughly two-thirds reduction in income".[23]

Because of state-investor arbitration clauses, investors began to sue the Argentine government. Of the 85 cases pending before ICSID as of February 2004, 35 of the cases were brought against Argentina, accounting for nearly half of the total investment arbitration caseload worldwide,[24] a magnitude unheard of in the history of arbitration. Currently, Argentina still has 31 cases pending before the ICSID, amounting to twenty eight percent of its total caseload.[25]

Such a large caseload for one country constitutes a significant burden, politically as well as financially. The average legal fee to defend a single investment treaty-based arbitration is estimated to be one to two million US dollars, in addition to which are costs for the arbitration tribunals amounting to roughly US $400,000.[26] Therefore, Argentina will have to pay tens of millions of dollars annually in order to defend these cases. Should Argentina lose every case, it would owe compensation amounting to roughly 17 billion dollars,[27] which, as alleged by Argentina, exceeds its annual budget.[28] Facing such severe legal challenges, Argentina has tried to cope by using procedural tactics.[29]

---

〔21〕 UNCTAD data show that Argentina signed 58 BITs by June 1, 2006, which is more than any other country in Latin America. *See* UNCTAD, Country Specific List of BITs, *available at* http://www.unctad.org/Templates/Page.asp?intItemID=2344&lang=1, last accessed on March 27, 2007.

〔22〕 Law No. 25561, Jan. 6, 2002, B. O. Articles 2–5, and 8–9. For English sources *see* Cremades, *supra* note 20, at 81; Patricia C. Mastropierro, Larry B. Pascal, ALERT: Argentine Devaluation Law, *available at* http://www.haynesboone.com/knowledge/knowledge_detail.asp?groupid=all&page=pubs&pubid=380 (last visit on March 27, 2007); M. & M Bomchil ABogados, Public Emergency Regulations on Public Works and Utilities Contracts and Licenses, *available at* http://www.ag-internet.com/bullet_iln_one_five/Bulletin-ContractsLicenses.doc (last visit on March 27, 2007).

〔23〕 Paolo Di Rosa, *The Recent Wave of Arbitrations against Argentina under Bilateral Investment Treaties: Background and Principal Legal Issues*, 36 U. MIAMI INTER-AM. L. REV., 41, 48 (2004).

〔24〕 Id. at 43.

〔25〕 *See* List of Pending Cases, *available at* http://www.worldbank.org/icsid/cases/pending.htm, last accessed March 27, 2007 (showing that 31 out of the 110 pending cases are against Argentina).

〔26〕 The legal costs to claimants are approximately the same as for defendants. *See* UNCTAD, *Issues Related to Investment Arrangements: Investor-State Disputes and Policy Implication*, 7, TD/B/COM.2/62 (January 14, 2005), *available at* http://www.unctad.org/en/docs/c2d62_en.pdf.

〔27〕 Indeed, the CMS award, the first of the many Argentine cases, has required Argentina to pay the company $1.33 billion. *See* UNCTAD, *Latest Developments in Investor-State Disputes Settlement*, 6, IIA Monitor No. 4, UNCTAD/WEB/ITE/IIT/2005/2 (2005); *see also* Luke Peterson, *Argentina Moves to Annul Award in Dispute with CMS Company Over Financial Crisis*, INVESTMENT TREATY NEWS (International Institute for Sustainable Development, Winnipeg, Canada), October 26, 2005, at 4–6, *available at* http://www.iisd.org/pdf/2005/investment_investsd_oct26_2005.pdf (accessed March 27, 2007).

〔28〕 *See* Peterson, *supra* note 27.

〔29〕 *See infra* Part I. 1. a.

Meanwhile, it has challenged the constitutionality of investment treaties and treaty-based arbitration.[30] Finally, Argentina has taken legislative measure to tackle the problem, and is currently considering further legislative measures.[31]

a) Procedural Tactics

In dealing with these cases, the Argentine government first makes every effort to reach a negotiated settlement with the disputant investors.[32] If this fails, the Government then almost always challenges the arbitrator's jurisdiction.[33] So far, the Government has failed to win a single jurisdictional challenge.[34]

These jurisdictional challenges have been launched on various grounds, some of which relate to "Calvo clauses" in BITs and/or concession agreements. In *Lanco International Inc. v. Argentine Republic*, a U. S. investor sued Argentina at the ICSID, based on a "fork-in-the-road clause" in a 1991 US-Argentina BIT allowing a choice among local remedies, agreed channels and international arbitration.[35] The Argentine government challenged ICSID's jurisdiction, arguing that Argentina had not given the necessary written consent to grant the ICSID jurisdiction and that the dispute should be settled by the Federal Contentious Administrative Tribunal of Buenos Aires, as provided in the Concession agreement between the parties.[36] The tribunal held, however, that the BIT constituted an open offer by the government and "consent" for the purposes of Article 25 (1) of the ICSID Convention.[37] The tribunal made the later much-debated distinction between the contract claim and the treaty claim, and ruled that the Argentine government's consent to the BIT had not been withdrawn by its subsequent execution of the Concession Agreement with the investor concerned.[38]

Subsequently in *CMS Gas Transmission Co. v. Argentine Republic*,[39] the Argentine government again challenged ICSID's jurisdiction. This time the government claimed, *inter alia*, that the license the Government granted to TNG[40] contained a separate dispute settlement mechanism vesting exclusive jurisdiction in the Federal Court of Buenos Aires. The Tribunal nevertheless upheld the investors' right to ICSID arbitration, reasoning that CMS was not bound by the license as it was not a party to it. But the Tribunal went fur-

---

[30] *See infra* Part I. 1. b.

[31] *See infra* Part I. 1. c.

[32] *See* Cremades, *supra* note 20, at 81.

[33] *See* Yanru Wei, *On the Impropriety of China's Recent Acceptance of Full ICSID Jurisdiction*, 13 J. INT' L ECON. LAW (in Chinese) 108, at 139 – 140.

[34] Id.

[35] Argentina-US BIT, Article 7, as cited in *Lanco International, Inc. v. Argentine Republic* (Case No. ARB/97/6), Preliminary Decision on Jurisdiction of December 8, 1998, 40 ILM 457 (2001), § 20.

[36] Clause 12, the Conssession Agreement for the Port Terminal No. 3, as cited in *Lanco International, Inc. v. Argentine Republic, id,* § 6.

[37] Lanco International, *Inc. v. Argentine Republic*, id, § § 32 – 33.

[38] Lanco International, *Inc. v. Argentine Republic, id,* § § 34 – 40. For further analyses on the distinction and relationship between contractual claims and treaty claims, see Yuval Shany, *Contract Claims vs. Treaty Claims: Mapping Conflicts between ICSID Decisions on Multisourced Investment Claim*, 99 AM. J. INT'l L. 835.

[39] *CMS Gas Transmission Co. v. Republic of Argentina*, Decision on Objections to Jurisdiction, ICSID ARB/01/8, 42 ILM 788 (2003).

[40] TNG is the company in which the claimant had 29.42% of the shares.

ther and ruled out altogether the legal effect of such "Calvo clauses" by saying "... referring certain kinds of disputes to the local courts... [is] not a bar to the assertion of jurisdiction by an ICSID tribunal under the treaty, as the functions of these various instrument are different."[41]

While a full discussion of this issue could merit a doctoral dissertation, it is sufficient to note here that Argentina was unsuccessful in challenging the jurisdiction of the ICSID tribunal. The government then attempted a further procedural technique to tackle the problem: applying for annulment of the ICSID award once the award is made. Thus in September 2005, Argentina applied for annulment of the award on the merits of the *CMS* case.[42] As of this article's submission, the annulment case is still pending before the ICSID.

b) The Unconstitutionality Argument

The Argentine government has recently challenged the constitutionality of BITs and, consequently, the BIT-based arbitration process.[43] The Argentine prosecutor, for example, argued in a hearing in the *CMS Gas Transmission Co. vs. Republica Argentina* case that:

a) Bilateral treaties do not supersede the National Constitution and therefore a company can not invoke such treaty to avoid trying the case in Argentina before local courts and violate the right of defense in court of the Argentine State.

b) A company that is engaged in the rendering of public services can not impose a limitation on the sovereign right of the government to change its economic policy or the

[41] *CMS Gas Transmission Co. v. Republic of Argentina*, *supra* note 35, para 76.

[42] The annulment proceeding can at least provide some additional time for Argentina before the payment has to be made. *See* Peterson, *supra* note 27.

[43] There are two lines of argument for the unconstitutionality of the ICSID Convention and its awards. One is the position actually adopted by the Argentine Government. The other is a more recent and also more radical argument, which has not been adopted by the Argentine Government. It holds that both BITs and the ICSID regime are unconstitutional because they were approved in violation of the process established in the Argentine Constitution as reformed in 1994.

Since the ICSID Convention was ratified and hence entered into force after the constitutional reforms took effect, and the domestic implementation bill was also subsequently published, the new constitutional provisions should apply. Additionally, the new Constitution requires a special and very stringent procedure for "treaties of integration which delegate powers and jurisdiction to supranational organizations." It is argued that since the acceptance of the arbitral jurisdiction of the ICSID requires transfer of sovereign power of domestic jurisdiction to be transferred to the ICSID, the ICSID Convention has "integration" purposes and as such must be subjected to the special constitutional procedure. Because such a procedure has never been undertaken, the validity requirement under the new system has not been completed and consequently any arbitration carried out by the ICSID against Argentina can be declared null and void by a domestic court.

The argument goes further that the special procedure required by the new Constitution is mandatory, and as a result, such treaties delegating powers and jurisdiction to international bodies as the ICSID Convention should be rendered null and void *per se* with the enactment of the reform.

For further details of the arguments, *See* Carlos E. Alfaro & Pedro M. Lorenti, *The Growing Opposition of Argentina to ICSID Arbitral Tribunals: A Conflict between International and Domestic* Law? 6 J. WORLD INVEST. & TRADE 3, 417, 425 – 429 (2005). Alfaro and Lorenti consider that the ICSID Convention is merely a treaty of "co-operation", not an "integration treaty", and therefore does not require the fulfilment of the special procedure required by the new constitution. Id, at 429 – 430.

tariffs.[44]

The Prosecutor also conducted a public campaign advocating the readoption of the Calvo and Drago[45] doctrines and attacking BITs and the ICSID by stating that Argentina should never again agree to submit a contractual dispute to a system with ICSID characteristics.[46]

The foundation of the constitutional argument is Sections 27 and 75 of the Constitution of Argentina. Section 75.22 set forth the legal status of international treaties as beneath the Constitution, but above the laws, excepting certain human rights treaties, as expressly stipulated in the Constitution, which enjoy constitutional status.[47] In short, most treaties, such as BITs and the ICSID Convention are subordinate to the Constitution. Section 27 further subjects such treaties to "the principles of public law laid down by this Constitution."[48] As a result, two commentator argue, "the validity of the ICSID Convention in Argentina could be tested by ascertaining its compatibility with said 'public law principles' of the Constitution."[49] The commentators continue by saying that the same 'public law principles' test could be applied to arbitration awards ren-

---

〔44〕 Carlos E. Alfaro, 'The Battle of the Century: Argentina Against the ICSID Arbitration and the BITs', World Law Group E-news Issue No. 31 (November 2004), *available at* http://www.imakenews.com/bcastro/e_66201_86528.pdf.

〔45〕 The Drago Doctrine was announced in 1902 by the Argentinean Minister of Foreign Affairs Luis Maria Drago, arguing mainly that no foreign power, including the United States, could use force to collect debt. *See* Wikipedia, the Free Encyclopedia, *Drago Doctrine*, *available at* http://en.wikipedia.org/wiki/Drago_Doctrine (last visited Jan. 22, 2007).

〔46〕 See Wikipedia, *available at* https://en.wikipedia.org/wiki/Calvo_Doctrine.

〔47〕 Chapter IV Section 75.22 of the Constitution of the Argentine Nation reads, "[t]reaties and concordats have a higher hierarchy than laws."

The American Declaration of the Rights and Duties of Man; the Universal Declaration of Human Rights; the American Convention on Human Rights; the International Pact on Economic, Social and Cultural Rights; the International Pact on Civil and Political Rights and its empowering Protocol; the Convention on the Prevention and Punishment of Genocide; the International Convention on the Elimination of all Forms of Racial Discrimination; the Convention on the Elimination of all Forms of Discrimination against Woman; the Convention against Torture and other Cruel, Inhuman or Degrading Treatments or Punishments; the Convention on the Rights of the Child; in the full force of their provisions, they have constitutional hierarchy, do no repeal any section of the First Part of this Constitution and are to be understood as complementing the rights and guarantees recognized herein. They shall only be denounced, in such event, by the National Executive Power after the approval of two-thirds of all the members of each House.

In order to attain constitutional hierarchy, the other treaties and conventions on human rights shall require the vote of two-thirds of all the members of each House, after their approval by Congress.

CONST. ARG. § 75.22, *available at* http://www.argentina.gov.ar/argentina/portal/documentos/constitucion_ingles.pdf.

〔48〕 Section 27 of the Argentine Constitution reads, "[t]he Federal Government is under the obligation to strengthen its relationships of peace and trade with foreign powers, by means of treaties in accordance with the principles of public law laid down by this Constitution." Id. § 27.

〔49〕 However, Alfaro and Lorenti seem to have entertained an expansive interpretation on the concept of "public law principles in the constitution" by extending them to cover all "matters of public law," with which the author of the present paper does not agree. *See* Carlos E. Alfaro & Pedro M. Lorenti, *supra* note 39, at 420, 423–25.

dered by the ICSID tribunals because they are the "products" of the ICSID.[50] Therefore, the Congress should not have ratified treaties such as the ICSID Convention that conflict with the Constitution's "public law principles" of the Constitution, nor should the President have negotiated the treaty in the first place.[51] The power to review treaties for unconstitutionality, however, lies in the hands of the Judiciary and, ultimately, the Federal Supreme Court of Argentina.[52]

In this connection, it is relevant to note that the Argentine judiciary recently echoed the Administration's position in a landmark case that, in matters of public policy, the Argentine courts may review the reasonability, fairness and constitutionality, i. e., the merits, of an arbitration award.[53] The case, *Jose Cartellone Construcciones Civiles S. A. v. Hidroelectrica Norpatagonica S. A.*, reportedly concerned a domestic arbitration involving a public services contract between a private Argentine company and a state-owned enterprise.[54] The contract had an arbitration provision excluding any appeal to courts.[55] The Federal Supreme Court of Argentina decided that the Court may "review arbitral awards if 'unconstitutional' 'unreasonable' or 'illegal', even when the parties involved have specifically agreed to waive the right to appeal."[56] This decision "reaffirmed the Supreme Court's role of '*guardian*' of the Constitution and of *public policy*, even in those cases that ha[d] been previously submitted to arbitrators and where judicial review ha[d] not been admitted by the parties."[57] In supporting the decision, the Supreme Court invoked Article 872 of the Civil Code, which states that "rights granted with aim at public policy cannot be waived."[58] With this, the Court effectively rejected the possibility of any parties' agreement restricting review over matters of public policy.

This decision implies that an award rendered by an international arbitration tribunal may be challenged in Argentina as "unreasonable" or "unconstitutional." This decision "is already influencing Argentine lower courts in connection with international arbitrations."[59]

---

[50] However, Alfaro and Lorenti seem to have entertained an expansive interpretation on the concept of "public law principles in the constitution" by extending them to cover all "matters of public law," with which the author of the present paper does not agree. *See* Carlos E. Alfaro & Pedro M. Lorenti, *supra* note 39, at 420, 423 – 25.

[51] Id. at 421.

[52] Id.

[53] Corte Suprema de Justicia [CSJN], 1/June/2004, "Jose Cartellone Construcciones Civiles S. A. v. Hidroelectrica Norpatagonica S. A./, La Ley [L. L.] (Causa J – 87, XXXVII R. O.) (Arg.), the Decision in Spanish is available at the Court's website: < http://www.csjn.gov.ar/documentos/cfal3/toc_fallos.jsp > (last visit on 17 March 2007).

[54] Carlos E. Alfaro, *Argentina: ICSID Arbitration and BITs Challenged by the Argentine Government*, Alfaro-Abogados, Dec. 21, 2004, http://www.alfarolaw.com/ima/tapa/alfaro3.htm.

[55] Id.

[56] Id.

[57] Id.

[58] Id. (reporting on Corte Suprema de Justicia [CSJN], 1/June/2004, "Jose Cartellone Construcciones Civiles S. A. v. Hidroelectrica Norpatagonica S. A./, La Ley [L. L.] (Causa J – 87, XXXVII R. O.) (Arg.) (citing 11 Cód. Civ. 872 (Arg.))

[59] Horacio A. Grigera Naon, *Arbitration in Latin America: Progress and Setbacks*, 21 ABR. INT' L 127, 165 (2005).

From an international law point of view, the aforementioned constitutionality argument is hardly tenable. The Vienna Convention on the Law of Treaties establishes that a state may not invoke the provisions of its internal law as justification for its failure to perform according to treaty.[60] Likewise, a state may not assert that its consent to be bound was expressed in violation of a provision of the state's internal law requiring competence to conclude treaties, unless violation of the provision was manifest and concerned a rule of its internal law of fundamental importance.[61] In the case of Argentina, establishing that the consent given by the Argentine Congress in BIT practice has been in "manifest" violation of a provision of Argentine internal law would be very difficult. Even if the "violation" could be established, it could hardly be shown that the violation was "manifest," as a violation is only "manifest" if "objectively evident to any state conducting itself in the matter in accordance with normal practice and in good faith."[62]

Judicial review for ICSID awards is more straightforward, as the ICSID Convention clearly requires member states to recognize ICSID awards as binding and enforce them as if they were final judgment of a court in that state.[63] Nevertheless, the issue may arise for investment arbitrations rendered by other arbitration tribunals such as International Chamber of Commerce (ICC) Court of Arbitration or *ad hoc* tribunals established in accordance with the rules of the United Nations Commission on International Trade Law (UNCITRAL). Thus Argentine courts could review the merits of such awards and set aside them on the ground that they were "unreasonable" or "unconstitutional."

c) Legislative Measures

While using procedural tactics to suspend and delay the arbitration process and the unconstitutionality argument to defend its position, the Argentine government has also taken and is considering taking further legislative measures to limit and prevent further investment arbitration cases. To further this end, the government has canceled a 1996 decree[64] and is contemplating a new law to control international arbitration.

---

[60] Vienna Convention on the Law of Treaties arts. 27, Jan. 27, 1980, 1155 U. N. T. S. 331, *available at* http://untreaty.un.org/ilc/texts/instruments/english/conventions/1_1_1969.pdf.

[61] Vienna Convention on the Law of Treaties art. 46, Jan. 27, 1980, 1155 U. N. T. S. 331, available at http://untreaty.un.org/ilc/texts/instruments/english/conventions/1_1_1969.pdf. SomeArgentine constitutional scholars have also noted such limitations imposed by international law. For example, Nestor Sagues has pointed out that the unconstitutionality of an international treaty could only be declared in the case where such a treaty violates the competence rule as set forth in the Article 46 of the Vienna Convention on the Law of Treaties. See Alfaro & Lorenti, *supra* note 39, at 422.

[62] Vienna Convention on the Law of Treaties art. 26(2), Jan. 27, 1980, 1155 U. N. T. S. 331, *available at* http://untreaty.un.org/ilc/texts/instruments/english/conventions/1_1_1969.pdf. The aforementioned *Ceskoslovenska Obchodni Banka, A. S. v. The Slovak Republic* case also touched upon Article 46, but held it irrelevant as it is about "invalidity of treaties," because the BIT at issue did not actually enter into force. Case No. ARB/97/4 *Ceskoslovenska Obchodni Banka, A. S. v. Slovak Republic Decision of the Tribunal on the Objections to Jurisdiction of May* 24, 1999, 14 ICSID REV. —FOREIGN INV. L. J. 251, 265 (2000), *available at* http://www.worldbank.org/icsid/cases/csob.pdf

[63] ICSID Convention art. 54(1), *available at* http://www.worldbank.org/icsid/basicdoc/CRR_English-final.pdf.

[64] Decreto N° 1021/96 of 6 September 1996, *available at* <http://www.boletinoficial.gov.ar/bora.portal/PrimeraSecci%C3%B3n/BusquedaRapida/tabid/81/Default.aspx> (last visit on 17 Mar. 07).

In 2003, the Argentine government passed a new decree terminating a 1996 Menen administration decision, which authorized the submission of disputes between Argentine government and certain foreign investors to international arbitration tribunals.[65] The new decree pointed out that referring such disputes to international arbitration "presented a series of difficulties from the legal, political and economic point of view."[66]

This was not the end of the story, but rather the first step of the government's attempt to "renationalise" state-investor disputes.[67] Horacio Rosatti, then head of the office of the Attorney General in the Treasury, reportedly said that the aim of the government was to "recover the jurisdiction of national courts."[68] Further, he said that the government was considering measures to bring other state-investor disputes back within Argentina's ambit, including measures to ensure that, first, that the companies had "exhausted all legal channels in Argentina" and second, "that the final decisions of international tribunals should then undergo 'analysis' by the local courts."[69]

Following a speech by President Kirchner on March 2005, which severely questioned eventual decisions of international or arbitration tribunals on state-investor claims,[70] two House Representatives of the ruling party reportedly promoted a bill aimed at limiting the intervention of national or international arbitral tribunals in cases involving the State, State agencies or enterprises.[71] The proposed bill prohibits access to international arbitration in such cases unless: a) an appeal of their decisions before Argentine federal courts is provided, b) the State's counterparty in the dispute is a foreign state (state-state disputes), or c) the Congress has exempted the case through a specific statute.[72] The bill also requests the Executive to inform the appropriate authorities of Argentina's repeal of any treaty accepting such jurisdiction; and, meanwhile, demands that the Executive, its agencies and enterprises issue necessary orders or decisions in order to annul prior agreements or decisions contrary to such provisions.[73] Since the bill generally requires all state-investor arbitration cases to be subject to the ultimate control of national courts, it would effectively abolish the finality and hence the autonomy of arbitration.

---

[65] Decreto N° 966/2003 of 28 October 2003, *available at* http://www.saij.jus.gov.ar/news/files/decreto966.html > (last visit on 17 March 2007). *See also* Laurence Norman, *Government Reopens 7 - Year-Old Case Vs Oil Group*, DOW JONES INT'L NEWS, Oct. 28, 2003 (reporting the 2003 decree annulling the 1996 executive order), *available at* < http://www.latinpetroleum.com/printer_2375.shtml > (retrieved 27 Jan 2005); Cremades, *supra note* 20 (discussing the same event citing the same source as above), at 81.

[66] Decreto 966/2003, id.

[67] Norman, *supra* note 61.

[68] Id.

[69] Id.

[70] Guido Santiago Tawil (M. & M. Bomchil), *Is Calvo finally back*? 3 TRANSNAT' L DISP. MGMT., 3 (2005).

[71] Id.

[72] Id.

[73] Id.

Other bills of similar nature have reportedly been introduced before the Argentine Congress since 2004.[74] For instance, a bill introduced in September 2004 in the House of Deputies would "subject all disputes to which the State is a party to the exclusive jurisdiction of the Argentine courts and would prohibit any clause to the contrary."[75] The bill would also require the denunciation of treaties in which the State had agreed to the jurisdiction of judicial or arbitral tribunals.[76] Another bill introduced in August 2005 would demand that matters relating to "economic policy and determinations by Argentine courts concerning direct or indirect expropriation should not be subject to review by international courts or tribunals."[77] The August 2005 bill would also require that a provision "to that effect be included in each investment treaty as a condition for approval."[78] If such bills are adopted, the Calvo Doctrine can be said to have finally returned to its birthplace. It remains to be seen, however, whether the bills are mere rhetoric or will be ultimately adopted.

2. *Brazil*

Brazil, the Latin American giant, had long been resistant to arbitration until 1996 when the Arbitration Act was adopted *to facilitate arbitration practice*.[79] In 2002, Brazil ratified the New York Convention and paved the way for recognition and enforcement of foreign arbitration awards.[80] Yet Brazil remains suspicious of international arbitration on some level. This is witnessed first by a constitutionality challenge against the Arbitration Act and more recently by the restrictive approach taken in the 2004 Public-Private Partnership Law (the PPP Law).

a) The Constitutionality Challenge

In October 1996, soon after the Arbitration Act was approved, an appeal (MBV v. Resil) was brought before the Brazilian Federal Supreme Court challenging the validity of the Arbitration Act as a violation of the Constitution.[81] As the first case concerning

---

[74] *See* Oscar M. Garibaldi, *Carlos Calvo Redivivus: The Rediscovery of the Calvo Doctrine in the Era of Investment Treaties*, TRANSNAT' L DIS. MGMT., December 2006, at 1.

[75] Id.

[76] Id.

[77] Id. at. 43 – 44.

[78] Id. at 44.

[79] Before 1996, arbitration in Brazil were subject to a number of restrictions. For instance, pre-dispute submission to arbitration by contract were unenforceable unless both parties agreed to enter into another arbitration agreement after the dispute actually raised. Foreign arbitration awards would not be recognised or enforced until two court imprimaturs had been obtained, one from the court at the sea of arbitration and one from the Brazilian Federal Supreme Court. For further details, *see* Noah D. Rubins, Investment Arbitration in Brazil, 4 J. WORLD INVESTMENT & TRADE 1071, 1084 – 1087 (2003).

[80] Brazil joined the New York Convention in 2002, by Decree No. 4311 of 23 July 2002. Id, at 1075 n. 16.

[81] For details of the case, *see* Joao Bosco Lee, *Brazil*, *in* INTERNATIONAL ARBITRATION IN LATIN AMERICA 61, 63 – 66 (Nigel Blackaby et al. eds., 2002); *see also* Guido Santiago Tawil, THE ROLE OF ARBITRATION AND INTERNATIONAL, REGIONAL, SUBREGIONAL AND BILATERAL TREATIES IN LATIN AMERICA1, *available at* http://www.bomchil.com/cas/articulos/The% 20role% 20of% 20arbitration% 20and% 20international.pdf(last visited May 22, 2006) (need parenthetical explaining how this is relevant).

the Arbitration Act, the case was brought to the attention of the eleven justices of the Court.[82] The case originated in a request of enforcement for a foreign arbitration award issued in Barcelona, Spain.[83] The Court, however, took the opportunity to review the constitutionality of the entire Act.[84]

Initially, the reporting justice (Min. Sepúlveda Pertence) considered that certain articles (including Articles 6 and 7, admitting specific performance of the arbitration clause, Article 41, providing the exclusion of courts when faced with an arbitration clause, and Article 42, listing the circumstances under which an appeal might be made against a judgement given under Article 7) of the Arbitration Act were unconstitutional, mainly because they would represent a general denial of access to the judicial review provided for in Article 5, XXXV of the 1998 Constitution.[85] After more than five years of discussion, however, the position of the reporting judge was defeated in December 2001 by a seven to four decision, and the Arbitration Act was declared constitutional.[86]

Although the final decision was pro-arbitration, the position of the reporting judge and the other three dissenting judges, as well as the long deliberation, have demonstrated Brazil's suspicion and hesitation towards international arbitration.

b) The PPP Law

On December 30, 2004, Brazil adopted Federal Law No. 11079, establishing a legal framework for Brazilian public-private partnerships (PPPs) and forbiddance and concession agreements within the scope of federal, state and local governments (the PPP Law).[87] The PPP Law permits parties to choose arbitration as a means to settle any dispute arising from PPP contracts.[88] It requires, however, that the seat of the arbitration be in Brazil and the proceedings be conducted in Portuguese.[89] Furthermore, the PPP Law only accepts domestic arbitration and prohibits the submission of any disputes in relation to a PPP contract to international arbitration. Foreign investors therefore can only seek redress before local courts or arbitration tribunals applying Brazilian law. This affirms the reluctance of the Brazilian Government to subject cases involving public enti-

---

[82] Tawil, *supra* note 75, at 14.

[83] Id.

[84] In Brazil, the Supreme Court takes charge of the control of constitutionality, and has jurisdiction to examine the constitutionality of the entire law in case one of its provisions is called into question. Therefore, even though the matter of the validity of the arbitration clause was not argued in the enforcement procedure, the Court raised the issue in its own initiative. *See* Lee, *supra* note 75, at 64 n. 15.

[85] Article 5, XXXV of the Constitution provides that "the law shall not exclude from review by the Judiciary any violation of or threat to a right." Constituição Federal [C. F.] [Constitution] art. 5, XXXV (Braz.). For further details of the reporting justice's reasoning, see Lee, *supra* note 75, at 63 – 64. *See also* Tawil, *supra* note 75, at 14 – 15.

[86] *See* Tawil, *supra* note 75, at 15.

[87] Lei No. 11. 079, de 30 de dezembro de 2004, *available at* https://www.planalto.gov.br/ccivil_03/_Ato2004 – 2006/2004/Lei/L11079.htm. An English version is available at http://www.planejamento.gov.br/arquivos_down/ppp/legislacao/lei_11079_301204_eng.pdf.

[88] Id., art. 11, III.

[89] Id.

ties, such as state-investor disputes, to international arbitration.[90]

3. *Venezuela*

Certain events which occurred in Venezuela in recent years have also been regarded as evidence of the resurgence of the Calvo Doctrine;[91] most notably, the Exploration Round Case and the MINCA Case.

a) The Exploration Round Case

"In December 1995 a petition was filed with the Venezuelan Supreme Court asking for a ruling on the constitutionality of 'arbitration provisions' in the Congressional Accord approving the 1995 Exploration Bidding Round."[92] One provision in the Congress Accord (Condition 17) stated that all disputes arising from Association Agreements (i. e., oil exploration agreements with investors concluded following the bid) will be resolved by binding arbitration.[93] A group of Venezuelan citizens, however, challenged that this provision violated Article 127 of the Venezuelan Constitution, which, they believed, gave local courts exclusive jurisdiction over such contracts.[94] Article 127 of the 1961 Venezuelan Constitution states as follows:

in contracts of public interest, even when not expressly stated, there is considered to be incorporated, if not against the nature of the contract, a clause pursuant to which any doubt or dispute that may arise in connection with such contracts and which cannot be amicably resolved by the parties, shall be decided by the competent courts of the Republic, in accordance with its laws, and may not give cause or reason to foreign claims.[95]

Since the validity of arbitration had never been decided by the Supreme Court and there had been contradictory opinions from the Attorney General's office on this issue,[96] the case was rather controversial.

On August 17, 1999, "the Venezuelan Supreme Court rendered a milestone decision in the Exploration Round Case,"[97] upholding the constitutionality of the arbitration clause in the Accord. The Supreme Court held that although the agreements were "contracts of public interest," they fell within the exception in Article 127, which waived the application of the local courtjurisdiction requirement in case such application

---

[90] As noted by Rubins, the only path towards international arbitration recognised in Brazil is by carefully drafted arbitration clauses in contracts between a foreign investor and the Brazilian Government, as "Brazil lacks the legal infrastructure that in many other countries of Latin America give foreign investors explicit guarantees of equitable treatment and access to international arbitration." *See* Noah D. Rubins, *Investment Arbitration in Brazil*, 4 J. WORLD INVESTMENT & TRADE 1071, 1080 – 1081, 1091 (2003).

[91] *See* Cremades, *supra* note 20, at 81.

[92] Elisabeth E. Elijuri, *Oil Opening: A Constitutional Challenge* (1996), *available at* http://www.natlaw.com/pubs/spveen1.htm.

[93] *See* id.

[94] See Cremades, *supra note* 20, at 81.

[95] Id.

[96] *See* Elijuri, *supra* note 86.

[97] Cremades, *supra* note 20, at 83 (citing Supreme Court Decision of August 17, 1999, File No. 812 – 829).

would be "against the nature of the contract."[98] The Court held that this exception "enabled the [g]overnment, subject to subsequent congressional approval, to decide—on a case-by-case basis—whether to include an arbitration clause in a contract of public interest."[99] The Court justified its conclusion by stating that, in the present case, "an eventual arbitral tribunal would not be confronted with issues concerning 'the national interest.'"[100]

Although the Exploration Round Case was resolved in favour of arbitration and foreign investors, the uncertainty of the constitutionality of arbitration has not been eradicated, given that the Venezuelan Supreme Court did little to clarify the ambiguity surrounding the "nature of the contract" exception. The new Constitution, adopted in 1999, after the case was settled, did nothing to resolve the question. Contrary to what foreign investors have hoped for, the new Constitution retains Article 127's existing language along with its exception, but renumbered it as Article 151.[101]

Further, the President of Venezuela issued, in March 2001, Instructive Order No. 4 "to regulate the internal review mechanisms of public interest contracts to be executed by the Republic, particularly, in connection with the inclusion of international arbitration clauses".[102] According to this Order, contracts concerning public interests must be submitted to the Attorney General of the Republic for an opinion with regard to the legality of the arbitration clause in light of Article 151 of the new Constitution.[103]

Additionally, as new members of a recently-established Supreme Tribunal of Justice have been appointed, the Supreme Court's previous favorable ruling upholding the constitutionality of an arbitration clause in a public contract might also be changed.[104] This perception seems to have been confirmed in the *Minera las Cristinas, C. A. (MINCA) v. Corporación Venezolana de Guyana (CVG)* case ("MINCA Case"),[105] a discussion of which follows.

b) The MINCA Case

The MINCA Case involved a 1992 mining agreement between CVG, an agency of Venezuelan Government, and MINCA, a Venezuelan company ninety-five percent owned by a Canadian company, Vannessa Ventures Ltd. The agreement was for the exploration,

---

[98] Cremades, *supra* note 20, at 83 (citing Supreme Court Decision of August 17, 1999, File No. 812 – 829).

[99] Id.

[100] Id.

[101] Constitution of the Bolivarian Republic of Venezuela, Article 151. An unofficial English translation of the Constitution can be found at the Australia Venezuela Solidarity Network Chavez website: < http://www.venezuela-solidarity.org/?q=node/53 > (last visit on 17 March 2007).

[102] Bernardo Weininger & David M. Lindsey, *Venezuela*, *in* INTERNATIONAL ARBITRATION IN LATIN AMERICA 223, 235 (Nigel Blackaby et al., eds., 2002).

[103] Id. at 235 – 236.

[104] *See* Cremades, *supra* note 20, at 83.

[105] Bernardo M. Cremades, *Resurgence of the Calvo Doctrine in Latin America*, 7 Business Law International 53, 65 (2006) (citing Decision No. 0083 of the Political Administrative Chamber of the Supreme Court, of 15 July 2004).

development and exploitation of gold and copper in an area called "Las Cristinas."[106] The agreement contained a dispute resolution provision requiring "that any dispute between parties would be referred to an arbitration seating in Venezuela, in accordance with the ICC Arbitration Rules and the Venezuelan Code of Civil Procedure."[107] A dispute arising in 2001 between the two parties resulted in the CVG terminating the mining agreement and then taking physical control of the site.[108] Later the Ministry of Energy and Mines passed a resolution to terminate the mining agreement and the government "issued a Presidential Decree declaring the area of Las Cristinas reserved to the National Government."[109]

MINCA first challenged CVG's action, and then the ministerial resolution and the Presidential Decree before domestic courts, but all its requests for judicial review were dismissed.[110] In May 2002, MINCA filed a petition in front of the Supreme Court of Justice, "requesting the enforcement of the arbitration clause."[111] The Supreme Court dismissed MINCA's petition on the ground that the subject matter concerned state assets and therefore could not be subject to arbitration.[112] The Court founded its decisions on, *inter alia*, the aforementioned Article 151 of the Constitution, which generally subjects contracts of public interests to the exclusive jurisdiction of local courts.[113] It thus resurrected the uncertainty of Venezuela's position towards international arbitration.

The aforementioned events in Argentina, Brazil and Venezuela, together with similar events in other Latin American states,[114] such as Ecuador's cancellation of oil contacts with Occidental petroleum[115] and Bolivia's nationalisation of its hydrocarbons sector,[116] clearly suggest that the tide of investment policy seems to be turning. No longer are Latin

[106] Bernardo M. Cremades, *Resurgence of the Calvo Doctrine in Latin America*, 7 Business Law International 53, 65 (2006) (citing Decision No. 0083 of the Political Administrative Chamber of the Supreme Court, of 15 July 2004).

[107] Id. at 66.

[108] Id.

[109] Id.

[110] Id.

[111] Id.

[112] Id.

[113] Id. at 67.

[114] Apart from the said three states, other Latin American states have also expressed increasing dissatisfaction in international arbitration. For example, the Attorney General of Ecuador has reportedly said that he is studying whether Ecuador should terminate the BIT with the United States. Di Rosa, *supra* note 23, at 74 n. 88.

[115] Luke E. Peterson, *Ecuador Moves Against Occidental Petroleum Contract and Assets*, INVESTMENT-TREATYNEWS, May. 16, 2006, *available at* http://www.iisd.org/pdf/2006/itn_may16_2006.pdf.

[116] In May 2006, Bolivia issued a decree through which natural hydrocarbon resources were nationalized. The decree stipulates that companies conducting activities in the gas and petroleum production industry have to turn over the entire production of hydrocarbons to "Yacimientos Petroliferos Fiscales Bolivianos" (YPFB), "which will control the distribution of these resources, and will also determine the amount and conditions at which gas and petroleum will be allocated to the domestic and foreign markets." *Bolivia: Presidential Supreme Decree* 28701 *(Nationalization of Hydrocarbons Sector) (May* 1, 2006*)*, INTERNATIONAL LAW IN BRIEF (AM. SOC'Y OF INT'L L., Wash., D.C.), May 25, 2006, http://www.asil.org/ilib/2006/05/ilib060525.htm#l1.

American states as eager to embrace neo-liberalism. Rather, a more conservative or nationalistic approach seems to be gaining the upper hand in these states.[117] As a result, Calvo does not seem to be dead, as many assumed or predicted, but rather alive and well.

II. The Revival of the Calvo Doctrine: Beyond Latin America

The resurgence of the Calvo Doctrine identified above is not confined to Latin America. Indeed, Latin American states' recent Calvo move coincided with a worldwide trend reflecting, revising and rejecting neo-liberalist investment instruments, while embracing a more conservative and balanced regime for international investment. Thus, firstly, to everyone's surprise, the Calvo Doctrine "suddenly is in vogue again... in the U. S. Congress" ![118] Mounting cases against the U. S. government before international arbitration tribunals, particularly North American Free Trade Agreement ("NAFTA") tribunals, has put the United States, a long-time unreserved advocate of investment liberalism, on defence, and forced it to re-examine investment treaties and treaty-based arbitration for the first time in history from a defendant's position. It has been noted that, since the mid – 1990s, there has been "a gradual, relatively moderate (but unmistakable) weakening" in the U. S. of the commitment to the traditional high standard of investment protection.[119] Thus in 1994 the Clinton administration dropped in its model BIT the "Umbrella clause", a provision requiring the state to observe obligations it had assumed in relation to the foreign investment.[120] In 2001, the three NAFTA member states, led by the U. S., adopted a binding interpretation declaring that "[t]he concept of 'fair and equitable treatment' and 'full protection and security' do not require treatment in addition to or beyond that which is required by the customary international law minimum standard of treatment of aliens,"[121] in an effort to eliminate the undesired influence of the *Pope & Talbot Inc. v. Canada*[122] jurisprudence. A bill was enacted in 2002 regarding the Executive's authority to negotiate trade and investment treaties, which requires that,

---

[117] The "revival" or "resurgence" of the Calvo Doctrine in Latin America has attracted wide attention. For instance, in September 2005, the Washington D. C. Bar organized a timely seminar entitled "The Resurgence of the Calvo Doctrine?" District of Columbia Bar, "The Resurgence of the Calvo Doctrine?" seminar program, *available at* http://www.bg-consulting.com/docs/calvo_program.jpg (last visited Feb. 15, 2007).

[118] David Schneiderman, *Calvo in Congress: The Migration of Constitution-Like Investment Rules*, *available at* http://www.ualberta.ca/GLOBALISM/pdf/Aus%20pdfs/schneidermanab.pdf (last visited Feb. 15, 2007).

[119] Garibaldi noted that such change might be the result of a political compromise between the country's traditional position and the pressure from the circumstantial alliance of at least three political forces, namely the pro-regulation interests on the left, the legal defence interest and the antiinternationalist interests on the right. Garibaldi, *supra* note 70, section 1.03 [3] [c].

[120] Ibid.

[121] Ibid.

[122] Pope & Talbot Inc. v. Canada, 13 World Trade & Arb. Mat'l 61 (Apr. 10, 2001), *available at* http://www.dfait-maeci.gc.ca/tna-nac/documents/Award_Merits-e.pdf. The Award held that fair and equitable treatment and full protection and security standards imposed an additional obligation to the international minimum standard of treatment under general international law. Id. at ¶ 111.

"...the principal negotiating objectives of the United States regarding foreign investment are to reduce or eliminate artificial or trade-distorting barriers to foreign investment, *while ensuring that foreign investors in the United States are not accorded greater substantive rights with respect to investment protections than United States investors in the United States*, and to secure for investors important rights comparable to those that would be available under *United States legal principles and practice*."[123] (emphasis added)

This bill was regarded as "Calvo in the Congress" because it adopted language very similar to the Calvo Doctrine as policy in international investment treaty-making practice. As a result, the U. S. government recently revised its Model BIT[124] and adopted a more conservative approach in its BIT practice. A narrower definition of "investment," for example, was adopted in the US-Uruguay BIT signed in December 2004, the very first after the 2004 Model BIT was adopted.[125] Indirect expropriation has been clarified and redefined so that mere adverse effect on the economic value of an investment does not constitute an indirect expropriation and that, except in rare circumstances, non-discriminatory regulatory actions by a party aimed at protecting legitimate public welfare objectives, such as public health, safety, and the environment, do not constitute indirect expropriations. A special procedure was devised in the US-Uruguay BIT at the early stages of the dispute settlement process, with a view to discarding "frivolous" claims.[126] Moreover, the BIT envisions the possibility of setting up a mechanism for appellate review, in order to ensure greater consistency in arbitral awards.[127]

Secondly, many other states, like Canada, Japan and certain Latin American states, are following the steps of the U. S. Thus, James McIlroy has observed that Canada's new model BIT is noteworthy "because it steps back from a current high water mark of private investor protection".[128] Further, an UNCTAD study has discovered that a "new

---

[123] Trade Act of 2002, Pub. L. No. 107 - 210, § 2102 (b)(3), 116 Stat. 995.

[124] TREATY BETWEEN THE GOV'T OF THE UNITED STATES OF AM. AND THE GOV'T OF [COUNTRY] CONCERNING THE ENCOURAGEMENT AND RECIPROCAL PROT. OF INV. (2004 Model BIT) (United States Trade Representative), *available at* http://www.ustr.gov/assets/Trade_Sectors/Investment/Model_BIT/asset_upload_file847_6897.pdf (last visited Jan. 22, 2007).

[125] Instead of the previously used open asset-based definition of investment, the US-Uruguay BIT has opted to define the term "investment" in economic terms, which in principle covers every asset that an investor owns and controls, but adds the qualification that such assets must have the "characteristics of an investment," such as "the commitment of capital or other resources, the expectation of gain or profit, or the assumption of risk." Treaty between the United States of Am. and the Oriental Republic of Uruguay Concerning the Encouragement and Reciprocal Prot. of Inv., U. S. - Uru, [Date of Treaty], *available at* http://www.ustr.gov/assets/Trade_Agreements/BIT/Uruguay/asset_upload_file748_9005.pdf (last visited Feb. 15, 2007) at § A, Art. 1 [hereinafter US-Uruguay BIT]. This is complemented by exclusions of several kinds of assets (e. g. certain debt instruments). Id.

[126] U. N. Conference on Trade and Development [UNCTAD], *Recent Developments in International Investment Agreements*, UNCTAD/WEB/ITE/IIT/2005/1, IIA MONITOR NO. 2 (2005), at 5, *available at* http://www.unctad.org/Templates/Download.asp?docid=6294&lang=1&intItemID=3784.

[127] Id.

[128] James McIlroy, *Canada's New Foreign Investment Protection and Promotion Agreement: Two Steps Forward, One Step Back?*, 5 J. WORLD INVESTMENT & TRADE 621, 646 (2004).

generation of BITs" has actually emerged, modelled after the new U. S. and Canadian Model BITs.[129] These new BITs exhibit four main features, most of which have the effect of either narrowing down substantive obligations, or tightening-up access to the state-investor dispute settlement mechanism.[130]

Thirdly, worldwide efforts have failed and again to create a global mechanism that protects and liberalizes investment flows. The debacle of the Multilateral Agreement on Investment (MAI)[131] within the OECD demonstrated that a liberal approach toward international investment was not viable even among developed countries, namely the OECD member states.[132] The Cancun ministerial conference, which led to the abandonment of the talks on a MAI within the WTO framework,[133] in turn, clearly refused another major effort to set forth a liberal investment regime on a global scale.

Finally, the change of governmental attitude towards investment liberalization is also reflected in domestic legal changes and BIT growth trends. As Table 1 shows, restrictive measures have been on the surge since 2000. In 2000, only 2% of the legal changes were geared toward more restrictions—this increased to 7% in 2001. In 2003 it reached 10%, followed in 2004 by an additional three point increase. The only drop during this period occurred in 2002, from 7% to 5%, and did not change the general conservative trend. (*Table 1: Restrictive Measure Adopted* 2000 – 2004) While there are still new BITs concluded each year, the general trend of newly-signed BITs has declined since 2001, as shown in Chart 1.

Table 1 Restrictive Measure Adopted 2000 – 2004

Year	Number of Legal Changes	Number of more restrictive measures adopted	Percentage of in total changes
2000	150	3	(2%)
2001	208	14	(7%)
2002	248	12	(5%)
2003	244	24	(10%)
2004	271	36	(13%)

The international investment regime tide has been turning even beyond Latin America: neo-liberalism is no longer unreservedly favoured by all countries, developed and

[129] UNCTAD, *supra* note 120, at 4.

[130] Id. at 4 – 6.

[131] Organisation for Economic Co-Operation and Development (OECD), Multilateral Agreement on Investment: Documentation From the Negotiations, http://www1.oecd.org/daf/mai/(last visited Jan. 22, 2007).

[132] Id.

[133] Decision Adopted by the General Council, *Doha Work Programme*, § (1) (g), WT/L/579 (Aug. 2 2004), *available at* http://www.wto.org/english/tratop_e/dda_e/ddadraft_31jul04_e.pdf.

developing states alike.[134] On the contrary, now even developed states, including the strongest advocates of a liberal investment regime, such as the United States, have started to rethink the roles and functions of international investment treaties and to redesign their BIT programs in order to contain the threats posed by the previously unfettered liberal investment regimes.[135] Calvo is regaining ground in the battle of international investment law.

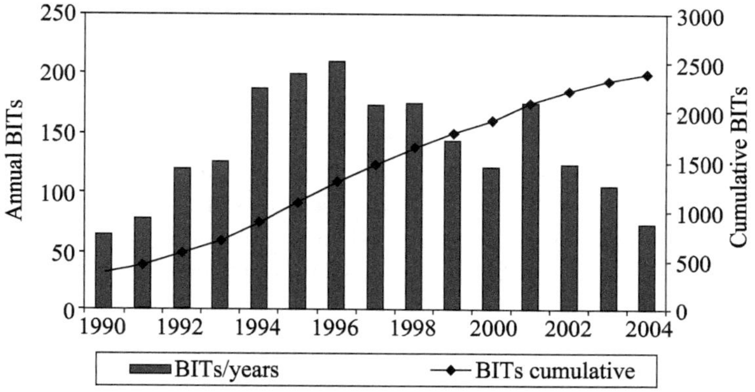

Chart 1 Number of BITs concluded, cumulative and year by year, 1990 – 2004[136]

III. The Future of International Investment Law: A Third Way between Neo-Liberalism and the Calvo Doctrine?

The resurgence of the Calvo Doctrine demonstrates that the neo-liberalist ideology underpinning international investment instruments exemplified by existing BITs[137] is neither ideal nor sustainable. However, it is unclear whether the current trend is going to eventually lead to, and sustain, a complete restoration of the Calvo Doctrine in its original form, or whether it is only a transitory phenomenon, which will soon die off. In other words, it is uncertain whether the political economy of international investment law will be

---

[134] The 1990s may be regarded as an era of 'neo-liberalism'. In that period, investment and trade liberalisation had gain almost universal support in all states, developed or developing. A best manifestation of this was that even the staunchest advocates and supporters of Calvo Doctrine in Latin America had changed their attitude toward foreign investment and had started to enter into BITs that embrace investment liberalism. For details of these changes, see SHAN, *supra note* 13, Sections II-VI.

[135] The aforementioned 'Calvo in Congress' episode is a best example of such change of attitude in developed states.

[136] *Source:* UNCTAD (www.unctad.org/iia).

[137] BITs present themselves as liberalist instruments, as evidenced by the goals typically referred to in their preambles, i.e., to create favourable conditions for investment and to increase economic prosperity. The history of the birth and development of BITs also shows that, as observed by Kenneth Vandevelde, "a principal inducement for states to enter into a BIT has been precisely that it affirms liberalism." Kenneth J. Vandevelde, *The Political Economy of a Bilateral Investment Treaty*, 92 AM. J. INT' L L. 621, 627 (1998). This nature of BITs, as embodied in their preambles, has actually been acknowledged by arbitration tribunals and has had an impact in the interpretation of BIT provisions. Id. at 627 – 28.

completely replaced by the Calvo Doctrine (as an example of "economic nationalism"), or will continue to be dominated by neo-liberalism (or "economic liberalism").[138]

The current trend is likely to continue, but unlikely to restore Calvo in its original form. Rather, Calvo will be revived in a modified form, striking a balance between the rights and interests of the investors and those of the states. There are two reasons for the sustainability of this trend. First, as elaborated above, the resurgence of Calvo is not a single event happening in one country or one region. Rather, it has been echoed throughout the world. Such a global trend is unlikely to quickly disappear. Second and more fundamentally, the decline and resurgence of Calvo has exposed a fundamental flaw in both the previous classical Calvo regime and the current dominant neo-liberal regime: the imbalance of the rights and obligations between the host state and foreign investors.

Before the 1980s, when Calvo dominated Latin America and indeed international forums such as the United Nations General Assembly, states had every power and no substantial international law restraints,[139] while investors took great commercial and noncommercial risks without sufficient international legal protection. There was an imbalance in favor of the states. Since the 1980s, and particularly in the 1990s when states—including Latin American states—embraced the neo-liberalistic investment regime, foreign investors have enjoyed every "constitution-like" guarantee and privilege derived from BITs and other investment instruments,[140] while governments were forced

---

[138] According to Vandevelde, who pioneered studies in the political economy of BITs, there are three dominant political economic theories relevant to BITs: economic nationalism, economic liberalism and Marxist economics. Among them, Marxist economics is generally hostile to foreign investment, considering it a tool of neo-colonialism that subjects local economies to foreign control and promotes underdevelopment. Following the collapse of the Soviet Bloc and the reforms in China and other formerly Communist states, this theory is no longer practised. "Economic nationalism" holds that international investment should be regulated to ensure that it promotes national political policy. Economic nationalist developing states therefore have sought to control inward and outward investment flows through interventionist measures—such as protective tariffs, tax incentives, investment screening, and performance requirements. The goals are to attract those foreign investments that would further their development policy, to prevent establishment of those investments that would not, and to ensure that investment, once established, would continue to operate in accord with national policy. Calvo Doctrine is a typical reflection of this theory, particularly in developing states. Economic liberalism posits that free markets, unfettered by state regulation, would result in the greatest prosperity for all. Accordingly, liberalism also advocates the free movement of capital across borders, which in essence holds that the state should permit the market to determine the direction of international investment flows. This theory is generally favoured by developed capital exporting states, which have actively promoted BIT programmes, particularly since the 1970s, as an essential neo-liberalist tool. For a good analysis of the basic features of these theories, and BITs as quintessentially liberalist instruments, *see* id. at 621 – 28.

[139] For details of the origin of Calvo Doctrine and its international influence before 1980s, see SHAN, *supra note* 13, Section I.

[140] Some scholars have argued that BITs and other investment treaties display the characteristics of domestic constitutions in that they bind governments over long periods of time to constitution-like rules designed to protect the private property of individuals and firms against discriminatory treatment or takings of investment interests, and that they generate constitution-like entitlements legally enforceable before tribunals and courts. *See* David Schneiderman, NAFTA's Takings Rule: American Constitutionalism Comes to Canada, 46 U OF TORONTO L. J. 499 (1996). *See also* Stephen Clarkson, Somewhat Less Than Meets the Eye: NAFTA as Constitution, Address at the International Sociological Association Annual Meeting (Jul. 27, 1998), *available at* http://www.chass.utoronto.ca/~clarkson/manuscripts/ecconstitution98.html.

to retreat—there was too much of an imbalance favoring foreign investors. Neither regime is ideal, although both of them may have some merit.

Calvo is unlikely to be completely restored because no country can now afford to be entirely cut off from interactions with the world in this era of globalization. With intensified international interactions, there come more extensive international rules, setting forth international substantive standards and procedural remedies. To reject such standards and remedies altogether, as Calvo originally advocated, would be neither plausible nor desirable. The classical Calvo Doctrine no longer fits the world as it is now, if it ever fit the world before. On the other hand, the neo-liberal regime must be reformed to avoid repeating the "Catch - 22" situations that Argentina and many other Latin American states have faced in recent years.[141] An ideal FDI regime, therefore, might have to be found somewhere between the two previously existing regimes, perhaps a "Third Way" in international investment law.

The new generation of BITs, exemplified by the new U. S. and Canadian model BITs, may be regarded as a step in that direction.[142] They nevertheless demonstrate only small changes within the previous liberalist paradigm of BITs. These changes do not alter the fundamental character of these investment treaties as quintessential liberalist instruments, which only protect and "empower" investors without sufficient consideration of the rights of host states and the duties of the investors.[143]

To fully address the problem of the imbalance of rights and obligations between investors and states, a more radical, and even revolutionary solution is needed. There are two alternative possibilities: one is to complement the current liberalist or capitalist BITs with binding instruments, in the form of bilateral, or preferably global, agreements on the rights of states and the obligations of foreign investors (a "complementary approach"). Efforts of this nature have been made at global and multilateral levels, but with only very limited success.[144] Hence, within the OECD, the Guidelines for Multinational Enterprises have been adopted to regulate the conduct of multinational corpora-

---

〔141〕 In the annulment application, for example, Argentina argued that the judgment by the ICSID in the CMS case placed the country in a "Catch - 22" when facing an emergency economic situation: a state may either do nothing and let the economy collapse, or do something to rescue the economy but then go bankrupt paying huge compensation to investors affected by such rescuing efforts. *See* Luke Peterson, *Argentina Moves to Annul Award in Dispute with CMS Company over Financial Crisis*, INVESTMENT TREATY NEWS (ITN) (Int' l Inst. Sustainable Dev., Winnipeg, Manitoba, Canada), Oct. 26, 2005, at § 4, para. 14, *available at* http://www.iisd.org/pdf/2005/investment_investsd_oct26_2005.pdf.

〔142〕 For instance, James Mcllroy has noted that the new Canadian model BIT attempts to "strike a balance between private investors' rights and the right of a sovereign State to regulate in public interest." Mcllroy, *supra* note 122, at 644 - 45.

〔143〕 Brewer and Young, for example, observed in the 1990s that the focus of investment law making had been shifted from an emphasis on "firms' obligations and governments' rights" to an emphasis on "firms' rights and governments' obligations". *See* Brewer, Tomas L., and Young, Stephen, *Towards a Multilateral Framework for Foreign Direct Investment: Issues and Scenarios*, Transnational Corporations, vol. 4, no. 1 (April 1995), at 74 - 75.

〔144〕 *See* WENHUA SHAN, THE LEGAL FRAMEWORK OF EU-CHINA INVESTMENT RELATIONS (2005), at 274.

tions, but lack binding force.[145] Globally, the UN Code of Conduct on Transnational Corporations had been drafted and discussed intensively in the 1970s and 1980s, but was finally abandoned in the 1990s during the heatwave of global investment liberalization.[146] It may be easier to simply resume work on the UN Code of Conduct with a view to establishing a binding global treaty on the regulation of the duties and responsibilities of international investors.

The other possibility, which might be called a "consolidated approach," is to add provisions on the responsibilities of foreign investors to the existing bilateral or multilateral investment instruments. This would effectively redefine the nature and ideology of BITs, moving from a one-sided liberalist instrument assuring and empowering foreign investors, toward a more rational instrument that balances the interests, rights and responsibilities of all parties concerned, particularly between host state and foreign investors. In this regard, one has to refer to the impressive work done by the International Institute for Sustainable Development ("IISD"), which developed the IISD Model International Agreement on Investment for Sustainable Development ("IISD Model Investment Agreement").[147] The IISD Model Investment Agreement marks the first major attempt to construct such a consolidated instrument on international investment. It aims to address the balance of interests among foreign investors, the host states and the home state. In a separate article entitled "Objective," it sets out its objectives "[promoting] foreign investment that supports sustainable development, in particular in developing and least developed countries."[148] The goal of promoting investment is no longer a singular objective, but one that is complemented and qualified by the goal of sustainable development. Also, the Preamble clearly states that it seeks "an overall balance of rights and obligations in international investment between investors, host countries and home countries."[149] To strike such a balance, the text of the IISD Model Investment Agreement provides for sets of substantive rights and obligation for each of the actors, as shown in Table 2 below. The Agreement also sets out three mechanisms to implement such rights and obligations. It encourages states to incorporate the rights and obligations in the agreement into domestic laws, which eventually enables domestic remedies to be

[145] For the text and further information about the Guidelines, *available at* <http://www.oecd.org/document/28/0,2340,en_2649_34889_2397532_1_1_1_1,00.html> (last visit on 17 March 2007).

[146] The last draft version was completed in 1988, but work on it was suspended in early 1990. For further details of the draft code, *see* M Sornarajah, *The International Law on Foreign Investment*, Camrbidge University Press, 275–283 (2004).

[147] The Model Agreement, together with a negotiators' handbook, is available on the International Institute for Sustainable Development (IISD) website: <http://www.iisd.org/publications/publication_list.aspx?themeid=7> (last visit on 17 March 2007). The Model Agreement was also published in 20 ICSID REV. – FOREIGN INVESTMENT L. J. 91, (2005).

[148] IISD MODEL INTERNATIONAL AGREEMENT ON INVESTMENT FOR SUSTAINABLE DEVELOPMENT (Int'l Inst. Sustainable Dev. (IISD) 2005), art. 1, 20 ICSID REV. – FOREIGN INVESTMENT L. J. 91, (2005) [hereinafter IISD MODEL AGREEMENT].

[149] Id.

brought to bear on investors.[150] It allows host states to raise the issues of compliance with the obligations in front of the international dispute settlement mechanism devised therein, either by a direct claim by a host state to annul rights of an investor under this agreement due to persistent failure to comply with the obligations, or a counterclaim to an investor-state claim based on the breach of an obligation by an investor.[151] Finally, it models the OECD Guidelines on Multinational Enterprises and provides for a national authority to thoroughly investigate civil society complaints of non-compliance in the host or home state.[152]

The IISD Model Investment Agreement notably contains some interesting innovations. For example, allowing a direct claim by host states against foreign investors for failing to comply with their investor obligations is a novel approach.[153] Although it is yet unknown whether and how it might work in practice, it is indeed a "logical corollary" of the one-sided investor-state dispute settlement regime that exists for current international investment instruments.[154] Despite that it is still in an early stages of development and that there is certainly room for further improvement,[155] the IISD Model Agreement represents the first genuine effort to strike a balance between the rights and obligations of host states and foreign investors and therefore deserves serious consideration.

Table 2 Summary of Key Rights and Obligations of Foreign Investors, Host States and Home States[156]

Parties	Rights	Obligations
Foreign Investors	National treatment Mostfavored nation Minimum international standards No expropriation without compensation Senior management Transfer of assets	Comply with local laws Pre-establishment impact assessment Anti corruption Environmental management/international environmental obligations Human rights protection Core labor standards Provision and publication of information Investor civil liability

[150] Howard Mann, *The IISD Model International Agreement on Investment for Sustainable Development: An Introductory Note*, 20 ICSID Rev. – Foreign Investment L. J. 84, 86 (2005).

[151] Mann, *supra* note 144, at 86.

[152] Id., at 87.

[153] IISD MODEL AGREEMENT, *supra* note 142, at art. 18(C).

[154] Mann, *supra* note 144, at 86.

[155] For example, Articles 11(A) and (B) might be improved by referring to the overriding effect of binding international law, particularly international treaty obligations, when asserting the applicability of local laws and local jurisdiction of the host state. *See* IISD MODEL AGREEMENT, *supra* note 142, art. 11(A) –(B).

[156] Mann, *supra* note 144, at 88.

Parties	Rights	Obligations
Host States	Inherent right of states to regulate, articulate development policy Right to performance requirements (exception from national treatment) Investment promotion Access to investor information	Procedural fairness Maintenance of environmental standards, labor standards Minimum standards for: environmental assessment, core labor, human rights Anti-corruption Publication of information
Home States	Claim protection of in vestor rights in dispute settlement	Assistance to facilitate foreign investment Provide information on investors Ensure procedural laws allow for hearing on investor liability Anti-corruption

VI. Concluding Remarks: From A "North-South Divide" to A "Private-Public Debate"

The revival of Calvo in and beyond Latin America not only signals a significant change of attitude and ideology toward the international investment regime, but also marks a noticeable shift of tension in international investment law, indicating progress. In previous debates on international investment instruments, such as UN General Assembly Resolutions[157] and BITs, the tension was primarily between developed states, with capital-exporting countries representing the interests of foreign investors, and developing states, and with capital-importing countries representing the interests of host states.[158]

---

[157] Resolutions 1803 and 3281 are the most important resolutions relating to the standard of treatment for international investment, particularly on the issue of expropriation and its compensation. The two instruments are traditionally read as taking contrasting stands and having different legal effects. The author is, however, of the view that the two resolutions should be read together as one emerging standard of two different development stages, carrying the same legal implications. *See* SHAN, supra note 138, at 181 – 87. *See also* Declaration on Permanent Sovereignty over Natural Resources, G. A. Res. 1803 (XVII), at 223, U. N. Doc. A/RES/1803 (XVII) (Dec. 14, 1962); Charter of Economic Rights and Duties of States, G. A. Res. 3281 (XXIX), at 251, U. N. Doc. A/RES/3281(XXIX) (Jan. 15, 1975).

[158] The literature on this debate has been tremendous. *See, e. g.*, S. FRIEDMAN, EXPROPRIATION IN INTERNATIONAL LAW (1953); Charles N. Brower, *Current Developments in the Law of Expropriation and Compensation: a Preliminary Survey of Awards of the Iran-United States Claims Tribunal*, 21 INT' L LAW. 639 (1987); Rudolf Dolzer, *New Foundations of the Law of Expropriation of Alien Property*, 75 AM. J. INT' L L. 553 (1981); Francesco Francioni, *Compensation for Nationalisation of Foreign Property: The Borderland Between Law and Equity*, 24 INT' L AND COMP. L. Q. 255 (1975); Rosalyn Higgins, *The Taking of Property by the State: Recent Developments in International Law*, 176 RECUEIL DES COURS 263 (1982); Eduardo Jiménez de Aréchaga, *State Responsibility for the Nationalisation of Foreign Owned Property*, 11 N. Y. U. J. INT' L L. & POL. 179 (1978); Davis R. Robinson, Notes and Comments, *Expropriation in the Restatement (Revised)*, 78 AM. J. INT' L L. 176 (1984); Oscar Schachter, *Compensation for Expropriation*, *id.* at 121; M. Sornarajah, *State Responsibility and Bilateral Investment Treaties*, 20 J. WORLD TRADE L. 79 (1986); F. A. Mann, *British Treaties for the Promotion and Protection of Investments*, 52 BRITISH YEARBOOK INT' L L. 241 (1981).

In other words, the previous international investment law-making process has been dominated and characterized by a North-South divide, with developed states trying to push for a neo-liberalist agenda, and developing states attempting to resist such an agenda and maintain their inherent rights to regulate and control foreign investment. The picture has recently changed and become much more complicated. The North-South divide has narrowed from what it was three or four decades ago. Currently, a more dominant issue seems to be the conflict between the private interests of foreign investors and the public interests of states, namely host states. In other words, the featured debate of international investment law-making seems to have shifted from a "North-South Divide" to a "Private-Public Debate." The following four major factors might have contributed to this shift.

The first factor is the shift, or the realization, of the role of leading developed states with regard to international investment. Before 1990s, developed states such as the U. S. and Canada had viewed themselves, and rightly so, as capital-exporting states and representatives of foreign investors, and therefore had fought hard to secure highest possible standard of protection for their investors abroad by pushing ahead BIT and multilateral investment treaty programmes. Since 1990s, particularly after a series of North America Free Trade Agreement (NAFTA) Chapter 11 cases, these countries have woken up realising that they are also major capital-importing states and therefore also have every reason to defend their interest as host states, just like what the developing states had done in the 1960s and 1970s. According to Todd Weiler, so far there have been 16 NAFTA cases against the U. S. and 13 against Canada.[159] Such litigation has forced the two governments into the shoes of capital-importing states, a standing point that used to be exclusive to developing states. Consequently, as mentioned above, they have stepped back from their previously unfettered liberal approach and have started to revise their BIT programs. Such a change by leading developed states helps to establish a shared understanding and a common interest between them and developing states: the need to effectively tame and regulate foreign investors and their investment in the international investment law-making process.

The second factor is that the role of developing countries in the international investment process has also been undergoing change. A number of developing countries have become more and more important foreign investment suppliers in the world. In its *World Investment Report* 2004, the United Nations Conference on Trade and Development (UNCTAD) highlighted that "outward FDI from developing countries is becoming important."[160] The report noted that some developing economies such as Malaysia, South Korea, and Singapore had already developed an established track record in outward investment.[161] Others, such as Chile, Mexico and South Africa, have become players rela-

---

〔159〕 *See* Todd Weiler, Naftaclaims. com, *available at* http://www. naftaclaims. com/disputes_canada. htm; *id.*, http://www. naftaclaims. com/disputes_us. htm (last visited Jul. 31, 2006).

〔160〕 U. N. CONFERENCE ON TRADE AND DEVELOPMENT [UNCTAD], WORLD INVESTMENT REPORT 2004: THE SHIFT TOWARDS SERVICES, at 19, U. N. Doc. UNCTAD/WIR/2005, U. N. Sales No. E. 04. II. D. 33(2004). *See also* Chart 2.

〔161〕 Id.

tively recently.[162] Others, such as Brazil, China and India, are at the take-off stage.[163] Viewed in relation to gross fixed capital formation, a number of developing economies, such as Singapore, Hong Kong (China) and Taiwan(China) rank higher than a number of developed countries (Germany, Japan, the United States) in FDI outflow. In other words, a number of developing countries, relatively speaking, are already among top investors.[164] Moreover, annual FDI outflows from developing countries have grown faster over the past 15 years than those from developed countries—from negligible up until the end of the 1980s, to over one-tenth of the world total stock and some 6% of world total flows in 2003 ($0.9 trillion and $36 billion, respectively).[165] Some developing economies are now large investors by global standards.[166]

Such an increased role in outward investment in those developing states has already has an impact on their international investment law-making practices. China, for example, has, since the late 1990s, significantly upgraded its substantive protection for foreign investment and provided wider access for foreign investors to resort to international arbitration forums, partly owing to its growing outward investment.[167]

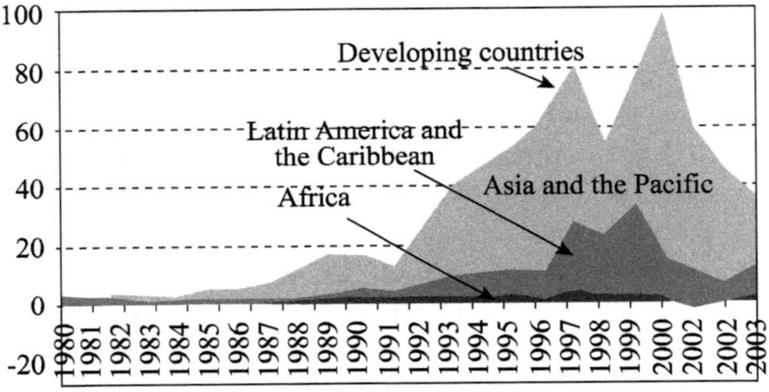

Chart 2 FDI outflows from developing countries by region1980 – 2003[168]

(Billions of dollars)

The changing role of developing states is also witnessed by a notable increase of

[162] U. N. CONFERENCE ON TRADE AND DEVELOPMENT [UNCTAD], WORLD INVESTMENT REPORT 2004: THE SHIFT TOWARDS SERVICES, at 19, U. N. Doc. UNCTAD/WIR/2005, U. N. Sales No. E. 04. II. D. 33(2004). *See also* Chart 2.

[163] Id.

[164] Id.

[165] UNCTAD, WORLD INVESTMENT REPORT 2004: THE SHIFT TOWARDS SERVICES, at 19, U. N. Doc. UNCTAD/WIR/2005, U. N. Sales No. E. 04. II. D. 33(2004). *See also* Chart 2.

[166] In 2003, for instance, Hong Kong (China) had a larger outward FDI stock than Sweden, even if round tripping and indirect FDI is taken into account. Also, transnational corporations (TNCs) from Hong Kong figure prominently among the leading TNCs from the developing world, along with those from Singapore, Mexico and South Africa. Id.

[167] Since 1998, China has widened its acceptance of international arbitration as a means of stateinvestor dispute settlement, by accepting all investment disputes to be automatically submitted to international arbitration including the ICSID. So far four BITs with such provisions have come into effect, another 16 are in the ratification process. One of the main reasons for China's opening-up in this area is that Chinese investment abroad has been increasing rapidly over the last few years and the government is actively encouraging domestic companies to do so.

[168] Source: UNCTAD, FDI/TNC database (www.unctad.org/fdistatistics).

South-South BITs in recent years. The 2005 World Investment Report, for example, noted that the largest number of the new BITs signed during 2004 were between developing states.[169] The change in the role of developing states thus echos similar changes in the role of the developed states identified above, and further enhances the shared understanding and interest in international investment law-making between the two groups.

The third factor is that the domestic legal infrastructure in developing states for the protection and promotion of foreign investment has been significantly improved, as a result of the extensive legal changes that favoured foreign investment and the massive BIT networks established, particularly during the 1990s. According to the 2005 World Investment Report, since 1991, an average of 64 states in every single year have made some changes to their FDI laws and regulations. Among the 2,156 changes made during that period, 2,006 were changes aimed toward a more liberal investment regime, accounting for 93% of the total changes (*see* Table 3).[170] Meanwhile, there has been an explosive

Table 3 Changes in Domestic Legislations(1991 – 2004)[171]

Year	Number of countries changed FDI laws	Number of changes made to FDI laws	Changes in favour of foreign investors	Changes detrimental to foreign investors
1991	35	82	80	2
1992	43	79	79	0
1993	57	102	101	1
1994	49	110	108	2
1995	64	112	106	6
1996	65	114	98	16
1997	76	151	135	16
1998	60	145	136	9
1999	63	140	131	9
2000	69	150	147	3
2001	71	208	194	14
2002	70	248	236	12
2003	82	244	220	24
2004	102	271	235	36

[169] The Report noted that there were 28 BITs signed between developing states accounting for 38 percent of the total, followed closely by the 27 BITs between developed and developing states. *See* UNCTAD, WORLD INVESTMENT REPORT 2005: TRANSNATIONAL CORPORATIONS AND INTERNATIONALIZATION OF R&D, at 24, U. N. Doc. UNCTAD/WIR/2005, U. N. Sales No. E. 05. II. D. 10 (2005).

[170] Id. at 28.

[171] Source: UNCTAD World Investment Report 2005, p. 26.

expansion of the BIT network in the world. UNCTAD statistics show that by the end of 2004, the number of BITs world wide had reached 2, 392, among which 2, 010 were concluded in the 1990s (*see* Chart I). [172] Moreover, states had been very active in entering into bilateral, regional and trans-regional preferential trade and investment agreements (PTIAs). By April 2005, 212 such agreements had also been concluded, among which approximately 87% were signed in the 1990s. [173] Such changes in domestic law, together with the extensive international investment treaty network, have significantly narrowed the gap between developed and developing countries in terms of the legal protection and promotion of international investment. Although the gap admittedly still exists, it is by far less significant than it was three decades ago. Consequently, the need for further legal protection of foreign investment has been greatly reduced, as has the tension between developed and developing states in intentional investment law making process. This obviously paved the way for a shift of attention to the more universal question, namely the conflict between public and private interests.

The fourth and final factor is that the increased participation of civil society in the international investment law-making process has significantly contributed to highlight the need for and importance of regulating international investment. Earlier NAFTA cases on investment arbitration, particularly the controversial *Metalclad Case*, [174] have focused the attention of many non-governmental organisations (NGOs) on international investment treaties and related arbitration practice. The debate on the Draft Multilateral Agreement on Investment within the OECD and the discussions on a multilateral agreement on investment within the WTO framework in the Doha Round have demonstrated the width and depth of NGO participation in the global investment law-making processes. Whilst different NGOs have different missions and therefore foci, they all share a main concern that investment liberalisation cannot be achieved at the expense of important public interests, such as human rights, environmental, and labour standards. In other words, they have helped highlight the importance of regulating foreign investment for the public good. Such voices from NGOs, most of which are actually based in developed states, have over the years become more and more influential in domestic and international law and policy making. As a result, they have helped to raise the awareness of the general public, particularly in the developed world, of the need to regulate foreign investment, and thus contributed to the shift of tension in international investment law making.

To conclude, recent years have witnessed a shift of tension on international investment law-making, from "*strong states*" versus "*weak states*", i. e., a "North-South divide", towards "*state sovereignty*" versus "*corporate sovereignty*", [175] i. e., a "Private-

---

[172] Source: UNCTAD World Investment Report 2005, p. 26.

[173] Id.

[174] *Metalclad Corp. v. United Mexican States*, ICSID Case No. ARB(AF)/97/1, ICSID REV. – FOR. INVESTMENT L. J. 168 (2001).

[175] Given the size and strength of some transnational corporations and that they are now often equipped with the standing to directly bring lawsuit again host governments before international forums such as the ICSID under BITs and other investment instruments, it is not too much an exaggeration to say that they enjoy certain elements of 'sovereignty', which may be referred to as 'corporate sovereignty'.

Public debate." If this is what is happening, there should be a better chance to strike a sensible global deal on the protection as well as supervision, and promotion as well as regulation of international investment for the general good of the world.

从"南北矛盾"到"公私冲突":卡尔沃主义的复苏与国际投资法的新视野*

统治了拉美乃至世界已有一个多世纪的卡尔沃主义往往被断定为已经"死亡",[1]这种观点在全球经济自由化浪潮涌动的20世纪90年代尤其盛行。然而,最近在拉丁美洲内外的一系列事件表明,该主义并没有死亡,而是正在逐渐复苏。卡尔沃主义的复苏现象从一个侧面反映了当代国际投资法的重大转向,新自由主义不再是国际投资立法的支配力量,一种更为均衡,或者说更为保守和更为"国家主义"的法律观正悄然登场。

本文通过探寻这一系列事件,分析卡尔沃主义在何种程度上已经复苏以及国际投资法理念正在发生怎样的变化。文章第一和二部分探究拉美及其他地区标志着卡尔沃主义复苏的一系列事件,并在此基础上揭示了国际投资法发展的最新趋势。第三部分在批判分析卡尔沃主义与新自由主义两种制度的弊病的基础上探讨了国际投资法的前景和出路。第四部分总结全文,提出国际投资法的

---

* 本文发表在《国际经济法学刊》(第15卷)2008年第4期。

[1] 例如,Shea早在20世纪50年代就在他的一部研究卡尔沃条款的专著中宣告了卡尔沃主义死亡。当然他是基于该条款遭到欧美国家拒绝这一事实得出这个结论的。最近,Giesze则断言,"实际上,卡尔沃主义在绝大多数拉丁美洲国家而言是一个已经消亡的词汇。" Shihata也认为卡尔沃主义与当今世界是不相干的。See Donald Shea, The Calvo Clause: A Problem Of Inter-America And International Law And Diplomacy (Mineapolis, University of Minnesota Press, 1955), at 20; Craig R. Giesze, Helms-Burton in Light of The Common Law And Civil Law Legal Traditions: Is Legal Analysis Alone Sufficient to Settle Controversies Arising Under International Law on The Eve Of The Second Summit Of The Americas?, 32 International Lawyer 51, 77 (1998), and Ibrahim F. I. Shihata, "Towards a Greater Depoliticization of Investment Disputes: The Roles of ICSID and MIGA", ICSID Review-Foreign Investment Law Journal, at 3-4 (1986). 在1995年发表的一篇文章中,Manning-Cabrol也认为卡尔沃主义"行将就木"(imminent death),见 Denise Manning-Cabrol, The Imminent Death of the Calvo Clause and the Rebirth of the Calvo Principle: Equality of Foreign and National Investors', 26 Law and Policy of International Business1169, (1995).

主旋律已经发生重要变化:由过去的“南北矛盾”转变为如今的“公私冲突”。

一、卡尔沃主义的复苏:拉美之内

一百多年来,拉丁美洲各国一直遵行卡尔沃主义(此名源于19世纪阿根廷知名法学家、外交家Calos Calvo的著作)。卡尔沃主义的核心在于强调“不干预内政和内外国国民的绝对平等这两个概念”,[2]尤其着重强调拒绝西方列强及其国民所寻求和享有的帝国主义特权和超级待遇。卡尔沃主义具体包括三个要素,即“反超国民待遇标准”、排他的国内管辖以及拒绝外交保护。[3]

尽管欧洲及北美国家[4]并不承认卡尔沃主义的法律效力,但拉丁美洲国家[5]“热情地拥抱”了卡尔沃主义。在拉美各国的宪法、国内立法、国际条约及拉美各国与外国政府及外国投资者签订的条约中处处可见卡尔沃主义的影子。卡尔沃主义早期的影响远远超出了拉丁美洲,在发展中国家中间,尤其是在那些在反殖民运动过程中新独立的亚洲和非洲国家中间拥有大批拥护者。当建立国际经济新秩序(NIEO)运动达到顶峰时,卡尔沃主义的一些原则一度被写入一系列联合国大会的重要决议之中。[6]

卡尔沃主义在全球经济自由化浪潮汹涌的20世纪90年代遭遇到了严重挑战,以至于有人推断或预言卡尔沃主义已经或即将死亡。[7] 对卡尔沃主义的挑战主要来自于越来越多的BIT(双边投资协定),尤其是拉美各国所签署的BIT。联合国贸易与发展委员会(UNCTAD)统计数字表明,拉美国家直到20世纪80年代末开始纷纷签署BIT。截至20世纪90年代,拉美国家共加入了300个BIT,其中93%签订于90年代。[8] 从区域层次而言,南锥体共同市场遵循的是BIT的投

---

〔2〕 Shea, *supra* note 1, at 19 - 20.

〔3〕 Wenhua Shan, Is Calvo Dead? 54 AM. J. COMP. L. (2007), section I. 1; See also Manning-Cabrol, *supra* note 1, at 1173.

〔4〕 卡尔沃主义之所以不能得到来自欧美法律界的支持,部分是因为,“尽管该主义排除了外交保护的滥用,但是该主义排除了该制度自身,而没有提供一个替代它的机制”。Shea, *supra* note 1, at 20.

〔5〕 Shea, *supra* note 1, at 21 - 32.

〔6〕 例如,Lillich就曾指出,拉美国家对宪章的努力“只不过是想把卡尔沃主义引入其中,这一尝试昭然若揭”。Richard Lillich, The Diplomatic Protection of Nationals Abroad: An Elementary Principle of International Law Under Attack, 69 Am. J. INT' LL. 359, 361 (1975). 另有评论家则认为卡尔沃主义是“国际经济新秩序(UNGA 3171 ofthe1973)和联合国《经济权利和国家义务宪章》(1974)的核心所在”。David Schneiderman, Investment Rules and The New Constitutionalism, 25 LAW& SOC. INQUIRY757, 766 (Summer2000); see also KennethJ. Vandevelde, Sustainable Liberalism and the International Investment Regime, 19MICH. J. INT' LL. 373, 384 (1998)。

〔7〕 Shea, *supra* note 1, at 19 - 20.

〔8〕 UNCTAD, Bilateral Investment Treaties 1959 - 1999, *supra* note 8.

资自由化方法,[9]同时,安第斯条约也几经修改,增加了灵活性,使其成员国有权采取偏离卡尔沃主义的法律措施。大多数拉美国家也接受了为解决国家与私人投资者之间投资争端提供国际仲裁机制的《ICSID 公约》,允许国家行使代位求偿权的《MIGA 公约》,以及为在世界范围内承认和执行外国仲裁裁决提供便利的《纽约公约》。与此同时,拉美各国也都修改了国内的法律法规,接受了国际待遇标准和国际争端解决机制,以保护和促进外国投资。[10] 尽管断言卡尔沃已经完全"死亡"的说法并不准确,但20 世纪 90 年代以来大量的为解决投资争端提供国际平台的投资条约的签署,的确使得卡尔沃主义已经面目全非,搁浅在岸。[11]

然而,国际投资自由化大潮近年来似乎正在转向。卡尔沃主义正在重返国际舞台,这一点在拉美表现尤其突出。出现这种现象的大背景是投资者依据投资条约提起的仲裁案件此起彼伏,迫使世界上许多国家,尤其是拉美国家,开始反思投资自由化的总体策略与接受国际仲裁庭的管辖权这一具体政策。根据联合国贸易发展委员会统计,截至2006 年年底,已有至少 259 个依据投资条约提起的仲裁案件,其中 70% 以上是在 2002 年之后提起的。[12] 换言之,在过去的 4 年里,平均每年约有 1430 件案子。几乎所有这些案件都是投资者起诉东道国的。[13] 并且大多数被告国家都是发展中国家(70 个被告国家中有 58 个)。目前为止拉美国家是被起诉次数最多的国家。[14] 其中阿根廷被起诉的次数最多,为 42 次,这几

---

〔9〕 南锥体共同市场是由阿根廷、巴西、巴拉圭和乌拉圭拉美四国于 1991 年创建的南美共同市场。南锥体共同市场关于国际投资的条约有两个:一个是管辖成员国之间投资的 Colonia Protocol,一个是管辖成员国与非成员国之间投资的 Buenos Aires Protocol,两个议定书的规定大体相同。布宜诺斯艾利斯议定书第 2 条第 3 项规定了对外国投资者实施国民待遇、最惠国待遇和"公正与平等待遇"。其中,关于国民待遇、最惠国待遇的条款采用的是典型的 BIT 用语,即"不应低于"给予该缔约一方国民和公司的待遇或不应低于给予第三国国民和公司的待遇。关于东道国与外国投资者投资争端的解决,该议定书第 2 条第 8 项规定了"岔路口"条款,即投资者可以既可将争端提交东道国法院审理,也可以提交国际常设仲裁机构或特设仲裁机构仲裁。这里,布宜诺斯艾利斯议定书只把当地救济规定为国际仲裁的可替代途径之一,而不是唯一的排他性途径,显然与卡尔沃主义的"绝对当地救济"原则相去甚远。See Protocol on Promotion and Protection of Investment Proceeding from Non-Member Countries of the MERCOSUL, March26, 1991, available at http://www.cvm.gov.br/ingl/inter/mercosul/buenos-e.asp.

〔10〕 Wenhua Shan, Is Calvo Dead?, 54 AM. J. COMP. L. (2007), Section IV; see also Manning-Cabriel, *supra* note 1, at 1181 - 1190; Eduardo A. Wiesner, ANCOM: A New Attitude toward Foreign Investment?, 24 U. MIAMIINTER-AM. L. REV. 435, 449 - 464 (1993).

〔11〕 作者通过对拉美主要的 9 个国家的法律和法规的系统调查发现,在拒绝外交保护和平等的国民待遇方面,大多数国家仍然坚守卡尔沃原则。因此认定卡尔沃原则完全消亡无疑是不确切的。然而,随着大多数拉美国家缔结国际条约,规定把国家与投资者之间的争端可以提交国际仲裁的,可以说,在拒绝外国与国际救济方面,卡尔沃主义已经在很大程度上被抛弃。因此,笔者认为,卡尔沃主义当时并没有"完全消亡",只是暂时搁浅了而已。See SHAN, *supra* note 13. Section V.

〔12〕 UNCTAD, Investor-State Disputes Settlement and Implications on Investment Rule-making, 7 - 8, (UNCTAD/ITE/IIA/2007/3).

〔13〕 Ibid.

〔14〕 Ibid., at 3.

乎占到案件总量的20%。墨西哥紧随其后,为17次。[15] 另外,来自ICSID的数据表明,截至2008年4月10日,ICSID未审结的案件有128个,其中就有61个是针对拉美国家,几乎占到了总量的近一半。[16]

国际投资条约仲裁案件的汹涌浪潮已经展示了投资条约存在的巨大破坏性能量,引起了世界各国政府的高度关注。有着卡尔沃主义传统的拉美国家已经或在酝酿采取措施限制国际投资条约仲裁并将这类案件收归国内管辖。其中表现最为突出的是阿根廷、巴西和委内瑞拉三个国家。

(一)阿根廷

阿根廷是卡尔沃主义的首倡者,卡罗斯·卡尔沃的故乡。然而,它也是通过缔结双边投资条约(BIT)背弃卡尔沃主义最积极的拉美国家之一。到目前为止,它已签订了59个BIT,是签订BIT数量最多的拉美国家。[17] 阿根廷近年来的投资条约仲裁案件的激增肇源于2002年1月阿根廷通过的《紧急状态法》(第25561号法令)。为了应对经济危机,该法规定直到2003年12月1日阿根廷处于公共紧急状态,同时冻结公用事业行业收费费率,废除1比索兑换1美元的兑换体制。[18] 这些措施对在已经私有化的国有企业里拥有股份的外国投资者产生了重大的负面影响。有观察家指出,这些措施对公共事业公司产生的后果是使它们"减少了大约三分之二的收入"。[19]

受到影响的这些投资者根据投资条约中的国家与私人投资者争端解决仲裁条款开始起诉阿根廷政府。在2004年2月ICSID中心悬而未决的85例案件中有35例是针对阿根廷的,占到了世界范围内全部投资争端仲裁案件的40%,[20] 可以说是创造了世界仲裁史上的一个神话!目前,阿根廷在ICSID中心还有36起

---

〔15〕 UNCTAD, Investor-State Disputes Settlement and Implications on Investment Rule-making, 7 - 8, (UNCTAD/ITE/IIA/2007/3), at3.

〔16〕 See list of pending cases at http://icsid. worldbank. org/ICSID/Front-Servlet? RequestType = CasesRH&actionVal = ListPending.

〔17〕 UNCTAD data show that Argentina signed 59 BITs by June 1, 2007, which is more than any other country in Latin America. See UNCTAD, Country specific List of BITs, available at http://www. unctad. org/Templates/Page. asp? intItemID = 2344&lang = 1, last accessed on April 10, 2008.

〔18〕 Law No. 25561, Jan. 6, 2002, B. O. Articles 2 - 5, and 8 - 9. For English sources see Bernardo M. Cremades, Disputes Arising out of Foreign Direct Investment in Latin America: A New Look at the Calvo Doctrine and Other Jurisdictional Issue', 59 Dispute Resolution Journa 178, May-July, 2004, at 81; Patricia C. Mastropierro, Larry B. Pascal, ALERT: Argentine Devaluation Law, available at http://www. haynesboone. com/knowledge/knowledge detail. asp? groupid = all&page = pubs&pubid = 380(last visit on April10, 2008); M. & M BomchilABogados, Public Emergency Regulations on Public Works and Utilities Contracts and Licenses, available at http://www. ag-internet. com/bulletin one five/Bulletin-Contracts Licenses. doc(lastvisit on April 10, 2008).

〔19〕 Paolo Di Rosa, The Recent Wave of Arbitrations against Argentina under Bilateral Investment Treaties: Background and Principal Legal Issues, 36 U. MIAMIINTER-AM. L. REV., 41, 48 (2004).

〔20〕 Ibid. at 43.

案件未了结,占到其待处理案件总数的28%。[21] 如此巨大的案件量对于一国而言,不论是在政治上,还是在财政上,都是一个沉重的负担。据统计,这些投资仲裁案件平均每件单单律师费用等法律费用就要耗费政府一两百万美元,仲裁庭的费用还需40万美元左右。[22] 换言之,近几年阿根廷仅仅为应付投资仲裁的花费每年就达数千万美元之巨。更严重的是,一旦败诉,国家对每个案件的赔偿负担就可能达到数亿美元,累计可达170亿美元。[23] 阿根廷表示这已经超过了其每年的财政预算。[24] 面对如此严峻的法律挑战,阿根廷采用三层战略:首先运用一些程序上的策略如管辖权异议来对付这些案件。[25] 另外,质疑投资条约和基于投资条约的仲裁的合宪性。[26] 最后,阿根廷还在酝酿并采纳一些相应的立法措施。[27]

1. 程序策略。为处理这些案件,阿政府首先尽一切努力争取与争端一方的投资者通过谈判来解决问题。[28] 如果此法不奏效,政府就对仲裁庭的管辖权提出异议。[29] 但迄今为止,阿根廷尚未在任何一起管辖权的案件中胜出。[30] 对管辖权提出异议的理由各种各样,其中有一些与BIT中或者许可协议中的"卡尔沃条款"有关,因此有必要在这里提及。在"蓝科国际公司诉阿根廷共和国"一案中(Lanco International Inc v. the Argentine Republic),一个美国投资者援引1991年美国—阿根廷BIT中的"岔路口条款"将阿根廷诉诸ICSID。依据该条款,争端当事方可以选择当地救济、双方同意的其他方式以及国际仲裁来解决争端。[31] 该案中,阿根廷政府对ICSID的管辖权提出了异议,主张阿根廷并没有对ICSID的

[21] See List of Pending Cases, available at http://www.worldbank.org/icsid/cases/pending.htm, lastaccessedApril10,2008 (showing that 36 outofthe128 pending cases are against Argentina).

[22] 申请人和被申请人在这方面的花费大体相同。See UNCTAD, Issues Related to Investment Arrangements: Investor-State Dispute sand Policy Implication, 7, TD/B/COM.2/62 (January14, 2005), available at http://www.unctad.org/en/docs/c2d62 en.pdf.

[23] Indeed, the CMS award, the first of the many Argentine cases, has required Argentina to pay the company $1.33 billion. See UNCTAD, Latest Developments in Investor-State Disputes Settlement, 6, IIA Monitor No. 4, UNCTAD/WEB/ITE/IIT/2005/2 (2005); see also Luke Peterson, Argentina Moves to Annul Award in Dispute with CMS Company Over Financial Crisis, INVESTMENTTREATYNEWS (International Institute for Sustainable Development, Winnipeg, Canada), October 26, 2005, at4 – 6, available at http://www.iisd.org/pdf/2005/investment investsd oct 26 2005.pdf (accessed April 10, 2008).

[24] See Peterson, *supra* note 26.

[25] See infra Part I. 1. a.

[26] See infra Part I. 1. b.

[27] See infra Part I. 1. c.

[28] See Cremades, *supra* note 21, at 81.

[29] See YanruWei, On the Impropriety of China's Recent Acceptance of Full ICSID Jurisdiction, 13 J. INT'LECON. LAW (in Chinese) 108, at139 – 140.

[30] Ibid.

[31] Argentina-USBIT, Article 7, as cited in Lanco International, Inc. v. Argentine Republic (Case No. ARB/97/6), Preliminary Decision on Jurisdiction of December 8, 1998, 40 ILM 457 (2001), § 20.

管辖权作出必要的同意,依据双方的书面许可协议,该争端必须受布宜诺斯艾利斯联邦行政争议庭管辖。[32] 然而,仲裁庭认为,该 BIT 构成政府的公开要约,因此构成符合《ICSID 公约》第 25 条第 1 款规定的"同意"。[33] 之后仲裁庭区分了后来颇具争议的条约诉求与合同诉求,并裁定:阿根廷后来与投资者达成并履行的许可协议并没有撤回在 BIT 中所作出的同意。[34]

在随后的"CMS 天然气运输公司诉阿根廷共和国"案中(CMS Gas Transmission Co. v. The Republic of Argentina case),[35] 阿根廷政府又一次对 ICSID 的管辖权提出了异议,主张政府授予 TNG[36] 公司的许可协议中含有一个独立的争端解决机制,即相关争端受布宜诺斯艾利斯联邦法庭的排他性管辖。然而仲裁庭仍然支持了投资者的诉求,裁决认为 CMS 不受该许可协议的约束,因为它不是该许可协议的一方当事人。仲裁庭进而就此类"卡尔沃条款"的法律效力评论道:

"……规定把某些争端交由国内法院管辖……并不能妨碍 ICSID 仲裁庭主张其管辖权,因为不同的法律文件有着不同的功能。"[37]

要对管辖权问题进行详细论述可能需要一篇专门的博士论文。在这里我们需要注意到的事实是:阿根廷在 ICSID 管辖权异议上是不成功的。于是,阿政府又采用了进一步的程序策略来处理该问题,那就是一旦 ICSID 作出裁决,则申请撤销该仲裁裁决。因此在 2005 年 9 月当 CMS 一案判决作出后,阿根廷就申请撤销该案裁决。2007 年 8 月 21 日,裁决撤销专门委员会对撤销申请做出判决,指出尽管 CMS 一案仲裁庭裁决在实体上存在错误,但是阿根廷仍需履行仲裁庭裁决中的赔偿义务。也就是要赔偿给 CMS 公司 2, 148, 100 美元。[38]

---

[32] Clause12, the Concession Agreement for the Port Terminal No. 3, as cited in Lanco International, Inc. v. Argentine Republic, id, § 6.

[33] Lanco International, Inc. v. Argentine Republic, id, § § 32 – 33.

[34] Lanco International, Inc. v. Argentine Republic, id, § § 34 – 40. 关于合同之诉与违约之诉的区别和联系, see Yuval Shany, Contract Claims vs. Treaty Claims: Mapping Conflicts Between ICSID Decisions on Multi-sourced Investment Claim, 99 Am. J. Int'l L. 835.

[35] CMS Gas Transmission Co. v. Republic of Argentina, Decision on Objections to Jurisdiction, ICSIDARB/01/8, 42 ILM 788 (2003).

[36] 申请人拥有 TNG 公司 29.42% 的股份。

[37] CMS Gas Transmission Co. v. Republic of Argentina, *supra* note 38, para. 76.

[38] Decision on the ad hoc committee on the application for annulment of the Argentine republic, available at http://icsid.worldbank.org/ICSID/FrontServlet?requestType=CasesRH&actionVal=showDoc&docId=DC687En&caseId=C4 (last visited April 10, 2008). 迄今为止,阿根廷一共对 6 起案件的仲裁庭判决提出了撤销申请,除了以上 CMS 一案已审结外,其余 5 起仍未审结。这 5 起案件是:Compañíade Aguasdel Aconquija S. A. and Vivendi Universal v. Argentine Republic (ICSID Case No. ARB/97/3)(阿根廷两次提出撤销申请);Enron Corporation and Ponderosa Assets, L. P. v. Argentine Republic (ICSID Case No. ARB/01/3);Azurix Corp. v. Argentine Republic (ICSID Case No. ARB/01/12);SiemensA. G. v. Argentine Republic (ICSID Case No. ARB/02/8);Sempra Energy International v. Argentine Republic (ICSID Case No. ARB/02/16).

2. 违宪审查。阿根廷政府近来对 BIT 以及依据 BIT 提起国际仲裁程序的合宪性问题也提出了质疑。[39] 例如,阿根廷代表在 CMS 天然气运输公司诉阿根廷共和国案(CMS Gas Transmission Company v. Republica Argentina)的听审会上指出:

(1)根据阿根廷宪法,双边投资条约的效力低于宪法。外国投资者不能援引双边投资条约规避阿根廷宪法的规定,将投资争端提交国际仲裁庭,从而剥夺阿根廷司法机关审理案件的机会。

(2)公用事业部门的外国投资者不能限制阿根廷享有的改变经济政策或限制公共事业收费标准的经济主权权利。[40]

该公诉人还发起了一个公共运动,倡议重新采用卡尔沃主义与德拉果主义,[41] 批判 BIT 与 ICSID,宣称阿根廷再也不应该同意将合同纠纷提交给 ICSID 之类的争端解决机制。[42] 主张投资条约违宪的主要依据是阿根廷《宪法》第 27 条与第 75 条。第 75 条第 22 款规定除了明文规定的特定的人权公约享受与宪法同等的法律地位之外,其余所有国际条约的法律地位都在宪法之下,法律之上。[43] 换言之,一般的国际条约,例如 BIT 与 ICSID 公约的效力都低于《宪法》。第 27 条

---

[39] 对于 ICSID 公约及其裁决的违宪问题有两种不同的观点。一种观点是阿根廷政府所持的观点,这在上文中已经阐述过。另一种观点是更新并且更激进的观点,该观点没有为阿根廷政府所采用。该观点认为 BIT 与 ICSID 制度都是违宪的,因为两者都被证明违反了 1994 年修订宪法所规定的程序。因为 ICSID 公约及其国内的具体实施法案是 1994 年修订宪法生效后才得到批准并生效,因此新宪法在这里应该得到适用。新宪法对“将权力与管辖权授予超国家组织的一体化条约”规定了一个特别严格的程序。因为对 ICSID 的仲裁管辖权的接受构成国内管辖权这一主权权力向 ICSID 的转移,因此 ICSID 公约有“一体化”的目的而必须受该宪法特别程序的约束。因为《ICSID 公约》并没有经过该特别程序,因此它也就尚未满足新宪法要求的生效条件。据此在 ICSID 中心对阿根廷提起的任何仲裁“可以被国内法院宣告无效”。该观点进一步认为新宪法所要求的该特别程序具有强制性的效力。因此,将权力与管辖权授予国际组织的国际条约如 ICSID 公约是无效的。然而,ICSID 公约是否构成这样一种“一体化条约”还有争论。例如,Alfaro 和 Lorenti 认为该公约只是一个“合作性”的条约而不是一个“一体化协定”,因此并不需要经过新宪法所要求的特别程序。关于该二人的观点和推理的细节,见 Carlos E. Alfaroand Pedro M. Lorenti,The Growing Opposition of Argentina to ICSID Arbitral Tribunals:A Conflict between International and Domestic Law? The Journal of World Investment & Trade,(Vol. 6,No. 3,June,2005),at 426 – 427,428 – 430.

[40] Carlos E. Alfaro,‘The Battle o fthe Century:Argentina Against the ICSID Arbitration and the BITs’, World Law Group E-news Issue No. 31 (November 2004), posted at http://www. imakenews. com/bcastro/eArt000332318. cfm? x = b11,0,w(visited on 9 July 2006).

[41] 德拉果主义由阿根廷外交部长 Luis Maria Drago 于 1902 年提出,该主义主张包括美国在内的任何外国势力,都不得使用武力来实现其债权。See Wikipedia,the Free Encyclopedia,Drago Doctrine,posted at http://en. wikipedia. org/wiki/Drago Doctrine(last visited April 10,2008).

[42] Alfaro,note 43 above.

[43] 阿根廷《宪法》第 75 条第 22 部分规定如下:“条约与协定的效力高于法律。《关于人的权利与义务的美国宣言》、《世界人权宣言》、《经济、社会与文化权利国际公约》、《公民权利与政治权利国际公约》及其议定书,《防止及惩治灭绝种族公约》、《消除一切形式种族歧视国际公约》、《消除对妇女一切形式歧视国际公约》、《禁止酷刑和其他残忍、不人道或有辱人格的待遇或处罚公约》、《儿童权利公约》;以上这些公约的效力与宪法等同,但与宪法第一部分的所有规定不得冲突,并且应理解为是对该条款所认可的权利和保证的补充。只有在征得议会三分之二以上成员同意的情况下,以上公约才能被政府撤消。为获得宪法地位,其他关于人权的条约与公约必须先获得参议院的同意,并需获得三分之二以上的议会成员通过。”

进一步要求这样的条约受“宪法所规定的公法原则”的制约。[44] 因此，有评论家这样认为，“《ICSID 公约》的有效性可通过考察其与宪法所规定的‘公法原则’是否相符来予以检验”。[45] 同样地，该“公法原则”也可以用来检验作为“ICSID 产物”的 ICSID 仲裁裁决。[46] 据此，国会本不应该批准像《ICSID 公约》这样的违背《宪法》“公法原则”的条约，而政府也本不应就这些条约进行谈判。[47] 然而，无论是国会或是政府都没有条约违宪审查权——这项权力在司法机关，最终也就是在国家最高法院手中。[48] 在这里，值得注意的是，阿根廷司法机构最近在审理一个重要案件时响应了政府的上述主张。该案判决指出，若涉及公共政策，阿根廷法院可以审查条约的合理性、公平性和合宪性，也就是仲裁裁决的实体内容。[49] 该案，Jose Cartellone Construcciones v. Hidro electrica Norpatagonica S. A.，针对的是因一个阿根廷私人公司与某国有企业间的公共服务合同的履行而引发的国内仲裁判决。[50] 该合同包含一个规定双方不能就仲裁判决向任何法院上诉的仲裁条款。[51] 阿根廷联邦最高法院判决认为：如果仲裁裁决存在“违宪”“不合理”或“非法”的情况，法院可以对仲裁裁决进行审查，即使当事人双方已经特别约定放弃就仲裁裁决向法院上诉的权利。[52] 该判决再一次确认了即使是在案件已经被提交给仲裁庭解决并且双方当事人已排除司法审查的情况下，[53] 最高法院仍可行使作为宪法与公共政策的“守护人”的权力。为支持其决定，最高法院引用了《民法典》第 872 条。该条规定，“为实施公共政策而赋予的权力不能被排除”。据此，法院可以否决当事人达成的任何限制对公共政策事务进行司法审查的协议。

这一判决表明国际仲裁庭做出的判决在阿根廷可因其“不合理”或者“违

---

〔44〕 阿根廷《宪法》第 27 条规定如下：“联邦政府负有这样的义务，即根据本宪法所规定的公法原则通过缔结条约的方式来与其他国家发展和平与贸易关系。”

〔45〕 然而，AlfaroandLorenti 看来对“宪法规定的公法原则”的概念做了一个很宽泛的解释，将该原则加以拓展使其覆盖了所有的“公法事务”。对此，笔者并不赞同。See Carlos E. Alfaroand Pedro M. Lorenti, note 42 above, at 420, 423 - 425.

〔46〕 Ibid.

〔47〕 Ibid., at 421.

〔48〕 Ibid.

〔49〕 Corte Suprema de Justicia[CSJN], 1/June/2004, Jose Cartellone Construcciones Civiles S. A. v. Hidro-electrica Norpatagonica S. A./, LaLey[L. L.] (CausaJ - 87, XXXVIIR. O.) (Arg.), the Decisionin Spanish is a-vailable at the Court's website: http://www.csjn.gov.ar/documentos/cfal3/toc fallos.jsp (last visit on April 10, 2008).

〔50〕 Carlos E. Alfaro, Argentina: ICSID Arbitration and BITs Challenged by the Argentine Government, Alfaro-Abogados, Dec. 21, 2004, available at http://www.alfarolaw.com/ima/tapa/alfaro3.htm.

〔51〕 Ibid.

〔52〕 Ibid.

〔53〕 Ibid.

宪”而提起司法审查。而实践中，该案判决已经“对国内低级法院处理与国际仲裁相关的类似案件产生了影响……”。[54]

从国际法的角度来看，前文所提到的违宪审查的主张是很难站得住脚的。因为正如《维也纳条约法公约》所规定的，一国不能援引其国内法规定来拒绝履行条约义务。[55] 同理，一国不能以其接受某条约约束的同意违反了其国内法关于缔约权限的规定来宣告该同意无效，除非这种违反是明显的，并且涉及具有根本重要性的国内法规定。[56] 在已发生的案件中，很难说阿根廷国会在BIT实践中所作出的同意“明显”（manifestly）违反了阿根廷国内法。即使该种同意“违反”国内法的论点成立，也很难证明这种违反是“明显的”，因为这需要证明该种“违反”是“根据通常实践和善意原则，对于任何国家而言在客观上都是明显的”。[57]

主张对ICSID仲裁判决进行司法审查在实践上也是难以成立的，因为《ICSID公约》明确要求成员国将ICSID的仲裁裁决作为国内法院的最终判决来承认和执行。[58] 然而，如果仲裁裁决由其他的仲裁机构作出，如国际商会（ICC）和根据联合国国际贸易法委员会（UNCITRAL）规则设立的仲裁庭，那么司法审查问题就可能出现。阿根廷法院可以对这些机构（国际商会仲裁院等）的裁决进行审查，并以其“不合理”或“违宪”作为理由撤销或拒绝执行。

3. 立法措施。在运用程序策略延缓仲裁程序和提起违宪主张进行抗辩的同时，阿根廷已经采取并正在酝酿进一步的立法措施来限制和防止投资仲裁案件的发生。为此，政府取消了1996年的一个法令[59]并酝酿一项旨在控制国际仲裁的新法。2003年阿根廷政府通过了一个新法令废除了梅内姆政府在1996年颁发的

---

〔54〕 Hirocio Grigera Naon, Arbitration in Latin America: Progress and Setbacks', 2004 Fresh fields Lecture, Arbitration International, Vol. 21, No. 2 (2005), at 165.

〔55〕 Vienna Convention on the Law of Treaties arts. 27, Jan. 27, 1980, 1155 U. N. T. S. 331, available at http://untreaty. un. org/ilc/texts/instruments/english/conventions/1 1 1969. pdf.

〔56〕 Vienna Convention on the Law of Treaties art. 46, Jan. 27, 1980, 1155 U. N. T. S. 331, available at http://untreaty. un. org/ilc/texts/instruments/english/conventions/1 1 1969. pdf. 一些阿根廷宪法学者也注意到了国际法所施加的此类限制。比如，Nestor Sagues 指出只有在国际条约违反了《维也纳公约》第46条规定的权限规则时，才能宣称这类条约违反了国内《宪法》。See Alfaro & Lorenti, *supra* note 42, at 422.

〔57〕 Vienna Convention on the Law of Treaties art. 26(2), Jan. 27, 1980, 1155 U. N. T. S. 331, available at http://untreaty. un. org/ilc/texts/instruments/english/conventions/1 1 1969. pdf. 在 Ceskoslovenska Obchodni Banka, A. S. v. The Slovak Republic 一案裁决中也涉及《维也纳公约》第46条，但是仲裁庭认为该案并不能适用此条款，因为这里涉及的是“条约的失效”，因为实际上该案所涉条约并未生效。Case No. ARB/97/4 Ceskoslovenska Obchodni Banka, A. S. v. Slovak Republic Decision of the Tribunal on the Objections to Jurisdiction of May24, 1999, 14ICSIDREV. —FOREIGNINV. L. J. 251, 265 (2000), available at http://www. worldbank. org/icsid/cases/csob. pdf.

〔58〕 ICSID Convention art. 54(1), available at http://www. worldbank. org/icsid/basicdoc/CRR English-final. pdf.

〔59〕 Decree to No 1021/96 of 6 September1996, available at http://www. boletinoficial. gov. ar/bora. portal/PrimeraSecci% C3% B3n/BusquedaRapida/tabid/81/Default. aspx (last visiton 17 Mar. 07).

一项命令,该命令规定有关阿根廷政府与保格罗尼集团(Bulgheroni Group)之间的投资争端提交给国际仲裁庭解决。[60] 新法令指出,将这样的争端提交给国际仲裁庭解决“无论从法律、政治还是经济的角度看都存在一系列的困难”。[61]

这一措施不是故事的结尾而只是政府尝试“重新国有化”国家与投资者之间争端的第一步。[62] 据报道,阿根廷财政部法律顾问 HoracioRosatti 称政府的目标是“恢复国内法院的管辖权”。[63] 他表示,阿根廷政府正在研究办法,以收回国家对涉及政府与企业的争议的管辖权与控制权。具体措施可能包括一方面要求这些公司在提起国际仲裁之前先“用尽当地救济”,另一方面“让本国法院对国际仲裁庭的裁决进行审查”。[64]

据报道,科奇纳总统(Kirchner)在其于 2005 年 3 月发表的一份演说中,对由国际仲裁庭最终裁决外国投资者与阿根廷政府的损害赔偿案件的实践提出了严重的质疑。[65] 随后,执政党的两名议员提出了一份旨在限制国内外仲裁庭管辖涉及政府的案件的议案。根据该议案,国际与国内仲裁庭不得审理、裁决涉及政府、政府机构以及国有企业的案件,[66]除非:(1)可以就有关仲裁裁决向阿根廷联邦法院提起上诉;(2)案件的对方当事人是一个国家(即属于国家与国家之间的纠纷的仲裁);或(3)国会通过具体立法规定该案可以是一个例外。[67] 该法案还要求:一方面,政府应将阿根廷废除已经接受的有关仲裁管辖权的国际条约的意愿告知各相应的当事国;[68]另一方面,政府、政府机构以及其企业应颁布命令或决定,以废除先前缔结或制订的与本法案相抵触的合同或决定。[69] 鉴于该法案

---

〔60〕 Decree to No 966/2003 of 28 October 2003, available at http://www.saij.jus.gov.ar/news/files/decreto966.html(last visit onApril10,2008). See also Laurence Norman, Government Reopens 7 - Year-Old Case Vs Oil Group, DOW JONESINT'LNEWS, Oct. 28, 2003(reporting the 2003 decree annulling the 1996 executive order), available at http://www.latinpetroleum.com/printer 2375.shtml(retrieved 27 Jan 2005); Cremades, *supra* note 21, at 81.

〔61〕 Decre to 966/2003, Ibid.

〔62〕 Norman, *supra* note 63.

〔63〕 Ibid.

〔64〕 Ibid.

〔65〕 Guido Santiago Tawil (M. & M. Bomchil), Is Calvo finally back? 3 TRANSNAT' LDISP. MGMT., 3 (2005).

〔66〕 Ibid.

〔67〕 Ibid.

〔68〕 实践中,已经有拉美国家向世界银行提出了撤销《ICSID 公约》的申请。2007 年 5 月 2 日,世界银行收到了玻利维亚提交的要求撤销《ICSID 公约》的书面通知。根据《ICSID 公约》第 71 条的规定,撤销在收到玻利维亚书面通知后的 6 个月后即 2007 年 11 月 3 日生效。而中心也依据《ICSID 公约》第 75 条规定,将此撤销通知了其成员国。See Bolivia Submits a Notice under Article 71 of the ICSID Convention, available at http://icsid.worldbank.org/ICSID/FrontServlet? requestType = CasesRH&actionVal = OpenPage&PageType = AnnouncementsFrame&FromPage = NewsReleases&pageName = Announcement3(last visit:2008/04/10).

〔69〕 Ibid.

要求所有的国家与投资者间的仲裁案件接受本国法院的最终控制，它将在实质上否定仲裁的终局性和自主性。

据有关报道，2004 年以来，还有一些类似性质的法案也已经向阿根廷国会提出。[70] 例如，2004 年 9 月的一项法案要求“涉及阿根廷政府的所有争端必须受本国法院的完全控制，并拒绝任何有相反规定的条款”。[71] 该法案同时要求废除条约中那些同意仲裁管辖的条款。[72] 2005 年 8 月提出的一项法案声称“阿根廷法院做出的涉及直接或间接征收的经济政策或决定，不受任何国际法院或仲裁庭的审查”。[73] 该法案同时提出“为达此目的，每个投资条约都应包含有上述效果的条款，并以此作为阿根廷政府批准该条约的条件”。[74] 如果此类法案被采纳，可以说卡尔沃主义已经完全重归故里。显然，仍需假以时日才能清楚这些法案究竟只是舆论宣传还是将被最终采纳。

（二）巴西

拉美巨人巴西，在很长一段时间内一直对仲裁采取抵制态度。1996 年仲裁法案通过后，才为仲裁实践提供了方便之门。[75] 2002 年，巴西批准了《纽约公约》，为外国仲裁裁决的承认与执行铺平了道路。[76] 然而巴西对国际仲裁仍心存芥蒂。这种态度可在对仲裁法案的违宪审查案与 2004 年公私合伙法中限制仲裁的规定中清楚看到。

1. 违宪审查案。1996 年 10 月，在仲裁法案得到批准后不久，巴西联邦最高法院就接到了一个以该法案违宪为由质疑该法案有效性的诉讼。[77] 作为第一个涉及仲裁法案的案件，该案件由 11 位法官参与审理。[78] 案件起因于一个要求执行

---

〔70〕 See Oscar M. Garibaldi, Carlos Calvo Redivivus: The Rediscovery of the Calvo Doctrine in the Era of Investment Treaties, TRANSNAT' LDIS. MGMT., December 2006, at 1.

〔71〕 Ibid.

〔72〕 Ibid.

〔73〕 Ibid. at. 43 – 44.

〔74〕 Ibid. at 44.

〔75〕 在 1996 年以前，仲裁在巴西受到一系列的限制。比如，在争端发生前依合同规定提请仲裁，所做裁决不具有执行力，除非当事人在争端发生后重新缔结一个仲裁协定；外国仲裁裁决要得到承认和执行，必须得到仲裁地的法院和巴西联邦最高法院的许可。Noah D. Rubins Investment Arbitration in Brazil, 4 J. WORLD INVESTMENT& TRADE 1071, 1084 – 1087 (2003).

〔76〕 巴西于 2002 年加入《纽约公约》，所依据的法令是 Decree No. 4311 of 23 July 2002. Ibid, at 1075 n. 16.

〔77〕 关于本案细节，参见 Joao Bosco Lee, ‘Brazil’, in International arbitration in Latin America, edited by Nigel Blackaby, David M. Lindsey and Alessandro Spinillo, Kluwer (2002), at 63 – 66; Guido Santiago Tawil, The Role of Arbitration and International, Regional, Subregional and Bilateral Treaties in Latin America, posted at http://66.249.93.104/search? q = cache: xjw8Vj40l7wJ: www. bomchilgroup. org/argdec02. html + + brazil + ratified + colonia + protocol + mercosur&hl = zh-CN&ct = clnk&cd = 9(22/05/2006).

〔78〕 Tawil, *supra* note 79, at 14.

在西班牙巴塞罗那作出的外国仲裁裁决的申请。[79] 而最高法院也借此机会对整个法案的合宪性进行了审查。[80]

开始时,案件的主审法官(Min. Sepúlveda Pertence)认为该仲裁法案中的某些条款(包括承认仲裁条款的特别适用效力的第6条与第7条,规定在存在仲裁条款情况下排除法院管辖权的第41条,列举出对根据第7条规定所作的某判决提起上诉的条件的第42条)违反了宪法,因为这些条款是对1998年《宪法》第35章第5条规定的司法审查权的否定。[81] 然而,经过了5年的讨论,主审法官的观点被以7比4通过的宣告该法案合宪的裁决所推翻。[82]

虽然最终判决是有利于仲裁的,然而主审法官与其他三名持反对意见的法官的观点,以及围绕着这一问题所展开的长时间的争论,都表明了巴西对国际仲裁的怀疑和犹豫态度。

2. 公私合伙法(The PPP Law)。2004年12月30日,巴西通过了第11079号法案,该法案为巴西公私合伙企业(PPPs)以及在联邦、州和当地政府范围内的投标与许可协议建构了一个法律框架(PPPs法)。[83] 该法允许公私合伙合同双方就合同所产生的任何争端选择仲裁作为解决方式。[84] 然而,该法同时要求仲裁在巴西境内进行而且仲裁程序必须使用葡萄牙语。[85] 更为重要的是,该法只接受国内仲裁而禁止将与公私合伙合同相关的争端提交给国际仲裁庭解决。因此,外国投资者只能在本国法院提起损害赔偿请求,或是将争端提交适用巴西法的仲裁庭。该法表明巴西政府不愿意把涉及公共实体的案件(诸如国家与投资者之间的争端)提交国际仲裁。[86] 巴西的BIT实践也印证了这一点:尽管该国已经签署了一些BIT,至今尚无一个BIT获准生效。

---

〔79〕 Tawil, *supra* note 79, at 14.

〔80〕 在巴西,最高法院拥有违宪审查问题的控制权,并且有权在某个条款产生问题的情况下对整部法律的合宪性问题进行审查。因此,即使在执行程序中仲裁条款的有效性问题并没有被提起,法院也可以主动提起该问题。See Lee, note 79 above, at 64 note 15.

〔81〕 该《宪法》第5条第35款规定"该法不能排除司法机关对某项权利的违反与威胁的情况的审查"。关于所称的法官的推理的更详细情况,见 Joao Bosco Lee, Ibid, at 63 - 64. See also Tawil, note 79 above。

〔82〕 Tawil, ibid.

〔83〕 该法可见于巴西计划、预算与管理部的网站: https://www. planalto. gov. br/ccivil 03/Ato2004 - 2006/2004/Lei/L11079. htm(visited on 22 June 2006)。英语版本可在下列网址中搜索到: http://www. planejamento. gov. br/arquivos down/ppp/legislacao/lei 11079301204 eng. pdf(visited on22 June2006)。

〔84〕 Art11 III, the PPP Law, Ibid.

〔85〕 Ibid.

〔86〕 Rubins 指出,要使国际仲裁判决在巴西得到承认,唯一的办法是在外国投资者与阿根廷政府之间的合同中订立一个仲裁条款。因为"与那些给予外国投资者平等待遇和诉诸国际仲裁的明确保证的拉美国家不同,巴西没有这样的规定"。See Noah D. Rubins, Investment Arbitration in Brazil, 4 J. WORLD INVESTMENT & TRADE 1071, 1080 - 1081, 1091 (2003).

（三）委内瑞拉

近年来在委内瑞拉发生的某些事件也被认为是卡尔沃主义复苏的明证。[87] 其中，勘探回合案（Exploration Round Case）与 MINCA 案最为引人注目。

1. 勘探回合案。1995 年 12 月，一群委内瑞拉国民向委内瑞拉最高法院起诉，质疑委内瑞拉国会一项批件中的仲裁条款的合宪性。[88] 该批件批准了 1995 年的一项石油勘探投标安排。该批件所批准的若干个"条件"中有一条（第 17 项条件）规定，"所有由关联协议引起的争议均应由有拘束力的仲裁来解决"。[89] 起诉方认为该项批件违反了委内瑞拉《宪法》第 127 条的规定，他们认为《宪法》第 127 条赋予了本国法院对于这类合同的排他性的管辖权。[90] 1961 年委内瑞拉《宪法》第 127 条规定如下：

"在公共利益合同中，除依合同的性质无法适用的情形外，应视为内含了这样一个条款（即使该条款在合同中并未被明确规定）：即有关这类合同的任何争议或纠纷，如不能由合同双方协商解决，则应该由委内瑞拉有管辖权的法院，根据其法律来解决，而不得诉诸国际求偿。"[91]

因为最高法院从未曾就仲裁的合宪性作出过判决，而且此前律政司就这一问题意见也颇不一致，[92] 因此该案吸引了广泛的关注。

1999 年 8 月 17 日，最高法院对该案作出了判决，[93] 认为该批件中的仲裁条款是合乎《宪法》的。最高法院认为虽然这些协议是"涉及公共利益的合同"，但是符合第 127 条所规定的例外条件。该条款规定在"依合同的性质无法适用的情形"[94] 下，可以排除本国法院管辖权。法院认为，该例外实际上使得政府可以通过国会批件的形式，在个案基础上决定在某一具体公共利益合同中可否包含仲裁条款。[95] 最后，法院还认为，在本案中，仲裁庭所作出的最后裁决不会牵涉到"国家利益"。[96] 虽然勘探回合案最终的裁决有利于仲裁与外国投资者，但是关于仲裁的合宪性问题并没有根本解决，因为最高法院并没有就关于"合同性质"例外的模糊性作出任何澄清。而在 1999 年通过的新宪法也未能解决该问题。出

---

〔87〕 See Cremades, *supra* note 21, at 81.

〔88〕 Elisabeth E. Elijuri (Caracas), Oil Opening: A Constitutional Challenge, posted at http://www.natlaw.com/pubs/spveen1.htm (visited on 12 February 2006).

〔89〕 Ibid.

〔90〕 See Cremades, *supra* note 21, at 81.

〔91〕 Ibid.

〔92〕 See Elijuri, *supra* note 90.

〔93〕 Cremades, *supra* note 21, at 83 (citing Supreme Court Decision of August17, 1999, File No. 812 – 829).

〔94〕 Ibid.

〔95〕 Ibid.

〔96〕 Ibid.

乎外国投资者的意料,原《宪法》第127条被原封不动地保留了下来,只是重新将其编号为第151条。[97]

2001年3月,委内瑞拉总统签发了第4号指令,对由国家履行的涉及公共利益的合同,尤其是包含国际仲裁条款的合同的国内审查机制作出规定。[98] 根据该指令,关于公共利益合同中的仲裁条款是否符合新《宪法》第151条的问题,必须提交给律政司进行审查。[99]

另外,随着最高法院的新法官宣誓就任,人们怀疑最高法院先前作出的肯定公共利益合同中的仲裁条款符合《宪法》的判决也可能会改变。[100] 这种怀疑似乎已被 Mineral as Cristinas, C. A. (MINCA) v. Corporation Venezuelana de Guyana 案 (MINCA Case)[101] 所证实。

2. MINCA案。该案涉及委内瑞拉政府机构CVG与加拿大Vannessa Ventures Ltd.公司持有其95%股份的委内瑞拉公司MINCA公司之间的采矿协议。该协议于1992年达成,是关于拉斯克里斯蒂那(LasCristinas)地区的金矿与铜矿的勘探与开采的。[102] 该协议包含一个争端解决条款,要求双方当事人之间的任何争端都要提交给位于委内瑞拉境内的仲裁庭解决,仲裁依据ICC仲裁规则与委内瑞拉《民事诉讼法典》作出。[103] 双方于2001年产生纠纷,这导致CVG终止了该采矿协议并对该矿实施了事实控制。[104] 随后,能源与矿业部发布了一个决议终止了该采矿协议,并且政府也发布了一项总统令,将拉斯克里蒂那矿区收归国有。[105]

MINCA公司在委内瑞拉法院先后对CVG的行为,以及该部门决议和总统法令提起诉讼。但这些司法审查请求权都被驳回。[106] 2002年5月,MINCA又向最高法院提交了申请书,请求执行协议中的仲裁条款。[107] 而最高法院以该行为涉

[97] Constitution of the Bolivarian Republic of Venezuela, Article 151. An unofficial English translation of the Constitution can be found at the Australia Venezuela Solidarity Network Chavez website: http://www.venezuelasolidarity.org/? q = node/53 (last visiton April 10, 2008).

[98] Bernardo Werningerand David M. Lindsey, 'Venezuela', in International Arbitration in Latin America, edited by Nigel Blackaby, David M. Lindsey and Alessandro Spinillo, Kluwer (2002), at 223, 235.

[99] Ibid. at 235 – 236.

[100] Cremades, note 21 above, at 83.

[101] Bernardo M. Cremades, Resurgence of the Calvo Doctrine in Latin America, 7 Business Law International 53, 65 (2006) (citing Decision No. 0083 of the Political Administrative Chamber of the Supreme Court, of 15 July 2004).

[102] Ibid.

[103] Ibid. at 66.

[104] Ibid.

[105] Ibid.

[106] Ibid.

[107] Ibid.

及国家财产因而不受仲裁约束为由又一次驳回了 MINCA 公司的请求。[108] 在陈述判决理由时,法院表示前文提到的《宪法》第 151 条是判决的主要依据之一。[109] 无疑,这个案子证实了委内瑞拉对于国际仲裁的立场的不确定性。

阿根廷、巴西与委内瑞拉所发生的这些事件,以及在其他的拉美国家所发生的相似的事件,如玻利维亚退出《ICSID 公约》,[110] 厄瓜多尔终止其已经签订的多个 BIT[111] 等,清楚表明投资政策的浪潮正在转向。拉美国家不再一味热衷于实行投资自由化,相反地,一种更加保守的,倾向于国家主义的方法看来正在占据上风。[112] 换言之,卡尔沃主义并不像许多人推断的那样在拉美已经消亡,而是仍然活着并且日趋活跃。

二、卡尔沃主义的复苏:拉美之外

卡尔沃主义的复苏现象并不局限于拉丁美洲。实际上,拉美卡尔沃主义复苏现象只是世界范围内的对投资自由主义制度进行反思、修正甚至抛弃的新潮流的一部分。

因此,首先,令所有人吃惊的是,卡尔沃主义发现其"在美国国会突然流行起来"![113] 一系列针对美国政府的投资案件被提交到国际仲裁庭,尤其是 NAFTA 仲裁庭,将向来竭力鼓吹毫无保留的投资自由化的美国推到被告席上,迫使其站在被告东道国的立场上开始对投资条约与建立在条约基础上的国际仲裁进行审

---

[108] Bernardo M. Cremades, Resurgence of the Calvo Doctrine in Latin America, 7 Business Law International 53, 65 (2006) (citing Decision No. 0083 of the Political Administrative Chamber of the Supreme Court, of 15 July 2004), at 66.

[109] Ibid. at 67.

[110] 据报道,玻利维亚政府已于 2007 年 5 月 1 日正式通知 ICSID 要求退出该公约。这是该公约缔结以来,第一次出现的要求退出该公约的现象。同时,该国政府还表示要修改已经签订的 BIT 的投资定义、业绩要求与争端解决等条款,以确保国家利益与国内法院的管辖权。详见 Damon Vis-Dunbar, Luke Eric Peterson and Fernando Cabrera Diaz, Bolivia notifies World Bank of withdrawal from ICSID, pursues BIT revisions, Investment Treaty News(ITN)(May 9, 2007), published by the International Institute for Sustainable Development(www.iisd.org/investment/itn)。

[111] 2007 年 9 月,厄瓜多尔政府宣布将终止与美国的 BIT。10 月,厄瓜多尔政府宣布不再同意将有关石油和采矿部门的投资争议提交 ICSID 仲裁。最近,厄瓜多尔政府又宣布将终止其与九个国家签订的 BIT。参见 Luke Eric Peterson, Ecuador announces that it wants out of US investment treaty, Investment Treaty News(ITN)(May 9, 2007), published by the International Institute for Sustainable Development(www.iisd.org/investment/itn); LATIN AMERICA ADVISOR, Ecuador and Investment Treaties, posted at http://203.208.37.104/search? q = cache:XoT27oFBw1cJ:www.latinbusinesschronicle.com/app/article.aspx% 3Fid% 3D2129 + us + ecuador + investment + treaty + terminate&hl = zh-CN&ct = clnk&cd = 5&gl = cn&st usg = ALhdy28IbmMK8AQgBp54 pWPeJvNY7K51A(last visit on 25 June 2008).

[112] 卡尔沃主义在拉美的"复活"或"重生"问题已经引起了广泛的关注。比如,在 2005 年 9 月,华盛顿律师协会适时组织了一个名为"卡尔沃主义的重生"的研讨会。District of Columbia Bar, "The Resurgence of the Calvo Doctrine?" seminar program, available at http://www.bg-consulting.com/docs/calvo program.jpg (last visited Feb. 15, 2007).

[113] David Schneiderman, Calvo in Congress: The Migration of Constitution-Like Investment Rules, http://www.ualberta.ca/GLOBALISM/pdf/Aus% 20pdfs/schneidermanab.pdf(last visited Feb. 15, 2007).

视。人们发现，自从20世纪90年代中期以来，美国传统的高标准的投资保护的承诺已经发生“逐渐的、相对缓和(但很清晰)的弱化现象”。[114] 例如，1994年，克林顿政府在其当时修订的BIT范本中放弃了要求国家恪守其对外国投资者所作出的承诺的所谓“保护伞条约”(umbrella clause)。[115] 2001年，北美自由贸易协议中的三个成员国在美国的带动下，正式通过了一项有约束力的解释性声明，指出“‘公正与公平待遇’和‘完全的保护与安全’(full protection and security)只能理解为国际法关于外商投资的最低待遇标准”，[116]而不是更高的待遇，试图以此削弱 *Pope Talbot Inc.* v. *Canada*[117] 案判决等所带来的不利影响。2002年，国会通过一项有关政府在贸易与投资条约方面谈判的权力的法案，要求：

“……美国就外国投资方面谈判的基本目标是减少或消除对外国投资所设置的人为的或者有贸易歪曲(trade-distorting)效果的法律障碍，同时确保在投资保护方面外国投资者所享受的实体权利不应高于本国投资者，并且保护投资者享有可与依据美国法的原则与实践所享有的权利相比拟的一些重要的权利。”[118]

有人称这项法案为“国会中的卡尔沃”法案，因为它所确立的国际投资立法政策采用的是与卡尔沃主义非常类似的语言。根据这种新政策，美国政府2004年对其BIT范本[119]进行了修正并在其BIT实践中采取了一些更加保守的做法。例如，美国与乌拉圭之间签订的BIT是自范本修订之后美国签订的第一个BIT。该BIT缩小了“投资”的范围，[120]对间接征收进行了界定与澄清，规定仅是对某投资的经济价值造成负面影响并不构成一项间接征收，并且除非有特殊情况，一方为实现保护合法的公共福利的目标比如公共健康、安全和环境而采取的非歧视性的管制措施并不构成间接征收。此外，在美乌BIT中还规定了一个特别程序，防

---

〔114〕 Garibaldi, supra note 72, section1.03[3][c].

〔115〕 Ibid.

〔116〕 Ibid.

〔117〕 Pope & Talbot Inc. v. Canada, 13 World Trade & Arb. Mat' l 61 (Apr. 10, 2001), available at http://www.dfait-maeci.gc.ca/tna-nac/documents/Award Merits-e.pdf. 裁决主张公正和平等待遇以及完全的保护和安全是一般国际法规定的国际最低标准待遇之外的另一种义务。

〔118〕 Trade Act of 2002, Pub. L. No. 107-210, § 2102(b)(3), 116 Stat. 995.

〔119〕 TREATY BETWEEN THE GOV' T OF THE UNITED STATES OF AM. AND THE GOV' TOF [COUNTRY] CONCERNING THE ENCOURAGEMENT AND RECIPROCAL PROT. OF INV. (2004 ModelBIT) (United States Trade Representative), available at http://www.ustr.gov/assets/Trade Sectors/Investment/Model BIT/asset upload file847 6897.pdf (last visited April 10, 2008).

〔120〕 与此前的以财产为基础对投资进行定义不同，美国—乌拉圭BIT选择用经济学术语来界定“投资”，该定义原则上包含了投资者拥有和控制的任何财产。但是该定义同时又规定这些财产必须“具有投资属性”，比如“有资本和其他资源的投入、具有收益预期以及风险的承担”。Treaty between the United States of Am. And the Oriental Republic of Uruguay Concerning the Encouragement and Reciprocal Prot. ofInv., U.S. - Uru, [Date of Treaty], http://www.ustr.gov/assets/Trade Agreements/BIT/Uruguay/asset upload file748 9005.pdf (last visited Feb. 15, 2007) at § A, Art. 1 [hereinafter US-Uruguay BIT].

止在争端解决过程中出现滥诉的情形。[121] 并且,该 BIT 还规定要建立一个上诉审查机制对仲裁裁决进行审查,以保证裁决的一致性。[122]

其次,许多其他国家,比如加拿大、日本和某些拉美国家,正紧步美国后尘。因此有人认为加拿大新的 BIT 范本引人注目,"因为它标志着在以往对私人投资者提供的过高保护水平的基础上有所回退"。[123] 与此同时,联合国贸易发展委员会(UNCTAD)的一份报告则称以美国与加拿大新 BIT 范本为代表的"新一代 BIT"实际上已经诞生。[124] 这些 BIT 呈现出四个主要特征,其主要趋向在于一方面缩减了实体义务范围,另一方面对诉诸国家与投资者之间的争端的解决机制施加了更严格的控制。[125]

再者,在世界范围内建立一个保护并使投资自由化的多边条约的努力一而再、再而三的遭到挫败。OECD 内 MAI[126] 的失败表明即使在发达国家,如 OECD 成员国之间,国际投资自由化也不能实现。[127] 而在坎昆部长级会议上,在 WTO 框架下进行 MAI 谈判也遭到了否决,[128] 这意味着在全球范围内建立一个自由化的投资制度的又一次重要努力再次流产。

最后,政府对投资自由化态度的转变同样可以从国内立法的变化和 BIT 的增长趋势中反映出来。如表 1 所示,自 2000 年以来,限制性的国内法措施处于上升势头。2000 年,只有 2% 的法律上的改变是限制性的,而这种改变 2001 年则上升到 7%,2003 年达到了 10%,而 2004 年又增长了 3%。在这段时间,唯一下降的年份是 2002 年,但是这种下降的幅度是非常小的(从 7% 到 5%),并不能改变总体趋势。同时,值得注意的是,尽管每年仍然有相当数量的 BIT 缔结,从 1996 年以来新缔结的 BIT 总体上呈明显减少趋势(见表 1)。

---

[121] U. N. Conference on Trade and Development [UNCTAD], Recent Developments in International Investment Agreements, UNCTAD/WEB/ITE/IIT/2005/1, IIA MONITOR NO. 2 (2005), at 5, available at http://www.unctad.org/Templates/Download.asp? docid = 6294&lang = 1&intItemID = 3784.

[122] Ibid.

[123] James McIlroy, Canada's New Foreign Investment Protection and Promotion Agreement: Two Steps Forward, One Step Back?, 5 J. WORLD INVESTMENT & TRADE 621, 646 (2004).

[124] UNCTAD, *supra* note 8, at 4.

[125] Ibid. at 4 – 6.

[126] Organisation for Economic Co-Operation and Development (OECD), Multilateral Agreement on Investment: Documentation From the Negotiations, http://www1.oecd.org/daf/mai/ (last visited Jan. 22, 2007).

[127] Ibid.

[128] Decision Adopted by the General Council, Doha Work Programme, § (1) (g), WT/L/579 (Aug. 2 2004), available at http://www.wto.org/english/tratop e/dda e/ddadraft 31jul04 e.pdf.

表 1　2000～2004 年所采取的限制性的措施

年份	法律变化的为数量（条）	采取更具限制性措施的法律变化的数量（条）	限制性措施在法律变化中的百分比（%）
2000	150	3	2
2001	208	14	7
2002	248	12	5
2003	244	24	10
2004	271	36	13

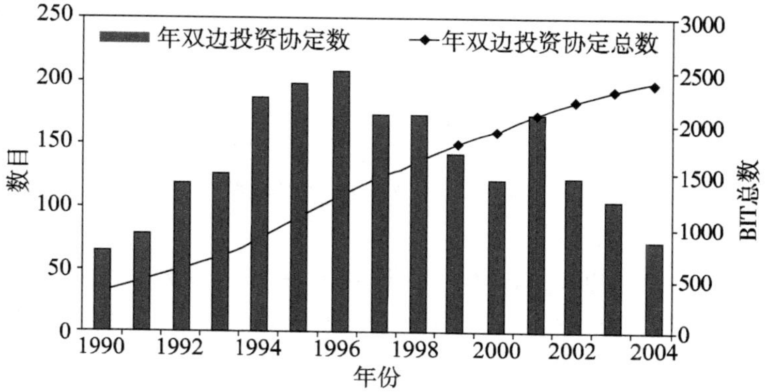

图 1　1990～2004 年缔结的 BIT 的数量　单位：件[129]

可见，即使在拉美之外，国际投资浪潮也正在转向，无论是发达国家还是发展中国家都无一例外地不再完全热衷于投资新自由主义。[130] 相反，即使是以往作为自由投资体制的最狂热支持者的发达国家，如美国，也已开始重新思考国际投资条约的作用和功能，并重新设计他们的 BIT 计划以克服先前的自由投资体制所带来的不利因素。[131] 卡沃尔似乎正在国际投资争端解决的硝烟中逐渐收复失地。

〔129〕 Source：UNCTAD（www. unctad. org/iia）.

〔130〕 20 世纪 90 年代可被称为“新自由主义”时代。在那一时期，投资和贸易自由化几乎获得了世界上所有国家的支持。不论是发达国家还是发展中国家。最好的例证就是曾是卡尔沃主义最忠实的拥护者和支持者的拉美国家都改变了对外国投资的态度并且开始缔结象征投资自由化的 BIT。SHAN，*supra* note 13，SectionsII-VI.

〔131〕 上述“国会卡尔沃”法案就是发达国家改变其态度的最好例证。

三、未来的国际投资法：介于经济自由主义和卡尔沃主义之间的第三条道路

卡尔沃主义的复苏现象表明以 BIT 为代表的国际投资条约所体现的投资自由化理念，既不理想，也难以为继。[132] 然而，人们仍然不能确知卡尔沃主义的复苏现象会不会只是昙花一现，会转瞬即逝，还是将一直持续下去，直到完全复活并重新统治世界？换句话说，国际投资法的政治经济学究竟是会被卡尔沃主义所象征的“经济国家主义”所完全取代，还是会继续由新自由主义所统治？对这个问题的答案，目前仍不甚明了。[133]

笔者认为，在可预见的未来，卡尔沃主义复苏的潮流将会继续，不过它不可能完全恢复到它最初的状态。它会以一种修正后的模式复活，最终达到投资者与东道国之间的利益与权利的平衡。理由有两方面：一方面，已如前述，卡尔沃主义的复苏不单是发生在某一国家或者某一地区的现象，而是在世界范围内发生的一个比较普遍的现象。这样一种全球性潮流是不太可能在短时间内逆转和消失的；另一方面，从根本意义上说，卡尔沃主义死亡与再生的经历暴露了传统的卡尔沃制度以及现行的占主导地位的投资自由主义制度的根本缺陷：东道国与外国投资者之间权利与义务的不平衡性。

在 20 世纪 80 年代以前，当卡尔沃主义在拉丁美洲及国际场合——如联合国大会——占统治地位的时候，东道国对外资拥有绝对的权力，几乎不受国际法的约束，[134] 而投资者无法得到任何国际法的保护而必须承担巨大的风险和负担，这时候的国际体制明显地偏向于东道国。从 20 世纪 80 年代起，特别是在 90 年代，当包括拉美国家在内的世界各国全心全意拥抱新自由主义投资制度之后，外国投

---

〔132〕 BIT 往往将其自身界定为自由主义的协定。这从规定其目标的序言中可以看出。比如，他们大都规定缔约目的是为投资创造有利条件并推动经济繁荣。正如 Kenneth Vandevelde 所指出的，BIT 产生和发展的历史“表明吸引国家缔结 BIT 的主要原因之一就是它支持自由主义主张”。Kenneth J. Vandevelde, The Political Economy of a Bilateral Investment Treaty, 92 AM. J. INT' LL. 621, 627 (1998). BITs 的自由主义性质已在实践中被仲裁庭所承认并且影响到了对 BIT 条款的解释。Id., at 627 – 28.

〔133〕 Vandevelde 是最早研究 BIT 政治经济学的学者之一。根据他的观点，与 BIT 有关的有三个主要的政治经济学理论：经济民族主义理论、经济自由主义理论和马克思主义经济理论。其中，马克思主义经济理论对外国投资采取敌对态度，认为它们是推行新自由主义的工具，会使本国经济受到外国的控制并导致经济倒退。随着苏联的瓦解和中国以及其他社会主义国家的改革，这一理论不再流行。经济民族主义理论主张对国际投资进行规制，以保证其为服务于国内政治需要。主张经济民族主义的发展中国家通常通过制定干预政策来对控制外资的进出流量。这类干预政策包括保护性关税、税收鼓励、投资审核以及履行要求等，目的是吸引那些会加快本国发展的外商投资，同时禁止那些不利于发展的投资，同时确保投资设立以后，其运营也符合国家政策。卡尔沃主义就是这一理论的典型代表。经济自由主义理论主张乌国家干预的自由市场能导致价值的最大化。相应的，自由主义理论倡导资本自由跨界流动，本质上主张国家应当允许由市场来决定国际投资的流向。要更进一步理解这些理论基本特征，详见 Vandevelde, Id., at 621 – 28.

〔134〕 更多有关卡尔沃主义的缘起以及在 20 世纪 80 年代之前该理论的影响，参见 SHAN, *supra* note 13, Section I。

资者享受到了 BIT 及其他法律文件所赋予“类宪法”的保障与特权,[135]而东道国政府则被迫步步退让——这也是一种不平衡,只不过这种不平衡是偏向外国投资者的。由此可见,这两种国际投资制度,虽然各自有其价值,但都不是理想的制度。

卡尔沃主义不可能完全恢复到最初的状态,因为在全球化时代,没有一个国家能完全故步自封,游离于世界之外。日渐密切的国际交流必然导致日趋完备的国际规则,以确立有关的国际实体标准与程序救济措施。卡尔沃主义原先所倡导的对这种国际标准与国际救济的完全反对的态度既不现实,亦非必要。传统的卡尔沃主义与当今世界是不相容的,即使它曾经是适应这个世界的。反过来,新自由主义的投资制度也必须改革,以避免阿根廷与其他拉美国家近年来所遭遇的“进退两难”的困境。[136] 一个理想的外国投资制度,必须在先前这两种制度间寻求一个平衡点——我们或许可以称为国际投资法的“第三条道路”。

以美国和加拿大 BIT 范本为例的新一代 BIT 或许可被认为是朝上述方向迈进的一步。[137] 然而它们只是对 BIT 作了很小的改动,这些小改动并没有从根本上改变其以新自由主义为精髓的本质特征。这类投资条约只注重保护投资者并且赋予其更多的权利而未能充分考虑东道国的权利和投资者的义务。[138]

为了彻底解决投资者与东道国之间权利与义务的不平衡问题,需要采取一种更为激进的甚至革命的方案。有两个可供选择的可能性:第一种可能,是就国家的权利和外国投资者的义务制定双边的,最好是全球性的协议,作为现有的自由主义的 BIT 及相关法律的补充。这种方法或许可以称为“补充法”

---

[135] 有些学者认为双边投资条约以及其他的投资条约体现了国内宪法的某些特征,因为它们要求政府受类似宪法的规则约束。这些规则要求国家保护自然人和公司的私人财产不受歧视待遇,他们的投资所获利益不应被征收。而且这些规定也产生了类似宪法的义务,可以由仲裁庭和法院予以强制实施。See David Schneiderman, NAFTA's Takings Rule: American Constitutionalism Comesto Canada, 46 U OF TORONTO L. J. 499 (1996). See also Stephen Clarkson, Somewhat Less Than Meets the Eye: NAFTA as Constitution, address at the International Sociological Association Annual Meeting (Jul. 27, 1998), http://www.chass.utoronto.ca/~clarkson/manuscripts/ecconstitution98.html.

[136] 在撤销裁决的申请中,阿根廷主张 ICSID 在 CMS 一案的判决事实上使处在经济危机中的阿根廷陷入“两难”的境地:要么坐等本国经济崩溃,要么采取措施来挽救经济,但这却意味着要给因此受到影响的投资者以巨额赔偿,同样会导致国家破产。See Luke Peterson, Argentina Moves to Annul Award in Dispute with CMS Company over Financial Crisis, INVESTMENT TREATYNEWS (ITN) (Int' lInst. SustainableDev., Winnipeg, Manitoba, Canada), Oct. 26, 2005, at § 4, para. 14, http://www.iisd.org/pdf/2005/investment invested oct 26 2005.pdf.

[137] 例如,James McIlroy 指出加拿大新的 BIT 范本试图“在私人投资者利益与主权国家基于公共利益规制投资的权利之间寻求平衡”。McIlroy, *supra* note 126, at 644-45.

[138] 例如 Brewerand Young 在 90 年代曾撰文指出国际投资立法的重心已经由“强调公司的义务和政府的权利”转移到“强调公司的权利和政府的义务”上来。See Brewer, Tomas L., and Young, Stephen, Towards a Multilateral Framework for Foreign Direct Investment: Issues and Scenarios, Transnational Corporations, vol. 4, no. 1 (April 1995), at 74-75.

(complimentary approach)。类似措施已经在全球及多边层面上屡有尝试，但却收效甚微。[139] 我们可以看到，多边层面上，OECD 制定了《多国企业指南》来规范和引导成员国多国企业的经营管理。但该指南没有强制约束力。在全球层面上，联合国曾公布了其草拟的《跨国公司行动守则草案》。该守则在 20 世纪七八十年代曾引起人们的广泛讨论，但却在 90 年代的全球投资自由化的浪潮中被迫放弃。[140] 最简单的办法也许就是恢复制定该守则的工作，并在其基础上建立一个规范外国投资者义务和责任的有约束力的全球公约。

表 2 《IISD 范本》外国投资本、东道国和母国主要权利和义务一览表[141]

当事主	权利	义　务
外国投资者	国民待遇 最惠国待遇 国际最低待遇标准 无赔偿不得征收 有效管理 财产自由转移	遵守国内法 投资前的影响评估 反腐败 环保以及遵守国际环境法义务 保护人权 遵守核心劳工标准 信息公开 投资者作为国民/居民应尽的义务
东道国	国家固有的规制权 和发展政策制定权 制定履行要求(国民待遇的例外) 保护投资 获取投资者信息	程序公平 统一的环保和劳工标准 履行环保、劳工和人权的最低标准要求 反腐败 信息公布
母国	在争端解决过程中呼吁保护本国投资者	为本国投资者海外投资提供便利 提供有关投资者的信息 确保本国程序法允许就投资者的责任举行听证会 反腐败

第二种方法或许可以称为“综合法”(consolidated approach)，即在双边或多边投资文件中增加有关东道国权利和外国投资者义务的规定。这将会实质性地

〔139〕 See WENHUA SHAN, THE LEGAL FRAMEWORK OF EU-CHINA INVESTMENT RELATIONS (2005), at 274.

〔140〕 最后的修改在 1988 年完成，但是该项工作在 1990 年年初终止了。M. Sornarajah, The International Law on Foreign Investment, Cambridge University Press, 275 – 283 (2004).

〔141〕 Mann, *supra* note 147, at 88.

改变 BIT 的性质与理念,使其由片面保障和授权外国投资者的自由主义条约转化为一个能够平衡各方,特别是东道国与外国投资者的利益、权利和义务的一种更为合理的条约。在这方面我们可以参考"可持续发展国际研究所"(IISD)所制定的"可持续发展国际投资协议"范本,它是在构建一个"综合性"的国际投资协定方面所作出的第一个有力的尝试。[142] 它旨在寻求外国投资者、东道国及母国之间的利益平衡。该范本将其目标规定为:促进支持可持续发展的外商投资,特别是对发展中国家以及欠发达国家的这种投资。[143] 据此,鼓励投资不再是单一的目标,该目标必须受到另一个目标,即可持续发展目标的检验和限制。而且,IISD 范本协议前言明确提出其宗旨在于寻求"投资者、东道国与母国在国际投资中权利与义务的完全平衡"。[144] 为达此目标,IISD 范本正文中列出了相关各方的一系列实体性的权利与义务(详见表 2)。协议同时还给出了三项措施以确保这些权利与义务的实施。第一,它鼓励各国将协议中的各项权利与义务写入各国国内法,从而使得国家可以针对投资者提起国内救济措施。[145] 再者,东道国可以向范本所设计的国际投资争端解决机构控诉投资者不履行义务:东道国一方面可以以投资者长期未履行规定的义务为由要求撤销其条约项下的权利;另一方面,也可以在投资者起诉其违反东道国义务时提出反诉。[146] 最后,该范本还效仿经合组织《多国企业指南》的做法,规定建立一个国内机构负责调查公民社会所提起的有关跨国公司未在母国或东道国履行义务的控诉。[147]

IISD 投资协议范本包含一些很有趣的创新点。例如,允许东道国就外国投资者未能履行义务而提起直接诉讼就不失为一项颇有创新的举措。虽然目前尚不知此项举措在实践中能否奏效以及应如何运作,但是它的确可以说是目前国际投资条约中这种一边倒的投资者/东道国争端解决机制的一个"合乎逻辑的推论"。[148] 尽管该范本目前还只是处于初级阶段,有许多地方都有待于进一步的研

---

[142] The Model Agreement, together with a negotiators' handbook, is available on the International Institute for Sustainable Development(IISD) website: http://www. iisd. org/publications/publication list. aspx? themeid = 7 (last visiton 10 April 2008). The Model Agreement was also published in 20 ICSID REV. – FOREIGN INVESTMENTL. J. 91, (2005).

[143] IISD MODELINTERNATIONALAGREEMENTON INVESTMENT FOR SUSTAINABLE DEVELOPMENT (Int' lInst. Sustainable Dev. (IISD) 2005), art. 1, 20 ICSID REV. – FOREIGN INVESTMENT L. J. 91, (2005) [hereinafterIISD MODELAGREEMENT].

[144] Id.

[145] Howard Mann, The IISD Model International Agreement on Investment for Sustainable Development: An Introductory Note, 20 ICSID Rev. – Foreign Investment L. J. 84, 86 (2005).

[146] Id., at 86.

[147] Id., at 87.

[148] Id., at 86.

究改进,[149]但它是在东道国与投资者之间寻求权利与义务平衡的一次有影响的尝试,值得深入和认真地研究。

四、结论:从"南北矛盾"到"公私冲突"

卡尔沃主义在拉美内外的复苏不仅仅表明了世界各国对待国际投资制度的态度和理念发生了重大转变,同时也体现了国际投资法领域论争焦点的一大转变。之前关于国际投资法律文件,例如联大有关决议[150]和 BIT 的争论,体现的是作为资本输出国代表投资者利益的发达国家,与作为资本输入国代表东道国利益的发展中国家之间的矛盾。[151] 换言之,也就是说先前的国际投资立法的主要焦点集中在南北关系上,表现为南北国家之间的分歧与对立关系。发达国家企图推进投资自由化,而发展中国家则试图对此进行抵制并维护其对外国投资进行限制和控制的权利。最近,情形发生了变化,变得更加复杂。跟三四十年前不同的是,南北分歧缩小了,显得已经不那么明显和重要。同时,外国投资者的私人利益与东道国公共利益之间的冲突却日显突出,已经成为争论的主要焦点。简言之,国际投资立法争论的焦点与主要特征似乎已经由先前的"南北矛盾"转为如今的"公私冲突"。促成这一转变的原因是多方面的,究其要,主要有如下四个方面。

第一个原因是,发达国家在国际投资方面的角色的转变,或者说"觉醒"。20世纪 90 年代之前,包括美国、加拿大在内的发达国家,只将自己视为资本输出国

---

[149] 例如,范本第 11 条第 A、B 两款在主张适用国内法和国内法院管辖的同时,应该指出该项规定尚且受制于有约束力的国际法,特别是国际条约义务的约束。See IISD MODEL AGREEMENT, *supra* note 145, art. 11(A) - (B).

[150] 第 1803 号决议和第 3281 号决议是有关国际投资待遇标准的最为重要的联大决议,特别是在征收及其赔偿方面。通常人们认为这两个决议立场互相对立,并且法律效果也不相同。然而,笔者主张这两个决议需要结合在一起考虑,因为两个决议是同一种形成中的国际法规则在不同的发展阶段的成果表现,应该具有同等的法律效果。See SHAN, *supra* note142, at 181 - 87. See also Declaration on Permanent Sovereignty over Natural Resources, G. A. Res. 1803 (XVII), at223, U. N. Doc. A/RES/1803 (XVII) (Dec. 14, 1962); Charter of Economic Rights and Duties of States, G. A. Res. 3281 (XXIX), at 251, U. N. Doc. A/RES/3281 (XXIX) (Jan. 15, 1975).

[151] 有关于这一方面的文章数不胜数。See, e. g., S. FRIEDMAN, EXPROPRIATION IN INTERNATIONAL LAW(1953); Charles N. Brower, Current Developments in the Law of Expropriation and Compensation: a Preliminary Survey of Awards of the Iran-United States Claims Tribunal, 21 INT'L LAW. 639 (1987); Rudolf Dolzer, New Foundations of the Law of Expropriation of Alien Property, 75 AM. J. INT'L L. 553 (1981); Francesco Francioni, Compensation for Nationalisation of Foreign Property: The Borderland Between Law and Equity, 24 INT' LANDCOMP. L. Q. 255 (1975); Rosalyn Higgins, The Taking of Property by the State: Recent Developments in International Law, 176 RECUEIL DES COURS 263 (1982); Eduardo Jiménezde Aréchaga, State Responsibility for the Nationalisation of Foreign Owned Property, 11 N. Y. U. J. INT' LL. & POL. 179 (1978); Davis R. Robinson, Notesand Comments, Expropriation in the Restatement(Revised), 78 AM. J. INT' LL. 176 (1984); Oscar Schachter, Compensation for Expropriation, id. at121; M. Sornarajah, State Responsibility and Bilateral Investment Treaties, 20 J. WORLDTRADEL. 79 (1986); F. A. Mann, British Treaties for the Promotion and Protection of Investments, 52 BRITISH YEARBOOKINT' LL. 241 (1981).

(尽管从绝对价值量上看它们同时也是主要的资本输入国),代表的是外国投资者的利益。因此它们积极推进双边或多边投资条约项目,不遗余力地为其在国外的投资者提供最大可能的保护。90 年代以来,尤其是投资者依据《北美自由贸易协定》(NAFTA)第十一章的提起一系列的仲裁案件发生之后,一些国家已经开始意识到自己同时也是主要的资本输入国这一事实。它们竭尽全力保护自己作为东道国的权利和利益,正如发展中国家在 20 世纪六七十年代所做过的那样。根据 Todd Weiler 的统计,迄今为止针对美国的案件至少有 16 起,针对加拿大的至少有 13 起。[152] 这些案件迫使两国政府站在资本输入国的立场上来思考问题,这在以前似乎只是发展中国家的事情。正因如此,才会有这些发达国家修正它们的 BIT 项目,增强对国家权力保护的做法。主要发达国家的此种转变使得它们与发展中国家之间有了更好的相互理解和利益趋同:作为投资东道国,它们都同样地需要在国际投资立法中确保他们能有效地管理和规范外国投资者及其投资。

第二个原因是,发展中国家在国际投资中的角色也发生了改变。不少发展中国家已经成为世界上日益重要的外国投资者。联合国贸易与发展委员会(UNCTAD)在《2004 年世界投资报告》中着重强调指出"发展中国家外国直接投资流量已经变得越来越重要"。[153] 报告同时指出,一些发展中国家,诸如马来西亚、韩国以及新加坡,在对外投资方面已经摸索出了自己的路子。[154] 其他国家,诸如智利、墨西哥及南非等国也都参与进来,[155] 巴西、中国、印度等国也都先后效仿,开始起步。[156] 相对而言,一些发展中国家和地区,如新加坡、我国香港和台湾地区,对外直接投资已位居一些发达国家(如德国、日本、美国)前列。[157] 而且,在过去的 15 年中,发展中国家的对外直接投资的增速已经超过了发达国家——截止到 20 世纪 80 年代,发展中国家的对外投资额微乎其微,而 2003 年却占世界外资总储量的 10% 以上,当年世界外资流量的差不多 6% 的比重(分别为 9000 亿美

---

[152] See Todd Weiler, Naftaclaims. com, http://www. naftaclaims. com/disputes canada. htm; Ibid. , http://www. naftaclaims. com/disputes us. htm(last visited Jul. 31, 2006).

[153] U. N. CONFERENCE ON TRADE AND DEVELOPMENT[UNCTAD], WORLD INVESTMENT REPORT 2004: THE SHIFT TOWARDS SERVICES, at19, U. N. Doc. UNCTAD/WIR/2005, U. N. Sales No. E. 04. II. D. 33 (2004). See also Chart 2.

[154] Ibid.

[155] Ibid.

[156] Ibid.

[157] Ibid.

元和 360 亿美元)。[158] 即使按全球标准来衡量,一些发展中国家已经成为重要的国际投资者。[159]

发展中国家在对外投资方面地位的上升已经对它们在国际投资立法中的实践产生了影响。例如,从 20 世纪 90 年代后期以来,中国已经明显提高了其对外国投资的实体保护,同时放宽了外国投资者将争议诉诸国际仲裁法庭的限制,这些变化与其日益增长的对外投资是分不开的。[160]

近年来,发展中国家间缔结的 BIT 数量的增长也表明了发展中国家角色的转变。例如,《2005 年世界投资报告》指出,2004 年缔结的 BIT,绝大多数是发展中国家之间缔结的。[161] 这表明不少发展中国家已走向了“自主的自由化”道路,其角色与发达国家日渐趋同。发展中国家角色的改变与前面提到的发达国家类似的角色转换交相辉映,进一步增进了双方在国际投资立法中的相互理解,拓展了双方的共同利益。

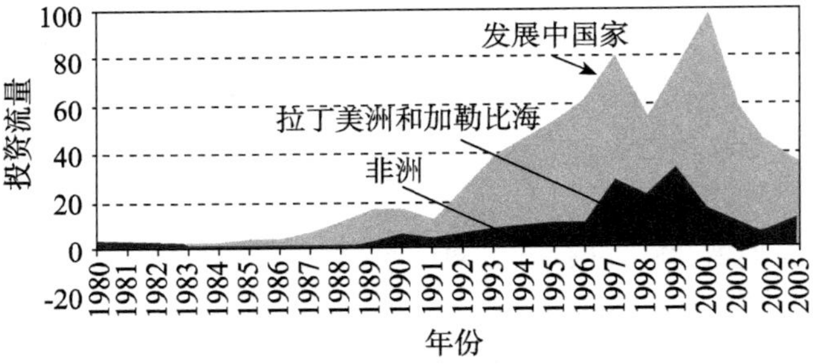

图 2 1980~2003 年发展中国家所在地区对外直接投资流量(单位:10 亿美元)[162]

[158] U. N. CONFERENCE ON TRADE AND DEVELOPMENT[UNCTAD],WORLD INVESTMENT REPORT 2004: THE SHIFT TOWARDS SERVICES,at 19,U. N. Doc. UNCTAD/WIR/2005,U. N. Sales No. E. 04. II. D. 33 (2004). See also Chart 2.

[159] 比如,在 2003 年,中国香港的对外直接投资额比瑞典高。即便将“迂回投资”和非直接投资计算在内也是如此。此外,香港的跨国公司数量也很突出。其他发展中国家,如新加坡、墨西哥和南非,也是如此。Id.

[160] 1998 年以来,中国已经有越来越多的 BIT 允许将外国投资者与东道国之间的投资争端提交国际仲裁。不少甚至规定所有的投资争端都可以自动提交包括 ICSID 在内的国际仲裁。迄今为止,4 个含有此类条款的 BIT 已经生效,另外有 16 个有待批准。中国开放此领域的一个主要原因就是在过去几年里中国的海外投资有大幅增长,同时政府也积极鼓励国内企业“走出去”。

[161] 报告指出,有 28 个 BIT 是在发展中国之间签订,占总量的 38%。See UNCTAD,WORLD INVESTMENT REPORT 2005:TRANSNATIONAL CORPORATIONS AND INTERNATIONALIZATION OFR&D,at 24,U. N. Doc. UNCTAD/WIR/2005,U. N. Sales No. E. 05. II. D. 10 (2005).

[162] Source:UNCTAD,FDI/TNCd atabase(www. unctad. org/fdistatistics).

表 3　1991～2004 年国内立法的改变[163]

年份	修改外国直接投资法律的国家(个)	对外国直接投资法律的修改数量(部)	对外国投资者有利的修改(部)	对外国投资者不利的修改(部)
1991	35	82	80	2
1992	43	79	79	0
1993	57	102	101	1
1994	49	110	108	2
1995	64	112	106	6
1996	65	114	98	16
1997	76	151	135	16
1998	60	145	136	9
1999	63	140	131	9
2000	69	150	147	3
2001	71	208	194	14
2002	70	248	236	12
2003	82	244	220	24
2004	102	271	235	36

第三个原因可能是,发展中国家为保护和促进外国直接投资的国内法律基础设施已有显著改善和提高。这一变化主要应归因于各国多年来不断修订完善其国内立法并缔结大量投资协定(尤其在 90 年代签订的)的努力。根据《2005 年世界投资报告》,从 1991 年起,每年平均有 64 个国家都对自己的 FDI 法规做出调整。在此期间做出的 2156 个修订中,促进投资自由化的修订就有 2006 个,占到了总变化数量的 93%(参照表 3)。[164] 投资自由化的另一个重要因素是双边投资协定(BITs)的大量签订。联合国贸易与发展委员会(UNCTDA)统计数字表明,截至 2004 年底,世界范围内的 BIT 总数已达到 2392 个,其中 2010 个签订于 90 年代(见图 1)。[165] 而且,各国还积极参与双边的、区域的及跨区域的贸易与投资协定(PTIAS)的谈判。到 2005 年为止,已签署此项协议 212 个,其中大约 87% 是在 20 世纪 90 年代签署的。[166] 国内法律的这些修改,连同大量的国际投资条约的签

---

[163] Source: UNCTAD World Investment Report 2005, p. 26.
[164] Id. at 28.
[165] Id.
[166] Id.

订,显著缩小了发展中国家与发达国家在国际投资法律保护方面的差距。诚然,差距仍然存在,但是比起30年前来说,形势已大有改观。因此,对外国投资进行进一步的法律保护的需要不再像从前那么迫切,发展中国家与发达国家在国际投资立法中争论的问题也日渐减少。因此,这就使人们的注意力转移到了一个更为普遍的问题上来,即公私利益的冲突。

第四个原因是,非政府组织在国际投资立法中的广泛参与提高了人们对规制国际投资的重要性和必要性的认识。早期的NAFTA关于投资仲裁的案例,尤其是颇有争议的Metalclad v. Mexico〔167〕等案件,使很多非政府组织将注意力集中到国际投资条约及相关仲裁实践上。OECD《多边投资协议》草案的谈判和多哈回合中关于WTO框架下的多边投资协议的谈判,都清楚表明了非政府组织在国际投资法立法中参与的广度与深度。诚然,不同的非政府组织有着不同的使命,其观察问题的角度也有所不同。但是它们却共同关注到一点:投资自由化不能以重要的公共利益诸如人权、环境以及劳动标准等为代价。简而言之,它们突出强调了为维护公共利益而规制外国投资的重要性。近年来,这些组织(大部分建立在发达国家)在国际与国内法律与政策的制定过程中发挥着越来越明显的影响。相应地,它们帮助提高了公众(尤其发达国家的民众)对管理和规范外国投资必要性的认识,从而客观上有助于国际投资法立法重心的转向。综上所述,近年来,国际投资法立法的争议焦点似乎已经发生了重要转变:从“强国”与“弱国”的对立,即“南北矛盾”,转向“国家主权”对“公司主权”〔168〕的对立,即“公私冲突”。果如是,则人们有理由相信,缔结一个利益均衡的全球性的投资条约,或许为期不会太远。

---

〔167〕 *Metalclad Corporation* v. *The United Mexican States*, ICSID Case No. ARB (AF)/97/1 (30 August 2000).

〔168〕 考虑到大型跨国公司的规模,以及它们现在根据BIT可以直接状告东道国政府的事实,可以说他们实质上已经享受了某些“主权”权利,具备了某些“主权”特征。称为“公司主权”,或不为过。

China and International Investment Law*

I. Introduction

China's success in attracting foreign direct investment (FDI) is undisputed and unprecedented. It now ranks second in the world in attracting FDI inflows and fifth in exporting foreign investment. This success is driven primarily by China's significant economic progress but has been facilitated by China's effort in streamlining the legal framework, including the establishment of the world's secondlargest network of bilateral investment treaties (BITs).

This chapter attempts to analyze the role of law in China's international investment activities. After an introduction regarding the historical development of FDI both in China and out of China, the chapter explores the legal framework governing such investments. It then moves on to analyze the most important legal issues involved in international investment, namely the admission regime, the general standards of treatment, expropriation and compensation, transfer, and dispute resolution. The chapter discusses the interaction between China's international and domestic norms in regulating foreign investment activities. It also demonstrates whether and to what extent the European-styled BIT prototype has been revised to fit "Chinese characteristics".

The chapter concludes that although the extensive regulatory framework has contributed to China's success in foreign investment activities, China has to do more to further strengthen the framework and be fully prepared for the change of role from a participant to a leader in international investment activities.

---

* In Leon Trakman and Nicola Ranieri (eds.), *Regionalism in International Investment Law*, Oxford University Press, 2013.

This chapter is written based on several previously published works including in particular the books CHINESE INVESTMENT TREATIES: POLICIES AND PRACTICE (Norah Gallagher & Wenhua Shan eds., 2009) and WENHU A SHAN, THE LEGAL FRAMEWORK OF EU-CHINA INVESTMENT RELATIONS: A CRITICAL APPRAISAL (2005), and the chapter on China in COMMENTARIES ON SELECTED MODEL INVESTMENT TREATIES (Chester Brown & Devashish Krishan eds., forthcoming).

1. China, International Investment, and the Law

1.1 China's International Investment and the Role of Law

a. FDI in China

As the second largest FDI recipient since 1992,[1] China presents a great success story in attracting FDI inflows.[2] However, China had been very hostile to FDI from its foundation in 1949 to the late 1970s, during which period many foreign enterprises in China were expropriated.[3] This situation was, nevertheless, changed in 1979 when the open-up policy was adopted to restore the collapsing economy after ten years of social disorder caused by the "Great Proletarian Cultural Revolution" (1966 – 1976). As an important part of the open-up policy, attracting FDI became the focus of work of the government, and numerous FDI-friendly measures at both international and national levels were adopted to create a competitive and attractive foreign investment environment.

As illustrated in Chart 1, FDI in China had been steadily increasing since the late 1970s until the early 1990s, when it experienced the first surge after Deng Xiaoping pronounced that China was to establish a "Socialist Market Economy." A second surge happened in the early twenty-first century mainly due to China's accession to the WTO in 2001. The chart also shows that China has generally maintained a high speed of growth in FDI inflow despite the global financial crisis, except for a slight drop in 2009. In 2010 China experienced a 17 percent increase in FDI inflow, proof of China's rapid recovery from the global crisis.

It can be expected that China will keep its position as a most popular FDI destination in the future. A series of UNCTAD surveys reveal that China is the top destination for FDI in 2010 – 2012 for transnational corporations (TNCs).[4] Moreover, a survey held by the American Chamber of Commerce confirms that U. S. companies remain optimistic about their China outlook in the medium term.[5] (p. 216)

---

[1] UNCTAD, *World Investment Report* 2010*: Investing in a Low-Carbon Economy* 4 (WIR series, U nited Nations, New York and Geneva 2010).

[2] UNCTAD, *World Investment Report* 2011*: Non-Equity Modes of International Production and Development* 4 (WIR series, United Nations, New York and Geneva 2010).

[3] *See* CHINESE INVESTMENT TREATIES, *supra* note 1, at 4 – 5.

[4] UNCATD, *supra* note 2, at 25.

[5] AMCHAM-CHINA, 2010 CHINA BUSINESS CLIMATE SURVEY REPORT 3 (2011), *available at* http://www. amchamchina. org/upload/cmsfile/2011/03/22/efb2ab9d3806269fc343f640cb33baf9. pdf (last visited Nov. 8, 2011). It is pointed out that 91% of the respondent companies reported their business outlook in China is "slightly optimistic" or "optimistic". Id.

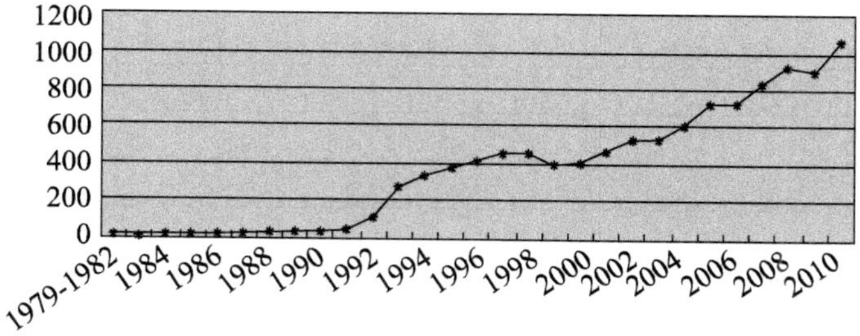

Chart 1 FDI in China 1979 – 2010 (Unit: US $ 100 million)

Source: compiled by the author in accordance with data from China's official FDI Web site: www. fdi. gov. cn.

b. ODI from China

China's performance in stimulating outward direct investment (ODI) in recent years is equally if not even more spectacular. According to UNCTAD, investors from South, East, and Southeast Asia and Latin America were the major contributors to the strong growth in global FDI outflows.[6] In 2010, outflows from China reached their historical high of $ 68 billion, and China has overtaken Japan in total outward FDI to become the fifth-largest home economy.[7]

As demonstrated in Chart 2, before 2000, Chinese outward investment was insignificant, despite a perceivable increase in the early 1990s following the announcement of the "Socialist Market Economy". In contrast, there has been a steep increase in ODI from China since 2000 when the "going abroad" policy was pronounced.[8] According to the recently published statistics, the ODI from China has been rapidly increasing in the last nine years with an average growth rate of 49. 9 percent. By the end of 2010, more than 13, 000 domestic entities had established around 16, 000 overseas enterprises, covering 178 countries/regions.[9] (p. 217)

---

[6] UNCTAD, *supra* note 3, at 7.

[7] Id. at 7 – 9.

[8] The "going abroad" policy was first proposed in 1998, which aimed to explore international market and take advantage of resources abroad. This strategy was written in the Outline of the Tenth Five-Year Plan for National Economy and Social Development in 2001. Accordingly, the Chinese government took various measures to promote ODI. For details, please see Cai Congyan, *Outward Foreign Direct Investment Protection and the Effectiveness of Chinese BIT Practice*, 7 J. WORLD INV. & TRADE 621, 627 – 31 (2006).

[9] Ministry of Commerce, 2010 *Statistical Bulletin of China's Outward Foreign Direct Investment* (2011), *available at* http://hz s. mofcom. gov. cn/accessory/201109/1316069658609. pdf (last visited Nov. 8, 2011). Some scholars, however, questioned the accuracy of China's ODI date and pointed out that there were some distortions, though they admitted that China's ODI has reached significant levels commercially and geoeconomically and has begun to challenge international investment norms and affect international relations. *See* Daniel H. Rosen & Thilo Hanemann, *China's Changing Outbound Foreign Direct Investment Profile: Drivers and Policy Implications, Policy Brief of Peterson Institute for International Economics* 2 – 7 (June 2009), http://www. iie. com/publications/pb/pb09 – 14. pdf (last visited Nov. 8, 2011).

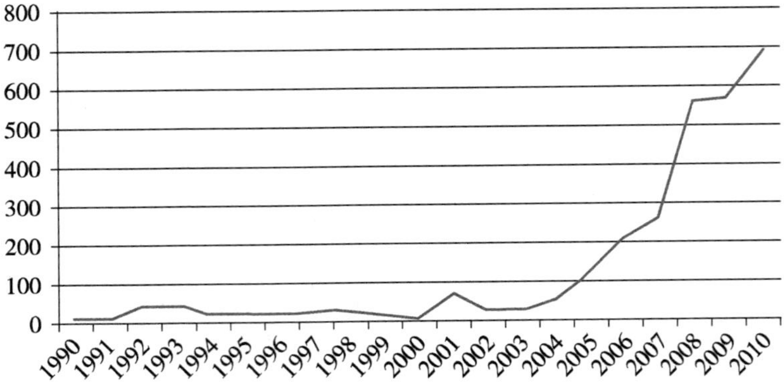

Chart 2 ODI from China 1990 – 2010 (U nit: U S $ 100 million)

Source: compiled by the author in accordance with data from China's official FDI Web site: www. fdi. gov. cn.

c. Role of Law in Attracting FDI to China: Empirical Evidences

It is generally believed that law, among other things such as economic determinants and business facilitation, has contributed to China's success in attracting FDI and promoting ODI, especially after China's accession into the WTO.[10] However, empirical studies on the extent to which the law has played a role are rare. To fill the gap, the author conducted two empirical studies in 2001 and 2008. The first one aimed to study the role of law in EU investors' decisions as to whether to invest in China,[11] whereas the (p. 218) second one was conducted in the SuZhou Industrial Park (SIP)[12] to investigate the role of law in foreign investment activities in the SIP. Both of the surveys have confirmed that the law has played an increasingly important role when the investment decisions were made. Specifically, the 2001 survey shows that 83 percent of the investors

---

〔10〕 *See, e. g.*, Hui Huang, *The Regulation of Foreign Investment in Post-WTO China: A Political Economy Analysis*, 23 COL. J. ASIAN L, , 185 (Fall 2009); Stephan W. Schill, *Tearing Down the Great Wall: The New Generation Investment Treaties of the People's Republic of China*, 15 CORDOZO J. INT'L & COMP. L. 73 (2007); Jessica Zoe Renwald, *Foreign Investment Law in the People's Republic of China: What to Expect from Enterprise Establishment to Dispute Resolution*, 16 IND. INT'L & COMP. L. REV. 453 (2006); Shaukat Ali & Wei Guo, *Determinants of FDI in China*, 1(2) J. GLOBAL BU S. & TECH. 21 (Fall 2005); Qun Li, *Tax Incentive Policies for Foreign-Invested Enterprises in China and Their Influence on Foreign Investment*, 18(1) REVENU E L. J., Article 5 (2008); Chen Yongmei, *The Legal Climate for Foreign Investment in China after Its WTO Accession*, 20(1) BOND L. REV., Article 2 (2008); Jordan Brandt, *Comparing Foreign Investment in China, Post-WTO Accession, with Foreign Investment in the United States, Post* – 9/11, 16 PACIFIC RIM L. & POL. J. 285 (Mar. 2007).

〔11〕 Comprehensive analysis of this investigation may be found in SHAN, THE LEGAL FRAMEWORK OF EU-CHINA INVESTMENT RELATIONS, *supra* NOTE 1, at 247 – 64; Wenhua Shan, *Law and Foreign Investment in China: General Role of Law and Substantive Issues*, 2(3) MANCHESTER J. INT'L ECON. L. 41 (2005); Wenhua Shan, *Law and Foreign Investment in China: Effectiveness of the Chinese FDI Legal System*, 3(1) MANCHESTER J. INT'L ECON. L. 51 (2006).

〔12〕 Though all of the respondent companies are from the Suz hou Industrial Park, they represent almost all the companies investing in Mainland China. For details, please see Wenhua Shan & Sheng Zhang, *FDI in China and the Role of Law: An Empirical Approach*, 12 J. WORLD INV. & TRADE 457 (2011).

saw the legal framework as an element of substantial importance,[13] and in a 2008 survey this number rose to 88 percent.[14]

1.2 The Regulatory Framework

a. The Framework

The general regulatory framework concerning FDI in China is composed of both domestic and international laws. Between them Chinese domestic laws and regulations constitute the most important source of law because these lay down the basic conditions for the entry and operation of FDI in China. Until now, there has not been a unified FDI code in China. Foreign investors have to refer to a series of national and subnational laws and regulations that apply to FDI activities, which together constitute the domestic FDI legal system.

The other source is international law, which serves to protect and promote foreign investment. China has the second-largest BIT network in the world and has sought to participate in regional economic integration arrangements since the beginning of the twenty-first century. China currently has entered into nine FTAs, including two Closer Economic Partnership Arrangements (2003) signed separately with Hong Kong and Macao. The remaining seven FTAs each have an investment chapter.[15] China is also in ongoing FTA negotiations with the Gulf Cooperation Council, Australia, Iceland, Norway, and the Southern African Customs Union. Feasibility studies are being conducted with India, Korea, Japan, and Switzerland on potential FTAs. On the other hand, China has signed more than ninety Double Taxation Avoidance Treaties (DTTS),[16] and is also a contracting party to relevant multilateral treaties such as the ICSID Convention (the Convention on the Settlement of Investment Disputes between States and Nationals of Other States), the Convention on Multilateral Insurance Guaranty Agency (MIGA), and the WTO agreements. This following section provides some further discussions on these elements of the regulatory framework.

b. Interaction between the International and Domestic Norms[17]

No constitutional rules in China have been enacted as yet to govern the relationship between international treaties and domestic law. The Chinese constitution merely pro-

---

[13] SHAN, LEGAL FRAMEWORK OF EU-CHINA INVESTMENT RELATIONS, *supra* note 1, at 248.

[14] Wenhua Shan & Sheng Zhang, *supra* note 13.

[15] China-Costa Rica FTA (2010) Chapter 9; China-New Zealand FTA (2008) Chapter 11; China-Pakistan FTA (2006) Chapter IX; China-Peru FTA (2010) Chapter 10; China-Singapore FTA (2008) Chapter 10. The China-ASEAN FTA has an entire agreement on investment signed in 2009. Full texts are available online at http://fta.mofcom.gov.cn/english/index.shtml (last visited Nov. 8, 2011). The China-Chile FTA (2005) has an article on the promotion of investment and a commitment to negotiation of a future agreement on trade in services and investment. The supplementary Agreement on Trade in Service was signed with Chile in 2008; the negotiations on investment are pending. The China-Singapore FTA chapter on investment does not contain any provisions but confirms that the ASEAN China Investment Agreement will be incorporated into the FTA.

[16] As of May 2011, China has signed ninety-six DTTs, ninety of which have entered into force. A list of these DTTs may be found on the following Web site of the State Administration of Taxation of China, http://www.chinatax.gov.cn/n8136506/n8136593/n8137537/n8687294/8688432.html (last visited Nov. 8, 2011).

[17] SHAN, THE LEGAL FRAMEWORK OF EU-CHINA INVESTMENT RELATIONS, *supra* note 1, pp. 106–08.

vides for general rules on treaty making and ratification[18] but is silent on these treaties' their legal status within the municipal legal system. Numerous laws and regulations do however provide that in case of conflict between international treaty and domestic law, international treaty provisions shall prevail. Thus the General Principles of Civil Law (GPCL) stipulates that:

If an international treaty concluded or acceded to by the PRC contains provisions differing from those in the civil laws of the PRC, the provisions of the international treaty shall apply, unless the provisions are ones on which the PRC has made reservations thereon.[19]

Similar provisions can be found in as many as seventy laws and regulations, ranging from civil law and civil procedures law to administrative procedures law, patent law, wildlife preservation law, and postal administration.[20] The Regulations on Some Issues in Handling Foreign-Related Cases, jointly promulgated in August 1987 by the Ministry of Foreign Affairs, the Supreme People's Court, the Supreme People's Procuratorate, the Ministry of Public Security, Ministry of State Security and the Ministry of Justice, provide that:

When domestic legislation or internal regulations are in conflict with obligations undertaken by China under an international treaty, rules of the international treaty shall be applied. Provisions of domestic legislation shall not be invoked as justification for the refusal to perform the obligations undertaken by China under the international treaty.

These provisions have been cited as evidence that China has already accepted the superiority of treaties over all municipal laws and regulations,[21] but most Chinese international lawyers believe that such provisions are merely an expression of China's willingness to accept the superiority of treaties within the legal hierarchy in specific areas, such as foreign-related civil and commercial, civil procedural, and administrative procedural areas rather than over the entirety of Chinese law.[22] As a result it is unclear whether the overriding effect of international treaties over domestic law can be main-

---

〔18〕 The Chinese Constitution provides that the State Council shall sign treaties and agreements with other countries, while the Standing Committee of the National People's Congress (SCNPC) shall decide to ratify or abolish these treaties and agreements, and the Head of State shall approve or abolish these treaties and agreements in line with the decisions of the SCNPC. The treaty-making procedure is similar to the procedure for domestic legislation. Such similarity suggests that international treaties have the same legal effect as domestic legislation. *See* Articles 89, 67, and 81, the Constitution of the People's Republic of China. *See also* judge TIEYA WANG, INTERNATIONAL LAW 33 (1995) 33; Lingliang Zeng, *Application of WTO Agreements in China and a Revolution of China's Legal Construction*, 6 CHINESE LEGAL SCI. [*Zhongguo Faxue*] 42 (2000).

〔19〕 Article 142, General Principles of Civil Law.

〔20〕 Hanfeng Chen, Weiguo Zhou & Jao Jiang Hao, *The Relationship between International Treaties and Municipal Law and the Practices of China*, 2 TRIBU NE POLITICAL SCI. & L. 122 [*Zhengfa Luntan*] (2000); WANG, *supra* note 19, at 33.

〔21〕 *See, e. g.*, Xiaoyong He, *On the Application of WTO Agreements in Chinese Courts*, 3 J. INT'L TRADE 50 [*Guoji Maoyi* Went] (2001).

〔22〕 *See, e. g.*, WANG, *supra* note 19, at 33; Zeng, *supra* note 19, at 45; Chen et al., *supra* note 21, at 122.

tained in the absence of further constitutional clarification.[23]

Whether the aforementioned investment-related multilateral and bilateral agreements (hereinafter "investment treaties") override domestic law is accordingly debatable. As a matter of fact, all major Chinese laws and regulations on foreign trade and FDI do not mention the status of international treaties vis – à – vis domestic law. Scholarly debates about the application of the WTO agreement in China have suggested that certain issues in the WTO Agreement relating to tariffs, antidumping, market access of financial services, and trade-related investment measures are not subject to the principle of the superiority of international treaties over national law.[24] With regard to the general status of the WTO Agreement within the Chinese legal system, Xiaoyong has argued that the place of WTO agreements should be equal to laws made by the Standing Committee of the National People's Congress (SCNPC) —that is, higher within the overall legal hierarchy than administrative regulations and local regulations but lower than the constitution and basic laws made by the National People's Congress (NPC).[25] Lingliang Zeng has further argued that should conflicts arise between WTO agreements and Laws, the principles of *lex posterior derogate priori* or *lex speciali derogate generalis* ought to apply.[26]

Indeed, under international law and as restated in the Vienna Convention on the Law of Treaties,[27] China may not "invoke the provisions of its internal law as justification for its failure to carry out an international agreement."[28] In other words China must guarantee that the treaties and agreements it concludes or to which it accedes have binding force in China. Furthermore as observed by Judge Tieya Wang, the sheer fact that a series of laws covering a wide range of areas has adopted the principle of superiority of international treaties over domestic law indicates a clear legislative policy trend and has made it possible for the principle to become a general principle of law in China.[29]

However, this does not mean that international treaty provisions can be directly applied before Chinese courts (or have "direct effect" in an EU law term). According to a recent regulation stipulated by the Supreme People's Court (SPC)[30], when adjudicating administrative cases involving international trade, Chinese courts should apply only Chinese national and local laws and regulations.[31] The authority's explanations of the reg-

---

[23] It has been further pointed out that, given that the right to interpret rules on applicable laws rests in the hands of the Standing Committee of the National People's Congress (SCNPC), the general binding effect of the Regulations is debatable. *See* He, *supra* note 22.

[24] Id.

[25] Id. at 50 – 51.

[26] Zeng, *supra* note 19, at 45; *see also* He, *supra* note 22, at. 51.

[27] According to the Chinese Ministry of Foreign Affairs, China deposited the protocol of accession on Sept. 3, 1997, which took effect in China on Oct. 3, 1997.

[28] Article 26, Vienna Convention on the Law of Treaties.

[29] WANG, *supra* note 19, at 33.

[30] The Provisions on Some Issues on the Adjudication of Administrative Cases Concerning International Trade (The Trade Cases Provisions), promulgated by the SPC on Aug. 29, 2002.

[31] Id. Articles 7 and 8.

ulation clarify that this regulation also applies to international investment administrative cases.[32] Such a regulation is said to be compatible with the commitments that China made in the course of WTO accession negotiations.[33] It is therefore clear that, at least from a judicial point of view, international trade and investment agreements to which China is a party must be transformed into Chinese law before they can be applied and implemented. Nonetheless the regulation also requires that the domestic laws and regulations implementing international trade and investment treaties should be interpreted in a manner consistent with international treaties if there should be more than one interpretation of any specific provision of those domestic laws and regulations.[34]

c. Multilateral Agreements

As mentioned above, China is concurrently a member state of the ICSID Convention, MIGA Convention, and WTO Agreement. These multilateral agreements play an increasingly important role in China's international investment activities, in particular given the increasing use of the ICSID and WTO dispute settlement systems.

i. ICSID Convention

The ICSID Convention was signed in 1965 under the auspices of the World Bank. The Convention was signed to remove major impediments to the free international flows of private investment posed by noncommercial risks against the absence of specializ ed international methods for investment dispute settlement. The International Centre for the Settlement of Investment Disputes (ICSID), which was created in accordance with the ICSID Convention, is an autonomous institution with 140 member states now, and is the leading international arbitration institution in investor-state dispute settlement.

China signed the convention in February 1990, and this Convention has been effective in China since February 1993. Before the signature, there were fierce debates over whether China should enter into the ICSID Convention.[35] Chinese traditional skepticism toward international law made China become very cautious on such an international commitment. However, the references to ICSID arbitration were already provided in some Chinese BITs before China entered into the ICSID Convention. Article 6 of the Protocol of the China-Belgian-Luxembourg BIT, for example, provides that international tribunals may use, as a guideline, the arbitral rules of the ICSID mechanism. The MoU (Memorandum of Understanding) of the China-Malaysia BIT (1988) also provides that the contracting parties should hold negotiations on the enlargements of the extent of the investor-state disputes submitted to the ICSID provided both of the contracting parties become members of the ICSID Convention. Nevertheless it was not possible to allow investor-state disputes to be referred to the ICSID for resolution until the convention became applicable to China in 1993. Recent years have witnessed increasing use of the ICSID mechanism by foreign and Chinese investors. So far the first and only case against the

---

[32] Ji Tian & Zhi Lin, *Judicial Review of Administrative Actions Involving International Trade*, PEOPLE'S DAILY (overseas edition), Sept. 7, 2002, at 3.

[33] Id.

[34] Article 9, the Trade Cases Provisions, *supra* note 31.

[35] For details, please see COMMENTS ON ICSID (Chen An ed., 1990).

Chinese government registered at the ICSID was *Ekran Berhad v. China*,[36] which is suspended at the moment. Earlier on a Hong Kong investor successfully made use of the Convention and the China-Peru BIT to sue the Peruvian government at the ICSID.[37] In September 2012, another case initiated by an Insurance Company of China, Ping An Life Insurance Company, against the Republic of Belgium was registered by ICSID.[38]

ii. MIGA Convention

The Convention Establishing the Multilateral Insurance Guaranty Agency (MIGA Convention) was signed in October 1985 and entered into force in 1988. The MIGA created by the MIGA Convention aims to promote the flows of FDI to and among (p. 223) developing countries by providing political risk insurance to foreign private investors against the risks of expropriation, transfer restriction, breach of contract, and war and civil disturbance. As of September 2011, the MIGA has 175 member countries, among which 25 are industrial countries while the rest of the 150 are developing countries.[39]

From the beginning China has taken a positive attitude toward MIGA. It signed and ratified the Convention as early as 1988. China is the fifth-largest shareholder in MIGA, and the largest shareholder among developing states.[40] As a developing state, China is an eligible host state under MIGA Convention. Until now MIGA has issued about forty guarantees for investment in China from 1993. Currently, ten investment projects are under MIGA guarantee with a total limit of liability of about US $ 240 million.[41] Moreover, MIGA is closely cooperating with China to facilitate Chinese ODI. It is reported that in June 2005, MIGA signed a Memorandum of Understanding with China's only policy-related insurance company, China Export & Credit Insurance Corporation (Sinosure) , on cooperation in marketing and coinsurance of Chinese outward investment.[42]

iii. WTO Agreements

Most of the WTO agreements are the result of the General Agreement on Tariff and Trade (GATT) Uruguay Round negotiations, and were signed at the Marrakesh ministerial meeting in April 1994. Developed from the GATT system, the WTO system was mainly intended to cover intentional trade. However, much effort has been made to include the investment issue within the framework of the multilateral trade system because

---

[36] *Ekran Berhad v. People's Republic of China* (ICSID Case No. ARB/11/15) .

[37] *Tz a Yap Shum v. Republic of Peru* (ICSID Case No. ARB/07/6) .

[38] *Ping An Life Insurance Company of China, Limited and Ping An Insurance (Group) Company of China, Limited v. Kingdom of Belgium* (ICSID Case No. ARB/12/29)

[39] MIGA, MIGA Member Countries, *available at* http: //www. miga. org/whoweare/index. cfm? stid = 1789, (last visited Nov. 8, 2011) .

[40] Shan, THE LEGAL FRAMEWORK OF EU-CHINA INVESTMENT RELATIONS, *supra* note 1, at 100.

[41] MIGA, Projects in Asia and the Pacific, *available at* http: //www. miga. org/projects/advsearchresults. cfm? srch = s&hctry = 2r&hregioncode = 2&dispset = 10&sortorder = asc&sortby = hctry&srow = 11&erow = 20 (last visited Nov. 8, 2011) .

[42] Actually this MOU is designed to deepen the cooperation. The former one was signed in Beijing on August 27, 2002. For details, please see Highbeam Business, *Sinosure Signs Cooperation MOU with MIGA*, June 13, 2005, *available at* http: //business. highbeam. com/436093/article – 1G1 – 133188796/sinosure-signs-cooperation-mou-miga (last visited Nov. 8, 2011) .

of the close link between trade and investment.[43] Among various WTO agreements, the Agreement on Trade-Related Investment Measures (the TRIMs Agreement) and the General Agreement on Trade in Service (GATS) are the prominent ones for investment. Some other WTO agreements, for instance, the Agreement on Subsidies and Countervailing Measures (SCM Agreement) and the Agreement on Trade-Related Aspects of Intellectual Property Rights (TRIPS) are also closely related to investment activities.

China was officially accepted as a WTO member on December 1, 2001. In order to comply with various WTO obligations, China made great efforts to reform its FDI regime. After its accession, China has been active in the participation in the Working Group on the Relationship between Trade and Investment, and China has proposed at least two Communications of the potential multilateral framework of investment (MFI).[44]

d. Bilateral Investment Treaties (BITs)

Since the first BIT with Sweden in 1982, China has signed 130 BITs, among which 100 have entered into effect.[45] These BITs cover most of the developed states except the U nited States, and Ireland. Currently China is negotiating BITs with the U nited States.[46] The China-Canada BIT was signed in September 2012, ending a long negotiation spanning eighteen years since 1994. In July 2011, it was reported that China and the European Union (EU) had agreed to negotiate a BIT,[47] which was regarded as signaling a redirection of foreign investment to Europe.[48]

Generally Chinese BIT practice can be divided into two phases. The first phase of BITs was signed with major European states. Admittedly China also signed BITs with other developing states and transition economies, but such BITs were signed more for diplomatic purposes than for investment protection because the Chinese economy was not strong enough to invest abroad.[49] The contents of the BITs signed during that period

---

[43] SHAN, THE LEGAL FRAMEWORK OF EU-CHINA INVESTMENT RELATIONS, *supra* note 1, at 103.

[44] WTO Working Group on the Relationship between Trade and Investment, Communication from China, WT/WGTI/W/159, Apr. 15, 2003; Communication from China, Cuba, India, Kenya, Pakistan and Zimbabwe, WT/WGTI/W/152, Nov. 19, 2002.

[45] Ling Li, *Chinese Bilateral Investment Treaties: Practice and Challenges* (2010) 17 J. INT'L ECON. L. [in Chinese] 1, 2 (2010).

[46] The U. S. – China BIT negotiation may be dated back to as early as the 1980s. However, the first round of negotiation ended with no result because of disputes over the core issues such as national treatment and the investor-state disputes settlement mechanism. The second round of negotiation was launched in 2008, After exchanging their drafts in 2010, China and the United States formally pronounced the launching of the BIT negotiation in the 4th Strategic and Economic Dialogue held in May 2012. For more about China-U. S. BIT negotiations, see Cai Congyan, *China – US BIT Negotiations and the Future of Investment Treaty Regime about China – Canada BIT negotiations—A Grand Bilateral Bargain with Multilateral Implications*(2009) 12 J. INT'L ECON. L. 457 (2009).

[47] CHINADAILY, *China, EU to Seek Bilateral Investment Treaty*, July 14, 2011, *available at* http://www.chinadaily.com.cn/china/2011-07/14/content_12906429.htm (last visited Nov. 8, 2011).

[48] Michael S. Snarr, *Europe Leaps Ahead of United States in Bilateral Investment Treaty Negotiations with China*, July 20, 2011, *available at* http://www.chinaustradelawblog.com/tags/bilateral-investment-treaty/(last visited Nov. 8, 2011).

[49] *See, e. g.*, the Chinese BITs with Romania (1983), Thailand (1985), Sri Lanka (1986), and Poland (1988). Ling Li, Chinese BIT Practice and Challenges, Address before the 2010 Chinese Society of International Economic Law Annual Conference, Oct. 16, Nanjing, China.

were accordingly rather conservative: only disputes concerning the amount of compensation for expropriation were allowed to be submitted for arbitration, while no substantial national treatment was committed.[50] It is therefore clear that the investment policy orientation of Chinese BITs at that time was to promote inward foreign investment rather than protect outward investment.

This policy orientation changed in 1998 when the Chinese government decided to implement a "Going Abroad" strategy focusing on investing abroad. In 2001, the "Going Abroad" strategy for the first time was written in the Outline of the Tenth Five-Year Plan for National Economy and Social Development. Various measures were accordingly implemented.[51] Against this background, a more liberal BIT regime was adopted by China beginning in 1998, which notably included access to (ICSID) arbitration for all investor-state disputes and a substantial national treatment commitment.[52] Clearly the new BIT policy is geared to the promotion and protection of both inward and outward investments.

e. Domestic Laws

The Chinese domestic legal system governing FDI has three distinct features, namely foreign-oriented, enterprise-focused, and unsystematic. It is "foreign-oriented" because it is a system that is generally separated from the legal regime governing domestic investments. Its rules primarily address issues of foreign invested enterprises, and hence are "enterprise-focused." Finally, it is unsystematic because its rules are found in numerous laws and regulations, and there is no general FDI code to hold them together. This long-established and relatively well-developed distinct legal regime for FIEs has its historical and political reasons.[53]

Specifically the FDI legal system consists of a series of national and local laws. Among the national legislation, the constitution is the highest. Since 1982, China amended its constitution to allow for FDI. Article 18 of the constitution stipulates that China "permits foreign enterprises, other foreign economic organiz ations and individual foreigners to invest in China and to enter into various forms of economic cooperation with Chinese enterprises and other Chinese economic organiz ations in accordance with the law of the People's Republic of China", and that the lawful rights and interests of foreign enterprises, other foreign economic organiz ations as well as Chinese-foreign joint ventures "are protected by Chinese law".

Apart from the constitution, China has enacted a number of laws and regulations exclusively applicable to FDI. Among them some are "Laws" (*Falu*), which are enacted by the National People's Congress (NPC) (including its Standing Committee). The most important among them include (1) the Chinese-Foreign Equity joint venture Law (EJVL), which was first adopted in 1979 and has been amended several times afterwards; (2) the Chinese-Foreign Contractual Joint Venture Law (CJVL), which was first

[50] Li, id.

[51] *See* Cai, *supra* note 9.

[52] Details can be found in CHINESE INVESTMENT TREATIES, *supra* note 1, ¶¶ 1.77 – 1.82.

[53] Huang, *supra* note 11, at 202 – 03.

adopted on April 13, 1988 (hereinafter referred to as "CJVL"); (3) the Wholly Foreign Owned Enterprises Law, which was first adopted on April 12, 1986 (hereinafter referred to as "WFEL"); (4) Income Tax for Foreign Invested Enterprises and Foreign Enterprises, which was adopted on April 9, 1991 but was replaced by Enterprise Income Tax (hereinafter referred to as "Enterprise Income Tax Law 2007") in 2007 implementing an equal tax regime on both domestic and foreign invested enterprises. Such laws are considered the basic laws for FDI activities in China.

Apart from these basic laws, there are more general laws adopted by the NPC that apply to FDI in the same way as they do to domestic investments. In other words, they apply to FDI on a nonexclusive basis. They include for instance the Foreign Trade Law 1995, Contract Law 1999, Negotiable Instrument Law 1995, Insurance Law 1995, Guarantee Law 1995, Maritime Law 1992, Customs Law 1987, and so forth. Below these NPC legislations, the Central government (the State Council) promulgates "Administrative Regulations" (*Xingzheng Fagui*), which provide more detailed rules on FDI activities, some of which are in the form of implementing regulations of the basic FIE laws. The most important ones include Implementing Regulations for EJVL 1979, first adopted on September 20, 1983; Implementing Regulation for CJVL 1988, first adopted in August 1995; Implementing Regulation for WFEL 1986, first adopted in October 1990; State Council Provisions for Encouraging Foreign Investment, adopted in October 1986; and Provision on Guidance on the Direction of Foreign Investment, adopted in February 2002.

Still lower on the hierarchy than national legislation are the rules issued by various departments of the State Council, which are named as "Department Rules" (*Bumen Guizhang*) in the Chinese legal system. They mainly include: Interim Provisions on the Takeover of Domestic Enterprises by Foreign Investors (August 2008);[54] Measures for Strategic Investment by Foreign Investors upon Listed Companies (January 2006);[55] Provisions Concerning the Administration of Foreign-Funded Venture Enterprises (January 2003);[56] Interim Provisions on the Merger and Acquisition (M&A) of Domestic Enterprises by Foreign Investors (March 2003, hereinafter referred to as "M&A Provisions 2003");[57] Interim Provisions on Restructuring State-Owned Enterprises with For-

[54] It was co-adopted by the Ministry of Commerce (MOFCOM), State Assets Supervision and Administration Commission of the State Council (SASAC), State Administration of Taxation (SAT), State Administration for Industry and Commerce (SAIC), China Securities Regulatory Commission (CSRC), and State Administration of Foreign Exchange (SAFE).

[55] It was co-adopted by the Ministry of Commerce (MOFCOM), China Securities Regulatory Commission (CSRC), State Taxation Administration (STA), State Administration of Industry and Commerce (SAIC), and State Administration of Foreign Exchange (SAFE).

[56] It was co-promulgated by the Ministry of Foreign Trade and Economic Cooperation (now MOFCOM) JMinistry of Science and Technology (MOST), State Administration for Industry and Commerce (SAIC), State Administration of Taxation (SAT), and State Administration of Foreign Exchange (SAFE).

[57] It was co-promulgated by the Ministry of Foreign Trade and Economic Cooperation (MOFTEC, now MOFCOM), State Administration of Taxation (SAT), State Administration of Industry and Commerce (SAIC), and the State Administration of Foreign Exchange (SAFE).

eign Investment (November 2002);[58] and Tentative Provisions on Guidance on the Direction of Foreign Investment (hereinafter referred to as "Investment Guidance 1995") (June 1995).[59]

According to the Law on Legislation 2000, some local governments and local People's Congresses are authorized to enact laws applicable at the local level, known in the Chinese legal system respectively as "Local Regulations" (*Difang Fagui*) and "Local Governmental Rules" (*Difang Zhengfu Guizhang*).[60] For instance, governments of provinces, Minority Autonomous Areas (MMAs), and Special Economic Zones (SEZ) may enact Local Regulations (*Difang Fagui*). Although these local laws, according to the Law on Legislation 2000, are required to conform to "Law" (*Falu*) by the NPC and "Administrative Regulation" (*Xingzheng Fagui*) by the State Council,[61] in some cases they might actually deviate from these national laws and regulations.[62]

There is therefore a sophisticated and multitiered domestic law regulating foreign investment in China. The types of foreign investment permitted are clearly defined, and once approved would then qualify as a covered investment for the purposes of applicable laws and regulations.

II. Admission

1. Under Multilateral Agreement

Under the scheme of the WTO Agreement, both the TRIMS Agreement and GATS include admission-related provisions. The TRIMS Agreement eliminates some Performance Requirements (PRs), and the GATS provides the admission of investment in services sectors in the attachment of "specific commitments" on "market access."

Article 2 of the TRIMS Agreement requires that members not apply any Trade-Related Investment Measures (TRIMS) that are inconsistent with the principles of "national treatment" and "the general elimination of quantitative restrictions" of GATT. Article 5 also requires each member to notify the Council of Trade in Goods under the Agreement of all their TRIMS within ninety days of the Agreement's entry into force, and eliminate them within a certain period of time. The TRIMS Agreement provides an illustrative list of restrictive measures that "are mandatory or enforceable under domestic law or under administrative rulings or with which it is necessary to comply for advantage" in its annex, and these include the local content requirement, trade-balancing requirement,

---

[58] It was co-promulgated by State Economic and Trade Commission, China (SETC), Ministry of Finance (MOF), State Administration for Industry and Commerce (SAIC), and State Administration of Foreign Exchange (SAFE).

[59] It is jointly issued by the State Planning Commission (SPC), State Economic and Trade Commission (SETC), and Ministry of Foreign Trade and Economic Cooperation (MOFTEC, now MOFCOM).

In addition, there are two special catalogs (i.e., the Catalogue of Encourage Industries for Foreign Investment in the Middle and Western Areas, which is aimed to promote investment in the middle and western areas of China, and the Catalogue of Encouraged High-Tech Products for Foreign Investment).

[60] Law on Legislation 2000, articles 63, 65, 66, 73.

[61] *See, e.g.*, Law on Legislation 2000, article 63.

[62] SHAN, THE LEGAL FRAMEWORK OF EU-CHINA INVESTMENT RELATIONS, *supra* note 1, at 36.

general and trade-balancing importation restriction, forex (foreign exchange) balancing requirement, and exportation restriction.[63] According to the Protocol on the Accession of the People's Republic of China, China not only undertakes to comply with the TRIMS Agreement without any transnational arrangement, but also goes beyond to undertake to abolish the export or performance requirements besides these requirements provided in the illustrative list. Moreover, China modified its FDI laws and regulations to ensure compatibility with the TRIMS Agreement.[64]

GATS is considered to be a set of "Rules for Growth and Investment" or "investor's agreement."[65] According to this agreement, investment is also stipulated because one of the four modes of trade in service in through "commercial presence," and this includes "any type of business or professional establishment" either in the form of a judicial person, or a branch or representative office. The GATS substantive rules may be divided into three parts. The first part provides the "general obligations and disciplines," including MFN, transparency, a number of traditional GATT-type exceptions, competition, business practices, and government procurement. The second part is provided in the "specific commitments," and it establishes the framework for a schedule of commitments from each member; three categories of commitments are included: limitations on market access, limitations on national treatment and additional commitments. The third part includes several articles on "progressive liberalization," and it mainly deals with further negotiations on the various specific commitments to be included in the schedules. The "specific commitments" provided in the second part on market access for admission of investment in the services sectors are of vital importance for investors. China makes "horizontal commitments" and "specific commitments" in the Schedule of Specific Commitments on Services as Part II of the Report of the Working Party on the Accession of China. The horizontal commitments apply to all sectors included in the schedule,[66] whereas the specific commitments apply to the specific sectors or subsectors that they address.[67] As with its compliance with the TRIMS Agreement, China also amended its domestic laws and made numerous new regulations to implement its "specific commitments" on market access in services sectors.[68]

2. Under BITs

General international law does not compel states to admit foreign investment. Terri-

---

〔63〕 *See* Annex: Illustrative List, to the TRIMS Agreement.

〔64〕 SHAN, THE LEGAL FRAMEWORK OF EU-CHINA INVESTMENT RELATIONS, *supra* note 1, at 119-21.

〔65〕 WORLD TRADE ORGANIZATION: TRADING INTO THE FUTURE 21 (2d ed. 1998).

〔66〕 It specifically covers forms of investment, term limitations on land use, and entry and staying of key personnel with a service presence in China. *See* Schedule CLII-The People's Republic of China Part II—Schedule of Specific Commitments on Service, List of Article II MFN Exemptions, WT/ACC/CHN/49/Add. 2, at 2-4.

〔67〕 Specific commitments cover professional services, computing and related services, real estate services, other business services, communication services, construction and related engineering services, distribution, educational services, environmental services, financial services, tourism and travel-related services, and transport services. Several annexes on basic telecommunication, distribution services, and insurance services are also included. Id., at 5-48.

〔68〕 For more, please see SHAN, THE LEGAL FRAMEWORK OF EU-CHINA INVESTMENT RELATIONS, *supra* note 1, at 121-23.

torial sovereignty entitles the governments to decide whether to close the national economy to foreign investors or whether to open it up, fully or with restrictions.[69] In BIT practice, there are basically two different approaches to dealing with admission and establishment. Thus BITs concluded by European countries tend to maintain the traditional sovereignty right of the host state concerning admission. A typical clause provides that each contracting state shall in its territory promote as far as possible investments by investors of the other contracting state and admit such investments in accordance with its legislation. This type of admission clause does not expose the host state to any substantive obligation to revise its domestic laws of admission after the ratification of the BIT.[70] However, the BITs negotiated by the United States, Canada, and Japan, to some extent, impose market access obligations, and these obligations are combined with most-favored-nation (MFN) and national treatment (NT) clauses.[71] The Chinese BITs have generally followed the European prototype leaving control and protection of the admission stage to the discretion of the host country.[72] This is largely due to the fact that BITs were not originally crafted as "market access" treaties but rather to protect investments once they had been made in the host state. Under Chinese BITs, foreign investments are encouraged and admitted in accordance with the laws and regulations of the host state.[73] They also require that, subject to its laws and regulations, the contracting parties must facilitate the obtaining of visas and working permits for personnel engaging in investment-related activities.[74]

3. Under Chinese Law

China still implements a "one-by-one" approval system on foreign direct investment admission, which requires each and every foreign investment project to be approved by relevant authorities before it can be established. Two instruments are most important to ascertain whether a particular investment project is permitted in China, namely (1) the Guidance on the Direction of Foreign Investment (Investment Guidance),[75] and (2) the attached Guiding Catalogue of Industries for Foreign Investment (Guiding Catalogue).[76] The Chinese government first issued the Investment Guidance and the Guiding Catalogue in 1995, which adopted the "negative list" approach. Both regulations are

---

[69] RUDOLF DOLZER & CHRISOPH SCHREUER, PRINCIPLES OF INTERNATIONAL INVESTMENT LAW 79 - 80 (2008).

[70] Id. at 81.

[71] Id.

[72] The U. S. BITs, notably, do impose obligations on investment admission by the combination of the MFN and national treatment clauses. *See* RUDOLF DOLZER & MARGRETE STEVENS, BILATERAL INVESTMENT TREATIES 49 (1995). *See also* UNCTAD, Key Issue I, at 143 - 44.

[73] *See, e. g.*, China-Germany BIT 1983, Article 2; China-Switz erland BIT, Article 2. For details of investment admission under Chinese law, see SHAN, THE LEGAL FRAMEWORK OF EU-CHINA INVESTMENT RELATIONS, *supra* note 1, ch. 4 (Admission and Establishment).

[74] *See, e. g.*, China-Russia BIT, Article 2(3).

[75] Guidance on the Direction of Foreign Investment (Investment Guidance, promulgated by the State Council Decree No. 346 on Feb. 21, 2002 and entered into force on Apr. 1, 2002).

[76] Guiding Catalogue of Industries for Foreign Investment ("Guiding Catalogue," first promulgated in 2002, latest revision took place in 2007 and entered into force on Dec. 1, 2007).

subject to periodic revisions. The Guidance has so far only been revised once, in 2002, soon after China's WTO accession. The Catalogue, however, has been subject to frequent revisions, and the latest version was published in December 2011.

The Guidance and the Catalogue classify all the foreign investment projects (FIPs) into four sub-catalogues: Encouraged, Restricted, Prohibited, and Permitted. The Encouraged, Restricted, and Prohibited industries are specifically defined while all others are classified as Permitted industries by default. FIPs in the Encouraged Catalogue enjoy certain special incentives, such as tax incentives. FIPs in the Restricted Catalogue are, on the contrary, subject to certain restrictions. Some of the restrictions are linked to the modes of investment. Basically there are three modes of foreign investment in China: EJVs (Equity Joint Ventures), CJVs (Contractual Joint Ventures) and WFEs (Wholly Foreign Owned Enterprises). The Catalogue, however, requires some FIPs take the form of either the CJV or EJV, not the WFE. Some FIPs are subject to more stringent conditions requiring "Chinese Partners Equity Control" (CPEC), or "Chinese Partners Relative Equity Control" (CPREC). The former requires that all Chinese partners taken together control 51 percent or more of the total equity of the FIE, whereas the latter only requires all the Chinese partners taken together to have more equity than any one of the foreign investors.[77] Such restrictions also apply to foreign invested merger and acquisition (M&A) activities.[78] In accordance with Article 4 of the 2006 Provisions of Merger and Acquisition of Domestic Enterprises by Foreign Investors, in sectors that require "JV only," or CPEC or CPREC, the enterprises should maintain their status as a JV, CPEC, or CPREC after such M&A takes place. Likewise, in sectors where foreign investments are prohibited, foreign investors are not allowed to conduct M&A activities.

In this connection, it should be noted that, in addition to the general Catalogue, China has also adopted a Catalogue of Encouraged Industries for Foreign Investment in the Middle and Western Areas ("Western Catalogue")[79] and a Catalogue of Encouraged High-Tech Products for Foreign Investment ("High-Tech Catalogue").[80] The High-Tech Catalogue has been integrated into the general Catalogue, though the Western Catalogue continues to take effect.

Recent years have witnessed China's effort to ensure the security of M&A activities by foreign investors. Alongside the antimonopoly review provided in the abovementioned 2006 Provisions on M&A, China adopted the Antimonopoly Law in August 2007. Accom-

---

[77] The Guidance on the Direction of Foreign Investment (Investment Guidance), Article 8.

[78] Article 4, Provisions of Merger and Acquisition of Domestic Enterprises by Foreign Investors (published jointly by MOFCOM and six other ministries in August 2006), which entered into force on Sept. 8, 2006). This regulation was drafted on the basis of the Provisional Regulations on Mergers and Acquisitions of Domestic Enterprises by Foreign Investors promulgated on Mar. 7, 2003. The revised regulation provides detailed guidelines on the requirements and the application process for foreign companies wishing to engage in M&A of China's domestic enterprises.

[79] This Catalogue was first published in June 2000 jointly by the former State Economic and Commerce Commission, the State Planning Commission, and the Ministry of Foreign Trade and Economic Cooperation (MOFTEC). It was revised in July 2004 by the SDRC, and has been in force since Sept. 1, 2004.

[80] This Catalogue was originally promulgated in July 2003 jointly by the MOFCOM and the Ministry of Science and Technology (MOST). The recent revision was issued on Dec. 31, 2006.

panied this law, Provisions on the Criteria for Reporting Concentration of Undertakings was issued by the State Council on August 2008. In February 2011, the State Council issued the Notice of the General Office of the State Council concerning Security Review of Mergers and Acquisitions of Domestic Enterprises by Foreign Investors, which takes a rather broad definition of covered sectors.[81] To implement the Notice, the Ministry of Commerce accordingly issued its Provisions on Implementing a Security Review System for Mergers and Acquisitions of Domestic Enterprises by Foreign Investors. After the entry into force of the above-mentioned Provisions in September 2011, China has formally established its security review system to review M&A activities by foreign investors.[82]

III. General Standards of Treatment

General standards of treatment are often found in China's international investment treaties. Some of them are also stipulated in Chinese legislation. The most common standards include fair and equitable treatment (FET), national treatment (NT), and most-favored-nation treatment (MFN). Together they define the general level of treatment foreign investors and their investment may receive in China.

1. Fair and Equitable Treatment

Fair and Equitable Treatment (FET) has been the most commonly used standard of treatment under BITs, and is the most frequently invoked standard in investment disputes.[83] The content and nature of the FET remains difficult to define despite the fact that it is included in most investment treaties.[84] It is reported by the UNCTAD that at least four approaches were taken in defining the concept of FET.[85]

FET is also the most commonly used substantive protection in Chinese BITs.[86] All three versions of the Model BIT contain this standard, accompanied by the provision of "protection" or "constant protection and security". The effect of the FET may differ according to its location in the BIT. It is believed that it may have only a hortatory effect and not create concrete legal obligations if appears only in the preamble,[87] as it does in the first BIT with Sweden.

Some earlier Chinese BITs incorporate it with both the MFN and national treatment

---

[81] European Union Chamber of Commerce in China, European Chamber Comments on State Council's Notice on Mergers and Acquisitions, Feb. 16, 2011, *available at* http://www.europeanchamber.com.cn/view/media/fullview?cid=8000 (last visited Nov. 8, 2011).

[82] Wenhua Shan, Norah Gallagher & Sheng Zhang, *National Treatment for Foreign Investment in China: A Changing Landscape*, 27(1) ICSID REV. 120 (2012); *see also* Sheng Zhang, *The Energy Charter Treaty: Member or Bystander?*, 13(4) J. WORLD INV. & TRADE 597, 612 (2012).

[83] DOLZER & SCHREU ER, *supra* note 70, at 119.

[84] *See, e.g.*, DOLZER & STEVENS, *supra* note 73, at 58 - 61.

[85] UNCTAD, Fair and Equitable Treatment, UNCTAD Series on issues in international investment agreements, UNCTAD/ITE/IIT/11 (Vol. III), United Nations, New York, and Geneva, 1999, at 1 - 2.

[86] CHINESE INVESTMENT TREATIES, *supra* note 1, at 126. Some Chinese BITs, such as the BITs with Japan, former Czechoslovakia, Romania (both 1983 and 1994 versions) and Belarus, however, do not include FET.

[87] Id., at 127.

standards,[88] or with at least one of the latter standards.[89] An UNCTAD study considers that such provision provided foreign investors with both noncontingent and contingent forms of protection. Under such provision, national and MFN treatment protect each beneficiary of those standards by ensuring equality or nondiscrimination for that beneficiary vis - ὰ - vis other investments.[90] Other Chinese BITs however do not make express reference to a particular body of law or other standards. In such cases, the FET provision should first be considered against other explicit provisions of the treaty, then general international law and/or domestic law of the host state.[91] In applying general/customary international law, it should be taken into account that many principles of general/customary international law emerged and were developed in the context of Europe and among developed states, with little or no participation at all of China in the process.[92] It is therefore unsurprising that there has been only a limited familiarity with and consequently a certain degree of resistance to such principles by China.

Indeed, some earlier writings by eminent Chinese scholars have flatly denied the existence and the applicability of international acprof: oso/minimum standard. Meiz hen Yao, for instance, wrote that the international (acprof: oso/minimum) standard "is essentially an imperialist and colonialist theory, and does not conform to contemporary international law", and therefore "cannot be accepted either in theory or in practice."[93] Accordingly, earlier Chinese BITs have tried as far as possible to avoid any reference to "international law", either as the law for the interpretation of FET, or the applicable law for the settlement of investment disputes. In the rare cases when reference is made, it is substantially qualified by confining such international law to be only those that have been "generally recognised" and that have also been "accepted" by both contracting parties.[94] Acceptance of such principles without qualifications did not appear in Chinese BITs until recent years. Therefore, it can be expected that there will be disagreements between China and its counterparts as to the exact scope and contents of "general/customary international law," even though the concept has been accepted. China's more recent treaties have included express reference to general principles of international law; for example, Article 9(7) China-Cyprus BIT (2001) refers to the "applicable principles of international law".[95] Article 9(5) of the China-Czech Republic BIT (2005) refers to the "general principles of international law," indicating a shift over the

---

[88] *See, e. g.*, the China-Morocco BIT, Art 3(1) and the China-Yemen BIT, Art 2(2).

[89] Art 3 (2) of the China-Poland BIT, for instance, incorporates FET with MFN. The China-Syria BIT is a little interesting because it uses the MFN standard for China and NT standard for Syria when defining the minimum threshold for the FET.

[90] UNCTAD, *supra* note 86, at 15 - 16.

[91] CHINESE INVESTMENT TREATIES, *supra* note 1, at 108 - 10.

[92] For an overview of China's changing attitude to international law, see Junwu Pan, *Chinese Philosophy and International Law*, 1 ASIAN J. INT'L L. 233 (2010).

[93] MEIZHEN YAO, INTERNATIONAL INVESTMENT LAW 334 - 38 [in Chinese] (1987).

[94] *See, e. g.*, China-BLEU BIT 1984, Article 7 of the Protocol.

[95] Other treaties refer to "principles of international law recognised by both Contracting Parties." Article 8 (5) China-Germany BIT (2003).

years in China's approach to the application of these principles.

More states have incorporated qualifications into their treaties in particular relating to this standard of protection. The United States as a direct result of its experience under NAFTA has done so in its Model BIT.[96] More recently China in the BIT with Mexico also incorporated qualifying language similar to that of the NAFTA Free Trade Commission at Article 5(2). It confirms that the fair and equitable treatment does not require anything "in addition to or beyond that which is required by the international law minimum standard of treatment of aliens ..."[97] Thereby it acknowledges the international minimum standard for the fair and equitable treatment provision.

2. National Treatment

National treatment (NT) is the other main standard that underpins the principle of nondiscrimination under investment treaties.[98] The purpose of this clause is to oblige a host state to make no negative differentiation between foreign and national investors.[99] However, the NT clause is not as common as the MFN clause in the BITs. In China's 130 BITs, for example, less than half of them have an NT provision. However, given that all the Chinese BITs contain a MFN clause, the investors and investments covered by a BIT without an NT clause may be entitled to NT by virtue of the MFN clause.[100]

a. Under BITs

Due to the planned economy legacy in China, the National Treatment (NT) standard has not been widely used in Chinese BIT practice. It is worth noting that the OECD Draft Convention 1967 did not contain a NT provision either.[101] China did not accept NT in its BIT practice until 1986 when the China-UK BIT 1986 was signed including a "best endeavours" NT provision. Among the three Model BITs, the first version did not have such a clause at all. The second version contained only a "best endeavors" or soft NT provision, whereas the third subjects the NT to local laws and regulations. However, a qualification in Version III subjecting NT to domestic laws and regulations has been modified by some recent BITs.[102] These BITs removed the "domestic laws and regulations" qualification from the treaty text, but retain a "grandfather provision" or "freez ing clause" in their Protocols applicable to China, allowing it to maintain and modify existing nonconforming measures inconsistent with the NT

---

[96] Article 5(2) U. S. Model BIT (2004).

[97] Article 5(2) China-Mexico BIT (2008). No such qualifying language appears in the investment Chapter 11 of the China-New Zealand FTA (2008) (see Article 143) or in the China-ASEAN Investment Agreement (2009) although both treaties do include what a breach of fair and equitable treatment means. Article 7(2) (a) of the China-ASEAN Investment Agreement confirms that "fair and equitable treatment refers to the obligation of each Party not to deny justice in any legal or administrative proceedings."

[98] CHINESE INVESTMENT TREATIES, *supra* note 1, at 157.

[99] DOLZER & SCHREU ER, *supra* note 70, at 178.

[100] CHINESE INVESTMENT TREATIES, *supra* note 1, at 157.

[101] In the 1960s there was no consistent or "typical" format of NT; *see* K. J. VANDEVELDE, BILATERAL INVESTMENT TREATIES: HISTORY, POLICY AND INTERPRETATION 374 (2010).

[102] *See, e. g.*, Articles 3(1) of the China-Bosnia and Herz egovina BIT 2002, 2(2) of the China-Germany BIT 2003, and 3(2) of the China-Finland BIT 2004.

standard, as long as this will not increase the general level of inconsistency. China also agrees in these BITs to gradually phase out such inconsistent measures.[103] The national treatment provision was one of the stumbling blocks for the failed BIT negotiations between the United States and China in the 1980s.[104] This may not be such an issue in the resumed talks on a BIT with the United States as China, since 2008, has shown its willingness to accept national treatment protections.

b. Under Chinese Law

NT is generally an inherent element of the market economy. This treatment is, nevertheless, unfeasible under the Planned Economy system that used to be implemented in China. During that period, foreign investors in China were accorded "inferior" NT in some respects, while they enjoyed "superior" NT in some other aspects such as tax and other preferential measures. This situation changed when China began to develop its market economy system in the early 1990s. With its economic growth and enormous achievements in the past two decades, China gradually has made efforts to provide a level playing field for both domestic and foreign investors. Affirmative evidence is the enactment of the Enterprise Income Tax Law 2007, which unifies the tax burden between domestic investors and foreign investors. The Property Law adopted in 2007 also provides that "equal legal status and the right to development of all market subjects shall be protected."[105] In 2010, Premier Jiabao Wen also said that China will make institutional agreements to provide a "fair playing ground" for foreign investors and grant them "national treatment."[106]

3. Most-Favored-Nation Treatment

The most-favored-nation (MFN) standard of treatment is the most commonly adopted standard in investment treaties. Under such a standard, the relevant parties undertake to treat each other in a manner that is at least as favorable as they treat third parties. The purpose of this standard therefore is to create a level playing field among different foreign states by prohibiting discrimination on the basis of different foreign nationalities.[107] The MFN treatment in most of the BITs and FTAs is restricted to the post-establishment phase of an investment. However, in the recent BIT practice by the United States and Canada, this treatment is extended to cover the establishment stage of foreign investment.[108]

---

[103] For further details, please see CHINESE INVESTMENT TREATIES, *supra* note 1, ¶¶ 4.65 – 4.90.

[104] *See* T. A. Steinert, *If the BIT Fits: The Proposed Bilateral Investment Treaty between the United States and the People's Republic of China*, 2 J. ASIAN L. 405 (2008).

[105] Property Law 2007, article 3(3).

[106] Xinhua Press, *Wen Promises to Grant Foreign Enterprises "National Treatment"*, Mar. 14, 2010, *available at* http://www.china.org.cn/china/NPC_CPPCC_2010/2010-03/14/content_19606081.htm (last visited Nov. 8, 2011).

[107] CHINESE INVESTMENT TREATIES, *supra* note 1, at 140.

[108] Article 4 "most-favored-nation treatment" of the U. S. Model BIT 2004 provides that "Each Party shall accord to investors of the other Party treatment no less favorable than it accords, in like circumstances, to investors of any non-Party with respect to the establishment, acquisition, expansion, management, conduct, operation, and sale or other disposition of investments in its territory." Article 4 of the Canada Model BIT 2004 has almost the same stipulation with that of the United States.

Under BITs

Unlike the NT standard, MFN treatment is common in all Chinese BITs. This is perhaps not surprising given the long history of the MFN provision in treaties.[109] Some of China's earlier BITs are limited in scope and cover only investments in their MFN clause, without direct reference to "investment-related activities."[110] All three Model BITs, however, have a similar MFN clause covering both investments and investment-related activities. Unlike many other Model BITs, the Chinese BITs do not cover both investors and investments in separate provisions. This may begin to change as the China-Mexico BIT does expressly refer to both protection of investors and investments in Article 4(1) and (2) respectively. It is not clear yet whether this is a new trend for China or a concession made to Mexico as the language is similar to that of Article 1105 of the NAFTA. Chapter 11 of the China-New Zealand FTA (2008) does not have a separate provision in Article 139, nor does the China-ASEAN Investment Agreement (2009) in Article 5. The MFN provision requires foreign investments to be treated no worse than investments made by investors from any other country, thereby preventing discrimination on the ground of nationality.[111]

Most Chinese BITs have not included the "in like circumstances" wording in the MFN provision, yet this is appearing in the more recent treaties signed by China; see for example Article 4 of the China-Mexico BIT (2008). Preadmission activities are covered by MFN clauses in some recent BITs, for example the China-Finland BIT (2004). As is typical in most MFN provisions, there are certain important exceptions. For example, the China-Germany BIT (2003) does not apply to any membership of customs unions, free trade zones, economic unions, or common markets, or to any double taxation agreements.[112] The MFN clause does not expressly refer to dispute resolution, as is made clear, for example, in the UK Model BIT. It is not certain whether the MFN provision in China's current Model BIT could therefore be extended to refer to substantive as well as procedural rights of the treaty. In light of the recent changes made to the dispute resolution provisions in Chinese BITs that now permit resort to ICSID arbitration for investor-state disputes, the exact scope and application of the MFN clause has significance for foreign investors in China.[113]

The tribunal in *Tza Yap Shum v Peru*, the first tribunal dealing with the interpretation of a Chinese BIT, considered the claimant's assertion that it could invoke the MFN in the China-Peru BIT to rely on Article 12 of the Peru-Colombia BIT to extend the

---

[109] For a discussion of the origins of MFN protection, see VANDEVELDE, *supra* note 102, at 352 - 57. The MFN standard has been included in "virtually all investment treaties"; DOLZER & SCHREU ER, *supra* note 70, at 186. *See also* ILC Draft Article on Most-Favoured-Nation Clauses 2(2) Y. B. ILC (1978) and C. MCLACHLAN, L. SHORE & M. WEINIGER, INTERNATIONAL INVESTMENT ARBITRATION: SU BSTANTIVE PRINCIPLES 254 - 57 (2007).

[110] *See, e. g.*, Article 2(2) of the China-Sweden BIT 1982.

[111] Article 3(3) of the current Model BIT.

[112] Article 3(4) of the China-Germany BIT 2003.

[113] For further details see CHINESE INVESTMENT TREATIES, *supra* note 1, at 145 - 57.

scope of its ICSID claim. The tribunal ultimately rejected the claimant's argument, finding that "Article 3 cannot be interpreted so as to extend the jurisdiction of the Centre as a basis for an independent source of competence of the Tribunal."[114] There are other Chinese treaties that also include this provision, thus broadly limiting the application of the MFN clause.[115] This outcome in *Tza Yap Shum* would not necessarily preclude a tribunal from adopting the broader application of the MFN provision in China's treaties that do not contain this additional language. In its more recent treaties, China has been including an express provision excluding the application of the MFN provision to dispute resolution provisions. The China-ASEAN Investment Agreement (2009), for example, provides at Article 5(4) that:

For greater certainty, the obligation in this Article does not encompass a requirement for a Party to extend to investors of another Party dispute resolution procedures other than those set out in this Agreement.[116]

IV. Expropriation and Compensation

Expropriation has long been of central concern to foreign investors because it is the most severe form of interference with property.[117] Hence modern international law does not prevent a state from expropriating property of foreign investors located within its territory.[118] Expropriation per se is not illegal so long as certain requirements are fulfilled. Under customary international law and typical international investment agreements, four principal requirements need to be considered to determine whether expropriation is lawful: public purpose, due process of law, nondiscrimination, and against compensation. In practice, it is difficult to differentiate expropriation from legitimate regulation in the context of international investment law. Its conclusions can be assessed and the quantum debated, but whether an expropriation exists at all will be decided case by case.[119]

---

[114] *Tza Yap Shum v Peru*, ICSID Case No. ARB/07/6 220 (unofficial translation). *See also Plama Consortium Ltd. v Bulgaria*, ICSID Case No. ARB/03/24 Award on Jurisdiction, Feb. 8, 2005, *Berschader v. Russia*, SCC Case No. 080/2004 Award, Apr. 21, 2006 and Telenor Mobile Commc'ns A. S. v. Republic of Hungary ICSID Case No. ARB/04/15.

[115] *See, e. g.*, Article 10(2) China-Greek BIT (1992). *See, e. g.*, a broader application of the MFN provision in Maffez ini v. Spain, ICSID Case No. ARB/97/7 Award on Jurisdiction, Jan. 25, 2000 and Gas Natural SDG SA v. Argentina, ICSID Case No. ARB/03/10, Award on Jurisdiction, June 17, 2005 and commentary in UNCTAD Series II MFN, at 66 – 92.

[116] *See also* Article 139(2) of the China-New Zealand FTA (2008), which also includes an express exclusion of procedural rights in similar terms. It provides: "For greater certainty, the obligation in this Article does not encompass a requirement to extend to investors of the other Party dispute resolution procedures other than those set out in this Chapter."

[117] DOLZER & SCHREU ER, *supra* note 70, at 89. For a general statement on expropriation, please see VANDEVELDE, *supra* note 102, at 271; J. W. SALACU SE, THE LAW OF INVESTMENT TREATIES CH. 12 (2010); A. Reinisch, *Expropriation, in* THE OXFORD HANDBOOK OF INTERNATIONAL INVESTMENT LAW 408 (P. Muchlinski, F. Ortino & C. Schreuer eds., 2008); MCLACHLAN ET AL., *supra* note 110, at 265. *See, e. g.*, Art 4 (1) of the China-Poland BIT (1988).

[118] DOLZER & SCHREU ER, *supra* note 70, at 89.

[119] CHINESE INVESTMENT TREATIES, *supra* note 1, at 253 – 54.

1. Under BITs

Expropriation constitutes perhaps the most controversial part of the Chinese attitude toward foreign investment.[120] All Chinese BITs include a clause regarding expropriation. It is also not surprising that all three of China's Model BITs have such a clause. The expropriation clause in earlier Chinese BITs is rather simple. The China-UK BIT (1986), for example, provides only two paragraphs on the subject. Most BITs stipulate only that each Contracting Party may nationalize, expropriate, or take similar measures against investments of investors of the other Contracting Party, but the BITS lack a definition of expropriation. In particular, indirect expropriation is not explicitly mentioned in the traditional investment treaties. The China-India BIT (2006) for the first time sought to clarify indirect expropriation.[121] A close examination of the definition included in this BIT reveals that it largely resumes the provision included in the 2004 U. S. Model BIT,[122] but only makes some modifications to make this provision more predictable. A definition of indirect expropriation may also be found in the China-New Zealand FTA (2008), along with a list of some circumstances where indirect expropriation most probably occurs.[123]

---

[120] Qingjiang Kong, *Bilateral Investment Treaties: The Chinese Approach and Practice*, 8 ASIAN Y. B. INT'L L. 106, 125 (1998 – 99).

[121] The Protocol of the China-India BIT provides:

With regard to the interpretation of expropriation under Article 5, the Contracting Parties confirm their shared understanding that:

1. A measure of expropriation includes, apart from direct expropriation or nationaliz ation through formal transfer of title or outright seiz ure, a measure or series of measures taken intentionally by a Party to create a situation whereby the investment of an investor may be rendered substantially unproductive and incapable of yielding a return without a formal transfer of title or outright seiz ure.

2. The determination of whether a measure or a series of measures of a Party in a specific situation, constitute measures as outlined in paragraph 1 above requires a case by case, fact based inquiry that considers, among other factors:

i. the economic impact of the measure or a series of measures, although the fact that a measure or series of measures by a Party has an adverse effect on the economic value of an investment, standing alone, does not establish that expropriation or nationaliz ation, has occurred;

ii. the extent to which the measures are discriminatory either in scope or in application with respect to a Party or an investor or an enterprise;

iii. the extent to which the measures or series of measures interfere with distinct, reasonable, investment-backed expectations;

iv. the character and intent of the measures or series of measures, whether they are for bona fide public interest purposes or not and whether there is a reasonable nexus between them and the intention to expropriate.

3. Except in rare circumstances, non-discriminatory regulatory measures adopted by a Contracting Party in pursuit of public interest, including measures pursuant to awards of general application rendered by judicial bodies, do not constitute indirect expropriation or nationaliz ation.

[122] *See* U. S. 2004 BIT Model, Annex B.

[123] Annex 13 "Expropriation" of this FTA provides that:

3. In order to constitute indirect expropriation, the state's deprivation of the investor's property must be:

(a) either severe or for an indefinite period; and (b) disproportionate to the public purpose.

4. A deprivation of property shall be particularly likely to constitute indirect expropriation where it is either:

(a) discriminatory in its effect, either as against the particular investor or against a class of which the investor forms part; or

(b) in breach of the state's prior binding written commitment to the investor, whether by contract, licence, or other legal document.

With respect to the conditions to be satisfied, most Chinese BITs follow the typical international practice and provide the abovementioned four conditions. However, there are some slight changes. For instance, most Chinese BITs refer to "due process of domestic law," but not "due process of law" or "legal order."[124] It is said that the "due process of law" might be interpreted as "due process of international law," which is considered fairer than "due process of domestic law" because there are a few international conventions concerning judicial procedure.[125] It is not clear whether this would result in any significant difference were a case to arise as the domestic law in China relating to expropriation does require that the same conditions be met. Expropriations have occurred in China as evidenced by the takings in the early years after the establishment of the People's Republic of China.[126] Investor disputes and disagreements also arose,[127] but none that have resulted in an international award against China. To date, ICSID has rendered its award in *Tza Yap Shum v. Peru* in July 2011, in which the tribunal ruled that it was not the audit taken by the Peruvian tax authority but the imposition of interim measures that constituted an indirect expropriation.[128] This is the first public award concerning the expropriation clause included in a Chinese BIT.

As to standard of compensation for expropriation, China has traditionally rejected using the Hull rule (i. e., prompt, adequate, and effective compensation). Occasionally Chinese BITs refer to concepts such as "fair and equitable compensation",[129] "fair, effective and non-discriminatory compensation",[130] and "fair and reasonable compensation".[131] In terms of calculating the damages payable, some of China's BITs refer to the "real", "actual", or "market" value. Arbitral tribunals have interpreted these terms to

---

[124] *See, e. g.*, China-Yemen BIT, article 4(1); China-Ukraine BIT, article 4(1).

[125] These international conventions especially include the relevant human rights conventions, for example International Covenant on Civil and Political Rights [General Assembly resolution 2200A (XXI) of Dec. 16, 1966]. According to article 14 of the Convention, all persons shall be equal before the courts and tribunals and everyone shall be entitled to a fair and public hearing by a competent, independent and impartial tribunal established by law. Dolz er and Stevens also suggested that domestic law not be accepted as an ultimate standard of the legality of expropriation because "the lack of reference to domestic law reflects the very purpose of BIT." DOLZER & STEVENS, *supra* note 73, at 106.

[126] P. K. Chew, *Political Risk and U. S. Investment in China: Chimera of Protection and Predictability?*, 34 VA. J. INT'L L. 615, 626 (1994), where it states that "China began a 'slow motion nationaliz ation' program resulting in the virtual termination of all direct foreign investment by 1957." *See generally* SHAN, THE LEGAL FRAMEWORK OF EU-CHINA INVESTMENT RELATIONS, *supra* note 1, at 8; LianLian Lin & John R. Allison, *An Analysis of Expropriation and Nationalization Risk in China*, 19 YALE J. INT'L L. 135 (1994); A. JEROME & H. CHIU, PEOPLE'S CHINA AND INTERNATIONAL LAW 686 (1974).

[127] For example, the *Changchun Huijin* case; *see* CHINESE INVESTMENT TREATIES, *supra* note 1, ch. 8, ¶¶ 168 – 71. *See also* the *Huang Qiao* case mentioned in SHOU SHU ANG LI, THE LEGAL ENVIRONMENT AND RISKS FOR FOREIGN INVESTMENT IN CHINA 115 (2007).

[128] International Arbitration Case Law, Summary of the award of *Tza Yap Shum v. Republic of Peru* (ICSID Case No. ARB/07/6), case report by Kenneth Juan Figueroa, at 5 – 6, available at http://italaw.com/documents/TzaYapShumAwardIACLSummary.pdf (last visited Nov. 8, 2011). The final award on Merits (in Spanish) was rendered on July 7, 2011.

[129] *E. g.*, Article 5(1) of the China-India BIT 2006.

[130] *E. g.*, Article 6(1) of the China-EAU BIT.

[131] *E. g.*, Article 5(1) of the China-Kuwait BIT 1985.

mean the "fair market value" of the investment.

Nevertheless, in practical terms, Chinese BITs do not depart significantly from general BIT practice. First, on the amount of compensation, although they do not refer to "adequate" or "full" compensation, they require it to be "equivalent to the value of the expropriated investments",[132] or calculated on the basis of "market value".[133] Such value shall be determined in accordance with "generally recogniz ed principles of valuation,"[134] such as capital invested, depreciation, capital repatriated, replacement value, and other relevant elements.[135] This standard of compensation is not substantially different from the "adequate" compensation requirement under the "Hull formula". Second, with regard to the time and method of payment, Chinese BITs require compensation to be made "without delay, be effectively realiz able and freely transferable", which is not that different from the "prompt" and "effective" compensation required under the "Hull formula". Although most of China's BITs require expropriation to be carried out in accordance with the host state laws, there are few if any additional limitations under China's law. On balance, it seems that China's position on expropriation and the laws that an international tribunal would apply are not so different as compared to most other states.[136]

It is worth pointing out that some Chinese BITs contain a provision at the end of the expropriation section confirming that the contracting parties agree to provide MFN treatment relating to the expropriation provisions specifically.[137] Article 4(4) of the China-Italy BIT (1985), for instance, provides that:

Nationals or companies of either Contracting Party shall enjoy *most favoured-nation treatment* in the territory of the other Contracting Party in respect of the matters provided for in the present Article.

In *Tza Yap Shum*, the tribunal also took the opportunity to interpret the meaning of "appropriate compensation" included in the China-Peru BIT. In the view of the tribunal, appropriate compensation means the amount needed should place the claimant in the same position he or she would have been without the act of expropriation.[138] Finally, the tribunal rejected the request proposed by the claimant that damages should be based on the discounted cash flow, but adopted the respondent's position that appropriate compensation should be based on the adjusted book value.[139]

2. Under Chinese Law

China was relatively slow in enacting legislation on expropriation and compensation. The Law of Legislation provides that the expropriation of non-state-owned proper-

---

[132] Art 4(2) of the third version of the Chinese Model BIT.

[133] Art 4(2) of the second version of the Chinese Model BIT.

[134] Art 4(2) of the third version of the Chinese Model BIT.

[135] Art 4(2) of the second version of the Chinese Model BIT.

[136] For further details, see CHINESE INVESTMENT TREATIES, *supra* note 1, ch. 7.

[137] Id. at 286.

[138] Figueroa, *supra* note 129, at 8.

[139] Id.

ties must be laid down in the form of "Law" (*Falv*), [140] which means it must be formulated by the National People's Congress or its Standing Committee. [141] When the EJVL was adopted back in 1979, it was silent on expropriation. In the REOFF for offshore exploitation concessions, China included a limited right to expropriate in the event of war or other emergency. [142] It was only over twenty years ago that China first introduced a specific expropriation provision in the WFEL. Article 5 confirms that:

China does not carry out expropriations or nationalisations of WFE's. Under special circumstances, in the public interest, WFEs can be expropriated in accordance with legal procedures and appropriate compensation will be provided.

This provision was followed in subsequent legislation relating to FIEs except the CJVL. [143] It is not very prescriptive other than to confirm the general position against expropriation. It leaves open the question of what "special circumstances" means. Other than that, it contains three of the four conditions commonly found in China's BITs: expropriation must be in the public interest, it must be in accordance with legal procedures, and payment of appropriate compensation is required.

A key concept here is "appropriate compensation, " which again is not further defined in Chinese law. A reasonable interpretation of this standard may be twofold: if there is an applicable BIT to the expropriation, the standard of compensation should be compatible with that stipulated in the BIT; in other cases, "appropriate compensation" requires the amount of compensation to be determined, taking into account "all circumstances" that are "pertinent". [144] As a result, the actual compensation may or may not be equivalent to the "Hull Formula" standard of compensation traditionally asserted by some Western countries. [145] Chinese foreign investment laws do not go any further in defining expropriation, its conditions, or the standard of compensation.

The 2007 Property Law, which applies to both public and private properties, sets forth general principles on the issue of expropriation of collectively owned land, premises of enterprises and individuals, and other immovable properties. [146] The law requires that

---

[140] Article 8, the *Law of Legislation*, passed on Mar. 15, 2000 by the National People's Congress.

[141] Article 7, the *Law of Legislation*.

[142] Article 26, REOFF. The article reads:

In the course of war, threat of war or other emergencies, the Chinese Government has the right to requisition or expropriate a part or all of the oil that the foreign contractors earn or buy.

[143] *See* Article 2(3) EJVL as amended in 1990.

[144] Such circumstances may include, as Judge Aréchaga has once suggested, "Whether the initial investment has been recovered, whether there has been undue enrichment as a result of the colonial situation, whether the profits obtained have been excessive, the contribution of the enterprise to the economic and social development of the country, its respect for labour laws and its investment policies. " *See* Eduardo Jiménez de Aréchaga, *State Responsibility for the Nationalisation of Foreign Owned Property*, 11 N. Y. U. J. INT'L L. & POLITICS 179, 185 (1978).

[145] For instance, the United States voted in favor of UN Res. 1803 and asserted that in its view the "appropriate compensation" therein was equivalent to the "Hull Formula" (namely "prompt, adequate and effective" compensation) it had advocated since 1938. *See* 2 RESTATEMENT (THIRD) OF THE FOREIGN RELATIONS LAW OF THE U NITED STATES § 206 (1986).

[146] According to Article 4, the law protects properties of the state, collectives, individuals, and other proprietors. *See* Property Law of the People's Republic of China (adopted at the 5th session of the Tenth National People's Congress on Mar. 16, 2007). The expropriation clause is located in Article 42.

expropriation of such properties take place for public interests and in accordance with the procedures stipulated under the law.[147] The law points out the general scope of compensation for the expropriation of such properties, without giving any further details as to the specific standards of compensation.[148] Such standards are said to be laid down in other more specific laws and regulations.[149] Reference must therefore be made to applicable BITs to find a clearer answer on the matter of calculation of compensation on expropriation.

V. Transfer

The ability to freely transfer capital and profits is central to the investment protection paradigm as "an investor expects to be able to repatriate his capital and his profits."[150] It is unlikely an investor would risk making an investment if a profit could not be generated and freely transferred without undue exchange control restrictions, taxes, or additional permissions being imposed. The balancing interest is that of the host state in controlling and protecting its currency and foreign reserves.[151]

1. Under BITs

As with the expropriation clause, all the Chinese BITs contain a provision on free transfers. Earlier Chinese BITs provide that free transfer is "subject to its laws and regulations ..."[152] to allow for China's foreign exchange controls. However, some of China's more recent treaties, such as China-Germany BIT (2003), have not referred to this restriction.[153] The Protocol to China-Germany BIT (2003) however contains a clarification with regard to China only that transfer of funds under Article 6(1)(c) is allowed so long as it complies "with the relevant formalities stipulated by the present Chinese laws and regulations relating to exchange control".[154] Besides, all Chinese treaties provide that the transfer shall be "fully convertible"[155] under the "prevailing make rate of exchange".[156]

Some of China's BITs include not just a list of the types of payments that are freely

---

[147] Id., Article 42, ¶ 1.

[148] Id., Article 42, ¶¶ 2 - 4.

[149] XINHU ANET, *Protecting the Rights of the Expropriated, the Property Law Detailed Rules on Expropriation*, Mar. 8, 2007, available at http://news.xinhuanet.com/misc/2007-03/08/content_5819987.htm (last visited Nov. 8, 2011).

[150] F. A. Mann, *British Treaties for the Promotion and Protection of Investments*, 52 BRIT. Y. B. INT'L L. 241, 243 (1981).

[151] K. J. VANDEVELDE, UNITED STATES INVESTMENT TREATIES: POLICY AND PRACTICE 143 (1992). *See also generally* UNCTAD, TRANSFER OF FUNDS (2000) and UNCTAD, INTERNATIONAL INVESTMENT AGREEMENTS: KEY ISSUES 257 (2004); DOLZER & STEVENS, *supra* note 73, at 85.

[152] *See, e. g.*, Art. 6 of the China-Italy BIT (1985).

[153] Article 6(1) Germany BIT (2003). *See also* Article 6 Finland BIT (2004).

[154] German BIT (2003) Protocol Ad Article 5; *see also* Finland BIT (2004) Ad Article 6.

[155] *See, e. g.*, 2003 China BIT Model, Article 6(3).

[156] *See, e. g.*, 2003 China BIT Model, Article 6(3). If a market rate of exchange does exist, the rate of exchange shall correspond to the cross rate obtained from those rates, which would be applied by the IMF; *see, i. e.*, China-Portugal BIT, Article 6, ¶ 2.

transferable, but also specific exclusions where transfer can be prevented or delayed. One of the more detailed transfer provisions is the ASEAN-China Investment Agreement (2009), which permits a state to prevent a transfer if applying in a fair way its laws relating to:

(a) bankruptcy, loss of ability or capacity to make payments, or protection of the right of creditors;

(b) non-fulfilment of the host Party's transfer requirements in respect of trading or dealing in securities, futures, options or derivatives;

(c) non-fulfilment of tax obligations ...[157]

Some recent BITs also include a provision on the "balance of payments." Article 8 (3) of the Mexico BIT, for example, provides:

In case of a serious balance of payments difficulty or of a threat thereof, each Contracting Party may temporarily restrict transfers provided that such a Contracting Party implements measures or a program in accordance with international standards. These restrictions should be imposed on an equitable, non-discriminatory and in good faith basis.[158]

Despite the significance of the transfer provisions, they have still not featured much in the cases after the global economic crisis when restrictions on capital flows would have been expected. However, these provisions did receive some attention since the European Commission successfully took proceedings against Austria, Finland, and Sweden under Article 226 EC Treaty as some of their BITs (predating accession to the EU) were incompatible with the EC Treaty as they did not have an express carve-out for restrictions that might be imposed by the European Council on free movement of capital. The Commission was concerned that the treaties might limit the powers of the EU Council to impose restrictions on the free movement of capital. The infringement proceedings under Article 226 were successful from the Commission's point of view as the European Court of Justice found the countries had failed to comply with their obligation under Article 307. This required the states to take appropriate steps to remove any incompatibilities from preexisting treaties once those states become members of the EU.[159] The ECJ found a breach in all three cases, and the member states must now take appropriate action, either by entering a new treaty or revising the existing ones, to comply with their EU obligations. The ECJ "added that, as follows from the judgment delivered today in Case C – 205/06 *Commission v Austria* [2009] ECR I – 0000, the incompatibilities with the Treaty to which the investment agreements with third countries give rise and which militate against the application of the restrictions on move-

---

[157] Article 10(3)(a) –(h) China-ASEAN Investment Agreement (2009). *See also* Article 8(3) Mexico BIT (2008). *See also* A. Kolo & T. Wälde, *Capital Transfer Restrictions under Modern Investment Treaties*, *in* STANDARDS OF INVESTMENT PROTECTION 205 (A. Reinish ed., 2008).

[158] *See also* Protocol to Slovakia BIT, Article 7(4); Uganda BIT (2004), Article 8(3); Sri Lanka BIT (1986).

[159] *Commission v. Austria* Case C – 205/06, Judgment of Mar. 3, 2009 [2009] ECR I – 01303, *Commission v. Sweden*, Case C – 249/06, Judgment of Mar. 3, 2009 and *Commission v. Republic of Finland*, Case C – 118/07 Judgment of Nov. 19, 2009. *See* E. Denz a, *Bilateral Investment Treaties and EU Rules on Free Transfer: Comment on Commission v Austria, Commission v. Sweden and Commission v. Finland*, 35(2) EU R. L. REV. 263 (2010).

ment of capital and on payments which the Council may adopt under Articles 57(2) EC, 59 EC and 60(1) EC are not limited to the Member State which is the defendant in the present case. "[160] China will now have to engage with these states as their European counterparts seek to comply with these obligations. This may result in a revised version of the transfer provisions in China's next Model BIT.

2. Under Chinese Law

China has taken an increasingly liberal approach toward the issue of monetary transfer. Nowadays the RMB, the Chinese currency, is fully convertible under current (p. 244) transactions,[161] though not under capital transactions. In this respect, foreign exchange transactions on China's capital account require a case-by-case review.

All the basic FIE laws and regulations have general guarantees on the rights of repatriation of investments and returns. Article 11 of the EJVL, for example, provides that foreign joint ventures' net profit and other funds may be remitted abroad in accordance with the foreign exchange regulations and in the currency specified in the joint venture contract. Likewise, article 12 of the EJVL also allows foreign employees of an FIE to remit their salary and other legitimate incomes out of China. Moreover, since 1996 FIEs were allowed to open forex accounts to hold foreign-invested capital and sell from these accounts upon the approval of SAFE. FIEs may also borrow forex directly from domestic and overseas banks provided that they shall register with SAFE afterwards and obtain approval for debt repayment and services. Upon approval by SAFE, FIEs could make payments from their forex accounts or in forex purchased from designated forex banks after liquidation.[162]

Nowadays, there is a strong recommendation that China need to further liberalize monetary transfer rules to fully facilitate FDI activities. In this connection, it is noted that Yi Gang, head of the State Administration of Foreign Exchanges, mentioned in early 2011 that China would progressively make its currency, RMB, convertible on the capital account in the next five years as China pushes for deeper internationalization of the currency.[163]

---

[160] Id. C – 249/06 ¶ 43. See also C – 205/06 ¶¶ 43 and C – 118/07 ¶ 34 where the ECJ noted that its findings in the earlier cases were not limited to the defendant member state. For consideration of the extra-and intra-EU BIT obligations, see Eureko BV v Slovakia, PCA Case No. 2008 – 13, UNCITRAL Award on Jurisdiction, Oct. 23, 2010, ¶¶ 57 – 83.

[161] Official RMB exchange rates were unified with the market rates in 1994, and since then China has adopted a single and managed floating exchange rate regime based on market. China formally undertook the IMF obligations in 1996, thus making RMB fully convertible on current accounts. On Jan. 1, 1994, official RMB exchange rates were unified with the market rates and thereby China had adopted a single and managed floating exchange rate regime based on supply and demand. On Dec. 1, 1996, China formally accepted the obligations of Article VIII of the IMF's Articles of Agreement, making RMB fully convertible on current accounts. *See* Congyan Cai. *Jurisdictional Report of China*, *in* THE LEGAL PROTECTION OF FOREIGN INVESTMENT: A COMPARATIVE STUDY 243 – 86. (Wenhua Shan ed., 2005).

[162] WTO, Report of the Working Party on the Accession of China, WT/ACC/CHN/49, Oct. 1, 2001, ¶ 33.

[163] *See* CHINA DAILY, *China to Make RMB Convertible on Capital Account in* 5 *Years*, Jan. 19, 2011, available at http://www.chinadaily.com.cn/biz china/2011 – 01/19/content_11878739.htm (last visited Nov. 8, 2011).

VI. Settlement of Disputes

The greatest breakthrough in the area of international investment law is the creation of an investor-state dispute settlement mechanism enabling foreign investors to sue the host government. Without a fair and effective dispute settlement mechanism, the substantive provisions of a BIT would be meaningless.[164]

1. Under BITs

The investor-state dispute resolution provisions in China's BITs have generated much debate and speculation over the years. This is largely due to China's initial reluctance to accept international arbitration as a means of settling investment disputes. Earlier Chinese BITs, especially those signed before 1998, provide for "disputes involving the amount of compensation for expropriation" to be referred to ad hoc arbitration comprised of a three-member tribunal.[165] Originally it was assumed that this wording would preclude a tribunal from deciding whether an actual expropriation had occurred and limit its remit to questions of quantum only.[166]

Yet recent jurisprudence indicates that this is not the case. In the *Tza Yap Shum* matter the Chinese investor persuaded the tribunal, relying on earlier cases, that this same wording in the Peru BIT did allow it not only to "determine the amount but also any other issues normally inherent to an expropriation, including whether the property was actually expropriated in accordance with the BIT provisions and requirements, as well as the determination of the amount of compensation due ..."[167] The tribunal felt to decide otherwise would render obsolete the last sentence of Article 8(3)—the fork-in-the-road provision confirming that if a party refers a dispute to the national courts, the arbitration provision does not apply. Presumably the tribunal felt that if the investor had referred the dispute on whether an expropriation had in fact occurred to the local courts of China, but not the question of quantum, this would activate the final sentence of Article 3 and exclude arbitration altogether. Another possible interpretation is that the final sentence relates only to the question of quantum; if the claimant had argued the damages before the national courts, it could not do so before an investment tribunal at a later time.

---

[164] Steinert, *supra* note 105, at 405.

[165] *See, e. g.*, Article 8(3) Mongolia BIT. Other examples include: Article 8(3) Argentina BIT (1992); Article IX(3) Indonesia BIT (1994); Article 13(3) Sri Lanka BIT (1986); Article 8(3) Lebanon BIT (1996); Article 9(3) Syria BIT (1996), Article 9(3) Cambodia BIT (1996).

[166] Kong, *supra* note 121, at 130. *See also* M. C. E. Heymann, *International Law and the Settlement of Investment Disputes relating to China*, 11 J. INT'L ECON. L. 507, 515 (2008); T. G. Nielson, *Investor State Arbitration and Investment Treaty Protection: The South-East Asian Angle*, 28 Australian Res. & Energy L, J. 213 (2009). *See generally* on investor-state arbitration VANDEVELDE, *supra* note 102, ch. 15; DOLZER & SCHREU ER, *supra* note 70, chs. X and C; MCLACHLAN ET AL., *supra* note 110, ch. 3.

[167] Tza Yap Shum v Peru ICSID Case No. ARB/07/6, Award on Jurisdiction, June 19, 2009 ¶ 188 (unofficial translation). *See also* decision of the English Court in European Media Ventures v Czech Republic [2007] EWHC 2851 upholding a similar finding of the tribunal that it did have jurisdiction to decide on expropriation even though the BIT referred to disputes "concerning compensation."

Some BITs also provide that "other disputes shall be submitted to ICSID on agreement between the parties."[168] This additional wording relating to "other disputes" (meaning other than involving compensation) appears in a significant number of China's treaties, and also appeared in the China-Peru BIT in the *Tza Yap Shum* case. The tribunal in that matter rejected the submission of the claimant that he could rely on the MFN provision to extend the scope of the arbitration clause by invoking Article 12 of the Peru-Columbia BIT. The claimant wanted the tribunal to have jurisdiction to consider other breaches of the treaty, for example fair and equitable treatment and full protection. The tribunal noted that the application of the MFN is one of the "*quaestiones vexatae*" of investment arbitration. After reviewing the numerous conflicting awards on this issue, the tribunal concluded that Article 8(3) of the China-Peru BIT was restricted in nature. The parties had agreed to two things; that expropriate matters would be arbitrated, and that other disputes could—if agreed upon—be referred to ICSID. In accordance with Article 31 of the Vienna Convention, the tribunal held the correct interpretation was that this specific agreement should prevail over the more general language in the MFN clause. The tribunal "does not accept the arguments presented by the Claimant relating to the interpretation of the MFN clause in the BIT (Article 3)." The tribunal "finds that Article 3 can not be interpreted to extend the jurisdiction of the Centre or as an independent source of competence for the Tribunal."[169] It is not certain given the existing divergent jurisprudence whether a future tribunal would also refuse to apply the MFN in the face of the additional wording on future disputes.

It is only in the last decade that China has included a broad or expansive investor state dispute resolution option. These third-generation BITs cover "all disputes" or all "disputes relating to an investment" and are consistent with global BIT practice. This shift in modern BITs only really started in earnest in the early 1980s. The Protocol to China's first BIT with Sweden refers to ICSID and the possibility of reaching agreement on mandatory arbitration in the future. The Finland BIT (2004) is an example of this new wording in the current Model BIT providing at Article 9(1) "Any dispute arising out of an investment between one Contracting Party and an investor of the other Contracting ..." can, at the investor's choice, be referred to international arbitration (ICSID or ad hoc). Other treaties such as the Uganda BIT (2004) provides for "Any legal dispute ... in connection with an investment"[170] The Mexico BIT has one of the most detailed investor-state dispute resolution provision in Section III, which is based more on NAFTA Chapter 11 than the China Model BIT. Article 13 covers any alleged breach of obligation

---

[168] *See, e. g.*, Art 11(2) of the China-Japan BIT (1988).

[169] Tza Yap Shum v Peru, Award on Jurisdiction, ¶ 220: the tribunal specifically endorses the approach in Plama v. Bulgaria. ICSID Case No. ARB/03/24, noting that in *Plama* "they actually took into account the warnings set out in paragraph 63 of the Award in *Maffezini*." [unofficial translation] *See generally* P. J. Turner & M. Mangan, *China's Investment Treaties: Substantive and Procedural Rights*, ASIAN COUNSEL (May 2007) and Y. Radi, *The Application of the Most-Favoured-Nation Clause to the Dispute Settlement Provisions of Bilateral Investment Treaties: Domesticating the "Trojan Horse"*, 18 EU R. J. INT' LAW 757 (2007).

[170] Article 8(1); *see also* Article 10(1) Jordan BIT (2005). There are now close to forty BITs that China has signed that contain these expansive dispute resolution provisions.

in Chapter II, the substantive protections.[171] These third-generation treaties do as does the Model BIT include a provision, either in the clause itself or in a Protocol, that the investor "shall go through the domestic administrative review procedures as specified by the laws and regulations of the disputing Contracting Party before the submission to international arbitration ..."[172] There is often a time limit within which to pursue this domestic administrative review; for example, no more than three months in the Finland BIT and four months in the Mexico version. A tribunal might be persuaded to forgo this requirement as in *Maffezini*, although this is not certain.[173] There is also a question of whether a future tribunal would apply the MFN clause to extend the scope of a restrictive Chinese BIT to the broader one in the third-generation treaties. Clearly this could only happen now if there was no specific wording in the principle treaty investment-dispute clause relating to "other disputes" as in *Tza Yap Shum*.

China became a contracting state of the ICSID Convention in 1993, and so it is not surprising the reference in the first two Model BITs was to ad hoc arbitration. They both do, however refer to ICSID as the appointing authority if the tribunal has not been constituted within four months from the notice of application. China when it ratified the ICSID Convention filed a notification under Article 25(4) of the Convention confirming that:

Pursuant to Article 25(4) of the Convention, the Chinese Government would only consider submitting to the jurisdiction of the International Centre for Settlement of Investment Disputes disputes over compensation resulting from expropriation and nationaliz ation.[174]

This notification does not amount to a consent (or lack thereof) for the purposes of ICSID jurisdiction, nor does it prevent a state from consenting to ICSID arbitration subsequent to the notification. China did so for the first time when it consented to arbitrate all disputes in its BIT with Barbados in 1998. The significance now of the notification made by China appears to have limited if any impact although it has been suggested that if a consent to arbitrate was unclear, it might be "interpreted by reference to a prior notification of classes of disputes in respect of which the host State has expressed its intentions."[175] There would be a presumption that the state intended to stay within the confines of the notification. China has also entered into BITs that provide for ICSID Additional Facility, for example with India, not yet a signatory to the ICSID Convention. There are also references to the UNCITRAL Arbitration Rules and the Stockholm Cham-

---

[171] Article 13 (1) Mexico BIT(2008); *see also* Article 14(4) China-ASEAN Investment Agreement (2009).

[172] Annex C to Article 13(5) Mexico BIT (2008). Other examples include the Protocol to the Finland and Germany BITs.

[173] In *Maffez ini v Spain*, ICSID Case No. ARB/97/7, Award on Jurisdiction, Oct. 28, 1999, the tribunal applied the MFN to permit the claimant to proceed directly to international arbitration without having to attempt to resolve the dispute in the local courts for eighteen months as stipulated in the basic treaty. In contrast, the opposite finding was made in *Wintershall v Argentina*, ICSID Case No. ARB/04/14, Award, Dec. 8, 2009.

[174] Notification of China, Jan. 7 January, 1993, available at www. worldbank. org/icsid (last visited Nov. 8, 2011).

[175] C. H. SCHREU ER, LORETTA MALINTOPPI, AU GU ST REINISCH, & ANTHONY SINCLAIR, THE ICSID CONVENTION: A COMMENTARY (2009) (discussion re: Article 25).

ber of Commerce as an appointing authority.[176]

On May 24, 2011, ICSID registered a case initiated by a Malaysian investor against China. This case, *Ekran Berhad v. People's Republic of China* (ICSID Case No. ARB/11/15) is the first one ever filed before the ICSID against the Chinese government. The dispute concerns rights to a leasehold over land in the Province of Hainan held by a subsidiary of Erkan Berhad, Sino Malaysia Art & Culture, and revoked by the local authorities in Hainan. However, according to ICSID, the proceeding was suspended pursuant to the parties' agreement on July 22, 2011 even before the constitution of the tribunal.[177]

2. Under Chinese Law

Chinese law regarding dispute settlement, particularly its administrative procedures, plays a very important role in settling investment disputes.[178] Normally Chinese BITs may require an administrative review process before a party may resort to international arbitration.[179] In China, state-investor disputes are normally handled through administrative channels, namely "administrative review" (*Xingzheng Fuyi*) and/or "administrative litigation" (*Xingzheng Susong*).[180]

The most relevant procedure to Chinese BIT is the "administrative review" because it is imposed in almost every new-generation BIT as the only local control over investor-state disputes. It is a hierarchical supervision mechanism within the administrative system permitting administrative organs of a higher level to review any specific administrative acts of lower-level organs for legality and propriety, upon request by any citizens, legal persons, and other organiz ations. The Chinese NPC adopted the Administrative Review Law of the People's Republic of China ("Administrative Review Law of 1999") on April 29, 1999, which replaced the Administrative Review Regulations of 1990.

Article 6 of the Administrative Review Law lists a series of "specific administrative acts" under review. Moreover, administrative review may also be conducted against "provisions" (guiding) adopted by lower-level administrative authorities, if they are the basis of a specific administrative act in question. These provisions are provided in Article 7. In this respect, it can be seen that the scope of review is relatively wide, covering not only "specific administrative acts", but also "abstract administrative acts". Again, the threshold for review is also relatively high, as it not only reviews "illegal" acts but also "improper" ones. The time limit for administrative review is normally sixty days, with ninety days as the maximum time allowed. This is probably the ground for China's insistence on the three-month, or ninety-day, maximum administrative review time limit in its BITs. An ad-

---

[176] *See* BITs with Cuba, Kuwait, Norway (Protocol), and Austria (Protocol).

[177] Available at http://icsid.worldbank.org/ICSID/FrontServlet (last visited Nov. 8, 2011).

[178] SHAN, THE LEGAL FRAMEWORK OF EU-CHINA INVESTMENT RELATIONS, *supra* note 1, at 223.

[179] For instance, Article 6 of the Protocol of the China-Germany BIT (2003) provides: With respect to investments in the People's Republic of China an investor of the Federal Republic of Germany may submit a dispute for arbitration under the following conditions only: (a) the investor has referred the issue to an administrative review procedure according to Chinese law, (b) the dispute still exists three months after he has brought the issue to the review procedure, and (c) in case the issue has been brought to a Chinese court, it can be withdrawn by the investor according to Chinese law. Similar content can also be found in the Protocol of the China/Finland BIT (2005).

[180] CHINESE INVESTMENT TREATIES, *supra* note 1, at 367.

ministrative review decision, however, may be challenged by bringing an administrative lawsuit to a Chinese court, unless otherwise stipulated by the law. Further details with regard to the implementation of the law are contained in the Implementing Regulations for the Administrative Review Law adopted in 2007.[181]

On the other hand, the administrative litigation procedure will also apply because Chinese courts are the default remedy for most investor-state disputes in China under Chinese BITs. Unlike administrative review, which is essentially an internal supervision mechanism conducted within the administrative system, an administrative process, or remedy, administrative litigation is conducted within the general judicial system and is therefore part of the formal judicial process. Since 1989, the promulgation of the Administrative Procedures Law (APL) has made it possible for all citizens, juridical persons, and other organiz ations to bring an action before a court against "specific administrative acts" by administrative authorities. Such acts are rather broadly defined in Article 11 to cover all "specific" regulatory activities by the government authorities on foreign investment. However, *abstract administrative acts* such as administrative regulations, rules, or decisions and orders with general binding force formulated by administrative organs, including provisions that may be reviewed under the administrative review process, are not subject to administrative proceedings.[182]

Many Chinese BITs have a fork-in-the-road provision requiring a choice between domestic court and international arbitration. Some BITs, such as the China-Germany BIT (2003), allow for further flexibility by permitting submission to international arbitration after a case has been submitted to a local court, provided that the investor withdraws the case from such court procedures before submitting it to international arbitration. However, if the local court procedures have been completed and a final ruling has been made, the investor cannot resort to international arbitration.[183]

3. Calvo in China?

The Calvo Doctrine is a foreign policy doctrine that arose from the idea of Carlos Calvo, an Argentine jurist. The essence of this doctrine is "anti-super-national-treatment," which focuses on the opposition and rejection of any discriminatory treatment by Western powers against weak, developing host states and their nationals, as compared to the treatment those Western powers accord each other and demand for their citizens in these host states.[184] The "anti-super-national-treatment" approach is reified in the widely used "Calvo Clauses" in domestic constitutions and laws, and in bilateral and regional treaties.[185] In context, such clauses often highlight that the treatment of foreigners and foreign investors should be "no more favorable than" that accorded to nationals and national investors.[186] The Calvo Doctrine was enthusiastically received by Latin American

---

[181] CHINESE INVESTMENT TREATIES, *supra* note 1, at 367 - 69.

[182] Id. at 369 - 70.

[183] Id. at 391.

[184] Wenhua Shan, *Is Calvo Dead?*, 55 AM. J. COMP. L. 123, 124 (2007).

[185] Id. at 125.

[186] Id.

states, and these states refer to the Calvo Clause to enforce this doctrine as a countermeasure to the rejection of the doctrine by Western powers.[187]

Though first embraced by Latin American states, after World War II the influence of this doctrine has gone well beyond them to be accepted by other states, such as a number of new ones that have emerged in Asia and Africa as the result of the decoloniz ation process. A Calvo Clause was also included in the United Nations General Assembly resolutions when the New International Economic Order movement reached its summit.[188] In the 1990s, the "imminent death" of this doctrine was declared due to changing attitudes in Latin American states toward foreign investment as witnessed in their international and domestic lawmaking practice.[189] However, although Calvo is not completely dead, it has largely been deactivated. It is still alive respecting rejection of diplomatic protection, yet in others ways it is greatly transformed.[190]

As with the Latin American States, China traditionally accepted the Calvo Doctrine. China was also actively participated in establishing the "New International Economic Order" that emphasiz ed state sovereignty over natural resources and denied any substantial protection of foreign investment under international law.[191] During the period before 1979, China's foreign policy was characteriz ed by the "Five Principles of Peaceful Co-Existence," a set of principles similar to the Calvo Doctrine.[192] "Five Principles of Peaceful Co-Existence" consist of "mutual respect for each other's sovereignty and territorial integrity, mutual non-aggression, non-interference in each other's internal affairs, equality and mutual benefit and peaceful coexistence."[193] In the sphere of foreign investment, these five principles were specified to have the following requirements: (1) states have the sovereign right to control the entry of FDI and to regulate the activities of foreign investors in their territory; (2) the right of the state to nationaliz e foreign property is an inherent attribute of national territorial sovereignty, and the exercise of this fundamental right is not subject to any precondition such as: public interest, due process of law, nondiscrimination, and against compensation; (3) state contracts or concessions are to be observed, subject to the sovereign power of host countries to mandate renegotiation, revision, or even unilateral modification on the basis of changed circumstances or public interests.[194]

However, China's attitude toward FDI has been changed fundamentally since its open-up policy. China's notion of sovereignty changed with its attempt to attract FDI. Nowadays, a more liberal approach is taken by China in negotiating BITs, evidenced by the inclusion of national treatment and full access to ICSID arbitration. Its domestic laws

---

[187] Wenhua Shan, *Is Calvo Dead?*, 55 AM. J. COMP. L. 123, 124 (2007), at 127.

[188] Id. at 129.

[189] Denise Manning-Cabrol, *The Imminent Death of the Calvo Clause and the Rebirth of the Calvo Principle: Equality of Foreign and National Investors*, 26 L. & POL'Y INT'L BU S. 1169 (1995).

[190] For more, please see Shan, *supra* note 185.

[191] Schill, *supra* note 11, at 78.

[192] Id.

[193] Kong, *supra* note 121, at 109.

[194] Id. *See also* Schill, *supra* note 11, at 78.

and regulations have also changed, especially after its access to the WTO. In general, the Calvo Doctrine and the Calvo Clause are derogated in China, yet they still have some place in China's FDI legal framework.

In China's domestic law, there is still a "Calvo Clause" in its law dealing with the foreign-related contracts since 1989, and as it stands today. It is provided that all Sino-foreign equity joint venture contracts, Sino-foreign cooperative joint venture contracts, and Sino-foreign contacts for the joint exploration and development of natural resources shall be governed by Chinese law and subject to the exclusive jurisdiction of Chinese courts.[195]

When it comes to Chinese BIT practice, the situation is a little complicated. According to Schreuer, the exhaustion of local remedies is taken as Calvo's children and grandchildren.[196] As mentioned above, among Chinese investment treaties allowing all invest disputes to be submitted to international arbitration, a few investment treaties authoriz e China as host country can demand that foreign investors seek a local remedy (e. g., administrative review procedure) before resorting to international arbitration. On the other hand, some Chinese BITs with the inclusion of full access to international arbitration have a "fork-in-the road" clause, which aims to preclude an investor from commencing other legal remedies having been chosen. Article 9(3) of the Sino-Russia BIT, for instance, provides:

Once the investor has submitted the dispute to the competent court of the concerned Contracting Party or to the Centre or to the ad hoc arbitration court, the choice of one of the three procedures shall be final.

Therefore, if an investor decides to resort to legal remedies in China, he or she may not be able to submit an investment dispute to international arbitration.[197]

VII. Conclusion

China's success in attracting FDI is undisputed and unprecedented, partly owing to its efforts in strengthening the legal framework, both international and domestic. Recent years have witnessed some significant changes in both China's domestic FDI law and BITs practice. In the sphere of domestic law, a unified and balanced approach is taking shape. The enactment of the Enterprise Tax Law 2007 and the application of the company law system to FIEs[198] illustrate a move toward convergence of the long-established

---

[195] Article 126 of the Contract Law of the People's Republic of China provides that such contracts should be governed only by Chinese law, and Article 246 of the Civil Procedure Law of the People's Republic of China states that any disputes arising out of such contracts should be subject only to the jurisdiction of Chinese courts.

[196] Christoph Schreuer, *Calvo's Grandchildren: The Return of Local Remedies in Investment Arbitration*, 1 L. & PRAC. INT'L CTS. & TRIBS. 1, 3 (2005).

[197] It should be admitted that the "fork-in-the road" clause appears not to prevent investors from resorting to international arbitration even though the investor has chosen national court proceeding. *See*, *e. g.*, Alex Genin, Eastern Credit Limited, Inc. and A. S. Baltoil v. The Republic of Estonia, ICSID Case No. ARB/99/2.

[198] Article 218 of the Company Law of the People's Republic of China (revised in 2005) provides that "The limited liability companies and joint stock limited companies invested by foreign investors shall be governed by the present Law. Where there are otherwise different provisions in any law regarding foreign investment, such provisions shall prevail."

dual systems of enterprise regulation. However, the establishment of the security review system further confirms that China is moving forward from its single focus on the amount of FDI to emphasiz ing both the quantity and the quality of FDI, trying to achieve a sustainable development of the economy. On the international stage, China is beginning to challenge existing international investment norms.[199] Its role has been developing from a participant to a leader in the world economy in general, and in international investment in particular.[200]

Yet China needs to do more to be fully prepared for the change in its role. On the one hand, the domestic legal framework relating to FDI is not sufficient to be effective.[201] On the other hand, China's success in attracting FDI is likely to result in the proliferation of FDI disputes between international investors and local governments, in addition to disputes involving China's central government. Given the magnitude of the FDI and the scale of investments in China, the ability to effectively deal with these disputes will not only affect China's ability to keep attracting and regulating FDI, but will also impact on the growing interconnection between the Chinese and the global economies. The future of China's investment program will depend not only on continuing adjustment of the notions of sovereignty and its actual exercise, but also on whether and how China may continue to cede control over aspects of its social and economic programs in order to continue attracting FDI in an increasingly interdependent world.

---

[199] Rosen & Hanemann, *supra* note 10.

[200] Guiguo Wang, *China's Practice in International Investment Law: From Participation to Leadership in the World Economy*, 34 YALE J. INT'L L. 575 (2009).

[201] Shan & Zhang, *supra* note 13.

Chinese Model BITs*

I. Introduction

China is one of the fastest growing economies in the world.[1] It is also the most populous country in the world. This combination has made it an attractive location for foreign investors resulting in a shift in the international financial markets to the East. China is now referred to as 'manufacturer to the world' which has resulted in an increased interconnectedness in the global economy.[2] This change was recent and rapid. China presents an unprecedented success story in attracting foreign direct investment ('FDI') inflows over the last three decades and is becoming a major player in exporting capital to the rest of the world. As China develops, the Chinese model bilateral investment treaty ('BIT') has witnessed several changes of focus and content, yet still displays certain unique characteristics.

This chapter intends to provide an article-by-article commentary on the Chinese Model BIT with extensive reference to actual BIT and arbitration practice. To facilitate better understanding of the content of the current model and BITs adopted, it also details and discusses the unique evolution of China's investment policies, from a closed economy to a more open one and now as one of the larger outward direct investment nations. This dramatic shift has changed the focus and interests of China as she now needs to protect her own investors abroad. This chapter will also review the overall BIT and free trade agreement ('FTA') activities and the internal procedures for treaty negotiation.

II. Chinese Investment Policy

A. Policy-orientation: from Capital-import to both Capital-import and Capital-export

China is now the second largest economy in the world. She is also the second largest

---

* In Chester Brown et al. (eds), *Commentaries on Selected Model Investment Treaties*, Chapter 4, Oxford University Press, 2013.

[1] UN Secretary-General Ban Ki-moon's remarks at Nanjing University, Nanjing, China, 31 October 2010, 'Hailing China as World's Fastest Growing Economy, Secretary-General Urges Chinese Government to Put Greater Emphasis on Social Equity, Environmental Sustainability'. He also noted that 'China is on the cusp between the developing and developed worlds': UN SG/SM/13219.

[2] P Marsh, 'China noses ahead as top goods producer', *Financial Times* (13 March 2011), noting that this puts China back 'to the position it occupied in the early 19th century and ending the US's 110 – year run as the largest goods producer'.

recipient of foreign investment and the sixth in terms of outward direct investment.[3] It is therefore unsurprising that the current Chinese investment policy-orientation is to promote both capital imports and capital exports. However, this was not the case until 1998, when China decided to 'go abroad' encouraging her companies to invest abroad. The policy has been maintained despite the economic crisis, and further large scale investment is expected, for example, in the energy industry as China has now overtaken the United States as the world's largest energy consumer.[4]

When China first adopted the 'open-door' policy in the late 1970s, attracting foreign direct investment ('FDI') was among the top priorities. For this purpose, the Chinese Government promulgated numerous FDI laws whilst entering into bilateral investment treaties ('BITs'). Naturally these earlier BITs mainly targeted industrialized States, or capital-exporting States.[5] Thus the first BIT was signed in 1982 with Sweden, followed by BITs with other major European States. Admittedly China also signed BITs with other developing States and transition economies, but such BITs were signed more for diplomatic purposes than for investment protection since the Chinese economy was not strong enough to invest abroad.[6] The contents of the BITs signed during that period were accordingly rather conservative: only disputes concerning the amount of compensation for expropriation were allowed to be submitted for arbitration, whilst no substantive national treatment obligation was included.[7] It is therefore clear that the investment policy orientation of Chinese BITs at that time was to promote inward foreign investment, rather than protect outward investment.

This policy orientation changed in 1998 when the Chinese Government decided to implement a 'Going Abroad' strategy focussing on investing abroad. In 2001, the 'Going Abroad' strategy for the first time was written in the Outline of the Tenth Five-Year Plan for National Economy and Social Development. Various measures were accordingly

---

[3] UNCTAD, *World Investment Report* 2011, available at < www.unctad.org > (last accessed 12 November 2012). China's ranking as an ODI State is set to rise in the coming years with the increase in consumer demand of a growing middle class. China has been a net importer of oil, gas, and coal for several years and is investing around the world to secure energy supplies to meet this demand in Africa, South America, and Asia. See 'China Tops US in Energy Use', *Wall Street Journal* (18 July 2010). Recently, Petrochina purchased a 50 per cent stake from EnCana in natural gas deposits in Western Canada: *Financial Times* (10 February 2011).

[4] World Energy Outlook report of the International Energy Agency, 9 November 2010. *See also* D H Rosen and T Hanemann, *China's Changing Outbound Foreign Direct Investment Profile: Drivers and Policy Implications* (Peterson Institute for International Economics, 2009). China is not a State party to the Energy Charter Treaty (a multilateral treaty covering all energy related investments), but it does have observer status see < www.encharter.org > (last accessed 27 December 2011).

[5] N Gallagher and W Shan, *Chinese Investment Treaties: Policies and Practice* (Oxford University Press, 2009), pp. 35 – 6.

[6] See eg, China-Romania BIT (1983), China-Thailand (1985), China-Sri Lanka (1986) and China-Poland (1988). L Li, *Chinese BIT Practice and Challenges,* Address at the 2010 Chinese Society of International Economic Law Annual Conference (16 October 2011, Nanjing, China), (2010) 17(4) *Chinese Journal of International Economic Law* 114 – 25.

[7] Li, *Chinese BIT Practice.*

implemented.[8] Against this background, a more liberal BIT regime was adopted by China since 1998, which notably included access to arbitration at the International Centre for Settlement of Investment Disputes ('ICSID') for all investor-State disputes and a substantive national treatment commitment.[9] Clearly the new BIT policy is geared to the promotion and protection of both inward and outward investments [reflecting China's shift to a siz eable outward direct investment ('ODI') nation] although arguably with slightly more focus on inward investments.

B. Definition of Foreign Investment

According to the statistics of the Department of Foreign Trade of the Ministry of Commerce ('MOFCOM'), foreign investment is divided into two categories. One is FDI, which includes equity joint ventures, contractual joint ventures, wholly foreign-owned enterprises, holding companies with foreign investment, joint exploration, and others, and the other category is named 'other foreign investments' (*Wai Shang Qi Ta Tou Zi*), which includes shares, international lease, compensation trade, and processing and assembling.[10] It is noted that the concept of 'other foreign investments' is wider than that of portfolio investments. According to Sornarajah, portfolio investments are instruments which are either directly connected with the companies (such as shares) or are only indirectly connected with the companies (such as promissory notes and bonds).[11]

C. Historical Foreign Investment Inflows

As Chart 1 shows, FDI in China had been steadily increasing from the late 1970s until the early 1990s, when it experienced the first surge after Mr Deng Xiaoping pronounced that China was to establish a 'Socialist Market Economy'. A second surge happened in the early 21st century mainly due to China's accession to the WTO in 2001. FDI in China reached its peak in 2008 at a level of US $92,395 million, which was slightly less in 2009 as a result of the global financial crisis. It however picked up again in 2010 with an increase of over 17 percent by the end of 2010, which was proof of China's rapid recovery from the crisis. According to the UNCTAD World Investment Report 2010, China has retained its position as number two on the list of countries in attracting foreign direct investment since 1992. It is believed that the extensive BIT network that China has established since 1982 has helped to achieve this huge success.[12]

---

[8] See C Congyan, 'Outward Foreign Direct Investment Protection and the Effectiveness of Chinese BIT Practice' (2006) 7 *The Journal of World Investment & Trade* 621, 627 – 37.

[9] Details can be found in N Gallagher and W Shan, *Chinese Investment Treaties*, paras 1.77 – 1.82.

[10] An example of this statistic may be found in the following website, Investment in China, 'Statistics about Utilisation of Foreign Investment in China from Jan to Oct 2010' (16 November 2010), *available at* www.fdi.gov.cn/pub/FDI/wz tj/wstz tj/lywz tj/t20101116_128338.htm (last accessed 29 December 2011).

[11] M Sornarajah, *The International Law on Foreign Investment* (3rd edn, Cambridge University Press, 2010), p. 196.

[12] China has one of the most extensive BIT networks in the world having entered into almost 130 treaties with countries. Only Germany has more BITs: see list (with full text) *available at* www.dis-arb.de/materialien/indexbiinvest.html (last accessed 29 December 2011).

D. Historical Outward Investment Flows

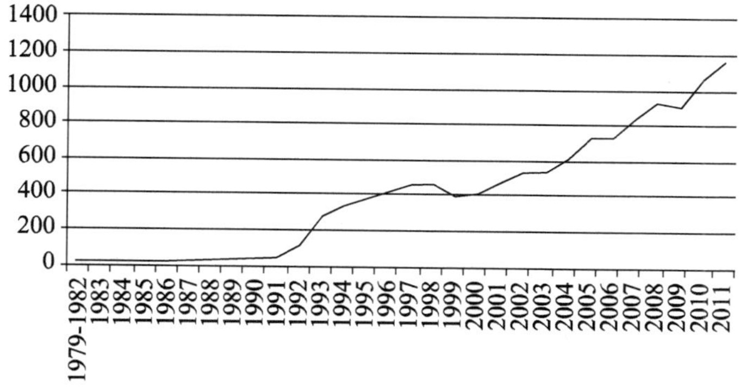

Viewfull-sized figure

Chart 1　FDI in China 1979 – 2011 (Unit: US $ 100 million)

Source: Compiled by the authors in accordance with MOFCOM data posted at: Invest in China: < www. fdi. gov. cn/pub/FDI/wz tj/default. htm > (last accessed 20 January 2012).

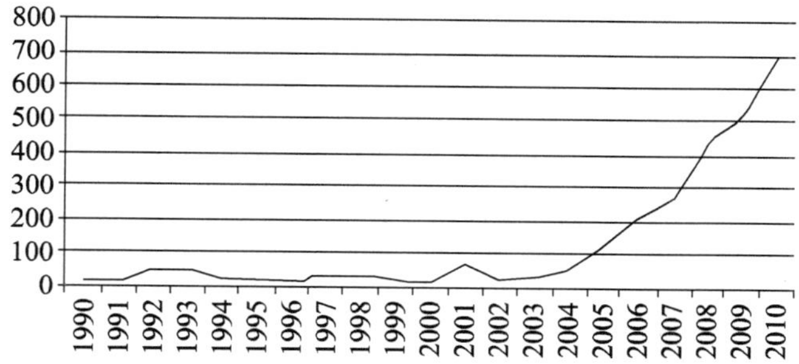

Viewfull-sized figure

Chart 2　ODI from China 1990 – 2010 (Unit: US $ 100 million)

Source: Compiled by the authors in accordance with MOFCOM data, posted at: Invest in China: < www. fdi. gov. cn/pub/FDI/wz tj/jwtz tj/default. htm > (last accessed 20 January 2012).

As demonstrated in Chart 2, prior to the 21st century, Chinese ODI was insignificant, despite a perceivable increase in the early 1990s following the announcement of the 'Socialist Market Economy'. In contrast, since 2000, particularly in the last five years, there has been a steep increase in ODI from China, from less than US $ 10 billion before 2004 to over US $ 50 billion in 2009. Indeed, according to the UNCTAD statistics, China ranked sixth in the world investors' league table with her US $ 52 billion in ODI. This clearly explains why China has to rethink and reshape her BIT strategy to accommodate the need of protecting and promoting this significant yet rapidly increasing outward investment.[13]

E. Domestic Legislative and Policy Regime Relating to Foreign Investment

In China, a series of national and local laws and regulations apply to FDI activities which together constitute the FDI legal regime. In the hierarchy of national laws, the Constitution sits at the apex. In 1982, China amended its Constitution to allow for FDI. Article 18 of the Constitution stipulates that China ' permits foreign enterprises, other foreign economic organizations and individual foreigners to invest in China and to enter into various forms of economic cooperation with Chinese enterprises and other Chinese economic organizations in accordance with the law of the People's Republic of China' and that the lawful rights and interests of foreign enterprises, other foreign economic organizations as well as Chinese-foreign joint ventures ' are protected by Chinese law' .

Apart from the Constitution, China has enacted a number of laws and regulations exclusively applicable to FDI. Among these laws, some, known as ' Law' (*Falv*) in the Chinese legal system, are enacted by the National People's Congress (' NPC') (including its Standing Committee). They mainly include: (1) the Chinese-Foreign Equity Joint Venture Law (' EJVL'), which was first adopted in 1979 and has been amended several times afterwards; (2) the Chinese-Foreign Contractual Joint Venture Law (' CJVL'), which was first adopted on 13 April 1988; (3) the Wholly Foreign Owned Enterprises Law (' WFEL'), which was first adopted on 12 April 1986; (4) Income Tax for Foreign Invested Enterprises and Foreign Enterprises, which was adopted on 9 April 1991, and which was replaced by the Enterprise Income Tax Law in 2007 (' Enterprise Income Tax Law 2007'), which implemented an equal tax regime on both domestic and foreign invested enterprises. These laws are the basic laws for FDI activities in China. Apart from these basic laws, there are more general laws adopted by the NPC that apply to FDI in the same way as they do to domestic investments. They include for instance the Foreign Trade Law 1995, the Contract Law 1999, the Negotiable Instruments Law 1995, the Insurance Law 1995, the Guarantee Law 1995, the Maritime Law 1992, and the Customs Law 1987, among others. At a lower level of national legislation within the Central Government, the State Council also promulgates ' Administrative Regulations' (*Xinzhen Fagui*), which provide more detailed rules for the basic laws. These mainly include: (1) Implementing Regulations for EJVL 1979 first adopted on 20 September 1983; (2) Implementing Regulation for CJVL 1988 first adopted in August 1995; (3) Implementing Regulation for WFEL 1986 first adopted in October 1990; (4) State Council Provisions for Encouraging Foreign Investment adopted in October 1986; (5) Guidance on the Direction of Foreign Investment adopted in February 2002 (' Investment Guidance 2002').

---

[13] In addition, there had been a shift in the global economic powerbase with China owning $1, 160 billion of US Government debt: ' China's US Treasuries Holdings Revised' , *Reuters* (28 February 2011). Although the official amount of China's investment in the US is still relatively small, this looks set to change in the coming decades: D Pilling, ' Why We Should Hail China's Spending Spree' , *Financial Times* (13 May 2011), and D H Rosen and T Hanemann, *An American Open Door? Maximising the Benefits of Chinese Foreign Direct Investment* (Asia Society Report, 2011) p. 22, *available at* http://asiasociety.org/policy/center-us-china-relations/american-open-door (last accessed 29 December 2011).

Further national legislation which is of lower status are the rules issued by various Departments of the State Council, which are named as 'Department Rules' (*Bumen Guizhang*). They mainly include: (1) Interim Provisions on the Takeover of Domestic Enterprises by Foreign Investors (August 2008);[14] (2) Measures for Strategic Investment by Foreign Investors upon Listed Companies (January 2006);[15] (3) Provisions Concerning the Administration of Foreign-funded Venture Enterprises (January 2003);[16] (4) Interim Provisions on the Merger and Acquisition (M&A) of Domestic Enterprises by Foreign Investors (March 2003), ('M&A Provisions 2003');[17] (5) Interim Provisions on Restructuring State-owned Enterprises with Foreign Investment (November 2002);[18] Tentative Provisions on Guidance on the Direction of Foreign Investment ('June 1995') ('Investment Guidance 1995').[19]

According to the Law on Legislation 2000, certain local governments and local parliaments are authorized to enact laws applicable at the local level, which are known as 'Local Regulations' (*Difang Fagui*) and 'Governmental Rules' (*Zhengfu Guizhang*) respectively.[20] For instance, governments of provinces, Minority Autonomous Areas ('MMAs'), Special Economic Zones ('SEZs') may enact 'Local Regulation' (*Difang Fagui*). Although these local laws, according to the Law on Legislation 2000, are required to conform to 'Law' (*Falv*) by the NPC and 'Administrative Regulation' (*Xingzheng Fagui*) by the State Council,[21] it is not uncommon that they deviate from those laws and regulations.[22] There is therefore a sophisticated and multi-tiered domestic law regulating foreign investment in China. The types of foreign investment permitted are clearly defined and once approved would then qualify as a covered investment for the purposes of an applicable investment treaty.

F. Portfolio Investment Regulation

The legislative regime mentioned above is for foreign direct investment, not for foreign portfolio investment. Indeed, there is no specific regulation devoted to foreign portfolio investment.[23] Some generally applicable laws notably the Company Law cover such

---

[14] This was co-adopted by the Ministry of Commerce ('MOFCOM'), the State Assets Supervision and Administration Commission of the State Council ('SASAC'), the State Administration of Taxation ('SAT'), the State Administration for Industry and Commerce ('SAIC'), the China Securities Regulatory Commission ('CSRC') and the State Administration of Foreign Exchange ('SAFE').

[15] This was co-adopted by the MOFCOM, the CSRC, the SAT, the SAIC, and the SAFE.

[16] This was co-promulgated by the Ministry of Foreign Trade and Economic Cooperation ('MOFTEC') (now MOFCOM), the Ministry of Science and Technology ('MOST'), the SAIC, the SAT, and the SAFE.

[17] This was co-promulgated by the MOFTEC (now MOFCOM), the SAT, the SAIC, and the SAFE.

[18] This was co-promulgated by the State Economic and Trade Commission, China ('SETC'), the Ministry of Finance ('MOF'), the SAIC, and the SAFE.

[19] This is jointly issued by the State Planning Commission ('SPC'), the State Economic and Trade Commission ('SETC') and the MOFTEC (now MOFCOM).

[20] Law on Legislation 2000, Arts 63, 65 - 6, 73.

[21] *See*, eg, Law on Legislation 2000, Art 63.

[22] W Shan, *The Legal Framework of EU-China Investment Relations: A Critical Appraisal* (Hart Publishing, Oxford and Portland, 2005), p. 36.

[23] Whether these portfolio investments would be covered by China's BITs would depend on its term. In *Gruslin v Malaysia* (ICSID Case No ARB/99/3, Award of 27 November 2000), the Tribunal held that the claimant's portfolio investment listed in the KL Stock Exchange did not comprise an 'approved project' under the treaty (para 26.1).

investment. According to Article 218 of the Company Law, ' joint stock limited companies invested by foreign investors shall be governed by the present Law' . The rights and obligation of foreign portfolio investors are therefore stipulated in the Company Law. Other laws, such as the Individual Income Tax Law, may also apply to such investors.

G. Market Access and Price Control

China still implements a ' one-by-one' approval system on foreign direct investment admission, which requires each and every foreign investment project to be approved by relevant authorities before it can be established. To find out whether a particular investment project is permitted in China, it is necessary to check the two most important instruments, namely: (1) the Investment Guidance 2002;[24] and (2) the attached Guiding Catalogue of Industries for Foreign Investment (' Guiding Catalogue').[25] The Chinese Government first issued the Investment Guidance and the Guiding Catalogue in 1995, which adopted the ' negative list' approach. Both regulations are subject to periodic revisions. The Guidance has so far only been revised once, in 2002, soon after China's accession to the WTO. The Guiding Catalogue, however, has been subject to more frequent revisions; as at the time of writing it has been amended four times.[26] The first revision took place in 1997 in the aftermath of the ' Asian Financial Crisis' . More tax incentives were introduced in order to mitigate the negative effects of the crisis. The Catalogue was revised again in 2002, incorporating China's commitments to the WTO, which China joined in 2001. The third revision took place in 2004 when incentives for certain areas such as steel, cement, and electrolytic aluminium were abolished to implement the State policies of macro-economic adjustment. The 2007 revision is the most recent and reflects both the latest development of macro-economic policies such as the ' Eleventh Five-year Plan on the Utiliz ation of Foreign Investments published in 2006' (' the 2006 Plan'),[27] as well as the need to further open-up after the completion of the WTO transition period. It is reported that this revision process started two years ago and had considered opinions from 41 governmental departments, 16 key trade associations,

---

[24] Guidance on the Direction of Foreign Investment (' Investment Guidance 2002' , promulgated by the State Council Decree No 346 on 21 February 2002, entered into force 1 April 2002).

[25] Guiding Catalogue of Industries for Foreign Investment (' Guiding Catalogue' , first promulgated in 2002, latest revision took place in 2007, entered into force 1 December 2007).

[26] Y Hongming, ' Interpreting the New Revision of the FDI Catalogue' , *China Investment* (in Chinese), *available at* www. sina. com. cn (last accessed 28 December 2011).

[27] The Eleventh Five-year Plan on Utiliz ation of Foreign Investments, (State Development and Reform Commission (' SDRC') (6 November 2006) (' 2006 Plan'). The 2006 Plan was the first plan published by the Chinese Government on foreign investment. The key word in the 2006 Plan is ' quality' , as opposed to ' quantity' . Using the language in the 2006 Plan, the government will ' propel the utiliz ation of foreign investments to be fundamentally converted from "quantity oriented" to "quality oriented" ' , practically transferring the focus from making up deficiencies of funds and foreign exchanges to bringing in advanced technologies, management experiences and skilful personnel. In other words, a ' selective approach' has been introduced in this plan. Two other significant features of the Plan include ' environment-friendliness' and ' innovation-orientation' . Thus the plan emphasizes that China will ' pay more attention to ecological construction, environmental protection, conservation and comprehensive utilization of resources and energies' , whilst promoting ' the improvement of the integrated innovation ability and the re-innovation ability' . See Gallagher and Shan, *Chinese Investment Treaties*, para 1. 18; and the 2006 Plan, particularly Section 2.

and a large number of experts and scholars. [28]

The Investment Guidance and the Guiding Catalogue classify all the foreign investment projects ('FIPs') into four subcategories: 'Encouraged', 'Restricted', 'Prohibited', and 'Permitted'. The 'Encouraged', 'Restricted', and 'Prohibited' industries are specifically defined, while all others are classified as 'Permitted' industries by default. FIPs in the 'Encouraged' category enjoy certain special incentives, such as tax incentives. FIPs in the 'Restricted' category are, on the contrary, subject to certain restrictions. Some of the restrictions are linked to the modes of investment. Basically there are three modes of foreign investment in China, EJVs, CJVs, and WFEs. The Guiding Catalogue, however, requires that some FIPs take the form of either a CJV or an EJV. Some FIPs are subject to more stringent conditions requiring 'Chinese Partners Equity Control' ('CPEC'), or 'Chinese Partners Relative Equity Control' ('CPREC'). The former requires that all Chinese partners taken together control 51 per cent or more of the total equity of the Foreign Invested Enterprise ('FIE'), whilst the latter only requires all the Chinese partners taken together to have more equity than any one of the foreign investors. [29] Such restrictions also apply to foreign invested M&A activities. [30] In accordance with Article 4 of the 2006 Provisions of Merger and Acquisition of Domestic Enterprises by Foreign Investors, in sectors which require 'JV only', or CPEC, or CPREC, the enterprises should maintain their status as a JV, or CPEC, or CPREC, after the merger or acquisition takes place. Likewise, in sectors where foreign investments are prohibited, foreign investors are not allowed to conduct merger and acquisition activities.

In this connection, it should be noted that, in addition to the general Guiding Catalogue, China has also adopted a Catalogue of Encouraged Industries for Foreign Investment in the Middle and Western Areas ('Western Catalogue')[31] and a Catalogue of Encouraged High-Tech Products for Foreign Investment ('High-Tech Catalogue'). [32] The High-Tech Catalogue has been integrated into the revised Guiding Catalogue, though the Western Catalogue continues to operate and is yet to be updated.

With regard to price control, China generally does not impose price control on foreign invested enterprises. Article 38 of the Implementing Regulation for CJVL, for instance, expressly states:

The joint ventures set the prices of their products for themselves according to the law. Chinese legislation, however, does prohibit foreign invested enterprises from engaging in unreasonable pricing behaviour by inflating the price when importing goods and

---

[28] Y Hongming, 'Interpreting the New Revision of the FDI Catalogue', *China Investment* (in Chinese), *available at* www.sina.com.cn (last accessed 28 December 2011).

[29] Investment Guidance, Art 8.

[30] Provisions of Merger and Acquisition of Domestic Enterprises by Foreign Investors, Art 4 (published jointly by MOFCOM and six other ministries in August 2006, entered into force 8 September 2006).

[31] This Catalogue was first published in June 2000 jointly by the former State Economic and Commerce Commission, the State Planning Commission, and the Ministry of Foreign Trade and Economic Cooperation ('MOFTEC'). It was revised in July 2004 by the SDRC, and has been in force since 1 September 2004.

[32] This Catalogue was originally promulgated in July 2003, jointly by the MOFCOM and the Ministry of Science and Technology ('MOST'). It was revised on 31 December 2006.

materials and cutting the price when exporting products. The Implementing Regulation for CJVL, for example, has such a requirement in Article 40:

The joint ventures must not export their products in prices obviously lower than reasonable international prices, neither can they import goods and materials in prices obviously higher than international prices.[33]

It is therefore clear that foreign investors and their enterprises are generally free to set the price.

H. Domestic Legal Position on Expropriation

China was relatively slow in enacting legislation on expropriation and compensation. The Law of Legislation provides that the expropriation of non-State-owned properties must be laid down in the form of 'Law' (*Falv*),[34] which means it must be formulated by the National People's Congress or its Standing Committee.[35] When the EJVL was adopted back in 1979, it was silent on expropriation. In the Regulations on the (p. 139) Exploration of Offshore Petroleum Resources in Cooperation with Foreign Enterprises 1982 ('REOFF') for offshore exploitation concessions, China included a limited right to expropriate in the event of war or other emergency.[36] It was just over 20 years ago that China first introduced a specific expropriation provision in the WFEL. Article 5 confirms that:

China does not carry out expropriations or nationalisations of WFEs. Under special circumstances, in the public interest, WFEs can be expropriated in accordance with legal procedures and appropriate compensation will be provided.

This provision was followed in subsequent legislation relating to FIEs except the CJVL.[37] It is not very prescriptive other than to confirm the general position against expropriation. It leaves open the question of what 'special circumstances' means. Other than that it contains three of the four conditions commonly found in China's BITs: expropriation must be in the public interest, in accordance with legal procedures, and payment of appropriate compensation is required.

A key concept here is 'appropriate compensation', which again is not further defined in Chinese law. A reasonable interpretation of this standard may be two-fold: if there is an applicable BIT to the expropriation, the standard of compensation should be compatible with that stipulated in the BIT; in other cases, 'appropriate compensation'

---

[33] The WFEL Implementing Regulation also has similar requirements. Art 46 of the Regulation provides that:

The price of goods and materials and any technical service imported by the foreign-funded enterprise shall not be higher than the normal price for goods and materials and technical services of the same kind in international market at that time. The price for the export products of a foreign-funded enterprise shall be determined by the enterprise itself in the light of the relevant prices in international market at that time, provided that they shall not be lower than reasonable export prices. If any enterprise evades taxes by importing products at a high price or exporting products at a low price, the legal responsibility of the relevant enterprise shall be investigated according to tax law by the tax authority.

[34] Law of Legislation, Art 8 (passed 15 March 2000 by the National People's Congress).

[35] Law of Legislation, Art 7.

[36] REOFF, Art 7, which states: 'In the course of war, threat of war or other emergencies, the Chinese Government has the right to requisition or expropriate a part or all of the oil that the foreign contractors earn or buy.'

[37] See EJVL, Art 2(3), as amended in 1990.

requires the amount of compensation to be determined, taking into account ' all circumstances' that are ' pertinent'.[38] As a result, the actual compensation may or may not be equivalent to the ' Hull Formula' standard of compensation traditionally asserted by some Western countries.[39] Chinese foreign investment laws do not go any further in defining expropriation, its conditions, and the standard of compensation.

The 2007 Property Law, which applies to both public and private properties, sets forth general principles on the issue of expropriation of collectively owned land, premises of enterprises and individuals, and other immovable properties.[40] The law requires that expropriation of such properties take place for public interests and in accordance with the procedures stipulated under the law.[41] The law points out the general scope of compensation for the expropriation of such properties, without giving any further details as to the specific standards of compensation.[42] Such standards are said to be laid down in other more specific laws and regulations.[43] Reference must therefore be made to applicable BITs to find a clearer answer on the matter of calculation of compensation on expropriation.

III. China's Investment Treaties and Free Trade Agreements

The changes in the domestic regime on investment combined with the ' open-door' policy of the 1970s mentioned earlier prompted China to take further steps to encourage foreign investment to help rebuild its economy.[44] As a result, China's BIT programme

---

[38] Such circumstances may include, as Judge Jiménez de Aréchaga once suggested: ' Whether the initial investment has been recovered, whether there has been undue enrichment as a result of the colonial situation, whether the profits obtained have been excessive, the contribution of the enterprise to the economic and social development of the country, its respect for labour laws and its investment policies' : E Jiménez de Aréchaga, ' State Responsibility for the Nationalisation of Foreign Owned Property' (1978) 11 *New York University Journal of International Law and Politics* 179, 185.

[39] For instance, the US voted in favour of UNGA Res 1803 and asserted that in its view the ' appropriate compensation' therein was equivalent to the ' Hull Formula' (namely ' prompt, adequate and effective' compensation) it had advocated since 1938: American Law Institute, *Restatement of the Foreign Relations Law of the United States* (3rd rev, 1986), vol II, p. 206.

[40] According to Art 4, the law protects properties of the State, collectives, individuals and other proprietors. See Property Law of the People's Republic of China (adopted at the 5th session of the Tenth National People's Congress, 16 March 2007) (' Property Law'). The expropriation clause is located in Art 42.

[41] Property Law, Art 42(1).

[42] Property Law, Art 42(2) - (4).

[43] For example, the Regulation on the Compensation for Expropriation of Houses on State Owned Land was promulgated on 19 January 2011. The full text of the regulation can be *accessed at* www. gov. cn/z wgk/2011 - 01/21/content_1790111. htm (last accessed 15 September 2012).

[44] It is contested whether BITs do impact the levels of FDI with Brazil being cited as an example of a State that has signed no BITs but has attracted FDI. That said, it is undisputed that the combined approach taken by China of domestic legal changes, opening up their economy and entering in to BITs seems to have succeeded. China now can accept quality investment over quantity. See for more general discussion K Sauvant and L E Sachs, *The Effect of Treaties on Foreign Direct Investment: Bilateral Investment Treaties, Double Taxation Treaties, and Investment Flows* (Oxford University Press, 2009), J W Salacuse and N P Sullivan, ' Do BITs Really Work? An Evaluation of Bilateral Investment Treaties and their Grand Bargain' (2005) 46 *Harvard International Law Journal* 67, D L Swenson, ' Why Do Developing Countries Sign BITs?' (2005) 12 *University of California Davis Journal of International Law & Policy* 131, and UNCTAD, *Bilateral Investment Treaties in the Mid - 1990s* (United Nations, 1998), p. 6.

was launched 30 years ago. The first modern style BIT being signed in Beijing on 29 March 1982 with Sweden. This BIT provided for many of the now standard protections including provisions on fair and equitable treatment, most-favoured-nation treatment, no expropriation without compensation, and a guarantee concerning the free transfer of funds. It only provided for inter-State arbitration for disputes on the interpretation and application of the treaty but noted in a letter from the Swedish Government that once China became a member of the ICSID Convention, then the parties would supplement the treaty to provide for binding arbitration for investor-State disputes.

China's BIT programme was launched in 1982, being the same year that the United States of America completed its first modern investment treaty.[45] Unlike the USA and other countries there was no historic use of Friendship, Commerce and Navigation ('FCN') treaties by China. The USA entered into over 100 such FCN treaties starting with the Treaty of Amity and Commerce with France in 1782 and continuing on well after World War II.[46] China has a mixed history relating to international treaties with many 'unequal treaties' being imposed on it by foreign States in the period after the first Opium War between Great Britain and China, such as the Treaty of Nanking of 1842; the Treaty of Wanghia of 1844 with the US; and the Treaty of Huangpu of 1844 with France.[47] The Treaty of Wanghia and the Treaty of Huangpu granted most-favoured-nation ('MFN') treatment to US and French nationals. As a result of these 'unequal treaties', China was slow to forget its 'bitter experience of imperialist oppression and foreign intervention'[48] and did not have any early experience with FCN treaties.

In the period after World War II, China entered into several treaties concerning consular relations (for example, with Sweden).[49] It also signed a Treaty of Friendship, Alliance and Mutual Assistance with the Soviet Union on 14 February 1950. Article 5 of

---

[45] The US BIT programme was launched in 1977 but its first BITs were completed in 1982 with Egypt and Panama, K J Vandevelde, *Bilateral Investment Treaties: History Policy and Interpretation* (Oxford University Press, 2010), p. 57. See also K J Vandevelde, 'The Bilateral Investment Treaty Program of the United States' (1988) 21 *Cornell International Law Journal* 201, 208 – 11. The UK programme started earlier in 1974; see S Brooks and E Denza, 'Investment Protection Treaties: United Kingdom Experience' (1987) 36 *International and Comparative Law Quarterly* 908; and C Brown and A Sheppard, 'United Kingdom', in this volume.

[46] See H Walker Jr, 'Modern Treaties of Friendship, Commerce and Navigation' (1957 – 58) 42 *Minnesota Law Review* 805 for a discussion of the 16 FCNs entered into by the US since 1946. See generally on the evolution of BITs: J Salacuse, *The Law of Investment Treaties* (Oxford University Press, 2010), pp. 81 – 95.

[47] Treaty of Nanking, signed 29 August 1842 (for historical background, see J K Fairbank, 'Chinese Diplomacy and the Treaty of Nanking, 1842' (1940) 12 *Journal of Modern History* 1); Treaty of Wanghia, signed 3 July 1844, reproduced in *Treaties, Conventions, etc between China and Foreign States* (2nd edn, Shanghai, 1917), vol I, pp. 677 – 712; Treaty of Huangpu, signed 24 October 1844; S Hoe and D Roebuck, *The Taking of Hong Kong: Charles and Clara Elliot in China Waters* (Routledge, 1999), p. 203; See I C Y Hsü, *The Rise of Modern China* (6th edn, Oxford University Press, 2000), p. 168; and for general information see D Wang, *China's Unequal Treaties: Narrating National History* (Lanham, MD, United States: Lexington Books, 2005).

[48] Q Kong, 'Bilateral Investment Treaties: The Chinese Approach and Practice' (1998 – 99) 8 *Asian Yearbook of International Law* 105, 108; see also T Wang 'International Law in China: Historical and Contemporary Perspectives' (1991) 1 *Chinese Yearbook of International Law* 1.

[49] Exchange of notes constituting an Agreement between Sweden and the People's Republic of China on the Establishment of Consular Relations, signed 26 June 1955 228(11) UNTS 3148.

this treaty provided that the Contracting Parties would 'develop and strengthen the economic and cultural ties' between the two nations.[50] A Treaty of Trade and Navigation was signed in 1958 with the former Soviet Union which granted MFN treatment to the Contracting Parties in all trade, navigation, and 'other economic relations'[51] between the States. Article 16 provides that the two States guarantee enforcement of arbitral awards 'with regard to disputes arising out of the commercial or other contracts of their corporate bodies or institutions, where the Parties have duly agreed to refer the dispute to an ad hoc or permanent arbitral tribunal for settlement'.

China also, for example, entered into a Trade Agreement as early as 1978 with the European Community which set out general commitments to foster economic relations.[52] This early treaty was replaced in 1985 by the Agreement for Trade and Economic Cooperation between the EEC and China. Article 12 called on the parties to 'promote and encourage greater and mutually beneficial investment'.[53] The US did not have an FCN treaty with China but did sign an FCN treaty with the Republic of China (Taiwan) in Nanking on 4 November 1946 which entered into force in November 1948.[54] It was not until 1979, after the restoration of diplomatic relations with the United States, before China signed an Agreement on Trade Relations with the United States, which contained an MFN clause.[55] A double taxation treaty was also signed,[56] but no agreement on a BIT was ever reached.[57] In June 2008, however, both countries declared the launch of new BIT negotiations as part of the Strategic Economic Dialogue between the two States,

---

[50] Treaty of Friendship, Alliance and Mutual Assistance between the Union of Soviet Socialist Republics and the People's Republic of China, signed 14 February 1950, UNTS 3103, Art 5 (entered in force 11 April 1950).

[51] Treaty of Trade and Navigation between the Union of Soviet Socialist States and the People's Republic of China, signed 23 April 1958, UNTS 4534, Art 2 (entered into force 25 July 1958).

[52] Trade Agreement between the EEC and the People's Republic of China ([1978] OJ L123, 11/05/1978). For a detailed account of China-EU agreements see F Snyder, *The European Union and China, 1949 – 2008: Basic Documents and Commentary* (Hart Publishing, 2009).

[53] Agreement on Trade and Economic Cooperation between the EEC and the People's Republic of China ([1985] OJ L250 19/09/1985), Art 12(1).

[54] Treaty of Friendship, Commerce and Navigation (with Protocols), signed on 4 November 1946, 25 UNTS 69 (entered into force 30 November 1948). See for a list of US FCN Treaties: (1981) 20 ILM 565. Another example is the FCN Treaty signed between Republic of China and Spain on 19 February 1953 (replacing the earlier 1928 Treaty) which provided for arbitration of disputes if diplomatic channels failed: see Art IV. See generally K J Vandevelde, 'A Brief History of International Investment Agreements' (2005 – 06) 12 *University of California Davis Journal of International Law & Policy* 157.

[55] Agreement on Trade Relations between the United States of America and Republic of China, signed 7 July 1979, TIAS 9630, 31 UST 4651; see also W S Morrison, 'China-US Trade Issues' in *Congressional Research Service* (30 September 2011) available at www.fas.org/sgp/crs/row/RL33536.pdf (last accessed 29 December 2011); M R Weiner and S Ying, 'The Need for a Bilateral Investment Treaty between the United States of America and the People's Republic of China' (1990) 2 *International Legal Perspectives* 33, 41.

[56] Agreement on for the Avoidance of Double Taxation and the Prevention of Tax Evasion with respect to Taxes on Income, signed 30 April 1984, available at www.irs.gov/pub/irs-trty/china.pdf (entered into force 1 January 1987).

[57] One of the main reasons there was no consensus was the national treatment provision which the US Model BIT included at the pre-establishment phase: see T A Steinert, 'If the BIT Fits: The Proposed Bilateral Investment Treaty between the United States and the People's Republic of China' (Fall 1988) 2 *Journal of Chinese Law* 405.

although no consensus has yet been reached.[58] It has been suggested that given the 'varying interests of the two nations, the huge investment potential and the clash of the two parties' positions, the BIT negotiation is destined to be the most difficult one in history'.[59] The most recent meeting was in May 2010 with no apparent conclusion reached. This was mainly because the US was revising its Model BIT. That process was completed in May 2012 so until this had been achieved no substantive negotiation could have started with China on any future BIT. This may now become a priority as Canada formally signed a BIT with China on 9 September 2012 (after over 18 years of negotiations).[60] This is certainly an impetus for the US negotiations. Other recent investment treaties—such as the investment protocol of the China-Chile FTA which was signed on 9 September 2012,[61] and the China-Japan-Korea investment treaty[62]—also have many similarities with the US Model BIT, so perhaps an agreement may be reached in the near future.

China has signed BITs with 130 countries,[63] and as at the time of writing, 101 of them have entered into force.[64] Most of these treaties are similar in form to the Model BIT in force at the time of completion with some variations due to the negotiation process with each State. China currently has entered into nine free trade agreements ('FTAs') although two of these—known as the 'Closer Economic Partnership Arrangements' (2003)—are with Hong Kong and Macao. The remaining seven FTAs each have an investment chapter,[65] except for the China-Chile FTA (2005) which has an article on the promotion of investment and a commitment to negotiation of a future agreement on trade in services and investment. A supplementary Agreement on Trade in Service was signed with Chile in 2008, and the negotiations on investment are pending. The chapter on in-

---

[58] Pre-establishment was also an issue although perhaps will be less of a stumbling block this time round. See C Congyan, 'China-US BIT Negotiations and the future of Investment Treaty Regime: a grand bilateral bargain with multilateral implications' (2009) *Journal of International Economic Law* 457 and generally Q Kong, *US-China Bilateral Investment Treaty Negotiations* (East Asian Institute, NUS, 2010).

[59] Q Kong, *US-China Bilateral Investment Treaty Negotiations* (East Asia Institute Brief No 507, 2010), p. ii. The US Chamber of Commerce has urged the government to enter in to more BITs in particular with China and India: *China Daily* (14 January 2012).

[60] The text of the BIT was made public just prior to publication: *see* http://www.international.gc.ca/trade-agreements-accords-commerciaux/agr-acc/fipa-apie/china-text-chine.aspx?lang=en&view=d (last accessed 14 November 2012). For comments on the BIT from China's Minister of Commerce, *see* http://english.mofcom.gov.cn/article/newsrelease/significantnews/201209/97801996451907.html (last accessed 14 November 2012).

[61] *See* 'MOFCOM Explains the Investment Protocol of the China-Chile FTA', *available at* www.gov.cn/gzdt/2012-09/10/content_2220655.htm (last accessed 15 September 2012).

[62] MOFA, 'Signing of the Japan-China-Korea Trilateral Investment Agreement', *available at* http://www.mofa.go.jp/announce/announce/2012/5/0513_01.html (last accessed 15 September 2012).

[63] Li, *Chinese BIT Practice*. A list of BITs with the dates of their signature and entry into force is on the MOFCOM website, *available at* http://tfs.mofcom.gov.cn/column/2010.shtml (last accessed 29 December 2011). The list is updated from time to time.

[64] Li, *Chinese BIT Practice*.

[65] China-Costa Rica FTA (2010), Chapter 9; China-New Zealand FTA (2008), Chapter 11; China-Pakistan FTA (2006), Chapter IX; China-Peru (2010) FTA, Chapter 10; China-Singapore FTA (2008), Chapter 10. There is a separate Agreement on Investment which is part of the China-ASEAN FTA, which was signed in 2009. Full texts *available at* http://fta.mofcom.gov.cn/english/index.shtml (last accessed 29 December 2011).

vestment in the China-Singapore FTA does not contain any provisions save to confirm that the ASEAN-China Investment Agreement will be incorporated into the FTA.

China is also engaged in ongoing FTA negotiations with the Gulf Cooperation Council, Australia, Iceland, Norway, and the Southern African Customs Union. Feasibility studies are being conducted with India, Korea, Japan, and Switzerland to establish where there was potential for any future agreements on trade. China seems set to expand its existing recent FTA coverage in the future.

China has a Model BIT, which is now the third version of the original Model that was used in the 1980s. The first Model BIT (' Version I') was amended towards the end of the 1980s, and the second version of the Chinese Model BIT was adopted in the early 1990s. This second Model BIT (' Version II') was used until the late 1990s when the current Model BIT was implemented. The changes to the provisions are in some instances only of a minor significance. Many of these are referred to throughout the commentary on the Model BIT below. One of the more notable changes in the third (current) version of the Model BIT (' Version III') was that it allowed international arbitration of all disputes and not just the question of quantum. There has been some discussion that China will adopt a further new Model BIT, but no text has been made public.

IV. Internal Government Issues

In practice, the making of an investment treaty in China is primarily undertaken by the Directorate-General of Treaty and Law (' DGTL') within the MOFCOM.[66] The DGTL also participates in the negotiation of FTAs, although it does not take the lead role.

In China, BIT negotiations normally involve the following nine steps.

Step 1: Request for Authorization (*Qingshi*): when there is a need to negotiate a new BIT, MOFCOM (normally initiated and drafted by the DGTL, more specifically by the officials in charge of investment treaties within the Directorate-General) will, after consultation with the Ministry of Foreign Affairs (' MFA'), make a joint application with the MFA to the State Council, asking for permission for the negotiation of such an agreement.

Step 2: Approval (*Pifu*): The State Council, if it approves of such *Qingshi* by the MOFCOM and the MFA, will issue a Reply of Approval (*Pifu*).

Step 3: Negotiations (*Tanpan*): With the *Pifu*, the MOFCOM officials conduct negotiations with the foreign counterparty. Such negotiations normally take place in Beijing and the capital of the counterparty in turn.

Step 4: Initialling (*Caoqian*): After an agreement is reached, the heads of the two delegations of negotiation initial the agreed treaty text.

Step 5: Formal Request for Authorization (*Zhenshi Qingshi*): MOFCOM will then, again jointly with the MFA, make a formal application to the State Council for formal signature of the agreement. In the application, the initialled treaty text and the proposed activities of signature (including the proposed event and the person who will sign the

[66] Gallagher and Shan, *Chinese Investment Treaties*, p. 33.

treaty) are normally attached.

Step 6: Formal Signature: After an approval has been obtained from the State Council, the investment agreement can be formally signed, normally by an official of ministerial level or above. There is usually a ceremony for the signature.

Step 7: Record: According to practice, investment treaties do not need formal ratification by the Standing Committee of the NPC, or further approval by the State Council. Rather, it is only required to be submitted (by MOFCOM) to the State Council for the record. In practice, they are submitted to the MFA only for the record. The domestic legal procedure for the treaty to be effective is hence completed.

Step 8: Exchange of Diplomatic Notes: The MFA will then notify the foreign counterpart with a diplomatic note of the fact that China has fulfilled the domestic legal procedures for the treaty. The foreign counterpart may issue a similar note in exchange.

Step 9: Entry into Force: The treaty normally enters into force within a certain time after the exchange of notes, depending on the treaty provisions.[67]

As mentioned above, China has, to date, signed BITs with 130 countries,[68] and 101 of them have entered into force.[69] Since there is no formal ratification requirement there is no data on the date of ratification on the Chinese side. However, according to data provided by MOFCOM, the average time taken from signature to entry into force of Chinese BITs is 741 days, that is, slightly over two years. At one extreme, the China-Israel BIT, took nearly 14 years, followed by the China-Gabon BIT, which took about 12 years. Several of the older BITs entered into force immediately, such as the BITs with Sweden, UK, Denmark, and Australia.

Most Chinese BITs are now available at the MOFCOM website.[70] They are also registered as a matter of course with the UN Treaty Section, as required by the Procedural Law of the People's Republic of China on the Conclusion of Treaties.[71]

In accordance with the 'Procedural Law of the People's Republic of China on the Conclusion of Treaties', official texts of signed BITs must be deposited with the MFA although they do not have to be made available to the public.[72] However, the text of the BITs may be accessed from the abovementioned website of the DGTL.

---

〔67〕 Gallagher and Shan, *Chinese Investment Treaties*, pp. 33 – 4.

〔68〕 Li, *Chinese BIT Practice*.

〔69〕 Li, *Chinese BIT Practice*.

〔70〕 Available at http://tfs.mofcom.gov.cn/column/2010.shtml (last accessed 29 December 2011).

〔71〕 Art 17 of the Law provides: 'Treaties and agreements concluded by the People's Republic of China shall be registered with the Secretariat of the United Nations by the Ministry of Foreign Affairs in accordance with the relevant provisions of the United Nations Charter.'

〔72〕 Art 14 of the 'The Procedural Law of the People's Republic of China on Conclusion of Treaties' stipulates as follows:

Signed originals of bilateral treaties and agreements concluded in the name of the People's Republic of China or the Government of the People's Republic of China and copies of multilateral treaties and agreements certified as true by the depositary States or international organiz ations concerned shall be deposited with the Ministry of Foreign Affairs. Signed originals of bilateral agreements concluded in the name of the government departments of the People's Republic of China shall be deposited with these departments.

V. Commentary on the Model BIT

The aims and purposes of a BIT are usually reflected in the preamble. Its terms are often used by arbitral tribunals as an aid in the interpretation of treaty clauses.[73] There has been no change to the wording in the three versions of the Chinese Model BIT.[74] The principles in the Model BITs are not as extensive or specific (the principles do not contain, for instance, a transfer of technology obligation) as the preambles of some other countries BITs, such as France.

The preamble of the current Chinese Model BIT provides as follows:

Preamble

The Government of the People's Republic of China and the Government of ____ (hereinafter referred to as the Contracting Parties), Intending to create favorable conditions for investments by investors of one Contracting Party in the territory of the other Contracting Party; Recognizing that the reciprocal encouragement, promotion and protection of such investments will be conducive to stimulating business initiative of the investors and will increase prosperity in both States; Desiring to intensify the economic cooperation of both States on the basis of equality and mutual benefits ...

In other words, China's Model BIT includes three principles in the preamble, namely to (i) facilitate and attract investment; (ii) contribute to the prosperity of both Contracting States; and (iii) cooperate on the basis of equality and mutual benefits. Thus, it can be said that although the primary purpose of the BIT is to promote and protect foreign investment, it is also essential that such investment shall be beneficial to the host country.[75] This can be seen from elements of the last two principles, namely the need to contribute to the 'prosperity of both States' and the principle of 'equality and mutual benefit'.

Although the Model BITs have remained unchanged, some of China's early BITs have simpler provisions in the preamble. The 1982 Sweden BIT, the very first Chinese BIT, has only one sentence stating that the aim of the BIT is to 'maintain fair and equi-

---

〔73〕 This is natural as the Vienna Convention of the Law of Treaties, opened for signature 23 May 1969, 1155 UNTS 311, Art 31(1) (entered into force 27 January 1980), widely viewed as a codification of customary international law on treaty interpretation, requires that: 'A treaty shall be interpreted in good faith in accordance with the ordinary meaning to be given to the terms of the treaty in their context and in the light of its object and purpose.'

See also SGS Société Générale de Surveillance SA v Republic of the Philippines (ICSID Case No ARB/02/6, Decision on Jurisdiction of 29 January 2004), para 116, which confirmed that the object and purpose of the BIT mandated an effective interpretation of the umbrella clause. The aim of the BIT was to promote investment. The Tribunal noted that according to 'the preamble it is intended "to create and maintain favourable conditions for investments by investors of one Contracting Party in the territory of the other". It is legitimate to resolve uncertainties in its interpretation so as to favour the protection of covered investments.'

〔74〕 *See* Preambles in the three versions of the Chinese Model BITs respectively.

〔75〕 This emphasis on balancing the interests of the investor with those of the host State were also included in the proposed draft Norway Model BIT (2007). Investors' rights were to be protected whilst recognizing the legitimate interest of the host State to regulate health, safety, environmental protections and labour rights: see Norway Model BIT (2007) Preamble, and the Preamble of the US Model BIT, both available at http://italaw.com/investment-treaties (last accessed 12 September 2012).

table treatment for investments'.[76] The second BIT entered into by China, the 1983 Germany BIT, also had a very short preamble of only one sentence. It was however the first treaty that introduced a clear 'pro-investor' purpose for the BIT. The signature of that BIT was based on the parties' desire 'to develop economic cooperation between both States' and 'to create favourable conditions for investment'.[77] The 1984 Belgium-Luxembourg Economic Union ('BLEU') BIT seems to be the first BIT that embedded the current preamble prototype,[78] which has been followed by the vast majority of Chinese BITs signed since then.

Some of the Chinese BITs, particularly the recent ones, have a more balanced approach in the preamble to investment protection and host State interests. The preamble in the Australia BIT signed in 1988, for example, expressly recognizes that investment should be made in accordance with domestic laws and regulations of the host State, in addition to the aforementioned standard objectives, the formulation of which is slightly amended.[79] The Sino-Nigeria BIT of 1997 also has a sentence in the preamble recogniz ing that investors are obliged to respect the sovereignty and laws of the host State. This obligation was repeated in China's BITs with Trinidad and Tobago (2002), Guyana (2003), and Benin (2004). These recent BITs with Trinidad and Tobago and Guyana have gone a step further in that their preambles include an 'exception clause'. It acknowledges that the BIT's objectives, namely the promotion and protection of investment can be achieved without 'relaxing health, safety and environmental measures of general application'.[80] This should impact the interpretation by a future tribunal of the substantive clauses, in particular, fair and equitable treatment and expropriation. An expansive interpretation of those substantive protections to cover all measures regardless of their nature and public

---

[76] China-Sweden BIT (1982), Preamble. In fact this BIT is currently under review as the EU was successful before the European Court of Justice in claiming its terms were incompatible with Community law as it contained no exception in the freedom of transfer provisions to comply with EU regulations that might be imposed: see *Commission v Sweden* [2009] ECR I-1335.

[77] China-Germany BIT (1983), Preamble. Although positive for an investor, the host State would also benefit from economic development and the BIT aims to make this a mutual benefit; just as the obligations are reciprocal so too are the benefits. The China-Germany BIT (2003) adopts the Model BIT wordings in its Preamble.

[78] China-Belgium-Luxembourg BIT (1984), Preamble.

[79] The Preamble to the China-Australia BIT states that Contracting Parties signed the treaty:

RECOGNISING the importance of promoting the flow of capital for economic activity and development and aware of its role in expanding economic relations and technical co-operation between them, particularly with respect to investment by nationals of one Contracting Party in the territory of the other Contracting Party;

CONSIDERING that investment relations should be promoted and economic co-operation strengthened in accordance with the internationally accepted principles of mutual respect for sovereignty, equality, mutual benefit, non-discrimination and mutual confidence;

ACKNOWLEDGING that investments of nationals of one Contracting Party in the territory of the other Contracting Party would be made within the framework of laws of that other Contracting Party; and

RECOGNISING that pursuit of these objectives would be facilitated by a clear statement of principles relating to the protection of investments and associated activities, combined with rules designed to render more effective the application of these principles within the territories of the Contracting Parties ...

[80] *See* Preambles in both the China-Trinidad and Tobago and China-Guyana BITs respectively.

See also the recently signed (but not yet ratified) tripartite investment agreement between China, Japan, and Korea, signed on 13 May 2012, which also contains this provision on health, safety, and environmental measures.

welfare effects is less likely where such provisions are included in the preamble.

A. Definitions

The definition article in the Chinese Model BIT defines only three terms, namely ' investment' ' investor' and ' return' . Since the definition for ' return' is rather straightforward,[81] this section focuses on the first two terms.

Article 1: Definition of ' Investment'

1. The term ' investment' means every kind of asset invested by investors of one Contracting Party in accordance with the laws and regulations of the other Contracting Party in the territory of the latter, and in particularly, though not exclusively, includes:

(a) movable and immovable property and other property rights such as mortgages pledges and similar rights;

(b) shares, debentures, stock and any other kind of participation in companies;

(c) claims to money or to any other performance having an economic value associated with an investment;

(d) intellectual property rights, in particularly copyrights, patents, trade-marks, trade-names, technical process, know-how and good-will;

(e) business concessions conferred by law or under contract permitted by law, including concessions to search for, cultivate, extract or exploit natural resources.

Any change in the form in which assets are invested does not affect their character as investments provided that such change is in accordance with the laws and regulations of the Contracting Party in whose territory the investment has been made.

It can be seen that the Chinese Model BIT adopts the generally used asset-based definition of ' investment' . It is quite broad in scope and is not a finite list as for example is contained in the Canadian Model BIT.[82] Version I defines ' investment' as including: ' every kind of asset' with a non-exhaustive list of examples. Version II did not make any change to this definition. However, Version III contained some changes in detail. Thus the term ' similar rights' is added to expand the list of examples of property rights; a reference to ' debentures' is included in parallel to ' shares' and ' stock' as another example of corporate participation; ' claims to money and other performance having an economic value' is qualified by the phrase ' associated with an investment' . These changes to the definition should help to clarify that for the purposes of the treaty these forms of assets must relate to an underlying investment. A further change is that business concessions covered by the BIT are expanded from only ' those conferred by law' to include also those conferred ' under contract permitted by law' . Finally, Version

---

[81] The definition provides:

3. The term ' returns' means the amounts yielded from investments, including profits, dividends, interests, capital gains, royalties, fees and other legitimate income.

See Version III of the Chinese Model BIT, Art 1(3).

[82] Art 1 of the 2004 Canadian Model Foreign Investment Promotion Agreement (' FIPA'), available at http://italaw.com/investmenttreaties.htm (last accessed 29 December 2011). Interestingly, the recent Mexico BIT has a finite list definition of investment. This is likely to have been included at the behest of Mexico in light of its extensive NAFTA experience. See NAFTA, Art 1139. See also the newly signed China-Canada BIT (2012), Art 1(i).

III added a paragraph clarifying that any change in the form in which assets are invested shall not affect the nature of the investment as long as such change is made in accordance with the laws and regulations of the host State. This clarification is likely to be significant as more foreign invested enterprises change the form of their original investment, for example, from a joint venture to a wholly foreign owned enterprise (*duzihua*) .[83] Such foreign investors in China will want to ensure that they will continue to be protected by applicable BITs.

The ' in accordance with its laws and regulations' requirement is the only generally applied qualification on the definition in Chinese BITs,[84] the importance of which has been demonstrated in some recent cases, such as *Inceysa Vallisoletana v El Salvador*[85] and *Fraport v Philippines*.[86] However, some recent Chinese BITs have removed the ' in accordance with its laws and regulations' requirement from the definition of ' investment' . Examples include the 2003 Germany BIT and the 2004 Uganda BIT. Both BITs nevertheless maintain in another provision that each Contracting Party shall ' admit such investments in accordance with its laws and regulations' .[87] Thus it can be said that the ' in accordance with its laws and regulations' requirement still exists in both BITs. It is relatively easy to determine whether a foreign investment has been made ' in accordance with Chinese laws' , given that China has been practising a ' one-by-one approval' regime.[88] Presumably if a foreign investment has obtained approval from the relevant competent government authorities, the investment can be deemed to have been made in accordance with local law.

The Chinese Model BIT does not follow the US Model BIT in imposing objective qualifications on the definition of ' investment' . However, the China-Germany BIT (2003) stands out, again, in that it has an explanation in the Protocol stating:

For the avoidance of doubt, the Contracting Parties agree that investments as de-

---

[83] A 2005 MOFCOM survey among transnational corporation shows that, whilst 82 percent of them intended to expand their investment in China during 2005 – 07, 57 percent of them planned to adopt the form of WFE. This is most obvious among large transnational corporations. See ' Whose Cheese Has Been Moved by the WFE Transformation of FIEs?' (in Chinese), *available at* http://finance.sina.com.cn/review/20061128/09413115559.shtml (last accessed 28 December 2011).

[84] The China-Germany BIT (2003) has a provision that provides certain objective tests for the definition of ' investment' , which is so far the only exception.

[85] *Inceysa Vallisoletana SL v Republic of El Salvador* (ICSID Case No ARB/03/26, Award of 2 August 2006). In this case, the Tribunal decided that El Salvador's consent to ICSID jurisdiction embodied in the BIT between El Salvador and Spain (1995) did not extend to investments that were made fraudulently, and therefore not in accordance with the law.

[86] *Fraport AG Frankfurt Airport Services Worldwide v Philippines* (ICSID Case No ARB/03/25, Award of 16 August 2007). In this case, the Tribunal declined its jurisdiction based on the BIT between Germany and the Philippines (1997) after having established that the claimant had not made an investment ' in accordance with the laws of the Philippines' .

[87] China-Germany BIT (2003), Art 2(1); and China-Uganda BIT (2004), Art 2(1).

[88] The ASEAN-China Investment Agreement (2009) only applies to investments made in Thailand that have been approved in writing ' by the competent authorities' (Art 3(3)). The approval of the investment under Art II(3) of the 1987 ASEAN Agreement proved to be fatal to the claimant's case in *Yaung Chi Oo Trading Pte Ltd v Government of the Union of Myanmar* (ASEAN ID Case No ARB/01/1, Final Award of 31 March 2003), paras 53 – 63.

fined in Article 1 are those made for the purpose of establishing lasting economic relations in connection with an enterprise, especially those which allow to exercise effective influence in its management.[89]

The BIT thus introduces three additional ' objective tests' to the term ' investment' defined under the ' definition' provision, namely ' lasting economic relations' ' connection with an enterprise' and ' effective influence in management' tests. Although the three criteria are different from what seem to have emerged from recent arbitration jurisprudence[90] and what have been adopted in the US Model BIT 2012,[91] it marks a breakthrough in Chinese BIT practice. However, it remains to be seen whether such an approach will be adopted in future Chinese BIT negotiations as several European BITs signed after this BIT have not followed suit.[92] That said, in May 2012 China signed an investment agreement with Japan and Korea which follows the US Model BIT 2012 definition very closely. It provides that an investment means ' every kind of asset that an investor owns or controls, directly or indirectly, which has the characteristics of an investment, such as the commitment of capital or other resources, the expectation of gain or profit, or the assumption of risk. Forms that investments may include ...'[93] This provision clearly reflects the ICSID jurisprudence and is similar to the US Model BIT terminology.

The new Germany BIT in force since November 2005 is also distinctive in that it expressly defines ' investment' to cover every kind of asset ' invested directly or indirectly' in the host State. It further clarifies in the Protocol that ' invested indirectly' means ' invested by an investor of one Contracting Party through a company which is fully or partially owned by the investor and having its seat in the territory of the other Contracting Party' . The main implication of this revision to the definition of ' invested indirectly' appears to be that investments made through holding companies will be covered by the BIT.

---

[89] China-Germany BIT (2003), Protocol Ad Art 1(a).

[90] Most relevant cases include *Fedax v Venezuela* (ICSID Case No ARB/96/3, Decision on Jurisdiction of 11 July 1997); *Salini Costruttori SpA and Italstrade SpA v Kingdom of Morocco* (ICSID Case No ARB/00/4, Decision on Jurisdiction of 23 July 2001), *Joy Mining Machinery Limited v Egypt* (ICSID Case No ARB/03/11, Award on Jurisdiction of 6 August 2004); *Saipem SpA v Bangladesh* (ICSID Case No ARB/05/07, Decision on Jurisdiction and Recommendation on Provisional Measures of 21 March 2007); *MCI Power Group LC and New Turbine, Inc v Ecuador* (ICSID Case No ARB/03/6, Award of 31 July 2007); *Malaysian Historical Salvors, SDN, BHD v Malaysia* (ICSID Case No ARB/05/10, Award on Jurisdiction of 17 May 2007); *Biwater Gauff (Tanzania) Ltd v Tanzania* (ICSID Case No ARB/05/22, Award of 24 July 2008); *GEA Group Aktiengesellschaft v Ukraine* (ICSID Case No ARB/08/16 Award of 31 March 2011), and *Sergei Paushok, CJSC Golden East Company and CJSC Vostokneftegaz Company v Mongolia* (Award on Jurisdiction and Liability of 28 April 2011).

[91] The current US Model BIT defines ' investment' as:

' investment' means every asset that an investor owns or controls, directly or indirectly, that has the characteristics of an investment, including such characteristics as the commitment of capital or other resources, the expectation of gain or profit, or the assumption of risk. Forms that an investment may take include...

US Model BIT 2012, Art 1. See also Norway Model BIT, Art 1(2).

[92] See eg China-Finland BIT (2004) Art 1(1), China-Belgium-Luxembourg BIT (2005) Art 1(2) and China-Spain BIT (2005) Art 1(1).

[93] China-Japan-Korea Trilateral Investment Agreement, signed 13 May 2012, Art 1, available at www.mofa.go.jp/announce/announce/2012/5/0513_01.html (last accessed 17 September 2012).

The 2007 Seychelles BIT generally follows the 2003 Germany BIT in its definition of ' investment' and also has a definition of ' invested indirectly' . Its definition of the latter, however, differs from the 2003 Germany BIT in that it covers not only investments by FIEs by investors of the other Contracting Party in China, but also those FIEs set up by legal persons of third States in China, which are owned or controlled by investors of the other Contracting Party.[94] However, the latter form of investment is protected by the BIT only when ' such third State has no right or abandons the right to claim compensation after the investment had been expropriated by the other Contracting Party' .[95] In other words, to benefit from treaty protection, two conditions must be met: one is that it is confined to expropriation and compensation cases; the other is that the third State has no right or has abandoned its right to make such a claim for compensation. This should be helpful in resolving problems such as those raised in the *Barcelona Traction* case, in which the ICJ decided that the Belgian Government was not allowed to exercise diplomatic protection against Spain for its citizens who owned the majority of the shares in a Canadian company, which invested in Spain and allegedly was expropriated by the Spanish Government.[96]

Similar to the approach adopted in many modern BITs, the general definition of ' investment' in the Chinese Model BIT is supplemented by an illustrative list of particular assets that are covered by the BIT. They include five categories of investments, namely movable and immovable property, interests in companies, contractual rights, intellectual property rights, and business concessions. This is followed in all but two BITs, namely the China-Poland and China-Bulgaria BITs,[97] which included only the first four categories of investment but exclude business concessions. Although the exact reasons for such exceptions are unclear, it is believed that their mutual dislike of business concessions with China as a legacy of their shared communist regime must have played an important, if not decisive, role. Such exclusion of concessions in the list in both BITs, however, may not necessarily mean that such business concessions cannot be covered by them. On the contrary, considering that the list is only illustrative and that all three countries have now accepted business concessions in their BIT practices, it is probably safe to argue that such concessions should also be protected by the two BITs.[98] The

---

[94] The China-Seychelles BIT reads:

2. ' Invested indirectly' includes:

1) invested by an investor of one Contracting Party through a company which is fully or partially owned by the investor and having its seat in the territory of the other Contracting Party, and

2) investments of legal persons of a third State which are owned or controlled by investors of one Contracting Party and which have been in the territory of the other Contracting Party in accordance with the laws and regulations of the latter. The relevant provisions of this Agreement shall apply to such investments only when such third State has no right or abandons the right to claim compensation after the investment had been expropriated by the other Contracting Party.

See the China-Seychelles BIT, Art 1(1).

[95] See also China-New Zealand FTA (2008), Art 135.

[96] *Barcelona Traction, Light and Power Company Ltd (Belgium v Spain) (Second Phase)* [1970] ICJ Rep 3. It should be noted that there have been many cases at ICSID where *Barcelona Traction* has no relevance to cases decided under a BIT. See, eg, *Rompetrol Group NV v Romania* (ICSID Case No ARB/06/3, Decision on Jurisdiction and Admissibility of 18 April 2008), paras 101, 107.

[97] China-Poland BIT, Art 1; and China-Bulgaria BIT, Art 1.

[98] For a close examination of the five categories of assets cover under the Model BIT, see Gallagher and Shan, *Chinese Investment Treaties*, paras 2.13 – 2.26.

ASEAN-China Investment Agreement sets out some examples of what ' business concessions' include in a footnote. It confirms that it covers ' contractual rights such as those under turnkey, construction or management contracts, production or revenue sharing contracts, concessions, or other similar contracts and can include investment funds for projects such as Build-Operate and Transfer (BOT) and Build-Operate and Own (BOO) schemes' . The China-Mexico BIT (2008) has additional categories set out in the definition of ' investment' and also specifically excludes certain types of transactions for example claims to money arising from a contract for the sale of goods.[99] This is a move away from the list provided in the Model BIT but clearly follows the North American Free Trade Agreement (' NAFTA') wording in Article 1139 with the categories set out in (a) to (h) and express exclusions in the following subsections.

To summarize, the Chinese Model BIT adopts a broad asset-based definition of ' investment' , which is only subject to the general requirement that such investments (p. 151) have to be made in accordance with the laws and regulations of the host State. Objective qualifications on what constitutes an ' investment' are not included in China's Model BIT, although the China-Germany BIT (2003) does include such criteria. It is not clear whether the inclusion of these objective criteria as applied by tribunals in ICSID arbitration in the context of Article 25 of the ICSID Convention will become a common feature of China's future BITs. Like other Model BITs, China's Model BIT contains a list of five categories of ' assets' that are deemed to be covered ' investments' . Whilst the list serves to clarify the meaning of ' investment' , it is important to bear in mind that the list is merely illustrative, and absence from the list of any particular asset does not necessarily mean that they are excluded from BIT protection.[100]

In view of the sharp increase in investment treaty based arbitration in recent years and the countermeasures taken by developed and developing States alike, it is advisable for China to carefully reassess the wording of such definitions, to avoid ' frivolous claims' . One way forward might be the introduction of qualifications and limitations introduced in, for example, the recent US Model BIT 2012. They include the ' characteristics of investment' requirement in the ' chapeau' part of the provision and the qualifications and clarifications on the listed forms of investment, such as the footnotes on debts and licences. A clarification on the scope of indirect investment holdings and controlling interest might also be useful.

Article 1: Definition of ' Investor'

2. The term ' investor' means,

(a) natural persons who have nationality of either Contracting Party in accordance with the laws of that Contracting Party;

---

[99] It is a finite list definition similar to that adopted in the NAFTA, Art 1; China-Mexico BIT (2008) (in force since 6 June 2009).

[100] An UNCTAD study comments:

the term ' investment' as used in investment agreements is a legal term of art. It is given a certain scope in order to accomplish the economic and political purposes of the treaty parties. It is not necessarily synonymous with the word ' investment' as used in other contexts, such as in national income accounting, or with other, related economic terms, such as ' capital' .

UNCTAD, *International Investment Agreements: Key Issues* (2004), vol I, p. 121.

(b) legal entities, including companies, associations, partnerships and other organizations, incorporated or constituted under the laws and regulations of either Contracting Party and have their seats in that Contracting Party.

Clearly the current Model BIT adopts a 'unified' approach and defines 'investors' both as natural persons and legal entities for either Contracting Party. This is in contrast with the first two Model BITs, which adopted a 'separate approach', defining investors from the two Contracting Parties separately. As a result, earlier Chinese BITs followed Version I and defined the term 'investor' separately (eg Sweden BIT 1982) for each Contracting State, whilst BITs signed from the late 1990s onwards generally follow Version III adopting the 'unified approach' (eg Finland BIT 2004).

1. *Natural Persons*

In all of China's Model BITs, 'nationality' is used as the identifying factor for 'investors' who are natural persons. Accordingly, most Chinese BITs only require a singular link with a Contracting Party, and the most often used link is nationality (citizenship).[101] The BIT with India, for example, provides in Article 1(a)(i) that nationals 'mean persons of either Contracting Party deriving their status as nationals of that Contracting Party from its laws in force.'[102] However, some BITs (eg the China-Australia, China-Bosnia and Herz egovina, China-Canada, China-Israel BITs and the China-New Zealand FTA) extend protection to permanent residents of a Contracting Party and therefore use 'permanent residency' as an alternative to nationality.[103] Other BITs use a combination of different links for individual investors, normally a combination

---

[101] 'Nationality' and 'citizenship' usually mean the same thing and are therefore often used interchangeably. However, there are subtle differences between the two terms, and there are cases where their scopes are rather different. In UK, for example, 'British Citizen' is only one among the several categories of citizenships, which are collectively referred to as 'British Nationals'; see, eg, UK Border Agency, 'What is British Citizenship?', available at www.ukba.homeoffice.gov.uk/britishcitizenship/aboutcitizenship (last accessed 27 December 2011). The China-UK BIT applies to UK nationals as defined by UK law who have the right of abode in the UK or in any territory to which the BIT has been agreed to extend in accordance with Art 10 of the treaty. According to Art 10, by exchange of notes the BIT protection can be extended to such 'territory' for whose international relations the UK Government is responsible, including, eg, the Virgin Islands and the Cayman Islands. As a matter of fact, however, so far, no such exchange of notes has been entered into. Therefore, investments from such islands are not eligible for the protection of the China-UK BIT.

[102] China-India BIT, signed 21 November 2006 (entered into force 1 August 2007). For the purposes of an ICSID arbitration the requirements of Art 25(2)(a) would still have to be met see R Wisner and N Gallus, 'Nationality Requirements in Investor-State Arbitration' (2004) 5(6) *Journal of World Investment and Trade* 927, 933.

[103] The China-Australia BIT applies to permanent residents except that (a) the provisions of an investment protection agreement between the other Contracting Party and the country of which the person is a citizen have already been invoked in respect of the same matter; or (b) the person is a citizen of the other Contracting Party. The China-New Zealand FTA also covers permanent residents as well as nationals, but on the condition that: '[U]ntil such time as China enacts its domestic law on the treatment of permanent residents of foreign countries, this Chapter does not impose obligations on a Party with respect to the permanent residents of the other Party except for the obligations in Arts 142, 143, 144, 145 and 148.' This is obviously for reciprocity considerations as China is yet to put in place a law on permanent residency: China-Australia BIT, Art 1(1)(d); China-New Zealand FTA, Art 135. See also Protocol to the China-Israel BIT, which states that Israeli permanent residents enjoy the same rights as Israeli nationals and are protected under this BIT. For general discussion on nationality links see UNCTAD, *Scope and Definition* (UNCTAD Series on Issues in International Investment Agreements II, 2011), pp. 73-6.

of nationality with other factor such as domicile,[104] residence (right of abode),[105] or place of business.[106] The purpose of imposing such additional requirements is apparently to add some substantial link to the home State, since sometimes nationality may be a rather superficial link.[107]

The Chinese Model BIT does not deal with the issue of dual/multiple nationality, but some Chinese BITs do so by expressly denying protection to nationals of the host State. The China-Iran BIT, for instance, stipulates that the covered 'natural persons' shall not have 'the nationality of the host Contracting Party'.[108] The China-Australia BIT, whilst covering Australian permanent residents, also excludes from them those having nationality of the host State.[109] In this connection, it should be noted that the Chinese Nationality Law does not recognize the dual nationality of Chinese citizens.[110] Chinese citizens who have settled abroad and have voluntarily acceded or otherwise obtained nationality of any other country automatically lose their Chinese nationality.[111] It should also be noted that the ICSID Convention contains clear rules excluding from ICSID jurisdiction such holders of dual nationality.[112] This has been confirmed in cases such as

---

[104] The China-Former Yugoslavia BIT (1995), for example, requires natural persons to have both the nationality of and be 'resident and domiciled' in former Yugoslavia, to be eligible as an investor under the BIT: China-Former Yugoslavia BIT, Art 1(2).

[105] China-Former Yugoslavia BIT; see also China-UK BIT, Art 1 (1) (requiring both nationality and right of abode). The recent Amendment to the Cuban BIT also has a provision requiring both nationality and 'permanent residency' as the link for natural person investors covered under the BIT: China-Cuba BIT Amendments (20 April 2007), Ad Art 1.

[106] The China-Bosnia and Herz egovina BIT requires that, for Bosnia and Herz egovina natural persons to become covered investors, they need to have either 'permanent residence' or 'main place of business' in Bosnia Herz egovina, on top of its citizenship: China-Bosnia and Herz egovina BIT, Art 1(2).

[107] Although the test for real and effective nationality as understood by the ICJ in *Nottebohm Guatemala v Liechtenstein) (Second Phase)* [1955] ICJ Rep 4 has been distinguished for the purposes of arbitration under BITs: see, eg, *Champion Trading Company, Ameritrade International, Inc, James T Wahba, John B Wahba, Timothy T Wahba v Egypt* (ICSID Case No ARB/02/9, Decision on Jurisdiction of 21 October 2003); *Soufraki v United Arab Emirates* (ICSID Case No ARB/02/7, Award of 7 July 2004); *Olguin v Paraguay* (ICSID Case No ARB/98/5, Decision on Jurisdiction of 8 August 2000); and *Ioan Micula, Viorel Micula, SC European Food SA, SC Starmill SRL and SC Multipack SRL v Romania* (ICSID Case No ARB/05/20, Decision on Jurisdiction and Admissibility of 24 September 2008), where the Tribunal confirmed that the burden of proof was on the party seeking to challenge the nationality asserted by the investor. This was accepted by the Tribunal in *Tza Yap Shum v Republic of Peru* (ICSID Case No ARB/07/6, Decision on Jurisdiction and Competence of 19 June 2009) ('*Tza Yap Shum v Republic of Peru*') where the Tribunal accepted that the claimant had produced sufficient evidence to confirm his Chinese nationality: see paras 55 – 66.

[108] China-Iran BIT, Art 1 (2)(a).

[109] China-Australia BIT, Art 1 (3).

[110] Art 3 of the Nationality Law of the People's Republic of China, passed by the National People's Congress on 10 September 1980.

[111] Nationality Law of the People's Republic of China, Art 9.

[112] Art 25(2)(a) of the ICSID Convention provides:

(2) 'National of another Contracting State' means: any natural person who had the nationality of a Contracting State other than the State party to the dispute on the date on which the parties consented to submit such dispute to conciliation or arbitration as well as on the date on which the request was registered pursuant to paragraph (3) of Article 28 or paragraph (3) of Article 36, *but does not include any person who on either date also had the nationality of the Contracting State party to the dispute* ... (emphasis added)

Champion Trading v Egypt and *Soufraki v United Arab Emirates*. In *Micula v Romania* the ICSID Tribunal questioned the applicability of the 'genuine link test' to the Romania-Sweden BIT noting that the parties 'are free to agree whether any conditional standards must be applied to the determination of nationality'.[113] The issue of dual nationality could be dealt with in the next revision of the China Model BIT to clarify their position.

A nuance with regard to nationality arises from the creation of Special Administrative Regions ('SARs') of China. The question is whether investors from SARs such as Hong Kong and Macau may make use of Chinese BITs for investment protection. The problem arises out of the fact that although the SARs are legally a part of China, they enjoy a high degree of autonomy and continue to practice a capitalist system and way of life for 50 years (different from the socialist system practiced in Mainland China).[114] In particular, the SAR Governments have the power to enter into international agreements in trade and investment areas,[115] and Hong Kong has already entered into a dozen BITs with other countries.[116]

It is submitted that the above-mentioned autonomy and competence of the SARs should not become a bar to SAR investors seeking to benefit from an applicable Chinese BIT. Such autonomy and competence were designed for the benefit of SAR residents, protecting their interests and way of life, not the reverse. A SAR investor may invoke a relevant Chinese BIT to protect his or her investment abroad, as long as the Chinese BIT covers the Hong Kong investor, for example in its definition of 'investors'. Indeed, a Hong Kong investor has already successfully brought a case before ICSID, on the basis of the China-Peru BIT (*Tza Yap Shum v Peru*).[117] The Tribunal in *Tza Yap Shum* rejected the assertion by Peru that even if the claimant was a Chinese national because of his residence in Hong Kong he was not protected by the BIT. There was no express exclusion of

---

[113] *Micula v Romania*, para 101.

[114] The Basic Law of the Hong Kong Special Administrative Region of the People's Republic of China, adopted on 4 April 1990 by the Seventh National People's Congress of the People's Republic of China at its Third Session, Arts 2 and 5.

[115] The Basic Law of the Hong Kong Special Administrative Region of the People's Republic of China, Art 151, which reads:

The Hong Kong Special Administrative Region may on its own, using the name 'Hong Kong, China', maintain and develop relations and conclude and implement agreements with foreign States and regions and relevant international organiz ations in the appropriate fields, including the economic, trade, financial and monetary, shipping, communications, tourism, cultural and sports fields.

[116] UNCTAD has a list of the BITs it is aware of that Hong Kong has signed, available at www. unctad. org/sections/dite_pcbb/docs/bits_hk_china. pdf (last accessed 29 December 2011).

The Hong Kong-Australia BIT has been invoked in the claim presented by Philip Morris Asia Ltd against the Government of Australia (see Philip Morris Asia Ltd's Notification of Claim of 22 June 2011, available at www. ag. gov. au. tobaccoplainpackaging (last accessed 29 December 2011).

[117] *Tza Yap Shum v Republic of Peru* (ICSID Case No ARB/07/6). The case was brought on the basis of the China-Peru BIT of 1994. For further details of the case, see F C Diaz, 'Chinese Investor Launches BIT Claim against Peru at ICSID', *Investment Treaty News* (2 March 2007); and A Chen, 'Queries to the Recent ICSID Decision on Jurisdiction Upon the Case of *Tza Yap Shum v Republic of Peru*: Should China-Peru BIT 1994 Be Applied to Hong Kong SAR under the "One Country Two Systems" Policy' (2009) 10(6) *Journal of World Investment & Trade* 829.

Chinese nationals with Hong Kong residence in the BIT itself nor did Article 25 of the ICSID Convention require anything more than nationality. Article 1(2)(a) of the China-Peru BIT is similar to the Model BIT providing that an investor means any 'Natural persons who have nationality of the People's Republic of China in accordance with its laws'. The tribunal 'believes that Respondent has not proven convincingly that the parties to the BIT intended to exclude Hong Kong residents from its scope of application'.[118] In addition, China had not excluded Hong Kong by written notice under Article 70 of the ICSID Convention.[119] In this connection, it should be noted that the aforementioned Chinese Nationality Law is among the few national laws that apply to Hong Kong,[120] which, as explained by the NPC,[121] grants Chinese nationality to a wide range of Hong Kong residents, including holders of the 'British Dependent Territories Citizens passport', 'British Nationals (Overseas) passport', or British Citizenship acquired through the 'British Nationality Selection Scheme'.[122]

It should also be noted that the issue of treaty coverage on persons (and entities) is different from the question of a treaty's territorial coverage. Although they are related, they perform different functions and their scopes may not necessarily be the same. In investment treaty arbitration, for example, the former determines the scope of application of a treaty to persons and entities (covered investors), whilst the latter decides its application to activities occurring in certain territorial areas (covered territories). A Chinese BIT covering all Chinese nationals may protect Hong Kong or Macau investors even when the BIT expressly excludes its application to both SARs, as does the China-Russia BIT.[123] For the same reason it cannot be argued that a Chinese BIT could not be used to protect SAR investors because it does not apply to the SARs failing to go through cer-

---

[118] *Tza Yap Shum v Republic of Peru* (ICSID Case No ARB/07/6, Decision on Jurisdiction and Competence of 19 June 2009), para 74 (unofficial translation). Annulment proceedings commenced by Peru are currently pending in this case.

[119] *Tza Yap Shum v Republic of Peru*, paras 67 – 77.

[120] Basic Law of Hong Kong, Art 18.

[121] Explanations of some questions by the Standing Committee of the National People's Congress concerning the implementation of the Nationality Law of the People's Republic of China in the Hong Kong Special Administrative Region (Adopted at the Nineteenth Session of the Standing Committee of the Eighth National People's Congress on 15 May 1996).

[122] Explanations of some questions by Standing Committee of National People's Congress concerning implementation of Nationality Law of People's Republic of China in Hong Kong Special Administrative Region.

[123] The China-Russia BIT expressly excludes its application to Chinese SARs including both Hong Kong and Macau. It states:

1. Unless otherwise agreed by both Contracting Parties, the Agreement does not apply to the Hong Kong Special Administrative Region of the People's Republic of China and the Macao Special Administrative Region of People's Republic of China.

It is submitted that such a provision only excludes protection of Russian investments in the two SARs, but not necessarily protection of investors from the two regions. As long as they qualify as Chinese 'national' under Art 1(2)(a) of the BIT, they are eligible for its protection. See China-Russia BIT Protocol, Ad Art 1.

tain formalities.[124]

2. Corporate Entities

For corporate entities, the Chinese Model BIT combines place of incorporation and domicile or seat as the connecting factors for identifying their nationality. In practice, Chinese BITs uses ‘incorporation’ ‘seat’ and ‘control’ as the basic criteria in establishing nationality of corporate entities. Some BITs combine two of the criteria, with a view to restricting the application of the treaty to companies. Others use them as alternatives, thereby broadening the scope of the application of the treaty concerned. Some BITs limit the BIT application by requiring Chinese companies to have been approved or qualified to conduct foreign economic activities. Others broaden the application by including companies that are not formulated in the form of a legal person, or a commercial entity, or a limited liability company.[125] The definition in the Model BIT would also cover State-owned or controlled entities as well as sovereign wealth funds. This has yet to be tested, but may be significant in future claims given the amount and size of investments made by Chinese State-owned entities and its sovereign wealth fund.

The position of SAR corporate entities under Chinese investment treaties is similar to that of natural persons, but it carries more complexity. The complexity lies in the applicable legal regime; the determination of the nationality of SAR natural persons is governed by a uniform law of China, the Chinese Nationality Law; whilst the incorporation of corporate entities in the two SARs is governed by separate laws in each SAR respectively. Nevertheless, laws of the SARs are also considered to be part of the law of China. Entities incorporated under the law of Hong Kong SAR, for example, are also entities incorporated under Chinese law.

A closer look at some of the BITs makes this clearer. Taking the China-Norway BIT as an example, it defines ‘companies’ in respect of China as ‘economic bodies incorporated and domiciled in the territory of the PRC in accordance with its laws’.[126] The use of the term ‘laws’, rather than ‘law’, gives a strong indication that such laws include all forms of laws of China, including the laws of SARs, which are also part of the ‘territory of China’. The language adopted in the China-UK BIT is less ambiguous; it defines ‘companies’ in respect of China as such entities ‘incorporated or constituted under the law in force in any part of the People's Republic of China’.[127] The reference to ‘any part’ of China clearly indicates that SARs such as Hong Kong and Macau are covered. This interpretation is supported by the legal situation in the UK, which also has a few different jurisdictions such as England and Wales, Scotland, and

---

[124] The Basic Law of Hong Kong, for example, requires a consultation procedure with the Hong Kong Government, before any decision is made by the central government as to whether a particular treaty participated by China shall apply to Hong Kong SAR. The relevant Article (Art 153) reads:

The application to the Hong Kong Special Administrative Region of international agreements to which the People's Republic of China is or becomes a party shall be decided by the Central People's Government, in accordance with the circumstances and needs of the Region, and after seeking the views of the government of the Region.

[125] For further details see Gallagher and Shan, *Chinese Investment Treaties*, 2.50 – 2.75.

[126] China-Norway BIT, Art 1(4).

[127] China-UK BIT, Art 1(1)(d).

Northern Ireland. The same wording was used in the definition of UK ' companies' and it is clearly the intention of such wording to treat all companies of UK, irrespective of whether they are incorporated under English law or laws of other jurisdictions within the UK, as covered ' investors' . It would certainly be absurd that it should be interpreted differently in the case of China.

Likewise, SAR corporate entities are also covered by Chinese BITs in cases where the ' seat' test is employed, because a seat in Hong Kong means a seat in the territory of China, unless SARs are expressly excluded from the scope of application of the BIT, as they are under the China-Russia BIT.[128] In addition, China BITs may also cover SAR entities by way of the ' control' criteria. This would be very useful for the numerous Chinese invested companies in Hong Kong and Macau. This vehicle, however, is only available when the applicable Chinese BIT adopts the ' control' test as an alternative test to corporate nationality.

B. Promotion and Protection of Investments

Article 2: Promotion and Protection of Investments

3. Each Contracting Party shall encourage investors of the other Contracting Party to make investments in its territory and admit such investments in accordance with its laws and regulations.

4. Investments of the investors of either Contracting Party shall enjoy the constant protection and security in the territory of the other Contracting Party.

5. Without prejudice to its laws and regulations, neither Contracting Party shall take any unreasonable or discriminatory measures against the management, maintenance, use, enjoyment and disposal of the investments by the investors of the other Contracting Party.

6. Subject to its laws and regulations, one Contracting Party shall provide assistance in and facilities for obtaining visas and working permit to nationals of the other Contracting Party engaging in activities associated with investments made in the territory of that Contracting Party.

This article sets out some of the most fundamental standards for the promotion and protection of foreign investment. It covers investment admission, constant protection and security, and non-discrimination obligations. It does not include the fair and equitable treatment (' FET') standard, which is found in Article 3 (standards of treatment).[129]

1. *Admission*

It is obvious that the Chinese Model BIT has followed the European prototype leaving control and protection of the admission stage to the discretion of the host country.[130] This is largely due to the fact that BITs were not originally crafted as ' market access'

---

[128] Russia BIT, Protocol, Point 1.

[129] Version II of the Model BIT did include the FET standard in Art 2. See Chinese Model BIT Version II (1989), Art 2.

[130] Notably, US BITs impose obligations on investment admission by the combination of the MFN and national treatment clauses. See R Dolzer and M Stevens, *Bilateral Investment Treaties* (Martinus Nijhoff, 1995), p. 49. *See also* UNCTAD, Key Issue I, at 143 - 4.

treaties, but rather to protect investments once they had been made in the host State. This approach has been followed in Chinese BIT practice. Under Chinese BITs, foreign investments are encouraged and admitted in accordance with the laws and regulations of the host State.[131] The Model BIT also requires that, subject to its laws and regulations, the Contracting Parties must facilitate the obtaining of visas and working permits for personnel engaging in investment-related activities.[132]

2. *Constant Protection and Security*

The inclusion of qualifiers such as 'full' 'adequate' or 'constant' on the protection and security obligation has been interpreted as suggesting a stronger commitment or wider coverage. In *Azurix v Argentina*,[133] for example, the tribunal considered that 'when the terms "protection and security" are qualified by "full" and no other adjective or explanation, they extend, in their ordinary meaning, the content of this standard beyond physical security'.[134] In other words, the addition of the adjective 'full' has the effect of extending the scope of protection, from physical protection to non-physical interference. As a result, the standard has often been merged by arbitral tribunals with the FET standard. As mentioned above, such an extension of coverage and merging of the two standards has become a trend in recent arbitration practice, though it remains to be seen whether this trend will be sustained.[135]

3. *Non-Discriminatory Treatment*

There was no such provision in Version I of the Chinese Model BIT, but it appeared in Version II in Article 2(3).[136] The Chinese Model BIT subjects the guarantee of non-arbitrariness and non-discrimination to the laws and regulations of the host State. Interpreted textually, such a reservation in respect of laws and regulations of the host State appears to allow the host government to maintain or introduce, in its legislation, measures that could otherwise be considered 'unreasonable' or 'discriminatory'.[137] However, this type of provision would still prevent unreasonable and discriminatory measures that are imposed by means other than laws and regulations, for example by individual acts of State officials or State agencies.

---

[131] See, eg, China-Germany BIT (1983), Art 2; China-Switzerland BIT (1986), Art 2; China-Japan-Korea Trilateral Investment Agreement (2012), Art 3, and China-Canada BIT (2012). For details of investment admission under Chinese law, see W Shan, *Legal Framework*, Chapter 4 (Admission and Establishment).

[132] Which is followed in some BITs. See, eg, China-Russia BIT (2006), Art 2(3).

[133] Azurix v. Argentine Republic (*ICISD Case No ARB/01/12, Award of 14 July 2006*).

[134] Azurix v. Argentine Republic, *para* 408.

[135] See for a discussion on the scope of the full protection and security provision in international law *Frontier Petroleum Services Ltd v Czech Republic* (Award of 10 November 2010) (not public), paras 260 – 73. See also *National Grid plc v Argentine Republic* (Award of 3 November 2008) and *Siemens v Argentine Republic* (ICSID Case No ARB/02/8, Award of 6 February 2007).

[136] This is consistent with the evolution of this standard in other treaties for example Denmark added this protection to its BIT in late 1980s. See Vandevelde, *Bilateral Investment Treaties*, pp. 215 – 19 and R Dolzer and C Schreuer, *Principles of International Investment Law* (Oxford University Press, 2008), pp. 173 – 8.

[137] Similar reservations are sometimes made in the national treatment clauses.

C. Treatment of Investments

Article 3: Treatment of Investment

1. Investments of investors of each Contracting Party shall all the time be accorded fair and equitable treatment in the territory of the other Contracting Party.

2. Without prejudice to its laws and regulations, each Contracting Party shall accord to investments and activities associated with such investments by the investors of the other Contracting Party treatment not less favorable than that accorded to the investments and associated activities by its own investors.

3. Neither Contracting Party shall subject investments and activities associated with such investments by the investors of the other Contracting Party to treatment less favorable than that accorded to the investments and associated activities by the investors of any third State.

4. The provisions of Paragraph 3 of this Article shall not be construed so as to oblige one Contracting Party to extend to the investors of the other Contracting Party the benefit of any treatment, preference or privilege by virtue of:

(a) any customs union, free trade zone, economic union and any international agreement resulting in such unions, or similar institutions;

(b) any international agreement or arrangement relating wholly or mainly to taxation;

(c) any arrangements for facilitating small scale frontier trade in border areas.

This article establishes the general standards of treatment accorded to foreign investors including FET, national treatment ('NT') and MFN treatment.

1. *Fair and Equitable Treatment*

All three versions of the Model BIT contain this standard, which is accompanied by the provision of 'protection' (in Version I) or 'constant protection and security' (in Versions II and III). Although the wording is not identical it is similar to Article 1 of the Draft OECD Convention of 1967.[138] In Version I this provision was stated in Article 3 (on standards of treatment). In Version II, it was moved to Article 2 on general investment promotion and protection, suggesting a standing offer applicable to both the admission and operation stages of foreign investment. In Version III, the current Model BIT, it has again been moved, this time to Article 3 on standards of treatment but with the additional wording 'all the time'.[139] There was some speculation on whether this meant it would apply to both the admission and operation stages. However, the protection relates to investments of investors which means that it would only apply once an 'investment'

---

[138] See Notes and Comments to Art 1 confirming that three rules in Art 1 emanated from the 'well-established general principle of international law' that a State had to protect property of other nationals including the fair and equitable treatment. For general discussion on the origins of the fair and equitable standard of treatment see Vandevelde, *Bilateral Investment Treaties*, pp. 195 - 202.

[139] This states that: Investments of investors of each Contracting Party shall all the time be accorded fair and equitable treatment in the territory of the other Contracting Party.

See Model Text, Version III, Art 3.

had actually been made. This version is also different in that it separated the provision on fair and equitable treatment from the ' constant protection and security' obligation which is stipulated in Article 2.

The Chinese Model BIT does not make express reference to a particular body of law or other standards. Accordingly, the FET provision should first be considered against other provisions of the treaty, then general international law, and/or domestic law of the host State.[140] In applying general or customary international law, it might be a consideration that many principles of general or customary international law have emerged and been developed in the context of Europe and among developed States, and China has not participated fully in this process.[141] As a result, there has been a limited familiarity with and consequently a certain degree of resistance to such principles in China.

Indeed, some earlier writings by eminent Chinese scholars have flatly denied the existence and the applicability of the international law standard (or ' international minimum standard'). Yao, for instance, wrote that the international (law/minimum) standard ' is essentially an imperialist and colonialist theory, and does not conform to contemporary international law' , and therefore ' cannot be accepted either in theory or in practice' .[142] Accordingly, earlier Chinese BITs have tried as far as possible to avoid any reference to ' international law' , either as the law for the interpretation of FET, or the applicable law for the settlement of investment disputes. In the rare cases when reference is made, it is substantially qualified, by confining such international law to be only these that have been ' generally recognized' and that have also been ' accepted' by both Contracting Parties.[143] Acceptance of such principles without qualifications did not appear in Chinese BITs until recent years. Therefore, it can be expected that there will be disagreements between China and its counterparts as to the exact scope and contents of ' general or customary international law' , even though the concept has now been accepted. China's more recent treaties have included express reference to general principles of international law for example Article 9(7) China-Cyprus BIT (2001) refers to the ' applicable principles of international law' .[144] Article 9(5) of the China-Czech Republic BIT (2005) refers to the ' general principles of international law' indicating a shift in China's approach to the application of these principles over the years.

More States are incorporating qualifications into their treaties in particular relating to this standard of protection. The United States as a direct result of its experience under

---

[140] Gallagher and Shan, *Chinese Investment Treaties*, paras 3.8 – 3.13.

[141] For an overview of China's changing attitude to international law, see Junwu Pan, ' Chinese Philosophy and International Law' (2011) 1 *Asian Journal of International Law* 233.

[142] Y Meiz hen, *International Investment Law* (Wuhan University Press, 1987) (in Chinese), pp. 334 – 8.

[143] See, eg, Chin-Belgium-Luxembourg BIT 1984, Art 7 of the Protocol.

[144] Other treaties refer to ' principles of international law recognised by both Contracting Parties' : China-Germany BIT (2003), Art 8(5).

NAFTA has done so in its Model BIT.[145] More recently China in the BIT with Mexico also incorporated qualifying language similar to that of the NAFTA Free Trade Commission at Article 5(2). It confirms that the fair and equitable treatment does not require anything 'in addition to or beyond that which is required by the international law minimum standard of treatment of aliens'.[146] The China-Colombia BIT, which was signed on 22 November 2008, makes similar provision.[147]

2. *National Treatment*

Due to the planned economy legacy in China, the NT standard has not been widely used in Chinese BIT practice. It is worth noting that the OECD Draft Convention 1967 did not contain a NT provision either.[148] Version I of the Chinese Model BIT did not have such a clause at all; Version II contains only a 'best endeavours' or soft NT provision. Version III has a NT standard but it is subject to local laws and regulations. The NT provision is not drafted in a broad manner and only applies to 'investments' of investors, and not to 'investors' and 'investments' as independent obligations (as is the case in, for example, Article 3 of the Canadian Model BIT).

China did not accept NT in its BIT practice until 1986 when the China-UK BIT 1986 was signed including a 'best endeavours' NT provision. The qualification in Version III subjecting NT to domestic laws and regulations has been modified by some recent BITs.[149] These BITs removed the 'domestic laws and regulations' qualification from the treaty text, but retain a 'grandfather provision' or 'freez ing clause' in their Protocols applicable to China, allowing it to maintain and modify existing non-conforming measures inconsistent with the NT standard, as long as this will not increase the general level of inconsistency. China also agrees in these BITs to gradually phase out such inconsistent measures.[150] The NT provision was one of the stumbling blocks for the failed BIT negotiations between the United States and China in the 1980s.[151] This

---

[145] US Model BIT (2012), Art 5(2). For a critical review of the standard applied by the tribunals under Art 1105 in the NAFTA cases see Judge Stephen Schwebel, 'Is *Neer* Far From Fair and Equitable?' (2011) 27 *Arbitration International* 555.

[146] China-Mexico BIT (2008), Art 5(2). No such qualifying language appears in the China-New Zealand FTA (2008) (Art 143), or in the ASEAN-China Cooperation Agreement (2009), although both treaties do include examples of what a breach of fair and equitable treatment means. Art 7(2) (a) of ASEAN-China Cooperation Agreement confirms that 'fair and equitable treatment refers to the obligation of each Party not to deny justice in any legal or administrative proceedings'.

[147] China-Colombia BIT, Art 2(3) – (4). See also China-Japan-Korea Trilateral Investment Agreement (2012), Art 5(1), which provides that 'the concepts of "fair and equitable treatment" and "full protection and security" do not require treatment in addition to or beyond any reasonable and appropriate standard of treatment accorded in accordance with generally accepted rules of international law'. See also the China-Canada BIT (2012), Art 4.

[148] In the 1960s there was no consistent or 'typical' format of NT: see Vandevelde, *Bilateral Investment Treaties*, p. 374.

[149] See, eg, China-Bosnia and Herzegovina BIT (2002), Art 3(1); Germany-China BIT (2003), Art 2(2); and Finland-China BIT (2004), Art 3(2).

[150] For further details please see Gallagher and Shan, *Chinese Investment Treaties*, paras 4.65 – 4.90; see also China-Japan-Korea Trilateral Investment Agreement, (2012), Art 3(2) – (3) (not yet in force).

[151] See T A Steiner, 'If the BIT Fits: The Proposed Bilateral Investment Treaty between the United States and the People's Republic of China' (1988) 2 *Journal of Chinese Law* 405.

may not be such an issue in the resumed talks on a BIT with the United States, as China has now shown its willingness to accept NT protections.

3. *Most-Favoured Nation ('MFN') Standard*

Unlike the NT standard, MFN treatment is common in all Chinese BITs. This is perhaps not surprising given the long history of the MFN provision in treaties.[152] All three Versions of the Chinese Model BIT have a similar MFN clause covering both 'investments' and 'activities associated with such investments'. Unlike many other Model BITs the Chinese BITs do not cover both investors and investments in separate provisions. This may begin to change as the China-Mexico BIT does expressly refer to both protection of investors and investments in Article 4(1) and (2) respectively, as does the China-Canada BIT (2012). It is not clear yet whether this is a new trend for China or a concession made to Mexico as the language is similar to that of Article 1105 of the NAFTA. Chapter 11 of the China-New Zealand FTA (2008) does not have a separate provision in Article 139, nor does the China – Colombia BIT (2008) in Article 3, or the ASEAN-China Investment Agreement (2009) in Article 5. The MFN provision requires foreign investments to be treated no worse than investments made by investors from any other country thereby preventing discrimination on the ground of nationality.[153] Some of China's earlier BITs are limited in scope and cover only investments in their MFN clause, without direct reference to 'investment-related activities'.[154] There are also treaties that follow the format of China's first Model BIT which links the MFN to the FET protection in the previous subparagraph (1). Article 3(2) states that 'the treatment and protection referred to in Paragraph 1 of this Article shall not be less favourable than that accorded to investments and activities associated with such investments of investors of a third State'.[155]

None of the Chinese Model BITs have included the 'in like circumstances' wording in the MFN provision, yet this is appearing in the more recent treaties signed by China.[156] This provision has been applied in the context of national treatment provisions under NAFTA Article 1102 for example in the case of *Methanex v USA*. The tribunal confirmed that the comparators should be 'in the most "like circumstances" and not ... in less "like circumstances". It would be a forced application of Article 1102 if a Tribu-

---

[152] See for a discussion of the origins of MFN protection Vandevelde *Bilateral Investment Treaties*, pp. 352 – 7. The MFN standard has been included in 'virtually all investment treaties': Dolzer and Schreuer *Principles of International Investment Law*, p. 186. See also ILC, 'Draft Articles on Most-Favoured-Nation Clauses' *Yearbook of the International Law Commission* (1978), vol II(2) and C McLachlan, L Shore, and M Weiniger, *International Investment Arbitration: Substantive Principles* (Oxford University Press, 2007), pp. 254 – 7.

[153] Art 3(3) of the current Model BIT.

[154] See eg, Art 2(2) of the China-Sweden BIT (1982).

[155] Art 3(2) Chinese Model BIT I. See also Art 3(2) of the China-Poland BIT (1988) and Art 3(2) of the China-Pakistan BIT (1989).

[156] See, eg, China-Mexico BIT (2008), Art 4; China-Japan-Korea Trilateral Investment Agreement (2012), Art 4(1), and China-Canada BIT (2012), Art 5.

nal were to ignore the identical comparator'.[157] The tribunal concluded that Methanex did not receive treatment less favourable than that received by the identical domestic comparators.

Pre-admission activities are covered by MFN clauses in some recent BITs, such as the Finland-China BIT (2004). As is typical in most MFN provisions, there are certain important exceptions. For example the Germany-China BIT 2003 does not apply to any membership of customs unions, free trade zones, economic unions or common markets, or to any double taxation agreements.[158] The MFN clause does not expressly refer to dispute resolution, as is made clear for example in the UK Model BIT. It is not certain whether the MFN provision in China's current Model BIT could therefore be extended to refer to substantive as well as procedural rights of the treaty. In light of the recent changes made to the dispute resolution provisions in Chinese BITs which now permit resort to ICSID arbitration for investor-State disputes, the exact scope and application of the MFN clause has significance for foreign investors in China.[159]

The tribunal in *Tza Yap Shum v Peru* considered the claimant's assertion that it could invoke the MFN in the China-Peru BIT to rely on Article 12 of the Peru-Colombia BIT to extend the scope of its ICSID claim. The tribunal ultimately rejected the claimant's argument finding that ' Article 3 cannot be interpreted so as to extend the jurisdiction of the Centre as a basis for an independent source of competence of the Tribunal'.[160] This was largely based on the restrictive wording of Article 8(3) and the fact that it specifically stated that the parties could agree to have other disputes decided at ICSID. The second part of Article 8(3) of the China-Peru BIT states:

Any disputes concerning other matters between an investor of either Contracting Party and the other Contracting Party may be submitted to the Centre if the parties to the disputes so agree.

This provision precluded the tribunal applying the MFN clause to widen the scope of the consent to arbitration. There are other Chinese treaties that also include this provision which limit the broad application of the MFN clause.[161] The China-Malaysia BIT (1988) which forms the basis of the claim filed by a Malaysian investor against China also has

---

[157] *Methanex Corporation v United States of America* (Final Award of 3 August 2005), Part IV, Chapter B, para 19. See also other NAFTA cases: *GAMI Investments Inc v Mexico* (Final Award of 15 November 2004); and *United Parcel Service of America Inc v Canada* (Award of 24 May 2007) where the dissenting arbitrator disagreed with the application of Art 1102. For a detailed review see UNCTAD, *Most-Favoured-Nation Treatment*, UNCTAD Series on Issues in International Investment Agreements II (United Nations, 2010) (' UNCTAD Series II MFN'), pp. 21 – 37.

[158] China-Germany BIT (2003), Art 3(4).

[159] For further details see Gallagher and Shan, *Chinese Investment Treaties*, paras 4. 17 – 4. 42.

[160] *Tza Yap Shum v Peru* (ICSID Case No ARB/07/6, Decision on Jurisdiction and Competence of 19 June 2009), para 220 (unofficial translation). See also *Plama v Bulgaria* (ICSID Case No ARB/03/24, Decision on Jurisdiction of 8 February 2005); *Berschader v Russia* (Award of 21 April 2006) and *Telenor Mobile Communications AS v Republic of Hungary* (ICSID Case No ARB/04/15, Award of 13 September 2006).

[161] See, eg, China-Greece BIT (1992), Art 10(2). See for an example of a broader application of the MFN provision *Emilio Agustín Maffezini v Kingdom of Spain* (ICSID Case No ARB/97/7, Decision on Jurisdiction of 25 January 2000), and *Gas Natural SDG, SA v Argentine Republic* (ICSID Case No ARB/03/10, Decision on Jurisdiction of 17 June 2005), and commentary in UNCTAD, *Series II MFN*, pp. 66 – 92.

this qualifying language. This would seem to preclude an expansive application of the MFN provision in Article 3.[162] But the outcome in *Tza Yap Shum* would not necessarily preclude a tribunal from adopting the broader application of the MFN provision in China's treaties that do not contain this additional language. For instance, in a claim against Slovakia where the BIT was also restrictive in nature, being limited to disputes 'concerning the amount or the conditions of payment of a compensation' under Article 4 (expropriation), the tribunal declined jurisdiction as the clause was intentionally narrow.[163] The award was not unanimous leaving open the possibility that China in the future might be able to exclude jurisdiction. In its more recent treaties, China has included an express provision excluding the application of the MFN provision to dispute resolution provisions. The ASEAN-China Investment Agreement (2009), for example, provides at Article 5(4) that: 'For greater certainty, the obligation in this Article does not encompass a requirement for a Party to extend to investors of another Party dispute resolution procedures other than those set out in this Agreement.'[164]

D. Expropriation

Article 4: Expropriation

1. Neither Contracting Party shall expropriate, nationalize or take other similar measures (hereinafter referred to as 'expropriation') against the investments of the investors of the other Contracting Party in its territory, unless the following conditions are met:

(a) for the public interests;

(b) under domestic legal procedure;

(c) without discrimination;

(d) against compensation.

2. The compensation mentioned in Paragraph 1 of this Article shall be equivalent to the value of the expropriated investments immediately before the expropriation is taken or the impending expropriation becomes public knowledge, whichever is earlier. The value shall be determined in accordance with generally recognized principles of valuation. The compensation shall include interest at a normal commercial rate from the date of expropriation until the date of payment. The compensation shall also be made without delay, be effectively realizable and freely transferable.

It is not surprising that each of Versions I, II, and III of China's Model BIT has an

---

[162] *Ekran Berhad v People's Republic of China* (ICSID Case No ARB/11/15). Art 7(4) of the Malaysia-China BIT provides that disputes 'relating to the amount of compensation and any other disputes agreed upon by both parties may be submitted to an International Arbitral Tribunal.'

[163] *Austrian Airlines AG v The Slovak Republic* (Award of 9 October 2009); cf Dissenting Opinion of Charles Brower on the application of the MFN provision.

[164] See also China-New Zealand FTA (2008), Art 139(2) which expressly excludes procedural rights in similar terms. It provides: 'For greater certainty, the obligation in this Article does not encompass a requirement to extend to investors of the other Party dispute resolution procedures other than those set out in this Chapter.' See also China-Canada BIT (2012), Art 5(3).

expropriation clause. It is a 'central issue of the international law on investment as well as the most controversial part of the Chinese attitude towards foreign investment'.[165] Expropriation per se is not illegal so long as certain requirements are fulfilled. The conditions included in the Chinese Models are also fairly typical.[166] This model sets out the basic structure of expropriation clauses in BITs actually entered into by China. Four conditions are attached to expropriation, namely, that it must be: (i) for the public interest; (ii) in accordance with domestic legal procedure; (iii) on a non-discriminatory basis; and (iv) compensation must be paid. A notable absence from the wording is a guarantee that an expropriation must be in accordance with due process. The requirement in the Chinese Model BITs is that the expropriation be carried out in accordance with the 'local legal procedure'.[167] This is in contrast to the more common reference in other countries BITs to an expropriation being made in accordance with 'due process of law'. It is not clear whether this would result in any significant difference were a case to arise, for as has been seen earlier, the domestic law in China relating to expropriation does require that the usual conditions be met including consideration of the public interest and payment of appropriate compensation. To date, there is only one public award concerning expropriation under a Chinese BIT.[168] This is not to say that expropriations have not occurred in China prior to this claim being presented under the China-Peru BIT, as is evidenced by the takings in the early years after the cultural revolution in the 1950s.[169] There have been investor disputes and disagreements,[170] but only one that

[165] Q Kong, 'Bilateral Investment Treaties: The Chinese Approach and Practice' (1998 – 99) 8 *Asian Yearbook of International Law*, p. 106, 125. See generally on expropriation, Vandevelde, *Bilateral Investment Treaties*, p. 271; Salacuse, *The Law of Investment Treaties*, ch 12; A Reinisch, 'Expropriation', in P Muchlinski, F Ortino, and C Schreuer (eds), *The Oxford Handbook of International Investment Law* (Oxford University Press, 2008), p. 408; Dolzer and Schreuer, *Principles of International Investment Law*, p. 89; C McLachlan, L Shore, and M Weiniger, *International Investment Arbitration*, p. 265.

[166] See Art 4(1) of the current Model BIT cited above. It has been noted that 'large scale nationaliz ation will not occur in China unless the institutions of government undergo a fundamental change': S Li, *The Legal Environment and Risks for Foreign Investment in China* (Springer-Verlag, 2007), p. 113. Schreuer suggests that indirect expropriations are more common in: C Schreuer, 'The Concept of Expropriation under the ECT and Other Investment Protection Treaties' in Clarisse Ribeiro (ed), *Investment Arbitration and the Energy Charter Treaty* (Juris, 2006), p. 105.

[167] Art 4(1)(b). Art 4(1)(b) of Version II refers to 'under appropriate legal procedure' and Model 1 is the same as the current Model referring only to domestic procedure. Most recently, in the China-Japan-Korea Trilateral Investment Agreement (2012), Art 11(1)(c), China has incorporated a condition that expropriation be 'in accordance with its laws and international standard of due process of law'.

[168] In *Tza Yap Shum v Peru* it was the Chinese investor that filed the claim for expropriation of its assets in Peru under the China-Peru BIT.

[169] P K Chew, 'Political Risk and US Investment in China: Chimera of Protection and Predictability?' (1994) 34 *Virginia Journal of International Law* 615, 626, where Chew states, 'China began a "slow motion nationaliz ation" program resulting in the virtual termination of all direct foreign investment by 1957'. See generally W Shan, *The Legal Framework of EU-China Investment Relations* (Hart Publishing, 2005), p. 8; L Lin and J R Allison, 'An Analysis of Expropriation and Nationaliz ation Risk in China' (1994) 19 *Yale Journal of International Law*, p. 135; A Jerome and H Chiu, *People's China and International Law: A Documentary Study* (Princeton University Press, 1974), p. 686.

[170] For example the *Changchun Huijin* case; see Gallagher and Shan, *Chinese Investment Treaties*, paras 168 – 71. See also *Huang Qiao* case mentioned in Li, *The Legal Environment*, p. 115.

has resulted in an international award against China. In *Tza Yap Shum v Peru*, the Chinese investor, Mr Tza Yap Shum, alleged that the Peruvian taxation authority had by its actions breached the expropriation provision of the China-Peru BIT. The tribunal concluded that the imposition of interim measures by the tax authority was arbitrary as they had not complied with their own internal procedures.[171] As a result, the tribunal concluded that this would impact the manner in which the compensation would be calculated (see discussion below). The first investment case to be filed against China was registered by ICSID on 24 May 2011. The exact nature of the dispute is still not known, but it relates to the development of land (over 900 hectares) in Hainan Province. The proceedings are currently suspended pending the parties' attempt to reach an amicable settlement.[172] It is interesting to note that in the recent BIT with Japan and Korea, China included a Protocol relating to the expropriation provisions in Article 4. The Protocol deals with indirect expropriation and what factors should be taken into consideration by a tribunal. In addition, it confirms that except in rare cases where a series of actions is severe or disproportionate 'non-discriminatory regulatory actions adopted by the Contracting Party for the purpose of legitimate public welfare do not constitute indirect expropriation'.[173] This wording is similar, though not identical, to the qualification in Annex B to the US Model BIT (2012) and clearly indicates that the parties are attempting to retain some legitimate regulatory space should there be any dispute in the future.

With regard to the standard of compensation, Chinese BITs tend to avoid any reference to principles such as 'prompt, adequate and effective compensation' ('the Hull formula'). The Draft OECD Convention 1967 did not include the Hull formula either, providing instead in Article 3 for 'just compensation' representing the 'genuine value of the property affected'.[174] Version III of the Chinese Model BIT does not equate 'compensation' to the 'genuine value' of the expropriated assets. It merely confirms that the amount payable will be decided in accordance with generally recognized principles of

---

[171] *Tza Yap Shum v Peru*, para 218. Article 4(1) of the China-Peru BIT provides: Neither Contracting Party shall expropriate, nationalize or take similar measures (hereinafter referred to as "expropriation") against investment of investors of the other Contracting Party in its territory, unless the following conditions are met:

(a) for the public interest;

(b) under domestic legal procedure;

(c) without discrimination;

(d) against compensation.

[172] *Ekran Berhad v People's Republic of China* (ICSID Case No ARB/11/15), proceedings suspended pursuant to the parties' agreement on 22 July 2011. At the time of writing, no progress had been reported of an agreement so a tribunal may still be appointed to consider the claim.

[173] China-Japan-Korea Trilateral Investment Agreement (2012), Art 2(c). See also China-Canada BIT (2012), Annex B. 10.

[174] For a discussion of 'just compensation' and 'genuine value', see *CME Czech Republic BV v Czech Republic* (Final Award of 14 March 2003, Sep Op Professor Ian Brownlie).

valuation.[175] These principles are applied by tribunals and some of these have been identified in the World Bank Guidelines on the Treatment of Foreign Direct Investment. Occasionally, Chinese BITs refer to concepts such as 'fair and equitable compensation',[176] 'fair, effective and non-discriminatory compensation',[177] and 'fair and reasonable compensation'.[178] In terms of calculating the damages payable, some of China's BITs refer to the 'real', 'actual', or 'market' value. Arbitral tribunals have interpreted these terms to mean the 'fair market value' of the investment. The China-Japan-Korea Trilateral Investment Agreement (2012) refers specifically to the 'fair market value of the expropriated investments at the time when the expropriation was publicly announced or when the expropriation occurred'.[179]

Nevertheless, in practical terms, Chinese BITs do not part significantly from general BIT practice. First, on the amount of compensation, although they do not refer to 'adequate' or 'full' compensation, they require it to be 'equivalent to the value of the expropriated investments' (Versions I and III), or calculated on the basis of 'market value' (Version II). Such value is to be determined in accordance with 'generally recognized principles of valuation' (Versions II and III), such as capital invested, depreciation, capital repatriated, replacement value, and other relevant elements (Version II). This standard of compensation is not substantially different from the 'adequate' compensation requirement under the 'Hull formula'. Second, with regard to the time and method of payment, Chinese BITs require compensation to be made 'without delay, be effectively realizable and freely transferable', which is not that different from the 'prompt' and 'effective' compensation required under the 'Hull formula'. Although most of China's BITs require expropriation to be carried out in accordance with the host State laws, there are few if any additional limitations under China's law. On balance, it seems that China's position on expropriation and the laws that an international tribunal would apply are not so different to most other States.[180]

In its Decision on Jurisdiction and Competence in *Tza Yap Shum v Peru*, the ICSID Tribunal found that a prima facie case was made by the claimant for an indirect expropriation.[181] In its Award of 7 July 2011, the ICSID Tribunal concluded that there had

---

[175] Recent BITs reflect this wording in the current Model see for example China-Portugal BIT (2005), China-Finland BIT (2004), China-Latvia BIT (2004), and the China-Spain BIT (2005). For a detailed review on quantum calculations under BITs, see S Ripinsky with K Williams, *Damages in International Investment Law* (London: BIICL, 2008) and I Marboe, *Calculation of Compensation and Damages in International Investment Law* (Oxford University Press, 2009).

[176] Eg, China-India BIT (2006), Art 5(1).

[177] Eg, China-UAE BIT (1993), Art 6(1).

[178] Eg, China-Kuwait BIT (1985), Art 5(1).

[179] China-Japan-Korea Trilateral Investment Agreement (2012), Art 11(2).

[180] For further details see Gallagher and Shan, *Chinese Investment Treaties*, ch 7.

[181] *Tza Yap Shum v Peru* (ICSID Case No ARB/07/6, Decision on Jurisdiction and Competence of 19 June 2009), paras 116 – 28. The Tribunal did note in footnote 119 of the Decision on Jurisdiction and Competence that it did not have jurisdiction to consider restitution or declaratory relief consistent with the decision in *European Media Ventures SA v Czech Republic* [2007] EWHC 2851 (Comm) (5 December 2007), paras 50 – 51.

been an indirect expropriation, and awarded compensation to Tza Yap Shum.[182] In *Tza Yap Shum*, Article 4 of the China-Peru BIT follows the wording of Version 1 of the Model BIT providing that:

3. The compensation mentioned in Paragraph 1(d) of this Article shall be equivalent to the value of the expropriated investments at the time when expropriation is proclaimed, be convertible and freely transferable. The compensation shall be paid without unreasonable delay.

The tribunal, however, found that as the expropriatory measures did not meet the criteria set down in Article 4 of the Peru BIT the damages should be calculated on the basis of customary international law and not Article 4.[183] So this specific provision of the BIT was not applied. The tribunal rejected the claimants discounted cash flow method of calculating the damages as the business had only been running for a few years. It accepted that the more appropriate method of calculating the damages was the 'libros ajustado o valor contable ajustado (Adjusted Book Value en inglés)'[184] The tribunal proceeded to award Tza Yap Shum 90 percent of the adjusted book value as he owned 90 percent of the share of the holding company. The tribunal awarded the claimant the sum of US $ 786,306.24 being 90 per cent of the market price of the investment company on 31 December 2004. No moral damages were awarded as the tribunal felt the principles applied in *Lemire v Ukraine* were not met.

The valuation date is consistent throughout China's BITs as being the date of the taking. Although the China-Peru BIT only provides for a limited investor-State dispute resolution provision relating to the 'amount of compensation for expropriation' the tribunal confirmed in its Decision on Jurisdiction and Competence of 19 June 2009 that this wording included not just the determination of the amount due but also whether in fact there had been an expropriation under the BIT (discussed further below).[185]

E. Compensation for Damages and Losses

Article 5: Compensation for Damages and Losses

Investors of one Contracting Party whose investments in the territory of the other Contracting Party suffer losses owing to war, a state of national emergency, insurrection, riot or other similar events in the territory of the latter Contracting Party, shall be accorded by the latter Contracting Party treatment, as regards restitution, indemnification, compensation and other settlements no less favorable than that accorded to the investors of its own or any third State, whichever is more favorable to the investor concerned.

Versions I, II, and III of the Chinese Model BIT have a provision dealing with compensation for losses due to armed conflict or internal disorder. This is one of the early treaty provisions and appears in most of the modern (ie post 1959) BITs. Historically,

---

[182] *Tza Yap Shum v Peru* (ICSID Case No ARB/07/6, Award of 7 July 2011), paras 140 – 70.

[183] *Tza Yap Shum v Peru*, para 253.

[184] *Tza Yap Shum v Peru*, para 260.

[185] *Tza Yap Shum v Peru* (ICSID Case No ARB/07/6, Decision on Jurisdiction and Competence of 19 June 2009), paras 143 – 88.

interference by the host State ' with foreign property typically occurred, if at all, during periods of war or civil disturbance'.[186] Despite this fact, the Draft OECD Convention did not include a compensation for losses clause. China's first BIT with Sweden also does not contain this provision even though it appeared in Version I of the Chinese Model BIT. All of the three Versions of the Chinese Model BIT are the same in that they guarantee MFN treatment for compensation of such losses. Version III does not follow Version II, but generally adopts the approach of Version I. The only substantial difference between Version I and Version III is that the latter grants national treatment to such compensation, in addition to the MFN treatment.

The provisions of the Model BITs are reflected in China's BIT practice. Thus, earlier BITs follow Version I requiring only MFN treatment on compensation for losses.[187] Subsequently, many BITs signed in the late 1980s or 1990s have compensation for losses provisions similar to Version II.[188] More recent BITs have followed Version III providing both MFN and NT treatment on compensation for losses.[189] However, some recent BITs still follow Version II.[190] Although it might seem that this provision is no longer required in BITs today, they still continue to appear, for example in the ASEAN-China Investment Agreement (2009).[191]

F. Repatriation of Investments and Returns

Article 6: Repatriation of Investments and Returns

1. Each Contracting Party shall, subject to its laws and regulations, guarantee to the investors of the other Contracting Party the transfer of their investments and returns held in its territory, including:

(a) profits, dividends, interests and other legitimate income;

(b) proceeds obtained from the total or partial sale or liquidation of investments;

(c) payments made pursuant to a loan agreement in connection with investment;

(d) royalties in relation to the matters in Paragraph 1(d) of Article 1;

(e) payments of technical assistance or technical service fee, management fee;

(f) payments in connection with contracting projects;

(g) earnings of nationals of the other Contracting Party who work in connection with an investment in its territory.

2. Nothing in Paragraph 1 of this Article shall affect the free transfer of compensa-

---

[186] Vandevelde, *Bilateral Investment Treaties*, p. 309. See also *AAPL v Sri Lanka* (ICSID Case No ARB/87/3, Award of 27 June 1990) where this provision in the Sri Lanka-UK treaty was invoked unsuccessfully by the claimant, and *AMT v Democratic Republic of Congo* (ICSID Case No ARB/93/1 Award of 21 February 1997) to which is appended an interesting dissenting opinion on the issue of what was meant by the word ' forces' in the compensation for losses provision at Art IV(1) of the BIT.

[187] See, eg, China-France BIT (1984), Art 4.

[188] See, eg, China-UK BIT (1986), Art 4; Czech Republic-China BIT (2005), Art 5.

[189] See, eg, Germany-China BIT (2003), Art 5; China-Portugal BIT (1992), Art 5, and China-Canada BIT (2012), Art 11.

[190] See, eg, China-Spain BIT (2005), Art 5; and Czech Republic-China BIT (2005), Art 5.

[191] See Art 9; see also China-Mexico BIT (2008), Art 8.

tion paid under Article 4 and 5 of this Agreement.

3. The transfer mentioned above shall be made in a freely convertible currency and at the prevailing market rate of exchange applicable within the Contracting Party accepting the investments and on the date of transfer.

The ability to transfer capital and profits freely is central to the investment protection paradigm as ' an investor expects to be able to repatriate his capital and his profits' .[192] It is unlikely that an investor would risk making an investment if a profit could not be generated and freely transferred without undue exchange control restrictions, taxes, or additional permissions being imposed. The balancing interest is that of the host State in controlling and protecting its currency and foreign reserves.[193] All three versions of China's Model BIT contain a provision on free transfers. Versions I and II were almost identical, and the current Version III has an extra subparagraph 6(2) confirming that the provision does not ' affect the free transfer of compensation paid under Article 4 and 5' . The obligation in the transfer provision is mandatory unlike the ' recommendation' contained in Article 4 of the Draft OECD Convention 1967. The parties recognized the freedom of transfer and would ' endeavour to grant the necessary authorisations for such a transfer' .[194] The China Model obligation on free transfers is ' subject to its laws and regulations' to allow for China's foreign exchange controls.

There have been comparatively few cases where the transfer provision has been considered by investment tribunals. In *Biwater Gauff (Tanzania) Ltd v Tanzania*, the ICSID Tribunal confirmed that the transfer provision does not guarantee that there will be funds to be transferred; rather, the ' free transfer principle is aimed at measures that would restrict the possibility to transfer, such as currency control restrictions or other measures taken by the host State which effectively imprison the investors' funds, typically in the host State of the investment' .[195] China's more recent treaties, such as the China-Germany BIT, have not included the ' subject to its laws and regulations' restriction.[196] The Protocol to the China-Germany BIT, however, contains a clarification with regard to China only, namely that transfers of funds under Article 6(1)(c) are permitted so long as such transfers comply ' with the relevant formalities stipulated by the present Chinese laws and regulations relating to exchange control' .[197]

Some of China's BITs include not just a list of the types of payments that are freely

---

[192] F A Mann, ' British Treaties for the Promotion and Protection of Investments' (1981) 52 *British Yearbook of International Law*, p. 241, 243.

[193] Vandevelde, *United States Investment Treaties: Policy and Practice*, 143; See also generally UNCTAD, *Transfer of Funds*, UNCTAD Series on Issues in International Investment Agreements (United Nations, 2000) and UNCTAD, *International Investment Agreements: Key Issues* (2004), p. 257; Dolzer and Stevens, *Bilateral Investment Treaties*, p. 85.

[194] Draft OECD Convention 1967, Art 4, *available at* www. oecd. org/dataoecd/35/4/39286571. pdf (last accessed 28 December 2011).

[195] See *Biwater Gauff (Tanzania) Ltd v Tanzania* (ICSID Case No ARB/05/22, Award of 24 July 2008), para 735.

[196] China-Germany BIT (2003), Art 6(1); see also China-Finland BIT (2004), Art 6.

[197] China-Germany BIT (2003), Protocol, Ad Art 5; see also China-Finland BIT (2004), Ad Art 6; and China-Canada BIT (2012), Annex B. 12.

transferable like in Article 6(1) of Version III, but also include specific exclusions where transfer can be prevented or delayed. One of the more detailed transfer provisions is the ASEAN-China Investment Agreement (2009) which permits a State to prevent a transfer if applying in a fair way its laws relating to:

(a) bankruptcy, loss of ability or capacity to make payments, or protection of the right of creditors;

(b) non-fulfilment of the host Party's transfer requirements in respect of trading or dealing in securities, futures, options or derivatives;

(c) non-fulfilment of tax obligations ...[198]

Like the Draft OECD Convention, Version III of the Model BIT does not contain a provision on the 'balance of payments'. These provisions do however appear in some of China's BITs, such as Article 8(3) of the China-Mexico BIT which provides:

In case of a serious balance of payments difficulty or of a threat thereof, each Contracting Party may temporarily restrict transfers provided that such a Contracting Party implements measures or a program in accordance with international standards. These restrictions should be imposed on an equitable, non-discriminatory and in good faith basis.[199]

Despite the significance of the transfer provision, they have still not featured heavily in investment treaty claims, even after the global financial crisis when restrictions on capital flows might have been expected. However, these provisions did receive some attention since the European Commission successfully took proceedings against Austria, Finland, and Sweden under Article 226 of the EC Treaty as some of their BITs (which predated their accession to the EU) were incompatible with the ECT Treaty as they did not have an express carve out for restrictions that might be imposed by the European Council on free movement of capital. The Commission was concerned that the treaties might limit the powers of the EU Council to impose restrictions on the free movement of capital. The infringement proceedings under Article 226 were successful from the Commission's point of view as the European Court of Justice found the countries had failed to comply with their obligation under Article 307. This required the States to take appropriate steps to remove any incompatibilities from pre-existing treaties once they become members of the EU.[200] The ECJ found a breach in all three cases and the Member States were required to take appropriate action, either by entering a new treaty or revising the existing ones, to comply with their EU obligations. The ECJ added:

---

[198] ASEAN-China Investment Agreement (2009), Art 10(3)(a) – (h); See also China-Mexico BIT (2008), Art 8(3); See also A Kolo and T Wälde, 'Capital Transfer Restrictions under Modern Investment Treaties' in A Reinish (ed), *Standards of Investment Protection* (Oxford University Press, 2008), p. 205.

[199] See also China-Slovakia BIT (1991), Protocol, Art 6; China-Uganda BIT (2004), Art 7(4); China-Sri Lanka BIT (1986), Art 8(3); China-Japan-Korea Trilateral Investment Agreement (2012), Art 19; and China-Canada BIT (2012), Art 12(4).

[200] *Commission v. Austria* Case C – 205/06, Judgment of 3 March 2009 [2009] ECR I – 01303; *Commission v. Sweden* Case C – 249/06, Judgment of 3 March 2009; and *Commission v. Republic of Finland* Case C – 118/07, Judgment of 19 November 2009. See E Denza, 'Bilateral Investment Treaties and EU Rules on Free Transfer: Comment on *Commission v. Austria, Commission v. Sweden* and *Commission v. Finland*' (2010) 35(2) *European Law Review*, p. 263.

As follows from the judgment delivered today in Case C - 205/06 *Commission v. Austria* [2009] ECR I - 0000, the incompatibilities with the Treaty to which the investment agreements with third countries give rise and which militate against the application of the restrictions on movement of capital and on payments which the Council may adopt under Articles 57(2) EC, 59 EC and 60(1) EC are not limited to the Member State which is the defendant in the present case.[201]

China will have to engage with these States as their European counterparts seek to comply with these obligations. This may result in a revised version of the transfer provisions in China's next Model BIT.

G. Subrogation

Article 7: Subrogation

If one Contracting Party or its designed agency makes a payment to its investors under a guarantee or a contract of insurance against non-commercial risks it has accorded in respect of an investment made in the territory of the other Contracting Party, the latter Contracting Party shall recognize: the assignment, whether under the law or pursuant to a legal transaction in the former Contracting Party, of any rights or claims by the investors to the former Contracting Party or to its designated agency, as well as, that the former Contracting Party or its designated agency is entitled by virtue of subrogation to exercise the rights and enforce the claims of that investor and assume the obligations related to the investment to the same extent as the investor.

All of the Chinese Model BITs contained a subrogation clause. Version III confirms that the parties will recognize any assignment of rights or claims by the investors.[202] No subrogation clause appeared in the Draft OECD Convention, but other countries such as the United States and UK started using them in the early 1980s. It also appears in Article 13 of the China-Canada BIT (2012).

H. Dispute Settlement

Article 8: Settlement of Disputes between Contracting Parties

1. Any dispute between the Contracting Parties concerning the interpretation or application of this Agreement shall, as far as possible, be settled with consultation through diplomatic channel.

2. If a dispute cannot thus be settled within six months, it shall, upon the request of either Contracting Party, be submitted to an ad hoc arbitral tribunal.

---

[201] *Commission v Sweden Case*, C - 249/06, para 43. See also C - 205/06, para 43 and C - 118/07, para 34, where the ECJ noted that its findings in the earlier cases were not limited to the defendant Member State. For consideration of the extra and intra-EU BIT obligations see *Eureko BV v Slovakia* (Award on Jurisdiction of 23 October 2010), paras 57 - 83.

[202] China's stance is consistent with general practice in this area as noted that there was no problem negotiating this provision with the UK 'since the UK and China took broadly the same approach'. E Denza and S Brooks, 'Investment Protection Treaties: United Kingdom Experience' (1987) 36 *International and Comparative Law Quarterly*, p. 908, 921.

3. Such tribunal comprises of three arbitrators. Within two months of the receipt of the written notice requesting arbitration, each Contracting Party shall appoint one arbitrator. Those two arbitrators shall, within further two months, together select a national of a third State having diplomatic relations with both Contracting Parties as Chairman of the arbitral tribunal.

4. If the arbitral tribunal has not been constituted within four months from the receipt of the written notice requesting arbitration, either Contracting Party may, in the absence of any other agreement, invite the President of the International Court of Justice to make any necessary appointments. If the President is a national of either Contracting Party or is otherwise prevented from discharging the said functions, the Member of the International Court of Justice next in seniority who is not a national of either Contracting Party or is not otherwise prevented from discharging the said function shall be invited to make such necessary appointments.

5. The arbitral tribunal shall determine its own procedure. The arbitral tribunal shall reach its award in accordance with the provisions of this Agreement and the principles of international law recognized by both Contracting Parties.

6. The tribunal shall reach its award by a majority of votes. Such award shall be final and binding on both Contracting Parties. The arbitral tribunal shall, upon the request of either Contracting Party, explain the reasons of its award.

7. Each Contracting Party shall bear the costs of its appointed arbitrator and of its representation in arbitral proceedings. The relevant costs of the Chairman and tribunal shall be borne in equal parts by the Contracting Parties.

Most investment treaties include a provision on the settlement of disputes between the two Contracting Parties.[203] Consistent with this trend, all three of China's Model BITs include a State-State dispute resolution provision. They are substantially similar in form and content with each comprising seven subsections. It reflects many of the provisions of the Draft OECD Convention 1967 Article 7 and Annex.[204] The scope of the State-State provision is set out in the first paragraph and relates to the 'interpretation or application' of the treaty.[205] To date there has only been one reported case under these inter-State dispute resolution procedures.[206]

The first obligation on the Contracting States is to try to reach an amicable settle-

---

[203] Salacuse, *The Law of Investment Treaties*, p. 360; Vandevelde, *Bilateral Investment Treaties*, p. 499.

[204] Text and commentary on Draft OECD Convention, *available at* www. oecd. org/dataoecd/35/4/39286571. pdf (last accessed 28 December 2011).

[205] See, eg, China-Switzerland BIT (1986), Art 11(1); China-Australia BIT (1988), Art 13(2); China-Turkey BIT (1990), Art 8(1); China-Mongolia BIT (1991), Art 7(1); China-Greece BIT (1992) Art 9(1); China-Korea BIT (1992), Art 10(1); China-Oman BIT (1995), Art 8(1); China-Zambia BIT (1996), Art 8(1) and China-Bangladesh (1996), Art 8(1).

[206] *Italian Republic v Republic of Cuba* (Ad Hoc State-State arbitration, Interim Award of 15 March 2005); in *Lucchetti v Peru* (ICSID Case No ARB/03/4, Award of 7 February 2005), para 9, Peru commenced a case against Chile and requested a suspension of the investor-State proceedings. At the first session held on 15 September 2003 the Tribunal declined to suspend the arbitration as the conditions were not met; see also *Lucchetti v Peru* (ICSID Case No ARB/03/4, Decision on Annulment of 5 September 2007), Dissenting Opinion of Sir Franklin Berman QC, para 11. The inter-State claim was ultimately discontinued.

ment through diplomatic channels. There are some variations in China's BITs from the wording set forth in the Model. For example the China-Turkey BIT, in Article VI, calls for consultation to try to settle ' any disputes arising' under the treaty and to discuss any matters relating to the interpretation and application of the treaty. There is also then a separate provision in Article VIII which requires ' direct and meaningful negotiations' to try to reach a solution.[207] If the negotiation efforts fail then after a certain time period, usually six months, the dispute shall be referred to arbitration. Not all of China's BITs provide for a six-month time period within which to reach a negotiated settlement. The China-Australia BIT (1988) has a 60 – day limit and the arbitral procedure is set out in Annex B in more detail than the Model BIT. Article 10(2) of the China-Korea BIT stipulates a three-month negotiation period while other treaties have no time limit at all, for example Article 9(2) of the China-Kuwait BIT.[208] Interestingly the China-Indonesia BIT (1994) provides for diplomatic negotiations only.[209] There is nothing to preclude the parties agreeing to arbitrate should a dispute arise, but there is no obligation to do so under the terms of the treaty.

The Model BITs and treaties are mostly consistent on the procedure for a three member ad hoc tribunal to decide the case. Minor variations do appear; for example, Article 8(5) of the China-Qatar BIT provides that the tribunal shall apply the UNCITRAL Rules and it also specifies a choice of venue at The Hague or Stockholm. Although the majority of treaties follow the wording on the allocation of costs in the Model BIT, others have additional wording giving discretion to the tribunal to allocate costs against one State.[210] The China-Mexico BIT (2008) is the most prescriptive on arbitral procedure. The China-Trinidad and Tobago BIT includes a back-stop date of six months from the selection of the chairman for all submissions and hearings to be completed. This was no doubt included in the interest of time and cost considerations. One final distinction from the Model BIT appears in the China-Uganda BIT. Under Article 9(4), a joint committee can be set up by the Contracting Parties ' comprising relevant experts to resolve the dispute'. If this Joint Committee can not reach a settlement then the dispute may be referred to ad hoc arbitration.

Article 9: Settlement of Disputes between an Investor and a Host State

1. Any legal dispute between an investor of one Contracting Party and the other

---

[207] See discussion in Q Kong, ' Bilateral Investment Treaties: The Chinese Approach and Practice' (1998 – 99) 8 *Asian Yearbook of International Law*, pp. 105, 129

[208] See also China-Sweden (1982), Art 6(2); China-Sri Lanka BIT (1986), Art 14(2); China-New Zealand BIT (1988), Art 14 (2); China-Turkey BIT (1990), Art VIII(1); China-Papua New Guinea BIT (1991), Art 9(2); China-UAE BIT (1993) Art 10(2); and China-Mauritius BIT (1996), Art 14(2); see also Art 27 of the Energy Charter Treaty which has no specific time period but refers to a ' reasonable period of time'.

[209] China-Indonesia BIT (1994), Art X, provides: ' Disputes concerning the interpretation or implementation of this Agreement shall be settled amicably through diplomatic negotiation between the Contracting Parties.'

[210] China-Bosnia and Herzegovina BIT, Art 9(7), provides: ' The Tribunal may ... direct that a higher proportion of costs shall be bourne by one of the two Contracting Parties'. See also China-Bahrain BIT (1999), Art 19 (5); China-Brunei BIT (2000), Art 8(7); China-Guyana BIT (2003), Art 8(7); China-Lao BIT (1993), Art 7(7); China-Lebanon BIT (1996), Art 9(9); China-Singapore BIT (1985) Art 14(7), and China-UAE (1993), Art 10(5).

Contracting Party in connection with an investment in the territory of the other Contracting Party shall, as far as possible, be settled amicably through negotiations between the parties to the dispute.

2. If the dispute cannot be settled through negotiations within six months from the date it has been raised by either party to the dispute, it shall be submitted by the choice of the investor:

(a) to the competent court of the Contracting Party that is a party to the disputes;

(b) to International Centre for Settlement of Investment Disputes (ICSID) under the Convention on the Settlement of Disputes between States and Nationals of Other States, done at Washington on March 18, 1965, provided that the Contracting Party involved in the dispute may require the investor concerned to go through the domestic administrative review procedures specified by the laws and regulations of that Contracting Party before the submission to the ICSID.

Once the investor has submitted the dispute to the competent court of the Contracting Party concerned or to the ICSID, the choice of one of the two procedures shall be final.

3. The arbitration award shall be based on the law of the Contracting Party to the dispute including its rules on the conflict of laws, the provisions of this Agreement as well as the universally accepted principles of international law.

4. The arbitration award shall be final and binding upon both parties to the dispute. Both Contracting Parties shall commit themselves to the enforcement of the award.

The investor-State dispute resolution provisions in China's BITs have generated much debate and speculation over the years. This is largely due to China's initial reluctance to accept international arbitration as a means of settling investment disputes. This is clear from the format of Versions I and II of China's Model BITs which provide for 'disputes involving the amount of compensation for expropriation' to be referred to ad hoc arbitration comprised of a three member tribunal. Originally it was assumed that this wording would preclude a tribunal from deciding whether an actual expropriation had occurred and limit its remit to questions of quantum only.[211] Yet recent jurisprudence indicates that this is not the case. In the *Tza Yap Shum* case, the Chinese investor persuaded the tribunal, relying on earlier cases, that this same wording in the China-Peru BIT did allow it not only to 'determine the amount but also any other issues normally inherent to an expropriation, including whether the property was actually expropriated in accordance with the BIT provisions and requirements, as well as the determination of the

[211] Q Kong, 'Bilateral Investment Treaties: The Chinese Approach and Practice' (1998 – 99) 8 *Asian Yearbook of International Law* 130; see also M C E Heymann, 'International Law and the Settlement of Investment Disputes relating to China' (2008) 11 *Journal of International Economic Law* 507, 515; T G Nelson, 'Investor-State Arbitration and Investment Treaty Protection: The South-East Asian Angle' (2009) 28 *Australian Resources and Energy Law Journal* 213. On investor-State arbitration, see generally Vandevelde, *Bilateral Investment Treaties*; Salacuse, *The Law of Investment Treaties*, ch 15; Dolzer and Schreuer *Principles of International Investment Law*, ch X; and McLachlan, Shore, and Weiniger, *International Investment Arbitration*, ch 3.

amount of compensation due'.[212] The tribunal considered to decide otherwise would render the last sentence of Article 8(3)—the 'fork-in-the-road' provision confirming that if a party refers a dispute to the national courts, the arbitration provision does not apply—obsolete. Presumably the tribunal felt that if the investor had referred the dispute on whether an expropriation had in fact occurred to the local courts of China but not the question of quantum, this would activate the final sentence of Article 3 and exclude arbitration altogether.

Another possible interpretation is that the final sentence only relates to the question of quantum; if the claimant had argued the damages before the national courts it could not do so before an investment tribunal at a later time. In any event, it might be difficult for China to make this argument in future cases as it was a Chinese investor that successfully ran this argument. Nearly all of China's older BITs follow a similar format to Versions I and II (see, for example, Article 8(3) of the China-Mongolia BIT).[213] This was the case up until the late 1990s as even in the China-Yemen BIT in 1998 the parties agreed to arbitrate disputes relating to the amount of compensation. The clause also provides that 'other disputes shall be submitted to ICSID on agreement between the parties'. This additional wording relating to 'other disputes' (meaning other than involving compensation) appears in a significant number of China's BITs and also appears in the China-Peru BIT which was invoked in the *Tza Yap Shum* case. The tribunal in that case rejected the submission of the claimant that he could rely on the MFN provision to extend the scope of the arbitration clause by invoking Article 12 of the Peru-Columbia BIT. The claimant wanted the tribunal to have jurisdiction to consider other breaches of the BIT, including fair and equitable treatment, and full protection.

The tribunal noted that the application of the MFN is one of the '*quaestiones vexatae*' of investment arbitration. After reviewing the numerous conflicting awards on this issue the tribunal concluded that Article 8(3) of the China-Peru BIT was restricted in nature. The parties had agreed to two things; arbitration of expropriation matters and that other disputes could—if agreed—be referred to ICSID. In accordance with Article 31 of the Vienna Convention the tribunal held the correct interpretation was that this specific agreement should prevail over the more general language in the MFN clause. The tribunal held that it did 'not accept the arguments presented by the Claimant relating to the interpretation of the MFN clause in the BIT (Article 3)', and it found that 'Article 3 cannot be interpreted to extend the jurisdiction of the Centre or as an independent

[212] *Tza Yap Shum v Peru* (ICSID Case No ARB/07/6, Decision on Jurisdiction and Competence of 19 June 2009), para 188 (unofficial translation). See also decision of the English Court in *European Media Ventures v Czech Republic* [2007] EWHC 2851 upholding a similar finding of the Tribunal that it did have jurisdiction to decide on expropriation even though the BIT referred to disputes 'concerning compensation'.

[213] Other examples include: China-Argentina BIT (1992), Art 8(3); China-Indonesia BIT (1994), Art IX (3); China-Sri Lanka BIT (1986), Art 13(3); China-Lebanon BIT (1996), Art 8(3); China-Syria BIT (1996), Art 9 (3); and China-Cambodia BIT (1996), Art 9(3).

source of competence for the Tribunal'.[214] It is not certain given the existing divergent jurisprudence whether a future tribunal would also refuse to apply the MFN in the face of the additional wording on future disputes. There is no doubt that if the *Ekran* case proceeds that this same argument will be made by China. Ekran, a Sarawak-based construction company, alleges that China is in breach of the China-Malaysia BIT (1988) in force since March 1990. It asserts that the revocation by the local authority of its interest in lands in Hainan for failure to develop it as required amounted to expropriation contrary to the BIT. The China-Malaysia BIT has a restrictive investor-State dispute resolution provision similar to the Peru-China BIT relied on in *Tza Yap Shum*. Article 7 of the China-Malaysia BIT gives the investor the right to take a dispute to the local administrative authority (Article 7(3)(1)) or the local courts (Article 7(3)(2)). Disputes on the amount of compensation for an expropriated investment may be referred to international arbitration.[215] If the *Ekran* case does proceed there will surely be a jurisdictional challenge by China that there is no consent to ICSID arbitration in the treaty. It will also be difficult for the claimant to try to extend the jurisdiction of the tribunal beyond questions of expropriation as in *Tza Yap Shum*, given the additional language in Article 7(4) of the BIT.

It is only in the last decade that China has included a broad or expansive investor-State dispute resolution option. These 'third generation' BITs cover 'all disputes' or all 'disputes relating to an investment' and are consistent with global BIT practice. This shift in modern BITs only really started in earnest in the early 1980s. The Protocol to China's first BIT with Sweden refers to ICSID and the possibility of reaching agreement on mandatory arbitration in the future. The China-Finland BIT (2004) is an example of this new wording in the current Version III Model BIT, providing at Article 9(1): 'Any dispute arising out of an investment between one Contracting Party and an investor of the other Contracting Party' can, at the investor's choice, be referred to international arbitration. Other treaties such as the China-Uganda BIT (2004) provides for '[a]ny legal dispute ... in connection with an investment'.[216] The China-Mexico BIT has one of the most detailed investor-State dispute resolution provisions in Section III, which is based more on NAFTA Chapter 11 than the China Model BIT. Article 13 covers any alleged

[214] In *Tza Yap Shum v Peru* (ICSID Case No ARB/07/6, Decision on Jurisdiction and Competence of 19 June 2009), para 220, the Tribunal specifically endorsed the approach in *Plama v Bulgaria* (ICSID Case No ARB/03/24) noting that in *Plama*, the Tribunal 'actually took into account the warnings set out in paragraph 63 of the Award in *Maffezini*' (unofficial translation); see generally P J Turner and M Mangan, 'China's Investment Treaties: Substantive and Procedural Rights' *Asian Counsel* (May 2007); Y Radi, 'The Application of the Most-Favoured-Nation Clause to the Dispute Settlement Provisions of Bilateral Investment Treaties: Domesticating the "Trojan Horse"' (2007) 18 *European Journal of International Law*, p. 757.

[215] China-Malaysia BIT (1988), Art 7(4). There is also a letter signed the same day as the treaty confirming that once China becomes a party to the ICSID Convention the parties would 'promptly enter into negotiations on the possibility to expand the area of investment disputes which may be submitted for conciliation and arbitration by [ICSID]', which does not appear to have been done.

[216] Art 8(1); see also China-Jordan BIT (2005), Art 10(1). There are now close to 40 BITs that China has signed that contain these expansive dispute resolution provisions.

breach of obligation in Chapter II, the substantive protections.[217] Most recently, the China-Japan-Korea Trilateral Investment Agreement (2012) defines what an investment dispute means as ' a dispute between a Contracting Party and an investor of another Contracting Party that has incurred loss or damage by reason of, or arising out of, an alleged breach of any obligation of the former Contracting Party under this Agreement with respect to the investor or its investments in the territory of the former Contracting Party'.[218] These third generation treaties do, like the Model BIT, include a proviso, either in the clause itself or in a Protocol, that the investor ' shall go through the domestic (p. 175) administrative review procedures as specified by the laws and regulations of the disputing Contracting Party before the submission to international arbitration'.[219] There is often a time limit within which to pursue this domestic administrative review, for example no more than three months in the China-Finland BIT and four months in the China-Mexico BIT. A tribunal might be persuaded to forgo this requirement by invocation of the MFN provision (as occurred in *Maffezini v Spain*), although this is not certain.[220] Consideration must now also be given to the possibility of an award being set aside for failure to comply with such an obligation in a treaty to pursue a domestic remedy after a US Appeals court vacated an award against Argentina on that basis.[221] There is also a question of whether a future tribunal would apply the MFN clause to extend the scope of a restrictive Chinese BIT to the broader one in Version III. Clearly this could only happen now if there was no specific wording in the principle treaty investment dispute clause relating to ' other disputes' as in *Tza Yap Shum.*

China became a Contracting State of the ICSID Convention in 1993 and so it is not surprising the reference in the first two Model BITs was to ad hoc arbitration. They both do, however, refer to ICSID as the appointing authority if the tribunal has not been constituted within four months from the notice of application. China when it ratified the ICSID Convention filed a notification under Article 25(4) of the Convention confirming that:

---

[217] China-Mexico BIT (2008), Art 13 (1); see also China-ASEAN Investment Agreement (2009), Art 14(4).

[218] China-Japan-Korea Trilateral Investment Agreement (2012), Art 15(1). The China-Canada BIT (2012) has an entire Part C dedicated to investor-State disputes.

[219] Annex C to China-Mexico BIT (2008), Art 13(5); Other examples include the China-Japan-Korea Trilateral Investment Agreement (2012), Art 15(7); the Protocol to the China-Finland BIT and China-Germany BIT.

[220] In *Maffezini v Spain* (ICSID Case No ARB/97/7, Award on Jurisdiction of 25 January 2000), the Tribunal applied the MFN provision to permit the claimant to proceed directly to international arbitration without having to attempt to resolve the dispute in the local courts for 18 months as stipulated in the basic treaty. In contrast, the opposite finding was made in *WintershallAktiengesellschaft v Argentine Republic* (ICSID Case No ARB/04/14, Award of 8 December 2008).

[221] *Argentina v BG Group Plc* (Judgment of 17 January 2012 of the District of Columbia Circuit, USCA Case No 11 -7021), which considered Art 8(1) of the Argentina-UK BIT and decided that: ' Because the Treaty provides that a precondition to arbitration of an investor's claim is an initial resort to a contracting party's court, and the Treaty is silent on who decides arbitrability when that precondition is disregarded, we hold that the question of arbitrability is an independent question of law for the court to decide' (p. 13). The Court concluded that the award should be vacated as BG Group plc was required under the BIT to commence proceedings in Argentina for 18 months before proceeding to international arbitration.

[P]ursuant to Article 25(4) of the Convention, the Chinese Government would only consider submitting to the jurisdiction of the International Centre for Settlement of Investment Disputes disputes over compensation resulting from expropriation and nationaliz ation.[222]

This notification does not amount to a consent (or lack thereof) for the purposes of ICSID jurisdiction, and nor does it prevent a State from consenting to ICSID arbitration subsequent to the notification. China did so for the first time when it consented to arbitrate all disputes in its BIT with Barbados in 1998. The significance now of the notification made by China appears to have limited if any impact although it has been suggested that if a consent to arbitrate was unclear it might be 'interpreted by reference to a prior notification of classes of disputes in respect of which the host State has expressed its intentions'.[223] There would be a presumption that the State intended to stay within the confines of the notification. China has also entered into BITs that provide for ICSID Additional Facility, for example with India, which is not yet a State Party to the ICSID Convention. There are also references to the UNCITRAL Arbitration Rules and the Stockholm Chamber of Commerce as an appointing authority.[224]

I. Other Obligations

Article 10: Other Obligations

1. If the legislation of either Contracting Party or international obligations existing at present or established hereafter between the Contracting Parties result in a position entitling investments by investors of the other Contracting Party to a treatment more favorable than is provided for by the Agreement, such position shall not be affected by this Agreement.

2. Each Contracting Party shall observe any commitments it may have entered into with the investors of the other Contracting Party as regards to their investments.

Paragraph 1 is a so-called 'preservation of rights' clause, which preserves the rights of the investors resulting from domestic legislation or other international obligations making sure that investors will still enjoy such rights as long as they are more favourable than the rights they enjoy under the applicable BIT. This provision is not intended to 'increase the security of investment, but to ensure that the BIT does not detract from existing investment protection'.[225] The use of 'international obligations' suggests a broader undertaking than 'international treaties'. The difference, however, might not be so significant given the qualification 'existing at present or established hereafter between the Contracting Parties', which suggests that such international obligations

---

[222] Notification of China, 7 January 1993, *available at* www. worldbank. org/icsid (last accessed 28 December 2011).

[223] C Schreuer, with L Malintoppi, A Reinisch, and A Sinclair, *The ICSID Convention: A Commentary* (2nd edn, Cambridge University Press, 2009), p. 346.

[224] See China-Cuba BIT; China-Kuwait BIT; China-Norway BIT (Protocol); and China-Austria BIT (Protocol).

[225] Vandevelde, *Bilateral Investment Treaties*, p. 333.

should mainly refer to treaty obligations.

Paragraph 2 is an observance of obligations clause or ' umbrella clause' .[226] It was absent from Version I, but added in Version II and retained in Version III. Less than half of the 130 Chinese BITs have an umbrella clause. Although the OECD Draft Convention did include an umbrella or ' observation of undertakings' clause, this provision does not have a very long history in international investment law.[227] The OECD Commentary on Article 2 confirms that this clause represents the ' application of the general principle of *pacta sunt servanda*' .[228] In Chinese BITs, there are five categories of restrictive formulations: First, several BITs subject such obligation or commitments to the laws of the host State.[229] Second, some BITs limit the protection of the clause to ' written obligations' .[230] Third, some BITs require Contracting Parties to observe only ' specific commitments' . Fourth, the China-Austria BIT (1985) and the Jordan-China BIT (2001) have a special qualification on the ' obligation' , which confines it to ' any contractual obligations' with regard to investments ' approved' by the host State. The fifth and last substantive limitation on ' obligation' can be found in the China-Kuwait BIT (1985) and the China-United Arab Emirates BIT (1993). Like the China-Austria BIT and the Jordan-China BIT, these two BITs also link the umbrella clause to the approval of the investment project. However, they do not limit the obligation covered by the umbrella clause only to that based on ' approved investment contracts' , but also extend it to cover any obligation that may be included in the ' document of approval of investments' .

In contrast, several BITs take an expansive approach in the umbrella clause adopting a broader formulation. The China-New Zealand BIT (1988), for instance, attempts to do so by bringing both ' any obligations, whether general or specific' under this protection. It appears that legislation of general applicability would be covered by this clause. Tribunals have applied the umbrella clause in a less than uniform manner.[231] The umbrella clause in the Model would most likely be found to elevate a contractual obligation to a treaty breach. The tribunal would of course have to consider the limits of the provision including whether the specific acts were attributable to the State,[232] whether the investor relied on the undertaking to its detriment, as well as considering the

[226] See A Sinclair, ' The Origins of the Umbrella Clause in the International Law of Investment Protection' (2004) 20 *Arbitration International*, p. 411.

[227] Vandevelde, *Bilateral Investment Treaties*, p. 260. One of the earliest examples of this clause was used in the Anglo Iranian Consortium Agreement of 1954.

[228] OECD Notes and Commentary to Art 2, para 1. It states at para 3 that an undertaking can be in a contract or concession.

[229] See, eg, China-Belgium-Luxembourg BIT (2005), Art 9.

[230] See, eg, China-Australia BIT (1988) and China-Japan-Korea Trilateral Investment Agreement (2012).

[231] See Salacuse, *The Law of Investment Treaties*, p. 280, D Foster, ' Umbrella Clauses: A Retreat from the Philippines?' , (2006) 9(4) *International Arbitration Law Review* 100; and B Kunoy, ' Singing in the Rain: Developments in the Interpretation of Umbrella Clauses' , (2006) 7 *The Journal of World Investment and Trade*, p. 275.

[232] See, eg, *CMS Gas Transmission Company v Argentina* (ICSID Case No ARB/01/8, Decision on Annulment of 25 September 2007), paras 89 - 100.

precise wording of the treaty provision.[233]

J. Scope of Application

Article 11: Application

This Agreement shall apply to investment made prior to or after its entry into force by investors of one Contracting Party in the territory of the other Contracting Party in accordance with the laws and regulations of the Contracting Party concerned, but not apply to the dispute arose before its entry into force.

Version I and Version II stipulated that: '[T]his Agreement shall apply to investments which are made prior to or after its entry into force by investors of either Contracting Party in accordance with the laws and regulations of the other Contracting Party in the territory of the Latter.' Version III, however, has an additional qualification excluding its applicability to 'disputes that arose before its entry into force'.[234] This is in line with other Model BITs; for example the Draft OECD Convention 1967 and the US Model BIT. Most Chinese BITs follow the particular Model BIT in place at that time, whilst others have special provisions. The China-Japan BIT, for example, applies to investments and returns invested 'prior to the entering into force of the present Agreement and on or after 29 September 1972'.[235]

1. *Territorial Extension*

The term 'territory' has not been defined in any of the Versions I, II, or III of the Chinese Model BIT. However, in some existing BITs, it is defined. Article 1(4) of the Finland-China BIT (2004), for example, defines the term.[236]

There are also some Chinese BITs that include a separate definition of territory for each Contracting State. Article 1(1) of the China-Belgium/Luxembourg Economic Union BIT is an example. It is interesting to note the minor distinction in this BIT between the definition for Chinese territory where the applicable law is 'Chinese law and international law', whilst only 'international law' is the law applied in defining the territory of Belgium and Luxembourg. The significance of such a variation would depend on whether

---

[233] See for a recent discussion on umbrella clauses where the claimant sought unsuccessfully to import the provision by application of the MFN in *Paushok v Mongolia* (Award of 28 April 2011), para 573.

[234] This can be significant: see *Lucchetti v Peru* (ICSID Case No ARB/03/4, Award of 7 February 2005), where the Tribunal declined jurisdiction as the dispute pre-existed the entry into force of the Chile-Peru BIT. See also *ATA Construction, Industrial and Trading Company v Jordan* (ICSID Case No ARB/08/2, Award of 18 May 2010), where the tribunal also declined jurisdiction over part of the claim as the dispute arose before the BIT entered into force.

[235] China-Japan BIT (1988), Art 9. This was the 'date of recognition by Japan of the People's Republic of China'; H Golsong, 'China-Japan: Agreement Concerning the Encouragement and Reciprocal Protection of Investment' (1989) 28 *International Legal Materials*, p. 575, 578; see also Joint Communiqué of the Government of Japan and the Government of the People's Republic of China (19 September 1972), *available at* www.mofa.go.jp/region/asia-paci/china/joint72.html (last accessed 29 December 2011).

[236] Art 1(4) states: 'The term "territory" means the territory of either Contracting Party, including the land area, internal waters and territorial sea and the airspace above them under the sovereignty of that Contracting Party, as well as any maritime area beyond the territorial sea of that Contracting Party, over which that Contracting Party exercises sovereign rights or jurisdiction in accordance with domestic and international law.' See also China-Canada BIT (2012), Art 1(22).

the investment was made in an area where sovereignty was disputed.[237]

K. Consultations

Article 12: Consultations

1. The representatives of the Contracting Parties shall hold meetings from time to time for the purpose of:

(a) reviewing the implementation of this Agreement;

(b) exchanging legal information and investment opportunities;

(c) resolving disputes arising out of investments;

(d) forwarding proposals on promotion of investment;

(e) studying other issues in connection with investment.

2. Where either Contracting Party requests consultation on any matter of Paragraph 1 of this Article, the other Contracting Party shall give prompt response and the consultation be held alternatively in Beijing and [ ].

All three Versions of China's Model BITs include a consultation provision which is not a common provision in other Model BITs. The inclusion of the consultation provision may reflect the Chinese preference of diplomatic rather than legal resolution of State-State investment disputes. However, hardly any evidence can be found as to how this actually turned out in practice.

A small number of China's BITs also have a mechanism for review on the implementation of the treaty provisions. The China-Japan BIT is one of the more detailed providing for the creation of a Joint Committee to review the implementation of the treaty and to hold consultations on its operation.[238] At the time this was seen as a 'most striking feature' of the treaty as it built into the treaty a 'dynamic element'.[239] This was an innovation in treaty practice at that time offering the Contracting States 'a structured framework for a continuing dialogue on investment policy and the laws governing reciprocal investments'.[240] This provision appears in many of China's BITs and its FTAs. Article 30 of the China-Mexico BIT, for example, provides that the Contracting Parties can consult 'on any matter relating to this Agreement'. The following provision on denial of benefits refers to these consultations and that the parties can decide to deny the

---

[237] For example the Spratly Islands in the South China Sea. See China's letter of 14 April 2011 to the Joint Submission of Malaysia and Vietnam of 6 May 2009, *available at* www.un.org/Depts/los/clcs_new/submissions_files/submission_mysvnm_33_2009.htm(last accessed 29 December 2011).

[238] China-Japan BIT (1988), Art 14; see also China-Bulgaria BIT (1989), Art 12; China-Turkey BIT (1990), Art VI; China-Vietnam BIT (1992), Art 11; China-Croatia BIT (1993), Art 11; China-Zimbabwe BIT (1996), Art 11; China-Myanmar BIT (2001), Art 13; China-Benin BIT (2004), Art 12; China-Korea BIT (2005), Art 13; China-Mexico BIT (2008), Art 30 and China-Japan-Korea Trilateral Investment Agreement (2012), Art 24.

[239] H Golsong, 'China-Japan: Agreement Concerning the Encouragement and Reciprocal Protection of Investment' (1989) 28 *International Legal Materials*, pp. 575, 567. These types of provisions do now appear in other Model BITs, for example the Denmark Model BIT, and although not in the USA Model 2004 their FTAs do in the 'Administration' chapter provide for a Free Trade Commission to be established: see, eg, Chile-USA FTA, ch 21.

[240] Golsong, 'China-Japan: Agreement Concerning the Encouragement and Reciprocal Protection of Investment', p. 576. See further China-Canada BIT (2012), Art 18.

benefit of the treaty ' if a natural person or enterprise of a non-Contracting Party owns or controls such enterprise'.[241]

L. Final Provisions

Article 13: Entry into Force, Duration and Termination

1. This Agreement shall enter into force on the first day of the following month after the date on which both Contracting Parties have notified each other in writing that their respective internal legal procedures necessary therefore have been fulfilled and remain in force for a period of ten years.

2. This Agreement shall continue to be in force unless either Contracting Party has given a written notice to the other Contracting Party to terminate this Agreement one year before the expiration of the initial ten year period or at any time thereafter.

3. With respect to investments made prior to the date of termination of this Agreement, the provisions of Article 1 to 12 shall continue to be effective for a further period of ten years from such date of termination.

4. This Agreement may be amended by written agreement between the Contracting Parties. Any amendment shall enter into force under the same procedures required for entry into force of the present Agreement.

All three Versions of the Chinese Model BIT stipulate that the treaty shall enter into force on the first day of the following month after the date on which both Contracting Parties have notified each other in writing that their respective internal legal procedures have been fulfilled, and shall remain in force for a period of five years (ten years for Version III).

Most Chinese BITs follow Version III on commencement and termination. However, some BITs stipulate that the treaty enters into force in a month or 30 days from the date on which both Contracting Parties notify each other in writing that their respective internal legal procedures have been fulfilled. Article 13.1 of the Germany-China BIT (2003) is an example of the former and Article 15.1 of the Finland-China BIT (2004) of the latter. Also, whilst most Chinese BITs have ten years as their initial effective period, some have longer or shorter terms. For example, the China-Ukraine BIT (1992) has only five years as the initial term, whilst the China-Sweden BIT (1982) has an initial term of 15 years. The Finland-China BIT (2004) has the longest initial term, which lasts 20 years. All versions of the Model BITs confirm that the protections continue to apply to investments made while the treaty was in force. This is a common provision to ensure protection for investment made under the legal regime at the time. Some States are now

---

[241] China-Mexico BIT (2008). Art 31. China's Model BITs do not include a ' Denial of Benefits' clause although it is appearing in recent treaties; see China-New Zealand FTA, Art 149; China-Japan-Korea Trilateral Investment Agreement (2012), Art 22; and China-Canada BIT (2012), Art 16.

trying to renegotiate or terminate their BITs,[242] but this provision ensures protection for investors for ten years.

M. Exceptions

There is no ' exceptions' clause in China's Model BIT. This might however change in any revision to the Model BIT. The ASEAN-China Cooperation Agreement (2009) includes a very detailed exception provision at Article 16 with a reference to GATS.[243] In addition, the language of the security exception in Article 17 provides for a self judging standard by the State.[244] This is seen again in the China-Japan-Korea Trilateral Investment Agreement where it confirms that each Contracting Party can take any measure:

(a) which it considers necessary for the protection of its essential security interests; (i) taken in time of war, or armed conflict, or other emergency in that Contracting Party or in international relations; or

(ii) relating to the implementation of national policies or international agreements respecting the non-proliferation of weapons;

(b) in pursuance of its obligations under the United Nations Charter for the maintenance of international peace and security.[245]

VI. Concluding Remarks

China has experienced much change in the recent decades relating to foreign investment. It has opened its economy and become one of the more attractive host nations in the world. As a direct result it has revised its laws on investment both domestic and international. The evolution of its BITs can be traced since China signed its first BIT in 1982. The investment treaties it has entered into largely reflect the provisions of the Model BIT current at the time. China, like the United States of America recently did in May 2012, is considering adopting an updated Model BIT. This would no doubt reflect its recent practice in its BITs and FTAs and might also include some clarifications on what comprises an investment, for example, or dual nationality. It is expected that.

progress will be made in negotiations with the US, although as China has already

---

[242] Including Bolivia, Venezuela, Czech Republic, and Poland: see M Sornarajah ' Toward Normlessness: The Ravage and Retreat of Neo-Liberalism in International Investment Law', in K P Sauvant (ed), *Yearbook on International Investment Law and Policy* (Oxford University Press, 2009 – 10), p. 635; and M Sornarajah, ' Evolution or Revolution in International Investment Arbitration: The Descent into Normlessness' in C Brown and K Miles (eds), *Evolution in Investment Treaty Law and Arbitration* (Cambridge University Press, 2011), p. 631. See also the Energy Charter Treaty, Art 47(3) which provides for a 20 – year period.

[243] See Art 16(1)(a) of the ASEAN-China Cooperation Agreement (2009) which incorporated at footnote 5 Art XIV GATS; see also China-Mexico BIT (2008), Art 10.

[244] ASEAN China Investment Agreement (2009), Art 17(b) provides: ' Nothing in this Agreement shall be construed: to prevent any Party from taking any action *which it considers necessary* for the protection of its essential security interests, including ...' (emphasis added)

[245] China-Japan-Korea Trilateral Investment Agreement (2012), Art 18(1). See also China-Canada BIT (2012), Art 8.

attracted FDI successfully it should not be under any pressure to conclude a treaty with the US. The conclusion of a China-US BIT may be more likely in light of the conclusion of a BIT with Canada, and also as China has signed a Trilateral Investment Agreement with Japan and Korea that is similar in many aspects to the US Model BIT, including a Protocol which provides clarification on regulatory expropriation. It also seems likely that, like many other States, China will continue to negotiate more comprehensive FTAs which include an investment chapter.

China continues to be the second most prolific state for investment treaties after Germany. Despite the fact that the first claim has been filed against it at ICSID, it seems unlikely that this position will change in the near future. China is a growing ODI nation and as such will want its treaties to provide sufficient protection for its investors abroad. Although the claimant in *Tza Yap Shum* was awarded only a fraction of the damages he sought, he was ultimately successful in his treaty claim. It is not yet certain whether the *Ekran Berhad* claim will proceed against China but there will be an uncomfortable realiz ation that the obligations in these investment treaties are reciprocal. China would no doubt prefer to have the case settled to maintain the ' MianZi' that is its reputation in the international stage as never having a case filed against it at ICSID but this may not be realistic given its extensive treaty regime. China is expected to defend its position vigorously should the ongoing settlement negotiations fail and has already discussed the claim with several international law firms with a view to retaining experienced counsel. On the other hand, as in the *Tza Yap Shum* case, Chinese investors abroad benefit from this regime.[246] This tension will persist as China continues to focus on investment abroad.

Select Bibliography

Ministry of Commerce (formerly the Ministry of Foreign Trade and Economic Cooperation)

(ed), Collection of International Investment Treaties *(Guoji Touzi Tiaoyue Huibian) (Jingguan Jiaoyu Press, Beijing,* 1998*)*

Santiago Montt, State Liability in Investment Treaty Arbitration: Global Constitutional and Administrative Law in the BIT Generation *(Hart,* 2009*)*

Michael Moser, Managing Business Disputes in Today's China: Duelling with Dragons *(Kluwer,* 2007*)*, 233 – 52

Tza Yap Shum v Peru *(ICSID Case No ARB/*07/6, *Decision on Jurisdiction and Competence of* 19 *June* 2009, *Award of* 7 *July* 2011*)*

Tza Yap Shum v Peru *(ICSID Case No ARB/*07/6 *Award,* 7 *July* 2011*)*

Ekran Berhad v People's Republic of China *(ICSID Case No ARB/*11/15*)*

China Heilongjiang International Economic & Technical Cooperative Corp. , *et al* v. Mongolia *PCA Case (China-Mongolia BIT* 1991*)*

---

[246] Another example of this is the PCA arbitration case against Mongolia brought by three mainland Chinese companies. See *China Heilongjiang International Economic & Technical Cooperative Corp. , et al v. Mongolia, posted at* www. pca-cpa. org/showpage. asp?pag_id = 1378(last accessed 24 January 2012).

Wenhua Shan, The Legal Framework of EU-China Investment Relations: A Critical Appraisal (*Hart Publishing*, 2005)

Wenhua Shan and Norah Gallagher, Chinese Investment Treaties: Policy and Practice (*Oxford University Press*, 2009)

National Treatment and Foreign Investment in China: A Changing Landscape*

I. Introduction

National treatment ('NT') is an important standard of treatment since it provides a clear criterion for the manner in which foreign investors should be treated. By allowing foreign investors to enjoy the same treatment as local investors, foreign investors can not only enjoy the benefits of local entities but also can feel more 'at home' when investing abroad.[1] As such, NT is a relative standard of treatment, as the host State must treat foreign investors no less favourable than national investors. Much has been written on this 'key feature of most investment agreements'.[2] This treatment has developed in a relatively short period of time as an important feature in both domestic and international legislation. In a rapidly globalizing world, granting NT to foreign investors has become more and more popular and as a result is now common practice.[3] This article does not

---

* *ICSID Review*, Volume 27 No. 1, Spring 2012. The authors are Shan Wenhua, Norah Gallagher and Zhang Sheng.

[1] Norah Gallagher and Wenhua Shan, Chinese Investment Treaties: Policy and Practice 173 (Oxford University Press 2009).

[2] Andrea K Bjorklund, 'The National Treatment Obligation' in Katia Yannaca-Small (ed), Arbitration under International Investment Agreements: A Guide to the Key Issues 411 (Oxford University Press 2010); see also Jeswald W Salacuse, The Law of Investment Treaties 245 - 51 (Oxford University Press 2010); Andrew Newcombe and Lluís Paradell 'National Treatment' in Andrew Newcombe and Lluís Paradell, Law and Practice of Investment Treaties:

Standards of Treatment 147 (Kluwer Law International 2009); Todd J Grierson-Weiler and Ian A Laird, 'Standards of Treatment' in Peter Muchlinski, Federico Ortino and Christoph Schreuer (eds), The Oxford Handbook of International Investment Law 290 (Oxford University Press 2008); Rudolf Dolzer and Christoph Schreuer, Principles of International Investment Law 178 - 86 (Oxford University Press 2008); Ian A Laird and Borzu Sabahi, 'Trends in International Investment Disputes' in Karl P Savant (ed), Yearbook on International Investment Law and Policy 2008 - 2009 79 (Oxford University Press 2009); Campbell McLachlan, Laurence Shore and Matthew Weiniger, International Investment Arbitration: Substantive Principles paras 7.152 - 7.160 (Oxford University Press 2007).

[3] Gallagher and Shan (n 4) 165.

propose to analyse the writings and case law[4] on the application of NT, but instead will look at how China has changed its approach to this international legal standard in both domestic and international regimes.

China had been reluctant to adopt the NT standard because of its former planned economy.[5] This situation has, nevertheless, been changing since the 'opening-up' policy adopted in the late 1970s. As China seeks to integrate into the world, economically and otherwise, it has become more and more willing to grant NT to foreign investors by reducing restrictions imposed on foreign investments ('inferior-national treatment').[6] In recent years, however, the principle has been used to cut certain incentives previously enjoyed only by foreign investors ('superior-national treatment'). Notably, in December 2010, China started to levy urban maintenance and construction tax and educational surcharges on foreign invested enterprises, a move widely regarded as signalling the end of the 'superior-national treatment' of foreign investments in China.[7]

This article will explore the recent policy shift and resulting domestic and international legal changes in China's implementation of NT protection for foreign investors. It will set out a brief introduction to China's changing policy toward foreign direct investment ('FDI') and proceed to analyse the establishment and development of NT in China in both domestic legislation and international investment treaties. It will also focus on the recent measures to eliminate 'superior NT' in domestic legislation and China's changing approach in international investment law. The article concludes with a discussion on the future agenda of China's NT policy with special reference to the ongoing bilateral investment treaty ('BIT') negotiations with the European Union ('EU') and the

---

[4] See eg GEA Group Aktiengesellschaft v Ukraine, ICSID *Case No ARB/08/16, Award (*31 *March* 2011*); AES Summit Generation Limited and AES-Tisza Ero¨mu¨ Kft v Hungary*, ICSID *Case No ARB/07/22, Award* (23 September 2010); GAMI Investments, *Inc v The Government of the United Mexican States*, UNCITRAL, Final Award (15 November 2004). The early North American Free Trade Agreement (NAFTA) cases were significant in developing a 'methodology for applying the national treatment standard'. Christopher F Dugan et al, Investor-State Arbitration 400 fn 19 (Oxford University Press 2008). See further Meg N Kinnear, Andrea K Bjorklund and John F G Hannaford, Investment Disputes under NAFTA: An Annotated Guide to NAFTA Chapter 11 art 1102 (2006).

[5] This article will focus on the evolution of the NT standard for foreign investment after the founding of the People's Republic of China ('PRC') in 1949. There are, nevertheless, some articles that discuss the NT standard in China that date back to the First Opium War in 1840. See Wei Wang, 'Historical Evolution of National Treatment in China' (2005) 39 Intl Lawyer 759; see also Wei Wang, 'Super-National Treatment: A Misconception or a Creation with Chinese Characteristics?' (2010) 5(3) Frontiers of Law in China 376.

[6] Gallagher and Shan (n 4) 165; see also Wenhua Shan, 'National Treatment and the Transformation of FDI Laws and Policies in China' (2000) 6(1) Intl Trade L Reg 21.

[7] Circular on Unifying the System for Urban Maintenance and Construction Tax and Educational Surcharge on Chinese and Foreign Investment Enterprises and Individuals, promulgated by the State Council (18 October 2010, entered into effect 1 December 2010). See also Han Jie and Xu Rui, 'Domestic and Foreign Tax Expert Analysis Significance of a Comprehensive Unified' China Daily (21 October 2010), *available at* http://www.china-daily.org/China-News/Domestic-and-foreign-tax-expert-analysis-significance-of-a-comprehensive-unified, accessed 10 May 2012. For more details see Section II. B.

United States.[8]

II. China's Recent Fdi Policy: A Shift of Focus

China's attitude toward FDI, to a large extent, determines the features of its domestic legislation and its practice in the field of international law. This section will investigate the evolution of China's attitude toward FDI and its resulting impact on the development of NT protection for foreign investment. Two different stages, based on the changes of policy orientation, can be identified in this respect, namely (A) China's pre – 2005 position, and (B) its post – 2006 approach to FDI.

1. China's FDI Policy: Before 2005

The very notion of NT is based on a market economy instead of a planned economy. There is no doubt that NT could not be traced in China's FDI policy in the first few decades following its establishment in 1949. Notions and concepts of private property and individual economic initiative were treated as elements of the 'blamed' capitalism and vigorously rejected. Ideologically, these concepts were incompatible with the Soviet style of socialism, evident in China in the post-World War II era. It was during this period that foreign investment also encountered gradual confiscation or creeping expropriations without any compensation, particularly by the adoption of the so-called 'socialist transformation of capitalist industry and commerce' over a period of seven years in the 1950s.[9] As with the Latin American States, China traditionally accepted the Calvo Doctrine,[10] and China was also an active participant in establishing the 'New International Economic Order' that emphasized State sovereignty over natural resources and limited any sub-

---

[8] These talks have been ongoing since the 1980s when no consensus could be reached between the States on the terms of a BIT. Talks were re-commenced in 2008 and are at a preliminary stage but ongoing. It will be interesting to see whether the signature by Canada of a 'Declaration of Intent' to sign a BIT with China will speed up the process with the United States. The terms of the China-Canada BIT are not yet public. See generally on the negotiations Justin Carter, 'The Protracted Bargain: Negotiating the Canada-China FIPA' (2009) 47 Can YB Intl L 197.

[9] For further details, see Wenhua Shan, The Legal Framework of EU-China Investment Relations—A Critical Appraisal 1 – 4 (Hart Publishing 2005). See also Thomas N Thompson, 'China's Nationalisation of Foreign Firms: The Politics of Hostage Taking 1949 – 1957' (1979) 27(6) University of Maryland School of Law Occasional Papers/Reprints Series in Contemporary Asian Studies (1979), *available at* http://digitalcommons.law.umaryland.edu/cgi/viewcontent.cgi?article=1026&context=mscas, accessed 5 August 2012; Gallagher and Shan (n 4) 4 – 5.

[10] The Calvo Doctrine is a foreign policy doctrine based on the ideology of Carlos Calvo, an Argentine jurist. The essence of this doctrine is 'anti-super-national-treatment', which focuses on the opposition and rejection of any discriminatory treatment by western powers against weak, developing host States and their nationals, as compared to the treatment western powers accord to each other and demand for their citizens in these host States. See Wenhua Shan, 'Is Calvo Dead?' (2007) 55 Am J Comp L 123, 124. For a historical review of the Calvo doctrine, see Santiago Montt, State Liability in Investment Treaty Arbitration: Global Constitutional and Administrative Law in the BIT Generation ch 1 (Hart Publishing 2009). In the 1990s, the 'imminent death' of this doctrine was declared due to changing attitudes in Latin American States toward foreign investment as witnessed in their international and domestic law-making practice. See Denise Manning-Cabrol, 'The Imminent Death of the Calvo Clause and the Rebirth of the Calvo Principle: Equality of Foreign and National Investors' (1995) 26 L Policy Intl Bus 1169. However, Calvo is not completely dead, but has largely been deactivated. It is still alive with respect to the rejection of diplomatic protection, yet in others ways is greatly transformed. See Shan (n 13) 124.

stantial protection of foreign investment under international law.[11]

During the period before 1979, China's foreign policy was characterized by the 'Five Principles of Peaceful Co-existence', which were similar to the 'anti-super-national-treatment' approach embodied in the Calvo Doctrine.[12] These five principles consisted of 'mutual respect for each other's sovereignty and territorial integrity, mutual non-aggression, non-interference in internal affairs, equality and mutual benefit and peaceful coexistence'.[13] Within the sphere of foreign investment, these five principles were understood to have the following elements: (i) the State had a sovereign right to control the entry of FDI and to regulate the activities of foreign investors in its territory; (ii) the right to nationalize foreign property was an inherent attribute of national territorial sovereignty, and the exercise of this fundamental right was not subject to any preconditions being met, such as a requirement that the nationalization be made in the public interest, in accordance with due process of law and non-discrimination, and against payment of compensation; and (iii) State contracts or concessions would be observed, subject to the sovereign power of host States to mandate renegotiation, revision or even unilateral modification on the basis of changed circumstances or public interests.[14]

Slowly, China realised that a State that wants and needs to encourage further development cannot just depend on itself and remain isolated from the international market. So began the 'opening-up' policy from 1979. After a decade of market-oriented reform and opening-up to the outside, the constitu-tional status of the 'Socialist Market Economy' was finally established in 1993. Later that same year, China embarked on an effort to 'create facilities and conditions to implement the national treatment for foreign-invested enterprises'.[15] The Chinese attitude toward FDI was further developed into the so-called 'three guiding principles' of international economic co-operation and exchange, namely, the principles of sovereignty, equality and mutual benefit, and reference to international practice.[16] These 'three guiding principles' were developed and refined from the above-mentioned 'Five Principles of Peaceful Co-existence' and resembled them to some extent. One important facet of the principle of 'equality and mutual benefit' was,

---

[11] Stephan W Schill, 'Tearing Down the Great Wall: the New Generation Investment Treaties of the People's Republic of China', (2007) 15 Cardozo J Intl Comp L 73, 78. See generally the Charter of Economic Rights and Duties of States, UNGA Res 3281 (XXIX) (12 December 1974), UN Doc A/RES/29/3281; Declaration on the Establishment of a New International Economic Order, UNGA Res 3201 (S-VI) (1 May 1974), UN Doc A/RES/S - 6/3201; Charles N Brower, and John B Tepe Jr, 'The Charter of Economic Rights and Duties of States: A Reflection or Rejection of International Law?', (1975) 9 Intl L 295; Stephen M Schwebel, 'The Story of the UN's Declaration on Permanent Sovereignty over Natural Resources', (1963) ABA J 463.

[12] Shan (n 13) 124.

[13] Qingjiang Kong, 'Bilateral Investment Treaties: The Chinese Approach and Practice' (2003) 8 Asian YB Intl L 105, 109.

[14] Ibid., see also Schill (n 14) 78.

[15] See The Central Committee of the Communist Party of China, Decision of the CPC Central Committee on Some Issues Related to the Establishment of the Socialist Market Economy, adopted at the Third Plenary Session of the 14th Central Committee (November 1993). It proposed reforms in key areas, including in the fiscal and banking system, as well as in the foreign exchange control system.

[16] Meizhen Yao, 'Legal Protection of International Investment' in Chinese Society of International Law (ed), Selected Articles from Chinese Yearbook of International Law 169 - 186 (China Translation & Publishing Corp 1983). See also Kong (n 16) 110.

in relation to FDI, the equality between nationals and corporations of different countries.[17] Clearly this revision was evidence of a shift by China to a more moderate stance on international practice, which would include treatment of foreign investors.[18] It demonstrated China's desire to establish NT in both its domestic and international spheres.

With rapid economic growth, including a sharp increase in FDI, trade surplus, and foreign exchange ('forex') reserves, China started to seriously consider an outward direct investment ('ODI') strategy. This concept was first put forward in 1998 as a strategy that was aimed at encouraging China's enterprises to invest overseas. The 'Going Abroad' policy encourages entities to actively explore international markets and take advantage of resources to strengthen the develop-ment impetus and potential of the Chinese economy. In 2001, the 'Going Abroad' strategy was for the first time included in the country's 10th Five-year Plan ('FYP') and was formally established as a separate national economic strategy. On 4 October 2003, the Central Committee of the Communist Party of China ('CCCPC') repeated its commitment to the implementation of the 'Going Abroad' policy. Undoubtedly, this policy has played a significant role in China's determination to take a more liberal approach in its BIT practice, including a more liberal NT clause. China is no longer entirely focused on inward direct investment, and it is now just as likely Chinese investors abroad would seek to rely on a BIT.[19]

A more liberal approach was taken by China especially after its accession to the World Trade Organization ('WTO'). Needless to say, China's membership in the WTO most certainly facilitates the implementation of NT in both domestic laws and international investment laws. Notwithstanding its role focusing on trade, the WTO also embraces some investment issues. The Agreement on Trade-related Investment Measures ('TRIMs Agreement') and the General Agreement on Trade in Service (GATS) have now become major sources of investment rules within the WTO framework.[20] It is observed that there are virtually identical rules between the WTO investment-related agreements and the Chinese BITs.[21]

2. China's FDI Policy: After 2006

With its undisputable and unprecedented success in attracting FDI, what concerns

---

〔17〕 Kong (n 16) 111.

〔18〕 Ibid.

〔19〕 See, for example, the arbitration taken by a Hong Kong investor under the China-Peru BIT. Tza Yap Shum v Republic of Peru, ICSID Case No ARB/07/6, Decision on Jurisdiction and Competence (19 June 2009) and Award (7 July 2011). For commentary see Wei Shen, 'The Good, the Bad or the Ugly? A Critique of the Decision on Jurisdiction and Competence in Tza Yap Shum v The Republic of Peru' (2011) 10(1) Chin J Intl L 55. See also the pending claim taken by another Chinese investor under the China-Mongolia BIT in China Heilongjiang International Economic & Technical Cooperative Corp, Beijing Shougang Mining Investment Company Ltd, and Qinhuangdaoshi Qinlong International Industrial Co Ltd v Mongolia, UNCITRAL.

〔20〕 Michael Gestrin and Alan Rugman, 'Rules for Foreign Direct Investment at the WTO: Building on Regional Trade Agreement' in Patrick FJ Macrory et al. (eds), The World Trade Organization: Legal, Economic and Political Analysis 313 – 23 (Springer 2005); see also Kevin C Kennedy, 'A WTO Agreement on Investment: A Solution in Search of a Problem?' (2003) 24 U Pa J Intl Econ L 77; Thomas L Brewer et al, 'Investment Issues at the WTO: The Architecture of Rules and the Settlement of Disputes' (1998) 1 J Intl Econ L 457.

〔21〕 Kong (n 16) 133.

the Chinese Government now is no longer how to attract additional FDI, but how to attract FDI of higher ' quality' . This change in emphasis has been most clearly demonstrated in the 11th FYP on Foreign Capital Utilization published in November 2006.[22] It is believed to be the indication of the next logical step in China's FDI policy, placing more emphasis on domestic development in accordance with the country's development requirements and WTO commitments.[23] The 11th FYP was the first plan on foreign investment published by the Chinese Government. Using the language ' quality' over ' quantity' , the FYP asserts that the Government will:

propel the fundamental conversion of the foreign capital utilization from ' being quantity oriented' to ' being quality oriented' ; to conscientiously transfer the emphasis of the foreign capital utilization from making up the shortage of funds and foreign exchange to introducing advanced technologies, management experience, and high-quality talents; and to focus more on ecological construction, environmental protection, conservation, and comprehensive utilization of resources and energies.[24]

In other words, a ' selective approach' was introduced by this plan.[25]

In April 2010, the State Council issued its ' Several Opinions of the State Council on Further Utilizing Foreign Capital' .[26] Although the starting position is that foreign investment is welcomed by China, it has been observed that these opinions also reflect a change in Chinese Government policy from attracting foreign capital without any differentiation to selective utilization.[27] Considering the situation that foreign investments are always welcomed and enjoy superior NT with more preferential treatment when compared with some national companies in certain areas, the opinions also demonstrate the trend that the Chinese Government will adopt more specific measures to regulate foreign investment with this selective utilization mode.[28] Also in 2010, the Premier Wen Jiabao said that China will make institutional agreements to provide a ' fair playing ground' for foreign investors and grant them ' national treatment' .[29] Moreover, the changes to the FDI policy orientation from quantity to quality are reiterated in the 12th FYP for Nation-

---

〔22〕 The State Development and Reform Commission (' SDFC'), The 11th Five-year Plan on Foreign Capital Utilization (10 November 2006) , *available at* www. fdi. gov. cn/pub/FDI_EN/Laws/GeneralLawsandRegulations/MinisterialRulings/t20061220_68109. jsp, accessed 10 May 2012.

〔23〕 Françoise Nicolas, ' China and Foreign Investors: The End of a Beautiful Friendship?' Asie Visions No 4, 19 (Institut Français des Relations Internationales, April 2008) , *available at* www. ifri. org/downloads/Asie_Visions_4_Nicolas. pdf, accessed 10 May 2012.

〔24〕 11th FYP (n 25) s 2, ' Guiding Ideology and Overall Strategic Objective of Foreign Capital Utilization of China during the 11th Five-year Plan Period' .

〔25〕 Gallagher and Shan (n 4) 28.

〔26〕 The State Council, Several Opinions of the State Council on Further Utilizing Foreign Capital (6 April 2010), *available at* http://english. mofcom. gov. cn/aarticle/policyrelease/announcement/201006/20100606982859. html, accessed 10 May 2012.

〔27〕 Global Trade Alert, ' China: General Analysis on Several Opinions of the State Council on Further Utilizing Foreign Capital' (30 November 2010), *available at* http://www. globaltradealert. org/measure/china-general-analysis-several-opinions-state-council-further-utilizing-foreign-capital, accessed 10 May 2012.

〔28〕 Ibid.

〔29〕 ' Wen Promises to Grant Foreign Enterprises "National Treatment"' , Xinhua (14 March 2010), *available at* http://www. china. org. cn/china/NPC_CPPCC_2010/2010 - 03/14/content_19606081. htm, accessed 10 May 2012.

al Economic and Social Development of the People's Republic of China ('PRC').[30]

At the same time, the policy of 'peaceful development' has been shaped to create a peaceful international and regional environment for China. The policy was first proposed by Chinese leaders in 2003 to counter international fears about China's growing economic and political might. This policy was reaffirmed in 2004 by Premier Wen Jiabao that China's rise 'will not stand in the way of any other country, nor pose a threat to any other country, nor at the cost of any other country'.[31] The 'peaceful development' policy proposes that China will develop economically by taking advantage of the peaceful international environment while maintaining and contributing to world peace through development.[32] It is according to this policy that China shaped its attitude toward regionalism and took steps to develop its free trade agreements ('FTAs').[33]

III. National Treatment in Domestic Legislation

NT is generally, as already stated, an inherent element of a market economy. This treatment is, nevertheless, unfeasible under the planned economy system that used to be implemented in China. During that period, foreign investors in China were accorded 'inferior' NT in some respects, while they enjoyed 'superior' NT in certain respects such as tax and other preferential measures. This situation began to change once China began to develop its market economy system in the early 1990s. With the economic growth and enormous achievements in attracting FDI and its rapidly growing ODI in the past two decades, China has gradually made efforts to provide a level playing field for both domestic and foreign investors. This part will delve into the development of the concept of NT in China's domestic legislation and China's recent efforts toward the implementation

---

[30] The 12th Five-Year Plan for National Economic and Social Development of the PRC (2011 – 15), adopted by the Fourth Session of the 11th National People's Congress ('NPC') (14 March 2011), *available at* http://www.gov.cn/2011lh/content_1825838.htm, accessed 10 May 2012. The Plan provides that China will 'improve the soft environment for investment and protect legitimate rights and interests of investors' (translation by authors). It is believed that if the 12th FYP is fully implemented, China will be a fairer, greener society by 2015. See Alan Wheatley, 'Why the World Should Heed China's Five-Year Plan', Reuters (7 March 2011), *available at* http://www.reuters.com/article/2011/03/07/us-china-economy-plan-idUSTRE7261J820110307, accessed 30 April 2012.

[31] See 'Chinese Premier on Foreign Relations', Xinhua (14 March 2004), *available at* http://news.xinhuanet.com/english/2004-03/14/content_1365726.htm, accessed 10 May 2012. This was to alleviate concern in certain quarters on the rapid rise of China. The US House of Representatives was concerned over national security when the State-owned China National Offshore Oil Corporation (CNOOC) bid to control UNOCAL. See He Yi, 'National Security Review System for Foreign Merger & Acquisitions in America—Taking CNNOC's Acquisition of Unocal as an Example' (2007) 14(1) Chin J Intl Econ L 45. For the impact this had on Chinese entities, see Albert Bressand, 'Foreign Direct Investment in the Oil and Gas Sector: Recent Trends and Strategic Drivers' (2009) YB Intl Invest L Policy 117, 190. The race between India and China for investment opportunities in Africa has also generated some misconceptions and concerns. See Anil K Gupta and Haiyan Wang, 'Myths about China and India's Africa Race', Bloomberg Insight (12 October 2011), *available at* http://www.businessweek.com/asia/myths-about-china-and-indias-africa-race-09222011.html, accessed 28 June 2012.

[32] Guiguo Wang, 'China's FTAs: Legal Characteristics and Implications' (2011) 105 Am J Intl L 493, 495 fn 12; see also Esther Pan, 'The Promise and Pitfalls of China's "Peaceful Rise"', Council on Foreign Relations (14 April 2006), *available at* http://www.cfr.org/china/promise-pitfalls-chinas-peaceful-rise/p10446, accessed 28 June 2012.

[33] Wang (n 35) 495.

of full NT for FDI.

1. The Development of NT in Domestic Laws and Regulations

In accordance with China's planned economy and its rejection of private property before 1979, the notion and concept of private ownership regarding the means of production did not appear in any of the three consecutive constitutions separately promulgated in 1954, 1975 and 1978.[34] None of these constitutions provided any protection or standards of treatment for foreign investors in China. This situation was, nevertheless, changed when China adopted the 'opening-up policy' in 1978. One year later, China normalized its relations with the United States and also in that year promulgated the Sino-Foreign Equity Joint Venture Law ('EJVL') to encourage and protect foreign investment in China.[35] The 1979 EJVL itself did not contain an article on NT. However, it was the first piece of national legislation relating to FDI in China and laid the foundation for subsequent NT legislation.[36] The constitutional status of NT for foreign investors was established in the 1982 Constitution,[37] which allowed foreigners and foreign enterprises to invest in China, to enter into various forms of economic cooperation, and provided them with legal protections.[38]

Traditionally, NT for foreign investors covers two factors, namely, civil and commercial rights (substantive rights) and judicial administrative rights (proced-ural rights). It is observed that the NT legislation in China started from procedural law and was extended to substantive law, within which NT was extended from civil law to trade law.[39] A clear NT clause first appeared in the Interim Civil Procedure Law in 1982.[40] Article 186 of this Law provided that foreign nationals and stateless persons shall have the same litigation rights and obligations as Chinese citizens while foreign enterprises and organizations only have litigation rights and obligations specifically provided by the Law. Based on these different statements, it seems that NT was only granted to foreign individuals, but not to foreign enterprises or organizations. This kind of discrimination between foreign individuals and foreign enterprises was eliminated after the enactment of the 1982 Constitution. NT with respect to administrative procedures was provided in the Adminis-

[34] Since it was founded in 1949, China has issued four consecutive constitutions: those of 1954, 1975, 1978 and 1982. To date, the current version, the 1982 Constitution, has been amended four separate times in 1988, 1993, 1999 and 2004.

[35] Sino-Foreign Equity Joint Venture Law of the PRC, promulgated by the NPC (1 July 1979, entered into effect 1 July 1979, amended 15 March 2001). Three years later, China signed its first BIT with Sweden on 29 March 1982.

[36] Wang (n 8) 773.

[37] Constitution of the PRC, promulgated by the NPC (12 April 1982, entered into effect 12 April 1982, amended 12 April 1988, 29 March 1993, 15 March 1999 and 14 March 2004) ('1982 Constitution').

[38] Ibid Arts 18, 32.

[39] Wang (n 8) 773.

[40] Interim Civil Procedure Law of the PRC, promulgated by the NPC Order No 8 (8 March 1982 entered into effect 1 October 1982, repealed 9 April 1991).

trative Procedure Law 1989.[41] NT within the field of civil procedure was also extended to foreign enterprises and organizations in the 1991 Civil Procedure Law, which replaced the above-mentioned Interim Civil Procedure Law.[42]

However, it was not until the enactment of the Foreign Trade Law[43] in 1994 that the term 'national treatment' was first introduced. Article 6 of the Foreign Trade Law reads:

[T]he People's Republic of China, shall, under international treaties or agreements to which it is a contracting party or a participating party, grant within the field of foreign trade most favoured nation treatment and the national treatment to the other contracting parties or participating parties under the principle of mutual benefit and reciprocity.[44]

Also in this Law, Article 23 addresses the application of NT within the field of international trade in services, which provides that,

[W]ith respect to international trade in services, the People's Republic of China shall, pursuant to the commitments made in international treaties or agreements to which it is a contracting party or a participating party, grant the other contracting parties and the other participating parties' market access or *national treatment*.[45]

As can be seen, these two articles will not directly grant NT to foreign investors and enterprises. They merely confirm that China will observe its commitments, provided that NT is required under international treaties or agreements. At the same time, the inclusion of the phrase relating to 'the principle of mutual benefit and reciprocity' in Article 6 illustrates China's FDI policy of 'three guiding principles' mentioned in Section I above. Also, China's NT is not unconditional, but subject to China's reservations under treaties or agreements.[46]

In contrast to the clear inclusion of the term 'national treatment' in trade law, the term was not found in any single basic law relating to foreign investment. Apart from the EJVL, China has enacted a number of laws and regulations exclusively applicable to FDI. These laws and regulations, including the Sino-Foreign Contractual Joint Venture Law ('CJVL'),[47] the Wholly Foreign Owned Enterprises Law ('WFEL'),[48] Income Tax for Foreign In-

---

[41] Administrative Procedure Law of the PRC, promulgated by the NPC (4 April 1989, entered into effect 1 October 1990). The first paragraph of Article 71 reads:

[F]oreign nationals, stateless persons and foreign organizations that are engaged in administrative suits in the People's Republic of China shall have the same litigation rights and obligations as citizens and organizations of the People's Republic of China.

[42] Civil Procedural Law of the PRC, Art 5, promulgated by the NPC (9 April 1991, entered into effect 9 April 1991, amended 28 October 2007).

[43] Foreign Trade Law of the PRC, promulgated by the NPC (12 May 1994, entered into effect 1 July 1994, amended 6 April 2004).

[44] Ibid Art 6 (emphasis added).

[45] Ibid Art 23. This Article remained in the Foreign Trade Law amended in 2004 but was renumbered as Article 24.

[46] See also Wang (n 8) 775.

[47] Sino-Foreign Contractual Joint Venture Law of the PRC, promulgated by the NPC (13 April 1988, entered into effect 13 April 1988, amended 31 October 2000).

[48] The Wholly Foreign Owned Enterprises Law of the PRC, promulgated by the NPC (12 April 1986, entered into effect 12 April 1986, amended 31 October 2000).

vested Enterprises ('FIEs') and Foreign Enterprises,[49] and their respective implementing regulations, are considered to be the basic laws for FDI activities in China. However, for a long time, the Chinese Government did not accept the concept of NT for FDI, and the basic laws and regulations relating to FDI were mostly about some special preferential or restrictive measures.[50] The absence of the word 'national treatment' does not mean the notion of NT is not provided in some other laws relating to FDI.[51] Article 18 of the Company Law in 1993,[52] for example, provides that both foreign invested and locally invested limited liability companies are subject to the Company Law.[53] In contrast with many western States where the single legal framework relating to corporation and partnership law generally provides the requirements for both domestic and foreign investors, China has a long-established and relatively well-developed distinct legal regime for FIEs. It is observed that this legal system has its historical and political reasons.[54] This traditional position where the regimes were separate perhaps goes some way toward explaining why the notion of NT was rarely found.

The beginning of the 21st century has witnessed a profound reform in the Chinese FDI legal regime.[55] The reasons behind this change are two-fold. On the one hand, China had to remove those non-conforming investment measures in order to meet various requirements imposed by the WTO agreements, in particular the TRIMs Agreement. On the other hand, China needed to modernize its governance regime, including its investment regime, to facilitate the rapid growth of the Chinese economy and to improve the business competitiveness of domestic enterprises.

Against this background, China made an effort to create and develop a consistent and systematic regulatory framework to facilitate FDI. It also strived to make or amend FDI legislation to conform to international agreements and rules, especially those of the WTO. China's membership in the WTO had a positive impact on its FDI legal framework, particularly with respect to NT. During this period, the National People's Congress ('NPC') amended the CJVL and WFEL in 2000, followed by the amendments

---

[49] Income Tax for Foreign Invested Enterprises and Foreign Enterprises of the PRC, promulgated by the NPC (9 April 1991, entered into effect 1 July 1991, replaced by Enterprise Income Tax Law in 2007).

[50] Shan (n 9) 21.

[51] Indeed, the term 'national treatment' appears in some local government rules (Difang Zhengfu Guizhang), which are much lower down the hierarchy in China's legislation law system. The Government of Shandong Province, for example, issued its 'Notice of the People's Government of Shandong Province on Implementing the National Treatment for Foreign Investment Enterprises' on 14 February 1998 to improve the investment environment and make it more attractive to foreign investment. Of course, this kind of notice is only targeted at the FIEs, not in creating a general obligation of NT for both foreign individuals and enterprises.

[52] Company Law of the PRC, promulgated by the NPC (29 December 1993, entered into effect on 1 July 1994, amended 25 December 1999, 28 August 2004 and 27 October 2005).

[53] Article 18 of the 1993 Company Law reads:

[T]his Law shall be applicable to foreign-invested companies with limited liability; and where laws concerning Sino-Foreign equity joint ventures, Sino-Foreign Contractual Joint Ventures and Sino-Owned Enterprises provide otherwise, the provisions there shall be applicable.

[54] Hui Huang, 'The Regulation of Foreign Investment in Post-WTO China: A Political Economy Analysis' (2009) 23 Colum J Asian L 185, 201 - 02.

[55] This does not mean that there was no amendment before 2000. For instance, the EJVL 1979 was amended for the first time in April 1990.

of the EJVL in March 2001. Accordingly, the State Council approved the amendments to the Implementing Regulations of the WFEL and EJVL in April and July 2001, respectively. Among the four main groups of amendments,[56] the abolition of the direct performance requirements, such as local purchase priority requirements, foreign exchange balance requirements, export performance and domestic sales restrictions, were more remarkable. These types of performance requirements had often been criticized by foreign investors as an indication of ' inferior NT' imposed on them.

Alongside these amendments, China also developed its laws and regulations to form a systematic and comprehensive regulatory framework to facilitate and regulate FDI. For example, the Interim Provisions on Mergers and Acquisitions of Domestic Enterprises by Foreign Investors,[57] issued in 2003, was the first comprehensive set of regulations on cross-border mergers and acquisitions (' M&As') in China. The Chinese Government also promulgated the Guidance on the Direction of Foreign Investment in 2002.[58] This Guidance, together with the periodically revised Guiding Catalogue of Industries for Foreign Investment,[59] comprises the two most important instruments on investment admission in China.

2. Recent Reforms Emphasising ' Quality' Over ' Quantity'

In line with its new trend of FDI policy since 2006, China has also made efforts to further reform its domestic laws and regulations. One of the most obvious changes was the promulgation of the Enterprise Income Tax Law in 2007,[60] which repealed the FIEs Income Tax Law of 1991. The new tax law, which was designed to equalize enterprise income tax imposed on local and foreign enterprises, put an end to the preferential rate enjoyed by foreign enterprises for about 30 years.[61] According to the new Income Tax Law, a single tax rate of 25 percent is levied on all enterprises, changing the long-established situation where Chinese enterprises were taxed at up to 33 percent, while foreign

---

[56] See Shan (n 12) 49 – 50.

[57] Interim Provisions on Mergers and Acquisitions of Domestic Enterprises by Foreign Investors, jointly promulgated by the Ministry of Foreign Trade and Economic Cooperation (' MOFTEC') (now the Ministry of Finance (' MOFCOM')), the State Tax Bureau, the State Industry and Commerce Bureau and the State Foreign Exchange Bureau (January 2003, entered into effect 12 April 2003, amended 8 August 2006).

[58] Guidance on the Direction of Foreign investment, promulgated by the State Council, Decree No 346 (21 February 2002, entered into effect 1 April 2002).

[59] Guiding Catalogue of Industries for Foreign Investment (promulgated 1995, revised most recently 24 December 2011 by Decree No 12 of the State Development and Reform Commission and the Ministry of Commerce of the PRC, entered into effect 30 January 2012). In addition to this catalogue, China has also adopted a Catalogue of Encouraged Industries for Foreign Investment in the Middle and Western Area (published June 2000, revised July 2004 and 2008) and a Catalogue of Encouraged High-Tech Products for Foreign Investments (published July 2003, revised 31 December 2006).

[60] Enterprise Income Tax Law of the PRC, promulgated by the NPC (16 March 2007, entered into effect 1 January 2008).

[61] For details of the tax incentives, see Zhaodong Jiang, ' China's Tax Preferences to Foreign Investment' (1998) 18 Northwest J Intl L Bus 549. It is argued that the extensive tax incentives that used to be offered to FDI enterprises had significant drawbacks; it not only distorted domestic capital markets, creating incentives for round-tripping FDI, but also created unfair competition between domestic and foreign enterprises. See Chunlai Chen, ' The Development of China's FDI Laws and Policies after WTO Accession' in Jane Golley and Ligang Song (eds), Rising China: Global Challenges and Opportunities 92 (Australian National University Press 2011).

enterprises had been subject to as little as 15 percent. Indeed, the beginning of the national tax treatment for foreign and Chinese enterprises may be traced back to 2006, when the State Council for the first time levied foreign enterprises with the Urban and Town Land Use Tax[62] and Vehicle and Vessel Usage Tax.[63] In 2007 and 2009, China also separately unified the Urban Real Estate Tax[64] and Farmland Occupation Tax.[65]

The Urban Maintenance and Construction Tax and Education Surcharges[66] in 2010 is the last reform effort in unifying the tax system in China. This tax standardization echoes the proposition that ' we will unify the taxation systems for both domestic and foreign-funded enterprises', as promised in the 11th FYP on the Utilization of Foreign Investments and the Decision of the Central Committee of the Chinese Communist Party (' CCP') on Improving the Socialist Market Economic System. Given China's economic and social development and the improvement of the market economy, unifying the taxation systems for enterprises of all types constitutes a necessary requirement of achieving equity in terms of tax burden and promoting fair competition. The unification was adopted against some positive fiscal policies, which include a series of structural tax reduction policies, in order to maintain economic growth and to tackle the financial crisis prevailing since 2009. It is expected that this unification would not have a negative impact on the levels of foreign investment. With sustainable development throughout the years, China has built a multi-dimensional, multi-tiered, and wide-ranging pattern of opening-up and has maintained many favourable conditions that continue to attract foreign investment. Moreover, China's unification aimed at creating a tax system and investment environment encourages fair competition without increasing the burden on FIEs.[67]

The fourth revision of the Guiding Catalogue of Industries for Foreign Investment was also an important step in implementing the ' selective' and ' quality oriented' approach adopted in the above-mentioned 11th FYP on the Utilization of Foreign Investments.[68] This approach is further endorsed in the recent 2011 revision of the Guiding Catalogue of Industries for Foreign Investment,[69] which was revised according to the

---

[62] Decision of the State Council on Amending the Interim Regulations of the PRC on Urban and Town Land Use Tax, promulgated by the State Council (31 December 2006, entered into effect 1 January 2007).

[63] Interim Regulations of the PRC on Vehicle and Vessel Tax, promulgated by the State Council (29 December 2006, entered into effect 1 January 2007, repealed by Law of the PRC on Vehicle and Vessel Tax, promulgated by the NPC 25 February 2011, entered into effect 1 January 2012). Note that the unified tax requirement is retained.

[64] Notice of the Ministry of Finance and the State Administration of Taxation on Issues Concerning the Collection of the Real Estate Tax from Foreign Invested Enterprises and Foreign Individuals, promulgated by the Ministry of Finance and State Administration (12 January 2009, entered into effect 12 January 2009).

[65] Interim Regulations of the PRC on Farmland Occupation Tax, promulgated by the State Council (1 December 2007, entered into effect 1 January 2008).

[66] Unifying the System (n 10).

[67] State Administration of Taxation of the PRC, ' Relevant Authorities of the Ministry of Finance and the SAT Answered the Reporters' Questions with Respect to Extending the Urban Maintenance and Construction Tax and Education Surcharges to Foreign Enterprises and Nationals' (16 November 2010), *available at* http://www.chinatax.gov.cn/n6669073/n6669118/10387049.html, accessed 10 May 2012.

[68] For details, see Gallagher and Shan (n 4) 25 – 8; see also Nicolas (n 26) 21 – 5.

[69] Guiding Catalogue of Industries for Foreign Investment (n 62) (amended 2011).

2010 'Several Opinions of the State Council on Further Utilizing Foreign Capital'.[70]

Another effort by China to secure the quality of foreign investment was the establishment of the security review system to monitor M&A activities by foreign investors. Alongside the anti-monopoly review provided in the Provisions of Merger and Acquisition of Domestic Enterprises by Foreign Investors, China adopted the Anti-monopoly Law in 2007.[71] Accompanied by this law, Provisions on the Criteria for Reporting Concentration of Undertakings was issued by the State Council on August 2008. In February 2011, the State Council issued the Circular of the General Office of the State Council concerning Security Review of Mergers and Acquisitions of Domestic Enterprises by Foreign Investors, which takes a rather broad definition of covered sectors.[72] Accordingly, the Ministry of Commerce ('MOFCOM') issued its Provisions on Implementing a Security Review System for Mergers and Acquisitions of Domestic Enterprises by Foreign Investors to implement the Notice. After the entry into force of the abovementioned Provisions of the MOFCOM in September 2011, China formally established its security system to systematically review M&A activities by foreign investors.

At the same time, the extent of NT for foreign investment has been further expanded. For example, the Property Law, adopted in 2007, provides that 'equal legal status and the right to development of all market subjects shall be protected'.[73] The abovementioned Anti-Monopoly Law also makes no distinction between foreign and domestic investors.[74]

---

[70] Compared with the 2007 revision, five adjustments may be found in the 2011 revision: firstly, the opening up has been further expanded; secondly, reconstruction and promotion of the manufacturing industry are more encouraged; thirdly, foreign investors encouraged to invest in strategic emerging industries; fourthly, the service industry is more encouraged and finally more emphasis is put on the coordinated development of regions. See 'China Encourages Foreign Investment in Emerging Industries' People's Daily Online (06 January 2012), *available at* http://english.people.com.cn/102774/7697820.html, accessed 30 April 2012. For further details see Guiding Catalogue of Industries for Foreign Investment (n 62) (amended 2011).

[71] The Anti-Monopoly Law of the PRC, promulgated by the NPC (30 August 2007, entered into effect 1 August 2008).

[72] The European Union Chamber of Commerce in China, Chamber in the News, Economic Observer, 'European Chamber: M&A Review Causes Concern' (16 February 2011) (in Chinese), *available at* http://www.europeanchamber.com.cn/en/chamber-in-news/317, accessed 10 May 2012. The scope of security review of mergers and acquisitions is the merger and acquisition by foreign investors of domestic military-industrial and military-related enterprises, neighbouring enterprises of key and sensitive military facilities and other units concerning national security; and such domestic enterprisers as major farm products, energy and resources, infrastructure, transportation services, key technologies and major equipment manufacturing involving in the national security and whose actual control right may be gained by foreign investors. See General Office of the State Council Circular on Security Review of Mergers and Acquisitions of Domestic Enterprises by Foreign Investors promulgated by the General Office of the State Council, [2011] Guo Ban Fa No 6, *available at* http://www.fdi.gov.cn/pub/FDI_EN/Laws/GeneralLawsandRegulations/Ministerial-Rulings/P020110222352839068480.pdf, accessed 10 May 2012.

[73] Property Law of the PRC Art 6, promulgated by the NPC (16 March 2007, entered into effect 1 October 2007).

[74] Before the Anti-Monopoly Law, there already existed some legislation regulating the cross-border M&A activities by foreign investors. See Interim Provisions on Mergers and Acquisitions of Domestic Enterprises by Foreign Investors (n 60) and accompanying text. After the enactment of the Anti-Monopoly Law, the Chinese Government amended the Provisions in 2009 to ensure its compliance with the Anti-Monopoly Law.

3. Summary

Undoubtedly, the evolution of the NT standard in Chinese domestic law reflects the development of the unique economic system in China. Domestic legislation with regard to FDI has been developing from being incentive-based, mixed with complicated fiscal incentives and other incentives, to becoming focused on providing a level playing field for both foreign and national investors. Its emphasis on the quality of the FDI, coupled with its removal of incentives, demonstrates China's efforts to gradually establish a full-market economy and implement NT protection.

China's domestic legal FDI regime not only helps to implement its BIT programme. It may also help to clarify the content and extent of the NT standard, especially where the provision is 'subject to its laws and regulations' in the relevant treaty. There is no doubt that most of the Chinese investment treaties containing a NT clause and the latest Model BIT make the NT standard contingent on the domestic legislation of the host State.[75]

IV. National Treatment in International Investment Treaties

The NT standard and most-favoured-nation (MFN) treatment, which together comprise the main non-discriminatory protections for foreign investors, are the most important relative or contingent standards of treatment provided for in investment treaties. The combination of the NT and MFN standards has the effect of levelling the playing field for all investors, regardless of their original nationality. It should be pointed out that the wording of the NT provisions in international investment treaties are not always the same as those contained in domestic law. The words 'no less favourable than', used in most Chinese BITs, illustrate that only 'inferior national treatment' is prohibited while 'superior national treatment' may still occur.[76]

1. NT in BITs

Since its first BIT concluded with Sweden in 1982, China has signed 130 BITs, of which 100 have entered into force.[77] These BITs cover most of the developed world except for the United States, Canada[78] and Ireland. Currently, China is negotiating the

[75] See eg China-Spain BIT, art 3(4) (1992) and Model Text Version III, Art 3(2).

[76] Shan (n 9) 22.

[77] LI Ling, 'Chinese Bilateral Investment Treaties: Practice and Challenges' (2010) 17 J Intl Econ L 1, 2 (in Chinese).

[78] In February 2012, Canada and China signed a 'Declaration of Intent' to enter into an agreed BIT (Canada refers to it as a Foreign Investment Promotion and Protection Agreement) after 20 years of talks. The text of the agreed BIT has not yet been signed and is not public. See Press Release, Foreign Affairs and International Trade Canada, Minister Fast Highlights Successes of Prime Minister Harper-led Trade Mission to China (22 February 2012), *available at* http://www.international.gc.ca/media_commerce/comm/news-communiques/2012/02/22a.aspx?lang=eng&view=d, accessed 10 May 2012.

terms of BITs with the United States[79] and Canada.[80] On 8 February 2012, the conclusion of the China-Canada BIT was announced, thereby ending the 18 years of on-and-off negotiations between those two States.[81] However, it remains to be seen when this BIT will be signed and ratified by both parties. Some also question the overly optimistic view by citing the announcement from Canada's Prime Minister's Office that 'both countries will need to conduct a legal review of the agreement and then sign and ratify it'.[82] This seems to suggest that there may be further legal discussion on the content of the BIT provisions.

The China-EU BIT, which was regarded as signalling a redirection of foreign investment to Europe,[83] is also on the negotiation schedule.[84] At the 14th EU-China Summit in Beijing on 14 February 2012, the parties agreed that a China-EU BIT was important as it would promote and facilitate investment in both directions. Negotiations towards this agreement would include all issues of interest to either side, without prejudice to the final outcome. They agreed to work towards the start of the negotiation as soon as possible.[85]

Any such treaty would clearly have implications for all of the existing treaties be-

---

[79] The United States-China BIT negotiations can be dated back to the early 1980s. However, the first round of negotiations ended in a stalemate because of disputes over core issues such as NT and the investor-State dispute settlement mechanism. The second round of negotiations was launched in 2008, and the sixth round of negotiations took place in 2010 when China and the United States exchanged their draft treaties. For a discussion on the China-United States BIT negotiations, see Cai Congyan, 'China-US BIT Negotiations and the Future of Investment Treaty Regime About China-Canada BIT negotiations—A Grand Bilateral Bargain with Multilateral Implications' (2009) 12 J Intl Econ L 457. In the fourth round of the China-United States Strategic and Economic Dialogue, which was held from 3 to 4 May 2012, the two sides pledged to schedule a seventh and subsequent negotiating round on the BIT. See 'Interview: China-U. S. Strategic and Economic Dialogue Productive: Expert', Xinhua (5 May 2012), *available at* http://news. xinhuanet. com/english/china/2012 – 05/05/c_131569583. htm, accessed 10 May 2012.

[80] For general information on the China-Canada BIT negotiations, see Foreign Affairs and International Trade Canada, 'Canada-China Foreign Investment Promotion and Protection Agreement (FIPA) Negotiations' (4 April 2012), *available at* http://www. international. gc. ca/trade-agreements-accords-commerciaux/agr-acc/fipa-apie/china-chine. aspx? lang = eng&view = d, accessed 10 May 2012. A wikileaks file also reveals that China-Canada BIT talks were slowed by China-United States negotiations. See 'Canada-China BIT Talks Slowed by United States-China Negotiations', *available at* http://wikileaks. ch/cable/2008/12/08BEIJING4612. html, accessed 10 May 2012.

[81] 'Joint List of Outcomes of Canadian Prime Minister Stephan Harper's Visit to China', Xinhua (9 February 2012), *available at* http://news. xinhuanet. com/english/china/2012 – 02/09/c_131401449. htm, accessed 10 May 2012.

[82] Luke Eric Peterson, 'Canada Announces Conclusion of Investment Treaty with China, but There's an Asterisk', Invest Arb Rep (16 February 2012), *available at* http://www. iareporter. com/articles/20120216, accessed 10 May 2012.

[83] Michael S Snarr, 'Europe Leaps Ahead of United States in Bilateral Investment Treaty Negotiations with China', China-US Trade Law Blog (20 July 2011), *available at* http://www. chinaustradelawblog. com/tags/bilateral-investment-treaty, accessed 10 May 2012.

[84] 'China, EU to Seek Bilateral Investment Treaty', China Daily (14 July 2011), *available at* http://www. chinadaily. com. cn/china/2011 – 07/14/content_12906429. htm, accessed 10 May 2012.

[85] See Leopoldo Rubinacci, EU-China Investment Relationship: Update on State of Play (European Commission 7 March 2012), *available at* http://trade. ec. europa. eu/doclib/docs/2012/march/tradoc_149185. pdf; see also 'Joint Press Communiqueé, 14th China-EU Summit', Xinhua (14 February 2012), *available at* http://news. xinhuanet. com/english/china/2012 – 02/14/c_131410070. htm, accessed 10 May 2012.

tween China and the EU Member States.

Though all the Chinese BITs include an MFN clause, the NT clause is not a frequent occurrence. Among the 130 – strong Chinese investment treaties that the authors have identified, less than half have a NT provision. Specifically, most of the earlier Chinese BITs do not offer any NT protection. Therefore, the inclusion of an NT standard, together with full access to international arbitration, is termed as the characteristics of the third and most recent generation of Chinese BIT practice.[86] According to the authors' observations elsewhere, six different approaches can be identified among Chinese investment treaties containing a NT clause.[87]

The China-UK BIT of 1986,[88] the first Chinese BIT to include a NT clause, provides a 'best effort' approach. The third paragraph of Article 3 of this BIT promulgates that:

either Contracting Party shall to the extent possible, accord treatment in accordance with the stipulations of its laws and regulations to the investment of nationals or companies of the other Contracting Party the same treatment as that accorded to its own nationals or companies.[89]

The 'best effort' requirement, symbolized by the inclusion of the phrase 'to the extent possible' is a substantial qualification. Ibrahim FI Shihata observed that such a qualified NT provision does not require existing discriminatory measures to be eliminated, nor does it prohibit new discriminatory actions from being taken, provided that they are in the form of domestic 'laws and regulations'.[90] This kind of NT provision imposes no material restrictions on the manner in which a host State treats foreign investments. The framing of this provision, in essence, remained largely symbolic by reducing its normative content to make goodwill efforts to treat the foreign investors equally.[91] However, despite its limited application, it was a first step for China toward adopting the NT standard in its BITs. It showed a subtle shift in China's willingness to accept international law concepts that were becoming more widespread.

The China-Japan BIT of 1988,[92] the second BIT to include a NT clause, appears to provide a straightforward NT standard. It is representative of the second approach of a substantially qualified NT. Though, neither of the two restrictions contained in the China-UK BIT is attached in the text,[93] the restriction and qualification of 'in accordance with

---

〔86〕 For more details, see Gallagher and Shan (n 4) 39 – 43.

〔87〕 Ibid., 166 – 71.

〔88〕 Agreement between the Government of the United Kingdom of Great Britain and Northern Ireland and the Government of the People's Republic of China Concerning the Promotion and Reciprocal Protection of Investments (15 May 1986) ('China-UK BIT').

〔89〕 Ibid art 3(3).

〔90〕 Ibrahim FI Shihata, 'Recent Trends Relating to Entry of Foreign Direct Investment' (1994) 9 ICSID Rev—FILJ 47, 55.

〔91〕 Schill (n 14) 95.

〔92〕 Agreement between Japan and the People's Republic of China Concerning the Encouragement and Reciprocal Protection of Investment (1 August 1988) ('China-Japan BIT').

〔93〕 See ibid Art 3.

its laws and regulations' is relocated in the China-Japan BIT's Protocol.[94] Moreover, the exceptions for 'public order, national security or sound development of national economy' allow considerable latitude for the Contracting Parties to uphold existing and to introduce new discriminatory measures against foreign investors.[95]

The third approach, that of 'NT Subject to Local Law', is most commonly used in Chinese BIT practice and is reflected in the latest Model Text.[96] The China-Latvia BIT of 2004, for example, provides that the NT standard is given subject to the condition that it is 'without prejudice to its laws and regulations'.[97] In this way, the laws of the host State remain applicable with regard to foreign investors and their treatment by that State.

The fourth approach, which provides for NT subject to a 'grandfather clause', appears in a number of recently concluded BITs. This practice started with the China-Cyprus BIT of 2001,[98] and was followed by a few more recent BITs, particularly some renegotiated European BITs.[99] A typical example of such a grandfather clause can be found in the China-Germany BIT of 2003:

---

[94] 'For the purpose of the provisions of paragraph 2 of Article 3 of the Agreement, it shall not be deemed "treatment less favourable" for either Contracting Party to accord discriminatory treatment, in accordance with its applicable laws and regulations, to nationals and companies of the other Contracting Party, in case it is really necessary for the reason of public order, national security or sound development of national economy.' Ibid Protocol Art 3.

[95] Schill (n 14) 96.

[96] Model Text Version III, Art 3(2).

[97] Agreement between the Government of the People's Republic of China and the Government of the Republic of Latvia on the Promotion and Protection of Investments, Art 3(2) (14 April 2004). Article 3(2) reads: 'Without prejudice to its laws and regulations, each Contracting Party shall accord to investments and activities associated with such investments by the investors of the other Contracting Party treatment not less favourable than that accorded to the investments and associated activities by its own investors'.

[98] Agreement between the People's Republic of China and Cyprus on the Reciprocal Promotion and Protection of Investments Art 3(3), Protocol ad Art 3 (15 January 2001).

[99] Agreement between the Kingdom of Spain and People's Republic of China on the Reciprocal Promotion and Protection of Investments (14 November 2005, entered into force 1 July 2008); Agreement between the Government of the People's Republic of China and the Government of the Portuguese Republic on the Promotion and Protection of Investments (9 December 2005, entered into force 26 July 2008); Agreement between the Government of the People's Republic of China and the Belgo-Luxembourg Economic Union on the Promotion and Protection of Investments (6 June 2005, entered into force 1 December 2009); Agreement between the Czech Republic and the People's Republic of China for the Promotion and Protection of Investments (8 December 2005, entered into force 1 September 2006) ('China-Czech Republic BIT'); Agreement between the Government of the Republic of Finland and the Government of the People's Republic of China on the Encouragement and Reciprocal Protection of Investments (15 November 2004, entered into force 15 November 2006) ('China-Finland BIT'); Agreement between the People's Republic of China and the Federal Republic of Germany on the Encouragement and Reciprocal Protection of Investments (1 December 2003, entered into force 11 November 2005) ('China-Germany BIT'); Agreement on the Encouragement and Reciprocal Protection of Investments between the Government of the People's Republic of China and the Government of the Kingdom of the Netherlands (26 November 2001, entered into force 1 August 2004); Protocol(7 December 2005, entered into force 25 May 2007) to the Agreement between the Government of the Czech and Slovak Federal Republic and the Government of the People's Republic of China for the Promotion and Reciprocal Protection of Investments (4 December 1991). The only exception is the renegotiated Agreement between the Government of the People's Republic of China and the Government of the Republic of France on the Encouragement and Reciprocal Protection of Investments (26 November 2007, entered into force 20 August 2010) ('China-France BIT') which takes the third approach of 'NT Subject to Local Law'. See China-France BIT, Art 3(1).

With regard to the People's Republic of China paragraph 3 of Article 2 and paragraph 2 of Article 3 do not apply to:

(a) any existing non-conforming measures maintained within its territory;

(b) the continuation of any such non-conforming measure;

(c) any amendment to any such non-conforming measure to the extent that the amendment does not increase the non-conformity of these measures.

The People's Republic of China will take all appropriate steps in order to progressively remove the non-conforming measures.[100]

A first observation on this clause is that it establishes a right for China, but not Germany, to maintain non-conforming measures. A closer look at the treaty illustrates that the scope of exception granted by this approach is narrower than the one established in the third approach discussed above, because it prohibits the adoption of new non-conforming measures or changes to existing non-conforming measures that would increase the degree of discrimination. This kind of clause further requires that China should commit to progressively removing the non-conforming measures.[101] However, it appears from the language and the context of the provision that this commitment to phase out non-conforming measures is of the 'best effort' non-binding variety and cannot be legally enforced.[102] The China-Mexico BIT concluded in 2008 also adopts the same grandfather clause approach but with a slight variation to the language used. It provides instead that NT is granted 'without prejudice to its laws and regulations at the time the investment is made'.[103] This shows a further step by China toward an acceptance of the NT standard of protection and its commitment to respect international legal principles.

The fifth approach, the full post-admission NT approach, is located in only one BIT, the China-Seychelles BIT of 2006. Unconditional full post-admission NT is provided in this treaty without any reservation.[104] The NT clause applies only after the estab-

[100] China-Germany BIT (n 102) Art 3 and Protocol ad Arts 2 and 3 (emphasis added).

[101] This is also termed as 'standstill' or 'rollback', which are used by the Organization for Economic Cooperation and Development ('OECD') to designate the comparable principles governing non-discrimination.

[102] See Gallagher and Shan (n 4) 169.

[103] Agreement between the Government of the United Mexican States and the Government of the People's Republic of China on the Promotion and Reciprocal Protection of Investments, Art 3(1), (11 July 2008) ('China-Mexico BIT'). Another noteworthy characteristic of the China-Mexico BIT is the adoption of the phrase 'like circumstances', which is rare in Chinese BIT practice but commonly used in other investment treaties, for example the US BITs and in Article 1102 of the NAFTA. For discussion on the application of this comparator principle, see Laird and Sabahi (n 5) 96-7:

'Although tribunals have largely agreed that malicious intent is not required to demonstrate a breach of the national treatment standard, much as we have seen in the application of the fair and equitable treatment standards tribunals are holding that a proportionality or balancing test may be applied to determine whether a like circumstances holding is justified'.

[104] The first paragraph of Article 5 of the China-Seychelles BIT provides that:

'Each Contracting Party shall apply on its territory to the investors of the other Party, with respect to their investments and activities related to the investments, a treatment not less favourable than that granted to its investors, or the treatment granted to the investors of the most favoured nation, if the latter is more favourable...'

Agreement between the Government of the People's Republic of China and the Government of the Republic of Seychelles on the Reciprocal Promotion and Protection of Investments, Art 3 (10 February 2007).

lishment of an investment, given that it includes a standard admission clause requiring investments to be admitted ' in accordance with its legislations'.[105] Given China's reluctance to grant full post-establishment NT in its BIT practice, and its attempt to preserve a limited right to discriminate between domestic and foreign investors, it is doubtful whether China's acceptance of such an unqualified NT in the Seychelles BIT was a wise move. This is especially true because the broad NT obligation of this treaty could be invoked by non-Seychelles investors by way of the MFN clause, which appears in all of the Chinese BITs.[106] China, nevertheless, can continue to avoid this kind of risk in a treaty claim, at least temporarily, considering the China-Seychelles BIT has not yet entered into force.

In cases where both MFN and NT standards are referred to, most treaties uniformly apply the two standards to both parties, while a few apply them on a non-reciprocal basis. This sixth and final kind of ' non-reciprocal' approach appears in the BITs separately concluded with Syria, Peru and South Africa. The China-Syria BIT of 1996 provides MFN obligations for China but NT obligations for Syria.[107] The Protocol to the China-Peru BIT of 1994 attaches an additional NT obligation on the Peruvian side, whilst under the treaty text MFN is the uniform obligation of both sides.[108] The China-South Africa BIT of 1997 also has a provision in the text that is similar to the China-Peru BIT, but with an exception to the NT obligation with regard to South Africa's black empowerment scheme.[109]

An interesting finding is that Chinese BITs with developed States, especially the renegotiated ones with European States, take the fourth approach, which provide slightly higher levels of investment protection than the BITs with developing countries following the approach of ' NT Subject to Local Law'. This may be due to the different negotiation powers between developed and developing States. However, this slight difference may be more symbolic than real. Given that all Chinese BITs contain an MFN clause, the investors and their investments from developing States might be entitled to the higher treatment by virtue of the MFN clause. Some BITs also incorporate the fair and equitable treatment (' FET') standard with both NT and MFN standards or with at least one of the latter

[105] Ibid.

[106] Gallagher and Shan (n 4) 170. See eg Bayindir Insaat Turizm Ticaret Ve Sanayi AS v Islamic Republic of Pakistan, ICSID Case No ARB/03/29, Award (27 August 2009) (The Tribunal imported the FET standard into the basic treaty by operation of the MFN clause, although no breach was ultimately found).

[107] See Agreement between the Government of the People's Republic of China and the Government of the Syrian Arab Republic Concerning the Reciprocal Promotion and Protection of Investments Protocol, Art 1 (9 December 1996, entered into force 1 November 2001).

[108] Agreement between the Government of the Republic of Peru and the Government of the People's Republic of China Concerning the Encouragement and Reciprocal Protection of Investments, Art 3 and Protocol (9 June 1994, entered into force 1 February 1995).

[109] See Agreement between the Government of the People's Republic of China and the Government of the Republic of South Africa on the Promotion and Protection of Investments, Art 3 (30 December 1997, entered into force 1 April 1998).

standards.[110] This approach is similar to the majority of investment instruments around the world.[111] According to the United Nations Conference on Trade and Development ('UNCTAD'), the incorporation of the non-contingent or absolute standard (FET) with the contingent or relative standards (NT and MFN) provides foreign investors with sufficient protection because the FET standard will prevent discrimination against the beneficiary of NT or MFN standards if discrimination would amount to unfairness or inequity in the circumstances, while the NT or MFN standards ensure that the FET standard is provided on a non-discriminatory basis.[112] With respect to the scope of application of the NT standard, some BITs grant the protection to 'investors', some to 'investments of investors' and others to 'investments and activities associated with investments'.[113] The term 'investments and activities' potentially offers a broader scope than that of 'investments', even though it is difficult to identify the precise difference between the two formulas. Some BITs, such as the China-Japan BIT of 1988, the China-Korea BIT of 1992 (renegotiated in 2005), and the China-Botswana BIT of 2000, extend the obligation to other aspects such as legal remedies and compensation for losses due to war.[114] To address the measures that would be considered inconsistent with the NT obligation, some BITs provide for an illustrative list. The China-Germany BIT of 2003, for example, stipulates in its Protocol that,

The following shall, in particular, be deemed 'treatment less favourable' within the meaning of Article 3: unequal treatment in the case of restrictions on the purchase of raw or auxiliary materials, of energy or fuel or of means of production or operation of any kind as well as any other measures having similar effects.[115]

---

[110] See eg China-Czech Republic BIT (n 102) Art 3(1):

'Each Contracting Party shall in its territory accord to investments and returns of investors of the other Contracting Party treatment which is fair and equitable and not less favourable than that which it accords to investments and returns of its own investors or to investments and returns of investors of any third State, whichever is more favourable'.

[111] United Nations Conference on Trade and Development ('UNCTAD'), 'Fair and Equitable Treatment', 3 IIA Issues 15, UN Doc UNCTAD/ITE/IIT/11 (1999).

[112] Ibid 15 – 16.

[113] Some BITs have a definition of the concept 'activities associated with investment'. The China-Germany BIT (n 102) defines 'associated activities' in a non-exhaustive manner in its Protocol, which provides that it means 'the management, maintenance, use, enjoyment, and disposal of an investment'. Article 3(2) of the China-Finland BIT (n 102) provides, in an exhaustive manner, that the NT obligations apply 'with respect to the operation, management, maintenance, use, enjoyment, expansion, sale or other disposal of investments that have been made'.

[114] See China-Japan BIT (n 95) Art 4; Agreement on the Encouragement and Reciprocal Promotion of Investments between the Government of the People's Republic of China and the Government of the Republic of Korea, Art 4 (30 September 1992, entered into force 4 December 1992); Agreement between the Government of the People's Republic of China and the Government of the Republic of Korea on the Promotion and Protection of Investments, Arts 3(4), 5(1) (7 September 2007, entered into force 1 December 2007); Agreement between the Government of the Republic of Botswana and the Government of the People's Republic of China on Promotion and Protection of Investments, Art 5 (12 June 2000).

[115] China-Germany BIT (n 102) Protocol ad Art 3.

A similar list is also provided in the Agreed Minutes of the China-Japan BIT of 1988.[116] The 'illustrative list' approach enables the Contracting Parties to rule out whether a specific measure or measures can be treated as a breach of the NT obligation. This approach makes the NT obligation more 'tangible' and gives it a more specific content. It is important to make clear that the list is non-exhaustive.[117]

Finally, there has been no arbitration award where a NT provision in a Chinese BIT has been considered, although there is no doubt that their application in any future claim would be consistent with the existing jurisprudence.[118]

2. NT in the Investment Chapters of China's FTAs

Although China's FTAs are not as vast in terms of quantity when compared with the State's BITs, they have been deemed by the Chinese Government as:

> a new platform to further opening up to the outside and speeding up domestic reforms, an effective approach to integrate into [the] global economy and strengthen economic cooperation with other economies, as well as particularly an important supplement to the multilateral trading system.[119]

China has, currently, 14 FTA partners, which are comprised of 31 economies. Among these, nine agreements have already been signed.[120]

Six of the nine signed FTAs have a specialized chapter on investment, namely the China-Pakistan FTA of 2006, the China-New Zealand FTA of 2008, the China-Singapore FTA of 2008, the China-Peru FTA of 2009, the China-Costa Rica FTA of 2008, and the China-Association of Southeast Asian Nations (ASEAN) FTA of 2009.[121] However, two

---

[116] The Agreed Minutes state that such NT obligation shall also apply to measures restricting or impeding the following activities:

'the purchase of raw or auxiliary materials, of power or fuel, or of means of production or operation of any kind; the marketing of products inside or outside the country; the obtaining of loans inside or outside the country; the introduction of technology; and the establishment of branches or offices of resident representatives outside the country.'

China-Japan BIT (n 95) Agreed Minutes, Point 2.

[117] Gallagher and Shan (n 4) 172.

[118] In the ICSID case *Tza Yap Shum v Republic of Peru*, the Tribunal in its Award of July 2011 found that the Respondent had expropriated the Claimant's assets and awarded compensation. *Tza Yap Shum v Republic of Peru*, Award (n 22). For a discussion of this case, see Shen (n 22). No award has been made in China Heilongjiang (n 22).

[119] MOFCOM, China FTA Network, *available at* http://fta.mofcom.gov.cn/english/index.shtml, accessed 21 February 2012.

[120] Up to February 2012, China had signed FTAs with the Association of Southeast Asian Nations ('ASEAN'), Pakistan, Chile, New Zealand, Singapore, Peru, Hong Kong, Macau and Costa Rica. The FTAs with the Gulf Cooperation Council ('GCC'), Australia, Iceland, Norway and Southern African Customs Union ('SACU') are under negotiation, while the FTAs with India, South Korea, Japan, South Korea and Switzerland are under consideration. Moreover, China is also a member of the Asia-Pacific Trade Agreement ('APTA'). See ibid.

[121] Even those FTAs which do not include a chapter on investment impose a requirement to promote investment. The Free Trade Agreement between the Government of the People's Republic of China and the Government of the Republic of Chile, Art 112 (18 November 2005), for example, requires the Contracting Parties to explore the possibility of establishing investment promotion mechanisms and to provide national information for the potential investors and on investment cooperative parties. See generally, on China's FTAs, Wang (n 35). For a discussion on the dispute resolution provisions in China's FTAs, see Wei Shen, 'Is This a Great Leap Forward? A Comparative Review of the Investor-State Arbitration Clause in the ASEAN-China Investment Treaty: From BIT Jurisprudential and Practical Perspectives' (2010) 27(4) J Intl Arb 379.

of these six FTAs do not include substantive protections. The FTA with Singapore only confirms that the provisions of the China-ASEAN Investment Agreement will be incorporated upon its conclusion.[122] The FTA with Costa Rica reaffirms the contracting parties' commitments under the China-Costa Rica BIT of 2007.[123] The NT provisions included in the investment chapter of the remaining four FTAs follow the approaches taken by China in its BIT practice. The NT clause in the China-Pakistan FTA follows the approach of 'NT Subject to Local Law' by requiring the NT protection to be accorded 'without prejudice to its laws and regulations'. The NT clauses in the other three FTAs, namely the FTAs with New Zealand, Peru and ASEAN, follow the 'NT subject to grandfather clause' approach.[124] Article 141 of the China-New Zealand FTA, which is believed to be the most comprehensive investment chapter in any Chinese FTA, also goes further to stress its compatibility with existing BIT practice, providing that the NT shall not 'apply to any measure, which with respect to each Party, would not be within the scope of the national treatment obligations in any of that Party's existing bilateral investment treaties'.[125] This is an attempt to ensure that the FTA does not go beyond the existing regime for NT in China's investment treaties.

Consistent with the European approach, most Chinese BITs tend not to include a 'like circumstance' qualification for NT, except in the China-Mexico BIT[126] and China-Colombia BIT signed in 2008.[127] However, the qualification of like circumstance is commonly used in FTAs with New Zealand, Peru and ASEAN. Some tribunals, particularly North American Free Trade Agreement ('NAFTA') tribunals, use 'in like circumstance' to qualify the 'comparator' investors and to allow for justifications of State measures. This test 'involves a comparative test—whereby the claimant is required to identify a comparator (either a national or another foreigner) in receipt of better treatment than it has received from the respondent state'.[128] It has been noted that it is:

difficult to understand the nature of such a limitation in the context of investment.

---

[122] Free Trade Agreement between the Government of the People's Republic of China and the Government of the Republic of Singapore, ch 10, Art 84(1) (23 October 2008).

[123] China-Costa Rica Free Trade Agreement, ch 9, Art 89, s A (8 April 2010, entered into force 1 August 2011).

[124] Free Trade Agreement between the Government of New Zealand and the Government of the People's Republic of China ch 11, Arts 138, 141 (7 April 2008, entered into force 1 October 2008) ('China-New Zealand FTA'); Free Trade Agreement between the Government of the People's Republic of China and the Government of the Republic of Peru, ch 10, Arts 129 – 30 (28 April 2009, entered into force 1 March 2010); Agreement on Investment of the Framework Agreement on Comprehensive Economic Cooperation between the People's Republic of China and the Association of Southeast Asian Nations Arts 4, 6 (signed 15 August 2009).

[125] China-New Zealand FTA (n 127) ch 11, Art 141(3).

[126] Agreement between the Government of the United Mexican States and the Government of the People's Republic of China on the Promotion and Reciprocal Protection of Investments, Art 3(1) (11 July 2008).

[127] Bilateral Agreement for the Promotion and Protection of Investments between the Government of the Republic of Colombia and the Government of the People's Republic of China, Art 3(1) (22 November 2008).

[128] Grierson-Weiler and Laird (n 5) 262. For further discussion on the comparative test, see Dugan et al (n 7) 400 – 8; Bjorklund (n 5) 419 – 30; Salacuse (n 5) 248.

A large multinational corporation as an investor is never in ' like circumstances' because of its size and vertically integrated global organisation.[129]

In the absence of this phrase, the textual interpretation may suggest that the comparison may be made to a broader group of domestic investors.[130]

3. NT in Multilateral Treaties

China acceded to the WTO in 2001.[131] Developed from the GATT system, the WTO system was mainly intended to cover international trade. However, much effort has been made to include investment issues within the framework of the multilateral trade system because of the close link between trade and investment.[132] Among various WTO agreements, the TRIMs Agreement and the GATS are the prominent ones for investment. Some other WTO agreements, for instance the Agreement on Subsidies and Countervailing Measures (' SCM Agreement') and the Agreement on Trade-Related Aspects of Intellectual Property Rights (' TRIPS Agreement'), are also closely related to investment activities. Under the GATS, NT, like admission (or ' market access' to use the GATS phrase) is a ' specific commitment', which applies only to the services sectors described in the host State's services schedule and which is subject to conditions set out therein.[133] Thus, a ' bottom-up' approach is adopted, and it cannot be justified that a general obligation of NT has been established.[134] When interpreting the NT obligation in investment arbitration, some tribunals also refer to the NT juris-

---

[129] M Sornarajah, The International Law on Foreign Investment 235 (2nd edn, Cambridge University Press 2004).

[130] Gallagher and Shan (n 4) 173. There are some recent awards where tribunals have considered the scope and application of the ' in like circumstances' qualification. See eg *Merrill & Ring Forestry LP v The Government of Canada*, UNCITRAL, Award, paras 79 - 94 (31 March 2010); *Total SA v Argentine Republic*, ICSID Case No ARB/04/1, Decision on Liability, paras 210 - 17 (27 December 2010); *Grand River Enterprises Six Nations, Ltd, and others v United States of America*, UNCITRAL/NAFTA, Award, paras 158 - 71 (12 January 2011).

[131] China became one of the 23 original Contracting Parties to the General Agreement on Tariffs and Trade (' GATT') in 1947, which was the predecessor of the WTO. In this respect, the NT obligation included in the GATT was binding on China. It is pointed out that when entering the GATT, the then-Government of the Republic of China (' ROC') (Taiwan) engaged in a comprehensive study of the effect of the NT clause. See Nationalist Government, Ministry of Foreign Affairs, Guanyu Shijie Maoyi Xianzhang Cao' an ji Guanshui ji Maoyi Zongxieding zhi Shuotie (On the Charter of World Trade (Draft) and the Memorandum of General Agreement on Tariffs and Trade) (2003) 2 Republican Archives 40, 41. In 1950, to prevent the PRC from making use of the preferential benefits provided under the GATT, the ROC Government (Taiwan) announced its withdrawal (in the name of China) from the treaty, whereas some countries, such as Czechoslovakia, questioned the legality of this action. From then on, China did not resume its status as a Contracting Party of the GATT. Some, nevertheless, argued that Taiwan's withdrawal from the GATT was illegal and invalid because the Government of ROC had no right to represent China from 1 October 1949. For details, see Yang Guohua and Cheng Jin, ' The Process of China's Access into the WTO' (2001) 4(2) J Intl Econ L 297, 298 - 9.

[132] Shan (n 12) 103.

[133] General Agreement on Trade in Services, Art 17(1) (adopted 15 April 1994, entered into force 1 January 1995).

[134] Shan (n 12) 156.

prudence developed by the WTO.[135]

4. Summary

Before 1998, NT was rarely found in China's BIT practice. This has, nevertheless, changed since China began to implement the 'Going Abroad' policy. On a review of all of China's BITs gathered by the authors, six different approaches to the NT obligation can be identified. In parallel with its BIT practice, China also participated in the FTA programme in recognition of the emerging 'new regionalism'.[136] The use of 'like circumstance' in its recent FTAs also illustrates the slight difference between FTAs and BITs. However, this difference should not result in any conflict between the treaties as expressly confirmed in the China-New Zealand FTA.[137]

More importantly, the regime set up by international investment treaties, particularly the new generation BITs and FTAs, also impacts China's domestic institutions and procedures whilst benefitting foreign investors in China. This is due to the fact that China's international investment treaties exercise 'significant influences on the development of the domestic legal and economic structures in the host State'.[138] In particular, NT, together with MFN treatment, aims at ensuring a level playing field with respect to economic activity of foreign and domestic economic actors, which is a 'prerequisite for competition'.[139] Besides, the contents of investment treaties should thus support the legal reform in China by contributing to good governance.[140] It is also believed that the investment treaties are 'likely to have spill-over effects on the domestic legal system' by creating 'an incentive for the PRC to promote liberal values on a broader basis by letting domestic economic factors benefit from the overall changes in the economic and legal system'.[141]

V. Conclusion

The success of China in attracting FDI is undisputed and unprecedented. After decades of development, China's attitude toward FDI is developing from generally welcomed to effectively utilized. The 11th FYP on the Utilization of Foreign Investments marked the beginning of a new trend with more emphasis on domestic development. The objective of China's FDI policy currently is to promote the quality of investment rather than

---

[135] See respectively *SD Myers Inc v The Government of Canada*, UNCITRAL, Partial Award, paras 244 – 7 (13 November 2000); *Pope & Talbot Inc v The Government of Canada*, UNCITRAL, Award on the Merits of Phase 2, paras 45 – 63, 68 – 9 (10 April 2001); *Marvin Roy Feldman Karpa v United Mexican States*, ICSID Case No ARB (AF)/99/1, Award, para 165 (16 December 2002).

[136] Luis Abugattas Majluf, 'Swimming in the Spaghetti Bowl: Challenges for Developing Countries Under the "New Regionalism"' in UNCTAD, Policy Issues in International Trade and Commodities Study Series No 27 (United Nations 2004), *available at* http://www.unctad.org/en/docs/itcdtab28_en.pdf, accessed 10 May 2012.

[137] China-New Zealand FTA (n 127) ch 11, Art 141(3).

[138] Schill (n 14) 116.

[139] Ibid.

[140] Ibid. 117; see also Rudolf Dolzer, 'The Impact of International Investment Treaties on Domestic Administrative Law' (2005) 37 NYU J Intl L Politics 953, 954.

[141] Schill (n 14) 117.

sheer quantity. This changing policy orientation also affects the NT of foreign investment in domestic legislation. The changes at the domestic level are more obvious than at the international level. However, China's more liberal approach in the practice of international investment law will continue to be the dominant feature of its policy for the foreseeable future.[142] China is beginning to challenge existing international investment norms.[143] Its role has been developing from a participant toward a leader in the world economy in general and in international investment in particular.[144]

Whether China will stick to the post-establishment NT clause in its future BIT negotiations, in particular with the United States and the European Union, is a critical issue and has profound implications. As mentioned above, even under the more liberal approach, there is no Chinese BIT in force providing for pre-establishment NT. It is argued that Chinese outward FDI de facto will be awarded pre-establishment NT by virtue of the 'multiplying effect' of the MFN clause, which is commonly found in Chinese BITs, and by relying on the BITs signed by those countries that have already taken the pre-establishment NT approach.[145] However, this de facto effect is limited to those States that have already signed BITs with China and are also the recipients of China's vast ODI flows.

The ongoing BIT talks with the United States and the European Union will test China's position favouring post-establishment NT. The China-United States BIT talks were first launched as early as the mid – 1980s but were shelved for over 20 years because of stark disagreement between the States on almost all critical issues. The revival of the China-United States BIT negotiation was officially relaunched in 2008 with the conclusion of the fourth China-United States Strategic Economic Dialogue. There is, nevertheless, no consensus among scholars on the conclusion of this BIT. Some argue that it will be concluded successfully, while others believe the outcome looks rather bleak.[146] Some US panelists and advisory committee members including Kevin Gallagher, Owen Herrnstadt and Linda Andros also share the view that it was good for the China-United States BIT negotia-

---

[142] However, some argue that China should reconsider its current policy to better protect domestic enterprises from increasing competition from foreign investors. An Chen, for example, argues that a liberal dispute settlement mechanism will leave China worse off when China is still in a transitional phase enjoying high investment inflows. See An Chen, 'Should the Four Great Safeguards in Sino-Foreign BITs Be Hastily Dismantled? Comments on Provisions Concerning Dispute Settlement in Model U. S. and Canadian BITs' (2006) 7 J World Invest Trade 899; see also An Chen, 'Distinguishing Two Types of Countries and Properly Granting Differential Reciprocity Treatment: Re-comments on the Four Safeguards in Sino-Foreign BITs Not to Be Hastily and Completely Dismantled' (2007) 8 J World Invest Trade 771.

[143] Daniel H Rosen and Thilo Hanemann, Policy Brief: China's Changing Outbound Foreign Direct Investment Profile: Drivers and Policy Implications 1, 2 – 7 (Peterson Institute for International Economics, June 2009), *available at* http://www.iie.com/publications/pb/pb09-14.pdf, accessed 10 May 2012.

[144] Guiguo Wang, 'China's Practice in International Investment Law: From Participation to Leadership in the World Economy' (2009) 34 Yale J Intl L 575.

[145] Axel Berger, 'China's New Bilateral Investment Treaty Programme: Substance Rational and Implications for International Investment Law Making' 12 (2008 unpublished manuscript), *available at* http://www.asil.org/files/ielconferencepapers/berger.pdf, accessed 13 May 2012.

[146] Cai Congyan, for example, shed positive light on the China-United States BIT talks. See Congyan (n 82). However, Alex Berger took the opposite view. See Berger (n 148).

tions to be delayed.[147] There is no doubt that the terms of the China-Canada BIT, when made public, will have some impact on negotiations with the United States.

Despite the absence of a general resolution on the implication of the inclusion of FDI in the Common Commercial Policy after the Treaty of Lisbon, the EU has strived to launch BIT talks. The China-EU BIT, whose negotiations were announced in July 2011[148] and reaffirmed in the 14th China-EU summit,[149] will be the first BIT to testify to the EU's exclusive competence over FDI. Though the post-establishment NT is commonly adopted by its Member States,[150] the EU has already incorporated the pre-establishment NT approach in several agreements. The EC-Chile Association Agreement, for example, grants full NT at the pre-and post-entry stages for both natural and legal persons of the other contracting party, together with consent to State-to-State arbitration as the means of dispute settlement.[151] The joint report concerning the economic and trade relationship published by the EU and Canada in February 2009 also provides that investment rules might ' cover pre-and post-establishment in all sectors in order to improve market access and provide for the non-discriminatory treatment of investors and invest-

---

[147] Amy Tsui, ' Negotiations on US-China BIT Likely to Be Long, Public Interest Advocate Says' , Bureau of National Affairs (14 December 2009), *available at* http://www.ase.tufts.edu/gdae/Pubs/rp/BNABIT.pdf, accessed 10 May 2012.

[148] ' China, EU to Seek Bilateral Investment Treaty' China Daily (14 July 2011), *available at* http://www.chinadaily.com.cn/china/2011-07/14/content_12906429.htm, accessed 10 May 2012.

[149] ' Full Text of Joint Press Communiqueé of the 14th China-EU Summit' , Xinhua (15 February 2012), *available at* http://news.xinhuanet.com/english/china/2012-02/15/c_131411130.htm, accessed 10 May 2012.

[150] The post-establishment NT approach is still taken under both the 2008 German Model BIT and the 2005 UK Model BIT.

Articles 2 and 3 of the 2008 German Model BIT provide:

Article 2

Admission and protection of investments

(1) Each Contracting State shall in its territory promote as far as possible investments by investors of the other Contracting State and admit such investments in accordance with its legislation.

...

Article 3

National and most-favoured-nation treatment

(1) Neither Contracting State shall in its territory subject investments owned or controlled by investors of the other Contracting State to treatment less favourable than it accords to investments of its own investors or to investments of investors of any third State.

...

Article 3 of the 2005 UK Model BIT also states:

Article 3

National Treatment and Most-favoured-nation Provisions

(1) Neither Contracting Party shall in its territory subject investments or returns of nationals or companies of the other Contracting Party to treatment less favourable than that which it accords to investments or returns of its own nationals or companies or to investments or returns of nationals or companies of any third State.

(2) Neither Contracting Party shall in its territory subject nationals or companies of the other Contracting Party, as regards their management, maintenance, use, enjoyment or disposal of their investments, to treatment less favour-able than that which it accords to its own nationals or companies or to nationals or companies of any third State.

[151] Agreement Establishing an Association between the European Community and its Member States, of the One Part, and the Republic of Chile, of the Other Part (18 November 2002), *available at* http://eur-lex.europa.eu/LexUriServ/LexUriServ.do?uri=OJ:L:2002:352:0003:1439:EN:PDF, accessed 10 May 2012.

ments, and to improve transparency.' [152]

The determination of the application of the NT obligation is still evolving in the relevant international jurisprudence. There is no requirement under customary international law that States should grant NT to aliens. In this respect, States will have to balance multiple considerations when deciding whether or how to accord NT. If China adopts the pre-establishment NT in its BITs with the EU or the United States, the implementation of such a clause would result in the entire overhaul of China's foreign investment regime, which features an industrial policy orientation and case-by-case approval for prospective FDI. [153] China should be more cautious on this subject. Furthermore, in contrast to other developing States, which may accept the Model BIT proposed by the developed States, China's increasing negotiating power enables it to stand equally against the EU and the United States. As argued elsewhere, if China wants to make a breakthrough in the NT clause in its future BIT negotiations with the United States and the EU, it is better advised to take the 'positive list' approach similar to the NT obligations under GATS, but not the United States-style 'negative list' approach. [154]

However, China still needs some time to implement the full NT for foreign investors and investment. Its will to implement such NT between foreign and domestic investors depends not only on a full-market economy, but more importantly on whether the general economic power of the State is strong enough to compete fairly and freely with other nations. To date, China has not obtained recognition as a full-market economy from the main global economies such as the United States, the EU and Japan. [155] Even though China will automatically obtain full-market economy status 15 years after joining the WTO in accordance with the WTO's rules, this will not happen until 2016, and an earlier recognition could benefit both Chinese and foreign investors. On the other hand, although Chinese enterprises have been making great progress in recent years, they are far from being high performance businesses, not to mention becoming enterprises of international competiveness. [156]

All in all, China's will to implement NT was reaffirmed by Premier WEN Jiabao on 13 September 2010 when he stated that:

---

[152] Joint Report on the EU-Canada Scoping Exercise 5 – 6 (5 March 2009), *available at* http://trade.ec.europa.eu/doclib/docs/2009/march/tradoc_142470.pdf, accessed 28 March 2012.

[153] See Qingjiang Kong, 'US-China Bilateral Investment Treaty Negotiations', EAI Background Brief No 507 (25 February 2010), *available at* http://www.eai.nus.edu.sg/BB507.pdf, accessed 10 May 2012.

[154] Gallagher and Shan (n 4) 394.

[155] 'Hu Calls for Early Recognition of China's Full-Market Economy Status', Xinhua (11 December 2011), *available at* http://news.xinhuanet.com/english/china/2011 – 12/11/c_131299814.htm; see also 'No Need to Nit-pick Over China's Market Economy Status', People Daily (28 September 2011), *available at* http://english.peopledaily.com.cn/90780/7606975.html, 10 May 2012.

[156] Accenture, 'Dancing on the Stage of a Multi-Polar World: The Path to Globalization for Chinese Enterprises', Executive Summary (2010), *available at* http://www.accenture.com/SiteCollectionDocuments/PDF/Accenture_The_Path_to_Globalization_for_Chinese_Enterprises_Exec_Sum.pdf, accessed 10 May 2012; see also Gong Li, Bo Wang and Yali Peng, 'Can Chinese Companies Win in the Global Big Leagues?', Accenture (October 2011), *available at* http://www.accenture.com/us-en/outlook/Pages/outlook-journal – 2011 – can-chinese-companies-win-globally.aspx, accessed 10 May 2012.

I wish to reiterate here that all enterprises registered in China in accordance with law are Chinese enterprises... China will treat foreign-invested enterprises and local companies equally and fairly in government procurement.[157]

It is also evident in numerous other high profile statements indicating that foreign enterprises are to be treated the same as domestic enterprises in China.[158] It is expected that these commitments will send a strong signal to the world that China intends to continue to reform its domestic legal FDI system while pursing a liberal approach in its international investment treaties.

---

[157] 'China's Wen Promises Fair Play for Foreign Investors', Reuters (13 September 2010), *available at* http://www.reuters.com/article/2010/09/13/china-investment-wen-idUSTOE68C08620100913, accessed 10 May 2012.

[158] See, for example, Qin Jize, 'China Welcomes Foreign Investment', China Daily (22 March 2011), *available at* http://www.chinadaily.com.cn/business/2011-03/22/content_12206914.htm, accessed 10 May 2012; see also PRC Ministry of Foreign Affairs, 'Premier Wen Jiabao Attends the Sixth Chinese-German Forum for Economic and Technological Cooperation and Delivers Speech' (29 June 2011), *available at* http://www.fmprc.gov.cn/eng/wjdt/zyjh/t835348.htm, accessed 10 May 2012.

FDI in China and the Role of Law: An Empirical Approach*

The success of the People's Republic of China (China) in attracting foreign direct investment (FDI)[1] in the last three decades is undisputed and unprecedented. UNCTAD statistics show that China has maintained its position as the second largest FDI recipient since early 1990s.[2] In the year 2010, FDI in China reached USD 105.735 billion.[3] As illustrated in *Chart* 1, there has been rapid increase of FDI in China, particularly in the first decade of the 21st century, despite the recent global financial crisis. Indeed, a recent survey by the European Chamber of Commerce in China demonstrates that the financial crisis has actually amplified the importance of China in the respondent companies' global strategies.[4] A series of UNCTAD surveys also reveal that China is the top destination for FDI in 2010 – 2012 for transnational corporations (TNCs).[5] The 2010 Business Climate Survey by the American Chamber of Commerce further confirms that US companies remain optimistic about

---

* Shan Wenhua, Zhang Sheng, *The Journal of World Investment and Trade*, Volume 12 No. 4, August 2011.

The authors would like to thank the organizer Professor Jiangyu Wang and all participants of the "Research Symposium on the Legal Dimension of China's Development Model", particularly Professor David C. Donald, Professor Jacques de Lisle, Professor Randall P. Peerenboom and Professor Lee Yong-Shik. for the wonderful event and the very helpful comments and suggestions received during and after the conference. The authors shall, of course, remain responsible for all the possible errors and omissions in the essay.

[1] Norah Gallagher and Wenhua Shan, Chinese Investment Treaties: Policies and Practice, Oxford Un. iversity Press, 2009, p. I.

[2] UNCTAD, World Investment Report 2010: Investing in a Low-Carbon Economy, United Nations, New York and Geneva, p. 4.

[3] Investment in China, News Release of National Assimilation of FDI from January to December 2010, January 17. 2011. *available at* http://www.fdi.gov.cn/pub/FDI_EN/Statistics/FD Statistics/ExpressofForeign Investment/t201IOI17_130201.htm (last visited on 21June 2011).

[4] European Union Chamber of Commerce in China, European Chamber Business Confidence Survey 2010, pp. 3 – 4, *available at* http://www.europeananchamber.com.cn/view/static/? sid = 7370 (last visited on 21 June2011).

[5] UNCTAD, World Investment Report 2010, *supra* note 2, p. 25.

their China outlook in the medium term.[6]

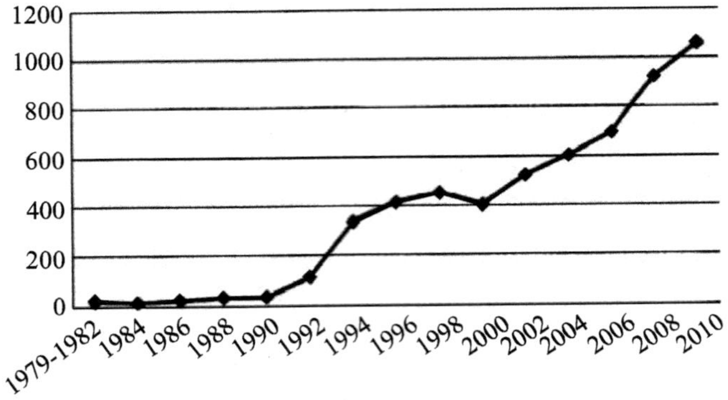

Chart 1 AMOUNT OF FDI IN CHINA (1979 – 2010)
(UNIT: US $ 100 MILLION)

Source: www. fdi. gov. cn.

Such huge FDI inflow makes a great contribution to the overall economic development of China. At the World Investment Forum 2010 held last September in Xiamen, for example, Vice President Xi Jinping acknowledged that "in China, 22 percent of tax revenues, 28 percent of added industrial value, 55 percent of technology import and some 45 million job opportunities are contributed by foreign invested enterprises".[7]

FDI flows into host countries are determined by a variety of factors. It has been pointed out that whether or not an FDI project will be made in a specific country is determined by a combination of these factors, which may be generally classified into three categories: the policy framework for FDI, economic determinants and business facilitation.[8] Although "economic" determinants may be playing a primary role in attracting FDI much attention has been paid to examine policy and institutional characteristics of host countries as FDI determinants.[9] In the case of China, scholarly work can be found on the law and policy of FDI,

---

[6] AmCham-China, 2010 China Business Climate Survey Report, p. 3. *available at* http: //www. amc. ham china. orglupload/cmsfile/2011/03/22/efb2ab9d3806269fc343f640cb33baf9. pdf(Last visited on 21June 2011) . It is pointed out that 91% of the respondent companies reporting their business outlook in China is "slightly optimistic" or "optimistic", Id.

[7] Chinese Government's Official Web Portal, Full text of Chinese Vice President Xi Jinping's speech at World Investment Forum 2010. September 7, 2010. *available at* http: //www. gov. cn/cng) ish/2010 – 09/07/content_1697902. htm (last visited on 21 June 2011) .

[8] UNCTAD, The Role of International Investment Agreements in Attracting Foreign Direct Investment to Development Countries. UNCTAD Series on International Investment Policies for Development, United Nations, New York and Geneva, 2 < Y. J9, p. 5.

[9] Id. , p. 12.

especially after China's access into the WTO.[10] However, most of the existing studies tend to be entertaining purely theoretical and/or ideological analysis, with little empirical support. In 2001, the author had conducted an empirical study on the role of law in EU investors' decisions as to whether or not to invest in China.[11] Seven years later, another study was conducted in the SuZhou Industrial Park (SIP'),[12] to investigate the role of law in foreign investment activities in the SIP.

This article focuses on the 2008 SIP study, as compared with the previous study of 2001. It first analyzes the general role that the law had played when foreign investors decided whether or not to invest. Then it discusses the various specific aspects affecting the effectiveness of the Chinese legal system, which is measured against the Ideal Institutional Paradigm developed by the World Bank. Then a comparative study on the two sets of empirical evidence is provided. The article concludes by pointing out that the legal environment for FDI in China has been significantly improved during 2001 – 2008 though much more needs to be done to further strengthen the Chinese FDI regime.

I. THE 2001 AND 2008 EMPIRICAL STUDIES

The 2001 study was part of a PhD research project conducted at the University of Cambridge, which has been published as a book entitled The Legal Framework of EU-China Investment Relations: A Critical Appraisal. Briefly it was a combination of questionnaire and interviews among EU investors, which show that law played an important role in China's success in attracting EU investment, evidenced by in-depth pre-investment investigation on the legal environment by most

---

[10] See, for example, Hui Huang, the Regulation of Foreign Investment in Post-WTO China: a Political Economy Analysis, 23 *Columbia Journal of Asian Law* 185, Fall 2009; Stephan W. Schill, Tearing Down the Great Wall: the New Generation Investment Treaties of the People's Republic of China, 15 *Cordozo Journal of International and Comparative Law* 73, 2007; Jessica Zoe Renwald, Foreign Investment Law in the People's Republic of China: What to Expect from Enterprise Establishment to Dispute *Resolution*, 16 *Indian International and Comparative Law Review* 453. 2006; Shaukat Ali and Wei Guo, Determinants of F1 > 1 in China, Journal of Global Business 2nd Technology, Y· Vol. I, No. 2, FU 2005; Qun Li, Tax Incentive Policies for Foreign-Invested Enterprises in China and their Influence on Foreign Investment. *Revenue Law Journal*, Vol. 18, Issue I, Article 5. 2008; Chen Yongmei, the Legal Climate for Foreign Investment in China afier its WTO Accession, *Bond Law Review*. Vol. 20, IssueI. Article 2. 2008 and Jordan Brandt, Comparing Foreign Investment in China. Post-WTO Accession, with Foreign Investment in the United States, Post – 9111, 16 Pacific Rim Law and Policy Journal 285. March 2007.

[11] Comprehensive analysis of this investigation may be found in Wenhua Shan. The Legal Framework of EU-China Investment Relations: A Critical Approach, Hart Publishing. 2005, pp. 247 – 264: Wenhua Shan, Law and Foreign Investment in China: General Role of Law and Substantive Issues, *Manchester Journal of International Economic Law*. Vol. 2. Issue 3, 2005 and Wenhua Shan, Law and Foreign Investment in China: Effectiveness of the Chinese FDI Legal System, *Manchester Journal of International Economic Law*, Vol. 3. Issue I, 2006.

[12] Though all of the respondent companies are from the Suzhou Industrial Park, they almost represent all the companies investing in the Mainland China. A comprehensive analysis may be found below.

investors.[13] At the same time, it demonstrates that further improvement was demanded on the Chinese For regime, which was perceived as generally "ineffective".[14]

The 2008 study generally followed the 2001 approach by using a similar questionnaire. The SIP was chosen mainly because it was very successful in attracting FDI and was manageable for the survey to be effectively carried out. As a co-operative program jointly developed by the governments of China and Singapore, SIP was established in 1994. According to Chinese official statistics, SIP was the second largest one among the 32 eastern national economic development zones in terms of the amount of FDI in 2007.[15] By now 76 out of the top 500 companies in the world have set up 119 companies or branches in the park.[16] It is beyond doubt that the SIP is one of the best locations for such an empirical study to be implemented.

Questionnaires were sent to 100 FIEs chosen by way of simple random sampling, firstly via emails then followed by phone calls or visit to secure responses. As a result, 61 effective responses were received.[17] Among the 61 respondents, 5 are Joint Venture Enterprises(JVEs) , and the remaining 56 are Wholly Foreign-Owned Enterprises (WFOEs) . Th. is conforms to the general picture of the forms of FDI in China now characterized by the enormous preference of WFOE over JVs.[18] In 2009, for example, WFOES constituted 80% of the total number of Fol projects while Equity Joint Ventures (EJVs) and Contract Joint Ventures (CJVs)

[13] See Shan, *supra* note 11, pp. 247 – 8. See also Wenhua Shan, *Law and Foreign Investment in China: General Role of Law and Substantive Issues*, Manchester Journal of International Economic Law, Vol. 2. Issue 3. 2005, p. 76.

[14] See Shan, *supra* note 11, pp. 261 – 4. See also Wenhua Shan, *Law and Foreign Investment in China: Effectiveness of the Chinese FDI Legal System*, Manchester Journal or International Economic Law, Vol. 3, Issue I, 2006, p. 65.

[15] Invest in China, Charts of the Amount of the Actual Use of Foreign Investment among the National Economic Development Zones in 2007. (2007 *nian guo jia jing ji kai fa qu* shi ji shi yong wai zi e qing kuang biao) May 21, 2008, *available at* http://www.fdi.gov.cn/pub/FDI/wztj/kfqtj/2007kfqtj/t2008052 1_93066.htm (last visited on 21 June 2011).

[16] Top 500 Enterprises in the Suzhou Industrial Park, *available at* http://www.sipac.gov.cn/tunltzcg/200807/t20080720_28780.htm (last visited on 21 June 2011).

[17] Such an amount is very positive. Our program got a high support from the local government. We guess that a letter of introduction by the local government did a great favor in this respect. Moreover, this may also demonstrate that most of them were concerned about the FDI legal framework in China.

[18] A lot of studies or report also confirm this trend. See Lutz-Christian Wolff, China's Private International Investment Law: One-Way Street into PRC Law, 56 American Journal Comparative Law 1039, 2008. at 1043; Hui Huang. *supra* note 10, pp. 205 – 209; Jessica Zoe Renwald. *supra* note 10. p. 464. Moreover, it was pointed out by the American Chamber of Commerce in its 2010 Business Climate Survey Report that WFOES were still the most popular structure for American companies in China. see the 2010 Business Climate Survey Report. *Supra* note 6, p. 2. In the Business Confidence Survey Report held by the European Chamber of Commerce, it was also pointed out that WFOEs were again the most common legal entity registered in Mainland China with half of all respondents reporting a WFOE in 2010. Furthermore, the WFOE legal entity registration is most commonly found in companies chat have been operating in China for 11 – 20 years. See the Business Confidence Survey Report 2010, *supra* note 4, p. 25.

each represented 18% and 2% separately; in terms of actual value of investment, the figures were 75%, 19% and 6% for WFOEs, EJVs and CJVs respectively.[19]

Among the 61 FIES, 13 enterprises were from Hong Kong or Taiwan, 15 from the European Union, 6 from America (United States), another 22 from other Asian Jurisdictions (including one jointly invested by Japan and Taiwan and one by Taiwan and Singapore), 2 jointly invested by Japan and the United States, and another 3 from the British Virgin Islands (BVI). A close look at the responses demonstrates the representative quality of the respondent companies. The bulk of the respondents (42 of the 61) were from the top 9 economies investing in Mainland China,[20] including Hong Kong (6), Japan (7), BVI (3), United States (6), Taiwan (7). South Korea (5), Singapore (2), Britain (2) and Germany (4).[21] Most importantly, as *Chart* 2 illustrates, the distribution of respondent investors also generally conforms to the distribution of foreign investors in China as a whole. Thus the results from the survey in the SIP in a way reflect the general situation of FDI.

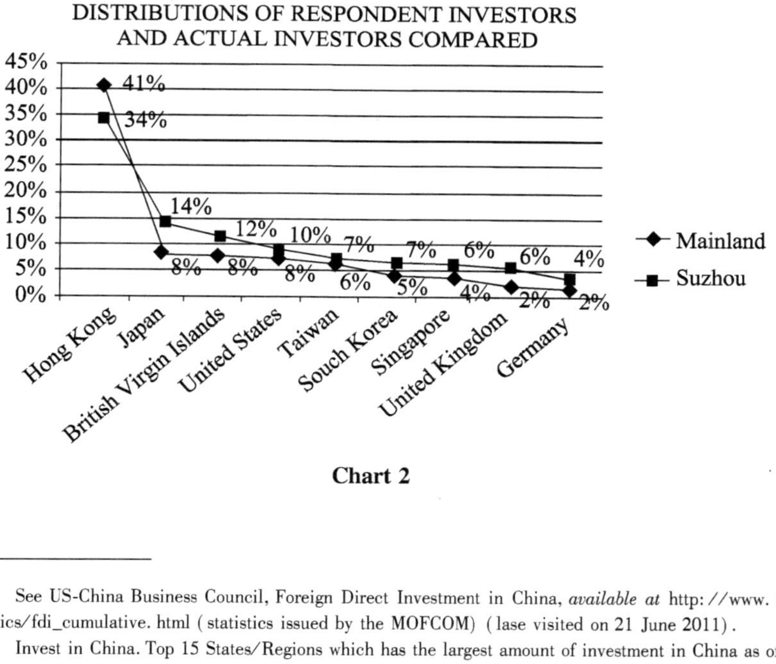

Chart 2

[19] See US-China Business Council, Foreign Direct Investment in China, *available at* http://www.uschina.org/statistics/fdi_cumulative.html (statistics issued by the MOFCOM) (lase visited on 21 June 2011).

[20] Invest in China. Top 15 States/Regions which has the largest amount of investment in China as of the end of 2006 *(jie zhi* 2006 *nian dui hua tou zi qian shi wu wei guo jia/di qu qing kuang)*, September 27. 2007, *available at* http://www.fdi.gov.cn/pub/FOI/wztj/lntjsj/wstzsj/2006nzgwztj/t200 70927_85191.htm (last visited on 21 June 2011).

[21] Actually, these nine Jurisdictions' positions as the cop source of origin with respect to FDI flows to China are only slightly changed in recent years. For example. according to the China Commerce Yearbook 2010, the top 10 Country/Economy concerning the FDI flows to Chin for 2009 are Hong Kong, British Virgin Islands, Japan, Singapore, South Korea, Cayman Islands, United States, Samoa, Taiwan, and Germany. When it comes to the cumulative FDI for 2009 by source of origin, the top ten are Hong Kong, British Virgin Islands, Japan, United States, Taiwan, South Korea, Singapore, Cayman Islands, United Kingdom and Germany. See the Editorial Board of the China Commerce Yearbook, the China Commerce Yearbook 2010, China Business Press, 2010.

II. GENERAL ROLE OF LAW

In this questionnaire, three questions were designed to determine to what extent the Law or the legal framework has played a role in foreign investors' decision whether or not to invest in China. The first is about the foreign investors' perceptions on the general role of law when they made the investment decision, followed by a series of sub-questions asking to what extent they had investigated the governing legal framework before the decisions were made. The last one is about the significance of investment incentives in their decision-making.[22]

1. *RELATIVE IMPORTANCE OF LAW AS A DETERMINANT OF INVESTMENT DECISION*

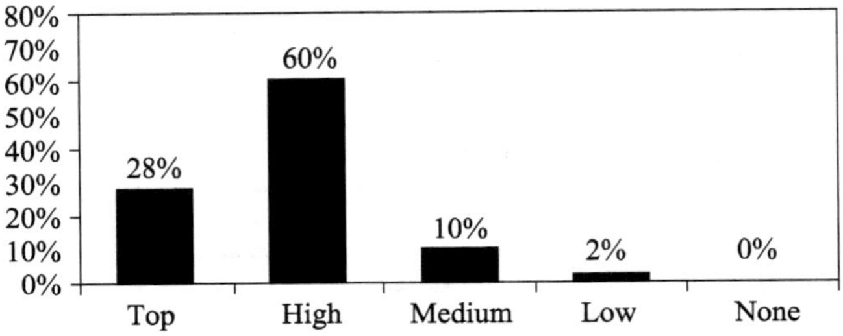

Chart 3 THE ROLE OF LAW IN INVESTMENT DECISION-MAKING

In the first question, investors were asked what priority they gave the nature of legal framework when deciding whether or not to invest in China, relative to other factors, such as market size, labour costs, environmental costs and raw material supply (top, high, medium, low or none) . The results *(Chart 3)* demonstrate that when deciding to invest, most respondents (88 percent) took legal framework as an element of substantial importance (top or high) . Among them, 28 percent of the respondents considered law as of "top" importance in investment decision-making, while 60 percent of them chose "high". 10 percent of the respondents regarded the legal framework as of "medium" importance. Only 2 percent of the respondents considered law of no significance.

It should be pointed out that this result was rather high and much higher than the

---

[22] According to UNCTAD, among the three groups influencing the flows of FDI (the policy framework for FDI, *economic* determinants and business facilitation), incentive policies as part of business facilitation, is separated from the policy framework. See UNCTAD, *supra* note 8, p. 5. However, most of the incentives in China are provided by laws and regulations. China takes a separate legal framework for foreign investment which facilitates to grant foreign investors preferential treatment. Tax incentives may be found in the EJV Law, CJV law and WFOE Law, Article 17 of the WFOE Law, for example, provides that pursuant to the taxation-refaced provisions of the State, WFOEs shall pay taxes and may be entitled to the preferential treatment of tax reduction or exemption.

result in the 2001 study.[23] This result might be explained by considering the following factors. First, China is a developing country, in which policy and institutional determinants arc especially important, as noted by an UNCTAD study.[24] UNCTAD investor surveys find out chat in developing states, foreign investors tend to focus on policy and other economic factors, disregarding questions concerning motives for entry such as market size, cost reduction or accessing natural resources were often disregarded by them.[25] In case of China, an OECD study confirmed that China's success in attracting FDI was partly owing to its efforts to "bring regulation s in line with international standards."[26] The second reason might be that the SIP, as a joint initiative by the Chinese and Singaporean governments, enjoys a higher reputation for its strong policy and institutional framework. Finally, a more direct reason might be related to the fact that thequestionnaire survey was supported by the SIP authority. In particular, it was pointed out in the introductory part of the questionnaire that the questionnaire report would be submitted to the SIP authority for reference. Nevertheless, this result should be considered as a confirmation that law does play a significant role in the decision making of foreign investors in China in general and in the SIP in particular. Moreover, the fact that this result is much higher than the 2001 result suggests that the status of law and institution has been significantly improved during the first decade of the 21st century after China's access to the WTO.

2. *INVESTIGATION OF LAW BEFORE INVESTMENT*

In order co find out whether or not the foreign investors actually carried out investigations of the legal framework before deciding to invest, four sub-questions were included. The first question was to inquire whether they had investigated the legal elements of investment. All the respondents made the choice of "yes", including those who regarded law as of low importance in the previous question. In this respect, all the foreign investors made their investigation into the legal system of China before their investment, and they only differ in their attitude coward the importance of the law. Actually, it is hard to believe that any investment is made without any investigation of law. The laws and regulations concerning the establishment or admission are at least to be known.

The following sub-question was about the actual evidence used in investigating the legal environment, i. e., whether they had investigated only the written law ("law on paper") or both the written law and the law in action (e. g., levels of enforcement). As shown in *Chart* 4, most investors (61 percent) paid an in-depth study, i. e., investigated both the written law and the law in action. In contrast, a substantial portion of investors (39 percent) merely examined the written law. This result reveals chat most investors have

---

〔23〕 In that survey, the figures were 5 percent and 36 percent for the choice of "top" or "high" respectively. See Shan, *supra* note 11, p. 248.

〔24〕 UNCTAD, *supra* note 8, pp. 12 – 3.

〔25〕 Id., p. 13.

〔26〕 See OECD, Reforms Could Boost China's Ability to Attract Foreign Investment, July 3, 2003, *available at* http://wwwoecd.org/document/8/0,3746,en_21571361_44315115_3240968_1_1_1_1,00.html (last visited on 21 June 2011).

conducted an in-depth study on the legal framework, while written law was put in a relatively higher priority when compared with law enforcement. This may partly result from the fact that written law is much easier to be acquired than law in action.

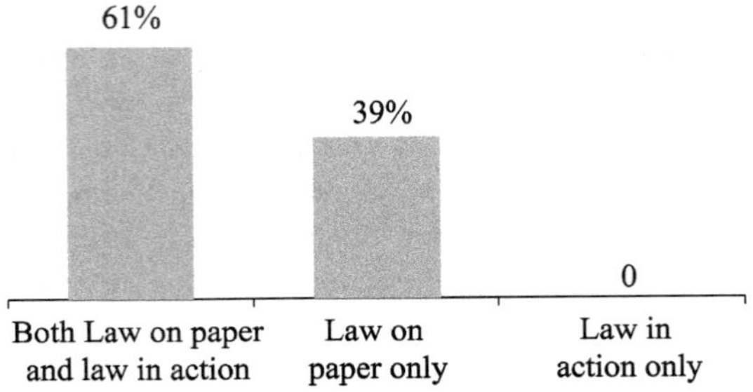

Chart 4　EVIDENCE OF LAW INVESTIGATED

Chart 5　CHINESE LAW AND INTERNATIONAL TREATIES CONSIDERED

The third sub-question on law investigation deals with the scope of laws that were under investigation, i. e., whether they had investigated both domestic law and applicable international investment treaties, or either or none of them. As *Chart* 5 shows, more than half of the respondents (54 percent) investigated both the Chinese law and the applicable investment treaties, while the rest only investigated the Chinese law. This result shows that, in the eyes of the foreign investors, domestic law nevertheless plays a much more important role than international law.

The following sub-question is the last of this series, which aimed to find the specific international investment-related treaties that have affected foreign investment decision making. As illustrated in *Chart* 6, among the foreign investors who considered both Chinese law and international treaties, most (75 percent) were aware of bilateral treaties devoted to the avoidance of double taxation (DTTs), as cost of investment was obviously the primary concern for them, followed by the bilateral investment treaties known by 63 percent of the respondents. Fewer investors knew MIGA Convention (44 percent) or ICSID Convention (35 percent).

However, compared with the 2001 study, the general level of awareness of these investment related treaties has been significantly increased. Like the 2008 study, DDT topped the list but with slightly lower score (68 percent). More significant increase is seen on the awareness of BITs (a nearly 20 percent increase from 18 percent in 2001), and MIGA an ICSID Conventions (9 percent and 18 percent respectively in 2001). This result demonstrates that international treaties are playing an increasingly important role in foreign investment activities in China.[27]

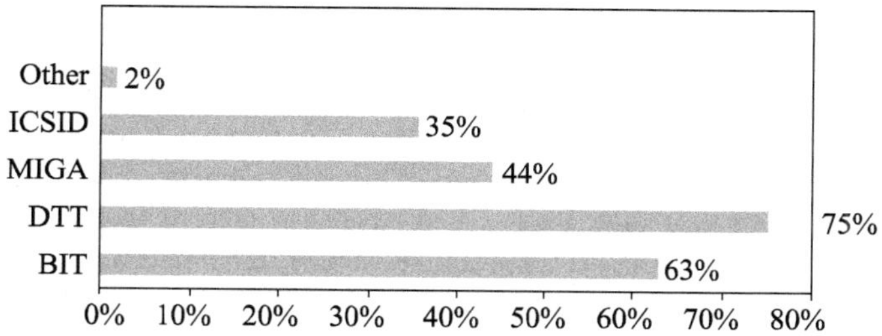

Chart 6 AWARENESS OF INTERNATIONAL TREATIES

The relative low awareness of the ICSID Convention might be explained by the fact that most of the bilateral investment treaties signed by China were done in earlier years, which provided for no or only very limited (limited to disputes concerning the amount of compensation) access to ICSID arbitration.

3. *IMPORTANCE OF INCENTIVES ON INVESTMENT DECISION-MAKING*

Two sub-questions aimed at determining whether the incentive measures that the Chinese Government used to attract foreign investment had worked. The first one asked the respondents what importance they put on the incentives (such as tax exemptions for foreign investors generally, or specifically to those in the SIP). As shown in *Chart* 7, 87 percent of them regarded the investment incentives of top or high importance. Among them, 13 percent made the choice of "top", and the rest chose "high". This confirms that China's investment incentives have worked in attracting foreign investors.[28]

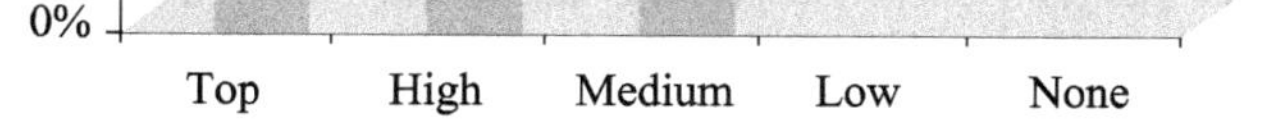

Chart 7 IMPORTANCE Of INCENTIVES

[27] An UNCTAD survey also confirmed that BIT coverage in host developing countries and transition economics plays a role in making a final decision on where to invest. See UNCTAD. *supra* note 8. p. xiv.

[28] The importance of a. x incentives in attracting foreign investment disputes was confirmed in many other articles. Such as Stephan W. Schill, *supra* note 10, p. 79. See also Yigang Pan, The Inflows of Foreign Direct Investment to China: the Impact of Country-Specific Factors. 56 Journal of Business Restatement 829, 2003, p. 833. A survey carried out by Shaukat Ali and Wei Guo also shows the incentives as an important determinant to Fill, the score of which ranked second among the 11variables. See Shaukat Ali and Wei Guo. Determinants of FDI in China, *supra* note 10, p. 28.

The second sub-question was designed to investigate the effect of the Enterprise Income Tax Law of the People's Republic of China promulgated on January 1, 2008. This specific law unifies the income tax treatment between domestic and foreign enterprises by consolidating the Provisional Regulations on Enterprise Income Tax and the Law on the Income Tax for Foreign-Invested Enterprises and Foreign Enterprises, eliminating some existing preferential treatment granted to FIEs. As illustrated in *Chart* 8, 79 percent of the respondents said that this law had adversely affected them, of whom 22 percent believed that the law had a very negative impact. Similar complaints can also be found in, for example, the Business Confidence Survey Report 2010 by the European Chamber of Commerce.[29]

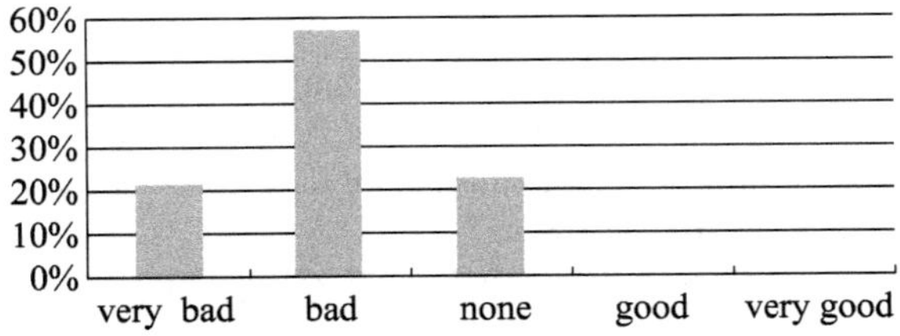

Chart 8 EFFECTS Of THE "ENTERPRISE INCOME TAX LAW"

Interestingly, there are 21 percent of the respondents saying that this law had little impact on them. This may be explained by the fact that tax incentives are also provided in the new Enterprise Income Tax Law. There are for instance reduced income tax given to key industries and projects whose development is supported and encouraged by the State such as industries of energy conservation, water-saving and those implementing a comprehensive utilization of resources, high-tech industries, the construction of infrastructure projects, and coal mine safety equipment. Also, regional tax concessions are available to foster development of disadvantaged regions.[30] Indeed the new Enterprise Income Tax Law has, to a certain extent, demostrated a more balanced and sustainable approach adopted by the Chinese government toward FDI.

III. KEY SUBSTANTIVE ISSUES

In order to determine whether the FDI legal system in China is adequate and sufficient in protecting and promoting FDI, a series of questions were designed to ask the experience of foreign investors on some of the key legal issues such as investment safety, expropriation, national treatment, intellectual property rights (IPR) protection, monetary transfer, performance requirement, and legal disputes.

1. *INVESTMENT SAFETY*

Three questions were included to explore the issue of investment safety. The first one asked the foreign investors whether or not they think it was safe to invest or reinvest

[29] European Chamber of Commerce in China, *supra* note 4, p. 14.

[30] See Qun Li, . supra note 10, pp. 18 – 24.

in China, and 59 out of the 61 respondents (up to 97 percent) chose the answer "yes". This confirms that in general foreign investors feel that China is a safe place to invest.[31]

The second question asked what the most important source of confidence was when they decided to invest or reinvest in China. The options provided were legal protection provided by domestic and international law, investment insurance against political risks, and political promise and social stability. As shown in *Chart* 9, 41 percent of the investors considered that the legal protection provided by the domestic and international law was the most important source of confidence, while 39 percent believed the political promise and social stability were more significant.[32] Only 10 percent selected "Investment insurance against political risk". This result is generally consistent with the 2001 result, as legal and political factors continue to play the most significant role in boosting investors' confidence. However, the relative importance of political and legal factors has been changed. In the 2001 study, political promise and social stability was considered by 40 percent of investors as the most important element whilst only 30 percent of investors voted for legal protection.[33] This change further confirms the increasingly important role that law has played in FDI activities in China, particularly in SIP.

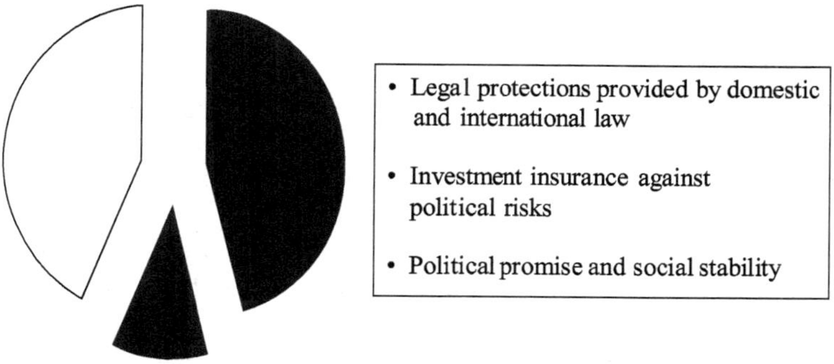

Chart 9 SOURCE OF INVESTMENT SAFETY

The issue of expropriation is of great concern to foreign investors because it is the single greatest threat to investment security.[34] Thus the third question asked whether foreign investors considered it possible for them to suffer nationalization or expropriation

---

[31] In the 2001 study, 81 percent of respondent EU i11vescors replied "yes" to the investment safety question. See Shan, *supra* note 13, p. 60.

[32] A worldwide survey jointly held by UNCTAD and World Association of Investment Promotion Agencies also reveals that macroeconomic stability and political stability were considered the most important. However, the options provided did not include the legal policy but other factors such as the quality of telecommunications, the supply and cost of skilled labour, corporate taxes and the quality of banking and other financial services. See UNCTAD, Worldwide Survey of foreign affiliates, Occasional Note, Geneva, 5 November. UNCTADIWEBIITE/IIA/2007/5. Also the UNCTAD, *supra* note 8, p. 13.

[33] See Shan, *supra* note 13, p. 61.

[34] Kenneth J. Vandevelde, *Bilateral Investment Treaties: History*, Policy, and Interpretation, Oxford University Press. 2010, p. 271.

in the next five years. *Chart* 10 shows that 72 percent of the surveyed investors gave a negative answer ("rarely" or "never"), while 12 percent believed it was "possible" and 6 percent thought it would "always" happen. There are another 10 percent choosing "don't know". This further confirms the increased confidence of foreign investors in China, as the vast majority believed that no expropriation would take place in the five years to follow.

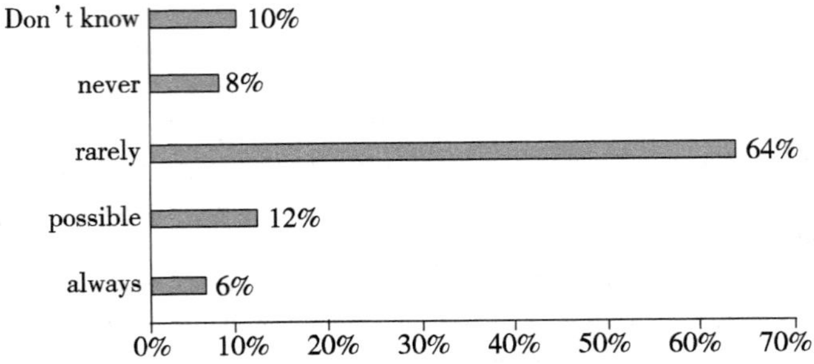

Chart 10 THE POSSIBILITY OF EXPROPRIATION IN THE NEXT FIVE YEARS

2. *NATIONAL TREATMENT*

National treatment, aiming at constructing a level playing field for investors irrespective of their origins, used to be resisted or denied by China. In China, domestic and foreign invested enterprises are traditionally segregated, subject to different laws with different requirements for their establishment and operation. There are historical and political reasons for this dual legal system.[35] It is rare to find articles of national treatment provided in China's earlier bilateral investment treaties. However, in recent years, China has been taking measures to implement the national treatment. The dual legal system in domestic level is converging as witnessed by the enactment of the aforementioned Enterprise Income Tax Law. In the sphere of international law, national treatment is granted in its recent BIT practice particularly those signed since 1998.[36] A question was therefore included in the questionnaire to explore the impact of the new national treatment policy.

As shown in *Chart* 11, the majority of the respondents (64 percent) believed that the national treatment had a "significant" or "some" beneficial impact on their investment. In contrast, 25 percent of the respondents were much less optimistic thinking it of only "a little" help, and 8 percent of them thought it would not help at all. This result suggests that national treatment was generally favored by the foreigners while some believed it would have negative effect on their investment such as the abolition of the tax

[35] Hui Huang, *supra* note 10, pp. 202 – 3.

[36] The inclusions of national treatment and a comprehensive investor-state dispute settlement mechanism (specially a full access to international arbitration) were seen as the main characteristics of the new generation of the Chinese BIT. See Stephan W. Schill. *supra* note 10, p. 82.

and other incentives it might result in.

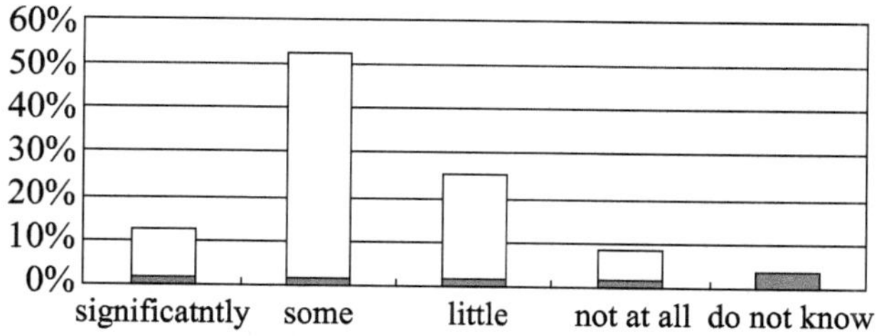

Chart 11 IMPACT OF THE NATIONAL TREATMENT POLICY

3. *INTELLECTUAL PROPERTY RIGHTS PROTECTION*

China has long been criticized by foreign investors, industrial associations, and western states for its weak protection of the Intellectual Property Rights (IPRs). US, for example, filed a WTO complaint against China in 2007, partly targeting at Article 4 of China's Copyright Law. The US alleged that the first sentence of this article, which provides that the publication or distribution of which is prohibited by law shall not be protected by this Law, denies protection and enforcement to works that have not been authorized for publication or distribution within China. In 2009, the Panel established under the Dispute Settlement Body (DSB) concluded that the first sentence of Article 4 of China's Copyright Law was inconsistent with its obligations under the TRIPS.[37]

Even though China has updated many of its laws and regulations to comply with the Agreement on Trade-Related Aspects of Intellectual Property (TRIPS), it is still pointed out by some western countries, such as US, that the enforcement of the laws and regulations is insufficient.[38] The feedbacks on the two questions concerning the IPR protection legal system in China confirmed this view. As illustrated in *Chart* 12, more than half of the respondents said they were "less" (38 percent) or "least" (20 percent) satisfied

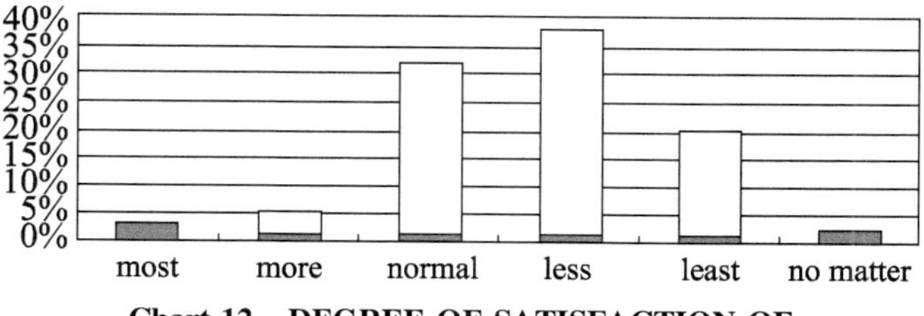

Chart 12 DEGREE OF SATISFACTION OF THEIPR PROTECTION SYSTEM

[37] WTO, China-Measures Affecting the Protection and Enforcement of Intellectual Property Rights, Dispute Settlement: Dispute DS362, *available at* http://www.wto.org/english/tr: uop_e/dispu_e/cases_c/ds362_c.htm (last visited on 21 June 2011).

[38] US Department of State, 2011 Investment Climate Statement-China, *available at* http://www.mw.gov/e/eeb/rls/othr/ics/201 1/157258.htm (last visited on 21 June 2011).

with the IPR legal system. Similar result was received in the 2001 study.[39]

The following question went on to ask for comments by the foreign investors on China's IPR protection legal system.[40] Four options were provided: comprehensive legislation and good enforcement, comprehensive legislation but poor enforcement, poor legislation but good enforcement, and poor legislation and enforcement. Seventy seven percent of the investors considered that Chinese IPR laws and regulations were comprehensive but their implementation was ineffective. This seems to be consistent with findings by major western business communities. In the Business Confidence Survey Report by the European Chamber of Commerce, most European companies (66 percent) believed that written IPR laws in China were adequate or excellent, while only 22 percent felt that the enforcement of laws and regulations were adequate.[41] It is also reported by the American Chamber of Commerce in its Business Climate Survey Report 2010 that 74 percent of US companies reporting that enforcement of intellectual property rights is "totally ineffective" or "ineffective".[42] It is mentioned in the 2011 white paper that AmCham South China's perception of China's IPR protection has for many years been that the legislative and regulatory foundations of the same were sound, although uneven application of those laws and regulations continued to be a source of frustration for some enterprises operating in the Mainland.[43]

4. *MONETARY TRANSFER*

Monetary transfer may become the most important concern of foreign investors, because they must be able co exchange the currency in which the returns are generated for a currency that they can use for their other transactions.[44] The provision of monetary transfer is accordingly one of the most important articles of an investment treaty.[45] China has taken an increasingly liberal approach toward the issue of monetary transfer. Nowadays the RMB, the Chinese currency, is fully convertible under current transactions, though not under capital transactions. In this respect, foreign exchange transactions on China's capital account require a case-by-case review. A question on transfer is therefore included in the questionnaire to ascertain whether foreign investors still have difficulty in making investment related transfers.

According to *Chart* 13, nearly half of the respondents said they "rarely" had problems in monetary transfer, and 7 percent of the respondents said they "never" encoun-

---

〔39〕 In the 2001 study, 58 percent of the respondent investors were unsatisfied by the Chinese IPR legal system. See Shan, *supra* note 13, pp. 68 – 9.

〔40〕 The options are comprehensive legislation and good enforcement, comprehensive legislation bur poor enforcement, poor legislation but good enforcement, and poor legislation and enforcement.

〔41〕 European Chamber of Commerce in China, *supra* note 4, p. 15. It is also pointed our in this report that companies' perception of enforcement levels has improved, albeit slightly, from 15 percent in 2008 to 22 percent today.

〔42〕 American Chamber of Commerce, *supra* note 6, p. 11.

〔43〕 The American Chamber of Commerce in South China. "2011 White Paper on the Business Environment in China", 2 February 2011, p. 26., *available at* http: //v. rww. amcham-sourhchina. orglamcham/static/publications/whitepaper. jsp (last visited on 21 June 2011).

〔44〕 KennerhJ-Vandevelde, *supra* note 35, p. 316.

〔45〕 Gallagher and Shan, *supra* note I, p. 175.

tered difficulty. However, 44 percent of them "sometimes" (33 percent) or "frequently" (11percent) experienced difficulties in transferring investment and profit out of China. Clearly from the foreign investors' perspective, China needs to further liberalize monetary transfer rules to fully facilitate FDI activities. In this connection, it is noted that Yi Gang, head of the State Administration of Foreign Exchanges, mentioned in early 2011 that China would progressively make its currency, RMB, convertible on the capiul account in the next five years as China pushes for the deeper internationalization of the currency.[46]

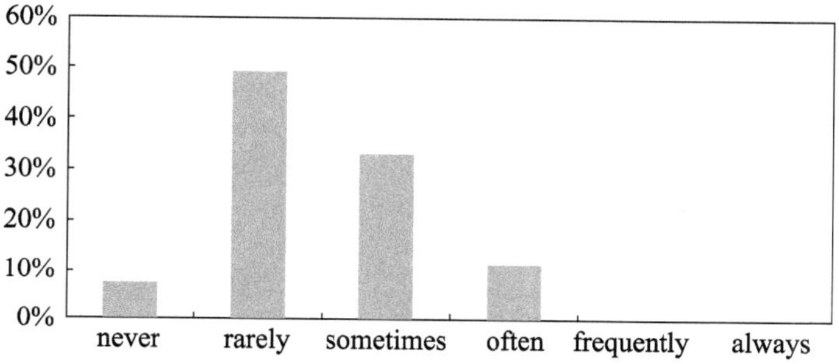

Chart 13　DIFFICULTY IN MONETARY TRANSFER.

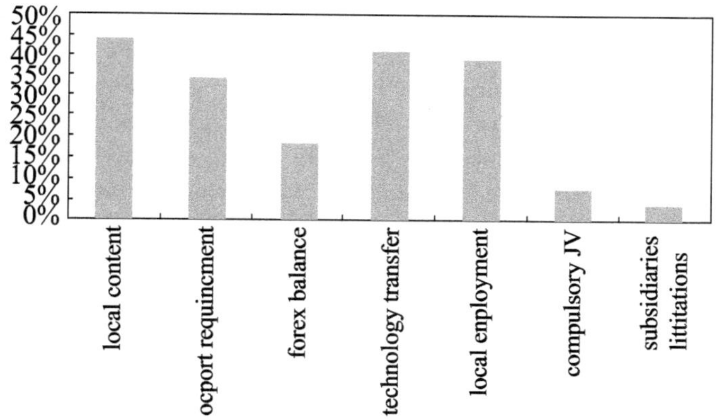

Chart 14　FREQUENCY OF PERFORMANCE REQUIREMENTS ENCOUNTERED

5. PERFORMANCE REQUIREMENTS

Performance requirements have two basic forms: either as a condition of admission (or direct performance requirements) or linked to an advantage (or indirect performance

---

[46] See China Daily, China to make RMB convertible on capital account in 5 years, January 19, 2011, *available at* http: //www. chinacbily. com. cnfbizchina/2011 01/19/content_1 187873'. 1. htm (last visited on 21 June 2011).

requirements). As a WTO member, China has committed to eliminate the performance requirements prohibited by the Agreement on Trade Related Investment Measures (TRIMs) such as export performance, trade and foreign exchange balancing, and local content requirements. Moreover, China takes measure to abolish the requirement of technology transfer. However, the effect of these measures need to he tested in practice, thus a question was designed to ask the foreign investors whether and to what extent they had been exposed to perfomance requirements.

A revealed in *Chart* 14, most of the foreign investors were subject to some performance requirements. The most widely used was local content requirement, with 44 percent of the respondents confirming its existence. Other performance requirements imposed were transfer of technology requirement (41 percent), local employment (39 percent), export performance (34 percent), forex balance (18 percent), compulsory JV (7 percent), and subsidiaries limitation (3 percent). It should be noted that some of those requirements and limitations, such as local content requirements, forex balancing requirements, and export performance, have been lifted or relaxed by recent amendment to FDI laws and regulations. However, they may still exist in the form of indirect performance requirements. Tax benefits and other incentives are still offered to FIES and domestic enterprises together with export, local content, technology transfer, or other requirements. The "Provisions Guiding the Direction of Foreign Investment" (Foreign Investment Guiding Provisions), for example, provides that foreign investment classified as "permitted projects" will be treated as "encouraged projects" if all their products are directly exported.[47] Moreover, projects classified as "restricted" may be treated as "permitted" upon approval by the relevant authorities if their product export sales amount to more than 70 percent of their total product sales, and projects classified as "permitted" or even "restricted" can enjoy the same treatment as "encouraged" projects if they are considered to be particularly conducive to economic development in western and central China.[48] In the 2007 version of the Catalogue for the Guidance of Foreign Investment Industries, certain projects are required to be carried only in the form of Joint Venture.[49]

6. *DISPUTES WITH CHINESE GOVERNMENT*

Foreign investors may encounter many kinds of disputes with local government authorities, thus the frequency of investor-state disputes can be an important indicator of the general investment climate of the host country. In this respect, two questions were designed to investigate whether the respondents had disputes with the government. 9 out of 61 respondents said "yes", taking a percentage of 15 (*Chart* 15). Among the 9 respondents, 3 are from Hong Kong, 3 from South Korea, 2 from Britain and 1 from Spain.

---

[47] Order of the State Council on Promulgation of Provisions on Guiding the Orientation of Foreign Investment, promulgated by the State Council, Feb. 11, 2002. effective Apr. 1, 2002. Article 10.

[48] Id, Articles 10 and 11.

[49] See "Catalogue of Restricted Foreign Investment Industry" in Catalogue for the Guidance of Foreign Investment Industries (Amended in 2007), *available at* http://www.fdi.gov.cn/pub/FDI_EN/uws/law_en_infojsp?docid=87372 (lase visited on 21 June 2011).

The 9 respondents were then asked to choose their ways to solve the disputes. Among the four choices "negotiate", "resort to local court", "submit to international arbitration" ; ind "other ways to be illustrated", 5 of the 9 respondents chose "negotiation" and the other 4 chose "resort to local court". It is a little surprising that none submitted the dispute to international arbitration. One possible reason is that most BITs between the home states of the 9 respondents and China provide that only amount concerning expropriation may be submitted to international arbitration.[50]

Chart 15 DISPUTES WITH THE CHINESE GOVERNMENT

To summarise, the present study demonstrates that law had played a significant role in China's success in attracting foreign investment. Most foreign investors considered China as a safe place to make investment and the most important source of such confidence was the legal protection provided by domestic and international laws. The implementation of national treatment to foreign investment was welcomed by most foreign investors, though some of them were concerned with the negative effect it might bring about by reducing existing tax incentives. However, China's weak regime in protecting intellectual property rights was criticized by foreign investors. Most respondents considered that although the relevant intellectual property laws and regulations were comprehensive and sound they were not effectively enforced. Also, indirect performance requirements still existed even though China had abolished the direct requirements of local content, export performance, and forex balance in the newly amended FIES laws and regulations. Moreover, further liberalization of the monetary transfer regime was demanded. These are the areas of the Chinese Fm legal framework in which China might wish to improve.

IV. EFFECTIVENESS OF THE LEGAL SYSTEM

According to the World Bank, an effective legal system for foreign investment normally has five features. First, it provides a set of rules ' known' to foreign investors in advance. Thus the law should be published (accessible) and clear. Second, it relies upon rules which are actually implemented, and not just ' on the books' . Third, it ensures that rules arc consistently applied. The discretionary power of state officials should, therefore, be limited to the narrowest possible field, in order to avoid abuse. Fourth, there must be an effective, independent mechanism for dispute resolution. The judiciary must be protected from intervention by other branches of the government, so that the

[50] Though full auess to international arbitration are both provided in the newly signed sino-Spain BIT and the Sino-South BIT, these two new BITs separately came into force on July 1, 2008 and Pecember 1, 2007. However, our servey was carried out during the period between late 2007 and early 2008.

government itself can be the subject of laws. Further, the judicial process must not be incapacitated by physical constraints due to poor facilities, unreasonable delays, prohibitive cost or uncertainty. Lastly, it has clear procedures for the amendments of rules, to prevent any arbitrary introduction or rejection of rules, and to clear out irrelevant rules.[51] Based on the above mentioned set of criteria, the World Bank and other development agencies developed an Ideal Institutional Paradigm (IIP) to give developing countries law reform advices.[52]

Based on these criteria identified by the World Bank, 9 questions were included in the Questionnaire to examine the effectiveness of the Chinese FDI legal system. These questions focus on five aspects, including the accessibility and stability of the law, the enforcement of law by government departments and courts and the enforcement of court and arbitration decisions.

1. *ACCESSIBILITY OF LAW*

The first question investigates the transparency and accessibility of China's FDI laws and the legal policies. The respondents were asked whether they thought the FDI laws and policies were easily accessible. As *Chart* 16 illustrates, more than half (55 percent) of the respondents said that laws and policies are "always" or "mostly" accessible while 12 percent answered negatively (choosing "rarely" or "never"). Another 33 percent replied that law was only "sometimes" accessible. This marks a considerable improvement compared with the 2001 result, in which only 40 percent replied positively and 22 percent replied negatively. In recent years, particularly after WTO accession in 2001, China has made great effort to make the laws and regulations accessible. This result should be considered as a confirmation of such efforts. However, there is still substantial room for improvement as 33 percent respondents reported that law was "sometimes" inaccessible.

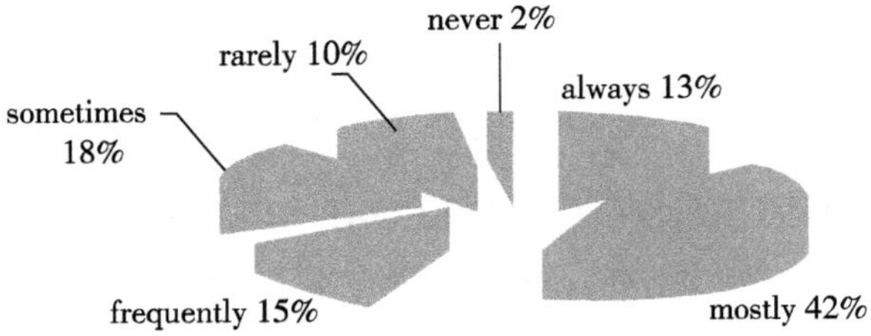

Chart 16 ACCESSIBILITY OF LAW AND POLICY

2. *STABILITY OF LAW*

The second question was included to determine, from the foreign investors' experience, whether Chinese FDI law and policies had been changed unexpectedly. The result of

---

[51] World Bank, Governance and Development. Washington D. C.: World Bank, 1992, p. 4. See Shan, *supra* nore I 1, at p. 293.

[52] Amanda Perry. An Ideal Legal System for Attracting Foreign Direct Investment? Some Theory and Reality, American University International Law Review, 15 (6), 2000, pp. 1628 – 1632.

this question is illustrated in the following *Chart* 17. Ten percent of the respondents said that in China law and policies were "always", "mostly" or "frequently" changed unexpectedly, while 46 percent reported that unexpected changes of law and policies "sometimes" happened. On the other hand, 41 percent of the respondents said that they "rarely encountered unexpected changes, while only 3 percent reported the laws and policies were "never" unexpectedly changed. This provides a sharp contrast to the 2001 result, in which 41 percent investors reported negatively ("always", "mostly" or "frequently") and only 5 percent gave a positive reply ("rarely").[53] The 2008 result should be taken as an acknowledgment of the improvement made by the Chinese government in encouraging democratic and public participation in the law draft and revision process. Now public consultation has become common practice particularly when important laws such as the Land Expropriation Regulations and Personal Income Tax Law are being drafted or revised.

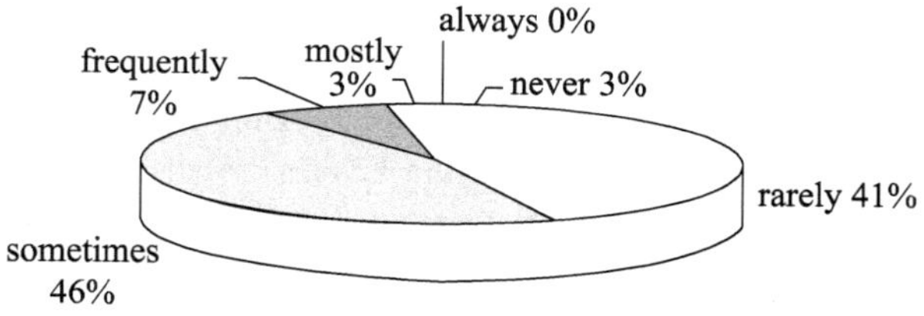

Chart 17 UNEXPECTED CHANCES OF LAW AND POLICY

3. *GOVERNMENT ENFORCEMENT OF LAW*

Two questions were designed, in this respect, to ask the foreign investors whether they were satisfied with the enforcement of laws by government departments: one is on the consistency of enforcement and the other on the need to bribe government officials.

3.1 CONSISTENCY OF GOVERNMENT LAW ENFORCEMENT

As the following *Chart* 18 shows, foreign investors thought positively of the government law enforcement. More than a half (68 percent) of the respondents thought that laws and policies "always" or "mostly" or "frequently" were enforced consistently, whilst only 12 percent of them complained that such consistency had "rarely" been achieved. Another 20 percent reported that this "sometimes" happened. This, again, demonstrates a significant improvement as compared with the result of the 2001 study, in which only 23% replied positively, whilst 14 percent did negatively ("rarely") and 35 percent gave a vague answer ("sometimes").[54]

3.2 NECESSITY OF BRIBERY TO DEAL WITH GOVERNMENT OFFICIALS

Experience shows that this question was not easy to answer, given that OECD and some home states of the foreign investor have laws and regulations that strictly prevent

---

[53] Amanda Perry. An Ideal Legal System for Attracting Foreign Direct Investment? Some Theory and Reality, American University International Law Review, 15 (6), 2000, pp. 254 – 5.

[54] Id., pp. 255 – 6.

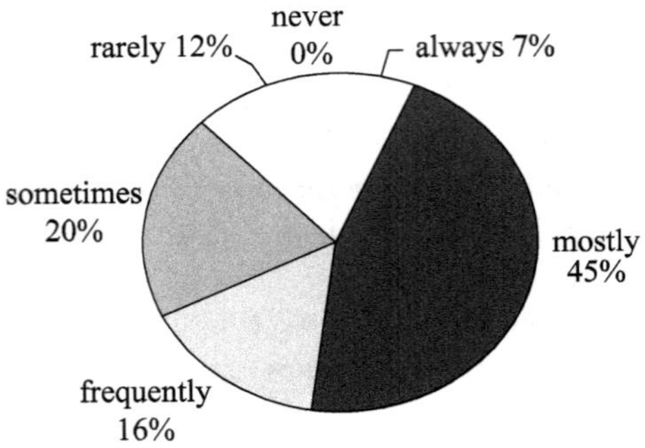

Chart 18 CONSISTENCY OF GOVERNMENT IN THE ENFORCEMENT OF LAW

their investors from engaging bribery practice abroad.[55] For this reason, rather than asking them whether there is need to give bribery, investors were asked "whether it was useful to provide economic benefit to make the business easily achieved when dealing with government officials". Forty-three percent of the respondents said that there had "never" or "rarely" been a need co use bribery when dealing with government officials. Only 14 percent of them answered that bribery was "frequently" or "mostly" used, while 34 percent of the respondents found it "sometimes" necessary. (*Chart* 19: Need of bribery for officials). Even though a more euphonious way was used in this question, about 10 percent of the respondents still refused to answer this question.[56]

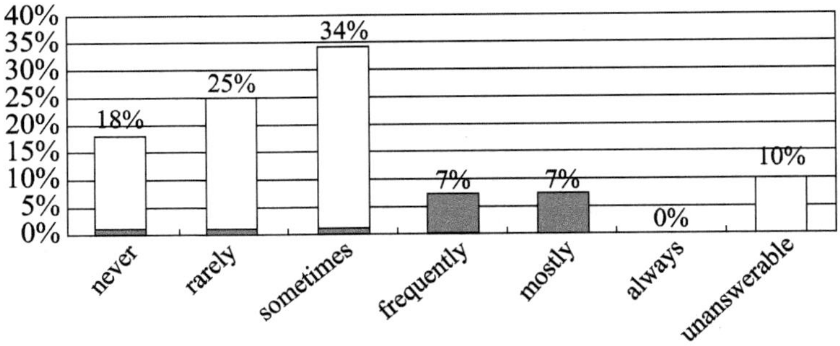

Chart 19 NECESSITY OF BRIBERY FOROFFICIALS

In this connection, it is noted that a most recent case of bribery in China relates to IBM. In 2011 American regulators filed a lawsuit in federal district court, alleging em-

---

〔55〕 US, for example, has the Foreign Corrupt Practices Act to ban payment of bribes of its MNES to foreign officials.

〔56〕 Far less (59 percent) respondents answered this question in the 2001 study which was phrased more directly. 45% replied that bribery was "never" or "rarely" needed, whilst 5% said it was "always" needed. See Shan, *supra* note 11, p. 256.

ployees of IBM's subsidiaries in China and South Korea, as well as a South Korean joint venture, paid government officials cash bribes, provided free computers and covered their entertainment costs as a means to secure sales. Now a settlement has been reached by the IBM and die U. S. Securities and Exchange Commission, according to which IBM will pay 10 million US dollars.[57] The case shows that bribery practice continues to exist in FDI activities in China.

4. *COURT ENFORCEMENT OF LAW*

The courts are the centre of all law enforcement activities. Therefore, five subquestions were designed to examine the record of law enforcement by and around the Chinese courts: the objectivity of law enforcement by the courts, the possibility of bribery impacting on court judgments, political interference on court decisions, unreasonable delays of court procedures, and unreasonable delays of court in enforcing its awards.

4.1 OBJECTIVITY OF THE LAW ENFORCEMENT DY COURT

On the question of the objectivity of law enforcement by court, as *Chart* 20 shows, only a few of the respondents replied positively. 15 percent of them said that this objectivity was "always" (6 percent) or "mostly" (9 percent) achieved, whilst 9 percent of them replied negatively (3 percent "rarely" and 6 percent "never"). 10 percent of them said that objectivity was "sometimes" achieved. Compared with the 2001 result, the ratio of positive replies is similar (18 percent in 2001), but that of negative replies decreased (from 19 percent in 2001)[58]. This suggests a slight improvement in this aspect.

On the other hand, more than half "did not know" the question, which may suggest that they had neither experience nor had any knowledge of Chinese courts enforcement. This seems to apply to all the rest of the court-related questions.

4.2 POSSIBILITY OF BR IBING THE JUDGES

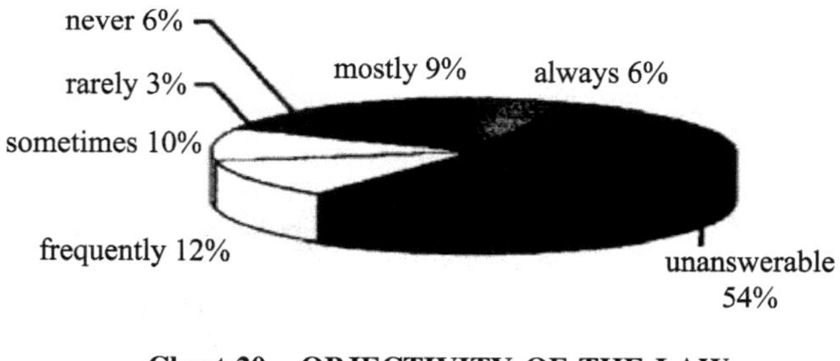

Chart 20 OBJECTIVITY OF THE LAW ENFORCEMENT BY COURT

The question on the possibility of bribing judges was also proved to be a difficult one. As with the previous question, half of the respondents (30 percent) did not answer this question. Twenty three percent of the respondents said there "never" (5 percent) or

[57] Ritsuko Ando, IBM pays $ 10 million to settle bribery complaint, March 18, 2011, *available at* http: l/ www. reuters. com/anicle/2011/03/18/ibm-idUSNJ8103187201 10318(last visited on 21June 2011).

[58] See Shan, *supra* note 11, p. 258.

"rarely" (18 percent) existed possibility of bribing judges. Fifteen percent of them replied negatively ("always", "mostly" or "frequently"). Twelve percent of the respondents replied that bribery "sometimes" could be used to influence judge's decision.[59] (*Chart* 21; Possibility of Bribing the Judges to Influence the Court Decisions) Compared with the 2001 result, there are more meaningful answers including more positive replies (only 13 percent in total in 2001) as well as more negative ones (10 percent in 2001).[60]

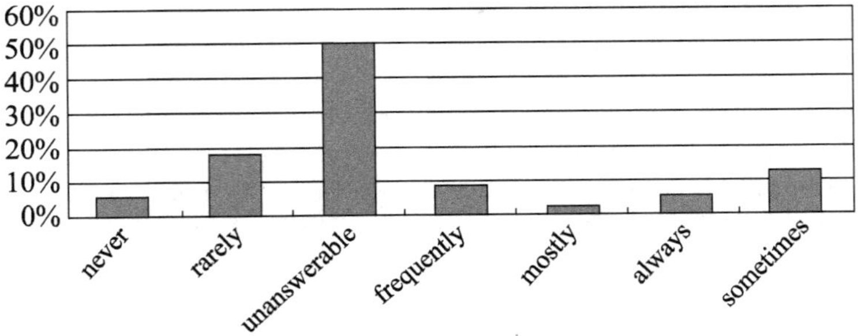

Chart 21 POSSIBILITY OF BRIBING THE JUDGES TO INFLUENCE THE COURT DECISIONS

4.3 POLITICAL INTERFERENCE IN COURT DECISIONS

Similarly to the previous question, forty-nine percent of the respondents did not answer the question. Among the rest respondents, twenty percent said the court decisions were "always" or "mostly" or "frequently" intervened by politicians. On the contrary, 24 percent of the respondents reported they "rarely" or "never" encountered political interference. Seven percent said political interference "sometimes" happened(*Chart* 22: Political interference in court decisions). This suggests a modest improvement on the 2001 result, in which there were slightly more negative replies (10 percent) than positive ones (9 percent) whilst a much larger portion of vague replies (18 percent).[61]

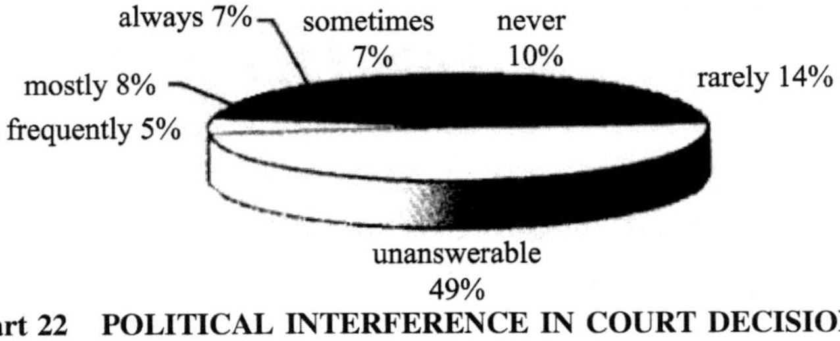

Chart 22 POLITICAL INTERFERENCE IN COURT DECISIONS

---

〔59〕 A well known bribery case happened in recent years is the Wuhan court bribery case, which was investigated in late 2002 and went co trial in 2004. It is pointed out chat this case exposed 3 sophisticated scheme of corruption within the court system and multiple levels of judges and administrator were involved. For details please see, HRIC, The Wuhan Court Bribery Case, China Rights Reform, No. 1, 2005, *available at* http://www.hrichina.org/sic. – s/dcfault/fiks/oldsitc/PDFs/CRF.1.2005/1.2005TheWuhanCoun.pdf (last visited on 21June 2011).

〔60〕 See Shan, *supra* note 11, p. 258.

〔61〕 Id, p. 259.

4.4 DELAYS IN COURT PROCEDURES

Again, 49 percent of the respondents did not answer this question. As *Chart* 23 shows, among those who did give their answers, 14 percent pointed out clearly that there was "always" or "mostly" or "frequently" delay in court procedures. Another 14 percent said the delays "rarely" or "never" happened. However, 23 percent reported that it was "sometimes" the case. This marks a clear improvement since the 2001 study, in which there was no clearly positive reply at all but 15 percent replied negatively and 22 percent said this "sometimes" happened.[62]

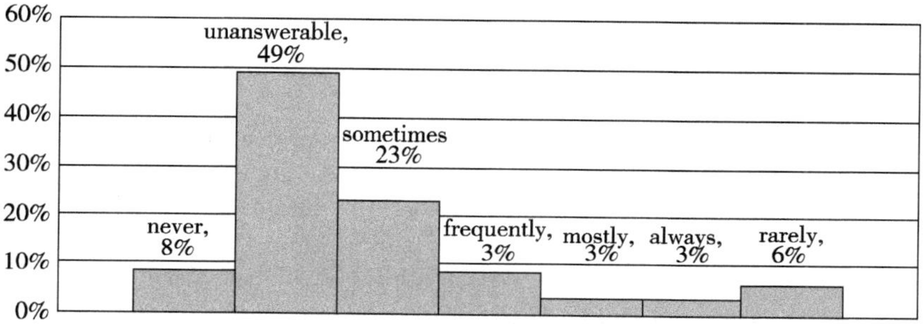

Chart 23 UNREASONABLE DELAYS IN COURT PROCEDURES

4.5 ENFORCEMENT OF COURT DECISION

As *Chart* 24 illustrates, again, 49 percent of them chose not to answer it. On the other hand, there are far more positive answer (21 percent, "always" or "mostly") than negative ones (5 percent, "never" or "rarely"). Another 10 percent of the respondents said that court decisions were "sometimes" enforced by the court. Compared with the 2001 result, the situation has been remarkably improved: There were then far more negative replies (19%) than positive ones (9%).[63] This is yet another signal of improvement in the Chinese legal system.

5. MEASURING THE FDI LEGAL SYSTEM IN CHINA AGAINST THE IDEAL INSTITUTION PARADIGM

In order to compare the FDI legal system in China as experienced by the respondents with the Ideal Institutional Paradigm (IIP), responses to the questions on the effectiveness of the legal system were converted into a score based on a scale between 0 and 5, with 5 representing maximum conformity with the IIP. Thus, for instance, on accessibility of law, the response 'always' obtains the maximum score (5) and 'never' receives the minimum (0). 'Mostly', 'frequently', 'sometimes', 'rarely' receive 4, 3, 2 and 1 respectively.[64]

Based on this conversion, the average score for each element (feature) was calcu-

[62] See Shan, *supra* note 11, pp. 259 - 260.

[63] Id., pp. 260 - 1.

[64] Unanswerable choices are excluded in the conversion and calculation as they do not bear any quantitative meanings.

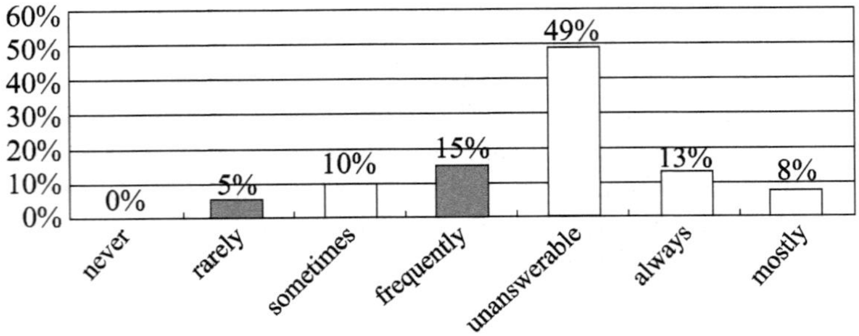

Chart 24 ENFORCEMENT OF THE COURT DECISIONS

lated. An average score for the legal system as a whole was generated on the basis of the average scores of the three major components, namely the laws, the bureaucracy and the courts. Elements scored 4 or above are described as ' effective', whilst others an described a ' borderline' (=3 & <4), ' ineffective (=2 & <3), ' seriously ineffective (<2). Details of the scores are presented in Table 1 and *Chart* 25 below.

Table 1 FDI LEGAL SYSTEM IN CHINA MEASURED AGAINST THE INSTITUTIONAL PARADIGM

Institution	Feature	Score	Effectiveness
Laws (Average Score: 3.29)	Accessibility	3.24	Borderline
	Predictability	3.34	Borderline
Bureaucracy (Average Score: 3.18)	Consistency	3.15	Borderline
	Corruption	3.21	Borderline
Courts (Average Score: 2.96)	Objectivity	2.72	Ineffective
	Corruption	2.98	Ineffective
	Independency	2.84	Ineffective
	Efficiency	2.98	Ineffective
Legal System as a whole	Enforceability	3.27	Borderline
	/	3.14	Borderline

As can be seen from Table 1 and Chart 24, the FDI legal system in China as perceived by respondents maintains a considerable gap from the Ideal Institution Paradigm, as its overall performance as well as all of the individual criteria fall on the "borderline" (3.19) and well under an ' effective' mark. Indeed all but two elements (except objectivity and independence of court) are on a "borderline" mark. However, as revealed below, this result, although not ideal, evidenced commendable progress in the Chinese FDI legal system since 2001.

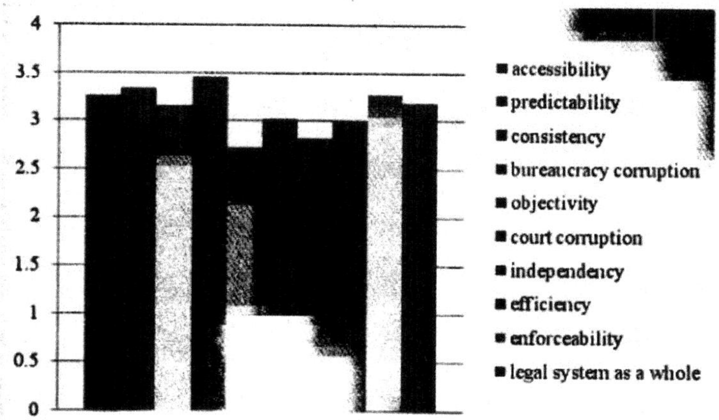

Chart 25 THE EFFECTIVENESS OF CHINA'S FDI LEGAL SYSTEM

6. *THE* 2008 *AND* 2001 *STUDIES COMPARED-AN IMPROVING FDI LEGAL SYSTEM*

Comparing the result of the present study with that of the 2001 study (*Table* 2), it can be easily seen that significant improvement has been achieved in the effectiveness of the legal system in China. On the whole, the legal system has been improved from "ineffective" in 2001 (2.68) to "borderline" in 2008 (3.14). In the 9 specific factors, all but two factors[65] witnessed increase in grade, with 5 of them (accessibility, predictability, consistency, court efficiency and decision enforceability) improved from "ineffective" to "borderline" or very close thereto, and one (objectivity) improved from "seriously ineffective" to "ineffective". On average, the grade on every factor has been increased by 23.61 percent. Such a change is undoubtedly remarkable and commendable. Much credit should go to the Chinese Government's effort to improve its governance of the country including the management of FDI activities. In the 2011 Government Report to the People's Congress, for instance, Premier Wen Jiabao stated that, in the past 5 years, "We constantly deepened reform of the administrative system. We accelerated the transformation of government functions, completed a new round of reforms of government agencies, intensively carried out administration in accordance with the law, developed law-based government, made the government more service-oriented, made government affairs

[65] The two factors are on questions relating to corruption of governmental officials and courts, in which the 2001 study result in higher marks than the 2008 study. One reason might be that the 2001 study were targeted at EU investors who were subject to strict anti-bribery regulations by the OECD and their home states. Another reason might be that the question had been asked too frankly in the 2001 study, which have frightened off some of the respondents from offering honest answers.

more open, improved the administrative accountability system, tirelessly combated corruption, and made positive progress in government capacity building. "[66] Clearly such efforts have had its effects. More specifically, the following elements might have contributed to such changes:

Firstly, China's accession into the WTO has resulted in the internationalization of many of her laws and regulations. China has been actively fulfilling its WTO commitments including elimination of unnecessary intervention in the economy, improvement of the legal system, and protection of intellectual property and so on. In the process of implementing WTO rules into the domestic laws and regulations, the transparency of the government has been greatly increased. The National People's Congress (NPC) and its Standing Committee and the State Council, for instance, tried to clean up the trade related laws and regulations to bring them in line with the WTO rules. Further, the State Council issued a circular requiring the local government to do the same with local government regulations and measures. At the same time, new laws are promulgated to meet the requirements of WTO. The Administrative Licensing Law, for example, was issued in 2004 to regulate licensing activities at national and local levels. Also the Regulation of the People's Republic of China on the Disclosure of Government Information was promulgated in 2007, which has greatly enhanced the transparency of regulatory activities whilst strengthening the protection of political rights of citizens.

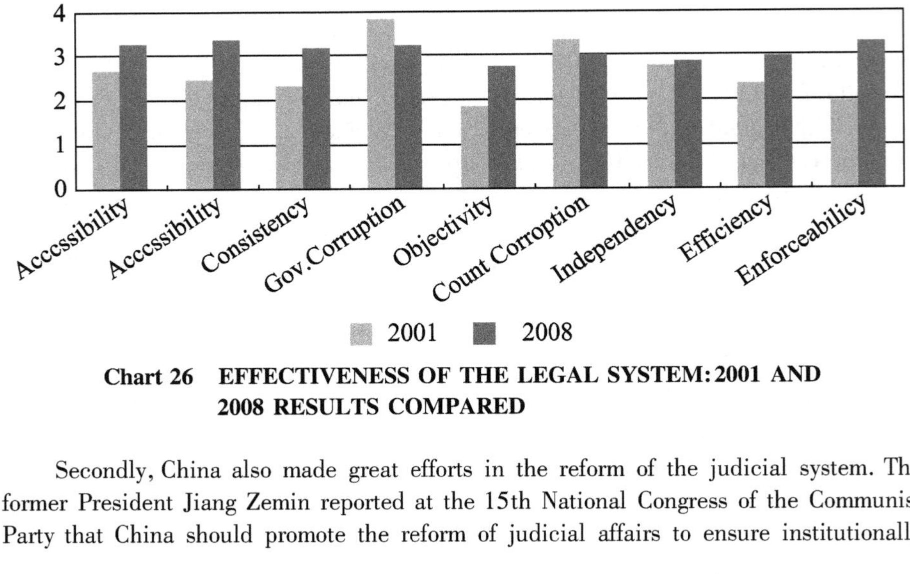

Chart 26 EFFECTIVENESS OF THE LEGAL SYSTEM: 2001 AND 2008 RESULTS COMPARED

Secondly, China also made great efforts in the reform of the judicial system. The former President Jiang Zemin reported at the 15th National Congress of the Communist Party that China should promote the reform of judicial affairs to ensure institutionally

[66] Wen Jiabao, Report on the Work of the Government, delivered at the Fourth Session of the Eleventh National People's Congress on March 5. 2011, *available at* http: //www. gov. cn/english/official/2011 – 03/15/, 1mtent_1 825268. htm (last visited on 21 June 2011).

that the judicial organs are in a position to exercise adjudicative and inspective powers in dependently and fairly according to law, and establish a system for investigating and prosecuting anyone who is held responsible for unjust or misjudged cases.[67] The same plan was reaffirmed in his report to the 16th National Congress.[68] As a result, the First 5 – Year Plan for Judicial Reform was carried out to enhance the independence of the judges, judicial credibility and reconstruction of a professional judiciary. The Supreme People's Court issued some judicial interpretations to achieve these goals.[69] In 2004 the Judicial Reform Steering Committee was established, which put forward 35 tasks to be finished covering ten aspects. By now the reform of the judicial system has resulted in remarkable achievements,[70] despite some upheavals in more recent years.

Last but not least, the effect of the BITs signed between China and other States could not be underestimated, especially when China's recent treaty practice introduces a generation of BITs transforming them into effective and powerful tools of investment protection.[71] Originally China was rather hesitant with regard to further liberalization of her BIT regime, particularly Oil the acceptance of national treatment standard and full access to international arbitration. However, the competition for FDI from the former USSR states, the Eastern European states, and the Latin American states since late 1990s, and the fact that China was emerging as an increasingly important export of foreign investment, notably to Asia and Africa, have led to a more liberal approach being adopted by the Chinese government. Thus in almost all newly signed investment treaties by China, all disputes arising from investment, rather than only disputes concerning amount of compensation for expropriation, have been allowed to be submitted to international arbitration without case by case consent by the host state. Furthermore, broader treatment standards are also provided.[72] These new generation BITs not only further strengthen the confidence of foreign investors by promising a safer and more reliable in-

---

〔67〕 The report, entitled "Hold High the Great Banner of Deng Xiaoping Theory for an All-round Advancement of the Cause of Building Socialism with Chinese Characteristics to the 21st Century", was delivered at the 15ch National Congress of the Communist Party of China (CPC) on September 12, 1997, *Available at* lmp: //www. china. org. cn/english/features/4560 7. htm (last visited on 21 June2011).

〔68〕 Jiang Zemin, Build a Well-off Society in an All-Round Way and Create a New Situation in Building Socialism with Chinese Characteristics, delivered at the 16th National Congress of the Communist Party of China on November 8, 2002, *available at* http: //news. xinhuanet. com/english/2002 – 11/17/content_632330. htm (last visited 011 21 June 2011).

〔69〕 These judicial interpretations include, such as Several Provisions of the Supreme People's Court on Strictly Enforce die System of Public Trial (enacted on March 8, 1999) and Measures of Supreme People's Court on the Management of Publication of Judgment Documents (effective as of June 15, 2000).

〔70〕 See Lang Guiguo and Ou Qiang. Judicial Reform in China. July 2007. Washington D. C., *available at* http: //www. iies. org/pubhcation/2b48df4c8dd0d36194e39ar28bl) 69a4/The% 20peopIes% 20courts% 20of% 20china% 20% 20% 20% 20duqing" /ĺ, 201angguimei% 20% 200722. pdf (last visited on 21 June 2011).

〔71〕 Stephan W. Schill, *supra* note 10, p. 77.

〔72〕 Comprehensive studies on the concept of the new generation of China s BIT may be found in the following articles. see. for example, Stephan Schill, supra note 10, 83 et seq; Callagher and Shan. supra note I. and Cai Congyan, *China-US BIT Negotiations and the Future of Investment Treaty Regime: A Grand Bilateral Bargain with Multilateral Implications*, Journal of International Economic Law, 2009, vol. 12. issue 2, pp. 457 – 506.

vestment climate based on notions of stability, reliability, and predictability,[73] but also help to transform China's domestic legal system supporting her transition to a market economy, and strengthening her further integration into the global economy.[74] It is expected that the role of China with regard to international investment law is being changed from a participant to a leader.[75]

V. CONCLUSIONS: TOWARDS A MORE EFFECTIVE FDI LEGAL SYSTEM IN CHINA

China's success in attracting FDI is undisputed, so is her effort to improve the FDI legal system. With her accession to the WTO and the reform of the governmental structure and the judicial reform, a rule-based governance structure is taking shape. As a result, foreign investors have growing confidence in the system, which is confimed in the 2008 survey.

However, China's current FDI legal system is yet to be considered as a fully "effective" legal system, let alone an ideal one or a "model". This finding from the 2008 study is affimed by some recent reports by leading business associations in China. A most recent report by the Millennium Challenge Corporation (MCC), for instance, reveals that China's performances in its control of corruption, rule of law and voice and accountability arc still under the level of median.[76] American Chamber of Commerce's 2010 business climate survey also reported that the top business challenge in China include: inconsistent regulatory interpretation, management-level human resources constraints, obtaining required licenses, national protectionism, bureaucracy, unclear regulations, lack of transparency, intellectual property rights, infringements, non management-level human resources constraints, visa difficulty for Chinese citizens traveling to the US.[77] In particular, foreign investors ranked inconsistent and arbitrary regulatory enforcement and lack of transparency among the major problems they face in China's market.[78] Clearly much more needs to be done.

In this connection, it is encouraging to see that the Chinese government seems to be taking some of the key issues very seriously. For example, the combat of corruption has been high on the political agenda and has achieved remarkable results. In his 2011 report to the People's Congress, for example, Premier Wen jiabao admitted that there was rampant corruption in some areas and that one of the important work of the government was to make further efforts to promote clean government and combat corruption.[79] The

---

〔73〕 Stephan W. Schill. *supra* note 10, p. 113.

〔74〕 Stephan W. Schill. *supra* note 10, p. 73.

〔75〕 Wang Guiguo, *China's Practice in International Investment Law: From Participation to Leadership in the World Economy*, 34 Yale journal of International Law 574, 2009.

〔76〕 Millennium Challenge Corporation Country Scorebook 2011, p. 82, *availble at* http://www.111cc.gov/documents/reports/reference-2010001042001-fyl 1-scorebook.pdf (last visited on 21 June 2011).

〔77〕 American Chamber of Commerce, *supra* note 6, p. 10.

〔78〕 US Department of states, 2011 Investment Climate Statement-China, *supra* note 39.

〔79〕 Wen jiabao, *supra* note 68.

11.1 The draft was finally adopted by the NPC, see Xinhua net, NPC adopt. s 12th Five-Year Plan, March 14, 2011, *available at* http://www.npcgov.cn/pc/11_4/2011-03/14/content_1646714.htm (last viewed on 21 June 2011).

draft of China 's 12th Five-Year Plan (2011 – 2015) also emphasizes that the government will resolutely prevent and punish corruption. 112 Clearly there is strong will in further improving the governance; hopefully there will also be ways to get it delivered.

Umbrella Clause and Investment Contracts under Chinese BITs: Are the Later Covered by the Former? *

1. Introduction

Recent arbitration practice shows that the umbrella clause has become one of the most challenging provisions in bilateral investment treaties (BITs). The clause takes its name from its main objective, namely bringing obligations of a host state to foreign investors under the protective umbrella of an applicable BIT or a multilateral investment treaty.[1] The umbrella clause can have far-reaching implications, the exact boundary of which is yet to be delimitated. Recent conflicting decisions by different arbitration tribunals on this matter suggest that the extent to which such clauses might "elevate" contractual obligations between a host stare and a foreign investor to the level of treaty obligations is far from settled.

Umbrella clauses arguably cover both contractual and non-contractual obligations.[2] However, it is undisputed that this clause is most closely associated with investment contracts, namely state contracts or "concession agreements." Guaranteeing rights under state contracts is arguably the primary purpose of the clause.[3] Hence it is better to address the two issues together.

China has now entered into more than 120 BITs and at least 50 of them have an um-

---

* *Journal of World Investment and Trade,* No. 2, 2010.

[1] The Energy Charter Treaty for example has an umbrella clause in the last sentence of Article 10(1).

[2] Umbrella clauses can potentially extend protection to non-contractual obligations undertaken by host states towards foreign investors in the form of. For instance, laws, regulations or licenses. For example, a UNCTAD research notes that 'the language of the provision is so broad that it could be interpreted to cover all kinds of obligations, explicit or implied, contractual or non-contractual. undertaken with respect to investment generally. A provision of this kind might possibly alter the legal regime and make the agreement subject to the rules of international law'. UNCTAD, 'Bilateral Investment Treaties. in the mid – 1990. (United Nations, 1998), 56.

[3] It has been noted that the concept of umbrella clause was first conceived by Sir Elihu Lauterpacht when he was advising the Anglo-Iranian Oil Company in early 1950s. And the purposes of such a device were to ensure that the host state observe its commitment towards foreign investor under a particular investment contract. AC Sinclair, 'The Origins of the Umbrella Clause in the International Law of Investment Protection', 20 Arbitration International(2004, No. 4), 414 – 418. See also T Walde, The "Umbrella Clause" in Investment Arbitration: A Comment on Original Intentions and Recent Cases, The journal of World Investment and Trade (Vol. 6, April2005 No. 2), 200 – 209.

brella clause. Meanwhile, there has been extensive practice of investment contract in China, particularly in the context of joint venture, joint exploitation (of petroleum resources) and build-operate-transfer operations. Although luckily so far there has been no case against China in international forum testing the application of such BIT provisions, it is important to analyse them now given that there have already been such cases in domestic courts and tribunals[4] and that there is huge potential of such cases in international forums in the wake of recent open access to international arbitration granted in recent BITs.[5]

This article therefore attempt to examine the umbrella clauses in Chinese BITs and investment contracts in China by mainly referring to jurisprudence in arbitration and court cases. It will first examine the umbrella clauses in Chinese BITs and discuss their legal implications by referring to jurisprudence of recent arbitration cases. It then moves on to analyse the main issues relating to investment contracts in China, including their nature, governing law, stabilization clause, governmental guarantees and dispute settlement. It concludes that whilst joint venture contracts normally are not states contracts, joint exploitation and BOT contracts are likely to be considered as state contract subject to the protection of umbrella clause under applicable investment treaties.

2. UMBRELLA CLAUSES IN CHINESE BITS

Among China's 120 strong BITs, only less than half of them (50) have a standard umbrella clause[6] or observation of obligations provision. This percentage is similar to the result of a survey on general BITs, which revealed that only about 40% of the BITs had such a clause?[7] The following section examines these clauses in Chinese BITs, including the standard and non-standard (broader or narrower) formulations, and its interaction with other BIT provisions such as "preservation of rights" clauses and the most-favoured-nation clause (the MFN Clause).

2.1 *THE STANDARD FORMULATION*

The standard formulation of umbrella clause in Chinese BITs[8] follows the Euro-

---

[4] See eg Changchun Huijin and Fuzhou Xingyuan cases. the details of which can be found in Wenhua Shan, The Legal Framework of EU-China Investment Relations: A Critical Appraisal, Oxford Hart Publishing 2005, p. 418.

[5] Since 1998, China has started to sign BITs with open access to international arbitration including ICSID arbitration. Under such BITS, not only previously allowed disputes concerning amount of compensation can be submitted to ICSID arbitration, all other investment dispute can also be submitted. For details see: Wenhua Shan and Norah Gallagher, Chinese Investment Treaties: Policy and Practices 2009, paras. 177 - 180 and 8.49 - 8.55.

[6] A few other BITs contain a "preservation of rights" clause, which has similar effect to an umbrella clause. See section 1.3.1 below.

[7] J Gill et al., 'Contractual Claims and Bilateral Investment Treaties: A Comparative Review of the SGS Cases' 21 J. Int'l. ARE. 397, 403 fn 31 (2004) (finding that approximately 40% of a sample of Brrs taken from investment treaties (ICSID ed., 2003) contained umbrella clauses).

[8] Both the 1980 and the 1990 Model BIT of China maintain a same umbrella clause, which states that "each contracting party shall observe any commitments it may have entered into with the investors of the other contracting party as regards to their investment". See Art. 2 (2). 1980 Model BIT and Art. 10 (2). 1990 Model BIT. It is interesting that the later Model BIT of China of 1994 does not appear to have any umbrella clause at all, see text online at: www. unctad. org/sections/diteliia/don/Compendium//n/64%20volum%203. pdf.

pean model.[9] A typical clause can be found, for example, in Article 2 (2) of the Sino-UK BIT, which states:

"Each Contracting Party shall observe any obligation it may have entered into with regard to investments of nationals or companies of the other contracting party."[10]

In most Chinese BITs that contain an umbrella clause, the language used includes "shall observe" or "shall respect" suggesting the imposition of a mandatory legal obligation. However, some BITs do have incorporated less strident language. The umbrella clause of the Sino-Iran BIT, for instance, only requires that either contracting parties "shall guarantee the observance of the commitments". This is similar to but even weaker than the language used in the Switzerland-Pakistan BIT, which requires the parties to "constantly guarantee the observance of the commitments".[11] The latter formula was regarded as "more ambiguous and may leave room for different interpretation".[12]

With regard to the scope of application, most Chinese BITs use very broad phrases such as "any obligation", "any commitments", or "any other obligation". Such phrases suggest a broader coverage of State undertakings. In the Partial Award rendered in *Eureko v Poland*, the tribunal held that "' Any' obligations is capacious; it means not only obligations of a certain type, but ' any' – that is to say, all-obligations..."[13] Likewise, the tribunal in the SGS v. Philippines case considered that the phrase "any obligation it has assumed with regard to specific investments in its territory" in Article x(2) of the Swiss-Philippines BIT was clearer and categorical than the umbrella clause in the Swiss-Pakistan BIT. Article 11 of that BIT obliged the Contracting Parties to observe "the commitments it has entered into with respect to the investments."[14]

Whilst most Chinese BITs refer to obligations "entered into" by a state, others refer to obligations "assumed"[15] by the state. The Sino-Australia BIT refers to "undertakings given by a competent authority". Such variations in wording probably do not make much difference to their meaning and application. Although it has been argued that the phrase "obligations entered into" may be interpreted as limiting the obligations in question to those undertaken vis – à – vis the other Contracting Party,[16] this view can hardly be sustained given that most umbrella clauses, including these in Chinese BITs, directly refer to obligations entered into by the State "with regard to investments of nationals or

---

[9] The 1991 Model BITs of UK (Art 2(2)), the 2000 Model BIT of Denmark (Art. 2. 3), the 2002 Model BIT of Sweden (Art. 2 (4)), for example, all follow this model. UNCTAD IIA Issue Papers: ' State Contract' (2004) 20.

[10] Art 2 (2). Sino-UK BIT, *available at* www. unctad. org/sections/dite/iia/docs/bitl/u k_china. pdf.

[11] Art 11. Swiss-Pakistan BIT.

[12] Katia Ya nuaca-Small, "Interpretation of the Umbrella Clause in the Investment Treaties", OECD Working Papers on International Investment (No. 2006/3. On 2006), p. 3.

[13] *Eurck B. V. v. Poland*, Partial Award 19 August 2005 para. 246.

[14] *SGS v. Philippines*, para. 119.

[15] See e. g., art 10. 2, Sino-Lebanon BIT; art 10. 2, Sino-Brunei BIT.

[16] W. Ben Hamida, La clause relative au respect des engagements dans les traites d'investissement, lnstitut des Hautes Etudes interna tionals, May 2005 at 2. 1, as cited in Yannaca-Small, 2006, pp. 10 – 11.

companies of the other contracting party".[17] Indeed, the Tribunal in *SGS v Pakistan* found the language "commitments entered into" broad enough to encompass both contractual obligations and unilateral obligations, including municipal acts and administrative measures.[18]

Despite this very broad formulation in BITs, however, it must be aware that not all obligations or commitments of a state are covered thereby. Purely commercial contracts, for instance, should not be covered. However, obligations assumed by the state as sovereign will be covered. This view finds support by both eminent scholars and jurisprudence of investment arbitration tribunals. Brower, for instance, commented that umbrella clauses should only apply "specifically to large-scale investment and concession contracts-in the making of which the state is deliberately 'exercising its sovereignty' – and thus it might be argued that the ordinary commercial contracts are an implied exception to the general rule..."[19] Walde is also of the view that the BIT and umbrella clause.. has no role" in case of "normal" contract disputes, i. e., "[I]f the core or centre of gravity of a dispute is not about the exercise of governmental powers... but about "normal" contract disputes.[20] The two SGS tribunals also declined to exercise jurisdiction in the cases, mainly on the ground that the disputes wen: : based essentially on a commercial contract, which gave local courts exclusive jurisdiction.[21] In *El Paso v Argentina* the tribunal concluded that,

> "in view of the necessity to distinguish the State as a merchant, especially when it acts through instrumentalities. from the State as a sovereign, the Tribunal considers that the "umbrella clause" in the Argentine-US BIT...can be interpreted in the light of Article VII(1) which clearly includes among the investment disputes under the Treaty all disputes resulting from a violation of a commitment given by the State as a sovereign State, either through an agreement, an authorization, or the BIT... Interpreted in this way, the *umbrella clause read in conjunction –with Article* VII, *will not extend the Treaty protection to breaches of at ordinary commercial contract entered into by the State or a State-owned entity,* but *will cover additional investment protections contractually agreed by the State as a sovereign –*

[17] This interpretation might be relevant when the umbrella clause refers to "obligations entered into with regard to investments", rather than "obligations entered into with regard to investments of investors of the other contracting party". Whilst European BITs tend to use the latter, earlier USA BIT as examplified by Article 2 (2)(c) of the US-Argentina BIT adopted the former formation. Article 2 (2)(c) of the US-Argentina BIT reads, "[E]ach Patty shall observe any obligation it may have entered into with regard to investments."

[18] *SGS v Pakistan* 163-166.

[19] Charles N. Brower, "The Future of Foreign Investment-Recent Developments in the International Law of Expropriation and Compensation", in V. S. Cameron (eds). Private Investors Abroad-Problems and Solutions in International Business in 1975 (Southwestern Legal Foundation symposium Series, Private Investors Abroad. Matthew Bender. New York, 1976), pp. 93. 105 n. 27 as cited by Antony Sinclair, " "The Origins of the Umbrella Clause in the International Law of Investment Protection", Arbitration International 2004, Vol. 20, No 4, pp. 411 – 434.

[20] Thomas Walde, "The Umbrella Clause in Investment Arbitration-A Comment on Original Intentions and Recent Cases', The Journal of World Investment and Trade, Vol. 6 No 2, April 2005, p. 236.

[21] The former tribunal held that it does toot have jurisdiction at all on the contractual disputes, whilst the latter considered it had jurisdiction but could not admit the case and therefore decided to stay the proceeding directing the parties to seek remedies first from the local courts designated in the underlying contract. See *SGS "Pakistan* and *SGS v Philippines.*

such as stabilization clause-inserted in an investment agreement."[22]

It is not the function of the umbrella clause to tum min or disagreements under a contract into a breach under international law. Clearly treaty provisions may only be invoked where there is a "specific breach of rights and violation of contract rights protected under the treaty."[23] Several requirements must be fulfilled before an umbrella clause might be invoked: there must be an investment, the state must have assumed a commitment or legal obligation towards that specific investment and the investor must have relied on those commitments in making or continuing its investment. In addition, the claimant must have the capacity to invoke the obligations assumed under the applicable law. If this is lacking, a BIT cannot be used to avoid the provisions of the contract including applicable law and any forum selection provision. It is therefore submitted that a standard umbrella clause should only apply to specific commitments and not to laws of general application.[24] The tribunal in *LG & E* did not analyse in any detail the fact that the obligation assumed "must have been assumed vis – à – vis the specific investment-not as a matter of the application of some legal obligation of a general character."[25] This is a key issue in applying the umbrella clause as the GAS Law may not have been covered if it did not target a ' specific investment' . This distinction would, correctly, preclude most municipal legislation from being covered by the umbrella clause.[26]

---

[22] *El Paso Energy international Company v Argeulina* ICSID Case No. ARB/03/15, Award on Jurisdiction, 27 April 2006. para 81. This view was endorsed by the tribunal (comprised of two of the same members as in El Paso) in *Pan American Energy LLC and BP Argentina Exploration Company Argentina* ICSID Case No. ARB/03/13 and *BP America Production Co. and other v Argentina ICSID* Case No. ARD/04/8 Award on Jurisdiction 27July 2006 at para. 108 where it confirmed "it was necessary to distinguish the State as a merchant from the State as a sovereign." There has been some concern voiced over the reliance by the tribunal on Article VII (the investor/ state dispute resolution provision) to interpret and essentially define the scope of a substantive provision of the treaty.

[23] *CMS v* Argentina, Jurisdiction. Para. 299.

[24] However, as discussed below, general obligations in the form of legislative acts may be caught by the Umbrella clause in case the applicable umbrella clause expressly covers both "general and specific" obligation/commitments, such as Article 3. 3 of the New Zealand BIT.

Withregard to the specific forms of specific obligation/commitments by host states. Fatouros considers that they include three types of commitments, namely approval instruments, concession agreements and guarantee contracts. Among them. both concession agreement and guarantee contracts are contractual commitments. whilst only approval instruments (or license/authorisation) are non-contractual instruments For further details see AA Fatouros. *Government* Guarantees to fo*reign investors* (Columbia University Press 1962), pp. 120 – 128.

[25] SGS v. Philippines, para. 121.

[26] It is a complex issue to ascertain whether a particular piece of legislation creates specific commitments towards certain investments or investors. The decisive criterion should be whether the target "investments or investors" are specific, not whether the commitments contained in the legislation are specific. In other words, if an act only applies to one or certain expressly identified foreign investors or foreign investments projects, as the special local regulation in the *Changchun Huijiu* case discussed below, it may be said that the act is targeting at those investors or investments identified and may therefor create specific obligation toward them. On the contrary, if an act does not expressly target any specific investment or investor, it may be assumed that it does not create specific commitments vis – à – vis those investments or investor, Unless it can be proved that the act actually targeted a certain specific investment project or investors which can be clearly identified at the time of the adoption of the act. The LG & E tribunal seemed to have missed the point here as it mainly analysed the: contents of the Gas Law and concluded that it created specific commitments. without sufficiently looking into the question whether the law actually targeted a particular investment project.

2.2 *NON-STANDARD FORMULATIONS*

2.2.1 NARROWER FORMATIONS

Whilst most BITs adopted by China include the standard format, a considerable number of them adopt a narrower formulation by imposing substantive limitations on the scope of application of the umbrella clause. There are mainly five categories of restrictive formulations, imposing restrictions such as "subject to local laws", "written obligation", "specific investments", "contractual obligation" concerning "approved investments", and "approved investment contracts" and "documents of approval". Details of these more restrictive formulations follow.

First of all, several BITs subject such obligation or commitments to the laws of the host state. The Sino-Belgium-Luxemburg BIT immediately after a standard umbrella clause in Article 9, adds that,

"The above special contracts or obligations shall be in conformity with the laws of the contracting parties accepting the investment and the provisions of this agreement."

Similar "domestic laws" limitation can be found in Sino-Thailand BIT[27] and Sino-Australia BIT.[28] The old Sino-Germany BIT is special in this context in that although it does not generally subject the umbrella clause to domestic law it guarantees that "the right of each contracting party to amend its general law shall remain unaffected."[29] The Sino-Thailand BIT not only subjects such obligation to the domestic law of the host state, but also requires that, in the event of any change of such laws of one contracting party, investors from the other contracting party "shall observe the new laws", but the former contracting party "shall make responsible arrangements for the appropriate interest" of the investors.[30] These BITs therefore make clear that host states are not precluded by the BITs from laying down new laws and regulations on foreign investment, though under the Sino-Thailand BIT, appropriate measures of adjustment must be made. However tempting, it would be a step too far to argue that without an express statement, host states would be prohibited from passing new laws, particularly those of general applicability rather than targeted specifically at the investors or investment concerned.[31] The implementation of legislation is an essential function of any government. As such it would be unthinkable that a BIT provision could deprive a sovereign government of this function. It is not inconceivable that certain laws of general application might have a significant impact on certain investors, . and as such, might give rise to the protection under

---

[27] Art 4.2 Sino-Thailand BIT.

[28] An 11, Sino-Australia BIT.

[29] Art 8 (2). Sino-Germany BIT (19R). This BIT is still currently effective. as the new one signed in 2003 is yet to be ratified and to take effect. In the new BIT, the "legal change" limitation is lifted. See Article 10 (2). 2003 Sino-Germany BIT.

[30] Art 4.2, Sino-Thailand BIT.

[31] It was partly for the avoidance of such consequences that the *SGs v Pakistan* tribunal denied the "elevator effect'" of the umbrella clause in the Swiss-Pakistan BIT. The *SGs v Pakistan* tribunal disagreed with *SGs "Pakistan* on the exact scope of application of the clause. it nevertheless shared the same concern and held that the umbrella clause only applied to a legal obligation that a host state assumed "vis – ὰ – vis the specific investment-not as a matter of the application of some legal obligation of a general character". *SGs v Pakistan.* para 166, *SGS v Philippines,* para. 121.

the umbrella clause.[32] The issue of whether and to what extent domestic legislation might be subject to the jurisdiction of the umbrella clause will be further examined in Section 2.2 below.

A second substantive qualification on the "obligation" requires that it be in "written" form. In this regard, the only example seems to be the Sino-Australia BIT, which stipulates,

"A contracting party shall, *subject to its law,* adhere to *any written undertakings* given by a competent authority to a national of the other contracting parry with regard to an investment *in accordance with its law and provisi ons of this agreement.* "[33] (emphasis added)

The intention of this qualification is obviously to exclude any obligation that may be granted in forms other than a written document, for example an oral promise. It is observed that some other Australian BITs[34] and a number of Mexican BITs[35] also have this requirement.

Thirdly, some BITs require contracting parties to observe only "specific commitments". As discussed below, a proper construction of an umbrella clause probably should confine its application to specific obligations/commitments, rather than extending it to obligations/commitments of a general nature[36]. Such a formulation nevertheless has the merit of clarifying it and as such preventing the adoption of a broader interpretation approach.

Fourthly, the Sino-Austria BIT[37] and the Sino-Jordan BIT[38] have a special qualification on the "obligation", which confines it to "any contractual obligations" with regard to investments "approved" by the host state. This wording would exclude any non-contractual obligation and any contractual obligation relating to an investment that has not been properly "approved" by the host state. Any unilateral measures by the host state that might give rise to its obligation towards foreign investors, such as a piece of

---

〔32〕 For example, the LG & E tribunal held that for the investment of the lG & E, the Gas Law and its regulations were not law of general nature, but were "very specific in relation to LG & E's investment in Argentina. so that their violation would he a violation of the umbrella clause". *LG & E v Argentina,* para. 174.

〔33〕 As can be seen in the provision and as said above, the BIT also attaches a double "domestic law" limitation. Art 11, Sino-Australia BIT.

〔34〕 Other such Australian BITs include theses signed with Chile, Papua New Guinea, and Poland. See Yannaca-Small, 2006, p. 11.

〔35〕 Including Mexican BITS entered into with Austria, Belgium-Luxemburg, Germany, Greece and France. Ibid.

〔36〕 The 1967 OECD draft Convention on the Protection of Foreign Property (Article 2). for example, adopted a rather broad ge neral formulation with its umbrella clause, which says: "(E) ach Party shall at all times ensure the observance of undertakings given by it in relation to property of nationals of any other Party. " However, its accompanying commentary insists that undertakings to be covered by this clause "must relate to the property concerned; it is not sufficient if the link is incidental". "Draft Convention on the protection of foreign property and Resolution of the Council of the OECD on the Draft Convention", OECD Publication No 23081, November 1967. Notes and Comments to Article 2, para. 3(a). Dolzer and Stevens also considered that these clauses "seek to ensure that each party to the treaty will respect specific undertakings towards nationals of the other party. " (Emphasis added) See R. Dolzer and M. Stevens "Bilateral Investment: Treaties". Kluwer Law, 1995, pp. 81 – 82.

〔37〕 Art 8. 2. Sino-Austria BIT.

〔38〕 Art 9. 2. Sino-Jordan BIT.

legislation providing certain incentives or guarantees for investments or a letter of guarantee from the government fall outside the reach of this clause. Only contractual obligation, such as a concession agreement, which is approved by the host state, is protected by this umbrella clause.

The fifth and last substantive limitation on "obligation" can be found in the Sino-Kuwait[39] and the Sino-United Arab Emirates BIT.[40] Like the Sino-Austria BIT and the Sino-Jordan BIT, these two BITs also link the umbrella clause to the approval of the investment project. However, they do not limit the obligation covered by the umbrella clause only to that based on "approved investment contracts", but also extend it to cover any obligation that may be included in the "document of approval of investments". What such "approved investment contracts" and "approval documents" are remains unclear and yet to be tested. However, when necessary the definitions on "investment authorisation" and "investment contract" in Model US BIT might be useful references.[41]

2.2.2 BROADER FORMULATIONS

A few BITs take an expansive approach in the umbrella clause adopting a broader formulation than the standard one. The Sino-New Zealand BIT, for instance, attempts to do so by bringing both "any obligations, whether general or specific" under this protection. Since it is yet to be tested in any case, it is unclear whether and to what extent the addition of the "whether general or specific" would affect the exact scope of application of the clause.

Another type of expansionary umbrella clause is where it covers not only investor-state contracts, but also contracts between foreign investors and domestic private parties.[42] The Sino-Singapore BIT, for example, stipulates that,

"Each contracting party shall observe any commitment in accordance with its laws additional to chose specified in this agreement *entered into by the contracting party, its nationals or companies With nationals or companies of the other contractin g party as re-*

---

[39] Art 2.2. Sino-Kuwait BIT.

[40] Art 2.3. Sino-United Arab Emirates BIT.

[41] The 2004 US Model BIT defines the two terms as follows:

"investment agreement" means a written agreement between a national authority of a Party and a covered investment or an investor of the other Party, on which the covered investment or the investor relics in establishing or acquiring-a covered investment other than the written agreement itself: that grants rights to the covered investment or investor:

(a) with respect to natural resources that a national authority controls. such as for their exploration, extraction, refining, transportation, distribution. or sale;

(b) to supply services to the public on behalf of the Party, such as power generation or distribution, water treatment or distribution. or telecommunications; or

(c) to undertake infrastructure projects. such as the construction of roads. bridges. canals. dams, or pipelines, that are not for the exclusive or predominant use and benefit of the government.

"investment authorization' means an authorization that the foreign investment authority of a Party grants to a covered investment or an investor of the other Party."

See Art 1. US Model BIT 2004.

[42] Art 15. Sino-Singapore U1T; Art 15. Sino-Sri Lanka BIT; Art 10. Sino-Yugoslavia BIT.

gards their investment."[43]

At first reading the provision looks rather strange if not absurd: whilst it is easy to understand that a host state should observe any commitment it entered into with private parties of the other contracting party, it seems excessive to require it to likewise "observe" "any commitment" entered into between two private parties without any particular involvement of the host state. A requirement of the host state to respect the freedom of contract and to refrain from interfering with the contractual relationship between two private parties of the two contracting parties might be what was called for under such a clause. This seems to have been confirmed by a similar provision included again by Singapore, but ten years later with the Czech Republic, which reads,

"(2) Each Contracting Party shall observe commitments, additional to those specified in this Agreement it has entered into with respect to investments of the investors of the other Contracting Party. Each Contracting Party shall not interfere with any commitments, additional to those specified in this Agreement, *entered into by nationals or companies with the nationals or companies of the other contracting Party as regards their investments*" (emphasis added).

This BIT thus separates the host state's obligation under a typical umbrella clause from its obligation vis – à – vis a private-private contractual relationship, which is not to interfere therewith. In a way, it might be regarded as a remote echo to Professor Walde's viewpoint and the *CMS v Argentina* award, which require the host state not only to observe the obligations and commitments it has specifically undertaken toward investments, but also to respect the freedom of contract and not to interfere with the rights of foreign investors under a commercial contract. It remains to be seen what the exact legal effect of this provision would be, in particular, whether any breach of the second obligation relating to private parties would give rise to a treaty breach.

2.3 *INTERACTION WITH OTHER RELEVANT BIT PROVISIONS*

2.3.1 UMBRELLA CLAUSE AND THE "PRESERVATION OF RICHTS CLAUSE"

In addition to the 50 BITs of China that contain an umbrella clause, there are six BITs that contain a "preservation of rights" clause. These clauses have a similar effect to an umbrella clause.[44] Among them, the Sino-France BIT is unique in that it is targeted only to special commitments given by the host state. More specifically, it stipulates that if an investment is made in accordance with a special commitment made by the host government, and the special commitment is more favorable than treatment under the present BIT, then the investment should be treated in accordance with the conditions under the special commitment.[45] The other five BITs deal with both "special commitments" and domestic laws. A good example can be found in Article 10 of the Sino-Qatar BIT, which stipulates that:

"If the treatment to be accorded by one contracting party in accordance with its laws and regulations or based on an undertaking or a special agreement to investors or activities associated with such investments of investors of the other investors of the other

---

[43] Art 15. Sino-Singapore BIT.

[44] Such BITs include these with France (art 9), Czech (2005, art 10.2), Korea (art 12.2), Cambodia (art 10), Qatar (art 10). Zimbabwe (art 10).

[45] Art 9. Sino-France BIT.

contracting party is more favorable than the treatment provided for in this agreement, the more favorable treatment shall be applicable."

Unlike the umbrella clauses, which address the issue (of assurance of special investment projects) from the perspective of the host state by forcing it to observe its obligations/commitment towards investments, these "preservation of rights" clauses address the same issue from the angle of the foreign investors, by entitling them to the more favorable treatment under such special undertakings or commitment. In other words, both of them serve the same aim, although the routes taken to achieve it are different. It would be hard to tell which way is more effective. However, by directly comparing treatment under a special "undertaking or special commitments" with that under an international treaty (the present BIT) and placing the former in a prevailing position, the "preservation of right" route seems to impose a stronger international obligation in the case of any breach of such standard of treatment.

There are also five further BITs that provide for such "preservation of rights" guarantee, in addition to a proper umbrella clause.[46] The combined effect should further enhance the assurance that special commitments made to foreign investors by host governments would be effective under international law.

2.3.2 UMBRELLA CLAUSE AND THE MFN CLAUSE

As mentioned above, less than half of the Chinese BITs have an umbrella clause. This raises a question of whether an "umbrella clause" can be "multiplied" by applying the most favored nation treatment clause (MFN clause). The interaction between the umbrella clause and the MFN clause is a very interesting topic, even though it is yet to be tested in practice. In the international investment treaty framework, the two clauses are distinctive in that both of them serve as leverage. The MFN clause is like a "multiplier", in that it can extend rights in one BIT to other BITs entered into by the same state[47] Likewise, the umbrella clause is somehow like an "elevator", as argued by SGS in its case against Pakistan,[48] in that it "elevates" obligations normally under domestic law and subject to domestic jurisdiction, to these under international law and subject to international jurisdiction. Both mechanisms, the multiplier and the elevator, are understandably subject to qualifications and limitations,[49] although the exact boundary of

---

[46] They are BITs concluded with Kuwait (arts 2.2 and 11). United Arab Emeritus(arts 2.3 and 13), Egypt (arts 2.2 and 13), Tunisia (arts 10.1 -3) and Argentina (arts 3.1 and 9).

[47] See for example *Maffezini v. Spain*, ICSID Case No. ARB/97/7 where the tribunal endorsed the view that the investor could avail of more favorable dispute Solution provision in another BIT.

[48] *SGS v Pakistan*, para. 163.

[49] For instance, it is settled that the MFN clause should be applied to benefits resulting from legal instruments of the same nature *(ejusdem generis)* to a BIT, rather than treaties of any kind. Often, it is also subject to express, exceptions stipulated in BITs such as customs unions, free trade areas, double-taxation treaties, etc. Likewise, it is suggested that umbrella clauses should only cover obligations/commitments towards a "specific investment"rather than universally applicable obligation or commitments. Shan, legal framework (stating limitations on MFN clause application). 151; *SGS v Philippines*, para 121 (stating that: [F]or Article x(2) to be applicable, the host State must have assumed a legal obligation, and it must have been assumed vis - à - vis the specific investment not as a matter of the application of some legal obligation of a general character). This is very far from elevating to the international level all "the municipal legislative or administrative or other unilateral measures of a Contracting Party".

each is unclear. One of the key current debates on MFN clauses is whether it should cover benefits resulting from procedural and jurisdictional provisions, on which different tribunals have reached different or even conflicting interpretations. It is settled that substantive provisions under BITs are eligible to benefit from the MFN clause. It is thus necessary to ascertain whether an umbrella clause might be classified as a substantive provision. The tribunal in the *SGS v Pakistan* case arrived at a negative conclusion partly on the ground of the location in the BIT of the umbrella clause. It was located towards the end after the bulk of substantive provisions.[50] In contrast, in the *SGS v Philippines* case the tribunal answered this question in the positive. It held that whilst the location of the clause is relevant it is not decisive. Further, it stated:

"In particular, it is difficult to accept that the same language in other Philippines BITs is legally operative but that it is legally inoperative in the Swiss-Philippines BIT merely because of its location."

In this regard, it is interesting to discover that among the 50 Chinese BITs with umbrella clauses, 34BITs place the clause towards the end of the text whilst only a small number of BITs (16) do so in the earlier part.[51] It is submitted that the *SGs v Philippines* tribunal's position should be upheld and that whether or not an umbrella clause is substantive and therefore operative should not be decided by the mere fact of its location in the BIT text. As a result, one could not simply say that they should operate and can be multiplied in the first 34 BITs but not in the other 16 BITs. A better approach to this issue of interpretation is to leave it for the tribunal to decide on a case-by-case basis by taking into account the relevant circumstances, particularly the specific obligation/commitment at issue. In theory, an umbrella clause can cover both substantive and procedural obligation/commitments. Whether or not the clause is "substantive" should therefore be judged on the particular obligation/commitment involved. If the obligation is of "substantive" nature, e. g. a tax incentive, it can be multiplied by the operation of the MFN clause, if the obligation at issue is to do with a "procedural/jurisdictional" obligation, such as a wider range of choices of international arbitration, it may or may not be multiplied by employing the MFN clause. As the question of whether an umbrella clause would work as an elevator remains unresolved, one can hardly imagine that foreign investors would venture to sue a host state based on a BIT without such a clause but an MFN clause.

---

[50] The tribunal reasoned that: "Given the above structure and sequence of the rest of the Treaty, we consider that, had Switzerland and Pakistan intended Article 11 to embody a substantive "first order" standard obligation. they would logically have placed Article II among the substantive "first order" obligations set out in Articles 3 to 7. The separation of Article II from those obligations by the subrogation article and the two dispute settlement provisions (Articles 9 and 10), indicates to our mind that Article 11 was not meant to project a substantive obligation like those set om in Articles 3 to 7, let alone one that could, when read as SGS asks us to read it, supersede and render largely redundant the substantive obligations provided for in Articles 3 to 7."

See *SGS v pakistan*, para 170.

[51] They include the BITs with Denmark (art 3.1), Netherlands (200 1. art 3.4), UK (an 2.2). Switzerland (art 5), Hungary (art 3.1), Spain (1992, art 3.1), Greece (an: 2.6), Iceland (art 2.2), Macedonia (art 2.3). Bosnia Herzegovina (art 3.2), Thailand (art 4.2), Kuwait (art 2.2), United Emirates (art 2.3), New Zealand (art 3.3), Egypt (art 2.2) and Argentina (art 3.1).

3. INVESTMENT CONTRACTS IN CHINA AND THE ASSOCIATED LEGAL ISSUES

Depending on the level of involvement of the government authorities, invesml ent contracts in China can be categorized into three types, namely joint venture contracts (JV contracts), joint exploitation of petroleum resources contracts (Joint exploitation contracts) and build-operate-transfer (BOT) contracts. Joint venture contracts and joint exploitation contracts do not directly involve a state party (i. e., the central or local governments), whilst in BOT contracts a governmental authority is directly involved as a contracting party. The major difference between a JV contract and joint exploitation contract is that the Chinese party involved in the latter is one of the three state enterprises with a monopoly on the rights to develop petroleum resources,[52] rather than normal private companies, as in most of the JV contracts. In other words, there is little if any, involvement of governmental authorities in a normal JV contract, whilst there is more such involvement in a joint exploitation contract, and most in a BOT contract. Further details on these types of contracts follow.

3.1 *JOINT VENTURES CONTRACTS*

3.1.1 JOINT VENTURES IN CHINA

A joint venture is one of the main forms of foreign investment in China.[53] By the end of 2005, joint ventures were still the most commonly used structure for FDI, which has been used in 317,438 investment projects bringing in 32.86 billion US $ of actual investment, amounting to 57% and 52% of the total number of investment projects and amount of actual investment in the country respectively.[54] (Table 1) If a foreign investor wants to invest in China but for some reason does not want to take on all the risks, he/she may decide to cooperate with a local Chinese firm and set up a Sino-foreign joint venture. The joint venture can be an equity joint venture (EJV), under which the rights and obligations of the JV partners are divided in accordance with the equity (shares) they possess, or a contractual joint venture (CJV), under which everything is defined by the JV contract between the partners.[55] With the change in the investment law in 1979, China started to accept foreign investment.[56] Originally, EJVS were the only

---

[52] See Article 5 of the State Responsibility Articles. See also *Wintershall A. G. et al. v. Government of Qatar* (1989). Partial Award on Liability of 5 February 1988, 28 I LM 795 (1989). section 2.

[53] Other forms include wholly foreign owned enterprises (WFEs), joint exploration of oil resources, build-operate-transfer, foreign invested holding companies, foreign invested merger and acquisition, etc. For further details, see Shan, Legal Framework, pp. 39 – 46.

[54] However, it is noticeable that WFEs have increased significantly in recent years and have already brought in the most investment in China according 10 contractual value. Hence it can be anticipated that WFE will soon replace JVs and become the most common form of investment in China. See Table for details of statistics.

[55] In general, CJV is less regulated by the state and allows more flexbility for the partners in determining their JV relationship. For more, see Shan. ibid., pp. 39 – 41.

[56] China's first law of foreign investment, which also legally signalled China's decision to embrace a "opening-up" policy, was the Law of Sino-Foreign Equiry Joint Ventures (hereinafter referred to as "EJVL"), adopted at the Second Session of the Fifth National People's Congress on 1 July 1979.

form of foreign investment in China until 1986, when a new law[57] was promulgated to allow wholly foreign owned enterprises to be set up in China. CJV investment was made legally possible in 1988 when the Law of Sino-Foreign Contractual Joint Ventures was a-dopted.[58]

Table 1 FDI IN CHINA BY FORM OF INVESTMENT (BY THE END OF 2005)

Unit: 100 million US $

Foml	Projects		Contractual Investment		Actual Investment	
	Number	Percentage	Amount	Percentage	Amount	Percentage
Total	552. %0	100	12, 856. 73	100	6. 345. 06	100
JV total	317, 43R	57. 4 1	5, 991. 98	46. 61	3, 285. 90	51. 79
EJV	260. 4 17	47. 10	4, 119. 20	32. 04	2, 370. 27	37. 36
CJV	157. 021	10. 31	1, 872. 78	14. 57	915. 63	14. 43
WFE	235. 124	42. 52	6, 773. 32	52. 68	2, 821. 83	44. 47
FISC*	157	0. 03	42. 51	0. 33	32. 47	0. 51
JE	191	0. 03	47. 40	0. 37	75. 07	1. 18
Others	50	0. 01	1. 52	0. 01	129. 79	2. 05

* FISC stands for "foreign invested stock company'", a stock company with at least 25 per-cent of the total shares being owned by foreign investors.

Source: FDI Statistics, Ministry of Commerce, China, *available at* http: //www. fdi. gov. cn/pub/FDI/wztj/lntjsj/wstzsj/2005nzgwztj/t20060906_6133 7. htm (last visited on 26 December 2008).

3.1.2 JOINT VENTURE CONTRACTS

In either an EJV or a CJV investment, a contract between the two JV partners is essential. According to relevant Chinese legislation, such JV contracts have to be ap-proved by the central or local authorities, before they take effect.[59] Such legislation also generally requires the JV parties to conclude an "agreement" (Xieyi), in addition to the contract (Hetong).[60] The agreement is a written document between the JV parties

[57] The Law of Wholly Foreign Owned Enterprises (here after referred to as "WFEL"), adopted at the Fourth Session oft he Sixth People's Congress, promulgated by Order No. 39 of the President of the People's Republic of China and took effect on 12 April 1986.

[58] The Law of Sino-Foreign joint Ventures (hereafter referred to as "CJVL"), adopted at the First Session of the Seventh National People's Congress and promulgated by the Order No. 4 of the President of the People's Republic of China 13 April 1988, and took effect on the same day.

[59] Art. 3, EJVL: Art. 5, CJVL, For further details on the approval process. See Shan. ibid., pp. 123 – 136.

[60] For example, CJVL, EJVL and their implementing regulations general require the JV parties to submit both the "agreement" and the "contract" for approval. See Art 3, EJVL and Art. 7 of its implementing regulations, and Art 5. CJVL and Art. 7 of its implementing regulations.

with regard to the principles and main aspects on the establishment of the JV business,[61] which the parties normally formulate at an earlier stage of their negotiation. In contrast, the JV contract is normally formulated at a later stage, which stipulates the detailed rights and obligations of the parties with regard to the establishment of a JV enterprise.[62] In case of any conflict between the two instruments, the contract prevails.[63] The duality of contractual instruments obviously may result in confusion among foreign investors. Chinese legislation nevertheless provides that the JV parties may opt out of such a requirement if they so agree.[64]

3.1.3 THE NATURE OF J0INT VENTURE CONTRACTS

The content of JV contracts, together with the fact that both contracting parties are independent commercial entities rather than the government or its agencies, demonstrates that JV contracts are generally commercial contracts,[65] not state contract. In this connection, it would be useful to recall the decisions in the *Egypt* V. *Spp* case by two French courts, the Court of Appeal of Paris and the Court of Cassation, which set aside an award rendered by an International Chamber of Commerce (ICC) arbitration tribunal, on the ground that the Egyptian Government was a party to a contract between the claimant (SPP, et al.) and an Egyptian public company (the EGOTH), which included an arbitration clause submitting disputes to Ice arbitration tribunals.[66] In reaching this conclusion, the Court of Appeal reasoned that, first of all, "[E]gyptian State did not appear among the persons having the capacity of parties to the transaction and, conse-

---

[61] Art 10, implementting Regulations of the EJVL, and Art. 10 of the implementing Regulations of the CJVL.

[62] Ibid.

[63] Ibid.

[64] Ibid.

[65] Despite a legacy of a restricted economy. more than two decades of economic: reform has significantly transformed Chinese companies to independent legal entities undertaking obligations in their own names. Most of them are no longer an auxiliary to a governmental department, nor do they exercise any public authority. Therefor, the contracts they enter into with foreign investors should generally be regarded as purely commercial contracts, rather than state contracts. See M Yao. Textbook on Foreign investment Enterprises (Law Press China. 1990), pp. 72 - 73.

There are, nevertheless, still certain State Owned Enterprises (SOEs) that may he exercising some elements of governmental authority, which will be discussed later.

[66] The Ice tribunal arrived at decision in favour of the foreign investors, SPP and *SPP* ME. and held that Egypt should be considered as a party to the contract. The tribunal reasoned that: "In our view, the requirement of the Minister's signature m ant and was understood to mean by the panics that through the signature of the Minister, not only was the Government confirming its approval of all contractual obligations undertaken by EGOTH in compliance with the laws of Egypt, *but it was also guaranteeing to the investor its continuing agreement and support if the project.* By the Minister signing not only "approved" but also "agreed" (which clearly means the undertaking of an obligation of its own) *the government also became a contractual party to the December Agreement.* " (Emphasis added) For further details of the award, see International Chamber of Commerce Court of Arbitration: Award in the Arbitration between S. P. P. (Middle East) Limited. Southern Pacific Properties Limited and the Arab Republic *or* Egypt, The Egyptian General Company for Tourism and Hotels (March 11, 1983), 22 International Legal Materials (ILM) 752, pp. 766 - 767. para. 46.

quently, was not bound by it".[67]

However, there are two main complications that may arise. The first complication is that it is possible that some local JV partners may be state owned enterprises (SOEs). Whilst most SOEs are independent commercial entities that do not· exercise any governmental authorities, other SOEs may have been "empowered" by domestic law to "exercise elements of governmental authority". If the latter is the case, in light of the ILC Articles on Responsibility of States for Internationally Wrongful Act (State Responsibility Articles), the conduct of such SOE JV partners "shall be considered as an act of the State under international law", provided that they are "acting in that capacity m the particular instance".[68] Consequently, JV contracts between foreign investors and such SOE JV partners may be considered as "state contracts".[69] Such contracts may cover a wide range of areas such as "loan agreements, purchase contracts for supplies or services, contract of employment, or large infrastructure projects, such as the construction of highways, ports or dams".[70] Atypical state contract of this category may be found in China's joint exploitation contracts with foreign enterprises examined below.

The second complication is that, as indicated above, Chinese laws require that all JV contracts, including any amendments thereto, be approved by the competent governmental authorities, before they can take effect.[71] A question thus arises as to whet her or not such act of approval will result in the Chinese government becoming a party to the contract and therefore the contract becoming a state contract.

The answer to this question should be in the negative. This is because, first of all, the act of approval is a regular exercise of governmental authority. It is not intended to alter the specific terms and conditions under a JV contract, but to oversee such con tracts making sure that they are in line with the public interests. In the aforementioned *SPP v Egypt* case, for example. the Court of Appeal of Paris considered the signature of the Minister of Tourism "approving, agreeing and ratifying" the contract constitute "not a solemn commitment by the State to enter into the contract, but specifically the material manifestation of approval by the supervising authority".

Secondly, a closer examination of approval criteria under relevant Chinese laws confirms that the required approval is not intended to interfere with the freedom of contract of the parties, but to exercise the supervisory power of the government. Whilst such

---

〔67〕 France: Court of Appeals of Paris Decision in *Arab Republic of Egypt* v. *Southern pacific properties, Ltd. et al.* (Appellate Review of Arbitral Awards between States and Private Parties), 23 International Legal Materials (ILM) 1004, 1056: France: *Court of Cassatiou Derision in Southern Pacific Properties Ltd. et al. v Arab Republic of Egypt* (Appellate Review *or* Arbitral Awards Between States: And Private Parties, January 6, 1987), 26 International Legal Materials (ILM) 1004. 1007.

〔68〕 ILA State Responsibility Articles. art 5.

〔69〕 In this connection, it is useful to recall a recent UNCTAL definition on state contracts, which include not only contracts concluded by a state, but also contracts entered into by ' an entity of the State. which... may be defined as any organization created by statute within a State that is given control over an economic activity'. See UNCTAD Series on issues in international investment agreements: *State Contracts* (UNCTADIITE/IJT/2004/11) 3.

〔70〕 Ibid.

〔71〕 Art. 3, EJVL; Art. 5, CJVL. For further details on the approval process. See Shan, ibid., pp. 123 – 136.

laws do not specify the criteria against which a JV project is approved, they do provide for certain conditions under which a JV contract may not be approved. The Implementing Regulations of the EJV Law, therefore, stipulate that a JV project will not be approved, if it is: (1) detrimental to Chinese State Sovereignty; or (2) against Chinese law; or (3) incompatible with the needs of China's national economic development; or (4) causing pollution to the environment; or (5) the agreement, contract and articles of association concluded are apparently unfair *(Xianshi Gongping)* and detrimental to the interests of one party.[72] The Implementing Regulations of the CJVL have a similar provision, although it deleted the fifth condition and added to the list JV projects that are detrimental to public interests or state security.[73] Apart from the fifth requirement, all of the conditions are clearly related to public interests, rather than private interests of the contracting parties. Even the fifth condition could be considered a public interest condition, because it is aimed at ensuring the balance of interests between the contracting parties, and hence achieving the public policy of "fairness" in JV contractual relations. It is nor intended to enable governmental authorities to interfere at will with specific contractual arrangement. Indeed, a similar public policy clause can be found in China's Contract Law, which stipulates that "apparently unfair" *("xianshi gongping")* contracts can be changed or terminated.[74] It would be absurd to say that because of such a clause, the Chinese government shall be responsible for all breaches of such contracts.

The contents of a Certificate of Approval, thirdly and finally, demonstrate that by approving a JV contract the Chinese government does nor commit itself to any contractual relationship with the foreign investor concerned, unlike the Egyptian Minister of Tourism's approval of the contract in the *SPP v Egypt* case, which directly affixed to the end of the contract,[75] a standard Certificate of Approval in China takes the form of a separate document, which includes items such as names in Chinese and English, address, type of business, name of investors and their place of incorporation, general amount of investment, registered capital, capital contributions of parties, and scope of

---

〔72〕 The Implementing Regulations of EJVL, art 4.

〔73〕 Ibid., art 9.

〔74〕 Contract law of the People's Republic of China, art 54 (2).

〔75〕 This factor was interpreted by the lee tribunal as signaling the government's willingness to be bound by the contract and become a parry to it, but was subsequently rejected by the Paris Court of Appeal, which held that: "even if it is not common for a supervisory authority to affix his authorization directly on the document submitted for his supervision, the exceptional nature of the negotiations in question could be sufficient to explain this circumstance" and that "on the contrary, it should be emphasized that the parties carefully separated their signatures and that the Minister's signature was affixed separately and clearly placed at the end of the contract".

See International Chamber of Commerce Court of Arbitration: Award in the Arbitration between S. P. P. (Middle East) limited. Southern Pacific Properties limited and the Arab Republic Of Egypt. The Egyptian General Company for Tourism and Hotels (March 1 I. 1983), 22 international Legal Materials (ILM) 752, p. 766, para 44; and France: court of *appeals of par is decision in Ara b Republic of Egypt v* Southern *Pacific Properties. Ltd. et al.* (Appellate Review of Arbitral Awards between Stares and Private Parties), 23 International Legal Materials (ILM) 1004, 1058.

business.[76] It does not include any commitment or guarantees of the government[77] Thus one cannot establish a contractual relationship between the foreign investor and the government, from either the JV contract itself or issuing the certificate of approval. Indeed, it would be absurd to argue that the mere act of approval would make the Chinese government a party to a myriad of JV contracts[78] and assume state responsibility for any breach of such contracts.

The same approach should also be applied to the interpretation of the umbrella clauses in the Sino-Kuwait[79] and the Sino-United Arab Emirates BIT.[80] They require the host state to observe "any obligation it may have entered into in the documents of approval of investments or the approved investment contracts" of investors of the home state. Such provisions should not be construed so as to render the host state a party to a normal JV contract and responsible for any breach. Rather, they should be understood to cover only such approved investment contracts, whether or not in JV form, in which the state has somehow committed itself to undertake certain obligations. More specifically, they probably refer to investment contracts entered into by local companies (in most cases SOEs) that are "empowered to exercise element of governmental authority", as discussed above. For example, in a dispute between Jiangsu Provincial Government and an American company with regard to a purchase agreement between three local electricity companies and the American company, MIGA's General Counsel LS Weisenfield considered that conduct of the local companies could be attributed to the Chinese government. As such, the unilateral decision to alter electricity tariffs amounted to breach of contract by the Government.[81]

Likewise, whilst a standard Certificate of Approval of a JV project may not render

---

[76] MOFTEC (now MOFCOM) Notice on the Adoption of the New Vision of the "Certificate of Foreign Invested Enterprises of the People's Republic of China", adopted by the MOFTEC on 5 October 1993, which attaches a standard Certificate of Approval.

[77] In this connection, it is interesting to note that the Icc tribunal on the *Spp v Egypt* case has attempted to set out certain specific obligations that Egyptian government had committed by the signature of approval of Minister of Tourism:

"By the signature of the Minister the government undertook the following obligations:

1. It reaffirmed in the context of the redefinition of the Agreement between SPP and EGOTH the support of the Government promised in the September Agreement.

2. It committed the. Government to the support of the project as defined in both Agreements.

3. It consequently committed the Government not to take any steps which would prevent that project being carried through to completion."

Whilst it is commendable to make effort to clarify such obligations. it perhaps has gone a step too far in subjecting the host government to such an extensive list of obligations, particularly those under item Nos. 2& 3. See International Chamber of Commerce Court of Arbitration: Award in the Arbitration between S. P. P. (Middle East) Limited, Southern Pacific Properties Limited and the Arab Republic of Egypt. The Egyptian General Company for Tourism and Hotels (March 11, 1983). 22 International legal Materials (ILM) 752, p. 766, para. 46.

[78] As can be Seen from Table 1. by the end of 2005, there have been 317.43M JV projects and hence at least the same number of JV contracts that have been signed between foreign and local JV partners in China.

[79] Art 2.2. Sino-Kuwait BIT.

[80] Art 2.3. Sino-United Arab Emirates BIT.

[81] A Chen. Monograph on International Economic Law (Higher Education press China, 2002. in Chinese), pp. 642 – 643.

the state accountable for breach of the JV contract covered by the Certificate, the state might be held accountable if it includes in the Certificate substantive commitments or guarantees towards foreign investors or the approved foreign invested enterprise. As Fatouros noted, an instrument of approval might have been "preceded by official or semi-official negotiations and constitute, in fact and in spice of their form, a kind of agreement between the state and the investor, providing for the granting of guarantees to the latter and for his corresponding obligations".[82] To illustrate it, he refers to an investment of approval by the Greek Government in May 1956 as an example.[83] The investment took the form of a Royal Decree, which is irrevocable and cannot be modified except with the investor's consent in accordance with local legislation pursuant to which the decree was issued.[84] The decree starts with a statement of approval of the investment, but includes in it a number of guarantees.[85] For example, the investing company is allowed to transfer abroad, without limitation, the capital imported and its profits. It is entitled to exemptions from import duties and other charges on the machinery imported by it, as well as all city and other local taxes and charges, during the initial period of ten years. It may, furthermore, employ foreign personnel up to one-forth of the total employees.[86] If the same kind of guarantees or commitments were included in a certificate of approval of a JV project, then the Chinese government would have to honour them. Otherwise, it could be held responsible for breach of the "umbrella clause" in the Sino-Kuwait and Sino-United Arab Emeritus BITS. However, in most cases this will not occur, since a standard Certificate of Approval, as mentioned above, does not contain any such guarantees.

3.1.4 APPLICABLE LAW

A second legal issue relating to JV contracts is the law that governs such contracts. In this regard, Chinese laws require that Chinese law be the governing law of JV contracts, including their formation, effect, interpretation, execution and the settlement of any disputes related thereto.[87] Such a requirement is mandatory and cannot be contracted out by the parties. Chinese scholars have argued that there are two main reasons

[82] AA Fatouros, Government Guarantees to Foreign Investors, Columbia University Press, 1962, pp. 123 – 124. It must be noted that different states adopt different met hods of approving foreign investment projects. Whilst some countries, such as China, distance itself from direct involvement in the JV contractual relationship, other countries tend to substantially involved therein. For example, in some African states, important foreign investment projects are subject to the same approval procedures as international treaties. In other African states such as Ghana, the review and approval process does not only involve passive assessment of the eligibility of the projects, but also positive suggestions and proposed changes. which would amount to ' a kind of agreement between the state and the investor', as described by Fatouros. Indeed, the Capital Investment Act of Ghana requires that the approval granted by its Foreign Investment Commission be transformed into an official agreement between the foreign investor and the Ministry of Finance. Ghana: Capital Investment Act 1963, Section Z (3), as cited in M Yao, Comparative Foreign Investment Law (Wuhan University Press, 1993, in Chinese), 557.

[83] Royal Decree of 30 May/23 June 1956, concerning the approval of an investment on the exploitation of asbestos in Greece by an American company, Kennecott Copper Corporation. as cited in Fatouros. ibid., pp. 124 – 219.

[84] Ibid., 124.

[85] Ibid., 124 – 125.

[86] Ibid.

[87] The Implementing Regulations of EJVL, art 12; the Implementing Regulations of the CJVL. art 55; and Contract law. art 126.

supporting such a seemingly arbitrary rule:[88] (1) petroleum resources are natural resources and therefore are subject to the "permanent sovereignty over natural resources" of the host state, China;[89] and (2) such contracts have the closest connection with China, because all of the major connecting factors point toward China: (a) they are concluded in accordance with Chinese law and approved by Chinese government; (b) they are entered into in China; (c) the subject matter lies in and belong; to China; (d) they are performed in China.[90] Indeed, a survey by the author among EU investors has shown that a half of the JV respondents actually expressed "satisfaction" with such a rule.[91]

However, Chinese law also respects international treaty obligations. For example, Article 142 of the General Principles of Civil Law (GPCL), whilst stipulating that the applicable law of foreign-related civil relations shall be governed by provisions of the present chapter of the GPCL, confirms that:

"In case international treaties to which China is a contracting party have rules that are different from those of civil laws of China, rules of the international treaties shall be applied, unless China has declared a reservation to such rules."

The question then is whether there are such international treaties that establish rules of applicable law to JV contracts. For the purposes of the present study, the more precise question is whether Chinese BITs and the ICSID Convention apply to such contracts. The answer to this question is obviously contingent on the nature of JV contracts. If the JV contracts are purely commercial contracts, they should be subject to Chinese law only and have nothing to do with BITS or the ICSID Convention. On the contrary, if it can be established that they are actually state contracts covered by the BITs, particularly the umbrella clause, then the BITs and the ICSID Convention, if it is applicable, will come into play.

3.1.5 DISPUTE SETTLEMENT

A final related issue is the settlement of disputes under JV contracts. Again, Chinese laws generally subject all disputes arising under a JV contract to the jurisdiction of Chinese courts, unless the parties have agreed to submit the disputes to arbitration.[92] More specifically, under relevant Chinese laws, JV parties shall first endeavour to settle the disputes by negotiation or conciliation.[93] Failing this, the parties may submit the

---

[88] M Yao, Textbook, 74; J Yu, International Investment law, p. 99.

[89] J Yu, Ibid, p. 99.

[90] M Yao, Textbook, 74; J Yu, ibid, p. 99.

[91] Meanwhile about 40% JV respondents expressed dissatisfaction. W Shan. 'Law and Foreign Investment in China: General Role of Law and Substantive Issues', Manchester Journal of International Economic Law (Vol 2 No. 3, 2005), p. 36.

[92] The implementing Regulations of the EJVL. art 99; CJVL, art 26; Civil Procedural Law of the People's Republic of China, art 246.

[93] There seems to have been a slight difference between the different investment laws with regard to the need of negotiation and conciliation. The Implementing Regulations of the EJVL and the Regulations on the Joint Exploration of Offshore Petroleum Resources appear to make negotiation and conciliation a compulsory procedure before resorting: to arbitration or litigation. In contrast, the Contract Law and CJVL seem to be more flexible in this regard as it stipulates that JV parties may turn to other options in case the parties do not want to settle through negotiation or conciliation or fail to arrive at a settlement through such channels. See Implementing Regulations of the EJVL, art 97; REOFF, art 27: CJVI, art 26 and Contract Law, art 128.

case to arbitration if they agree to do so.[94] In case the parties do not agree on arbitration, either of the parties may submit the case to a Chinese court.[95] It should be noted that here the assumption of the Chinese laws is that JV contracts are normal domestic law contracts, not state contract that could be subject to international law. Otherwise, it would have been impossible for the Chinese legislature to have approved to submit all such contracts to arbitration including arbitration at international forums, which may imply public international law arbitration facilities such as those conducted under the auspices of the Permanent Court of Arbitration, and the mixed arbitration facility such as ICSID arbitration.[96] For this reason, the arbitration option referred to in the Chinese laws must be domestic or international commercial arbitration only, and could not include public international law or mixed arbitration. However, again, if it can be established that there is an element of state commitment to the JV contract that renders a breach of the JV contract. also a breach of an effective BIT, then the case can be submitted to the ICSIU, if it is applicable, or a public international law forum for the settlement of the disputes. Clearly this route would be based on a relevant BIT, rather than the aforementioned provisions of Chinese law.

3.2 *JOINT EXPL OITATION OF PETROLEUM RESOURCES CONTRACTS*

3.2.1 JOINT EXPLOITATION IN CHINA

Since the early 1980s, China started to lay down laws accepting and attracting foreign investment in joint exploitation of its onshore and offshore oil resources. In 1982, the first of such laws, the Regulations on the Exploration of Offshore Petroleum Resources in Cooperation with Foreign Enterprises (hereinafter the "REOFF"), was promulgated to allow foreign investors to participate in joint exploitation and development of China's offshore oil resources.[97] Eleven years later, China passed the Regulations on the Exploration of Onshore Petroleum Resources in Cooperation with Foreign Enterprises (hereinafter REON) to regulate joint exploitation operations with foreign companies on

---

[94] There seems to have been a slight difference between the different investment laws with regard to the need of negotiation and conciliation. The Implementing Regulations of the EJVL and the Regulations on the Joint Exploration of Offshore Petroleum Resources appear to make negotiation and conciliation a compulsory procedure before resorting: to arbitration or litigation. In contrast, the Contract Law and CJVL seem to be more flexible in this regard as it stipulates that JV parties may turn to other options in case the parties do not want to settle through negotiation or conciliation or fail to arrive at a settlement through such channels. See Implementing Regulations of the EJVL, art 97; REOFF, art 27: CJVI, art 26 and Contract Law, art 128.

[95] Ibid.

[96] Chinese scholars have unanimously and consistently voiced dissent against what they consider to be the "western view" that JV contracts and JE contracts are state contracts and that state contracts shall he subject to international law. See e. g. . M Yao. International Investment Law (Wuhan University Press 1987). pp. 360 – 376; M Yao, Textbook on Foreign Invested Enterprises law (Law Press China 1992), pp. 72 – 75; J Yu, International Investment Law (Law Press China 2003), pp. 84 – 101.

[97] This Regulation was promulgated by the State Council on 30 January 1982 and entered into force on the same date. It was amended on 23 September 2001 by the State Council to bring it in conformity with China's WTO commitments.

onshore oil resources.[98] Both regulations were amended in 2001 by the State Council, in an effort to bring them into conformity with China's WTO Commitments.[99]

Apart from the two main regulations, there are a range of laws and regulations that are also relevant to the joint exploitation of oil and gas resources.[100]

As can be seen in Table 1, 191 joint exploitation projects had been set up in China by the end of 2005, contributing 7.5 billion million US $ of capital[101] Whilst joint exploitation accounted for only about one percent (1.18%) of the total foreign direct investment in China, the average amount contributed in JE investment had been substantial (39.3 million US $). The following is to take joint exploitation of offshore petroleum resources as an example to examine the legal aspects of a joint exploitation arrangement.[102]

In accordance with REOFF, foreign investments, profits, and other legitimate rights of foreign enterprises and their offshore cooperative exploitation activities are protected by the law.[103] Likewise the Law of Mineral Resources also stipulates that "the state shall guarantee the lawful rights and interests of mining enterprises established according to law in the exploitation of mineral resources."[104] The REOFF also generally guarantees that China will not expropriate the investment and income of foreign enterprises, and that appropriate compensation will be given in case of expropriation under exceptional circumstances.[105] On the other hand, the REOFF requires all joint exploitation activities shall be conducted in accordance with relevant Chinese laws and regulations, and that foreign enterprises and individuals are subject to Chinese law and shall accept inspection and supervision by competent Chinese authorities.[106]

3.2.2 THE JOINT EXPLOITATION CONTRACT

The specific mode of joint exploitation in China seems to be a combination of "risk

---

〔98〕 REON was promulgated by the State Council Decree No. 131 on 7 October 1993 and entered into force on the same date. It was amended on 23 September 2001 by the State Council, to bring it in conformity with China's WTO commitments.

〔99〕 In the REOFF, for example, some restrictive provisions, in particular relating to technology transfer, sales of production, purchase of raw materials, and employment, were deleted or amended. Meanwhile, the Guiding Catalogue of Industries for Foreign Investment adopted in 2002 lists exploration and exploitation of oil and gas and development of related new technologies as an area where foreigners are encouraged to invest.

〔100〕 Such laws include the Law of Mineral Resources (1986, amended in 1996). Law on Marine Environmental Protection (1982, amended in 2000), Regulations Concerning Environmental Protection in Offshore Oil Exploration and Exploitation (1983), etc. For a fuller list of such legislation particularly those relating to joint exploitation of offshore oil resources, see K Zou, 'China's Governance over Offshore Oil and Gas Development and Management', 35 Ocean Development & International Law 339 (2004), Table 2 in Page 343.

〔101〕 It is interesting to note that, as Table 1 shows, the actual investment made in this form actually exceeded the contractual investment (4.7 billion US $). This probably implies that foreign investors have made follow-up investment in addition to the original amount stipulated in the JE contract.

〔102〕 For a good introduction of the law of joint exploitation of onshore petroleum resources, see KM Wolf, 'The Legal Framework for Joint Development of China's Onshore Oil resources: Negotiation Strategies and Future Prospects', 9 *journal of Chinese law*, pp. 141 –205.

〔103〕 REOFF, art 3.

〔104〕 The Law of Mineral Resources, art 4.

〔105〕 REOFF, art 4.

〔106〕 REOFF, art 3.

contract" and "product sharing contract".[107] The most authoritative definition of such contractual relationship is found in Article 8 of the REOFF:

The China National Offshore Oil Corporation (CNOOC) may cooperate with foreign enterprises to exploit offshore petroleum resources by means of entering into petroleum contracts, and unless otherwise stipulated by laws and administrative regulations or specified in a petroleum contract, the foreign enterprise which is one party to the petroleum contract (hereinafter "foreign contractor") shall provide the investment to carry Out exploration, be responsible for exploration operation and bear all exploration risks; after a commercial oil (gas) field is discovered, both the foreign contractor and CNOOC shall provide the investment for their cooperative development, and the foreign contractor shall be responsible for development operations and production operations until CNOOC takes over the production operations when conditions permit as provided in the petroleum contract. The foreign contractor, in accordance with the provisions of the petroleum contract. may recover its investment and expenses and receive remuneration out of the petroleum produced.[108]

Thus the joint exploitation is arranged by a "petroleum contract" between a Chinese party, the CNOOC, and a foreign contractor, which covers two stages of operation: exploration and exploitation.[109] At the exploration stage, foreign companies shall provide all the capital and take all the risks. If the exploration fails, the investment will not be recoverable. In this sense, it is a risk contract. However, once oil fields with commercial values are found, both the Chinese and foreign sides shall jointly provide the exploitation capital to develop and produce the oil/gas fields, and the foreign contractor may recover its investment and expenses and receive profit out of the petroleum produced. In this sense, it is a "product sharing contract" (Psc). Indeed, some recent official documents have directly referred to this term as a model of joint exploitation contracts.[110] For instance, the CNOOC signed in May 2001 a Psc with Santa Fe Energy Resources (China) Ltd., which covers the exploration area of Block 27/10 in the Pearl River basin

---

[107] Such a choice was made after a very careful study by the Chinese government. It is reported that, during 1978 and 1979, China sent delegations to various countries including the United States, the United Kingdom, France, Brazil, Norway, and Japan, and invited 23 foreign oil companies to China. Such a contractual arrangement was chosen after an analysis of more than 120 contact samples and legal materials from 125 countries. See Lai Wanzhong, "Launch Foreign Cooperation and Speed up Offshore Oil and Gas Development," China Institute for Marine Development Strategy (ed.). Law and Policy in Marine Affairs, Vol. 2 (Beijing: Ocean Press. 1992) (in Chinese), 160, as cited in K Zou, ' China's Governance over offshore Oil and Gas Development and Management'. 35 *Ocean Development* & International *Law* 339 (2004), 349. see also J Yu, international investment law (Law Press China, 2003), p. 98.

[108] REOFF, art 8.

[109] The implementing Regulations of the Law of Mineral Resources define the right to explore mineral resources within the prescribed scope of the License (contract). whereas the latter refers to the right to exploit and acquire mineral resources within the prescribed scope of the granted license (contract). Such definition would be helpful in defining the two terms. See the Implementing regulations of the Law of Mineral Resources, p. 6.

[110] See eg. Information Office of the State Council ' China's Policy on Mineral Resources . *People's Daily* (in Chinese). 24 December 2003, p. 6.

of 6,546 square kilometers.[111]

In the joint exploitation contract, most of the terms and conditions are fixed and only three areas are open for further discussion: the work program, the X factor (which determines the percentage of production a company receives as profit) and other contributions.[112] Such contracts cannot enter into effect until they are officially approved by the Chinese Ministry of Commerce. The contract may run for a period as agreed by both parties, though the upper ceiling normally is seven years for an exploration contract and thirty years for production from the effective date of the contract.[113]

3.2.3 THE ROLE OF THE CNOOC AND THE NATURE OF THE JOINT EXPLOITATION CONTRACT

The nature of the joint exploitation contracts, in particular, whether such contracts should be regarded as concession agreements or state contract is controversial. And such controversies are closely associated with the role CNOOC plays in such contract.

Created in February 1982, right after the REOFF was adopted, CNOOC is a state-owned Chinese enterprise taking overall charge of the joint exploitation operations in co-operation with foreign enterprises.[114] It has an independent legal personality, but was granted by the state the exclusive right to explore, exploit, produce, and sell the petroleum extracted from cooperative blocks.[115] In the exploitation contract, CNOOC has the right to own 51% of the shares in the joint venture or joint project, though has the option to take less percentage of working interest.[116] Under the joint exploitation contract, CNOOC "has hardly any substantive obligations towards foreign companies",[117] but assists the contractor in opening accounts with the Bank of China; expediting foreign exchange formalities; obtaining office space and supplies, accommodations, and communications; dealing with customs; obtaining permits to export data and samples for analysis or processing; and arranging purchases of data available from relevant Chinese departments.[118] Such background information helps in gaining a better understanding of the role of the CNOOC and the nature of the joint exploitation contracts.

Chinese scholars have argued that, joint exploitation contracts are not state contracts or concession agreements or "Internationalized" contracts, but contracts subject to Chinese national law. There are three main reasons to support this argument.[119] First of all, CNOOC is an independent legal person, not a governmental department, and is not

[111] National Program on Marine Economic Development' China ocean news (in Chinese), 6 February 2004, p. 2.

[112] Zhi guo Gao, internation*al Petroleum Contracts:* Current *Trends and New Directions* (London: Graham & Trotman/Martinus Nijhoff, 1994), p. 157.

[113] Ibid., p. 163.

[114] REOFF, art 6.

[115] Ibid.

[116] For example, CNOOC owns 51% interests in the Penglai 19 - 3 oil field. while Phillips China Ltd. am as the operator. See "China's largest offshore oilfield is in production" China Ocean News (in Chinese). 7 January 2003; Zhiguo Gao, above, p. 167.

[117] Zhiguo Gao, Ibid., p. 169.

[118] Ibid.

[119] J Yu, ibid.

acting in the capacity as the sovereign, hence the contracts it enters into cannot be regarded as state contracts. Secondly, such contracts are concluded in China and approved by Chinese authorities. Such approval does not result in China becoming a parry to the contracts. Thirdly, such contracts are governed by Chinese law as required by relevant laws and regulations. The whole point of detaching such contracts from state contracts is obviously to avoid state responsibility of China in case there is any dispute arising out of them. One Chinese scholar has made this clear by confirming that.

The contract signed between a foreign company and the CNOOC is a commercial contract, not a government agreement. This helps *the Chinese government avoid any state responsibility if there is a dispute concerning the implementation of the contract.* [120] (emphasis added)

However, it might be too optimistic to argue that the Chinese government could be immune from any international responsibilities in the event of a breach of such contracts. It might be argued that the Chinese contracting party, the CNOOC, has been legally empowered "to exercise elements of the governmental authority", which is covered by Article 5 of the State Responsibility Articles. The Article reads as follows:

Article5

Conduct of persons or entities exercising elements of governmental authority.

The conduct of a person or entity which is not an organ of the State under article 4 but which is empowered by the law of that State to exercise elements of the governmental authority shall be considered an act of the State under international law, provided the person or entity is acting in that capacity in the particular instance.

Under REOFF, as mentioned above, the CNOOC is a state enterprise empowered by the state to exercise the exclusive right to enter into agreement with foreign investors and to explore, exploit, produce and distribute offshore petroleum resources. Such exclusive right on petroleum resources is normally exercised by a governmental department and is likely to be considered as an "element of governmental authority". The *Wintershall A. G., et al. v. Government of Qatar* case is a case in point. In this case, the tribunal considered the Qatar General Petroleum Corporation (QGPC), a wholly state-owned company, was acting as an agent of the Government of Qatar, and therefore, all actions attributed to QGPC were attributed to the Government. The tribunal appreciated that the QGPC was created as a separate independent legal personality under Qatari law, but nevertheless concluded that "as a matter of Qatari law it is clear that QGPC operates as an arm or agent of the Government in respect of the concession cares held by it. "[121] Indeed, a recent UNCTAD report on international investment agreements seems to suggest a broader definition of "state contract":

A "State contract" can be defined as a contract made between the State, *or an entity of the State, which, for present purposes, may be defined as any organization created by statue within a State that is given control over an economic activity, and a foreign nation-*

---

[120] K Zou, above, p. 348.

[121] *Wintershall* A. G, *et al.*, *v*. *Government if Qatar* (1989), Partial Award on Liability of 5 February 1988. 28 ILM 795 (1989).

al or a legal person of foreign nationality. State contracts can cover a wide range of issues, including loan agreements, purchase contracts for supplies or services, contracts of employment, or large infrastructure projects, such as the construction of highways, port or dams. One of the commonest forms of State contracts is the natural resource exploitation contract, sometimes referred to as a "concession agreement", though this is not a strict term of art (Brownlie, 2003, p. 522).[122]

This definition seems to be broad enough to catch CNOOC's joint exploitation contracts. Nevertheless, classifying such contracts as state contracts may not necessarily invoke the state responsibility of China on a breach of such contractual obligations. As a generally accepted rule, the mere fact that a state is a party to a contract *per se* will not necessarily make the contract subject to international law. Whether or not the contract would be subject to international law depends on all of the circumstances, including the terms and conditions of the contract and whether there are any applicable international treaties in place.

3.2.4 APPLICABLE LAW AND DISPUTE SETTLEMENT

The rules on applicable law and dispute settlement of joint exploitation contracts are similar to those on joint venture contracts, which are discussed above. Thus in principle Chinese law is the governing law,[123] whilst applicable international treaty obligations prevail where they are in conflict with Chinese law. In case of any disputes arising out of a joint exploitation contract, the parties should first seek resolutions through friendly negotiation.[124] Failing this, the case may be submitted to arbitration or conciliation by Chinese arbitration agencies, or other arbitration institutions as agreed by the parties concerned.[125] The case may also be submitted to litigation, in which case Chinese courts have exclusive jurisdiction.[126] However, if applicable international treaties have alternative dispute resolution options, such treaty rules will come into play. Thus if it can be established that a joint exploitation contract is a state contract covered by a relevant BIT, then the BIT rules of dispute settlement will be applicable.

3.2.5 STALISING AND ADJUSTMENT CLAUSES

One of the features of joint exploitation contracts are that they tend to be long-term contracts involving significant commercial risks. During such a long period of time, the political, economic and other conditions of a state may undergo significant or fundamental changes, which may result in governments changing their laws or regulations, or specific commitments made to foreign investors. In an effort to restrict such changes by the host stare, foreign investor sometime insert a "stabilising clause" in their investment contracts with the host state. Some governments also guarantee such stability in their do-

---

[122] UNCTAD Series on issues in international investment agreements: *State Contracts* (UNCTAD/ITE/IIT/2004/11) 3.

[123] R. F. OFF, art 3; Contract Law, art 126.

[124] R. FOFF, art 24.

[125] Ibid.

[126] Civil Procedural Law, art 246.

mestic laws. and regulations.[127] However, modern stabilisation clauses seem to have-transformed into renegotiation and adjustment clauses, providing that if the government changes the law in ways that affect the economic equilibrium of the investment project, the contract may be adjusted to maintain the economics of the project as originally a-greed.[128]

The same transformation may also have taken place in Chinese law with regard to stabilising clauses. In the early years of attracting foreign investment, the Chinese government introduced certain "stabilising clauses" in domestic laws and regulations. For example, the Ministry of Finance promulgated a decision in 1982 stipulating that join t venture contracts concluded before the joint venture income tax law took effect could still pay income tax in accordance with their original contractual terms, until the term of the contract expired.[129] More significantly, the Foreign Economic Contract Law adopted and entered into effect in 1985 provided that,

"If new legal provisions have been adopted whilst contracts for Sine-foreign equity joint ventures, Sino-Foreign contractual joint ventures, or Sino-foreign joint exploitation of natural resources, which have been concluded with the approval of the state, are being performed within the territory of the People's Republic of China, *such contracts can still be performed on the basis of the terms of the contracts.*"[130] (emphasis added)

The Law also stipulated that it can apply to contracts concluded before it went into effect in case the parties to the contract so agreed.[131] Such provisions vividly demonstrate that the Chinese government was eager to assure foreign investors that the legal environment of FDI in China would be sound and stable. Yet the implication of such "stabilisation" commitment in a national law has been so significant that it substantially limit government's power to effectively regulate foreign investment. As a result, these stabilising clauses in the Foreign Economic Contract Law were repealed when the law was amended and amalgamated into a new unified Contract Law in 1999.

Chinese standard petroleum contracts, nevertheless, still contain a modem stabilising clause, or a re-negotiation and adjustment clause. The following provision from a contract for exploration in the Sichuan Basin is a good example:

"If a material change occurs to the Contractor's economic benefit after the effec-

---

〔127〕 For example, in 1999 Russia adopted a new foreign investment law (No. 160 – FZ. which became effective on July 14 1999), one of the few features of which is the tax stabilization clause stipulated in Article 9. For certain companies and projects, the article prohibits increases in the rates of certain import duties and federal taxes until initial investments have been recouped. See B Zimbler and K Arbatova, ' Russia: The new Russian foreign investment law , *available at* http://www.iflr.com/?Page = 10&PUBID 33&ISS = 11977&SID = 508948 TYPE = 20 (last visited on 26 December 2008).

〔128〕 RD Bishop. J Crawford and WM Reisman, Foreign Investment Disputes: Cases, Materials and Commentary (Kluwer Law International, 2005) 15.

〔129〕 M Yao. Textbook. 71.

〔130〕 Foreign Economic Contract Law (adopted by the Tenth Meeting of the Standing Committee of the Sixth Session of the National people's Congress on 21 March 1985 and entered into forth on 1 July 1985) art 40. This law was replaced by the Contract Law adopted on 15 March 1999, by the Second Meeting of the Ninth Session of the National People's Congress, and entered into force on I October 1999), which has not maintained this provision.

〔131〕 Ibid., art. 41.

tive date of the Contract due to the promulgation of new laws, decree, rules and regulations or any amendment to the applicable laws, decrees, rules and regtu lations made by the Government of the People's Republic of China. the Parties hall consult promptly and make necessary revisions and adjustments to the relevant provisions of the Contract in order to maintain the Contractor's reasonable economic benefits here under. "[132]

In this connection, it is useful to recall that some Chinese BITs have also included relevant provisions either affirming the host state's rights to change their laws and regulations,[133] or requiring contracting parties to "make responsible arrangements for the appropriate interest" of the foreign investors.[134] Indeed, the Chinese Government attempts to make any legal changes as smooth as possible by providing transition arrangements. For example, the former Income Tax Law of Foreign Invested Enterprises and Foreign Enterprises stipulated that:

"Where any foreign invested enterprises which was established before the promulgation of this Law would, in accordance With the provisions of this Law, otherwise be subject to higher tax rates or enjoy less preferential treatment of tax exemption or reduction than that they were subject to before the entry into force of this Law, the law and relevant regulations of the State Council in effect before the entry into force of this Law shall continue to apply to such enterprises within it approved period of operation. If any such enterprises have no approved period of operation, such law and relevant regulations of the State Council in effect before the entry into force of this Law shall apply within the period prescribed by the State Council Specific measures shall be drawn up by the State Council to implement this provision. "[135]

Similar transition arrangements have also been included in a new income tax law, which was adopted in 2007 and applies to both domestic and foreign invested enterprises.[136]

3. 3 *BUILD-OPERATE-TRANSFER (BOT) CONTRACT*

BOT contracts are one of the very few foreign investment contracts to which the

---

[132] Art 29 (2), Contract for Exploration, Development and Production in Zitong Block, Sichuan Basin of the People's Republic Of China between China National Petroleum Corporation and Pan-China Resources Ltd. (Beijing. China. 19 September 2002). Available at http://contracts. onecle. com/ivanhoe/cnpc. zitong. 2002. 09. 19. shtml (last visit on 25 December 2008). See also M Yao, Textbook. 72 (noting that recent Chinese petroleum contracts contain such re-negotiation and adjustment provisions).

[133] Art 8(2). Sino-Germany BIT(1983). As noted above, this BIT is still currently effective, and is to be repla ced by the new one signed in 2003, in which thus provision has been removed.

[134] Art 4. 2. Sino-Thailand BIT.

[135] Income: Tax Law of Foreign Invested enterprises and Foreign Enterprises (adopted by the Fourth Meeting of the Seventh Session of the National People's Congress on9 April 1991), art 27.

[136] Xinhua New Agency, Enterprise: Income Tax Law in Focus: A Two-in-One' Law for both Domestic and Foreign Invested Enterprise (24 December 2006. in Chinese, *available at* http://news. xinhuanet. com/legal/2006 - 12/24/content_5526401. htm (last visit on 26 December 2008).

Chinese governmental authorities are directly involved as a contracting parry.[137] Given the cautious attitude towards state contracts and concession agreements, the move of the Chinese government to adopt BOT investment has been a significant one.[138] This section discusses such contract practice in China and the legal controversies related to such contracts and concession agreements in general.

3.3.1 BOT INVESTMENT IN CHINA

BOT investment is a relatively new form of investment, often used for large infrastructure and public utility projects such as highways, ports, dams, mass transit system, power plants, water supply systems and industrial estates.[139] A typical definition of a BoT investment is as follows:

The BOT scheme is a contractual arrangement between the government and the private contractor The contractor undertakes the construction and financing of an infrastructure facility for the government that the contractor shall operate and maintain the facility for an agreed period of time. During the agreed period, the contractor shall be allowed to charge the facility users, tolls, fees and other charges to enable him to recover both his investment and operating expenses plus a reasonable rate of return. The facility is turned-over to the government when the agreed period ends.[140]

A BOT project is different from a turn-key project, in that the contractor operates the facility in order to recover its costs and profit thereafter.[141]

The first BOT project in China was introduced in 1995, and since then it has been

---

[137] Another form of concession agreement is arguably track land development contracts between a foreign investor and a local land administrative authority. The governing laws are the Interim Measures for the Administration of the Foreign-Invested Development and Management of Tracts of land (adopted by Decree No. 56 of the Sure Council of the People's Republic of China on 19 May 1990). See also J Yu, International Investment Law. 105 (arguing that such contracts may be considered a form of concession agreements, but nevertheless are domestic law contracts, not international agreements or 'Internationalised' contract' subject to international law.)

[138] The Chinese government has tried as far as possible not to be directly involved in a contractual relationship with a foreign investor to avoid the complex legal problems associated with such state contracts, or concession agreements. This is demonstrated by China's approach to joint exploitation contracts examined above, where the government is not directly involved as a party even though it hold the ultimate control over such activities. This may go some way in explaining the dearth of investment arbitrations against China despite the vast amount of FDI. Likewise, Chinese scholars views with regard to the legal issues associated with state contracts and concession agreements, such as their nature, applicable law and jurisdiction. are significantly different from these of western scholars. Such views are to be discussed below.

[139] M Sornarajah, The Settlement of Foreign Investment Disputes (Kluwer Law International. 2000). ch 2 - 2.7. However, BOT is now also used in the off-shoring and out: sourcing of knowledge work. In these cases there is usually no government or public finding involved. Typically, a Western customer contracts with an Indian or Chinese vendor and the vendor builds and operates a customer call center or other business process for anextended period of time. However, the client retains the right to take over the operation ("transfer") at any time based on certain conditions and certain payments to the offshore partner. See Wikipedia: 'Build-Operate-Transfer', *available at* http://en.wikipedia.org/wiki/Build-Operate-Transfer (last visit on 26 December 2008).

[140] Sornarajah, ibid.

[141] Ibid.

commonly used in energy, transport, communication and environment projects.[142] The first Chinese law dealing with BOT projects is the MOFCOM (then MOFTEC) Notice on Some Issues about Utilising Foreign Investment in the Form of BOT (the MOFCOM BOT Notice) adopted in January 1995. Later in the year, the Notice on Issues about Approval Procedures of Foreign Invested Concession Projects jointly promulgated by the State Planning Commission, the Ministry of Electricity and the Ministry of Transportation (the Joint BOT Notice). The Interim Measures on the Administration of Overseas Project Financing Activities adopted in 1997[143] is also an important law that is closely related to BOT investment.

According to the Joint BOT Notice, a BOT project in China is not different from the general BOT practice worldwide. The Notice defines it as a scheme under which a government authority enters into a concession agreement with a Project Company set up by foreign investors for the purpose of the BOT project.[144] Under the agreement, the Project Company is responsible for the investment and finance, engineering design, construction, equipment purchase, operation management and fees charged, a well as the maintenance of the project equipment and facilities.[145] The government authority supervise examines and audits the BOT project and may penalise the Project Company if it is behaving inconsistently with the Concession Agreement.[146] The MOFCOM BOT Notice requires the Project Company to be established in the form of an EJV, CJV or a WFE.[147]

The aforementioned legislation constitutes a legal framework for BOT investment. However, this legal framework is marred by incompleteness, relatively low ranking within the legal system and inconsistency.[148] It is incomplete because a range of important issues have not been covered, such as the nature of governmental guarantees, applicable law, and dispute settlement.[149] Also, such legislation all take the form of departmental regulations *(Bumen Guizhang)*, which rank very low in the Chinese hierarchy of legislation.[150] Finally, some provisions are contradictory. For instance, the stipulations on governmental guarantees are different and conflicting between the two Notices, as observed

---

〔142〕 For Chinese literature on BOT investment in China. See G Meng, "Legal Nature of the BOT Concession Agreement and the Legislative structure, (Chinese) Journal of International Economic Law (Vol 13. No 3. 2006). 206 – 237; A Yu. *Foreign Invested BOT Projects and Administrative Contract Law* (Law Press China. 1998); C Sun and W Shen, *"BOT Investment the Legal Confilics and Analysis"*, Chinese Legal Science (Zhongguo faxue, 1997), No. I; S Zhu and W Lin, *"The Legal nature of BOT concession agreement'*, Chinese Legal Science (Zhongguo Faxue, 1999). No. 4; Beijing Engineering Consultancy, Guidelines *to BOT Projects* (Dizhen Press, 1995); L Xie, Government intervention *and the legislation on BOT Concession Agreements"*. Law Review (Faxue Pinglun. 1999). No. 4.

〔143〕 This instruments was jointly adopted by the State Planning Commission (now the State Development and Reform Commission. the SDRC) and the Suit Administration of Foreign Exchange (SAFE) on 16 April1997. Which has details about the approval and financing of such projects.

〔144〕 Point I. the Joint BOT Notice.

〔145〕 Id.

〔146〕 Id.

〔147〕 Point I, the MOFCOM BOT Notice.

〔148〕 See also Meng, above, pp. 223 – 224.

〔149〕 Ibid.

〔150〕 Ibid.

below.

3.3.2 GOVERNMENTA L GUARANTE ES UNDER BOT CONTRACTS AND UMBRELLA CLAUSE

With regard to government guarantees, the two BOT Notices are somewhat inconsistent. The MOFCOM BOT Notice stipulates that government authorities normally shall not offer any guarantees or promises to the project (e.g.. guarantees on forex convertibility and loans).[151] By contrast, the Joint BOT Notice provides that the State will guarantee the conversion and repatriation of foreign exchange that the Project Company pays back on loan principals, interests or dividends.[152] It also maintains that in case the Project Company suffers significant economic loss due to China 's policy changes, the Project Company will be allowed to raise the charging standard or extend the concession period.[153] Nevertheless, the Joint BOT Notice does not permit guarantees on the rate of return[154] and domestic financial institutions are not allowed to provide guarantees for the project's finance.[155]

A Central question is whether such governmental guarantees constitute the obligations/commitments covered by the umbrella clauses in the BITs. There are two factors that complicate the answer; (1) the governmental authority involved in the BOT contract is normally a department of a local government; and (2) the other contracting party is the Project Company, which more often than not will have registered as a Chinese legal person in the form of either a JV or a WFE.[156] Despite such complications, however, the answer to this question should probably be in the affirmative. First, it is well established that conduct of state organs, of central or local government, should be attributed to the state. This is confirmed in the ILC State Responsibility Articles[157] and ju-

---

[151] See also Meng, above, p. 3.

[152] Id.

[153] Pojnt 2, the joint BOT Notice.

[154] In practice, this has not always been the case, In a reported case, the Chengdu Municipality government offered a 12% profit rate for a BOT water factory according to a co-operation agreement with French company and Japanese company. See the *First BOT Water Project has started to pvovide water,* posted at http://www.cctv.com(visited on 26July 2001 at 18:21).

[155] Point 2. the Joint BOT Notice.

[156] Chinese scholars have argued that since Chinese BOT contract is made between a Chinese entity and a local government department. it is purely domestic concession contract subject to domestic law. Rather than international concession agreement or state contract. J Yu, International Investment Law (2003). 110. The Issue of the nature of such BoT contracts and its Applicable law will be further discussed later in this article.

[157] See Article 4 of the ILC State Responsibility Articles:

'Article 4 Conduct of organs of a State

1. The conduct of any Stare organ shall be considered an act of that State under international law, whether the organ exercises legislative, executive, judicial or any other functions, whatever position it holds in the organization of the Stale, and whatever its character as an organ of the central government or of a territorial unit of the State.

2. An organ includes any person or entity which has that Status in accordance With the internal law of the Stare.'

Such local governmental department under Chinese BOT contracts should fall within the organ of a territorial unit of the State'.

risprudence from investment treaty arbitration cases.[158] Second, umbrella clauses under Chinese BITs tend to cover "any obligations/commitment entered into with regard to investments of investors from the other contracting party". In other words, *to* benefit from this clause, the commitments do not have to be made directly to the foreign investors. As long as such commitment are related to their investments. they are entitled to protection under the umbrella clause. In the present case, any guarantees given to the Project Company under a BOT contract, would become a kind of obligation or commitment entered into with regard to the foreign investment concerned. It would be eligible for protection of the umbrella clause, as long as the home state of the foreign investors has an effective BIT with China containing such a clause.[159]

3.3.3 THE NATURE OF AND THE APPLICABLE LAW TO BOT CONTRACTS

The nature of BOT contracts is an issue that has been subject to intensive debate within China.[160] The essential point of such debate is to ascertain whether such contacts should be governed by domestic law, international law, or both. So far Chinese law has been silent on such issues leaving them open for interpretation and discussion. There seem to have been three schools of thoughts in China on the issue.

The first school of Chinese scholars account for the vast majority, which consider BOT contracts and concession agreements as domestic law contracts.[161] Among them, Yao is the most eminent and influential.[162] In his writings he gives two main reasons supporting this view.[163] First, concession agreements deal with state-investor relations, not relations between two subjects of international law, and therefore should be regarded as contracts under domestic law. He relied on the PCIJ decision in the 1929 *Serbian loan* case, which states that "[A] ny contract that is not a contract between states in their capacity as subjects of international law is based on the municipal law of some country."[164] Yao contended that to be qualified as a subject of any legal relationship an entity must meet certain legally defined conditions, and such status could not be acquiesced to or granted by any other parties. Thus one cannot argue that private parties can

---

[158] Recent cases include *Metalclad cooperation* v mexico (2002). lCSID Case No. ARB(AF)/97/1(NAFTA), Award of 30 August 2000. 40 ILM 36 (which held that Mexico was internationally responsible for the acts of SLP and Guadalcazar respectively a State and a Municipality of the Mexico); and campania de aguas del aconquija S. A and vivendi universal v argentine republic ICSID Case No ARB/97/3, Award 21 November 2000 (which held that acts of officials of the provinces of Tucuman could be attributed to the federal government).

[159] As discussed above, it might also be possible to establish such an umbrella clause by the operation of the MFN clause in an applicable Sino-Foreign BIT: although this theory remain untested.

[160] G Meng, 'Legal nature of BOT concession Agreement. New Interpretation' Journal of Wuhan University (Social Scise Edition in Chinese) (Vol 56, No. 5. 2006), pp. 857 – 861.

[161] Meng has observed that this view represents of the view of most developing country scholars. Including chinese scholars, diplomats and legal officers. G Meng. above, p. 210.

[162] Yao was a professor of Law at Wuhan University and the founding President of the chinese Society of International Economic Law. His writings in international investment law are still today widely citedly by Chinese scholars as authorities.

[163] M Yao, International investment Law, Wuhan University Press. 1987, in Chinese, pp. 360 – 363.

[164] Case concerning the payment of Various Serbian Loans insured in france (*France v Kingdom of Serbs. Croats and Slovens*) 1929 PCIJ(ser A) No. 20/21 (July 12), p. 46.

become subjects of international law on the ground of consent or acquiescence by a state parry concerned.[165] Secondly, all concession agreements are entered into in accordant" with the law of the host country in order to establish the rights and obligations of parties, and are approved by the host government.[166] As a result, they are contracts under domestic law, not international law.

Secondly, an opposite view to the previous one has emerged in recent years, which argues that concession agreements should be acknowledged as state contracts subject to international law.[167] This view takes into account recent developments such as individu-al s becoming subjects of international law, Chinese practice with regard to bilateral and multilateral investment treaties acknowledging state responsibility in state-investor relations, and concludes that the majority view is now outdated and should be abandoned.[168] However, such a view seems to have won little support to date among Chinese scholar.

A third hybrid approach has been taken by some Chinese scholars, which argues that concession agreements should be regarded as a separate, new category of agreement (agreement *sui generis*).[169] This view considers that concession agreements are generally not state contracts of international law, but display certain characters of state contract, such as the indispensability of a state party involved, the governmental guarantees and the methods of dispute settlement.[170] Further, it contends that a domestic law definition of the nature of such concession agreements as dometic law contracts is meaningless when in conflict with overriding international treaty obligations.[171] It is therefore better to classify it as agreement *sui generis*, and subject it to special rules.[172]

It is submitted that BOT contracts, together with other concession agreements, should all be regarded as forms of state contracts. However, such state contracts may or may not be subject to international law. In the absence of any international treaty obligations, such contracts should be subject to the domestic law of the host state. However, in case there are treaty obligations, eg, under a BIT, it is possible that such domestic law obligations may become obligations under international law. Two provision s are particularly important in this regard. One is the umbrella clause discussed above, which may lift, *inter alia*, obligations under concession agreement to international law obligation. The other is the definition clause, which tend to include "concession agreements" as a form of "investment" cov-

---

[165] Yao, above 362.

[166] Ibid, p. 363.

[167] W Li, 'Legal Issues of BOT Concession Agreements' (in Chinese), *available at* http;//www. colaw. cn/Wenku/bot/questions. htm (last visit 26 December 2008).

[168] Ibid.

[169] This view seems to be in general agreement with the 'transnational agreement, argument advocated by Fatouros. which consider that such agreements display elements of both domestic law contracts and international Agreements, Fatouros. , above, 34.

[170] Meng. A bove, 215 - 221.

[171] Ibid, pp. 220 - 221.

[172] Ibid, pp. 221 - 235 (discussing the need and contents of such a special law on BOT concession agreements).

ered by the BIT. In this connection, it is noted chat almost all Chinese BITs have adopted such a definition.[173]

3.3.4 DISPUTES SETTLEMENT AND RECENT CASES

Chinese law is again silent on the methods of settling disputes under BOT contracts. Presumably, since such contracts are between two Chinese entities, local remedies will apply, unless such contracts are also subject to any overriding treaty obligation. Apart from amicable solutions such as negotiation, consultation and mediation, such local remedies normally include arbitration, litigation and administrative review.[174] Resorting to international remedies such as ICSID or ad hoc arbitration is possible if the home state of the foreign investor has entered into a BIT with China agreeing to submit such disputes to international forums. However, since most Chinese BITs only allow the submission of disputes over the amount of compensation for expropriation to international arbitration.[175] and the effect of MFN clause on such provisions is uncertain,[176] in most cases, foreign investors may find out that they have to or should resort to local remedies, rather than testing their luck by bringing the cases before an international arbitration tribunal. Recently, there have already been some investment disputes, which have all been settled through domestic courts or tribunals. *Changchun Huijin* case and the *Fuzhou Xinyuan* case are two examples.[177]

4. CONCLUSIONS

Umbrella clauses are important provisions under investment treaties and have raised a number of questions and controversies in investment law and arbitration practice. Chinese BITs are no exception to this. At least 50 Chinese BITs contain this provision and a further 6 BITs contain a preservation of rights clause that has similar but per-

---

〔173〕 Among the 120 plus Chinese BITs, all but Sino-Poland BIT expressly refer to concession agreements as a form of ' investment' covered by the treaty. For further details on the definition of ' investment' under Chinese BITs, see Chapter 4 in Chinese investment *Treaties: Policy and Practice* (OUP forthcoming).

〔174〕 See Chapter 9 Section 9.7 in Chinese investment *Treaties: Policy and Practice* (OUP forthcoming) for details of dispute resolution under Chinese law.

〔175〕 So far only half a dozen of effective Chinese BITS have set up a mechanism for the international settlement of any/all investment disputes'. All the rest BIT either limit the scope of submission to amount of compensation disputes, or have a broader scope but arc yet to be ratified. See Chapter 9 in Chinese Investment Treaties: Policy and Practice (OUP forthcoming) for further details.

〔176〕 The Maffezini tribunal has confirmed that the MFN provision could be extended to benefits of procedural provisions. and this has been followed by some other cases such as *Siemens, Camuzzi*. More recent cases such as *Salini* and p*lama* took an opposite view rejecting such effect of the MFN clause. *See Emilio Agustin Maffezini v Kingdom of Spain (*Case No. ARB./97/7), Decision on Objections to jurisdiction of January 25, 2000 *(Maffezini v. Spain)*, paras 38–64; *Siemens A. C. v. Argentine Republic* (Case No. ARII/02/8). Decision on Jurisdiction of August 3, 2004 *(Siemens v. Argentina)*, para. 103; *Camuzzi International S. A. v. Argentina Republic* (Case No. ARB/03/7), Decision on Jurisdiction of May 11, 2005, paras. 120–121; *Salini Constrottori S. p. A. attd Italstrade S. . p. A. v. . the Hashemite Kingdom of Jordan* (Case No. ARB/02/13), Decision of the Tribunal on Jurisdiction of November 29, 2004 *(salini v. Jordan)*, paras. 117–118; *Plama Consortium United v. Republic of Bulgaria (*Case No. ARB/03/24), Decision on Jurisdiction of February 8. 2005 *(Plama v. Bulgaria)*, paras. 183–227.

〔177〕 Detail of the two cases can be found in Wenhua Shan. The Legal Framework of EU-China Investment Relations, Hart Publishing Oxford. 2005, pp. 227–229.

haps stronger effect. Whether or not the MFN provision has the effect of multiplying the umbrella clause depends on the attending circumstances of the case.

Among the 50 BITs, most BITs adopt the standard formulation requiring the host state to observe any or all obligation/commitments she undertakes towards foreign investors. Purely commercial obligations should nevertheless not be covered by this clause. Also, it is argued that legislative measures of general application which does not target at any specific investment should be excluded from it application.

It is observed that a considerable number of Chinese BITs specifically adopt a more restrictive approach imposing substantive limitations on the scope of application of the umbrella clause. Some subject such obligation or commitments to the laws of the host state, others confine the obligation or commitments to only "written obligation", obligation relating to "specific investments", "contractual obligation" concerning "approved investments", or "approved investment contracts". The inclusion of these restrictions helps to more accurately define the scope of application of this provision.

On the contrary, the Sino-Singapore BIT requires the host state to "observe" "any commitment" entered into between two private parties of the two contracting states, in addition to any commitment the host state has entered into with private parties of the other contracting party. It is argued that this addition commitment can only be interpreted as requiring the host state to respect the freedom of contract and to refrain from interfering with the contractual relationship between two private parties of the two contracting parties and nothing more than that.

Contractual obligations are the main targets of this clause and their main manifestation in China include contracts for joint ventures, joint exploitations and BOT projects. After careful examination and analyses, it is concluded that normal joint venture contracts are purely commercial contracts and as such should not be covered by the umbrella clauses. The fact that Chinese governmental authorities examine and approve every and all joint venture contracts should not render them liable for any breach of such contracts, because they merely exercise regulatory powers and contracts remain commercial contracts between the two joint venture partners.

In contrast, joint exploitation contracts are very likely to be considered as state contract and therefore subject to the umbrella clauses, since they are signed by designated state enterprises exercising certain governmental authorities. BOT contracts are likewise state contracts because of direct involvement of governmental agencies as their parties.

In most cases all these three types of contracts are subject to only Chinese laws and local remedies. In case they are covered by a valid investment treaty, however, international law and international remedies may come into play. For this reason, it is necessary and indeed important to enhance the studies on these treaties, particularly their application in arbitration practice.

Law and Foreign Investment in China: Effectiveness of the Legal System*

I. Introduction

It has become a consensus among development agencies and commentators that the effectiveness of the host country's legal system can to some extent determine the inflow of FDI.[1] Such a legal system includes not only laws and courts, but also other institutions and officials that are involved in the creation and implementation of law, such as bureaucrats and politicians.[2] According to the World Bank, an effective legal system for foreign investment normally has five features.[3] First, it provides a set of rules "known" to foreign investors in advance. Thus the law should be published (accessible) and clear. Second, it relies upon rules which are actually implemented, and not just stay "on the books". Third, it ensures that rules are consistently applied. The discretionary power of state officials should, therefore, be limited to the narrowest possible field, in order to avoid abuse. Fourth, there must be an effective, independent mechanism for dispute resolution. The judiciary must be protected from intervention by other branches of the government, so that the government itself can be the subject of laws. Further, the judicial process must not be incapacitated by physical constraints due to poor facilities, unreasonable delays, prohibitive cost or uncertainty. Lastly, it has clear procedures for

---

* *Manchester Journal of International Economic Law,* Volume 3 No. 1, 2006.

The author would like to also thank Professor Sir Elihu Lauterpacht CBE QC, Mr. Daniel Bethlehem QC, Lord Leon Brittan, Mr. Peter Nightingale and Miss Amanda Perry for their help and support on the Questionnaire and interviews conducted for this research. He would also like to thank Professor Thomas Walde and Professor Peter Edge for their comments on earlier versions of this article.

[1] See UNCTAD, *Effectiveness of Foreign Direct Investment Policy Measures* (Note by the UNCTAD Secretariat), TD/B/COM. 2/EM. 13/2 (22 April 2003), p. 4; UNCTAD, *World Investment Report* 1995: *Trends and Determinants* (1995); Geneva, United Nations; UNCTC, *The Determinants of Foreign Direct Investment: Survey of the Evidence* (1992a), New York, United Nations. See also Meier, Gerald M, *Leading Issues in Economic Development*, OUP(1995), pp. 247 – 251; Todaro, Michael P, *Economics for a Developing World,* Longman (19920, pp. 379 – 400; Perry, Amanda, *Effective Legal System and Foreign Direct Investment: In Search of the Evidence*, 49 *ICLQ* 779, p. 779.

[2] Perry, ibid, p. 781.

[3] World Bank, *Governance and Development*, Washington DC: World Bank, 1992, p. 4. See also Perry, Amanda J., *Legal Systems as a Determinant of Foreign Direct Investment: The Case of Sri Lanka*, London School of Economics PhD Dissertation, 2000, (hereinafter as Perry, PhD Dissertation), p. 95, 96.

the amendments of rules, to prevent any arbitrary introduction or rejection of rules, and to clear out irrelevant rules.[4]

Such a set of criteria constitute the core components of the Ideal Institutional Paradigm (IIP) that the World Bank and other development agencies are offering to developing countries when giving law reform advice.[5] The essence of such a set of standards is to apply the ' normative Coase theorem' , to reduce those ' costs endogenous to the legal system' , and to ' lubricate' private bargaining by providing useful solutions to reduce market transaction costs.[6]

Based on these criteria, nine questions were included in the Questionnaire to examine and assess the effectiveness of the legal system that governs foreign investment in China. These questions focus on five aspects, including the accessibility and stability of the law, the enforcement of law by government departments, courts and arbitration tribunals, and the enforcement of court/arbitration decisions. These questions were also asked during the interviews conducted by the author with foreign investors, chamber of commerce officers and governmental officials. The article, as the second half of a study on the role of law in China's success in attracting foreign direct investment (FDI), is to present and analyse the general results on these aspects and measure such results against the above mentioned IIP criteria. This is followed by an analysis on the breakdown results. For details of the Questionnaire and the interview processes, as well as findings and discussions on general role of law and substantive issues, see the first half of this study, which was published in the previous issue of this journal.

II. The Effectiveness of the Chinese FDI Legal System: General Results

This section presents and comments on the general result on the five main aspects, namely the accessibility and stability of the law, the enforcement of law by government departments, courts and arbitration tribunals, and the enforcement of court/arbitration decisions.

1. Accessibility of Law

The Chinese legal system has long been criticised for a lack of transparency.[7] The Chinese Government has therefore made great efforts to solve this problem. For in-

---

[4] World Bank, id.

[5] Perry, PhD Dissertation, note 3 above, pp. 94, 195 - 199.

[6] Cooter, Robert D and Ulen, Thomas, Law and Economics Reading Massachusetts: Addison-Wesley Longman (1997), p. 89.

[7] An article published at the Harvard Law Review observed that, "[T]he chief problem for students of modern Chinese law has often been one of finding it." See *Concepts of Law in the Chinese Anti-Crime Campaign*, 98 Harvard Law Review 1890, June 1985, p. 1890. Also, a number of studies on China's WTO accession have examined the problem of transparency in the Chinese legal system. See e. g., Ostry, Sylvia, *China and the WTO: The Transparency Issue*, 3 UCLA Journal of International Law and Foreign Affairs 1, in particular pp. 12 - 15, (Summer, 1998); Hu, Patrick H., *The China* 301 *on Market Access: A Prelude to GATT Membership*? 3 Minnesota Journal of Global Trade 131, p. 143, (Spring 1994); Blumental, David, *"Reform" Or "Opening" ? Reform of China's State-Owned Enterprises and WTO Accession—The Dilemma of Applying GATT to Marketizing Economies*, 16 UCLA Pacific Basin Law Journal 198, (Spring, 1998), p. 234; Yuan, Anyuan, *China's Entry into the WTO: Impact on China's Regulating Regime of Foreign Direct Investment*, 35 Int'l Law. 195, (Spring, 2001), p. 217.

stance, the Guidance on the Direction of Foreign Investment (the Investment Guidance) and its attached Guiding Catalogue of Industries for Foreign Investment (Guiding Catalogue) have been published to direct FDI admission and a Gazette of MOFTEC (now MOFCOM) is also available to publish new laws and regulations in a timely manner. However, there has been no empirical evidence as to how the foreign investors view the transparency and accessibility of law. Thus, in the Questionnaire, they were asked whether they thought FDI laws and policies were easily accessible. As *Chart* 1 demonstrates, forty percent of the foreign investors replied that laws and regulations are "always" or "mostly" accessible while twenty three percent of them answered negatively ("rarely" or "never" accessible). Another twenty three percent replied that law was only "sometimes" accessible, which suggested that in most of the time it was inaccessible (*Chart* 1). In general, the Questionnaire shows that further improvement on transparency and accessibility of the law is needed[8], as a substantial portion of foreign investors still regarded access to the law as difficult.

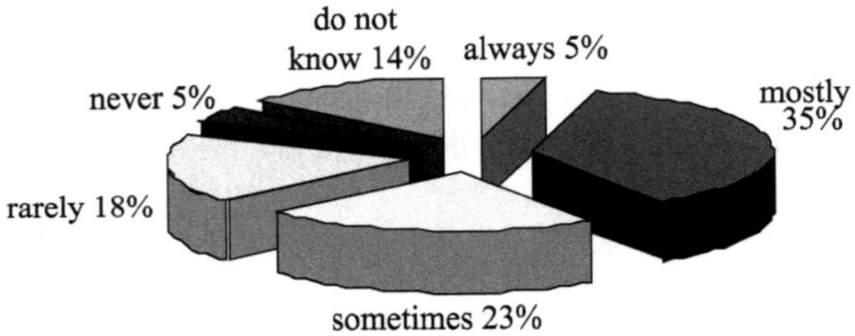

Chart 1 Accessibility of Law and Policy

2. Stability of Law

The stability of the law in China is another problem that is often raised[9]. Thus another question was included to determine, from the foreign investors' experience, whether Chinese FDI laws and policies had been changed unexpectedly. The Questionnaire results confirm that stability of FDI law and policy was still perceived as a major problem. More than forty percent of the surveyed investors replied that in China law and policies are "always", "mostly" or "frequently" changed unexpectedly, while about half (49%) reported that unexpected changes of law are "sometimes" experienced. Only five percent stated that they had "rarely" encountered unexpected changes of law (*Chart* 2). Admittedly, as a country in transition, changes in law and policies are inevitable and are not necessarily unfavourable for investors. However, the high frequency of "unexpected" changes of law shows that public participation in the law drafting and revision processes

[8] The recent OECD policy review also suggested that China increase transparency and adopt clear, open rules on matters like taxation and labour benefits. It also suggested that China align official FDI statistics with international standards such as those recommended by the IMF and OECD. See OECD Policy Brief, *Attarcting Investment to China*, (September 2003), pp. 3 – 7.

[9] See e. g., Zheng, Henry R., *The Sino-U. S. Income Tax Treaty and Its Effect on Chinese Taxation of American Economic Interests*, 40 Tax Lawyer 733 (Spring, 1987), p. 773.

has been a continuous problem and needs to be improved[10]. The *Changchun Huijin* and *Fuzhou Xinyuan* cases mentioned in the first part of the study highlighted the severity of this problem.

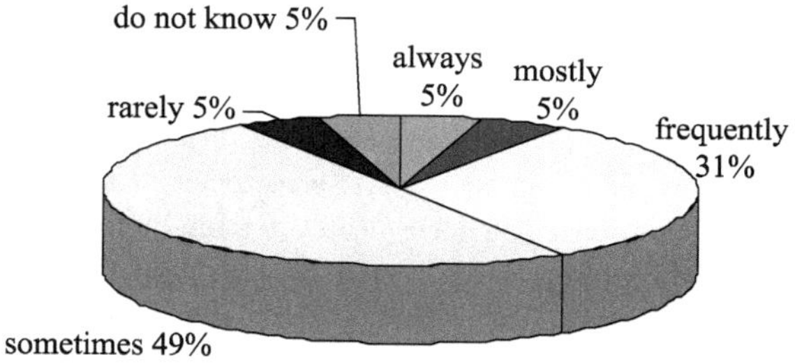

Chart 2 Unexpected Changes of Law and Policy

3. Government Enforcement of Law

Two questions were devised to establish the experience with the enforcement of laws by government departments (the *Bureaucracy*): one was on the consistency of enforcement and the other was on corruption.

3.1 Consistency of Government Law Enforcement

It is said that in China laws are interpreted and implemented inconsistently by different departments and in different regions[11]. This perception was confirmed by this Questionnaire. As *Chart* 3 shows, thirty five percent of respondents thought the law only "sometimes" was enforced consistently, whilst fourteen percent of them complained that such consistency had "never" or "rarely" been achieved. Only twenty three percent of respondents reported that laws were "mostly" and "frequently" enforced in a consistent way (*Chart* 3). The substantial percentage who distrusted the enforcement of law by the bureaucracy shows that improvement should be made.

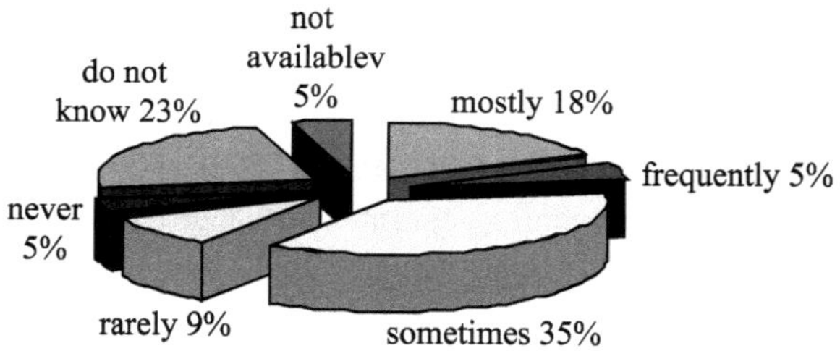

Chart 3 Consistency of Governm ent Law Enforcem ent

[10] Again, the recent OCED policy review observed such a problem and suggested that China increase transparency in the process of formulating laws and regulations. See OECD Policy Brief, *Attracting Investment to China*, (September 2003), p. 4.

[11] See Blumental, David, *note* 7 *above*, p. 237. See also Kong, Kevin T. S., *Prospects For Asset Securitization within China's Legal Framework: The Two-Tiered Model*, 32 Cornell International Law Journal 237 (1998), p. 271.

3.2 Necessity of Bribery to Deal with Government Officials

In order to explore the role of bribery in relations between investors and government officials, the question was asked whether it was "necessary" to bribe government officials. The responses have shown that in dealing with government officials, bribery was normally unnecessary. Forty five percent of surveyed foreign investors reported that there had "never" (40%)[12] or "rarely" (5%) been a need to use bribery when dealing with government officials. Only five percent answered that bribery was "always" needed, while around nine percent found it necessary "sometimes" (*Chart* 4). Meanwhile, it must be noted that this question might have been too straightforward for some investors to answer honestly, probably due to certain regulations in their home countries and from the OECD with regard to bribery. Thus, there was a rather high percentage (31%) of "do not know" responses and a five percent of "unanswerable" reply.[13] Also, in an interview with the head of a Chamber of Commerce, doubt was expressed about the number of honest answers to this question.[14]

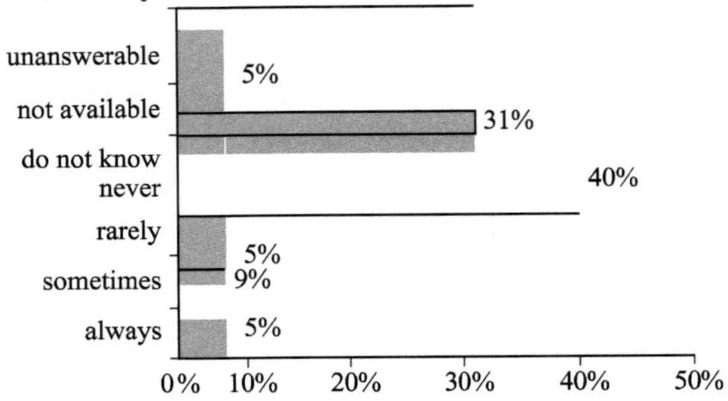

Chart 4 Need of Bribery for Officials

4. Court Enforcement of Law

The Courts are the centre of all law enforcement activities. Therefore, five questions were designed to examine the record of law enforcement by and around the Chinese courts: the objectivity of law enforcement by the courts,[15] the possibility of bribery impacting on court judgements, political interference on court decisions, unreasonable delays of court and arbitration procedures and enforcement of court and arbitration decisions.

---

[12] Among those who replied that bribery had "never" been necessary, 2 (9%) suspected that others might have used it.

[13] The actual answer was "Do you really want an answer?"

[14] The interviewee commented, "this question is good and straightforward, but I do not know how many of them will answer honestly." See Interview No. 1.

[15] It has been widely held that the Chinese court system cannot effectively resolve disputes and enforce its judgments. See Blumental, *note* 7 *above*, at 236. See also Clarke, Donald C., *The Execution of Civil Judgments in China, in China's Legal Reforms*, pp. 65 – 81 (Stanley Lubman ed., 1996). Snyder, Kelley Brooke, *Denial Of Enforcement of Chinese Arbitral Awards on Public Policy Grounds: The View From Hong Kong*, 42 Virginia Journal of International Law 339, (Fall 2001), p. 340, note 10.

4.1 Objectivity of Courts Law Enforcement

On the question of the objectivity of court law enforcement, as *Chart* 5 shows, the answers were negative. About eighteen percent of surveyed foreign investors gave clearly positive replies ("mostly" and "frequently"), while forty two percent of them replied negatively ("never", "rarely" or "sometimes"). However, a large portion of respondents "did not know" (31%) the question, which might suggest that they had neither direct nor indirect experience of law enforcement by Chinese courts. The other nine percent did not answer the question (*Chart* 5).

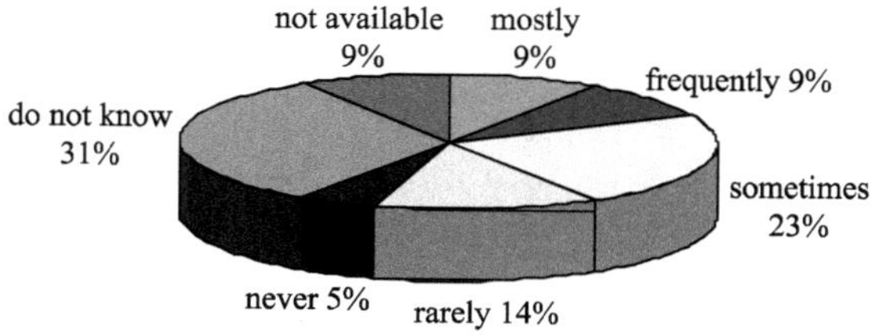

Chart 5 Objectivity of Court Enforcement of Law

4.2 Possibility of Bribing Judges

The question on the possibility of bribing judges has proved to be even more difficult to answer than that on bribing officials[16]. About ten percent of respondents answered positively ("always" and "frequently"), though they claimed that they based their answers on suspicion or belief of other companies' behaviour, rather than their own experience. Another five percent replied that bribery "sometimes" could be used to influence judge's decisions. Thirteen percent of the respondents stated that this had "never" happened to them, but they suspected that other companies might have participated in bribery. Another nine percent did not answer at all. Finally, there was also one response who directly challenged the propriety of the question, by asking "do you really want an answer?" In short, like the question about bribery to officials, this question might have been too provocative to have solicited honest answers (*Chart* 6).

4.3 Political Interference in Court Decisions

Similar to the previous question, most investors ticked "do not know" (54%) or simply did not answer (9%) the question on whether politicians interfered in court decisions. Among these who did give answers, ten percent did positively ("always" or "frequently"), whilst nine percent negatively ("rarely"). Another eighteen percent indicated that political interference "sometimes" happened. No one ticked "never" (*Chart* 7). It might be said that whilst most of the investors did not have court experience, those who had experience tend to believe that political interference in court decisions was not rare.

---

[16] Snyder, ibid.

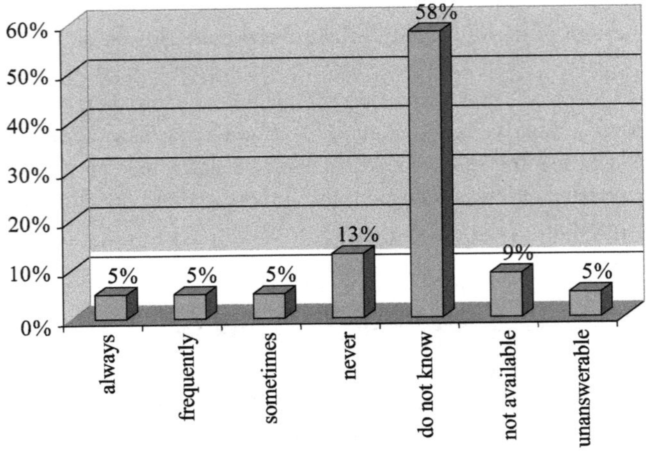

Chart 6 Possibility of Bribery Impacting on Court Decisions

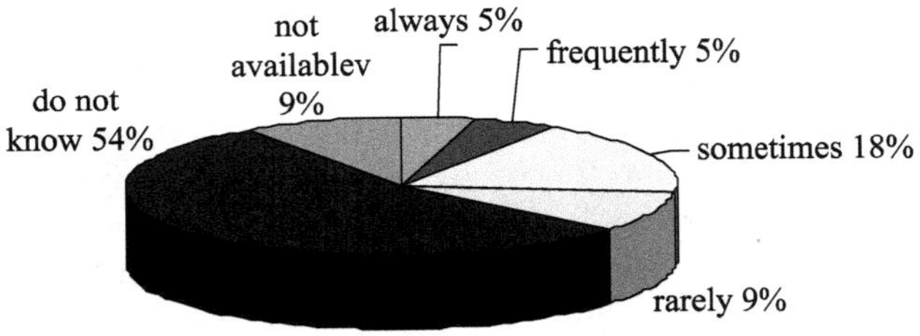

Chart 7 Political Interference in Court Decisions

4.4 Delays in Court and Arbitration Procedures

Answers to the question on the frequency of delays in court and arbitration procedures are clearer, although, similarly, more than a half (54%) of respondents "did not know" the answer and nine percent did not answer it. In the thirty seven percent that did answered the question, fifteen percent clearly said yes ("always", "mostly" or "frequently") while twenty two percent reported that it was "sometimes" the case (*Chart* 8). The fact that no one replied negatively has signalled the seriousness of this problem.

One interesting phenomenon in the responses to all those questions on court enforcement of law is that there was always nine percent who did not answer any of them, whilst there was a substantial but varied percentage (31% for the first one and more than 50% for the latter three) of "do not know" answers. The former may be simply explained as that they did not feel the questions were appropriate, or were not sure how to answer them. The reasons for the latter might be two fold. On the one hand, the substantial portion of foreign investors "did not know" the answer probably shows that they had no court experience at all. On the other hand, however, the differences in the exact percentages implies that some respondents might be unwilling, rather than unable, to answer

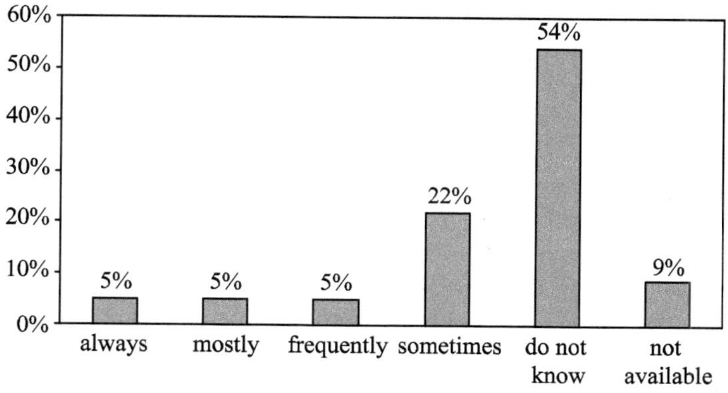

Chart 8 Unreasonable Delays in Court/Arbitration Procedures

some of the questions.

4.5 Enforcement of Court and Arbitration Decisions

In China, the problem over enforcement of court and arbitration decisions have been so prevalent[17] that a special terminology has been developed to describe it—"the Difficulty of Enforcement" (*Zhixing Nan*). As *Chart* 9 shows, the experience of foreign investors confirmed that such a problem did exist. Although there were still more "do not know" answers (45%) than real answers, among the real answers, there were more negative ones (19%, "never" and "rarely") than positive ones (9%, "mostly") No one said that it was "always" the case. As with the previous questions, eighteen percent of replies state that court and arbitration decisions are "sometimes" enforced by the courts. Further, one of the interviewees had expressed desperation over the non-enforcement of the arbitration award he had won[18] (*Chart* 9).

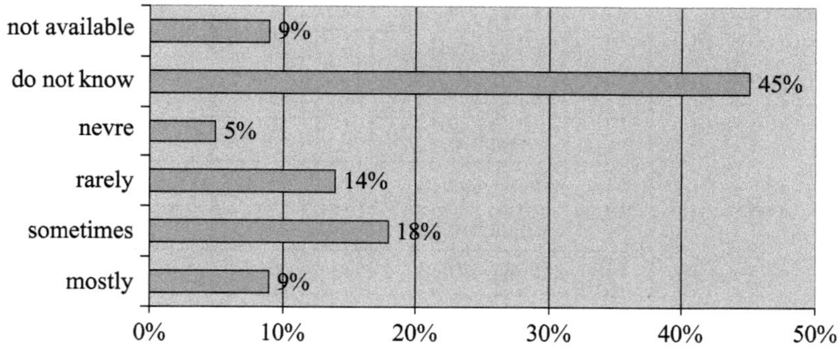

Chart 9 Enforcem ent of Court/Arbitration Decisions

---

〔17〕 See Blumental, *note* 7 *above*, p. 236. See also Clarke, Donald C., *The Execution of Civil Judgments in China, in China's Legal Reforms*, pp. 65 – 81 (Stanley Lubman ed., 1996). Snyder, ibid.

〔18〕 Interview No. 2.

Ⅲ. Measuring the FDI Legal System in China against the Ideal Institutional Paradigm: General Results

In order to compare the FDI legal system in China as experienced by the respondents with the Ideal Institutional Paradigm (IIP), responses to each of the nine questions on the effectiveness of the legal system were converted into a score based on a scale between 0 and 5, with 5 representing maximum conformity with the IIP[19]. Thus, for instance, on accessibility of law, the response "always" obtains the maximum score (5) and "never" receives the minimum (0). "Mostly", "frequently", "sometimes", "rarely" receive 4, 3, 2 and 1 respectively.[20] Details are included in *Annex I: Scores Allocated to Questionnaire Responses to the Effectiveness of the FDI Legal System in China*. Based on this conversion, the average score for each element (feature) was calculated. An average score for the legal system as a whole was generated on the basis of the average scores of the three major components, namely the laws, the bureaucracy and the courts. Elements scored 4 or above are described as "effective", whilst others are described as "borderline" (3 & <4), "ineffective" (2 & <3), "seriously ineffective" (<2). Details of the scores are presented in *Table* 1 below, followed by *Tables* 2 – 3 showing the breakdown results by home state, establishing date and form of investment.

Table 1 FDI Legal System in China Measured against the Ideal Institutional Paradigm

Institution	Feature	Score	Descriptor
Laws	Accessibility	2.65	Ineffective
	Predictability	2.45	Ineffective
	Laws Average	2.55	Ineffective
Bureaucracy	Consistency	2.29	Ineffective
	Corruption	4.23	effective
	Bureaucracy Average	3.26	Borderline
Courts	Objectivity	1.85	Seriously Ineffective
	Corruption	3.33	Borderline
	Independency	2.75	Ineffective
	Efficiency	2.25	Ineffective
	Enforceability	2.00	Ineffective
	Courts Average	2.44	Ineffective
Legal System as a Whole	/	2.75	Ineffective

[19] Perry has conducted a similar comparison in her case study on the effectiveness of Sri Lanka legal system. Perry, PhD dissertation, note 3 above, pp. 195 – 199.

[20] "Do not know" and "do not understand" or blank responses are excluded in the conversion and calculation as they do not bear any quantitative meanings.

As can be seen from *Table* 1, the FDI legal system in China as perceived by respondents, in general, does not conform to the IIP. Only two features, namely corruption by bureaucracy and courts, were on the *effective* or *borderline* category, the accuracy of which as explained above is doubtful. All the other seven factors were well below the *borderline* and were either *ineffective* or *seriously ineffective*. These included accessibility and predictability of laws, consistency in bureaucracy law enforcement, and objectivity, independence, efficiency and enforceability in courts' law enforcement. The worst situation was on objectivity in courts' enforcement of laws, which was *seriously ineffective*, followed by the poor enforcement of courts and arbitration decisions. Overall, the FDI legal system in China was perceived as *ineffective*, with a score of 2.68.

Such a finding was further confirmed by "further comments" of respondents. Of the nine "further comments" received, six were related to the weakness in the enforcement of laws, rather than in the laws *per se*. One respondent said that "[K] ey issue is not only 'regulations', but their implementation." Another commented that "[T] he legal environment is actually not that bad, the problematic part is the enforcement side."[21] One respondent, nevertheless, acknowledged that "there are significant improvements on the legal environment development and the enforcement development."

It can therefore be said that, despite significant improvements, the FDI legal system in China remains ineffective, as it is sometimes inaccessible, often subject to unexpected changes, sometimes inconsistently and often subjectively enforced by government officials and courts, and that court and arbitration decisions are not well carried out.

Ⅳ. Measuring the FDI Legal System in China against the Ideal Institutional Paradigm: Breakdown Of Results

In order to have a more accurate view of the effectiveness of FDI legal system in China, the questionnaire data were broken down by home state, establishing date and form of investment. The following is to present the results of such a breakdown analysis.

First of all, a comparison between British and Continental investors (*Table* 2) shows that Continental investors had, in general, a slightly more positive view on the FDI legal system in China, with a higher overall score (2.83 vs. 2.63). Continental investors were, in particular, more satisfied in the accessibility of laws, the consistency in bureaucracy law enforcement, the corruption and independence of courts and the enforcement record of judicial decisions. The fact that the Chinese legal system is modelled on the Continental legal system might be a reason underpinning such a distinction in perceptions. British investors voted, nevertheless, more positively on the predictability of laws and objectivity in courts law enforcement.

---

〔21〕 Other comments included: "It is utmost important that China evolves towards a real state of law..." "1. Elimination of corruption-Chinese and foreign investors-by clear law fully enforced; 2, Law separated from central politics—see US Constitution!!" "The only frustrating part of doing business in China is that what you have been advised, initially, as being achievable by local authority representatives invariably ends up with several reasons why it is NO longer possible, usually at an advanced stage." "Arbitration process are improving in China, but enforcement of court ruling often deficient."

The comparison between investors in 1990s and 2000s[22] shows that investors in 2000s investors (*Table* 3) were generally much more satisfied with the Chinese FDI system, despite the fact that they were much less experienced than the older investors. The inexperience of the investors in 2000s can be seen from their inability to answer most of the questions on court law enforcement. Nevertheless, as Table 3 shows, wherever they did answer questions, particularly those on laws and bureaucracy, they consistently rated them much more highly than the 1990s investors. On the legal system as a whole, the investors in 2000s rated it within the *borderline* (3. 67), much higher than the *ineffective* score given by the investors in 1990s (2. 38). This might be read as a confirmation of improvement by the Chinese Government over the last couple of decades.

The breakdown data also show that JV investors were much more satisfactory with the legal system than WFE investors. On all aspects except predictability of legal changes, JV investors gave considerably higher scores than those by WFE investors. As a result, the general score given by JV investors was approaching the *borderline* (2. 98), which is a sharp contrast with the *seriously ineffective* score given by WFE investors (1. 79). This further confirms that, compared with WFE, JV is an investment vehicle better attuned to the local legal system.

Table 2　Comparison between British and European Continental Investors

Institution	Feature	Scores		
		British Investors	Continental Investor	All Investors Average
Laws	Accessibility	2. 30	3. 11	2. 65
	Predictability	2. 42	2. 00	2. 45
	Laws Average	2. 36	2. 56	2. 55
Bureaucracy	Consistency	2. 13	2. 50	2. 29
	Corruption	4. 38	4	4. 23
	Bureaucracy Average	3. 26	3. 25	3. 26
Courts	Objectivity	2. 25	1. 5	1. 85
	Corruption	2. 50	4. 33	3. 33
	Independency	2. 50	3. 00	2. 75
	Efficiency	2. 25	2. 25	2. 25
	Enforceability	1. 80	2. 25	2. 0
	Courts Average	2. 26	2. 67	2. 44
Legal System as a Whole	General Score	2. 63	2. 83	2. 75
	Descriptor	Ineffective	Ineffective	Ineffective

〔22〕 Since they were only two respondents established in 1980s and one of them did not answered most of the questions regarding the effectiveness of the legal system, the 1980s data thereon are not included in this comparison as they are not representative enough to demonstrate the general views of the 1980s investors. It is nevertheless noted that, interestingly, when they did answer the questions, they rated most of the factors higher than the 1990s did (except for consistency in bureaucracy law enforcement where they rated 2 in contrast of 2. 08 by 1990s investors) and their score for the overall legal system reached the borderline (3. 00).

Table 3　Comparison between Investors in 1990s and 2000s

Institution	Feature	Score		
		1990s Investor	2000s Investors	All Investors Average
Laws	Accessibility	2.54	3.00	2.65
	Predictability	2.20	3.33	2.45
	Laws Average	2.37	3.17	2.55
Bureaucracy	Consistency	2.08	3.33	2.29
	Corruption	2.80	4.33	4.23
	Bureaucracy Average	2.44	3.83	3.26
Courts	Objectivity	2.00	4.00	1.85
	Corruption	3.33	n/a	3.33
	Independency	2.57	n/a	2.75
	Efficiency	2.14	n/a	2.25
	Enforceability	1.63	n/a	2.0
	Courts Average	2.33	4.00	2.44
Legal System as a Whole	Score	2.38	3.67	2.75
	Descriptor	Ineffective	Borderline	Ineffective

Table 4　Comparison between JV and WFE Investors

Institution	Feature	Score		
		WFE Investors	JV Investors	All Investors Average
Laws	Accessibility	1.75	3.00	2.65
	Predictability	2.80	2.50	2.45
	Laws Average	2.28	2.75	2.55
Bureaucracy	Consistency	2.00	2.38	2.29
	Corruption	3.25	4.67	4.23
	Bureaucracy Average	2.63	3.53	3.26
Courts	Objectivity	1.00	2.17	1.85
	Corruption	0.00	3.33	3.33
	Independency	0.00	3.25	2.75
	Efficiency	0.00	3.00	2.25
	Enforceability	1.33	1.50	2.0
	Courts Average	0.46	2.65	2.44
Legal System as a Whole	Score	1.79	2.98	2.75
	Descriptor	Seriously Ineffective	Ineffective	Ineffective

Ⅴ. Conclusion and Implications

The comparison of foreign investors' perception of the FDI legal system in China with the Ideal Institutional Paradigm reveals that, despite significant advancement in many aspects, the FDI legal system in China remained ineffective. Laws are sometimes inaccessible and often subject to unexpected changes. Government officials sometimes implemented laws inconsistently, whilst courts often implemented laws subjectively, rather than objectively. Court judgements were sometimes interfered by politicians, and court proceedings often subject to delays. To make it worse, decisions by courts and arbitration tribunals were often poorly enforced. In addition, the breakdown data suggest that, relative to British, WFE and earlier investors, Continental, JV and later investors were more satisfied by the effectiveness of the FDI legal system in China, which is in conformity with a previous finding that they were also more concerned with the nature of the legal system.

This finding, read together with the great importance that foreign investors attached to the law and the general satisfaction by the substantive aspects of the law mentioned in the first part of this study, demonstrates that, foreign investors had observed a wide gap between the substance of the laws and the enforcement of the these laws. As a result, investors will probably continue to take advantage of the favourable substance of existing laws and regulation, particularly those granting them investment incentives and better treatment, whilst trying to avoid as far as possible the formal dispute resolution system in China.[23] It can thus be anticipated that foreign investors will be inclined to resort to international forums for settling their disputes, particularly those involving Chinese government authorities. As China has widened the access to international investment dispute settlement mechanisms such as ICSID in its BIT practice,[24] it is very likely that international investment dispute involving the Chinese government will be on the rise. *Chanchun Huijin case* and *Fuzhou Xinyuan case* are clear manifestations of this trend.

From the perspectives of the Chinese government, the implications of this investigation are that it should work harder to strengthen the legal system, in particular, its law enforcement mechanism, including the courts and the bureaucracy. The courts and judges should be empowered to ensure independence.[25] The qualification of judges

---

〔23〕 An alternative to this might be that foreign investors learn the Chinese legal and administrative culture and adapt themselves to the local circumstances. However, this takes time and "real" foreign investors can not compete with overseas Chinese investors in this regard.

〔24〕 For instance, in the new Sino-Germany BIT singed in December 2003, China agreed that foreign investors might automatically submit "all investment disputes" to the ICSID for arbitration, rather than only disputes over amount of compensation for expropriation as old version stated. See Article 9 of the new Sino-Germany BIT and compare it with Point 4 of the Protocol to the old Sino-Germany BIT singed in 1983.

〔25〕 This could be done institutionally by raising the status of courts and judges in relation to government departments and party officials, and financially by increasing the salaries of judges and other key personnel. That might reduce their vulnerability to both administrative powers and private briberies. See also OECD Policy Brief, *Attracting Investment to China*, note 30 above, p. 7.

should be enhanced by raising appointment threshold and intensifying professional training.[26] Likewise, government agencies involved in law enforcement should be well empowered and staffed. Politicians, as well as the general public, should be made fully aware of the importance of judicial independence.[27] A national and regional mechanism might be established to enhance the enforcement of court decisions.[28] All these aspects contribute to a general theme, which is the establishment of the rule of law in China. Undoubtedly, it could be a painful process and would take years, if not decades, to achieve. However, it is believed that such a painful course is worth taking, because it is in the interests of not only foreign investors, but even more so, the Chinese government and the Chinese people.

ANNEX I

SCORES ALLOCATED TO QUESTIONNAIRE RESPONSES TO THE EFFECTIVENESS OF FDI LEGAL SYSTEM IN CHINA

16. Are Chinese FDI laws and policies easily accessible in China?

0 __	Never	4 __	Mostly
1 __	Rarely	5 __	Always
2 __	Sometimes		
3 __	Frequently		

17. Are the laws and/or policies of China changed unexpectedly?

5 __	Never	1 __	Mostly
4 __	Rarely	0 __	Always
3 __	Sometimes		
2 __	Frequently		

18. Do government officials enforce laws consistently?

0 __	Never	4 __	Mostly
1 __	Rarely	5 __	Always
2 __	Sometimes		
3 __	Frequently		

[26] In Chinese primary courts, most judges had not received proper legal training before they started their judicial practice. Most of them are former military officers who returned their home provinces after completing military services. Only few judges were university graduates who may or may not have a law degree. The situation seems to have been improved as a national examination has been introduced to qualify judges and existing judges have been undergoing legal training. Yet their overall quality seems to remain low. For an insightful discussion on this issues, among other issues relating to grass-root judicial system in China, see ZHU, Suli, *Sending Law to the Country: An Inquiry into the Judicial System at the Grass-root Level* (in Chinese), China Political Science and Law University Press (2000), particularly Chapter 10.

[27] This may prove to be the most difficult part, since China had a long tradition that local governors also acted as local judges and current government officials tend to consider them in charge of everything in the localities, including judicial matters. Accordingly, China's general public usually consider the courts a part of the government.

[28] China's Supreme Court has made effort to improve the enforcement record of court judgements. However, the problem still exists as a huge back-log of un-enforced cases can not be dealt with overnight. See OECD Policy Brief, *Attarcting Investment to China*, (September 2003), p. 7.

19. Is it necessary to use bribery when dealing with government officials?

5 __ Never
4 __ Rarely
3 __ Sometimes
2 __ Frequently
1 __ Mostly
0 __ Always

20. Do the Chinese courts enforce law objectively according to published rules?

0 __ Never
1 __ Rarely
2 __ Sometimes
3 Frequently
4 __ Mostly
5 __ Always

21. Is it possible to use bribery to impact on judge's decisions?

5 __ Never
4 __ Rarely
3 __ Sometimes
2 __ Frequently
1 __ Mostly
0 __ Always

22. Do politicians interfere in court decisions?

5 __ Never
4 __ Rarely
3 __ Sometimes
2 __ Frequently
1 __ Mostly
0 __ Always

23. Are court/arbitration procedures subject to unreasonable delays?

5 __ Never
4 __ Rarely
3 __ Sometimes
2 __ Frequently
1 __ Mostly
0 __ Always

24. Are the decisions of courts and arbitrators well enforced by Chinese authorities?

0 __ Never
1 __ Rarely
2 __ Sometimes
3 __ Frequently
4 __ Mostly
5 __ Always

Law and Foreign Investment in China: General Role of Law and Substantive Issues*

The empirical evidence shows that law had played a very important role in investor's decision-making process. Most investors had conducted an in-depth research on the legal environment before they invested, including not only the written law but law in action; not only Chinese laws and regulations but also applicable international agreements. Contrary to what is commonly believed, an overwhelming majority of foreign investors considered incentives a very important factor when they decided to invest in China. The survey also confirms the positive impact of China's accession to the WTO and a potential new investment treaty in improving the investment conditions.

The study also demonstrates that foreign investors considered China as a safe place to invest. They appreciated the great efforts the Chinese government had made to attract FDI, particularly the implementation of national treatment, the elimination of certain performance requirements, the relaxation of foreign exchange regime, and the strengthening of IPR law and enforcement. However, they also thought that a better investment could be achieved by, in particular, strictly enforcing IPR laws.

The success of the People's Republic of China (hereinafter referred to as "China") in attracting foreign direct investment (FDI) in the last decade is unprecedented. Since 1993, China has maintained its position as the second largest FDI recipient in the world for at least six years, and the single largest among developing countries for ten consecutive years.[1] In

---

* *Manchester Journal of International Economic Law*, Vol. 2, No. 3, 2005.

The author would like to also thank Professor Sir Elihu Lauterpacht CBE QC, Mr. Daniel Bethlehem QC, Lord Leon Brittan, Mr. Peter Nightingale and Miss Amanda Perry for their help and support on the Questionnaire and interviews conducted for this research. He would also like to thank Professor Thomas Walde and Professor Peter Edge for their comments on earlier versions of this article.

[1] According to Rubens Ricupero, by 1998 China had been the top FDI recipient in developing countries and second largest in the world for five consecutive years. See Ricupero, Rubens (Secretary General of UNCTAD), *Recent Development in FDI Trends and Policies and Their Implications for Developing* Counties, Forum on Direct Investment Strategies of the Multinational Corporations.

2003, China outstripped the United States and became the largest FDI recipient in the world.[2] The growth rate of its FDI stock over the past decade has outpaced that of all other major economies in the world[3], with the total stock reaching $ 562 billion by the end of 2004[4]. Undoubtedly, China serves as the best example of success among the developing (if not all) countries in effectively attracting and utilising FDI.[5]

It has been unclear, however, whether and to what extent law[6] has played a role in China's success in attracting FDI. On the one hand, outsiders tend to discount the importance of law in the light of East Asian history, particularly that of China after World War II.[7] On the other hand, law has been regarded as one of the most important factors contributed to the Pacific economic boom.[8] China's efforts to strengthen its FDI regulatory regime, in particular, have often been considered as one of the most important factors that have fuelled China's success in attracting FDI.[9] However, there is little empirical evidence demonstrating such an interrelationship between FDI activities in China and the governing domestic and international laws. Considering that the Chinese legal system is generally characterized by a significant gap between law and reality,[10] ascertaining the law as experienced by foreign invest-

---

[2] It was widely reported that China had already become the number one FDI recipient in 2002. However, according to the OECD, a revision of data revealed that China was actually still in the second place in the FDI recipient league table in 2002, next to the United States. In consequence, 2003 became the first year on record in which China surpassed the US as the world's largest FDI recipient. See OECD, *Trends and Recent Development in Foreign Direct Investment, June* 2004, p. 3, 5, availble at < http://www.oecd.org/dataoecd/52/11/2958722.pdf > (visited on 10 July 2004). For previous reports on China's performance in attracting FDI in 2002, see OECD: *Trends and Recent Developments in Foreign Direct Investment*, June 2003, availble at < http://www.oecd.org/pdf/M00042000/M00042212.pdf > (visited on 1 July 2003); *UNCTAD* Predicts 27% Drop in FDI Inflow this Year and China May Outstrip U.S. as World's Largest FDI Recipient, UNCTAD Press Release TAD/INF/PR/63 (24/10/02). See also QIAN Weizeng, *International Investors Favours China the Most*, CE, Yuming, *China Received FDI 52.7 Billion Last Year*, and YANG Qing, *Sharp Increase of Investment Opportunities in China for Multinationals*, in People's Daily (overseas edition), 28 June 2003, at 5, 15 January 2003, at 1 and 24 May 2003, at 5 respectively.

[3] Ricupero, note 1 above, p. 7.

[4] Gong, Wen, 621 *Billion FDI Is Not Too Much*, Global Times (Huanqiu Shibao, in Chinese), 28 January 2005, p. 13.

[5] China accounted for over half of the FDI inflows into Asia—twice as much as Central and Eastern Europe and Africa combined—and 11 per cent of the world total in 1997. Ricupero, note 1 above, p. 7.

[6] "Law" here refers to the legal environment in general, including not only the law on paper such as IPR laws and investment incentives, but also the law in action, i. e., the enforcement of laws and regulations.

[7] Emilou, Nicholas and O'Keeffe, David, *The European Union and the World Trade Law: after the Uruguay Round*, John Wiley & Sons Ltd, 1996, p. 363.

[8] Ibid.

[9] Other factors include the country's large and continuously growing market; its export-oriented strategy and successful penetration of world markets; significant improvement of its macro-economic environment; the spill-over effects of industrial upgrading in neighbouring economies. See Ricupero, Rubens, note 1 above, p. 6 and OECD Press Release: *Reforms Could Boost China's Ability to Attract Foreign Investment*, availble at < http://www.oecd.org/document/8/0,2340,en_2649_37467_3240968_1_1_1_37467,00.html > (visited 10 July 2004). See also Emilou, Nicholas and O'Keeffe, David, *The European Union and the World Trade Law: after the Uruguay Round*, John Wiley & Sons Ltd, 1996, p. 363.

[10] For general discussion of such a gap, see Corne, Peter Howard, *Foreign Investment in China: the Administrative Legal System*, Transnational Publishers, 1997, pp. 1 – 50.

ors, rather than the law as intended and designed by the government, is of essential importance[11]. Such a study may also contribute to the studies of general international investment law and development, where empirical research is essential yet empirical evidence remains rare[12].

The present study considers the practical implications of the law governing foreign investment in China, through the experiences of European Union (EU) investors. EU investors were chosen not only because the author has been residing in the EU and therefore it is more convenient to conduct such a study, but also because EU investors might be more representative. They are more representative than Asian investors, such as overseas Chinese investors from Hong Kong, Macau, Taiwan and south-east Asian countries, since they tend to be genuine "foreign" investors. EU investors are also more representative than US or Japanese investors as they represent investors from 15 (now 25) countries rather than only one country.

To that end, the author designed a Questionnaire (*Annex I*) and circulated it to EU investors in China. The author also conducted interviews with EU investors, representatives of European chambers of commerce and government officials from both China and the EU.

As the first half of the study, this article first briefly introduces the Questionnaire and interview processes. It will then present the main findings out of the Questionnaire and interview, with regard to the general role of law in investment decision making process and some key substantive legal issues involved in the life cycle of foreign investment. In this process, the questionnaire data will first be looked at as a whole to obtain a general view of EU and foreign investors. Then they are broken down into three factors, namely the country of origin, date of establishment and the form of investment, to see whether there factors could further explain some of the variations in opinions between European investors. (See *Annex II* for further details on country of origin, date of establishment and type of foreign investment of the respondent investors.) The second half of this study explores and examines the question of the effectiveness of the Chinese FDI legal system, which is to be published in the following issue of this journal.

---

〔11〕 Indeed, as the European Bank of Reconstruction and Development (EBRD) rightly pointed out in the *Transition Report* 1996, "as important as what rules say...is what they mean in practice. A pristine statute on investment that is unknown, unadministered and unenforced is ineffective." European Bank of Reconstruction and Development (EBRD), *Transition Report*, 1996, London: EBRD, p. 101.

〔12〕 For instance, a recent report by the UNCTAD Secretariat addressing the issues of effectiveness of FDI laws and policies concluded that specialised studies are required to answer the question, among others, "What are private sector views on effective FDI policy measures and the role of investment promotion institutions?", Perry also observed that there was "little empirical evidence" to support the argument that the effectiveness of a legal system should be a determinant of FDI. On the lack of evidence in development studies, an area closely associated with international investment, Joseph Stiglitz, the former chief economist of the World Bank wrote, "if we believe our policies were helping East Asia, where was the evidence? As a participant in these debates, I got to see the evidence. There was none." See UNCTAD, *Effectiveness of Foreign Direct Investment Policy Measures* (Note by the UNCTAD Secretariat), TD/B/COM. 2/EM. 13/2 (22 April 2003). Perry, Amanda, *Effective Legal System and Foreign Direct Investment: In Search of the Evidence*, 49 ICLQ 779 (hereinafter as "Perry, ICLQ"), p. 779; J. Stiglitz, *What I Learned at the World Economic Crisis*, The New Republic (April 2000).

I. The Questionnaire and the Interviews

1. The Questionnaire

The Questionnaire[13] consisted of three parts which contain twenty seven questions, in addition to some basic information about the investor being surveyed. Because contact information for foreign investors in China was not publicly available, the survey was carried out among members of chambers of commerce connected with EU investment in China. From April to July 2001, 549 questionnaires were therefore sent to members of the China-Britain Business Council (CBBC), European Union Chamber of Commerce in China (EUCCC) and the British Chamber of Commerce in China (BCCC). Among those, 203 questionnaires were sent by post to CBBC members in Britain, 174 were sent via email to EUCCC members and 162 to BCCC members that were not CBBC members. The Questionnaire was sent out in English, accompanied by an introduction and a cover letter from the author explaining the objectives of the survey. Companies which did not respond were contacted either by telephones (for those in Britain and Europe) or by further emails (for those in China).

Of the fifty four responses received, twenty two were usable[14]. The ten percent response rate was not low compared with other similar postal questionnaire surveys[15]. The number of usable responses was rather small, mainly because many of these chamber members were not engaged in direct investment in China.[16] Such a small sample size suggests that it be more appropriate treating the questionnaire results as a step towards definitive answers on the surveyed issues, rather than such answers *per se*.

A close look at the responses, nevertheless, shows that the representative quality of the twenty two usable responses should not be underestimated. Firstly, the responses covered seven major EU countries, which accounted for ninety five percent of total EU investment in China, including Britain, Germany, France, Italy, Netherlands, Denmark and Luxembourg.[17] As *Chart* 1 shows, the country distribution of surveyed EU invest-

---

[13] In the designing of the Questionnaire, references have been made to Perry's Questionnaire on laws and law enforcement in Sri Lanka and the "*Survey of the Attitudes of the European Business Community to International Investment Rules*" by TN SOFRES Consulting. See Perry, Amanda J., *Legal Systems as a Determinant of Foreign Direct Investment: The Case of Sri Lanka*, London School of Economics PhD Dissertation, 2000, (Hereinafter as Perry PhD Dissertation) Appendix 2: Questionnaire; TN SOFRES Consulting (on behalf of the European Commission DG Trade), *Survey of the Attitudes of the European Business Community to International Investment Rules: Final Report*, April 2000 (hereinafter referred as the TN SOFRES Survey).

[14] A Swiss response was discarded, as Switzerland is not a member state of the EU even though it is in Europe.

[15] For instance, the TN SOFRES Survey supported by the European Commission had achieved only a seven percent response rate. See TN SOFRES Survey, note 13 above, p. 1.

[16] Most of the unusable responses stated that they would like to help but this Questionnaire did not apply to them as they did not directly invest in China. Some of them are not precisely EU investment but investment from the US or other places like Switzerland. Some expressed that they were not in the best position to answer the questions and would pass the Questionnaire to better-positioned persons, which resulted in no further communication. Few companies simply said that they were too busy to participate in this exercise.

[17] Britain may be relatively "over-represented" for obvious reasons. However, this is still justifiable as Britain is the largest EU investor in China.

ments was generally consistent with that of actual EU investments in China (*Chart* 1). Also, these responses covered all the three major industries and many different sectors of the economy, including agriculture, manufacturing, infrastructure, energy and service sectors. From *Chart* 2, one can see that the industry distribution of the surveyed EU investments actually coincided with that of the general foreign investment in China[18] (*Chart* 2). Thirdly, investment sizes of the responding companies range from £ 100,000 to one billion Deutschmarks (approximately £ 357 million).[19] Fourthly, although most of the investment projects were situated in eastern China, some were located in western China (including central China). As can be seen from *Chart* 3, the location distribution of the surveyed EU investments was also in conformity with that of actual foreign investment in China (*Chart* 3). Moreover, whilst most of the EU investments were established in the 1990s, some were set up as early as the 1980s and some as late as 2001 (*Chart* 4). Finally, other elements, such as investment duration, foreign equity and foreign participation in management, also demonstrated that these responses generally reflected the overall picture of EU and foreign investment in China.[20]

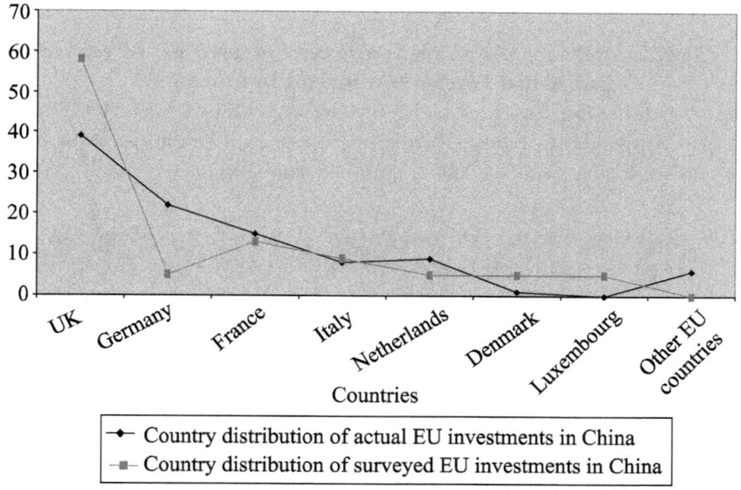

Chart 1 Country Distributions between Surveyed EU Investments and Actual EU Investment in China (%)

Source of country distribution of EU investments in China: *Yearbook of China Customs Statistics*, 1980 – 1999.

[18] Unfortunately, the data on EU investment in these industries and sectors is not available.

[19] This conversion is in accordance with the conversion rate published in Financial Times on 1 July 2003. See http://mwprices.ft.com/custom/ft-com/currency.asp (visited 1 July 2003).

[20] Details of the profiles of those surveyed investors are included in "*Appendix II: Profiles of Surveyed Investors*" in the author's PhD dissertation completed at the University of Cambridge (2004).

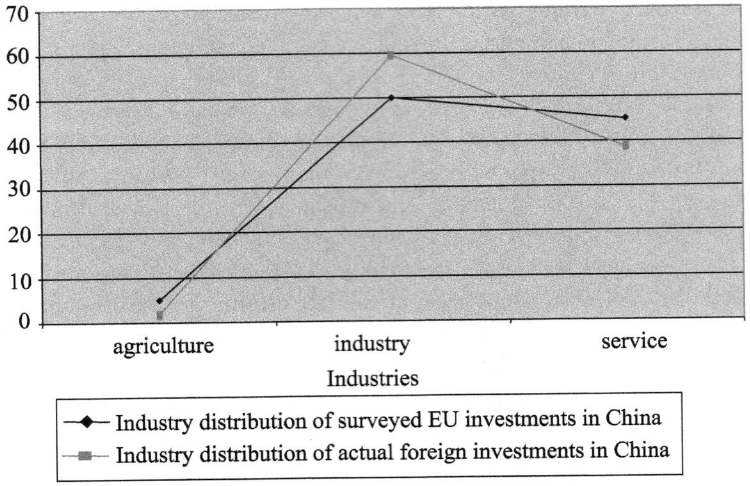

Chart 2 Industry Distributions between Surveyed EU Investments and Actual Foreign Investments in China (%)

Source of industry distribution of foreign investment in China is from MOFTEC FDI Statistics: Industry Distribution of Foreign Direct Investment by 1999, available at http://www.moftec.gov.cn/moftec_cn/tjsj/wztj/2000_9-22-23.html (visited on 15 July 2002).

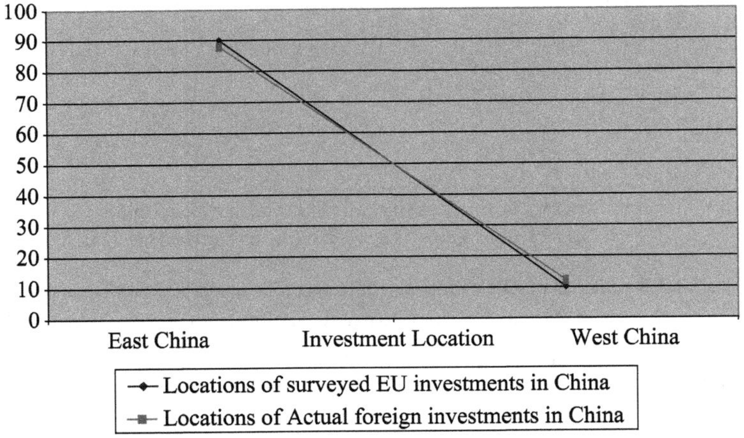

Chart 3 Location Distributions between Surveyed EU Investments and Actual Foreign Investments in China (%)

Source of location distribution of foreign investment in China is from MOFTEC FDI Statistics: Foreign Direct Investment in the East, West and Middle China by 1999, available at <http://www.moftec.gov.cn/moftec_cn/tjsj/wztj/2000_9-22-28.html> (visited on 15 July 2002). Here the FDI in the West and the Middle China are counted together as foreign investment in the Western China.

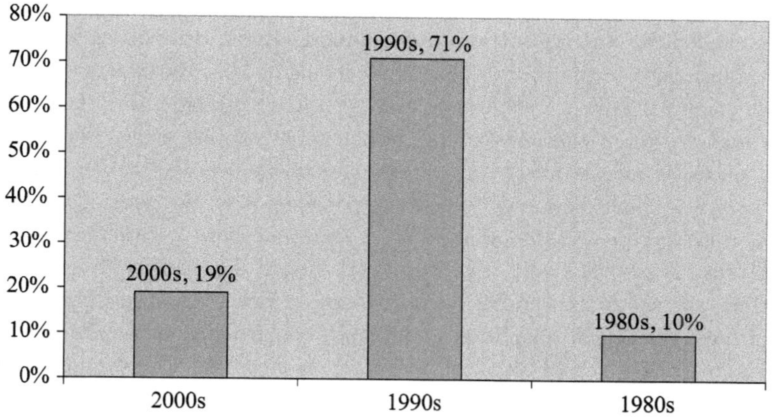

Chart 4　Establishing Dates of Respondent Investors

2. The Interviews

The interviews conducted within this research fell into three categories: interviews with government officials, interviews with investment promotion agencies and interviews with private companies. In June 2001, the author went to Brussels and interviewed officials in charge of the Community's investment or China business issues, including two of the major negotiators from the EU in the EU-China WTO talks. Several officials from the Ministry of Foreign Trade and Economic Co-operation (MOFTEC, now the Ministry of Commerce (MOFCOM)) were also interviewed in 2001 by email and via telephone conversations.

Interviews with investment promotion agencies included those with the Chief Executive Officer (CEO) of China-Britain Business Council (CBBC), the Chief Representative of the Representative Office of the China Commission for the Promotion of International Trade (CCPIT)[21] in the EU, and the China Manager of the Asia Invest, a privately run European Union programme. The author also followed up questionnaire responses with interviews with London-based companies which had invested in China.

All interviews were based on semi-structured questions similar to those in the Questionnaire. The questions were slightly adapted to suit the special circumstances of interviewees. The interviews revealed the attitudes of the business communities and government agencies towards the legal environment of EU investment in China, and their concerns and preferences on the subject of its direction in future development.

II. The General Role of Law in Investment Decision-Making

Shihata, the former General Counsel of the World Bank, once commented that "a legal and regulatory framework...is a fundamental element in the stability and flexibility

[21] CCPIT is the oldest and biggest trade and investment promotion agency of China.

needed for the investment environment."[22] In the case of China, a recent OECD research concluded that China's success in attracting FDI was partly owing to its efforts to "bringing regulations in line with international standards"[23]. However, so far there has been little empirical evidence confirming such a positive co-relationship. Thus the Questionnaire included three questions aiming to determine to what extent the legal framework has played a role in foreign investors' investment decision-making process. The first question was about the foreign investors' perceptions on the general role of law in the decision-making process, followed by a series of questions on whether and to what extent they had investigated the legal framework before the decisions were made. The last question was about the significance of investment incentives in making their investment decisions. Further, another three questions were included to ascertain EU investors' perceptions of the implication of WTO accession on the Chinese investment climate, the significance of concluding a bilateral or multilateral investment agreement to which China and the EU are parties, and their preferences of important provisions to be included in the potential agreement.

1. Relative Importance of Law as a Determinant of Investment Decision

In the first question, investors were asked what priority they gave the nature of the legal system in deciding whether or not to invest in China, relative to other factors, such as market size, labour costs, environmental costs and raw material supply. The Questionnaire results (*Chart* 5) show that when deciding to invest in China, most respondents (83%) considered law (nature of the legal system) as an element of substantial importance (top, high or medium). Among them, five percent of the respondents regarded law as of "top" importance in investment decision-making, while most of them considered it as of high (36%) or medium (40%) importance. Only one respondent considered law of no significance at all. However, the respondent wrote in the Questionnaire margin that it "shall be top now".

Admittedly, this result was rather high and might be higher than in reality, as those who answered this Questionnaire entitled "Law and EU Investment in China" might be those who were more concerned about the legal environment and had therefore paid more attention to the law whilst making the investment decisions. However, this might also be explained by the fact that the EU investors were generally unfamiliar with the legal climate of foreign investment in China and were therefore more concerned about it.

The home country breakdown shows that British investors placed slightly less importance to law than their European Continental counterparts, as only seventy seven percent of British investors considered law of substantial importance, compared with a near ninety percent of Continental investors who shared this view. All respondents from France, Italy, Netherlands, Denmark and Luxemburg considered law of substantial importance. This contrasts the Perry's finding in her Sri Lanka study which suggested a

---

〔22〕 Shihata, Abrahim F I, *World Bank in a Changing World* (1995), Martinus Nijhoff, p. 234.

〔23〕 OECD Press Release, *Reforms Could Boost China's Ability to Attract Foreign Investment*, note 9 above.

higher importance attached to law by British investors than other European investors[24]. Interestingly, however, one German respondent attached only "low" importance to the nature of law. This might be explained by the fact that the company was established in China in 1980s when a sophisticated legal system has not yet been established in China. The company's "over 100 years of experience" of doing business with China might be another reason, which this investor specifically highlighted as a source of confidence in investing in China, as we will see later.

The establishing date breakdown confirms that earlier investors tended to discount the importance of law. All respondents established in 1980s considered law of only "low" or "medium" importance. On the contrary, seventy five percent of investors established in or after 2000 attached "high" importance to law. Investors established in 1990s varied in their responses, which are consistent with the general picture mentioned above. The underlying reason, as said above, might be that a sophisticated FDI law system had not been constructed until middle 1990s.

The breakdown by the form of investment demonstrates that joint venture (JV) investors were slightly more concerned with the law than wholly foreign owned enterprise (WFE) investors. A half of the straight JV respondents attached "high" importance to law, whilst only one third straight WFE respondents did the same. Some respondents invested in both JV and WFE forms and their replies were mixed: two third of them thought law of "high" value and the rest of "low" value. The finding that JV investors attached higher importance to law than WFE investors is interesting and somewhat unexpected, as it is often believed that due to the availability of local participation and then local resources in the venture, JV investors are less sensitive to the nature of the legal system in the host country. One explanation could be that JV investments are more complicated and therefore more reliant on a sophisticated legal system.

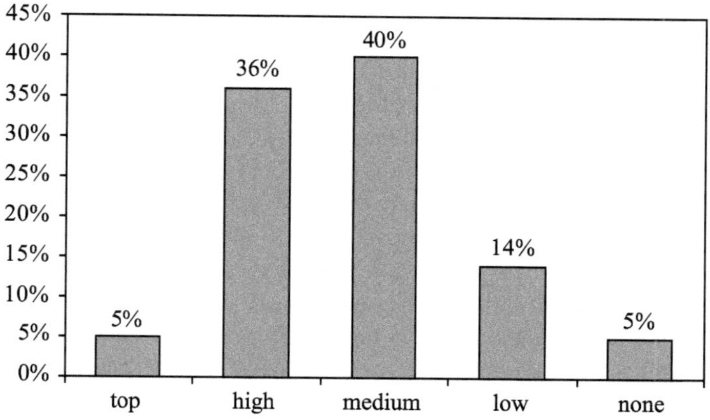

Chart 5 Relative Importance of Law in Investment Decision Making

[24] Perry, ICLQ, note 12 above, p. 794.

2. Investigation of Law before Investment

The second question consisted of a series of sub-questions designed to find out whether or not foreign investors actually carried out investigations of the legal environment before the investment decisions were made. The first question was to inquire whether they had investigated the legal elements of investment, including legal measures of investment promotion (e. g., tax incentives) and protection (e. g., expropriation and compensation and investment insurance). The answers (*Chart* 6) to this question corresponded to answers to the previous one, which confirms that the vast majority of investors had done such an investigation when decided to invest. All those who considered law as of "high" or "top" importance had conducted such studies. On the contrary, those who did not study law when are those who considered law of "medium" (17%) or "low" (5%) importance. It is interesting to note that, however, some investors (9%) did such a study although they considered law of "low" importance.

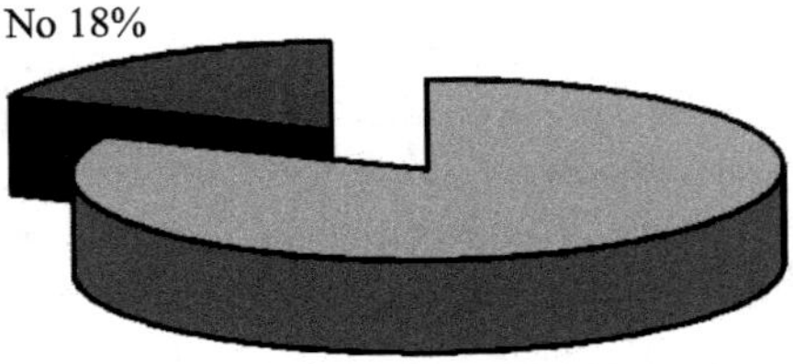

Chart 6 Investigation of Law before Making Investment

On this point, the three breakdown results are general correspondent to those to the previous question. In other words, European, later and JV investors were more active in studying law than British, earlier and WFE investors respectively.

The following sub-question was about the evidence used in investigating the legal environment, i. e., whether they had investigated only the written law ("law on paper") or both the written law and the law in action (e. g., levels of enforcement). As shown in *Chart* 7, in investigating the legal environment, most (55%) investors paid an *in-depth study*, i. e., investigated both the written law and the law in action. In contrast, a substantial portion of investor (39%) merely examined the written law (a *superficial study*). This result reveals that, on the one hand, most investors has conducted an in-depth investigation on the legal environment, and that, on the other hand, written law was put in a relatively higher priority when compared with law enforcement.

A closer look at this issue using the breakdown prism demonstrates that earlier and JV investors tended to conduct in-depth studies, whilst more recent and WFE investors tended to do only a superficial study. (In this regard, there is no perceivable difference between investors from difference origins, particularly between British and Continental investors.) Sixty percent of the investors established in 1990s studied both the written law and the law enforcement, whilst only twenty percent of the investors entered in China in 2000s did the same thing. There might be two reasons: one is that law enforcement has been improved considerably over the decades; the other is that laws and regulation

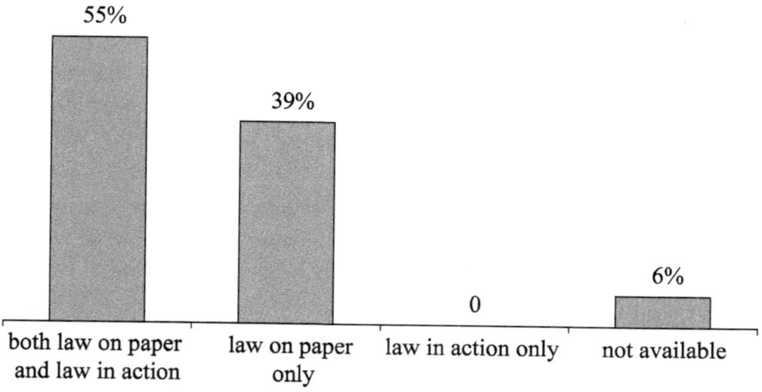

Chart 7 Evidence of Law Investigated

on FDI have been increased so significantly over the years that recent investors could no longer afford to investigate beyond the written law. Among the straight WFE respondents, only less than twenty percent (17%) examined both written law and law enforcement, a sharp contrast with the eighty percent of such investigation conducted by straight JV investors. This result conforms with the previous finding that JV investors tended to be more concerned with the nature of the legal system.

Furthermore, as *Chart* 8 reveals, about a half (49%) of those who investigated the legal environment made a *comprehensive study*, i. e., studied both the Chinese law and the applicable international treaties. About forty percent of these investors, however, studied only Chinese law whilst only six percent of them investigated international treaties only (*partial study*). This shows that, compared with international treaties, domestic law played a much more important role (*Chart* 8).

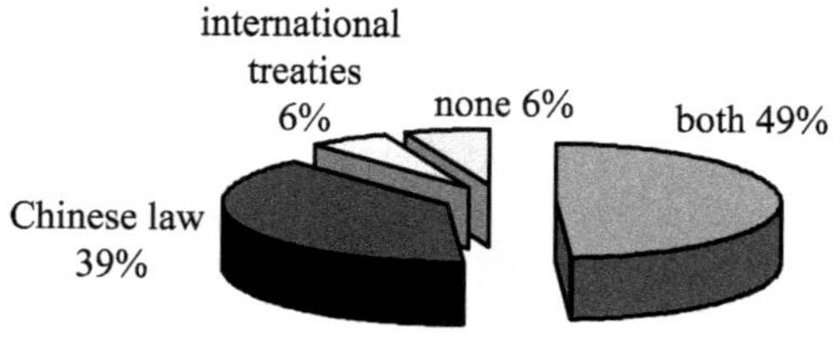

Chart 8 Chinese Law and International Treaties Considered

The breakdown data show that earlier and JV investors tended to take a comprehensive approach, which confirms their more active attitude towards the study of law in general. More than a half of the 1990s investors did a comprehensive study, whilst one a quarter of 2000s investors did the same study. This seems to suggest a decrease of the influence of investment treaties over the last decades, relative to Chinese laws in the investment decision making process. One explanation of this might be the rapid advancement of Chinese FDI laws and regulations, particularly since early 1990s, which have become more and more in line with international agreements and standards. As a result, existing investment treaties between China and the home states of the foreign investors have become, relatively, less and less significant to them.

Among the JV investors, seventy percent did a comprehensive research, whilst only seventeen percent of WFE investors conducted such research. As said, this result conforms to the previous finding that JV investors tended to be more emphatic on the nature of the legal system.

Chart 9 further disclosed that, among the relevant international treaties, most investors (68%) were aware of bilateral treaties devoted to the avoidance of double taxation (DTTs).[25] About a half (45%) of them knew that there were bilateral investment treaties (BITs) between China and their home states.[26] The two important global conventions on investment protection, namely the Convention Establishing the International Centre for the Settlement of Investment Disputes between States and Nationals of Other States (ICSID Convention)[27] and the Convention Establishing the Multilateral Investment Guarantee Agency (MIGA Convention)[28] were known to many fewer investors (18% and 9% respectively). Furthermore, one respondent added the New York Convention on the Recognition and Enforcement of Foreign Arbitration Awards (New York Convention) as another international treaty that has great importance on foreign investment in China (*Chart* 9). The fact that more investors knew of DTTs than BITs demonstrates that economic concern (i. e. taxation and cost) was always put at a much higher priority than legal concern (i. e. investment protection). The limited publicity of ICSID Convention and MIGA Convention highlighted the limitation of the two instruments: they are probably too specialised to be even generally known of.

The home state breakdown study shows that EU continental investors had better knowledge of BITs than British investors, although both of them highlighted the importance of DTTs. Only twenty three percent of British investors were aware of the Sino-Britain BIT whilst seventy eight percent of investors from the European Continent reported knowledge of applicable BITs. One reason of such a difference might be that UK is

---

[25] By 2000, China has signed 66 DTTs with other states, including 24 of the 25 EU member states (except Greece). See ZHU, Qing, *International Taxation*, China People's University Press, 2001, pp. 225 – 231. Details of these DTTs could be found at http://www. abacn. com/csfg/index. php? lei = ssxd (visited on 16 July 2004).

[26] According to MOFTEC (now MOFCOM) officials, China had concluded 106 BITs by March 2003, including 22 of the 25 EU member states (except Ireland, Latvia and Malta). See XU, Chunlin, *Investment Protection on Fast Track of Development in China*, available at < http://www. fdi. gov. cn/common/frnreport. jsp? id = CENSOFT0000000007375 > (visited on 4 June 2003). See also ICSID, *Bilateral Investment Treaties*, available at < http://www. worldbank. org/icsid/treaties/china. htm > (visited on 14 July 2004); UNCTAD, *Bilateral Investment Treaties for China*, available at < http://stats. unctad. org/fdi/treaties/bits/China. htm > (visited on 14 July 2004).

[27] As of November 2003, 154 States had signed the ICSID Convention, 139 of which have already deposited their instruments of ratification. Both China and 24 of the 25 EU member states (except Poland) are members of the convention. ICSID, *List of Contracting States and other Signatories of the Convention* (as of Nov. 3, 2003), available at < http://www. worldbank. org/icsid/constate/c-states-en. htm > (visited on 14 July 2004).

[28] As of 25 June 2003, the number of member countries reached 162, and 8 additional countries were in the process of fulfilling the membership requirements. Both China and all the 25 EU member states are members of the MIGA Convention. MIGA, *MIGA Member Countries*, available at < http://www. miga. org/screens/about/members/members. htm > (visited on 14 July 2004).

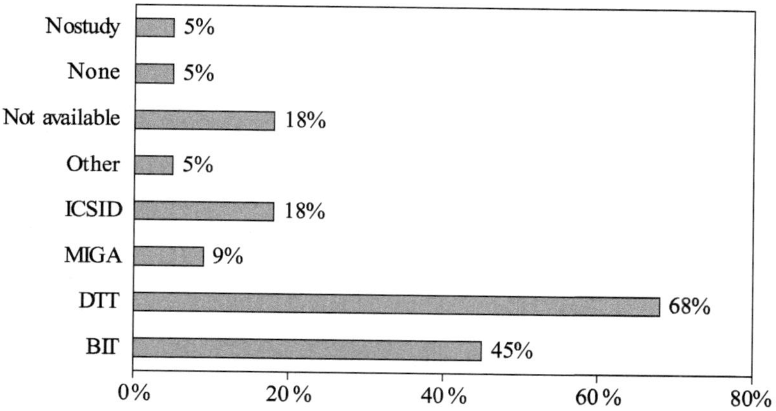

Chart 9 International Treaties Aware of

relatively a newcomer in BIT practice, compared with its Continental partners. The date of establishment breakdown study further confirms the decreasing influence of BITs in investors' decision making process. Only twenty five percent of investors established in 2000s knew of BITs, a sharp drop compared with a fifty three percent among 1990s investors. The breakdown of data by the type of investment has shown no significant difference between WFEs and JV in their knowledge applicable international treaties: they both had a much better knowledge of DTTs than BITs.

3. Importance of Incentives on Investment Decision-Making

The third question aimed at determining whether the incentive measures that the Chinese Government used to attract FDI had been effective. Thus it asked what importance foreign investors put on investment incentive (such as tax exemptions for foreign investors generally, or specifically to those in particular industrial sectors or zones), when they made the investment decision. The Questionnaire shows that an overwhelming majority of foreign investors (91%) put investment incentives on medium or higher position when deciding to invest. Forty one percent of them considered incentives as highly important factors in making their investment decision, while nine percent of them considered it of the highest importance (*Chart* 10). This was further confirmed by one respondent in his/her "further comments" at the end of the Questionnaire[29]. This result is in sharp contrast with the common view that foreign investors, particularly OECD investors, prefer a secure, stable and predictable legal environment, rather than preferential treatment such as tax incentives[30].

The home state breakdown shows that continental EU investors placed higher im-

---

[29] The respondent commented that "the beneficial tax treatment that FDI are enjoying at the moment" was actually "an important incentive for investing in China".

[30] For example, a recent OECD policy review indicated that "[I]ndeed, recent surveys show that foreign investors are much more concerned about the overall regulatory regime than about incentives, and that they prefer to locate investments, especially large, long term ones, in countries with predictable policy regimes". See OECD Policy Brief, *Attarcting Investment to China*, (September 2003), p. 3.

portance on incentives than their counterparts from the British Isles. A great majority (78%) of continental investors attached "high" or "top" importance to investment incentives, whilst less than one third (31%) of UK investors considered incentive of such significance. The establishing date breakdown reveals an increasing emphasis on investment incentives. All the 1980s investors considered incentives of "medium" importance. However, near a half 1990s investors (47%) 1990s thought incentive of "high" or top significance. The percentage has increased to three-forth among 2000s investors. The breakdown analysis discloses, furthermore, that JV investors tended to view incentives more highly than WFE investors, as a half of straight JV investors placed them at "high" importance, whilst only one third of straight WFE investors did the same.

The high and even growing importance that foreign investors have attached to investment incentives is a rather striking finding, which suggests that a re-consideration or a further investigation of the use of incentives is necessary. The widely held assumption that western investors do not care much about incentives is probably based on the opinions and experiences of large multinationals, which accounts for the vast majority among international investors in terms of the amount of their investment, but a tiny minority in terms of their number. Since this questionnaire is based on *number of investors* rather than *amount of investment*, it is unsurprising that its result is not in conformity with such assumption. Therefore it is probably more accurate to say that although incentives do not play a much important role in attracting large *amount* of FDI, which essentially means investment by multinationals, it does have a great role to play in attracting large number of foreign investors, particularly small and medium sized enterprises (SMEs). In the latter sense, it might be concluded that China's investment incentives had worked in attracting foreign investment.

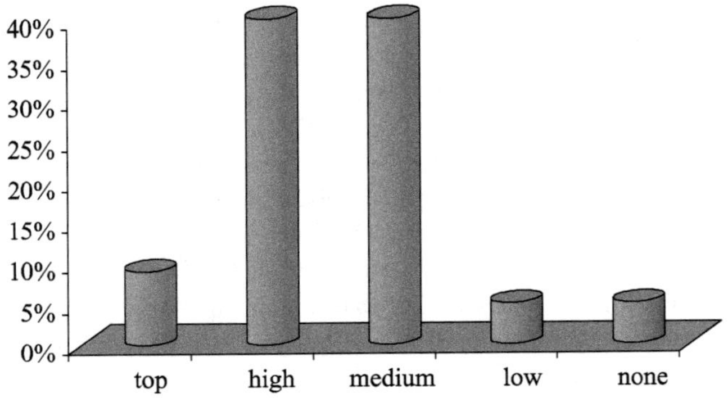

Chart 10　Importance of Incentives

4. Implication of WTO on Chinese FDI Environment

The survey (*Chart* 11) shows that an overwhelming majority of respondents (93%) believed that the WTO accession will be very (73%) or fairly (20%) useful in improving the conditions of foreign investment in China. No one responded negatively to this question. Although the breakdown in establishing date and form of investment has not resulted in any notable finding, the home state breakdown shows that British investors appeared to be more optimistic than their Continental counterparts with regard to the positive impact brought about by the WTO admission. All British investors that answered this question thought it would be "very useful" whilst only 63% of Continental investors voted in the same way (the rest nevertheless thought it would be "fairly useful"). These results, in general, give a clear endorsement on the positive impact of WTO accession onto the improvement of the FDI environment in China.

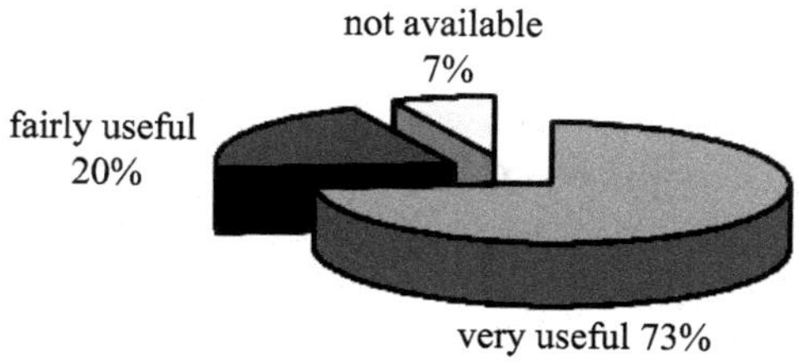

Chart 11 WTO to Improve Investment Climate

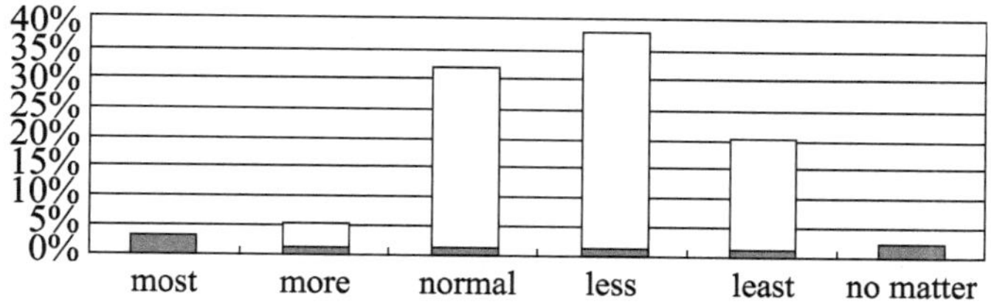

Chart 12 Significance of a New EU-China Investment Agreement

5. Significance of a New Investment Agreement

As the following chart (*Chart* 12) shows, despite the potential improvement brought about by China's admission to the WTO, most respondents (76%) still believed that it would be very (36%) or fairly (40%) useful to sign a new bilateral or multilateral investment agreement to which China and the EU are parties, while only less than 15% of them considered such an agreement as "not very useful" or "not useful at all". This result confirms that investment treaties are useful instruments in improving investment climate.[31] The breakdown analysis shows that, firstly, British investors were less positive

[31] Whether and to what extent BITs contribute to improve state's investment environment seems to be a question. Despite the lack of empirical evidence, however, many commentators tend to consider that the answer should be positive. For example, Vandevelde claimed that BITs did "reduce risks for foreign investors by stabilising the legal framework within which the investment operate", even although he acknowledged that the claim that BITs increased the general economic prosperity was not supported by empirical evidence. Also, a recent UNCTAD study surveyed ten countries' laws, policies and practices on foreign investment and concluded that "extensive treaty network, including major and regional home countries" were an "optimal" policy choice in effective attracting FDI. See Vandevelde, *Investment Liberalisation and Economic Development: the Role of Bilateral Investment Treaties*, 36 Columbia Journal of International Law 501, p. 525. UNCTAD, *Effectiveness of Foreign Direct Investment Policy Measures* (Note by the UNCTAD Secretariat), TD/B/COM. 2/EM. 13/2 (22 April 2003), p. 4. See also, 2, ICLQ, note 12 above, p. 784.

than Continental investors on the usefulness of an EU-China BIT. All respondents from the European Continent considered such a BIT either "very useful" (56%) or "fairly useful" (44%), whilst only slight over sixty percent of British investors (62%) shared such a view with much less of them considered it "very useful" (23%). This result is in conformity with the abovementioned finding on the awareness of BITs when making investment decisions. Secondly, newer investors were more enthusiastic about the potential new BIT than "older" investors. Seventy five percent of investors established in 2000s thought it would be "very useful" with the rest considered it "fairly useful". This provides a sharp contrast with the twenty seven percent of "very useful" and forty seven percent "fairly useful" votes by investors established in 1990s. Reading together with the earlier finding that BITs were less known to later investors than earlier investors, it seems to indicate a growing dissatisfaction with existing BITs, rather than with the usefulness of BITs in general. Finally, the breakdown analysis shows that joint venture investors were more emphatic on the usefulness of such a new BIT than WFE investors. A half of the JV investors replied that such a new BIT would be "very useful", contrasting with an only seventeen percent of WFE investors did so. This result, again, complies with the aforementioned result on investigation of international agreements, relative to Chinese law, which demonstrated that JV investors were more active in studying international treaties (and Chinese law) than WFE investors.

With regard to preferred provisions in the future agreement, respondents considered free monetary transfer provision the most useful, followed by provisions of full compensation, most favoured nation (MFN) treatment, pre-admission national treatment (NT) and post-admission NT. This confirms what was observed above that the respondents preferred concrete measures (e. g., free monetary transfer, full compensation) to abstract principles (e. g., MFN, NT, etc) on investment protection and facilitation. (*Chart* 13)

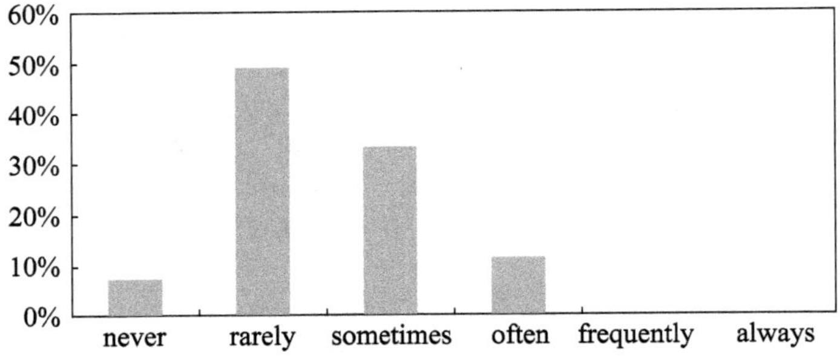

Chart 13 Useful Provisions in the Future Investment Agreement

6. Summary

The preceding investigations demonstrate that law had played a very important role in investor's decision-making. The vast majority of foreign investors had investigated the legal environment before they made their investment decisions. Among those investigated the legal environment, most conducted an in-depth research by looking into both the written law and the law in action whilst others had studied the written law. About half of these investors did a comprehensive study looking into both Chinese law and applicable international treaties, whilst others investigated only the Chinese law. The most well-known international treaties were DTTs, followed by BITs, ICSID Convention and MIGA Convention. The fact that more foreign investors were aware of the DTTs than proper investment protection treaties such as BITs and ICSID, MIGA Conventions demonstrates that foreign investors always pay more attention to treaties bringing in direct benefit (such as tax avoidance or reduction), than to treaties bringing only indirect benefits (such as a high standard of treatment and protection). This observation is further confirmed by the finding that, contrary to what was commonly believed, an overwhelming majority of respondents considered investment incentives to be a factor of substantial importance when they decided to invest in China.

The breakdown analysis shows that European Continental investors were more concerned with the legal system than British investors, contrary to what is found in other studies. European investors were accordingly more active in pre-investment studies in the governing laws, particularly applicable international treaties. Another breakdown finding that is again unexpected is that foreign investors invested in collaboration with a local partner, i. e., JV investors paid more attention to the nature of legal system and were more positive in conducting in-depth and comprehensive pre-admission studies of such legal system. Thirdly, the establishing date breakdown gives a conflicting picture: one the one hand, later investors seemed to be more concerned with the nature of the legal system than earlier ones; on the other hand, earlier investors seemed to be more enthusiastic in pre-admission legal investigations. It is argued that the rapid increase of FDI laws and the improvement in legal enforcement in China over the last decades might be the explanations.

However, despite above mentioned decrease of influence of existing BITs, the survey confirms that the vast majority of foreign investors thought that China's accession to the WTO would significantly improve the investment conditions, as it indeed did. Furthermore, most of them still considered it of substantial use to enter into a new bilateral or multilateral investment agreement to protect their investment. As to the specific provisions that they would like to see included in the agreement, concrete measures such as free monetary transfer and full compensation for expropriated properties were most wanted, while important principles, including MFN treatment, pre-and post-admission NT, compulsory ICSID jurisdiction over state-investor disputes, are also generally considered very useful.

III. Some Substantive Aspects of the FDI Legal System

This part intends to determine whether the FDI legal system in China was adequate and sufficient in protecting and promoting FDI, by examining the experience of foreign investors on some most important substantive issues of the legal system[32]. These issues include investment safety, expropriation and compensation, national treatment (NT) policy, transfer of funds, intellectual property rights (IPR) protection, investment insurance, state-investor dispute settlement, Chinese law governing contracts and performance requirements.

1. The Question of Investment Safety

Safety is the primary concern of investors when making an investment decision, particularly when the investment is to be made in a previously unfamiliar country such as China. Hence, the first question on the substance of the Chinese FDI law was directed to the question of safety and confidence.

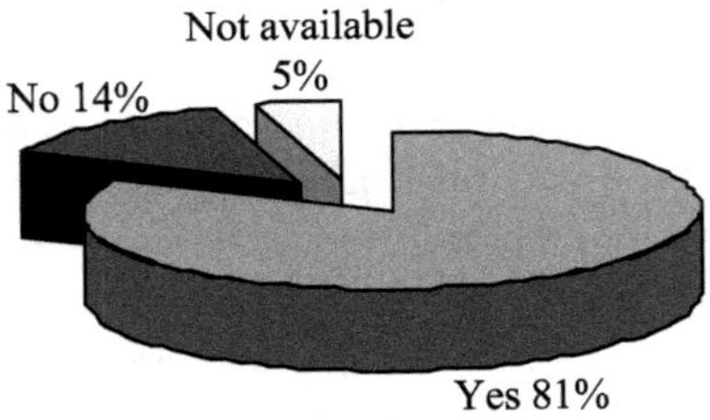

Chart 14 Question of Investment Safety

As demonstrated in Chart 14, eighty one percent of the surveyed foreign investors felt it safe to invest or re-invest in China while only fourteen percent of them felt the opposite. Such a result is not surprising as the survey was carried out amongst existing investors, rather than potential investors who might be much more sceptical and concerned. Nevertheless, the high rate of confidence should be read as an affirmation of many other surveys considering China as one of the most popular places to invest in[33]. For instance, a Survey of chief executives from the world's 1000 biggest companies carried out by A. T. Kearney in 2001 showed that China was the second in the table of FDI confidence, only after the United States[34]. The latest UNCTAD survey among major multinationals also suggested that China was one of the top locations in terms of FDI

---

〔32〕 Apart from aforementioned international treaties, Chinese laws and regulations are a most important component of the FDI legal system in China and are many in number. Essential Chinese laws and regulations are reprinted in the *Handbook of Foreign Economic Law* (in both Chinese and English) (edited by the State council), Volumes 1 and 2, Law Press, 1997. An updated publication is *The New Compilation of Laws, Regulations and Ministerial Rules on Foreign Trade and Economic Co-operation of the People's Republic of China*, edited by the Ministry of Foreign Trade and Economic Co-operation (now the Ministry of Commerce, the MOFCOM), in Chinese, Law Press, 2002. For a convenient, web-based source, see Invest in China (a MOFCOM website): *Laws and Regulations*, available at < http://www.fdi.gov.cn/ltlawpackage/index.jsp?app=1&language=en > (visited on 15 July 2004).

〔33〕 These surveys include surveys done by the American Chamber of Commerce in China, German Chamber of Commerce in China, Multilateral Investment Guarantee Agency and Goldman Sachs. For an overview of these surveys, see UNCTAD, *China: WTO Accession and Growing FDI Inflows*, 11 December 2002, p. 5, available at < http://r0.unctad.org/en/subsites/dite/pdfs/PRChina.pdf > (visited on 18 July 2003).

〔34〕 Kevin Brown, *China Moves up Investors Table*, available at < www.FT.com >, visited on February 12 2001 20:01 GMT.

prospects and opportunities.[35]

The breakdown data show that British (85%) and JV investors (90%) felt more confident in the safety of investing in China, than the Continental (67%) and WFE investors (67%). All investors established in both 1980s and 2000s voted positively for the safety question, whilst about twenty percent of investors established in 1990s responded in the negative.

The immediate following question might contribute to explain the results on the question of safety and confidence. This question asked what the most important source of confidence was when they decided to invest or re-invest in China. The options were legal protection provided by domestic and international law, investment insurance against political risks, political promise and social stability, and others, in the latter case investors were asked to specify the sources.

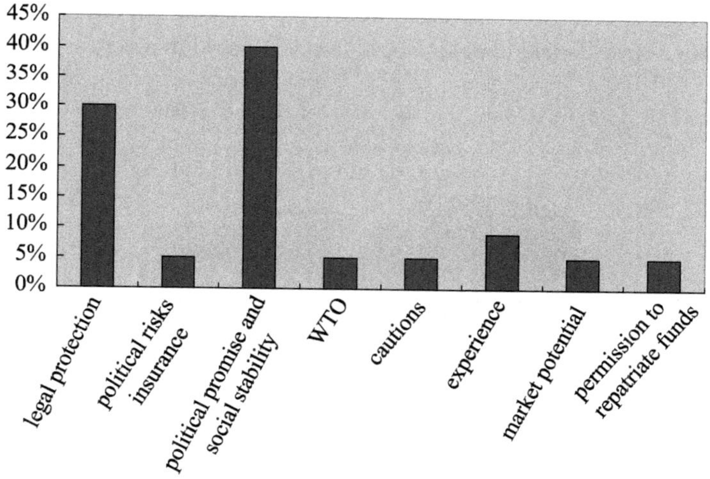

Chart 15 Sources of Confidence

The feedback (*Chart* 15) shows that political promise and social stability, and legal protection were by far the two most significant sources of confidence, which was not surprising. What seems to be surprising, however, was that investors considered political factors (40%) of greater importance than legal protection (30%) in boosting their confidence. This coincides with Perry's Sri Lanka Study, which shows that "Western" investors "usually place greater emphasis on political stability".[36] Nevertheless, none of the WFE investors viewed political stability as the most important source of confidence, a sharp contrast with the responses from JV investors with sixty percent of them replied positively thereon. This probably reflect the fact the, compared with JV investors, WFE investors have less access to local political resources because of the absence of a local partner. In addition, few investors (less than 5%) credited in-

---

[35] UNCTAD, *Prospects for FDI Flows and TNC Strategies* (2004 – 2007), TD (XI)/BP/14 (7 June 2004), p. 5.

[36] See Perry, ICLQ, note 12 above, p. 793.

vestment insurance against political risks as the most important source of confidence. Other sources as specifically added by respondents included experience, WTO membership, market potential and permission to repatriate funds from China.

2. Expropriation and Compensation

The issue of expropriation and its compensation is of great concern to foreign investors, as it by and large decides the extent of risks involved in an investment project. It has also been one of the most controversial issues in modern international law[37] and a wealth of literature on the subject has been created by international lawyers.[38]

In the period immediately after the People's Republic of China was established, China conducted large scale nationalisation of private industrial and commercial enterprises including foreign funded enterprises.[39] However, it is unclear whether expropriation or nationalization has taken place after China started to attract FDI in late 1970s. The widely reported McDonald incident[40] has shown that foreign investors are still deeply concerned with this issue. The following three questions therefore aimed to ascertain whether foreign investor had suffered or heard of any kind of expropriations of foreign investment in the last 20 years, and if so, what were the standards of their compensations.

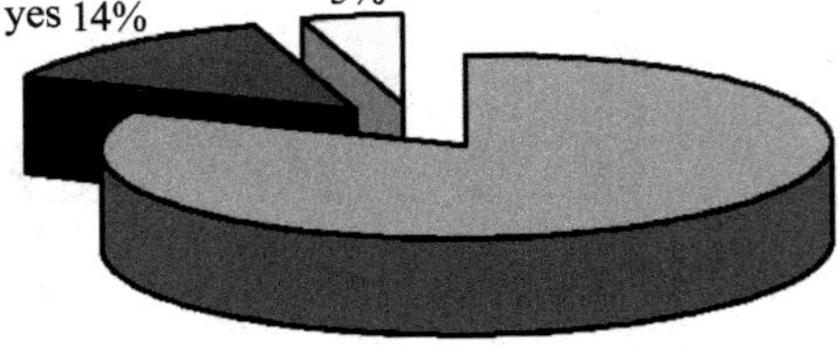

Chart 16 Expropriation Suffered

---

[37] Oscar Schachter wrote that "apart from the use of force, no question of international law seemed to have aroused as much debate—and often strong feelings-as the question of the standard for payment of compensation when foreign property is expropriated". See Schachter, Oscar, *Compensation for Expropriation*, Editorial Comment, 78 American Journal of International Law (AJIL), 121 (1984).

[38] The most important publications on this topic include *Oppenheim's International Law*, 8th edition (Lauterpacht, H., ed. Longmans, 1955), pp. 350 – 357, 9th edition (Jennings and Watts eds., Longman, 1992), pp. 910 – 927; Higgins, Rosalyn, *The Taking of Property by the State: Recent Developments in International Law*, 176 Recueil des Cours 263 (1982); Aréchaga, Eduardo Jiménez de, *State Responsibility for the Nationalisation of Foreign Owned Property*, 11 New York University Journal of International Law and Politics 179(Fall, 1978); Schachter, *Compensation for Expropriation*, id; Robinson, Davis R., *Expropriation in the Restatement (Revised)*, 78 AJIL 176 (1984); Mann, F. A., *British Treaties for the Promotion and Protection of Investments*, 52 British Yearbook of International Law (BYIL) 241 (1981); Dolzer, Rudolf, *New Foundations of the Law of Expropriation of Alien Property*, 75 AJIL, 553 (1981); Friedman, S., *Expropriation in International Law*, 1953; Lauterpacht, Sir Elihu, *International Law and Private Foreign Investment*, 4 Global Legal Studies Journal, 257 (1996).

[39] For more details, see SHAN, Wenhu, *A Critical Appraisal of the Legal Framework Governing EU Investment in China*, University of Cambridge PhD Dissertation 2004, pp. 4 – 6.

[40] See U. S. and Foreign Commercial Service (US&FCS) (Telegraphic Report from the American Embassy in Beijing): *China: Investment Climate Statement for* 1997. See also Friedman, Thomas L., *Fed up*, New York Times, 04 – 12 – 1996, p. 29.

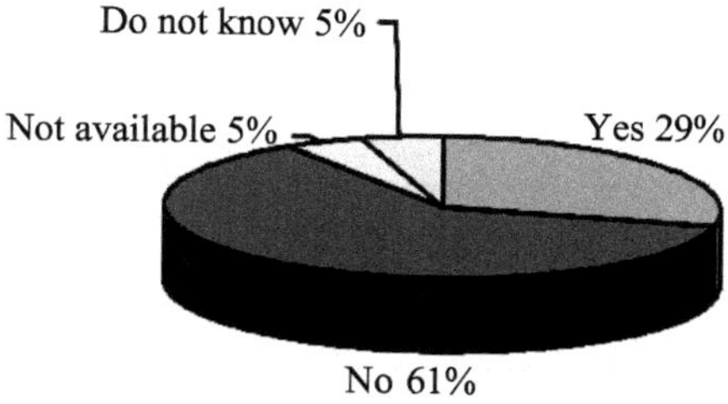

Chart 17 Expropriation Heard of

The survey (*Chart* 16 *and Chart* 17) shows that most foreign investors had not suffered (81%) or heard of (61%) any kind of expropriation in the last 20 years. However, it also shows that fourteen percent of the respondents have actually suffered expropriation and twenty nine percent of them had heard of expropriation cases. It is noted that none of the JV investors had reported suffering from expropriation though some of them did hear from such cases of other companies. On the contrary, thirty three percent of WFE investors reportedly have suffered expropriation. This seems to suggest that WFE investors are more vulnerable and perhaps also more sensitive to expropriation and similar measures.

This relatively high portion of expropriation cases suffered and heard of, however, must at least partly attribute to an extra-wide definition of "expropriation" that the investors tend to take. For instance, the author has interviewed a respondent who claimed to have suffered from expropriation in his returned questionnaire.[41] It turned out that the "expropriation" he meant was actually breach of contracts by Chinese State-run entities, which were legal and financially independent from the Chinese government.[42] However, taking into account the widely reported McDonald case, one may conclude that some form of expropriation, as broadly defined, may have happened in China since the late 1970s.

As far as compensation for expropriation was concerned, more than half of the respondents said that they did not know whether "adequate, prompt and effective" (or "full") compensation had been paid to the expropriated companies. Five percent of them gave positive answers ("always") whilst fourteen percent provided negative answers ("rarely" or "never"). Another fourteen percent of the surveyed investors stated that full compensation was "sometimes" paid. Therefore, it might be concluded that although China had paid full or "adequate, prompt and effective" compensation for some expropriation cases, it had not become common practice. Another explanation might be that investors' expectation of "full compensation" was higher than they could reasonably

---

[41] Interview no. 2.

[42] Ibid.

obtain[43]. (*Chart* 18)

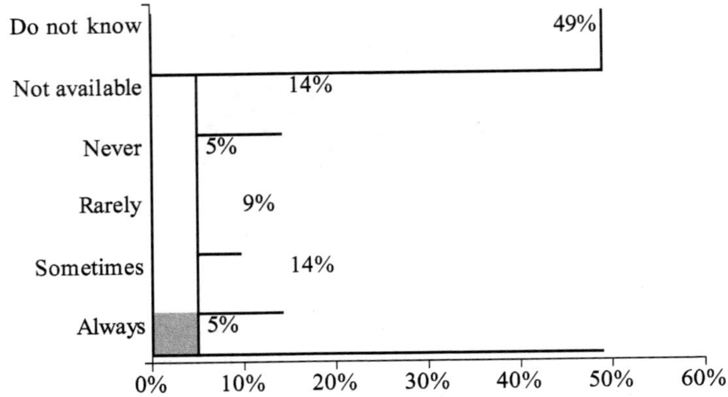

Chart 18 "Adequate, Prompt and Effective" Compensation

3. National Treatment for Foreign Investors

China's laws and policies on foreign invested enterprises (FIE) have been featured a combination of special privileges (superior national treatment) on the one hand and special restrictions on the other (inferior national treatment), compared with the FDI regime of western countries.[44] In 1992, China decided to establish a "Socialist Market Economy".[45] As a result, it embarked on the implementation of "national treatment" (NT),[46] a standard of treatment it had resisted and denied for half a century.[47] As a new FDI policy, it aimed at granting FIEs the same treatment as that to domestic enterprises and therefore constructing a level playing field for investors irrespective of their origins. At a technical level, this meant that limitations and restrictions would be relaxed

---

〔43〕 It is not unusual that in international investment cases, a "full" compensation awarded by the arbitration tribunals was substantially lower than what the investors originally claimed for. For details and discussions of some of the cases, see e. g., Westberg, John A., *Compensation in Cases of Expropriation and Nationalisation: Awards of the Iran-United States Claims Tribunal*, 5 ICSID Review—FILJ 256 (1990); Amerasinghe, C. F., *Issues of Compensation for the Taking of Alien Property in the Light of Recent Cases and Practice*, 41 ICLQ 22 (1992); Dolzer, Rudolf, *New Foundations of the Law of Expropriation of Alien Property*, 75 AJIL, 553 (1981); Francioni, Francesco, *Compensation for Nationalisation of Foreign Property: The Borderland between Law and Equity*, 24 ICLQ 255 (1975).

〔44〕 For details about superior national treatment and inferior national treatment, see SHAN, Wenhua, *National Treatment and the Transformation Of FDI Laws and Policies in China*, International Trade Laws and Regulations, Vol. 6, No. 1, 2000;

〔45〕 See *The Central Committee of the Chinese Communist Party (CCCPC) Decision on Some Issues Related to the Establishment of the Socialist Market Economy*, published on the People's Daily, 7 November 1993, p. 1.

〔46〕 SHAN, Wenhua, *Market Economy and the National Treatment for Foreign Invested Enterprises*, Chinese legal Science, No. 5, 1994, p. 89; See also ZHANG, Mo, *China's Move toward National Treatment of Foreign Investors: New Shenzhen Regulations*, 18 East Asia Executive Report 9, 15 November 1996, No. 11, p. 9.

〔47〕 For instance, in the China-US negotiation of a BIT, one of the stickiest points was the NT clause. See Steinert, Timothy A., *If the BIT Fits: The Proposed Bilateral Investment Treaty between the United States and the People's Republic of China*, 2 Journal of Chinese Law, fall 1988, p. 434.

whilst privileges and incentives might also be removed[48]. For example, since 1992 foreign investment had gained access to wider business areas such as banking, insurance and commercial retailing markets[49]. On the other hand, exemption of import duties for materials purchased by FIEs as an investment contribution, an important incentive for FIEs, was once abolished[50]. A question was therefore included in the Questionnaire to elicit the response from foreign investors on the impact of the NT policy.

The Questionnaire (*Chart* 19) shows that the vast majority (77%) of respondents believed that the NT policy would help to improve the investment climate for FIEs, although the degree of impact varied. Forty-one percent of them were very positive and considered that NT policy would "significantly" improve the investment environment. Among them, the Continental investors (78%) seemed to be much more positive than the British investors (15%) on the positive effect ("significantly") of the NT policy. Likewise, WFE investors (50%) were more positive than JV investors (30%).

In contrast, thirty six percent of the respondents were much less optimistic thinking it of only "a little" help. Nine percent of all the respondents, however, thought it would not help at all. One respondent stated in the "further comments" that the NT policy "will positively mean access by FDI in sectors only allowed for domestic enterprises. However, it has a negative impact due to the reduction of the beneficial tax treatment that FDI currently enjoy, which is, in fact, an important incentive for investing in China."

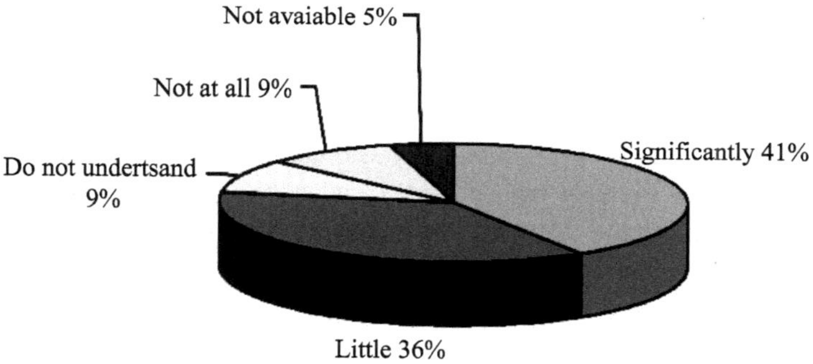

Chart 19 Improvement by Provision of National Treatment

This result, in general, suggests that whilst most investors generally favoured the new policy move, many of them were concerned about the negative effects it might result

[48] SHAN, Wenhua, *Market Economy and the National Treatment for Foreign Invested Enterprises*, Chinese legal Science, No. 5, 1994, p. 89.

[49] For details of changes brought about by the introduction of the NT policy, see SHAN, Wenhua, *A Critical Appraisal of the Legal Framework Governing EU Investment in China*, University of Cambridge PhD Dissertation 2004, pp. 168 – 170.

[50] Ibid.

in, namely the abolition of tax incentives. This result also reaffirms the finding on the great importance investors had attached to investment incentives. It is noteworthy that the aforementioned tax exemption was reinstated in late 1997, as FDI influx dropped sharply in the two years, partly due to this change in preferential tax policy and partly to the Asian financial crisis.[51]

4. Transfer of Investment and Profit

Monetary transfer is another key concern of foreign investors, because it affects the feasibility, implementation and profitability of any investment project. The foreign exchange (forex) regime in China has undergone rapid changes since 1979[52]. A rather liberal regime has existed since December 1996 when the Regulations of Foreign Exchange Administration (RFEA) were adopted. China has since then also formally accepted the obligations of Article VIII of the IMF Articles of Agreement, removing exchange restrictions on current account transactions.[53] Accordingly, China has freed all the payments and transfers of current transactions, which covers import and export transactions of the FIEs, profits, dividends and interests of foreign investors and salaries and other legitimate income of foreign employees.[54] Now RMB, the Chinese currency, is fully convertible under current transactions, but not under capital transactions. Under pressures from other states and the international business community, China has committed to make RMB a fully convertible international currency, i. e., convertible under both current and capital accounts, in the future.[55] The question on transfer intended to ascertain whether foreign investors still have difficulty in making investment related transfers.

According to the Questionnaire (*Chart* 20), only ten percent of investors "always" or "frequently" experienced difficulties in transferring investment and profit out of China. Eighteen percent of them occasionally experienced problems. Forty five percent of them have never or rarely encountered any transfer problem. This result shows that China's effort to relax the forex regime has been effective and it is now relatively free for foreign investors to conduct monetary transfer. Further liberalisation, however, is still considered necessary to fully facilitate FDI activities in China.

---

[51] *Foreign Investment in China—I: Changing Trends and Policies*, East Asia Executive Report, Vol. 20, No. 4, (April 15, 1998). at 8.

[52] A brief outline of the history of China's forex regime reform can be found in World Trade Organisation Working Party on the Accession of China: *Report of the Working Party on the Accession of China (hereinafter "Working Party Report")*, WT/ACC/CHN/49 (1 October 2001). at 5 – 6.

[53] World Trade Organisation Working Party on the Accession of China: *Report of the Working Party on the Accession of China (hereinafter "Working Party Report")*, WT/ACC/CHN/49 (1 October 2001), pp. 6 – 7.

[54] Art. 21 – 25, Regulations on Sale and Purchase of and Payment in Foreign Exchange.

[55] ZHANG, Weimin, *Maintaining the Balance of International Payment, Proceeding to Full Convertibility of RMB*, People's Daily (overseas edition), November 15, 2001, p. 4.

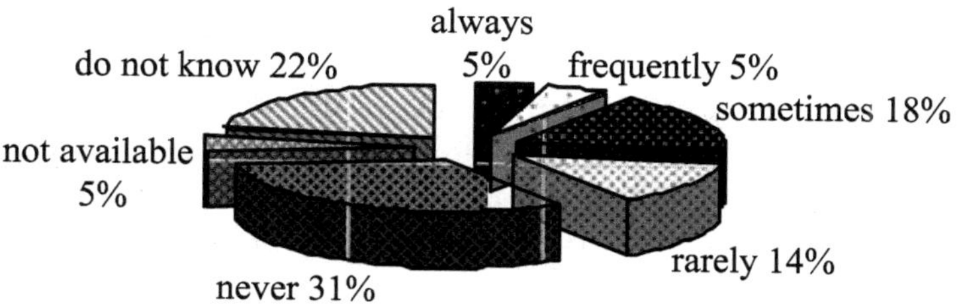

Chart 20　Difficulty in Monetary Transfer

5. Intellectual Property Rights Protection

China has long been criticised by western countries for its weak protection of international intellectual property rights (IPR).[56] The US government, in particular, threatened China with a $ 1.1 billion retaliation list in 1994 and a $ 2 billion in 1996, on the ground that China failed to protect US IPR.[57] After that, more notably after it acceded to the WTO in 2001, China has made significant progress in strengthening IPR protection[58] which has been acknowledged by international community including the WTO and the US government.[59] However, the US government and the EU still hold that the enforcement of IPR protection in China remains insufficient.[60] A question was therefore asked whether foreign investors were satisfied with the Chinese system of intellectual

[56] Whilst the United States has long been active in advocating the improvement of China's IPR protection, the EU has also long been concerned over China's IPR law enforcement. See Congressional Research Services (CRS) Issue Brief for Congress: *China-U. S. Trade Issues* (16 May 2003), pp. 12 – 14, available at <http://fpc. state. gov/documents/organization/21120. pdf> (visitedon21July2004). Seealso Communication from the Commission, "*Building a Comprehensive Partnership with China*", Section C. 1. 3, COM (1998) 181 (25. 03. 1998).

[57] For more details on the US-China IPR disputes, see Congressional Research Services (CRS) Issue Brief for Congress: *China-U. S. Trade Issues* (16 May 2003), ibid, pp. 12 – 14.

[58] China has laid down numerous new IPR laws and regulations and modified existing laws with a view to improving the protection standards. China has also enhanced the administrative and judicial systems in order to strengthen the legal protection of IPR rights. In a bid to guarantee trial standards, for example, the Supreme People's Court stipulated that only the country's 400 or so intermediate people's courts were qualified to accept cases concerning alleged trademark or copyright infringements, and only 47 of these were authorized to accept lawsuits on alleged patent infringements. See *Intellectual property disputes on the rise* (last updated on December 18, 2003), available at <http://english. peopledaily. com. cn/200312/18/eng20031218_130653. shtml> (visited on 21 July 2004). See also, *China paying increasing attention to protection of IPR: Wu Yi* (Last updated on November 19, 2003), available at <http://english. peopledaily. com. cn/200312/09/eng20031209_129949. shtml> (visited on 21 July 2004).

[59] The US Trade Representative has stated that China has made "great strides" in improving IPR protection regimes. In September 2002, WTO members issued a positive review of the China's new IPR laws in relation to the Agreement on Trade-Related Aspects of Intellectual Property Rights (TRIPS). It has also been reported that foreign investors are now less worried about IPR infringement due to an improved IPR protection system in China. See Congressional Research Services (CRS) Issue Brief for Congress: China-U. S. Trade Issues (16 May 2003), note 56 above, pp. 12 – 14. See also *Efforts in IPR protection praised by foreign investors* (last updated on December 09, 2003), available at <http://english. peopledaily. com. cn/200312/09/eng20031209_129949. shtml> (visited on 21 July 2004).

[60] See Congressional Research Services (CRS) Issue Brief for Congress: China-U. S. Trade Issues (16 May 2003), note 56 above, pp. 12 – 14. Likewise, the EU still has concerns over the enforcement of IPR protection laws, See Commission Policy Paper for Transmission to the Council and the European Parliament: *A maturing partnership-shared interest and challenges in EU-China relations*, COM (2003), 533 fin., p. 16.

property rights protection.

The result on this question (*Chart* 21) is not surprising. Only seven percent of the respondents expressed satisfaction whilst more than a half of investors (58%) were not satisfied with the Chinese system of IPR protection. In an interview with a respondent, very strong criticism thereon was expressed. The investor resold TV programs to central and local TV stations that were all state-run. However, according to the investor, as soon as the stations gained all the hardware, software and necessary know-how, they refused to pay the fees agreed in the contract. To make things worse, an arbitral award that the investor won against one of the TV stations was unable to be enforced, as a result of "local protectionism". This story might have highlighted the worst possible scenario of IPR protection in China. Despite the improvement after China' accession to the WTO, it can be anticipated that China still has a long way to go to be able to protect IPR in a sufficient and effective manner, as it depends on the improvement on the law enforcement system in general, which remains inadequate, as perceived by foreign investor.[61]

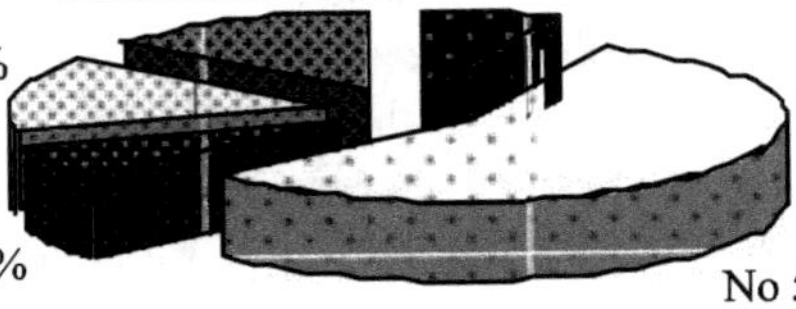

Chart 21 Satisfaction by Chinese IPR Protection System

6. Investment Insurance

Although investment insurance had been treated in a previous question about sources of confidence, another question is included here, to reveal how many investors have actually insured their investments against political risks based on the MIGA Convention or any applicable BIT.

The Questionnaire (*Chart* 22) shows that most (67%) foreign investors did not insure their investments against political risks. Only five percent of the respondents had done so. This result, together with that of the previous question related to investment insurance, has demonstrated that investment insurance had not been widely used by foreign investors in China.[62]

---

[61] See Part IV below.

[62] Statistics from the MIGA show that from 1993 till 1999 every year there were only half a dozen or less investment projects in China that were insured by MIGA. This is indeed a very small fraction out of the tens of thousand of investment projects China attracted each year (for example, by 2002, China had approved 424, 196 FDI projects and during 2002 China had approved 34, 171 FDI projects). For details of MIGA guaranteed investment in China, see *Guarantees Issued in FY* 1995, *Guarantees Issued in FY* 1996, *Guarantees Issued in FY* 1997, *Guarantees Issued in FY* 1998 and *Guarantees Issued in FY* 1999, all available at MIGA website: < http://www.miga.org/welcome.htm > (visited on 29 October 1999). The information of fiscal year 1993 and 1994 are based on Lorin s. Weisenfeld, *The Co-operation between MIGA and China and its Potentials*, in MIGA and China: Comments on the Multilateral Investment Guarantee Agency (CHEN An edited), Fujian People's Press, 1995, pp. 496 – 498. For statistics of FDI in China in and by 2002, see < http://www.fdi.gov.cn/common/info.jsp?id=ABC00000000000004548 > (visited on 21 July 2004).

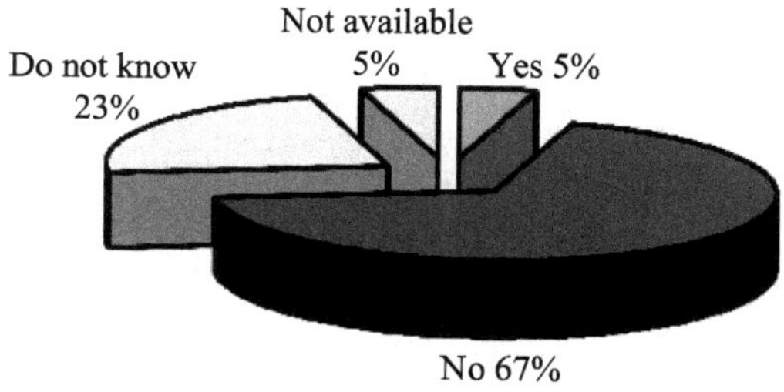

Chart 22 Political Risks Insurance Based on MIGA or a BIT

7. Disputes with Chinese Government

Apart from expropriation, foreign investors might come cross many kinds of disputes with local government authorities, particularly when licenses and permissions are required. The frequency of state-investor disputes can also be an important indicator of the general investment climate of the host country. This question thus intended to establish the frequency of disputes between investors and the Chinese government and the use of ICSID mechanism in case of dispute.

The responses (*Chart* 23 *and Chart* 24) shows that an overwhelming majority of investors (91%) had not had any disputes with the Chinese Government.[63] Only nine percent of them claimed to have had a dispute with the Chinese government. However, according to the author's interview conducted after the Questionnaire, one respondent actually mistook his contractual disputes with China's state-run enterprises as disputes with the Chinese government *per se*.[64] The respondent also mistook his case before the International Economic and Trade Arbitration Commission (CIETAC) of China as arbitration by the ICSID.[65] Apart from this falsely reported case, no respondent had reported any case submitted to the ICSID. Indeed, ICSID data confirm that so far there has been no case against China before the ICSID[66]. The breakdown data show that no JV had been exposed to a dispute with local governments, compared with a 17% of such incidents with WFEs.

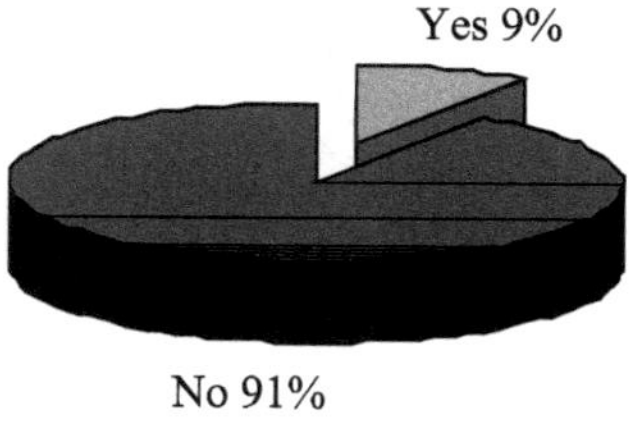

Chart 23 Disputes with the Chinese Government

[63] TN SOFRES Survey, pp. 8 -9.

[64] Interview No. 2.

[65] Ibid.

[66] Details of ICSID cases are *available at* http://www.worldbank.org/icsid/cases/cases.htm (visited on 22 July 2004). For a compilation of reported ICSID cases, see ICSID Reports, edited by James Crawford and Karen Lee, and published by Cambridge University Press. Its most recent volume, the 7th volume, was published in October 2004.

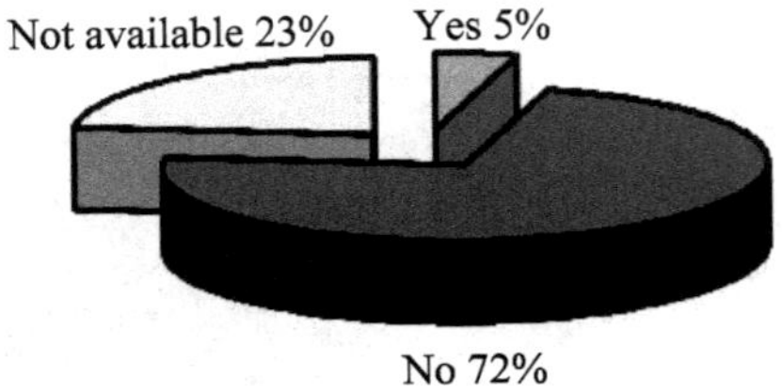

Chart 24 Submission to ICSID

The generally low dispute rate with Chinese government might have shown that, on the one hand, Chinese government has handled the requests from foreign investors with greatest care and accommodation, in order to keep its image as a FDI-friendly country. On the other hand, foreign investors might have also learned to cooperate, rather than to confront, with Chinese government authorities. As a result, most problems and issues might have been dealt with by friendly consultation and negotiation, before they became a serious state-investor "dispute". It is therefore logical that formal legal resolution including ICSID arbitration was not often resorted to, because of such a low dispute rate, and such a cooperative relationship between the government and the foreign investors.

However, this situation seems to have been under rapid change. Recently, three cases between foreign investors and local governments have drawn wide attention, namely the *Changchun Huijin Case*[67], the *Fuzhou Xinyuan Case*[68] and the *Beijing Jialilai case*[69]. It is yet to know the results of these recent disputes. However, what seems to become clear is that the no-dispute honey-moon between foreign investors and local gov-

---

〔67〕 The Changchun Huijin (CWC) Case is reportedly the first litigation case between a foreign invested enterprise (FIE) and a local government. In this case, Changchun Huijin, the FIE, sued Changchun city Government at local courts for breach of governmental guarantee. For details, see YANG, Mei, *A Hong Kong Investor is Suing the City Government of Changchun (in Chinese)*, available at <http://rainbow. www46. cnidc. cn/cgi-bin/wz/ab3. cgi? menu = show&id = lyutao&slttitle = 20040131195350&see = 14> (03/10/2004). Seealso WANG, Ling, *TheRiseadFallofWater-Market(inChinese)*, available at <http://www. hqcj. com/docs/2004_05/gb/content/fmgs2. htm> (03/10/2004).

〔68〕 This case has been accepted by the China International Economic and Trade Arbitration Commission (CIETAC), China's primary arbitration institution for international trade disputes. IN this case Fuzhou Xinyuan City Bridges Ltd (*Xinyuan*) sued the Fuzhou City Government, on the basis of a concession agreement concluded between the two sides in 1997. For details, see, "*The Case of Hong Kong China Travel Service BOT Project*", Legal Daily (in Chinese), available at <http://www. legaldaily. com. cn/zb/2004 - 09/02/content_130048. htm> (04/10/2004). Other reports of the case include *Who Should Pay for the Loss of this Hong Kong investment*?, available at <http://www. legaldaily. com. cn/bm/2004 - 07/13/content_116067. htm> (04/10/2004); *A Foreign Investor is Suing Fuzhou City Government for* Breach of Contract, available at <http://www. sznews. com/n1/ca1044229. htm> (03/10/2004); Fuzhou Government Facing Dispute of 900 Million for Blindly Introducing Foreign Investment, available at <http://info. news. hc360. com/html/001/002/003/013/61066. htm> (03/10/2004).

〔69〕 This is a dispute between a Beijing local authority and, again, a Hong Kong investors concerning the transfer of equity of the latter to another Hong Kong investor. See, e. g., Kang, Shouyong, *What Does the Jialilai Equity Transfer case Imply*? Economic Daily, 4 February 2004.

ernments is over[70]. The next stage might be a rise of investment cases submitted to the ICSID and other international tribunals, as a result China's open acceptance to international arbitration and in viewing of the general ineffectiveness of the Chinese dispute settlement system, as perceived by foreign investors[71].

8. Chinese Law as Governing Law

According to Chinese law, Sino-foreign joint ventures (including equity joint ventures and contractual joint ventures) contracts and Sino-foreign natural resources joint exploration contracts that are carried out in China must be governed by Chinese law[72]. This rule is in contrast to the general Chinese rule applicable to "normal" contracts, under which contracting parties can choose the applicable law that can be non-Chinese law[73]. This special rule applicable to joint venture (JV) and joint exploration (JE) contracts seems to be unique and inflexible. The following question therefore asked whether investors were satisfied with such a rule.

As *Chart* 25 shows, the responses seem to be mixed, as both "yes" and "no" answers received around forty percent of the votes each, with a slightly higher positive votes (41%) than the negative ones (36%). Nine percent of respondents said that they did not care about it. The responses seem to suggest that whilst many foreign investors were unhappy with such an inflexible rule, most of them understood the reason behind it[74] and had accepted it. This is confirmed by the breakdown data, which show that, even among JV investors, there were more positive votes (50%) than negative ones (40%). What is interesting, however, is that British investors (23%) seemed to have been less worried about this rule than their fellow Continental investors (55%). The different legal cultures between the two must be an explanation.

9. Performance Requirements

The term "performance requirements" (PRs) is normally regarded as deriving from US BIT practice[75]. It is generally defined as certain commitments or obligations undertaken by foreign investors imposed by the host country as conditions for mere permission of investment entry or for enjoyment of certain special advantages or privileges[76]. PRs

---

[70] Itis estimated that there have been more than 200 "fixed return projects" similar to Fuzhou Xinyuan and Changchun Huijin, most of which are yet to be settled. Thus it can be reasonably predicted that more such cases will arise in near future. See *Fuzhou Government Facing Dispute of* 900 *Million for Blindly Introducing Foreign Investment*, available at <http://info.news.hc360.com/html/001/002/003/013/61066.htm> (03/10/2004).

[71] Details follow in Section IV.

[72] Article 126, para. 2, the *Contract Law of the People's Republic of China*, passed by the National People's Congress on 15 March 1999 and took effect on 1 October 1999. Same rule could be found in the abolished *Foreign Economic Contract Law of the People's Republic of China*, passed by the National People's Congress Standing Committee on 21 March 1985 and took effect on 1 July 1985. The latter was replaced by the former on 1 October 1999.

[73] Article 126, para. 1, the *Contract Law of the People's Republic of China*, passed by the National People's Congress on 15 March 1999 and took effect on 1 October 1999.

[74] The JV and JE contracts are special contracts and are subject to approval by the Chinese government authorities before they can be carried out. Also, as they are normally signed and carried out in China, they can be regarded as "most closely connected" to China. Therefore, it is not unreasonable to apply Chinese law to such contracts.

[75] ZENG, Huaqun, *International Investment Law* (in Chinese), Peking University Press, 1999, p. 424.

[76] Vendevelde, K., *United States Investment Treaties: policy and practice*, Kluwer, 1992, p. 110.

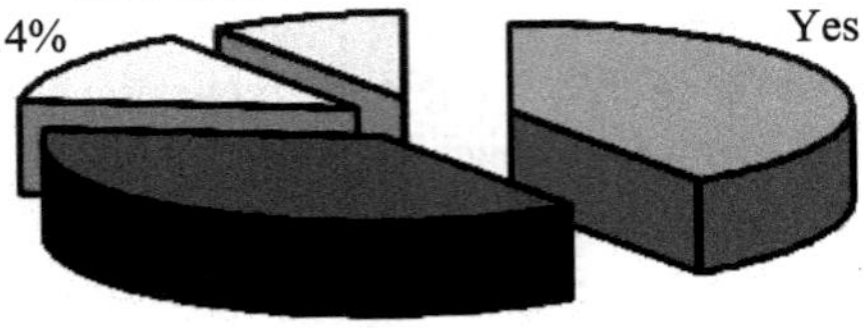

Chart 25 Satisfaction by the Requirement of Chinese Law Governing FDI Contracts

have two basic forms: either as a condition of admission (which may be called "direct PRs"); or linked to an advantage (which may be called "indirect PRs").[77] Developed countries, led by the US, take a liberal approach towards investment admission and attack the use of PRs and other screening measures as conservative and inward-looking, because they interfere with market forces and invite corruption. In contrast, developing and transition countries including China have long viewed PRs as essential and effective tools to control FDI inflows, making sure that they are conducive rather than harmful to the national economy and society.

In a recent survey conducted under the auspices of the European Commission, China was singled out as the country having the highest number of barriers to EU investment.[78] It is recorded that China favoured performance requirements such as compulsory joint venture requirements, local content requirements, and restrictions on the right to acquire full ownership of local subsidiaries and export performance requirements.[79] This question was thus designed to further investigate this issue.

The Questionnaire (*Chart* 26) shows that most foreign investors had been subjected to some performance requirements. The most widely used was transfer of technology requirements, with half of the respondents reported that such requirements were imposed. Other performance requirements imposed included export performance (36%), local content (27%), forex balance (27%), compulsory JV (27%), subsidiaries limitations (23%) and local employment (14%). About forty one percent of them had also experienced other forms of performance requirements that they did not specify. The breakdown data show that, apart from local employment requirement which was more often imposed

[77] Also, PRs are sometimes divided into those imposed on the admission stage and those imposed on the operation stage. However, this division may prove to be false, since PRs imposed on admission stage will inevitably be carried onto the operation stage of a foreign investment projects, and, PRs imposed on FDI operation may also be regarded as a part of the general conditions of investment admission—because admission of every foreign investment in every host country is conditional on foreign investors abiding by its laws and regulations, including those affecting investment operations. Therefore, in this article, they are all treated together, even though some of those (e. g., local employment requirements) discussed are mainly concerned with investment operations. Gudgon also thinks that such a division is relative. See Gudgeon, Nancy, *United States Bilateral Investment Treaties: Comments on their Origin, Purposes and General Treatment Standards*, 4 International Tax and Business Law, 1986, pp. 118, 120.

[78] TN SOFRES Survey, pp. 8 –9.

[79] Ibid.

on WFE investors (17%) than on JV investors (10%0, the latter were more frequently required than the former, to fulfil PRs in local content (20% vs. 17%), export performance (60% vs. 0%), forex balancing (40% vs. 0%), technology transfer (70% vs 0%) and limitation on subsidiaries ownership (20% vs. 17%). This seems to suggest that WFE be a better vehicle of investment to avoid PRs.

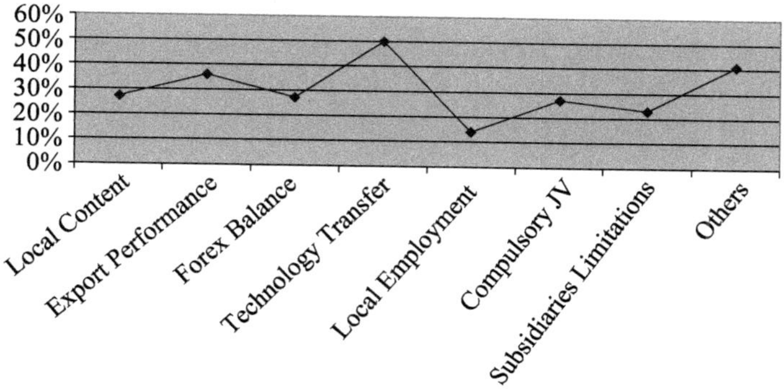

Chart 26 Frequency of Performance Requirements Encountered

The Questionnaire, in general, confirms the finding of the TN SOFRES that extensive direct and indirect PRs were attached in case of China. However, it must be noted that some of those requirements and limitations, such as local content requirements, forex balancing requirements, export performance and technology transfer requirements, have been lifted or relaxed by recent amendments to FDI laws and regulations[80].

10. Summary

The finding from the above questions on key substantive issues can be summarised as follows. First of all, most foreign investors considered China as a safe place to make investment. Political promise and social stability and legal protection were the major important sources of confidence. Secondly, performances requirements (PRs) were widely used as conditions for either approval or obtaining special advantages. The most widely used PRs were transfer of technology requirements, followed by export performance, local content, forex balancing, compulsory JV, subsidiaries limitations and local employment. Thirdly, expropriation of foreign investment had rarely taken place in China in the last 20 years.

Fourthly, the implementation of national treatment to foreign investment was welcomed by most foreign investors, though some of them were concerned with the negative effect it might bring about by reducing existing tax incentives. As far as monetary transfer is concerned, fifthly, most foreign investors encountered no or little difficulty, which suggest that the continuous liberalisation efforts thereon had been successful. Sixthly, however, China's weak regime in protecting intellectual property rights was criticised by foreign investors. Investment insurance, seventhly, only plays a very limited role in FDI

[80] For details of the amendments, including their background and outlook, see SHAN, Wenhua, *Towards a Level Playing Field for Foreign Investment in China*, 3 The Journal of World Investment (JWI) 2, 2002.

in China. Eighthly, the vast majority of foreign investors had not come across any disputes with the Chinese government and none of these disputes had actually been submitted to the ICSID for arbitration.

Finally, mixed responses were received on the compulsory rule that Chinese law applied to all JV and JE contracts. Whilst over forty percent of foreign investors were happy with such a rule, another thirty six percent were dissatisfied with it. This result demonstrates that the requirement is understandable and acceptable to many foreign investors despite its "arbitrary" appearance. The survey also shows that British investors were less worried about this requirement.

IV. Conclusion

The present study demonstrates that law had played a significant role in China's success in attracting foreign investment. Most investors had conducted an in-depth research on the legal environment before they invested, including not only the written law but law in action; not only Chinese laws and regulations but also applicable international agreements. Contrary to what is commonly believed, investment incentives were considered a very important factor when foreign investors made investment decisions. The survey also confirms the positive impact of China's accession to the WTO and a potential new investment treaty in improving the investment conditions.

The study, furthermore, shows that China was generally regarded as a safe place to invest or re-invest. Foreign investors appreciated the efforts the Chinese government had made to create a more conducive legal climate for foreign investment, particularly the implementation of national treatment, the elimination of certain performance requirements, the relaxation of foreign exchange regime, and the strengthening of IPR law and enforcement. However, it was thought that the investment conditions could be further improved by, for example, strictly enforcing intellectual property rights laws.

ANNEX I QUESTIONNAIRE ON LAW AND EUROPEAN INVESTMENT IN CHINA

PLEASE answer all questions and return to the address below. MANY THANKS for your support.

Your Profile

Your designation: ______________ Nationality of your company ______________

Location of investment ______________ Industrial sector of investment ______________

Date investment established: ______________ Intended duration of investment (year): ______________

Investment amount (£): ______________ Foreign equity participation (%): ______________

Foreign participation in management: ______________

1. *General Role of Law in Investment Decision Making*

1. In making the decision to invest in China, how important was the nature of the

legal system to your company, relative to other issues (e. g. market size, labor costs, environmental costs, raw materials etc.) ?

__ Top　　__ None
__ High　　__ Do not know
__ Medium　　__ Do not understand
__ Low

2. Did your company investigate the general legal environment for investment from the EU (e. g. tax incentives, protection from expropriation, investment insurance etc.) before deciding to invest?

__ Yes　　__ Do not know
__ No　　__ Do not understand

3. In making the decision to invest in China, what importance did your company put on foreign investment incentives (such as tax exemptions for foreign investors generally, or specifically to those in particular industrial sectors or zones) offered by China?

__ Top　　__ None
__ High　　__ Do not know
__ Medium　　__ Do not understand
__ Low

4. If your company did investigate the legal environment before investing, what evidence did it use? Please tick all that apply:

__ Law on the paper　　__ Do not understand
__ Law in action (e. g. levels of enforcement)　　__ Do not know

5. If your company did investigate the legal environment before investing, which laws were considered? Please tick all that apply:

__ Domestic (Chinese) law　　__ Do not understand
__ International investment treaties　　__ Do not know

6. Which of the following investment protection and promotion treaties between China and your company's home country was your company aware of when making the decision to invest? Please tick all that apply:

Bilateral Investment Treaty (BIT)[81]

Bilateral Double Taxation Treaty (DTT)[82]

__ Convention Establishing the Multilateral Investment Guarantee Agency(MIGA Convention)

__ Convention on the Settlement of Investment Disputes between States and Nationals of Other States (ICSID Convention)

__ Other International Investment Rules (Please specify)

2. Experience of Chinese FDI Legal System

7. Does your company feel safe to invest or re-invest in China?

---

[81] Bilateral treaties that aim to promote and protect mutual investment, e. g. , the UK-China BIT signed in 1986.

[82] Bilateral treaties that aim to avoid double taxation on trans-border business.

__ Yes __ Do not know

__ No __ Do not understand

If "Yes", which of the following instruments (if any) has contributed the most to your company's sense of safety? Please tick ONE:

__ Legal protection provided by domestic and international law

__ Investment insurance against political risks

__ Political promise and social stability

__ Others (please specify)

8. Has your company suffered from any sort of nationalization or expropriation in China in the last 20 years?

__ Yes __ Do not know

__ No __ Do not understand

Have you heard of any other company which has suffered from any sort of nationalization or expropriation in China in the last 20 years?

__ Yes __ Do not know

__ No __ Do not understand

Have those nationalizations or expropriations that your company or other companies have suffered been compensated "adequately, promptly and effectively"[83]?

__ Never __ Mostly

__ Rarely __ Always

__ Sometimes __ Do not know

__ Frequently __ Do not understand

9. In recent years, the Chinese government has been trying to implement national treatment for foreign investors. To what extent would you think the new policy might improve the investment climate?

__ Significantly __ Do not know

__ A little __ Do not understand

__ Not at all

10. Has your company encountered any difficulty in transferring its investment or profit out of China?

__ Never __ Mostly

__ Rarely __ Always

__ Sometimes __ Do not know

__ Frequently __ Do not understand

11. Is your company satisfied with the Chinese system of intellectual property rights protection?

__ Yes __ Do not know

__ No __ Do not understand

__ Not relevant

---

〔83〕 This means that the compensation shall be able to put the expropriated enterprise in the same financial situation as if it had not been expropriated. The compensation shall also be paid in convertible currency and without undue delay.

12. Has your company insured your investment against political risks based on MIGA or a BIT?

__ Yes __ Do not know

__ No __ Do not understand

13. Has your company has had any legal disputes with the Chinese Government?

__ Yes __ Do not know

__ No __ Do not understand

If yes, has such a dispute been submitted to the ICSID for arbitration, according to the ICSID Convention and the applicable BIT (see Question 6)?

__ Yes __ Do not know

__ No __ Do not understand

14. Are you satisfied with the rule that Chinese law must govern all joint venture and joint exploitation contracts?

__ Yes __ Do not know

__ No __ Do not understand

__ Do not care

15. Has the Chinese government insisted on the inclusion of any of the following performance requirements in legal documents as a prerequisite for giving approval and/or preferential treatment to your company? Please tick all that apply:

Local content requirement[84]

Export performance requirement[85]

Foreign exchange balancing requirem ent[86]

__ Technology transfer requirement

__ Local employment requirement

__ Compulsory joint venture requirement

__ Limitation on ownership of local subsidiaries

__ Other performance requirements, please specify:

16. Are Chinese FDI laws and policies easily accessible in China?

Never Mostly

Rarely Always

__ Sometimes __ Do not know

__ Frequently __ Do not understand

17. Are the laws and/or policies of China changed unexpectedly?

__ Never __ Mostly

__ Rarely __ Always

__ Sometimes __ Do not know

__ Frequently __ Do not understand

18. Do government officials enforce laws consistently?

__ Never __ Mostly

---

[84] An obligation on foreign funded enterprises to obtain all or part of their supplies from local suppliers.

[85] An obligation of exporting a minimum level of products manufactured by foreign funded enterprises.

[86] A requirement by host government on foreign funded enterprises to maintain foreign exchange balance.

__ Rarely __ Always
__ Sometimes __ Do not know
__ Frequently __ Do not understand

19. Is it necessary to use bribery when dealing with government officials?

__ Never __ Mostly
__ Rarely __ Always
__ Sometimes __ Do not know
__ Frequently __ Do not understand

20. Do the Chinese courts enforce law objectively according to published rules?

__ Never __ Mostly
__ Rarely __ Always
__ Sometimes __ Do not know
__ Frequently __ Do not understand

21. Is it possible to use bribery to impact on judge's decisions?

__ Never __ Mostly
__ Rarely __ Always
__ Sometimes __ Do not know
__ Frequently __ Do not understand

22. Do politicians interfere in court decisions?

__ Never __ Mostly
__ Rarely __ Always
__ Sometimes __ Do not know
__ Frequently __ Do not understand

23. Are court/arbitration procedures subject to unreasonable delays?

__ Never __ Mostly
__ Rarely __ Always
__ Sometimes __ Do not know
__ Frequently __ Do not understand

24. Are the decisions of courts and arbitrators well enforced by Chinese authorities?

__ Never __ Mostly
__ Rarely __ Always
__ Sometimes __ Do not know
__ Frequently __ Do not understand

III. A Possible Investment Agreement to which the EU and China are Parties?

25. How useful would the Chinese joining into the World Trade Organisation (WTO) be to improve the legal environment for foreign investment?

__ Very useful __ Not at all useful
__ Fairly useful __ Do not understand
__ Not very useful __ Do not know

26. How useful would a new bilateral or multilateral investment agreement to which China and the EU are parties be to improve the legal environment for foreign investment?

__ Very useful
__ Fairly useful
__ Not very useful
__ Not at all useful
__ Do not understand
__ Do not know

27. How useful do you think the inclusion of each of the following provisions into a new international agreement would be?

Provisions	*Very useful*	*Fairly useful*	*Not very useful*	*Not useful at all*	*Do not know*	*Do not under-stand*
Most Favoured Nation (MFN) Treatment[87]						
Pre-establishment National Treatment[88]						
Post-establishment National Treatment[89]						
Adequate, prompt, effective compensation[90] in the event of expropriation						
Free transfer of property and profit						
Compulsory jurisdiction of ICSID over state-investor investment disputes[91]						
Other provisions (please specify)						

Do you have any further comments to make on the legal environment of FDI in China?

ANNEX II RESPONDENT INVESTORS

Company	Home State	Date of Establishment	Type of Investment
1	France	1990s (Since 1990s)	Joint Venture (JV)
2	Britain	2000s (Summer 2000)	JV
3	France	1990s (1996)	Wholly Foreign Funded Enterprise (WFE)
4	Britain	2000s (end 2001)	JV
5	Italy	1990s (1996)	Representative Office
6	Italy	1990s (1995)	JV and WFE

[87] A treatment by a host country (China) granted to investment or investors from another country that is not less favourable than that accorded to investment and investors from any third country.

[88] A treatment by a host country applied to investors or investment of another country that is not less favourable than that accorded to its domestic investors and their investment. If this treatment only applies to the post-establishment stage of investment, e. g., the operation, management, maintenance, use, possession and sale or any other form of disposal, it is called "post-establishment national treatment". On the other hand, if it applies to the pre-establishment stage of investment, e. g., the establishment, acquisition, or expansion, it is called "pre-establishment national treatment".

[89] See note 8.

[90] See note 3.

[91] This means that in the event of a dispute between an investor and the host country (China), the investor can brings a claim before the ICSID against the country without its consent.

续表

Company	Home State	Date of Establishment	Type of Investment
7	Britain	Not Available (N/A)	WFE
8	Britain	1990s (1994)	JV
9	Britain	2000s (Aug. 2000)	WFE
10	Britain	1990s (1996)	WFE
11	Luxembourg	1990s (since 1996)	JV
12	Britain	1990s (1996)	JV
13	Britain	1990s (1996)	(N/A)
14	Britain	1980s (1989)	JV
15	Britain	1990s (1996)	N/A
16	Britain	1990s (1999)	WFE
17	Denmark	1990s (1997)	JV
18	Netherlands	2000s (Jan. 2000)	WFE
19	France	1990s (since 1995)	JV and WFE
20	Germany	1980 (early 1980)	JV and WFE
21	Britain	1990s (1994)	JV
22	Britain	1990s (1995)	JV

Towards a Level Playing Field of Foreign Investment in China*

From October 2000 to July 2001, Chinese foreign direct investment (FDI) laws and regulations underwent massive amendment. Three basic FDI laws, namely the China-Foreign Equity Joint Venture Law (EJVL), the China-Foreign Contractual Joint Venture Law (CJVL) and the Wholly Foreign-Funded Enterprises Law (WFEL) were revised. Two of the three Implementing Regulations of these basic laws, i. e. those of the EJVL and the WFEL, were modified.[1] The amendments have understandably drawn much attention in business and legal circles both within and outside Mainland China.[2]

As a participant in this legal process and one of the original advocates of the main

* *Journal of World Investment* (Geneva), Vol. 3, No. 2, April 2002.

[1] The third Implementing Regulation, that of eh "CJVL, has not been changed, probably because" it was promulgated in 1995 and therefore updated enough to stay as it is.

[2] For related reports in English, see, for example, *China Publishes Amended Foreign Investment Enterprise Law,* Hong Kong Economic Journal, 1November 2000; China: Congress Drafts Further Changes to Joint Venture Law, Xinhua News Agency. Beijing, 0230 GMT, 14 March 2001, BBC Monitoring; China: Congress Passes Amendment to Joint Venture Law as Commitment to WTO, Xinhua News Agency, Beijing, 0813 GMT. 15 March 2001, l: BBC Monitoring; China Drafts legislation Easing Restrictions on Foreign Investors, Xinhua News Agency, Beijing, 1335 GMT, 31 October 2000, BBC Monitoring. For similar reports in Chinese, see, for example, Chinese Tirade Minister Explains Draft Amendments to Foreign Enterprise Laws, Xinhua News Agency Domestic Service, Beijing, 0856 GMT, 23 October 2000, But Monitoring; China: Premier Zhu Rongji Signs Bills to Revise Foreign-funded Enterprise Law, Xinhua News Agency for Hong Kong, Beijing, 0642 GMT, 23 October 2000, But Monitoring; Chinese State Council Eases Regulations oil Foreign Investment, Xinhua News Agency Domestic Service, Beijing, 0439 GMT, 2 August 2001, BBC Monitoring; FIEs Welcome the Amendments to the Fin Law, 12 December 2000, available at http: //www. pu-doiig. coiii/jxx/200012/jxx_001204. htm. The Amendments to the EJVL Will Benefit Hong Kong Investors Significantly, 17 March 2001, available at http: //ticws. cliiiia. coni/zh-cii/hnit/1004/20010317/145251. html; Lu Ciarong and Zhang Bingsheng, NPC Deputies Discuss the Proposed Arrrendrnents to the "Chitta-Foreign Equity Joint Venture Law", 14 March 2001, available at http: //dailynews. sina. com. cn/c/207560. html. Liu Jiangfeng, Combining the Three FIE Law, or Including them into the Company Law? 15 March 2001, available at http: //nnance. sina. com. cn/g/43903. html. Wu Yu, China has Generally Finished the Checking-up and Amendments fuzz Laws and Regulations related tn Foreign Trade and Economic Relations, 18 May 2001, available at http: //financc. sina. com. cn/g/61985. htmh.

amendments,[3] the author is delighted to see that what was studied and proposed has been seriously considered by the Legislature and largely adopted in the new laws and regulations. It is therefore a great pleasure to share with those who may be interested in this field the author's understanding of this amendment of Chinese FDI law, including its background and content, and to discuss possible directions of further development.

I. BACKGROUND OF THE AMENDMENT

Why does the Chinese government choose this time to modify its FDI laws and regulations? A quick answer is that China had to fulfill the promises made to the World Trade Organization Members, with its own membership imminent.[4] This answer is certainly correct in that WTO membership and the commitments that China has made have to a large extent impacted on this amendment, in particular on its timing. However, a closer look at the changes and their background would show that this is only half of the truth. The other, probably more fundamental, half is the market-oriented economic reform and opening-up policies that China has carried out consistently for over twenty years.

It is obvious that this amendment has been pushed by the prospect of Chinese admission to the WTO. After fifteen years of "long march",[5] China has finally finished all the bilateral negotiations and sorted out all substantive and procedural problems on its way to Geneva.[6] On 10 November 2001, when WTO Member Ministers met in Doha, Qatar, China was officially accepted as a new Member, with its membership taking effect on 11 December 2001. Therefore, there had indeed not been very much time left for the Chinese government to review and revise its FDI laws and regulations in line with its promises made in the bilateral talks. For example, in the China-United States bilateral Market Access Agreement, China agreed to abolish upon its WTO accession all trade-related investment measures (TRIMs) prohibited by the Agreement on Trade-Related

---

[3] Since 1993, the author has published a series articles in leading Chinese law journals on the necessity for, possibility of and measures required to implement national treatment for FDI in line with the" establishment of a "socialist market economy". In 1996, the Ministry of Foreign Trade and Economic Co-operation (MOFTEC) encrusted the author's Instituteto carry out a more detailed research on chis topic. As a result, he wrote the Final Research Report, in which he proposed some necessary amendments to the main FDI Laws and regulations, which seem by and large to have been adopted in the recent amendments. For further details of the author's earlier research, see (in Chinese), Shan Wenhua, *Market Economy and National Treatment for Foreign Funded Enterprises,* Chinese Legal Science *(Zhongguo Faxue)*. No. 5, 1994; The Development *and Perfection of National Treatment for FDI in China,* CASS Journal of Law *(Faxue Yanjiu)*, 1995, No. 5; *National Treatment for FDI and its Conditions for Implementation,* Social Sciences in *China (Zhongguo Shehui Kexue), No. 5, 1998. For a recent publication in English, See idem, National Treatment and the Transformation of Chinese FDI Laws and Policies,* International Trade Laws and Regulations (ITLR.), Vol. 6, issue 1, March 2000.

[4] See, for example, *China: Congress Passes Amendment to Joint Venture Law as Commitment to WTO,* Xinhua News Agency, Beijing, 0813 GMT, 15 March 2001, BBC Monitoring.

[5] Since China formally applied for membership in the General Agreement on Tariffs anti Trade, predecessor to the WTO, in 1986, fifteen years have passed, which is about twice the length of time the Communist Party spent on its retreat march to western China-the "Long March". For details of the background, see Scan Leonard, The Dragon Awakens: China's Long March to Geneva, Camcron May, London, 1999.

[6] Frances Williams, China and Taiwan Join World Trade Today, Financial Times, 11 December 2001.

Investment Measures (TRIMs Agreement), including local content requirements, trade balancing requirements and export performance requirements, so as to be in conformity with the national treatment (NT) requirement of the General Agreement on Tariffs and Trade (GATT) 1994.[7] Therefore, immediate measures had to be taken by China to bring its FDI law into harmony with WTO rules and its promises.

At the same time, however, the internal need of further reform and opening-up has also played a very, if not much more, important role in this legal change. This can be easily seen with a closer look at the contents of this amendment. Take the amendments to the EJVL-the oldest and most important FDI law-as an example. These amendments have mainly touched three issues: the production and operation plan, the right to amend the Law and the purchase of domestic materials.

As explained by Mr. Gu Angran in the National People's Congress (NPC) before it was passed,[8] the first change-the deletion of the requirement for equity joint ventures (EJVS) to submit their production and operation plans to authorities concerned and to carry them out "by means of economic contracts" – is because China has already shifted from a centrally planned economy to the socialist market economy.[9] The second change, that of shifting the right to amend the EJVL from the foll NPC to its Standing Committee, was made purely so that the Standing Committee can amend the Law in a timely manner as reform and the opening-up policy so require.[10] In other words, the first two changes are both responses to the economic reform and opening-up and are not directly related to WTO membership.

Although it appears that the third amendment-the deletion of the domestic purchase priority requirement-was to conform with the NT requirement of the TRIMS Agreement, it is also based on the need for establishing a market economy. Mr. Gu said:

"The main consideration of this amendment is that: under the socialist market economy, enterprises' purchases of supplies should be decided by enterprises according to the market situation and the principle of fairness and reasonableness; the Government shall not interfere. Foreign-invested enterprises (FIEs), like other national enterprises, shall have such purchasing rights. Meanwhile, according to the TRIMS Agreement of the WTO and Article 1 of its Annex 'Illustrative List', Members shall not by any means restrict enterprises to purchase, use products produced locally or originated therefrom. Our Government has made a commitment to abolish the 'local content requirement' during the WTO admission negotiations..."[11]

---

[7] United States-China WTO Market Access Agreement, available at http://www.uschina.org/public/wt0/market/227237.pdf, 21 August 2001. Among these performance requirements that China promised to remove, the export performance requirement is beyond the scope of WTO rules, as the TRIMS Agreement does prohibit export performance requirements in general; see U. S. International Trade Commission, *Assessment of the Economic Effects on the United States of* China's Accession *to the WTO*. Publication No. 3229, September 1999, p. xiii.

[8] Gu Angran, *The Amendments to the China-Foreign EWL are to Adapt to the Development of Circumstances*, People's Daily, Overseas Edition, 10 March 2001, p. 2.

[9] Id.

[10] Id.

[11] Id.

Here it can be seen that the internal needs for China to carry on reform and opening-up and, at the end, to establish a "socialist market economy" are deeper and more fundamental reasons for these amendments. If China was not committed to establish a market economy, it should not have made these commitments at all.

Moreover, as a matter of fact, China had committed to provide NT for FIEs far earlier than when it signed the bilateral WTO agreement with the United States. As early as 1992, China announced that it would create "facilities and conditions to implement national treatment for FIEs".[12] And in 1996, President Jiang Zemin clearly mentioned in the Central Economical Meeting that:

"The basic laws of utilizing foreign investment were made in the early years of our reform and opening-up policy. They have played very important, positive roles. Nevertheless, it is necessary to amend and perfect them with urgency, in accordance with the new circumstances as they develop."[13]

As argued elsewhere, a market economy requires NT for FIEs, which is impossible to be realized within a centrally planned economy.[14] Under a planned economy, every company is but an executing symbol and a statistical unit of the omnipotent central plan.[15] As a result, State-owned enterprises have to undertake special responsibilities, such as carrying out national plans, providing public services and taking lifelong care of their staff and workers, and consequently enjoy special rights and privileges, such as material supply, financial loans and subsidies.[16] Neither of these responsibilities and rights could be applied to FIEs, which are operated on a market and competition basis. Thus there is no ground for implementing NT for FIEs under a planned economy, just as we have seen in the former Soviet Union and other socialist countries.

On the contrary, under a market economy, where the market and competition allocate resources, it is not only possible but also necessary to implement NT for FIEs.[17] On the one hand, a market economy needs a level playing field-a market-on which different enterprises can compete with each other on an equal footing. In other words, a market economy needs a united market for all kinds of domestic enterprises to enjoy "fair play" ; and such a domestic level playground is indeed the very condition of implementing NT for FIES. On the other hand, in today's world economy, one market has to be indispensably linked to other markets and thus form a level playing field worldwide-a world or global market. This means that one country shall not just treat its domestic enterprises equally, but also treat foreign companies in the same way as domestic companies; in other words, to provide NT for FIEs.

The twenty years of market-oriented reform and opening-up of China has been a

〔12〕 Shan, 1994, supra, footnote 3.

〔13〕 Zhang Mei, The Unification of Foreign Invested Enterprises, in Legal Aspects of Doing Business in China, (Zhongguo touzi falu zhinan), Vol. 1, Law Press, Beijing, 1999, pp. 69 – 70 and 244.

〔14〕 Shan, 1994, supra, footnote 3.

〔15〕 Id.

〔16〕 Id.

〔17〕 Id.

very vivid and telling footnote to this conclusion. Before 1979, when the central plans dominated everything in the whole country, there was virtually no foreign trade and investment in China. From 1979 on, in pace with the market-oriented economic reform and opening-up to the outside world, the market has played a more and more important role in China. As a result, more and more FDI was attracted to the country and was well treated by the Chinese authorities with relaxed entry conditions and preferential tax arrangements. However, NT for FIES had never been formally mentioned until 1992, when Deng Xiaoping, the *de facto* leader of the country, took a historical tour to South China and remarked that "a socialist country may also implement a market economy". From then on, the Chinese government has persistently stressed the need "to create conditions and facilities for implementing NT for FIEs".[18] NT for F1Es has indeed been the flag and symbol of a new stage of FDI policy in China which carries wide and profound implications.[19]

Undoubtedly, the recent massive amendment of FDI laws and regulations is a continuity and development of this consistent process of creating conditions for implementing NT of FIES, although it is also a well-timed preparation for the Chinese entry into the WTO. Nevertheless, it is necessary to stress that the two sides-the internal side of establishing a market economy and the external side of entering into the WTO-are in harmony, rather than in contradiction. Both of them are market-and rule-based. Meanwhile, the WTO may be used as a powerful instrument to carry out massive, radical economic and social changes.

II. THE CHANGED RULES

This amendment of FDI laws and regulations started in October 2000, when the 18th Session of the Ninth NPC Standing Committee reviewed and passed the amendments to the WFEL and the CJVL. In April, the State Council approved the modifications to the Implementing Regulations of the WFEL accordingly. In March 2001, the 4th Meeting of the Ninth NPC reviewed and passed the amendments to the EJVL. Subsequently, in July 2001, the State Council approved the amendments to the Implementing Regulations of the EJVL. The detailed changes of these laws and regulations are as follows:

A. THE AMENDMENTS TO THE EJVL AND ITS IMPLEMENTING REGULATIONS

1. *Amendment s to the EJVL*

Although there are only three major changes in the EJVL, there are quite a few technical amendments. Details of these changes are:

Article 2, Paragraph 2 was changed to read: "All activities of the EJV shall observe the rules of the laws and regulations of the People's Republic of China (PRC)." Here, "laws and regulations" replaced the previous wording of "laws, decrees and pertinent

---

[18] Shan, 1994, supra, footnote 3.

[19] Shan, 2000, supra, footnote 3, pp. 26 – 27.

regulations" so as to conform to other related laws, such as the CJVL and the WFEL.

Article 6, Paragraph 4 was changed to read: "Matters concerning the staff and workers of a joint venture, such as appointment, dismissal, remuneration, fringe benefits, labour protection and labour insurance, should be laid down in contracts concluded in accordance with the law." The intentions of this amendment were to supplement the provision by subsequently enacted legal provisions and to provide a legal requirement for labour protection and labour insurance.

A clause was added as Article 7 of the new EJVL. It reads: "The staff and workers of a joint venture may establish trade unions, engage in trade union activities and protect the legitimate rights and interests of staff and workers... A joint venture shall provide necessary conditions for the activities of its own trade unions." This addition was made to be in line with other related laws, including the WFEL and the CJVL.

Article 8 was changed to be Article 9. Its Paragraph 4 was modified as: "The various kinds of insurance coverage of a joint venture shall be furnished by insurers in China." The change of "Chinese insurers" to "insurers in China", which makes sure that foreign-funded insurers in China will enjoy the same rights as domestic insurers in this sense (NT), is also in line with the WFEL, the CJVL and the Insurance Law.

Article 9 was renumbered as Article 10. The first paragraph, which said: "Production and operation plans of a joint venture shall be reported to authorities concerned for the record", was deleted and the second paragraph was renumbered as the first paragraph and changed to read as: "Raw materials, fuels and other resources required by a joint venture within its approved business scope can, according to the principles of fairness and reasonableness, be purchased from either the domestic market or the international market." These changes, as mentioned previously (Section 1), were made to adapt to the new situations of establishing a market economy and preparing for admission to the WTO.

Article 14 was changed to be Article 15 and a paragraph was added as the second paragraph, which reads: "If the venture partners have not concluded an arbitration clause in the contract or have not reached a written arbitration agreement, either of them can bring a lawsuit before the People's Court." This revision was made to be in line with other related laws, including the Arbitration Law, and to clarify that the possibility of litigation exist if necessary.

Article 15 was renumbered as Article 16 and the second sentence therein was deleted. The previous sentence read: "The right to revise this law belongs to the National People 's Congress...", which was to guarantee the stability of this Law. It fact made it impossible to amend the three basic FDI laws in one go in October 2000.

The number and order of some provisions were changed accordingly.[20]

· *Amendments to the EJVL Implementing Regulations*

Unlike amendments to other laws and regulations, the amendments to the EJVL Im-

---

[20] The Decision of the National People's 's Congress Concerning Amendments of the "Law of the People's Republic of china on Equity Joint Ventures" (adopted by the National People's Congress on 15 March 2001), People's Daily, Overseas Edition, 21 March 2001, p. 2.

plementing Regulations are massive and significant. In total, forty-five changes have been made and nineteen Articles and provisions were deleted.[21] According to officials from the Ministry of Foreign Trade and Economic Co-operation (MOFTEC) and other departments concerned, these amendment to the Implementing Regulations can be classified into four main aspects:

· *Amendment s in accordance with the changes to the EJVL:* These include deletion of provisions of export performance requirements and domestic sales restrictions; deletion of provisions for EJVS production and operational plans to be reported; deletion of the provision for EJVS to "as far as possible" give priority to purchasing in China; and deletion of the provision requiring EJVS to maintain a balance betwteen their foreign exchange income and expenditure.

· *Amendments of clauses inconsistent with WTO rules and China's external commitments:* Deleted from the "Implementing Regulations" were the provision for machines and equipment contributed as investment by the foreign joint venture partner to be import-substituting machines and equipment and the provision requiring industrial property rights contributed as investment by the foreign joint venture partner to be capable of producing exports. It has been stipulated, in accordance with China's external commitments, that industries in which Sino foreign joint ventures arc allowed shall be determined according to State Provisions Guiding the Direction of Foreign Investment (PGDFI) and the Guiding Catalogue of Industries with Foreign Investment (GCIFI).

· *Amendments of clauses clearly inconsistent with laws, administrative laws and regulations and relevant State Council rules currently in effect:* These have mainly amended the provisions on industrial and commercial registration. land use right acquisition and transfer, tariff and industrial and commercial consolidated tax reduction or exemption, labour management, the joint venture term of EJVS and the liquidation of EJVS to keep the Implementing Regulations in conformity with relevant laws and administrative laws and regulations in effect. Also, in accordance with the provisions in relevant laws such as the Company Law, the Accounting Law, the Income Tax Law for Enterprises with Foreign Investment and Foreign Enterprises, and the Legislation Law, they also have amended the provision that EJVS shall not reduce their registered capital, provisions on accounting in foreign currency and financial and accounting reports, provisions on income clearing and tax payment by Sino-foreign joint ventures and the provision on the power to interpret the Implementing Regulations.

· *Amendment of some provisions clearly unsuitable to new circumstances in reform and development:* These have deleted, in accordance with the reform of government institutions and the change of their functions, the provisions on a Department in charge of an EJV. They have also deleted the provisions on channels through which foreign investors may seek co-operative partners, on EJVS' capital construction plans and funds, on goods and materials supply, and on marketing channels for products to suit the requirements of

---

[21] For details, see The Decision of the State Council Concerning Amendment of the "Implementing Regulations for the Law f the People's Republic of China on Equity joint Ventures (promulgated and entered into force on 22 July 2001), People's Daily, Overseas Edition, 6 August 2001, p. 5.

a market economy. At the same time, they have amended, in the light of the new circumstances after the structural reforms in foreign exchange control and financial administration, the provisions on foreign exchange rates, on account opening and foreign exchange receipt and expenses administration, on loans, and on outward remittances. Finally, in view of the fact that enterprises have enjoyed under the law the right to fix product prices by themselves according to the principles of structural reform in price control, they have deleted the provision for price control on EJVS.[22]

B. THE AMENDMENTS TO THE WFEL AND ITS IMPLEMENTING REGULATIONS

1. *Amendments to the WFEL*

These include:

Article 3, Paragraph 1 was changed to read: "The establishment of a wholly foreign-funded enterprise (WFE) must be conducive to the development of the Chinese national economy. The State encourages the establishment of product-exporting and technology-advanced WFEs." The compulsory condition for all WFEs to be export-oriented or technologically advanced was therefore abolished in accordance with the TRIMs Agreement.

As in the EJVL, the previous Article 11, Paragraph 1, which read: "The production and operation plans of a WFE shall be reported to its department in charge..." was deleted.

Similarly, Article 15 was modified as "Raw materials, fuels, and other resources required by a joint venture within its approved business scope can, according to the principles of fairness and reasonableness, be purchased from either the domestic market or the international market."

Article 18, Paragraph 3 was deleted. It said: "A WFE shall maintain the foreign exchange balance by itself. If a WFE sells its products in the Chinese market as approved by authorities concerned, and thus causes an imbalance of foreign exchange, the authority that approved the domestic sale shall be responsible for solving the problem."

The order of some provisions was also rearranged.[23]

2. *Amendments to the Implementing Regulations of the WFEL*

These were quite extensive and included the following:

Article 3 was changed to read: "The establishment of a WFE must be conducive to the development of the Chinese national economy and can attain significant economic effect. The State encourages WFEs to apply advanced technology and equipment, to engage in new product development, to upgrade products and to save energy and raw materials; it also encourages the establishment of export-oriented WFEs."

---

[22] MOFIEC and State Council Legislative Affairs Bureau Officials Answer Questions Raised by journalist on the Amendments to the Implementing Regulations of the EJVL, People's Daily, Overseas Edition, 13 August 2001, p.5.

[23] The Decision of the Standing Committee of the National People's Congress Concerning Amendment of the "Law of the People's Republic of China on Wholly Foreign-Funded Enterprises" (adopted and effected on 31 October 2000); available at http://www.chinalawinfo.com/newlaw/reportshowcontent.asp?ID=2577, 6 November 2000.

Articles 3 and 4 were combined and revised as, "Industries in which WFEs are prohibited or restricted to establish shall be implemented in accordance with the PGDFI and the GCIFI."

The words: "... the portion of the sale of products in the Chinese and foreign markets..." in Article 10 were deleted.

The words: "... and the portion of the sale in the Chinese and foreign markets..." in Article 15 were deleted.

Article 22 was changed to read: "A WFE shall not reduce its registered capital. However, if it is indeed necessary to reduce the registered capital due to changes of the total investment amount and its scale of production and operation, it must be approved by the approval authorities."

Article 27, Paragraph 1 was changed to read: "If a foreign investor makes the investment with machines and equipment as evaluated, the machines and equipment shall be that required for the production of the WFE."

Article 28, Paragraph 1 was modified to read: "If a foreign investor makes the investment with its industrial rights and know-how as evaluated, the industrial rights and know-how shall be that belonging to the foreign investor."

Article 43 was deleted.

Article 45 was changed to read: "A WFE may sell its products in the Chinese market. The State encourages WFEs to export products they produce."

Article 46, Paragraph 2 was changed to read: "A WFE may sell its products in China by itself or through commercial agencies on a commission basis."

Article 48, Paragraphs 2 and 3 were deleted.

The provision: "If a WFE imports materials as follows, it can be exempt from customs tariff, and industrial and commercial consolidation tax..." in Artide 52 was replaced by this provision: "If a WFE imports materials as follows, it may enjoy tax reduction or exemption in accordance with related rules of the Chinese tax law."

Article 53 was changed to read: "Export products made by WFEs, except those subject to export restrictions by the State, shall enjoy tax reduction, exemption or refund in accordance with Chinese tax law."

Article 56 was deleted.

Article 84 was modified to read: "If a WFE signs a contract with another company, enterprise or economic organization or individual, the contract shall be subject to the Contract Law of the People's Republic of China."

Article 87 was deleted.

Some provisions were modified in terms of the wording, while the order of some provisions was also adjusted.[24]

C. THE AMENDMENTS TO THE CJVL

The amendments to the CJVL are the simplest and are similar to those of the previ-

---

[24] The Decision of the State Council Concerning Amendment of the "Detailed Implementing Rules for the Law of the People's Republic of China on Wholly Foreign Contractual Enterprises" (issued and entered into force on 12 April 2000), People's Daily, Overseas Edition, 26 April 2001, p. 5.

ous two laws.

Article 19 was modified to read: "A contractual joint venture (CJV) can, within its business scope as approved, import materials it needs and export the products it makes. Raw materials, fuels, and other resources required by a joint venture within its approved business scope can, according to the principles of fairness and reasonableness, be purchased from either the domestic market or the international market."

Article 20 was deleted. It read: "A CJV shall maintain foreign exchange balance by itself. If a CJV cannot maintain foreign exchange balance, it can apply for assistance from authorities concerned, according to national rules."

The order of some provisions was also rearranged.[25]

III. AN EVALUATION OF THE AMENDMENT

The amendment of these FDI laws and regulations has been, naturally, very warmly welcomed by foreign investors in China, as it entitles FIEs to more freedom in activities such as production planning, purchasing and sales.[26] It is a very positive sign which demonstrates that China is treating its WTO commitments very seriously and positively. However, it can clearly be seen that the amendments are tactical and technical changes rather than a fundamental shift and, therefore, their limitations are obvious.

Firstly, in some places, changes were made just to match the changes that had already taken place in practice.[27] Mr. Gu Angran also mentioned in his report that, as China was establishing a market economy, FIEs were not, in practice, required to submit their production and operation plans as required by previous laws and regulations.[28]

Secondly, this amendment has not addressed many important aspects of FDI law, some of which have been raised by the NPC deputies. During NPC discussions on the amendments to the EJVL, for example, some Deputies proposed that Chinese joint venture partners should also include individuals; that joint ventures should also take the form of shareholding companies; that the proportion of the investment contributed by the foreign joint venture partner need not necessarily be no less than 25 percent; and that the positions of president, vice-president, general manager and deputy general manager need not necessarily be assumed by the joint venture partners.[29] The Law Committee,[30] how-

---

〔25〕 The Decision of the Standing Committee of the National People Congress Concerning Amendment of the "Law of the People's Republics of China on Chinese-Foreign Contractual Joint Ventures", (adopted and effected on 31 October 2000); available at: http://www.cliiiialawiiifo.com/iiewlaw/reportshowcoiiteiit.asp? ID = 2575, , , 6 November 2000.

〔26〕 See, for example, China: Congress Passes Amendment to Joint Venture Law as Commitment to WTO, Xinhua News Agency, Beijing, (in English), 0813 GMT, 15 March 2001, BBC Monitoring; FIEs Welcome the Amendments to the FIE Laws, 12 December 2000, available at http://www.pu-dong.com/ijxx/200012/ijxx_OOI204.htm; T7te Amendments to the EJVL Will Benefit Hong Kong Investors Significantly, 17 March 2001, available at http://news.china.com/zh_cn/hmt/1004/20010317/145251.html.

〔27〕 See, for example, PIES Welcome Amendments, ibid.

〔28〕 Gu, supra, footnote 8, p. 2.

〔29〕 China Congress Amends Sino-Foreign Equity joint Venture Law, Xinhua News Agency Domestic Service, Beijing, (in Chinese), 0324 GMT, 14 March 2001, BBC Monitoring.

〔30〕 The special department in charge of the preparation and reviewing of laws within the NPC.

ever, "considering the complexity and the number of problems involved, and considering that some questions have to do with CJVL and WFEL", believes that, in order to make the decisions, "more thorough investigations and fuller discussions are required". These changes, however, arc all sensible, necessary and important, though they may need to be considered together with the change of the FDI legal framework, an issue which is treated in succeeding sections of this article.

Moreover, even in the seemingly radical and resolute changes, such as those of local content requirements, trade-balancing requirements and export performance requirements, some are not as thorough as they should and could be. For instance, while abolishing the compulsory requirement for all WFEs to be either export-oriented or technologically advanced, the WFEL still explicitly states that: "the State encourages the establishment of product-exporting and technology-awarded WFEs",[31] which may turn out to be measures having the same effect as the previous WFEL provisions. Or, if that is not the case, people will then challenge the necessity to maintain this restrictive "rubber provision".

Last, but not least, there has been no change of the general FDI legal framework as some scholars and legislators have argued and proposed.[32] In other words, the changes are only deliberate changes of details without couching the general regime, or "new wine in an old battle" *(jiu ping zhuang xin jiu)*, as the Chinese might say it. For example, the problem of the application of the Company Law to FIEs has not been touched at all, which ha caused much difficulty for judges and officials in handling FIE cases.[33]

All in all, it can be argued that the changes may be able to satisfy the immediate needs of WTO admission and completed economic reform projects, but they cannot meet the rapid changes in prospect as China establishes a real market economy and further integrates into the world economy.

IV. A UNIFIED FDI CODE OR A UNIVERSALLY APPLIED COMPANY LAW

It is certain that, in a not too distant future, China will need to further amend its For laws and regulations, from details to the general framework. As for the general framework, two issues in this regard are of particular importance and have been hotly debated. The first is the unification of FDI laws and the other is the application of the Company Law to FIES.

A. A UNIFIED FDI CODE

As mentioned, China now has three basic FDI laws and three Implementing Regulations, respectively governing EJVs, CJVs and WFEs. In addition, there are some single pieces of regulations, either governing specific kinds of investment, such as foreign-in-

[31] Article 3, Paragraph 1 of the WFEL. See also the Implementing Regulations of the WFEL, Articles 3, 45 and 53.

[32] Liu, supra, footnote 2. See also Yang Zhongxiao, Report of the Conference on "How to Apply Company Law to Joint ventures", Legal Science (Faxue), No. 8, 1998.

[33] Yang, ibid.

vested holding companies, foreign-invested stock companies or foreign-participated build-operate-transfer (BOT) projects, or governing specific aspects of investment, such as directions of investment, investment input, liquidation, contracting operations, etc. Moreover, there are numerous laws and regulations that are not devoted to FDI activities but relate to them in some way, such as the Foreign Exchange Supervision Regulations, the Contract Law, the Accounting Law, etc. Finally, there are local regulations and rules on FDI issues. All these laws and regulations combined make up the general legal framework governing FDI in China, with the basic laws and regulation s sitting at the core.

Now some contents of the core have been changed, but nothing has been done with the structure-the framework. Although the contents are important and their perfection would be welcome, without a proper structure they probably cannot work well. It is therefore argued that China should consolidate its three basic FDI laws and their implementing regulations to make a unified FDI law.[34] This argument is supported by several very good reasons.

First of all, a unified law would remove all the repetitions that arc prevalent in the three laws and regulations. Since the three laws and regulations are different rules, governing in parallel more or less similar FIEs, they are bound to be similar in both structure and content. These similarities and repetitions are more common between the EJVL and the CJVL, as they are more similar in nature. For instance, the three basic laws have the same provision s on the purposes of the laws and the protection of FIEs. In legal form, they are all limited liability companies if only they satisfy the legal requirements therefor. In terms of approval mechanism, the approval authority, approval term, approval competence and procedure and the required documentation, all are the same. In short, it can be observed that, in the three laws and their implementing regulations, there are more similar provisions than different ones.[35] On aspects such as establishment, organization and management, registered capital and enterprise conduct, there are numerous repetitious provisions.[36] These repetitions are certainly a huge waste of legal resources and are reflections of the immaturity of legislative skills. Hence a unified and consolidated law is justified.

Secondly, and more importantly, a unified law would avoid legal loopholes and contradictions. In the current legal system, there are not only repetitious provisions, but also many legal gaps and contradictions. For example, there is no provision in any of the three laws and their implementing regulations defining the general legal treatment to be accorded to foreign investors and their investments. On investment protection, while there are provisions on nationalization and compensation in the EJVL and WFEL, there is no such rule in the CJVL or its Implementing Regulations. A unified FDI code could be expected to have a chapter of general rules on the purposes of the law, definition of FIEs and the general treatment and protection standards of all kinds of FIEs, etc., which

---

〔34〕 Shan Wenhua, Towards a New Legal Framework for EU-China Investment Relations, 34 J. W. T. 5, September 2000, p. 137, pp. 166 – 167. See also Zhang, supra, footnote 13, pp. 70 – 74.

〔35〕 Zhang, id.

〔36〕 Id.

would in turn make the law much more comprehensive and coordinated.[37] On the other hand, in practice, there are a number of legal problems that the current laws have not dealt with.[38] For instance, can the foreign investor invest with the shares he/she has in other enterprises? In practice, if the directors of one partner do not turn up at the Board of Directors meeting, the Board may not be able to make any effective decision, as it could not meet the legally required number of attending directors. How to solve this dilemma? The existing law is silent thereon. In a new unified law, these loopholes could be fixed.

Thirdly, it would be sensible to consolidate and coordinate the numerous For laws, regulations and rules by making a unified FDI code. At the moment, the number of Chinese Fm laws and regulations remains a mystery. Even the officials in charge would have difficulty enumerating them all. Not counting the infamous "inside rules", the published regulations on FDI have been tremendous. Take EJV regulations as an example. On the single issue of EJV term, there are Article 12 of the EJVL and Article 100 of the EJVL Implementing Regulations, both of which are on the topic but too simple to be applied in practice. Therefore, the Government had to promulgate an individual regulation-the Provisional Rules on the Joint Venture Terms of China-Foreign EJVS. And, in order to solve some problems raised in the implementation of this Provisional Rule, the Government issued a Notice Concerning Problems in the Implementation of the "Provisional Rules on the joint Venture Terms of China-Foreign EJVs". Together with the fact that laws and regulations are neither formally compiled nor easily available, these numerous laws and regulations add substantially to the legal costs of investing in China. While it might be impossible to anticipate every aspect and detail and put all of them into a single code, it would be worthwhile and practical to consolidate these mature but scattered rules and form a unified and coordinated law. In this sense, the codification of the unified Contract Law can offer valuable experience.[39]

Lastly, most complementary single regulations and related laws and regulations address F1Es collectively, rather than treating them separately. For example, the regulations about investment directions, capital contribution, contracting operation and liquidation arc all aimed at all FIEs. In addition, unlike those in earlier years, many newly promulgated FDI – related laws apply to both FIEs and domestic investors and their enterp rises. Since 1994, for instance, China has adopted a new tax system which addresses all enterprises in China in the same way. On foreign exchange the Foreign Exchange Supervision Regulations apply to all financial institutions, FIEs and other institutions and individuals in China. The recently amended Contract Law applies not only to domestic transactions, but also to foreign transactions, including joint venture contracts which were previously governed by a special contract law-the Foreign Economic Contract Law.

---

〔37〕 Shan, supra, footnote 34, pp. 166 – 167.

〔38〕 Zhang, supra, footnote 13, pp. 70 – 74.

〔39〕 The Contract Law promulgated in 1999 not only unified the former Economic Law, Foreign Economic Law and Technology Contract Law but also consolidated and combined many related regulations and rules and has been well received as a success.

The FDI laws and regulations should therefore be unified co be in agreement with these laws and practices. On the other hand, the experience of the unification of these laws and regulations can be a good reference for the unification of FDI laws and regulations.

In summary, a unified FDI code may be justifiable, as it will eliminate the repetitions, avoid contradictions and legal loopholes, consolidate and simplify rules and be in harmony which ocher new laws. However, some people may consider this change still to be a transitional change and may prefer a more radical and fundamental change to abolish the FDI laws and regulations altogether and apply the Company Law universally to FIEs just as to the domestic companies.

B. A UNIVERSALLY APPLIED COMPANY LAW

The relationship of FIEs to the Company Law has been a problem ever since the Company Law came into being in 1993. The problem starts at Article 18 of the Company Law, which states: "This law applies to foreign-funded limited liability companies. However, if the EJVL, CJVL or WFEL have different rules thereon, these rules shall be applied." The interpretations of this provision have been so controversial that in 1998 a conference was arranged to discuss it in depth.[40] Some scholars argued that this provision had in fact enabled FIEs to choose the method of incorporation, in accordance with either the EJVL, CJVL or WFEL, or the Company Law, as the two sets of laws were not necessarily contradictory.[41] However, most scholars believed that their relationship was the relationship between "special law" (the three basic FIE laws) and "general law" (the Company Law) and that, accordingly, the principle of "special law dominates general law" should apply.[42] In practice, since the FIE laws were published (with the EJVL published as early as 1979) and executed much earlier than the Company Law, FIEs have almost all followed the FIE laws rather than the Company Law when incorporating.[43] In 1995, MOFTEC published the Provisional Rules on Some Problems Related to the Establishment of Foreign-Funded Stock Companies, which made it possible for foreign investors to adopt an advanced form of company-a stock company in accordance with the Company Law. Nevertheless, under the current system, FIEs still cannot establish limited liability companies (LLCs) in accordance with the Company Law.

Under the Company Law, the governance structure of an LLC is far different from that of an LLC under the FIE laws, especially the EJVL and the CJVL. The basic governance model of an LLC under the Company Law is a triple level structure: shareholders meeting, Board of Directors, Manager. At the shareholders' meeting, all shareholders represent themselves as the owners of the company and, in proportion to their capital contributions, they vote in every meeting and decide all the most important issues of the LLC. The Board of Directors, in turn, is the executive arm of the company, with all of the

---

〔40〕 Yang, supra, footnote 32.

〔41〕 Ibid., pp. 63 – 64.

〔42〕 See for example, Xu Chongli, From China-Foreign joint Venture Enterprises to China-Foreign joint Capital Companies: The Multiplication of the Internal Organization Structure System, Political Science and Law Forum (Zhengfa Luntan), No. 5, 2000, p. 135.

〔43〕 Id.

Directors appointed by and reporting to the shareholders' meeting. In theory, Directors shall therefore be loyal to the company only, not to any specific shareholder(s). Appointed by and reporting to the Board of Directors, the Manager handles all the daily operations of the company. Under the EJVL and the CJVL, however, the management structure is only a dual level system: Board of Directors and the General Manager(s), both of which are different from the Board of Directors and manager of an LLC under the Company Law. Since there is no shareholders' meeting, under the EJVL and the CJVL the Board of Directors actually acts as the shareholders' meeting as well as the Board of Directors in an LLC under the Company Law. Appointed by the joint venture partners "in reference" to the proportion of their capital contributions, the Directors have to be loyal to the company as well as to the appointing partner. In many cases, the partners themselves serve as the Directors. Like the manager in an LLC incorporated under the Company Law, the General Managers are in charge of daily operations of the company. However, as it often happens, Directors may also be appointed as the General Managers, which at the end may be the partners themselves. Thus, unlike an LLC under the Company Law, in an LLC incorporated under the EJVL or the CJVL, the company owners are not separated from the operator (manager), which may cause the problem of "dual loyalty", which may in turn, as it frequently happens, impair the smooth running of the company.

With this in mind, many scholars argue that, in the future, China should abolish the LLC model of FIEs altogether and let the Company Law govern all companies in China, including LLC FIEs.[44] However, it has also been argued that, however old-fashioned it might be, this design has its own value even nowadays and therefore should be kept as an option.[45] This argument maintains that this management model not only allows the investment partners to have direct control of the management, but also serves the "public purpose" of learning advanced management skills from the foreign managers through Chinese partners directly participating in company management.[46]

On the other hand, it may not be necessary to keep this as an option of company form if the Company Law were to govern all LLC FIEs. Firstly, it is not a good idea to have several kinds of LLC within a single legal system which will complicate the law and confuse investors. Also, decades of experience in attracting FDI has made it much less important to learn management skills by directly participating in management. Lastly, investors who still want to learn from the other co-operation partners and to take direct control over the enterprise may utilize the business form of partnership, which is governed by the Law of Partnership Enterprises.

C. A UNIFIED FDI CODE PLUS A UNIVERSALLY APPLIED COMPANY LAW

However, would it necessarily lead, as some people have suggested, to a total aboli-

---

[44] Yang, supra, footnote 32.

[45] See Xu, supra, footnote 42, pp. 131 – 132, 136.

[46] Ibid., p. 132.

tion of all FDI laws and regulations once the Company Law applies to all FIES in the form of companies? The answer is no. FDI laws, as they are in many developing countries, are mainly laws of government regulations over FDI, rather than laws of corporate governance, i. e. FIE laws. In China, the reason that FDI laws served as FIE laws for decades is because at the very beginning there was no Company Law at all. Therefore, the application of the Company Law to FIEs is just to reshape the FDI laws as they should have been and will not necessarily cause those laws to disappear. Nevertheless, with the company law sections removed, this change should make the unification and codification of FDI laws and regulations much easier. If this is the case, it can be anticipated that a universally applied Company Law will go hand in hand with a unified FDI code as China marches towards a real market economy and further integrates into the world.

National Treatment and the Transformation of FDI Laws and Policies in China*

China has experienced an unprecedented boom in Foreign Direct Investment (FDI) inflows over the past two decades, with total flows reaching more than $250 billion.[1] It is no exaggeration to say that, among the developing countries, China serves as the best example of success in effectively attracting and utilising FDI: China accounted for over half of the FDI inflows into Asia-twice as much as Central and Eastern Europe and Africa combined-and 11 per cent of the world total in 1997. For five consecutive years, China has maintained its position as the second largest FDI recipient in the world and the single largest among developing countries. The growth rate of its FDI stock over the past decade has outpaced that of all other major economies in the wo rld. FDI has been, as the Chinese Government has realised, one of the important elements of the whole national economy and a key point of its economic growth.[2]

This achievement has been fuelled by various factors, including: the country's large and continuously growing market; its export-oriented strategy and successful penetration of world markets; significant improvement in its macroeconomic environment; the spillover effects of industrial upgrading in neighbouring economies; and, outstandingly, the liberalisation of its FDI regime.[3]

The core of the FDI regime is the general treatment standard, as it decides the fundamental legal status of all the FDIs. The common standards include equity and fair trealment, nondiscrimination, national treatment, most-favoured-nation treatment and the international standard treatment, among which the national treatment and the most-favoured-nation (hereinafter referred to as MFN) treatment are most commonly used.

---

* *International Trade Law and Regulation* (London), Vol. 6, No. 1, 2000.

This article was prepared during the author's Visiting Fellowship (Sept. 1998 – *Sept.* 1999*) at the Lauterpacht Research Centre for International Law of Cambridge University. The author would like to thank Professor Vincent Johnson and Miss Cairo Robb for their insightful comments on the early drafts of this article.*

[1] This is the general amount of the actual inflows of foreign direct investment; the contractual inflows amount is $560.5 billion. See "Our country has attracted $560.5 billion foreign investment since starting the policy of reform and opening-up to the outside", in the *People 's Daily (Renming Ribao)*, Nov. 27, 1998.

[2] See Striving for a growth in difficulties: An exclusive year-end interview to Minister Shi Guansheng of the MOFTEC by a correspondent of the People's Daily, published in: www. moftec. gov. cn.

[3] Rubens Ricupero, n. 2 above, p. 6.

For a long time, the Chinese Government did not accept the concept of national treatment for FDI (hereinafter referred to as the NTFDI). The normal treatment standards for FDI reflected in the Sino-Foreign bilateral investment treaties (BITs) were "Fair and Reasonable Treatment" and "Most-Favoured-Nation Treatment", while the laws and regulations relating to FDI were mostly about some special preferential or restrictive measures. In 1993, the Chinese Government embarked on an effort to "create facilities and conditions to implement the national treatment for foreign-invested enterprises".[4] More recently, in a Report on the 15th CPC (Communist Party of China) Assembly, President Jiang Zemin announced that China, in order to "protect the rights and interests of foreign investors", would "implement national treatment".[5] Obviously, providing NTFDI is a key component in the current transformation of, Chinese FDI laws and policies, which is very likely to be speeded up by the promising prospect of its entry into the World Trade Organisation (WTO).[6]

National treatment: a preliminary definition

What is national treatment (hereinafter referred to as NT)? In general, national treatme nt is a treatment standard for aliens under international law, which means that the host state treats aliens as it does its own nationals. Here the term "aliens" may have two different meanings. The narrow definition of "aliens" includes only citizens or legal persons with a foreign nationality, while the broad definition embraces not only the citizens or legal persons with a foreign nationality, but also those legal persons which, although not having a foreign nationality, are subject to a certain extent of foreign control. In the field of FDI, foreign-invested enterprises normally have the nationality of the host state, though they are controlled by foreign investors to a certain extent. Thus they cannot be counted as "aliens" under the narrow definition, but do fall within the broad definition. Therefore, when the Chinese Government declared the implementation of NT for "foreign invested enterprises", they took the viewpoint of the broad definition.

This basic definition of NT has been commonly accepted by domestic legislation. For example, in as early as 1804, the Civil Code of France provided in Article 11 that "An alien shall enjoy in France the same civil rights as those which are or will be accorded to Frenchmen by treaties of the nation to which the alien belongs". Later, in 1829, the Civil Code of Netherlands said in Article 2, that "All people in the territory of the Kingdom are liberal persons and can enjoy the civil rights." The Foreign Relations Law of the United States, a representative of the Anglo-American law system, in section 722 (1) stipulates that: "An alien in the United States is entitled to the guarantees of the United States Constitution other than those expressly reserved for citizens." Among these

---

[4] See "The CCCPC Decision on Some Issues Related to the Establishment of the Socialist Market Economy", published in the *People 's Daily*, Nov. 7, 1993, p. 1.

[5] See Jiang Zernin, *Report on the 15th National Representatives Assembly of CPC*, s. 5.

[6] In November 1999, China finalised the bilateral negotiation with America about the Chinese entry into the World Trade Organisation, which paved the way for China to gain WTO membership and would greatly promote its market-oriented reform and establishment of the rule of law.

domestic provisions on NT, the French provision emphasises that NT shall be based on the principle of reciprocity, while the Netherlands and U. S. provisions emphasise simply the equal treatment between the national and non-nationals without the condition of reciprocity based on treaties. Therefore the former approach is called a "reciprocalism" NT provision and the latter approach is called an "equalism" NT provision.[7] Regardless of this distinction, the basic spirit of national treatment stresses the equity of rights between nationals and non-nationals: both special restrictions (which may be called "Inferior National Treatment") and special rights and privileges (which may be called "Superior National Treatment") against or for aliens are abolished.[8]

The wordings of the NT provisions in international investment treaties are not always the same as those contained in domestic laws. Many BITs use the words "no less favourable than" (*e. g.* Article 3 of the Sino-Japan investment treaty) instead of the phrase "the same as" (*e. g.* Article 3 (3) of the Sino-Britain investment treaty). According to this kind of NT provision, only "inferior national treatment" is prohibited while "superior national treatment" may still occur. This kind of NT provision, which may be called the "noninferior national treatment provision", is not a new definition of the national treatment different from the usual definition; the wording merely reflects the special purpose of BITs. The main concern of a BIT is to guarantee the full protection of overseas investors and investment, rather than to provide a general standard of treatment, which normally is one of the functions of a basic civil law. From the point of view of the host countries, such a wording would not withstand the exercise of the sovereign right of the host countries to grant the FDI special preferential treatment. Anyway, however, the "no less favourable than" wording itself does not imply that the host country shall provide "superior national treatments" to FDI.

In China, there is a special issue related to this definition. According to the principle of "one country, two systems" and its practice in Hong Kong and Macao, Hong Kong, Macao and Taiwan belong to the same country-China (one country), but can carry out a social system different from Mainland China (two systems). Logically, there is no problem of "national" treatment for investors from the three territories and the enterprises established with their investments, but only a problem of "territorial people treatment" or "resident treatment" (if any). Of course this is a sensitive topic deserving specific study, which is outside the scope of this article. However, it is worth noting that the Chinese Government often "refers to" the principle of NTFDI when handling these kinds of issues.

Market economy: the economic ground of the NTFDI

Why did the Chinese Government recently decide to provide NTFDI? The answer to this question lies in the fact that the NTFDI, as a legal principle, is based on a market e-

---

[7] As to details of the differences and relations between the two kinds of NT provisions, see Mei Zhongxie, *New Analysis on Private International Law (Guoji Sifa Xinlun)* (Taiwan Sanmin Bookstore, 1980), p. 143.

[8] See also Yao Meizhen, *International Investment Law (Guoji Touzi Fa)* (Wuhan University Press, 1987), p. 287.

conomy instead of a planned economy. Without the establishment of a market economy, the NTFDI could not be implemented.

NTFDI is not compatible with a planned economy. Under a planned economy, it is the central plan, instead of market, that acts as the fundamental means of allocating resources. Inevitably, this type of economic system emphasises the unconditional compliance of all economic entities with the central plan. The system denies the importance of independent economic entities and therefore excludes the merits of competition and the markets based thereon. "Nationals" therefore are not the masters of the market, but merely the executing symbols and statistical units of the central plan. The nature of "national" treatment is therefore completely different from the way that foreign investors, which normally run business on a market-oriented basis, would wish to be treated. It would be improper and impractical under a planned economy, to impose the principle of national treatment on foreign investors. This is why there were no NT provisions in most of the BITs between the Western countries and the Socialist countries. Even though there were several such BITs with NT provisions, what those provisions established is not the real "principle" of NT.[9] For example, in 1990, the United States and Poland concluded an investment treaty with a provision on NT. But in the Annex to the Treaty, there is a long list of "Exceptions" to it which, as an American scholar said, "are so broad that they almost dwarf the 'absolute' national treatment set forth in the body of the treaty".[10]

On the contrary, a market economy system, with its features of equity, competitiveness, internationality, transparency and stability, lays a suitable economic soil for the implementation of NTFDI.[11] On one side, market economy, as an advanced form of commodity economy, requires a united market subjects system in which the market subjects with different ownership and other social status are treated equally and compete fairly. It is self-evident that such equal treatment embraces the NTFDI, the equal treatment between national invested enterprises and foreign invested enterprises. A market economy, as developed to date, is a huge economy with transitional dimensions. A country that wants to develop further can not just depend on itself and isolate itself from the international market. This is a truth that has been proved by experience, and it is the basis of China's opening-up policy. In a world with increasing internationality, a "national" is more and more a "world citizen". Just as products from different countries are treated equally in the international market, it is rational and natural for a country to grant nationals of other countries the same treatment as its own nationals.

General legislatien and practices around the world support this judgment. Almost all market economy countries, whether developing or developed countries, are providing

---

[9] Robert K. Paterson, "Canadian Investment Promotion and Protection Treaties", *The Canadian Yearbook of International Law* (UBC Press, 1992), Vol. 24.

[10] Nancy J. Goodman, "International Trade: Poland Bilateral Investment Treay-A Reflection of United States Efforts to Shape the Economic Development of Eastern Europe" (1991) 32 *Harvard International Law Journal*, 257.

[11] See Shan Wenhua, "Studies on the Market Economy and National Treatment for Foreign Invested Enterprises" (1994) *China Legal Sciences (Zhongguo Faxue)* No. 5.

or endeavouring to provide NTFDI. It is well known that in developed countries, like the United States, Sweden, the United Kingdom, Germany and France, NTFDI is generally guaranteed. In 1991, a survey of legislation o n FDI demonstrated that 31 of the 51 developing countries surveyed provided NTFDI (although subject to certain restrictions). These countries, including Korea, the Philippines and Yemen in Asia, Bulgaria, Hungary, Romania and Yugoslavia· in Europe, Argentina, Bolivia, Colombia, Haiti, Paraguay in Latin America and the Caribbean, and Burundi, Cameroon, Chad, Congo, Egypt and 14 other African countries, are all market economy countries.[12]

Like the common situation of socialistcapitalist BITs, most of the Sino-Foreign BITs concluded prior to the 1990s did not have a NT provision. Even in some exceptional treaties, such as the Sino-Japan BIT and Sino-Britain BIT, China and its counterparts did not undertake a substantive obligation to provide NT, although there were NT provisions in these agreements. The fundamental explanation for the absence of NT in China's pre – 1990 BITs is that China, at that time, carried on a highly centralised planned economy and the market was limited to such a very small scope that it was not a fundamental way of allocating resources. In such an economy, the national-invested enterprises, significantly the state-managed enterprises, undertake special obligations in the fields of production, trans. action and distribution, so as to guarantee the implementation of the national plan. Obviously, such obligations cannot be imposed on foreign invested enterprises.[13] At the same time, the Government gave national invested enterprises special support with respect to such matters as salaries, prices, material supplies, financial loans and subsidiaries. Those forms of support were not enjoyed by the foreign invested enterprises with different ownership. Furthermore, there are different forms of national invested enterprises, including state-owned enterprises, collectively owned enterprises, and recently emerged private enterprises and they are treated differently. Deciding which kind of "national" treatment shall be accorded to the FDI is apparently another difficulty under a centralised planned economy.

In 1993, China finally established, after a decade of market-oriented reform and opening-up to the outside, the constitutional status of the "Socialist Market Economy".[14] Later, the Chinese Government officially embarked on the plan to "create facilities and conditions to implement the National Treatment for foreign-invested enterprises".[15] This fact strongly suggested that a market economy is the economic basis of the NTFDI.

NTFDI: its basic scope of application

How far does the NTFDI extend and what is its scope of application? These ques-

---

[12] See Antonio R. Parra, "Principles Governing Foreign Investment, as Reflected in National Investment Codes" (1992) 7 *ICSID Review-Foreign Investment Law Journal* No. 2, p. 436.

[13] Palitha T. B. Kohona, "Investment Protection Agreements: An Australian Perspective" (1987) 21 *Journal of World Trade Law*, No. 2, p. 93.

[14] See Art. 7 of the Amendments to the Constitution of the People's Republic of China.

[15] See "The CCCPC Decision on Some Issues Related to the Establishment of the Socialist Market Economy", published in the *People 's Daily*, Nov. 7, 1993, p. 1.

tions are of common concern to both foreign and domestic investors in China.

Traditional fields of the NTFDI

Traditionally, NTFDI covers only two aspects: civil and commercial rights and judicial and administrative remedies.

Civil and commercial rights are fundamental rights that lay the legal basis for a market economy. Thus the NT of these rights is normally guaranteed in market economy countries. In China, after 20 years of reform and development, the law largely guarantees this form of NT. The Constitution, as the basis of the legal system, not only permits aliens to invest in China, but also provides that the legal rights and interests of foreign invested enterprises shall be protected by the law of the P. R. China. The Chinese-Foreign Equity Joint Ventures Law, the first and most important law for foreign invested enterprises, further clarifies this matter as follows:

"The Chinese Government shall protect, according to the law, the investment of foreign joint ventures, the profits due them and their other lawful rights and· interests in an equity joint venture, pursuant to the agreement, contract and articles of association approved by the Chinese Government...

The State shall not nationalise or requisition any equity joint ventures. Under special circumstances, when public interest requires, equity joint ventures may be requisitioned by following legal procedures and appropriate compensation shall be made."

At the same time, according to the Trade Mark Law, the Patent Law, the Copyright Law, the Ordinance for Protecting Computer Software and other intellectual property laws, the NT for the protection of intellectual properties is accorded for foreign investors and their enterprises. Moreover, the General Principles of Civil Law, the Economic Contract Law, the Foreign Economic Contract Law, the Security Law, the Negotiable Instruments Law, the Insurance Law and other important civil and commercial laws do not differentiate foreign invested enterprises from the other enterprises. Therefore the NT in the field of civil and commercial rights, including both the property rights and the creditor's rights, is sufficiently guaranteed.[16]

The NT with respect to judicial and administrative remedies was the first field of NT afforded to the aliens. The creation of the NT was initially intended to change the hostile attitude towards aliens and to guarantee the fundamental protection of human persons by providing the judicial and administrative remedies thereto. The NT in this respect is now a universal custom observed by most countries. In China, in accordance with the Law of Civil Procedures [Article 15(1)], aliens, stateless persons, foreign enterprises and organisations can enjoy the same litigation rights as those of Chinese citizens, legal persons and other organisations. As another example, Article 16 of the Regu-

---

[16] It is noticeable that the division of contract law into Economic Contract Law and the Foreign Economic Contract Law does not mean the discrimination between national invested enterprises and foreign invested enterprises. Because just the same as the national invested enterprises, the foreign invested enterprises must observe the Economic Contract Law as to their domestic contract relations and observe the. Foreign Economic Contract Law as to their foreign contract relations.

lation for Encouraging Foreign Investment provides that the foreign invested enterprises may refuse to pay any improper fee and can complain to Local Authorities, and even to the State Authority. Obviously, the NT for foreign invested enterprises in this respect provided by the Chinese Government is adequate.

Governmental management and the NTFDI

The governmental management of FDI, which may be divided into the admission and postadmission management, used to be a matter of policy left to the discretion of the host country without any general legal obligation in these respects.[17] It was regarded as a kind of sovereignty right, which had been accepted in international instruments like the UN General Assembly Resolution of 1962 on Permanent Sovereignty Over Natural Resources (Resolution 1803)[18] and the Charter of Economic Rights and Duties of States (Resolution 3281).[19]

However, in the last few decades, this situation seems to have been changing. The management of FDI has also been the main object of scholarly debate and of international negotiations and agreements. This shift in the focus of concern was the result of complex changes in the world economy, political conditions and national policies. The debate has significantly shifted to pragmatic, policy-oriented considerations: not so much what the law is, nor even which legal principles or rules are correct, but what policies and measures are effective in promoting international flows of capital and technology, under present conditions. This shift of approach has resulted in an emphasis on international agreements as an important source of pertinent legal regulation and in increased concern over the specific aspects (*e. g.* the "performance requirements") of FDI operations.[20]

Until 1993, however, such international agreements remained on the bilateral level (BITs) or regional level (*e. g.* NAFTA). In 1993, the first global instrument in this field was concluded. That was the final act of the Uruguay Round negotiation of GATT, among which the General Agreement of Trade in Services (GATS) and the Agreement of Trade-related Investment Measures (TRIMs) are of great value to FDI law. The "market access" and "national treatment" rules of GATS regulate the admission and treatment of

[17] See Ibrahim F. I. Shihata, "Recent Trends relating to Entry of Foreign Direct Investment" (1994) 9 *ICSID Review-Foreign Investment Law Journal*, No. 1, p. 47. See also A. A. Fatouros, "Towards an International Agreement on Foreign Direct Investment? (1995) 12 *ICSID Revie w-Foreign Investment Law Journal*, No. 2, p. 181.

[18] The Resolution 1803 provides, in I(2), that: "The exploration, development and disposition of such resources, as well as the import of the foreign capital required for these purposes, should be in conformity with the rules and conditions which the peoples and the nations freely consider to be necessary or desirable with regard to the authorisation, restriction or prohibition of such activities."

[19] The Resolution 3281 stipulates further in Chap. II Art. 2 that:

"Each state has the right: to regulate and exercise authority over foreign investment within its national jurisdiction in accordance with its laws and regulations and in conformity with its national objectives and priorities. No State shall be compelled to grant preferential treatment to foreign investment;

To regulate and supervise the activities of transnational corporations within its national jurisdiction and take measures to ensure that such activities comply with its laws, rules and regulations and to conform with its economic and social policies. Transnational corporations shall not intervene in the internal affairs of a host country..."

[20] See A. A. Fatouros, n. 17 above, pp. 182 - 183.

FDI in services directly, although they are of "specific commitments", which may be decided by a host state based on negotiations with other states. At the same time, the TRIMs agreement is an agreement regulating the trade-related investment measures, some of which are the above-mentioned "performance requirements". Among the measures prohibited by the agreement, the local content requirement and the trade-balancing requirement are regarded as the measures against the principle of NT established by GATT.[21]

Like other developing countries, China used to have no clear definition on the exact fields opened or closed to FDI, which prompted complaints by foreign investors and their home countries. In order to enhance the transparency, the Chinese Government promulgated, in 1995, "Interim Provisions for Guiding Foreign Investment Direction" and an annex thereto named "Catalogue for the Guidelines of Foreign Investment". The two regulations specify categories of the "Encouraged", "Restricted" and "Prohibited" industries for FDI. All the other industries are "Permitted" industries. The two regulations not only clarified, but also enlarged, the fields for FDI.[22] For instance, China used to prohibit FDI in the fields such as commercial retail and wholesale, foreign trade and international trade in services-all of which are very attractive to foreign investors due to the huge market in China. Now the two new regulations list them in the "Restricted Catalogue", rather than in the "Prohibited Catalogue".

It is also worth mentioning that, according to the two regulations, the access for FDI in China is much wider and deeper than that in most developing counties. Many developing countries, especially those with small economies, usually prohibit FDI in the fields of telecommunication, transportation, and mining, which are perceived to be essential for their national security and economic autonomy. In China, however, under provisions of the two new regulations, those fields are part of the "Encouraged Catalogue" and therefore enjoy special advantages.

However, some of China's regulations and practices may still be considered TRIMs against the principle of NT, which are prohibited in the TRIMs agreement.[23] For example, certain regulations and practices may be viewed as "local content requirements". In some basic FDI laws there are requirements[24] that foreign-funded enterprises shall give priority. to purchase in China any of their required raw and semiprocessed materials, fuels, auxiliary equipment, etc. In the course of reviewing proposed FDI projects, the central and local governmental decisionmakers typically require the enterprises to buy a certain amount of domestic products and make this requirement as a condition for approving

---

〔21〕 See Ernmanuel Opoku Awuku, "How Do the Results of the Uruguay Round Affect the North-South Trade?" (1994) 28 *Journal of World Trade*, No. 2, p. 8.

〔22〕 See "The Responsible Person of the State Planning Commission 's Answers to the Correspondents' Questions About the Implementation of the 'Interim Provisions for Guiding Foreign Investment Direction' and the 'Catalogue for the Guidelines of Foreign Investment' ", *Xinhua News Agency*, Beijing, June 27, 1995.

〔23〕 Shan Wenhua, "The Development and Completion of National Treatment System for Foreign Investment in China" (1995) 6 *Faxue Yanjiu (Studies in Law*, now the *CASS Journal of Law)*.

〔24〕 See, *e. g.*, Art. 15 of the Law of Foreign-Capital Enterprises and Art. 9 of the Law of the Chinese-Foreign Equity Joint Ventures.

the project or for allowing the project to enjoy preferential treatment. In practice, for instance, certain local content has been qne of the prerequisites for approval of foreign invested car projects. Some governmental regulations make the percentage of local content the main criterion in applying discriminative taxes. A higher tax rate may be applied to those who do not meet the requirements for local content.

On the other hand, some existing investment rules may be regarded as trade balancing measures. One is the requirement relating to foreign exchange revenue and expenditures. The Implementation Regulations of the Law of the Chinese-Foreign Equity Joint Ventures stipulate in Article 75 that, the Chinese-Foreign Equity Joint Ventures shall generally maintain the balance of foreign exchange revenue and expenditure. Article 16 of the Law of Foreign-Capital Enterprises and Article 3 of its Implementation Regulations require, as a condition for approval, that the Foreign Capital Enterprises must solve the balance of foreign exchange revenue and expenditure problem by themselves. There is also a rule about taking the exports as a prerequisite for accepting imports. Article 13 of the Rule for Encouraging Foreign Investment, for example, provides that:

"Machinery and equipment, vehicles used in production, raw materials, fuel, bulk parts, spare parts, machine component parts and fittings (including imports restricted by the state), which enterprises with foreign investment need to import in order to carry out their export contracts do not require further applications for examination and approval and are exempt from the requirement for import licences. The customs shall exercise supervision and control, and shall inspect and release such imports on the basis of the enterprises contracts or the importexport contracts.

The imported materials and items mentioned above are restricted to use by the enterprise itself and may not be sold on the domestic market. If they are used as products to be sold on the domestic market, import procedures shall be gone through in accordance with relevant regulations."

Although not requiring the equivalent amount or value of imports and exports, those provisions are likely to be considered as trade balancing requirements.

China does not have to modify those provisions because it is still not a part of the WTO. However, if China really wants to be fully integrated into the world economy, sooner or later, it will have to eliminate them. As to such flexible provisions as "foreign-funded enterprises shall give priority to purchase in China in their purchase of required raw and semi-processed materials, fuels, auxiliary equipment, etc.", they should be removed as soon as possible.

Towards a "full" NT FDI in China

As discussed above, the establishment of the constitutional status of the market economy in China has laid down the fundamental economic ground for the NTFDI. However, is it sufficient to justify calls for China to implement "full" NTFDI now?

In 1992, Guidelines on the Treatment of Foreign Direct Investment (hereinafter referred to as the Guidelines) were issued by the Development Committee, a joint ministerial committee of the Boards of Governors of the International Monetary Fund and the World Bank. This instrument broadened the application of NTFDI without any substantive limitation to numerous related areas, including "the establishment, operation, management, control, and exercise of rights in such an investment, as well as such other associated activities necessary therefor or incidental thereto".[25] This pronouncement goes too far to be generally accepted (at least by most developing countries) as an accurate reflection of present international law, although it announces in its Progress Report that it is based on a series of background studies (BITs, Multilateral Instruments, National Legislation, Awards and International Law Literature), and could serve as "a legal basis for generally accepted customary international law".[26] Nevertheless, the Guidelines may serve as a good model for "full" NTFDI.

However, in every sense, it is impractical for China to implement "full" NTFDI at its current stage. A market economy is an important and necessary condition for NTFDI, but is not a sufficient condition for a "full" NTFDI. The implementation of "full" NTFDI relies on the achievement of another important economic condition, namely the general economic power of the country strong enough to compete fairly and freely with other countries. "Full" NTFDI materially means the elimination of protections for national capital and of restrictions on FDI. It therefore means that the national capital has to confront challenges from FDI without any protection. If the general economic power and the national capital of a countr y are adequately developed and sufficiently strong, it can take advantage of the FDI to supplement and enrich the internal market without the need to worry about threats and injuries to the national economy. At the same time, national capital can make use of the NT arrangement to move freely in the world market, picking the best business opportunities and pursuing the greatest profits. This is actually why the major developed countries are involved in carrying out and promoting the NTFDI around the world. However, if a country only has limited national capital and little economic power, it is dangerous for it to afford aliens "full" or "absolute" NTFDI. It would be like "introducing a wolf into one's home" or "smashing a stone with an egg". Such an insight is the very reason why the developing countries have declined to provide general NTFDI for so long.

From 1979 on, China started its marketoriented reform. In the national economy, the plan-controlled parts are getting smaller while the market-controlled parts are getting larger. In 1993, the principle of a "Socialist Market Economy System" was finally set forth in the Constitution. By then the amount of the general economic power had accumulated considerably, and therefore the Chinese Government could announce its intention to grant the NTFDI. Nevertheless, it must be recognised that in China thus far a market economy has not been fully established, and the quality and efficiency of national capital and the national economy are still quite low. In particular, there is still quite a long way to go to reform the State-Owned Enterprises (SOEs) into real market entities and to establish the rule of law in China. Therefore, one cannot expect an instant realisation of a "full" NTFDI, but can expect the Chinese Government to "create facilities and conditions" to carry it out gradually but substantially.

---

〔25〕 See S. 3 of the Guidelines for details.

〔26〕 See "Progress Report on the 'Legal Framework for the Treatment of Foreign Investment' ", (1992) 7 *ICSID Review: Foreign In vestment La w journal*, No. 2, p. 308.

Anyway, the Chinese decision to provide NTFDI is significant and influential. On the most superficial level, such a decision means that certain specific regulations may be made, particular restrictions may be removed and certain preferential arrangements may be phased out. Furthermore, this decision necessitates a material change of Chinese FDI policy, from the preliminary stage FDI policy that featured "tax concession" towards the senior stage FDI policy that features as "fair play". Thirdly, this decision may catalogue not only the adjustment of FDI policy and regulations, but also the further reform of national funded enterprises and national industries, especially the state-owned enterprises. Facing FDI with the guarantee of NT, these enterprises have to be restructured as real players at the market. It may be necessary "to find a solution through ' the markets' instead of ' the mayors' ".[27] Gradually, it could be expected that a full NTFDI in China would be implemented, as China is heading for a real market economy and a rule of law system, and its national economy is becoming stronger and stronger.

[27] During the planned economy era, when in difficulties, the state-owned enterprise used to ask for help from the administrative authorities, normally "the mayors" who were the best representatives. Now in the "Socialist Market Economy", these enterprises have to solve their difficulties basically through "the market". Therefore there is a new saying that "Looking for the mayors is less useful than looking for the markets".

美国投资条约新范本及其可接受性问题研究*

美国 BIT 新范本是中美 BIT 谈判的主要文本基础，而中美 BIT 谈判因为其涉及中美两个世界上最大却又最具差异性的经济体而备受海内外关注，将其称为"世纪 BIT 谈判"或"中国第二次入世"均不为过。中美 BIT 谈判经历七轮磋商，已渐入实质。因此，系统研究美国 BIT 新范本并探讨其对于中国的可接受性，无论是对于妥善应对中美 BIT 谈判，还是对于深化国际投资法学研究，均具重要意义。

有鉴于此，本文以美国 BIT 范本的历史发展为基点，研究美国投资协定项目的起源与流变，分析投资协定项目发展背后所体现出的美国经济和投资政策，进而重点分析 2012 年新 BIT 范本的主要变化以及新特点，并考察它们所体现出的投资条约政策的调整。在此基础上，本文从中美双边投资关系与中国的政策取向角度探讨美国 BIT 范本可接受性的判断标准。

一、美国投资协定计划的起源与流变

与德国等欧洲国家比起来，美国的投资条约实践开始得并不算早。"二战"后，随着一系列外资征收事件的发生，以及越来越多的国家对征收需要提供全部赔偿这一习惯国际法提出质疑和挑战，美国于 1977 年开始启动其投资条约计划。[1] 在此之前，一些欧洲国家已经签订了许多 BITs，其中，德国与巴基斯坦于 1959 年签订的 BIT 更是开启了现代 BIT 的先河。美国希望借助双边投资条约来弥补习惯国际法在保护外资方面的不足，推动外国投资保护的国家实践的发展，并建立一个机制，保证在无须美国政府介入的情况下，其对外投资在遭受东道国

---

* 本文发表在《现代法学》2013 年第 5 期。作者单文华、张生。

[1] Kenneth J. Vandevelde, U. S. International Investment Agreements, Oxford: Oxford University Press, 2009.

非法侵害后能够得到补偿。[2]

目前美国已经签订了47个BITs,其中39个已经生效。[3] 同时,美国还签订了14个自由贸易协定,涵盖美国与加拿大、墨西哥等19个国家的贸易与投资。在已经生效的13个自由贸易协定中,有11个都包含投资条款。[4]

仔细考察美国所签订的47个BITs后可以发现,签署这些协定的国家都是发展中国家,这反映了美国实施BIT项目主要用于保护美国私人对外投资的首要目的。基于此,美国BIT从一开始就包含4大条款:(1)确定外资在东道国享有最低标准的待遇,包括公平公正待遇等绝对待遇标准和国民待遇、最惠国待遇等相对待遇标准;(2)对东道国征收外资的行为设定若干条件,并要求提供"及时、充分和有效"的补偿;(3)保证与投资有关的资金自由和不迟延地汇进或汇出东道国;(4)保证外国投资者可以将其与东道国的投资争端诉诸中立的国际仲裁机构。此外,美国BIT的常见条款还有:禁止业绩要求(如当地成分要求或出口配额要求)条款;允许外国投资者自由选择公司高管条款;透明度条款;战争与内乱损失补偿条款;国家与国家争端解决条款等。[5]

BIT条款的内容并非一成不变,一些在早期BIT中出现的条款,如保证投资者有权诉诸国内法庭条款、授权签发投资者签证条款、缔约方就条约事项谘商条款以及要求东道国确保内外资享受同等竞争条件条款,在后来的条约范本或者投资协定中被逐渐摒弃。[6] 最早的BIT还有一般例外的规定,包括公共秩序例外、重大安全利益例外以及履行维护国际和平与安全义务例外。后期的范本在删去公共秩序例外的同时,加上了关于金融服务、税收等方面的例外规定。[7]

到目前为止,美国还从来不曾成为其订立的BIT项下的被告。所有针对美国的国际投资仲裁都是依据《北美自由贸易协定》(NAFTA)提起的,但是迄今为止,

---

〔2〕 Kenneth J. Vandevelde, U. S. International Investment Agreements, Oxford: Oxford University Press, 2009, p. 1.

〔3〕 截至2012年6月,美国与阿尔巴尼亚、阿根廷、亚美尼亚、阿塞拜疆、巴林、孟加拉国、玻利维亚、保加利亚、喀麦隆、刚果(布)、刚果(金)、克罗地亚、捷克、厄瓜多尔、埃及、爱沙尼亚、格鲁吉亚、格林纳达、洪都拉斯、牙买加、约旦、哈萨克斯坦、吉尔吉斯斯坦、拉脱维亚、立陶宛、摩尔多瓦、蒙古、摩洛哥、莫桑比克、巴拿马、罗马尼亚、塞内加尔、斯洛伐克、斯里兰卡、特立尼达多巴哥、突尼斯、土耳其、乌克兰和乌拉圭等39个国家签订的双边协定已生效;与尼加拉瓜、喀麦隆、海地、波兰、俄罗斯、白俄罗斯、萨尔瓦和卢旺达等8个国家签订的协定仍未生效。

〔4〕 截至2012年6月,美国与加拿大和墨西哥(NAFTA)、以色列、约旦、巴林、摩洛哥、新加坡、智利、多美尼加和中美洲五国(哥斯达黎加、萨尔瓦多、危地马拉、洪都拉斯和尼加拉瓜,CAFTA-DR)、秘鲁、阿曼、哥伦比亚、巴拿马和韩国等19个国家签署了14个自贸协定。除了与巴拿马的协定,其他13个协定已全部生效。其中,除了与巴林、以色列和约旦的协定未涉及投资外,其余11个都包含专门的投资条款。

〔5〕 Kenneth J. Vandevelde, U. S. International Investment Agreements, Oxford: Oxford University Press, 2009, pp. 3 – 5.

〔6〕 Ibid.

〔7〕 Ibid.

美国未曾输掉一起官司。可以说,无论是从科学应对中美 BIT 谈判的角度,还是从研习借鉴美国 BIT 经验的角度,系统深入地研究美国 BIT 均具有重要意义。

从历史的角度来看,依据缔约政策背景和内容的不同,可以大体将历史上美国的 BIT 实践划分为四个阶段。[8]

(一)第一阶段(1980~1986 年)

这一阶段是美国 BIT 的起步和探索阶段,一共签订了 10 个 BITs,缔约对象除土耳其外,都是来自非洲和拉美地区的发展中国家。[9] 考虑到只有得到参议院的支持才能缔结大量 BITs,国务院于 1986 年初将最初签订的这 10 个 BITs 提交给参议院审议和通过。

美国启动 BIT 项目主要基于一系列经济、法律和政治角度的考量:经济方面主要是想通过 BIT 保护美国投资免于歧视待遇、外汇管制和征收等威胁;法律方面主要是想通过 BIT 弥补习惯国际法在保护外资方面的不足;政治方面则是因为美国政府需要向美国国会和美国企业表明其保护海外投资的决心和态度。[10]

相比较而言,当时法律和经济上的考虑远甚于政治上的考虑,其中,法律的考量又重于经济的考虑。[11] 经济上的政策目标比较单一:"保护"美国海外投资,并不涉及对海外投资的促进和鼓励。它反映出美国政府的政策是既不鼓励也不限制对外投资,而只是想为已有的对外投资提供一个稳定的和可预见的环境。这种政策选择体现出浓厚的经济学色彩:投资决策主要取决于市场考量,而不是政府干预。此外,这样的选择也体现出政治上的妥协:这一阶段时值卡特总统执政,美国劳工对对外投资普遍持反对态度,因此,一个仅仅保护而不是鼓励对外投资的折中温和政策可以减少人们对 BIT 项目的排斥和反对。[12]

从 BIT 项目启动伊始,国务院的法律顾问部就在其中发挥核心作用。它的作用不仅仅是起草法律文件,事实上,它是整个 BIT 政策制定和发展的推动力量。正因为它的坚持,美国的 BIT 谈判从一开始就表现出一种不肯妥协的立场:如果外国不愿意基本上按照美国模式签订 BIT,美国宁可不要这个 BIT。一

---

〔8〕 Kenneth J. Vandevelde, U. S. International Investment Agreements, Oxford: Oxford University Press, 2009, pp. 30-82. 有学者如 Vandevelde 将美国的投资条约发展归纳为三个阶段,即美国投资条约的"三次浪潮"。我们认为,自 2009 年以来,美国 BIT 实质上进入了第四个阶段,或者说"第四次浪潮"。

〔9〕 这 10 个 BITs 由美国分别与孟加拉国、喀麦隆、刚果(金)、埃及、格林纳达、海地、摩洛哥、巴拿马、塞内加尔和土耳其签订。

〔10〕 Kenneth J. Vandevelde, U. S. International Investment Agreements, Oxford: Oxford University Press, 2009, p. 31

〔11〕 Ibid.

〔12〕 Ibid., pp. 31-41.

个千疮百孔的 BIT 达不到美国所要确立的目标——投资保护，这也就可以解释为什么在这一阶段美国只签订了 10 个 BITs。[13] 相应地，这一阶段投资条约的核心条款主要涉及以下 4 个方面的内容：规定最低待遇标准和非歧视待遇；保证征收后的补偿；确保资金可以自由转移；规定外国投资者—东道国投资争端解决机制。[14]

（二）第二阶段（1989～1999 年）

在得到参议院的支持后，国务院于 1989 年重新启动了 BIT 项目。当时国际社会的政治经济秩序发生了巨大的变化：政治方面体现为前苏联解体和社会主义阵营分崩离析；经济方面则表现为在自由化经济浪潮的影响下，一些发展中国家也意识到外国投资对本国经济发展的推动作用，纷纷签订自由化的投资协定。也正因为如此，大多数缔约国都同意依据美国提供的范本进行 BIT 谈判，这样可以表明这些国家对原有政治体制的摒弃。BIT 的谈判也得到了美国国会的支持——在国会看来，签订投资条约也是推动这些新兴独联体国家国内民主的重要手段。[15]

在这一阶段，美国共签订了 35 个投资协定，其中包括 21 个刚从苏联社会主义阵营中脱离出来的过渡经济体国家。[16] 在这一时期，美国也与来自拉美和加勒比海地区的 8 个国家签订了 BITs。[17] 在 20 世纪 90 年代初期，由于新自由主义经济理论的影响，拉美国家纷纷放弃以前坚守的“卡尔沃主义”，并通过缔结投资条约的方式吸引外国投资。[18] 此外，美国还与其他 6 个国家签订了 BITs，其中 4 个是非洲国家。[19]

与此同时，基于投资条约的实践，美国也开始着手签订自由贸易协定，并在其中专门就投资作出规定。美国与加拿大、墨西哥于 1992 年签订了 NAFTA，之后即启动了与其他国家的自贸协定谈判。不过，让美国意想不到的是，NAFTA 在为美国创造优惠对外贸易和投资条件的同时，也将美国推向了国际投资仲裁的“被告

---

〔13〕 Kenneth J. Vandevelde, U. S. International Investment Agreements, Oxford: Oxford University Press, 2009, pp. 31－41.

〔14〕 Ibid.

〔15〕 Ibid., 2009, p. 42.

〔16〕 这 21 个国家包括阿尔巴尼亚、亚美尼亚、阿塞拜疆、白俄罗斯、保加利亚、捷克、克罗地亚、爱沙尼亚、格鲁吉亚、哈萨克斯坦、吉尔吉斯斯坦、拉脱维亚、立陶宛、摩尔多瓦、蒙古国、波兰、罗马尼亚、俄罗斯、斯洛伐克、乌克兰和乌兹别克斯坦。

〔17〕 这 8 个国家是阿根廷、玻利维亚、厄瓜多尔、萨尔瓦多、洪都拉斯、牙买加、尼加拉瓜和特立尼达和多巴哥。

〔18〕 单文华：《从“南北矛盾”到“公私冲突”：卡尔沃主义的复苏与国际投资法的新视野》，张生译，载《西安交通大学学报》2008 年第 28 卷第 4 期。

〔19〕 它们分别是：刚果（布）、莫桑比克、突尼斯、巴林、约旦和斯里兰卡。

席”。1998年,来自加拿大的投资公司 The Loewen Group Inc. 依据 NAFTA 第11章的规定,提起了针对美国的仲裁请求,使美国首次成为国际投资仲裁的“被告”。之后,陆续有其他外国投资者根据 NAFTA 提起针对美国的国际投资仲裁请求,这迫使美国开始重新审视和反思其投资协定。于是在1999年,美国再次暂停了 BIT 谈判,开始着手总结美国参与国际投资仲裁的经验,并据此对 BIT 范本进行重新评估,并调和 NAFTA 和美国 BIT 范本文本间的差异。[20]

这一时期美国 BIT 政策的一个突出特征在于其政治色彩显著增强,BIT 日益成为推动美国对外政策的重要工具。[21] 这在美国与前苏联东欧国家签订的 BITs 中表现最为明显,因为这些 BITs 成了美国支持这些国家民主与市场经济转型的政策工具,既具象征意义,又有实质意义。其他 BITs 如与巴拿马、刚果 BITs 的签订,均具有很明显的政治色彩。即使是 NAFTA 的签订也充满着政治色彩:一个重要的方面就是要改善与墨西哥的关系,以创造解决困扰两国关系的非法移民、毒品走私以及环境保护等政治问题的机会。[22]

第二阶段的投资条约虽然开始强调对外资的促进,但投资保护仍然是 BITs 的重点。不过与第一阶段相比,投资条约在内容方面更加丰富,已经不再局限于第一阶段 BITs 的4个方面核心内容,而且这个时期的投资条约在主要内容和目标上已经和美国当前的投资条约极为接近。1992年3月16日,美国国务卿在一封提交给众议院的关于斯里兰卡 BIT 的信件中,对美国 BIT 的目标进行了详细阐述,总结了美国投资条约所要实现的6大目标及主要特征:(1)在准入和准入后阶段,缔约一国国民和公司的投资在缔约另一国境内的投资要享有在类似情况下(in like circumstances)不低于该国给予本国国民和第三国国民的待遇;(2)保证不给外资施加业绩要求;(3)外资公司可以自由确定公司高管,缔约一方不得施加国籍限制;(4)征收必须符合国际标准,即非歧视、公共利益以及充分、及时和有效的补偿;(5)除非一国遭遇严重的汇兑不平衡,外国投资的资金可以自由使用的货币不受限制地转移;(6)在发生投资争端后,缔约一方投资者可以将投资争端提交国际仲裁而不用诉诸东道国国内法院。[23] 这6个新的核心目标一直贯彻实施到2004年范本推出。[24]

---

〔20〕 Kenneth J. Vandevelde, U. S. International Investment Agreements, Oxford: Oxford University Press, 2009, pp. 2 – 3.

〔21〕 Ibid., p. 45.

〔22〕 Ibid., pp. 45 – 46.

〔23〕 Ibid., pp. 52 – 53.

〔24〕 Ibid., pp. 52 – 54.

（三）第三阶段（1999～2009年）

NAFTA框架下"被诉"的经历使美国开始反思其投资协定政策，在此之前，美国在制定投资协定范本时，都是从保护美国的对外投资出发，几乎没有考虑到美国会成为国际投资仲裁的被请求人。一方面，考虑到与美国缔结BITs的国家都是拥有极少外国直接投资份额的发展中国家；另一方面，美国对其国内法律环境有着极大的信心。不过，NAFTA却与美国着手签订的双边投资协定不同，因为成员国之一的加拿大是美国国内外国投资的主要来源地。NAFTA的仲裁经历使美国开始站在资本输入国而非资本输出国的角度去考虑其投资协定。

在这一阶段，美国更看重投资对贸易的促进作用，因此将投资协定谈判的重心转移到包含投资条款的自由贸易协定的谈判上。在2002年，美国出台了《两党贸易促进授权法案》（Bipartisan Trade Promotion Authority Act），规定国会对于政府提交的贸易协定，不能再进行修订，只能作出批准或不批准的决定。该法案既简化了国会对政府签署的贸易协定的审批程序，又降低了因国会要求修改贸易协定而使协定谈判重启的风险，极大地提升了美国政府进行自贸协定谈判的积极性。仅在2002年到2005年间，美国政府就签订了10个自贸协定。[25] 在内容方面，上述《两党贸易促进授权法案》规定自由贸易协定的投资条款要体现3大目标：确保在美国的外国投资者所享有的待遇不得高于美国国内投资者依据美国国内法所享有的待遇；消除影响投资流动的人为障碍或贸易扭曲措施；保护美国的对外投资。[26] 此时，美国的BIT政策已发生了重大变化：过去的首要目的（保护海外投资）虽然仍在，但其重要性却下降到了第三位。鼓励投资特别是消除影响投资流动的贸易措施成了第二重要的目的，突出了鼓励投资和贸易的主旨。其中最重要的目的，却是过去闻所未闻的，即确保在美国的外国投资者不能享受超国民待遇。也许美国从来就不曾给予外国投资者以超国民待遇，但它也从来不曾将其作为首要投资政策来规定。有人因此认为，这一规定实际上正是美国版的"卡尔沃主义"。[27]

相形之下，美国在BIT方面却鲜有收获。美国在总结之前的投资协定和自贸协定谈判和参与国际仲裁实践的基础上，于2004年推出了新的投资条约范本。该范本除了继续坚持为美国的对外投资提供保护外，在内容方面体现出更多新特

---

〔25〕 这些自贸协定由美国分别与新加坡、智利、澳大利亚、摩洛哥、中南美洲五国和多美尼加、秘鲁、阿曼、哥伦比亚、巴拿马和韩国等国签订。

〔26〕 Kenneth J. Vandevelde, U. S. International Investment Agreements, Oxford: Oxford University Press, 2009, p. 73.

〔27〕 单文华：《卡尔沃主义死了吗》，张生等译，载《国际经济法学刊》2008年第15卷第2期。

点，体现出美国政府、跨国公司和非政府组织的广泛诉求，对于具体条款的规定更加细化和具体，比如，关于公平与公正待遇的规定就借鉴了 NAFTA 自由贸易委员会的解释，对容易引起争议的“间接征收”进行了详细界定。另一方面，范本吸纳了非政府组织的一些诉求，注重保护外国投资和东道国国内利益的均衡。[28] 最后，在争端解决程序方面，范本一方面对投资者的“滥诉”进行规制，同时进一步提高了仲裁程序的透明度要求，并通过考虑设立上诉机制的规定保证仲裁裁决的公正性。在 2004 年范本推出后，美国先后与乌拉圭和卢旺达签署投资协定，这两个 BITs 在内容上完全照搬了 2004 范本。

（四）第四阶段（2009 年至今）

2004 年推出的投资条约范本既为美国对外投资提供了充分的保障和高标准的保护，也对东道国在维护环境、安全等公共利益方面的公权力表示了充分尊重。但是，一些非政府保护组织仍然认为该范本在维护缔约国公共利益方面做得不够，另一方面，一些政府议员则认为条约范本过分侧重于维护公共利益、提倡高标准的劳工标准和人权保护，有可能阻碍投资条约的谈判。还有人则抱怨 BIT 范本在推动美国 BIT 谈判方面作用有限，因为美国至今仍未与中国、印度等主要经济体签订双边投资协定。

2007 年始于美国的金融危机使美国政府再次审视其投资条约政策。有学者指出，2004 年范本在资本控制方面的规定已经过时，并指出在全球化的时代，应当给予缔约国政府更大政策空间以应对金融危机，而且当前的金融危机已经表明，美国政府需要制定新的协定以应对将来可能还会发生的危机，并创设一个稳定的和可持续发展的环境。[29] 日益高涨的呼声使奥巴马政府于 2009 年组建了一个国际经济政策咨询委员会（ACIEP）来审查 2004 年 BIT 范本，以实现奥巴马政府作出的“确保外国投资者的权利受到严格限制，并保证缔约国维护安全和促进公共利益的权力”的承诺。2009 年 9 月，ACIEP 向国务院递交了对 2004 年范本

---

〔28〕 Susan D. Franck. The Legitimacy Crisis in Investment Treaty Arbitration: Privatizing Public International Law through Inconsistent Decisions, Fordham Law Review, 2005, 73(4): 1521 - 1625. 随着国际投资仲裁受理越来越多的案件，人们对仲裁裁决的质疑也越来越多，这一方面起因于不同的仲裁庭在处理基于类似事实和相似条款的争端时作出不同甚至截然相反的裁决；另一方面，仲裁庭在解释投资协定时，往往作出倾向于保护外国投资者的认定，这也极大限制了东道国在维护公共利益方面的公权力。有学者就将这些问题进行归纳，并指出这些问题引发了国际投资仲裁的“合法性危机”。

〔29〕 Sarah Anderson, Comments on the U. S. Model Bilateral Investment Treaty (2009 - 07 - 17), available at http://www.ips-dc.org/files/1366/IPS% 20comments% 20on% 20Model% 20Bilateral% 20Investment% 20Treaty.pdf (2012 - 10 - 30).

的审查报告。[30] 在此基础上,美国于 2012 年 4 月公布了最新的投资条约范本。不过,与 2004 年范本以及大众的期待相比,2012 年范本的改变似乎并不显著。

二、2012 年新范本:新在何处

2009 年,ACIEP 在对 2004 年范本进行审查时,曾广泛听取了来自于国会议员、企业、商业组织、劳工组织、环保组织等非政府组织和学者的意见。但新推出的 2012 年范本在改动上显得不温不火:它秉承了 2004 范本的大多数内容,只在很少方面做了改动,此举也招致了一些学者和非政府组织的强烈反对。2009 年,ACIEP 投资分委员会关于 BIT 新范本的报告[31]出台以后,一些学者和非政府组织曾就 2004 年范本的完善提出了 17 条建议,但是这些建议中仅有 2 条被采纳。[32] 这也就不难理解为什么新范本在推出后会遭到一些非政府组织的猛烈批评。[33] 即便如此,比起 2004 年范本,2012 年范本在内容方面仍然有不少亮点:

第一,范本在透明度方面提出了更高的要求。与其他改动相比,新范本在这方面的动作很大。(1)新范本要求缔约方定期就如何完善有关投资的法律法规以及措施的制定与实施过程中、投资者—东道国投资仲裁过程中的透明度实践进行磋商。[34] (2)新范本对于投资法规的发布提出了严格的具体要求。一方面,对于缔约方拟发布的法规,新范本要求必须通过官方刊物进行公布;公布中应当包含关于法规制定目的和依据的说明;在发布前留有足够的(60 天以上)公众评论期限;且在最终通过法规时,应当对评论期间收到的重大、实质性评论进行处理,并对任何实质性的修改进行说明。[35] (3)新范本要求缔约方允许缔约另一方的投资者参与到标准的制订中,任一缔约方应当在其中央政府机构标准或技术法规的制订过程中允许另一缔约方的人参与,缔约方应建议其领土内的非政府标准机构允许另一缔约方的人参与制订标准的过程。不过范本也规定标准制订的要求不适用于 WTO 协议中的卫生与检疫措施和政府采购措施。[36]

第二,新范本加强了缔约方在保护环境和实施劳工标准方面的义务。(1)在环境保护方面,新范本首先强调了缔约国国内环境法律和政策以及缔约方共同参

---

〔30〕 ACIEP, Report of the Subcommittee on Investment of the Advisory Committee on International Economic Policy Regarding the Model Bilateral Investment Treaty(2009 - 09 - 30), available at http://www.state.gov/e/eb/rls/othr/2009/131118.htm(2012 - 10 - 30).

〔31〕 Ibid.

〔32〕 Null. Public Interest Groups Issue Strong Critique of New US Model Bilateral Investment Treaty(2012 - 05 - 15), available at http://www.bilaterals.org/spip.php? article21484&lang = en(2012 - 10 - 30).

〔33〕 Ibid.

〔34〕 参见美国 2012 年范本第 11 条第 1 款。

〔35〕 参见美国 2012 年范本第 11 条第 3 款、第 4 款,该两款为新增加内容。

〔36〕 参见美国 2012 年范本第 11 条第 8 款,该款为新增加内容。

与的多边环境协定的重要性。(2)缔约双方要确保(shall ensure)不得为吸引外资而豁免或降低(waive or otherwise derogate)其国内环境法律的要求,也不得为吸引外资而不去有效实施(effectively enforce)其国内环境立法。[37] 2004年范本规定缔约双方要努力确保(shall strive to ensure)缔约国豁免或降低其国内的环境法律或其有效实施,[38]显而易见,2012年范本在措词上更为严格,已构成一项硬性法律义务。(3)新范本还明确承认了缔约双方在处理环保事项和资源分配的决策方面的自由裁量权,但条件须是缔约方的作为或不作为属于对该自由裁量权的合理使用,或者属于资源分配方面的善意决定。[39] (4)新范本还对协定中出现的"环境法"进行了解释。[40] (5)新范本规定缔约一方可以就有关环保的任何事项向另一缔约方提出磋商的书面请求,缔约另一方需要在规定的时间(30天)内作出回应,之后缔约双方应当努力达成彼此满意的结果。[41] (6)新范本规定要为因环保问题产生的事项提供公众参与的机会。[42]

在劳工保护方面,新范本规定协定不会影响缔约双方作为国际劳工组织成员的义务,以及缔约双方在《国际劳工组织的基本原则和权利宣言及后续工作》项下的承诺。[43] 与环保方面的规定相似,新范本也强调不得为吸引外资而豁免或降低(waive or otherwise derogate)其国内劳工法律的要求,或者不去有效实施(effectively enforce)其国内劳工立法。[44] 与2004年范本相比,2012年范本扩大了"劳动法"所指的对象范围。[45] 同时,新范本也包含了缔约双方进行磋商以及保证公众参与机会的规定。[46]

第三,针对所谓的"国家主导经济"(stateled economies),即一国经济活动的组织在很大程度上建立于其国有企业(SOEs)或其他国家控制或影响机制基础之上的经济,新范本提出了几个新的规定。(1)范本在一个脚注中明确了如何认定一缔约方是否将政府权力(governmental authority)授权给一家国有企业或者其他个

[37] 参见美国2012年范本第12条第2款。
[38] 参见美国2004年范本第12条第1款,该款为新增加内容。
[39] 参见美国2012年范本第12条第3款,该款为新增加内容。
[40] 参见美国2012年范本第12条第4款,该款为新增加内容。
[41] 参见美国2012年范本第12条第6款,该款为新增加内容。
[42] 参见美国2012年范本第12条第7款,该款为新增加内容。
[43] 参见美国2012年范本第13条第1款。
[44] 参见美国2012年范本第13条第2款。
[45] 参见美国2012年范本第13条第3款。
[46] 参见美国2012年范本第13条第4款和第5款,该两款为新增内容。

人或实体,以确保这类企业与实体完全处于 BIT 条约义务的覆盖之下。[47] (2)范本禁止东道国要求采取“国内技术要求”,即在购买、使用、授惠方面对国内研发的技术予以倾斜的措施。[48] 不过,范本同时指出它不适用于缔约方履行 WTO 框架下的 TRIPS 协定义务或政府采购,也不应被解释为对缔约方适用或维持环境保护措施造成阻碍。[49] 如前所述,范本要求在标准制定方面,缔约方要给对方投资者在非歧视的基础上参与的机会。

第四,在投资协定的适用范围方面,新范本不仅明确了对美国来说“领土”的具体含义,还对“领土”中的海洋部分进行了明确界定,指出其适用的地域范围不仅包括领海,还包括领海之外根据《联合国海洋法公约》所反映的习惯国际法可行使主权或管辖权的任何区域。[50]

第五,就投资者—东道国争端解决机制而言,2012 年范本基本上没有改动,唯一的例外便是关于上诉机制的规定。2004 年范本在附件四中规定要在协定生效之日起 3 年内,缔约方应当考虑是否建立一个双边上诉机构或类似机制来处理有关投资仲裁案件裁决的再审。[51] 新范本并没有将上诉机制放在附件中进行规定,而是直接在第 28 条“仲裁程序的进行”中作出规定。在内容方面,新范本并没有规定设立上诉机制的期限,而是规定将来如果其他机制性安排建立了上诉机制,缔约方应当考虑国际投资仲裁裁决是否适用于上诉机制,同时要求缔约方要保证该上诉机制的透明度。[52]

三、2012 年新范本:主要特点

美国 2012 年范本进一步保证了法律法规和仲裁程序的透明度,强调了缔约国在保护环境和劳工方面的义务,并强化了对国有企业的规制。但与美国国内各界针对 2004 范本的热烈讨论以及 ACIEP 投资分委员会于 2009 年提出的咨询报告相比,2012 年范本在很多方面的“动作幅度”并不大,在内容上大体承袭了 2004 年范本的规定。总体而言,2012 范本体现了以下几个方面的特点:

---

〔47〕 2012 年范本关于授权条款脚注 8 指出,“为明确起见,被授权的政府权力包括向国有企业或其他个人转移政府权力或授予其行使政府权力的立法许可、政府命令、指令或行为”。笔者认为本脚注存在笔误,其原意应该是“为明确起见,政府权力的授权方式包括向国有企业或其他个人转移政府权力或授予其行使政府权力的立法许可、政府命令、指令或行为”。

〔48〕 参见美国 2012 年范本第 8 条第 1 款第 8 项,该项为新增加内容。

〔49〕 参见美国 2012 年范本第 8 条第 3 款。

〔50〕 参见美国 2012 年年范本第 1 条。

〔51〕 参见美国 2004 年范本附件四。在规定上诉机制的考虑期限方面,美国在投资协定和自由贸易协定方面并不一致。在与中南美洲和多美尼加的自贸协定(CAFTA-DR)中,该期限为 3 个月,而美国和卢旺达投资协定则沿用了 2004 年范本的规定,将期限设置为 3 年。

〔52〕 参见美国 2012 年范本第 28 条第 10 款。

（一）新范本仍然继承了“高标准”外资保护的传统

尽管一些非政府组织曾经抨击美国投资协定赋予外国投资者比本国投资者更多的权利，并进而要求美国在投资协定中不再规定投资者—东道国投资争端解决机制，而是将此类争端交由缔约国间的争端处理机制解决，新范本并未采纳这些建议。保护外国投资仍然是2012年范本的首要目的。[53] 在这方面，非政府组织在考虑美国的投资条约时显得有些极端，它过多地站在美国是资本输入国的角度考虑问题，忽略了美国同时也是世界上重要的资本输出国这一事实，而且美国现有的投资协定大部分都是和发展中国家或者过渡经济体签订的，保护美国的对外投资也极为重要，甚至更加重要。事实上，美国近期正在启动或者考虑启动与“金砖四国”（巴西、俄罗斯、印度、中国）的投资协定谈判，新范本正好可以为这些谈判提供依据，也会为美国在这些国家的投资提供强有力的保护。

（二）新范本在“社会化”方面进展显著

“社会化”是当前世界投资法发展的一大趋势，[54] 2012范本在这方面表现得很突出。新范本两个最显著的变化即在于环境与劳工保护义务和透明度责任均得到大大加强，堪称BIT“社会化”的最新成果。但是，它并没有像一些学者所建议的那样，将因环保措施和劳工保护措施引起的争议完全排除在国际投资争端解决范围之外，更没有完全废除投资者—东道国争端解决机制，而是小心地寻求保护外资和维护公共利益方面的平衡，当然，这种平衡要完全实现并不容易。挪威2007年公布的投资条约范本就是一个例证，尽管该范本在维持利益平衡方面作出了很多努力和尝试，但仍然无法同时满足政府、投资者和非政府组织的要求，结果只好搁浅。[55] 这样的争论在2012年范本公布后各方的反应中也可见一斑。非政府组织批评新范本在维护公共利益方面不够“给力”，而投资界则认为范本中的社会化条款走得太远，不仅会影响美国与中国等国家的投资协定谈判进度，还会影响国际投资的积极性。

（三）新范本朝着所谓的“竞争中立”政策方向迈进了一步

近年以来，面对以中国为代表的以国有经济为主导的经济体的崛起，以美国

---

〔53〕 Office of the United States Trade Representative. Bilateral Investment Treaties, available at http://www.ustr.gov/trade-agreements/bilateral-investment-treaties(2012 -10 -30).

〔54〕 Wenhua Shan, Towards a Balanced Liberal Investment Regime: General Report on the Protection of Investment for the XVIIIth International Congress of Comparative Law 2010 Washington DC, ICSID Review: Foreign Investment Law Journal, 2010, 25(2): pp. 421 -497.

Wenhua Shan. Legal Protection of Foreign Investment: A Comparative Study, Oxford: Hart Publishing, 2012.

〔55〕 Dammon Vis-Dunbar, Norway Shelves Its Draft Model Bilateral Investment Treaty(2009 -06 -08), http://www.iisd.org/itn/2009/06/08/norway-shelves-its-proposed-model-bilateral-in-vestment-treaty/(2012 -10 -30).

和欧盟为代表的西方国家加紧协调立场,酝酿策划各种应对措施。其中最为突出的对策,莫过于所谓的“竞争中立”(com-petitive neutrality)政策。例如,在美国和欧盟联合提出的《美国—欧盟国际投资共同原则申明》中,一个最重要的原则便是“竞争中立”。该原则强调国有企业应该和私有企业处于同样的外部环境,以保证他们在同等市场条件下公平竞争。[56] 从表面看来,该原则只是要求公平待遇,它在实质上却意图在国际社会中加强对国有企业的约束,甚至是围堵,对我国这样以国有经济占主导地位的国家十分不利。在以前,这种政策尚未在美国投资条约或其范本中具体体现。2012年范本对国有企业的行为可能导致“国家责任”进行了明确界定,以及对东道国“国内技术要求”的禁止和对外资参与国内标准制定的强调,均可视为“竞争中立”政策在范本中的具体化。尽管目前其内容尚且不十分“尖锐”,但其所代表的方向对我国的国有经济特别是我国巨大的国有对外投资来说,将构成巨大的潜在威胁。

(四)新范本更多借鉴了BIT而非FTA谈判经验

近年以来,美国在自由贸易协定的谈判中十分积极,在投资协定谈判和签订方面则进展比较缓慢。相比较而言,新范本更多借鉴了BIT的经验,而不是FTA的经验。例如,新范本在某些方面(如金融服务)借鉴了美国与卢旺达BIT的文本,美国自贸协定的某些最新重大发展却没有在新范本中体现。例如,在维护缔约国公共利益方面,一些自贸协定的规定要比2012年范本更为直接和有效。再如,在美国与韩国、巴拿马、哥伦比亚和秘鲁的自贸协定中都规定,有关环保和劳工保护方面的争端应当通过缔约国之间的争端解决机制解决。[57] 此外,有的自贸协定也规定主权债务重组中的债权人仅享有国民待遇和最惠国待遇。[58] 2012年范本并未就这些内容作出规定,而是将该问题交给协定的缔约双方自由决定。

(五)新范本意味着TPPA谈判仍需更多协调

在投资争端解决方面,2012年范本几乎照搬了2004年范本的规定。这招致了一些消费者和环境保护组织的猛烈抨击,他们认为BIT中的这种投资者—东道国争端解决机制赋予了外国投资者比本国投资者更多的权利,因为外国投资者可以依据BIT通过国际投资仲裁向东道国实施的保护公共利益的法律规

---

〔56〕 European Commission, Statement of the European Union and the United States of America on Shared Principles for International Investment(2012-04-10), available at http://trade.ec.europa.eu/doclib/html/149331.htm(2012-10-30).

〔57〕 Charlene Barshefsky and Others. United States to Resume Bilateral Investment Treaty Negotiations on the Basis of a Revised Model Treaty(2012-05-12), available at http://www.wilmerhale.com/publications/wh-Pubs-Detail.aspx? publication=10150(2012-10-30).

〔58〕 如《美国—智利自贸协定》Annex 10B。

章或措施提出控诉并得到赔偿，而国内投资者无权诉诸国际仲裁解决同样的诉求。[59] 反过来，参与《跨太平洋战略经济伙伴关系协议》(Trans-Pacific Strategic Economic Partnership Agreement, TPPA)谈判的另一个重要国家澳大利亚对待此类机制的态度则硬朗得多。2011年4月，吉拉德政府在一次贸易政策陈述中就明确指出，澳大利亚不会在FTA中引入投资者—东道国争端解决机制。[60] 在2012年5月签署的《澳大利亚—马来西亚自贸协定》中，也没有规定国际投资仲裁机制。

一些学者也通过公开信的方式呼吁TPPA不应当包含投资者—东道国争端解决机制。[61] 在这种背景下，如果美国基于2012年范本展开与其他国家的TPPA谈判，如何协调各方在国际投资争端解决机制方面的态度，无疑是一大挑战。

四、美国范本的可接受性问题

经贸关系是中美关系的重要组成部分，也是中美关系发展的重要基础和推动力。自1979年建交以来，中美双边经贸关系发展迅速，合作领域不断扩大，内涵日益丰富，中美之间相互依存持续加深，已经形成"你中有我，我中有你"的利益交融格局。[62] 就贸易规模而言，中美已互为第二大贸易伙伴，而且双边投资关系也日益密切，但迄今为止，中美之间并没有签订一个BIT。事实上，早在20世纪80年代初，中美之间就曾开展BIT谈判，但当时双方几乎在每一个条款上都存在争执，到最后条约谈判被迫搁置。[63] 2008年，中美双方决定重启双边投资协定的谈判，在2012年5月开展的中美战略与经济对话中，中美双方决定正式启动谈判工作，目前已经进行了多轮技术层面的磋商。鉴于美国BIT谈判以严苛著称，尽管中国与加拿大已于2012年9月签署双边投资协定，中美BIT谈判仍将是一场

---

〔59〕 Earth Justice, Friends of the Earth, Institute for Policy Studies, Public Citizen and Sierra Club Key Elements of Damaging U. S. Trade Agreement Investment Rules That Must Not Be Replicated in TPP, available at http://www. citizen. org/documents/tpp-investment-fixes. pdf(2012 - 10 - 30).

〔60〕 Australian Government Department of Foreign Affairs and Trade. Gillard Government Trade Policy Statement: Trading Our Way to More Jobs and Prosperity, available at http://www. dfat. gov. au/publications/trade/trading-our-way-to-more-jobs-and-prosperi-ty. html#investor-state(2012 - 10 - 30).

〔61〕 TPP Legal, An Open Letter from Lawyers to the Negotiators of the Trans-Pacific Partnership Urging the Re-jection of Investor-State Dispute Settlement(2012 - 05 - 08), available at http://tpplegal. wordpress. com/open-letter/(2012 - 10 - 30).

〔62〕 中国驻美国大使馆经商参赞处：《投资美国指南》(2012 - 02 - 13)，载 http://us. mofcom. gov. cn/aarticle/subject/investguide/lanmutwo/201201/20120107935078. html，2012年10月30日访问。

〔63〕 Cai Congyan, China-US BIT Negotiations and the Future of Investment Treaty Regime about China-Canada BIT Negotiations-A Grand Bilateral Bargain with Multilateral Impli-cations, Journal of International Economic Law, 2009, 12(2): pp. 457 - 506.

硬仗,一场不折不扣的 BIT“世纪谈判”。[64]

在中美 BIT 谈判过程中,包括在我们研究制定谈判对策的过程中,我们一方面需要深入准确地研究、把握对方的目标和意图,另一方面需要弄清我们自己的“家底”和需要,做到“知己知彼”,方能“百战不殆”。为此,我们有必要对中美投资关系的现状和发展趋势进行分析,以明确彼此所处的地位(如主要是投资输出国还是输入国),并在此基础上提出如何判断某一具体条款是否可以接受的依据或者标准。

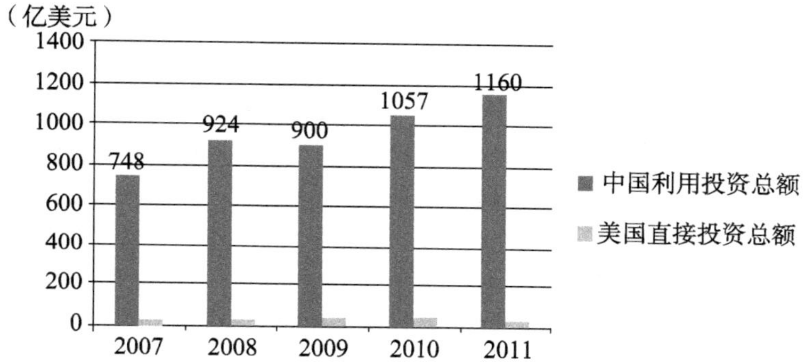

图 1　美国在中国的非金融类直接投资(2007 ~ 2011 年)[65]

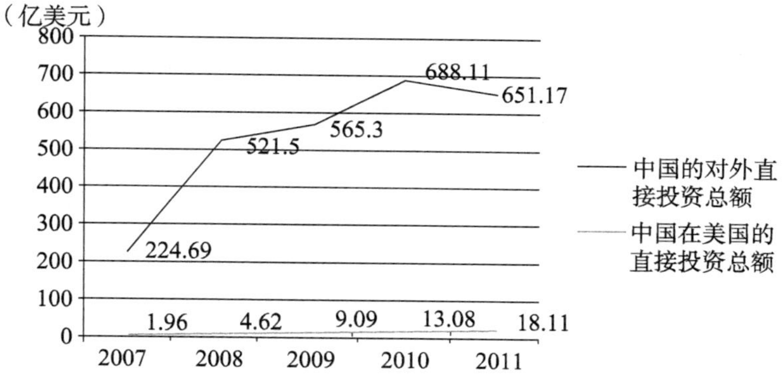

图 2　中国在美国的直接投资统计(2007 ~ 2011 年)[66]

(一)中美双边投资关系与中国的对美 BIT 政策取向:外资管理与投资保护的均衡

从图 1 和图 2 可以看出,中美投资关系具有双重特征:一方面,从数量或静

---

〔64〕 单文华、诺拉·伽拉赫:《和谐世界理念和中国 BIT 范本建设——一个“和谐 BIT 范本”建议案》,陈虹睿、王朝恩译,载《国际经济法学刊》2010 年第 17 卷第 1 期。

〔65〕 数据来源:中国投资指南网,http://www.fdi.gov.cn/,

〔66〕 同上。

态角度来看,美国在中国的投资,无论是在流量还是存量上,要远大于中国在美国的投资。从流量上看,在过去5年间,美国对华投资均在26亿美元以上,平均每年投资额达32.4亿美元;我国同期对美最高年度投资额不过18亿美元,最低则不到2亿美元,平均不到10亿美元。另据商务部统计,截至2010年底,美国在华投资累计已达652亿美元;截至2011年上半年,我国在美投资总计53.1亿美元。换言之,从近年流量看,中国对美投资尚不到美在华投资的1/3;从存量看,中国在美投资不到美国在华投资的1/10。可见,从绝对数量看,在中美之间,美国仍然主要是资本输出国,我国则主要是资本输入国。

另一方面,从趋势或动态上看,中国对美投资增速强劲,远远高于美国对华投资增长水平。突出表现在近5年来,美国对华投资比较平稳,而我国对美投资急剧增长。在过去5年里,美国对华投资有增有降,但起伏很小;我国对美投资则直线上升,增长了9倍之多。其结果是,到2011年,我国对美投资超过了18亿美元,达到了美国当年对华投资的一半以上。如果双方照这种势头持续下去,在不久的将来,中美之间的投资流量或许很快就能够实现平衡甚至逆转。

中美投资关系是中美BIT的出发点和归宿。中美投资关系的双重特点对中美BIT谈判不可避免地将产生深刻影响。一方面,目前我国主要是资本输入国而美国是输出国,中美BIT谈判的焦点和重心首先在于如何解决高标准严要求地保护美国在华投资和有效维护我国外资管理主权之间的矛盾。这在实践中并非易事,因为保护外资往往会在某些程度上影响我国对外资的管理权限。长久以来,我国的外资管理制度一直受到外国投资者的批判,如根据2012年中国美国商会进行的《商务环境调查》结果,大多数美国企业认为在华运营所面临的第二大挑战便是法规解释相互矛盾和法律不明确,此外,取得许可证困难、腐败、官僚主义以及各种形式的保护主义也都被不少美国投资者看作很大的挑战。[67] 调查结果还显示,不少投资者对行政许可申请以及限制性的市场准入制度都有不同程度的抱怨。[68] 从这个角度看,有必要借助投资条约增强外国投资者的信心,进一步推动外商投资在中国的发展。但同时,对于来自发达资本输出国的高度自由化的要求,我们也要有所应对,适当保护我国外资的管理权限。

另一方面,我国对美投资流量飞速增长并快速接近美国对华投资流量的事实

---

〔67〕 中国美国商会:《2012年美国企业在中国白皮书》,载 http://web.resource.amcham-china.org/cmsfile/2012/04/26/cd626ad14b98c 259cfb187f4576b4d79.pdf,2012年10月30日访问,第4页。

〔68〕 同上,第8页。

也表明，我们在重视保护外资管理权的同时，也必须重视我国对美投资的有效和有力保护。归结起来，在中美投资条约谈判中，保护我国对外资管理权限的效果是重心，而保护和发展我国对美投资也同样重要，必须予以高度重视，不可偏废。

(二)美国2012年范本可接受性的判断基于上述认识

我们认为，判断美国2012年范本或者其任何具体条文是否可接受的标准大致有三个层面，分别对应我国国际投资利益的三个层面：外来投资管理权力的维护、对外投资权益的保护和促进、中国参与国际投资制度和价值建构的贡献。具体而言，这三重标准是指：

1. 外资管理权之维护

前已述及，尽管美国2012年新范本在很多方面体现了保护外国投资者利益与东道国公共利益的均衡，但是新范本仍然继承了"高标准"外资保护的传统。对于美国新范本的这一特点，中国应当小心应对，避免中美BIT不适当地限制我国对外资的管理权限。以投资准入为例，美国一直主张投资条约要涵盖投资准入，而习惯国际法则认为，一国有权自主决定是否接受外资。目前，所有的中国BITs大都只规定了投资保护，尚未承担实质性的投资准入义务。如果中国在与美国的BIT中接受投资准入制度，将有可能改变中国的整个外商投资法律制度结构和方向。正因为如此，在2012年2月签署的中国—日本—韩国三方投资条约中，尽管日本和韩国力主在该条约中加入投资准入条款，但是在中国的坚持下，最后不得不放弃该主张。[69] 在2012年9月签署的中—加BIT也未涉及准入前国民待遇要求，甚至没有规定不符措施的负面清单。可以预见，以准入阶段国民待遇为核心的争议条款将成为双方艰苦谈判的重中之重。

2. 对外投资之保护与促进

从图3中我们可以看出，近年以来，特别是自2005年以来，中国的对外直接投资有了快速发展。根据贸发会的统计，2011年，中国已成为世界上对外投资第五大经济体。[70] 这一新发展使得我国在国际投资中的角色定位发生了重大转变：由一个主要投资输入国变成一个兼具投资输入国和输出国双重身份的国家。

---

〔69〕 Null, Korea, China, Japan to Conclude Investment Pact after 5 Years (2012 - 02 - 28), http://www.bilaterals.org/spip.php? article21112 (2012 - 10 - 30).

〔70〕 UNCTAD, World Investment Report 2011: Non-Equity Modes of International Production and Development, United Nations: New York and Geneva, 2011, p. 9.

但是,我国现有的投资条约框架并不能够真正有效地保护中国的对外投资。[71]尤其是我国的对外投资流入国大都不具有完善的国内法制并存有较高的风险,特别需要国际法的保护。从这个角度讲,中美 BIT 谈判也为确保我国对外投资得到有效保护和促进提供了一个很好的契机。

毫无疑问,美国高标准的 BIT 模式完全能够对一般性的投资提供充分的保护。但是,我国的对外投资又有其十分突出的特点:在对外投资者构成中,国有企业占有很大比重。商务部《2011 年度对外直接投资统计公报》显示,截至 2011 年底,在我国非金融类对外直接投资存量中,国有企业投资占 62.7%。[72] 虽然该报告没有关于我国在美投资者构成的数据,但相信不会与我国对外直接投资的总体状况相差太远。我国大规模的国有对外投资已经引起以美欧为首的西方国家的高度关注,在近年来的 OECD 等场合中,它们往往以"竞争中立"为借口,力图制约国有企业的投资贸易活动,《欧盟美国国际投资共同政策声明》就是一个突出的例证。在这种背景下,如何确保我国的国有企业对外投资在中美 BIT 中得到充分有效的保护,将是一个十分突出的问题,不能有效保护我国对外投资者的 BIT 将很难说是一个成功的 BIT。

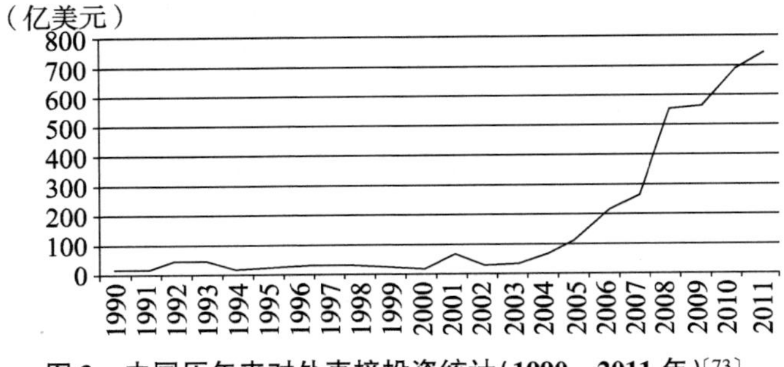

图 3　中国历年来对外直接投资统计(1990 ~ 2011 年)[73]

3. 国际投资制度与价值之建构

国际投资法正处于大变革、大转型的时代,各国都在思考、探讨、酝酿改革的方向。在这个大背景下,中美 BIT 作为世界上两个最大且最具代表性的经济体之间签订的 BIT,无疑将对国际投资法的发展产生影响。一个好的中美 BIT 完全有

〔71〕 Sheng Zhang. The Energy Charter Treaty and China: Member or Bystander? Journal of World Investment & Trade, 2012, 13(4): pp. 597 - 617. Cai Congyan, Outward Foreign Direct Investment Protection and the Effectiveness of Chinese BIT Practice, Journal of World Investment & Trade, 2006, 7(5): pp. 621 - 652.

〔72〕 商务部、国家统计局、国家外管局:《2011 年度对外直接投资统计公报》,中国统计出版社 2012 年版,第 17 页。

〔73〕 数据来源:中国投资指南网,http://www.fdi.gov.cn/。

可能成为未来世界投资法典的基础,因此,中美 BIT 不仅仅是关涉中美双边投资关系(由于事实上是中外投资关系总体,因为所有的中外投资协定均含有“最惠国待遇”条款,可以产生多边自动传导效应)的大事,也是可望影响世界投资法发展大局的“盛事”。换言之,谈判中美 BIT 不仅仅是我国加强引进美(外)资和保护对美(外)投资的重大战略行动,更是我国影响国际投资立法与价值建构的重要战略机遇。

在这方面,我们应该贯彻“和谐世界”的理念,致力于缔结一个有助于“和谐世界”建设的中美 BIT。中美 BIT 的谈判首先要立足于中国作为重要投资接受国和来源国这一双重身份。从功利主义或实用主义角度讲,中美 BIT 一方面要能够应对美国范本中的高度自由化要求,适当保护我国对外商投资的管理权力,而另一方面则需要为中国在美国的投资提供有力的法律支持。这两个方面的要求看似相互矛盾且无法调和,但是如果将“和谐世界”的理念引入中美 BIT 的谈判,则能够较好地化解上述矛盾,并对世界投资法的发展起到引领作用。[74] 在“和谐世界”理念的指引下,中美 BIT 要坚持“平衡原则”,致力于平衡东道国与外国投资者之间的权利和义务关系,[75]同时该条约也要坚持“绿色主义”,强化外国投资者的责任,努力使投资与经济繁荣同社会发展与环境保护相协调。[76] 如果中美 BIT 能够实现上述制度设计与价值目标,不仅能彰显我国对国际投资条约的政策与价值取向,还将为我国争取未来多边国际投资立法的话语权奠定基础。

在上述三个标准中,即维护对外来投资的管理权、保护我国对外投资、推动国际投资制度和价值建构,如果能够实现第一个目标,可以认为达到了最低(或曰“及格”)标准;如果能够实现前二者,可以认为达到了“良好”标准;如果三个目标均得以实现,就可以说达到了最高(“理想”)标准。考虑到美国 BIT 的高标准、严要求以及其谈判态度十分苛刻的特点,要在中美 BIT 谈判中实现理想目标,无疑将是非常艰难的,但并不是不可能的。

---

〔74〕 单文华、诺拉伽拉赫:《和谐世界理念和中国 BIT 范本建设——一个“和谐 BIT 范本”建议案》,陈虹睿、王朝恩译,载《国际经济法学刊》2010 年第 17 卷第 1 期。

〔75〕 同上。

〔76〕 同上。

美国 2012 年 BIT 范本中的投资定义条款及中国的对策研究*

一、导论

“投资”定义决定双边投资条约(以下简称 BIT)保护的对象范围,构成投资仲裁管辖权的基础,在条约特别是其定义条款中居于核心地位。[1] 因此,几乎所有的国际投资条约都对“投资”的概念进行了界定。由于国际投资争端解决中心(以下简称 ICSID)仅仅接受“投资”争端,而其所赖以成立的《华盛顿公约》却并未对“投资”作任何定义,[2]因此 BIT 关于“投资”定义的重要性更加凸显。在仲裁实践中,关于一个项目是否构成“投资”从而受到 BIT 保护的争议层出不穷,对“投资”的认定问题往往成为确定投资仲裁管辖权的关键和先决性问题。

鉴于中美在世界经济政治体系中的领导地位,中美 BIT 谈判不仅受到国内学术界的高度重视,也引起了国际投资法学界的高度关注。[3] 2012 年 5 月,中美两国正式宣布重启中美双边投资保护协定的谈判工作,并于 10 月进行了第七

* 本文发表在《国际经济法学刊》(第 20 卷)2013 年第 3 期,作者单文华、王璐。

本文系在商务部“第六届国际投资保护协定研讨会”会议报告的基础上整理而成,并受到国家社科基金项目“双边投资保护协定核心条款的法解释学研究”(项目号 10BFX091)的资助。

〔1〕 一般来说,只有符合国际投资条约规定的“投资”才受到该条约的保护,进而能够适用条约中的实体权利义务和争端解决程序的相关规范。国际投资条约中对“投资”的定义直接反映了缔约国能够对外国投资者的资产或利益提供保护的范围。UNCTAD, Scope and Definition: UNCTAD Series on Issues in International Investment Agreement II, United Nation, New York and Geneva, UN Publication, 2010, p. 111; Mahnaz Malik, Recent Developments in the Definition of Investment in InternationalInvestment Agreements, 2nd Annual Forum for Developing Country Investment Negotiators, held in Marrakech, Morocco, 2008, p. 1.

〔2〕 ICSID Convention, Article 25(1).

〔3〕 单文华、[英]诺拉·伽拉赫:《和谐世界理念和中国 BIT 范本建设——一个“和谐 BIT 范本”建议案》,陈虹睿、王超恩译,载《国际经济法学刊》第 17 卷第 1 期。

轮谈判。[4] 随后，第八、九轮谈判也已经结束。据了解，中美 BIT 谈判将主要以美国在2012 年4 月公布的 BIT 新范本为基础。[5] 与2004 年范本相比，2012 年范本对投资定义条款的内容未作改动，整个定义条款的修订仅涉及“领土”定义一项。[6]

二、美国 BIT 范本中投资定义条款的制定背景

美国 BIT 既是其《友好通商航海条约》(FCN)的延续，同时也是认真借鉴欧洲既有 BIT 实践的结果。然而，美国的 FCN 并没有对“投资”进行界定。因此，BIT 范本的起草者们所面临的首要问题是要不要对“投资”这个术语进行界定。[7]

在这一点上，核心的问题是如何在“投资”这个概念的确定性和灵活性之间达到平衡。一方面，对“投资”定义的关键问题在于如何确保新的投资形式同样得到条约的保护。长久以来，投资类型不断扩张，早已远远超越了传统的投资形式，而这些新的投资形式在 BIT 缔结的早期根本无法为起草者所预见。因此，他们希望确保那些在条约起草时没能被预见但未来可能出现的投资形式能够被 BIT 的投资定义所涵盖，即要有足够的灵活性。另一方面，对投资定义的无约束的泛泛规定同样存在风险，因为仲裁庭可能对“投资”进行过窄的解释，使得显然需要保护的投资无法得到保护。最终，起草者感到一定程度上的确定性比完全的灵活性更加重要，因此，他们决定对“投资”进行定义，一方面规定“投资”必不可少的核心内容以防止仲裁庭对定义的过窄解释。

另一方面保留一定的空间以适应未来发展的需要。[8] 其结果是，美国 BIT 的投资定义模式与欧洲模式相差无几，即一方面规定一个较宽泛的概括性定义，另一方面列举一个非穷尽式的保护清单，对已经能够认定的投资形式予以明确。

自 1981 年美国推出第一个 BIT 范本以来，其投资定义条款经历了多次修订。其中，修订幅度最大的是2004 年的范本。[9] 2009 年，美国政府开始着手对该范本进行逐条审查和修订，以适应美国投资政策的需要。其间，美国各界对 2004

---

〔4〕 参见《中美重启双边投资保护协定谈判，抵制贸易保护主义》，载中国新闻网，http://fi－nance. chinanews. com/cj/2012/05－04/3866678. shtml，2012 年 10 月 23 日。

〔5〕 商务部：《美国政府公布新的“双边投资协定”示范文本》，载 http://newyork. mofcom. gov. on/aarticle/jmxw/201204/20120408087889. html，2012 年 10 月 23 日访问。

〔6〕 2012 年范本不仅明确规定了美国领土的含义，同时也对领海和所适用的海洋区域也进行了界定。

〔7〕 Kenneth J. Vandervelde, U. S. International Investment Agreements, Oxford University Press, 2009, p. 114.

〔8〕 Ibid.

〔9〕 截至目前，美国先后有 10 个 BIT 范本，其中对投资定义条款修改较多的分别是 1984 年范本、1991 年范本、1994 年范本和 2004 年范本。

年 BIT 范本的修订进行了广泛的探讨，特别是从保护公共利益的角度提出了多项建议。[10] 具体到投资定义条款方面，美国国际经济政策咨询委员会（ACIEP）在向政府提交的咨询报告中建议，投资定义应该明确，非营利性的海外收购如基于环保目的的收购，也具备“投资”的特征。[11] 此外，在讨论范本附件 B 第 2 款（关于投资征收所涉及的投资财产权利或财产利益）的规定时，委员会进一步讨论了范本的投资定义条款。有委员指出，范本的宽泛定义条款很有必要，而附件 B 第 2 款的规定有可能被解释为不包括不产生财产权利或利益的金融或其他形式的投资，如债券、期货和合同权利等。为此，他们建议删除本款，或者明确这些形式的投资也属于被保护的财产权利或利益之列。反之，有委员则表示，2004 年范本中对投资定义条款的规定过于宽泛，超过了美国宪法保护的财产范畴，建议将其缩小，以便与后者保持一致。[12] 据此，投资定义条款中对收益或利润期待和风险承担的规定应予排除，知识产权以外的无形财产以及期货、期权等金融衍生工具也不在保护之列。同时，他们还建议将国际碳补偿合同排除在“投资”定义之外，以免破坏美国在环保方面的努力。[13] 可以说，咨询委员会见仁见智，对“投资”定义相关问题作了认真深入的探讨，也提出了相应的意见和建议。然而，美国政府最终并没有采纳上述建议。结果是，2012 年新范本在投资定义条款方面未作任何修改，完全接受 2004 年范本的规定。[14]

下文将对美国 2012 年 BIT 范本中“投资”定义的具体规定及其含义予以更详细的论析。

三、2012 年范本中投资定义条款的含义解读

据美国 2012 年 BIT 范本的规定“投资”系指一个投资者直接或者间接拥有或控制的具有投资特征的各种资产，这些特征包括资本或其他资源的投入、收益或利润的期待、风险的承担等。投资的形式可能包括：

（1）企业；

---

〔10〕 2009 年 5 月，美国国务院（State Department）和贸易代表办公室（USTR）要求成立官方咨询委员会（Subcommittee），作为其国际经济政策咨询委员会（ACIEP）的下设委员会，开始对 2004 年 BIT 范本进行审查。下设委员会的成员范围十分广泛，包括国际经济政策咨询委员会的代表，来自商界、学界、劳工组织、NGO 的代表以及法律专家。

〔11〕 Report of the Subcommittee on Investment of the Advisory Committee on International Economic Policy Regarding the Model Bilateral Investment Treaty, available at http://www.state.gov/e/eb/rls/othr/2009/131098.htm, Jan. 24, 2013.

〔12〕 Ibid.

〔13〕 Ibid.

〔14〕 Model Bilateral Investment Treaty, available at http://www.state.gov/r/pa/prs/ps/2012/04/188199.htm, Jan. 24, 2013.

(2)企业中的股份、股票和其他形式的参股;

(3)债券、无担保债券、其他债务和贷款;

(4)期货、期权和其他衍生权利;

(5)交钥匙、建设、管理、生产、特许、收益分享及其他类似合同;

(6)知识产权;

(7)许可、授权、允许和其他根据国内法所授予的类似权利;

(8)其他有形或无形财产、动产或不动产,以及相关财产权利,如租赁、抵押、质押和保证。可见,美国BIT中的投资定义条款包括两个部分,即概括性规定和列举式清单。下面就从这两个方面分别解读其文本含义。

(一)概括性规定

美国2012年BIT范本的概括性规定具有三个要点,即资产、投资特征,以及"所有和控制"。以下逐一论之。

(1)资产。长期以来,美国BIT范本的投资定义都是循环定义,即以"所有形式的投资"作为对"投资"的定义。但2004年的范本却改变了这一惯常做法,首次引入欧式BIT以"资产"为基础的投资定义,不仅解决了循环定义的问题,也使其定义条款的表述与国际普遍做法相一致。

(2)投资特征。已如前述,这是美国BIT范本投资定义条款的最大特色,也是其长期以来的做法。[15] 所不同的是,从2004年范本开始,美国BIT范本开始明确提出一些具体的特征要求,包括资本或其他资源的投入、收益或利润的期待和风险的承担。有趣的是,美国范本所提出来的投资特征与国际投资条约仲裁实践特别是ICSID仲裁实践中所普遍接受的投资特征的要素(Salini test)并不完全一致。后者要求"投资"应该包括四个要素,即"一定的投入、一定的持续期间、一定的风险和对东道国经济的贡献"[16]两相比较,在"资本投入"和"风险承担"这两点上,美国BIT范本的规定与仲裁实践的态度是一致的,反映出"投资"的两个最本质的特征。然而,美国范本中的"对收益或利润的期待"在"Salini test"里面并没有出现。反过来,"Salini test"中的"一定的持续期间"和"对东道国经济的贡献"这两个要素在美国BIT范本中也没有规定。这说明二者各有侧重。值得注意的是,在具体的ICSID案件中,ICSID的管辖要求同时满足BIT与《华盛顿公约》中关于

---

〔15〕 尽管美国BIT范本直到2004年才明确规定了"投资"应该具备投资的特征以及投资特征的具体内容,但根据其定义条款一贯采取循环定义的做法,可以看出先前BIT范本普遍认为投资特征是"投资"毋庸置疑的暗含条件。

〔16〕 Salini Costruttori S. p. A. and Italstrade S. p. A. v. Kingdom of Morocco(ICSID Case No. ARB/00/4), Decision on Jurisdiction of July 23, 2001, English translations published in 42 ILM 609(2003), 6 ICSID Rep. 400(2004), para. 52.

“投资”的条件要求。这意味着,即使美国 BIT 中没有规定某项条件,要构成 ICSID 的管辖也仍需满足《华盛顿公约》对“投资”的条件要求。例如,在 Patrick Mitchell v. DR Congo 案的撤销仲裁裁决阶段,撤销专门委员会认为,美国与刚果的 BIT 除了规定“所有形式的投资”之外实际上并没有对“投资”作任何进一步的界定。[17] 同时委员会认为,ICSID 的案件已经明确表明投资包括四个特征,即资本投入、持续时间、风险和对经济发展的贡献。[18] 委员会进而指出,该 BIT 的序言中提到了“就投资待遇达成协议将能够促进缔约国间私人资本的流动和经济的发展”[19] 在判断经济发展这一要素的本质时,委员会认为对发展的贡献不必总是巨大的或成功的,而且“对经济发展的贡献”这一概念“不仅非常宽泛,而且也会因为案情而各不相同”[20] 就该案而言,原仲裁裁决已经认定了美国投资者律师事务所中的动产,包括专业知识、商誉和法律执业的权利等,不仅属于《华盛顿公约》中的“投资”,而且属于 BIT 投资定义条款项下资产清单中所列举的“投资”。[21] 然而,委员会也指出,尽管原仲裁裁决认定投资者的律师事务所曾经就美国在刚果的投资提供法律咨询服务,但是原裁决并没有进一步解释该律所如何对经济发展作出了贡献。[22] 正是基于这一点,委员会最终撤销了仲裁庭的裁决。[23]

(3)“所有和控制”。美国 BIT 范本要求投资必须是投资者“所有或控制”的资产,而大多数的欧式和中式 BIT 则采用投资者“投入”的资产的表述。美式 BIT 的效果一方面是使投资定义的规定更加明确,因为“所有或控制”在法律上显然比“投入”更加容易界定;另一方面也使 BIT 所保护的范围尽可能扩大,以涵盖直接或间接控制的资产。事实上,对“所有或控制”的规定在美国第一个 BIT 范本中就已经存在。[24] 从历史背景来看,这一规定也是美国对 Barcelona Traction 案裁决的一种回应。在该案中,国际法院认为,一个在加拿大成立但主要由比利时人所有的公司不能由比利时来提供外交保护。其依据是,根据习惯国际法,公司只受到设立地国家而不是所有者国家的保护。[25] 但美国 BIT 范本关于“所有或控制”

---

〔17〕 Patrick Mitchell v. Democratic Republic of the Congo(ICSID Case No. ARB/99/7),Decision on the Application for Annulment of the Award,February 9,2004,para. 26.

〔18〕 Ibid.,para. 27.

〔19〕 Ibid.,para. 32.

〔20〕 Ibid.,para. 33.

〔21〕 Ibid.,para. 35.

〔22〕 Ibid.,para. 40.

〔23〕 Ibid.,para. 46.

〔24〕 1983 US Model BIT,Article 1(d).

〔25〕 Barcelona Traction,Light and Power Company,Ltd.(Belgium v. Spain),ICJ Report 1970,p. 3.

的规定则表明,美国国民所有或控制的投资都属于 BIT 项下的投资,无论该投资是否由根据其他国家法律设立的公司所有或控制。

在 1983 年范本中,对“所有或控制”还作了进一步的定义,表明它包括通过子公司或分公司所实现的所有或控制,而不论子公司或分公司位于何地。[26] 据此,如果一个美国公司依据法国法成立了一家子公司,并且在 BIT 缔约另一方境内投资,那么该投资就应该受到 BIT 的保护。换句话说,直接控制或所有的投资和通过中间公司所有或控制的投资均受到保护,毫无二致。同时,美国 BIT 也不要求投资最终由美国国民或公司所有或控制。事实上,由一个或多个外国投资者所有或控制的美国公司,仍然是美国 BIT 项下受到条约保护的适格的“投资”。换句话说,BIT 项下的“所有或控制”仅仅要求投资者具备实施控制的法律能力,即使该投资者并没有在事实上对“投资”实施控制。不过,在 Loewen v. United States 案中,美国政府却成功地主张,案中的加拿大投资者仅仅是一个借壳公司,该公司成立的唯一目的是向 NAFTA 提交仲裁申请。该案中加拿大投资者完全由美国公司控制,因此不能算作独立于美国公司的公司。相应地,该项诉求事实上也是由美国投资者提出的,而不是加拿大投资者的诉求。

需要注意的是,1983 年的美国 BIT 范本并没有规定认定“所有和控制”的具体方式,因此对这一事实的判断仍然需要视个案具体情况而定。而在 1983 年范本之后,上述对“所有或控制”的进一步规定即被删除,尽管这一删除在事实上并没有对条约产生实质性的影响。“所有或控制”的含义在一些仲裁案件中得到了进一步明确。例如,在 International Thunderbird v. Mexico 案中,仲裁庭需要考察其在 NAFTA 第 1117 条项下是否有管辖权,该条款允许投资者对其“所有或控制”的投资提交仲裁申请。[27] 仲裁庭认为,如果能证明有效的或事实上的控制,则“控制”可以成立,尽管仲裁庭也认为,如果不存在法定控制,则有效控制的证明必须达到不存在任何合理怀疑的程度。在该案中,美国投资者只拥有公司的少数股份。但仲裁庭认定,投资者能够对公司决定的作出施加重要影响,而且投资者是该公司在墨西哥从事商业活动的持续的推动力量。更具体地说,仲裁庭发现,该案中的美国投资者就是被投资企业的核心管理人员,而且该投资项目最初的开支、设备的专有技术、供应商的选择以及预期回报等都是由投资者提供或决定的。因此,美国投资者有权就其“投资”依据 NAFTA 第 1117 条提出仲裁请求在 Mondev v. United States 案中,仲裁庭认为,美国 BIT 对“所有或控制”的定义是为

〔26〕 Supra note 30, Article 1(c).

〔27〕 NAFTA, Chapter 11, Article 1117.

了避免出现 Barcelona Traction 案中阻碍股东诉权的裁决结果。因此,仲裁庭指出,对 NAFTA 的解释不应该依照 Barcelona Traction 案的判决。S. D. Myers v. Canada 案中,投资者是一家名为 S. D. Myers International 的美国公司,而实际投资者则是一个独立的加拿大公司 Myers Canada。S. D. Myers International 并不拥有 Myers Canada,但这两家公司事实上却是由同一家族所有并控制的。依据条约文本,所有或控制权可以是"间接的",因此仲裁庭认为 S. D. Myers International 可以视为是在加拿大存在所有或控制投资的美国投资者。仲裁庭进而指出,公司形式的选择并不是一个决定性的因素,对"投资"的要考察其背后的经济现实,即两家公司由同一所有人控制的事实,[28] 可见,"直接或间接所有或控制"的提法为仲裁庭对"投资"作宽泛解读提供了依据。

(二)列举式清单

和大多数的 BITs 一样,美国 BIT 范本规定了一个非穷尽的列举式的"投资"所包括的利益清单。清单中的规定大量借用了欧式 BIT 文本的语言。清单的目的在于一方面规定"投资"必不可少的核心内容,另一方面以列举的方式表明这一概念的大体范畴。需要注意的是,在 1994 年以前的范本中,除了清单中有规定之外,还在概括性规定中也列举了四种类型的资产,包括股权、债务、服务合同和投资合同。而在清单中,这四种投资形式再次得到重申。[29] 上述四类资产类型在概括性规定中的列举旨在显示投资定义的广度,例如对股权和债务的列举明确表明了投资同时保护所有权和非所有权利益,以及间接投资和直接投资。对服务合同和投资合同的列举则表明,基于财产产生的权利和基于合同产生的权利都属于"投资"。概括性规定中对这四种型的规定在 1994 年范本修订时得以删除。[30]

美国 2012 年 BIT 范本的资产清单共列举了 8 种类型的资产,包括企业、股权、债权、金融衍生权利、合同权利、知识产权、依法授权权益和其他财产权益。

1. 企业

已如前述,美国 BIT 范本在清单方面的一个特点在于它明确规定了"企业"本身就是一种"投资"。不过,"企业"的概念是在 2004 年范本中才被引入的,并非从一开始就有。此前 BIT 所使用的概念是"公司"。根据范本定义,"企业"系指"根据所适用的法律所组建的任何实体,无论其是否以营利为目的,无论其是由私人或政府所有或掌控,包括公司、信托、合伙、个人独资企业、合营企业、社团或类

---

〔28〕 S. D. Myers, Inc. v. Canada, UNCITRAL(NAFTA), Partial Award, November 13, 2000, paras. 227, 229.

〔29〕 Supra note 30, Article 1(c).

〔30〕 1994 US Model BIT, Article 1(d).

似组织,以及企业的分支机构”。[31] “企业”的概念在NAFTA以及美国和智利、新加坡签订的FTA中曾使用过。[32] 较之“公司”,“企业”概念的优势在于其内涵更加广泛,而且也可以避免定义中出现公司包括“公司”这样的循环定义。此外,根据2004年以前的范本规定,公司的“分支机构”往往由于未曾独立成立,缺乏独立的公司存在形式,因此可能会被排除在条约保护的范围之外。但在2004年范本中,“公司”这一术语被修改为“企业”,而“企业”又被定义为明确包括“企业的分支机构”,因此没有独立公司存在形式的企业分支机构仍然可以算是一个“企业”,仍然在条约保护的“投资”范畴之内。更重要的是,根据2004年BIT范本的规定,缺乏公司存在形式的分支机构同时也是适格的“投资者”。该范本规定“缔约一方投资者”包括“一方的企业”,而“一方的企业”又包括“在缔约一方领域内从事商业活动的分支机构”。[33] 因此,在2004年范本项下,缺乏独立的公司存在形式的分支机构仍是母国的投资者,只要它位于母国境内并且在其中从事商业活动。该规定在2012范本中得到继承。[34]

2. 股权

这是最常见的投资资产类型之一。美国先前范本中的提法是“公司”股权,2004年范本中将其修改成了“企业”股权,包括企业的股份、股票或其他股权参与形式。实践表明,认定公司(或企业)股权构成投资几乎不存在困难。例如,在Continental Casualty v. Argentina案中,美国投资者拥有当地公司99.995%的股权,因此仲裁庭认定存在投资。[35] 又如,在Lanco v. Argentina案中,虽然美国投资者只拥有阿根廷公司的少数股份,但仲裁庭认为,阿根廷与美国BIT“并没有规定投资者在股权方面控制公司的管理或者占有多数份额,因此尽管美国投资者只拥有18.3%的股权,也是条约项下的投资者”。该案中,美国投资者正好是引发争端的特许协议的一方,因此该特许协议也被视为一项投资。[36] 相同地,在CMS Gas

---

〔31〕 *Supra* note 20“enterprise”means any entity constituted or organized under applicable law, whether or not for profit, and whether privately or governmentally owned or controlled, inclu-ding a corporation, trust, partnership, sole proprietorship, joint venture, association, or similar or-ganization; and a branch of an enterprise.

〔32〕 *Supra* note 34, Article 1139; US-Singapore FTA, Article 15.1.13; US-Chile FTA, Article 10.27.

〔33〕 *Supra* note 20“investor of a Party”means a Party or state enterprise thereof, or a national or an enterprise of a Party, that attempts to make, is making, or has made an investment in the territory of the other Party; provided, however, that a natural person who is a dual national shall be deemed to be exclusively a national of the State of his or her dominant and effective nationality; “en-terprise of a Party”means an enterprise constituted or organized under the law of a Party, and a branch located in the territory of a Party and carrying out business activities there.

〔34〕 *Supra* note 14, Article1.

〔35〕 Continental Casualty Company v. The Argentine Republic(ICSID Case No. ARB/03/9), Decisions on Jurisdiction, February 22, 2006, paras. 42, 78 – 79.

〔36〕 Lanco International Inc. v. The Argentine Republic(ICSID Case No. ARB/97/6), Preliminary Decision on Jurisdiction, December 8, 1998, § 10, 15.

Transmission v. Argentina 案中，美国投资者拥有一家阿根廷公司 29.42% 的股份，该公司从州政府取得了销售天然气的许可证。仲裁庭认为，美国投资者在公司的股份构成"投资"。投资者是否是许可证或特许协议的一方对其构成"投资"无关紧要。[37] 这一观点也被 LG & E v. Argentina 案的仲裁庭采纳。[38] 另外，在 GAMI Investments v. Mexico 案中，仲裁庭认为 14.18% 的公司股份也构成"投资"。美国投资者认为，墨西哥征收了其所有的 5 个糖厂（实质上是公司的全部资产），致使其股份一文不值。尽管仲裁庭最终否决了 GAMI 的实体性权利主张，但仲裁庭却认为，GAMI 的股份属于"投资"，因此 GAMI 有权提出股份价值受损的主张。[39] 由此可见，仲裁庭普遍认为股权属于"投资"，不论其份额大小。

3. 债权

现行范本中的债权涵盖"债券、无担保债券、其他债务和贷款"。这一规定也是 2004 年最新修订的，它和此前的范本很相似，只是增加了"贷款"。OECD 制定的多边投资协定（MAI）草案中也曾使用过"贷款"的概念。[40] 鉴于"贷款"可以是短期的，并且可以用于贸易融资，因此美国 BIT 的起草者就此增加了一个脚注。该脚注规定，"一些形式的债务，如证券、债券、远期票据往往更具有投资的特征，而其他形式的债务，如源于货物或服务贸易的立即支付便不太具有投资的特征"。[41] 这一规定是为了保证"投资"定义项下的资产具备投资的经济特征，从而排除基于普通商业交易产生的债务，如用于采购货物或服务的融资安排。在仲裁实践中，某些债权构成"投资"也得到了确认。例如，在 Link-Trading v. Moldova 案中，仲裁庭支持了美国投资者关于债务融资是"投资"的主张。[42]

4. 金融衍生权利

这是 2004 年范本新增加的投资类型，旨在保护美国在海外的金融利益。其所列举的权利包括期货、期权和其他衍生权利。对这一资产类型，仲裁实践中暂没有相关的案件。

---

〔37〕 CMS Gas Transmission Company v. The Republic of Argentina (ICSID Case No. ARB/01/8), Decision on Jurisdiction, July 17, 2003, paras. 19, 65, 68.

〔38〕 LG&E Energy Corp., LG&E Capital Corp. and LG&E International Inc. v. Argentina (ICSID Case No. ARB/02/1), Decision on Jurisdiction, April 30, 2004, para. 60.

〔39〕 GAMI Investments Inc. v. United Mexican States, UNCITRAL (NAFTA), Award, November 15, 2004, paras. 26 - 27, 33.

〔40〕 OECD, The Multilateral Agreement on Investment (Draft Consolidated Text), Chapter II: Scope and Application: Definitions, DAFFE/MAI(98)7/REV1, p. 11, April 22, 1998, at http://www1.oecd.org/daf/mai/pdf/ng/ng987r1e.pdf, Sep. 26, 2012.

〔41〕 *Supra* note 20, footnote 1.

〔42〕 Link-Trading Joint Stock Company v. Moldova, UNCITRAL (US/Moldova BIT), Award on Jurisdiction, 2001, p. 8.

5. 合同权利

这也是常见的清单列举中的投资类型之一。最近的修改也是在2004年BIT范本之中。2012年范本不再在一般意义上提到合同,而是列举了合同的具体类型包括"交钥匙、建设、管理、生产、特许、收入分享及其他类似合同"。这一规定在实质上和此前的范本并无二致,只是修改后的资产类型更加明晰。修改的目的在于排除普通的商事合同和不具备"投资特征"的合同,而只有同清单中所列举的合同类型一样具有"投资特征"的合同才能构成"投资"。实践中不少仲裁庭讨论并确认了合同权利构成"投资"。在Azurix v. Argentina案中,仲裁庭认为特许合同属于"投资"。如果一项特许合同是由当地公司取得的,那么只要外国投资者对当地公司拥有所有权或控制权,该合同就构成外国投资者的"投资"。仲裁庭指出,投资者是真正的利益攸关方,BIT中"投资"定义的目的是保护真正攸关方的利益。在该案中,美国投资者拥有阿根廷公司90%的股份,而该公司正是引发投资争端的特许协议的一方当事人。因此,尽管争端是由特许协议引发的,而美国投资者不是合同的一方当事人,但仲裁庭仍然认为该争端是由美国投资者的"投资"所引发的争端。[43] 在Lanco v. Ar-gentina案中,美国投资者Lanco是持有公司少数股份的股东,该公司有经营港口码头的特许权。在案件中,美国投资者虽然不是特许协议的合同一方,但却作为担保人在特许协议上签了字。由于投资者在特许协议下承担连带的投资义务,因此仲裁庭认为该特许协议本身也构成美国投资者的"投资"[44] 在PSEG v. Turkey案中,特许合同也被认为是"投资"。在该案中,美国投资者主张其与土耳其政府签订的建设运营褐煤发电厂的合同是"投资",但土耳其政府却认为双方之间的合同无效,并提出了管辖权异议。仲裁庭认为,双方事实上已经达成了协议,而且该协议构成"投资"。[45]

6. 知识产权

美国BIT范本关于知识产权的规定几经修订,以适应知识产权发展与保护的需要。例如,在1983年范本中,该类型被规定为"知识及工业产权",包括版权、专利、商标、商号、商业秘密、工业设计、专门技术和商誉。[46]

在2004年范本以后,该文本得到了极大的简化,取消了先前列举式的举例,

---

〔43〕 Azurix Corp. v. The Argentine Republic(ICSID Case No. ARB/01/12), Decision on Jurisdiction, December 8, 2003, paras. 62–66.

〔44〕 Supra note 45, § 10–16.

〔45〕 PSEG Global, Inc., The North American Coal Corporation, and Konya Ingin Electrik üretim ve Ticaret Limited Sirketi v. Republic of Turkey(ICSID Case No. ARB/02/5), Decision on Jurisdiction, June 4, 2004, paras. 66, 69, 77, 80, 104.

〔46〕 *Supra* note 30, Article 1(c)(iv).

而仅仅规定了"知识产权"。[47] 这和 MAI 草案的定义方式是一样的。[48]

7. 依法授权权益

过去美国的 BIT 范本将这类权益和合同权利归为一类。[49] 1994 年范本将二者分开。[50] 2004 年范本则对其进行了最新的进一步修改。2012 年范本仅规定了"许可、授权、允许和其他根据国内法所授予的类似权利"。这一条款还包括了两个脚注,即脚注②和③。脚注②规定:"一个特定形式的许可、授权、允许或类似文件(包括具有这类文件性质的特许)是否具有投资的特征取决于持有者依据该缔约方的法律所享有的权利的性质和范围等因素。那些根据国内法不产生任何权利的许可、授权、允许和类似工具不具有投资特征。为了进一步明确,前述规定不影响对任何与许可、授权、允许或类似文件相联系的资产是否具有投资特征的认定。"[51] 从表面上看来,那些依据国内法不能产生任何权利的文件似乎在任何情况下都不可能属于"投资",因此这一规定显得多余。不过,脚注②的主旨与作用在于明确并非所有的许可、授权、允许和类似文件都属于"投资"。同时,脚注②的最后一句话明确表明,许可或授权不是投资的事实并不意味着与该许可或授权相关的资产必然不属于"投资",对资产是否具备投资特征的判断要根据个案单独进行。脚注③则进一步规定,"投资"这一术语不包括司法或者行政诉讼过程中所作出的判决或命令。[52] 对此,美国 BIT 权威专家范德维尔德认为,这一规定不能完全按照字面意思去理解。BIT 实践已界定"投资"至少包括某些请求权,不能说一项请求权构成"投资",而当它经过法庭确认后反而不能被当成"投资"。因此他认为,如果一项判决或命令确认了某项法律上的利益构成"投资",则该判决和命令也应该被视为"投资"。[53] 然而在笔者看来,这里范德维尔德不一定正确,因为确认投资的判决不等于"投资"本身。因此,该规定即使按照字面含义解释,也是适当的,甚至是更合理的。

仲裁实践中,依法授权权益也得到过确认。例如,在 MCI Power v. Ecuador 案中,仲裁庭认为美国投资者主张的经营许可证(和应收账款)构成"投资"。[54] 在 Generation Ukraine v. Ukraine 案中,仲裁庭认为,尚未产生法律效力的土地分配决

---

〔47〕 *Supra* note 20.

〔48〕 *Supra* note 49.

〔49〕 See e. g. ,1984 US Model BIT, Article 1(1).

〔50〕 *Supra* note 39, Article 1(1)(a)(iii), Article 1(1)(a)(v).

〔51〕 *Supra* note 14, footnote 2.

〔52〕 Ibid. , footnote 3.

〔53〕 *Supra* note 7, p. 124.

〔54〕 M. C. I. Power Group L. C. and New Turbine, Inc. v. Republic of Ecuador(ICSID Case No. ARB/03/6), Award, July 31, 2007, para. 164.

定书、未产生可执行权利的意向书、记录了投资计划但实际并未投资的登记证书，都不构成“投资”，因为这些都没有产生法律上可执行的权利；但是，一项土地分配的命令能够给予美国投资者取得租契的权利，因此构成“投资”；此外，美国投资者的建筑许可证也属于“投资”定义下的资产类型。[55]

8. 其他财产权益

这里包括其他有形或无形财产、动产或不动产以及相关财产权益，如租赁、抵押、质押和保证。最新的修改也在2004年范本中完成。新范本主要是将过去“有形资产和无形资产”的规定修改为“动产或不动产”。这一提法原本属于大陆法系的概念，在美国对外BIT谈判中相对方有时也会提出增加这一术语的要求。MAI草案也采用了这一提法。[56] 因此，这一术语的加入使美国BIT和其他法律体系的普遍做法保持了一致，但并不意味着其定义范围有实质性的变化。一些仲裁实践也确认了有形财产和无形财产均可以构成“投资”。例如，在ADF Group v. United States案中，仲裁庭认为，投资者在美国购买的用于在美建筑项目的钢材属于在美国境内的“投资”。[57] 在MCI Power v. Ecuador案中，仲裁庭认为，应收账款（和经营许可证）是美国投资者在厄瓜多尔境内的“投资”。[58]

四、2012年范本中投资定义条款的主要特点

从上面的分析可以看出，相较欧式BIT和中国的BIT文本，[59] 美国2012年BIT范本中的“投资”定义条款有四个比较突出的特点：

第一，明确了投资必须具有投资的“特征”，并对一些特征作了列举。

从1983年第一个范本开始，美式BIT范本就要求投资必须是“投资”，而不是所有的“资产”。[60] 因此，美国在2004年以前的范本中均规定投资是“所有形式的投资”。虽然这一定义是典型的循环定义，从语言学的角度来说显属不佳。但是，它却表明美国从BIT起草之初就坚持认为投资就是“投资”，不包括不属于投资的“资产”。与将投资定义为“所有形式的资产”的欧式和中式投资定义条款相比，美国BIT的投资定义条款明确排除了不具有投资属性的资产，其范围明显较

---

〔55〕 Generation Ukraine, Inc. v. Ukraine (ICSID Case No. ARB/00/9), Award, September 16, 2003, para. 18. 22.

〔56〕 *Supra* note 49.

〔57〕 ADF Group Inc. v. United States of America (ICSID Case No. ARB (AF)/00/1), Award, January 9, 2003, paras. 152, 154.

〔58〕 Supra note 63.

〔59〕 参见单文华、[英]诺拉·伽拉赫：《和谐世界理念和中国BIT范本建议——一个“和谐BIT范本”建议案》，陈虹睿、王起恩译，载《国际经济法学刊》第17卷第1期。See 2003 China Model BIT, Article 1.

〔60〕 *Supra* note 30, Article 1(c).

窄。这一规定在实质上也构成美式 BIT 投资定义条款的最大特征。

第二,投资定义条款的清单以“企业”为基础,而且规定比较详细,共有八项之多。

欧式和中式 BIT 中的投资定义条款均没有将“企业”直接规定为投资的一种,其清单仅仅是列举具体的“资产”类型,大多为五项,不包括“企业”和期货等衍生权利,对其他类型的组成规定也有所不同。[61]

第三,美国 BIT 范本没有规定“根据东道国法律”的要求。在中式 BIT 和不少欧式 BIT 中,投资定义条款均要求资产是“根据东道国法律法规”投入的。[62] 但美国 BIT 范本的投资定义条款则从一开始就排除了这一规定,体现出强烈的“非国内化”的政策取向。对此,范德维尔德认为,美国的做法是故意为之。因为他们认为外国投资法律法规可能是复杂且模糊的,而东道国可能以对本国法律的微小违反作为借口而拒绝对投资提供条约保护。[63] 因此,在美国 BIT 范本项下,只要投资在条约涵盖范围之内,就应该受到条约的保护,而无论其是否是依据东道国法律建立的,甚至无论其是否是依据东道国法律经营的。美国实践的这一做法与其 BIT 计划的宗旨是一脉相承的。事实上,美国积极倡导 BIT 实践不仅仅是为了保护投资,更是为了修复关于投资的国际法。质言之,就是试图通过一系列体现其所认同的所谓“习惯国际法”标准的国际条约,构筑国际法的新实践,以抵制和消解“国际经济新秩序”中确立的“国内化”的投资规范,进而恢复此前所谓的传统国际法规范。

第四,美国 BIT 范本将“投资”与“涵盖投资”并列规定在定义条款中,即将投资的一般定义与条约所保护的缔约一方投资者的投资区分开来,显得更加严谨。[64] 在欧式 BIT 和我国的 BIT 中,“投资”的定义均仅仅涵盖“缔约一方的投资”,其内涵显然与国民待遇条款中提及的本国国民的“投资”是不一致的。

---

〔61〕 See e. g. , BLEU-Sudan BIT, Article 1(2); Netherlands-Ethiopia BIT, Article 1(a); Germany-Timor-Leste BIT, Article 1(1); Switzerland-Algeria BIT, Article 1(2); Italy-Nicaragua BIT, Article 1(1).

〔62〕 See e. g. , Cambodia-Vietnam BIT, Article 1(1); Lebanon-Chile BIT, Article 1(2); Indonesia-Algeria BIT, Article 1(1); Italy-Nicaragua BIT, Article 1(1); Finland-Armenia BIT, Ar-ticle 1(1); Sweden-Kazakhstan BIT, Article 1(1); Australia-India BIT, Article 1(c); Chile-In-donesia BIT, Article2.

〔63〕 *Supra* note 7, p. 118.

〔64〕 *Supra* note 14 “covered investment” means, with respect to a Party, an investment in its territory of an investor of the other Party in existence as of the date of entry into force of this Treaty or established, acquired, or expanded thereafter. 需要注意的是,1994 年范本第 1 条第 5 款中也规定了“涵盖投资”的定义。

五、中国的对策

作为世界上最为重要的两个经济大国，中美之间的跨国直接投资活动十分活跃。[65] 随着中国"走出去"战略的不断推进实施，中国对外直接投资也迅猛发展。[66] 在这样的背景下，吸引高质量的海外投资，同时保护本国投资者在外国的投资，是中美两国进行投资协定谈判的共同目标和利益取向。在 BIT 实践方面，中国目前已经缔结了 130 多个 BIT，建立了仅次于德国的世界第二大 BIT 网络，而美国也已经签订了 48 个 BIT。[67] 在此次重启的中美 BIT 谈判中，双方约定以美国 2012 年新范本作为主要基础。本部分拟在中美 BIT 范本[68] 比较的基础上，提出我们应对美国基于 2012 年 BIT 范本中的投资定义条款谈判的相应对策。

（一）中美 BIT 范本投资定义条款的比较

比较中美现行投资条约范本，可以发现有同有异。其中，相同点主要有二：一是两个范本均采用了以资产为基础的宽泛的投资定义；二是两者均采用了概括性规定加列举式清单的定义模式。但比较而言，其不同之处更加明显。

在概括性规定方面，首先，美国范本有"投资特征"的限制而中国范本没有；其次，中国范本有"符合东道国法律要求"的条件而美国范本没有；再次，美国范本采用的是较宽泛的"直接或间接所有或控制"的措辞而中国范本采用的是"投入"的措辞；最后，美国范本采取的是"投资"与"涵盖投资"定义并存的规定方式，而中国范本中仅有"投资"的定义。在列举式清单方面，首先，美国范本包括"企业"而我国范本没有明确提及；其次，美国范本包括"期货、期权和其他衍生权利"而我国范本没有提及；最后，美国范本其他清单资产的规定详略及其排列组合与我国范本有所不同，例如对知识产权的规定美国范本的表述更加宽泛，而对合同权利的规定中国范本的表述更为宽泛。总体来说，列举式清单部分的技术性差异

---

〔65〕 根据美国贸易代表办公室公布的统计数据显示，2010 年美国对华直接投资达到 605 亿美元，比 2009 年增加 21.4%，中国对美直接投资达到 32 亿美元，比 2009 年增加 171.6%，参见 http://www.ustr.gov/countries-regions/china，2012 年 10 月 23 日。

〔66〕 根据《2011 年度中国对外直接投资统计公报》显示，"2011 年，中国对外接直投资实现了自 2003 年权威发布年度数据以来连续十年的增长，达到 746.5 亿美元，同比增长 8.5%，再次刷新年度投资流量纪录。20022011 年，中国对外直接投资年均增长速度为 44.6%"。参见商务部、国家统计局、国家外汇管理局编：《2011 年度中国对外直接投资统计公报》，中国统计出版社 2012 年版，第 56 页。

〔67〕 其中包括已签订但未批准的 7 个 BIT，参见 http://tcc.export.gov/Trade_Agreements/Bilateral_Investment_Treaties/index.asp，2012 年 10 月 24 日访问。

〔68〕 我国除 1984 年范本之外没有其他正式的 BIT 范本。BIT 谈判工作大多以先前缔结的条约作为工作文本。目前的基本 BIT 谈判工作文本是 1997 年以后确立的第三代文本。故本部分的比较探讨以此第三代工作文本为基础展开。参见单文华、[英]诺拉·伽拉赫：《和谐世界理念和中国 BIT 范本建议——一个"和谐 BIT 范本"建议案》，陈虹睿、王起恩译，载《国际经济法学刊》第 17 卷第 1 期。关于该文本英文版，详见 Norah Gallagher, Wenhua Shan, Chinese Investment Treaties: Policies and Practice, Oxford University Press, 2009, Appendix IV, pp. 433 – 438.

较大,实质性的区别并不明显。

（二）对美国 BIT 投资定义条款谈判的对策建议

基于上述对比,笔者提出以下对策建议,作为对美国范本投资定义条款可接受性的探讨。

1. 概括性规定方面

（1）关于投资特征。笔者认为,这是一条中性条款,是对“投资”宽泛定义的必要和有效的限制,不仅可以接受,而且应该明确。不过,对于投资特征的具体内容,笔者认为应该有所取舍,没必要照单全收。具体来说,美国范本中的“资本投入”和“风险承担”两个要素体现了“投资”的两个最本质的特征,应予保留。“收益或利润的期待”虽然对绝大多数投资适用,但是排除了非营利性的投资项目,不利于我国对某些对外投资项目的保护。同时,这一要求事实上也与美国 BIT 关于“企业”涵盖非营利企业的规定自相矛盾。因此,建议删去。另外,“Salini test”中的另外两项特征,即“一定的时期”和“对东道国经济发展的贡献”也可以考虑接受。其中,第一点“一定的时期”符合投资的本质属性,不妨保留。第二点“对东道国经济发展的贡献”虽然本身并不是“投资”的题中之义,而更多的是出于平衡投资者与东道国利益的需要,但考虑到目前在中美之间中国主要是投资接受国的现状,似乎也以接受为宜。

（2）关于“符合东道国法律”。笔者认为,目前还是保留为宜。主要理由是两方面。一方面,对于外来投资,包括美国投资,我国目前实行严格的“逐项审批”制。因此,取消对“符合东道国法律”要求的规定可能对我国的外资审批权构成障碍,不利于国家对外来投资的监管。另一方面,保留“符合东道国法律”要求的规定也有利于对我国对外投资的保护,符合 BIT 促进和保护投资的要求,在适用 BIT 保护时更为妥当。同时,我们应该鼓励“走出去”的企业多了解和研究外国法律,并在遵守外国法律的基础上投资兴业。只有这样,企业才可能得到可持续发展。此外,虽然这一条件可以说是 BIT 的暗含条件,但是有条约的明确规定显然还是更加明确有力。

（3）关于“直接或间接所有或控制”。笔者认为,这一规定可以接受,但需要同时设置“安全阀”以排除没有实质关联的投资。在美国条约中,这个安全阀就是“拒绝利益”条款。[69]

2. 列举式清单方面关于列举式清单,笔者有如下两项建议:

（1）关于“企业”。一方面,笔者认为这里以“法律实体”的概念来取代“企

---

〔69〕 *Supra* note 14, Article 17: Denial of Benefits.

业”的概念更为妥当。因为前者不仅含义广泛，可以很好地涵盖这些经济组织形式，而且它不是一个经常得到各国法律界定的概念，能更有效地避免各国既有立法定义所导致的概念混淆和解释分歧。[70] 另一方面，就具体实体形式的列举而言，本条规定的企业形式与我国的企业形式基本对应。而且这里的企业形式列表仅仅是列举式的，无需穷尽，因此基本可以接受。不过，考虑到我国有国有企业利益需要保护，可以考虑在列表正文或附加一个脚注特别说明这里被保护的企业包括“国有企业”，或者说包括“公有和私有企业”。需要指出的是，虽然美国 BIT 范本中的“企业”定义已经涵盖了“由私人或政府所有或控制”的企业，但笔者认为在“投资”定义中明确规定“国有企业”能有力加强对这些企业的保护。

(2)关于“债权”。笔者认为，美国范本的表述总体属于中性，可以接受，但出于保护我国重大经济利益的需要，建议在这里明确将对政府国债的投资，包括一国主权财富基金对外国国债的投资涵盖在条约的保护范围之内。由于我国国有企业的对外投资和国债投资是我国对外投资的重要形式和主要组成部分，笔者认为，在投资定义条款中明确对二者的保护具有重大意义。即使不能成功纳入，这两点至少也可以成为我们对美谈判的重要筹码，值得引起重视。

从总体上看，笔者认为，对美国 2012 年 BIT 范本中的投资定义条款的可接受性分析，需要从利益和制度价值多个层面来综合考虑。我国必须立足国际投资领域双重角色的定位，在吸引外资和对外投资两方面找到利益保障的平衡点，一方面要避免不适当地限制我国对外资的管理权限，维护国家外资管理权的实现，另一方面也要确保我国对外投资得到有效保护和适当促进。与此同时，鉴于中美两国在国际投资领域的重要地位，中美 BIT 势必会在国际投资立法中产生重要影响，因此我国更应该以此为契机，彰显我国对国际投资条约的政策与价值取向，为争取未来多边国际投资立法的话语权奠定基础。

---

〔70〕 Norah Gallagher, Wenhua Shan, *supra* note 77, paras. 9.22 – 31.

和谐世界理念和中国 BIT 范本建设：一个“和谐 BIT 范本”建议案*

中国国际投资条约实践和理论目前面临着前所未有的挑战。这种挑战主要表现在三个方面。首先，这种挑战来源于目前正在进行的中美双边投资条约(811)谈判。鉴于中美在世界经济政治体系中的领导地位，中美 BIT 谈判不仅受到了国内学术界的高度重视，也引起了国际投资法学界的高度关注。将中美 BIT 谈判称为 BIT 的“世纪谈判”，或不为过。从技术层面上看，我国过去长期以来实践的是欧洲式的，即“简式”BIT 模式，与内容纷繁的美式的 BIT 模式相去甚远。因此，中美谈判意味着我们要面对许多新问题、新情况，需要理论上与实践中的新思路和新对策。这无疑是一大严峻挑战。其次，这种挑战源自我国对外投资快速发展这一新现实。我国在近几年对外投资飞速发展，在最近国际金融危机导致世界投资总体普遍下降的国际大形势下，尤其令人瞩目，也引起了相当的国际关注。特别是，我国的对外投资大都发生在国内法制不太完备、风险较高的国家和地区，特别需要国际法律保护。这一新发展使得我国在国际投资中的角色定位发生了重大改变：由一个主要投资输入国变成一个兼具投资输入和输出国双重身份的国家。相应地，我们的投资条约政策也需要进行调整，以适应这一重大变化。这是第二重严峻挑战。最后，近年来，世界许多国家都在反思国际投资条约政策，不断修订其投资条约范本。以 2004 年美国 BIT 范本和 2004 加拿大 BIT 范本为代表的

---

* 本文发表在《国际经济法学刊》2010 年第 17 卷第 1 期，作者单文华、[英]诺拉 · 伽拉赫，译者陈虹睿、王朝恩。

本文是在笔者合作撰写的 Chinese Investment Treaties: Policies and Practice(Oxford university Press,2009，以下简称 Chinese Investment Treaties)专著的最后一章和书后所附的我们起草的中国 BIT 新范本的基础上写成的。本文后附中国 BIT 范本，该范本也载于 Chinese Investment Treaties 一书中。

新一代 BIT 已经出现并颇具特色。[1] 全球国际投资条约理论和实践也面临着调整和转型。在这一国际背景之下,如何学习借鉴其他国家的相关理论和实践成果,并对国际技资条约理论与实践的发展作出贡献,构成了我国投资条约理论与实践界所面临的第三大挑战。

挑战往往孕育着机遇。上述严峻挑战同时也为我国国际投资条约理论与实践的加速发展提供了极好的机遇。在全面深入认识我国已有条约的基础上,结合我国对外投资发展和中美谈判和国际转向的实际,深入反思我国的条约政策,明确其未来发展路向,此其时也!这种政策的反思与明确将不仅对我国的对外投资条约实践和理论研究具有重要的指导意义,随着中国国际经济地位的快速提升,它对世界国际投资条约理论与实践的发展的影响力也将日益彰显。[2]

一国的 BIT 范本往往是其投资条约政策的最重要的国际展示。BIT 范本兼具规范性和宣示性,但其宣示性的效果往往大于规范性的意义,因为决定性的规则最终体现在真实条约的具体条款之中,而这些条款则取决于具体的谈判过程。世界主要资本输出国都经历三次大的修订。目前采用的文本是2004 年修订的,但对它的再次修订已正在进行之中。长期以来,我国政府为了吸引外资,十分重视 BIT 的缔约工作。到目前为止,已经签订了近 130 个 BIT,是世界上签订 BIT 最多的国家之一。但相对这一积极的实践而言,我们对 BIT 范本的制定工作,似乎显得重视不够、投入不足。据了解,到目前为止,我国正式制定的 BIT 范本只有一个 1984 年的范本。这个范本以欧洲早期的 BIT 范本和 20 世纪 80 年代我国的实际情况为依据,对我国早期的 BIT 缔约工作发挥了重要的指导作用。此后,我国的 BIT 谈判多以此前缔结的 BIT 作为工作基础,或工作文本,对正式的范本,则未能及时更新。这种做法,能够有效应对缔约实践的需要。但由于它以与个别国家的个案谈判为主要依归,存在相对性和局部性,因此,全局性、主体性和主动性相对欠缺。

面对上述新形势,商务部目前正在酝酿拟定新的 BIT 范本,这无疑是大势所趋、人心所向,令人振奋。为响应这一号召,笔者合作起草了一个我们认为适合我国新时代需要的 BIT 范本,附在我们新近由英国牛津出版社出版的一本专著后面(附件五),并且在最后一章(第九章)对其作了简要评述。本文在扼要地综合评

[1] 这类新 BIT 表现出四个主要特征,它们大多具有缩减实体义务或强化实施投资者—东道国争端解决机制的效果。具体参见 UNCTAD, *Recent Development 13 in International Investment Agreemen*13, UNCTAD/WEB/ITE/IIT/2005/1, IIA Monitor No. 2 (2005), pp. 4 - 6, available at http://www. unctad. Org/Templates/Down1oad. asp? docid = 6294&lang = 1&intItemID = 3784, 2009 年 10 月 10 日访问。

[2] 事实上,中国在最近签署的条约中所表现出来的自由主义倾向已经导致一些学者的论和批评。有人认为这些条约的内容构成了对国家主权的诸多限制。例见陈安主编:《国际投资发得新发展与中国两边国际条约的新实践》,复旦大学出版社 2007 年版。

价中国 BIT 的条约实践之后，着重对我们起草的范本的总体考虑和具体条文（在对照我国现行的基本 BIT 谈判工作文本，即 2003 年的第三代文本[3]的基础上）逐条作简要评析，尝试提出一个能够比较妥善平衡东道国和投资者权益从而有利于各国和谐共处、持续发展的“和谐 BIT 范本”，期能为我国 BIT 政策研讨和范本建设抛砖引玉。

一、中国现有国际投资条约简评

中国是世界上缔结国际投资条约最活跃的国家之一。自 1982 年与瑞典缔结第二个双边投资协定以来，中国已与世界上近 130 个国家缔结了 BIT。事实上，中国有着仅次于德国的庞大 BIT 网络。随着与美国和加拿大谈判的进行，中国的 BIT 网络有望变得涵盖范围更为全面，而且其在发展中国对外投资关系中所起的作用也将更显突出。

长期以来，中国虽然积极缔结 BIT，但一直对一个具有全面执行力的外资国际法保护制度持保留态度。[4] 但自 20 世纪 90 年代末期开始，情况有了重大变化。自那时起中国缔结了一批新一代 BIT，即我们所称的“第三代 BIT”。在这些 BIT 中，中国突破了其长期坚持的关于给外资以实质性的国民待遇和全面的投资者—东道国争端解决方案的保留。2001 年同塞浦路斯和荷兰签订的 BIT 以及 2003 年同德国签订的 BIT 是这一变化的突出标志。尽管还留有部分限制，这些条约“在主要方面都与由全世界约 2500 个 BIT 的标准条约实践”并无二致。[5]

在新一代 BIT 中，中国作出了两个主要改变。一方面，增加了投资者 - 东道国争端的国际仲裁解决机制。现在中国允许投资者在满足 3 个月的当地行政复议程序的限制之后可以将任何争端直接提交仲裁，而不仅仅是有关赔偿数额的争端。另一方面，除了“祖父条款”限制之外，中国给予投资者标准的国民待遇。中国之所以在新一代的 BIT 中增加这些保障，可能主要是出于保护其海外投资的需要。[6]

---

〔3〕 对中国 BIT 版本的划分参见 Norah Gallagher &Wenhua Shan, *Chinese Investment Trealies: Policies and Practice*, Oxford University Press, 2009, paras. 1.65 - 1.77.

〔4〕 尽管中国在 20 世纪 80 年代和 90 年代都缔结过双边投资条约（中国的第一个双边投资条约是 1982 年同瑞典签订的），但这些老一代 BIT 没有建立确保主要条款可执行性的机制。

〔5〕 S. W. Schill, Tearing Down the Great Wall: The New Generation In vestment treaties of the People's Republic of China, *Cardozo J. of lnt'l & Comp* Law, Vol. 15, 2007, pp. 73, 76.

〔6〕 中国正在逐渐成为世界上最大的资本输出国之一，因此其利益需求很可能会转向更高层次的投资保护。26 年中国在非洲下撒哈拉地区的投资额为 117 亿美元，主要投资于安哥拉、乍得、尼日利亚和苏丹的石油生产和出口业。See The Lawyer Special Report, August 6, 2007, p. 18. 如此大量的投资不可避免会带来争端的发生，ICSID 已收到第一起由中国投资者提起的仲裁案件：Tza Yap Shum v. Peru, ICSID Case No. ARB/07/6.

在其他实体性权利方面，诸如对直接和间接征收的保护、公正与公平待遇、充分的保护与安全、利润兑换与汇出自由等方面，新一代 BIT 没有明显变化。不过，全面的投资者—东道国争端解决机制的引入，立刻使得这些权利变成了可兑现、可执行的现实权利。

通过全面详细地考察中国的 BIT，可以发现：国际投资条约领域的快速发展与变化在中国也同样有所反映。这一点从 20 世纪 90 年代中国缔结的 BIT 的类型和数量即可看出。尽管事实上所有的 BITs 都包含大致相同的事项，但每个条约又各有其特点。认为所有中国（或者说任何一个国家）的 BIT 是整齐划一的看法是不正确的。要想探索任何条约约文的真谛，审视各条约约文在遣词造句、定义等上的细微差别永远是很有必要的。

显然，中国现有 BIT 中关于最惠国待遇的规定会对未来的投资者—东道国仲裁产生非常重要的影响。投资者可以通过这一机制得以利用新的第三代 BIT 中的更有利的争端解决条款。如果基础条约只允许有限的国际仲裁，比如说只允许就征收赔偿数额进行仲裁，而仲裁庭准许投资者利用基础条约中的最惠国待遇条款，那么投资者将有可能将整个投资争端提交仲裁，而无需首先将实体性争端交由国内法院判决。

目前，几乎所有的中国 BIT 都要求在发动仲裁程序前用尽“争端缔约方法律和法规所规定的国内行政复议程序”。[7] 有的 BIT 还规定了 3 个月或 90 天的最长时间限制。当然，有的 BIT 规定的时间要长一些，如 2008 年签订的中国—墨西哥 BIT 要求的是 4 个月；同时有些 BIT 则没有明确时间限制。中国—伊朗 BIT 没有明确规定将“用尽当地救济”作为国际仲裁的先决条件：该条约第 12 条第 2 款的规定允许当事方“根据其相关的法律和规定”将争端提交一个三人仲裁庭。在此情形下，投资者有可能通过援引最惠国待遇条款，绕过了基础条约中“当地救济”要求，这样的结果已经在某些案件中得到肯定。

总体而论，现有的中国投资条约属于“投资保护”型，因为它们重在保护已为东道国接受的投资，而在“市场准入”方面并不能创造更多的机会。如果希望把 BIT 当作市场准入的工具，则有必要重新考虑这种条约立法方式。正如美国和加拿大那样，把国民待遇和最惠国待遇义务延伸至企业准入前的阶段，可以实现 BIT 作为市场准入工具的作用。为此，中国不妨采用谨慎的积极列举清单的方

---

〔7〕《中国—墨西哥双边投资协定》附件三（关于第 13 条第 5 款之附件）。其他所有新一代 BIT 或在争端解决条款中或在条约议定书中都规定有类似但书。

式,也即可以指明向外资开放的产业领域。[8]

这方面最值得关注的是中美 BIT 谈判。2008 年 6 月 18 日正式启动的这一谈判进程,是在“中美两国政府经过 17 个月的试探性磋商”[9]后的结果。如果未来中美 BIT 中规定了美国强烈希望的“市场准入”内容的话,其他投资者将可望通过引用中国现有各投资条约中的最惠国待遇条款而从中受益。

另一方面,我们认为中国也到了该更新其投资条约范本的时候了。事实上,中国有关部门已着手考虑起草一部新的投资条约范本。以下章节是我们在这方面的一些初步考虑。

二、新 BIT 范本的总体考虑

(一)指导思想

如前所论,中国 BIT 新范本是在面临着三大挑战的大背景下的一次重要的国际投资法理论与实践活动。在这三大背景中,最突出的背景是我国在国际投资活动中角色变迁这一重大事实。同时,国际投资法世界潮流的转向和中美 BIT 谈判也无疑是重要的影响因素。因此,我们起草 BIT 新范本,首先要立足于中国作为重要投资接受国和来源国这一双重身份。从功利主义或实用主义的角度来看,也就是我们的 BIT 范本要能同时胜任看似矛盾的双重使命,或者通俗地说,要能够指导中国打赢关于 BIT 的两场战争:一方面,要能够应对来自发达资本输出国的高度自由化要求,适当保护对外来投资的管理权力;另一方面,又要能够适应我国对外投资的时代需要,为我国企业在海外开拓、创业和经营提供有力的法律支持。表面看来,二者的矛盾是明显的:前者要求我们的 BIT 范本以东道国权益为出发点和归宿,因此应该是保守的、“防御性”的;后者则要求范本能以投资者权益作为出发点和归宿,因此应该是积极地、“进攻性”的。也就是说,从纯功利主义的角度我们无法制定一个能够胜任这双重使命的 BIT 范本。

然而,如果我们跳出纯功利主义的桎梏,而从中国领导人新近提出的“和谐世

---

[8] 如果一国给予他国此类待遇,第三国可以依据各自条约中的最惠国待遇条款要求将此类待遇适用于本国投资者。鉴于中国签订了大量的双边投资条约,第三国由此要求类似待遇的数量会是非常巨大的,所以中国可能不愿采取这种处理方式。

[9] 参见美国贸易代表办公室的新闻通告,载 http://www. uslr. Gov/assels/Document_Library/Fact-Sheets2008/asset-upload - _file993 - 14943. pdf,2008 年 6 月 30 日访问。前期谈判困在国民待遇等问题上存在分歧而未能达成双边投资协议。有关以前中美 BIT 谈判的分析,参见 T. A. Sleinert, If The BIT Fils: The Proposed Bilaleral Investment Treaty between the United States and the People's Republic of China, *Journal of Chinese Law*, Vol. 2, Fall 1988。

界”[10]的理念的角度去考察 BIT 范本建设，就会发现：实现这双重使命的统一不仅是完全可能的，而且是很自然的。

“和谐世界”的理念是在 2005 年 9 月举行的纪念联合国成立 60 周年全球峰会上，由胡锦涛主席在题为“努力建设持久和平、共同繁荣的和谐世界”的演讲中首次提出的。此后，中国政府和领导人在多种场合对构建和谐世界的目标、原则和实现路径等进行了提炼总结，自此形成了比较完整的构建和谐世界的理论。[11]自此，和谐世界理念已成为中国政府处理国际关系的核心理念。

让世界更加“和谐”的思想，首先是一种美好的政治愿景，代表了“人类实现普遍和平、共同发展的理想”。作为各人类文明所共同追求的一种价值诉求，“和谐”思想具有普世性。以和谐为出发点，应该成为处理国际关系的基本指导准则。但“和谐世界”理念不仅仅是一种政治愿景，而且也是对发展对外关系的指导原则的深刻概括，具有更加丰富的内涵。“推动建设和谐世界……要致力于同各国相互尊重、扩大共识、和谐相处，尊重各国人民自主选择社会制度和发展道路的权利，坚持各国平等参与国际事务，促道国际关系民主化；致力于同各国深化合作、共同发展、互利共赢，推动共享经济全球化和科技进步的成果，促进世界普遍繁荣；致力于促进不同文明加强交流、增进了解、相互促进，倡导世界多样性，推动人类文明发展进步；致力于同各国加深互信、加强对话、增强合作，共同应对人类面临的各种全球性问题，促进和平解决国际争端，维护世界和地区安全稳定。”[12]

由此可见，“和谐世界”理念并不是无视各国的利益冲突和文化差异，而是强调在相互尊重对方利益诉求和文化多样性的基础上，求同存异，寻求共识，实现共赢。“和谐世界”理念也不排斥对功利的追求，自然更不反对发展本身。但是，她强调一国及其国民对其利益和发展的追求应该与他国或其国民的利益和发展诉求互相协调，互相促进，而不是互相对立，更不是“以邻为整”，互相破坏。“和谐世界”理念在强调“推动共享经济全球化和科技进步的成果，促进世界普遍繁荣”的同时，还注重加强各国间的合作，以共同应对发展过程中所产生的环境恶化、能源安全等全球性问题。总之，以“和谐世界”理念为指导，有助于实现和平与发展问题的解决，有助于公正合理的国际新秩序的实现。

就国际投资领域而言，外国投资既有促进经济繁荣的积极效果，也有着投资

---

〔10〕 在 2005 年 9 月的纪念联合国成立 60 周年全球峰会上，胡锦涛主席在演讲中首次提出这一理念。关于该理念的权威解读可参见王逸舟：《和谐世界：一个重大的国际倡议》，载《人民日报》（海外版）2005 年 9 月 24 日。

〔11〕 有关和谐世界理念的发展脉络可参见岳晓勇：《对推动建设和谐世界理论的初步认识》，载《国际问题研究》2007 年第 4 期。

〔12〕 《中央外事工作会议在京举行》，载《人民日报》2006 年 8 月 24 日，第 1 版。

本性所决定的偏重经济利益、忽略社会影响的负面效果。外国投资者、投资者母国和东道国之间在对待投资的态度和利益诉求上,既有重合、交会的一面,也有着分歧、矛盾的一面。因此如何协调、实现三者之间的利益和权利平衡,是我们设计BIT 范本时所必须予以权衡考虑的根本问题。对此,我们认为,就不能单从利益博弈的角度来考虑,而应当以强调合作共赢的"和谐世界"理念为指导,使得我们的新 BIT 范本能够有利于促进世界的和谐发展。具体来说,"和谐世界"理念要求我们处理好两对关系:一是东道国与投资者的关系,实现二者权利和利益的平衡;二是要处理好投资活动与当地自然和社会条件之间的关系,使前者有助于后者的持续发展。简言之,就是要坚持后文所论的"平衡原则"和"绿色主义"。做到了这两点,就可以说我们的 BIT 范本站到了国际技资关系的"道德高地",不仅可以突破功利主义下 BIT 范本双重角色冲突的困扰,还可以向世界昭示弘扬我国的"和谐世界"理念,在当前世界 BIT 前路晦暗不明的情况下,不啻为一盏明灯,或可引领世界走出 BIT 缔约与仲裁实践中的种种误区。

(二)基本原则

关于中国的新 BIT 范本,我们认为要坚持三个原则。第一,应该坚持单一范本原则而不是多重范本原则,即坚持"单一性"。有一种观点认为,中国应采用至少两种不同的 BIT 范本。一个用于和发达的资本输出国的 BIT 谈判,另一个用于同苏丹、安哥拉等中国已有或将有重大投资的发展中国家的 BIT 谈判。前者应坚持中国传统坚持的比较保守的"防御性"立场以保护中国的管理境内外资的主权权力,后者则应采用更自由或曰"进攻性"的立场以保护和促进中国在当地的投资。这种提法似乎很有吸引力但却是行不通的。因为,首先,这种做法与世界各国通常的条约实践不符。通常一个国家制定 BIT 范本是希望以此为基础与所有其他国家进行谈判。尽管根据缔约相对方的特定需要,具体条约中可以对范本进行修改,但基本的底线应与标准文本相同,至少在其公布的 BIT 范本中,似乎还没有一个国家采用过这种二元/多元范本的进路。此外,这种二元/多元范本进路也违反了根植于绝大多数 BIT 中的非歧视原则和最惠国待遇原则。事实上,任何一个 BIT 中的标准最惠国待遇条款都可以使"防御性"BIT 中的种种限制变得形同虚设,因为通过最惠国待遇条款可以将别的"进攻性"BIT 中的自由主义条款引入其中。当然,在立法技术上也存在这种可能性,即可以把这些自由主义的 BIT 作为例外,排除在保守主义的 BIT 的最惠国待遇条款的适用范围之外。[13] 不过,这

---

〔13〕 此类最惠国待遇条款例外的例子参见 2008 年挪威 BIT 范本的附件二,以及可持续发展国际研究所(IISD):《基于可持续发展的投资协定范本》,载 www. iisd. org/pdf/2005/investment_model_int_agreement. pdf,2009 年 10 月 14 日访问。

种做法无疑会显得十分奇怪,而且也很可能会遭到条约相对方的拒绝。

第二,新范本应该致力于平衡东道国与外国投资者之间的权利义务关系,即要坚持“平衡原则”。尽管BIT是国家间的条约,但它们主要处理的是东道国与外国投资者之间的关系,这一点是毋庸置疑的。长期以来,资本输出国把BIT作为保护其海外投资的手段,而根本不考虑东道国管理外国投资的权利。始料未及的是,依据《北美自由贸易协定》提起的针对美、加等资本输出国的国际仲裁案,却把这些传统的资本输出国推到了被诉方的地位。〔14〕通过这些案件,美、加等发达资本输出国认识到,除了外国投资者的权利和利益需要保护之外,〔15〕东道国的管理权也同样需要加以保护。〔16〕为此,它们修改了各自的BIT范本以适应这种国家需要。美国还将进一步修订以更充分地反映这种需要。当前中国作为重要的资本输入者的同时,正在迅速崛起为重要的国际资本输出者,其在国际投资领域内的角色越来越接近发达的资本输出国。同大多数资本输出国一样,中国的双重角色要求其BIT范本兼顾两种需求,即维护国家对在华外国投资的管理权的需要和保护本国海外投资者权利的需要。尽管在真正谈判过程中,具体条约条款可以调整以适应具体情况需要,但作为兼具规范性和宣示性作用的BIT范本,有必要一开始就保持这种权利义务的总体平衡。

第三,与“平衡”原则相适应,新范本应强化投资者的社会责任,努力使投资与经济繁荣同社会发展与环境保护相协调一致,即坚持“持续发展原则”或“绿色主义”。为此,正如在下文所能看到的,我们的新BIT范本不仅包括保护投资者权益和保障东道国管理投资权利的条款,也包括强化外国投资者责任的条款。〔17〕我们认为,一个BIT范本只有当它能够保证东道国与投资者权利义务平衡,并保证投资活动与当地社会环境协调发展,才可以成为一个先进的BIT范本,一个符合时代要求并可能引领世界潮流的BIT范本。因此,我们的“和谐BIT范本”也可以说是一种“绿色BIT范本”。

(三)总体架构

新范本共分五节。第一节包括两个条款,分别界定基本术语和条约适用范围;第二节规定了给予外国投资的待遇标准,包括一般性标准和更具体的标准;第

---

〔14〕 对发达国家立场调整的分析,特别是对美国和加拿大的分析,参见 W. Shan,“From North-South Divide to private-public Debate: Revival of the Calvo Doctrine and the Changing Landscape of International Investment Law”, Northwestern Journal of International Law and Business, Vol. 27(3), 2007. pp. 631 – 64。

〔15〕 Ibid.

〔16〕 Ibid.

〔17〕 这种平衡立场已为2008年挪威BIT范本和可持续发展国际研究所《IISDH基于可持续发展的投资协定范本》所采用。

三、四节规定了投资争端解决机制，分别针对的是投资者一东道国争端和国家间争端；第五节作为最后一节，规定的是条约的最后条款，如条约的生效、有效期和终止等事项。至于范本的具体内容，则可见下文。

三、新 BIT 范本的条文评述

从新范本文本中可以看出，相对于现行的我国的第三代 BIT 文本（“现行文本”），大多数条款都进行了修改，新增了相当数量的条文。本部分详列出各条款的建议案文，并简要说明在现有文本基础上修改的地方和理由：

（一）序言

新范本继承了现行文本的三项原则：（1）便利和吸引投资的原则；（2）促进缔约国繁荣的原则；（3）加强在平等互利基础上合作的原则。在此基础上，新范本作了四处改动。第一，将“在平等互利基础上合作”的原则调整到序言的第一段。主要是因为在论文一开头就表明最一般的原则更符合逻辑。同时，该举措也有助于强调“平等互利”这一具有“中国特色”的国际法原则，该原则在诸多中国 BIT 的序言中都有所体现。[18] 第二，强调了建立保护和促进投资法律框架体系的共同意愿。尽管签订条约本身已经隐含了这种意愿，但在序言中申明这一点更能强化其重要性。特别是考虑到在根据《维也纳条约法公约》第 31 条解释条约的“目的与宗旨”时，仲裁庭可能会依据条约序言进行解释时，就显得尤为必要。[19] 第三，强调保护和促进投资不能妨碍对健康、安全和环境的保护，以及对国际公认的劳工权利的促进。换言之，尽管 BIT 的主要目的是保护和促进外国投资，但条约不应当妨碍东道国采取措施以保护健康、安全和环境以及促进国际公认的劳工权利标准的权利。这样规定起到了保障东道国权利并进而实现上述外国投资者和东道国权利平衡的作用。类似条款已被最近的多个 BIT 范本所采纳，[20] 并也已被部分地吸收进中国最近几个 BIT 条约中。[21] 第四，在序言中还明确强调了公司的社会责任。它和其他措施一道旨在确保条约能够达到平衡双方利益和促进经济社会持续协调发展的效果。[22]

---

〔18〕 该原则源自中国政府在 20 世纪 50 年代起倡导的“和平共处五项基本原则”。五项基本原则具体是相互尊重主权和领土完整、互不侵犯、互不干涉内政、平等互利、和平共处。有关其起源和内容参见《中国国际法学刊》（Chinese JIL）2004 年第 3 卷的系列文章。

〔19〕 例如，在 SGS v. Philippines 案中，仲裁庭考察了保护伞条款的解释后认定“双边投资条约是促进和双边保护投资的条约[……]有理由对其中的不确定事项作有利于被保护的投资的解释”。

〔20〕 参见 2004 年美国 BIT 范本的序言和 2008 年挪威 BIT 范本。

〔21〕 中国—特立尼达和多巴哥 BIT、中国—圭亚那 BIT。

〔22〕 类似的序言条款可参见 2008 年挪威 BIT 范本。

(二)第一节　定义和适用

通常BIT在开头部分都会对主要概念进行定义。关于条约的适用范围条款在中国现行文本中则被安排在最后一节。然而,本文认为条约的适用范围条款亦应当放在第一节中,因为它和定义条款一样,都是主要用来确定条约的适用范围。

新BIT范本中对五个重要的概念进行了定义,其中包括三个现行文本已定义的术语,即"投资者""投资"和"收益"。为了更准确地界定"投资者"和"投资"两个术语,新范本采用了"法律实体"(legal entity)的概念,并对该概念进行了定义。与现行文本不同的是,为了便于理解,新范本首先定义了"(缔约一方)投资者",然后才定义"法律实体""技资"和"领土"。"收益"一词使用了与现行文本的基本相同的定义,故下文将不再对其进行分析。以下逐个分析各个定义。

1."缔约一方投资者"

关于"投资者"的定义有三个主要的变化。第一个变化是增加"永久居留权"作为自然人国籍的一个替代标准。这反映了当前在这一问题上国际条约实践的发展趋势。[23] 这种做法也已为《中国新西兰自由贸易协定》所采用。[24]

第二个变化是增加了一个备选条文,即通过采用"主要和有效国籍标准"来限制双重国籍的人利用条约的保护机制。[25] 在与承认双重国籍的国家签订双边投资条约时,这种规定会特别有用的。

第三个主要变化体现在认定构成"缔约一方投资者"的法律实体的国籍标准方面。现行文本中采用的是"设立地"与"住所地"的双重标准。在新范本中,用"实质性经营"代替了"住所地"标准,从而更具灵活性。这种做法也已为中国墨西哥双边投资条约所采用。[26] 然而,新范本并没有像中国墨西哥双边投资条约那样采用"企业"(enterprise)的概念,也没有像其他中国的BIT那样采用"公司"(company)或"法人"(legal persons)的概念。这是因为这些术语各自对应的中国法律术语(即企业、公司和法人)有着不同于双边投资条约用法的国内法含义。[27] 为避免不必要的混乱,本范本采用了"法律实体"(legal entity)这一术语。该术语比上述三个术语的内涵更广,并且还没有在中国任何主要的法律文件中被定义过。为清楚起见,新范本随后对此术语进行了界定。

"法律实体"为了使其涵盖全面,有必要对"法律实体"采用一个更广义的定

〔23〕 参见2008年挪威BIT范本第I条。

〔24〕 《中国新西兰自由贸易协定》第135条。

〔25〕 参见2004年美国BIT范本第1条("缔约一方投资者"的定义)。

〔26〕 中国墨西哥BIT第1条。

〔27〕 "法人"的定义见我国《民法通则》;各类型企业的定义见我国《个人独资企业法》《合伙企业法》和《中外合资企业法》《中外合作企业法》和《外商独资企业法》等有关法律;各类公司的定义见我国《公司法》。

义，确保其包含所有营利和非营利实体，以及公共和私人实体。可以看出，本定义采用了类似于2004年美国BIT范本中的“企业”的定义方式。这种做法在中国—墨西哥BIT中也有所体现。[28]

2. “投资”

在“投资”的定义方面有几处变化。这些变化目的在于使该定义更显严谨。正如新近几个仲裁案件所表明的那样，作出改变的这几处在决定仲裁庭的管辖权时是至关重要的。第一，最明显的变化是引入了“投资特征”这一概念来限定该定义的范围。这一限定源自仲裁实践，并已为晚近的几个BIT范本所采纳。[29] 第二，为使其含义更加明确，新范本用“所有的或控制的”（owned or controlled）取代了“投入的”（invested）这一用语。[30] 第三，加上了“直接或间接”这一短语来修饰“所有的或控制的”以扩展其涵盖范围。就此处的修订而言，可以看出中国新近的几个BIT已经将保护的范围扩大到“非直接投资”（indirect investment），其中有些条约还就“非直接投资的”（invested indirectly）这一短语作了进一步的界定。[31] 这种进一步的解释使得约文更具确定性。最后，该定义中包含了一个相对较长的列举清单，以保证其涵盖范围更加全面。[32]

3. “领土”

现行文本并没有定义“领土”一词的含义。不过我国有些BIT中则使用了上述定义。[33] 关于香港和澳门特别行政区的特殊地位问题将在后面予以讨论。

4. 适用范围

本范本条款从适用的标的物、时间和地域范围三个方面界定了本条约的适用范围。现行BIT范本仅规定了其涵盖的“投资”范围和适用的时间范围，而没有定义其涵盖的“措施”以及其适用的地域范围。

新范本沿袭了现行文本中对涵盖“投资”范围和适用的时间范围的规定。条约不适用于条约生效前已经发生的争议的规定也与现行文本的规定相同。至于其涵盖的政府措施，新范本明确表明仅包括“本协定生效后缔约一方对缔约另一方投资者或其投资所采取或维持的措施”。换言之，在该问题上，条约不具有溯及力。

至于地域适用范围问题，新范本规定适用第1条“定义”中的“领土”规定。

---

〔28〕 参见2004年美国BIT范本第1条、2008年挪威BIT范本第1条。

〔29〕 参见2004年美国BIT范本第1条、2008年挪威BIT范本第1条。有关仲裁实践参见 *supra* note 3, para. 2. 18。

〔30〕 该做法已为中国墨西哥BIT第I条采用。

〔31〕 详情参见 *supra* note 3, para. 2. 28。

〔32〕 类似清单见2008年挪威BIT范本。

〔33〕 有关中国BIT中“领土”定义的详情参见 *supra* note 3, para. 2. 81。

不过,为明确起见,缔约双方可以考虑增加一个解释性说明,以明确特定条约对中国的特别行政区的适用效力。正如在中国—墨西哥 BIT 中所作的那样:

经中华人民共和国中央政府的授权,香港和澳门特别行政区政府可以自己另行与墨西哥政府谈判和签署促进和相互保护投资协定。[34]

如缔约双方无意将本 BIT 适用于香港和澳门特别行政区,则可采用中俄 BIT 的做法,并使用如下表述:

除非缔约双方另行约定,本协定不适用于中华人民共和国香港特别行政区和中华人民共和国澳门特别行政区。

(三)第二节

待遇标准条约的第二节规定了投资待遇的实体性标准,既包括一般标准也包括具体标准。一般待遇标准包括公正与公平待遇、保护与安全、最惠国待遇和国民待遇。具体待遇标准既包括传统的投资保护和促进条款,如投资准入、征收、损失赔偿、转移、代位和"权利保留"条款,也包括这些标准的例外和投资者的社会责任条款。

一般待遇标准投资条约中有必要规定一般待遇标准以对明示性待遇标准的起到"补白"(gap-filling)作用。考虑到在"习惯国际法"和"国际最低待遇标准"等概念的发展过程中,中国的认知和参与有限,建议采用"普遍接受的国际法原则"这一更为中性的表述。这意味着这些国际法原则应是那些事实上为国际社会所普遍接受的原则,而非只被有限数量的国家承认的原则。[35] 第 2 款和美国 2004 年范本有关规定一样,是根据《北美自由贸易协定》的经验起草的。[36] 该标准应适用于投资准入和运营阶段,但和本范本其他条款一样,应受制于第 12 条规定的例外的限制。最惠国待遇此处,对现行文本的第一个改变是最惠国待遇涵盖了投资运营和准入两个阶段,在文本上表现为引入投资"准入、扩张"的概念。[37] 改变是增加了"相同情况下"的限定语以明确该条款的适用。第三个改变是明确

---

〔34〕 该解释条文适用的内涵参见 *supra* note 3, para. 2.90。

〔35〕 由于中国和绝大多数发展中国家一样,对近现代国际法发展进程参与有限,认识不足,如果援引"习惯国际法……出现纠纷,国际法院仲裁庭往往会参考既有法律实践,在许多情况下即发达国家的法律实践,来解释有关习惯国际法规则,这往往会使得中国和其他发展中国家处于不利的相对地位。例如,在论述……习惯国际法"待遇或"国际最低标准"待遇时,国际仲裁庭往往会援引美国的 Neer 案、Robinson 案等案件来论证其内涵。而对于这些案例实践,中国律师无论如何认真研究也很难达到与美国律师完全一样的认识水平。反过来,采用"普遍接受的国际法律原则"这一提法则相对中性,尽管也不乏争议性,但毕竟可能可以给中国这样的发展中国家的意志和实践以相对较大的尊重。关于"普遍接受的国际法律原则"以及其在中外投资条约的具体实践,可参见 *Chinese Investment Treaties* 第 3.68 – 3.74 节。

值得注意的是中国—墨西哥 BIT 实际上采用了"最低待遇标准"的用语,类似于《北美自由贸易协定》第 11 章和 2004 年美国 BIT 范本的措辞。然而正如上面陈述的理由,这并不是一个好的做法,不值得仿效。参见中国—墨西哥 BIT 第 5 条。

〔36〕 2004 年美国 BIT 范本第 5 条第 2 款和第 3 款。

〔37〕 中国—芬兰 BIT 第 3 条第 3 项是最近的将建立阶段涵盖在最惠国待遇条款之中的实例。

将争端解决问题排除出最惠国待遇的适用范围。如果缔约方希望最惠国待遇条款涵盖争端解决机制,则可以相应地修改第3款。最后一个改变是在第2款规定了两个常见的最惠国待遇例外,即自由贸易区和边境贸易例外,但不包括国际税收协定。后者作为一般适用例外规定在第12条第5款中。

1. 国民待遇

在新范本中,除了“祖父条款”的限制外,对准入之后的投资给予充分的国民待遇。2001年后中国签订的一些BIT规定了“祖父条款”。[38] 至于准入阶段的适用,新范本采用了类似WTO《服务贸易总协定》的“积极列举”式的方式。与最惠国待遇条文一样,本条也明确规定了“相同情况下”的限制。另外,该标准也同样受第12条规定的普遍接受的例外的限制。

2. 投资准入

除了本条约和其他条约规定的义务限制外,投资准入通常属于东道国自由裁量的范围。例如,在新范本中,公正与公平待遇和最惠国待遇以及部分国民待遇义务都适用于准入阶段。与投资准入相关的一个重要问题是与投资有关的人员的准入问题。新范本中,该问题的决定权保留在东道国手中,东道国只承担给予便利的义务。

3. 征收

与现行文本的规定相比,本条款对征收提供了更强的保护,主要表现在将“正当法律程序”(而非“国内法律程序”)作为征收的前提条件,并将“公平市场价值”(而非“同等”价值)作为补偿标准。“正当法律程序”意味着有义务既遵循国内法也遵循国际法所要求的正当程序。[39] “公平市场价值”表明赔偿应是充分的赔偿而不能是较低的赔偿。另一方面,增加了第三款用来保障东道国为公共福利目的管理投资活动的合法权利。[40] 缔约方如希望进一步定义“直接与间接征收”等概念,则可以参考2004年美国范本的做法。[41]

4. 转移

与现行文本的相应条款相比,本条更加周密并更能符合时代要求。首先,“在不损害缔约一方法律和法规规定的任何可适用的手续要求之前提下”这一更宽松的表述取代了“依据缔约一方法律和法规”的表述。接着,这一限制又被第二款规定的

---

〔38〕 参见中国—塞浦路斯BIT议定书。

〔39〕 关于将正当程序明确扩展到国际法层面的利弊的分析,可参见*Chinese Investment Treaties*,第7.42～7.45节。

〔40〕 有关例证如2008年挪威BIT范本第12条、2004年美国BIT范本附件二第4款第2项。

〔41〕 参见2004年美国BIT范本附件二。

“冻结”(stand-still)和“回退”(roll-back)规定进一步加以约束。[42] 第二,对货币和汇率都作了清楚的规定,从而更加明确。第三,本条第四款和第五款分别规定了普遍接受的例外和在严重收支困难情况下采取临时性安全措施的例外规定。[43]

5.“权利保留”条款

“权利保留”条款旨在确保外国投资者可以享受到任何本 BIT 所提供的特权和利益之外的权利和利益。这种“更优惠待遇”的来源非常广泛,可以是国内法律和实践,也可以是国际规范和任何特定承诺。其中,特定承诺又包括投资授权和投资协议等形式。本范本对后两个术语也进行了界定,以便明晰其含义。[44] 特别是考虑到它涵盖了“投资协议”,本条款也可以看作是一种“保护伞条款”的变形。“保护伞条款”通过给东道国施加条约义务,以确保东道国履行其在特定投资项目中的义务,而“权利保留”条款通过保留投资者得以享受其在某项特定投资项目中获取更加优惠待遇,以确保该特定投资项目得以正常履行。从功能上两类条款是相似,所不同的是实现该功能的方法和角度不同:一个是对东道国施加义务;另一个是对投资者保留权利。一方面,由于“权利保留”条款的权利来源基础更加广泛,可以说它给东道国附加的国际义务相对更多些,但是对于投资者来说要证明争议事项属于“更加优惠”的利益却并非易事。[45] 但另一方面,由于“权利保留”条款采用的是消极保留而不像“保护伞条款”那样采用的是积极赋权的方式,可以认为,它不像“保护伞条款”,没有将非本条约权利的违反必然上升到国际法层面的效力。[46]

6.例外

较之于贸易协定,国际投资条约对东道国的经济、社会和政治状况具有更加深远的影响。然而,传统投资条约仅对东道国施加义务,却没有对东道国的合法权利和利益提供充分的保障措施。这也是致力于该领域的非政府组织所秉持的主要观点之一:条约过分偏重于投资者的利益,而无视东道国基于环境保护、公共安全等众多合法理由治理国家的权力。[47] 尤其是相对于贸易条约而言,双边投资条约中的例外条款一直没有得到发展。因此有必要在投资条约中引入上述例外条款以保障东道国的此类权益。

---

〔42〕 这符合中国新近的双边投资条约实践,参见中国—德国 BIT 第 6 条及附加议定书第 6 条。

〔43〕 中国最近的一些投资条约已开始采取这种措施。参见《中国—新西兰自贸协定》第 142 条第 4 款和中国—墨西哥 BIT 第 8 条第 3 款、第 5 款。

〔44〕 本条与 2004 年美国 BIT 第 1 条(定义)和第 16 条(非减损)非常类似。

〔45〕 相关内容参见 *Chinese Investemt Treaties*,第 6.50 ~ 6.52 节。

〔46〕 故新范本没有单独的“保护伞条款”。

〔47〕 M. Mahnaz, Time for a Change: Germany's Bilateral Investment Treaty Programme and Development Policy, *Dialogue on Globalization Occasional Papers*, No. 27, Fried rich Ebert Stiftung, November 2006, available at http://library.fes.de/pdf-files/iez/global/04138.pdf.

基于这些因素的考虑，也受到挪威、加拿大、美国[48]等国新近采用的双边投资条约泡本的启发，在这个新的范本中包含了五种例外。其一，增加了一“般例外”条款。这些例外与《服务贸易总协定》第14条、《关税及贸易总协定》(1947年)第20条类似。其二，它包含一项“安全例外”条款，该条款与《服务贸易总协定》第14条、《关税及贸易总协定》(1947年)第21条类似。其三，鉴于中国是一个拥有丰富文化和传统的国家，所以加入了“文化例外”。但是，该文化例外条款不会影响各方依据著作权及邻接权相关的国际规则、国内立法、协定的规定而承享的权利和义务。其四，金融审慎监管例外，即缔约国出于对本国的财政体系审慎监管目的而采取的某些措施不在条约约束之列。这一例外也纳入了《服务贸易总协定》金融服务附件之中。最后，新范本原则上不适用于缔约国课征直接、间接税收的行为，也不适用于任何国际税收协定所衍生的利益。另外，就前面提及的国内税收措施的豁免范围如果存在潜在争议，范本也为这类争议的解决设计了一种特殊的机制。[49]

7. 企业社会责任

已如前论，双边投资条约不应当是单方面给投资者赋权的法律文件，它应该寻求在东道国与投资者的权利、利益之间建立一种平衡。因此增加的这一条款是向投资者的母国施加义务，要求他们采取措施，鼓励他们的海外投资者以一种对社会负责的方式开展经营活动，具体措施包括遵循《经济合作与发展组织(OECD)跨国企业准则》和加入《联合国全球契约》等。[50]

(四)第三节　投资者与国家之间的争端解决

与现行投资条约范本相比，新范本的技资者与东道国争端解决条款更加具体并有了很大的扩充，这遵循了新近的双边投资条约实践。[51] 现行投资条约范本关于投资者与东道国争端解决的条文只有1条4款；而新范本中以完整的一节来处理投资者与东道国争端，这一节包含9条，且较之于现行文本，这9条中大部分条款都是新增加的。虽然一些国家可能不倾向于在BIT中规定详细的争议解决条款，但是这些条款至少可以作为磋商缔约当事国备选的参考。下面对照现行文

---

〔48〕 参见2008年挪威BIT范本第五节第24～28条可待续发展国际研究所范本第十部分第49～51条。

〔49〕 此处借鉴了2008年挪威BIT范本第28条。至于更宽泛的方式参见2004年美国BIT范本第21条。本段中使用的术语的具体含义，参见OECD税收协定范本(OECD Model Taxation Convention)及其评论。

〔50〕 例如2008年挪威BIT范本第32条。

〔51〕 参见最近的双边投资条约范本，如美国24年双边投资条约范本[包括两节，即处理国家间纠纷的第二节(Section B)和处理国家间争端的第三节(Section C)。这两节包含了关于解决纠纷的15项条款]。此外还有挪威2008年双边投资条约(整整一节包含10项条款)。近年来，中国双边投资条约中也包含大量纠纷解决条款，参见2008年《中国与墨商哥签订的双边投资条约》第三章第11条至第28条，以及《中国与新西兰签订的自由贸易协定》第十一章第二节第152条至第158条。

本，对建议条文进行简要的分析。

1. 适用

该条是新增条款，它阐明了援引该节需要满足的三个条件。第一，该争议须存在于缔约国与另一个缔约国的投资者之间。第二，诉求必须基于违反本条约的义务而产生。第三，对条约义务的违反已经导致了损害。通过设定这些条件，该条款可产生阻却向仲裁庭提出“轻率”诉求的效果。

2. 磋商和意向通知

该条款强调了通过磋商友好解决争端的重要性，规定磋商总是首选、是争议各方应当在第一时间诉诸的解决手段。同时该条款确认这一过程以“意向通知书”为初始程序[52]为明确计，该条还罗列了通知2010年书应当列明的具体内容。强调磋商是首选的解决纠纷的手段，这一点与现行文本一脉相承，但是“意向通知书”程序是新增内容。

3. 提交仲裁

较之于现行文本，该条款规定更加细致和缜密。第一，条款缩小了提交仲裁的争议范围，从“任何争议”限缩到满足前述三个条件的争议。第二，条款未明示列出国内法庭为争端解决备选方式，因为这里专门讲的是“提交仲裁”。显然，如果当事方想要选用国内法庭解决争端，也完全是可以的，用不着在这里明示规定。[53] 第三，条文将国际仲裁拓展到ICSID以外的仲裁机制，比如ICSID附加便利机制、联合国国际贸易法委员会仲裁机制，或其他任何特别仲裁庭，因此给投资者提供了最广泛的选择。第四，条款要求存在争端的投资者要明示同意仲裁并放弃其他的救济方式。第五，条款确定从知道纠纷存在起的3年是援引该条款的时效。第六，条款为小股东代表诉讼设定特殊的限制——如果缔约方想保护小股东，那么小股东可以且只能对他们的直接损失提出诉请。中国一贯坚持的先行行政复议制度通过附件B得以维持。显然，如果中国不再打算保留这项制度，也可以将其取消。

4. 争端各方的同意

该条文确认缔约方无条件同意将投资者与东道国争端提交国际仲裁庭解决，该同意须满足《华盛顿公约》《解决投资争端国际中心附加便利规则》或《纽约公约》(1958年)等条约的同意要求。虽然从投资者与东道国争端解决程序的规定中援引上述公约这一事实可能就意味着当事人的同意，但为更明确计，最好还是明示规定。同意是《华盛顿公约》的基石，如果没有清楚的同意，仲裁庭也就缺乏

---

〔52〕 类似条款参见《中国—墨西哥双边投资条约》第12条。

〔53〕 参见Rudolf Dolzer and Christoph Schreuer, *Principles of International Investment Law*, Oxford University Press, 2008, pp. 215 - 216；同时参见 *Chinese investment Treaties*，第8.143～8.153节。

对诉求的管辖权。在现行文本中是不包含此类条款的，虽然这在一些其他国家条约范本中普遍存在。[54]

5. 仲裁庭的组成

该条款是新范本中新增的款项。它规定了技资者与东道国争端仲裁案件中仲裁员委任的程序和要求。对于依据《华盛顿公约》《解决投资争端国际中心附加便利规则》或《纽约公约(1958 年)等既定条约设立的仲裁而言，本款对这些条约中与本范本不相符合的规则具有修正效力。[55]

6. 合并仲裁

合并仲裁已经成为近年来一个争议的话题，这主要是由于近年来涌现出来的仲裁案件中有的案件的事实是互相关联的。由于仲裁是完全基于双方意愿的程序，所以相关诉求的合并不是强制性的，除非所有仲裁当事方同意这么做。[56] 除非有特别规定，将像阿根廷金融危机所引发的一系列仲裁案件那样的类似案件进行合并仲裁是不可能的。事实上，由于所有相关方都予以同意，有几起涉及阿根廷的仲裁请求非正式地得到了合并审理。[57] 《北美自由贸易协定》(NAFTA)第十一章第 26 条是最早也是最著名的引入了合并审理条款的范例。[58] 晚近的中国—墨西哥 BIT

〔54〕 例见美国和加拿大的 BIT 范本。挪威 BIT 范本只规定同意提交 ICSID 仲裁。中国—墨西哥 BIT 中也有明示同意的条款，即第 14 条。

〔55〕 参见新范本第 16 条第 5 款。

〔56〕 例如，在 Lauder. Czech Republic 案中，被诉方拒绝进行合并审理，参见 UNCITRAL Award (Final), September 3, 2001, para. 173. 一般性论述可参见 P. Friedland 的著作 *Arbitralion Clauses for Inlemalional Conlracls* (2000)第 6 至 8 章和附录 27 关于多方协议的论述，以及 J. Carver, "How to Avoid Conflicting Awards: the Lauder and CME Cases", *J World Investment & Trade*, Vol. 5, 2004, pp. 23 - 29; H. Bagner, "How to Avoid Conflicting Awards: the Lauder and CME Cases", *J World Investment & Trade*, Vol. 5, 2004, pp. 31 - 35; W. Kahn, "How to Avoid Conflicting Awards: the Laud er and CME Cases", *World Investment & Trade*, Vol. 5, 2004, pp. 7 - 17; and N. Gallagher, "Parallel Proceedings, Res Judicata and Lis Pendens: Problems and Possible Solutions" in L. A. Mistelis and J. D. M. Lew (eds), *Pervasive Problems in International Arbitration*, 2006, pp. 329 - 356.

〔57〕 涉及水务特许协议的几个案件可参见：Aguas Provinciales de Santa Fe, SA, Suez, Sociedad General de Aguas de Barcelona, SA and Interagua Seruiaos Integrales de Agua, SA v. Argentina, ICSID Case No. *ARB*/03/17; Aguas Cordobesas, SA, Suez, and Sociedad General de Aguas de Barcelona, SA v. Argentina, ICSID Case No. *ARB*/03/18; and Aguas A rgentinas, SA, Suez, Sociedad General de Aguas de Barcelona, SA and Vivendi Universal, SA v. Argentina, ICSID Case No. *ARB*/03/19 该仲裁庭实际上也同时在依据 UNCITRAL 规则审理一个由 Anglian Water Group 提起并交由 ICSID 管理的特别仲裁案。

〔58〕 例见在 25 年 9 月 7 日的合并仲裁庭决定(the Order of the Consolidation Tribunal)中，NAFTA 合并仲裁庭决定合并审理 Canfor Corporation, Tembec Investments 和 Terminal Forest Products Limited 等加拿大软木材企业与美国政府间的争议。然而在软饮料甜味剂生产商 Com Produ cts International 和 ADM-Archer Daniels Midland s Company 以及 Tate & Lyle iIl 提起对墨西哥政府的两个仲裁案中，历史上首次组建的 NAFTA 合并仲裁庭却驳回墨西哥政府要求合并审理的请求。详情参见 Order of the Consolidation Tribunal, May 20, 2005。上述两个决定均载 http://www.naftaclaims.com。

以及中国—新西兰自由贸易协定都引入了有关合并审理的条款。[59] 本范本采纳了中国—新西兰自由贸易协定的模式,因为该模式以相关方的同意为基础,具有可操作性。一些缔约国可能希望在合并仲裁方面能有更具体的规定,这可以参照 NAFTA 第十一章第 26 条以及 2004 年美国 BIT 范本第 33 条的规定。[60]

7. 仲裁的进行

本条也是新增内容。它涉及仲裁过程中某些重要的事项。其一,范本确认缔约方自主确定仲裁地点的权利。如果缔约方未就仲裁地点达成协议,仲裁庭可以在《纽约公约》成员国内挑选仲裁地点,以确保仲裁裁决得以承认和执行。显然,这对非 ICSID 仲裁至关重要。[61] 其二,作为一个可供选择的条款,范本允许仲裁庭可以接受和考虑来自相关第三方提供的法庭之友意见(*amicus curiae* submissions),并且给争端方提供对上述意见发表评论的机会。[62] 其三,范本确认投资者的诉诸争端解决机制的权利不因他们缔结过的任何保险或保证合约而受到影响。[63] 其四,范本允许仲裁庭采取临时措施,包括对由争端方所有或控制的证据采取保全措施。[64]

---

〔59〕 该条约规定:

“第 16 条　合并如果由解决投资争端国际中心秘书长指定组建的合并仲裁庭认为依第 15 条组建的两个或两个以上仲裁庭受理的诉求具有共同的事实或法律问题,为了公正和有效地解决这些诉求,该合并仲裁庭可依所涵盖的所有争端各方的协议合并仲裁程序。”

〔60〕 参见美国 BIT 范本第 33 条。

〔61〕 根据(ICSID 公约)第 54 条,不论仲裁地点如何,(ICSID 公约)裁决具有当然的与本国判决一样的执行力。

〔62〕 需要注意的是,这里仲裁庭“可以”接受和考虑,并不等于它“应该”接受和考虑法庭之友意见。仲裁庭首次接受法庭之友意见是依贸发会(UNCITRAL)规则审理的 Methanex 仲裁案。此后,ICSID 仲裁规则进行修改,规定了法庭之友的情形。此外,诸多 BIT 范本也规定了这种情形,如美国、挪威和可持续发展国际研究所的 BIT 范本等。如果想要对仲裁庭此种权利施加限制,则美国 BIT 范本的有关最新修改建议可供参考。

该建议文本如下:

“非争议当事方的个人或者团体(“法庭之友”)向仲裁庭就当事方未曾提交的、与案件有关联的提交的事实情况会对仲裁庭的审理提供相当的帮助。在咨询当事方以后,仲裁庭可以允许这些个人或团体就争议范围内的有关事项向法庭提交书画意见。

仲裁庭在决定是否允许提交法庭之友意见时,除考虑其他事项外,应当考虑以下情形:

(1)法庭之友意见会对仲裁庭判定事实法律事项时提供的观点,尤其是不同于争端方的知识和见解;

(2)法庭之友对争议范围内的事项发表意见;

(3)法庭之友对诉讼具备重要利益。仲裁庭需要确保法庭之友意见不会破坏诉讼过程,也不会给争端任一方引致不当的负担或者不公正的歧视,同时仲裁庭还须保证争端双方有机会对法庭之友意见发表各自的评论。”

详见 Report of The Subcommittee on Investment of the Advisory Committee on International Economic Policy Regarding The Model Bilateral Investment Treaty, September 30, 2009, pp. 8 – 9, 载 http://www. investment treaty news. org/cfs-filesystemfile. ashx/_key/Community Server. Components Site Files/ACIEP-report-model-BIT. pdf, 2010 年 1 月 30 日访问。

〔63〕 中国—墨西哥 BIT 中即包含此类条款。参见中国—墨西哥 BIT 范本第 18 条。

〔64〕 参见中国—墨西哥 BIT 范本第 21 条。

8. 准据法

大部分中国 BIT 中都包括法律适用的条款。[65] 虽然这些条款有详有略，准据法范围有宽有窄，它们一般都指向东道国国内法之规定。事实上，《华盛顿公约》第 42 条也认可仲裁庭可适用东道国国内法。新范本对现行文本进行了两处修改。一方面，新范本去掉了东道国内国法作为准据法的选项——现行文本则将东道国内国法作为可适用的法律之一——理由是既然这里讲的是用国际仲裁方式解决国际投资争端，则适用国际法规范当为题中应有之义。实践中，国际仲裁庭很少援引国内法，即使偶尔提及也大都是作为案件事实问题被援引，而不是作为准据法来援引国内法。[66] 另一方面，新范本注意到很可能存在对条约文本解释的需要，因此范本规定由缔约各方共同制定的关于条约条款的解释对根据本节成立的仲裁庭具备约束力。NAFTA 的经验表明这样的机制对于保持条约标准适用的一致性往往是非常必要的。[67]

9. 裁决与执行

较之现行文本，除了第 3 款外，这一条基本是全新的条文。不过，有关内容在中国—墨西哥 BIT 中已有体现。增加该条文的目的是为了使该条文更加明晰和确定，以防止东道国在最后执行阶段提出反对意见。范本在诸如违约救济、仲裁裁决的公开与执行等多个方面进行了详尽的陈述。它规定对违反条约义务的首要的救济方式应当是金钱赔偿。只有在恢复原状的裁决可以以金钱赔偿的方式进行履行时方可作出恢复原状的判决。仲裁庭不可作出惩罚性的裁决。仲裁裁决应当公开以便于公众知悉。此外，范本还有其他一些有关仲裁执行程序的细节规定。

（五）第四节　国家之间的争端解决

较之于投资者与东道国争端解决条款，中国现行文本在国家间争端解决方面的规定显得相对细致一些。不过，为了使条文更加明晰并强化其效果，新范本对该部分仍进行了许多修正，以确保在实务中更便于操作。

---

〔65〕 典型的例子是中国—捷克 BIT 第 9 条第 5 款。其规定如下：仲裁庭应当考虑以下因素依法裁决：（1）有关缔约方的生效法律；（2）本协议的条款，以及缔约方之间的其他相关协议；（3）缔约一方与缔约另一方投资者之间签订的关于投资的特定合同的条款；（4）国际法的普遍原则。

〔66〕 这种做法已被中国—墨西哥 BIT 第 19 条所采纳。

〔67〕 例如，NAFTA 的自由贸易委员会（Free Trad e Commission，FTC）对诸如公正与公平待遇等重要概念即作出过解释。参见 NAFTA-FTC，*North American Free Trade Agreement Notes of Interpretation of Certain Chapter 11 Provisions*（adopted on 31 July 2001），available at http://www.sice.oas.org/TPD/NAFTA/Commission/CHl1understanding_e.asp，2008 年 10 月 10 日访问。不过，在双边条件下，要双方联合对条约解释作出声明恐怕会更困难，特别是在争端已经产生的情况下，尤为困难。

1. 适用

本条款属于新增条款。它解决了两个问题：一方面，它确定本节的适用范围，另一方面，它确定了本节与前面一节在适用上的关系。原则上，投资者与东道国之间的争端不得适用国家之间的争端解决机制。根据该范本规定，只有当缔约方没有遵守根据第三节规定作出的仲裁裁决，才可以行使本节（第四节）提供的方法来保护投资者的利益。这就相应地限制了国家之间的争端解决机制适用的范围。〔68〕

2. 磋商

该条款与现行文本没有实质的区别。两者不同之处在于根据新范本的规定国家之间的条约争端有可能通过常设的国际法庭来解决。只要缔约国一致同意，就可以将争端提交常设的国际法庭进行裁决。

3. 仲裁庭的组成

本款比现行文本中对应条款规定的更加明细，更具有可操作性。〔69〕

新增的重要具体规定主要包括：启动程序的意向通知，以及当指定的仲裁员辞职或者不能履行职责时委派替代仲裁员的程序。〔70〕

4. 仲裁的进行

本条中大量的款项是新增内容。〔71〕本条除了确认仲裁庭有权决定仲裁地点以及仲裁起始的时间外，还明确规定在争端解决过程中的任何阶段，仲裁庭都可以建议和解。此外，本条强调在仲裁过程中公平听诉的重要性。

5. 准据法

本条款与现行文本总体相近。但是，它不再将可适用的“国际法原则”限定于“缔约双方认可的”的范围之内，而只要求它们必须是普遍认可的国际法原则。

6. 裁决

较之于现行文本，本条唯一的变化在于将裁决书须陈述其法律和事实依据作为一项强制性要求。现行文本仅要求仲裁庭“根据缔约国任何一方的要求”而说明其裁决的“理由”。〔72〕

---

〔68〕 尽管如此，到目前为止此类国家之间的争端解决条款很少被适用，比如在 the Empresas Lucchetti, S. A. and Lucchetti Peru, SA v. Peru 案（ICSID Case No. ARB/03/4）中，秘鲁与智利政府间虽然启动了仲裁程序，但仲裁程序却中止着，一直在等待投资者与东道国仲裁的结果。一般认为《能源宪章条约》27 条（国家间争端）被适用的可能性会大些，因为毕竟在未来，能源供应将成为各国关注的重点。

〔69〕 中国 BIT 范本（2003 年版）第 8 条第 3 款、第 4 款。

〔70〕 中国—墨西哥 BIT 第 24 条。

〔71〕 不包括第 2 款关于仲裁庭有权决定其程序的规定。该规则在现行文本的第 8 条第 5 款也予以规定。

〔72〕 中国 BIT 范本（2003 年）第 8 条第 2 款。

7. 费用

本节中最后这一条阐明缔约国承担仲裁员费用的方式。这是现行文本中所欠缺的内容。许多中国 BIT 都有类似规定,这也与中国早期采用的 BIT 范本的规定相一致。[73]

(六) 第五节　最后条款

最后一节由一系列常见的 BIT 中最后条款组成。这些最后条款包括:磋商条款、拒绝授惠条款以及条约的生效、有效期和终止条款。

1. 磋商

该规定与现行文本相同。在必要的时候,尤其是当条约涉及一个重要的相对国的时候,磋商也可以发展成为缔约双方的一项适当的制度性安排。此类磋商结果可能会导致前述关于某一条约条文的解释。已如前述,[74] 这种对条文的解释对根据第三节组建的仲裁庭具有约束力。

2. 拒绝授惠

本条为新增条款,缔约国可以凭借该条款拒绝向某项由非成员方。

投资者控制或者所有的投资提供条约保护。该条不同于 2004 年美国范本的规定,前者要求"共同"而非"单方面"拒绝授惠。根据本条规定,拒绝授惠应由缔约双方共同作出。两相比较,美国的方式相对更加宽松:在某种情况发生以后,缔约一方可以单方面作出拒绝授惠的决定。[75] 在新范本中采纳更加严格的方式是为了确保 BIT 中提供的保护不会轻易被剥夺。中国—墨西哥 BIT 也采纳了这样的条款。

3. 生效、有效期租终止

除第 1 款外,本条各款与现行文本基本保持了一致,只作了一些技术性的修改。第 1 款是新增条款,该款规定缔约国有义务在完成使本协定批准和生效所必需的国内法律程序后通知另一缔约方。该条也许可以加快 BIT 获得批准的速度,

---

〔73〕 中国 BIT 范本(第 1 版)第 8 条第 7 款。亦可参见中国比利时卢森堡经济联盟 BIT 第 9 条。

〔74〕 见本文中就"准据法"的相关论述。

〔75〕 参见 2004 年美国 BIT 范本第 17 条、中国—墨西哥 BIT 第 31 条。2004 年美国 BIT 范本相关条款为:

"第 17 条　拒绝授惠

一、缔约一方可以拒绝将本条约之利益授予缔约另一方之企业投资者及该投资者之投资,如果该企业系由非缔约方之人员拥有或控制且拒绝授益方

(一) 与该非缔约方元外交关系;或

(二) 对该非缔约方或非缔约方之人员采取或维持禁止与该企业进行交易之措施,或者授予该企业或其投资本条约之利益将违反或规避此类措施。

二、缔约一方可以拒绝将本条约之利益授予缔约另一方之企业投资者及该投资者之投资,如果该企业在该缔约另一方领土内无实质性经营且系由非缔约方或拒绝授惠方之人员拥有或控制。"

并提高获批 BIT 在已签订 BIT 中的比率。在大量已经签订的 BIT 未获批准的国际大背景之下，这一规定的意义更显突出。

四、结论

近十几年来，中国一直是全球最重要的外资输入国之一。在最近几年里，她正迅速成为一个重要的资本输出国。这种角色的重大转变，以及中美 BIT 谈判和国际 BIT 转型等因素，使中国起草一个独立自主并具有前瞻性的 BIT 范本的条件更见成熟。

鉴于晚近的发展已经证明传统的那种片面维护投资者利益的 BIT 将难以为继，我们在新范本草案中贯彻"和谐世界"理念，在权益平衡和环境、社会协调发展的基础上实现投资促进与保护，故称为"和谐 BIT 范本"或"绿色 BIT 范本"。新范本由 5 节 32 个条款组成，除序言外，涉及定义和适用范围、实体性待遇标准、投资者与东道国争端解决、国家之间的争端解决以及最后条款等五大方面。在起草这个范本时，我们不仅注意使条约能与 BIT 的最新和最佳国际实践相接轨，而且还致力保持 BIT 项下最主要的两个主体，即外国投资者与东道国，二者之间权利和义务的总体平衡。因此，该范本不仅仅更新与强化传统意义上的投资保护与促进条款，而且增加了维护东道国在管制外国投资，督促外国技资者承担社会责任等方面的权利的条款。我们相信，随着中国的进一步繁荣发展，以及构建"和谐世界"的努力的进一步实施，新范本将不仅能够最大限度地服务于中国的利益，并可能影响其他国家的 BIT 条约与仲裁实践，进而对世界普遍福利的增进，有所裨益。

附：中国双边投资条约（BIT）范本建议文本（2010 中文本）

中华人民共和国政府和____国政府
关于鼓励和相互保护投资协定

中华人民共和国政府和____国政府（以下称缔约双方）愿意在平等互利原则的基础上，加强两国间的经济合作，为缔约一方的投资者在缔约另一方领土内的投资创造有利条件，认识到相互鼓励、促进和保护此类投资将有利于增强投资者投资的积极性和增进两国的繁荣，期望建立一个有利于促进相互投资的规则框架，并确保在一缔约方领土内另一缔约方投资的保护与安全，希望通过与保护健康、安全和环境以及促进国际承认的劳工权利之目的相一致的方式达成上述目标，强调公司社会责任的重要性，达成协议如下：

第一节　定义和适用

第一条　定义

本协定内，

一、“缔约一方投资者”一词系指：在缔约另一方领土内已拥有投资的，(一)根据缔约一方可适用的法律，具有其国籍或永久居留权的自然人，然而具有双重国籍的自然人只能视为其主要或有效国籍国的国民；或(二)根据缔约一方的法律设立或组建并在该缔约一方领土内开展实质性经营活动的法律实体。

二、“法律实体”一词系指根据可适用的法律设立或组建的任何实体，不论是否以营利为目的，不论是私人所有还是国家所有，包括任何公司、信托、合伙、独资企业、合资企业和其他组织。

三、“投资”一词系指由缔约一方投资者依照缔约另一方法律和法规直接或间接所有或控制的任何资产，包括但不限于：

(一)法律实体；

(二)股份、股票和对企业的其他形式的股权参与，以及由此产生的任何权利；

(三)债券、票据、贷款和其他形式的债权，以及由此产生的任何权利；

(四)合同项下的权利，包括交钥匙工程、建筑、管理、生产或收入分成；

(五)合同；

(六)金钱请求权和行为请求权；

(七)知识产权；

(八)依据法律或合同所获得的权利，诸如特许经营、执照、授权和许可等；

(九)任何有形财产、无形财产、动产、不动产及其他有关财产权利，如租赁权、抵押权、留置权和质权。任何构成本协定所述投资的财产，必须具备投资的特征，包括资本或其他资源的投入，收入或利润的预期或者风险的承担。

作为投资的财产发生任何形式上的变化，不影响其作为投资的性质，只要这种变化符合投资所在的缔约方的法律和法规。

四、“收益”一词系指投资所得，包括利润、分红、利息、资本收益、提成费、收费和其他合法收入。

五、“领土”一词：

(一)在中华人民共和国方面，系指中华人民共和国领土(包括领海及其领空)，以及根据中国法律和国际法，在其领海以外中华人民共和国拥有勘探和开发海床和底土资源及其上覆水域资源的主权权利的任何区域。[76]

（二）在________国方面，系指[　　]

第二条　适用范围

一、本协定适用于本协定生效后缔约一方对缔约另一方投资者或其投资所采取或维持的措施。第三节（争端解决）之规定不适用于基于本协定生效前业已存在之事端而产生的争议。

二、本协定适用本协定生效之前或之后依据有关缔约方法律和法规进行的投资。

三、本协定适用于第一条第五款所规定的缔约方的领土范围。

第二节　待 遇 标 准

第三条　一般待遇标准

一、缔约一方应始终根据普遍接受的国际法原则给予缔约另一方投资者的投资以待遇，包括公正和公平待遇以及完全的保护和安全。

二、“公正和公平待遇”和“完全的保护和安全”这两个概念并不要求给予普遍接受的国际法原则所要求的待遇标准之上或额外的待遇。违反本协定的其他条款或其他国际协定的条款，不构成对本条的违反。

第四条　最惠国待遇

一、缔约一方应给予缔约另一方投资者及其投资在投资准入、扩大、经营、管理、维持、使用、享有以及处分方面不低于其在相同情况下给予任何第三国投资者及其投资的待遇。

二、上述第一款所述的待遇，不得解释为缔约一方有义务将基于下列原因产生的待遇、优惠或特权方面的利益给予缔约另一方投资者：

（一）任何关税同盟、自由贸易区、经济联盟和任何设立此类联盟的国际协定，以及任何类似制度安排；

（二）任何便利边境地区的小额边境贸易的安排。

三、第一款所指的待遇不包括本协定及其他国际协定规定的争端解决机制。

第五条　国民待遇

一、在不损害投资时缔约一方已有法律和法规的前提下，缔约一方应给予缔

---

[76]　此处可像中墨协定一样加入如下解解性语句：

“经中华人民共和国中央政府的授权，香港和澳门特别行政区政府可以自己另行与一国政府谈判和签署促进和相互保护投资协定。

如缔约双方无意将本条约适用于香港和澳门特别行政区，协定可采用中俄 BIT 的做法，并使用如下表述：除非缔约双方另行约定，本协定不适用于中华人民共和国香港特别行政区和中华人民共和国澳门特别行政区。”

约另一方投资者及其投资在投资经营、管理、维持、使用、享有以及处分方面不低于其在相同情况下给予其本国投资者及其投资的待遇。[77]

二、在附件A所列部门之内,并在符合该附件所设定之条件或要求的前提之下,缔约一方应给予缔约另一方投资者在投资设立、扩大和兼并方面不低于其在相同情况下给予其本国投资者的待遇。

第六条　投资的准入

一、除非本协定和其他可适用的条约另有规定,缔约一方可依照其可适用的法律和法规接受缔约另一方投资者所进行之投资。

二、缔约一方应依据其法律和法规,为在其领土内从事与投资有关活动的缔约另一方国民获得签证和工作许可提供帮助和便利。

第七条　征收

一、缔约一方不得直接地或通过类似于征收或国有化的措施间接地对投资实施征收或国有化(下文简称征收),除非:

(一)为了公共利益;

(二)在非歧视的基础上;

(三)根据法律的正当程序;并且

(四)根据下文第二款给予补偿。

二、补偿应:

(一)相当于征收前一刻被征收投资的公平市场价值,该公平市场价值不应反映由于征收事先为公众所知而发生的价值变化;

(二)包括自征收之日起到实际支付之日止按照合理的商业利率计算的利息;

(三)毫不迟延地支付;以及

(四)可以充分兑现和自由转移。

三、除在极少数情况下外,缔约一方旨在保护诸如公共健康、安全和环境等合理的公共福利目标的非歧视性管理行为,不构成间接征收。

第八条　损失赔偿

缔约一方投资者在缔约另一方领土内的投资,因在缔约另一方领土内发生的

---

〔77〕 中国也可以考虑通过在议定书或附件中加入"祖父条款"以继续维持不符措施,正如在中德BIT议定书中的那样:

"中华人民共和国方面,第二条第三款和第三条第二款不适用于:

(一)任何现存的在其境内维持的不符措施;

(二)这种不符措施的持续;

(三)任何对这种不符措施的修改,但修改不能增加措施的不符程度。

中华人民共和国将采取所有适当的措施逐渐地撤除这些不符合措施。"

战争、全国紧急状态、暴动、骚乱或其他类似事件而遭受损失，缔约另一方给予该投资者在恢复原状、赔偿、补偿或其他解决方案方面的待遇，不应低于其给予本国或任何第三国投资者的待遇，两者中以对有关投资者更为有利者为准。

第九条　转移

一、在不损害缔约一方法律和法规规定的任何可适用的手续要求之前提下，缔约一方应保证缔约另一方投资者可以毫不迟延地自由汇入或汇出所有与其领土内的投资有关的款项。这类汇兑应包括，但不限于：

（一）设立、维持或扩大投资所必需的数额；

（二）利润、利息、分红、资本收益、提成费和其他与知识产权和工业产权有关的收费；

（三）依照包括贷款协议在内的合同所付的款项；

（四）全部或部分出售或清算投资所获得的收入；

（五）从事与投资有关活动的缔约另一方国民的收入和薪酬；

（六）投资者依照第五条和第六条所拥布的任何补偿；以及

（七）依照第三节的争端解决获得的款项。

二、本条第一款涉及的手续要求：

（一）不应严于本协定生效时的要求；

（二）不应在本协定生效后施加新的限制；

（三）不应作为规避本条项下缔约方的承诺和义务的方式。

三、除非本条另有规定，缔约一方不应阻止以国际货币基金组织列举的可自由兑换的货币按照汇兑当日通行的市场汇率的汇兑得以毫不迟延的履行。

四、缔约一方可以通过公平、非歧视和善意地适用该国关于以下事项的法律，禁止汇兑：

（一）破产、清算或保护债权人利益；

（二）债券的发行、买卖或交易；

（三）刑事犯罪和行政违法；

（四）汇兑货币或其他货币工具的报告；或者（五）保证司法程序中判决的实现。

五、在面临严重的国际收支困难或严重的国际收支困难之威胁时，缔约一方可以暂时限制汇兑，只要该国是依照国际标准实施某些措施或方案。这些限制应在公平、非歧视和善意的基础上进行。

第十条　代位

如果缔约一方或其指定的代理机构依照其对在另一缔约方领土内投资的非

商业风险所做的担保或保险合同向其投资者进行了支付，另一缔约方应当承认：

（一）不论转让是依据缔约他方的法律还是合法交易，该投资者的任何权利和请求都已转让给了该缔约他方或其指定的代理机构；并且

（二）该缔约他方或其指定的代理机构有权在与投资者同等的范围内，代位行使投资者的权利，实施投资者的诉求权，并履行与投资相关的义务。

第十一条　权利保留

一、本协定不得减损基于以下任何规定而赋予一方投资者或其投资以比本协定所规定的待遇更高的待遇：

（一）一方的法律、法规，行政惯例或程序，或行政决定和司法裁判；

（二）一方的国际法律义务；或者

（三）一方承担的义务，包括投资授权和投资协议中所涉之义务。

二、为此目的，本协定中：

（一）“投资授权”一词系指缔约一方的对外投资主管机构对缔约另一方的投资者或其投资的授权。

（二）“投资协议”一词系指由缔约一方的国家主管机构与缔约另一方的投资者或其投资所达成的书面协议。该协议构成了该投资者或其投资所据以设立或获取（除了该协议本身以外的）投资项目的基础。该协议授予该投资者或其投资以下列权利之一：

（1）对一国家主管机构控制的自然资源的权利，包括勘探、开采、提炼、运输、分配和销售的权利；

（2）代表国家一方提供公共服务的权利，包括开展电力生产及销售、水处理及销售和电信业务的权利；或

（3）进行并非完全或主要由政府使用与收益的建筑施工的权利，包括建设道路、桥梁、隧道、水坝和管网的权利。

第十二条　例外

一、在不构成对投资和投资者故意或不合理的歧视，且不对国际投资构成变相的限制的前提下，本协定的任何规定不得解释为阻碍一方采取或执行必要措施以：

（一）保护公共利益和维护公共秩序；

（二）保护人类、动物或植物的生命与健康；

（三）维护不与本协定相冲突的法律和法规；

（四）保护具有艺术、历史或考古价值的国家财物；或（五）保护环境

二、本协定的任何规定不得解释为：

（一）要求任何一方提供其认为如披露则会违背其基本安全利益的任何信

息;或者

(二)阻止一方采取其认为对保护国家基本安全利益所必需的任何行为:

(1)与防卫和安全部门有关的投资行为:

(2)与裂变和聚变物质或衍生这些物质的物质有关的行为:

(3)在战时或国际关系中其他紧急情况下采取的行动。

(三)阻止一方为履行其包括《联合国宪章》项下义务在内的维护国际和平与安全的义务而采取的任何行动。

三、本协定各条款不适用于一方为保护语言与文化多样性、文化与音像制品政策所特别制定的法律和措施,亦不适用于一方与知识产权及其邻接权有关的国内法律和措施以及其作为知识产权及其邻接权的国际协定的缔约方所承享的权利义务。

四、本协定的任何其他条款不得阻止一方为审慎原因而采取措施,包括为保护投资者、存款人、保单持有人或金融服务提供者对其负有信托责任的人而采取的措施,或为保证金融体系完整和稳定而采取的措施,或为促进市场竞争而采取的措施,包括所有权控制或限制措施。

如此类措施不符合本协定的规定,则不得用作规避该方在本协定项下的承诺或义务的手段。

五、税收

(一)本协定的任何规定不得影响一方直接或间接税的课税、征收;

(二)本协定的任何条款均未设定于缔约一方签署的避免双重征税条约中得益的权利;

(三)任何因第一款和第二款所生争端都只能诉诸于一方税收主管机构或国内法院、上诉机构解决,不得适用本协定第三节[投资者与国家之间的争端解决]。

(四)若经过第三款规定的程序后,一方税收主管机构认为争端不适用上列第一款的规定,而认定案件应适用[征收]一条的规定,则该争端可以适用本协定第三节[投资者与国家之间的争端解决]。

第十三条　企业的社会责任

缔约方同意通过鼓励投资者遵循《经济合作与发展组织(OECD)跨国企业准则》加入《联合国全球契约》等符合其社会责任的方式,进行投资活动。

第三节　投资者与国家之间的争端解决

第十四条　适用范围

本节应适用于缔约一方与缔约另一方的投资者之间由于声称违反本协定第

二节规定之义务且造成损失或损害而产生的争端。

第十五条　磋商和意向通知

一、争端双方应首先努力通过磋商或谈判解决争端。

二、为友好解决诉求，争端投资者应至少在提交仲裁前6个月向争端缔约方递交书面的拟将诉求提交仲裁的意向通知书。该通知书应载明：

（一）争端投资者的名称和住所，以及企业的名称和住所（如果投资者是为该企业所遭受的损失或损害提起诉求）；

（二）第二节中被声称违反的条款以及任何其他相关条款；

（三）争议问题及诉求的事实和法律依据；以及

（四）所寻求的救济以及[如果可能]所要求赔偿的大概数额。

第十六条　提交仲裁

一、在满足附件B的情况下，缔约一方投资者可将缔约另一方违反第二节规定之义务且该投资者由于或源于该违反行为而蒙受损失或损害的诉求提交仲裁。

二、争端投资者可以根据下列规则将诉求提交仲裁：

（一）(解决国家和他国国民之间投资争端公约)（以下简称《华盛顿公约》）；倘若争端缔约方与投资者所属缔约方都系《华盛顿公约》的缔约方；

（二）解决投资争端国际中心附加便利规则，倘若争端缔约方或投资者所属缔约方中一方而不是双方系《华盛顿公约》的缔约方；

（三）联合国国际贸易法委员会仲裁规则；或者

（四）争端各方同意的任何其他仲裁规则。

三、争端投资者可将诉求提交仲裁，仅当：

（一）投资者同意根据本节规定的程序进行仲裁；且

（二）投资者和企业（如果诉求是为投资者拥有或控制的缔约另一方企业法人的利益所遭受的损失或损害而提起）放弃启动或继续与争端缔约方被指控违反第二节的措施有关的、根据缔约一方法律在行政法庭或法院，或者依其他争端解决方式的任何争端解决程序。但根据争端缔约方的法律在行政法庭或法院寻求禁止性、确权性或其他不涉及损害赔偿的类似救济的程序除外。

四、本条所指的同意和弃权应以书面形式递交给争端缔约方，并应附在仲裁请求书中。

五、除本节修改的地方外，可适用的仲裁规则应适用于仲裁。

六、在不损害第十五条的前提下，投资者可以于其首次获悉或应当获悉产生该争端的事件之日起3年内将争端提交仲裁。

七、缔约双方承认，根据本条规定，无控制权的小投资者仅有资格就其自己作为投资者的法律利益遭受的直接损失或损害提出诉求。

第十七条　缔约方的同意

一、缔约各方在此无条件同意依据本节将相关争端提交国际仲裁。

二、上述第一款的同意和争端投资者将诉求提交仲裁的申请应满足《华盛顿公约》第二章(中心的管辖权)或《解决投资争端国际中心附加便利规则》的要求或《纽约公约》第二条关于争端各方书面同意的要求。

第十八条　仲裁庭的组建

一、除非争端双方另有约定,仲裁庭应由3名仲裁员组成。争端各方应各指定一名仲裁员,争端双方应协商决定第三名仲裁员,并由其出任仲裁庭主席。

二、上述第一款所指的仲裁员应具有国际法和国际投资事务方面的经验。

三、如果因为争端一方未能指定仲裁员或者争端双方未能就仲裁庭主席人选达成一致,致使仲裁庭不能在仲裁请求提出之日起90日内组建,则应任一争端方的请求,解决投资争端国际中心秘书长应自由指定尚待指定的仲裁员。但解决投资争端国际中心秘书长应确保其所指定的仲裁庭主席系非缔约双方的国民。

第十九条　合并

若两个或更多投资者表明提交仲裁意图,且所提交的仲裁请求源于同一事件或情状且存在共同的法律或事实问题,则在所有争端方均同意合并仲裁请求的情况下,争端方应当就此进行磋商,以协调应当适用的程序,包括选择审理争端的机构。

第二十条　仲裁的进行

一、争端方应依据适用的仲裁规则对仲裁地点达成合意。如争端各方未能就此达成协议,仲裁庭得依据适用的仲裁规则确定仲裁地点,惟其必须位于《纽约公约》之任一缔约国领土内。

二、在仲裁庭认为来自非争端方的个人或实体的书面意见与正在审理的事实和法律问题有直接关系时,仲裁庭有权接受和考虑此类书面意见。仲裁庭应确保争端各方在这方面机会均等,并应确保争端各方以及缔约另一方有对此类书面意见进行辩驳的机会。

三、在依本节进行的仲裁中,争端缔约方不应将争端投资者依据保险合同或保证合同就其所主张的全部或部分损害已经获得或将要获得保险赔付或其他补偿作为一种抗辩、反请求、抵销权或其他主张。

四、仲裁庭可建议采取临时保全措施以保护争端一方的权利,或确保仲裁庭管辖权得到充分有效行使,包括建议保存争端一方拥有或控制的证据或保护仲裁庭的管辖权。但仲裁庭不得建议扣押财产或者禁止被指控违反第十六条的措施的施行。

第二十一条　可适用的法律

一、依本节组建的仲裁庭应根据本协定和普遍接受的国际法原则对所提交争端中的各争议问题作出裁决。

二、缔约双方共同作出或一致同意的关于本协定的任何条款的解释应对依本节组建的仲裁庭具有拘束力。

第二十二条　裁决与执行

一、除非争端双方另有约定,裁定缔约一方违反依本协定承担之义务的裁决,只可单独或一并判定:

(一)金钱赔偿及任何适当的利息;或者

(二)恢复原状,前提是恢复原状的判决可以以支付金钱补偿的方式履行。

二、如果是为企业所遭受的损失或损害将诉求提交仲裁:

(一)恢复原状的判决之救济应向企业提供;

(二)判定金钱赔偿及任何适当利息的裁决应规定该赔偿应该向该企业支付;以及

(三)裁决应规定,本裁决的作出不损害任何人依据可适用的国内法可能享有救济的任何权利。

三、仲裁裁决应当且仅对争端各方和该特定案件具有终局性和拘束力。

四、仲裁裁决应当公开,除非争端各方另有约定。

五、仲裁庭不得判定惩罚性的赔偿。

六、缔约各方应在其领土内采取一切必要措施以有效执行依本条作出的裁决,并应为在其为当事一方的程序中作出的任何裁决的执行提供便利。

七、只有在下列情况下,争端一方才可寻求执行一项终局裁决:

(一)当终局裁决是依《华盛顿公约》作出时:

(1)自裁决作出之日起已超过120日且无任一争端方请求修改或撤销该裁决;或者

(2)修改或撤销程序已经完结;以及

(二)当终局裁决是依解决投资争端国际中心附加便利规则、联合国国际贸易法委员会仲裁规则或争端双方选择的任何其他仲裁规则作出时:

(1)自裁决作出之日起已超过3个月且无一争端方启动修改、取消或撤销该裁决的程序;或者

(2)法院已经驳回或同意修改、取消或撤销裁决的申请且没有进一步上诉的可能。

第四节　国家之间的争端解决

第二十三条　适用范围

一、本节适用于缔约双方之间因本协定条款的解释或适用而产生的争端。

二、缔约一方不得依本节就侵害投资者权利的有关争端启动程序，除非缔约另一方未能遵守或履行就该投资者依第三节提交的争端所作之终局裁决。在这种情况下，依本节组建的仲裁庭，应争端投资者所属缔约方之请求，可：

（一）声明不遵守或不履行终局裁决不符合本协定规定之义务；以及

（二）建议缔约另一方遵守或履行该终局裁决。

第二十四条　磋商和谈判

一、如果缔约双方因本协定之解释或适用产生争端，则该争端应尽可能通过磋商和谈判友好解决。

二、如果争端未能在书面请求谈判或磋商之日起6个月内通过上述方式解决，缔约一方可将争端提交给依本节规定组建的仲裁庭，或提交给缔约双方同意的任何其他国际法庭。

第二十五条　仲裁庭的组建

一、缔约一方（申请方）通过外交途径将书面通知递交给缔约另一方（被申请方），则仲裁程序启动。该通知应包含关于其诉求之法律和事实基础的陈述，依第二十四条进行之磋商和谈判的经过和结果的概述，申请方依本节启动仲裁程序的意向，以及该申请方指定之仲裁员的姓名。

二、在该通知递交后30日内，被申请方应通知申请方其所指定之仲裁员的姓名。

三、在第二名仲裁员被指定之日后30日内，缔约双方指定的仲裁员应共同协商指定第三名仲裁员，该仲裁员经缔约双方同意应担任首席仲裁员。如果本款所指之同意未能在指定第三名仲裁员之日后30日内作出，则适用下述第四款的规定。

四、若在上述第二款和第三款规定的期限内，未按要求指定仲裁员或作出同意，缔约一方可邀请国际法院院长指定尚未指定的仲裁员。如果院长是缔约一方的公民或永久居民，或由于其他原因院长无法指定仲裁员，则应邀请国际法院副院长进行指定。如果副院长是缔约一方的公民或永久居民，或由于其他原因副院长无法指定仲裁员，则应邀请国际法院中不属于缔约一方的公民或永久居民的最资深法官进行必要的指定。

五、如果按本条规定指定的仲裁员辞职或不能履行职责，则应以指定原仲裁员的相同方式指定继任仲裁员，且该继任者拥有与原仲裁员相同的权力和责任。

第二十六条 仲裁的进行

一、经首席仲裁员召集，仲裁庭应决定仲裁地点和启动仲裁程序的日期。

二、仲裁庭应决定与其管辖权相关的所有问题，并在不违反缔约双方的约定的前提下，决定自己的程序。

三、在程序进行的任何阶段和在作出任何裁决前，仲裁庭均可建议缔约双方友好解决该争端。

四、在任何时候，仲裁庭都应给予缔约双方公平听证的机会。

第二十七条 可适用的法律

依本节组建的仲裁庭应根据本协定和公认的国际法原则对争议问题作出裁决。

第二十八条 裁决

一、仲裁庭应依多数票作出裁决。裁决应以书面形式作出且应包含所适用的事实和法律认定。裁决作出后应当送达缔约各方。

二、裁决对缔约双方具有终局性和拘束力。

第二十九条 费用

缔约各方应各自承担所指定仲裁员及仲裁程序中的律师代理费用。首席仲裁员的费用和与仲裁活动有关的其他费用应由缔约双方平均分担，除非仲裁庭裁定缔约一方应承担较高比例的费用。

第五节 最后条款

第三十条 磋商

缔约一方可以建议缔约另一方就与本协定有关的任何问题举行磋商。此类磋商应在缔约双方同意的时间和地点举行。

第三十一条 拒绝受惠

缔约双方可以共同磋商决定拒绝将本协定之利益授予缔约另一方之企业及其投资，如果该企业系由非缔约方之自然人或企业拥有或控制。

第三十二条 生效、有效期和终止

一、缔约双方应相互书面通知对方其已完成使本协定批准和生效所必需的国内法律程序。

二、本协定应自缔约双方通过外交渠道所发出本条第一款关于国内要求完成的较后一份通知发出之日起30日后生效。

三、本协定有效期10年。之后，除非缔约一方提前12个月通过外交途径书面通知另一缔约方其终止本协定的决定，本协定应永久有效。

四、对于本协定终止之前作出的投资，本协定之规定应自终止之日起10年内继续有效。

五、经缔约双方同意可对本协定作出修改,修改应根据上述第一款和第二款规定的程序生效。

下列签字人经各自政府授权在本协定上签字,以昭信守。

本协定于________年____月____日在________签订,一式两份,每份都用中文、________文和英文写成,三种文本同等作准。如对文本的解释发生分歧,以英文本为准。

中华人民共和国政府

________国政府

代表

代表

外资国民待遇及其实施条件*

本文认为，外资国民待遇是指一国给予外国人以与其本国国民同等的待遇，但在国际立法实践中，东道国往往还可以维持一些特殊的外资国民待遇例外与限制。比如，在外资准入阶段，各国都划定了禁止或限制外资进入的领域，而且一般都规定了外资准入的资格条件；而在外资运营阶段，国民待遇则主要体现在司法行政救济、民事权益保护和宏观管理等几个方面。由于实行国民待遇原则必须建立在市场经济体制之上，并且要求一国总体经济实力的充分发展壮大，因此文章认为，在我国实行外资国民待遇，不仅仅意味着外资政策与法律的调整，同时还意味着内资企业与民族工业发展路向的调整，意味着社会主义市场经济体制改革向纵深发展以及我国综合国力的不断增强。

外资待遇问题实质上就是外资的法律地位问题，它构成一国投资法律环境的基础与核心。因此，它一直是国际投资者关注的焦点，也是各国缔结国际投资条约时争议的焦点之一。目前，国际上比较常见的待遇标准有公平合理待遇、非歧视待遇、国民待遇、最惠国待遇以及"国际标准待遇"等，其中，最常用的又是最惠国待遇与国民待遇两个标准。

长期以来，在我国与外国缔结的双边投资保护协定中，一般只提"公平合理待遇"与"最惠国待遇"，而很少明确提及"国民待遇"，有关的国内立法也更多的是关于外商投资企业种种特殊优惠与限制的规定，而鲜有国民待遇的内容。1993年底，我国正式提出要"创造条件，逐步对外商投资企业实行国民待遇"。[1] 1997年9月，江泽民同志在"十五大"所作的报告则进一步提出，要"依法保护外商投

---

* 本文发表在《中国社会科学》1998年第5期。

本文的写作得到了厦门大学陈安教授和徐崇利教授的悉心指导和热忱襄助，谨此致以衷心的感谢。

〔1〕 参见《中共中央关于建立社会主义市场经济体制若干问题的决定》，载《人民日报》1993年11月7日，第1版。

资企业的权益,实行国民待遇”。[2] 可见,对外资实行国民待遇已成为新时期我国外资立法政策调整的主要标志之一。

一、外资国民待遇的基本内涵

大而言之,国民待遇是国际法上外国人待遇标准中的一种,它大体指一国给予外国人以与其本国国民同等的待遇。[3] 这一定义我们不妨称为“自然定义”。在这里,“国民”一般包括法人与自然人(公民),“外国人”则有广狭两种含义。狭义的“外国人”一般仅指具有外国国籍的法人或自然人;广义的“外国人”则不仅包括具有外国国籍的法人或自然人,而且包括虽不具有外国国籍,甚至取得了本国国籍,却存在外国控制因素的法人。显然,应用到外商投资领域,如果从上述狭义的“外国人”界定出发,则只存在“外国投资者”的国民待遇,而不存在“外商投资企业”的国民待遇;只有从广义的“外国人”界定出发,才既存在“外国投资者”的国民待遇,也存在“外商投资企业”的国民待遇。因为外商投资企业(法人)虽然大都已取得东道国本国国籍,但仍不同程度地存在外国控制因素,故其虽不能算作狭义的“外国人”,但却可以作为广义上的“外国人”。不过,由于“外国投资者”的国民待遇与“外商投资企业”的国民待遇在实践上往往又难以完全分离,所以本文以“外资国民待遇”笼统称之,尽管着重探讨的是后者。

在我国,按“一国两制”的方针及其在香港、澳门地区的实践,香港、澳门与台湾和祖国大陆同属中华人民共和国(“一国”),但实行不同于大陆的经济制度与法律制度(“两制”)。因此,对港、澳、台地区居民及其在大陆地区投资设立的企业,不存在“国民”待遇问题,而只存在“区民”待遇或“居民”待遇问题。这一问题值得另辟专题加以研究。当然,在某些具体待遇措施方面,也不妨参照外资国民待遇原则进行处理。

国民待遇的上述自然定义,为各国国内法所普遍主张与肯定。例如,1804 年《法国民法典》第 11 条规定:“外国人,如其本国和法国订有条约允许法国人在其国内享有某些民事权利者,在法国亦得享有同样的民事权利。”1829 年《荷兰民法典》第 2 条则规定:“凡在王国之领土内者,皆为自由之人,均保有私权享受之能力。”作为英美法系的代表,美国的《对外关系法》第 722 条也规定:除非法律另有规定,外国人在美国可享受与本国国民同等的保护。在这三种关于国民待遇的国内立法模式中,《法国民法典》的规定强调以条约互惠作为前提,被称为“互惠主

---

〔2〕 江泽民:《高举邓小平理论伟大旗帜,把建设有中国特色的社会主义事业全面推向二十一世纪——在中国共产党第十五次全国代表大会上的报告》第五之(七)部分。

〔3〕 参见[英]罗伯特·麦克里宁:《国际法教程》1993 年英文版,第 148 页。

义”的国民待遇条款，是国民待遇条款的早期模式；荷兰与美国的有关规定则旨在倡导内、外国民的平等对待，而不以互惠为前提，故又称“平等主义”的国民待遇条款，是国民待遇条款的现代模式。[4] 显然这两种国内立法模式的主要区别仅在于是否以互惠作为国民待遇的前提，其基本精神乃是一致的，那就是强调内、外国民的权利平等，一方面反对对外国人的歧视，即“次国民待遇”，另一方面反对对外国人的特权，即“超国民待遇”。[5]

历史上，国民待遇曾成为发展中国家反对发达国家以所谓的“国际标准主义”为幌子的特权要求，而倡导“国内标准主义”的法理依据。过去，西方一些学者，以发展中国家政治不良、法制不善、行政低效为借口，主张对外国投资者的保护仅依据国民待遇标准是不够的，而应使外国投资者享受高于本国国民的“国际最低标准”的保护，如此方为“公平合理”，否则便构成“国家责任”。[6] 这种霸权主义逻辑自然遭到广大发展中国家的有力反驳。如南美著名法学家卡尔沃就明确提出，国家主权平等，“属于一国领土内的外国人同该国国民有同等受保护的权利，而不应要求更大的保护；当受到任何侵害时，应依赖所在国政府来解决，而不应由外国人的本国出面要求任何金钱补偿……政府对外国人的责任不能超过其对本国国民的责任”。[7] 也就是说，外国人在一国境内所享有的权利与保护，应以本国国民所享有的权利与保护为准，而不应要求高于本国国民的待遇，此即为国内标准主义的基本内涵，其实质就是主张实行国民待遇，而强调反对“超国民”的特权。

发展中国家坚持国内标准主义与国民待遇，并不意味着完全排斥有关国际法律规则的适用。事实上，外资国民待遇既有国内法律渊源，也有国际法律渊源。而且，从发展来看，似乎其国际法律基础有不断强化的趋势。众所周知，长期以来，南北国家聚讼纷纷，国民待遇条款只能在双边条约与某些区域性（如欧盟、北美、东盟）国际条约中得以体现，在全球性国际投资条约如《多边投资担保机构公约》（MIGA 公约）与《解决国家与他国国民间投资争端公约》（ICSID 公约）中，国民待遇条款一直被迫搁置一旁。但是，在 1993 年底达成的乌拉圭回合“一揽子”协定中，却事实上纳入了许多关于外资国民待遇的规范。它们集中体现在《与贸

---

〔4〕 关于“互惠主义”与“平等主义”的国民待遇之分野与承继，详见梅仲协：《国际私法新论》，台湾三民书局 1980 年版，第 143 页。

〔5〕 姚梅镇教授也曾强调指出，国民待遇的主要精神是从国际法上的平等原则出发，既反对对外国投资者的歧视，也反对对外国投资者的特权。参见姚梅镇：《国际投资法》，武汉大学出版社 1987 年版，第 287 页。

〔6〕 例见费陀洛斯：《对外国投资者的政府保证》，1962 年英文版，第 214～215 页；柯伦费尔：《外国投资的保护》，1972 年英文版，第 59 页。

〔7〕 卡尔沃：《卡尔沃条款》，西娅英译本（1955），第 18、19 页。

易有关的投资措施协议》(TRIMs)和《服务贸易总协定》(GATS)之中,其他协议,如《与贸易有关的知识产权协议》(TRIPS)及《争端解决规则与程序谅解》(DSU)中的国民待遇规则事实上也与外资国民待遇密切相关。[8] 不仅如此,发达国家还"乘胜追击",意图在世贸组织的框架内制定一项国际多边投资协议,并以国民待遇作为基本原则之一。尽管这种多边投资协议的达成断非一蹴而就,但在世界经济一体化的大潮之下,也未必全无可能。对此,发展中国家,包括我国,应有充分的思想准备。

不过,在国际条约中有关国民待遇的规定却往往与上述国内法规定不尽相同。以双边投资保护协定为例,世界各国的双边投资保护协定中的国民待遇条款大致有两种模式:一种指东道国给予外国投资的待遇应等同于(as the same favourable as) 其给予本国国民的待遇;另一种则指东道国给予外国投资的待遇应不低于(no less favourable than) 其给予本国投资的待遇。前者如中国与英国签订的双边投资保护协定(以下简称中英协定);后者如中国与日本签订的双边投资保护协定(以下简称中日协定)。显然,前一种规定与上述各国国内法的有关规定是一致的,而后一种规定则与各国国内法的有关规定有重大差别。如前所述,各国国内立法上的国民待遇倡导的是内、外国民的平等对待,既反对歧视,也反对特权;而按上述后一种规定,则"国民待遇"成为最低标准待遇,换言之,它只反对对外国人的歧视,而不反对给外国人以特权,只反对"次国民待遇",而不反对"超国民待遇"。

我们认为,双边投资保护协定中的后一种国民待遇规定并不是要给国民待遇下一个有别于其自然定义与有关国内立法的新定义,而只是国民待遇条款的一种特殊的表述方式,我们不妨称这种条款为"非次国民待遇条款"。"非次国民待遇条款"措辞上的这种特殊性主要是由双边投资条约的特点决定的:与国内立法不同,双边投资条约更侧重于强调对缔约国海外侨民(投资者)的尽可能充分的保护,使其免受歧视待遇;从另一个角度来说,采用这种措辞,也是为了不妨碍东道国在特定时期,基于特定政策需要而施予外国人以某种特别优惠与便利的主权权利的正当行使。它本身并不暗示东道国"应"给予外国投资者以高于本国国民的"国际最低标准"待遇。

实际上,即便是上述双边投资保护协定关于国民待遇的第一种规定,也并不妨碍东道国在特殊情况下对外国投资者提供特殊的优惠与便利。许多订有国民待遇条款的双边投资保护协定都同时规定,该协定(包括其国民待遇条款)并不

---

〔8〕 参见单文华:《世界贸易组织协定中的国际投资规范评析》,载《法学研究》1996 年第 2 期。

妨碍缔约一方根据其国内法和国际法给予缔约另一方投资者以更优惠待遇。[9]中国与摩洛哥签订的投资保护协定(以下简称中摩协定)第8条就有此类"权利保留条款"(preservation-of-rights clauses)。即便是条约中并没有这种明确的规定,各东道国也可以从国家主权原则出发,做出这种特惠规定与安排,而事实上任何外国投资者及其母国均不会以"国民待遇"的条款义务为由来反对这种求之不得的优惠。所以,可以说,国民待遇与特惠待遇在条约上与实践中均是相容的,尽管在概念上与理论上可能是相悖的。这就意味着我国取消对外资的种种优惠政策与措施,并不是基于国民待遇的条约义务,而主要是基于发展国民经济与深化改革开放的现实需要。

进而言之,国民待遇甚至也并不完全排除东道国对外国投资施以特别的限制。首先,对于外资国民待遇,国际上存在两项公认的"一般例外":[10]第一,在外资准入(即投资领域)方面,东道国一般都可以对外国投资加以特殊的限制。这种例外有时在双边投资保护协定中有明确表示,如中日协定第2条第1款规定,缔约一方有权根据其本国的有关法律与法规,决定对缔约另一方国民与公司在其境内投资的许可;更多时候则表现为各国国内立法的具体规定。一般来说,发达国家禁止或限制外资准入的领域多为公用事业、交通、矿业、银行、保险、国防、原子能工业等等;而发展中国家则多集中于公用事业、航空、内陆运输、电信、国防、武器弹药、印刷、无线电与电视等领域。[11] 1995年,我国发布了《指导外商投资方向的暂行规定》和《外商投资产业指导目录》,具体列明了禁止、限制与鼓励外商投资的产业目录,并规定,此三类所列之外的则全部为"允许类"的外商投资项目。其中关于禁止与限制外商投资的产业目录实质上就是外资准入方面的国民待遇例外的具体表现形式。外资国民待遇的第二个一般例外便是公共秩序保留例外,即东道国可以以维护公共秩序(社会公共利益)与保证国家安全为由,对外国投资实行差别待遇。中日协定附加议定书第3条就包括了这一内容。事实上,外资准入方面的国民待遇例外很多就是基于公共秩序与国家安全的考虑,所以,这里的"公共秩序例外"应主要指外资进入以后,在对其实施监督管理方面的公共秩序例外。

除上述两项"一般例外"外,根据双边投资保护协定与各国外资立法,东道国往往还可以维持一些特殊的外资国民待遇例外与限制。如中日协定附加议定书第3条规定,缔约一方为了国民经济的正常发展,在实际需要时,可以对缔约另一

---

[9] 参见联合国跨国公司中心:《双边投资条约》,1988年英文版,第55页。

[10] 同上书,第46~47页。

[11] 参见陈安:《国际投资法》,鹭江出版社1987年版,第142~144页。

方的投资者实行差别待遇;中英协定第3条第3款则规定缔约任何一方应尽量根据其法律和法规的规定给予国民待遇。在这两个协定中,“正常发展”“实际需要”与“尽量给予”等极富弹性的概念,无疑为东道国实施国民待遇的例外与限制留下了极大的空间。可以认为,这些弹性概念的纳入,使得缔约任何一方均无需承担国民待遇的实质性义务。因而,这两个协定的有关条款,只能说是体现了国民待遇的一定内容,但尚不能说是确定了国民待遇的“原则”或“标准”。即据此缔约一方投资者在缔约另一方只享有内容十分有限的国民待遇,而不是全面的、只存在少量例外的国民待遇。从各国国内立法与实践来看,这些特殊的例外与限制主要指董事或经理人员国籍限制、当地股权要求、外资逐步退出要求、外汇管制措施、国产化率要求、内销比例要求、出口实绩要求、外汇平衡要求、当地雇佣要求等。[12] 其中,不少属于所谓的“履行要求”(performance requirements)。[13] 当然,这些例外与限制的具体内容是不断变化的,目前总的趋势是不断减少。例如,根据乌拉圭回合谈判达成的《与贸易有关的投资措施协议》(TRIMs),许多国家都修改了其外资立法中关于当地成分(国产化率)要求、贸易平衡要求、出口实绩要求等方面的规定,使之与TRIMs的规定相吻合。

在国际经贸条约中,国民待遇条款与最惠国待遇条款往往是结合起来使用的。国民待遇条款旨在确保内、外国民之间的平等,最惠国待遇则旨在确保外国国民之间的平等。二者相互为用,构成“不歧视原则”不可缺一的两翼。值得强调的是,即使甲、乙两国(例如中、德两国)之间的投资保护协定只提相互给予最惠国待遇,而未提国民待遇,但甲国与丙国的双边投资保护协定(如中日协定)却规定相互提供国民待遇标准的话,则按最惠国待遇的原理,乙国(德国)也应享有甲国(中国)的国民待遇。因此,即使一国在对外条约中不泛提国民待遇而泛提最惠国待遇,只要该国给予任何一国以国民待遇标准,则这种国民待遇应立即自动和无条件地给予其他与其确立了最惠国待遇关系的国家。最惠国待遇条款的这种法律效应,我们不妨称为“多边自动传导效应”。然而,如果据此认为我国与日本、英国等国已确立了相互间的投资国民待遇原则,则这一待遇原则将自动适用于与我国订有双边投资保护协定的近80个国家,[14] 从而意味着我国已普遍确立国民待遇标准。[15] 这显然与事实是不相符合的。这也从反面说明中日、中英

〔12〕 参见姚梅镇:《比较外资法》,武汉大学出版社1993年版,第302页。

〔13〕 关于“履行要求”,详见本文第二部分。

〔14〕 这类双边投资保护协定都含有最惠国待遇的规定。

〔15〕 参见斯坦纳特:《假如双边投资条约奏效:美国与中国之间的双边投资条约建议案评析》,载《中国法学刊》(英文版)1988年第2期;参见联合国跨国公司中心《双边投资条约》1988年英文版,第48页。

协定所确立的只是有限的国民待遇，而不是国民待遇原则或标准。

二、外资国民待遇的外延

究竟在什么范围内对外资实行国民待遇，这是当前国人最关心的一个相关问题。而且，应该承认，这同时也是一个难以简单作答的问题。实际上，上文关于国民待遇内涵的界定已在一定程度上勾勒了外资国民待遇的初步轮廓，这里拟对其作进一步剖析。

外国投资活动以外国投资机构建立为准，大致可划分为两个阶段，即外资准入（Admission of Foreign Investment）阶段与外资运营阶段（Operation of Foreign Investment）。[16] 前一阶段处于外国投资机构建立之前，后一阶段则处于外国投资机构建立之后。

（一）外资准入与国民待遇

如前所述，外资准入是外资国民待遇的一般例外之一。近年来，尽管各国对外资准入有逐步放宽的趋势，但无论发达国家抑或发展中国家，都保留了不同程度的外资准入限制权。在乌拉圭回合关于《服务贸易总协定》的谈判中，服务领域的"市场准入"与"国民待遇"都只是"具体承诺义务"（specific commitment），而不是一般义务。即各国经过与他国谈判，可以自主确定服务市场准入与国民待遇的领域、资格与条件限制。在双边投资条约中，绝大多数国家都没有提出对外资准入实行国民待遇的要求。只有美国例外，它为尽可能撬开他国的市场大门，在对外双边投资条约谈判中，往往会提出对外资准入方面实行国民待遇。然而由于发展中国家的普遍抵制，美国的这种"非分"要求收效不大。[17] 又如前述，在中日协定与中英协定中，尽管有国民待遇条款，但都同时有外资准入的国民待遇例外的规定（中英协定第2条第1款，中日协定第2条第1款）。

在实践中，各国对外资准入的限制主要表现在两个方面：一方面，各国都划定了禁止或限制外资进入的领域；另一方面，各国一般都规定了外资准入的资格条件。目前，无论是发达国家还是发展中国家，在一些关系国计民生的经济敏感部门，如公用事业、交通运输、国防工业、金融业等，一般都对外国直接投资作禁止或限制性规定，保证本国资本在这些要害部门的所有权优势，以确保本国对这些部

〔16〕 参见米切勒·P. 达登：《美国双边投资条约》，载《国际学刊》（英文版）1993年第3期；迈克尔·R. 雷丁：《东盟的双边投资条约：比较分析》，载《杜克法律学刊》（英文版）1992年第42卷。

〔17〕 参见帕马拉·B. 肯：《美国双边投资条约计划》，《斯坦福国际法学刊》（英文版）1985年第2期；艾里诺·罗伯特·赖维斯：《美国—波兰有关商务与经济关系的条约》，载《国际商务法律与政策》（英文版）1991年第22卷第3期。

门的控制权。这对维护本国经济主权具有重要的意义。[18] 在这方面,即便是声称对外资最为开放的美国也不例外。过去在航空运输、远洋和沿海航运、银行业、保险业、政府特许行业、政府保险和信贷计划、能源和电力开发、土地和自然资源的利用、代客报关服务行、不动产所有权、电台和电视台广播、电报和电话服务、海底电传服务、卫星通信等领域,美国或禁止或限制外资进入。在这些领域,外资是无国民待遇可言的。[19]

以往对禁止或限制设立中外合资经营企业、中外合作经营企业的行业,我国的外资立法均无具体的规定。对于外商投资企业,虽有这方面的限定,但仍然不够明确,其中采用了像"中国政府规定禁止设立外资企业的其他行业"之类的弹性条款。[20] 总之,过去我国对外商投资方向的管制一直透明度不够,这也是近年来许多发展中国家外资立法的通病。[21] 为了增加我国外资政策的透明度,以及贯彻国家产业政策,积极引导外商投资,1995 年 6 月,我国同时发布了《指导外商投资方向的暂行规定》(以下简称《暂行规定》)和《外商投资产业指导目录》(以下简称《指导目录》),把外商投资项目分为鼓励、允许、限制和禁止四类。鼓励类、限制类和禁止类的外商投资项目分别由《指导目录》具体列明。除此之外,均为允许类的外商投资项目。从这两个法律文件的规定来看,我国明确划定了目前限制或禁止外商投资的产业,这表明在投资方向上我国也没有对外资全面实行国民待遇。但是,为了体现进一步扩大开放的政策,较之以往的外资立法与实践,这两个法律文件却又相对拓宽了外商投资的领域。[22]

拓宽外商投资领域,一方面是基于我国合理有效地利用外资的需要,另一方面也反映了外国投资者的要求。例如,以往,我国的商业零售和批发、对外贸易以及服务等行业,均不允许外资涉足。然而,中国巨大的潜在市场对外商极具吸引力。由此,许多发达国家不断向我国施压,要求我国开放这些投资领域。但考虑到我国国内企业竞争力有限,为了对国内市场实行必要的保护,对发达国家的这些要求,过去我国一概予以拒绝,这曾经成为中美双边投资保护协定谈判搁浅的

---

〔18〕 参见曾华群:《国际投资法概论》,厦门大学出版社 1995 年版,第 143 页。

〔19〕 参见琼斯费·帕特森:《美国—埃及双边投资条约:一个供将来谈判之用的样板》,《康奈尔国际法学刊》(英文版)1985 年第 2 期。

〔20〕 参见《外资企业法实施细则》,第 4 条、第 5 条。

〔21〕 参见亚伯拉罕·F. I. 希哈塔:《有关外国直接投资准入的最新趋向》,载《ICSID 评论——外国投资法学刊》(英文版)1994 年第 1 期。

〔22〕 参见《就发布实施我国〈指导外商投资方向暂行规定〉和〈外商投资产业指导目录〉,国家计委负责人答记者问》,新华社北京 1995 年 6 月 27 日电。

主要原因之一。[23] 现在,《指导目录》已将这些以前属于禁止外商投资的行业转变为只是限制外商投资,而且,随着各项条件的进一步成熟,我国还将逐步放宽对这些外商投资领域的限制。

值得一提的是,从总体上看,我国对外商投资领域的开放度明显高于许多发展中国家。例如,不少发展中国家,尤其是那些弱小的发展中国家,为了维护本国的经济命脉和国家安全,往往把交通运输、邮电通信以及矿产开发等行业列为限制或禁止外商投资的领域。但是,根据《指导目录》,这些行业在我国基本上属于鼓励类的外商投资行业。这是由我国的具体国情所决定的,适当放宽对外商投资领域的限制,并不会危及我国的经济主权和根本利益。

在划定限制外资准入领域的同时,目前无论是发展中国家,还是发达国家,均在不同程度上设立了外资准入的条件,在这方面不对外国投资者实行国民待遇。从发展中国家的立法实践来看,它们一般都建立了外资的审查和甄别制度。例如,一些投资环境较差的非洲国家,为了吸引更多的外资,虽然没有开列限制外资流入的各种条件,但是至少都订有外国投资不得损害东道国公共道德、公共健康以及不得造成环境污染等条款。大多数发展中国家(包括中国)对外资的进入都设立了各种限制性条件。事实上,即便是发达国家也都有外资准入的程序性规定。像日本、西班牙等发达国家的法律规定,外国投资需经事先登记;英国和美国的做法与之类似;而澳大利亚、加拿大、新西兰、法国等发达国家的法律则规定,所有新的外国投资都须经过事先审批。无论采用哪一种程序制度,这些发达国家都保留了在一定条件下拒绝接受外资的权力。[24] 目前,在外资准入方面,发达国家与发展中国家争议的焦点是发展中国家就此设置的各种"履行要求"(perf ormance requirements)的问题。所谓"履行要求",是指东道国把外国投资者允诺承担某项特定的义务作为批准该项外国投资进入的前提条件,具体包括当地成分要求、外汇平衡要求以及当地股权要求等。[25] 1992 年,由世界银行和国际货币基金组织联合设立的行政委员会(即发展委员会)制定了一项《外国直接投资待遇指南》。该指南从保护发达国家的利益出发,要求各国注意各种"履行要求"对国际投资的阻碍作用以及可能给东道国带来的法律规避问题和腐败问题(该指南第2

---

〔23〕 参见斯坦纳特:《假如双边投资条约奏效:美国与中国之间的双边投资条约建议案评析》,载《中国法学刊》(英文版)1988 年第 2 期。

〔24〕 参见安东尼·帕拉:《反映在各国投资法中的外资管理原则》,载《ICSID 评论——外国投资法学刊》(英文版)1992 年第 2 期。

〔25〕 参见琼斯沃尔德·W. 沙拉克斯:《正在形成之中的一个有关外国直接投资的新条约构架》,载《航空法与商务学刊》1985 年第 50 卷;威廉·E. 古林:《美国双边投资条约:是对履行要求的回答吗?》,载巴特·S. 费哈与杰弗·塔纳主编:《对各国企业的管理:来自国内与国际的挑战》,1983 年英文版,第 129 ~ 142 页。

部分第3条)。然而,这些“履行要求”直接关系到发展中国家利用外资的根本利益和宗旨,因此,它们是不会被轻易放弃的。例如,在与各发展中国家所进行的双边投资保护协定的谈判中,美国以对外资准入实行国民待遇为由,要求这些发展中国家取消已有的各种“履行要求”,但均未奏效或未完全奏效。[26] 大部分发展中国家(如埃及、海地、扎伊尔、摩洛哥、孟加拉国、突尼斯以及土耳其等国)都拒绝承担取消各种“履行要求”的强制性义务,只是承诺:“应努力”(shall endeavor)而为之;另一些发展中国家(如斯里兰卡、阿根廷和巴拿马等国)则以其他方式对美国式协定中的样板条款作了变通或设置了例外。当然,作为一种相互妥协的结果,发展中国家也会在“履行要求”的问题上对发达国家做出一定程度上的妥协与让步,《与贸易有关的投资措施协议》(TRIMs)之达成就是很好的例证。事实上,TRIMs协议所禁止的投资措施,如当地成分要求、贸易平衡要求、外汇平衡要求以及国内销售要求等均为所谓的“履行要求”。对于这些措施,世贸组织的发展中成员也将不得不及时予以裁撤。其中的当地成分要求和贸易平衡要求就通常被认为是违反了关贸总协定规定的国民待遇原则。[27]

在我国目前的一些外资立法与实践中,也存在一些与TRIMs协议不相符合的“履行要求”措施。[28] 首先,当地成分要求方面,我国有关法律虽没有明确的“当地成分要求”条款,但有关法律却有外商投资企业所需的设备、原材料、燃料、零配件等物资应当尽量在中国购买的规定,如《外资企业法》第15条及《中外合资经营企业法》第9条及其实施条例第57条即是。在审批外资项目时,我国各级政府往往也有规定要求购买一定数量的国内产品作为生产投入,并以此作为项目获得批准或享受优惠的先决条件。例如,我国在审批外商投资汽车项目时,就把国产化程度作为要件之一。还有的文件则以国产化率高低作为适用差别税率的主要依据,对不按期实现国产化计划的企业征收高税率。在国家批准的建设期内,对按合同规定国产化计划进度进口散件组装轿车时,关税可适当调减,对不按期实现国产化计划的,则适用高税率。同时,合资企业向国内用户收取的外汇必须与合同中规定的国产化计划相一致,进口散件总量严格控制在合同规定的范围内。此外,在实际工作中,有关部门也把国产化程度高作为一种实绩予以肯定和鼓励,如在考核外商投资企业是否为产品出口型或技术先进型企业时,就把国产化程度

---

〔26〕 参见肯尼斯·J.范德费尔德:《美国双边投资条约:第二次浪潮》,载《密歇根国际法学刊》(英文版)1993年第14卷。

〔27〕 参见埃马努勒·奥普库·阿乌库:《乌拉圭回合的成果将对南、北贸易产生何种影响》,载《世界贸易法学刊》(英文版)1994年第2期,第85页。

〔28〕 参见单文华:《我国外资国民待遇制度的发展与完善》,载《法学研究》1995年第6期。

列为逐年考核的依据之一。[29]

其次,贸易平衡要求方面。这在我国主要有两种表现形式,最明显的是外汇平衡要求。我国《外资企业法》第 16 条及其实施细则第 3 条均要求外资企业自行解决外汇平衡问题,并以此作为允许设立的基本条件之一。《中外合资经营企业法实施条例》第 75 条则要求中外合资经营企业一般应保持外汇收支平衡;国务院关于中外合资企业外汇收支平衡问题的规定也要求“中外合资企业生产的产品多出口、多创汇,做到外汇收支平衡”。与此同时,我国还有以出口为进口先决条件的规定,如《国务院关于鼓励外商投资的规定》第 13 条第 1 款规定,外商投资企业为履行“产品出口合同”需要进口机械设备、原材料、零部件等,不再报请审批,免领进口许可证,由海关凭企业合同或进出口合同验放。而且,上述进口料件,只限于本企业自用,不得在国内市场出售。诚然,上述规定并无进出口数额或价值对等的要求,但以履行出口合同作为进口和免证放行的前提,可被视为贸易平衡要求。

最后,在我国外资立法中,还有许多“出口实绩要求”的规定。例如,我国《外资企业法》第 3 条明确规定设立外资企业的前提条件之一就是“产品全部出口或大部分出口”,该法的实施细则进一步明确该条件意为“年出口产品的产值达到当年全部产值 50% 以上,实现外汇收支平衡或有结余”。同时,我国在审批外商投资企业时,一般要求在外商投资企业合同中,就其产品的内外销比例或内销比例做出具体承诺。例如,《中外合资经营企业法实施条例》第 14 条规定,合资企业合同中应包括“产品在中国境内和境外销售的比例”;新近颁布的《中外合作经营企业法实施细则》第 12 条规定中外合作经营企业也应载明“产品在中国境内销售和境外销售的安排”,虽然避免了“比例”一词,但同样易被视为外销比例要求;《外资企业法实施细则》第 45 条则规定“外资企业在中国市场销售其产品,应当依照批准的销售比例进行”;相应地,外经贸部 1993 年 10 月发布的《关于外商投资企业合同、章程的审查原则和审查要点》则将“产品内外销的比例、方式、定价原则”作为审查要点之一。所有这些规定,都可视为“限制性”的出口实绩要求。

与此同时,我国外资立法中还有不少“引导性”的出口实绩要求。例如,《中外合资经营企业法》第 9 条与《中外合作经营企业法》第 4 条都有鼓励产品出口的一般规定。最为明显的是,我国对外商投资的产品出口企业所提供的一系列特别优惠措施,包括减免关税与降低所得税税率等。例如,《外商投资企业和外国企业所得税法实施细则》第 75 条规定:“外商投资举办的产品出口企业,在依照税法

---

〔29〕 参见单文华:《我国外资国民待遇制度的发展与完善》,载《法学研究》1995 年第 6 期。

规定免征、减征企业所得税期满后，凡当年出口产品产值达到当年企业产品产值百分之七十以上的，可以按照税法规定的税率减半征收企业所得税；经济特区和经济技术开发区以及其他已经按百分之十五的税率缴纳企业所得税的产品出口企业，符合上述条件的，按百分之十的税率征收企业所得税。”此外，1995 年 6 月，国家计委、经委与外经贸部联合发布的《指导外商投资方向暂行规定》第 11 条规定，属于限制类（甲）的外商投资项目，如产品出口销售额占其产品总销售额 70%以上的，经批准可以视为允许类外商投资项目，而不受该规定第 9 条的限制，即可不约定企业经营期限，中方投资中的固定资产部分也可不使用中方投资者自有资金或属于中方投资者所有的资产。这也是一种很明显的出口实绩要求措施。

我国外资立法中的上述与 TRIMs 协议的国民待遇原则不相符的投资措施中，当地成分要求与贸易平衡要求二项是为 TRIMs 协议附件清单所一律禁绝的，故如果我国“复关”成功，则有必要在过渡期（对发展中国家，为《世界贸易组织协定》生效后 5 年）内，逐步修改有关法令，取消有关条款。至于出口实绩要求，则并未为 TRIMs 协定所特别列举，因而不属于一律禁绝的措施，只有结合个案的具体情况，才能界定是否应予取消。这就是说，即使我国成为世贸组织的一员，我们仍可维持有关出口实绩的要求，只是应加以适当的限制。在目前我国尚未加入世贸组织的情况下，上述要求与措施从法理上仍可以维持，但从与世贸组织的国际规范相接轨的角度来考虑，似也应创造条件，逐步减少，及至最后取消。特别是某些含混而缺乏实效的规定如“合资企业所需原材料、燃料、零配件应尽量在中国购买”“鼓励合营企业向境外销售产品”等口号式的条款，徒然授人以柄，不如尽早删除。

（二）外资运营与国民待遇

与外资准入阶段相反，在外资运营阶段，许多国家往往要求提供国民待遇，这一国民待遇，实质上就是指“外商投资企业的国民待遇”。按中外立法与有关条约，外资运营阶段国民待遇主要体现三个方面：司法行政救济方面、民事权益保护方面及宏观管理方面。

司法行政救济方面的国民待遇指因投资而产生的司法审理与行政申诉方面的内外资平等待遇。它可分为两种类型，一种是关于投资经营活动中所发生的普通民事经济纠纷的司法行政救济，如对经济合同、劳动争议的申诉、仲裁与审理，等等；另一种则指涉及国家责任的投资争端的司法行政救济，即在外国投资被国有化、征收或由于战争、武装冲突或东道国的禁兑行为，使投资者丧失对其投资的有效控制从而蒙受损失的情况下，外国投资者所可望获得的东道国的司法与行政救济。[30] 司法行政救济方面的国民待遇实质上是国民待遇最早涉及的领域。国民待遇创设之初,其主旨就是为杜绝视外国人为仇敌的野蛮做法,使外国人与本国人一样,在人身与司法行政救济方面得到最基本的保护。发展到现在,这方面的国民待遇可以说已成为一项国际惯例,世界各国普遍遵循。我国也不例外。例如,我国《民事诉讼法》第15条第1款规定,外国人、无国籍人、外国企业和组织在人民法院起诉、应诉,同中国公民、法人和其他经济组织有同等的诉讼权利。又如,国务院《关于鼓励外商投资的规定》第16条规定,外商投资企业凡遇不合理收费情况,可以拒交或向当地经济委员会直至国家经济委员会申诉。可见,我国在司法行政救济方面为外商投资企业提供的国民待遇是比较充分的。

民事权益保护方面的国民待遇主要包括物权保护方面的国民待遇与债权保护方面的国民待遇。物权保护方面的国民待遇主要指对外商投资企业的投资财产及其收益的控制权与处分权,应与内资企业一样予以保护。这里的"投资财产",可以包括东道国法律所允许的任何股权,债权或类似的请求权、专利权、商标权等工业产权和专有技术权,关于动产与不动产的权利及勘探、开采自然资源的特许权等。这里的"收益"可以包括投资所产生的任何价值形式,如利润、利息、股息、特许权使用费和手续费等。[31] 债权保护方面的国民待遇则指对外商投资企业在与其他企业或公民进行交易流转过程中所发生的债权(如合同权利)的保护应与内资企业所受的保护一样,不受歧视。由于物权、债权等民事权利是任何市场经济都赖以生存发展的基础权利,同时它们又多与国家主权无涉,所以,目前各国一般都对内、外资企业的这两种民事权益平等对待,不分轩轾,外商投资企业一般都享有较充分的国民待遇。事实上,不少国家为了吸引外资甚至会做出特别承诺,为外资提供高于本国投资企业的特殊保护,如承诺不实行国有化、特别保护国外著作权等。我国对外商投资企业的财产保护方面的国民待遇也是比较充分的。我国《宪法》作为国家根本大法,不仅允许外商投资中国,并规定外商投资企业的"合法权利与利益受中华人民共和国法律的保护"。我国《民法通则》第5条也规定"公民、法人的合法民事权益受法律保护";第8条进而规定:除另有规定外,该法关于公民的规定,于中国人、外国人与无国籍人同等适用。这意味着《民法通则》对所有权、债权、知识产权等民事权益的保护一般均及于外国投资者及其投资设立或参与设立的外商投资企业。《中外合资经营企业法》作为最早的与最基本的外商投资企业立法,进一步明确"中国政府依法保护外国合营者按照经中

〔30〕 参见单文华:《市场经济与外商投资企业的国民待遇研究》,载《中国法学》1994年第5期。
〔31〕 同上。

国政府批准的协议、合同、章程在合营企业的投资、应分得的利润和其他合法权益”。该法还特别承诺:“国家对合营企业不实行国有化或征收;在特殊情况下,根据社会公共利益的需要,对合营企业可以依照法律程序实行征收,并给予相应的补偿。”我国对外商投资企业民事财产与权益保护之充分恳切,于此可见一斑。与此同时,根据《商标法》《专利法》《著作权法》《计算机软件保护条例》等知识产权立法,外商与外商投资企业在知识产权这种特殊产权的保护方面也享有国民待遇。在债权保护方面,除上述《民法通则》所提供的同等保护外,《经济合同法》《涉外经济合同法》《担保法》《票据法》《保险法》等重要立法均未将外商投资企业与国内投资企业区别对待,即外商投资企业也享有国民待遇。〔32〕

宏观管理方面的外资国民待遇是指东道国在对外商投资企业经营活动的管理与干预方面应与内资企业一视同仁,不分彼此。具体来说,它包括东道国在人、财、物、产、供、销等各个方面与各个环节对外商投资企业实施的监督与管理措施应与对内资企业的有关措施一般无二,毫无歧视。据此,举凡雇佣限制、利润汇出限制、物资采购限制(当地成分要求)、生产限制、销售限制(如外销比例要求)等措施,如系专门针对外商投资企业,则构成违反国民待遇原则。显然,这里的不少措施实质上就是前面提到的“履行要求”,但这并不意味着重复或矛盾,因为这类“履行要求”措施既可以用于外资准入阶段,也可用于外资运营阶段。〔33〕 已如前述,由于外商投资企业不同程度地存在“外国控制因素”,其对东道国的效忠程度往往与内资企业有一定区别,因此,各国一般都对其施以必要的引导、管理与限制,以使其与本国的现实需要相符合。这种对外资进行的管理的主权权力对有着长期殖民地历史的发展中国家尤为重要,在实践上也是在发展中国家实施得较为普遍与广泛。事实上,这一主权权力也得到了《各国经济权利与义务宪章》(以下简称《宪章》)等国际法律文件的充分肯定。〔34〕 但是,一些发达国家却试图凭借其经济优势,利用发展中国家急需外资“输血”的现实,迫使发展中国家实行“绝对的”国民待遇标准,从而限制乃至取消发展中国家对其境内外商投资企业进行管理的主权权力。例如,在1983年开始的中美双边投资保护协定的谈判中,美方就不顾中国的经济现实,不切实际地要求一步到位,给予美国在华投资以广泛的国

---

〔32〕 值得注意的是,我国就国内经济合同与涉外经济合同分别立法,并不意味着对外商投资企业实行歧视待遇,因为在这方面外商投资企业与内资企业一样,就其国内经济合同关系适用《经济合同法》,而就其涉外经济合同关系适用《涉外经济合同法》,二者并不分轩轾。

〔33〕 参见斯坦纳特:《假如双边投资条约奏效:美国与中国之间的双边投资条约建议案评析》,载《中国法学刊》(英文版)1988年第2期。

〔34〕 该《宪章》第2条第2款明确规定:“每个国家都有权根据本国的法律与条例,按本国的国家目标以及本国优先权的原则,在国内管辖权范围内,对外国投资者加以管理并行使权力。”

民待遇。[35] 事实上,正是由于美方在国民待遇及国有化补偿标准等方面索价过高而致使谈判自 1987 年起搁浅至今。

少数发达国家在双边投资条约中提出过分要求的同时,还试图将其双边条约有关条款多边化,从而使外资国民待遇成为一项几无限制的多边国际法律义务。在乌拉圭回合关于 TRIMs 与 GATS 等协议的谈判中,这些发达国家就曾表明了这一意向,只是由于发展中国家的坚决抵制而未能得逞。在世贸组织的第一次部长会议即新加坡部长会议期间,这些国家老调重弹,又提出了建立一个世贸组织框架内的多边投资协议的动议,并将这一动议列入了世贸组织的研究议题之中。但是,很明显,这距离真正的多边国际投资协议仍很遥远。

在这方面,还有必要提及的是世界银行发展委员会 1992 年制定的《外国直接投资待遇指南》(以下简称《指南》)。这份由世界银行集团各成员机构的法律顾问们所起草的文件的序言声称,它是在对全世界各国有关外资的立法、双边条约、多边条约以及各种学说、判例进行广泛考察之后制定的,是普遍接受的国际习惯法演进过程中的重要一步。[36] 但究其实质,它主要反映的仍只是发达国家的意志与利益。这份指南不仅要求东道国对外国投资者的人身、财产权利与利益、进出口许可、劳动雇佣、出入境与居留以及其他相关事项实行国民待遇,而且要求东道国对外国投资企业的建立、经营、管理、控制、权利的行使以及其他相关活动等方面都实行国民待遇。无疑,这是一项范围极广的国民待遇规则,并且对该国民待遇原则未规定任何实质性的限制条件。[37] 这显然是为广大发展中国家所不可接受的。对于该指南的实质,指南起草小组召集人、世行法律总顾问希哈塔先生曾一语道破,他指出:目前,各发展中国家都保有对外资进行管理的权利,然而,该起草小组制订的指南不仅仅是对现有法律文件所体现出的一般趋势的肯定,而且是对其有所超越,即从中抽取所谓的“最好实践”(best practice)制定而成的。言外之意,这个世行的智囊团在起草该指南时,并不是全面、客观、公正地反映各国,尤其是发展中国家的立法与实践,而是按发达国家所惬意的标准与尺度,对有关规则与实践进行了“加工”与“取舍”。显然,这样制定出来的文件不可能是国际习惯法的编纂,而且恐怕也很难算得上是有关习惯法演进的中间环节。因为,外资国民待遇,尤其是外资管理方面的国民待遇的实施,取决于东道国的经济体制与经济发展水平这两个前提条件的现状,而这两个经济前提在各国的发展状况参

---

〔35〕《呈报发展委员会的有关外国投资待遇法律框架的最终报告》,载《ICSID 评论——外国投资法学刊》(英文版)1992 年第 2 期。

〔36〕 参见约翰·弗雷斯比:《投资条约陷入僵局》,载《中国商务评论》1986 年 9 ~ 10 月号。

〔37〕 详见该《指南》第三部分。

差不齐,国际投资市场也远未成熟到可以完全自由流动的地步,所以,《指南》的这种几近无限的外资国民待遇原则目前只能是少数国家的超前理论预设而已。全面的国民待遇,特别是外资管理方面的国民待遇,目前仍旧只是发展深化中的外资待遇准则,而不是世界各国的普遍实践,当然更谈不上国际习惯法。

三、对外资实行国民待遇的基本前提

经济基础决定上层建筑。外资国民待遇制度作为上层建筑的一种表现形式也不例外,它也需要一个相应的经济基础作为前提。事实上,这既是我国过去不“泛提”国民待遇的根本原因,也是我国现在倡导国民待遇的主要依据。[38]

首先,从经济体制层面来看,外资国民待遇,尤其是外资管理方面的国民待遇必须建立在市场经济体制之上。

从根本上说,计划经济体制与外资国民待遇制度是不相容的。计划经济体制的基本特征是以高度集中统一的计划而不是市场作为配置资源的基本手段。由于这种体制过分强调各类经济主体对国家计划的严格服从,实质上完全否定了不同经济主体独立的经济利益,进而也就否定了建立在这种独立利益之上的竞争与市场的意义。换言之,在计划经济体制下,由于排除经济主体的独立利益,因而不存在真正的市场,也就不存在真正的市场主体之间的竞争。既然“国民”不是市场主体,而只是国家计划的执行单位与计算符号,那么这样的“国民待遇”毫无意义可言。正因如此,传统上,西方国家与社会主义国家签订的双边投资保护协定,都没有列入有关国民待遇的条款,即使列入,实行的也不是真正意义上的国民待遇原则。[39] 例如,1989 年加拿大与前苏联缔结的此类协定就只规定,缔约一方应“尽量地、并根据其法律和法规”给予缔结另一方投资者以国民待遇(第 3 条第 4 款)。这样的规定与前述中英协定的条款如出一辙。又如,1990 年美国与波兰缔结的双边投资保护协定虽然原则上规定了国民待遇原则,但在该协定的附件中,波兰一方开列了大量的“例外”,美国学者古德曼认为,这些例外几乎使该协定本来规定的“绝对”国民待遇变成了“侏儒”。[40] 过去的中外双边投资保护协定也不例外。如前所述,在我国对外签订的双边投资保护协定中,一般都不泛提国民待遇,即使在提及国民待遇的协定如中日协定及中英协定中,也并未承担国民待遇的实质性义务。究其原因,主要是因为我国过去实行的是集中程度较高的计划

---

〔38〕 参见单文华:《市场经济与外商投资企业国民待遇研究》,载《中国法学》1994 年第 5 期。

〔39〕 参见罗伯特·K. 帕特森:《加拿大投资促进和保护条约》,载《加拿大国际法年刊·1991 年》(英文版)。

〔40〕 参见南希·J. 古德曼:《国际交易:波兰双边投资条约——美国力图架构东欧经济发展的一大表现》,载《哈佛国际法学刊》(英文版)1991 年第 32 卷。

经济模式，市场只在很小范围内存在，根本谈不上是配置资源的基础性手段。具体而言，过去，为了保证国家计划的实现，国内企业尤其是国营企业，在生产、流通、分配等各个领域对国家负有特殊的义务，显然这些特殊的义务不可能一并施加于外商投资企业；[41]另一方面，国家在要求国内企业承担更过义务的同时，在工资、价格、物资供应、信贷以及政府补贴等方面，也给它们以特殊的支持，当然这些特殊的支持也不可能由外商投资企业来分享；加之，这些待遇本身在国内全民、集体和私营企业之间并不一致，加入对外商投资企业的经营活动实行国民待遇，也缺乏一项统一的参照标准。

与此相反，市场经济体制所具有的平等性、竞争性、国际性、透明性与规范性等特性，则使得国民待遇的实行有了理论的基础与现实的可能。[42] 首先，市场经济作为商品经济发展的较高级形态，平等性依旧是其最基本的特征之一。它首先要求存在一个统一的、一视同仁的市场主体体系，不论这些主体的所有制性质或其他社会属性，在市场上一律得以平等对待、公平竞争。显然，这里也包括对内资企业和外商投资企业的平等待遇。其次，竞争是市场的全部动力与活力的源泉，竞争的前提就是主体间权利义务的平等性；在不平等的主体之间是不存在竞争的，至少不存在完全意义上的竞争。竞争呼唤平权，平权也就意味着国民待遇有了法理的基础。再次，市场经济发展到今天，早已形成了跨越国界的规模化的大经济，任何国家要想发展经济，就不能孤立于国际大市场之外。这是为中外的无数现实所反复印证了的真理，也是我国重启国门对外不断开放的主要理论依据。在经济国际化日益加深的形势下，“国民”也越来越有“世界公民”的意味，犹如在国际大市场中对任何一国的产品都应平等对待一样，在当代国际大家庭中，给予其他国家国民以本国国民同等的待遇，也是情理之中的事情。

最后，当代国际投资的历史表明：在国际资本市场上，投资者往往更愿意将资本投放在一个虽然没有明显优惠待遇，但却有很高的政策、法律的透明度并能获得公平待遇的地区，而不是投向一个看起来待遇优惠，却充满着“内部规定”和歧视待遇的地区。这主要是因为当今国际经济交往日益频繁、日趋快捷，在瞬息万变的国际市场上，投资的安全性成了投资决策的首要参考因素。相对而言，国民待遇以国内立法与国际条约为依据，其可操作性、规范性与透明度远较其他待遇标准为佳，故必然更契合国际化市场经济的需要。

从世界各国的立法与实践来看，大凡实行市场经济的国家，一般都提倡给外

---

〔41〕 参见巴利沙·T. B. 科洪纳：《投资保护条约：一个澳大利亚人的看法》，载《世界贸易法学刊》（英文版）1987年第21卷。

〔42〕 参见单文华：《市场经济与外商投资企业的国民待遇研究》，载《中国法学》1994年第5期。

资以国民待遇，如美国、瑞士、英国、德国、法国等发达市场经济国家，对内、外资基本上做到了平等对待。即使是发展中国家，只要是实行了市场经济，一般也都实行或趋向于实行外资国民待遇。1991 年，解决投资争端国际中心（ICSID）对 51 个发展中国家外资立法的调研表明，大多数发展中国家（31 个）给外资以国民待遇，而这些国家又都是推行或已转向市场经济的国家，如亚洲的韩国、菲律宾、也门；欧洲的保加利亚、匈牙利、南斯拉夫；南美的阿根廷、哥伦比亚、巴拉圭等；非洲的埃及、喀麦隆等国。〔43〕 1993 年，我国正式确立了“社会主义市场经济”的宪法地位，〔44〕随后，我国政府即提出要“创造条件，逐步对外商投资企业实行国民待遇”，〔45〕这一时间上的先后承继绝非偶然，而恰恰是市场经济是国民待遇的体制基础这一客观规律的最好注脚。

但是，市场经济体制只是外资国民待遇必要的体制前提，而不是其实现的充分条件，要全面与充分地实施外资国民待遇，尚取决于另一方面的经济基础成就，那就是一国的总体经济实力的充分发展壮大已足以与其他国家分庭抗礼、平等竞争、从宏观上说，对外资实行全面的国民待遇就意味着对一国的民族资本与外国资本一视同仁，其实质就是要解除对民族产业的特殊保护与对外来投资的特别限制，而使两种资本在国内甚至国际市场上迎面相击、平等竞争。换言之，就是要让民族资本“赤膊上阵”，去接受国际资本的挑战和洗礼。这无疑须以民族资本的充分成长发育作为前提。实质上，发达国家之所以能够实行且急于在世界范围内推行较广泛的外资国民待遇，从根本上说，是由于其民族资本与综合国力已十分强大。这样，一方面，享有其国民待遇的外来资本一般不仅不会构成对民族经济的威胁，而且能成为民族经济很好的补充；另一方面，本国资本借助“国民待遇”安排，则可以在世界市场上自由流动，选择最佳商机，赚取最大利润。反过来，如果一发展中国家民族资本尚未壮大，民族经济尚未振兴，却一味侈谈对外资实行全面的国民待遇，则是极不相宜的。因为那样无异于“引狼入室”“以卵击石”，有百害而无一利。发展中国家（包括中国）之所以长期反对给外资以广泛的国民待遇，正是基于这种深刻的认识。

1979 年以后，我国开始了市场取向的改革，国民经济的计划性不断减少，市场性不断增强。但长期以来，市场并未取代计划而成为配置资源（尤其是重要资源）的基础性手段。在这种条件下，可以说，我国对外资实行较为全面的国民待遇

---

〔43〕 参见斯坦纳特：《假如双边投资条约奏效：美国与中国之间的双边投资条约建议案评析》，载《中国法学刊》（英文版）1988 年第 2 期。

〔44〕 参见《宪法》修正案（1993 年 3 月 29 日八届人大一次会议通过）第七条。

〔45〕 参见中共中央《关于建立社会主义市场经济体制若干问题的决定》第七部分。

的两个前提无一具备，因此，我国从不“泛提”国民待遇，即使少数双边投资保护协定，如中日协定、中英协定偶尔提及，也都极有节制，极为谨慎。1993年，我国提出确立社会主义市场经济体制模式，国民经济总量也有了较大的发展，外资国民待遇实施的两个条件中的第一个条件已初步具备，第二个条件也已达到了一定的水准，因此，我国方能明确提出要对外商投资企业实行国民待遇。然而，应该承认，迄今为止，我国的市场经济体制并未完全建立，民族资本与民族经济的发育在质量与效益上仍很有限，因此可以说，全面的外资国民待遇的两个前提在我国仍未完全具备，所以，我们只能“创造条件”“逐步”地实行，而不是说也不能说是已“万事俱备”，可以一蹴而就。

可见，对于“对外商投资企业实行国民待遇”这一重大国策，我们不能简单地、片面地理解，而应作全面与深入的分析。首先，从利用外资的角度来看，这一决策不仅意味着我国对外资具体法律与措施要进行调整，如某些限制的取消与某些优惠的淡化；更意味着我国外资政策的重大转向，即适应引进外资成熟期的实际需要，将外资政策由“减税让利”式的初级外资政策逐步转向“平等竞争”式的高级外资政策。进而言之，这一决策也不仅仅意味着外资政策与法律的调整，它同时还意味着内资企业与民族工业发展路向的调整，意味着改革开放向纵深发展、社会主义市场经济体制的全面建设与贯彻落实，意味着社会生产力的巨大发展与综合国力的不断增强。只要置于这样一个大环境、大背景之下，才能全面准确地理解与认识“对外商投资企业实行国民待遇”这一重大国策，也只有这样，才能正确地与逐步地实施和完善这一重大国策。

世界贸易组织协定中的国际投资规范评析*

《世界贸易组织协定》[1]（以下简称《WTO 协定》）不仅仅是一个全球性的多边贸易协定，由于它首次对与贸易有关的投资措施（TRIMs）及与贸易有关的知识产权（TRIPS）进行了规范，因而，从一定意义上说，它又是4个新的多边投资协定和多边知识产权协定。据此，可以预见，世界贸易组织（WTO）将不仅是世界贸易自由化的主要载体，还是未来世界经济自由化与一体化的主要依托。正如《马拉喀什宣言》所指出的，"世界贸易组织的建立，开创了全球经济合作的新纪元"。

投资问题最初并不是乌拉圭回合谈判的议题，然而，在经过长达八年的谈判所达成的《WTO 协定》中，却存在着大量规范国际投资的条款。这些国际投资规范不仅仅指真《与贸易有关的投资措施协议》（以下简称《TRIMs 协议》），它是指包含在世界贸易组织"一揽子"协议中的，所有具有促进与保护国际投资意义的规定。[2] 显然，《TRIMs 协议》是其主干与核心，此外规范还较集中地体现在《服务贸易总协定》（GATS）、《与贸易有关的知识产权协议》（以下简称《TRIPs 协议》、《争端解决规则与程序谅解》（英文简称 DSU）等其他《WTO 协定》的附属协议之中。可以说，这些国际投资规范是国际投资法领域中最新的、重大的发展。

本文拟对这几个协议中的国际投资规范进行初步评析，期能于我国国际投资法研究及我国涉外投资的立法与实践有所助益。

---

* 本文发表在《法学研究》1996 年第 2 期。

〔1〕 指乌拉圭回合谈判所达成的，以《建立世界贸易组织协定》（Agreement Establishing The World Trade Organization）为主，包括其所有附属协议（如多边货物贸易协定、服务贸易总协定、与贸易有关的知识产权协议）在内的一揽子协议。

〔2〕 由于国际贸易与国际投资的密切关联，严格地说，《WTO 协定》中的所有条款都将对国际投资流动产生直接或间接的影响，本文所讨论的只能是其中的很少一部分，即能促进或保护国际投资从而直接影响国际投资决策与投资活动的那些规范。

一、与贸易有关的投资措施协议

《TRIMs 协议》是乌拉圭回合所首次提出来的《关税与贸易总协定》(GATT)的新议题(或曰"新领域之一")。在 GATT 的历史上,该协议第一次将投资问题纳入世界多边贸易体制之中,使 GATT(WTO)第一次具备了规范国际投资的职能,进而在一定意义兼有了国际投资组织的性质。尽管其适用范围十分有限(仅适用与货物有关的特定投资措施),但其意义将是极为深远的。

《TRIMs 协议》开门见山地明确指出,某些投资措施对国际贸易存在限制性和扭曲性作用。为此,协议禁止任何成员采取与《1994 年关贸总协定》(《GATT 1994》)第 3 条(国民待遇)及第 11 条(数量限制的一般取消)不相符的 TRIMs。具体来说,根据该协议后所附的解释性清单规定,下列 TRIMs 是与上述条款完全不符的,应予以一律禁绝:(1)要求企业购买或使用原产于国内或来自于任何国内来源的产品,无论是规定具体产品、产品的数量或价值,还是规定当地生产的数量或价值的比例(所谓的"当地成分要求")(2)根据当地产品出口的数量或价值限制企业购买或使用进口产品(即所谓的"贸易平衡要求");[3](3)全面地或根据当地产品的数量或价值限制企业进口用于当地生产或与当地生产有关的产品;(4)根据企业创收外汇的数量,通过限制其获得外汇,限制企业进口用于当地生产或与当地生产有关的产品;(5)限制企业出口产品或为出口而销售产品,无论是规定特定产品、产品的数量或价值,还是当地生产的数量或价值的比例。[4]

上列禁止使用 TRIMs 清单中,第(1)、(2)项是属于违反《GATT 1994》第 3 条第 4 款国民待遇原则的,第(3)、(4)、(5)项则是违反其第 11 条第 1 款数量限制的一般取消义务的。除了明确列举出来的这五项之外,该协议还一般性地规定禁止与上述条款不符的,根据国内法或行政规章而采取的义务性或强制性的措施,以及那些"为获得利益所必需"的措施。至于何谓"利益",协议未予明定,一般认为应包括所有形式的"利益"(包括与税收有关的利益)。显然,这比《补贴与反补贴协议》所界定的"补贴",在含义上更为广泛。由此可见,《TRIMs 协议》附件清单是一种描述性与列举性相结合的规范,其所禁止的 TRIMs 并不限于上述五项,而包括所有与国民待遇及数量限制的一般取消条款不相符的措施或做法,其他有类似作用的 TRIMs(如出口实绩要求、当地股份要求)之所以未曾明列禁绝,在原因上是由于发展中国家的坚决反对。在法律后果上则意味着它们不是一律禁绝的,而是需结合个案的具体情况,分别加以认定与处理。国

---

[3] 分别见《TRIMs 协议》附件《解释性清单》之第 1 条(a)、(b)款。

[4] 分别见《TRIMs 协议》附件《解释性清单》之第 2 条(a)、(b)、(c)款。

内许多相关论述认为《TRJMs 协议》所禁止的 TRIMs 仅指上列五项,这种理解是不全面的。

此外,为贯彻透明度原则,《TRIMs 协议》还规定了成员通报其在全国范围内或地区范围内所维持着的与上列清单不符的 TRIMs 的强制性义务。同时,协议进一步要求所有这些 TRIMs 必须限期取消。这个期限视各国经济发展水平而定:对发达国家为《WTO 协定》生效后 2 年,对发展中国家为 5 年,对最不发达国家则为 7 年。

为了监督协议义务的履行,《TRIMs 协议》还决定成立与贸易有关的投资措施委员会。另外,有关的磋商及争端解决事宜则由 WTO 的综合性争端解决机制来执行。《WTO 协定》生效后 5 年内,将由货物贸易理事会对该协议进行审议,在适当的情况下,该理事会还将进而提出对该协议文本的修改建议(如扩充清单内容),并考虑有关投资政策与竞争政策的补充性条款的范围。

《TRIMs 协议》的主要内容大体如上,从中可以看出它确是一个十分简明的框架性协议。

然而如前所述,该协议的意义与影响是非常重大而深刻的。首先,它将特定范围的投资规范纳入了 WTO(GATT)的多边贸易体制,揭示了国际贸易与国际投资之间的密切关系,拓宽了 GATT 的范围,推动了多边贸易体制与国际贸易法的发展。其次,它将 GATT 的重要法律原则(如国民待遇、数量限制的一般取消、透明度等原则)引入了国际投资领域,丰富与发展了国际投资法的内容。尤其是国民待遇制度的引入,在某种意义上,可以说是突破了国际投资法领域关于投资待遇问题的长期争执的僵局。再次,协议的达成使限制与扭曲贸易的若干 TRIMs 被限期取消,这无论是对国际贸易,还是对国际投资的自由化、国际化都可以起到很大的促进作用。最后,站在发展中国家的立场来看,该协议给发展中成员(国)较长的过班期,并特别允许发展中成员(国)按照《GATT 1994》第 18 条、《关于 GATT 1994 国际收支条款的谅解》和《关于为国际收支目的而实施的贸易措施的宣言》等文件的规定,暂时背离上述国民待遇与取消数量限制的要求,这在一定程度上照顾了发展中成员(国)的特殊情况,也具有一定的进步意义与实际价值。

当然,在看到该协议的种种积极意义的同时,我们也应看到,该协议是发达国家极力推动的产物,发展中国家的参与具有一定的被动性与局限性,这就决定了该协定在表面上兼顾发展中成员(国)利益的同时,实质上仍对发展中成员(国)存在较大的负面影响。例如,当地成分要求(包括国产化要求)与贸易平衡要求往往是发展中国家保护真幼稚民族工业所必需的,在短期内完全取消是比较困难的；又如，上述清单采取的列举式与描述式并用的方法，使得被禁止TRIMs的范围有极大的弹性，很容易作扩大的解释。与此同时，该协议仅适用于货物贸易，对服务贸易则不适用。实际上，正如后文将论述到的，服务贸易与投资之间关系至为密切，将服务贸易排除在《TRIMs协议》适用范围之外，未免失之褊狭。此外，该协议总共才9条，过于简单缺乏系统性、完整性与可操作性。所有这些，都有待于进一步谈判磋商，需要发展中国家的共同努力方能解决。

二、服务贸易总协定

服务贸易是目前世界贸易中发展最快的一个重要部分。在乌拉圭回合谈判之前，它一再游离于GATT体制之外；《服务贸易总协定》(GATS)的签订使它第一次并入了世界多边贸易体制之中。服务贸易与投资是密不可分的，因为国际服务的最主要和最受欢迎的提供方式是通过外国直接投资所建立的服务性“商业存在”。通过对商业存在服务提供方式的规范，GATS实质上蕴含着WTO“一揽子”协议中分量最大的国际投资规范。

GATS主要包括三大方面的内容：其一为一般义务框架规则，包括最惠国待遇、透明度、发展中国家的更多参与、国内规定等具体内容，它们适用于所有成员的所有服务部门(为实施政府职能而提供的服务[5]除外，下同)。其二为成员关于具体部门或分部门的市场准入与国民待遇的具体承诺及真细目表(它们亟待继续谈判以进一步“自由化”)；其三则包括一系列关于特定部门或特定方面问题的附件，前者如关于空运、金融、海运、电讯等部门服务的附件，后者如关于最惠国例外、自然人(服务提供者)流动的附件等。

由于谈判各方无法就服务贸易的定义达成一致的意见，GATS只得采用列举方式来解决其概念与适用范围问题。它规定服务贸易包括通过四种服务提供方式所提供的服务，其中最重要的便是通过商业存在方式所提供的服务。[6] 这里，“商业存在”指任何类型的商业或专业机构，包括为提供服务而在一成员境内组建、取得或维持的法人或创办或维持的分支机构或代表处。显然，它不仅包括已经建立的机构，也包括尚未成立的机构；既包括既有的投资，也包括再投资。这种范围，与双边投资保护协定或《北美自由贸易协定》(NAFTA)根据资产而界定的

[5] 它指既非在商业基础上，也非在一个或多个服务提供者相竞争的情况下所提供的服务

[6] 另外三种服务提供方式分别为：(1)过境提供如金融及视听服务等；(2)消费者流动，如旅游、留学、就医等；提供者流动如外国律师、会计师、医师的服务，等等。

“投资”比起来，要狭窄得多。[7]

简言之，GATS 的适用范围大致如下图所示：

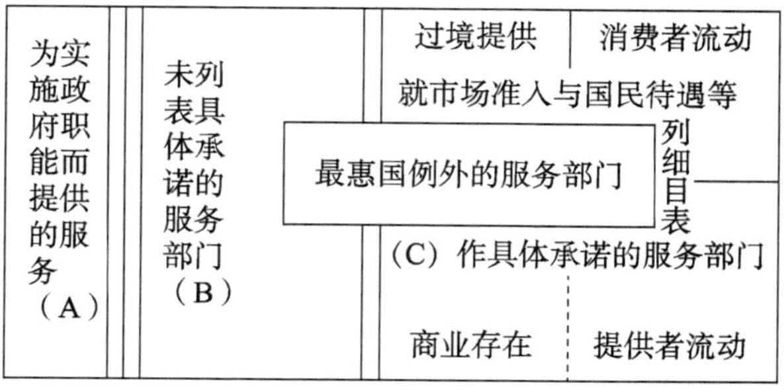

图 1　GATS 适用范围

注：整个图包括了所有的服务部门，它分 A、B、C 三部分。其中，A 部分被排除在 GATS 适用范围之外；B 与 C 部分则在此内，它们又存在属于最惠国例外的服务部门；同时，C 部分还须受成员在其具体承诺细目表上所列的条件、限制与资格要求的约束。

从上图可以看出，要准确勾画 GATS 的适用范围是十分困难的。虽然 GATS 适用于除为实施政府职能而提供的服务之外的所有部门的所有服务，但对于市场准入、国民待遇及一系列一般义务（如关于支付与转移的义务）等的具体承诺则仅适用于各成员所提交的具体承诺细目表上所列的部门、分部门或服务提供方式。不仅如此，该适用范围的界定还有赖于各成员对最惠国例外部门的圈定。[8]

尽管对协定范围的精确界定有待于对各成员具体承诺细目表的深入考察，但只要考虑到商业存在方式较其他方式更有利于东道国总体经济实力的增强与监督管理的实施这一公认事实，我们就可以推知，各成员所承担的具体承诺中的最大部门是关于商业存在方式的服务的承诺。当然，各种服务提供方式之间并非都是截然分开、互不关联的。例如，提供者（如律师、会计师、工程师、经理人员或专家）流动有助于商业存在的建立与发展，商业存在也可以反过来促进提供者流动量的增加；消费者流动可以促进商业存在（如餐旅业）的发展，商业存在的发展又可能导致更多的消费者流动；过境提供是种基础性、中介性的服务提供方式，它与

〔7〕 据资产定义的“投资”，除直接投资外，一般还包括证券投资、债券及其他金融资产（如贷款等），包括有形的与无形的财产，少数股票以及合同利益等。GATS 对商业存在的界定则似乎仅包括外国直接投资，而不包括证券、债券等间接投资。

〔8〕 这种圈定并不是没有限度的。按 GATS 规定，这种例外须在乌拉圭回合谈判最后文件达成之日即（1994 年 4 月 15 日）前通知所有谈判方。

另外三种方式之间的关系也是互利互动、互相补充的。不过,相对而言,商业存在与提供者流动之间关系最为密切,因为一个驻外服务机构的建立与运营,一定离不开经理人员、专家、律师、会计师、工程师等“服务提供者”的流动。正因如此,上因在此二者之间所划的是虚线。

GATS 对国际投资的促进具有重大意义,这主要是由于服务“贸易”与机构之间关系十分密切。如前所述,商业存在方式的服务更有利于东道国的管理与发展,这极有可能使东道国采取类似于 TRIMs 的限制与引导措施.迫使外国服务提供者不得不以商业存在的建立作为国际服务提供的基本前提,这在客观上可以促进商业存在方式的服务的发展。GATS 对商业存在方式提供的服务的促进,无疑即是对国际直接投资的促进。

GATS 最核心、最重要的投资促进性条款包括第 2 条(最惠国待遇)、第 3 条(透明度)、第 16 条(市场准入)与第 17 条(国民待遇)。民中,最惠国待遇与透明度条款是适用于所有成员、所有部门的一般性义务(尽管各成员可以设定关于最惠国待遇的种种例外)GATS 第 16 条并未给“市场准入”下一个严格的定义,但谈判各方就六个方面的市场准入措施达成了一致意见,除非经各成员的承诺细目表所特别列明,原则上这六类限制性的市场准入的措施均应予禁止。这种列举出来的措施在实质上勾勒出了 GATS 市场准入概念的大致轮廓。其中有两大类与商业存在关系比较密切:(1)限制或要求服务提供者通过特定形式的法人实体或合资企业提供服务;(2)限制外国资本参与的最高股权额或一笔投资或累计投资总额。[9] 其实质是对外国投资法律形式与股权的限制。该条第 1 款的注释进一步明确指出,如果一成员对通过商业布在方式的服务作出市场准入的承诺,则该成员应允许有关资本进入其境内。可见,市场准入实质上就是各国投资法中的投资领域开放问题。不过,该条没有提到有关商业存在的资本输出(如清算所得的汇出)的待遇,这不能不说是一个漏洞。

GATS 第 17 条第 1 款对服务贸易的国民待遇定义为“在其承诺细目表所列的服务部门中,每一成员按该表所列的任何资格和条件,在影响服务的提供的所有措施方面,给予任何其他成员国的服务和服务提供者以不低于民类似国内服务和服务提供者的待遇”。第(2)、(3)款进而澄清,国民待遇并不要求与其适用于国内机构的待遇在形式上完全一样,而只要求民不至于损害外国服务提供者的竞争条件(当然也不意味着对外国投资的固有竞争劣势进行特别弥补)。依前论,对商业存在服务的待遇实质上就是对外国直接投资的待遇。因而,GATS 关于最惠

---

[9] 参见 GATS 第 16 条第 2 款第(e)、(f)项。

国待遇与国民待遇的规定对国际投资的意义并不亚于《TRIMs 协议》的有关规定。

与《TRIMs 协议》及《TRIPs 协议》不同的是，GATS 允许成员维持既存的、与 GATS 义务不相符的措施。在作出了具体承诺的部门中，这种措施必须在细目表上列举出来；在未作具体承诺的部门（尽管它们仍觉最惠国待遇条款的约束）以及最惠国例外的部门中，成员还可以享有采取新的歧视措施的自由。此外 GATS 还设有一般例外条款（包括对与直接税和双边税收协定有关措施的例外）和与 GATT 的货物贸易协定相类似的安全例外条款。同时，GATS 也考虑到了未来对服务贸易中的紧急保障措施，及有扭曲贸易作用的补贴问题进行进一步的谈判与磋商的必要性。GATS 未对投资审查措施及投资活动限制措施作直接规定，但这些都将受制于各成员的承诺细目表所设的条件的约束。[10]

GATS 还要求其成员采取措施，确保其境内的垄断贸易提供者按最惠国待遇、透明度及具体承诺的要求行事，不得滥用其垄断地位，破坏正常的竞争秩序。在判断谁应享受 GATS 利益时，该协定采用“实际业务运作”这一标准。具体到商业存在方式，则根据所有权（指拥有 50% 以上的股权）和控制（指有权任命其大多数董事或在法律上有权指导其业务活动）两个标准。这样，未能“控制”的外国少数股权所有者就不能算是 GATS 另一成员的法人。

相对来说，GATS 投资保护方面的规施比较少，也比较薄弱。其第 8 条关于支付与转让的规定不是一项一般义务，而仅仅是一项受制于具体承诺的义务。该条规定，成员一般不得限制其具体承诺部门中的国际转让与支付。不过，在发生国际收支和对外金融地位严重困难或有此威胁时，成员可经就此作一定的限制。[11] 这种限制必须在多边监督之下实施，以确保其限制是临时的、非歧视性的和适度的。只要成员不对任何资金交易采取与其有关承诺不一致的限制，GATS 将不影响国际货币基金组织（OMF）成员在基金组织协定条款中所享有的权利与承担的义务。

GATS 未直接规定双边投资保护协定中常见的国有化及其补偿问题。一旦 WTO 争端解决机构（DSB）调查后认定一成员应得的利益受到了抵消（nullified）或损害（impaired），则受害成员将被授权采取相当措施，以弥补其损失，具体程序则由争端解决谅解（DSU）规定，这一点与《TRIMs 协议》是一致的。

值得一提的是，投资促进与投资保护措施在这里并不是完全割裂、泾渭分明

---

〔10〕 这两者均可能构成对市场准入的违反。例如，一项包括数量限制内容的投资审查措施将违反 GATS 第 16 条第（2）款（b）项的规定，而一项只许以法人实体而不允许以分支机构的形式开办外资银行的要求同样会构成对 GATS 第 16 条第（2）款（e）项的违反。显然，这两者均不得违反是惠国待遇条款。

〔11〕 参见 GATS 第 12 条第（1）款。

的，此处作为投资促进措施介绍的最惠国待遇与国民待遇条款，往往构成双边投资保护协定的核心内容之一，从这个意义来看，则 GATS 保护投资的条款也并不贫乏。

综上所述，GATS 不仅拓展了世界多边贸易体制的视野，更增强和丰富了国际投资的法律规范，其对国际投资法的意义并不逊于《TRIMs 协议》。与此同时，GATS 另一个突出的特点，便是它比《TRIMs 协议》及《TRIPs 协议》更多地顾及了发展中国家的利益。首先，它规定了对发展中国家的许多保留，如透明度、经济一体化、逐步自由化等，特别是 GATS 明确将一般义务与市场准入、国民待遇和附属协议义务的具体承诺分开，使发展中国家可以根据其发展战略提出自由化的服务部门，从而减少了对关键产业的冲击；其次，它规定了发达国家向发展中国家提供技术援助的义务，有助于发展中国家有关行业技术水平的提高；最后，部分服务行业的发展必然带动服务业整体的发展，从而可望形成较坚实的服务业基础，这有助于发展中国家三大产业的协调发展及整体经济的稳定增长。所有这些，反映了发展中国家国际法律地位提高及国际经济新秩序的不断发展。这对国际投资及国际投资法发展都是富有积极意义的。

三、与贸易有关的知识产权协议

与《TRIMs 协议》及 GATS 一样，《TRIPs 协议》也是 GATT 乌拉圭回合谈判的崭新成果之一。毋庸讳言，《TRIPs 协议》中并无直接规范投资问题的条文，然而，知识产权本身就是国际投资的一种表现形式；[12] 知识产权保护更是国际投资法制中的重要内容与常见争议问题之一，在大多数双边投资保护协定中，一般都要就知识产权保护问题作出规定，而各国之间关于外国投资者的知识产权保护问题的争端更是层出不穷、屡见不鲜《TRIPs 协议》作为一个全新的关于知识产权保护的国际协定，对国际投资，特别是知识与技术密集型的投资，无疑是具有十分突出的促进与保护意义的。

《TRIPs 协议》强调指出，由于各国对知识产权保护水准相去甚远以及缺乏一个惩处冒牌商品的多边原则、规则框架，已经衍生出了许多国际争端，并构成了国际经济关系中的一种新的不稳定因素。很显然，协议的达成及其中的这种明确的强调，使得世界各国均深刻认识到一国知识产权保护程度对国际投资流动的质与量，尤其是对国际高新技术投资的流动的决定性影响，从而有助于国际投资障碍的逐步消除及国际投资的更大发展。

---

〔12〕 例如，按我国《中外合资经营企业法》第 5 条规定，知识产权中的主体部分“工业产权”是可供选择的外商投资形式之一。

概言之,《TRIPs 协议》主要包括下列几方面内容:

1. GATT 有关原则(如最惠国待遇和国民待遇)及有关国际知识产权协定[13]原则的适用性;

2. 关于知识产权效力、范围及使用的标准的规定,如对版权、商标、地理标志、工业设计(即外观设计)、专利、集成电路的外观设计及未公开信息的保护,以及在合同许可中对反竞争行为的控制等条款;

3. 关于知识产权的执法,主要规定国内法中关于确保知识产权能为外国或本国权利持有人所有效实施的程序及救济方法;

4. 关于在 WTO 综合争端解决机制下防止与解决知识产权争端的规定;

5. 根据不同经济发展水平而设定的逐步实施该协议的过渡期安排(对发达国家为 WTO 协定生效后 1 年;对发展中国家为 5 年;对最不发达国家为 7 年)。[14]

《TRIPs 协议》与 GATS 一道,使 GATT 的“管辖”范围从单纯的国际货物贸易发展到国际货物、技术与服务贸易三位一体的新格局,大大促进了国际贸易的多元化与国际知识产权保护的加强。不仅如此,《TRIPs 协议》还一改过去国际公法的“软法”性质,扩大和强化了知识产权的多边保护,并特别强调建立严格的法律制裁机制及其他有力措施,不仅加大了保护力度,对相关的争端解决也奠定了坚实的法律基础。此外,考虑到发展中国家的实际困难,协议明确规定发达国家对发展中国家提供相关援助是一项国际义务,还特别为发展中国家设定了较长的过渡期,这也有一定的进步意义.然而,稍微了解乌拉圭回合谈判背景的人都知道,乌拉圭回合谈判追求的是“在广泛的贸易领域和谈判议题范围内,寻求平衡的减让”、发展中国家在某些协议中所得到的优惠或“特惠”,是以在其他协议中作较大的让步作为代价的。TRIPS 问题是发展中国家最初反对最为强烈的一个新议题,[15]但在“平衡的减让”的旗帜下,发展中国家最终就此作出了较大的让步——事实上,要求技术普遍严重落后的发展中国家在短期内达到知识产权保护的“国际标准”,确是一件十分困难的事情。

无论如何,《TRIPs 协议》对国际投资的促进与保护意义还是显而易见、不可抹杀的。

---

〔13〕 如《巴黎公约》《伯尔尼公约》《罗马公约》《集成电路知识产权公约》。

〔14〕 如果根据本协定发展中成员(国)有义务在本协定生效之日将产品专利扩大到境内尚未予以保护的技术领域,则该发展中成员(国)对该技术领域的保护可再延长 5 年,即在本协定生效后 10 年内开始执行。

〔15〕 例如,巴西代表在谈判中曾经尖锐地指出,把知识产权等问题纳入 GATT 之中,就像把病毒输入计算机一样,其结果只会是进一步加剧国际贸易中既有的不平衡。参见郑成思:《关贸总协定与世界贸易组织中的知识产权》,北京出版社 1994 年版,第 7 页。

四、争端解决规则和程序谅解

WTO“一揽子”协议中的《争端解决规则与程序谅解》(DSU)并没有专门针对国际投资的规定,但作为所有WTO“一揽子”协议下的综合争端解决机制,该谅解对违反其中的国际投资规范而引发的所有争端,也当然地具有管辖权,这使得它在一定意义上具备了国际投资争端解决机制的意义。

DSU继承了GATT争端解决机制的某些内容,但更重要的是,它在此基础上作了重大的改革,大大强化了其解决多边争端的能力。其主要改革与创新体现在:(1)自动设立专家组程序,指除非争端解决机构(DSB)一致反对,否则应当事方的请求,DSB应随之设立专家组。[16] (2)专家组报告的自动采纳,即除非DSB一致反对,DSB应采纳专家组所提出的调查报告。(3)上诉程序的设立与上诉机构审议结论的自动采纳。谅解还特设了常设上诉机构对专家组报告的审议程序,非经DSB一致反对,该审议结论是终局有效的。(4)跨部门的交叉报复措施。谅解规定,只要DSB认定成员的利益被抵消;或损害了,则可授权受害当事方实施报告——中止协定项下的减让与义务,且这种报复可以跨部门、跨协议进行。[17] (5)由有关成员建议“合理执行期限”[18]这有利于专家组建议的尽快执行。

简单地说,DSU所确立的争端解决程序大致为:有关成员之间的磋商→专家组的建立(应请求)→(在争议方所提出的书面陈述的基础上进行的)第一、二次专家组听证→专家组报告的公布与采纳→(应请求)常设上诉机构的审议→建议的执行与监督。

DSU对上述每一步均设有严格的时间限制。整个程序不得超过6~9个月,在有上诉的情况下,总时限也不得超过12个月。如果专家组的建议未获执行,受损害一方经缔约方全体授权,可以实施相当的贸易报复。除非另有特别规定,DSU允许受害方在WTO“一揽子”协议框架范围之内,实施跨部门、跨领域(协议)的交叉报复。

此外,值得指出的是,DSU并未规定私人(如投资者对东道国)可以向DSB请求救济。它仅仅适用于争议成员(包括“国家”或“独立关税区”)之间的争端。可

---

〔16〕 参见联合国贸易与发展会议秘书处:《乌拉圭回合成果:初步估计》,1994年英文版,第205页。该书认为,一致反对设在专家组的可能性极小,因而这实质上“是一种自动设主专家组程序,这就超出了GATT过去的做法,标志着争端解决机制的一大进步”。

〔17〕 详见DSU第21、22条。

〔18〕 同上。

见，它的职能与解决投资争端国际中心（ICSID）[19]的职能正好可以相互补充、相互配合。

DSU的上述创新，不仅是GATT争端解决机制的完善，也可以说是国际投资争端解决机制的发展与创新。

五、结论

通过上述分析可以看出，尽管《埃斯特角城宣言》并未列入投资议题，但乌拉圭回合谈判最后达成的《WTO协定》中却确实存在大量的国际投资规范。其核心固然体现为《TRIMs协议》，但分量最大的部分却蕴含在GATS对商业存在方式的服务贸易的规范之中；与此同时，《TRIPs协议》及DSU关于知识产权保护和争端解决的多边规范也弥补了既存国际投资规范在有关方面的不足。所有这些蕴藏在WTO"一揽子"协议中的国际投资规范无疑是国际投资法领域中最新的、重大的成果，是对实体与程序方面的多边规范均严重缺乏的国际投资法的重大发展。在国际投资法的发展史上，必将有着重大而深远的历史意义。

之所以会在贸易协定中规定投资问题，从主观上看，它固然离不开发达国家保护海外投资的迫切需要和发展中国家引进外资、发展经济的现实考虑；从客观上看，则主要是由于国际投资与国际贸易唇齿相依、密不可分的相互关系。国际投资原本是在国际贸易的基础上发展起来，国际投资反过来又促进了国际贸易的发展；与此同时，随着国际投资市场竞争的激化，各国纷纷制定了大量的鼓励与保护投资的措施，其中有些投资措施不免对国际贸易的既存秩序产生一定的限制性与扭曲性的影响，在缺乏详备有力的国际投资法律规范可资援用，以消除这种限制与扭曲的情况下，各国退而求其次，转向求助于较完备的GATT多边贸易体制规范的想法与做法，是很自然的。可以预见. 只要国际投资不断发展而国际多边投资规范未能同步强化，这种贸易协定规范投资问题的现象仍将持续，并且会进一步强化。

中国是世界上最大的也是最具潜力的发展中国家。世界多边贸易体制离不开中国的支持与参与，否则，它永远不能成为真正的"世界"贸易体制；与此同时，中国还是一个正在建立社会主义市场经济的国家，这决定它必须不断深化改革、扩大开放，进一步融入国际市场经济体系之中，与国际规则与惯例接轨。中国长期游离于WTO之外，是不可能的。可以说，中国与WTO之间互相需要，合则两利、分则两伤，早已是大势所趋，是不可逆转的。

---

〔19〕 该中心是专门解决国家与他国国民（即"外国投资"）的投资争端的国际投资争端解决机构。详见陈安：《"解决投资争端国际中心"述评》，鹭江出版社1990年版，第53页。

退一步来说，即便是我国短期内未能就成为WTO的创始会员国地位问题达成协议，我们仍需按市场经济的一般规律，继续大力引进外资，进一步“优化环境、拓宽领域、引导投向、优化结构”。[20] 这就意味着，我们有必要加紧对WTO“一揽子”协议，特别是其中的国际投资规范的研究，并在掌握其基本制度框架与具体运作规范的基础上，结合我国国情，提出相应的趋利避害的法律对策来。只有这样，才能真正推动我国外资立法的科学化、完善化，进而促进以引进外资为核心的对外开放事业稳定、健康地发展。

---

〔20〕《中共中央关于制定国民经济和社会发展“九五”计划的建议》第4部分第29段。

我国外资国民待遇制度的发展与完善*

外国投资(以下简称外资)在东道国的待遇标准实质上决定了外国投资在东道国的法律地位。它不仅直接关系到外国投资者的利益与东道国的权益,而且与国家主权、征收与国有化、外交保护、国家责任等一系列敏感的国际政治法律问题也密切相关,因而它又是国际投资关系中的先决条件问题。[1] 有鉴于此,世界各国都在其制定的国内法或与外国缔结的国际条约中对此作出专门的规定。比较常见的待遇标准有公平合理待遇、不歧视待遇、国民待遇、最惠国待遇及所谓的“国际标准待遇”等。其中,国民待遇与最惠国待遇两个标准又使用得最为普遍。

长期以来,由于计划经济体制的影响,我国与外国缔结的双边投资保护协定一般只提“公平合理待遇”与“最惠国待遇”,而很少提及“国民待遇”,[2]有关的国内法更多的是关于外商投资企业的种种特殊优惠与限制的规定,而鲜有“国民待遇”的内容。为适应“公平、公正、公开”的市场机制的需要,中共中央在1993年底明确提出要创造条件对外商投资企业实行国民待遇。[3] 这意味着我国即将进入内外资企业平等竞争的新时代。本文拟在剖析外资的国民待遇及其在中国的实践情况的基础上,探讨其发展的方向与完善的对策。

一

“国民待遇”是一个使用非常广泛、含义十分丰富的概念,它泛指一国授于外国人(包括自然人与法人)在投资、贸易、知识产权保护、出入境管理等方面享有

---

* 本文发表在《法学研究》1995年第6期。

〔1〕 姚梅镇:《国际投资法》,武汉大学出版社1986年版,第330页。

〔2〕 据对外贸易经济合作部统计,截至1994年6月,我国已与外国签订了61个双边投资保护协定,其中采用“国民待遇”标准的只有“中英协定”与“中日协定”等少数几个。

〔3〕 参见《中共中央关于建立社会主义市场经济体制若干问题的决定》,载《人民日报》1993年11月7日。

不低于本国人(包括自然人与法人)的待遇。作为外国投资待遇标准的一种,外资的国民待遇主要指一主权国家在条约或互惠的基础上,授与外国国民或法人在投资财产、投资活动及有关的司法行政救济方面以不低于本国国民或法人的待遇。它大致包括"外国投资者的国民待遇"与"外商投资企业的国民待遇"两个方面,但在实践中对外国自然人与企业的待遇之区别往往并不十分明确,所以这里采用"外资国民待遇"的提法,尽管本文着重探讨的是后一方面。

值得强调的是,国民待遇并不意味着对外资与内资在待遇上的绝对平等。在目前的国际条件下,还没有任何一个国家能给予外国投资与国内投资完全相同的待遇。外资的国民待遇只可能在一定范围内适用。例如,就投资领域而言,各国对内外资从来都是有区别的。许多关涉国家安全与国计民生的领域,一般都不允许外资涉足;即使是非关键的经济部门,也可能基于国家经济规划与发展目标而对外资的引进有所先后、有所厚薄。这种限制,发达国家与发展中国家同样存在,毫无例外。在号称对外资最开放的美国,其在国内航运、原子能、水电等行业中同样禁止外资投入;在通信与航空、矿业等领域则只允许外资拥有少数股权参与。〔4〕 一般来说,发达国家禁止或限制外资的领域集中在公用事业、交通、矿业、银行、国防工业、保险业、原子能工业等;而发展中国家禁止或限制外资的领域则集中在公用事业、航空、内陆运输、电信、国防、武器弹药、印刷、无线电与电视等行业。〔5〕 此外,这种差别待遇还可能包括对外资的审批手续与监督、雇佣限制、投资期限与本地化要求等。这些适当的限制与例外不仅为一国经济社会发展所必需,也是国家主权的一种体现。当然,这种限制与例外应以不与既存有效的国际法规则相抵触为前提。

另一方面,绝大多数发展中国家为吸引外资纷纷制定了许多优惠政策,使外资企业在税收、经营管理权等方面甚至享有比本国公司和国民更优惠的"超国民待遇"。这与国民待遇原则也是相容的。所以,各国间的双边投资保护协定关于国民待遇的措辞,都是用"不低于本回国民或公司"的待遇,而不是"完全等同于"本国国民或公司的待遇。事实上,这同样也是国家主权的一种表征。不过,从理论上说,国民待遇原则是不鼓励"超国民"的优惠待遇的。

国民待遇标准较之于其他待遇标准,具有不可替代的优点。公平合理待遇只是一个抽象的照则,具体的内容有待于结合其他标准(一般是国民待遇标准和最惠国待遇标准)来明确。最惠国待遇标准必须参照有关第三国所获得的优惠,方

---

〔4〕 姚梅镇:《国际投资法》,武汉大学出版社1987年版,第43~57页。
〔5〕 陈安主编:《国际投资法》,鹭江出版社1987年版,第142~144页。

能间接获得。一国不给任何国家以优遇,则最惠国照样是无惠国。至于所谓的“国际文明标准”,则不仅有“内容抽象、含义模糊、无以为据的明显缺陷”,而且它是以西方资产阶级文明为基础的,有明显的特权思想与霸权主义的痕迹。因而,它不仅为广大发展中国家所坚决反对,就连许多资产阶级学者也不得不承认该标准在国际社会中实难求同、达成妥协。相反,国民待遇标准通过双边或多边条约确定,以国内法进一步明确其透明度、可靠性与可操作性是其他待遇标准所不具有的。进一步来说,国民待遇标准是与国内标准主义一脉相承的,它不仅符合国家主权的最高原则,也符合世界上大多数国家的意志与利益。也正因为国民待遇这些不可替代的优越性,使得它越来越多、越来越广泛和深入地适用于市场经济的国际交往之中。

当今世界上,但凡实行市场经济的国家,一般都提倡给外资以国民待遇;大凡实行计划经济的国家,都不提或很少提及国民待遇。前者如美国、英国、瑞士、德国、法国等发达的市场经济国家,对内资与外资基本上做到了平等对待;后者如前苏联、东欧国家和改革开放前的中国,由于实行高度集中的计划经济,没有也无法实行国民待遇。即使是发展中国家,只要是实行了市场经济体制,一般都实行或趋向于实行国民待遇。1992 年,解决投资争端国际中心(ICSID)对 51 个发展中国家外资立法的调查表明:大多数发展中国家(31 个)给外资以国民待遇,而这些国家又都是推行或正转向市场经济的国家,如亚洲的韩国、菲律宾、也门,欧洲的保加利亚、匈牙利、南斯拉夫;南美的阿根廷、哥伦比亚、巴拉圭及非洲的埃及、喀麦隆等国。〔6〕

1979 年中外合资经营企业法颁布以来,我国开始了市场取向的改革,并积极推行对外开放,大力引进外资。对外资的国民待遇问题从此产生,并且在一定范围内得到适用与实行,从下列国内立法与双边条约中可以清楚地看到这一点。

我国《宪法》在允许外商来华投资的同时,还规定它的合法权利和利益受到中国法律的保护。〔7〕《民法通则》规定,凡在中国境内设立的外商投资企业,具备法定条件的,可取得“中国法人”资格。〔8〕《中外合资经营企业法实施条例》进一步规定,在中国境内设立的中外合资经营企业是“中国法人”,受中国法律管辖和保护。〔9〕在中国国内立法中已体现出的外资国民待遇主要包括三个方面:第一,司法行政救济上的国民待遇。这方面是比较充分的。例如,《民事诉讼法》规定,

〔6〕 解决投资争端国际中心资料,参见《外国投资法杂志》1992 年英文版,第 436 页。
〔7〕 参见《宪法》第 18、32 条。
〔8〕 参见《民法通则》第 41 条第 2 款。
〔9〕 参见《中外合资经营企业法实施细则》第 2 条。

外国人、无国籍人、外国企业和组织在人民法院起诉、应诉,同中国公民、法人和其他经济组织有同等的诉讼权利。[10] 再如,国务院《关于鼓励外商投资的规定》针对向外商投资企业摊派的现象,规定外商投资企业凡遇有不合理收费情况,可以拒交或向当地经济委员会直至国家经济委员会申诉。[11] 第二,投资活动方面一定范围内的国民待遇。例如,国务院《关于鼓励外商投资的规定》规定,对产品出口企业和先进技术企业所提供的水、电、运输条件和通讯设施,按当地国营企业收费标准计收费用。[12] 第三,在投资财产保护的某些方面,也适用国民待遇。例如,《商标法》、《专利法》、《著作权法》和《计算机软件保护条例》等知识产权法律、法规,均以类似的文字规定,外商与外商投资企业在上述知识产权的保护方面,享有国民待遇。[13] 此外,根据普通法与特别法关系的原理,在其他法律没有特殊规定的领域,外商投资企业根据民法通则等普通适用的法律还可享有广泛的实体权利(如财产所有权)上的国民待遇。

值得一提的是,1988 年国务院发布了《关于鼓励投资开发海南岛的规定》,该规定最引人注目之处在于,它不分境内与境外投资者,提供完全相同的待遇,一视同仁。例如该规定第 3 条规定:"国家鼓励境内外的企业、其他经济组织或个人(以下简称为投资者)投资开发海南岛……"这种统一以投资者身份完全平等对待境内外投资者的做法在中国投资立法史上是绝无仅有的。它表明中国政府在当时就已尝试在局部地区实行较为全面的国民待遇,反映了在对外资法律保护标准上与国际通行做法接轨的政策取向。

从中国与外国签订的双边投资保护协定来看,中国尚很少给予外国投资以国民待遇。1986 年中英签订的《关于促进和相互保护投资协定》(以下简称中英协定),是中国在双边投资保护协定中给外国投资提供国民待遇的初次尝试。根据中英协定,中国"应尽量根据其法律和法规的规定"给予英国的国民或公司以国民待遇。[14] 1988 年中日签订的《关于鼓励和相互保护投资协定》就投资、投资活动及有关的司法行政救济方面,相互给予对方国民或公司以国民待遇。[15] 以上两个协定是中外投资保护协定中明确规定外资国民待遇的两例,反映出中国政府在国民待遇的给予上的谨慎立场。另外,中国与瑞士两国《关于相互促进和保护投资协定》虽没有明确的国民待遇条文,但从其议定书第 3 项的规定之措词来看,

[10] 参见《民事诉讼法》第 15 条第 1 款。
[11] 参见国务院《关于鼓励外商投资的规定》第 16 条。
[12] 参见国务院《关于鼓励外商投资的规定》第 5 条。
[13] 参见《商标法》第 9 条,《专利法》第 18 条,《著作权法》第 3 条,《计算机软件保护条例》第 6 条。
[14] 参见该协定第 3 条第 3 款。
[15] 参见该协定第 3 条第 2、3 款。

该协定也隐含国民待遇的意向。[16]

由此可见,市场经济体制确立以前,我国虽未“泛提”国民待遇,但也并非完全拒绝提供国民待遇,而是采取了灵活与谨慎的态度,在一定范围内或一定地区内、一定程度上给予外资以国民待遇。当然,很明显地,由于计划经济体制的限制,国民待遇的适用范围与实际执行都是很有限的。在很多方面,外商投资企业所获得的待遇与内资企业的待遇迥然有异,外商投资企业往往同时处于“超国民”和“次国民”的地位。譬如,相对于内资企业而言,外商投资企业一般享有较低的税负、较高的经营管理自主权和较多的优惠,但同时在投资领域、审批手续、销售方向等方面又受到较多的限制。

随着市场经济体制的确立与对外开放、经济国际化程度的不断加深,这种有限的国民待遇显然已不适应形势发展的需要,给外商投资企业提供较为全面的国民待遇的呼声日高一日。这是因为:市场经济必然要求各类市场主体平等待遇、公平竞争。目前内资企业与外商投资企业待遇相差悬殊,不仅不利于吸引外资,对内资企业的发展也极为不利。由于待遇不同,目前全国到处流行着形形色色的“假三资企业”。这些显然都是为市场经济的基本精神——平等竞争所不容的。所以说,给外商投资企业提供国民待遇,首先是市场经济发展的必然需要。从世界各国的立法与实践来看,对外资提供国民待遇已不仅是少数发达国家的主张,面对新的世界政治、经济形势,广大发展中国家也纷纷改变立场,转向提供国民待遇。中国如不及时调整策略,实行国民待遇,将既不利于吸引外资,也不符合与国际通行做法衔接的需要。从国际法的角度来看,刚刚结束的乌拉圭回合的谈判的成果使得投资领域也被纳入关贸总协定的体制之内,而国民待遇是总协定的基本原则之一,其结果,必然是投资领域的国民待遇将成为一项极为广泛的国际义务。中国要“复关”,并要成为世界贸易组织(WTO)的创始成员国,就必须及时调整对外资的立法和政策,走上国民待遇的道路。正是基于对这种国内与国际形势的清醒认识。中共中央不失时机地提出要创造条件对外商技资企业实行国民待遇。这一决定明确宣告了中国在对外资的保护方面将更全面、更广泛地采用国际通行的法律保护标准;标志着国民待遇在中国的外资领域由零星的、局部的规定进入全面提供和逐步完善的阶段。

1993 年以来,中国在立法主朝着这一方向已经作出了重大的努力。例如,不

[16] 该项规定为:“尽管由于两国间的经济和法律制度不间以及由于中华人民共和国经济发展的需要,瑞士投资者对其在中国进行的投资不能要求在各方面都享有与中国投资者相同的待遇,但中国政府应尽量注意使给予瑞士投资者的待遇在整体上是公平的。”

久前通过的《公司法》规定，该法同样适用于外商投资的有限责任公司。[17] 这样，它以中国市场主体基本法的形式宣告了内资企业与外商投资企业待遇的平等性，可以说是朝着全面的国民待遇迈出了坚实的、根本性的第一步。又如，新近通过的《对外贸易法》明确提出，中国在对外贸易方面将根据有关条约规定或互惠精神给予外方以国民待遇。[18] 再如，八届人大常委会决定：新颁布的增值税、消费税和营业税三个税收暂行条例从1994年1月1日起适用于外商投资企业与外国企业，同时废止原先适用的《工商统一税条例(草案)》。[19] 这一决定使内、外资企业在税负上统一起来，从实体利益上平等了待遇，是朝着国民待遇方向所作的又一次重大的努力。另据《法制日报》：1994年起，我国人大和国务院制定的有关安全生产的部分法规将适用于"三资"企业，这些法规包括《矿山安全法》《工厂安全卫生规程》《女职工保护条例》等24个单行法律、法规，涉及有关安全生产与职工保护的几乎所有领域。[20] 此外，《经济合同法》的修订，汇率并轨等重大政策与法律举措都为国民待遇的实行创造了有利的法律条件。

然而迄今为止，我国外资的国民待遇仍然是不够的，与国际通行的做法及乌拉圭回合达成的《与贸易有关的投资措施协议》(以下简称《TRIMs协议》)的要求还有很大差距，突出表现在：

一方面，外商投资企业仍享有许多"超国民"待遇。例如，就所得税而言，内资企业所得税税率现改为33%，[21]表面上与外商投资企业的所得税税率持平，但按照外商投资企业和外国企业所得税法的规定，外商投资企业的所得税税率根据设立地区(如经济特区、经济技术开发区、高新技术产业开发区等)、企业性质(如生产性企业)和所属行业(如基础设施或第一产业等)的不同，可以减按24%或15%甚至更低的税率征收，同时，它们还可以享有"免二减三"的待遇，[22]其实际税负仍比内资企业低很多。就企业的生产经营自主权而言，虽然经过了种种转换机制的努力，内资企业的经营自主权仍难以落实；而外商投资企业一开始就享有比较广泛和充分的生产、采购、销售、人事、资金、物资等各方面的自主经营管理权，特别优厚的是，它们可以享有一般内资企业难以企盼的进出口经营权。[23] 与此同时，外商投资企业在关税等方面还享有比较优惠的待遇。例如，按照《中外合

---

[17] 参见《公司法》第18条。

[18] 参见《对外贸易法》第6、23条。

[19] 参见八届人大常委会第五次会议《关于外商投资企业和外国企业适用增值税、消费税和营业税暂行条例的决定》。

[20] 详见1994年1月29日《法制日报》。

[21] 参见《企业所得税暂行条例》第3条。

[22] 参见《外商投资企业与外国企业所得税法》第5、7、8条规定。

[23] 这种差别在新通过的对外贸易法中仍得到肯定。参见《对外贸易法》第9条。

资经营企业法实施条例》,合营企业进口四类物资免征关税和工商统一税(现已改为增值税、消费税和营业税,下同),合营企业生产的出口产品,一般免征工商统一税。[24]《外资企业法实施细则》也有类似的税收优惠规定。[25] 此外,根据国务院《关于鼓励外商投资的规定》(俗称"二十二条")和《中外合资经营企业法实施条例》等法规与文件,我国对外商投资设立的进口替代项目与以产顶进项目还可享受特殊优惠待遇。[26]

另外,外商投资企业在享受种种优惠的同时,又受到较多限制,居于"次国民"的地位。这主要体现为:(1)投资领域的限制,主要是对外资投向服务业的限制。(2)审批手续与服务收费方面。对外商投资企业的审批手续问题,虽经再简化,但仍然比较复杂和严格,加之官僚主义的影响,使审批延误事件时有发生。在服务收费方面,前面提到对于外商投资企业所购买的物料或为其所提供的公共设施,其收费一般应与国有企业相同,但在实践中,却常常有悖于此。例如,邮电部曾规定外商投资企业的电话费必须用外汇支付,在人民币汇率并轨后,又规定原用外汇券支付的费用,现用人民币支付时,需加收50%。此外,外国投资者和其他外籍管理人员在购买机票、车票、各种门票等时也需支付高于中国国民的费用。(3)当地成分要求。"当地成分要求"是《TRIMs 协议》所禁止的投资措施之一,即"求企业购买或使用原产于国内或来自于任何国内来源的产品"。[27] 我国有关法律虽没有明确规定"当地成分要求"的条款,但有关法律却有要求外商投资企业所需的设备、原材料、燃料、配套件等物资,应当(尽先)在中国购买的规定。[28] 在审批项目中,我国各级政府往往又有各种规定,要求购买一定数量的国内产品作为生产投入,并以此为项目获得批准或享受优惠的先决条件。如我国在审批外商投资汽车项目时,都把国产化程度作为要件之一。而国产化要求无疑是当地成分要求的一种表现形式。它在我国虽同样未被法律所明确规定,却为有关文件所硬性要求。(4)出口实绩要求。我国《外资企业法》明确规定设立外资企业的前提条件之一种就是"产品全部出口或大部分出口"。[29] 该法的实施细则进一步明确该条件意为"年出口产品的产值达到当年全部产品产值50%以上,实现外汇收支

---

〔24〕 参见该实施条例第71、72条。

〔25〕 参见该实施细则第52、53条。

〔26〕 例如《国务院关于鼓励外商投资的规定》第2条,《中外合资企业法实施条例》第61条,以及《海关对外商投资企业履行产品出口合同所需进口料件管理办法》第5条等。

〔27〕 参见《TRIMs 协定》附件清单之1(a)项。

〔28〕 参见《外资企业法》第15条,《中外合资经营企业法》第9条及其实施条例之第57条。

〔29〕 参见该法第3条。

平衡或有结余”。[30]《中外合作经营企业法》[31]和《中外合资经营企业法》[32]也都有鼓励产品出口的规定。相应地，我国对产品出口型企业还提供了一系列优惠措施，包括进出口减免关税、降低所得税税率等。如《外商投资企业和外国企业所得税法实施细则》规定，“外商投资举办的产品出口企业，在依照税法规定免征、减征企业所得税期满后，凡当年出口产品产值达到当年企业产品产值70%以上的，可以按照税法规定的税率减半征收企业所得税。但经济特区和经济技术开发区以及其他已经按百分之十五的税率缴纳企业所得税的产品出口企业，符合上述条件的，按百分之十的税率征收企业所得税”。[33] 以上规定实际上是引导性的出口实绩要求措施。尽管出口实绩要求未列入《TRIMs 协议》所一般禁止的措施之列，但在个案中它仍较容易被当作对贸易有限制和扭曲作用的措施，故需引起重视和防范。(5)贸易平衡要求。“贸易平衡要求”也是《TRIMs 协定》所禁止的投资措施之一，它指的是一国根据企业出口国内产品的实绩，规定其进口的数量或价值。我国现行涉外经济法规中未发现这类明文规定，但有以出口为先决条件才可进口的规定。

二

从上面的分析可以看出，尽管我国已做出了重大努力，为外资国民待遇的实行创造了许多有利的法律条件，但是许多有关外资的法律与政策与国民待遇原则仍是不相符合的，有的则直接与关贸总协定乌拉圭回合新达成的《TRIMs 协议》的有关要求相抵触。为此，我们有必要根据市场经济国际惯例及有关国际条约的要求，结合我国的发展中国家现实地位及国家经济发展战略的需要，有计划、有步骤地对这些外资法律与政策进行进一步的修订。

对于那些既明显违背国民待遇原则与《TRIMs 协议》要求，又不适应国内经济运行现实及发展战略需要的规定，我们应该尽快予以修改。从目前看来，这种修改主要应包括两个方面：一方面，要淡化优惠、公平税负。如前所述，现阶段我国外资法律与政策仍停留在“优惠导向”“减税让利”的初级阶段。然而，随着外商投资的不断发展壮大，外商投资的成熟期已经到来，而成熟期的外资政策应当是侧重于创设一个稳定和公平的投资环境，而不再是简单地减免税收。所以，要进一步调整外资法律与政策，首要的任务便是淡化优惠，公平税

---

〔30〕 参见该细则第3条。
〔31〕 参见该法第4条。
〔32〕 参见该法第9条
〔33〕 参见该细则第75条。

负。这既是外资流动的一般规律,也是市场经济与“复关”的客观要求。要公平税负,目前主要是要统一税收政策和税率水平,杜绝各种各样的税收减免攀比行为。现阶段我国除经济特区、经济技术开发区等特别经济区外,在内地也存在着各种各样的减免税优惠政策,有的擅自延长减免期,有的则将所得税税率降到极低的地步,这种盲目攀比的“优惠大战”不仅破坏了国家税收政策的统一性,对引进外资也是极为不利的。因为外商更看重的是一个可预测、可把握的投资环境,而不是一个混乱不堪的“税收天堂”。此外,对关税等的减免也应统一起来,平等对待。

另一方面,要减少限制,取消不平等待遇。首先,对外商投资企业服务多收费用的规定,虽然是个别部门所为,但影响极坏,应予立即纠正,否则将因为部门利益而影响我国整体的投资环境。我国《外商投资法》中涉及当地成分要求、贸易平衡要求的规定,属于《TRIMs 协定》中规定应予禁止的投资措施,最好从有关法律中删除,有关内容不妨在合同中商定。至于“外资企业在批准的经营范围内需要的原材料、燃料等物资,可以在中国购买,也可以在国际市场购买;但在同等条件下,应当在中国购买”,[34]“合资企业所需原材料、燃料、配套件等,应尽先在中国购买”[35]等比较含糊笼统的规定,不仅没有实效,反而授人以柄,不如删去。关于出口实绩要求的条款,既不符合国际投资规范,也缺乏约束力,同样不宜在法律中明文规定。鼓励外资企业出口,可以采取出口退税的办法,这样做也可以使内外资企业享有同等待遇。在外商投资领域方面的某些限制,既违反了互惠互利原则,又不符合我国现实需要,应予修改。实际上这也与我国的实际做法不符。近年我国已经有限度地向外商开放了金融、贸易、外贸、交通和通讯等行业。另外,随着我国外汇体制的改革,外汇调剂市场的建立,外资法中有些关于外汇管制的规定已逐渐变得没有多大实际意义,也可考虑修改。

在尽快修改那些完全不合时宜的规定的同时,对于那些虽然与国民待遇原则及《TRIMs 协议》要求不相符,但却为我国经济发展的现实水平所必需,并为世界贸易组织一揽子协议中的例外与保障条款及对发展中国家特别优惠政策的条款所允许的规定,我们应当给以时日,逐步修订。例如,我国向外商开放金融领域,允许外商在沿海开放城市开办外资银行或办事处,但在目前人民币不能自由兑换和中、外资银行税负不一的条件下,我们仍不能允许外资银行经营人民币业务。这一规定虽然不符合国民待遇原则的要求,但它却是《服务贸易总协定》(GATS)

---

〔34〕 参见《外资企业法》第 15 条。

〔35〕 参见《中外合资经营企业法》第 9 条。

的有关规定所允许的。[36] 不过，我们可以扩大金融领域的开放，允许外商在内地开办银行或办事处，对外资银行经营人民币业务做出明确承诺，在一定时间内放开。另外，我国也可以援引世界贸易组织“一揽子”协议的例外和保障条款，为了保持我国的国际收支平衡而对外资企业进行一定的外汇管制和进口限制。同样的，我们可以取消外资法律中有关当地成分要求的条文，但对某些幼稚工业，如汽车业，仍可以在一定期限内采取按国产化程度给予税收优惠的政策。当然，这些措施只能是临时性的，一旦我国的这些产业发展到一定程度，或者导致援引保障和例外条款的其他条件消失，有关不适当的、会对贸易造成扭曲或限制作用的投资措施也应立即取消。

从长远来看，要完全适应市场经济条件下外资国民待遇原则的需要，我国外商投资法律与政策的调整不能仅仅是局部的或暂时性的，而应当是根本性的变动，即应当是以外资国民待遇制度为核心来构起“对内、对外统一”的技资法律体系。当今世界，在大多数发达国家，一般都只有一套经济法律体系，或称“对内对外统一”的立法模式。这既是市场经济超越国界的必然结果，是经济发展到一定水平的产物，也反映了一种进步的、文明的国际化意识与气魄。中国是发展中的大国，历史上，它曾有过“不拒外”的恢宏气概。如今中国再度走向世界，加入国际经济大循环之中，并要成为其中积极的一员，只有敞开国门，接纳来自五大洲四大洋的一切文明。在这“走出去，请进来”的国际交往中，我国的法律规范必然要逐步国际化，要“与国际惯例接轨”，其必然的结果是：对内、外的法律法规逐步趋向统一。相应地，对内、对外的投资法规必将趋向一致，最终将建立一种统一的投资法律制度，从而使外资的国民待遇在法律上得到全面的实现。

此外，值得强调的是，在我国，要全面提供并完善外资国民待遇制度，还需要一段时间。因为外资国民待遇实现的范围与程度，不仅表现为对内、对外法律法规的一体化，更取决于一国经济市场化、国际化的程度。从目前我国的现实来看，外资国民待遇的提供必须与内资现代企业制度的建设结合起来。理由是：国民待遇的实行，一方面意味着内资企业，尤其是国有企业与集体企业生产力的重大解放，这一点从税负的公平化与经营自主权的下放与进一步落实上得到了证实。另一方面，由于外商投资企业一般都采用先进的技术与先进的管理方法，并往往拥有雄厚的资金与广泛的国际营销管道，与刚刚从旧体制中摆脱出来的相对幼稚、脆弱的内资企业相比，其优势是明显的。在这种情况下实行国民待遇无疑会对内

---

〔36〕 按该协定，服务贸易的自由化并不是一揽子归功给予的，而是建立在谈判与个别承诺基础上的渐进过程，该进程“应充分考虑具体成员的国家政策目标和发展水平”“根据其发展状况逐步扩大市场准入”。参见《服务贸易总协定》(GATS)第19条。

资企业构成一定的压力,甚至对部分产业的生存构成严重威胁。所以,待以时日并给予相应的扶持是很有必要的。当然,给内资企业以适当的压力对现代企业的催育也是很有必要的,但必须注意在动力与压力之间保持一种平衡。这里,国家强有力的宏观调控也就变得非常重要。简言之,外资国民待遇问题虽然主要表现为法律的调整与完善,但并不仅仅限于法律问题;外资国民待遇的提供必须与现代企业制度之建立、民族经济实力的增强结合起来,逐步实行,渐趋完善。

市场经济与外商投资企业的国民待遇研究*

一、国民待遇的基本界定

“国民待遇”是一个使用极为广泛的概念，它泛指一主权国家授予外国人（包括自然人与法人）在投资、贸易、知识产权保护等方面享有不低于本国国民的待遇。作为外国投资待遇标准的一种，国民待遇主要指一主权国家在互惠的基础上，授予他国国民或公司在投资财产、投资活动及有关的司法行政救济上以不低于本国国民或公司的待遇，简称为“外资的国民待遇”。根据具体适用对象的不同，它大致可分为“外国投资者的国民待遇”和“外商投资企业的国民待遇”，本文着重探讨后者。

在国内立法上，关于外资的国民待遇，一般都只表现为笼统的规定。例如，1804 年《法国民法典》第 11 条规定，“外国人，如其本国和法国订有条约允许法国人在其国内享有某些民事权利者，在法国亦得享有同样的民事权利”。这条在互惠基础上一定范围内的国民待遇规定后来成了各国国民待遇立法的起源。有的国家（主要是发展中国家），在其外资立法中专门规定给予外资以国民待遇，例如近年来拉美许多国家新修订的外资法就采用了这一做法。[1] 这种规定仅仅适用于外资领域，较前者专门得多，但它们依旧是原则性的规定，并未明确外资的国民待遇的具体内涵。

在实践中，关于外资的国民待遇的详细规定，更多地见诸国与国之间的双边投资保护协定之中。尽管不同的双边投资保护协定有不同的措词，但归纳起来，对外资的国民待遇的具体适用范围的规定大致可分为三大类：第一类是最狭窄

---

* 本文发表在《中国法学》1994 年第 5 期。

〔1〕 参见张森根等：《拉美国家外资政策的调整》，载《国际经济合作》1993 年第 2 期。

的,即规定国民待遇仅适用于“投资”。中国与英国的双边投资保护协定采用的就是这种模式,该协定第3条第3款规定“除本条第1、2款规定外,缔约任何一方应尽量根据其法律和法规的规定给予缔约另一方的国民或公司的投资与其给予本国国民或公司的相同的待遇”。第二类规定国民待遇仅适用于“投资”及“投资活动”,例如,1970年《联邦德国与印度尼西亚关于促进与相互保护投资协定》第3章规定:(1)除非协议另有规定,缔约任何一方对他方国民或公司在其境内所享有或控制的投资,应给予不低于本国国民或公司,或第三国国民或公司所拥有的投资的待遇;(2)除非协议另有规定,缔约一方对他方国民或公司在其境内与投资有关的活动,应给予不低于其本国国民或公司,或第三国国民或公司投资活动的待遇。〔2〕 第三类国民待遇的适用范围是最广泛的,它不仅适用于“投资”及“投资活动”,还适用于有关的“司法行政救济”方面。例如,中、日两国政府1988年签订的双边投资保护协定第3条第2款规定:“缔约任何一方在其境内给予缔约另一方国民和公司就投资财产、收益及与投资有关的业务活动的待遇,不应低于给予该缔约另一方国民与公司的待遇。”协定第4条接着规定:“缔约任何一方国民和公司在缔约另一方境内,为行使和维护自身的权利,在请求或接受法院审理和向行政机构提出申诉的权利方面的待遇,不应低于该缔约另一方给予其国民和公司或第三国国民和公司的待遇。”〔3〕

三种不同的适用范围,反映了各国政府对国民待遇的基本态度及其妥协的程度。目前第一种类型的已极为鲜见,第二种类型的较为普遍,第三种类型的,即对此做广义适用的正在增多,这反映了国际经济自由化的时代趋势。事实上,在国际法的历史中,国民待遇首先适用的领域就是外国人的人身与诉讼权利,〔4〕司法行政救济上的国民待遇已基本形成了一项国际惯例。将与投资有关的司法行政救济纳入双边投资保护协定的国民待遇条款之中,仅仅是这一国际惯例在双边条约中的落实与强化,并非有关当事国的创新。所以,笔者采用广义的适用范围说,认为对外国投资者的国民待遇不仅适用于“投资”和“投资活动”,也适用于有关的“司法行政救济”。

综观各国的双边投资保护协定(或条约),国民待遇的具体涵盖范围一般包括:

1. 对投资财产及其收益的控制权与处分权。这里“投资财产”包括东道国法

---

〔2〕 参见《世界投资法(发展中国家:印度尼西亚)》,1973年英文版。

〔3〕 参见《中华人民共和国和日本国关于鼓励和相互保护投资的协定》第3、4条,转引自《中华人民共和国商贸投资指南》,经济科学出版社1992年版。

〔4〕 参见日本国际法学会编:《国际法辞典》,世界知识出版社1985年版,第476页。

律所允许的任何股份权、金钱债权或类似的请求权、专利权、商标权等工业产权和专有技术权，关于动产与不动产的权利及勘探、开采自然资源的特许权等。这里“收益”是指投资财产所产生的任何价值形式，包括利润、利息、股息、特许权使用费和手续费等。对投资财产及其收益的控制权与处分权主要表现为对资金投向、投资形式的选择权，在必要时候转让或收回本金的权利，对所得收益的汇出的权利等。

2. 与投资有关的业务活动。又称“投资活动”，系指投资者对投资产业所进行的日常经营、管理活动。按中日鼓励与保护投资协定的解释，这种活动包括：(1)设立和维持分公司、代理店、办事处、工厂和其他用于业务活动的适当的设施；(2)控制和经营自己设立或取得的公司；(3)雇佣和解雇专家，包括技术工人、高级职员和律师及其他职工刊的缔结和履行合同〔5〕，等。

3. 与投资有关的司法行政救济措施。也即因投资而产生的纠纷的司法审理与行政申诉等方面的平等待遇。这里应分为两个方面：一方面，是关于投资经营活动中发生的普通民事、经济纠纷的司法行政救济，例如对合同纠纷的仲裁与审理，对劳动争议的行政申诉与司法审理，等等。另一方面，涉及国家责任的投资争端的司法行政救济，指在外国投资被国有化、征收或由于战争、武装冲突或东道国的禁兑行为，使投资者丧失对其投资的有效控制，从而蒙受损失的情况下，外国投资者所可望获得的东道国的司法与行政救济。当然，在这一问题上，尤其是在关于赔偿的标准问题上，国际性会一直莫衷一是。与国民待遇一脉相连的“国内标准主义”得到了世界上大多数国家的赞同，这同时也是我国的一贯立场。

值得强调的是，国民待遇并不意味着在对内资与外资待遇上的绝对平等。在目前的国际条件下，还没有任何一个国家能给予外国投资与国内投资完全相同的待遇。外资的国民待遇只可能在一定范围内适用。例如，就投资领域而言，各国对内、外资从来都是有区别的。许多关乎国家安全与国计民生的领域，一般都不允许外资涉足；即使是非关键的经济部门，也可能基于国家经济规划与发展目标而对外资的引进有所先后，有所厚薄。这种限制，发达国家与发展中国家同样存在，毫无例外。一般来说，发达国家禁止或限制外资的领域集中在公用事业、交通、矿业、银行、国防工业、保险业、原子能工业，等等；而发展中国家禁止或限制外资的领域则集中在公用事业、航空、内陆运输、电讯、国防、武器弹药、印刷、无线电与电视等行业。〔6〕 此外，这种适当的差别待遇还可能包括对外资的审批手续与

---

〔5〕 参见前引中日协定第3条第3款。

〔6〕 参见陈安主编：《国际投资法》，鹭江出版社1987年版，第142～144页。

监督、雇佣限制、投资期限与本地化要求,等等。这种限制与合理的例外不仅为一国经济社会发展所必需,也是国家主权的一种体现。

国民待遇也并不意味对外资优惠待遇的普遍取消。绝大多数发展中国家为了吸引外资,纷纷制定了许多优惠政策,使外资企业在税收、经营管理权等方面甚至是有比本国公司和国民更优惠的"超国民待遇"。这与国民待遇原则也是相容的。所以,在各国间的双边投资保护协定关于国民待遇的措辞,都是用"不低于本国国民或公司"的待遇,而不是"完全等同于"本国国民或公司的待遇。事实上,这同样也是国家主权的一种表证。

二、市场经济与国民待遇的实行

国民待遇的实行并非毫无条件的,它需要一个相应的经济基础作为前提。这既是我国过去不泛提国民待遇的根本原因,也是我国现在适应新的形势而逐步实行国民待遇的主要依据。

过去,我国在中外双边投资保护协定中,很少提及国民待遇,主要是因为:长期以来,我国企业是按所有制形式划分的,作为"内资企业"的有全民所有制企业、集体所有制企业、私营企业三种所有制形式。不同类型的企业在经济上的权利义务千差万别。根据我国颁布的一系列的企业法与有关的法规与政策,不同所有制的企业在资金来源、物资供应、产品销售、劳动人事、财政信贷、税收、工资福利等方面各不相同。"内资"企业之间的待遇尚且相差如此悬殊,又何谈内、外资企业的同等待遇?即使真要实行国民待遇,又以哪一种企业作为参照系呢?同时,我国的工资体制、物价体系及国家补贴政策与其他国家有很大区别,特别是国营企业,由于对国家负有特殊的义务,因而受到国家的严格控制与保护,如果将这些待遇一并给予外商投资企业,则在执行中势必造成很大困难。此外,对国民待遇理解的不全面恐怕也是一个因素。例如,有人认为,国民待遇就是对待内、外资绝对平等,如此,则国家安全无以保障,国家规划无以实现;有的人则反过来,认为国民待遇就意味着外商投资企业优惠措施的一律取消,如此则吸引不了外资,从而影响经济的正常发展。

上述三个方面的原因均可归因于计划经济体制的影响。市场主体待遇的不平等,市场机制的缺乏或不健全,都是计划经济体制特征的直接体现,思想上的误区也与计划经济的思维方式密切相关。

与此相反,市场经济体制所具有的平等性、竞争性、国际性、透明性和规范性等特性,使国民待遇的提出与实行有了理论的基础与现实的可能:首先,市场经济作为商品经济发展的一种较高级的形态,平等性依旧是其最基本的特征之一。它首先要求存在一个统一的、一视同仁的市场主体体系，不论这些主体的所有制性质或其他社会属性，在市场上一律得以平等对待、公平竞争。显然，这里也包括对内资企业和外商投资企业的平等待遇。其次，竞争是市场的全部动力与活力的源泉，竞争的前提就是主体间权利义务的平等性；在不平等的主体之间是不存在竞争的，至少不存在完全意义上的竞争。竞争呼唤平权，平权也就意味着国民待遇有了法律的基础。再者，市场经济发展到今天，早已形成了跨越国界的规模化的大经济。任何国家要想发展经济，就不能孤立于国际大市场之外，这是为中外的元数现实所反复验证了的真理，也是我国重启国门，对外不断开放的主要理论依据。在经济国际性日益加强的形势下，"国民"也越来越有"世界公民"的意味，犹如在国际大市场中对任何一国的产品都应平等对待一样，在当代国际大家庭中，给予其他国家国民以本国国民同等的待遇，也是情理之中的事情。最后，当代国际投资的历史表明：在国际资金市场上，投资者往往更愿意将资金投放在一个虽然没有明显优惠待遇，但具有很高的政策、法律的透明度并能获得公平待遇的地区，而不是投向一个看起来待遇优惠，却充满着"内部规定"和歧视待遇的地区。这主要因为当今国际经济交往日益频繁、日趋快捷，在瞬息万变的国际市场上，投资的安全性成了首要的影响因素。相对而言，国民待遇以国内立法与国际条约为依据，其可操作性、规范性与透明度远较其他待遇标准为佳，故必然更契合国际化市场经济的需要。

当今世界上，大凡实行市场经济的国家，一般都提倡给外资以国民待遇；大凡实行计划经济的国家，都不提或很少提及国民待遇。前者如美国、英国、瑞士、德国、法国等发达的市场经济国家，对内资与外资基本上做到了平等对待；后者如前苏联、东欧国家和改革开放前的中国，由于实行高度集中的计划经济，没有也无法实行国民待遇。即使是发展中国家，只要是实行了市场经济体制，一般都实行或趋向于实行国民待遇。1991 年，解决投资争端国际中心（lCSID）对 51 个发展中国家外资立法的调查表明：绝大多数发展中国家（31 个）给外资以国民待遇，而这些国家又都是推行或已转向市场经济的国家，如亚洲的韩国、菲律宾、也门；欧洲的保加利亚、匈牙利、南斯拉夫；南美的阿根廷、哥伦比亚、巴拉圭及非洲的埃及、喀麦隆等国。〔7〕

三、国民待遇在中国的实践及其发展

1979 年《中外合资经营企业法》颁布以来，中国开始积极推行对外开放，大力

〔7〕 参见《解决投资争端国际中心评论——外国投资法杂志》1992 年英文版，总第 7 卷第 2 号，第 436 页。

引进外资。对外资的国民待遇问题从此产生,并且在一定范围内得到适用与实行,从下列国内立法与双边条约中可以清楚地看到这一点。

中国《宪法》在允许外商来华投资的同时,还规定它的合法权利和利益受到"中国法律"的保护。[8] 这里提供的国内标准的法律保护为国民待遇的适用奠定了《宪法》基础。可《民法通则》规定,凡在中国境内设立的外商投资企业,具备法人条件的,可取得"中国法人"资格。[9] 《中外合资经营企业法实施条例》进一步规定,在中国境内设立的中外合资经营企业是"中国法人",受中国法律管辖和保护。[10] 这两个重要的法律明确了外商投资企业的法律地位可以是"中国法人",显然隐含了其享有国民待遇的可能性。具体来说,在中国国内立法中已体现出的外资国民待遇主要包括三个方面:第一,司法行政救济上的国民待遇。这方面是比较充分的。例如,《民事诉讼法》规定,外国人、无国籍人、外国企业和组织在人民法院起诉、应诉,同中国公民、法人和其他经济组织有同等的诉讼权利。[11] 再如,国务院《关于鼓励外商投资的规定》针对向外商投资企业摊派的现象,规定外商投资企业凡遇有不合理收费情况,可以拒交或向当地经济委员会直至国家经济委员会申诉。[12] 第二,投资活动方面一定范围的国民待遇。例如,国务院《关于鼓励外商投资的规定》规定,对产品出口企业和先进技术企业所提供的水、电、运输条件和通讯设施,按当地国营企业收费标准计收费用。[13] 实践中,在一些对中国国家安全与社会公共利益没有不利影响的领域,中国一般都给予外商投资企业以国民待遇,例如允许中外合资企业与内资企业一样参加国内举办的各种出口商品交易会,并享有广泛的成交权;在配额等方面,也享有与国有企业同等的待遇;等等。第三,在投资财产保护的某些方面,也适用国民待遇。例如,《商标法》《专利法》《著作权法》和《计算机软件保护条例》等知识产权法律、法规,均以类似的文字规定,外商与外商投资企业在上述知识产权的保护方面,享有国民待遇。[14] 此外,根据普通法与特别法关系的原理,在其他法律没有特殊规定的领域,外商投资企业根据《民法通则》等普遍适用的法律还可享有广泛的实体权利上(如财产所有权)的国民待遇。

值得一提的是,1988 年国务院发布了《关于鼓励投资开发海南岛的规定》,该

---

〔8〕 参见《宪法》第 4、32 条。
〔9〕 参见《民法通则》第 41 条第 2 款。
〔10〕 参见《中外合资经营企业法实施细则》第 2 条。
〔11〕 参见《民事诉讼法》第 15 条第 1 款。
〔12〕 参见国务院《关于鼓励外商投资的规定》第 16 条。
〔13〕 同第 5 条。
〔14〕 参见《中华人民共和国商标法》第 9 条;《中华人民共和国专利法》第 18 条;《中华人民共和国著作权法》第 3 条;《计算机软件保护条例》第 6 条。

规定最引人注目之处在于，它不分境内与境外投资者，提供完全相同的待遇，一视同仁。例如，其第3条规定："国家鼓励境内外的企业、其他经济组织或个人（以下简称为投资者）投资开发海南岛……"这种统一以投资者身份完全平等对待境内外投资者的做法在中国投资立法史上是绝无仅有的。它表明中国政府在当时就已尝试在局部地区实行较为全面的国民待遇，反映了在对外资法律保护标准上与国际通行做法接轨的政策取向。

从中国与外国签订的双边投资保护协定来看，中国很少给予外国投资者以国民待遇。1986年签订的中英《关于促进和相互保护投资协定》（以下简称"中英协定"），是中国在双边投资保护协定中给外国投资者提供国民待遇的初次尝试。根据中英协定，中国"应尽量根据其法律和法规的规定"给予英国的国民或公司以国民待遇。〔15〕在此基础上，1988年签订的中日《关于鼓励和相互保护投资协定》就投资、投资活动及有关的司法行政救济方面，相互给予对方国民或公司以国民待遇。〔16〕以上两个协定是中外投资保护协定中仅见的明确规定国民待遇的两例，反映出中国政府在国民待遇的给予上的谨慎立场。另外，中国与瑞士两国《关于相互促进和保护投资协定》虽没有明确的国民待遇条文，但从其议定书第3项规定的措辞来看，该协定也隐含国民待遇的意向。〔17〕由此可见，过去，我国虽未"泛提"国民待遇，但也并非完全拒绝提供国民待遇，而是采取了相当灵活与谨慎的态度，在一定范围内或一定地区内，一定程度上给予外商投资企业国民待遇。当然，很明显地，由于计划经济体制的限制，国民待遇的适用范围与实际执行都是很有限的。在很多方面，外商投资企业所获得的待遇与内资企业的待遇迥然不同，外商投资企业往往同时处于"超国民"和"次国民"的地位。前者的表现如：相对于内资企业而言，外商投资企业一般享有较低的税负，较高的经营管理自主权和较多的优惠；后者的表现如在投资领域、投资转让、审批手续、销售方向等方面对外商投资企业又有较多的限制。随着市场经济体制的确立与对外开放、经济国际化程度的不断加深，这种极为有限的国民待遇显然已不适应形势发展的需要，给外商投资企业提供较为全面的国民待遇的呼声日高一日。从世界各国的立法与实践来看，对外资提供国民待遇已不仅是少数发达国家的主张；面对新的世界政治、经济形势，广大发展中国家也纷纷改变立场，转向提供国民待遇，就连以"卡

---

〔15〕 参见该协定第3条第3款。

〔16〕 参见该协定第3条第2、3款。

〔17〕 该项规定为"尽管由于两国间的经济和法律制度不同以及由于中华人民共和国经济发展的需要，瑞士投资者对其在中国进行的投资不能要求在各方面都享有与中国投资者相同的待遇，但中国政府应尽量注意使给予瑞士投资者的待遇在整体上是公平的"。

尔沃主义”闻名于世的南美诸国也不例外。[18] 我国如不及时调整策略，实行国民待遇，将既不利于吸引外资也不符合与国际通行做法衔接的需要。从国际法的角度来看，刚刚结束的乌拉圭回合的谈判的成果使得投资领域也被纳入关贸总协定的体制之内，而国民待遇是总协定基本原则之一，其结果，必然是投资领域的国民待遇将成为一项极为广泛的国际义务。我国要“复关”，并要成为世界贸易组织（WTO）的创始成员国，就必须及时调整对外资的立法和政策，走上国民待遇的道路。

朝着这一方向，1993 年以来，我国在立法上已经作出了重大的努力。例如，新近通过的《公司法》规定，该法同样适用于外商投资的有限责任公司。[19] 这样，它以中国市场主体基本法的形式宣告了内资企业与外商投资企业待遇的平等性，可以说是朝着全面的国民待遇迈出了坚实的、根本性的第一步。又如，八届人大常委会决定新颁布的增值税、消费税和营业税三个税收暂行条例从 1994 年 1 月 1 日起适用于外商投资企业与外国企业，同时废止原先适用的《工商统一税条例（草案）》。[20] 这一决定使内、外资企业在税负上首次统一起来，从实体利益上平等了待遇，是朝着国民待遇方向所作的又一次重大的努力。另据报道，1994 年起，我国人大和国务院制订的有关安全生产的部分法规将适用于“三资”企业，这些法规包括《矿山安全法》《工厂安全卫生规程》《女职工保护条例》等 24 个单行法律、法规，涉及有关安全生产与职工保护的几乎所有领域。[21] 此外，经济合同法的修订，汇率并轨等重大政策与法律举措都为国民待遇的实行创造了有利条件。

但是，全面提供并完善对外商投资企业的国民待遇，还需要相当长的一段时间，因为国民待遇实现的范围与程度，不仅取决于经济市场化、国际化的程度，也与一国政治、法律，乃至文化的发展程度紧密相关。就目前而言，我国至少在如下几个方面有待于更大的努力：

第一，围绕公司法的施行，加快企业制度改革，着力塑造“自主经营、自负盈亏、自我约束、自我发展”的中国现代内资企业。国民待遇的实行，一方面意味着内资企业，尤其是国有企业与集体企业生产力的重大解放，这一点从税负的公平化与经营自主权的下放与进一步落实上得到了证实。另一方面，由于外商投资企

---

〔18〕 参见张森根等：《拉美国家外资政策的调整》，载《国际经济合作》1993 年第 7 期。

〔19〕 参见《公司法》第 18 条。

〔20〕 参见八届人大常委会第五次会议《关于外商投资企业和外国企业适用增值税、消费税和营业税暂行条例的决定》。

〔21〕 详见《法制日报》1994 年 1 月 29 日，第 6 版。

业一般都采用先进的技术与先进的管理方法,并往往拥有雄厚的资金与广泛的国际销售渠道,与刚刚从旧体制中摆脱出来的,相对幼稚、脆弱的内资企业相比,其优势是明显的。在这种情况下实行国民待遇无疑会对内资企业构成一定的压力,甚至,对部分产业的生存构成严重威胁。所以,待以时日并给予相应的扶持是很有必要的。否则,盲目地、草率地实行国民待遇,无异于“引狼入室”“以卵击石”。当然,给内资企业以适当的压力对现代企业的催育也是很有必要的,但必须注意在动刀与压力之间保持一种平衡。这里,国家强有力的宏观调控也就变得非常重要。一句话,国民待遇的给予必须与现代企业制度改革,民族经济实力的增强相结合,逐步实行,逐步完善,不能操之过急,也不能坐失良机。

第二,结合产业结构的调整,适当让出部分国内市场。对于来华投资者来说,最大的诱因莫过于中国巨大的潜在市场。中国经济的迅速、稳定发展与人民生活水平的提高,越来越引起国际投资者的密切关注,中国国内市场日益成为中国吸引外资的“王牌”。在这种有利的形势下,进一步向外商投资的高新技术、高附加值的项目或产品提供部分国内市场,不仅有利于国内产业结构的优化和产品质量的提高,也是符合国民待遇的一种积极表示。

第三,继续拓宽外商投资的领域,放宽对外资的限制。根据世界银行集团外国投资咨询服务公司专家们的研究,发展中国家吸引外国直接投资时,对投资领域应尽量做到“肯定的名单”要长,“否定的名单”要短,要允许外国资本大体上能不受限制地进入,要将那些必须严格限制的项目或不允许的项目缩小到极小的范围并要作出明确规定。目前,许多发展中国家也都纷纷放宽了对外资进入领域的限制,许多原先不允许外资进入的领域,如基础工业、银行业、保险业及零售商业等已逐步对外资开放,原先风行的国有化和征收的做法,事实上早已不复存在。[22] 在我国,目前外资也已经进入绝大多数的领域,金融、保险、百货零售、保税区内外贸公司以合资建设开发区等外商技资项目,正在试验之中,外商投资股份公司也有了进一步的发展。[23] 今后,我们还将进一步在国内商业、旅游业、房地产业、航运业、资源开发等方面进行兴办外商投资企业的试点,积累经验后再加以推广。投资领域的拓展与限制的缩减是国民待遇走向成熟的体现。

第四,进一步改革税制,保证税负公平与税收优惠。首先要统一内、外资企业的税负,不宜有所偏颇;同时要维护并改善对外商投资企业的税收优惠措施,要将税收优惠与产业结构调整结合起来;要将优惠措施统一化、透明化;要确保税率合

---

〔22〕 参见王海军:《近年来发展中国家吸引外资的主要措施》,载《国际贸易》1993 年第 4 期。

〔23〕 参见经贸部外资司:《外商来华投资新特点》,载《中华人民共和国对外经济贸易合作部新闻公报》1993 年第 4 期。

理而优惠,尽量避免使用难以操作的免税期的做法等。税制改革是企业制度改革中的一个大课题,也是优化投资环境的重要依托,税负公平、合理,则国民待遇易于操作。

第五,进一步改革审批制度,提高办事效率。对于外资的审批,向来在各发展中国家都是要求比较严格的,加之官僚主义等因素的影响,使审批延误,办事低效率的情况时有发生。近年来,许多发展中国家都简化了审批手续,有的干脆改审批制为注册登记制(如委内瑞拉、阿根廷),有的实行逾期自动批准制(如墨西哥、印度)。中国的《公司法》大致采用的是以登记制为原则,辅以审批制的方式,这是顺乎国际潮流的。但是,由于《公司法》第 18 条的规定,使《公司法》与外商投资企业的法律有普通法与特别法的关系,所以,修改外资立法,使之与公司法趋于一致也就成为迫切的需要。

第六,完善经济法制,逐步实行内外法律并轨。当今世界,在大多数发达国家,一般都只有一套经济法律体系,或称"对内对外统一"的立法模式。这既是市场经济超越国界的必然结果,是经济发展到一定水平的产物,也反映了一种进步的、文明的国际化意识与气魄。中国是发展中的大国,要加入到国际经济大循环之中,并成为其中积极的一员,只有敞开国门,接纳来自四大洋的一切文明。在这"走出去,请进来"的国际交往中,我国的法律规范要逐步国际化,要"与国际惯例接轨",其必然的结果是:对内、对外的法律、法规逐步趋向统一。相应地,对外商及其投资的企业的国民待遇也将得到不断扩充、渐臻成熟与完善。

国有化补偿理论与实践的发展及中国的对策*

国有化及其补偿问题是国际投资法律理论与实践的中心问题之一,[1]也是国际投资法领域中最为敏感、最富争议的问题。[2] 关于国有化问题,特别是国有化补偿问题的争论,随着投资国际化的发展及有关国际仲裁实践的进行,已被逐步引向深入,有了进一步的发展。

中国已经坚定不移地走上了市场经济的道路。中国对这个问题的立场将是十分引人注目的。对此,国内有的学者已提出一些新的看法。[3] 本文拟在简析国有化补偿诸般理论的基础上,结合世界各国的立法与实践,探讨这一问题的发展走向,相应地提出中国的有关立场与对策,以供商榷。

一、国有化补偿标准的诸般理论介评

国有化补偿标准问题,即对外国人财产实施征收或国有化之后,是否和在何种程度上给予补偿的问题在国际社会中尤其是在发达国家与发展中国家之间一直是各执一词、聚讼不已的。大致说来,这些理论主张可分为三大类:

(一)"赫尔规则"(Hull Rule)

长期以来,西方发达国家和部分西方学者坚持认为,根据"国际法",实行国有化的国家有义务以"充分(adquate)、有效(effective)和及时(prompt)"的方式赔偿被国有化的外国人的一切损失,并认为这是"国际最低标准"。这一补偿标准

---

* 本文发表在《法律科学》1995 年第 4 期。

[1] 参见陈安主编:《国际投资法》,鹭江出版社 1987 年版,第 85 页。

[2] 正如著名国际法学者沙赫特指出的,"除使用武力外,国际法中似乎没有任何问题像外国财产被征收时支付补偿那样引起如此多的争论,而且往往带有强烈的身事情色彩"。参见奥斯卡·沙赫特:《征收外国人财产的补偿问题》,载《美国国际法杂志》第 78 卷。中译本见《外国法学译丛》1986 年第 1 期,第 1 页。

[3] 有学者认为,中国在这一问题上对发达国家作了妥协,而接受了"充分补偿"的标准。参见徐崇利:《国际投资法中的重大争议问题与中国的对策》,载《中国社会科学》1994 年第 1 期。

说因由美国国务卿赫尔1938年写给墨西哥政府的著名函件所首次明确而被称为“赫尔规则”。这一规则的实质就是从赔偿数量、支付方式及支付时间三个方面要求获得完全的赔偿,即全部赔偿(Full Compensation),以确保投资者的既得权益不受损害。持这种观点的人往往还要求赔偿包括预期利润在内的间接损失。[4]其法理依据一为既得权学说,一为不当得利理论,二者均引自资产阶级民法的基本原理。诚然,尊重既得权是资本主义国家民法的根基,不当得利原则也是近现代民法的基本原则之一,但正如德国著名学者多尔泽所说的,“在某些一般原则的国际约束力得到确认以前,必须考虑在国内法与国际法领域是否具备实施这些原则的同样的条件。‘尊重既得权’和‘不当得利’原则从国内法转移到国际法是大有问题的”。[5] 更何况,“尊重既得权”与“不当得利”原则只能适用于无法律依据的行为,把它们作为补偿标准的理论依据,无疑意味着把国有化这一合法行为视同非法行为。[6] 在国有化权利得到广泛承认的今天,这种理论显然是自相矛盾、无法自圆其说的。从实践中看,这种理论也是行不通的。

从国际仲裁实践来看,虽然有一些案件仲裁裁决采用了“充分、及时、有效”的补偿标准,但在实际赔偿数额与支付方式、时间上从来都不是完全按发达国家的主张给予全部补偿的。在大量“一次总付协定”的国家补偿实践中,则几乎没有全部赔偿的例子。由于后面将详细论及,这里不作展开。

尽管“赫尔规则”在理论上自相矛盾,在实践中也未得到承认,但少数发达国家和部分西方学者在国际公开场合仍旧坚持这种补偿模式。究其原因,无非是为的在国际仲裁或协商谈判中取得相对有利的谈判地位,[7]以最大限度地获取补偿。它更多的是基于政治与经济的考虑,而不是基于对法理与实践的客观分析。实际上,“将‘赫尔规则’称为最低标准……这在目前情况下是误用了这个名词;在国内法方面,今天‘赫尔规则’是‘最高标准’,并且在主要的资本输出国也未完全遵守这个规则”。[8]

(二)“卡尔沃主义”(Calvo Doctrine)

“卡尔沃主义”是发展中国家针对欧美列强滥用外交保护权而提出的一种理论,是由曾任阿根廷外长的南美著名法学家卡洛·卡尔沃(Carol Calvo)于1868年在其所著的《国际法的理论与实践》一书中提出的,归纳起来,卡尔沃主义有两大

---

〔4〕 柯伦佛尔:《外国投资的保护》1972年英文版,第105页。

〔5〕 鲁道夫·多尔泽:《征收外国人财产的法律新基础》,载《美国际法杂志》1981年英文版,第569页。

〔6〕 参见余劲松:《论国际投资法中国有化补偿的根据》,载《中国社会科学》1986年第2期。

〔7〕 参见阿梅拉森赫:《从最近的案例和实践看征收外国人财产的补偿问题》,载《国际法与比较法季刊》1991年春季英文版第41卷。

〔8〕 鲁道夫·多尔泽:《征收外国人财产的法律新基础》,载《美国际法杂志》1981年英文版。

要点：(1)基于主权平等的原则，独立国家可以自由地享受不受任何外国干涉的权利；(2)外国人一旦进入所在国，应视为默许作为该国国民看待，不得享受不同于该国国民的权利和特权，只能依靠所在国国内救济，不得行使外交保护。表现在国有化及其补偿问题上，“卡尔沃主义”认为：国有化及其补偿是一国国内法上的事情，完全不受任何形式的国际法的约束。一国有国有化或征收的主权权利，而不存在补偿的国家责任；是否补偿，补偿数额、支付方式与时间及争议的解决等项，完全是国有化国家的国内事务，只能据国内法加以裁决，而排斥一切国内法之外的干涉。其实质是无赔偿国家责任理论。其法理依据一为国家主权原则、一为国民待遇原则。“卡尔沃主义”得到了广大发展中国家尤其是拉美国家和前苏联东欧国家的支持与拥护，在联合国大会讨论《关于自然资源的永久主权的决议》期间，广大发展中国家一直坚持这一观点。

值得一提的是，国有化补偿问题上的“卡尔沃主义”并不等于国内外学术界流行的“不予补偿”理论。实质上，不予补偿只是卡尔沃主义的一种极端表现形式，其本身并非一种补偿理论。从国家主权和国民待遇原则也不能必然地推出“不予补偿”的结论，而只能得出根据国内法决定补偿或不补偿（“卡尔沃主义”）的结论。而且，从战后的实践来看，也并未发生非战争时期征收外国人财产而不予补偿的事件。[9]

“卡尔沃主义”在历史上对维护发展中国家的主权权益产生过相当大的积极作用，而且，从理论上说，基于国家主权和国民待遇原则而提出应由国内法管辖国有化及其补偿问题，这种论点是颇为有力的。但是，国际法发展的历史表明，国家主权并非绝对不受限制的。基于相互合作和发展的需要，各主权国家须放弃某些主权权利，而接受国际条约以及国际习惯的约束。在国有化补偿问题上一国完全排斥国际法的约束，这是不现实的。各国实践还表明，国民待遇从来都是受到相当限制的，在政治权利及某些经济、文化领域，国民待遇一般不对外国人开放，[10]在这种情况下，为了确保国外侨民的安全与利益，基于互惠或国际法上的安排而给外国人提供一定的外交保护权，这不仅合乎法理，也是为各国的实践所公认的。从实用的角度来讲，过分强调国家主权，完全拒绝接受国际法上对外资进行保护的义务，只会削弱一国吸引外资的各种努力，而不会带来任何实质性的好处。因而，目前已很难找到突出强调国有化补偿问题上的“卡尔沃主义”的实例。相反，大量双边投资保护协定及“一次总付协定”的国家实践都表明：“卡尔沃主义”在

[9] 关于1959年以前的有关实践的总结，参见《国际法年刊》1959年英文版，第136页。
[10] 单文华：《市场经济与外商投资企业的国民待遇研究》，载《中国法学》1994年第5期。

目前的国有化领域实在难以坚持。

(三)适当补偿(Appropriate Compensation)

适当补偿原则是在国家赔偿实践发展的基础上,由1962年通过的《关于自然资源的永久主权的宣言》和1974年通过的《各国经济权利与义务宪章》所逐步明确的一种新的补偿标准理论。适当补偿原则包括下列三层含义:第一,原则上,国有化补偿应根据东道国国内法来决定。即关于补偿数额、支付方式与支付时间及争议的解决等通常都应由东道国按其有关法律规章来规定。第二,如果当事国之间存在双边投资保护协定或其他双方均承认的有关国际法规则,则应按该协定或规则裁决国有化补偿事宜。第三,在缺乏有关生效的国内或国际法规则或有关规定过于抽象的情况下,则应在充分协商的基础上,按"公平原则"确定补偿的数额、支付方式与时限等问题。

显然,这里适当补偿并不等于部分补偿。在东道国财政能力允许,被征收财产并不属东道国国民经济中的支柱部门,且被征收外国人并无不法行为的情况下,在充分协商的基础上,仅根据"公平原则"也可能得出"全部赔偿"的结论。况且,如果双方当事国之间现存有效的国际法规则或东道国国内法有关规则存在"全部赔偿"的要求或承诺,也自然会得出同样的结论。但是,在大多数情况下,部分补偿却最能体现出适当补偿的原则精神,这与"全部赔偿"比较集中地反映了"赫尔规则"的要求,而"卡尔沃主义"更多地被用来支持"不予补偿"的实践在道理上是一样的。

至于适当补偿原则的法理依据,西方学者认为是"针对不当得利的公平原则和善意原则",[11]中国学者则一般认为是"公平互利原则"与"自然资源永久主权原则"。[12] 笔者赞同国内学者的看法,同时认为适当补偿原则的第三个法理依据是"国际合作共谋发展"的国际经济法基本原则。"国际合作共谋发展原则"是所有国家的共同目标和共同义务,也是《联合国宪章》的主要宗旨[13]和原则之一,它要求世界各国进行合作,以促进较为公平合理的国际经济关系,并在一个均衡的世界经济的条件下鼓励结构变革,要符合所有国家特别是发展中国家的需要和利益,并为此目的采取适当措施。[14] 这就意味着在国有化补偿问题上,一方面,被国有化外国人及其母国(一般为发达国家)应充分考虑到国有化国家(一般是发

〔11〕 参见1982年国际法协会蒙特利尔会议《关于国际经济新秩序法律问题的国际委员会的报告》,第17～18页。

〔12〕 详见陈安主编:《国际投资法》,鹭江出版社1987年版,第94～95页。另见姚梅镇主编:《比较外资法》,武汉大学出版社1993年版,第805～807页。

〔13〕 参见《联合国宪章》第1条第3项。

〔14〕 参见《各国经济权利与义务宪章》第8条。

展中国家)实施国有化的历史渊源及其对本国政治独立、经济发展和社会进步的重大意义,考虑到国有化补偿可能给东道国带来的财政负担与东道国的实际承受能力以及与发展中国家进一步合作、共同发展的需要等现实因素,不应单凭一己之私,一味地、盲目地强调自己蒙受的损失与补偿的“充分、有效和即时”。另一方面,国有化国家应考虑到外国投资者的财产损失的事实与双方进一步合作,引进外资以发展经济、文明社会的客观需要,给予被国有化外国人以适当补偿。在全球经济一体化日趋明显,南北国家之间经济依赖性日益加强的今天,基于“国际合作共谋发展”的需要适当补偿国有化的财产损失,对东道国与投资者及其母国都是有益的。至于“公平互利原则”与“自然资源永久主权原则”,国内学者已多有论述,兹不赘述。

综上所述,“赫尔规则”与“卡尔沃主义”实质上只是南北国家之间、东西国家之间的政治经济斗争的产物,从法理上都失之偏颇。而且,在南北矛盾、东西矛盾渐趋缓和,和平与发展成为世界性主题的今天,两者在实践中也都难以坚持。适当补偿原则作为实践中产生的新理论,尽管内容,有待进一步确定,参数体系有待进一步充实,但它合乎公平互利的法理原则和建立国际经济新秩序时代要求,反映了大多数国家的意志,故仍不失为最具活力、最有价值的一种指导原则。

二、国有化补偿法律与实践的发展及其对有关国际法的影响

(一)国内法、双边条约及联大决议的有关规定及其效力

如前所述,传统上,发展中国家一般采用“卡尔沃主义”。反对国有化补偿问题上所谓的“充分、有效与及时”补偿的“国际最低标准”,坚持国有化是否补偿及如何补偿应完全由国内法规定。然而,进入 80 年代以来,随着世界政治、经济形势的显著变化,发展中国家对外资的态度已有了很大的转变,各国在加强国内改革的同时都竞相开放市场、引进外资。这种转变首先反映在发展中国家国内立法上. 大多数发展中国家的法律采取了较为灵活的做法,允诺一般地提供“补偿”或“公正补偿”“公平补偿”。但是,上述被调查的国家中,尚无任何一国的法律声明直接采用“全部补偿”或“充分、有效、即时”补偿的。同时,多数发展中国家在国内法上的“沉默”态度,也都表明:尽管发展中国家已不株守原先的立场,趋向灵活,但仍不失原则,并未接受经济强国挟求的“赫尔规则”。

从发达国家这方面来看,尽管少数发达国家在其宪法和其他有关立法中仍坚持在任何情况下都应全部赔偿的观点,但有的发达国家的国内法也接受了

“公正而非全部”(Less than full but just)的补偿原则。[15] 在态度最为强硬的美国,在其第二巡回上诉法院1981年对古巴国家银行诉大通曼哈顿银行案的判决中,亦没有坚持“赫尔规则”,而承认“要求征收国支付适当补偿……更接近于反映国际法的要求”。可见,基于现实的考虑,发达国家对国有化补偿标准的态度在国内法上也有所变化,与发展中国家的有关转变相呼应,双方更趋向于一种更为实际、更为灵活的标准,这就是“适当补偿标准”,或称“公平补偿标准”。

1991年,解决投资争端国际中心对335个发达国家与发展中国家之间签订的双边投资保护条约进行了调查统计发现:不少条约(191个)直接采用了“充分、有效和即时”补偿的标准,有些条约(47个)则采用“公正”“全部”“合理”或“公平”补偿的措辞。同时,有近250个条约还规定了补偿的计算方法。其中,有92个为“征收之日价值”,70个为“实际价值”,83个为“市场价值”,3个为“公平价值”。[16] 表面看来,似乎双边投资保护条约大都接受了“赫尔规则”的补偿模式,但这并不意味着“赫尔规则”就反映了国际习惯法的要求(尽管少数发达国家一直坚持这种看法)。事实上,双边条约或协定作为证实国家习惯法存在的证据,它的法律价值须视具体情况来判定,一般说来,至少要证明各国长期重复一致的行为,而且各国重复类似行为时有一种必须这么做,否则就构成非法的法律义务感。[17] 以此衡量上述被统计的双边条约,则可以发现至少有三个层面的理由表明“赫尔规则”并不能代表目前的国际习惯法。首先,上述条约全部是南北国家之间签订的投资保护条约、这种条约在很大程度上反映了东道国吸引外资以助于国内经济改革与社会发展的客观需要与主观意愿,以及投资国竭力保护海外资本安全与利益进而试图以大量类似的标准协定来表面造成所谓“国际习惯法”的既成事实的主客观需要。客观地讲,在发展中国家纷纷转变政策,竞相引进外资的新形势下签订的这种大量类似的条约,与其说是反映了发展中国家有按发达国家主张的标准全部补偿国有化损失的法律义务感,不如说是体现了这些国家吸引外资以发展经济的时代紧迫感。其次,即使是在这样的背景下,也并不是所有条约都无一例外地采用了“充分、有效和即时”补偿的赫尔规则,大量条约并没有关于补偿一般标准的规定,有相当数量的条约采用的仅仅是“补偿”或较灵活的“公

---

〔15〕 例见欧洲人权法庭:《利斯高判例案》(Lighgow Case)1986年卷系列A,第102页。又见曼德尔逊:《联合国固有化案例与欧洲人权公约》1986年英文版,载《英国国际法年刊》第57卷,第33、44~63页。

〔16〕 详见《外国投资法杂志》1992年秋英文版,第7卷第2号,第366~367页。

〔17〕 参见[英]布朗利:《国际法原理》1979年英文版,第5~14页。

平”“合理”“公平”补偿的原则,而这些标准并不等于赫尔规则。[18] 最后,证之以上述各国国内立法,则更可看出“赫尔规则”绝非发展中国家业已一般接受的主张,这一事实同时也证实了发展中国家在签订这些条约时并无那种“法律义务感”或“法律信念”。

从多边措施的角度来看,目前似乎尚无为发达国家和发展中国家一致接受的国际公约。联合国大会1803号决议(1962年《关于自然资源永久主权的宣言》)兼采了国内法与国际法两个标准,[19]因而得到了绝大多数成员国的赞同,它实质上是“西方市场经济国家与受苏联东欧社会主义国家支持的发展中国家间的一个精心设计的折衷产物,特别是对征收问题而言”。[20] 1974年联合国大会通过的《各国经济权利与义务宪章》(以下简称《宪章》)规定:“实行国有化的国家,应当考虑到本国的法律、条例以及本国认为有关的一切情况,给予适当补偿。”少数发达国家对该款的主要反对理由是它“完全排斥国际法……因此,国内法本身就使国家可以掌握一切手段避免所规定的义务”。[21] 事实上,只要细读该《宪章》第2条的全文并考虑到作为文件整体的其他部分以及国际法基本原则,得出的结论便会完全不同。在用尽国有化的救济方法之后,财产被征收的所有者的国籍国根据现行国际法规则,有权受理其国民的案件,并可代表其国民索赔,理由是该宪章规定的、支付“适当补偿”的国际义务未得到履行。[22] 再证之以1986年联合国大会一致通过的《关于国际经济新秩序的国际公法原则的逐步发展的宣言》(汉城宣言)[23]和同年通过的《非洲人权和民族权利宪章》,[24]则更可以得知:适当赔偿原则已经成为世界大多数国家公认的补偿原则。同时,发展中国家也已经不否认在国有化补偿问题上国际法的存在及其效力。

关于联合国大会决议的法律效力,少数西方国家与西方法学家是持否定态度

---

〔18〕 参见阿梅拉森赫:《从最近的案例与实践看征收外国人财产的补偿问题》,载《国际法与比较法季刊》1992年英文版第41卷,第30页。另见多尔泽:《征收外国人财产的法律新基础》,载《美国国际法杂志》1981年英文版,第15卷。

〔19〕 该宣言规定,实际国有化或征收时,“应依据采取措施以行使主权的国家的现行法规并依据国际法”给予所有人“适当补偿”,参见《联合国第17届大会决议集》1963年英文版,第15页。

〔20〕 参见米兰·布拉伊奇:《国际发展法原则》,中国对外翻译出版公司1989年版,第269页。

〔21〕 参见弗尔:《国际公法综合杂志》(1975)。转引自米兰·布拉伊奇:《国际发展法原则》,中国对外翻译出版公司1989年版,第274页及注284。

〔22〕 参见阿雷查加:《将外国人所有的财产收归国有的国家责任》,载《纽约大学国际法与国际政治杂志》1978年英文版,第11卷,第7~8页。

〔23〕 该宣言第515节在肯定国有化权利的同时,规定国有化“应根据国际法的要求给予适当补偿,遵守可适用的条约”。

〔24〕 该《宪章》规定各民族在自由处置财产与自然资源时,“不得损害基于相互尊重、公平交易和国际法原则的促进国际经济合作的义务”,参见非洲统一组织文件CAB/LEC/67/5,第4页;该《宪章》第21条第1~3款。

的。理由是它仅仅是“政治性表态”,而没有法律上的意义,或者只涉及将来的法体。[25] 然而事实表明,联大所进行的广泛辩论所涉及的不仅仅是政治观点,也包括法律意见,而且,《各国经济权利与义务宪章》的名称及其获得通过的事实也清楚地表明决议的法律性质。[26] 就算这些条款只着眼于将来,但有这么多国家的支持,“将来”也很快可以变成现实。可见,联大决议的法律意义是不容置疑的,它至少反映了国际法发展的方向。而作为纯粹“政治性表态”的只怕正是这些西方国家与西方法学家及其所主张的“赫尔规则”。

(二)国际判例及国家补偿实践

受传统国际法的影响,早期的国际判例一般是支持“全部赔偿”的。[27] 20 世纪 70 年代以来,随着国有化案的大量涌现及发展中国家集体力量的壮大,“全部赔偿”的案例实践已出现了“偏离”,有一些案例甚至完全否定了全部赔偿原则,而采纳了“公平原则”或“适当补偿”标准。在著名的利美公司(Liamco)仲裁案中,仲裁员在详细考查国内法与国际法及其实践之后,认为“即时、充分和有效”的补偿标准只是“最高标准”,在实践中它已被“公平”补偿的标准所取代。其裁决从公平原则出发,否定利美公司对预期利润的赔偿要求。[28] 在“科威特石油国有化案”(Aminoil Arbitation)中,仲裁庭从“适当补偿”原则出发,尽管考虑到该美国公司是“兴旺企业”,最终仍以 8300 万美元补偿金结束了这场标的为 30 亿美元的争端,较大地背离了所谓的“全部赔偿”标准。[29] 晚近,在解决投资争端国际中心(ICSID)和美国—伊朗争端仲裁庭(即海牙仲裁庭,Hague Tribunal)所仲裁的国有化补偿案中,都适用了“全部赔偿”标准。[30] 这一方面因为这些国有化大都违反了“契约义务”;另一方面主要(特别是在美—伊仲裁案中)是因为双方当事国的友好通商航海和领事权利协定规定征收国应给予被征收者完全等于“其被征收财产价值的补偿”。[31] 即使如此,这两个现在仍活跃着的国际仲裁机构也并不排

---

〔25〕 例见德士古(Texaco)海外石油公司和加州亚细埃迪克(Asiatic)石油公司诉利比亚政府案的仲裁裁决,载《国际法律资料》1978 年英文版第 17 卷,第 330 页及注 87,另见阿梅拉森赫:《从最近案例和实践看征收外国人财产的补偿问题》,载《国际法与比较法季刊》1991 年春季英文版第 41 卷。

〔26〕 阿雷查加:前引文,第 184 页。

〔27〕 参见姚梅镇主编:《比较外资法》,武汉大学出版社 1993 年版,第 798 ~ 799 页。

〔28〕 参见《国际法报告》第 53 卷,另见姚梅镇主编:《国际投资法成案研究》,武汉大学出版社 1989 年版,第 47 ~ 88 页。

〔29〕 参见《国际法律资料》1982 年英文版第 21 卷,第 1033 页。另见姚梅镇主编:《国际投资法成案研究》,武汉大学出版社 1989 年版,第 117 ~ 148 页。

〔30〕 参见约翰·欧·魏斯特伯格:《征收案中的法律适用、征收式措施及补偿:解决投资争端国际中心与美国—伊朗争端仲裁庭的判例比较》,载《外国投资法杂志》1993 年英文版第 8 卷,第 1 号,第 15 页。

〔31〕 参见罗布沃:《征收及其赔偿法律的新发展:伊朗—美国争端仲裁庭裁决的初步分析》,载《国际律师》1987 年英文版第 21 卷,第 3 号,第 661 ~ 662 页。

除在特定条件下，采取部分或者说“公正而非全部”的补偿的可能。在解决投资争端国际中心主持的“AGIP公司诉刚果政府”一案中，仲裁庭的“附带性意见”指出在特定条件下，部分补偿是可行的。[32] 而在美—伊争端仲裁庭主持的“INA公司诉伊朗政府”一案中，仲裁员拉杰格林（Lagergren）认为体现了“赫尔规则”的全部赔偿原则在仲裁实践中已只能获得“比较少的支持”，而“在由于国家政治体制和经济结构发生根本性变化或深刻的社会改革导致大规模的对私人财产的干预时”，现代的标准允许只提供“部分补偿”。[33]

由上可见，在基本上仍为传统国际法理论所支配的国际仲裁实践中，全部赔偿理论也并非无一例外地得到坚持。相反，根据具体情况，给予“部分赔偿”或“适当赔偿”的观点正得到越来越多的判例支持。与此同时，越来越多的西方学者也认为“适当”补偿更能反映该领域中的国际一致意见。[34]

从国家补偿实践来看，适当补偿原则更是得到了压倒性的支持。据联合国秘书处向联合国大会提出的一份报告显示：1966年至1974年中期，62个国家的875起国有化或征收案件均未按“赫尔规则”进行补偿，补偿支付均按“账面价值”而不是“市场价值”，支付期间更非“即时”，而是15～30年的长期。[35] 西方学者布林在研究了1953年至1976年间关于国有化的30宗案例后，断定只有3宗提供的补偿符合“充分”的要求，却也并不及时。联合国跨国公司中心对发展中国家70年代发生的154宗征收案所作的研究也得出了类似的结论。[36] 这些补偿案件绝大多数是通过“一次总付协定”的方式达成的。[37] 例如，1948年南斯拉夫与美国达成补偿协议，由南一次性补偿1700万美元，相当于美方求偿额的42.5%。在英国与许多国家达成的类似协定中，也都是采用部分补偿的方法。[38] 如前所述，部分补偿不等于适当补偿，但在事实上却正是适当补偿原则的实践基础与集中体现。

三、中国对国有化补偿问题的立场与对策

作为发展中国家中的大国，中国一贯支持广大发展中国家为经济独立与社会

---

〔32〕 参见《国际法律资料》1982年英文版第21卷，第726～729页。

〔33〕 参见《伊朗—美国争端仲裁庭报告》1985年英文版第8卷，第373页。

〔34〕 例见布林：《发展中国家对保护外国人财产的国际习惯法的影响》，载《斯堪的纳维亚法律研究》1980年版，第99～132页；多尔泽：《征用与国有化》，载《国际公法百科全书》1985年英文版第8卷，第218、219页。又见杜普伊在“德士古仲裁案”中的裁决，载《国际法律资料》1978年第17卷。

〔35〕 参见汪渲：《国家对自然资源的永久主权》，载《中国国际法年刊》（1982年）。

〔36〕 参见布林：《发展中国家对保护外国人财产的国际习惯法的影响》，载《斯堪的纳维亚法律研究》1980年版。

〔37〕 根据李利奇的统计，战后国有化补偿有95%是通过一次总付协定解决的。参见李利奇：《国际求偿：通过一次总付协定解决》1975年英文版，第35页。

〔38〕 参见法托罗斯：《对外国投资者的政策保证》1962年英文版，第308页。

发展而采取的国有化措施，这从1958年中国政府关于苏伊士运河问题的声明[39]与1974年在联合国大会第六次特别会议上中国代表邓小平同志的发言[40]等国际场合的表态中都可以看出。至于国有化的补偿标准，1986年颁布的《外资企业法》第5条和1990年修订的《中外合资经营企业法》第2条均规定为"相应的补偿"。对于"相应的补偿"的具体所指，我国法律未作进一步规定。有学者基于对中国与外国签订的双边投资协定的考查及国际法优先的原理推定，上述"相应的补偿"即为"充分补偿"。笔者认为，将我国法律中的"相应的补偿"的原则立场等于同"赫尔规则"中的"充分补偿"，这无论从理论上还是从实践中都是不妥当的；相反，在这里，"相应的补偿"正应该是适当补偿原则的一种具体表现形式。

首先，从字面上看，"相应的"意为"相适当的"或"相呼应的"。[41] 换言之，"相应的补偿"应为与征收或国有化的具体情况相适应的补偿，意即在补偿额、支付方式与支付时间等方面均应视双方当事国的关系，国有化事件整体及具体个案的各种情况而定，其义实质上与前面所述的适当补偿原则几乎一样，而无论如何也与要求按所谓"国际最低标准"进行足够的或尽量的（甚至包括预期利润）的补偿的"充分补偿"标准相去甚远。其次，纵观所有中外双边投资协定，几乎每一协定都有"补偿应使投资者处于未被征收或国有化相同的财政地位"（如中国与瑞典、日本的协定）或"补偿额应等于被征收的投资或收益在征收或即将进行的征收已为公众所知的前一刻的价值"。（如中国与丹麦、挪威、新加坡、英国、意大利、波兰等近20个国家的协定）[42]之类的条文，而且这些条文与美国双边投资保护条约（样本）关于"充分"补偿的规定非常接近，甚至于"几近相同"。[43] 但是，如前所述，双边投资保护协定对发展中国家而言更多地反映的是吸引外资、发展经济的内在迫切需要，它往往并不反映该国对这一问题的一般立场。撇开国际社会对充分补偿的种种争议与分歧不论，就算这些协定的有关条文与某些发达国家对"充分补偿"的理解真的"几乎相近"，它也不能说明我国在国有化补偿标准问题上已完全放弃了原先的立场，而一般地接受了西方国家所坚持的标准。何况，截至1992年初，在我国与外国签订的28个双边投资保护协定中，没有一个协定言明采用"充分补偿"，倒是有四个协定（中国与法国、泰国、瑞士及巴布新几内亚

---

〔39〕 该声明指出，埃及将苏伊士运河收归国有的行为"无论从法律上还是从道义上"都是"完全正确"的。参见《人民日报》1956年8月15日。

〔40〕 该发言鲜明指出，中国支持发展中国家"对一切外因资本特别是'跨国公司'进行控制和管理，甚至把它们收归国有"。参见《我国代表团出席联合国有关会议文件集》（1973、7～1974、7）第11页。

〔41〕 参见《古今汉语实用辞典》，四川人民出版社1986年版，第796页。

〔42〕 参见《中华人民共和国商贸技资指南》，经济科学出版社1992年版。

〔43〕 参见徐崇利：《国际投资法重大争议问题与中国的对策》，载《中国社会科学》1994年第1期。

之间的有关协定）提到了“适当的补偿”“适当价值”或“补偿应是适当”等措辞。[44]

与此同时，我国国有化补偿的实践也并不支持充分补偿理论；相反，这正反映了中国政府所一贯坚持的适当补偿的坚定立场。例如，在1979年中美两国政府达成的关于国有化求偿问题的协定中，中国同意支付8.050万美元作为对解放初期被国有化的美国资产的补偿，相当于被国有化美资总额的41%，分6年还清。同时，美国政府将所冻结的中国资产全部予以解冻。[45] 此外，从中国政府在联合国的一贯主张，尤其是从投票赞成《关于自然资源永久主权的宣言》和《各国经济权利与义务宪章》这一事实，也可以推知中国政府在国有化补偿问题上坚持的是“适当补偿”原则，而不是“充分补偿”标准。

反过来，如果把中国外资立传中“相应的补偿”的原则等同于某些西方国家所株守的“充分补偿”标准，就意味着中国放弃了适当补偿的原则立场而投向西方，完全接受了西方发达国家的赔偿标准。这一方面不符合中国经济发展的实际现状，势必给未来的补偿实践事业带来不利，使中国在未来的补偿争议中处于被动的地位；另一方面，作为引进外资最多的发展中国家，中国的有关立场的骤然转变必将在广大发展中国家造成巨大的反响；在有关政治经济条件尚未成熟，绝大多数发展中国家仍坚持原有立场与原则的前提下，中国的这种立场的转变可能对中国同其他发展中国家的政治合作与经济交流产生消极影响。而且，值得一提的是，至少在目前，发展中国家群体仍旧是中国坚实的政治基础与外交后盾；同时，随着广大发展中国家经济的振兴和南南合作的加强，发展与其他发展中国家的经济合作以促进中国经济建设和社会进步也将变得越来越重要。可见，将“相应的补偿”原则等同于“充分补偿”标准不仅在理论上难以自圆其说，在实践中对中国也是不利的。中外双边投资保护协定中有关接近“充分补偿”的条文，只是适当补偿原则在双边场合的一种表现形式，而不是对适当补偿的背离，更不是中国政府在补偿标准问题上新的政策取向；我国有关外资立法中的“相应的补偿”则正是适当补偿的另一措辞。

当然，在坚持适当补偿原则立场的同时，在具体的立法与实践中采取比较灵活的措施不仅为适当补偿原则所允许，也是中国对当前国际国内政治经济形势的必要反应。双边投资保护协定就是一种比较好的反应形式，它既能为双方提供切实有效的保护，又不至于构成一般立场的变化，而恰恰是适当补偿原则在双边范

---

〔44〕 参见《中华人民共和国商贸投资指南》，经济科学出版社1992年版。

〔45〕 详见《国际法律资料》1979年英文版第18卷，第551页。

围内的丰富与充实。从目前的情况来看，将来在发达国家与发展中国家之间订立多边投资保护公约也是可能的，中国作为引进外资最多的发展中国家，决不能袖手旁观，只是在补偿标准问题上，恐怕仍只能跟广大发展中国家站在一起，坚持“适当补偿”原则。相应的，在国内立法上，不妨先以较低层次的立法形式明确国有化补偿的具体范围、计算方法及支付方式、期限等具体事项，再根据形势发展的需要，及时修订，逐步提高，以利于更多更好地吸引、利用外资和发展海外投资，促进国民经济的持续、稳定与健康地发展。随着国力的增强，外汇储备的增加及海外投资的发展，中国在互惠的基础上，向外国普遍提供比较充分的国有化补偿也并不是不可能的。

多边投资担保机构的投资促进业务与附带权力*

诚然，MIGA 的主要职能是为跨国投资的非商业性风险提供担保。然而，MIGA 的担保业务本身并不能直接为投资决策提供依据。要全面实现其“鼓励生产性投资在成员国之间尤其是向发展中国家成员国流动”的宗旨，[1]必须赋予 MIGA 以担保业务之外的补充性和附带性的职能。

为此，《汉城公约》在规定其担保业务的同时，还为 MIGA 设定了研究、信息传播、技术咨询和援助、政策磋商、谈判和建议等投资促进业务和捐赠、借款、管理基金、建立分公司等附带权力。[2] 这些职能，尤其是其中的投资促进业务能直接有效地服务于国际投资环境的改善与投资机会的推介，并具有系统性、协调性与稳定性等特点，因而对 MIGA 目标的全面实现有着特别重要的意义。

近年来，世界政治经济形势发生了显著的变化，国际资金需求量急剧增大，发展中国家与发达国家之间，发展中国家相互之间吸引外资的竞争日趋激化，MIGA 的投资促进业务越来越受到视。开业数年来，其业务量迅速上升，业务面不断拓展。[3] 实践证明，这些非担保业务对扩大 MIGA 的影响，促进 MIGA 宗旨的全面实现是卓有成效的。

---

* 本文原载陈安主编：《MIGA 与中国：多边投资担保机构述评》，第 10 章，福建人民出版社 1995 年版，第 408 ~ 448 页。

〔1〕 参见《汉城公约》第 2 条。

〔2〕 附带权力（incidental powers）指虽未为 MIGA 所赖以产生的条约所明文规定，但为实现该条约确立的目标所必须的权力。或称“暗含权力”（implied powers）。详见本章第 3 节。

〔3〕 以外国投资咨询服务为例，1989 年，MIGA 完成的投资咨询项目为 9 项，1993 年则激增至 30 多项；从项目分布的国家来看，1989 年集中在东欧 5 个国家，1993 年则发展到 39 个国家，遍及发展中世界的所有地区。详见《MIGA1993 年度报告》（英文版），第 29、30 页。

第一节　多边投资担保机构的投资促进业务的特性

一、多边投资担保机构投资促进业务的主要特征

众所周知，MIGA 并不是促进国际投资流动的唯一机构。实际上，早在 MIGA 成立之前已有许多开发性金融组织将促进投资国际流动作为其目标之一。[4] 但是从总体上说，现有其他国际金融机构在这一领域的活动主要限于它们以直接贷款方式或股权所有人的身份对特定投资所进行的融资合作，具有分散性与不协调等缺点。相反，MIGA 作为第一个以促进投资为唯一宗旨的国际机构的特点，这些特点同时也是 MIGA 的优点之所在。

（一）MIGA 投资促进业务的系统性

在 MIGA 成立之前，许多国际机构都已部分地、零星地设有促进投资流动的职能。例如，世界银行通过基建筹资和为各国借用机构提供信用额度等活动间接地便利投资；联合国贸易与发展会议定期发布一些关于某些发展中国家，尤其是非洲国家的外国投资法和发展中国家之间的合资经营企业的研究报告；联合国跨国公司中心主持着一项含有咨询培训和信息服务内容的技术合作方案，旨在增强发展中国家处理跨国公司事务的能力；解决投资争端国际中心的有关业务主要是出版有关投资法律条约与案例等书刊，以弥补有关法律资料的空缺；国际金融公司的投资促进方面的授权比较广泛，然而其项目资助者的传统定位却限制了它有关业务的发展，其实际促进活动仅表现为给国际投资者提供发展中国家潜在资金市场的电脑数据资料。[5] 可见，这些国际机构的投资促进活动，仅仅是为满足各自主要业务的需要而零星地、分散地进行的，缺乏一个长期的、系统的制度性安排。

与此相反，MIGA 的投资促进业务则多种多样，既有信息资料的搜集、传播，又有支持性的研究；既有政策性的磋商与建议，也有技术性的咨询与援助；可以说是涵盖了投资促进业务的所有领域。同时，各种促进活动互相支持、互相促进，共同构成一个促进国际投资的业务系统。支持性研究既以信息资料工作为基础，又以技术咨询和援助、政策磋商、谈判及建议为服务对象；信息服务既是研究、技术咨询与援助、政策磋商以及谈判的记录、汇集与传播，又为这些活动提供背景材料；技术咨询与援助则必须以信息服务为根据，以支持性研究为依据，才能有的放矢，

---

〔4〕 例见《国际复兴开发银行协定》第 1 条、《国际金融公司协定》第 1 条和《亚洲开发银行协定》第 2 条，分别载《联合国条约集》（英文版）第 2 卷第 134 页，第 264 卷第 117 页，第 571 卷第 123 页。

〔5〕 参见希哈塔：《MIGA 与外国投资》1988 年英文版，第 192 ~ 195 页。

取得实效，而另一方面，它又可能是政策谈判与磋商、建议的结果。所以说，MIGA的各项投资促进业务既相对独立，各有所司；又紧密联系，互为体用，它们共同构成了一个有效的投资促进业务体系。

（二）MIGA 投资促进业务的协调性现存的其他国际机构的促进业务除了有分散的缺点外，还严重缺乏协调

例如，国际金融公司关于发展中国家潜在的资金市场的电脑数据库与联合国工业发展组织的“投资促进信息系统”（Investment Promotion Information System）的投资项目数据库就有交叉，而两者之间并无必要的联系与交流。再如，解决投资争端国际中心、联合国贸易与发展会议都发布一些关于发展中国家外国投资法的研究报告，但两机构之间也缺乏合作与协调。

MIGA 的投资促进业务则不同，它从一开始就与其他相关国际机构有着密切的合作与广泛的交流。MIGA 本身就是世界银行、国际金融公司、解决投资争端国际中心等国际机构积极支持和配合下的产物，属世界银行集团的一员。MIGA 建立以后，通过人员交换、资金参与等途径与这些机构建立了经常性的、广泛的互助合作关系。借此，它得以利用世界银行、国际金融公司的专家、捐款与管理经验，可以利用解决投资争端国际中心的有关出版物，还可以利用联合国工业发展组织在各发达国家的办事机构，等等。相应地，其他机构则可从它的专业化、系统化的投资促进活动中得到全面的回馈。这种协调性还集中表现在 MIGA 与国际金融公司及世界银行的紧密合作上。目前，这三个互相独立又互相支持的机构共同投资开办着一项名为“外国投资咨询服务”（Foreign Investment Advisory Services）的业务。该业务本来只由机构与国际金融公司合营，1992 年世界银行的加入更增加了它的实力与影响。此外，MIGA 投资促进业务的协调性还表现在其与担保业务的互补性上。

（三）MIGA 投资促进业务的稳定性现有的其他国际机构的促进活动一般很不定型，大多数属于临时性质，针对某一特定项目而展开，项目完成即意味着业务的结束

相应地，其促进活动的时效也较短，有的只延续两到三年。更重要的其促进活动的经费往往得不到充分的保障，缺乏一个制度性的、长期的资金安排。这些限制使许多机构的促进活动时断时续，难以为继；有的机构（如国际金融公司）虽有广泛的促进业务权限，也不得不大大收缩其业务范围。事实表明，现有国际机构这种不稳定的促进方案对投资决策影响不大，在改进外国投资立法方面也收效

甚微。[6]

MIGA 是以促进投资为唯一目的的国际机构,这使它能着眼于长远利益,有计划地、稳定地发展其投资促进业务。尽管 MIGA 成立不久,促进业务尚未发展成熟,却已基本上形成了较为定型的研究、信息传播、技术咨询和援助、政策磋商、谈判和建议等五大类活动,并在初期的实践中显示出了不凡的成效。同时 MIGA 作为专业性的投资促进机构,其促进活动有着稳定和可靠的经费来源。这种来源包括世界银行和国际开发协会的拨款、各种渠道的捐款、MIGA 自身的年度分红、保险费用附加和请求国际资助,等等。[7] 总而言之,稳定的经费来源,相对定型的业务范围和长远的业务目标是 MIGA 促进业务稳定、高效运转的可靠保证。

MIGA 将其投资促进业务的系统性、协调性与稳定性结合起来,就充分显示出其促进投资的专业性。它说明了该机构的投资促进业务不是其他国际机构有关业务的简单重复,而是一种前所未有的、高度系统化和专业化的新型业务模式,具有十分明显的相对优势。这种优势是由 MIGA 自身的宗旨决定的,同时也得益于 MIGA 与兄弟机构的紧密合作以及机构内部两大类业务间的密切配合。

二、多边投资担保机构的投资促进业务与投资担保业务之间的关系

MIGA 的核心职能是投资担保业务,而且对非商业性风险的担保在某种意义上也可以促使一个踌躇观望的投资者最终决定投资;但担保业务本身并不能为投资决策提供依据,而恰恰是研究、信息传播、技术援助、政策磋商等投资促进业务能直接为投资决策提供所需的信息资料扩进而直接服务于机构宗旨的全面实现。促进业务与担保业务的这种功能上的差异性决定了二者的互补性。

如果说投资担保业务是 MIGA 业务中心点的话,那么 MIGA 的投资促进活动是其业务所扩及与延伸到的面。“点”是“面”的中心与依托,没有担保业务,促进业务就失去了一个强有力的支柱,MIGA 就变成了单纯的投资促进机构,这不仅使 MIGA 名不符实,也会使其促进业务流于一般化、空泛化,甚至难以为继;“面”是“点”的扩展与深化,没有投资促进业务,MIGA 就成了纯粹的投资担保机构,从而会使其失之狭隘与脆弱,更谈不上促进跨国投资流动的宏旨的全面实现。只有将“点”与“面”有机地统一起来,使之互相强化、互相配合,才能有效消除国际投资流动的障碍,达到有效促进国际投资流动的目的。

正是基于这一点,MIGA 的设计者们将 MIGA 的业务划分为两大类,并使它们

---

〔6〕 详见美洲国家理事会:《1980 年美洲国家理事会成员国调查》,载《解决危机:美国投资与拉美的持续性经济问题》1987 年英文版,第 26 ~ 27 页。

〔7〕 详见本章第 2 节。

优势互补。这首先从 MIGA 的有关规定可以看出来。《MIGA 投资促进业务细则》(以下简称《业务细则》)强调 MIGA 的促进方案应与其他开发性机构的类似方案相协调,从而将 MIGA 的促进活动引向鼓励外国投资,包括减少投资障碍的方向。〔8〕《汉城公约》第 23 条(a)款(ii)项则规定这些障碍将通过"在发达国家与发展中国家"进行持续对话与协商,由 MIGA 提出来解决。这样,《汉城公约》与《业务细则》明确了 MIGA 的投资促进服务将集中于那些其他机构未能充分提供,而 MIGA 拥有相对优势的领域。这种"相对优势"主要源自三个方面:即成员国的请求;专门知识与资金的充分供应以及它通过其担保方案与研究方案的实施和各种多边与双边磋商等渠道所得来的对投资促进问题的深刻了解。〔9〕其中,第二方面的优势清楚表明了 MIGA 投资担保业务对其促进业务的积极意义。

与此同时,《业务细则》也强调了 MIGA 促进业务对担保业务的积极作用。它规定这些方案"应通过加强对承保的投资在各东道国获得公平和稳定的待遇的保证以及扩大潜在投资者对在发展中国家成员国中进行投资的机会的了解,来支持机构的担保业务"。〔10〕

《业务细则》还以下述例证进一步阐明了 MIGA 两大类业务间的高度协调性:"研究工作既可服务于担保方案的业务需要,同时也可从担保业务中吸取适用于机构技术咨询和技术援助服务的经验。信息方案应同时促进投资者对进行投资的兴趣和机构对进行担保服务的兴趣。"〔11〕

具体说来,这种互补性表现为两个方面:一方面,MIGA 的担保业务活动必然促进和便利投资促进业务的开展。MIGA 在执行担保业务的过程中,必然与投资者、投资者母国及投资东道国紧密合作。为此,MIGA 必须熟悉投资者的兴趣、投资决策因素、决策程序以及东道国关于促进、吸引和管理外国投资的政策与行政管理体制。这就使 MIGA 有必要发展一个专业化的知识体系,使之能为成员国政府提供建议与技术援助,例如,加强管理引进和监管外资的程序规定;改善外国投资者与当地政府间的日常交流;提高促进项目的效益;等等。同时,也正是这种与商业团体的日常交往为 MIGA 推介发展中国家的投资机会提供了有效的和可靠的途径;此外,作为东道国与投资者母国之间可靠的中介,MIGA 也应尽量为二者间的投资政策磋商提供便利条件。这一点已为世界银行的经验所证实。作为一个金融中介机构,世界银行成功地实现了与发展中成员国之间的积极有效的政策

---

〔8〕《多边投资担保机构业务细则》第 7.01、7.04、7.03 条。

〔9〕同上。

〔10〕同上。

〔11〕同上。

协商对话。另一方面,MIGA 的投资促进业务活动对担保业务的作用也是很明显的:投资机会的甄别与推介增加了各国对 MIGA 担保业务的需求量;研究与咨询:雷动所得来的知识使 MIGA 能做出更明智的担保决策;政策磋商有利于稳定投资环境,从而减少 MIGA 所承担的风险进而促成 MIGA 成长成为一个公认的开发性机构。同样,这里世界银行的经验表明,[12]这种国际承认可以有效避免东道国对 MIGA 所担保的投资采取对立措施,促进投资争端的和平解决,并减少损失的发生。

通过综合这两大类业务活动,使之互相补充、互相协调、互相促进,MIGA 就能组织起一种前所未有的高度专业化和系统化的投资促进服务。这种服务既着眼于东道国创设适宜和富有吸引力的投资环境的需要,也充分考虑有关外国投资者的利益,从而能有效激发双方的热情与信心,进而达到促进投资跨国流动的目的。

第二节　多边投资担保机构的投资促进业务

一、多边投资担保机构投资促进业务的基本内容

《汉城公约》第 23 条列举了 MIGA 拟提供的投资促进服务的业务项目,并规定了相应的原则与方针。另外,它还用大致相同的措词明确了这些业务的目的所在:情报、研究等目的在于改善投资环境,促进外国投资向发展中国家流动;技术咨询和援助则旨在改善成员国境内的投资条件。[13]《业务细则》则通过剖析它们与 MIGA 担保业务的关系及它们与其他国际机构有关服务的相互关系,进一步界定了这些业务及《汉城公约》第 23 条提到的其他业务,规定了 MIGA 在执行这些职能的过程中所应遵循的原则和宗旨。

根据《业务细则》第 7.02 条的规定,MIGA 的投资促进业务包括五个方面的活动:(1)研究;(2)信息传播;(3)技术咨询和援助;(4)就投资政策和方案与对此感兴趣的国家或在对此感兴趣的国家之间进行磋商;(5)就机构与各成员国之间有关代位取得已被予补偿的投资者进行索赔的权利或有关给予被担保的投资的待遇的协议进行谈判。

(一)研究(Research)

研究工作从一开始就被认为是 MIGA 的一种内在需求。正如《业务细则》所

---

〔12〕 由于世界银行在世界上享有卓越的声誉,迄今为止,在它所提供的所有贷款中,尚未出现不偿还的记录。参见沃斯:《多边投资担保机构:地位、权限、概念、特征和本质》,载《世界贸易法杂志》1987 年英文版第 21 卷第 5 期,第 14 页。

〔13〕 《汉城公约》第 23 条(a)款。

强调指出的:“机构自身的需求将引导机构首先研究如何获得有关制定并实施有效可行的担保方案所需的基本知识,例如对东道国投资政策的评估,包括国有化以及该东道国曾与其他投资担保人之间有过的任何争端;税务和管理制度,解决争端的司法机制和其他机制;人力资源和自然资源的禀赋;以及与未来的被担保投资有关的其他经济因素。”[14]

大致说来,MIGA 所要进行的研究活动可分为三个方面:一是直接支持担保业务的研究,例如对存在 MIGA 担保投资的国家的外国投资环境的资料的汇辑与评论等;二是支持政策磋商和建议业务的研究,如对不同国家间关于影响外国直接投资的国内激励因素与阻碍因素的比较研究;三是支持技术援助业务的研究,如对成员国与各种类型的投资促进机构的交往的经历,对成员国投资审查和管理程序等问题的分析研究。而所有这些研究活动都会支持 MIGA 为各国政府与投资者提供的情报方案。

实际上,对于 MIGA 在某一成员国的投资担保而言,有关具体国家、具体部门和具体行业的知识是重要的前提条件。当然,这种广泛的研究有赖于对有关成员国的全面了解及该国与其他国际机构的密切配合。这样,MIGA 不仅能利用该回国内的资料,也可以利用其他国际机构(如世界银行和国际金融公司)的研究成果。此外,它还可以有选择地汲取与特定国家有长期稳定关系并对该固有深入了解的某些国内机构的经验。

事实表明,这种针对具体国家的研究还有助于 MIGA 与众多成员国的合作性研究的发展。这种研究包括对不同国家间具体投资促进与管理措施的比较评价,还可以涉及特定国家或部门的某些方面,诸如影响外国投资的鼓励或阻碍因素体系、对投资促进活动的行政管理及对所引进外资的管理,等等。

MIGA 的研究还可以通过改造世界银行和国际金融公司现有的部门研究计划或扩展它们的研究范围以纳入外国投资问题的方式得到实现。当然,这要求 MIGA 将其研究、咨询和技术援助活动与其他意图改善投资环境的其他机构的活动结合起来,使之互相协调、密切配合。值得强调的是,对投资者特别关心的领域的研究和对它们的意见、部门偏好及销售方向等问题的调查,应与对制约投资或影响某特定国家的外国投资的预期利益的因素的研究结合起来。显然,这三者是紧密相连、不可分割的。只有将具体部门的研究与对投资者和东道国有关态度与措施的研究结合起来,才能使研究工作得以扩大和深化,而不至于失之偏颇和浅陋。

---

〔14〕《业务细则》第 7.07 条。

此外，MIGA对特定国家外资政策或措施的特定方面的研究，还可以在该国政府的委托下进行。这种研究可以作为一项独立的专门活动，也可以作为改善该国总体投资条件的技术援助项目的一部分。相应地，MIGA将把研究工作的结论提供给有关国家；经过该国同意，也可以提供给世界银行或国际金融公司，甚至其他投资促进机构。

从实践中看，研究活动是MIGA最早开展的活动之一。MIGA本身在一定意义上就是研究、论证的结果。MIGA成立数年以来，研究工作已取得相当的进展。起初，研究工作集中在宏观的经济问题上，例如关于国家货币、财政、税收、汇率等宏观经济政策对外资流动的影响等。近年来，这种研究已转向从微观经济的角度探讨外国投资问题，例如对关于发展中国家投资机会的推介及便利外来投资的机制的研究等。如1991年度MIGA的主要研究成果是一份关于"某些工业固影响私人资本投向发展中国家的政策评价"的报告。报告指出：工业化国家大量宏观经济政策，特别是财政、货币、汇率政策对资本的输出有着重大影响；同时，许多微观经济措施，如双边税收协定等也正被用作投资激励措施，从而对资本输出产生着越来越大的影响。研究还表明工业化国家促进对外直接投资的政府机构和制度尚需提高效率并加强引导。[15] 这种深入细致的研究无疑对发展中国家还是对投资者与发达国家甚至机构自身无疑都是很有裨益的。

（二）信息传播（Dissemination of Information）

投资促进业务的重要组成部分之一就是汇辑有关投资机会和东道国投资环境等信息资料并提供给潜在的外国投资者；同时，也为东道国提供有关外国投资者的情报资料。这两方面就构成了MIGA的信息传播业务。

MIGA信息传播业务的实现是多渠道的。在MIGA活动的初期，这些活动主要通过与其他从事投资促进的机构合作的方式来进行。例如，MIGA可以与国际金融公司和联合国工业开发组织合作，将各自的资料库系统开发成一个共通性设施，使之既能为外国投资者所接受，又能适应有关机构及利害关系国促进投资的需要。该资料库系统还将联络并利用从事投资促进活动的其他国际或国内机构的资料系统，也可以利用有关私人机构的数据资料。同时，在逐步发展的信息网中，特别是在世界银行、国际金融公司的紧密合作下，MIGA还可以对大量当时并无投资促进意义的专门资料进行分析研究并使之协调一致，MIGA将因而逐步成长为其成员国的完整的投资信息资料的编辑与分析中心。这样，一旦投资者向MIGA提出信息服务的请求，MIGA就可以将他引向某个合适的国际或国内机

〔15〕 参见《MIGA1991年度报告》（英文版），第21页。

构——该机构在其专业领域内,能够帮助和支持对意向投资项目的分析研究。

从长期来看,作为鼓励外国投资流动方面最重要的机构,MIGA仅仅提供上述信息服务是远远不够的。面对成员国日益扩大的需求,一种更为周到和便捷的信息服务将显得越来越重要。这些信息服务包括:

1. 具体国家的综合性投资指南,它将详细说明有关国家的投资条件,包括它的经济、影响外国投资的立法(不仅仅是投资法典)、金融与投资制度、商业习惯及其他有关事项。

2. 为潜在投资者提供特定国家或国家群体中有关某一部门或分部门的详细资料,即所谓"具体部门的研究"。

3. 影响外国投资的综合性的各国法律法规大全,这将是比解决投资争端国际中心的《世界投资法》全面得多的一份工具书。前者只发布投资法典,后者则还包括其他有关资料,诸如劳动法、贸易法、税务、土地使用、技术转让和许可及往往包括在其他法律和法规中的争端解决适用制度,等等。

4. 关于部分工业化国家资本输出障碍的综合研究,以便人们更清楚地了解这种障碍因素以及消除它们的必要性。

5. 关于不同国家建立在相关法律和条约基础上的适用于外国投资的待遇标准的比较资料及其分析,以助于外国投资待遇的标准模式或国际统一标准的进一步发展和逐步法典化。

6. 有关外国投资者激起东道国采取消极措施,致使投资条件恶化,因而阻碍外国投资的输入的实证研究。

7. 特定成员国与现存的和潜在的外国投资者在政策磋商场合进行有效谈判所需的情报资料。这些谈判可能是针对双方关心的广泛的议题,也可能是针对象如何完满筹备一项特定的新投资之类的具体问题。

8. 一个关于外国投资问题的专门的世界性图书馆和一份关于这些问题的非法学刊物,以补充解决投资争端国际中心的《外国投资法杂志》之不足。

一般而言,MIGA的信息服务对于自身拥有的信息量有限的中小型公司是颇有价值的。特别是它的关于为巨大的潜在投资者群体所不熟悉的发展中国家的投资机会的信息资料将是最有意义的。此外,它还有助于发展中国家之间的投资流动。从近几年的实践来看,作为一项基础性的促进活动,MIGA的信息服务大都结合在该机构主持的技术咨询和援助、政策磋商与谈判及研究工作之中。例如,在前面提到的"某些工业国影响私人资本投向发展中国家的政策评价"及后面将提到的"外国投资政策圆桌会议"等活动中,无不可以发现信息传播工作的踪迹。此外,MIGA年度报告的编辑与出版也可以看作它信息活动的一个重要表现。

(三)技术咨询和援助(Technical Advice and Assistance)

根据《汉城公约》第 23 条的规定,MIGA 应成员国的请求可以为该国吸引外国直接投资提供技术咨询和援助服务。这种业务的范围非常广泛,小到帮助促进在某一特定行业或项目的外国投资,大到协助修订该固有关外国投资的制度框架或加强其国家投资促进机构的建设。当然,MIGA 这种广泛的业务权限必须与实际情况结合起来,尤其是必须与世界银行、国际金融公司及其他国际机构的有关活动协调起来,从而使其技术服务集中于它的其他促进业务及担保业务使之具有比较优势的项目上。

据此,有人提出 MIGA 的技术援助应致力于对成员国促进或管理外国投资的制度或方案提供专门化和实质性的帮助。因为这种制度建设性技术援助可以充分利用 MIGA 自身得天独厚的优越条件,那就是通过担保业务、合作性研究、政策磋商及谈判等活动,MIGA 对外国投资的有关问题有细致的研究和深刻的了解。这也正是其"比较优势"之所在。由于只有制度建设性的技术援助才能对投资决策构成普遍而深刻的影响,因而这种技术援助比对某一具体项目的促进有价值得多。

另外,MIGA 对成员国提出的技术援助的请求应进行审查,以免徒然重复其他机构的有关业务。同时,MIGA 还应保持与世界银行、国际金融公司的紧密联系与合作,以确保其建议与援助与后二者协调一致。特别是当 MIGA 的建议可能与成员国对世行所作的全面开发政策的承诺相互矛盾时,这种联系与合作将尤为重要。[16] 为此,有必要建立起这样一种合作关系,以便 MIGA 的专家直接参加到世界银行和国际金融公司的技术援助项目中去,或者互相分享从各自完成的项目中所获得的资料和成果。从某种意义上讲,"外国投资咨询服务"就是这样一种合作的产物。该业务项目现为 MIGA 与国际金融公司及世界银行合资开办,共同经营。其主要职能是就投资法律的内容和管理及影响外国直接投资(Foreign Direct Investment)的政策与方案,向有关国家的政府提供技术性咨询意见。同时,它还协助有关调处外国投资事务的国内机梅的重建与强化,以提高其效率。[17] 1990 年度(MIGA 的第一个完整的业务年度),该项目的业务量已达 17 项,1991 年度增加到 21 项,1993 年度则达到了 31 项之多。[18] 1992 年,该机构还组织力量再次考

---

〔16〕 世界银行的贷款中,有 25% 左右是政策导向型贷款,它通常要求借款国作出有效改善其整个投资环境或与特定部门或特定投资有关的投资环境的承诺。参见希哈塔:《MIGA 与外国投资》1988 年英文版,第 5 章,注[20]。

〔17〕 参见《MIGA1990 年度报告》英文版,第 16 页。

〔18〕 分别见于《MIGA1990 年度报告》第 16 页,《MIGA1991 年度报告》第 22 页,《MIGA1993 年度报告》第 23 页。

察了中国吸引外资的障碍因素——哪些在五年之后仍然存在,又有哪些新的障碍出现,等等。1993 年,“外国投资咨询服务”机构在中国开办了一个“投资促进研讨班”,旨在向政府官员们介绍国际上投资促进的先进机制与技术,同时考察各省的投资促进措施。1994 年,该机构专家组还具体考察了中国的外资审批程序,并设计了一种更友善的审批体制,以简化手续、提高效率,并增强中国政府督察引进重点与保障国家权益的能力。业务量的不断上升,不仅表明该项业务是卓有成效的,也从侧面反映了国际投资市场竞争日渐剧烈的客观事实。

(四)政策磋商、谈判和建议(Policy Consultations、Negotiations and Advices)

政策磋商、谈判和建议是 MIGA 帮助改善外国直接投资的政策环境的核心活动,它能对国际投资流动产生广泛而积极的直接影响。MIGA 这类活动的主要依据同样是促进生产性投资的国际流动,尤其是流向发展中国家的机构主旨。《汉城公约》第 23 条(b)款为其铺垫了更直接的法律基础,该款规定 MIGA 应“推动和促进成员国之间缔结有关促进和保护投资的协定”。并在 MIGA 作为特定投资担保者的利益所必需的时候达成机构与某一成员国间的协定。为达成这种协定,MIGA 管理部门与 MIGA 成员国必须就影响投资者信心的各种因素进行磋商。这些影响因素包括契约性安排的稳定程度及影响投资决策的其他政府保证等。此外,研究工作也会提出这方面的许多新问题,从而为 MIGA 的政策建议服务奠定基础。

一般而言,政策建议自然最好是在成员国之间就某些具体政策实践进行多边磋商的过程中,由它们相互提出来。这种磋商可能是由 MIGA 召集的专家小组主持,也可能在 MIGA 董事会或理事会内进行。按《业务细则》的规定,这种磋商主要集中在实用的问题上。例如,哪些投资措施或方案对于发展中国家国内目标的实现最为有利?哪些激励措施证明是有效可行的?哪种法律保护方式对吸引外资是最为成功的?等等。在特定情况下,这种磋商也可能导致成员国之间就外国投资者待遇标准或投资者行为的协议的磋商和谈判,或者 MIGA 管理部门与某一成员国之间就 MIGA 担保投资的个别协议的磋商和谈判。[19]

政策磋商、谈判和建议活动的目的自然主要是改善发展中国家的投资政策环境,但它也可以检查发达国家制约流向发展中国家的投资的流量、流向和构成的国内政策的影响。《汉城公约》第 23 条(a)款(iii)项规定 MIGA 应“努力消除在发达国家成员固和发展中国家成员闺中存在的影响投资流向发展中国家成员国的障碍”。因此,磋商、谈判和建议工作应引导投资者母国采取促进投资自由化,

---

〔19〕 参见希哈塔:《MIGA 与外国投资》1988 年英文版,第 6 章。

并鼓励和推进向外投资的措施,而这对发展中国家外资的引进是很有积极意义的。这样,在对影响国际投资环境的措施进行深入细致的研究的基础上,那些有积极意义的政策将作为经验不断被总结出来,并作为建议得到进一步的推广和使用。

当然,与技术援助等其他促进活动一样,MIGA 的政策磋商、谈判和建议服务将尊重世界银行、国际金融公司、解决投资争端国际中心等机构在该领域内已有的业务活动,并与之协调起来。不难看出,MIGA 在有关国家投资环境的法律、管理、会计和争端解决等方面将拥有越来越多的专业知识和专业人才。因此,它将能提供关于特定法律、规章、鼓励与阻碍措施等因素对外国投资者决策的影响的知识与资料,以便资金和技术的提供与特定成员国既定的发展目标相一致。显然,这些知识和资料对国际金融公司和其他机构从各自的经验中得来的知识是一个很好的补充。政策建议通常是与政策咨询结合在一起的,所以,从某种意义上讲,"外国投资咨询服务"项目也可以说是政策建议业务的一种具体体现。

从实践的角度来看,成员国获得详尽而可靠的政策建议的最佳渠道是多方面听取建议并通过 MIGA 安排的磋商、谈判等场合与其他会员国交流经验教训。近年来,MIGA 先后在加纳(1990 年 9 月)、匈牙利(1990 年 9 月)、牙买加(1991 年 2 月)、巴基斯坦(1991 年 11 月)等国发起"投资促进会议"(Investment Promotion Conference),帮助这些国家开发并推介投资机会,有力地加快了这些国家引进外资的步伐。1992 年 6 月,MIGA 还在博茨瓦纳发起了首次"外国投资政策圆桌会议"(Foreign Investment Policy Roundtable),意在为发展中国家提供一个分享吸引外国直接投资的经验的机会。来自非洲与其他地区的 16 个部长和其他高级政府官员出席了会议,并交流了各自在吸引外资方面的成功政策和方案。许多跨国公司的高级管理人员也应邀参加了会议并互相探讨了影响其投资决策的经济与政策因素。[20] 显然,这种多层次、多角度的大型交流活动,对全球直接投资的流动,特别是流向发展中国家是颇有裨益的。更进一层来看,这些磋商、谈判和建议的结果且通过信息传播业务公之于众,势必在更大范围内,更深刻地发挥其影响力。

二、多边投资担保机构投资促进业务的筹资方案

任何业务的开展都离不开资金的支持,MIGA 的投资促进业务也不例外,而且由于促进业务从总体上具有非商业的性质,故而其筹资问题显得更加突出。大致说来,有的活动,如研究、信息服务等,是完成 MIGA 业务所必不可少的,故完全应

〔20〕 详见《MIGA1992 年度报告》英文版,第 25 页。

当从 MIGA 的行政预算中列支；有的活动，尤其是技术援助与特定投资机会的推介活动，主要是应个别成员国的请求而提供的，故一般应由其他渠道，包括受益国自身来筹集资金。当然，到目前为止，MIGA 的促进业务的完整筹资模式与运作机制尚未形成。随着经验的不断积累和财力的不断增加，MIGA 将逐步形成一套完整而科学的筹资体制。而这显然是 MIGA 日益扩大的促进业务高效运转的前提。

在筹备 MIGA 公约期间，当世界银行董事会全体委员会讨论 MIGA 促进活动的筹资问题时，该委员会主席希哈塔提出：MIGA 不妨将不同类型的服务与接受者区别开来，分别对待。[21] 那些事关 MIGA 成败的基础性服务活动和提供给最贫穷的成员国的服务的开支，可以由 MIGA 自身承担；那些提供给其他成员国的服务的开支则应由它们自己或它们所得到的捐赠来承担。这种观点不仅得到委员会的赞同，还进一步反映到了《业务细则》的规定之中："由几个单位共同进行的技术和顾问服务应由一个特别账户支付。该特别账户由受服务人的付费、成员国的资助和其他捐助以及机构和国际金融公司的预算拨款组成。机构对该特别账户的拨款不应超过投资顾问服务处为机构成员国利益而规划的方案和项目所需的支出。有关技术、顾问及咨询活动的计划及财务估算应由总裁制定并列入年度预算，然后……报送董事会批准，但是，在不增加机构本身资金支出的情况下，总裁可以增加批准项目。"[22] 为确保投资促进业务的顺利实现，MIGA 董事会已经考虑设立一项特别基金。其筹资渠道大致包括：(1)世界银行或/和国际开发协会(International Development Assotiation)的开办拨款；(2)MIGA 根据盈利情况及提取储备金的需要，从 MIGA 的毛利中提取的年度分红(在 MIGA 审批其年度预算时，由董事会决定)；(3)其他机构或个人的捐款，包括联合国开发计划署等多边机构的捐款、双边捐助者(潜在投资者的东道国)的捐款以及私人捐赠者(基金会、商业协会等)的无条件捐款；(4)MIGA 担保投资的投资者或所有人所支付的保险费之外的附加费用。

经验表明，如果对投资促进业务的资金筹措缺乏一个制度性的安排，有关业务将很难开展。除上述方案外，为节约起见，MIGA 还应参加到其他有关机构，特别是世界银行和国际金融公司的方案中去，以分摊与这些机构有共同关联的研究与服务的成本费用。同理，它不应重复其他机构业已能完满提供的服务。此外，为最大限度地降低成本，它还应尽可能地借助于这些机构的设施，如世界银行、国际金融公司和联合国开发计划署的驻地办事处及联合国工业开发组织在工业化

---

〔21〕 参见世界银行执行董事会：《全体委员会会议记录》英文版第 1 卷，第 163 页。

〔22〕 《业务细则》第 7.09 条。

国家的办事处。

从其他现存的投资担保机构的实践来看，促进活动的筹资问题通常是由机构自有资金来解决的。在美国，海外私人投资公司是自负盈亏的，它以自己的收入来维持其促进活动的开支并积累了大量的储备金；阿拉伯投资保证公司也是以自己的盈利来资助其日益扩大的信息与促进业务的。所以说，从长远来看，MIGA 的筹资问题主要也应依靠自身的努力来解决，这不仅有赖于一个健全科学的筹资制度安排，更取决于 MIGA 的发展壮大及其财力的相应增强。

第三节　多边投资担保机构投资促进业务的实践与发展

一、多边投资担保机构投资促进业务的实践概览

关于 MIGA 的投资促进业务的必要性，在其成立之初许多人颇有异议。他们提出，如果一国的政策与体制环境对外国投资没有吸引力，再促进也无济于事；反之，如果一国的投资环境十分优越，也就用不着 MIGA 去促进投资。他们甚至推论道，这种褊狭的促进活动，不仅于事无补，反而会耽误一国政府对其国内政策与措施作及时和必要的调整。然而，MIGA 第一个五年的实践有力地驳斥了这种观点。

在 MIGA 的第一个五年里，由于国际投资市场上的竞争日益加剧，许多发展中国家纷纷改善其投资环境，增强对外资的吸引力。但是，国与国之间在外资政策及其实施上的差别仍然存在，而这正是一个谨慎的投资者所必须认真考虑的。这种国际比较评估往往需要在许多竞争国家中，就某一特定行业或部门进行系统、深入的调查分析。然而，绝大多数投资者，即使是大型的跨国公司，也无法获得进行这种评估所需的全部信息资料。它们只有借助于一个功能强大而相对独立的国际投资机构，才能获得所需的全部信息材料，并对这些信息，特别是有关的法律、政策和规章进行鉴别、分析、提炼和掌握。该机构同时也可以帮助投资者检查东道国所许诺的设施、服务和激励措施的实际供应情况。必要的时候，它还可以建议有关政府当局和金融机构采取有效措施，以弥补其吸引外资政策中的种种缺点与不足，从而避免投资者转向其他的竞争国家。

实践证明，MIGA 的投资促进活动不仅是必要的，而且是卓有成效的。

1990 年，“外国投资咨询服务”机构组织专家对投资促进活动的实践与效用进行了调查研究，提出一份名为《推销一个国家：作为吸引外资有力工具的促进活动》的研究报告。报告指出，投资促进活动对增强发达思家与发展中国家对外资

的吸引力大有裨益。具体说来,促进活动与 18 个国家外国直接投资的流入有直接的、密切的关系。另一项对 32 个发展中国家的统计调查结果虽然不十分明确,但也得出了一些积极的结论。例如,研究者们经过对 5 个发达国家和 5 个发展中国家的 10 个投资促进机构(Investment Promotion Agencies)的调查访问,发现在 30 项投资决策中,投资促进机构的促进活动对 11 项投资决策有“显著影响”,而对 9 项决策具有“一定影响”。而且上述 11 个案例都是属于出口导向型的投资,这可能是因为这种投资较进口替代型的投资有着更多需要了解和核实的复杂因素,使得训练有素的投资促进机构的援助变得尤有价值。

上述研究和“外国投资咨询服务”“政策与咨询服务”(Policy and Advisory Services)以及其他项目的经验还表明,不同的促进技术对于实现投资促进机构的不同目标有着重要的意义。在 10 个上述促进活动有“显著影响”的投资中,投资者反映投资促进机构的代表们曾直接介入,并在整个项目评估过程中与他们并肩工作,有的甚至会跟踪服务相当一段时间。只有 1 项投资决策是受到一次促进研讨会的“显著影响”,该研讨会是专门针对一个工业部门的公司而召开的。“外国投资咨询服务”和“政策与咨询服务”据此得出结论,认为如果旨在创造投资,这种高度集中的直接推销方式是投资少、收效明显的途径。1990 年“外国投资咨询服务调查报告”还表明一项典型的投资促进活动在创造就业方面的成本效益远远高于免税期政策的成本效益。

正是由于实践有力地证明了投资促进业务的巨大价值,使各国政府和投资者对 MIGA 促进业务的需求量逐年激增,很快超过了 MIGA 有限财力所及的范围。这使 MIGA 不得不重新审视自己在投资促进方面过于广泛的活动范围,对之作适当的调整,以适应财力及与“外国投资咨询服务”等机构分工合作的需要。

几乎在 MIGA 开始业务的同时,它与国际金融公司已达成协议,将“外国投资咨询服务”建设成为这两个世界银行集团成员机构的合营项目。与此相应,MIGA《业务细则》也做了修订,以赋予“外国投资咨询服务”向发展中成员国提供咨询、增强其吸引外资的能力的权利与义务。同时,《业务细则》赋予“政策与咨询服务”以“着重服务于机构成员国整体或支持其担保业务的其他技术、建议与咨询活动”。显然,这一分工条款是十分含糊的。但是,MIGA 数年的业务实践已在事实上解决了这一问题,即将“政策与咨询服务”的业务主要集中于协助东道自促进投资的业务性的方面,而把就吸引外资中的政策与体制建设问题向第二类国家提供咨询与建议的任务留给“外国投资咨询服务”。

至于 MIGA 投资促进活动的具体范围,有关的 MIGA 文件并未明确。有人认为,促进仅仅意味着进行广告或宣传活动以使外国投资者积极地看待一国的投资机会或吸引措施。这种观点未免失之褊狭。反之,如果认为,投资促进意味着实施《汉城公约》第23条所授权的全部活动,包括有关政策、法律和规章的修订和执行,有关机制的健全,构成"投资环境"的基础设施和其他服务的提供,以及引导和协调外国投资者利用这些"条件"等,那又未免失之空泛。它不切实际地包括了世界银行、国际金融公司和"外国投资咨询服务"提供的许多援助活动。

对MIGA投资促进活动范围的普遍接受的界定是介于上述二者之间的。它主要包括:(1)改善一国的形象或作为对外资富有吸引力的地区的认同感;(2)通过信息与推广活动,使经挑选出来的潜在投资者能直接接触到特定部门的或更窄范围的投资机会,从而达到创造投资的目的;(3)通过促成申请与审批及其他服务,将投资者暂时的兴趣转化为坚定的承诺。〔23〕此外,如果一个促进机构或促进项目能向政府当局,提供潜在投资者认为有助于加强该国在国际投资市场上的竞争力的政策及政策执行方面的完善措施的反馈信息的话,投资促进活动还可以进一步间接地影响到一国的政策与法律环境。

投资促进业务中的技术性援助则主要指开发和提高"投资促进机构"和其他诸如地区性或国家产业协会或政府专门机构之类的,从事促进方面的活动的机构的能力和效率的所有建议性或技术性服务。它还包括任何技术援助机构所直接参与的、促进在某国的投资的活动,以及它与其他机构合作开展的促进活动,而不论这些活动是否明确宣称具有机构建设的自的。

关于促进业务的筹资,MIGA的设计者们希望依靠其投资收入来承担其内在的、必需的促进活动的费用开支,而对其向成员国提供的技术性与咨询性服务,则期望通过外来资金,如使用费、赞助等来承担。几年的实践表明,MIGA所设想的种种筹资方案中,有的被证明是切实可行的,只是行政开支偏离;有的则未见明显成效,致使筹资问题日益突出,成了困扰MIGA促进业务发展的大难题。

为此,MIGA管理机构已采取了一项临时性措施。其要点在:首先,将MIGA对"政策与咨询服务"的拨款限定在1993年度的水平上即170万美元,并按通胀率逐年调整,以节约资金来壮大行政力量,确保对技术性服务的规划、协商、设计和监督的顺利实施,并使之能覆盖更多的成员国。其次,积极寻求对每项活动的外来资助(如捐款、受益人分摊、其他赞助及使用费等)以支付业务活动所需的费用,包括资料费、短期咨询费、活动所需的设备开支及有关的差旅费等。〔24〕从长

〔23〕 参见卢瑟福·M.波茨:《MIGA第一个五年的回顾和未来的展望》(以下简称回顾和展望),世界银行1994年英文版,第28、30、30~32页。

〔24〕 同上。

远来看,MIGA 还是应着眼于依靠自身的投资收入来资助对低收入成员国的技术服务活动,并与中等或高收入成员国共同分摊有关服务的开支。

二、多边投资担保机构政策与咨询服务项目的主要活动及其发展

根据 1993 年 5 月提交给 MIGA 董事会的一份“MIGA 的政策和咨询服务项目评估”报告及前面提到的波茨的报告,在开业的头几年里,作为 MIGA 核心促进业务的“政策与咨询服务”(现已更名为“投资推介服务”)项目经历了一个不断探索和发展的过程。

1989 年至 1992 年四年间,“政策与咨询服务”主要承担了四种技术援助活动:(1)组织“投资促进会议”(Investment Promotion Conferences)。分别在加纳、匈牙利、牙买加和巴基斯坦四个国家举行,还在美国为萨尔瓦多举办了为期一天的投资促进会议;(2)举办“高级职员开发计划”研讨会。分别在里斯本(为 5 个非洲国家)、布达佩斯、布拉格和卢旺达进行,旨在培养这些国家的商界(政界)人士就组建合营企业事宜与外国投资者进行谈判的能力;(3)组织“投资政策圆桌会议”,在博茨瓦纳为 10 个撒哈拉以南自家召开。会上来自其他几个吸引外资较为成功的国家的 6 位专家介绍了他们的成功经验。(4)出版了一份研究报告。“政策与咨询服务”的高级职员中大部分还参与了其他一些投资促进活动的策划工作,只是这些活动有的被有关政府取消了,有的则被推迟了。

经过对“政策与咨询服务”四年里上述主要活动的深入考查与认真评估,专家们总结出了一些经验与教训:

第一,尽管在计划所有活动时都考虑到了要避免其他机构早期促进活动中的通病,但“政策与咨询服务”在概念明确、时机选择及具体执行等方面依然存在一定的缺陷与不足。

第二,除 1992 年的十国部长圆桌会议外,该项目每年只能服务于少数几个国家。在大多数情况下,由于 MIGA 人力、物力有限,又缺乏像“外国投资咨询服务”信托基金那样雄厚的外来资金的支持,“政策与咨询服务”不得不选择可以相对集中人力、节约财力的单国促进项目。1991 年至 1992 年间,“政策与咨询服务”有几个私人项目由于得到了第一类成员国与跨国机构的赞助与使用费的支持,因而也能如期举行。在以后的技术性服务活动中,MIGA 应优先考虑那些可以同时服务于一大批成员国,甚至于所有成员国的“批发”式促进活动,或者那些能吸引世界银行其他成员机构、其他赞助商和服务用户提供资助的项目。

第三,早期的“政策与咨询服务”项目很少用于加强国内投资促进机构的能力,也极少采取后续措施,以确保促进会议或研讨会上所得出的结论和提出的建

议得到有关部门和外部机构的重视和实施。将来 MIGA 技术援助与咨询服务的震心应转向增强第二类成员国吸引并促进外资流入的能力上来,这就意味着在咨询之外,相互间还要进行业务性的合作,并伴有培训与后续的顾问服务。

第四,有两项“投资促进会议”在增强东道国对外资的吸引力方面是卓有成效的。这是因为东道国最近据此对其私人企业与外商投资企业的经营环境进行了综合性的改革;反之,由于有关国家未能将会议成果落到实处,另外的两项“投资促进会议”则收效不大。“政策与咨询服务”还曾试图将“投资促进会议”集中针对某些有发展前途的部门,从而吸引相关的投资者,但这种努力有时会因东道国政府当局的压力或某些难以预料的事件而搁浅。有时,东道国政府与“政策与咨询服务”都过高地估计了促进活动对外资流入所产生的立竿见影的成效。如果 MIGA 将来还要举办“投资促进会议”活动,它应协助一个当地的有经验的从事投资促进方面活动的机构进行,该“投资促进会议”应专门针对某一部门,同时还需要聘请一名该部门的专家来鉴别和帮助征集本国与外国的商界人士与会。经验表明,如果“投资促进会议”在主要的潜在投资者的本土内举行的话,与会的投资者会更多一些。此外,值得注意的是,只有在一回已经明显地改善了其外资环境的情况下,这种针对单一部门的“投资促进会议”才能有较大的成效。

第五,对高级职员的技术培训有利于培养更多的、适合于与外国投资者开办合资经营企业的当地合作伙伴。但这种培训往往需要与本地的需要结合起来,并应多次重复才能达到应有的效果。其最佳实现途径是 MIGA 帮助国内的投资促进机构或其他类似机构,使它们将这种培训活动纳入其日常服务项目之中去。在此,MIGA 最恰当的角色不过是给这些投资促进机构或其他机构提供培训资料,包括以成本价提供的一般性和特定部门的录像资料。

第六,“政策与咨询服务”与“外国投资咨询服务”之间的分工已经尽可能地避免了重复,但是,无论如何,它们仍旧是在大致相同的领域内开展活动。所以,它们必须互相沟通,共事观点、信息,并在必要的时候,共享其人力资源。[25]

在总结了“政策与咨询服务”四年实践的经验和教训的基础上,1993 年,MIGA 开始对其“政策与咨询服务”进行战略调整。在 1993 年这过渡性的一年里,新组阁的由 3 名高级职员和数名顾问组成的“政策与咨询服务”项目小组向 MIGA 提交了一份雄心勃勃的活动计划。根据该计划,“政策与咨询服务”在 1993 年财政年度内,实施了 15 项活动,并为 24 个以上的成员国提供技术援助。这些活动主要指:

---

〔25〕 参见《回顾和展望》,世界银行 1994 年英文版,第 28、30、30～32 页。

1. 一项在博茨瓦纳的“投资促进会议”。与以往不同的是，它包括一次南部非洲相邻国家关于旅游业的次区域性会议；为办好这次会议，“政策与咨询服务”还在纳米比亚、赞比亚、斯威士兰和莱索托举办了一系列高级职员培训活动。

2. 在“政策与咨询服务”与“外国投资咨询服务”和一些国内投资促进机构及其他东道国政府的共同组织下，在乌干达、坦桑尼亚和津巴布韦举办了三次关于投资环境改革方案的实施问题的专题研讨会；这些研讨会主要是应那些参加了1992 年的“投资政策圆桌会议”的非洲部长们的要求而举行的。

3. 在南美举行的一次规模宏大的旅游业“投资促进会议”。它由 MIGA、美国商务部、巴西工商与旅游部、泛美酒店协会联合组织，并得到了另外 9 个南美国家的旅游和酒店部门、几个其他机构以及国际金融公司的共同资助。

4. 一项关于巴西旅游业投资促进的后续活动。

5. 推介“外国投资咨询服务”所开发的电脑软件，供各国的投资促进机构采用，以改进它们的管理信息系统（Management Information Systems），该系统现主要包括一项投资者跟踪系统（Investor Tracking System）的标准数据库和一项商业运营环境（Business Operating Conditions）数据库。“政策与咨询服务”还与“外国投资咨询服务”合作，在马拉维和委内瑞拉试装了这种管理信息系统。

6. 拟建一个关于成员国的投资促进机构的顾问型协会“IPA 网络”（IPA-Network），作为它们交流“怎么做”的业务经验的场所。同时，还伴有一项名为“IPA 网”（IPA Net）的计划，以便通过电子途径把协会的成员国、感兴趣的私人投资者和相关机构与 MIGA 及其他机构联结在一起。专家们通过审阅有关资料及采访“政策与咨询服务”职员及其他机构的有关人士，对 1993 年的基本活动作出了系统的评估和细致的考察，主要结论与建议如下：总的来说，“政策与咨询服务”的过渡期项目是根据其早期的活动受到的主要批评而作出的相应的调整。它比早期“政策与咨询服务”项目服务的国家更多，且大都有明显的“机构建设”的特征。此外，为保证和强化关于成员菌的政策、机构或项目等方面的技术援助成果的施行和落实，“政策与咨询服务”还举办了一些后续活动。同时绝大多数促进活动集中于某一部门，并启用了专业化的部门性团体与专家从事征集与会人士的工作。

过渡期“政策与咨询服务”各项活动的具体情况及其评估如下：

第一，关于落实改革措施的研讨会。

1993 年度在坦桑尼亚、乌干达及津巴布韦召开的投资政策改革措施落实研讨会可算是将初始咨询建议转化为具体政策措施的有效途径。与会的官方和商界人士一致认为，在见识广博而又利益超脱的当地会计师事务所和顾问们的帮助下起草的各项议题阐明了扩大吸收外资的主要障碍及政府可以解决的实际问题。

它们对时机的把握也非常恰当，既利用了政府新近颁布的政策，又恰好赶在政府起草下一个财政年度的预算报告之前。一些官员称赞这三个专题研讨会大大推动了改革的进程，对在几个有争议的问题上作出积极的决策起了决定性的作用。另外有些与会人士则认为，像进口自由化、放宽外汇限制、取消管制和私有化等政策措施，并不是研讨会直接影响的结果。还有一些人士则指出研讨会的主题报告及 MIGA 邀请来的印度尼西亚和巴基斯坦高级官员们的发言对政府决策部门的态度产生了及时有效的影响，从而有力地改善了国内有关决策程序。结论是：尽管任何单项活动都不可能起到决定性的作用，但是，一次安排妥当、准备充分，而且将政府要员们的注意力集中于可解决问题的改革措施实施问题上的专题研讨会确实可以产生极大的推动作用。这几个研讨会都是“政策与咨询服务”和“外国投资咨询服务”联合举办的，二者的合作一直十分愉快。

第二，关于“投资促进会议”。

1. 旅游业。1993 年 10 月 10 日至 12 日，在巴西的佛塔拉泽（Fortaleza）召开的“南美酒店与旅游业投资者论坛”聚集了 10 个南美国家 70 个旅游项目的促进者、潜在投资者，来自该地区和发达国家的其他公司，以及相关国内和国际机构的官员们，具体包括巴西及泛美酒店协会、世界旅游组织、国际酒店协会、国际商会等国际机构和智利、阿根廷、巴拉圭、乌拉圭、哥伦比亚、委内瑞拉、玻利维亚、秘鲁、厄瓜多尔以及巴西的旅游和其他部门的部长们。会议期间开展了 30 个项目展示会和 I 个私人介绍会，还召开了数个关于政策、产业及金融问题的专题研讨会。这些研讨会大都致力于在 MIGA 的南美成员国中发展新的旅游业投资促进机构或相关的官方或民间机构。据美国商务部与会人士调查统计，这次投资促进会议产生了至少 7 项投资决策和此后三个月内的一系列设计、建设和供应合同。MIGA 因而得到了商界和政界人士的广泛赞誉。一位未曾参与组织但出席了该会的 MIGA 律师评论该会是他“从事这类活动 16 年以来所见过的组织得最好的一次”。

2. 采矿业。在参与纳米比亚采矿业“投资促进会议”的过程中以及在与纳米比亚政府及采矿公司的合作中，“政策与咨询服务”吸取了其早期活动的教训。“政策与咨询服务”加强了纳米比亚采矿部与纳米比亚投资中心在筹划该“投资促进会议”及征集外地公司、投资银行及其他与会人士等方面的准备工作。大约有 40 名投资者是“政策与咨询服务”所直接邀请到的。MIGA 负责担保业务的副总裁在会上作了主题发言，并向投资者们推销了 MIGA 的担保服务。“政策与咨询服务”的地区专家自始至终都在为纳米比亚官员们提供技术方面的建议。该会的主要组织者，也即后来的纳米比亚投资中心主任在接受评估人的采访时指出

“不仅在会议期间,就在会议前后,MIGA 与‘外国投资咨询服务’都给我们提供了颇有价值的投资政策建议和措施。”他说该次会议成功地向国际采矿业界介绍了纳米比亚,并导致了 8 ~ 10 个与会公司的进一步实地考查和数个投资项目的谈判。简言之,这一项目是对“政策与咨询服务”有限资源的有效的和高效益地运用,既强化了机构能力,促进了投资,又推销了 MIGA 的担保业务,且有良好的后续效应。

第三,关于为“投资促进机构”提供的“管理信息系统”。

第二类国家的“投资促进机构”和其他从事促进、便利和控制外国投资的国内机构的计算机管理信息系统的主体部分是由“外国投资咨询服务”所开发,并由“外国投资咨询服务”和“政策与咨询服务”于 1993 年联合推出的。目前“外国投资咨询服务”正准备将“管理信息系统”软件的推销工作转移给“投资促进机构”,同时开展进一步的开发研究。该软件主要包括一固的投资者跟踪系统和国内商业经营环境数据库两项内容。投资者跟踪系统软件是用以规范报道和训练投资促进机构职员们或其他从事投资促进活动的机构的职员们的促进工作的。它主要收录关于上述机构吸引外资的推销方法,个别公司间的业务往来,投资者考虑中的项目与实地考察的项目,东道国拟议中的和已提供给投资者的激励措施或服务项目及其对取得土地和设施的协助、审查与批准程序以及其他与投资者有关的事项。同时,投资者跟踪系统还希望能提供关于促进措施和推销战略的效果的信息反馈,以指导东道国进一步完善其吸引外资的政策与措施。

商业运营环境软件的用途是记录和更新关于一国商贸投资与经营的环境的数据资料,如政治体制、法律制度、税收、激励措施、基础设施、自然资源、教育、劳动市场、外汇交易状况与管制、国内金融体制,等等。“政策与咨询服务”希望所获取这些信息和来自国际货币基金组织、世界银行及私人会计师事务所或其他公司等独立机构的资料,以建立更为可靠的资料库,供合作成员以及潜在投资者使用。“政策与咨询服务”还曾提出它将帮助投资促进机构将商业运营环境资料,特别是有关特定部门的投资机会与环境的资料转化成像激光视盘这样的现代促进工具。这一提议正在实施之中,据《MIGA1994 年度报告》,MIGA 正在开发这种交互式、多媒体的激光视盘,以帮助南美旅游部门与撒哈拉以南的非洲的采矿部门推销投资机会。由“政策与咨询服务”和“外国投资咨询服务”所发明的管理信息系统软件深受投资促进机构的欢迎。其最初的两套软件已于 1993 年在马拉维和委内瑞拉试装,同时还伴随着使用和适应性培训服务。其他的安装则始于 1994 年。该系统的造价十分昂贵,每安装一套至少要花费 13 万美元,包括硬件、软件、培训及后续技术服务费用要最大限度地利用管理信息系统的推销和其他功能则还需要更多的费用开支如“政策与咨询服务”和其他机构的技术服务费等。不过，管理信息系统的倡导者们相信，它将有力地增强成员国投资促进服务的能力，并提高其效益。其实际效果究竟如何，首先取决于“政策与咨询服务”能否取得支持低收入国家安装这一设备的捐助以及所有购买这一软件的投资促进机构所支付的工本费。其次则看投资促进机构如何使用该系统以及“政策与咨询服务”能否提供确保所安装的这一设施长期有效运转的后续服务。

第四，关于“IPA 网络”（“IPA”Network）。

“政策与咨询服务”1993 年度的另一个补充性的创造便是为一个由所有感兴趣的成员国的投资促进机构组成的协会，即“IPA 网络”，提供秘书处服务。通过便利成员国之间信息和经验的交流以及为其职员们提供共通的培训服务。它将有助于增强成员国促进国际投资流入的能力。

与此同时，为加强“IPA 网络”成员间，以及它们与其他从事促进方面的活动的机构之间的信息交换，MIGA 还提议建立一项全球电子网络，将它们彼此联络起来。它将可以为任何成员提供给所有成员的信息，或传递给一个或几个接受者的电子邮件提供由密码控制的路径。那些向项目赞助人和其他投资者提供服务的公司、投资银行、会计师事务所及其他专业性公司将购买该网络的进入权，以便推销服务、传递信息。“政策与咨询服务”的设想是：由其他机构和公司投资开办该电子网络，并由它们与投资促进机构支付网络的使用费，故从长远看来，MIGA 完全无须支付任何费用。从 1993 年 9 月举行的世界银行——基金年会上的初步调查与对部分潜在投资者调查来看，这种设想倒并非异想天开。不过，除了资金问题外，该电子网络的成效将取决于作为秘书处与管理者的 MIGA 及其“政策与咨询服务”的服务质量，特别是它能否提供关于投资者、投资机会及经济与金融环境的全球性资料。

三、多边投资担保机构投资促进业务新方案及其前景展望

MIGA 与“政策与咨询服务”为最大限度地发挥促进投资的功用，已做出了种种不懈的努力，也取得了明显的成效。然而，问题并没有因此而完全解决；尤其是资金来源问题，仍旧在很大程度上限制着 MIGA 促进业务的质和量。有鉴于此，1994 年 2 月 25 日，MIGA 管理部门向董事会提交了一份建议，要求 MIGA 退出与世界银行及国际金融公司就“外国投资咨询服务”所进行的合资经营，今后不再资助和管理该项目，以便从 1995 年度起，将其技术援助集中于帮助第二类成员回开展投资促进活动的各项服务活动。其依据是，通过免除对“外国投资咨询服务”每年 100 万美元的拨款，MIGA 可以在一定程度上缓解资金紧张，并扩大保险

储备金存量。MIGA 将通过继续实施《汉城公约》第 23 条(a)款所规定的“义务性”服务活动,履行它对成员国的法定义务,而将其中的“任意性”的政策咨询服务项目留给“外国投资咨询服务”。这样,“政策与咨询服务”的主要项目包括:

(1)促进活动,如投资促进会议、投资促进研讨会、当地高级职员培训研修班之类;

(2)传播关于投资机会的信息。为实现上述职能,“政策与咨询服务”将致力于加强其与投资促进机构(包括发展中国家官方的和非官方的投资促进机构,例如投资委员会、商会,等等)的联系并增强其实力。因此,“政策与咨询服务”项目的重点将是对一个国家的促进(即把一国作为一个对外国直接投资富有吸引力的东道因而推销出去),而不是对个别项目的促进。[26]

1994 年 3 月,MIGA 管理部门曾向董事会提交一份报告,详细开列了新方案的具体内容。在这份报告中,管理部门建议将“政策与咨询服务”改名为“投资推介服务”(Investment Marketing Services)。目前,这一更名已被正式通过。[27]

根据上述报告,新方案的活动主要是服务于机构建设的目的;在有些活动中,这一目的将与其他目的结合在一起。这项探索性的方案列举了 25 项促进、培训、技术咨询和其他活动。同时,“政策与咨询服务”的工作人员亦已扩大至 13 名,包括顾问,来自成员国政府的两名高级职员,以及其他工作人员。

MIGA 对该方案的预算拨款将维持在 1994 年度的 170 万美元的水平上,并按通胀率作年度调整。实际上,这决定了所有方案中的业务活动都必须依靠外部资金的资助。如果这一方案中的所有活动都如约实施的话,其年预算外资金需求量将高达 700 万美元。从 1994 年财政年度上半年的情况来看,这大概是 MIGA 能实际获得的外部资金的 8 倍。[28]

这些活动将在所有的地区展开,每个地区都有专家负责开发工作。其中,最主要的三项活动都与投资促进机构有关:(1)管理信息系统软件的提供,包括协助安装、相关培训等;(2)“IPA 网络”或协会的组织与秘书处工作;(3)联结参加的投资促进机构、相关政府机构、私人企业及其他与外国直接投资有关的机构的电子服务活动。传统的促进活动,如集中子个别部门的投资促进会议、对投资促进机构及其他相关机构的技术援助等,将扩大到更多的成员国。

通过对 MIGA 在其第一个五年里投资促进活动的全部、系统、深入的调查、分

---

〔26〕 参见《回顾和展望》,第 32 ~ 36 页。

〔27〕 详见《MIGA1994 年度报告》英文版,第 26 页。

〔28〕 参见《回顾和展望》,第 37 ~ 39 页。

析和研究,专家们得出了下列结论,并提出了相应的建议:

第一,投资促进活动的技术援助是 MIGA 的法定义务之一。对这种服务的迫切需求已为许多第二类国家的投资促进机构和相关机构所充分表达出来。管理部门对 MIGA 技术援助工作的近期调整与 1993 年 4 月对投资促进机构项目的评估是相吻合的。

第二,在目前的条件下,管理部门集中 MIGA 有限的技术援助实力,以增强第二类国家投资促进业务的效率的做法是切合实际的。因此,MIGA 的技术援助服务将与"外国投资咨询服务"的活动互相补充。在今后相当一段时间里,"外国投资咨询服务"仍将一如既往地向请求服务的 MIGA 成员国提供高质量的政策咨询服务。新近界定的关于 MIGA 的技术援助服务与"外国投资咨询服务"之间的责任分工应在修订 MIGA《业务细则》时予以确定下来。当然,任何分工也无法完全避免这两个世界银行集团机构在协助促进投资工作上某种程度的交叉。例如,当一成员国请求"外国投资咨询服务"帮助它实施其关于本国吸引外资的制度方面的建议,如请求"外国投资咨询服务"提供顾问参与某项促进活动时,"外国投资咨询服务"难免要重复 MIGA 有关的业务性工作。同样地步当"政策与咨询服务"("投资推介服务")作为秘书处组织"IPA 网络"的咨询会议时,它将也不免在投资促进的业务性活动之外,涉足政策与法律咨询方面的事务。所以,MIGA 与"外国投资咨询服务"都有必要认清自己的相对优势之所在,而将自己知识和能力范围之外的有关请求事项引向另一方。何时,二者还有必要经常进行个案会商,并实行人力资源的共同分享。

第三,由于资金与人力的限制,MIGA 将不得不对其未来的技术援助服务活动进行精选。为此,专家们提出下列指导意见:

(1)MIGA 技术援助工作的重心应是帮助增强第二类国家的投资促进机构和相关机构的能力,使它们能更有效地促进投资。因此,前面提到的有关投资促进机构的三项服务措施(管理信息系统软件、"IPA 网络"和有关机构的电子联通)应成为 MIGA 技术援助活动的核心,在人力等资源的供应上应优先得到保障。但是,在设计、征集加入者与资助电子联网时,MIGA 一方面应注意避免因过分依赖现代科技而影响总体的容量,另一方面也应注意不要偏离增强成员国吸引外资能力的主旨。

(2)所有技术援助活动都应服务于帮助发展中国家提高其促进投资效率的目的,并着重致力于有关机构促进能力的增强。如果发展中国家的投资促进机构和相关机构能参与组织会议并参加实施有关会议成果的活动的话,MIGA 与这种国内或国际机构联合举办的针对某一部门的(最好是地区性的)投资促进会议也能够达到上述目的。

(3)除非 MIGA 的收入或其取得项目资助的能力大为改观,否则,MIGA 只能将其活动限定在受益人愿意付酬或个人赞助愿意资助的项目范围之内。当然,MIGA 仍不能放弃其对低收入成员固的基础性技术援助服务,这就要求它继续寻求赞助者们对具体活动,甚至是支援方案中的主体活动进行资助。MIGA 同时还应就争取项目赞助事宜与"外国投资咨询服务"交流经验、交换意见。

(4)在充分考虑到可能获得的外部资金支持之外,MIGA 确定其技术援助范围时还应充分顾及到其有限的工作人员提供高质量的服务的实际可能。因为即使资金问题解决了,MIGA 仍免不了要承担规划、磋商、设计和监督促进项目的责任,这些都是需要投入大量人力、物力的。此外,争取资助、推销赞助商资格、收取费用、争取外援等必要的行政管理活动也将是不可避免的繁重任务。

(5)MIGA 可用来开展技术援助的有限资源可以通过与世界银行的相关单位、与国际金融公司及"外国投资咨询服务"的合作得到扩大和延伸。这种协作的基本目的都是为了全面实现世界银行发展私人企业的广泛承诺。

第四,MIGA 的所有技术援助项目都应有助于促进其担保业务的发展。[29]

第四节　多边投资担保机构的附带权力

一项建立一个长期性的国际机构的公约是不可能预见该机构为实现其宗旨所需开展的全部活动的。所以,国际法上早就承认一个国际机构"必须被认为具有那些未在其宪章中规定,但为履行其职能所必需的潜在权利"。[30] 从权威国际法学家的论点出发,[31] 国际法院认为这种潜在的权力并不受那些被认为至关重要的权力的限制,而包括为实现机构目标所需采取的任何"必要的"或"合适的"行动(当然,它必须不违反该机构赖以创立的法律的任何条款)。[32] 这一原则早

---

〔29〕 参见《回顾和展望》,第 37 ~ 39 页。

〔30〕 参见《联合国服务活动中所受损害的赔偿》,载《国际法院》1949 年卷,第 174、182 页(4 月 11 日国际法院的咨询意见);此外,当年国际常设法院在国际劳工组织临时管理员的个人劳动的权力上也持相近的观点,参见《国际常设法院》1926 年卷、系列 B 卷第 13 号,第 18 页(7 月 23 日的咨询意见)。

〔31〕 例见被威特:《国际机构的法律》1982 年英文第 4 版,第 338 页;卢梭:《国际公法》1974 年法文版,第 470 ~ 472 页。

〔32〕 参见《联合国行政仲裁院所作的赔偿额决定的效力》,载《国际法院》1954 年卷,第 47、56 ~ 77 页(7 月 13 日的咨询意见);《联合国的特定费用》(《宪章》第 2 段第 17 条),载《国际法院》1962 年卷,第 151、168 页(7 月 20 日的咨询意见)。

已为世界银行的实践所肯定,而世界银行公约中也没有附带权力的规定。

遵循《国际金融公司协定》和《国际开发协会协定》的先例,《汉城公约》明确规定了 MIGA 实施公约列举的活动之外而可能是“必要的”和“适宜的”活动的权力。《汉城公约》第 2 条在罗列了 MIGA 的各项职能(包括担保业务和促进业务)之后,还授权 MIGA 可以“为进一步实现目标,使用其他必要的和适宜的权力”。显然,这种宽泛的授权使得 MIGA 的职能的执行有着很大的自由度,而且,这类活动大都是事先无法预料到的。但是,其他国际金融机构的经验表明,下列权力相对来说是比较典型,也比较重要的:

第一,捐赠权。这种权力早已为世界银行的实践所承认,该行曾从其毛收入(从执行董事会批准的行政预算中列支)中给许多特别项目提供捐赠,也曾从其纯收入中给国际开发协会等机构提供捐款。同时,这种权力也暗含在 MIGA 给最贫穷成员国的技术援助之中,这是公约的筹备性文件(第 23 条)和《业务细则》的正本所明确承认的。但是,这种从纯收入中捐赠的权力,只有在 MIGA 储备金已达到《汉城公约》第 27 条(a)款所规定的水平,即为本机构认缴资本的 5 倍时,才能出理事会行使。这时,“理事会应决定本机构的净收入是否及按何比例作为储备金、或分派给本机构的成员国、或作其他用途”。[33]

第二,建立分公司的权力。1984~1985 年,这一权力在世界银行内部已被详细讨论过。当时世界银行正考虑建立一个全部或部分为其所拥有的投资银行,并按某一成员国法律或世界银行与某一成员国的协定的安排而组建成公司法人。世界银行法律部就此所得出的结论是:(1)只要它全部或部分地服务于世界银行的宗旨,世界银行有权建立这样的分公司;(2)该公司可以不受该行业务的世界银行协定条款的约束(如资金合格率要求),但该公司的章程必须确保它通过其活动,促成该行目标的实现;并且(3)在一般情况下,世界银行无须为该分公司承担责任,但如果世界银行不适当地控制该分公司,使之成为世界银行纯粹的工具或代理机构,则世界银行可以在一定范围内承担这种责任。[34] 不久前,国际金融公司也曾考虑依照马里兰州法律,建立一个可以以经纪商身份在美国证券市场活动的全资国内分公司。实际上,MIGA 建立一个分公司至少能使机构投资促进业务的实施有一个独立的资金安排,因而完全是有必要的。当然,从法律上讲,这一权力的行使须征得 MIGA 理事会的同意。

第三,管理专用基金的权力。这一权力也早为世界银行和国际开发协会的实

〔33〕 参见《汉城公约》第 27 条(b)款。

〔34〕 参见世界银行法律部报告(1987 年 7 月 5 日):《世界银行分公司的设立——法律问题探讨》。

践所认可。20 世纪 70 年代，世界银行为欧洲委员会管理过一项专用基金；国际开发协会在一个特别安排下也管理过非洲专用基金，这一安排确保该资金贷款将偿还给国际开发协会，而不是捐款人本身。世界银行和国际金融公司同时都还是许多特别安排下的其他官方捐款的管理者。MIGA 管理专用基金的权力隐含在《汉城公约》第 45 条的规定之中，该条将 MIGA 的豁免权范围扩及其"所管理的基金"，管理专用基金的权力在 MIGA 根据它与某些商业银行的协议而接受对一系列商业贷款的担保进行管理时，将显得尤为重要。[35] 事实证明，将基金的管理委托给 MIGA，较之为此建立一个新的国际机构更加实际，也更加合算。所以，MIGA 成员国希望将来建立这样一种体制是顺理成章的。同样的，这似乎亦须征得机构理事会的批准。

第四，借款的权力。关于 MIGA 是否有权向其成员国或市场借款，公约未作规定，晚近在对农业开发国际基金（International Fund for Agricultural Development）的讨论中，推定借款的权力也隐含于其国际金融机构的性质之中，尽管其公约并未就此作出规定。《汉城公约》及其财务细则对于 MIGA 是否拥有借款权同样未作规定。诚然，《汉城公约》第 7 条（ii）项规定机构"在需清偿其债务时"，可以催缴 MIGA 股份中的可催缴的部分，并不受债务性质的限制，但《汉城公约解说》第 7 条和《业务细则》第 4.01 条（i）款都认为，求助于可催缴资本的情形通常不会发生；而且，这无论如何也不意味着这种资本可以用来担保 MIGA 的借款。然而，为了使 MIGA 能进行其日常业务所必需的短期借款（例如，MIGA 以与担保业务所产生的义务有关的付款通知书的形式来进行的清偿前的临时性融资就是其表现形式之一），原则上确立这样一种权力是很有必要的。而其他形式的借款则须在对它可能产生的财务影响进行仔细评估之后，经 MIGA 理事会批准后才能进行，其大前提是它们所导致的 MIGA 总体费用开支（包括其担保金额的总数在内）的增加不至于超过《汉城公约》第 27 条所规定的限度。

MIGA 关于鼓励成员国之间的投资流动，特别是流向发展中国家的宗旨要求它在担保业务之外，实施一系列补充性和附带性的活动。这些活动中，有的在《汉城公约》第 23 条已明确提到，如实施有关的支持性研究工作，将信息情报传播给投资者和东道国，应请求提供技术服务和政策建议等投资促进活动，意图改善投资条件，推介投资机会，消除投资流动障碍，和平解决投资争端并便利关于外国投资者待遇的协议的达成。这些活动由于能直接影响投资决策，因而较之担保业务更能促成 MIGA 目标的全面实现。几年的业务实践表明，MIGA 投资促进业务很

---

〔35〕 参见希哈塔：《MIGA 与外国投资》1988 年英文版，第 192～195 页。

能适应发展中国家的需要，对投资者与发达国家也颇有裨益。投资促进的筹资目前应由 MIGA 自身、东道国和第三方共同承担，并应区别不同类型的服务及对象因而分别对待。当然，如果 MIGA 能成功地建立一个专用基金并能从其他渠道获得资金帮助的话，它的投资促进业务必能更为广泛、更有成效。

与此同时，在与 MIGA 的目标相关并与《汉城公约》相一致的前提下，MIGA 根据惯例还可以进行公约明确提到的业务以外的"必要的"和"适当的"活动，这些活动包括捐赠、建立分公司、管理专用基金和借款等。由于这些活动可能导致 MIGA 财务开支的明显增加，所以它们的实施除了在实体上要与机构的宗旨和财力相吻合外，在程序上还必须征得 MIGA 理事会的批准。